OFFICIAL PGA TOUR FAN GUIDE

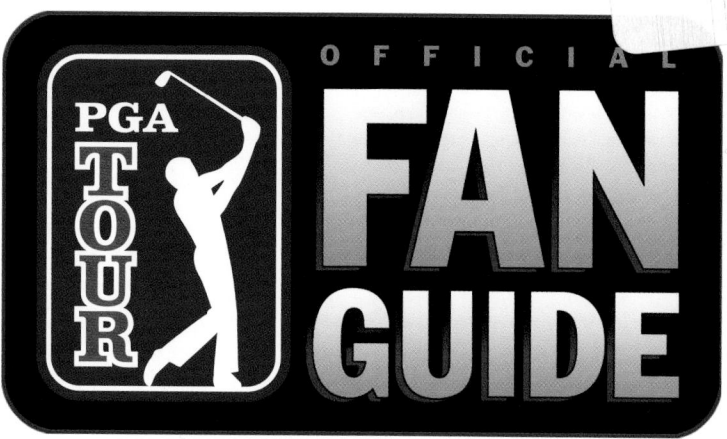

2005 EDITION

TEHABI
sports

The 2005 PGA TOUR Official Fan Guide

The 2005 PGA TOUR Official Fan Guide was developed and published by Tehabi Sports, an imprint of Tehabi Books, Inc. Tehabi is the official book publishing licensee of the PGA TOUR and has produced and published many award-winning sports and other non-fiction books that are recognized for their strong literary and visual content. Tehabi works with national and international brands, corporations, institutions, and nonprofit groups to identify, develop, and implement comprehensive publishing programs. Tehabi Books is located in San Diego, California. www.tehabi.com

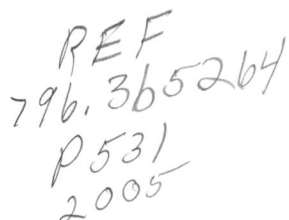

President and Publisher: Chris Capen
Senior Vice President: Sam Lewis
Vice President and Creative Director: Karla Olson
Director, PGA TOUR Publishing Program: Marci Weinberg

Design: Switch Studio, Tempe, Arizona
Production: PGA TOUR Creative Services

Editor: Terry Spohn
Editorial Assistant: Emily Henning

Introduction written by Dave Shedloski

With special thanks to key individuals at the PGA TOUR for their invaluable contributions in the creation of *The 2005 PGA TOUR Official Fan Guide*: Donna Orender, Senior Vice President, Strategic Development; Robert J. Combs, Senior Vice President, Public Relations and Communications; Ward Clayton, Director, Editorial Services; John Rice, Production/Systems Manager; Jana Arnold, Print Production Artist; Mike Smith, Senior Graphic Designer; Laury Livsey, Manager of Corporate Communications; and Maureen Feeley, Publications Assistant. And a special thanks to Bob Rosen and Jennifer Unter of RLR Associates.

ISBN 1-933208-01-5

U.S. Edition
Printed by RR Donnelley

10 9 8 7 6 5 4 3 2 1

Table of Contents

Letter from the Commissioner

Commissioner Tim Finchem and player Fred Funk

Dear Fans,

Welcome to the inaugural edition of *The PGA TOUR Official Fan Guide,* a comprehensive look at the players, tournaments, and records of the PGA TOUR.

We have combined information on our three Tours, the PGA TOUR, Champions Tour and Nationwide Tour, into one publication so that you can more easily follow the upcoming seasons. It will be an exciting book for both longtime golf fans and those who are new to our sport.

The fan base for PGA TOUR golf continues to grow, both on site at our 100-plus tournaments and via our international broadcasts throughout the year. Our core group of dedicated fans continues to develop and is increasingly being joined by more women, children, and minorities. These new fans are rapidly getting involved in the game, creating new levels of interest in golf.

The PGA TOUR reflects this expansion with nearly 78 international players representing almost 22 countries in our membership this season. More than half of the winners in 2004 hailed from outside the United States. Television extends the TOUR's global reach, with our broadcasts reaching 140 countries and 200 million households with translation into 32 languages.

Through this publication you can learn more about our players, tournaments, courses, television broadcasts, all-time records, the greats of the game, and how the PGA TOUR is structured. Find out who holds the all-time record for 18 holes, which brothers have won on the PGA TOUR, and the 104 members of the World Golf Hall of Fame. It's all in here.

The 2004 PGA TOUR season was as thrilling as any in memory. From Craig Parry's hole-out from the fairway to win a playoff at the Ford Championship at Doral, to Player of the Year Vijay Singh's record-setting year, to pressure-packed major championship victories by Phil Mickelson, Todd Hamilton, and Retief Goosen, 2004 was a year to remember.

Whether it's watching the young stars like 2004 PLAYERS Championship winner Adam Scott or Sergio Garcia or following ageless veterans like Fred Funk and Jay Haas, the level of competition on the PGA TOUR continues to strengthen each year.

The upcoming season promises to continue this surge. The new Tournament Players Club of Louisiana, a classic Pete Dye-designed course, will debut as the site of the Zurich Classic of New Orleans. Congressional Country Club, one of the world's top courses, will be the site of the Booz Allen Classic near Washington, D.C. San Francisco's Harding Park Golf Course, one of the best public facilities in the nation, will be the site of the World Golf Championships-American Express Championship in the fall. The Presidents Cup team competition, which ended in a deadlock in South Africa in late 2003, returns this fall with World Golf Hall of Famers Jack Nicklaus and Gary Player back as captains of the United States and International squads, respectively.

The Champions Tour is the most fan-friendly professional league in all of sports, allowing fans to get closer to the game at tournaments and through tournament broadcasts and by giving game-improvement tips. Two-time U.S. Open champion Curtis Strange and two-time British Open winner Greg Norman lead a group of newcomers who will find stiff competition in 2004 Player of the Year Craig Stadler and 2004 Charles Schwab Cup winner Hale Irwin, among others.

On the Nationwide Tour, fans can see the stars of tomorrow as they prepare during a full season of play. The excellence of the Nationwide Tour is showcased by the fact that five of the 20 graduates of the 2003 Nationwide Tour class won on the PGA TOUR in 2004. Former Nationwide Tour players have won nearly 160 times on the PGA TOUR.

The PGA TOUR is also extremely proud of what our tournaments and players do for charity, with proceeds expected to reach $1 billion by 2006. Fans contribute mightily to this effort, with approximately 80,000 volunteers annually working at our tournaments as marshals, in transportation, with support staff and other areas. The donation of their time allows us to drive significantly more money to charity each week.

Needless to say, we are also focused on entertaining you, the fan, with outstanding tournaments and golf action. Here's hoping you get more involved in our sport through reading this publication and attending or watching the broadcast of many of our outstanding tournaments this year.

I think you will agree with me that the 2005 season promises one of the most dynamic and fascinating seasons in TOUR history.

Sincerely,

Timothy W. Finchem

Timothy W. Finchem
Commissioner
PGA TOUR

2005 PGA TOUR Schedule

DATE	TOURNAMENT	TELEVISION	GOLF COURSE(S)	LOCATION
JAN 3-9	Mercedes Championships ‡	ESPN	Plantation Course at Kapalua	Kapalua, HI
10-16	Sony Open in Hawaii ‡	ESPN	Waialae Country Club	Honolulu, HI
17-23	Buick Invitational ‡	USA/ABC	Torrey Pines Golf Course (**South Course, North Course)	San Diego, CA
24-30	Bob Hope Chrysler Classic ‡	USA/ABC	**PGA West- Palmer Private, Tamarisk CC, LaQuinta CC, Bermuda Dunes CC	La Quinta, CA
31-6	FBR Open ‡	USA/CBS	Tournament Players Club of Scottsdale	Scottsdale, AZ
FEB 7-13	AT&T Pebble Beach National Pro-Am ‡	USA/CBS	"**Pebble Beach Golf Links, Spyglass Hill, Poppy Hills	Pebble Beach, CA
14-20	Nissan Open ‡	USA/ABC	Riviera Country Club	Pacific Palisades, CA
21-27	WGC-Accenture Match Play Championship ‡	ESPN/ABC	La Costa Resort and Spa	Carlsbad, CA
	Chrysler Classic of Tucson ‡	USA	Omni Tucson National Golf Resort and Spa	Tucson, AZ
28-6	Ford Championship at Doral	USA/NBC	Doral Golf Resort and Spa (Blue Course)	Miami, FL
MAR 7-13	The Honda Classic	USA/NBC	Country Club at Mirasol (Sunrise Course)	Palm Beach Gardens, FL
14-20	Bay Hill Invitational presented by MasterCard	USA/NBC	Bay Hill Golf Club and Lodge	Orlando, FL
21-27	THE PLAYERS Championship	ESPN/NBC	Tournament Players Club at Sawgrass	Ponte Vedra Beach, FL
28-3	BellSouth Classic	USA/NBC	Tournament Players Club at Sugarloaf	Duluth, GA
APR 4-10	The Masters	USA/CBS	Augusta National Golf Club	Augusta, GA
11-17	MCI Heritage	USA/CBS	Harbour Town Golf Links	Hilton Head Island, SC
18-24	Shell Houston Open	USA/CBS	Redstone Golf Club (Jacobsen/Hardy Course)	Houston, TX
25-1	Zurich Classic of New Orleans	USA/CBS	Tournament Players Club of Louisiana	Avondale, LA
MAY 2-8	Wachovia Championship	USA/CBS	Quail Hollow Club	Charlotte, NC
9-15	EDS Byron Nelson Championship	USA/CBS	**Tournament Players Course at Four Seasons Resort and Cottonwood Valley	Irving, TX
16-22	Bank of America Colonial	USA/CBS	Colonial Country Club	Fort Worth, TX
23-29	FedEx St. Jude Classic	USA/CBS	Tournament Players Club at Southwind	Memphis, TN
30-5	the Memorial Tournament	ESPN/CBS	Muirfield Village Golf Club	Dublin, OH
JUN 6-12	Booz Allen Classic	USA/ABC	Congressional Country Club (Blue Course)	Potomac, MD
13-19	U. S. Open	ESPN/NBC	Pinehurst Resort (Pinehurst #2 Course)	Pinehurst, NC
20-26	Barclays Classic	USA/ABC	Westchester Country Club	Harrison, NY
27-3	Cialis Western Open	USA/ABC	Cog Hill Golf and Country Club	Lemont, IL
JUL 4-10	John Deere Classic	USA/ABC	Tournament Players Club at Deere Run	Silvis, IL
11-17	British Open	TNT/ABC	St. Andrews Links (Old Course)	St. Andrews, Fife, Scotland
	B. C. Open	USA	En-Joie Golf Club	Endicott, NY
18-24	U.S. Bank Championship in Milwaukee	USA/CBS	Brown Deer Park Golf Course	Milwaukee, WI
25-31	Buick Open	USA/CBS	Warwick Hills Golf and Country Club	Grand Blanc, MI
AUG 1-7	The INTERNATIONAL	USA/CBS	Castle Pines Golf Club	Castle Rock, CO
8-14	PGA Championship	TNT/CBS	Baltusrol Golf Club	Springfield, NJ
15-21	WGC-NEC Invitational	ESPN/CBS	Firestone Country Club (South Course)	Akron, OH
	Reno Tahoe Open	TGC	Montreux Golf and Country Club	Reno, NV
22-28	Buick Championship	USA/CBS	Tournament Players Club at River Highlands	Cromwell, CT
29-5	Deutsche Bank Championship §	USA/ABC	Tournament Players Club of Boston	Norton, MA
SEP 5-11	Bell Canadian Open §	ESPN	Shaughnessy Golf & Country Club	Vancouver, BC, Canada
12-18	84 LUMBER Classic §	ESPN	Nemacolin Woodlands Resort & Spa (Mystic Rock Course)	Farmington, PA
19-25	The Presidents Cup	TNT/NBC	Robert Trent Jones Golf Club	Lake Manassas, VA
	Valero Texas Open §	ESPN	LaCantera Golf Club	San Antonio, TX
26-2	Chrysler Classic of Greensboro §	USA/ABC+	Forest Oaks Country Club	Greensboro, NC
OCT 3-9	WGC-American Express Championship §	ESPN/ABC	Harding Park Golf Course	San Francisco, CA
	Southern Farm Bureau Classic §	TGC	Annandale Golf Club	Madison, MS
10-16	Michelin Championship at Las Vegas §	USA/ABC+	** Tournament Players Club at Summerlin,TPC at The Canyons	Las Vegas, NV
17-23	FUNAI Classic at WALT DISNEY WORLD Resort §	ESPN/ABC+	Walt Disney World Resort (**Magnolia Course, Palm Course)	Lake Buena Vista, FL
24-30	Chrysler Championship §	USA/ABC+	Westin Innisbrook Resort (Copperhead Course)	Tampa Bay, FL
31-6	THE TOUR Championship presented by Coca-Cola §	ESPN/ABC	East Lake Golf Club	Atlanta, GA
NOV 7-13	Franklin Templeton Shootout *	USA/CBS	Tiburon Golf Club	Naples, FL
7-8	Tommy Bahama Challenge (Airs 1/2-6/06) *	CBS	Grayhawk Golf Club	Scottsdale, AZ
14-20	UBS Cup *	TGC	TBD	TBD
	WGC-Algarve World Cup *	ESPN/ABC	The Vilamoura Resort, Victoria Golf Course	Algarve, Portugal
21-27	Merrill Lynch Skins Game *	ABC	Trilogy Golf Club at La Quinta	La Quinta, CA
22-23	PGA Grand Slam of Golf *	TNT	Poipu Bay Golf Course & Hyatt Regency Resort & Spa	Kauai, HI
28-Dec 4	Father/Son Challenge *	NBC	ChampionsGate Golf Course	Orlando, FL
30-Dec 5	PGA TOUR Qualifying Tournament *	TGC	Orange County National Golf Center and Lodge	Orlando, FL
DEC 5-11	Target World Challenge *	USA/ABC	Sherwood Country Club	Thousand Oaks, CA
12-18	Wendy's 3-Tour Challenge (Airs 12/12-18/05) *	ABC	Lake Las Vegas, South Shore Course	Henderson, NV
24-25	ADT Golf Skills Challenge (Airs 12/25-26/05) *	NBC	Trump International	Palm Beach, FL

Television coverage subject to change
WGC is World Golf Championships abbreviated due to space restrictions

* Challenge Event
‡ West Coast Swing presented by Allianz
§ Fall Finish presented by Pricewaterhouse Coopers

\+ Sunday Only
** Host Course

SECTION 1 INTRODUCTION

Champions Tour Tournament Schedule

Champions Tour

DATE		TOURNAMENT	TELEVISION	GOLF COURSE	LOCATION
JAN	17-23	MasterCard Championship	TGC	Hualalai Golf Club	Ka'upulehu-Kona, HI
	24-30	Turtle Bay Championship	TGC	Palmer Course at Turtle Bay Resort	Kahuku, HI
FEB	5-6	Wendy's Champions Skins Game +	ABC	Wailea Resort (Gold Course)	Wailea, HI
	14-20	The ACE Group Classic	TGC	TwinEagles Golf Club	Naples, FL
	21-27	Outback Steakhouse Pro-Am	TGC	TPC of Tampa Bay	Tampa, FL
MAR	7-13	SBC Classic	TGC	Valencia Country Club	Los Angeles, CA
	14-20	Toshiba Senior Classic *	TGC	Newport Beach Country Club	Orange County, CA
APR	18-24	Liberty Mutual Legends of Golf	ESPN/ABC	Westin Savannah Harbor Golf Resort & Spa	Savannah, GA
	25-1	FedEx Kinko's Classic *	TGC	The Hills Country Club	Austin, TX
MAY	9-15	Blue Angels Classic	TGC	The Moors Golf Club	Pensacola, FL
	16-22	Bruno's Memorial Classic *	TGC	Greystone Golf & Country Club	Birmingham, AL
	23-29	Senior PGA Championship	ESPN2/NBC	Laurel Valley Golf Club	Pittsburgh. PA
	30-5	Allianz Championship	TGC	Tournament Club of Iowa	Des Moines, IA
JUN	6-12	Bayer Advantage Classic	TGC	Nicklaus Golf Club at LionsGate	Kansas City, KS
	20-26	Bank of America Championship *	TGC	Nashawtuc Country Club	Boston, MA
	27-3	Commerce Bank Championship	TGC	Red Course at Eisenhower Park	Long Island, NY
JUL	4-10	Ford Senior Players Championship	USA/CBS	TPC of Michigan	Detroit, MI
	18-24	Senior British Open Championship	TNT/ABC	TBD	TBD
	25-31	U.S. Senior Open Championship	ESPN/NBC	NCR Country Club	Dayton, OH
AUG	1-7	3M Championship	TGC	TPC of the Twin Cities	Minneapolis, MN
	15-21	Greater Seattle Champions Classic	TGC	TPC at Snoqualmie Ridge	Seattle, WA
	22-28	JELD-WEN Tradition	TGC	The Reserve Vineyards & Golf Club	Portland, OR
	29-4	The First Tee Open at Pebble Beach presented by Wal-Mart	TGC/NBC	Pebble Beach Golf Links/Bayonet Golf Club	Pebble Beach, CA
SEP	12-18	Constellation Energy Classic *	TGC	Hayfields Country Club	Baltimore, MD
	26-2	SAS Championship	TGC	Prestonwood Country Club	Raleigh, NC
OCT	3-9	Greater Hickory Classic at Rock Barn	TGC	Rock Barn Golf & Spa	Hickory, NC
	10-16	Administaff Small Business Classic	TGC	Augusta Pines Golf Club	Houston, TX
	17-23	SBC Championship	TGC	Oak Hills Country Club	San Antonio, TX
	24-30	Charles Schwab Cup Championship	TGC	Sonoma Golf Club	Sonoma, CA
NOV	14-20	UBS Cup +	TGC	TBD	TBD
	14-21	National Qualifying Tournament Finals +		PGA Southern California Golf Course (Champions)	Riverside, CA
	28-4	Father/Son Challenge +	NBC	ChampionsGate Golf Club (International)	Orlando, FL
DEC	17-18	Wendy's 3-Tour Challenge +	ABC	South Shore Course at Lake Las Vegas	Henderson, NV

* Georgia-Pacific Grand Champions events (5), plus Championship (Site TBD)

\+ Challenge Event

Pebble Beach Golf Links

Nationwide Tour Tournament Schedule

Nationwide Tour

DATE		TOURNAMENT	TELEVISION	GOLF COURSE	LOCATION
JAN	24-30	BellSouth Panama Championship		Club de Golf de Panama	Panama City, Rep. of Panama
FEB	14-20	Jacob's Creek Open	TGC	Royal Adelaide Golf Club	Adelaide, So. Australia, Australia
	21-27	ING New Zealand PGA Championship	TGC	Clearwater Golf Club	Christchurch, New Zealand
MAR	21-27	Chitimacha Louisiana Open presented by Dynamic Industries		Le Triomphe Country Club	Broussard, LA
APR	18-24	Virginia Beach Open presented by ACS Systems & Engineering		TPC at Virginia Beach	Virginia Beach, VA
	25-1	BMW Charity Pro-Am at The Cliffs	TGC	The Cliffs - Valley (Host Course); Keowee Vineyards; Walnut Cove	Greenville, SC
MAY	2-8	Carolina Classic		TPC at Wakefield Plantation	Raleigh, NC
	9-15	Rheem Classic presented by Times Record	TGC	Hardscrabble Country Club	Fort Smith, AR
	16-22	Henrico County Open	TGC	The Dominion Club	Richmond, VA
	23-29	Reese's Cup Classic		Hershey Golf Club	Hershey, PA
	30-5	Chattanooga Classic		Black Creek Club	Chattanooga, TN
JUN	6-12	LaSalle Bank Open	TGC	The Glen Club	Glen View, IL
	13-19	Knoxville Classic presented by Food City		Fox Den Country Club	Knoxville, TN
	20-26	Northeast Pennsylvania Classic		Glenmaura National Golf Club	Scranton, PA
	27-3	Lake Erie Charity Classic	TGC	Peek'n Peak Resort - Upper Course	Findley Lake, NY
JUL	4-10	Pete Dye West Virginia Classic presented by National Mining Association	TGC	Pete Dye Golf Club	Bridgeport, WV
	11-17	Scholarship America Showdown	TGC	Troy Burne Golf Club	Hudson, WI
	18-24	Canadian PGA Championship presented by MasterCard	TGC	Whistle Bear Golf Club	Cambridge, Ontario, Canada
	25-31	Preferred Health Systems Wichita Open		Crestview Country Club	Wichita, KS
AUG	1-7	Cox Classic	TGC	Champions Run Golf Club	Omaha, NE
	8-14	Price Cutter Charity Championship		Highland Springs Country Club	Springfield, MO
	15-21	Xerox Classic	TGC	Irondequiot Country Club	Rochester, NY
	29-4	Alberta Classic	TGC	TBD	Calgary, Alberta, Canada
SEPT	5-11	Envirocare Utah Classic		Willow Creek Country Club	Sandy, UT
	12-18	Mark Christopher Charity Classic presented by Adelphia		Empire Lakes Golf Club	Rancho Cucamonga, CA
	19-25	Albertsons Boise Open presented by First Health	TGC	Hillcrest Country Club	Boise, ID
	26-2	Oregon Classic presented by Kendall Automotive Group		Shadow Hills Country Club	Junction City, OR
OCT	3-9	The Arizona Desert Championship presented by The Executive Council		TBD	Phoenix, AZ
	10-16	Permian Basin Charity Classic		Midland Country Club	Midland, TX
	17-23	Miccosukee Championship	TGC	Miccosukee Golf & Country Club	Miami, FL
	24-30	Nationwide Tour Championship	TGC	TBD	TBD

Tournament Players Club at Wakefield Plantation

What is the PGA TOUR?

The PGA TOUR is a tax-exempt organization composed of professional golfers who play more than 100 tournaments a year on three Tours: the namesake PGA TOUR; Champions Tour, which is for golfers 50 years and older; and the Nationwide Tour. Headquartered in Ponte Vedra Beach, FL, the PGA TOUR was affiliated with the PGA of America until 1968, when the tournament players, who made up a subdivision of the PGA membership, sought to control their finances and schedule and broke away to form the Tournament Players Division. The Tournament Players Division was renamed the PGA TOUR in 1975.

The PGA is different than the PGA TOUR. The PGA is the Professional Golfers' Association of America, a membership organization for the nation's club professionals. The PGA runs the PGA Championship, Senior PGA Championship, and Ryder Cup Matches, among other championships.

• • •

How do you become a member of the PGA TOUR?

Easy. Become one of the 150 or so best players in the world.

Actually, there are five ways to become eligible to compete in events held under the auspices of the TOUR and subject to TOUR regulations: Finish within the top 30 and ties at the annual National Qualifying Tournament; win a co-sponsored or approved TOUR event; finish among the top 150 players on the official money list in a year (through sponsor exemptions, foreign exemptions, open qualifying, or section qualifying); win official money equal to the amount won in the preceding year by the 150th finisher on the official money list; or finish in the top 20 on the official Nationwide Tour money list.

• • •

Is there an age requirement?

If you're 18, then you can join the TOUR. There is no upper-age restriction.

• • •

How do you become a member of the Champions Tour?

Players must be at least 50 years old prior to the first tournament entered. Those eligible for membership or tournament entry include: the top 30 players available from the prior year's money list (with a floor of 50); the top 30 players from the All-Time Money List who are not exempt in the previous category; four players in the Career Victory Category, age 50–51 not otherwise exempt; seven players from the Champions Tour National Qualifying Tournament; five tournament invitees; two players each week through open qualifying.

• • •

How do you become a member of the Nationwide Tour?

The Nationwide Tour has become a great stepping stone to the PGA TOUR. Tour membership and tournament spots can be gained several ways: winning Nationwide Tour co-sponsored events in the last calendar year or during the current year; being a past champion; finishing 21st to 60th on the final official Nationwide Tour money list; reaching the PGA TOUR National Qualifying Tournament finals; being a former exempt PGA TOUR member; being PGA TOUR members 48–49 years old; winning weekly open qualifying; gaining a sponsor exemption; finishing in the top 25 at the previous Nationwide Tour event; possessing veteran member standing on the PGA TOUR or Nationwide Tour.

• • •

What is the Nationwide Tour?

Some players need seasoning before taking on the world's best. Nationwide Tour grads have accounted for 159 PGA TOUR victories since 1990, including major winners like Ernie Els, John Daly, David Duval, Tom Lehman, Jim Furyk, and David Toms.

• • •

What is Monday qualifying?

Most PGA TOUR events conduct a one-day open qualifying round with the four lowest scores earning those players a spot in the tournament. This opening qualifying round is normally held the Monday of tournament week and is open to all professionals and amateurs with a United States Golf Association handicap of no more than two. In conjunction, the PGA of America section holds qualifying for all its section members, with two spots available.

• • •

What is Q-School?

The PGA TOUR National Qualifying Tournament is the process by which professionals have an "open" chance through their performance to gain access to the PGA TOUR. Q-School, as it is also known, is conducted annually in three stages in the final two months of the season. The top 30 places and ties from the final stage (contested over six rounds and 108 holes) gain membership and playing eligibility for the subsequent calendar year on the PGA TOUR. The number of players who advance from the first and second stages (over 72 holes each) is determined by the number of players in the field at that particular site. Entry fees are as follows: first-stage qualifying is $4,500, second-stage qualifying is $4,000, and the final is $3,500. The next 50 or so finishers after the top 30 and ties in the final stage earn Nationwide Tour status. The remainder of those from the final have conditional status on the Nationwide Tour, allowing them to enter Nationwide Tour events after all players ahead of them on the eligibility list have had a chance to enter.

• • •

Does the Champions Tour have its own Q-School?

Yes, the Champions Tour has a separate Qualifying Tournament, which includes two stages. The final also is played over 108 holes. Seven players earn exempt status and eight more get conditional status.

• • •

How are pairings at PGA TOUR tournaments decided?

Groupings are drawn in threesomes for the first two rounds based on categories. They are paired up accordingly. For instance, tournament winners, PGA TOUR Life members, those in the top 25 on the TOUR career money list, and non-members with a TOUR victory would be grouped together. Another category includes former winners of TOUR events and former winners of THE PLAYERS Championship, Masters Tournament, U.S. Open, British Open, and PGA Championship. Members who placed among the top 125 on the previous year's money list, players with 50 or more career cuts, and players within the top 50 on the Official World Golf Ranking would make up another group. Following the cut, unless otherwise determined by the tournament director, groupings are drawn in twosomes in the order of the players' scores, with the lowest scores (leaders) going out last each day.

Champions Tour Player Peter Jacobsen

• • •

How are tournament venues selected?

The local tournament organization that owns the event chooses the golf course on which to hold the competition, but the PGA TOUR must approve its selection. First and foremost, the site must have a non-discriminatory membership policy. The TOUR then looks at a variety of factors including: the quality of the layout strategically and agronomy-wise; size and quality of the practice range; quality of the clubhouse and other structures; flow of holes for competitors who all must walk; its ability to accommodate spectators and parking; and business aspects such as sponsorship, hospitality, and community support.

• • •

How is a golf course set up for a tournament?

Preparation for the tournament begins months in advance when TOUR officials consult with the course superintendent to achieve certain playing conditions. As a general rule, the TOUR always seeks to have a golf course firm and fast during tournament week because these conditions provide for the best challenge and separate good play from poor play. Because of varying strains of grass and other conditions such as weather, there is no uniform grass height. Rough can be nearly non-existent, as it is at Harbour Town Golf Links for the MCI Heritage, or it can be 4–5 inches high, as at Brown Deer Park for the U.S. Bank Championship in Milwaukee. Fairway heights range from about three-eighths to seven-sixteenths of an inch. Greens should roll at about 10 or faster on a Stimpmeter.

• • •

What is a Stimpmeter?

A Stimpmeter is a device first created about 60 years ago by Edward S. Stimpson, a former Massachusetts Amateur champion, to achieve a standard measurement for the speed of greens. Modified by the United States Golf Association in the 1970s, the Stimpmeter is essentially a small aluminum bar ramp 36 inches long and set at an angle of approximately 20 degrees. A ball released about 30 inches from the green is rolled down the ramp and onto the green. The distance that the ball rolls on the green before coming to rest establishes its Stimpmeter reading. If the ball rolls 10 feet, then it is said to be rolling at 10 on the Stimpmeter. The farther a ball rolls, the faster the green speed.

• • •

What about establishing the location of holes on each green?

Two PGA TOUR Rules Officials arrive prior to the tournament to establish the final setup of the course, including prospective hole locations for

THE PLAYERS Championship, Tournament Players Club at Sawgrass

each of the tournament rounds. One official is assigned to the front nine and the other to the back nine. The officials look at the course's design and playing characteristics, such as placement of bunkers, trees, the shape and slope of a green. They then determine hole locations based on what kinds of clubs (short iron, long iron, etc.) the players would be hitting into the green if they drove it in the fairway. The officials identify four optimum hole locations but wait until the day before each round to "cut" the hole. Changing weather conditions, such as wind or rain, can force an official to alter the order of the hole locations or even select a new hole location. By the same token, tee markers, which identify where players must begin each hole, can be changed based on playing conditions. Unlike hole locations, the tee marker locations are determined each morning before the round begins.

• • •

What is the Official World Golf Ranking?

Using a mathematical formula based on factors such as player performance, strength of field at recognized tournaments, and the number of starts a player makes, the Official World Golf Ranking (OWGR) determines an order of the game's professional competitors. At the end of 2004, Vijay Singh was determined by the OWGR to be the No. 1 player in the world. The Official World Golf Ranking helps determine who is eligible to play in marquee events such as World Golf Championships tournaments and the four major championships—the Masters, U.S. Open, British Open, and PGA Championship.

• • •

What is the format of competition at official money PGA TOUR tournaments?

Generally the format is total strokes over 72 holes, but there are exceptions. Some tournaments are contested over 90 holes. The World Golf Championships-Accenture Match Play Championship is contested at match play, meaning a winner is determined by the number of holes he wins against an opponent over 18 holes instead of by the number of strokes attempted. The INTERNATIONAL uses a format called the Modified Stableford System, which awards points for eagles and birdies and subtracts for bogeys and worse. The winner is the player with the most points after 72 holes.

• • •

What are the World Golf Championships?

The four World Golf Championships (WGC) feature players from around the world competing against one another in varied formats (match play, stroke, and team competition). The championships are staged at various venues worldwide, in the U.S. and in countries represented by the International Federation of PGA Tours, which is composed of golf's organizing bodies. WGC events were developed to enhance the competitive structure of professional golf worldwide while preserving the traditions and strengths of the individual Tours and their events. The first three jointly sanctioned championships—the Accenture Match Play Championship, NEC Invitational, and American Express Championship—were launched in 1999. The addition of the World Cup, a two-man team event, debuted in 2000.

• • •

How are purses at PGA TOUR events distributed?

The standard formula for PGA TOUR events provides a first prize of 18 percent of the total purse all the way to 0.200 percent for 70th place. For example, a tournament with a $4-million purse would award $720,000 for first place and $8,000 for 70th place. If more than 70 players make the cut, then the remaining cash is divided among those finishing 70th or lower.

• • •

How is the cut determined?

It varies, depending on the tournament, but at most PGA TOUR events the players with the 70 lowest scores, including ties, after 36 holes advance to the final two rounds and earn a paycheck. At the U.S. Open, it's the low 60 and ties. At The Masters, it's the low 44 scores and ties and any player within 10 shots of the lead. If a player fails to make the cut he doesn't earn a cent.

• • •

How can I purchase tickets to a TOUR event?

You can phone the tournament office or you can buy tickets on-line at PGATOUR.COM by clicking on "Tournaments" and then clicking on the event you want to attend.

• • •

What's the best way to watch a TOUR event in person?

There are several ways to view the golfers during tournament action. Some people prefer to follow one group if it includes one of their favorite players; on the weekend they might just follow the final group, which would include the tournament leader. Others bounce around the golf course to see a variety of players. Still other members of the gallery prefer to sit at one hole and watch all the players come through and see how each handles the challenges of a particular hole. No matter what you choose, remember to remain still upon request by a player, caddie, or marshal; do not talk above a whisper or make startling noises during play; never pick up a golf ball or interfere with the line of play; watch out for errant shots (they do happen); and be respectful of all the competitors no matter to whom you might have an allegiance.

• • •

What am I allowed to bring to a TOUR event?

Start with the premise that you should not bring anything to a golf tournament that you would not be allowed to carry on an airplane. Cameras are usually permitted during practice rounds but strictly prohibited once a tournament begins. Wear proper attire, including hats and good walking shoes and make sure you have essentials like analgesics, bug spray, and sunscreen.

Champions Tour's Mastercard Championship, Hualalai Golf Course

The PGA TOUR is Searching for the Ultimate TOUR Fan!

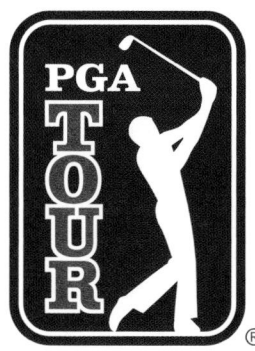

2005 FAN OF THE YEAR

Submit your story TODAY!

We Want to Hear from You!

In 2005, the PGA TOUR will select and recognize a Fan of the Year through a nomination process. Are you the ultimate PGA TOUR fan? Or do you know someone who is? Do you attend TOUR events on a regular basis? Do you watch broadcasts religiously? Has your collection of PGA TOUR memorabilia surpassed your collection of family photos? Has a PGA TOUR event or player had a significant impact on your life? Whatever your experience has been—whether humorous or heart-felt—we want to hear about it!

Nominate Yourself or a Friend.

All you have to do is write us an essay explaining, in 500 words or less, why this person should be selected as the 2005 PGA TOUR Fan of the Year.

How to Submit Your Nomination.

Submit your nomination either:

- On-line at www.PGATOURFanOfTheYear.com, or
- By sending it on a single 8-1/2" x 11" sheet via regular mail to:

  2005 PGA TOUR Fan of the Year
  c/o Tehabi Books
  4920 Carroll Canyon Road, Suite 200
  San Diego, CA 92121

Be sure to include your name, address, phone number, and email address (if available), as well as the same information for the person you are nominating (if not yourself).

Deadline.

Nominations will be accepted between January 17, 2005 and September 30, 2005. All nominations submitted on-line must be received before 5pm (PDT) on September 30, 2005, and nominations submitted via regular mail must be postmarked by September 30, 2005.

Selection Process.

Nominations will be reviewed by a panel and evaluated based on one or more of the following criteria: *passion* (i.e., the ways in which the nominee demonstrates his or her passion for the TOUR and/or TOUR players); *knowledge* (i.e., how the nominee demonstrates and shares his or her knowledge of the TOUR and/or TOUR players); *support* (i.e., the ways in which the nominee supports TOUR events and/or players); and *impact* (i.e., how the nominee's life or golfing experience has been impacted by the TOUR and/or its players). Through this process, the panel will select the top five candidates for the 2005 PGA TOUR Fan of the Year. From these top five candidates, TOUR players will be invited to select the ultimate 2005 Fan of the Year.

Notification and Announcement.

Prior to October 21, 2005, the nominee that is selected as the 2005 PGA TOUR Fan of the Year will be notified and the announcement of the 2005 Fan of the Year will be made at THE TOUR Championship Presented by Coca-Cola in Atlanta, GA, sometime between October 31 and November 6, 2005.

Recognition.

The 2005 PGA TOUR Fan of the Year will be profiled on PGATOUR.COM during the fall of 2005 and featured in the 2006 edition of the *PGA TOUR Official Fan Guide*. Additional media profiles and features on the Fan of the Year will be pursued by the PGA TOUR. The 2005 Fan of the Year will also receive two (2) PGA TOUR VIP Special Guest passes granting the Fan of the Year and a guest either Clubhouse or grounds access to all 2006 PGA TOUR, Champions Tour and Nationwide Tours events.* Passes may be transferred to others throughout 2006.

* Includes PGA TOUR events, Champions Tour, Nationwide Tour, World Golf Championships, and Challenge Season events. Does not include The Masters, U.S. Open, British Open, or PGA Championship. For a full PGA TOUR schedule visit www.PGATOUR.COM.

Official Rules.

HOW TO ENTER: Send 500-word essay nomination on 5" x 7" index card to 2005 PGA TOUR Fan of the Year, c/o Tehabi Books, 4920 Carroll Canyon Road, Suite 200, San Diego, CA 92121 or at www.PGATOURFanOfTheYear.com. Only one nomination per person. Incomplete entries will be disqualified. No correspondence will be entered into. All entries must be received or postmarked by September 30, 2005.

WINNER: No purchase necessary. A purchase will not increase your chance of being selected. The 2005 Fan of the Year will be selected from all eligible entries received. The selected nominee will be notified by mail or e-mail by October 21, 2005 by a representative of Tehabi Books. The nominee selected will be required to complete and return an Affidavit of Eligibility and Liability Release and, where legal, a Publicity Release form within ten days of receipt; or selection and VIP Special Guest passes may be forfeited and awarded to an alternate. Passes are transferable but are not exchangeable for cash. If selection is refused or notification is returned or deemed undeliverable, an alternate winner will be selected.

RULES: Nominees must be at least 18 years old prior to September 30, 2005. Nominees must be legal residents of the United States or Canada. Employees of the PGA TOUR, Inc. and Tehabi Books, Inc., their parents, affiliates, subsidiaries, advertising and promotion agencies, persons living in the same household, and the families of each are not eligible. PGA TOUR and Tehabi Books reserve the right to print the name and story of the selected Fan of the Year in magazines, web sites, and books, take a photo of the selected individual which may be used in such magazines, web sites, and books as well as in advertising and publicity at its sole discretion without further compensation unless prohibited by law. Void where prohibited. All federal, state, and local laws and regulations apply.

CONDITIONS: By submitting a nomination, participants (a) agree to these rules and the decisions of the judges which shall be final in all respects, and (b) release PGA TOUR and Tehabi Books, their respective divisions, subsidiaries, affiliates, and advertising and promotion agencies and their respective directors, officers, and employees from any and all liability for any injuries, losses, or damages of any kind caused by their participation or resulting from acceptance, possession, use, or misuse of the 2006 VIP Special Guest Passes. Noncompliance with the official rules will result in disqualification.

2006 VIP SPECIAL GUEST PASSES: Two (2) PGA TOUR VIP Special Guest passes granting the Fan of the Year and a guest either Clubhouse or grounds access to all 2006 PGA TOUR, Champions Tour, and Nationwide Tours events, excluding The Masters, U.S. Open, British Open, and PGA Championship. Passes may be transferred to others throughout 2006. No substitution permitted. Not redeemable for cash or credit. The failure of the selected Fan of the Year to execute and return an Affidavit of Eligibility/Release within ten (10) days from the date of notification, the return of a notification or a prize as undeliverable, or any other non-compliance with rules and/or conditions will result in a disqualification and the selection of an alternate. Non-compliance within this time period may result in disqualification and forfeiture of Passes.

Year In Review

Defining the dimensions of a dominant season is easier explained than attained. Vijay Singh couldn't be outplayed in 2004 primarily because he couldn't be outworked. The result was a PGA TOUR season that few have matched.

Viewed through the prism of history, Singh's 2004 campaign takes on a notable veneer of magnificence. Since 1916 there have been 27 seasons when one player won at least seven times; 17 men share that distinction. But bringing Singh's season into sharper focus are these facts:

Among those 27 seasons, a player has led in victories, earnings, and stroke average on 13 occasions. Eight men have done it: Harry Cooper, Paul Runyan, Sam Snead, Byron Nelson, Ben Hogan, Arnold Palmer, Tiger Woods, and Singh.

Among that group are six who also won a major championship that year: Runyan, Nelson, Hogan, Palmer, Woods, and Singh.

The oldest among them, by more than five years, is Vijay Singh.

Singh has never seemed constrained by age, just the amount of daylight in which he can pour himself into practice.

However, Singh was not alone in the spotlight.

Phil Mickelson recovered from a sub-par year in 2003 to win the Masters, thanks to five birdies in the final seven holes, including a walk-off birdie at the 72nd hole to end his 0-for-42 streak in the majors. He registered multiple wins in a season for the eighth time, and his 69.16 scoring average, fourth on the TOUR, was more than a stroke better than in 2003.

Ernie Els had a shot to win all four majors, though he won none of them. However, he still captured three titles with marquee wins at the Memorial Tournament and the World Golf Championships-American Express Championship, in addition to defending his Sony Open in Hawaii crown. Els and Mickelson were the lone players to finish in the top-10 in all four majors.

Woods, undergoing swing changes, didn't take a stroke-play event for the first time in his career, but his victory at the WGC-Accenture Match Play Championship extended his string of consecutive years with a win to nine—more than halfway to the record of 17 straight shared by Palmer and Jack Nicklaus.

The PGA TOUR's best rookie, like its Player of the Year, used experience to his advantage. Todd Hamilton, who spent a decade competing in the Far East, won twice, including a marble-jawed playoff triumph over Els at the British Open at Royal Troon. Hamilton and Zach Johnson, who won the BellSouth Classic, became the first two rookies in TOUR history to surpass $2 million in earnings. Andre Stolz, who won the Michelin Championship at Las Vegas, Vaughn Taylor (Reno-Tahoe Open), and Ryan Palmer (FUNAI Classic at WALT DISNEY WORLD Resort) joined in to set a TOUR record for rookie victories. Palmer's 62 at Disney was the low final round by a winner.

Golf's contemporary Ice Mon, Retief Goosen, won multiple titles on the TOUR for the first time, and his timing was good, finishing first at the U.S. Open and THE TOUR Championship presented by Coca-Cola. The quiet South African became the 21st player to win at least two U.S. Open titles after finishing two strokes ahead of Mickelson at sinister and sun-baked Shinnecock Hills Golf Club.

The youngest player to win was Adam Scott, who, at 23, captured THE PLAYERS Championship after getting short-game lessons from his idol, fellow Aussie Greg Norman. Further accolades were earned when Scott fired a TOUR-best 128 over the first 36 holes on the way to the Booz Allen Classic crown.

At 48, Fred Funk was the oldest winner at the Southern Farm Bureau Classic, which marked his first victory since winning the same event in 1998.

Speaking of victory gaps, John Daly hadn't won since the 1995 British Open before he beat Luke Donald and Chris Riley in a playoff at the Buick Invitational. Daly, the Comeback Player of the Year, arrived at the Buick Invitational ranked 299th in the world. After tying his career-high with five top-10s, Daly ended the official season ranked 43rd.

Joey Sindelar won the Wachovia Championship in a playoff over Arron Oberholser for his first victory since 1990, ending a string of 370 tournaments.

Brent Geiberger's victory at the Chrysler Classic of Greensboro made him and his father Al the first father-son tandem to win the same tournament in modern history. In winning the Valero Texas Open, Bart Bryant joined his brother Brad in the victory column, marking the 11th brother duo to win on the TOUR.

Player of the Year Vijay Singh was one of four players to repeat as statistical leaders. Hank Kuehne was the longest driver again, averaging 314.4 yards, Funk won his third straight driving-accuracy crown (and seventh overall), and Joe Durant repeated as leader in greens in regulation. Stewart Cink led the TOUR in putting and became the first player to use a non-traditional length putter and win that title. A record 77 players earned at least $1 million.

International players claimed the upper hand on American soil for the majority of the year. Foreign-born players won 26 of the 48 official money events on the PGA TOUR, and Europe registered a record-tying 9–point victory in the 35th Ryder Cup matches at Oakland Hills Country Club in Bloomfield Hills, MI. The shot of the year belonged to an Aussie: At the Ford Championship at Doral, Craig Parry holed out for eagle with a 6-iron from 176 yards to defeat Scott Verplank on the first sudden-death playoff hole. The top 125 money winners, who earned full exemptions for 2005, included players from 17 countries.

Phil Mickelson (far left) came back from a mediocre 2003 to win his first major, the 2004 Masters.

Tiger Woods (above) had a challenging year with only one win, the World Golf Championships-Accenture Match Play Championship.

Vijay Singh (left), PGA TOUR Player of the Year, had nine victories and over $10 million in earnings, a PGA TOUR record.

Year In Review

Craig Stadler established himself as the man to beat on the Champions Tour in 2005. Hale Irwin, who for years entrenched himself in that role, dug deep in the closing weeks to make foes aware that he shouldn't be overlooked or forgotten.

Stadler, a former Masters champion, won the Jack Nicklaus Trophy as the Champions Tour Player of Year on the strength of five victories, including his second major title and a career-high $2,306,066 in earnings, which won him the Arnold Palmer Award as the leading money winner, and the Byron Nelson Award for low-stroke average. Among his victories was the inaugural First Tee Open held at Pebble Beach. At 51, Stadler became the third player to win money titles on both the PGA TOUR and the Champions Tour. Lee Trevino is the only other man to pull off this feat.

Irwin, however, wasn't about to let Stadler claim all the goodies on the Champions Tour. Irwin, who turned 59 in June, added to his career victory record by winning twice in 2004, including his fourth Senior PGA Championship. Furthermore, despite a neck injury late in the season, Irwin had 14 top-10s, including consecutive second-place finishes, to claim his second Charles Schwab Cup, the year-long bonus competition worth $2.1 million in annuities to its five leaders. Irwin edged Stadler by a mere 39 points, with the competition coming down to the final hole of the final round of the season-ending Charles Schwab Cup Championship.

"The caliber of play on the Tour this year has been spectacular," Irwin, who won a $1 million annuity, said. "If you're intending to keep up with that play, you have to step on it yourself."

For a decade Irwin has been senior golf's bellweather. His $2,035,397 in earnings gave him seven seasons of at least $2 million in prize money. His victory total stands at 40 after completing his record 10th season with multiple victories; no one else had done that more than six times. After 10 seasons on the Champions Tour, the three-time U.S. Open winner has played in 228 events and 722 rounds. Nearly half his finishes (98) have been in the top three while his top-10s number 168—nearly three-quarters of the time.

A marathon five-day affair at the Senior PGA Championship at weather-plagued Valhalla Golf Club in Louisville, KY, saw Irwin outlast rookie Jay Haas, who, at 50 years old, played

In 2004, Craig Stadler (far left) became only the second golfer in history to win money titles on both the PGA TOUR and the Champions Tour.

Hale Irwin (top) won two Champions Tour events in 2004, including the Senior PGA Championship.

Mark McNulty (left) won three Champions Tour events in 2004, his rookie year.

Peter Jacobsen (above), another rookie, won the U.S. Senior Open only eight weeks after hip surgery.

well enough to make the Ryder Cup team and finish among the top 30 money winners on the PGA TOUR. Irwin, who had a Tour-best 40 rounds in the 60s in 2004, was three days shy of his 59th birthday when he won his seventh senior major and became the oldest man to win a major title on the Champions Tour.

Stadler distinguished himself with the lowest stroke average on the Champions Tour and five wins, including a come-from-behind triumph at the JELD-WEN Tradition that featured a rare double-eagle in the third round and four straight birdies to end the final round. He won three straight events in the fall, the first man to do that since Gil Morgan in 1997. Also of note: he and his son Kevin became only the second father-son duo (after Bob and David Duval in 1999) to win PGA TOUR-sponsored tournaments on the same day. In June, father won the Bank of America Championship and son claimed a playoff victory in the Nationwide Tour's Lake Erie Charity Classic.

Stadler and Irwin were among six multiple winners on the Champions Tour in 2004, one more than the 2003 total, while overall 20 different players posted wins.

Rookie Mark McNulty became the first international player since David Graham in 1997 to win three Champions Tour titles. He closed the year with consecutive triumphs at the SBC Championship and the Charles Schwab Cup Championship. The Zimbabwe native also won the Outback Steakhouse Pro-Am in his Champions Tour debut. He jumped to fifth in the final Schwab Cup race behind Irwin, Stadler, Tom Kite, and Peter Jacobsen.

McNulty was one of four rookies to triumph—but the others, Jacobsen, Mark James, and Pete Oakley, all won majors.

Jacobsen was the surprise winner of the U.S. Senior Open at Bellerive Country Club in St. Louis. A versatile personality, Jacobsen was only eight weeks removed from hip surgery when he survived a 36-hole final day in searing heat to edge Kite.

Another rookie, Oakley, was an even more unlikely major winner. He held off Kite, Eduardo Romero, and James to win the Senior British Open by one stroke at Royal Portrush in Northern Ireland. England's James had won the Ford Senior Players Championship at the Tournament Players Club of Michigan two weeks before. A club pro from Rehoboth Beach, DE, Oakley became the first qualifier in the tournament's 18-year history to capture the title.

Tom Purtzer was the only player to successfully defend a statistical title when he led again in driving distance. D. A. Weibring rang up a Tour-best 15 top-10 finishes.

Dana Quigley and Graham Marsh were the Champions Tour ironmen, each playing all 30 events. This is nothing new to Quigley, who has played in every event for the last seven years and takes a streak of 262 starts into 2005.

Nationwide Tour

Year In Review

The skill level of professional golfers seems to be on a perpetual rise, and competition has become as exceptionally fierce. One needed only to watch the Nationwide Tour in 2004 for proof of that.

The PGA TOUR-sponsored circuit was founded in 1990 and continues to attract many of the world's most promising performers. A record 372 players earned money on the Nationwide Tour in 2004—the fifth straight year the number of money winners increased from the year prior. That figure was just two short of the PGA TOUR record of 374 players who cashed a check in 1996.

Though only the top twenty money winners earned their PGA TOUR cards for 2005, a number of players distinguished themselves with bursts of brilliance or with season-long displays of skill and steadiness.

While leading money-winner and Player of the Year Jimmy Walker, who led the Tour with $371,346, didn't come close to Zach Johnson's $494,882 haul from last year, he was one of a record five players to earn at least $300,000. Eighteen players earned more than $200,000, and the amount of cash required to earn the last of the 20 automatic berths on the PGA TOUR jumped by nearly $20,000. Still another record 60 men won at least $100,000.

Walker, in his second full year on the Nationwide Tour, was one of five multiple winners, with titles at the season-opening BellSouth Panama Championship and the Chitimacha Louisiana Open. At age 25, the San Antonio resident became the second-youngest player to win Player of the Year honors. Stewart Cink was 23 when he won the award in 1996.

A few former PGA TOUR members set significant statistical records. Scott Gump established the Nationwide Tour's driving accuracy standard by hitting 81.4 percent of his fairways in 2004. Jeff Gove bettered the record for greens in regulation by reaching them 74.3 percent of the time.

Daniel Chopra set an all-time Nationwide Tour mark when his 30-under-par won the Henrico Country Open. The Swede, 31, was a member of the PGA TOUR who made three Nationwide Tour starts and won two of them, including his Henrico heroics.

Records were set just about any way imaginable. Paul Gow didn't win a tournament in 2004, but his three losses in playoffs tied the all-time mark set by Franklin Langham in 1995. Bubba Watson hit the longest recorded drive in Nationwide Tour history with a 422-yard blast at the Gila River Golf Classic.

Five of this year's graduating class are moving up for the second time via season earnings: Langham (who led the Nationwide Tour in scoring with a 69.80 stroke average), Gow, Darron Stiles, Michael Long, and Gavin Coles. Among the 10 first-time TOUR qualifiers, three started the year with no status at all on the Nationwide Tour: Brendan Jones, Kevin Stadler, and Euan Walters.

Stadler, the son of former Masters champion Craig Stadler, was one of the chief newsmakers on the Tour. In late June, Stadler, 24, of Scottsdale, AZ, won the Lake Erie Charity Classic in a four-hole playoff not long after his dad completed a rally from four strokes back with a final-round 64 to capture the Bank of America Championship. They became the second father-son duo to win PGA TOUR-sponsored tournaments the same day, following Bob and David Duval in 1999.

Golf legend Jack Nicklaus played a handful of tournaments in 2004, but he again competed on all three tours, including his second start in the BMW Charity Pro-Am at The Cliffs in Greenville, SC. This time fellow Champions Tour member and close friend Gary Player joined him.

Paul Claxton was the Tour's ironman, playing 100 rounds by making 22 of 28 cuts. Stiles had the most top-ten finishes with nine and the most rounds in the 60s (43). Still more proof that the competition is as fierce as ever.

Jimmy Walker (left) is the second-youngest player to win Player of the Year honors on the Nationwide Tour.

Kevin Stadler (above) and his dad, Champions Tour Player of the Year Craig Stadler, in 2004 became only the second father-son duo to win PGA TOUR-sponsored events in the same day.

Paul Claxton (below) played 100 rounds in 2004, making 22 out of 28 cuts on the Nationwide Tour.

2004 Nationwide Tour Champions	
BellSouth Panama Championship	Jimmy Walker
Jacob's Creek Open Championship	Euan Walters
New Zealand PGA Championship	Gavin Coles
Chitimacha Louisiana Open	Jimmy Walker
First Tee Arkansas Classic	Daniel Chopra
Rheem Classic	Franklin Langham
BMW Charity Pro-Am at The Cliffs	Ryuji Imada
Chattanooga Classic	Justin Bolli
Henrico County Open	Daniel Chopra
SAS Carolina Classic	Chris Anderson
Knoxville Open	Hunter Haas
LaSalle Bank Open	Brendan Jones
Northeast Pennsylvania Classic	D.A. Points
Lake Erie Charity Classic	Kevin Stadler
The Reese's Cup Classic	Ben Bates
Scholarship America Showdown	Kevin Stadler
Pete Dye West Virginia Classic	D.A. Points
Samsung Canadian PGA Championship	Charles Warren
Preferred Health Systems Wichita Open	Bradley Hughes
Cox Classic	Charles Warren
Price Cutter Charity Championship	Brad Ott
Alberta Classic	David Hearn
Envirocare Utah Classic	Brett Wetterich
Virginia Beach Open	James Driscoll
Oregon Classic	Jeff Quinney
Albertsons Boise Open	Scott Gump
Mark Christopher Charity Classic	Scott Dunlap
Gila River Golf Classic	Chris Nallen
Permian Basin Charity Golf Classic	Charley Hoffman
Miccosukee Championship	D.J. Trahan
Nationwide Tour Championship presented by Hyundai	Nick Watney

2004 Players of the Year

Jack Nicklaus Trophy

The Jack Nicklaus Trophy is presented annually to the Player of the Year on each of the three Tours: the PGA TOUR, the Champions Tour, and the Nationwide Tour. Winners are determined by a vote of the eligible membership of those Tours. An eligible member of the PGA TOUR is defined as any player who has competed in a minimum of 15 events. Voting privileges on the Champions Tour and Nationwide Tour require at least 12 starts. Players are restricted to voting only on the Tour(s) for which they are members.

PGA TOUR	
1990	Wayne Levi
1991	Fred Couples
1992	Fred Couples
1993	Nick Price
1994	Nick Price
1995	Greg Norman
1996	Tom Lehman
1997	Tiger Woods
1998	Mark O'Meara
1999	Tiger Woods
2000	Tiger Woods
2001	Tiger Woods
2002	Tiger Woods
2003	Tiger Woods
2004	Vijay Singh

Champions Tour	
1990	Lee Trevino
1991	Mike Hill/George Archer
1992	Lee Trevino
1993	Dave Stockton
1994	Lee Trevino
1995	Jim Colbert
1996	Jim Colbert
1997	Hale Irwin
1998	Hale Irwin
1999	Bruce Fleisher
2000	Larry Nelson
2001	Allen Doyle
2002	Hale Irwin
2003	Tom Watson
2004	Craig Stadler

Nationwide Tour	
1990	Jeff Maggert
1991	Tom Lehman
1992	John Flannery
1993	Sean Murphy
1994	Chris Perry
1995	Jerry Kelly
1996	Stewart Cink
1997	Chris Smith
1998	Bob Burns
1999	Carl Paulson
2000	Spike McRoy
2001	Chad Campbell
2002	Patrick Moore
2003	Zach Johnson
2004	Jimmy Walker

PGA TOUR Player of the Year

Vijay Singh

Seldom does a player enjoy as much success as Vijay Singh did in 2004, and rarer still is a golfer of his age assembling one of the great seasons in PGA TOUR history—a season remarkable for more than just the record $10,905,166 he earned in his 29 starts.

Turning 41 in February, the native of Fiji won nine times, including the PGA Championship, his third major title. The nine victories equal the fifth-best season record since 1916. Singh is the only player in his 40s to accomplish the feat.

Singh's victories include six titles in eight weeks. In addition to his second straight money title, Singh won his first Byron Nelson Award for lowest adjusted stroke average, 68.84. He also led the TOUR in top-10 finishes, with 18.

For his astounding consistency Singh was rewarded with the ultimate affirmation of his standing in the game: overtaking Woods as the No. 1 player in the Official World Golf Ranking to break Woods' 334-week stranglehold on the position.

"You don't wake up one day and think you're going to be able to play like I did this year," Singh, of Ponte Vedra Beach, FL, said. "It's a build-up to it. You win one and then you win another one. You get more confident, like snowballing. You can't wait for the next hole and to play better. That's how it's been. I can't wait for the next year to start."

Champions Tour Player of the Year

Craig Stadler

With earnings of $2,306,066, Stadler became the third man in history—and the second in as many years after Tom Watson—to win a money title on both the PGA TOUR and Champions Tour.

The former Masters champion won five times among a dozen top-10 finishes in 2004, but a three-week, late-summer stretch undoubtedly sealed top honors for Stadler, 51, of Evergreen, CO. He earned his second Champions Tour major title when he closed with four straight birdies to capture the JELD-WEN Tradition, a victory memorable for a rare double eagle at the par-5 16th hole in the third round. The following week The Walrus captured the inaugural First Tee Open at Pebble Beach presented by Wal-Mart, and then he posted a wire-to-wire victory at the SAS Championship. No one had won three straight tournaments since Gil Morgan in 1997. The latter win was his ninth title in 14 months, including the 2003 B.C. Open on the PGA TOUR.

Stadler's other conquests included a playoff victory at The ACE Group Classic and the Bank of America Championship, which came on the same day that his son Kevin claimed the Nationwide Tour's Lake Erie Charity Classic. That made the Stadlers the second father-son duo to win on the same day in PGA TOUR-sponsored tournaments.

Statistics reveal Stadler's year-round consistency. He placed first in scoring average, at 69.30, birdies, eagles, and the all-around category. He was second in total driving, fourth in greens in regulation, and a close second to Hale Irwin in the Charles Schwab Cup race.

Nationwide Tour Player of the Year

Jimmy Walker

A victory in the season-opening BellSouth Panama Championship was a harbinger of things to come for Jimmy Walker, who at the end of the year found himself in a similar position–atop the Nationwide Tour.

"If you would have told me at the beginning of the year that this was going to happen," Walker said, "I would have taken it, said 'thanks a lot' and run with it. But it was fun to go through it, and I wouldn't have changed anything."

In only his second year on the Nationwide Tour, Walker, 25, of San Antonio, TX, was the leading money winner, with $371,346, and won twice among his seven top-10 finishes. A former Baylor University All-American, Walker also won the first domestic event of the year, the Chitimacha Louisiana Open. He added a pair of runner-up finishes at the Virginia Beach Open and the Albertsons Boise Open.

Previously a winner on the Gateway Tour and Tight Lies Tour, Walker is the 15th player to earn Nationwide Tour Player of the Year honors. In 2005 he faces the challenge of upholding a proud tradition: 10 of the previous 14 Players of the Year have gone on to win on the PGA TOUR. "I think it's pretty big footsteps to follow. It shows the depth of the Nationwide Tour and what we're about," said Walker, who finished tied for 52nd in his only U.S. Open appearance in 2001. "I look forward to continuing the tradition of playing well out there and keeping it going."

The underpinning to Walker's season, which included making 20 of 25 cuts, was his rank of second in the all-around stats category. He also ranked fifth in scoring average, at 70.06, and was among the leaders in birdies and eagles. In all, Walker ranked among the top 10 in 15 statistical categories.

2004 Wall of Champions

PGA TOUR

Stuart Appleby
Mercedes Championships

Ernie Els
Sony Open in Hawaii

Phil Mickelson
Bob Hope Chrysler Classic

Jonathan Kaye
FBR Open

Vijay Singh
AT&T Pebble Beach National Pro-Am

John Daly
Buick Invitational

Mike Weir
Nissan Open

Tiger Woods
WGC-Accenture Match Play Championship

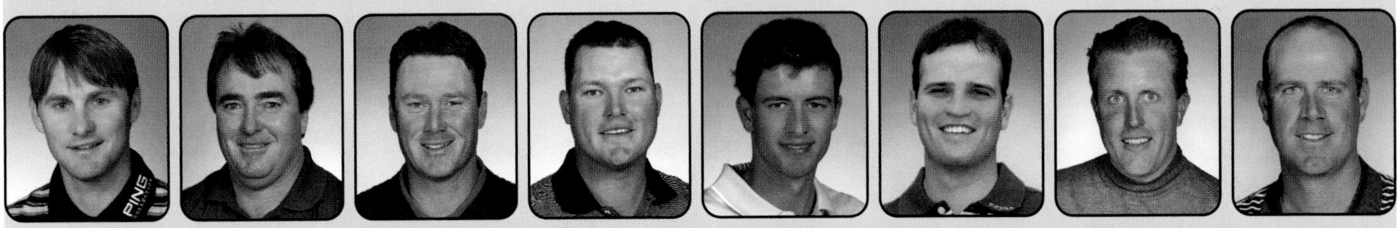

Heath Slocum
Chrysler Classic of Tucson

Craig Parry
Ford Championship at Doral

Todd Hamilton
The Honda Classic

Chad Campbell
Bay Hill Invitational presented by MasterCard

Adam Scott
THE PLAYERS Championship

Zach Johnson
BellSouth Classic

Phil Mickelson
The Masters

Stewart Cink
MCI Heritage

Vijay Singh
Shell Houston Open

Vijay Singh
Zurich Classic of New Orleans

Joey Sindelar
Wachovia Championship

Sergio Garcia
EDS Byron Nelson Championship

Steve Flesch
Bank of America Colonial

David Toms
FedEx St. Jude Classic

Ernie Els
the Memorial Tournament

Sergio Garcia
Barclays Classic

Retief Goosen
U.S. Open

Adam Scott
Booz Allen Classic

Stephen Ames
Cialis Western Open

Mark Hensby
John Deere Classic

Todd Hamilton
British Open

Jonathan Byrd
B.C. Open

Carlos Franco
U.S. Bank Championship in Milwaukee

Vijay Singh
Buick Open

Rod Pampling
The INTERNATIONAL

Vijay Singh
PGA Championship

Stewart Cink
WGC-NEC Invitational

Vaughn Taylor
Reno-Tahoe Open

Woody Austin
Buick Championship

Vijay Singh
Deutsche Bank Championship

Vijay Singh
Bell Canadian Open

Bart Bryant
Valero Texas Open

Vijay Singh
84 LUMBER Classic

Ernie Els
WGC-American Express Championship

Fred Funk
Southern Farm Bureau Classic

Andre Stolz
Michelin Championship at Las Vegas

Brent Geiberger
Chrysler Classic of Greensboro

Ryan Palmer
FUNAI Classic at WALT DISNEY WORLD Resort

Vijay Singh
Chrysler Championship

Retief Goosen
THE TOUR Championship presented by Coca-Cola

2004 Wall of Champions

CHAMPIONS TOUR

Fuzzy Zoeller
MasterCard Championship

Bruce Fleisher
Royal Caribbean Golf Classic

Craig Stadler
The ACE Group Classic

Mark McNulty
Outback Steakhouse Pro-Am

Ed Fiori
MasterCard Classic

Gil Morgan
SBC Classic

Tom Purtzer
Toshiba Senior Classic

Tom Jenkins
Blue Angels Classic

Hale Irwin
Liberty Mutual Legends of Golf

Bruce Fleisher
Bruno's Memorial Classic

Larry Nelson
FedEx Kinko's Classic

D.A. Weibring
Allianz Championship

Hale Irwin
Senior PGA Championship

Jim Thorpe
Farmers Charity Classic

Allen Doyle
Bayer Advantage Celebrity Pro-Am

Craig Stadler
Bank of America Championship

Jim Thorpe
Commerce Bank Long Island Classic

Mark James
Ford Senior Players Championship

Pete Oakley
Senior British Open

Peter Jacobsen
U.S. Senior Open

Tom Kite
3M Championship

Doug Tewell
Greater Hickory Classic at Rock Barn

Craig Stadler
JELD-WEN Tradition

Craig Stadler
The First Tee Open at Pebble Beach presented by Wal-Mart

Bruce Summerhays
Kroger Classic

Craig Stadler
SAS Championship

Wayne Levi
Constellation Energy Classic

Larry Nelson
Administaff Small Business Classic

Mark McNulty
SBC Championship

Mark McNulty
Charles Schwab Cup Championship

Nationwide Tour Graduates

The latest class of Nationwide Tour graduates includes 10 newcomers to the PGA TOUR and 10 who have had at least one year of experience at golf's elite level. They range in age from 22-year-old Nick Watney to three players who are 36 years old—Gavin Coles, Franklin Langham, and Michael Long—and they hail from four different countries, including 13 from the U.S. Fifteen logged victories in 2004, including University of Georgia attendees Langham, Ryuji Imada, and Justin Bolli. Together they accounted for 19 triumphs.

Jimmy Walker, 25 events, $371,346

In his second full season, Walker, age 25, of San Antonio, TX, won the season-opening BellSouth Panama Championship and the Chitimacha Louisiana Open. He added a pair of seconds and finished in the top-10 seven times while making 20 cuts. Best statistical categories were All-Around (second) and scoring (fifth, with a 70.06 average). Other notable achievements include finishing tied for 58th at the 2001 U.S. Open and victories on the Gateway Tour and Tight Lies Tour. A former All-American at Baylor University, Walker learned the game from his father, who was a scratch golfer. He joins the PGA TOUR for the first time.

D.A. Points, 24, $332,815

Twice a winner in a three-week span with victories at the Northeast Pennsylvania Classic and the Pete Dye West Virginia Classic, Points, of Orlando, FL, gained his PGA TOUR card for the first time. The 28-year-old had four top-10 finishes, including runner-up at the LaSalle Bank Open the week prior to his victory run. He led the Tour with a 4.38 birdie average. A third-team All-American at the University of Illinois, Points lost to eventual winner Tiger Woods in the quarterfinals of the 1996 U.S. Amateur. Other professional credits include victory at the 2001 Inland Empire Open in his rookie season.

Ryuji Imada, 24, $313,185

Imada broke through to earn his first PGA TOUR card in his fifth season on the Nationwide Tour, thanks to his second career win in a playoff at the BMW Charity Pro-Am at The Cliffs, three other top-three finishes, and seven top-10s. A native of Japan now residing in Tampa, FL, Imada finished fourth in scoring average, with a career-best 70.00 average. He ranked first in scrambling, and his season earnings were more than double his previous best year. He is a former All-American at the University of Georgia, where he helped the Bulldogs win the 1999 NCAA Division I title.

Franklin Langham, 23, $312,896

The graduate with the most PGA TOUR experience played like a veteran in 2004. Langham, 36, of Peachtree City, GA, shot a career-low 61 on the way to his second Nationwide Tour victory at the Rheem Classic, and he added seven other top-10s (with two second places) and 13 top-25s. A member of the PGA TOUR for six seasons with four career second-place finishes and one Masters berth, Langham led the Nationwide Tour in stroke average at 69.80, was second in greens in regulation, third in putting, and finished in the top 10 in 14 statistical categories in all.

Nick Watney, 25, $301, 988

The youngest of the Nationwide Tour grads, Watney, 22, made the cut in 15 of his last 16 starts and capped his rookie season by finishing second at the Miccosukee Championship and first at the Nationwide Tour Championship with a combined score of 29-under par. A native of Sacramento, CA, Watney ended up with eight top-10 finishes, 11 top-25s, and was second on Tour in total driving. Before turning professional, Watney was a three-time All-American at Fresno State University, where his uncle Mike was the coach. Watney was also Western Athletic Conference Player of the Year a record three times.

Brendan Jones, 8, $292,714

A native of Canberra, Australia, Jones appeared on five tours in 2004 and made the most of his opportunities. He won twice in Japan to double his career total there. Though he missed the cut in his first appearances in the U.S. Open, British Open, and PGA Championship, Jones, 29, truly excelled on the Nationwide Tour, with five finishes among the top four—three of them seconds—as well as a victory at the LaSalle Bank Open. He lacked enough starts to be ranked in the Nationwide Tour statistical categories but would have placed among the top 40 in driving distance, greens in regulation, and putting.

James Driscoll, 24, $281,161

Some prominent amateur near-misses haven't carried over to Driscoll's professional career. He's embarking on his first trip to the PGA TOUR after winning the Virginia Beach Open, among 12 top-25 finishes in 24 Nationwide Tour starts. A former University of Virginia All-American, Driscoll, 27, of Brookline, MA, had five top-four finishes, highlighted by a 65-63 weekend at the Henrico County Open, tied-for low-final 36 holes of 2004. He ranked fifth in birdie conversion percentage. Driscoll was runner-up in the 2000 U.S. Amateur, but the consolation prize was a berth in the 2001 Masters.

Charles Warren, 26, $275,138

Warren returns to the PGA TOUR for the first time since 1999 after a stellar two-win Nationwide Tour campaign in which he won back-to-back starts, only the eighth man to turn the trick. His seven-stroke win at the Samsung Canadian PGA Championship was the second-largest winning margin of the season. The following week the Columbia, SC, resident captured the Cox Classic. His victories extended an odd streak: eight years in a row that a Clemson alumnus has won a Nationwide Tour title. Warren, 29, ranked sixth in total driving and ninth in bounce-back and ball-striking in 2004.

Justin Bolli, 26, $273,387

Never taking no for an answer, Bolli, who walked onto the University of Georgia golf team three times, earned his PGA TOUR card in his first full season on the Nationwide Tour. The leader in the all-around ranking and second in eagles, Bolli, 28, had the second most top-10 finishes (eight), including the Chattanooga Classic title that was won with a 63-65—128 weekend that tied for low final 36 holes of the year. Bolli, a fitness devotee from Roswell, GA, also lost a playoff at the Knoxville Open, and was third at the First Tee Arkansas Classic.

Brett Wetterich, 28, $253,637

Putting on golf's version of a finishing kick, Wetterich earned more than half his money in his final eight starts, with a victory in late August at the Envirocare Utah Classic and second place at the Nationwide Tour Championship, which lifted him 13 spots. A member of the PGA TOUR from 2000–02, Wetterich, 31, of Palm Beach Gardens, FL, had five top-10s while finishing in the money 16 times. The Wallace State Community College alumni finished second in total eagles and third in driving distance, averaging 315.9 yards. He first qualified for the PGA TOUR at the 1999 National Qualifying Tournament.

Nationwide Tour Graduates

Paul Gow, 27, $247,218

This rugby enthusiast got involved in several scrums that resulted in three second-place finishes and helped him achieve a return to the PGA TOUR. Gow, 34, of Sydney, Australia, has three years' experience on the TOUR (2001–03), with a second place at the B.C. Open his best effort. The Nationwide Tour leader in sand saves, Gow had seven top-10s, including playoff losses at the BMW Charity Pro-Am at The Cliffs, SAS Carolina Classic, and The Reese's Cup Classic. Recovered from a bout of vertigo, this two-time Nationwide Tour champ set the Australian PGA scoring record with a 60 at the 2001 Canon Challenge.

Bradley Hughes, 26, $233,968

An Australian native living in Farmington, CT, Hughes, 34, has experience on every major tour in the world. With a win and a runner-up on the 2004 Nationwide Tour, he returns to the PGA TOUR, where he played full-time from 1997–2002. A winner of five international titles with experience in The Presidents Cup and World Cup, Hughes won the Preferred Health Systems Wichita Open. His statistical strengths came in total driving (ranked fourth) and greens in regulation (fifth).

Kevin Stadler, 13, $228,001

The son of former Masters champion Craig Stadler had a busy but productive rookie season that included two victories and 11 top-10s. Stadler, 24, of Scottsdale, AZ, followed his father's win on the Champions Tour with a playoff victory in his first start at the Lake Erie Charity Classic, making them the second father-son duo to win PGA TOUR-sponsored tournaments the same day. Including a 65th at the U.S. Open, Stadler made four of five cuts on the PGA TOUR. His Scholarship America Showdown win also came after a playoff. A product of USC, Stadler led the Nationwide Tour in putting average.

Euan Walters, 20, $213,554

Driving distance is closely watched in the upper echelon of professional golf, but Walters, 34, of Melbourne, Australia, ranked only 143rd in that category on the Nationwide Tour. Fortunately, he was seventh most accurate off the tee. Even more fortunate was his decision to drive a car with 250,000 miles on it from Sydney to Adelaide to enter the Jacob's Creek Open Championship. A professional for a decade, Walters collected a Tour record $145,587 when he won it, then he tied for fifth the next week at the New Zealand PGA Championship to essentially sew up his first PGA TOUR card.

Darron Stiles, 27, $212,894

Stiles, who has three career victories on the Nationwide Tour, returns to the PGA TOUR after a one-year hiatus, thanks to a season that didn't include a win but was among the most consistent. Stiles, 31, of Asheville, NC, notched a Tour-high nine top-10 finishes, including third at the Pete Dye West Virginia Classic. Third in scoring and fourth in the All-Around category, the former All-American at Division II Florida Southern University knows about rebounds. In 1989 Stiles underwent successful surgery to remove a cancerous tumor from his jaw and then had bone grafted from his hip to repair it.

Hunter Haas, 27, $212,065

One of seven golfing siblings, Haas, 27, of Dallas, TX, gears up for his second PGA TOUR campaign, thanks primarily to a Nationwide Tour season featuring disparate playoff results: a victory in the Knoxville Open and a loss six weeks later at the Preferred Health Systems Wichita Open. A University of Oklahoma product, Haas won the 1999 U.S. Public Links Championship to qualify for the Masters. The following week he won the prestigious Porter Cup. Haas, a TOUR member in 2001, ranked second in scrambling, and sixth in total birdies in 2004 while collecting five top-10s and 22 checks in 27 tournaments.

Scott Gutschewski, 25, $206,308

Five top-five finishes, including three in his last five starts, pushed Gutschewski over the top and onto the PGA TOUR. A University of Nebraska product who lives in Omaha, Gutschewski, 28, came close to a second Nationwide Tour victory when he placed second at the Mark Christopher Charity Classic. Gutschewski, who was introduced to the game by his father and grandfather, has played professionally since 1999. His 17 eagles led the Nationwide Tour, thanks to his strength off the tee (he ranked fifth in total driving, sixth in driving distance at 309.6). He ranked 11th in the all-around category.

Chris Anderson, 25, $203,794

The 12th-year pro returns to the PGA TOUR for a second time after a breakout Nationwide Tour season that included a marathon eight-hole playoff victory in the SAS Carolina Classic. Anderson, 34, of Covina, CA, added a tie for second at the Chattanooga Classic after having never finished higher than seventh in his Nationwide Tour career. His eight top-25s more than doubled his career total. He juggled jobs in golf and at the family-owned forklift business before making his way to the TOUR in 2003 via Q-School. His 70.27 scoring average, 12th on Tour, was more than a stroke lower than his previous best.

Michael Long, 28, $199,943

Long was a longshot to make the PGA TOUR, not because of a dearth of skill but because he's lucky to be playing competitive golf after a 1999 accident resulted in a broken neck. A Kiwi native living in Perth, Australia, the 36-year-old Long had a pair of runner-up finishes and four other top-10s as he made the most of his opportunities despite his absence in the top 10 in any statistical category. He's the only man to win each of the four New Zealand Golf Association titles. Other pro credits include competing in three British Opens and representing New Zealand in the 1997 World Cup.

Gavin Coles, 25, $198,683

For the second time in three years, the key for Coles's step up to the PGA TOUR was achieving success Down Under. Thanks to a final-round 68, the native of New South Wales, Australia, won the New Zealand PGA Championship by three shots, one of his two top-10 finishes. In 2002, the 36-year-old Coles captured the Jacob's Creek Open Championship in Adelaide, South Australia, on the way to earning his TOUR card for the first time. A professional since 1992, Coles shot a career-low 63 in the first round of the Price Cutter Charity Championship.

World Golf Hall of Fame Members

Name	Induction Year	Birthplace	Birth and Death Dates
Amy Alcott	1999	Kansas City, Missouri	Feb. 22, 1956–
Willie Anderson	1975	North Berwick, Scotland	1878–Oct. 25, 1910
Isao Aoki	2004	Abiko, Chiba, Japan	Aug. 31, 1942–-
Tommy Armour	1976	Edinburgh, Scotland	Sept. 24, 1894–Sept. 12, 1968
John Ball	1977	Hoylake, England	Dec. 24, 1861–Dec. 2, 1940
Severiano Ballesteros	1997	Pedrena, Spain	April 9, 1957–
Jim Barnes	1989	Lelant, Cornwall, England	1886–March 25, 1966
Judy Bell	2001	Wichita, Kansas	Sept. 23, 1936—
Deane Beman	2000	Washington, DC	April 22, 1938–
Patty Berg	1974	Minneapolis, Minnesota	Feb. 3, 1918–
Tommy Bolt	2002	Haworth, Oklahoma	March 31, 1918–
Sir Michael Bonallack	2000	Chigwell, Essex, England	Dec. 31, 1934–
Julius Boros	1982	Fairfield, Connecticut	March 3, 1920–May 28, 1994
Pat Bradley	1991	Westford, Massachusetts	March 24, 1951–
James Braid	1976	Earlsferry, Fifeshire, Scotland	Feb. 6, 1870–Nov. 27, 1950
Jack Burke, Jr.	2000	Ft. Worth, Texas	Jan. 29, 1930–
William Campbell	1990	Huntington, West Virginia	May 23, 1923–
Donna Caponi	2001	Detroit, Michigan	Jan. 29, 1945–
JoAnne Gunderson Carner	1985	Kirkland, Washington	April 4, 1939–
Billy Casper	1978	San Diego, California	June 24, 1931–
Neil Coles	2000	London, England	Sept. 26, 1934–
Harry Cooper	1992	Leatherhead, England	Aug. 4, 1904–Oct. 17, 2000
Fred Corcoran	1975	Cambridge, Massachusetts	April 4, 1905–June 23, 1977
Henry Cotton	1980	Holmes Chapel, Cheshire, England	Jan. 28, 1907–Dec. 22, 1987
Ben Crenshaw	2002	Austin, Texas	Jan. 11, 1952–
Bing Crosby	1978	Tacoma, Washington	May 2, 1904–Oct. 14, 1977
Beth Daniel	1999	Charleston, South Carolina	Oct. 14, 1956–
Jimmy Demaret	1983	Houston, Texas	May 24, 1910–Dec. 28, 1983
Roberto De Vicenzo	1989	Buenos Aires, Argentina	April 14, 1923–
Joseph C. Dey	1975	Norfolk, Virginia	Nov. 17, 1907–March 3, 1991
Leo Diegel	2003	Detroit, Michigan	April 27, 1899–May 8, 1951
Chick Evans	1975	Indianapolis, Indiana	July 8, 1890–Nov. 6, 1979
Nick Faldo	1997	Welwyn Garden City, Hertfordshire, England	July 18, 1957–
Raymond Floyd	1989	Fort Bragg, North Carolina	Sept. 4, 1942–
Herb Graffis	1977	Logansport, Indiana	May 31, 1893–Feb. 13, 1989
Ralph Guldahl	1981	Dallas, Texas	Nov. 22, 1911–June 11, 1987
Walter Hagen	1974	Rochester, New York	Dec. 21, 1892–Oct. 5, 1969
Marlene Bauer Hagge	2002	Eureka, South Dakota	Feb. 16, 1934–
Bob Harlow	1988	Newburyport, Massachusetts	Oct. 21, 1899–Nov. 15, 1954
Sandra Haynie	1977	Ft. Worth, Texas	June 4, 1943–
Hisako "Chako" Higuchi	2003	Kawagoe City, Saitama Prefecture, Japan	Oct. 13, 1945–
Harold Hilton	1978	West Kirby, England	Jan. 14, 1869–March 5, 1942
Ben Hogan	1974	Dublin, Texas	Aug. 13, 1912–July 29, 1997
Bob Hope	1983	Eltham, England	May 29, 1903–July 27, 2003
Dorothy Campbell Hurd Howe	1978	Edinburgh, Scotland	March 24,1883–March 20, 1945
Juli Inkster	2000	Santa Cruz, California	June 24, 1960–
Hale Irwin	1992	Joplin, Missouri	June 3, 1945–
Tony Jacklin	2002	Scunthorpe, England	July 7, 1944–
John Jacobs	2000	Lindrick, Yorkshire, England	March 14, 1925–
Betty Jameson	1951	Norman, Oklahoma	May 19, 1919–
Robert Trent Jones, Sr.	1987	Ince, Lancanshire, England	June 20, 1906-June 14, 2000
Bobby Jones	1974	Atlanta, Georgia	March 17, 1902–Dec. 18, 1971
Betsy King	1995	Reading, Pennsylvania	Aug. 13, 1955–
Tom Kite	2004	Austin, Texas	Dec. 9, 1949–
Bernhard Langer	2002	Anhausen, Germany	Aug. 27, 1957–
Lawson Little	1980	Newport, Rhode Island	June 23, 1910–Feb. 1, 1968
Gene Littler	1990	San Diego, California	July 21, 1930–
Bobby Locke	1977	Germiston, Transvaal, South Africa	Nov. 20, 1917–March 9, 1987

World Golf Hall of Fame Members

Name	Induction Year	Birthplace	Birth/Death Dates
Nancy Lopez	1989	Torrance, California	Jan. 6, 1957–
Lloyd Mangrum	1998	Trenton, Texas	Aug. 1, 1914–Nov. 17, 1973
Carol Mann	1977	Buffalo, New York	Feb. 3, 1941–
Cary Middlecoff	1986	Halls, Tennessee	Jan. 6, 1921–Sept. 1, 1998
Johnny Miller	1996	San Francisco, California	April 29, 1947
Tom Morris, Jr.	1975	St. Andrews, Scotland	April 20, 1851–Dec. 25, 1875
Tom Morris, Sr.	1976	St. Andrews, Scotland	June 16, 1821–May 24, 1908
Byron Nelson	1974	Long Branch, Texas	Feb. 4, 1912–
Jack Nicklaus	1974	Columbus, Ohio	Jan. 21, 1940–
Greg Norman	2001	Mt. Isa, Queensland, Australia	Feb. 10, 1955–
Francis Ouimet	1974	Brookline, Massachusetts	May 8, 1893–Sept. 2, 1967
Arnold Palmer	1974	Latrobe, Pennsylvania	Sept. 10, 1929–
Harvey Penick	2002	Austin, Texas	Oct. 23, 1904–April 2, 1995
Gary Player	1974	Johannesburg, South Africa	Nov. 1, 1935–-
Nick Price	2003	Durban, South Africa	Jan. 28, 1957–
Judy Rankin	2000	St. Louis, Missouri	Feb. 18, 1945–
Betsy Rawls	1987	Spartanburg, South Carolina	May 4, 1928–
Clifford Roberts	1978	Morning Sun, Iowa	March 6, 1894–Sept. 29, 1977
Allan Robertson	2001	St. Andrews, Scotland	Sept. 11, 1815–Sept. 1, 1859
Chi Chi Rodriguez	1992	Rio Pledras, Puerto Rico	Oct. 23, 1935–
Donald Ross	1977	Dornoch, Scotland	Nov. 23, 1872–April 26, 1948
Paul Runyan	1990	Hot Springs, Arkansas	July 12, 1908–March 17, 2002
Gene Sarazen	1974	Harrison, New York	Feb. 27, 1902–May 3, 1999
Patty Sheehan	1993	Middlebury, Vermont	Oct. 27, 1956–
Dinah Shore	1994	Winchester, Tennessee	Feb. 29, 1916–Feb. 24, 1994
Charlie Sifford	2004	Kingwood, Texas	June 2, 1922–
Horton Smith	1990	Detroit, Michigan	May 22, 1908–Oct. 15, 1963
Sam Snead	1974	Hot Springs, Virginia	May 27, 1912–May 23, 2002
Karsten Solheim	2001	Bergen, Norway	Sept. 15, 1911–Feb. 16, 2000
Annika Sörenstam	2003	Stockholm, Sweden	Oct. 10, 1970–
Payne Stewart	2001	Springfield, Missouri	Jan. 30, 1957–Oct. 25, 1999
Marlene Stewart Streit	2004	Cereal, Alberta, Canada	March 9, 1934–
Louise Suggs	1979	Lithia Springs, Georgia	Sept. 7, 1923–
J. H. Taylor	1975	Northam, North Devon, England	March 18, 1871–Feb. 10, 1963
Peter Thomson	1998	Melbourne, Australia	Aug. 23, 1929–
Jerry Travers	1976	New York, New York	May 19, 1887–March 29, 1951
Walter Travis	1979	Malden, Victoria, Australia	Jan. 10, 1862–July 31, 1927
Lee Trevino	1981	Dallas, Texas	Dec. 1, 1939–
Richard Tufts	1992	Medford, Massachusetts	March 16, 1896–Dec. 17, 1980
Harry Vardon	1974	Grouville, Isle of Jersey, England	May 9, 1870–March 20, 1937
Glenna Collett Vare	1975	New Haven, Connecticut	June 20, 1903–Feb. 3, 1989
Tom Watson	1988	Kansas City, Missouri	Sept. 4, 1949–
Joyce Wethered	1975	Devon, England	Nov. 17, 1901–Nov. 18, 1997
Kathy Whitworth	1982	Monohans, Texas	Sept. 27, 1939–
Mickey Wright	1976	San Diego, California	Feb. 14, 1935–
"Babe" Didrikson Zaharias	1974	Port Arthur, Texas	June 26, 1914–Sept. 27, 1956

2004 Inductees

With 73 career victories, including 56 in his native Japan, **Isao Aoki** became the second Japanese member of the Hall of Fame. He is the only Japanese player to win on six tours, including one PGA TOUR title, the 1983 Hawaiian Open, and nine Champions Tour titles.

A native of Austin, TX, **Tom Kite**'s combination of talent and tenacity enabled him to win 19 PGA TOUR titles, including the 1992 U.S. Open. A trailblazer by becoming the first player to put a third wedge in his bag, Kite in 1989 won THE PLAYERS Championship and was the PGA Player of the Year. He also has won six times on the Champions Tour. Kite captained the 1997 U.S. Ryder Cup team and played on seven American teams in the biennial competition.

The Jackie Robinson of golf, **Charlie Sifford** broke the race barrier in professional golf by competing on the PGA TOUR full time in 1961, the first African-American to do so. Sifford, who grew up in Charlotte, NC, won twice on the PGA TOUR, at the 1967 Greater Hartford Open and the '69 Los Angeles Open. An original member of the Champions Tour, he added the Senior PGA Championship in 1975 among his two senior titles.

Marlene Stewart Streit is the only golfer to have won the Australian, British, Canadian, and United States women's amateur championships. Between 1951 and 2003, Streit won 30 national or international championships, at least one in each decade. She won 11 Canadian Ladies Open Amateurs, nine Canadian Ladies Close Amateurs, and four Canadian Ladies Senior Women's Amateur tournaments.

The World Golf Hall of Fame is in Saint Augustine, FL. www.wgv.com

PGA TOUR player K.J. Choi (above) visits with children at the St. Michaels Special School in New Orleans, which is beneficiary of the Zurich Classic of New Orleans.

Phil Mickelson (second from the left) and his partners, Ford and BearingPoint, present a check to the Special Operations Warrior Foundation.

TOUR Tournaments Approach $1 Billion Threshold

Since the Palm Beach Invitational donated $10,000 in 1938, the PGA TOUR has generated more than $900 million for charitable causes large and small. Proceeds come through the TOUR's member tournaments, with help from generous sponsors and conscientious, civic-minded volunteers, not to mention the players themselves. Charitable giving from TOUR tournaments rose to more than $80 million in 2004.

Just one of many examples was the first-year initiative of pharmaceutical company AstraZeneca, maker of CRESTOR, which donated $2.7 million on behalf of TOUR players to health care and PGA TOUR charities nationwide.

Philanthropic efforts don't end with PGA TOUR-sponsored tournaments. The players, through special tournaments and events and their own foundations, add significantly to the overall mix. The Tiger Woods Foundation, through its high-profile namesake, has been a force in various causes since Woods turned professional in 1996, and many other players, such as Vijay Singh and Phil Mickelson, have started their own foundations. In 2004 Mickelson raised more than $100,000 for the Special Operations Warrior Fund, which finances college educations for the children of U.S. Special Operations military personnel killed in operational or training missions. He also lent his name and energy to a nationwide education initiative that ExxonMobile Corp. underwrites.

"You look at what Tiger does with his foundation, his Tiger Jam, his clinics … those things almost go unnoticed, but he gives a great deal of himself," Mickelson said. "I haven't really been in a position to reach people like I can now, and it's something I feel is part of my responsibility."

GIVING BACK
THE HEART OF THE PGA TOUR

The First Tee

One more element to golf's giving happens when each of the governing bodies unite behind important programs like The First Tee. Well beyond the obvious mission of introducing children of all backgrounds to golf is the more important role it plays in education and life-skills training.

Created in 1997, The First Tee is a World Golf Foundation initiative dedicated to providing young people an opportunity to develop life-enhancing values through golf and character education. These core values include honesty, integrity, communication, and sportsmanship. With more than 100 facilities in the United States, The First Tee's intent is to improve each participating child's quality of life, and to increase their potential for success.

The First Tee program is overseen and supported not only by the PGA TOUR, but also by members of the U.S. Golf Association, the Ladies Professional Golf Association, the PGA of America, and the Augusta National Golf Club. Former President George H. W. Bush serves as Honorary Chairman. Each year The First Tee has exceeded its goals both in the number of facilities and the number of participating youngsters.

The First Tee Life Skills Experience differentiates The First Tee from other junior golf programs. Through the Life Skills Education, participants are taught the importance of maintaining a positive attitude, how to make decisions by thinking about potential consequences, how to define and set goals, and how to transfer these skills from the golf course to everyday life.

The First Tee epitomizes the commitment of PGA TOUR tournaments, sponsors, players, and volunteers to the cause of giving, and to golf's overarching mission of spreading privileges to the lives of those outside the game as well as those lucky enough to be in it.

The First Tee Life Skills & Golf Experience seamlessly incorporates nine life skills into its golf lessons.

Official Marketing Partners of the PGA TOUR

The PGA TOUR enjoys significant marketing relationships with some of the world's leading corporations whose support contributes to the growth of the game and to the PGA TOUR's charitable donations of more than $80 million in 2004.

Accusplit
The Official Pedometer of the PGA TOUR and Champions Tour

Anheuser-Busch
An Official Sponsor of the PGA TOUR including the Michelob Ultra and O'Doul's brands

Michelob ULTRA
The Official Beer of the PGA TOUR and Champions Tour

O'Doul's
The Official Non-Alcohol Brew of the PGA TOUR and Champions Tour

Buick
The Official Car of the PGA TOUR

Canon
The Official Copier, Fax, Multi-Function Products, Printer, Scanner, Camera, and Binocular of the PGA TOUR and Champions Tour

Carey
The Official Chauffeured Transportation Provider of the PGA TOUR and Champions Tour

Celebrex®
An Official Sponsor of the PGA TOUR and Champions Tour

Charles Schwab & Co., Inc.
The Official Investment Firm of the PGA TOUR and Champions Tour

Cialis
An Official Sponsor of the PGA TOUR and Champions Tour

Cingular
The Official Wireless Communication Service Provider of the PGA TOUR, Champions Tour, and Nationwide Tour

Coca-Cola
The Official Soft Drink, Isotonic Beverage, Sports Drink, Energy Drink, and Water of the PGA TOUR, Champions Tour, and the Nationwide Tour

CRESTOR
An Official Sponsor of the PGA TOUR and Champions Tour

John Deere
The Official Golf Course Equipment Supplier, Landscape Product Supplier and Golf Course Equipment Leasing Company of the PGA TOUR

Delta Air Lines
The Official Airline of the PGA TOUR and Champions Tour

Official Marketing Partners of the PGA TOUR

FedEx Kinko's
The Official Document Services Provider of the PGA TOUR and Champions Tour

Bombardier Flexjet
The Official Aviation Solutions Provider of the PGA TOUR and the Champions Tour

Forbes
The Official Business Publication of the PGA TOUR

Georgia-Pacific
The Official Forest Products Provider of the PGA TOUR and Champions Tour

Golf Digest
Official Marketing Partnership with PGA TOUR and Champions Tour

Golf Magazine
Produces *PGA TOUR Magazine*, an official publication of the PGA TOUR, and *Champions Tour Magazine*, an official publication of the Champions Tour

Guide to Golf
Publisher of PGA TOUR Branded Regional Golf Guide

Hawaii Tourism Authority
An Official Marketing Relationship with the PGA TOUR

IBM
The Official Information Technology Sponsor for the PGA TOUR

JELD-WEN
The Official Door, Window, and Millwork Provider of the PGA TOUR and Champions Tour

Mastercard
The Official Payment System of the PGA TOUR and Champions Tour

North American Membership Group
Manages and markets the PGA TOUR Partners Club on behalf of the PGA TOUR

National Car Rental
The Official Car Rental Company of the PGA TOUR and Champions Tour

Nature Valley Granola Bars
The Official Natural Energy Bar of the PGA TOUR, Champions Tour, and Nationwide Tour

www.omegawatches.com

OMEGA
The Official Timekeeper of the PGA TOUR and Champions Tour

Official Marketing Partners of the PGA TOUR

Outback Steakhouse
The Official Restaurant of the PGA TOUR and Champions Tour

Palm, Inc.
Official ShotLink Provider of the PGA TOUR and Champions Tour

PricewaterhouseCoopers
The Official Professional Services Firm of the PGA TOUR

Southern Company
The Official Energy Company of the PGA TOUR and Champions Tour

Starwood Hotels & Resorts
The Official Hotels and Resorts of the PGA TOUR

Stryker Physiotherapy Associates
Sponsor of the Player Fitness and Therapy Program of the PGA TOUR and Champions Tour

ThermaCare
The Official Back Pain Therapy of the PGA TOUR and Champions Tour

TourTurf
The Official Synthetic Golf Turf of the PGA TOUR and Champions Tour

The Weather Channel
The Official Forecaster for the PGA TOUR, Champions Tour, and Nationwide Tour

About the Rules: Q & A

During PGA TOUR tournament play, the Rules of Golf are strictly upheld. Sometimes even the best players in the world must stop and ask for guidance from rules officials or their playing partners before taking an action that might cost them a stroke or two, or, in extreme cases, lead to their disqualification – even if they commit an honest mistake.

The United States Golf Association and the Royal and Ancient Golf Club of St. Andrews have worked jointly since 1952 to produce a uniform code for the sport. Through an agreement with the R&A, USGA jurisdiction of the rules is restricted to the U.S. and Mexico. All other competitions around the world are overseen by the R&A. For a complete set of rules, as well as a rundown of recent decisions made in competition regarding those rules, go to usga.org/playing/rules/rules_of_golf.html.com

Here are a few common – and not-so common – rules questions and the answers to them:

During competition, who plays first?

Play order on the first hole is determined by draw. On subsequent holes, the player who makes the lowest score on the just-completed hole has the honor. If two players make the same score, they tee off in the order of the previous hole. During play of a hole, the player whose ball is farthest from the hole plays first. If balls are equidistant from the hole, play order is determined by mutual agreement or by a draw.

• • •

How many clubs may a player have in his bag during competition?

No more than 14. A player may add clubs if he started with fewer than 14, but he may not substitute any of the clubs with which he started the round – unless a club breaks during the round under the normal course of play. If a player breaks a club by slamming it down or knocking it against a tree or some other action not considered normal course of play, he cannot replace the damaged club. If a player exceeds 14 clubs, he must remove the extra club or clubs and he is assessed a two-stroke penalty for each hole completed with the extra clubs, with a maximum of four strokes per round. Standing at the second tee while tied for the lead in the 2001 British Open at Royal Lytham and St. Annes, England, Ian Woosnam discovered he had 15 clubs in his bag. He incurred a two-stroke penalty for playing the first hole with an extra club.

• • •

May a player ask his fellow competitor which club he used to make a shot before he makes his stroke?

No. The player may only ask his caddie or, in match play, his partner, for advice. The penalty for this in match play is loss of the hole. The penalty in stroke play is two strokes.

• • •

What are "loose impediments" and what can a golfer do about them?

"Loose impediments" are naturally occurring objects such as stones, leaves, twigs, branches, dung, worms, insects, and the like. Sand and loose soil are considered loose impediments on the putting green, but not elsewhere. Although snow and ice are considered loose impediments, dew and frost are not. This is important in determining whether a player can remove impediments on or around his ball before playing his next shot. Any time a player wishes to remove loose impediments from on or around his ball while not on the putting green, he must do so without moving the ball. If the ball moves, he must replace it in its original spot, and he incurs a one-stroke penalty. If while removing loose impediments around a ball on the green the ball moves, there is no penalty but the ball must still be replaced. If a ball and a loose impediment touch the same hazard, the impediment cannot be removed.

• • •

What is an "obstruction?"

An "obstruction" is anything artificial on the course, including signs, scoreboards, the surfaces of cart paths and roads or other materials that interfere with a golfer's intended line of play, his stance, or his swing. Anything that defines "out of bounds," such as walls, fences, stakes, or railings, is not considered an obstruction but is integral to the course. A "movable obstruction" consists of some object that can be moved without unreasonable effort, without delaying play, and without causing damage to the course. Otherwise such objects are considered "immovable obstructions" and a player is entitled to lift his ball and, without penalty, drop it within one club length of the nearest point of relief as long as it isn't nearer the hole.

• • •

Is a player allowed to bend back the branches of a tree in order to get a better shot?

No, a player cannot bend or break anything fixed or growing in order to improve his lie, stance, or area of intended swing. He also cannot do anything that would create or eliminate irregularities of surface, remove or press down sand, loose soil, replaced divots, or other cut turf placed in position, or remove dew, frost, or water.

• • •

When looking for a ball, can a player move grass, branches, or leaves out of his way?

A player may touch or bend any impediments such as long grass, bushes, or branches, but only so he can identify that the ball he intends to play is his. He may not alter any natural objects to improve the lie of the ball or his stance, swing, or line of play.

• • •

Can a player smooth down the line of a putt?

The player may not touch any part of the line of the putt except to remove loose impediments and to repair ball marks or plugs. He cannot press anything down, including spike marks, in order to improve the surface or assist with the putt. He may place the club in front the ball to measure or gain perspective only. Also, he may not test the green by rolling a ball or scraping the grass with his club or shoes.

• • •

Who decides if a ball is unplayable?

The player is the only person who can judge whether or not his ball is unplayable, and he can do so anywhere on the course except in a water hazard. If he decides that his ball is unplayable he must take a penalty stroke and play a new ball as near as possible to the spot from which he took the original shot. Or he can drop a ball behind the point where the ball lay, with no limit on how far behind he can place the ball, or he can drop a ball two club-lengths from the spot where the ball lay, but not nearer the hole.

• • •

A shot comes to a stop in an impossible lie and the player declares his ball unplayable, takes a one-stroke penalty, measures two club-lengths from the original lie, and drops his ball. The ball is dropped legally, but rolls back to the same unplayable lie. What is the ruling?

The ball must be played as it lays or the player must declare it unplayable and accept another one-stroke penalty.

• • •

A ball hangs on the lip of the cup. How long can a player wait before having to make another stroke?

A player can wait ten seconds after arriving at the ball to see if the ball will fall in. After that, he must play the next stroke. If he waits longer than ten seconds and the ball falls in, he must assess himself a one-stroke penalty.

• • •

Can a player place anything on the ground to stand or kneel on while making a shot?

No, that would be considered building a stance. In 1987, at the Shearson Lehman Brothers Andy Williams Open at Torrey Pines Golf Club in La Jolla, CA, Craig Stadler had to kneel to play a shot from under a low-hanging evergreen tree, and he put a towel down on the wet grass to protect his light blue slacks. He should have been assessed a two-stroke penalty, but the infraction did not come to light until after he signed his scorecard, thereby leading to his disqualification.

PGATOUR.COM

The New Media division of the PGA TOUR is the intersection at which the ancient game of golf crosses paths with state-of-the-art technology to enhance understanding of the game for all who appreciate it and greater access for those who want to get closer to it.

A key component of New Media is PGATOUR.COM, which is the top global online-golf destination. The Official Website of the PGA TOUR, Champions Tour, and Nationwide Tour, PGATOUR.COM keeps fans connected to the game through real-time scoring, in-depth tournament coverage, extensive player information, real-time fantasy games, instruction tips, travel and real estate features, and the exclusive TOUR Pass premium access package. This membership package allows fans inside-the-ropes access to a variety of live events, video highlights, audio interviews and the revolutionary TOURCast application, powered by ShotLink.

Two other significant offerings from PGATOUR.COM are the Official Online Store and the Official Online Auctions. The Official Online Store, developed through a partnership with The Golf Warehouse, features top-line equipment, apparel, accessories, memorabilia, multimedia products such as books, videos, and DVDs—and merchandise emblazoned with the PGA TOUR logo. The Official Online Auctions site, facilitated through an alliance with eBay, helps raise money for charity through daily on-line auctions of autographed memorabilia provided by PGA TOUR players.

ShotLink

A revolutionary technological creation is the ShotLink Scoring System. Created by the PGA TOUR in collaboration with IBM, ShotLink gathers, collates, and disseminates statistics in real time. Through a combination of lasers, global-positioning satellites, and hand-held Palm computers used by volunteers, the TOUR can record the distance, direction, lie, stance, club, and result of every shot struck. This data is fed into many applications, including Tournament Tracker, a disseminating program for ShotLink, which has been available to players, the media, and television networks for more than two years. The result is a panoramic statistical picture of all the players in the field as well as the field on which they are competing.

In addition to greater reliability in charting basic statistics such as driving distance and accuracy, greens in regulation, and putting, ShotLink enables a new and more complete analysis of the game and how it is played on the PGA TOUR. New uses for ShotLink data include assessing statistics to help determine how the PGA TOUR field staff sets up a golf course for a tournament; redesigning tournament courses based on statistics; allowing TOUR players to compare their statistics from different time periods as a teaching tool; and creating on-site video board content that provides myriad pieces of tournament information to fans in attendance at TOUR events.

Imagine fans having access to driving distance for each player on a particular hole and the distance each has remaining to the green, who has hit the longest drive on that hole, who has hit it closest to the pin, or how many birdies, pars, and bogeys have been made. It is the first step to bringing a full spectrum of media enhancements to the tournament fan's live golf experience.

SHOTLink
AN IBM ON DEMAND BUSINESS SOLUTION

South Africa's **Ernie Els** won a career-high three times on the PGA TOUR in 2004 and placed second on the money list, another career high finish, with $5,787,225 in earnings.

All-Exempt TOUR Priority Rankings

Each PGA TOUR player has earned a position on the priority ranking system that will be used to select tournament fields. The complete ranking system, in order of priority, is as follows:

1. Winners of PGA Championship or U.S. Open prior to 1970 or in the last 10 calendar years. (Beginning in 1998, this is a five-year exemption.):

Rich Beem	**Jim Furyk**	**Jack Nicklaus**
Mark Brooks	**Al Geiberger**	**Arnold Palmer**
Jack Burke, Jr.	**Retief Goosen**	**Corey Pavin**
Billy Casper	**Don January**	**Gary Player**
Steve Elkington	**Steve Jones**	**Bob Rosburg**
Ernie Els	**Gene Littler**	**Vijay Singh**
Dow Finsterwald	**Davis Love III**	**David Toms**
Jack Fleck	**Shaun Micheel**	**Lee Trevino**
Ray Floyd	**Orville Moody**	**Ken Venturi**
Doug Ford	**Bobby Nichols**	**Tiger Woods**

2. Winners of THE PLAYERS Championship in the last 10 calendar years. (Beginning in 1998, this is a five-year exemption.):

Fred Couples	**Craig Perks**	**Hal Sutton**
Lee Janzen	**Adam Scott**	

3. Winners of the Masters Tournament in the last 10 calendar years. (Beginning in 1998, this is a five-year exemption.):

Ben Crenshaw	**Mike Weir**
Phil Mickelson	

4. Winners of the British Open in the last 10 calendar years. (Beginning in 1998, this is a five-year exemption.):

Ben Curtis	**David Duval**	**Tom Lehman**
John Daly	**Todd Hamilton**	**Justin Leonard**

5. Winners of the World Series of Golf from 1995 to 1997. (Ten-year exemption.):
   Greg Norman

6. THE TOUR Championship winners in the last three years, beginning with the 2002 winner:
   Chad Campbell

7. Winners of offiical money World Golf Championship events in the last three years:

Stewart Cink	**Craig Parry**
Darren Clarke	**Kevin Sutherland**

8. The leader in PGA TOUR official earnings in each of the last five calendar years.

9. Winners of PGA TOUR co-sponsored or approved events (except team events) within the last two calendar years, or during the current year; winners receive an additional year of exemption for each additional win, up to five years:

Stephen Ames	**Brent Geiberger**	**Ryan Palmer**
Stuart Appleby	**Mark Hensby**	**Rod Pampling**
Tommy Armour III	**Scott Hoch**	**Kenny Perry**
Woody Austin	**John Huston**	**Rory Sabbatini**
Bart Bryant	**Peter Jacobsen**	**Joey Sindelar**
Jonathan Byrd	**Zach Johnson**	**Heath Slocum**
K.J. Choi	**Jonathan Kaye**	**Craig Stadler**
Ben Crane	**Jerry Kelly**	**Andre Stolz**
Steve Flesch	**J.L. Lewis**	**Vaughn Taylor**
Carlos Franco	**Frank Lickliter II**	**Kirk Triplett**
Fred Funk	**Shigeki Maruyama**	**Bob Tway**
Sergio Garcia	**Len Mattiace**	

10. A. Members of the last-named U.S. Presidents Cup Team.

Chris DiMarco	**Jay Haas**	**Charles Howell III**

B. Members of the last-named International Presidents Cup Team provided they were a PGA TOUR member at the time they were named to the team.

Robert Allenby	**Stephen Leaney**	**Nick Price**
Tim Clark	**Peter Lonard**	

C. Members of the last-named U.S. Ryder Cup team provided they were a PGA TOUR member at the time they were named to the team.
Chris Riley

D. Members of the last-named European Ryder Cup Team.

Paul Casey	**Thomas Levet**	**Ian Poulter**
Luke Donald	**Padraig Harrington**	

11. Leaders in official PGA TOUR career earnings, as follows:
A. Players among the top 50 in career earnings as of the end of the preceding calendar year may elect to use a one-time, one-year exemption for the next year.

John Cook	**Billy Mayfair**
Tom Kite	**Rocco Mediate**

B. Players among the Top 25 in career earnings as of the end of the preceding calendar year may elect to use this special exemption for a second year, provided that the player remains among the Top 25 on the career money list.

12. Sponsor exemptions (a maximum of eight, which may include amateurs with scratch handicaps or less), on the following basis:
A. Not less than two sponsor invitees shall be PGA TOUR members not otherwise exempt for the event.

B. Not less than two of the top 30 finishers and ties from the last Qualifying Tournament, as well as 2-20 from the 2004 Nationwide Tour money list, if not all of them can otherwise be accommodated. (Note: PGA TOUR members may receive an unlimited number of sponsor invitations. Non-TOUR members may receive a maximum of seven per year).

13. Two international players designated by the Commissioner.

14. The current PGA Club Professional Champion for a maximum of six open events (three must be from open tournaments held opposite the British Open and the World Golf Championships), in addition to any sponsor selections.
Bob Sowards

15. PGA Section Champion or Player of the Year of the Section in which the tournament is played.

16. Two members of the PGA Section in which the tournament is played, who qualify through sectional qualifying competitions.

17. Four low scorers at Open Qualifying which shall normally be held on Monday of tournament week.

18. Past champions of the particular event being contested that week, if co-sponsored by the PGA TOUR and the same tournament sponsor (except for Team events), as follows:
A. Winners prior to July 28, 1970: unlimited exemptions for such events.

B. Winners after July 28, 1970 and prior to Jan. 1, 2000: 10 years of exemptions for such events.

C. Winners after Jan. 1, 2000: five years of exemptions for such events.

19. Life Members (who have been active members of the PGA TOUR for 15 years and have won at least 20 co-sponsored events).

Hale Irwin	**Tom Watson**

20. Top 125 on previous year's Official Money List: If not exempt under "Special Exemptions," the top 125 PGA TOUR members on the previous year's Official Money List, in order of their position:

Scott Verplank	**Briny Baird**	**Scott McCarron**
Tim Herron	**Bob Estes**	**Jose Coceres**
Ted Purdy	**Brad Faxon**	**Cameron Beckman**
Bo Van Pelt	**Jeff Sluman**	**Daniel Chopra**
Jesper Parnevik	**Loren Roberts**	**John Rollins**
Jeff Maggert	**Joe Durant**	**Robert Gamez**
Duffy Waldorf	**Bernhard Langer**	**Pat Perez**
Tom Pernice, Jr.	**Robert Damron**	**Mark Calcavecchia**
Harrison Frazar	**Brian Bateman**	**Neal Lancaster**
Joe Ogilvie	**Kevin Na**	**John Senden**
Carl Pettersson	**Michael Allen**	**Chris Smith**
Arron Oberholser	**Tom Byrum**	**Dennis Paulson**
Alex Cejka	**Dudley Hart**	**Kent Jones**
Fredrik Jacobson	**J.J. Henry**	**Jay Williamson**
Geoff Ogilvy	**Todd Fischer**	**Steve Allan**
Justin Rose	**Brett Quigley**	**Brian Gay**
Patrick Sheehan	**Matt Gogel**	**Aaron Baddeley**
Skip Kendall	**Hank Kuehne**	**Billy Andrade**
Tim Petrovic	**Hunter Mahan**	**Tag Ridings**
Steve Lowery	**Hidemichi Tanaka**	

21. Players who earned more than the 125th place finsher on 2004 PGA TOUR Money List as non-members:
Lee Westwood

22. Major Medical Extension: If granted by the Commissioner, if not otherwise eligible, and if needed to fill the field, Major Medical Extension:

Chris Perry	**Andrew Magee**	**John Riegger**
Notah Begay III	**Brandt Jobe**	**Marco Dawson**
Paul Stankowski	**Paul Goydos**	**Fulton Allem**
Phil Tataurangi	**Ian Leggatt**	
David Berganio, Jr.	**Glen Hnatiuk**	

23. Leading Money Winner from 2004 Nationwide Tour:
Jimmy Walker **Patrick Moore** *

24. Top 10 and Ties among professionals from the previous open tournament whose victory has official status are exempt into the next open tournament whose victory has official status.

25. Top 30 and Ties from the previous year's PGA TOUR Qualifying Tournament, in order of their finish, and players 2-20 on the 2004 Nationwide Tour money list:

Brian Davis	**D.J. Trahan**	**Hideto Tanihara**
D.A. Points	**Bradley Hughes**	**Mario Tiziani**
Rob Rashell	**Matt Davidson**	**David Hearn**
Ryuji Imada	**Kevin Stadler**	**Omar Uresti**
Danny Briggs	**D.J. Brigman**	**Mark Wilson**
Franklin Langham	**Euan Walters**	**Craig Barlow**
Paul Claxton	**Jason Allred**	**Doug Barron**
Nick Watney	**Darron Stiles**	**Tom Gillis**
Sean O'Hair	**Joey Snyder III**	**Lucas Glover**
Brendan Jones	**Hunter Haas**	**Charlie Wi**
Bill Glasson	**Dean Wilson**	**Scott Hend**
James Driscoll	**Scott Gutschewski**	**Jeff Hart**
John Elliott	**Jim Carter**	**Will MacKenzie**
Charles Warren	**Chris M. Anderson**	**Tjaart van der Walt** *
Greg Owen	**Phillip Price**	**Wes Short, Jr.** *
Justin Bolli	**Michael Long**	**Ken Green** *
Jason Bohn	**Carl Paulson**	**Brad Lardon** *
Brett Wetterich	**Gavin Coles**	**Boyd Summerhays** *
Roland Thatcher	**Jeff Brehaut**	**John Maginnes** *
Paul Gow	**Bob Heintz**	**Brian Watts** *

* - Medical exemption

26. Players winning three Nationwide Tour events in the current year, in priority determined by the date they win their third event.

27. Minor Medical Extension:

David Peoples	**Tripp Isenhour**
Mark O'Meara	**James H. McLean**

28. Next 25 members after the Top 125 members from previous year's Official Money List. If needed to fill the field, the next 25 PGA TOUR members after the top 125 PGA TOUR members from the previous year's Official Money List, in order of their position on the list:

Paul Azinger	**Glen Day**	**John E. Morgan**
Olin Browne	**Matt Kuchar**	**Arjun Atwal**
Bob Burns	**Jose M. Olazabal**	**Richard S. Johnson**
Mathias Gronberg	**Craig Bowden**	
Brenden Pappas	**Danny Ellis**	

29. Non-Exempt, Major Medical Extension:

Bob May	**Ted Tryba**	**Per-Ulrik Johansson**
Frank Nobilo		

30. Past Champions, Team Tournament Winners and Veteran Members Beyond 150 on Money List: If not otherwise eligible and as needed to fill the field, Past Champion members, Team Tournament Winners and Veteran members beyond 150th place on the previous year's Money List, in order of their combined official PGA TOUR and Nationwide Tour earnings in the previous year.

31. Past Champion Members: If not otherwise eligible and if needed to fill the field, Past Champion members, in order of the total number of co-sponsored or approved events won, excluding Team events. If two or more players are tied, the player who is higher on the PGA TOUR Career Money List shall be eligible.

32. Special Temporary: If during the course of a PGA TOUR season, a non-member of the PGA TOUR wins an amount of official money (e.g., by playing in PGA TOUR events through sponsor exemptions, Open Qualifying, etc.) equal to the amount won in the preceding year by the 150th finisher on the official money list, he will be eligible for the remainder of the year.

33. Team Tournament Winners: If not otherwise eligible and if needed to fill the field, winners of co-sponsored team championships, in order of the total number of team championship tournaments won. If two or more players are tied based on the number of such tournaments won, the player who is higher on the official PGA TOUR Career Money List shall be eligible.

34. Veteran Members: If not otherwise eligible and if needed to fill the field, Veteran members (players who have made a minimum of 150 cuts during their career), in order of their standing on the PGA TOUR Career Money List.

Steve Allan

EXEMPT STATUS: 121st on 2004 money list
FULL NAME: Steve Douglas Allan
HEIGHT: 5-9
WEIGHT: 170
BIRTHDATE: October 18, 1973
BIRTHPLACE: Melbourne, Australia
RESIDENCE: Melbourne, Australia
FAMILY: Single

SPECIAL INTERESTS: Golf course design, all sports
TURNED PROFESSIONAL: 1996
Q SCHOOL: 2000

BEST PGA TOUR CAREER FINISHES:

T2—2003 Greater Milwaukee Open, 2004 Reno-Tahoe Open.

INTERNATIONAL VICTORIES (2):

1998 German Open [Eur]. **2002** Holden Australian Open Championship [Aus].

BEST 2004 PGA TOUR FINISH:

T2—Reno-Tahoe Open.

2004 SEASON:

Earned fully-exempt status for the second time in his four-year career. Made a career-high 33 starts and 18 made cuts. . .Had a two-stroke lead heading to the 72nd hole of regulation at the Reno-Tahoe Open. His third shot, from a greenside bunker, flew 10 yards over the green. He missed a 4-foot putt for bogey and made double-bogey, dropping to 10-under and into a four-man playoff. Rookie Vaughn Taylor claimed his first PGA TOUR victory, rolling in an 11-foot birdie putt on the first extra hole. Allan's T2 finish matched his career-best finish on the PGA TOUR. . .Opened the year tying the Waialae Country Club's course record at the Sony Open in Hawaii with a second-round 8-under-par 62. Held the 36-hole lead by one over Harrison Frazar, but shot 70-74 to finish T27. . .Ended the season on a high note by making the cut at the FUNAI Classic at the WALT DISNEY WORLD Resort, firing a final-round 6-under 66 to move from T62 to T33. Collected $21,263 for a $648,480 total, pushing him over the $623,262 needed to finish in the top 125 on the final season money list.

CAREER HIGHLIGHTS:

2003: Played in just 18 events but managed to put together back-to-back top-10s for the first time in his career on TOUR...Missed seven of first eight cuts before finishing one stroke behind winner Kenny Perry at the Greater Milwaukee Open. Finished the final round with a one-stroke advantage over Perry, but Perry birdied the final two holes to edge him by a stroke...Followed the next week with a T5 at the B.C. Open. Earned $406,250 over those two weeks. Was 28-under par during that period. **2002:** Won the 2002 Holden Australian Open at the Victoria GC just five minutes from where he honed his golf game at the Woodlands Club. Shot a final-round 68 to beat Rich Beem, Aaron Baddeley and Craig Parry by one shot. He received a spot in the field only on an invitation from the Australian Golf Union...Made nine cuts in his last 11 starts of the season, including four rounds in the 60s for the first time in his career at the Valero Texas Open, where he finished T14. **2001:** Retained PGA TOUR exempt status for 2002 with a T19 at 2001 PGA TOUR Qualifying Tournament...In rookie season on the PGA TOUR, played in 31 events and made 12 cuts. **2000:** Struggled with a hip injury, but had several high finishes on the European Tour before coming to the U.S. Won the 2000 PGA TOUR Qualifying Tournament with a 32-under-par 400 total. Member of the European PGA Tour from 1997-2000. **1999:** Qualified for U.S. Open and British Open, finishing T42 and T49, respectively. **1998:** His first victory came at the German Open at The Sporting Club in Berlin. Victory assisted him in finishing 16th on the European Tour Order of Merit. **1997:** Finished 11th in the 1996 European Tour Qualifying School and went on to T4 in 1997 Portuguese Open in first season on that tour...Underlined his potential by just losing to José Maria Olazábal in the Dubai Desert Classic. . .Finished 82nd in 1997 Order of Merit.

PERSONAL:

Enjoys a long-distance relationship with his coach, Dale Lynch, by e-mailing videos of his swing to Australia for assessment once a week. . .Parents emigrated from Edinburgh to Australia in 1970. Spent several summers visiting relatives in the UK and playing amateur tournaments as a youngster.

PLAYER STATISTICS

2004 PGA TOUR STATISTICS

Scoring Average	71.32	(118)
Driving Distance	301.2	(11)
Driving Accuracy Percentage	59.3%	(158)
Total Driving	169	(61)
Greens in Regulation Pct.	66.8%	(50)
Putting Average	1.795	(142)
Sand Save Percentage	48.9%	(101)
Eagles (Holes per)	222.8	(87)
Birdie Average	3.57	(85)
All-Around Ranking	752	(95)
Scoring Avg. Before Cut	71.06	(104)
Round 3 Scoring Avg.	69.89	(29)
Final Round Scoring Average	71.75	(110)
Birdie Conversion Percentage	28.9%	(101)
Par Breakers	20.3%	(83)

MISCELLANEOUS PGA TOUR STATISTICS

2004 Low Round/Round: 62–Sony Open in Hawaii/2
Career Low Round/Round: 62–2004 Sony Open in Hawaii/2
Career Largest Paycheck/Finish: $308,000–2003 Greater Milwaukee Open/T2

PGA TOUR CAREER SUMMARY — PLAYOFF RECORD: 0-1

Year	Events Played	Cuts Made	1st	2nd	3rd	Top 10	Top 25	Earnings	Rank
1996A	1								
1998	1								
1999	2	2						$26,343	247
2001	31	12					1	156,686	185
2002	30	16					5	359,655	149
2003	18	8		1		2	4	616,325	105
2004	33	18		1		1	5	648,480	121
Total	116	56		2		3	15	1,807,489	
NATIONWIDE TOUR									
2003	5	3			1	1	2	32,336	113
Total	5	3			1	1	2	32,336	

PGA TOUR TOP TOURNAMENT SUMMARY

Year	96	97	98	99	00	01	02	03	04
U.S. Open				T42					CUT
British Open	CUT		CUT	T49					
THE PLAYERS									CUT
WGC-NEC Invitational								T46	

Fulton Allem

EXEMPT STATUS: Major Medical Extension
FULL NAME: Fulton Peter Allem
HEIGHT: 5-11
WEIGHT: 215
BIRTHDATE: September 15, 1957
BIRTHPLACE: Kroonstad, South Africa
RESIDENCE: Heathrow, FL

FAMILY: Wife, Jennifer; Nadia (7/7/86), Nicholas (1/1/91), Sybil Mary (1/14/01)
SPECIAL INTERESTS: Riding horses, breeding horses, fishing and hunting
TURNED PROFESSIONAL: 1976
JOINED TOUR: 1987

PGA TOUR VICTORIES (3):

1991 Independent Insurance Agent Open. **1993** Southwestern Bell Colonial, NEC World Series of Golf.

INTERNATIONAL VICTORIES (14):

1985 Palaborwa Classic, Million Dollar Challenge. **1986** Minolta Match Play Championship, Palaborwa Classic, South African PGA. **1987** South African PGA, Palaborwa Classic. **1988** Palaborwa Classic, Million Dollar Challenge. **1989** Minolta Match Play Championship. **1990** Lexington PGA Championship, Twee Jongezellen Masters, Goodyear Classic. **1991** ICL International [all South Africa].

BEST 2004 PGA TOUR FINISH:

74—HP Classic of New Orleans.

2004 SEASON:

Coupled with $28,883 earned in 28 events in 2003-04, has the opportunity to play in one event with a Major Medical Extension and earn $458,612 to match the $487,495 in winnings of 2003's No. 125, Esteban Toledo. If he does so, will play out of the Major Medical Extension category for the remainder of the season. Made only one cut and finished 74th at the HP Classic of New Orleans.

CAREER HIGHLIGHTS:

2003: In final season of 10-year exemption for winning the 1993 NEC World Series of Golf, played in only 15 events due to wrist surgery (July 14) and degenerative discs in his back. **2002:** Best finish was T23 at the Compaq Classic of New Orleans. **2001:** Finished in the top-25 four times in only seven cuts made...Opened with 66 at the Honda Classic and stood one stroke back of the lead. Finished T11. **2000:** Best finish of the year came at the Buick Invitational with a T21, earning $29,014, his largest check of the season. **1997:** One of his best seasons since winning twice in 1993. Had four top-10s including top-fives at the Doral-Ryder Open (T5) and Greater Milwaukee Open (T5). **1996:** Best finish was a T4 at Doral-Ryder Open. Closing 66 left him five strokes behind winner Greg Norman. **1994:** Captain's Choice for International Team at Presidents Cup. Was 1-3 in foursomes and four-ball before halving singles match with Phil Mickelson. **1993:** Pair of victories came on two of the TOUR's most storied courses: Colonial and Firestone. Moved into contention with second-round 63 at Colonial National Invitation, then closed with 67 to defeat Greg Norman by one stroke. The victory earned a place in the NEC World Series of Golf, where final-round 62 earned him $360,000 first-place check and a 10-year PGA TOUR exemption. **1991:** First TOUR victory came at Independent Insurance Agent Open, played in October after tournament had been postponed because of rain in April. Played final two rounds in 11-under par to defeat Billy Ray Brown, Mike Hulbert and Tom Kite by one stroke. **1988:** Finished 65-68 on weekend for T3 at THE PLAYERS Championship. **1987:** Joined PGA TOUR after finishing second at NEC World Series of Golf, three strokes behind Curtis Strange. **1985:** Had 18 runner-up finishes on Southern Africa Tour before gaining first victory there...Won Palaborwa Classic and Million Dollar Challenge.

PERSONAL:

Started playing golf at age 7 with encouragement from father...Countryman Gary Player had large influence on his early career.

PLAYER STATISTICS

2004 PGA TOUR STATISTICS

Scoring Average	74.92	(N/A)
Driving Distance	271.0	(N/A)
Driving Accuracy Percentage	65.5%	(N/A)
Total Driving	(N/A)	(N/A)
Greens in Regulation Pct.	52.9%	(N/A)
Putting Average	1.883	(N/A)
Sand Save Percentage	52.6%	(N/A)
Eagles (Holes per)	243.0	(N/A)
Birdie Average	2.00	(N/A)
Scoring Avg. Before Cut	74.56	(N/A)
Round 3 Scoring Avg.	78.00	(N/A)
Final Round Scoring Average	74.00	(N/A)
Birdie Conversion Percentage	19.6%	(N/A)
Par Breakers	11.5%	(N/A)

MISCELLANEOUS PGA TOUR STATISTICS

2004 Low Round/Round: 67–HP Classic of New Orleans/2
Career Low Round/Round: 62–1993 NEC World Series of Golf/4
Career Largest Paycheck/Finish: $360,000–1993 NEC World Series of Golf/1

PGA TOUR CAREER SUMMARY — PLAYOFF RECORD: 0-0

Year	Events Played	Cuts Made	1st	2nd	3rd	Top 10	Top 25	Earnings	Rank
1986	2								
1987	6	3		1		1	1	88,734	105
1988	22	12			1	3	5	163,911	73
1989	26	18					10	134,706	104
1990	23	14				1	5	132,493	116
1991	23	13	1			2	5	229,702	71
1992	29	21				2	7	209,982	74
1993	28	19	2			4	8	851,345	9
1994	28	17				1	3	166,144	109
1995	21	8					2	54,239	199
1996	18	10				1	3	162,515	132
1997	21	10				4	5	237,051	102
1998	21	9				1	1	118,714	176
1999	26	12					1	112,215	192
2000	25	12					1	119,626	187
2001	21	7					4	241,680	160
2002	26	6					1	92,379	201
2003	15	2						19,091	242
2004	13	1						9,792	255
Total	394	194	3	1	1	20	62	3,144,319	

PGA TOUR TOP TOURNAMENT SUMMARY

Year	86	87	88	89	90	91	92	93	94	95	96	97	98
Masters							T52		T38				
U.S. Open						CUT		T52	T33	CUT			
British Open	CUT	T44				T44		CUT	CUT				
PGA			CUT	CUT			T40	T31	T47				
THE PLAYERS			T3	T14	T11	CUT	CUT	T20	T55	CUT	CUT	CUT	CUT
TOUR Championship								T12					

Year	99	00	01	02	03
THE PLAYERS	T77	T66	CUT	CUT	CUT

NATIONAL TEAMS: Dunhill Cup, 1993; The Presidents Cup, 1994.

Michael Allen

EXEMPT STATUS: 88th on 2004 money list
FULL NAME: Michael Louis Allen
HEIGHT: 6-0
WEIGHT: 195
BIRTHDATE: January 31, 1959
BIRTHPLACE: San Mateo, CA
RESIDENCE: Scottsdale, AZ; plays out of Mesa CC
FAMILY: Wife, Cynthia; Christy (12/8/93), Michelle (6/3/97)
EDUCATION: University of Nevada (1982, Horticulture)
SPECIAL INTERESTS: Sports, wine, reading, politics, motorcycles
TURNED PROFESSIONAL: 1984
Q SCHOOL: 1989, 1990, 1991, 1992, 1994, 2001, 2003
Nationwide Tour Alumnus

BEST PGA TOUR CAREER FINISH:
2—2004 Chrysler Classic of Greensboro.

NATIONWIDE TOUR VICTORIES (1):
1998 Greater Austin Open.

INTERNATIONAL VICTORIES (1):
1989 Bell's Scottish Open.

BEST 2004 PGA TOUR FINISHES:
2—Chrysler Classic of Greensboro; T9—Reno-Tahoe Open.

2004 SEASON:
Finished in the top 125 on the money list for just the second time in his career and first since finishing 73rd in 1993. His $882,872 earnings were more than he had earned in his first 187 events on TOUR ($740,360). First top-10 of the season was T9 at the Reno-Tahoe Open. Last time he finished in the top-10 on the PGA TOUR was at the 1995 Quad Cities Open, where he finished T5…Posted a hole-in-one on the 193-yard par-3 fourth hole with a 6-iron in the third round at the FedEx St. Jude Classic…Posted career-best finish with a solo second at the Chrysler Classic of Greensboro. Birdie putt on the 72nd hole that put him in solo second was worth $92,000 and payday of $496,800 jumped position on money list from No. 153 to No. 84.

CAREER HIGHLIGHTS:
2003: Successfully qualified at PGA TOUR Qualifying Tournament for the seventh time in his career (1989-92, 1994, 2001, 2003) with a third-place finish. Marked the 11th time he had been to Q-School finals...Played primarily on the Nationwide Tour, where he was also a member from 1997-2001, with two top-10s in 24 events. Finished T2 at the Monterey Peninsula Classic. **1998:** Using a long putter, earned his first career Nationwide Tour victory at the Greater Austin Open, shooting a final-round 76 as winds in excess of 40 mph dropped the wind chill into the low 20s. His 4-over-par 76 was the highest finish by a winner on the Nationwide Tour that season. **1995:** Posted third career TOUR top-10 with a T5 at the weather-shortened Quad Cities Open. **1993:** Then-career-best PGA TOUR finishes came back-to-back in his first two events of the season, a T3 in Northern Telecom and Phoenix Opens. **1992:** Made his TOUR card for fourth straight season via Q-School finals. **1989:** Won Bell's Scottish Open on European Tour. Fired a 9-under-par 63 in the final round to defeat Ian Woosnam and Jose Maria Olazabal by two strokes at Gleneagles. Had only 22 putts during the final round, which saw him hole two chips and a bunker shot en route to a 30 on the back nine. Later in the year, finished second in the Scandinavian Open. Finished 15th on European Tour Order of Merit.

PERSONAL:
Was planning to be a stockbroker before turning to golf as a profession...Most memorable moment was winning the 2003 Southern Arizona Open with daughter Christy caddying.

PLAYER STATISTICS

2004 PGA TOUR STATISTICS

Scoring Average	71.28	(114)
Driving Distance	291.1	(60)
Driving Accuracy Percentage	56.5%	(179)
Total Driving	239	(160)
Greens in Regulation Pct.	64.2%	(115)
Putting Average	1.763	(52)
Sand Save Percentage	48.9%	(101)
Eagles (Holes per)	218.6	(81)
Birdie Average	3.56	(89)
All-Around Ranking	791	(104)
Scoring Avg. Before Cut	70.95	(88)
Round 3 Scoring Avg.	70.69	(71)
Final Round Scoring Average	71.67	(103)
Birdie Conversion Percentage	30.1%	(66)
Par Breakers	20.3%	(83)

MISCELLANEOUS PGA TOUR STATISTICS

2004 Low Round/Round: 65–Sony Open in Hawaii/3
Career Low Round/Round: 63–1990 Nissan Los Angeles Open/1
Career Largest Paycheck/Finish: $496,800–2004 Chrysler Classic of Greensboro/2

PGA TOUR CAREER SUMMARY — PLAYOFF RECORD: 0-0

Year	Events Played	Cuts Made	1st	2nd	3rd	Top 10	Top 25	Earnings	Rank
1988	1								
1990	30	16					4	$95,319	140
1991	29	15					2	47,626	177
1992	16	4						11,455	233
1993	27	15			2	3	6	231,072	73
1994	32	17					2	91,191	162
1995	21	7				1	1	55,825	197
1996	1	1						2,425	362
1999	1								
2000	1	1						4,936	
2001	1	1					1	91,734	
2002	29	9					1	108,777	197
2004	28	15		1		2	4	882,872	88
Total	217	101		1	2	6	21	1,623,232	
NATIONWIDE TOUR									
1992	1	1						1,125	219
1995	5	3					1	4,840	158
1997	20	9				3	4	26,792	75
1998	21	10	1			4	7	67,482	42
1999	24	10				1	3	22,871	93
2000	11	8		1		3	6	103,373	49
2001	21	13				2	4	59,864	71
2003	24	14		1		2	7	89,201	55
Total	127	68	1	2		15	32	375,548	

PGA TOUR TOP TOURNAMENT SUMMARY

Year	88	89	90	91	92	93	94	95	96	97	98	99	00
U.S. Open							DQ						
British Open	CUT	T52	T53										
PGA						T61							
THE PLAYERS			CUT				T62						

Year	01	02
U.S. Open	T12	CUT

Robert Allenby

EXEMPT STATUS: 2003 International Presidents Cup Team Member (through 2005)
FULL NAME: Robert Allenby
HEIGHT: 6-1
WEIGHT: 178
BIRTHDATE: July 12, 1971
BIRTHPLACE: Melbourne, Australia
RESIDENCE: Melbourne, Australia
FAMILY: Wife, Sandy; Harry Jack (9/20/99); Lily Bella (1/17/02)
SPECIAL INTERESTS: Fishing, fast boats
TURNED PROFESSIONAL: 1991
Q SCHOOL: 1998

PGA TOUR VICTORIES (4):

2000 Shell Houston Open, Advil Western Open. **2001** Nissan Open, Marconi Pennsylvania Classic.

INTERNATIONAL VICTORIES (12):

1992 Perak Masters [Aus], Johnnie Walker Classic [Aus]. **1993** Optus Players Championship [Aus]. **1994** Heineken Australian Open [Aus], Honda Open [Eur]. **1995** Heineken Classic [Aus]. **1996** Alamo English Open [Eur], Peugeot Open de France [Eur], One2One British Masters [Eur]. **2000** Australian PGA Championship [Aus]. **2001** Australian PGA Championship [Aus]. **2003** MasterCard Australian Masters [Aus].

BEST 2004 PGA TOUR FINISHES:

T4—The Honda Classic; T6—Chrysler Championship; T7—U.S. Open Championship; T9—PGA Championship, WGC-NEC Invitational.

2004 SEASON:

Although he dropped below $2 million in earnings for the first time since 2000, finished in the top 50 on the money list and earned over $1 million for the fifth straight season. . .First top-10, a T4 at The Honda Classic, came in his fifth start of the season. . .Next top-10 did not come until four months later, a T7 at the U.S. Open, his best career finish in a major. It was his third top-10 in 33 major championship appearances and his first since a T10 at the 2002 PGA. His final-round, even-par 70 was the only round of par or better on the day. . .Added another top-10 at the PGA with a T9. One of 10 players to record multiple top-10s in the major championships in 2004. . .Continued strong play at WGC-NEC Invitational, as T9 was third top-10 in five starts at the NEC event. . .Final top-10 came in last full-field event of the season, a T6 at the Chrysler Championship.

CAREER HIGHLIGHTS:

A four-time winner on the PGA TOUR, has also earned eight PGA Tour of Australasia victories and four European Tour titles. Twice led the PGA Tour of Australasia Order of Merit ('92 and '94) and participated in four Presidents Cup competitions. **2003:** Posted a career-best nine top-10s, placing in the top 30 in earnings for the fourth consecutive season...Best finish was third at the EDS Byron Nelson Championship. Also won at the MasterCard Australian Masters. **2002:** Finished 27th on the money list despite not winning for the first time since 1999...T2 at WGC-NEC Invitational at Sahalee Country Club. Earnings pushed him past the $2-million mark for the second consecutive season. **2001:** His second consecutive top-30 finish in earnings (16th) was driven by two victories...Beat Brandel Chamblee, Toshi Izawa, Dennis Paulson, Jeff Sluman and Bob Tway in a playoff at the Nissan Open with birdie on first extra hole when he laced a 3-wood through a cold rain to five feet and made the putt. Owns a 3-0 playoff record on the PGA TOUR and career 8-0 mark...Later in the year, earned second title at the Marconi Pennsylvania Classic with a three-stroke victory. Took the lead after second round and cruised to three-stroke victory...Was one of nine multiple winners on the year. **2000:** Earned first two PGA TOUR victories and, at same time, kept intact his string of playoff successes...Posted first TOUR win at Shell Houston Open. Despite placing one shot in water and another in grandstand, defeated Craig Stadler in four-hole playoff. Received on-course support from countryman, defending champion and good friend Stuart Appleby, who had missed cut...Second win came on first hole of playoff with Nick Price at Advil Western Open. Joined elite company after second victory, becoming one of only six players to win multiple times...Participated in his third career Presidents Cup as member of International Team, combining for 0-3 record in losing effort...Edged Steve Conrad by one stroke to win the Australian PGA Championship in December. **1999:** In rookie season on TOUR, finished just outside the top 125 in earnings (No. 126). **1998:** Earned exempt status for 1999 by finishing 17th at PGA TOUR Qualifying School. **1997:** Posted first top-10 in a major with T10 at the British Open. **1996:** Won three times on European Tour. Alamo English Open, Peugeot French Open and One2One British Masters...to finish third on European Tour Order of Merit. **1995:** Claimed Heineken Classic title...Member of World Cup team for second time. **1994:** Member of Presidents Cup Team...Won Heineken Australian Open and European Tour's Honda Open...Led PGA Tour of Australasia Order of Merit for second time in career. **1993:** Captured Optus Players Championship and named PGA Tour of Australasia Most Consistent Player...Member World Cup team and participated in Dunhill Cup. **1992:** Won Perak Masters and Johnnie Walker Classic to lead Australasian Tour Order of Merit...Named PGA Tour of Australasia Rookie of the Year. **1991:** Won Riversdale Cup for second consecutive year. **Amateur:** Began career as one of Australia's finest young amateurs. Won Riversdale Cup and Victorian Amateur Championship. In 1990, represented Australia in Eisenhower Cup and on World Amateur Team.

PERSONAL:

1996 season on European Tour, when he finished third on Order of Merit, ended prematurely in October, when he suffered a broken sternum and facial injuries in a traffic accident in Spain. Was presented 2001 Ben Hogan Award by the Golf Writers Association of America for recovering from that accident. . .Patron and spokesperson for Challenge Cancer Support Network, which aids children with cancer and blood disorders, since 1993.

PLAYER STATISTICS

2004 PGA TOUR STATISTICS

Scoring Average	70.32	(26)
Driving Distance	294.9	(34)
Driving Accuracy Percentage	65.0%	(80)
Total Driving	114	(10)
Greens in Regulation Pct.	70.3%	(8)
Putting Average	1.798	(157)
Sand Save Percentage	46.5%	(134)
Eagles (Holes per)	528.0	(179)
Birdie Average	3.67	(65)
All-Around Ranking	683	(71)
Scoring Avg. Before Cut	70.59	(46)
Round 3 Scoring Avg.	71.20	(113)
Final Round Scoring Average	70.70	(38)
Birdie Conversion Percentage	28.4%	(112)
Par Breakers	20.6%	(70)

MISCELLANEOUS PGA TOUR STATISTICS

2004 Low Round/Round: 65–Cialis Western Open/1
Career Low Round/Round: 62–2002 Air Canada Championship/2
Career Largest Paycheck/Finish: $612,000–2001 Nissan Open/1

PGA TOUR CAREER SUMMARY — PLAYOFF RECORD: 3-0

Year	Events Played	Cuts Made	1st	2nd	3rd	Top 10	Top 25	Earnings	Rank
1993	6	1						$11,052	235
1994	1	1							
1995	9	5					3	73,288	176
1996	7	2						15,932	252
1997	8	3				1	2	69,990	185
1998	9	7				1	4	191,867	141
1999	27	17					4	321,507	126
2000	26	22	2	1		3	10	1,968,685	16
2001	29	25	2			5	14	2,309,029	16
2002	27	22		2	1	8	14	2,115,771	20
2003	24	21			1	9	13	2,176,452	24
2004	26	22				5	11	1,513,537	44
Total	199	148	4	3	2	32	75	10,767,108	
EUROPEAN TOUR									
2004	1	1					1	52,527	

PGA TOUR TOP TOURNAMENT SUMMARY

Year	91	92	93	94	95	96	97	98	99	00	01	02	03
Masters							CUT				47	T29	T39
U.S. Open			T33				CUT		T46		CUT	T12	CUT
British Open	CUT		CUT	T60	T15	T55	T10	T19		T36	T47	CUT	T43
PGA			CUT		CUT	CUT	T49	T13	CUT	T19	T16	T10	T39
THE PLAYERS					73	CUT	CUT			T53	T21	T11	T4
TOUR Championship										T16	T22	T22	T13
WGC-Accenture Match Play											T17	T33	T9
WGC-NEC Invitational										T12	T23	T2	T6
WGC-American Express Champ										T25	CNL	T31	T21

Year	04
Masters	CUT
U.S. Open	T7
British Open	CUT
PGA	T9
THE PLAYERS	T33
WGC-Accenture Match Play	T17
WGC-NEC Invitational	T9
WGC-American Express Champ	T54

NATIONAL TEAMS: Presidents Cup (4) 1994, 1996, 2000, 2003; World Cup (2) 1993, 1995; Dunhill Cup, 1993

SECTION 2 PLAYER BIOGRAPHIES

Stephen Ames (Aims)

EXEMPT STATUS: 2004 tournament winner (through 2006)
FULL NAME: Stephen Michael Ames
HEIGHT: 6-1
WEIGHT: 165
BIRTHDATE: April 28, 1964
BIRTHPLACE: San Fernando, Trinidad
RESIDENCE: Calgary, Alberta, Canada

FAMILY: Wife, Jodi; Justin (2/28/97), Ryan Michael (5/25/99)
EDUCATION: Boca Raton (Business Administration)
SPECIAL INTERESTS: Reading, films, sports
TURNED PROFESSIONAL: 1987
Q SCHOOL: 1997
Nationwide Tour Alumnus

PGA TOUR VICTORIES (1):
2004 Cialis Western Open.

NATIONWIDE TOUR VICTORIES (1):
1991 Pensacola Open.

INTERNATIONAL VICTORIES (3):
1989 Trinidad and Tobago Open. **1994** Open V33 [Eur]. **1996** Benson and Hedges International Open [Eur].

BEST 2004 PGA TOUR FINISHES:
1—Cialis Western Open; 3—Bank of America Colonial; T4—Shell Houston Open, THE TOUR Championship presented by Coca-Cola; T6—Bay Hill Invitational Presented by MasterCard, the Memorial Tournament; T7—MCI Heritage, HP Classic of New Orleans; T8—Sony Open in Hawaii; T9—U.S. Open Championship, PGA Championship.

2004 SEASON:
Recorded a career year on the PGA TOUR, finishing eighth on the TOUR money list. Compiled a career-best 11 top-10s, including his first TOUR victory. Made 21 cuts in 27 tournaments entered and made over $3 million in a single season for the first time in his career...At age 40, captured his initial TOUR win at the Cialis Western Open by two strokes over Steve Lowery. Became first player 40-over to capture initial win since Brad Bryant at the 1995 Walt Disney World /Oldsmobile Golf Classic. Earned career-best paycheck of $864,000 and pushed season's earnings over $2 million for the first time. Shared third-round lead with Mark Hensby at 9-under 204 prior to his final-round 1-under 70. Was one of 10 first-time winners during the season and first at Cog Hill since Joe Durant in 1998. Win capped a period of eight top-10s in his last 10 starts and moved him to a career-best 17th in the Official World Golf Ranking...In first start of season, finished T8 with Craig Barlow at the Sony Open in Hawaii...Finished T6 at the Bay Hill Invitational, aided by a tournament-best 7-under 65 during the second round...Posted back-to-back top-10s for the first time in career, a T7 at MCI Heritage and T4 at the Shell Houston Open...Followed up with T7 the next week at the HP Classic of New Orleans, thanks to a final-round 65...Three weeks later, finished third at the Bank of America Colonial...Added another top-10, for five in row, with a T6 finish at the Memorial Tournament. Was one back of the lead through the first 18 holes and shared the 36-hole lead with Justin Rose and 2003 British Open champion Ben Curtis...Two weeks later, added his seventh top-10 in last nine starts with a T7 at the U.S. Open...Added a third career top-10 in a major with his T9 at the PGA Championship. One of 10 players to record multiple top-10s in the majors in 2004...Earned a spot in the TOUR Championship for the first time in his career and finished T4...Began the season 96th on Official World Golf Ranking list and had moved up to 21st through THE TOUR Championship.

CAREER HIGHLIGHTS:
Member of the PGA TOUR since 1997. Played European Tour from 1993 through 1997 and had three consecutive stints on Nationwide Tour starting in 1990. **2003:** The 72nd and last player to earn $1 million on the PGA TOUR during season...Shared first- and third-round leads before finishing T8 at Bob Hope Chrysler Classic. First-round 63 was his low round of the season, and best since a 63 at the 2001 B.C. Open...Season's best finish was a T5 at the Chrysler Classic of Greensboro. **2002:** Finished among the top 50 in earnings for the first time...Runner-up to Craig Perks at THE PLAYERS Championship. After starting the final round T21, recorded seven birdies (including four straight on Nos. 9-12) en route to 67, the second-lowest score of the day...One month later, cracked the $1-million mark for the first time in career with a T7 at the Greater Greensboro Chrysler Classic...Playing with younger brother Robert, finished T17 representing Trinidad and Tobago at the World Cup in Puerto Vallarta. **2001:** Finished 89th in earnings, the fourth consecutive year in the top 100...Recorded T8 at Compaq Classic of New Orleans and T6 in the B.C. Open...Low round of the year was a closing 63 at the B.C. Open. **2000:** Finished among the top 70 on the money list for the first time...Was two strokes off the lead heading into final round of the Bob Hope Chrysler Classic, but had to withdraw Sunday morning due to a pulled muscle in right shoulder...Recorded course-record 61 at "Blue Monster" course in second round of Doral-Ryder Open and was three back through 36 holes. Finished eighth...Best week of the season was Compaq Classic when he sat two strokes behind Carlos Franco after 36 holes and finished T4. Also, received word on a two-year extension on visa...Shared first-round lead with four others in The INTERNATIONAL and posted third top 10 with an eighth in Colorado...Final top 10 of the year was T5 in the Michelob Championship...Teamed with younger brother Robert in the World Cup, where they finished 19th. **1999:** Due to visa problems was unable to start the 1999 season until May. Made the most of the 18 events entered, making 11 cuts and finishing among top 10 four times...His debut came at the Kemper Open where he finished T44 after closing with 68. Missed birth of his second child during tournament week...Matched then-career-best finish with third at '99 Sprint International. **1998:** Was first rookie to post a top 10 on the year with a solo third at Nissan Open. **1997:** Finished third at the PGA TOUR Qualifying Tournament to earn exempt status for following season. **1996:** Claimed second European Tour title at the Benson and Hedges International Open. **1994:** Won first European Tour titile in the Open V33. **1991:** Earned only Nationwide Tour victory in the Pensacola Open. **1989:** Winner of Trinidad and Tobago Open.

PERSONAL:
Both parents were born in Trinidad and Tobago (father of English ancestry, mother of Portuguese)...He is the first touring professional to emerge from Trinidad and Tobago...Grandmother was a two-time Trinidad and Tobago champion...Met his Canadian wife, Jodi, a former flight attendant, on a flight between tournaments...Younger brother Robert, who has competed in three WGC-World Cups with Stephen, serves as his caddie.

PLAYER STATISTICS

2004 PGA TOUR STATISTICS

Scoring Average	69.90	(8)
Driving Distance	287.9	(89)
Driving Accuracy Percentage	65.0%	(80)
Total Driving	169	(61)
Greens in Regulation Pct.	68.4%	(23)
Putting Average	1.755	(33)
Sand Save Percentage	54.5%	(30)
Eagles (Holes per)	244.3	(95)
Birdie Average	3.95	(12)
All-Around Ranking	370	(5)
Scoring Avg. Before Cut	70.24	(20)
Round 3 Scoring Avg.	69.48	(11)
Final Round Scoring Average	70.00	(7)
Birdie Conversion Percentage	30.8%	(44)
Par Breakers	22.3%	(12)

MISCELLANEOUS PGA TOUR STATISTICS

2004 Low Round/Round: 64–4 times, most recent Cialis Western Open/3
Career Low Round/Round: 61–2000 Doral-Ryder Open/2
Career Largest Paycheck/Finish: $864,000–2004 Cialis Western Open/1

PGA TOUR CAREER SUMMARY — PLAYOFF RECORD: 0-0

Year	Events Played	Cuts Made	1st	2nd	3rd	Top 10	Top 25	Earnings	Rank
1996	1	1						$8,816	282
1997	2	2				1	1	110,461	163
1998	16	10			1	3	7	357,859	83
1999	18	11			1	4	5	460,760	84
2000	31	19				4	9	747,312	63
2001	26	19				2	8	574,451	89
2002	28	17		1		4	9	1,278,037	46
2003	27	19				4	9	1,005,959	72
2004	27	21	1		1	11	16	3,303,205	8
Total	176	119	1	1	3	33	64	7,846,860	
NATIONWIDE TOUR									
1990	24	20				5	15	32,226	28
1991	23	14	1	1	1	5	9	58,415	8
1992	20	10				3	5	25,906	58
Total	67	44	1	1	1	13	29	116,547	

PGA TOUR TOP TOURNAMENT SUMMARY

Year	93	94	95	96	97	98	99	00	01	02	03	04
U.S. Open					T68					DQ		T9
British Open	T51			T55	T5	T24				T69		CUT
PGA								T30		W/D	CUT	T9
THE PLAYERS						CUT		T42	CUT	2	T17	T13
TOUR Championship												T4
WGC-NEC Invitational												T22
WGC-American Express Champ												T36

NATIONAL TEAMS: WGC-World Cup, (3) 2000, 2002, 2003.

Billy Andrade (ANN-drade)

EXEMPT STATUS: 124th on 2004 money list
FULL NAME: William Thomas Andrade
HEIGHT: 5-8
WEIGHT: 155
BIRTHDATE: January 25, 1964
BIRTHPLACE: Bristol, RI
RESIDENCE: Bristol, RI and Atlanta, GA
FAMILY: Wife, Jody; Cameron James (4/5/94); Grace (4/7/97)
EDUCATION: Wake Forest University (1987, Sociology)
SPECIAL INTERESTS: All sports, Billy Andrade/ Brad Faxon Charities for Children
TURNED PROFESSIONAL: 1987
Q SCHOOL: 1987, 1988

PGA TOUR VICTORIES (4):
1991 Kemper Open, Buick Classic. **1998** Bell Canadian Open. **2000** Invensys Classic at Las Vegas.

OTHER VICTORIES (3):
1992 Fred Meyer Challenge [with Tom Kite]. **1999** Fred Meyer Challenge [with Brad Faxon]. **2001** Fred Meyer Challenge [with Brad Faxon].

BEST 2004 PGA TOUR FINISH:
T4—U.S. Bank Championship in Milwaukee.

2004 SEASON:
Finished among the top 125 for 16th consecutive season...On the bubble for fully exempt status in the latter part of the season, made six of last seven cuts to finish No. 124. Best finish during this stretch was T11 at the Bell Canadian Open, worth $103,500...Lone top-10 of the season was T4 at the U.S. Bank Championship in Milwaukee, best on TOUR since a T2 at the 2002 SEI Pennsylvania Classic...Held a share of the 36-hole lead with Jim Furyk and Vijay Singh at the Buick Open. Finished T15 after rounds of 73-70 on the weekend.

CAREER HIGHLIGHTS:
2003: First top-10 of the season, a T10, came at the Bay Hill Invitational...Entered the PGA Championship as the No. 5 alternate, replaced injured Larry Nelson in the field, and finished T10...Finished solo eighth at Las Vegas Invitational to jump into the top 100 on the money list and secure card for 2004...Aced the fourth hole at Forest Oaks CC with a 6-iron from 191 yards during the third round of the Chrysler Classic of Greensboro, his first ace on TOUR since the final round of the 1987 British Open. **2002:** Was top-50 on the money list for ninth time in his career with a career-best earnings of $1,365,707...With T4 finish at The Honda Classic, was one of three players (Brad Faxon and Brett Quigley) from Rhode Island to finish in the top four there...Career-best finish at THE PLAYERS Championship, with T4, four strokes behind champion Craig Perks...Held the outright lead for three rounds at the SEI Pennsylvania Classic. Closing round of 69 one back of winner Dan Forsman, who eagled the final hole. His runner up check of $290,400 lifted him over the $1-million mark for the third consecutive season. **2001:** In June, posted top-3 finishes in back-to-back weeks, at the Buick Classic (T3) and Canon Greater Hartford Open (second)...Closing 66 at PGA Championship produced sixth-place finish, his best showing in a major since a T6 at the 1992 U.S. Open. **2000:** Made one of the year's most dramatic moves up the money list after earning $765,000 for his win at the Invensys Classic at Las Vegas, the largest single payday of his career. Winning week at Las Vegas moved him from 159th to 43rd on the money list. Third-round 9-under-par 63 was his lowest 18-hole score of the year. **1998:** Came from behind to collect his third title at Bell Canadian Open. Rolled in 30-foot putt for par to secure a playoff with 54-hole leader Bob Friend. Won playoff with par on first extra hole. **1997:** In closest race ever for top 30, his season earnings of $665,602 missed qualifying for THE TOUR Championship by $5. Entered final week of season 30th on money list, $22,595 behind Andrew Magee, who was 29th. Fell to 31st when Bill Glasson jumped from 54th to 27th with Las Vegas Invitational victory. **1995:** Set then-course-record 62 at TPC at River Highlands at the Canon Greater Hartford Open (broken by Kirk Triplett with 61 in 2000). **1993:** At Buick Southern Open, part of five-man playoff won by John Inman. **1991:** In June 1991, became the first player in six years to win first two TOUR titles in consecutive weeks. Bernhard Langer (1985 Masters-Heritage) was previous player...Birdied first playoff hole to defeat Jeff Sluman at Kemper Open after both had carded a tournament-record 21-under-par 263...Defeated Brad Bryant by one stroke the following week in Buick Classic. **Amateur:** Three-time All-American at Wake Forest, where he was member of 1986 NCAA Championship team along with current TOUR player Len Mattiace...Winner of 1986 Sunnehanna Amateur and North and South Amateur...Top-ranked junior in country in 1981.

PERSONAL:
Along with Brad Faxon, runs Billy Andrade/Brad Faxon Charities for Children, Inc., which was formed in 1991 and has donated more than $4 million to children in Rhode Island and southeastern Massachusetts. In 1999, duo was honored by Golf Writers Association of America.

PLAYER STATISTICS

2004 PGA TOUR STATISTICS

Scoring Average	71.43	(132)
Driving Distance	283.5	(128)
Driving Accuracy Percentage	59.7%	(155)
Total Driving	283	(186)
Greens in Regulation Pct.	64.4%	(112)
Putting Average	1.773	(82)
Sand Save Percentage	50.5%	(78)
Eagles (Holes per)	208.0	(73)
Birdie Average	3.57	(85)
All-Around Ranking	845	(120)
Scoring Avg. Before Cut	71.14	(118)
Round 3 Scoring Avg.	71.71	(150)
Final Round Scoring Average	71.15	(69)
Birdie Conversion Percentage	29.8%	(74)
Par Breakers	20.3%	(83)

MISCELLANEOUS PGA TOUR STATISTICS

2004 Low Round/Round: 63–Bob Hope Chrysler Classic/4
Career Low Round/Round: 62–1995 Canon Greater Hartford Open/3
Career Largest Paycheck/Finish: $765,000–2000 Invensys Classic at Las Vegas/1

PGA TOUR CAREER SUMMARY — PLAYOFF RECORD: 2-1

Year	Events Played	Cuts Made	1st	2nd	3rd	Top 10	Top 25	Earnings	Rank
1983A	1								
1986A	2	2					2		
1987A	1								
1987	4	3						$4,001	235
1988	34	17				1	7	74,950	134
1989	31	17		1		3	6	202,242	69
1990	28	25				1	12	231,362	64
1991	29	19	2			4	10	615,765	14
1992	28	16			1	2	8	202,509	76
1993	29	18		1	1	7	10	365,759	40
1994	26	18		1	1	3	5	342,208	48
1995	29	16				3	8	276,494	69
1996	28	18		1		3	9	433,157	46
1997	28	23				4	14	665,602	31
1998	30	18	1			3	6	705,434	41
1999	29	17					7	345,801	118
2000	31	12	1			2	6	1,004,827	45
2001	27	14		1	1	6	8	1,313,047	40
2002	31	20		1		5	11	1,365,707	42
2003	29	19				3	5	659,694	97
2004	31	20				1	5	631,143	124
Total	506	312	4	6	4	51	139	9,439,702	

PGA TOUR TOP TOURNAMENT SUMMARY

Year	87	88	89	90	91	92	93	94	95	96	97	98	99
Masters	CUT					T54	61					CUT	T38
U.S. Open		CUT			CUT	T6	T33		T21	T23	T13	CUT	
British Open	T54					T25	CUT		CUT		70		CUT
PGA			CUT	T14	T32	T12	CUT	T47	CUT	CUT	CUT	T44	CUT
THE PLAYERS				CUT	T27	CUT	T20	CUT	T8	CUT	5	T35	T62
TOUR Championship					T13								

Year	00	01	02	03	04
Masters			CUT		
U.S. Open		CUT	CUT	CUT	
British Open		T13	CUT		
PGA		6	CUT	T10	CUT
THE PLAYERS	CUT	T44	T4	T48	CUT
WGC-Accenture Match Play			T33		
WGC-American Express Champ		CNL			

NATIONAL TEAMS: Junior World Cup, 1981 (won team title with Sam Randolph at Portmarnock, Ireland); World Amateur Team Championship, 1986; Walker Cup, 1987.

Stuart Appleby

EXEMPT STATUS: 2004 tournament winner (through 2006)
FULL NAME: Stuart Appleby
HEIGHT: 6-1
WEIGHT: 195
BIRTHDATE: May 1, 1971
BIRTHPLACE: Cohuna, Australia
RESIDENCE: Orlando, FL

FAMILY: Wife, Ashley
SPECIAL INTERESTS: Action sports, motor racing
TURNED PROFESSIONAL: 1992
Q SCHOOL: 1996
Nationwide Tour Alumnus

PGA TOUR VICTORIES (5):

1997 Honda Classic. **1998** Kemper Open. **1999** Shell Houston Open. **2003** Las Vegas Invitational. **2004** Mercedes Championships.

NATIONWIDE TOUR VICTORIES (2):

1995 Monterrey Open, Sonoma County Open.

INTERNATIONAL VICTORIES (2):

1998 Coolum Classic [Aus]. **2001** Holden Australian Open.

OTHER VICTORIES (1):

1999 CVS Charity Classic [with Jeff Sluman].

BEST 2004 PGA TOUR FINISHES:

1—Mercedes Championships; 2—Bay Hill Invitational Presented by MasterCard; 3—Nissan Open; T5—Cialis Western Open; T9—WGC-NEC Invitational.

2004 SEASON:

Finished in the top 20 (No. 13) on the PGA TOUR money list for the third time in his career and second consecutive season. Also won for second straight season. Earned fifth career PGA TOUR victory at the Mercedes Championships, becoming the third consecutive international player to capture the TOUR's season-opening event (Sergio Garcia, 2002; Ernie Els, 2003). Carded rounds of 66-67-66-71—270 to top Vijay Singh by one stroke, earning a career-best $1,060,000. Held first- and third-round leads...At the Nissan Open got within three shots of the lead on the back nine, but finished with six straight pars for 66 to finish alone in third three shots back of winner Mike Weir...Held four-stroke lead through 54 holes at the Bay Hill Invitational but a final-round 76 left him six strokes behind winner Chad Campbell. His second runner-up finish at Bay Hill gave him six top-3 finishes in his last 11 events on TOUR...Next top-10 did not come until July, a T5 at the Cialis Western Open...Finished T9 at WGC-NEC Invitational for second career NEC top-10 in six starts...Finished season with a T15 at THE TOUR Championship presented by Coca-Cola.

CAREER HIGHLIGHTS:

2003: Season punctuated by fourth career PGA TOUR victory at the Las Vegas Invitational, his first TOUR win since 1999. Finished a career-best 12th on the TOUR money list and represented the International team at The Presidents Cup in South Africa. Surpassed the $10-million mark in career TOUR earnings with victory at Las Vegas Invitational. Defeated Scott McCarron in playoff after the two set a tournament record with scores of 31-under 328, including career-low 62 in first round...Prior to win, had finished T2 three times earlier in the year, Shell Houston Open, 84 Lumber Classic of Pennsylvania and the WGC-American Express Championship. **2002:** Moved back into top 50 in season TOUR earnings with then-career-best $1,729,459, highlighted by near-miss at British Open. Best career finish in a major, T2, at the 131st British Open at Muirfield. After posting final-round 65 to join Ernie Els, Thomas Levet and Steve Elkington in playoff, bogeyed the fourth and final hole of the playoff to be eliminated...Second runner-up finish came at the Invensys Classic at Las Vegas, one stroke shy of Phil Tataurangi, who posted a final-round 62 in winning effort. **2001:** Despite four top-10s, fell out of the top 30, at 55th, for the first time since 1998. **2000:** Although winless for first time in four seasons, stood 24th on PGA TOUR official money list with earnings of $1,642,221 in 24 starts. Money total marked his best in five years on TOUR to date, and third time in which he surpassed $1 million...Best of five top-10 finishes came in his second start, as runner-up to Paul Azinger at Sony Open in Hawaii...Four sub-par rounds at PGA Championship produced 12-under-par 276, good for career-best T4 finish at that event...Participated in second career Presidents Cup as member of International Team, compiling 0-3 record. **1999:** Earned his third PGA TOUR title in as many seasons with Shell Houston Open win. Stood two strokes back after 36 holes and three back through 54 holes. Closing 71, the highest final round by a winner in 15 years at TPC at the Woodlands, was good for one-stroke victory over John Cook and Hal Sutton. Credited his late wife Renay with giving him the strength to win his first title since her death in the previous year. **1998:** Earned his second TOUR victory at Kemper Open. Trailed by one through 54 holes and survived windswept Sunday with closing 72, one stroke better than Scott Hoch. **1997:** Established himself as one of TOUR's young stars, becoming the first Q-School graduate to earn more than $1 million the following year...Won the Honda Classic, finished second twice and earned trip to THE TOUR Championship...Held one-stroke lead over Payne Stewart after 54 holes at Honda Classic. Closing 71 on windy Sunday enough for one-stroke victory over Stewart and Michael Bradley. **1995:** Became eighth player to win first Nationwide Tour event with victory at Monterrey Open...Earned place on PGA TOUR in 1996 by finishing fifth on the Nationwide Tour money list.

PERSONAL:

Raised on dairy farm, where he used to hit golf shots from paddock to paddock once his chores were completed...Former Australian Rules football player before turning to pro golf in 1992 and playing in Australia before coming to the United States in 1995.

PLAYER STATISTICS

2004 PGA TOUR STATISTICS

Scoring Average	70.47	(32)
Driving Distance	293.2	(42)
Driving Accuracy Percentage	62.5%	(125)
Total Driving	167	(58)
Greens in Regulation Pct.	65.1%	(95)
Putting Average	1.764	(56)
Sand Save Percentage	51.4%	(65)
Eagles (Holes per)	200.6	(70)
Birdie Average	3.76	(37)
All-Around Ranking	522	(26)
Scoring Avg. Before Cut	70.60	(48)
Round 3 Scoring Avg.	69.88	(26)
Final Round Scoring Average	71.69	(106)
Birdie Conversion Percentage	30.9%	(39)
Par Breakers	21.4%	(37)

MISCELLANEOUS PGA TOUR STATISTICS

2004 Low Round/Round: 64–Nissan Open/2
Career Low Round/Round: 62–2003 Las Vegas Invitational/1
Career Largest Paycheck/Finish: $1,060,000–2004 Mercedes Championships/1

PGA TOUR CAREER SUMMARY — PLAYOFF RECORD: 1-1

Year	Events Played	Cuts Made	1st	2nd	3rd	Top 10	Top 25	Earnings	Rank
1996	30	18				1	5	$164,483	130
1997	23	18	1	2		5	12	1,003,356	18
1998	22	12	1			5	7	717,962	40
1999	29	21	1	1		5	12	1,359,724	25
2000	24	20		1	1	5	15	1,642,221	24
2001	29	23				4	8	1,004,528	55
2002	28	21		2		4	10	1,729,459	32
2003	27	19	1	3		5	13	2,662,538	12
2004	25	18	1	1	1	5	14	2,949,235	13
Total	237	170	5	10	2	39	96	13,233,506	
NATIONWIDE TOUR									
1995	22	18	2	1		7	15	144,419	5
Total	22	18	2	1		7	15	144,419	
EUROPEAN TOUR									
2004	1	1					1	19,610	

PGA TOUR TOP TOURNAMENT SUMMARY

Year	97	98	99	00	01	02	03	04
Masters	T21	CUT	CUT	CUT	T31	CUT	CUT	T22
U.S. Open	T36	T10	CUT	CUT	CUT	T37	CUT	CUT
British Open	T20	CUT	CUT	T11	61	T2	T15	T36
PGA	T61	CUT	CUT	T4	T16	T17	T23	T17
THE PLAYERS	T14	CUT	CUT	T22	T33	T28	T21	CUT
TOUR Championship	T22		T26	7			27	T15
WGC-Accenture Match Play			T33	T33	T9	T33	T33	T17
WGC-NEC Invitational			T23	T20	T5	T42	T46	T9

NATIONAL TEAMS: The Presidents Cup (3), 1998, 2000, 2003; Dunhill Cup (3), 1997, 1998, 1999; World Cup, 2003.

Tommy Armour III

EXEMPT STATUS: 2003 tournament winner (through 2005)
FULL NAME: Thomas Dickson Armour III
HEIGHT: 6-2
WEIGHT: 190
BIRTHDATE: October 8, 1959
BIRTHPLACE: Denver, CO
RESIDENCE: Dallas, TX

FAMILY: Tommy (10/16/89)
EDUCATION: University of New Mexico
SPECIAL INTERESTS: Music, sports
TURNED PROFESSIONAL: 1981
Q SCHOOL: Fall 1981, 1987, 1996, 2001
Nationwide Tour Alumnus

PGA TOUR VICTORIES (2):

1990 Phoenix Open. **2003** Valero Texas Open.

NATIONWIDE TOUR VICTORIES (2):

1994 Miami Valley Open, Cleveland Open.

INTERNATIONAL VICTORIES (1):

1993 Mexican Open.

BEST 2004 PGA TOUR FINISHES:

T2—Chrysler Championship; T9—The Honda Classic.

2004 SEASON:

With two-year exemption in hand after winning the 2003 Valero Texas Open, struggled most of the season, posting two top-10s and three top-25s...Finished T9 at The Honda Classic, for his first top-10 since winning the Valero Texas Open...Finished T2 at Chrysler Championship, the last full-field event of the year, to jump from 153rd to 95th on the money list. Paycheck in Tampa ($440,000) was more than half of season's earnings ($844,634).

CAREER HIGHLIGHTS:

2003: After playing with partial status most of season, turned it around in September with second career victory at the Valero Texas Open, done in record-setting fashion with rounds of 64-62-63-65—254. The 254 total (26-under-par) broke Mark Calcavecchia's 72-hole PGA TOUR mark of 256 he set in winning at the 2001 Phoenix Open. The 54-hole total of 189 matched the OUR record shared by Calcavecchia and John Cook (1996 FedEx St. Jude Classic). Did not post a bogey until the back nine on Sunday. Was attempting to become the first player since Lee Trevino (1974 New Orleans Open) to win a TOUR event without a bogey. The 13 years and eight months and 366 starts between victories (1990 Phoenix Open) was the third-longest time between victories in TOUR history. At age 43 years, 11 months and 20 days, was one of 11 players age 40 or above to win on TOUR during the year. In relation to par for a par-70 golf course, also broke the TOUR record of 22-under-par set by Donnie Hammond at the 1989 Texas Open. Win was worth $630,000, the largest payday of career. **2002:** Picked up first top-10 finish since the 2000 Byron Nelson Classic with a T7 at the Sony Open in Hawaii...Led Greater Milwaukee Open after opening-round 63, lowest round on TOUR since 60 during second round of 1999 Las Vegas Invitational. Finished T8. **2001:** Finished 161st on the money list, returned to Qualifying Tournament and finished T8 to retain his card for the 2002 season. Played in 32 PGA TOUR events and posted three top-25s. **2000:** Earned full-exempt status for the third consecutive season on the strength of two top-10s. Best finish was T5 at the Nissan Open. **1999:** Came close to winning his first TOUR title since 1990 Phoenix Open when he lost a playoff to Gabriel Hjertstedt at the Touchstone Energy Tucson Open. Hjertstedt won playoff on the first extra hole with a birdie...Fired second-round 60 at Las Vegas CC in Las Vegas Invitational. His 12-under-par 60 included a missed two and one-half foot putt on 14. He became the only player 40 or older to shoot a 60 on a par-72 course. **1998:** Finished among the top-60 on the TOUR money list for the first time since 1990...Shot final-round 64 to finish T2 at Phoenix Open for first runner-up finish since 1990. **1994:** Found success on Nationwide Tour, winning Miami Valley and Cleveland Opens in consecutive weeks to become first player to win back-to-back Nationwide Tour events. Finished seventh on Nationwide Tour money list to gain spot on 1995 PGA TOUR...Played in 1994 U.S. Open at Oakmont CC, site of grandfather's 1927 U.S. Open victory. **1990:** Enjoyed success and consistency on the TOUR from 1988 through 1990, including a victory at the Phoenix Open. Phoenix was his first start of the season and he earned a five-stroke victory over Jim Thorpe...Nearly won again three weeks later, fin-

PGA TOUR CAREER SUMMARY — PLAYOFF RECORD: 0-1

Year	Events Played	Cuts Made	1st	2nd	3rd	Top 10	Top 25	Earnings	Rank
1982	14	5						$4,254	220
1983	1								
1984	3	1						781	267
1985	2								
1986	3	1				1	1	9,675	209
1987	3	1						970	290
1988	31	17		1		4	9	175,461	66
1989	32	21		1		2	7	185,018	81
1990	31	16	1	1		2	6	348,658	35
1991	31	15				1	3	90,478	140
1992	30	11					3	47,218	180
1993	20	7				1	2	52,011	181
1994	9	6			1	2	5	112,778	147
1995	30	16				1	5	134,407	141
1996	21	6				1	2	79,616	178
1997	30	18					7	163,664	131
1998	28	16		1		4	10	554,650	52
1999	28	16		1	1	5	6	782,185	54
2000	30	14				2	6	397,610	122
2001	32	14					3	238,091	161
2002	30	13				3	3	379,191	145
2003	23	11	1			1	4	932,984	76
2004	28	15		1		2	3	844,634	95
Total	490	240	2	6	2	32	85	5,534,333	
NATIONWIDE TOUR									
1992	1								
1993	5	3					2	3,529	159
1994	19	14	2	1	1	5	7	126,620	7
1996	6	2					1	1,838	194
1998	1	1			1	1	1	14,813	106
2003	1								
Total	33	20	2	1	2	6	11	146,799	

PGA TOUR TOP TOURNAMENT SUMMARY

Year	86	87	88	89	90	91	92	93	94	95	96	97	98
Masters					CUT								
U.S. Open				CUT					T55	T67			
British Open	T46		T28	T39	CUT								
PGA				T24	CUT								CUT
THE PLAYERS				CUT	CUT	71							T31

Year	99	00	01	02	03	04
U.S. Open		CUT			CUT	
PGA	CUT					T45
THE PLAYERS	CUT	CUT	W/D			CUT
WGC-NEC Invitational						T50

Tommy Armour III (Continued)

ishing second, two strokes behind Shearson Lehman Hutton champion Dan Forsman. Played on European and Asian Tours until fall of 1987. **1983:** Winner of the Mexican Open. **1982:** Qualified for the TOUR in 1981, but earned only $4,254 in 1982. **Amateur:** Winner of the 1981 New Mexico State Amateur.

PERSONAL:

Grandfather, known as "The Silver Scot," won the U.S. Open, British Open and PGA Championship...Started playing golf with his mom and dad when he was 10...Played golf and baseball in high school but decided to stick with golf because both seasons were during same time...After record-setting performance at the 2003 Valero Texas Open, commented on colorful career, "You only get one trip around life. Golf is just something that I love to do. I don't play for the money, I never have. I've made a lot of good friends through golf over the last 22 years playing golf professionally." Father Tommy, a surgeon and the son of "The Silver Scot," passed away on March 4, 2003.

PLAYER STATISTICS

2004 PGA TOUR STATISTICS

Scoring Average	71.72	(156)
Driving Distance	290.5	(70)
Driving Accuracy Percentage	62.4%	(129)
Total Driving	199	(104)
Greens in Regulation Pct.	65.1%	(95)
Putting Average	1.807	(173)
Sand Save Percentage	43.6%	(164)
Eagles (Holes per)	391.5	(165)
Birdie Average	3.30	(148)
All-Around Ranking	1,100	(178)
Scoring Avg. Before Cut	71.60	(151)
Round 3 Scoring Avg.	71.41	(137)
Final Round Scoring Average	71.60	(95)
Birdie Conversion Percentage	27.2%	(159)
Par Breakers	18.6%	(156)

MISCELLANEOUS PGA TOUR STATISTICS

2004 Low Round/Round: 64–Chrysler Championship/2
Career Low Round/Round: 60–1999 Las Vegas Invitational/2
Career Largest Paycheck/Finish: $630,000–2003 Valero Texas Open/1

SHOTLink
AN IBM ON DEMAND BUSINESS SOLUTION

HOT SHOTS

Long Hole

Plantation Course at Kapalua
18th Hole, Par 5, 663 Yards
Mercedes Championships

The par-5 18th hole at The Plantation Course at Kapalua can measure 692 yards from the back tee box. However, a severe drop from the tee to the fairway creates extraordinary distance for drives off the tee. A quick look at the hole:

DRIVING DISTANCE	AVERAGE (YARDS)
Round 1	391.5
Round 2	374.4
Round 3	390
Round 4	408.7
Total	**391.2**

In 2003, the average drive was 364.8 yards.

Longest holes on TOUR

EVENT/COURSE NAME	PAR	HOLE	TOUR SCORECARD YARDAGE
WGC-NEC Invitational Firestone CC (South Course)	5	16	667
Valero Texas Open LaCantera GC	5	1	665
Mercedes Championships Plantation Course at Kapalua	5	18	663
The INTERNATIONAL Castle Pines GC	5	1	644
Reno-Tahoe Open Montreux G&CC	5	17	636

The par-5 18th hole at The Plantation Course at Kapalua, site of the Mercedes Championships.

Woody Austin

EXEMPT STATUS: 2004 tournament winner (through 2006)
FULL NAME: Albert Woody Austin
HEIGHT: 6-0
WEIGHT: 190
BIRTHDATE: January 27, 1964
BIRTHPLACE: Tampa, FL
RESIDENCE: Derby, KS; plays out of Wolfcreek and Wichita CC
FAMILY: Wife, Shannon; Parker (3/31/98), Peyton (3/14/00)
EDUCATION: University of Miami (1986, Business Administration)
TURNED PROFESSIONAL: 1986
Q SCHOOL: 1994, 2002
Nationwide Tour Alumnus

PGA TOUR VICTORIES (2):

1995 Buick Open; **2004** Buick Championship

BEST 2004 PGA TOUR FINISHES:

1—Buick Championship; T4—The Honda Classic; 8—Reno-Tahoe Open.

2004 SEASON:

Earned a victory for the first time since his rookie season of 1995, a period of more than nine years, and went over the $1-million mark for the second straight season. . .Second TOUR victory came in August at the Buick Championship, his 301st career start. After opening 68-70-66, trailed leader Fred Funk by three strokes entering the final round. Posted a 4-under-par 66 on Sunday to finish tied with Tim Herron at 10-under-par 270. Defeated Herron with a birdie-3 on the first hole of a sudden-death playoff. Earned a career-best paycheck of $756,000. . .Recorded first top-10 of season, a T4, at The Honda Classic. . .Second top-10 was solo eighth at Reno-Tahoe Open, which came one week before his victory in Cromwell, CT.

CAREER HIGHLIGHTS:

2003: Finished in the top-50 for the first time since 1996. Earned over $1 million for the first time in his career, with $1,518,707...Runner-up to Davis Love III at MCI Heritage, falling on the fourth hole of a sudden-death playoff. Missed two putts inside 10 feet that would have clinched title on second and third playoff holes. Payday of $486,000 was a career high, and runner-up finish was best since playoff win over Mike Brisky at 1995 Buick Open. **2002:** With four sub-par rounds, finished T10 at the Reno-Tahoe Open, first top-10 since T8 at the 2001 INTERNATIONAL. Finished T26 at the Qualifying Tournament to return to the PGA TOUR in 2003. **2001:** A late surge earned playing card for 2002 by finishing 125th in earnings; second time in last three years he retained playing privileges with good play late in season. Made cut in his last three events, including T16 in National Car Rental Golf Classic at Walt Disney World...Only two top-10s came in consecutive starts, a T8 at John Deere Classic followed by a solo eighth in The INTERNATIONAL. **2000:** Collected $485,589 in prize money and had three top-10s...Missed the cut in his first six tournaments. Finished T7 in seventh start at the Touchstone Energy Tucson Open...At Buick Open, 1995 winner finished T4, worth $118,000, moving from 108th on the TOUR money list to 81st, enough to keep his card. **1999:** Made successful return to PGA TOUR, playing in 30 events and making the cut in 20 of those...Lone top-10 of the year came at the Reno-Tahoe Open where he finished T9...Finished 121st on the money list to retain his card. **1998:** Played mainly on Nationwide Tour and was first in scoring average (69.61) on way to eighth-place finish on money list to regain TOUR playing privileges. **1997:** Lost his card after finishing 180th on the money list. **1996:** Was among top-25 in 15 events and among top-10 in five events...Shared U.S. Open first-round lead with Payne Stewart after a 67...In defense of title, finished T3 at Buick Open. **1995:** Earned PGA TOUR Rookie of the Year honors. One of three rookies to qualify for THE TOUR Championship...Highlight was a playoff victory over Mike Brisky at Buick Open. Opening 63 gave him two-stroke lead, but lost his advantage to Payne Stewart after second round. Final-round 68 earned spot in playoff, which he won with par on first extra hole. Win was worth $216,000...Made 10 of 12 cuts leading up to TOUR Championship, where he finished fourth. **1994:** Made his debut on TOUR by capturing the 1994 PGA TOUR Qualifying Tournament. Finished 23rd on Nationwide Tour money list. . .Played in Japan (1989-90) and on mini-tours (1992-93).

PERSONAL:

Tore tendons and cartilage in left knee during 1987 Qualifying Tournament. Injury sidelined him for two years. Originally injured knee as 11-year old playing Little League baseball. . .Worked for years as credit-union teller during off-season. Also worked in supplies department at Eckerd Drug. . .After falling to Davis Love III in a playoff at the 2003 MCI Heritage, said of his previous struggles: "It's just so much fun to actually be in the game again and show people that I do know how to play the game and hit quality shots. I had numerous chances, and it just wasn't my day."

PLAYER STATISTICS

2004 PGA TOUR STATISTICS

Scoring Average	71.04	(85)
Driving Distance	291.3	(56)
Driving Accuracy Percentage	63.3%	(112)
Total Driving	168	(60)
Greens in Regulation Pct.	68.1%	(25)
Putting Average	1.775	(86)
Sand Save Percentage	46.9%	(129)
Eagles (Holes per)	282.0	(120)
Birdie Average	3.96	(9)
All-Around Ranking	622	(51)
Scoring Avg. Before Cut	71.07	(105)
Round 3 Scoring Avg.	70.33	(49)
Final Round Scoring Average	71.11	(66)
Birdie Conversion Percentage	31.1%	(34)
Par Breakers	22.3%	(12)

MISCELLANEOUS PGA TOUR STATISTICS

2004 Low Round/Round: 64–Southern Farm Bureau Classic/2
Career Low Round/Round: 63–4 times, most recent 2003 FUNAI Classic at the WALT DISNEY WORLD Resort/2
Career Largest Paycheck/Finish: $756,000–2004 Buick Championship/1

PGA TOUR CAREER SUMMARY — PLAYOFF RECORD: 2-1

Year	Events Played	Cuts Made	1st	2nd	3rd	Top 10	Top 25	Earnings	Rank
1992	1								
1995	34	22	1			7	12	$736,497	24
1996	35	26			1	5	15	539,397	32
1997	35	7				1	2	75,151	180
1998	10	5					1	56,028	203
1999	30	20				1	5	338,045	121
2000	32	19				3	5	485,589	100
2001	34	14				2	5	406,352	125
2002	36	14				1	3	307,348	156
2003	31	23		1		4	10	1,518,707	44
2004	29	18	1			3	8	1,495,980	45
Total	307	168	2	1	1	27	66	5,959,094	
NATIONWIDE TOUR									
1990	1								
1993	1	1						383	274
1994	26	18		1	1	6	10	72,206	23
1995	1								
1998	23	17		2	2	9	15	140,955	8
1999	1	1				1	1	8,250	135
Total	53	37		3	3	16	26	221,793	

PGA TOUR TOP TOURNAMENT SUMMARY

Year	95	96	97	98	99	00	01	02	03	04
Masters		CUT								
U.S. Open		T23				T37		CUT	T48	
British Open		CUT								
PGA	T23	T69							T27	T62
THE PLAYERS		T67	CUT			T61	CUT	CUT		T16
TOUR Championship	T4									

Aaron Baddeley (BAD-a-Lay)

EXEMPT STATUS: 123rd on 2004 money list
FULL NAME: Aaron John Baddeley
HEIGHT: 6-1
WEIGHT: 182
BIRTHDATE: March 17, 1981
BIRTHPLACE: Lebanon, NH
RESIDENCE: Scottsdale, AZ; plays out of Moonah Links GC (Victoria, Australia)

FAMILY: Single
SPECIAL INTERESTS: Music, fitness
TURNED PROFESSIONAL: 2000
JOINED TOUR: 2003
Nationwide Tour Alumnus

BEST PGA TOUR CAREER FINISHES:
2—2003 Sony Open in Hawaii, 2004 Chrysler Classic of Tucson.

INTERNATIONAL VICTORIES (3):
1999 Holden Australian Open [Aus]. **2000** Holden Australian Open [Aus]. **2001** Greg Norman Holden International [Aus].

BEST 2004 PGA TOUR FINISH:
2—Chrysler Classic of Tucson.

2004 SEASON:
Started his sophomore season with a bang making 70 percent of his season earnings during the West Coast Swing ($445,509, six tournaments), thanks to a runner-up finish in Tucson...In 38th career professional start finished second to Heath Slocum at the Chrysler Classic of Tucson. Had not made a bogey since the second round at the Omni Tucson National Golf Resort and Spa, but a three-putt on the 72nd green ended the streak and his chance at victory. Ironically, posted a season TOUR-low 95 putts in the tournament... Other top-25 finishes included a T21 at The Honda Classic, where he made his first career TOUR start in 2000 as an amateur and a T15 at the Sony Open in Hawaii...Needed to make the cut at the season-ending Chrysler Championship to secure a spot inside the top-125 on the final money list and placed 67th in Tampa.

CAREER HIGHLIGHTS:
2003: PGA TOUR rookie had a strong debut thanks to three top-10s, including losing in a playoff at the Sony Open in Hawaii. Finished the highest on the TOUR money list among the six Nationwide Tour graduates from the class of 2002 to retain TOUR cards, finishing 73rd...Made a 10-foot birdie putt on the 72nd hole at the Sony Open in Hawaii for a final-round 69 to get into a playoff with Ernie Els. On the second playoff hole at Waialae Country Club, Els made a 43-foot birdie putt from the fringe of the 10th green. Baddeley left his 20-foot birdie putt on the edge. The runner-up spot was his first career top-10 and worth a career-best $432,000...Missed the better part of three months during the year due to ankle injury suffered playing ultimate frisbee after the Bay Hill Invitational in late March. He was out of action from THE PLAYERS Championship until coming back at the FedEx St. Jude Classic, where he finished T53...Opened and closed with career-best 62s at the Valero Texas Open to finish fifth. **2002:** Earned his way on to the PGA TOUR via a 10th-place finish on the Nationwide Tour money list. Posted three runner-up finishes, at the Knoxville Open, Bank of America Monterey Peninsula Classic and the Gila River Classic. Closed out season with four top-15s to earn Player of the Month (October) honors. Made the cut in two of his three PGA TOUR appearances with his best finish, a T44 at the Reno-Tahoe Open. **2001:** Played in nine TOUR events and teamed with Adam Scott for a T14 at the WGC-EMC World Cup. Winner of the Greg Norman Holden International. Finished as the 2000-01 PGA TOUR of Australasia Order of Merit Champion and did not miss a cut on the PGA Tour of Australasia that year. **Amateur:** In 2000, made one cut, a T57 at Honda Classic, in nine TOUR appearances as an amateur. Stayed with countryman Greg Norman during The Honda Classic, his first TOUR start. Highlight of the year came when he defended his Holden Australian Open title...In 1999, won the Holden Australian Open as an amateur, becoming the youngest player to win that event and the first amateur since Bruce Devlin in 1959...First amateur to receive a special invitation to the Masters since 1976...Was selected to the Eisenhower World Team, becoming the youngest Australian to represent his country in any world team event.

PERSONAL:
Born in New Hampshire before family moved back to Australia when Aaron was only 2. Father Ron served as chief mechanic for Mario Andretti's race team in New Hampshire. Holds dual American and Australian citizenship...Introduced to golf at age 8 by his grandmother, Jean Baddeley...Counts fashion as one of his hobbies along with fitness, food and music. Is seen wearing fashion designer Johan Lindeberg clothing, both on and off the course...If he didn't become a professional golfer wanted to be the best fitness trainer in the world...Has his own golf tournament, the Aaron Baddeley Junior World Championship, held in Fiji last year with 40 players from five countries...Web site www.Badds.com.

PLAYER STATISTICS

2004 PGA TOUR STATISTICS

Scoring Average	71.61	(146)
Driving Distance	288.0	(87)
Driving Accuracy Percentage	53.1%	(191)
Total Driving	278	(184)
Greens in Regulation Pct.	58.2%	(195)
Putting Average	1.767	(64)
Sand Save Percentage	50.9%	(71)
Eagles (Holes per)	255.0	(104)
Birdie Average	3.34	(140)
All-Around Ranking	998	(155)
Scoring Avg. Before Cut	71.68	(160)
Round 3 Scoring Avg.	72.12	(171)
Final Round Scoring Average	72.63	(164)
Birdie Conversion Percentage	30.1%	(66)
Par Breakers	19.0%	(140)

MISCELLANEOUS PGA TOUR STATISTICS

2004 Low Round/Round: 64–Chrysler Classic of Tucson/3
Career Low Round/Round: 62–2 times, most recent 2003 Valero Texas Open/4
Career Largest Paycheck/Finish: $486,000–2003 Sony Open in Hawaii/2

PGA TOUR CAREER SUMMARY — PLAYOFF RECORD: 0-1

Year	Events Played	Cuts Made	1st	2nd	3rd	Top 10	Top 25	Earnings	Rank
2000A	9	1							
2001	9	2						$19,435	
2002	3	2						16,380	
2003	20	15		1		3	4	989,168	73
2004	27	16		1		1	3	632,876	123
Total	68	36		2		4	7	1,657,859	
NATIONWIDE TOUR									
2001	1	1						1,413	279
2002	17	11		3	1	5	9	216,536	10
Total	18	12		3	1	5	9	217,949	
EUROPEAN TOUR									
2003	1	1						5,350	

PGA TOUR TOP TOURNAMENT SUMMARY

Year	00	01	02	03	04
Masters	CUT	CUT			
U.S. Open	CUT				CUT
British Open		CUT			CUT
PGA				T57	
THE PLAYERS					CUT
WGC-American Express Champ		CNL			

NATIONAL TEAMS: World Cup, 2001.Eisenhower Cup, 2000.

Briny Baird

EXEMPT STATUS: 69th on 2004 money list
FULL NAME: Michael Jancey Baird
HEIGHT: 5-11
WEIGHT: 170
BIRTHDATE: May 11, 1972
BIRTHPLACE: Miami Beach, FL
RESIDENCE: Jupiter, FL
FAMILY: Wife, Laura; Madison Kaye (3/10/03)
EDUCATION: Valdosta State University (1995, Communications)
SPECIAL INTERESTS: Fishing
TURNED PROFESSIONAL: 1995
Q SCHOOL: 1998
Nationwide Tour Alumnus

BEST PGA TOUR CAREER FINISHES:
2—2001 John Deere Classic, T2—2003 Buick Open, 2004 FUNAI Classic at the WALT DISNEY WORLD Resort.

NATIONWIDE TOUR VICTORIES (1):
2000 Monterrey Open.

BEST 2004 PGA TOUR FINISHES:
T2—FUNAI Classic at the WALT DISNEY WORLD Resort; T5—Sony Open in Hawaii; T10—Nissan Open.

2004 SEASON:
Finished in the top-100 on the final money list for the fourth consecutive season. Posted three top-10s in 30 TOUR starts, including a T2 finish...Posted a T5 finish in first full-field event of the season at the Sony Open in Hawaii, carding four rounds in the 60s to finish five shots out of the Ernie Els-Harrison Frazar playoff...Was one back of the lead through 36 holes at the Nissan Open after firing a 9-under-par 62 in the second round and finished T10...Made his first start in a World Golf Championships event at the Accenture Match Play Championship. Lost to Davis Love III in the first round, 1-up...Made a hole-in-one on the third hole during the first round of the Buick Open with a 4-iron from 197 yards. His father, Butch, made the first hole-in-one at the Buick Open in 1962 on the same hole...Held the lead through 36 and 54 holes at the FUNAI Classic at WALT DISNEY WORLD Resort. Finished T2 after Ryan Palmer came from five strokes back with a 62. It was the third runner-up finish of his career. Collected a career-best $369,600 which pushed him over the $1-million mark for the second straight season.

CAREER HIGHLIGHTS:
2003: Finished a career-best 22nd on the final money list with a career-high seven top-10s...Posted a top-10 in his first start of the season at the Sony Open in Hawaii, with T7...Finished T4 at Buick Invitational, six strokes behind champion Tiger Woods...Posted back-to-back top-10s for the first time in his career at the HP Classic of New Orleans (T8) and EDS Byron Nelson Championship (T9)...Held first- and second-round leads and shared third-round lead with Skip Kendall, Jonathan Kaye and John Rollins at the Buick Classic. Finished T30 after a final-round 77...Aided by rounds of 65-66 on the weekend, finished T2 at Buick Open, two shots behind champion Jim Furyk...Tied a TOUR birdie-eagle streak record during the second round of the FUNAI Classic at the WALT DISNEY WORLD Resort. Began streak with an eagle on the 15th hole and then birdied the next seven holes for a total of 9-under over eight holes. Billy Mayfair set the mark at the 2001 Buick Open...Finished T13 in his first trip to THE TOUR Championship. **2002:** Recorded two top-10s and earned $817,514...Best finish of the year was a T3 at the Bob Hope Chrysler Classic at 28-under-par 332, two strokes behind champion Phil Mickelson and David Berganio Jr. **2001:** Made most of return to TOUR by finishing 63rd on the final season money list...Runner-up at John Deere Classic, where he finished one stroke behind first-time winner David Gossett. Second-place check worth $302,400 or $27,306 less than father Butch Baird won in 20-plus years on PGA TOUR. **2000:** Graduated to the PGA TOUR with fourth-place finish on the Nationwide Tour money list...Won the Monterey Open with tournament-record 20-under par. **1999:** Finished 186th on the money list as a TOUR rookie. **1998:** Finished 12th at PGA TOUR Qualifying School to earn his first TOUR card. **Amateur:** 1994 and 1995 Division II champion and Player of the Year at Valdosta (GA) State...Winner of Press Thornton Future Masters in 1989.

PERSONAL:
Beginning in 2003, in cooperation with Canon, U.S.A., Inc., and the National Center for Missing & Exploited Children (NCMEC), placed a photo of a local missing child on his golf bag at every PGA TOUR event to raise awareness of missing children in the United States. As an additional component of Canon4Kids, for each birdie registered by Baird, Canon donates $100 to NCMEC, with additional donations for eagles and aces...Was MVP of high school soccer team...Father, Butch Baird, is a Champions Tour player...Says his biggest thrill in golf was "repeating as Division II champion and ending amateur career with a win."

PLAYER STATISTICS

2004 PGA TOUR STATISTICS

Scoring Average	70.79	(56)
Driving Distance	289.4	(73)
Driving Accuracy Percentage	65.0%	(80)
Total Driving	153	(38)
Greens in Regulation Pct.	70.6%	(5)
Putting Average	1.780	(107)
Sand Save Percentage	42.1%	(178)
Eagles (Holes per)	291.0	(124)
Birdie Average	3.62	(72)
All-Around Ranking	695	(78)
Scoring Avg. Before Cut	70.34	(26)
Round 3 Scoring Avg.	70.62	(67)
Final Round Scoring Average	71.80	(117)
Birdie Conversion Percentage	28.0%	(132)
Par Breakers	20.4%	(80)

MISCELLANEOUS PGA TOUR STATISTICS
2004 Low Round/Round: 62–Nissan Open/2
Career Low Round/Round: 62–2 times, most recent 2004 Nissan Open/2
Career Largest Paycheck/Finish: $369,600–2004 FUNAI Classic at the WALT DISNEY WORLD Resort/T2

SECTION 2 PLAYER BIOGRAPHIES

PGA TOUR CAREER SUMMARY — PLAYOFF RECORD: 0-0

Year	Events Played	Cuts Made	1st	2nd	3rd	Top 10	Top 25	Earnings	Rank
1999	28	12						$115,357	186
2001	31	22		1		2	6	812,001	63
2002	33	22			1	2	6	817,514	82
2003	33	24		1	1	7	16	2,202,519	22
2004	30	21		1		3	9	1,156,517	69
Total	155	101		3	2	14	37	5,103,908	
NATIONWIDE TOUR									
1996	22	8					2	11,369	115
1997	23	11				2	7	33,433	58
2000	26	19	1	1		9	14	271,897	4
Total	71	38	1	1		11	23	316,699	

PGA TOUR TOP TOURNAMENT SUMMARY

Year	01	02	03	04
Masters				CUT
U.S. Open	T40			CUT
PGA	T22	T43	T39	T37
THE PLAYERS		T49	T11	T33
TOUR Championship			T13	
WGC-Accenture Match Play				T33

Craig Barlow

EXEMPT STATUS: Minor Medical Extension
FULL NAME: Craig Alan Barlow
HEIGHT: 5-11
WEIGHT: 205
BIRTHDATE: July 23, 1972
BIRTHPLACE: Henderson, NV
RESIDENCE: Henderson, NV; plays out of Reflection Bay at Lake Las Vegas
FAMILY: Wife, Lee Ann; Joel Nino, Jason Nino, Jeremy Nino
SPECIAL INTERESTS: Table tennis, tennis
TURNED PROFESSIONAL: 1995
Q SCHOOL: 1997, 1998, 2000

BEST PGA TOUR CAREER FINISH:

T3—1999 Buick Challenge, 2002 Air Canada Championship.

BEST 2004 PGA TOUR FINISH:

T8—Sony Open in Hawaii.

2004 SEASON:

After finishing No. 128 on the money list in 2004, improved status for 2005 with a T26 finish at PGA TOUR Qualifying Tournament. Will also receive a Minor Medical Extension for 2005 due to time missed (April-June) with hip and wrist injuries. Coupled with $595,820 earned in 25 events in 2004, has the opportunity to play in four events to earn $27,442 and match the $623,262 in earnings of 2004's No. 125, Tag Ridings. If he does so, will play out of the Major Medical Extension category for the remainder of the season...Began the year with four rounds in the 60s to finish T8 at the Sony Open in Hawaii...Best finish the rest of the way was T12 at the Buick Open...Entered the season's final full-field event, the Chrysler Championship, No. 126 on the money list but missed the cut to finish No. 128.

CAREER HIGHLIGHTS:

2003: Career highs in money earned ($638,721) and money list position (100th). Finished in the top 125 for the third consecutive season and the fourth overall...In late July compiled first top-10, T4 at the Greater Hartford Open. Finished four shots behind Peter Jacobsen with four rounds in the 60s...Nevada native tied for the 54-hole lead with Tim Herron at the Reno-Tahoe Open. Final-round 75 dropped finish to T6...Solidified his job for 2004 with a T8 finish at the 84 Lumber Classic of Pennsylvania. Entered week 120th on the money list and $120,000 paycheck moved him to No. 103 ($552,374). **2002:** Got off to a late start due to hip and shoulder surgery in fall of 2001 to finish just inside top 125 to secure TOUR card for 2003...Withdrew from first event back from surgery at Honda Classic in March, where suspension of play would have forced 36 holes of play on Saturday...First top-10 did not come until August, when he finished T7 at The INTERNATIONAL. Held third-round lead by one point...At the Air Canada Championship, a T3 matched best TOUR finish of T3 at the 1999 Buick Challenge. The $182,000 payday in Vancouver was the best of his career...Finished T7 at Tampa Bay Classic, boosting official earnings inside top 125 (120th, $486,288) for the first time all season...Never fell out of top 125 for the rest of the season, despite missing cuts in three of final four events. **2001:** Made first nine cuts of season, then made just five the remainder of the way...From first week of February through first week of March earned three of his four top-25s...Only top-10 came at AT&T Pebble Beach National Pro-Am. **2000:** Best effort of the season came at the Tampa Bay Classic where he finished T10...After finishing 137th on the money list went to Qualifying Tournament and improved his position on TOUR by finishing T21. **1999:** Successful sophomore season on the PGA TOUR...Highlight of the year was T4 at the Compaq Classic of New Orleans...His career best came late in the season at the Buick Challenge where he finished T3. Prior to the week, was 153rd on the money list, but earned $93,600 and moved to 126th on money list...In hometown, took first-round lead in Las Vegas Invitational after shooting career-best 11-under-par 61. Finished T9. Check worth $32,500 helped secure 2000 card. **1998:** Best finish was T14 at the Kemper Open...Failed to retain playing privileges by finishing 183rd on TOUR money list...Returned to Qualifying Tournament and finished 18th. **1997:** Earned TOUR status for 1998 after finishing 28th at the PGA TOUR Qualifying Tournament. **Amateur:** Winner of the 1994 Nevada State Amateur Championship...Qualified for the 1994 U.S. Open as an amateur...Named 1994 Southern Nevada Golf Association Player of the Year...1995 Nevada State Match Play Champion.

PERSONAL:

About injuries that plagued him in his career: "It's been frustrating, but I promised myself through this whole thing that I was going to be patient. It's hard to perform against the best golfers in the world when your body is not allowing you to do it."...As a kid, served as standard-bearer for the Las Vegas Invitational. Later, worked on tournament operations staff...Ranked fifth in state of Nevada as high school tennis player in 1990...Worked at Pizza Hut for five years before playing on PGA TOUR.

PLAYER STATISTICS

2004 PGA TOUR STATISTICS

Scoring Average	70.99	(79)
Driving Distance	291.0	(61)
Driving Accuracy Percentage	67.8%	(49)
Total Driving	110	(8)
Greens in Regulation Pct.	67.7%	(31)
Putting Average	1.787	(119)
Sand Save Percentage	52.9%	(43)
Eagles (Holes per)	140.4	(23)
Birdie Average	3.65	(67)
All-Around Ranking	472	(18)
Scoring Avg. Before Cut	70.77	(63)
Round 3 Scoring Avg.	70.47	(57)
Final Round Scoring Average	71.14	(68)
Birdie Conversion Percentage	29.7%	(80)
Par Breakers	21.0%	(58)

MISCELLANEOUS PGA TOUR STATISTICS

2004 Low Round/Round: 66–5 times, most recent Michelin Championship at Las Vegas/1
Career Low Round/Round: 61–1999 Las Vegas Invitational/1
Career Largest Paycheck/Finish: $182,000–2002 Air Canada Championship/T3

PGA TOUR CAREER SUMMARY — PLAYOFF RECORD: 0-0

Year	Events Played	Cuts Made	1st	2nd	3rd	Top 10	Top 25	Earnings	Rank
1994A	1								
1998	29	13					2	$98,111	183
1999	28	16			1	2	3	327,393	124
2000	31	19				1	4	297,672	137
2001	23	14				1	4	414,139	122
2002	22	9			1	3	5	528,569	124
2003	29	17				3	5	638,721	100
2004	25	14				1	7	595,820	128
Total	188	102			2	11	30	2,900,425	
NATIONWIDE TOUR									
1998	2	1					1	1,748	209
Total	2	1					1	1,748	

PGA TOUR TOP TOURNAMENT SUMMARY

Year	94	95	96	97	98	99	00	01	02	03	04
U.S. Open	CUT										
THE PLAYERS							T57		CUT	CUT	CUT

Brian Bateman

EXEMPT STATUS: 86th on 2004 money list
FULL NAME: Brian Bateman
HEIGHT: 5-10
WEIGHT: 185
BIRTHDATE: February 25, 1973
BIRTHPLACE: Monroe, LA
RESIDENCE: Monroe, LA; plays out of Bayou de Siard CC
FAMILY: Wife, Dawn
EDUCATION: Louisiana State University (1996, Marketing)
SPECIAL INTERESTS: Duck hunting, fishing, cooking, wine, Deuce (dog)
TURNED PROFESSIONAL: 1996
Q SCHOOL: 2001, 2002, 2003
Nationwide Tour Alumnus

BEST PGA TOUR CAREER FINISH:
3—2004 The Honda Classic.

NATIONWIDE TOUR VICTORIES (1):
1998 Carolina Classic.

BEST 2004 PGA TOUR FINISHES:
3—The Honda Classic; T7—HP Classic of New Orleans.

2004 SEASON:
Finished in the top 125 for the first time in his three-year PGA TOUR career. Year included his first two top-10s on TOUR and a career-high six top-25s...Solid play allowed him to jump up the Official World Golf Ranking list from No. 428 to No. 176 after THE TOUR Championship...Finished third at The Honda Classic for first career top-10 in his 66th career start. Previous best was T11 at the 2003 HP Classic of New Orleans. Collected $340,000, which topped his best year on TOUR in 2002, when he made 31 starts and earned $281,421...Louisiana native and LSU graduate posted four rounds in the 60s to finish T7 at the HP Classic of New Orleans.

CAREER HIGHLIGHTS:
2003: Earned PGA TOUR card for third consecutive season through TOUR Qualifying Tournament where he finished T12. Made 10 cuts in 26 starts in 2003, with one top-25, a T11 in home state at HP Classic of New Orleans. **2002:** Rookie season, making just over half of his cuts and posting four top-25s, including a then-career-best T15 at the SEI Pennsylvania Classic. Earned return trip to TOUR via a T8 finish at the Qualifying Tournament. **2001:** Member of Nationwide Tour for fifth straight season. Finished 58th on Nationwide Tour money list but earned first TOUR card by finishing T32 at TOUR Qualifying Tournament. **1998:** Best season on Nationwide Tour when he finished 20th on the money list with $107,590 in earnings. Picked up first career victory at Carolina Classic in Raleigh, NC, coming from behind to defeat Jimmy Green by one stroke. Lost playoff to Matt Gogel later that year at Tri-Cities Open. **Amateur:** NCAA All-America selection in 1996...NCAA Academic All-America in 1995...Three-time All-Southeastern Conference selection, as well as three-time Academic All-SEC selection...Winner of 1992 Louisiana State Amateur Championship...Louisiana state junior champion in 1990 and state high school champion in 1989.

PERSONAL:
A big wine enthusiast with an extensive collection. He and his wife travel to the California wine country often...Avid LSU football and Atlanta Braves baseball fan...Has five nieces and two nephews...Loves TV Food Network and to cook...Collects famous musician's memorabilia...Avid reader, especially Clive Cussler novels.

PLAYER STATISTICS

2004 PGA TOUR STATISTICS

Scoring Average	70.95	(75)
Driving Distance	292.2	(48)
Driving Accuracy Percentage	66.1%	(65)
Total Driving	113	(9)
Greens in Regulation Pct.	66.6%	(54)
Putting Average	1.766	(61)
Sand Save Percentage	48.5%	(106)
Eagles (Holes per)	160.0	(44)
Birdie Average	3.63	(70)
All-Around Ranking	523	(27)
Scoring Avg. Before Cut	70.55	(43)
Round 3 Scoring Avg.	71.47	(140)
Final Round Scoring Average	71.06	(60)
Birdie Conversion Percentage	30.3%	(58)
Par Breakers	20.8%	(65)

MISCELLANEOUS PGA TOUR STATISTICS

2004 Low Round/Round: 65–FedEx St. Jude Classic/2
Career Low Round/Round: 65–2004 FedEx St. Jude Classic/2
Career Largest Paycheck/Finish: $340,000–2004 The Honda Classic/3

PGA TOUR CAREER SUMMARY — PLAYOFF RECORD: 0-0

Year	Events Played	Cuts Made	1st	2nd	3rd	Top 10	Top 25	Earnings	Rank
1991	1								
1997	1								
1998	1								
2002	31	16					4	281,421	159
2003	26	10					1	217,150	173
2004	24	18			1	2	6	919,255	86
Total	84	44			1	2	11	1,417,826	
NATIONWIDE TOUR									
1997	20	8				2	2	16,735	96
1998	26	17	1	1		5	10	107,590	20
1999	22	8					3	13,059	115
2000	18	9					4	37,607	101
2001	24	17				2	10	75,343	58
Total	110	59	1	1		9	29	250,334	

PGA TOUR TOP TOURNAMENT SUMMARY

Year	04
PGA	CUT

Cameron Beckman

EXEMPT STATUS: 107th on 2004 money list
FULL NAME: Cameron Reid Beckman
HEIGHT: 6-1
WEIGHT: 205
BIRTHDATE: February 15, 1970
BIRTHPLACE: Minneapolis, MN
RESIDENCE: San Antonio, TX
FAMILY: Wife, Jennifer; Hannah Reid (10/16/02)

EDUCATION: Texas Lutheran University (1993, Art)
SPECIAL INTERESTS: Art, movies, time with friends
TURNED PROFESSIONAL: 1993
Q SCHOOL: 1998, 1999, 2000
Nationwide Tour Alumnus

PGA TOUR VICTORIES (1):

2001 Southern Farm Bureau Classic.

BEST 2004 PGA TOUR FINISHES:

T4—FUNAI Classic at the WALT DISNEY WORLD Resort; T9—Buick Classic.

2004 SEASON:

Finished in the top 125 for the third consecutive season. Ended the season on a high mark, making five cuts in last six starts, including T4 in the FUNAI Classic at WALT DISNEY WORLD Resort...Held a one-stroke lead at the MCI Heritage after a first-round 67 but followed with three rounds in the 70s to finish T45...First of only two top-10s of the season came in June, T9 at the Buick Classic. Was one back of the lead through 54 holes but a closing 75 at Westchester Country Club dropped him to T9...Enjoyed a strong end of the season, starting with a T13 at the 84 LUMBER Classic. Fifth consecutive cut made at the event...In mid-October finished T16 at the Chrysler Championship of Greensboro...The next week headed into the FUNAI Classic at the WALT DISNEY WORLD Resort ranked 103rd on the season money list. Sat two strokes back through 54 holes, closed with 69 to finish T4, his best finish since finishing T3 at the 2002 Bob Hope Chrysler Classic. Collected a season-best $184,800 at the FUNAI Classic to secure his card for the 2005 season with only one full-field tournament remaining.

CAREER HIGHLIGHTS:

2003: Shared second-round lead with Robert Damron at the 84 Lumber Classic of Pennsylvania and held two-stroke advantage through 54 holes prior to picking up his only top-10 of the season, a T5. Entered the week No. 117 on money list, earnings of $146,000 moved him to 95th on the money list, thus securing his card for another season...Had a bulging disc late in the season that kept him from competition. Doctors recommended that he should spend the end of the season doing an extensive workout program so he could be healthy for the 2004 season. His last event of the year was the Valero Texas Open in late September. **2002:** Finished comfortably inside the top 100 in earnings, 72nd...Logged best finish of season with T3 at the Bob Hope Chrysler Classic at 28-under-par 332, two strokes behind the playoff of Phil Mickelson and David Berganio, Jr. **2001:** Ended the year strong by earning first TOUR victory to finish a career-high 50th on money list. Despite nearly withdrawing from the Southern Farm Bureau Classic, the last full-field official money event of the year, because of a stiff neck, fired consecutive 67s to edge Chad Campbell by one stroke. Down the stretch, birdied three of the final five holes to make up a three-stroke deficit and record a 19-under 269 total. **2000:** Finished in the Top-25 six times, including back-to-back T14s at the Westin Texas Open and Buick Challenge...Shared the first-round lead at Michelob Championship at Kingsmill after an opening 66. Was two back after 54 holes. Closing 73 produced T15. **1999:** Posted three top-25s in 28 PGA TOUR events...Posted four consecutive rounds at or below par at the Buick Challenge on the way to a season-best finish of T13. **1998:** Member of the Nationwide Tour for the second consecutive year. **1994:** Lone Star Tour Player of the Year. **Amateur:** 1991 NAIA individual champion at Texas Lutheran.

PLAYER STATISTICS

2004 PGA TOUR STATISTICS

Statistic	Value	Rank
Scoring Average	70.77	(52)
Driving Distance	291.2	(59)
Driving Accuracy Percentage	66.5%	(62)
Total Driving	121	(15)
Greens in Regulation Pct.	67.0%	(44)
Putting Average	1.771	(79)
Sand Save Percentage	47.3%	(122)
Eagles (Holes per)	144.0	(27)
Birdie Average	3.72	(56)
All-Around Ranking	501	(23)
Scoring Avg. Before Cut	70.32	(23)
Round 3 Scoring Avg.	70.68	(70)
Final Round Scoring Average	71.05	(58)
Birdie Conversion Percentage	29.9%	(71)
Par Breakers	21.4%	(37)

MISCELLANEOUS PGA TOUR STATISTICS

2004 Low Round/Round: 65–2 times, most recent FUNAI Classic at the WALT DISNEY WORLD Resort/2
Career Low Round/Round: 63–2 times, most recent 2003 Valero Texas Open/1
Career Largest Paycheck/Finish: $432,000–2001 Southern Farm Bureau Classic/1

PGA TOUR CAREER SUMMARY — PLAYOFF RECORD: 0-0

Year	Events Played	Cuts Made	1st	2nd	3rd	Top 10	Top 25	Earnings	Rank
1993	1								
1997	1	1						$5,185	305
1998	1								
1999	28	12					3	147,036	172
2000	26	14					6	291,515	139
2001	29	23	1			4	7	1,071,343	50
2002	26	18			1	3	9	907,740	72
2003	26	18				1	6	608,981	106
2004	30	20				2	4	779,189	107
Total	168	106	1		1	10	35	3,810,988	
NATIONWIDE TOUR									
1995	3	2					1	2,416	198
1997	23	8				1	2	11,089	117
1998	3								
1999	1								
2000	4	3						6,948	190
Total	34	13				1	3	20,454	

PGA TOUR TOP TOURNAMENT SUMMARY

Year	00	01	02	03	04
U.S. Open	CUT				
British Open					CUT
PGA			T53		
THE PLAYERS			CUT	CUT	T26

Rich Beem

EXEMPT STATUS: Winner, 2002 PGA Championship (through 2007)
FULL NAME: Richard Michael Beem
HEIGHT: 5-8
WEIGHT: 165
BIRTHDATE: August 24, 1970
BIRTHPLACE: Phoenix, AZ
RESIDENCE: Austin, TX

FAMILY: Wife, Sara; Michael Waide (7/23/03)
EDUCATION: New Mexico State University (1993, Marketing)
SPECIAL INTERESTS: Music, water sports, cooking
TURNED PROFESSIONAL: 1994
Q SCHOOL: 1998

PGA TOUR VICTORIES (3):

1999 Kemper Open. **2002** The INTERNATIONAL Presented by Qwest, PGA Championship.

OTHER VICTORIES (1):

2002 Hyundai Team Matches [with Peter Lonard].

BEST 2004 PGA TOUR FINISHES:

T33—WGC-Accenture Match Play Championship, FedEx St. Jude Classic

2004 SEASON:

Did not post a top-25 for first time in six seasons on the PGA TOUR…Top finishes were T33 at WGC-Accenture Match Play Championship and FedEx St. Jude Classic…Past champion opened with 7-under 64 at the Booz Allen Classic and was three back of leader Charles Howell III. Finished T51…Second place through 36 holes at the U.S. Bank Championship in Milwaukee after opening 66-66, but placed T57.

CAREER HIGHLIGHTS:

2003: Collected his first top-10 of the season with a T10 at the Nissan Open...Playing in the Masters for the first time, finished T15...Finished second to Tiger Woods at the Western Open, aided by rounds of 65-67 on the weekend. **2002:** Had a career year on TOUR, seventh place on the money list with season earnings of $2,938,365 and consecutive victories, including a major championship title at the PGA...Early in the season posted a solo fourth at Genuity Championship...Runner-up finish at Kemper Insurance Open was best finish since capturing the Kemper in 1999, carding four rounds in the 60s for only the third time in his career on the PGA TOUR. Finished one stroke behind champion Bob Estes...Collected $810,000 for winning The INTERNATIONAL, his second career victory, more than he had made in any of his previous three seasons on TOUR. Recorded 19 points on Sunday to come from three back of third-round leader Craig Barlow and defeat Steve Lowery by a stroke. Eagle on No. 17 offset Lowery's double eagle there later...In next start, won his first major title with a one-stroke victory over Tiger Woods at the PGA. Shared the lead through 36 holes with four other players and was three back of Justin Leonard playing in the final pairing on Sunday. With a 66, he became the first final-round, come-from-behind winner in a major since the 1999 British Open, when Paul Lawrie came from 10 back to win a playoff at Carnoustie. Eagled the 13th hole and made a 35-foot birdie putt on the 16th hole to hold off Woods. Became the first player during the year to win in consecutive starts...Including T6 at WGC-NEC Invitational, totaled $1,950,00 in three August starts. **2001:** Opened the year with a bang in the first full-field event, finishing T9 at Touchstone Energy Tucson Open...Second top-10 came near the end of the season, a T7 at the Michelob Championship. His $101,850 paycheck in Williamsburg secured a 2002 card. **2000:** Made 13 cuts in 29 starts and finished with two top-25s...Best outing of the year came at the Bob Hope Chrysler Classic with a T12 finish. **1999:** Nominated for Rookie of the Year honors after earning his first TOUR victory at the Kemper Open in only his 12th start on TOUR. Opened with a 66 for a one-stroke lead, which he extended to three with a second-round 67. Third-round 71 left him tied for lead with Tommy Armour III. Closing 70 produced a one-stroke victory over Bradley Hughes and Bill Glasson worth $450,000. Prior to winning Kemper Open, biggest first-place check was $5,000 he earned for winning 1998 Conrad Hilton Open in Socorro, NM. **1998:** Earned status on the PGA TOUR for the 1999 season with a T8 finish at the Qualifying Tournament in Palm Springs, CA...Played mini-tour events in the Sun Country PGA Section and was named Player of the Year after victories in Soccoro and Truth Or Consequences. **Amateur:** Member of the New Mexico State University golf team.

PERSONAL:

Quit the game temporarily in 1995 and sold cellular phones and car stereo systems in Seattle…Watched fellow El Paso, TX resident J.P. Hayes win 1998 Buick Classic and gained renewed interest…Worked in pro shop at El Paso CC prior to joining TOUR…Father, Larry, retired as golf coach at New Mexico State in 2004.

PLAYER STATISTICS

2004 PGA TOUR STATISTICS

Scoring Average	71.76	(163)
Driving Distance	296.7	(22)
Driving Accuracy Percentage	61.7%	(136)
Total Driving	158	(45)
Greens in Regulation Pct.	63.7%	(129)
Putting Average	1.814	(188)
Sand Save Percentage	56.4%	(15)
Eagles (Holes per)	173.3	(55)
Birdie Average	3.40	(131)
All-Around Ranking	839	(119)
Scoring Avg. Before Cut	71.38	(140)
Round 3 Scoring Avg.	71.85	(157)
Final Round Scoring Average	74.58	(194)
Birdie Conversion Percentage	28.9%	(101)
Par Breakers	19.5%	(122)

MISCELLANEOUS PGA TOUR STATISTICS

2004 Low Round/Round: 64–2 times, most recent Booz Allen Classic/1
Career Low Round/Round: 63–2 times, most recent 2003 Las Vegas Invitational/1
Career Largest Paycheck/Finish: $990,000–2002 PGA Championship/1

PGA TOUR CAREER SUMMARY — PLAYOFF RECORD: 0-0

Year	Events Played	Cuts Made	1st	2nd	3rd	Top 10	Top 25	Earnings	Rank
1999	24	9	1			2	3	$610,555	67
2000	29	13					2	249,881	146
2001	31	15				2	5	460,565	109
2002	30	19	2	1		5	8	2,938,365	7
2003	26	14		1		2	5	1,013,950	71
2004	28	14						230,499	183
Total	168	84	3	2		11	23	5,503,816	
EUROPEAN TOUR									
2004	1	1						14,728	

PGA TOUR TOP TOURNAMENT SUMMARY

Year	99	00	01	02	03	04
Masters					T15	CUT
U.S. Open			CUT		CUT	CUT
British Open	CUT				T43	T71
PGA	T70			1	CUT	CUT
THE PLAYERS		CUT		T44	CUT	CUT
TOUR Championship				T26		
WGC-Accenture Match Play					T33	T33
WGC-NEC Invitational				T6	T67	
WGC-American Express Champ				T49	T59	

Notah Begay III

EXEMPT STATUS: Major Medical Extension
FULL NAME: Notah Ryan Begay III
HEIGHT: 5-11
WEIGHT: 195
BIRTHDATE: September 14, 1972
BIRTHPLACE: Albuquerque, NM
RESIDENCE: Albuquerque, NM; plays out of Las Campanas, Santa Fe, NM

FAMILY: Single
EDUCATION: Stanford University (1995, Economics)
SPECIAL INTERESTS: Notah Begay III Scholarship Fund Boys and Girls Club
TURNED PROFESSIONAL: 1995
JOINED TOUR: 1999
Nationwide Tour Alumnus

PGA TOUR VICTORIES (4):

1999 Reno-Tahoe Open, Michelob Championship at Kingsmill. **2000** FedEx St. Jude Classic, Canon Greater Hartford Open.

BEST 2004 PGA TOUR FINISHES:

T3—B.C. Open; T5—Wachovia Championship.

2004 SEASON:

After finishing No. 129 on the money list, will receive a Major Medical Extension for 2005 due to chronic back problems. Did not play after Reno-Tahoe Open in late August. Coupled with $583,537 earned in 23 events in 2004, has the opportunity to play in six events to earn $42,725 and match the $623,262 winnings of 2004's No. 125, Tag Ridings. If he does so, will play out of the Major Medical Extension category for the remainder of the season. . .Finished T5 at the Wachovia Championship, his best finish since a T5 at the 2003 Honda Classic. . .One shot back of the lead heading into the final round of the B.C. Open after opening the tournament with 1-over 73. Fired a final round 69 to finish T3.

CAREER HIGHLIGHTS:

2003: Made 30 starts on the PGA TOUR, the most in a season in his career...First top-10 finish came in early March, a T5 at The Honda Classic after posting four rounds in the 60s. Co-leader through 18 and 36 holes. Post-round thoughts were on brother Greg, 20, a third-generation U.S. Marine stationed in the Middle East. "We are on the brink of war, but maybe I can go out and win the golf tournament, my younger brother might read it somewhere in the paper." Reunited with Greg after return from Middle East at the FedEx St. Jude Classic, where he finished T13...Posted a T8 at John Deere Classic. Two shots behind Chris Riley and J.L. Lewis through 54 holes after third-round 65. Needing to secure TOUR card for 2004 with Top-125 finish on money list, jumped from 117th to 103rd with $105,000 paycheck. **2002:** Continued comeback from annular tears of L-4 and L-5 discs in lower back that limited him to 12 events in 2001. Improved from 197th in 2001 to 108th on the TOUR money list. **2001:** Made only four cuts in 12 starts to finish 197th in earnings because of injured back. Attributed lower-back injury to over-exuberance in off-season conditioning, with rest being the only cure. Took off two months between the Masters in April and the FedEx St. Jude Classic in June. **2000:** Eclipsed first-year earnings with $1,819,323, 20th on PGA TOUR official money list...Became the first player to win in back-to-back weeks since former Stanford teammate Tiger Woods in 1999...Rebounded from five missed cuts in 10 starts with third career victory, one-stroke win at the FedEx St. Jude Classic. Followed with second consecutive victory and fourth of career, by one stroke over Mark Calcavecchia at Canon Greater Hartford Open. That victory marked his fourth in 12 months...PGA Championship eighth lifted him to eighth place in U.S. Team eligibility and into the Presidents Cup where he compiled a 3-2 record, playing in team matches with Woods. **1999:** Nominated for Rookie of the Year honors after winning his first two TOUR titles. Joined Carlos Franco as rookies with two victories...First victory and first top 10 on TOUR came at Reno-Tahoe Open, the 23rd start of his career. Became the first Native American to win TOUR event since Rod Curl at 1974 Colonial...Second TOUR victory came at Michelob Championship at Kingsmill. Birdied final two holes in regulation to force playoff with Tom Byrum. Defeated Byrum with par on second extra hole. **1998:** Became first Nationwide Tour player to record a 59 in tournament play. The 13-under-par round included a 27 (9-under) on the second nine of his second round at the Dominion Open. Recorded nine birdies and two eagles (one of which was a hole-in-one)...Placed 10th on Nationwide Tour money list and earned exempt status on 1999 PGA TOUR. **1996:** Medalist at Canadian Tour Qualifying Tournament. **Amateur:** Member of U.S. Walker Cup team. Member of Stanford's 1994 NCAA Championship team, along with Casey Martin...where he was an all-America selection for third time...Holder of record for lowest 18-hole score in NCAA Championship history with 62 in the second round of the 1994 tournament. Winner of 15 major junior and amateur titles.

PERSONAL:

Began playing golf at age 6. Father played in a business league while working for the Bureau of Indian Affairs. Notah would tag along for the twilight, nine-hole competition. In summer would save spare change for bucket of range balls and then asked head pro at Ladera Golf Course near his home if he could work at course for playing privileges. . .Most successful Native American golfer, with four TOUR victories. Half Navajo, one-quarter San Felipe and one-quarter Isleta. . .In a continuing effort to honor heritage, conducted a junior clinic in Philadelphia, MS, home to the Choctaw Indian Reservation, two weeks prior to the 2002 Southern Farm Bureau Classic. "I hope to sort of continue to help (Native American) junior programs along, and work with them to increase the diabetes awareness within their community. These are some of the pivotal issues that are an integral part of my agenda as reaching out to Native American groups.". . .Has putted left- and right-handed, depending upon direction the putt breaks. . .Brother Clint caddied in his two 2000 victories. . .The movie, "Windtalkers," starring Nicolas Cage and Christian Slater, tells the story of the 375 Navajo Indians recruited to help in intelligence during World War II. Begay's grandfather, the late Notah Begay, was one of the Navajos recruited to assist the U.S. government. His grandfather was a radioman and was stationed on the front line.

PLAYER STATISTICS

2004 PGA TOUR STATISTICS

Scoring Average	71.25	(108)
Driving Distance	285.8	(110)
Driving Accuracy Percentage	69.5%	(31)
Total Driving	141	(27)
Greens in Regulation Pct.	66.2%	(64)
Putting Average	1.771	(79)
Sand Save Percentage	44.2%	(155)
Eagles (Holes per)	301.5	(130)
Birdie Average	3.69	(60)
All-Around Ranking	737	(91)
Scoring Avg. Before Cut	71.22	(128)
Round 3 Scoring Avg.	70.09	(36)
Final Round Scoring Average	71.09	(63)
Birdie Conversion Percentage	30.2%	(62)
Par Breakers	20.8%	(65)

MISCELLANEOUS PGA TOUR STATISTICS

2004 Low Round/Round: 62–B.C. Open/2
Career Low Round/Round: 62–2004 B.C. Open/2
Career Largest Paycheck/Finish: $540,000–2000 FedEx St. Jude Classic/1

PGA TOUR CAREER SUMMARY — PLAYOFF RECORD: 1-0

Year	Events Played	Cuts Made	1st	2nd	3rd	Top 10	Top 25	Earnings	Rank
1996	1								
1999	29	22	2			2	5	$1,255,314	31
2000	24	17	2			4	10	1,819,323	20
2001	12	4						100,538	197
2002	26	11			1	3	5	624,026	108
2003	30	15				2	6	565,572	119
2004	23	12			1	2	4	583,537	129
Total	145	81	4		2	13	30	4,948,309	
NATIONWIDE TOUR									
1994A	1								
1995	3	1					1	2,400	199
1996	5	1						570	261
1997	2								
1998	22	15		4		6	11	136,289	10
Total	33	17		4		6	12	139,259	

PGA TOUR TOP TOURNAMENT SUMMARY

Year	99	00	01	02	03	04
Masters		T37	CUT			
U.S. Open	CUT	22	CUT			
British Open		T20				
PGA		8	CUT			
THE PLAYERS		CUT	CUT	CUT	T56	CUT
TOUR Championship	T15	29				
WGC-NEC Invitational		T17	T31	T52		
WGC-American Express Champ	T46					

NATIONAL TEAMS: Walker Cup, 1995; Presidents Cup, 2000.

David Berganio, Jr.

EXEMPT STATUS: Major Medical Extension
FULL NAME: David Berganio, Jr.
HEIGHT: 5-11
WEIGHT: 170
BIRTHDATE: January 14, 1969
BIRTHPLACE: Los Angeles, CA
RESIDENCE: Sylmar, CA
FAMILY: Single

EDUCATION: University of Arizona
SPECIAL INTERESTS: Basketball
TURNED PROFESSIONAL: 1993
JOINED TOUR: 1997
Nationwide Tour Alumnus

BEST PGA TOUR CAREER FINISH:
2—2002 Bob Hope Chrysler Classic.

NATIONWIDE TOUR VICTORIES (3):
1996 Monterrey Open. **1999** Permian Basin Open. **2000** Omaha Classic.

2004 SEASON:
Will receive second consecutive Major Medical Extension after playing in only two events in 2004 due to disk problems. Coupled with $124,065 earned in 17 events over the last two years, has the opportunity to play in 12 events to earn $363,430 and match the $487,495 winnings of 2003's No. 125, Esteban Toledo. If he does so, will play out of the Major Medical Extension category for the remainder of the season...Missed the cut in both appearances, the Nissan Open and the Chrysler Classic of Tucson.

CAREER HIGHLIGHTS:
2003: Limited to only 15 starts due to a bulging disk. Did not play again after a first-round withdrawal at the FedEx St. Jude Classic in late June. Granted a Major Medical Exension...Lone top-25 in 15 starts was a T19 at the EDS Byron Nelson Championship, aided by a final-round 66. **2002:** Earned career-best finish (2nd) and largest paycheck ($432,000) after losing to Phil Mickelson in a one-hole playoff at the Bob Hope Chrysler Classic. Birdied the final hole of regulation to tie Mickelson at 30-under-par 330. Fourth-round 64 tied TOUR career low. **2001:** Finished in the top 100 on the TOUR money list for the first time...Had just one career top-10 entering the year and added four more, including a career-best T3 at the Canon Greater Hartford Open...Held first-round lead in AT&T Pebble Beach National Pro-Am after tying Spyglass Hill course record with 8-under 64. **2000:** Finished 11th on the Nationwide Tour money list to regain his PGA TOUR card. Captured the Omaha Classic by shooting a 67 in the final round to tie Ahmad Bateman. Used a par-4 on the second playoff hole to capture his third career victory. **1999:** Picked up his second title with a two-stroke win over Dicky Thompson and Paul Gow at the Permian Basin Open. **1997:** As a rookie, finished just outside of keeping his conditional card on the PGA TOUR at No. 155 on the money list. **1996:** Final-round 66 gave him a one-stroke victory over four others at the Monterey Open on the Nationwide Tour. Also had three runners-up finishes... Earned his initial TOUR card for the 1997 season by finishing 4th on the Nationwide Tour money list. **Amateur:** Winner of the 1991 and 1993 U.S. Amateur Public Links Championships.

PERSONAL:
Played on the same college team at Arizona as PGA TOUR member Jim Furyk...Was introduced to the game while growing up in an economically depressed area of Los Angeles by a local priest who gave him his first set of clubs.

PLAYER STATISTICS

2004 PGA TOUR STATISTICS

Scoring Average	73.25	(N/A)
Driving Distance	291.1	(N/A)
Driving Accuracy Percentage	67.9%	(N/A)
Total Driving	(N/A)	(N/A)
Greens in Regulation Pct.	59.7%	(N/A)
Putting Average	1.767	(N/A)
Sand Save Percentage	0%	(N/A)
Birdie Average	3.00	(N/A)
Scoring Avg. Before Cut	72.25	(N/A)
Birdie Conversion Percentage	27.9%	(N/A)
Par Breakers	16.7%	(N/A)

MISCELLANEOUS PGA TOUR STATISTICS

2004 Low Round/Round: 71–Nissan Open/2
Career Low Round/Round: 63–1997 GTE Byron Nelson Golf Classic/2
Career Largest Paycheck/Finish: $432,000–2002 Bob Hope Chrysler Classic/2

PGA TOUR CAREER SUMMARY — PLAYOFF RECORD: 0-1

Year	Events Played	Cuts Made	1st	2nd	3rd	Top 10	Top 25	Earnings	Rank
1991A	1								
1992A	2								
1993A	2	1							
1993	2	1						$2,486	302
1994	4	1						5,105	273
1996	4	2					1	36,590	211
1997	30	14				1	3	118,290	155
1998	3	1						6,487	300
1999	5	4						48,015	228
2000	4	3						34,625	
2001	25	16			1	4	6	685,082	76
2002	30	13		1		1	2	573,151	115
2003	15	6					1	124,065	197
2004	2								
Total	129	62		1	1	6	13	1,633,897	
NATIONWIDE TOUR									
1993	1								
1994	5	4					2	6,830	123
1995	4								
1996	21	17	1	3		7	12	146,047	4
1998	20	14				6	8	76,969	32
1999	21	10	1		1	3	7	80,399	29
2000	24	17	1			4	14	196,512	11
2004	1	1							
Total	97	63	3	3	1	20	43	506,757	

PGA TOUR TOP TOURNAMENT SUMMARY

Year	92	93	94	95	96	97	98	99	00	01	02	03
Masters	CUT					CUT						
U.S. Open		CUT	T47		T16			T28	CUT			
THE PLAYERS											W/D	T56

NATIONAL TEAMS: Walker Cup, 1993.

SECTION 2 PLAYER BIOGRAPHIES

Mark Brooks

EXEMPT STATUS: Winner, 1996 PGA Championship (through 2006)
FULL NAME: Mark David Brooks
HEIGHT: 5-9
WEIGHT: 150
BIRTHDATE: March 25, 1961
BIRTHPLACE: Fort Worth, TX
RESIDENCE: Fort Worth, TX

FAMILY: Wife, Cynthia; Lyndsay (1/24/86), Hallie (9/20/89)
EDUCATION: University of Texas
SPECIAL INTERESTS: Golf course design, collecting antique golf architecture books and historic golf prints, all sports, cooking and drawing
TURNED PROFESSIONAL: 1983
Q SCHOOL: 1983, 1984, 1985, 1986, 1987

PGA TOUR VICTORIES (7):

1988 Canon Sammy Davis Jr.-Greater Hartford Open. **1991** Kmart Greater Greensboro Open, Greater Milwaukee Open. **1994** Kemper Open. **1996** Bob Hope Chrysler Classic, Shell Houston Open, PGA Championship.

BEST 2004 PGA TOUR FINISH:

T9—Bank of America Colonial.

2004 SEASON:

Lowest finish on money list (No. 173) since joining TOUR in 1984, with only five made cuts in 31 starts…Notched one top-10, a T9 at the Bank of America Colonial, his first since a solo third at the 2002 Tampa Bay Classic.

CAREER HIGHLIGHTS:

2003: Finished the season outside the top 125 for the first time since 1987 (No. 167)...Best finish was a T18 at the Las Vegas Invitational. **2002:** Maintained his position in the Top 100 on the money list for the 11th time in his last 13 seasons...His two top-10 finishes were thirds at The INTERNATIONAL and the Tampa Bay Classic. **2001:** Had highest finish on PGA TOUR money list (60) since finishing third in 1996...Made playoff at U.S. Open after Retief Goosen three-putted 72nd hole. Brooks also three-putted 18th hole in group ahead of Goosen. Lost by two strokes, 70-72, in 18-hole Monday playoff. Shared 36-hole lead and was one back after 54 holes. **2000:** Finished T5 at the Shell Houston Open, his first top-five on TOUR since winning the 1996 PGA. **1999:** Returned to top 75 on TOUR money list for the first time since 1996...Earned first top-10 since a T7 at the 1997 THE PLAYERS Championship with a T9 at Nissan Open. **1996:** Enjoyed his best season on TOUR with three victories, including his first major title, the PGA...First victory of year came in his second start. Had five consecutive sub-par rounds to win Bob Hope Chrysler Classic. His 23-under-par 337 total was one stroke better than John Huston...Won Shell Houston Open in a playoff over fellow Texan and hometown favorite Jeff Maggert. Rolled in 50-foot birdie putt on first playoff hole for victory, the first in his home state...Birdied 72nd hole at PGA at Valhalla GC to force playoff with Kenny Perry, then birdied first extra hole to earn title. **1995:** Tied for third with Steven Bottomley and Michael Campbell at British Open, one stroke out of John Daly-Constantino Rocco playoff. **1994:** Won the Kemper Open by three strokes over D.A. Weibring and Bobby Wadkins. **1993:** Was part of a five-man playoff at Buick Southern Open won by John Inman. **1991:** Won twice. Shot a closing 64 to catch Gene Sauers at Kmart Greater Greensboro Open, then parred third playoff hole for victory. Edged Robert Gamez by one stroke at Greater Milwaukee Open after opening with 63. **1988:** His first TOUR victory, at Canon Sammy Davis, Jr.-Greater Hartford Open, came with 10-foot putt on second playoff hole with Dave Barr and Joey Sindelar. **Amateur:** Three-time All-American at University of Texas...Winner of 1979 and 1981 Texas State Amateurs, 1979 Southern Amateur and 1979 Trans-Mississippi Amateur.

PERSONAL:

Served as host of W. Hal Brooks Memorial Golf Tournament and Gala, in honor of his father. Event was held for 11 years in his hometown and benefited hundreds of youth and teenage programs…Partner in Knott-Linn-Brooks House, a golf course design company based in Palo Alto, CA…His first start-to-finish project, Southern Oaks GC outside Fort Worth, TX, opened to rave reviews in 1999.

PLAYER STATISTICS

2004 PGA TOUR STATISTICS

Scoring Average	72.58	(190)
Driving Distance	273.8	(184)
Driving Accuracy Percentage	66.8%	(59)
Total Driving	243	(165)
Greens in Regulation Pct.	59.8%	(190)
Putting Average	1.796	(147)
Sand Save Percentage	43.5%	(165)
Eagles (Holes per)	630.0	(187)
Birdie Average	3.03	(185)
All-Around Ranking	1,307	(195)
Scoring Avg. Before Cut	72.66	(192)
Round 3 Scoring Avg.	68.33	(2)
Final Round Scoring Average	72.00	(131)
Birdie Conversion Percentage	27.0%	(165)
Par Breakers	17.0%	(187)

MISCELLANEOUS PGA TOUR STATISTICS

2004 Low Round/Round: 64–Michelin Championship at Las Vegas/3
Career Low Round/Round: 61–1990 Shearson Lehman Hutton Open/2
Career Largest Paycheck/Finish: $530,000–2001 U.S. Open Championship/2

PGA TOUR CAREER SUMMARY — PLAYOFF RECORD: 4-3

Year	Events Played	Cuts Made	1st	2nd	3rd	Top 10	Top 25	Earnings	Rank
1983A	1								
1983	6	2					1	$6,924	194
1984	35	17				1	4	40,438	122
1985	32	11					3	32,094	141
1986	32	19				1	5	47,264	140
1987	32	17					2	42,100	165
1988	30	22	1	1		2	11	280,636	36
1989	30	15				1	3	112,838	115
1990	33	23			2	5	10	307,948	45
1991	30	24	2			5	11	667,263	11
1992	29	24			3	11	16	629,754	21
1993	31	19		1		3	10	249,696	66
1994	33	23	1			4	8	523,285	31
1995	29	17			1	3	10	366,860	48
1996	29	23	3	1		8	12	1,429,396	3
1997	30	15				1	3	213,516	108
1998	30	18					5	219,570	129
1999	33	24				3	7	557,037	74
2000	29	17				3	4	528,959	90
2001	27	16		1		2	5	899,444	60
2002	32	16			2	2	5	731,671	95
2003	31	14					2	236,489	167
2004	31	5				1	2	264,076	173
Total	655	381	7	4	8	56	139	8,387,257	

PGA TOUR TOP TOURNAMENT SUMMARY

Year	84	85	86	87	88	89	90	91	92	93	94	95	96
Masters						CUT		T35	CUT	CUT		CUT	CUT
U.S. Open	CUT		CUT	CUT	CUT		T5	T19	T44	T46	CUT		T16
British Open								T80	T55		T20	T3	T5
PGA					CUT	CUT	T26	CUT	T15	CUT	CUT	T31	1
THE PLAYERS	CUT	CUT		T63		CUT	T36	CUT	T9	CUT	CUT	CUT	CUT
TOUR Championship								T24	T27		T29		T27

Year	97	98	99	00	01	02	03	04
Masters	CUT	CUT	T38	T40	T31	T24		
U.S. Open	CUT	57	CUT	CUT	2	CUT		CUT
British Open	CUT	T66	T62	CUT	CUT			
PGA	CUT	T56	T16	CUT	CUT	CUT	CUT	CUT
THE PLAYERS	T7	CUT	T10	T57	T65	T57	T62	CUT

NATIONAL TEAMS: The Presidents Cup, 1996.

Bart Bryant

EXEMPT STATUS: 2004 tournament winner (through 2006)
FULL NAME: Barton Holan Bryant
HEIGHT: 6-0
WEIGHT: 195
BIRTHDATE: November 18, 1962
BIRTHPLACE: Gatesville, TX
RESIDENCE: Ocoee, FL

FAMILY: Wife, Cathy; Kristen (8/1/88), Michelle (1/11/94)
EDUCATION: New Mexico State University
SPECIAL INTERESTS: Movies, spending time with friends
TURNED PROFESSIONAL: 1986
Q SCHOOL: 1990, 1994, 1995, 1999, 2000, 2002
Nationwide Tour Alumnus

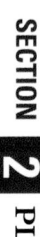

PGA TOUR VICTORIES (1):
2004 Valero Texas Open.

BEST 2004 PGA TOUR FINISH:
1—Valero Texas Open.

2004 SEASON:
Earned job security through 2006 with first PGA TOUR victory at the Valero Texas Open. Oft-injured Texan entered 2004 having played only six full seasons on the PGA TOUR since 1991, with six successful trips to Q-School during his career. Playing in 18th (of 23) events on 2004 Major Medical Extension, captured the Valero event in 187th career start at the age of 41 years, 10 months and one day. Posted rounds of 67-67-60-67—261 to finish three strokes ahead of Patrick Sheehan, taking home a career-best $630,000. Took the 54-hole lead after setting the Resort Course at LaCantera course record with a 10-under-par 60 in the third round. Oldest first-time winner since Ed Dougherty won the 1995 Deposit Guaranty Golf Classic at the age of 47 years, eight months and 19 days. Set 2004 PGA TOUR mark for low 54- and 72-hole totals at 194 (67-67-60) and 261 (67-67-60-67), respectively, and third-round 60 tied Robert Gamez for low round of the season. The victory was only fifth career top-10 in. Teamed with brother Brad (T37) as the duo played in their 743rd combined event on TOUR. The brothers have two wins between them—Brad at the Walt Disney World/Oldsmobile Classic and Bart at the 2004 Valero Texas Open. The two were the 11th brother combination to win on the PGA TOUR.

CAREER HIGHLIGHTS:
2003: Lone top-25 in 2003 was T24 at the FUNAI Classic at The WALT DISNEY WORLD Resort. Played in only six events after earning TOUR card through Q-School for the sixth time. Season was cut short due to elbow surgery (March 4). Did not play after Sony Open in Hawaii until Reno-Tahoe Open in August. Received Major Medical Extension for 2004. **2002:** T9 at Kemper Insurance Open was fourth top 10 of career and first since 1992 Hardee's Golf Classic. **2001:** Missed first half of season due to rehabilitation from elbow surgery that occurred in December 2000. Did not play in a PGA TOUR event until June at the FedEx St. Jude Classic and made only 10 starts. **1995:** Posted career-best five top-25s. **1993:** Played full-time on the Nationwide Tour, with 21 starts. **1991:** Career-best two top-10 finishes in rookie season. **1986:** Turned professional and won the 1988 Florida Open. **Amateur:** Winner of 1984 UCLA Billy Bryant Invitational and 1983-84 Sun Country Amateur. Two-time All-American at New Mexico State.

PERSONAL:
Older brother Brad is a past PGA TOUR champion and will be a member of the Champions Tour in 2005.

PLAYER STATISTICS

2004 PGA TOUR STATISTICS

Scoring Average	70.53	(34)
Driving Distance	282.1	(138)
Driving Accuracy Percentage	74.2%	(7)
Total Driving	145	(30)
Greens in Regulation Pct.	68.9%	(12)
Putting Average	1.777	(99)
Sand Save Percentage	40.4%	(190)
Eagles (Holes per)	310.5	(136)
Birdie Average	3.62	(72)
All-Around Ranking	688	(74)
Scoring Avg. Before Cut	70.78	(66)
Round 3 Scoring Avg.	69.15	(3)
Final Round Scoring Average	70.08	(9)
Birdie Conversion Percentage	28.9%	(101)
Par Breakers	20.5%	(72)

MISCELLANEOUS PGA TOUR STATISTICS

2004 Low Round/Round: 60–Valero Texas Open/3
Career Low Round/Round: 60–2004 Valero Texas Open/3
Career Largest Paycheck/Finish: $630,000–2004 Valero Texas Open/1

PGA TOUR CAREER SUMMARY — PLAYOFF RECORD: 0-0

Year	Events Played	Cuts Made	1st	2nd	3rd	Top 10	Top 25	Earnings	Rank
1986	1	1						$2,076	251
1987	1								
1991	31	17				2	5	119,931	124
1992	19	10				1	1	52,075	172
1993	2								
1994	1								
1995	27	13					5	119,201	146
1996	26	14					3	88,788	172
2000	25	11						85,797	201
2001	10	7					1	73,884	206
2002	20	15				1	3	309,880	155
2003	6	6					1	78,966	215
2004	23	13	1			1	4	962,167	80
Total	192	107	1			5	23	1,892,765	
NATIONWIDE TOUR									
1990	6	5				1	4	8,251	94
1991	1	1					1	1,563	193
1993	21	9				1	2	10,255	108
1994	4	1						570	257
1995	1								
1998	1								
2001	1	1						1,825	258
2002	2	1					1	3,690	237
2003	2	2				2	2	28,170	118
2004	3	2				1	2	21,395	147
Total	42	22				5	12	75,718	

PGA TOUR TOP TOURNAMENT SUMMARY

Year	87	88	89	90	91	92	93	94
U.S. Open	CUT							CUT
THE PLAYERS					CUT	CUT		

SECTION 2 PLAYER BIOGRAPHIES

Jonathan Byrd

EXEMPT STATUS: 2004 tournament winner (through 2006)
FULL NAME: Jonathan Currie Byrd
HEIGHT: 5-9
WEIGHT: 160
BIRTHDATE: January 27, 1978
BIRTHPLACE: Anderson, SC
RESIDENCE: St. Simons Island, GA; plays out of Sea Island Golf Club
FAMILY: Wife, Amanda
EDUCATION: Clemson University (2000, Marketing)
SPECIAL INTERESTS: Working out, Clemson athletics, College Golf Fellowship, fishing, hanging out with wife at home
TURNED PROFESSIONAL: 2000
JOINED TOUR: 2002
Nationwide Tour Alumnus

PGA TOUR VICTORIES (2):
2002 Buick Challenge. **2004** B.C. Open.

NATIONWIDE TOUR VICTORIES (1):
2001 Charity Pro-Am at The Cliffs.

BEST 2004 PGA TOUR FINISHES:
1—B.C. Open; T3—84 LUMBER Classic; T8—Southern Farm Bureau Classic.

2004 SEASON:
Struggled early in the year due to a hip injury, but bounced back with a strong finish after undergoing surgery…Had hip surgery on Feb. 15 in Pittsburgh because of two tears in the labrum front and back. The surgery tightened up the looseness and instability. Returned for THE PLAYERS Championship at the end of March…Entered the final round of the B.C. Open with a one-stroke lead, but had to withstand a six-hour rain delay before capturing his second PGA TOUR victory. The win was his first top-10 of the season and came 1 year, 8 months, 21 days after his first victory at the 2002 Buick Challenge, a span of 45 events…Second top-10 of the season was a third at the 84 LUMBER Classic. His $201,600 payday pushed him over $1 million for the third time in his career…The next week finished T8 at the Southern Farm Bureau Classic, marking back-to-back top-10s for just the second time in his career (2002 Buick Challenge, Southern Farm Bureau Classic/T5).

CAREER HIGHLIGHTS:
2003: Made more than $1.4 million for second straight season and posted career-high five top-10s...Aided by a 10-under-par 63 on Sunday, finished T6 at season-opening Mercedes Championships. One of four first-time participants to finish in the top 10 at Kapalua...Made most of his first appearance in a major with a T8 at the Masters, the best finish by any of the 16 first-timers in Augusta...Best finish of season was a T2 at John Deere Classic, four strokes behind Vijay Singh. Tied with J.L. Lewis for lead through 18 holes. **2002:** Became first rookie to win on the PGA TOUR since Jose Coceres in early 2001 with his victory at the Buick Challenge. Began season 404th in the Official World Golf Ranking and by the end of the season had improved to 72nd. Defeated David Toms by one stroke at the Buick Challenge. Had five-stroke lead through 15 holes on Sunday thanks to eagle-birdie-birdie-birdie-eagle (tied for season's best) stretch. Bogey on next hole and eagle by Toms cut that to two but Byrd hung on for the win in his 32nd start on TOUR. Score of 27-under par 261 set tournament record by three strokes. **2001:** Earned first TOUR card by finishing eighth on the Nationwide Tour money list...Lone victory came at the BMW Charity Pro-Am at The Cliffs in Traveler's Rest, SC, not far from his hometown of Elgin, SC. **2000:** T36 at the Michelob Championship at Kingsmill after turning professional in September after graduating from Clemson University. **Amateur:** Member of 1999 Walker Cup Team...Winner of Northeast Amateur and Carolinas Amateur...Was an All-America selection in three of his four years at Clemson, including first team in 1999...First-team Academic All-America in 1999.

PERSONAL:
Dad introduced him and his brother to golf at age 3.

PLAYER STATISTICS

2004 PGA TOUR STATISTICS

Scoring Average	70.88	(67)
Driving Distance	295.8	(28)
Driving Accuracy Percentage	62.1%	(133)
Total Driving	161	(47)
Greens in Regulation Pct.	61.4%	(180)
Putting Average	1.760	(48)
Sand Save Percentage	56.0%	(20)
Eagles (Holes per)	213.4	(78)
Birdie Average	3.81	(28)
All-Around Ranking	582	(43)
Scoring Avg. Before Cut	71.13	(115)
Round 3 Scoring Avg.	70.69	(71)
Final Round Scoring Average	71.80	(117)
Birdie Conversion Percentage	32.5%	(12)
Par Breakers	21.6%	(28)

MISCELLANEOUS PGA TOUR STATISTICS
2004 Low Round/Round: 65–2 times, most recent Southern Farm Bureau Classic/4
Career Low Round/Round: 63–2 times, most recent 2003 Mercedes Championships/4
Career Largest Paycheck/Finish: $666,000–2002 Buick Challenge/1

PGA TOUR CAREER SUMMARY — PLAYOFF RECORD: 0-0

Year	Events Played	Cuts Made	1st	2nd	3rd	Top 10	Top 25	Earnings	Rank
2000	1	1						14,130	
2001	1	1						8,400	
2002	32	15	1		1	4	10	1,462,713	39
2003	29	21		1		5	9	1,430,538	47
2004	27	15	1		1	3	5	1,133,165	70
Total	90	53	2	1	2	12	24	4,048,946	
NATIONWIDE TOUR									
2000A	1	1							
2001	20	16	1	1	1	5	11	222,244	8
Total	21	17	1	1	1	5	11	222,244	

PGA TOUR TOP TOURNAMENT SUMMARY

Year	03	04
Masters	T8	CUT
U.S. Open	T15	CUT
PGA	CUT	CUT
THE PLAYERS	CUT	CUT
WGC-NEC Invitational	T71	

NATIONAL TEAMS: Walker Cup, 1999.

Tom Byrum

EXEMPT STATUS: 91st on 2004 money list
FULL NAME: Thomas Elliott Byrum
HEIGHT: 5-10
WEIGHT: 175
BIRTHDATE: September 28, 1960
BIRTHPLACE: Onida, SD
RESIDENCE: Sugar Land, TX
FAMILY: Wife, Dana; Brittni Rene (4/2/88), Corinne (1/29/91)
EDUCATION: New Mexico State University
SPECIAL INTERESTS: Hunting, fishing, all sports
TURNED PROFESSIONAL: 1984
Q SCHOOL: 1985, 1991, 1992, 1996
Nationwide Tour Alumnus

PGA TOUR VICTORIES (1):

1989 Kemper Open.

BEST 2004 PGA TOUR FINISHES:

T4—Buick Classic; T9—Buick Championship.

2004 SEASON:

Earned a career-best $873,139. Position on money list (91st) was best since 1999. . .Finished T4 at the Buick Classic, his first top-10 since a T6 at the 2002 Buick Open and best finish since a playoff loss to Notah Begay III at the 1999 Michelob Championship at Kingsmill. . .Playing in his 400th event since last TOUR victory, finished T9 at the Buick Championship. Entered final round trailing Fred Funk by one stroke, but dropped from contention after double bogey on No. 16 in the final round.

CAREER HIGHLIGHTS:

2003: Finished 109th on the money list for the second straight season...Did not have a top-10 for only the second time in his 18-year career, but posted seven top-25s...Best effort of the season was T13 at the Chrysler Classic of Tucson. **2002:** Regained fully exempt status...Recorded first top-10 in five appearances at the U.S. Open with a T8 finish...Playing in 460th career TOUR event, recorded first (second of career) TOUR hole-in-one in the second round of the Reno-Tahoe Open. Ace was the first in the four-year history of the tournament. **2001:** Involved in what is believed to be the first ace on a par 4 in TOUR history at Phoenix Open when Andrew Magee's drive on the 333-yard, par-4 17th hole caromed off his putter and went into the hole. Byrum was lining up a putt when the ball deflected off his putter and rolled about eight feet into the hole. **2000:** Ended season with two top-10s in his last two starts worth a total of $183,610 to secure his card for the 2001 season. **1999:** Lost to Notah Begay III in playoff at Michelob Championship, when Begay parred second extra hole. **1997:** Nominated for Comeback Player of the Year after posting back-to-back runner-up finishes at the Canon Greater Hartford Open and Buick Open. **1989:** Lone PGA TOUR victory came at Kemper Open. Took two-stroke lead after third-round 65, then shot closing 68 for five-stroke win over Tommy Armour III, Billy Ray Brown and Jim Thorpe. Brother Curt won Hardee's Golf Classic that year, making them the first brothers to win in same year since Mike and Dave Hill in 1972. **Amateur:** After graduating from high school in Onida, SD, joined brother Curt in Albuquerque, NM, where Tom worked at country club and was a walk-on with University of New Mexico golf team. After two years, transferred to New Mexico State in Las Cruces.

PERSONAL:

Older brother Curt, a former PGA TOUR winner, works as an analyst for The Golf Channel. . .Involved with nine-hole course, The Training Station, where golfers of all ages play three, six or nine holes.

PLAYER STATISTICS

2004 PGA TOUR STATISTICS

Scoring Average	70.55	(37)
Driving Distance	272.6	(190)
Driving Accuracy Percentage	74.7%	(5)
Total Driving	195	(95)
Greens in Regulation Pct.	63.7%	(129)
Putting Average	1.776	(91)
Sand Save Percentage	52.5%	(48)
Eagles (Holes per)	373.5	(159)
Birdie Average	3.35	(137)
All-Around Ranking	796	(105)
Scoring Avg. Before Cut	70.98	(94)
Round 3 Scoring Avg.	69.53	(12)
Final Round Scoring Average	70.76	(42)
Birdie Conversion Percentage	27.9%	(136)
Par Breakers	18.9%	(143)

MISCELLANEOUS PGA TOUR STATISTICS

2004 Low Round/Round: 64–Buick Classic/2
Career Low Round/Round: 62–1993 Anheuser-Busch Golf Classic/2
Career Largest Paycheck/Finish: $270,000–1999 Michelob Championship at Kingsmill/2

PGA TOUR CAREER SUMMARY — PLAYOFF RECORD: 0-2

Year	Events Played	Cuts Made	1st	2nd	3rd	Top 10	Top 25	Earnings	Rank
1985	1	1						$935	257
1986	34	18		1		4	5	89,739	93
1987	33	23			1	5	8	146,384	76
1988	34	23		1		2	11	174,378	67
1989	32	17	1			4	7	320,939	32
1990	32	14			1	1	3	136,910	113
1991	33	16					2	68,871	153
1992	29	10			1	1	2	94,399	136
1993	26	12				1	2	82,355	154
1994	12	7		1		1	3	112,259	148
1995	14	10			1	2	3	145,427	132
1996	26	12			1	2	4	166,500	126
1997	27	21		2		5	11	525,161	42
1998	30	15				2	5	252,832	116
1999	27	17		1		2	5	495,319	80
2000	27	18				3	6	514,193	93
2001	27	15				1	5	391,925	129
2002	23	15				3	8	620,280	109
2003	31	17					7	590,720	109
2004	25	17				2	7	873,139	91
Total	523	298	1	6	5	41	104	5,802,666	
NATIONWIDE TOUR									
1993	2	1						600	250
1994	8	6				2	4	21,120	68
1995	8	8		1		1	6	29,983	63
1996	1	1						650	252
Total	19	16		1		3	10	52,354	

PGA TOUR TOP TOURNAMENT SUMMARY

Year	86	87	88	89	90	91	92	93	94	95	96	97	98
Masters					CUT								
U.S. Open	CUT				T33	CUT							
PGA		T47	CUT	CUT								9	T62
THE PLAYERS		CUT	CUT	T67	CUT	CUT							CUT

Year	99	00	01	02	03	04
Masters					CUT	
U.S. Open			T44	T8	T15	CUT
British Open					T43	
PGA						T24
THE PLAYERS	70	CUT	T55		CUT	T16

Mark Calcavecchia (cal-kuh-VEK-ee-UH)

EXEMPT STATUS: 112th on 2004 money list
FULL NAME: Mark John Calcavecchia
HEIGHT: 6-0
WEIGHT: 225
BIRTHDATE: June 12, 1960
BIRTHPLACE: Laurel, NE
RESIDENCE: West Palm Beach, FL

FAMILY: Wife, Brenda; Britney Jo (8/8/89), Eric Jordan (1/1/94)
EDUCATION: University of Florida
SPECIAL INTERESTS: Bowling, music, guitar
TURNED PROFESSIONAL: 1981
Q SCHOOL: Spring 1981, 1983

PGA TOUR VICTORIES (11):

1986 Southwest Golf Classic. **1987** Honda Classic. **1988** Bank of Boston Classic. **1989** Phoenix Open, Nissan Los Angeles Open, British Open Championship. **1992** Phoenix Open. **1995** BellSouth Classic. **1997** Greater Vancouver Open. **1998** Honda Classic. **2001** Phoenix Open.

INTERNATIONAL VICTORIES (5):

1988 Australian Open [Aust]. **1993** Argentine Open. **1995** Argentine Open. **1997** Subaru Sarazen World Open. **2004** Maekyung Open [Kor].

OTHER VICTORIES (3):

1995 Franklin Templeton Shootout [with Steve Elkington]. **2001** CVS Charity Classic [with Nick Price], Hyundai Team Matches [with Fred Couples].

BEST 2004 PGA TOUR FINISHES:

T6—FUNAI Classic at the WALT DISNEY WORLD Resort; T9—Ford Championship at Doral.

2004 SEASON:

Did not secure his card until the second-to-last tournament of the season. A T6 at the FUNAI Classic at the WALT DISNEY WORLD Resort jumped him from No. 129 to No. 111 on the money list. Finished season No. 112, the first time he has been out of the top 65 since 1985, when he finished No. 162…First top-10, a T9, came at the Ford Championship at Doral.

CAREER HIGHLIGHTS:

2003: Surpassed $1 million in earnings for the sixth time in seven years despite battling various back and knee injuries. Surpassed $15 million in career earnings and ranked 12th all-time in that department entering 2004…Had knee surgery to repair damaged cartilage in his right knee he injured playing in the pro-am at the Phoenix Open two days after a T7 at Buick Invitational...Finished T2 behind Fred Couples at the Shell Houston Open. **2002:** Finished outside the top 50 on the PGA TOUR money list for only the second time since 1987. Experimented with combination of long putter and "claw" grip at several events...Top finish of season was runner-up at the Greater Greensboro Chrysler Classic. Tied PGA TOUR record for fewest putts in a 72-hole event (Kenny Knox, 1989 MCI Heritage Classic) with 93...Opened with rounds of 70-68 at the PGA Championship to share the 36-hole lead. Finished solo seventh, his best finish in a major championship since he won the 1989 British Open...Member of the U.S. Ryder Cup Team and has compiled a record of 6-7-1 in four Ryder Cup appearances. **2001:** Earned a personal best $1,991,576. Claimed first victory since 1998...Set or tied seven PGA TOUR scoring records in winning the Phoenix Open with 28-under-par 256. Broke Mike Souchak's 46-year-old mark of 257 and also established a record for lowest consecutive 36-holes with middle rounds of 60-64—124. An all-time TOUR-high 32 birdies enabled him to tie marks for lowest score in relation to par (28-under), lowest opening 54 holes (189), lowest consecutive 54 holes (189) and lowest opening 36 holes (125). Took lead after second-round 60. Has won the Phoenix Open three times, each in a different decade, starting in 1989. Has eight top-10 finishes in Phoenix and posted three seconds in Tucson...Finished third two starts later in the Bob Hope Chrysler Classic...Had arthroscopic surgery on left knee after the Bob Hope Chrysler Classic. Returned to action at Honda Classic and finished T2. Started final round three shots off the pace and closed with 70 to finish one behind Jesper Parnevik...Putting improvement key to season. Used the "Claw" putting grip which he began experimenting with early in the 2000 season. **2000:** Earned $1,597,317 to finish 23rd on the official money list and qualify for his 11th TOUR Championship...Finished second at the Canon Greater Hartford Open and T2 at the SEI Pennsylvania Classic, marking his sixth career season with multiple runner-up finishes...Nine top-10 finishes was most since nine in 1990...Finished T9 at WGC-Accenture Match Play Championship after posting victories in matches over Nick Price and Jose Maria Olazabal. Eventually lost to Paul Lawrie...Became the 10th player in TOUR history to top the $10-million mark in career earnings after winning $84,390 for T7 finish at the Honda Classic...Continued recent trend of fine play at Canon Greater Hartford Open with his fourth top-five finish in last five years at TPC at River Highlands. **1998:** Earned ninth TOUR title at Honda Classic after closing 68-65 and winning by three strokes...Shot final-round 66 to finish second by one stroke at Las Vegas Invitational. **1995:** After trailing Jim Gallagher, Jr. and Stephen Keppler by two

PGA TOUR CAREER SUMMARY — PLAYOFF RECORD: 0-3

Year	Events Played	Cuts Made	1st	2nd	3rd	Top 10	Top 25	Earnings	Rank
1981	7	1						$404	313
1982	25	14				1	5	25,064	135
1983	20	9				1	2	16,313	161
1984	25	14				1	1	29,660	140
1985	15	7					2	15,957	162
1986	17	9	1			5	8	155,012	58
1987	26	20	1	2	3	9	12	522,398	10
1988	33	28	1	4	1	12	18	751,912	6
1989	25	18	3	1	2	10	13	807,741	5
1990	27	22		5	1	9	14	834,281	7
1991	24	17			1	6	8	323,621	50
1992	27	22	1			4	6	377,234	39
1993	30	20		3		6	13	630,366	21
1994	27	18		1	2	6	13	533,201	30
1995	29	25	1	2		6	13	843,552	13
1996	29	24			2	6	12	628,851	29
1997	27	23	1	1		7	17	1,117,365	14
1998	27	22	1	1	1	7	13	1,368,554	12
1999	29	22			1	4	10	733,971	59
2000	28	21		2	2	9	14	1,702,317	23
2001	23	16	1	1	1	5	8	1,991,576	17
2002	25	16		1		5	8	1,162,509	53
2003	24	19		1		3	8	1,121,069	65
2004	24	17				2	6	717,876	112
Total	593	424	11	25	17	124	224	16,410,803	
EUROPEAN TOUR									
2004	1	1						6,068	

PGA TOUR TOP TOURNAMENT SUMMARY

Year	86	87	88	89	90	91	92	93	94	95	96	97	98
Masters		T17	2	T31	T20	T12	T31	T17	CUT	T41	T15	T17	T16
U.S. Open	14	T17	T62	T61	CUT	T37	T33	T25	CUT	CUT	CUT	CUT	CUT
British Open		T11	CUT	1	CUT	CUT	T28	T14	T11	T24	T40	T10	T35
PGA		CUT	T17		CUT	T32	T48	T31	CUT	CUT	T36	T23	T44
THE PLAYERS		T50	T64	CUT	2	CUT	73	CUT	T23	T18	T29	T24	4
TOUR Championship		T5	T3	T9	T14			T7	T24	T27	T15	T4	29

Year	99	00	01	02	03	04
Masters	CUT		T4	CUT		
U.S. Open	CUT		T24	CUT	T20	T20
British Open	CUT	T26	T54	T80	CUT	T11
PGA	T61	T34	T4	7	T39	DQ
THE PLAYERS	T10	CUT	CUT	T69	T11	T66
TOUR Championship		T11	19			
WGC-Accenture Match Play	T33	T9		T9		
WGC-NEC Invitational	T12		T36	74	T53	
WGC-American Express Champ		10	CNL	T33		

NATIONAL TEAMS: Ryder Cup (4), 1987, 1989, 1991, 2002; Kirin Cup 1987; Asahi Glass Four Tours World Championship of Golf (2), 1989, 1990; Dunhill Cup (2), 1989, 1990; The Presidents Cup, 1998.

Mark Calcavecchia (Continued)

entering final day, closed with 66 for two-stroke victory at BellSouth Classic...Teamed with Steve Elkington to win the Franklin Templeton Shootout. **1994:** December 1993 skiing accident hampered him early in year, but came back to finish T9 at Buick Invitational of California after cartilage damage and torn ACL were surgically repaired. **1992:** Won Phoenix Open for the second time following final-round 63. Set Augusta National back-nine record at Masters with 29, a record shared with David Toms. **1989:** Won British Open at Royal Troon. Defeated Wayne Grady and Greg Norman in first playoff using Royal & Ancient's multi-hole system. Sealed victory with 5-iron shot to seven feet on fourth and final hole...Won twice in U.S. earlier that year. Closed with 65-64 to win Phoenix Open by seven strokes over Chip Beck. Trailed Sandy Lyle by two strokes after third round of Nissan Los Angeles Open. Closing 68 was good for one-stroke victory. **1988:** Runner-up to Sandy Lyle in Masters...Earned third career victory in the Bank of Boston Classic. **1986:** First TOUR victory came at Southwest Golf Classic by three over Tom Byrum. **Amateur:** First-team all-SEC in 1979...Winner of 1976 Florida State Junior and Orange Bowl Championships...Member of inaugural AJGA All-America team in 1978.

PERSONAL:

Treated for sleep apnea after 2002 season that included fatigue, weight gain and "general lack of focus." Began wearing oxygen mask to bed following Ryder Cup...In 2002, inducted into Phoenix Open Hall of Fame, becoming only the 15th person and sixth golfer put into the Hall which was established in 1985. Other golfers include Arnold Palmer, Gene Littler, Byron Nelson, Ben Hogan and Ken Venturi...Father was bowling center proprietor. At age 13, Mark had 185 average...Concentrated on golf when family moved from Nebraska to Florida. Played as many as 72 holes a day during the summer months.

PLAYER STATISTICS

2004 PGA TOUR STATISTICS

Scoring Average	71.12	(99)
Driving Distance	291.3	(56)
Driving Accuracy Percentage	64.5%	(91)
Total Driving	147	(32)
Greens in Regulation Pct.	64.9%	(100)
Putting Average	1.765	(59)
Sand Save Percentage	52.3%	(52)
Eagles (Holes per)	175.5	(57)
Birdie Average	3.77	(34)
All-Around Ranking	548	(38)
Scoring Avg. Before Cut	70.65	(53)
Round 3 Scoring Avg.	71.56	(144)
Final Round Scoring Average	72.75	(168)
Birdie Conversion Percentage	30.9%	(39)
Par Breakers	21.5%	(32)

MISCELLANEOUS PGA TOUR STATISTICS

2004 Low Round/Round: 65–2 times, most recent FUNAI Classic at the WALT DISNEY WORLD Resort/3

Career Low Round/Round: 60–2001 Phoenix Open/2

Career Largest Paycheck/Finish: $720,000–2001 Phoenix Open/1

SHOTLink
AN IBM ON DEMAND BUSINESS SOLUTION

HOT SHOTS

Short Hole

Tournament Players Club at Scottsdale

17th Hole, Par 4, 332 Yards

FBR Open

The drivable par-4 17th at the Tournament Players Club at Scottsdale is tempting. Andrew Magee made the only ace on a par 4 in TOUR history here in 2001 when his tee shot bounced onto the green, caromed off Tom Byrum's putter and went into the hole. The 332-yard hole is one of the shortest on TOUR but requires great touch around the elevated green. A quick look at how the hole played in 2004:

PLAYERS THAT DROVE THE GREEN	
Round 1	6 (4 birdies and 2 pars)
Round 2	3 (1 birdie and 2 pars)
Round 3	7 (5 birdies and 2 pars)
Round 4	1 (par)
Total	**17**

Of the 17 players that drove the green, none of them made eagle and seven of them three-putted.

REACHABLE PAR 4s ON THE PGA TOUR

No.16 La Cantera G.C. – 380 Yards
44 of 441 tee shots were attempted at the green (10%)
Six of those 44 tee shots successfully reached the green (14%)

No.14 TPC at Deere Run – 361 Yards
88 of 456 tee shots were attempted at the green (19%)
10 of those 88 tee shots successfully reached the green (11%)

No.15 TPC at Summerlin – 341 Yards
174 of 214 tee shots were attempted at the green (81%)
21 of those 174 tee shots successfully reached the green (12%)

No.17 TPC of Scottsdale – 332 Yards
291 of 402 tee shots were attempted at the green (72%)
17 of those 291 tee shots successfully reached the green (6%)

No. 7 Westchester Country Club – 326 Yards
192 of 474 tee shots were attempted at the green (41%)
Six of those 192 tee shots successfully reached the green (3%)

No.14 Warwick Hills G & C.C. – 322 Yards
146 of 454 tee shots were attempted at the green (32%)
Five of those 146 tee shots successfully reached the green (3%)

No. 10 Riviera Country Club – 315 Yards
139 of 442 tee shots were attempted at the green (31%)
Six of those 139 tee shots successfully reached the green (4%)

No.10 Westchester Country Club – 314 Yards
242 of 474 tee shots were attempted at the green (51%)
10 of those 242 tee shots successfully reached the green (4%)

No. 15 TPC at Sugarloaf – 310 Yards
174 of 214 tee shots were attempted at the green (81%)
21 of those 174 tee shots successfully reached the green (12%)

No.14 Plantation Course at Kapalua – 305 Yards
40 of 120 tee shots were attempted at the green (33%)
Four of those 40 tee shots successfully reached the green (10%)

No.14 TPC at Avenel – 301 Yards
96 of 464 tee shots were attempted at the green (21%)
14 of those 96 tee shots successfully reached the green (15%)

No.15 TPC at River Highlands – 296 Yards
388 of 464 tee shots were attempted at the green (84%)
37 of those 388 tee shots successfully reached the green (10%)

17th Hole-TPC at Scottsdale

SECTION 2 PLAYER BIOGRAPHIES

Chad Campbell

EXEMPT STATUS: Winner, 2003 TOUR Championship (through 2006)
FULL NAME: David Chad Campbell
HEIGHT: 6-1
WEIGHT: 205
BIRTHDATE: May 31, 1974
BIRTHPLACE: Andrews, TX
RESIDENCE: Lewisville, TX

FAMILY: Wife, Amy
EDUCATION: University of Nevada-Las Vegas (1996, Hotel Administration)
SPECIAL INTERESTS: Hunting
TURNED PROFESSIONAL: 1996
JOINED TOUR: 2001
Nationwide Tour Alumnus

PGA TOUR VICTORIES (2):

2003 THE TOUR Championship presented by Coca-Cola. **2004** Bay Hill Invitational presented by MasterCard.

NATIONWIDE TOUR VICTORIES (3):

2001 Richmond Open, Permian Basin Open, Monterey Peninsula Classic.

BEST 2004 PGA TOUR FINISHES:

1—Bay Hill Invitational Presented by MasterCard; 2—Bank of America Colonial; T9—WGC-Accenture Match Play Championship, The Honda Classic.

2004 SEASON:

Finished in the top 30 on the TOUR money list and collected victory for the second straight season…Came from four strokes back of Stuart Appleby at the Bay Hill Invitational presented by MasterCard and defeated him by six strokes. It was his second win in last 10 events on TOUR after winning 2003 season-ending TOUR Championship. Largest come-from-behind victory at Bay Hill since 1984 when Gary Koch made up six shots to win. Final-round 6-under 66 was the best by a winner at Bay Hill since Phil Mickelson fired a 7-under 65 in 1997, and he was first to come-from-behind and win there since Mickelson's victory. Shared the first-round lead with Darren Clarke and Shigeki Maruyama after opening with a 66…Leading into the win at Bay Hill, finished T9 at the WGC-Accenture Match Play Championship after losing to Jerry Kelly in the third round (1-up)…In next TOUR start, finished T9 at The Honda Classic…Did not have another top-10 after March victory until mid-May, when he finished one stroke behind winner Steve Flesch at the Bank of America Colonial. Shared the third-round lead with Flesch and Brian Gay…Finished seventh on the Ryder Cup Team points list to make his first Ryder Cup Team…Made second straight TOUR Championship but had to withdraw at the halfway point due to a personal family illness.

CAREER HIGHLIGHTS:

2003: Banner year for the sophomore, becoming the first player in TOUR history to record his first win at the season-ending TOUR Championship. Fired personal best, course and tournament record 10-under 61 in third round to take a one-stroke lead over Charles Howell III. Final-round 68 was good for three-stroke victory over Howell and $1,080,000 check. Became seventh first-time winner of season...With season's earnings over $3.9 million, tripled his earnings from his 2002 rookie campaign...Recorded 12 top-10s in two-plus years on TOUR (68 events)...Runner-up to Shaun Micheel at PGA Championship at Oak Hill CC in Rochester, NY. Tied for the lead with Micheel entering the final round, was outdone on 72nd hole as Micheel's 7-iron shot from 175 yards rolled within inches of the cup to clinch a two-stroke victory...Led TOUR in ball striking...Improved from 164 World No. in world at beginning of season to 26th after his victory. **2002:** TOUR rookie had strong first season thanks to two top-10s...Had a second, T3 and fourth in his first 41 TOUR events...Picked up a T3 at the Greater Greensboro Chrysler Classic, thanks in part to a third-round 6-under 66. **2001:** Second of three Nationwide Tour players to earn PGA TOUR card by winning three events (Heath Slocum and Pat Bates the others)...Named Nationwide Tour Player of the Year...Set two Nationwide Tour records: Hit 66 greens in regulation at the Permian Basin Open and earned $394,552, highest single-season earnings by one player at the time...Captured his first victory at the Richmond Open. Shared third-round lead with PGA TOUR member J.J. Henry before defeating Kelly Gibson by three strokes...His 21-under-par total through 54 holes at the Permian Basin Open broke the tournament record by three strokes and tied the Nationwide Tour record for most shots under par after three rounds (Chris Smith, 1997 Omaha Classic). Also broke tournament 72-hole mark with 24-under 264, besting old mark (Paul Gow, 1997) by three strokes...One month later, became second player and third in Nationwide Tour history to earn "promotion" to PGA TOUR during the season. Captured the Monterey Peninsula Classic with a birdie on the 72nd hole to defeat Deane Pappas by one stroke...Held third-round lead at PGA TOUR's Southern Farm Bureau Classic before placing second behind Cameron Beckman. **2000:** Leading money winner on the Hooters Tour for third time in career. Captured eight of the first 16 tournaments on the way to earning $188,279. Closest competitor was over $110,000 behind...Has 13 career victories on that tour...Named Player of the Year for third consecutive year. **1997:** Named Rookie of the Year on the Hooters Tour. **Amateur:** Member of UNLV golf team that placed second at the 1996 NCAA Championships...Teammates at UNLV included PGA TOUR member Chris Riley and former Nationwide Tour member Ted Oh...First-team Junior College All-America at Midland (Texas) College.

PERSONAL:

Started playing golf with his father and brother in Andrews, TX…Older brother Mike is the golf coach at Abilene Christian…While playing golf at UNLV, worked at a coffee shop with other teammates to earn spending money…Has three holes-in-one during competitive rounds…Voted by his peers as "player most likely to win a major" in 2003 issue of Sports Illustrated.

PLAYER STATISTICS

2004 PGA TOUR STATISTICS

Scoring Average	70.81	(60)
Driving Distance	288.0	(87)
Driving Accuracy Percentage	63.9%	(102)
Total Driving	189	(83)
Greens in Regulation Pct.	67.7%	(31)
Putting Average	1.799	(160)
Sand Save Percentage	46.1%	(139)
Eagles (Holes per)	186.0	(62)
Birdie Average	3.32	(145)
All-Around Ranking	786	(103)
Scoring Avg. Before Cut	71.24	(130)
Round 3 Scoring Avg.	70.00	(32)
Final Round Scoring Average	71.45	(86)
Birdie Conversion Percentage	26.1%	(182)
Par Breakers	19.0%	(140)

MISCELLANEOUS PGA TOUR STATISTICS

2004 Low Round/Round: 61–Bank of America Colonial/3
Career Low Round/Round: 61–2 times, most recent 2004 Bank of America Colonial/3
Career Largest Paycheck/Finish: $1,080,000–2003 THE TOUR Championship presented by Coca–Cola/1

PGA TOUR CAREER SUMMARY — PLAYOFF RECORD: 0-0

Year	Events Played	Cuts Made	1st	2nd	3rd	Top 10	Top 25	Earnings	Rank
1998	1	1						4,332	321
1999	2	1						11,038	281
2000	1								
2001	3	1		1		1	1	259,200	
2002	34	21			1	2	7	825,474	81
2003	27	25	1	3		9	15	3,912,064	7
2004	28	23	1	1		4	9	2,264,985	24
Total	96	72	2	5	1	16	32	7,277,092	
NATIONWIDE TOUR									
1993A	1								
1996	2	1					1	2,050	193
1997	1								
1998	1	1						1,451	222
1999	2	2						1,879	197
2000	1								
2001	23	21	3	1		8	13	394,552	1
Total	31	25	3	1		8	14	399,932	

PGA TOUR TOP TOURNAMENT SUMMARY

Year	99	00	01	02	03	04
Masters					CUT	CUT
U.S. Open	CUT	CUT	CUT		T35	CUT
British Open					T15	CUT
PGA				CUT	2	T24
THE PLAYERS					T6	T42
TOUR Championship					1	W/D
WGC-Accenture Match Play						T9
WGC-NEC Invitational					T53	T69
WGC-American Express Champ					T59	T50

NATIONAL TEAMS: Ryder Cup, 2004.

Paul Casey

EXEMPT STATUS: 2004 European Ryder Cup Team member (through 2006)
FULL NAME: Paul Alexander Casey
HEIGHT: 5-10
WEIGHT: 180
BIRTHDATE: July 21, 1977
BIRTHPLACE: Cheltenham, England
RESIDENCE: Scottsdale, AZ and Weybridge, England
FAMILY: Single
EDUCATION: Arizona State University
SPECIAL INTERESTS: Cars, motor racing
TURNED PROFESSIONAL: 2000
JOINED TOUR: 2004

BEST PGA TOUR CAREER FINISH:
T6—2004 Masters Tournament.

INTERNATIONAL VICTORIES (3):
2001 Gleneagles Scottish PGA. **2003** ANZ Championship [Eur], Benson and Hedges International Open [Eur].

OTHER VICTORIES (1):
2004 WGC-World Cup [with Luke Donald].

BEST 2004 PGA TOUR FINISHES:
T6—Masters Tournament; T10—THE PLAYERS Championship.

2004 SEASON:
Joined the PGA TOUR in late April as a Special Temporary Member and earned privileges for the 2005 season via making the 2004 Ryder Cup Team...Made the cut in seven of 11 events, posting top-25s in six of them...In first start at THE PLAYERS Championship, finished T10 to lead the 17 first-time participants...Finished T6 at the Masters in first appearance. Entered final round one back of co-leaders Chris DiMarco and Phil Mickelson, but shot 74...Shared the first-round lead with Thomas Levet (5-under 66) at the British Open in Scotland before finishing T20...Finished 14th on the European Tour's Volvo Order of Merit, his second straight season in the top 20, which included seconds at the ANZ Championship and The Celtic Manor Wales Open...Teamed with Luke Donald to win WGC-World Cup in Spain in mid-November.

CAREER HIGHLIGHTS:
2003: Began season quickly with two victories outside the U.S., the first in the ANZ Championship at New South Wales Golf Club in Sydney where he carded a final-round 71 to finish with 45 points under the Modified Stableford System, the second in the final Benson and Hedges International Open at the De Vere Belfry where he won by four shots...Top PGA TOUR finishes were a T10 at The INTERNATIONAL and T8 at the WGC-American Express Championship. **2001:** Finishing 22nd on the European Tour's Volvo Order of Merit Award helped him win the Sir Henry Cotton Rookie of the Year. **Amateur:** Coached by Peter Kostis...His amateur highlight came as one of the stalwarts of Great Britain and Ireland's Walker Cup victory at Narin in 1999, becoming one of only three players in 77 years to record four victories without a defeat...He won the English Amateur and the Pac-10 Championship at Arizona State back to back in 1999 and 2000. Victory in the 2000 Pac-10 Championships broke the scoring record held by Tiger Woods (18-under par) with a 23-under-par 265. By winning he became the first player to win three successive Pac-10 Championships. Other records he has broken include the scoring average for Arizona State University, previously held by Phil Mickelson.

PLAYER STATISTICS

2004 PGA TOUR STATISTICS

Scoring Average	70.48	(N/A)
Driving Distance	291.9	(N/A)
Driving Accuracy Percentage	62.2%	(N/A)
Total Driving	(N/A)	(N/A)
Greens in Regulation Pct.	66.1%	(N/A)
Putting Average	1.797	(N/A)
Sand Save Percentage	59.5%	(N/A)
Eagles (Holes per)	558.0	(N/A)
Birdie Average	3.71	(N/A)
Scoring Avg. Before Cut	71.95	(N/A)
Round 3 Scoring Avg.	69.17	(N/A)
Final Round Scoring Average	71.17	(N/A)
Birdie Conversion Percentage	29.3%	(N/A)
Par Breakers	20.8%	(N/A)

MISCELLANEOUS PGA TOUR STATISTICS

2004 Low Round/Round: 66–2 times, most recent Buick Open/2
Career Low Round/Round: 66–5 times, most recent 2004 Buick Open/2
Career Largest Paycheck/Finish: $200,000–2004 THE PLAYERS Championship/T10

PGA TOUR CAREER SUMMARY — PLAYOFF RECORD: 0-0

Year	Events Played	Cuts Made	1st	2nd	3rd	Top 10	Top 25	Earnings	Rank
2001	3	1						$8,580	
2002	9	4					1	55,921	
2003	7	5				2	3	136,700	
2004	11	7				2	6	517,939	
Total	30	17				4	10	719,140	
NATIONWIDE TOUR									
2001	1								
Total	1								
EUROPEAN TOUR									
2004	14	13		2	1	6	9	1,055,449	

PGA TOUR TOP TOURNAMENT SUMMARY

Year	02	03	04
Masters			T6
U.S. Open		CUT	CUT
British Open	CUT	CUT	T20
PGA	CUT	66	CUT
THE PLAYERS			T10
WGC-Accenture Match Play		T33	T33
WGC-NEC Invitational		T17	T16
WGC-American Express Champ		T8	T21

NATIONAL TEAMS: Ryder Cup, 2004. WGC-World Cup (4), 2001, 2002, 2003, 2004. Walker Cup, 1999.

Alex Cejka (CHAY-kuh)

EXEMPT STATUS: 54th on 2004 money list
FULL NAME: Alexander Cejka
HEIGHT: 5-8
WEIGHT: 170
BIRTHDATE: December 2, 1970
BIRTHPLACE: Marienbad, Czech Republic (of German nationality)
RESIDENCE: Boca Raton, FL

FAMILY: Children, Alexander, Felix
SPECIAL INTERESTS: Fishing, fast cars, jet skiing, pool
TURNED PROFESSIONAL: 1989
Q SCHOOL: 2002

BEST PGA TOUR CAREER FINISHES:

2—2004 The INTERNATIONAL, T2—2003 B.C. Open.

INTERNATIONAL VICTORIES (11):

1990 Czech Open. **1991** Audi Quattro Trophy. **1992** Czech Open. **1993** Audi Open. **1995** Turespana Open Andalucia [Eur], Hohe Brucke Open [Eur], Volvo Masters [Eur]. **1997** KB Golf Challenge. **1998** Lancia Golf Pokal. **2002** Trophee Lancome [Eur], Galeria Kaufhof Pokal Challenge.

BEST 2004 PGA TOUR FINISHES:

2—The INTERNATIONAL; T7—Booz Allen Classic; T9—WGC-NEC Invitational.

2004 SEASON:

Followed rookie season with a solid sophomore campaign, making a career-best $1,313,483 and posting three top-10s, including a runner-up finish at The INTERNATIONAL... Opened the year with three top-20s early, the FBR Open (T14), WGC- Accenture Match Play Championship (T17) and Ford Championship at Doral (T15)...Picked up his first top-10 in June at the Booz Allen Classic, finishing T7. Recorded a career-best 8-under 63 in round two after opening with a 3-over 74. Weekend rounds of 67-69 moved him into the top-10 at TPC of Avenel...Posted best finish of his career, in his 65th TOUR start, a solo second at The INTERNATIONAL. Trailed by one point in the tournament's Modified Stableford scoring system heading into the final round, but was passed by Rod Pampling who made eagle on the 71st hole to collect five points. His $540,000 paycheck was largest of TOUR career....Two weeks later, in second career WGC-NEC Invitational start, finished T9. Shared low final-round honors with a 4-under-par 66.

CAREER HIGHLIGHTS:

2003: Second-highest finishing rookie on the money list, 60th, behind Ben Curtis (No. 46)...Picked up first top-10 finish as a member of the TOUR with a T7 at the Phoenix Open. Only other previous TOUR top-10 was a T6 at the 1996 NEC World Series of Golf...Posted career-best, runner-up finish at the B.C. Open, helping to solidify his playing privileges for 2004...Finished solo fourth at PGA Championship for first career top-10 at a major championship. **2002:** Finished T2 at the PGA TOUR Qualifying Tournament to earn his first TOUR card...Collected his fourth victory on the European Tour, where he has been a member since 1992, at the 2002 Trophee Lancome...Finished 23rd on the Volvo Order of Merit, making the cut in 12 of 18 events...Also picked up a victory at the Galeria Kaufhof Pokal Challenge on the European Challenge Tour, his fourth on that tour. **1999:** Finished 17th on the Volvo Order of Merit. **1998:** Led the European Tour in Greens in Regulation. **1996:** Made the cut in all four majors, highlighted by a T11 showing at the British Open at Royal Lytham & St. Annes. **1995:** Finished sixth on the 1995 Order of Merit...Won three times that year, including the prestigious Volvo Masters. The others were the Turespana Open Andalucia and the Hohe Brucke Open. Set course record with a 61 during the Hohe Brucke event. **1992:** Won Czech Open for second time in career.

PERSONAL:

Escaped Communist Czechoslovakia at age 9 with his father through Yugoslavia, Italy and Switzerland before settling in Germany. Returned to Prague in 1997 to settle there with his family. On obtaining his PGA TOUR card in 2002, has settled in America. He is of German nationality.

PLAYER STATISTICS

2004 PGA TOUR STATISTICS

Scoring Average	71.15	(101)
Driving Distance	285.8	(110)
Driving Accuracy Percentage	64.2%	(100)
Total Driving	210	(122)
Greens in Regulation Pct.	63.8%	(126)
Putting Average	1.795	(142)
Sand Save Percentage	50.7%	(75)
Eagles (Holes per)	210.0	(75)
Birdie Average	3.44	(121)
All-Around Ranking	850	(121)
Scoring Avg. Before Cut	71.18	(123)
Round 3 Scoring Avg.	71.21	(118)
Final Round Scoring Average	73.23	(184)
Birdie Conversion Percentage	28.8%	(104)
Par Breakers	19.6%	(116)

MISCELLANEOUS PGA TOUR STATISTICS

2004 Low Round/Round: 63–Booz Allen Classic/2
Career Low Round/Round: 63–2004 Booz Allen Classic/2
Career Largest Paycheck/Finish: $540,000–2004 The INTERNATIONAL/2

PGA TOUR CAREER SUMMARY — PLAYOFF RECORD: 0-0

Year	Events Played	Cuts Made	1st	2nd	3rd	Top 10	Top 25	Earnings	Rank
1996	10	5				1	2	$134,961	143
1997	1								
1999	2	2						6,800	304
2000	1								
2001	1	1					1	57,310	
2002	1								
2003	30	20		1		4	7	1,182,883	60
2004	24	16		1		3	7	1,313,483	54
Total	70	44		2		8	17	2,695,437	
NATIONWIDE TOUR									
2002	5	3				1	2	33,967	104
Total	5	3				1	2	33,967	
EUROPEAN TOUR									
2004	5	4			1	3	4	366,519	

PGA TOUR TOP TOURNAMENT SUMMARY

Year	96	97	98	99	00	01	02	03	04
Masters	44								26
U.S. Open	T50							T61	T60
British Open	T11	CUT			CUT	T13	CUT		
PGA	T52			T65				4	CUT
THE PLAYERS									T33
WGC-Accenture Match Play								T9	T17
WGC-NEC Invitational								T42	T9
WGC-American Express Champ				T55				T12	T28

NATIONAL TEAMS: Dunhill Cup (4), 1994, 1995, 1997, 1998. World Cup (7) 1995, 1996, 1997, 1999, 2000, 2001, 2003. The Seve Trophy (3), 2000, 2002, 2003.

K.J. Choi (choy)

EXEMPT STATUS: 2002 two-time tournament winner (through 2005)
FULL NAME: Kyoung-Ju Choi
HEIGHT: 5-8
WEIGHT: 185
BIRTHDATE: May 19, 1968
BIRTHPLACE: Wando, South Korea
RESIDENCE: The Woodlands, TX
FAMILY: Wife, Hyunjung Kim; Hohjun "David" (5/9/97), Amanda (3/4/02), Daniel (12/26/03)
SPECIAL INTERESTS: Movies
TURNED PROFESSIONAL: 1994
Q SCHOOL: 1999, 2000

PGA TOUR VICTORIES (2):

2002 Compaq Classic of New Orleans, Tampa Bay Classic presented by Buick.

INTERNATIONAL VICTORIES (6):

1996 Korean Open. **1999** Ube Kosan Open [Jpn], Kirin Open [Jpn], Kolon Korean Open. **2003** Linde German Masters [Eur], S.K. Telecom Open [Asia].

BEST 2004 PGA TOUR FINISHES:

3—Masters Tournament; T4—AT&T Pebble Beach National Pro-Am; 5—the Memorial Tournament, Ford Championship at Doral; T6—PGA Championship; T7—HP Classic of New Orleans, 84 LUMBER Classic.

2004 SEASON:

Another consistent season on the PGA TOUR, making 19 cuts in 24 starts. Earned over $2 million and matched his season best total in top-10s with seven...Picked up first top-10 of season in his second start, a T4 at the AT&T Pebble Beach National Pro-Am...Finished T5 at the Ford Championship at Doral. Was two-strokes back of the lead through 54 holes...In second Masters appearance, finished solo third, three strokes behind champion Phil Mickelson. Had a 30 on the front nine in second round and 31 on the back nine in final round. Final round included an eagle on the par-4 11th hole...Past champion finished T7 at the HP Classic of New Orleans. Was one of only five players to post four rounds in the 60s at English Turn...Was among the leaders all week at the Memorial Tournament, and posted a final-round 72 to finish fifth...Earned second top-10 in a major with a T6 at the PGA Championship. One of only 10 players to record multiple top-10s in the majors...Finished T7 at the 84 LUMBER Classic, his seventh top-10 of the season.

CAREER HIGHLIGHTS:

2003: Finished in top 30 for second consecutive season on strength of six top-10s, including a runner-up in the season-opening Mercedes Championships, earning $450,000. Fired course-record 11-under-par 62 in third round, and entered final round two strokes back of Ernie Els. Finished eight strokes back of Els after even-par round of 73 on Sunday...Ran off five consecutive top-10s, including a win on the European Tour, beginning with a T4 at the Bell Canadian Open. Posted a final-round 67 to capture the Linde German Masters, his first career victory on the European Tour. The next week in United States recorded an 8-under-par 62 in the second round, good for T7 in San Antonio, and followed that with a T6 at the WGC-American Express Championship...Was chosen by Gary Player as a captain's pick for the 2003 Presidents Cup. **2002:** Third season on PGA TOUR proved to be the breakthrough, as he was one of three first-time winners to win twice...Jumped from 192nd on the Official World Golf Ranking at end of 2001 to 49th at season's end...Became the first South Korean winner in TOUR history, closing with 5-under-par 67 for a four-stroke victory in the Compaq Classic of New Orleans. Fourth Asian to win on the TOUR, joining Isao Aoki and Shigeki Maruyama of Japan and T.C. Chen of Taiwan. Donated 10 percent of his $810,000 check to underprivileged South Koreans back home and to the Christian church his family attends near Houston...Earned his second victory in his 86th career start at the Tampa Bay Classic. Became the second player to record wire-to-wire victory during the year, joining Tiger Woods (U.S. Open, WGC-American Express Championship). First-place check of $468,000 jumped him from 31st to 17th. Became the second Asian-born player to win multiple events on the TOUR, joining Shigeki Maruyama of Japan, who earlier in the year earned his second victory at the Verizon Byron Nelson Classic...On Sept. 23, a day after his win in Tampa, had an inflamed appendix removed in Houston. Began suffering stomach pain on the eve of the final round at Tampa Bay. **2001:** Finished season inside Top 125 for first time in his career...Earned card by surviving the Qualifying Tournament for second consecutive season, finishing T31. **2000:** Rookie on PGA TOUR after T35 finish at the 1999 Qualifying Tournament. Finished 134th on the money list and picked up his only top-10 with a T8 at the Air Canada Championship.

PERSONAL:

Interest in golf grew after one of his high school teachers recommended he try the sport. Began studying videos of Jack Nicklaus and spent long hours hitting practice balls on his island home's only practice range. Later studied under Phil Ritson...First Korean to earn PGA TOUR card.

PLAYER STATISTICS

2004 PGA TOUR STATISTICS

Scoring Average	70.54	(36)
Driving Distance	285.0	(120)
Driving Accuracy Percentage	61.2%	(146)
Total Driving	266	(180)
Greens in Regulation Pct.	65.9%	(76)
Putting Average	1.770	(77)
Sand Save Percentage	45.8%	(142)
Eagles (Holes per)	210.9	(76)
Birdie Average	3.55	(90)
All-Around Ranking	763	(97)
Scoring Avg. Before Cut	70.91	(84)
Round 3 Scoring Avg.	71.44	(139)
Final Round Scoring Average	71.33	(76)
Birdie Conversion Percentage	29.4%	(87)
Par Breakers	20.2%	(90)

MISCELLANEOUS PGA TOUR STATISTICS

2004 Low Round/Round: 65–84 LUMBER Classic/4
Career Low Round/Round: 62–2 times, most recent 2003 Valero Texas Open/2
Career Largest Paycheck/Finish: $810,000–2002 Compaq Classic of New Orleans/1

PGA TOUR CAREER SUMMARY — PLAYOFF RECORD: 0-0

Year	Events Played	Cuts Made	1st	2nd	3rd	Top 10	Top 25	Earnings	Rank
1998	1								
1999	2	2					1	$31,457	241
2000	30	16				1	4	305,745	134
2001	29	19				5	8	800,326	65
2002	27	19	2			7	11	2,204,907	17
2003	32	25		1		6	13	1,999,663	30
2004	24	19			1	7	10	2,077,775	26
Total	145	100	2	1	1	26	47	7,419,874	
EUROPEAN TOUR									
2004	4	4				3	3	209,538	

PGA TOUR TOP TOURNAMENT SUMMARY

Year	98	99	00	01	02	03	04
Masters						T15	3
U.S. Open				CUT	T30	CUT	T31
British Open	CUT	T49			CUT	T22	T16
PGA				T29	CUT	T69	T6
THE PLAYERS					T28	CUT	T42
TOUR Championship					T9	T19	27
WGC-Accenture Match Play						T17	T33
WGC-NEC Invitational					T19	T53	T58
WGC-American Express Champ						T6	T57

NATIONAL TEAMS: WGC-World Cup (2), 2002, 2003; Presidents Cup, 2003.

Daniel Chopra (chope-RAH)

EXEMPT STATUS: 108th on 2004 money list
FULL NAME: Daniel Samir Chopra
HEIGHT: 6-0
WEIGHT: 180
BIRTHDATE: December 23, 1973
BIRTHPLACE: Stockholm, Sweden
RESIDENCE: Perth, Australia
FAMILY: Wife, Samantha

SPECIAL INTERESTS: Television, reading, film, snooker
TURNED PROFESSIONAL: 1992
Q SCHOOL: 2003
Nationwide Tour Alumnus

BEST PGA TOUR CAREER FINISH:
T4—2004 Deutsche Bank Championship.

NATIONWIDE TOUR VICTORIES (2):
2004 First Tee Arkansas Classic, Henrico County Open.

INTERNATIONAL VICTORIES (1):
2001 Mercuries Masters [Asia].

BEST 2004 PGA TOUR FINISHES:
T4—Deutsche Bank Championship; T8—Buick Open; T9—Reno-Tahoe Open.

2004 SEASON:
Finished in top 125 in rookie season on PGA TOUR while posting three top-10s...Made huge leap up the Official World Golf Ranking list from 504th to 208th by season's end...Initial success of season actually came on Nationwide Tour, where he finished 21st on the money list the prior year. Was not eligible for the MCI Heritage in April, so took advantage of a return to the Nationwide Tour where he won the First Tee Arkansas Classic. A month later, did not qualify for the Bank of America Colonial and broke the 72-hole tournament record on the Nationwide Tour with a record 30-under-par 258 at the Henrico County Open in Glen Allen, VA. He broke the Tour mark by four strokes...Made his first start in a major at the U.S. Open and finished T24...Finished T8 for first career top-10 on the TOUR at the Buick Open, earning a then career-best $135,000...Continued his consistent play with T9 at the Reno-Tahoe Open...Posted third top-10 in last five outings, a career-best T4 at the Deutsche Bank Championship, giving him enough money to keep his card for the 2005 season.

CAREER HIGHLIGHTS:
2003: Finished sixth at PGA TOUR Qualifying Tournament, earning his first TOUR card. Made the cut in 19 of 22 events on the 2003 Nationwide Tour. Finished the season No. 21 on the money list with $178,799, just $1,164 behind Tommy Tolles for the final 2004 PGA TOUR card. Best finish came at the LaSalle Bank Open (T3). **2002:** Finished No. 90 on the Nationwide Tour money list, his rookie season. Posted his only top-10s in consecutive weeks, finishing T7 at the Dayton Open followed by a T5 at the Fort Smith Classic. Won the Mercuries Masters on the Asian Tour at the Taiwan G&CC after gaining entry on a sponsor invitation. Posted a 4-under 284 total to win by one and collect the $69,565 first-place check. **2000:** Finished T3 at the Tour Players Championship on the Japan Golf Tour. Member of the European Tour 1996-2000.

PERSONAL:
Moved to India at age 7 and was raised by grandparents. Won the All-India Junior Golf Championship at age 14. Won two more Indian Junior titles plus the Doug Sanders World Junior title. Born to a Swedish mother and Indian father...Claims to be the first person to hit a golf ball off the Great Wall of China, in 1995.

PLAYER STATISTICS

2004 PGA TOUR STATISTICS

Scoring Average	70.93	(72)
Driving Distance	295.9	(26)
Driving Accuracy Percentage	58.6%	(169)
Total Driving	195	(95)
Greens in Regulation Pct.	63.9%	(122)
Putting Average	1.748	(19)
Sand Save Percentage	52.2%	(53)
Eagles (Holes per)	190.8	(65)
Birdie Average	3.79	(31)
All-Around Ranking	557	(39)
Scoring Avg. Before Cut	70.50	(39)
Round 3 Scoring Avg.	70.43	(56)
Final Round Scoring Average	72.20	(143)
Birdie Conversion Percentage	32.0%	(15)
Par Breakers	21.6%	(28)

MISCELLANEOUS PGA TOUR STATISTICS

2004 Low Round/Round: 64–2 times, most recent Michelin Championship at Las Vegas/2
Career Low Round/Round: 64–2 times, most recent 2004 Michelin Championship at Las Vegas/2
Career Largest Paycheck/Finish: $220,000–2004 Deutsche Bank Championship/T4

PGA TOUR CAREER SUMMARY — PLAYOFF RECORD: 0-0

Year	Events Played	Cuts Made	1st	2nd	3rd	Top 10	Top 25	Earnings	Rank
2004	33	20				3	5	$763,253	108
Total	33	20				3	5	763,253	
NATIONWIDE TOUR									
2002	25	8				2	3	41,269	90
2003	22	19			1	7	13	178,799	21
2004	3	3	2			2	3	182,130	27
Total	50	30	2		1	11	19	402,198	

PGA TOUR TOP TOURNAMENT SUMMARY

Year	04
U.S. Open	T24

Stewart Cink (sink)

EXEMPT STATUS: 2004 World Golf Championships winner (through 2007)
FULL NAME: Stewart Ernest Cink
HEIGHT: 6-4
WEIGHT: 205
BIRTHDATE: May 21, 1973
BIRTHPLACE: Huntsville, AL
RESIDENCE: Duluth, GA; plays out of East Lake GC

FAMILY: Wife, Lisa; Connor Stewart (9/13/93), Reagan Braswell (4/8/97)
EDUCATION: Georgia Tech (1995, Management)
SPECIAL INTERESTS: Family, boating, water sports, hiking, BBQ, snow skiing
TURNED PROFESSIONAL: 1995
JOINED TOUR: 1997
Nationwide Tour Alumnus

PGA TOUR VICTORIES (4):

1997 Canon Greater Hartford Open. **2000** MCI Classic. **2004** MCI Heritage, WGC-NEC Invitational.

NATIONWIDE TOUR VICTORIES (3):

1996 Ozarks Open, Colorado Classic, TOUR Championship.

INTERNATIONAL VICTORIES (2):

1996 Mexican Open. **1999** Mexican Open.

BEST 2004 PGA TOUR FINISHES:

1—MCI Heritage, WGC-NEC Invitational; 2—84 LUMBER Classic; T4—Bell Canadian Open; 5—Buick Open, FedEx St. Jude Classic; T6—The INTERNATIONAL; T8—BellSouth Classic, John Deere Classic; T10—Buick Invitational.

2004 SEASON:

Career season included multiple TOUR victories for the first time, a career-best fifth-place finish on the money list, and a spot on the U.S. Ryder Cup squad…Jumped to No. 10 in Official World Golf Ranking after THE TOUR Championship from outside the top 50 at start of season…Led the TOUR in Putting Average (1.723) …Held two-stroke lead through 36 holes at the Buick Invitational before finishing T10. His second-round, 9-under 63 matched his career best, which came during the final round of the 2000 NEC Invitational…Playing in the BellSouth Classic at his home course, the TPC at Sugarloaf, posted his sixth top-10 in eight appearances, finishing T8…Earned third career victory and first in four years by defeating Ted Purdy in a five-hole playoff at the MCI Heritage. Made birdie on the fifth playoff hole, the par-4 16th, to win. Became seventh player to win the tournament more than once (2000) and had the largest come-from-behind win on TOUR, nine strokes, since Paul Lawrie won the 1999 British Open by coming from 10 strokes back at the start of the final round. The final-round, 7-under 64 was a tournament record for low finish by a winner, topping the 6-under 65 he posted in his 2000 win for second time this year or season…Posted fourth top-10 with a T5 at the FedEx St. Jude Classic…Fifth top-10 was T8 at the John Deere Classic, three shots out of the Mark Hensby-John E. Morgan playoff…Finished solo fifth at the Buick Open, five shots behind champion Vijay Singh…Finished eagle-birdie on Nos. 17-18 in the final round at The INTERNATIONAL for T6 finish…Along with Jay Haas, selected by Hal Sutton as a Captain's pick for the 2004 Ryder Cup Team, his second appearance on the team. Next week, recorded wire-to-wire victory at WGC-NEC Invitational, posting rounds of 63-68-68-70—269. Four-stroke victory over Rory Sabbatini and Tiger Woods was worth a career-best $1.2 million. First-round 63 matched career low on the TOUR. First player of 2004 to win wire-to-wire and first since Davis Love III at 2003 INTERNATIONAL…Tuned up for the Ryder Cup Matches with a T4 at the Bell Canadian Open, his first start since the victory in Akron, Ohio…Finished runner-up to Vijay Singh at the 84 LUMBER Classic for a career-best 10th top-10 of the season. Eclipsed the $4-million mark in season earnings for the first time in his career with his $453,600 payday in Pennsylvania.

CAREER HIGHLIGHTS:

2003: Returned to the top 40 on the money list after falling out in 2002. Runner-up at Bay Hill Invitational and FUNAI Classic at the WALT DISNEY WORLD Resort...36- and 54-hole leader at the MCI Heritage. Final-round 73 dropped finish to T10 for the MCI Heritage past champion...Solo sixth-place finish at the Memorial Tournament. Surpassed $1 million in earnings for fourth time in career with $180,000 payday at Muirfield Village...Set two course records in one day with 62-61 U.S. Open sectional qualifying scores on June 2 in Columbus, OH. Bogeyed the first hole then recorded 22 birdies to win the qualifier by nine strokes. **2002:** Without a top-10 finish through first 13 events, recorded back-to-back top 10s at the Memorial Tournament (T9) and Buick Classic (T5)...Recorded his fifth top-10 at a major championship, T10 at PGA Championship...Made his Ryder Cup debut with a 1-2-0 record...Ended the season on a high note when he recorded four rounds in the 60s for the first time during the season and finished T7 at the Buick Challenge. **2001:** Highlight of the season came when he posted three top-fives in June, including missing the 18-hole playoff at the U.S. Open with Mark Brooks and Retief Goosen. Started the month with a solo fourth at The Memorial Tournament. Two weeks later finished alone in third at the U.S. Open, where he was tied for the lead through 54 holes. Closing 72, including a double bogey on 18, left him one shy of the playoff on Monday morning. The next week an opening-round 65 at the Buick Classic gave him a one-stroke lead over Scott Hoch and Vijay Singh. Finished T3...Earned a spot as a first-time member of the U.S. Ryder Cup team. **2000:** Earned second PGA TOUR victory at MCI Classic. Shot final-round 65, which included birdies on three of final four holes. Two-stroke win over Tom Lehman was worth $540,000...Followed with T2 at MasterCard Colonial, where he held three-stroke lead through 54 holes. Closing 71 left him two strokes behind Phil Mickelson...Was solo seventh at WGC-NEC Invitational, where he closed with a 63...Member of U.S. Presidents Cup team where he was 4-0-0 in first appearance...Closed the year with T3 at the Invensys Classic at Las Vegas. **1999:** Missed earning a place in THE TOUR Championship by one spot. Was 31st on the money list after finishing T11 at National Car Rental Golf Classic at Disney World Resort, $14,600 behind Duffy Waldorf...Defeated Payne Stewart and Craig Parry before losing to Tiger Woods in the third round of the WGC-Accenture Match Play Championship...Earned a share of the 54-hole lead at the BellSouth Classic, but closing 70 left him one stroke behind winner David Duval, who shot 67...At PGA Championship, shot 69-70-68-73, was one stroke out of 54-hole lead and finished T3. **1998:** Recorded six top-10s and almost became first to successfully defend a Canon GHO. A final-round 67 moved him into playoff with Olin Browne and Larry Mize. Browne won with a chip-in birdie. **1997:** Voted PGA TOUR Rookie of the Year after victory at the Canon Greater Hartford Open and $809,580 in earn-

SECTION 2 PLAYER BIOGRAPHIES

PGA TOUR CAREER SUMMARY — PLAYOFF RECORD: 1-1

Year	Events Played	Cuts Made	1st	2nd	3rd	Top 10	Top 25	Earnings	Rank
1995A	1	1							
1995	5	4				1	2	$58,426	192
1996	5	5				1	4	108,710	158
1997	31	19	1	1		4	13	809,580	29
1998	28	23		1		6	15	833,648	31
1999	27	21		1	1	8	14	1,255,100	32
2000	27	23	1	1	1	9	15	2,169,727	10
2001	29	22			2	6	14	1,743,028	26
2002	27	20				4	8	894,212	73
2003	28	23		2		6	14	1,781,885	35
2004	28	24	2	1		10	20	4,450,270	5
Total	236	185	4	7	4	55	119	14,104,588	
NATIONWIDE TOUR									
1995	3	1					1	2,936	180
1996	21	18	3	2	1	14	17	251,699	1
Total	24	19	3	2	1	14	18	254,635	

PGA TOUR TOP TOURNAMENT SUMMARY

Year	96	97	98	99	00	01	02	03	04
Masters		CUT	T23	T27	T28	CUT	T24		T17
U.S. Open	T16	T13	T10	T32	T8	3	CUT	T28	CUT
British Open			T66	CUT	T41	T30	T59	T34	T14
PGA		CUT	CUT	T3	T15	T59	T10	CUT	T17
THE PLAYERS			T42	CUT	T33	CUT	CUT	T39	T22
TOUR Championship		24			T18	T13			T21
WGC-Accenture Match Play				T9	T33	T33	T33		T17
WGC-NEC Invitational					7	T13	T47	T61	1
WGC-American Express Champ				T4		CNL			T23

NATIONAL TEAMS: The Presidents Cup, 2000; Ryder Cup (2), 2002, 2004.

Stewart Cink (Continued)

ings...Was only rookie to qualify for THE TOUR Championship and finished season ranked 29th in official earnings...First player to be named Nationwide Tour Player of the Year and PGA TOUR Rookie of the Year in successive seasons...Came from behind to earn his first TOUR victory. Started final round in fifth place, four strokes behind leader Jeff Maggert. Closing 66 good for one-stroke victory over Brandel Chamblee, Tom Byrum and Maggert. **1996:** Named Nationwide Tour Player of the Year after his record-setting season. Established Nationwide Tour record for earnings in a season with $251,699. Won three tournaments—Ozarks Open, Colorado Classic and TOUR Championship...Tied for 16th at U.S. Open to earn invitation to 1997 Masters Tournament. **1995:** Tied for 18th in first professional start at Canon Greater Hartford Open. **Amateur:** A three-time All-American (1993-95) at Georgia Tech...Received 1995 Dave Williams, Haskins and Jack Nicklaus Awards as country's top collegiate golfer...Beat Tiger Woods 3 and 2 in an exhibition match in 1995 in Atlanta the week before the Masters...AJGA All-American in 1990.

PERSONAL:

Took up game when his parents, single-digit handicappers, left him at driving range before he was old enough to go on the course…Was a husband and a father while still at Georgia Tech…Member of East Lake GC, site of THE TOUR Championship…A big Atlanta Thrashers hockey fan. Enjoys roller hockey…Enjoys hiking in the mountains and goes for a week each summer with a group of friends.

PLAYER STATISTICS

2004 PGA TOUR STATISTICS

Scoring Average	69.82	(7)
Driving Distance	290.5	(70)
Driving Accuracy Percentage	58.7%	(167)
Total Driving	237	(157)
Greens in Regulation Pct.	66.4%	(60)
Putting Average	1.723	(1)
Sand Save Percentage	56.1%	(18)
Eagles (Holes per)	249.4	(98)
Birdie Average	3.86	(18)
All-Around Ranking	439	(12)
Scoring Avg. Before Cut	70.33	(24)
Round 3 Scoring Avg.	69.77	(18)
Final Round Scoring Average	69.77	(5)
Birdie Conversion Percentage	31.3%	(29)
Par Breakers	21.8%	(21)

MISCELLANEOUS PGA TOUR STATISTICS

2004 Low Round/Round: 63–2 times, most recent WGC-NEC Invitational/1
Career Low Round/Round: 63–3 times, most recent 2004 WGC-NEC Invitational/1
Career Largest Paycheck/Finish: $1,200,000–2004 WGC–NEC Invitational/1

SHOTLink — AN IBM ON DEMAND BUSINESS SOLUTION

HOT SHOTS

Toughest Courses (2004)

Event Name	Course Name	To Par
U.S. Open Championship	Shinnecock Hills GC	+4.07
British Open Championship	Royal Troon GC	+2.21
Masters Tournament	Augusta National GC	+1.97
Bell Canadian Open	Glen Abbey GC	+1.73
Buick Invitational	Torrey Pines (South Course)**	+1.41

** = Multiple-course tournament

TPC at Summerlin

Easiest Courses (2004)

Event Name	Course Name	To Par
Bob Hope Chrysler Classic	Indian Wells CC**	-3.93
Bob Hope Chrysler Classic	Bermuda Dunes CC**	-3.41
Bob Hope Chrysler Classic	PGA West (Palmer Course)**	-2.75
Michelin Champ at Las Vegas	TPC at Summerlin**	-2.59
Michelin Champ at Las Vegas	Bear's Best**	-2.17

Tim Clark

EXEMPT STATUS: 2003 International Presidents Cup Team Member (through 2005)
FULL NAME: Timothy Henry Clark
HEIGHT: 5-7
WEIGHT: 150
BIRTHDATE: December 17, 1975
BIRTHPLACE: Durban, South Africa
RESIDENCE: Scottsdale, AZ

FAMILY: Single
EDUCATION: North Carolina State University
SPECIAL INTERESTS: Music, travel
TURNED PROFESSIONAL: 1998
JOINED TOUR: 2001
Nationwide Tour Alumnus

BEST PGA TOUR CAREER FINISH:

3—2003 PGA Championship.

NATIONWIDE TOUR VICTORIES (2):

2000 Fort Smith Classic, Boise Open.

INTERNATIONAL VICTORIES (1):

2002 Bell's South African Open.

BEST 2004 PGA TOUR FINISHES:

T5—Valero Texas Open; T6—FUNAI Classic at the WALT DISNEY WORLD Resort; T8—Chrysler Classic of Tucson, Southern Farm Bureau Classic; T9—Buick Classic; T10—Nissan Open.

2004 SEASON:

Continued his strong play in his third full season as a member of the PGA TOUR. Recorded a career-high six top-10s and made 16 cuts in 26 TOUR starts. . . Collected first top-10 of the season with a T10 finish at the Nissan Open. . . The next week at the Chrysler Classic of Tucson finished T8. First time since he joined the TOUR in 2001 that he has recorded back-to-back top-10s. . . First top-10 after the West Coast Swing came at the Buick Classic in early June, finished T9. . . In just his second career appearance at the U.S. Open finished T13. . . Recorded a T5 finish at The Barclays Scottish Open on the European Tour the week before the British Open. . . Best finish of the season on the PGA TOUR was T5 at the Valero Texas Open. . . Two weeks later, added a T8 at the Southern Farm Bureau Classic thanks to four rounds in the 60s. . . Posted four rounds in the 60s at the FUNAI Classic at the WALT DISNEY WORLD Resort, finished T6. His $120,000 payday lifted him over $1 million for the second consecutive season.

CAREER HIGHLIGHTS:

2003: In defense of first European Tour title, finished second to Trevor Immelman at the South African Airways Open in early January...Named to The Presidents Cup team by International Captain Gary Player after third-place finish at PGA Championship, best career finish in a major. Trailed co-leaders Shaun Micheel and Chad Campbell by four entering final round, but a 1-under-par 69 fell three strokes short of Micheel. Earned a career-best paycheck of $408,000. **2002:** Took advantage of Major Medical Extension due to wrist injury that cut his 2001 campaign to three events. Had 26 events to earn $384,602 and almost doubled that with $632,609...Won the Bell's South African Open on the European Tour/Southern Africa Tour in January. Won the pre-qualifying tournament earlier in the week, becoming the first qualifier to win on the European Tour since Paul Lawrie captured the 1999 British Open...Captured the Southern Africa Tour Order of Merit based on five top-10s and one victory...Collected his first top-10 finish in only his eighth professional TOUR start, with a T9 at the Compaq Classic of New Orleans...His T6 finish and $119,788-check at the Michelob Championship at Kingsmill moved him past the $384,602 that he needed to receive fully-exempt Major Medical Extension status for the last three events of the season...Added another T6 two weeks later at the Disney Golf Classic, after carding four rounds in the 60s. Jumped up the TOUR money list from a bubble-position of No. 126 to No. 106 to clinch TOUR card for 2003. **2001:** Withdrew after first-round 79 at the AT&T Pebble Beach National Pro-Am, effectively ending season in which he played just three events. **2000:** Earned first PGA TOUR card by finishing third on the Nationwide Tour money list. Captured two titles, Fort Smith Classic and Boise Open. **1999:** Made the Nationwide Tour Championship and finished T23 after opening with a 77. **1998:** Missed cut as an amateur at his first PGA TOUR event, the Masters, where he earned a spot via 1997 Public Links title...Won back-to-back events on the Canadian Tour, New Brunswick Open and CPGA Championship. **Amateur:** 1997 U.S. Public Links Champion. Two-time NCAA East Regional Individual Champion (1996 and 1997)...1997 ACC Player of the Year...T5 at 1996 NCAA Championship and T7 in 1998 NCAAs...1996 CGAA National Freshman of the Year...Won 1997 Cardinal Amateur Championship (Greensboro, NC).

PERSONAL:

Recorded his first hole-in-one when he was age 8.

PLAYER STATISTICS

2004 PGA TOUR STATISTICS

Statistic	Value	Rank
Scoring Average	70.53	(34)
Driving Distance	278.8	(168)
Driving Accuracy Percentage	72.0%	(13)
Total Driving	181	(74)
Greens in Regulation Pct.	65.8%	(78)
Putting Average	1.764	(56)
Sand Save Percentage	53.3%	(40)
Eagles (Holes per)	378.0	(161)
Birdie Average	3.63	(70)
All-Around Ranking	620	(50)
Scoring Avg. Before Cut	71.08	(108)
Round 3 Scoring Avg.	69.19	(5)
Final Round Scoring Average	71.25	(73)
Birdie Conversion Percentage	29.9%	(71)
Par Breakers	20.4%	(80)

MISCELLANEOUS PGA TOUR STATISTICS

2004 Low Round/Round: 64–4 times, most recent FUNAI Classic at the WALT DISNEY WORLD Resort/3
Career Low Round/Round: 63–2003 Valero Texas Open/2
Career Largest Paycheck/Finish: $408,000–2003 PGA Championship/3

PGA TOUR CAREER SUMMARY — PLAYOFF RECORD: 0-0

Year	Events Played	Cuts Made	1st	2nd	3rd	Top 10	Top 25	Earnings	Rank
1998A	1								
2001	3	1						$21,750	227
2002	23	15				3	7	632,609	107
2003	25	16			1	3	10	1,253,690	53
2004	26	16				6	9	1,108,190	71
Total	78	48			1	12	26	3,016,239	
NATIONWIDE TOUR									
1998A	1	1							
1998	1								
1999	25	14			1	3	6	57,220	46
2000	27	16	2		1	7	11	288,056	3
2001	4	1				1	1	16,200	147
Total	58	32	2		2	11	18	361,476	
EUROPEAN TOUR									
2004	1	1				1	1	125,708	

PGA TOUR TOP TOURNAMENT SUMMARY

Year	98	99	00	01	02	03	04
Masters	CUT					T13	CUT
U.S. Open						CUT	T13
British Open					CUT		CUT
PGA					T53	3	CUT
THE PLAYERS						T21	CUT
WGC-Accenture Match Play						T33	
WGC-NEC Invitational						T64	T48
WGC-American Express Champ					62		

NATIONAL TEAMS: WGC-World Cup, 2002; The Presidents Cup, 2003.

Darren Clarke

EXEMPT STATUS: 2003 World Golf Championship winner (through 2006)
FULL NAME: Darren Christopher Clarke
HEIGHT: 6-2
WEIGHT: 215
BIRTHDATE: August 14, 1968
BIRTHPLACE: Dungannon, Northern Ireland
RESIDENCE: Surrey, England
FAMILY: Wife, Heather; Tyrone (1998), Conor (2000)
SPECIAL INTERESTS: Films, reading, cars, fishing
TURNED PROFESSIONAL: 1990
JOINED TOUR: 2003

PGA TOUR VICTORIES (2):

2000 WGC-Accenture Match Play Championship. **2003** WGC-NEC Invitational.

INTERNATIONAL VICTORIES (11):

1993 Alfred Dunhill Open [Eur]. **1996** Linde German Masters [Eur]. **1998** Benson and Hedges International Open [Eur], Volvo Masters [Eur]. **1999** Compass Group English Open [Eur]. **2000** Compass Group English Open [Eur]. **2001** Dimension Data Pro-Am [SAf], The Chunichi Crowns [Jpn], Smurfit European Open [Eur]. **2002** Compass Group English Open. **2003** Northern Ireland Masters [EurChall]. **2004** Mitsui Sumitomo VISA Taiheiyo Masters [Jpn].

BEST 2004 PGA TOUR FINISHES:

3—Mercedes Championships, WGC-Accenture Match Play Championship; T4—WGC-American Express Championship; T6—Bay Hill Invitational Presented by MasterCard.

2004 SEASON:

Finished in the top 30 (No. 28) on the PGA TOUR money list but won in Japan…Making his Mercedes Championships debut, finished third at the TOUR's season-opening event, five strokes behind champion Stuart Appleby. One of three first-timers to finish in the top 10 (Adam Scott, Ben Crane) at Kapalua…Past champion finished third at the WGC-Accenture Match Play Championship, falling to Davis Love III in 21 holes in the semifinals. In consolation finals, beat Stephen Leaney 2 and 1 to secure paycheck of $530,000. Career record at Accenture event is 14-4…Shared first-round lead with eventual winner Chad Campbell and Shigeki Maruyama at the Bay Hill Invitational. Finished the event T6…Held one-stroke lead after opening with a 7-under 65 at the PGA Championship but finished T13 after closing with a 76. The 65 was his best career round in a major, topping the 66 in second round of the 1997 British Open, where he finished T2…His last top-10 was a T4 at the WGC-American Express Championship in Ireland for his fourth top-10 of the season…Finished eighth on the European Tour's Volvo Order of Merit with sevent top-10s…Had 3-1-1 record for Europe's victorious Ryder Cup team…Ended TOUR season with a T15 at THE TOUR Championship...Captured the Masters on the Japan Golf Tour by four shots.

CAREER HIGHLIGHTS:

2003: Won the WGC-NEC Invitational at Firestone CC in Akron, OH, joining Tiger Woods as the only players to win multiple WGC events...Totaled five top-10s in a career-high 16 events on the PGA TOUR...Eight-time European Tour winner failed to win in Europe for the first time since 1997, but racked up six top-10s in 11 starts on the European Tour, including a T2 at The Barclays Scottish Open…Joined the PGA TOUR as a Special Temporary Member on April 9...Earned second career World Golf Championships victory with four-shot win at WGC-NEC Invitational at Firestone CC, earning a career-best $1,050,000. Held one-shot lead over Jonathan Kaye entering final round. First European non-PGA TOUR member to win on the PGA TOUR since Retief Goosen won the U.S. Open in 2001...Made THE TOUR Championship field by $9,768, with a total of $1,896,931 official/unofficial money earned (including $1,250,000 in WGC earnings), ranking 29th on the PGA TOUR Money List. By finishing among the top 30 with his combination of official/unofficial money, the field increased to 31 players. **2002:** Playing in his fourth PGA TOUR event of the year, was runner-up to Vijay Singh in the Shell Houston Open...Placed in the top 25 at the Masters and U.S. Open...In June, became the first person to win The Compass Group English Open three times. **2001:** Won in South Africa for the first time, capturing the Dimension Data Pro-Am...Also won in Japan at the Chunichi Crowns before capturing his first European Tour title of the year on home soil in the Smurfit European Open at The K Club, the first Irishman to win in Ireland since John O'Leary 19 years earlier. Finished T3 at British Open...Posted another third-place finish at 2001 NEC Invitational, three behind Tiger Woods-Jim Furyk playoff. **2000:** Became first European to win World Golf Championships event. Defeated David Duval in semifinals and Tiger Woods in final to capture WGC-Accenture Match Play Championship... Followed that early season victory and $1-million payday in June by retaining the Compass Group English Open. Came from six strokes back in final round. **1999:** Won the Compass Group European Open title…Followed that victory by becoming, at Smurfit European Open, first player on European Tour to shoot 60 twice (first 60 came at 1992 European Monte Carlo Open). Equaled three records: most birdies (12), consecutive birdies (eight) and low round on European Tour (ninth time 60 had been shot). **1998:** Won Benson and Hedges International Open en route to second-place finish on Volvo Order of Merit. Runner-up placing came after capturing Volvo Masters with record-equaling 63. **1997:** Tied for runner-up honors to Justin Leonard at the 1997 British Open at Royal Troon. **Amateur:** Winner of the 1989 East of Ireland Amateur. In 1990, captured the Spanish Open Amateur Championship, Irish Amateur Championship, North of Ireland Amateur and the South of Ireland Amateur.

PERSONAL:

Drives Ferrari that bears the registration DC 60 in reference to his two low rounds…New fitness regime in 2003 was so successful that the Northern Ireland native had to shed his wardrobe of around 200 golf shirts and 100 pairs of trousers. Worked with former rugby league professional Steve Hampson, losing 30 pounds in the process.

PLAYER STATISTICS

2004 PGA TOUR STATISTICS

Scoring Average	70.33	(27)
Driving Distance	289.0	(78)
Driving Accuracy Percentage	62.3%	(130)
Total Driving	208	(119)
Greens in Regulation Pct.	64.0%	(120)
Putting Average	1.745	(13)
Sand Save Percentage	46.2%	(137)
Eagles (Holes per)	172.8	(54)
Birdie Average	3.77	(34)
All-Around Ranking	593	(44)
Scoring Avg. Before Cut	71.00	(96)
Round 3 Scoring Avg.	70.56	(66)
Final Round Scoring Average	70.44	(23)
Birdie Conversion Percentage	32.1%	(14)
Par Breakers	21.5%	(32)

MISCELLANEOUS PGA TOUR STATISTICS

2004 Low Round/Round: 65–2 times, most recent WGC-American Express Championship/3
Career Low Round/Round: 63–2003 Las Vegas Invitational/1
Career Largest Paycheck/Finish: $1,050,000–2003 WGC–NEC Invitational/1

PGA TOUR CAREER SUMMARY — PLAYOFF RECORD: 0-0

Year	Events Played	Cuts Made	1st	2nd	3rd	Top 10	Top 25	Earnings	Rank
1994	1								
1995	1	1						$12,955	249
1996	2	1					1	41,850	202
1997	4	3		1		1	2	282,816	87
1998	6	4				1	2	121,628	175
1999	10	7				1	2	139,118	176
2000	10	8	1			3	5	254,114	
2001	7	5			2	2	3	330,870	
2002	11	8		1		2	5	665,911	
2003	16	15	1			5	6	763,931	85
2004	16	10			2	4	9	2,009,819	28
Total	84	62	2	2	4	19	35	4,623,011	
EUROPEAN TOUR									
2004	11	9			1	4	6	722,603	

PGA TOUR TOP TOURNAMENT SUMMARY

Year	91	92	93	94	95	96	97	98	99	00	01	02	03
Masters								T8	CUT	T40	24	T20	T28
U.S. Open				CUT		CUT	T43	T43	T10	T53	T30	T24	T42
British Open	T64	CUT	T39	T38	T31	T11	T2	CUT	T30	T7	T3	T37	T59
PGA							CUT		CUT	T9	CUT	CUT	CUT
THE PLAYERS								CUT	T71	CUT	T26	CUT	T6
TOUR Championship													18
WGC-Accenture Match Play									T33	1		T33	T5
WGC-NEC Invitational									T36	T17	3	T19	1
WGC-American Express Champ									T40	T17	CNL	63	T38

Year	04
Masters	CUT
U.S. Open	CUT
British Open	T11
PGA	T13
THE PLAYERS	T26
TOUR Championship	T15
WGC-Accenture Match Play	3
WGC-NEC Invitational	T14
WGC-American Express Champ	T4

NATIONAL TEAMS: Ryder Cup (4), 1997, 1999, 2002, 2004; World Cup (3), 1994, 1995, 1996; Dunhill Cup (6), 1994, 1995, 1996, 1997, 1998, 1999.

Jose Coceres (coh-SEAR-us)

EXEMPT STATUS: 106th on 2004 money list
FULL NAME: Jose Eusebio Coceres
HEIGHT: 5-11
WEIGHT: 170
BIRTHDATE: August 14, 1963
BIRTHPLACE: Chaco, Argentina
RESIDENCE: Buenos Aires, Argentina
FAMILY: Wife, Monica; Maria Belen (1992), Marcos Jose (1995), Maria Jose
SPECIAL INTERESTS: All sports, soccer
TURNED PROFESSIONAL: 1986
JOINED TOUR: 2001

PGA TOUR VICTORIES (2):

2001 WORLDCOM CLASSIC - The Heritage of Golf, National Car Rental Golf Classic at the WALT DISNEY WORLD Resort.

INTERNATIONAL VICTORIES (8):

1991 Pinemar Open [Arg]. **1992** Montevideo Open [Ura], Los Cardales Challenge [Arg]. **1993** Pinemar Open [Arg]. **1994** Heineken Open Catalonia [Eur]. **1995** Tournament of Champions [Arg]. **1996** Los Leones Open [Chile]. **2000** Dubai Desert Classic [Eur].

BEST 2004 PGA TOUR FINISHES:

3—John Deere Classic; T6—Shell Houston Open.

2004 SEASON:

Finished among the top 125 for the first time since earning two wins in 2001…In fourth start of season, finished T6 at the Shell Houston Open. One off the lead of Vijay Singh and John Huston through 54 holes, but slipped with final-round 73…Solo third at John Deere Classic was best finish since winning the 2002 National Car Rental Golf Classic at the WALT DISNEY WORLD Resort. Round of 9-under-par 62 in the first round was one off the TPC at Deere Run course record. On track through 54 holes to become the first wire-to-wire winner on TOUR since Davis Love III did so at the 2003 INTERNATIONAL, but a double-bogey on the eighth hole in the final round dropped him from the lead.

CAREER HIGHLIGHTS:

2003: Inconsistent season, continuing to battle back from broken arm suffered prior to 2002 campaign...Finished strong, posting top-25s in two of three starts at the end of the year...Lone top-10 came in October when he finished T7 at the Southern Farm Bureau Classic..**2002:** Limited to 16 events due to a broken bone in right arm suffered in pickup soccer game in native Argentina. Did not played first tournament until early April at BellSouth Classic...After missing three of his first four cuts, made three consecutive cuts, finishing T18 at the Buick Classic, his best finish since breaking his arm...Recorded lone top-10 of the season at the PGA Championship in August, a T10, his best career finish in a major championship. **2001:** Became the first Argentine to win on TOUR since Roberto De Vicenzo at the 1968 Houston Champions Invitational. One of nine players to claim multiple victories en route to finishing 34th in earnings in only 19 starts...Became one of nine first-time winners with a par on the fifth playoff hole to defeat Billy Mayfair at the WORLDCOM CLASSIC. Stood two strokes off the lead after 54 holes and closed with 71 to tie Mayfair at 11-under 273. Two playoff holes were contested Sunday before darkness forced a postponement until Monday. Saved par from greenside bunker on fourth playoff hole, No 17, before a dramatic recovery for par from the marsh alongside the closing lighthouse hole at Harbour Town Golf Links. Speaks little English and held a hand-made pillowcase that said, "For my family and my friends and for all the Argentineans, a million thanks."...Became first international player to win the National Car Rental Golf Classic at Disney World Resort. Led by three after 54 holes and closed with a 68 to defeat Davis Love III by one. Win came on Mother's Day in Argentina so he used a pillowcase for a sign that read, "Happy Mother's Day for all the mothers." **2000:** Won the Dubai Classic. **1999:** Passed six figures for fifth time in seven years on European Tour to become member of Millionaires Club. Had five top-10 finishes that season, ending with an eighth-place finish at Sarazen World Open and T10 in Volvo Masters...Closed his year by tying for second in Argentine Open. **1995:** Won Tournament of Champions, his fourth career victory in Argentina. **1994:** Won the Heineken Open Catalonia in Europe. **1992:** Won $50,000 for hole-in-one at Dubai Desert Classic.

PERSONAL:

Voted highest sporting award, "The Olympian," in native Argentina in 2002, only the third golfer to receive the award…One of 11 children and an ex-caddie who taught himself the game. Took control of his family's finances after father died in motor accident. Used to sleep five or six to a bed in family's two-bedroom home. Four brothers also are professionals. Took up game when one brother cut branches off tree and fashioned golf club. Started playing by hitting rocks…Makes it a point to walk to a religious shrine near his hometown after every victory.

PLAYER STATISTICS

2004 PGA TOUR STATISTICS

Scoring Average	70.98	(77)
Driving Distance	279.4	(166)
Driving Accuracy Percentage	74.3%	(6)
Total Driving	172	(65)
Greens in Regulation Pct.	63.3%	(139)
Putting Average	1.754	(32)
Sand Save Percentage	61.7%	(2)
Eagles (Holes per)	576.0	(185)
Birdie Average	3.61	(76)
All-Around Ranking	683	(71)
Scoring Avg. Before Cut	70.15	(18)
Round 3 Scoring Avg.	70.54	(64)
Final Round Scoring Average	73.08	(178)
Birdie Conversion Percentage	30.9%	(39)
Par Breakers	20.2%	(90)

MISCELLANEOUS PGA TOUR STATISTICS

2004 Low Round/Round: 62–John Deere Classic/1
Career Low Round/Round: 62–2004 John Deere Classic/1
Career Largest Paycheck/Finish: $630,000–2001 WORLDCOM CLASSIC – The Heritage of Golf/1

PGA TOUR CAREER SUMMARY — PLAYOFF RECORD: 1-0

Year	Events Played	Cuts Made	1st	2nd	3rd	Top 10	Top 25	Earnings	Rank
1995	1	1						$6,380	288
1996	1								
1997	1	1						11,812	261
2000	3	2					1	21,256	
2001	19	12	2			2	5	1,502,888	34
2002	16	9				1	2	286,552	157
2003	21	11				1	3	337,682	153
2004	20	14			1	2	6	779,196	106
Total	82	50	2		1	6	17	2,945,767	

PGA TOUR TOP TOURNAMENT SUMMARY

Year	92	93	94	95	96	97	98	99	00	01	02	03
Masters										CUT	CUT	
U.S. Open										T52	CUT	
British Open	T45			T96	CUT	T44			T36	CUT	CUT	T34
PGA									CUT	T16	T10	T51
THE PLAYERS												W/D
WGC-Accenture Match Play										T33		
WGC-NEC Invitational											T75	
WGC-American Express Champ									T14	CNL	T36	

John Cook

EXEMPT STATUS: Top 50 on PGA TOUR Career Money List
FULL NAME: John Neuman Cook
HEIGHT: 6-0
WEIGHT: 175
BIRTHDATE: October 2, 1957
BIRTHPLACE: Toledo, OH
RESIDENCE: Windermere, FL

FAMILY: Wife, Jan; Kristin (7/20/81), Courtney (4/11/84), Jason (1/10/86)
EDUCATION: Ohio State University
SPECIAL INTERESTS: Auto racing, skiing, all sports
TURNED PROFESSIONAL: 1979
Q SCHOOL: Fall 1979

PGA TOUR VICTORIES (11):

1981 Bing Crosby National Pro-Am. **1983** Canadian Open. **1987** The International. **1992** Bob Hope Chrysler Classic, United Airlines Hawaiian Open, Las Vegas Invitational. **1996** FedEx St. Jude Classic, CVS Charity Classic. **1997** Bob Hope Chrysler Classic. **1998** GTE Byron Nelson Golf Classic. **2001** Reno-Tahoe Open.

INTERNATIONAL VICTORIES (2):

1982 Sao Paulo Open [Brazil]. **1995** Mexican Open

OTHER VICTORIES (3):

1983 World Cup [with Rex Caldwell. **1994** Fred Meyer Challenge [with Mark O'Meara]. **2000** Fred Meyer Challenge [with Mark O'Meara].

BEST 2004 PGA TOUR FINISHES:

T19—the Memorial Tournament; T24—The INTERNATIONAL.

2004 SEASON:

Played in the 19 events he was eligible via his Major Medical Extension but did not earn enough money to keep his card for the remainder of the season…Finished outside the top 125 (No. 189) on the PGA TOUR money list for just the third time in his 25-year career…Posted two top-25s, a T19 at the Memorial Tournament and a T24 at The INTERNATIONAL…Served as a broadcaster for the USA Network's early round coverage of the TOUR and on the "PGA TOUR Sunday" show.

CAREER HIGHLIGHTS:

2003: Limited to 10 events due a torn labrum and several cysts in his right shoulder. After missing the cut at the Masters, underwent surgery in Orlando that put him out of action until a rehab assignment at the Albertsons Boise Open on the Nationwide Tour in September. Played two more events in October, missing the cut in each. Received a Major Medical Extension for 2004. Coupled with $78,931 earned in 10 events in 2003, had the opportunity to play in 19 events to earn $408,564 and match the $487,495 winnings of 2003's No. 125, Esteban Toledo. **2002:** Posted six top-10s for the first time since 1998...Finished one stroke behind Jerry Kelly at the Sony Open in Hawaii for his first runner-up finish since the 1999 Shell Houston Open. Set course record with 8-under 62 on way to second-round lead. Score of 12-under 128 through two rounds was one behind the season's best turned in by Chris DiMarco (17-under 127) at the Disney Golf Classic...Finished T9 in WGC-Accenture Match Play Championship after losing to Brad Faxon (3 and 2) in the third round....T4 at the Compaq Classic of New Orleans was worth $177,188, pushing career earnings past $10 million to $10,168,829...Added second runner-up finish of the season with a T2 at the Memorial Tournament. First time since 1992, that he has posted two seconds in a season. **2001:** Collected first victory since 1998 at Reno-Tahoe Open and had highest finish on TOUR money list (No. 54) since that same year. Victory was 11th of his career. Was six strokes behind Jerry Kelly after third-round 74 but closed with 64 to overtake Kelly by a stroke for his first victory since the 1998 GTE Byron Nelson Classic. The $540,000 check was the largest payday of 22-year career. **2000:** Finished among the top-100 on the money list for the 19th time in his 21-year career on the PGA TOUR. **1999:** Streak of three straight seasons with a victory ended. **1998:** Earned his 10th TOUR victory at GTE Byron Nelson Classic after entering the final round four strokes behind Fred Couples. They were tied at 17th hole but Couples found water and made triple bogey. Cook won by three. **1997:** At Bob Hope Chrysler Classic, trailed leader Mark Calcavecchia by five after third round, but matched then-PGA TOUR record for consecutive rounds when he closed with 62-63 for one-stroke victory. Total of 125 also matched Ron Streck for best 36-hole finish. **1996:** At FedEx St. Jude Classic, tied then all-time PGA TOUR record with opening rounds of 16-under-par 126 (64-62) and added third-round 63 to tie TOUR record for first 54 holes of 24-under-par 189. Closed with a 69 to fall one stroke shy of all-time 72-hole record, but won tournament by seven over John Adams...Added second victory of year at CVS Charity Classic by three strokes over Russ Cochran. **1995:** Won Ernst Championship. **1994:** Finished in the top five at two of the majors, U.S. Open (5) and PGA Championship (T4). **1992:** Surpassed $1 million in season earnings, winning three times. Captured five-man playoff at Bob Hope Chrysler Classic, outlasting Gene Sauers with three birdies and an eagle over four holes. Posted two-stroke victories at United Airlines Hawaiian Open and Las Vegas Invitational...Finished as runner-up at the British

PGA TOUR CAREER SUMMARY — PLAYOFF RECORD: 3-3

Year	Events Played	Cuts Made	1st	2nd	3rd	Top 10	Top 25	Earnings	Rank
1978A	1	1					1		
1979A	3	3							
1980	30	19				2	6	$43,316	80
1981	30	23	1			3	12	127,608	25
1982	28	21				3	6	57,483	79
1983	28	27	1		2	7	12	216,868	16
1984	28	20				1	5	65,710	90
1985	29	17				1	5	63,573	106
1986	30	20		2	1	6	13	255,126	27
1987	32	19	1			6	10	333,184	29
1988	29	21				2	9	139,916	84
1989	12	6				1	2	39,445	172
1990	27	20		2		4	10	448,112	28
1991	25	21		1	2	8	12	546,984	26
1992	21	18	3	2	1	8	13	1,165,606	3
1993	23	19				5	13	342,321	45
1994	24	16			1	6	11	429,725	37
1995	27	17				1	5	186,977	97
1996	26	19	2			5	10	831,260	19
1997	28	21	1		1	6	11	815,903	28
1998	26	19	1			6	12	1,145,511	22
1999	26	16		1		2	5	567,168	71
2000	28	15				3	6	537,105	89
2001	25	21	1			2	3	1,022,778	54
2002	25	16		2		6	7	1,624,095	35
2003	10	6						78,931	216
2004	19	9					2	210,448	189
Total	640	450	11	10	8	94	201	11,295,153	
NATIONWIDE TOUR									
2003	1	1						1,935	298
Total	1	1						1,935	

PGA TOUR TOP TOURNAMENT SUMMARY

Year	74	75	76	77	78	79	80	81	82	83	84	85	86
Masters						39		T21	CUT		CUT		
U.S. Open						T53	T51	T4	CUT		CUT	CUT	T35
British Open	T39						CUT						
PGA								T19	T34	T20	CUT		T53
THE PLAYERS								CUT	T41	T3	T44	CUT	T7

Year	87	88	89	90	91	92	93	94	95	96	97	98	99
Masters	T24	CUT			CUT	T54	T39	T46	CUT		CUT	43	CUT
U.S. Open	T36	T50			T19	T13	T25	5	T62	T16	T36	CUT	T60
British Open						2	CUT	T55	T40		CUT		
PGA	T28	T48			CUT	T2	T6	T4	CUT	T47	T23	9	CUT
THE PLAYERS	CUT	CUT	CUT		T3	CUT	CUT	T23	W/D	CUT	T22	T13	T58
TOUR Championship				T22	28	T13				11	T20	T21	
WGC-Accenture Match Play													T33

Year	00	01	02	03
Masters				CUT
U.S. Open	CUT		CUT	
British Open			CUT	
PGA			CUT	
THE PLAYERS	CUT	T55	CUT	W/D
WGC-Accenture Match Play			T9	T33
WGC-NEC Invitational			T28	
WGC-American Express Champ			T49	

NATIONAL TEAMS: World Amateur Team Championship, 1978; World Cup, 1983; Ryder Cup, 1993.

John Cook (Continued)

Open and tied for second at PGA Championship. **1990:** Had two playoff losses, to Tom Kite on the first extra hole at Federal Express St. Jude Classic and to Bob Tway on first extra hole at Las Vegas Invitational. **1989:** Underwent hand surgery. **1987:** Won The International. **1986:** Final-round 66s left Cook and Donnie Hammond, who were one back heading into the final round, tied after 90 holes at the Bob Hope Chrysler Classic. Hammond won playoff with birdie on first extra hole. **1983:** At Canadian Open, defeated Johnny Miller on sixth extra hole for victory...Teamed with Rex Caldwell to win World Cup. **1981:** First TOUR victory came in five-man playoff at 1981 Bing Crosby National Pro-Am. Parred third extra hole to defeat Bobby Clampett, Ben Crenshaw, Hale Irwin and Barney Thompson. **Amateur:** 1978 U.S. Amateur Champion, beating PGA TOUR member Scott Hoch in the championship match...Three-time All-American at Ohio State (1977-79) and member of 1979 NCAA Championship team.

PERSONAL:

Born in Ohio, but grew up in Southern California... Persuaded by Jack Nicklaus and Tom Weiskopf to attend Ohio State...John's father, Jim, was a longtime tournament director on the PGA TOUR...Joined the USA Network's "PGA TOUR Sunday" as an analyst in 2003. Son Jason plays golf at Pepperdine.

PLAYER STATISTICS

2004 PGA TOUR STATISTICS

Scoring Average	71.68	(153)
Driving Distance	270.2	(194)
Driving Accuracy Percentage	73.4%	(9)
Total Driving	203	(109)
Greens in Regulation Pct.	66.5%	(57)
Putting Average	1.789	(127)
Sand Save Percentage	50.0%	(80)
Eagles (Holes per)	954.0	(193)
Birdie Average	3.21	(168)
All-Around Ranking	981	(152)
Scoring Avg. Before Cut	71.59	(150)
Round 3 Scoring Avg.	69.67	(16)
Final Round Scoring Average	71.63	(97)
Birdie Conversion Percentage	25.4%	(188)
Par Breakers	17.9%	(179)

MISCELLANEOUS PGA TOUR STATISTICS

2004 Low Round/Round: 66–U.S. Bank Championship in Milwaukee/2

Career Low Round/Round: 62–5 times, most recent 2002 Sony Open in Hawaii/2

Career Largest Paycheck/Finish: $540,000–2001 Reno–Tahoe Open/1

SHOTLink
AN IBM ON DEMAND BUSINESS SOLUTION

HOT SHOTS

Hardest Hole

Doral Golf Resort & Spa

Hole No. 18

Par 4, 467 Yards

The 18th hole at Doral was ranked most difficult out of 1,007 holes in 2004.The finishing hole also was the scene of one of the most dramatic finishes of the season when Australian Craig Parry holed his second shot for an eagle-2 in a playoff to defeat Scott Verplank and win the Ford Championship at Doral. The hole was lengthened by nearly 30 yards to 467 yards before last year's tournament.

Round	Greens in Reg.	Fairways Hit	Scoring Avg.
1	23.60%	43.10%	4.743
2	33.80%	55.60%	4.500
3	32.90%	58.20%	4.291
4	58.20%	63.30%	4.291
Total	**34.70%**	**53.40%**	**4.48**

- *In 2003, 74 percent of all second shots were from inside 175 yards.*
- *In 2004, only 30 percent of all second shots were from inside 175 yards.*

OFF THE TEE

Driving Average	271.3 yards (8th on the week)
Longest Drive	336 (9th)
Driving Accuracy	237/ 444 53% (9th)

- *The 47 percent of the field that missed the fairway averaged 1.026 over par.*
- *The 53 of 444 (12 percent) players who hit shots in the water averaged 1.566 over par.*

APPROACH TO THE GREEN

Greens in Regulation	154/ 444 35% (17th)
Avg. Distance to Pin	64 ft 10 in

- *The 18th green was the ninth-most difficult green to hit on TOUR.*

DIFFICULT AROUND THE GREEN

Sand Saves	27/ 64 (15th)
Scrambling	114/ 290 (18th)

- *Of the 65 percent of the field that missed the green only 39.3 percent were able to salvage par.*

SCORING

Average Score	4.48
Eagles	—*
Birdies	31
Pars	231
Bogeys	125
Double Bogeys	53
Other	4
Rank	1

Parry's eagle occurred in a playoff.

The field was a combined 213-over par on the 18th hole at Doral.

18th Hole-Doral Golf Resort & Spa

Fred Couples

EXEMPT STATUS: Winner, 1996 PLAYERS Championship (through 2006)
FULL NAME: Frederick Steven Couples
HEIGHT: 5-11
WEIGHT: 185
BIRTHDATE: October 3, 1959
BIRTHPLACE: Seattle, WA
RESIDENCE: Santa Barbara, CA

FAMILY: Wife, Thais; GiGi and Oliver
EDUCATION: University of Houston
SPECIAL INTERESTS: All sports, tennis, antiques, bicycling, vintage cars
TURNED PROFESSIONAL: 1980
Q SCHOOL: Fall 1980

PGA TOUR VICTORIES (15):

1983 Kemper Open. **1984** Tournament Players Championship. **1987** Byron Nelson Golf Classic. **1990** Nissan Los Angeles Open. **1991** Federal Express St. Jude Classic, B.C. Open. **1992** Nissan Los Angeles Open, Nestle Invitational, Masters Tournament. **1993** Honda Classic. **1994** Buick Open. **1996** THE PLAYERS Championship. **1998** Bob Hope Chrysler Classic, Memorial Tournament. **2003** Shell Houston Open.

INTERNATIONAL VICTORIES (5):

1991 Johnnie Walker World Championship. **1994** World Cup [Indiv]. **1995** Dubai Desert Classic [Eur], Johnnie Walker Classic [Eur], Johnnie Walker World Championship [Eur].

OTHER VICTORIES (17):

1990 Franklin Templeton Shark Shootout [with Raymond Floyd], Sazale Classic, RMCC Invitational. **1992** World Cup [with Davis Love III]. **1993** World Cup [with Davis Love III]. **1994** Franklin Templeton Shark Shootout [with Brad Faxon], World Cup [with Davis Love III]. **1995** Skins Game, World Cup [with Davis Love III]. **1996** Skins Game. **1999** Franklin Templeton Shark Shootout [with David Duval], Skins Game. **2001** Hyundai Team Matches [with Mark Calcavecchia]. **2003** Skins Game, Tylenol Par-3 Shootout at Treetops Resort. **2004** Tylenol Par-3 Shootout at Treetops Resort, Merrill Lynch Skins Game.

BEST 2004 PGA TOUR FINISHES:

2—the Memorial Tournament; T4—Buick Classic; T6—Masters Tournament.

2004 SEASON:

Continued to play limited schedule due to back problems, but posted three top-10s in 16 starts…Finished T6 at Masters for ninth career top-10 in 20 starts for 1992 champion. Holds longest active cut streak at Augusta, having never missed in 20 starts dating back to 1983…Past champion was unable to catch Ernie Els on the weekend at the Memorial Tournament. Finished solo second thanks to four rounds in the 60s, only the seventh time and Couples' second time that a player has put together four rounds in the 60s at Muirfield Village…The following week recorded a T4 finish at the Buick Classic. Posted a bogey-free 6-under 65 in the second round for a one-stroke lead through 36 holes, but third-round 74 derailed title hopes. Posted back-to-back top-10 finishes for the first time since 2000.

CAREER HIGHLIGHTS:

2003: Candidate for Comeback Player of the Year won for the first time since 1998 at the Shell Houston Open, where he played collegiately. Missed just one cut in 18 starts...Began season at No. 147 in the Official World Golf Ranking and was No. 36 by season's end...Discouraged with his game, hooked up with Butch Harmon during the AT&T Pebble Beach National Pro-Am. The two worked for six hours one day, with Couples shortening his swing to take some pressure off his tender back. From there, the former Masters champion rediscovered his game with the win in Houston. "I have been practicing," he said after his win in Houston. "I never really thought I'd win this quickly, but I thought I could win again if I practiced and played." Held first- and third-round leads before defeating runners-up Mark Calcavecchia, Stuart Appleby and Hank Kuehne by four strokes. Win was the first victory in 87 events, dating back to the 1998 Memorial Tournament. Became the first player from the University of Houston and the sixth player over age 40 to win the Shell Houston Open...Shared first-round lead at THE PLAYERS Championship and was two back of lead through 54 holes. A 74 on the final day dropped him to solo 10th, his sixth top-10 in event...No. 32 on the money list entering the Chrysler Championship with hopes of jumping into the top 30, was forced to WD with back injury during pro-am. **2002:** Climbed back into the top 125 after nearly doubling his earnings from the prior season...T9 at Nissan Open, first top-10 finish since a sixth at 2000 British Open...In first career appearance at Valero Texas Open, fired rounds of 65-64 on the weekend to finish T2, best since win at 1998 Memorial Tournament. **2001:** Finished outside top 125 for first time in his career. Previous low finish was 76th in 1986...Continued as only Masters champion who has never missed a cut with an T36 finish. **2000:** Earned eighth career top-10 finish in British Open with solo sixth...Ranked first in Sand Saves (67 percent) and fifth in Greens In Regulation (71.1 percent). **1998:** For third time in career collected two victories. Final-round 66 earned playoff spot with Bruce Lietzke at Bob Hope Chrysler Classic, which he won with birdie on first extra hole at Bermuda Dunes. Earned 14th TOUR title with four-stroke win over Andrew Magee at Memorial Tournament...Fell one stroke shy of winning his second Masters after leading each of first three rounds. **1996:** Became first player to win two PLAYERS Championships at TPC at Sawgrass. Trailed Tommy Tolles by four strokes through 54 holes, but closing

PGA TOUR CAREER SUMMARY — PLAYOFF RECORD: 5-4

Year	Events Played	Cuts Made	1st	2nd	3rd	Top 10	Top 25	Earnings	Rank
1979A	1	1							
1981	25	19		1	1	4	9	$78,939	54
1982	28	18			1	2	9	77,606	54
1983	30	23	1		1	7	15	209,733	19
1984	26	24	1		2	9	19	334,573	7
1985	26	23				7	10	171,272	38
1986	26	16		1		1	6	116,065	76
1987	27	21	1			9	15	441,025	19
1988	27	25		1	1	10	19	489,822	21
1989	24	21		1	2	9	17	653,944	11
1990	22	17	1	1	3	9	12	757,999	9
1991	21	20	2		4	9	12	791,749	3
1992	22	20	3	2	3	12	19	1,344,188	1
1993	19	17	1	2		9	15	796,579	10
1994	15	15	1	2		4	7	625,654	23
1995	15	12				4	7	299,259	63
1996	18	16	1	1		9	12	1,248,694	6
1997	15	13				7	7	448,385	55
1998	17	16	2	2	1	5	10	1,650,389	9
1999	16	13				6	7	769,192	56
2000	19	17				5	11	990,215	47
2001	19	14					4	385,984	131
2002	18	13		1		2	7	646,703	103
2003	18	17	1			4	9	1,820,495	34
2004	16	12		1		3	8	1,396,109	50
Total	510	423	15	16	19	146	266	16,544,574	
EUROPEAN TOUR									
2004	1	1				1	1	132,075	

PGA TOUR TOP TOURNAMENT SUMMARY

Year	79	80	81	82	83	84	85	86	87	88	89	90	91
Masters					T32	10	T10	T31		T5	T11	5	T35
U.S. Open	T48			CUT	CUT	T9	T39		T46	T10	T21	CUT	T3
British Open						T4		T46	T40	T4	T6	T25	T3
PGA				T3	T23	T20	T6	T36	CUT	CUT	CUT	2	T27
THE PLAYERS				CUT	CUT	1	T49	CUT	CUT	T23	T4	CUT	T23
TOUR Championship									T12	7	T7	T22	T16

Year	92	93	94	95	96	97	98	99	00	01	02	03	04
Masters	1	T21		T10	T15	T7	T2	T27	T11	26	T36	T28	T6
U.S. Open	T17	T16	T16	CUT		T52	T53	CUT	T16	CUT		T66	CUT
British Open	CUT	T9			T7	T7	T66		6	CUT		T46	
PGA	T21	T31	T39	T31	T41	T29	T13	T26	CUT	T37		T34	
THE PLAYERS	T13	T39		T29	1	T10	T42	T4	T33	T58	CUT	10	CUT
TOUR Championship	T5	T10	T29		5		T24						
WGC-Accenture Match Play								T9	T33				T17
WGC-NEC Invitational								T15				T21	T32
WGC-American Express Champ												T10	T36

NATIONAL TEAMS: USA vs. Japan, 1984; Ryder Cup (5), 1989, 1991, 1993, 1995, 1997; Asahi Glass Four Tours World Championship of Golf (2), 1990, 1991; Dunhill Cup (4), 1991, 1992, 1993, 1994; World Cup (4), 1992, 1993, 1994, 1995; The Presidents Cup (3), 1994, 1996, 1998.

Fred Couples (Continued)

64, featuring eagle at 16 and birdie at 17, sealed victory. **1995:** Recorded back-to-back victories on PGA European Tour, first American to do so since Charles Coody in 1973...Teamed with Davis Love III to win four consecutive World Cup of Golf titles (1992-95). **1994:** Opened the season with a playoff loss to Phil Mickelson at the Mercedes Championship when Mickelson parred the second extra hole...Missed three months due to tear in outer layer of disc in lower back...Edged Corey Pavin with a two-stroke win over him at the Buick Open in August...Won unofficial Lincoln-Mercury Kapalua Invitational for second consecutive year. **1993:** Earned 10th career victory at the wind-shortened (54 holes) Honda Classic. Closed with a 70 to tie Robert Gamez. Holed a bunker shot on 17th hole to force the playoff. Won with par on second extra hole. **1992:** Career year, winning three tournaments, including the Masters, and earned more than $1.3 million to finish No. 1 on the money list for the only time in his career...Earned his second consecutive Player of the Year Award as voted by the players...Entered final round of Masters trailing Craig Parry by one stroke. Closing 70 good for two-stroke victory. Masters completed remarkable streak during which he won three tournaments and finished second twice in six starts...Defeated Davis Love III with a birdie on the second playoff hole to win his second Nissan Los Angeles Open title...Three weeks later, decimated the field at the Nestle Invitational, winning by nine strokes...Third-round 63 set the course record at the TPC at Sawgrass during THE PLAYERS CHAMPIONSHIP...Winner of Vardon Trophy for second consecutive year...Winner of Arnold Palmer Award and PGA of America Player of the Year. **1991:** Took lead at Federal Express St. Jude Classic with third-round 66 and went on to three-stroke victory over Rick Fehr. Won B.C. Open by three strokes as well. **1990:** After equaling the then-course record with a 9-under 62 during the third round, defeated Gil Morgan by three strokes at the Nissan Los Angeles Open...Finished second at the PGA Championship and fifth at the Masters Tournament. **1988:** Lost playoff to Sandy Lyle at the Phoenix Open when Lyle bogeyed the third extra hole. **1987:** Defeated Mark Calcavecchia with a par on the third extra hole at Byron Nelson Golf Classic. **1984:** Edged Lee Trevino by a stroke to earn his first Tournament Players Championship. Featured second-round 64. **1983:** First TOUR victory came in five-man playoff at Kemper Open. Birdied second playoff hole to defeat T.C. Chen, Barry Jaeckel, Gil Morgan and Scott Simpson.

PERSONAL:

Roomed with Blaine McCallister and CBS broadcaster Jim Nantz at University of Houston...His charity is Millie Medlin Violet Sobich Couples Fund, in memory of mother...Serves as host of the Fred Couples Invitational, a charity event in hometown of Seattle...Introduced to game by his father, who worked in Seattle Parks and Recreation Department.

PLAYER STATISTICS

2004 PGA TOUR STATISTICS

Scoring Average	70.92	(71)
Driving Distance	294.5	(35)
Driving Accuracy Percentage	58.8%	(166)
Total Driving	201	(105)
Greens in Regulation Pct.	66.3%	(62)
Putting Average	1.781	(112)
Sand Save Percentage	47.1%	(124)
Eagles (Holes per)	133.7	(18)
Birdie Average	3.75	(41)
All-Around Ranking	629	(55)
Scoring Avg. Before Cut	71.13	(115)
Round 3 Scoring Avg.	72.00	(164)
Final Round Scoring Average	72.00	(131)
Birdie Conversion Percentage	30.3%	(58)
Par Breakers	21.6%	(28)

MISCELLANEOUS PGA TOUR STATISTICS

2004 Low Round/Round: 65–Buick Classic/2

Career Low Round/Round: 62–1990 Nissan Los Angeles Open/3

Career Largest Paycheck/Finish: $810,000–2003 Shell Houston Open/1

SHOTLink
AN IBM ON DEMAND BUSINESS SOLUTION

HOT SHOTS

Easiest Hole

Tournament Players Club at Summerlin

Hole No. 3

Par 5, 492 Yards (Multi-course event)

3rd Hole-TPC at Summerlin

Hole No. 3 at TPC Summerlin was the easiest hole on TOUR, among the 1,007 holes played last year.

Under par from anywhere

No. 3 TPC Summerlin

OFF THE TEE

Driving Average	286.8 (14th on the week)
Longest Drive	343 (12th)
Driving Accuracy	151/ 214 71% (T26th)
Left Rough	30 (-.467)
Right Rough	20 (-.550)
Fairway Bunker	10 (-.100)

APPROACH TO THE GREEN

Greens in Regulation	198/ 211 93% (2nd)
Left Rough	15/ 20 (T4th)
Right Rough	10/ 18 (11th)
Avg. Distance to Pin	33'09"

- *Out of 214 attempts only 16 shots missed the green*

GOING FOR GREEN

Attempts	199/ 214 93% (1st)
Success	109/ 199 55% (2nd)

- *Risk/Reward: 93 percent of the field attempted to go for it in two and 55 percent were successful.*

SCORING

Average Score	4.257
Eagles	19
Birdies	129
Pars	59
Bogeys	6
Double Bogeys	1
Other	—
Actual Yardage	492
Rank	18

The field was a combined 159-under par on hole No. 3 at the TPC Summerlin.

Ben Crane

EXEMPT STATUS: 2003 tournament winner (through 2005)
FULL NAME: Benjamin McCully Crane
HEIGHT: 5-10
WEIGHT: 165
BIRTHDATE: March 6, 1976
BIRTHPLACE: Portland, OR
RESIDENCE: Westlake, TX

FAMILY: Wife, Heather
EDUCATION: University of Oregon (1999, Sociology)
SPECIAL INTERESTS: Fishing, Bible study, fitness, ping-pong
TURNED PROFESSIONAL: 1999
JOINED TOUR: 2002
Nationwide Tour Alumnus

PGA TOUR VICTORIES (1):

2003 BellSouth Classic.

NATIONWIDE TOUR VICTORIES (2):

2000 Wichita Open. **2001** Gila River Classic at Wild Horse Pass Development.

BEST 2004 PGA TOUR FINISHES:

T5—Bob Hope Chrysler Classic; T6—BellSouth Classic; T8—Chrysler Classic of Greensboro; T9—Mercedes Championships, PGA Championship.

2004 SEASON:

Posted a career-best five top-10s and finished in the top 75 on the money list for the third straight season. Made 19 cuts in 27 starts…In making Mercedes Championships debut, finished T9 at the PGA TOUR's season-opening event. One of three first-timers to finish in the top-10 (along with Darren Clarke and Adam Scott) at Kapalua…Carded five rounds in the 60s to finish T5 at the Bob Hope Chrysler Classic, four shots out of playoff between Phil Mickelson and Skip Kendall…In defense of BellSouth Classic title, finished T6, six strokes behind winner Zach Johnson…Recorded first career top-10 in a major championship with his T9 at the PGA Championship. Top-10 came in his fourth appearance in a major and only major appearance of the season…Fifth top-10 of the season was a T8 at the Chrysler Classic of Greensboro. His $110,975 payday pushed him over $1 million for the second consecutive season.

CAREER HIGHLIGHTS:

2003: The first of seven first-time winners on the PGA TOUR, capturing the BellSouth Classic...In 40th career start, carded rounds of 64-63 on the weekend to come from six strokes back of 54-hole leader Lee Janzen to capture the BellSouth Classic. Final-round, 9-under-par 63 punctuated by an eagle-3 on the 72nd hole after a 357-yard drive, matching TPC at Sugarloaf course record held by Tiger Woods (1998) and later matched by Duffy Waldorf (1999). Opened 73-73 to make the cut by only one stroke. Earned a career-high paycheck of $720,000. **2002:** One of several rookies that found success on the PGA TOUR after posting wins during Nationwide Tour career...After struggling early, finished second to Shigeki Maruyama at the Verizon Byron Nelson Classic. Closed on Sunday with a 65, matching Tiger Woods' low round of the day. Recorded an eagle and birdie on final three holes that closed gap to two strokes. Earned $518,400 six days before his wedding, enough to secure card for 2003. **2001:** Earned his first TOUR card by virtue of T5 at the PGA TOUR Qualifying Tournament...Won a three-man playoff which included Bo Van Pelt and Jason Caron at the Gila River Classic (Nationwide Tour) on the fourth extra hole. Shared first- and second-round leads with Van Pelt and held one-stroke advantage at the 54-hole mark. The victory and a T5 at the Nationwide Tour Championship moved him to 23rd on the final money list. **2000:** Gained membership on Nationwide Tour with victory at the 2000 Wichita Open. Was the 12th Monday qualifier to win a Nationwide Tour title. **Amateur:** Won the 1998 Pacific Coast Amateur...Three-time All-Pac-10 selection at the University of Oregon...Originally attended Baylor University, but did not play golf.

PERSONAL:

Was age 5 when his grandfather taught him how to play golf…Doesn't like to know who he will be paired with, saying, "I looked up to a lot of these guys who I'm now playing with. So, I didn't want to have to go to sleep thinking about it. And so that's kind of been my routine. I never want to know who I'm playing with. Just tell me the time. In 2002, at the Byron Nelson I played with Ernie Els in the final round, it worked good, because I watched Ernie play a lot of golf on TV. So we just kind of kept that routine going. I just never look and find out on the first tee."

PLAYER STATISTICS

2004 PGA TOUR STATISTICS

Statistic	Value	Rank
Scoring Average	71.01	(82)
Driving Distance	283.8	(125)
Driving Accuracy Percentage	64.4%	(93)
Total Driving	218	(135)
Greens in Regulation Pct.	64.2%	(115)
Putting Average	1.740	(9)
Sand Save Percentage	53.8%	(35)
Eagles (Holes per)	276.0	(118)
Birdie Average	3.73	(50)
All-Around Ranking	627	(53)
Scoring Avg. Before Cut	70.66	(54)
Round 3 Scoring Avg.	70.32	(48)
Final Round Scoring Average	71.21	(72)
Birdie Conversion Percentage	31.1%	(34)
Par Breakers	21.1%	(53)

MISCELLANEOUS PGA TOUR STATISTICS

2004 Low Round/Round: 64–Bob Hope Chrysler Classic/2
Career Low Round/Round: 63–2003 BellSouth Classic/4
Career Largest Paycheck/Finish: $720,000–2003 BellSouth Classic/1

PGA TOUR CAREER SUMMARY — PLAYOFF RECORD: 0-0

Year	Events Played	Cuts Made	1st	2nd	3rd	Top 10	Top 25	Earnings	Rank
2002	30	16		1		2	7	$921,076	70
2003	27	19	1			3	8	1,419,070	48
2004	27	19				5	7	1,036,958	75
Total	84	54	1	1		10	22	3,377,104	

NATIONWIDE TOUR

Year	Events Played	Cuts Made	1st	2nd	3rd	Top 10	Top 25	Earnings	Rank
1998A	1								
1999A	1								
1999	1								
2000	18	11	1			1	4	103,651	48
2001	26	14	1			4	6	147,474	23
Total	47	25	2			5	10	251,125	

PGA TOUR TOP TOURNAMENT SUMMARY

Year	02	03	04
U.S. Open	CUT		
British Open		CUT	
PGA		T48	T9
THE PLAYERS		CUT	T66
WGC-NEC Invitational		T42	

Ben Crenshaw

WORLD GOLF HALL OF FAME MEMBER (Inducted 2002)
EXEMPT STATUS: Winner, 1995 Masters Tournament (through 2005)
FULL NAME: Ben Daniel Crenshaw
HEIGHT: 5-9
WEIGHT: 157
BIRTHDATE: January 11, 1952
BIRTHPLACE: Austin, TX
RESIDENCE: Austin, TX; plays out of Austin GC
FAMILY: Wife, Julie; Katherine Vail (10/6/87), Claire Susan (4/23/92), Anna Riley (2/12/98)
EDUCATION: University of Texas
SPECIAL INTERESTS: Fishing, bird watching, collecting golf artifacts, golf course architecture, country music
TURNED PROFESSIONAL: 1973
Q SCHOOL: 1973

PGA TOUR VICTORIES (19):
1973 San Antonio Texas Open. **1976** Bing Crosby National Pro-Am, Hawaiian Open, Ohio Kings Island Open. **1977** Colonial National Invitation. **1979** Phoenix Open, Walt Disney World National Team Championship. **1980** Anheuser-Busch Golf Classic. **1983** Byron Nelson Golf Classic. **1984** Masters Tournament. **1986** Buick Open, Vantage Championship. **1987** USF&G Classic. **1988** Doral-Ryder Open. **1990** Southwestern Bell Colonial. **1992** Centel Western Open. **1993** Nestle Invitational. **1994** Freeport-McMoRan Classic. **1995** Masters Tournament.

INTERNATIONAL VICTORIES (4):
1976 Irish Open [Eur]. **1981** Mexican Open. **1988** World Cup [indiv], World Cup [with Mark McCumber].

OTHER VICTORIES (2):
1985 Shootout at Jeremy Ranch [with Miller Barber]. **1995** PGA Grand Slam of Golf.

BEST 2004 CHAMPIONS TOUR FINISHES:
T20—Bruno's Memorial Classic; T23—Toshiba Senior Classic

2004 SEASON:
Played in his 33rd consecutive Masters but missed the cut with rounds of 74-75…On the Champions Tour, played in 18 events and finished among the top 25 twice during a three-tournament span early in the season (T20 at the Bruno's Memorial Classic in May and T23 in late March at the Toshiba Senior Classic).

CAREER HIGHLIGHTS:
2003: Played in the Masters, missing the cut with rounds of 79-76...On the Champions Tour, played in 18 events with two top-10s. Turned in his best Champions Tour performance with a T4 at the 3M Championship in August. **2002:** On Nov. 15, inducted into the World Golf Hall of Fame via the PGA TOUR Ballot...Played in only two PGA TOUR events at the age of 50, concentrating on Champions Tour career, where he made 20 starts. **2001:** Honored with Payne Stewart Award at THE TOUR Championship. **1999:** Spent most of the season preparing for Ryder Cup. Captain of U.S. team which staged greatest comeback in event's history, winning 8 points in singles matches on final day to come from four points back for victory. Crenshaw's team was the first U.S. squad to win Ryder Cup since 1993...Appeared in 13 TOUR events but did not make a cut. **1997:** Underwent foot surgery. **1995:** Prior to being named Ryder Cup Captain, most memorable moment in golf came in winning second Masters. Earlier in week had served as pallbearer at funeral of long-time mentor, friend and teacher Harvey Penick. Closed with a 68 to defeat Davis Love III by one stroke...Produced a victory each year from 1992 through 1995. From July 1992 until April 1994, his only three top-10 finishes were victories. **1991:** Won Bob Jones Award from USGA. **1990:** Earned second Colonial title. Victory was his fifth in home state of Texas among 19 TOUR victories.

PGA TOUR CAREER SUMMARY — PLAYOFF RECORD: 0-8

Year	Events Played	Cuts Made	1st	2nd	3rd	Top 10	Top 25	Earnings	Rank
1970A	1	1							
1971A	3	3				1	2		
1972A	4	4			1	1	4		
1973A	3	3				1	3		
1973	6	5	1	1		3	4	$76,374	32
1974	27	22		2		6	11	66,825	32
1975	28	20			3	6	8	63,528	32
1976	28	27	3	3		14	17	257,760	2
1977	26	19	1	1	2	6	11	123,841	16
1978	27	24		1	2	5	12	108,305	21
1979	26	21	2	4		8	16	236,770	5
1980	26	24	1	2	1	10	13	237,727	5
1981	25	20		2	1	9	14	151,038	20
1982	22	15				2	8	54,277	85
1983	21	18	1	2	2	9	14	275,474	7
1984	24	20	1		1	9	13	270,989	16
1985	22	8					2	25,814	149
1986	26	22	2			5	12	388,169	8
1987	24	19	1	1	1	14	15	638,194	3
1988	26	25	1	1	1	8	21	696,895	8
1989	23	18		1	1	5	12	443,095	21
1990	21	15	1			2	8	351,193	33
1991	21	10			2	4	7	224,563	75
1992	24	19	1	1		4	7	439,071	31
1993	22	15	1			1	7	318,605	51
1994	24	20	1			6	13	659,252	21
1995	23	17	1		1	4	7	737,475	23
1996	19	11				1	5	176,857	119
1997	17	5					1	42,513	213
1998	15	2						11,393	268
1999	13								
2000	13	1						7,400	240
2001	11	1						7,770	244
2002	2								
2003	1								
2004	1								
Total	645	454	19	22	19	144	267	7,091,166	

CHAMPIONS TOUR CAREER SUMMARY — PLAYOFF RECORD: 0-0

Year	Events Played	Cuts Made	1st	2nd	3rd	Top 10	Top 25	Earnings	Rank
2002	20					1	4	204,528	71
2003	19					2	3	231,512	58
2004	18						2	113,343	83
Total	57					3	9	549,382	

PGA TOUR TOP TOURNAMENT SUMMARY

Year	70	71	72	73	74	75	76	77	78	79	80	81	82
Masters			T19	T24	T22	T30	2	T8	T37	CUT	T6	T8	T24
U.S. Open	T36	T27				T3	T8	T49	CUT	T11	T31	T11	T19
British Open					T28			T5	T2	T2	3	T8	T15
PGA					T63	T10	T8	W/D	T16	2	T41	CUT	CUT
THE PLAYERS					T39	T55	T70	CUT	T4	CUT	2	T63	CUT

Year	83	84	85	86	87	88	89	90	91	92	93	94	95
Masters	T2	1	T57	T16	T4	4	T3	T14	T3	46	CUT	T18	1
U.S. Open	CUT	CUT	CUT	T6	T4	T12	CUT	CUT				T33	T71
British Open	CUT	T22	T35	T21	T4	T16	T52	T31	T80		CUT	T77	T15
PGA	T9	CUT	T59	T11	T7	T17	T17	T31	W/D	T73	T61	T9	T44
THE PLAYERS	T10	T26	T33	T54	T9	T11	T11	CUT	CUT	T29	CUT	T19	CUT
TOUR Championship					T5	T21	T14					T13	T25

Year	96	97	98	99	00	01	02	03	04
Masters	CUT	45	CUT	CUT	CUT	CUT	CUT	CUT	CUT
U.S. Open	CUT	T65	CUT	CUT					
British Open	T26		CUT						
PGA	T69	CUT	CUT	CUT	W/D				
THE PLAYERS	T73	CUT	CUT	CUT	CUT	CUT			

CHAMPIONS TOUR TOP TOURNAMENT SUMMARY

Year	02	03	04
Senior PGA Championship	T27	CUT	W/D
U.S. Senior Open	CUT	CUT	CUT
Ford Senior Players Championship	T53	T61	T56
Senior British Open			CUT
JELD-WEN Tradition	T64	T33	T55

NATIONAL TEAMS: World Amateur Team Championship, 1972; Ryder Cup (4), 1981, 1983, 1987, 1995, 1999 (Captain); U.S. vs. Japan, 1983; World Cup (2), 1987, 1988; Kirin Cup (Captain), 1988; Dunhill Cup, 1995.

Ben Crenshaw (Continued)

1989: Won William Richardson Award, given by Golf Writers Association of America. **1987:** Placed third on the money list and recorded 14 top-10s. **1986:** Won Vantage Championship (now THE TOUR Championship) at Oak Hills CC in San Antonio. **1984:** Earned first Masters victory. Two strokes off lead entering final round, shot closing 68 to defeat Tom Watson by two strokes. **1983:** Prevailed again in Texas with a win in the Byron Nelson Classic. **1977:** Claimed the first of two Colonial National Invitation titles. **1976:** Won three events and finished second three times on way to second-place finish on money list behind Jack Nicklaus...Despite opening 75, won Bing Crosby National Pro-Am by two over Mike Morley...The following week, closed with rounds of 65-66 to win Hawaiian Open by four over Larry Nelson and Hale Irwin...Third victory came at Ohio Kings Island Open. **1973:** Won Qualifying Tournament by then-record 12-stroke margin...In his first start as a PGA TOUR member, defeated Orville Moody by two strokes in the San Antonio-Texas Open. **Amateur:** Winner of 1971-72-73 NCAA Championships, sharing title with University of Texas teammate Tom Kite in 1972...Winner of Fred Haskins Award as nation's outstanding collegiate golfer each of those years.

PERSONAL:

Noted golf historian...Introduced to golf by his father and won his first tournament as a fourth-grader...Fought winning battle against Graves Disease in mid-1980s...1996 PGA National Golf Day Honorary Chairperson...His book, "A Feel for the Game," reached No. 25 on the New York Times best-seller list in 2001...Named as a Player Ambassador for the World Golf Hall of Fame in 2003.

PLAYER STATISTICS

2004 PGA TOUR STATISTICS

Scoring Average	72.02	(N/A)
Driving Distance	271.5	(N/A)
Driving Accuracy Percentage	67.9%	(N/A)
Total Driving	1,998	(N/A)
Greens in Regulation Pct.	55.6%	(N/A)
Putting Average	1.850	(N/A)
Sand Save Percentage	40.0%	(N/A)
Birdie Average	2.50	(N/A)
Scoring Avg. Before Cut	74.50	(N/A)
Birdie Conversion Percentage	20.0%	(N/A)
Par Breakers	13.9%	(N/A)

MISCELLANEOUS PGA TOUR STATISTICS

2004 Low Round/Round: 74–Masters Tournament/1
Career Low Round/Round: 61–1979 Phoenix Open/2
Career Largest Paycheck/Finish: $396,000–1995 Masters Tournament/1

2004 CHAMPIONS TOUR STATISTICS:

Scoring Average	72.72	(64)
Driving Distance	263.2	(67)
Driving Accuracy Percentage	63.4%	(68)
Total Driving	135	(78)
Greens in Regulation Pct.	56.7%	(77)
Putting Average	1.772	(16)
Sand Save Percentage	50.0%	(20)
Eagles (Holes per)	324.0	(38)
Birdie Average	2.83	(62)
All-Around Ranking	412	(61)

MISCELLANEOUS CHAMPIONS TOUR STATISTICS

2004 Low Round: 68–Toshiba Senior Classic/2.
Career Low Round: 65–2002 Kroger Senior Classic/2
Career Largest Paycheck: $85,750–2003 3M Championship/T4

SHOTLink. AN IBM ON DEMAND BUSINESS SOLUTION

HOT SHOTS

2004 Best Single-Event Statistics

TOTAL FEET IN PUTTS MADE (PER ROUND)

Rank	Player	Tournament	Stat	Finish
1	Lee Janzen	Honda Classic	141 ft 8 in	T-9th
2	Tiger Woods	WGC-American Express Champ	122 ft 10 in	9th
3	Duffy Waldorf	Sony Open	122 ft 2 in	T-36th
4	Kent Jones	Chrysler Championship	121 ft 0 in	T-17th
5	Rich Barcelo	Buick Open	120 ft 6 in	T-30th
6	Brendan Pappas	Southern Farm Bureau Classic	118 ft 2 in	T-46th
7	Zach Johnson	84 Lumber Classic	116 ft 10 in	T-3rd
8	Brendan Pappas	FBR Open	114 ft 3 in	T-14th
9	Adam Scott	Booz Allen Classic	112 ft 11 in	1st
10	Michael Bradley	FedEx St. Jude Classic	110 ft 6 in	T-13th

PUTTING FROM 10-15 FEET

Rank	Player	Tournament	Stat	Finish
1	Tim Herron	Bay Hill Invitational	100.00%	T-24th
2	Aaron Baddeley	Buick Championship	80.00%	T-61st
	Carlos Franco	WGC-AmEx Championship	80.00%	T-28th
4	Hidemichi Tanaka	Chrysler Classic of Tucson	77.80%	T-20th
	Fred Couples	Honda Classic	77.80%	T-25th
	Gabriel Hjertstedt	B.C. Open	77.80%	T-35th
	Brian Watts	Valero Texas Open	77.80%	T-52nd

PLAYERS WHO DIDN'T MISS A PUTT FROM 4-8 FEET

No.	Player	Tournament	Finish
1	Danny Ellis	Ford Championship at Doral	T-9th
2	Spike McRoy	MCI Heritage	T-39th
3	Daniel Chopra	HP Classic of New Orleans	T-34th
4	Brad Faxon	Bank of America Colonial	T-50th
5	Jeff Maggert	Bank of America Colonial	T-9th
6	Stephen Leaney	the Memorial	T-11th
7	Luke Donald	Buick Classic	7th
8	Tim Herron	Booz Allen Classic	T-4th
9	Ben Crane	John Deere Classic	T-32nd
10	Hank Kuehne	B.C. Open	T-13th
11	Bob Burns	Buick Open	T-30th
12	Bill Glasson	Buick Open	42nd
13	Thomas Levet	WGC-NEC Invitational	T-32nd
14	Brad Faxon	WGC-American Express Championship	T-13th
15	Brent Geiberger	Southern Farm Bureau Classic	T-19th
16	Jay Haas	The TOUR Championship	T-7th

PUTTS IN A TOURNAMENT

Rank	Player	Tournament	Statistic	Finish
1	Aaron Baddeley	Chrysler Classic of Tucson	95 putts	2nd
2	Cliff Kresge	Ford Championship	96 putts	T-34th
3	Justin Rose	H.P. Classic of New Orleans	98 putts	T-5th
	Carl Pettersson	Reno-Tahoe Open	98 putts	T-5th
5	Mike Weir	Nissan Open	99 putts	1st
	Cliff Kresge	MCI Heritage	99 putts	T-16th
	Greg Chalmers	John Deere Classic	99 putts	T-4th
8	Kevin Na	EDS Byron Nelson Championship	100 putts	T-34th
	Bob Estes	FedEx St. Jude Classic	100 putts	2nd
	Ernie Els	the Memorial	100 putts	1st
	Jonathan Byrd	84 Lumber Classic	100 putts	T-3rd

Ben Curtis

EXEMPT STATUS: Winner, 2003 British Open (through 2008)
FULL NAME: Ben Clifford Curtis
HEIGHT: 5-11
WEIGHT: 175
BIRTHDATE: May 26, 1977
BIRTHPLACE: Columbus, OH
RESIDENCE: Stow, OH
FAMILY: Wife, Candace
EDUCATION: Kent State University (2000, Recreation Management)
SPECIAL INTERESTS: Family
TURNED PROFESSIONAL: 2000
Q SCHOOL: 2002

PGA TOUR VICTORIES (1):

2003 British Open Championship.

BEST 2004 PGA TOUR FINISH:

T8—the Memorial Tournament.

2004 SEASON:

After a career season in 2003, collected his only top-10 in 2004 with a T8 at the Memorial Tournament...Held a one-stroke lead through two rounds at the MCI Heritage, but finished T25 after rounds of 75-73 on the weekend...Shared the 18- and 36-hole lead at the Memorial Tournament, only 18 miles from where he grew up in Ostrander, Ohio. Finished with rounds of 73-72 at Muirfield Village Golf Club for a T8 finish, the second top-10 of his career (34 events) and the first since his victory at the 2003 British Open...Was two back of Vijay Singh through 36 holes at the 84 LUMBER Classic, but closing 81-68 dropped him to T32. Recorded a hole-in-one on the par-3 12th hole in the final round.

CAREER HIGHLIGHTS:

2003: Voted PGA TOUR Rookie of the Year. Pulled one of the greatest upsets in golf history, capturing the British Open in the first major championship start of his career. Rounds of 72-72-70-69—283 topped Vijay Singh and Thomas Bjorn by one shot. Entered final round tied for third, but grabbed lead with birdies on six of first 11 holes on Sunday, putting him two up on Bjorn, three on Singh and four on Tiger Woods. Went to No. 18 three behind Bjorn after bogeys at Nos. 12, 14, 15 and 17. Saved par with 10-foot putt on No. 18, and earned title when Bjorn finished 4-over par on the final four holes. First player since Francis Ouimet at the 1913 U.S. Open to win a major in his first try. First player to win first British Open start since Tom Watson in 1975. Youngest British Open winner at 26 years, 1 month, 24 days, since Tiger Woods won in 2000 at the age of 24 years, 6 months, and 23 days. Jumped from 396th to 35th in the Official World Golf Ranking, the biggest jump since the Ranking began in 1986. One of four first-time major champions in 2003, joining Mike Weir (Masters), Jim Furyk (U.S. Open), and Shaun Micheel (PGA). Qualified for the British Open via a T13 finish at the 100th Western Open, his best career finish to date and first career top-25 finish...Just one month after British Open triumph, returned to home state to play in the WGC-NEC Invitational at Firestone CC in Akron. First-round co-leader with Sergio Garcia after a 6-under-par 64. Married Candace Beatty in Kent on Saturday evening, Aug. 23 after the completion of the third round. Finished T30. **2002:** Played the Hooters Tour for a second consecutive season, finishing 10th on the money list and winning in Myrtle Beach, SC...Placed T26 at the PGA TOUR Qualifying Tournament. **Amateur:** Three-time All-American at Kent State...Won the Ohio Amateur in 1999 and 2000. Second win came by 17 strokes, joining the PGA TOUR's John Cook and Arnold Palmer as the tournament's only back-to-back winners. That same year, Curtis finished runner-up at the Western Amateur and won the Players' Amateur to become the No. 1-ranked amateur golfer in the world by Golfweek.

PERSONAL:

Grew up only 50 yards from the practice putting green of Mill Creek GC in Ostrander, OH, where grandfather built the course and where his father is superintendent...Started playing golf at age 3, but says he didn't get serious about golf until high school. Won the Division II state title his junior and senior years of high school...The week after British Open victory, was a guest on David Letterman, hitting wedge shots rooftop-to-rooftop during broadcast, and visited President Bush in the White House...Caddie for most of 2003 was former Kent State University teammate Danny Fahl. Andy Sutton, a long-time caddie on the European Tour, worked for Curtis at the British Open...Signed an endorsement contract in 2004 with Reebok to wear its NFL apparel at PGA TOUR events, the first player to do that since the late Payne Stewart.

PLAYER STATISTICS

2004 PGA TOUR STATISTICS

Scoring Average	71.58	(143)
Driving Distance	282.1	(138)
Driving Accuracy Percentage	64.3%	(96)
Total Driving	234	(155)
Greens in Regulation Pct.	63.4%	(136)
Putting Average	1.809	(177)
Sand Save Percentage	42.2%	(176)
Eagles (Holes per)	156.0	(38)
Birdie Average	3.08	(182)
All-Around Ranking	1,086	(174)
Scoring Avg. Before Cut	71.61	(153)
Round 3 Scoring Avg.	73.50	(193)
Final Round Scoring Average	72.25	(146)
Birdie Conversion Percentage	25.1%	(189)
Par Breakers	17.7%	(182)

MISCELLANEOUS PGA TOUR STATISTICS

2004 Low Round/Round: 66–3 times, most recent FUNAI Classic at the WALT DISNEY WORLD Resort/3
Career Low Round/Round: 64–2003 WGC-NEC Invitational/1
Career Largest Paycheck/Finish: $1,112,720–2003 British Open Championship/1

PGA TOUR CAREER SUMMARY — PLAYOFF RECORD: 0-0

Year	Events Played	Cuts Made	1st	2nd	3rd	Top 10	Top 25	Earnings	Rank
2000	1								
2001	1	1						$6,020	
2003	21	13	1			1	3	1,434,911	46
2004	20	9				1	4	500,818	141
Total	43	23	1			2	7	1,941,748	
NATIONWIDE TOUR									
1997	1								
2001	2	1					1	6,847	194
2002	4	2					1	6,470	200
2003	1	1					1	5,146	229
Total	8	4					3	18,463	
EUROPEAN TOUR									
2004	6	2						26,663	

PGA TOUR TOP TOURNAMENT SUMMARY

Year	03	04
Masters		CUT
U.S. Open		30
British Open	1	CUT
PGA	CUT	CUT
THE PLAYERS		CUT
WGC-Accenture Match Play		T17
WGC-NEC Invitational	T30	
WGC-American Express Champ	T66	

NATIONAL TEAMS: World Amateur Team Championship, 2000.

John Daly

EXEMPT STATUS: Winner, 1995 British Open (through 2005)
FULL NAME: John Patrick Daly
HEIGHT: 5-11
WEIGHT: 220
BIRTHDATE: April 28, 1966
BIRTHPLACE: Carmichael, CA
RESIDENCE: Rogers, AR

FAMILY: Wife, Sherrie; Shynah Hale (6/10/92), Sierra Lynn (6/1/95), Austin (3/8/99), John Patrick (7/23/03)
EDUCATION: University of Arkansas
SPECIAL INTERESTS: Most sports
TURNED PROFESSIONAL: 1987
Q SCHOOL: 1990
Nationwide Tour Alumnus

PGA TOUR VICTORIES (5):

1991 PGA Championship. **1992** B.C. Open. **1994** BellSouth Classic. **1995** British Open Championship. **2004** Buick Invitational.

NATIONWIDE TOUR VICTORIES (1):

1990 Utah Classic.

INTERNATIONAL VICTORIES (4):

1990 AECI Charity Classic [SAf], Hollard Royal Swazi Sun Classic [SAf]. **2001** BMW International Open [Eur]. **2003** Kolon Korean Open [Asia].

OTHER VICTORIES (2):

2002 Champions Challenge [with Pat Perez]. **2003** Callaway Golf Pebble Beach Invitational.

BEST 2004 PGA TOUR FINISHES:

1—Buick Invitational; 2—Buick Open; 4—Nissan Open; T6—Shell Houston Open; T10—Bay Hill Invitational Presented by MasterCard.

2004 SEASON:

Rebirth of career started with first PGA TOUR victory since 1995, capped by first TOUR Championship appearance since rookie year in 1991. Most consistent season ever – with a career-best 17 made cuts in 22 starts. Among the leaders in several categories, including Driving Distance (third), Putting Average (fifth) and All-Around (fourth)...Won for the first time since the 1995 British Open with his playoff victory at the Buick Invitational, a span of 189 starts and 8 years, 6 months, 22 days between PGA TOUR wins. Defeated Chris Riley and Luke Donald on the first extra hole by knocking a 99-foot bunker shot to within seven inches and sinking the birdie. Won after holding third-round lead for the fourth time in five tries on TOUR. Rolled in 32-foot eagle putt on Saturday to take the 54-hole lead by one over Stewart Cink. Win earned career-best $864,000 payday and made him more money than he had in any of his previous 13 years on TOUR. His previous high was $828,914 (2001). Became first winner since Steve Pate at the 1991 Honda Classic to shoot 3-over-par 75 in the final round and go on to victory. Win moved him from 299th on Official World Golf Ranking to 85th...In the fourth round of the Bob Hope Chrysler Classic, recorded a double eagle on the par-5 second hole, holing out from 220 yards with a 5-iron. Marked the sixth time since 1970, when the PGA TOUR started tracking the record, a player has posted an albatross at the Hope. Finished T30...After winning the Buick Invitational, finished T4 at the Nissan Open, posting back-to-back top-10s in consecutive starts for the first time since finishing T4 at the 2002 Phoenix Open and solo fourth at the Buick Invitational. The last time he finished in the top 10 in consecutive weeks was in 1994 (T7 at the Shell Houston Open and first at the BellSouth Classic)...Added a third top-10 with a T10 at the Bay Hill Invitational... Finished T6 at the Shell Houston Open despite a first-round 76...Finished runner-up to Vijay Singh at the Buick Open, moving into the top 50 in the Official World Golf Ranking (No. 57 to 36). Entered the final round two shots behind Singh after opening 70-64-66 and took early lead with three birdies and an eagle on the first four holes. Finished with a 6-under-par 66, one stroke behind Singh...Underwent surgery on his right heel on Sept. 30 to remove bone spurs...Ended TOUR season No. 43 in the Official World Golf Ranking.

CAREER HIGHLIGHTS:

2003: Fell out of the top 125 from No. 112 to No. 171 with only one top-10 in 22 starts. Missed cut or was disqualified at final seven events of 2003...Averaged a career-best 314.3 yards off the tee, but failed to win ninth consecutive Driving Distance crown. Rookie Hank Kuehne averaged 321.4 yards...Won the Kolon Korean Open on the Asian PGA Tour. It was his first victory since the 2001 BMW International Open in Germany. **2002:** Slipped from 61st to 112th on TOUR money list, but won his 11th Driving Distance crown with a record mark of 306.8 yards per drive, topping his own 2001 mark of 306.7 yards. Daly's 11th category win surpassed the mark of Calvin Peete, who won 10 Driving Accuracy titles in his career...Returned to Masters after one-year hiatus. Qualified for Augusta as No. 43 in the Official World Golf Ranking after The Honda Classic...T4 with Lee Janzen at Phoenix Open, two shots behind champion Chris DiMarco...Finished fourth at the Buick Invitational, two strokes behind champion Jose Maria Olazabal. Back-to-back top-10s jumped Official World Golf Ranking to season-best No. 40, and were his first consecutive top-10s since a pair of T4s at the 1998 Nissan Open and Honda Classic. **2001:** Returned to old form with a career-high $828,914 in earnings and four top-10 finishes. Finished 61st on the money list, his highest since 1995. Began the season ranked 507th in the Official World Golf Ranking and reached the top 50 by the end of the official PGA TOUR season...Closed with a 66 at the Phoenix Open to post a T9, his first top-10 since T4 in the 1998 Honda Classic...Stood one stroke off 54-hole lead after a third-round 63 in the FedEx St. Jude Classic, best round since 63 at the 1991 Las Vegas Invitational. Closed with a 73 to record a T5...Captured European Tour's BMW International Open, his first victory since the 1995 British Open. **2000:** Played in 26 events and seemed to find some consistency at end of the year, making four straight cuts for his best stretch of the year...With rounds of 80-73—153, missed Masters cut for first time in eight appearances and his five-year exemption to Augusta National, earned with victory in 1995 British Open, expired. **1998:** Joined Mark O'Meara and Tiger Woods to represent

PGA TOUR CAREER SUMMARY — PLAYOFF RECORD: 2-0

Year	Events Played	Cuts Made	1st	2nd	3rd	Top 10	Top 25	Earnings	Rank
1986	1								
1989	6	3					1	$14,689	200
1990	3	2					1	10,000	230
1991	33	21	1		2	4	11	574,783	17
1992	25	15	1	1		5	8	387,455	37
1993	24	15			1	1	5	225,591	76
1994	17	9	1			3	4	340,034	49
1995	23	15	1			1	4	321,748	57
1996	23	14				1	3	173,557	121
1997	17	9				1	2	106,762	165
1998	25	14				2	6	393,740	77
1999	22	11					3	186,215	158
2000	26	10					1	115,460	188
2001	25	16				4	8	828,914	61
2002	21	12				2	4	593,595	112
2003	22	8				1	1	220,647	171
2004	22	17	1	1		5	8	2,359,507	21
Total	335	191	5	2	3	30	70	6,852,695	
NATIONWIDE TOUR									
1990	19	14	1	3		6	11	64,692	9
1991	1	1						673	276
Total	20	15	1	3		6	11	65,365	
EUROPEAN TOUR									
2004	1	1					1	35,333	

PGA TOUR TOP TOURNAMENT SUMMARY

Year	86	87	88	89	90	91	92	93	94	95	96	97	98
Masters							T19	T3	T48	T45	T29		T33
U.S. Open	CUT			T69			CUT	T33	CUT	T45	T27	W/D	T53
British Open							75	T14	81	1	T66		CUT
PGA						1	82	T51	CUT	CUT	CUT	T29	CUT
THE PLAYERS						CUT	72	CUT	CUT		T19	W/D	T16
TOUR Championship						3							

Year	99	00	01	02	03	04
Masters	T52	CUT		T32		CUT
U.S. Open	68	W/D		T70		
British Open		CUT	CUT	CUT	T72	CUT
PGA		CUT	CUT	CUT	CUT	CUT
THE PLAYERS	W/D	T48	CUT	CUT	T56	79
TOUR Championship						18
WGC-Accenture Match Play				T33		
WGC-NEC Invitational				73		T43

NATIONAL TEAMS: Dunhill Cup (3), 1993, 1998, 2000.

John Daly (Continued)

U.S. in Dunhill Cup, where he was unbeaten in four matches. **1995:** Added second major title with victory at British Open at St. Andrews. After holding 36-hole lead, fell to fourth with third-round 73. Appeared to have one-stroke victory after closing 71, but Costantino Rocca holed 70-foot putt from "Valley of Sin" short of 18th green. Daly won playoff by four strokes, thanks largely to Rocca's 7 at par-4 17th...Became youngest active player on TOUR (at the time) with two major championship titles and fourth American since World War II to win two majors before his 30th birthday, joining Jack Nicklaus, Tom Watson and Johnny Miller. **1994:** After serving suspension early in season, earned third TOUR victory at BellSouth Classic. Grabbed lead with second-round 64, then withstood challenges of Nolan Henke and Brian Henninger. **1992:** Won B.C. Open by six strokes for second career victory. **1991:** Delighted golf world with surprising victory at 1991 PGA Championship. As ninth and final alternate into field at Crooked Stick, shot opening 69 without benefit of practice round. Added rounds of 67-69-71 for three-stroke victory over Bruce Lietzke. Named PGA TOUR Rookie of the Year. **1990:** Played Nationwide Tour, won Utah Classic and finished ninth on money list.

PERSONAL:

Enjoys writing lyrics and playing guitar. . .Recorded a largely autobiographical album entitled "My Life," featuring guest performances by Darius Rucker, Willie Nelson, Johnny Lee and Daron Norwood. . .Instead of flying to tournament sites, purchased large RV and drives to many events. . .Involved in many charitable causes, most notably Make-a-Wish Foundation and Boys & Girls Clubs of America. . .Donated $25,000 to Nationwide Tour's Mark Christopher Charity Classic in 2002 and 2003.

PLAYER STATISTICS

2004 PGA TOUR STATISTICS

Statistic	Value	Rank
Scoring Average	70.82	(61)
Driving Distance	306.0	(3)
Driving Accuracy Percentage	53.0%	(192)
Total Driving	195	(95)
Greens in Regulation Pct.	66.4%	(60)
Putting Average	1.736	(5)
Sand Save Percentage	54.8%	(27)
Eagles (Holes per)	101.6	(4)
Birdie Average	3.99	(7)
All-Around Ranking	359	(4)
Scoring Avg. Before Cut	70.33	(24)
Round 3 Scoring Avg.	71.24	(121)
Final Round Scoring Average	71.35	(78)
Birdie Conversion Percentage	33.3%	(2)
Par Breakers	23.1%	(5)

MISCELLANEOUS PGA TOUR STATISTICS

2004 Low Round/Round: 64–2 times, most recent Buick Open/2

Career Low Round/Round: 62–2001 Invensys Classic at Las Vegas/2

Career Largest Paycheck/Finish: $864,000–2004 Buick Invitational/1

SHOTLink — AN IBM ON DEMAND BUSINESS SOLUTION

HOT SHOTS

2004 Best Single-Event Statistics

DRIVING ACCURACY

Rank	Player	Tournament	Stat	Tourn Finish
1	Jim Furyk	Buick Open	96.40%	T-6th
2	Scott Verplank	Michelin Champ at Las Vegas	94.60%	T-15th
3	Fred Funk	THE PLAYERS Championship	92.90%	T-10th
	Hidemichi Tanaka	Reno-Tahoe Open	92.90%	T-24th
5	John Cook	Reno-Tahoe Open	91.10%	T-35th
	Jose Coceres	Michelin Champ at Las Vegas	91.10%	T-15th
7	David Edwards	AT&T Pebble Beach	90.90%	T-41st
	Jeff Maggert	AT&T Pebble Beach	90.90%	2nd
	Kevin Sutherland	AT&T Pebble Beach	90.90%	T-54th

DRIVING DISTANCE

Rank	Player	Tournament	Stat	Tourn Finish
1	Hank Kuehne	FedEx St. Jude Classic	341.0	T-23rd
2	Scott Hend	Reno-Tahoe Open	338.4	71st
3	Roger Tambellini	Reno-Tahoe Open	337.6	T-50th
4	Dennis Paulson	Reno-Tahoe Open	337.4	T-9th
5	Scott Hend	BellSouth Classic	334.8	3rd
	Steve Allan	Reno-Tahoe Open	334.8	2nd
7	J.J. Henry	Reno-Tahoe Open	333.5	T-29th
8	Vaughn Taylor	Reno-Tahoe Open	332.0	1st
9	Craig Barlow	Reno-Tahoe Open	331.9	T-18th
10	Scott Hend	Bank of America Colonial	331.3	T-61st

DRIVING PERCENTAGE 300+ (ALL DRIVES)

Rank	Player	Tournament	Stat	Tourn Finish
1	John Daly	84 Lumber Classic	80.40%	T-13th
2	Scott Hend	Wachovia Championship	73.20%	T-44th
3	Hank Kuehne	Cialis Western Open	71.40%	T-63rd
	Mike Heinen	Reno-Tahoe Open	71.40%	T-56th
	Tag Ridings	84 Lumber Classic	71.40%	T-13th
6	Hank Kuehne	Buick Open	69.60%	T-18th
	Chris Smith	84 Lumber Classic	69.40%	T-20th
8	Rich Beem	Reno-Tahoe Open	67.90%	T-35th
	Vijay Singh	Deutsche Bank Championship	67.90%	1st
10	Bill Haas	Reno-Tahoe Open	66.70%	T-45th

SCRAMBLING (Getting up and down for par or better after missing green in regulation)

Rank	Player	Tournament	Stat	Tourn Finish
1	Vijay Singh	Mercedes Championships	100.00%	2nd
	Heath Slocum	Chrysler Classic of Tucson	100.00%	1st
	Patrick Sheehan	Valero Texas Open	100.00%	2nd
4	Steve Allan	Funai Classic	95.00%	T-33rd
5	Glen Day	Southern Farm Bureau Classic	94.10%	T-3rd
6	Loren Roberts	Bob Hope Chrysler Classic	92.30%	T-20th
	Tiger Woods	Buick Open	92.30%	T-3rd
8	Shigeki Maruyama	Ford Championship	91.30%	T-11th
9	Joe Ogilvie	HP Classic of New Orleans	90.90%	T-2nd
	Carl Pettersson	Chrysler Championship	90.90%	T-8th

SECTION 2 PLAYER BIOGRAPHIES

Robert Damron

EXEMPT STATUS: 84th on 2004 money list
FULL NAME: Robert Douglas Damron
HEIGHT: 5-8
WEIGHT: 185
BIRTHDATE: October 27, 1972
BIRTHPLACE: Pikeville, KY
RESIDENCE: Orlando, FL
FAMILY: Wife, Molly; Katherine Rose (9/30/02), William Bernard (3/29/04)
EDUCATION: University of Central Florida
SPECIAL INTERESTS: Sports
TURNED PROFESSIONAL: 1994
Q SCHOOL: 1996

PGA TOUR VICTORIES (1):

2001 Verizon Byron Nelson Classic.

BEST 2004 PGA TOUR FINISHES:

T2—EDS Byron Nelson Championship; 8—Bell Canadian Open.

2004 SEASON:

Finished in the top 100 on the PGA TOUR money list for the first time since 2001. Lost in a three-way playoff at the EDS Byron Nelson Championship was his best finish on TOUR since his victory at Las Colinas in 2001. Playoff record on TOUR fell to 1-1, the first coming at the 2001 Verizon Byron Nelson Classic where he topped Scott Verplank on the fourth extra hole…Only other top-10 came three months later, an eighth at the Bell Canadian Open, thanks to a final-round 66.

CAREER HIGHLIGHTS:

2003: A T7 at the Greater Hartford Open was his best finish since lone TOUR victory at the 2001 Verizon Byron Nelson Classic. **2002:** Ended season making nine of the last 11 cuts, including his only top-10 in hometown of Orlando at Disney Golf Classic...Set career-low mark with 63 during second round of Greater Milwaukee Open. **2001:** First victory of his five-year PGA TOUR career at Verizon Byron Nelson Classic led to best finish on money list (51st). After sharing 54-hole lead with Scott Verplank, used birdie on fourth extra hole to defeat Verplank. Victory worth $810,000, more than he had won in any of four previous TOUR seasons. Second-round 64 matched his career best, done three times previously. **2000:** Matched career-best 18-hole score in his first round of the year at the Bob Hope Chrysler Classic with a 64...Matched previous career-best finish with a T3 at THE PLAYERS Championship after rebounding from disastrous opening-round 78 with three consecutive sub-par scores (70-66-70) to finish six shots behind winner Hal Sutton...Matched career-low round again at the FedEx St. Jude Classic with a second-round 64. **1999:** Highlight of season included a fourth-place finish in front of hometown fans at Bay Hill Invitational after receiving a sponsor's exemption from host Arnold Palmer. **1997:** Impressive rookie season earned him nomination for Rookie of the Year honors...Finished year 53rd on money list on strength of four top-five finishes...Second only to Rookie of the Year Stewart Cink in first-year earnings. **Amateur:** Winner of five collegiate events while at University of Central Florida, where he was a three-time All-America.

PERSONAL:

Father moved family to Orlando for warmer winter weather after retiring from Kentucky coal business. Winter house was at Bay Hill Club, where Robert met Arnold Palmer and gained early advice about golf. Palmer helped him get sponsor's exemption to 1997 Bob Hope Chrysler Classic.

PLAYER STATISTICS

2004 PGA TOUR STATISTICS

Scoring Average	71.45	(133)
Driving Distance	277.2	(178)
Driving Accuracy Percentage	70.0%	(24)
Total Driving	202	(108)
Greens in Regulation Pct.	63.8%	(126)
Putting Average	1.792	(137)
Sand Save Percentage	49.4%	(88)
Eagles (Holes per)	552.0	(183)
Birdie Average	3.42	(125)
All-Around Ranking	994	(154)
Scoring Avg. Before Cut	71.03	(102)
Round 3 Scoring Avg.	71.72	(152)
Final Round Scoring Average	72.29	(150)
Birdie Conversion Percentage	28.4%	(112)
Par Breakers	19.2%	(131)

MISCELLANEOUS PGA TOUR STATISTICS

2004 Low Round/Round: 64–Bob Hope Chrysler Classic/3
Career Low Round/Round: 63–2002 Greater Milwaukee Open/2
Career Largest Paycheck/Finish: $810,000–2001 Verizon Byron Nelson Classic/1

PGA TOUR CAREER SUMMARY — PLAYOFF RECORD: 1-1

Year	Events Played	Cuts Made	1st	2nd	3rd	Top 10	Top 25	Earnings	Rank
1994	1								
1997	32	17			2	4	8	$455,604	53
1998	28	19				1	8	370,211	81
1999	30	24				3	4	434,157	90
2000	28	17			1	3	6	724,580	67
2001	27	18	1			1	4	1,059,187	51
2002	28	15				1	4	391,867	141
2003	32	16				2	6	580,087	115
2004	28	17		1		2	5	933,388	84
Total	234	143	1	1	3	17	45	4,949,080	
NATIONWIDE TOUR									
1995	4	1						410	274
Total	4	1						410	

PGA TOUR TOP TOURNAMENT SUMMARY

Year	97	98	99	00	01	02	03	04
U.S. Open				63	CUT		T20	
British Open	CUT							
PGA	CUT	CUT		T74	T66			
THE PLAYERS	T53	CUT	T52	T3	CUT	74	CUT	CUT

Marco Dawson

EXEMPT STATUS: Major Medical Extension
FULL NAME: Marco Thomas Dawson
HEIGHT: 6-0
WEIGHT: 200
BIRTHDATE: November 17, 1963
BIRTHPLACE: Freising, Germany
RESIDENCE: Lakeland, FL; plays out of Grasslands CC
FAMILY: Wife, Heather

EDUCATION: Florida Southern College (1985, Marketing)
SPECIAL INTERESTS: Fishing
TURNED PROFESSIONAL: 1985
Q SCHOOL: 1991, 1992, 1994
Nationwide Tour Alumnus

BEST PGA TOUR CAREER FINISH:
2—1995 Greater Milwaukee Open.

NATIONWIDE TOUR VICTORIES (1):
2002 LaSalle Bank Open.

BEST 2004 PGA TOUR FINISH:
T27—FBR Open.

2004 SEASON:
Made six starts before season was cut short due to back surgery in April. Will receive a Major Medical Extension for 2005. Coupled with $59,550 earned in six events in 2004, has the opportunity to play in 23 events to earn $595,820 and match the $623,262 in earnings of 2004's No. 125, Tag Ridings. If he does so, will play out of the Major Medical Extension category for the remainder of the season.

CAREER HIGHLIGHTS:
2003: One of six Nationwide Tour graduates from the class of 2002 to retain TOUR card, finishing in top 125 for the first time since 1996...Best finish of the year was a T7 at the Buick Invitational, his first top-10 since T6 at Buick Challenge in 1996, a span of 68 events. Collected a career-best $130,950...Followed with a T10 the next week at the Nissan Open. **2002:** Continued to play under Major Medical Extension carryover from 2001 season. After playing in 19 events in 2001, had one remaining event in 2002 to earn $174,047 and keep Major Medical Extension status for the remainder of the season. Missed cut at the Touchstone Energy Tucson Open, then spent the remainder of the year on the Nationwide Tour where he finished eighth and picked up his first win at the LaSalle Bank Open in Chicago. Win came in his 309th combined start on the Nationwide Tour/PGA TOUR. Added runners-up finishes at the Dayton Open and the Oregon Classic. **2001:** Playing on a Medical Extension, earned $172,738 in 19 events. Made 10 cuts and had two top-25 finishes. **2000:** Only played in 10 TOUR events before undergoing back surgery on May 30. **1999:** Became the first player in Nationwide Tour history to earn more than $200,000 without benefit of a victory. Finished third on Nationwide Tour money list to earn PGA TOUR card for 2000. Carded a 69 in the final round of the Nationwide Tour Championship, the only sub-70 on the last day, and forced a playoff with eventual winner Bob Heintz. **1998:** Spent most of the season retooling his game, changing from a right-to-left approach to a preferred left-to-right style. Played in only one tournament. **1996:** Finished in top 100 for second consecutive season. Posted three top-10 finishes, including a T3 at the Buick Invitational and T4 at CVS Charity Classic. **1995:** Finished No. 71 on TOUR money list. Closest brush with victory on the PGA TOUR came at the Greater Milwaukee Open where final-round 67 left him in second place, three behind winner Scott Hoch, for a $108,000 payday.

PERSONAL:
Was a teammate of Lee Janzen and Rocco Mediate at Florida Southern College...Took up golf at age 9 after his family moved to Coral Springs, FL and lived adjacent to a course.

PLAYER STATISTICS

2004 PGA TOUR STATISTICS

Scoring Average	71.93	(N/A)
Driving Distance	290.9	(N/A)
Driving Accuracy Percentage	53.6%	(N/A)
Total Driving	(N/A)	(N/A)
Greens in Regulation Pct.	65.2%	(N/A)
Putting Average	1.771	(N/A)
Sand Save Percentage	48.3%	(N/A)
Eagles (Holes per)	171.0	(N/A)
Birdie Average	3.79	(N/A)
Scoring Avg. Before Cut	71.50	(N/A)
Round 3 Scoring Avg.	68.25	(N/A)
Final Round Scoring Average	70.33	(N/A)
Birdie Conversion Percentage	32.0%	(N/A)
Par Breakers	21.6%	(N/A)

MISCELLANEOUS PGA TOUR STATISTICS

2004 Low Round/Round: 66–Bob Hope Chrysler Classic/4
Career Low Round/Round: 61–1991 Chattanooga Classic/1
Career Largest Paycheck/Finish: $130,950–2003 Buick Invitational/T7

PGA TOUR CAREER SUMMARY — PLAYOFF RECORD: 0-0

Year	Events Played	Cuts Made	1st	2nd	3rd	Top 10	Top 25	Earnings	Rank
1986	1	1					1	$2,080	249
1990	2	1						2,154	272
1991	29	12				2	3	96,756	137
1992	28	14				2	4	113,464	123
1993	32	21				1	4	120,462	124
1994	30	13				1	4	121,025	139
1995	25	14		1		2	7	261,214	71
1996	28	17			1	3	7	261,661	82
1997	31	13					2	100,110	168
1998	1	1						3,173	340
2000	11	5						44,290	217
2001	19	10					2	172,738	182
2002	1								
2003	31	11				2	6	601,729	107
2004	6	3						59,550	227
Total	275	136		1	1	13	40	1,960,405	
NATIONWIDE TOUR									
1990	24	15			1	3	12	29,972	31
1991	4	3				3	3	9,071	102
1998	1								
1999	21	19		2	2	11	16	201,219	3
2000	5	4					3	19,696	143
2002	23	17	1	2	1	5	9	227,590	8
Total	78	58	1	4	4	22	43	487,548	

PGA TOUR TOP TOURNAMENT SUMMARY

Year	93	94	95	96	97	98	99	00	01	02	03
U.S. Open					83						T48
PGA				75							
THE PLAYERS	T46	CUT		T33	CUT						

SECTION 2 PLAYER BIOGRAPHIES

Chris DiMarco

EXEMPT STATUS: 2004 U.S. Ryder Cup Team Member (through 2006)
FULL NAME: Christian Dean DiMarco
HEIGHT: 6-0
WEIGHT: 180
BIRTHDATE: August 23, 1968
BIRTHPLACE: Huntington, NY
RESIDENCE: Orlando, FL; plays out of The CC of Heathrow

FAMILY: Wife, Amy; Cristian Alexander (2/11/96), Amanda Elizabeth (1/28/98), Abigale Brooke (1/8/04)
EDUCATION: University of Florida
SPECIAL INTERESTS: Family, sports
TURNED PROFESSIONAL: 1990
JOINED TOUR: 1994
Nationwide Tour Alumnus

PGA TOUR VICTORIES (3):

2000 SEI Pennsylvania Classic. **2001** Buick Challenge. **2002** Phoenix Open.

NATIONWIDE TOUR VICTORIES (1):

1997 Ozarks Open.

OTHER VICTORIES (1):

2002 CVS Charity Classic [with Dudley Hart].

BEST 2004 PGA TOUR FINISHES:

2—FBR Open, PGA Championship; T3—84 LUMBER Classic; T6—Masters Tournament, The INTERNATIONAL, WGC-NEC Invitational; T9—WGC-Accenture Match Play Championship, Buick Classic, U.S. Open Championship.

2004 SEASON:

Finished in the top 20 (No. 12) on the PGA TOUR money list for the fifth straight season and earned a career-high $2,971,842…In his second event of the season, was runner-up to Jonathan Kaye at the FBR Open after the pair shared the third-round lead. Was two back of Kaye and Phil Mickelson through nine holes but made six straight birdies to begin the back nine to sit even with Kaye with three holes to play. Bogeyed two of three coming in to lose by two strokes…Co-leader at 6-under-par with Phil Mickelson through 54 holes at the Masters. Final-round 76 dropped finish to T6, second career top-10 in four starts at Augusta National. Posted first ace of the week with a 5-iron at the 180-yard sixth hole…Playing in the Buick Classic for the first time since the 1999 season, finished T9. In first four starts at Westchester Country Club (1994, '95, '98,'99) missed the cut…Collected his first top-10 in his fifth U.S. Open with a T9 and posted back-to-back top-10s in majors for the first time in his career. One of three players (Phil Mickelson and Ernie Els) to post top-10s in the first two majors of the season…The 36-hole leader at the INTERNATIONAL after opening with 14 and 17 points in the Modified Stableford scoring system. Had a nine-point lead heading into the weekend, but minus-7 points on the weekend dropped him to T6 at Castle Pines…Followed that finish with a T2 the next week at the PGA Championship. Entered three-man, three-hole playoff with Justin Leonard and Vijay Singh when Leonard missed a 12-footer for par on the 72nd hole. Tied for second after Singh recorded the only birdie of the playoff. The T2 was his best finish in 20 major championships and his third top-10 in a major in 2004. The finish moved him to eighth on the final Ryder Cup Team list, allowing him to make his first Ryder Cup Team…Third straight top-10 came at WGC-NEC Invitational, a T6, six strokes behind champion Stewart Cink. First top-10 in three career NEC Invitational starts…Collected 2 1/2 points at Oakland Hills, the most points for the U.S. Team at the Ryder Cup, with his 2-1-1 record…Past champion of the 84 LUMBER Classic finished T3 for his third top-10 in five starts in Pennsylvania. One of only four players who has made the cut in the five 84 LUMBER Classic tournaments.

CAREER HIGHLIGHTS:

2003: Did not win for the first time since 1999, but racked up 10 top-10s to tie career best...Ranked third on the PGA TOUR in Putting Average at 1.723...Played for the United States at The Presidents Cup in South Africa. **2002:** Won for third consecutive season and compiled career-high earnings of $2,615,363...Captured third career PGA TOUR title at the Phoenix Open with rounds of 68-64-66-69. Four-shot lead with eight to play evaporated with a double bogey and two bogeys (Nos. 11-13). Recovered with a birdie on par-3 16th hole that provided one-shot margin of victory over Kaname Yokoo and Kenny Perry. Payday of $720,000 was largest of career…Winner of West Coast Swing presented by The St. Paul, earning a bonus of $500,000...Climbed to career-best No. 9 position in Official World Golf Ranking after T23 finish at BellSouth Classic. **2001:** Won once and had nine other top-10s to crack the single-season $2-million mark for the first time with $2,595,201...In 29 starts, never went more than five events without a top-10...At the Buick Challenge, was one stroke off the lead after 36 holes. After a third-round 71, rebounded by making a 15-foot birdie putt on the final hole to shoot 65 and force a playoff with David Duval at 21-under-par 267. Proceeded to make par on the first extra hole to win on TOUR for the second consecutive season...Opened with 65 to claim a one stroke-lead in Masters. Was the third consecutive Masters rookie to lead after 18 holes. Followed with a 69 to claim a two-stroke margin over Tiger Woods and Phil Mickelson after 36. Finished T10. **2000:** For the first time in his career finished in the top 30 on the money list on the strength of five top-10s and a victory. Made 25 cuts in 33 tournaments entered and made over $1 million in a single season for the first time in his career, $1,842,221...Was one of nine first-time winners on the PGA TOUR with his victory at the inaugural SEI Pennsylvania Classic. Won in record fashion with a six-stroke victory over five players. $576,000 payday put him over $1.4 million for the season, jumped him to 16th on TOUR money list and secured a spot in THE TOUR Championship, where he finished T18. Victory on the PGA TOUR came in his 159th career start. Also had two T2 finishes. **1999:** Posted three top-10s, including a second and a third...Closed the year with best finish in his first five sea-

PGA TOUR CAREER SUMMARY — PLAYOFF RECORD: 1-1

Year	Events Played	Cuts Made	1st	2nd	3rd	Top 10	Top 25	Earnings	Rank
1989A	1	1							
1990	1								
1992	1								
1994	29	16			1	4	5	$216,839	85
1995	33	13					3	74,698	174
1996	5	3						18,678	245
1998	31	17				2	5	260,334	111
1999	31	20		1	1	3	8	672,503	62
2000	33	25	1	2		5	13	1,842,221	19
2001	29	26	1	1	2	10	18	2,595,201	12
2002	29	27	1	1		7	16	2,606,430	11
2003	27	23		1	2	10	14	2,350,630	18
2004	27	25		2	1	9	17	2,971,842	12
Total	277	196	3	8	7	50	99	13,609,377	
NATIONWIDE TOUR									
1991	29	13				4	7	23,333	53
1992	1								
1993	29	19		2		10	15	90,687	9
1994	1	1						460	276
1996	1								
1997	27	23	1	2	1	8	15	135,513	3
Total	88	56	1	4	1	22	37	249,993	

PGA TOUR TOP TOURNAMENT SUMMARY

Year	95	96	97	98	99	00	01	02	03	04
Masters							T10	T12	W/D	T6
U.S. Open				T32			T16	T24	T35	T9
British Open						CUT	T47	T66	CUT	T63
PGA					T41	T15	T16	T39	56	T2
THE PLAYERS	CUT				T46	CUT	T55	T36	T21	CUT
TOUR Championship						T18	T10	T7	T21	T24
WGC-Accenture Match Play							T33	T17	T33	T9
WGC-NEC Invitational								T28	T33	T6
WGC-American Express Champ						T25	CNL	T11	T70	T36

NATIONAL TEAMS: Presidents Cup, 2003; Ryder Cup, 2004.

Chris DiMarco (Continued)

sons on TOUR with a second at the Southern Farm Bureau Classic. **1998:** Manufactured a pair of top-10s in the fall to help retain his playing privileges, T9 at Bell Canadian Open and B.C. Open in consecutive weeks. **1997:** Returned to the Nationwide Tour after finishing 86th at the Qualifying Tournament. Won Ozarks Open and had seven other top-10s to place third on Nationwide Tour money list and earn exempt status for 1998 PGA TOUR. **1994:** Rookie year on PGA TOUR an impressive one as he finished eighth in rookie earnings. Pair of back-to-back top-10s, T3 at Deposit Guaranty Golf Classic and solo fourth in New England Classic, helped him retain exempt status. **1993:** Earned playing privileges on the Nationwide Tour, where he finished ninth in earnings. **1992:** Winner of Canadian Order of Merit. Also led Canadian Tour with 69.52 stroke average.**1991:** Nationwide Tour member, finishing 53rd with $23,333. **Amateur:** All-American and SEC Player of the Year 1990. All-SEC 1989-90. Winner of 1989 SEC Championship.

PERSONAL:

Played on same college team at the University of Florida with TOUR members Dudley Hart and Pat Bates...Raised more than $400,000 for R.O.C.K (Reach Out for Cancer Kids) through his charity golf tournament in fall 2004.

PLAYER STATISTICS

2004 PGA TOUR STATISTICS

Scoring Average	70.28	(24)
Driving Distance	277.3	(176)
Driving Accuracy Percentage	68.6%	(40)
Total Driving	216	(133)
Greens in Regulation Pct.	67.1%	(41)
Putting Average	1.752	(28)
Sand Save Percentage	50.6%	(76)
Eagles (Holes per)	294.0	(125)
Birdie Average	3.74	(47)
All-Around Ranking	557	(39)
Scoring Avg. Before Cut	70.04	(13)
Round 3 Scoring Avg.	70.92	(93)
Final Round Scoring Average	71.39	(82)
Birdie Conversion Percentage	29.5%	(83)
Par Breakers	21.1%	(53)

MISCELLANEOUS PGA TOUR STATISTICS

2004 Low Round/Round: 64–FBR Open/3
Career Low Round/Round: 61–2001 Invensys Classic at Las Vegas/2
Career Largest Paycheck/Finish: $720,000–2002 Phoenix Open/1

SHOTLink
AN IBM ON DEMAND BUSINESS SOLUTION

HOT SHOTS

2004 Best Single-Event Statistics

GREENS IN REGULATION

Rank	Player	Tournament	Stat	Finish
1	Jim Furyk	Mercedes Championships	90.30%	11th
	Kevin Na	Southern Farm Bureau Classic	90.30%	T-3rd
3	Bart Bryant	Valero Texas Open	88.90%	1st
4	Woody Austin	Buick Open	87.50%	T-24th
	Mark Wilson	Michelin Champ at Las Vegas	87.50%	T-15th
	Billy Andrade	Southern Farm Bureau Classic	87.50%	T-34th
	Shaun Micheel	Mercedes Championships	87.50%	T-13th
	Scott Hoch	Mercedes Championships	87.50%	8th

FAIRWAY PROXIMITY

Rank	Player	Tournament	Stat (Avg.)	Finish
1	Kent Jones	Valero Texas Open	17 ft 7 in	T-37th
2	Chris DiMarco	Buick Open	18 ft 2 in	T-15th
3	Kevin Na	Southern Farm Bureau Classic	18 ft 5 in	T-3rd
	Todd Fischer	Valero Texas Open	18 ft 5 in	T-3rd
5	Chris Riley	Sony Open	18 ft 11 in	T-30th
6	Fred Funk	Southern Farm Bureau Classic	19 ft 0 in	1st
7	Ernie Els	Sony Open	19 ft 5 in	1st
8	J.J. Henry	Southern Farm Bureau Classic	19 ft 7 in	T-3rd
	Justin Leonard	Valero Texas Open	19 ft 7 in	T-10th
10	Justin Rose	Valero Texas Open	19 ft 9 in	T-17th

APPROACHES FROM 125-150 YDS

Rank	Player	Tournament	Stat (Avg.)	Finish
1	Mark O'Meara	WGC-NEC Invitational	6 ft 1 in	T-72nd
2	Patrick Sheehan	Chrysler Championship	8 ft 5 in	T-50th
3	Shigeki Maruyama	Wachovia Championship	8 ft 6 in	T-56th
4	Notah Begay III	Chrysler Classic of Tucson	9 ft 1 in	T-15th
5	Frank Lickliter II	84 Lumber Classic	9 ft 2 in	T-9th
6	Matt Gogel	Nissan Open	9 ft 5 in	T-74th
7	Padraig Harrington	THE TOUR Championship	9 ft 8 in	14th
8	Steve Stricker	U.S. Bank Championship	10 ft 6 in	T-36th
9	Vijay Singh	Buick Open	10 ft 10 in	1st
	Bob Burns	Buick Open	10 ft 10 in	T-30th

APPROACHES FROM 150-175 YDS

Rank	Player	Tournament	Stat (Avg.)	Finish
1	Geoff Ogilvy	Shell Houston Open	11 ft 11 in	10th
2	Fredrik Jacobson	Buick Classic	12 ft 0 in	8th
3	Chris DiMarco	Buick Open	12 ft 6 in	T-15th
4	Jeff Sluman	Wachovia Championship	12 ft 10 in	T-44th
5	Scott McCarron	John Deere Classic	13 ft 11 in	T-14th
6	Padraig Harrington	WGC-NEC Invitational	14 ft 4 in	74th
7	Richard Johnson	B.C. Open	14 ft 6 in	T-35th
8	Harrison Frazar	Chrysler Championship	14 ft 11 in	T-30th
9	Adam Meyer	Valero Texas Open	15 ft 6 in	T-61st
10	Jerry Kelly	Bay Hill Invitational	16 ft 4 in	5th

Luke Donald

EXEMPT STATUS: 2004 European Ryder Cup Team Member (through 2006)
FULL NAME: Luke Campbell Donald
HEIGHT: 5-9
WEIGHT: 160
BIRTHDATE: December 7, 1977
BIRTHPLACE: Hempstead, England
RESIDENCE: Chicago, IL
FAMILY: Single
EDUCATION: Northwestern University (2001, Art Theory and Practice)
SPECIAL INTERESTS: Art
TURNED PROFESSIONAL: 2001
Q SCHOOL: 2001

PGA TOUR VICTORIES (1):
2002 Southern Farm Bureau Classic.

INTERNATIONAL VICTORIES (2):
2004 Scandinavian Masters [Eur], Omega European Masters [Eur].

OTHER VICTORIES (1):
2004 WGC-World Cup [with Paul Casey].

BEST 2004 PGA TOUR FINISHES:
T2—Buick Invitational; T3—Cialis Western Open; 7—Buick Classic; T8—BellSouth Classic.

2004 SEASON:
Won two times on the European Tour and collected a career-best four top-10s on the PGA TOUR, including season-high $1,646,268. Earned a spot on the European Ryder Cup Team after his consistent play on both the PGA TOUR and the European Tour…Led by one stroke over three players after 36 holes at the AT&T Pebble Beach National Pro-Am, opening 69-65. Finished T17…Lost in a three-way playoff (along with Chris Riley) to John Daly at the Buick Invitational in fourth start of season. Sank a 10-foot birdie putt on the 72nd hole to force a sudden-death playoff. On the first extra hole, Donald and Riley both missed birdie putts inside 10 feet while Daly splashed a 99-foot bunker shot to tap-in range for birdie to claim the title…Second top-10 came at the BellSouth Classic, a T8…Surpassed the $1-million mark in a single-season earnings for the second time in his career with his seventh-place finish at the Buick Classic…T3 at the Cialis Western Open was the fourth top-10 of the season, one more than he had combined for in his first two seasons. Final-round 4-under 67 for the Chicago resident jumped him nine spots from his T12 place through 54 holes… Claimed his first European Tour victory after carding a 3-under 69 in the final round for a five-shot victory at the Scandinavian Masters…Collected a second victory on the European Tour at the Omega European Masters, just a week before making his first appearance in the Ryder Cup Matches in the United States. Teamed with Paul Casey to win WGC-World Cup for England in Spain.

CAREER HIGHLIGHTS:
2003: Posted eight top-25 finishes in the 17 cuts made for the season. First top-10 came in third start, a T7 at the Buick Invitational, seven strokes behind champion Tiger Woods...Next top-10 did not come until eight months later in October, when as defending champion of the Southern Farm Bureau Classic, he finished T10. **2002:** First start as a member of the PGA TOUR was a T13 at the Sony Open in Hawaii...Earned first PGA TOUR title in rookie season at Southern Farm Bureau Classic, joining Jonathan Byrd as only rookies to win that season...Earned first career PGA TOUR victory in his 37th professional start. Tournament reduced to 54 holes due to unplayable conditions. Carded rounds of 66-68-67—201 to win by one over Deane Pappas. Trailed Brad Elder by one after 18 holes and two through 36 holes. Birdied Nos. 15-17 and finished with 4-under-par 32 on back nine Saturday afternoon to take the lead from Elder for the first time. Play was suspended prior to Sunday tee time of 10:10 a.m., and was deemed a 54-hole tournament on Monday morning. Collected first-place check of $468,000, the largest paycheck of his career. Became the 11th rookie in TOUR history to earn $1 million in his first season and the 61st millionaire of 2002. **2001:** Turned professional in August, making his debut at the Reno-Tahoe Open on a sponsor exemption. Earned sponsor exemptions into six other events and managed to make four cuts. Best finish was a T18 at the Bell Canadian Open...Only 2001 college graduate to make it through all three stages of Qualifying Tournament. **Amateur:** Led the GB&I Walker Cup team to a 15-9 victory in 1999 and 12 -11 victory in 2001, going 7-1 in match play over two competitions...Won the 1999 NCAA individual title. Two-time Big Ten Individual Champion (1999 and 2000). Won the 1999 Fred Haskins Award for top collegiate golfer. Won 1999 Jack Nicklaus Award as collegiate men's golf's player of the year, which earned him a spot in the field at the 2000 Memorial Tournament, where he finished T51. Broke Tiger Woods' Golfstat Cup record for lowest stroke average (70.45) in 1999. Three-time (1999, 2000, 2001) first-team All-American.

PERSONAL:
Brother Christian caddies for Luke…An avid painter. Earned degree in art theory and practice at Northwestern. Donated one of his paintings to the PGATOUR.COM auction and the winning bid was $1,640, which was split between PGA TOUR Charities and junior golf charity in Chicago.

PLAYER STATISTICS

2004 PGA TOUR STATISTICS

Scoring Average	70.11	(15)
Driving Distance	279.8	(162)
Driving Accuracy Percentage	69.6%	(30)
Total Driving	192	(91)
Greens in Regulation Pct.	69.4%	(11)
Putting Average	1.791	(133)
Sand Save Percentage	52.2%	(53)
Eagles (Holes per)	432.0	(171)
Birdie Average	3.49	(105)
All-Around Ranking	680	(70)
Scoring Avg. Before Cut	70.44	(36)
Round 3 Scoring Avg.	70.73	(76)
Final Round Scoring Average	70.93	(52)
Birdie Conversion Percentage	26.6%	(178)
Par Breakers	19.6%	(116)

MISCELLANEOUS PGA TOUR STATISTICS

2004 Low Round/Round: 64–EDS Byron Nelson Championship/3
Career Low Round/Round: 64–3 times, most recent 2004 EDS Byron Nelson Championship/3
Career Largest Paycheck/Finish: $468,000–2002 Southern Farm Bureau Classic/1

PGA TOUR CAREER SUMMARY — PLAYOFF RECORD: 0-1

Year	Events Played	Cuts Made	1st	2nd	3rd	Top 10	Top 25	Earnings	Rank
1999A	2								
2000A	3	1							
2001	7	3					1	$80,747	
2002	30	23	1			1	11	1,088,205	58
2003	27	17				2	8	705,121	90
2004	21	15		1	1	4	12	1,646,268	35
Total	90	59	1	1	1	7	32	3,520,340	
EUROPEAN TOUR									
2004	6	6	2		1	3	6	1,021,495	

PGA TOUR TOP TOURNAMENT SUMMARY

Year	99	00	01	02	03	04
U.S. Open				T18		
British Open	CUT	CUT		CUT	CUT	CUT
PGA					T23	T24
THE PLAYERS					CUT	CUT
WGC-NEC Invitational						T16
WGC-American Express Champ						T11

NATIONAL TEAMS: Ryder Cup, 2004. WGC-World Cup, 2004. Walker Cup (2), 1999, 2000.

Joe Durant

EXEMPT STATUS: 81st on 2004 money list
FULL NAME: Joseph Scott Durant
HEIGHT: 5-10
WEIGHT: 170
BIRTHDATE: April 7, 1964
BIRTHPLACE: Pensacola, FL
RESIDENCE: Molino, FL; plays out of Steelwood GC
FAMILY: Wife, Tracey; Connor (8/4/91), Hayes (2/27/98)

EDUCATION: Huntingdon (AL) College (1987, Marketing)
SPECIAL INTERESTS: Sports, reading, music
TURNED PROFESSIONAL: 1987
Q SCHOOL: 1992
Nationwide Tour Alumnus

PGA TOUR VICTORIES (3):

1998 Motorola Western Open. **2001** Bob Hope Chrysler Classic, Genuity Championship.

NATIONWIDE TOUR VICTORIES (1):

1996 Mississippi Gulf Coast Classic.

BEST 2004 PGA TOUR FINISHES:

4—Ford Championship at Doral, Chrysler Championship; T10—HP Classic of New Orleans.

2004 SEASON:

Finished in the top 100 on the PGA TOUR money list for the fifth time in his nine-year career, including second straight…Past champion recorded his first top-10 of the season with fourth at the Ford Championship at Doral. Added T10 at the HP Classic of New Orleans in May. A 63 in the final round at the Chrysler Championship gave him his final top-10 of the season, a solo fourth…Finished first on TOUR in Greens in Regulation for second consecutive season, fourth in Driving Accuracy and fifth in Total Driving. Finished in top 10 in Greens in Regulation for the sixth straight season.

CAREER HIGHLIGHTS:

2003: Posted four top-10s and finished in the top 75 on the money list for just the third time in his eight-year career. Led TOUR in Greens in Regulation (72.9%)...A T2 at the FBR Capital Open was his best finish on TOUR since a T2 at the 2001 Shell Houston Open. **2002:** T11 at the Honda Classic was his best finish of season. **2001:** Finished in Top 15 on TOUR money list for first time in career...After missing first cut at Touchstone Energy Tucson Open, ran off string of eight consecutive cuts made including four top-10s, two victories and rewrote several TOUR records...Earned more money in first nine starts of season ($1,778,672) than in entire TOUR career ($1,696,838), which covered 128 events...Indian Wells course-record-tying 61, his career low, in round two of Bob Hope Chrysler Classic gave him three-stroke lead. 136 and 193 were 36- and 54-hole tournament records. Fourth-round 66 lifted him to 29-under 256, establishing PGA TOUR record for most strokes under par through 72 holes. Closing 65 brought 90-hole records for most strokes under par (36) and fewest strokes (324), breaking marks established by Tom Kite in winning 1993 Bob Hope Chrysler Classic...Continued winning trend in Miami at Genuity Championship, where closing 65 brought his third TOUR title. Began final round four strokes off lead. $810,000 paycheck lifted him to top of money list with $1,493,267 for three weeks...Shared first-round lead at Shell Houston Open and held one-stroke advantage through 54 holes. Closing 74 dropped him to T2, three strokes behind Hal Sutton. Runner-up finish pushed him past $2 million for season. Joined Tiger Woods (1992) as only players to better $2 million without first having $1-million campaign. **2000:** Returned to the Top 100 after falling out in 1999 due to an injured rib that hindered his play most of the season. **1999:** Won Par-3 Contest at Masters...In February at AT&T Pebble Beach National Pro-Am, thought he suffered a muscle pull trying to throw duffel bag over his shoulder. Took six weeks off to heal, during which time was diagnosed with a fractured rib. **1998:** Became the fifth of eight first-time winners with victory at the Motorola Western Open. Shot 66 for 17-under 271 and two-stroke victory over Vijay Singh. Broke a tie with Singh with birdies at Nos. 14, 15 and 17. **1997:** Had successful return to PGA TOUR, finishing 100th on the money list on strength of three top-10s…Led TOUR in Total Driving. **1996:** Finished third on Nationwide Tour money list with four top-three finishes. Won Mississippi Gulf Coast Classic by one stroke over Dave Rummells and Brett Quigley. **1992:** Earned first PGA TOUR card at Qualifying Tournament. **Amateur:** 1992 T.C. Jordan Tour Player of the Year...Three-time NAIA All-American and medalist at 1987 NAIA Championship while at Huntingdon College.

PERSONAL:

Took six months away from golf after 1991 Nationwide Tour season. Received license to sell insurance but sold no policies. Also took job at golf equipment retail house, filling orders and stacking boxes. Before returning to TOUR golf, received lecture from wife Tracey about changing his negative outlook on golf course…Gave Chrysler (Town & Country Limited) received for victory at Bob Hope Chrysler Classic to Coachella Valley (CA) Youth Center and Boxing Club…Owns four horses.

PLAYER STATISTICS

2004 PGA TOUR STATISTICS

Scoring Average	70.75	(50)
Driving Distance	287.2	(97)
Driving Accuracy Percentage	75.1%	(4)
Total Driving	101	(5)
Greens in Regulation Pct.	73.3%	(1)
Putting Average	1.798	(157)
Sand Save Percentage	41.7%	(182)
Eagles (Holes per)	218.6	(81)
Birdie Average	3.60	(79)
All-Around Ranking	651	(62)
Scoring Avg. Before Cut	70.83	(74)
Round 3 Scoring Avg.	69.88	(26)
Final Round Scoring Average	69.56	(4)
Birdie Conversion Percentage	27.0%	(165)
Par Breakers	20.5%	(72)

MISCELLANEOUS PGA TOUR STATISTICS

2004 Low Round/Round: 63–Chrysler Championship/4
Career Low Round/Round: 61–2001 Bob Hope Chrysler Classic/2
Career Largest Paycheck/Finish: $810,000–2001 Genuity Championship/1

PGA TOUR CAREER SUMMARY — PLAYOFF RECORD: 0-0

Year	Events Played	Cuts Made	1st	2nd	3rd	Top 10	Top 25	Earnings	Rank
1987	1								
1993	18	2						$4,055	279
1997	31	19				3	7	240,936	100
1998	24	15	1			2	6	651,803	43
1999	26	13					2	187,062	157
2000	28	18				4	7	612,882	76
2001	25	14	2	1		6	9	2,381,684	14
2002	28	16					5	427,217	137
2003	28	19		1		4	7	1,119,002	66
2004	26	16				3	7	952,547	81
Total	235	132	3	2		22	50	6,577,188	
NATIONWIDE TOUR									
1990	4	3						1,930	166
1991	27	16				1	6	16,095	67
1992	5	4				1	3	7,025	122
1993	11	4				1	1	6,398	127
1994	24	12				1	8	20,340	71
1995	27	20		1		7	12	81,697	20
1996	27	23	1	1	2	8	17	159,386	3
Total	125	82	1	2	2	19	47	292,871	

PGA TOUR TOP TOURNAMENT SUMMARY

Year	97	98	99	00	01	02	03	04
Masters			CUT		CUT	CUT		
U.S. Open		T32	CUT		T24	CUT	CUT	
British Open		CUT			CUT	T59	CUT	
PGA		T40			T51	T60	T39	CUT
THE PLAYERS	CUT	CUT	76		T10	CUT	T62	T58
TOUR Championship					T10			
WGC-Accenture Match Play						T33		
WGC-American Express Champ					CNL			

David Duval

EXEMPT STATUS: Winner, 2001 British Open (through 2006)
FULL NAME: David Robert Duval
HEIGHT: 6-0
WEIGHT: 180
BIRTHDATE: November 9, 1971
BIRTHPLACE: Jacksonville, FL
RESIDENCE: Denver, CO
FAMILY: Wife, Susie; Deano, Nick, Shalene
EDUCATION: Georgia Tech
SPECIAL INTERESTS: Reading, fly fishing, surfing, skiing, baseball, snowboarding
TURNED PROFESSIONAL: 1993
JOINED TOUR: 1995
Nationwide Tour Alumnus

PGA TOUR VICTORIES (13):
1997 Michelob Championship at Kingsmill, Walt Disney World/Oldsmobile Classic, THE TOUR Championship. **1998** Tucson Chrysler Classic, Shell Houston Open, NEC World Series of Golf, Michelob Championship at Kingsmill. **1999** Mercedes Championships, Bob Hope Chrysler Classic, THE PLAYERS Championship, BellSouth Classic. **2000** Buick Challenge. **2001** British Open Championship.

NATIONWIDE TOUR VICTORIES (2):
1993 Wichita Open, TOUR Championship.

INTERNATIONAL VICTORIES (1):
2001 Dunlop Phoenix [Jpn].

OTHER VICTORIES (3):
1998 Fred Meyer Challenge [with Jim Furyk]. **1999** Franklin Templeton Shootout [with Fred Couples]. **2000** EMC World Cup [with Tiger Woods].

BEST 2004 PGA TOUR FINISH:
T13—Deutsche Bank Championship.

2004 SEASON:
Made comeback after seven-month break with his first start of the season at the U.S. Open at Shinnecock Hills, his first pro competition since he withdrew from a tournament in Japan in November 2003. Had not played on the PGA TOUR since he missed the cut in Las Vegas in October 2003. Missed cut at U.S. Open shooting 83-82. . .Finished T13 at Deutsche Bank Championship, his best finish since a T6 at the 2002 Invensys Classic at Las Vegas, and first cut made since 2003 FBR Capital Open.

CAREER HIGHLIGHTS:
2003: Fell from 80th to 211th on the money list, making only four cuts in 20 starts...Set course record at TPC at Avenel with 9-under 62 during second round of the FBR Capital Open. Finished T28 for best finish of campaign. **2002:** Failed to win for the first time since 1996 and had his lowest position on the money list (No. 80) since 1994. Recorded two top-10s, at the Memorial (T4) and Invensys Classic at Las Vegas (T6). Member of the U.S. Ryder Cup team and has compiled a 2-3-2 record in two appearances. **2001:** Overcame early season wrist injury to win the first major of his career at the British Open...Finished eighth in earnings, the sixth consecutive year in the Top 10 and the fourth time to top $2-million mark...Forced to withdraw from Bay Hill Classic and THE PLAYERS Championship due to tendinitis in right wrist...Returned to action, after a five-week layoff, to post a second in the Masters. It was his second runner-up finish and the fourth consecutive top-10. Trailed by three strokes after 36 and 54 holes. Finished two behind Tiger Woods after a closing 67 where he was tied for the lead on the back nine at Augusta National until a bogey at No. 16...In his 27th attempt, won first major at the British Open. Third-round 65 put him in a four-way tie for the lead. Closing 67 produced a three-shot victory over Niclas Fasth. Took the lead for good with a birdie on hole No. 6 at Royal Lytham & St. Annes...Finished T10 in the PGA Championship. A T16 in the U.S. Open prevented him from posting a top-10 in all four majors...Lost a one-hole playoff to Chris DiMarco in the Buick Challenge after firing a closing 63. **2000:** Sidelined for 10 weeks by back problems. Rebounded with 12th TOUR victory at the Buick Challenge. Made birdie on three of last four holes for a two-stroke victory at the Mountain View Course at Callaway Gardens, GA. With $414,000 paycheck, went over $2 million in a season for third time in career...Season impacted by back problems. First felt back pain following U.S. Open and was forced to withdraw during first round of INTERNATIONAL. Problem described as "persistent and painful ligament-related damage in lower and middle back." Continuing pain caused withdrawals from PGA Championship and WGC-NEC Invitational. PGA was first major championship missed since rookie year of 1995, when not eligible for Masters. Since then, had made 22 consecutive starts in majors, finishing in the top-10 six times...Defeated Davis Love III, 4 and 2, for third place in WGC-Accenture Match Play Championship....Subsequent top-10s came at Doral-Ryder Open (T4), Masters (T3), where second-round 65, best of tournament, gave him 36-hole lead. . .In June, lost Buick Classic in playoff with Dennis Paulson; the next week T8 at U.S. Open. . .Ended season with a sixth-place finish at THE TOUR Championship, an event he lead by one stroke after 36 holes...Member of his third Presidents Cup Team. 2000 Presidents Cup record 3-2-0 for a three-year total of 7-6-1...Completed the year by teaming with Tiger Woods in the WGC-EMC World Cup in Argentina. **1999:** Became first player since Johnny Miller in 1974 to win four times before the Masters...Also first player since Nick Price (1993-94) to earn at least four victories in consecutive years...Eagled last hole to win Bob Hope Chrysler Classic and shoot 59, which matched Al Geiberger (1977) and Chip Beck (1991)...PLAYERS Championship victory came same day father Bob won Emerald Coast Classic on Champions Tour. $900,000 paycheck made David earliest to win $2 million in season...Moved to No. 1 in Official World Golf Ranking, snapping Tiger Woods' string of 41 consecutive weeks in first...First to surpass $3 million in season after T10 at Buick Classic...Played on first Ryder Cup team with 1-2-1 record. **1998:** Led Presidents Cup Team eligibility list...Earned the Byron Nelson Award and Vardon Trophy with lowest scoring average (69.13) and the Arnold Palmer Award for earnings ($2,591,031). **1997:** Won last three events to finish second in official earnings. Won Michelob Championship at Kingsmill for first TOUR title, followed with win at Walt Disney World/Oldsmobile Classic and then won THE TOUR Championship...Became first player since Nick Price in 1993 to win three consecutive starts...First

PGA TOUR CAREER SUMMARY — PLAYOFF RECORD: 2-2

Year	Events Played	Cuts Made	1st	2nd	3rd	Top 10	Top 25	Earnings	Rank
1990A	1	1							
1992A	5	2					2		
1993	5	4					1	$27,181	201
1994	6	4				1	1	44,006	195
1995	26	20		3	1	8	14	881,436	11
1996	23	16		2	3	6	11	977,079	10
1997	29	21	3	2		7	14	1,885,308	2
1998	23	19	4	1	1	12	17	2,591,031	1
1999	21	20	4	1	1	12	17	3,641,906	2
2000	19	18	1	1	3	9	14	2,462,846	7
2001	20	18	1	2	1	7	11	2,801,760	8
2002	24	16				2	7	838,045	80
2003	20	4						84,708	212
2004	9	3					1	121,044	210
Total	231	166	13	12	10	64	110	16,356,349	
NATIONWIDE TOUR									
1993	9	8	2		1	5	6	85,882	11
1994	22	17		1	3	10	15	126,430	8
Total	31	25	2	1	4	15	21	212,312	

PGA TOUR TOP TOURNAMENT SUMMARY

Year	90	91	92	93	94	95	96	97	98	99	00	01	02
Masters							T18	CUT	T2	T6	T3	2	CUT
U.S. Open	T56		CUT			T28	T67	T48	T7	T7	T8	T16	CUT
British Open						T20	T14	T33	T11	T62	T11	1	T22
PGA						CUT	T41	T13	CUT	T10		T10	T34
THE PLAYERS						CUT	T4	T43	T18	1	T13		T28
TOUR Championship						T9	T15	1	T8	T15	6	T7	
WGC-Accenture Match Play										T17	3		T33
WGC-NEC Invitational										T27		27	T28
WGC-American Express Champ												CNL	T46

Year	03	04
Masters	CUT	
U.S. Open	CUT	CUT
British Open	CUT	
PGA	W/D	CUT
THE PLAYERS	CUT	
WGC-Accenture Match Play	T33	

NATIONAL TEAMS: World Amateur Team Championship (2), 1990, 1992; Walker Cup, 1991; The Presidents Cup (3), 1996, 1998, 2000; Ryder Cup (2), 1999, 2001; World Cup (2), 2000, 2001.

David Duval (Continued)

player in PGA TOUR history to win playoffs in consecutive weeks...Also became first player since Billy Andrade in 1991 to win his first two titles back-to-back...Had seven seconds and four thirds in 86 starts before winning his first TOUR event. **1995:** In rookie season, finished second three times, at AT&T Pebble Beach National Pro-Am, Bob Hope Chrysler Classic and Memorial Tournament, and finished season with eight top-10s and a then-rookie earnings record. **1993:** Finished 11th on Nationwide Tour money list despite playing in only nine events. Won '93 Wichita Open and Nationwide Tour Championship. **Amateur:** 1993 Collegiate Player of the Year and winner of Dave Williams Award...Held two-stroke lead through 54 holes at 1992 BellSouth Classic before closing with 79 and finishing T13. While at Georgia Tech, joined Wake Forest's Gary Hallberg, Arizona State's Phil Mickelson and Georgia Tech's Bryce Molder as only four-time Division I first-team All-Americans...1989 U.S. Junior Amateur champion.

PERSONAL:

Father, Bob, is a Champions Tour player. They have teamed in such events as the Fred Meyer Challenge. David caddied for his dad at 1996 Transamerica, Bob's first Champions Tour event.

PLAYER STATISTICS

2004 PGA TOUR STATISTICS

Scoring Average	72.90	(N/A)
Driving Distance	288.2	(N/A)
Driving Accuracy Percentage	50.6%	(N/A)
Total Driving	(N/A)	(N/A)
Greens in Regulation Pct.	58.3%	(N/A)
Putting Average	1.784	(N/A)
Sand Save Percentage	40.8%	(N/A)
Eagles (Holes per)	99.0	(N/A)
Birdie Average	3.27	(N/A)
Scoring Avg. Before Cut	73.47	(N/A)
Round 3 Scoring Avg.	71.33	(N/A)
Final Round Scoring Average	69.67	(N/A)
Birdie Conversion Percentage	29.6%	(N/A)
Par Breakers	19.2%	(N/A)

MISCELLANEOUS PGA TOUR STATISTICS

2004 Low Round/Round: 67–2 times, most recent Michelin Championship at Las Vegas/1

Career Low Round/Round: 59–1999 Bob Hope Chrysler Classic/5

Career Largest Paycheck/Finish: $900,000–1999 THE PLAYERS Championship/1

SHOTLink
AN IBM ON DEMAND BUSINESS SOLUTION

HOT SHOTS

2004 TOUR Averages

OFF THE TEE	TOUR Average
Driving Distance (Two Holes)	287.3
Driving Distance (All Drives)	279.4
Driving Accuracy	64.2%
Left Rough Tendency	13.3%
Right Rough Tendency	14.2%

APPROACH TO THE GREEN	TOUR Average
Greens in Regulation	65.1%
Going for the Green (Par 5s)	38.8%
Going for the Green-Success	21.7%
Proximity to Hole	32 ft 2 in
Rough Proximity	42 ft 5 in
Left Rough Proximity	42 ft 4 in
Right Rough Proximity	42 ft 5 in
Fairway Proximity	24 ft 11 in
Approaches from Inside 75 Yds	16 ft 5 in
Approaches from 75-100 Yds	18 ft 1 in
Approaches from 100-125 Yds	20 ft 8 in
Approaches from 125-150 Yds	23 ft 11 in
Approaches from 150-175 Yds	28 ft 10 in
Approaches from 175-200 Yds	34 ft 4 in
Approaches from Over 200 Yds	42 ft 7 in

AROUND THE GREEN	TOUR Average
Sand Save Percentage	49.1%
Proximity to Hole from Sand	9 ft 10 in
Scrambling	58.3%
Scrambling From the Fringe	85.3%
Scrambling From the Rough	53.8%
Scrambling From Over 30 Yds	26.8%
Scrambling From 20-30 Yds	47.9%
Scrambling From 10-20 Yds	61.3%

PUTTING	TOUR Average
Putting Average (Greens in Regulation)	1.777
Overall Putting Average	1.620
One-Putt Percentage	38.7%
3-Putt Avoidance	3.3%
Putts per Round	29.08
Putting from Inside 3 Feet	99.1%
Putting from 3-4 Feet	90.9%
Putting from 4-5 Feet	80.8%
Putting from 5-6 Feet	69.8%
Putting from 6-7 Feet	61.6%
Putting from 7-8 Feet	54.0%
Putting from 8-9 Feet	47.0%
Putting from 9-10 Feet	42.2%
Putting from 4-8 Feet	68.8%
Putting from Inside 10 Feet	86.9%
Putting from 10-15 Feet	31.0%
Putting from 15-20 Feet	18.9%
Putting from 20-25 Feet	13.2%
Putting from Over 25 Feet	5.8%
Approach Putt Performance	2 ft 5 in
Average Distance of Putts Made per Day	74 ft 7 in

SCORING	TOUR Average
Scoring Average (Adjusted)	71.07
Scoring Average (Actual)	71.30
Birdie Average (per Round)	3.45
Round 1 Scoring Average	71.16
Round 2 Scoring Average	71.08
Round 3 Scoring Average	70.94
Round 4 Scoring Average	71.63
Front 9 Scoring Average	35.65
Back 9 Scoring Average	35.79
Early Scoring Average	71.37
Late Scoring Average	71.53
Eagles (Holes per)	222.1
Par 3 Birdie Average	13.0%
Par 4 Birdie Average	15.9%
Par 5 Birdie Average	39.0%

Steve Elkington

EXEMPT STATUS: Winner, 1995 PGA Championship (through 2005)
FULL NAME: Stephen John Elkington
HEIGHT: 6-2
WEIGHT: 190
BIRTHDATE: December 8, 1962
BIRTHPLACE: Inverell, Australia
RESIDENCE: Sydney, Australia and Houston, TX; plays out of Champions GC
FAMILY: Wife, Lisa; Annie Elizabeth (3/24/95); Samuel Ross (2/25/97)
EDUCATION: University of Houston (1985, Recreation)
SPECIAL INTERESTS: Caricature drawing, fishing, hunting, gardening
TURNED PROFESSIONAL: 1985
Q SCHOOL: 1986

PGA TOUR VICTORIES (10):

1990 KMart Greater Greensboro Open. **1991** THE PLAYERS Championship. **1992** Infiniti Tournament of Champions. **1994** Buick Southern Open. **1995** Mercedes Championships, PGA Championship. **1997** Doral-Ryder Open, THE PLAYERS Championship. **1998** Buick Challenge. **1999** Doral-Ryder Open.

INTERNATIONAL VICTORIES (2):

1992 Australian Open [Aus]. **1996** Honda Invitational [Asia].

OTHER VICTORIES (4):

1993, **1995**, **1998** Franklin Templeton Shootout [with Raymond Floyd, Mark Calcavecchia and Greg Norman, respectively]. **1997** Diners Club Matches [with Jeff Maggert].

BEST 2004 PGA TOUR FINISH:

T18—Reno-Tahoe Open.

2004 SEASON:

Played a limited schedule of 20 events, but managed to make 15 cuts. Started out the year making all five cuts in five starts during the eight-week stretch of the West Coast Swing…Best finish of the season was T18 at the Reno-Tahoe Open.

CAREER HIGHLIGHTS:

2003: His 14 appearances were least of his career, finished 187th on money list, lowest since joining the PGA TOUR full-time in 1987...Withdrew after first-round 86 at the British Open, and did not play the remainder of the season...Best finish was T17 at the Nissan Open, site of his 1995 PGA Championship at Riviera. **2002:** Finished in the top 100 (59th) on the PGA TOUR money list, his highest finish since 1999 (35th). High point was a T2 at the British Open, his best finish at a major since third at the 1998 PGA. Closed with rounds of 68-66 to join eventual champion Ernie Els, Stuart Appleby and Thomas Levet in four-hole playoff at 6-under-par 278. Eliminated after missing 6-foot par putt on fourth and final hole of playoff...A T5 at the Genuity Championship was his best finish on the PGA TOUR since his 1999 victory at Doral. **2001:** Lingering injuries limited effective play early in the year. Was 117th on the money list...Played well late in the season. Had back-to-back T6s in the Marconi Pennsylvania Classic and Texas Open. Made the cut in his last six starts. **2000:** Year riddled with injuries and ailments. Made only 17 appearances...When playing, remained consistent, missing only two cuts during the season...Lone top-10 was T10 at the Buick Challenge... Injured wrist in first round of Greater Greensboro Chrysler Classic, where he missed cut, then withdrew from the next week's Shell Houston Open. WD was second in a row in his adopted hometown. Sinus history forced withdrawals from THE PLAYERS Championship and U.S. Open...Underwent surgery on Aug. 11, three days before PGA, to repair torn hip and ball socket...A Captain's Pick by Peter Thomson for the International's Presidents Cup team. **1999:** Appeared in winner's circle for third straight year with victory at the Doral-Ryder Open, which included a closing 64 that featured six consecutive birdies. **1998:** Captured ninth TOUR title and second Buick Challenge win in a playoff over Fred Funk. **1997:** Reached top-10 again thanks to two more victories. Trailed David Duval by two strokes entering final round of Doral-Ryder Open before earning two-stroke victory with closing 69. Three weeks later was dominant at THE PLAYERS Championship with wire-to-wire seven-stroke victory over Scott Hoch. At the time, joined Jack Nicklaus and Fred Couples as only two-time winners at TPC at Sawgrass. **1995:** First top-10 finish on the money list, when he won twice and finished second twice... Opened year with second Mercedes Championships title. Birdied second playoff hole to defeat Bruce Lietzke...Trailed Ernie Els by six strokes entering final

PGA TOUR CAREER SUMMARY — PLAYOFF RECORD: 4-4

Year	Events Played	Cuts Made	1st	2nd	3rd	Top 10	Top 25	Earnings	Rank
1984A	1	1							
1985A	2	2							
1985	5	5					1	$9,897	180
1986	5	3					1	12,705	194
1987	35	19				2	7	75,738	118
1988	29	19				2	9	149,972	79
1989	29	21		1	1	3	9	231,062	61
1990	26	24	1			4	14	548,564	18
1991	28	17	1			4	10	549,120	25
1992	24	21	1	2	3	9	14	746,352	12
1993	23	23		1	1	8	14	675,383	17
1994	20	15	1			2	5	294,943	62
1995	21	16	2	2		7	11	1,254,352	5
1996	19	15		1	1	5	9	459,637	42
1997	17	14	2		1	3	9	1,320,411	8
1998	16	10	1		1	4	5	695,775	42
1999	21	18	1			3	7	1,086,376	35
2000	17	15				1	2	232,785	154
2001	20	14				2	4	437,200	117
2002	23	17		1	1	3	5	1,084,535	59
2003	14	6					2	154,124	187
2004	20	15					1	243,238	179
Total	415	310	10	8	9	62	139	10,262,170	

EUROPEAN TOUR

Year	Events Played
2004	1

PGA TOUR TOP TOURNAMENT SUMMARY

Year	87	88	89	90	91	92	93	94	95	96	97	98	99
Masters					T22	T37	T3	CUT	T5	CUT	T12	30	T11
U.S. Open			T21	T21	T55	CUT	T33		T36	T40	T24	CUT	T51
British Open				CUT	T44	T34	T48	T67	T6	CUT	CUT	W/D	CUT
PGA		T31	T41	CUT	T32	T18	T14	T7	1	T3	T45	3	
THE PLAYERS	CUT	T54	CUT	T16	1	CUT	T16	T51	W/D	T19	1		T38
TOUR Championship				10	9	T22	T23		T2		T17		
WGC-Accenture Match Play													T33
WGC-NEC Invitational													39
WGC-American Express Champ													T34

Year	00	01	02	03	04
Masters	T52			CUT	
British Open	T60	CUT	T2	W/D	
PGA		W/D	T48		
THE PLAYERS			T63	CUT	T26
WGC-Accenture Match Play	T33				
WGC-NEC Invitational		T23	T68		

NATIONAL TEAMS: Presidents Cup (4), 1994, 1996, 1998, 2000; World Cup, 1994; Dunhill Cup (4), 1994, 1995, 1996, 1997.

Steve Elkington (Continued)

round of PGA at Riviera. Shot front-nine 31 on way to final-round 64 to force playoff with Colin Montgomerie. Sank 25-foot putt on first extra hole to win first major title...Won Vardon Trophy with 69.62 scoring average. **1994:** Missed part of season after sinus surgery, but came back for T7 at PGA Championship and notched five-stroke victory at Buick Southern Open. **1993:** Made all 23 cuts. Lost playoff to Rocco Mediate at Kmart Greater Greensboro Open and T3 at Masters Tournament. **1992:** Won Infiniti Tournament of Champions in playoff over Brad Faxon, one of six top-three finishes. **1991:** Outdueled Fuzzy Zoeller to win THE PLAYERS Championship. **1990:** First TOUR victory came at Kmart Greater Greensboro Open, where final-round 66 brought him from seven strokes back. **Amateur:** Won 1980 Australia-New Zealand Amateur...Winner 1981 Australian Amateur and Doug Sanders Junior...Two-time All-American at University of Houston, where teammate was Billy Ray Brown...Two-time Southwest Conference champion... Member of NCAA Championship teams in 1984 and 1985.

PERSONAL:

Idol growing up was fellow Australian Bruce Devlin...An avid gardener and accomplished caricaturist...A member of Champions GC, site of 1990, 1997, 1999, 2001 and 2003 TOUR Championships...In 2003 while rehabbing his shoulder was a youth instructor at Yeager Elementary School in Houston where his children are students. He helped out kids struggling with a subjects such as math and English.

PLAYER STATISTICS

2004 PGA TOUR STATISTICS

Scoring Average	71.27	(111)
Driving Distance	287.1	(100)
Driving Accuracy Percentage	68.2%	(45)
Total Driving	145	(30)
Greens in Regulation Pct.	66.1%	(69)
Putting Average	1.796	(147)
Sand Save Percentage	49.0%	(98)
Eagles (Holes per)	549.0	(182)
Birdie Average	3.41	(127)
All-Around Ranking	879	(128)
Scoring Avg. Before Cut	71.55	(147)
Round 3 Scoring Avg.	70.50	(58)
Final Round Scoring Average	71.36	(79)
Birdie Conversion Percentage	27.2%	(159)
Par Breakers	19.1%	(134)

MISCELLANEOUS PGA TOUR STATISTICS

2004 Low Round/Round: 66–Chrysler Classic of Tucson/2
Career Low Round/Round: 62–3 times, most recent 1991 Southwestern Bell Colonial/3
Career Largest Paycheck/Finish: $630,000–1997 THE PLAYERS Championship/1

SHOTLink — AN IBM ON DEMAND BUSINESS SOLUTION

HOT SHOTS

Statistical Keys to Victory in 2004

Note: Does not include WGC-Accenture Match Play Championship and The INTERNATIONAL.

SCORING

Seven winners led the field in first-round scoring
12 winners led the field in second-round scoring
Seven winners led the field in third-round scoring
Seven winners led the field in final-round scoring

FRONT-NINE/BACK-NINE SCORING

12 winners led the field in front-nine scoring
26 winners were among the top three in front-nine scoring
16 winners led the field in back-nine scoring
32 winners were among the top three in back-nine scoring

ALL AROUND

26 winners finished in the top 10 in driving distance
14 winners finished in the top 10 in driving accuracy
26 winners finished in the top 10 in greens in regulation
15 winners led the field in greens in regulation (Only eight of 46 winners in 2003 led the field in greens in regulation)

Vijay Singh's nine victories included a high ranking in all scoring.

Ernie Els (Else)

EXEMPT STATUS: Winner, 1997 U.S. Open (through 2007)
FULL NAME: Theodore Ernest Els
HEIGHT: 6-3
WEIGHT: 210
BIRTHDATE: October 17, 1969
BIRTHPLACE: Johannesburg, South Africa
RESIDENCE: Wentworth, England

FAMILY: Wife, Liezl; Samantha (5/26/99), Ben (10/6/02)
SPECIAL INTERESTS: Movies, reading, sports
TURNED PROFESSIONAL: 1989
JOINED TOUR: 1994
Nationwide Tour Alumnus

PGA TOUR VICTORIES (15):

1994 U.S. Open Championship. **1995** GTE Byron Nelson Golf Classic. **1996** Buick Classic. **1997** U.S. Open Championship, Buick Classic. **1998** Bay Hill Invitational. **1999** Nissan Open. **2000** The International Presented by Qwest. **2002** Genuity Championship, British Open Championship. **2003** Mercedes Championships, Sony Open in Hawaii. **2004** Sony Open in Hawaii, the Memorial Tournament, WGC-American Express Championship.

INTERNATIONAL VICTORIES (38):

1991 Amatola Classic [SAf].**1992** Protea Assurance South Africa Open [SAf], Lexington PGA Championship [SAf], South African Masters [SAf], Hollard Royal Swazi Sun Classic [SAf], FNB Players' Championship [SAf], Goodyear Classic [SAf]. **1993** Dunlop Phoenix Tournament [Jpn]. **1994** Dubai Desert Classic [Eur], Toyota World Match Play Championship [Eur], Johnnie Walker World Championship [Eur], Sarazen World Open. **1995** Lexington South African PGA Championship [SAf], Toyota World Match Play [Eur], Bells Cup [SAf]. **1996** South African Open [SAf], Toyota World Match Play [Eur], Johnnie Walker Super Tour Event, World Cup [indiv]. **1997** Johnnie Walker Classic [Aus], World Cup [indiv]. **1998** South African Open [SAf] **1999** Alfred Dunhill PGA Championship [SAf], Sun City Nedbank Challenge [SAf]. **2000** Standard Life Loch Lomond [Eur], Nedbank Challenge [SAf]. **2001** Vodacom Players Championship [SAf]. **2002** Heineken Classic [Eur], Dubai Desert Classic [Eur], Cisco World Match Play [Eur], Nedbank Challenge [SAf]. **2003** Heineken Classic [Eur], Johnnie Walker Classic [Eur], The Barclay's Scottish Open [Eur], Omega European Masters [Eur], World Match Play Championship [Eur]. **2004** Heineken Classic [Eur], HSBC World Match Play Championship [Eur].

OTHER VICTORIES (4):

1997 PGA Grand Slam of Golf, Dunhill Cup [with David Frost, Retief Goosen]. **1998** Dunhill Cup [with David Frost, Retief Goosen]. **2001** WGC-World Cup [with Retief Goosen].

BEST 2004 PGA TOUR FINISHES:

1—Sony Open in Hawaii, the Memorial Tournament, WGC-American Express Championship; 2—Masters Tournament, British Open Championship; T3—MCI Heritage; T4—PGA Championship; T7—EDS Byron Nelson Championship; T9—U.S. Open Championship; T10—THE TOUR Championship presented by Coca-Cola.

2004 SEASON:

Season included three PGA TOUR victories and top-10 finishes in all four majors, including near-misses at the Masters and British Open. Also captured two events on the European Tour...Holed a 30-foot birdie putt on the third playoff hole to beat Harrison Frazar for 13th career PGA TOUR victory at the Sony Open in Hawaii. Became the first back-to-back winner of the Sony event since Corey Pavin (1986-87) and the first player since Tiger Woods to successfully defend a PGA TOUR title (WGC-American Express Championship, 2002-2003). Started one shot off the lead of Frazar after opening 67-64-66, but posted final-round 65, his 16th consecutive round in the 60s at Waialae Country Club, to force the playoff...Became the fifth player on the European Tour to win a tournament in three consecutive years by capturing the Heineken Classic. Opened with a European Tour record-tying 12-under-par 60 at Royal Melbourne, and went wire-to-wire to beat Adam Scott by a stroke and become first player to win that event three times...Finished runner-up to Phil Mickelson at the Masters for fifth straight top-10 in Augusta, sixth overall. After opening 70-72-71, started the final round three back of Mickelson and co-leader Chris DiMarco. Took the lead after eagle-3 on No. 8 and another eagle-3 on No. 13 and posted final-round 5-under-par 67 to take the clubhouse lead at 8-under-par 280. Edged by one when Mickelson holed 18-foot putt on 72nd hole...Posted back-to-back top-10s on TOUR for the first time in 2004 with a T3 at the MCI Heritage, two out of the playoff between Stewart Cink and Ted Purdy. One of just two players (Fred Funk) to record four sub-par rounds at Harbour Town Golf Links...With rounds of 66-67 on the weekend wrapped up his third straight top-10 finish with a T7 at the EDS Byron Nelson Championship. The 1995 champion has recorded three top-10s in Dallas in six career starts...Won the Memorial Tournament with a pair of 66s on the weekend for a four-stoke victory over Fred Couples. He needed 100 putts to win his second tournament of the season. Overtook Vijay Singh for second in the Official World Golf Ranking. Five of his 15 titles have come in the month of June...Posted his seventh top-10 finish in 12 U.S. Open appearances with a T9 at Shinnecock Hills Golf Club, his fifth top-10 in last six majors...Finished as the runner-up for the second time in a major during the season, losing to Todd Hamilton in a four-hole playoff at the British Open. Birdied two of the last three holes and tied Hamilton on the 72nd hole when Hamilton bogeyed the hole. Hamilton posted four pars to Els' three pars and a bogey (17th hole) to win the playoff. Recorded a hole-in-one during round one on the "Postage Stamp," the par-3 eighth hole by using a wedge from 123 yards. Became the sixth player in tournament history to post four rounds in the 60s and did it for the second time (1993). Took over the lead on the European Tour's Volvo Order of Merit and ended up winning his second consecutive Order of Merit Award...Fourth top-10 in a major was a T4 at the PGA Championship. One of two players (Phil Mickelson) to record top-10s in all four majors and the only player to post a top-10 in the last five majors (T5-2003 PGA

PGA TOUR CAREER SUMMARY — PLAYOFF RECORD: 4-3

Year	Events Played	Cuts Made	1st	2nd	3rd	Top 10	Top 25	Earnings	Rank
1990	1								
1991	1	1						$2,647	274
1992	3	2						18,420	213
1993	6	2				1	1	38,185	190
1994	11	10	1	1		4	6	684,440	19
1995	18	14	1	1	2	6	10	842,590	14
1996	18	17	1	1		6	11	906,944	14
1997	19	15	2	1		7	11	1,243,008	9
1998	15	12	1			4	8	763,783	36
1999	18	16	1	1	1	7	10	1,710,756	15
2000	20	20	1	5	2	10	15	3,469,405	3
2001	19	15		1	5	9	11	2,336,456	15
2002	18	17	2			7	14	3,291,895	5
2003	17	17	2			7	14	3,371,237	9
2004	16	15	3	2	1	10	12	5,787,225	2
Total	200	173	15	13	11	78	123	24,466,992	
NATIONWIDE TOUR									
1991	8	5				1	2	6,143	123
Total	8	5				1	2	6,143	
EUROPEAN TOUR									
2004	9	9	2		2	9	9	1,857,647	

PGA TOUR TOP TOURNAMENT SUMMARY

Year	89	90	91	92	93	94	95	96	97	98	99	00	01
Masters						T8	CUT	T12	T17	T16	T27	2	T6
U.S. Open					T7	1	CUT	T5	1	T49	CUT	T2	T66
British Open	CUT			T5	T6	T24	T11	T2	T10	T29	T24	T2	T3
PGA				CUT	CUT	T25	T3	T61	T53	T21	CUT	T34	T13
THE PLAYERS					CUT	T45	T68	T8	T10	T11	T17	T20	CUT
TOUR Championship						T17	T16	T6	T26		T26	T3	T2
WGC-Accenture Match Play											T33	T17	4
WGC-NEC Invitational											5	T12	T8
WGC-American Express Champ											T40	W/D	CNL

Year	02	03	04
Masters	T5	T6	2
U.S. Open	T24	T5	T9
British Open	1	T18	2
PGA	T34	T5	T4
THE PLAYERS	T44		T26
TOUR Championship	T13	17	T10
WGC-Accenture Match Play	T17	T33	
WGC-NEC Invitational	T15	T17	T65
WGC-American Express Champ	T23	T12	1

NATIONAL TEAMS: Dunhill Cup (9), 1992, 1993, 1994, 1995, 1996, 1997, 1998, 1999, 2000; World Cup (5), 1992, 1993, 1996, 1997, 2001; Presidents Cup (4), 1996, 1998, 2000, 2003.

Ernie Els (Continued)

Championship). First time in his career that he has finished in the top 10 in all four majors...Added his third win on the PGA TOUR and first in a World Golf Championship at the WGC-American Express Championship in Ireland. Led by two strokes after the second and third rounds and defeated Thomas Bjorn by a stroke after a final-round 69 to collect the $1.2 million check. Moved back into second, past Tiger Woods, in the Official World Golf Ranking...Two weeks later, won the HSBC World Match Play title on the European Tour for a record sixth time. On his 35th birthday, beat Lee Westwood 2 and 1 Sunday to capture $1.8 million...After T10 finish at THE TOUR Championship, dropped to No. 3 in Official World Golf Ranking behind Tiger Woods.

CAREER HIGHLIGHTS:

2003: Played 17 PGA TOUR and nine European Tour events. In addition to winning twice on the PGA TOUR in Hawaii and finishing ninth on the TOUR's money list, compiled four official European Tour wins (in Australia, Austria, Scotland) and won the European Tour Order of Merit. Also won his fifth career HSBC World Match Play Championship, a European Tour-approved special event. One of three players (along with Mike Weir and Kenny Perry) that posted three top-10s in majors. T6 at Masters, T5 at U.S. Open and T5 at PGA Championship...Became the first player since Steve Jones in 1989 to capture the first two tournaments of the season when he won the Mercedes Championships and Sony Open in Hawaii in early January. Only Byron Nelson (1946), Lloyd Mangrum (1953), Johnny Miller (1974, three events; and 1975), Gil Morgan (1983), Jones and Els have accomplished that among modern-day players...Captured season-opening Mercedes Championships in record fashion, finishing at 31-under-par 261. Total in relation to par broke Mark Calcavecchia's 72-hole tournament TOUR record of 28-under set at the 2001 Phoenix Open. Eight-stroke margin of victory over K.J. Choi and Rocco Mediate was largest on TOUR since Calcavecchia's eight-stroke Phoenix victory in 2001...Sank a 43-foot birdie putt on the 10th hole, the second playoff hole, to beat Aaron Baddeley at the Sony Open in Hawaii. Both players finished at 16-under-par after Baddeley birdied the 72nd hole...Played in homeland of South Africa at The Presidents Cup, competing for The International Team. **2002:** A year to remember with the birth of a son and third career major victory at the British Open...Won four official events worldwide, including twice on the PGA TOUR, solidifying No. 3 Official World Golf Ranking. Won the Heineken Classic in Melbourne, Australia on the European Tour by five strokes for his ninth European Tour victory...Collected first PGA TOUR victory since 2000 at the Genuity Championship. Rounds of 66-67-66 gave him an eight-stroke lead with 18 holes to play. Final-round 72 earned a two-stroke victory over Tiger Woods and a paycheck of $846,000...Won again the following week at the Dubai Desert Classic, becoming the first multiple winner in the tournament's 14-year history after posting all four rounds in the 60s...Earned third career major victory at the 131st British Open at Muirfield with scores of 70-66-72-70—278. Tied for the lead with Shigeki Maruyama, Padraig Harrington, Duffy Waldorf and Bob Tway after 36 holes at 6-under-par. Held 54-hole lead at 5-under-par, two strokes ahead of Soren Hansen. After losing a three-shot lead on the back nine on Sunday, Els survived a playoff with Thomas Levet, Steve Elkington and Stuart Appleby to earn the Claret Jug. After parring his way through the four-hole playoff, made a par out of the greenside bunker on the first hole of sudden death against Levet. With his right foot anchored on the top of a bunker left of the 18th green, blasted out to five feet and made the putt to secure the victory. **2001:** In a year full of streaks, didn't win for the first time since joining TOUR in 1994...Ranked in top 30 for seventh time in eight years with 1998 the only year he failed to qualify for THE TOUR Championship...His nine top-10s were second only to 10 in 2000...Best chance to win was a playoff loss at THE TOUR Championship. Closed with 68 to tie eventual winner Mike Weir, Sergio Garcia and David Toms at 14-under 270...Finished T6 at Masters Tournament, second consecutive year in top 10...Completed year in November by teaming with Retief Goosen to win World Cup in Japan. Els and Goosen beat three others teams, including Americans Tiger Woods and David Duval, in a playoff.. **2000:** Victory at The INTERNATIONAL extended to seven years his string of years with wins on PGA TOUR. Defeated Phil Mickelson by four points to earn his eighth TOUR title. 48 points, under Modified Stableford scoring system, tied tournament record Mickelson set in 1997...Also finished second five times, most since Jack Nicklaus and Arnold Palmer in 1964 (six). Record is 13 by Harold (Jug) McSpaden (1945). Began with playoff loss to Tiger Woods at Mercedes Championships and then had seconds at Masters, U.S. Open and British Open. First player to finish second in three consecutive majors in same season. Jack Nicklaus (1964) was previous player to have three majors' runners-up in same year. **1999:** Earned two-stroke victory over Ted Tryba, Tiger Woods and Davis Love III at Nissan Open. **1998:** Claimed sixth career TOUR victory at Bay Hill. Rains forced 36-hole finish Sunday and third-round 65 vaulted him to six-stroke lead while closing 73 good for four-stroke win...After T16 at Masters, ranked No.1 in world for several weeks...Member of victorious Presidents Cup team in 1998 with a 3-1-1 individual record. **1997:** Became first foreign player since Alex Smith (1906 and 1910) to win U.S. Open more than once with victory at Congressional CC. Trailed Tom Lehman by one stroke after 36 holes and by two after 54. Final-round 69, including decisive par on 71st hole, secured victory by one stroke over Colin Montgomerie...Successfully defended Buick Classic title the following week in wire-to-wire fashion. First repeat wire-to-wire winner since Tom Watson won Tournament of Champions in 1979-80. **1996:** Won Buick Classic for third TOUR title...Won third consecutive Toyota World Match Play Championship (1994-96)...Was 3-1-1 as member of International Team in Presidents Cup. **1995:** Earned second title at GTE Byron Nelson Classic on strength of second-round 61, a course record at Cottonwood Valley. His 263 total broke Sam Snead's 38-year-old tournament record...At PGA Championship at Riviera, equaled 36-hole tournament record with 131 and set 54-hole record with 197. Held three-stroke lead entering final round, but shot 72 to finish two strokes out of Steve Elkington-Colin Montgomerie playoff. **1994:** Victorious at U.S. Open in a playoff over Loren Roberts and Colin Montgomerie. Held two-stroke lead entering final round, but closed with a 73. Montgomerie eliminated from 18-hole playoff after 78. Els and Roberts each shot 74 and Els won with 4 on 20th hole. **1993:** Became first player to record four rounds in 60s at the British Open, finishing T6. **1992:** Won six events on Southern African Tour...Joined Gary Player that year as only players to win South African Open, South Africa PGA and South African Masters in same year. **Amateur:** Was a scratch golfer at age 14, when he won the world under-14 title at San Diego.

PERSONAL:

Started playing golf at age 9...An accomplished junior tennis player, turned full attention to golf at age 14...Heavily involved in junior golf of South Africa and Cancer Society of South Africa...Hosts Ernie Els Invitational in South Africa to raise money for charity. Ernie Els Foundation formed in early 1999, with the purpose of providing full support to disadvantaged children. Proceeds from the Ernie Els Invitational go to four charities and the Foundation...In December 1998, received lifetime membership on European Tour—other non-Europeans so honored are Bob Charles, Arnold Palmer and Gary Player...In 2002, the 2000 Engelbrecht-Els wine was released and received the highest rating yet given to a South African wine...Third Ernie Els design signature golf course near George in South Africa proved to be a great success in opening year...Web site is ernieels.com.

PLAYER STATISTICS

2004 PGA TOUR STATISTICS

Scoring Average	68.98	(2)
Driving Distance	298.0	(19)
Driving Accuracy Percentage	55.5%	(185)
Total Driving	204	(112)
Greens in Regulation Pct.	65.6%	(83)
Putting Average	1.740	(9)
Sand Save Percentage	47.9%	(113)
Eagles (Holes per)	149.1	(33)
Birdie Average	4.07	(4)
All-Around Ranking	448	(14)
Scoring Avg. Before Cut	69.57	(6)
Round 3 Scoring Avg.	69.43	(9)
Final Round Scoring Average	70.21	(13)
Birdie Conversion Percentage	33.3%	(2)
Par Breakers	23.3%	(4)

MISCELLANEOUS PGA TOUR STATISTICS

2004 Low Round/Round: 64–2 times, most recent WGC-American Express Championship/2

Career Low Round/Round: 61–1995 GTE Byron Nelson Golf Classic/2

Career Largest Paycheck/Finish: $1,200,000–2004 WGC–American Express Championship/1

SECTION 2 PLAYER BIOGRAPHIES

Bob Estes (ES-tis)

EXEMPT STATUS: 74th on the 2004 money list
FULL NAME: Bob Alan Estes
HEIGHT: 6-2
WEIGHT: 180
BIRTHDATE: February 2, 1966
BIRTHPLACE: Graham, TX
RESIDENCE: Austin, TX
FAMILY: Single

EDUCATION: University of Texas
SPECIAL INTERESTS: Music, hunting, physical fitness
TURNED PROFESSIONAL: 1988
Q SCHOOL: 1988

PGA TOUR VICTORIES (4):

1994 Texas Open. **2001** FedEx St. Jude Classic, Invensys Classic at Las Vegas. **2002** Kemper Insurance Open.

BEST 2004 PGA TOUR FINISH:

2—FedEx St. Jude Classic.

2004 SEASON:

Finished in the top-100 on the money list for the 13th time in his career, including each of the last eight years...Only top-10 of the season came in 13th start, a solo second at the FedEx St. Jude Classic where he won in 2001. Opened with a 3-over-par 74 but bounced back with three rounds in the 60s to finish six strokes behind David Toms. Unusual second-round 64 included a bogey on No. 10, a triple-bogey on No. 11, followed by seven consecutive birdies (Nos. 12-18) for a back-nine 32. Second-place finish was best since a T2 at the 2003 HP Classic of New Orleans...At the Michelin Championship at Las Vegas, a T11 finish pushed him over the $1-million mark in earnings in Las Vegas with his $88,000 payday. Ranks third on the tournament money list behind Jim Furyk and Stuart Appleby.

CAREER HIGHLIGHTS:

2003: Despite not winning for the first time since 2000, finished among the top 40 on the money list for the third straight season thanks to six top-10s...Trailed Ernie Els by three strokes after opening Mercedes Championships with rounds of 66-66 and finished T6...Narrowly missed fifth career PGA TOUR title at the HP Classic of New Orleans, losing in a sudden-death playoff to Steve Flesch. On the first extra hole, Flesch rolled in a birdie putt on the par-4 18th hole from 40 feet. Playoff record fell to 0-3 for TOUR career. **2002:** Earned fourth career TOUR victory and eight top-10s...Streak of 29 consecutive rounds at par or better was snapped at first round of Phoenix Open...Captured fourth career TOUR title (third in last 26 events) at the Kemper Insurance Open. Paycheck of $648,000 was second largest of career. Shared lead at 10-under-par with Bob Burns after 54 holes, and finished one stroke ahead of runner-up Rich Beem. Recorded 17 pars and one birdie in final-round 70. **2001:** Posted two victories and ended season with six consecutive top-10s to place career-high ninth on money list. The $2,795,477 in earnings was also a personal best...One of nine multiple winners on TOUR...Opened with 61 in the Fed Ex St. Jude Classic, a season low start by a winner on TOUR, and never trailed en route to winning by one stroke over Bernhard Langer. It was the season's only wire-to-wire victory...In contrast, never led after a round until winning the Invensys Classic at Las Vegas by one stroke over Tom Lehman. Was five shots off the pace after 72 holes and closed with a 63, which tied for low finish by winner on the year...Won the Fall Finish presented by PricewaterhouseCoopers with late-season rush and the $500,000 bonus money. Was TOUR Player of the Month for October-November. **2000:** Fell out of the top-30 on the PGA TOUR money list for the first time in two seasons. Recorded seven top-25s and three top-10s and was among the Top 100 on the money list. **1999:** Started the season on a positive note with a T4 at Bob Hope Chrysler Classic and by season's end missed only one cut in 28 starts. His nine top-10s were a career high and for third time in his career finished among top-30 on the TOUR money list. Combined with consistent 1998 season, had chance to make first U.S. Ryder Cup team. Needed to finish in the top five at the PGA Championship, but finished T6 and 11th in eligibility rankings, one shy of automatic selection...Posted T4 at Masters Tournament, best career finish in a major. **1998:** Put together seven top-10s that included a second and third. T2 at Bay Hill Invitational followed by solo third at Greater Greensboro Chrysler Classic. Shared 54-hole lead in Greensboro and at FedEx St. Jude Classic **1997:** Rebounded with $340,057 in earnings in 19 starts. His 25 consecutive rounds of par or better (from fourth round of Motorola Western Open through fourth round of CVS Charity Classic) was second-longest on TOUR for the year. Also that year, set a TOUR record in sand saves with 70.3 percent and was first in scrambling. **1996:** Lost fully exempt status after finishing 149th on money list. **1994:** Earned first PGA TOUR victory at Texas Open. Opened with course-record-tying 62 at Oak Hills CC, then cruised to wire-to-wire victory. **1993:** Held lead briefly during final round of 1993 PGA Championship before finishing T6...Was part of five-man playoff at Buick Southern Open, won by John Inman...In final full-field event, a T3 at Las Vegas Invitational, left him $1,135 out of top 30 and berth in TOUR Championship. **1989:** Came close to victory in rookie season when he lost playoff to Mike Hulbert at B.C. Open.

PERSONAL:

First played golf at age 4 and set sight on PGA TOUR at age 12...High school teammate of Mike Standly...Once worked for Charles Coody in bag room of Fairway Oaks Golf & Racquet Club...Serves as host for annual FCA Tom Landry Memorial Golf Tournament in Austin, TX...Works with personal trainer, former world-class pole vaulter Scott Hennig. Follows a strict routine that includes weightlifting, agility exercises, diet and short-distance sprints...Played basketball in high school...Has been a season ticket holder for University of Texas football since 1989.

PLAYER STATISTICS

2004 PGA TOUR STATISTICS

Scoring Average	70.79	(56)
Driving Distance	278.2	(170)
Driving Accuracy Percentage	63.9%	(102)
Total Driving	272	(181)
Greens in Regulation Pct.	64.2%	(115)
Putting Average	1.756	(36)
Sand Save Percentage	44.8%	(153)
Eagles (Holes per)	426.0	(169)
Birdie Average	3.52	(99)
All-Around Ranking	900	(133)
Scoring Avg. Before Cut	70.89	(81)
Round 3 Scoring Avg.	70.08	(35)
Final Round Scoring Average	70.15	(11)
Birdie Conversion Percentage	29.0%	(98)
Par Breakers	19.8%	(107)

MISCELLANEOUS PGA TOUR STATISTICS

2004 Low Round/Round: 64–FedEx St. Jude Classic/2
Career Low Round/Round: 61–2 times, most recent 2001 FedEx St. Jude Classic/1
Career Largest Paycheck/Finish: $810,000–2001 Invensys Classic at Las Vegas/1

PGA TOUR CAREER SUMMARY — PLAYOFF RECORD: 0-3

Year	Events Played	Cuts Made	1st	2nd	3rd	Top 10	Top 25	Earnings	Rank
1988	5	4						$5,968	237
1989	27	14		1		2	5	135,628	102
1990	28	18				4	9	212,090	69
1991	32	19				1	7	147,364	105
1992	28	18			1	2	4	190,778	80
1993	28	23		1	1	5	12	447,187	32
1994	27	23	1	1	1	8	17	765,360	14
1995	24	21				5	12	433,992	41
1996	26	7			1	1	2	123,100	149
1997	19	15			1	3	8	340,057	69
1998	29	23		1	1	7	14	987,930	28
1999	28	27				9	15	1,357,618	26
2000	21	12				3	7	538,706	88
2001	26	20	2	1	1	8	12	2,795,477	9
2002	26	20	1			8	14	1,934,600	26
2003	25	22		1	1	6	10	1,824,414	33
2004	23	14		1		1	7	1,046,064	74
Total	422	300	4	7	8	73	155	13,286,333	
NATIONWIDE TOUR									
1997	3	2				1	2	8,674	131
Total	3	2				1	2	8,674	

PGA TOUR TOP TOURNAMENT SUMMARY

Year	90	91	92	93	94	95	96	97	98	99	00	01	02
Masters					CUT	T29	T27			T4	T19		45
U.S. Open		CUT	T44	T52		CUT				T30	CUT	T30	CUT
British Open	CUT				T24	T8	CUT		T24	T49	T20	T25	T18
PGA	CUT		T76	T6	T47	T6	CUT		T34	T6	CUT	T37	CUT
THE PLAYERS	T70	CUT	T70	T20	T35	T34	CUT		T42	T62	CUT	CUT	T44
TOUR Championship					T15				28	25		T7	T11
WGC-Accenture Match Play										T33	T9	T33	T5
WGC-NEC Invitational													T19
WGC-American Express Champ										T11			T9

Year	03	04
Masters	22	T31
U.S. Open	CUT	CUT
British Open	T34	T20
PGA	T57	CUT
THE PLAYERS	31	CUT
WGC-Accenture Match Play	T33	T17
WGC-NEC Invitational	T46	
WGC-American Express Champ	T25	

Brad Faxon (FAX-un)

EXEMPT STATUS: 76th on 2004 money list
FULL NAME: Bradford John Faxon, Jr.
HEIGHT: 6-1
WEIGHT: 180
BIRTHDATE: August 1, 1961
BIRTHPLACE: Oceanport, NJ
RESIDENCE: Barrington, RI

FAMILY: Wife, Dory; Melanie (1/3/89), Emily (5/13/91), Sophie Lee (9/10/95), Charlotte Dorothea (1/18/02)
EDUCATION: Furman University (1983, Economics)
SPECIAL INTERESTS: All sports, golf course design, family
TURNED PROFESSIONAL: 1983
Q SCHOOL: Fall 1983

PGA TOUR VICTORIES (7):

1991 Buick Open. **1992** New England Classic, The International. **1997** Freeport-McDermott Classic. **1999** B.C. Open. **2000** B.C. Open. **2001** Sony Open in Hawaii.

INTERNATIONAL VICTORIES (1):

1993 Heineken Australian Open [Aus].

OTHER VICTORIES (10):

1986 Provident Classic. **1994** Franklin Templeton Shootout [with Fred Couples]. **1995** Fred Meyer Challenge [with Greg Norman]. **1996** Fred Meyer Challenge [with Greg Norman]. **1997** Fred Meyer Challenge [with Greg Norman]. **1999** Fred Meyer Challenge [with Billy Andrade]. **2001** Fred Meyer Challenge [with Billy Andrade], Franklin Templeton Shootout [with Scott McCarron]. **2002** Franklin Templeton Shootout [with Scott McCarron].

BEST 2004 PGA TOUR FINISHES:

8—The Honda Classic; T9—Deutsche Bank Championship.

2004 SEASON:

Slow start to the season due to an injury in the off-season. Missed the first month of the season rehabilitating a torn right anterior cruciate ligament without surgery. Made his first start at the AT&T Pebble Beach National Pro Am on February 5, where he missed the cut...First cut made for the season came in March (fourth stroke-play tournament) at The Honda Classic, finished T8...Active PLAYERS Championship consecutive cuts leader (1992-95; skipped 1996; 1997-2004) made the cut for his 12th straight year, tying Tom Kite and Bernhard Langer for the most consecutive cuts made all-time at the event. Finished T42...Made eighth consecutive cut of season at the Deutsche Bank Championship and posted first top-10 since March with a T9 thanks to closing rounds of 68...Had a stretch of 362 consecutive holes without a three-putt, the longest on TOUR in five years. Streak lasted 19 rounds, from PGA in August to Chrysler Classic of Greensboro in mid-October.

CAREER HIGHLIGHTS:

2003: Notched eight top-10s spread over seven months with career-best earnings of $2,718,445...Finished third at the Buick Invitational, fourth career top-10 at Torrey Pines. Tied with Marco Dawson for 36-hole lead at 10-under par after opening 70-64. One off Tiger Woods' lead after 54 holes...Added second top-three finish of the season with a T2 at the Bay Hill Invitational...Made three consecutive birdies on Nos. 13-15 in the final round to get into a playoff with Bob Tway at the Bell Canadian Open. Lost in a three-hole playoff...Earned third runner-up finish of the season, his most since 1997, with a second at the Chrysler Classic of Greensboro. Only player in field with four rounds in the 60s. **2002:** Despite not winning on TOUR for the first time since 1998, finished season 31st on TOUR money list with $1,814,672...Finished T2 at Nissan Open, one stroke behind winner Len Mattiace...Lost to eventual winner Kevin Sutherland in the semifinals of the World Golf Championships-Accenture Match Play Championship. Finished third after defeating Paul Azinger on the 19th hole in the consolation match...Picked up third consecutive top-three finish of the season at The Honda Classic with a T2, two strokes behind Matt Kuchar...Did not post another top 10 until season-ending Southern Farm Bureau Classic, a T5 in 54-hole, rain-shortened event. **2001:** Returned to the top 30 on money list (18th) for first time since 1997. Earned a victory for third consecutive year...Won Sony Open in Hawaii by four strokes. Made an eagle during each round. Had five-shot cushion after 36 holes and was three up going into the final round. Cruised to $720,000 paycheck, the largest of his career, with a closing 65. **2000:** Became the first player in B.C. Open history to successfully defend his title with a one-stroke victory over Esteban Toledo. Spent July 16-17 in Scotland, attempting to qualify for British Open. After failing, he caught a flight back to United States to play in B.C. Open. Started with a 68-66 and was T2 through 36 holes, trailing Toledo by three strokes. Third-round 68 lifted him into tie for 54-hole lead. Closed with a 68 for his seventh TOUR title. Won B.C. Open twice while age 38—in 1999 tournament held in the fall and in 2000 event played in summer...First top-10 of year came at Mercedes Championships, where he finished T8...Also T6 at Buick Open and Tampa Bay Classic...Earned his third putting title. Led the TOUR in Putting Average in 1996 and 1999 and in 2000 had a 1.704 average (new record). **1999:** Won B.C. Open in playoff over Fred Funk. Trailed Funk by five strokes through 36 holes, closed with 70-67 to force playoff. Due to Hurricane Floyd, final 36 holes played Sunday. Due to darkness, playoff held Monday morning when he won playoff with par on second extra hole...Won Fred Meyer Challenge with Billy Andrade. **1997:** Earned first victory since 1992 at Freeport-McDermott Classic. Gained one-stroke lead with third-round 66 and secured a three-stroke victory over Bill Glasson and Jesper Parnevik with final-round 69. Posted runner-up finishes at Greater Greensboro Chrysler Classic, MCI Classic and MasterCard Colonial and for second straight year finished among top-10 on TOUR money list...Teamed with Greg Norman to win Fred Meyer

PGA TOUR CAREER SUMMARY — PLAYOFF RECORD: 2-6

Year	Events Played	Cuts Made	1st	2nd	3rd	Top 10	Top 25	Earnings	Rank
1981A	1	1							
1983A	1	1							
1983	8	5				1	2	$16,526	160
1984	33	19			1	2	6	71,688	82
1985	31	15				1	6	46,813	124
1986	34	16				1	2	92,716	90
1987	28	19				2	10	113,534	90
1988	29	15			1	3	8	162,656	74
1989	28	20		2		2	5	222,076	63
1990	28	16			1	3	8	197,118	81
1991	28	23	1		1	4	11	422,088	34
1992	26	20	2	2		7	12	812,093	8
1993	25	20				4	11	312,023	55
1994	25	23			2	6	10	612,847	24
1995	25	19		1		5	8	471,887	37
1996	22	22		4		9	14	1,055,050	8
1997	23	17	1	3		6	10	1,233,505	10
1998	25	19				1	8	401,496	74
1999	21	15	1			1	7	582,691	68
2000	29	20	1			5	9	999,460	46
2001	26	21	1			6	12	1,951,412	18
2002	25	21		2	1	5	10	1,814,672	31
2003	27	22		3	1	8	15	2,718,445	11
2004	28	20				2	8	1,016,898	76
Total	576	409	7	17	8	84	192	15,327,693	

PGA TOUR TOP TOURNAMENT SUMMARY

Year	83	84	85	86	87	88	89	90	91	92	93	94	95
Masters										T31	T9	T15	T17
U.S. Open	T50		57			CUT	T33	66	CUT	CUT	T68	T33	T56
British Open			CUT			T11	T73				CUT	7	T15
PGA			CUT	CUT	CUT	CUT	CUT	CUT	T48	T15	T14	T30	5
THE PLAYERS		T33	CUT	CUT	CUT	CUT	T17	T70	CUT	T67	DQ	T6	T49
TOUR Championship										T7		T26	

Year	96	97	98	99	00	01	02	03	04
Masters	T25	CUT	T26	T24		T10	T12	T23	T31
U.S. Open	T82	T65	T49		CUT	CUT	T66	CUT	CUT
British Open	T32	T20	T11			T47	CUT	T46	T60
PGA	T17	CUT	T13	T61	T27	T59	T29	CUT	T13
THE PLAYERS		4	T35	T46	T77	T26	T36	T11	T42
TOUR Championship	2	T6				T26		T21	
WGC-Accenture Match Play				T33		T5	3	T17	T33
WGC-NEC Invitational							T63	T9	T32
WGC-American Express Champ						CNL	T49	T16	T13

NATIONAL TEAMS: Walker Cup, 1983; Ryder Cup (2), 1995, 1997; Dunhill Cup, 1997.

Brad Faxon (Continued)

Challenges. **1996:** Surpassed $1 million in earnings for first time on strength of four runner-up finishes. Made all 22 cuts...Lost playoff to Jim Furyk at United Airlines Hawaiian Open, finished three behind Steve Stricker at Kemper Open, lost playoff at Sprint International to Clarence Rose and closed with 68 for second at THE TOUR Championship. **1995:** Featured five top-10s and first selection to Ryder Cup Team...Shot front-nine 28 in final round of PGA Championship, the second 28 in major championship history (Denis Durnian, 1983 British Open). **1992:** Earned two PGA TOUR victories. Defeated Phil Mickelson by two strokes at New England Classic...14-point final round good for two-point victory over Lee Janzen at The INTERNATIONAL...Also lost two playoffs, to Steve Elkington at Infiniti Tournament of Champions and to Dan Forsman at Buick Open. **1991:** Defeated Chip Beck in playoff for first official TOUR win at Buick Open. **1986:** Earned unofficial victory at Provident Classic when he defeated Scott Hoch by one. **Amateur:** Winner 1983 Fred Haskins, Golf magazine and NCAA Coaches Awards as nation's outstanding golfer...1982-83 All-America selection at Furman...Winner of 1980-81 New England Amateurs and 1979-80 Rhode Island Amateurs.

PERSONAL:

Along with Billy Andrade, runs Billy Andrade/Brad Faxon Charities for Children, Inc., which was formed in 1991 and has donated more than $3 million to youngsters in Rhode Island and southeastern Massachusetts. Organization was honored in 1999 with Golf Writers Association of America's Charlie Bartlett Award, given to playing professionals for their unselfish contributions to society...Along with Andrade, serves as host for CVS Charity Classic...Created own junior golf foundation and hosts its annual tournament in Rhode Island. Co-Chair, with Andrade, of Button Hole, a short course that serves as a teaching and learning center for kids.

PLAYER STATISTICS

2004 PGA TOUR STATISTICS

Scoring Average	70.72	(48)
Driving Distance	273.7	(185)
Driving Accuracy Percentage	61.6%	(140)
Total Driving	325	(194)
Greens in Regulation Pct.	61.4%	(180)
Putting Average	1.749	(21)
Sand Save Percentage	52.9%	(43)
Eagles (Holes per)	320.4	(139)
Birdie Average	3.34	(140)
All-Around Ranking	896	(132)
Scoring Avg. Before Cut	71.11	(113)
Round 3 Scoring Avg.	72.00	(164)
Final Round Scoring Average	70.72	(39)
Birdie Conversion Percentage	29.2%	(91)
Par Breakers	18.9%	(143)

MISCELLANEOUS PGA TOUR STATISTICS

2004 Low Round/Round: 66–2 times, most recent Booz Allen Classic/2

Career Low Round/Round: 62–1986 Provident Classic/2

Career Largest Paycheck/Finish: $720,000–2001 Sony Open in Hawaii/1

SHOTLink
AN IBM ON DEMAND BUSINESS SOLUTION

HOT SHOTS

Statistical Keys to Victory in 2004

Note: Does not include WGC-Accenture Match Play Championship and The INTERNATIONAL.

PUTTING

35 winners didn't miss a putt from inside 3 feet the entire week
25 winners didn't miss a putt from inside 4 feet the entire week
Seven winners didn't miss a putt from inside 5 feet the entire week
11 winners led the field in putting from 8-9 feet
10 winners finished in the top 10 in putting from 4-8 feet
12 winners finished in the top 10 in putting from 10-15 feet
11 winners finished in the top 10 in putting from 15-20 feet
14 winners finished in the top 10 in putting from 20-25 feet
Eight winners finished in the top 10 in putting from over 25 feet
14 winners had no three-putts

AROUND THE GREEN

25 winners finished in the top 10 in scrambling
Eight winners led the field in scrambling from 10 – 20 yards
18 winners led the field in scrambling from 20 – 30 yards
Five winners led the field in scrambling from over 30 yards

APPROACH TO THE GREEN

25 winners finished in the top 10 in proximity to the hole
Nine winners led the field in proximity to the hole
Three winners finished in the top 10 in approaches inside 75 yards
Seven winners finished in the top 10 in approaches 75-100 yards
11 winners finished in the top 10 in approaches 100-125 yards
14 winners finished in the top 10 in approaches 125-150 yards
14 winners finished in the top 10 in approaches 150-175 yards
12 winners finished in the top 10 in approaches 175-200 yards
14 winners finished in the top 10 in approaches over 200 yards

Stewart Cink ranked high in the short game in his victories.

Todd Fischer

EXEMPT STATUS: 94th on 2004 money list
FULL NAME: Todd David Fischer
HEIGHT: 6-0
WEIGHT: 160
BIRTHDATE: August 23, 1969
BIRTHPLACE: Columbus, OH
RESIDENCE: Pleasanton, CA
FAMILY: Single

EDUCATION: University of San Francisco (1993, Exercise and Sports Science)
SPECIAL INTERESTS: Travel, all sports
TURNED PROFESSIONAL: 1993
JOINED TOUR: 2003
Nationwide Tour Alumunus

BEST PGA TOUR CAREER FINISH:

3—2003 Greater Hartford Open, T3—2004 B.C. Open, Valero Texas Open.

NATIONWIDE TOUR VICTORIES (1):

2002 Fort Smith Classic.

BEST 2004 PGA TOUR FINISHES:

T3—B.C. Open, Valero Texas Open; T8—Chrysler Classic of Tucson; T9—Buick Championship.

2004 SEASON:

Followed up his rookie season with a solid sophomore campaign, making $847,996 and posting a career-high four top-10s...Recorded four rounds in the 60s at the Omni Tucson National Golf Resort to finish T8 at the Chrysler Classic of Tucson, his first top-10 of the season and only the third of his career...Opened and closed with 65s at the B.C. Open to finish T3. The next week shared U.S. Bank Championship in Milwaukee first-round lead at 5-under 65 with seven others, tying a TOUR record for players sharing the lead through 18 holes (2000 Honda Classic) before finishing T18...Posted second consecutive top-10 at the Buick Championship. Closing 66 moved him into the top-10. Finished T9...Fourth top-10 was T3 at Valero Texas Open that featured four rounds in the 60s, including a third-round 63. Finished four strokes behind champion Bart Bryant.

CAREER HIGHLIGHTS:

2003: Made the cut in 15 of his 32 events during his rookie season...Finished a career-best third, three strokes behind Peter Jacobsen, at the Greater Hartford Open, thanks to four rounds in the 60s. **2002:** Finished seventh on the Nationwide Tour money list with $234,777 and had seven top-10s to earn his first PGA TOUR card. Named Nationwide Tour Player of the Month for July after winning the Fort Smith Classic. In only his fourth PGA TOUR event of his career and sole 2002 start, posted T15 at the AT&T Pebble Beach National Pro-Am for his first career made cut. **2001:** Finished 33rd on the Nationwide Tour money list. Earned his way through Monday Qualifying, top-25 finishes and sponsor exemptions. Made the cut in 11 of 12 events and posted four top-10s. **2000:** Qualified for the U.S. Open at Pebble Beach. Forced to stop play due to weather after six holes during the second round, returned to the course on Saturday morning and aced the par-3 seventh hole on his first swing. Bogeyed the 18th hole to miss the cut by one shot. **Amateur:** Four-time All-West Coast Conference selection at University of San Francisco. Second-Team All-American in 1992. Won the 1992 Western Intercollegiate championship and the Pacific Coast Amateur Championship...Won the 1991 West Coast Conference Individual title.

PERSONAL:

Lists his father David as his hero...Father introduced him to golf at age 7...Basically a self-taught player...Has had three competitive career holes-in-one...Says his biggest thrill in golf is walking between the ropes and being a professional golfer.

PLAYER STATISTICS

2004 PGA TOUR STATISTICS

Scoring Average	71.16	(102)
Driving Distance	280.1	(157)
Driving Accuracy Percentage	61.7%	(136)
Total Driving	293	(189)
Greens in Regulation Pct.	63.9%	(122)
Putting Average	1.769	(70)
Sand Save Percentage	46.7%	(131)
Eagles (Holes per)	262.3	(110)
Birdie Average	3.49	(105)
All-Around Ranking	933	(144)
Scoring Avg. Before Cut	71.07	(105)
Round 3 Scoring Avg.	70.42	(54)
Final Round Scoring Average	71.00	(53)
Birdie Conversion Percentage	28.6%	(107)
Par Breakers	19.8%	(107)

MISCELLANEOUS PGA TOUR STATISTICS

2004 Low Round/Round: 63–2 times, most recent Valero Texas Open/3
Career Low Round/Round: 63–2 times, most recent 2004 Valero Texas Open/3
Career Largest Paycheck/Finish: $272,000–2003 Greater Hartford Open/3

PGA TOUR CAREER SUMMARY — PLAYOFF RECORD: 0-0

Year	Events Played	Cuts Made	1st	2nd	3rd	Top 10	Top 25	Earnings	Rank
1995	1								
2000	1								
2001	1								
2002	1	1					1	$60,000	
2003	32	15			1	2	4	621,398	102
2004	33	18			2	4	7	847,996	94
Total	69	34			3	6	12	1,529,395	
NATIONWIDE TOUR									
1998	1	1						1,499	217
1999	1								
2000	3								
2001	12	11		1		4	5	118,622	33
2002	26	18	1	1		7	10	234,777	7
Total	43	30	1	2		11	15	354,898	

PGA TOUR TOP TOURNAMENT SUMMARY

Year	00	01	02	03	04
U.S. Open	CUT	CUT			
THE PLAYERS					CUT

Steve Flesch

EXEMPT STATUS: 2004 tournament winner (through 2006)
FULL NAME: Stephen J. Flesch
HEIGHT: 5-11
WEIGHT: 155
BIRTHDATE: May 23, 1967
BIRTHPLACE: Cincinnati, OH
RESIDENCE: Union, KY; plays out of Triple Crown CC

FAMILY: Wife, Lisa; Griffin McCarty (10/6/98), Lily Katelin (12/20/01)
EDUCATION: University of Kentucky
SPECIAL INTERESTS: Skiing, movies
TURNED PROFESSIONAL: 1990
JOINED TOUR: 1998
Nationwide Tour Alumnus

PGA TOUR VICTORIES (2):

2003 HP Classic of New Orleans. **2004** Bank of America Colonial.

NATIONWIDE TOUR VICTORIES (1):

1997 TOUR Championship.

INTERNATIONAL VICTORIES (1):

1996 Benson & Hedges Malaysian Open [Asia].

BEST 2004 PGA TOUR FINISHES:

1—Bank of America Colonial; T3—FBR Open; T5—Wachovia Championship; T7—U.S. Open Championship.

2004 SEASON:

Surpassed $2 million in earnings and won for the second consecutive season…Has finished in the top 75 on the money list in each of his seven years on TOUR. His No. 18 finish on the money list was second best in his career behind the No. 13 finish in 2000…Earned second career PGA TOUR win at the Bank of America Colonial in May on his 37th birthday, defeating Chad Campbell by a stroke. Shared third-round lead with Campbell and Brian Gay. Turned third-round lead into victory for first time in six tries. Only player in field to post four rounds in the 60s. Win moved him to ninth on the money list and career-best 24th in the world. Surpassed $1-million mark in earnings for fifth consecutive season and moved into the top 50 on TOUR's career money list, with almost $10 million in earnings…Picked up the sixth top-three finish of his career with a T3 at the FBR Open. One of three left-handers to finish in the top 10 along with Mike Weir (T5) and Phil Mickelson (T7)…Was paired with two left-handers, Russ Cochran and Greg Chalmers, in the final round of the HP Classic of New Orleans…Finished T5 with Mickelson at the Wachovia Championship after firing rounds of 66-69 on the weekend in Charlotte…Named Player of the Month in May for his two top-five finishes during the month…Collected first top-10 in a major (19 appearances) with his T7 at the U.S. Open…Made his third trip to THE TOUR Championship and finished T21.

CAREER HIGHLIGHTS:

2003: Earned a then-career-high $2,269,630 thanks to nine top-10s...Sank a 35-footer for birdie on the first extra hole of a playoff at the HP Classic of New Orleans to defeat Bob Estes and earn his first career victory in his 174th start on the PGA TOUR. Became the seventh left-hander to win on the PGA TOUR and the second of the season, joining Mike Weir. Win came after finishing second in New Orleans in 1998 and 1999...A 10-under-par 62 in the first round at Southern Highlands during the Las Vegas Invitational was career low on the PGA TOUR. **2002:** Posted T4 at the Bell Canadian Open, one stroke out of a three-way playoff (champion John Rollins, Neal Lancaster and Justin Leonard), one of seven top-10s during the season. **2001:** Finished in the top 50 on the money list for third time in four years as a member thanks to six top-10s. At the National Car Rental Golf Classic at Walt Disney World Resort, opened with a 73 to sit T110. Closed 65-66-65 for T5, his best finish of the season. **2000:** Ranked second behind Tiger Woods in top-10s during the season with 13...Best opportunity for victory came at National Car Rental Golf Classic at Walt Disney World. Had two-stroke lead over Woods going into final round. He and Woods shot final-round 69s but Duffy Waldorf fired 62 to take victory. Marked second career solo second for Flesch. **1999:** Season interrupted when he fractured right forearm falling down stairs after leaving Tucson. Made first start since injury at THE PLAYERS Championship and went on to post three top-10s...Held 54-hole lead at Compaq Classic of New Orleans before finishing second, two strokes behind Carlos Franco. **1998:** Voted PGA TOUR Rookie of the Year by his peers. First left-hander to receive honor, keyed by seven consecutive top-25s in the spring, including a second and a third. **1997:** Won Nationwide Tour Championship to vault from 24th to fourth place on money list and earn exempt status on PGA TOUR in 1998. **1996:** Finished top-10 on Asian Tour Order of Merit for the third time in his career; others came in 1993-94...Won Benson & Hedges Malaysian Open to earn spot in Sarazen World Open, where he T9 and earned $47,000. **1993:** Winner of the Kentucky Open for second time in career; other came in 1991.

PERSONAL:

Began game right-handed before switching over to natural left side…One of two left-handers (Vic Wilk the other) to win on Nationwide Tour…Die-hard Cincinnati Reds fan and Kentucky Wildcats basketball fan…Has workshop in his basement where he works on his own clubs…Interested in getting involved in golf course design.

PLAYER STATISTICS

2004 PGA TOUR STATISTICS

Scoring Average	70.85	(64)
Driving Distance	279.9	(161)
Driving Accuracy Percentage	65.8%	(68)
Total Driving	229	(150)
Greens in Regulation Pct.	65.8%	(78)
Putting Average	1.763	(52)
Sand Save Percentage	49.0%	(98)
Eagles (Holes per)	171.8	(53)
Birdie Average	3.69	(60)
All-Around Ranking	634	(57)
Scoring Avg. Before Cut	70.85	(76)
Round 3 Scoring Avg.	70.33	(49)
Final Round Scoring Average	71.78	(115)
Birdie Conversion Percentage	30.3%	(58)
Par Breakers	21.1%	(53)

MISCELLANEOUS PGA TOUR STATISTICS

2004 Low Round/Round: 63–Bob Hope Chrysler Classic/3
Career Low Round/Round: 62–2003 Las Vegas Invitational/1
Career Largest Paycheck/Finish: $954,000–2004 Bank of America Colonial/1

PGA TOUR CAREER SUMMARY — PLAYOFF RECORD: 1-0

Year	Events Played	Cuts Made	1st	2nd	3rd	Top 10	Top 25	Earnings	Rank
1993	2	2						$6,786	252
1994	1								
1996	1								
1998	29	23		1	1	5	14	777,186	35
1999	31	20		1		3	6	552,346	75
2000	32	29		1		13	21	2,025,781	13
2001	32	24				6	14	1,207,552	44
2002	32	22				7	11	1,192,341	52
2003	33	21	1			9	12	2,269,630	21
2004	31	24	1		1	4	11	2,461,787	18
Total	224	165	2	3	2	47	89	10,493,408	
NATIONWIDE TOUR									
1990	1	1					1	1,400	182
1991	2	1						570	297
1994	1	1						360	292
1997	27	19	1	1		9	14	133,190	4
1998	1	1		1		1	1	34,050	63
Total	32	23	1	2		10	16	169,570	
EUROPEAN TOUR									
2004	1	1				1	1	75,945	

PGA TOUR TOP TOURNAMENT SUMMARY

Year	93	94	95	96	97	98	99	00	01	02	03	04
Masters									CUT			T17
U.S. Open	84	CUT		CUT			CUT		CUT	T18	CUT	T7
British Open								T20	CUT		CUT	T54
PGA						T13	T34	CUT	T13	T17	CUT	T37
THE PLAYERS							CUT	T38	T40	CUT	T39	CUT
TOUR Championship								15			T9	T21
WGC-Accenture Match Play									T33	T9		T17
WGC-NEC Invitational											T11	T48
WGC-American Express Champ								T11			T21	T23

Raymond Floyd

WORLD GOLF HALL OF FAME MEMBER (Inducted 1989)
EXEMPT STATUS: Winner, 1969 PGA Championship (Lifetime)
FULL NAME: Raymond Loran Floyd
HEIGHT: 6-1
WEIGHT: 200
BIRTHDATE: September 4, 1942
BIRTHPLACE: Fort Bragg, NC
RESIDENCE: Palm Beach, FL
FAMILY: Wife, Maria; Raymond, Jr. (9/20/74), Robert Loran (1/23/76), Christina Loran (8/29/79)
EDUCATION: University of North Carolina
SPECIAL INTERESTS: Sports, golf course design
TURNED PROFESSIONAL: 1961
JOINED TOUR: 1963

PGA TOUR VICTORIES (22):

1963 St. Petersburg Open Invitational. **1965** St. Paul Open Invitational. **1969** Greater Jacksonville Open, American Golf Classic, PGA Championship. **1975** Kemper Open. **1976** Masters Tournament, World Open Golf Championship. **1977** Byron Nelson Golf Classic, Pleasant Valley Classic. **1979** Greater Greensboro Open. **1980** Doral-Eastern Open. **1981** Doral-Eastern Open, Tournament Players Championship, Manufacturers Hanover Westchester Classic. **1982** Memorial Tournament, Danny Thomas Memphis Classic, PGA Championship. **1985** Houston Open. **1986** U.S. Open Championship, Walt Disney World/Oldsmobile Classic. **1992** Doral-Ryder Open.

CHAMPIONS TOUR VICTORIES (14):

1992 GTE North Classic, Ralphs Senior Classic, SENIOR TOUR Championship. **1993** Gulfstream Aerospace Invitational, Northville Long Island Classic. **1994** The Tradition, Las Vegas Senior Classic, Cadillac NFL Golf Classic, GOLF MAGAZINE SENIOR TOUR Championship.

PGA TOUR CAREER SUMMARY — PLAYOFF RECORD: 5-10

Year	Events Played	Cuts Made	1st	2nd	3rd	Top 10	Top 25	Earnings	Rank
1963	17	17	1	1		3	5	$10,529	
1964	21	21			2	4	11	21,407	30
1965	19	19	1			3	9	36,692	25
1966	19	19		1	1	6	11	29,713	33
1967	23	23			1	3	9	25,254	
1968	20	20		1	2	6	14	56,490	
1969	25	20	3			6	9	104,814	6
1970	23	17			1	3	11	43,591	45
1971	28	19		1		4	10	49,846	45
1972	24	18				4	7	32,579	71
1973	24	19		1		2	7	38,751	75
1974	26	22		3	1	8	14	116,385	17
1975	25	20	1	1		5	12	103,628	13
1976	23	21	2	1	1	9	16	178,318	7
1977	24	23	2			8	15	163,261	7
1978	26	20		1		4	14	77,595	30
1979	26	19	1			6	10	122,872	26
1980	27	24	1	1		9	15	192,993	10
1981	23	23	3	2		14	18	359,360	2
1982	23	18	3	3		9	16	386,809	2
1983	22	22		1		8	18	208,353	20
1984	23	18				2	8	102,813	68
1985	22	20	1	2	1	9	15	378,989	5
1986	23	19	2	1		5	15	380,508	9
1987	20	12				2	9	122,880	86
1988	19	16				3	8	169,549	69
1989	17	13				1	2	74,699	145
1990	17	11		1	1	3	6	264,078	55
1991	17	15			1	5	10	284,897	56
1992	15	15	1	2	1	5	11	741,918	13
1993	6	5				2	4	126,516	120
1994	4	4				1	3	95,017	158
1995	4	4					2	65,031	180
1996	2	2				1	2	67,800	184
1997	3	2						7,811	284
1998	2	1					1	31,000	229
1999	2	2						22,480	253
2000	3								
2001	2								
2002	2								
2003	1								
2004	2								
Total	694	583	22	24	13	163	347	5,323,075	

CHAMPIONS TOUR CAREER SUMMARY — PLAYOFF RECORD: 3-1

Year	Events Played	1st	2nd	3rd	Top 10	Top 25	Earnings	Rank
1992	7	3	1		6	6	$436,991	14
1993	14	2	4	2	12	14	713,168	9
1994	20	4	5	2	17	20	1,382,762	2
1995	21	3	7	1	19	21	1,419,545	2
1996	23	1		4	16	20	1,043,051	8
1997	20			3	10	16	584,755	23
1998	21		1	1	10	18	702,472	19
1999	19		2	1	9	15	683,314	27
2000	17	1			6	9	717,258	26
2001	14		2		5	9	546,190	34
2002	11					7	205,718	70
2003	11				2	5	201,675	66
2004	11				2	2	169,679	69
Total	209	14	22	14	114	162	8,806,576	

PGA TOUR TOP TOURNAMENT SUMMARY

Year	63	64	65	66	67	68	69	70	71	72	73	74	75
Masters				T8		T7	T35	CUT	T13	CUT	54	T22	T30
U.S. Open		T14	T6		T38		T13	T22	8	CUT	16	T15	T12
British Open							T34	CUT					T23
PGA	T57		T17	T18	T20	T41	1	T8	CUT	T4	T35	T11	T10
THE PLAYERS												T24	T21

Year	76	77	78	79	80	81	82	83	84	85	86	87	88
Masters	1	T8	T16	T17	T17	T8	T7	T4	T15	T2	CUT	CUT	T11
U.S. Open	13	T47	T12	CUT	T45	T37	T49	T13	T52	T23	1	T43	T17
British Open	4	8	T2	T36		T3	T15	T14	CUT		T16	T17	CUT
PGA	T2	T40	T50	T62	T17	T19	1	T20	13	CUT	CUT	T14	T9
THE PLAYERS	T12	T13	CUT	T14	CUT	1	T22	T23	T12	T33	T21	CUT	DQ

Year	89	90	91	92	93	94	95	96	97	98	99	00	01
Masters	T38	2	T17	2	T11	T10	T17	T25	CUT	CUT	T38	CUT	CUT
U.S. Open	T26	CUT	T8	T44	T7		T36						
British Open	T42	T39	CUT	T12	T34		T58						
PGA	T46	T49	T7	T48	CUT	T61							
THE PLAYERS	CUT	CUT											
TOUR Championship				T5									

Year	02	03	04
Masters	CUT	CUT	CUT
U.S. Open			CUT

CHAMPIONS TOUR TOP TOURNAMENT SUMMARY

Year	92	93	94	95	96	97	98	99	00	01	02	03	04
Senior PGA Championship		T13	T3	1	19	T35	15	T24	T51	T40	T15	T17	T10
U.S. Senior Open		T7	12	T8	3	T44	3	T11	4	T16	T21	T19	CUT
Ford Senior Players Championship		2	T3	T10	1	T19	T19	T9	1	T6	T17		
JELD-WEN Tradition		T3	1	T6	3	T19	5	T20	W/D	T16	T21		
Charles Schwab Cup Champ	1	T2	1	2	T14	T9	T11	8	T14				

Raymond Floyd (Continued)

1995 PGA Seniors' Championship, Burnet Senior Classic, Emerald Coast Classic. **1996** FORD SENIOR PLAYERS Championship. **2000** FORD SENIOR PLAYERS Championship.

INTERNATIONAL VICTORIES (4):

1978 Brazilian Open. **1979** Costa Rica Open. **1981** Canadian PGA [Can]. **1992** Fuji Electric Grand Slam [Jpn].

OTHER VICTORIES (11):

1985 Chrysler Team Championship. **1988** Skins Game. **1990** Franklin Templeton Shootout [with Fred Couples]. **1993** Franklin Templeton Shootout [with Steve Elkington]. **1990** RMCC Invitational. **1994** Diners Club Matches [with Dave Eichelberger]. **1995** Office Depot Father-Son Challenge [with Raymond Jr.]. **1996** Office Depot Father-Son Challenge [with Raymond Jr.]. **1997** Office Depot Father-Son Challenge [with Raymond Jr.]. **2000** Office Depot Father-Son Challenge [with Robert]. **2001** Office Depot Father-Son Challenge [with Robert].

BEST 2004 CHAMPIONS TOUR FINISHES:

T4—Allianz Championship; T10—Senior PGA Championship

2004 SEASON:

Missed the cut in two PGA TOUR starts at the Masters and U.S. Open. . .Limited his schedule on the Champions Tour to just 12 events, with best finishes being a T4 at the Allianz Championship and T10 at Senior PGA. . .Second to Mike Hill in the season-ending Georgia-Pacific Grand Champions Championship.

CAREER HIGHLIGHTS:

2003: Missed cut at the Masters, his only TOUR event of the season...Posted a pair of T9s on the Champions Tour and finished T2 at the Georgia-Pacific Grand Champions Championship...Underwent successful prostate cancer surgery at Johns Hopkins Medical Center in late December 2002. **2002:** Missed cuts at the Masters and Western Open but recorded a pair of 72s at the Chicago event...Finished 70th on the Champions Tour money list with seven top-25s. **2001:** Did not make cut for second consecutive year...Made 14 starts on Champions Tour and finished No. 34 on the money list, his lowest finish since turning 50 in 1992. **2000:** Captured his fourth Champions Tour major at the Ford Senior Players Championship. **1992:** Collected most recent PGA TOUR victory at the Doral-Ryder Open, which he won at age 49. After turning 50 later that year, captured GTE North Classic on Champions Tour, becoming first to win on both Tours in same year...He and Sam Snead are only players in PGA TOUR history to win in four decades. **1989:** Ryder Cup Captain, culmination of Ryder Cup career that included eight Ryder Cup teams...Inducted into World Golf Hall of Fame. **1986:** Shot closing 66 to win U.S. Open at Shinnecock Hills by two over Chip Beck and Lanny Wadkins. **1983:** Won Vardon Trophy. **1982:** Defeated Lanny Wadkins by three strokes at PGA Championship. **1981:** Won Tournament Players Championship in playoff over Barry Jaeckel and Curtis Strange, the year before the tournament moved to the TPC at Sawgrass. **1976:** Wire-to-wire winner of the Masters. **1969:** Won PGA by one stroke over Gary Player.

PERSONAL:

His family was named by Golfweek as the 1994 "Golf Family of the Year." Also selected Golf World's "Man of the Year" for 1992. . .The son of a career Army man, he was exposed to golf at an early age but chose to pursue baseball until capturing the National Jaycees golf title in 1960. . .Remains a devoted Chicago Cubs fan. . .Has two sons. Raymond, Jr., a Wake Forest graduate, works at the investment firm Weeden Capital in Greenwich, CT, and Robert is pursuing a pro golf career. Daughter Christina, a Wake Forest graduate, works for Sotheby's in New York City.

PLAYER STATISTICS

2004 PGA TOUR STATISTICS

Scoring Average	71.91	(N/A)
Driving Distance	272.4	(N/A)
Driving Accuracy Percentage	64.3%	(N/A)
Total Driving	(N/A)	(N/A)
Greens in Regulation Pct.	52.8%	(N/A)
Putting Average	1.974	(N/A)
Sand Save Percentage	20.0%	(N/A)
Birdie Average	1.75	(N/A)
Scoring Avg. Before Cut	74.75	(N/A)
Birdie Conversion Percentage	13.2%	(N/A)
Par Breakers	9.7%	(N/A)

MISCELLANEOUS PGA TOUR STATISTICS

2004 Low Round/Round: 73–Masters Tournament/1
Career Low Round/Round: 63–2 times, most recent 1992 MCI Heritage Golf Classic/2
Career Largest Paycheck/Finish: $252,000–1992 Doral–Ryder Open/1

2004 CHAMPIONS TOUR STATISTICS

Scoring Average	72.15	(N/A)
Driving Distance	272.8	(N/A)
Driving Accuracy Percentage	71.2%	(N/A)
Total Driving	(N/A)	(N/A)
Greens in Regulation Pct.	68.9%	(N/A)
Putting Average	1.841	(N/A)
Sand Save Percentage	56.8%	(N/A)
Eagles (Holes per)	297.0	(N/A)
Birdie Average	2.91	(N/A)
All-Around Ranking	1,569	(N/A)

MISCELLANEOUS CHAMPIONS TOUR STATISTICS

2004 Low Round: 66–Allianz Championship/3.
Career Low Round: 62–1992 Ralphs Senior Classic/3
Career Largest Paycheck: $345,000–2000 FORD SENIOR PLAYERS Championship/1

SHOTLink
AN IBM ON DEMAND BUSINESS SOLUTION

HOT SHOTS

Pebble Beach Golf Links

18th Hole-Pebble Beach Golf Links

18th Hole, Par 5, 543 Yards

The par-5 18th hole at Pebble Beach Golf Links is one of the most famous holes in all of golf. In 2004, here were vital statistics on the final hole at the AT&T Pebble Beach National Pro-Am:

- The average drive was only 251.2 yards
- 49 players went for the green in two with only five successfully reaching
- The closest to the hole in two shots for the week was Dennis Paulson, at 14 feet, 10 inches in the final round. He two-putted for birdie.
- Only 14 of 40 putts from 4-8 feet were made (35 percent). The 2004 PGA TOUR average from 4-8 feet was 68.8 percent.

Carlos Franco

EXEMPT STATUS: 2004 tournament winner (through 2006)
FULL NAME: Carlos Daniel Franco
HEIGHT: 5-9
WEIGHT: 165
BIRTHDATE: May 24, 1965
BIRTHPLACE: Asuncion, Paraguay
RESIDENCE: Asuncion, Paraguay

FAMILY: Wife, Celsa; Carlos, Alcides, Jessenia Catalina
SPECIAL INTERESTS: Charity, fishing
TURNED PROFESSIONAL: 1986
Q SCHOOL: 1998

PGA TOUR VICTORIES (4):

1999 COMPAQ Classic of New Orleans, Greater Milwaukee Open. **2000** COMPAQ Classic of New Orleans. **2004** U.S. Bank Championship in Milwaukee.

INTERNATIONAL VICTORIES (27):

1994 Jun Classic [Jpn]. **1995** Sapporo Tokyo Open [Jpn]. **1996** ANA Open [Jpn]. **1998** Just System KSB Open [Jpn], Fuji Sankei Classic [Jpn]. **1999** Philippines Open. [Also won 21 times in South America].

BEST 2004 PGA TOUR FINISHES:

1—U.S. Bank Championship in Milwaukee; T3—Wachovia Championship, Buick Open; T8—Chrysler Classic of Tucson.

2004 SEASON:

Returned to the winner's circle with victory at the U.S. Bank Championship in Milwaukee, and earned a spot in the season-ending TOUR Championship for the first time since 2000...Grabbed the first-round lead at the Sony Open in Hawaii with a 7-under-par 63, finished T20...Finished T8 at the Chrysler Classic of Tucson. Second top-10 was T3 at the Wachovia Championship, one shot out of Joey Sindelar-Aaron Oberholser playoff...Won for the first time in more than four years at the U.S. Bank Championship in Milwaukee. Became the seventh player in tournament history to win the event twice, having won it first in 1999. One of two players to record four rounds in the 60s, which he did in 1999 as well. Held second-round lead by a stroke and shared third-round lead with Brett Quigley and Patrick Sheehan before defeating Fred Funk and Quigley by two strokes. Was one back of the lead through 54 holes and posted 2-under-par 70 for his first top-10 of the season...Finished T3 at the Buick Open, two shots behind champion Vijay Singh. Posted four rounds in the 60s for the second consecutive week.

CAREER HIGHLIGHTS:

2003: Finished in the top 125 on the money list for the fifth consecutive season...Made nine straight cuts beginning with his lone top-10 at the Chrysler Classic of Tucson...Led the TOUR in eagles with 22...Represented Paraguay in the World Cup for the second time in his career (1992). **2002:** Late rally to jump from 131st to 102nd on money list in final five events. Push aided by top-10s in two of final three events, only top-10s of the season. **2001:** Didn't win or post a top-10 for the first time since joining the TOUR in 1999...Ranked 104th in money with $486,665, both career lows. **2000:** In defense of first PGA TOUR title, at the Compaq Classic of New Orleans, shared second- and third-round leads with Blaine McCallister, then both closed with 68. Won playoff with three-foot par putt on second extra hole. Became first TOUR player to successfully defend since Jim Furyk won 1998-99 Las Vegas Invitationals. New Orleans victory gave him three victories in 12 months, exceeded at that time only by Tiger Woods...First player in TOUR history to earn more than $1 million in each of first two years ($1,864,584 in 1999)...A member of International Team at Presidents Cup, defeating Hal Sutton in singles and teaming with Shigeki Maruyama in four-ball to beat Tiger Woods and Notah Begay III. **1999:** Selected PGA TOUR Rookie of the Year by his peers...Invited to Masters for first time and was three strokes out of the lead through 54 holes. Final-round 73 good for T6 and another invitation for 2000. Following performance, Paraguay threw a parade for him...In his next appearance, won Compaq Classic of New Orleans. Rounds of 66-69-68 had him two strokes off 54-hole lead. Closing 66 produced two-stroke victory over Steve Flesch and Harrison Frazar, worth $468,000. Also became first South American to win on TOUR since Roberto De Vicenzo in Houston in 1968...Earned second victory of rookie season at Greater Milwaukee Open with two-stroke victory over Tom Lehman and set another tournament record. Became only the eighth rookie to win twice since 1960. With victory became first rookie to surpass $1 million in a season and moved to seventh on money list. First player since Greg Norman in 1989 to win GMO on first try. **1998:** Member of the victorious International team at Presidents Cup. Halved with Phil Mickelson in singles...Gained exempt status on PGA TOUR in fall of 1998 by finishing 36th at TOUR Qualifying Tournament. **1997:** Finished sixth at 1997 World Series of Golf at Firestone in third event ever on PGA TOUR. **1993:** Made first big impact outside South America with victory over Sam Torrance at Dunhill Cup when Paraguay defeated host Scotland on opening day.

PERSONAL:

Grew up in poverty in Paraguay. Family of nine shared a one-room, dirt-floor home...Father was a greens superintendent and caddie at course in Asuncion...All five of his brothers became golf professionals. Brother Angel won the 1993 Dominion Open on Nationwide Tour...Appointed Minister De Deportes (Minister of Sports) in 1999...Has raised more than $700,000 for needy patients at hospitals in Asuncion, including victims from the Aug. 1, 2004 fire that claimed nearly 500 lives.

PLAYER STATISTICS

2004 PGA TOUR STATISTICS

Scoring Average	70.77	(52)
Driving Distance	290.6	(69)
Driving Accuracy Percentage	59.3%	(158)
Total Driving	227	(145)
Greens in Regulation Pct.	68.5%	(20)
Putting Average	1.798	(157)
Sand Save Percentage	47.1%	(124)
Eagles (Holes per)	178.2	(60)
Birdie Average	3.61	(76)
All-Around Ranking	716	(86)
Scoring Avg. Before Cut	70.06	(14)
Round 3 Scoring Avg.	70.92	(93)
Final Round Scoring Average	71.13	(67)
Birdie Conversion Percentage	28.4%	(112)
Par Breakers	20.6%	(70)

MISCELLANEOUS PGA TOUR STATISTICS

2004 Low Round/Round: 63–2 times, most recent U.S. Bank Championship in Milwaukee/2
Career Low Round/Round: 63–2 times, most recent 2004 U.S. Bank Championship in Milwaukee/2
Career Largest Paycheck/Finish: $630,000–2004 U.S. Bank Championship in Milwaukee/1

PGA TOUR CAREER SUMMARY — PLAYOFF RECORD: 1-0

Year	Events Played	Cuts Made	1st	2nd	3rd	Top 10	Top 25	Earnings	Rank
1994	1								
1997	2	2				1	1	$74,950	181
1998	2	2						21,079	242
1999	22	15	2		3	7	10	1,864,584	11
2000	24	20	1			6	11	1,550,592	30
2001	27	17					8	486,665	104
2002	31	22				2	8	652,147	102
2003	30	19				1	7	672,022	94
2004	27	23	1		2	4	10	1,955,395	29
Total	166	120	4		5	21	55	7,277,434	

PGA TOUR TOP TOURNAMENT SUMMARY

Year	94	95	96	97	98	99	00	01	02	03	04
Masters						T6	T7	46			
U.S. Open						T34	T61	CUT			W/D
British Open	CUT				T64	CUT	CUT	T54			
PGA				70	T40	T26	T58	T29		T18	T31
THE PLAYERS						CUT	T27	CUT	T22	T48	T58
TOUR Championship						T15	24				T24
WGC-Accenture Match Play						T17	T33				
WGC-NEC Invitational						T7	T27	20	T42		T58
WGC-American Express Champ						T48	T45				T28

NATIONAL TEAMS: World Cup (3), 1992, 2000, 2003; The Presidents Cup (2) 1998, 2000.

SECTION 2 PLAYER BIOGRAPHIES

Harrison Frazar (FRAY-zur)

EXEMPT STATUS: 48th on 2004 money list
FULL NAME: Harrison Frazar
HEIGHT: 6-0
WEIGHT: 190
BIRTHDATE: July 29, 1971
BIRTHPLACE: Dallas, TX
RESIDENCE: Dallas, TX

FAMILY: Wife, Allison; William Harrison (12/2/99), Charles "Ford" (8/7/02)
EDUCATION: University of Texas (1996, Psychology and Business Foundations)
SPECIAL INTERESTS: Sports, fishing, hunting
TURNED PROFESSIONAL: 1996
JOINED TOUR: 1998
Nationwide Tour Alumnus

BEST PGA TOUR CAREER FINISHES:

2—2004 Sony Open in Hawaii, T2—1998 GTE Byron Nelson Golf Classic, 1999 COMPAQ Classic of New Orleans,2004 Michelin Championship at Las Vegas.

NATIONWIDE TOUR VICTORIES (1):

1997 South Carolina Classic.

BEST 2004 PGA TOUR FINISHES:

2—Sony Open in Hawaii, Michelin Championship at Las Vegas; T3—Chrysler Classic of Tucson; T9—Bob Hope Chrysler Classic.

2004 SEASON:

Cracked $1 million in earnings for the first time in seven-year PGA TOUR career, finishing a career-best 48th on the money list…With four rounds in the 60s, finished runner-up in first start of season at the Sony Open in Hawaii, falling to Ernie Els in a three-hole playoff. Entered the final round with a one-shot lead over Els after opening 67-63-66. Paired with Els for the final round, lost the lead on the front nine but regained a share with four consecutive birdies on Nos. 9-12. Trailing Els at the 71st hole, finished birdie-birdie to shoot 66 and force the playoff, the 10th in Sony Open in Hawaii history. Earned a personal-best $518,400 with top finish of PGA TOUR career…One week later, finished T9 at the Bob Hope Chrysler Classic. Opened with a 1-over-par 73 but posted four sub-70 rounds to finish six shots out of play-off between Phil Mickelson and Skip Kendall. Recorded three eagles in the fourth round at Indian Wells CC…Finished T3 at the Chrysler Classic of Tucson, his third top-10 in first five starts of season…Shared first-round lead (with Glen Day and John Senden) and second-round lead (with Steve Pate) at Southern Farm Bureau Classic before finishing T34. Posted four eagles in a tournament for the second time in the season (Bob Hope Chrysler Classic), the most by any player in a tournament during year…Added his fourth career runner-up finish with a T2 at the Michelin Championship at Las Vegas. One of six players to share the fist-round lead and finished one stroke behind winner Andre Stolz. One of 10 players in the field to post four rounds in the 60s.

CAREER HIGHLIGHTS:

2003: Inside the top 100 in earnings for the sixth consecutive season on TOUR...Held outright lead through 18 and 54 holes at the Phoenix Open and shared 36-hole lead before finishing T3. It was his highest finish since a third at 2000 Compaq Classic of New Orleans. **2002:** Finished T4 at the Memorial Tournament; was one stroke off the lead after 36 holes...Followed effort at the Memorial with a T7 at the Kemper Insurance Open, second time in career posted back-to-back top-10s. **2001:** Best year on TOUR since rookie season, despite missing two months due to Aug. 8 surgery to repair torn ligaments in right hip. Earned a career best $792,456...Was one shot back after 36 holes and three off the pace through 54 holes in the Compaq Classic of New Orleans. Closed with 71 for solo fourth...Tied career low score with third-round 62 at Greater Milwaukee Open. **2000:** Recorded a pair of third-place finishes and was among the top 100 on the PGA TOUR money list for the third consecutive season...Posted T3 finish at rain-shortened BellSouth Classic, two strokes shy of playoff between Phil Mickelson and Gary Nicklaus...Second third-place finish came at Compaq Classic of New Orleans. **1999:** A successful sophomore season on TOUR produced three top-10s and six top-25s...Matched career-best finish at Compaq Classic of New Orleans with a T2. Two strokes off 54-hole lead. Closing 68 left him two strokes behind Carlos Franco. Starting with runner-up finish in New Orleans, only missed two cuts in final 17 starts. **1998:** Nominated for Rookie of the Year honors on strength of three top-10s, including a runner-up finish at GTE Byron Nelson Classic...Earned $461,633, making 16 of 26 cuts and was the second-highest-ranked rookie on the money list at 63rd. After missing five cuts in first 10 starts, rounds of 64-68-66-70 good for three-way T2 at GTE Byron Nelson with Fred Couples and Hal Sutton. Stood one off first- and second-round leads, two off third-round lead. A week later, recorded second top-10 with solo fourth at MasterCard Colonial. **1997:** Parlayed the first 36-hole Sunday in Nationwide Tour history into a three-stroke victory over R.W. Eaks at the South Carolina Classic. Finished 13th on Nationwide Tour money list to earn first PGA TOUR card. **1996:** Turned professional in June. His only event prior to 1997 was T49 in 1996 Wichita Open. **Amateur:** Three-time All-American at University of Texas from 1993-95.

PERSONAL:

Grew up in Abilene, TX and moved to Dallas in 1985. Was a three-time all-state player and won two state championships with Highland Park High from 1986-1990…Graduated from University of Texas in 1996 with a degree in Psychology and Business Foundations. Went to work in Dallas for a commercial real-estate firm working as an analyst for office, retail and industrial acquisitions and development, as well as golf course management and development…Recently began designing golf courses in Texas…Enjoys spending time with friends and family.

PLAYER STATISTICS

2004 PGA TOUR STATISTICS

Statistic	Value	Rank
Scoring Average	70.90	(69)
Driving Distance	298.8	(18)
Driving Accuracy Percentage	64.3%	(96)
Total Driving	114	(10)
Greens in Regulation Pct.	65.2%	(94)
Putting Average	1.748	(19)
Sand Save Percentage	51.7%	(61)
Eagles (Holes per)	92.3	(3)
Birdie Average	3.88	(15)
All-Around Ranking	375	(7)
Scoring Avg. Before Cut	70.52	(42)
Round 3 Scoring Avg.	69.88	(26)
Final Round Scoring Average	70.56	(30)
Birdie Conversion Percentage	32.7%	(10)
Par Breakers	22.6%	(10)

MISCELLANEOUS PGA TOUR STATISTICS

2004 Low Round/Round: 63–2 times, most recent Bob Hope Chrysler Classic/4
Career Low Round/Round: 62–4 times, most recent 2003 Bob Hope Chrysler Classic/2
Career Largest Paycheck/Finish: $518,400–2004 Sony Open in Hawaii/2

PGA TOUR CAREER SUMMARY — PLAYOFF RECORD: 0-1

Year	Events Played	Cuts Made	1st	2nd	3rd	Top 10	Top 25	Earnings	Rank
1997	1								
1998	26	16		1		3	5	$461,633	63
1999	29	19		1		2	6	530,971	79
2000	24	12			2	2	5	608,535	79
2001	25	18				4	9	792,456	66
2002	28	15				5	6	731,295	96
2003	27	17			1	4	5	776,876	83
2004	25	17		2	1	4	7	1,446,764	48
Total	185	114		4	4	24	43	5,348,529	
NATIONWIDE TOUR									
1996	1	1						570	261
1997	25	17	1		1	6	13	104,023	13
1998	1	1						473	288
Total	27	19	1		1	6	13	105,066	

PGA TOUR TOP TOURNAMENT SUMMARY

Year	98	99	00	01	02	03	04
U.S. Open				T66	T54		
PGA	CUT	CUT	CUT	CUT			CUT
THE PLAYERS		CUT	T33	CUT	T44	CUT	CUT

Fred Funk

EXEMPT STATUS: 2004 tournament winner (through 2006)
FULL NAME: Frederick Funk
HEIGHT: 5-8
WEIGHT: 165
BIRTHDATE: June 14, 1956
BIRTHPLACE: Takoma Park, MD
RESIDENCE: Ponte Vedra Beach, FL

FAMILY: Wife, Sharon; Eric (8/2/91), Taylor Christian (10/30/95), Perri Leigh (12/16/99)
EDUCATION: University of Maryland (1980, Law Enforcement)
SPECIAL INTERESTS: Water and snow skiing
TURNED PROFESSIONAL: 1981
Q SCHOOL: 1988, 1989

PGA TOUR VICTORIES (6):

1992 Shell Houston Open. **1995** Ideon Classic at Pleasant Valley, Buick Challenge. **1996** B.C. Open. **1998** Deposit Guaranty Golf Classic. **2004** Southern Farm Bureau Classic.

INTERNATIONAL VICTORIES (1):

1993 Mexican Open.

BEST 2004 PGA TOUR FINISHES:

1—Southern Farm Bureau Classic; T2—U.S. Bank Championship in Milwaukee; T3—Buick Championship; 6—MCI Heritage, U.S. Open Championship; T10—THE PLAYERS Championship.

2004 SEASON:

Finished in the top 30 (No. 25) on the PGA TOUR money list for the third straight season and went over the $2-million mark for the third consecutive year...Won for first time in over six years with victory at the Southern Farm Bureau Classic, the site of his last victory in July 1998. The drought spanned 196 tournaments and included 10 runner-up finishes. Became second two-time winner of the tournament after making birdie on the final hole to defeat rookie Ryan Palmer by one stroke (Brian Henninger 1994, 1999). Led by one stroke through 54 holes. Tied 72-hole tournament record on current course with 22-under 266 total (Steve Lowery, Skip Kendall/2000). Was his sixth top-10 in 11 appearances at the tournament which became an official TOUR event in 1994 and is the all-time leading money winner with $1,028,465...In eighth start of season, notched first top-10 with a T10 at THE PLAYERS Championship. Top-10 was first in 14 starts at the TPC at Sawgrass for Ponte Vedra Beach resident...One of just two players in the MCI Heritage field to post four rounds under par. Finished week in sixth for his second top-10 of season...Posted best career finish at a U.S. Open with his sixth-place finish, topping the T7 in 1993. Was second-best finish in a major behind a T4 at the 2002 PGA Championship and fifth top-10 in a major in 43 appearances. Jumped from 15th to ninth in Ryder Cup standings with eight qualifying events remaining...His T2 at the U.S. Bank Championship in Milwaukee was his best finish since a T2 at the 2003 FBR Capital Open and gave him crucial Ryder Cup points to solidify his eighth spot in the rankings with three weeks to go before the team was selected. Final-round, 4-under 66 jumped him five spots on Sunday...Finished ninth on the 2004 Ryder Cup Team points list to make his first Ryder Cup Team at age 48, oldest player to finish in top 10 for U.S. Ryder Cup points... Finished T3 at the Buick Championship, one stroke out of the Woody Austin-Tim Herron playoff. Co-leader through 36 holes and solo leader through 54 holes. Opened a two-stroke lead on Sunday after a birdie on the 11th hole, but dropped from contention with three straight bogeys (Nos. 12-14)...Entered THE TOUR Championship .10 ahead of Scott Verplank in Driving Accuracy and hit one more fairway than Verplank during the week to edge him out for the title at 77.23-77.13 percent. Funk captured his seventh Driving Accuracy title in his 16-year career, including his third straight.

CAREER HIGHLIGHTS:

2003: Posted a career-high nine top-10s, including a T2 at the FBR Capital Open in Potomac, MD...On the strength of T7 finish at PGA Championship, was named as Captain's Pick by Jack Nicklaus to 2003 U.S. Presidents Cup team...Made a hole-in-one in the final round of the Bell Canadian Open. **2002:** Had his best earnings season ever, topping the $2 million for the first time and earning his highest placement on the money list, 13th. Had four runner-up finishes, a career best. The last players to have that many runner-up finishes in a year without winning were Davis Love III and Tom Lehman in 1999...T4 at PGA after taking halfway lead and then placed T2 the following week at the WGC-NEC Invitational in Seattle. **2001:** Finished in the top 20 10 times, including a T3 at the Air Canada Championship and a third at the Southern Farm Bureau Classic. **2000:** Recorded at least four top-10s for the eighth time in his last 10 seasons...Suffered a tear in right knee which required surgery in September, but rebounded by making his last six cuts of the year, including back-to-back top-10s to end the season, a T4 at National Car Rental Golf Classic at Walt Disney World Resort and T6 at Southern Farm Bureau Classic. **1999:** Finished second three times and posted eight top-10s. Runner-up at MasterCard Colonial, Air Canada Championship and B.C. Open (losing Monday playoff to Brad Faxon). **1998:** Collected his fifth PGA TOUR victory and for the first time in his 10-year career eclipsed the $1-million mark in earnings. Made 25 of 32 cuts on his way to $1,121,988 season in which he was among top 10 eight

PGA TOUR CAREER SUMMARY — PLAYOFF RECORD: 1-3

Year	Events Played	Cuts Made	1st	2nd	3rd	Top 10	Top 25	Earnings	Rank
1982	3	2						$1,779	251
1985	1	1					1	6,345	196
1986	3								
1987	2	1						2,400	255
1988	2	1						1,552	286
1989	29	17			1	2	3	59,695	157
1990	29	13			1	3	7	179,346	91
1991	31	17				5	9	226,915	73
1992	32	24	1		1	3	9	416,930	34
1993	34	24				5	11	309,435	56
1994	30	23				4	8	281,905	67
1995	32	26	2			4	11	717,232	26
1996	31	23	1	1	2	8	13	814,334	21
1997	33	25			1	3	10	544,419	38
1998	32	25	1	1	1	8	17	1,121,988	23
1999	34	27		3		8	14	1,638,881	16
2000	32	24				4	10	827,691	58
2001	33	27			2	4	13	1,237,004	43
2002	29	24		4		7	19	2,383,071	13
2003	33	25		1	1	9	12	2,144,653	27
2004	29	20	1	1	1	6	8	2,103,731	25
Total	514	369	6	11	11	83	175	15,019,306	

PGA TOUR TOP TOURNAMENT SUMMARY

Year	85	86	87	88	89	90	91	92	93	94	95	96	97
Masters									CUT	T38		T36	T17
U.S. Open	T23	CUT	CUT		CUT		CUT	T33	T7	T44	CUT	CUT	T43
British Open								73					
PGA			T47				T57	CUT	T44	T55	T39	T26	T61
THE PLAYERS							CUT	T60	T39	T78	T61	T13	T14
TOUR Championship											T27	14	

Year	98	99	00	01	02	03	04
Masters	CUT	CUT	T37			CUT	CUT
U.S. Open		CUT	CUT	T44		T35	6
British Open		W/D	CUT			CUT	
PGA	T23	73	T9	T70	T4	T7	CUT
THE PLAYERS	T69	T38	T13	T33	CUT	T45	T10
TOUR Championship	T24	T5			T24	T9	T24
WGC-Accenture Match Play		T33	T33	T33		T33	T33
WGC-NEC Invitational					T2	T14	T61
WGC-American Express Champ		T7			T49	T40	

NATIONAL TEAMS: The Presidents Cup, 2003; Ryder Cup, 2004.

Fred Funk (Continued)

times and top 25 17 times. Along with victory, also finished second and third...Earned two-stroke win at Deposit Guaranty Golf Classic. After rounds of 69-64, stood one off 36-hole lead. Third-round 69 produced share of the lead. Birdied four holes on Sunday back nine on way to 66...Nearly became two-time winner for first time since 1995 at Buick Challenge, losing a playoff when Steve Elkington parred first extra hole. **1996:** Earned fourth victory in five-year stretch, at B.C. Open. Third-round 63 moved him into share of lead with Pete Jordan. After birdieing four of six holes on Sunday, round was canceled due to rain and tournament was reduced to 54 holes. Hit 7-iron approach on first extra hole to within 10 inches to secure victory...Nearly won again the following week when rain reduced Buick Challenge to 36 holes. Was part of five-man playoff won by Michael Bradley. **1995:** Opened four-stroke lead through 54 holes of Ideon Classic. Won by one stroke over Jim McGovern after closing 73...Entered final round of Buick Challenge tied with Steve Stricker before closing 67 gave him one-stroke victory over John Morse and Loren Roberts. **1992:** First TOUR victory came at Shell Houston Open. Grabbed one-stroke lead with course-record 62 in third round, then shot closing 70 for two-stroke victory over Kirk Triplett. Shot 59 on TPC at Scottsdale (Desert Course) during pro-am at Phoenix Open. **1989:** Rookie on the PGA TOUR. **1984:** Won Foot-Joy National Assistant Pro Championship.

PERSONAL:

Golf coach at University of Maryland from 1982 through 1988...Also worked as newspaper circulation supervisor before joining TOUR...One of the first TOUR players to have LASIK surgery.

PLAYER STATISTICS

2004 PGA TOUR STATISTICS

Scoring Average	70.45	(31)
Driving Distance	271.9	(192)
Driving Accuracy Percentage	77.2%	(1)
Total Driving	193	(93)
Greens in Regulation Pct.	65.5%	(86)
Putting Average	1.769	(70)
Sand Save Percentage	54.6%	(28)
Eagles (Holes per)	288.0	(122)
Birdie Average	3.52	(99)
All-Around Ranking	629	(55)
Scoring Avg. Before Cut	70.78	(66)
Round 3 Scoring Avg.	70.50	(58)
Final Round Scoring Average	70.42	(22)
Birdie Conversion Percentage	28.4%	(112)
Par Breakers	19.9%	(105)

MISCELLANEOUS PGA TOUR STATISTICS

2004 Low Round/Round: 64–2 times, most recent Southern Farm Bureau Classic/3
Career Low Round/Round: 61–1999 B.C. Open/2
Career Largest Paycheck/Finish: $540,000–2004 Southern Farm Bureau Classic/1

SHOTLink
AN IBM ON DEMAND BUSINESS SOLUTION

HOT SHOTS

Bay Hill Club and Lodge

Chad Campbell won the 2004 Bay Hill Invitational

18th Hole, Par 4, 441 Yards

The par-4 18th hole at Bay Hill offers quite a test because of the water hazard that guards the green. As a result, driving the ball into the fairway is a must, as shown by statistics at the 2004 Bay Hill Invitational presented by MasterCard:

(Final Round)

DRIVING	PLAYERS	SCORING AVG.
Hit Fairway	48	4.23
Left Rough	3	5.00
Right Rough	22	4.77

- Only three birdies were made all week by a player that missed the 18th fairway.

Jim Furyk (FYUR-ik)

EXEMPT STATUS: Winner, 2003 U.S. Open (through 2008)
FULL NAME: James Michael Furyk
HEIGHT: 6-2
WEIGHT: 185
BIRTHDATE: May 12, 1970
BIRTHPLACE: West Chester, PA
RESIDENCE: Ponte Vedra Beach, FL

FAMILY: Wife, Tabitha; Caleigh Lynn (6/24/02); Tanner James (12/12/03)
EDUCATION: University of Arizona
SPECIAL INTERESTS: All sports
TURNED PROFESSIONAL: 1992
Q SCHOOL: 1993
Nationwide Tour Alumnus

PGA TOUR VICTORIES (9):
1995 Las Vegas Invitational. **1996** United Airlines Hawaiian Open. **1998** Las Vegas Invitational. **1999** Las Vegas Invitational. **2000** Doral-Ryder Open. **2001** Mercedes Championships. **2002** Memorial Tournament. **2003** U.S. Open Championship, Buick Open.

NATIONWIDE TOUR VICTORIES (1):
1993 Mississippi Gulf Coast Classic.

INTERNATIONAL VICTORIES (1):
1997 Argentine Open.

OTHER VICTORIES (2):
1998 Fred Meyer Challenge [with David Duval]. **2003** PGA Grand Slam of Golf.

BEST 2004 PGA TOUR FINISHES:
T6—Buick Open; T7—Cialis Western Open.

2004 SEASON:
Did not have a win for the first time since the 1997 season, ending the second-best current win streak on the PGA TOUR…Had arthroscopic surgery to repair cartilage damage in his left wrist on March 22, which sidelined him for nearly three months. Played in 14 events, the lowest total in his 11-year TOUR career and finished outside the top 100 on the money list for the first time. Played in the first two events of the season in Hawaii. Decided the week of the Bay Hill Invitational to have surgery after sitting out more than two months…At THE PLAYERS Championship, did some work during the first two rounds as a commentator with ESPN…In second start since return at U.S. Open, picked up his first top-10 of the season, a T7, at the Cialis Western Open. The T7 was his fifth top-10 at Cog Hill in his last six appearances…In defense of Buick Open title, was tied for 36-hole lead with Billy Andrade and Vijay Singh after opening 66-67. Finished T6 for fourth straight top-10 at the Buick Open. Has posted 25 consecutive rounds of par or better at Warwick Hills G&CC, dating back to the final round in 1997…Finished fourth on the Ryder Cup Team points list to make his fourth Ryder Cup Team…Played the last five weeks of the season trying to get a win but missed his last three cuts and could finish no higher than a T11 at the Michelin Championship at Las Vegas during that period.

CAREER HIGHLIGHTS:
2003: Collected first major championship of his career, the U.S. Open at Olympia Fields near Chicago. Claimed a victory in sixth consecutive season. Became 57th player to make the U.S. Open his first career major championship. Shared second-round and held third-round lead. Set 36-hole record (133), along with Vijay Singh. Set 54-hole mark (200) and tied 72-hole record (272). The $1,000,008 check, largest of his career, pushed him over the $3-million mark in season's earnings for first time in his career...Four rounds in the 60s produced runner-up finish at the Ford Championship at Doral. Playoff record dropped to 1-4 when Scott Hoch sank birdie putt on the third extra hole on Monday after play was suspended due to darkness on Sunday night...With four rounds in the 60s, captured Buick Open to win twice for first time in a season and jumped to a career-best No. 3 in the Official World Golf Ranking. Held 54-hole lead and with a final-round 68, completed two-stroke victory over a group of four players that included Tiger Woods...Became only the fourth player to earn over $5 million in a single season in TOUR history...Played on his third U.S Presidents Cup team. **2002:** Won the Memorial Tournament thanks to a final-round 65 that included a chip-in for birdie on the par-3 12th hole and an eagle from the front bunker on the par-5 15th. Won by two strokes over John Cook and David Peoples, marking the fifth consecutive season with a victory. Recorded third-round ace with 5-iron from 192 yards on No. 4...Made his third appearance as a member of the U.S. Ryder Cup team and compiled a 1-2-2 record. **2001:** Earned sixth PGA TOUR title at Mercedes Championships. Was four strokes down to start the final round in Maui. Holed a 10-foot birdie putt on 72nd hole in Kapalua that put him in the lead as Rory Sabbatini missed three-foot birdie that would have forced a playoff. Victory came after slight cartilage tear in right wrist forced him to withdraw from 2000 TOUR Championship, 2001 WGC-American Express Championship and Accenture Match Play Championship. Suffered injury the previous fall while trying to intercept a pass in the parking lot of a Baltimore Ravens-Pittsburgh Steelers NFL game...Lost in a playoff on the seventh extra hole at the WGC-NEC Invitational. With scores of 65-66-66, he held the lead for the first three rounds. Closing 71 produced playoff with Tiger Woods, who closed with 69. Holed bunker shot for par on first playoff hole to extend the match. **2000:** Posted eight top-10s, including a victory at the Doral-Ryder Open. For the second time in his career, missed only one cut all season, at SEI Pennsylvania Classic. In 1999, missed cut at AT&T Pebble Beach National Pro-Am...Earned fifth PGA TOUR victory at the Doral-Ryder Open. Shared first-round lead after opening with a 7-under-par 65. Was three strokes back of Franklin Langham after 54 holes. Trailed Langham by six with seven holes to play. Shot 30 on back nine for a final-round 65 and equaled tournament record with 23-under-par 265...Member of his second U.S. Presidents Cup Team. Presidents Cup record was 3-1-0 for a two-year total of 4-4-0. **1999:** Earned third Las Vegas Invitational title, becoming first successful defender. Victory started with rounds of 67-64-63 for a share of 54-hole lead. After awakening to early morning earthquake, played in 40-mph winds and shot 71 to

SECTION 2 PLAYER BIOGRAPHIES

PGA TOUR CAREER SUMMARY — PLAYOFF RECORD: 1-4

Year	Events Played	Cuts Made	1st	2nd	3rd	Top 10	Top 25	Earnings	Rank
1988A	1								
1990A	1								
1991A	1								
1993	1								
1994	31	17				3	7	$236,603	78
1995	31	22	1			3	10	535,380	33
1996	28	24	1			3	13	738,950	26
1997	27	24		3	1	13	17	1,619,480	4
1998	28	24	1	2	2	12	19	2,054,334	3
1999	25	24	1	1		8	17	1,827,593	12
2000	25	24	1		1	8	15	1,940,519	17
2001	24	19	1	2		8	16	2,540,734	13
2002	25	19	1			9	14	2,363,250	14
2003	27	25	2	1	1	15	22	5,182,865	4
2004	14	8				2	5	691,675	116
Total	289	230	9	9	5	84	155	19,731,382	
NATIONWIDE TOUR									
1993	25	13	1	1		3	6	58,240	26
1994	1	1				1	1	3,815	153
Total	26	14	1	1		4	7	62,055	

PGA TOUR TOP TOURNAMENT SUMMARY

Year	94	95	96	97	98	99	00	01	02	03	04
Masters			T29	T28	4	T14	T14	T6	CUT	4	
U.S. Open	T28		T5	T5	T14	T17	60	T62	CUT	1	T48
British Open			T44	4	T4	T10	T41	CUT	CUT	CUT	CUT
PGA		T13	T17	T6	CUT	T8	T72	T7	9	T18	CUT
THE PLAYERS		CUT	T13	T53	T35	T17	T61	T21	T14	T4	
TOUR Championship			T15	2	T3	T15	DNS	T7	T18	8	
WGC-Accenture Match Play						T33	T9		T9	T9	
WGC-NEC Invitational						T10	T4	2	T6	T6	T22
WGC-American Express Champ						T11		CNL	T33	T12	T36

NATIONAL TEAMS: Ryder Cup (4), 1997, 1999, 2002, 2004; The Presidents Cup (3), 1998, 2000, 2003; World Cup, 2003.

Jim Furyk (Continued)

build a three-stroke lead. Final-round 66 good enough to edge Jonathan Kaye by one stroke...A member of victorious U.S. Ryder Cup team, notching a key 4-and-3 singles victory over Sergio Garcia in Sunday's matches. **1998:** His 12 top-10s matched David Duval for second most on TOUR (one behind Tiger Woods) and his $2,054,334, good for third on TOUR money list...Made cut in 24 of his 28 appearances, including a win, two seconds, two thirds and three fourths...Closed year by becoming the first player to win the Las Vegas Invitational twice. Rounds of 67-68-69-63 put him in first place after 72 holes, three strokes ahead of Mark Calcavecchia. Closed with a 68 to Calcavecchia's 66 for one-stroke victory. **1997:** Set then-TOUR record for most money earned without a victory with $1,619,480, fourth on money list...His 13 top-10 finishes, including eight straight, matched Davis Love III for most on TOUR...Nearly had successful defense at United Airlines Hawaiian Open, shooting 66-68 on weekend to force playoff with Paul Stankowski and Mike Reid. Stankowski won playoff...Had an impressive stretch of top-10s in majors: T5 at U.S. Open, fourth at British Open and T6 at PGA Championship. **1996:** Kept winning streak alive in Hawaii three months later with second official victory at United Airlines Hawaiian Open. After trailing by one stroke through 54 holes, shot final-round 69 to take clubhouse lead, only to see Brad Faxon hole 50-foot eagle putt on 72nd hole to force playoff. Birdied third extra hole for victory. **1995:** Recorded first PGA TOUR victory at Las Vegas Invitational. Grabbed share of lead with David Edwards after third-round 65 at TPC at Summerlin. Following fourth-round 67, shared lead with Billy Mayfair. Went on to one-stroke victory over Mayfair...Three weeks later, earned unofficial victory at Lincoln-Mercury Kapalua International. **1994:** Recorded three top-10s as a rookie, including T7 at Northern Telecom Open, his first start of the year. **1993:** Member of the Nationwide Tour, won Mississippi Gulf Coast Classic in playoff over Bob Friend...Qualified for TOUR by finishing T37 at Qualifying Tournament. **Amateur:** Twice named All-Pac 10 Conference and All-America at University of Arizona.

PERSONAL:

Possesses one of the PGA TOUR's less orthodox swings. . . His father, Mike, has been his only swing instructor. . . Started putting cross-handed at age 7. . . Never played high school football, although did play basketball as a sophomore. Played midget football until age 13. . . Owns a home on The Plantation Course at Kapalua, home of the Mercedes Championships.

PLAYER STATISTICS

2004 PGA TOUR STATISTICS

Scoring Average	70.78	(N/A)
Driving Distance	278.5	(N/A)
Driving Accuracy Percentage	74.3%	(N/A)
Total Driving	(N/A)	(N/A)
Greens in Regulation Pct.	69.4%	(N/A)
Putting Average	1.782	(N/A)
Sand Save Percentage	43.3%	(N/A)
Eagles (Holes per)	264.0	(N/A)
Birdie Average	3.20	(N/A)
Scoring Avg. Before Cut	70.69	(N/A)
Round 3 Scoring Avg.	71.25	(N/A)
Final Round Scoring Average	71.50	(N/A)
Birdie Conversion Percentage	25.9%	(N/A)
Par Breakers	18.2%	(N/A)

MISCELLANEOUS PGA TOUR STATISTICS

2004 Low Round/Round: 66–2 times, most recent Michelin Championship at Las Vegas/4

Career Low Round/Round: 62–3 times, most recent 2001 THE TOUR Championship/3

Career Largest Paycheck/Finish: $1,080,000–2003 U.S. Open Championship/1

SHOTLink — AN IBM ON DEMAND BUSINESS SOLUTION

HOT SHOTS

Riviera Country Club

18th Hole-Riviera Country Club

18th Hole, Par 4, 475 Yards

The par-4 18th hole at Riviera Country Club, the site of the Nissan Open, is one of the most demanding finishing holes on the PGA TOUR. The dogleg right begins with a blind tee shot to a fairway that slopes from left to right. The bunkerless green sits below amphitheater seating for the gallery. Some information on why it is necessary to drive accurately on the closing hole, from the 2004 Nissan Open:

18th Hole - Par 4, 475 Yards

Hit Fairway	67.40%	4.08 Avg.
Left Rough	6.20%	4.41 Avg. (0 birdies)
Right Rough	26.40%	4.28 Avg.

Of the 27 tee shots hit into the left rough during the week, only three players managed to hit the green in regulation.
For the week, only 44.1 percent of the field hit the green in regulation.

Robert Gamez (GAM-ez)

EXEMPT STATUS: 110th on 2004 money list
FULL NAME: Robert Anthony Gamez
HEIGHT: 5-9
WEIGHT: 180
BIRTHDATE: July 21, 1968
BIRTHPLACE: Las Vegas, NV
RESIDENCE: Orlando, FL
FAMILY: Single

EDUCATION: University of Arizona
SPECIAL INTERESTS: Music, movies and going to Disney Theme Parks
TURNED PROFESSIONAL: 1989
Q SCHOOL: 1989

PGA TOUR VICTORIES (2):
1990 Northern Telecom Tucson Open, Nestle Invitational.

BEST 2004 PGA TOUR FINISHES:
T5—Bank of America Colonial; T10—B.C. Open.

2004 SEASON:
Finished in the top 125 for the third straight season...Set the course record at Indian Wells CC in the third round of the Bob Hope Chrysler Classic with a 12-under 60. On the front nine (his back nine), had seven birdies and an eagle to turn with an 8-under 27, which set the nine-hole tournament record and tied the PGA TOUR record. Finished T50....First top-10 of the season came in his 14th event, a T5 at the Bank of America Colonial...Opened with 3-over 75 at the B.C. Open, but set a tournament record for best back-to-back rounds by shooting 61-65. One off the lead of Jonathan Byrd through 54 holes, but final-round 71 dropped to finish T10...Shared the U.S. Bank Championship in Milwaukee first-round lead at 5-under 65 with seven others, tying a TOUR record for players sharing the lead through 18 holes (2000 Honda Classic) before finishing T36...Posted an ace during the second round of the PGA Championship with a 5-iron from 228 yards on the par-3 17th hole at Whistling Straits.

CAREER HIGHLIGHTS:
2003: Comeback from 1998 car accident complete after a career-best $1,519,804 in earnings. Finished 43rd on the money list for best finish since rookie season in 1990 when he finished 27th...Consistent all season, making 25 cuts in 31 start, including a T3 at the Phoenix Open and a T2 at the Wachovia Championship, two strokes behind David Toms. **2002:** After missing qualifying for TOUR by one stroke at Q-School in fall of 2001, regained card by finishing in the top 125 (85th) for the first time since 1997...Earned his first top-10 since a T5 at the 1997 B.C. Open with a T7 at the Greater Greensboro Chrysler Classic, a span of 96 starts between top-10s. Entered the week as the seventh alternate...T3 at B.C. Open, two shots behind champion Spike McRoy, was best finish since T2 at 1997 Quad City Classic...The following week, placed second at the John Deere Classic. **2001:** Played in 22 events and made only six cuts. Closing 61 at Palmer Private Course/PGA West lifted him to T11 in Bob Hope Chrysler Classic, two strokes shy of top 10. **1999:** In addition to 19 PGA TOUR events, played in six events on the Nationwide Tour. **1998:** Injuries suffered in car accident at 1998 Kemper Open kept him out of action for more than a month as he fell from 85th to 195th on TOUR money list. Did not post a top-10 for first time in career, dating back to rookie season of 1990. **1997:** Posted three top-10s, T5 at The Honda Classic, T2 at Quad City Classic and T5 at B.C. Open. **1996:** T4 at Bay Hill Invitational, site of second TOUR win in 1990, and solo third at Walt Disney World/Oldsmobile Classic. **1995:** Posted three top-10s, at the Bob Hope Chrysler Classic (sixth), Memorial Tournament (T5) and the Greater Milwaukee Open (T10). **1994:** Runner-up at Las Vegas Invitational to Bruce Lietzke, one of a career-best five top-10 finishes on the season, at the Northern Telecom Open (T7), Memorial Tournament (sixth), Kemper Open (T10) and Walt Disney World/Oldsmobile Classic (sixth)...Defeated Scott Hoch by four strokes for lone international victory at 1994 Casio World Open in Japan. **1993:** Lost playoff to Fred Couples at The Honda Classic...Posted top-10s at Northern Telecom Open (T8) and Las Vegas Invitational (T10). **1992:** Runner-up at FedEx St. Jude Classic to Jay Haas...T7 at Shell Houston Open and finished seventh in hometown at Las Vegas Invitational. **1991:** Runner-up twice, at Greater Milwaukee Open, after opening-round 61 at Tuckaway CC, and at Southern Open. **1990:** Won his first official start on PGA TOUR, capturing Northern Telecom Tucson Open by four strokes over Mark Calcavecchia...Two months later, holed 7-iron shot from 176 yards for eagle-2 on 72nd hole of Nestle Invitational for one-stroke victory over Greg Norman. Two wins and $461,407 in earnings led to PGA TOUR Rookie of the Year honors. **Amateur:** Winner of 1994 Casio World Open in Japan...Winner of 1989 Fred Haskins and Jack Nicklaus Awards as collegiate player of the year...Winner of 1989 Porter Cup.

PERSONAL:
Annual charity tournament in Celebration, FL benefits Robert Gamez Foundation...Brother Randy was caddie for both of Robert's victories...Drove home from Tampa to Orlando area after second round of Chrysler Championship on October 31, 2003 to pass out candy to more than 500 trick-or-treaters on Halloween.

PLAYER STATISTICS

2004 PGA TOUR STATISTICS

Scoring Average	71.11	(96)
Driving Distance	288.1	(85)
Driving Accuracy Percentage	65.2%	(77)
Total Driving	162	(50)
Greens in Regulation Pct.	65.7%	(82)
Putting Average	1.767	(64)
Sand Save Percentage	48.3%	(109)
Eagles (Holes per)	264.9	(112)
Birdie Average	3.68	(62)
All-Around Ranking	687	(73)
Scoring Avg. Before Cut	70.42	(34)
Round 3 Scoring Avg.	71.10	(110)
Final Round Scoring Average	72.05	(137)
Birdie Conversion Percentage	29.6%	(81)
Par Breakers	20.8%	(65)

MISCELLANEOUS PGA TOUR STATISTICS

2004 Low Round/Round: 60–Bob Hope Chrysler Classic/3
Career Low Round/Round: 60–2004 Bob Hope Chrysler Classic/3
Career Largest Paycheck/Finish: $418,133–2003 Wachovia Championship/T2

PGA TOUR CAREER SUMMARY — PLAYOFF RECORD: 0-1

Year	Events Played	Cuts Made	1st	2nd	3rd	Top 10	Top 25	Earnings	Rank
1988A	1	1							
1989	3	1					1	$4,827	237
1990	25	16	2			2	6	461,407	27
1991	27	13		2		3	7	280,349	59
1992	25	13		1		3	3	215,648	72
1993	25	15		1		3	4	236,458	70
1994	23	15		1		5	7	380,353	44
1995	27	13				3	5	206,588	89
1996	25	12			1	2	6	249,227	89
1997	28	12		1		3	5	283,434	86
1998	24	9					1	76,148	195
1999	19	11						71,236	208
2000	26	11					5	259,305	145
2001	22	6					2	193,525	175
2002	21	13		1	1	4	5	807,892	85
2003	31	25		1	1	2	12	1,519,804	43
2004	31	20				2	6	725,368	110
Total	383	206	2	8	3	32	75	5,971,568	
NATIONWIDE TOUR									
1999	5	2					1	2,790	174
2000	6	5				1	3	23,280	130
2001	3	1						2,520	241
2002	3								
Total	17	8				1	4	28,590	

PGA TOUR TOP TOURNAMENT SUMMARY

Year	90	91	92	93	94	95	96	97	98	99	00	01	02
Masters	CUT	CUT											
U.S. Open	T61	CUT		88	CUT	CUT					CUT	CUT	
British Open	T12	T44											
PGA	T49		T79	CUT		CUT		CUT					CUT
THE PLAYERS	T46	CUT	CUT	CUT	84	T49	T29	T24	T63				
TOUR Championship	30												

Year	03	04
PGA	T14	T68
THE PLAYERS	T69	CUT

NATIONAL TEAMS: Walker Cup, 1989.

Sergio Garcia

EXEMPT STATUS: 2004 two-time tournament winner (through 2007)
FULL NAME: Sergio Garcia Fernandez
HEIGHT: 5-10
WEIGHT: 160
BIRTHDATE: January 9, 1980
BIRTHPLACE: Castellon, Spain
RESIDENCE: Borriol, Spain

FAMILY: Single
SPECIAL INTERESTS: Real Madrid FC (soccer), kids, tennis
TURNED PROFESSIONAL: 1999
JOINED TOUR: 1999

PGA TOUR VICTORIES (5):

2001 MasterCard Colonial, Buick Classic. **2002** Mercedes Championships. **2004** EDS Byron Nelson Championship, Buick Classic.

INTERNATIONAL VICTORIES (9):

1997 Catalonian Open Championship. **1999** Murphy's Irish Open [Eur], Linde German Masters [Eur]. **2001** Trophee Lancome [Eur], Nedbank Golf Challenge [SAf]. **2002** Canarias Open de Espana [Eur], Kolon Cup Korean Open [Asia]. **2003** Nedbank Golf Challenge [SAf]. **2004** Mallorca Classic [Eur].

BEST 2004 PGA TOUR FINISHES:

1—EDS Byron Nelson Championship, Buick Classic; T4—Masters Tournament, WGC-American Express Championship; T9—FBR Open.

2004 SEASON:

Ninth in the Official World Golf Ranking after THE TOUR Championship, on the strength of two PGA TOUR wins and one European Tour victory. . .Posted a top-10 in his first start of the season with a T9 at the FBR Open, first top-10 on TOUR since T10 at the 2003 British Open. . .In sixth Masters appearance, logged a T4 for second career top-10 in Augusta, aided by low final round, a 6-under-par 66, that included a double bogey on the par-3 sixth hole. . .Collected his third career TOUR title at the EDS Byron Nelson Championship after winning a three-way playoff on the first hole over Dudley Hart and Robert Damron. Became the 13th player to win both the Byron Nelson and the Bank of America Colonial in a career. . .Won a three-man playoff for the second time in five weeks on the third extra hole at the Buick Classic. Victory over Rory Sabbatini and Padraig Harrington improved his playoff record to 3-1. The two-time Buick Classic champion has four consecutive top-10s at Westchester. His final round of 4-under 67 extended his streak of consecutive rounds of par or better in the Buick Classic to 19. . .Posted his fourth top-10 finish in five appearances at the WGC-American Express Championship with his T4 finish in Ireland. . .Playing in his third Ryder Cup, had a 4-0-1 record for the victorious European squad. Career record in Ryder Cup is 10-3-2. . .Earned fifth career European Tour victory in Spain at the Mallorca Classic at Pula Golf Club. Posted final-round 67 to win by four shots. . .Fell to Ian Poulter in a playoff at the European Tour's season-ending Volvo Masters Andalucia in Spain. Played in his first WGC-World Cup. Paired with Miguel Angel Jimenez and finished second.

CAREER HIGHLIGHTS:

2003: Managed two top-10s in 20 starts...Posted a T4 at the Buick Classic, his third straight top-10 at the tournament. A past champion of the event, was one back of the four leaders heading into the final round. . .T10 at British Open. **2002:** Began year with a victory at the season-opening Mercedes Championship, and top-10 finishes in all four majors, the only player to do so...Posted a 3-2-0 record in Europe's winning Ryder Cup effort...Captured the Canarias Open de Espana on the European Tour, the fourth career European Tour victory for the Spanish native and his first professional win in Spain...Birdied the 18th hole on The Plantation Course at the Mercedes Championships to set up playoff with David Toms, then birdied same hole again to earn third PGA TOUR title. Overcame a four-shot deficit with a final round 9-under-par 64, for the best final-round finish at The Plantation Course. The last first-time champion to win the event was Tiger Woods in 1997. **2001:** Recorded two victories to crack the top 10 in earnings at sixth...Became first player born in 1980s to win on TOUR with a two-stroke victory in the MasterCard Colonial. Starting the final round five off the lead and closed with a 63, which tied Davis Love III at the AT&T Pebble Beach National Pro-Am and Bob Estes at the Invensys Classic at Las Vegas for season's low finish by winner...Three starts after first win, became one of nine multiple winners on TOUR with a victory in Buick Classic. Tied for lead after 36 holes and led by two after 54. Closed with 67 to win by three. Become youngest player to win $2 million in a season...Lost a four-man playoff to at THE TOUR Championship (Ernie Els, David Toms and winner Mike Weir)...Was a Captain's Choice for European Ryder Cup team...Earned third European title at Trophee Lancome, edging Retief Goosen by one stroke. **2000:** A successful sophomore season on TOUR which produced five top-10s and eight top-25s...Played in 16 events during the year, making 14 cuts. **1999:** Made the cut in seven of nine starts, finishing among top-10 four times with a runner-up and third-place finish...Nominated for Rookie of the Year honors (qualified by finishing top-125 on money list)...In first PGA TOUR start as a professional and second start as a professional, finished T3 at GTE Byron Nelson Classic. Opening 62 left him one stroke behind Tiger Woods' 18-hole lead. Remained one back through 36 holes after 67 and followed with 71-69 to finish seven strokes out of Loren Roberts-Steve Pate playoff...Following Memorial payday of $58,650, had $202,650 in TOUR earnings and joined TOUR as special temporary member...Runner-up finish at PGA Championship assured berth on European Ryder Cup Team. Opening-round 66 gave him first-round lead at Medinah CC. Was youngest player to lead PGA Championship since tournament went to stroke play in 1958. On Sunday, trailed Tiger Woods by two strokes with three holes to play, and tee shot on 16 came to rest against a root behind large tree, then hit a 6-iron, with eyes closed, safely on green and ran down fairway to watch recovery shot. Finished one stroke behind Woods for solo second...Youngest Ryder Cup participant ever at age 19 years, 8 months, 15 days (more than five months younger than Nick Faldo in 1977), where he posted a 3-1-1 overall record...Won first professional event on July 4, 1999 at Murphy's Irish Open in his sixth professional start. Became European Tour's fourth-youngest winner (youngest was South African Dale Hayes, 18, when he won 1971 Spanish Open)...Earned second European Tour victory at Linde

PGA TOUR CAREER SUMMARY — PLAYOFF RECORD: 3-1

Year	Events Played	Cuts Made	1st	2nd	3rd	Top 10	Top 25	Earnings	Rank
1996A	1								
1998A	1	1							
1999A	1	1							
1999	8	6		1	1	4	6	$784,917	53
2000	16	14			2	5	8	1,054,338	42
2001	18	14	2	2		8	12	2,898,635	6
2002	21	19	1			9	14	2,401,993	12
2003	20	12				2	4	666,386	95
2004	18	16	2			5	10	3,239,215	9
Total	104	83	5	3	3	33	54	11,045,484	
NATIONWIDE TOUR									
1998A	3	2			1	1	2		
Total	3	2			1	1	2		
EUROPEAN TOUR									
2004	4	4	1	1	1	3	4	862,702	

PGA TOUR TOP TOURNAMENT SUMMARY

Year	96	97	98	99	00	01	02	03	04
Masters				T38	T40	CUT	8	T28	T4
U.S. Open					T46	T12	4	T35	T20
British Open	CUT		T29	CUT	T36	T9	T8	T10	CUT
PGA				2	T34	CUT	T10	CUT	CUT
THE PLAYERS					CUT	T50	T4	CUT	T53
TOUR Championship						T2	28		T15
WGC-Accenture Match Play					T9		T9	T33	T33
WGC-NEC Invitational				T7			T58	T30	T16
WGC-American Express Champ				T7	T5	CNL	7	T12	T4

NATIONAL TEAMS: Ryder Cup (3), 1999, 2002, 2004; Dunhill Cup (2), 1999, 2000. WGC-World Cup, 2004.

Sergio Garcia (Continued)

German Masters on Oct. 3. Sank 15-foot birdie putt on second playoff hole to defeat Padraig Harrington...Joined Jose Maria Olazabal and Miguel Angel Jimenez to capture Spain's first Dunhill Cup title. **Amateur:** Turned pro on April 21, 1999 after playing in 28 professional events as an amateur...Was first British Amateur champion to finish as low amateur in Masters (1999)...Winner of 19 events as an amateur and also a professional event, the Catalonian Open, at age 17...Made the cut in 12 of 18 European Tour events entered before turning professional...At age 14, made his first cut in a European Tour event, the 1995 Turespana Open Mediterranea. Set a European Tour record as youngest player to make a cut...Won the 1995 European Amateur Championship, the youngest winner of the event.

PERSONAL:

Nicknamed 'El Nino'. . .Father, Victor, is his teacher and the teaching professional at home club, the Club de Golf de Mediterraneo. Father has played in eight career Champions Tour events. . .Started playing golf at age 3 and became club champion at age 12. . .Said this about the swing change he undertook in 2003, "I knew what I was doing and I just thought take it slow, because it might take some time. But you've got to realize those things, and just wait, and that's what I did."

PLAYER STATISTICS

2004 PGA TOUR STATISTICS

Scoring Average	69.80	(6)
Driving Distance	295.1	(33)
Driving Accuracy Percentage	58.5%	(170)
Total Driving	203	(109)
Greens in Regulation Pct.	70.8%	(4)
Putting Average	1.790	(129)
Sand Save Percentage	48.1%	(111)
Eagles (Holes per)	144.0	(27)
Birdie Average	3.78	(32)
All-Around Ranking	512	(24)
Scoring Avg. Before Cut	70.12	(17)
Round 3 Scoring Avg.	70.53	(62)
Final Round Scoring Average	71.60	(95)
Birdie Conversion Percentage	29.5%	(83)
Par Breakers	21.7%	(25)

MISCELLANEOUS PGA TOUR STATISTICS

2004 Low Round/Round: 65–3 times, most recent EDS Byron Nelson Championship/3
Career Low Round/Round: 62–2 times, most recent 2002 WGC-American Express Championship/4
Career Largest Paycheck/Finish: $1,044,000–2004 EDS Byron Nelson Championship/1

SHOTLink
AN IBM ON DEMAND BUSINESS SOLUTION

HOT SHOTS

Hardest Par 3 on Tour

Tournament Players Club at Southwind

11th Hole, 185 Yards

11th Hole-TPC at Southwind

This hole is a version of the famous 17th at the Tournament Players Club at Sawgrass, but with its own uniqueness. This hole requires an iron over water to an island green with a small pot bunker that guards the front edge of the green.

SCORING

Average Score	3.442
Birdies	52
Pars	249
Bogeys	85
Double Bogeys	51
Other	18
Actual Yardage	185
Rank	1

The field was a combined 201-over par on this hole.

APPROACH TO THE GREEN

Greens in Regulation	242/ 455 53%
Average Distance to Pin	31 ft 2 in

AROUND THE GREEN

Sand Saves	30/ 62 (12th)
Scrambling	78/ 213 (18th)

47 percent of the field missed the green and only 36.6 percent of those players were able to make par.

PENALTY

Round 1	60 (+2.117)
Round 2	17 (+1.765)
Round 3	6 (+1.833)
Round 4	10 (+2.300)
Total	93 (+2.054)

1 in every 5 players to tee off on No. 11 hit the ball in the water.

Brian Gay

EXEMPT STATUS: 122nd on 2004 money list
FULL NAME: Joseph Brian Gay
HEIGHT: 5-10
WEIGHT: 155
BIRTHDATE: December 14, 1971
BIRTHPLACE: Ft. Worth, TX
RESIDENCE: Windermere, FL; plays out of Keene's Pointe
FAMILY: Wife, Kimberly; Makinley Kathryn (9/27/99), Brantley Olivia (2/3/04)
EDUCATION: University of Florida
SPECIAL INTERESTS: Stock market, reading
TURNED PROFESSIONAL: 1994
Q SCHOOL: 1998, 1999, 2003
Nationwide Tour Alumnus

BEST PGA TOUR CAREER FINISHES:
T2—2001 MasterCard Colonial, 2002 Buick Open.

BEST 2004 PGA TOUR FINISH:
T5—FedEx St. Jude Classic.

2004 SEASON:
After finishing out of the top-125 in 2003, managed to get back into the top-125 with five top-20s, including one top-10...Posted final-round ace on the par-3 third hole at Redstone GC at the Shell Houston Open...Finished T14 at the BellSouth Classic, best finish since finishing T8 at the 2003 Honda Classic....Bank of America Colonial Sponsor Exemption selection shared third-round lead for first time in career (172nd event) with eventual winner Steve Flesch and runner-up Chad Campbell. Final-round 75 left him T14...Played in final group on Sunday for the second consecutive week at the FedEx St. Jude Classic. Opened final round eight strokes behind David Toms and posted 73 to finish T5. Collected a season-best $165,088...Ended the season with a strong finish at the Michelin Championship at Las Vegas. Weekend rounds of 65-67 at TPC of Summerlin pushed him to T11...Needed to make one cut with three tournaments remaining for the season to secure his card for 2005. Managed to make the cut near his home at the FUNAI Classic at the WALT DISNEY WORLD resort, finishing T41.

CAREER HIGHLIGHTS:
2003: Finished out of the top 125 for the first time since 1998, his rookie season. Returned to the Qualifying Tournament and finished T28. Only top-10 of the season was a T8 at The Honda Classic after four rounds of 67. **2002:** Played in 34 events, making 24 cuts, and finishing the top-10 four times. Best finish was a T2 at the Buick Open, four strokes behind champion Tiger Woods. **2001:** Had career-highs in money earned and money list position. Surpassed the $1-million mark for the first time, thanks to a career-high five top-10s. At the MasterCard Colonial, finished T2 on the strength of a closing 65, two strokes behind Sergio Garcia. His $352,000 paycheck was largest of his career. **2000:** On strength of eight top-25s, placed among Top 125 on TOUR Money List for first time...First career top-10 came at Honda Classic, a T4. Part of eight-way first-round tie for lead after 7-under-par 65 in Coral Springs. Stood two strokes back through 54 holes and pulled within one of champion Dudley Hart heading to 17th hole Sunday. Gay's 30-foot birdie putt stopped on the edge of the front lip and fell in, but Gay waited longer than the allowed 10 seconds to tap ball in and was assessed one-stroke penalty (Rule 16-2) after play was completed, giving him a par. He bogeyed 18th hole and finished two strokes behind Hart. **1999:** In first career full PGA TOUR season, played in 26 events and made eight cuts...Best finish of the season was T24 at the Reno-Tahoe Open...Retained PGA TOUR exempt status with T10 at PGA TOUR Qualifying Tournament. **1998:** Member of the Nationwide Tour...Earned status on the PGA TOUR for the next season with T31 finish at Qualifying Tournament in Palm Springs. **1997:** Three-time winner on Golden Bear Tour, a two-time winner on Sunshine Players Tour and a four-time winner on South Florida Tour. **1996:** Lone PGA TOUR event was U.S. Open...Finished second on Golden Bear Tour money list after winning Golden Bear Tour Championship. **1995:** Played in 40 mini-tour tournaments and won nine times, including victories on the Emerald Coast Golf Tour, Gulf Coast Tour, Gary Player Tour and Tommy Armour Tour. **Amateur:** Member of 1993 U.S. Walker Cup team...Medalist at the 1993 U.S. Amateur...Two-time All-America selection and a three-time All-SEC selection of the University of Florida. Only player to win the SEC Championship twice. Also, SEC Freshman of the Year...College teammate of TOUR players Pat Bates and Chris Couch.

PERSONAL:
Father was a scratch golfer and played for the all-Army team. Dad got him started in golf when he was 9.

PLAYER STATISTICS

2004 PGA TOUR STATISTICS

Scoring Average	70.85	(64)
Driving Distance	279.7	(163)
Driving Accuracy Percentage	64.8%	(85)
Total Driving	248	(168)
Greens in Regulation Pct.	61.5%	(177)
Putting Average	1.737	(6)
Sand Save Percentage	52.2%	(53)
Eagles (Holes per)	338.4	(149)
Birdie Average	3.59	(82)
All-Around Ranking	779	(99)
Scoring Avg. Before Cut	70.81	(70)
Round 3 Scoring Avg.	69.19	(5)
Final Round Scoring Average	72.25	(146)
Birdie Conversion Percentage	30.4%	(55)
Par Breakers	20.2%	(90)

MISCELLANEOUS PGA TOUR STATISTICS

2004 Low Round/Round: 65–3 times, most recent Michelin Championship at Las Vegas/3
Career Low Round/Round: 64–2 times, most recent 2002 Valero Texas Open/2
Career Largest Paycheck/Finish: $352,000–2001 MasterCard Colonial/T2

PGA TOUR CAREER SUMMARY — PLAYOFF RECORD: 0-0

Year	Events Played	Cuts Made	1st	2nd	3rd	Top 10	Top 25	Earnings	Rank
1996	1								
1999	26	8					1	$74,329	206
2000	33	17				1	8	482,028	102
2001	32	23		1		5	12	1,299,361	41
2002	34	24		1		4	10	926,735	69
2003	34	15				1	4	447,647	137
2004	32	16				1	6	645,194	122
Total	192	103		2		12	41	3,875,295	
NATIONWIDE TOUR									
1994	2								
1996	4	1						740	245
1998	23	16				1	4	24,591	80
1999	1	1						1,380	206
Total	30	18				1	4	26,711	

PGA TOUR TOP TOURNAMENT SUMMARY

Year	96	97	98	99	00	01	02	03	04
U.S. Open	CUT				CUT		CUT	CUT	CUT
British Open						CUT			
PGA						T22	T53	T51	
THE PLAYERS						T40	T63	CUT	

NATIONAL TEAMS: Walker Cup, 1993.

Brent Geiberger

EXEMPT STATUS: 2004 tournament winner (through 2006)
FULL NAME: Brent Andrew Geiberger
HEIGHT: 6-4
WEIGHT: 200
BIRTHDATE: May 22, 1968
BIRTHPLACE: Santa Barbara, CA
RESIDENCE: Palm Desert, CA

FAMILY: Single
EDUCATION: Pepperdine University
SPECIAL INTERESTS: Hockey, basketball
TURNED PROFESSIONAL: 1993
Q SCHOOL: 1996
Nationwide Tour Alumnus

PGA TOUR VICTORIES (2):

1999 Canon Greater Hartford Open. **2004** Chrysler Classic of Greensboro.

BEST 2004 PGA TOUR FINISH:

1—Chrysler Classic of Greensboro.

2004 SEASON:

Season highlight was winning same PGA TOUR event, Chrysler Classic of Greensboro, as father Al did in 1976...Withdrew from the Ford Championship at Doral and after 10 holes at THE PLAYERS Championship because of a back injury...Captured second career TOUR victory at the Chrysler Classic of Greensboro. Brent and Al became first father-son combination to win same TOUR event on American soil. Tom Morris Sr. and Jr. and Willie Park Sr. and Jr. all won the British Open in the 1800s. Entered the week at No. 144 on TOUR money list looking to secure card for 2005. With win, earned two-year exemption and jumped to No. 52 with $828,000 payday. Opened 66-67-71 and held a share of the lead at 12-under-par with Tom Lehman entering the final round. Posted final-round, bogey-free 66 to secure two-stroke victory over Michael Allen.

CAREER HIGHLIGHTS:

2003: Finished among the top-125 on the money list for the seventh consecutive season with $588,533. Missed most of the season due to a foot injury...Only top-10 came at the Wachovia Championship, T2, two strokes back of winner David Toms. Finish was best since winning the 1999 Canon Greater Hartford Open. One of only two players on the week to card all four rounds under-par at Quail Hollow Club...Withdrew after the first round of the FedEx St. Jude Classic due to plantar fasciitis (pain in bottom of the foot). Was rehabbing foot and three weeks later severely sprained his left ankle. Sat out rest of year. **2002:** Best effort of the season came at the SEI Pennsylvania Classic where four rounds in the 60s good for T7...Earned $60,600 with his T19 finish at the Invensys Classic at Las Vegas to secure his card for the 2003 season. **2001:** Opening 64 gave him first-round lead in Buick Invitational, finished T5...Also finished T5 at the Greater Milwaukee Open and Air Canada Championship. **2000:** Started the year with a T8 at the Mercedes Championships...Shot final-round 68 to move into T10 at the Buick Invitational...Ended season on a strong note, finishing T8 at Air Canada Championship and T5 at Buick Challenge. **1999:** First PGA TOUR victory came at the Canon Greater Hartford Open. Victory also marked first time a son of former TOUR champion had won on TOUR since Guy Boros (son of Julius) captured 1996 Greater Vancouver Open. Won in record fashion after rounds of 66-63-66-67 produced three-stroke victory over Skip Kendall. Shared 36-hole lead at 11-under-par 129. Held 54-hole lead at 15-under 195, which established tournament record. 262 total bettered 72-hole record by four. Became the first player since Justin Leonard in 1996 Buick Open to win tournament in which he had hole-in-one...In start before victory, finished third at Motorola Western Open...Also finished third at the Westin Texas Open, one stroke out of Duffy Waldorf-Ted Tryba playoff...Ended the season with a third-place finish at THE TOUR Championship. Was only player other than champion Tiger Woods with all four rounds in the 60s at Champions GC. Finished moved him to 47th in Official World Golf Ranking. **1998:** Cracked the top-50 on TOUR money list with $573,098 and missed only seven cuts in 26 appearances...Closed with 66 at Phoenix Open to finish T2, three strokes behind Jesper Parnevik...Closed 68-65 at the National Car Rental Golf Classic for third-place finish. **1997:** Rookie season was highlighted by runner-up finish at LaCantera Texas Open. **1996:** Improved to 11th on Nationwide Tour money list with $103,817, missing top-10 money list finish that would have earned place on PGA TOUR by $112. Earned TOUR spot anyway with seventh-place finish at 1996 Qualifying Tournament. **1995:** Rookie on the Nationwide Tour...Had six top-10s in 28 starts on way to 23rd-place finish on money list with $74,274. **Amateur:** Winner of eight junior college tournaments while attending College of the Desert in Palm Springs, CA.

PERSONAL:

Father Al, winner of 11 PGA TOUR events and nine Champions Tour titles, was the first to shoot 59 in PGA TOUR history (1977 Memphis Classic)...Brother John is the coach of the Pepperdine University golf team that won 1997 NCAA Championship...In 1998, made PGA Championship history when he and father Al became first father-son combo to compete in same PGA.

PLAYER STATISTICS

2004 PGA TOUR STATISTICS

Scoring Average	70.88	(67)
Driving Distance	291.3	(56)
Driving Accuracy Percentage	64.8%	(85)
Total Driving	141	(27)
Greens in Regulation Pct.	65.6%	(83)
Putting Average	1.775	(86)
Sand Save Percentage	49.3%	(92)
Eagles (Holes per)	327.6	(144)
Birdie Average	3.60	(79)
All-Around Ranking	692	(77)
Scoring Avg. Before Cut	70.51	(41)
Round 3 Scoring Avg.	71.05	(106)
Final Round Scoring Average	70.53	(29)
Birdie Conversion Percentage	29.3%	(90)
Par Breakers	20.3%	(83)

MISCELLANEOUS PGA TOUR STATISTICS

2004 Low Round/Round: 65–Southern Farm Bureau Classic/4
Career Low Round/Round: 61–2000 Bob Hope Chrysler Classic/2
Career Largest Paycheck/Finish: $828,000–2004 Chrysler Classic of Greensboro/1

PGA TOUR CAREER SUMMARY — PLAYOFF RECORD: 0-0

Year	Events Played	Cuts Made	1st	2nd	3rd	Top 10	Top 25	Earnings	Rank
1997	29	19		1		1	11	$395,472	62
1998	26	19		1	1	4	7	573,098	49
1999	30	21	1		3	6	11	1,541,409	19
2000	24	17				4	7	564,918	85
2001	25	18				3	7	711,194	74
2002	29	18				2	8	582,592	113
2003	16	9		1		1	2	588,533	111
2004	31	18	1			1	4	1,259,779	57
Total	210	139	2	3	4	22	57	6,216,995	
NATIONWIDE TOUR									
1993	1								
1995	28	17			2	6	10	74,274	23
1996	28	21			2	8	15	103,817	11
Total	57	38			4	14	25	178,091	

PGA TOUR TOP TOURNAMENT SUMMARY

Year	98	99	00	01	02	03	04
Masters			CUT				
U.S. Open	CUT		CUT		CUT		
PGA	T71	CUT	CUT				
THE PLAYERS	CUT	T46	CUT	T70	CUT	CUT	W/D
TOUR Championship		3					
WGC-Accenture Match Play			T33	T33			
WGC-American Express Champ		T55					

Matt Gogel

EXEMPT STATUS: 98th on 2004 money list
FULL NAME: Matthew John Gogel
HEIGHT: 5-10
WEIGHT: 175
BIRTHDATE: February 9, 1971
BIRTHPLACE: Denver, CO
RESIDENCE: Mission Hills, KS
FAMILY: Wife, Blair; Kimball Ann (8/14/01), Thomas Matthew (7/8/04)

EDUCATION: University of Kansas (1994, Communications)
SPECIAL INTERESTS: Thoroughbred racing, fly fishing, skiing
TURNED PROFESSIONAL: 1994
JOINED TOUR: 2000
Nationwide Tour Alumunus

PGA TOUR VICTORIES (1):

2002 AT&T Pebble Beach National Pro-Am.

NATIONWIDE TOUR VICTORIES (6):

1996 Boise Open. **1997** Laurel Creek Classic. **1998** Omaha Classic, Tri-Cities Open. **1999** Louisiana Open, Cleveland Open.

BEST 2004 PGA TOUR FINISHES:

T6—Buick Championship; T8—Chrysler Classic of Greensboro.

2004 SEASON:

Finished in the top-100 on the money list for the fifth consecutive season, thanks to two late-season top-10s. Earned 45 percent of his season earnings in his last five starts of the season, which included a missed cut…Shared second-round lead (6-under 136) with Steve Lowery and Charles Howell III at the Cialis Western Open thanks to second-round 7-under 64. Finished T17…Recorded two top-10s beginning with the Buick Championship at the end of August. Only player to post four rounds in the 60s en route to first top-10 of season, a T6 at the Buick Championship…Three strokes back of Vijay Singh at the 84 LUMBER Classic through 54-holes, closing 72 dropped him T11…One stroke off the lead entering the final round of the Chrysler Classic of Greensboro in mid-October. Final-round even-par 72 dropped finish to T8. Collected $110,975, enough to move him inside the top-100 on the final season money list. It was his second consecutive top-10 in Greensboro. He finished third in 2003.

CAREER HIGHLIGHTS:

2003: Aced the 163-yard 16th hole at Riviera CC with a 6-iron in the second round of the Nissan Open, his first on TOUR...Posted second ace of the season, on the sixth hole at Westchester CC during the Buick Classic...Posted best finish on TOUR since his victory at 2002 Pebble Beach National Pro Am with a third at the Chrysler Classic of Greensboro. **2002:** Captured his first TOUR victory at the AT&T Pebble Beach National Pro-Am two years after finishing T2 and being overtaken by Tiger Woods on the back nine. This time he came from four back after 54 holes to overtake Pat Perez. Nailed a 35-foot putt for birdie on the 18th hole at Pebble Beach Golf Links to tie Perez for the lead and won the event moments later after Perez triple-bogeyed the hole. **2001:** Earned full exempt status on the strength of four top-10s and seven top-25s. Made nine cuts out of his last 12 starts. Finished 70th on the final TOUR money list. **2000:** Made an impressive and successful transition from Nationwide Tour to rookie season on PGA TOUR...Earned respect early with a pair of top-10s on the West Coast Swing...Rounds of 69-68-67 gained share of third-round lead with Mark Brooks at AT&T Pebble Beach National Pro-Am. Due to weather, final round played on Monday and Gogel opened with three straight birdies, but a back-nine 40 and Tiger Woods' eagle-birdie-par-birdie finish earned Woods the victory and Gogel a T2 one stroke back. **1999:** Finished seventh on the Nationwide Tour money list to earn PGA TOUR card after consecutive near-misses the past two seasons. Recorded $180,173 in earnings thanks to wins at the Louisiana Open and Cleveland Open. Those wins gave him six career Nationwide Tour victories, which ties Sean Murphy for the record. First player in Nationwide Tour history to win in four consecutive years (1996-99)...Defeated Casey Martin in Cleveland with a birdie on the second extra hole, running his career playoff record to 3-0, also a Nationwide Tour record...Member of the Nationwide Tour team at the Ganter Cup Challenge. Won the individual stroke play with a 7-under-par 65 and defeated Craig Stadler in the match-play portion of the event. **1998:** Finished 16th on the Nationwide Tour money list on the strength of two victories, at the Omaha Classic and Tri-Cities Open. **1997:** Finished 19th on the Nationwide Tour money list...Winner of the Laurel Creek Classic in Moorestown, NJ. **1996:** Collected his first Nationwide Tour title at the Boise Open. **1995:** Winner of the Kansas Open...Played the Asian Tour. Best finishes were fourth place at the China Open and Korea Shinhan Open. **Amateur:** NCAA All-American at Kansas in 1994.

PERSONAL:

While playing the 1996 Indian Open in Calcutta, met Mother Teresa…Dad purchased tickets for Matt and his brother to attend the 1982 PGA Championship at Southern Hills CC in Tulsa where he watched Tom Watson and became hooked on golf…Honorary Coach of the Kansas delegation to the 2003 Special Olympics in Dublin, Ireland…Is involved in many Kansas City community activities, including Turning Point - an outreach and counseling program for people whose relatives have been stricken with cancer…Has become an avid fan of thoroughbred horse racing.

PLAYER STATISTICS

2004 PGA TOUR STATISTICS

Scoring Average	71.04	(85)
Driving Distance	285.6	(113)
Driving Accuracy Percentage	68.5%	(42)
Total Driving	155	(41)
Greens in Regulation Pct.	63.2%	(142)
Putting Average	1.749	(21)
Sand Save Percentage	53.3%	(40)
Eagles (Holes per)	252.0	(99)
Birdie Average	3.62	(72)
All-Around Ranking	614	(47)
Scoring Avg. Before Cut	70.92	(86)
Round 3 Scoring Avg.	70.21	(41)
Final Round Scoring Average	71.75	(110)
Birdie Conversion Percentage	30.8%	(44)
Par Breakers	20.5%	(72)

MISCELLANEOUS PGA TOUR STATISTICS

2004 Low Round/Round: 64–2 times, most recent Cialis Western Open/2
Career Low Round/Round: 62–2001 AT&T Pebble Beach National Pro-Am/2
Career Largest Paycheck/Finish: $720,000–2002 AT&T Pebble Beach National Pro–Am/1

PGA TOUR CAREER SUMMARY — PLAYOFF RECORD: 0-0

Year	Events Played	Cuts Made	1st	2nd	3rd	Top 10	Top 25	Earnings	Rank
1992A	1								
1995	1	1						$5,843	296
1997	1								
2000	30	12		1		2	4	604,199	80
2001	26	14				4	7	729,783	70
2002	25	14	1			3	4	1,089,482	57
2003	25	13			1	3	6	897,410	78
2004	25	16				2	7	817,117	98
Total	134	70	1	1	1	14	28	4,143,835	
NATIONWIDE TOUR									
1994	1								
1995	1								
1996	12	5	1			2	2	53,840	35
1997	24	16	1	1		5	8	91,429	19
1998	26	13	2			4	7	119,899	16
1999	26	17	2	1		7	12	180,173	7
Total	90	51	6	2		18	29	445,342	

PGA TOUR TOP TOURNAMENT SUMMARY

Year	92	93	94	95	96	97	98	99	00	01	02	03	04
U.S. Open	CUT			T51		CUT			CUT	T12	CUT		CUT
British Open										T47			
PGA											T64		T17
THE PLAYERS									CUT	CUT	CUT	T66	T53
WGC-Accenture Match Play											T9		
WGC-NEC Invitational											T9		

Retief Goosen (re-TEEF GOO-sen)

EXEMPT STATUS: 2004 U.S. Open winner (through 2009)
FULL NAME: Retief Goosen
HEIGHT: 6-0
WEIGHT: 175
BIRTHDATE: February 3, 1969
BIRTHPLACE: Pietersburg, South Africa

RESIDENCE: Pietersburg, South Africa; South Ascot, England; Orlando, FL
FAMILY: Wife, Tracy; Leo (3/8/03), Ella Ann (11/18/04)
SPECIAL INTERESTS: Water skiing, all sports
TURNED PROFESSIONAL: 1990
JOINED TOUR: 2001

PGA TOUR VICTORIES (5):

2001 U.S. Open Championship. **2002** BellSouth Classic. **2003** Chrysler Championship. **2004** U.S. Open Championship, THE TOUR Championship presented by Coca-Cola.

INTERNATIONAL VICTORIES (17):

1991 Iscor Newcastle Classic [SAf]. **1992** Spoornet Classic [SAf], Bushveld Classic [SAf], Witbank Classic [SAf]. **1993** Mount Edgecombe Trophy [SAf]. **1995** Phillips South African Open [SAf]. **1996** Slaley Hall Northumberland Challenge [Eur]. **1997** Peugeot Open de France [Eur]. **1999** Novotel Perrier Open de France [Eur]. **2000** Trophée Lancôme [Eur]. **2001** The Scottish Open at Loch Lomond [Eur], Telefonica Open de Madrid [Eur], EMC World Cup [with Ernie Els]. **2002** Johnnie Walker Classic [Eur], Dimension Data Pro-Am [SAf]. **2003** Trophee Lancome [Eur]. **2004** Smurfit European Open [Eur], Nedbank Challenge.

OTHER VICTORIES (3):

1997 Dunhill Cup [with Ernie Els, David Frost]. **1998** Dunhill Cup [with Ernie Els, David Frost]. **2001** WGC-World Cup [with Ernie Els].

BEST 2004 PGA TOUR FINISHES:

1—U.S. Open Championship, THE TOUR Championship presented by Coca-Cola; 3—Ford Championship at Doral; T4—Mercedes Championships; T6—WGC-American Express Championship; T7—British Open Championship; T8—the Memorial Tournament; T9—FBR Open; T10—Sony Open in Hawaii.

2004 SEASON:

On the strength of U.S. Open and TOUR Championship victories, finished a career-best sixth on TOUR money list despite missing time due to injury. One of only two players to collect a win in each of the last four seasons on TOUR (Tiger Woods - nine straight)...Began the season with a tie for fourth at the season-opening Mercedes Championships. Was third consecutive top-five finish dating back to 2003 Chrysler Championship...One week later, finished T10 at the Sony Open in Hawaii, posting four rounds in the 60s...Added his third top-10 in first four starts with a T9 at the FBR Open...Closed with a 6-under-par 66 at the Ford Championship at Doral to finish alone in third, one stroke out of the playoff with Craig Parry and Scott Verplank. It was his fourth top-10 in only six starts for the season...Played his first 22 rounds of the season at par or better (most on TOUR in 2004) and last 30 dating back to end of the 2003 season before posting a 2-over 74 in second round of the Bay Hill Invitational...Finished top-10 at the Memorial Tournament for the second consecutive year (T8)...Became the 21st player to win multiple U.S. Opens after finishing two strokes ahead of Phil Mickelson at Shinnecock Hills. Became the sixth straight third-round leader to win the U.S. Open. After holding two-stroke 54-hole lead over Mickelson and Ernie Els, trailed Mickelson by one stroke with three holes to play. Took lead for good when Mickelson double bogeyed the par-3 17th hole and he birdied the par-5 16th hole. Needed only 24 putts, including 11 one-putts, in the final round and recorded 32 one-putts for the tournament...Won the Smurfit European Open by five strokes, two weeks after taking the U.S. Open. Became the first player to win his first start after claiming a major since Tiger Woods took the PGA Championship title and won the WGC-NEC Invitational in 2000...Posted his third consecutive top-10 on TOUR and back-to-back top-10s in a major with his T7 finish at the British Open in Scotland... Injured in a jet-ski accident in Barbados in late July that caused him to pull out of The INTERNATIONAL and the PGA...Next top-10 did not come until October, a T6 at the WGC-American Express Championship in Ireland...Captured the season-ending TOUR Championship presented by Coca-Cola at East Lake Golf Club. Entered final round four shots off the lead of Tiger Woods and Jay Haas after opening 70-66-69. Posted a bogey-free, 6-under-par 64 on Sunday to win by four shots and collect a paycheck of $1.08 million.

CAREER HIGHLIGHTS:

2003: Rode second- and third-round leads to a three-stroke victory over Vijay Singh at the Chrysler Championship, the third win of his career on the PGA TOUR...Continued a decade of consistency on the European Tour, winning the 34th and final Lancome Trophy to continue a string of nine consecutive years with at least one victory. **2002:** Won on three different Tours and three different continents - PGA TOUR, European Tour and Southern Africa Tour...Won Volvo Order of Merit on European Tour for second straight season...From his victory at the 2001 U.S. Open to his win at the 2002 BellSouth Classic, captured six of his last 24 official worldwide events: two on the PGA TOUR, three on the European Tour and one on the Southern Africa Tour. He also had three runner-up finishes among the 24 events...Won the Johnnie Walker Classic in Australia on the European Tour by eight strokes. Fired a course-record, third-round 63 and led by 13 entering the final round...Won the Dimension Data Pro-Am at the Gary Player CC, his second win in as many weeks...Third-round 68 moved him to 14-under 202 and gave him a two-shot lead over Phil Mickelson at the BellSouth Classic. Closed with a 70 to earn a four-stroke victory over Jesper Parnevik. Moved up to career-best No. 4 in Official World Golf Ranking following the BellSouth Classic. **2001:** Earned over $1.1 million in 10 starts during official rookie campaign on PGA TOUR. Became fourth rookie in TOUR history to earn $1 million in his first season...Won U.S. Open in 38th start in PGA TOUR event, defeating Mark Brooks, 70-72, in 18-hole Monday playoff at Southern Hills CC. Overcame three-putt on 72nd hole on Sunday to become

PGA TOUR CAREER SUMMARY — PLAYOFF RECORD: 1-0

Year	Events Played	Cuts Made	1st	2nd	3rd	Top 10	Top 25	Earnings	Rank
1995	3	3						$20,652	237
1996	1	1						7,363	297
1997	5	2				1	1	45,048	209
1998	6								
1999	4	2				1	2	54,368	222
2000	13	9					4	196,093	
2001	10	7	1			2	4	1,126,985	47
2002	15	14	1	2		5	13	2,617,004	10
2003	19	17	1	1	3	9	14	3,166,373	10
2004	16	13	2		1	9	11	3,885,573	6
Total	92	68	5	3	4	27	49	11,119,459	
EUROPEAN TOUR									
2004	8	8	1			4	7	1,128,125	
JAPAN GOLF TOUR									
2004	1	1				1	1	$25,933	

PGA TOUR TOP TOURNAMENT SUMMARY

Year	93	94	95	96	97	98	99	00	01	02	03	04
Masters						CUT		T40	CUT	2	T13	T13
U.S. Open						CUT	CUT	T12	1	CUT	T42	1
British Open	CUT			75	T10	CUT	T10	T41	T13	T8	T10	T7
PGA					T61	CUT	CUT	CUT	T37	T23	CUT	
THE PLAYERS						CUT		CUT	CUT	T14	CUT	CUT
TOUR Championship										T9	3	**1**
WGC-Accenture Match Play								T17	T17	T17	T33	T33
WGC-NEC Invitational	T24	10	T11	T17	DNS							
WGC-American Express Champ							T25	T35	CNL	2	T8	T6

NATIONAL TEAMS: Dunhill Cup (6), 1995, 1996, 1997, 1998, 1999, 2000; World Cup (4), 1993, 1995, 2000, 2001; Presidents Cup (2), 2000, 2003.

Retief Goosen (Continued)

the eighth player in past 50 years to make U.S. Open first TOUR title. Held first-round lead and shared second- and third-round leads...Joined TOUR as member week of July 30...Won Volvo Order of Merit on European Tour, first South African winner since 1975 (Dale Hayes). **2000:** Continued love affair with France by winning Trophée Lancôme, his third on French soil...Won the Nelson Mandela Invitational with Alan Henning. **1999:** Suffered broken left arm in skiing accident in Switzerland prior to season...After linking up with Belgian psychologist Jos Vanstiphout, won third European Tour title - Novotel Perrier Open de France - in playoff with Greg Turner. **1997:** Won Peugeot Open de France. **1996:** First European Tour win came at Staley Hall Northumberland Challenge. **1995:** Collected sixth victory on Southern Africa Tour at the Philips South African Open. **1991:** Southern Africa Tour Rookie of Year. **Amateur:** Won 1990 South African Amateur Championship.

PERSONAL:

Regarded as one of South Africa's brightest young prospects in generation that included Ernie Els. However, after being struck by lightning as an amateur in South Africa, had to deal with ongoing health problems… Introduced to golf at age 11 by his estate agent father, a 10-handicapper…After U.S. Open win in 2004, made a media tour that included an appearance on Regis and Kelly among other shows.

PLAYER STATISTICS

2004 PGA TOUR STATISTICS

Scoring Average	69.32	(5)
Driving Distance	294.2	(38)
Driving Accuracy Percentage	62.5%	(125)
Total Driving	163	(53)
Greens in Regulation Pct.	68.7%	(17)
Putting Average	1.743	(11)
Sand Save Percentage	54.6%	(28)
Eagles (Holes per)	330.0	(145)
Birdie Average	4.05	(5)
All-Around Ranking	374	(6)
Scoring Avg. Before Cut	70.19	(19)
Round 3 Scoring Avg.	68.08	(1)
Final Round Scoring Average	69.50	(2)
Birdie Conversion Percentage	32.0%	(15)
Par Breakers	22.8%	(8)

MISCELLANEOUS PGA TOUR STATISTICS

2004 Low Round/Round: 64–3 times, most recent THE TOUR Championship presented by Coca-Cola/4

Career Low Round/Round: 62–2002 WGC-American Express Championship/4

Career Largest Paycheck/Finish: $1,125,000–2004 U.S. Open Championship/1

SHOTLink

AN IBM ON DEMAND BUSINESS SOLUTION

HOT SHOTS

Easiest Par 3 on Tour (2004)

Indian Wells Country Club
6th Hole, 140 Yards
Bob Hope Chrysler Classic

HOLE 6 - INDIAN WELLS

Stroke Average	2.719
Avg. over/under par	-0.281
Birdies	41
Pars	82
Bogeys	5
Yardage	140

The 2004 field was a combined 36-under par on this hole.

(Part of multi-course event – no laser data)

Easiest Par 4 on Tour (2004)

Bermuda Dunes Country Club
11th Hole, 382 Yards
Bob Hope Chrysler Classic

HOLE 11 - BERMUDA DUNES

Stroke Average	3.535
Avg. over/under par	-0.465
Eagles	2
Birdies	56
Pars	68
Bogeys	1
Yardage	382

The 2004 field was a combined 59-under par on this hole.

(Part of multi-course event – no laser data)

Hardest Par 5 on Tour (2004)

Whistling Straits
11th Hole, 618 Yards
PGA Championship

HOLE 11 - WHISTLING STRAITS

Stroke Average	5.205
Avg. over/under par	0.205
Eagles	2
Birdies	59
Pars	264
Bogeys	105
Double bogeys	21
Other	3

The field was a combined 93-over par on this hole.

(Part of multi-course event – no laser data)

Paul Goydos

EXEMPT STATUS: Major Medical Extension
FULL NAME: Paul David Goydos
HEIGHT: 5-9
WEIGHT: 190
BIRTHDATE: June 20, 1964
BIRTHPLACE: Long Beach, CA
RESIDENCE: Long Beach, CA; plays out of Virginia CC
FAMILY: Chelsea (8/21/90), Courtney (9/8/92)
EDUCATION: Long Beach State University (1988, Finance)
SPECIAL INTERESTS: Sports
TURNED PROFESSIONAL: 1989
Q SCHOOL: 1992, 1993, 2002
Nationwide Tour Alumnus

PGA TOUR VICTORIES (1):
1996 Bay Hill Invitational.

NATIONWIDE TOUR VICTORIES (1):
1992 Yuma Open.

BEST 2004 PGA TOUR FINISH:
T49—FUNAI Classic at the WALT DISNEY WORLD Resort.

2004 SEASON:
Limited to only two starts at the end of the year because of hip surgery and sinus problems. Will receive a Major Medical Extension for 2005. Coupled with $19,366 earned in two events in 2004 has the opportunity to play in 27 events to earn $603,896 and match the $623,262 winnings of 2004's No. 125, Tag Ridings. If he does so, will play out of the Major Medical Extension category for the remainder of the season.

CAREER HIGHLIGHTS:
2003: Moved back into top 100 on the money list for the first time since 1999 when he finished 61st...Posted first top-10 with a T6 finish at the Buick Open, carding four rounds in the 60s...Second top-10 came at the Valero Texas Open where four rounds in the 60s were good for T7 finish, securing his position in the top 125…Made cut in last 11 tournaments. **2002:** Managed to get into 20 tournaments after finishing 132nd on the money list in 2001...Finished between 126-150 for the second straight season with two top-10s. **2001:** Fell out of the top 100 for the first time in five seasons (No. 121), but still managed to finish in top-10 three times in 30 appearances. **1999:** Accumulated at least four top-10s for the third time in his career...Recorded his career-best round with 62 in opening round of GTE Byron Nelson Classic. Was one back of Tiger Woods' tournament-leading 61...A week later, rounds of 70-68-69-66 earned him a five-way T2 at MasterCard Colonial, one stroke behind champion Olin Browne...Shared first-round lead at U.S. Open after opening 67. **1998:** Finished second at Deposit Guaranty Golf Classic, where he was two behind winner Fred Funk. **1997:** Followed winning season with consistent 1997, highlighted by five top-10 finishes.**1996:** First TOUR victory came at 1996 Bay Hill Invitational. With rounds of 67-74-67, was two strokes behind Guy Boros and Patrick Burke entering final round. Shot closing 67 to defeat Jeff Maggert by one stroke and earn $216,000. **1995:** Earned $10,212 in final tournament of 1995, LaCantera Texas Open, to finish 129th and remain exempt. **1994:** Finished 75th on money list on strength of three top-10 finishes. **1993:** Earned $87,804 in rookie season for 152nd place, but regained card at Qualifying Tournament that fall. **1992:** First earned PGA TOUR playing privileges with T13 finish at 1992 Qualifying Tournament. Won the Yuma Open on the Nationwide Tour.

PERSONAL:
Was substitute teacher in Long Beach, CA, at time of 1992 Yuma Open victory…1996 EA Sports Golf Challenge champion.

PLAYER STATISTICS

2004 PGA TOUR STATISTICS

Scoring Average	71.32	(N/A)
Driving Distance	280.6	(N/A)
Driving Accuracy Percentage	77.7%	(N/A)
Total Driving	(N/A)	(N/A)
Greens in Regulation Pct.	72.9%	(N/A)
Putting Average	1.705	(N/A)
Sand Save Percentage	50.0%	(N/A)
Birdie Average	4.88	(N/A)
Scoring Avg. Before Cut	68.80	(N/A)
Round 3 Scoring Avg.	68.00	(N/A)
Final Round Scoring Average	72.00	(N/A)
Birdie Conversion Percentage	34.3%	(N/A)
Par Breakers	27.1%	(N/A)

MISCELLANEOUS PGA TOUR STATISTICS

2004 Low Round/Round: 66–2 times, most recent FUNAI Classic at the WALT DISNEY WORLD Resort/3
Career Low Round/Round: 62–1999 GTE Byron Nelson Classic/1
Career Largest Paycheck/Finish: $216,000–1996 Bay Hill Invitational/1

PGA TOUR CAREER SUMMARY — PLAYOFF RECORD: 0-0

Year	Events Played	Cuts Made	1st	2nd	3rd	Top 10	Top 25	Earnings	Rank
1993	30	18					4	$87,804	152
1994	31	22				3	9	241,107	75
1995	35	21					6	146,423	129
1996	29	15	1			4	7	438,111	44
1997	30	21				5	9	396,241	61
1998	31	20		1		2	5	368,413	82
1999	29	20		1		4	8	695,052	61
2000	30	19				3	5	398,393	121
2001	29	12				2	3	375,557	132
2002	20	13				2	4	407,345	139
2003	25	18				2	7	734,284	88
2004	2	2						19,366	246
Total	321	201	1	2		27	67	4,308,097	
NATIONWIDE TOUR									
1991	25	13		1		4	7	30,237	39
1992	29	17	1		2	3	8	61,104	17
1993	2	2						615	246
2002	1	1					1	3,690	237
2004	1	1						1,305	361
Total	58	34	1	1	2	7	16	96,950	

PGA TOUR TOP TOURNAMENT SUMMARY

Year	94	95	96	97	98	99	00	01	02
Masters			CUT						
U.S. Open	T44	T62	CUT	T28		T12	CUT	CUT	CUT
PGA			T73	T29	T34	T31			
THE PLAYERS	T62	T49	CUT	CUT	T57	T38	CUT	T68	

Jay Haas

EXEMPT STATUS: 2003 U.S. Presidents Cup Team Member (through 2005)
FULL NAME: Jay Dean Haas
HEIGHT: 5-10
WEIGHT: 180
BIRTHDATE: December 2, 1953
BIRTHPLACE: St. Louis, MO
RESIDENCE: Greenville, SC

FAMILY: Wife, Janice; Jay, Jr. (3/8/81), William Harlan (5/24/82), Winona Haley (1/18/84); Emily Frances (9/25/87), Georgia Ann (3/12/92)
EDUCATION: Wake Forest University
SPECIAL INTERESTS: All sports
TURNED PROFESSIONAL: 1976
Q SCHOOL: Fall 1976

PGA TOUR VICTORIES (9):

1978 Andy Williams-San Diego Open Invitational. **1981** Greater Milwaukee Open, B.C. Open. **1982** Hall Of Fame, Texas Open. **1987** Big "I" Houston Open. **1988** Bob Hope Chrysler Classic. **1992** Federal Express St. Jude Classic. **1993** H.E.B. Texas Open.

INTERNATIONAL VICTORIES (1):

1991 Mexican Open.

OTHER VICTORIES (2):

1996 Franklin Templeton Shootout [with Tom Kite]. **2004** CVS Charity Classic [with son Bill].

BEST 2004 PGA TOUR FINISHES:

3—Bob Hope Chrysler Classic; 5—The INTERNATIONAL; T6—THE PLAYERS Championship; T7—MCI Heritage, THE TOUR Championship presented by Coca-Cola; T8—the Memorial Tournament; T9—U.S. Open Championship; T10—Buick Invitational.

BEST 2004 CHAMPIONS TOUR FINISHES:

2—Senior PGA Championship, The First Tee Open at Pebble Beach presented by Wal-Mart; T3—U.S. Senior Open

2004 SEASON:

In first start of 2004, past champion earned second consecutive top-three finish at the Bob Hope Chrysler Classic, posting five rounds in the 60s to finish one stroke out of playoff with Phil Mickelson and Skip Kendall...Added a T10 three weeks later at the Buick Invitational...With a T6 at THE PLAYERS Championship, posted second consecutive top-10 finish and the sixth of career in 27 starts. The record for appearances at THE PLAYERS is 28 by Tom Kite and Ben Crenshaw. One of three players over the age of 50 that played the 2004 PLAYERS, along with Craig Stadler and Peter Jacobsen. All three made the cut...Made ninth straight cut of season without a miss and finished T7 at the MCI Heritage for his fourth top-10. The $144,600 paycheck moved him over the $1-million mark for just the second time in his 28 years on TOUR...Playing in his first Champions Tour event after turning 50 last December lost to Hale Irwin by one stroke at the Senior PGA Championship. Sitting in the scoring tent Haas watched as Irwin birdied the 72nd hole of regulation to win the weather-plagued tournament...Finished T8 at the Memorial Tournament...Son Bill qualified for the U.S. Open at Shinnecock Hills GC to join Jay as the first father-son duo to compete in the same U.S. Open twice...Collected his fifth career top-10 at the U.S. Open in 25 appearances with his T9 and his first since a T5 in 1997. Shared first-round lead after opening 4-under 66 with Shigeki Maruyama and Angel Cabrera...Sank a 12-foot birdie putt on the 18th hole to give he and son Bill a victory in the two-day CVS Charity Classic at Rhode Island CC in late June...A week after making his second start on the Champions Tour at the U.S. Senior Open (T3), collected his seventh top-10 with a fifth-place finish at The INTERNATIONAL, moving him into the top-10 in Ryder Cup points with only one week remaining...Passed by Chris DiMarco

PGA TOUR CAREER SUMMARY — PLAYOFF RECORD: 3-0

Year	Events Played	Cuts Made	1st	2nd	3rd	Top 10	Top 25	Earnings	Rank
1973A	1	1							
1974A	1	1							
1975A	1	1					1		
1976	4	4					1	$2,911	192
1977	30	18				2	5	32,326	77
1978	29	20	1			4	9	77,176	31
1979	28	20		1		7	12	102,515	34
1980	30	26			1	7	14	114,102	35
1981	30	25	2			6	13	181,894	15
1982	29	27	2		1	10	15	229,746	13
1983	28	25		2	1	8	15	191,735	23
1984	27	20		1	1	3	12	146,514	45
1985	29	20				3	7	121,488	69
1986	29	17				7	12	189,204	45
1987	29	24	1			5	10	270,347	37
1988	29	22	1	1		6	12	490,409	20
1989	30	17		2		5	8	248,831	54
1990	28	17		1		1	5	180,023	89
1991	29	18			1	3	8	200,637	84
1992	28	24	1	1	1	6	16	632,628	20
1993	29	27	1			6	15	601,603	26
1994	30	25			1	5	14	593,386	25
1995	27	18		1	2	11	14	822,259	16
1996	26	21		1		4	11	523,019	36
1997	24	18				4	11	437,895	57
1998	25	17		1		4	7	515,454	56
1999	24	16			2	5	7	696,861	60
2000	26	13					4	265,755	144
2001	21	16				2	8	565,141	92
2002	24	18				1	9	722,782	98
2003	25	19		2		8	13	2,563,545	15
2004	23	20			1	8	11	2,071,626	27
Total	773	575	9	14	12	141	299	13,791,809	
NATIONWIDE TOUR									
2001	1								
Total	1								

CHAMPIONS TOUR CAREER SUMMARY — PLAYOFF RECORD: 0-0

Year	Events Played	1st	2nd	3rd	Top 10	Top 25	Earnings	Rank
2004	3		2	1	3	3	$541,920	34
Total	3		2	1	3	3	541,920	

PGA TOUR TOP TOURNAMENT SUMMARY

Year	74	75	76	77	78	79	80	81	82	83	84	85	86
Masters					T47		T17	T31	44	T27	T21	5	T6
U.S. Open	T54	T18		T5	CUT		T25	CUT	T6	T43	T11	T15	CUT
British Open									T27	T19	T36		
PGA					T58	T7	T50	T19	T5	T9	T39	T38	T53
THE PLAYERS				CUT	T57	T9	T8	T29	T27	W/D	T29	T55	T7

Year	87	88	89	90	91	92	93	94	95	96	97	98	99
Masters	T7	CUT	T46				38	T5	T3	T36		T12	T44
U.S. Open		T25	CUT	CUT		T23	T77	CUT	T4	T90	T5	CUT	T17
British Open	T35	T38							T79	T22	T24		
PGA	T28	T38	CUT	CUT		T62	T20	14	T8	T31	T61	T40	T3
THE PLAYERS	T50	DQ	CUT	CUT	CUT	CUT	T20	T55	CUT	T8	T43	CUT	CUT
TOUR Championship		T14				T7	T10	6	T20				

Year	00	01	02	03	04
Masters	T37			CUT	T17
U.S. Open			T12	CUT	T9
British Open				CUT	CUT
PGA	T64		CUT	T5	T37
THE PLAYERS	CUT		T49	T2	T6
TOUR Championship				29	T7
WGC-Accenture Match Play				T5	T33
WGC-NEC Invitational				T17	T41
WGC-American Express Champ				T54	T43

CHAMPIONS TOUR TOP TOURNAMENT SUMMARY

Year	04
Senior PGA Championship	2
U.S. Senior Open	T3

NATIONAL TEAMS: Walker Cup, 1975; Ryder Cup (3), 1983, 1995, 2004; The Presidents Cup (2), 1994, 2003.

Jay Haas (Continued)

and Chris Riley to finish 12th on the Ryder Cup Team points list but selected by Hal Sutton as one of two Captain's Choices. His third Ryder Cup appearance and first since 1995. Closed season with a T7 at THE TOUR Championship presented by Coca-Cola. Held second-round lead and shard thrid-round lead with Tiger Woods before posting a final-round 5-over 75.

CAREER HIGHLIGHTS:

2003: Finished in the Top 30 on the money list for the first time since 1995 and his 15th-place finish on the list was the highest since he finished 13th in 1982...Although he did not win, the 49-year old posted two runner-up finishes, at the Bob Hope Chrysler Classic and THE PLAYERS Championship...Was named to Presidents Cup team as a Captain's Choice by Jack Nicklaus after T5 finish at PGA Championship. Earnings of $214,000 pushed season winnings over $2 million for the first time in career. **2002:** Made 10 of his first 11 cuts on the way to then-second-best earnings year of career...First-round co-leader at the Bob Hope Chrysler Classic after career-tying low of 63. Outright leader by one stroke over Cameron Beckman and Kenny Perry after fourth round with second 63 of tournament. Final-round 74 produced T16...Son Bill, a sophomore at Wake Forest, received sponsor exemption into Greater Greensboro Chrysler Classic. Duo became first father-son tandem to compete in a TOUR event since Raymond and Robert Floyd at the 2000 Advil Western Open. **2001:** Regained full exempt status by finishing 92nd on money list. **2000:** Finished outside the top 125 on the money list for the first time since turning pro in 1976. **1999:** Earned five top-10s, including a pair of third-place finishes for first time since 1995—T3 at Doral-Ryder Open and PGA Championship. Best finish at a major since T3 at 1995 Masters. **1996:** Won Par-3 Contest at Masters as he had 20 years earlier as an amateur...Tied then-record of nine for most consecutive rounds of par or better at Masters (1994-96). **1994:** Captain's Choice for Presidents Cup Team, where his record was 3-2. **1993:** Collected ninth TOUR victory at the H-E-B Texas Open in a playoff with Bob Lohr. **1992:** Shot weekend rounds of 64-64 for three-stroke victory over Dan Forsman and Robert Gamez at Federal Express St. Jude Classic. **1988:** Shot opening 63 on way to Bob Hope Chrysler Classic crown. **1987:** After four years without a victory, sank 70-foot putt on final hole of Big "I" Houston Open to force playoff with Buddy Gardner, then won playoff. **1982:** Had back-to-back two-win seasons. Won playoff at Hall of Fame Classic with John Adams and defeated Curtis Strange by three strokes at Texas Open. **1981:** Three-stroke victories over Chi Chi Rodriguez at Greater Milwaukee Open and Tom Kite at B.C. Open. **1978:** Earned first TOUR victory at Andy Williams-San Diego Open by three strokes. **Amateur:** Won 1975 NCAA Championship at Wake Forest and received Fred Haskins Award that year...1975-76 All-America selection. Teammates included Curtis Strange and Scott Hoch.

PERSONAL:

Introduced to golf by uncle, 1968 Masters Tournament winner Bob Goalby...Won first trophy at National Pee Wee Championship in Orlando at age 7...Brother Jerry is the golf coach at Wake Forest...Brother-in-law Dillard Pruitt played PGA TOUR and is now a TOUR Rules Official...Appeared in a Hootie and the Blowfish music video...Older son Jay, Jr. caddied for him in 1999 PGA Championship. Second son, Bill, was an All-America player at Wake Forest, Jay's alma mater. Bill was the medalist and a semifinalist at the 2002 U.S. Amateur at Oakland Hills and a 2003 Walker Cup member. He is a 2005 member of the Nationwide Tour.

PLAYER STATISTICS

2004 PGA TOUR STATISTICS

Scoring Average	70.05	(10)
Driving Distance	274.5	(183)
Driving Accuracy Percentage	65.4%	(75)
Total Driving	258	(174)
Greens in Regulation Pct.	66.9%	(47)
Putting Average	1.758	(40)
Sand Save Percentage	56.1%	(18)
Eagles (Holes per)	177.8	(58)
Birdie Average	3.54	(94)
All-Around Ranking	525	(29)
Scoring Avg. Before Cut	69.89	(11)
Round 3 Scoring Avg.	69.83	(22)
Final Round Scoring Average	71.72	(108)
Birdie Conversion Percentage	28.2%	(127)
Par Breakers	20.3%	(83)

MISCELLANEOUS PGA TOUR STATISTICS

2004 Low Round/Round: 64–Bob Hope Chrysler Classic/3
Career Low Round/Round: 61–2003 Bob Hope Chrysler Classic/2
Career Largest Paycheck/Finish: $572,000–2003 THE PLAYERS Championship/T2

2004 CHAMPIONS TOUR STATISTICS:

Scoring Average	68.64	(N/A)
Driving Distance	274.5	(N/A)
Driving Accuracy Percentage	74.0%	(N/A)
Total Driving	1,998	(N/A)
Greens in Regulation Pct.	73.7%	(N/A)
Putting Average	1.753	(N/A)
Sand Save Percentage	75.0%	(N/A)
Birdie Average	4.18	(N/A)
All-Around Ranking	1,569	(N/A)

MISCELLANEOUS CHAMPIONS TOUR STATISTICS

2004 Low Round: 66–The First Tee Open at Pebble Beach presented by Wal-Mart/2.
Career Low Round: 66–2004 The First Tee Open at Pebble Beach presented by Wal-Mart/2
Career Largest Paycheck: $216,000–2004 Senior PGA Championship/2

Todd Hamilton

EXEMPT STATUS: Winner, 2004 British Open (through 2009)
FULL NAME: William Todd Hamilton
HEIGHT: 6-1
WEIGHT: 195
BIRTHDATE: October 18, 1965
BIRTHPLACE: Galesburg, IL
RESIDENCE: McKinney, TX; plays out of Vaquero GC (Westlake, TX)
FAMILY: Wife: Jacque; Tyler (4/2/98), Kaylee (6/20/00), Drake (4/18/03)
EDUCATION: University of Oklahoma
SPECIAL INTERESTS: Crossword puzzles, hockey, basketball
TURNED PROFESSIONAL: 1987
Q SCHOOL: 2003

PGA TOUR VICTORIES (2):

2004 The Honda Classic, British Open Championship.

INTERNATIONAL VICTORIES (14):

1992 Singapore Rolex Masters [Asia], Maekyung Open [Asia], Maruman Open [Jpn]. **1993** Acom International [Jpn]. **1994** PGA Philanthropy [Jpn], Japan PGA Matchplay Championship [Jpn], Thailand Open [Asia]. **1995** Token Corporation Cup [Jpn]. **1996** Japan PGA Philanthropy [Jpn]. **1998** Gene Sarazen Jun Classic [Jpn]. **2003** Fujisankei Classic [Jpn], Diamond Cup [Jpn], Gateway to the Mizuno Open [Jpn], Japan PGA Matchplay Championship [Jpn].

BEST 2004 PGA TOUR FINISHES:

1—The Honda Classic, British Open Championship; T6—WGC-American Express Championship.

2004 SEASON:

Surprise story of 2004 in the golf world. At the age of 38, named PGA TOUR Rookie of the Year on the strength of two wins, including dramatic playoff victory over Ernie Els at the British Open…Entered the season with only 12 TOUR events under his belt, having played primarily in Japan over the last decade, with 14 international victories during that period…Birdied the 71st and 72nd holes at The CC at Mirasol's Sunrise Course to win The Honda Classic. Opened the final round with a four-stroke lead and finished at 12-under 274 to defeat Davis Love III by one shot. Made a 10-foot birdie putt on No. 17 and a four-footer on No. 18 after an 8-iron from 162 yards. Earned his first career TOUR victory in his 18th career start on the TOUR. First rookie to win on the TOUR since Adam Scott at the 2003 Deutsche Bank Championship…Captured first major championship at the British Open at Royal Troon…Held a one-stroke lead over Ernie Els and two over Phil Mickelson and Retief Goosen through 54 holes. Bogeyed the 72nd hole to fall into a tie with Els, who birdied two of the last three holes, at 10-under. Defeated Els in the four-hole playoff by parring all four holes, while Els bogeyed the third (17th hole). The 38-year old became second consecutive rookie to win the British Open and the first rookie since Jose Coceres in 2001 to win twice in his first season on TOUR. The $1,348,272 paycheck was the second-highest in TOUR history behind Adam Scott's $1,440,000 at the 2004 PLAYERS Championship. Became the eighth American player in the last 10 years to win the British Open…Held first-round lead at the WGC-American Express Championship in Ireland after an opening-round 66 and finished T6 for his first top-10 in three WGC events…Entered THE TOUR Championship 10th on money list, attempting to become the first rookie to finish among the top 10 since Jerry Pate (1976). Finished 28th at East Lake to drop one spot to No. 11.

CAREER HIGHLIGHTS:

2003: Earned first TOUR card on eighth attempt with a T16 finish at the PGA TOUR Qualifying Tournament...Led the Japan Golf Tour with four wins, and finished third on the Japan Golf Tour Official Money List…Also placed 72nd in the WGC-American Express Championship. **1993-2002:** Captured seven events on Japan Golf Tour during this period. Typically would make five trips back and forth between the United States and Japan during a season—playing four weeks and then returning home to Dallas for two weeks. **1992:** Won 1992 Asian Tour Order of Merit, thereby earning an exemption onto the Japan Golf Tour. Won the Asian Tour's Thailand Open, Singapore Rolex Masters and Korean Open that year. **1991:** Playing on the Nationwide Tour, making one cut in four starts. **Amateur:** Three-time NCAA All-American at Oklahoma and roomed with fellow TOUR member Grant Waite.

PERSONAL:

Lists Jack Nicklaus as his hero…Credits his father for giving him his start in golf…His wife was his high school sweetheart at Union High School in Biggsville, IL…Almost quit golf prior to winning the 1992 Asian Tour Order of Merit…Grew up playing on a nine-hole course in Biggs, IL

PLAYER STATISTICS

2004 PGA TOUR STATISTICS

Scoring Average	71.04	(85)
Driving Distance	283.5	(128)
Driving Accuracy Percentage	58.7%	(167)
Total Driving	295	(191)
Greens in Regulation Pct.	62.7%	(157)
Putting Average	1.774	(84)
Sand Save Percentage	44.6%	(154)
Eagles (Holes per)	396.0	(166)
Birdie Average	3.28	(156)
All-Around Ranking	1,097	(177)
Scoring Avg. Before Cut	71.00	(96)
Round 3 Scoring Avg.	71.94	(161)
Final Round Scoring Average	72.22	(145)
Birdie Conversion Percentage	27.7%	(143)
Par Breakers	18.5%	(158)

MISCELLANEOUS PGA TOUR STATISTICS

2004 Low Round/Round: 65–EDS Byron Nelson Championship/2
Career Low Round/Round: 65–2004 EDS Byron Nelson Championship/2
Career Largest Paycheck/Finish: $1,348,272–2004 British Open Championship/1

PGA TOUR CAREER SUMMARY — PLAYOFF RECORD: 1-0

Year	Events Played	Cuts Made	1st	2nd	3rd	Top 10	Top 25	Earnings	Rank
1986A	1								
1987	3								
1988	1	1						$1,074	305
1992	1								
1993	1								
1994	1								
1996	1	1						9,920	276
2003	3	2						36,600	
2004	27	19	2			3	8	3,063,778	11
Total	39	23	2			3	8	3,111,372	
NATIONWIDE TOUR									
1991	4	1					1	1,204	208
Total	4	1					1	1,204	
EUROPEAN TOUR									
2004	2	1				1	1	75,945	

PGA TOUR TOP TOURNAMENT SUMMARY

Year	92	93	94	95	96	97	98	99	00	01	02	03	04
Masters													40
U.S. Open													CUT
British Open	CUT				T44							CUT	**1**
PGA												T29	T37
THE PLAYERS													T58
TOUR Championship													28
WGC-NEC Invitational													21
WGC-American Express Champ												72	T6

Padraig Harrington (PAW-drig)

EXEMPT STATUS: 2004 European Ryder Cup Team Member (through 2006)
FULL NAME: Padraig Harrington
HEIGHT: 6-1
WEIGHT: 196
BIRTHDATE: August 31, 1971
BIRTHPLACE: Dublin, Ireland
RESIDENCE: Dublin, Ireland

FAMILY: Wife, Caroline; Patrick (2003)
SPECIAL INTERESTS: Snooker, tennis, all sports
TURNED PROFESSIONAL: 1995
JOINED TOUR: 2003

BEST PGA TOUR CAREER FINISH:

2—2004 THE PLAYERS Championship, T2—2003 THE PLAYERS Championship,2004 Buick Classic.

INTERNATIONAL VICTORIES (9):

1996 Peugeot Spanish Open. **2000** Brazil Sao Paulo 500 Years Open, BBVA Open Turespaña Masters Comunidad de Madrid. **2001** Volvo Masters. **2002** Dunhill Links Championship, BMW Asian Open. **2003** Deutsche Bank - SAP Open TPC of Europe [Eur], Omega Hong Kong Open [Eur]. **2004** Linde German Masters [Eur].

BEST 2004 PGA TOUR FINISHES:

2—THE PLAYERS Championship, Buick Classic; 4—BellSouth Classic; T5—WGC-Accenture Match Play Championship; T6—WGC-American Express Championship.

2004 SEASON:

Irishman split time between the PGA TOUR and the European Tour...Finished No. 1 on the non-member list on the PGA TOUR and No. 3 on the European Tour's Volvo Order of Merit...In first TOUR start of 2004, finished T5 at the WGC-Accenture Match Play Championship, falling in the fourth round to eventual champion Tiger Woods, 2 and 1...Earned second consecutive runner-up finish at THE PLAYERS Championship, one stroke behind champion Adam Scott. Shot a final-round, 6-under-par 66 that included a back-nine 30, the first 30 posted on the back nine since Taylor Smith did so in the first round in 1997...Finished fourth at the BellSouth Classic to become the first non-member to earn $1 million in 2004. Entered final round three strokes behind Zach Johnson. Even-par 72 on Sunday did not include a par until the seventh hole. Finished the day with one eagle, five birdies, three bogeys, two double bogeys and seven pars...Posted an ace on the par-3 16th hole on Sunday at the Masters en route to a T13 finish. Also captured the annual Par-3 Contest on Wednesday at 4-under par...In late May, became a Special Temporary Member of the PGA TOUR for the remainder of 2004...Was part of a three-man playoff with Sergio Garcia and Rory Sabbatini at the Buick Classic. Garcia won on the third extra hole. Harrington, who was eliminated with a bogey on the second playoff hole, was the only player in the field to post four rounds in the 60s at Westchester CC. Garcia and Harrington also were in a three-way playoff with Ian Woosnam in the 1999 German Masters. Garcia won on the second extra hole...Next top-10, a T6, came at the WGC-American Express Championship in Ireland...Won the Linde German Masters on the European Tour in September and a week later was a member of the winning European Ryder Cup Team...As non-member had enough earnings to be included in the season-ending TOUR Championship presented by Coca-Cola as a 31st player, where he finished 14th.

CAREER HIGHLIGHTS:

2003: Solo 36-hole leader at THE PLAYERS Championship by two strokes over eventual champion Davis Love III and defending champion Craig Perks. Third-round 70 gave him share of lead with Jay Haas. Final-round 72 good for T2 finish...Joined the TOUR as a Special Temporary Member after collecting $572,000 at THE PLAYERS Championship...Posted seventh career European Tour victory at the Deutsche Bank-SAP Open and had two other top-10 finishes. **2002:** Picked up his first top-10 on the PGA TOUR since a T6 at the 2001 Buick Open with a T8 at the BellSouth Classic...Continued momentum one week later with a T5 finish at the Masters, six shots behind champion Tiger Woods...Second top 10 in 2002 majors was T8 finish at the U.S. Open. In second place after opening 70-68, three strokes off the lead. Paired with leader Tiger Woods on Saturday, carded a 3-over-par 73 to drop six strokes behind the eventual champion...Also finished T5 at British Open, after sharing the 36-hole lead....Earned two points for the victorious European Team at the Ryder Cup, including a singles victory over Mark Calcavecchia...Won the Dunhill Links Championship in October with a birdie on the last hole at St. Andrews and then the second playoff hole to beat Argentina's Eduardo Romero. **2001:** Won the season-ending Volvo Masters and placing second six other times to finish second on the European Tour Order of Merit behind Retief Goosen. **2000:** Will remember season for two victories and one that might have been. Disqualified from Benson and Hedges International Open, while holding five-stroke lead through 54 holes, after failing to sign first-round scorecard...Ended run of nine second-place finishes (seven in 11 months between April 1999 and March 2000) since first European Tour victory at 1996 Peugeot Open de France by winning 2000 Brazil Sao Paulo 500 Years Open. Also won the BBVA Open Turespana Masters. **1999:** Earned 10th and last automatic place on 1999 European Ryder Cup Team by finishing second in both West of Ireland Classic and BMW International, last two events in which ranking points were available. Collected 1 point in Ryder Cup debut at The Country Club at Brookline, MA, defeating Mark O'Meara in singles. **1998:** Won the Irish PGA Championship. **Amateur:** Played on winning Walker Cup side against USA at Royal Porthcawl in 1995.

PERSONAL:

Began fitness program at start of 2000 season and made swing adjustments that added distance...Coached by Bob Torrance, father of 2002 European Ryder Cup Captain Sam Torrance...Completed accountancy degree before turning professional...Distant cousin of Detroit Lions quarterback Joey Harrington...Web site is padraigharrington.com.

PLAYER STATISTICS

2004 PGA TOUR STATISTICS

Scoring Average	70.05	(N/A)
Driving Distance	290.0	(N/A)
Driving Accuracy Percentage	60.0%	(N/A)
Total Driving	(N/A)	(N/A)
Greens in Regulation Pct.	62.0%	(N/A)
Putting Average	1.753	(N/A)
Sand Save Percentage	49.3%	(N/A)
Eagles (Holes per)	126.0	(N/A)
Birdie Average	3.67	(N/A)
Scoring Avg. Before Cut	71.32	(N/A)
Round 3 Scoring Avg.	70.20	(N/A)
Final Round Scoring Average	71.80	(N/A)
Birdie Conversion Percentage	31.7%	(N/A)
Par Breakers	21.2%	(N/A)

MISCELLANEOUS PGA TOUR STATISTICS

2004 Low Round/Round: 66–2 times, most recent WGC-American Express Championship/3
Career Low Round/Round: 65–3 times, most recent 2002 BellSouth Classic/2
Career Largest Paycheck/Finish: $864,000–2004 THE PLAYERS Championship/2

PGA TOUR CAREER SUMMARY — PLAYOFF RECORD: 0-1

Year	Events Played	Cuts Made	1st	2nd	3rd	Top 10	Top 25	Earnings	Rank
1996	1	1					1	$24,025	232
1997	3	1				1	1	104,719	166
1998	3	2						23,352	238
1999	4	4					2	51,491	224
2000	8	7				2	4	265,313	
2001	9	8				1	2	240,426	
2002	9	9				4	7	806,797	
2003	11	9		1		3	7	961,235	
2004	12	11		2		5	7	1,882,276	
Total	60	52		3		16	31	4,359,634	
EUROPEAN TOUR									
2004	12	10	1	2	1	4	6	1,583,161	

PGA TOUR TOP TOURNAMENT SUMMARY

Year	96	97	98	99	00	01	02	03	04
Masters					T19	T27	T5	CUT	T13
U.S. Open		CUT	T32		T5	T30	T8	T10	T31
British Open	T18	T5	CUT	29	T20	T37	T5	T22	CUT
PGA		CUT			T58	CUT	T17	T29	T45
THE PLAYERS						T33	T22	T2	2
TOUR Championship									14
WGC-Accenture Match Play					T33	T33	T33	T17	T5
WGC-NEC Invitational				T12	T27	T17	T47	T39	74
WGC-American Express Champ				T30	T5	CNL	21	T6	T6

NATIONAL TEAMS: Ryder Cup (3), 1999, 2002, 2004; WGC-World Cup (9), 1996, 1997, 1998, 1999, 2000, 2001, 2002, 2003, 2004; Dunhill Cup (5), 1996, 1997, 1998, 1999, 2000.

Dudley Hart

EXEMPT STATUS: 92nd on 2004 money list
FULL NAME: Howard Dudley Hart
HEIGHT: 5-10
WEIGHT: 180
BIRTHDATE: August 4, 1968
BIRTHPLACE: Rochester, NY
RESIDENCE: Fort Lauderdale, FL

FAMILY: Wife, Suzanne; Abigail, Rachel and Ryan (12/6/01)
EDUCATION: University of Florida
SPECIAL INTERESTS: Hockey, reading, fishing
TURNED PROFESSIONAL: 1990
Q SCHOOL: 1990
JOINED TOUR: 1991

PGA TOUR VICTORIES (2):
1996 Bell Canadian Open. **2000** Honda Classic.

INTERNATIONAL VICTORIES (1):
1998 Subaru Sarazen World Open.

OTHER VICTORIES (1):
2002 CVS Charity Classic [with Chris DiMarco].

BEST 2004 PGA TOUR FINISHES:
T2—EDS Byron Nelson Championship; T4—Shell Houston Open.

2004 SEASON:
Returned to form by finishing among the top 100 for the eighth time in nine years. Earned 85 percent of his season earnings during a three-week stretch in April and May...In sixth start, finished T4 at the Shell Houston Open the last week of April, to earn $220,000 to remain in the Major Medical Extension category for the remainder of the season. Two weeks later a final-round 67 at the EDS Byron Nelson Championship put him in first career sudden-death playoff with Sergio Garcia and Robert Damron; lost to Garcia on the first playoff hole. His T2 finish was his best since finishing T2 at the 2002 Compaq Classic of New Orleans. His payday of $510,400, for his T2 finish, is the second-largest payday of his career behind the $522,000 he won for his victory at the 2000 Honda Classic.

CAREER HIGHLIGHTS:
2003: Limited to 22 starts due to herniated disc in his back. Received a Major Medical Extension for 2004...Lone top-10 was T8 at the 100th Western Open, first since a solo fourth at the 2002 MasterCard Colonial...Missed the cut at the British Open in next start, and then was forced to WD from three straight events (Greater Hartford Open, Buick Open, Reno-Tahoe Open) before shutting it down for the remainder of 2003. **2002:** Finished in the top 60 on the money list for the seventh consecutive season and had career high in earnings ($1,161,080)...Made 10 straight cuts beginning at THE PLAYERS Championship, which included all three of his top-10s, a seventh at the BellSouth Classic, T2 at the Compaq Classic of New Orleans, four strokes behind champion K.J. Choi, and fourth at the MasterCard Colonial, thanks to second and final rounds of 65. **2001:** Fired second- and final-round 63s to earn T3 at Canon Greater Hartford Open. The pair of 63s matched his career low which had come during the fourth round of the 1998 Motorola Open. **2000:** Included among three top-10 finishes was a victory in hometown area at The Honda Classic and a share of third place at the Greater Greensboro Chrysler Classic. Started final round at Honda four strokes behind leader J.P. Hayes and birdied last four holes to edge Hayes and Kevin Wentworth by one stroke. **1999:** For the first time in his career finished in the top 30 on the PGA TOUR money list on the strength of a career-high eight top-10s and three third-place finishes...Injured his ribs at AT&T Pebble Beach National Pro-Am and missed just two weeks of action...First of career-best trio of third-place finishes came at Bell Canadian Open, site of first TOUR victory...Placed solo third at Las Vegas Invitational. After impressive run, just missed top-30 qualification for THE TOUR Championship, finishing 36th. Jumped into top-30 on money list next week at WGC-American Express Championship with solo third and moved to 29th on final TOUR money list. **1998:** Closed year by winning unofficial Subaru Sarazen World Open. Collected $360,000, which helped finance delayed honeymoon with wife Suzanne at Mexico's Cabo San Lucas. **1997:** Nearly collected second TOUR victory at 1997 FedEx St. Jude Classic. Shot 66-66 during 36-hole Sunday and posted a 15-under-par 266 total and led in the clubhouse. Had to settle for second when Greg Norman birdied final three holes for one-stroke victory. **1996:** Earned his first PGA TOUR victory at the Bell Canadian Open. Trailed by three strokes after two rounds. After Saturday rain reduced tournament to 54 holes, shot closing 70 to defeat David Duval by one stroke. **1995:** Injured wrist by hitting root at Canon Greater Hartford Open. After two months in a cast and another two in rehab, finally underwent surgery to repair torn ligaments prior to 1996 season. **1993:** Finished 52nd on money list thanks to T3s at Northern Telecom Open and Kmart Greater Greensboro Open. **1992:** Recorded his first career top-3 finish, T3 at Greater Milwaukee Open. **1990:** Turned professional and won Florida Open and Louisiana Open...Finished 21st at the National Qualifying Tournament to earn PGA TOUR card.

PERSONAL:
Proud father of triplets (Ryan, Rachel and Abigail born 12/6/01) who often travel on TOUR...With his father, Chuck, and Jeff Sluman purchased Lake Shore GC on Lake Ontario in Rochester, NY...Season-ticket holder for the NHL's Florida Panthers and huge fan of the Buffalo Sabres. Is a close friend of Sabres head coach Lindy Ruff.

PLAYER STATISTICS

2004 PGA TOUR STATISTICS

Scoring Average	70.98	(77)
Driving Distance	285.6	(113)
Driving Accuracy Percentage	63.1%	(115)
Total Driving	228	(149)
Greens in Regulation Pct.	65.3%	(91)
Putting Average	1.784	(115)
Sand Save Percentage	45.6%	(148)
Eagles (Holes per)	149.1	(33)
Birdie Average	3.41	(127)
All-Around Ranking	819	(114)
Scoring Avg. Before Cut	71.16	(120)
Round 3 Scoring Avg.	69.33	(8)
Final Round Scoring Average	72.00	(131)
Birdie Conversion Percentage	28.5%	(109)
Par Breakers	19.6%	(116)

MISCELLANEOUS PGA TOUR STATISTICS

2004 Low Round/Round: 65–2 times, most recent Michelin Championship at Las Vegas/3
Career Low Round/Round: 63–3 times, most recent 2001 Canon Greater Hartford Open/4
Career Largest Paycheck/Finish: $522,000–2000 Honda Classic/1

PGA TOUR CAREER SUMMARY — PLAYOFF RECORD: 0-1

Year	Events Played	Cuts Made	1st	2nd	3rd	Top 10	Top 25	Earnings	Rank
1991	31	17				2	7	$126,217	120
1992	29	19			1	3	10	254,903	61
1993	30	16			2	4	8	316,750	52
1994	31	12				2	3	126,313	135
1995	30	18					4	116,334	148
1996	13	10	1			3	7	422,198	47
1997	28	14		1		3	6	410,188	60
1998	25	19			1	3	8	553,729	53
1999	27	23			3	8	12	1,267,994	29
2000	24	16	1		1	3	6	1,048,166	43
2001	25	16			1	5	11	1,035,710	53
2002	26	18		1		3	7	1,161,080	54
2003	22	13				1	1	381,735	144
2004	23	8		1		2	2	854,638	92
Total	364	219	2	3	9	42	92	8,075,956	

NATIONWIDE TOUR

Year	Events Played	Cuts Made
1991	1	1
Total	1	1

PGA TOUR TOP TOURNAMENT SUMMARY

Year	92	93	94	95	96	97	98	99	00	01	02	03	04
Masters			CUT			CUT			T28	T43			
U.S. Open	T23						W/D	T17	CUT	T62	T12	CUT	T53
British Open						CUT	81	T37	W/D	T37	CUT	CUT	
PGA	CUT	T6	T55			CUT	T44	CUT	W/D	T16	CUT		W/D
THE PLAYERS	CUT	W/D	CUT			CUT	T25	T38	W/D	CUT	T49	T62	
WGC-Accenture Match Play								T33	T33	T9			
WGC-American Express Champ								3	T48	CNL			

J.J. Henry

EXEMPT STATUS: 93rd on 2004 money list
FULL NAME: J. J. Henry
HEIGHT: 6-3
WEIGHT: 190
BIRTHDATE: April 2, 1975
BIRTHPLACE: Fairfield, CT
RESIDENCE: Fort Worth, TX ; plays out of Mira Vista (Fort Worth, TX) and The Patterson Club (Fairfield, CT)

FAMILY: Wife, Lee, Connor Joseph (7/27/2004)
EDUCATION: Texas Christian University (1998, Marketing)
SPECIAL INTERESTS: All Sports
TURNED PROFESSIONAL: 1998
JOINED TOUR: 2000
Nationwide Tour Alumnus

BEST PGA TOUR CAREER FINISHES:

2—2001 Kemper Insurance Open, T2—Texas Open at LaCantera.

NATIONWIDE TOUR VICTORIES (1):

2000 Knoxville Open.

BEST 2004 PGA TOUR FINISHES:

T3—Southern Farm Bureau Classic; T5—Valero Texas Open; T7—Nissan Open.

2004 SEASON:

Finished among the top-125 on the official money list for the fourth consecutive season...Shared first-round lead with Matt Kuchar at the AT&T Pebble Beach National Pro-Am before finishing T41...Posted his first top-10, with a T7 finish at the Nissan Open...Finished T5 in adopted home state at the Valero Texas Open with four rounds in the 60s, five shots behind champion Bart Bryant. Collected $118,650 for his T5 finish, enough to secure his TOUR card for 2005...Two weeks later, matched his best TOUR finish in over two years (T3 at the 2002 Reno-Tahoe Open) with a T3 at the Southern Farm Bureau Classic, thanks in part to closing rounds of 66-65...Recorded four top-25 finishes during the middle of the season—Wachovia Championship (T21), Buick Classic (T16), Booz Allen Classic (T18) and Cialis Western Open (23).

CAREER HIGHLIGHTS:

2003: Only top-10 of 2003 was T9 at the BellSouth Classic. Top-10 was first since a T3 at the 2002 Reno-Tahoe Open...Season best payday came at the Wachovia Championship with T11 and $111,200...Put together back to back top-20 finishes in August to help secure his card for the 2004 season. Made both cuts at The INTERNATIONAL, under the Modified Stableford scoring system to finish 18th, worth $75,000. Opened Reno-Tahoe Open with a 6-under-par 66 and a share of the lead, but drifted to T16, collected $45,000. **2002:** Had a slow start to the year but two top-10s along with 11 straight cuts in the second half of the season was the key to his season...After almost withdrawing due to mother-in-law's cancer diagnosis, dedicated week of Buick Open to her, finishing T10 for first top-10 of season...Carded four sub-par rounds at the Reno-Tahoe Open for second top-10 of year, T3. Best paycheck of the year $174,000. **2001:** Had a successful rookie campaign on PGA TOUR, making 15 of 28 cuts and earning $1,073,847 good for 49th on the TOUR money list. First-year earnings were fourth among 2001 rookies. Had five top-10s, including two seconds, at Kemper Insurance Open and Texas Open. **2000:** Member of the Nationwide Tour. Entered 29 Nationwide Tour tournaments and finished five times in the top-10...Earned his first career title at the Nationwide Tour Knoxville Open, defeating four others by one stroke and collected the $72,000 first-place check...Had a hole in one on the second hole in the first round of the Nationwide Tour Greater Cleveland Open. Notched his second ace of the year on hole No. 17 in the final round at Tri-Cities, joining Deane Pappas as the only players with two holes-in-one for the year. **1999:** Finished T2, one stroke behind Glen Hnatiuk at the Nationwide Tour Tri-Cities Open...Posted four consecutive rounds in the 60s to finish T4 at the Nationwide Tour Greensboro Open. **1998:** Turned professional in the summer after finishing at TCU. **Amateur:** 1998 Golfweek/Taylor Made Co-College Player of the Year...Named to the 1998 Palmer Cup team...1998 WAC Player of the Year...WAC Championship tournament medalist...Individual runner-up at the 1998 NCAA Championships...1998 First team All-American...Winner 1998 New England Amateur...1996 Connecticut Player of the Year...Winner of the 1994, 1995 and 1998 Connecticut State Amateur...Member of the 1995 Stoddard Cup team.

PERSONAL:

A talented junior athlete in many sports...Exposed to high-level golf at a young age from his Father, who played in numerous British and U.S. Amateur Championships... Awarded the 1998 CSWA Bill Lee Award given to the state's Male Athlete of the Year by the Connecticut Sportswriters Association...Biggest thrill in golf was his hole-in-one on the 17th hole in the last round of the 1998 WAC Championship to win both the team and individual title.

PLAYER STATISTICS

2004 PGA TOUR STATISTICS

Statistic	Value	Rank
Scoring Average	70.83	(62)
Driving Distance	301.3	(10)
Driving Accuracy Percentage	64.5%	(91)
Total Driving	101	(5)
Greens in Regulation Pct.	66.6%	(54)
Putting Average	1.788	(122)
Sand Save Percentage	41.7%	(182)
Eagles (Holes per)	309.0	(133)
Birdie Average	3.49	(105)
All-Around Ranking	759	(96)
Scoring Avg. Before Cut	70.81	(70)
Round 3 Scoring Avg.	71.33	(132)
Final Round Scoring Average	71.10	(65)
Birdie Conversion Percentage	28.3%	(121)
Par Breakers	19.7%	(110)

MISCELLANEOUS PGA TOUR STATISTICS

2004 Low Round/Round: 64–Valero Texas Open/1
Career Low Round/Round: 64–2 times, most recent 2004 Valero Texas Open/1
Career Largest Paycheck/Finish: $378,000–2001 Kemper Insurance Open/2

PGA TOUR CAREER SUMMARY — PLAYOFF RECORD: 0-0

Year	Events Played	Cuts Made	1st	2nd	3rd	Top 10	Top 25	Earnings	Rank
1998A	1	1							
1998	2	2						$6,871	299
1999	2								
2001	28	15		2		5	6	1,073,847	49
2002	34	21			1	2	5	569,875	116
2003	31	18				1	7	660,341	96
2004	30	21			1	3	7	848,823	93
Total	128	78		2	2	11	25	3,159,757	
NATIONWIDE TOUR									
1999	28	19		1		3	8	67,300	36
2000	29	21	1		1	5	12	192,287	13
2001	1	1				1	1	20,400	137
Total	58	41	1	1	1	9	21	279,987	

PGA TOUR TOP TOURNAMENT SUMMARY

Year	02	03	04
U.S. Open			64
PGA	63		
THE PLAYERS	CUT	CUT	CUT

Mark Hensby

EXEMPT STATUS: 2004 tournament winner (through 2006)
FULL NAME: Mark Adam Hensby
HEIGHT: 5-8
WEIGHT: 150
BIRTHDATE: June 29, 1971
BIRTHPLACE: Melbourne, Australia
RESIDENCE: Mesa, AZ

FAMILY: Wife, Jillian; Chase (2/7/00)
SPECIAL INTERESTS: Cars, movies
TURNED PROFESSIONAL: 1995
JOINED TOUR: 2000
Nationwide Tour Alumnus

PGA TOUR VICTORIES (1):
2004 John Deere Classic.

NATIONWIDE TOUR VICTORIES (3):
1998 Fort Smith Classic. **2000** Carolina Classic. **2003** Henrico County Open.

BEST 2004 PGA TOUR FINISHES:
1—John Deere Classic; 2—BellSouth Classic; T3—Chrysler Classic of Tucson, Cialis Western Open; T4—THE TOUR Championship presented by Coca-Cola; T6—FUNAI Classic at the WALT DISNEY WORLD Resort; T7—AT&T Pebble Beach National Pro-Am; T9—Bell Canadian Open.

2004 SEASON:
Returned for a second time to the PGA TOUR after finishing seventh on the Nationwide Tour money list in 2003. Responded by finishing 15th on the TOUR money list with a playoff victory at the John Deere Classic...In second start of season at the Bob Hope Chrysler Classic, first-round co-leader with Skip Kendall after posting a 9-under-par 63 at Indian Wells CC. Missed the 72-hole cut...Picked up first top-10 of the season with a T7 at the AT&T Pebble Beach National Pro-Am. Previous best was a T9 at the 2001 Touchstone Energy Tucson Open...Second top-10 of season was T3 at the Chrysler Classic of Tucson. Was one back of the lead through 54 holes, posted 4-under-par 68 to finish in the top five for the first time in his career...Runner-up finish at BellSouth Classic, one stroke behind Zach Johnson. Sunday's 67 was low round of the day and one of only four rounds in the 60s that day...Fourth top-10, a T3, came at the Cialis Western Open at Cog Hill. Shared third-round lead with Stephen Ames at 9-under 204 before finishing three back of Ames after final-round 73...Earned first PGA TOUR victory with a par-3 on the second sudden-death playoff hole to beat John E. Morgan at the John Deere Classic. Posted rounds of 68-65-69-66—268, overcoming four-shot lead of Jose Coceres in the final round, earning a career-best $684,000. Became the 16th first-time winner in John Deere Classic history. Recorded an ace in the first round, becoming the first player since Jim Furyk (2002 Memorial Tournament) to post an ace and win in the same week...First top-10 since win came two months later, a T9 at the Bell Canadian Open...T6 at FUNAI Classic at the WALT DISNEY WORLD Resort...In first TOUR Championship appearance, finished T4 to jump to No. 40 in the Official World Golf Ranking.

CAREER HIGHLIGHTS:
2003: Made the cut in 17 of 23 events on the 2003 Nationwide Tour. Collected $276,519 to finish No. 7 on the final money list...Earned his third career victory at the Henrico County Open. Posted a final-round 9-under 63 to finish regulation tied with Zach Johnson at 20-under-par. Went on to birdie the first playoff hole for the victory...Had a hole-in-one in the first round of the Miccosukee Championship. Finished the 2003 season No. 2 all-time on the Nationwide Tour career money list with $832,916 (1997-2000, 2002-03). **2001:** In first season on TOUR, finished 186th on money list and recorded only top-10, a T9 at the Touchstone Energy Tucson Open, during his first event as a member. **2000:** Second Nationwide Tour victory came during the 2000 at the Carolina Classic. Defeated Manny Zerman on seventh extra playoff hole. **1998:** Set tournament mark with 20-under 260 at Fort Smith Classic, his first Nationwide Tour victory...Winner of numerous other tournaments, including the 1996 Illinois Open by eight strokes and the 1994 Illinois State Amateur.

PERSONAL:
Lived in Chicago with acquaintances in 1994. For a few weeks in December 1994, after the people moved, lived in his car in the parking lot at Cog Hill, home of the TOUR's Cialis Western Open.

PLAYER STATISTICS

2004 PGA TOUR STATISTICS

Scoring Average	70.63	(41)
Driving Distance	284.6	(122)
Driving Accuracy Percentage	67.7%	(51)
Total Driving	173	(66)
Greens in Regulation Pct.	63.3%	(139)
Putting Average	1.738	(7)
Sand Save Percentage	54.0%	(32)
Eagles (Holes per)	186.0	(62)
Birdie Average	3.75	(41)
All-Around Ranking	495	(21)
Scoring Avg. Before Cut	71.03	(102)
Round 3 Scoring Avg.	70.42	(54)
Final Round Scoring Average	70.44	(23)
Birdie Conversion Percentage	31.5%	(24)
Par Breakers	21.4%	(37)

MISCELLANEOUS PGA TOUR STATISTICS
2004 Low Round/Round: 63–Bob Hope Chrysler Classic/1
Career Low Round/Round: 63–2004 Bob Hope Chrysler Classic/1
Career Largest Paycheck/Finish: $684,000–2004 John Deere Classic/1

PGA TOUR CAREER SUMMARY — PLAYOFF RECORD: 1-0

Year	Events Played	Cuts Made	1st	2nd	3rd	Top 10	Top 25	Earnings	Rank
1995	1								
1996	1	1						$3,799	332
1997	1								
2001	29	7				1	2	155,629	186
2003	1	1						8,880	
2004	29	19	1	1	2	8	12	2,718,766	15
Total	62	28	1	1	2	9	14	2,887,073	
NATIONWIDE TOUR									
1997	17	11					4	16,401	100
1998	25	12	1			4	6	75,359	33
1999	25	9			1	3	7	49,054	52
2000	25	18	1	3		7	14	291,757	2
2002	19	12		1		4	8	123,825	33
2003	23	17	1	2		7	12	276,519	7
Total	134	79	3	6	1	25	51	832,916	

PGA TOUR TOP TOURNAMENT SUMMARY

Year	04
PGA	T68
TOUR Championship	T4
WGC-NEC Invitational	T65
WGC-American Express Champ	T11

Tim Herron (HAIR-en)

EXEMPT STATUS: 32nd on 2004 money list
FULL NAME: Timothy Daniel Herron
HEIGHT: 5-10
WEIGHT: 210
BIRTHDATE: February 6, 1970
BIRTHPLACE: Minneapolis, MN
RESIDENCE: Scottsdale, AZ; plays out of Rush Creek GC
FAMILY: Wife, Ann; Carson Magne (7/24/2002)
EDUCATION: University of New Mexico
SPECIAL INTERESTS: Fishing, pool, snow skiing
TURNED PROFESSIONAL: 1993
Q SCHOOL: 1995
Nationwide Tour Alumnus

PGA TOUR VICTORIES (3):

1996 Honda Classic. **1997** LaCantera Texas Open. **1999** Bay Hill Invitational.

BEST 2004 PGA TOUR FINISHES:

2—Buick Championship; T3—FedEx St. Jude Classic; T4—EDS Byron Nelson Championship, Booz Allen Classic.

2004 SEASON:

Finished in the top 50 on the PGA TOUR money list for the fifth time in nine-year career and for second straight season. . .Recorded his first top-10 of the season at the EDS Byron Nelson Championship in May. Finished T4 thanks to a final-round 64. . .Second top-10 was a T3 at the FedEx St. Jude Classic, seven strokes behind David Toms. . .Finished T13 at the US Open, his best showing in a major since a sixth at the 1999 U.S. Open. . .Recorded his third top-five of the season with T4 finish at the Booz Allen Classic thanks to four rounds in the 60s. . .Finished second to Woody Austin at Buick Championship as Austin posted a birdie-3 on the first hole of sudden death to claim the title. Drained a 20-foot birdie putt on the 72nd hole to force the playoff. Earned a career-best $453,600. . .Was diagnosed with Lyme Disease in late July and suffered chronic fatigue the remainder of the season. . .Ten top-25s were the most since the 2001 season (10).

CAREER HIGHLIGHTS:

2003: Enjoyed one of best seasons on TOUR, finishing 25th on the money list along with a second career appearance in THE TOUR Championship...Had a second (Reno-Tahoe Open), T2 (WGC-American Express Championship) and two T3s (Bob Hope Chrysler Classic and AT&T Pebble Beach National Pro-Am)...Shot career-best 61 in third round at PGA West at the Hope, entered final round four shots ahead of the field. Shot a final-round 75 which included a quadruple bogey on the par-4 16th hole...Solo second came after tie for the lead after 36 and 54 holes, but was overcome by Kirk Triplett's final-round 63. **2002:** Finished 67th on money list. With four rounds in the 60s, picked up his first top-10 of the season, a T2, at the Greater Milwaukee Open...After GMO, did not play again until August due to the birth of daughter Carson Magne on July 24. **2001:** In a solid season, improved standing on the money list from 65th in 2000 to 57th...Managed three top-10s. **2000:** First of four top-10s was T10 at Bay Hill Invitational. Although unable to repeat, continued fine play at Bay Hill, marking third top-10 in last four years there...Four sub-par rounds at Kemper Insurance Open were good for T7. . .Tallied six birdies on the way to posting a 6-under-par 29 on the back nine at the Air Canada Championship, matching the PGA TOUR season mark for low nine...Finished ninth in final appearance of year at Tampa Bay Classic. **1999:** Captured his third PGA TOUR title in four years with playoff victory over Tom Lehman at Bay Hill Invitational. Victory was highlight of season in which he finished among the top 25 on TOUR money list for first time in career...Posted a career-high seven top-10s, including first career runner-up finishes at MasterCard Colonial and FedEx St. Jude Classic...Led or shared lead after each round of Bay Hill Invitational.. Held one-stroke, first-round lead over Steve Lowery and shared second- and third-round leads with Davis Love III. Closing 71 by Lehman to his 72 produced playoff which he won with birdie on second extra hole...At MasterCard Colonial used a final-round 67 to move into five-way T2, one stroke behind Olin Browne...In a four-way tie for the lead through 54 holes at FedEx St. Jude Classic. Closing 68 good for T2, two strokes shy of Ted Tryba. . .Finished solo sixth at U.S. Open, marking best career finish in a major championship. **1997:** Second victory came at LaCantera Texas Open. After grabbing one-stroke lead with third-round 64, went on to two-stroke victory over Rick Fehr and Brent Geiberger after closing 69. **1996:** Was the first of 13 first-time winners, with wire-to-wire victory at Honda Classic. Tied TPC at Eagle Trace course record with opening 10-under-par 62. Held six-stroke lead after second-round 68 and led by three after Saturday 72. Closing 69 in steady rain secured four-stroke win and $234,000 check. **1995:** Spent season on Nationwide Tour, where he finished 25th on money list. Best finish was T3 at Mississippi Gulf Coast Classic. **Amateur:** 1992-93 first-team All-American at University of New Mexico, where he won five tournaments...Went undefeated in three matches as member of victorious 1993 U.S. Walker Cup Team...1988 Minnesota junior player of the year...Defeated 15-year-old Tiger Woods in second round of 1992 U.S. Amateur, one of only two defeats Woods suffered in 23 U.S. Amateur matches.

PERSONAL:

Nicknamed "Lumpy" first day on job at golf course in Wayzata, MN. Nickname stood at golf course, but not at school ("There already was a 'Lumpy' at school"). . .Says ice fishing was way to pass time during Minnesota winters. . .Grandfather, Carson Lee Herron, played in 1934 U.S. Open and won state titles in Minnesota and Iowa. Father, also named Carson, played in 1963 U.S. Open. . .Herron, Tom Lehman and Lee Janzen are Minnesotans who have won more than once on TOUR. . .Sister Alissa won 1999 U.S. Mid-Amateur and is a three-time Minnesota Amateur champion.

PLAYER STATISTICS

2004 PGA TOUR STATISTICS

Scoring Average	70.79	(56)
Driving Distance	293.8	(40)
Driving Accuracy Percentage	58.0%	(173)
Total Driving	213	(129)
Greens in Regulation Pct.	65.1%	(95)
Putting Average	1.787	(119)
Sand Save Percentage	47.8%	(115)
Eagles (Holes per)	166.0	(48)
Birdie Average	3.28	(156)
All-Around Ranking	802	(106)
Scoring Avg. Before Cut	71.66	(158)
Round 3 Scoring Avg.	70.00	(32)
Final Round Scoring Average	71.00	(53)
Birdie Conversion Percentage	27.0%	(165)
Par Breakers	18.8%	(149)

MISCELLANEOUS PGA TOUR STATISTICS

2004 Low Round/Round: 64–3 times, most recent FedEx St. Jude Classic/2
Career Low Round/Round: 61–2003 Bob Hope Chrysler Classic/3
Career Largest Paycheck/Finish: $453,600–2004 Buick Championship/2

PGA TOUR CAREER SUMMARY — PLAYOFF RECORD: 1-1

Year	Events Played	Cuts Made	1st	2nd	3rd	Top 10	Top 25	Earnings	Rank
1995	1								
1996	31	22	1			3	7	$475,670	39
1997	31	21	1			6	11	640,997	33
1998	29	21				4	10	525,373	54
1999	29	21	1	2		7	11	1,511,202	22
2000	28	21				4	10	731,925	65
2001	29	20			1	3	10	945,441	57
2002	30	21		1		3	7	954,917	67
2003	29	21		2	2	6	9	2,176,390	25
2004	26	17		1	1	4	10	1,727,577	32
Total	263	185	3	6	4	40	85	9,689,490	
NATIONWIDE TOUR									
1994	4	4					3	6,894	121
1995	27	21			1	6	16	69,534	25
Total	31	25			1	6	19	76,429	

PGA TOUR TOP TOURNAMENT SUMMARY

Year	95	96	97	98	99	00	01	02	03	04
Masters		CUT		CUT	T44	CUT				CUT
U.S. Open	CUT	CUT		T53	6	CUT	T40	T50		T13
British Open		CUT			T30	CUT				CUT
PGA		T31	T13	75	CUT	CUT	CUT	CUT	T14	CUT
THE PLAYERS		T19	CUT	CUT	CUT	CUT	T21	T28	T54	CUT
TOUR Championship					T9				31	
WGC-Accenture Match Play						T17	T17			T33
WGC-American Express Champ					T16				T2	T54

NATIONAL TEAMS: Walker Cup, 1993.

Glen Hnatiuk (NATCH-ik)

EXEMPT STATUS: Major Medical Extension
FULL NAME: Glen Anthony Hnatiuk
HEIGHT: 6-2
WEIGHT: 185
BIRTHDATE: May 15, 1965
BIRTHPLACE: Selkirk, Manitoba, Canada
RESIDENCE: Homosassa, FL; plays out of World Woods GC
FAMILY: Wife, Julia; Aileen Caitlin (2/6/96), Morgan Mary (12/28/97)
EDUCATION: University of Southern Mississippi
SPECIAL INTERESTS: Family, sports
TURNED PROFESSIONAL: 1990
JOINED TOUR: 1998
Nationwide Tour Alumnus

BEST PGA TOUR CAREER FINISH:
T3—2000 B.C. Open.

NATIONWIDE TOUR VICTORIES (4):
1992 Gulf Coast Classic. **1995** Utah Classic. **1996** Carolina Classic. **1999** Tri-Cities Open.

BEST 2004 PGA TOUR FINISH:
T20—BellSouth Classic.

2004 SEASON:
Limited to nine events due to lateral epicondylitis, or "tennis elbow," in his left arm. Did not play after the MCI Heritage in April. Underwent surgery to correct problem in May. Top finish was T20 at the BellSouth Classic. Will receive a Major Medical Extension for 2005. Coupled with $103,500 earned in nine events in 2004 has the opportunity to play in 20 events to earn $519,762 and match the $623,262 winnings of 2004's No. 125, Tag Ridings. If he does so, will play out of the Major Medical Extension category for the remainder of the season.

CAREER HIGHLIGHTS:
2003: Canadian secured status for 2004 in final full-field event of 2003 at the Chrysler Championship. Rebounded from first-round 74 to finish T49, jumping from 130th to 124th on the PGA TOUR Money List with a paycheck of $11,976. Hnatiuk bumped Per-Ulrik Johansson to No. 126...First top-10 came in ninth start, a T10 at the MCI Heritage, thanks to four rounds in the 60s...Late in September recorded a T7 at the Valero Texas Open for his best finish on TOUR since T3 at the 2000 B.C. Open. **2002:** Made 19 cuts in 28 starts and finished 120th on the Official Money List with $558,940...Earned highest PGA TOUR finish since 2000 with a T8 at the WORLDCOM CLASSIC...Shared the first-round lead at the FedEx St. Jude Classic after opening with 65. Was the outright leader through 36 and 54 holes at the TPC at Southwind, including a four-stroke lead heading into the final round. Shot a closing 77 for T14. **2001:** Began the year on a positive note with a T15 at the Touchstone Energy Tucson Open. Entered final round tied for second, two strokes back of the lead...Best effort of the season (T9) came at the Marconi Pennsylvania Classic. **2000:** T3 at the B.C. Open, career-best finish, and T6 at The INTERNATIONAL earned his largest TOUR paycheck, $121,625. **1999:** Member of the Nationwide Tour...Made a 12-foot birdie putt on 72nd hole for one-stroke win at the Tri-Cities, his first 72-hole victory. Victory assured a return to PGA TOUR in 2000 moving him to 11th on Nationwide Tour money list, where he eventually finished eighth...Joined Matt Gogel as one of two players to win Nationwide events in four separate years. **1998:** Finished 165th on PGA TOUR money list and returned to Nationwide Tour...Top finish was T14 at the Tucson Chrysler Classic. **1997:** Eight top-10s helped him earn the 10th spot on the Nationwide Tour money list and move on to the PGA TOUR the next season. **1996:** Earned his third career title at the rain-shortened Nationwide Tour Carolina Classic, thanks to a final-round 8-under-par 64. **1995:** Member of the Nationwide Tour...Won the Utah Classic in a playoff over Franklin Langham and Harry Rudolph. **1992:** First Nationwide Tour win came as a Monday qualifier at the Mississippi Gulf Coast Classic. **Amateur:** 1988 All-Metro Conference selection at University of Southern Mississippi.

PERSONAL:
Was a member of the Western Canadian Junior "B" championship hockey team prior to moving to the United States.

PLAYER STATISTICS

2004 PGA TOUR STATISTICS

Scoring Average	72.32	(N/A)
Driving Distance	274.8	(N/A)
Driving Accuracy Percentage	69.6%	(N/A)
Total Driving	1,998	(N/A)
Greens in Regulation Pct.	66.2%	(N/A)
Putting Average	1.835	(N/A)
Sand Save Percentage	50.0%	(N/A)
Eagles (Holes per)	156.0	(N/A)
Birdie Average	3.08	(N/A)
Scoring Avg. Before Cut	72.16	(N/A)
Round 3 Scoring Avg.	68.50	(N/A)
Final Round Scoring Average	73.25	(N/A)
Birdie Conversion Percentage	25.6%	(N/A)
Par Breakers	17.7%	(N/A)

MISCELLANEOUS PGA TOUR STATISTICS

2004 Low Round/Round: 65–Bob Hope Chrysler Classic/3
Career Low Round/Round: 64–5 times, most recent 2003 Valero Texas Open/3
Career Largest Paycheck/Finish: $121,625–2000 The International Presented by Qwest/T6

PGA TOUR CAREER SUMMARY — PLAYOFF RECORD: 0-0

Year	Events Played	Cuts Made	1st	2nd	3rd	Top 10	Top 25	Earnings	Rank
1997	2	2						$8,625	281
1998	30	15					3	148,098	165
2000	30	16			1	2	5	482,744	101
2001	31	23				1	5	434,524	119
2002	28	19				1	8	558,940	120
2003	29	18				2	4	488,429	124
2004	9	4					1	103,500	215
Total	159	97			1	6	26	2,224,861	
NATIONWIDE TOUR									
1992	19	6	1			1	2	30,234	52
1993	28	4					1	4,376	146
1994	26	13				1	4	18,526	76
1995	27	18	1	1		4	11	102,547	14
1996	23	16	1		1	4	6	79,700	23
1997	24	19		1	1	8	14	116,381	10
1999	25	20	1	3		9	14	176,085	8
Total	172	96	4	5	2	27	52	527,849	

PGA TOUR TOP TOURNAMENT SUMMARY

Year	01	02	03	04
THE PLAYERS	T58	CUT	T39	CUT

NATIONAL TEAMS: World Cup, 2000.

Scott Hoch (hoak)

EXEMPT STATUS: 2003 tournament winner (through 2005)
FULL NAME: Scott Mabon Hoch
HEIGHT: 5-11
WEIGHT: 170
BIRTHDATE: November 24, 1955
BIRTHPLACE: Raleigh, NC
RESIDENCE: Orlando, FL

FAMILY: Wife, Sally; Cameron (5/1/84), Katie (5/16/86)
EDUCATION: Wake Forest University (1978, Communications)
SPECIAL INTERESTS: All sports
TURNED PROFESSIONAL: 1979
Q SCHOOL: Fall 1979

PGA TOUR VICTORIES (11):

1980 Quad Cities Open. **1982** USF&G Classic. **1984** Miller High Life QCO. **1989** Las Vegas Invitational. **1994** Bob Hope Chrysler Classic. **1995** Greater Milwaukee Open. **1996** Michelob Championship at Kingsmill. **1997** Greater Milwaukee Open. **2001** Greater Greensboro Chrysler Classic, Advil Western Open. **2003** Ford Championship at Doral.

INTERNATIONAL VICTORIES (6):

1982 Pacific Masters [Jpn], Casio World Open [Jpn]. **1986** Casio World Open [Jpn]. **1990** Korean Open [Asia]. **1991** Korean Open [Asia]. **1995** Heineken Dutch Open [Eur].

BEST 2004 PGA TOUR FINISHES:

2—Shell Houston Open; T7—MCI Heritage; 8—Mercedes Championships; 10—U.S. Bank Championship in Milwaukee.

2004 SEASON:

Was having another consistent year, with four top-10s in 16 starts, until an injury at the PGA Championship sidelined him for the rest of the season. Managed to surpass the $1-million mark for the ninth consecutive season...After playing in just four 2003 events after July due to nagging wrist injury, finished eighth at 2004's season-opening Mercedes Championships...Played in his 22nd MCI Heritage and had second-best finish at the tournament, a T7, behind his 1996 third-place performance...One week later, finished runner-up to Vijay Singh at the Shell Houston Open. Along with Singh, only player without a bogey in the final round. Back-to-back top-10s were first since 2003 (T5 at the WGC-Acccenture Match Play Championship and a victory at the Ford Championship at Doral)...Posted one of three aces during second round of Cialis Western Open. Used 4-iron from 196 yards on the 14th hole. The 2001 winner finished T11...Recorded four rounds of 68 at the John Deere Classic to finish T11...Picked first top-10 in five months with a T10 at the U.S. Bank Championship in Milwaukee, his fifth career top-10 in 17 starts in Milwaukee. Made his 12th consecutive cut in Milwaukee, one behind Dave Eichelberger for the all-time tournament record...During the second round of the PGA Championship in August fell walking off a tee box. The ground (sand) gave way, causing him to fall backward. He put his hands out to break fall and ended up with a sprained left wrist. Played about three more holes and then withdrew.

CAREER HIGHLIGHTS:

Perhaps the PGA TOUR's most consistent performer since joining in 1980. Has collected 160 top-10s in his career. **2003:** In his second tournament of the season finished T5 at the WGC-Accenture Match Play Championship after losing to eventual champion Tiger Woods in the quarterfinals (5 and 4)...Following week won the Ford Championship at Doral, for his 11th career victory and fifth since turning 40. Shared third-round lead with Bob Tway, then went on to defeat Jim Furyk with birdie on the third extra hole to even his career playoff record at 2-2. Play was suspended due to darkness on Sunday night while both players were on the green of the second playoff hole. First Monday finish since the 2001 Buick Classic. $900,000 paycheck was largest of career. Now holds the 10th-longest span between first and last victories (22 years, seven months and 21 days) in TOUR history. At beginning of the week was going to pull out of the Ford Championship due to wrist injury...Played off and on the rest of the season due to a nagging right wrist injury. Made only five cuts in the 13 starts after his win in Miami. Missed six straight cuts in the middle of the season. His longest stretch of consecutive cuts missed in his 23 year TOUR career was four in a row coming into the 2003 season. He missed four consecutive cuts in each of the first two seasons on the TOUR, 1980 and 1981. **2002:** T4 at THE PLAYERS Championship was fifth top-10 there in the last six years...Did not defend his title at the Greater Greensboro Chrysler Classic due to trouble with right eye from LASIK surgery. Had two surgeries over last four months to fix an astigmatism...Tied career best with a T5 finish at the U.S. Open, closing with a 1-under-par 69. On Sunday, sporting a stars and stripes golf shirt dedicated to New York City, recorded an ace with a 3-iron on the 207-yard 17th hole, one of three holes-in-one on the week...In only fifth career British Open appearance, finished T8 for low American, aided by a final-round 66. Total of 280 was only two strokes out of a four-man playoff. Previous best finish at British Open had been T68 in 1995, missing cut in three others...Finished Ryder Cup with 0-3-1 record. Along with Jim Furyk, tied Darren Clarke and Paul McGinley during Saturday's Four-Ball contest...Picked up T2 at the Michelob Championship at Kingsmill. Made the cut 19 of 20 times at Kingsmill GC, including a win, T2, third and T3, T4, fifth and a sixth-place finish. Also had a T9, which gave him more top-10 finishes than any other player in the history of that event. **2001:** At 45, had a career year in money earned with $2,875,319 (seventh on money list) and tournament titles (two) in a single season. First 45-year old to win twice in same season since Hale Irwin in 1990. Only Julius Boros (age 47 and 48 in 1967 and '68), Sam Snead (age 47 in 1960) and Irwin had won multiple times at age 45 or older...Held third-round lead at Greater Greensboro Chrysler Classic. Closing 69 brought him his ninth TOUR title, first in last 94 starts. At age 45 years, 5 months and 5 days, oldest TOUR winner since Tom Watson won the 1998 MasterCard Colonial at age 48. Also supplanted defending champion Hal Sutton (age 41) as oldest Greater Greensboro Chrysler Classic winner since 52-year-old Sam Snead...Closing 64 at Advil Western Open produced 10th TOUR title and second of season. Edged 36- and 54-hole leader David Love III by

SECTION 2 PLAYER BIOGRAPHIES

PGA TOUR CAREER SUMMARY — PLAYOFF RECORD: 2-2

Year	Events Played	Cuts Made	1st	2nd	3rd	Top 10	Top 25	Earnings	Rank
1979A	1	1							
1980	18	6	1			1	4	$45,600	77
1981	31	19				2	7	49,606	87
1982	28	23	1	1		8	17	193,862	16
1983	25	20			1	7	11	144,605	37
1984	26	22	1	1	3	7	13	224,345	27
1985	30	24		1	1	6	13	186,020	35
1986	28	23		1	3	6	13	222,077	36
1987	27	23			4	8	12	391,747	20
1988	31	26				10	18	397,599	26
1989	27	21	1	1	1	6	12	670,680	10
1990	26	19			1	7	13	333,978	40
1991	31	26		1	1	9	14	520,038	27
1992	16	13					3	84,798	146
1993	28	18			1	6	15	403,742	37
1994	28	21	1	1	2	7	14	804,559	11
1995	28	23	1	1	1	8	14	792,643	18
1996	27	23	1	2	3	8	14	1,039,564	9
1997	22	22	1	1	1	11	15	1,393,788	6
1998	27	22		2		9	17	1,237,053	17
1999	27	24				6	17	1,172,692	33
2000	29	24		1		7	17	1,368,888	33
2001	24	17	2	1		10	14	2,875,319	7
2002	21	16		1		7	11	1,465,173	38
2003	17	8	1			2	2	1,198,250	59
2004	17	11		1		4	6	1,239,360	60
Total	640	495	11	17	23	162	306	18,455,984	

PGA TOUR TOP TOURNAMENT SUMMARY

Year	79	80	81	82	83	84	85	86	87	88	89	90	91
Masters	T34		T37		T27		T53			CUT	2	T14	T35
U.S. Open			CUT	W/D	T48		T34		T36	T21	T13	T8	6
British Open												CUT	
PGA		CUT	CUT		T61	T48	T12	T41	T3	T25	T7	T49	T43
THE PLAYERS			T37	T13	CUT	T44	CUT	T14	T39	CUT	CUT	W/D	CUT
TOUR Championship									T12	28	T7		T21

Year	92	93	94	95	96	97	98	99	00	01	02	03	04
Masters			CUT	T7	T5	38	T16	T44	CUT	T37	CUT	CUT	
U.S. Open	CUT	T5	T13	T56	T7	T10	CUT	CUT	T16	T16	T5	CUT	T53
British Open				T68			CUT			CUT	T8		
PGA	CUT	T6	CUT	CUT	T61	T6	T29	T21	T74	T7	CUT	T57	W/D
THE PLAYERS		CUT	CUT	W/D	T19	2	T5	T6	T13	T7	T4	W/D	T42
TOUR Championship			T20	T27	T18	T10	T21			29			
WGC-Accenture Match Play								T17	T5		T33	T5	T33
WGC-NEC Invitational								T23		T21	T55	T51	
WGC-American Express Champ								T7	T17	CNL	T23	T70	

NATIONAL TEAMS: World Amateur Team Championship, 1978; Walker Cup, 1979; The Presidents Cup (3), 1994, 1996, 1998; Ryder Cup (2), 1997, 2002.

Scott Hoch (Continued)

one stroke. His 267 total broke tournament record set by Sam Snead in 1949 and equaled by Chi Chi Rodriguez in 1964. **2000:** First of seven top-10s came at WGC-Accenture Match Play Championship, where he defeated Stuart Appleby, Lee Westwood and Jesper Parnevik before a 5-and-4 quarterfinal loss to David Duval...Shot a final-round 65 to finish runner-up at SEI Pennsylvania Classic. **1999:** Another consistent season making 24 cuts in 27 starts and finished No. 33 on the final PGA TOUR money list...Had six top-10s and 17 top-25s. **1998:** Finished second at Kemper Open and CVS Charity Classic. **1997:** Won second Greater Milwaukee Open...That year had career-high 11 top-10s, including second at THE PLAYERS Championship, third at Nissan Open, T4 at Shell Houston Open and Memorial Tournament, fifth at Michelob Championship, T6 at PGA Championship, T9 at Bob Hope Chrysler Classic and MCI Classic, T10 at U.S. Open and THE TOUR Championship. Was the second oldest (Lee Elder) Ryder Cup rookie. **1996:** Six top-three finishes, topped by wire-to-wire victory at Michelob Championship at Kingsmill...Won Vardon Trophy with 70.08 scoring average. **1995:** Shot back-to-back 65s on weekend at Greater Milwaukee Open for three-stroke victory...Lost playoff to Payne Stewart at Shell Houston Open after holding five-stroke lead through 54 holes. **1994:** After four years without a victory, captured Bob Hope Chrysler Classic...Later that year, runner-up to Jose Maria Olazabal at NEC World Series of Golf. **1989:** Lost on second hole of sudden-death playoff to Nick Faldo at Masters. Three weeks later, won Las Vegas Invitational in playoff over Robert Wrenn...Had first money list top-10 finish (No.10), earning $670,680. **1986:** Winner of Chrysler Team Championship with Gary Hallberg. **1984:** Won third TOUR title, at the Miller Lite Quad Cities Open by five strokes. **1982:** Won second TOUR title at the USF&G Classic in New Orleans, beating Bob Shearer and Tom Watson by two strokes in the weather-shortened 54-hole tournament. **1980:** First victory came in rookie season, winning first of two Quad Cities Opens. **Amateur:** Runner-up to John Cook at 1978 U.S. Amateur...Member of 1975 national championship team at Wake Forest...An All-America selection in 1977 and 1978 when he won Atlantic Coast Conference title.

PERSONAL:

Donated $100,000 of 1989 Las Vegas Invitational winnings to Arnold Palmer Children's Hospital in Orlando. Has a floor named after him at the Arnold Palmer Hospital thanks to his family's donations. Although son Cameron was successfully treated elsewhere for rare bone infection in right leg, he and wife Sally are strong supporters of Orlando facility. . .Family has also made large donations to area hospitals and churches. . .Brother Buddy was a professional bowler, while their father won All-American honors in baseball at Wake Forest.

PLAYER STATISTICS

2004 PGA TOUR STATISTICS

Scoring Average	70.57	(38)
Driving Distance	280.4	(154)
Driving Accuracy Percentage	68.8%	(37)
Total Driving	191	(87)
Greens in Regulation Pct.	68.6%	(18)
Putting Average	1.786	(117)
Sand Save Percentage	50.0%	(80)
Eagles (Holes per)	229.5	(93)
Birdie Average	3.53	(97)
All-Around Ranking	634	(57)
Scoring Avg. Before Cut	70.77	(63)
Round 3 Scoring Avg.	71.40	(134)
Final Round Scoring Average	70.50	(27)
Birdie Conversion Percentage	27.5%	(151)
Par Breakers	20.0%	(103)

MISCELLANEOUS PGA TOUR STATISTICS

2004 Low Round/Round: 65–U.S. Bank Championship in Milwaukee/2

Career Low Round/Round: 62–1994 Bob Hope Chrysler Classic/2

Career Largest Paycheck/Finish: $900,000–2003 Ford Championship at Doral/1

SHOTLink
AN IBM ON DEMAND BUSINESS SOLUTION

HOT SHOTS

The Final 3...

(Holes 16-18 at the TPC at Sawgrass)

The final three holes on The Stadium Course at the Tournament Players Club at Sawgrass, site of THE PLAYERS Championship, make up one of the most dramatic finishes in all of golf. A look at those holes, beginning with the par-5 16th, followed by the par-3 17th (page 95) and the par-4 18th (page 114).

16th Hole-TPC at Sawgrass

Tournament Players Club at Sawgrass
(Stadium Course)

16th Hole, 507 Yards

No. 16 at the TPC Sawgrass was 50th of the 56 toughest 16th holes on TOUR and ranked 931st/1,007 toughest holes on TOUR.

Hole 16	
Driving Average	278.2 (5th)
Longest Drive	339 (6th)
Driving Accuracy	288/ 459 63% (9th)
Greens in Regulation	359/ 459 78% (T1st)

GOING FOR GREEN	
Attempts	289/ 459 63% (2nd)
Success	65/ 289 23% (1st)

Risk/Reward: Only 23 percent of the field succeeded out of the 63 percent who attempted to hit 16 in two shots.

Driving Distance	Total Drives	Total %	Total Par Relative	Scoring Avg
320+	1	1.20%	2 under	3
300-320	10	12.00%	10 under	4
280-300	34	41.00%	21 under	4.38
260-280	28	33.70%	5 under	4.82
240-260	5	6.00%	2 under	4.6
<240	5	6.00%	1 over	5.2

DISTANCE TO PIN	
200+	58 ft 05 in (2nd)
175-200	48 ft 00 in (4th)
150-175	64 ft 01 in (12th)
125-150	29 ft 11 in (6th)
0-125	21 ft 11 in (4th)

From 175-200 yards the field averaged 48 feet from the pin. From 150-175 yards the average distance to the pin increased by 16 ft 1 in.

SCORING	
Average Score	4.641
Eagles	18
Birdies	179
Pars	213
Bogeys	48
Double Bogeys	1
Rank	18

PLAYERS GOING FOR IT	DISTANCE (YARDS)	SCORE
Daly	179	Eagle
Scott	187	Par
Cink	191	Birdie
McRoy	192	Birdie
Perry	195	Birdie
Harrington	196	Eagle
Haas	197	Birdie
Els	198	Par
Love III	198	Eagle
Rose	201	Birdie

Charles Howell III

EXEMPT STATUS: 2003 United States Presidents Cup team member (through 2005)
FULL NAME: Charles Gordon Howell III
HEIGHT: 5-11
WEIGHT: 155
BIRTHDATE: June 20, 1979
BIRTHPLACE: Augusta, GA
RESIDENCE: Orlando, FL
FAMILY: Wife, Heather
EDUCATION: Oklahoma State University
SPECIAL INTERESTS: Fitness, nutrition, fishing
TURNED PROFESSIONAL: 2000
JOINED TOUR: 2001

PGA TOUR VICTORIES (1):

2002 Michelob Championship at Kingsmill.

BEST 2004 PGA TOUR FINISHES:

2—Booz Allen Classic; T5—HP Classic of New Orleans; T9—FedEx St. Jude Classic, WGC-NEC Invitational, Deutsche Bank Championship.

2004 SEASON:

Continued his consistent play on the PGA TOUR, recording five top-10s and finishing in the top 40 for the third consecutive season...Recorded a career-best T13 in his third start at the Masters in hometown of Augusta...First top-10 of year was a T5 at the HP Classic of New Orleans, five strokes behind Vijay Singh...Second top-10 was a T9 at the FedEx St. Jude Classic, aided by rounds of 68-69 on the weekend...Fired a TPC of Avenel course-record, a career-best, 10-under 61 to take a three-stroke lead after 18 holes at the Booz Allen Classic. Recorded five consecutive birdies on the back nine Sunday to put pressure on leader Adam Scott, who started the day with a six-stroke lead. Ended the day alone in second, the fifth runner-up finish of his career...Shared second-round lead (6-under 136) with Steve Lowery and Matt Gogel at Cialis Western Open before finishing T17...Posted back-to-back T9s at WGC-NEC Invitational and Deutsche Bank Championship. First back-to-back top-10s since August 2003.

CAREER HIGHLIGHTS:

2003: Made the cut in 29 of 31 starts and...Lost to Mike Weir in a playoff at the Nissan Open after Weir birdied the second extra hole. Was second- and third-round leader, and held three-shot lead heading into Sunday, but finished with 2-over 73 to tie Weir at the end of regulation...Grabbed first-round lead at the Memorial Tournament with an 8-under-par 64, finished T27...Posted first career top-10 at a major with a T10 at the PGA Championship. Clinched 10th and final spot on 2003 Presidents Cup team with PGA Championship finish...Held the 36-hole lead at the Bell Canadian Open and was two back through 54 holes. Closing round of 74 dropped him into T14...Ended the year on a high note with his second runner-up finish at the TOUR Championship. Finished two back of Vijay Singh in Atlanta in 2002 and three back of Chad Campbell in Houston in 2003...Earned a spot on The Presidents Cup for the United States. **2002:** Followed a successful rookie campaign with an even better sophomore season, thanks to a victory and ninth-place finish on the season money list with $2,702,747...Picked up his first career victory in his 68th TOUR event at the Michelob Championship at Kingsmill. Began final round two strokes behind leader Brandt Jobe and final-round 67 gave him the two-stroke victory...Tied Waialea CC course record with a second-round 62 on way to his first top-10 finish of the season, a T4 at the Sony Open in Hawaii...Tied Riviera CC record with front-nine, 7-under 28 in third round of Nissan Open for a 64 and eventual T6...Made his first appearance in the Masters Tournament, local favorite finished T29...Runner-up to Vijay Singh in season-ending TOUR Championship. Held second-round lead. Only player in field to post four rounds in the 60s and finished season with 16 consecutive rounds in the 60s. **2001:** Rookie of the Year. Earned his 2002 PGA TOUR card by playing TOUR events via sponsor exemptions. Earned Special Temporary Member status for the second consecutive season...Ranked first in PGA TOUR non-member earnings with $1,520,632. Earnings would have ranked 33rd on TOUR official money list...Five top-10s on the season...First top-10 came at the BellSouth Classic, a T6...Lost in sudden-death playoff at Greater Milwaukee Open to Shigeki Maruyama. Birdied six of last seven holes of regulation to shoot 64 and force playoff but bogeyed first sudden-death hole as Maruyama made birdie. **2000:** Earned Special Temporary Member status in only six events after turning professional on June 26. Made the cut in seven of 11 official TOUR events...Best effort of the season came at the John Deere Classic, a solo third...Week before turning professional, turned in a second-place finish at the Greensboro Open, the highest amateur finish in Nationwide Tour history. **Amateur:** 2000 NCAA champion as a junior at Oklahoma State. Winning total of 23-under-par set NCAA Championship scoring record...Two-time first-team All-American...Recipient of Jack Nicklaus and Fred Haskins Awards...Big 12 Champion and Big 12 Player of the Year in 2000...Represented United States at 2000 Palmer Cup...1996 AJGA Player of the Year...Three-time first-team AJGA All-American...Captured 1996 Rolex Tournament of Champions.

PERSONAL:

Grew up near Augusta National GC, home of the Masters, and was a member of Augusta CC, which is adjacent to Amen Corner...Next-door neighbor was the first person who introduced him to golf...Started playing golf at age 7 and won five tournaments before his 11th birthday...Shot his first sub-70 tournament round at age 10, the same age at which he began taking lessons from instructor David Leadbetter...Father is a pediatric surgeon.

PLAYER STATISTICS

2004 PGA TOUR STATISTICS

Scoring Average	70.77	(52)
Driving Distance	288.5	(82)
Driving Accuracy Percentage	64.3%	(96)
Total Driving	178	(71)
Greens in Regulation Pct.	66.1%	(69)
Putting Average	1.802	(164)
Sand Save Percentage	48.9%	(101)
Eagles (Holes per)	227.3	(91)
Birdie Average	3.26	(161)
All-Around Ranking	816	(113)
Scoring Avg. Before Cut	70.73	(59)
Round 3 Scoring Avg.	71.48	(141)
Final Round Scoring Average	71.48	(90)
Birdie Conversion Percentage	26.7%	(175)
Par Breakers	18.5%	(158)

MISCELLANEOUS PGA TOUR STATISTICS

2004 Low Round/Round: 61–Booz Allen Classic/1
Career Low Round/Round: 61–2004 Booz Allen Classic/1
Career Largest Paycheck/Finish: $666,000–2002 Michelob Championship at Kingsmill/1

PGA TOUR CAREER SUMMARY — PLAYOFF RECORD: 0-2

Year	Events Played	Cuts Made	1st	2nd	3rd	Top 10	Top 25	Earnings	Rank
1996A	1								
1997A	1								
2000	13	7			1	1	2	$263,533	
2001	24	20		1	1	5	14	1,520,632	
2002	32	27	1	1	1	7	16	2,702,747	9
2003	31	29		2		6	16	2,568,955	14
2004	30	22		1		5	10	1,703,485	33
Total	132	105	1	5	3	24	58	8,759,352	
NATIONWIDE TOUR									
2000A	1	1		1		1	1		
Total	1	1		1		1	1		

PGA TOUR TOP TOURNAMENT SUMMARY

Year	01	02	03	04
Masters		T29	T28	T13
U.S. Open	CUT	T18	T53	T36
British Open			T65	T42
PGA	T22	T17	T10	T31
THE PLAYERS		T60	T32	CUT
TOUR Championship		2	2	
WGC-Accenture Match Play		T17	T33	T33
WGC-NEC Invitational			T21	T9
WGC-American Express Champ			T21	T59

NATIONAL TEAMS: The Presidents Cup, 2003.

SECTION 2 PLAYER BIOGRAPHIES

John Huston

EXEMPT STATUS: 2003 tournament winner (through 2005)
FULL NAME: Johnny Ray Huston
HEIGHT: 5-10
WEIGHT: 155
BIRTHDATE: June 1, 1961
BIRTHPLACE: Mt. Vernon, IL

RESIDENCE: Palm Harbor, FL; plays out of Westin Innisbrook Golf Resort
FAMILY: Wife, Suzanne; Jessica (11/9/87), Travis (3/29/93)
EDUCATION: Auburn University
SPECIAL INTERESTS: All sports
TURNED PROFESSIONAL: 1983
Q SCHOOL: Fall 1987

PGA TOUR VICTORIES (7):

1990 Honda Classic. **1992** Walt Disney World/Oldsmobile Classic. **1994** Doral-Ryder Open. **1998** United Airlines Hawaiian Open, National Car Rental Golf Classic/Disney. **2000** Tampa Bay Classic. **2003** Southern Farm Bureau Classic.

OTHER VICTORIES (1):

1988 JCPenney Classic.

BEST 2004 PGA TOUR FINISHES:

3—Shell Houston Open; T9—WGC-Accenture Match Play Championship; T10—Sony Open in Hawaii, FUNAI Classic at the WALT DISNEY WORLD Resort.

2004 SEASON:

Finished inside the top 100 on the PGA TOUR money list for the seventh straight season and the 16th time in his 17-year career. . .Past champion (1998) carded four rounds in the 60s to finish T10 at the Sony Open in Hawaii. . .Turned in his best finish in a World Golf Championships event with a T9 at the WGC-Accenture Match Play Championship. Upset No. 5 Retief Goosen in first round, and No. 28 Peter Lonard in second before losing to No. 44 Ian Poulter in third round, 2 and 1. . .Held a share of the 54-hole lead with Vijay Singh at the Shell Houston Open at 7-under-par. Finished solo third in Monday finish after final-round 71, three strokes behind Singh. . .Made only one cut from the Shell Houston Open in April through the FUNAI Classic at the WALT DISNEY WORLD Resort. Opened with 64 at the Disney Magnolia Course and was two strokes out of the lead. Collected his fourth top-10 at Disney with his T10 finish.

CAREER HIGHLIGHTS:

2003: Won for the second time in the 2000s with his victory at the Southern Farm Bureau Classic, his seventh career victory. Shared first-round lead and held second- and third-round leads while firing four rounds in the 60s. Birdied three of final four holes to defeat Brenden Pappas, who shot a final-round 10-under 62, by a stroke...Began year making seven straight cuts, including a second at the Phoenix Open. **2002:** Began the season making 15 consecutive cuts and missed just three of 26 cuts, the least in his 15-year TOUR career...Was ninth in All-Around Ranking, a year after finishing 72nd in the same category...Third-round 11-under-par 61, a career low, moved him into a tie for the lead with Tim Herron through 54 holes at the Buick Challenge. The 61 tied J.P. Hayes and Garrett Willis for low round of the season. Finished T4 after final-round 70. **2001:** After three consecutive years in top 25 on TOUR money list, finished No. 100. **2000:** Collected his sixth PGA TOUR victory and for the third consecutive season eclipsed $1.5 million in earnings...Was among the top-10 eight times, including his first two starts of the season...Earned three-stroke victory at the inaugural Tampa Bay Classic, his fifth victory in the state of Florida. In final round, birdied three of the last four holes en route to a 65. Win occurred on home course, Innisbrook Resort's Copperhead Course...Shared the 54-hole lead with Davis Love III at GTE Byron Nelson Classic. Closing 70 left him T4, one stroke out of three-man playoff...Posted his best finish at the U.S. Open, solo fourth...Ranked seventh in par-4 birdie average (18.6 percent). **1999:** Although without a victory, posted three third-place finishes...Earned over $700,000 in first four starts of season on strength of back-to-back third-place finishes at Bob Hope Chrysler Classic and WGC-Accenture Match Play Championship. Won consolation match at Accenture, defeating Steve Pate 5 and 4 for $400,000 payday. **1998:** A memorable season from start to finish...Best four-day performance at the time by any player on TOUR at United Airlines Hawaiian Open, where he broke the 72-hole scoring record in relation to par with a 28-under-par 260 to capture his fourth TOUR title. Rounds of 63-65-66-66 included 31 birdies and only three bogeys. Broke record shared by Ben Hogan and Mike Souchak which had stood for 43 years. Joe Durant's 29-under in 2001 broke Huston's record. Shared first-round lead with David Ogrin before breaking away with tournament record-tying 16-under 128 total through 36 holes. Shot tournament-record 22-under 194 through 54 holes...Closed year with fifth TOUR victory at National Car Rental Golf Classic at Walt Disney World Resort and for first time in career earned two wins in a season. Closing 66 produced his second title at Disney...Shot closing 67 to earn T2 at Doral-Ryder Open...The finish in Miami marked four top-10s with earnings of $636,250 after six starts and earned him top spot on TOUR money list. It was his best start ever...Ranked first in all-around stats category (151), third in birdie average (3.96), fourth in putting (1.730) and third in third-round scoring average (69.29). **1997:** Fell out of top 125 for first time in

PGA TOUR CAREER SUMMARY — PLAYOFF RECORD: 0-1

Year	Events Played	Cuts Made	1st	2nd	3rd	Top 10	Top 25	Earnings	Rank
1987	1	1						$1,055	287
1988	31	17			1	2	6	150,301	78
1989	29	14		1		2	5	203,207	68
1990	25	16	1		1	3	7	435,690	30
1991	27	23			1	5	13	395,853	40
1992	32	23	1		1	4	15	515,453	26
1993	30	26		2		6	15	681,441	15
1994	25	19	1		1	8	11	731,499	16
1995	27	15				5	7	294,574	64
1996	25	18		1		6	9	506,173	37
1997	29	12				1	3	151,840	141
1998	25	21	2	1		8	16	1,544,110	10
1999	23	17			3	7	11	1,519,387	21
2000	23	19	1		1	8	11	1,631,695	25
2001	20	14				1	7	505,252	100
2002	26	23			1	5	12	1,299,053	45
2003	23	17	1	1		2	8	1,565,119	42
2004	20	11			1	4	5	874,280	90
Total	441	306	7	6	11	77	161	13,005,980	

PGA TOUR TOP TOURNAMENT SUMMARY

Year	88	89	90	91	92	93	94	95	96	97	98	99	00
Masters			T3	T29	T25	59	T10	T17	17	T21	T23	T36	T14
U.S. Open		CUT	T14	CUT		CUT	CUT	CUT	T82		T32	T17	4
British Open			CUT			T48	CUT	T31			T11	T68	CUT
PGA		CUT	T57	T7	T18	T44	CUT	DQ	CUT		T13	CUT	71
THE PLAYERS	68	CUT		T15	T40	CUT	T35	CUT	CUT	T68	CUT	T20	CUT
TOUR Championship			T28		T13	T2	T10				T11	T5	T25
WGC-Accenture Match Play												3	T33
WGC-NEC Invitational												T33	
WGC-American Express Champ												T34	

Year	01	02	03	04
Masters	T20		CUT	
U.S. Open	CUT	CUT		
British Open	CUT			CUT
PGA	72	T39	W/D	CUT
THE PLAYERS	CUT	T9	W/D	T26
WGC-Accenture Match Play	T33		T33	T9
WGC-American Express Champ	CNL			

NATIONAL TEAMS: The Presidents Cup (2) , 1994, 1998.

John Huston (Continued)

career, finishing 141st. **1996:** Shot course-record 61 at Muirfield Village GC during second round of Memorial Tournament. **1994:** Earned third victory at 1994 Doral-Ryder Open. Entered final round four strokes behind, but closing 66 good for three-stroke victory. **1993:** Lost playoff to Jim McGovern at Shell Houston Open...T2 with Greg Norman, Scott Simpson and David Frost at 1993 TOUR Championship, one stroke behind Jim Gallagher, Jr. **1992:** Fired closing 62 to overtake Mark O'Meara and win the Walt Disney World/Oldsmobile Classic, where winning total of 26-under-par 262 was one off TOUR record for most strokes below par in 72-hole event. **1990:** Earned first PGA TOUR victory at windswept Honda Classic, where he held off strong Mark Calcavecchia challenge to win by two strokes. **1987:** Medalist at Qualifying Tournament. **1985:** Won Florida Open (non-TOUR event).

PERSONAL:

Sister Julie Jones caddied for him during record-breaking performance at 1997 United Airlines Hawaiian Open. "She never said one word to me all week, she was scared stiff," Huston said...With daughter Jessica, won the Father-Daughter tournament at 1997 National Car Rental Golf Classic at Walt Disney World Resort...Suffered with bursitis in left shoulder in 1997. Sleeps on magnetic mattress cover and wears magnets in soles of shoes for relief.

PLAYER STATISTICS

2004 PGA TOUR STATISTICS

Scoring Average	71.57	(141)
Driving Distance	286.4	(103)
Driving Accuracy Percentage	65.9%	(67)
Total Driving	170	(63)
Greens in Regulation Pct.	68.8%	(15)
Putting Average	1.804	(169)
Sand Save Percentage	55.9%	(21)
Eagles (Holes per)	336.0	(147)
Birdie Average	3.82	(27)
All-Around Ranking	690	(76)
Scoring Avg. Before Cut	70.97	(92)
Round 3 Scoring Avg.	70.20	(40)
Final Round Scoring Average	72.44	(159)
Birdie Conversion Percentage	29.5%	(83)
Par Breakers	21.5%	(32)

MISCELLANEOUS PGA TOUR STATISTICS

2004 Low Round/Round: 64–FUNAI Classic at the WALT DISNEY WORLD Resort/1

Career Low Round/Round: 61–2 times, most recent 2002 Buick Challenge/3

Career Largest Paycheck/Finish: $540,000–2003 Southern Farm Bureau Classic/1

SECTION 2 PLAYER BIOGRAPHIES

SHOTLink
AN IBM ON DEMAND BUSINESS SOLUTION

HOT SHOTS

The Final 3...

(Holes 16-18 at the TPC at Sawgrass)

The final three holes on The Stadium Course at the Tournament Players Club at Sawgrass, site of THE PLAYERS Championship, make up one of the most dramatic finishes in all of golf. A look at those holes, beginning with the par-5 16th (page 92) followed by the par-3 17th (below) and the par-4 18th (page 114).

Tournament Players Club at Sawgrass
(Stadium Course)

17th Hole, 134 Yards

HOLE 17 – STATISTICS (2004)

Greens in Regulation	359/ 459 78% (T1st)
Avg. Distance to Pin	24 ft 08 in

27/459 or 5.9 percent of the players hit their tee shot in the water on 17. Three players hit the greenside bunker, none of which were able to get up and down for par. When missing the green (water) players averaged 1.889 strokes over par.

PUTTING	TOTAL (RANK)
Average Putts	1.850 (12th)
Total One Putts	138 (17th)
Three putts	25 (T4th)
SCORING	
Average Score	3.024
Holes in One	—
Birdies	81
Pars	310
Bogeys	51
Double Bogeys	12
Other	5
Actual Yardage	137
Rank	12

No. 17 on The Stadium Course at the TPC at Sawgrass ranked 30th/56 toughest hole 17s on TOUR in 2004 and was the 496th/1,007 toughest holes on TOUR.

17th Hole-TPC at Sawgrass

Hale Irwin

WORLD GOLF HALL OF FAME MEMBER (Inducted 1992)
EXEMPT STATUS: Life Member
FULL NAME: Hale S. Irwin
HEIGHT: 6-0
WEIGHT: 185
BIRTHDATE: June 3, 1945
BIRTHPLACE: Joplin, MO
RESIDENCE: Paradise Valley, AZ
FAMILY: Wife, Sally; Becky (12/15/71), Steven (8/6/74); one grandchild
EDUCATION: University of Colorado (1967, Marketing)
SPECIAL INTERESTS: Photography, golf course design
TURNED PROFESSIONAL: 1968
JOINED TOUR: 1968

PGA TOUR VICTORIES (20):

1971 Sea Pines Heritage Classic. **1973** Sea Pines Heritage Classic. **1974** U.S. Open Championship. **1975** Atlanta Classic, Western Open. **1976** Glen Campbell-Los Angeles Open, Florida Citrus Open. **1977** Atlanta Classic, Colgate Hall of Fame Golf Classic, San Antonio Texas Open. **1979** U.S. Open Championship. **1981** Hawaiian Open, Buick Open. **1982** Honda Inverrary Classic. **1983** Memorial Tournament. **1984** Bing Crosby National Pro-Am. **1985** Memorial Tournament. **1990** U.S. Open Championship, Buick Classic. **1994** MCI Heritage Golf Classic.

CHAMPIONS TOUR VICTORIES (40):

1995 Ameritech Senior Open, Vantage Championship. **1996** American Express Invitational, PGA Seniors' Championship. **1997** MasterCard Championship, LG Championship, PGA Seniors' Championship, Las Vegas Senior Classic, Burnet Senior Classic, BankBoston Classic, Boone Valley Classic, Vantage Championship, Hyatt Regency Maui Kaanapali Classic. **1998** Toshiba Senior Classic, PGA Seniors' Championship, Las Vegas Senior Classic, Ameritech Senior Open, U.S. Senior Open, BankBoston Classic, Energizer SENIOR TOUR Championship. **1999** Nationwide Championship, Boone Valley Classic, FORD SENIOR PLAYERS Championship, Ameritech Senior Open, Coldwell Banker Burnet Classic. **2000** Nationwide Championship, BellSouth Senior Classic at Opryland, U.S. Senior Open, EMC Kaanapali Classic. **2001** Siebel Classic in Silicon Valley, Bruno's Memorial Classic, Turtle Bay Championship. **2002** ACE Group Classic, Toshiba Senior Classic, 3M Championship, Turtle Bay Championship. **2003** Kinko's Classic of Austin, Turtle Bay Championship. **2004** Liberty Mutual Legends of Golf, Senior PGA Championship.

PGA TOUR CAREER SUMMARY — PLAYOFF RECORD: 4-5

Year	Events Played	Cuts Made	1st	2nd	3rd	Top 10	Top 25	Earnings	Rank
1966A	1	1							
1967A	1	1							
1968	17	11					3	$5,129	
1969	29	21				1	7	18,211	83
1970	32	24		1		4	14	44,101	44
1971	35	28	1	2	1	7	13	96,695	12
1972	34	27		3	3	11	17	107,140	14
1973	32	25	1	1	1	12	18	128,353	7
1974	23	21	1	2		8	15	150,068	6
1975	22	21	2	1	1	14	17	205,380	4
1976	21	21	2	3	2	12	17	252,719	3
1977	23	23	3	1	1	8	13	221,456	4
1978	22	22		2	4	13	17	191,666	7
1979	22	17	1		3	6	12	154,168	19
1980	25	18			1	9	14	109,810	38
1981	23	21	2	4	1	8	12	276,499	7
1982	23	20	1	1		4	11	173,719	19
1983	20	20	1			9	15	232,567	13
1984	20	16	1			6	11	183,384	31
1985	20	14	1			2	8	195,007	31
1986	25	15				1	3	59,983	128
1987	22	14				2	7	100,825	96
1988	23	14		1		2	7	164,996	72
1989	19	14			1	2	6	150,977	93
1990	17	15	2	1	2	6	11	838,249	6
1991	17	15		1	2	6	7	422,652	33
1992	20	13				1	2	98,208	131
1993	21	15				2	9	252,686	65
1994	22	19	1	1	1	6	11	814,436	10
1995	14	11				2	5	190,961	95
1996	3	3						31,550	218
1997	3	2						20,764	240
1998	2	1						5,244	309
1999	2	1						11,250	280
2000	1	1						34,066	223
2001	1	1						13,164	234
2002	1								
2004	1								
Total	659	526	20	25	24	164	302	5,966,031	

CHAMPIONS TOUR CAREER SUMMARY — PLAYOFF RECORD: 2-6

Year	Events Played	1st	2nd	3rd	Top 10	Top 25	Earnings	Rank
1995	12	2	3		11	12	$799,175	10
1996	23	2	7	2	21	23	1,615,769	2
1997	23	9	3	1	18	22	2,343,364	1
1998	22	7	6	2	20	22	2,861,945	1
1999	26	5	2	3	14	23	2,025,232	2
2000	24	4	4	1	17	23	2,128,968	3
2001	26	3	2	4	18	24	2,147,422	3
2002	27	4	6	4	22	27	3,028,304	1
2003	22	2	2	2	13	19	1,607,391	5
2004	23	2	3	1	14	20	2,035,397	2
Total	228	40	38	20	168	215	20,592,965	

PGA TOUR TOP TOURNAMENT SUMMARY

Year	66	67	68	69	70	71	72	73	74	75	76	77	78
Masters						T13	CUT		T4	T4	T5	5	8
U.S. Open	T61					T19	T36	T20	1	T3	T26	T41	T4
British Open									T24	9	T32	T46	T24
PGA					T31	T22	T11	T9	W/D	T5	T34	T44	T12
THE PLAYERS									T34	7	T17	T3	T42

Year	79	80	81	82	83	84	85	86	87	88	89	90	91
Masters	T23	CUT	T25	CUT	T6	T21	T36	CUT					T10
U.S. Open	**1**	T8	T58	T39	T39	6	14	CUT	CUT	T17	T54	**1**	T11
British Open	6				T2	T14						T53	T57
PGA	CUT	T30	T16	T42	T14	T25	T32	T26		T38		T12	T73
THE PLAYERS	CUT	T14	T51	T19	T49	T15	T5	CUT	T24	CUT	CUT	T5	T27
TOUR Championship												T19	

Year	92	93	94	95	96	97	98	99	00	01	02	03	04
Masters	47	T27	T18	T14	T29								
U.S. Open	T51	T62	T18	CUT	T50	T52	CUT	W/D	T27	T52	CUT		
British Open	T19												
PGA	T66	T6	T39	T54		T29		T41					CUT
THE PLAYERS	CUT	CUT	4	T55	T46								
TOUR Championship			T22										

CHAMPIONS TOUR TOP TOURNAMENT SUMMARY

Year	95	96	97	98	99	00	01	02	03	04
Senior PGA Championship		**1**	**1**	**1**	T11	T2	T5	T2	T15	**1**
U.S. Senior Open	T5	2	T5	**1**	T3	**1**	T11	T11		2
Ford Senior Players Championship	T10	2	T19	2	**1**	T4	3	T6	T12	T9
JELD-WEN Tradition		2	T13	4	T20	T37	3	6	T10	13
Charles Schwab Cup Champ	T8	T10	2	**1**	T18	T24	T7	4	T4	T7

NATIONAL TEAMS: World Cup (2), 1974, 1979 (indiv. title 1979); Ryder Cup (5), 1975, 1977, 1979, 1981, 1991; U.S. vs. Japan, 1983; The Presidents Cup, 1994 (playing captain).

Hale Irwin (Continued)

INTERNATIONAL VICTORIES (8):
1974 Piccadilly World Match Play [Eur]. **1975** Piccadilly World Match Play [Eur]. **1978** Australian PGA [Aus]. **1979** South African PGA [SAf]. **1979** World Cup [indiv]. **1981** Bridgestone Classic [Jpn]. **1982** Brazilian Open. **1986** Bahamas Classic.

OTHER VICTORIES (1):
2003 Office Depot Father-Son Challenge [with Steve].

BEST 2004 CHAMPIONS TOUR FINISHES:
1—Liberty Mutual Legends of Golf, Senior PGA Championship; 2—U.S. Senior Open, Constellation Energy Classic, Administaff Small Business Classic presented by KBR; T3—The First Tee Open at Pebble Beach presented by Wal-Mart; T6—Farmers Charity Classic; T7—The MasterCard Classic, SBC Classic, Kroger Classic, Charles Schwab Cup Championship; T9—Ford Senior Players Championship; T10—Commerce Bank Long Island Classic, SBC Championship

2004 SEASON:
Is playing under the category of Life Member in 2005. To be eligible under this category, a Life Member must maintain a scoring average no greater than three strokes above the field average for the rounds of golf in which he has played during each calendar year...Posted an ace during the first round of the PGA Championship at Whistling Straits. Used a 3-iron from 185 yards on the par-3 seventh hole. Missed the cut by a stroke, ending his PGA consecutive-made-cut streak at 16. Also marked only the second time in his career he has missed the cut at the PGA, the other being 1979...Did not participate in the U.S. Open Championship, ending a streak of 33 consecutive appearances in the event...Continued to defy the odds on the Champions Tour and again put together a remarkable season that contained multiple victories including his fourth Senior PGA Championship. Had to deal with a balky lower back and assorted neck and shoulder pain throughout the year...Held off Craig Stadler by a mere 39 points in the season's final event to earn his second Charles Schwab Cup...Finished among the top 10 in 14 of 23 events, including three top-10 efforts in four of the senior major championships he entered...Won multiple titles for an unprecedented 10th straight season.

CAREER HIGHLIGHTS:
2003: Earned a special exemption into the U.S. Open, his 33rd consecutive appearance in the event, but was forced to withdraw after 11 holes in the opening round with severe back spasms. First time since 1966 that he did not finish at least one tournament on the PGA TOUR...Continued to work on his Champions Tour career. Despite a back injury for the final four months of the season, earned at least $1 million for the eighth straight year, finishing fifth on the money list with $1,607,391. **2002:** Concentrating on Champions Tour career, played in only one TOUR event, missing the cut at U.S. Open at Bethpage State Park's Black Course...Set a new Champions Tour record for earnings in a season with $3,028,304, breaking his own mark of $2,861,945 and in the process became the oldest player to win the money title (Arnold Palmer Award) at age 57. **1995:** Joined Champions Tour on June 3. **1994:** First and last TOUR win came at MCI Heritage Classic where he defeated Greg Norman by two shots. First win was at Harbour Town GL in 1971...Selected as first captain of the U.S. Presidents Cup Team and earned spot on team that defeated International squad 20-12. Posted a 2-1 record in the competition. **1990:** Illustrious 29-year PGA TOUR career was highlighted by three U.S. Open titles, the last of which came in a grueling 19-hole playoff with Mike Donald at Medinah. Sank a 45-foot putt on the final hole to force overtime the next day, and then eventually won with a 10-foot birdie putt. Victory at 45 made him the oldest to win a U.S. Open...Followed that win with another the next week at the Buick Classic, and went on to have his finest earnings year on the PGA TOUR (sixth/ $838,249). **1985:** Won for the second time in three starts at the Memorial Tournament. **1979:** Captured second U.S. Open victory at Inverness Club. **1977:** Won for the second time in three starts at the Atlanta Classic. **1975:** Started a streak of 86 tournaments without missing a cut that ended in 1978. It is the third-best streak on TOUR for consecutive events in the money. **1974:** First of three U.S. Open victories came at Winged Foot GC.

PERSONAL:
Unusual two-sport participant at the University of Colorado: 1967 NCAA champion in golf and two-time All-Big Eight selection as a football defensive back. Also played quarterback early in his collegiate career...Was also an academic All-American...Member of Colorado's All-Century Football Team...Son Steve also played on the Colorado golf team...Got his start in golf at age 4 through his father...Actively involved in his own course design business, including the TPC at Wakefield Plantation, the site of the Carolina Classic on the Nationwide Tour...Inducted into the World Golf Hall of Fame in 1992...Biggest thrills in golf were his first TOUR win in 1971 at Hilton Head Island, SC, his three U.S. Open victories, his two U.S. Senior Open wins and playing on the victorious U.S. Ryder Cup team in 1991...Participates in a charity golf tournament in St. Louis each year to benefit the St. Louis Children's Hospital and Hale Irwin Center for Pediatric Hematology/Oncology at the facility that bears his name.

PLAYER STATISTICS

2004 PGA TOUR STATISTICS

Scoring Average	73.00	(N/A)
Driving Distance	274.5	(N/A)
Driving Accuracy Percentage	53.6%	(N/A)
Total Driving	(N/A)	(N/A)
Greens in Regulation Pct.	58.3%	(N/A)
Putting Average	1.905	(N/A)
Sand Save Percentage	0%	(N/A)
Eagles (Holes per)	36.0	(N/A)
Birdie Average	50	(N/A)
Scoring Avg. Before Cut	73.00	(N/A)
Birdie Conversion Percentage	5.0%	(N/A)
Par Breakers	5.6%	(N/A)

MISCELLANEOUS PGA TOUR STATISTICS
2004 Low Round/Round: 73–PGA Championship/2
Career Low Round/Round: 61–1982 Southern Open/4
Career Largest Paycheck/Finish: $225,000–1994 MCI Heritage Golf Classic/1

2004 CHAMPIONS TOUR STATISTICS

Scoring Average	69.58	(2)
Driving Distance	269.8	(51)
Driving Accuracy Percentage	80.9%	(5)
Total Driving	56	(13)
Greens in Regulation Pct.	76.0%	(1)
Putting Average	1.753	(5)
Sand Save Percentage	40.4%	(64)
Eagles (Holes per)	328.5	(39)
Birdie Average	4.14	(2)
All-Around Ranking	169	(8)

MISCELLANEOUS CHAMPIONS TOUR STATISTICS
2004 Low Round: 64–Constellation Energy Classic/3.
Career Low Round: 62–4 times, most recent 2000 EMC Kaanapali Classic/2
Career Largest Paycheck: $400,000–2000 U.S. Senior Open/1

SECTION 2 PLAYER BIOGRAPHIES

Peter Jacobsen

EXEMPT STATUS: 2003 tournament winner (through 2005)
FULL NAME: Peter Erling Jacobsen
HEIGHT: 6-2
WEIGHT: 220
BIRTHDATE: March 4, 1954
BIRTHPLACE: Portland, OR
RESIDENCE: Bonita Springs, FL; Lake Oswego, OR

FAMILY: Wife, Jan; Amy (7/19/80), Kristen (2/23/82), Mick (10/12/84)
EDUCATION: University of Oregon
SPECIAL INTERESTS: Music
TURNED PROFESSIONAL: 1976
Q SCHOOL: Fall 1976

PGA TOUR VICTORIES (7):

1980 Buick-Goodwrench Open. **1984** Colonial National Invitation, Sammy Davis Jr.-Greater Hartford Open. **1990** Bob Hope Chrysler Classic. **1995** AT&T Pebble Beach National Pro-Am, Buick Invitational of California. **2003** Greater Hartford Open.

CHAMPIONS TOUR VICTORIES (1):

2004 U.S. Senior Open.

INTERNATIONAL VICTORIES (3):

1979 Western Australian Open [Aus]. **1981** Johnnie Walker Cup [Eur]. **1982** Johnnie Walker Cup [Eur].

BEST 2004 PGA TOUR FINISHES:

T14—AT&T Pebble Beach National Pro-Am; T15—Mercedes Championships.

BEST 2004 CHAMPIONS TOUR FINISHES:

1—U.S. Senior Open; 3—SBC Classic, Administaff Small Business Classic presented by KBR; 4—Charles Schwab Cup Championship, JELD-WEN Tradition; T9—The First Tee Open at Pebble Beach presented by Wal-Mart

2004 SEASON:

Split time between the PGA TOUR and the Champions Tour, where he gained eligibility in March…Opened the season with a T15 finish at the season-opening Mercedes Championships…With his T50 finish at the Bob Hope Chrylser Classic, extended his tournament record for made cuts to 23 in 26 starts in Palm Springs…Best PGA TOUR finish came at the AT&T Pebble Beach National Pro-Am, a T14…Played in only two PGA TOUR events after turning 50 on March 4…Had hip surgery on April 20th to repair a torn labrum. Missed six weeks…Returned to the Champions Tour and collected his first title in June with a victory at the U.S. Senior Open.

CAREER HIGHLIGHTS:

2003: Voted PGA TOUR Comeback Player of the Year. Began the season with partial status, but became one of the year's top golf stories with a victory at the Greater Hartford Open. Having finished outside the top 125 in previous four seasons, 49-year-old won a career-best $1,162,726 to finish 62nd on the money list, best since finishing seventh in 1995...Thanks to four rounds in the 60s, finished T10 at MCI Heritage for first top-10 since at T9 at the 2002 Tampa Bay Classic...Posted another top-10 the next week in Houston with a T9 at the Shell Houston Open. The last time he recorded back-to-back top-10s was in 1995 with a T2 at the Doral-Ryder Open and third at Nestle Invitational...Earned seventh career PGA TOUR victory in his 27th season (624th career tournament) at the Greater Hartford Open. Held at least a share of the lead for all four rounds in carding four rounds in the 60s. Oldest winner on TOUR (49 years, 4 months, 23 days) since Craig Stadler (50 years, 1 month, 18 days) the week before at the B.C. Open. Nineteen years since last victory in Hartford (1984). Earned a career-high first-place check of $720,000. The first-place check was exactly 10 times more than he earned for his first GHO victory in 1984 ($72,000)...Set the first-round tournament record with a 9-under 63 at the Chrysler Classic of Greensboro before finishing T30. **2002:** Three top-10s were the most since five (including two wins) in 1995. T8 at The Honda Classic was his first top-10 finish since a solo ninth-place finish at the 1999 B.C. Open…Also logged top-10s at the John Deere Classic and the Tampa Bay Classic. **1995:** Enjoyed best season of his career with two victories and more than $1 million in earnings, finishing seventh on the money list...Victories came in successive weeks at AT&T

PGA TOUR CAREER SUMMARY — PLAYOFF RECORD: 1-3

Year	Events Played	Cuts Made	1st	2nd	3rd	Top 10	Top 25	Earnings	Rank
1977	23	10					3	$12,608	130
1978	25	14			1	2	4	34,188	83
1979	33	23				2	6	49,439	78
1980	28	23	1	1		5	12	138,562	26
1981	23	17		1		3	7	85,624	51
1982	24	23		2		7	10	145,832	25
1983	26	22			1	5	12	158,765	29
1984	23	20	2		1	6	12	295,025	10
1985	21	16		2		7	13	214,959	23
1986	23	17			1	1	5	112,964	78
1987	25	19				1	5	79,924	111
1988	25	19		3		6	11	526,765	16
1989	24	20		1		3	9	267,241	48
1990	22	20	1		2	5	12	547,279	19
1991	23	13		2		2	5	263,180	64
1992	27	18					4	106,100	127
1993	23	17				3	9	222,291	77
1994	19	15				3	7	211,762	88
1995	25	22	2	2	1	5	13	1,075,057	7
1996	19	14				1	3	127,197	146
1997	25	19			1	2	9	294,931	82
1998	22	12		1		1	5	327,336	92
1999	22	15				1	5	285,461	138
2000	22	10					1	141,484	181
2001	17	7						64,297	209
2002	21	11				3	5	389,123	144
2003	22	14	1			3	5	1,162,726	62
2004	10	6					2	232,851	182
Total	642	456	7	15	8	77	194	7,572,970	

CHAMPIONS TOUR CAREER SUMMARY — PLAYOFF RECORD: 0-0

Year	Events Played	1st	2nd	3rd	Top 10	Top 25	Earnings	Rank
2004	9	1		2	6	7	$1,040,690	16
Total	9	1		2	6	7	1,040,690	

PGA TOUR TOP TOURNAMENT SUMMARY

Year	78	79	80	81	82	83	84	85	86	87	88	89	90
Masters				T11	T20	T20	T25	CUT	T25			T34	T30
U.S. Open			T22	T37		T34	T7	T31	T59	T24	T21	8	CUT
British Open						T12	T22	T11	CUT	W/D		T30	T16
PGA		T23	T10	T27	T34	3	T18	T10	3	20	47	T27	T26
THE PLAYERS	T52	T14	T5	CUT	T27	T16	T51	CUT	T33	CUT	T16	T70	T29
TOUR Championship											6		T19

Year	91	92	93	94	95	96	97	98	99	00	01	02	03
Masters	T17	T61			T31								
U.S. Open	T31	63	CUT		T51	T23							
British Open	T73			T24	T31	T44							
PGA		T28	T28		T23	W/D	T67						CUT
THE PLAYERS	CUT	CUT		CUT	T29	CUT	T48		CUT				
TOUR Championship					T16								
WGC-NEC Invitational													T14

Year	04
THE PLAYERS	80

CHAMPIONS TOUR TOP TOURNAMENT SUMMARY

Year	04
U.S. Senior Open	**1**
JELD-WEN Tradition	T4
Charles Schwab Cup Champ	4

NATIONAL TEAMS: U.S. vs. Japan, 1984; Ryder Cup (2), 1985, 1995; Dunhill Cup, 1995.

Peter Jacobsen (Continued)

Pebble Beach National Pro-Am and Buick Invitational of California. Was tied for 20th after two rounds at AT&T before moving into a tie for second with third-round 66. Closing 65 gave him two-stroke victory over David Duval...The next week took lead at Buick Invitational with third-round 68, then added another in final round for four-stroke victory...Passed on chance to win three straight at Bob Hope Chrysler Classic, opting for wife Jan's 40th birthday party instead. **1990:** Defeated Scott Simpson by one stroke for 1990 Bob Hope Chrysler Classic title. **1986:** Won Fred Meyer Challenge with Curtis Strange. **1984:** First two-victory season on TOUR. Defeated Payne Stewart in playoff for Colonial National Invitation title, which he dedicated to his father, who had just undergone serious surgery...Two-stroke victory over Mark O'Meara at Sammy Davis, Jr.-Greater Hartford Open later that year was highlighted by third-round 63. **1980:** Came from six strokes off pace in final round for first TOUR victory at Buick-Goodwrench Open. **1976:** First two professional titles were Oregon Open and Northern California Open. **Amateur:** Three-time All-American at University of Oregon...Won 1974 Pac-8 Conference title.

PERSONAL:

Has own event management company, Peter Jacobsen Productions, Inc. (www.pjp.com), which conducts the CVS Charity Classic, the Save Mart Shootout and two Champions Tour events, The JELD-WEN Tradition and the Constellation Energy Classic. PJP also conducted the 2003 U.S. Women's Open...Founded Jake Trout and the Flounders musical group, featuring Mark Lye and the late Payne Stewart...Has served two terms as PGA TOUR Player Director...Co-owns Jacobsen Hardy Golf Design Co (jacobsenhardy.com) with former TOUR player Jim Hardy...Hosts variety show, "Peter Jacobsen Unplugged," on The Golf Channel with "Signboy" Matt Griesser...One of the great ambassadors of golf, played 16 years at the AT&T Pebble Beach National Pro-Am with actor Jack Lemmon until the Oscar winner's death in 2001.

PLAYER STATISTICS

2004 PGA TOUR STATISTICS

Scoring Average	71.84	(N/A)
Driving Distance	271.6	(N/A)
Driving Accuracy Percentage	73.8%	(N/A)
Total Driving	(N/A)	(N/A)
Greens in Regulation Pct.	67.9%	(N/A)
Putting Average	1.802	(N/A)
Sand Save Percentage	52.3%	(N/A)
Eagles (Holes per)	558.0	(N/A)
Birdie Average	3.32	(N/A)
Scoring Avg. Before Cut	71.00	(N/A)
Round 3 Scoring Avg.	70.83	(N/A)
Final Round Scoring Average	72.50	(N/A)
Birdie Conversion Percentage	27.0%	(N/A)
Par Breakers	18.6%	(N/A)

MISCELLANEOUS PGA TOUR STATISTICS

2004 Low Round/Round: 67–3 times, most recent Nissan Open/2

Career Low Round/Round: 62–1982 Manufacturers Hanover Westchester Classic/2

Career Largest Paycheck/Finish: $720,000–2003 Greater Hartford Open/1

2004 CHAMPIONS TOUR STATISTICS

Scoring Average	69.40	(N/A)
Driving Distance	282.3	(N/A)
Driving Accuracy Percentage	73.3%	(N/A)
Total Driving	(N/A)	(N/A)
Greens in Regulation Pct.	76.3%	(N/A)
Putting Average	1.772	(N/A)
Sand Save Percentage	29.6%	(N/A)
Eagles (Holes per)	180.0	(N/A)
Birdie Average	4.37	(N/A)
All-Around Ranking	1,569	(N/A)

MISCELLANEOUS CHAMPIONS TOUR STATISTICS

2004 Low Round: 64–Commerce Bank Long Island Classic/1.

Career Low Round: 64–2004 Commerce Bank Long Island Classic/1

Career Largest Paycheck: $470,000–2004 U.S. Senior Open/1

SHOTLink
AN IBM ON DEMAND BUSINESS SOLUTION

HOT SHOTS

Toughest Bunkers on TOUR (2004)

Event/Course Name	Hole	Par	Saves	Sand Tries	%
84 LUMBER Classic Nemacolin - Mystic Rock Course	4	4	0	8	0
AT&T Pebble Beach National Pro-Am Pebble Beach Golf Links**	16	4	0	4	0
AT&T Pebble Beach National Pro-Am Poppy Hills**	17	3	0	2	0
AT&T Pebble Beach National Pro-Am Pebble Beach Golf Links**	13	4	0	1	0
AT&T Pebble Beach National Pro-Am Poppy Hills**	5	4	0	1	0

Easiest Bunkers on TOUR (2004)

Event/Course Name	Hole	Par	Saves	Sand Tries	%
B.C. Open En-Joie GC	8	5	21	21	100
Bay Hill Invitational Presented by MasterCard Bay Hill Club & Lodge	13	4	5	5	100
AT&T Pebble Beach National Pro-Am Poppy Hills**	10	5	3	3	100
AT&T Pebble Beach National Pro-Am Spyglass Hill GC**	2	4	2	2	100
AT&T Pebble Beach National Pro-Am Spyglass Hill GC**	15	3	2	2	100

** - Multiple-course tournament

Fredrik Jacobson (YOCK-ub-son)

EXEMPT STATUS: 59th on 2004 money list
FULL NAME: Fredrik Ulf Yngve Jacobson
HEIGHT: 6-1
WEIGHT: 178
BIRTHDATE: September 26, 1974
BIRTHPLACE: Gothenburg, Sweden
RESIDENCE: Monte Carlo, Monaco; plays out of Kungsbacua GC

FAMILY: Wife, Erika, Alice Sophia J. (5/07/04)
SPECIAL INTERESTS: Boating, skiing, sports
TURNED PROFESSIONAL: 1994
JOINED TOUR: 2003

BEST PGA TOUR CAREER FINISH:
T3—2003 FedEx St. Jude Classic.

INTERNATIONAL VICTORIES (3):
2003 Omega Hong Kong Open [Eur], Algarve Open de Portugal [Eur], Volvo Masters [Eur].

BEST 2004 PGA TOUR FINISHES:
T4—The Honda Classic; T5—FedEx St. Jude Classic; 8—Buick Classic; T9—FBR Open, WGC-Accenture Match Play Championship.

2004 SEASON:
Continued consistent play in just his second season on the PGA TOUR. Recorded five top-10 finishes and collected over $1 million in season earnings...Earned first top-10, a T9, in his second start of the season at the FBR Open...Finished T9 at the WGC-Accenture Match Play Championship after losing to eventual winner Tiger Woods in the third round (5 and 4)...In next start recorded his third top-10 finish, a T4 at The Honda Classic...Fired a first round, 6-under 66 at the Wachovia Championship and was only two strokes off the lead. Withdrew and flew home at 5:30 a.m. on Friday as his wife, Erika, had gone into premature labor with the couple's first child at Jupiter Hospital near their home in Hobe Sound, FL. Just missed witnessing the birth of Alice Sofia on May 7...In first tournament back after daughter's birth, earned second consecutive top-10 at the FedEx St. Jude Classic, finishing T5...Two weeks later finished eighth at the Buick Classic and collected $162,750. Surpassed the $1-million mark in a single season in only his 13th event during first full season on the PGA TOUR. Was only one back of the lead after 18 and 36 holes at Westchester CC...Finished T17 at the Masters Tournament and PGA Championship...Played with Joakim Haeggman at the WGC-World Cup in Spain.

CAREER HIGHLIGHTS:
Played virtually full-time on the European Tour from 1997-2002, with 17-plus starts each of those seasons. Totaled six runner-up finishes and 16 top-10s during that time. **2003:** Had three wins on the European Tour, along with top-10 finishes at both the U.S. Open and the British Open, looks to be one of the rising stars in golf...Placed fourth in the European Tour Order of Merit and finished third in PGA TOUR non-member earnings with $786,771, with four top-10s in only eight starts. Joined the TOUR having finished among the top 125 as a non-member. Also added another $66,821 in two World Golf Championships appearances...Playing in his first U.S. Open, finished T5 and shared top first-time honors with Justin Rose...Two weeks later, finished T3 at the FedEx St. Jude Classic, four shots behind David Toms. Earned top-10 exemption in the following week's 100th Western Open, where he finished T8. In just four starts, was eligible to join the PGA TOUR as a Special Temporary Member, having earned ($572,970) more than the No. 150 player (Tom Scherrer, $356,657) from the 2002 TOUR money list...Finished T6 at the British Open, three shots behind Ben Curtis...After 160 events as a professional, claimed his breakthrough victory on The European Tour when he won the Omega Hong Kong Open, the second event of the 2003 season...Won again three tournaments later in the Algarve Open de Portugal. Victory was all the more remarkable considering it was his first start back after a 10-week layoff due to a wrist injury...Ended European Tour season with third victory of 2003 at the Volvo Masters at Valerrama, defeating Spain's Carlos Rodiles in a four-hole playoff. **2002:** Lost to Eduardo Romero in a playoff at the Barclays Scottish Open. Finished 30th on the Volvo Order of Merit. **2001:** Was fifth at the Omega European Masters. **2000:** Progressed to 25th on the Volvo Order of Merit, his highest prior to 2003. **1999:** Had to return to the Qualifying School, but finished seventh to stay on Tour. **1998:** With one week remaining, he lay in 124th position in the Volvo Order of Merit but played superbly and only lost in a play-off for the Belgacom Open to Lee Westwood. Moved to 75th place and rescued his card.

PERSONAL:
A promising ice hockey player at age 10. However one of the players at his club, Per Nellbeck, was also the local golf professional and taught the entire Jacobson family to play. First handicap was 40, but reached scratch five years later at age 15...Love of ice hockey was to delay his start to 2000 season. Missed first three months after breaking left thumb playing hockey for golf professionals vs. tennis players in 1999. Needed operation and returned in March to finish third, second and second in successive starts...Won several notable titles in amateur golf before turning professional in 1994. Was ranked top 30 in Swedish table tennis at age 14-15.

PLAYER STATISTICS

2004 PGA TOUR STATISTICS

Scoring Average	70.71	(47)
Driving Distance	287.9	(89)
Driving Accuracy Percentage	55.6%	(184)
Total Driving	273	(182)
Greens in Regulation Pct.	64.4%	(112)
Putting Average	1.750	(25)
Sand Save Percentage	43.9%	(158)
Eagles (Holes per)	144.0	(27)
Birdie Average	3.84	(24)
All-Around Ranking	666	(68)
Scoring Avg. Before Cut	70.81	(70)
Round 3 Scoring Avg.	69.82	(21)
Final Round Scoring Average	71.53	(92)
Birdie Conversion Percentage	32.8%	(9)
Par Breakers	22.0%	(18)

MISCELLANEOUS PGA TOUR STATISTICS

2004 Low Round/Round: 64–3 times, most recent Valero Texas Open/3
Career Low Round/Round: 64–3 times, most recent 2004 Valero Texas Open/3
Career Largest Paycheck/Finish: $234,000–2003 FedEx St. Jude Classic/T3

PGA TOUR CAREER SUMMARY — PLAYOFF RECORD: 0-0

Year	Events Played	Cuts Made	1st	2nd	3rd	Top 10	Top 25	Earnings	Rank
1998	1	1						$8,965	285
2000	1								
2001	1								
2002	1								
2003	8	7			1	4	4	786,771	
2004	24	18				5	9	1,259,048	59
Total	36	26			1	9	13	2,054,784	
EUROPEAN TOUR									
2004	3	2				1	1	86,899	

PGA TOUR TOP TOURNAMENT SUMMARY

Year	98	99	00	01	02	03	04
Masters							T17
U.S. Open						T5	CUT
British Open	76		CUT	CUT	CUT	T6	CUT
PGA						CUT	T17
THE PLAYERS							CUT
WGC-Accenture Match Play							T9
WGC-NEC Invitational						84	T32
WGC-American Express Champ						T28	T59

NATIONAL TEAMS: World Cup (2), 2003, 2004.

Lee Janzen

EXEMPT STATUS: Winner, 1995 PLAYERS Championship (through 2005)
FULL NAME: Lee MacLeod Janzen
HEIGHT: 6-0
WEIGHT: 175
BIRTHDATE: August 28, 1964
BIRTHPLACE: Austin, MN
RESIDENCE: Orlando, FL

FAMILY: Wife, Beverly; Connor MacLeod (10/20/93)
EDUCATION: Florida Southern College (1986, Marketing)
SPECIAL INTERESTS: Christian music, reading, snow skiing and comedy
TURNED PROFESSIONAL: 1986
Q SCHOOL: 1989

PGA TOUR VICTORIES (8):

1992 Northern Telecom Open. **1993** Phoenix Open, U.S. Open Championship. **1994** Buick Classic. **1995** THE PLAYERS Championship, Kemper Open, Sprint International. **1998** U.S. Open Championship.

OTHER VICTORIES (1):

2000 Franklin Templeton Shootout [with Rocco Mediate].

BEST 2004 PGA TOUR FINISHES:

T6—BellSouth Classic; T7—Michelin Championship at Las Vegas; T9—The Honda Classic.

2004 SEASON:

Finished inside the top 100 on the PGA TOUR money list for the 14th straight time in his 15-year career. . .First top-10 of the season was a T9 at The Honda Classic. . .Recovered from first-round 75 to compile second top-10 of season, a T6 at BellSouth Classic, six strokes behind Zach Johnson. . .Third and last top-10 of season did not come until October, a T7 at the Michelin Championship at Las Vegas.

CAREER HIGHLIGHTS:

2003: Managed to exceed the $1-million mark for the fourth time in his career with $1,132,001...At the BellSouth Classic, held the 54-hole lead by one stroke over Bob Tway. Closed with a 5-over-par 77 to finish T13...Recorded his first top-10 of the season with solo second at the Memorial Tournament...Held or shared the lead on several occasions during Sunday's final round of the FedEx St. Jude Classic. Stumbled with bogeys on three of the last five holes to finish T6. **2002:** Finished T4 at the Phoenix Open. The 64-64—128 total on Saturday-Sunday matched the lowest final 36 holes in Phoenix Open history...Topped the previous week's finish with a T3 at the AT&T Pebble Beach National Pro-Am, four strokes behind Matt Gogel. **2001:** Best showing of the year occurred at the Shell Houston Open, where he shared first-round lead after opening with 67. Followed with 68 for one-stroke lead through 36-holes. Stood one back after 54 holes following a third-round 73. Closing 73 on Sunday produced T2, three strokes behind Hal Sutton. **2000:** First top-10 came at THE PLAYERS Championship, a T9. Also marked his first top-10 finish in THE PLAYERS Championship since winning the event in 1995...Best finish of the season came at Tampa Bay Classic, a T6. **1999:** Slipped out of the top 40 on the PGA TOUR money list for the first time in five seasons...At GTE Byron Nelson Classic, final-round 69 was good for T3...Shared first-round lead at Bell Canadian Open after opening with 66. Took outright lead with third-round 68 before closing 76 left him T3. **1998:** Captured his second U.S. Open title in six years by recording the best final-round U.S. Open comeback in 25 years. Was five strokes behind Payne Stewart through 54 holes. Closed with 68 to win by one over Stewart, who closed with 74 at Olympic Club. Five-stroke comeback best since Johnny Miller came from six back to win 1973 U.S. Open. It was his first victory on TOUR since 1995 and eighth career win. **1997:** Posted seven top-10 finishes, including two seconds, and earned a fourth trip to THE TOUR Championship. **1995:** Won three times—THE PLAYERS Championship, Kemper Open and Sprint International...Trailed Bernhard Langer and Corey Pavin by one entering final round at TPC at Sawgrass. Shot closing 71 for one-stroke victory...Birdied 72nd hole at Kemper Open to tie Pavin then birdied 18th again to win playoff...Birdied holes 14-17 on Sunday to overtake Ernie Els and win Sprint by one point under Modified Stableford scoring system. **1994:** Won Buick Classic by three strokes over Els, who won U.S. Open the following week. **1993:** First U.S. Open title came in head-to-head battle with Payne Stewart at Baltusrol GC. Shot 67-67-69-69—272 to equal U.S. Open scoring record set by Jack Nicklaus in 1980 and defeat Stewart by two strokes...Earlier that year, defeated Andrew Magee by two strokes for Phoenix Open title. **1992:** First TOUR victory came at Northern Telecom Open. Closing 65 gave him one-stroke win over Bill Britton. **1989:** Leading money winner on U.S. Golf Tour. **Amateur:** Won 1986 Division II national championship while at Florida Southern. First-team All-American in 1985-86.

PERSONAL:

Began to take golf seriously at age 14 after family moved to Florida from Maryland, where he played Little League baseball. Still avid Baltimore Orioles fan. . .Won first tournament at 15 as member of Greater Tampa Junior Golf Association.

PLAYER STATISTICS

2004 PGA TOUR STATISTICS

Scoring Average	70.77	(52)
Driving Distance	286.1	(106)
Driving Accuracy Percentage	62.2%	(131)
Total Driving	237	(157)
Greens in Regulation Pct.	67.8%	(30)
Putting Average	1.781	(112)
Sand Save Percentage	51.5%	(64)
Eagles (Holes per)	147.6	(31)
Birdie Average	3.73	(50)
All-Around Ranking	576	(42)
Scoring Avg. Before Cut	70.36	(31)
Round 3 Scoring Avg.	71.06	(108)
Final Round Scoring Average	71.65	(102)
Birdie Conversion Percentage	30.1%	(66)
Par Breakers	21.4%	(37)

MISCELLANEOUS PGA TOUR STATISTICS

2004 Low Round/Round: 65–Michelin Championship at Las Vegas/4
Career Low Round/Round: 61–1993 Southwestern Bell Colonial/4
Career Largest Paycheck/Finish: $540,000–2 times, most recent 2003 the Memorial Tournament/2

PGA TOUR CAREER SUMMARY — PLAYOFF RECORD: 1-0

Year	Events Played	Cuts Made	1st	2nd	3rd	Top 10	Top 25	Earnings	Rank
1985	1								
1988	2	1					1	$3,686	256
1989	2	1						5,100	233
1990	30	20				2	6	132,986	115
1991	33	23				2	11	228,242	72
1992	32	21	1	2	1	6	15	795,279	9
1993	26	23	2		1	7	15	932,335	7
1994	26	19	1			2	8	442,588	35
1995	28	22	3			4	14	1,378,966	3
1996	27	21		1	1	7	13	540,916	31
1997	27	24		2		7	15	877,832	24
1998	24	20	1		1	3	12	1,155,314	20
1999	26	18			2	5	11	849,994	48
2000	27	20				2	9	753,709	62
2001	29	18		1		2	9	905,628	59
2002	29	22			1	4	9	1,127,740	56
2003	25	16		1		2	6	1,132,001	64
2004	25	17				3	6	837,482	96
Total	419	306	8	7	7	58	160	12,099,798	
NATIONWIDE TOUR									
1990	2	1					1	1,125	204
Total	2	1					1	1,125	

PGA TOUR TOP TOURNAMENT SUMMARY

Year	85	86	87	88	89	90	91	92	93	94	95	96	97
Masters								T54	T39	T30	T12	T12	T26
U.S. Open	CUT						CUT	CUT	1	CUT	T13	T10	T52
British Open								T39	T48	T35	T24	CUT	CUT
PGA								T21	T22	T66	T23	T8	4
THE PLAYERS							CUT	CUT	T34	T35	1	T46	T37
TOUR Championship								T2	22		T20		T26

Year	98	99	00	01	02	03	04
Masters	T33	T14	CUT	T31	CUT	CUT	
U.S. Open	**1**	T46	T37	CUT	CUT	T55	T24
British Open	T24	70	CUT		T80	CUT	
PGA	CUT	CUT	T19	CUT	T53	T34	
THE PLAYERS	T13	CUT	T9	T18	CUT	68	CUT
TOUR Championship	T24						
WGC-Accenture Match Play		T17	T33		T33		
WGC-NEC Invitational		T30					

NATIONAL TEAMS: Ryder Cup (2), 1993, 1997; Dunhill Cup, 1995; The Presidents Cup, 1998.

SECTION 2 PLAYER BIOGRAPHIES

Brandt Jobe

EXEMPT STATUS: Major Medical Extension
FULL NAME: Brandt William Jobe
HEIGHT: 5-11
WEIGHT: 180
BIRTHDATE: August 1, 1965
BIRTHPLACE: Oklahoma City, OK
RESIDENCE: Southlake, TX

FAMILY: Wife, Jennifer; Brittan Catherine (5/7/00), Jackson William (7/30/02)
EDUCATION: UCLA (1988, History)
SPECIAL INTERESTS: Skiing, basketball, baseball, fishing
TURNED PROFESSIONAL: 1988
Q SCHOOL: 1990

BEST PGA TOUR CAREER FINISH:
T2—2002 Michelob Championship at Kingsmill.

INTERNATIONAL VICTORIES (9):
1990 British Columbia Open [Can]. **1991** Payless Classic [Can]. **1994** Thailand Open [Asia]. **1995** Mitsubishi Galant Tournament [Jpn]. **1997** Tokai Classic [Jpn], Golf Digest Tournament [Jpn]. **1998** Japan PGA Championship [Jpn], UBE Kosan Open [Jpn], Mizuno Open [Jpn].

BEST 2004 PGA TOUR FINISH:
T10—Buick Invitational.

2004 SEASON:
Limited to nine events due to lingering left wrist problems after 2003 surgery. Will receive a Major Medical Extension for 2005. Coupled with $247,911 earned in nine events in 2004 has the opportunity to play in 20 events to earn $375,351 and match the $623,262 winnings of 2004's No. 125, Tag Ridings. If he does so, will play out of the Major Medical Extension category for the remainder of the season. Picked up first top-10 of the season in his third event, a T10 at the Buick Invitational...Missed five weeks after THE PLAYERS Championship due to a recurring injury to his left hand. Dallas-area resident played EDS Byron Nelson Championship and Bank of America Colonial before shutting it down for the remainder of the season.

CAREER HIGHLIGHTS:
2003: Although he recorded just one top-10, finished in the top 100 on the money list for a second straight season...At the Bank of America Colonial, a final-round 64 produced a fourth-place finish, his only top-10 of the season...Withdrew from the 100th Western Open with a shattered hook of left hamate bone (palm of hand). Did not play again until the Valero Texas Open in late September. **2002:** Finished in the top 100 for the first time in his five-year career, aided by a career-high three top-10s and earnings just shy of $1 million. Made more in 2002 than in previous two seasons combined...Recorded a T2 finish at the Michelob Championship at Kingsmill, where he held a one-stroke lead over Billy Mayfair heading into Sunday. Final-round 72 left him two strokes behind winner Charles Howell III, tied with Scott Hoch for second. **2001:** For second consecutive year kept his card with a strong finish in the season-ending Southern Farm Bureau Classic. Rounds of 67-66 put him in a tie for first, but closed 69-78, which still earned $14,960 and a T28 finish that was enough to move him into the top 125. **2000:** In first full season on PGA TOUR since 1991, retained fully-exempt playing privileges with strong finish to rank 120th on money list...At the Phoenix Open, posted his best final-round score of the year, 65, to finish T4. **1999:** Joined PGA TOUR as special temporary member in September...Had first two career top-20s in major championships with T14 at Masters Tournament and T16 at PGA Championship. Qualified for the Masters Tournament by virtue of being in top 50 in Official World Golf Ranking...Played on the Japan Golf Tour from 1995-1999 with six victories and a pair of runner-up finishes. **1996:** Was 20th on Japan Golf Tour Order of Merit with 70.99 scoring average. **1995:** Finished 25th on Japan Golf Tour Order of Merit and was ranked third in scoring with 70.24 average. **1991:** First earned PGA TOUR playing privileges with sixth-place finish at PGA TOUR Qualifying Tournament. **1990:** Played Canadian Tour where he won the British Columbia Open and finished first on the Order of Merit while compiling the low scoring average for the year.

Amateur: Named All-American 1986-88, All Pac-10 Conference 1986-87...Member of 1988 NCAA Championship Team while at UCLA.

PERSONAL:
Interest in golf stemmed from his attendance at 1978 U.S. Open at Cherry Hills CC in Denver.

PLAYER STATISTICS

2004 PGA TOUR STATISTICS

Scoring Average	71.37	(N/A)
Driving Distance	296.3	(N/A)
Driving Accuracy Percentage	58.9%	(N/A)
Total Driving	1,998	(N/A)
Greens in Regulation Pct.	66.1%	(N/A)
Putting Average	1.798	(N/A)
Sand Save Percentage	44.6%	(N/A)
Eagles (Holes per)	108.0	(N/A)
Birdie Average	3.77	(N/A)
Scoring Avg. Before Cut	70.95	(N/A)
Round 3 Scoring Avg.	71.67	(N/A)
Final Round Scoring Average	72.00	(N/A)
Birdie Conversion Percentage	30.3%	(N/A)
Par Breakers	21.9%	(N/A)

MISCELLANEOUS PGA TOUR STATISTICS
2004 Low Round/Round: 64–Bob Hope Chrysler Classic/2
Career Low Round/Round: 63–1999 Air Canada Championship/1
Career Largest Paycheck/Finish: $325,600–2002 Michelob Championship at Kingsmill/T2

PGA TOUR CAREER SUMMARY — PLAYOFF RECORD: 0-0

Year	Events Played	Cuts Made	1st	2nd	3rd	Top 10	Top 25	Earnings	Rank
1987A	1								
1990	1								
1991	27	5					2	$37,502	189
1992	2	1						6,340	257
1993	1								
1994	1	1						8,006	258
1995	4	1						3,969	313
1996	2								
1997	1								
1998	4	3				1	2	114,285	177
1999	13	10				1	4	272,100	141
2000	32	14				2	5	402,017	120
2001	30	17					5	407,065	124
2002	28	18		1	1	3	6	972,479	62
2003	22	16				1	4	691,604	91
2004	9	5				1	2	247,911	178
Total	178	91		1	1	9	30	3,163,278	
NATIONWIDE TOUR									
1991	1								
Total	1								
JAPAN GOLF TOUR									
2004	2	2					1	23,041	

PGA TOUR TOP TOURNAMENT SUMMARY

Year	90	91	92	93	94	95	96	97	98	99	00	01	02
Masters										T14	48		
U.S. Open	CUT		CUT		T39	T62	CUT				CUT	T52	
British Open						CUT			T52	CUT			
PGA									CUT	T16			
THE PLAYERS										CUT		CUT	CUT
WGC-Accenture Match Play										T17	T33		

Year	03	04
U.S. Open	T35	
THE PLAYERS	T32	T74

Zach Johnson

EXEMPT STATUS: 2004 tournament winner (through 2006)
FULL NAME: Zachary Harris Johnson
HEIGHT: 5-11
WEIGHT: 160
BIRTHDATE: February 24, 1976
BIRTHPLACE: Iowa City, IA
RESIDENCE: Lake Mary, FL
FAMILY: Wife, Kimala

EDUCATION: Drake University (1998, Business Management/Marketing)
SPECIAL INTERESTS: Movies, all sports, downhill skiing, relaxing with wife and friends, University of Iowa athletics
TURNED PROFESSIONAL: 1998
JOINED TOUR: 2004
Nationwide Tour Alumnus

PGA TOUR VICTORIES (1):
2004 BellSouth Classic.

NATIONWIDE TOUR VICTORIES (2):
2003 Rheem Classic, Envirocare Utah Classic.

BEST 2004 PGA TOUR FINISHES:
1—BellSouth Classic; T3—Buick Championship, 84 LUMBER Classic; T6—Bay Hill Invitational Presented by MasterCard; 10—WGC-American Express Championship.

2004 SEASON:
Became just the second player in PGA TOUR history to surpass $2 million in earnings in his first season. Made 24 of 30 cuts and picked up his first TOUR win in just his 13th career tournament. Along with Todd Hamilton, became the first pair of rookies to make THE TOUR Championship since 1999, when Notah Begay III and Carlos Franco finished inside the top 30. Began season outside the top 200 on the Official World Golf Ranking (207th) and ended the season at No. 41. . .Captured BellSouth Classic in April at the age of 28 years, 1 month and 10 days, and in doing so jumped from 126th to 49th in the Official World Golf Ranking with victory. Held the 36- and 54-hole leads after opening 69-66-68. Rollercoaster round on Sunday, with birdies on five of first 10 holes, followed by four bogeys in five holes. Converted pars on final three holes to edge runner-up Mark Hensby by one stroke. Earned a career-best $810,000, becoming just the fourth player to win BellSouth Classic for maiden TOUR victory, joining Tommy Aaron (1970), Paul Stankowski (1996) and Ben Crane (2003). . .Earned first top-10 of his TOUR career with a T6 at the Bay Hill Invitational Presented by MasterCard in March. Was three back through 36 holes but was derailed by a third-round 75. . .Held a share of the 36-hole lead at the Shell Houston Open after opening 71-68. Finished T11. . .Continued strong rookie season with T3 at Buick Championship. Co-leader with Fred Funk through 36 holes after opening 67-65. . .Finished T3 at the 84 LUMBER Classic, his fourth top-10 of the season, which enabled him to pass the $2-million mark. . .Posted his first top-10 in a WGC event with a 10th at the WGC-American Express Championship in Ireland. It was the fifth top-10 of his rookie season, the most since Pat Perez posted six as a rookie in 2002. . .Finished sixth in Total Birdies, with 403, and was one of seven players to surpass the 400 mark in 2004.

CAREER HIGHLIGHTS:
2003: Earned Nationwide Tour Player of the Year honors after making the cut in 19 of 20 events, including the last 17 and finishing first on the final money list with a record $494,882. Produced two wins, a Tour-leading 11 top-10s and 16 top-25s...Opened season with three top-5 finishes...Recorded his first career win at the Rheem Classic. Made a par on the first extra hole to defeat veteran Steve Haskins after beginning the round six shots behind 54-hole leader Franklin Langham...Voted April's Nationwide Tour Player of the Month...Tied a Nationwide Tour record with three consecutive runner-up performances — The Reese's Cup Classic, dropping a playoff to Mark Hensby at the Henrico County Open and the Dayton Open...July Player of the Month...Second victory came at the Envirocare Utah Classic, posting weekend rounds of 65-65 to finish one stroke ahead of Bobby Gage. In the process he broke the Tour's all-time, single-season money record and became the first player in Tour history to top the $400,000 mark in earnings...Finished third at the season-ending Nationwide Tour Championship, giving him nine top-three finishes, the best single-season performance in Nationwide Tour history...Posted 68 of 78 rounds during the season at par or better...Led Tour with a record scoring average of 68.97 and finished first in putting average and all around ranking. **2002:** Won once (Tulsa, OK) on the Hooters Tour. Recorded five top-five finishes, nine top-10s and finished second on the money list. **2001:** Won final three regular-season events on Hooters Tour, earning the nickname "Back-to-Back-to-Back-Zach." Finished the season as the tour's leading money winner and Player of the Year. **2000:** Rookie on the Nationwide Tour...Missed the first six cuts of the year but rebounded by making four of the final five cuts with T25 at the Tri-Cities Open his best showing. **1999:** Finished third on Prairie Golf Tour after winning twice. **1998:** Won once on the Prairie Golf Tour and finished sixth on the money list.

PERSONAL:
Began playing golf at age 10. . .Lists his father and mother among his heroes. . .Father is a chiropractor. . .Married Kim Barclay on Feb. 8, 2003. . .Huge Iowa Hawkeye football and basketball fan. . .The gallery at BellSouth Classic at first TOUR victory included a group of about 10 men from Iowa who gave him financial support early in his career. Some were seeing him play as a pro for the first time. "It started out as a business, but it ended up as a business family," Johnson said of his relationship with them. "It's unbelievable having them here."

PLAYER STATISTICS

2004 PGA TOUR STATISTICS

Scoring Average	70.18	(17)
Driving Distance	285.6	(113)
Driving Accuracy Percentage	71.9%	(15)
Total Driving	128	(21)
Greens in Regulation Pct.	67.9%	(29)
Putting Average	1.751	(26)
Sand Save Percentage	45.3%	(150)
Eagles (Holes per)	321.0	(140)
Birdie Average	3.77	(34)
All-Around Ranking	524	(28)
Scoring Avg. Before Cut	70.08	(15)
Round 3 Scoring Avg.	71.00	(101)
Final Round Scoring Average	71.04	(57)
Birdie Conversion Percentage	30.2%	(62)
Par Breakers	21.2%	(49)

MISCELLANEOUS PGA TOUR STATISTICS

2004 Low Round/Round: 65–4 times, most recent Buick Championship/2
Career Low Round/Round: 65–4 times, most recent 2004 Buick Championship/2
Career Largest Paycheck/Finish: $810,000–2004 BellSouth Classic/1

PGA TOUR CAREER SUMMARY — PLAYOFF RECORD: 0-0

Year	Events Played	Cuts Made	1st	2nd	3rd	Top 10	Top 25	Earnings	Rank
2001	1								
2002	2	1					1	$57,000	
2003	1								
2004	30	24	1		2	5	15	2,417,685	19
Total	34	25	1		2	5	16	2,474,685	
NATIONWIDE TOUR									
1999	2	1						945	227
2000	11	4					1	10,280	174
2003	20	19	2	4	3	11	16	494,882	1
Total	33	24	2	4	3	11	17	506,107	

PGA TOUR TOP TOURNAMENT SUMMARY

Year	04
U.S. Open	T48
British Open	CUT
PGA	T37
TOUR Championship	13
WGC-NEC Invitational	T22
WGC-American Express Champ	10

Kent Jones

EXEMPT STATUS: 119th on 2004 money list
FULL NAME: Stephen Kent Jones
HEIGHT: 5-8
WEIGHT: 150
BIRTHDATE: January 8, 1967
BIRTHPLACE: Portales, NM
RESIDENCE: Albuquerque, NM
FAMILY: Wife, JoAnna; Lauren Marie (10/11/00), Samuel Kent (10/8/02)
EDUCATION: University of New Mexico (1990, Business Administration) (1991, Masters in Business Admininstration)
SPECIAL INTERESTS: Reading, fishing
TURNED PROFESSIONAL: 1992
Q SCHOOL: 1997
Nationwide Tour Alumnus

BEST PGA TOUR CAREER FINISH:
T8—2002 AT&T Pebble Beach National Pro-Am.

NATIONWIDE TOUR VICTORIES (2):
2000 Shreveport Open, Greensboro Open.

BEST 2004 PGA TOUR FINISHES:
T9—Bob Hope Chrysler Classic; T10—AT&T Pebble Beach National Pro-Am.

2004 SEASON:
Finished inside the top 125 for the second straight season, thanks in part to a T17 at the final full-field event of the season, the Chrysler Championship. Came into the event No. 124 on the money list and improved to No. 119...Had career-high two top-10s...Posted five sub-70 rounds en route to T9 finish at the Bob Hope Chrysler Classic, second top-10 of career and first since 2002 campaign...Added another top-10 (T10) two weeks later at the AT&T Pebble Beach National Pro-Am. One of five players with rounds in the 60s (69) during Sunday's final round...Shared the first-round lead with six others at the Michelin Championship at Las Vegas prior to finishing T15. The $58,100 check moved him to 120th on the TOUR money list.

CAREER HIGHLIGHTS:
2003: Entered the season with conditional status after finishing 131st on 2002 money list...Seven top-25s allowed him to finish inside the the top 125 on the money list for the first time in his career. Finished the season with four consecutive made cuts, moving from 143rd to 122nd during that stretch. **2002:** Made the most of 33 events entered, making 19 cuts. Earned first top-10 of TOUR career at the AT&T Pebble Beach National Pro-Am with a T8...Led after 18 holes at the Buick Open at 7-under-par 65, before finishing T14. **2001:** Only top-25 was a T15 at John Deere Classic. **2000:** Was two-time winner on Nationwide Tour at Shreveport Open and Greensboro Open. Set tournament record by three strokes in Greensboro with a 17-under 263. **1998:** Rookie on TOUR, was one shot off the lead after 36 holes of the Buick Open, finished T12.

PERSONAL:
College teammate of PGA TOUR member Tim Herron...Season ticketholder for New Mexico basketball...Traveled with his wife and dog for three years in recreational vehicle while playing the Canadian Tour (1993-94) and the Hooters Tour (1995). Finally sold the truck after putting more than 200,000 miles on it...Was inducted in the Carlsbad (NM) Athletic Hall of Fame.

PLAYER STATISTICS

2004 PGA TOUR STATISTICS

Scoring Average	71.06	(90)
Driving Distance	286.4	(103)
Driving Accuracy Percentage	69.8%	(27)
Total Driving	130	(23)
Greens in Regulation Pct.	67.4%	(39)
Putting Average	1.776	(91)
Sand Save Percentage	46.5%	(134)
Eagles (Holes per)	158.7	(42)
Birdie Average	3.55	(90)
All-Around Ranking	616	(49)
Scoring Avg. Before Cut	70.95	(88)
Round 3 Scoring Avg.	70.71	(74)
Final Round Scoring Average	70.35	(20)
Birdie Conversion Percentage	29.1%	(95)
Par Breakers	20.3%	(83)

MISCELLANEOUS PGA TOUR STATISTICS

2004 Low Round/Round: 64–2 times, most recent Chrysler Championship/1
Career Low Round/Round: 64–3 times, most recent 2004 Chrysler Championship/1
Career Largest Paycheck/Finish: $127,200–2004 AT&T Pebble Beach National Pro–Am/T10

PGA TOUR CAREER SUMMARY — PLAYOFF RECORD: 0-0

Year	Events Played	Cuts Made	1st	2nd	3rd	Top 10	Top 25	Earnings	Rank
1996	1	1						$5,415	309
1997	1								
1998	29	17					2	133,339	171
1999	26	7					1	64,217	218
2001	28	7					1	87,308	201
2002	33	19				1	6	489,879	131
2003	23	13					7	539,737	122
2004	32	17				2	6	674,909	119
Total	173	81				3	23	1,994,805	
NATIONWIDE TOUR									
1992	1								
1993	2	2						846	222
1994	2								
1996	25	10				1	3	14,830	101
1997	27	17		1		3	9	45,689	46
1998	1								
1999	1	1						953	226
2000	25	17	2			4	11	220,081	7
2001	1								
2003	2	1						1,520	313
Total	87	48	2	1		8	23	283,918	

PGA TOUR TOP TOURNAMENT SUMMARY

Year	96	97	98	99	00	01	02	03	04
U.S. Open	T82	CUT					T68	CUT	
THE PLAYERS									CUT

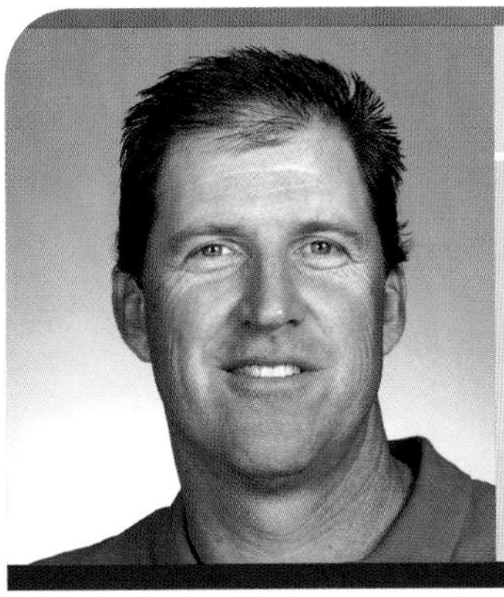

Steve Jones

EXEMPT STATUS: Winner, 1996 U.S. Open (through 2006)
FULL NAME: Steven Glen Jones
HEIGHT: 6-4
WEIGHT: 200
BIRTHDATE: December 27, 1958
BIRTHPLACE: Artesia, NM
RESIDENCE: Bozeman, MT; plays out of Valley View GC
FAMILY: Wife, Bonnie Buckingham; Cy Edmond (2/27/91), Stacey Jane (2/21/93)
EDUCATION: University of Colorado
SPECIAL INTERESTS: Basketball, fly fishing, snow skiing, hunting
TURNED PROFESSIONAL: 1981
Q SCHOOL: 1981, 1984, 1986

PGA TOUR VICTORIES (8):

1988 AT&T Pebble Beach National Pro-Am. **1989** MONY Tournament of Champions, Bob Hope Chrysler Classic, Canadian Open. **1996** U.S. Open Championship. **1997** Phoenix Open, Bell Canadian Open. **1998** Quad City Classic.

BEST 2004 PGA TOUR FINISH:

T33—BellSouth Classic.

2004 SEASON:

Served as Hal Sutton's Assistant Captain for the 2004 Ryder Cup at Oakland Hills, where Jones won the 1996 U.S. Open. Plans to start the 2005 season after being sidelined for part of the 2003 season and all of 2004 following elbow surgery in 2003.

CAREER HIGHLIGHTS:

2003: Made five cuts in 11 appearance early in the season. Last event he played in was the Wachovia Championship in early May. Missed the rest of the season due to tennis elbow in his right elbow. Was having problems with both elbows throughout the summer and finally had surgery on his right elbow on August 7. Continued rehabilitation on both elbows throughout the season. **2002:** Troubled by an irregular heartbeat, called superventricular tachycardia, for most of the past four seasons. Underwent a laser procedure to correct the condition on Aug. 14...Was one back of the lead through first round of the British Open after opening with 67, finished T43...Shared the first round lead at the Invensys Classic at Las Vegas, finished T42. **2001:** Best effort was T15 at John Deere Classic...Placed T20 at The INTERNATIONAL...His T27 finish at Masters was sixth top-30 finish in nine trips to Augusta National. **2000:** Continued to regain old form after battling through injury-plagued 1999 season...Finished with two top-10s and ranked 87th on PGA TOUR official money list...Recorded best opening score of season with 66 at Touchstone Energy Tucson Open. Finished 70-67-69 to earn T5 and season-best $114,000...Three starts later, matched that finish with another T5 at weather-shortened BellSouth Classic. **1999:** Recorded three top-10 finishes in abbreviated season in which he logged 19 appearances. Suffered from an irregular heartbeat first two months of season and a shoulder injury sidelined him from Masters Tournament through John Deere Classic, with exception of U.S. Open. After missing cut at Augusta National, did not touch a club during nine weeks of shoulder rehab. **1998:** Won for third straight year with victory at the Quad City Classic. Started final round in four-way tie for third and had share of 36-hole tournament record with Frank Lickliter II at 11-under-par 129 closed with 66 for one-stroke victory over Scott Gump. **1997:** Followed up U.S. Open victory with second multiple-victory season of career...Dominated Phoenix Open, winning by 11 strokes over Jesper Parnevik. Total of 258 equaled third-lowest 72-hole score in PGA TOUR history...Lead after 36 holes (126), was one stroke off 54-hole mark and held one-stroke lead through 54 holes at Bell Canadian Open. Closed with 69 for one-stroke victory over Greg Norman. **1996:** After spending nearly three years off TOUR due to ligament and joint damage to left ring finger suffered on Nov. 25, 1991 in dirt-bike accident, completed comeback with victory in U.S. Open at Oakland Hills. Became first sectional qualifier to win since Jerry Pate in 1976. After opening-round 74, shot 66-69 to trail Tom Lehman by one stroke through 54 holes. Led by one after 71 holes, then parred 18 to defeat Lehman and Davis Love III by a stroke. Winning score of 2-under-par 278 was lowest in a U.S. Open at Oakland Hills. **1989:** Won three times, opening year with back-to-back wins. Defeated Jay Haas and David Frost by two at MONY Tournament of Champions and followed with playoff win over Paul Azinger and Sandy Lyle at Bob Hope Chrysler Classic. Third win came at Canadian Open. **1988:** Earned first TOUR victory in playoff over Bob Tway at AT&T Pebble Beach National Pro-Am. **1986:** Medalist at PGA TOUR Qualifying Tournament. **Amateur:** Second-team All-American at University of Colorado...Semifinalist at 1976 U.S. Junior Amateur.

PERSONAL:

Reverse overlap grip he uses is by-product of injury to left index finger two years after original injury to left ring finger...Play at U.S. Open inspired by Ben Hogan book sent to him by friend... In addition to golf, ran track and was an all-state basketball player in high school...A two-time Colorado State sand greens champion...On Aug. 14, 2002, underwent surgery to correct a heart condition called superventricular tachycardia, an ailment that isn't life-threatening, but mirrors the symptoms of a heart attack. Phil Tataurangi underwent the procedure a month earlier in 2002.

PLAYER STATISTICS

MISCELLANEOUS PGA TOUR STATISTICS

Career Low Round/Round: 62–2 times, most recent 2002 Invensys Classic at Las Vegas/1
Career Largest Paycheck/Finish: $425,000–1996 U.S. Open Championship/1

PGA TOUR CAREER SUMMARY — PLAYOFF RECORD: 2-1

Year	Events Played	Cuts Made	1st	2nd	3rd	Top 10	Top 25	Earnings	Rank
1982	12	3						$1,986	250
1984	1	1						788	264
1985	21	12				1	7	43,379	129
1986	23	14				2	5	51,473	136
1987	30	20		1		2	6	154,918	66
1988	25	19	1			3	6	241,877	45
1989	26	22	3			6	11	745,578	8
1990	24	16		1	1	5	12	350,982	34
1991	27	19			1	4	11	294,961	54
1994	2	2						8,740	254
1995	24	16				2	9	234,749	79
1996	25	18	1		1	6	10	810,644	22
1997	24	16	2	1		6	9	959,108	20
1998	23	19	1			2	11	741,544	38
1999	19	11				3	8	360,706	116
2000	21	16				2	7	548,070	87
2001	25	12					2	264,456	155
2002	24	12						169,315	180
2003	11	5						68,756	222
Total	387	253	8	3	3	44	114	6,052,026	
NATIONWIDE TOUR									
1994	2	2				1	1	5,195	140
Total	2	2				1	1	5,195	

PGA TOUR TOP TOURNAMENT SUMMARY

Year	87	88	89	90	91	92	93	94	95	96	97	98	99
Masters		T30	T31	T20	CUT						CUT	T26	CUT
U.S. Open			T46	T8	CUT					1	T60	CUT	CUT
British Open			CUT	T16	T64					CUT	T48	T57	
PGA	T61	T9	T51	CUT						CUT	T41		CUT
THE PLAYERS	T15	T48	T41	T3	T41					T33	CUT	T25	CUT
TOUR Championship			T14							T18	25		
WGC-Accenture Match Play													T9

Year	00	01	02	03
Masters	T25	T27		
U.S. Open	T27	T30	CUT	
British Open	T31	CUT	T43	
PGA	T24			
THE PLAYERS	T27	T50	CUT	T62

NATIONAL TEAMS: Ryder Cup, 2004 (Captain's Assistant); World Cup, 1996.

SECTION 2 PLAYER BIOGRAPHIES

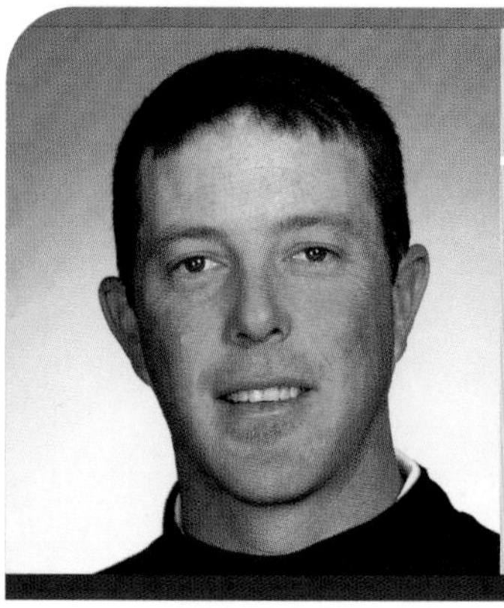

Jonathan Kaye

EXEMPT STATUS: 2004 tournament winner (through 2006)
FULL NAME: Jonathan Andrew Kaye
HEIGHT: 5-11
WEIGHT: 165
BIRTHDATE: August 2, 1970
BIRTHPLACE: Denver, CO
RESIDENCE: Phoenix, AZ
FAMILY: Wife, Jennifer
EDUCATION: University of Colorado
SPECIAL INTERESTS: Cooking, avid indoorsman
TURNED PROFESSIONAL: 1993
Q SCHOOL: 1994

PGA TOUR VICTORIES (2):

2003 Buick Classic. **2004** FBR Open.

BEST 2004 PGA TOUR FINISHES:

1—FBR Open; 4—Bob Hope Chrysler Classic.

2004 SEASON:

Finished inside the top 80 on the PGA TOUR money list for the sixth straight year…In third start of season, posted solo fourth at the Bob Hope Chrysler Classic, including rounds of 65-64 on the weekend to finish two strokes out of Phil Mickelson-Skip Kendall playoff… The next week collected second TOUR title of his career at the FBR Open. Picked up $936,000 with his victory and moved to the top of the PGA TOUR season money list for the first time in his career. Win was second in his last 14 starts on TOUR. His wife, Jennifer, won the Wives Golf Classic held early in the week with players caddying for the wives…Recorded just three top-20s the remainder of the season but was dealing with back pain, which occurred during his first match of the WGC-Accenture Match Play Championship, and a bad wrist, which he aggravated prior to The INTERNATIONAL.

CAREER HIGHLIGHTS:

2003: Captured first career victory in his 195th start on TOUR at the Buick Classic. Defeated John Rollins with an eagle-3 on the first extra hole to raise his playoff record to 1-1. Birdied 72nd hole to force playoff. Shared third-round lead with Briny Baird, Skip Kendall and John Rollins. Due to rain-shortened Saturday, played 30 holes on Sunday...Earned first top-10 at a major championship with a T10 at the U.S. Open...In only second World Golf Championships appearance, finished second at NEC Invitational, four shots behind Darren Clarke. Paired with Clarke in final group on Sunday, fell four shots behind on par-5 second hole with a bogey along with a Clarke eagle. Final-round 70 wrapped up solo second, earning $550,000 to surpass $2 million on season for the first time...Ended the season on a high note with T7 finish at the TOUR Championship, his first appearance in the event. **2002:** Posted T2 at the Canon Greater Hartford Open. Held first 54-hole lead of career at 13-under-par, one stroke ahead of Scott Verplank. Carded final-round 70, missing birdie putt on 72nd hole that would have forced a playoff with winner Phil Mickelson…Lost in a playoff to Chris Riley at the Reno-Tahoe Open. Tied with Riley and Steve Flesch for the lead through 54 holes, missed eight-footer for birdie on 72nd hole that would have clinched first PGA TOUR victory. **2001:** Had only one top-10 (third at B.C. Open) but was able to parlay making 26 cuts in 33 starts into a very respectable year...Took first-round lead in the Canon Greater Hartford Open with an opening 62 after coming close to withdrawing due to a pinched nerve. Round featured a 29 on the front nine. Fell off the pace to finish T29. **2000:** Surpassed the $1-million mark for the first time since joining the PGA TOUR on the strength of a career-high 11 top-25 finishes and four top-10s, including a second and third...Posted best finish of the year at inaugural SEI Pennsylvania Classic, a T2 worth $192,000...Tied the TPC at Summerlin course record with a 10-under-par 62 on the final day at the Invensys Classic at Las Vegas. Finished T3 and won $246,500. **1999:** Had five top-10s, including a second at Las Vegas Invitational, three behind winner Jim Furyk...Opened with 64, one off first-round lead at Bob Hope Chrysler Classic. Followed with second-round 83 and next round shot 62 to tie Tamarisk course record. His 21-stroke improvement from second round to third was best turnaround since Bob Murphy shot 88-69 in first two rounds to improve 19 strokes at 1985 Bing Crosby National Pro-Am. **1998:** Regained PGA TOUR membership with T2 at PGA TOUR Qualifying Tournament. **1997:** Played under special medical extension. **1996:** Had rotator cuff surgery in February. Missed majority of 1996 and 1997 seasons but played several times on PGA TOUR and Nationwide Tour. **1995:** Had brush with first PGA TOUR victory at Quad City Classic. In tournament shortened to 54 holes due to weather, stood on final tee leading D.A. Weibring by one stroke. When he bogeyed and Weibring birdied from off the green, fell to second. Earned $108,000 to clinch TOUR card. **Amateur:** Won 1992 Ping Intercollegiate in playoff over Phil Mickelson.

PERSONAL:

A self-taught player.

PLAYER STATISTICS

2004 PGA TOUR STATISTICS

Scoring Average	71.47	(135)
Driving Distance	290.9	(62)
Driving Accuracy Percentage	64.7%	(90)
Total Driving	152	(37)
Greens in Regulation Pct.	66.5%	(57)
Putting Average	1.803	(167)
Sand Save Percentage	42.2%	(176)
Eagles (Holes per)	171.0	(51)
Birdie Average	3.41	(127)
All-Around Ranking	865	(123)
Scoring Avg. Before Cut	71.18	(123)
Round 3 Scoring Avg.	70.53	(62)
Final Round Scoring Average	73.00	(174)
Birdie Conversion Percentage	27.8%	(140)
Par Breakers	19.5%	(122)

MISCELLANEOUS PGA TOUR STATISTICS

2004 Low Round/Round: 64–2 times, most recent Chrysler Championship/1
Career Low Round/Round: 62–3 times, most recent 2001 Canon Greater Hartford Open/1
Career Largest Paycheck/Finish: $936,000–2004 FBR Open/1

PGA TOUR CAREER SUMMARY — PLAYOFF RECORD: 1-1

Year	Events Played	Cuts Made	1st	2nd	3rd	Top 10	Top 25	Earnings	Rank
1995	25	8		1		2	4	$191,883	94
1996	3	1						5,070	318
1997	2	1					1	10,693	266
1998	21	12					1	86,496	190
1999	32	24		1		5	10	845,051	49
2000	34	24		1	1	4	11	1,096,131	40
2001	33	26			1	1	6	683,210	79
2002	27	15		2		4	5	1,082,803	60
2003	27	18	1	1		8	9	2,474,837	16
2004	25	16	1			2	6	1,695,332	34
Total	229	145	2	6	2	26	53	8,171,506	
NATIONWIDE TOUR									
1995	3	2				1	2	6,747	142
1997	3	2					1	3,382	163
Total	6	4				1	3	10,129	

PGA TOUR TOP TOURNAMENT SUMMARY

Year	00	01	02	03	04
Masters		T43			CUT
U.S. Open	CUT			T10	CUT
British Open			CUT	CUT	CUT
PGA	T51	T63	CUT	T61	CUT
THE PLAYERS	CUT	T18	T57	T32	CUT
TOUR Championship				7	
WGC-Accenture Match Play		T33			T33
WGC-NEC Invitational				2	T65
WGC-American Express Champ				20	T59

Jerry Kelly

EXEMPT STATUS: 2002 two-time tournament winner (through 2005)
FULL NAME: Jerome Patrick Kelly
HEIGHT: 5-11
WEIGHT: 165
BIRTHDATE: November 23, 1966
BIRTHPLACE: Madison, WI
RESIDENCE: Madison, WI

FAMILY: Wife, Carol; Cooper Patrick (8/14/98)
EDUCATION: University of Hartford (Finance and Insurance, 1989)
SPECIAL INTERESTS: Hockey, all sports
TURNED PROFESSIONAL: 1989
JOINED TOUR: 1996
Nationwide Tour Alumnus

PGA TOUR VICTORIES (2):

2002 Sony Open in Hawaii, Advil Western Open.

NATIONWIDE TOUR VICTORIES (2):

1995 Alabama Classic, Buffalo Open.

BEST 2004 PGA TOUR FINISHES:

3—THE TOUR Championship presented by Coca-Cola; 5—Bay Hill Invitational Presented by MasterCard, Sony Open in Hawaii, WGC-Accenture Match Play Championship, Valero Texas Open; T6—THE PLAYERS Championship; T8—Buick Open, Chrysler Classic of Greensboro.

2004 SEASON:

Finished inside the top 30 and made over $2 million for the third straight season…Did not post a win but matched his career-high in top-10s (2003) with eight…Best finish came at the season-ending TOUR Championship, where he closed with a 5-under 65 to finish solo third, five strokes behind winner Retief Goosen…In season's first start, past champion finished T5 at the Sony Open in Hawaii, posting four rounds in the 60s…Finished T5 at the WGC-Accenture Match Play Championship, falling to Darren Clarke, 5 and 3, in the fourth round. In first three matches, topped Sergio Garcia, Vijay Singh and Chad Campbell…Despite fighting a stomach virus throughout the tourament, he picked up his third top-10 of the season by finishing fifth at the Bay Hill Invitational Presented by MasterCard…Held a share of the 36-hole lead with Kevin Sutherland at THE PLAYERS Championship after opening 69-66. Finished T6 after rounds of 74-72 on the weekend…Added a T8 at the Buick Open in August…Following week, saw streak of 27 straight made cuts come to an end when he missed the cut at the PGA Championship. At the time, was second-longest current streak behind Tiger Woods (128)…Next top-10 was T5 at the Valero Texas Open, aided by four rounds in the 60s. Finished five strokes behind champion Bart Bryant…Seventh top-10 was T8 at the Chrysler Classic of Greensboro…Finished tied for second on TOUR with 46 Rounds in the 60s and fourth on TOUR in Total Birdies with 409…Contemplated off-season left shoulder surgery (AC joint) but decided to try and rehab rather than go under the knife.

CAREER HIGHLIGHTS:

2003: Earned a career-best 10 top-10s...Finished T8 at The Honda Classic, setting The CC at Mirasol Sunset Course record with a second-round 10-under 62. Round of 62 also tied 18-hole tournament record...T3 in defense of 100th Western Open title...Tied the PGA TOUR record for consecutive birdies with eight in the third round of the Las Vegas Invitational at the TPC at Summerlin, posting birdies on Nos. 7-14 on Friday. Bob Goalby set the record at the 1961 St. Petersburg Open, and was later tied by Fuzzy Zoeller (1976 Quad Cities Open), Dewey Arnette (1987 Buick Open), Edward Fryatt (2000 Doral-Ryder Open) and J.P. Hayes (2003 Bob Hope Chrysler Classic)...Earned spot on the U.S. Presidents Cup team. **2002:** Finished top 10 on the TOUR money list for the first time in his career...Earned first career victory in 200th career PGA TOUR start at the Sony Open in Hawaii. Shared first-round lead and held third-round lead outright on way to defeating John Cook by one stroke...Second TOUR victory came just 18 events after the first at the Advil Western Open.Four rounds in the 60s, including a final-round 65, gave him the come-from-behind win. Kelly began the day three strokes back of third-round leader Robert Allenby and finished two strokes ahead of runner-up Davis Love III. **2001:** Made more than $1 million in a season for the first time in his career, $1,491,607 (35th). For sixth consecutive year, played in 30-plus events...Led THE PLAYERS Championship through the second and third rounds. Closing 73 dropped him to fourth, four strokes behind Tiger Woods...After opening with rounds of 66-68-67, held one-stroke third-round lead in Reno-Tahoe Open. Closed with 71 and lost by one stroke to John Cook's final-round 64. **2000:** Finished 59th on the TOUR money list with $784,754. Ranking equaled previous career best when he won $336,748 in 1996...At AT&T Pebble Beach National Pro-Am, had season-best T4. **1999:** Played 34 events during the year and made the cut in 22 of those...Posted first third-place finish of career at Greater Milwaukee Open. Started with 66-65-66 to earn third-round lead before final-round 71 dropped to solo third, four strokes behind Carlos Franco...Recorded the first of five double eagles on TOUR at Bob Hope Chrysler Classic on 14th hole at Indian Wells CC. **1996:** Madison, WI native nearly captured first PGA TOUR title in front of home-state fans. Trailed by three strokes entering final round of Greater Milwaukee Open. Shot closing 64 to catch Loren Roberts and force playoff after each shot tournament-record 265. Roberts birdied first extra hole for victory. Finished rookie season 59th on money list. **1995:** Named Nationwide Tour Player of the Year. Was leading money-winner with $188,878. Won Alabama Classic and Buffalo Open. **1992:** Won 1992 Wisconsin State Open.

PERSONAL:

All-city hockey selection in high school. Says hockey background may have hurt his golf in past, because he brings aggressiveness to the game…Wife Carol's brother, Jim Schuman, played on Nationwide Tour from 1990-93.

PLAYER STATISTICS

2004 PGA TOUR STATISTICS

Scoring Average	70.09	(12)
Driving Distance	278.1	(172)
Driving Accuracy Percentage	70.4%	(21)
Total Driving	193	(93)
Greens in Regulation Pct.	68.0%	(27)
Putting Average	1.763	(52)
Sand Save Percentage	52.8%	(46)
Eagles (Holes per)	327.0	(143)
Birdie Average	3.75	(41)
All-Around Ranking	514	(25)
Scoring Avg. Before Cut	70.00	(12)
Round 3 Scoring Avg.	70.65	(68)
Final Round Scoring Average	70.31	(17)
Birdie Conversion Percentage	29.6%	(81)
Par Breakers	21.2%	(49)

MISCELLANEOUS PGA TOUR STATISTICS

2004 Low Round/Round: 64–WGC-NEC Invitational/3
Career Low Round/Round: 62–2003 The Honda Classic/2
Career Largest Paycheck/Finish: $720,000–2 times, most recent 2002 Advil Western Open/1

PGA TOUR CAREER SUMMARY — PLAYOFF RECORD: 0-1

Year	Events Played	Cuts Made	1st	2nd	3rd	Top 10	Top 25	Earnings	Rank
1991	1								
1992	1								
1993	2								
1995	2	1						$4,733	306
1996	31	17		1		4	5	336,748	59
1997	34	13				3	7	234,257	103
1998	31	17				2	8	340,144	87
1999	34	22			1	2	8	533,702	77
2000	32	23				3	12	784,754	59
2001	31	21		1		7	11	1,491,607	35
2002	29	21	2			8	14	2,946,889	6
2003	30	23			1	10	16	2,158,342	26
2004	29	27			1	8	15	2,496,222	17
Total	287	185	2	2	3	47	96	11,327,398	
NATIONWIDE TOUR									
1993	28	15		1		3	10	61,074	25
1994	26	19				8	11	60,928	26
1995	28	23	2	1		15	19	188,878	1
Total	82	57	2	2		26	40	310,881	

PGA TOUR TOP TOURNAMENT SUMMARY

Year	96	97	98	99	00	01	02	03	04
Masters							T20	48	T31
U.S. Open				T57	T37		CUT	CUT	T40
British Open		T44				CUT	T28	W/D	T47
PGA		CUT	W/D	T26	CUT	T44	CUT	CUT	CUT
THE PLAYERS	CUT	CUT	T31	CUT	T42	4	T11	CUT	T6
TOUR Championship							4	T13	3
WGC-Accenture Match Play							T33	T5	T5
WGC-NEC Invitational							77	T53	T19
WGC-American Express Champ						CNL	T4	T21	T16

Skip Kendall

EXEMPT STATUS: 64th on 2004 money list
FULL NAME: Jules I. Kendall
HEIGHT: 5-8
WEIGHT: 150
BIRTHDATE: September 9, 1964
BIRTHPLACE: Milwaukee, WI
RESIDENCE: Windermere, FL
FAMILY: Wife, Traci; Noah Jules (6/4/98)

EDUCATION: University of Nevada-Las Vegas (1987, Business Education)
SPECIAL INTERESTS: Reading, sports, Green Bay Packers, gardening
TURNED PROFESSIONAL: 1987
Q SCHOOL: 1992
Nationwide Tour Alumnus

BEST PGA TOUR CAREER FINISH:

2—**1998** Buick Invitational, **1999** Canon Greater Hartford Open, **2000** Southern Farm Bureau Classic, **2004** Bob Hope Chrysler Classic.

NATIONWIDE TOUR VICTORIES (2):

1994 Inland Empire Open, Carolina Classic.

BEST 2004 PGA TOUR FINISHES:

2—Bob Hope Chrysler Classic; T5—Bank of America Colonial.

2004 SEASON:

Finished inside the top 125 on the PGA TOUR money list for the eighth straight season. No. 64 was highest finish on TOUR since finishing No. 50 in 2000…Career high in earnings, with $1,206,438, passing $1-million mark for second year in a row…Earned fourth career runner-up finish in second start of season at the Bob Hope Chrysler Classic, falling to Phil Mickelson on the first playoff hole. Shared the 18-hole lead with Mark Hensby after a first-round 63 and finished 68-68-66-65—330 to earn a career-best paycheck of $486,000…Next top-10 did not come until May, a T5 at the Bank of America Colonial…Held a one-stroke lead over Thomas Levet after 36 holes of the British Open in Scotland before finishing T11.

CAREER HIGHLIGHTS:

2003: Had only two top-10s, but was able to parlay making 24 cuts in 30 starts into a very respectable year in which he earned over $1 million for the first time in his career...Two days before the start of the Memorial Tournament, cut most of the top of his left index finger above the first knuckle off while cutting a bagel for breakfast. He put the finger tip on ice and rushed to a Columbus, OH, hospital and had a two-hour procedure to reattach the finger, complete with 16 stitches. Ten days later, was able to resume practice. Three weeks after the accident, returned to the TOUR with a reverse overlap grip at the Buick Open, was tied for the third-round lead and finished in a season-best T4. **2002:** Managed to stay in the top 125 on the TOUR money list with two top-10s and eight top-25s...First top-10 of season did not come until June when he finished T7 at Canon Greater Hartford Open. Trailed Brett Quigley and Hidemichi Tanaka by one stroke after opening with a 5-under-par 65...Added T10 at the Greater Milwaukee Open. Aced the 215-yard, par-3 seventh hole with a 5-iron during the final round. His $80,600 payday in Milwaukee moved him over the $600,000 mark to secure his TOUR card for 2003. **2001:** Made 23 cuts in a career-high 33 starts...Only top-10 was a T6 in the National Car Rental Golf Classic at Walt Disney World Resort. Performance was highlighted by a third-round 64. **2000:** Recorded third consecutive top-50 finish on the official money list. Three top-10s included runner-up finish for third consecutive year, which came in season's final week at Southern Farm Bureau Classic. Started the final day four strokes behind leader Steve Lowery, then posted a 66 on Sunday to force a playoff. Lost when Lowery sank a 45-foot putt from off the fringe for birdie on first playoff hole. Along with Lowery, established new tournament record for low 72 holes with 266. **1999:** At Canon Greater Hartford Open, shared first-round lead after opening 63. Closed with 68-68-66 for second career runner-up finish, three strokes behind Brent Geiberger...Set competitive course record at Medinah with 65 in second round of PGA Championship. **1998:** Posted first career runner-up finish, losing playoff to Scott Simpson in Buick Invitational. Birdied final hole from nine feet to force playoff. **1997:** Earned more than he had in first five TOUR seasons combined—$320,800. Best finish, a third-place showing, came at Sprint International. **1996:** Returned to Nationwide Tour and finished ninth on money list, thanks to nine top-10s, including second at Tri-Cities Open. **1994:** Finished fifth in earnings on Nationwide Tour money list. Won Inland Empire Open and Carolina Classic. **1993:** First year on TOUR after earning co-medalist honors at 1992 Qualifying Tournament, despite opening-round 79. Best finish of year was eighth at Sprint International. **Amateur:** Winner of 1988 and 1989 Wisconsin State Opens.

PERSONAL:

In 1994, became first Nationwide Tour player to serve as host of "Inside the PGA TOUR."…Serves as host for the Children's Hospital of Wisconsin/Skip Kendall Pro-Am for Kids, which began in 2000…Credited with showing the "claw" putting grip to Chris DiMarco in 1995. Putts with conventional grip.

PLAYER STATISTICS

2004 PGA TOUR STATISTICS

Scoring Average	71.03	(84)
Driving Distance	281.3	(146)
Driving Accuracy Percentage	68.2%	(45)
Total Driving	191	(87)
Greens in Regulation Pct.	62.7%	(157)
Putting Average	1.767	(64)
Sand Save Percentage	48.3%	(109)
Eagles (Holes per)	254.6	(103)
Birdie Average	3.46	(119)
All-Around Ranking	827	(115)
Scoring Avg. Before Cut	70.56	(45)
Round 3 Scoring Avg.	71.20	(113)
Final Round Scoring Average	72.35	(156)
Birdie Conversion Percentage	29.1%	(95)
Par Breakers	19.6%	(116)

MISCELLANEOUS PGA TOUR STATISTICS

2004 Low Round/Round: 63–Bob Hope Chrysler Classic/1
Career Low Round/Round: 63–6 times, most recent 2004 Bob Hope Chrysler Classic/1
Career Largest Paycheck/Finish: $486,000–2004 Bob Hope Chrysler Classic/2

PGA TOUR CAREER SUMMARY — PLAYOFF RECORD: 0-3

Year	Events Played	Cuts Made	1st	2nd	3rd	Top 10	Top 25	Earnings	Rank
1987	1								
1988	1								
1990	1	1						$2,118	275
1991	1								
1992	1								
1993	32	18				1	3	115,189	129
1994	4	2						8,392	257
1995	31	18				1	1	93,606	164
1996	2	1						5,415	309
1997	31	22			1	2	7	320,800	74
1998	30	22		1		5	13	796,564	32
1999	31	24		1		4	13	962,642	38
2000	32	24		1	1	3	7	947,118	50
2001	33	23				1	12	753,701	67
2002	31	20				2	8	653,594	101
2003	30	24				2	12	1,022,244	70
2004	29	20		1		2	7	1,206,438	64
Total	321	219		4	2	23	83	6,887,822	
NATIONWIDE TOUR									
1991	10	4			1	2	3	17,660	65
1992	22	17		1	1	4	10	54,178	23
1993	2	2			1	2	2	16,500	86
1994	26	20	2		2	5	13	131,067	5
1995	2	2				1	2	12,367	109
1996	26	20		1	1	9	16	107,396	9
Total	88	65	2	2	6	23	46	339,168	

PGA TOUR TOP TOURNAMENT SUMMARY

Year	92	93	94	95	96	97	98	99	00	01	02	03	04
Masters									56				
U.S. Open	CUT				T82					CUT			T17
British Open							CUT					T59	T11
PGA							T10	T21	T27	T63	CUT	CUT	73
THE PLAYERS							68	T10	CUT	T26	CUT	T32	CUT
WGC-Accenture Match Play										T33			

Tom Kite

WORLD GOLF HALL OF FAME MEMBER (Inducted 2004)
EXEMPT STATUS: Top 50 on PGA TOUR Career Money List
FULL NAME: Thomas Oliver Kite, Jr.
HEIGHT: 5-9
WEIGHT: 170
BIRTHDATE: December 9, 1949
BIRTHPLACE: McKinney, TX
RESIDENCE: Austin, TX
FAMILY: Wife, Christy; Stephanie Lee (10/7/81), twins David Thomas and Paul Christopher (9/1/84)
EDUCATION: University of Texas (1972, Business Administration)
SPECIAL INTERESTS: Landscaping
TURNED PROFESSIONAL: 1972
Q SCHOOL: Fall 1972
JOINED TOUR: 1972

PGA TOUR VICTORIES (19):

1976 IVB-Bicentennial Golf Classic. **1978** B.C. Open. **1981** American Motors Inverrary Classic. **1982** Bay Hill Classic. **1983** Bing Crosby National Pro-Am. **1984** Doral-Eastern Open, Georgia-Pacific Atlanta Golf Classic. **1985** MONY Tournament of Champions. **1986** Western Open. **1987** Kemper Open. **1989** Nestle Invitational, THE PLAYERS Championship, Nabisco Championship. **1990** Federal Express St. Jude Classic. **1991** Infiniti Tournament of Champions. **1992** BellSouth Classic, U.S. Open Championship. **1993** Bob Hope Chrysler Classic, Nissan Los Angeles Open.

CHAMPIONS TOUR VICTORIES (7):

2000 The Countrywide Tradition, SBC Senior Open. **2001** Gold Rush Classic. **2002** MasterCard Championship, SBC Senior Classic, Napa Valley Championship presented by Beringer Vineyards. **2004** 3M Championship.

INTERNATIONAL VICTORIES (3):

1974 New Zealand Open. **1980** European Open. **1986** Oki Pro-Am [Spain].

BEST 2004 PGA TOUR FINISH:

T57—U.S. Open Championship.

BEST 2004 CHAMPIONS TOUR FINISHES:

1—3M Championship; 2—Charles Schwab Cup Championship, Bank of America Championship, Senior British Open; T3—U.S. Senior Open, The First Tee Open at Pebble Beach presented by Wal-Mart; T4—Allianz Championship, JELD-WEN Tradition, SBC Championship; T5—Bruno's Memorial Classic; T7—Ford Senior Players Championship; T8—Administaff Small Business Classic presented by KBR; T9—Royal Caribbean Golf Classic

2004 SEASON:

Became one of the oldest players to earn a spot in the U.S. Open when he earned a berth at a qualifying tournament near Houston. Made the field in the prestigious event for the 31st consecutive year and 33rd time overall, tying Arnold Palmer and Gene Sarazen for third all-time in appearances. Made the cut at Shinnecock Hills and finished T57...Inducted into the World Golf Hall of Fame in November, along with Charlie Sifford, Marlene Streit and Isao Aoki...Started slowly on the Champions Tour but went on to finish third on the final earnings list, his highest standing ever. Made more than $1.8 million, a career best. Also placed third on the final Charles Schwab Cup points list...Had more top-five finishes than any other Champions Tour player, with all 10 top-fives coming after the start of May...Ended a 22-month victory drought by winning the

PGA TOUR CAREER SUMMARY — PLAYOFF RECORD: 6-4

Year	Events Played	Cuts Made	1st	2nd	3rd	Top 10	Top 25	Earnings	Rank
1971A	1	1							
1972A	4	4					2		
1972	2	2						$2,132	216
1973	34	31				2	15	51,219	55
1974	28	27			1	8	18	78,677	25
1975	26	21		1	1	9	14	87,046	18
1976	27	25	1			8	15	116,181	20
1977	29	27		1	3	7	16	125,204	14
1978	28	25	1	1	3	8	15	161,370	11
1979	28	24			3	11	15	166,878	17
1980	26	22		1		10	18	152,490	20
1981	26	26	1	3	3	21	24	375,699	1
1982	25	24	1	4	1	15	17	341,081	3
1983	25	21	1	2		8	16	257,066	9
1984	25	21	2	1		10	14	348,640	5
1985	24	21	1	1	1	6	11	258,793	14
1986	26	24	1	1	1	9	13	394,164	7
1987	24	21	1	2		11	18	525,516	8
1988	25	21		3	1	10	16	760,405	5
1989	23	23	3	1		10	14	1,395,278	1
1990	22	21	1		1	9	15	658,202	15
1991	25	19	1	1	1	4	9	396,580	39
1992	23	22	2	1	1	9	17	957,445	6
1993	20	14	2	2		8	10	887,811	8
1994	23	18		1	1	8	12	658,689	22
1995	25	21				1	4	178,580	104
1996	21	15		1		1	5	319,326	66
1997	22	15		1		5	8	631,252	35
1998	22	12					3	161,295	159
1999	21	7					1	85,630	200
2000	6	6					1	121,605	186
2001	5	3				1	1	211,252	168
2002	5	2					1	54,350	214
2003	1								
2004	1	1						17,304	247
Total	698	587	19	29	22	209	358	10,937,613	

CHAMPIONS TOUR CAREER SUMMARY — PLAYOFF RECORD: 2-0

Year	Events Played	1st	2nd	3rd	Top 10	Top 25	Earnings	Rank
2000	20	2	1	1	9	18	$1,199,658	11
2001	23	1		4	16	22	1,398,802	10
2002	23	3		1	14	21	1,631,930	4
2003	27		4	1	12	20	1,549,819	6
2004	27	1	3	2	13	23	1,831,211	3
Total	120	7	8	9	64	104	7,611,419	

PGA TOUR TOP TOURNAMENT SUMMARY

Year	71	72	73	74	75	76	77	78	79	80	81	82	83
Masters	T42	T27			T10	T5	T3	T18	5	T6	T5	T5	T2
U.S. Open		T19		T8	CUT	CUT	T27	T20	CUT	CUT	T20	29	T20
British Open						T5		T2	T30	T27		CUT	T29
PGA				T39	T33	T13	T13	CUT	T35	T20	T4	T9	T67
THE PLAYERS				T19	T40	T17	CUT	T28	T9	T31	DNS	T27	T27

Year	84	85	86	87	88	89	90	91	92	93	94	95	96
Masters	T6	CUT	T2	T24	44	T18	T14	56		CUT	4	CUT	CUT
U.S. Open	CUT	13	T35	T46	T36	T9	T56	T37	**1**	CUT	T33	T67	T82
British Open	T22	T8	CUT	T72	T20	T19	CUT	T44	T19	T14	T8	T58	T26
PGA	T34	T12	T26	T10	T4	T34	T40	T52	T21	T56	T9	T54	CUT
THE PLAYERS	T51	T64	T4	T9	T11	**1**	T5	CUT	T35	CUT	T9	T43	CUT
TOUR Championship				T17	2	**1**	18		T13	T7	T22		

Year	97	98	99	00	01	02	03	04
Masters	2	38				CUT		
U.S. Open	T68	T43	T60	T32	T5	CUT	CUT	T57
British Open	T10	T38		T70				
PGA	5	CUT	CUT	T19	CUT			
THE PLAYERS	CUT	T25	T77	T66	T44	T36		

CHAMPIONS TOUR TOP TOURNAMENT SUMMARY

Year	00	01	02	03	04
Senior PGA Championship	T2	T23	T15	T10	T21
U.S. Senior Open	3	15	3	T12	T3
Ford Senior Players Championship	6	T10	T10	T2	T7
Senior British Open				4	T2
JELD-WEN Tradition	**1**	T24	T7	T2	T4
Charles Schwab Cup Champ	T8	T7	T21	3	2

NATIONAL TEAMS: World Amateur Team Championship.

Tom Kite (Continued)

3M Championship, his seventh overall title on the Champions Tour. One-stroke win over Craig Stadler at the TPC of the Twin Cities came during the midst of five consecutive top-five performances. It was his first victory in 47 official starts on the Champions Tour.

CAREER HIGHLIGHTS:

2003: Played in the U.S. Open at Olympia Fields, but missed the cut...Finished sixth on the Champions Tour money list despite not winning an event for the first time in four seasons on the Champions Tour. **2002:** Played in five PGA TOUR events, including his first Masters since 1998, but missed the cut at Augusta National...Finished T36 at THE PLAYERS championship, the 23rd time he made the cut in the event, a tourament record...Also missed the cut at the U.S. Open at Bethpage...Moved up six spots on the Champions Tour money list and had a career-best with $1.6 million and three victories, equaling the total of his first two years on the circut. **2001:** Missed the cut at the PGA Championship at the Atlanta Athletic Club, ending a run of nine consecutive cuts made on the PGA TOUR since becoming a senior, and also missed the cut at the Southern Farm Bureau Classic. Was among the top-10 in over two-thirds of his starts on the Champions Tour. Finished third in four events before winning the Gold Rush Classic by one stroke over Allen Doyle. **2000:** Played in six PGA TOUR events, making the cut every time. Best finish was T19 at the PGA Championship...Won twice on the SENIOR TOUR in his rookie season, at The Countrywide Tradition, with a playoff victory over Larry Nelson and Tom Watson and at the SBC Senior Open. **1997:** 35th-place money-list finish best since 1994...Five top-10s, including three in majors...After an opening 77 at the Masters, closed 69-68-70 to finish second to Tiger Woods...His $291,600 paycheck made him the second player in PGA TOUR history to surpass $10 million in career earnings...Selected as Captain of Ryder Cup squad at Valderamma in Spain. **1995:** Did not win for the second consecutive season, the first time he had gone two full seasons without a victory since 1979-80...Led the TOUR in career earnings from Oct. 29, 1989 until Aug. 27, 1995...Was the first player in PGA TOUR history to reach $6 million, $7 million, $8 million and $9 million in career earnings. **1994:** Streak of 13 consecutive years (1981-93) with at least one PGA TOUR victory was halted. **1993:** Captured two PGA TOUR victories, the Bob Hope Chrysler Classic and Nissan Los Angeles Open...At the Bob Hope, set a then-90 hole record by shooting 35-under-par 325. Record was broken by Joe Durant's 36-under-par in 2001...Represented United States at Ryder Cup for the seventh time. **1992:** Recorded greatest triumph at U.S. Open at Pebble Beach. Even-par 72 in final round in difficult conditions earned a two-stroke victory over Jeff Sluman...Also captured BellSouth Classic and finished sixth on PGA TOUR Official Money List with $957,445. **1991:** Four top-10s was highlighted by title at Infiniti Tournament of Champions. **1990:** Nine top-10s...Earned victory at FedEx St. Jude Classic in a playoff over John Cook. **1989:** PGA TOUR Player of the Year...PGA of America Player of the Year...Earned Arnold Palmer Award for leading PGA TOUR in Official Money for second time with a record $1,395,278...Three PGA TOUR victories...Triumphed at Nestle Invitational at Bay Hill in a playoff over Davis Love III...One week later, continued hot streak with victory at THE PLAYERS Championship... Season-ending title at the Nabisco Championship in a playoff victory over Payne Stewart was worth $625,000, including a $175,000 season-long bonus. **1988:** Ten top-10 finishes in 25 starts, including three runner-up finishes. **1987:** Won Kemper Open by seven shots to extend his TOUR-leading streak of consecutive years with at least one win to seven. **1986:** Made the cut in 24 of 26 PGA TOUR events and finished seventh on money list...Western Open champion in a playoff...T2 at the Masters. **1985:** Earned title at MONY Tournament of Champions by six shots. **1984:** Fifth on money list with $348,640...Two victories, including Doral-Eastern Open an Georgia-Pacific Atlanta Classic. **1983:** Victory at the Bing Crosby Pro-Am included a course-record 62 at Pebble Beach. **1982:** Earned second consecutive Vardon Trophy Award...Bay Hill Classic playoff win over Jack Nicklaus and Denis Watson was catalyst to season winnings of $341,081, third on the money list. **1981:** Joined PGA TOUR elite with breakout season...PGA TOUR Player of the Year with 21 top-10s in 26 events...Made the cut at all 26 events and extended streak to 35 consecutive events...Captured Vardon Trophy with a 69.80 stroke average, ending Tom Watson's four-year reign at the top...Received Arnold Palmer Award as leading money winner on the TOUR with $375,699...Winner of American Motors-Inverrary Classic. **1979:** Named to first of seven Ryder Cup squads...Recipient of Bobby Jones Award from the USGA. **1978:** Earned second PGA TOUR title at the B.C. Open. **1976:** First career TOUR victory at the IVB-Bicentennial Golf Classic. **1973:** PGA TOUR Rookie of the Year with earnings of $54,270. **Amateur:** Shared NCAA title with Texas teammate Ben Crenshaw in 1972.

PERSONAL:

After wearing glasses since age 12, he had LASIK surgery in late January 1998 to correct acute nearsightedness... Serves as a spokesman for Chrysler Junior Golf Scholarship program...Started playing golf at age 6 by following his father around and won his first tournament at 11...Biggest thrill in golf was being selected as the U.S. Ryder Cup captain in 1997...Has worked with such teachers as Harvey Penick, Bob Toski, Peter Kostis, Chuck Cook and Dave Philips...His daughter, Stephanie, was a gymnast at the University of Alabama.

PLAYER STATISTICS

2004 PGA TOUR STATISTICS

Scoring Average	70.84	(N/A)
Driving Distance	278.1	(N/A)
Driving Accuracy Percentage	41.1%	(N/A)
Total Driving	(N/A)	(N/A)
Greens in Regulation Pct.	43.1%	(N/A)
Putting Average	1.871	(N/A)
Sand Save Percentage	42.9%	(N/A)
Birdie Average	1.50	(N/A)
Scoring Avg. Before Cut	71.50	(N/A)
Round 3 Scoring Avg.	75.00	(N/A)
Final Round Scoring Average	84.00	(N/A)
Birdie Conversion Percentage	19.4%	(N/A)
Par Breakers	8.3%	(N/A)

MISCELLANEOUS PGA TOUR STATISTICS

2004 Low Round/Round: 71–U.S. Open Championship/2
Career Low Round/Round: 62–4 times, most recent 1993 Bob Hope Chrysler Classic/5
Career Largest Paycheck/Finish: $450,000–1989 Nabisco Championship/1

2004 CHAMPIONS TOUR STATISTICS

Scoring Average	69.98	(4)
Driving Distance	278.4	(19)
Driving Accuracy Percentage	72.8%	(27)
Total Driving	46	(4)
Greens in Regulation Pct.	73.3%	(6)
Putting Average	1.785	(25)
Sand Save Percentage	53.1%	(14)
Eagles (Holes per)	172.0	(13)
Birdie Average	4.03	(6)
All-Around Ranking	114	(3)

MISCELLANEOUS CHAMPIONS TOUR STATISTICS

2004 Low Round: 63–Outback Steakhouse Pro-Am/1.
Career Low Round: 61–2003 SAS Championship Presented by BusinessWeek/3
Career Largest Paycheck: $262,500–2004 3M Championship/1

Hank Kuehne (KEE-knee)

EXEMPT STATUS: 99th on 2004 money list
FULL NAME: Henry August Kuehne II
HEIGHT: 6-2
WEIGHT: 205
BIRTHDATE: September 11, 1975
BIRTHPLACE: Dallas, TX
RESIDENCE: Palm Beach Gardens, FL; plays out of Old Palm

FAMILY: Wife, Nicole
EDUCATION: Southern Methodist University (1999, Communications)
SPECIAL INTERESTS: Fishing, meditation
TURNED PROFESSIONAL: 1999
JOINED TOUR: 2003

BEST PGA TOUR CAREER FINISH:
T2—**2003** Shell Houston Open.

INTERNATIONAL VICTORIES (2):
2002 Texas Challenge [Can], TELUS Quebec Open [Can].

OTHER VICTORIES: (2):
2003 Franklin Templeton Shootout [with Jeff Sluman]. **2004** Franklin Templeton Shootout [with Jeff Sluman].

BEST 2004 PGA TOUR FINISHES:
5—Nissan Open; T6—Deutsche Bank Championship.

2004 SEASON:
Followed up a strong rookie campaign with a successful second season, recorded two top-10s and finished inside the top-100 on the final season money list…First top-10 of the season was a solo fifth at the Nissan Open, in his first career start at Riveria. His best finish on PGA TOUR since he finished T5 at the 2003 B.C. Open…Next top-10 did not come until September, a T6 at the Deutsche Bank Championship…Managed to finish in the top-20 in four events in the second half of the season to help him secure his card for 2005—B.C. Open (T13), Buick Open (T18), Buick Championship (T13) and Chrysler Classic of Greensboro (T19).

CAREER HIGHLIGHTS:
2003: Earned TOUR card for 2004 with $872,139 in earnings as a non-member playing primarily on Sponsor Exemptions. Began the season with partial status on the Nationwide Tour...Topped TOUR in Driving Distance, averaging a record 321.4 yards, unseating John Daly, who had won eight consecutive Driving Distance titles...Playing in 24th career TOUR event as a Sponsor Exemption, finished T3 at the BellSouth Classic to earn a paycheck of $208,000. Carded hole-in-one during third round on the 131-yard second hole with a 52-degree wedge...Earned top-10 exemption into Shell Houston Open for his T3 finish at BellSouth. Posted a T2 in Houston ($356,657) and earned enough money to push him past the 150th player (Tom Scherrer) on the 2002 PGA TOUR money list and enabled him to become a Special Temporary Member of the TOUR. The top-10 finish also earned him entrance into the next week's HP Classic of New Orleans...Posted third top-10 of season with a T9 at the FedEx St. Jude Classic...Recorded his fourth and final top-10 of the season with a T5 finish at the B.C. Open. **2002:** Made the cut in four of six tournaments, including top-25 finishes at the B.C. Open (T19) and the Kemper Insurance Open (T23)...2002 Order of Merit champion on the Canadian Tour. Posted two victories, at the Texas Challenge and the TELUS Quebec Open...Earned International Rookie of the Year honors. **2000:** Made the cut in two of six tournaments, with a T13 at the GTE Byron Nelson Classic, his best showing. **1999:** Turned pro midway through the year and made two cuts in six starts, with a T29 at the Bell Canadian Open his best result. **Amateur:** Missed the cut at the 1999 Masters...1998 U.S. Amateur champion, defeating Tom McKnight, 2 and 1, in the finals at Oak Hill CC in Rochester, NY...Began college career at Oklahoma State but later transferred to Southern Methodist University. Second-team All-American as a junior at SMU…Winner of two individual titles during the 1996-97 season...Tied SMU's all-time low 54-hole total of 208 at the Dr Pepper Intercollegiate and established a school record for low round, firing a 63 at the Golf World Invitational.

PERSONAL:
Lists playing in the 1999 Masters and winning the 1998 U.S. Amateur, with older brother Trip as his caddie, as his biggest thrills in golf…Credits his father for giving him his start in golf…Lists Fred Couples as his hero…Sister, Kelli, was a two-time U.S. Women's Amateur champion and currently plays on the LPGA. Brother, Trip, a former All-American at Oklahoma State, was the U.S. Amateur runner-up to Tiger Woods in 1994 and remains an amateur.

PLAYER STATISTICS

2004 PGA TOUR STATISTICS

Scoring Average	71.36	(122)
Driving Distance	314.4	(1)
Driving Accuracy Percentage	49.9%	(196)
Total Driving	197	(102)
Greens in Regulation Pct.	62.9%	(152)
Putting Average	1.765	(59)
Sand Save Percentage	59.3%	(7)
Eagles (Holes per)	123.2	(11)
Birdie Average	3.55	(90)
All-Around Ranking	638	(59)
Scoring Avg. Before Cut	71.56	(148)
Round 3 Scoring Avg.	70.50	(58)
Final Round Scoring Average	71.20	(70)
Birdie Conversion Percentage	31.1%	(34)
Par Breakers	20.5%	(72)

MISCELLANEOUS PGA TOUR STATISTICS

2004 Low Round/Round: 64–FUNAI Classic at the WALT DISNEY WORLD Resort/2
Career Low Round/Round: 63–2002 B.C. Open/2
Career Largest Paycheck/Finish: $336,000–2003 Shell Houston Open/T2

SECTION 2 PLAYER BIOGRAPHIES

PGA TOUR CAREER SUMMARY — PLAYOFF RECORD: 0-0

Year	Events Played	Cuts Made	1st	2nd	3rd	Top 10	Top 25	Earnings	Rank
1998A	1								
1999A	2	1							
1999	6	2						$19,869	258
2000	6	2					1	85,656	
2002	6	4					2	80,840	
2003	23	14		1	1	4	5	872,139	
2004	30	15				2	8	816,889	99
Total	74	38		1	1	6	16	1,875,392	
NATIONWIDE TOUR									
2000	4	1						2,337	241
2001	2								
2002	4								
Total	10	1						2,337	

PGA TOUR TOP TOURNAMENT SUMMARY

Year	99	00	01	02	03	04
Masters	CUT					
U.S. Open	65					
PGA					CUT	
THE PLAYERS						CUT

NATIONAL TEAMS: World Amateur Team Championship, 1998.

Neal Lancaster

EXEMPT STATUS: 113th on 2004 money list
FULL NAME: Grady Neal Lancaster
HEIGHT: 6-0
WEIGHT: 170
BIRTHDATE: September 13, 1962
BIRTHPLACE: Smithfield, NC
RESIDENCE: Smithfield, NC; plays out of Johnston CC
FAMILY: Single

SPECIAL INTERESTS: Fishing, movies, auto racing
TURNED PROFESSIONAL: 1985
Q SCHOOL: 1989, 1990, 1999

PGA TOUR VICTORIES (1):

1994 GTE Byron Nelson Golf Classic.

BEST 2004 PGA TOUR FINISHES:

T7—B.C. Open; T10—FUNAI Classic at the WALT DISNEY WORLD Resort.

2004 SEASON:

Finished inside the top 125 for the fifth straight season and 12th time in 15-year TOUR career…Posted first top-10 of the season at the B.C. Open in July, thanks to four rounds in the 60s for only the fourth time in his career…Finished T11 at the Ford Championship at Doral after closing with 65…Recorded seven straight birdies (Nos. 15-3) during the first round of the U.S. Bank Championship in Milwaukee to tie the top mark of the season…Second top-10 finish of the season, a T10 finish at the FUNAI Classic at WALT DISNEY WORLD Resort, did not come until late October. He collected $93,100 and improved his season earnings to $689,203, good enough to secure his card for the 2005 season.

CAREER HIGHLIGHTS:

2003: His lone top-10 was a T6 at the Buick Open, thanks to four rounds in the 60s. First top-10 since a playoff loss to John Rollins at the 2002 Bell Canadian Open...Posted consecutive top-20 finishes late in the year—T17 at Valero Texas Open and T19 at Southern Farm Bureau Classic—to help him secure his card for the 2004 season. **2002:** Continued a four-year progression of earning more money than the previous year with a career-high $813,230 in earnings...Lost in three-man playoff at Bell Canadian Open when John Rollins birdied the first extra hole. T2 was best finish on TOUR since his 1994 playoff victory and the only runner-up finish of his 13-year career. Made double bogey on the final hole of regulation to force the playoff with Rollins and Justin Leonard...Posted back-to-back top-10s on the PGA TOUR for only the second time in his career and first since 1991 (T5-Greater Milwaukee Open, T8-Canadian Open) with a T9 at the FedEx St. Jude Classic and a T5 at the Advil Western Open. **2001:** Turned in best season on TOUR since 1994 when he finished No. 58...Two top-10s and one top-15 in last five starts left him at No. 80 on money list and secured his TOUR card for another season. Made $345,450 of his $657,580 during that period. **2000:** Finished T4 at the Bay Hill Invitational for the best effort of the season...T8 at the John Deere Classic after posting four rounds in the 60s for the first time in his career in a single tournament. **1999:** Finished out of the top 125 on the official money list for the first time since joining the TOUR in 1990, with 139th-place ranking. Forced to earn full playing privileges for the 2000 season through third-place finish at PGA TOUR Qualifying Tournament. **1998:** Was 86th on the final season money list with $346,563. **1997:** Finished right on the number of 125th on the final season money list to earn playing privileges for 1998. **1996:** Made history for second time at U.S. Open. Appeared on way to missing the cut after playing first 27 holes 7-over par. Posted a 29 on back nine at Oakland Hills to easily qualify for final two rounds. The 29 was made possible with a birdie on hole 11, eagle on 12 and birdies from 13 through 15. **1995:** During U.S. Open at Shinnecock Hills, became first player to shoot 29 in U.S. Open for nine holes. Moved from 46th-place tie to fourth on final day after posting 36-29—65 to finish four strokes behind Corey Pavin. Birdied holes 11-14, 16 and 17. **1994:** Lone PGA TOUR victory came at rain-shortened GTE Byron Nelson Classic. Birdied the final two holes in regulation to join in TOUR-record, six-man playoff. Birdied first extra hole to defeat David Edwards, Tom Byrum, Mark Carnevale, David Ogrin and Yoshinori Mizumaki. **1989:** Winner of Pine Tree Open in Birmingham, AL, and the Utah Open.

PERSONAL:

Didn't take first golf lesson until 1992. Was self-taught until then. First lesson was given to him by L.B. Floyd, father of Raymond Floyd…With $93 bankroll and driving a van, gave mini-tours a try in 1989. Earned $96,000 in four months before going to Qualifying Tournament.

PLAYER STATISTICS

2004 PGA TOUR STATISTICS

Scoring Average	71.27	(111)
Driving Distance	291.6	(52)
Driving Accuracy Percentage	57.6%	(175)
Total Driving	227	(145)
Greens in Regulation Pct.	65.9%	(76)
Putting Average	1.781	(112)
Sand Save Percentage	52.4%	(50)
Eagles (Holes per)	132.4	(17)
Birdie Average	3.48	(112)
All-Around Ranking	705	(84)
Scoring Avg. Before Cut	71.02	(100)
Round 3 Scoring Avg.	71.71	(150)
Final Round Scoring Average	71.20	(70)
Birdie Conversion Percentage	29.0%	(98)
Par Breakers	20.1%	(96)

MISCELLANEOUS PGA TOUR STATISTICS

2004 Low Round/Round: 65–Ford Championship at Doral/4
Career Low Round/Round: 63–1998 Canon Greater Hartford Open/2
Career Largest Paycheck/Finish: $352,000–2002 Bell Canadian Open/T2

PGA TOUR CAREER SUMMARY — PLAYOFF RECORD: 1-1

Year	Events Played	Cuts Made	1st	2nd	3rd	Top 10	Top 25	Earnings	Rank
1990	26	11				2	7	$85,769	142
1991	33	22				3	5	180,037	90
1992	35	23				1	4	146,867	103
1993	32	19				2	5	149,381	107
1994	29	19	1			1	2	305,038	58
1995	29	18				1	4	182,219	101
1996	32	22				2	6	210,000	104
1997	34	19					4	179,273	125
1998	28	18				2	7	346,563	86
1999	35	13				1	3	283,140	139
2000	31	19				2	5	466,712	105
2001	36	18			1	3	6	657,580	80
2002	31	20		1		3	4	813,230	83
2003	35	21				1	6	590,627	110
2004	33	21				2	6	701,239	113
Total	479	283	1	1	1	26	74	5,297,675	
NATIONWIDE TOUR									
1990	4	4				2	2	4,516	118
2003	1								
Total	5	4				2	2	4,516	

PGA TOUR TOP TOURNAMENT SUMMARY

Year	91	92	93	94	95	96	97	98	99	00	01	02	03
Masters					CUT	CUT							
U.S. Open					T4	T82							CUT
British Open												T37	
PGA		T84		T44		T52		CUT				T34	
THE PLAYERS	T20	T40	CUT	T35	CUT	T53	CUT	CUT	CUT		CUT	68	T27

Year	04
THE PLAYERS	83

Bernhard Langer

WORLD GOLF HALL OF FAME MEMBER (Inducted in 2002)
EXEMPT STATUS: 83rd on 2004 money list
FULL NAME: Bernhard Langer
HEIGHT: 5-9
WEIGHT: 155
BIRTHDATE: August 27, 1957
BIRTHPLACE: Anhausen, Germany
RESIDENCE: Anhausen, Germany
FAMILY: Wife, Vikki; Jackie (7/9/86); Stefan (6/8/90), Christina (2/3/93), Jason (3/20/00)
SPECIAL INTERESTS: Skiing, football, tennis, cycle riding
TURNED PROFESSIONAL: 1972
JOINED TOUR: 1985, 2001

PGA TOUR VICTORIES (3):

1985 Masters Tournament, Sea Pines Heritage. **1993** Masters Tournament.

INTERNATIONAL VICTORIES (58):

1974 German National Open Championship [Am]. **1977** German National Open Championship. **1979** German National Open Championship. **1980** Dunlop Masters, Colombian Open. **1981** German Open, Bob Hope British Classic. **1982** Lufthansa German Open. **1983** Italian Open, Glasgow Golf Classic, St. Mellion Timeshare TPC, Casio World Open [Jpn]. **1984** Peugeot Open de France, KLM Dutch Open, Carroll's Irish Open, Benson & Hedges Spanish Open, German National Open Championship. **1985** Lufthansa German Open, Panasonic European Open, Australian Masters [Aus], German National Open Championship. **1986** German Open, Lancome Trophy, German National Open Championship. **1987** Whyte & Mackay PGA Championship, Carroll's Irish Open, German National Open Championship. **1988** Epson Grand Prix of Europe, German National Open Championship. **1989** Peugeot Spanish Open, German Masters, German National Open Championship. **1990** Cepsa Madrid Open, Austrian Open, German National Open Championship. **1991** Benson & Hedges International Open, Mercedes German Masters, German National Open Championship, Hong Kong Open. **1992** Heineken Dutch Open, Honda Open, German National Open Championship. **1993** Volvo PGA Championship, Volvo German Open. **1994** Murphy's Irish Open, Volvo Masters. **1995** Volvo PGA Championship, Deutsche Bank Open TPC of Europe, Smurfit European Open. **1996** Alfred Dunhill Masters. **1997** Conte Of Florence Italian Open, Benson & Hedges International Open, Chemapol Trophy Czech Open, Linde German Masters, Argentinian Masters [SA]. **2001** The TNT Open [Eur], Linde German Masters. **2002** Volvo Masters [Eur/shared with Colin Montgomerie].

BEST 2004 PGA TOUR FINISHES:

T4—Masters Tournament; T5—Ford Championship at Doral; 8—Bob Hope Chrysler Classic; T9—The INTERNATIONAL.

2004 SEASON:

Highlight of the season was leading the European Ryder Cup team to a record 18 1/2 to 9 1/2 victory over the Americans in the 35th Ryder Cup matches held at Oakland Hills CC in Bloomfield, MI…Despite carrying the extra burdens of his captaincy, finished inside the top 100 (83rd) on the PGA TOUR money list for just the third time in his last 10 seasons. Four top-10s on the PGA TOUR were most since seven in 2001. In first start of season, posted five rounds in the 60s to finish solo eighth at the Bob Hope Chrysler Classic…Made 18th cut at THE PLAYERS Championship, passing Hale Irwin and Gil Morgan for solo third all-time in made cuts at the event behind Tom Kite (23) and Tom Watson (21). Finished T77…Playing in his 22nd Masters, two-time champion finished T4. Co-leader early on Sunday after opening birdie-birdie. Within three strokes of leader Ernie Els on the par-5 15th hole, 4-iron second shot from pine straw found the green but trickled back into water for a double bogey, dashing hopes for third green jacket…Fourth top-10 of the season was T9 at The INTERNATIONAL at Castle Pines…After the Ryder Cup, added a T5 at the HSBC World Match Play Championship on the European Tour by defeating World No. 1 Vijay Singh in the first round and losing to Miguel Angel Jimenez on the fourth extra hole of the 36-hole match in round two…Following week, came back to the States for his first start on TOUR since leading the European Ryder Cup Team to victory and missed the cut at the FUNAI Classic at the WALT DISNEY WORLD Resort, ending a streak of 14 straight cuts made, which was the fourth-longest current streak on TOUR.

CAREER HIGHLIGHTS:

2003: Named 2004 Ryder Cup Captain in July. "It's a fabulous honor to be named European captain. I've never made a secret of how much I enjoy being part of the Ryder Cup, and to be the captain makes me feel very proud, especially as the first German golfer to hold this prestigious role." A stalwart of the European Ryder Cup team, lying second behind Nick Faldo with 10 tournament appearances. In that time he has picked up 24 points out of a possible 42, including 3 1/2 of 4 points at The Belfry in 2002...Competed in 21 PGA TOUR events, tying the 1986 season for most starts of PGA TOUR career, but managed only two top-10s...A T5 at the FBR Capital Open and a T10 at the John Deere Classic...Streak of 19 consecutive made cuts at the Masters came to an end with rounds of 79-76. **2002:** Although he missed just three of 16 cuts, his lone top top-10 was a fourth-place finish at the WORLDCOM CLASSIC, aided by a second-round 65...Finished European Tour season as co-

PGA TOUR CAREER SUMMARY — PLAYOFF RECORD: 1-1

Year	Events Played	Cuts Made	1st	2nd	3rd	Top 10	Top 25	Earnings	Rank
1981	1	1				1	1	$14,500	154
1982	6	2						1,356	263
1983	3								
1984	8	8			1	3	5	82,465	75
1985	16	12	2			4	7	271,044	13
1986	21	18		2	2	8	15	379,800	10
1987	15	13		2	1	7	12	366,430	23
1988	15	8				3	4	100,635	111
1989	14	13		1	1	3	5	195,973	73
1990	5	1				1	1	35,150	187
1991	7	5				2	3	112,539	129
1992	5	5					1	41,211	183
1993	6	4	1	1		3	4	626,938	23
1994	6	6				1	5	118,241	142
1995	7	7		1		1	3	394,877	46
1996	7	3					1	34,183	212
1997	7	6				1	3	158,508	136
1998	8	4				1	3	141,715	168
1999	9	8				1	3	162,257	169
2000	10	9					2	189,955	
2001	17	15		1	3	7	9	1,810,363	22
2002	16	13				1	3	559,395	119
2003	21	13				2	4	555,981	121
2004	15	14				4	5	943,589	83
Total	245	188	3	8	8	54	99	7,297,104	
EUROPEAN TOUR									
2004	3	1				1	1	145,516	

PGA TOUR TOP TOURNAMENT SUMMARY

Year	76	77	78	79	80	81	82	83	84	85	86	87	88
Masters							CUT		T31	**1**	T16	T7	T9
U.S. Open							CUT			CUT	T8	T4	CUT
British Open	CUT		CUT		T51	2	T13	T56	T2	T3	T3	T17	70
PGA										T32	CUT	T21	CUT
THE PLAYERS									T29	T7	T40	T24	T16
TOUR Championship												T17	

Year	89	90	91	92	93	94	95	96	97	98	99	00	01
Masters	T26	T7	T32	T31	**1**	T25	T31	T36	T7	T39	T11	T28	T6
U.S. Open	T59	CUT	CUT	T23	CUT	T23	T36	DQ	CUT	CUT		CUT	T40
British Open	80	T48	T9	T59	3	T60	T24	W/D	T38	CUT	T18	T11	T3
PGA	T61	CUT	CUT	T40	CUT	T25		76	T23		T61	T46	CUT
THE PLAYERS	T67		T6	T29	2	T27	2		T31	CUT	T38	T42	3
TOUR Championship													T10
WGC-Accenture Match Play											T9	T33	T33
WGC-NEC Invitational													T11
WGC-American Express Champ											T48	T35	CNL

Year	02	03	04
Masters	T32	CUT	T4
U.S. Open	T35	T42	
British Open	T28	CUT	
PGA	T23	T57	T66
THE PLAYERS	T22	T48	T77
WGC-Accenture Match Play	T33	T33	
WGC-NEC Invitational	T38	T11	T61
WGC-American Express Champ	T33		

NATIONAL TEAMS: World Cup (11), 1976-1980, 90-96; Hennesy Cognac Cup (4), 1976, 1978, 1980, 1982; Ryder Cup (10), 1981, 1983, 1985, 1987, 1989, 1991, 1993, 1995, 1997, 2002; Nissan Cup (2), 1985-86; Asahi Glass Four Tours (2), 1989-90; Dunhill Cup (2), 1992, 2000; Ryder Cup (Captain), 2004.

Bernhard Langer (Continued)

champion of Volvo Masters with Colin Montgomerie. The pair was declared co-champions after posting identical 3-under 281, then playing two sudden-death holes before darkness...Inducted into World Golf Hall of Fame. **2001:** Posted seven top-10s on TOUR for first time since 1987 season including a second and three third-place finishes - THE PLAYERS Championship, WORLDCOM CLASSIC and British Open...First German to be elected to the World Golf Hall of Fame via International Ballot and was slated for induction in the Fall of 2002...Second-place finish at FedEx St. Jude Classic, one stroke behind Bob Estes. Best finish at TOUR event since runner-up at 1995 THE PLAYERS Championship...Week later won The TNT Open, his 38th victory on the European Tour and 64th worldwide...Won Linde German Masters, boosting him to third on the Volvo Order of Merit. He finished the year sixth on the European Tour money list. **2000:** Made appearances in 10 PGA TOUR events, the most since 14 in 1988.Participated in 12 events on the European Tour where he finished runner-up twice — TNT Dutch Open and the BMW International Open — the only event held in Germany he has yet to win. **1999:** Made a bold bid for a 10th successive Ryder Cup appearance, but finished 14th in the qualifying table. **1996:** The only time he has been outside the top 30 in the Volvo Order of Merit since 1980, finishing 39th. **1993:** Won his second Masters, by four strokes over Chip Beck. **1992:** Won German National Open Championship for 12th time in his career. **1985:** Won the Masters, by two over Seve Ballesteros, Raymond Floyd and Curtis Strange, and followed with a win at the Sea Pines Heritage Classic, the last man to win the Masters and the event afterward.

PERSONAL:

One of the most remarkably consistent and resilient professionals in golf...Conquered adversity in the form of the putting 'yips' to reach the top, and has hovered in the upper echelons of the game for over 20 years. Played the last eight years with a long putter that he began using at the end of the 1996 season...Father settled in Bavaria after jumping a Russian prisoner-of-war train bound for Siberia...Developed "fever cramps" several times as a child (ages 2-5) and nearly died as a result. Took up golf at age 7 through caddying, turned pro at 15...Developed back problems when he was 19, during an 18-month stint as a member of the German Air Force. Marching with 30-pound pack and rifle led to two stress fractures and bulging discs...Devout Christian, helped organize the regular meetings of the European Tour Bible Class...Web site is bernhardlanger.de...Started skiing at age 4 and would say he's a "scratch skier" Also enjoys driving fast cars.

PLAYER STATISTICS

2004 PGA TOUR STATISTICS

Scoring Average	71.25	(108)
Driving Distance	282.2	(136)
Driving Accuracy Percentage	62.6%	(124)
Total Driving	260	(175)
Greens in Regulation Pct.	65.3%	(91)
Putting Average	1.777	(99)
Sand Save Percentage	47.7%	(117)
Eagles (Holes per)	247.5	(96)
Birdie Average	3.44	(121)
All-Around Ranking	892	(131)
Scoring Avg. Before Cut	70.77	(63)
Round 3 Scoring Avg.	70.85	(89)
Final Round Scoring Average	72.46	(161)
Birdie Conversion Percentage	27.7%	(143)
Par Breakers	19.5%	(122)

MISCELLANEOUS PGA TOUR STATISTICS

2004 Low Round/Round: 64–Bob Hope Chrysler Classic/5
Career Low Round/Round: 64–3 times, most recent 2004 Bob Hope Chrysler Classic/5
Career Largest Paycheck/Finish: $408,000–2001 THE PLAYERS Championship/3

SHOTLink
AN IBM ON DEMAND BUSINESS SOLUTION

HOT SHOTS

The Final 3...

(Holes 16-18 at the TPC at Sawgrass)

The final three holes on The Stadium Course at the Tournament Players Club at Sawgrass, site of THE PLAYERS Championship, make up one of the most dramatic finishes in all of golf. A look at those holes, beginning with the par-5 16th (page 92) followed by the par-3 17th (page 95) and the par-4 18th (below).

18th Hole-TPC at Sawgrass

Tournament Players Club at Sawgrass (Stadium Course)
18th Hole

The 18th hole is the hardest of the three finishing holes at the TPC at Sawgrass. It ranks 12th/56 toughest hole 18s and 101st/1,007 toughest holes on TOUR.

The final three holes at the TPC at Sawgrass averaged -.1 under par, ranking 25th/56 toughest three finishing holes.

HOLE 18 – STATISTICS (2004)

Driving Average	272.4 (9th)
Longest Drive	324 (T9th)
Driving Accuracy	291/ 459 63% (8th)

32/459 (7 percent) of the field hit tee shots in the water averaging 1.625 over par.

Driving Accuracy	Total Drives	Total %	Total Par Relative	Scoring Avg
Fairway	291	63.40%	26 under	3.91
Left Rough	8	1.70%	1 over	4.13
Right Rough	125	27.20%	79 over	4.63
Other	35	7.60%	54 over	5.54

APPROACH TO THE GREEN

Greens in Regulation	223/ 459 49% (16th)
Avg. Distance to Pin	60 ft 0 in

AROUND THE GREEN

Sand Saves	9/ 15 (3rd)
Scrambling	104/ 236 (16th)

236/459 (51 percent) of the field missed the green and only 44 percent were able to get up and down for par on 18.

SCORING

Average Score	4.235
Eagles	—
Birdies	78
Pars	237
Bogeys	107
Double Bogeys	33
Other	4
Actual Yardage	447
Rank	4

Stephen Leaney (LEE-knee)

EXEMPT STATUS: 2003 International Presidents Cup Team Member (through 2005)
FULL NAME: Stephen John Leaney
HEIGHT: 6-0
WEIGHT: 172
BIRTHDATE: March 10, 1969
BIRTHPLACE: Busselton, Australia
RESIDENCE: Perth, Australia

FAMILY: Wife, Tracey; Sebastian (9/19/03)
SPECIAL INTERESTS: Cars, wine, family
TURNED PROFESSIONAL: 1992
JOINED TOUR: 2003

BEST PGA TOUR CAREER FINISH:

2—2003 U.S. Open Championship.

INTERNATIONAL VICTORIES (7):

1995 Victorian Open [Aus]. **1997** Victorian Open [Aus]. **1998** Moroccan Open [Eur], TNT Dutch Open [Eur], ANZ Players Championship [Aus]. **2000** TNT Dutch Open [Eur]. **2002** Linde German Masters [Eur].

BEST 2004 PGA TOUR FINISHES:

4—WGC-Accenture Match Play Championship; T7—EDS Byron Nelson Championship.

2004 SEASON:

Finished 68th on the PGA TOUR money list in his first official season as a member. Season included two top-10s, six top-25s and over $1 million in earnings…Finished fourth at the WGC-Accenture Match Play Championship, falling to Tiger Woods in the semifinals, 2 and 1. In consolation final, lost to Darren Clarke, 1-up. Four wins came over Fred Funk, Mike Weir, Colin Montgomerie and Ian Poulter. Paycheck of $430,000 was second-largest of career…Recorded four rounds in the 60s at the EDS Byron Nelson Championship to finish T7…Posted just two top-25s from June through the end of the season, a T11 at the Memorial Tournament and a T22 at the WGC-NEC Invitational.

CAREER HIGHLIGHTS:

2003: Joined the PGA TOUR as a Special Temporary Member prior to the Western Open, having earned $709,600 in five events, exceeding the No. 150 (Tom Scherrer/$356,657) from the 2002 TOUR money list...Recorded his first top-10 on the PGA TOUR with T9 at WGC-Accenture Match Play Championship after losing to eventual champion Tiger Woods (7 and 6). Defeated Justin Leonard and Bob Estes in the first two rounds...Posted best TOUR finish, with a runner-up at the U.S. Open, three strokes back of Jim Furyk...Represented Australia with Stuart Appleby at the World Cup and played for the International Team at The Presidents Cup in South Africa. **2002:** Ensured a five-year exemption on the European Tour when he won the Linde German Masters. **2001:** Took a six-week break after The TNT Open when he returned home to Adelaide to get married. **2000:** Collected a second TNT Dutch Open title in three years, leading from start to finish and making just one bogey all week. **1998:** Won twice on the European Tour and finished 11th in Volvo Order of Merit. Won Moroccan Open by eight strokes to record maiden victory in Europe. Added TNT Dutch Open which he dedicated victory to his close friend, Stuart Appleby, whose wife died in Paris earlier that week...Captured the ANZ Players Championship in homeland of Australia. **1997:** Captured second career Victorian Open. **1995:** First professional title of note at the Victorian Open in Australia.

PERSONAL:

Two ribs cut out in December 1993 after doctors diagnosed blood clot. Took 18 months to recover…Has twice missed earning a PGA TOUR card by one stroke at the finals of Qualifying School (1998 and 2000).

PLAYER STATISTICS

2004 PGA TOUR STATISTICS

Scoring Average	71.00	(80)
Driving Distance	282.3	(135)
Driving Accuracy Percentage	64.8%	(85)
Total Driving	220	(137)
Greens in Regulation Pct.	64.8%	(104)
Putting Average	1.805	(170)
Sand Save Percentage	55.3%	(25)
Eagles (Holes per)	168.8	(49)
Birdie Average	2.97	(188)
All-Around Ranking	836	(117)
Scoring Avg. Before Cut	71.15	(119)
Round 3 Scoring Avg.	70.93	(95)
Final Round Scoring Average	72.53	(162)
Birdie Conversion Percentage	24.7%	(190)
Par Breakers	17.1%	(186)

MISCELLANEOUS PGA TOUR STATISTICS

2004 Low Round/Round: 65–Buick Invitational/2
Career Low Round/Round: 65–2004 Buick Invitational/2
Career Largest Paycheck/Finish: $650,000–2003 U.S. Open Championship/2

PGA TOUR CAREER SUMMARY — PLAYOFF RECORD: 0-0

Year	Events Played	Cuts Made	1st	2nd	3rd	Top 10	Top 25	Earnings	Rank
1995	1								
1998	2	1						$5,650	306
1999	4	1							
2000	1								
2001	1								
2002	2	2					1	26,732	
2003	9	6		1		2	3	723,986	
2004	24	17				2	6	1,166,560	68
Total	44	27		1		4	10	1,922,927	
NATIONWIDE TOUR									
2002	2	2				1	2	28,477	121
Total	2	2				1	2	28,477	
EUROPEAN TOUR									
2003	11	10		1		2	4	475,551	

PGA TOUR TOP TOURNAMENT SUMMARY

Year	95	96	97	98	99	00	01	02	03	04
Masters										T17
U.S. Open					CUT				2	T40
British Open	CUT			CUT	CUT	CUT	CUT	T37	T65	CUT
PGA				68	CUT				CUT	CUT
THE PLAYERS									CUT	CUT
WGC-Accenture Match Play					T33				T9	4
WGC-NEC Invitational									T71	T22
WGC-American Express Champ								T23		63

NATIONAL TEAMS: WGC-World Cup (2), 2003, 2004; The Presidents Cup, 2003; Dunhill Cup (2), 1999, 2000.

SECTION 2 PLAYER BIOGRAPHIES

Ian Leggatt

EXEMPT STATUS: Major Medical Extension
FULL NAME: Ian Donald Leggatt
HEIGHT: 6-0
WEIGHT: 170
BIRTHDATE: September 23, 1965
BIRTHPLACE: Cambridge, Ontario, Canada
RESIDENCE: Scottsdale, AZ; plays out of Galt CC
FAMILY: Wife, Lori; Mia Riess (4/25/2002), Aidan (9/25/04)
EDUCATION: Texas Wesleyan University (1990, Sports Management)
SPECIAL INTERESTS: Cars, fishing, movies, reading
TURNED PROFESSIONAL: 1990
JOINED TOUR: 2001
Nationwide Tour Alumnus

PGA TOUR VICTORIES (1):
2002 Touchstone Energy Tucson Open.

NATIONWIDE TOUR VICTORIES (1):
2000 Dayton Open.

BEST 2004 PGA TOUR FINISH:
78—Bob Hope Chrysler Classic.

2004 SEASON:
Limited to five events due to carpal tunnel syndrome in his left wrist. Did not play after withdrawing from the Chrysler Classic of Tucson and had wrist surgery on April 7th. Will receive a Major Medical Extension for 2005. Coupled with $8,280 earned in five events in 2004 has the opportunity to play in 24 events to earn $614,982 and match the $623,262 winnings of 2004's No. 125, Tag Ridings. If he does so, will play out of the Major Medical Extension category for the remainder of the season.

CAREER HIGHLIGHTS:
2003: Suffered through injury-plagued season after capturing his first TOUR title in 2002...Played in the first three events of the season, missing the cut at the Sony Open in Hawaii and the Phoenix Open. Sidelined for the next two weeks with a bad sinus infection that interfered with his oxygen intake. Also nursed a tendon problem in his left elbow and had to wear a brace...Best finish of the season was a T20 at the U.S. Open at Olympia Fields. **2002:** Beat Loren Roberts and David Peoples by two shots to capture his first PGA TOUR title in his 46th start on TOUR at the Touchstone Energy Tucson Open. Final-round 64 was a career low and 20-under-par 268 total was the lowest score at Tucson since David Frost shot 266 in 1988. $540,000 winner's check was more than his combined earnings since turning pro...In June was T5 at the Buick Classic, earning $112,875...Surpassed the $1-million mark for the first time in his career with a $108,000 payday for his T11 finish at The INTERNATIONAL Presented by Qwest...Stood one back through 36 holes following opening rounds of 70-65 at the SEI Pennsylvania Classic. Finished T7...Teamed with Mike Weir at the WGC-EMC World Cup in Puerto Vallarta, Mexico. **2001:** Retained PGA TOUR card for 2002 with T5 finish at 2001 Qualifying School...PGA TOUR rookie made 12 cuts in 29 starts with two top-10s and three top-25s...Rounded into form in late July with a T5 at the John Deere Classic, earning a season-high $106,400...One week later, T8 at Buick Open. **2000:** Rookie member of the Nationwide Tour, finishing fifth on the money list...Made the cut at 18 of 23 events with six top-10s and 10 top-25s...Became the TOUR's second rookie to win in 2000 with a playoff victory over Chris Smith at the Dayton Open. Fourth Canadian at the time to win on the Nationwide Tour (Jerry Anderson, Glen Hnatiuk and Rick Todd). **Amateur:** Member of the Canadian World Cup Team, which played in New Zealand...NAIA All-American at Texas Wesleyan in 1988-89.

PERSONAL:
Served as Athletic Director for the Cerebral Palsy Foundation of Tarrant County in Fort Worth, TX...Works with kids with disabilities and is sponsored by the Ronald McDonald Children's Charities to raise money for kids. Worldwide ambassador for Ronald McDonald Children's Charities of Canada...Father got him started in the game...Provincial and national speed skating champion in Canada.

PLAYER STATISTICS

2004 PGA TOUR STATISTICS

Scoring Average	73.58	(N/A)
Driving Distance	272.8	(N/A)
Driving Accuracy Percentage	59.8%	(N/A)
Total Driving	1,998	(N/A)
Greens in Regulation Pct.	63.7%	(N/A)
Putting Average	1.799	(N/A)
Sand Save Percentage	41.2%	(N/A)
Eagles (Holes per)	234.0	(N/A)
Birdie Average	3.08	(N/A)
Scoring Avg. Before Cut	72.33	(N/A)
Round 3 Scoring Avg.	72.00	(N/A)
Final Round Scoring Average	75.00	(N/A)
Birdie Conversion Percentage	25.7%	(N/A)
Par Breakers	17.5%	(N/A)

MISCELLANEOUS PGA TOUR STATISTICS
2004 Low Round/Round: 65–Bob Hope Chrysler Classic/4
Career Low Round/Round: 64–4 times, most recent 2002 Buick Challenge/2
Career Largest Paycheck/Finish: $540,000–2002 Touchstone Energy Tucson Open/1

PGA TOUR CAREER SUMMARY — PLAYOFF RECORD: 0-0

Year	Events Played	Cuts Made	1st	2nd	3rd	Top 10	Top 25	Earnings	Rank
1992	1								
1994	1								
1995	1								
1996	2	2						$4,780	323
1998	2	1						4,420	319
1999	2	1						4,725	329
2000	2								
2001	29	12				2	3	368,862	133
2002	29	20	1			3	8	1,245,048	47
2003	26	11					3	271,014	161
2004	5	1						8,280	256
Total	100	48	1			5	14	1,907,129	
NATIONWIDE TOUR									
1990	1	1						661	255
1995	1								
2000	23	18	1	2	1	6	10	259,724	5
2001	1	1						2,044	249
2004	1								
Total	27	20	1	2	1	6	10	262,429	

PGA TOUR TOP TOURNAMENT SUMMARY

Year	02	03
U.S. Open	T54	T20
PGA	CUT	
THE PLAYERS	CUT	W/D

NATIONAL TEAMS: WGC-World Cup (2), 2001, 2002.

Tom Lehman (LAY-mun)

EXEMPT STATUS: Winner, 1996 British Open (through 2006)
FULL NAME: Thomas Edward Lehman
HEIGHT: 6-2
WEIGHT: 215
BIRTHDATE: March 7, 1959
BIRTHPLACE: Austin, MN
RESIDENCE: Scottsdale, AZ; plays out of DC Ranch
FAMILY: Wife, Melissa; Rachael (5/30/90), Holly (8/13/92), Thomas Andrew (7/24/95), Sean (3/18/03)
EDUCATION: University of Minnesota
SPECIAL INTERESTS: Fly fishing, golf course design, hunting, all sports
TURNED PROFESSIONAL: 1982
Q SCHOOL: 1983, 1984
Nationwide Tour Alumnus

PGA TOUR VICTORIES (5):
1994 Memorial Tournament. **1995** Colonial National Invitation. **1996** British Open Championship, THE TOUR Championship. **2000** Phoenix Open.

NATIONWIDE TOUR VICTORIES (4):
1990 Reflection Ridge. **1991** Gulf Coast Classic, South Carolina Classic, Santa Rosa Open.

INTERNATIONAL VICTORIES (2):
1993 Casio World Open [Jpn]. **1997** Loch Lomond World Invitational [Eur].

OTHER VICTORIES (7):
1995 Hyundai Team Matches [with Duffy Waldorf]. **1996** Hyundai Team Matches [with Duffy Waldorf], PGA Grand Slam of Golf, Skins Game. **1997** Skins Game, Wendy's Three-Tour Challenge. **1999** Target World Challenge presented by Williams. **2000** Hyundai Team Matches [with Duffy Waldorf].

BEST 2004 PGA TOUR FINISHES:
T2—Michelin Championship at Las Vegas; T4—Bell Canadian Open, Chrysler Classic of Greensboro; T6—FUNAI Classic at the WALT DISNEY WORLD Resort.

2004 SEASON:
On Nov. 3, was named 2006 Ryder Cup captain by the PGA of America. Three-time Ryder Cup team member (1995, '97, '99) has a career record of 5-3-2. After struggling most of the year, posted top-10s in four of last five starts. In final three starts, held at least a share of the lead entering the final round. . .Aided by a final-round 64, posted his first top-10 of the year, a T4 at the Bell Canadian Open and the first since a T8 at the 2003 Buick Classic. . .A month later at the Michelin Championship at Las Vegas, finished T2, one back of winner Andre Stolz. Held one-stroke lead over Stolz and Dicky Pride through 54 holes, his first third-round lead since the 1999 Buick Open. Second time in four years (2001, Bob Estes) that he has finished one stroke behind the winner in Las Vegas. . .Entered final round of Chrysler Classic of Greensboro tied for the lead with Brent Geiberger at 12-under. Unfortunate start to final round, as he was penalized one stroke on No. 2 as ball moved while addressing a tap-in putt and later four-putted the sixth green. Recovered to post 2-under 70 for T4 finish. . .Tied for the lead with Briny Baird entering the final round of the FUNAI Classic at the WALT DISNEY WORLD Resort, but was overtaken by rookie Ryan Palmer's final-round 62. Finished T6 with a 72 on Sunday.

CAREER HIGHLIGHTS:
2003: Finished in top 100 on money list for 12th straight season...Earned first top-10 with solo second at AT&T Pebble Beach National Pro-Am, his best finish since T2 at the 2001 Invensys Classic at Las Vegas. Entered 72nd hole tied with Davis Love III at 13-under-par. Love two-putted 18 for birdie to claim one-shot victory **2002:** 74th on the money list was the lowest since he returned to the TOUR full-time in 1992...Earned T5 in WGC-Accenture Match Play Championship after losing to Scott McCarron (4 and 3) in the quarterfinals...Converted to a long putter at the WORLDCOM CLASSIC in April. **2001:** Finished in the top 25 on PGA TOUR money list for ninth time since regaining his TOUR card in 1992...Runner-up at Sony Open in Hawaii...Winner of Charles Bartlett Award, given by GWAA for unselfish contributions to golf. Has raised $3.5 million through his charity tournament in Minneapolis and is involved with "Match Point," a Phoenix program that matches adults with troubled children...With opening rounds of 63-62 (career low) in Invensys Classic, shared first-round lead and held second-round lead outright. Finished T2, one-stroke behind Bob Estes. First two rounds tied PGA TOUR record for opening two rounds. **2000:** Had most financially rewarding season of 12-year career with earnings of $2,068,499 and a 12th-place finish on the TOUR money list...Kicked off the season in red-hot fashion with three consecutive top-10s, including his first official money TOUR victory since winning the 1996 THE TOUR Championship...At the Phoenix Open, earned his fifth PGA TOUR title. Drained 10-foot putt for par on final hole then watched Robert Allenby miss a five-footer that would have forced a playoff...Came close at MCI Classic, where he held clubhouse lead on Sunday after shooting 65. Stewart Cink's own closing 65 snatched away win...Withdrew from INTERNATIONAL due to torn cartilage in right knee, then underwent surgery prior to PGA Championship...Participated in third Presidents Cup and compiled a 3-2 record while lending support to victorious United States team...Prior to official money season, was victorious in unofficial Williams World Challenge. **1999:** Made successful return to form from off-season shoulder surgery...Four runner-up finishes that year—Bay Hill Invitational, Greater Milwaukee Open, FedEx St. Jude Classic and Buick Open—were most ever for him in a single season. **1998:** Turned in T2 at THE PLAYERS Championship...Claimed a solo third at the Buick Classic and was a T5 at the U.S. Open, his third straight top-five finish in the event...Did not make the cut at the British Open after suffering a separated right shoulder just prior to the event while on a family outing in England. Was attempting a handstand for his children when the mishap occurred and played with the injury the remainder of the year before undergoing surgery in November in the Los Angeles area. **1997:** Tied with Tiger Woods after 54 holes at the Mercedes Championships and after final round was canceled, the two played off at the par-3 seventh hole. Lehman hit his tee shot

SECTION 2 PLAYER BIOGRAPHIES

PGA TOUR CAREER SUMMARY — PLAYOFF RECORD: 0-2

Year	Events Played	Cuts Made	1st	2nd	3rd	Top 10	Top 25	Earnings	Rank
1983	22	9					1	$9,413	182
1984	26	9						9,382	184
1985	26	10					2	20,232	158
1986	2								
1987	1								
1990	1								
1992	29	25		1	1	9	15	579,093	24
1993	27	20			1	6	12	422,761	33
1994	23	21	1	1	1	9	15	1,031,144	4
1995	18	16	1	1	1	5	12	830,231	15
1996	22	20	2	2	1	13	19	1,780,159	1
1997	21	18		1	1	9	14	960,584	19
1998	23	18		1	1	5	12	1,033,673	25
1999	23	19		4		5	9	1,435,564	24
2000	21	18	1	1		7	13	2,068,499	12
2001	23	18		2	1	5	12	1,907,660	20
2002	22	17				3	8	868,632	74
2003	25	19		1		2	9	1,173,237	61
2004	19	16		1		4	11	1,343,277	53
Total	374	273	5	16	8	82	164	15,473,541	
NATIONWIDE TOUR									
1990	19	12	1			5	8	41,338	17
1991	28	27	3	3		11	24	141,934	1
Total	47	39	4	3		16	32	183,272	
EUROPEAN TOUR									
2004	1	1					1	$60,905	

PGA TOUR TOP TOURNAMENT SUMMARY

Year	86	87	88	89	90	91	92	93	94	95	96	97	98
Masters								T3	2	40	T18	T12	CUT
U.S. Open	CUT	CUT			CUT		T6	T19	T33	3	T2	3	T5
British Open								T59	T24		**1**	T24	CUT
PGA								CUT	T39	CUT	T14	T10	T29
THE PLAYERS							T13	T11	CUT	T14	T8	6	T2
TOUR Championship							T13		28	12	**1**	T15	15

Year	99	00	01	02	03	04
Masters	T31	6	T18	CUT	CUT	
U.S. Open	T28	T23	T24	T45		
British Open	CUT	T4	CUT	CUT	T46	CUT
PGA	T34	W/D	CUT	T29	CUT	
THE PLAYERS	CUT	8	T12	T28	T39	CUT
TOUR Championship	T15	T18	T15			
WGC-Accenture Match Play	T33	T17	T9	T5	T33	
WGC-NEC Invitational	T15	T31		T38		
WGC-American Express Champ	T25		CNL	T39		

NATIONAL TEAMS: The Presidents Cup (3), 1994, 1996, 2000; Ryder Cup (3), 1995, 1997, 1999; World Cup, 1996; Dunhill Cup (2) 1999, 2000.

Tom Lehman (Continued)

in the water, Woods then hit to tap-in range for victory...At U.S. Open, water at 71st hole kept him from chance at victory and finished third, two strokes behind Ernie Els. Joined Bobby Jones as only player to lead U.S. Open after three rounds three straight years...With T4 at MCI Classic, moved into first place on Official World Golf Ranking. Only second player from U.S. to lead World Ranking at the time, following Fred Couples, who led for 15 weeks in 1992. Relinquished spot the next week when Greg Norman was second at Spanish Open. **1996:** PGA TOUR Player of the Year...Leading money-winner with then-record $1,780,159...First victory came at British Open at Royal Lytham and St. Annes. After consecutive 67s, shared 36-hole lead with Paul McGinley. Followed with a course-record 64 in third round to lead Nick Faldo by six strokes and his closing round 73 was enough for a two-stroke victory over Ernie Els and Mark McCumber. First American professional to win at that venue and the first since amateur Bobby Jones in 1926...Closed out year with dominant performance at TOUR Championship. After sharing first-round lead with Vijay Singh at 66, shot 67 to open a four-stroke margin after 36 holes. Led by nine after bogey-free 64, eventually winning by six over Brad Faxon. **1995:** Earned second win at Colonial National Invitation...Opened that season with second at United Airlines Hawaiian Open...After MCI Classic, missed a month of the season due to colon surgery...Third at U.S. Open after sharing 54-hole lead with Greg Norman. **1994:** First served notice of things to come with breakthrough season that included his first TOUR victory at Memorial Tournament. That win helped him secure first $1-million season on TOUR...Earlier that year was runner-up to Jose Maria Olazabal at Masters. **1992:** In first year back on PGA TOUR was 24th on money list, including T2 at Hardee's Golf Classic. **1991:** Won three times on the Nationwide Tour...Was that tour's top money-winner and Player of the Year. **1990:** Won once on the Nationwide Tour in 1990. **1985:** After three lukewarm seasons on TOUR from 1983-85, played in Asia, South Africa and elsewhere for the rest of the 1980s.

PERSONAL:

Credits marriage with giving him focus to do well on TOUR...Hosted Dayton's Challenge 1993-2002...Brother, Jim Lehman, Jr., is his agent...Honorary Chairman for PGA of America's National Golf Day in 1997...His wife, Melissa, was enlisted as his caddie at 1998 Nissan Open when regular caddie Andy Martinez suffered two broken ribs in a pickup basketball game the night before the start of the event. Went to a lighter carry bag instead of the heavier TOUR version...Lehman Design Group had 15 golf course deisgn projects ongoing or complete in 2004. They include the Troy Burne Golf Club in Hudson, WI, site of the Nationwide Tour's Scholarship America Showdown (where he serves as the host near his native Minnesota); the TPC of the Twin Cities, done with Arnold Palmer, as the site of the 3M Championship on the Champions Tour in Minneapolis; and The Gallery Golf Club in Tucson, AZ, co-designed with John Fought, which was part of the Chrysler Classic of Tucson tournament in 2002.

PLAYER STATISTICS

2004 PGA TOUR STATISTICS

Scoring Average	70.10	(13)
Driving Distance	287.2	(97)
Driving Accuracy Percentage	69.7%	(29)
Total Driving	126	(19)
Greens in Regulation Pct.	71.4%	(3)
Putting Average	1.778	(102)
Sand Save Percentage	44.0%	(157)
Eagles (Holes per)	118.8	(10)
Birdie Average	3.88	(15)
All-Around Ranking	426	(9)
Scoring Avg. Before Cut	69.82	(9)
Round 3 Scoring Avg.	69.87	(25)
Final Round Scoring Average	70.33	(19)
Birdie Conversion Percentage	30.2%	(62)
Par Breakers	22.4%	(11)

MISCELLANEOUS PGA TOUR STATISTICS

2004 Low Round/Round: 64–2 times, most recent Michelin Championship at Las Vegas/1

Career Low Round/Round: 62–2001 Invensys Classic at Las Vegas/2

Career Largest Paycheck/Finish: $576,000–2000 Phoenix Open/1

SHOTLink

AN IBM ON DEMAND BUSINESS SOLUTION

HOT SHOTS

Vijay Singh

Money List – 2004 Statistical Comparison (Top 10)

TOP 10 PLAYERS ON THE MONEY LIST (with ranking in parentheses)

Rank	Player	Driving Distance	Driving Accuracy %	Putting 4-8 ft	Proximity to the Hole	Appr. from 125-150 Yds
1	Vijay Singh	300.8 (13th)	60.4% (T149th)	63.3% (185th)	27′ 11″ (1st)	20′ 4″ (2nd)
2	Ernie Els	298 (19th)	55.5% (185th)	69.7% (T89th)	31′ 2″ (T62nd)	22′ (T29th)
3	Phil Mickelson	295.4 (T30th)	62.9% (T120th)	66.1% (T155th)	30′ 5″ (T30th)	21′ 4″ (T14th)
4	Tiger Woods	301.9 (9th)	56.1% (T182nd)	71.1% (T55th)	31′ 6″ (T74th)	23′ 6″ (T82nd)
5	Stewart Cink	290.5 (T70th)	58.7% (T167th)	71.8% (T38th)	30′ 6″ (T34th)	21′ 0″ (T7th)
6	Retief Goosen	294.2 (38th)	62.5% (T125th)	72.4% (T29th)	29′ 11″ (T18th)	22′ 5″ (T45th)
7	Adam Scott	295.4 (T30th)	57.7% (174th)	76.8% (2nd)	31′ 1″ (T56th)	20′ 6″ (4th)
8	Stephen Ames	287.9 (T89th)	65% (T80th)	74.6% (T10th)	30′ 2″ (T24th)	21′ 11″ (T26th)
9	Sergio Garcia	295.1 (33rd)	58.5% (T170th)	62.9% (T186th)	29′ 11″ (T18th)	19′ 0″ (1st)
10	Davis Love III	300.1 (T14th)	60.1% (T151st)	69.1% (T107th)	31′ 11″ (T88th)	24′ 1″ (T112th)

Justin Leonard

EXEMPT STATUS: Winner, 1997 British Open (through 2007)
FULL NAME: Justin Charles Garrett Leonard
HEIGHT: 5-9
WEIGHT: 170
BIRTHDATE: June 15, 1972
BIRTHPLACE: Dallas, TX
RESIDENCE: Dallas, TX

FAMILY: Wife, Amanda; Reese Ella (9/14/03)
EDUCATION: University of Texas (1994, Business)
SPECIAL INTERESTS: Fishing, hiking, skiing
TURNED PROFESSIONAL: 1994
JOINED TOUR: 1994

PGA TOUR VICTORIES (8):

1996 Buick Open. **1997** Kemper Open, British Open Championship. **1998** THE PLAYERS Championship. **2000** Westin Texas Open at LaCantera. **2001** Texas Open at LaCantera. **2002** WORLDCOM CLASSIC - The Heritage of Golf. **2003** The Honda Classic.

OTHER VICTORIES (1):

2000 CVS Charity Classic [with Davis Love III].

BEST 2004 PGA TOUR FINISHES:

T2—PGA Championship; T9—FBR Open; T10—Valero Texas Open.

2004 SEASON:

Near-miss at PGA Championship characterized season as Texan had lowest finish on money list (42nd) since joining the TOUR full-time in 1995...In third start of the season, finished T9 at the FBR Open, aided by six consecutive birdies (Nos. 13-18) to finish the third round...Shared second-round lead with J.L. Lewis at the Bank of America Colonial before finishing T14...Next top-10 did not come until August at the PGA Championship. Shared second-round lead with Vijay Singh at 9-under 135 and was one back of Singh through 54 holes. Held one-stroke lead over Chris DiMarco and Singh through 71 holes but missed a 12-footer for par on the 72nd hole to force a three-man, three-hole playoff. Finished T2 after Singh was only one of the three to record a birdie during the playoff...Finished T10 at Valero Texas Open, fifth top-10 in eight starts at the San Antonio event.

CAREER HIGHLIGHTS:

2003: Successful season, with eighth career PGA TOUR victory at The Honda Classic and the birth of a daughter...Earned come-from-behind win at The Honda Classic with rounds of 63-70-64-67—264. Earned a career-best payday of $900,00. Co-leader through 18 holes with Notah Begay III and Jeff Brehaut. Entered final round one stroke behind Davis Love III, and carded 5-under 67 to earn one-stroke win over Love and Chad Campbell. Winning 72-hole total of 264 broke previous Honda Classic record of 266 set by Blaine McCallister in 1989...At the Bank of America Colonial, was 10-under-par through 17 holes in final round with a chance to post a 59 with a birdie. Bogeyed the 18th hole to finish with a 9-under 61, tying the course record, and finished T2. Also holds a share of the course record (61) at the TPC at Las Colinas, one of the two host courses of the EDS Byron Nelson Championship...Teamed with American Jim Furyk at World Cup and played on his third Presidents Cup squad. **2002:** Re-established himself as one of the world's premier players, finishing with earnings of $2,738,235, $714,770 better than previous career best. Finished in the top 10 in earnings for the first time since 1999 and captured TOUR event for third consecutive season...Picked up seventh career victory at the WORLDCOM CLASSIC. Closed with a 73 to edge Heath Slocum by one stroke. Became first player to shoot over-par in the final round and win since Scott McCarron at the 2001 BellSouth Classic. Also the first without a birdie in the final round and win since Vijay Singh at the 1995 Buick Classic. Singh won with a playoff birdie...Opened with rounds of 72-66 to shared the 36-hole lead at the PGA. Had a three-shot lead over eventual champion Rich Beem after posting the only round in the 60s, shooting a third-round 69 amid winds gusting to 40 mph. Closing 77 dropped him to T4. **2001:** After struggling early in the season with a swing change, rallied to once again qualify for THE TOUR Championship for the seventh consecutive time by earning $1,783,842. Had a very successful year playing in Texas by winning once and added three other top-10s in as many starts. Was able to defend his title in the Texas Open at La Cantera. Became the first player to win in consecutive years at the Texas Open since Arnold Palmer won three in a row (1960-62). Led by three strokes after 36 holes and held that lead to capture sixth victory by two strokes over J.J. Henry and Matt Kuchar. Earlier in the year, posted a T4 at Shell Houston Open, a T6 at the Verizon Byron Nelson Classic and a T5 in the MasterCard Colonial. **2000:** Returned to the winner's circle after a one-year drought...Along with a victory, also finished second three times...Earned a five-stroke victory at Westin Texas Open. Shot 66-67 and stood one back through 36 holes. Third-round 71 produced share of the lead. His 66 on Sunday ended 2 -year victory drought and earned fifth PGA TOUR career title. First victory since 1998 PLAYERS Championship and first title in home state. **1999:** Didn't record a victory for first time in three years, but was still among the top 10 of money list for third consecutive year...Posted seven top 10s, including his first three starts...Nearly won his second British Open in July, losing to Paul Lawrie in three-way playoff with Jean Van de Velde...His 45-foot putt on 17th hole at The Country Club during Sunday singles match with Jose Maria Olazabal earned decisive half-point that regained Ryder Cup for U.S. Won four consecutive holes (12-15) to square match and set up his 17th-hole heroics. **1998:** Won a tournament for third year in a row and earned $1,671,823 to finish eighth on money list...Nabbed one of the year's biggest prizes in March, when he came from five strokes back to overtake Lee Janzen on the final day at THE PLAYERS Championship. Opened with a 72 and followed with rounds of 69-70 before firing a 5-under-par 67 Sunday for a two-stroke victory over Tom Lehman and Glen Day. Victory was worth $720,000, at that point the largest payday of his career. Five-stroke comeback was largest ever on Stadium Course at TPC at Sawgrass and was one shy of Raymond Floyd's tournament record established in 1981 at Sawgrass CC. **1997:** Won first major championship at British Open. After opening with 67 in blustery conditions at Royal Troon, trailed Jim Furyk and Darren Clarke by two strokes. Remained two back after second-round 66, but fell five behind Jesper Parnevik after three rounds. Closing 65 was only round in 60s by a player who began round under par. Won by three strokes over Parnevik and Clarke. At age 25, was youngest British Open

SECTION 2 PLAYER BIOGRAPHIES

PGA TOUR CAREER SUMMARY — PLAYOFF RECORD: 0-4

Year	Events Played	Cuts Made	1st	2nd	3rd	Top 10	Top 25	Earnings	Rank
1993A	7	5					1		
1994	13	5			1	2	4	$140,413	126
1995	31	25		2		7	13	748,793	22
1996	29	23	1	1		8	13	943,140	11
1997	29	25	2	1	1	8	13	1,587,531	5
1998	28	22	1	2		8	13	1,671,823	8
1999	28	26		2	2	7	25	2,020,991	8
2000	28	22	1	3		4	14	2,023,465	14
2001	30	22	1			9	12	1,783,842	25
2002	26	23	1	1		7	17	2,738,235	8
2003	23	19	1	1		4	13	2,450,525	17
2004	25	21		1		3	9	1,531,023	42
Total	297	238	8	14	4	67	147	17,639,781	

PGA TOUR TOP TOURNAMENT SUMMARY

Year	93	94	95	96	97	98	99	00	01	02	03	04
Masters	CUT			T27	T7	T8	T18	T28	T27	T20	CUT	T35
U.S. Open	T68			T50	T36	T40	T15	T16	CUT	T12	T20	CUT
British Open			T58	CUT	**1**	T57	T2	T41	CUT	T14	CUT	T16
PGA			T8	T5	2	CUT	CUT	T41	T10	T4	CUT	T2
THE PLAYERS			T34	T65	T37	**1**	T23	T22	CUT	T44	T21	T42
TOUR Championship			T7	T6	T8	T5	T12	T16	T22	T18	T21	
WGC-Accenture Match Play							T17	T17	T9	T33	T17	T33
WGC-NEC Invitational							20	T2		T28	T23	T50
WGC-American Express Champ							T11	T25	CNL	T11		T28

NATIONAL TEAMS: World Amateur Team Championship, 1992; Walker Cup, 1993; The Presidents Cup (3), 1996, 1998, 2003; Ryder Cup (2), 1997, 1999; Dunhill Cup, 1997; World Cup (2), 1997, 2003.

Justin Leonard (Continued)

champion since Seve Ballesteros won in 1979 at 22...Nearly earned second major title at PGA Championship. Shared third-round lead with Davis Love III after course-record 65 and stood seven strokes in front of next-closest rival. Closing 71 left him alone in second, five strokes behind Love...Member of U.S. Ryder Cup team. **1996:** First PGA TOUR victory came at Buick Open. Shot 65-64-69 to lead by one after 54 holes. Closed with 68 to win by five strokes over Chip Beck. Became first player since Mark Calcavecchia at 1992 Phoenix Open to win tournament in which he had hole-in-one...First victory nearly came earlier that year at Phoenix Open where he lost in playoff to Phil Mickelson...Played on Presidents Cup team. **1995:** Runner-up twice. Was one stroke shy of Billy Mayfair at Motorola Western Open and finished second to Duffy Waldorf at LaCantera Texas Open. Finish vaulted him to first TOUR Championship appearance. **1994:** Earned TOUR privileges without making trip to Qualifying Tournament by finishing third at Anheuser-Busch Golf Classic, his third professional start. **Amateur:** Played in eight TOUR events as an amateur, making five cuts...Member of winning 1993 U.S. Walker Cup team...Only golfer in Southwest Conference history to win four consecutive conference championships...All-American at University of Texas in 1993-94...Winner of 1994 Dave Williams Award...1992 U.S. Amateur champion.

PERSONAL:

In late 2001, completed the White Rock Marathon in Dallas in 3 hours, 55 minutes. Wife, Amanda, has run several marathons, including New York City Marathon…Grew up playing at Royal Oaks CC in Dallas with Harrison Frazar, his roommate at the University of Texas…Host of AJGA's Justin Leonard/Deloitte & Touche Junior Team Championship at Northwood Club, with proceeds benefiting the Northern Texas PGA Junior Golf Foundation and AJGA…Web site is justinleonard.com.

PLAYER STATISTICS

2004 PGA TOUR STATISTICS

Scoring Average	70.61	(40)
Driving Distance	282.9	(134)
Driving Accuracy Percentage	67.4%	(53)
Total Driving	187	(80)
Greens in Regulation Pct.	66.1%	(69)
Putting Average	1.769	(70)
Sand Save Percentage	54.0%	(32)
Eagles (Holes per)	306.0	(131)
Birdie Average	3.42	(125)
All-Around Ranking	654	(63)
Scoring Avg. Before Cut	70.29	(21)
Round 3 Scoring Avg.	70.95	(98)
Final Round Scoring Average	71.47	(88)
Birdie Conversion Percentage	27.9%	(136)
Par Breakers	19.3%	(129)

MISCELLANEOUS PGA TOUR STATISTICS

2004 Low Round/Round: 64–Bank of America Colonial/2
Career Low Round/Round: 61–2 times, most recent 2003 Bank of America Colonial/4
Career Largest Paycheck/Finish: $900,000–2003 The Honda Classic/1

SHOTLink
AN IBM ON DEMAND BUSINESS SOLUTION

HOT SHOTS

Tag Ridings

Money List – 2004 Statistical Comparison

120-125 ON THE MONEY LIST (with ranking in parentheses)

Rank	Player	Driving Distance	Driving Accuracy %	Putting 4'8'	Proximity to the Hole	Appr. from 125-150 Yds
120	Jay Williamson	288.1 (T85th)	69.3% (T33rd)	64.9% (T172nd)	30' 1" (T21st)	23' 1" (T66th)
121	Steve Allan	301.2 (11th)	59.3% (T158th)	64% (T179th)	32' 4" (T109th)	23' 8" (T91st)
122	Brian Gay	279.7 (T163rd)	64.8% (T85th)	71.3% (52nd)	30' 10" (T42nd)	21' 2" (T10th)
123	Aaron Baddeley	288 (T87th)	53.1% (191st)	72.8% (25th)	35' 10" (193rd)	23' 2" (T70th)
124	Billy Andrade	283.5 (T128th)	59.7% (155th)	68.3% (T121st)	31' 7" (T77th)	23' 2" (T70th)
125	Tag Ridings	301 (12th)	56.4% (180th)	70.6% (T69th)	32' 11" (T137th)	25' 5" (T159th)

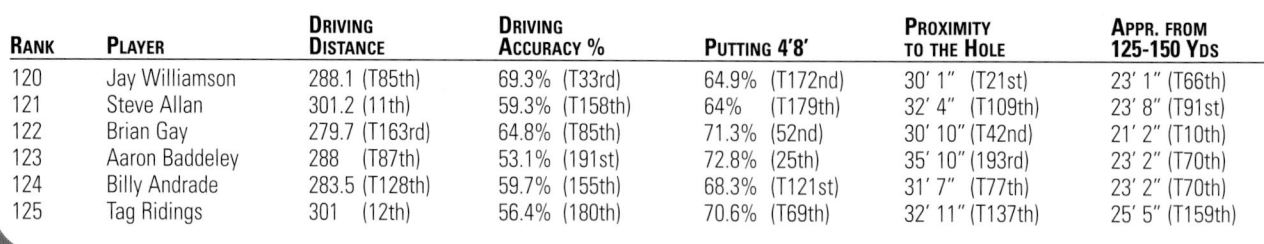

Thomas Levet (luh-VAY)

EXEMPT STATUS: 2004 European Ryder Cup Team Member (through 2006)
FULL NAME: Thomas Levet
HEIGHT: 5-9
WEIGHT: 160
BIRTHDATE: September 5, 1968
BIRTHPLACE: Paris, France
RESIDENCE: Berkshire, England
FAMILY: Caroline; Gregoire (1998), Juliette (2000), Charlotte (2004)
SPECIAL INTERESTS: Sports, animals, music, cars, social games
TURNED PROFESSIONAL: 1988
Q SCHOOL: 1993

BEST PGA TOUR CAREER FINISH:
T2—2002 British Open Championship.

INTERNATIONAL VICTORIES (9):
1988 French PGA Championship [Fr]. **1990** National Omnium [Fr]. **1991** French PGA Championship [Fr]. **1992** Championnat de France Pro [Eur Chall]. **1998** Cannes Open [Eur]. **1997** Toulouse Open [Fr], New Caledonia French Masters [Fr]. **2001** Victor Chandler British Masters [Eur]. **2004** Barclays Scottish Open [Eur].

BEST 2004 PGA TOUR FINISH:
T5—British Open Championship.

2004 SEASON:
Finished 154th on the money list after playing in just five PGA TOUR events as a conditional member. Made the European Ryder Cup team to secure his fully exempt status on TOUR for 2005. . .Spent a full season on the European Tour, where he posted his third career win and first since the 2001 season. Had seven other top-10 finishes on that circuit. . .Came from seven strokes back at the European Tour's Barclays Scottish Open in July by firing an 8-under 63 in the final round to defeat New Zealand's Michael Campbell by a stroke. Began the day in a tie for 14th, seven strokes behind 54-hole leaders Gregory Havret and Marcus Fraser. . . The win gave him an exemption into the following week's British Open in Scotland, where he finished T5. Shared the first-round lead with Paul Casey after an opening, 5-under 66 and trailed Skip Kendall by one at the halfway mark before finishing five strokes behind winner Todd Hamilton. . .The following month shared the 54-hole lead with Miguel Angel Jimenez at the BMW International Open, but posted a 68 to Jimenez's 66 and finished solo second.

CAREER HIGHLIGHTS:
2003: Only top 10 finish came in final event of the season, a T6 at the Chrylser Championship. Teammed with Raphael Jacquelin to finish T3 at the 2003 WGC-World Cup competition in Kiawah Island, SC. **2002:** Earned $532,186 as a non-member, inside the No. 125 total of $515,445, enabling him to have fully exempt status for the following year...T18 in U.S. Open and then T2 in British Open with rounds of 72-66-74-66—278, making four-way playoff with eventual winner Ernie Els, Stuart Appleby and Steve Elkington. Advanced with Els out of the four-hole playoff into sudden death, with Els winning on the first sudden-death hole, the 18th at Murifield, with a par. Earned career-best $452,990 for playoff runner-up. **2001:** Won his first title outside France, the Victor Chandler British Masters, after a four-way playoff at Woburn's Marquess Course. Became the first Frenchman to win on British soil since Arnaud Massy won the British Open in 1907...Posted five other top-10 finishes, and finished 19th in the European Tour Order of Merit with $706,776. **2000:** Finished T2 at Moroccan Open on European Tour. **1998:** After struggling on the European Tour for the better part of the mid-90s, received invite from French Federation to play in Europe One Cannes Open, and became first winner on home soil since Jean Garaialde took the French Open in 1969. **1994:** Became first Frenchman to earn PGA TOUR card after taking 18th place in Qualifying Tournament...Played in 10 events, making one cut and $2,200...Also played 19 European Tour events, with one top 10. **1992:** First full year on European Tour with one top 10 in 29 events.

PERSONAL:
Member of the French National 18-and-under field hockey team, and a nationally-ranked tennis player at the age of 14. . .Born into a true sporting family. His father, a Paris doctor, was a first-class hockey and tennis player, his mother played for France in volleyball and his grandfather was a professional cyclist.

PLAYER STATISTICS

Scoring Average	70.33	(N/A)
Driving Distance	280.9	(N/A)
Driving Accuracy Percentage	59.4%	(N/A)
Total Driving	(N/A)	(N/A)
Greens in Regulation Pct.	63.2%	(N/A)
Putting Average	1.764	(N/A)
Sand Save Percentage	34.8%	(N/A)
Eagles (Holes per)	144.0	(N/A)
Birdie Average	3.25	(N/A)
Scoring Avg. Before Cut	71.70	(N/A)
Round 3 Scoring Avg.	71.33	(N/A)
Final Round Scoring Average	71.00	(N/A)
Birdie Conversion Percentage	27.6%	(N/A)
Par Breakers	18.8%	(N/A)

MISCELLANEOUS PGA TOUR STATISTICS
2004 Low Round/Round: 66–British Open Championship/1
Career Low Round/Round: 65–2003 Southern Farm Bureau Classic/4
Career Largest Paycheck/Finish: $452,991–2002 British Open Championship/T2

PGA TOUR CAREER SUMMARY — PLAYOFF RECORD: 0-1

Year	Events Played	Cuts Made	1st	2nd	3rd	Top 10	Top 25	Earnings	Rank
1994	10	1						$2,200	310
1998	1								
1999	1	1						11,275	275
2001	1	1						11,766	
2002	3	3		1		1	2	532,186	
2003	26	16				1	4	470,021	133
2004	5	3				1	1	404,305	154
Total	47	25		1		3	7	1,431,753	
EUROPEAN TOUR									
2004	23	19	1	2	2	7	12	1,723,872	

PGA TOUR TOP TOURNAMENT SUMMARY

Year	98	99	00	01	02	03	04
Masters						CUT	
U.S. Open					T18		CUT
British Open	CUT	T49		T66	T2	T22	T5
PGA					71		CUT
THE PLAYERS						CUT	
WGC-NEC Invitational							T32
WGC-American Express Champ				CNL			T28

NATIONAL TEAMS: WGC-World Cup (5), 2000, 2001, 2002, 2003, 2004. Alfred Dunhill Cup (3) 1992, 1998, 2000. The Seve Trophy (1) 2002.

J.L. Lewis

EXEMPT STATUS: 2003 tournament winner (through 2005)
FULL NAME: John L. Lewis
HEIGHT: 6-3
WEIGHT: 200
BIRTHDATE: July 18, 1960
BIRTHPLACE: Emporia, KS
RESIDENCE: Horseshoe Bay, TX; plays out of Horseshoe Bay Resort
FAMILY: Wife, Dawn; Cole (5/12/84), Sherry (4/30/87)
EDUCATION: Southwest Texas State University
SPECIAL INTERESTS: Family, basketball
TURNED PROFESSIONAL: 1984
JOINED TOUR: 1989
Nationwide Tour Alumnus

PGA TOUR VICTORIES (2):

1999 John Deere Classic. **2003** 84 Lumber Classic of Pennsylvania.

BEST 2004 PGA TOUR FINISHES:

T9—Bob Hope Chrysler Classic; T10—Valero Texas Open.

2004 SEASON:

Finished inside the top 125 on the PGA TOUR money list for the seventh straight season. . .In second start of year, finished T9 at the Bob Hope Chrysler Classic, posting five rounds in the 60s. . .Carded a 64 in the first round of the EDS Byron Nelson Championship and shared the lead with Peter Lonard. A second-round 74 dropped him out of contention, and he finished T48. . .A week later, shared the second-round lead with Justin Leonard at the Bank of America Colonial before finishing T27. . .Finished T10 at Valero Texas Open, six strokes behind Bart Bryant. . .Held one-stroke lead over Chez Reavie through two rounds at the Michelin Championship at Las Vegas prior to finishing T23.

CAREER HIGHLIGHTS:

2003: Finished a career-best 28th on the PGA TOUR money list thanks to his second win, a career-high six top-10s and over $2 million in earnings. Had never earned over $1 million entering the season...First win in over four years came at the 84 Lumber Classic of Pennsylvania. Set course and tournament records with final-round, career-best 10-under 62 and 72-hole total of 22-under 266. Came from seven strokes back on a 36-hole Sunday...Week prior to victory, was leader or co-leader through first three rounds at rain-hampered John Deere Classic. Finished T2, four strokes behind Vijay Singh...Earnings were enough to qualify him for a place in his first TOUR Championship, where he finished 28th, and the 2004 Masters, where he missed the cut. **2002:** Had then-best season on TOUR in seven-year career with most top 10s (4), highest money list finish (65) and most earnings ($957,182)...T2 at the Buick Invitational, one stroke behind champion Jose Maria Olazabal. Shared lead following second and third rounds, but final-round 70 included a three-putt bogey on the tournament's 72nd hole...Fired only ace of Valero Texas Open on Sunday at the 182-yard 17th hole with a 7-iron. **2001:** Made over $500,000 for third consecutive season and kept his TOUR card for fourth straight year since playing 1997 season on Nationwide Tour...Tied career-low mark with 63 in fourth round of Bob Hope Chrysler Classic, which he set during second round of 1998 Greater Milwaukee Open. **2000:** Posted season-best T3 at Bob Hope Chrysler Classic. **1999:** Broke through to earn first PGA TOUR title, after 113 events, at the John Deere Classic. Birdied 72nd hole to force playoff with Mike Brisky, then birdied fifth playoff hole to earn $360,000. Holed bunker shot on second playoff hole (No. 16) for birdie. Brisky birdied from 12 feet to match him. Was 12th first-time winner at Oakwood CC. $622,883 he earned was more than he had earned in his career on the PGA TOUR and Nationwide Tour combined...Won the Honda Invitational in Guadalajara, Mexico. **1998:** Returned to the PGA TOUR after prior membership in 1989 and 1995...Finished 104th on the final money list, his first ever in the top 125. **1997:** Played the Nationwide Tour full-time and finished seventh on the final money list thanks, in part, to a third-place effort at the Nationwide Tour Championship. Set a Grand National Lake Course record in the third round when he fired a 6-under-par 66. **1994:** Member of winning PGA Cup team. **Amateur:** Member of 1983 NCAA Division II championship team...First team All-America in high school.

PERSONAL:

Named to the 1978 all-state high school basketball team and earned golf scholarship to Emporia State (KS) University. . .Later transferred to Texas State University on a golf scholarship; finished second in individual play that year. . .Wife, Dawn, caddied for him most of 1997. . .Worked as head professional at Forest Creek GC in Round Rock, TX, for three years before giving TOUR golf another shot. . .Three-time Player of the Year in South Texas Section of PGA and Player of the Year in Southwest Section PGA in Nevada. . .Introduced into Emporia High School Hall of Fame in 2001. . .Inducted into Texas State Hall of Honor in 2002.

PLAYER STATISTICS

2004 PGA TOUR STATISTICS

Scoring Average	71.21	(105)
Driving Distance	288.3	(83)
Driving Accuracy Percentage	65.5%	(73)
Total Driving	156	(42)
Greens in Regulation Pct.	66.5%	(57)
Putting Average	1.769	(70)
Sand Save Percentage	49.1%	(97)
Eagles (Holes per)	173.5	(56)
Birdie Average	3.59	(82)
All-Around Ranking	623	(52)
Scoring Avg. Before Cut	70.76	(61)
Round 3 Scoring Avg.	71.64	(147)
Final Round Scoring Average	71.05	(58)
Birdie Conversion Percentage	29.4%	(87)
Par Breakers	20.5%	(72)

MISCELLANEOUS PGA TOUR STATISTICS

2004 Low Round/Round: 62–FUNAI Classic at the WALT DISNEY WORLD Resort/1
Career Low Round/Round: 62–2 times, most recent 2004 FUNAI Classic at the WALT DISNEY WORLD Resort/1
Career Largest Paycheck/Finish: $720,000–2003 84 Lumber Classic of Pennsylvania/1

PGA TOUR CAREER SUMMARY — PLAYOFF RECORD: 1-0

Year	Events Played	Cuts Made	1st	2nd	3rd	Top 10	Top 25	Earnings	Rank
1985	1								
1989	21	4						$9,087	214
1992	2								
1993	3	2						5,965	261
1994	3	2						3,299	291
1995	28	13					1	59,750	190
1996	3	2					1	26,118	228
1998	32	15				2	6	287,753	104
1999	31	17	1			2	6	622,883	66
2000	30	21			1	2	5	610,432	78
2001	31	23				1	5	508,618	98
2002	31	17		1		4	9	957,182	65
2003	31	18	1	1		6	9	2,039,259	28
2004	32	21				2	9	807,345	102
Total	279	155	2	2	1	19	51	5,937,693	
NATIONWIDE TOUR									
1990	1	1						710	245
1991	1								
1992	1	1						913	239
1993	9	4					1	3,565	156
1994	3	1						315	297
1995	3	3			1	1	1	18,070	92
1996	3	2				1	1	10,673	120
1997	28	21		2	2	6	15	119,829	7
1998	3	2		1		2	2	31,819	69
1999	1								
Total	53	35		3	3	10	20	185,893	

PGA TOUR TOP TOURNAMENT SUMMARY

Year	93	94	95	96	97	98	99	00	01	02	03	04
Masters												CUT
U.S. Open				T40				CUT	T30			CUT
British Open											T22	
PGA	CUT	CUT					T21			CUT	T34	T24
THE PLAYERS							CUT	CUT	T73	T63	CUT	CUT
TOUR Championship											28	
WGC-NEC Invitational												T55
WGC-American Express Champ											T59	

Frank Lickliter II

EXEMPT STATUS: 2003 tournament winner (through 2005)
FULL NAME: Franklin Ray Lickliter II
HEIGHT: 6-1
WEIGHT: 200
BIRTHDATE: July 28, 1969
BIRTHPLACE: Middletown, OH
RESIDENCE: Ponte Vedra Beach, FL

FAMILY: Fiancee, Diane Owen
EDUCATION: Wright State University (1991, Sociology)
SPECIAL INTERESTS: Fishing, hunting, reading and playing chess
TURNED PROFESSIONAL: 1991
Q SCHOOL: 1995, 1996
Nationwide Tour Alumnus

PGA TOUR VICTORIES (2):

2001 Kemper Insurance Open. **2003** Chrysler Classic of Tucson.

NATIONWIDE TOUR VICTORIES (1):

1995 Boise Open.

BEST 2004 PGA TOUR FINISHES:

T3—THE PLAYERS Championship; 4—Sony Open in Hawaii; T9—Booz Allen Classic, 84 LUMBER Classic.

2004 SEASON:

Finished inside the top 125 on the PGA TOUR money list for the eighth time in his nine-year career and surpassed the $1-million mark for the third time...His four top-10s were the most since 2001, when he had eight...Tied the Waialae CC course record with a second-round, 8-under-par 62 en route to a fourth-place finish at the Sony Open in Hawaii. Started the final round two strokes behind Harrison Frazar but was unable to make up any ground after posting a 68 on Sunday...Held a two-shot lead through first round of the Chrysler Classic of Tucson after opening with 63. Was trying to become the fourth PGA TOUR player to successfully defend his title in 2004, but shot 73-72-69 to finish 27th...Posted second career top-10 at THE PLAYERS Championship, a T3, four strokes behind champion Adam Scott...Other two top-10s were a pair of T9s at the Booz Allen Classic in June and the 84 LUMBER Classic in September.

CAREER HIGHLIGHTS:

2003: Earned second career PGA TOUR victory in 219th start with two-shot win over Chad Campbell at Chrysler Classic of Tucson. Tournament leader after 36 and 54 holes. Nursing a one-stroke lead on the 72nd hole, was able to get up and down for par after hitting drive into water hazard skirting the 18th fairway. Earned $540,000 paycheck and jumped 40 spots in Official World Golf Ranking to No. 91...Waited almost seven months for his next top-10, but made it count with a T2 at the 84 Lumber Classic of Pennsylvania. Tied for clubhouse lead at 20-under before eventual winner J.L. Lewis birdied two of the last three holes to finish at 22-under. **2002:** First top top-10 did not come until May when he finished T8 at the Verizon Byron Nelson Classic aided by opening-round 64...Finished T7 at The INTERNATIONAL Presented by Qwest. Earned 24 of his 25-point total on the weekend...Tied for second, one stroke behind Loren Roberts through 54 holes at Valero Texas Open, before finishing T14. **2001:** Finished in the top 30 on the PGA TOUR money list for the first time on the strength of a career-high eight top-10s and a victory. Was one of 10 first-time winners. Rounds of 69-65-66-68 produced one-stroke victory over J.J. Henry at Kemper Insurance Open. Victory on the PGA TOUR came in his 168th career start...Nearly won early in the season until a triple bogey on third extra hole lost Buick Invitational playoff to Phil Mickelson. Closing round of 66 put him into extra holes with Mickelson and Davis Love III. **2000:** First shot at his first PGA TOUR victory came early in year at Phoenix Open. Moved into position with 67-64-69 and had one-stroke lead over Phil Mickelson heading into final round. Shot 74 to Tom Lehman's 67 and fell into T10...At Michelob Championship was one stroke off first and third-round leads before finishing T3...Two weeks later posted a T3 at Tampa Bay Classic. **1999:** Finished solo second at AT&T Pebble Beach National Pro-Am, one stroke behind Payne Stewart. Was three strokes behind Stewart after 36 holes. Stewart birdied his 54th hole to give him a one-stroke lead over Lickliter. The event was shortened to 54 holes when heavy rains moved in Saturday night and Sunday. **1998:** Breakthrough season with five top-10s and over $600,000 in earnings...Highlight of the season a T4 at the PGA Championship at Sahalee CC near Seattle. **1997:** Made first appearance in top 125...Got off to a slow start, but three top-10s in second half of season helped him retain his playing privileges for the next season. Began turnaround at Quad City Classic where he posted a third-round 63, his low round of the season, and trailed David Toms and Brad Fabel by one stroke. T5 after closing 68...Entered final round of Bell Canadian Open two strokes behind leader Steve Jones, then shot closing 70 for a T4. **1996:** First joined PGA TOUR after T20 at Qualifying Tournament...Lone top-10 his rookie season was a seventh at the BellSouth Classic. Contended at Greater Milwaukee Open with third-round 64 before finishing T12...Had opening-round 63 to share lead at Walt Disney World/Oldsmobile Classic, but finished T51...Returned to Q-School after finishing 138th on 1996 money list but regained TOUR card with 36th-place finish. **1995:** Played the Nationwide full-time and was 15th on the money list, including victory at Boise Open.

PERSONAL:

One of his biggest thrills in golf was making a double eagle while playing with former major league baseball player Chris Sabo...After he missed qualifying for PGA TOUR in 1993, took four months off and reconstructed his swing with former PGA TOUR player Mike McGee...Enjoyed a bear-hunting trip to Alaska with Fuzzy Zoeller in spring 2000 and fall 2003...Visited U.S. troops at Guantanamo Bay and in Korea.

PLAYER STATISTICS

2004 PGA TOUR STATISTICS

Scoring Average	71.07	(93)
Driving Distance	287.3	(94)
Driving Accuracy Percentage	66.6%	(60)
Total Driving	154	(39)
Greens in Regulation Pct.	64.8%	(104)
Putting Average	1.759	(43)
Sand Save Percentage	40.8%	(188)
Eagles (Holes per)	221.1	(85)
Birdie Average	3.85	(21)
All-Around Ranking	688	(74)
Scoring Avg. Before Cut	71.11	(113)
Round 3 Scoring Avg.	70.22	(42)
Final Round Scoring Average	71.76	(113)
Birdie Conversion Percentage	31.5%	(24)
Par Breakers	21.8%	(21)

MISCELLANEOUS PGA TOUR STATISTICS

2004 Low Round/Round: 62–Sony Open in Hawaii/2
Career Low Round/Round: 62–2 times, most recent 2004 Sony Open in Hawaii/2
Career Largest Paycheck/Finish: $630,000–2001 Kemper Insurance Open/1

PGA TOUR CAREER SUMMARY — PLAYOFF RECORD: 0-1

Year	Events Played	Cuts Made	1st	2nd	3rd	Top 10	Top 25	Earnings	Rank
1994	1								
1996	29	15				1	4	$138,847	138
1997	30	14				3	5	221,049	107
1998	32	22				5	12	600,847	45
1999	31	23		1		4	12	872,422	44
2000	31	22			2	6	9	889,153	53
2001	29	22	1	1		8	11	1,941,911	19
2002	30	19				2	8	740,460	93
2003	30	17	1	1		3	7	1,340,436	49
2004	27	19			1	4	7	1,259,234	58
Total	270	173	2	3	3	36	75	8,004,359	
NATIONWIDE TOUR									
1993	4	2					1	2,404	174
1994	4	2					1	3,920	151
1995	27	18	1		2	5	10	102,227	15
1996	1								
Total	36	22	1		2	5	12	108,551	

PGA TOUR TOP TOURNAMENT SUMMARY

Year	94	95	96	97	98	99	00	01	02	03	04
Masters						CUT			W/D		
U.S. Open	CUT		T67	CUT	T18		CUT	T52	T50		
British Open								T37	CUT		CUT
PGA					T4	CUT		T51	CUT	T29	W/D
THE PLAYERS					CUT	T23	T48	T7	T49	CUT	T3
TOUR Championship								T20			
WGC-Accenture Match Play									T33		
WGC-American Express Champ								CNL			

Peter Lonard (LAH-nard)

EXEMPT STATUS: 2003 International Presidents Cup Team Member (through 2005)
FULL NAME: Peter L. Lonard
HEIGHT: 6-0
WEIGHT: 225
BIRTHDATE: July 17, 1967
BIRTHPLACE: Sydney, Australia
RESIDENCE: Berkshire, England
FAMILY: Single
SPECIAL INTERESTS: Cars
TURNED PROFESSIONAL: 1989
Q SCHOOL: 2001

BEST PGA TOUR CAREER FINISH:

3—2002 Genuity Championship.

INTERNATIONAL VICTORIES (8):

1997 Ericsson Masters [Aus]. **2000** Ford Open Championship [Aus]. **2001** ANZ Championship [Aus]. **2002** Australian PGA Championship [shared with Jarrod Moseley], Australian MasterCard Masters. **2003** Australian Open. **2004** Australian Open, Australian PGA

OTHER VICTORIES (1):

2002 Hyundai Team Matches [with Rich Beem].

BEST 2004 PGA TOUR FINISH:

5—BellSouth Classic.

2004 SEASON:

Struggled in his third season on the PGA TOUR making only 12 cuts in 23 PGA TOUR starts...Notched first top-10 of season with solo fifth at BellSouth Classic, five strokes behind Zach Johnson...Held a one-stroke lead through the first round of the EDS Byron Nelson Championship. Was only two back after 36 holes but rounds of 71-74 dropped him to T48...Had a good showing at the Memorial Tournament with a T11 finish...Spent most of July in Europe and collected two top-five finishes on the European Tour during his visit—T5 at the Barclays Scottish Open and solo fourth at the Nissan Irish Open...First week of October collected $65,000 for his T23 finish at the WGC-American Express Championship in Ireland.

CAREER HIGHLIGHTS:

2003: Followed up spectacular rookie campaign with strong second season, finishing in the top 50 for the second consecutive season...Finished fourth at the WGC-Accenture Match Play Championship, earning $390,000. Defeated Kenny Perry, Phil Tataurangi, Robert Allenby and Darren Clarke before falling to eventual runner-up David Toms in the semifinals. Fell to Adam Scott in the consolation match...Posted four rounds in the 60s good for T9 at the EDS Byron Nelson Championship, his second top-10 of the season...Ended the season strong with a T9 at the Chrysler Championship...Played in his first Presidents Cup for International squad. **2002:** Rookie out of Qualifying School opened PGA TOUR career in workman-like fashion, making 22 consecutive cuts to start the season. For comparison, Tiger Woods opened his professional career with 25 consecutive made cuts...Became the ninth PGA TOUR rookie in history to surpass $1 million in earnings, finishing with $1,413,113...Picked up first career PGA TOUR top-10 with a third at the Genuity Championship...Second top 10 was T9 at Buick Classic, six strokes behind champion Chris Smith...Finished 11th at the U.S. Open for best career finish in a major championship, aided by a 3-under-par 67 on Sunday, the best final-round score among the 72 participants. Began the day T42...Surpassed $1 million in rookie-season earnings with his T5 check of $135,600 at the Advil Western Open...Only missed cut of the season was the Buick Challenge, despite shooting 4-under-par 140...Shared Australian PGA Championship with Jarrod Moseley when darkness ended playoff after one hole...Beat Gavin Coles and Adam Scott in playoff to win Australian MasterCard Masters for second time. **2001:** Started season in style by winning the ANZ Championship to finish second in the 2000-01 Australasian Tour Order of Merit...Finished 54th in European Tour Order of Merit, with one top 10 at the Moroccan Open (solo third)...Played in seven PGA TOUR events, with one top 25 at the Memorial Tournament (T15). Best finish in 15 career TOUR events before joining TOUR full-time in 2002. **2000:** Captured Ford Open on Australasian Tour. Missed portion of season after breaking a bone in his left wrist during the Volvo Scandinavian Masters in August...Had laser surgery on his eyes while recovering from injury. **1997:** Winner of Ericsson Australian Masters and topped Australasian Order of Merit in 1996-97.

PERSONAL:

In 1993-94, sidelined for nearly 18 months after contracting Ross River Fever, a mosquito-carried virus, which caused damage to the eyes. Developed conjunctivitis from over-wearing contact lenses...Club professional at Oatlands G&CC (1994-97) before playing way back onto PGA TOUR of Australasia and European Tour...Uses broom-handle putter...Enjoys motorsports including attending V8's at Bathurst...Lists fellow Aussies Greg Norman and tennis player Patrick Rafter as his heroes.

PLAYER STATISTICS

2004 PGA TOUR STATISTICS

Scoring Average	71.00	(80)
Driving Distance	291.4	(54)
Driving Accuracy Percentage	61.5%	(142)
Total Driving	196	(98)
Greens in Regulation Pct.	62.9%	(152)
Putting Average	1.819	(190)
Sand Save Percentage	47.1%	(124)
Eagles (Holes per)	169.7	(50)
Birdie Average	2.77	(195)
All-Around Ranking	987	(153)
Scoring Avg. Before Cut	71.95	(174)
Round 3 Scoring Avg.	70.91	(92)
Final Round Scoring Average	71.73	(109)
Birdie Conversion Percentage	23.9%	(195)
Par Breakers	16.0%	(194)

MISCELLANEOUS PGA TOUR STATISTICS

2004 Low Round/Round: 64–EDS Byron Nelson Championship/1
Career Low Round/Round: 64–2 times, most recent 2004 EDS Byron Nelson Championship/1
Career Largest Paycheck/Finish: $390,000–2003 WGC–Accenture Match Play Championship/4

PGA TOUR CAREER SUMMARY — PLAYOFF RECORD: 0-0

Year	Events Played	Cuts Made	1st	2nd	3rd	Top 10	Top 25	Earnings	Rank
1996	1								
1997	5	3					1	$37,537	221
1998	1								
1999	1	1						11,275	275
2001	7	3					1	91,172	
2002	24	23			1	4	14	1,413,113	41
2003	26	21				3	11	1,323,594	50
2004	23	12				1	5	675,189	118
Total	88	63			1	8	32	3,551,881	
EUROPEAN TOUR									
2004	4	4				2	2	304,033	

PGA TOUR TOP TOURNAMENT SUMMARY

Year	97	98	99	00	01	02	03	04
Masters							CUT	CUT
U.S. Open					T66	11	T20	T31
British Open	T24		T49		T47	T14	T59	CUT
PGA	CUT	CUT				T17	T29	CUT
THE PLAYERS							T56	CUT
WGC-Accenture Match Play							4	T17
WGC-NEC Invitational						T19	T23	T32
WGC-American Express Champ					CNL	T54	37	T23

NATIONAL TEAMS: The Presidents Cup, 2003.

Davis Love III

EXEMPT STATUS: Winner, 1997 PGA Championship (through 2007)
FULL NAME: Davis Milton Love III
HEIGHT: 6-3
WEIGHT: 175
BIRTHDATE: April 13, 1964
BIRTHPLACE: Charlotte, NC
RESIDENCE: Sea Island, GA; plays out of Sea Island

FAMILY: Wife, Robin; Alexia (6/5/88), Davis IV (12/4/93)
EDUCATION: University of North Carolina
SPECIAL INTERESTS: Fishing, reading novels, hunting, golf course architecture
TURNED PROFESSIONAL: 1985
Q SCHOOL: 1985

PGA TOUR VICTORIES (18):

1987 MCI Heritage Golf Classic. **1990** The International. **1991** MCI Heritage Golf Classic. **1992** THE PLAYERS Championship, MCI Heritage Golf Classic, KMart Greater Greensboro Open. **1993** Infiniti Tournament of Champions, Las Vegas Invitational. **1995** Freeport-McMoRan Classic. **1996** Buick Invitational. **1997** PGA Championship, Buick Challenge. **1998** MCI Classic. **2001** AT&T Pebble Beach National Pro-Am. **2003** AT&T Pebble Beach National Pro-Am, THE PLAYERS Championship, MCI Heritage, The INTERNATIONAL.

INTERNATIONAL VICTORIES (1):

1998 Chunichi Crowns [Jpn].

OTHER VICTORIES (8):

1992 World Cup of Golf [with Fred Couples]. **1993** World Cup of Golf [with Fred Couples]. **1994** World Cup of Golf [with Fred Couples]. **1995** World Cup of Golf [with Fred Couples], World Cup [indiv]. **2000** CVS Charity Classic [with Justin Leonard], Target World Challenge presented by Williams. **2003** Target World Challenge presented by Williams.

BEST 2004 PGA TOUR FINISHES:

2—WGC-Accenture Match Play Championship, The Honda Classic; 3—Sony Open in Hawaii; T4—WGC-NEC Invitational; T5—British Open Championship; T6—Masters Tournament; T7—Cialis Western Open; T9—Mercedes Championships.

2004 SEASON:

Surpassed the $2-million mark in earnings for the sixth straight season and went over $3 million for the second consecutive year. . .Highlight of season was two more runner-up finishes to bring his career total to 26, second-most by an active TOUR player behind Greg Norman's 31. . .Finished T9 to open season at Mercedes Championships, seventh top-10 in 11th career Mercedes start. . .One week later, posted second consecutive top-10 with a third-place finish at the Sony Open in Hawaii, aided by a third-round, 7-under 63. . .After missing cut in defense of AT&T Pebble Beach National Pro-Am title, came back strong at WGC-Accenture Match Play Championship, winning five matches (over Briny Baird, Fred Couples, Adam Scott, Phil Mickelson and Darren Clarke) before falling to Tiger Woods, 3 and 2, in the 36-hole championship match. Overall Accenture Match Play Championship record now stands at 11-6. . .Finished runner-up at The Honda Classic for the second straight time after closing with a 69. In 2003, lost the lead to hard-charging Justin Leonard. This time, applied the heat on 54-hole leader Todd Hamilton, playing mistake-free down the stretch, taking the lead on the 17th, and looked like the winner when he saved par on the 72nd hole of regulation. But Hamilton birdied the 17th and 18th holes to win by a stroke. . .Overcame first-round 75 to finish T6 at the Masters, sixth top-10 in Augusta in 15 starts. . .Earned fourth consecutive top-10 finish at Cog Hill, with a T7 at the Cialis Western Open in July. . .Posted his fifth top-10 in his last eight appearances at the British Open in Scotland, thanks in part to a final-round, 4-under 67, including an eagle-2 on the 18th hole, which jumped him from T15 to T5. . .Finished third on Ryder Cup team points list to make his sixth Ryder Cup squad. . .Finished T4 at the WGC-NEC Invitational, five strokes behind Stewart Cink. With paycheck of $282,500, became the third player in PGA TOUR history to exceed $3 million in earnings in a season without a victory. . .Pulled out of season-ending TOUR Championship with neck injury after 14 holes.

CAREER HIGHLIGHTS:

2003: Won a career-high four times and surpassed the $6-million mark in single-season earnings for first time in career. Led TOUR money list for 14 weeks and finished third overall...In second start of season, captured AT&T Pebble Beach National Pro-Am for the second time in three years, ending 44-tournament drought. Held two-stroke lead after 54 holes over Tom Lehman, Mike Weir and Rod Pampling with rounds of 72-67-67. Opened final round with bogeys on two of the first three holes, but battled back with seven birdies and only one bogey en route to a final-round 68. Clinched one-stroke victory over Lehman with two-putt birdie on par-5 18th hole after second shot approach with 4-iron from 224 yards settled to within 15 feet of cup...Finished T2 with Chad Campbell behind Justin Leonard at The Honda Classic. Held 54-hole lead by one over Leonard...Won his second PLAYERS Championship in 11 years. Paired with good friend Fred Couples on Sunday, tied final-round record with an 8-under 64 in windy conditions to come from two shots behind and win by six strokes over third-round leaders Jay Haas and Padraig Harrington...Captured fifth tartan jacket at the MCI Heritage at Harbour Town GL. Chipped in from 67 feet on 72nd hole to force sudden death with Woody Austin after four rounds in the 60s. Hit 6-iron approach on fourth playoff hole (No. 18) to three feet and converted birdie putt for third win of season...Became second player on the year to go wire-to-wire on his way to his second victory at The INTERNATIONAL (first came in 1990). Finished 12 points ahead of his nearest competitors—Retief Goosen and Vijay Singh. Surpassed $25-million mark in career earnings. Joined Phil Mickelson as only two players to win the Castle Pines, CO, event twice. Set the 36-hole point record with 36 points (Ernie Els/34 points/2000). Posted three eagles during the second round...Played in fifth Presidents Cup for the United States...Won second Target World Challenge in December and earned career-high paycheck (unofficial money) of $1.2 million. **2002:** Six top-10 finishes included posting runner-up finishes in back-to-back starts for the third time in his career with his T2 at the Canon Greater Hartford Open and second at the Advil Western Open. Final-round 66 in Chicago pulled him within two of winner Jerry Kelly. Second consecutive year he shot final-round 66 and placed second...Member of his fifth Ryder Cup team. Ryder Cup record was 2-1-1 for a five-year total of 8-9-3...Ended season with a T5 at THE TOUR Championship. Paycheck pushed him over the $2-million mark for the fourth consecutive season. **2001:** Returned to the winner's circle after a two-year drought. Earned first win since 1998 MCI Classic at AT&T Pebble Beach National Pro-Am. Entered final round seven strokes down and completed play one stroke up on Vijay Singh after 63. Front nine featured PGA TOUR record-tying birdie-eagle string: went

SECTION 2 PLAYER BIOGRAPHIES

PGA TOUR CAREER SUMMARY — PLAYOFF RECORD: 2-7

Year	Events Played	Cuts Made	1st	2nd	3rd	Top 10	Top 25	Earnings	Rank
1985A	1								
1986	31	22			1	2	7	$113,245	77
1987	26	18	1	1		4	9	297,378	33
1988	29	17				3	9	156,068	75
1989	24	17		1	1	4	10	278,760	44
1990	27	20	1		1	4	12	537,172	20
1991	28	23	1	1	1	8	14	686,361	8
1992	25	22	3	1	1	9	15	1,191,630	2
1993	26	23	2	1		5	12	777,059	12
1994	28	21		1		4	9	474,219	33
1995	24	22	1	1	1	9	15	1,111,999	6
1996	23	19	1	3		11	14	1,211,139	7
1997	25	24	2		1	13	17	1,635,953	3
1998	21	19	1	1	2	10	16	1,541,152	11
1999	23	21		4	2	13	17	2,475,328	3
2000	25	22		3	1	9	16	2,337,765	9
2001	20	17	1	3		12	15	3,169,463	5
2002	26	21		2		6	14	2,056,160	21
2003	23	20	4	1	1	11	16	6,081,896	3
2004	24	18		2	1	8	11	3,075,092	10
Total	479	386	18	26	14	145	248	29,207,838	

PGA TOUR TOP TOURNAMENT SUMMARY

Year	86	87	88	89	90	91	92	93	94	95	96	97	98
Masters			CUT			T42	T25	T54	CUT	2	T7	T7	T33
U.S. Open			CUT	T33		T11	T60	T33	T28	T4	T2	T16	CUT
British Open		CUT	CUT	T23	CUT	T44	CUT	CUT	T38	T98	CUT	T10	8
PGA	T47	CUT		T17	T40	T32	T33	T31	CUT	CUT	CUT	**1**	T7
THE PLAYERS	T14	CUT	DQ	CUT	T24	CUT	**1**	T67	T6	T6	T46	DQ	T57
TOUR Championship					T12	T19	T25	27		T16	13	3	T8

Year	99	00	01	02	03	04
Masters	2	T7	CUT	T14	T15	T6
U.S. Open	T12	CUT	T7	T24	CUT	CUT
British Open	T7	T11	T21	T14	T4	T5
PGA	T49	T9	T37	T48	CUT	CUT
THE PLAYERS	T10	T48	CUT	CUT	**1**	T33
TOUR Championship	2	T8	T15	T5	T5	W/D
WGC-Accenture Match Play	T33	4		T17	T17	2
WGC-NEC Invitational	T10	35	T5	T11	3	T4
WGC-American Express Champ	T16		CNL	8	T40	T41

NATIONAL TEAMS: Walker Cup, 1985; Dunhill Cup, 1992; World Cup (5), 1992, 1993, 1994, 1995, 1997; Ryder Cup (6), 1993, 1995, 1997, 1999, 2002, 2004; The Presidents Cup (5), 1994, 1996, 1998, 2000, 2003.

Davis Love III (Continued)

birdie-eagle-five birdies on holes 1-7. Seven-stroke comeback matched the best in tournament history (Bob Rosburg, 1961)...Decision to play in Buick Invitational was last minute, following his AT&T Pebble Beach National Pro-Am win. Fell just short in attempt at back-to-back wins. Stood one stroke back after first round, then moved into share of 36-hole lead. Closed with 67, forcing a three-way playoff with Phil Mickelson and Frank Lickliter II, eliminated with bogey on the second extra hole...Captured West Coast Swing presented by The St. Paul title...Withdrew from three events in May due to neck pain and disk problem that causes numbness in left arm and fingers. First experienced numbness at BellSouth Classic...After being off for two months, returned to T7 at U.S. Open...Lost head-to-head battle with Scott Hoch for Advil Western Open title. Held second- and third-round leads. Closing 66 left him one stroke shy of Hoch, who finished with 64. **2000:** A season of second- and third-place finishes. T18 at Phoenix Open, worth $41,728, moved him past Greg Norman and into first place on PGA TOUR career money list...Hold on career money position was short-lived, taken away by Tiger Woods, who finished T2 at Buick Invitational...En route to T3 finish at MCI Classic, toured course in 95 putts, tying for third-lowest total since TOUR began keeping stats in 1980...Shared first- and third-round lead and held second-round lead outright at GTE Byron Nelson Classic. Closing 69 resulted in a berth in the three-man playoff won by Jesper Parnevik...Member of his fourth President's Cup Team. 2000 President's Cup record 4-0-0 for a four-year total of 12-5-2...Won Williams World Challenge, shooting a final-round 64...Father Davis Love, Jr. selected posthumously as the recipient of Harvey Penick Teaching Award. **1999:** Though he went without a victory for the first time in four years, the season was still a success. Finished third on money list with career-high $2,475,328...13 top-10s included four runner-up finishes...Had to withdraw after three rounds of MCI Classic due to sore back. Was told to take week off, but as defending champion, wanted to play...Ailment diagnosed as recurring problem with lower back disk. Advised by doctors to take at least two weeks off between WGC-NEC Invitational and Ryder Cup to recover from pinched nerve in back. Injury first flared at Sprint International. Went 19 days without touching club. Pinched nerve caused pain in shoulder and back and numbness in fingers. **1998:** 13th career victory came at MCI Classic, which he had won three times previously. Posted a seven-stroke win over Glen Day. **1997:** Earned first major championship at PGA Championship at Winged Foot CC. Rounds of 66-71-66-66 gave him five-stroke victory over Justin Leonard...Earned second victory of year at the Buick Challenge where, after setting the 54-hole record at 189, he was a four-stroke winner over Stewart Cink. **1996:** In third start of season, trailed by four after 54 holes of Buick Invitational before posting final-round 64 for three-stroke win over Phil Mickelson...Three-time runner-up that year, finishing one behind Steve Jones at U.S. Open and losing playoffs to Michael Bradley at Buick Challenge and Tiger Woods at Las Vegas Invitational...Won World Cup individual title at TPC at Mission Hills in Shenzhen, China, defeating former PGA TOUR player Hisayuki Sasaki of Japan in a playoff. **1995:** After winless 1994, won Freeport-McMoRan Classic in playoff over Mike Heinen to earn place at the following week's Masters Tournament...At Augusta National, was T11, three strokes behind leaders through 54 holes, before closing with 66 to finish second, one behind Ben Crenshaw. **1993:** Won twice, at season-opening Infiniti Tournament of Champions and at year's final full-field event, Las Vegas Invitational. **1992:** First $1-million season, when he won three times in a five-week stretch: THE PLAYERS Championship, where he came from three strokes off the pace with closing 67 for four-stroke victory; third MCI Classic (previous wins 1987 and 1991); and Kmart Greater Greensboro Open. Erased three-stroke deficit entering final round of Kmart GGO with closing 62. **Amateur:** Winner of 1984 North and South Amateur and ACC Championship.

PERSONAL:

Father was highly regarded teacher who died in a plane crash in 1988. Davis III was born shortly after his father contended at 1964 Masters. Wrote book, "Every Shot I Take," to honor his dad's lessons and teachings on golf and life. Book was named recipient of 1997 USGA International Book Award...Conducts charity event to benefit Safe Harbour...Brother, Mark, has caddied for Davis and also involved in golf course design...Inducted into University of North Carolina Order of Merit in 1997...Named honorary chairman for PGA of America's National Golf Day in June 1998...Inducted into the Georgia Golf Hall of Fame in Augusta in January 2001...Owns and raises horses, with a seven-stall barn at home. Daughter, Lexie, is a nationally ranked competitive rider in the adult division on Paso Fino horses...Love Enterprises and Associates redesigned Forest Oaks CC, site of the Chrysler Classic of Greensboro, with the redesigned course debuting in 2003...Travels to many PGA TOUR events on Featherlite custom bus... Featured in episode of Orange County Chopper, a pop culture TV show. Love was given a custom-built motorcycle by his wife for his 40th birthday.

PLAYER STATISTICS

2004 PGA TOUR STATISTICS

Scoring Average	70.13	(16)
Driving Distance	300.1	(14)
Driving Accuracy Percentage	60.1%	(151)
Total Driving	165	(57)
Greens in Regulation Pct.	64.2%	(115)
Putting Average	1.753	(31)
Sand Save Percentage	51.9%	(57)
Eagles (Holes per)	150.0	(35)
Birdie Average	3.71	(57)
All-Around Ranking	476	(19)
Scoring Avg. Before Cut	71.19	(125)
Round 3 Scoring Avg.	69.94	(30)
Final Round Scoring Average	70.44	(23)
Birdie Conversion Percentage	30.8%	(44)
Par Breakers	21.3%	(42)

MISCELLANEOUS PGA TOUR STATISTICS

2004 Low Round/Round: 63–Sony Open in Hawaii/3
Career Low Round/Round: 60–1994 United Airlines Hawaiian Open/2
Career Largest Paycheck/Finish: $1,170,000–2003 THE PLAYERS Championship/1

Steve Lowery (LAU-ree)

EXEMPT STATUS: 66th on 2004 money list
FULL NAME: Stephen Brent Lowery
HEIGHT: 6-2
WEIGHT: 225
BIRTHDATE: October 12, 1960
BIRTHPLACE: Birmingham, AL
RESIDENCE: Birmingham, AL

FAMILY: Wife, Heather; Kristen Branch (12/27/91), Lauren Elizabeth (5/30/95), Stephen Brent, Jr. (1/25/98)
EDUCATION: University of Alabama
SPECIAL INTERESTS: Hunting, fishing, Alabama football
TURNED PROFESSIONAL: 1983
Q SCHOOL: 1987
Nationwide Tour Alumnus

PGA TOUR VICTORIES (2):
1994 Sprint International. **2000** Southern Farm Bureau Classic.

NATIONWIDE TOUR VICTORIES (1):
1992 Tulsa Open.

BEST 2004 PGA TOUR FINISHES:
2—Cialis Western Open; T3—FedEx St. Jude Classic.

2004 SEASON:
Finished in the top 100 (66th) for the 11th time in last 12 seasons on TOUR. . .Held a share of the 36-hole lead at the Shell Houston Open. Finished T19 after third-round 4-over-par 76. . .First top-10 came in 15th start at the FedEx St. Jude Classic. Closing 67 at the TPC of Southwind good for T3 in Memphis. . .Sank an eight-foot putt on the 72nd hole at the Cialis Western Open to finish solo second, earning one of the last exemptions into the British Open. Shared second-round lead with Matt Gogel and Charles Howell III at 6-under 136, and trailed by two at the 54-hole mark. His $518,400 payday marked a career-best for the 17-year veteran.

CAREER HIGHLIGHTS:
2003: Carded an ace on No. 6 at Indian Wells CC during the third round of the Bob Hope Chrysler Classic...Held the outright lead through the first three rounds of the B.C. Open but a closing 72 and a 9-under-par 63 by Champions Tour player Craig Stadler dropped Lowery into T2. Opened with a pair of 64s to match the 36-hole tournament record of 128 and matched the 54-hole record of 196...Finished solo third at Las Vegas Invitational, three behind Stuart Appleby and Scott McCarron. **2002:** Thanks to three runner-up finishes (Greater Milwaukee Open, The INTERNATIONAL and Air Canada), earned a career-best $1,885,553 and gained a spot in THE TOUR Championship for the third time in career...Missed 10-foot birdie putt on 18th hole at The INTERNATIONAL which would have given him the win by one over Rich Beem. In his final five holes, Lowery had a birdie on the par-5 14th after getting up and down from a water hazard, a hole-out eagle on the par-4 15th and hole-out double eagle on the par-5 17th (6-iron from 200 yards). **2001:** Returned to THE TOUR Championship for the first time since 1994 by placing 27th in earnings. It was only the second top-30 finish in his career...Finished third at PGA Championship, three strokes behind winner David Toms. The showing lifted him to 12th in the final Ryder Cup standings. **2000:** His second career victory at the Southern Farm Bureau Classic crowned a season that included nine top-10 finishes. In season-ending victory, opened with 64 for share of lead with Frank Lickliter. Followed with a 67 and 65 for solo lead through 36 and 54 holes. Took three-stroke lead into final round, shot 37 on the front nine and then birdied three of his final six holes to finish tied with Skip Kendall. In playoff, ran in 45-foot birdie putt from the fringe on the first extra hole for the title. **1997:** Challenged TOUR scoring record in final round at Buick Challenge where he was 10-under through 13 holes. He needed to birdie three of the final five holes to equal record but parred 14, 15 and 16 before birdies at 17 and 18 gave him a 60 and a third-place finish. It was the first 60 on TOUR since Grant Waite's at 1996 Phoenix Open. **1994:** First PGA TOUR victory came at the Sprint International. Tied with Rick Fehr with 35 points through 72 holes and then won playoff on first extra hole when Fehr's ball found water. Victory was worth $252,000, more than he had earned in any previous season on TOUR...Year also included T2 at Buick Invitational, one stroke behind Craig Stadler, and T3 at NEC World Series of Golf where he held a one-stroke lead through 54 holes at Firestone before closing 72 left him two behind winner Jose Maria Olazabal. **1992:** Used his play on 1992 Nationwide Tour to return to the PGA TOUR in 1993. Won Tulsa Open to finish third on the money list. **1990:** Earned Special Temporary Membership in 1990 and 1991 by earning as much as 150th-place finisher on previous year's money list. **1988:** Lost card after finishing 157th on money list. **1987:** First earned playing privileges at Qualifying Tournament. **Amateur:** 1982 and 1983 All-American and Southeastern Conference Player of the Year while at the University of Alabama.

PERSONAL:
Alabama Crimson Tide football and Atlanta Braves baseball fan. . .Received 1995 Singleton Award as Outstanding Professional Athlete in Alabama. . .Enjoys quail hunting in south Alabama and snow skiing in Beaver Creek, CO.

PLAYER STATISTICS

2004 PGA TOUR STATISTICS

Scoring Average	71.42	(130)
Driving Distance	288.8	(79)
Driving Accuracy Percentage	58.3%	(172)
Total Driving	251	(169)
Greens in Regulation Pct.	63.9%	(122)
Putting Average	1.769	(70)
Sand Save Percentage	43.8%	(161)
Eagles (Holes per)	228.9	(92)
Birdie Average	3.61	(76)
All-Around Ranking	902	(135)
Scoring Avg. Before Cut	71.36	(138)
Round 3 Scoring Avg.	71.56	(144)
Final Round Scoring Average	71.63	(97)
Birdie Conversion Percentage	30.6%	(50)
Par Breakers	20.5%	(72)

MISCELLANEOUS PGA TOUR STATISTICS

2004 Low Round/Round: 64–2 times, most recent Michelin Championship at Las Vegas/1
Career Low Round/Round: 60–1997 Buick Challenge/4
Career Largest Paycheck/Finish: $518,400–2004 Cialis Western Open/2

PGA TOUR CAREER SUMMARY — PLAYOFF RECORD: 2-0

Year	Events Played	Cuts Made	1st	2nd	3rd	Top 10	Top 25	Earnings	Rank
1983	2								
1984	1								
1986	1	1						$666	287
1987	4	2						4,190	233
1988	34	17					2	44,327	157
1989	11	7				3	3	38,699	174
1990	8	6				2	2	68,524	159
1991	10	7			1	2	3	87,597	143
1992	7	4					2	22,608	207
1993	32	25				1	8	188,287	92
1994	30	20	1	1	1	5	9	794,048	12
1995	30	25				6	15	463,858	38
1996	31	21				2	7	263,505	80
1997	30	20			2	5	9	480,467	44
1998	28	16			1	4	8	409,940	70
1999	30	19				2	6	385,937	104
2000	30	23	1	1		9	14	1,543,818	31
2001	28	23		1	2	6	11	1,738,820	27
2002	28	21		3		5	10	1,882,553	30
2003	29	15		1	1	2	5	932,293	77
2004	28	17		1	1	2	5	1,191,245	66
Total	432	289	2	8	9	56	119	10,541,382	
NATIONWIDE TOUR									
1990	3	2					1	1,420	179
1991	5	2		1		1	1	10,363	93
1992	21	19	1	2	1	7	14	114,553	3
Total	29	23	1	3	1	8	16	126,336	

PGA TOUR TOP TOURNAMENT SUMMARY

Year	88	89	90	91	92	93	94	95	96	97	98	99	00
Masters								CUT	T41				
U.S. Open	CUT					T33	T16	T56	T60			CUT	
British Open								T79					
PGA							CUT	T8	CUT	T58	T44		T51
THE PLAYERS							T6	DQ	T46	T65	CUT	CUT	T66
TOUR Championship							T8						

Year	01	02	03	04
Masters	T40	T40	CUT	
U.S. Open	T24	CUT	T42	
British Open				T36
PGA	3	T10	CUT	CUT
THE PLAYERS	CUT	T22	W/D	CUT
TOUR Championship	25	T13		
WGC-Accenture Match Play	T33	T17	T17	
WGC-NEC Invitational		8		
WGC-American Express Champ	CNL	T15		

Andrew Magee

EXEMPT STATUS: Major Medical Extension
FULL NAME: Andrew Donald Magee
HEIGHT: 6-0
WEIGHT: 180
BIRTHDATE: May 22, 1962
BIRTHPLACE: Paris, France
RESIDENCE: Paradise Valley, AZ
FAMILY: Wife, three children

EDUCATION: University of Oklahoma (1984)
SPECIAL INTERESTS: Travel, swimming, fishing, whistling
TURNED PROFESSIONAL: 1984
Q SCHOOL: 1984

PGA TOUR VICTORIES (4):

1988 Pensacola Open. **1991** Nestle Invitational, Las Vegas Invitational. **1994** Northern Telecom Open.

BEST 2004 PGA TOUR FINISHES:

T6—Chrysler Classic of Tucson; T8—Buick Open; T9—EDS Byron Nelson Championship.

2004 SEASON:

Did not play due to Achilles tendon surgery (Oct. 24, 2003) and subsequent rehabilitation. Will receive a Major Medical Extension for the 2005 campaign. Has the opportunity to play in 29 events and match the $623,262 winnings of 2004's No. 125, Tag Ridings. If he does so, will play out of the Major Medical Extension category for the remainder of the season.

CAREER HIGHLIGHTS:

2003: Finished among the top 125 for the 18th time in 19 seasons on TOUR...A final-round 68 at Omni Tucson National Golf Resort vaulted him to a T6 finish at the Chrysler Classic of Tucson, his best finish since a T3 at the 2002 AT&T Pebble Beach National Pro-Am...Recorded four rounds in the 60s at the EDS Byron Nelson Championship to finish T9, his second top-10 of the season...One week after withdrawing from Greater Hartford Open due to the death of his mother, finished T8 at the Buick Open, five shots behind champion Jim Furyk. **2002:** Used Top-50 career money winners exemption for 2002. Actually 51st, but with the ranking of the late Payne Stewart (No. 15), moved into top 50...T3 at the AT&T Pebble Beach National Pro-Am, his first top-10 on the PGA TOUR since the 2000 Tampa Bay Classic and first top-3 finish since the 2000 Greater Greensboro Chrysler Classic...Closed with 64 at the John Deere Classic good for T10, his second top-10 of the season. **2001:** Fell to 180th on the money list with uncharacteristic season...T25 at the Invensys Classic of Las Vegas produced lone top-25 finish of the season...Made history in the first round of the Phoenix Open, recording an ace on the 333-yard, par-4 17th hole. Magee's drive bounded onto the green at the TPC of Scottsdale, caromed off Tom Byrum's putter and went into the hole for what was believed to be the first hole-in-one on a par 4 in PGA TOUR history. "It looked like a hole-in-one and sounded like a hole-in-one. But I still wasn't sure it was one," Magee said. Byrum was squatting down looking over a putt when the ball deflected off his putter and rolled about 8 feet directly into the hole for a rare double-eagle ace. Magee's opening 66 was two strokes behind leaders Brad Elder, Scott Verplank and Tom Lehman. Finished T44. **2000:** Four top-10 finishes were most since 1998, while earnings of $867,372 were third most of his career and ranked 55th on official money list...Extended streak of years with a runner-up finish to five...Best finish of season came at Greater Greensboro Chrysler Classic where four sub-par rounds produced a lone second-place finish and season-high $324,000 payday. **1999:** Bulk of earnings came in one week when he finished second and earned $500,000 in the WGC-Accenture Match Play Championship. Had victories over Darren Clarke (1-up), Thomas Bjorn (2 and 1), Bill Glasson (1-up), Shigeki Maruyama (1-up) and John Huston (3 and 1) before losing to Jeff Maggert. **1998:** Earned career-best $964,302 and had one runner-up and a pair of third-place finishes. Finished 30th on official money list for second consecutive year...Rounds of 67-71-68-69 produced Memorial Tournament runner-up finish, four strokes behind Fred Couples. **1997:** Came close twice to first victory since 1994 Northern Telecom Open with second-place finishes at Greater Vancouver Open and B.C. Open. Held one-stroke lead in final round of B.C. Open, but bogey on No. 16 opened door for Gabriel Hjertstedt to claim title by one stroke...Seven top-10s his best since 1991, when he also had seven. **1996:** Ended the season with five top-10s. **1994:** Most recent victory came at Northern Telecom Open. Closing 67 gave him a two-stroke margin over Loren Roberts, Vijay Singh, Jay Don Blake and Steve Stricker. **1988:** First TOUR victory came at Pensacola Open, where he rallied from four strokes back on final day. **1991:** Strong early-season run culminated in second career victory at rain-shortened Nestle Invitational over Tom Sieckmann. 30-foot eagle putt at 16 on final day was margin of victory...Later that year, shot 31-under-par 329, then the 90-hole scoring record, to force playoff with D.A. Weibring at Las Vegas Invitational. Won playoff with par on second extra hole. **Amateur:** Three-time All-American at University of Oklahoma...Won 1979 Doug Sanders Junior Invitational.

PERSONAL:

Born in Paris, where his father worked in the oil business...With Gary McCord, conducts Santa Claus Open, annual charity pro-am at TPC of Scottsdale...With Scott Verplank and Brian Watts, runs ClubCorp Pro-Am in Dallas to benefit health clinic at his former junior high school...Finished third at the 1998 Bob Hope Chrysler Classic one week after tangling with chainsaw at his Phoenix home while cutting a limb. Saw slipped and hit his left index finger. In comment that typifies his unique sense of humor, remarked: "There are better ways to weaken the grip on your left hand, don't you think?"...Won 1999 Southern Company Citizenship Award for work with charities.

PLAYER STATISTICS

2004 PGA TOUR STATISTICS

Scoring Average	71.03	(89)
Driving Distance	299.3	(14)
Driving Accuracy Percentage	60.5%	(166)
Total Driving	180	(72)
Greens in Regulation Pct.	68.0%	(39)
Putting Average	1.783	(112)
Sand Save Percentage	51.5%	(75)
Eagles (Holes per)	133.5	(25)
Birdie Average	3.55	(110)
All-Around Ranking	630	(57)
Scoring Avg. Before Cut	70.48	(51)
Round 3 Scoring Avg.	70.53	(85)
Final Round Scoring Average	71.06	(93)
Birdie Conversion Percentage	28.7%	(128)
Par Breakers	20.5%	(100)

MISCELLANEOUS PGA TOUR STATISTICS

2004 Low Round/Round: 64–2 times, most recent Buick Open/2
Career Low Round/Round: 62–2 times, most recent 1996 Quad City Classic/4
Career Largest Paycheck/Finish: $500,000–1999 WGC–Accenture Match Play Championship/2

PGA TOUR CAREER SUMMARY — PLAYOFF RECORD: 1-0

Year	Events Played	Cuts Made	1st	2nd	3rd	Top 10	Top 25	Earnings	Rank
1984	3	1						$1,701	238
1985	31	18				4	5	75,593	99
1986	33	17				1	5	69,478	120
1987	33	18				2	7	94,598	99
1988	30	17	1		1	4	8	261,954	43
1989	33	19				3	5	126,770	109
1990	30	22				3	8	210,507	71
1991	28	19	2			7	12	750,082	5
1992	28	21				3	12	285,946	53
1993	25	14		1		2	7	269,986	62
1994	25	20	1			3	9	431,041	36
1995	27	18				3	5	256,918	72
1996	26	13		1	1	3	7	332,504	60
1997	29	23		2		7	15	752,007	30
1998	29	19		1	2	6	12	964,302	30
1999	27	17		1		2	8	911,565	42
2000	26	14		1		4	8	867,372	55
2001	31	16					1	175,108	180
2002	28	17			1	2	6	543,035	122
2003	26	19				3	4	578,558	116
Total	548	342	4	7	5	62	144	7,959,025	

PGA TOUR TOP TOURNAMENT SUMMARY

Year	85	86	87	88	89	90	91	92	93	94	95	96	97
Masters					CUT		T7	T19	T31	T41			
U.S. Open		CUT		CUT		CUT	CUT	T17			CUT		
British Open				CUT			T57	T5	T39	CUT			T36
PGA		CUT		69	CUT	T45	T13	T56	T51	T47			75
THE PLAYERS	CUT	CUT	CUT	CUT	CUT	T36	CUT	T17	T20	T45	T37	CUT	T53
TOUR Championship							T19						T15

Year	98	99	00	01	02	03
Masters	T31	T36				
U.S. Open	CUT	CUT	CUT			
British Open	CUT	CUT				
PGA	T21	T54	CUT			
THE PLAYERS	CUT	CUT	CUT	CUT		CUT
TOUR Championship	T21					
WGC-Accenture Match Play		2	T33			

Jeff Maggert (MAG-ert)

EXEMPT STATUS: 43rd on 2004 money list
FULL NAME: Jeffrey Allan Maggert
HEIGHT: 5-9
WEIGHT: 165
BIRTHDATE: February 20, 1964
BIRTHPLACE: Columbia, MO
RESIDENCE: Houston, TX
FAMILY: Wife, Michelle; five children
EDUCATION: Texas A&M
SPECIAL INTERESTS: Fishing, hunting, camping, sporting events
TURNED PROFESSIONAL: 1986
JOINED TOUR: 1991
Nationwide Tour Alumnus

PGA TOUR VICTORIES (2):

1993 Walt Disney World/Oldsmobile Classic. **1999** WGC-Accenture Match Play Championship.

NATIONWIDE TOUR VICTORIES (2):

1990 Knoxville Open, Buffalo Open.

INTERNATIONAL VICTORIES (2):

1989 Malaysian Open [Asia]. **1990** Vines Classic [Aus]

OTHER VICTORIES (2):

1994 Diners Club Matches [with Jim McGovern]. **1997** Diners Club Matches [with Steve Elkington].

BEST 2004 PGA TOUR FINISHES:

2—AT&T Pebble Beach National Pro-Am; 3—U.S. Open Championship; T5—Wachovia Championship; T9—Bank of America Colonial; T10—Nissan Open.

2004 SEASON:

With five top-10s, over $1.5 million in earnings and a No. 43 finish on the PGA TOUR money list, had his best season since 2000 when he posted six top-10s and finished 39th on the money list...Finished second, three strokes behind Vijay Singh at the AT&T Pebble Beach National Pro-Am. Final-round 69 was one of only five Sunday rounds in the 60s. His best effort since a T2 at the 2000 Buick Challenge—a span of 85 starts...Posted his second top-10 of the season, with a T10 finish at the Nissan Open...The next week withdrew after the first round from the Chrysler Classic of Tucson because of a sore left shoulder...Was among the leaders all week at the Wachovia Championship. Was only two back of the lead through 54 holes, but a final-round 72 dropped him to T5...Two weeks later, finished T9 at the Bank of America Colonial for his fourth top-10 of the season...Finished in the top-10 for the seventh time in 14 U.S. Open appearances with his third-place finish. Matched his previous best Open finish, a third in 2002, which also came in New York at Bethpage Black...Did not play much toward the end of the season due to the birth of his twins the week of the PGA Championship.

CAREER HIGHLIGHTS:

2003: Finished among the top 100 for the 13th consecutive season on TOUR...Solo third-round leader at Masters after a 66. Final-round 75 resulted in a career-best fifth-place finish and included a triple bogey on the par-4 third hole when his second shot out of a fairway bunker caromed into his body and an 8 on the par-3 12th when he hit the ball in Rae's Creek twice...Thanks to a tournament-tying course record 64 on Sunday he moved into a T6 at the Shell Houston Open to post back-to-back top-10s for the first time since the 2000 season. **2002:** Broke the $10-million barrier in career earnings, and entered 2003 season 28th all-time with $10,006,019...First top-10 of season at Phoenix Open. T8 finish earned $100,000 paycheck...Second-round hole-in-one on the 180-yard 17th hole with an 8-iron at the Compaq Classic of New Orleans...Earned sixth top-10 in his last nine U.S. Open appearances. Two-over-par total of 282 was good for solo third, five strokes behind champion Tiger Woods. Solo third finish matched previous best finish in a major at the 1997 PGA Championship. Earned season-best paycheck of $362,356. **2001:** Dropped to 72nd in earnings with four top-10s, the fewest since 1992...Season-best finish was T4 at the Greater Greensboro Chrysler Classic...Made double eagle on the par-5 sixth hole in the first round of the British Open to become first player with an albatross in the British Open and the Masters. Made double eagle on No. 13 at Augusta National in fourth round in 1994. **2000:** Earned second-best season total of 10-year career with $1,138,749. That total was good for 39th on money list and marked ninth consecutive year in which he has placed among the top-40. Had six top-10s, including T2 at Buick Challenge. **1999:** Notched second career win on the way to earning career-best $2,016,469. Became just the 10th player at that time to record $2 million in single-season earnings. As the 24th seed, won five matches on his way to the title in the inaugural WGC-Accenture Match Play Championship... Participated in his third Ryder Cup and had a record of 2-2-0 at Brookline. **1997:** A sterling final round at PGA Championship, where he closed with 65 to finish third, brought a position on that year's Ryder Cup team. **1996:** For the second time recorded nine top-10s, including three second-place finishes. **1995:** Posted a 2-2 record in the Ryder Cup. **1994:** Compiled a 2-2 record at Presidents Cup. **1994:** Teamed with Jim McGovern to win PGA TOUR division of Diners Club Matches. **1993:** Earned first PGA TOUR victory at Walt Disney World/Oldsmobile Classic by three strokes over Greg Kraft. Victory came under floodlights at the end of a day in which he played 36 holes due to weather delays earlier in the week. **1991:** Second only to John Daly in rookie earnings with $240,940. **1990:** Nationwide Tour Player of the Year with earnings of $108,644 and victories in Knoxville and Buffalo...Was Vines Classic (Australian Tour) champion. **1989:** Won Malaysian Open. **Amateur:** All-American at Texas A&M in 1986.

PLAYER STATISTICS

2004 PGA TOUR STATISTICS

Scoring Average	70.68	(44)
Driving Distance	281.2	(148)
Driving Accuracy Percentage	69.2%	(35)
Total Driving	183	(77)
Greens in Regulation Pct.	67.5%	(37)
Putting Average	1.789	(127)
Sand Save Percentage	49.5%	(87)
Eagles (Holes per)	216.0	(80)
Birdie Average	3.53	(97)
All-Around Ranking	655	(65)
Scoring Avg. Before Cut	70.60	(48)
Round 3 Scoring Avg.	71.00	(101)
Final Round Scoring Average	72.70	(165)
Birdie Conversion Percentage	28.5%	(109)
Par Breakers	20.1%	(96)

MISCELLANEOUS PGA TOUR STATISTICS

2004 Low Round/Round: 66–3 times, most recent Bank of America Colonial/1
Career Low Round/Round: 62–1999 Greater Greensboro Chrysler Classic/2
Career Largest Paycheck/Finish: $1,000,000–1999 WGC–Accenture Match Play Championship/1

PGA TOUR CAREER SUMMARY — PLAYOFF RECORD: 0-1

Year	Events Played	Cuts Made	1st	2nd	3rd	Top 10	Top 25	Earnings	Rank
1986	4	1				1	1	$13,400	192
1987	4	1						936	293
1990	2	1						2,060	277
1991	29	17				2	9	240,940	68
1992	26	19			2	4	9	377,408	38
1993	28	17	1	2	1	6	13	793,023	11
1994	26	22		2	2	11	14	814,475	9
1995	23	17		1	1	5	10	527,952	34
1996	26	20		3		9	12	804,955	23
1997	27	19		2	1	6	10	835,884	26
1998	24	18		2		8	12	992,964	27
1999	23	20	1	1	1	6	10	2,016,469	9
2000	27	17		1	1	6	11	1,138,749	39
2001	27	15				4	7	713,607	72
2002	27	14			1	2	5	733,198	94
2003	24	16				2	5	747,166	86
2004	20	11		1	1	5	5	1,527,884	43
Total	367	245	2	15	11	77	133	12,281,068	
NATIONWIDE TOUR									
1990	22	20	2	3	1	13	17	108,644	1
Total	22	20	2	3	1	13	17	108,644	
EUROPEAN TOUR									
2004	1	1				1	1	75,945	

PGA TOUR TOP TOURNAMENT SUMMARY

Year	86	87	88	89	90	91	92	93	94	95	96	97	98
Masters								T21	T50	CUT	T7	CUT	T23
U.S. Open	CUT	CUT						T52	T9	T4	T97	4	T7
British Open							CUT	CUT	T24	T68	T5	T51	CUT
PGA							6	T51	CUT	T3	T73	3	T44
THE PLAYERS						CUT	T54	CUT	3	T18	T53	CUT	T51
TOUR Championship								15	7		T27	29	16

Year	99	00	01	02	03	04
Masters	CUT	CUT	T20		5	CUT
U.S. Open	T7	CUT	T44	3	CUT	3
British Open	T30	T41	CUT	T47		
PGA	CUT	CUT	CUT	CUT	CUT	
THE PLAYERS	T46	T3	CUT	T14	T11	T33
TOUR Championship	20					
WGC-Accenture Match Play	**1**	T33				
WGC-NEC Invitational	T7	T24				
WGC-American Express Champ	T48	39				

NATIONAL TEAMS: The Presidents Cup, 1994; Ryder Cup (3), 1995, 1997, 1999.

Hunter Mahan (MAY-han)

EXEMPT STATUS: 100th on 2004 money list
FULL NAME: Hunter Myles Mahan
HEIGHT: 5-11
WEIGHT: 175
BIRTHDATE: May 17, 1982
BIRTHPLACE: Orange, CA
RESIDENCE: Keller, TX
FAMILY: Single

EDUCATION: Oklahoma State University
SPECIAL INTERESTS: Fishing, basketball
TURNED PROFESSIONAL: 2003
Q SCHOOL: 2003

BEST PGA TOUR CAREER FINISH:

T2—2004 Reno-Tahoe Open.

BEST 2004 PGA TOUR FINISHES:

T2—Reno-Tahoe Open; T4—Bell Canadian Open; T5—Valero Texas Open.

2004 SEASON:

At age 21 when the season kicked off, was second-youngest player on TOUR, behind fellow rookie Kevin Na. . .Finished 100th on the PGA TOUR money list on the strength of three top-five finishes. . .Posted his first career top-10 in his 29th professional PGA TOUR start with T2 finish at the Reno-Tahoe Open. Made a 14-foot putt to save par at the 72nd hole of regulation and qualify for the four-man playoff. Rookie Vaughn Taylor claimed his first TOUR victory, rolling in an 11-foot birdie putt on the first extra hole to win. . .Three weeks later, posted his second top-10, a T4 at the Bell Canadian Open. . .Posted second consecutive top-10 at the Valero Texas Open, aided by four rounds in the 60s. Entered final round in second place, thanks to third-round 62. Played in the last group on Sunday with eventual champion Bart Bryant and posted final-round 69 to finish T5.

CAREER HIGHLIGHTS:

2003: Finished T16 at 2003 PGA TOUR Qualifying Tournament to earn his first TOUR card for the following season...Made the cut and finished 28th at the Masters. Turned professional after missing the cut at the U.S. Open, and made four cuts in seven starts. **Amateur:** Co-recipient with Ricky Barnes of 2003 Ben Hogan Award and also won the Jack Nicklaus Award and Fred Haskins Award as top collegiate golfer in 2003...No. 1 Amateur in the Golfweek/Sagarin Ratings in 2003...Runner-up to Ricky Barnes at the 2002 U.S. Amateur and placed third at the 2002 NCAA Championships...Two-time member of the U.S. Palmer Cup team...Two-time first-team All-America selection at OSU...Two-time Big 12 Player of the Year (2002-03)...Began collegiate career at Southern California before transferring to OSU after earning second-team All-America honors, as well as Pac-10 Freshman of the Year in 2001...American Junior Golf Association Player of the Year in 1999 and a three-time AJGA All-American. Winner of 1999 U.S. Junior Amateur.

PLAYER STATISTICS

2004 PGA TOUR STATISTICS

Scoring Average	71.31	(117)
Driving Distance	293.0	(45)
Driving Accuracy Percentage	62.2%	(131)
Total Driving	176	(69)
Greens in Regulation Pct.	63.7%	(129)
Putting Average	1.775	(86)
Sand Save Percentage	45.8%	(142)
Eagles (Holes per)	188.0	(64)
Birdie Average	3.52	(99)
All-Around Ranking	813	(112)
Scoring Avg. Before Cut	71.44	(142)
Round 3 Scoring Avg.	71.22	(120)
Final Round Scoring Average	71.38	(81)
Birdie Conversion Percentage	29.8%	(74)
Par Breakers	20.1%	(96)

MISCELLANEOUS PGA TOUR STATISTICS

2004 Low Round/Round: 62–Valero Texas Open/3
Career Low Round/Round: 62–2004 Valero Texas Open/3
Career Largest Paycheck/Finish: $224,000–2004 Reno–Tahoe Open/T2

PGA TOUR CAREER SUMMARY — PLAYOFF RECORD: 0-1

Year	Events Played	Cuts Made	1st	2nd	3rd	Top 10	Top 25	Earnings	Rank
2000A	1								
2002A	1								
2003A	2	1							
2003	7	4					2	$106,300	
2004	30	16		1		3	6	813,089	100
Total	41	21		1		3	8	919,389	
EUROPEAN TOUR									
2003	1	1						10,159	

PGA TOUR TOP TOURNAMENT SUMMARY

Year	03	04
Masters	T28	
U.S. Open	CUT	
British Open		T36

NATIONAL TEAMS: World Amateur Team Championship, 2002.

Shigeki Maruyama

EXEMPT STATUS: 2003 tournament winner (through 2005)
FULL NAME: Shigeki Maruyama
HEIGHT: 5-7
WEIGHT: 185
BIRTHDATE: September 12, 1969
BIRTHPLACE: Chiba, Japan
RESIDENCE: Chiba, Japan; Los Angeles, CA

FAMILY: Wife, Mizuho; Sean (6/2/00)
EDUCATION: Nihon University
TURNED PROFESSIONAL: 1992
JOINED TOUR: 2000

PGA TOUR VICTORIES (3):
2001 Greater Milwaukee Open. **2002** Verizon Byron Nelson Classic. **2003** Chrysler Classic of Greensboro.

INTERNATIONAL VICTORIES (9):
1993 Pepsi Ubekousan [Jpn]. **1995** Bridgestone Open [Jpn]. **1996** Bridgestone Open [Jpn]. **1997** PGA Championship [Jpn], Pocari Sweat Yomiuri Open [Jpn], PGA Match Play Promise Cup [Jpn], Golf Nippon Hitachi Cup [Jpn]. **1998** PGA Philanthropy Open [Jpn]. **1999** Bridgestone Open [Jpn].

BEST 2004 PGA TOUR FINISHES:
2—Nissan Open; T4—Buick Invitational, U.S. Open Championship; T6—Bay Hill Invitational Presented by MasterCard, Deutsche Bank Championship; T7—EDS Byron Nelson Championship.

2004 SEASON:
Solidified claim as the most successful Japanese golfer in PGA TOUR history, finishing inside the top 30 for the second time in career...In his fourth event of the season, picked up his first top-10, a T4, at the Buick Invitational...Was five back of lead going into the final round of Nissan Open. Fired a closing-round 67 to finish one back of 54-hole leader Mike Weir. Missed a 12-foot par putt on the 72nd hole...Shared first-round lead with eventual winner Chad Campbell and Darren Clarke at the Bay Hill Invitational Presented by MasterCard. Also held second-round lead but finished T6 after rounds of 75-73 on the weekend...Pair of 66s on the weekend at the EDS Byron Nelson Championship good for T7 finish and his fourth top-10 of the season...Posted his career-best finish in a major and just his second top-10 (T5, 2002 British Open) with a T4 at the U.S. Open. Shared first-round lead with Jay Haas and Angel Cabrera after opening-round 4-under 66, and shared second-round lead with Phil Mickelson at 6-under 134...Posted his career-high sixth top-10, a T6 at the Deutsche Bank Championship, topping the five recorded during the 2000 season.

CAREER HIGHLIGHTS:
2003: Despite being plagued by nagging neck injury during the early season, finished 37th on money list for third time in four years on the strength of win at the Chrysler Classic of Greensboro...Opened season with a T7 at the Sony Open in Hawaii...recorded a hole-in-one for the third straight season when he aced the eighth hole with a 6-iron from 177 yards during the first round of the MasterCard Colonial...One of only five players to collect a win in each of the last three seasons (Tiger Woods, Justin Leonard, Jim Furyk and Retief Goosen) with his win in Greensboro. Became the third player in tournament history to finish the event at 20-under-par or better with his final score of 22-under-par 266. Held second- and third-round leads on way to victory. With $810,000 paycheck, became the first player in TOUR history to surpass $1 million in first four seasons. Other top-10s were T10 at the 84 Lumber Classic of Pennsylvania and third at the Southern Farm Bureau Classic. **2002:** Turned in best finish on money list in three-year career, along with most earnings...Won the Verizon Byron Nelson Classic and became the first Asian with multiple PGA TOUR victories. Closed with a 2-under 68 for a two-stroke victory over rookie Ben Crane...Posted the first ace of the 2002 U.S. Open, using an 8-iron from 154 yards on No. 14 at Bethpage Black...T5 at British Open, best career finish at a major. Tied for lead with eventual champion Ernie Els and three others after 36 holes at 6-under-par 136. Closed with 68 to solidify second career top-10 at the British Open...Withdrew from WGC-American Express Championship due to shoulder injury and played one more event, his first TOUR Championship, where he finished T13...Teamed with Toshi Izawa to win the World Cup. Team rebounded from double bogey to birdie 17th hole and par 18th to beat U.S. team by two strokes. **2001:** Finished in the top 40 on PGA TOUR money list in his first two years as a member and captured his first win at the Greater Milwaukee Open. Defeated Charles Howell III with birdie-4 on first playoff hole. Victory made him first Japanese player to win PGA TOUR event on U.S. mainland (Isao Aoki captured 1983 Hawaiian Open). **2000:** Became first Japanese player to top $1 million in one TOUR season...Had three top 5s included among seven top 10s, his best a T2 with Tiger Woods at Buick Invitational, four strokes behind Phil Mickelson...High point of year likely came during qualifying for U.S. Open. Shot 13-under 58 (11 birdies and one eagle) at Woodmont CC in Rockville, MD, during first round. Second round was 74, giving him total of 132 and second place at qualifier to medalist David Berganio, Jr.'s 130...Earned spot on International Presidents Cup team and finished with a 1-2-0 record. **1999:** Earned his 2000 PGA TOUR membership by virtue of his strong play in the World Golf Championships: WGC-Accenture Match Play Championship (T5) and WGC-NEC Invitational (sixth)...In October, won the Bridgestone Open on the Japan Golf Tour for the third time (first two came in 1995-96). **1998:** First came to attention of golf world when he was surprise star of Presidents Cup with a 5-0 record...Won PGA Philanthropy Open. **1997:** Won four times on the Japan Golf Tour—Japan PGA Championship, Pocari Sweat Yomiuri Open, PGA Match Play Promise Cup and Golf Nippon Hitachi Cup. **1993:** First victory came at Pepsi-Ubekousan.

PERSONAL:
Known for his ever-present smile on the golf course...First shot even-par at age 11...Early in career, made regular appearances on Japanese TV variety show called Yume-ga-MoriMori (Lots of Dreams)...Followed up on his dream with his father by launching his own junior golf foundation, which his company operates, in Japan.

PLAYER STATISTICS

2004 PGA TOUR STATISTICS

Scoring Average	70.23	(21)
Driving Distance	280.1	(157)
Driving Accuracy Percentage	63.7%	(105)
Total Driving	262	(178)
Greens in Regulation Pct.	64.6%	(108)
Putting Average	1.746	(17)
Sand Save Percentage	49.4%	(88)
Eagles (Holes per)	552.0	(183)
Birdie Average	3.75	(41)
All-Around Ranking	720	(87)
Scoring Avg. Before Cut	70.36	(31)
Round 3 Scoring Avg.	71.19	(112)
Final Round Scoring Average	70.67	(36)
Birdie Conversion Percentage	31.2%	(32)
Par Breakers	21.0%	(58)

MISCELLANEOUS PGA TOUR STATISTICS

2004 Low Round/Round: 64–Nissan Open/1
Career Low Round/Round: 63–2 times, most recent 2002 Verizon Byron Nelson Classic/2
Career Largest Paycheck/Finish: $864,000–2002 Verizon Byron Nelson Classic/1

PGA TOUR CAREER SUMMARY — PLAYOFF RECORD: 1-0

Year	Events Played	Cuts Made	1st	2nd	3rd	Top 10	Top 25	Earnings	Rank
1994	1								
1995	1								
1996	2	2					1	$50,588	196
1997	6	6				1	3	111,781	161
1998	6	4					1	78,556	193
1999	9	4				3	3	79,137	202
2000	26	19		1	1	7	11	1,207,104	37
2001	27	22	1			4	13	1,441,455	37
2002	24	21	1			5	13	2,214,794	16
2003	28	18	1		1	4	9	1,669,292	37
2004	26	22		1		6	13	2,301,692	23
Total	156	118	3	2	2	30	67	9,154,398	
JAPAN GOLF TOUR									
2004	1	1		1		1	1	86,163	

PGA TOUR TOP TOURNAMENT SUMMARY

Year	96	97	98	99	00	01	02	03	04
Masters			CUT	T31	T46	CUT	T14	CUT	CUT
U.S. Open					CUT		T16	CUT	T4
British Open	T14	T10	T29	CUT	T55	CUT	T5	CUT	T30
PGA		T23	T65	CUT	T46	T22	T43	T48	CUT
THE PLAYERS			CUT	CUT	W/D		T14	T45	T53
TOUR Championship							T13		T19
WGC-Accenture Match Play				T5	T9	T5		T17	T33
WGC-NEC Invitational				6	T15	T31	T36		T27
WGC-American Express Champ					T50		W/D		T16

NATIONAL TEAMS: The Presidents Cup (2), 1998, 2000; WGC-World Cup (5), 2000, 2001, 2002, 2003, 2004.

Len Mattiace (muh-TEECE)

EXEMPT STATUS: 2002 two-time tournament winner (2005)
FULL NAME: Leonard Earl Mattiace
HEIGHT: 6-1
WEIGHT: 185
BIRTHDATE: October 15, 1967
BIRTHPLACE: Mineola, NY
RESIDENCE: Jacksonville, FL
FAMILY: Wife, Kristen; Gracee Lauren (7/4/97), Noelle Anna (12/1/00)
EDUCATION: Wake Forest University (1990, Sociology)
SPECIAL INTERESTS: All sports
TURNED PROFESSIONAL: 1990
Q SCHOOL: 1992, 1995
Nationwide Tour Alumnus

PGA TOUR VICTORIES (2):

2002 Nissan Open, FedEx St. Jude Classic.

BEST 2004 PGA TOUR FINISH:

T20—John Deere Classic.

2004 SEASON:

Injured both knees in Dec. 2003 skiing in Vail. Following surgery, made his comback at The Honda Classic in March where he missed the cut…Made his first cut of the season at THE PLAYERS Championship two weeks later and finished T33…Did not post a top-10 for the first time in his 10-year PGA TOUR career and had just one top-25, a T20 at the John Deere Classic in July.

CAREER HIGHLIGHTS:

2003: Playing in his first Masters as a professional and first in 15 years (1988 as an amateur), fired the best round of the tournament, a 7-under 65, in the final round to tie Mike Weir and force the first Masters playoff since 1990. Mattiace began the day five strokes back of the third-round leader Jeff Maggert. Held a two-stroke lead over Weir during the back nine before he bogeyed the 18th hole and Weir birdied No. 15 and made a 6-footer for par on the 18th to force the playoff. Weir won the playoff with bogey on the first extra hole. Had never finished in the top-20 in his 10 previous majors **2002:** Finished in the top 30 on the TOUR money list for the first time on the strength of two victories. Made 25 cuts in 28 starts and collected over $2 million in a single season for the first time...Captured first career PGA TOUR victory at the Nissan Open in 220th start. Tied for the lead on the tournament's 72nd hole, he two-putted from 30 feet while co-leader Scott McCarron was unable to get up-and-down for par. Rounds of 69-65-67-68—269 was one better than McCarron, Brad Faxon and Rory Sabbatini...Won the Fed Ex St. Jude Classic by one stroke over Tim Petrovic. Was seven strokes off the pace after 54 holes and closed with a 64. Paycheck of $684,000 was largest of career. **2001:** Finished T6 in the Shell Houston Open...Shared second-round lead at Michelob Championship and closed with 74-67 for a solo fifth. **2000:** Steady play at The PLAYERS Championship earned him his second top-10 at that event. Was one stroke back of Hal Sutton after posting a 2-under-par 70 in the first round and finished T9...Second top-10 came at MasterCard Colonial, a T8...In contention after 18 and 36 holes at the Westin Texas Open. His 73-66 on the weekend produced T6 in San Antonio...Best effort of the season came at Tampa Bay Classic, a T3. Stood two strokes back of the lead after 36 and 54 holes. **1999:** Best finish of season came in his first start when he finished T2 at the Sony Open in Hawaii...Rest of the year was a struggle with only two more top-25 finishes until final event...In last start of the year, finished T9 at Southern Farm Bureau Classic. **1998:** Finished T5 at THE PLAYERS Championship. **1997:** Best finish came in second-to-last start of year at Walt Disney World/Oldsmobile Classic. Shot 67-66 and trailed Payne Stewart by one stroke through 36 holes. Third-round 65 produced two-stroke lead over David Duval. Posted final-round 74, falling two strokes shy of Duval-Dan Forsman playoff. **1996:** A second at Buick Challenge, along with T4 at LaCantera Texas Open, helped him retain playing privileges for 1997...Shot 68-68 at Callaway Gardens to share 36-hole lead. After final two rounds were canceled due to weather, parred first extra hole of five-man playoff, losing to Michael Bradley's birdie...Won first Compaq World Putting Championship. **1995:** Was 27th at Qualifying School, earning membership in 1996...Finished 69th on Nationwide Tour money list with $27,430, driven by T5s at Cleveland Open and Buffalo Open. **1992:** First qualified for TOUR at Qualifying Tournament. **Amateur:** Captured 1984 Florida High School Championship...Member of Wake Forest's 1986 NCAA Championship team, along with current PGA TOUR player Billy Andrade.

PERSONAL:

Was first encouraged to play golf by his father Louis at age 6…Is left-handed but plays golf right-handed…Has his own charitable organization, "Len's Friends" foundation, that aids Jacksonville, FL, charities with a series of golf events. Web site for event is lensfriends.org.

PLAYER STATISTICS

2004 PGA TOUR STATISTICS

Scoring Average	72.03	(173)
Driving Distance	278.0	(173)
Driving Accuracy Percentage	67.2%	(54)
Total Driving	227	(145)
Greens in Regulation Pct.	59.1%	(192)
Putting Average	1.792	(137)
Sand Save Percentage	60.2%	(5)
Eagles (Holes per)	337.5	(148)
Birdie Average	2.96	(189)
All-Around Ranking	1,071	(169)
Scoring Avg. Before Cut	72.04	(178)
Round 3 Scoring Avg.	72.46	(180)
Final Round Scoring Average	73.25	(185)
Birdie Conversion Percentage	26.8%	(173)
Par Breakers	16.7%	(189)

MISCELLANEOUS PGA TOUR STATISTICS

2004 Low Round/Round: 66–2 times, most recent Michelin Championship at Las Vegas/2
Career Low Round/Round: 64–7 times, most recent 2002 FedEx St. Jude Classic/4
Career Largest Paycheck/Finish: $684,000–2002 FedEx St. Jude Classic/1

PGA TOUR CAREER SUMMARY — PLAYOFF RECORD: 0-2

Year	Events Played	Cuts Made	1st	2nd	3rd	Top 10	Top 25	Earnings	Rank
1988	1								
1991	1								
1993	26	13				2	3	$74,521	160
1996	30	15		1		2	6	238,977	92
1997	35	18			1	1	12	315,656	77
1998	31	23				3	5	418,416	68
1999	31	17		1		2	4	403,115	100
2000	31	22			1	5	8	762,979	61
2001	30	19				2	6	592,781	84
2002	28	25	2		1	4	9	2,194,064	18
2003	27	21		1		2	4	1,221,476	56
2004	25	12					1	213,707	188
Total	296	185	2	3	3	23	58	6,435,692	
NATIONWIDE TOUR									
1991	3	1						495	315
1992	28	17				1	5	20,760	64
1993	2								
1994	1								
1995	19	10				2	5	27,430	69
1996	1	1					1	1,750	198
Total	54	29				3	11	50,435	

PGA TOUR TOP TOURNAMENT SUMMARY

Year	88	89	90	91	92	93	94	95	96	97	98	99	00
Masters	CUT												
U.S. Open										T24		T42	
British Open												T30	
PGA										CUT	CUT		
THE PLAYERS										T24	T5	CUT	T9

Year	01	02	03	04
Masters			2	CUT
U.S. Open		T68	T57	
British Open		T69	T65	
PGA	CUT	T48	T51	
THE PLAYERS	CUT	T69	CUT	T33
TOUR Championship		T18		
WGC-Accenture Match Play			T33	
WGC-NEC Invitational		T36	T30	
WGC-American Express Champ		T46	T54	

NATIONAL TEAMS: Walker Cup, 1987.

Billy Mayfair

EXEMPT STATUS: Top 50 on PGA TOUR Career Money List
FULL NAME: William Fred Mayfair
HEIGHT: 5-8
WEIGHT: 175
BIRTHDATE: August 6, 1966
BIRTHPLACE: Phoenix, AZ
RESIDENCE: Scottsdale, AZ; plays out of Estrella Mountain Ranch GC
FAMILY: Wife, Tammy; Maxwell (11/15/99)
EDUCATION: Arizona State University
SPECIAL INTERESTS: All sports
TURNED PROFESSIONAL: 1988
Q SCHOOL: 1988

PGA TOUR VICTORIES (5):
1993 Greater Milwaukee Open. **1995** Motorola Western Open, THE TOUR Championship. **1998** Nissan Open, Buick Open.

BEST 2004 PGA TOUR FINISH:
T10—Buick Invitational.

2004 SEASON:
Finished outside the top 125 (No. 140) on the PGA TOUR money list for the first time in his 16-year career. Previous low had been No. 116 in 1989, his rookie season...Made 22 of 32 cuts but posted just one top-10, his lowest output since recording one in 1997, and a career-low three top-25s...In his third event of the season, made his first cut and earned his only top-10, a T10, at the Buick Invitational...Shared first-round lead after an opening-round 64 at the Michelin Championship at Las Vegas prior to finishing T32...His other two top-25s, a T24 at the Cialis Western Open and a T13 at the 84 LUMBER Classic.

CAREER HIGHLIGHTS:
2003: Continued streak of finishing in the top 125 on the money list for all 15 years on TOUR...Earned season's best T5 finish at The Honda Classic...Posted his third top-10 in his last five U.S. Opens with a T10 at Olympia Fields CC in Olympia, IL (T10 in 1999, T5 in 2002). **2002:** Played in 31 events, the most since 1993 (32)...Earned second career top-10 at the U.S. Open with a T5 finish. **2001:** Made return visit to THE TOUR Championship for first time since 1998 after finishing in the top 30 on the money list...Just missed sixth PGA TOUR title at WORLDCOM CLASSIC. Opened with 65 to share first-round lead at Harbour Town. Closing 71 tied him with Jose Coceres at the end of regulation. Lost to Coceres on fifth playoff hole...Turned in best career performance at a major and first top-10 in one since a T7 at the 1998 PGA Championship with a T3 at the British Open...Closing 61, a tournament record, gave him T14 at Buick Open. Key to round was PGA TOUR record-tying 27 on back nine. 9-under 27 produced TOUR record in relation to par (nine holes). String of seven birdies and one eagle broke TOUR's best birdie-eagle streak of seven set by Al Geiberger in 1977 and matched by Webb Heintzelman in 1989. **2000:** Fell out of the top-100 money winners for just the third time in 12 full seasons on TOUR. **1999:** Top showing of season was a T2 at season-opening Mercedes Championships...Year ended on sad note when father, Dick, died of heart attack in early November. **1998:** Earned first of two victories that season at Nissan Open, where closing 67 forced playoff with Tiger Woods. Birdied first extra hole to defeat Woods...Nearly made it two wins in a row the following week at Doral-Ryder Open where he finished T2...Shared 54-hole lead at Buick Open following rounds of 70-69-65. Took lead for good on Sunday with first-hole birdie en route to closing 67. Dedicated his victory to Renay Appleby, the wife of TOUR player Stuart Appleby, who died tragically in July. **1997:** Season was wracked by illness and loss of confidence...His T2 performance in Las Vegas, the last full-field event of the season, proved to be his best showing of the year. **1996:** Seventh career runner-up finish came with a T2 at NEC World Series of Golf. **1995:** Enjoyed one of the best turnaround seasons in PGA TOUR history, recording two victories, three runner-up finishes and earning $1,543,192. Increase in earnings over previous year — $1,385,033 — stood at that time as TOUR record, since broken by Tiger Woods...Victories came at Motorola Western Open, where he shot a closing 67, and THE TOUR Championship, where he had a three-stroke lead through 54 holes and maintained that margin with closing 73...Runner-up finishes came at Phoenix Open, NEC World Series of Golf (both in playoffs) and Las Vegas Invitational. **1993:** Collected first victory on TOUR at Greater Milwaukee Open, where he defeated Mark Calcavecchia and Ted Schulz in a playoff...T2, one stroke behind Scott Simpson at the GTE Byron Nelson Classic. **1990:** T2 with Ed Dougherty after losing to Jim Gallagher, Jr. on first playoff hole at the Greater Milwaukee Open...Also lost to Jodie Mudd in season-ending Nabisco Championships when Mudd birdied first extra hole. **Amateur:** Won 1986 U.S. Public Links and 1987 U.S. Amateur titles. Also won Fred Haskins Award as nation's top collegiate player.

PERSONAL:
Married Tammy Gubin McIntire on 18th green at TPC at Las Colinas prior to 1994 GTE Byron Nelson Classic, explaining: "We're going to be spending the rest of our lives on golf courses. We thought we might as well be married on one."...Volunteered as standard bearer at Phoenix Open while in high school, usually working with the group of his idol, Jerry Pate...Inducted into Arizona State Sports Hall of Fame in November 1998...First golf course design, The Golf Club of Virginia, in Roanoke, opened in 2002.

PLAYER STATISTICS

2004 PGA TOUR STATISTICS

Scoring Average	71.61	(146)
Driving Distance	285.2	(118)
Driving Accuracy Percentage	70.1%	(22)
Total Driving	140	(26)
Greens in Regulation Pct.	66.0%	(75)
Putting Average	1.829	(193)
Sand Save Percentage	49.7%	(83)
Eagles (Holes per)	270.0	(116)
Birdie Average	3.18	(174)
All-Around Ranking	927	(143)
Scoring Avg. Before Cut	70.98	(94)
Round 3 Scoring Avg.	72.91	(188)
Final Round Scoring Average	72.90	(172)
Birdie Conversion Percentage	25.5%	(187)
Par Breakers	18.0%	(176)

MISCELLANEOUS PGA TOUR STATISTICS

2004 Low Round/Round: 64–Michelin Championship at Las Vegas/1
Career Low Round/Round: 61–2 times, most recent 2001 Buick Open/4
Career Largest Paycheck/Finish: $540,000–1995 THE TOUR Championship/1

PGA TOUR CAREER SUMMARY — PLAYOFF RECORD: 2-5

Year	Events Played	Cuts Made	1st	2nd	3rd	Top 10	Top 25	Earnings	Rank
1987A	3	1							
1988A	3	2					1		
1988	5	3					1	$8,433	220
1989	33	18					6	111,998	116
1990	32	23		2		7	15	693,658	12
1991	33	20				1	7	185,668	89
1992	33	23				1	9	191,878	79
1993	32	22	1	1		5	8	513,072	30
1994	32	18				1	7	158,159	113
1995	28	21	2	3		6	9	1,543,192	2
1996	28	18		1		1	8	357,654	55
1997	30	16		1		1	5	304,083	79
1998	27	20	2	1		5	9	1,281,685	16
1999	29	16		1		4	10	741,733	58
2000	29	18				2	6	466,345	106
2001	29	21		1	1	5	15	1,716,002	29
2002	31	19				3	6	864,745	75
2003	31	20				3	7	842,186	79
2004	32	22				1	3	503,251	140
Total	500	321	5	11	1	46	132	10,483,744	

PGA TOUR TOP TOURNAMENT SUMMARY

Year	88	89	90	91	92	93	94	95	96	97	98	99	00
Masters	CUT			T12	T42		CUT		CUT		CUT	CUT	
U.S. Open	T25	T33	CUT	T37	T23		CUT		T32			T10	CUT
British Open									T44		T52	CUT	
PGA			T5	CUT	CUT	T28	T39	T23	T52	T53	T7	T34	T74
THE PLAYERS		CUT	CUT	T73	T67	T52	CUT	T18	CUT	CUT	T42	CUT	T17
TOUR Championship			2			30		**1**			T13		
WGC-Accenture Match Play												T33	T17

Year	01	02	03	04
Masters		T32	T37	
U.S. Open		T5	T10	66
British Open	T3	CUT		
PGA	CUT	CUT	T61	
THE PLAYERS	T5	CUT	CUT	T58
TOUR Championship	T26			
WGC-Accenture Match Play		T33		
WGC-American Express Champ	CNL			

NATIONAL TEAMS: Walker Cup, 1987; Four Tours World Championship of Golf, 1991.

Scott McCarron

EXEMPT STATUS: 105th on 2004 money list
FULL NAME: Scott Michael McCarron
HEIGHT: 5-10
WEIGHT: 170
BIRTHDATE: July 10, 1965
BIRTHPLACE: Sacramento, CA
RESIDENCE: Reno, NV
FAMILY: Wife, Jennifer; Courtney (10/31/95), Cassidy (12/23/97)
EDUCATION: UCLA (1988, History)
SPECIAL INTERESTS: Flying, skiing, mountain biking, fly fishing, guitar
TURNED PROFESSIONAL: 1992
Q SCHOOL: 1994

PGA TOUR VICTORIES (3):

1996 Freeport-McDermott Classic. **1997** BellSouth Classic. **2001** BellSouth Classic.

OTHER VICTORIES (4):

1998 Franklin Templeton Shark Shootout [with Bruce Lietzke]. **2000** Franklin Templeton Shootout [with Brad Faxon]. **2001** Franklin Templeton Shootout [with Brad Faxon]. **2002** Fred Meyer Challenge [with Brian Henninger].

BEST 2004 PGA TOUR FINISHES:

T2—Reno-Tahoe Open; T10—AT&T Pebble Beach National Pro-Am.

2004 SEASON:

Failed to extend streak of $1-million seasons to four as money list position fell below No. 100 for the first time since 1999. . .Posted first top-10, a T10 at the AT&T Pebble Beach National Pro-Am, in his third event of the season. . .Part of a four-man playoff after closing with 1-under 71 at the Reno-Tahoe Open, one of only 11 players to post an under-par score on Sunday. Rookie Vaughn Taylor claimed his first PGA TOUR title when he rolled in an 11-foot birdie putt on the first extra hole to win the playoff.

CAREER HIGHLIGHTS:

2003: After eight top-25s in first 22 events, broke through in 23rd start, a T10 in adopted hometown at the Reno-Tahoe Open...Lost in sudden-death playoff to Stuart Appleby at the Las Vegas Invitational, posting rounds of 69-62-64-67-66—328. Came from three strokes back on final day to force the playoff with a 6-under-66. The 328 (31-under-par) total broke the tournament total of 329 by D.A. Weibring (1991), Andrew Magee (1991) and Bob Estes (2001). Collected $432,000 to surpass the $1-million mark in season earnings for the third consecutive season. **2002:** Made 23 cuts in 28 starts and earned a career-best $1,896,714...Began the season in superb style, earning $1,073,624 of his season earnings during the West Coast Swing...Opened with T5 at Mercedes Championships. Finished second at the Nissan Open. The next week was runner-up to fellow Sacramento, CA native Kevin Sutherland in the WGC-Accenture Match Play Championship...Defending champion at the BellSouth Classic made a charge on the back nine on Sunday, putting together four straight birdies, to finish alone in fourth...Did not post another top-10 until a solo sixth at the WGC-American Express Championship...Teamed with Brian Henninger to win the Fred Meyer Challenge. **2001:** Collected his third PGA TOUR victory and his second title in Atlanta...Opening rounds of 68-67 produced a share of lead at BellSouth Classic, with 36-hole final on Sunday. Took outright lead with third round 72, then closed with 73 for three-stroke victory over Mike Weir. Victory came in face of high winds on Sunday...Posted T3 at Fed Ex St. Jude Classic...Ended the season with two top-10s. At the 90-hole Invensys Classic at Las Vegas, held a fourth-round lead by three strokes over Tom Lehman. A 71 on Sunday dropped him to T4...Shared first-round lead at National Car Rental Golf Classic after opening with 65 and placed in a T6, his fourth top-10 of season. His $99,329 payday in Orlando moved him up the money list from No. 34 to No. 26. Finished in the top-30 for the first time since 1997 and secured a spot in THE TOUR Championship, where he finished 18th...Teamed with Brad Faxon to win the Franklin Templeton Shootout for the second consecutive season. **2000:** Compiled season earnings of $495,975, good for 97th on official money list...Two top-10 finishes came in final stretch of season, effectively securing full playing privileges...In final official money appearance of year, finished T5 at Invensys Classic of Las Vegas. Started off that week with four consecutive rounds in the 60s (67-66-66-66) to stand just one stroke off the 72-hole lead. However, a final day 70 dropped him to T5...Teamed with Brad Faxon to win the Franklin Templeton Shootout at the new Great White Course at Doral in November. **1999:** Fell out of the top 100 in season earnings for first time in four years with 101st-place finish. Lone top-10 came at Air Canada Championship where high finish was sparked by Northview G&CC course-record 10-under-par 61 in the final round. Began the day tied for 47th and, starting on the back nine, played his first nine holes in 5-under-par 30. He then birdied five consecutive holes on the front-nine for a 5-under-par 31. The 61 was two strokes better than his previous best. **1998:** Made 14 of 28 cuts, including three top-10s on way to 69th-place ranking on money list. **1997:** Captured his second PGA TOUR title, winning the BellSouth Classic. Opened 70-69 at TPC at Sugarloaf, then fired 66 for share of lead with David Duval. Final-round 69 secured three-stroke victory over Duval and Lee Janzen. Victory came after he pulled hamstring racing Dicky Pride during second-round rain delay. Injury forced him to keep swing shorter, and he credited Pride (at least in part) for the win...In pairing of long putters, teamed with Bruce Lietzke to capture unofficial money title Franklin Templeton Shark Shootout. **1996:** Became third consecutive first-time winner following Tim Herron (Honda Classic) and Paul Goydos (Bay Hill Invitational) with victory at Freeport-McDermott Classic. After opening 68-67 at English Turn G&CC, took one-stroke lead over Tommy Tolles with a third-round 69 and closed with 71 on windy Sunday for a five-stroke victory...Made seven of final nine cuts to finish 49th on money list. **1995:** Third-place finish at Las Vegas Invitational spared him a trip to Qualifying Tournament.

PERSONAL:

After college, gave up golf for four years to work with his father in the family clothing business. During that period, athletic focus was on flag football, softball, tennis and racquetball. Return to golf was sparked by 1991 visit to Raley's Senior Gold Rush, the Champions Tour event at Rancho Murieta, CA. After watching event, went home and built long putter in garage. Nearly won U.S. Mid-Amateur with homemade model later that year. Used more sophisticated version to win his three TOUR titles. . .In August 1999, made hole-in-one during first round of CVS Charity Classic immediately following ace by Lee Janzen on 17th hole at Rhode Island CC.

PLAYER STATISTICS

2004 PGA TOUR STATISTICS

Statistic	Value	Rank
Scoring Average	71.19	(103)
Driving Distance	294.1	(39)
Driving Accuracy Percentage	64.9%	(84)
Total Driving	123	(16)
Greens in Regulation Pct.	65.4%	(89)
Putting Average	1.772	(81)
Sand Save Percentage	49.7%	(83)
Eagles (Holes per)	309.6	(134)
Birdie Average	3.76	(37)
All-Around Ranking	650	(61)
Scoring Avg. Before Cut	70.64	(52)
Round 3 Scoring Avg.	70.76	(78)
Final Round Scoring Average	72.12	(141)
Birdie Conversion Percentage	30.9%	(39)
Par Breakers	21.2%	(49)

MISCELLANEOUS PGA TOUR STATISTICS

2004 Low Round/Round: 64–Bob Hope Chrysler Classic/2
Career Low Round/Round: 61–1999 Air Canada Championship/4
Career Largest Paycheck/Finish: $594,000–2001 BellSouth Classic/1

PGA TOUR CAREER SUMMARY — PLAYOFF RECORD: 0-2

Year	Events Played	Cuts Made	1st	2nd	3rd	Top 10	Top 25	Earnings	Rank
1995	25	12			1	1	2	$147,371	128
1996	27	17	1			2	5	404,329	49
1997	26	16	1			7	13	852,459	25
1998	28	14				3	7	414,247	69
1999	27	18				1	7	400,678	101
2000	30	19				2	4	495,975	97
2001	25	23	1		1	4	15	1,793,506	23
2002	28	23		2		5	10	1,896,714	29
2003	27	16		1		2	11	1,250,849	54
2004	27	17		1		2	7	790,720	105
Total	270	175	3	4	2	29	81	8,446,847	
NATIONWIDE TOUR									
1992	1	1						720	268
1995	3	1					1	1,950	204
Total	4	2					1	2,670	

PGA TOUR TOP TOURNAMENT SUMMARY

Year	96	97	98	99	00	01	02	03	04
Masters	T10	T30	T16	T18			CUT	T23	
U.S. Open	T82	T10	T40				T30	CUT	
British Open		CUT					T18	T34	
PGA	T47	T10	CUT			T70	T39	T14	CUT
THE PLAYERS	CUT	CUT	T35	CUT	T66	T44	CUT	CUT	T53
TOUR Championship		T12				18	T11		
WGC-Accenture Match Play							2	T33	
WGC-NEC Invitational							T75		
WGC-American Express Champ						CNL	6		

Rocco Mediate (MEE-de-ate)

EXEMPT STATUS: Top 50 on PGA TOUR Career Money List
FULL NAME: Rocco Anthony Mediate
HEIGHT: 6-1
WEIGHT: 190
BIRTHDATE: December 17, 1962
BIRTHPLACE: Greensburg, PA
RESIDENCE: Naples, FL
FAMILY: Wife, Linda; three children
EDUCATION: Florida Southern University
SPECIAL INTERESTS: Music, tennis, home theater
TURNED PROFESSIONAL: 1985
Q SCHOOL: Fall 1985, 1986

PGA TOUR VICTORIES (5):

1991 Doral-Ryder Open. **1993** KMart Greater Greensboro Open. **1999** Phoenix Open. **2000** Buick Open. **2002** Greater Greensboro Chrysler Classic.

INTERNATIONAL VICTORIES (1):

1992 Perrier French Open.

OTHER VICTORIES (3):

1999 Callaway Pebble Beach Invitational. **2002** Franklin Templeton Shootout [with Lee Janzen]. **2003** CVS Charity Classic [with Jeff Sluman].

BEST 2004 PGA TOUR FINISHES:

T15—The INTERNATIONAL; T16—Bob Hope Chrysler Classic.

2004 SEASON:

Continued to battle back problems throughout the season. . .Finished outside the 125 on the PGA TOUR money list for the fourth time in his 19-year career and for the first time since he finished No. 155 in 1995. . .Did not post a top-10 for the first time since 1989 and had just two-top-25s, a T16 in his first event of the season, the Bob Hope Chrysler Classic and a T15 at The INTERNATIONAL in August.

CAREER HIGHLIGHTS:

2003: Finished season 31st on money list and was bounced from the field for season-ending TOUR Championship after missing cut in final full-field event, the Chrysler Championship...Began season with two top-fives in first three events...Switched to conventional putter for season-opening Mercedes Championships, and finished T2 with K.J. Choi. Tied Jonathan Byrd for low final round, a 10-under 63...A couple weeks later, posted a T5 at AT&T Pebble Beach National Pro-Am...Fired rounds of 66-65 on the weekend to finish solo second, four shots behind Adam Scott, at the inaugural Deutsche Bank Championship. Paycheck of $540,000 pushed earnings over $1 million for fourth consecutive season...Withdrew from Las Vegas Invitational due to back spasms. **2002:** Earned over $2 million for the first time in his career and had best finish on the money list (22) since finishing 16th in 1993...Picked up first victory since the 2000 Buick Open with win at the Greater Greensboro Chrysler Classic. Had two-stroke lead over Mark Calcavecchia through 54 holes. Final-round 71 gained a three-stroke win over Calcavecchia and earned a career-high $684,000 paycheck...Finished third at THE PLAYERS Championship in hometown of Ponte Vedra Beach, FL...A sixth at the PGA was his second top-10 in a major. First was a solo fourth at the 2001 U.S. Open. **2001:** Shot 20-under 264 to finish second to Mark Calcavecchia's record-setting 28-under 256 at Phoenix Open. Finished 1-T2-2 in last three Phoenix Opens...Finished T2 at Marconi Pennsylvania Classic. Grew up about 20 miles from the Laurel Valley, PA course. **2000:** Earned his fourth career victory the way he won his first PGA TOUR title—with a birdie on the final hole at the Buick Open. It was the first time he had led the Buick Open all week. Birdied two of final three holes for one-stroke victory over 54-hole leader Chris Perry. Victory lifted him over $1-million mark in a single season for first time in his career...Earlier in season, fell one stroke short of his defense of 1999 Phoenix Open with rounds of 67-70-67-67 and finished T2...Following his victory, went to PGA Championship with high hopes but chair he was sitting in on clubhouse patio collapsed, he hit his head on a railing and wrenched his shoulder, neck and wrist in the fall. He withdrew after opening 77. **1999:** Made clear comeback from 1994 back surgery with victory at the Phoenix Open in only his second start of the season. Held season-best 54-hole lead of six strokes. Final-round 71 earned him two-stroke victory over Justin Leonard. **1997:** Made eight consecutive cuts near end of the year to retain full exempt status. **1996:** Returned to TOUR under special medical extension and promptly tied for sixth at Phoenix Open to earn $42,088 and regain full playing privileges. Had three other top-10s, including T4 at THE PLAYERS Championship, where he became the first player to birdie the final six holes at the TPC at Sawgrass on his way to a final-round 66. **1994:** Missed most of season with ruptured disk, for which he underwent surgery in July. **1993:** Second win came in playoff at Kmart GGO, where he birdied fourth playoff hole to defeat Steve Elkington...Tied for second, two strokes behind Ben Crenshaw at the Nestle Invitational. **1991:** Earned first PGA TOUR title in sixth season at Doral-Ryder Open. Sank 10-foot birdie putts on 71st and 72nd holes, forcing playoff with Curtis Strange. In Monday playoff, birdied first extra hole from five feet to win $252,000. Victory was one of six top-10s in his first seven starts of the year. **1990:** Final-round 66 jumped him into a T2 at the Canon Greater Hartford Open, two strokes back of Wayne Levi. **1987:** Was T2, one-stroke behind John Inman at the Provident Classic.

PERSONAL:

Gained interest in golf in high school after years of playing baseball. . .With help from Champions Tour member Jim Ferree during college, began to construct his swing. . .At Florida Southern, coach Charlie Matlock became large influence on his game. . .Started using long putter to save his back and became the first player to win on the PGA TOUR using a long putter when he won the 1991 Doral-Ryder Open. Back problems have been minimized in recent years due to improved fitness level, and switched back to conventional putter for 2003 Mercedes Championships.

PLAYER STATISTICS

2004 PGA TOUR STATISTICS

Scoring Average	71.90	(168)
Driving Distance	283.4	(131)
Driving Accuracy Percentage	69.9%	(25)
Total Driving	156	(42)
Greens in Regulation Pct.	65.5%	(86)
Putting Average	1.800	(162)
Sand Save Percentage	45.0%	(151)
Eagles (Holes per)	123.4	(12)
Birdie Average	3.29	(153)
All-Around Ranking	888	(130)
Scoring Avg. Before Cut	71.68	(160)
Round 3 Scoring Avg.	70.88	(90)
Final Round Scoring Average	71.83	(122)
Birdie Conversion Percentage	27.8%	(140)
Par Breakers	19.1%	(134)

MISCELLANEOUS PGA TOUR STATISTICS

2004 Low Round/Round: 65–Bob Hope Chrysler Classic/3
Career Low Round/Round: 62–2001 MasterCard Colonial/2
Career Largest Paycheck/Finish: $684,000–2002 Greater Greensboro Chrysler Classic/1

PGA TOUR CAREER SUMMARY — PLAYOFF RECORD: 2-0

Year	Events Played	Cuts Made	1st	2nd	3rd	Top 10	Top 25	Earnings	Rank
1984A	1								
1985	2								
1986	27	10				1	4	$20,670	174
1987	32	19		1		1	7	112,099	91
1988	32	25				1	9	129,829	92
1989	30	23					8	132,501	108
1990	27	17		1	1	3	5	240,625	62
1991	25	19	1			7	14	597,438	15
1992	25	17			2	6	8	301,896	49
1993	24	22	1	1		6	10	680,623	16
1994	6	4				1	2	45,940	193
1995	18	8				2	2	105,618	155
1996	21	15			1	4	10	475,255	40
1997	24	18				2	7	240,521	101
1998	24	20				2	9	389,996	78
1999	25	18	1			3	8	963,075	37
2000	24	18	1	1		3	7	1,320,278	34
2001	21	14		2		5	10	1,474,435	36
2002	23	17	1		2	4	11	2,040,676	22
2003	24	18		2		5	8	1,832,656	31
2004	19	8					2	257,692	176
Total	454	310	5	8	6	56	141	11,361,822	

PGA TOUR TOP TOURNAMENT SUMMARY

Year	84	85	86	87	88	89	90	91	92	93	94	95	96
Masters								T22	T37				
U.S. Open	CUT							CUT	T44	T25	W/D		
British Open								CUT	T45	T39			T18
PGA					T31		T69	T16	T40	T68			T36
THE PLAYERS				T50	CUT	T11	T11	T15	CUT	T6		T55	T4
TOUR Championship								T26		T23			

Year	97	98	99	00	01	02	03	04
Masters			T27	T52	T15	T36	T33	CUT
U.S. Open			T34	T32	4	T37	CUT	
British Open			CUT	T52	W/D	T47		
PGA		CUT	T49	W/D	T66	6	T18	CUT
THE PLAYERS	CUT	T57	CUT	CUT	T65	3	T45	
TOUR Championship						T13		
WGC-Accenture Match Play			T33	T33		T17	T17	T33
WGC-NEC Invitational						T24	T77	
WGC-American Express Champ				W/D	CNL	T15	T16	

NATIONAL TEAMS: UBS Cup, 2003.

SECTION 2 PLAYER BIOGRAPHIES

Shaun Micheel (MICK-heel)

EXEMPT STATUS: Winner, 2003 PGA Championship (through 2008)
FULL NAME: Shaun Micheel
HEIGHT: 6-0
WEIGHT: 180
BIRTHDATE: January 5, 1969
BIRTHPLACE: Orlando, FL

RESIDENCE: Memphis, TN, plays out of Ridgeway CC, TPC at Southwind, Colonial CC
FAMILY: Wife, Stephanie; Dade Palmer (11/20/03)
EDUCATION: Indiana University (1991)
SPECIAL INTERESTS: Flying, hunting, snowskiing
TURNED PROFESSIONAL: 1992
Q SCHOOL: 1993, 1996,
Nationwide Tour Alumnus

PGA TOUR VICTORIES (1):
2003 PGA Championship.

NATIONWIDE TOUR VICTORIES (1):
1999 Greensboro Open.

INTERNATIONAL VICTORIES (1):
1998 Singapore Open [Asia].

BEST 2004 PGA TOUR FINISH:
9—THE PLAYERS Championship.

2004 SEASON:
Cracked the top 100 on the money list for just the second time in eight seasons on TOUR, with 20 made cuts in 27 events...In seventh start of season, earned first top-10 since capturing the 2003 PGA Championship with a T9 at THE PLAYERS Championship...Made the cut in all four majors, finishing T24th in defense of PGA Championship. Posted a second-round 68 to make the cut after opening with a 77.

CAREER HIGHLIGHTS:
2003: Became fifth consecutive first-time major winner with his victory at the PGA Championship and finished 32nd on the money list, the highest in his six years on TOUR...Earned top-10s in back-to-back starts for the first time in his TOUR career with a T10 at the Nissan Open and a T8 at the Ford Championship at Doral...Stunned golf world by earning first career PGA TOUR victory in 164th PGA TOUR start (third career major start) at the PGA at Oak Hill CC in Rochester, NY. First player since John Daly (1991) to capture first PGA TOUR event at PGA. Jumped from 169th to 46th in the Official World Golf Ranking with the win. Held the lead outright after 36 holes and shared the lead with Chad Campbell through 54 holes. Playing 72nd hole with a one-shot lead, rifled 7-iron from 175 yards to within inches of the hole for a memorable birdie and a two-stroke victory over Campbell. Finished week 4-under-par with rounds of 69-68-69-70—276 and a $1,080,000 payday...Thanks to final-round 65, finished 10th at the Greater Hartford Open, six shots behind Peter Jacobsen...Four top-10s were a career-best. **2002:** Two top-10s nearly matched the three he had in his first 111 events on TOUR and one of those, a T3 at the B.C. Open, was the best previous finish of his career. Held a share of the lead through the first 54 holes, but carded a 2-over-par 74 on Sunday, with bogeys on two final holes, to finish T3 behind winner Spike McRoy. Finish was first top-10 since T5 at the 2000 Invensys Classic at Las Vegas. **2001:** T13 at Qualifying School to retain TOUR card following season. **2000:** Enjoyed his best season on the PGA TOUR thanks to a then-career-high three top-10s and four top-25s...After earning only $35,689 as a professional in 43 PGA TOUR events prior to 2000, nearly cracked the top 100 in earnings with $467,431 (No. 104) in 31 events. **1999:** Earned his first Nationwide Tour title at the Greensboro Open, edging Garrett Willis by one stroke. Was three strokes back of Willis with three holes to play in the final round but played the last three holes in 1-under par while Willis played them in 3-over. **1996:** T9 at PGA TOUR Qualifying Tournament to regain his TOUR card. **1993:** Earned first TOUR card with T37 at the PGA TOUR Qualifying Tournament.

PERSONAL:
Friendly with the rock band KISS and was a backstage guest of the band in Columbus, OH, the week following the PGA...Was honored with the 1994 Sons of Confederate Veterans Award for Bravery after saving two people from a sinking car while at a golf tournament in New Bern, NC...Wife, Stephanie, graduated from LSU and is an attorney...Recently retired father was one of the original pilots for FedEx in 1973...Shot 58 in the 1998 Omega PGA Championship pro-am in Hong Kong.

PLAYER STATISTICS

2004 PGA TOUR STATISTICS

Scoring Average	71.06	(90)
Driving Distance	287.5	(93)
Driving Accuracy Percentage	63.1%	(115)
Total Driving	208	(119)
Greens in Regulation Pct.	67.0%	(44)
Putting Average	1.793	(141)
Sand Save Percentage	47.2%	(123)
Eagles (Holes per)	163.8	(46)
Birdie Average	3.38	(132)
All-Around Ranking	784	(102)
Scoring Avg. Before Cut	71.08	(108)
Round 3 Scoring Avg.	71.00	(101)
Final Round Scoring Average	71.63	(97)
Birdie Conversion Percentage	27.4%	(153)
Par Breakers	19.4%	(127)

MISCELLANEOUS PGA TOUR STATISTICS

2004 Low Round/Round: 64–2 times, most recent Nissan Open/1
Career Low Round/Round: 63–2000 Invensys Classic at Las Vegas/4
Career Largest Paycheck/Finish: $1,080,000–2003 PGA Championship/1

PGA TOUR CAREER SUMMARY — PLAYOFF RECORD: 0-0

Year	Events Played	Cuts Made	1st	2nd	3rd	Top 10	Top 25	Earnings	Rank
1989	1								
1990A	1								
1991A	1								
1994	19	4						$12,252	247
1997	21	5						14,519	250
1998	2	2						8,918	286
1999	1								
2000	31	15				3	4	467,431	104
2001	34	18					3	351,095	136
2002	30	21			1	2	8	641,450	105
2003	28	21	1			4	7	1,827,000	32
2004	27	20				1	8	949,919	82
Total	196	106	1		1	10	30	4,272,582	
NATIONWIDE TOUR									
1994	3								
1996	27	15				1	5	22,007	82
1997	5	3				1	2	18,140	92
1999	25	19	1	1	2	6	13	173,411	9
Total	60	37	1	1	2	8	20	213,558	
EUROPEAN TOUR									
2004	1	1				1	1	61,468	

PGA TOUR TOP TOURNAMENT SUMMARY

Year	99	00	01	02	03	04
Masters						T22
U.S. Open	CUT		T40			T28
British Open						T47
PGA					**1**	T24
THE PLAYERS			CUT		T54	9
WGC-Accenture Match Play						T17
WGC-NEC Invitational					T23	T50
WGC-American Express Champ					T44	

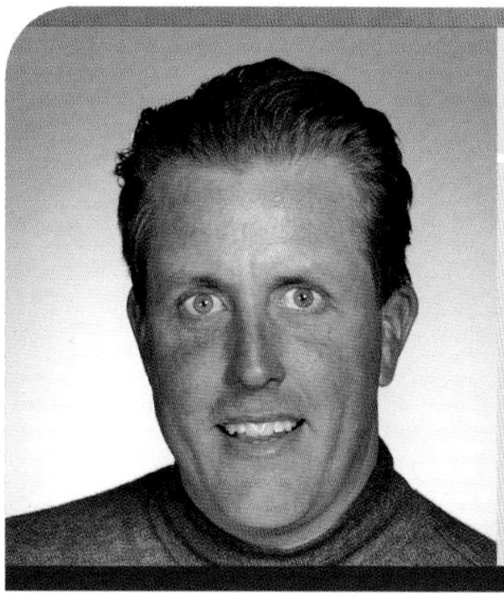

Phil Mickelson

EXEMPT STATUS: Winner, 2004 Masters Tournament (through 2009)
FULL NAME: Philip Alfred Mickelson
HEIGHT: 6-2
WEIGHT: 190
BIRTHDATE: June 16, 1970
BIRTHPLACE: San Diego, CA
RESIDENCE: Rancho Santa Fe, CA; plays out of Grayhawk GC
FAMILY: Wife, Amy; Amanda Brynn (6/21/99), Sophia Isabel (10/23/01), Evan Samuel (3/23/03)
EDUCATION: Arizona State University (Psychology, 1992)
SPECIAL INTERESTS: All sports, especially football; flying
TURNED PROFESSIONAL: 1992
JOINED TOUR: June 1992

PGA TOUR VICTORIES (23):

1991 Northern Telecom Open. **1993** Buick Invitational of California, The International. **1994** Mercedes Championships. **1995** Northern Telecom Open. **1996** Nortel Open, Phoenix Open, GTE Byron Nelson Golf Classic, NEC World Series of Golf. **1997** Bay Hill Invitational, Sprint International. **1998** Mercedes Championships, AT&T Pebble Beach National Pro-Am. **2000** Buick Invitational, BellSouth Classic, MasterCard Colonial, THE TOUR Championship. **2001** Buick Invitational, Canon Greater Hartford Open. **2002** Bob Hope Chrysler Classic, Canon Greater Hartford Open. **2004** Bob Hope Chrysler Classic, Masters Tournament.

INTERNATIONAL VICTORIES (1):

1993 Perrier Open [Eur].

OTHER VICTORIES (3):

2001 Tylenol Par-3 Shootout at Treetops Resort. **2004** TELUS Skins Game, PGA Grand Slam of Golf.

BEST 2004 PGA TOUR FINISHES:

1—Bob Hope Chrysler Classic, Masters Tournament; 2—U.S. Open Championship, HP Classic of New Orleans; 3—AT&T Pebble Beach National Pro-Am, British Open Championship, THE PLAYERS Championship; T4—Buick Invitational; T5—WGC-Accenture Match Play Championship, Wachovia Championship; T6—PGA Championship; T7—FBR Open; 10—BellSouth Classic.

2004 SEASON:

At the age of 33 years, 9 months and 26 days, captured first major championship in 47th attempt (43rd as a professional), winning the Masters Tournament. Climbed to No. 6 in the Official World Golf Ranking with the victory. Held a share of the 54-hole lead with Chris DiMarco after opening 72-69-69, one stroke ahead of Paul Casey. Stumbled early on Sunday with a front-nine of 2-over-par 38, while Ernie Els took a one-stroke lead with an eagle on the par-5 eighth hole. Fought back on final nine, posting a 5-under-par 31, punctuated by an 18-foot birdie putt on the 72nd hole to clinch the one-stroke win over Els. Only the fourth player in Masters history to win the event on the final putt of the tournament, joining Arnold Palmer (1960), Sandy Lyle (1988) and Mark O'Meara (1998). With the final-round 69, finished at 9-under-par 279. Eighth top-10 in 12 appearances in Augusta, including six consecutive dating back to 1999...Won in his first TOUR appearance of the season for the fifth time in career, capturing the Bob Hope Chrysler Classic. Totaled 37 birdies to lead the field, carding rounds of 68-63-64-67-68—330. Was 54-hole outright leader and co-leader with Kirk Triplett through 72 holes. Posted a birdie on first playoff hole to defeat Skip Kendall. Playoff record now stands at 6-1. The 2002 Hope champion became the seventh player to win the event multiple times...Held the second-round lead at the FBR Open and was one back through 54 holes before finishing T7...Notched third consecutive top-10, with a third at the AT&T Pebble Beach National Pro-Am, his third top-three finish at this event since 1998 (win in '98, T3 in 2001)...Following week, added a T4 at the Buick Invitational...Won three matches at the WGC-Accenture Match Play Championship before falling to Davis Love III in the fourth round, 1-up. All square with Love entering the par-5 18th hole but hooked a 3-wood from 255 yards right of the green and made bogey. Defeated Lee Westwood, Ben Curtis (7 and 6 to tie the tournament record for largest victory margin) and Chris DiMarco in the first three rounds...Posted rounds of 70-69-70-71—280 to finish T3 at THE PLAYERS Championship, best career finish at the TPC at Sawgrass...Past champion earned fifth career top-10 at the BellSouth Classic, finishing 10th. With seven top-10s in eight starts in 2004, jumped to No. 1 on the PGA TOUR Official Money List for the first time since 1998, with $2,318,600...In first start after Masters, finished T2 at HP Classic of New Orleans, one stroke behind Vijay Singh. Finish was third top-10 in New Orleans in five starts...Named PGA TOUR Player of the Month for April...Next start in Charlotte, NC, finished T5 at the Wachovia Championship his eighth top-five finish and 10th top-10 in 11 events in 2004...Finished second for the third time in last six years at the U.S. Open. Led Retief Goosen by one stroke with two holes to play. Lost lead when he three-putted the par-3 17th hole for double bogey and Goosen birdied the par-5 16th hole. Finished two strokes behind Goosen. The two were the only players to finish below par for the tournament...Won two ESPY Awards, for Best Championship Performance and Best Male Golfer...Collected his third top-three in a major championship with a third at the British Open to go with his win at the Masters and second at the U.S. Open...Earned fourth top-10 in a major with his T6 at the PGA Championship. First time in his career he finished in the top 10 in all four majors. Only he and Ernie Els accomplished the feat in 2004...Finished second on the Ryder Cup team points list to make his fifth U.S. Ryder Cup team...Shot 13-under par 59 to win PGA Grand Slam of Golf in late November. Made 11 birdies and one eagle.

CAREER HIGHLIGHTS:

2003: Uncharacteristic season, finishing outside the top 30 for first time in 11-year career. Still managed seven top-10s in 23 starts....For the third consecutive year finished third at the Masters (also finished third there in 1996). The top-10 was his 17th in a major championship. One of only five players to post a sub-par round on Sunday with his 4-under 68...First-round co-leader at the PGA after carding a 4-under-par 66. Finished T23...Played on fifth Presidents Cup team representing the United States. **2002:** Won multiple PGA TOUR events for seventh time in 10 years on TOUR...Second on TOUR with 12 top-10s in 26 starts...Became second player to top $20-million mark for career...Captured Bob Hope Chrysler Classic in first appearance of season and first TOUR start since August 2001. Overcame four-shot deficit with a 64 on the final day to finish tied with David Berganio, Jr., at 30-under-par 330. Made up and down from beside the green to birdie the finishing

PGA TOUR CAREER SUMMARY — PLAYOFF RECORD: 6-1

Year	Events Played	Cuts Made	1st	2nd	3rd	Top 10	Top 25	Earnings	Rank
1988A	2								
1989A	1								
1990A	2	2					1		
1991A	7	6	1			1	1		
1992A	7	1							
1992	10	7		1		2	4	$171,714	90
1993	24	14	2			4	7	628,735	22
1994	18	17	1		3	9	10	748,316	15
1995	24	15	1			4	9	655,777	28
1996	21	19	4	1	1	8	10	1,697,799	2
1997	21	19	2	1		5	15	1,225,390	11
1998	24	19	2	2	1	9	11	1,837,246	6
1999	23	20		2		6	14	1,722,681	14
2000	23	21	4	3		12	18	4,746,457	2
2001	23	20	2	4	4	13	13	4,403,883	2
2002	26	23	2	1	5	12	18	4,311,971	2
2003	23	20			1	7	10	1,623,137	38
2004	22	19	2	2	3	13	16	5,784,823	3
Total	301	242	23	17	18	105	157	29,557,928	
EUROPEAN TOUR									
2004	1								
JAPAN GOLF TOUR									
2003	1	1					1	9,239	

PGA TOUR TOP TOURNAMENT SUMMARY

Year	90	91	92	93	94	95	96	97	98	99	00	01	02
Masters		T46		T34		T7	3	CUT	T12	T6	T7	3	3
U.S. Open	T29	T55	CUT		T47	T4	T94	T43	T10	2	T16	T7	2
British Open		T73			CUT	T40	T40	T24	79	CUT	T11	T30	T66
PGA				T6	3	CUT	T8	T29	T34	T57	T9	2	T34
THE PLAYERS			CUT	CUT		T14	T33	CUT	T8	T32	CUT	T33	T28
TOUR Championship				28	T17	24	12	T22	17	T21	**1**		T5
WGC-Accenture Match Play										T9	T33		T33
WGC-NEC Invitational										2	T4	T8	T9
WGC-American Express Champ										T40		CNL	T23

Year	03	04
Masters	3	**1**
U.S. Open	T55	2
British Open	T59	3
PGA	T23	T6
THE PLAYERS		T3
TOUR Championship		T19
WGC-Accenture Match Play	T9	T5
WGC-NEC Invitational	T23	T43
WGC-American Express Champ	T38	

NATIONAL TEAMS: Walker Cup (2), 1989, 1991; World Amateur Team Championship, 1990; The Presidents Cup (5), 1994, 1996, 1998, 2000, 2003; Ryder Cup (5), 1995, 1997, 1999, 2001, 2004; Dunhill Cup, 1996. WGC-World Cup, 2002.

Phil Mickelson (Continued)

hole. Defeated Berganio with a birdie on the first playoff hole with another birdie, running his playoff record on the PGA TOUR to 5-1. Victory, worth $720,000, was the 20th of PGA TOUR career...Shot a final-round 64 at the Canon Greater Hartford Open, including a birdie on the final hole, to beat Davis Love III and Jonathan Kaye by one stroke. Became first player in 51 Hartford tournaments to win in consecutive years...Third-place finish at the Masters was sixth career top-10 at Augusta National and fourth consecutive top-10. After entering the final round four strokes behind Tiger Woods and Retief Goosen, birdied the first two holes to close within two strokes of Woods. Finished with 1-under-par 71, four behind Woods...Runner-up to Tiger Woods at the U.S. Open. Finishing even par, joined Woods as only two players at par or better on the week...Member of fourth Ryder Cup squad, compiling a 2-2-1 record. All-time record in Ryder Cup play is 8-5-3. **2001:** Continued to be among the game's top players, posting two PGA TOUR victories and finishing second on the money list ($4,403,883)...Won the Buick Invitational in hometown of San Diego in playoff with Frank Lickliter II and Davis Love III. Beat Lickliter with a double bogey on the third extra hole...Won for the second time on the season at Canon Greater Hartford Open, keyed by a third-round 61, his career low round...Shot three straight 66s to start the PGA at Atlanta Athletic Club. Came down to 18th hole one behind David Toms. Toms laid up short of the hazard in front of the green. Mickelson's long birdie putt from the back of the green was just short and Toms got up and down for par and the victory...Took remainder season off after NEC Invitational in September because of the birth of a second child, Sophia Isabel, on Oct. 23. **2000:** Enjoyed fifth multiple-win season and second four-win season, including ending Tiger Woods' consecutive victory string at six with four-stroke win at Buick Invitational and capturing the TOUR Championship at Atlanta's East Lake GC with a final-round 66. **1999:** Despite failing to win, posted another strong season and had memorable performance in the U.S.Open at Pinehurst. With wife Amy's delivery of their first child imminent, lost by one stroke to Payne Stewart. Couple's first child, Amanda Bryan, was born day after tournament finished...Had a 2-2-0 record in his third Ryder Cup, including a 4-and-3 defeat of Jarmo Sandelin in Sunday's singles. **1998:** Was able to hold off the charging pair of Mark O'Meara and Tiger Woods on Sunday with a final-round 68 to win Mercedes Championships...Also won the weather-postponed AT&T Pebble Beach National Pro-Am. **1997:** Two-time winner, with victories at Bay Hill Invitational and Sprint International. Finished in top 25 in 15 of 21 tournaments entered. **1996:** Won four times, including two of his first three starts, successfully defending Nortel Open title and defeating Justin Leonard in playoff to win Phoenix Open. Became first player since Johnny Miller in 1975 to win in Phoenix and Tucson in the same year...Won GTE Byron Nelson Classic and NEC World Series of Golf, taking the lead at both events after 36 holes. **1995:** Won Northern Telecom Open for the second time, following his 1991 victory as an amateur...Made first appearance as member of Ryder Cup team. **1994:** Won Mercedes Championships at La Costa, defeating Fred Couples in a playoff...Made first Presidents Cup team, finishing with 2-1-2 record. **1993:** Won first two titles as a professional, the Buick Invitational in hometown of San Diego, and The INTERNATIONAL. **Amateur:** Last amateur to win PGA TOUR event with victory at 1991 Northern Telecom Open, by one stroke over Tom Purtzer. Was the first amateur since Scott Verplank in 1985 at the Western Open to win PGA TOUR event...In 1990, became only left-handed player to win U.S. Amateur...One of only three golfers to win NCAA Championship and U.S. Amateur in same year. The other two are Jack Nicklaus and Tiger Woods...Along with Gary Hallberg, David Duval and Bryce Molder, only four-time first-team golf All-Americans.

PERSONAL:

After Masters victory in April of 2004, did media tour of New York and Los Angeles that included appearances on Late Night with David Letterman and The Tonight Show with Jay Leno. . .Started hitting golf balls at 18 months. . .Is right-handed in everything except golf. As his father demonstrated right-handed, he followed along left-handed. . .An avid pilot. . .With wife Amy, was involved with the Special Operations Warrior Foundation in 2004. Donated $100 for each birdie and $500 for each eagle Mickelson posted in 2004 to the Birdies for the Brave program to support U.S. troops and their families. . .Mother, Mary, was honored as March of Dimes Mother of the Year in November 1998. . .First golf course design project, Whisper Rock, near Scottsdale, AZ, opened in 2001. . .Web site is philmickelson.com. . .National Co-Chairman for American Junior Golf Association.

PLAYER STATISTICS

2004 PGA TOUR STATISTICS

Scoring Average	69.16	(4)
Driving Distance	295.4	(30)
Driving Accuracy Percentage	62.9%	(120)
Total Driving	150	(33)
Greens in Regulation Pct.	69.5%	(10)
Putting Average	1.759	(43)
Sand Save Percentage	56.4%	(15)
Eagles (Holes per)	203.1	(71)
Birdie Average	4.20	(3)
All-Around Ranking	296	(3)
Scoring Avg. Before Cut	69.22	(2)
Round 3 Scoring Avg.	69.61	(14)
Final Round Scoring Average	70.44	(23)
Birdie Conversion Percentage	32.9%	(6)
Par Breakers	23.8%	(3)

MISCELLANEOUS PGA TOUR STATISTICS

2004 Low Round/Round: 63–Bob Hope Chrysler Classic/2
Career Low Round/Round: 61–2001 Canon Greater Hartford Open/3
Career Largest Paycheck/Finish: $1,170,000–2004 Masters Tournament/1

Patrick Moore

EXEMPT STATUS: Major Medical Extension
FULL NAME: Patrick Joseph Moore
HEIGHT: 5-11
WEIGHT: 160
BIRTHDATE: April 28, 1970
BIRTHPLACE: Austin, MN
RESIDENCE: Mesa, AZ; plays out of Minot, ND
FAMILY: Wife, Jessica; Maggie (8/12/04)

EDUCATION: University of North Carolina (Industrial Relations, 1992)
TURNED PROFESSIONAL: 1993
JOINED TOUR: 2002
Nationwide Tour Alumnus

BEST PGA TOUR CAREER FINISH:
T49—2003 Phoenix Open.

NATIONWIDE TOUR VICTORIES (3):
2002 Greater Richmond Open, Lake Erie Charity Classic at Peek 'n Peak Resort, TOUR Championship.

BEST 2004 PGA TOUR FINISH:
T74—John Deere Classic.

2004 SEASON:
Due to continued problems with back that dates back to 2003, the 2002 Nationwide Tour Player of the Year was limited to only 14 events, playing on a Major Medical Extension. Coupled with $34,859 earned in 17 events in 2003-04, has the opportunity to play in six events to earn $452,636 and match the $487,495 winnings of 2003's No. 125, Esteban Toledo. If he does so, will play out of the Major Medical Extension category for the remainder of the season.

CAREER HIGHLIGHTS:
2002: Became just the fifth player in Nationwide Tour history to earn an immediate promotion to the PGA TOUR, based on victories at the Richmond Open, Lake Erie Charity Classic and the Nationwide Tour Championship...Finished first on the 2002 final money list with $381,965, overtaking Arron Oberholser in the year's season-ending event and earned Nationwide Tour Player of the Year honors...One of then-15 players in the history of the Nationwide Tour to win as a Monday Qualifier when he posted a tournament record-tying 20-under-par 268 at the Richmond Open. Made a 15-foot eagle putt on the final hole for victory...Used a birdie on the 17th hole at the Lake Erie Charity Classic to post a score of 9-under 275 after beginning the day two behind the three co-leaders and had to wait as the final groups failed to catch him...Birdied four of the last five holes in the third round of the TOUR Championship to move to 10-under-par. Inclement weather eventually shortened the tournament to 54 holes, giving Moore the victory...Did not make the cut in his first PGA TOUR event, Southern Farm Bureau Classic, after rounds of 68-76. **2001:** Finished T130 at the PGA TOUR Qualifying Tournament to earn conditional status on the Nationwide Tour for 2002...Played the Canadian Tour where his best finishes were T2s at the Barefoot Classic and the CanAm Days Championship. Finished 16th on Order of Merit. **2000:** Had two runners-up finishes on the Canadian Tour. **Amateur:** Three-time All-ACC selection at the University of North Carolina...1991 All-American...Selected honorable mention All-American in 1990 and 1992.

PERSONAL:
Got his start in golf by going to the practice range with his father in North Dakota...Cites the 1995 U.S. Open as his biggest thrill in golf.

PLAYER STATISTICS

2004 PGA TOUR STATISTICS

Scoring Average	74.02	(N/A)
Driving Distance	281.6	(N/A)
Driving Accuracy Percentage	62.9%	(N/A)
Total Driving	(N/A)	(N/A)
Greens in Regulation Pct.	58.2%	(N/A)
Putting Average	1.855	(N/A)
Sand Save Percentage	39.0%	(N/A)
Eagles (Holes per)	297.0	(N/A)
Birdie Average	2.82	(N/A)
Scoring Avg. Before Cut	73.53	(N/A)
Round 3 Scoring Avg.	68.00	(N/A)
Final Round Scoring Average	77.00	(N/A)
Birdie Conversion Percentage	25.4%	(N/A)
Par Breakers	16.0%	(N/A)

MISCELLANEOUS PGA TOUR STATISTICS

2004 Low Round/Round: 66–Bob Hope Chrysler Classic/4
Career Low Round/Round: 65–2003 Bob Hope Chrysler Classic/3
Career Largest Paycheck/Finish: $9,720–2003 Bob Hope Chrysler Classic/T61

PGA TOUR CAREER SUMMARY — PLAYOFF RECORD: 0-0

Year	Events Played	Cuts Made	1st	2nd	3rd	Top 10	Top 25	Earnings	Rank
2002	1								
2003	3	2						$19,411	240
2004	14	2						15,448	248
Total	18	4						34,859	
NATIONWIDE TOUR									
1992	1	1						735	261
1999	1	1						945	227
2002	20	16	3	1		9	11	381,965	1
2003	3	2						3,879	253
Total	25	20	3	1		9	11	387,524	

Kevin Na

EXEMPT STATUS: 87th on the 2004 money list
FULL NAME: Kevin Sangwook Na
HEIGHT: 5-11
WEIGHT: 167
BIRTHDATE: September 15, 1983
BIRTHPLACE: Seoul, South Korea
RESIDENCE: Rancho Cucamonga, CA
FAMILY: Single
TURNED PROFESSIONAL: 2001
Q SCHOOL: 2003

BEST PGA TOUR CAREER FINISH:

T3—2004 Southern Farm Bureau Classic.

INTERNATIONAL VICTORIES (1):

2002 Volvo Masters of Asia.

OTHER VICTORIES (1):

2002 Long Beach Open.

BEST 2004 PGA TOUR FINISHES:

T3—Southern Farm Bureau Classic; T4—The Honda Classic.

2004 SEASON:

The youngest member on the PGA TOUR in 2004...The TOUR rookie carded a final-day 69 at The Honda Classic to move up the leaderboard for a T4 finish. His first top-10 on the PGA TOUR in his 11th career start...Was among the leaders all week at the MCI Heritage, but closing 73 dropped him out of the top 10 to T11...Made one start on the Asian Tour at the Kolon Korean Open in September, finished T26...Next top-10 did not come until October, when rounds of 66-66 on the weekend helped him to a career-best T3 finish at the Southern Farm Bureau Classic...Ended the year on a high note with a T13 finish at the Chrysler Championship. His $93,750 payday in Tampa secured him a spot inside the top 100 on the final season money list. Finished T2 at the Shinhan Korea Golf Championship after the 2004 season. Collected career-best $325,000.

CAREER HIGHLIGHTS:

2003: Earned first PGA TOUR card at age 20 by finishing T21 at the 2003 Qualifying Tournament. Medalist by eight strokes at La Purisima CC in Lompoc, CA during first stage of tournament. Finished T3 in second stage at Oak Valley GC in Beaumont, CA. Played his second season on the Asian Tour and finished 46th on the Order of Merit. His win on the Asian Tour in 2002 qualified him for the 2003 WGC-NEC Invitational, where he finished T71. Also played in 11 events on the European Tour with one top-10, a T6 at the Dubai Desert Classic. **2002:** Played professionally on the Asian Tour, where he finished fourth on the Order of Merit. Became the third-youngest winner in Asian Tour history at 19 years and three months when he won the 2002 Volvo Masters of Asia by two strokes. Added five other top-10s that season.

PERSONAL:

At age 8, Na's family moved from South Korea to the United States. Took up the game a year later and by the time he left the junior golf program had become the number one junior player in the U.S. By-passed senior year of high school and college to turn professional at age 17.

PLAYER STATISTICS

2004 PGA TOUR STATISTICS

Scoring Average	71.21	(105)
Driving Distance	280.1	(157)
Driving Accuracy Percentage	68.7%	(39)
Total Driving	196	(98)
Greens in Regulation Pct.	64.7%	(107)
Putting Average	1.775	(86)
Sand Save Percentage	49.7%	(83)
Eagles (Holes per)	345.6	(152)
Birdie Average	3.49	(105)
All-Around Ranking	834	(116)
Scoring Avg. Before Cut	70.86	(78)
Round 3 Scoring Avg.	70.28	(44)
Final Round Scoring Average	71.41	(84)
Birdie Conversion Percentage	28.3%	(121)
Par Breakers	19.7%	(110)

MISCELLANEOUS PGA TOUR STATISTICS

2004 Low Round/Round: 64–Booz Allen Classic/3
Career Low Round/Round: 64–2004 Booz Allen Classic/3
Career Largest Paycheck/Finish: $196,875–2004 The Honda Classic/T4

PGA TOUR CAREER SUMMARY — PLAYOFF RECORD: 0-0

Year	Events Played	Cuts Made	1st	2nd	3rd	Top 10	Top 25	Earnings	Rank
2001	1								
2003	2	1							
2004	32	19			1	2	7	$901,158	87
Total	35	20			1	2	7	901,158	
NATIONWIDE TOUR									
2001	1								
Total	1								
EUROPEAN TOUR									
2003	11	9				1	4	207,471	
JAPAN GOLF TOUR									
2003	1	1						7,080	

PGA TOUR TOP TOURNAMENT SUMMARY

Year	03
WGC-NEC Invitational	T71

Jack Nicklaus (NICK-lus)

WORLD GOLF HALL of FAME

WORLD GOLF HALL OF FAME MEMBER (Inducted 1974)
EXEMPT STATUS: Winner, 1962 U.S. Open (Lifetime)
FULL NAME: Jack William Nicklaus
HEIGHT: 5-11
WEIGHT: 180
BIRTHDATE: January 21, 1940
BIRTHPLACE: Columbus, OH
RESIDENCE: North Palm Beach, FL
FAMILY: Wife, Barbara Bash; Jack II (9/23/61), Steven (4/11/63), Nancy Jean (5/5/65),Gary (1/15/69), Michael (7/24/73); 17 grandchildren
CLUB AFFILIATIONS: Muirfield VIllage GC (Dublin, OH), The Bear's Club (Jupiter, FL)
EDUCATION: Ohio State University
SPECIAL INTERESTS: Fishing, hunting, tennis
TURNED PROFESSIONAL: 1961
JOINED TOUR: 1962

PGA TOUR CAREER SUMMARY — PLAYOFF RECORD: 14-11

Year	Events Played	Cuts Made	1st	2nd	3rd	Top 10	Top 25	Earnings	Rank
1958A	2	2					1		
1959A	7	5					1		
1960A	3	3		1		1	2		
1961A	6	6				3	4		
1962	26	26	3	3	4	16	22	$61,869	3
1963	22	21	5	2	2	17	21	100,040	
1964	25	25	4	6	3	17	24	113,285	1
1965	23	23	5	4	1	17	17	140,752	1
1966	18	18	3	3	3	12	16	111,419	2
1967	21	19	5	2	3	13	14	188,998	
1968	19	19	2	3	1	12	18	148,168	
1969	23	21	3	1		10	15	131,990	3
1970	21	19	3	2	2	10	14	105,229	9
1971	18	18	5	3	3	15	15	241,873	1
1972	19	19	7	3		14	16	316,911	1
1973	18	18	7	1	1	16	17	305,463	1
1974	18	18	2	3		12	17	234,455	2
1975	16	16	5	1	3	14	16	298,149	1
1976	16	15	2	2	1	11	15	266,439	1
1977	18	16	3	2	1	14	16	284,509	2
1978	15	13	4	2		10	12	256,672	4
1979	12	12			1	3	6	59,434	71
1980	13	12	2	1		3	8	172,386	13
1981	16	15		3		8	13	178,213	16
1982	15	12	1	3	2	7	11	232,645	12
1983	15	14		3	1	8	11	256,158	10
1984	13	13	1	2	1	6	12	272,595	15
1985	15	14		2	1	4	8	165,456	43
1986	15	11	1			4	7	226,015	34
1987	11	9				1	5	64,686	127
1988	9	5					2	28,845	177
1989	10	9				2	4	96,595	129
1990	9	6				1	1	68,045	160
1991	8	7				1	4	123,797	122
1992	8	3						14,868	223
1993	10	4				1	1	51,532	182
1994	8	1						11,514	248
1995	11	4				1	1	68,180	179
1996	6	3						37,779	208
1997	7	4				1	1	85,383	174
1998	5	3				1	1	128,157	172
1999	2	1						5,075	322
2000	8	2						17,244	229
2001	4								
2002	1	1						8,910	241
2003	4								
2004	2	1						11,130	251
Total	591	506	73	58	34	286	389	5,734,322	

NATIONWIDE TOUR

Year	Events Played	Cuts Made	1st	2nd	3rd	Top 10	Top 25	Earnings	Rank
2003	1	1						2,113	293
2004	1								
Total	2	1						2,113	

CHAMPIONS TOUR CAREER SUMMARY — PLAYOFF RECORD: 2-1

Year	Events Played	1st	2nd	3rd	Top 10	Top 25	Earnings	Rank
1990	4	2	1	1	4	4	$340,000	15
1991	5	3			4	5	343,734	17
1992	4		1	1	3	3	114,548	53
1993	6	1			3	5	206,028	42
1994	6	1			5	5	239,278	34
1995	7	1	2	1	7	7	538,800	22
1996	7	2			3	7	360,861	38
1997	6		1		3	6	239,932	58
1998	6				3	5	205,723	61
1999	3					1	19,673	110
2000	7				1	5	166,422	74
2001	7				2	4	266,127	61
2002	2						1,880	176
2003	9				2	6	221,593	62
2004	4				1	2	105,464	84
Total	83	10	5	3	41	65	3,370,062	

PGA TOUR TOP TOURNAMENT SUMMARY

Year	58	59	60	61	62	63	64	65	66	67	68	69	70
Masters		CUT	T13	T7	T15	**1**	T2	**1**	**1**	CUT	T5	T23	8
U.S. Open	T41	CUT	2	T4	**1**	CUT	T23	T32	3	**1**	2	T25	T51
British Open					T34	3	2	T12	**1**	2	T2	T6	**1**
PGA					T3	**1**	T2	T2	T22	T3	CUT	T11	T6

Year	71	72	73	74	75	76	77	78	79	80	81	82	83
Masters	T2	**1**	T3	T4	**1**	T3	2	7	4	T33	T2	T15	W/D
U.S. Open	2	**1**	T4	T10	T7	T11	T10	T6	T9	**1**	T6	2	T43
British Open	T5	2	4	3	T3	T2	2	**1**	T2	T4	T23	T10	T29
PGA	**1**	T13	**1**	2	**1**	T4	3	CUT	T65	**1**	T4	T16	2
THE PLAYERS				**1**	T18	**1**	T5	**1**	T33	T14	T29	CUT	T19

Year	84	85	86	87	88	89	90	91	92	93	94	95	96
Masters	T18	T6	**1**	T7	T21	T18	6	T35	T42	T27	CUT	T35	T41
U.S. Open	T21	CUT	T8	T46	CUT	T43	T33	T46	CUT	T72	T28	CUT	T27
British Open	T31	CUT	T46	T72	T25	T30	T63	T44	CUT	CUT	CUT	T79	T44
PGA	T25	T32	T16	T24	CUT	T27	CUT	T23	CUT	CUT	CUT	T67	CUT
THE PLAYERS	T33	T17	CUT	CUT	CUT	T29	CUT					CUT	

Year	97	98	99	00	01	02	03	04
Masters	T39	T6		T54	CUT		CUT	CUT
U.S. Open	T52	T43	CUT	CUT				
British Open	T60			CUT				
PGA	CUT			CUT				

CHAMPIONS TOUR TOP TOURNAMENT SUMMARY

Year	90	91	92	93	94	95	96	97	98	99	00	01	02
Senior PGA Championship	T3	**1**	T10	T9	9	8	T22	T2	T6		T12	12	W/D
U.S. Senior Open	2	**1**	T3	**1**	T7	2	16	T5	T13		T21	T4	
Ford Senior Players Championship	**1**	T22		T22	T6	2	T24	T8	6	W/D	T34	W/D	
JELD-WEN Tradition	**1**	**1**	2	T9	T4	**1**	**1**	T25	T25		T9	T29	69

Year	03	04
Senior PGA Championship	CUT	W/D
U.S. Senior Open	T25	
Ford Senior Players Championship	T40	
Senior British Open	T14	
JELD-WEN Tradition	T10	

NATIONAL TEAMS: Walker Cup (2), 1959, 1961; World Amateur Team Championship, 1960; World Cup (6), 1963, 1964, 1966, 1967, 1971, 1973 (medalist three times); Ryder Cup (6), 1969, 1971, 1973, 1975, 1977, 1981; Ryder Cup Captain (2), 1983, 1987; The Presidents Cup Captain, 1998, 2003, 2005.

Jack Nicklaus (Continued)

PGA TOUR VICTORIES (73):

1962 U.S. Open Championship, Seattle World's Fair Open Invitational, Portland Open Invitational. **1963** Palm Springs Golf Classic, Masters Tournament, Tournament of Champions, PGA Championship, Sahara Invitational. **1964** Phoenix Open Invitational, Tournament of Champions, Whitemarsh Open Invitational, Portland Open Invitational. **1965** Masters Tournament, Memphis Open Invitational, Thunderbird Classic, Philadelphia Golf Classic, Portland Open Invitational. **1966** Masters Tournament, British Open Championship, Sahara Invitational. **1967** Bing Crosby National Pro-Am, U.S. Open Championship, Western Open, Westchester Classic, Sahara Invitational. **1968** Western Open, American Golf Classic. **1969** Andy Williams-San Diego Open Invitational, Sahara Invitational, Kaiser International Open Invitational. **1970** Byron Nelson Golf Classic, British Open Championship, National Four-Ball Championship [with Arnold Palmer]. **1971** PGA Championship, Tournament of Champions, Byron Nelson Golf Classic, National Team Championship [with Arnold Palmer], Walt Disney World Open Invitational. **1972** Bing Crosby National Pro-Am, Doral-Eastern Open, Masters Tournament, U.S. Open Championship, Westchester Classic, U.S. Professional Match Play Championship, Walt Disney World Open Invitational. **1973** Bing Crosby National Pro-Am, Greater New Orleans Open, Tournament of Champions, Atlanta Classic, PGA Championship, Ohio Kings Island Open, Walt Disney World Golf Classic. **1974** Hawaiian Open, Tournament Players Championship. **1975** Doral-Eastern Open, Sea Pines Heritage Classic, Masters Tournament, PGA Championship, World Open Golf Championship. **1976** Tournament Players Championship, World Series of Golf. **1977** Jackie Gleason-Inverrary Classic, MONY Tournament of Champions, Memorial Tournament. **1978** Jackie Gleason-Inverrary Classic, Tournament Players Championship, British Open Championship, IVB-Philadelphia Golf Classic. **1980** U.S. Open Championship, PGA Championship. **1982** Colonial National Invitation. **1984** Memorial Tournament. **1986** Masters Tournament.

CHAMPIONS TOUR VICTORIES (10):

1990 The Tradition at Desert Mountain, Mazda SENIOR TOURNAMENT PLAYERS Championship. **1991** The Tradition at Desert Mountain, PGA Seniors' Championship, U.S. Senior Open. **1993** U.S. Senior Open. **1994** Mercedes Championships. **1995** The Tradition. **1996** GTE Suncoast Classic, The Tradition.

INTERNATIONAL VICTORIES (11):

1963 Canada Cup [indiv]. **1964** Australian Open [Aus], Canada Cup [indiv]. **1968** Australian Open [Aus.]. **1970** Piccadily World Match Play Championship [Eur]. **1971** Australian Open [Aus], Dunlop International [Aus], World Cup [indiv]. **1975** Australian Open [Aus]. **1976** Australian Open [Aus]. **1978** Australian Open [Aus].

OTHER VICTORIES (9):

1963 Canada Cup [with Arnold Palmer]. **1964** Canada Cup [with Arnold Palmer]. **1966** PGA National Team Championship [with Arnold Palmer], Canada Cup [with Arnold Palmer]. **1967** World Cup [with Arnold Palmer]. **1971** World Cup [with Lee Trevino]. **1973** World Cup [with Johnny Miller]. **1999** Champions Tour-Hyundai Team Matches [with Tom Watson]. **2000** Champions Tour-Hyundai Team Matches [with Tom Watson].

BEST 2004 PGA TOUR FINISH:

T63—the Memorial Tournament.

BEST 2004 CHAMPIONS TOUR FINISH:

6—MasterCard Championship

2004 SEASON:

Made two starts, including one major championship, the Masters. Played as host of the Memorial Tournament, where he made the cut and finished T63...Made the cut in all four appearances on the Champions Tour. Best finish was sixth at the season-opening MasterCard Championship in Kona, HI...For the second consecutive year played in the BMW Charity Pro-Am on the Nationwide Tour near Greenville, SC, with his four sons, and missed the cut by one stroke despite shooting 69-71...Named to serve as Presidents Cup captain for a third time, scheduled for the fall of 2005.

CAREER HIGHLIGHTS:

"Golden Bear" considered by many the greatest player in the history of the sport...Along with Gene Sarazen, Ben Hogan, Gary Player and Tiger Woods, owns a career Grand Slam...Winner of 18 professional major championships: six Masters (1963, '65, '66, '72, '75, '86), five PGA Championships (1963, '71, '73, '75, '80), four U.S. Opens (1962, '67, '72, '80) and three British Opens (1966, '70, '78)...Shares with Arnold Palmer the record for most consecutive years with at least one TOUR victory: 17 (1962-78)...105 consecutive cuts made (11/70-9/76) is third only to Tiger Woods and Byron Nelson...Finished in top 10 in 243 of 357 TOUR events from 1962 to 1979 (68.1 percent)...From 1971-73, had 41 top-10s in 55 events (88.8 percent), including 19 victories and seven seconds...Also has 19 runner-up finishes in majors...Led TOUR in earnings eight times (1964, '65, '67, '71, '72, '73, '75, '76). **2003:** Made four starts, including one major championship, the Masters...Played in the Ford Championship at Doral, Bay Hill Invitational and as host of the Memorial Tournament...Appeared in more Champions Tour events than in any other previous season since joining the circuit in 1990...Made his debut on the Nationwide Tour at the BMW Charity Pro-Am at The Cliffs near Greenville, SC. Appearance at The Cliffs with four sons marked the first time all five played together in a professional event. He was the only Nicklaus to make the cut...Captained the U.S. Presidents Cup team for a second time in the matches in South Africa. **2002:** Announced on April 3 that a bad back would force him to miss the Masters, only the second time the six-time champion didn't start in the tournament since his debut in 1959. Hip replacement surgery forced him to miss the 1999 tournament...Made one start during the season as tournament host of the Memorial Tournament. His 71-74—145 two-round total was good enough to make his first cut on the PGA TOUR since the 2000 Memorial Tournament...Teamed with Tiger Woods to win the Battle of Bighorn over Sergio Garcia and Lee Trevino, 3 and 2. **2000:** Named "Golfer of the Century" by virtually every national and international media outlet...Named Sports Illustrated's Male Athlete of the Century and No. 9 on ESPN's list of 100 Greatest Athletes of the Century...Played in all four majors, possibly for the last time...U.S. Open site of Pebble Beach was home to his Open victory in 1972 and U.S. Amateur title in 1961...Received Distinguished Service Award at PGA Championship. **1998:** It was announced at the PGA TOUR Awards Dinner that PGA TOUR and Champions Tour Player of the Year Awards would be named in his honor (Nationwide Tour honor also holds that title now)...Streak of consecutive major championships played (146) and consecutive majors for which he was eligible (154) ended...Thrilled golf fans around world at the Masters, where he was in hunt down to the final moments...Final-round 68 was instrumental in making him, at 58, the oldest to post Masters top-10...Served as Presidents Cup captain. **1997:** Broke Sam Snead's record for most rounds played at Augusta National with 147. **1988:** First PGA TOUR player to reach $5 million (8/20/88). **1987:** Captain of Ryder Cup at his own Muirfield Village in Dublin, Ohio. **1986:** Became oldest player to win Masters (46), shooting a final-round 65, coming home in 30. Masters win was first major victory since capturing U.S. Open and PGA in 1980. **1983:** First PGA TOUR player to reach $4 million. **1980:** Captured U.S. Open and PGA...Named Sports Illustrated Sportsman of the Decade for the 1970s. **1979:** British Open champion for the third time. **1978:** Named Sports Illustrated Sportsman of the Year. **1977:** First PGA TOUR player to reach $3 million (5/2/77). **1976:** Named PGA Player of the Year for the fifth time (1967-72-73-75-76). **1975:** Captured five PGA TOUR events, including Masters and PGA Championship. **1974:** Tied previous year's career high for wins with seven...Inducted into World Golf Hall of Fame. **1973:** First PGA TOUR player to reach $2 million (12/1/73)...PGA Championship winner, one of career-high seven victories on the season in only 18 events. **1972:** Winner of Masters and U.S. Open, and runner-up at British Open, one of 19 second-place major finishes. **1969:** Playing in his first Ryder Cup Matches, conceded a two-footer to Tony Jacklin after making a four-footer for par on the last green, resulting in the first tie in the Matches' history. Considered one of golf's all-time gestures of sportsmanship. **1966:** Second consecutive Masters victory (and third in four years) and first British Open win. **1965:** 17 top-10s in 20 events...Five victories included second Masters win. **1964:** Runner-up finishes at Masters, British Open and PGA Championship...Led PGA TOUR in official earnings for the first time. **1963:** First Masters and PGA Championship victories...Posted 17 top-10s in 24 events, including five wins. **1962:** As a rookie, first professional victory came at U.S. Open at Oakmont CC, where he defeated Arnold Palmer in 18-hole playoff. **Amateur:** Won two U.S. Amateur titles, defeating Charles Coe 1-up in 1959 and Dudley Wysong 8 and 6 in 1961...Finished runner-up to Arnold Palmer in 1960 U.S. Open as an amateur, shooting 282...Won 1961 NCAA Championship at Ohio State.

PERSONAL:

One of golf's driving forces off the course...Founder and host of the Memorial Tournament...The Nicklaus Companies' global business includes golf course design, development and licensing...Alma mater, Ohio State, opened the Jack Nicklaus Museum on campus in May 2002...Named 1999 Father of Year by Minority Golf Association.

PLAYER STATISTICS

2004 PGA TOUR STATISTICS

Scoring Average	72.92	(N/A)
Driving Distance	260.2	(N/A)
Driving Accuracy Percentage	72.6%	(N/A)
Total Driving	(N/A)	(N/A)
Greens in Regulation Pct.	61.1%	(N/A)
Putting Average	1.894	(N/A)
Sand Save Percentage	60.0%	(N/A)
Birdie Average	2.00	(N/A)
Scoring Avg. Before Cut	74.25	(N/A)
Round 3 Scoring Avg.	77.00	(N/A)
Final Round Scoring Average	71.00	(N/A)
Birdie Conversion Percentage	18.2%	(N/A)
Par Breakers	11.1%	(N/A)

MISCELLANEOUS PGA TOUR STATISTICS

2004 Low Round/Round: 71–the Memorial Tournament/4
Career Low Round/Round: 62–2 times, most recent 1973 Ohio Kings Island Open/3
Career Largest Paycheck/Finish: $144,000–1986 Masters Tournament/1

2004 CHAMPIONS TOUR STATISTICS

Scoring Average	70.42	(N/A)
Driving Distance	270.0	(N/A)
Driving Accuracy Percentage	67.9%	(N/A)
Total Driving	(N/A)	(N/A)
Greens in Regulation Pct.	68.5%	(N/A)
Putting Average	1.743	(N/A)
Sand Save Percentage	55.0%	(N/A)
Eagles (Holes per)	108.0	(N/A)
Birdie Average	3.50	(N/A)
All-Around Ranking	1,569	(N/A)

MISCELLANEOUS CHAMPIONS TOUR STATISTICS

2004 Low Round: 66–MasterCard Championship/2.
Career Low Round: 64–2 times, most recent 1990 Mazda SENIOR TOURNAMENT PLAYERS Championship/4
Career Largest Paycheck: $150,000–3 times, most recent 1996 The Tradition/1

Greg Norman

WORLD GOLF HALL OF FAME MEMBER (Inducted 2001)
EXEMPT STATUS: Winner, 1997 NEC World Series of Golf (Through 2007)
FULL NAME: Gregory John Norman
HEIGHT: 6-0
WEIGHT: 180
BIRTHDATE: February 10, 1955
BIRTHPLACE: Mt. Isa, Queensland, Australia
RESIDENCE: Hobe Sound, FL; plays out of Medalist
FAMILY: Wife, Laura; Morgan-Leigh (10/5/82), Gregory (9/19/85)
SPECIAL INTERESTS: Fishing, hunting, scuba diving
TURNED PROFESSIONAL: 1976
JOINED TOUR: 1983

PGA TOUR VICTORIES (20):

1984 Kemper Open, Canadian Open. **1986** Panasonic Las Vegas Invitational, Kemper Open, British Open Championship. **1988** MCI Heritage Golf Classic. **1989** The International, Greater Milwaukee Open. **1990** Doral-Ryder Open, Memorial Tournament. **1992** Canadian Open. **1993** Doral-Ryder Open, British Open Championship. **1994** THE PLAYERS Championship. **1995** Memorial Tournament, Canon Greater Hartford Open, NEC World Series of Golf. **1996** Doral-Ryder Open. **1997** FedEx St. Jude Classic, NEC World Series of Golf.

INTERNATIONAL VICTORIES (68):

1976 Westlakes Classic [Aus]. **1977** Martini International [Eur], Kuzuhz International [Jpn]. **1978** New South Wales Open [Aus], Traralgon Classic [Aus], Caltex Festival of Sydney Open [Aus], South Seas Classic [Fiji]. **1979** Traralgon Classic [Aus], Martini International [Eur], Hong Kong Open. **1980** Australian Open [Aus], French Open [Eur], Scandinavian Open [Eur], Suntory World Match Play Championship [Eur], State Express Classic, Benson & Hedges International. **1981** Australian Masters [Aus], Martini International [Eur], Dunlop Masters [Eur]. **1982** Dunlop Masters [Eur], State Express Classic [Eur], Benson & Hedges International [Eur]. **1983** Australian Masters [Aus], Stefan Queensland Open [Aus], National Panasonic New South Wales Open [Aus], Hong Kong Open, Cannes Invitational [Eur], Suntory World Match Play Championship [Eur], Kapalua International. **1984** Victorian Open [Aus], Australian Masters [Aus], Australian PGA [Aus].**1985** Toshiba Australian PGA Championship [Aus], National Panasonic Australian Open [Aus], Dunhill Cup. **1986** Stefan Queensland Open [Aus], National Panasonic New South Wales Open [Aus], West End Jubilee South Australian Open [Aus], National Panasonic Western Australian Open [Aus], European Open [Eur], Suntory World Matchplay Championship [Eur], Dunhill Cup, PGA Grand Slam of Golf. **1987** Australian Masters [Aus], National Panasonic Australian Open [Aus]. **1988** Palm Meadows Cup [Aus], ESP Open [Aus], PGA National Tournament Players Championship [Aus], Panasonic New South Wales Open [Aus], Lancia Italian Open [Eur]. **1989** Australian Masters [Aus], PGA National Tournament Players Championship [Aus], Chunichi Crowns [Jpn]. **1990** Australian Masters [Aus]. **1993** Taiheyo Masters [Jpn], PGA Grand Slam of Golf. **1994** Johnnie Walker Asian Classic [Eur], PGA Grand Slam of Golf. **1995** Australian Open [Aus], Fred Meyer Challenge [with Brad Faxon]. **1996** Ford South Australian Open [Aus], Australian Open [Aus], Fred Meyer Challenge [with Brad Faxon]. **1997** Fred Meyer Challenge [with Brad Faxon], Andersen Consulting World Championship. **1998** Greg Norman Holden International [Aus], Franklin Templeton Shootout [with Steve Elkington]. **2001** Skins Game.

BEST 2004 PGA TOUR FINISH:

T81—THE PLAYERS Championship.

2004 SEASON:

Played in seven PGA TOUR events, making only one cut—at THE PLAYERS Championship (T81). Made one start in a major championship, at the British Open…Made two appearances on the European Tour.

CAREER HIGHLIGHTS:

2003: Made only seven starts on the PGA TOUR and played on the weekend four times...Opened up one stroke back of the lead after the first round of the British Open. Rounds of 79-74-68 dropped him into T18 for the tournament. Played in his 19th consecutive British Open without missing a cut dating back to 1981, the longest active streak. Did not participate four years during the streak (1988, 1998, 2000 and 2001). **2002:** Played in 13 PGA TOUR events in a reduced schedule, making the cut 10 times and withdrawing once...Turned in first top-10 since a T4 at the 2001 Bay Hill Invitational with a T4 at The INTERNATIONAL Presented by Qwest...Best worldwide finish was a T6 in the Heineken Classic in Australia. **2001:** Played in 11 PGA TOUR events in 2001, with a best finish of T4 at the Bay Hill Invitational...Inducted into World Golf Hall of Fame...Captured $1 million at the 2001 Skins Game, shutting out Tiger Woods, Colin Montgomerie and Jesper Parnevik. **2000:** Despite playing a reduced schedule due to medical reasons, still managed 84th-place ranking on official money list with $580,510...Earned first of two top-10s at Buick Classic. Fourth-place finish was best since third at 1999 Masters and just third top-10 since 1997 season...Sidelined by arthroscopic hip surgery June 28. Right hip had bothered him for a number of years. Pain linked to left shoulder problems that required reconstructive surgery in 1998. After missing cut at U.S. Open and with intense pain and discomfort, opted for surgery. In amazing show of physical perseverance, returned to action at INTERNATIONAL just five weeks later to record second top-10 of year. Finished alone in fourth with 38 points after returning to hitting balls just eight days prior to event...Member of International Presidents Cup team where he compiled 1-3 record in losing effort to American squad...Received honorary life membership on European Tour. **1999:** Played reduced schedule as he continued to recover from previous year's shoulder surgery. Began year at WGC-Accenture Match Play Championship where he lost in the second round and finished T17...Became first player to surpass $12 million in PGA TOUR career earnings when he won $29,000

PGA TOUR CAREER SUMMARY — PLAYOFF RECORD: 4-7

Year	Events Played	Cuts Made	1st	2nd	3rd	Top 10	Top 25	Earnings	Rank
1979	2	2						$3,653	208
1981	9	8				3	5	54,272	77
1982	4	3				1	2	22,671	142
1983	9	9		1		2	4	71,411	74
1984	16	15	2	2		7	10	310,230	9
1985	16	13		2		6	9	165,458	42
1986	19	17	3	4	1	10	12	653,296	1
1987	18	18		2	2	9	13	535,450	7
1988	14	12	1	2	1	7	11	514,854	17
1989	17	16	2	1	1	8	14	835,096	4
1990	17	16	2	2		11	15	1,165,477	1
1991	17	15		1		6	7	320,196	53
1992	16	15	1	2		8	10	676,443	18
1993	15	14	2	4	2	12	13	1,359,653	3
1994	16	16	1	3		11	14	1,330,307	2
1995	16	15	3	2	1	9	14	1,654,959	1
1996	17	12	1	1		5	10	891,237	15
1997	15	13	2	2	1	7	10	1,345,856	7
1998	3	1						25,925	235
1999	12	9			1	2	6	570,879	69
2000	12	10				2	4	580,510	84
2001	11	7				1	1	256,310	156
2002	13	10				1	4	467,988	
2003	7	4					2	119,799	199
2004	7	1						14,160	249
Total	318	271	20	31	10	128	190	13,946,089	
EUROPEAN TOUR									
2004	2	1						2,254	

PGA TOUR TOP TOURNAMENT SUMMARY

Year	77	78	79	80	81	82	83	84	85	86	87	88	89
Masters					4	T36	T30	T25	T47	T2	T2	T5	T3
U.S. Open			T48		T33		T50	2	T15	T12	T51	W/D	T33
British Open	CUT	T29	T10	CUT	T31	T27	T19	T6	T16	**1**	T35		T2
PGA					T4	T5	T42	T39	CUT	2	70	T9	T12
THE PLAYERS							T63	CUT	T49	T33	T4	T11	T4
TOUR Championship											3	30	T11

Year	90	91	92	93	94	95	96	97	98	99	00	01	02
Masters	CUT	CUT	T6	T31	T18	T3	2	CUT	CUT	3	T11	CUT	T36
U.S. Open	T5	W/D		CUT	T6	2	T10	CUT		CUT	CUT		T59
British Open	T6	T9	18	**1**	T11	T15	T7	T36		6			T18
PGA	T19	T32	T15	2	T4	T20	T17	T13		CUT	CUT	T29	T53
THE PLAYERS	T16	T63	T35	T3	**1**	T37	CUT	T53		CUT	T53	CUT	CUT
TOUR Championship	T7		T7	T2	T13	T9	W/D	T12					
WGC-Accenture Match Play										T17	T33		
WGC-NEC Invitational										T25	T31	35	T55

Year	03	04
British Open	T18	CUT
PGA	CUT	
THE PLAYERS	W/D	T81

NATIONAL TEAMS: Hennessy Cognac Cup, 1982; Nissan Cup (2), 1985, 1986; Dunhill Cup (10), 1985, 1986, 1987, 1988, 1989, 1990, 1992, 1994, 1995, 1996; Kirin Cup, 1987; Four Tours, 1989; The Presidents Cup (4), 1994 (withdrew due to illness), 1996, 1998, 2000.

Greg Norman (Continued)

for T19 at Doral-Ryder Open...Dueled eventual champion Jose Maria Olazabal down the stretch before finishing third at the Masters. In one of the most memorable moments of the tournament, his eagle at the 13th hole was answered by Olazabal's birdie...On September 12, fell out of top 50 in Official World Golf Ranking after exactly 700 weeks, or since ranking began. **1998:** April shoulder surgery cut his season short. Surgery was performed on April 22 by Dr. Richard Hawkins at the Steadman Hawkins Sports Medicine Foundation in Vail, CO. Procedure involved the shaving of bone spurs that caused tendinitis in his rotator cuff, and the use of a heat probe to shrink the shoulder socket capsule. Followed a seven-month rehabilitation period with a victory at the Franklin Templeton Shark Shootout, playing with Steve Elkington...Won the Greg Norman Holden International in Australia in February. Victory was his first in six tries at his own tournament. **1997:** Began year with victory in finals of Andersen Consulting World Championship of Golf...Season highlighted by two victories. First win came at FedEx St. Jude Classic, where in dramatic fashion he birdied final three holes for a 66 to earn one-stroke victory over Dudley Hart. 20th TOUR victory came at NEC World Series of Golf, where final-round 67 earned four-stroke victory over Phil Mickelson...Had two second-place finishes and one third and finished among top 15 on money list for third year in a row. **1996:** Became the first to surpass $10 million in career earnings...Missed consecutive cuts for first time on TOUR at Bay Hill Invitational and THE PLAYERS Championship...At Masters, shot record-tying 63 in opening round. Led by six entering final round, but lost when he shot 78 and Nick Faldo shot 67. It was the eighth time in his career that he finished as the runner-up in a major. **1995:** Won his third Arnold Palmer Award (1986, '90, '95)...Named PGA TOUR Player of the Year...First player to earn $1 million four times (1990, '93, '94, '95)...Did not miss a cut for the fourth time in his career (1983, '87, '94 and '95)...Won three titles—Memorial Tournament, Canon Greater Hartford Open and NEC World Series of Golf—and then-record $1,654,959. **1994:** Earned his third Vardon Trophy (1988, '89, '94). **1993:** At Royal St. George's, trailed Corey Pavin and Nick Faldo by one stroke after 54 holes, then closed with 64 to defeat Faldo. **1986:** Won his first British Open title at Turnberry. After an opening 74, shot tournament-record-tying 63 to take two-stroke lead. Closed with rounds of 74-69 to defeat Gordon Brand by two strokes...Led all four majors entering the final round but won just the British. **1984:** Finished in the top 10 on the money list for the first of nine times in his career. Defeated Mark O'Meara by five strokes for his initial TOUR win at the Kemper Open. Four weeks later, won again by two strokes over Jack Nicklaus at the Canadian Open.

PERSONAL:

Serves as Chairman and CEO of Great White Shark Enterprises, a multi-national corporation with offices in Jupiter, FL, and Sydney, Australia. The company's interests are primarily focused around golf and the golf lifestyle. Established in 1987, Greg Norman Golf Course Design is recognized as one of the premier signature design groups. Medalist Developments is an international developer of premier residential golf course communities. Established in 1995, Greg Norman Turf Company licenses proprietary turfgrasses for golf courses, athletic fields and home lawns. Greg Norman Collection is a leading worldwide marketer and distributor of men's sportswear, golf apparel and accessories. Greg Norman Estates produces a line of highly rated wines. Greg Norman's Australian Grille in North Myrtle Beach, S.C., offers indoor and outdoor dining with authentic Australian fare. The Greg Norman Production Company, which is devoted to event management, operates the Franklin Templeton Shootout...Began playing at age 16 caddieing for his mother. Scratch two years later...Initial ambition was to become a pilot in the Australian Air Force but opted for golf and took just four tournaments to record first of more than 80 titles worldwide.

PLAYER STATISTICS

2004 PGA TOUR STATISTICS

Scoring Average	73.46	(N/A)
Driving Distance	284.3	(N/A)
Driving Accuracy Percentage	56.0%	(N/A)
Total Driving	(N/A)	(N/A)
Greens in Regulation Pct.	52.1%	(N/A)
Putting Average	1.844	(N/A)
Sand Save Percentage	30.4%	(N/A)
Birdie Average	2.38	(N/A)
Scoring Avg. Before Cut	74.09	(N/A)
Round 3 Scoring Avg.	77.00	(N/A)
Final Round Scoring Average	79.00	(N/A)
Birdie Conversion Percentage	21.3%	(N/A)
Par Breakers	13.2%	(N/A)

MISCELLANEOUS PGA TOUR STATISTICS

2004 Low Round/Round: 72–4 times, most recent Cialis Western Open/1

Career Low Round/Round: 62–4 times, most recent 1993 Doral-Ryder Open/3

Career Largest Paycheck/Finish: $450,000–1994 THE PLAYERS Championship/1

SHOTLink
AN IBM ON DEMAND BUSINESS SOLUTION

HOT SHOTS

Toughest Fairways to Hit on TOUR (2004)

(Note: Most players on No. 6 at Kapalua went for the green from the tee)

EVENT/ COURSE NAME	HOLE	PAR	HIT FAIRWAY	TRIES	%
Mercedes Championships Plantation Course at Kapalua	6	4	2	120	1.70%
British Open Championship Royal Troon GC	10	4	120	458	26.20%
British Open Championship Royal Troon GC	15	4	132	458	28.80%
Wachovia Championship Quail Hollow Club	5	5	160	454	35.20%
U.S. Open Championship Shinnecock Hills Golf Club	16	5	157	442	35.50%

Easiest Fairways to Hit on the TOUR (2004)

EVENT/ COURSE NAME	HOLE	PAR	HIT FAIRWAY	TRIES	%
MCI Heritage Harbor Town Golf Links	18	4	393	408	96.30%
Mercedes Championships Plantation Course at Kapalua	5	5	115	120	95.80%
Mercedes Championships Plantation Course at Kapalua	7	4	111	120	92.50%
Mercedes Championships Plantation Course at Kapalua	17	4	109	120	90.80%
Buick Classic Westchester CC	8	4	426	473	90.10%

18th Hole-Harbor Town Golf Links

Mark O'Meara

EXEMPT STATUS: Minor Medical Extension
FULL NAME: Mark Francis O'Meara
HEIGHT: 6-0
WEIGHT: 180
BIRTHDATE: January 13, 1957
BIRTHPLACE: Goldsboro, NC
RESIDENCE: Windermere, FL

FAMILY: Wife, Alicia; Michelle (3/14/87), Shaun Robert (8/29/89)
EDUCATION: Long Beach State (1980, Marketing)
SPECIAL INTERESTS: Golf course design, fly tying, fly fishing
TURNED PROFESSIONAL: 1980
Q SCHOOL: Fall 1980

PGA TOUR VICTORIES (16):

1984 Greater Milwaukee Open. **1985** Bing Crosby National Pro-Am, Hawaiian Open. **1989** AT&T Pebble Beach National Pro-Am. **1990** AT&T Pebble Beach National Pro-Am, H.E.B. Texas Open. **1991** Walt Disney World/Oldsmobile Classic. **1992** AT&T Pebble Beach National Pro-Am. **1995** Honda Classic, Bell Canadian Open. **1996** Mercedes Championships, Greater Greensboro Chrysler Classic. **1997** AT&T Pebble Beach National Pro-Am, Buick Invitational. **1998** Masters Tournament, British Open Championship.

INTERNATIONAL VICTORIES (8):

1985 Fuji Sankei Classic [Jpn]. **1986** Australian Masters [Aus]. **1987** Lawrence Batley International [Eur]. **1992** Tokai Classic [Jpn]. **1994** Argentine Open. **1997** Trophee Lancome [Eur]. **1998** Cisco World Match Play Championship. **2004** Dubai Desert Classic [Eur].

OTHER VICTORIES:

1989 RMCC [with Curtis Strange]. **1998** Cisco World Match Play Championship, Skins Game. **1999** World Cup [with Tiger Woods]. **2000** Fred Meyer Challenge. **2002** Skins Game.

BEST 2004 PGA TOUR FINISH:

T10—Buick Open.

2004 SEASON:

Limited to 17 events due to wrist injury, did not play after Deutsche Bank Championship in early September. Will play on a Minor Medical Extension in 2005, with eight events needed to earn $79,396 (equal to 2004 No. 125). If he does so, he will play out of the Major Medical Extension category for the remainder of 2005…Won for the first time on any Tour since the 1998 British Open with his victory at the Dubai Desert Classic on the European Tour. Hit all 18 greens in regulation on Sunday and finished at 17-under, one stroke ahead of Paul McGinley after the two shared the 54-hole lead at 14-under…Was only one back of the leader Tiger Woods through 36 holes at the EDS Byron Nelson Championship. Closed with a pair of 70s to finish T11. Played with Woods in the final pairing on Saturday near Dallas…First top-10 on the season on the PGA TOUR was T10 at the Buick Open, posting four rounds of 70 or better. First top-10 since T8 at the 2003 Masters Tournament…Past champion made the cut at both the Masters Tournament (T27) and British Open (T30).

CAREER HIGHLIGHTS:

2003: Fell out of the top 125 for the first time since earning his card in 1981…Only top-10 of the season came at the Masters, his first top-10 in a major (T8) since a T4 at the 1998 PGA and his first top-10 at the Masters since his win in 1998..**2002:** Two runner-up finishes were the most since he had two in 1996...T2 with J.L. Lewis at Buick Invitational for first top-10 finish. Held share of the 54-hole lead, but final-round 70 came up one stroke short of champion Jose Maria Olazabal...Aided by rounds of 70-68 on the weekend, finished T2 at the Buick Open behind champion Tiger Woods...Won The ConAgra Foods Skins Game on Thanksgiving weekend. **2001:** Second-round 63 at PGA tied all-time low 18 for a major. Top-20 finish was fifth career top-20 at Augusta National for the former Masters champion. **2000:** Struggled through difficult season, which saw him fall out of the top 100 on the official money list for first time since 1982. **1999:** Lost to Colin Montgomerie, 3 and 2, in defense of Cisco World Match Play Championship... Represented the United States on his fifth Ryder Cup team and in Dunhill Cup and World Cup competitions. **1998:** At age 41, became the oldest player to win two major championships in the same year. As a reward, was chosen by his peers as PGA TOUR Player of the Year. Joined Nick Price and Nick Faldo as the only players in the 1990s to win two majors in one year...In April, closed birdie-birdie to edge Fred Couples and David Duval and win the Masters Tournament. Joined Arnold Palmer and Art Wall as the only players to birdie the last two holes and win at Augusta National. Won at Augusta on his 15th try, the most for any first-time champion. The fifth player in Masters history to win after not leading in the first three rounds...In July, cap-

PGA TOUR CAREER SUMMARY — PLAYOFF RECORD: 3-4

Year	Events Played	Cuts Made	1st	2nd	3rd	Top 10	Top 25	Earnings	Rank
1979A	1	1							
1981	34	22		1		4	9	$76,063	56
1982	35	19				1	4	31,711	120
1983	32	17		1		2	6	69,354	76
1984	32	24	1	5	3	15	19	465,873	2
1985	25	19	2		1	6	13	340,840	10
1986	25	22		1	4	5	12	252,827	30
1987	26	20		2	1	7	11	327,250	30
1988	27	20		2	1	7	12	438,311	22
1989	26	19	1	1	1	7	13	615,804	13
1990	25	20	2		1	6	14	707,175	10
1991	25	15	1	1		5	12	563,896	20
1992	23	18	1	2		9	15	759,648	11
1993	26	18			1	4	9	349,516	43
1994	29	17				3	8	214,070	86
1995	27	21	2			8	12	914,129	10
1996	21	19	2	2	2	8	14	1,255,749	5
1997	22	19	2		1	6	11	1,124,560	13
1998	19	15	2	1	1	7	11	1,786,699	7
1999	19	15		1	1	3	8	868,796	45
2000	19	12				1	5	424,309	112
2001	21	13				1	5	438,620	116
2002	24	9		2		2	5	730,132	97
2003	25	11				1	2	388,349	143
2004	17	12				1	4	543,866	135
Total	605	417	16	22	18	119	234	13,687,545	
EUROPEAN TOUR									
2004	1	1	1			1	1	331,589	

PGA TOUR TOP TOURNAMENT SUMMARY

Year	81	82	83	84	85	86	87	88	89	90	91	92	93
Masters					24	48	T24	T39	T11	CUT	T27	T4	T21
U.S. Open	CUT	58		T7	T15	T41	CUT	T3	CUT	CUT	CUT	CUT	CUT
British Open	T47				T3	T43	T66	27	T42	T48	T3	T12	CUT
PGA	T70		CUT	T25	T28	CUT	CUT	T9	CUT	T19	CUT	CUT	CUT
THE PLAYERS	T26	T77	T49	T5	T17	T33	3	CUT	CUT	W/D	CUT	T9	5
TOUR Championship							T10	29	6	T12	T16	29	

Year	94	95	96	97	98	99	00	01	02	03	04
Masters	T15	T31	T18	T30	**1**	T31	CUT	T20	CUT	T8	T27
U.S. Open	CUT		T16	T36	T32	CUT	T51	CUT	T18	T35	
British Open		T49	T32	T38	**1**	CUT	T26	T42	T22	T65	T30
PGA		T6	T26	T13	T4	T57	T46	T22	CUT	CUT	CUT
THE PLAYERS	CUT	CUT	T29	T70	T42	T6	T9	CUT	CUT	CUT	
TOUR Championship		T13	T18	T17	T13						
WGC-Accenture Match Play						T33	T17				
WGC-NEC Invitational						T25	T27				T72

NATIONAL TEAMS: U.S. vs. Japan, 1984; Ryder Cup (5), 1985, 1989, 1991, 1997, 1999; Nissan Cup, 1985; Dunhill Cup (7), 1985, 1986, 1987, 1996, 1997, 1998, 1999; The Presidents Cup (2), 1996, 1998; World Cup, 1999.

Mark O'Meara (Continued)

tured his second major at the British Open at Royal Birkdale. Trailed by two strokes through 54 holes but shot closing 68 to tie Brian Watts, then defeated Watts 17-19 in four-hole playoff...In October, defeated Tiger Woods in final of Cisco World Match Play Championship...Named PGA of America and Golf Writers Association of America Player of Year. **1997:** Posted back-to-back victories at AT&T Pebble Beach National Pro-Am and Buick Invitational. First player to win at Pebble Beach five times. Six of his victories have come in pro-am events: 1985-89-90-92-97 AT&T Pebble Beach National Pro-Ams and 1991 Walt Disney World/Oldsmobile Classic. **1996:** Captured Mercedes Championships and Greater Greensboro Chrysler Classic to earn $1 million in season for first time. **1995:** Posted first victory in three years with Honda Classic title, then parred first playoff hole to defeat Bob Lohr at Bell Canadian Open...Equaled PGA Championship 36-hole record with 131 at Riviera CC, but finished T7. **1994:** Victory in Argentine Open gave him victories on five continents: North America, South America, Asia, Europe and Australia. **1981:** PGA TOUR Rookie of the Year. Highlight of rookie season was playoff loss to Dave Eichelberger at Tallahassee Open. **Amateur:** Defeated John Cook in final of 1979 U.S. Amateur Championship.

PERSONAL:

Continues fund-raising efforts on behalf of long-time caddie Donnie Wanstall, diagnosed with multiple sclerosis during the 1994 PLAYERS Championship. . .Took up game at age 13, when family moved above a golf course in California. . .Avid fan of Orlando professional sports, including NBA Magic and minor-league hockey Solar Bears. . .Teamed with PGA TOUR Design Services to build TPC of Valencia (CA), which opened in 2003.

PLAYER STATISTICS

2004 PGA TOUR STATISTICS

Scoring Average	71.32	(118)
Driving Distance	272.9	(187)
Driving Accuracy Percentage	67.0%	(58)
Total Driving	245	(166)
Greens in Regulation Pct.	62.5%	(162)
Putting Average	1.768	(67)
Sand Save Percentage	53.7%	(36)
Eagles (Holes per)	522.0	(178)
Birdie Average	3.29	(153)
All-Around Ranking	959	(149)
Scoring Avg. Before Cut	70.95	(88)
Round 3 Scoring Avg.	72.42	(178)
Final Round Scoring Average	71.82	(121)
Birdie Conversion Percentage	28.4%	(112)
Par Breakers	18.5%	(158)

MISCELLANEOUS PGA TOUR STATISTICS

2004 Low Round/Round: 64–Bob Hope Chrysler Classic/5
Career Low Round/Round: 62–2 times, most recent 1996 Greater Greensboro Chrysler Classic/3
Career Largest Paycheck/Finish: $576,000–1998 Masters Tournament/1

SHOTLink
AN IBM ON DEMAND BUSINESS SOLUTION

HOT SHOTS

Toughest Greens to Hit in Regulation on TOUR (2004)

EVENT/ COURSE NAME	HOLE	PAR	HIT GREEN	TRIES	%
MCI Heritage					
Harbor Town Golf Links	8	4	117	408	28.70%
FUNAI Classic at the WALT DISNEY WORLD Resort					
Palm GC **	18	4	43	144	29.90%
Buick Invitational					
Torrey Pines (South Course) (MC)	12	4	98	316	31.00%
Buick Invitational					
Torrey Pines (South Course) **	15	4	101	316	32.00%
AT&T Pebble Beach National Pro-Am					
Spyglass Hill GC (MC)	13	4	58	179	32.40%

Easiest Greens to Hit in Regulation on TOUR (2004)

EVENT/ COURSE NAME	HOLE	PAR	HIT GREEN	TRIES	%
THE TOUR Championship presented by Coca-Cola					
East Lake GC	15	5	114	118	96.60%
Mercedes Championships					
Plantation Course at Kapalua	9	5	115	120	95.80%
Ford Championship at Doral					
Doral Golf Resort & Spa	1	5	424	444	95.50%
Bob Hope Chrysler Classic					
Indian Wells CC **	5	5	121	128	94.50%
Nissan Open					
Riviera CC	1	5	417	442	94.30%

** = Multiple course tournament

15th Hole-East Lake Golf Club

Arron Oberholser (Oh-BURR-hole-zur)

EXEMPT STATUS: 52nd on 2004 money list
FULL NAME: Arron Matthew Oberholser
HEIGHT: 6-0
WEIGHT: 180
BIRTHDATE: February 2, 1975
BIRTHPLACE: San Luis Obispo, CA
RESIDENCE: Scottsdale, AZ
FAMILY: Single

EDUCATION: San Jose State University (Broadcast Journalism, 1998)
SPECIAL INTERESTS: Fishing, hunting, music, fitness
TURNED PROFESSIONAL: 1998
JOINED TOUR: 2003
Nationwide Tour Alumnus

BEST PGA TOUR CAREER FINISH:
2—2004 Wachovia Championship.

NATIONWIDE TOUR VICTORIES (2):
2002 Samsung Canadian PGA Championship, Utah Classic.

OTHER VICTORIES (1):
2004 Shinhan Korea Golf Championship.

BEST 2004 PGA TOUR FINISHES:
2—Wachovia Championship; T4—AT&T Pebble Beach National Pro-Am, Booz Allen Classic.

2004 SEASON:
Followed his rookie season with a solid sophomore campaign, making over $1.3 million and posting a career-high three top-10s, including runner-up finish at the Wachovia Championship. Made 17 cuts in 23 TOUR starts...Shared the third-round lead with eventual winner Vijay Singh at the AT&T Pebble Beach National Pro-Am after opening with three rounds in the 60s. Final-round 76 left him T4...Had a one-stroke lead heading into the final round at the Wachovia Championship. A closing 72 put him into a playoff. Lost to Joey Sindelar on the second playoff hole. His runner-up finish was a career best, as was the paycheck of $604,800...Finished T4 at the Booz Allen Classic in his first appearance at the TPC at Avenel. His $198,400 payday pushed him over the $1-million mark in season earnings for the first time in his career...Made his first start in a major championship tournament at the PGA Championship in Whistling Straits, WI, finishing T13...Other top-20 finishes included a T20 at the BellSouth Classic...Began the season 188th on Official World Golf Ranking and moved up to 89th through THE TOUR Championship...Collected $1 million first prize when he won the Shinhan Korea Golf Championship.

CAREER HIGHLIGHTS:
2003: Began rookie campaign by making eight consecutive cuts including his only two top-10s. Earned 64 percent ($396,869) of his season's earnings during the stretch...In seventh career PGA TOUR start (fourth as a TOUR member), posted first top-10 of career with a T4 at the Buick Invitational. Held the first-round lead after opening with a 7-under-par 65 on the North Course at Torrey Pines...Added a second top-10 finish during the West Coast Swing with a T6 at the Chrysler Classic of Tucson...Posted career-low 64 on TOUR during the second round of The Honda Classic. **2002:** Finished second on the Nationwide Tour money list with $319,883. Led the money list for seven of the final eight weeks of the season until Patrick Moore's victory at the TOUR Championship...Posted first of two victories at the Samsung Canadian PGA Championship. Final-round 5-under-par 66 propelled him to a tournament record 16-under par 268, more than enough to move the former Canadian Tour member to his first career win...Second victory came at the rain-shortened Utah Classic. Shot a final-round 5-under-par 67 on Sunday after tournament had been shortened to 54 holes earlier that morning. Recorded three eagles in the second round on his way to an 8-under 64, only player on Nationwide Tour to accomplish feat in 2002. **2001:** Only played in three Nationwide Tour events, his first season on the Tour, due to a wrist injury. **2000:** Finished second on the Canadian Tour Order of Merit. **1999:** Named Ericsson Canadian Tour International Rookie of the Year after winning twice. Set Canadian Tour record for largest margin of victory (11 strokes) during his win at the Ontario Open.

PERSONAL:
Has helped as men's assistant golf coach at Santa Clara University.

PLAYER STATISTICS

2004 PGA TOUR STATISTICS

Scoring Average	71.01	(82)
Driving Distance	284.6	(122)
Driving Accuracy Percentage	68.8%	(37)
Total Driving	159	(46)
Greens in Regulation Pct.	67.0%	(44)
Putting Average	1.780	(107)
Sand Save Percentage	50.9%	(71)
Eagles (Holes per)	131.4	(16)
Birdie Average	3.30	(148)
All-Around Ranking	627	(53)
Scoring Avg. Before Cut	70.59	(46)
Round 3 Scoring Avg.	70.31	(45)
Final Round Scoring Average	73.20	(182)
Birdie Conversion Percentage	27.4%	(153)
Par Breakers	19.1%	(134)

MISCELLANEOUS PGA TOUR STATISTICS

2004 Low Round/Round: 65–Booz Allen Classic/2
Career Low Round/Round: 64–2003 The Honda Classic/2
Career Largest Paycheck/Finish: $604,800–2004 Wachovia Championship/2

PGA TOUR CAREER SUMMARY — PLAYOFF RECORD: 0-1

Year	Events Played	Cuts Made	1st	2nd	3rd	Top 10	Top 25	Earnings	Rank
1999	1								
2000	1								
2001	1								
2003	25	15				2	4	$619,865	103
2004	23	17		1		3	5	1,355,433	52
Total	51	32		1		5	9	1,975,299	
NATIONWIDE TOUR									
1996A	1								
1998	1								
2000	3	2				1	1	15,636	157
2001	3	2					1	10,720	167
2002	20	14	2	2	1	8	9	319,883	2
Total	28	18	2	2	1	9	11	346,239	

PGA TOUR TOP TOURNAMENT SUMMARY

Year	04
PGA	T13
THE PLAYERS	T66

Joe Ogilvie (OH-gil-vee)

EXEMPT STATUS: 49th on 2004 money list
FULL NAME: Norman Joseph Ogilvie
HEIGHT: 5-10
WEIGHT: 165
BIRTHDATE: April 8, 1974
BIRTHPLACE: Lancaster, OH
RESIDENCE: Austin, TX; plays out of Spanish Oaks GC (Bee Caves, TX)

FAMILY: Wife, Colleen; Lauren Brady (2/5/03)
EDUCATION: Duke University (1996, Economics)
SPECIAL INTERESTS: Travel, financial markets, politics
TURNED PROFESSIONAL: 1996
Nationwide Tour Alumnus

BEST PGA TOUR CAREER FINISH:
T2—2004 HP Classic of New Orleans.

NATIONWIDE TOUR VICTORIES (4):
1998 Monterrey Open, Greensboro Open. **2003** Jacob's Creek Open, The Reese's Cup Classic.

BEST 2004 PGA TOUR FINISHES:
T2—HP Classic of New Orleans; 3—Bell Canadian Open; T8—Chrysler Classic of Greensboro; T9—Reno-Tahoe Open.

2004 SEASON:
Made more money in 2004 ($1,443,363) than he had in his first four years on the PGA TOUR combined ($1,197,971)…Finished career-best 49th on the money list, while jumping from No. 308 at start of year to No. 120 in Official World Golf Ranking by season's end…Career-best T2 finish at the rain-soaked HP Classic of New Orleans. Held the 54-hole lead after opening 66-67-66, two strokes ahead of Charles Howell III and Phil Mickelson at 17-under-par. Despite posting a 4-under-par 68 in the final round Monday, was passed by Vijay Singh, who carded a 9-under 63 to earn a one-stroke victory. Nearly holed bunker shot on 72nd hole that would have forced a sudden-death playoff. Did not record a bogey over the final 36 holes. Previous best finish on TOUR was T4 at the 2000 FedEx St. Jude Classic, and the $448,800 was largest of career. Finish came one week after Shell Houston Open, where he was one stroke out of the lead after 54 holes, but shot a final-round 76 and fell to T19…Second top-10 of the season was a T9 at the Reno-Tahoe Open in August. Was only four back of the lead heading into the final round…Surpassed the $1-million mark for the first time in his five-year TOUR career with a T3 at the Bell Canadian Open, his second top-three finish of the season. The only player in the field to post four sub-par rounds during the week…One stroke off the lead entering the final round of the Chrysler Classic of Greensboro. Finished T8 after even-par 72 on Sunday.

CAREER HIGHLIGHTS:
2003: Made the cut in 21 of 23 events on the 2003 Nationwide Tour, with 16 top-25 finishes. Finished the season No. 2 on the money list with $392,337...Won the inaugural event at the Jacob's Creek Open Championship in Adelaide, Australia. Finished one stroke ahead of Shane Tait after sharing the 36-hole lead with Marcus Fraser and holding a two-shot lead over Tait through 54 holes. Collected a Nationwide Tour-record $115,007 for the win, the third of his career and his first since the 1998 Greensboro Open...Earned Nationwide Tour Player of the Month honors for his efforts...After losing in a playoff to Vaughn Taylor at the Knoxville Open, came back two weeks later and claimed his fourth career win on the Nationwide Tour at The Reese's Cup Classic. The win pushed his season earnings over $300,000, making him the fastest to earn $300,000 in Tour history. **2000:** Finished 92nd on the money list with a then-career high three top-10s, including a T4 at the FedEx St. Jude Classic. **1999:** Earned his first PGA TOUR top-10 finish at the Motorola Western Open with a T9 and a season-best $65,000 payday...First-year earnings of $287,346 were the 10th-best among rookies that year. **1998:** Two-time winner on the Nationwide Tour with victories at the Monterrey Open and Greensboro Open. **1997:** Earned fully exempt status on the Nationwide Tour for the following season in his second attempt at Qualifying School, where he missed the cut in 1996.

PERSONAL:
Lists Warren Buffet and Bill Gates as heroes…Follows the stock market extensively.

PLAYER STATISTICS

2004 PGA TOUR STATISTICS

Scoring Average	70.93	(72)
Driving Distance	288.8	(79)
Driving Accuracy Percentage	61.3%	(145)
Total Driving	224	(144)
Greens in Regulation Pct.	63.1%	(145)
Putting Average	1.755	(33)
Sand Save Percentage	47.7%	(117)
Eagles (Holes per)	612.0	(186)
Birdie Average	3.83	(26)
All-Around Ranking	803	(107)
Scoring Avg. Before Cut	70.89	(81)
Round 3 Scoring Avg.	70.24	(43)
Final Round Scoring Average	72.30	(151)
Birdie Conversion Percentage	31.8%	(19)
Par Breakers	21.5%	(32)

MISCELLANEOUS PGA TOUR STATISTICS

2004 Low Round/Round: 61–Valero Texas Open/3
Career Low Round/Round: 61–2004 Valero Texas Open/3
Career Largest Paycheck/Finish: $448,800–2004 HP Classic of New Orleans/T2

PGA TOUR CAREER SUMMARY — PLAYOFF RECORD: 0-0

Year	Events Played	Cuts Made	1st	2nd	3rd	Top 10	Top 25	Earnings	Rank
1996	1								
1998	1								
1999	31	14				2	5	$287,346	137
2000	30	17				3	7	519,740	92
2001	34	20					4	343,189	139
2002	20	5					1	47,696	216
2003	1								
2004	32	20		1	1	4	9	1,443,363	49
Total	150	76		1	1	9	26	2,641,334	
NATIONWIDE TOUR									
1998	30	19	2		1	7	10	157,812	3
1999	1	1						850	234
2002	5	3					1	12,690	161
2003	23	21	2	1		7	16	392,337	2
Total	59	44	4	1	1	14	27	563,689	

PGA TOUR TOP TOURNAMENT SUMMARY

Year	00	01	02	03	04
U.S. Open				CUT	T40
British Open		T25			
PGA	T58				T49
THE PLAYERS		CUT			

Geoff Ogilvy (OH-gil-vee)

EXEMPT STATUS: 61st on 2004 money list
FULL NAME: Geoff Charles Ogilvy
HEIGHT: 6-2
WEIGHT: 180
BIRTHDATE: June 11, 1977
BIRTHPLACE: Adelaide, South Australia
RESIDENCE: Melbourne, Australia; Scottsdale, AZ
FAMILY: Wife, Juli
SPECIAL INTERESTS: Australian Rules Football, reading, movies
TURNED PROFESSIONAL: 1998
Q SCHOOL: 2000

BEST PGA TOUR CAREER FINISHES:
T2—2001 Honda Classic, 2002 Compaq Classic of New Orleans, 2003 Buick Open.

BEST 2004 PGA TOUR FINISHES:
T5—Cialis Western Open; 10—Shell Houston Open, Wachovia Championship, FUNAI Classic at the WALT DISNEY WORLD Resort.

2004 SEASON:
Finished inside the top 100 on the PGA TOUR money list for the fourth consecutive season and once again earned over $1 million…First top-10 came in 10th start, a solo 10th at the Shell Houston Open…Two weeks later, was only one stroke back of the lead through 54 holes at the Wachovia Championship. Fired a final-round 72 and finished T10…Added a third top-10, a T5, at the Cialis Western Open, where he trailed by one after 36 and 54 holes and finished four back of winner Stephen Ames…Finished the year on a strong note with a T10 at the FUNAI Classic at the WALT DISNEY WORLD Resort…Led the TOUR in All-Around Ranking (276) and shared the title for Total Eagles with Vijay Singh after recording a career-high 17. Also finished second in Eagles (holes per), fourth in Sand Save Percentage, seventh in Driving Distance and eighth in Birdie Average.

CAREER HIGHLIGHTS:
2003: Improved his standing on the money list from 64th in 2002 to 45th and earned over $1 million for the first time in his career. Made 16 cuts and finished in top 25 10 times...Aided by final-round 65, tied career-best finish with T2 at Buick Open, two strokes behind champion Jim Furyk. **2002:** Slow start to the season until May when he recorded his second career T2 finish on the PGA TOUR at the Compaq Classic of New Orleans, earning career-best paycheck of $396,000...Second top-10 came at the Bell Canadian Open. Almost missed the cut with a second-round 74, but rounds of 64-68 on the weekend moved him up the leaderboard to finish T6...Was one out of the lead through 54 holes at the Michelob Championship at Kingsmill after third-round 66. Closing round of 70 gave him a solo fourth. **2001:** Had a successful rookie campaign on the PGA TOUR, with two top-five finishes and earnings of $525,338...Part of a six-man first-round lead at Touchstone Energy Tucson Open after a 67. Finished T3 in first PGA TOUR start...Earned second top-10 in fifth start, T2 at Honda Classic. Opened with 65 for share of first-round lead. **2000:** Joined Ben Ferguson and Stephen Allan as three Australians who survived PGA TOUR Qualifying School...Played on the Australasian, European and Southern African Tours...Four top-10s rocketed to him to fifth on PGA Tour of Australasia Order of Merit in second season...Finished second behind Tiger Woods in Johnnie Walker Classic. **1999:** Qualified to play in the British Open, his only PGA TOUR experience...Australian Rookie of the Year...Finished second place in the Johnnie Walker Classic behind Michael Campbell. **1998:** Gained card at first attempt on the European Tour and Australasian Tour. **Amateur:** Played full-time amateur golf before turning pro...Visited the UK with some success, finishing runner-up in the 1997 Brabazon Trophy and reaching the last eight of the 1998 British Amateur at Muirfield...Won 1997 Lake Macquarie Amateur.

PERSONAL:
A distant relative of Sir Angus Ogilvy, part of Britain's Royal Family and an even-more distant relative of Scotland's King of Bannockburn fame, Robert the Bruce…Was given a cut-down club by his dad at age 7 and progressed to a scratch handicap by age 16…Played full-time amateur golf before turning pro. Talented junior athlete in many sports…Numerous athletics medals at state and national level…Interested in history of golf.

PLAYER STATISTICS

2004 PGA TOUR STATISTICS

Scoring Average	70.80	(59)
Driving Distance	303.3	(7)
Driving Accuracy Percentage	63.2%	(113)
Total Driving	120	(14)
Greens in Regulation Pct.	66.9%	(47)
Putting Average	1.752	(28)
Sand Save Percentage	61.0%	(4)
Eagles (Holes per)	92.1	(2)
Birdie Average	3.97	(8)
All-Around Ranking	268	(1)
Scoring Avg. Before Cut	70.34	(26)
Round 3 Scoring Avg.	70.17	(39)
Final Round Scoring Average	70.89	(50)
Birdie Conversion Percentage	33.1%	(5)
Par Breakers	23.1%	(5)

MISCELLANEOUS PGA TOUR STATISTICS

2004 Low Round/Round: 63–Bob Hope Chrysler Classic/3
Career Low Round/Round: 63–2004 Bob Hope Chrysler Classic/3
Career Largest Paycheck/Finish: $396,000–2002 Compaq Classic of New Orleans/T2

PGA TOUR CAREER SUMMARY — PLAYOFF RECORD: 0-0

Year	Events Played	Cuts Made	1st	2nd	3rd	Top 10	Top 25	Earnings	Rank
1999	1								
2001	23	7		1	1	2	4	$525,338	95
2002	27	17		1		3	4	957,184	64
2003	26	16		1	1	7	10	1,477,246	45
2004	26	19				4	14	1,236,910	61
Total	103	59		3	2	16	32	4,196,678	

PGA TOUR TOP TOURNAMENT SUMMARY

Year	99	00	01	02	03	04
U.S. Open					CUT	
British Open	CUT		CUT			
PGA					T27	T24
THE PLAYERS				CUT	T21	T16

Arnold Palmer

WORLD GOLF HALL OF FAME MEMBER (Inducted 1974)
EXEMPT STATUS: Winner, 1960 U.S. Open (Lifetime)
FULL NAME: Arnold Daniel Palmer
HEIGHT: 5-10
WEIGHT: 185
BIRTHDATE: September 10, 1929
BIRTHPLACE: Latrobe, PA
RESIDENCE: Latrobe, PA; Bay Hill, FL
FAMILY: Peggy (2/26/56), Amy (8/4/58); seven grandchildren
EDUCATION: Wake Forest University
SPECIAL INTERESTS: Flying, business, clubmaking
TURNED PROFESSIONAL: 1954
JOINED TOUR: 1955

PGA TOUR CAREER SUMMARY — PLAYOFF RECORD: 14-10

Year	Events Played	Cuts Made	1st	2nd	3rd	Top 10	Top 25	Earnings	Rank
1949A	1	1							
1953A	2	1							
1954A	4	4				1	3		
1954	1								
1955	30	26	1		1	8	15	$7,958	32
1956	29	28	2	1		8	13	16,145	19
1957	31	28	4		2	13	20	27,803	5
1958	32	30	3	5	2	14	23	42,608	1
1959	31	31	3	1	3	16	25	32,462	
1960	27	26	8	1	2	19	24	75,263	1
1961	25	24	6	5	2	20	23	61,091	2
1962	21	21	8	1		13	19	81,448	1
1963	20	20	7	3		14	16	128,230	
1964	26	26	2	6	4	18	24	113,203	2
1965	21	19	1	3		6	13	57,771	10
1966	21	21	3	2	2	13	15	110,468	3
1967	25	22	4	4	1	16	19	184,065	
1968	23	20	2	2		8	13	87,496	
1969	26	25	2		1	10	16	95,267	9
1970	22	22	1	3	2	11	14	100,941	11
1971	24	24	4		1	10	20	162,896	3
1972	22	19		1	2	10	15	81,440	24
1973	22	20	1		1	7	15	87,275	27
1974	20	14				2	7	32,627	75
1975	20	16			1	5	12	59,018	36
1976	19	14					6	17,018	115
1977	21	17					7	21,950	102
1978	15	11				2	4	27,073	95
1979	16	9					1	9,276	159
1980	14	10					3	16,589	136
1981	13	7						4,164	204
1982	11	4					1	6,621	199
1983	11	6				1	1	16,904	159
1984	8	2						2,452	218
1985	6	2						3,327	214
1986	6								
1987	4	1						1,650	269
1988	5								
1989	4	1						2,290	253
1990	4								
1991	5	1					1	7,738	237
1992	5								
1993	5	1						1,970	316
1994	6								
1995	5								
1996	3								
1997	2								
1998	3								
1999	3								
2000	3								
2001	4								
2002	3								
2003	2								
2004	2								
Total	734	574	62	38	27	245	388	1,861,857	

NATIONAL TEAMS: World Cup (6), 1960, 1962, 1963, 1964, 1966, 1967; Ryder Cup (6), 1961, 1963, 1965, 1967, 1971, 1973; Ryder Cup Captain (2), 1963, 1975; Captain and member of Chrysler Cup Team (5), 1986, 1987, 1988, 1989, 1990; The Presidents Cup Captain, 1996; UBS Warburg Cup Captain and Player, 2001, 2002, 2003.

CHAMPIONS TOUR CAREER SUMMARY — PLAYOFF RECORD: 2-1

Year	Events Played	1st	2nd	3rd	Top 10	Top 25	Earnings	Rank
1980	1	1			1	1	$20,000	4
1981	4	1	1	2	4	4	55,100	4
1982	7	2		1	5	7	73,848	4
1983	12	1	1	1	8	12	106,590	6
1984	13	3	3		9	12	184,582	4
1985	13	1	1	2	9	12	137,024	11
1986	15		1	1	6	13	99,056	21
1987	17			1	8	13	128,910	19
1988	18	1		1	8	14	185,373	17
1989	17				4	11	119,907	38
1990	17					5	66,519	65
1991	17				4	7	143,967	46
1992	18					4	70,815	72
1993	18				1	5	106,232	64
1994	13					1	34,471	91
1995	12					1	51,526	86
1996	16					1	48,192	89
1997	13						29,052	101
1998	13						20,454	111
1999	10						8,185	135
2000	14						15,338	122
2001	7						4,384	167
2002	8						5,596	150
2003	9						19,311	126
2004	7						14,812	133
Total	309	10	7	9	67	123	1,749,244	

PGA TOUR TOP TOURNAMENT SUMMARY

Year	53	54	55	56	57	58	59	60	61	62	63	64	65
Masters			T10	21	T7	**1**	3	**1**	T2	**1**	T9	**1**	T2
U.S. Open	CUT	CUT	T21	7	CUT	T23	T5	**1**	T14	2	T2	T5	CUT
British Open								2	**1**	**1**	T26		16
PGA						T40	T14	T7	T5	T17	T40	T2	T33

Year	66	67	68	69	70	71	72	73	74	75	76	77	78
Masters	T4	4	CUT	26	T36	T18	T33	T24	T11	T13	CUT	T24	T37
U.S. Open	2	2	T59	T6	T54	T24	3	T4	T5	T9	T50	T19	CUT
British Open	T8		T10		12		T6	T14		T16	T55	7	T34
PGA	T6	T14	T2	W/D	T2	T18	T16	CUT	T28	T33	T15	T19	CUT
THE PLAYERS									CUT	CUT	T51	T40	T77

Year	79	80	81	82	83	84	85	86	87	88	89	90	91
Masters	CUT	T24	CUT	47	T36	CUT	CUT	CUT	CUT	CUT	CUT	CUT	CUT
U.S. Open	T59	61	CUT	CUT	T60								
British Open		CUT	T23	T27	T56	CUT			CUT		CUT	CUT	
PGA	CUT	T72	76	CUT	T67	CUT	T65	CUT	T65	CUT	T63	CUT	CUT
THE PLAYERS	T50		T45	CUT	T54	T66	T69	CUT					

Year	92	93	94	95	96	97	98	99	00	01	02	03	04
Masters	CUT	CUT	CUT	CUT	CUT	CUT	CUT	CUT	CUT	CUT	CUT	CUT	CUT
U.S. Open			CUT										
British Open				CUT									
PGA	CUT	CUT	CUT										

CHAMPIONS TOUR TOP TOURNAMENT SUMMARY

Year	80	81	82	83	84	85	86	87	88	89	90	91	92
Senior PGA Championship	**1**	2	T3		**1**			T16	T5	T11	T13	CUT	T47
U.S. Senior Open		**1**	6	T11	2	T11	T25	T14	T22	T53	CUT	CUT	T32
Ford Senior Players Championship				T5	**1**	**1**	T3	T5	T32	T4	T48	T43	T36
JELD-WEN Tradition										T26	T61		

Year	93	94	95	96	97	98	99	00	01	02	03	04
Senior PGA Championship	T27	CUT	CUT	CUT	CUT	CUT	CUT	CUT	CUT	CUT	CUT	W/D
U.S. Senior Open	T52	T57	T51	T43	68	51	CUT	CUT	CUT	CUT	CUT	CUT
Ford Senior Players Championship	T44	T65	T46									
Senior British Open											CUT	
JELD-WEN Tradition	T57		T25	T43								

Arnold Palmer (Continued)

PGA TOUR VICTORIES (62):

1955 Canadian Open. **1956** Insurance City Open, Eastern Open. **1957** Houston Open, Azalea Open Invitational, Rubber City Open Invitational, San Diego Open Invitational. **1958** St. Petersburg Open Invitational, Masters Tournament, Pepsi Championship. **1959** Thunderbird Invitational, Oklahoma City Open Invitational, West Palm Beach Open Invitational. **1960** Palm Springs Desert Golf Classic, Texas Open Invitational, Baton Rouge Open Invitational, Pensacola Open Invitational, Masters Tournament, U.S. Open Championship, Insurance City Open Invitational, Mobile Sertoma Open Invitational. **1961** San Diego Open Invitational, Phoenix Open Invitational, Baton Rouge Open Invitational, Texas Open Invitational, Western Open, British Open Championship. **1962** Palm Springs Golf Classic, Phoenix Open Invitational, Masters Tournament, Texas Open Invitational, Tournament of Champions, Colonial National Invitation, British Open Championship, American Golf Classic. **1963** Los Angeles Open, Phoenix Open Invitational, Pensacola Open Invitational, Thunderbird Classic Invitational, Cleveland Open Invitational, Western Open, Whitemarsh Open Invitational. **1964** Masters Tournament, Oklahoma City Open Invitational. **1965** Tournament of Champions. **1966** Los Angeles Open, Tournament of Champions, Houston Champions International. **1967** Los Angeles Open, Tucson Open Invitational, American Golf Classic, Thunderbird Classic. **1968** Bob Hope Desert Classic, Kemper Open. **1969** Heritage Golf Classic, Danny Thomas-Diplomat Classic. **1970** National Four-Ball Championship [with Jack Nicklaus]. **1971** Bob Hope Desert Classic, Florida Citrus Invitational, Westchester Classic, National Team Championship [with Jack Nicklaus]. **1973** Bob Hope Desert Classic.

CHAMPIONS TOUR VICTORIES (10):

1980 PGA Seniors' Championship. **1981** U.S. Senior Open. **1982** Marlboro Classic, Denver Post Champions of Golf. **1983** Boca Grove Classic. **1984** General Foods PGA Seniors' Championship, Senior Tournament Players Championship, Quadel Senior Classic. **1985** Senior Tournament Players Championship. **1988** Crestar Classic.

INTERNATIONAL VICTORIES (11):

1955 Panama Open, Colombia Open [S. America]. **1963** Australian Wills Masters [Aus]. **1964** Piccadilly World Match Play Championship [Eur]. **1966** Australian Open [Aus]. **1967** Piccadilly World Match Play Championship [Eur], World Cup [indiv]. **1971** Lancome Trophy [Eur]. **1975** Spanish Open [Eur], British PGA Championship [Eur]. **1980** Canadian PGA Championship [Can].

OTHER VICTORIES (9):

1960 Canada Cup [with Sam Snead]. **1962** Canada Cup [with Sam Snead]. **1963** Canada Cup [with Jack Nicklaus]. **1964** Canada Cup [with Jack Nicklaus]. **1966** Canada Cup [with Jack Nicklaus], PGA Team Championship [with Jack Nicklaus]. **1967** World Cup [with Jack Nicklaus]. **1984** Doug Sanders Celebrity Pro-Am. **1986** Unionmutual Classic.

BEST 2004 CHAMPIONS TOUR FINISH:

39—MasterCard Championship

2004 SEASON:

Celebrated his 50th year in professional golf. Announced that 2004 would be his final Augusta National appearance and recorded his 50th consecutive start at the Masters Tournament...Played in his 26th consecutive Bay Hill Invitational...Finished second to Tom Watson at the Wendy's Champions Skins Game, earning five skins and $140,000 at Wailea. Played with his grandson Sam Saunders at the Father/Son. Sam is one of the top-ranked juniors in the country...Served as captain of the U.S. team once again at the UBS Cup.

CAREER HIGHLIGHTS:

2003: Came back to Augusta National for his record 49th consecutive start at the Masters Tournament. Missed the cut there and at the Bay Hill Invitational...Played in nine Champions Tour events, with a season's best 36th at the MasterCard Championship in February. **2002:** Missed cut at Bob Hope Chrysler Classic, Bay Hill Invitational and the Masters. **2001:** Shot his age (71) in fourth round of Bob Hope Chrysler Classic. First player in his 70s to shoot his age or better on PGA TOUR since 77-year-old Jerry Barber had 71 in second round of 1994 Buick Invitational...Added another 71 during the first round of the Senior PGA Championship, but missed cut after second-round 83. **2000:** Reached milestone in July when he played in 1,000th combined PGA TOUR and Champions Tour event...Joined Jack Nicklaus and Byron Nelson as the first recipients of the Payne Stewart Award. **1998:** Named recipient of third PGA TOUR Lifetime Achievement Award at annual PGA TOUR Awards Dinner at La Costa on January 9. **1996:** Captained U.S. Presidents Cup Team to its second consecutive win in biennial series, 16 -15 victory over International Team at Robert Trent Jones GC. **1995:** Final British Open appearance at St. Andrews, came on 35th anniversary of his first time in event. **1994:** Played his last U.S. Open at Oakmont, 40 years after playing his first, and final PGA Championship at Southern Hills...Awarded PGA of America Distinguished Service Award. **1981:** Became first person to win U.S. Open and U.S. Senior Open. **1975:** Ryder Cup captain for second time in career (1963, 1975). **1973:** Last of 62 PGA TOUR victories came at Bob Hope Desert Classic by two strokes over Nicklaus and Johnny Miller. Trails only Sam Snead (81), Jack Nicklaus (70) and Ben Hogan (63) on all-time victory list. **1969:** Named Associated Press Athlete of the Decade for the 1960s. **1968:** Collected at least one victory for the 11th consecutive season, which ties him with Nicklaus for longest streak...First TOUR player to earn $1 million in his career (7/21/68). **1967:** Won his fourth Vardon Trophy (1961-62-64-67). **1964:** Captured his seventh major championship at the Masters (1958-60-62-64). Also won the 1961-62 British Opens and 1960 U.S. Open. **1963:** Led PGA TOUR in earnings for fourth time in career (1958-60-62-63) and is namesake of PGA TOUR and Champions Tour award for top money-winner...Won 29 tournaments between 1960 and 1963. **1962:** Named PGA Player of the Year for the second time (1960, 1962). **1960:** Final-round 65 at U.S. Open at Cherry Hills defeated amateur Nicklaus by two strokes...Named Hickock Professional Athlete of the Year and Sports Illustrated Sportsman of the Year. **Amateur:** 1954 U.S. Amateur Champion.

PERSONAL:

Maintains active business schedule with golf course design, construction and development...Principal owner of Bay Hill Club and Lodge, site of Bay Hill Invitational...Consultant to The Golf Channel...Pilot of considerable renown who set one aviation record...Received Francis Ouimet Award from Francis Ouimet Caddie Scholarship Foundation in Boston in January 1997...Received 1999 Donald Ross Award from the American Society of Golf Course Architects and Patriot Award from Congressional Medal of Honor Society in 2000...First former champion to become a member at Augusta National GC, joined by Jack Nicklaus in 2001...Latrobe, PA airport named after him in honor of 70th birthday...Family named Golf Family of the Year for 1999 by the National Golf Foundation.

PLAYER STATISTICS

2004 PGA TOUR STATISTICS

Scoring Average	82.56	(N/A)
Driving Distance	239.3	(N/A)
Driving Accuracy Percentage	64.3%	(N/A)
Total Driving	(N/A)	(N/A)
Greens in Regulation Pct.	20.8%	(N/A)
Putting Average	1.867	(N/A)
Sand Save Percentage	14.3%	(N/A)
Birdie Average	.75	(N/A)
Scoring Avg. Before Cut	83.75	(N/A)
Birdie Conversion Percentage	20.0%	(N/A)
Par Breakers	4.2%	(N/A)

MISCELLANEOUS PGA TOUR STATISTICS

2004 Low Round/Round: 79–Bay Hill Invitational Presented by MasterCard/2
Career Low Round/Round: 62–1966 Los Angeles Open/3
Career Largest Paycheck/Finish: $50,000–1971 Westchester Classic/1

2004 CHAMPIONS TOUR STATISTICS

Scoring Average	80.78	(N/A)
Driving Distance	232.4	(N/A)
Driving Accuracy Percentage	70.6%	(N/A)
Total Driving	(N/A)	(N/A)
Greens in Regulation Pct.	30.2%	(N/A)
Putting Average	1.939	(N/A)
Sand Save Percentage	48.9%	(N/A)
Birdie Average	1.33	(N/A)
All-Around Ranking	1,569	(N/A)

MISCELLANEOUS CHAMPIONS TOUR STATISTICS

2004 Low Round: 75–2 times, most recent 2004 Bank of America Championship/3.
Career Low Round: 63–1984 General Foods PGA Seniors' Championship/2
Career Largest Paycheck: $48,750–1988 Crestar Classic/1

Ryan Palmer

EXEMPT STATUS: 2004 tournament winner (through 2006)
FULL NAME: Ryan Hunter Palmer
HEIGHT: 5-11
WEIGHT: 175
BIRTHDATE: September 19, 1976
BIRTHPLACE: Amarillo, TX
RESIDENCE: Hurst, TX; plays out of Tascosa CC

FAMILY: Wife, Jennifer
EDUCATION: Texas A&M University (2000, Recreation)
SPECIAL INTERESTS: Cooking, racquetball, football
TURNED PROFESSIONAL: 2000
JOINED TOUR: 2004
Nationwide Tour Alumnus

PGA TOUR VICTORIES (1):

2004 FUNAI Classic at the WALT DISNEY WORLD Resort.

NATIONWIDE TOUR VICTORIES (1):

2003 Clearwater Classic.

BEST 2004 PGA TOUR FINISHES:

1—FUNAI Classic at the WALT DISNEY WORLD Resort; 2—Southern Farm Bureau Classic.

2004 SEASON:

The rookie posted his first tournament title in his 34th career start on the PGA TOUR at the FUNAI Classic at the WALT DISNEY WORLD Resort. Was fifth rookie and 10th first-time winner to win on TOUR during the year. Was five strokes back through 54 holes but closed with a career-best 62 to win by three...Recorded a hole-in-one with a pitching wedge on the par-3, 166-yard ninth hole at the TPC at Avenel. Finished T11 at the Booz Allen Classic...Shared first-round lead with Tiger Woods at Deutsche Bank Championship after opening-round 65. Eventually finished T17...Ended the season on a high note, beginning with a runner-up finish at the Southern Farm Bureau Classic. Posted four rounds in the 60s in a single event for the first time in his career, including a final-round 64 at Annandale GC. Three weeks later won his first tournament title in Orlando...Earns a spot into his first Masters Tournament in 2005, thanks to his 37th-place finish on the final season money list.

CAREER HIGHLIGHTS:

2003: Made the cut in 18 of 24 appearances on the Nationwide Tour and enjoyed six top-10 and 10 top-25 finishes. Finished the season No. 6 on the final money list with $286,066...Earned his first career Nationwide Tour win at the 2003 Clearwater Classic in New Zealand in just his second Tour start. Fired a course-record, 9-under 63 in the second round at the Clearwater Resort. **2002:** First start on the TOUR as a professional came at the 2002 Valero Texas Open...Played the 2002 Tight Lies Tour in 2002 and made the cut in all 15 events he entered. Won four times in 2002 on the Tight Lies Tour and was the leading money winner with $81,634. Won the Valley Open (Harlingen, TX) and Sprint PCS Open (Tyler, TX) in consecutive weeks. Added victories in Lake Charles, LA, and Hattiesburg, MS, to close the year. **Amateur:** Played practice round with Payne Stewart at the 1998 U.S. Open, where he posted rounds of 82-73 but missed the cut.

PLAYER STATISTICS

2004 PGA TOUR STATISTICS

Scoring Average	71.27	(111)
Driving Distance	295.6	(29)
Driving Accuracy Percentage	63.2%	(113)
Total Driving	142	(29)
Greens in Regulation Pct.	65.5%	(86)
Putting Average	1.768	(67)
Sand Save Percentage	51.3%	(66)
Eagles (Holes per)	163.6	(45)
Birdie Average	3.86	(18)
All-Around Ranking	535	(36)
Scoring Avg. Before Cut	71.07	(105)
Round 3 Scoring Avg.	70.83	(86)
Final Round Scoring Average	70.29	(16)
Birdie Conversion Percentage	31.5%	(24)
Par Breakers	22.1%	(15)

MISCELLANEOUS PGA TOUR STATISTICS

2004 Low Round/Round: 62–FUNAI Classic at the WALT DISNEY WORLD Resort/4
Career Low Round/Round: 62–2004 FUNAI Classic at the WALT DISNEY WORLD Resort/4
Career Largest Paycheck/Finish: $756,000–2004 FUNAI Classic at the WALT DISNEY WORLD Resort/1

PGA TOUR CAREER SUMMARY — PLAYOFF RECORD: 0-0

Year	Events Played	Cuts Made	1st	2nd	3rd	Top 10	Top 25	Earnings	Rank
1998A	1								
2002	1								
2004	33	18	1	1		2	6	$1,592,344	37
Total	35	18	1	1		2	6	1,592,344	
NATIONWIDE TOUR									
2003	24	18	1		3	6	10	286,066	6
2004	1	1						1,440	343
Total	25	19	1		3	6	10	287,506	

PGA TOUR TOP TOURNAMENT SUMMARY

Year	98
U.S. Open	CUT

Rod Pampling (PAM-pling)

EXEMPT STATUS: 2004 tournament winner (through 2006)
FULL NAME: Rodney Pampling
HEIGHT: 5-10
WEIGHT: 175
BIRTHDATE: September 23, 1969
BIRTHPLACE: Redcliffe, Queensland, Australia
RESIDENCE: Flower Mound, TX; Brisbane, Australia

FAMILY: Wife, Angela
SPECIAL INTERESTS: Sports
TURNED PROFESSIONAL: 1994
JOINED TOUR: 2002
Nationwide Tour Alumnus

PGA TOUR VICTORIES (1):
2004 The INTERNATIONAL.

INTERNATIONAL VICTORIES (1):
1999 Canon Challenge [Aus].

BEST 2004 PGA TOUR FINISHES:
1—The INTERNATIONAL; T9—Bob Hope Chrysler Classic.

2004 SEASON:
Made 22 cuts in 26 TOUR starts and earned a career-high $1,737,72. Began the season 111th in Official World Golf Ranking and had moved up to 65th through THE TOUR Championship. . .Recorded his first PGA TOUR victory in his 81st career start at The INTERNATIONAL. Curled in a 21-foot eagle putt from the fringe on the par-5, 71st hole, collecting five points in the tournament's Modified Stableford scoring system to move into a two-point lead over Alex Cejka. Went on to capture his first PGA TOUR title at Castle Pine GC in Castle Rock, CO. Was one of six Australians to win on the PGA TOUR in 2004, joining Stuart Appleby, Mark Hensby, Adam Scott, Andre Stolz and Craig Parry. . .In second start of season, finished T9 at the Bob Hope Chrysler Classic, aided by rounds of 66-66 on the weekend. . .First-round leader at the Shell Houston Open, with a 6-under-par 66. Despite a second-round 7-over-par 79, made the cut by a stroke. Finished T43. . .Qualified for the British Open at the qualifier held in the United States at Congressional CC. It was his first trip back to the British Open since 1999 when he held the first-round lead and then missed the cut. . .Made his first career-start in the WGC-NEC Invitational, finishing T14. . .Was T14 at the Southern Farm Bureau Classic after a final round, 8-under 64. . .His top-40 finish on the final money list earned him first ever invitation to the Masters Tournament in 2005.

CAREER HIGHLIGHTS:
2003: Recorded five top-10s and won over $1 million...First top-10, a T10 at the AT&T Pebble Beach National Pro-Am. T2 after 36 and 54 holes, but dropped out of hunt for first TOUR title after final-round 73...Added second top-10, a T8, at the Ford Championship at Doral. Led tournament through 18 holes after opening with a 8-under 64...Finished T10 at MCI Heritage...Missed eight out of nine cuts after the Heritage. Made a switched to a belly putter the week of the B.C. Open and posted a solo fourth. Carded a pair of 66s on the weekend and collected $144,000. Increased his season earnings to $637,614 to secure his card for the 2004 season...Overcame second-round 73 to finish T3 at the Reno-Tahoe Open for fifth top-10 of the season. Rebounded with rounds of 67-68 on the weekend and earn $174,000 and exceed $1 million in earnings on the season for the first time in his career. **2002:** One of six Nationwide Tour graduates from class of 2001 to retain TOUR card, finishing in the top 100 in rookie season...In third start as a member of the PGA TOUR, finished T8 at the Phoenix Open. Best showing of the season was a T4 at the Tampa Bay Classic. In second place after 18 and 36 holes. Dropped out of contention with third-round 2-over-par 73, seven strokes behind eventual champion K.J. Choi. **2001:** Led the Nationwide Tour in top-10s with nine but did not bring home a win in his second season on that tour...Earned $306,573, setting a record for earnings without a victory...Eight of his top-10s were top-fives, including three runner-up finishes and two thirds...Lost playoff to John Rollins at Hershey Open after matching course record with 7-under 64 during final round...Came out on short side of three-man playoff with Mark Wurtz and winner D.A. Points at Inland Empire Open...Continued to support PGA Tour of Australasia, playing in seven events with two top 10s...Made 46 of 49 cuts between 1996-2001 on PGA Tour of Australasia. **2000:** Played in 24 events on the Nationwide Tour, with three top-25 finishes. **1999:** First-round leader at the British Open. Shot an even-par 71 Carnoustie, Scotland, then missed the cut after posting a second-round 86...Won the Canon Challenge on the Australasian Tour. **1998:** Finished second at the New Zealand Open on the Australasian Tour.

PERSONAL:
Played the PGA Tour of Australasia during the winter and the Hooters Tour during the summer to support career before concentrating efforts primarily on the Nationwide Tour beginning in 2000. . .Playing primarily in the United States beginning in 2000, Aussie relocated to Flower Mound, TX. . .Wife Angela is a clinical psychologist. "She gets to see everything I do out there. I'm kind of lucky. I have a psychologist out there 24 hours a day. She doesn't lie. I can't kid myself."

PLAYER STATISTICS

2004 PGA TOUR STATISTICS

Scoring Average	70.75	(50)
Driving Distance	292.1	(50)
Driving Accuracy Percentage	59.8%	(154)
Total Driving	204	(112)
Greens in Regulation Pct.	66.1%	(69)
Putting Average	1.763	(52)
Sand Save Percentage	58.9%	(10)
Eagles (Holes per)	141.0	(24)
Birdie Average	3.71	(57)
All-Around Ranking	466	(17)
Scoring Avg. Before Cut	70.38	(33)
Round 3 Scoring Avg.	70.05	(34)
Final Round Scoring Average	71.81	(120)
Birdie Conversion Percentage	30.8%	(44)
Par Breakers	21.3%	(42)

MISCELLANEOUS PGA TOUR STATISTICS

2004 Low Round/Round: 64–Southern Farm Bureau Classic/4
Career Low Round/Round: 64–3 times, most recent 2004 Southern Farm Bureau Classic/4
Career Largest Paycheck/Finish: $900,000–2004 The INTERNATIONAL/1

PGA TOUR CAREER SUMMARY — PLAYOFF RECORD: 0-0

Year	Events Played	Cuts Made	1st	2nd	3rd	Top 10	Top 25	Earnings	Rank
1999	6	3						$17,476	263
2001	1								
2002	29	19				3	11	776,903	89
2003	27	16			1	5	9	1,064,974	68
2004	26	22	1			2	10	1,737,725	31
Total	89	60	1		1	10	30	3,597,078	
NATIONWIDE TOUR									
1997	5								
1998	1								
1999	3								
2000	24	8					3	25,591	121
2001	26	21		3	2	9	14	306,573	4
Total	59	29		3	2	9	17	332,164	

PGA TOUR TOP TOURNAMENT SUMMARY

Year	99	00	01	02	03	04
U.S. Open					CUT	
British Open	CUT					T27
PGA					T14	T55
THE PLAYERS					CUT	T58
WGC-NEC Invitational						T14
WGC-American Express Champ	T37					

SECTION 2 PLAYER BIOGRAPHIES

Jesper Parnevik (YES-per PAR-nuh-vick)

EXEMPT STATUS: 40th on 2004 money list
FULL NAME: Jesper Bo Parnevik
HEIGHT: 6-0
WEIGHT: 175
BIRTHDATE: March 7, 1965
BIRTHPLACE: Stockholm, Sweden
RESIDENCE: Jupiter, FL

FAMILY: Wife, Mia; Peg (9/3/95), Penny (5/9/97), Phillipa (5/16/99), Phoenix (2/16/01)
SPECIAL INTERESTS: Magic, vitamins, bridge, backgammon, yoga, yachting, tennis
TURNED PROFESSIONAL: 1986
Q SCHOOL: 1993

PGA TOUR VICTORIES (5):

1998 Phoenix Open. **1999** Greater Greensboro Chrysler Classic. **2000** Bob Hope Chrysler Classic, GTE Byron Nelson Classic. **2001** Honda Classic.

INTERNATIONAL VICTORIES (9):

1988 Odense Open [Sweden], Ramlosa Open [Sweden], Open Passing Shot [France]. **1990** Swedish Open [Eur]. **1993** Scottish Open [Eur]. **1995** Scandinavian Masters [Eur]. **1996** Trophee Lancome [Eur]. **1997** Johnnie Walker Super Tour [Asia]. **1998** Scandinavian Masters [Eur].

BEST 2004 PGA TOUR FINISHES:

T2—Chrysler Championship; T4—Buick Invitational; T5—Bob Hope Chrysler Classic; T7—AT&T Pebble Beach National Pro-Am; T9—Bell Canadian Open.

2004 SEASON:

After posting a total of three top-10 finishes during the 2002-03 seasons, opened the '04 year with three top-10s in his first five events. . .Five top-10s were most since nine in 2000, and his 40th-place finish on the PGA TOUR money list was his best since finishing 31st in 2001. . .Past champion posted five rounds in the 60s to finish T5 at the Bob Hope Chrysler Classic, four shots out of playoff between Phil Mickelson and Skip Kendall. . .Two weeks later, added a T7 at the AT&T Pebble Beach National Pro-Am. . .Followed that with a T4 at the Buick Invitational. His first back-to-back top-10 finishes on TOUR since a win at the 2000 GTE Byron Nelson Classic and a T5 at the Buick Classic and first back-to-back top-10 starts since April 2000 (MCI Classic, T9 and Greater Greensboro Chrysler Classic, T8). . .Posted his fourth top-10 of the season, a T9 at the Bell Canadian Open, his most top-10s since the 2001 season. . .Best finish came in the last full-field event of the season, a T2 at the Chrysler Championship. A birdie on the last hole, along with a bogey by Tommy Armour III on the 18th, gave him an extra $100,000 and allowed him to pass Joey Sindelar for the 40th spot on the list and gain an exemption into the 2005 Masters Tournament.

CAREER HIGHLIGHTS:

2003: Played in a career-high 31 PGA TOUR events. Sub-par year in which he slumped to $570,587 in earnings...Only top-10 of the season came in late September, T5 at the 84 Lumber Classic of Pennsylvania. **2002:** Did not crack the $1-million mark in earnings for the first time since 1996...Made an early-season pledge to play until earning TOUR victory...Playing in his ninth consecutive event at the Genuity Championship, picked up his first top-10 of the season...Did not play Bay Hill Invitational, having missed the cut playing 10th straight week in title defense of Honda Classic...Final-round 7-under 65 gave him a second-place finish at the BellSouth Classic, four strokes back of Retief Goosen...Played in third Ryder Cup, posting an 0-1-1 record. Career Ryder Cup record is 4-3-4. **2001:** Won a TOUR event for the fourth consecutive season to place 31st on the money list with $1,574,208...Shared first round lead at Honda Classic and led the remainder of the tournament for his fifth TOUR victory. Closed with a 72 to edge three players by one stroke and capture the $576,000 winner's paycheck...Was one off the lead after 54 holes in the British Open. Fired a final-round 71 to post a T9, the fourth top-10 in his last five British Open starts...Withdrew from defense of Bob Hope Chrysler Classic due to pending birth of fourth child...Was a Captain's Choice for the European Ryder Cup team, his third appearance. **2000:** Continued proving that he is one of the PGA TOUR's rising stars by posting first career multiple-win season despite dealing with increasing hip pain that eventually required corrective surgery...Eighth-place finish on money list was his first year among the top 10...Established or matched career marks for: single-season earnings ($2,413,345), top-10s (nine) and wins (two)...Started the season red-hot with six top-10 finishes in first seven events. Led Mercedes Championships by one stroke after opening 69 before dropping to T6 finish...Improved on performance the following week at SONY Open with a T3...Won first tournament of year at Bob Hope Chrysler Classic. Superlative week included five rounds in the 60s...Two starts later at Nissan Open, turned in only runner-up performance of year. Tournament highlight was birdie putt on 72nd hole that forced eventual winner Kirk Triplett to drain par putt for victory...Second win came at GTE Byron Nelson Classic in nail-biting fashion. Outlasted Davis Love III and Phil Mickelson with a par on third playoff hole to win largest winning purse of career ($720,000)...Began suffering from hip pain two weeks prior to U.S. Open. Underwent hip surgery to repair Labrum on Sept. 23. Surgery was performed by Dr. Marc Philippon, the same surgeon who operated on Greg Norman and Steve Elkington earlier in the year. **1999:** Earned his second career PGA TOUR title by two strokes over Jim Furyk at Greater Greensboro Chrysler Classic. Won in wire-to-wire fashion, becoming the first player since Ernie Els at the 1997 Buick Classic to accomplish the feat. Final-round 70 earned him the victory and tournament record. Lit victory cigar on 18th green before holing his final putt...In November, withdrew from WGC-American Express Championship due to an irregular heartbeat and took remainder of year off to undergo tests and rest...Was 3-1-1 as member of European Ryder Cup team. **1998:** First PGA TOUR title came at the Phoenix Open, a three-stroke victory over Tommy Armour III, Steve Pate, Brent Geiberger and Tom Watson. Earned distinction as second Swede to win on TOUR, following Gabriel Hjertstedt at 1997 B.C. Open. **1997:** Finished top-25 in 11 of 19 events entered. Posted five runner-up finishes and one third-place...Fired third-round 66 at British Open to open a

PGA TOUR CAREER SUMMARY — PLAYOFF RECORD: 1-0

Year	Events Played	Cuts Made	1st	2nd	3rd	Top 10	Top 25	Earnings	Rank
1994	17	12				2	4	$148,816	120
1995	19	15				2	7	222,458	84
1996	19	17			1	5	9	389,266	53
1997	19	16		5	1	9	11	1,217,587	12
1998	20	17	1		1	5	13	1,290,822	14
1999	20	17	1			4	10	1,055,468	36
2000	20	17	2	1	1	9	11	2,413,345	8
2001	25	21	1			4	13	1,574,208	31
2002	26	17		1		2	4	964,304	63
2003	31	20				1	5	570,587	118
2004	24	18		1		5	9	1,550,135	40
Total	240	187	5	8	4	48	96	11,396,995	
EUROPEAN TOUR									
2004	2	2				1	2	83,596	

PGA TOUR TOP TOURNAMENT SUMMARY

Year	93	94	95	96	97	98	99	00	01	02	03	04
Masters					T21	T31	CUT	T40	T20	T29		
U.S. Open					T48	T14	T17	CUT	T30	T54	CUT	
British Open	T21	2	T24	T44	T2	T4	T10	T36	T9	T28	DQ	
PGA		CUT	T20	T5	T45	CUT	T10	T51	T13	CUT	T34	CUT
THE PLAYERS			T49	T53	CUT	T25	T23	CUT	CUT	CUT	T48	T33
TOUR Championship					T6	T3		T22				
WGC-Accenture Match Play							T33	T9		T33		
WGC-NEC Invitational							T27			T71	T71	T22
WGC-American Express Champ								W/D	CNL			

NATIONAL TEAMS: Dunhill Cup (4), 1993, 1994, 1995, 1997; World Cup (2), 1994, 1995; Ryder Cup (3), 1997, 1999, 2002.

Jesper Parnevik (Continued)

two-stroke lead over Darren Clarke and five-stroke edge over Justin Leonard heading into final round. Sunday 73 not good enough to hold off Leonard, so settled for British Open second place for second time in career...Was 1-1-2 as member of European Ryder Cup team. **1996:** Won Lancome Trophy on PGA European Tour by five strokes over Colin Montgomerie. **1995:** Became first Swede to capture a European Tour event in Sweden with victory at Scandanavian Masters. **1994:** Marked first British Open near miss at Turnberry. Held two-stroke lead at final hole, but made bogey to finish 11-under-par 269. Nick Price went eagle-birdie-par on final three holes to capture one-stroke victory. **1993:** First European Tour win came at Bell's Scottish Open. **1992:** Joined TOUR after finishing T4 in 1993 Qualifying Tournament.

PERSONAL:

Wilson Golf donated $90 for every birdie that Parnevik made in the 2004 season to The First Tee program...Father, Bo, is Sweden's most famous comedian...First turned up bill of cap to get a tan on his face while playing. Also known for distinct golf attire, outfitted by J. Lindeberg... Learned game by hitting floating golf balls into lake behind family home...His company, Lifizz, Inc., markets and distributes effervescent vitamins in the United States...Son is named Phoenix, where Jesper first won on PGA TOUR in 1998.

PLAYER STATISTICS

2004 PGA TOUR STATISTICS

Scoring Average	70.20	(18)
Driving Distance	287.9	(89)
Driving Accuracy Percentage	60.0%	(153)
Total Driving	242	(164)
Greens in Regulation Pct.	66.1%	(69)
Putting Average	1.759	(43)
Sand Save Percentage	51.9%	(57)
Eagles (Holes per)	258.0	(107)
Birdie Average	3.76	(37)
All-Around Ranking	573	(41)
Scoring Avg. Before Cut	69.73	(7)
Round 3 Scoring Avg.	70.95	(98)
Final Round Scoring Average	70.67	(36)
Birdie Conversion Percentage	30.6%	(50)
Par Breakers	21.3%	(42)

MISCELLANEOUS PGA TOUR STATISTICS

2004 Low Round/Round: 65–6 times, most recent Michelin Championship at Las Vegas/1
Career Low Round/Round: 62–1997 Bob Hope Chrysler Classic/5
Career Largest Paycheck/Finish: $720,000–2000 GTE Byron Nelson Classic/1

SECTION 2 PLAYER BIOGRAPHIES

SHOTLink
AN IBM ON DEMAND BUSINESS SOLUTION

HOT SHOTS

Most Three-Putted Greens on TOUR (2004)

EVENT/COURSE NAME	HOLE	PAR	THREE PUTTS
PGA Championship Whistling Straits	18	4	50
Nissan Open Riviera CC	8	4	48
Nissan Open Riviera CC	6	3	44
BellSouth Classic TPC at Sugarloaf	1	4	43
BellSouth Classic TPC at Sugarloaf	2	3	40

Least Three-Putted Greens on TOUR (2004)

EVENT/COURSE NAME	HOLE	PAR	THREE PUTTS
AT&T Pebble Beach National Pro-Am Poppy Hills **	14	4	1
Bob Hope Chrysler Classic Bermuda Dunes CC **	2	4	1
Bob Hope Chrysler Classic Bermuda Dunes CC **	4	3	1
Bob Hope Chrysler Classic Bermuda Dunes CC **	11	4	1
Bob Hope Chrysler Classic Bermuda Dunes CC **	16	4	1

** = Multiple course tournament

1st Hole-TPC at Sugarloaf

Craig Parry

EXEMPT STATUS: 2002 World Golf Championships winner (through 2005)
FULL NAME: Craig David Parry
HEIGHT: 5-6
WEIGHT: 180
BIRTHDATE: January 12, 1966
BIRTHPLACE: Sunshine, Victoria, Australia
RESIDENCE: Sydney, Australia; Orlando, FL

FAMILY: Wife, Jenny; April, Ryan and Brendan
SPECIAL INTERESTS: Water sports, cricket, rugby, computers, Australian Rules Football, golf course design
TURNED PROFESSIONAL: 1985
JOINED TOUR: April 1992

PGA TOUR VICTORIES (2):
2002 WGC-NEC Invitational. **2004** Ford Championship at Doral.

INTERNATIONAL VICTORIES (19):
1987 New South Wales Open [Aus], Canadian TPC [Can]. **1989** German Open [Eur], Wang Four Stars Pro-Celebrity [Eur], Bridgestone ASO [Jpn]. **1991** Italian Open [Eur], Scottish Open [Eur]. **1992** Australian PGA Championship [Aus], New South Wales Open [Aus], Australian Masters [Aus]. **1994** Australian Masters [Aus]. **1995** Canon Challenge [Aus], Greg Norman's Holden Classic [Aus]. **1996** Australian Masters [Aus]. **1997** Satelindo Indonesia Open [Asia], Japan Open [Jpn], Coolum Classic [Aus]. **1999** Ford Open [Aus]. **2002** New Zealand Open.

BEST 2004 PGA TOUR FINISH:
1—Ford Championship at Doral.

2004 SEASON:
Made a miraculous eagle from the fairway, on the par-4 18th, the first playoff hole, to beat Scott Verplank and win the Ford Championship at Doral. His eagle, a 6-iron from 176 yards, came on the Blue Monster's signature hole. It was his first start on the PGA TOUR in 2004. Nearly missed first-round 7:54 a.m. tee time as he slept through his alarm. "My brother (Glenn) awoke me at 7:40 a.m. It was a mad dash to the 10th tee grabbing whatever clothes I could find in the wardrobe," Parry later explained. He went on to post a first-round 1-under-par 71. From there, Parry posted rounds of 67-65-68 to force the playoff with Verplank.

CAREER HIGHLIGHTS:
2003: Sub-par year as position on the season money list (165th) was lowest of career on the TOUR. Played in only 16 events and made 10 cuts...Best effort of the season was a T25 at the Mercedes Championships at the start of the season. **2002:** Had career-highs in money earned ($1,466,235) and money list position (37th)...Earned first PGA TOUR win in his 236th start at the WGC-NEC Invitational. Victory was 20th career victory worldwide, and second of 2002 (TelstraSaturn Hyundai New Zealand Open). Payday of $1 million exceeded any of his previous 10 full seasons on TOUR. Jumped into top 50 on Official World Golf Ranking from No. 118 to No. 45. After third-round 66, grabbed share of 54-hole lead with Robert Allenby. Closed out victory with final-round 66...In his last start of the season at the Buick Challenge, shared the 36-hole lead, but closing 66-69 dropped him to T4. **2001:** Finished outside the top 100 on the money list for the first time since he became a PGA TOUR member in April 1992...Only top-10 of season came in Invensys Classic at Las Vegas, a T7 worth $135,562 that lifted him to 93rd on money list. Held third-round lead by one stroke over Tom Lehman, helped by a double eagle during the round. **2000:** Fell to 95th on money list after finishing 39th the prior year...Lone top-10 of year was T7 at FedEx St. Jude Classic. **1999:** Enjoyed his best season on TOUR with more than $900,000 in earnings and 39th-place finish on money list...Finished T4 at the British Open. Third-round 67 matched low round of tournament...Posted his best finish of the year at the WGC-NEC Invitational in August when he finished T3...Won Ford Open on the PGA TOUR of Australasia. **1998:** Was member of third International Team for Presidents Cup Matches (1994, 1996, 1998). **1997:** Earned more than $200,000 for sixth consecutive year and eclipsed $300,000 mark for fourth time in six seasons. Also had four top-10s, his most since 1992...Won three international events - Satelindo Indonesia Open on Omega Tour, Japan Open and Coolum Classic in Australia. **1996:** Posted two runner-up finishes in 24 starts. At GTE Byron Nelson Classic, opened with 70-67 before shooting 65-65 to move from T23 to second. Later T2 at Buick Classic with three others. **1994:** First runner-up finish came at Honda Classic, where he closed with 67. Also finished second at Colonial National Invitation after leading through 36 and 54 holes. Final-round 71 relinquished lead and eventually victory to Tom Lehman by one stroke. **1992:** Became special temporary TOUR member in April. Finished T6 at THE PLAYERS Championship and Freeport-McMoRan Classic in consecutive weeks.

PERSONAL:
Nicknamed "Popeye" for his well-developed forearms. . .A computer enthusiast who often tinkers with his laptop at tournament sites. Built own Web site: www.craigparry.com.

PLAYER STATISTICS

2004 PGA TOUR STATISTICS

Scoring Average	71.41	(129)
Driving Distance	276.9	(179)
Driving Accuracy Percentage	63.5%	(109)
Total Driving	288	(188)
Greens in Regulation Pct.	60.7%	(184)
Putting Average	1.797	(152)
Sand Save Percentage	55.3%	(25)
Eagles (Holes per)	450.0	(173)
Birdie Average	3.00	(187)
All-Around Ranking	1,138	(182)
Scoring Avg. Before Cut	71.80	(166)
Round 3 Scoring Avg.	71.20	(113)
Final Round Scoring Average	74.10	(191)
Birdie Conversion Percentage	26.2%	(181)
Par Breakers	16.9%	(188)

MISCELLANEOUS PGA TOUR STATISTICS

2004 Low Round/Round: 64–THE PLAYERS Championship/3
Career Low Round/Round: 64–7 times, most recent 2004 THE PLAYERS Championship/3
Career Largest Paycheck/Finish: $1,000,000–2002 WGC–NEC Invitational/1

PGA TOUR CAREER SUMMARY — PLAYOFF RECORD: 1-0

Year	Events Played	Cuts Made	1st	2nd	3rd	Top 10	Top 25	Earnings	Rank
1987	1								
1988	1	1						$1,650	283
1990	8	6					2	43,351	181
1991	6	6					3	63,767	162
1992	13	11			1	4	6	241,901	64
1993	23	16			1	6	7	323,068	50
1994	20	15		1		3	8	354,602	46
1995	24	16		1		2	5	293,413	65
1996	24	19		2		3	7	454,203	43
1997	20	16			1	4	7	387,603	63
1998	16	10				4	6	312,710	98
1999	19	15			1	5	8	962,376	39
2000	22	16				1	5	507,308	95
2001	22	13				1	6	503,923	102
2002	21	13	1			2	6	1,466,235	37
2003	16	10					1	257,281	165
2004	16	10	1			1	4	1,308,586	55
Total	272	193	2	4	4	36	81	7,481,976	
NATIONWIDE TOUR									
2004	1	1				1	1	18,256	158
Total	1	1				1	1	18,256	
EUROPEAN TOUR									
2004	2	2						13,310	
JAPAN GOLF TOUR									
2003	2	2				2	2	50,791	

PGA TOUR TOP TOURNAMENT SUMMARY

Year	87	88	89	90	91	92	93	94	95	96	97	98	99
Masters				CUT		T13	T45	T30					T48
U.S. Open				46	T11	T33	T3	T25		T90	T43		T34
British Open	CUT	CUT		T22	8	T28	T59	T77	CUT	CUT	CUT	CUT	T4
PGA				T40	T43		T31	T19	CUT	T65	CUT	T71	CUT
THE PLAYERS				T61	T15	T6	CUT	T14	CUT	T53	T22	CUT	69
WGC-Accenture Match Play													T17
WGC-NEC Invitational													T3
WGC-American Express Champ													T20

Year	00	01	02	03	04
Masters	T25			T39	CUT
U.S. Open	T37		CUT	CUT	T60
British Open	T36		CUT	T59	CUT
PGA	CUT		CUT	CUT	T55
THE PLAYERS	T22	T33	T57	CUT	T13
WGC-Accenture Match Play	T33	T17		T33	
WGC-NEC Invitational			**1**	T64	T65
WGC-American Express Champ			T49	T54	

NATIONAL TEAMS: Kirin Cup, 1988; Four Tours World Championship of Golf (3), 1989, 1990, 1991; Dunhill Cup (5), 1993, 1995, 1996, 1998, 1999; The Presidents Cup (3), 1994, 1996, 1998; WGC-World Cup, 2002.

SECTION 2 PLAYER BIOGRAPHIES

Dennis Paulson

EXEMPT STATUS: 117th on 2004 money list
FULL NAME: Dennis Jay Paulson
HEIGHT: 6-0
WEIGHT: 200
BIRTHDATE: September 27, 1962
BIRTHPLACE: San Gabriel, CA
RESIDENCE: Encinitas, CA; plays out of Rancho Santa Fe (The Farms)
FAMILY: Wife, Linda; Dillon Jay (6/10/97), Ethan James (5/10/00)
EDUCATION: San Diego State University
SPECIAL INTERESTS: Hunting, fishing, being a great dad
TURNED PROFESSIONAL: 1988
Q SCHOOL: 1993
JOINED TOUR: 1994
Nationwide Tour Alumnus

PGA TOUR VICTORIES (1):
2000 Buick Classic.

NATIONWIDE TOUR VICTORIES (1):
1998 Huntsville Open.

INTERNATIONAL VICTORIES (1):
1990 Philippines Open [Asia]

BEST 2004 PGA TOUR FINISHES:
T9—Reno-Tahoe Open; T10—Bay Hill Invitational Presented by MasterCard.

2004 SEASON:
Finished inside the top 125 for the first time since the 2001 season. Made the cut in his first 12 TOUR starts of the year. . .Picked up first top-10 of the season with a T10 at the Bay Hill Invitational presented by MasterCard. . .Missed four straight cuts before the Reno-Tahoe Open. Finished T9 in Nevada after a 1-under 71 closing round, one of only nine players to record an under-par round Sunday. It marked his third top-10 in Reno in five career starts, T3 in 2003 and T7 in 1999. . .Recorded a T13 finish at the Deutsche Bank Championship and collected $93,750, enough to secure his card for the 2005 season as a fully-exempt member for the first time since the 2001 season.

CAREER HIGHLIGHTS:
2003: Spilt time on both the PGA TOUR and the Nationwide Tour in 2003. Made 15 starts on the PGA TOUR and five on the Nationwide Tour...In only his second appearance of the season finished T13 at the Buick Invitational...Finished T5 at the Greater Milwaukee Open, his first top-10 on TOUR since a T3 at the 2001 BellSouth Classic. In Milwaukee, was one of five players to post all four rounds in the 60s...Second top 10 was T3 at the Reno-Tahoe Open. Tied for 36-hole lead at 10-under-par 134, but third-round 73 de-railed title hopes. With final-round 69 thanks to two eagles, earned $174,000 to jump into top 125 on TOUR money list. **2002:** Finished outside the 125 for the first time since 1998 and without a top-10 for the first time in a season with 25 or more starts...Best finish was T11 at the B.C. Open, aided by rounds of 66-67 on the weekend...Earned a season-best payday of $74,480 after a T12 finish at the BellSouth Classic. **2001:** Earned a top-75 spot on the money list for the third consecutive year. Finished 67th in earnings courtesy of three top-10s and 13 cuts made in 25 starts...After starting the final day three shots off the lead, closed with a 70 in the Nissan Open to tie Robert Allenby, Brandel Chamblee, Toshi Izawa, Jeff Sluman and Bob Tway at 8-under 276. Allenby made birdie on the first extra hole to win, but Paulson earned his best finish on TOUR since winning the 2000 Buick Classic...Part of a five-man tie for the lead after an opening 66 in the Bay Hill Invitational. Followed rounds of 75-69-70 to post a T8...Trailed by two shots after both 36 and 54 holes at the BellSouth Classic. Shot 75 in the final round for a T3. **2000:** Despite a dropoff from previous year's breakthrough campaign in overall performance, registered finest career moment by capturing first PGA TOUR title...Finished season with just one top-10, yet managed to rank among the top 60 on money list for second consecutive year with $896,098 (51st)...Season's first memorable moment came in first career Masters appearance. Opened with 68 to hold solo first-round lead, but finished 76-73-72 for solid T14 showing...Found vindication at Buick Classic with playoff victory over David Duval nearly a year after having lost in a playoff to close friend Duffy Waldorf in previous year's event. Opened with 65-68 and held the lead through first two rounds. Third-round 75 dropped him to two strokes off 54-hole leader Waldorf. Final-day comeback was completed with 68 that forced a playoff with Duval. Par-4 on fourth extra hole brought his first TOUR victory and largest single career payday of $540,000. Became first player since Jim Furyk at 1996-97 Hawaiian Opens to participate in a playoff in the same event in consecutive years...Enjoyed his best finish at a major with a T11 at the British Open. **1999:** Breakthrough season came in his third as a TOUR member...Second-round 64 at Buick Invitational featured tournament-record-tying 29 on his first nine, the back nine of the South Course at Torrey Pines, and propelled him to T7 finish...In May, matched his then career-best finish with T4 in the Compaq Classic of New Orleans...Recorded three consecutive top-10s at the end of May: Kemper Open (T8), Memorial Tournament (6) and Buick Classic (P2). Lost playoff to Duffy Waldorf after finishing as clubhouse leader until Waldorf birdied his final two holes to force playoff...In September, finished second to Hal Sutton at the Bell Canadian Open. **1998:** Won Nationwide Tour Huntsville Open, defeating Brent Schwarzrock in playoff. Named Nationwide Tour Player of Month for May for victory and two other top-10s. **1996:** Posted three non-tour wins: Long Beach Open, Wyoming Open, California Open. **1994:** Finished T4 Freeport-McMoRan Classic after an English Turn G&CC record 10-under-par 62 in second round...Ranked second to Davis Love III in Driving Distance. **1993:** Persistence at PGA TOUR National Qualifying Tournament eventually rewarded after eight consecutive unsuccessful attempts beginning in 1985. Winner of Utah State Open. **1990:** Played three years on Asian Tour and won Philippines Open. Also, won the California State Open. **1985:** Won National Long Driving Championship.

PERSONAL:
Nickname "The Chief." Says some friends haven't called him by his first name since he picked up moniker. Wears nickname on back of hat. . .While ranked No. 1 in Southern California, quit golf in high school because of political issues involving scholarships. Didn't play for 18 months before going to San Diego State, where he missed making team. Tried again 18 months later and gained last spot via qualifying.

PLAYER STATISTICS

2004 PGA TOUR STATISTICS

Statistic	Value	Rank
Scoring Average	70.67	(42)
Driving Distance	300.1	(14)
Driving Accuracy Percentage	60.4%	(149)
Total Driving	163	(53)
Greens in Regulation Pct.	63.0%	(147)
Putting Average	1.774	(84)
Sand Save Percentage	61.1%	(3)
Eagles (Holes per)	426.0	(169)
Birdie Average	3.73	(50)
All-Around Ranking	658	(66)
Scoring Avg. Before Cut	70.88	(80)
Round 3 Scoring Avg.	70.93	(95)
Final Round Scoring Average	72.33	(154)
Birdie Conversion Percentage	31.6%	(23)
Par Breakers	21.0%	(58)

MISCELLANEOUS PGA TOUR STATISTICS
2004 Low Round/Round: 66–HP Classic of New Orleans/1
Career Low Round/Round: 62–1994 Freeport-McMoRan Classic/2
Career Largest Paycheck/Finish: $540,000–2000 Buick Classic/1

PGA TOUR CAREER SUMMARY — PLAYOFF RECORD: 1-2

Year	Events Played	Cuts Made	1st	2nd	3rd	Top 10	Top 25	Earnings	Rank
1985A	1								
1986	1								
1994	27	12				1	5	$142,515	125
1995	30	11				1	4	103,411	158
1998	1	1						4,557	317
1999	28	25		2		7	9	1,313,814	27
2000	26	15	1			1	5	896,098	51
2001	25	13		1	1	3	7	811,105	64
2002	30	13					4	344,121	151
2003	15	10			1	2	3	452,648	135
2004	21	15				2	9	677,035	117
Total	205	115	1	3	2	17	46	4,745,304	
NATIONWIDE TOUR									
1990	1	1					1	963	217
1992	1								
1997	25	18		2		5	13	81,344	25
1998	26	18	1	2		8	13	145,065	6
2003	5	3					2	11,161	185
Total	58	40	1	4		13	29	238,533	

PGA TOUR TOP TOURNAMENT SUMMARY

Year	95	96	97	98	99	00	01	02	03	04
Masters						T14	CUT			
U.S. Open						W/D	CUT			CUT
British Open					T58	T11	CUT			
PGA					CUT	T58	CUT			
THE PLAYERS	CUT					CUT	T31	CUT		
TOUR Championship					29					
WGC-Accenture Match Play						T33	T33			
WGC-American Express Champ					T20	T45				

Corey Pavin (PAY-vin)

EXEMPT STATUS: Winner, 1995 U.S. Open (through 2005)
FULL NAME: Corey Allen Pavin
HEIGHT: 5-9
WEIGHT: 155
BIRTHDATE: November 16, 1959
BIRTHPLACE: Oxnard, CA
RESIDENCE: Plano, TX

FAMILY: Wife, Lisa; Ryan (5/29/86), Austin (3/5/93)
EDUCATION: UCLA
SPECIAL INTERESTS: Basketball, snow skiing
TURNED PROFESSIONAL: 1982
Q SCHOOL: 1983

PGA TOUR VICTORIES (14):

1984 Houston Coca-Cola Open. **1985** Colonial National Invitation. **1986** Hawaiian Open, Greater Milwaukee Open. **1987** Bob Hope Chrysler Classic, Hawaiian Open. **1988** Texas Open. **1991** Bob Hope Chrysler Classic, BellSouth Atlanta Golf Classic. **1992** Honda Classic. **1994** Nissan Los Angeles Open. **1995** Nissan Open, U.S. Open Championship. **1996** MasterCard Colonial.

INTERNATIONAL VICTORIES (12):

1983 German Open [Eur], South African PGA Championship [SAfr], Calberson Classic [Eur]. **1984** New Zealand Open [Aus]. **1985** New Zealand Open [Aus], U.S. vs. Japan Matches [indiv.]. **1993** Toyota World Match Play Championship [Eur]. **1994** Tokai Classic [Jpn]. **1995** Asian Masters [Asia], Million Dollar Challenge [Afr]. **1996** Ssang Yong International Challenge [Korea]. **1999** Martel Skins Game [Taiwan].

BEST 2004 PGA TOUR FINISHES:

T6—Buick Championship; T10—AT&T Pebble Beach National Pro-Am.

2004 SEASON:

Two top-10s were the most since he posted three in 1998. Finished inside the top 100 (89th) on the PGA TOUR money list for the first time since that same year, when he was No. 70…Picked up first top-10 since a T6 at the 2002 Michelob Championship at Kingsmill with a T10 at the AT&T Pebble Beach National Pro-Am…Held the lead after 36-holes at the Reno-Tahoe Open, thanks to a second-round 64. Weekend round of 76-75 dropped finish to T14…Tied career low with a first-round 8-under 62 at the Buick Championship. Entered second round with a three-stroke lead over Bob Burns and Matt Weibring. Finished T6, two strokes out of Woody Austin-Tim Herron playoff.

CAREER HIGHLIGHTS:

2003: Made 18 cuts in 26 starts...His best effort of the season came in the first start of the year, a T15 at the Sony Open in Hawaii. **2002:** Only top-10 of the season came at the at Michelob Championship at Kingsmill. Was one back of the lead through 18 holes and only two back through 54 holes. A 73 on the final day dropped him to T6, his best finish since a T5 at the 1999 MCI Classic. **2001:** Rounds of 68-64 gave him 36-hole lead MasterCard Colonial. Closed with 73-68 for T8, first top-10 since T9 at 2000 Westin Texas Open. His 64 matched the second round he shot at Colonial in 1999. Finish produced largest payday, $116,000, since earning $270,000 for winning 1996 MasterCard Colonial. **2000:** Played in 25 events on PGA TOUR and finished among the top 25 in three tournaments, including a T9 at the Westin Texas Open...Tied PGA TOUR record with 18 putts in second round of Bell Canadian Open en route to 65...Finished T9 at Westin Texas Open. **1999:** After finishing outside of the top 150 on the money list in 1997-98, rebounded to finish 70th. Had as many top-10s (3) as he did in the two previous years combined. **1998:** Showed comeback was complete at end of season, when he posted top-10s in two late-season events, Westin Texas Open and the Michelob Championship at Kingsmill...Lost playoff to Stephen Leaney at ANZ Players Championship in Australia, where he shot course-record 66 in second round. **1996:** Made 21 of 22 cuts and won the MasterCard Colonial...Finished in the top-10 nine times and ranked 18th on the money list...Earned berth on second straight Presidents Cup squad. **1995:** After shooting 72-69-71, entered final round of U.S. Open at Shinnecock Hills three strokes behind Greg Norman. Closing 68 was highlighted by 228-yard 4-wood shot to 18th green, where ball came to rest five feet from hole. Two-putt par gave him his first major championship title...Became only the second player to win back-to-back at Riviera (Ben Hogan the other) when he successfully defended his Nissan Open title...Played on his third Ryder Cup team, compiling an career 8-5-0 record. **1991:** Won Arnold Palmer Award, the last player to win TOUR money title with less than $1 million. **1988:** Captured the Texas Open, shooting 21-under-par 259 to become fifth player in TOUR history to break 260. **1984:** Scored victories in each of his first five full years on TOUR, starting with his first win at the Coca-Cola Houston Open. **Amateur:** At UCLA, was a two-time first-team All-American (1979, 1982), won 11 collegiate tournaments, including the 1982 PAC-10 title, and was named 1982 college player of the year. Bruin teammates included former or current PGA TOUR members Steve Pate, Jay Delsing, Tom Pernice Jr. and Duffy Waldorf...At age 17, won the Junior World and Los Angeles City Amateur titles.

PERSONAL:

Corey and son Ryan won Disney's father-child event for Ryan's age group (1996)…Serves as host for Corey Pavin Golf Classic benefiting Big Brothers and Big Sisters in Ventura County, CA…Had LASIK surgery in November 1998…Caddied for former UCLA teammate Jay Delsing at 2003 PGA TOUR Qualifying Tournament, where Delsing earned his card for the 2004 TOUR season.

PLAYER STATISTICS

2004 PGA TOUR STATISTICS

Scoring Average	70.44	(30)
Driving Distance	268.2	(196)
Driving Accuracy Percentage	71.9%	(15)
Total Driving	211	(124)
Greens in Regulation Pct.	62.1%	(168)
Putting Average	1.762	(50)
Sand Save Percentage	57.4%	(13)
Eagles (Holes per)	158.0	(41)
Birdie Average	3.51	(102)
All-Around Ranking	615	(48)
Scoring Avg. Before Cut	70.10	(16)
Round 3 Scoring Avg.	71.29	(124)
Final Round Scoring Average	71.41	(84)
Birdie Conversion Percentage	29.2%	(91)
Par Breakers	20.1%	(96)

MISCELLANEOUS PGA TOUR STATISTICS

2004 Low Round/Round: 62–Buick Championship/1
Career Low Round/Round: 62–2 times, most recent 2004 Buick Championship/1
Career Largest Paycheck/Finish: $350,000–1995 U.S. Open Championship/1

PGA TOUR CAREER SUMMARY — PLAYOFF RECORD: 5-3

Year	Events Played	Cuts Made	1st	2nd	3rd	Top 10	Top 25	Earnings	Rank
1980A	1	1							
1983	3	1					1	$4,209	207
1984	29	26	1	2		5	14	260,536	18
1985	27	23	1	1	1	13	19	367,506	6
1986	28	23	2			6	14	304,558	19
1987	27	17	2			7	10	498,406	15
1988	26	17	1			3	7	216,768	50
1989	28	23				1	10	177,084	82
1990	29	26		1	1	6	13	468,830	26
1991	25	24	2	2	2	10	18	979,430	1
1992	25	20	1	3	2	7	13	980,934	5
1993	24	21		2		6	13	675,087	18
1994	20	16	1	3	1	9	11	906,305	8
1995	22	18	2	2	1	6	11	1,340,079	4
1996	22	21	1			9	14	851,320	18
1997	22	11				1	1	99,304	169
1998	23	12				2	3	168,485	155
1999	25	18				3	10	569,045	70
2000	25	11				1	3	209,883	160
2001	22	14				1	6	458,401	111
2002	24	14				1	2	362,012	148
2003	26	18					2	358,911	148
2004	23	18				2	8	881,938	89
Total	526	393	14	16	8	99	203	11,139,031	

PGA TOUR TOP TOURNAMENT SUMMARY

Year	83	84	85	86	87	88	89	90	91	92	93	94	95
Masters			T25	T11	T27	T42	50		T22	3	T11	T8	T17
U.S. Open	CUT		T9	CUT	W/D	CUT		T24	T8	CUT	T19	CUT	**1**
British Open		T22	T39	CUT	CUT	T38		T8	CUT	T34	T4	CUT	T8
PGA		T20	T6	T21	CUT	T17	CUT	T14	T32	T12	CUT	2	CUT
THE PLAYERS		CUT	CUT	T58	T50	T42	T34	CUT	T41	T46	T16	T78	T3
TOUR Championship					T5			21	T10	T2	T7	T10	T2

Year	96	97	98	99	00	01	02	03	04
Masters	T7	T43	T41	CUT	CUT				
U.S. Open	T40	CUT	CUT	T34	CUT	T19	T54	CUT	T17
British Open	T26	T51	CUT	CUT	CUT	CUT	T22	CUT	
PGA	T26		CUT	T10	CUT				
THE PLAYERS	T46	CUT	CUT	T71	T61	T21	CUT	T32	T33
TOUR Championship	T21								

NATIONAL TEAMS: Walker Cup, 1981; USA vs. Japan, 1982; Nissan Cup, 1985; Ryder Cup (3), 1991, 1993, 1995; The Presidents Cup (2), 1994, 1996.

David Peoples

EXEMPT STATUS: Minor Medical Extension
FULL NAME: David Roy Peoples
HEIGHT: 5-9
WEIGHT: 170
BIRTHDATE: January 9, 1960
BIRTHPLACE: Augusta, ME
RESIDENCE: Orlando, FL

FAMILY: Wife, Melissa; Andrew (10/20/89), Benjamin (6/4/92), Matthew (1/29/94)
EDUCATION: University of Florida
SPECIAL INTERESTS: Family activities, beach activities, sightseeing
TURNED PROFESSIONAL: 1981
Q SCHOOL: 1982, 1983, 1985, 1986, 1987, 1989, 1999
Nationwide Tour Alumnus

PGA TOUR VICTORIES (2):
1991 Buick Southern Open. **1992** Anheuser-Busch Golf Classic.

OTHER VICTORIES (1):
1990 Isuzu Kapalua International.

BEST 2004 PGA TOUR FINISHES:
T11—BellSouth Classic, Shell Houston Open; T25—Deutsche Bank Championship.

2004 SEASON:
Missed entire month of June along with first-half of July due to hernia surgery along with a rib injury. Will receive a Minor Medical Extension for 2005. Coupled with $479,464 earned in 26 events in 2004 has the opportunity to play in four events to earn $143,798 and match the $623,262 winnings of 2004's No. 125, Tag Ridings. If he does so, will play out of the Minor Medical Extension category for the remainder of the season…Finished No. 147 on money list, with T11s at both the BellSouth Classic and Shell Houston Open his best finishes.

CAREER HIGHLIGHTS:
2003: Finished in the top 100 for the third consecutive season, continuing to search for first win since 1992...Co-leader through 36 holes after opening 65-65 at The Honda Classic, marking the first time he held a 36-hole lead/co-lead since September 30, 1990 at the Buick Southern Open. Finished T21 after rounds of 71-69 on the weekend...One off the lead after the first round, finished eighth at the FedEx St. Jude Classic for first top-10 of 2003. Aced the par-3 eighth hole in the second round with an 8-iron from 174 yards...Clinched TOUR card with top-25 finishes in three of last five starts. **2002:** Earned career-best $1,243,774, $531,117 more than previous best season on the PGA TOUR...Finished 48th on money list, the third consecutive season in the top 125. Had not accomplished that feat since 1990-92. **2001:** Parlayed making 19 cuts, including two top-10s, in 31 starts into a 73rd position on the money list...Best finish of T3 came thanks to a final-round 66 in the National Car Rental Golf Classic at Walt Disney World Resort. The last time he had two top-10s in the same season was 1993. **2000:** Earned playing privileges in 2000 with T2 finish at the 1999 PGA TOUR Qualifying Tournament...Rebounded from lean years in the mid- to late-'90s on the strength of making 21 of 28 cuts. Had his best financial year on TOUR since 1992 with earnings of $459,812. **1999:** Played the Nationwide Tour. Made 11 cuts in 18 starts to finish 75th in earnings. **1992:** Won Anheuser-Busch Golf Classic, scoring a one-stroke victory over Bill Britton, Ed Dougherty and Jim Gallagher, Jr. **1991:** Captured Buick Southern Open at Callaway Gardens by one stroke over Robert Gamez. **1990:** Won Isuzu Kapalua International. Medalist at 1989 Qualifying Tournament. **Amateur:** Winner of Florida State Amateur.

PERSONAL:
Entered Qualifying school each year from 1981-89, earning his card six times.

PLAYER STATISTICS

2004 PGA TOUR STATISTICS

Scoring Average	71.05	(88)
Driving Distance	281.3	(146)
Driving Accuracy Percentage	63.7%	(105)
Total Driving	251	(169)
Greens in Regulation Pct.	64.0%	(120)
Putting Average	1.779	(106)
Sand Save Percentage	50.0%	(80)
Eagles (Holes per)	360.0	(155)
Birdie Average	3.50	(103)
All-Around Ranking	903	(136)
Scoring Avg. Before Cut	70.50	(39)
Round 3 Scoring Avg.	71.31	(128)
Final Round Scoring Average	71.67	(103)
Birdie Conversion Percentage	28.3%	(121)
Par Breakers	19.7%	(110)

MISCELLANEOUS PGA TOUR STATISTICS
2004 Low Round/Round: 64–Valero Texas Open/2
Career Low Round/Round: 62–2 times, most recent 1993 New England Classic/3
Career Largest Paycheck/Finish: $396,000–2002 Memorial Tournament/T2

SECTION 2 PLAYER BIOGRAPHIES

PGA TOUR CAREER SUMMARY — PLAYOFF RECORD: 0-0

Year	Events Played	Cuts Made	1st	2nd	3rd	Top 10	Top 25	Earnings	Rank
1983	32	13				1	2	$28,446	137
1984	27	9				1	1	18,124	160
1986	32	15					5	37,668	154
1987	30	10					3	31,234	180
1988	36	16					7	65,537	139
1989	20	12			1	2	5	82,624	140
1990	32	26			1	4	10	259,367	57
1991	29	21	1	1		4	9	414,346	35
1992	28	21	1		1	5	10	539,531	25
1993	29	15				2	3	105,309	142
1994	30	17				1	4	126,918	133
1995	15	11				1	2	86,679	169
1996	22	7					1	32,385	215
1997	8	4						13,740	253
1998	9	3					1	24,994	236
1999	7	6					3	112,965	191
2000	28	21				1	6	459,812	110
2001	31	19			1	2	7	712,657	73
2002	30	22		2		4	9	1,243,774	48
2003	30	18				1	8	674,222	93
2004	26	15					3	479,464	147
Total	531	301	2	3	4	29	99	5,549,795	

NATIONWIDE TOUR

Year	Events Played	Cuts Made	1st	2nd	3rd	Top 10	Top 25	Earnings	Rank
1995	5	3				1	2	7,252	139
1996	2								
1997	6	2						1,240	219
1998	6	3					1	4,721	157
1999	18	11				1	6	33,615	75
Total	37	19				2	9	46,828	

PGA TOUR TOP TOURNAMENT SUMMARY

Year	90	91	92	93	94	95	96	97	98	99	00	01	02
Masters			T54	T52									
U.S. Open				CUT								T66	
PGA	T57	T70	T69										CUT
THE PLAYERS	T68	72	CUT	CUT								CUT	CUT
TOUR Championship			T27										

Year	03	04
THE PLAYERS	W/D	T42

Pat Perez

EXEMPT STATUS: 111th on 2004 money list
FULL NAME: Pat Perez
HEIGHT: 6-0
WEIGHT: 180
BIRTHDATE: March 1, 1976
BIRTHPLACE: Phoenix, AZ
RESIDENCE: Scottsdale, AZ
FAMILY: Single

EDUCATION: Arizona State University
SPECIAL INTERESTS: Racing, boating, basketball, watching TV
TURNED PROFESSIONAL: 1997
Q SCHOOL: 2001
Nationwide Tour Alumnus

BEST PGA TOUR CAREER FINISHES:
2—2002 AT&T Pebble Beach National Pro-Am, T2—Buick Classic.

NATIONWIDE TOUR VICTORIES (1):
2000 Ozarks Open.

OTHER VICTORIES (1):
2002 Champions Challenge [with John Daly].

BEST 2004 PGA TOUR FINISH:
T3—84 LUMBER Classic.

2004 SEASON:
Started out the season slow making only three cuts in his first 12 TOUR starts. Ended the year with a bang, making 50 percent of his season earnings in his last five starts, including a T3 in Pennsylvania to secure his card for 2005...Was T35 heading into the final round of the Cialis Western Open and fired a closing 67 to finish T11...Ended the season on a high note, beginning with the Bell Canadian Open in mid-September, finishing T14...Two weeks later earned his first top-10 at the 84 LUMBER Classic. Was T3 after being one of only four players to record two rounds in the 60s on the weekend at Mystic Rock Course. His $201,600 payday in Pennsylvania lifted him over the mark to secure his card for the 2005 season, from $468,728 to $670,328 in season earning...Other top-25 finishes came at the HP Classic of New Orleans (T20), Wachovia Championship (T21), Valero Texas Open (T22) and Michelin Championship at Las Vegas (T23).

CAREER HIGHLIGHTS:
2003: Made the cut in just under half of his 33 starts during his sophomore campaign. First of two top-10s was T6 at Bob Hope Chrysler Classic. Set course record with 11-under-par 61, a TOUR career best, at Bermuda Dunes Country Club in second round...Second, a T10, came at the Bay Hill Invitational presented by Cooper Tires. **2002:** Only thing missing from his stellar rookie season was a victory but did qualify for his first Masters Tournament thanks to finishing 40th on the money list...Began season 507th on Official World Golf Ranking list and had moved up to 84th through THE TOUR Championship...Became eighth rookie in TOUR history to surpass $1 million...Finished second at the AT&T Pebble Beach National Pro-Am after holding a four-stroke advantage after 36 and 54 holes. Had the lead with one hole to play but triple-bogeyed the 18th hole at Pebble Beach to lose by three strokes to Matt Gogel...Second runner-up finish came at the Buick Classic, tied with David Gossett and Loren Roberts two strokes behind champion Chris Smith. Paycheck of $261,333 pushed season earnings over $1 million at $1,006,341...Recorded hole-in-one in the second round of the Reno-Tahoe Open, acing No. 7 with a 6-iron from 210 yards...Turned in the round of the tournament during the final round of the Bell Canadian Open with an Angus Glen Golf Club record 9-under-par 63. **2001:** Earned first PGA TOUR card by finishing as medalist at PGA TOUR Qualifying Tournament...T3 finish at the Samsung Canadian PGA Championship on the Nationwide Tour. **2000:** Picked up his first victory at the Ozarks Open on the Nationwide Tour where he defeated Pat Bates and Mike Heinen in a playoff with birdie on the first extra hole. Was 36-hole leader by three strokes and 54-hole leader by four strokes at the 2000 Monterey Peninsula Classic, won by Richard Johnson. **Amateur:** Member of Arizona State University's 1996 NCAA National Championship team...Won the 1993 Junior World title at Torrey Pines, where Tiger Woods finished fourth, eight strokes back. Won the 1993 Maxfli PGA Junior two weeks later at Pinehurst, NC.

PERSONAL:
Brother Mike played on the 2002 Nationwide Tour. They were the only brothers to play in the 2001 Qualifying Tournament finals at Bear Lakes CC in West Palm Beach, FL.

PLAYER STATISTICS

2004 PGA TOUR STATISTICS

Scoring Average	71.28	(114)
Driving Distance	291.4	(54)
Driving Accuracy Percentage	65.0%	(80)
Total Driving	134	(24)
Greens in Regulation Pct.	66.2%	(64)
Putting Average	1.780	(107)
Sand Save Percentage	51.1%	(70)
Eagles (Holes per)	300.0	(129)
Birdie Average	3.80	(29)
All-Around Ranking	647	(60)
Scoring Avg. Before Cut	71.32	(135)
Round 3 Scoring Avg.	70.70	(73)
Final Round Scoring Average	71.56	(94)
Birdie Conversion Percentage	30.8%	(44)
Par Breakers	21.4%	(37)

MISCELLANEOUS PGA TOUR STATISTICS

2004 Low Round/Round: 63–Valero Texas Open/3
Career Low Round/Round: 61–2003 Bob Hope Chrysler Classic/2
Career Largest Paycheck/Finish: $432,000–2002 AT&T Pebble Beach National Pro–Am/2

PGA TOUR CAREER SUMMARY — PLAYOFF RECORD: 0-0

Year	Events Played	Cuts Made	1st	2nd	3rd	Top 10	Top 25	Earnings	Rank
2002	30	14		2		6	10	$1,451,726	40
2003	33	16				2	5	578,141	117
2004	32	18			1	1	7	723,724	111
Total	95	48		2	1	9	22	2,753,592	
NATIONWIDE TOUR									
2000	19	11	1		1	4	5	148,094	26
2001	26	16			1	5	10	124,818	32
Total	45	27	1		2	9	15	272,912	

PGA TOUR TOP TOURNAMENT SUMMARY

Year	02	03	04
Masters		T45	
U.S. Open	CUT		T40
PGA	70		
THE PLAYERS		CUT	CUT

Craig Perks

EXEMPT STATUS: Winner, 2002 PLAYERS Championship (through 2007)
FULL NAME: Craig William Perks
HEIGHT: 6-2
WEIGHT: 200
BIRTHDATE: January 6, 1967
BIRTHPLACE: Palmerston North, New Zealand
RESIDENCE: Lafayette, LA

FAMILY: Wife, Maureen Elizabeth; Meghan Elizabeth (6/26/ 96), Nigel William (10/6/98)
EDUCATION: University of Southwestern Louisiana (1990, Behavioral Science)
SPECIAL INTERESTS: Family time
TURNED PROFESSIONAL: 1993
Q SCHOOL: 1999, 2000
Nationwide Tour Alumnus

PGA TOUR VICTORIES (1):

2002 THE PLAYERS Championship.

BEST 2004 PGA TOUR FINISH:

4—Bank of America Colonial.

2004 SEASON:

Finished outside the top 150 (152nd) on the PGA TOUR money list for the first time in his five-year TOUR career. . .Earned his highest finish since his win at the 2002 PLAYERS Championship with a fourth-place performance at the Bank of America Colonial. Held the first-round lead after an opening round, 6-under 64, his first lead on TOUR since his victory. . .Finished season on a strong note, making seven of his last eight cuts.

CAREER HIGHLIGHTS:

2003: Inconsistent season where he put together no more than a high of two consecutive cuts made and no top-10s...Finished in the top 150 for the fourth consecutive season. **2002:** Made more money by collecting his first victory at THE PLAYERS Championship than he had in his previous two years on TOUR combined and his three top-10s matched his career total in that category...Became the first player to win his first PGA TOUR event at THE PLAYERS Championship, earning $1,080,000 and the final invitation to the 2002 Masters (three-year exemption). Joined Jack Nicklaus (1974) and Hal Sutton (1983) as only players to win THE PLAYERS in first attempt. After opening with 71-68-69, entered final round one stroke behind leader Carl Paulson. Even-par 72 on Sunday included one putt over the final three holes (chip-in for eagle on par-5 16th, 28-foot birdie putt on par-3 17th and chip-in for par on par-4 18th). His 72-hole total of 280 was two strokes better than runner-up Stephen Ames. Entered the event ranked No. 203 in the Official World Golf Ranking, but moved up to No. 64 following victory...Named PGA TOUR Player of the Month for March. **2001:** Began second season on PGA TOUR in sophomore slump, making the cut in two of first 16 starts...Made the most of one of those cuts with a then career-best T2 at the Honda Classic. **2000:** Retained playing privileges with a T8 finish at the PGA TOUR Qualifying Tournament...Earned first PGA TOUR top-10 in 20th start of season, 21st of career. T4 at Bell Canadian Open...Played in one PGA TOUR of Australasia event and lost in a playoff to Michael Campbell at the Crown Lager New Zealand Open. **1999:** Posted second runner-up finish on Nationwide Tour at the Oregon Classic. **1996:** Lost one-hole playoff to Glen Hnatiuk at the Carolina Classic on the Nationwide Tour. **1995:** Collected fourth career Hooters Tour victory at Natchez, MS. **Amateur:** All-America selection at Oklahoma (1986) and Southwest Louisiana (1990).

PERSONAL:

Named 2002 New Zealand Sportsman of the Year. . .Was a two-time table tennis champion in New Zealand. . .Left New Zealand at age 18 to come to the United States to play college golf, where he was an All-America at Oklahoma and Southwestern Louisiana (now Louisiana-Lafayette). Followed countryman and PGA TOUR member Grant Waite to Oklahoma. . .Served as assistant pro for two years in early '90s at La Triomphe, home course of the Chitimacha Louisiana Open on the Nationwide Tour. . .Nine-time PGA TOUR Qualifying Tournament participant.

PLAYER STATISTICS

2004 PGA TOUR STATISTICS

Scoring Average	71.75	(158)
Driving Distance	289.4	(73)
Driving Accuracy Percentage	54.4%	(187)
Total Driving	260	(175)
Greens in Regulation Pct.	63.0%	(147)
Putting Average	1.815	(189)
Sand Save Percentage	50.5%	(78)
Eagles (Holes per)	259.2	(108)
Birdie Average	3.26	(161)
All-Around Ranking	1,101	(179)
Scoring Avg. Before Cut	71.92	(173)
Round 3 Scoring Avg.	71.90	(158)
Final Round Scoring Average	70.10	(10)
Birdie Conversion Percentage	27.3%	(157)
Par Breakers	18.5%	(158)

MISCELLANEOUS PGA TOUR STATISTICS

2004 Low Round/Round: 64–Bank of America Colonial/1
Career Low Round/Round: 64–3 times, most recent 2004 Bank of America Colonial/1
Career Largest Paycheck/Finish: $1,080,000–2002 THE PLAYERS Championship/1

PGA TOUR CAREER SUMMARY — PLAYOFF RECORD: 0-0

Year	Events Played	Cuts Made	1st	2nd	3rd	Top 10	Top 25	Earnings	Rank
1993	1								
2000	28	12				1	3	$297,912	136
2001	30	9		1		2	3	457,127	113
2002	28	17	1			3	4	1,632,042	34
2003	28	12					3	368,163	146
2004	27	11				1	1	423,748	152
Total	142	61	1	1		7	14	3,178,993	
NATIONWIDE TOUR									
1993	3	1						735	230
1994	1								
1995	2								
1996	19	7		1		1	2	27,383	70
1997	24	5					3	8,316	134
1998	21	16				3	5	33,613	64
1999	28	13		1		2	5	54,703	47
2000	4	1						1,380	263
Total	102	43		2		6	15	126,129	

PGA TOUR TOP TOURNAMENT SUMMARY

Year	02	03	04
Masters	CUT	CUT	CUT
U.S. Open	CUT		
British Open	T50	CUT	CUT
PGA	T29		
THE PLAYERS	**1**	T17	CUT
WGC-NEC Invitational	T42		
WGC-American Express Champ	61		

NATIONAL TEAMS: WGC-World Cup (3), 2001, 2002, 2004.

SECTION 2 PLAYER BIOGRAPHIES

Tom Pernice, Jr. (purr-NIECE)

EXEMPT STATUS: 47th on 2004 money list
FULL NAME: Thomas Charles Pernice, Jr.
HEIGHT: 5-10
WEIGHT: 160
BIRTHDATE: September 5, 1959
BIRTHPLACE: Kansas City, MO
RESIDENCE: Murrieta, CA.; plays out of Bear Creek GC

FAMILY: Wife, Sydney; Kristen (9/30/93), Brooke (3/7/95)
EDUCATION: UCLA (Economics, 1982)
SPECIAL INTERESTS: Gardening, TV, sports, politics, home decorating
TURNED PROFESSIONAL: 1983
Q SCHOOL: 1985, 1996, 1997
Nationwide Tour Alumnus

PGA TOUR VICTORIES (2):

1999 Buick Open. **2001** The INTERNATIONAL Presented by Qwest.

BEST 2004 PGA TOUR FINISHES:

3—The INTERNATIONAL, Buick Championship; 7—Chrysler Classic of Greensboro, AT&T Pebble Beach National Pro-Am; T10—Buick Invitational.

2004 SEASON:

Posted career-highs in top-10s (five) and earnings ($1,475,274) and matched his career-high in top-25s (nine)...Among the five top-10s were a career-high two third-place finishes...First top-10 of the season, a T7, came at the AT&T Pebble Beach National Pro-Am...Followed that with a T10 the next week at the Buick Invitational...Using an 8-iron from 160 yards on the 12th hole at Muirfield Village GC he recorded the ninth ace of the season during the second round of the Memorial Tournament...Best finish of the year was solo third at The INTERNATIONAL. The 2001 champion moved into a tie for the lead at 28 points through 10 holes, but dropped back with consecutive bogeys on Nos. 11 and 12...Aided by rounds of 68-67 on the weekend, finished T3 at the Buick Championship...In contention most of the week at Chrysler Classic of Greensboro before finishing solo seventh, six strokes behind champion Brent Geiberger.

CAREER HIGHLIGHTS:

2003: Played in 31 tournaments and made 21 cuts, including 11 consecutive at the end of the season, longest consecutive cuts streak of his career...Finished in the top-25 nine times, a career best...Third-place check for $285,000 at the Bell Canadian Open, a season's best payday, lifted him over the $1-million mark for only the second time in his 12-year career. **2002:** Struggled after a career season in 2001...First top-10 of the season came at the Shell Houston Open, his 10th start of the season, with a T6...Finished the year on a strong note with three top-15s, including a T7 at the Reno Tahoe Open. **2001:** Collected his second PGA TOUR victory and for the first time eclipsed the $1-million mark in season earnings with $1,273,902...At The INTERNATIONAL, accumulated 12 points in each of the first two rounds under Modified Stableford scoring system and led by two. Added nine points in round three and increased his lead to three. Recorded only one point in the final round, but was good enough for one-point victory over Chris Riley. Inspirational victory because his two daughters, Kristen and Brooke, were in attendance. Brooke, then age 6, is blind...Next week finished T4 at the Buick Open after posting rounds of 68-67-66-66. INTERNATIONAL first-place check for $720,000, combined with Buick Open payday ($136,400), gave him $856,400 in two weeks, more than he had earned in any of his nine previous seasons on TOUR. **2000:** Opened season at the Mercedes Championships with T8. His third-round 65 was the low round of the championship...His only other top-10 came at the rain-shortened BellSouth Classic, a T5. **1999:** Earned first PGA TOUR victory at Buick Open. His closing 65 brought one-stroke victory over Tom Lehman, Ted Tryba and Bob Tway. Shared 36-hole lead after opening 67-66 and stood five strokes back after third-round 72. Victory came in his 213th career start on the PGA TOUR. His $432,000 payday was more than he made the first 16 years as professional. **1998:** First season he earned full-exempt status....Although it took more than half a year because of tournament delay, enjoyed runner-up finish to Phil Mickelson at AT&T Pebble Beach National Pro-Am. Rounds of 67-69-67 were worth $270,000. **1997:** Earned more than $100,000 for the first time with $173,012, which placed him 127th on money list...Best finish was fourth at Greater Milwaukee Open...Finished 25th at PGA TOUR Qualifying Tournament to return to TOUR in 1998. **1996:** Had three top-10 Nationwide Tour finishes, including T6 at Miami Valley Open. **1992:** Best Nationwide Tour finish T3 at Hawkeye Open. **1986:** Earned status on the PGA TOUR with his second-place finish at the 1985 Qualifying Tournament...Made 12 cuts and finished 148th on the money list with $40,172. **Amateur:** Two-time All-American at UCLA. Pac-10 Player of Year in 1981.

PERSONAL:

Teammates at UCLA included Jay Delsing, Corey Pavin, Steve Pate and Duffy Waldorf...All-conference wrestler in high school...Daughter Brooke has a genetic disease, Leber's Amorosis, which causes blindness. Her retinas did not develop fully at birth. Tom and Brooke won the National Car Rental Golf Classic at Walt Disney World Resort father-child event for Brooke's age group in 2001...Player Director on the PGA TOUR Policy Board.

PLAYER STATISTICS

2004 PGA TOUR STATISTICS

Scoring Average	70.96	(76)
Driving Distance	286.0	(109)
Driving Accuracy Percentage	68.2%	(45)
Total Driving	154	(39)
Greens in Regulation Pct.	66.8%	(50)
Putting Average	1.778	(102)
Sand Save Percentage	55.4%	(24)
Eagles (Holes per)	222.8	(87)
Birdie Average	3.46	(119)
All-Around Ranking	612	(46)
Scoring Avg. Before Cut	70.84	(75)
Round 3 Scoring Avg.	69.95	(31)
Final Round Scoring Average	71.63	(97)
Birdie Conversion Percentage	28.3%	(121)
Par Breakers	19.7%	(110)

MISCELLANEOUS PGA TOUR STATISTICS

2004 Low Round/Round: 63–FedEx St. Jude Classic/3
Career Low Round/Round: 63–4 times, most recent 2004 FedEx St. Jude Classic/3
Career Largest Paycheck/Finish: $720,000–2001 The INTERNATIONAL Presented by Qwest/1

PGA TOUR CAREER SUMMARY — PLAYOFF RECORD: 0-0

Year	Events Played	Cuts Made	1st	2nd	3rd	Top 10	Top 25	Earnings	Rank
1983	1								
1986	33	12					5	$40,172	148
1987	20	5				1	1	15,431	195
1988	31	14				1	2	47,108	150
1989	22	10				2	5	81,863	142
1990	20	7					1	19,504	212
1991	3	1						1,824	306
1992	1								
1994	1								
1996	1	1						5,235	313
1997	30	12				1	5	173,012	127
1998	27	15		1		1	8	520,400	55
1999	31	14	1			1	5	656,140	65
2000	32	16				2	5	387,716	127
2001	33	19	1			4	6	1,318,762	39
2002	31	19				2	8	645,110	104
2003	31	21			1	4	9	1,210,541	57
2004	31	20			2	5	9	1,475,274	47
Total	379	186	2	1	3	24	69	6,598,090	
NATIONWIDE TOUR									
1990	10	7					3	6,077	108
1991	4	1						550	305
1992	12	2			1	2	2	12,500	95
1995	28	19				2	11	42,047	48
1996	24	12				3	8	34,224	58
1997	1	1						1,390	213
Total	79	42			1	7	24	96,788	

PGA TOUR TOP TOURNAMENT SUMMARY

Year	86	87	88	89	90	91	92	93	94	95	96	97	98
Masters					CUT								
U.S. Open	CUT			T13	CUT						T94		
British Open								T66					

Year	99	00	01	02	03	04
Masters				T24		
U.S. Open			CUT	CUT		CUT
PGA	CUT	T27	T51		T45	CUT
THE PLAYERS	CUT	CUT		T69	CUT	T72

Chris Perry

EXEMPT STATUS: Major Medical Extension
FULL NAME: James Christopher Perry
HEIGHT: 6-1
WEIGHT: 195
BIRTHDATE: September 27, 1961
BIRTHPLACE: Edenton, NC
RESIDENCE: Powell, OH
FAMILY: Wife, Katharine; Andrew Christopher (3/1/93), Emily Ann (3/10/96), Natalie Kay (12/31/97)
EDUCATION: Ohio State University
SPECIAL INTERESTS: All sports, especially Ohio State football, hockey, snow skiing, movies
TURNED PROFESSIONAL: 1984
Q SCHOOL: 1984
JOINED TOUR: 1985
Nationwide Tour Alumnus

PGA TOUR VICTORIES (1):
1998 B.C. Open.

NATIONWIDE TOUR VICTORIES (1):
1994 Utah Classic.

INTERNATIONAL VICTORIES (1):
1994 Mexican Open.

2004 SEASON:
Played in just one event, withdrawing after second round of Bob Hope Chrysler Classic as he continues to battle hand and wrist ailments. Will receive a Major Medical Extension for third consecutive year. Has the opportunity to play in 22 events to earn $515,445 and match the total winnings of 2002's No. 125. If he does so, will play out of the Major Medical Extension category for the remainder of the season.

CAREER HIGHLIGHTS:
2003: Received a second consecutive Major Medical Extension after playing in only three events due to hand and wrist injuries. Did not play the remainder of the year. **2002:** Did not finish in the top 125 for the first time since 1995. Schedule was limited to only five events due to lingering left hand and wrist injuries suffered at the 2001 British Open. Missed the cut in three and withdrew after first round from two. Received Major Medical Extension for 2003. **2001:** Posted lowest finish on TOUR money list, No. 91, since finishing No. 112 in 1996...Made cut in first nine events of season and posted eight top-25s in that stretch...Had a pair of T8s early in the season at Nissan Open and Bay Hill Invitational...Withdrew from THE PLAYERS Championship due to stomach virus...Knee and wrist injuries caused withdrawal after round one of British Open...Played in just five events the remainder of the year and did not make the cut in any of them. **2000:** Finished in the top 30 for the second consecutive year on the strength of two runner-up finishes and seven top-10s...Missed the cut at the Buick Invitational, ending his string of 30 consecutive cuts made that began at the '99 Buick Invitational...Won Par-3 contest at the Masters and finished T14 in tournament, his best finish in three appearances...65 in the third round gave him one-stroke 54-hole lead over eventual winner Rocco Mediate at Buick Open. Closed with 68 compared to 66 for Mediate to finish T2 worth $291,600, career payday...Second runner-up finish came at inaugural SEI Pennsylvania Classic, where he tied with four others. **1999:** Nearly tripled his best previous earnings year, ranked fifth on TOUR in earnings with $2,145,707 thanks to two second-place finishes...His 14 top-10 finishes were second only to Tiger Woods' 16...Came close to second TOUR title at MCI Classic, where he held one-stroke lead through 70 holes, but closed bogey-bogey for fourth-place finish...Closing 68 led to T2 at Reno-Tahoe Open and closing 66 led to T2 at SONY Open in Hawaii...Led PGA TOUR with 468 birdies that year. **1998:** Earned first PGA TOUR title in his 377th career start at B.C. Open, where he defeated Peter Jacobsen by three strokes. **1997:** For first time in career, finished among top 50 on money list...Finished T2, one stroke behind Gabriel Hjertstedt at the B.C. Open. **1996:** Along with Emlyn Aubrey and Woods, one of only three non-exempt players to earn full playing privileges for 1997...Made cut in 15 of 20 starts to earn $184,171 and finish 112th on 1996 money list. **1994:** Concentrated on Nationwide Tour and, in the process, earned Player of the Year honors...Topped Nationwide Tour money list with $167,148...Collected one victory (Utah Classic), two seconds and two thirds. Made cut in last 31 Nationwide Tour events he entered, a record...Won the Mexican Open. **1990:** Tied for second with three others, two strokes behind Wayne Levi at Canon Greater Hartford Open. **1987:** Earned first runner-up finish with T2, seven back of Tom Kite. **Amateur:** Three-time All-America selection at Ohio State, where he also captured the 1983 Big-10 Championship.

PERSONAL:
Also played baseball and hockey while growing up. . .Father, Jim Perry, pitched in major leagues for Cleveland, Minnesota, Detroit and Oakland. Uncle Gaylord Perry is a member of Baseball Hall of Fame.

PLAYER STATISTICS

2004 PGA TOUR STATISTICS

Scoring Average	77.11	(N/A)
Driving Distance	264.0	(N/A)
Driving Accuracy Percentage	53.6%	(N/A)
Total Driving	(N/A)	(N/A)
Greens in Regulation Pct.	47.2%	(N/A)
Putting Average	1.941	(N/A)
Sand Save Percentage	0%	(N/A)
Birdie Average	1.00	(N/A)
Scoring Avg. Before Cut	75.00	(N/A)
Birdie Conversion Percentage	11.8%	(N/A)
Par Breakers	5.6%	(N/A)

MISCELLANEOUS PGA TOUR STATISTICS
2004 Low Round/Round: 74–Bob Hope Chrysler Classic/1
Career Low Round/Round: 62–1998 Greater Milwaukee Open/2
Career Largest Paycheck/Finish: $291,600–2000 Buick Open/2

PGA TOUR CAREER SUMMARY — PLAYOFF RECORD: 0-0

Year	Events Played	Cuts Made	1st	2nd	3rd	Top 10	Top 25	Earnings	Rank
1984A	1								
1984	6	3					1	$5,086	201
1985	30	22				1	5	60,801	110
1986	33	22				1	5	75,213	114
1987	31	21		1		4	10	197,593	56
1988	33	21			1	1	3	85,546	121
1989	31	24			1	3	7	206,932	67
1990	30	20		1		3	8	259,108	58
1991	33	20				2	5	116,105	126
1992	29	11					3	53,943	171
1993	9	5					3	25,333	202
1994	2	1					1	14,840	237
1995	30	17					2	113,632	150
1996	20	15			1	2	5	184,171	112
1997	32	22		1		2	11	460,984	48
1998	31	24	1		1	4	12	730,171	39
1999	31	30		2	1	14	21	2,145,707	5
2000	31	25		2		7	15	1,563,115	28
2001	26	15				2	8	568,391	91
2002	5								
2003	3								
2004	1								
Total	478	318	1	7	5	46	125	6,866,671	
NATIONWIDE TOUR									
1993	13	10					3	13,337	94
1994	24	24	1	2	2	10	19	167,148	1
1995	1	1				1	1	6,000	150
1996	4	4				1	2	11,190	116
2002	4	2						3,273	243
2003	1								
Total	47	41	1	2	2	12	25	200,948	

PGA TOUR TOP TOURNAMENT SUMMARY

Year	84	85	86	87	88	89	90	91	92	93	94	95	96
Masters	CUT												
U.S. Open		CUT	CUT			T54		T31			CUT	T56	
PGA				T28		T17	T26						
THE PLAYERS		T55	T54	T20	T64	T21	T16	T27	CUT				

Year	97	98	99	00	01
Masters			T50	T14	T37
U.S. Open	T43	T25	T42	T32	T19
British Open	W/D			CUT	W/D
PGA	T49	74	T10	T34	CUT
THE PLAYERS	T31	CUT	T32	T33	
TOUR Championship			4	T8	
WGC-Accenture Match Play				T33	T17
WGC-American Express Champ			T7	16	

Kenny Perry

EXEMPT STATUS: 2003 three-time tournament winner (through 2007)
FULL NAME: James Kenneth Perry
HEIGHT: 6-2
WEIGHT: 220
BIRTHDATE: August 10, 1960
BIRTHPLACE: Elizabethtown, KY
RESIDENCE: Franklin, KY; plays out of Country Creek GC
FAMILY: Wife, Sandy; Lesslye (5/20/84), Justin (11/23/85), Lindsey (4/27/88)
EDUCATION: Western Kentucky University
SPECIAL INTERESTS: Drag racing, coaching high school golf team
TURNED PROFESSIONAL: 1982
Q SCHOOL: Fall 1986

PGA TOUR VICTORIES (7):

1991 Memorial Tournament. **1994** New England Classic. **1995** Bob Hope Chrysler Classic. **2001** Buick Open. **2003** Bank of America Colonial, the Memorial Tournament, Greater Milwaukee Open.

BEST 2004 PGA TOUR FINISHES:

T3—THE PLAYERS Championship; T5—Bob Hope Chrysler Classic; T6—the Memorial Tournament; T7—U.S. Bank Championship in Milwaukee; T8—Chrysler Championship; T9—WGC-Accenture Match Play Championship, Buick Classic.

2004 SEASON:

Followed up a career-best season with his fourth consecutive top-30 finish (No. 30) and seven more top-10s, the third-most in any of his 18 years on the PGA TOUR…Past champion held the 36-hole lead and went on to finish T5 at the Bob Hope Chrysler Classic, four shots out of Phil Mickelson-Skip Kendall playoff. Entered final round one shot out of the lead shared by Mickelson and Kirk Triplett but lost ground with final-round 71…With his 18-year-old son Justin on the bag, finished T3 at THE PLAYERS Championship, four strokes behind Adam Scott…2003 Memorial Tournament champion followed up his victory with a T6, thanks to four birdies in the final five holes on Sunday. It was his fourth top-10 finish in Dublin, OH, in 17 appearances…The next week closed with a 5-under 66 at the Buick Classic to finish T9. With the low round of the day moved from 46th position to the top-10 on the final day…Defending champion has finished in the top 10 in each of the last five years (T7 in 2004, win in 2003, fourth in 2002, T5 in 2001 and T3 in 2000) at the U.S. Bank Championship in Milwaukee…Finished fifth on the Ryder Cup team points list to make his first U.S. Ryder Cup squad…Did not play after the Ryder Cup until the final full-field event of the season, the Chrysler Championship. Came into event 31st on the money list and finished T8, good enough to pass Rod Pampling, who finished T62, for the final spot in THE TOUR Championship.

CAREER HIGHLIGHTS:

2003: Enjoyed most prolific season of career, with three wins and 10 top-10s in 26 starts, along with a career-best $4,400,122 in winnings. One of three players, along with Mike Weir and Ernie Els, to log top-10s in three major championships...Recorded a T2 at the Bay Hill Invitational... Picked up first win since the 2001 Buick Open with a six-stroke victory at the Bank of America Colonial. Set 54- and 72-hole tournament records while tying the course record with a third-round, 9-under 61. Held eight-stroke lead heading into Sunday prior to picking up his career-largest $900,000 paycheck...Picked up second victory of season one week later at the Memorial Tournament with rounds of 65-68-70-72. At the age of 42, became oldest player to win back-to-back weeks on the PGA TOUR since Hale Irwin won the U.S. Open and the Buick Classic in consecutive weeks at age 45 in 1990. Held solo lead after 36 and 54 holes. A winner at Muirfield Village in 1991, became the sixth player to capture multiple titles at the Memorial Tournament...Added third consecutive top-three finish with a T3 at the U.S. Open. Jumped from T33 to T3 on Sunday thanks to a final-round-best 3-under 67. Second time in his 17-year career that he has posted three consecutive top-threes...Picked up third win in four starts on TOUR at the Greater Milwaukee Open. Held third-round lead and won for fourth consecutive time after holding/sharing the 54-hole lead. Victory was his fourth straight top-five finish at the Greater Milwaukee Open (T3 in 2000, T5 in 2001 and fourth in 2002)...Represented the United States at The Presidents Cup in November. **2002:** Finished in the top 30 in earnings for fifth time in career. Of his six top-10s, three came in first four starts...Finished third, one stroke shy of the Sergio Garcia-David Toms playoff at the Mercedes Championships...T2 with Kaname Yokoo at Phoenix Open, one stroke behind champion Chris DiMarco...Second runner-up finish of the season at the MasterCard Colonial, five strokes (tied with David Toms) behind champion Nick Price. Earnings of $378,400 jumped season winnings over $1 million for the second time in career at $1,301,646...Sat 31st on the money list heading into the Buick Challenge, the last event before THE TOUR Championship. T7 finish vaulted him to No. 27 and earned him a spot in the season-ending event. **2001:** In finishing 24th on the money list with $1,786,066, surpassed the $1-million single-season earnings mark for the first time...Top-30 finish earned a spot in THE TOUR Championship for the first time since 1996...Year was driven by six top-10s...Captured his fourth TOUR title with an impressive two-shot victory in the Buick Open. A second-round 64, which included a 29 on the front nine of Warwick Hills G&CC, came on his 41st birthday and earned a three-stroke lead. Followed with another 64, this time with a 29 on the back nine, to extend his lead to five after 54 holes. Closed with a 69 to collect the $558,000 paycheck. **2000:** Consistent season, making 18 cuts in 20 tournaments entered and finishing third three times…Finished T3 finish at rain-shortened BellSouth Classic for best finish on TOUR since he lost in playoff at 1996 PGA Championship. **1999:** Though he surpassed $400,000 in earnings, finished 94th on the money list, his lowest ranking since joining the TOUR. **1998:** Rebounded from sub-standard 1997 season, entered 25 tournaments and finished in top 10 five times. **1997:** Not as spectacular a year as 1996, but still managed to retain full-exempt status for 11th consecutive season. **1996:** Earned nearly $1 million and 13th spot on money list with nine top-10s, including a second, one third, two fourths and a fifth...Nearly won PGA Championship at Valhalla GC in home state of Kentucky. Took lead with course-record opening 66, followed with 72-71 to fall four back with 18 to play. Fired 34 on front nine Sunday to take slim lead, but bogey-6 on final hole left him at 11-under-par 277. Mark Brooks forced playoff with closing birdie and won with birdie on 18 after Perry took four strokes to reach green. **1995:** Season highlighted by February stretch that featured T3 at AT&T Pebble Beach National Pro-Am, victory at Bob Hope Chrysler Classic and T2 at Nissan Open. Led all three tournaments entering final round. **1994:** Shot closing 65 at Pleasant Valley to win New England Classic by one stroke over David Feherty. Win helped him to 26th on money list

PGA TOUR CAREER SUMMARY — PLAYOFF RECORD: 1-1

Year	Events Played	Cuts Made	1st	2nd	3rd	Top 10	Top 25	Earnings	Rank
1984	1								
1985	1								
1987	27	15				1	5	$107,239	93
1988	32	20				3	7	139,421	85
1989	26	15		1		3	7	202,099	70
1990	23	17		1		2	9	279,881	50
1991	24	16	1			3	7	368,784	44
1992	25	17				3	9	190,455	81
1993	29	18				3	8	196,863	88
1994	30	22	1	1		4	10	585,941	26
1995	25	21	1	1	1	5	13	773,388	21
1996	25	17		1	1	9	13	925,079	13
1997	26	17				2	8	270,081	90
1998	25	16			1	5	7	487,551	58
1999	26	16				1	7	426,184	94
2000	20	18			3	4	9	889,381	52
2001	26	22	1			6	13	1,786,066	24
2002	27	23		2	1	6	13	1,928,598	27
2003	26	24	3	1	1	11	14	4,400,122	6
2004	23	17			1	7	13	1,952,043	30
Total	467	331	7	8	9	78	172	15,909,178	

PGA TOUR TOP TOURNAMENT SUMMARY

Year	88	89	90	91	92	93	94	95	96	97	98	99	00
Masters					CUT			T12	CUT	CUT			
U.S. Open	T55					T25		CUT	T50	CUT			
British Open				CUT									
PGA		T51	T49	77			T55	T49	2	T23	T10	T34	T30
THE PLAYERS	33	T21	T56	T57	W/D	T65	T62	T55	T4	CUT	CUT	W/D	T27
TOUR Championship							T26	T20	4				

Year	01	02	03	04
Masters		CUT	T39	CUT
U.S. Open		T45	T3	CUT
British Open			T8	T16
PGA	T44	T29	T10	CUT
THE PLAYERS	T18	T60	T32	T3
TOUR Championship	T5	T18	T9	29
WGC-Accenture Match Play	T33	T33	T33	T9
WGC-NEC Invitational		T24	T53	T27
WGC-American Express Champ	CNL	22	T28	

NATIONAL TEAMS: The Presidents Cup (2), 1996, 2003; Ryder Cup, 2004.

Kenny Perry (Continued)

and first trip to TOUR Championship. **1991:** Claimed first TOUR victory at Memorial Tournament. Moved into lead with then-course-record 9-under-par 63. Was forced into playoff when Hale Irwin shot 65-66 on weekend. Birdied first extra hole for victory.

PERSONAL:

Took up golf at age 7 with encouragement from his father, who spent hours teeing balls up for him...Member of Western Kentucky University Hall of Fame...Named winner of the 2002 Charles Bartlett Award, given to a professional golfer for his unselfish contributions to the betterment of society, by the Golf Writers Association of America. Perry donates five percent of his winnings to David Lipscomb University, his wife's alma mater, to fund a pair of scholarships. In addition, 11 years ago, Perry took out a loan to build Country Creek, a public course in his hometown of Franklin, KY. In 1995, Perry bought 142 acres of land and borrowed more than $2.5 million to design and build the only public course in the town in 1995. He designed it for mid-to-high handicappers and kept it affordable: 18 holes with a cart is $28; $12 without one...Takes a six-week break to serve as assistant coach for boys and girls golf at Simpson High School in Franklin, KY, a public school with about 800 students. His son, Justin, is a senior and his daughter, Lindsey, is a sophomore. In 2003, Simpson High finished fifth at the state tournament and Justin finished fifth individually, posting scores of 74-71—145.

PLAYER STATISTICS

2004 PGA TOUR STATISTICS

Scoring Average	70.26	(23)
Driving Distance	295.9	(26)
Driving Accuracy Percentage	62.5%	(125)
Total Driving	151	(35)
Greens in Regulation Pct.	68.6%	(18)
Putting Average	1.776	(91)
Sand Save Percentage	45.8%	(142)
Eagles (Holes per)	171.0	(51)
Birdie Average	3.84	(24)
All-Around Ranking	500	(22)
Scoring Avg. Before Cut	70.89	(81)
Round 3 Scoring Avg.	69.81	(20)
Final Round Scoring Average	70.06	(8)
Birdie Conversion Percentage	30.7%	(49)
Par Breakers	21.9%	(19)

MISCELLANEOUS PGA TOUR STATISTICS

2004 Low Round/Round: 64–2 times, most recent Bob Hope Chrysler Classic/4
Career Low Round/Round: 61–2003 Bank of America Colonial/3
Career Largest Paycheck/Finish: $900,000–2 times, most recent 2003 the Memorial Tournament/1

SECTION 2 PLAYER BIOGRAPHIES

SHOTLink
AN IBM ON DEMAND BUSINESS SOLUTION

HOT SHOTS

Holes with the Highest Scoring Average when Hitting the Fairway on TOUR (2004)

Event/Course Name	Hole	Par	Hit Fairway	Avg Score	Avg to Par
Buick Invitational Torrey Pines (South Course)*	12	4	143	4.33	0.33
Masters Tournament Augusta National GC	1	4	168	4.29	0.29
Masters Tournament Augusta National GC	18	4	197	4.25	0.25
EDS Byron Nelson Championship Cottonwood Valley GC*	1	4	95	4.25	0.25
BellSouth Classic TPC at Sugarloaf	15	4	250	4.25	0.25

**Multiple course tournament*

Holes with the Lowest Scoring Average when Hitting the Fairway on TOUR (2004)

Event/Course Name	Hole	Par	Hit Fairway	Avg Score	Avg to Par
Bob Hope Chrysler Classic Indian Wells CC*	14	5	54	4.09	-0.91
Sony Open in Hawaii Waialae CC	9	5	237	4.10	-0.90
Southern Farm Bureau Classic Annandale GC	5	5	194	4.12	-0.88
Michelin Championship at Las Vegas TPC at Summerlin*	3	5	151	4.13	-0.87
Michelin Championship at Las Vegas Bear's Best*	12	5	112	4.13	-0.87

3rd Hole-TPC at Summerlin

Tim Petrovic (peh-TRO-vick)

EXEMPT STATUS: 65th on 2004 money list
FULL NAME: Tim Petrovic
HEIGHT: 6-2
WEIGHT: 195
BIRTHDATE: August 16, 1966
BIRTHPLACE: Northampton, MA
RESIDENCE: Dade City, FL
FAMILY: Wife, Julie; Bayleigh, Mackenzie
EDUCATION: University of Hartford (1988, Communications)
SPECIAL INTERESTS: Autos, music, TV, film, antiques, sports
TURNED PROFESSIONAL: 1988
JOINED TOUR: 2002
Nationwide Tour Alumnus

BEST PGA TOUR CAREER FINISHES:

2—2002 FedEx St. Jude Classic, T2—2003 84 Lumber Classic of Pennsylvania.

BEST 2004 PGA TOUR FINISHES:

T5—Bank of America Colonial; T6—The INTERNATIONAL; T7—Michelin Championship at Las Vegas.

2004 SEASON:

Finished inside the top 100 for the third consecutive season. Made 23 cuts in 32 TOUR starts and finished in the top 10 three times…Was among the leaders after the first and second rounds of the BellSouth Classic. Was two back of the lead through 18 and 36 holes. Fired 75-72 on the weekend, finishing T11…Qualified for the Masters Tournament for the first time his career, after finishing in the top 40 on the money list in 2003. At Augusta National, made the cut and was T41…Was two back of the lead through the first round at the Bank of America Colonial and finished T5 after closing with rounds of 69-68…Made his third consecutive cut in three career starts at the U.S. Open, where he finished T24…Collected his second top-10 of the season at The INTERNATIONAL. Was T6 near Denver…Added a T7 at the Michelin Championship at Las Vegas in October, on the strength of four rounds in the 60s.

CAREER HIGHLIGHTS:

2003: Moved up 50 spots on the money list (86 to 36) in his sophomore season, more than doubling his income with earnings over $1.7 million and qualified for first Masters in 2004...Began season with 12 straight rounds in the 60s and a T3 at the Phoenix Open. Shared the second-round lead with Harrison Frazar...Finished T2 at the 84 Lumber Classic of Pennsylvania thanks to being one of four players to post four rounds in the 60s. **2002:** Rookie season included a career-high T2 finish at the FedEx St. Jude Classic. Led the first round after posting a career-best 6-under-par 65. Won $410,000, helping him earn a trip the British Open...Converted the second double eagle in Honda Classic tournament history on the 534-yard, par-5 16th hole at TPC at Heron Bay from 220 yards with a 4-iron. **2001:** Became fourth player in Nationwide Tour history to earn over $100,000 through first four events. Actually did it in three (T2, T2, 3rd), since he missed the first event of the season. **2000:** Named Player of the Year after finishing first on the Golden Bear Tour money list. **1997:** Finished third at Pelz World Putting Championship. **Amateur:** Division I All-America selection at the University of Hartford.

PERSONAL:

Inducted into the University of Hartford Hall of Fame…Devout fan of The Doors. Maintains a friendship with Robby Krieger, former Doors guitarist…Once worked as a pizza baker and delivery man…Lists Ben Crenshaw, Seve Ballesteros and Jim Morrison among his heroes. College teammates included Patrick Sheehan and Jerry Kelly.

PLAYER STATISTICS

2004 PGA TOUR STATISTICS

Scoring Average	70.91	(70)
Driving Distance	287.2	(97)
Driving Accuracy Percentage	63.6%	(108)
Total Driving	205	(115)
Greens in Regulation Pct.	63.4%	(136)
Putting Average	1.776	(91)
Sand Save Percentage	49.2%	(95)
Eagles (Holes per)	214.0	(79)
Birdie Average	3.37	(134)
All-Around Ranking	810	(110)
Scoring Avg. Before Cut	70.73	(59)
Round 3 Scoring Avg.	72.18	(172)
Final Round Scoring Average	71.45	(86)
Birdie Conversion Percentage	28.4%	(112)
Par Breakers	19.2%	(131)

MISCELLANEOUS PGA TOUR STATISTICS

2004 Low Round/Round: 65–Buick Championship/4
Career Low Round/Round: 63–2003 Phoenix Open/2
Career Largest Paycheck/Finish: $410,400–2002 FedEx St. Jude Classic/2

PGA TOUR CAREER SUMMARY — PLAYOFF RECORD: 0-0

Year	Events Played	Cuts Made	1st	2nd	3rd	Top 10	Top 25	Earnings	Rank
1988A	1								
1989	1	1						$2,569	249
1990	2								
1991	2								
1992	2								
1996	2	1						2,088	370
2001	1	1						11,443	
2002	31	15		1		1	5	797,206	86
2003	32	21		1	1	4	14	1,739,349	36
2004	32	23				3	11	1,193,354	65
Total	106	62		2	1	8	30	3,746,008	
NATIONWIDE TOUR									
1992	1	1						913	239
1993	13	4					1	3,066	167
1999	26	15				2	7	45,035	63
2001	23	18		2	2	7	12	239,010	7
Total	63	38		2	2	9	20	288,024	
EUROPEAN TOUR									
2004	1	1					1	42,837	
JAPAN GOLF TOUR									
2003	1	1					1	14,506	

PGA TOUR TOP TOURNAMENT SUMMARY

Year	01	02	03	04
Masters				T41
U.S. Open	T62		T15	T24
British Open		CUT		
PGA			CUT	CUT
THE PLAYERS			CUT	T53

Carl Pettersson (PEET-er-son)

EXEMPT STATUS: 51st on 2004 money list
FULL NAME: Carl Pettersson
HEIGHT: 5-11
WEIGHT: 195
BIRTHDATE: August 29, 1977
BIRTHPLACE: Gothenburg, Sweden
RESIDENCE: Raleigh, NC
FAMILY: Wife, DeAnna; Carlie (9/13/04)

EDUCATION: North Carolina State University
SPECIAL INTERESTS: Sports
TURNED PROFESSIONAL: 2000
Q SCHOOL: 2002

BEST PGA TOUR CAREER FINISH:
2—2003 Buick Invitational.

INTERNATIONAL VICTORIES (1):
2002 Algarve Open de Portugal [Eur].

BEST 2004 PGA TOUR FINISHES:
T3—MCI Heritage; T5—Reno-Tahoe Open, Michelin Championship at Las Vegas; T7—Cialis Western Open; T8—Chrysler Championship; T10—Southern Farm Bureau Classic, FUNAI Classic at the WALT DISNEY WORLD Resort.

2004 SEASON:
Followed his rookie season with a solid sophomore campaign, making over $1 million for the first time in his career and posting a personal-best seven top-10s...Recorded a hole-in-one on No. 14 at Riveria CC in the second round of the Nissan Open, the first of the season on the PGA TOUR...Held the first- and second-round lead at The Honda Classic, but weekend rounds of 76-75 dropped him to T13...Topped that with a T3 finish at the MCI Heritage, the second top-three finish of his career (second, 2003 Buick Invitational)...Next top-10, a T7, came at the Cialis Western Open in July...Ended the season with five top-10s in his last six starts, beginning with the Reno-Tahoe Open. Closed with a 3-under-par 69 in Reno, NV, to finish T5. Was just one of three players to post a round in the 60s Sunday at very windy Montreux G&CC...In October, added a T10 at the Southern Farm Bureau Classic, thanks to four rounds in the 60s...The next week at the Michelin Championship at Las Vegas finished T5. The first time in his career he has posted back-to-back-to-back top-10s. His $152,000 check in Las Vegas also pushed him over the $1-million mark for the first time in a single season...Aided by an 8-under 64 final-round, finished T10 at the FUNAI Classic at the WALT DISNEY WORLD Resort...Ended the season with a T8 finish at the Chrysler Championship, the last full-field event of the year, for a career-best seventh top-10 of the season...His season-ending streak of 21 straight rounds at par or better was tied for second-longest on TOUR for the season.

CAREER HIGHLIGHTS:
2003: Was just shy of earning $1 million in his rookie season and finished in the top 75 on the money list...Lone top-10 occured in fifth career TOUR start (second as a PGA TOUR member), finished second, four shots behind Tiger Woods, at Buick Invitational. Birdied final hole on Sunday to move into solo second, earning a career-best paycheck of $486,000. **2002:** Finished T21 at the PGA TOUR Qualifying Tournament to earn his first TOUR card...Fulfilled the early promise he showed on the European Tour by winning the Algarve Open de Portugal in a playoff with David Gilford...Also held a share of the first-round lead in the British Open with a 67. Finished T43. **2001:** Made a bright start to his European Tour career, finishing T7 in the Carlsberg Malaysian Open, his first career start and outright second in the Open de Argentina, his sixth career professional start on the European Tour. **2000:** Won the European Amateur Championship and represented Sweden in the Eisenhower Trophy before turning professional in September. **Amateur:** Won four tournaments while at North Carolina State University, including the NCAA East Regionals event by four strokes, but was disqualified for signing for an incorrect scorecard...Prior to attending North Carolina State, was two-time national junior college individual champion at Central Alabama Community College (1997-98).

PERSONAL:
Took up golf at age 10 near course where he lived in Gothenburg, Sweden...Father, Lars, a low-handicap golfer, was an executive for Volvo Trucks Division, resulting in Carl living in England between ages 10-14, then his current home of Raleigh, NC, when his father was transferred.

PLAYER STATISTICS

2004 PGA TOUR STATISTICS

Scoring Average	70.67	(42)
Driving Distance	290.8	(64)
Driving Accuracy Percentage	61.1%	(147)
Total Driving	211	(124)
Greens in Regulation Pct.	64.5%	(109)
Putting Average	1.733	(4)
Sand Save Percentage	52.9%	(43)
Eagles (Holes per)	158.7	(42)
Birdie Average	4.00	(6)
All-Around Ranking	457	(15)
Scoring Avg. Before Cut	70.34	(26)
Round 3 Scoring Avg.	70.81	(85)
Final Round Scoring Average	70.19	(12)
Birdie Conversion Percentage	33.2%	(4)
Par Breakers	22.9%	(7)

MISCELLANEOUS PGA TOUR STATISTICS

2004 Low Round/Round: 63–The Honda Classic/1
Career Low Round/Round: 63–2 times, most recent 2004 The Honda Classic/1
Career Largest Paycheck/Finish: $486,000–2003 Buick Invitational/2

PGA TOUR CAREER SUMMARY — PLAYOFF RECORD: 0-0

Year	Events Played	Cuts Made	1st	2nd	3rd	Top 10	Top 25	Earnings	Rank
2002	3	2						$21,728	
2003	26	15		1		1	6	977,076	74
2004	28	22			1	7	11	1,367,962	51
Total	57	39		1	1	8	17	2,366,765	

PGA TOUR TOP TOURNAMENT SUMMARY

Year	02	03	04
British Open	T43		T57
PGA	CUT	CUT	54
THE PLAYERS			CUT
WGC-Accenture Match Play		T33	
WGC-American Express Champ	T54		

Gary Player

WORLD GOLF HALL OF FAME MEMBER (Inducted 1974)
EXEMPT STATUS: Life Member
FULL NAME: Gary Player
HEIGHT: 5-7
WEIGHT: 146
BIRTHDATE: November 1, 1935
BIRTHPLACE: Johannesburg, South Africa
RESIDENCE: Johannesburg, South Africa; Palm Beach, FL

FAMILY: Wife, Vivienne Verwey; Jennifer, Marc, Wayne, Michele, Theresa, Amanda; 13 grandchildren
SPECIAL INTERESTS: Breeding thoroughbred race horses, ranching and farming, education, golf course design, family, health and fitness
TURNED PROFESSIONAL: 1953
JOINED TOUR: 1957

PGA TOUR VICTORIES (24):

1958 Kentucky Derby Open. **1959** British Open Championship. **1961** Lucky International Open, Sunshine Open Invitational, Masters Tournament. **1962** PGA Championship. **1963** San Diego Open Invitational. **1964** Pensacola Open Invitational, 500 Festival Open Invitation. **1965** U.S. Open Championship. **1968** British Open Championship. **1969** Tournament of Champions. **1970** Greater Greensboro Open. **1971** Greater Jacksonville Open, National Airlines Open Invitational. **1972** Greater New Orleans Open, PGA Championship. **1973** Southern Open. **1974** Masters Tournament, Danny Thomas Memphis Classic, British Open Championship. **1978** Masters Tournament, MONY Tournament of Champions, Houston Open.

CHAMPIONS TOUR VICTORIES (19):

1985 Quadel Senior Classic. **1986** General Foods PGA Seniors' Championship, United Hospitals Senior Golf

PGA TOUR CAREER SUMMARY — PLAYOFF RECORD: 3-10

Year	Events Played	Cuts Made	1st	2nd	3rd	Top 10	Top 25	Earnings	Rank
1957	9	9			1	1	6	$3,683	54
1958	14	13	1	2		9	11	18,591	12
1959	9	9	1	1		2	5	5,694	
1960	13	13		1		5	13	13,879	28
1961	28	28	3	2	4	20	25	64,540	1
1962	17	17	1	2	2	10	15	45,838	6
1963	22	22	1	6	1	18	21	55,455	
1964	17	17	2	1	2	9	14	61,450	7
1965	12	12	1	2		7	10	69,964	5
1966	10	10			2	4	7	26,391	39
1967	14	14		1	2	8	12	55,821	
1968	15	15	1	1		12	14	48,828	
1969	16	16	1	3	3	10	13	122,884	4
1970	17	15	1	1	2	8	12	99,267	12
1971	14	14	2	2	1	8	8	119,355	5
1972	15	15	2	1		8	13	118,041	7
1973	9	9	1			3	7	47,752	59
1974	14	13	3			5	10	105,986	19
1975	15	14		2		4	8	73,943	27
1976	16	15			1	4	10	53,669	53
1977	17	17		2		8	12	112,485	21
1978	17	17	3			7	10	177,336	9
1979	8	7		2		3	6	74,482	53
1980	11	10			1	3	4	45,471	78
1981	15	9					3	22,483	123
1982	11	6					3	22,059	147
1983	11	9					2	20,567	147
1984	13	10		1		1	5	93,258	70
1985	8	4					1	11,032	175
1986	1								
1987	1	1						4,257	231
1988	2								
1989	2								
1990	1	1					1	11,000	225
1991	1								
1992	1								
1993	1	1						3,700	281
1994	1								
1995	2	1						7,935	269
1996	2								
1997	2								
1998	2	1						11,200	270
1999	2								
2000	2								
2001	2								
2002	1								
2003	1								
2004	1								
Total	435	384	24	33	22	177	281	1,834,482	

NATIONWIDE TOUR

2004	1
Total	1

CHAMPIONS TOUR CAREER SUMMARY — PLAYOFF RECORD: 4-2

Year	Events Played	1st	2nd	3rd	Top 10	Top 25	Earnings	Rank
1985	1	1			1	1	$30,000	44
1986	17	3	4	2	13	17	291,190	5
1987	20	3	2	3	16	20	333,439	6
1988	20	5	2	3	16	18	435,914	2
1989	18	2	1	1	11	17	514,116	4
1990	22	1	4	2	13	20	507,268	9
1991	20	1	1	2	9	17	337,253	18
1992	21		2	3	9	16	346,798	23
1993	22	1	1		6	15	360,272	26
1994	22		1	1	4	12	309,776	30
1995	20	1			2	11	309,251	38
1996	23		3		7	13	494,714	24
1997	22				1	10	208,615	62
1998	18	1			5	15	455,206	37
1999	20				2	7	235,181	61
2000	21					7	199,579	70
2001	21				3	4	256,013	63
2002	18				1	1	109,006	90
2003	15					1	78,690	93
2004	15					1	62,287	96
Total	376	19	21	17	119	223	5,874,569	

PGA TOUR TOP TOURNAMENT SUMMARY

Year	56	57	58	59	60	61	62	63	64	65	66	67	68
Masters		T24	CUT	T8	T6	1	T2	T5	T5	T2	T28	T6	T7
U.S. Open			2	T15	T19	T9	T6	T8	T23	**1**	T15	T12	T16
British Open	4	T24	7	**1**	7	CUT	CUT	T7	T8	CUT	T4	T3	**1**
PGA						T39	**1**	T8	T13	T33	T3		

Year	69	70	71	72	73	74	75	76	77	78	79	80	81
Masters	T32	3	T6	T10		**1**	T30	T28	T19	**1**	T17	T6	T15
U.S. Open	T48	T44	T27	T15	12	T8	T43	T23	T10	T6	T2	CUT	T26
British Open	T23	CUT	T7	T6	T14	**1**	T32	T28	T22	T34	T19	CUT	CUT
PGA	2	T12	T4	**1**	T51	7	T33	T13	T31	T26	T23	T26	T49
THE PLAYERS						CUT	T21	T9	T13	T28	CUT	T8	CUT

Year	82	83	84	85	86	87	88	89	90	91	92	93	94
Masters	T15	CUT	T21	T36	CUT	T35	CUT	CUT	T24	CUT	CUT	60	CUT
U.S. Open	CUT	T20	T43				CUT	CUT					
British Open	T42	CUT	CUT	CUT	T35	T66	T61	CUT	CUT	T57	CUT	CUT	CUT
PGA	CUT	T42	T2	CUT									
THE PLAYERS	CUT		61										

Year	95	96	97	98	99	00	01	02	03	04
Masters	CUT	CUT	CUT	46	CUT	CUT	CUT	CUT	CUT	CUT
British Open	T68	CUT	CUT	CUT	CUT	CUT	CUT			

CHAMPIONS TOUR TOP TOURNAMENT SUMMARY

Year	86	87	88	89	90	91	92	93	94	95	96	97	98
Senior PGA Championship	**1**	8	**1**	T8	**1**	T8	5	T16	T19	T60	T31	T20	T39
U.S. Senior Open	2	**1**	**1**	T9	T3	T8	T3	T17	T13	T19	T60	T21	
Ford Senior Players Championship	T14	**1**	T3	3	T18	T43	T18	T33	T42		T49	T49	
JELD-WEN Tradition				2	2	T15	T20	T17	T27	T17	T9	T51	T17
Charles Schwab Cup Champ											T26		

Year	99	00	01	02	03	04
Senior PGA Championship	T43	T46	T8	T45	CUT	CUT
U.S. Senior Open		CUT	57	CUT	T54	CUT
Ford Senior Players Championship	T29	T57	T56			T58
Senior British Open					T51	CUT
JELD-WEN Tradition	T50	T34	T19	T62	75	T64

NATIONAL TEAMS: The Presidents Cup, 2003 (captain).

Gary Player (Continued)

Championship, Denver Post Champions of Golf. **1987** Mazda SENIOR TOURNAMENT PLAYERS Championship, U.S. Senior Open, PaineWebber World Seniors Invitational. **1988** General Foods PGA Seniors' Championship, Aetna Challenge, Southwestern Bell Classic, U.S. Senior Open, GTE North Classic. **1989** GTE North Classic, The RJR Championship. **1990** PGA Seniors' Championship. **1991** Royal Caribbean Classic. **1993** Bank One Classic. **1995** Bank One Classic. **1998** Northville Long Island Classic.

INTERNATIONAL VICTORIES (53):

1956 South African Open, East Rand Amateur and Open, Ampol Tournament. **1957** Australian PGA Championship. **1958** Australian Open. **1959** Transvaal Open. **1960** Sprite Tournament, Transvaal Open, South African Open. **1962** Australian Open, Transvaal Open. **1963** Australian Open, Transvaal Open. **1965** Australian Open, Piccadilly World Match Play Championship, South African Open, World Cup [indiv], World Cup [with Harold Henning], World Series of Golf. **1966** Piccadilly World Match Play Championship, Transvaal Open, South African Open. **1967** South African Open. **1968** Piccadilly World Match Play Championship, World Series of Golf, South African Open. **1969** Australian Open, South African Open, South African PGA Championship. **1970** Australian Open. **1971** South Africa Masters, Piccadilly World Match Play Championship, General Motors Open Golf Tournament. **1972** South African Masters, South African Open, Brazilian Open, World Series of Golf. **1973** Piccadilly World Match Play Championship. **1974** Australian Open, Brazilian Open, Ibergolf Tournament. **1975** Lancome Trophy, South African Open. **1976** South African Masters, South African Open. **1977** South African Open, World Cup [indiv]. **1979** South African Open. **1980** Chile Open, Trophy Felix Houphonet-Boigny. **1981** South African Open. **1984** Johnnie Walker. **1994** Skills Challenge.

BEST 2004 CHAMPIONS TOUR FINISH:

T24—Outback Steakhouse Pro-Am

CAREER HIGHLIGHTS:

2003: Was Captain of International Team in Presidents Cup in South Africa. Match ended in a tie. Will return as Captain against Jack Nicklaus' U.S. Team in Fall 2005. **2002:** Had entered the open qualifier for the British Open, but was forced to withdraw due to a pulled rib muscle. Broke streak of competing in 46 consecutive British Opens. **1985:** Joined the Champions Tour. **1978:** Earned the third Masters title of his career when he began the final round seven strokes behind Hubert Green and shot 64, winning by one after birdies on seven of the final 10 holes...Went on to win the Houston Open and Tournament of Champions the next two weeks for three wins in as many starts. They were his last victories on TOUR. He has the distinction of winning at least one TOUR event in five decades. **1974:** Captured both the second Masters title of his career and third British Open. Became the only player in the 20th century to win the British Open in three different decades...Inducted into the World Golf Hall of Fame. **1972:** Earned his second PGA Championship. **1968:** Second British Open title came at Carnoustie, Scotland with a two-stroke victory over Jack Nicklaus and Bob Charles. **1965:** Won his only U.S. Open Championship.Joins Gene Sarazen, Ben Hogan, Jack Nicklaus and Tiger Woods as winners of all four majors. He completed the Grand Slam at age 29. **1962:** Won the first of two PGA Championships. **1961:** Won his first of three Masters Tournaments...Also claimed two other victories for first muliti-win season. Was the leading money winner on TOUR for the only time in his career. **1959:** Claimed his first major title with victory at the British Open. **1958:** Won first TOUR event of his career at the Kentucky Derby Open.

PERSONAL:

Dubbed the Black Knight, Mr. Fitness and the International Ambassador of Golf...A renowned golf course architect with over 200 design projects located throughout the world. Designer of the course at the TPC at Jasna Polana near Princeton, NJ, and The Links at Fancourt in South Africa—the site of the 2003 Presidents Cup...Operates Black Knight International, which includes Gary Player Group, Gary Player Design, Gary Player Golf Academy and Gary Player Enterprises - aspects of which include licensing, publishing, videos, apparel, golf equipment and memorabilia...Gary Player Stud Farm has received worldwide acclaim for breeding top horses...Operates The Player Foundation, with its primary objective to promote education for underprivileged children. The Foundation built the Blair Atholl Schools in Johannesburg, South Africa, which has educational facilities for more than 500 students from kindergarten through the seventh grade and also supports other educational projects throughout the world...Says his biggest thrill in golf is being the third player in history after Gene Sarazen and Ben Hogan to win all four Grand Slam events...Has traveled more miles than any athlete in history - more than 14 million and counting...At one point in his career, traveled with his six children and more than 30 pieces of luggage that sometimes took as many as three taxis to transport...Among his heroes are Winston Churchill, Mother Teresa, Nelson Mandela and Mahatma Gandhi...Among his favorite golf courses are The Links at Fancourt in his native South Africa, Cypress Point, Carnoustie and the TPC at Jasna Polana...One of his superstitions or lucky charms is wearing black...Favorite athletes are Michael Jordan and Pele...Web site is GaryPlayer.com.

PLAYER STATISTICS

2004 PGA TOUR STATISTICS

Scoring Average	78.52	(N/A)
Driving Distance	254.8	(N/A)
Driving Accuracy Percentage	50.0%	(N/A)
Total Driving	(N/A)	(N/A)
Greens in Regulation Pct.	44.4%	(N/A)
Putting Average	2.125	(N/A)
Sand Save Percentage	42.9%	(N/A)
Birdie Average	1.00	(N/A)
Scoring Avg. Before Cut	81.00	(N/A)
Birdie Conversion Percentage	12.5%	(N/A)
Par Breakers	5.6%	(N/A)

MISCELLANEOUS PGA TOUR STATISTICS

2004 Low Round/Round: 80–Masters Tournament/2
Career Low Round/Round: 62–1976 Florida Citrus Open/3
Career Largest Paycheck/Finish: $62,500–1984 PGA Championship/T2

2004 CHAMPIONS TOUR STATISTICS

Scoring Average	74.39	(77)
Driving Distance	246.7	(80)
Driving Accuracy Percentage	73.5%	(24)
Total Driving	104	(69)
Greens in Regulation Pct.	55.1%	(79)
Putting Average	1.814	(52)
Sand Save Percentage	45.9%	(38)
Eagles (Holes per)	792.0	(68)
Birdie Average	2.50	(72)
All-Around Ranking	490	(74)

MISCELLANEOUS CHAMPIONS TOUR STATISTICS

2004 Low Round: 66–2004 Outback Steakhouse Pro-Am/3.
Career Low Round: 63–1993 GTE West Classic/1
Career Largest Paycheck: $202,500–1989 The RJR Championship/1

Ian Poulter

EXEMPT STATUS: 2004 European Ryder Cup Team Member (through 2006)
FULL NAME: Ian James Poulter
HEIGHT: 6-1
WEIGHT: 189
BIRTHDATE: January 10, 1976
BIRTHPLACE: Hitchin, England
RESIDENCE: Milton Keynes, England

FAMILY: Fiancee, Katie; Aimee-Leigh (2/1/02), Luke James (5/22/04)
EDUCATION: Barclay School
SPECIAL INTERESTS: Cars, all ball sports
TURNED PROFESSIONAL: 1995

BEST PGA TOUR CAREER FINISH:
T5—2004 WGC-Accenture Match Play Championship.

INTERNATIONAL VICTORIES (6):
2000 Italian Open [Eur]. **2001** Moroccan Open [Eur]. **2002** Italian Open [Eur]. **2003** Celtic Manor Resort Wales Open [Eur], Nordic Open [Eur]. **2004** Volvo Masters Andalucia [Eur].

OTHER VICTORIES (1):
1999 Open de Cote d'Ivoire.

BEST 2004 PGA TOUR FINISH:
T5—WGC-Accenture Match Play Championship.

2004 SEASON:
Has enjoyed a tremendous start to his European Tour career, winning at least one title in each of his first four seasons, including the 2004 season-ending Volvo Masters, where he defeated Sergio Garcia in a playoff…In first PGA TOUR start of 2004, finished T5 at the WGC-Accenture Match Play Championship, losing to Stephen Leaney, 1-up, in the fourth round. In first three rounds, defeated Chris Riley, Duffy Waldorf and John Huston. Earned $225,000, largest paycheck of PGA TOUR career…Posted a T25 at the British Open for his best finish in any of the four majors. Earned enough money ($60,391) to push him past the 150th player (Mike Grob) on the 2003 PGA TOUR money list and enabled him to become a Special Temporary Member of the TOUR. Officially joined the TOUR as a Special Temporary Member the week of August 4…Member of victorious European Ryder Cup squad and posted a 1-1 record in Ryder Cup debut…Finished ninth in European Tour's Volvo Order of Merit.

CAREER HIGHLIGHTS:
2003: Victorious twice in Europe at the Celtic Manor Resort Wales Open and the Nordic Open, and finished career-best fifth in Volvo Order of Merit. **2002:** Captured the the 59th Italian Open Telecom Italia. **2001:** Capped off successful sophomore campaign with victory at the Moroccan Open. **2000:** His first year culminated in winning the Sir Henry Cotton Rookie of the Year Award thanks to a first in the Italian Open in October, ultimately finishing 31st on the Volvo Order of Merit. **1999:** Played the European Challenge Tour with a win at teh Open de Cote d'Ivoire. On the way to a top-15, but tripped over golf bag leaving the BIL Luxembourg Open and suffered torn ligaments and tendons in an ankle, necessitating a lengthy recuperation and a trip to Q-School.

PERSONAL:
Took up the game at age 4 when his father, Terry, a single-digit handicapper, gave him a cut-down 3-wood…Older brother Danny is also a professional, serving as an assistant at Chadwell Springs, Ware, Hertfordshire…Grew up near the home of Nick Faldo and used Faldo's career as an inspiration…Noted for his colorful hairstyles and clothing, most notably the 2004 majors where he wore trousers that featured pink (Masters Tournament), Union Jack (British Open) and United States stars and stripes (PGA Championship) designs…Web site is ianpoulter.co.uk.

PLAYER STATISTICS

2004 PGA TOUR STATISTICS

Scoring Average	71.43	(N/A)
Driving Distance	284.4	(N/A)
Driving Accuracy Percentage	65.4%	(N/A)
Total Driving	(N/A)	(N/A)
Greens in Regulation Pct.	57.5%	(N/A)
Putting Average	1.807	(N/A)
Sand Save Percentage	40.0%	(N/A)
Eagles (Holes per)	468.0	(N/A)
Birdie Average	2.85	(N/A)
Scoring Avg. Before Cut	72.31	(N/A)
Round 3 Scoring Avg.	71.80	(N/A)
Final Round Scoring Average	73.20	(N/A)
Birdie Conversion Percentage	25.0%	(N/A)
Par Breakers	16.0%	(N/A)

MISCELLANEOUS PGA TOUR STATISTICS
2004 Low Round/Round: 70–5 times, most recent FUNAI Classic at the WALT DISNEY WORLD Resort/1
Career Low Round/Round: 67–2 times, most recent 2003 WGC-NEC Invitational/3
Career Largest Paycheck/Finish: $225,000–2004 WGC–Accenture Match Play Championship/T5

PGA TOUR CAREER SUMMARY — PLAYOFF RECORD: 0-0

Year	Events Played	Cuts Made	1st	2nd	3rd	Top 10	Top 25	Earnings	Rank
2000	1	1						$10,970	
2001	2	1					1		
2002	1	1						16,223	
2003	4	4						30,859	
2004	9	6				1	2	176,318	
Total	17	13				1	3	234,371	
EUROPEAN TOUR									
2004	20	15	1		1	8	13	1,568,382	

PGA TOUR TOP TOURNAMENT SUMMARY

Year	00	01	02	03	04
Masters					T31
U.S. Open					CUT
British Open	T64		T50	T46	T25
PGA		CUT		T61	T37
THE PLAYERS					T33
WGC-Accenture Match Play					T5
WGC-NEC Invitational		T13		T33	
WGC-American Express Champ		CNL		T44	

NATIONAL TEAMS: Ryder Cup, 2004, World Cup, 2001.

Nick Price

WORLD GOLF HALL OF FAME MEMBER (Inducted 2003)
EXEMPT STATUS: 2003 International Presidents Cup Team Member (through 2005)
FULL NAME: Nicholas Raymond Leige Price
HEIGHT: 6-0
WEIGHT: 190
BIRTHDATE: January 28, 1957
BIRTHPLACE: Durban, South Africa
RESIDENCE: Hobe Sound, FL; plays out of McArthur GC
FAMILY: Wife, Sue; Gregory (8/9/91), Robyn Frances (8/5/93), Kimberly Rae (9/9/96)
SPECIAL INTERESTS: Water skiing, tennis, fishing, flying, golf course architecture
TURNED PROFESSIONAL: 1977
Q SCHOOL: 1982

PGA TOUR VICTORIES (18):

1983 World Series of Golf. **1991** GTE Byron Nelson Golf Classic, Canadian Open. **1992** PGA Championship, H.E.B. Texas Open. **1993** THE PLAYERS Championship, Canon Greater Hartford Open, Sprint Western Open, Federal Express St. Jude Classic. **1994** Honda Classic, Southwestern Bell Colonial, Motorola Western Open, British Open Championship, PGA Championship, Bell Canadian Open. **1997** MCI Classic. **1998** FedEx St. Jude Classic. **2002** MasterCard Colonial.

INTERNATIONAL VICTORIES (24):

1979 Asseng Invitational [SAf]. **1980** Canon European Masters [Eur]. **1981** San Reno Masters [Eur], South African Masters [SAf]. **1982** Vaals Reef Open [SAf]. **1985** Trophee Lancome [Eur], ICL International [SAf]. **1989** West End South Australian Open [Aus]. **1992** Air New Zealand/Shell Open [Aus]. **1993** ICL International [SAf], Sun City Million Dollar Challenge [SAf]. **1994** British Open [Eur], ICL International [SAf]. **1995** Alfred Dunhill Challenge [SAf], Hassan II Golf Trophy [Morocco], Zimbabwe Open [SAf]. **1997** Dimension Data Pro-Am [Eur], Alfred Dunhill South African PGA [Eur], Zimbabwe Open [SAf], Million Dollar Challenge [SAf].**1998** Dimension Data Pro-Am [SAf], Zimbabwe Open [SAf], Million Dollar Challenge [SAf]. **1999** Suntory Open [Jpn].

OTHER VICTORIES (2):

1992 PGA Grand Slam of Golf. **2001** CVS Charity Classic [with Mark Calcavecchia].

BEST 2004 PGA TOUR FINISHES:

T6—Masters Tournament; T7—EDS Byron Nelson Championship.

2004 SEASON:

Played in a minimum 15 events for just the second time in his 22-year PGA TOUR career and made 12 consecutive cuts…Has finished inside top 105 in each of his 22 years…Made his 17th cut in 21 starts (including one disqualification) at THE PLAYERS Championship, tied for fourth most with Hale Irwin and Gil Morgan. Finished T42…Finished T6 at the Masters for fourth career top-10 in 19 starts at Augusta National…In only his eighth start of the season posted his third top-10, with a T7 finish at the EDS Byron Nelson Championship. He was one of five past champions to finish in the top-10 in Dallas…Named as recipient of the 2005 Bob Jones Award by the USGA, given in recognition of distinguished sportsmanship in golf.

CAREER HIGHLIGHTS:

Finished in the top 50 on the money list for 18 consecutive seasons (1986-2003). **2003:** Inducted into the World Golf Hall of Fame on October 20 at the World Golf Village in St. Augustine, FL...Finished in the top 20 (No. 20) and missed just one cut for the second consecutive season, marking the fifth time in his career he has only missed one cut in a season...Although did not win, picked up two runner-ups and a third on the way to earning over $2 million for the second straight year...Posted rounds of 66-65 on the weekend at the EDS Byron Nelson to finish two back of Vijay Singh. Ruuner-up finish moved him to the top spot on the EDS Byron Nelson Championship money list, with $1,464,808...Third top-five in four starts was a T5 at the U.S. Open...In his next start two weeks later, finished second to David Toms at the FedEx St. Jude Classic. Two-time winner in Memphis opened with a 2-over-par 73, but rebounded with rounds of 67-65-62. Final-round, 9-under-par 62 was his best competitive score at the TPC at Southwind in 64 rounds. Now has eight top-10 finishes at the FedEx event, tied for fourth all-time and leads the all-time money list with $1,436,615 in 17 starts...Climbed over the $1-million mark in official earnings for a PGA TOUR-best 10th time in his career (Davis Love III also has 10)...Earned a spot on International Team for The Presidents Cup contested near homeland of Zimbabwe in George, South Africa. **2002:** Surpassed earnings of $2 million for the first time in his career, while finishing fifth in scoring average (69.59)...Picked up his first win since the 1998 FedEx St. Jude Classic (a span of three years, nine months and 17 days). The first of five plus 40-year olds to win with his victory at the MasterCard Colonial. Earned paycheck of $774,000, $5,800 more than his combined winnings at his three major victories (1992 PGA Championship, 1994 British Open, 1994 PGA Championship). Co-leader after 36 holes with Esteban Toledo. Grabbed solo third-round lead by five strokes. Needed only 104 putts on the week en route to his second MasterCard Colonial title. Earned Player of the Month of May accolades for his win and two other top-10s...Made 14 consecutive cuts to begin the year prior to missing his only cut at the PGA Championship...Recipient of the 2002 Payne Stewart Award, presented at THE TOUR Championship. **2001:** Made 20 starts, the most since 1992...Led first round of the Marconi Pennsylvania Classic by one stroke after opening with a 66 but had fifth-place finish. **2000:** Earned third top-10 at Advil Western Open, led first round after opening with a course-record-tying 63. Closed with 72-70-69 that set up playoff with Robert Allenby. Allenby won with a par on first extra hole...Final-round 67 at TOUR Championship lifted him to a three-way T3...Member of his fourth International Presidents Cup Team, finishing with a 2-3-0 record for a four-year total of 6-9-4. **1999:** In March, second-round 67 led to third-place finish at THE PLAYERS Championship, his

SECTION 2 PLAYER BIOGRAPHIES

PGA TOUR CAREER SUMMARY — PLAYOFF RECORD: 3-3

Year	Events Played	Cuts Made	1st	2nd	3rd	Top 10	Top 25	Earnings	Rank
1983	21	14	1			2	5	$49,435	104
1984	19	15			1	4	6	109,480	66
1985	20	14				2	5	96,069	80
1986	25	17		1		6	11	225,373	35
1987	25	19		1		7	14	334,169	28
1988	24	20		1		4	10	266,300	42
1989	27	22			1	7	12	296,170	42
1990	28	22		2	1	6	13	520,777	22
1991	23	18	2			9	11	714,389	7
1992	26	24	2	1	2	13	19	1,135,773	4
1993	18	17	4	2		8	12	1,478,557	1
1994	19	14	6	1		8	10	1,499,927	1
1995	18	15		1	1	5	11	611,700	30
1996	15	12			2	5	7	402,467	50
1997	16	15	1	1	2	8	14	1,053,845	17
1998	18	15	1			6	9	1,019,404	26
1999	18	17			2	7	12	1,572,402	18
2000	18	15		2	3	6	11	1,804,433	21
2001	20	. 17			1	6	12	1,286,756	42
2002	18	17	1			8	14	2,170,912	19
2003	17	16		2	1	6	9	2,271,111	20
2004	15	12				2	6	796,086	103
Total	448	367	18	15	17	135	233	19,715,533	
EUROPEAN TOUR									
2004	1	1					1	61,889	
SOUTHERN AFRICA TOUR									
2004	1	1		1		1	1	25,866	

PGA TOUR TOP TOURNAMENT SUMMARY

Year	78	79	80	81	82	83	84	85	86	87	88	89	90
Masters							CUT		5	T22	T14	CUT	
U.S. Open						T48		CUT		T17	T40	CUT	
British Open	T39		T27	T23	T2	CUT	T44	CUT		T8	2	CUT	T25
PGA						T67	T54	5	CUT	T10	T17	T46	T63
THE PLAYERS							7	T22	T58	T24	DQ	CUT	T16
TOUR Championship										T5			5

Year	91	92	93	94	95	96	97	98	99	00	01	02	03
Masters	T49	T6	CUT	T35	CUT	T18	T24	CUT	T6	T11	CUT	T20	T23
U.S. Open	T19	T4	T11	CUT	T13		T19	4	T23	T27	CUT	T8	T5
British Open	T44	T51	T6	**1**	T40	T44	CUT	T29	T37	CUT	T21	T14	T28
PGA		**1**	T31	**1**	T39	T8	T13	T4	5	CUT	T29	CUT	
THE PLAYERS	T9	8	**1**	CUT	T37	T46	T24	T8	3	T3	T10	T9	CUT
TOUR Championship	T5	T13	T18	T20	30		T26	30	T21	T3		T22	30
WGC-Accenture Match Play									T17	T33		T9	T9
WGC-NEC Invitational									T3	T20	T29	T28	T42
WGC-American Express Champ									T4	T5	CNL	T15	T48

Year	04
Masters	T6
U.S. Open	T24
British Open	T30
THE PLAYERS	T42
WGC-Accenture Match Play	T33
WGC-NEC Invitational	T46

NATIONAL TEAMS: World Cup (2), 1978, 1993; Dunhill Cup (8), 1993, 1994, 1995, 1996, 1997, 1998, 1999, 2000; The Presidents Cup (5), 1994, 1996, 1998, 2000, 2003.

Nick Price (Continued)

sixth top-10 in 16 appearances in the event. **1998:** Earned 16th PGA TOUR title and 15th in decade of the '90s by making birdie on second playoff hole at TPC at Southwind to defeat Jeff Sluman and win FedEx St. Jude Classic. Along with Tiger Woods, 15 victories were the most by any player in the 1990s. **1997:** Returned to the form that golf fans are familiar with when he captured the MCI Classic. Climbed back into top 20 on money list for first time since 1994. The second of only three wire-to-wire winners on TOUR. **1994:** Had one of the most prolific years ever on TOUR. Captured six titles, including the British Open and PGA Championship. One of only three players in the 1990s to win two major titles in the same season, joining Nick Faldo in 1990 and Mark O'Meara in 1998. One of only seven players since 1945 to capture consecutive majors (Ben Hogan, Jack Nicklaus, Arnold Palmer, Lee Trevino, Tom Watson, Tiger Woods)...In British Open at Turnberry, played final three holes eagle-birdie-par to make up two-stroke deficit to Jesper Parnevik...Took five-stroke lead at PGA Championship at Southern Hills with second-round 65, then cruised to six-stroke win over Corey Pavin...PGA TOUR Player of the Year. **1993:** Posted four wins including a five-stroke victory at THE PLAYERS Championship...Later that year won three consecutive starts: Canon Greater Hartford Open, Sprint Western Open and Federal Express St. Jude Classic...First time named PGA TOUR Player of the Year. **1986:** Shot third-round 63 in Masters (with a bogey on the first hole) and shares Augusta National course record with Greg Norman. **1983:** Went wire-to-wire to defeat Jack Nicklaus by two strokes at the World Series of Golf for his first TOUR victory.

PERSONAL:

Published The Swing in 1997...Born in South Africa, moved to Rhodesia (now Zimbabwe) at an early age...Was the first recipient, in 2002, of the ASAP Sports/Jim Murray Award, given to a professional player for his cooperation, quotability and accommodation to the media, and for reflecting the most positive aspects of the working relationship between athlete and journalist...After a decade of collaborating with a variety of architects, formed his own design company, Nick Price Golf Course Design. Currently designing golf courses in South Africa, Dominican Republic and Cancun, Mexico...Web site is nickprice.com.

PLAYER STATISTICS

2004 PGA TOUR STATISTICS

Scoring Average	70.38	(28)
Driving Distance	272.8	(188)
Driving Accuracy Percentage	68.3%	(43)
Total Driving	231	(153)
Greens in Regulation Pct.	59.1%	(192)
Putting Average	1.746	(17)
Sand Save Percentage	58.7%	(11)
Eagles (Holes per)	90.0	(1)
Birdie Average	3.18	(174)
All-Around Ranking	654	(63)
Scoring Avg. Before Cut	71.36	(138)
Round 3 Scoring Avg.	70.55	(65)
Final Round Scoring Average	71.36	(79)
Birdie Conversion Percentage	29.2%	(91)
Par Breakers	18.8%	(149)

MISCELLANEOUS PGA TOUR STATISTICS

2004 Low Round/Round: 65–Ford Championship at Doral/3
Career Low Round/Round: 62–3 times, most recent 2003 FedEx St. Jude Classic/4
Career Largest Paycheck/Finish: $774,000–2002 MasterCard Colonial/1

SHOTLink
AN IBM ON DEMAND BUSINESS SOLUTION

HOT SHOTS

Holes with the Lowest Scoring Average when Missing the Fairway on TOUR (2004)

Event/ Course Name	Hole	Par	Missed Fairway	Avg Score	Avg to Par
Mercedes Championships					
Plantation Course at Kapalua	9	5	66	4.33	-0.67
THE TOUR Championship presented by Coca-Cola					
East Lake GC	15	5	48	4.44	-0.56
FUNAI Classic at the WALT DISNEY WORLD Resort					
Palm GC **	7	5	41	4.44	-0.56
Bob Hope Chrysler Classic					
PGA West (Palmer Course) **	2	5	52	4.46	-0.54
Buick Invitational					
Torrey Pines (North Course **	1	5	72	4.49	-0.51

** = Multiple course tournament

Holes with the Highest Scoring Average when Missing the Fairway on TOUR (2004)

Event/ Course Name	Hole	Par	Missed Fairway	Avg Score	Avg to Par
Reno-Tahoe Open					
Montreux G&CC	8	4	110	5.00	1.00
WAG-American Express Championship					
Mount Juliet	18	4	49	4.94	0.94
Ford Championship at Doral					
Doral Golf Resort & Spa	18	4	207	4.83	0.83
Buick Championship					
TPC at River Highlands	13	5	100	5.81	0.81
Buick Classic					
Westchester CC	8	4	47	4.81	0.81

9th Hole-Plantation Course at Kapalua

Ted Purdy (PER-dee)

EXEMPT STATUS: 36th on 2004 money list
FULL NAME: Theodore Townsend Purdy
HEIGHT: 5-10
WEIGHT: 175
BIRTHDATE: August 15, 1973
BIRTHPLACE: Phoenix, AZ
RESIDENCE: Phoenix, AZ; plays out of Moon Valley CC
FAMILY: Wife, Arlene Rebecca; Samuel (6/19/03)

EDUCATION: University of Arizona (1996, Finance)
SPECIAL INTERESTS: Stock market, skiing
TURNED PROFESSIONAL: 1996
Nationwide Tour Alumnus

BEST PGA TOUR CAREER FINISHES:
2—2004 MCI Heritage, B.C. Open.

NATIONWIDE TOUR VICTORIES (1):
2003 First Tee Arkansas Classic.

BEST 2004 PGA TOUR FINISHES:
2—MCI Heritage, B.C. Open; T5—Valero Texas Open; T8—Chrysler Classic of Greensboro.

2004 SEASON:
Had a career year on the PGA TOUR in just his second season as a full-time member. Played in 34 tournaments, making 22 cuts and posting a career-best four top-10s, including two runner-up finishes. . .Held a four-stroke lead over Heath Slocum heading into the final round of the MCI Heritage. Stewart Cink caught him by firing a final-round 64. Lost in a five-hole playoff to Cink. The runner-up finish was his career-best and his first top-10 in 41 career starts on the TOUR. His previous best was a T11 at the 2000 Touchstone Energy Tucson Open. Earned more money for second ($518,400) than he had combined in his first 40 starts ($288,351). Began the week 367th on Official World Golf Ranking and improved to 179th. . .Earned his second runner-up finish of the season at the B.C. Open. Moved within one shot of eventual winner Jonathan Byrd with a 13-foot birdie putt on the 71st hole of regulation, then missed the chance to force a playoff when he missed a three-foot birdie putt on the 72nd hole. . .First-round leader at the Valero Texas Open, with a course-record-tying, 9-under-par 61. Eventually finished T5. . .Posted low round of the week with a final round, 8-under-par 64 at the Chrysler Classic of Greensboro, aided by two eagles (Nos. 13 and 15). Jumped from T48 to finish T8. . .Will receive an invitation to his first Masters Tournament in 2005, thanks to finishing inside the top 40 on the final money list.

CAREER HIGHLIGHTS:
2003: Posted 11 top-25s in 25 starts to finish 15th on Nationwide Tour money list to earn his PGA TOUR card for the the second time...Notched initial career win at the First Tee Arkansas Classic by nipping Chris Tidland in a playoff. Rolled in a short birdie putt in near darkness on the third playoff hole to garner $85,500 first prize. Finished tied with Tidland at 13-under-par 275 at the end of regulation after being forced to play 36 holes Sunday when rain postponed most of Saturday's third round. Began the day six shots back of 36-hole leader Zach Johnson before making his charge...Finished T7 at the Volvo Masters of Asia in late December. **2002:** Played in 23 events on the Nationwide Tour finished 113th on the final money list. Finished T4 at the Caltex Singapore Masters on the European Tour. Played three events on the Asian PGA, finished T6 at the TLC Classic. **2000:** Played one PGA TOUR event the Touchstone Energy Tucson Classic, posted a T11 finish...Member of the Nationwide Tour. Collected two top-10s, T7 at the Oregon Classic and T5 Shreveport Open...Had four top-10s on the Asian PGA, including finishing T2 at the Casino Filipino Phillippine. **1999:** Made the cut in eight of 27 events during his rookie season on TOUR. Best finish was a T35 at the Buick Invitational. **1998:** Earned his 1999 TOUR card by virtue of a T14 finish at the 1998 Qualifying Tournament. **1997:** Indian Masters Champion. Named Rookie of the Year on the Asian PGA Tour. **Amateur:** Winner of the Arizona State Amateur...Two-time All-American at the University of Arizona. Roomed with former PGA TOUR player Jason Gore during freshman season in Tucson. . .Winner of the 1996 Ping Arizona Intercollegiate by six strokes over Stanford's Tiger Woods.

PERSONAL:
Says his mother and grandfather started him in the game of golf while he was still in diapers. . .Lists Jimmy Buffett as his hero.

PLAYER STATISTICS

2004 PGA TOUR STATISTICS

Statistic	Value	Rank
Scoring Average	70.69	(45)
Driving Distance	289.2	(76)
Driving Accuracy Percentage	70.1%	(22)
Total Driving	98	(3)
Greens in Regulation Pct.	67.4%	(39)
Putting Average	1.769	(70)
Sand Save Percentage	46.6%	(132)
Eagles (Holes per)	126.0	(13)
Birdie Average	3.75	(41)
All-Around Ranking	438	(11)
Scoring Avg. Before Cut	70.61	(51)
Round 3 Scoring Avg.	69.59	(13)
Final Round Scoring Average	71.09	(63)
Birdie Conversion Percentage	30.5%	(52)
Par Breakers	21.6%	(28)

MISCELLANEOUS PGA TOUR STATISTICS

2004 Low Round/Round: 61–Valero Texas Open/1
Career Low Round/Round: 61–2004 Valero Texas Open/1
Career Largest Paycheck/Finish: $518,400–2004 MCI Heritage/2

PGA TOUR CAREER SUMMARY — PLAYOFF RECORD: 0-1

Year	Events Played	Cuts Made	1st	2nd	3rd	Top 10	Top 25	Earnings	Rank
1998	1								
1999	27	8						$46,660	230
2000	1	1					1	72,000	
2003	2								
2004	35	22		2		4	12	1,636,876	36
Total	66	31		2		4	13	1,755,537	
NATIONWIDE TOUR									
1996	1								
1997	4	2					1	2,600	176
1999	1								
2000	23	8				2	3	45,176	92
2002	23	10					3	31,211	113
2003	25	16	1			6	11	206,584	15
Total	77	36	1			8	18	285,571	
EUROPEAN TOUR									
2003	3	1					1	10,516	
JAPAN GOLF TOUR									
2003	2	1						4,956	

PGA TOUR TOP TOURNAMENT SUMMARY

Year	04
PGA	CUT

SECTION 2 PLAYER BIOGRAPHIES

Brett Quigley

EXEMPT STATUS: 97th on 2004 money list
FULL NAME: Brett Cephas Quigley
HEIGHT: 5-11
WEIGHT: 160
BIRTHDATE: August 18, 1969
BIRTHPLACE: Ft. Devens, MA
RESIDENCE: Jupiter, FL; plays out of Rhode Island CC (Barrington, RI)

FAMILY: Wife, Amy
EDUCATION: University of South Carolina (1991)
SPECIAL INTERESTS: Surfing, reading, cars, motorcycles
TURNED PROFESSIONAL: 1991
Q SCHOOL: 2002
JOINED TOUR: 1997
Nationwide Tour Alumnus

BEST PGA TOUR CAREER FINISHES:

T2—2001 Greater Greensboro Chrysler Classic, 2004 U.S. Bank Championship in Milwaukee.

NATIONWIDE TOUR VICTORIES (2):

1996 Philadelphia Classic. **2001** Arkansas Classic.

BEST 2004 PGA TOUR FINISH:

T2—U.S. Bank Championship in Milwaukee.

2004 SEASON:

Cracked the top 100 on the money list for the third time in four years. . .Posted only top-10 of season, a T2 at the U.S. Bank Championship in Milwaukee, his first top-10 on TOUR since a fourth at the same event in 2003. Earned a career-best $308,000. Shared first-round lead with seven others, tying the PGA TOUR record for most players tied through 18 holes (2000 Honda Classic). Shared the third-round lead with Carlos Franco and fellow Rhode Islander Patrick Sheehan, prior to finishing two strokes back of Franco in a tie with Fred Funk.

CAREER HIGHLIGHTS:

2003: Finished in the top 125 for only the second time in his career on the PGA TOUR...Opened the season making six consecutive cuts. Resident of nearby Jupiter earned first top-10 in fifth start with T8 at The Honda Classic that included four rounds in the 60s. Finish was second straight top-10 at Honda event...Shared the first-round lead at the U.S. Open with Tom Watson at 5-under 65, finished T28...Two weeks after getting married, added second top-10 with a fourth-place finish at the Greater Milwaukee Open, his best TOUR finish since a T4 at the 2002 Honda Classic. $168,000 payday in Milwaukee secured his card for the 2004 season. **2002:** Only top-10 of the season, T4 at The Honda Classic. Was one stroke out of the lead with two holes to play but bogeyed the last two holes...Shared the first-round lead at Canon Greater Hartford Open. After opening with season-best 64, finished T20. **2001:** At 5-11, 160 pounds, is one of the longest drivers on the PGA TOUR, averaging 298.5 in 2001, second to John Daly in the Driving Distance category...Earned a career best $956,934 on the PGA TOUR on the strength of six top-10s, including a runner-up finish at the Greater Greensboro Chrysler Classic. Won a Nationwide Tour event early in the season and finished 56th on the PGA TOUR money list...On cold and rainy opening day at the Arkansas Classic, shot 31 on the front nine, finished with a 65, led wire-to-wire and won by three...The next week committed to the Greater Greensboro Chrysler Classic, shot 15-under-par and finished second to Scott Hoch...Month later earned second TOUR top-10 at MasterCard Colonial. Opened with three rounds in the 60s. Stood one stroke back after 36 holes and shared top of leaderboard with Phil Mickelson at 11-under-par 199 through 54 holes. Shot 73 on Sunday for T5...Following an opening 67 at the B.C. Open, a second-round 62 gave him a three-stroke lead. Closed with a pair of 72s for T8. **2000:** Split time on the Nationwide Tour and PGA TOUR...Made the cut in four of eight Nationwide Tour events early in the year with a T2 at the Nationwide South Carolina Classic and a T3 at the Nationwide Richmond Open...Did not play Nationwide Tour after mid-May...In 21 PGA TOUR events, made 10 cuts, including a T5 at the B.C. Open. **1999:** Kept status on the PGA TOUR for the next year by finishing 150th on the money list. **1998:** Recorded a T4 at the United Airlines Hawaiian Open. **1997:** Played in 34 events making 21 cuts...Best finish T12 at the Greater Vancouver Open. **1996:** Earned his first career title at the Philadelphia Classic on the Nationwide Tour, setting the Philmont CC course record with a 6-under-par 64 in the opening round....Had eight top-10s, including T2 at the Mississippi Gulf Coast Classic and the Boise Open. **Amateur:** Winner of the 1987 U. S. Junior Amateur...Named Academic All-American in 1990 and 1991 at University of South Carolina.

PERSONAL:

Caddied for his uncle, Dana Quigley, now a member of the Champions Tour, when Dana fired a 61 at the 1982 Greater Hartford Open. . .His dad, Paul, was one of New England's top amateur golfers.

PLAYER STATISTICS

2004 PGA TOUR STATISTICS

Scoring Average	71.05	(88)
Driving Distance	294.3	(37)
Driving Accuracy Percentage	57.2%	(177)
Total Driving	214	(132)
Greens in Regulation Pct.	65.8%	(78)
Putting Average	1.780	(107)
Sand Save Percentage	52.7%	(47)
Eagles (Holes per)	294.0	(125)
Birdie Average	3.57	(85)
All-Around Ranking	744	(92)
Scoring Avg. Before Cut	70.97	(92)
Round 3 Scoring Avg.	70.80	(84)
Final Round Scoring Average	72.06	(138)
Birdie Conversion Percentage	29.1%	(95)
Par Breakers	20.2%	(90)

MISCELLANEOUS PGA TOUR STATISTICS

2004 Low Round/Round: 64–U.S. Bank Championship in Milwaukee/3
Career Low Round/Round: 62–2001 B.C. Open/2
Career Largest Paycheck/Finish: $308,000–2 times, most recent 2004 U.S. Bank Championship in Milwaukee/T2

PGA TOUR CAREER SUMMARY — PLAYOFF RECORD: 0-0

Year	Events Played	Cuts Made	1st	2nd	3rd	Top 10	Top 25	Earnings	Rank
1991	2	1						$1,990	298
1992	1								
1997	34	21					4	172,023	128
1998	29	16				2	5	224,076	127
1999	22	12				2	3	209,318	152
2000	21	10				1	4	247,037	150
2001	21	13		1		6	8	956,934	56
2002	32	16				1	5	404,422	140
2003	27	19				2	7	786,294	82
2004	31	20		1		1	5	836,380	97
Total	220	128		2		15	41	3,838,473	
NATIONWIDE TOUR									
1992	15	7					1	7,518	119
1994	1								
1995	4	2				1	1	9,540	124
1996	28	17	1	2		8	10	123,763	5
1998	2								
1999	1	1					1	2,500	181
2000	8	4		1	1	2	2	56,766	79
2001	4	4	1			2	2	101,776	47
Total	63	35	2	3	1	13	17	301,864	

PGA TOUR TOP TOURNAMENT SUMMARY

Year	00	01	02	03	04
U.S. Open	CUT	CUT		T28	
PGA		CUT			T37
THE PLAYERS			CUT		T42

Tag Ridings

EXEMPT STATUS: 125th on 2004 money list
FULL NAME: Taggart Twain Ridings
HEIGHT: 6-1
WEIGHT: 185
BIRTHDATE: September 7, 1974
BIRTHPLACE: Oklahoma City, OK
RESIDENCE: Fayetteville, AR
FAMILY: Wife, Brenda

EDUCATION: University of Arkansas (1997, Marketing)
SPECIAL INTERESTS: Xbox, fishing, down-home cooking, enlightening books, entertaining movies
TURNED PROFESSIONAL: 1997
JOINED TOUR: 2003
Nationwide Tour Alumnus

BEST PGA TOUR CAREER FINISH:
T2—2004 Michelin Championship at Las Vegas.

NATIONWIDE TOUR VICTORIES (1):
2002 Permian Basin Open.

BEST 2004 PGA TOUR FINISH:
T2—Michelin Championship at Las Vegas.

2004 SEASON:
Playing on a Major Medical Extension, finished No. 125 on the money list to retain full playing privileges for the 2005 campaign. Recorded two eagles (Nos. 15 and 18) during the first round of the U.S. Bank Championship in Milwaukee…Earned his first top-10 on TOUR in 22 career events, a T2, thanks to a career-best, final-round, 11-under 61 at the Michelin Championship at Las Vegas. Began the final round tied for 54th, eight strokes behind third-round leader Tom Lehman and finished in a three-way T2, one stroke behind winner Andre Stolz. Played three of the four rounds without a bogey, including a 36-hole bogey-free stretch to begin the tournament. The $298,666 payday allowed him to jump from 191st on the money list to 136th with three weeks to play…Entered the season's final full-field event, the Chrysler Championship, No. 137 on the money list. Finished T11, aided by a final-round, 7-under-par 64, to earn $120,000 to slide into No. 125 position by $21,824.

CAREER HIGHLIGHTS:
2003: Rookie season was cut short to only six events due to a herniated disk in his back and a shoulder injury. Withdrew after a first-round 75 at The Honda Classic and did not play the remainder of the season. Received Major Medical Extension for 2004…Best finish in six events was T27 in initial start at the Sony Open in Hawaii. **2002:** Finished No. 14 on the final 2002 Nationwide Tour money list with $187,494 to earn TOUR card for 2003. Notched first career victory at the Permian Basin Open, where he holed out from 138 yards with a pitching wedge for an eagle on the first playoff hole to defeat Mark Hensby. **2001:** Played in three Nationwide Tour events. **Amateur:** Earned All-America and Scholastic All-America honors in 1997 at Arkansas. Named to the All-SEC Second Team from 1995-97.

PERSONAL:
Father is a club professional at South Lakes GC in Jenks, OK.

PLAYER STATISTICS

2004 PGA TOUR STATISTICS

Scoring Average	71.38	(123)
Driving Distance	301.0	(12)
Driving Accuracy Percentage	56.4%	(180)
Total Driving	192	(91)
Greens in Regulation Pct.	64.2%	(115)
Putting Average	1.751	(26)
Sand Save Percentage	49.4%	(88)
Eagles (Holes per)	450.0	(173)
Birdie Average	3.86	(18)
All-Around Ranking	735	(90)
Scoring Avg. Before Cut	71.51	(145)
Round 3 Scoring Avg.	72.33	(175)
Final Round Scoring Average	69.50	(2)
Birdie Conversion Percentage	32.0%	(15)
Par Breakers	21.7%	(25)

MISCELLANEOUS PGA TOUR STATISTICS

2004 Low Round/Round: 61–Michelin Championship at Las Vegas/4
Career Low Round/Round: 61–2004 Michelin Championship at Las Vegas/4
Career Largest Paycheck/Finish: $298,667–2004 Michelin Championship at Las Vegas/T2

PGA TOUR CAREER SUMMARY — PLAYOFF RECORD: 0-0

Year	Events Played	Cuts Made	1st	2nd	3rd	Top 10	Top 25	Earnings	Rank
2000	1								
2003	6	1						$31,275	234
2004	18	9		1		1	4	623,262	125
Total	25	10		1		1	4	654,537	
NATIONWIDE TOUR									
1998	2	1						1,637	213
1999	1								
2001	3	1						1,789	259
2002	25	16	1	1		5	9	187,494	14
2003	5	2				1	1	18,307	160
2004	1								
Total	37	20	1	1		6	10	209,227	

PGA TOUR TOP TOURNAMENT SUMMARY

Year	00
U.S. Open	CUT

John Riegger

EXEMPT STATUS: Major Medical Extension
FULL NAME: John Stewart Riegger
HEIGHT: 6-3
WEIGHT: 190
BIRTHDATE: June 13, 1963
BIRTHPLACE: Metropolis, IL
RESIDENCE: Las Vegas, NV

FAMILY: Wife, Jennie; Kalie (7/3/88), Tara (12/29/90), Jaxon (8/15/01)
EDUCATION: Lamar University (1985, Education)
SPECIAL INTERESTS: Hunting, fishing
TURNED PROFESSIONAL: 1985, 2003
JOINED TOUR: 1987
Nationwide Tour Alumnus

BEST PGA TOUR CAREER FINISH:
7—2004 Sony Open in Hawaii.

INTERNATIONAL VICTORIES (2):
1997 Colombian Open. **1988** Milan Open.

BEST 2004 PGA TOUR FINISH:
7—Sony Open in Hawaii.

2004 SEASON:
After finishing No. 153 on the money list, will receive a Major Medical Extension for 2005 due to injury. Withdrew after the first round of the Cialis Western Open and did not play the rest of the season. Coupled with $423,263 earned in 17 events in 2004 has the opportunity to play in 12 events to earn $199,999 and match the $623,262 winnings of 2004's No. 125, Tag Ridings. If he does so, will play out of the Major Medical Extension category for the remainder of the season…Began the 2004 season with Major Medical Extension, but also had posted fourth-place finish at PGA TOUR Qualifying School as a back-up…Seven made cuts in first eight starts, including a career-best seventh in first start of season at the Sony Open in Hawaii, posting four rounds in the 60s. Earned a personal-best $160,800 with the second top-10 of career (eighth at the 2002 Honda Classic).

CAREER HIGHLIGHTS:
2003: Suffered through season that included a torn rib cage muscle and a shoulder injury. Finished with 12 made cuts in 17 starts, with three top-25s at the Shell Houston Open (T13), HP Classic of New Orleans (T16) and FBR Capital Open (T22). Granted Major Medical Extension for 2004. **2002:** Finished 143rd on the 2002 money list with a career-high $390,675 in earnings. Logged his first career top-10 with a T8 at 2002 Honda Classic. Led tournament by two strokes after opening with a 9-under 63. Carried a one-stroke lead into the weekend after a second-round 69. His T8 was worth $101,500, a career payday. **2001:** Five top-25s led to 140th position on TOUR money list and partial status for 2002…Best finish was 14th at John Deere Classic. **2000:** Eight top-10s on the Nationwide Tour and a 10th-place position on the money list earned PGA TOUR card for 2001. **1999:** Full-time on Nationwide Tour with 22 starts, with a runner-up finish at the Mississippi Gulf Coast Classic. **1994:** Best finish in 17 Nationwide Tour starts was T3 Dominion Open. **1992:** After earning PGA TOUR card via Q-School, rookie's only top-25 was T21 at GTE Byron Nelson Golf Classic. **1991:** Played 12 events on the Nationwide Tour with one top-10.

PLAYER STATISTICS

2004 PGA TOUR STATISTICS

Scoring Average	71.42	(130)
Driving Distance	285.0	(120)
Driving Accuracy Percentage	61.4%	(144)
Total Driving	264	(179)
Greens in Regulation Pct.	67.1%	(41)
Putting Average	1.773	(82)
Sand Save Percentage	38.9%	(191)
Eagles (Holes per)	190.8	(65)
Birdie Average	3.36	(135)
All-Around Ranking	908	(139)
Scoring Avg. Before Cut	70.85	(76)
Round 3 Scoring Avg.	71.30	(126)
Final Round Scoring Average	72.40	(158)
Birdie Conversion Percentage	27.2%	(159)
Par Breakers	19.2%	(131)

MISCELLANEOUS PGA TOUR STATISTICS

2004 Low Round/Round: 63–Bob Hope Chrysler Classic/2
Career Low Round/Round: 63–2 times, most recent 2004 Bob Hope Chrysler Classic/2
Career Largest Paycheck/Finish: $160,800–2004 Sony Open in Hawaii/7

PGA TOUR CAREER SUMMARY — PLAYOFF RECORD: 0-0

Year	Events Played	Cuts Made	1st	2nd	3rd	Top 10	Top 25	Earnings	Rank
1987	23	6						$8,743	210
1988	1								
1990	1								
1992	28	10					1	33,980	192
1993	1	1					1	22,275	211
1995	1								
1998	29	16					3	150,874	162
2001	27	17					5	342,221	140
2002	29	16				1	4	390,675	143
2003	17	12					3	318,102	154
2004	17	10				1	3	423,263	153
Total	174	88				2	20	1,690,134	
NATIONWIDE TOUR									
1991	12	8				1	4	10,488	90
1992	1								
1994	17	7			1	1	1	17,389	80
1997	3	2						1,020	232
1998	1	1							
1999	22	13		1		2	8	65,889	39
2000	27	19		1	2	8	10	200,904	10
2003	2	1						2,328	285
Total	85	51		2	3	12	23	298,018	

PGA TOUR TOP TOURNAMENT SUMMARY

Year	02	03	04
British Open	CUT		
THE PLAYERS			CUT

Chris Riley

EXEMPT STATUS: 2004 U.S. Ryder Cup Team Member (through 2006)
FULL NAME: Chris J. Riley
HEIGHT: 5-11
WEIGHT: 160
BIRTHDATE: December 8, 1973
BIRTHPLACE: San Diego, CA
RESIDENCE: Las Vegas, NV
FAMILY: Wife, Michelle Louviere; Taylor Lynn (9/2/04)
EDUCATION: University of Nevada-Las Vegas (1996, Communications)
SPECIAL INTERESTS: San Diego Chargers
TURNED PROFESSIONAL: 1996
Q SCHOOL: 1998
Nationwide Tour Alumnus

PGA TOUR VICTORIES (1):

2002 Reno-Tahoe Open.

BEST 2004 PGA TOUR FINISHES:

T2—Buick Invitational; T4—PGA Championship; T9—Bob Hope Chrysler Classic.

2004 SEASON:

Fell out of the top 30 for the first time in three years to No. 56...Three top-10s and six top-25s were lowest since his rookie season of 1999, when he posted the same figures...Making second start of season, finished T9 at the Bob Hope Chrysler Classic, recording four-of-five rounds in the 60s...Finished T2 at the Buick Invitational after being involved in three-man playoff with John Daly and Luke Donald. His third runner-up finish in last seven months (2001 Greater Hartford Open, John Deere Classic). He and Donald were eliminated on first extra hole after Daly made birdie and Riley lipped out a putt from five feet. Finished the tournament first in Putts Per Round (25.5) and is 1-1 on TOUR in playoffs...Picked up second top-10 in 12 career major appearances, with a T4 at the PGA Championship; the other was a third at the 2002 PGA. A three-putt bogey on the 72nd hole left him one stroke out of the three-man playoff between winner Vijay Singh, Chris DiMarco and Justin Leonard. Finish enabled him to jump from 18th to 10th on the final Ryder Cup team points list and qualify for his first Ryder Cup squad.

CAREER HIGHLIGHTS:

2003: Finished in the top 30 for the second straight season. Collected a career-high six top-10s, including three top-3s. Carded rounds of 66-67 on the weekend to finish T3 at the MCI Heritage at Harbour Town Golf Links...Was one back of third-round leader Peter Jacobsen at the Greater Hartford Open. Closed with 68 to Jacobsen's 67 to finish alone in second...Shared the 36-hole lead at first WGC-NEC Invitational and was one back through 54 holes, but a closing 71 dropped T4...Shared 54-lead at the John Deere Classic and finished T2. It was his third top-five finish in Moline, IL. **2002:** Earned first PGA TOUR victory in his 109th career start at Reno-Tahoe Open after defeating Jonathan Kaye in a one-hole playoff. Tied for the lead with Kaye and Steve Flesch at 12-under-par after 54 holes, Riley came from two strokes down on the back nine Sunday to tie Kaye in regulation. With a two-putt par to win on the first hole of the playoff, Riley earned $540,000, his largest career paycheck in becoming the 12th of 18 first-time winners on the PGA TOUR...T5 at the Advil Western Open earned a spot in the British Open at Muirfield where he finished T22 with a final-round 66...PGA was his second major championship start of the season. Entered the final day T6. Posted a final-round, 2-under-par 70 good for solo third and his first ticket to the Masters for finishing in the top four and ties...Closed the year making 14 consecutive cuts. **2001:** Had a slow start after breaking out early in each of his first two seasons on the PGA TOUR. Eclipsed the $1-million mark in season earning for the first time in his career thanks to four top-10s...Best effort of the year runner-up finish at The INTERNATIONAL. Accumulated 32 points, under Modified Stableford scoring system, to finish one point behind Tom Pernice, Jr. **2000:** Four top-10s including two fourth-place finishes...Earned first top-10 of the season at John Deere Classic, where four rounds in the 60s gave him solo fourth-place finish worth, $124,800. **1999:** Earned top-10 in his first start as a member of the PGA TOUR, a T7 at Sony Open in Hawaii. Ironically, his first shot was out of bounds. Recovered to shoot 67. Matching 68s on the weekend led to T7. **1998:** Finished 28th at PGA TOUR Qualifying Tournament to earn status in 1999...Rookie on the Nationwide Tour...Finished second in only his second start as a Nationwide Tour member, two behind Eric Johnson at South Florida Classic. **Amateur:** Four-time All-America selection at UNLV...Teammate of Tiger Woods at 1995 Walker Cup at Royal Porthcawl.

PERSONAL:

Brother Kevin was member of Nationwide Tour in 1998-99. Riley brothers were second of three sets of brothers to be Nationwide Tour members in same year, joining Tom and Curt Byrum (1994) and Brenden and Deane Pappas (2001). The Pappas brothers both qualified for the 2002 PGA TOUR...Fred Brown, a retired teacher who coached the golf team at San Diego's Madison High when Chris was a student there, caddied for Chris in 1999 and 2000...Teammates at UNLV with Chad Campbell and Edward Fryatt...Married LPGA golfer Michelle Louviere on December 14, 2002 in New Orleans.

PLAYER STATISTICS

2004 PGA TOUR STATISTICS

Scoring Average	70.84	(63)
Driving Distance	277.3	(176)
Driving Accuracy Percentage	61.8%	(135)
Total Driving	311	(192)
Greens in Regulation Pct.	62.5%	(162)
Putting Average	1.766	(61)
Sand Save Percentage	51.6%	(63)
Eagles (Holes per)	333.0	(146)
Birdie Average	3.35	(137)
All-Around Ranking	943	(146)
Scoring Avg. Before Cut	70.60	(48)
Round 3 Scoring Avg.	71.31	(128)
Final Round Scoring Average	72.27	(149)
Birdie Conversion Percentage	27.7%	(143)
Par Breakers	18.9%	(143)

MISCELLANEOUS PGA TOUR STATISTICS

2004 Low Round/Round: 64–Bob Hope Chrysler Classic/2
Career Low Round/Round: 63–2 times, most recent 2003 Greater Hartford Open/3
Career Largest Paycheck/Finish: $540,000–2002 Reno–Tahoe Open/1

PGA TOUR CAREER SUMMARY — PLAYOFF RECORD: 1-1

Year	Events Played	Cuts Made	1st	2nd	3rd	Top 10	Top 25	Earnings	Rank
1995A	1								
1996	1								
1999	28	15				3	6	$367,805	112
2000	28	20				4	7	660,707	71
2001	30	21		1		4	11	1,198,225	45
2002	28	23	1		1	5	14	2,032,979	23
2003	29	19		2	1	7	13	2,178,133	23
2004	23	17		1		3	6	1,292,732	56
Total	168	115	1	4	2	26	57	7,730,581	
NATIONWIDE TOUR									
1998	24	11		2	1	4	5	74,239	35
Total	24	11		2	1	4	5	74,239	
EUROPEAN TOUR									
2004	1	1				1	1	75,945	

PGA TOUR TOP TOURNAMENT SUMMARY

Year	99	00	01	02	03	04
Masters					T23	44
U.S. Open	CUT				CUT	T48
British Open				T22	CUT	CUT
PGA			T51	3	CUT	T4
THE PLAYERS		T48	T58	T22	CUT	CUT
TOUR Championship				T26	4	
WGC-Accenture Match Play					T17	T33
WGC-NEC Invitational					T4	T43
WGC-American Express Champ				T39	T28	T50

NATIONAL TEAMS: Walker Cup, 1995; Ryder Cup, 2004.

SECTION 2 PLAYER BIOGRAPHIES

Loren Roberts

EXEMPT STATUS: 78th on 2004 money list
FULL NAME: Loren Lloyd Roberts
HEIGHT: 6-2
WEIGHT: 190
BIRTHDATE: June 24, 1955
BIRTHPLACE: San Luis Obispo, CA
RESIDENCE: Germantown, TN
FAMILY: Wife, Kimberly; Alexandria (10/14/86), Addison (10/15/91)
EDUCATION: Cal Poly-San Luis Obispo
SPECIAL INTERESTS: Clubmaking, hunting, all sports
TURNED PROFESSIONAL: 1975
Q SCHOOL: Fall 1980, 1982, 1983, 1986, 1987
JOINED TOUR: 1981

PGA TOUR VICTORIES (8):

1994 Nestle Invitational. **1995** Nestle Invitational. **1996** MCI Classic, Greater Milwaukee Open. **1997** CVS Charity Classic. **1999** GTE Byron Nelson Classic. **2000** Greater Milwaukee Open. **2002** Valero Texas Open.

BEST 2004 PGA TOUR FINISHES:

T3—Southern Farm Bureau Classic; T10—Nissan Open.

2004 SEASON:

Finished inside the top 100 for the 17th consecutive season…First top-10 of the season was a T10 at the Nissan Open…Fired a 7-under 64 in the third round of the Buick Classic to take a one-stroke, 54-hole lead, but a closing 78 at Westchester CC dropped finish to T16…Held first-round lead at Cialis Western Open after opening 7-under 64 then finished T11, thanks to final-round 68…Next top-10 came in October, a T3 at the Southern Farm Bureau Classic.

CAREER HIGHLIGHTS:

2003: While playing consistent golf (14 of 17 cuts made), did not post a top-10 until 18th event, a T7 at the PGA at Oak Hill, where he finished eight strokes back of champion Shaun Micheel...After a two-week break, recorded a T8 at the Bell Canadian Open…Defending champion at the Valero Texas Open closed with 62 to finish T2. The 62 tied his career low, which he had shot three times previously. His finish in San Antonio moved him into the top 50 on the Official World Golf Ranking and earned a spot in the WGC-American Express Championship in Atlanta the next week, where he finished T16. **2002:** Picked up victory and finished in the top 30 on the money list for the third time in the last four years...Captured Valero Texas Open for eighth career TOUR win and first since 2000 Greater Milwaukee Open. At 47 years, three months and five days, became oldest player to win TOUR event since 48-year-old Tom Watson won the 1998 MasterCard Colonial. 19-under-par total of 261 tied Jeff Sluman (Greater Milwaukee Open) and Jonathan Byrd (Buick Challenge) for low 72-hole total on TOUR that season. Co-leader through 36 holes with Pat Perez after 7-under-par 63, his best round since a 63 at the 2000 Greater Milwaukee Open. Entered final round with one-shot lead over Frank Lickliter II, Garrett Willis, Bob Tway and Matt Peterson. After trailing Fred Funk and Fred Couples by one making the turn, birdied four of final six holes to secure three-shot victory over Funk, Couples and Willis. Victory led to Player of the Month for September honors...Six of eight TOUR victories have occurred since turning age 40, tying Hal Sutton and Greg Norman for the lead among active players. **2001:** His 86th-place finish on the money list was the worst since finishing No. 89 in 1988. **2000:** Had most lucrative season on the PGA TOUR thanks to a victory and nine top-10s...Has been successful at Brown Deer Park GC in Greater Milwaukee Open. Won for second time there in five years, shooting tournament-record 260, breaking Carlos Franco's previous record by four strokes. His 260 total was the lowest score by player 45 or older. In four of his eight victories, set tournament records. Owns the tournament record at the MCI Classic and the Greater Milwaukee Open, shares it at GTE Byron Nelson Classic and held the 72-hole record for the CVS Charity Classic, which is no longer part of the TOUR schedule. In addition to 1996 playoff victory over Jerry Kelly, finished second at Brown Deer in 1994 and 1997...Recorded top 10s at three of the majors—Masters (T3), U.S. Open (T8) and British Open (T7)...Member of his second President's Cup Team (1994, 2000) with 2-1-0 record good for a two-year total of 4-2-1. **1999:** After failing to finish in the top 30 on the money list in 1998 for the first time since 1993, returned with a solid year...Third-round 62 matching career-low produced 54-hole lead at GTE Byron Nelson Classic and a tournament-record 16-under-par 194. Finished tied with Steve Pate with tournament record 18-under-par 262. Won playoff with par on first extra hole...His father, who spent 1998 looking after his Alzheimer's stricken wife, was in attendance for first time in nearly a year. He joined Loren when Byron Nelson presented championship trophy. **1997:** Earned fifth title in four years at CVS Charity Classic...Finished T2 at Greater Milwaukee Open after Scott

PGA TOUR CAREER SUMMARY — PLAYOFF RECORD: 2-1

Year	Events Played	Cuts Made	1st	2nd	3rd	Top 10	Top 25	Earnings	Rank
1981	21	8					2	$8,935	177
1982	2								
1983	24	8						7,724	189
1984	26	14				3	7	67,515	88
1985	32	22			1	3	5	92,761	83
1986	33	20				2	5	53,655	133
1987	31	13					4	57,489	138
1988	29	19				3	13	136,890	89
1989	30	28				5	11	275,882	46
1990	30	26			1	7	14	478,522	24
1991	29	23				4	12	281,174	58
1992	28	23		1	1	3	12	338,673	43
1993	28	19			1	4	9	316,506	53
1994	22	19	1	3	1	9	12	1,015,671	6
1995	23	19	1	1	1	5	10	678,335	27
1996	24	19	2			3	11	725,231	27
1997	24	17	1	1	1	9	14	1,089,140	15
1998	22	18				3	10	467,285	60
1999	26	20	1			7	10	1,258,745	30
2000	24	21	1		2	9	15	1,932,280	18
2001	25	17				2	6	584,072	86
2002	25	21	1	2		5	11	1,919,047	28
2003	24	21		1		3	10	1,297,739	52
2004	22	19			1	2	12	998,677	78
Total	604	434	8	9	10	91	215	14,081,948	

PGA TOUR TOP TOURNAMENT SUMMARY

Year	85	86	87	88	89	90	91	92	93	94	95	96	97
Masters							CUT			T5	T24	T23	CUT
U.S. Open	T34		CUT		CUT		T49		T11	T2	W/D	T40	T13
British Open										T24	CUT	T18	CUT
PGA	CUT				T34	T5	T27		T28	T9	T58	CUT	T49
THE PLAYERS	CUT	T40		CUT	T14	T46	T27	T21	CUT	T14	T34	T33	3
TOUR Championship						T14				T8	11	W/D	T8

Year	98	99	00	01	02	03	04
Masters		CUT	T3	T37		T33	
U.S. Open	T18		T8	T52		T42	
British Open	T29		T7	T13	T28		
PGA	T65	CUT	T58	CUT	T43	T7	T17
THE PLAYERS	CUT	CUT	CUT	CUT	T49	71	T66
TOUR Championship		T21	27		30		
WGC-Accenture Match Play		T9	T33			T33	T17
WGC-NEC Invitational			14	T29	T28		
WGC-American Express Champ		T40				T16	

NATIONAL TEAMS: The Presidents Cup (2) 1994, 2000; Ryder Cup, 1995.

Loren Roberts (Continued)

Hoch sank winning chip-in eagle on 72nd hole. **1996:** Won twice, at MCI Classic and Greater Milwaukee Open...At MCI Classic, 63 on Saturday captured third-round lead, and 265 total broke Hale Irwin's tournament record by one stroke...Birdied two of final three holes to break tournament record for the first time with a 265 at Greater Milwaukee Open, forcing playoff with Jerry Kelly. Birdie on first extra hole earned GMO victory. **1995:** First two PGA TOUR victories came at 1994 and 1995 Nestle Invitationals, making him the only player to successfully defend a title at Bay Hill Invitational until Tiger Woods joined him in 2001 and 2002. Became first player to win same event for first two TOUR victories since Calvin Peete (1979 and 1982 Greater Milwaukee Opens)...Member of Ryder Cup Team. **1994:** Won The Nestle Invitational with closing 67 to defeat Fuzzy Zoeller, Vijay Singh and Nick Price by one stroke...Had three top-10s in majors: T5 Masters, T2 U.S Open and T9 PGA Championship...Tied with Ernie Els after 18-hole playoff at U.S. Open, lost on 20th hole.

PERSONAL:

Nicknamed "Boss of the Moss" for his putting ability. Nickname coined by fellow TOUR member David Ogrin in 1985...Cary Middlecoff said of him in the mid-1980s: "We've got a kid back home (in Tennessee) who is just a beautiful putter. He'll just break your heart on the greens, he's so pure. If he ever gets to believing in himself, he could really be something to watch"...In 1998, was inducted into Cal Poly Athletic Hall of Fame.

PLAYER STATISTICS

2004 PGA TOUR STATISTICS

Scoring Average	70.22	(20)
Driving Distance	269.1	(195)
Driving Accuracy Percentage	69.8%	(27)
Total Driving	222	(143)
Greens in Regulation Pct.	66.6%	(54)
Putting Average	1.738	(7)
Sand Save Percentage	59.3%	(7)
Eagles (Holes per)	711.0	(189)
Birdie Average	3.80	(29)
All-Around Ranking	528	(30)
Scoring Avg. Before Cut	69.49	(4)
Round 3 Scoring Avg.	70.78	(81)
Final Round Scoring Average	70.78	(43)
Birdie Conversion Percentage	29.8%	(74)
Par Breakers	21.2%	(49)

MISCELLANEOUS PGA TOUR STATISTICS

2004 Low Round/Round: 64–2 times, most recent Cialis Western Open/1
Career Low Round/Round: 62–4 times, most recent 2003 Valero Texas Open/4
Career Largest Paycheck/Finish: $630,000–2002 Valero Texas Open/1

HOT SHOTS

Easiest Front Nine (2004)

Event Name	Course Name	To Par
Bob Hope Chrysler Classic	Indian Wells CC*	-1.98
Bob Hope Chrysler Classic	PGA West (Palmer Course)**	-1.93
Bob Hope Chrysler Classic	Bermuda Dunes CC**	-1.76
Michelin Champ at Las Vegas	Bear's Best**	-1.63
Michelin Champ at Las Vegas	TPC at Summerlin**	-1.55

Toughest Front Nine (2004)

Event Name	Course Name	To Par
U.S. Open Championship	Shinnecock Hills Golf Club	+1.84
British Open Championship	Royal Troon GC	+1.59
Buick Invitational	Torrey Pines (South Course)**	+1.14
FedEx St. Jude Classic	TPC at Southwind	+1.13
Masters Tournament	Augusta National GC	+1.00

** = Multiple course tournament

Easiest Back Nine (2004)

Event Name	Course Name	To Par
Bob Hope Chrysler Classic	Indian Wells CC**	-2.23
Bob Hope Chrysler Classic	Bermuda Dunes CC**	-1.83
FUNAI Classic at the WALT DISNEY WORLD Resort	Palm GC**	-1.52
Michelin Champ. at Las Vegas	TPC at The Canyons**	-1.33
Buick Invitational	Torrey Pines (North Course)**	-1.33

Toughest Back Nine (2004)

Event Name	Course Name	To Par
U.S. Open Championship	Shinnecock Hills Golf Club	+1.99
BellSouth Classic	TPC at Sugarloaf	+1.09
Cialis Western Open	Cog Hill G&CC	+0.94
Masters Tournament	Augusta National GC	+0.90

Torrey Pines Golf Course

John Rollins

EXEMPT STATUS: 109th on TOUR money list
FULL NAME: John Rollins
HEIGHT: 6-0
WEIGHT: 200
BIRTHDATE: June 25, 1975
BIRTHPLACE: Richmond, VA
RESIDENCE: Richmond, VA; plays out of Lake Chesdin GC
FAMILY: Isabella Armain (7/16/03)
EDUCATION: Virginia Commonwealth University (1997, Mass Communications)
SPECIAL INTERESTS: Playing guitar, billiards
TURNED PROFESSIONAL: 1997
Q SCHOOL: 1999
JOINED TOUR: 2000
Nationwide Tour Alumnus

PGA TOUR VICTORIES (1):

2002 Bell Canadian Open.

NATIONWIDE TOUR VICTORIES (1):

2001 Hershey Open.

BEST 2004 PGA TOUR FINISHES:

T4—Deutsche Bank Championship; T8—John Deere Classic.

2004 SEASON:

Finished inside the top 125 on the PGA TOUR money list for the third consecutive season and third time in four-year career...Had a rough start, making three of 14 cuts, but made 14 of 15 to end season, including both of his top-10s...Made his first appearance in the World Golf Championship-Accenture Match Play Championship. Took Tiger Woods 18 holes before falling, 1-up, to the eventual tournament winner...First top-10 came in 19th start of 2004, a T8 at the John Deere Classic. Posted four rounds in the 60s to finish three shots out of Mark Hensby-John E. Morgan playoff. Recorded an ace in the final round on No. 7 with a 7-iron from 169 yards...Posted a T4 at the Deutsche Bank Championship, his best finish since losing the Buick Classic playoff to Jonathan Kaye in June 2003.

CAREER HIGHLIGHTS:

2003: Made over $1 million for the second straight season thanks to five top-10s, including his first career runner-up finish...Lost to Jonathan Kaye on the first extra hole of a playoff at the Buick Classic. Birdied last hole to get to 13-under and hold clubhouse lead, while Kaye was standing on 18th tee. Played 29 holes on Sunday due to rain-shortened Saturday. Playoff record dropped to 1-1. Shared third-round lead with Briny Baird, Skip Kendall and Jonathan Kaye...Shared third-round lead with Vijay Singh, Stewart Cink and Scott Verplank at the FUNAI Classic at the WALT DISNEY WORLD Resort and finished T5. **2002:** Made most of second chance on PGA TOUR, earning his first victory and just shy of $2 million...Moved up from 408th on Official World Golf Ranking list to T67 through THE TOUR Championship...Six top-10s were five more than he had during his rookie season of 2000 and his 120 rounds were the most on TOUR...Won Bell Canadian Open with birdie on first extra hole of three-man playoff with Neal Lancaster and Justin Leonard. Shot final-round 65 and reached playoff when Lancaster double-bogeyed the 18th hole. Came from seven strokes behind on final day, tied with Len Mattiace (FedEx St. Jude Classic) and Spike McRoy (B.C. Open) for best comeback of season...Qualified for first TOUR Championship and finished T13. **2001:** Sixth-place finish on 2001 Nationwide Tour money list ensured return trip to PGA TOUR...Made just four cuts in first 12 Nationwide Tour starts but game clicked in July and finished by making 13 consecutive cuts, the most by any player during the 2001 Nationwide Tour season...Defeated Rod Pampling with birdie-3 on first extra hole at Hershey Open for first career win. Entering 2002, had played five TOUR-sanctioned events in Pennsylvania and has finished T13 or better including a T12 at the 2000 SEI Pennsylvania Classic. **2000:** First TOUR top-10 was a T9 at the Greater Milwaukee Open thanks to a final-round 8-under 63. **1999:** Earned first TOUR card by virtue of his T16 finish at the PGA TOUR Qualifying Tournament. **Amateur:** Two-time Virginia state amateur champion in 1996 and 1997. Honorable Mention All-America selection at Virginia Commonwealth.

PERSONAL:

Plays the guitar.

PLAYER STATISTICS

2004 PGA TOUR STATISTICS

Scoring Average	71.20	(104)
Driving Distance	286.7	(101)
Driving Accuracy Percentage	69.1%	(36)
Total Driving	137	(25)
Greens in Regulation Pct.	62.5%	(162)
Putting Average	1.764	(56)
Sand Save Percentage	46.1%	(139)
Eagles (Holes per)	255.0	(104)
Birdie Average	3.49	(105)
All-Around Ranking	807	(109)
Scoring Avg. Before Cut	71.30	(133)
Round 3 Scoring Avg.	72.06	(168)
Final Round Scoring Average	71.40	(83)
Birdie Conversion Percentage	29.9%	(71)
Par Breakers	19.8%	(107)

MISCELLANEOUS PGA TOUR STATISTICS

2004 Low Round/Round: 65–2 times, most recent Michelin Championship at Las Vegas/2
Career Low Round/Round: 63–2000 Greater Milwaukee Open/4
Career Largest Paycheck/Finish: $720,000–2002 Bell Canadian Open/1

PGA TOUR CAREER SUMMARY — PLAYOFF RECORD: 1-1

Year	Events Played	Cuts Made	1st	2nd	3rd	Top 10	Top 25	Earnings	Rank
1998	1								
2000	27	8				1	2	$169,570	171
2002	34	27	1			6	15	1,956,565	25
2003	27	17		1		5	8	1,612,314	39
2004	29	18				2	7	737,957	109
Total	118	70	1	1		14	32	4,476,406	
NATIONWIDE TOUR									
1997	2								
1998	1								
1999	20	6			1	1	4	28,736	82
2000	3								
2001	25	17	1		2	6	14	242,841	6
Total	51	23	1		3	7	18	271,577	
EUROPEAN TOUR									
2003	1	1						13,117	

PGA TOUR TOP TOURNAMENT SUMMARY

Year	02	03	04
Masters		47	CUT
U.S. Open		T53	T48
British Open		70	
PGA	CUT	CUT	
THE PLAYERS		CUT	CUT
TOUR Championship	T13		
WGC-Accenture Match Play			T33
WGC-NEC Invitational		T67	
WGC-American Express Champ	T43		

Justin Rose

EXEMPT STATUS: 62nd on TOUR money list
FULL NAME: Justin Rose
HEIGHT: 6-2
WEIGHT: 178
BIRTHDATE: July 30, 1980
BIRTHPLACE: Johannesburg, South Africa
RESIDENCE: London, England; Orlando, FL
FAMILY: Single
SPECIAL INTERESTS: Tennis, soccer, cricket, cars, music
TURNED PROFESSIONAL: 1998
JOINED TOUR: 2004

BEST PGA TOUR CAREER FINISH:

3—2003 Deutsche Bank Championship.

INTERNATIONAL VICTORIES (4):

2002 dunhill championship [Eur], Chunichi Crowns [Jpn], Nashau Masters [SAf], Victor Chandler British Masters [Eur].

BEST 2004 PGA TOUR FINISHES:

4—the Memorial Tournament, Bell Canadian Open; T5—HP Classic of New Orleans; T7—MCI Heritage.

2004 SEASON:

Fared well in his first season as an offical PGA TOUR member, making 18 of 22 cuts, including four top-10s and earning over $1 million...Making second Masters Tournament appearance, grabbed first-round lead with a 5-under-par 67. Led by two over Alex Cejka and Jose Maria Olazabal through 36 holes after a 71 for a 6-under 138 total. Faded from contention on Saturday, with a 9-over-par 81 and finished T22...Following week, posted his first top-10 of the season, a T7 at the MCI Heritage Classic...Two weeks later, earned second top-10 with a T5 at the HP Classic of New Orleans, five strokes behind champion Vijay Singh...Making his first appearance at the Memorial Tournament finished fourth. Shared the 36-hole lead with Stephen Ames and Ben Curtis and was only two strokes back of eventual champion Ernie Els through 54 holes...Tied his career-low round (63, first round, 2003 Deutsche Bank Championship) on the PGA TOUR with an 8-under 63 in the final round of the Bell Canadian Open, where he finished T4. The 63 was also the low round of the tournament and allowed him to make the largest jump of the day into the top 10, from T34 to T4...Recorded hole-in-one in first round of Chrysler Classic of Greensboro, acing the par-3 17th hole with a 3-iron from 232 yards.

CAREER HIGHLIGHTS:

2003: As a non-member, made more money than the 125th spot on the PGA TOUR money list to earn his initial PGA TOUR card...Playing in his first U.S. Open, finished T5 and shared honors with Frederik Jacobson for best finish by a first-time participant...Best PGA TOUR finish to date was solo third in 16th professional PGA TOUR start at the inaugural Deutsche Bank Championship. First-round 8-under-par 63 (also a career low on the PGA TOUR) set the TPC of Boston course record that was broken one day later by Adam Scott's 62. **2002:** Delivered the huge potential which first became apparent in the 1998 British Open by capturing the Dunhill Championship at the start of the season...Went on to win the Nashua Masters title in South Africa and the Crowns Tournament in Japan then claimed the Victor Chandler British Masters after a battle with friend Ian Poulter. **2001:** Begun the season with successive second-place finishes in South Africa, the country of his birth, to ensure his playing rights for this season. **2000:** Finished ninth at European Tour Qualifying tournament to retain playing privileges for next season after coming within five spots of retaining his card. **1999:** Finished fourth at European Tour Qualifying tournament to earn first card. **1998:** Pitched in at the last hole to tie for fourth in the British Open Championship at Royal Birkdale. Won Silver Medal as leading amateur. Turned professional the next day. **Amateur:** At age 17, was the youngest Walker Cup player ever at 1997 event.

PERSONAL:

Moved to England at age 5, when he started to play seriously at Hartley Wintney GC near his Hampshire home. First swung a club in back garden at 11 months when dad, Ken, handed him a plastic club...Broke 70 for the first time at age 11. Handicap of plus-3 at age 14 and played in 1997 Walker Cup at only 17...Brother Brandon is an ex-professional in South Africa...Father Ken passed away in September 2002 and he is remembered via the Ken Rose Foundation (kenrosefoundation.com)...Web site is justinrose.co.uk.

PLAYER STATISTICS

2004 PGA TOUR STATISTICS

Scoring Average	70.42	(29)
Driving Distance	290.7	(65)
Driving Accuracy Percentage	61.5%	(142)
Total Driving	207	(118)
Greens in Regulation Pct.	67.7%	(31)
Putting Average	1.762	(50)
Sand Save Percentage	49.4%	(88)
Eagles (Holes per)	259.2	(108)
Birdie Average	3.85	(21)
All-Around Ranking	534	(35)
Scoring Avg. Before Cut	70.68	(55)
Round 3 Scoring Avg.	70.31	(45)
Final Round Scoring Average	70.81	(46)
Birdie Conversion Percentage	30.3%	(58)
Par Breakers	21.8%	(21)

MISCELLANEOUS PGA TOUR STATISTICS

2004 Low Round/Round: 63–Bell Canadian Open/4
Career Low Round/Round: 63–2 times, most recent 2004 Bell Canadian Open/4
Career Largest Paycheck/Finish: $340,000–2003 Deutsche Bank Championship/3

PGA TOUR CAREER SUMMARY — PLAYOFF RECORD: 0-0

Year	Events Played	Cuts Made	1st	2nd	3rd	Top 10	Top 25	Earnings	Rank
1998A	1	1				1	1		
1999	1								
2001	1	1						$30,756	
2002	4	4				1	3	94,816	
2003	11	9			1	2	3	599,874	
2004	22	18				4	10	1,236,764	62
Total	40	33			1	8	17	1,962,211	
EUROPEAN TOUR									
2004	8	5					3	158,552	
JAPAN GOLF TOUR									
2003	1	1					1	14,495	
SOUTHERN AFRICA TOUR									
2003	1	1					1	2,442	

PGA TOUR TOP TOURNAMENT SUMMARY

Year	98	99	00	01	02	03	04
Masters						T39	T22
U.S. Open						T5	CUT
British Open	T4	CUT		T30	T22	CUT	
PGA					T23	CUT	CUT
THE PLAYERS						T39	T58
WGC-Accenture Match Play						T17	T33
WGC-NEC Invitational					5	T33	
WGC-American Express Champ					T46	T28	

NATIONAL TEAMS: WGC-World Cup (2), 2002, 2003.

Rory Sabbatini (SAB-ih-TEE-knee)

EXEMPT STATUS: 2003 tournament winner (through 2005)
FULL NAME: Rory Mario Trevor Sabbatini
HEIGHT: 5-10
WEIGHT: 160
BIRTHDATE: April 2, 1976
BIRTHPLACE: Durban, South Africa
RESIDENCE: Southlake, TX

FAMILY: Wife, Amy; Harley Aiden (8/28/03)
EDUCATION: University of Arizona
SPECIAL INTERESTS: Fast cars, fishing, scuba diving, fashion
TURNED PROFESSIONAL: 1998
Q SCHOOL: 1998
JOINED TOUR: 1999

PGA TOUR VICTORIES (2):

2000 Air Canada Championship. **2003** FBR Capital Open.

OTHER VICTORIES (1):

2003 WGC-World Cup [with Trevor Immelman].

BEST 2004 PGA TOUR FINISHES:

T2—Buick Classic, WGC-NEC Invitational; 3—Booz Allen Classic, Chrysler Classic of Tucson; T6—Shell Houston Open; T9—The Honda Classic; T10—THE TOUR Championship presented by Coca-Cola.

2004 SEASON:

Despite not winning had career-best season in just his sixth year as a full-time member of the PGA TOUR. Earned over $2.5 million for the first time in a single season and was ranked a career-best 16th on the final season money list. Made 19 cuts in 26 TOUR starts and had a personal-best six top-10s, including two runner-up finishes…First top-10 of the season came close to collegiate home with at T3 at the Chrysler Classic of Tucson, thanks to a final-round, 8-under-par 64…In his next start finished T9 at The Honda Classic. Last time he posted back-to-back top-10 finishes was in 2002 when he finished T5 at the Buick Invitational and T2 at the Nissan Open…Finished T6 at the Shell Houston Open, rebounding from a first-round 74…Was part of a three-man playoff with Sergio Garcia and Padraig Harrington at the Buick Classic. Garcia won with a birdie on the thrid extra hole. Was only one back of the lead through 54 holes and fired a closing round of 70 to get into the playoff at Westchester CC…Defending champion closed with a 5-under 66 to finish alone in third at the Booz Allen Classic…Earned a spot in the British Open by being the one of the top two players on a six-tournament money list that ended the week of the Cialis Western Open…In second career WGC-NEC Invitational start, posted T2 finish, four strokes behind champion Stewart Cink…Qualified for his first TOUR Championship and finished T10…Once again teamed with Trevor Immelman at the WGC-World Cup in Seville, Spain, to defend their 2003 title.

CAREER HIGHLIGHTS:

2003: Recorded his second career win in Washington, D.C. at the FBR Capital Open in June. Four-stroke margin was largest margin of victory at this event since Tom Byrum's five-stroke win in 1989. Held second- and third-round leads. Only player in field to post four rounds in the 60s and second player in 2003 to win a Monday finish. Saturday's third round was washed out and players were forced to play 18 holes on Sunday and Monday to finish the tournament…Teamed with countryman Trevor Immelman to win the World Golf Championships-World Cup at Kiawah Island, SC by four strokes over England's Justin Rose and Paul Casey. **2002:** More than half of season's earnings and three of his four top-10s came during four-week stretch (Phoenix Open to Nissan Open), which included a T2 at the Nissan Open, one stroke behind winner Len Mattiace. **2001:** Began season with 69-69-65 to take two-stroke lead at Mercedes Championships. Closing 72 left him one stroke behind winner Jim Furyk. Missed three-foot putt on 72nd hole denied playoff opportunity...Earned T2 finish, one stroke behind Bob Estes in the Invensys Classic at Las Vegas. **2000:** With win at Air Canada Championship, the 24-year old became the youngest player to win on the PGA TOUR since 21-year-old Tiger Woods won the 1996 Las Vegas Invitational. The victory made him the tournament's fourth first-time winner in its five-year history. Trailed Grant Waite by three strokes after 54 holes. Holed a 25-foot birdie putt on No. 17 to go a stroke ahead of playing partner Mark Calcavecchia. Added 30-foot birdie putt on final hole for victory...Had one-stroke lead through 72 holes at Bob Hope Chrysler Classic. Closed with 68 to finish one stroke behind Jesper Parnevik. **1999:** Had a successful rookie campaign on PGA TOUR...Held 36-hole lead on his 23rd birthday at BellSouth Classic, and finished T3 worth $145,000...Earned second third-place finish of season at B.C. Open. **1998:** Earned his first PGA TOUR membership by finishing 41st at PGA TOUR National Qualifying Tournament...Won Southern Arizona Open. **Amateur:** Won 1993 International Junior Masters...Three-time All-America and 1996 individual runner-up in the NCAA Tournament at Arizona.

PERSONAL:

Started playing game at age 4...Was youngest member of PGA TOUR in 1999 at age 22 when season started...Has never recorded an ace and took first lesson at age 22...Family travels with him in a RV with their miniature dachsunds, Chloe and Zoe...Best friend Kevin Fasbender has been his caddie for more than four years...Web site is rorysabbatini.com.

PLAYER STATISTICS

2004 PGA TOUR STATISTICS

Scoring Average	70.51	(33)
Driving Distance	292.2	(48)
Driving Accuracy Percentage	59.2%	(160)
Total Driving	208	(119)
Greens in Regulation Pct.	64.9%	(100)
Putting Average	1.792	(137)
Sand Save Percentage	48.9%	(101)
Eagles (Holes per)	516.0	(177)
Birdie Average	3.73	(50)
All-Around Ranking	806	(108)
Scoring Avg. Before Cut	71.00	(96)
Round 3 Scoring Avg.	70.95	(98)
Final Round Scoring Average	70.56	(30)
Birdie Conversion Percentage	30.0%	(70)
Par Breakers	20.9%	(61)

MISCELLANEOUS PGA TOUR STATISTICS

2004 Low Round/Round: 64–Chrysler Classic of Tucson/4
Career Low Round/Round: 63–2 times, most recent 2003 Valero Texas Open/1
Career Largest Paycheck/Finish: $810,000–2003 FBR Capital Open/1

PGA TOUR CAREER SUMMARY — PLAYOFF RECORD: 0-1

Year	Events Played	Cuts Made	1st	2nd	3rd	Top 10	Top 25	Earnings	Rank
1999	27	13			2	2	5	$381,322	108
2000	26	16	1	1		3	7	1,262,535	36
2001	23	13		2		3	3	1,038,590	52
2002	23	13		1		4	6	936,664	68
2003	27	20	1			5	6	1,604,701	41
2004	26	19		2	2	7	13	2,500,397	16
Total	152	94	2	6	4	24	40	7,724,208	

PGA TOUR TOP TOURNAMENT SUMMARY

Year	00	01	02	03	04
Masters		CUT	CUT		
U.S. Open	CUT			CUT	CUT
British Open		T54		T53	T66
PGA	77	CUT	CUT	68	CUT
THE PLAYERS	CUT	CUT	CUT	CUT	T42
TOUR Championship					T10
WGC-Accenture Match Play			T33		
WGC-NEC Invitational				T51	T2
WGC-American Express Champ					T21

NATIONAL TEAMS: WGC-World Cup (3), 2002, 2003, 2004.

Adam Scott

EXEMPT STATUS: Winner, 2004 PLAYERS Championship (through 2009)
FULL NAME: Adam Scott
HEIGHT: 6-0
WEIGHT: 170
BIRTHDATE: July 16, 1980
BIRTHPLACE: Adelaide, Australia
RESIDENCE: Crans sur Sierre, Switzerland

FAMILY: Single
EDUCATION: University of Nevada-Las Vegas
SPECIAL INTERESTS: All sports, biographies, fashion, surfing
TURNED PROFESSIONAL: 2000
JOINED TOUR: 2003

PGA TOUR VICTORIES (3):

2003 Deutsche Bank Championship. **2004** THE PLAYERS Championship, Booz Allen Classic.

INTERNATIONAL VICTORIES (4):

2001 Alfred Dunhill PGA Championship [SAf]. **2002** Qatar Masters [Eur], Gleneagles Scottish PGA Championship [Eur]. **2003** Scandic Carlsberg Scandinavian Masters [Eur].

BEST 2004 PGA TOUR FINISHES:

1—THE PLAYERS Championship, Booz Allen Classic; T2—Deutsche Bank Championship; T3—Bay Hill Invitational Presented by MasterCard; 7—Mercedes Championships; T9—WGC-Accenture Match Play Championship, PGA Championship.

2004 SEASON:

Young gun totaled two PGA TOUR wins, including dramatic victory at THE PLAYERS Championship. . .Totaled seven top-10s in only 16 starts. . .In Mercedes Championships debut, finished solo seventh at PGA TOUR's season-opening event, nine strokes behind winner Stuart Appleby. One of three first-timers to finish in the top 10 (Darren Clarke, Ben Crane) at Kapalua. . .Defeated Miguel Angel Jimenez and Robert Allenby before losing to Davis Love III and finishing T9 at the WGC-Accenture Match Play Championship. . .Picked up third top-10 in four TOUR starts with a T3 at the Bay Hill Invitational Presented by MasterCard. . .One week later, at the age of 23 years, 8 months and 12 days, became the youngest winner of THE PLAYERS Championship, with rounds of 65-72-69-70—276, one shot ahead of runner-up Padraig Harrington. Held the 18- and 54-hole leads and led by as many as five strokes in the final round. At the 72nd hole with a two-stroke lead over Harrington, pull-hooked 6-iron approach shot from 213 yards into water hazard, forcing up-and-down recovery from 39 yards. Clinched title with 10-foot bogey putt to earn $1.44 million, the largest first-place check in the history of the PGA TOUR. . .Won the Booz Allen Classic in his first appearance at TPC at Avenel. Equaled the tournament record of 21-under 263 held by Billy Andrade and Jeff Sluman in 1991. Has collected all three of his PGA TOUR victories on TPC courses—Deutsche Bank Championship (TPC of Boston) and THE PLAYERS Championship (TPC at Sawgrass). Improved to 7-1 when holding at least a share of the 54-hole lead in his professional career, including a 3-0 mark on the PGA TOUR. Moved two spots to No. 13 on the Offical World Golf Ranking, his best career position. . .Earned second career top-10 in a major with his T9 at the PGA Championship, matching the T9 at the 2002 Masters. . .Finished T2, three strokes behind Vijay Singh in defense of his first PGA TOUR title at the Deutsche Bank Championship. Fired a final-round best, 6-under 65, which included four consecutive birdies on the back nine to pull within a stroke of Singh at one point. . .Played in six European Tour events, with one runner-up finish at the Heineken Classic.

CAREER HIGHLIGHTS:

2003: Earned first PGA TOUR title in 34th career TOUR start at the age of 23 years, 1 month and 16 days (youngest since Sergio Garcia won the 2002 Mercedes Championships at 21 years, 11 months and 27 days) at the inaugural Deutsche Bank Championship. Led Vijay Singh by two strokes after 36 holes, thanks to a course record 9-under-par 62. Maintained three-stroke lead over Jonathan Kaye through 54 holes, and brought home a four-stroke victory over runner-up Rocco Mediate...Lost to eventual champion Tiger Woods in 20 holes in the semifinals of the World Golf Championship-Accenture Match Play Championship. Defeated Bernhard Langer, Rocco Mediate, defending champion Kevin Sutherland and Jay Haas in first four rounds. Finished third after defeating fellow Australian Peter Lonard 1-up in the consolation match...Joined the PGA TOUR as a Special Temporary Member in late April...Claimed his fourth European Tour victory with a final-round 3-under-par 69 to win the Scandic Carlsberg Scandinavian Masters by two shots over Nick Dougherty...Representing the International team, was the youngest player on either Presidents Cup squad. **2002:** Earned second European Tour victory at the Qatar Maters, with a 19-under-par 269...Earned Masters invitation based on being ranked in the top 50 in the Official World Golf Ranking at end of 2001. Finished T9 at Augusta National. Earnings of $151,200 put season PGA TOUR winnings at $288,642, earning an invitation to join the PGA TOUR as a Special Temporary Member for the remainder of the 2002 season...Also captured the Qatar Masters on the European Tour for second victory of the season. **2001:** Finished 13th in the Volvo Order of Merit in first full season on European Tour...In 16 European Tour events, compiled five top-10s, including three third-place finishes...Captured the Alfred Dunhill PGA Championship on the Southern Africa Tour...Also played in United States, Japan and Australia. **2000:** Secured European Tour card for 2001 in just eight starts as a professional, clinching his place with a T6 at the Linde German Masters in October. **Amateur:** As a junior, captured both Australian and New Zealand Junior titles, and fired a course-record 62 at Los Coyotes Country Club at the U.S. Junior Amateur...Spent one year playing collegiately at UNLV.

PERSONAL:

Golf hero is countryman Greg Norman, who along with coach Butch Harmon, urged Scott to play several seasons on the European Tour. . .Wears clothing by Burberry.

PLAYER STATISTICS

2004 PGA TOUR STATISTICS

Scoring Average	70.10	(13)
Driving Distance	295.4	(30)
Driving Accuracy Percentage	57.7%	(174)
Total Driving	204	(112)
Greens in Regulation Pct.	65.6%	(83)
Putting Average	1.757	(37)
Sand Save Percentage	59.3%	(7)
Eagles (Holes per)	936.0	(192)
Birdie Average	3.96	(9)
All-Around Ranking	545	(37)
Scoring Avg. Before Cut	70.80	(68)
Round 3 Scoring Avg.	70.36	(53)
Final Round Scoring Average	70.64	(34)
Birdie Conversion Percentage	32.9%	(6)
Par Breakers	22.1%	(15)

MISCELLANEOUS PGA TOUR STATISTICS

2004 Low Round/Round: 62–Booz Allen Classic/2
Career Low Round/Round: 62–3 times, most recent 2004 Booz Allen Classic/2
Career Largest Paycheck/Finish: $1,440,000–2004 THE PLAYERS Championship/1

PGA TOUR CAREER SUMMARY — PLAYOFF RECORD: 0-0

Year	Events Played	Cuts Made	1st	2nd	3rd	Top 10	Top 25	Earnings	Rank
2000	6	1						$10,200	
2001	6	4					1	93,026	
2002	10	7				2	4	339,157	
2003	14	11	1		1	2	6	1,238,736	55
2004	16	12	2	1	1	7	8	3,724,984	7
Total	52	35	3	1	2	11	19	5,406,103	
EUROPEAN TOUR									
2004	6	5		1		2	4	366,241	

PGA TOUR TOP TOURNAMENT SUMMARY

Year	00	01	02	03	04
Masters			T9	T23	CUT
U.S. Open			CUT	CUT	CUT
British Open	CUT	T47	CUT	CUT	T42
PGA		CUT	T23	T23	T9
THE PLAYERS			CUT	T17	**1**
TOUR Championship					T21
WGC-Accenture Match Play			T17	3	T9
WGC-NEC Invitational				T64	T55
WGC-American Express Champ		CNL	T39	T40	T36

NATIONAL TEAMS: The Presidents Cup, 2003; World Cup, 2002

John Senden

EXEMPT STATUS: 114th on 2004 money list
FULL NAME: John Gerard Senden
HEIGHT: 6-3
WEIGHT: 183
BIRTHDATE: April 20, 1971
BIRTHPLACE: Brisbane, Queensland, Australia
RESIDENCE: Brisbane, Queensland, Australia
FAMILY: Wife, Jackie; Jacob (4/6/04)

SPECIAL INTERESTS: Spending time at home
TURNED PROFESSIONAL: 1992
Q SCHOOL: 2001
JOINED TOUR: 2002

BEST PGA TOUR CAREER FINISHES:

T9—**2002** Air Canada Championship, **2004** Bank of America Colonial.

INTERNATIONAL VICTORIES (3):

1996 Indonesian PGA Championship. **1998** Interlaken Open [Eur Chall], Alliance Open [Eur Chall].

BEST 2004 PGA TOUR FINISHES:

T9—Bank of America Colonial; T10—B.C. Open.

2004 SEASON:

Consistent play was once again the key to his season. Secured his card by finishing inside the top 125 for the third straight season since joining the TOUR in 2002. Made 21 cuts in 28 starts on the PGA TOUR, incuding a career-high two top-10s. . .Jumped from T37 through three rounds to T5 finish at the Bank of America Colonial after a final-round, 5-under 65, his second career top-10 (T9, 2002 Air Canada Championship). . .Finished T10 at the B.C. Open in July for his second top-10 of the season. . .Was two strokes back of the lead through 36 holes at the Valero Texas Open after opening with rounds of 66-65. Finished 21st and collected $42,000, good enough to secure his card for the 2005 season. . .Shared first-round lead with Harrison Frazar and Glen Day at the Southern Farm Bureau Classic, but finished T14.

CAREER HIGHLIGHTS:

2003: Collected $601,670 in earnings and finished in top 125 for second straight season but did not post a top-10...Ran off streak of 11 consecutive cuts made beginning with the MCI Heritage in April...Best finish was a T13 at the inaugural Deutsche Bank Championship. **2002:** Half of the 22 rookies who began the season finished in the top 125, and the Australian was one of them, thanks to eight top-25s...Picked up first career top-10, a T9, in his 24th event at the Air Canada Championship in September. **2001:** Earned TOUR card at first trip to finals of PGA TOUR Qualifying Tournament...Member of European Tour 1999-2001 and has played at least half a dozen events per year on PGA TOUR of Australasia since 1992. **1999:** Highest finish on European Tour Order of Merit came when he was 69th. **1998:** Won twice on European Challenge Tour.

PLAYER STATISTICS

2004 PGA TOUR STATISTICS

Scoring Average	70.69	(45)
Driving Distance	296.6	(23)
Driving Accuracy Percentage	65.6%	(70)
Total Driving	93	(2)
Greens in Regulation Pct.	70.5%	(6)
Putting Average	1.791	(133)
Sand Save Percentage	50.6%	(76)
Eagles (Holes per)	108.0	(7)
Birdie Average	3.60	(79)
All-Around Ranking	439	(12)
Scoring Avg. Before Cut	70.34	(26)
Round 3 Scoring Avg.	70.67	(69)
Final Round Scoring Average	70.50	(27)
Birdie Conversion Percentage	28.8%	(104)
Par Breakers	20.9%	(61)

MISCELLANEOUS PGA TOUR STATISTICS

2004 Low Round/Round: 62–Bob Hope Chrysler Classic/3
Career Low Round/Round: 62–2004 Bob Hope Chrysler Classic/3
Career Largest Paycheck/Finish: $143,100–2004 Bank of America Colonial/T9

PGA TOUR CAREER SUMMARY — PLAYOFF RECORD: 0-0

Year	Events Played	Cuts Made	1st	2nd	3rd	Top 10	Top 25	Earnings	Rank
2002	30	18				1	8	$578,613	114
2003	33	22					5	601,670	108
2004	28	21				2	7	698,203	114
Total	91	61				3	20	1,878,485	

PGA TOUR TOP TOURNAMENT SUMMARY

Year	02	03	04
U.S. Open			CUT
British Open	CUT		
THE PLAYERS		CUT	T58

Patrick Sheehan (SHEE-han)

EXEMPT STATUS: 63rd on 2004 money list
FULL NAME: Patrick James Sheehan
HEIGHT: 5-11
WEIGHT: 190
BIRTHDATE: August 9, 1969
BIRTHPLACE: Providence, RI
RESIDENCE: Orlando, FL; plays out of Black Bear GC
FAMILY: Wife: Pamela; Emily (9/26/98), Kelly (12/30/01)
EDUCATION: University of Hartford (1992, Secondary Education)
SPECIAL INTERESTS: Family, music, movies
TURNED PROFESSIONAL: 1992
JOINED TOUR: 2003
Nationwide Tour Alumnus

BEST PGA TOUR CAREER FINISH:
2—2004 Valero Texas Open.

NATIONWIDE TOUR VICTORIES (1):
2002 Price Cutter Charity Championship.

BEST 2004 PGA TOUR FINISHES:
2—Valero Texas Open; T3—MCI Heritage; T4—U.S. Bank Championship in Milwaukee.

2004 SEASON:
Had a career year in just his second season as a full-time TOUR member. Made over $1 million and had three top-10s, incuding a runner-up finish...Notched his first top-10 of his career in his 46th TOUR start with a T3 at the MCI Heritage...Was one-stroke off the lead after 36 holes at the Shell Houston Open. Finished T11...Next top-10 came three months later, with a T4 at the U.S. Bank Championship in Milwaukee. Shared first-round lead with seven others, tying a TOUR record for players sharing the lead through 18 holes (2000 Honda Classic). Shared third-round lead with Carlos Franco and fellow Rhode Islander Brett Quigley prior to finishing three strokes behind Franco...Made his first-ever start in a major championship tournament, the PGA Championship at Whistling Straits, finishing T49...Recorded career-best runner-up finish to Bart Bryant at the Valero Texas Open, with four rounds in the 60s. Challenged Bryant until three-putt bogey on 15th hole derailed title hopes. Finished three strokes behind Bryant. Earned a career-best $378,000 to surpass $1 million for the season for the first time in his career.

CAREER HIGHLIGHTS:
2003: A 2002 graduate of the Nationwide Tour, rookie kept his TOUR card finishing 104th with $618,019 on the strength of seven top-25 finishes. One of six out of 15 Nationwide Tour graduates to finish among the top 125. **2002:** Earned his first PGA TOUR card by finishing 12th ($201,231) on the Nationwide Tour money list. Went wire-to-wire to win the Price Cutter Charity Championship for his first career victory...Missed the cut in his only PGA TOUR appearance at the 2002 BellSouth Classic. **2001:** Made the cut in nine of 23 tournaments on the Nationwide Tour. Had one top-10 and three top-25s, including a T5 at the Omaha Classic. **1998:** Golden Bear Tour Player of the Year. **1997:** Played in 13 Nationwide Tour events, making the cut in four. Best showing came at the Cleveland Open where he finished second, one stroke behind winner Mike Small.

PERSONAL:
Played junior hockey growing up in Rhode Island. Father got him started in golf. College teammate of Tim Petrovic and Jerry Kelly.

PLAYER STATISTICS

2004 PGA TOUR STATISTICS

Scoring Average	71.14	(100)
Driving Distance	290.3	(72)
Driving Accuracy Percentage	63.0%	(117)
Total Driving	189	(83)
Greens in Regulation Pct.	64.9%	(100)
Putting Average	1.759	(43)
Sand Save Percentage	43.0%	(170)
Eagles (Holes per)	666.0	(188)
Birdie Average	3.74	(47)
All-Around Ranking	837	(118)
Scoring Avg. Before Cut	70.43	(35)
Round 3 Scoring Avg.	71.65	(148)
Final Round Scoring Average	72.13	(142)
Birdie Conversion Percentage	30.5%	(52)
Par Breakers	20.9%	(61)

MISCELLANEOUS PGA TOUR STATISTICS

2004 Low Round/Round: 65–4 times, most recent Valero Texas Open/3
Career Low Round/Round: 64–2003 EDS Byron Nelson Championship/2
Career Largest Paycheck/Finish: $378,000–2004 Valero Texas Open/2

PGA TOUR CAREER SUMMARY — PLAYOFF RECORD: 0-0

Year	Events Played	Cuts Made	1st	2nd	3rd	Top 10	Top 25	Earnings	Rank
2002	1								
2003	32	20					7	$618,019	104
2004	33	23		1	1	3	7	1,234,344	63
Total	66	43		1	1	3	14	1,852,364	
NATIONWIDE TOUR									
1997	13	4		1		1	1	25,812	76
1998	1								
2000	1								
2001	23	9				1	3	39,395	93
2002	27	16	1			6	11	201,231	12
Total	65	29	1	1		8	15	266,438	

PGA TOUR TOP TOURNAMENT SUMMARY

Year	04
PGA	T49
THE PLAYERS	CUT

Joey Sindelar (SIN-dih-lahr)

EXEMPT STATUS: 2004 tournament winner (through 2006)
FULL NAME: Joseph Paul Sindelar
HEIGHT: 5-10
WEIGHT: 220
BIRTHDATE: March 30, 1958
BIRTHPLACE: Fort Knox, KY
RESIDENCE: Horseheads, NY
FAMILY: Wife, Suzanne Lee; Jamison Prescott (2/2/90), Ryan Joseph (5/13/93)
EDUCATION: Ohio State University
SPECIAL INTERESTS: Fishing, electronics
TURNED PROFESSIONAL: 1981
Q SCHOOL: Fall 1983

PGA TOUR VICTORIES (7):

1985 Greater Greensboro Open, B.C. Open. **1987** B.C. Open. **1988** Honda Classic, The International. **1990** Hardee's Golf Classic. **2004** Wachovia Championship.

BEST 2004 PGA TOUR FINISHES:

1—Wachovia Championship; T4—FUNAI Classic at the WALT DISNEY WORLD Resort.

2004 SEASON:

Enjoyed rebirth of career with his seventh PGA TOUR title at the Wachovia Championship in a two-hole playoff over Arron Oberholser, a span of 370 events since his last TOUR win at the 1990 Hardee's Golf Classic. The 13-year, 8-month span since previous win tied for third-longest in TOUR history. Collected the winner's check of $1,008,000 to surpass the $1-million mark in a single season for the first time in his 21-year career…Held one-stroke lead after 18 holes at the Bell Canadian Open, a tournament where he made the cut for the 10th consecutive year (finished T26)…Closed out the season with a T4 finish at the FUNAI Classic at the WALT DISNEY WORLD Resort, his second top-10 of the season.

CAREER HIGHLIGHTS:

2003: Finished in the top 125 for the 17th time in 20 seasons on TOUR...Posted four eagles during Bob Hope Chrysler Classic, tying the TOUR record for a 90-hole event dating back to 1980. Rich Beem last accomplished the feat at the 2002 Invensys Classic at Las Vegas. **2002:** Veteran finished in the top 100 for fourth time in last five years...Posted a T2 for the second consecutive season after having posted just one second-place finish or better from 1991-2000. This one came at The Honda Classic, where he finished in a tie with Brad Faxon, two strokes behind Matt Kuchar. Made only one bogey in the tournament, on the 71st hole. **2001:** Bounced back from a disappointing 2000 campaign to finish 81st in earnings with $654,864...Best finish on money list since placing 61st in 1998...Posted two top-10s and five top-25s....T2 at the Bell Canadian Open was best finish since a solo second at 1993 Sony Open. **2000:** Finished out of the top 125 on the money list for the first time since 1994 with 126th position. Was 125th heading into final official money event, the WGC-American Express Championship, but did not qualify for event and Joe Ozaki passed him on TOUR money list...First of two top-10s came at the BellSouth Classic where he opened with 68-66 and had a one-stroke lead through 36 holes. Shot 74 in the final round of the rain-shortened event and finished T5. It was his best finish since T4 at the 1995 Ideon Classic and ended a streak of six straight missed cuts to start his season. **1999:** Became the fourth player in tournament history to ace the par-3 17th hole at THE PLAYERS Championship. Ace came in first round...Had share of Shell Houston Open 36-hole lead with Hal Sutton but finished T10. **1998:** Had four top-10s, including a T9 at the Canon Greater Hartford Open when he shot a final-round 65 and a T6 at the Buick Open when he fired a final-round 64. **1997:** Recorded a T10 in the PGA Championship at Winged Foot. It was his best performance in a major since T6 finish at 1992 U.S. Open. **1992:** Inductee into Ohio State University Athletic Hall of Fame.**1990:** Won Hardee's Golf Classic, where he defeated Willie Wood in playoff. **1988:** Had best year when he posted 10 top-10 finishes, including two victories (Honda Classic and The INTERNATIONAL), two seconds and one third. $813,732 placed him third on money list. **1987:** Defeated Jeff Sluman for second B.C. Open title by four strokes at En-Joie GC. **1986:** Winner MCI Long Distance Driving competition. **1985:** Came from four strokes back to gain first TOUR title, at Greater Greensboro Open, by one over Isao Aoki and Craig Stadler...Won first of two B.C. Opens, by one stroke over Mike Reid. **Amateur:** Winner 1972 New York State Junior, 1980 New York State Amateur, 1981 New York State Open...Three-time All-American at Ohio State University and member of 1979 NCAA Championship team at Ohio State...Winner of 10 collegiate titles, including 1981 Big Ten Championship by 12 strokes...Named 1981 Ohio State Athlete of the Year.

PERSONAL:

Childhood friend of fellow PGA TOUR member Mike Hulbert…1992 inductee into Ohio State University Athletic Hall of Fame.

PLAYER STATISTICS

2004 PGA TOUR STATISTICS

Scoring Average	71.11	(96)
Driving Distance	291.5	(53)
Driving Accuracy Percentage	65.6%	(70)
Total Driving	123	(16)
Greens in Regulation Pct.	67.6%	(36)
Putting Average	1.811	(182)
Sand Save Percentage	35.1%	(193)
Eagles (Holes per)	294.0	(125)
Birdie Average	3.47	(114)
All-Around Ranking	869	(124)
Scoring Avg. Before Cut	71.10	(112)
Round 3 Scoring Avg.	70.84	(88)
Final Round Scoring Average	71.33	(76)
Birdie Conversion Percentage	27.3%	(157)
Par Breakers	19.6%	(116)

MISCELLANEOUS PGA TOUR STATISTICS

2004 Low Round/Round: 66–3 times, most recent FUNAI Classic at the WALT DISNEY WORLD Resort/1
Career Low Round/Round: 62–3 times, most recent 1987 Provident Classic/1
Career Largest Paycheck/Finish: $1,008,000–2004 Wachovia Championship/1

PGA TOUR CAREER SUMMARY — PLAYOFF RECORD: 2-1

Year	Events Played	Cuts Made	1st	2nd	3rd	Top 10	Top 25	Earnings	Rank
1982	2								
1983	3	2					1	$4,696	203
1984	33	23		1		3	9	116,528	59
1985	33	28	2		1	7	15	282,762	12
1986	35	29		2	2	7	17	341,231	14
1987	33	25	1	1		4	10	235,033	40
1988	30	27	2	2	1	10	16	813,732	3
1989	28	20				3	9	196,092	72
1990	27	15	1			3	5	307,207	46
1991	28	19				2	6	168,352	94
1992	32	22			1	6	13	395,354	35
1993	22	14		1	1	5	8	391,649	38
1994	22	12			1	1	3	114,563	145
1995	24	14				3	7	202,896	90
1996	28	18				3	7	275,531	77
1997	31	19				1	3	200,069	114
1998	27	22				4	10	466,797	61
1999	24	14				4	8	413,993	97
2000	30	14				2	4	388,341	126
2001	25	12		1		2	5	654,864	81
2002	32	19		1		3	6	790,750	87
2003	29	17			1	1	4	691,328	92
2004	31	18	1			2	3	1,536,881	41
Total	609	403	7	9	8	76	169	8,988,650	

PGA TOUR TOP TOURNAMENT SUMMARY

Year	82	83	84	85	86	87	88	89	90	91	92	93	94
Masters				T31	CUT	T35	T39	CUT		T46		T27	
U.S. Open	CUT			T15	T15	T51	T17	T33			T6	CUT	
British Open					CUT								
PGA			T62	T28	T53	CUT	CUT	CUT		T63	T56	W/D	
THE PLAYERS			CUT	T27	T17	T63	T16	T34	T46	T41	T46	T16	T35
TOUR Championship							T21						

Year	95	96	97	98	99	00	01	02	03	04
U.S. Open				T43	CUT			CUT	CUT	CUT
PGA		T14	T10	T40	W/D			T64		CUT
THE PLAYERS		CUT	T31	T61	T10	CUT		CUT	CUT	T74
WGC-NEC Invitational										T32

NATIONAL TEAMS: Kirin Cup, 1988; World Cup, 1991.

Vijay Singh (VEE-jay SING)

EXEMPT STATUS: Winner, 2004 PGA Championship (through 2009)
FULL NAME: Vijay Singh
HEIGHT: 6-2
WEIGHT: 198
BIRTHDATE: February 22, 1963
BIRTHPLACE: Lautoka, Fiji
RESIDENCE: Ponte Vedra Beach, FL

FAMILY: Wife, Ardena Seth; Qass Seth (6/19/90)
SPECIAL INTERESTS: Snooker, cricket, rugby, soccer
TURNED PROFESSIONAL: 1982
JOINED TOUR: Spring 1993

PGA TOUR VICTORIES (24):

1993 Buick Classic. **1995** Phoenix Open, Buick Classic. **1997** Memorial Tournament, Buick Open. **1998** PGA Championship, Sprint International. **1999** Honda Classic. **2000** Masters Tournament. **2002** Shell Houston Open, THE TOUR Championship presented by Coca-Cola. **2003** Phoenix Open, EDS Byron Nelson Championship, John Deere Classic, FUNAI Classic at the WALT DISNEY WORLD Resort. **2004** AT&T Pebble Beach National Pro-Am, Shell Houston Open, HP Classic of New Orleans, Buick Open, PGA Championship, Deutsche Bank Championship, Bell Canadian Open, 84 LUMBER Classic, Chrysler Championship.

INTERNATIONAL VICTORIES (22):

1984 Malaysian PGA Championship [Asia]. **1988** Nigerian Open [Afr], Swedish PGA. **1989** Volvo Open di Firenze [Eur], Ivory Coast Open [Afr], Nigerian Open [Afr], Zimbabwe Open [SAf]. **1990** El Bosque Open [Eur]. **1991** King Hassan Trophy [Morocco]. **1992** Turespana Masters Open de Andalucia [Eur], Malaysian Open [Asia], Volvo German Open [Eur]. **1993** Bells Cup [SAf]. **1994** Scandinavian Masters [Eur], Trophee Lancome [Eur]. **1995** Passport Open [Asia], **1997** South African Open [SAf], Toyota World Match Play Championship [Eur], **2000** Johnnie Walker Taiwan Open. **2001** Carlsberg Malaysian Open, Caltex Singapore Masters. **2003** TELUS Canadian Skins Game.

BEST 2004 PGA TOUR FINISHES:

1—AT&T Pebble Beach National Pro-Am, Shell Houston Open, HP Classic of New Orleans, Buick Open, PGA Championship, Deutsche Bank Championship, Bell Canadian Open, 84 LUMBER Classic, Chrysler Championship; 2—Mercedes Championships, FUNAI Classic at the WALT DISNEY WORLD Resort; T3—FBR Open; T4—Buick Classic, John Deere Classic; T6—Masters Tournament; 9—THE TOUR Championship presented by Coca-Cola; T10—Sony Open in Hawaii, Wachovia Championship.

2004 SEASON:

Player of the Year put together one of the finest seasons in golf history, posting nine wins and earning a PGA TOUR-record $10,905,166 while becoming No. 1 in the Official World Golf Ranking. Became just the sixth player in TOUR history to accumulate nine wins in a season and first since Tiger Woods in 2000. The others: Paul Runyan (9/1933), Byron Nelson (18/1945), Ben Hogan (13/1946, 10/1948) and Sam Snead (11/1950). Led the TOUR in top-10s for the second straight season with 18 in 29 events. The 36 over a two-year period (2003-2004) were the most since Tom Kite recorded 36 during the 1981 (21) and 1982 (15) seasons…Finished second, one stroke behind Stuart Appleby, at the season-opening Mercedes Championships for ninth consecutive top-10 dating back to the 2003 WGC-NEC Invitational. Posted a 9-under-par 64 in the second round, including seven consecutive birdies on Nos. 12-18, to take the 36-hole lead by one stroke over Appleby…The next week, finished T10 at the Sony Open in Hawaii, aided by four rounds in the 60s…Posted his 11th consecutive top-10 on the PGA TOUR, with a T3 at the FBR Open…Picked up a victory for the third consecutive year and sixth out of the last seven with his win at the AT&T Pebble Beach National Pro-Am. Shared third-round lead with Arron Oberholser before final-round 69 (one of just five rounds in the 60s Sunday) gave him a three-stroke victory over Jeff Maggert. Extended his consecutive top-10 streak to 12 straight, two behind Jack Nicklaus for the modern-day record and longest on TOUR since Nicklaus had 12 straight in 1975. Win jumped him to the top of the money list for the first time in 2004…Top-10 streak of 12 straight ended the next week after missed cut at Buick Invitational…Past champion recovered from opening rounds of 75-73 to finish T6 at the Masters. Rounds of 69-69 on the weekend and a 286 total were seven strokes shy of champion Phil Mickelson. Top-10 was fourth in 11 appearances at Augusta National, including three straight…With rounds of 74-66-69-68-277, won the Shell Houston Open for the second time in three years. Opening 74 was highest first-round score for winner on TOUR since Mark O'Meara posted 74 in opening round en route to victory at the 1998 Masters. Has seven top-10s in nine starts at Shell event, having never missed a cut. Monday finish after rain postponed the completion of the third round and the final round…First player since Kenny Perry to win PGA TOUR events in back-to-back weeks, coming from four strokes back in the final round to capture the HP Classic of New Orleans for 18th career TOUR victory. After opening 70-65-68, closed with a 9-under-par 63 (7-under-par 29 on back nine) that included a 30-foot birdie putt on the par-4 72nd hole to clip 54-hole leader Joe Ogilvie and Phil Mickelson by one stroke at 22-under-par. Second time with back-to-back TOUR victories (1998 PGA and International) and fourth Monday finish victory (1997 Memorial Tournament, 2003 John Deere Classic, 2004 Shell Houston Open). Surpassed $30-million in career earnings and re-took 2004 PGA TOUR Official Money List lead with $4,267,866…Finished T10 at the Wachovia Championship for his fourth consecutive top-10 and eighth top-10 in 12 starts during season…Opened with an 8-under 63 at the Buick Classic to take the first-round lead and then finished T4. It marked the 14th time that he had been a leader/co-leader through 18 holes…In defense of John Deere Classic, posted four rounds in the 60s to finish T4, two shots out of Mark Hensby-John E. Morgan playoff…Won fourth event of season at Buick Open, holding off John Daly by one shot and Tiger Woods by two. Grabbed the lead after 18 holes with a 9-under 63, using a traditional putter for the first time in several years. Also held a share of the 36-hole lead and entered final round with a two-stroke lead over Daly. On Sunday, Daly grabbed the early advantage by posting three birdies and an eagle in the first four holes. Singh responded with six birdies and a bogey en route to becoming just the third multiple winner of the Buick Open. Seventh win since turning 40, eclipsing Greg Norman, Loren Roberts and Hal Sutton for the lead among active players…Picked up his third major victory by defeating Chris DiMarco and Justin Leonard in a three-hole playoff in the PGA Championship at Whistling Straits. Shared second-round lead with Leonard and held one-stroke margin over Leonard through 54 holes.

PGA TOUR CAREER SUMMARY — PLAYOFF RECORD: 5-1

Year	Events Played	Cuts Made	1st	2nd	3rd	Top 10	Top 25	Earnings	Rank
1992	4	4				1	3	$70,680	156
1993	14	12	1	1		6	10	657,831	19
1994	21	16		2		3	7	325,959	52
1995	22	17	2			9	13	1,018,713	9
1996	24	24		1		9	16	855,140	17
1997	21	21	2			4	9	1,059,236	16
1998	26	23	2	3		7	18	2,238,998	2
1999	29	26	1	1	1	11	21	2,283,233	4
2000	26	24	1	1	3	8	15	2,573,835	5
2001	26	24		2	4	14	22	3,440,829	4
2002	28	24	2		2	11	17	3,756,563	3
2003	27	26	4	5		18	24	7,573,907	1
2004	29	28	9	2	1	18	24	10,905,166	1
Total	297	269	24	18	11	119	199	36,760,089	
EUROPEAN TOUR									
2004	3	3				1	3	199,725	

PGA TOUR TOP TOURNAMENT SUMMARY

Year	89	90	91	92	93	94	95	96	97	98	99	00	01
Masters						T27	CUT	T39	T17	CUT	T24	**1**	T18
U.S. Open					CUT		T10	T7	T77	T25	T3	T8	T7
British Open	T23	T12	T12	T51	T59	T20	T6	T11	T38	T19	CUT	T11	T13
PGA				T48	4	CUT	CUT	T5	T13	**1**	T49	CUT	T51
THE PLAYERS					T28	T55	T43	T8	T31	T54	T20	T33	2
TOUR Championship					T16		6	T9	T10	2	T9	T3	17
WGC-Accenture Match Play											T17	T33	T17
WGC-NEC Invitational											T15		T13
WGC-American Express Champ											T16	T3	CNL

Year	02	03	04
Masters	7	T6	T6
U.S. Open	T30	T20	T28
British Open	CUT	T2	T20
PGA	8	T34	**1**
THE PLAYERS	CUT	CUT	T13
TOUR Championship	**1**	T5	9
WGC-Accenture Match Play	T17		T17
WGC-NEC Invitational	T11	T6	T32
WGC-American Express Champ	3	T2	

NATIONAL TEAMS: The Presidents Cup (5), 1994, 1996, 1998, 2000, 2003; World Cup (2), 2001, 2002.

Vijay Singh (Continued)

Final-round 76 was good enough to get him into playoff after Leonard bogeyed the 72nd hole. Made the only birdie of the playoff on the first hole (par-4 10th) to secure his fourth playoff win in five tries. Became 18th player in PGA Championship history to win multiple titles. Final-round 4-over 76 was the highest 18-hole score by a PGA champion and the highest final-round score for a major winner since Reg Whitcombe shot a closing 78 at Royal St. George's to win the 1938 British Open...Jumped Ernie Els for No. 2 spot in the Official World Golf Ranking, 10 points behind No. 1 Tiger Woods...Moved to No. 1 with victory at the Deutsche Bank Championship, dueling Woods down the stretch before topping Woods and Adam Scott by three strokes for sixth TOUR victory of the year....The following week, win at the Bell Canadian Open took three extra holes versus Canadian Mike Weir. Trailed Weir by three strokes through 54 holes and posted final-round, 2-under 69 but did not get into playoff until Weir bogeyed the 72nd hole. Improved playoff record to 5-1...Earned wire-to-wire victory for the first time in his career at the 84 LUMBER Classic. Elevated his season earnings to $9,455,566, the most money earned in one season on TOUR, surpassing Woods' record of $9,188,321 in 2000...In defense of FUNAI Classic at THE WALT DISNEY WORLD Resort, finished T2 to Ryan Palmer...Broke the $10-million mark with ninth victory of season at the Chrysler Championship, posting four rounds in the 60s en route to record-setting 18-under-par performance...Season came to an end with a ninth-place finish at THE TOUR Championship presented by Coca-Cola. With his $180,000 paycheck, brought his TOUR-record, single-season earnings to $10,905,166. The top-10 was a record ninth in 11 appearances at THE TOUR Championship...Captured the Fall Finish presented by PricewaterhouseCoopers for the third consecutive year on the strength of four wins and a runner-up in six starts.

CAREER HIGHLIGHTS:

Has won in Malaysia, France, Nigeria, Ivory Coast, Morocco, Zimbabwe, Singapore, Spain, Germany, England, South Africa, Sweden, Taiwan, Canada and U.S. **2003:** A four-time winner on the PGA TOUR, clinched first career PGA TOUR money title at the season-ending TOUR Championship, where a T5 finish worth $228,000 brought total official money in 27 events to $7,573,907, topping Tiger Woods by $900,494. The season total was also second all-time, at the time, to Woods' $9,188,321 in 2000. A total of 18 top-10s were the most on TOUR since Tim Kite posted 21 top-10s in 26 starts in 1981...Picked up career victory No. 12 at the Phoenix Open, a tournament he also won in 1995. Fired final-round, 8-under 63 to come from two strokes back of Harrison Frazar after 54 holes to win by three strokes over John Huston. Bested his TOUR career low for total score (261) and in relation to par (23-under) with the victory...Held one-stroke lead through 36 and 54 holes at the EDS Byron Nelson Championship. Went on to win by two over Nick Price. Won for the first time in his 40s and recorded his fifth multiple-win season of his career. One of 11 players to win on the PGA TOUR over the age of 40...Along with Jim Furyk, set the U.S. Open record for best first 36 holes with a 7-under 133. His 7-under 63 during the second round tied Johnny Miller (1973), Jack Nicklaus and Tom Weiskopf (1980) for best 18-hole score in U.S. Open history. Finished event T20...Third victory of the season came at the John Deere Classic. Did not lead until final round but was within striking distance the entire tournament. Due to rainout of Saturday's third round, Singh played 23 holes on Sunday and the remaining 13 on Monday. Finished the day Sunday at 12-under in a tie for lead with J.L. Lewis. Pulled ahead on back nine Monday morning to win by four strokes. Victory moved him to No. 1 on the money list, a position he held for three weeks...Won fourth TOUR event of season by posting four rounds in the 60s at the FUNAI Classic at the WALT DISNEY WORLD Resort. Held second-round lead and shared third-round lead with Stewart Cink, John Rollins and Scott Verplank. Paycheck moved him into the top spot on the money list for second time during season. Became third player (Tiger Woods-5, Davis Love III-4) in 2003 to win at least four times, the first time since 1973 (Jack Nicklaus, 7; Tom Weiskopf, 5; Bruce Crampton, 4) three players had won at least four times...Played for the International squad at The Presidents Cup for the fifth time in career. **2002:** Returned to the victory circle after one-year hiatus. Won multiple events for the first time since 1998 (Shell Houston Open and THE TOUR Championship). Third-place finish on money list with $3,756,563 was best since finishing second in 1998...At the Shell Houston Open, collected his first PGA TOUR victory since the 2000 Masters, a span of 50 starts. Set a new 72-hole scoring record at the TPC at The Woodlands with a 22-under-par total. Rounds of 67-65-66-68—266 earned a six-stroke victory over Darren Clarke...Third-round leader at THE TOUR Championship for third consecutive time at East Lake GC (1998 and 2000) and won for first time by two strokes over Charles Howell III. **2001:** Despite failing to win for the first time in five years, put together a consistent season with a TOUR-best 14 top-10s and $3,440,829 in earnings, fourth on the money list. Finished second twice, at the AT&T Pebble Beach National Pro-Am, where he shot a final-round 69 but was passed by Davis Love III's 63, and at THE PLAYERS Championship, where he made triple-bogey-7 on the par-4 14th, eagle on the par-5 16th and birdie on the par-3 17th to complete a 68 and finish one stroke behind Tiger Woods. **2000:** Extended victory string to four straight seasons and captured his second major in 20-month period with victory in the Masters. Won by three strokes over Els...Had LASIK surgery on May 31. **1999:** Earned his eighth career TOUR victory in March at the Honda Classic. Stood nine strokes behind Eric Booker after 36 holes and five back through 54 holes but closed with 69 for two-stroke victory over Payne Stewart. **1998:** Recorded consecutive victories in summer at the PGA Championship and International in August. In PGA at Sahalee opened with even-par 70, followed by a course-record-tying 66 that produced a one-stroke lead. Third-round 67 brought tie for lead with Steve Stricker, and his closing 68 good for two-stroke win over Stricker. Became 10th winner in past 11 years to make PGA his first major victory...Consecutive cuts made streak ended at 53 at Masters. Previous missed cut came at 1995 PGA...A week after PGA victory, earned second win in two weeks and third top-10 in month of August with six-point win over Phil Mickelson and Willie Wood at International...Closed year at East Lake GC with playoff loss to Hal Sutton at THE TOUR Championship after opening week with course record 7-under-par 63. **1997:** Won two TOUR events and earned more than $1 million for second time in career...Made 24 consecutive cuts in 1996 and 21 in row in 1997...First victory came at the Memorial Tournament. Shot 70 in first round and stood four strokes out of lead. Followed with second-round 65 to pull to within three strokes of lead. Due to heavy rains, tournament was shortened to 54 holes. He fired final-round 67 to earn two-stroke victory over Jim Furyk and Greg Norman. Memorial was his first win without a playoff...Second victory came at Buick Open. Was his third win at Buick-sponsored event. Closing 66 matched low round of day and earned six-stroke victory over six players. **1996:** Season featured June-July hot streak: T7 U.S. Open, T8 Motorola Western Open, T11 British Open and T5 PGA Championship. **1995:** After being hampered by back and neck problems in 1994, came back to win twice at Phoenix Open and Buick Classic. **1993:** PGA TOUR Rookie of the Year based on Buick Classic victory in playoff over Mark Wiebe and T4 in PGA that included a second-round 63.

PERSONAL:

Fiji's only world-class golfer...Learned game from his father, an airplane technician who also taught golf...Admired Tom Weiskopf while growing up and used Weiskopf's swing as early model for his own...Noted for his rigorous practice routine...Once held a club professional position in Borneo...Of Indian ancestry, first name means "victory" in Hindi...Served as Honorary Chairperson for 1999 National Golf Day, PGA of America's annual fundraiser for junior golf...Teamed with son Qass in Office Depot Father-Son in 2003 and 2004...Established, with wife and son, the Vijay Singh Charitable Foundation, benefiting charities and non-profit agencies that provide assistance, shelter, counseling and support to women and children who are victims of domestic abuse. The Betty Griffin House of St John's County, FL (Safety Shelter of St. John's County) was one of the first beneficiaries of the foundation...Through the 2004 CRESTOR Charity Challenge, donated $150,000 to American Red Cross to support the victims of hurricanes in Florida.

PLAYER STATISTICS

2004 PGA TOUR STATISTICS

Scoring Average	68.84	(1)
Driving Distance	300.8	(13)
Driving Accuracy Percentage	60.4%	(149)
Total Driving	162	(50)
Greens in Regulation Pct.	73.0%	(2)
Putting Average	1.757	(37)
Sand Save Percentage	50.9%	(71)
Eagles (Holes per)	116.5	(8)
Birdie Average	4.40	(1)
All-Around Ranking	282	(2)
Scoring Avg. Before Cut	68.91	(1)
Round 3 Scoring Avg.	69.15	(3)
Final Round Scoring Average	69.78	(6)
Birdie Conversion Percentage	32.7%	(10)
Par Breakers	25.3%	(1)

MISCELLANEOUS PGA TOUR STATISTICS

2004 Low Round/Round: 63–5 times, most recent Deutsche Bank Championship/2

Career Low Round/Round: 62–1998 Canon Greater Hartford Open/4

Career Largest Paycheck/Finish: $1,125,000–2004 PGA Championship/1

Heath Slocum

EXEMPT STATUS: 2004 tournament winner (through 2006)
FULL NAME: Tyler Heath Slocum
HEIGHT: 5-8
WEIGHT: 150
BIRTHDATE: February 3, 1974
BIRTHPLACE: Baton Rouge, LA
RESIDENCE: Pensacola, FL; plays out of Steelwood (Loxley, AL) and Moors GC (Milton, FL)

FAMILY: Single
EDUCATION: University of South Alabama (1996, Physical Education)
SPECIAL INTERESTS: Fishing, hunting
TURNED PROFESSIONAL: 1996
JOINED TOUR: 2001
Nationwide Tour Alumunus

PGA TOUR VICTORIES (1):

2004 Chrysler Classic of Tucson.

NATIONWIDE TOUR VICTORIES (3):

2001 Greater Cleveland Open, Knoxville Open, Omaha Classic.

BEST 2004 PGA TOUR FINISHES:

1—Chrysler Classic of Tucson; T10—Wachovia Championship, Valero Texas Open.

2004 SEASON:

The first of 10 first-time winners on the PGA TOUR in 2004, capturing the Chrysler Classic of Tucson. In 78th career start he carried his 54-hole lead to a victory with a final-round 65. Becomes the third player who earned an immediate promotion from the Nationwide Tour to the PGA TOUR to win on TOUR, joining Chris Smith and Chad Campbell...Was among the leaders all week at the Wachovia Championship. Finished T10 in Charlotte, his second top-10 of the season and fifth of his career...Finished T10 at Valero Texas Open, six strokes behind champion Bart Bryant, posting four rounds in the 60s. His $84,000 payday in San Antonio pushed him over the $1-million mark in season earnings for the first time in his career.

CAREER HIGHLIGHTS:

2003: Got off to a slow start making the cut in just five of first 16 starts, but changed that in the second half of his season making 13 of 16...Second career runner-up finish was a T2 at the Greater Milwaukee Open, thanks to a final-round 66, which included a birdie on the final hole...Shared the first-round lead at the Valero Texas Open after posting a course record-tying, career-best 61. **2002:** Sixth-ranked player of the 11 rookies who ended the season in the top 125...Had one-stroke lead with three holes to play at the WORLDCOM CLASSIC-The Heritage of Golf but a double bogey on the 16th hole left him in second place, one stroke behind winner Justin Leonard. **2001:** Became second person since Chris Smith in 1997 to earn promotion to PGA TOUR by winning three Nationwide Tour events in same season—Greater Cleveland Open, Knoxville Open and Omaha Classic...Became second player in Nationwide Tour history to complete 72 holes without a bogey at Dayton Open, joining Clark Dennis, who accomplished the feat at the 1997 Upstate Classic...Nationwide Tour record of 106 consecutive holes without a bogey came to an end during the second round. He followed the three-putt bogey with another 37 consecutive holes without a bogey. Over the three-week period, finished 21-, 23- and 21-under and posted a scoring average of 66.41...Completed the trifecta with a victory at the Omaha Classic, where ironically Smith also earned his promotion. Held on to his 54-hole one-stroke lead to defeat Rod Pampling by a stroke. With $337,090, became the first player in Nationwide Tour history to surpass the $300,000 mark in a season. **2000:** Regained Nationwide Tour membership at TOUR Qualifying School. **Amateur:** Three-time All-America for South Alabama...Captured the Sun Belt Conference individual title to help the Jaguars capture the team championship.

PERSONAL:

Father is a golf professional and head of the DP TOUR...Contracted ulcerative colitis in November 1997 and dropped from 150 to 122 pounds. Missed the next year and one-half of golf...Played on the same high school golf team as former TOUR player Boo Weekley.

PLAYER STATISTICS

2004 PGA TOUR STATISTICS

Scoring Average	71.26	(110)
Driving Distance	280.1	(157)
Driving Accuracy Percentage	71.3%	(17)
Total Driving	174	(67)
Greens in Regulation Pct.	67.1%	(41)
Putting Average	1.788	(122)
Sand Save Percentage	54.3%	(31)
Eagles (Holes per)	324.0	(141)
Birdie Average	3.41	(127)
All-Around Ranking	746	(93)
Scoring Avg. Before Cut	71.23	(129)
Round 3 Scoring Avg.	70.33	(49)
Final Round Scoring Average	70.79	(45)
Birdie Conversion Percentage	27.1%	(162)
Par Breakers	19.3%	(129)

MISCELLANEOUS PGA TOUR STATISTICS

2004 Low Round/Round: 64–2 times, most recent Valero Texas Open/3
Career Low Round/Round: 61–2003 Valero Texas Open/1
Career Largest Paycheck/Finish: $540,000–2004 Chrysler Classic of Tucson/1

PGA TOUR CAREER SUMMARY — PLAYOFF RECORD: 0-0

Year	Events Played	Cuts Made	1st	2nd	3rd	Top 10	Top 25	Earnings	Rank
2001	8	6						$45,670	
2002	32	15		1		2	6	864,615	76
2003	32	18		1		2	5	815,812	80
2004	31	14	1			3	6	1,066,837	72
Total	103	53	1	2		7	17	2,792,933	
NATIONWIDE TOUR									
1997	19	5					2	6,567	142
2000	1								
2001	18	11	3		2	6	8	339,670	3
Total	38	16	3		2	6	10	346,237	

PGA TOUR TOP TOURNAMENT SUMMARY

Year	02	03	04
U.S. Open	CUT		
PGA	22		CUT
THE PLAYERS		CUT	T58

Jeff Sluman

EXEMPT STATUS: 77th on 2004 money list
FULL NAME: Jeffrey George Sluman
HEIGHT: 5-7
WEIGHT: 140
BIRTHDATE: September 11, 1957
BIRTHPLACE: Rochester, NY
RESIDENCE: Hinsdale, IL
FAMILY: Wife, Linda; Kathryn Doreen (4/22/98)
EDUCATION: Florida State University (1980, Finance)
SPECIAL INTERESTS: Old cars, stock market, Akitas, wine
TURNED PROFESSIONAL: 1980
Q SCHOOL: Fall 1982, 1984

PGA TOUR VICTORIES (6):

1988 PGA Championship. **1997** Tucson Chrysler Classic. **1998** Greater Milwaukee Open. **1999** Sony Open in Hawaii. **2001** B.C. Open. **2002** Greater Milwaukee Open.

OTHER VICTORIES (3):

1999 CVS Charity Classic [with Stuart Appleby]. **2003** CVS Charity Classic [with Rocco Mediate], Franklin Templeton Shark Shootout [with Hank Kuehne].

BEST 2004 PGA TOUR FINISHES:

T6—Buick Open; T8—John Deere Classic; T9—Buick Championship.

2004 SEASON:

Cracked the $1-million mark for fourth straight season and sixth in last seven years, although finish on money list (77th) was lowest since 1993...Was disqualified after four holes during the third round at the Buick Classic for playing a non-comforming ball under Rule 5-1. He recognized his golf ball did not have the proper markings after he hit his tee shot on No. 1 and notified a PGA TOUR Rules Official...Posted a T8 at the John Deere Classic for first top-10 since a solo third at the 2003 Bank of America Colonial...Second top-10 in three starts was T6 at the Buick Open, with rounds of 70-67-68-66—271. Finished six shots behind champion Vijay Singh...Third top-10 was T9 at the Buick Championship, aided by a career-tying, 8-under-par 62 in the final round.

CAREER HIGHLIGHTS:

2003: Played in at least 30 events for the sixth consecutive season...Recorded first top-10 of the season with a T7 at the Bay Hill Invitational...Entered final round at MCI Heritage one stroke behind Stewart Cink after third-round 7-under-par 64. Finished T10 after closing with a 72...Held the first-round lead at the EDS Byron Nelson Championship. One back of Vijay Singh through 54 holes, but a closing 73 dropped him into T14...Third at the Bank of America Colonial made it four straight tournaments finishing in the top 15...Named Captain's Assistant for The Presidents Cup team by Jack Nicklaus...T13 at the Chrysler Championship, the final full-field event of the season to move from 42nd to 40th on the final money list and qualify for his 15th trip to the Masters in 2004...Teamed with Hank Kuehne to win the Franklin Templeton Shark Shootout. Survived a three-team playoff with Chad Campbell/Shaun Micheel and Brad Faxon/Scott McCarron. Won with a birdie at the second extra hole. **2002:** Has won on TOUR in five of the last six seasons...Began Greater Milwaukee Open one back of Tommy Armour III after opening-round 64. Tied with Armour and Kirk Triplett for second-round lead at 12-under 130. Third-round 63 left him two strokes ahead of Steve Lowery and at 20-under-par 193 surpassed the GMO record of 19-under-par set by Loren Roberts in 2000. The 63 was one off his career low, a 62, at the 1992 GTE Byron Nelson Classic, and was his lowest round since a 63 during the third round of the 1998 GMO. Sunday 68 gave him four-stroke victory over Lowery and Tim Herron...Finished T2 at the Invensys Classic at Las Vegas, one shot behind champion Phil Tataurangi. Paycheck of $440,000 pushed season winnings to career-best $2,083,181, moving from 31st to 15th on the money list and clinching a spot in season-ending TOUR Championship. **2001:** T2 at Nissan Open was best finish since 1999. Lost in six-man playoff won by Robert Allenby at Riviera CC...Held 54-hole lead at Greater Milwaukee Open, which he won in 1998. Closing 72 dropped him to T10...Earned fifth PGA TOUR title and first playoff victory at B.C. Open. Career playoff record had been 0-6 coming into the event. Tied for 54-hole lead with Paul Gow. Each closed with 66, and Sluman won playoff with birdie on second extra hole. Win was third event since turning 40. Became fifth player with upstate New York ties to win B.C. Open. **2000:** Streak of three consecutive years with a victory ended...Was among the top-25 16 times in 32 starts. **1999:** Won at Sony Open in Hawaii, where he posted a two-stroke victory over Davis Love III, Jeff Maggert, Len Mattiace, Chris Perry and Tommy Tolles. Birdied final two holes to seal the victory...Lost in three-man playoff involving winner Glen Day and Payne Stewart at MCI Classic...Earned second runner-up finish at MasterCard Colonial where he was part of five-way T2, one behind Olin Browne...Led TOUR in Sand Saves with 67.3 percent. **1998:** Earned more than $1 million for the first time...Lost in playoff at FedEx St. Jude Classic, where Nick Price birdied second extra hole...Earned title at Greater Milwaukee Open where third-round 63 produced 54-hole tie for lead with Chris Perry. Closing 68 gave him one-stroke victory over Steve Stricker. Won with best friend Rick Bruder, a non-golfer, serving as a caddie for the first time. **1997:** Had eight second-place finishes in between first and second victories (1988-1997). Captured the Tucson Chrysler Classic after opening 75, when he stood nine strokes out of lead. Final-round 67 produced one-stroke victory over Steve Jones. His opening 75 was highest by winner since Mark O'Meara posted first-round 75 at 1996 Greater Greensboro Chrysler Classic. **1992:** Finished second at U.S. Open, where final-round 71 was one of only four

PGA TOUR CAREER SUMMARY — PLAYOFF RECORD: 1-6

Year	Events Played	Cuts Made	1st	2nd	3rd	Top 10	Top 25	Earnings	Rank
1983	20	11					2	$13,643	171
1984	1	1						603	282
1985	25	18				4	10	100,523	78
1986	34	24				7	12	154,129	60
1987	32	22		2		6	11	335,590	27
1988	32	30	1		1	6	15	503,321	18
1989	23	16				4	6	154,507	89
1990	31	22		1		2	6	264,012	56
1991	30	24		2		7	13	552,979	23
1992	30	26		2	1	8	17	729,027	14
1993	27	21				1	6	187,841	93
1994	30	16		1		4	8	301,178	59
1995	29	20		1	2	7	12	563,681	31
1996	30	23		1		7	14	650,128	28
1997	29	20	1		1	3	9	634,203	34
1998	30	25	1	1	1	5	11	1,148,375	21
1999	31	26	1	2		6	13	1,621,491	17
2000	32	25				1	16	877,390	54
2001	30	23	1	1	1	7	15	1,841,952	21
2002	32	27	1	1		6	15	2,250,187	15
2003	31	22			1	3	15	1,609,748	40
2004	28	23				3	8	1,007,635	77
Total	617	465	6	15	8	97	234	15,502,142	

PGA TOUR TOP TOURNAMENT SUMMARY

Year	86	87	88	89	90	91	92	93	94	95	96	97	98
Masters			T45	T8	T27	T29	T4	T17	T25	T41	CUT	T7	CUT
U.S. Open	T62		CUT	CUT	T14	CUT	2	T11	T9	T13	T50	T28	T10
British Open				CUT	T25	T101	CUT	CUT			T59		
PGA	T30	T14	**1**	T24	T31	T61	T12	T61	T25	T8	T41	CUT	T27
THE PLAYERS	T40	2	T45	CUT	CUT	CUT	T40	T46	CUT	T49	T41	CUT	CUT
TOUR Championship		T27	T26			T10	T13				T9		T11

Year	99	00	01	02	03	04
Masters	T31	18		T24	44	43
U.S. Open	CUT	CUT		T24	CUT	
British Open	T45	T60			CUT	
PGA	T54	T41	CUT	T23	CUT	T62
THE PLAYERS	T46	T17	T33	T4	T32	T26
TOUR Championship	T5		T20	T24		
WGC-Accenture Match Play	T33	T17	T17	T33	T17	T33
WGC-NEC Invitational					T39	
WGC-American Express Champ	T34		CNL	T43		

NATIONAL TEAMS: Presidents Cup, 2003 (Captain's Assistant).

Jeff Sluman (Continued)

sub-par rounds that day...Had earlier second-place finish in AT&T Pebble Beach National Pro-Am...Was T4 at Masters, where he became first player ever to ace fourth hole during opening-round 65 that produced tie for lead. **1991:** Finished one stroke behind Ted Schulz at Nissan Open and lost playoff to Billy Andrade at Kemper Open. **1988:** Won PGA Championship at Oak Tree GC with one of the finest closing rounds in tournament history. Trailed Paul Azinger by three strokes through 54 holes, then shot 6-under-par 65 to win by three.

PERSONAL:

Has been a Chicago Bulls season ticketholder since 1996...Loves Formula One auto racing...Big fan of the Florida State Seminoles, Chicago Bears and Chicago Cubs...Serious wine collector, owns about 2,000 bottles, dating back to 1957...Co-owner with Dudley Hart of Lakeshore GC in Rochester, NY, a course he played regularly growing up...Good friend of 1986 Indianapolis 500 winner Bobby Rahal...After disqualifying himself at 1996 Bay Hill Invitational, refused to take undue credit for act, quoting Bobby Jones: "It would be like congratulating someone for not robbing a bank."...Teamed up with office supply retailer OfficeMax to create The Jeff Sluman & OfficeMax "Drive for Hope"—a charity fund that is poised to raise $450,000 to $750,000 for the City of Hope and other charities.

PLAYER STATISTICS

2004 PGA TOUR STATISTICS

Scoring Average	70.74	(49)
Driving Distance	279.6	(165)
Driving Accuracy Percentage	67.9%	(48)
Total Driving	213	(129)
Greens in Regulation Pct.	68.8%	(15)
Putting Average	1.777	(99)
Sand Save Percentage	45.9%	(141)
Eagles (Holes per)	436.5	(172)
Birdie Average	3.71	(57)
All-Around Ranking	746	(93)
Scoring Avg. Before Cut	69.84	(10)
Round 3 Scoring Avg.	72.19	(173)
Final Round Scoring Average	70.86	(48)
Birdie Conversion Percentage	28.6%	(107)
Par Breakers	20.8%	(65)

MISCELLANEOUS PGA TOUR STATISTICS

2004 Low Round/Round: 62–2 times, most recent Chrysler Championship/1
Career Low Round/Round: 62–4 times, most recent 2004 Chrysler Championship/1
Career Largest Paycheck/Finish: $558,000–2002 Greater Milwaukee Open/1

SHOTLink
AN IBM ON DEMAND BUSINESS SOLUTION

HOT SHOTS

Easiest Three Finishing Holes (2004)

Event/Course Name	Hole	Par	Avg Score	Avg to Par
Bob Hope Chrysler Classic Indian Wells CC**	16	4	3.77	-0.23
Bob Hope Chrysler Classic Indian Wells CC**	17	4	3.80	-0.20
Bob Hope Chrysler Classic Indian Wells CC**	18	5	4.48	-0.52
Total				**-0.95**

Toughest Three Finishing Holes (2004)

Event/Course Name	Hole	Par	Avg Score	Avg to Par
THE TOUR Championship presented by Coca-Cola East Lake GC	16	4	4.36	+0.36
THE TOUR Championship presented by Coca-Cola East Lake GC	17	4	4.28	+0.28
THE TOUR Championship presented by Coca-Cola East Lake GC	18	3	3.26	+0.26
Total				**+0.91**

Hardest First Holes (2004)

Event/Course Name	Hole	Par	Avg Score	Avg to Par
U.S. Open Championship Shinnecock Hills Golf Club	10	4	4.45	0.45
EDS Byron Nelson Championship Cottonwood Valley GC**	1	4	4.38	0.38
Masters Tournament Augusta National GC	1	4	4.35	0.35
Sony Open in Hawaii Waialae CC	1	4	4.34	0.34
BellSouth Classic TPC at Sugarloaf	1	4	4.33	0.33

Easiest First Holes (2004)

Event/Course Name	Hole	Par	Avg Score	Avg to Par
Nissan Open Riviera CC	1	5	4.32	-0.68
Ford Championship at Doral Doral Golf Resort & Spa	1	5	4.33	-0.67
FUNAI Classic at the WALT DISNEY WORLD Resort Palm GC**	1	5	4.39	-0.61
FUNAI Classic at the WALT DISNEY WORLD Resort Magnolia GC**	10	5	4.46	-0.54
Buick Invitational Torrey Pines (North Course)**	1	5	4.47	-0.53

Chris Smith

EXEMPT STATUS: 115th on 2004 money list
FULL NAME: Christopher McClain Smith
HEIGHT: 5-11
WEIGHT: 190
BIRTHDATE: April 15, 1969
BIRTHPLACE: Indianapolis, IN
RESIDENCE: Peru, IN; plays out of Rock Hollow GC
FAMILY: Wife, Beth; Abigail (2/28/93), Cameron McClain (3/24/97)

EDUCATION: Ohio State University (1991, Economics)
SPECIAL INTERESTS: Rodeo, whistling show tunes, bowling, Internet checkers
TURNED PROFESSIONAL: 1991
Q SCHOOL: 1998
JOINED TOUR: 1996
Nationwide Tour Alumnus

PGA TOUR VICTORIES (1):

2002 Buick Classic.

NATIONWIDE TOUR VICTORIES (5):

1995 Gateway Classic, Dakota Dunes Open. **1997** Upstate Classic, Dakota Dunes Open, Omaha Classic.

BEST 2004 PGA TOUR FINISH:

3—Chrysler Classic of Greensboro.

2004 SEASON:

His consistent play late in the season secured him a spot inside the top 125, after falling out in 2003...Grabbed the first-round lead at the Ford Championship at Doral with a 7-under-par 65 despite a double-bogey 6 at the par-4 18th. He stood 10-under through 13 after running off six consecutive birdies, but closed out his day with a bogey-par-double bogey finish to end the day with a one-stroke lead. Closing rounds of 76-71-68 dropped him to T27...Was two-strokes off the lead through 36 holes at the B.C. Open and three back of the lead through 54 holes. Finished T13...Ended the year strong, with his lone top-10 of the season, a solo third at Chrysler Classic of Greensboro, three shots behind champion Brent Geiberger. Jumped from No. 152 to No. 110 on money list with $312,800 paycheck, securing TOUR card for 2005.

CAREER HIGHLIGHTS:

2003: Finished outside the top 125 for the first time since he regained his TOUR card in 2001...Struggled with back pain throughout the first half of the season and posted his only top-10, a T5, at the Greater Milwaukee Open, thanks, in part, to a final-round 64. **2002:** For the second straight season had five top-10s, but this time was able to punch through for his first TOUR victory at the Buick Classic in his 148th TOUR start...After opening 66-69 at the Buick Classic, grabbed sole possession of 54-hole lead at 11-under-par with a third-round 67. Sewed up first-place check of $630,000 with a 1-under-par 70 in the final round, two strokes ahead of runners-up David Gossett, Pat Perez and Loren Roberts. Jumped from 149th in World Ranking to 57th...Fired career-low 63 during third round of the Buick Challenge. **2001:** Best finish of career prior to win was a T3 at the BellSouth Classic. Was T41 heading into the 36-hole Sunday finish...Recorded five top-10s. **2000:** Established a Nationwide Tour record with five runner-up finishes and finished in the top-25 in 13 of his 20 starts...Sixth-place finish on money list earned his PGA TOUR card for 2000 season...Tore tendon in left wrist at Omaha Classic in August which sidelined him for seven weeks...Finished season as No. 1 on Nationwide Tour career money list with $605,332. **1999:** Ranked sixth in Driving Distance (287.2) and had the longest drive on TOUR that year, a 427-yard effort in the final round of the Honda Classic. That drive is the longest recorded drive at a PGA TOUR event since such record keeping began in 1980. **1997:** Earned three of his five Nationwide Tour victories, making him the first player to take advantage of a three-win promotion that awards PGA TOUR membership to any Nationwide Tour player who wins three times in a year. Won the Dakota Dunes Open and the Omaha Classic in back-to-back weeks, becoming only the third player in TOUR history to accomplish that feat. Win at Dakota Dunes made him the first player in TOUR history to win the same tournament twice (1995, 1997). Victory in Omaha was a record-setting affair. Set TOUR scoring records for 72-hole score with a 258, strokes-under-par at 26 and winning margin (11 strokes)...Week prior to his consecutive wins, lost to Ben Bates in four-man playoff at Wichita Open...Defeated Terry Price by three strokes at the Upstate Classic for first victory of season...Named Player of the Year after finishing No. 1 on the money list with $225,201 in just 17 events...After earning PGA TOUR spot on Aug. 10, made cut in all five of his TOUR appearances in the fall and finished in top-20 three times. **1995:** Finishes seventh on Nationwide Tour money list to graduate to PGA TOUR for first time...Two-time winner, earning wins at the Gateway Classic and the Dakota Dunes Open in a three-week period. **Amateur:** All-American at Ohio State in 1991 and Big-10 Conference Individual Champion...1990 Indiana State Amateur Champion and Player of the Year.

PERSONAL:

Lifelong St. Louis Cardinals fan, became friends with catcher Tom Pagnozzi the week of his 1995 Gateway Classic victory in St. Louis.

PLAYER STATISTICS

2004 PGA TOUR STATISTICS

Scoring Average	71.51	(138)
Driving Distance	304.0	(5)
Driving Accuracy Percentage	59.5%	(156)
Total Driving	161	(47)
Greens in Regulation Pct.	70.4%	(7)
Putting Average	1.811	(182)
Sand Save Percentage	33.2%	(195)
Eagles (Holes per)	135.0	(19)
Birdie Average	3.67	(65)
All-Around Ranking	767	(98)
Scoring Avg. Before Cut	71.16	(120)
Round 3 Scoring Avg.	71.00	(101)
Final Round Scoring Average	72.06	(138)
Birdie Conversion Percentage	29.0%	(98)
Par Breakers	21.1%	(53)

MISCELLANEOUS PGA TOUR STATISTICS

2004 Low Round/Round: 65–2 times, most recent B.C. Open/2
Career Low Round/Round: 63–2002 Buick Challenge/3
Career Largest Paycheck/Finish: $630,000–2002 Buick Classic/1

PGA TOUR CAREER SUMMARY — PLAYOFF RECORD: 0-0

Year	Events Played	Cuts Made	1st	2nd	3rd	Top 10	Top 25	Earnings	Rank
1987A	1								
1991	1								
1993	3	1				1	1	$24,000	207
1994	2	1						3,075	294
1996	28	12						41,112	206
1997	6	6				1	3	120,768	151
1998	31	16				2	2	184,933	144
1999	28	11					1	116,794	184
2001	30	20			1	5	8	932,810	58
2002	30	21	1			5	8	1,361,094	43
2003	30	15				1	6	479,523	131
2004	33	19			1	1	4	692,785	115
Total	223	122	1		2	16	33	3,956,893	
NATIONWIDE TOUR									
1992	1								
1993	1								
1995	28	14	2	2	1	7	10	143,200	7
1997	17	16	3	2	1	8	12	225,201	1
1998	1	1						390	297
2000	20	17		5		7	13	236,541	6
Total	68	48	5	9	2	22	35	605,332	

PGA TOUR TOP TOURNAMENT SUMMARY

Year	97	98	99	00	01	02	03	04
U.S. Open	T60		T62		CUT		CUT	CUT
British Open						T76	71	
PGA					T29	T53		
THE PLAYERS						CUT	CUT	CUT
WGC-NEC Invitational						T55		

Craig Stadler

EXEMPT STATUS: 2003 tournament winner (through 2005)
FULL NAME: Craig Robert Stadler
HEIGHT: 5-10
WEIGHT: 255
BIRTHDATE: June 2, 1953
BIRTHPLACE: San Diego, CA
RESIDENCE: Evergreen, CO

FAMILY: Wife, Sue; Kevin (2/5/80), Chris (11/23/82)
EDUCATION: University of Southern California (1975)
SPECIAL INTERESTS: Hunting, wine collecting
TURNED PROFESSIONAL: 1975
Q SCHOOL: Spring 1976
JOINED TOUR: 1977

PGA TOUR VICTORIES (13):

1980 Bob Hope Desert Classic, Greater Greensboro Open. **1981** Kemper Open. **1982** Joe Garagiola-Tucson Open, Masters Tournament, Kemper Open, World Series of Golf. **1984** Byron Nelson Golf Classic. **1991** THE TOUR Championship. **1992** NEC World Series of Golf. **1994** Buick Invitational of California. **1996** Nissan Open. **2003** B.C. Open.

CHAMPIONS TOUR VICTORIES (8):

2003 Ford Senior Players Championship, Greater Hickory Classic at Rock Barn, SBC Championship. **2004** The ACE Group Classic, Bank of America Championship, JELD-WEN Tradition, The First Tee Open at Pebble Beach presented by Wal-Mart, SAS Championship presented by Forbes.

INTERNATIONAL VICTORIES (4):

1985 Canon European Masters [Eur]. **1987** Dunlop Phoenix [Jpn]. **1990** Scandinavian Enterprise Open [Eur]. **1992** Argentine Open.

BEST 2004 PGA TOUR FINISH:

T21—B.C. Open.

BEST 2004 CHAMPIONS TOUR FINISHES:

1—The ACE Group Classic, Bank of America Championship, JELD-WEN Tradition, The First Tee Open at Pebble Beach presented by Wal-Mart, SAS Championship presented by Forbes; 2—3M Championship; 3—Senior PGA Championship, MasterCard Championship; T4—Liberty Mutual Legends of Golf; T7—SBC Classic, U.S. Senior Open, Charles Schwab Cup Championship

2004 SEASON:

The Champions Tour Player of the Year played in two PGA TOUR events in Hawaii prior to the Champions Tour's opening tournament, the MasterCard Classic. Was T28 at the Mercedes Championships and then missed the cut at the Sony Open in Hawaii…Also played in the AT&T Pebble Beach National Pro-Am with his son Kevin and finished T35…Made an appearance at THE PLAYERS Championship, where he made the cut and finished T66…Was T21 in defense of his title at the B.C. Open in July…Played in 21 Champions Tour events and collected a season-high five victories…Started the Champions Tour year by winning The ACE Group Classic in Naples…Became the first player since Gil Morgan to win three consecutive starts on the Champions Tour and posted his fifth victory in the process, the first player to win that many events since Larry Nelson in 2001…Rallied from four strokes back on the final day to win the Bank of America Championship near Boston by four shots. Win became extra special when son Kevin claimed the Lake Erie Charity Classic on the Nationwide Tour in a four-hole playoff just an hour later. It marked the second time a father and son won on the same day in PGA TOUR-sponsored events (David Duval/Bob Duval on 3/28/1999).

CAREER HIGHLIGHTS:

2003: Split year between PGA TOUR and Champions Tour, where he gained eligibility in June...Made the cut in four of 10 events on the PGA TOUR but made the most of them with his 13th TOUR victory at the B.C. Open. Fresh from his victory the week before at the Ford Senior Players Championship on the Champions Tour, Stadler came from eight strokes back on the final day to win the B.C. Open. He became just the second player in PGA TOUR history to win both a PGA TOUR and Champions Tour event in the same season, joining Raymond Floyd who won the Doral Ryder

PGA TOUR CAREER SUMMARY — PLAYOFF RECORD: 3-3

Year	Events Played	Cuts Made	1st	2nd	3rd	Top 10	Top 25	Earnings	Rank
1974A	1	1				1	1		
1975A	1	1					1		
1976	9	5						$2,702	194
1977	32	20				5	11	42,949	66
1978	28	21				6	12	63,486	49
1979	33	24				4	11	73,392	55
1980	24	21	2	1		7	11	206,291	8
1981	28	21	1	2	3	8	12	218,829	8
1982	25	23	4	2		11	18	446,462	1
1983	27	20		2	1	11	14	214,496	17
1984	22	20	1		3	8	16	324,241	8
1985	24	20		3		8	14	297,926	11
1986	26	17			1	8	10	170,076	53
1987	22	17		1		6	11	235,831	39
1988	21	16			2	5	11	278,313	37
1989	22	20		1	1	4	13	409,419	25
1990	19	16			1	5	9	278,482	52
1991	21	16	1	1	1	7	12	827,628	2
1992	25	18	1			4	10	487,460	28
1993	24	17		2	1	5	7	553,623	29
1994	22	15	1	1		4	8	474,831	32
1995	21	15			1	4	9	402,316	45
1996	18	12	1			1	4	336,820	58
1997	21	16		2		6	9	525,304	41
1998	18	15				2	7	350,091	85
1999	17	11			1	1	6	454,091	87
2000	21	13		1		2	6	631,752	74
2001	19	6				1	1	196,073	174
2002	22	13				1	6	505,778	127
2003	10	4	1			1	1	584,830	113
2004	6	4					1	137,475	205
Total	629	458	13	19	16	136	262	9,730,968	

CHAMPIONS TOUR CAREER SUMMARY — PLAYOFF RECORD: 1-0

Year	Events Played	1st	2nd	3rd	Top 10	Top 25	Earnings	Rank
2003	14	3			7	13	$1,192,278	14
2004	21	5	1	2	12	19	2,306,066	1
Total	35	8	1	2	19	32	3,498,344	

PGA TOUR TOP TOURNAMENT SUMMARY

Year	77	78	79	80	81	82	83	84	85	86	87	88	89
Masters			T7	T26	T43	**1**	T6	T35	T6	CUT	T17	3	CUT
U.S. Open			CUT	T16	T26	T22	T10	W/D	CUT	T15	T24	T25	
British Open				T6	CUT	T35	T12	T28	CUT	W/D	T8	T61	T13
PGA		6	CUT	T55	CUT	T16	T63	T18	T18	T30	T28	T15	T7
THE PLAYERS	CUT	CUT	T67	T67	CUT	T6	T63	T3	T13	CUT	CUT	T45	T21
TOUR Championship													T14

Year	90	91	92	93	94	95	96	97	98	99	00	01	02
Masters	T14	T12	T25	T34	CUT	CUT	T29	T26	T41	T38	CUT	CUT	T32
U.S. Open	T8	T19	T33	T33	CUT						CUT		T18
British Open	CUT	T101	T64		T24	CUT	T44	CUT					
PGA	T57	T7	T48	CUT	T19	T8	CUT	T53	T38	CUT	T64		
THE PLAYERS	T61	CUT	CUT	CUT	CUT	T14	T41	CUT	T31	T62	CUT	CUT	T36
TOUR Championship		**1**	T13	29									
WGC-Accenture Match Play										T17		T5	

Year	03	04
Masters	49	CUT
THE PLAYERS		T66

CHAMPIONS TOUR TOP TOURNAMENT SUMMARY

Year	03	04
Senior PGA Championship	T15	3
U.S. Senior Open	T10	T7
Ford Senior Players Championship	**1**	T18
Senior British Open	19	
JELD-WEN Tradition	T10	**1**
Charles Schwab Cup Champ	9	T7

NATIONAL TEAMS: Walker Cup, 1975; U.S. vs. Japan, 1982; Ryder Cup (2) 1983, 1985; UBS Cup, 2003.

Craig Stadler (Continued)

Open at age 49 and the GTE North Classic at 50 in 1992. At the age of 50 years, 1 month and 18 days he became the fifth-oldest player to win on the TOUR and the first player over the age of 50 to win since Art Wall won the 1975 Greater Milwaukee Open at the age of 51 years, 7 months and 10 days. With the win he collected $540,000, the largest of his professional career. His previous best was $375,000 the week before at the Ford Senior Players Championship. Stadler posted four rounds in the 60s in a single PGA TOUR event for the first time since the 1995 B.C. Open when he finished T3. It was a family affair for the Stadlers at the B.C. Open. His older son, Kevin, was playing on a sponsor exemption and missed the cut by one and younger son Chris served as his father's caddie...Won three times on the Champions Tour and had seven top-10s in 14 starts, and was voted Champions Tour Rookie of the Year. **2002:** Played with son Kevin for the first time in an official TOUR event at the B.C. Open. T50 at 6-under-par but Kevin missed cut by seven strokes...Used a 7-iron from 185 yards to ace No. 13 during the third round of THE PLAYERS Championship. **2001:** Finished outside the Top 100 for first time in his career...Used long putter for first time in career at the Shell Houston Open. **2000:** His $631,752 season earnings are the most he has won in a single year since 1991 when he made a career-best $827,628...Came into the season 50 pounds lighter than in 1999...Nearly won for the first time since the 1996 Nissan Open when he lost in a playoff on the fourth extra hole to Robert Allenby at the Shell Houston Open. One of six top-10s that year. **1999:** Played in only 17 events, the fewest since he joined the TOUR in the spring of 1976...Posted third-place finish at AT&T Pebble Beach National Pro-Am. **1997:** Posted three top-5s at Nissan Open (second), Buick Invitational (T2) and AT&T Pebble Beach National Pro-Am (T5). **1996:** Used front-nine 30 en route to Sunday 68 for one-stroke victory at Nissan Los Angeles Open. **1994:** Defeated Steve Lowery by a stroke at Buick Invitational of California. **1992:** Captured NEC World Series of Golf, 10 years after wining same event, by one stroke over Corey Pavin. **1991:** Finished second on money list after winning THE TOUR Championship at Pinehurst No. 2 in playoff with Russ Cochran, his first victory in seven years. **1985:** Finished runner-up a career-high three times. Lost playoff to Lanny Wadkins on fifth extra hole at Bob Hope Classic. Finished one behind Mark O'Meara at Hawaiian Open and T2 at Greater Greensboro Open. **1985:** Won Byron Nelson Classic by a stroke over David Edwards. **1982:** TOUR's leading money-winner, when he won four times...Captured season-opening Joe Garagiola Tucson Open by three strokes over Vance Heafner and John Mahaffey...After opening 75, won Masters in playoff over Dan Pohl...Scored seven-stroke victory over Seve Ballesteros at Kemper Open...Made up five strokes with closing 65 at World Series of Golf, then defeated Raymond Floyd in playoff. **1981:** Earned six-stroke victory at The Kemper Open. **1980:** First of 12 TOUR victories came at season-opening Bob Hope Desert Classic...Won Greater Greensboro Open by six strokes. **Amateur:** Two-time All-American at University of Southern California...Defeated David Strawn to win the 1973 U.S. Amateur at Inverness

PERSONAL:

Nicknamed "The Walrus," is one of golf's most colorful and popular personalities...A California native who lives in Denver, is ardent fan of NHL's Colorado Avalanche... Inducted into San Diego's Breithard Hall of Fame in February 1996...Son Kevin was a second-team All-American at Southern Cal in 2002 and won the 2002 Colorado Open in his professional debut. Kevin also played into the third round of match play at the 2002 U.S. Amateur at Oakland Hills. Kevin, a two-time winner on the 2004 Nationwide Tour, will be a rookie on the PGA TOUR in 2005.

PLAYER STATISTICS

2004 PGA TOUR STATISTICS

Scoring Average	72.09	(N/A)
Driving Distance	275.6	(N/A)
Driving Accuracy Percentage	67.5%	(N/A)
Total Driving	1,998	(N/A)
Greens in Regulation Pct.	64.4%	(N/A)
Putting Average	1.772	(N/A)
Sand Save Percentage	40.6%	(N/A)
Eagles (Holes per)	180.0	(N/A)
Birdie Average	3.50	(N/A)
Scoring Avg. Before Cut	71.92	(N/A)
Round 3 Scoring Avg.	71.00	(N/A)
Final Round Scoring Average	72.75	(N/A)
Birdie Conversion Percentage	28.1%	(N/A)
Par Breakers	20.0%	(N/A)

MISCELLANEOUS PGA TOUR STATISTICS

2004 Low Round/Round: 67–B.C. Open/1
Career Low Round/Round: 62–4 times, most recent 1987 Shearson Lehman Brothers Andy Williams Open/2
Career Largest Paycheck/Finish: $540,000–2003 B.C. Open/1

2004 CHAMPIONS TOUR STATISTICS

Scoring Average	69.30	(1)
Driving Distance	286.1	(7)
Driving Accuracy Percentage	70.6%	(37)
Total Driving	44	(2)
Greens in Regulation Pct.	73.8%	(4)
Putting Average	1.749	(3)
Sand Save Percentage	47.1%	(33)
Eagles (Holes per)	86.1	(1)
Birdie Average	4.18	(1)
All-Around Ranking	87	(1)

MISCELLANEOUS CHAMPIONS TOUR STATISTICS

2004 Low Round: 63–2 times, most recent 2004 The First Tee Open at Pebble Beach presented by Wal-Mart/2.
Career Low Round: 63–2 times, most recent 2004 The First Tee Open at Pebble Beach presented by Wal-Mart/2
Career Largest Paycheck: $375,000–2003 Ford Senior Players Championship/1

Paul Stankowski

EXEMPT STATUS: Major Medical Extension
FULL NAME: Paul Francis Stankowski
HEIGHT: 6-1
WEIGHT: 185
BIRTHDATE: December 2, 1969
BIRTHPLACE: Oxnard, CA
RESIDENCE: Flower Mound, TX

FAMILY: Wife, Regina; Joshua (8/11/99), Katelyn (2/25/02)
EDUCATION: University of Texas-El Paso
SPECIAL INTERESTS: Hunting, music, watching our children grow up
TURNED PROFESSIONAL: 1991
Q SCHOOL: 1993, 1995

PGA TOUR VICTORIES (2):

1996 BellSouth Classic. **1997** United Airlines Hawaiian Open.

NATIONWIDE TOUR VICTORIES (1):

1996 Louisiana Open.

INTERNATIONAL VICTORIES (2):

1996 Casio World Open [Jpn], Lincoln Mercury Kapalua International.

BEST 2004 PGA TOUR FINISH:

T9—FedEx St. Jude Classic.

2004 SEASON:

After finishing No. 150 on the money list, will receive a Major Medical Extension for 2005 due to injury and subsequent surgery to left wrist. Limited to 14 events and did not play after Booz Allen Open. Underwent surgery on his left wrist on August 17. Coupled with $442,872 earned in 14 events in 2004 has the opportunity to play in 15 events to earn $180,390 and match the $623,262 winnings of 2004's No. 125, Tag Ridings. If he does so, will play out of the Major Medical Extension category for the remainder of the season…Lone top-10 since a T4 at the 2003 Southern Farm Bureau Classic was a T9 at the FedEx St. Jude Classic.

CAREER HIGHLIGHTS:

2003: Earned a spot in the top 125 for the eighth consecutive season. Moved back into the top 100 by finishing 89th in earnings. Played in only 22 events, a career low for him on the PGA TOUR...Underwent right wrist surgery in May for torn cartilage after missing cut at EDS Byron Nelson Championship. Secured his position in the Top-125 for 2004, jumping from 110th to 96th on PGA TOUR Official Money List with his $127,000 payday at John Deere Classic. **2002:** His 31 starts tied his personal high. First top-10 of season, T10, came at Greater Greensboro Chrysler Classic, where he was one shot off the lead after an opening-round 66. Secured TOUR card for 2003 with T9 finish at the Invensys Classic at Las Vegas, best outing of the year. Jumped from 130th to 112th with $130,000 check. **2001:** Appeared in 27 tournaments and was among the top-10 twice, including a runner-up finish early in the season at the Bob Hope Chrysler Classic. **2000:** Recorded three top-10s and nine top-25s in 22 appearances. Top-10s came in Phoenix Open (T10), GTE Byron Nelson Classic (T10) and Bell Canadian Open (T10). **1999:** Came close to losing full exempt status on PGA TOUR. Was 140th on money list with only Southern Farm Bureau Classic to play. However, rounds of 70-69-67 produced T3 worth $104,000 which lifted him to 113th on final money list. **1998:** Was hampered to some degree by right shoulder injury sustained at Bay Hill Invitational. MRI showed slight cartilage irritation but no muscle tears. Was forced to withdraw during second round of THE PLAYERS Championship…T6 in final start of year, at Las Vegas Invitational, to earn $69,500 which led to 96th-place finish on final money list. **1997:** Qualified for THE TOUR Championship, where he finished T17...Scores of 71-66-64-70-271 forced playoff at United Airlines Hawaiian Open with Jim Furyk and Mike Reid. Reid was eliminated on first extra hole, and Stankowski defeated Furyk on fourth playoff hole to capture second PGA TOUR title...After Hawaii, finished T3 at Bob Hope Chrysler Classic and T5 at Honda Classic, Masters Tournament and GTE Byron Nelson Classic. **1996:** Unquestionably his breakthrough year, featuring his first victory on TOUR at BellSouth Classic in just his third full season. Started 68-71-70 for third place entering final round. Closing 71 forced playoff with Brandel Chamblee, which Stankowski won with birdie on first extra hole. Had arrived in Atlanta as sixth alternate after winning Natonwide Tour Louisiana Open the week before. Is the only player to win Nationwide Tour and PGA TOUR events back-to-back. Prior to Atlanta had missed five of six PGA TOUR cuts...After the season, posted a victory at unofficial Lincoln-Mercury Kapalua International, birdieing 72nd hole to earn one-stroke victory over Fred Couples...Later that month, captured Casio World Open on Japanese Tour. **1994:** First year on TOUR, achieved PGA TOUR exempt status following T26 finish at Qualifying Tournament. Played in 29 events, making 10 cuts. Finished in the top-10 three times and finished 106th on the PGA TOUR money list. **Amateur:** Three-time All-American at Texas El-Paso.

PERSONAL:

First played golf on Easter Sunday in 1978; 18 years later, won BellSouth Classic on Easter…Uncertain he would return to Masters, so bought souvenir glass, filled it with bunker sand and placed tee and ball inside as remembrance of first visit to Augusta National in 1996. Returned in 1997 and 1998…Underwent LASIK surgery in September 1998.

PLAYER STATISTICS

2004 PGA TOUR STATISTICS

Scoring Average	71.05	(N/A)
Driving Distance	292.0	(N/A)
Driving Accuracy Percentage	63.1%	(N/A)
Total Driving	1,998	(N/A)
Greens in Regulation Pct.	66.4%	(N/A)
Putting Average	1.805	(N/A)
Sand Save Percentage	54.4%	(N/A)
Eagles (Holes per)	96.8	(N/A)
Birdie Average	3.42	(N/A)
Scoring Avg. Before Cut	71.10	(N/A)
Round 3 Scoring Avg.	69.71	(N/A)
Final Round Scoring Average	71.86	(N/A)
Birdie Conversion Percentage	28.3%	(N/A)
Par Breakers	20.0%	(N/A)

MISCELLANEOUS PGA TOUR STATISTICS

2004 Low Round/Round: 66–THE PLAYERS Championship/3
Career Low Round/Round: 61–2001 Compaq Classic of New Orleans/1
Career Largest Paycheck/Finish: $378,000–2001 Bob Hope Chrysler Classic/2

PGA TOUR CAREER SUMMARY — PLAYOFF RECORD: 2-0

Year	Events Played	Cuts Made	1st	2nd	3rd	Top 10	Top 25	Earnings	Rank
1994	29	10				3	4	$170,393	106
1995	31	15				1	3	144,558	133
1996	25	11	1			3	3	390,575	52
1997	29	22	1		1	5	15	929,405	21
1998	26	14				2	6	322,036	96
1999	28	11			1	2	6	362,889	113
2000	22	16				3	9	669,709	70
2001	27	19		1		2	5	743,603	69
2002	31	18				2	6	565,294	118
2003	21	13				4	6	719,436	89
2004	14	7				1	4	442,872	150
Total	283	156	2	1	2	28	67	5,460,771	
NATIONWIDE TOUR									
1991	1	1						1,063	223
1992	3	1					1	1,296	212
1993	1	1						665	243
1994	1								
1996	2	2	1			1	2	46,800	43
Total	8	5	1			1	3	49,824	

PGA TOUR TOP TOURNAMENT SUMMARY

Year	94	95	96	97	98	99	00	01	02	03	04
Masters			CUT	T5	T39						
U.S. Open	CUT			T19	CUT				T62		
British Open				CUT							
PGA		CUT	T47	T67	CUT		T41	74			
THE PLAYERS		CUT		T14	W/D	CUT	CUT	T44	CUT	CUT	T16
TOUR Championship				T17							

Andre Stolz (stoles)

EXEMPT STATUS: 2004 tournament winner (through 2006)
FULL NAME: Andre Pierre Stolz
HEIGHT: 5-11
WEIGHT: 180
BIRTHDATE: May 10, 1970
BIRTHPLACE: Brisbane, Australia

RESIDENCE: Central Coast, New South Wales, Australia
FAMILY: Wife, Cathy; Zac (6/21/95), Shania (6/5/99)
SPECIAL INTERESTS: Snowboarding
TURNED PROFESSIONAL: 1992
Nationwide Tour Alumnus

PGA TOUR VICTORIES (1):
2004 Michelin Championship at Las Vegas.

NATIONWIDE TOUR VICTORIES (1):
2003 LaSalle Bank Open.

INTERNATIONAL VICTORIES (3):
2000 Tour Championship [Aus]. **2002** Queensland PGA Championship [Aus], Victoria Open Championship [Aus].

BEST 2004 PGA TOUR FINISH:
1—Michelin Championship at Las Vegas.

2004 SEASON:
Earned his first PGA TOUR victory in rookie season at Michelin Championship at Las Vegas, joining four other rookies to win in 2004. He was also one of five members of the 2003 Nationwide Tour graduating class to earn his initial TOUR victory in 2004…After posting just six rounds in the 60s the entire season, the rookie was one of 10 players in the field in Las Vegas to post four rounds in the 60s. The 34-year-old birdied the 16th hole at the TPC at Summerlin on Sunday to grab the outright lead and then made crucial pars at the final two holes to close with a five-under 67 that allowed him to come from one stroke back of third-round leader Tom Lehman. He become the sixth different Australian player to post a victory during the season, joining Stuart Appleby, Mark Hensby, Craig Parry, Adam Scott and Rod Pampling. The win moved him from 217th on the money list to 89th. Coming into the week he was 341st on the Official World Golf Ranking, but with his victory he moved to 136th. His best finish in 20 career TOUR events prior to the win was a T34 at the HP Classic of New Orleans…After win in mid-October did not play again for the remainder of the season.

CAREER HIGHLIGHTS:
2003: Had big year in 2003, placing second on the PGA Tour of Australasia's Order of Merit and also winning on the Nationwide Tour and the Japan Golf Tour. Finished 13th on the 2003 Nationwide Tour money list to earn his first TOUR card. Had seven top-25s in 16 starts on the Nationwide Tour, including his first win at the LaSalle Bank Open...Opened the season with an impressive start Down Under, finishing T6 at the Jacob's Creek Open and runner-up at the Clearwater Classic...Was a fixture inside the top 15 on the money list most of the season, thanks, in large part, to his victory at the LaSalle Bank Open. Rallied with five birdies in his last six holes to collect the $90,000 first-place prize...Won the Token Homemate Cup on the Japan Golf Tour...Finished T2 at the Johnnie Walker Classic on the European Tour behind champion Ernie Els. **2002:** Won twice on the PGA TOUR of Australasia — Queensland PGA and Victoria Open Championship...Missed cut in his first career start on the PGA TOUR at the 2002 PGA Championship. **2000:** Won the TOUR Championship on the PGA TOUR of Australasia.

PLAYER STATISTICS

2004 PGA TOUR STATISTICS

Scoring Average	72.34	(185)
Driving Distance	297.9	(20)
Driving Accuracy Percentage	59.0%	(162)
Total Driving	182	(76)
Greens in Regulation Pct.	63.0%	(147)
Putting Average	1.787	(119)
Sand Save Percentage	47.7%	(117)
Eagles (Holes per)	190.8	(65)
Birdie Average	3.26	(161)
All-Around Ranking	976	(150)
Scoring Avg. Before Cut	72.28	(188)
Round 3 Scoring Avg.	71.25	(122)
Final Round Scoring Average	71.71	(107)
Birdie Conversion Percentage	28.4%	(112)
Par Breakers	18.7%	(152)

MISCELLANEOUS PGA TOUR STATISTICS

2004 Low Round/Round: 65–Michelin Championship at Las Vegas/3
Career Low Round/Round: 65–2004 Michelin Championship at Las Vegas/3
Career Largest Paycheck/Finish: $720,000–2004 Michelin Championship at Las Vegas/1

PGA TOUR CAREER SUMMARY — PLAYOFF RECORD: 0-0

Year	Events Played	Cuts Made	1st	2nd	3rd	Top 10	Top 25	Earnings	Rank
2003	1								
2004	20	7	1			1	1	$808,373	101
Total	21	7	1			1	1	808,373	
NATIONWIDE TOUR									
1996	1	1						1,300	208
2000	1								
2002	2	2					1	15,244	157
2003	16	12	1	1		5	7	218,867	13
2004	2								
Total	22	15	1	1		5	8	235,411	
EUROPEAN TOUR									
2003	3	2		1		1	2	153,110	
JAPAN GOLF TOUR									
2003	3	3	1			1	2	187,385	
PGA TOUR OF AUSTRALASIA									
2003	1	1						2,374	

PGA TOUR TOP TOURNAMENT SUMMARY

Year	03	04
PGA	CUT	
WGC-American Express Champ		65

Kevin Sutherland

EXEMPT STATUS: 2002 World Golf Championships winner (through 2005)
FULL NAME: Kevin John Sutherland
HEIGHT: 6-1
WEIGHT: 185
BIRTHDATE: July 4, 1964
BIRTHPLACE: Sacramento, CA
RESIDENCE: Sacramento, CA

FAMILY: Wife, Mary; Keaton (8/28/00)
EDUCATION: Fresno State University (1987, Business)
SPECIAL INTERESTS: Basketball, baseball
TURNED PROFESSIONAL: 1987
Q SCHOOL: 1995, 1996
Nationwide Tour Alumnus

PGA TOUR VICTORIES (1):

2002 WGC-Accenture Match Play Championship.

BEST 2004 PGA TOUR FINISHES:

T6—THE PLAYERS Championship; T9—FBR Open, Buick Championship; T10—Wachovia Championship.

2004 SEASON:

Finished inside the top 100 on the PGA TOUR money list for the eighth consecutive season...His four top-10s were the most since he posted seven in 2001...In second start of season, earned a T9 at the FBR Open...Held a share of the 36-hole lead with Jerry Kelly at THE PLAYERS Championship after opening 66-69. Finished T6 after rounds of 73-73 on the weekend, five strokes behind champion Adam Scott...Posted four sub-par rounds at the Wachovia Championship and finished T10...Fourth top-10 was T9 at the Buick Championship, aided by rounds of 67-66 on the weekend.

CAREER HIGHLIGHTS:

2003: Surpassed $1 million in earnings for third consecutive season. Finished T9 at the WGC-Accenture Match Play Championship after losing to Adam Scott in the third round (2 and 1). Defeated Justin Rose and Sergio Garcia in the first two rounds. He holds the WGC-Accenture Match Play Championship record of eight consecutive winning matches won...Top finish of season was T5 at the John Deere Classic, five strokes behind Vijay Singh. **2002:** Earned first PGA TOUR title in his 184th career start. Became first player to make a World Golf Championships event his first career victory with a win at WGC-Accenture Match Play Championship. Beat fellow Sacramento, CA native Scott McCarron 1-up in the 36-hole final at La Costa Resort and Spa. Became the highest seed (No. 62) to win the tournament. Key shot was and up-and-down for par from the front bunker on the final hole. Used claw putting grip to win just one week after experimenting with it at Nissan Open. **2001:** Shattered previous mark for top-25s with 13 (previous best was 12 in 2000)...Opening 67 gave him six-way share of the first-round lead at Touchstone Energy Tucson Open. Closing 68 left him one shy of winner Garrett Willis. Managed to eclipse the $1-million mark in a single season for the first time in his career with T7 at the Advil Western Open, worth $112,200...Participated in the British Open for the first time and finished T9, his only top-10 in a major championship. **2000:** Best showing of year came at Buick Invitational. After opening with 1-over-par 73, closed 66-69-68 for T5 finish...At Canon Greater Hartford Open where a final-day 65, his lowest final-round score of the year, was good for a T9...Held first-round lead at Bell Canadian Open after opening 65. Entered the event as a last-minute commitment due to fact his wife, Mary, gave birth to their first child just 10 days prior to tournament. Eventually finished T10. **1999:** Finished with four top-10s and eight top-25s. Top-10s came in Bob Hope Chrysler Classic (T8), Buick Invitational (T4), FedEx St. Jude Classic (T6) and Las Vegas Invitational (T6). **1998:** At Buick Invitational, where rounds of 68-67-70 left him one stroke shy of second career playoff. **1997:** Came close to victory at Shell Houston Open, sharing 54-hole lead with Phil Blackmar. He and Blackmar shot final-round 70s before Blackmar won with a birdie on first playoff hole. **1991-92:** Member of Nationwide Tour. **Amateur:** Second-team All-American at Fresno State University.

PERSONAL:

Brother David is a member of PGA TOUR. The Sutherlands often can be seen practicing together at TOUR events. The two were paired together for the first time on TOUR during first two rounds of 1999 Compaq Classic of New Orleans...Won 1997 EA Sports Challenge Championship, defeating defending champion Paul Goydos.

PLAYER STATISTICS

2004 PGA TOUR STATISTICS

Scoring Average	70.94	(74)
Driving Distance	286.1	(106)
Driving Accuracy Percentage	67.1%	(56)
Total Driving	162	(50)
Greens in Regulation Pct.	63.8%	(126)
Putting Average	1.799	(160)
Sand Save Percentage	53.7%	(36)
Eagles (Holes per)	492.0	(175)
Birdie Average	3.35	(137)
All-Around Ranking	870	(126)
Scoring Avg. Before Cut	70.70	(56)
Round 3 Scoring Avg.	71.13	(111)
Final Round Scoring Average	71.93	(130)
Birdie Conversion Percentage	28.0%	(132)
Par Breakers	18.8%	(149)

MISCELLANEOUS PGA TOUR STATISTICS

2004 Low Round/Round: 65–FBR Open/2
Career Low Round/Round: 63–3 times, most recent 1999 Las Vegas Invitational/3
Career Largest Paycheck/Finish: $1,000,000–2002 WGC–Accenture Match Play Championship/1

PGA TOUR CAREER SUMMARY — PLAYOFF RECORD: 0-1

Year	Events Played	Cuts Made	1st	2nd	3rd	Top 10	Top 25	Earnings	Rank
1991	1	1						$2,030	296
1995	1								
1996	33	21				1	4	144,828	135
1997	27	17		1		4	6	455,860	52
1998	30	22			1	3	9	444,429	66
1999	29	21				4	8	663,891	63
2000	27	21				4	12	728,635	66
2001	30	21		1		7	13	1,523,573	32
2002	28	18	1			3	7	1,569,529	36
2003	27	21				3	9	1,092,918	67
2004	27	16				4	5	928,760	85
Total	260	179	1	2	1	33	73	7,554,453	
NATIONWIDE TOUR									
1990	2	1					1	1,475	176
1991	26	16		1		2	8	30,221	40
1992	15	6		1		2	4	21,444	63
1993	5	5				1	5	15,113	91
1994	4	3				1	2	10,130	106
1995	26	21				7	12	60,822	32
Total	78	52		2		13	32	139,205	

PGA TOUR TOP TOURNAMENT SUMMARY

Year	96	97	98	99	00	01	02	03	04
Masters							CUT	T33	
U.S. Open	CUT		CUT			T44	T37	T28	CUT
British Open						T9	CUT		
PGA		T76	T44	CUT	CUT	CUT	T43	T18	CUT
THE PLAYERS			T42	CUT	CUT	T58	CUT	T48	T6
WGC-Accenture Match Play						T33	**1**	T9	
WGC-NEC Invitational							T58		
WGC-American Express Champ							T27		

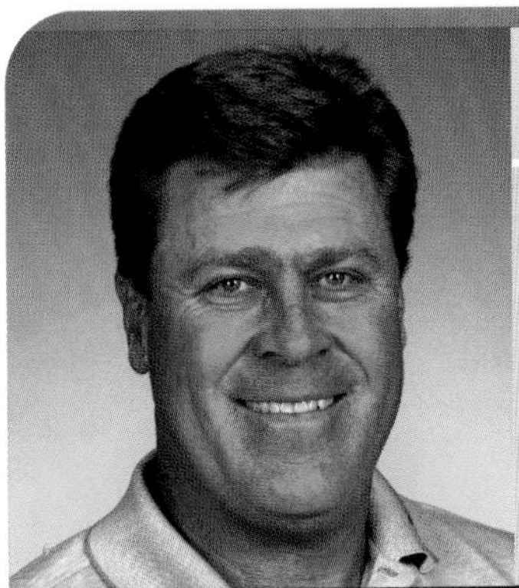

Hal Sutton

EXEMPT STATUS: Winner, 2000 PLAYERS Championship (through 2005)
FULL NAME: Hal Evan Sutton
HEIGHT: 6-1
WEIGHT: 210
BIRTHDATE: April 28, 1958
BIRTHPLACE: Shreveport, LA
RESIDENCE: Shreveport, LA

FAMILY: Wife, Ashley; Samantha Jean (11/24/96), Sara Rias and Sadie Ann (1/18/99), Holt Edwin (4/25/03)
EDUCATION: Centenary College (Business)
SPECIAL INTERESTS: Horses, hunting, fishing
TURNED PROFESSIONAL: 1981
Q SCHOOL: Fall 1981

PGA TOUR VICTORIES (14):

1982 Walt Disney World Golf Classic. **1983** Tournament Players Championship, PGA Championship. **1985** St. Jude Memphis Classic, Southwest Golf Classic. **1986** Phoenix Open, Memorial Tournament. **1995** B.C. Open. **1998** Westin Texas Open, THE TOUR Championship. **1999** Bell Canadian Open. **2000** THE PLAYERS Championship, Greater Greensboro Chrysler Classic. **2001** Shell Houston Open.

BEST 2004 PGA TOUR FINISH:

T25—HP Classic of New Orleans.

2004 SEASON:

Joined ABC Sports in January to provide commentary for nine PGA TOUR tournaments during the 2004 season…Between his obligations to the PGA of America as Ryder Cup Captain and broadcasting responsibilities, played in 16 events, making just five cuts…Captained the Ryder Cup team, which lost to the European Team, 18½ to 9½.

CAREER HIGHLIGHTS:

2003: A year after finishing outside the top 125 for the first time since 1993 and posting no top-10s, came back and finished 75th on the money list with four top-10s...Finished T3 at the MCI Heritage, first top-10 since winning the 2001 Shell Houston Open, a span of 50 events. Finished third on TOUR in Driving Accuracy. **2002:** Named by the PGA of America as the 2004 Ryder Cup Captain...Was member of Ryder Cup team and compiled a 1-1 record. **2001:** Won seven times in his 20s, once in his 30s, now six times in 40s with win at Shell Houston Open. Closing 69 at Shell Houston Open brought him from two strokes back to 14th title. $612,000 payday also lifted him over $1 million for fourth consecutive season... Suffering from sleep apnea he disclosed at the PGA Championship. **2000:** By season's end, had accumulated two victories for a total of five in a three-year stretch, the best run of his career...In first win, went head to head with Tiger Woods at THE PLAYERS Championship and came away with one-stroke, wire-to-wire win. Sutton and Woods played in the last group Sunday and Sutton held a three-stroke lead on the 12th hole when lightning suspended play for the day. On Monday morning, Woods fell four back but pulled to within one with an eagle on the par-5 16th hole before both players parred the closing two holes. Victory came 17 years after first PLAYERS win in '83...Second victory of season and 13th of PGA TOUR career came at Greater Greensboro Chrysler Classic with a three-stroke win over Andrew Magee...Fifth TOUR season in which he has had two victories...A member of the victorious U.S. Presidents Cup team with 2-2 record. **1999:** Had another super year with a career-best 13 top-10s, including a three-stroke victory over Dennis Paulson in Bell Canadian Open. Leader of Ryder Cup victory with 3-1-1 record. **1998:** Had best money-list finish since 1983, when he was first...Earned ninth PGA TOUR victory, first since 1995 B.C. Open, with one-stroke win over Justin Leonard and Jay Haas at Westin Texas Open. Defeated Vijay Singh in playoff with birdie on first extra hole to capture THE TOUR Championship at East Lake GC...Qualified for his first Presidents Cup Team, but subsequently was forced to withdraw due to his father-in-law's death. **1995:** Returned to winner's circle at B.C. Open. His closing 10-under-par 61 was best final round by winner since Johnny Miller at 1975 Dean Martin Tucson Open...Won twice in one season for the first time since '86. **1994:** Played under one-time exemption for being in top 50 in career earnings. Comeback began when he made $540,162 and twice finished second. **1992:** Winless for eight years after 1986, with low point coming, when earnings fell to $39,324. **1986:** Posted two more titles for the second consecutive season, Phoenix Open and Memorial Tournament. **1985:** Won two tournaments, St. Jude Memphis Classic and Southwest Classic. **1983:** Finished atop money list with $426,668 on strength of victories in THE PLAYERS Championship and PGA Championship...Led wire-to-wire at PGA Championship, defeating Jack Nicklaus by one stroke...Trailed John Cook by four strokes entering final round of THE PLAYERS Championship before closing 69 gave him one-stroke victory...PGA of America and GWAA Player of the Year. **1982:** Rookie year, posted three seconds, a third and, in final event of his season at Walt Disney World Golf Classic, his first victory. **Amateur:** Winner 1980 U.S. Amateur at CC of North Carolina...1980 Golf College Player of the Year.

PERSONAL:

As side business and hobby, rides and sells cutting horses…Family owns an oil company in hometown of Shreveport, LA…Developing a golf course design business. His first course, Old Oaks, opened in Bossier City, LA in October 1999…Donated $100,000 to his alma mater Centenary College and to United Way of Northeast Louisiana after earning $1,080,000 for 2000 PLAYERS Championship victory…Was awarded the Omar N. Bradley Spirit of Independence award, which he accepted at the Independence Ball on New Year's Day 2004.

PLAYER STATISTICS

2004 PGA TOUR STATISTICS

Scoring Average	72.11	(N/A)
Driving Distance	283.3	(N/A)
Driving Accuracy Percentage	64.4%	(N/A)
Total Driving	(N/A)	(N/A)
Greens in Regulation Pct.	65.6%	(N/A)
Putting Average	1.837	(N/A)
Sand Save Percentage	37.3%	(N/A)
Eagles (Holes per)	378.0	(N/A)
Birdie Average	3.38	(N/A)
Scoring Avg. Before Cut	71.94	(N/A)
Round 3 Scoring Avg.	73.50	(N/A)
Final Round Scoring Average	71.40	(N/A)
Birdie Conversion Percentage	27.7%	(N/A)
Par Breakers	19.0%	(N/A)

MISCELLANEOUS PGA TOUR STATISTICS

2004 Low Round/Round: 66–2 times, most recent HP Classic of New Orleans/4
Career Low Round/Round: 61–1995 B.C. Open/4
Career Largest Paycheck/Finish: $1,080,000–2000 THE PLAYERS Championship/1

PGA TOUR CAREER SUMMARY — PLAYOFF RECORD: 4-2

Year	Events Played	Cuts Made	1st	2nd	3rd	Top 10	Top 25	Earnings	Rank
1980A	1	1							
1981A	2	2							
1981	4								
1982	31	25	1	3	1	8	15	$237,434	11
1983	30	25	2	1	1	12	16	426,668	1
1984	26	23		1	1	11	16	227,949	26
1985	26	23	2	1	1	7	16	365,340	7
1986	28	23	2	1		9	11	429,434	6
1987	25	20		3		6	16	477,996	16
1988	27	16				1	8	137,296	88
1989	30	20		2		7	12	422,703	23
1990	28	18				4	8	207,084	75
1991	28	23			1	5	13	346,411	47
1992	29	8					1	39,234	185
1993	29	13				1	2	74,144	161
1994	29	23		2		4	15	540,162	29
1995	31	17	1	2		4	8	554,733	32
1996	29	17				1	7	193,723	109
1997	29	18			1	4	9	453,928	54
1998	30	22	2	1		9	16	1,838,740	5
1999	25	22	1	1		13	17	2,127,578	6
2000	25	20	2		1	11	14	3,061,444	4
2001	26	23	1		1	3	9	1,723,946	28
2002	26	11					3	320,002	153
2003	24	16			1	4	6	939,719	75
2004	16	5					1	103,698	214
Total	634	434	14	18	9	124	239	15,249,365	

PGA TOUR TOP TOURNAMENT SUMMARY

Year	81	82	83	84	85	86	87	88	89	90	91	92	93
Masters	CUT		T27	CUT	T31	CUT	CUT	CUT	CUT	CUT		CUT	
U.S. Open	CUT	T19	6	T16	T23	T4	T31	64	T29	CUT	CUT		
British Open	T47	CUT	T29	CUT			T11	CUT					
PGA		T29	**1**	T6	T65	T21	T28	T66	CUT	T49	T7	CUT	T31
THE PLAYERS			**1**	T41	T22	T7	T24	CUT	T29	CUT	T68	CUT	CUT
TOUR Championship							T5		T22				

Year	94	95	96	97	98	99	00	01	02	03	04
Masters		CUT	CUT			CUT	10	36			
U.S. Open		T36		T19		T7	T23	T24	CUT		
British Open						T10	CUT		CUT	CUT	
PGA	T55	CUT	CUT	CUT	T27	T26	CUT	T44	T60	T39	CUT
THE PLAYERS	T19	CUT	T53	T50	T18	T4	**1**	T5	CUT	CUT	CUT
TOUR Championship	T24				**1**	T9	T25	T26			
WGC-Accenture Match Play						T33	T5	T33	T33		
WGC-NEC Invitational						T15	T4	T11	T42	T33	
WGC-American Express Champ						19		CNL			

NATIONAL TEAMS: Walker Cup (2), 1979, 1981; World Amateur Team Championship, 1980; USA vs. Japan, 1983; Ryder Cup (4), 1985, 1987, 1999, 2002, Captain in 2004; Nissan Cup, 1986; The Presidents Cup, 1998 (withdrew), 2000; UBS Cup, 2003.

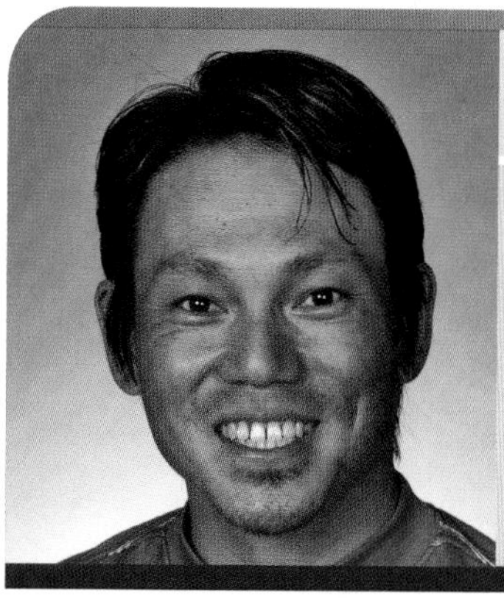

Hidemichi Tanaka (hid-uh-MEE-chee tuh-KNOCK-uh)

EXEMPT STATUS: 104th on 2004 money list
FULL NAME: Hidemichi Tanaka
HEIGHT: 5-6
WEIGHT: 136
BIRTHDATE: March 29, 1971
BIRTHPLACE: Hiroshima, Japan
RESIDENCE: Aichi, Japan; Newport Beach, CA
FAMILY: Wife, Yoshiko

SPECIAL INTERESTS: Music, cars
TURNED PROFESSIONAL: 1991
Q SCHOOL: 2001

BEST PGA TOUR CAREER FINISH:
T3—2004 B.C. Open.

INTERNATIONAL VICTORIES (15):
1995 Philip Morris Championship [Jpn], Mito Green Open [Jpn], Korakuen Cup No. 2 [Jpn]. **1996** Pepsi Ube-Kosan [Jpn], Hirao Masaaki Pro-Am [Jpn]. **1998** Japan Open, DDI Okinawa Open [Jpn], Aiful Cup [Jpn], Hirao Masaaki Pro-Am [Jpn]. **1999** Acom International [Jpn]. **2000** Dydo Drinco Shizuoka Open [Jpn], The Crowns [Jpn]. **2001** Tsuruya Open [Jpn], Gateway to the Open Mizuno Open [Jpn], Hawaii Pearl Open.

BEST 2004 PGA TOUR FINISHES:
T3—B.C. Open; 4—HP Classic of New Orleans.

2004 SEASON:
Finished inside the top 125 for the third consecutive season since joining the TOUR in 2002. Made 17 cuts and finished in the top-five twice…In 10th start of season, finished solo fourth at the HP Classic of New Orleans, his first top-five of the season. Collected a career-high $244,800…Recorded a career-best finish at the B.C. Open in July, posting four rounds in the 60s, including a final-round 66 for T3 finish…Other top-20 finishes came at the Chrysler Classic of Tucson (T20) and Buick Championship (T13)…Second time he has represented the Japan team with Shigeki Maruyama at the WGC-World Cup.

CAREER HIGHLIGHTS:
2003: Had a career year in money earned ($1,026,678) and position on the money list (69th)...Despite making 20 of first 22 cuts, first top-10 did not come until Reno-Tahoe Open in 23rd start, a T6...Two weeks later held the lead at the Bell Canadian Open after 18 and 54 holes. Had a two-stroke lead heading into the final round. Closing 1-over 71 dropped him into a T4...Posted third top-10 finish in four starts with a T5 at the John Deere Classic...Shared first-round lead at the Southern Farm Bureau Classic with eventual winner John Huston and Carlos Franco before finishing T4. His $124,000 payday in Mississippi lifted him over $1 million for the first time in his career...Represented the defending champion Japan team with Shigeki Maruyama at the WGC-World Cup in Kiawah Island, SC. Maruyama teamed with Toshi Izawa to win in 2002 in Mexico. **2002:** One of 11 rookies to finish in the top 125...Recorded first ace of TOUR season in the first round of the Sony Open of Hawaii on the par-3 seventh hole...Final-round 65 good for T7 finish at the SEI Pennsylvania Classic, his first top-10 in 48 career PGA TOUR starts...Two weeks later, owned share of the lead through 18 holes at the Disney Golf Classic, finished T4. Paycheck of $162,800 was best of the season...Made the last seven cuts of the season but withdrew from his final event, the Buick Challenge, prior to round three due to symptoms of vertigo. **2001:** T23 at PGA TOUR Qualifying Tournament to earn TOUR card for 2002...Played the Japan Golf Tour since 1995, with nine career victories. Notched 10 top-10s in 16 starts on the Japan Golf Tour, including wins at the Tsuruya Open and Gate Way to the Open Mizuno Open...Sixth in the Japan Golf Tour Order of Merit. **2000:** Won two of the first five events on the Japan Golf Tour

PERSONAL:
Lists veteran Japanese golfer Massy Kuramoto as his hero…Began playing golf by hitting balls in a vacant lot in his neighborhood…Known in Japan as the "Chibbiko" golfer, which means "little golfer."

PLAYER STATISTICS

2004 PGA TOUR STATISTICS

Scoring Average	71.08	(94)
Driving Distance	281.0	(150)
Driving Accuracy Percentage	72.3%	(11)
Total Driving	161	(47)
Greens in Regulation Pct.	66.1%	(69)
Putting Average	1.780	(107)
Sand Save Percentage	41.6%	(184)
Eagles (Holes per)	267.0	(113)
Birdie Average	3.30	(148)
All-Around Ranking	876	(127)
Scoring Avg. Before Cut	70.70	(56)
Round 3 Scoring Avg.	71.56	(144)
Final Round Scoring Average	72.61	(163)
Birdie Conversion Percentage	27.0%	(165)
Par Breakers	18.7%	(152)

MISCELLANEOUS PGA TOUR STATISTICS

2004 Low Round/Round: 64–HP Classic of New Orleans/2
Career Low Round/Round: 63–2002 Disney Golf Classic/1
Career Largest Paycheck/Finish: $244,800–2004 HP Classic of New Orleans/4

PGA TOUR CAREER SUMMARY — PLAYOFF RECORD: 0-0

Year	Events Played	Cuts Made	1st	2nd	3rd	Top 10	Top 25	Earnings	Rank
1996	4	4					1	$38,999	207
1997	2								
1998	1								
1999	5	1						5,075	322
2000	3	3					2	37,750	
2001	7	2					1	15,363	
2002	31	21				2	10	766,423	92
2003	30	25				4	9	1,024,678	69
2004	27	18			1	2	7	795,206	104
Total	110	74			1	8	30	2,683,494	

PGA TOUR TOP TOURNAMENT SUMMARY

Year	96	97	98	99	00	01	02	03	04
U.S. Open							T37	T15	T36
British Open	T32			CUT		CUT			
PGA				CUT	79	CUT			T55
THE PLAYERS								CUT	T81
WGC-Accenture Match Play						T17			
WGC-American Express Champ					T11	CNL			

NATIONAL TEAMS: WGC-World Cup (3), 2000, 2003, 2004

SECTION 2 PLAYER BIOGRAPHIES

Phil Tataurangi (TAT-uh-rang-ee)

EXEMPT STATUS: Major Medical Extension
FULL NAME: Phillip Mikaera Tataurangi
HEIGHT: 5-10
WEIGHT: 175
BIRTHDATE: October 31, 1971
BIRTHPLACE: Auckland, New Zealand
RESIDENCE: Taupo, New Zealand; plays out of Cape Kidnappers (Hawks Bay, New Zealand)
FAMILY: Wife, Melanie; Kahurangi Jack (6/30/00), Talia Aniwaniwa (5/1/04)
SPECIAL INTERESTS: Music, cooking, friends, sports
TURNED PROFESSIONAL: 1993
Q SCHOOL: 1993, 1996, 2001
Nationwide Tour Alumnus

PGA TOUR VICTORIES (1):
2002 Invensys Classic at Las Vegas.

NATIONWIDE TOUR VICTORIES (1):
1996 Tri-Cities Open.

INTERNATIONAL VICTORIES (1):
1996 MasterCard Australian PGA Championship [Aus].

BEST 2004 PGA TOUR FINISH:
T60—Reno-Tahoe Open.

2004 SEASON:
Limited to eight starts due to back injury. Will receive a Major Medical Extension for 2005. Coupled with $6,540 earned in eight events in 2004 has the opportunity to play in 21 events to earn $616,722 and match the $623,262 winnings of 2004's No. 125, Tag Ridings. If he does so, will play out of the Major Medical Extension category for the remainder of the season…Made only one made cut where he finished T60 at the Reno-Tahoe Open.

CAREER HIGHLIGHTS:
2003: Fresh off first PGA TOUR victory in 2002, missed a large portion of the season due to a herniated disc at the base of his spine. Limited to only 11 events. Did not compete between the Wachovia Championship and the Buick Open, a span of almost two months. Shut it down for the season after a T61 finish at the PGA in mid-August...In second start of season, finished T7 at AT&T Pebble Beach National Pro-Am, six shots behind Davis Love III...Entered WGC-Accenture Match Play Championship No. 65 in Official World Golf Ranking, upset No. 2 seed Ernie Els in 20 holes. Finished T17...Playing in first Masters, made the cut and finished T39. **2002:** One of a record 18 first-time winners, getting his victory at the Invensys Classic of Las Vegas...Finished 23rd in PGA TOUR Qualifying School in December 2001 to retain full status after injury-plagued 2001 campaign...Had heart surgery in July to control a heart condition that he has had for several years called superventricular tachycardia, a rapid heartbeat that occurs and disappears suddenly...Carded final-round 10-under 62 to capture first TOUR win at the Invensys Classic at Las Vegas. Started the day five shots behind leader David Duval, but posted 10 birdies without a bogey to claim a one-stroke victory at 29-under-par 330 over Stuart Appleby and Jeff Sluman. Key stretch was back nine, where birdies on Nos. 13, 15 and 16 built a three-shot lead. With a career-best paycheck of $900,000, jumped from 77th to 33rd on the TOUR money list for 2002. **2001:** Limited in 12 PGA TOUR events in 2001 due to lingering neck injury...Notched only top-25s of season at first two events, Greater Greensboro Chrysler Classic (T12) and Kemper Insurance Open (T17). Greensboro earnings of $68,600 represented season high. **2000:** Did not make a cut in four events on the PGA TOUR, but did make one cut in six events on Nationwide Tour...T30 at the Oregon Classic for his only payday of the year. **1999:** Finished T4 at the Bell Canadian Open after entering the final round just one stroke off the lead. Finished 150th on the money list with $232,078. **1998:** Posted a second consecutive season in the top 100 on the money list...Logged best career finish at 1998 Michelob Championship, a second, three strokes behind winner David Duval. **1997:** Finished third at Bell Canadian Open. **1996:** Earned his first career title at the Nationwide Tri-Cities Open, finishing at 21-under par and six strokes ahead of runner-up Skip Kendall...At end of the season won the Australian PGA Championship. Gained exempt status for the 1997 on the PGA TOUR by finishing T7 at PGA TOUR Qualifying Tournament. **1995:** On Nationwide Tour, had back-to-back weeks where he finished one stroke back of winner — at the Ozarks Open (T4) and Permian Basin Open (T2). **Amateur:** Medalist at 1992 World Amateur Team Championship as member of New Zealand's winning team. 1993 New Zealand Amateur Champion.

PERSONAL:
Father TeRoi played rugby for New Zealand's All Blacks between 1960-66…Started playing golf at age 7 after caddying for father…Extremely proud of Maori heritage…In July 2002, underwent surgery in Texas to correct a heart condition called superventricular tachycardia. The ailment is not life-threatening, but mirrors the symptoms of a heart attack. Steve Jones had the procedure done in August 2002.

PLAYER STATISTICS

2004 PGA TOUR STATISTICS

Scoring Average	73.95	(N/A)
Driving Distance	292.4	(N/A)
Driving Accuracy Percentage	55.7%	(N/A)
Total Driving	1,998	(N/A)
Greens in Regulation Pct.	54.8%	(N/A)
Putting Average	1.811	(N/A)
Sand Save Percentage	64.0%	(N/A)
Eagles (Holes per)	270.0	(N/A)
Birdie Average	2.47	(N/A)
Scoring Avg. Before Cut	73.77	(N/A)
Round 3 Scoring Avg.	71.00	(N/A)
Final Round Scoring Average	80.00	(N/A)
Birdie Conversion Percentage	23.6%	(N/A)
Par Breakers	14.1%	(N/A)

MISCELLANEOUS PGA TOUR STATISTICS
2004 Low Round/Round: 70–2 times, most recent Buick Championship/2
Career Low Round/Round: 62–2002 Invensys Classic at Las Vegas/5
Career Largest Paycheck/Finish: $900,000–2002 Invensys Classic at Las Vegas/1

PGA TOUR CAREER SUMMARY — PLAYOFF RECORD: 0-0

Year	Events Played	Cuts Made	1st	2nd	3rd	Top 10	Top 25	Earnings	Rank
1994	24	9					2	$47,587	190
1996	1	1						3,743	333
1997	28	12			1	2	6	256,930	96
1998	28	13		1		1	5	335,821	89
1999	29	8				2	3	232,078	150
2000	4								
2001	12	4					2	141,581	189
2002	25	19	1			4	8	1,643,686	33
2003	11	6				1	3	354,083	149
2004	8	1						6,540	258
Total	170	73	1	1	1	10	29	3,022,048	
NATIONWIDE TOUR									
1994	2	1					1	2,374	173
1995	24	13		1		2	5	39,579	50
1996	20	13	1		1	3	8	77,535	24
2000	6	1						2,604	231
2001	10	6			1	2	4	59,119	72
2004	4	2						4,826	242
Total	66	36	1	1	2	7	18	186,038	
PGA TOUR OF AUSTRALASIA									
2003	1	1						3,026	

PGA TOUR TOP TOURNAMENT SUMMARY

Year	98	99	00	01	02	03
Masters						T39
U.S. Open	CUT				CUT	
PGA						T61
THE PLAYERS	CUT	CUT				CUT
WGC-Accenture Match Play						T17

NATIONAL TEAMS: World Amateur Team Championship, 1992.

Vaughn Taylor

EXEMPT STATUS: 2004 tournament winner (through 2006)
FULL NAME: Vaughn Joseph Taylor
HEIGHT: 6-0
WEIGHT: 150
BIRTHDATE: March 9, 1976
BIRTHPLACE: Roanoke, VA
RESIDENCE: Augusta, GA; plays out of Goshen Plantation GC

FAMILY: Single
EDUCATION: Augusta State University (1999, Business Administration)
SPECIAL INTERESTS: Fishing
TURNED PROFESSIONAL: 1999
JOINED TOUR: 2004
Nationwide Tour Alumnus

PGA TOUR VICTORIES (1):

2004 Reno-Tahoe Open.

NATIONWIDE TOUR VICTORIES (1):

2003 Knoxville Open.

BEST 2004 PGA TOUR FINISHES:

1—Reno-Tahoe Open; T5—FedEx St. Jude Classic; T7—B.C. Open; T10—FUNAI Classic at the WALT DISNEY WORLD Resort.

2004 SEASON:

One of five rookies to win on the PGA TOUR in 2004 and one of four to earn over $1 million in his first season...Along with his win, posted three other top-10s...Stellar play in rookie season allowed him to jump from No. 418 in January to No. 133 in the Official World Golf Ranking after THE TOUR Championship Presented by Coca-Cola...Claimed his first TOUR victory by rolling in an 11-foot birdie putt on the first extra hole to win a four-way playoff at the Reno-Tahoe Open. Taylor made a 14-foot birdie putt on the last hole of regulation for a 3-over 75 and tied hometown favorite Scott McCarron, rookie Hunter Mahan and Australia's Steve Allan at 10-under 278. Taylor was the seventh first-time winner on TOUR last year and the third of the five rookies to claim a title....Earned first career top-10 in 12th professional start, a T5 at the FedEx St. Jude Classic. First-round leader after opening with a 5-under-par 66 in blustery conditions that included winds up to 25 mph. One off the lead of David Toms through 36 holes after a second-round 65 but finished 71-74 to fall from contention...Second top-10 came at the B.C. Open. Closing-round 66 moved him to T7...Added a T10 in October at the FUNAI Classic at the WALT DISNEY WORLD Resort...Finished fourth in Eagles (holes per) and tied for sixth in Total Eagles, with 14.

CAREER HIGHLIGHTS:

2003: Finished 11th on Nationwide Tour's final money list to earn his initial PGA TOUR card. Began season with no status, but stormed out of the gate in May by Monday qualifying at the Virginia Beach Open and finishing second. Based on his top-25 finish, made it into the field the following week at the SAS Carolina Classic, where he posted his second consecutive runner-up finish. Broke through for his first career win on the Nationwide Tour at the Knoxville Open. Shot a final-round, 8-under-par 64 and then won on the first playoff hole against Joe Ogilvie to collect a career-best $85,500. **2000:** Was a rookie on the Nationwide Tour in 2000. **Amateur:** Qualified for the 1998 U.S. Open at The Olympic Club in San Francisco. Posted rounds of 76-76 and missed the cut...Four-time winner on the Hooters Tour...Honorable Mention All-American during his senior season at Augusta State University.

PLAYER STATISTICS

2004 PGA TOUR STATISTICS

Statistic	Value	Rank
Scoring Average	70.87	(66)
Driving Distance	292.5	(46)
Driving Accuracy Percentage	65.1%	(78)
Total Driving	124	(18)
Greens in Regulation Pct.	68.4%	(23)
Putting Average	1.761	(49)
Sand Save Percentage	41.9%	(180)
Eagles (Holes per)	105.4	(5)
Birdie Average	3.94	(13)
All-Around Ranking	460	(16)
Scoring Avg. Before Cut	70.35	(30)
Round 3 Scoring Avg.	70.75	(77)
Final Round Scoring Average	71.87	(123)
Birdie Conversion Percentage	31.3%	(29)
Par Breakers	22.8%	(8)

MISCELLANEOUS PGA TOUR STATISTICS

2004 Low Round/Round: 63–John Deere Classic/1
Career Low Round/Round: 63–2004 John Deere Classic/1
Career Largest Paycheck/Finish: $540,000–2004 Reno–Tahoe Open/1

SECTION 2 PLAYER BIOGRAPHIES

PGA TOUR CAREER SUMMARY — PLAYOFF RECORD: 1-0

Year	Events Played	Cuts Made	1st	2nd	3rd	Top 10	Top 25	Earnings	Rank
1998A	1								
2000A	1								
2004	27	16	1			4	8	$1,176,434	67
Total	29	16	1			4	8	1,176,434	
NATIONWIDE TOUR									
2000	12	7				2	4	50,986	85
2001	1								
2002	10	5				1	2	24,798	127
2003	17	10	1	2		5	6	223,988	11
2004	1	1					1	7,250	214
Total	41	23	1	2		8	13	307,023	

PGA TOUR TOP TOURNAMENT SUMMARY

Year	98
U.S. Open	CUT

David Toms

EXEMPT STATUS: Winner, 2001 PGA Championship (through 2006)
FULL NAME: David Wayne Toms
HEIGHT: 5-10
WEIGHT: 160
BIRTHDATE: January 4, 1967
BIRTHPLACE: Monroe, LA
RESIDENCE: Shreveport, LA

FAMILY: Wife, Sonya; Carter Phillip (7/29/97)
EDUCATION: Louisiana State University
SPECIAL INTERESTS: Hunting, fishing
TURNED PROFESSIONAL: 1989
Q SCHOOL: 1991
JOINED TOUR: 1992
Nationwide Tour Alumnus

PGA TOUR VICTORIES (10):

1997 Quad City Classic. **1999** Sprint International, Buick Challenge. **2000** Michelob Championship at Kingsmill. **2001** Compaq Classic of New Orleans, PGA Championship, Michelob Championship at Kingsmill. **2003** Wachovia Championship, FedEx St. Jude Classic. **2004** FedEx St. Jude Classic.

NATIONWIDE TOUR VICTORIES (2):

1995 Greater Greenville Classic, Wichita Open.

BEST 2004 PGA TOUR FINISHES:

1—FedEx St. Jude Classic; T4—Chrysler Classic of Greensboro; T5—Ford Championship at Doral; T6—WGC-NEC Invitational, Chrysler Championship; T9—WGC-Accenture Match Play Championship; T10—THE TOUR Championship presented by Coca-Cola.

2004 SEASON:

Finished outside the top 10 (No. 22) on the PGA TOUR money list for the first time since 2000...Missed the Mercedes Championships due to December 9, 2003 surgery on left wrist (bone spurs)...Made his first appearance of the 2004 season at the Nissan Open in February and missed the cut by a shot...Making his third start since the surgery, missed a five-foot putt on No. 18 that dropped him into a four-way T5 at the Ford Championship at Doral...Defending champion became the third player to win back-to-back titles at the FedEx St. Jude Classic, joining Dave Hill (1969-70) and Lee Trevino (1971-72). Opened a seven-stroke lead entering the final round after opening 67-63-65. Posted final-round, 2-over 73 to end streak of 11 consecutive rounds in the 60s at the FedEx St. Jude Classic, but still captured event by six over runner-up Bob Estes. With 10th career victory, joined four others under 40 with 10 or more wins on the PGA TOUR—Tiger Woods (40), Phil Mickelson (23), Ernie Els (13) and David Duval (13)...Finished sixth on the Ryder Cup team points list to make his second U.S. Ryder Cup squad...Finished T6 at WGC-NEC Invitational for first NEC top-10 in four starts...Finished the season making his last 11 cuts, seventh-longest current streak on TOUR, which included top-10s in his final three events—T4 at Chrysler Classic of Greensboro, T6 at the Chrysler Championship and a T10 at THE TOUR Championship.

CAREER HIGHLIGHTS:

2003: Won twice, at the Wachovia Championship and FedEx St. Jude Classic, and had a third straight season inside the money list top 10...Despite severe food poisoning during the week, finished runner-up to Tiger Woods in the WGC-Accenture Match Play Championship. Was four down after 18 holes in the 36-hole final at La Costa Resort and Spa, and lost 2 and 1...Earned first victory in 42 starts at the inaugural Wachovia Championship, earning a career-best $1,008,000 paycheck. Leader by five strokes through 54 holes after opening 70-69-66. Despite a quadruple-bogey eight on the 72nd hole, held off Vijay Singh, Robert Gamez and Brent Geiberger by two shots for eighth career PGA TOUR title...Carded four rounds in the 60s to capture the FedEx St. Jude Classic. Has reached multiple TOUR victories in three seasons (1999, 2001, 2003). Used final-round 7-under 64 to overcome 54-hole leader Richard S. Johnson. With the victory and $810,000 paycheck, moved into 10th place on all-time TOUR money list...Underwent surgery on his left wrist on Dec. 9 to remove bone spurs. **2002:** Despite not winning for the first time on TOUR since 1998, finished fourth on TOUR money list with $3,461,794. Season earnings were a record for player without a victory...Earned a career-best 12 top-10 finishes, tied for second on TOUR, including three runner-up finishes (lost in playoff to Sergio Garcia at Mercedes Championships, T2 at Colonial and solo second at Buick Challenge)...In first Ryder Cup appearance, led U.S. squad with a 3-1-1 record, including a singles victory over Sergio Garcia...Finished T5 in WGC-Accenture Match Play Championship after losing to Kevin Sutherland (3 and 2) in the quarterfinals...Led TOUR in rounds in the 60s (56) and shared title for most eagles on the season (17) with Jonathan Byrd and J.J. Henry. **2001:** Best season on TOUR, with three victories (second only to Tiger Woods' five), nine top 10s and third place on money list ($3,791,595)...Captured first major, the PGA Championship, in dramatic fashion. Shot 66-65-65 to hold the 54-hole lead, which included an ace on the par-3 15th in Saturday's third round. Battled playing competitor Phil Mickelson in the final round. Holding a one-stroke lead over Mickelson on the par-4 18th hole, he chose to lay up short of a water hazard in front of the green after studying a poor lie from 213 yards away. He wedged to 12 feet and sank the par putt for the win after Mickelson's long birdie putt rolled just short...First victory of the season came on home soil at the Compaq Classic of New Orleans. With fellow LSU fans cheering him on, Toms shot 63-64 on the weekend to win by one stroke...Won third title of the season at the Michelob Championship at Kingsmill, shooting 67-68 on the weekend to win for the second consecutive year in Williamsburg, VA...Made four-man playoff at THE TOUR Championship, losing to Mike Weir's birdie on the first playoff hole...Qualified for spot on the Ryder Cup team, his first time representing the U.S. in international competition. **2000:** Earned fourth PGA TOUR title and for the first time in career won in consecutive seasons with playoff victory at Michelob Championship at Kingsmill. Made five-foot par putt on first playoff hole to beat Mike Weir. Victory marked first time he won by coming from behind (trailed by two entering final round)...Trailed Tiger Woods by three strokes through 36 holes in first appearance in British Open. Closed with a pair of 71s at St. Andrews for T4, his then-best finish in a major. **1999:** Breakthrough season where he was one of seven multiple winners on way to 10th-place finish on TOUR money list...Picked up second career TOUR title at Sprint International. Victory was second wire-to-wire win, same manner in which he won 1997 Quad City Classic. Birdied last two holes at Castle Pines GC to defeat David Duval by three points. Came close to wins in back-to-back weeks, finishing T2 at Reno-Tahoe Open...Played through back pain to earn third TOUR title at Buick Challenge. Rounds of 68-66 produced share of 36-hole lead. Another 66 provided three-stroke lead through 54 holes. Maintained three-stroke cushion over Stuart Appleby with final-round 71. Had to quit Wednesday pro-am after one hole due to

PGA TOUR CAREER SUMMARY — PLAYOFF RECORD: 1-2

Year	Events Played	Cuts Made	1st	2nd	3rd	Top 10	Top 25	Earnings	Rank
1989	5	1						$1,463	278
1990	3								
1992	30	14			1	1	4	148,712	101
1993	32	12				3	5	120,952	123
1994	32	16					4	87,607	164
1996	29	16				2	8	205,188	105
1997	27	17	1			2	7	460,355	49
1998	26	18		1		3	11	635,073	44
1999	32	21	2	1	1	7	17	1,959,672	10
2000	31	26	1		1	6	19	2,002,068	15
2001	28	23	3	1		9	16	3,791,595	3
2002	27	25		3	1	12	20	3,459,739	4
2003	26	19	2	1		7	11	3,710,905	8
2004	24	17	1			7	13	2,357,531	22
Total	352	225	10	7	4	59	135	18,940,861	
NATIONWIDE TOUR									
1990	26	12		1		1	5	20,943	49
1991	6	4					3	3,372	149
1993	1								
1995	27	18	2	1	2	10	15	174,892	3
Total	60	34	2	2	2	11	23	199,206	

PGA TOUR TOP TOURNAMENT SUMMARY

Year	92	93	94	95	96	97	98	99	00	01	02	03	04
Masters							T6	CUT	T49	T31	T36	T8	CUT
U.S. Open					CUT	W/D		CUT	T16	T66	T45	T5	T20
British Open									T4	CUT	83	CUT	T30
PGA						CUT	CUT	CUT	T41	**1**	CUT	T29	T17
THE PLAYERS	CUT	CUT	CUT		CUT	CUT	CUT	T20	T38	T12	T19	CUT	CUT
TOUR Championship								T12	T11	T2	3	T21	T10
WGC-Accenture Match Play									T17	T17	T5	2	T9
WGC-NEC Invitational										T13	T15	T33	T6
WGC-American Express Champ								T11	T25	CNL	T4	5	T13

NATIONAL TEAMS: Ryder Cup (2), 2002, 2004; The Presidents Cup, 2003; WGC-World Cup, 2002.

David Toms (Continued)

severe back pain. **1998:** Made an impression in first Masters Tournament appearance in 1998. Shot final-round 64, one off Augusta National course record and one shy of record for any major championship. Hot finish helped Masters rookie to T6 finish. Back-nine 29 tied tournament record, as did his six consecutive birdies on holes 12-17...With three consecutive 65s, took 54-hole lead in defense of Quad City Classic title but closing 71 produced fourth-place finish. **1997:** Captured first TOUR title at Quad City Classic. Shot 67-66 and trailed 36-hole leader Keith Fergus by two strokes. Added Saturday 67 to share one-stroke lead with Brad Fabel and final-round 65 earned three-stroke victory over three others. **1995:** Won Greenville Classic in playoff over Tom Scherrer...Won another playoff over E.J. Pfister at Wichita Open. **1992:** Opened Kemper Open with course-record-tying 63, first time he set foot on TPC at Avenel. **1991:** First qualified for TOUR by finishing 24th in Qualifying Tournament. **Amateur:** First-team All-American at LSU in 1988-89, when he was named Southeastern Conference Player of the Year...Won the Junior World Championship and the PGA Junior Championship as a junior golfer in 1984.

PERSONAL:

Honorary Captain at 2001 LSU-Tulane football game, participating in pre-game coin toss. Received a standing ovation from 90,000 fans at Tiger Stadium...Teammates at Louisiana State included Bob Friend, Emlyn Aubrey, Perry Moss and Greg Lesher, current or former PGA TOUR members...In 2003, created the David Toms Foundation. The foundation helps underprivileged, abused and abandoned children through funding programs that are designed to enhance a child's character, self-esteem and career possibilities...Grew up playing baseball with future major leaguers Ben McDonald and Albert Belle...Helped in re-design of Palmetto Dunes Club (Louisiana) in 1999....First David Toms signature course, Carter Plantation in Springfield, La., opened to the public in October of 2003...Currently working with Rees Jones on a new 18-hole course at Redstone that will be the site of the 2006 Shell Houston Open.

PLAYER STATISTICS

2004 PGA TOUR STATISTICS

Scoring Average	70.05	(10)
Driving Distance	285.3	(117)
Driving Accuracy Percentage	63.4%	(110)
Total Driving	227	(145)
Greens in Regulation Pct.	68.5%	(20)
Putting Average	1.758	(40)
Sand Save Percentage	55.7%	(22)
Eagles (Holes per)	222.0	(86)
Birdie Average	3.85	(21)
All-Around Ranking	426	(9)
Scoring Avg. Before Cut	71.09	(110)
Round 3 Scoring Avg.	69.47	(10)
Final Round Scoring Average	70.40	(21)
Birdie Conversion Percentage	31.0%	(38)
Par Breakers	21.8%	(21)

MISCELLANEOUS PGA TOUR STATISTICS

2004 Low Round/Round: 63–FedEx St. Jude Classic/2
Career Low Round/Round: 62–2001 Verizon Byron Nelson Classic/3
Career Largest Paycheck/Finish: $1,008,000–2003 Wachovia Championship/1

SHOTLink. AN IBM ON DEMAND BUSINESS SOLUTION

HOT SHOTS

Par 4s with the Longest Average Second Shot (2004)

Event/ Course Name	Hole	Par	Hole Yardage	2nd Shot Yards
WGC-American Express Championship Mount Juliet	18	4	480	227.40
Mercedes Championships Plantation Course at Kapalua	1	4	473	223.48
Buick Invitational Torrey Pines (South Course)**	12	4	477	217.11
Wachovia Championship Quail Hollow CC	9	4	491	212.86
EDS Byron Nelson Championship TPC at Four Seasons Resort**	3	4	490	211.37

Par 4s with the Shortest Average Second Shot (2004)

Event/ Course Name	Hole	Par	Hole Yardage	2nd Shot Yards
Buick Championship TPC at River Highlands	15	4	296	27.64
Michelin Championship at Las Vegas TPC at Summerlin**	15	4	341	39.28
Mercedes Championships Plantation Course at Kapalua	6	4	398	43.76
FBR Open TPC of Scottsdale	17	4	332	50.51
Buick Classic Westchester CC	10	4	314	51.58

15th Hole - TPC at River Highlands

Kirk Triplett (TRIP-lit)

EXEMPT STATUS: 2003 tournament winner (through 2005)
FULL NAME: Kirk Alan Triplett
HEIGHT: 6-3
WEIGHT: 200
BIRTHDATE: March 29, 1962
BIRTHPLACE: Moses Lake, WA
RESIDENCE: Scottsdale, AZ

FAMILY: Wife, Cathi; Conor Logan and Samuel Jacob (1/19/96), Alexis Marie (3/17/00), Kobe Thomas (5/14/02)
EDUCATION: University of Nevada (1985, Civil Engineering)
SPECIAL INTERESTS: Adoption
TURNED PROFESSIONAL: 1985
Q SCHOOL: 1989

PGA TOUR VICTORIES (2):
2000 Nissan Open. **2003** Reno-Tahoe Open.

INTERNATIONAL VICTORIES (1):
1988 Alberta Open [Can].

BEST 2004 PGA TOUR FINISHES:
5—Chrysler Championship; 6—Mercedes Championships, Nissan Open, Masters Tournament; 7—Southern Farm Bureau Classic; T9—Bob Hope Chrysler Classic.

2004 SEASON:
Once again consistent play was the key to his season. Made 19 cuts in 24 starts and collected six top-10s…In second career appearance at season-opening Mercedes Championships, finished sixth, eight strokes behind winner Stuart Appleby…Shared the 72-hole lead with Phil Mickelson at the Bob Hope Chrysler Classic, but balky putter on back nine on Sunday (21 putts) dashed hopes of victory as he struggled to a 2-over-par 74 and a T9 finish…Past champion of the Nissan Open finished sixth, his third top-10 in first five starts of the season…Finished T6 at Masters, tying a career-best in six starts at Augusta. Sunday's even-par 72 included an ace on the par-3 16th hole…Held the first-round lead at the Wachovia Championship after firing a course record, 8-under-par 64. Was two back of Tiger Woods through 36 holes, but rounds of 71-74 on the weekend dropped him to T15…Next top-10 came in October, a seventh at the Southern Farm Bureau Classic, thanks to four rounds in the 60s…Ended the season on a high note with a solo fifth-place finish at the Chrysler Championship. Opened with an 8-under 64 and was two-strokes back of the lead after 18 and 54 holes.

CAREER HIGHLIGHTS:
2003: Recorded first top-10 since the 2001 Michelob Championship with a T2 at the Bay Hill Invitational...The next week at THE PLAYERS Championship, a final-round 67 secured a T8 finish, and got him into the Masters as No. 49 in the Official World Golf Ranking...After withdrawing from the PGA Championship the week before, earned second career TOUR victory at the Reno-Tahoe Open. University of Nevada-Reno graduate tied the 72-hole tournament record of 17-under-par 271 thanks to a final-round 63...Earned a spot in the TOUR Championship for only the third time in his career, finished T21. Earned over $2 million for the second time since joining the TOUR in 1990. **2002:** First top-10 of season was T6 at the Bob Hope Chrysler Classic...Shared second-round lead at Greater Milwaukee Open, finished T8...Earned third top-five finish in last four years at the John Deere Classic with his third-place finish (T3-1999, second-2000). **2001:** Finished in the top-10 in three of the four majors. Did not play in British Open. Best finish in a major before this season included T13 at the PGA in 1995 and 1997...Began the defense of Nissan Open title with first-round 66, good for four-way share of lead. Skied to an 81 in second round and missed cut. First player to lead after the first round and miss cut since Rodney Pampling at 1999 British Open...First top-10 of season came at Masters Tournament, where rounds of 68-70-70-71 produced T6...Recorded a T7 in season's second major, U.S. Open at Southern Hills...Finished T7 at Canon Greater Hartford Open...Playing in his 10th PGA Championship, rounds of 68-70-71-66 were good for T10...Four rounds in the 60s produced Michelob Championship runner-up finish. **2000:** Earned first victory in 266th PGA TOUR start, a one-stroke win over Jesper Parnevik in Nissan Open. A clutch four-foot par putt on final hole at Riviera CC brought victory after watching Parnevik drain a birdie putt. Trailed 54-hole leader David Sutherland by one stroke before closing with 67….Almost won again at John Deere Classic, where he lost on fourth playoff hole to Michael Clark II, the 2000 Rookie of the Year. Shot third-round 62 at TPC at Deere Run, tying course record set day before by David Frost...Qualified for U.S. Presidents Cup team and was 3-0-1 in his first appearance in team competition. **1999:** Recorded his fifth and sixth third-place finishes at Touchstone Energy Tucson Open and John Deere Classic. **1998:** Posted four top-10s and 10 top-25s in 25 appearances. Top-10s came in Bob Hope Chrysler Classic (T10), Deposit Guaranty (T7) FedEx St. Jude Classic (T7) and Las Vegas Invitational (T8). **1997:** Played in 26 events, finished in the top-10 four times, including a solo third. Three of the top-10s came in consecutive starts at THE PLAYERS Championship (T10), Freeport-McDermott Classic (T4) and Greater Greensboro Classic (3). **1996:** Closed with a 68, one stroke shy of Willie Wood at the Deposit Guaranty Classic, for his fifth career runner-up finish...Won Merrill Lynch Pebble Beach Invitational. **1995:** First of two runner-up finishes came at Buick Invitational of California, where he placed four strokes behind Peter Jacobsen. He then finished two strokes behind Greg Norman, tying for second at Canon Greater Hartford Open. Also T3 at B.C. Open. **1994:** Was part of four-way T2 at AT&T Pebble Beach National Pro-Am, one stroke behind Johnny Miller. **1992:** Posted first second-place finish at Shell Houston Open. **1990:** Rookie on the PGA TOUR, earned status through the 1989 Qualifying Tournament. **1988:** Winner of Alberta Open, Sierra Nevada Open and Fort McMurray Open...Played Australian, Asian and Canadian Tours from 1987-89.

PERSONAL:
Says of days on foreign tours: "I wouldn't trade the experience for anything. I learned so much, not only about golf, but about myself. I'll be telling stories about Asia until the day I die."…Wife, Cathi, active in TOUR Wives Association, has served as his caddie on occasion…Known for his patented "bucket" golf hat…Active in promoting adoption through the Fore Adoption Foundation and the Dave Thomas Foundation. Places a photo of a local foster child on his golf bag at every PGA TOUR event to raise awareness for foster childern. Also spends one afternoon during the week with the local foster child at each TOUR stop.

PLAYER STATISTICS

2004 PGA TOUR STATISTICS

Scoring Average	70.31	(25)
Driving Distance	279.1	(167)
Driving Accuracy Percentage	72.1%	(12)
Total Driving	179	(73)
Greens in Regulation Pct.	67.7%	(31)
Putting Average	1.752	(28)
Sand Save Percentage	49.3%	(92)
Eagles (Holes per)	252.0	(99)
Birdie Average	3.76	(37)
All-Around Ranking	491	(20)
Scoring Avg. Before Cut	69.54	(5)
Round 3 Scoring Avg.	71.05	(106)
Final Round Scoring Average	71.50	(91)
Birdie Conversion Percentage	29.8%	(74)
Par Breakers	21.3%	(42)

MISCELLANEOUS PGA TOUR STATISTICS

2004 Low Round/Round: 63–Bob Hope Chrysler Classic/4
Career Low Round/Round: 61–2000 Canon Greater Hartford Open/3
Career Largest Paycheck/Finish: $558,000–2000 Nissan Open/1

PGA TOUR CAREER SUMMARY — PLAYOFF RECORD: 0-1

Year	Events Played	Cuts Made	1st	2nd	3rd	Top 10	Top 25	Earnings	Rank
1986	1								
1987	1								
1988	1								
1990	26	13			1	2	5	$183,464	88
1991	28	18					6	137,302	112
1992	25	10		1		1	2	175,868	85
1993	27	19			1	2	6	189,418	90
1994	26	19		1		8	15	422,171	38
1995	27	24		2	1	7	17	644,607	29
1996	22	16		1		3	8	321,714	65
1997	26	19			1	4	10	541,023	39
1998	25	18				4	10	472,145	59
1999	26	19			2	5	12	863,399	47
2000	28	21	1	1	1	10	14	2,099,943	11
2001	26	19		1		5	12	1,388,202	38
2002	25	18			1	3	8	843,273	79
2003	25	20	1	1		5	12	2,001,561	29
2004	24	19				6	13	1,566,426	38
Total	389	272	2	8	8	65	150	11,850,516	

PGA TOUR TOP TOURNAMENT SUMMARY

Year	86	87	88	89	90	91	92	93	94	95	96	97	98
Masters											CUT		
U.S. Open	CUT	CUT			T33	CUT	66	T52	T23		T40		CUT
British Open									CUT				
PGA					CUT		CUT		T15	T13	CUT	T13	CUT
THE PLAYERS					T36	T68	CUT	T39	T45	67	T19	T10	T35
TOUR Championship										T20			

Year	99	00	01	02	03	04
Masters		CUT	T6	T40	CUT	T6
U.S. Open	CUT	56	T7	CUT	T28	T20
British Open		T60				
PGA	T49	T69	T10	T29	W/D	CUT
THE PLAYERS	T38	T42	T31	CUT	T8	CUT
TOUR Championship		T8			T21	
WGC-Accenture Match Play			T33	T17		
WGC-NEC Invitational		T33	DQ	T28		T69
WGC-American Express Champ		T14	CNL		65	

NATIONAL TEAMS: The Presidents Cup (1), 2000

Bob Tway

EXEMPT STATUS: 2003 tournament winner (through 2005)
FULL NAME: Robert Raymond Tway
HEIGHT: 6-4
WEIGHT: 195
BIRTHDATE: May 4, 1959
BIRTHPLACE: Oklahoma City, OK
RESIDENCE: Edmond, OK; plays out of Oak Tree GC

FAMILY: Wife, Tammie; Kevin (7/23/88), Carly Paige (11/8/93)
EDUCATION: Oklahoma State University
SPECIAL INTERESTS: Snow skiing, fishing, all sports
TURNED PROFESSIONAL: 1981
Q SCHOOL: 1984

PGA TOUR VICTORIES (8):

1986 Shearson Lehman Brothers Andy Williams Open, Manufacturers Hanover Westchester Classic, Georgia-Pacific Atlanta Golf Classic, PGA Championship. **1989** Memorial Tournament. **1990** Las Vegas Invitational. **1995** MCI Classic. **2003** Bell Canadian Open.

BEST 2004 PGA TOUR FINISHES:

T6—WGC-NEC Invitational; T9—The INTERNATIONAL; T10—Nissan Open.

2004 SEASON:

Another consistent year on the PGA TOUR for the 20-year veteran who made 20 cuts in 26 TOUR starts. Recorded three top-10s, including a T6 at the WGC-NEC Invitational…First top-10 of the season was a T10 at the Nissan Open, his third top-10 in Los Angeles in 18 starts in Pacific Palisades…Finished T9 at The INTERNATIONAL. Only three points back of the leaders heading into the final round, but minus-three points on the final day dropped him to T9, his fourth top-10 at Castle Pines…Two weeks later, finished T6 in first start at WGC-NEC Invitational in Akron, OH, and only his fifth start in a World Golf Championships event…Finished T26 in defense of his title at the Bell Canadian Open…Selected to represent the United States team with Scott Verplank at the WGC-World Cup in Seville, Spain.

CAREER HIGHLIGHTS:

2003: Had career year, with $2,469,750 in earnings on the strength of a victory, four top-threes and seven top-10s...Won the Bell Canadian Open in a three-hole playoff over Brad Faxon. Improved his playoff record to 4-4. Win came 8 years, 4 months and 21 days from his last victory at the 1995 MCI Classic, a span of 233 events. His last three victories have come in playoffs. Collected a career-high $756,000 to put him over $2 million for the season for the first time in his career...Finished T4 at the Chrysler Classic of Tucson, giving him four consecutive top-10s in Tucson...Topped that with a third-place finish the following week at the Ford Championship at Doral. Held second-round lead and shared third-round lead with Scott Hoch before finishing two strokes out of the playoff between Hoch and Jim Furyk...Finished second at the BellSouth Classic. Tied for the lead after 36 holes and trailed Lee Janzen by one stroke after 54 holes. Playing in final threesome, grabbed early lead but was passed on the back nine by Ben Crane's 9-under 63...Finished T10 at The INTERNATIONAL...Playing in his first event since winning the Bell Canadian Open shared the first-round lead at the Valero Texas Open after posting a course record-tying 61. Finished T2. **2002:** Six top-10s were the most since posting nine in 1998. **2001:** After falling out of the top-100 in 2000 for the first time since 1994, managed to bonce back with $1,121,858, good for 48th on the money list. Made the cut in 25 of 29 events, including 11 consecutive to end the season. **2000:** Fell out of the top 100 money winners for just the fourth time in 16 seasons on TOUR...Made the cut in four of the last five tournaments, including T10 at Tampa Classic and T20 at Southern Farm Bureau Classic, to move from 130th to 114th on TOUR money list and regain full exempt status. **1999:** Enjoyed fifth consecutive standout season with $899,484 in earnings...In his last attempt to earn spot in THE TOUR Championship, had to win National Car Rental Golf Classic at Walt Disney World Resort. Shared 36- and 54-hole lead with eventual winner Tiger Woods before T3. **1998:** Surpassed $1 million in season earnings for the first time after playing in 18 events, finishing in top 10 nine times...Was in second place after second and third rounds of U.S. Open before final-round 73 at The Olympic Club produced third-place finish, his best in U.S. Open. **1997:** Five top-10s, including T5 at U.S. Open. **1995:** Returned to winner's circle after four-year hiatus (1991-94) at MCI Classic, defeating Nolan Henke and David Frost in playoff and finished year with eight top-10s...Had fallen on hard times, finishing as low as 179th on the money list in 1992...Shared lead at U.S. Open with nine holes to play, but fell to T10...Voted by peers as PGA TOUR Comeback Player of the Year. **1990:** Parred first playoff hole to defeat John Cook at Las Vegas Invitational. **1989:** Defeated Fuzzy Zoeller by two strokes at Memorial Tournament. **1986:** Collected four titles, including PGA Championship, while finishing second on money list...Holed out from green-side bunker on 18th hole at Inverness to win PGA Championship by two strokes over Greg Norman...Also won Shearson Lehman Brothers-Andy Williams Open, Manufacturers Hanover Westchester Classic and Georgia Pacific Atlanta Classic...Named PGA of America Player of the Year. **1985:** Rookie on the PGA TOUR and collected winnings of $164,023, 45th on the money list. **Amateur:** Three-time All-American at Oklahoma State and member of two national championship teams (1978, 1980)...Winner of 1981 Fred Haskins Award as nation's top college player...Winner of 1985 and 1987 Oklahoma State Opens.

PERSONAL:

Described 1995 MCI Classic victory as "better than any other win I've had, because I was down so low."…Introduced to golf at age 5, following his father and grandfather around course. Played his first tournament at age 7.

PLAYER STATISTICS

2004 PGA TOUR STATISTICS

Scoring Average	71.11	(96)
Driving Distance	278.2	(170)
Driving Accuracy Percentage	63.7%	(105)
Total Driving	275	(183)
Greens in Regulation Pct.	64.8%	(104)
Putting Average	1.788	(122)
Sand Save Percentage	46.9%	(129)
Eagles (Holes per)	382.5	(163)
Birdie Average	3.21	(168)
All-Around Ranking	1,057	(164)
Scoring Avg. Before Cut	71.02	(100)
Round 3 Scoring Avg.	70.79	(82)
Final Round Scoring Average	72.33	(154)
Birdie Conversion Percentage	26.3%	(179)
Par Breakers	18.1%	(173)

MISCELLANEOUS PGA TOUR STATISTICS

2004 Low Round/Round: 64–Valero Texas Open/3
Career Low Round/Round: 61–2 times, most recent 2003 Valero Texas Open/1
Career Largest Paycheck/Finish: $756,000–2003 Bell Canadian Open/1

PGA TOUR CAREER SUMMARY — PLAYOFF RECORD: 4-4

Year	Events Played	Cuts Made	1st	2nd	3rd	Top 10	Top 25	Earnings	Rank
1981A	1	1							
1981	2	1						$582	295
1982	9	7					1	9,039	177
1983	8	6					2	12,089	174
1984	2	1						1,719	237
1985	25	14		1	2	4	9	164,023	45
1986	33	28	4			13	21	652,780	2
1987	27	19			1	7	12	212,362	47
1988	30	25		2	1	4	13	381,966	29
1989	28	19	1	2		4	9	488,340	17
1990	29	20	1			5	8	495,862	23
1991	24	15		1		5	7	322,931	52
1992	21	12						47,632	179
1993	25	11				2	4	148,120	109
1994	29	13					4	114,176	146
1995	27	22	1			8	15	787,348	20
1996	25	17		1	1	5	11	529,456	35
1997	26	21				5	14	507,523	43
1998	28	24			1	9	18	1,073,447	24
1999	29	20		1	1	5	11	899,484	43
2000	30	16				1	8	417,646	114
2001	29	25		1	1	5	11	1,121,858	48
2002	28	22				6	10	1,160,399	55
2003	26	17	1	2	1	7	9	2,601,600	13
2004	26	20				3	6	966,553	79
Total	567	396	8	11	9	98	203	13,116,936	

PGA TOUR TOP TOURNAMENT SUMMARY

Year	86	87	88	89	90	91	92	93	94	95	96	97	98
Masters	T8	CUT	T33	CUT	T36	CUT					T12	CUT	CUT
U.S. Open	T8	T68	T25	CUT	T33	T26		CUT	CUT	T10	T67	T5	3
British Open	T46	T35	T20	T61	CUT	T5	CUT			CUT	CUT	CUT	CUT
PGA	**1**	T47	T48	CUT	T45	T66	T56	CUT	CUT	CUT	CUT	T13	T13
THE PLAYERS	T10	CUT	CUT	T29	CUT	T41	T70	CUT	CUT	T68	CUT	CUT	T18
TOUR Championship			T8	T22	T14					15			T8

Year	99	00	01	02	03	04
Masters	T52	CUT				T27
U.S. Open	T62		T52	T59	CUT	CUT
British Open	CUT	CUT		T50		70
PGA	T57	CUT	T29	CUT	CUT	T55
THE PLAYERS	CUT	CUT	T40	T28	T17	T77
TOUR Championship					T13	
WGC-Accenture Match Play	T17	T17				T33
WGC-NEC Invitational						T6
WGC-American Express Champ	T37				T59	T28

NATIONAL TEAMS: World Amateur Team Championship, 1980; Nissan Cup, 1986; Asahi Glass Four Tours, 1991; WGC-World Cup, 2004.

Bo Van Pelt

EXEMPT STATUS: 39th on TOUR money list
FULL NAME: Bo Van Pelt
HEIGHT: 6-4
WEIGHT: 200
BIRTHDATE: May 16, 1975
BIRTHPLACE: Richmond, IN
RESIDENCE: Tulsa, OK; plays out of GC of Oklahoma (Broken Arrow, OK)
FAMILY: Wife, Carrie; Olivia (5/26/01), Trace (11/26/02)
EDUCATION: Oklahoma State University (1998, General Business)
SPECIAL INTERESTS: Billiards, basketball, movies, watching sports
TURNED PROFESSIONAL: 1998
Q SCHOOL: 1998
Nationwide Tour Alumnus

BEST PGA TOUR CAREER FINISH:
T4—**2004** Buick Invitational, Booz Allen Classic.

NATIONWIDE TOUR VICTORIES (1):
2003 Omaha Classic.

BEST 2004 PGA TOUR FINISHES:
T4—Buick Invitational, Booz Allen Classic; T5—Bank of America Colonial; T7—U.S. Bank Championship in Milwaukee; T9—Buick Classic.

2004 SEASON:
Returned to PGA TOUR for a third time, the second via the Nationwide Tour money list, where he finished fifth in 2003…This time he made it count by finishing 39th on the money list and qualifying for his first trip to the Masters in 2005…Moved from No. 429 at start of season to No. 104 in the Official World Golf Ranking after THE TOUR Championship…Came into the season with no top-10s and two top-25s in 58 starts but recorded five top-10s and 13 top-25s, while making the cut in 23 of 30 events…Posted his first career top-10 finish on TOUR with a T4 at the Buick Invitational. Picked up $174,000, better than the $139,357 he earned for the entire 2002 season. Through five events in '04, already had doubled his career top-25s…A final-round, 5-under 65 gave him a T5 finish at the Bank of America Colonial, his eighth top-25 finish of the season…Two starts later finished T9 at the Buick Classic…Matched his career-best finish with a T4 at the Booz Allen Classic, thanks to being one of only four players with four rounds in the 60s. His $198,400 payday was a career best and lifted him over the $1-million mark in season earnings for the first time in his career…Added a fifth top-10 with a T7 at the U.S. Bank Championship in Milwaukee. Shared first-round lead with seven others, tying a TOUR record for players sharing the lead through 18 holes (2000 Honda Classic)…Finished tied for second on TOUR in Rounds in the 60s (46) and fourth in Total Birdies (406).

CAREER HIGHLIGHTS:
2003: Posted 16 top-25s in 24 events on the Nationwide Tour on way to fifth-place finish on money list. Finish allowed him to earn his PGA TOUR card for the third time in his career and second time via the Nationwide Tour...His 26-under 262 at the Omaha Classic equaled the low 72-hole score in Nationwide Tour history. It was his first win on the tour that he played in 2000-01 and 2003. Had a hole-in-one on No. 8 in the final round of the season-ending Nationwide Tour Championship. **2002:** Made the cut in 10 of 28 events on the PGA TOUR with his only top-25 a T25 at the BellSouth Classic. Fired career-low, final-round 63 at the Greater Milwaukee Open. **2001:** Finished 11th on Nationwide Tour money list to earn second TOUR card. Finished in top 25 in 10 of his 17 cuts made, including two runner-up finishes at the Dayton Open and Gila River Classic. Lost three-man playoff with Jason Caron and winner Ben Crane at Gila River. **1999:** Made only seven cuts in rookie season on the PGA TOUR in 1999, including a career-best T20 finish at the Bell Canadian Open. **1998:** Earned his first TOUR card with T17 finish at the 1998 PGA TOUR Qualifying Tournament.

PERSONAL:
Father, Bob, was fifth-round draft pick by the NFL's Philadelphia Eagles in 1967 after collegiate career at Indiana University.

PLAYER STATISTICS

2004 PGA TOUR STATISTICS

Scoring Average	70.24	(22)
Driving Distance	294.4	(36)
Driving Accuracy Percentage	65.1%	(78)
Total Driving	114	(10)
Greens in Regulation Pct.	67.7%	(31)
Putting Average	1.768	(67)
Sand Save Percentage	43.1%	(169)
Eagles (Holes per)	267.4	(114)
Birdie Average	3.90	(14)
All-Around Ranking	531	(33)
Scoring Avg. Before Cut	70.44	(36)
Round 3 Scoring Avg.	70.13	(37)
Final Round Scoring Average	70.32	(18)
Birdie Conversion Percentage	31.4%	(27)
Par Breakers	22.1%	(15)

MISCELLANEOUS PGA TOUR STATISTICS

2004 Low Round/Round: 65–4 times, most recent Michelin Championship at Las Vegas/3
Career Low Round/Round: 63–2002 Greater Milwaukee Open/4
Career Largest Paycheck/Finish: $198,400–2004 Booz Allen Classic/T4

PGA TOUR CAREER SUMMARY — PLAYOFF RECORD: 0-0

Year	Events Played	Cuts Made	1st	2nd	3rd	Top 10	Top 25	Earnings	Rank
1999	28	7					1	$70,080	210
2002	28	10					1	139,357	191
2004	30	23				5	13	1,553,825	39
Total	86	40				5	15	1,763,262	
NATIONWIDE TOUR									
1999	1	1					1	3,069	169
2000	27	16			1	3	6	84,064	62
2001	24	17		2		5	10	175,947	11
2002	1								
2003	24	19	1		1	7	16	289,248	5
Total	77	53	1	2	2	15	33	552,328	

PGA TOUR TOP TOURNAMENT SUMMARY

Year	04
U.S. Open	T31
British Open	T30
PGA	T31

Scott Verplank

EXEMPT STATUS: 20th on 2004 money list
FULL NAME: Scott Rachal Verplank
HEIGHT: 5-9
WEIGHT: 165
BIRTHDATE: July 9, 1964
BIRTHPLACE: Dallas, TX
RESIDENCE: Edmond, OK

FAMILY: Wife, Kim; Scottie (7/14/92), Hannah (1/26/95), Emma (8/15/97), Heidi Ann (2/12/04)
EDUCATION: Oklahoma State University (1986, Business)
SPECIAL INTERESTS: Playing with his kids, quail hunting, Oklahoma State football
TURNED PROFESSIONAL: 1986
JOINED TOUR: 1986

PGA TOUR VICTORIES (4):

1985 Western Open. **1988** Buick Open. **2000** Reno-Tahoe Open. **2001** Bell Canadian Open.

INTERNATIONAL VICTORIES (1):

1998 World Cup of Golf [indiv].

BEST 2004 PGA TOUR FINISHES:

2—Ford Championship at Doral; T3—Bay Hill Invitational Presented by MasterCard; T7—FBR Open, British Open Championship, THE TOUR Championship presented by Coca-Cola; T10—Buick Open.

2004 SEASON:

Despite suffering from plantar fasciitis, an ailment in his right foot for much of the year, finished among the top 30 money winners for the fourth time in five years...Led the FBR Open after first-round, 8-under 63, then finished seventh for his first top-10 of the season...His 5-under-par 67 final round at the Ford Championship at Doral forced a playoff with Craig Parry. On the first playoff hole, Parry holed his second shot from the fairway on the par-4 18th for an eagle and the victory over Verplank...Continued strong play during the Florida swing with a T3 at the Bay Hill Invitational...Matched his career-best performance in a major with a T7 at the British Open in Scotland. His other T7 came at the 2001 PGA Championship...Past champion finished T10 at the Buick Open, with four rounds of 70 or better, remaining at No. 12 in Ryder Cup standings for 2004 U.S. squad...Shared first-round lead with six others at the Michelin Championship at Las Vegas prior to finishing T15...Closed the season with a T7 at THE TOUR Championship, aided by rounds of 68-67 on the weekend.

CAREER HIGHLIGHTS:

2003: Recorded top-10s at THE PLAYERS Championship (T8), Masters (T8) and U.S. Open (T10)...Recorded first runner-up finish on TOUR since losing a playoff to Robert Damron at the 2001 EDS Byron Nelson Classic by finishing T2 at the FUNAI Classic at the WALT DISNEY WORLD Resort. **2002:** Named winner of the 2002 Ben Hogan Award, given by the Golf Writers Association of America to an individual who has continued to be active in golf despite a physical handicap or serious illness...One stroke back of the lead through 54 holes at the Canon Greater Hartford Open, finish solo fourth...Playing in his first Ryder Cup, posted a record of 2-1-0. **2001:** Finished in the top 10 on the money list and earned over $2 million for first time in his career, completing the season with a victory...Opened with an 8-under 62 to take first-round lead at Verizon Byron Nelson Classic. Shared second- and third-round leads after rounds of 67-68. Closing 66 produced playoff with Robert Damron. Damron won playoff with birdie on fourth extra hole...Following T7 at PGA Championship, selected by Curtis Strange as one of two Captain's Choices for Ryder Cup team. First Ryder Cup rookie to make team as Captain's Choice...Three weeks later, earned fourth PGA TOUR victory at Bell Canadian Open. Second-round 63, after opening 70, lifted him into contention. Third-round 66 put him one stroke ahead of Paul Gow and Dicky Pride. Closing 67 produced three-stroke victory over Bob Estes and Joey Sindelar. **2000:** Returned to the winner's circle for the first time since 1988 with victory at Reno-Tahoe Open. Trailed third-round leader Jean Van de Velde by five strokes after 54 holes. Final-round 67 earned a tie with Van de Velde, and Verplank won playoff with an eight-foot birdie putt on the fourth extra hole. **1999:** Made 26 starts, making cut in 19...Finished in the top 10 once during the year with solo eighth at the John Deere Classic. **1998:** Lost playoff to Trevor Dodds at Greater Greensboro Chrysler Classic on first extra hole...Finished fifth at THE TOUR Championship...Earnings of $1,223,436 placed him 18th on money list, highest finish by Q-School grad since John Daly was 17th in 1991...With Daly, represented United States in World Cup of Golf and won individual title with 9-under-par 279, one stroke better than Nick Faldo and Costantino Rocca...Chosen by his peers as PGA TOUR Comeback Player of the Year. **1997:** Finished as medalist at 1997 PGA TOUR Qualifying Tournament to regain PGA TOUR

PGA TOUR CAREER SUMMARY — PLAYOFF RECORD: 2-3

Year	Events Played	Cuts Made	1st	2nd	3rd	Top 10	Top 25	Earnings	Rank
1983A	1								
1984A	1	1							
1985A	5	2	1			1	1		
1986A	5	3				1	2		
1986	13	5				1	2	$19,757	177
1987	31	12					2	34,136	173
1988	28	19	1	1		3	9	366,045	31
1989	28	15				1	3	82,345	141
1990	27	18		1	1	4	7	303,589	47
1991	26	1						3,195	266
1992	13	1						1,760	309
1994	19	14				1	8	183,015	97
1995	25	20				4	10	332,886	55
1996	12	10					4	88,801	171
1997	21	10				1	4	113,254	159
1998	27	22		2	1	10	14	1,223,436	18
1999	26	19				1	8	474,260	82
2000	28	24	1			6	16	1,747,643	22
2001	26	24	1	1	1	8	16	2,783,401	10
2002	26	21				4	12	1,217,022	50
2003	26	23		1	1	8	13	2,306,714	19
2004	24	23		1	1	6	13	2,365,592	20
Total	438	287	4	7	5	60	144	13,646,851	
NATIONWIDE TOUR									
1992	1								
1994	1	1						220	309
Total	2	1						220	

PGA TOUR TOP TOURNAMENT SUMMARY

Year	85	86	87	88	89	90	91	92	93	94	95	96	97
Masters	CUT	CUT	CUT		CUT								
U.S. Open	T34	T15	CUT			T61				T18	T21		
British Open		CUT		CUT									
PGA				CUT	CUT	T31					CUT		
THE PLAYERS		CUT			CUT		CUT				CUT	W/D	
TOUR Championship				T8									

Year	98	99	00	01	02	03	04
Masters		CUT		CUT	43	T8	29
U.S. Open	T49	T17	T46	T22	CUT	T10	T40
British Open		T15	CUT	T30	T37	CUT	T7
PGA	T54	T34	CUT	T7	CUT	CUT	T62
THE PLAYERS	T11	T32	T20	T44	T28	T8	T26
TOUR Championship	T5		14	T5		T9	T7
WGC-Accenture Match Play		T17		T17	T17	T33	T33
WGC-NEC Invitational				T17	T58	T46	T19
WGC-American Express Champ			T48	CNL	T15	T51	T54

NATIONAL TEAMS: Walker Cup, 1985; Ryder Cup, 2002; WGC-World Cup, 1998, 2004.

Scott Verplank (Continued)

card. **1996:** Required surgery on elbow again and received special medical extension for 1997. **1994:** Played first part of season under special medical extension and was able to retain card by finishing 97th on money list. **1992:** Missed most of season and the prior year due to first elbow surgery. **1988:** Earned second TOUR title at the Buick Open, where a final-round 66 produced two-stroke victory over Doug Tewell. **1985:** Became first amateur in 29 years to win a PGA TOUR event (Doug Sanders at 1956 Canadian Open had been the last) when he defeated Jim Thorpe in a playoff at the Western Open. **Amateur:** 1984 U.S. Amateur and 1986 NCAA Championship winner...Four-time All-American at Oklahoma State...Played on the U.S. Walker Cup team in 1985.

PERSONAL:

Has diabetes and wears a MiniMed insulin pump while playing to regulate his medication. . .Co-chair of The Next Level campaign at Oklahoma State, designed to raise funds to improve the OSU football facilities.

PLAYER STATISTICS

2004 PGA TOUR STATISTICS

Scoring Average	69.92	(9)
Driving Distance	278.0	(173)
Driving Accuracy Percentage	77.1%	(2)
Total Driving	175	(68)
Greens in Regulation Pct.	68.5%	(20)
Putting Average	1.743	(11)
Sand Save Percentage	47.1%	(124)
Eagles (Holes per)	546.0	(181)
Birdie Average	3.96	(9)
All-Around Ranking	529	(31)
Scoring Avg. Before Cut	69.76	(8)
Round 3 Scoring Avg.	69.77	(18)
Final Round Scoring Average	70.73	(40)
Birdie Conversion Percentage	30.9%	(39)
Par Breakers	22.2%	(14)

MISCELLANEOUS PGA TOUR STATISTICS

2004 Low Round/Round: 63–FBR Open/1
Career Low Round/Round: 61–2001 Canon Greater Hartford Open/4
Career Largest Paycheck/Finish: $684,000–2001 Bell Canadian Open/1

SHOTLink
AN IBM ON DEMAND BUSINESS SOLUTION

HOT SHOTS

Holes with Most Birdies (2004)

Event/ Course Name	Par	Hole	Birdies
Sony Open in Hawaii Waialae CC	5	9	265
Ford Championship at Doral Doral Golf Resort & Spa	5	1	262
John Deere Classic TPC at Deere Run	5	2	254
Nissan Open Riviera CC	5	1	249
Chrysler Classic of Tucson Tucson Nat'l Golf	5	2	237

Holes with Most Eagles (2004)

Event/ Course Name	Par	Hole	Eagles
Nissan Open Riviera CC	5	1	36
Sony Open in Hawaii Waialae CC	5	9	30
Southern Farm Bureau Classic Annandale GC	5	5	25
Valero Texas Open LaCantera GC	5	14	24
Ford Championship at Doral Doral Golf Resort & Spa	5	1	23

Hole with Most Bogeys or Higher (2004)

Event/ Course Name	Par	Hole	Avg Score	Bogeys+
Bell Canadian Open Glen Abbey GC	4	16	5.13	188
U.S. Open Championship Shinnecock Hills Golf Club	4	10	5.26	187
Ford Championship at Doral Doral Golf Resort & Spa	4	18	5.34	182
U.S. Bank Championship in Milwaukee Brown Deer Park GC	4	4	5.09	180
PGA Championship Whistling Straits	4	15	5.15	178

Duffy Waldorf

EXEMPT STATUS: 46th on 2004 money list
FULL NAME: James Joseph Waldorf, Jr.
HEIGHT: 6-0
WEIGHT: 225
BIRTHDATE: August 20, 1962
BIRTHPLACE: Los Angeles, CA
RESIDENCE: Northridge, CA

FAMILY: Wife, Vicky; Tyler Lane (7/16/90), Shea Duffy (4/23/92), Kelli Ann (1/14/94), Justin James (7/20/96)
EDUCATION: UCLA (1985, Psychology)
SPECIAL INTERESTS: Wine collecting
TURNED PROFESSIONAL: 1985
Q SCHOOL: 1986, 1987, 1988, 1990

PGA TOUR VICTORIES (4):

1995 LaCantera Texas Open. **1999** Buick Classic, Westin Texas Open. **2000** National Car Rental Golf Classic at Walt Disney World Resort.

OTHER VICTORIES (3):

1995 Hyundai Team Matches [with Tom Lehman]. **1996** Hyundai Team Matches [with Tom Lehman]. **2000** Hyundai Team Matches [with Tom Lehman].

BEST 2004 PGA TOUR FINISHES:

4—The INTERNATIONAL, Buick Invitational, EDS Byron Nelson Championship; T5—FBR Open; T7—84 LUMBER Classic.

2004 SEASON:

Entered 26 tournaments and made 16 cuts. Finished 46th on the money list on the strength of four top-five finishes. . .Earned first top-five of the season with a T5 at the FBR Open in Phoenix, thanks in part to a final-round 6-under 65. . .In his next start two weeks later, had a T4 at the Buick Invitational. . .After withdrawing from the Shell Houston Open due to a back injury and missing the cut at the Wachovia Championship, bounced back with a T4 finish at the EDS Byron Nelson Championship. Missed the three-way playoff near Dallas by one stroke. . .Finished T11 at the Booz Allen Classic in June, just missing a chance for three consecutive top-10s at TPC of Avenel. Finished second in 2003 and T9 in 2002. . .Did not play again on the PGA TOUR until The INTERNATIONAL in Colorado the first week of August. Finished alone in fourth at Castle Pines. . .Four rounds in the 60s at the Valero Texas Open was good for T14. . .Finished T7 at the 84 LUMBER Classic on the strength of four under-par rounds at Mystic Rock Club. . .Was two strokes back of the lead through 54 holes at the Michelin Championship at Las Vegas. Fired a final round 70 to finish T11.

CAREER HIGHLIGHTS:

2003: Entered 25 tournaments and made 19 cuts. Finished among the top-10 three times and top-25 nine times...Making his 13th start at The PLAYERS Championship, posted a career-best finish with T11...Recorded a T2 at the FBR Capital Open in June. Would have finished alone in second but was penalized two strokes after he finished his round because of a rules infraction (13-2: Improving his line of play) that occurred in the 12th fairway...Two-time winner of the Valero Texas Open finished alone in fourth after closing rounds of 62-67. **2002:** Made 19 cuts in 27 starts, finished in top-10 four times and top-25 10 times...Led Phoenix Open after 36 and 54 holes. Final-round 73 dropped finish to sixth...Best outing of the year was a T5 at the Advil Western Open where he earned a spot in the British Open. The top-8 finishers from the Advil Western Open, not previously exempt, gained entry into British Open...Tied for 18- and 36-hole leads at the British Open. Fell out of contention with third-round 76, but recovered with final-round 69 for best career British Open finish, T18. **2001:** Earned his only top-10 of the year in 22nd start of the season in Reno-Tahoe Open, finished T5. **2000:** For the first time in his career, won in back-to-back seasons with victory at National Car Rental Golf Classic at Walt Disney World Resort. Came from six strokes back of 54-hole leaders Steve Flesch and Tiger Woods with a final-round 62 to win by one. Final round highlighted by 10 birdies, including the winning putt from 12 feet on the 18th green...In his next start, finished T3 at the WGC-American Express Championship. In his final two starts of the season, earned $827,000. **1999:** Had a career-first multiple-win season with victories at the Buick Classic and Westin Texas Open. Shared 54-hole lead at Buick Classic. Closed with 71, during which he birdied last two holes at Westchester CC to produce a playoff with Dennis Paulson. Birdied first extra hole. Became a two-time champion of Westin Texas Open, sinking a 45-foot birdie putt on first hole of playoff to defeat Ted Tryba. The two began final round two strokes behind Stephen Ames. **1997:** Had runner-up finishes at Michelob Championship at Kingsmill and at Buick Invitational. Had an opportunity to win at Kingsmill after leading the first two rounds by one stroke and by three after the third round. Final-round 70 not enough to hold off David Duval and Grant Waite, each of whom shot 67 to create three-man playoff. Duval birdied first extra hole to win. **1996:** Two runner-up finishes and second trip to THE TOUR Championship...Started year with T7 in his first Mercedes Championships...Finished solo second at Greater Greensboro Chrysler Classic and T2 at NEC World Series of Golf...T5 at Masters Tournament, his best finish in a major. **1995:** First PGA TOUR victory came in decisive fashion at LaCantera Texas Open. Held 36-hole lead after shooting back-to-back 66s and led Jay Don Blake by one stroke through 54 holes. Shot closing 65 to defeat runner-up Justin Leonard by six strokes and next-closest competitors by 12. **1994:** Finished in the top-10 eight times including a third at the Sprint International. **1993:** Held 54-hole lead at Buick Classic before closing 75 dropped him to T10. **1992:** Had runner-up finishes in Phoenix Open and Buick Classic. **1990:** Qualifying Tournament medalist in fourth attempt. **Amateur:** Winner of 1984 California State Amateur and Broadmoor Invitational...1985 College Player of the Year.

PERSONAL:

A connoisseur of fine wine. . .Enjoys wearing colorful caps and shirts. His wife and children mark, with messages and reminders, the golf balls he uses each week. Duffy adds a few designs too. During 2000 victory at Disney World Resort, drew a picture of Mickey Mouse on one side of his golf ball and on the other his wife wrote, "Mouse in the House.". . .Got his nickname Duffy from his grandparents when he was small. Tagged along on the golf course and they called him "Little Duffer."

PLAYER STATISTICS

2004 PGA TOUR STATISTICS

Scoring Average	70.60	(39)
Driving Distance	285.4	(116)
Driving Accuracy Percentage	68.6%	(40)
Total Driving	156	(42)
Greens in Regulation Pct.	69.9%	(9)
Putting Average	1.770	(77)
Sand Save Percentage	41.3%	(187)
Eagles (Holes per)	146.0	(30)
Birdie Average	3.78	(32)
All-Around Ranking	530	(32)
Scoring Avg. Before Cut	70.55	(43)
Round 3 Scoring Avg.	69.21	(7)
Final Round Scoring Average	71.07	(61)
Birdie Conversion Percentage	29.8%	(74)
Par Breakers	21.7%	(25)

MISCELLANEOUS PGA TOUR STATISTICS

2004 Low Round/Round: 65–3 times, most recent Michelin Championship at Las Vegas/1
Career Low Round/Round: 62–2 times, most recent 2003 Valero Texas Open/3
Career Largest Paycheck/Finish: $540,000–2000 National Car Rental Golf Classic Disney/1

PGA TOUR CAREER SUMMARY — PLAYOFF RECORD: 2-1

Year	Events Played	Cuts Made	1st	2nd	3rd	Top 10	Top 25	Earnings	Rank
1985A	1	1							
1985	1								
1986	3								
1987	32	17				1	4	$52,175	148
1988	29	16				1	3	58,221	143
1989	28	16			1	3	9	149,945	94
1990	28	16				1	2	71,674	157
1991	29	20				2	9	196,081	86
1992	25	19		2	2	8	12	582,120	23
1993	25	15				4	6	202,638	84
1994	26	14			1	4	8	274,971	71
1995	26	21	1	1		4	9	525,622	35
1996	21	12		2		5	6	604,382	30
1997	26	20		2		4	4	458,074	51
1998	26	15				2	6	290,092	103
1999	26	19	2			3	7	1,302,784	28
2000	23	17	1		1	6	9	1,384,508	32
2001	27	15				1	4	427,461	120
2002	27	19				4	10	909,003	71
2003	25	19		1		3	9	1,206,005	58
2004	26	16				5	11	1,487,912	46
Total	480	307	4	8	5	61	128	10,183,668	

PGA TOUR TOP TOURNAMENT SUMMARY

Year	87	88	89	90	91	92	93	94	95	96	97	98	99
Masters							T39		T24	T5	36		
U.S. Open	T58	CUT	CUT			T57	T72	T9	T13	CUT	T60		
British Open						T25	T39						T43
PGA						T9	CUT		T20	CUT	CUT	T38	T41
THE PLAYERS				T61		T35	T52	CUT	CUT	CUT	T43	CUT	T17
TOUR Championship						T7				26			T5
WGC-American Express Champ													T40

Year	00	01	02	03	04
Masters	CUT	T31			
U.S. Open	CUT	T44			CUT
British Open		T54	T18	T34	
PGA	T46	CUT	CUT	T45	T49
THE PLAYERS	CUT	CUT	CUT	T11	T74
WGC-Accenture Match Play	T9	T33			T17
WGC-American Express Champ	T3				

NATIONAL TEAMS: Walker Cup, 1985.

Jimmy Walker

EXEMPT STATUS: No. 1 on 2004 Nationwide Tour money list
FULL NAME: Jimmy M. Walker
HEIGHT: 6-2
WEIGHT: 180
BIRTHDATE: January 16, 1979
BIRTHPLACE: Oklahoma City, OK
RESIDENCE: San Antonio, TX; plays out of Oak Hills CC

FAMILY: Single
EDUCATION: Baylor University
SPECIAL INTERESTS: Fishing
TURNED PROFESSIONAL: 2001
JOINED TOUR: 2005
Nationwide Tour Alumnus

BEST PGA TOUR CAREER FINISH:

T52—2001 U.S. Open Championship.

NATIONWIDE TOUR VICTORIES (2):

2004 BellSouth Panama Championship, Chitimacha Louisiana Open.

2004 SEASON:

Became second-youngest player to earn Nationwide Tour Player of the Year honors after winning twice and finishing No. 1 on the money list with $371,346. At 25, trails only 1996 winner Stewart Cink, who was 23 when he won the award...Recorded seven top-10s and 12 top-25s, while making the cut in 20 of 25 tournaments entered...Captured his first career victory at the inaugural BellSouth Panama Championship, with rounds of 65-69-70-69, making him the only player to post par-or-better scores all four days. His 7-under 273 was good for a five-stroke victory over Tom Scherrer. Collected a career-best $90,000 for his efforts... Claimed his second title in only the fourth event of the year at the Chitimacha Louisiana Open, making him the quickest in Tour history to win two events so early in the season, topping the old mark set in 1990 by Dick Mast, who won his second title of the year in the season's eighth event. Entered the final round eight shots off of the lead in Louisiana, marking the second-largest, come-from-behind victory in Tour history. His victory helped secure Nationwide Tour Player of the Month honors for March...Posted runner-up finishes this season at the Virginia Beach Open and the Albertsons Boise Open. Other top-10 finishes were posted at the Jacob's Creek Open (T8), Henrico County Open (sixth) and the Knoxville Open (T4)...Finished second in All Around Ranking, fourth in Total Eagles, fifth in Birdie Average and Scoring Average, sixth in Putting Average and ninth in Driving Distance.

CAREER HIGHLIGHTS:

2003: Made the cut in 13 of 18 events on the 2003 Nationwide Tour, with 10 top-25 appearances. Finished the season No. 31 on the money list, with $146,516 and three top-5s, at the Permian Basin Charity Golf Classic (T2), Oregon Classic (T3) and Chattanooga Classic (T4)...Became just the eighth player in Tour history to post three eagles in a round, doing so during the third round of the Chattanooga Classic...Had the longest streak of consecutive rounds of par or better with 30...Ranked in the top 10 in 13 statistical categories...Also captured wins on the Tight Lies Tour. **2002:** Made the cut in eight of 10 starts on the Nationwide Tour, with a pair of top-10 finishes...Won the Scottsdale Swing at Eagle Mountain on the Canadian Tour...Won events on the Gateway Tour. **2001:** Played in the U.S. Open at Southern Hills, where he T52. His second-round 66 tied for the third-best round of the week, behind only 64s by Mark Brooks (second round) and Tom Kite (fourth round). **Amateur:** Was an All-American selection at Baylor University.

PERSONAL:

Learned the game from his father, who was a scratch golfer...Biggest thrill in golf so far has been playing in the 2001 U.S. Open.

CAREER STATISTICS

2004 PGA TOUR STATISTICS

Scoring Average	71.72	(N/A)
Driving Distance	323.8	(N/A)
Driving Accuracy Percentage	57.1%	(N/A)
Total Driving	1,998	(N/A)
Greens in Regulation Pct.	66.7%	(N/A)
Putting Average	1.875	(N/A)
Sand Save Percentage	50.0%	(N/A)
Eagles (Holes per)	18.0	(N/A)
Birdie Average	2.00	(N/A)
Scoring Avg. Before Cut	73.00	(N/A)
Birdie Conversion Percentage	25.0%	(N/A)
Par Breakers	16.7%	(N/A)

MISCELLANEOUS PGA TOUR STATISTICS

2004 Low Round/Round: 72–Shell Houston Open/2
Career Low Round/Round: 66–2001 U.S. Open Championship/2
Career Largest Paycheck/Finish: $13,164–2001 U.S. Open Championship/T52

PGA TOUR CAREER SUMMARY — PLAYOFF RECORD: 0-0

Year	Events Played	Cuts Made	1st	2nd	3rd	Top 10	Top 25	Earnings	Rank
2001	3	1						$13,164	
2002	1								
2003	1								
2004	1								
Total	6	1						13,164	
NATIONWIDE TOUR									
2001	3	2						2,728	233
2002	10	8				2	6	58,962	74
2003	18	13		1	1	5	10	146,516	31
2004	25	20	2	2		7	12	371,346	1
Total	56	43	2	3	1	14	28	579,551	

PGA TOUR TOP TOURNAMENT SUMMARY

Year	01	02
U.S. Open	T52	CUT

Tom Watson

WORLD GOLF HALL OF FAME MEMBER (Inducted 1988)
EXEMPT STATUS: Life member
FULL NAME: Thomas Sturges Watson
HEIGHT: 5-9
WEIGHT: 175
BIRTHDATE: September 4, 1949
BIRTHPLACE: Kansas City, MO
RESIDENCE: Stilwell, KS
FAMILY: Wife, Hilary; Meg (9/13/79), Michael Barrett (12/15/82), stepchildren Kyle (9/23/86), Paige (4/22/89), Ross (8/31/91)
EDUCATION: Stanford University (1971, Psychology)
SPECIAL INTERESTS: Current affairs, outdoor life
TURNED PROFESSIONAL: 1971
Q SCHOOL: Fall 1971

PGA TOUR VICTORIES (39):

1974 Western Open. **1975** Byron Nelson Golf Classic, British Open Championship. **1977** Bing Crosby National Pro-Am, Andy Williams-San Diego Open Invitational, Masters Tournament, Western Open, British Open Championship. **1978** Joe Garagiola-Tucson Open, Bing Crosby National Pro-Am, Byron Nelson Golf Classic, Colgate Hall of Fame Classic, Anheuser-Busch Golf Classic. **1979** Sea Pines Heritage Classic, MONY Tournament of Champions, Byron Nelson Golf Classic, Memorial Tournament, Colgate Hall of Fame Classic. **1980** Andy Williams-San Diego Open Invitational, Glen Campbell-Los Angeles Open, MONY Tournament of Champions, Greater New Orleans Open, Byron Nelson Golf Classic, British Open Championship, World Series of Golf. **1981** Masters Tournament, USF&G New Orleans Open, Atlanta Classic. **1982** Glen Campbell-Los Angeles Open, Sea Pines Heritage, U.S. Open Championship, British Open Championship. **1983** British Open Championship. **1984** Seiko-Tucson Match Play Championship, MONY Tournament of Champions, Western Open. **1987** Nabisco Championship. **1996** Memorial Tournament. **1998** MasterCard Colonial.

CHAMPIONS TOUR VICTORIES (6):

1999 Bank One Championship. **2000** IR SENIOR TOUR Championship. **2001** Senior PGA Championship. **2002** SENIOR TOUR Championship at Gaillardia. **2003** Senior British Open, JELD-WEN Tradition.

INTERNATIONAL VICTORIES (4):

Dunlop Phoenix [Jpn]. **1984** Australian Open [Aus]. **1992** Hong Kong Open [Asia]. **1997** Dunlop Phoenix [Jpn].

OTHER VICTORIES:

1999, **2000** Champions Tour Hyundai Team Matches. **1994** Skins Game.

BEST 2004 PGA TOUR FINISH:

T66—Bay Hill Invitational Presented by MasterCard.

BEST 2004 CHAMPIONS TOUR FINISHES:

T2—The ACE Group Classic; 3—Allianz Championship; T4—Senior PGA Championship; T9—FedEx Kinko's Classic; T10—Constellation Energy Classic

2004 SEASON:

Is playing under the category of Life Member in 2005. To be eligible under this category, a Life Member must maintain a scoring average no greater than three strokes above the field average for the rounds of golf in which they have played during each calendar year...Finished T66 at the Bay Hill Invitational and earned $10,350. It was his first made cut in a PGA TOUR event since the 2002 Bank of America Colonial...Also made a start at the Masters Tournament, but missed the cut...Played in 12 Champions Tour events and collected five top-10s...Won his first Wendy's Champions Skins Game on the third extra playoff hole. Collected 10 skins and $400,000 at Wailea...Continued to be snakebit at The ACE Group Classic, losing in a three-way

PGA TOUR CAREER SUMMARY — PLAYOFF RECORD: 8-4

Year	Events Played	Cuts Made	1st	2nd	3rd	Top 10	Top 25	Earnings	Rank
1968A	1	1							
1971	6	5					2	$2,185	191
1972	32	22		1		1	8	30,413	74
1973	31	23			2	8	13	73,692	35
1974	29	27	1	1		10	20	131,537	10
1975	25	22	2	1	1	12	21	153,796	7
1976	25	22		2	1	11	15	138,203	12
1977	23	22	5	1	3	17	19	310,653	1
1978	24	22	5	3	1	15	21	362,429	1
1979	21	20	5	4	1	15	18	462,636	1
1980	22	22	7	1	3	16	22	530,808	1
1981	21	19	3	3	1	10	16	347,660	3
1982	20	19	4	1	1	12	17	316,483	5
1983	17	16	1	2		10	14	237,519	12
1984	20	17	3	2	1	9	15	476,260	1
1985	19	17		1	1	7	11	226,778	18
1986	20	17			4	9	13	278,338	20
1987	20	15	1	1		5	12	616,351	5
1988	19	15		1		6	11	273,216	39
1989	18	13			1	2	7	185,398	80
1990	17	13				5	9	213,989	68
1991	16	12		1	1	6	10	354,877	45
1992	15	12		1		5	7	299,818	50
1993	16	14				4	9	342,023	46
1994	15	14		1		5	9	380,378	43
1995	16	14				3	7	320,785	58
1996	15	14	1	1		4	7	761,238	25
1997	16	12			1	5	8	479,146	45
1998	15	10	1	2		4	5	976,585	29
1999	13	7					1	141,410	174
2000	4	3				1	1	158,409	174
2001	4	1						9,950	240
2002	4	3				1	1	180,130	177
2003	4	2					1	108,017	204
2004	2	1						10,350	253
Total	585	488	39	31	23	218	350	9,892,128	

CHAMPIONS TOUR CAREER SUMMARY — PLAYOFF RECORD: 1-6

Year	Events Played	1st	2nd	3rd	Top 10	Top 25	Earnings	Rank
1999	2	1			1	2	$208,240	62
2000	13	1	4		10	13	1,146,361	13
2001	13	1	1		8	11	986,547	17
2002	14	1	5		10	12	1,522,437	8
2003	14	2	5		10	13	1,853,108	1
2004	12		1	1	5	7	475,203	42
Total	68	6	16	1	44	58	6,191,895	

PGA TOUR TOP TOURNAMENT SUMMARY

Year	72	73	74	75	76	77	78	79	80	81	82	83	84
Masters				T8	T33	**1**	T2	T2	T12	**1**	T5	T4	2
U.S. Open	T29	CUT	T5	T9	7	T7	T6	CUT	T3	T23	**1**	2	T11
British Open				**1**	CUT	**1**	T14	T26	**1**	T23	**1**	**1**	T2
PGA		T12	T11	9	T15	T6	T2	T12	T10	CUT	T9	T47	T39
THE PLAYERS			CUT	T8	T9	T5	CUT	2	T3	CUT	T6	T19	T8

Year	85	86	87	88	89	90	91	92	93	94	95	96	97
Masters	T10	T6	T7	T9	T14	T7	T3	T48	T45	13	T14	CUT	4
U.S. Open	CUT	T24	2	T36	T46	CUT	T16	CUT	T5	T6	T56	T13	64
British Open	T47	T35	7	T28	4	CUT	T26	CUT	CUT	T11	T31		T10
PGA	T6	T16	T14	T31	T9	T19	CUT	T62	5	T9	T58	T17	CUT
THE PLAYERS	T55	T58	CUT	CUT	T11	T36	T20	T2	10	T14	T29	T33	T53
TOUR Championship			**1**									T6	

Year	98	99	00	01	02	03	04
Masters	CUT	CUT	CUT	CUT	T40	CUT	CUT
U.S. Open	CUT	T57	T27			T28	
British Open	CUT	CUT	T55	CUT	CUT	T18	
PGA	CUT	CUT	T9	T66	T48	CUT	
THE PLAYERS	T35	T62					
TOUR Championship	T18						
WGC-Accenture Match Play		T33					

CHAMPIONS TOUR TOP TOURNAMENT SUMMARY

Year	00	01	02	03	04
Senior PGA Championship	T17	**1**	T18	T17	T4
U.S. Senior Open	T10	T16	2	2	T25
Ford Senior Players Championship	T18	T8		T2	
Senior British Open				**1**	T22
JELD-WEN Tradition	T2		5	**1**	T55
Charles Schwab Cup Champ	**1**	4	**1**	2	

NATIONAL TEAMS: Ryder Cup (5), 1977, 1981, 1983, 1989, 1993 (Captain); UBS Cup, 2003

SECTION 2 PLAYER BIOGRAPHIES

Tom Watson (Continued)

playoff with winner Craig Stadler and Gary Koch…Finished T4 at the Senior PGA Championship after being tied with Hale Irwin for the first-round lead at Valhalla. Has now finished among the top four in his last five majors on the Champions Tour…Had surgery on his right shoulder in October.

CAREER HIGHLIGHTS:

2003: Played in just four events for the fourth straight year on PGA TOUR but participated in all nine majors between the PGA TOUR and Champions Tour, a record for majors participation...Thanks to two major victories, named Champions Tour Player of the Year...Playing on a special exemption, the 53-year old shared the first-round lead at the U.S. Open with Brett Quigley at 5-under 65. Finished T28...Finished in top 10 in 10 of 14 events on the Champions Tour including two wins and five runner-ups. Wins came in two of the Champions Tour majors: Senior British Open and JELD-WEN Tradition...Finished first in Charles Schwab Cup points and donated entire $1-million bonus to ALS research, the disease his caddie Bruce Edwards suffers from...Also the recipient of the Card Walker Award and the Payne Stewart Award. **2002:** Made his 23rd cut in 29 appearances at the Masters and finished T40...Was the oldest player to make the cut at the PGA at Hazeltine National and finished T48. **2001:** PGA TOUR record string of consecutive years earning at least $100,000 stopped at 26 (1974-2000)...Picked up a win for third consecutive year on Champions Tour at Senior PGA Championship. **2000:** Made cut in three of four majors with a best finish of T9 in the PGA (missed Masters cut)...Won season-ending IR Champions Tour Championship...Went over $1-million mark in season earnings for first time in his career. **1998:** Earned 34th PGA TOUR title with victory at MasterCard Colonial. At 48, was oldest player to win event (previous oldest:46-year-old Ben Hogan when he captured his last of five Colonial titles)...Stretch between first win, the 1974 Western Open, and most recent (23 years, 11 months, 24 days) third longest in TOUR history. **1997:** Posted T3 at GTE Byron Nelson Classic and fourth at Masters Tournament. Best finish at Augusta National since 1991. **1996:** After nine-year absence, returned to the PGA TOUR winner's circle with victory at Memorial Tournament...Finished 25th on the money list, highest ranking since 1987, and made first trip to THE TOUR Championship since winning that event in 1987. **1993:** Captain of victorious Ryder Cup team. **1987:** Won season-ending Nabisco Championship (now THE TOUR Championship) and finished in top five on money list (No. 5) for last time in his career. **1984:** Finished in top-3 six times including three victories...First on final money list for fifth time in career...Won PGA of America Player of the Year Award for sixth time in career (1977, '78, '79, '80, '82, '84). **1983:** Won the last of his eight major championship crowns at the British Open. Also captured British Open titles in 1975, '77, '80, '82, Masters titles in 1977 and 1981 and the 1982 U.S. Open. **1982:** Won only U.S. Open title, chipping in on the 17th hole at Pebble Beach to nip Jack Nicklaus...For sixth consecutive year, captured at least three victories in a season. During that time (1977-82) posted 26 wins, 13 runners-up finishes and 10 thirds along with being the PGA TOURs leading money-winner four years in a row (1977-80)...Became one of six players to win U.S. and British Opens in same year (Bobby Jones, Gene Sarazen, Ben Hogan, Lee Trevino and Tiger Woods). **1980:** Became first player to earn $500,000 in a season when he captured six TOUR events to go along with third British Open...Was last player to win same event three consecutive years (1978-79-80 GTE Byron Nelson Classics) before Tiger Woods accomplished the feat twice in 2001. **1979:** Earned third consecutive Vardon Trophy (1977-79). **1974:** First victory came at Western Open, where he defeated Tom Weiskopf and J.C. Snead by two strokes.

PERSONAL:

Active in Kansas City-area charitable endeavors, including Children's Mercy Hospital and development of golf courses for junior players. Won the 2003 Card Walker Award as the result of his interest in junior golf…In 1999, named honorary member of the Royal & Ancient Golf Club of St. Andrews, joining fellow Americans Arnold Palmer, Jack Nicklaus, former President George Bush and Gene Sarazen…Led the effort to raise awareness of ALS, the disease that took the lives of longtime caddie Bruce Edwards and former TOUR player Jeff Julian. Web site is driving4life.org.

PLAYER STATISTICS

2004 PGA TOUR STATISTICS

Scoring Average	72.95	(N/A)
Driving Distance	277.7	(N/A)
Driving Accuracy Percentage	64.3%	(N/A)
Total Driving	(N/A)	(N/A)
Greens in Regulation Pct.	56.5%	(N/A)
Putting Average	1.820	(N/A)
Sand Save Percentage	33.3%	(N/A)
Eagles (Holes per)	108.0	(N/A)
Birdie Average	3.00	(N/A)
Scoring Avg. Before Cut	74.00	(N/A)
Round 3 Scoring Avg.	75.00	(N/A)
Final Round Scoring Average	73.00	(N/A)
Birdie Conversion Percentage	26.2%	(N/A)
Par Breakers	17.6%	(N/A)

MISCELLANEOUS PGA TOUR STATISTICS

2004 Low Round/Round: 70–Bay Hill Invitational Presented by MasterCard/1
Career Low Round/Round: 63–3 times, most recent 1992 Buick Invitational of California/1
Career Largest Paycheck/Finish: $414,000–1998 MasterCard Colonial/1

2004 CHAMPIONS TOUR STATISTICS

Scoring Average	71.36	(N/A)
Driving Distance	278.7	(N/A)
Driving Accuracy Percentage	75.2%	(N/A)
Total Driving	(N/A)	(N/A)
Greens in Regulation Pct.	71.9%	(N/A)
Putting Average	1.819	(N/A)
Sand Save Percentage	50.0%	(N/A)
Eagles (Holes per)	351.0	(N/A)
Birdie Average	3.36	(N/A)
All-Around Ranking	1,569	(N/A)

MISCELLANEOUS CHAMPIONS TOUR STATISTICS

2004 Low Round: 66–2004 MasterCard Championship/3.
Career Low Round: 62–2 times, most recent 2003 JELD-WEN Tradition/2
Career Largest Paycheck: $440,000–2002 SENIOR TOUR Championship at Gaillardia/1

Mike Weir

EXEMPT STATUS: Winner, 2003 Masters Tournament (through 2008)
FULL NAME: Michael Richard Weir
HEIGHT: 5-9
WEIGHT: 155
BIRTHDATE: May 12, 1970
BIRTHPLACE: Sarnia, Ontario, Canada
RESIDENCE: Draper, UT
FAMILY: Wife, Bricia; Elle Marisa (12/19/97), Lili (4/3/00)
EDUCATION: Brigham Young University (1993, Recreation Management)
SPECIAL INTERESTS: Hockey, fly fishing, skiing
TURNED PROFESSIONAL: 1992
Q SCHOOL: 1997, 1998

PGA TOUR VICTORIES (7):

1999 Air Canada Championship. **2000** WGC-American Express Championship. **2001** THE TOUR Championship. **2003** Bob Hope Chrysler Classic, Nissan Open, Masters Tournament. **2004** Nissan Open.

INTERNATIONAL VICTORIES (2):

1997 BC TEL Pacific Open [Can], Canadian Masters [Can].

OTHER VICTORIES (2):

2003 Champions Challenge [with Dean Wilson]. **2004** Champions Challenge [with Dean Wilson].

BEST 2004 PGA TOUR FINISHES:

1—Nissan Open; 2—Bell Canadian Open; T4—AT&T Pebble Beach National Pro-Am, U.S. Open Championship, THE TOUR Championship presented by Coca-Cola; T5—FBR Open; T9—British Open Championship.

2004 SEASON:

Maintained top-10 Official World Golf Ranking status on the strength of a victory at Nissan Open and top-10s in two majors…In third start of season, picked up his first top-10, a T5, at the FBR Open…Followed with another top-five (T4) the next week at the AT&T Pebble Beach National Pro-Am…Started the final round with a five-stroke lead and survived a rainy final round at Riviera to successfully defend his Nissan Open title. Won his previous six PGA TOUR events from behind and was 0-for-5 with a 54-hole lead. Closed with an even-par 71 and became the first back-to-back winner at Riviera since Corey Pavin in 1994-95. Became the second-winningest left-hander in PGA TOUR history with seven career wins, surpassing Bob Charles' six victories. Phil Mickelson leads in this category with 23 wins…Posted back-to-back top-10s at the U.S. Open with his T4 finish (T3 in 2003). Then posted back-to-back top10s in a major with a T9 at the British Open in Scotland…Finished as runner-up at the Bell Canadian Open after a bogey on the 72nd hole pushed him into a playoff with Vijay Singh. Missed a five-footer for birdie on the second extra hole to win and was defeated by Singh on the following hole after Weir's approach found the hazard just right of the green. Held the second- and third-round leads, including a three-stroke lead heading into Sunday's final round. His best finish and just the second top-10 in 14 starts in his national Open…Closed the season with a T4 at THE TOUR Championship to move to No. 6 in Official World Golf Ranking.

CAREER HIGHLIGHTS:

2003: Had breakthrough season on TOUR with three wins, matching his career total entering the season, including his first major title at the Masters. Missed just one cut all season for the fist time in his career. Fifth-place finish on money list and earnings over $4.8 million were career bests...Claimed fourth PGA TOUR title at Bob Hope Chrysler Classic. Entered final day four shots behind Tim Herron but final-round 67, tied for low final-round score, helped him edge Jay Haas by two strokes...Won for second time in four events at the Nissan Open, finishing strong with a final-round 5-under 66. Defeated Charles Howell III with a birdie on the second playoff hole after beginning the final round seven strokes behind Howell. Payday moved him past the $2-million mark for the third time in the last four seasons…After recording just the fourth bogey-free final-round by a winner in the 67-year history of the Masters (first since Doug Ford in 1957), defeated Len Mattiace in a playoff with a bogey on the first extra hole. Nailed a six-footer for par on the 18th hole to force the playoff. Became first left-hander since Bob Charles at the 1963 British Open to win a major...Finished season with top-10s in three of four majors…Edged Los Angeles Dodgers relief pitcher Eric Gagne to win The Canadian Press's male athlete of the year award for a third time (also 2000 and 2001). **2002:** Had 11 top-25s but did not have a top-10 finish for the first time in his five-year TOUR career...Tied The Plantation Course record with 10-under-par 63 before finishing T14 at the Mercedes Championships. His 63 was the lowest first-round score in Mercedes Championships history. **2001:** Earned over $2 million for second consecutive season and picked up a victory for the third straight year...Finished season by winning THE TOUR Championship. Final-round 68 put him in playoff with Ernie Els, Sergio Garcia and David Toms. Birdie-3 on first extra hole gave him his first playoff victory and made him first international player to win THE TOUR Championship. **2000:** First Canadian to play in Presidents Cup, where he led the international team with a 3-2-0 record...Collected his second victory on the PGA TOUR in the season-ending WGC-American Express Championship. A bogey-free 67 on Saturday and final-round 67 lifted him to his first WGC title. Career-best $1 million first prize moved him to sixth on the money list with $2,547,829, seventh player to surpass the $2.5 million mark in single-season earnings...Lost first TOUR playoff at Michelob Championship when David Toms sank a five-foot par putt on first extra hole. **1999:** Went from being medalist at 1998 PGA TOUR Qualifying Tournament to TOUR Championship...Earned first PGA TOUR title at Air Canada Championship with two-stroke victory over Fred Funk. Key

SECTION 2 PLAYER BIOGRAPHIES

PGA TOUR CAREER SUMMARY — PLAYOFF RECORD: 3-2

Year	Events Played	Cuts Made	1st	2nd	3rd	Top 10	Top 25	Earnings	Rank
1989A	1								
1992A	1								
1992	1								
1993	2	1						$1,940	317
1994	1								
1995	1								
1996	5	2				1	1	36,624	210
1997	4	1						7,709	287
1998	27	13				2	5	218,967	131
1999	30	20	1	1	1	7	12	1,491,139	23
2000	28	23	1	1		8	16	2,547,829	6
2001	23	20	1	2	1	6	13	2,777,936	11
2002	25	22					11	843,890	78
2003	21	20	3		4	10	16	4,918,910	5
2004	22	16	1	1		7	10	2,761,536	14
Total	192	138	7	5	6	41	84	15,606,480	
NATIONWIDE TOUR									
1993	1								
Total	1								
EUROPEAN TOUR									
2004	1	1				1	1	75,945	

PGA TOUR TOP TOURNAMENT SUMMARY

Year	99	00	01	02	03	04
Masters		T28	T27	T24	**1**	CUT
U.S. Open	CUT	T16	T19	CUT	T3	T4
British Open	T37	T52	CUT	T69	T28	T9
PGA	T10	T30	T16	T34	T7	CUT
THE PLAYERS		CUT	T44	T19	T27	CUT
TOUR Championship	T26	21	**1**		T19	T4
WGC-Accenture Match Play		T17		T17	T17	T17
WGC-NEC Invitational		T24	25	T24	T23	T41
WGC-American Express Champ	T30	**1**	CNL	T15	T28	

NATIONAL TEAMS: Presidents Cup (2), 2000, 2003; WGC-World Cup (3), 2000-2002.

Mike Weir (Continued)

to victory was eagle-2 from 147 yards on No. 14 during final round. First Canadian to win on native soil since Pat Fletcher won 1954 Canadian Open. First Canadian to win on TOUR since Richard Zokol won 1992 Greater Milwaukee Open. **1998:** As rookie, earned $218,967 to rank 131st on money list. **1997:** Led Canadian Tour Order of Merit after winning BC TEL Pacific Open and Canadian Masters. Was first Canadian to lead Order of Merit since Jerry Anderson in 1989. **1993:** Named Canadian Tour Rookie of the Year after winning Infiniti Tournament Players Championship. **Amateur:** Won 1990 Ontario Amateur Championship...Western Athletic Conference Player of Year and second-team All-American in 1992 at Brigham Young...Winner of 1988 Ontario Junior Championship and 1986 Canadian Juvenile Championship.

PERSONAL:

Dropped the ceremonial puck before the Toronto Maple Leafs playoff game against the Philadelphia Flyers on April 14, 2003. Prior to 2003 Presidents Cup, gave teammates Team Canada hockey jerseys complete with names stitched on the back…Is friend of Edmonton Oilers center Adam Oates. Practiced with NHL's Washington Capitals at beginning of two-week break in late September 1999…At age 13, sought advice from Jack Nicklaus. In a letter, asked whether he should switch to playing right-handed. Response was to stick to natural swing…Three-time recipient (2000-01 and 2003) of Lionel Conacher Award, given to Canada's Male Athlete of the Year. First golfer to be so honored since 1932…Enjoys taking family to Barnes & Noble for reading nights with his children…Web site is mikeweir.com.

PLAYER STATISTICS

2004 PGA TOUR STATISTICS

Scoring Average	70.20	(18)
Driving Distance	282.1	(138)
Driving Accuracy Percentage	64.1%	(101)
Total Driving	239	(160)
Greens in Regulation Pct.	65.1%	(95)
Putting Average	1.749	(21)
Sand Save Percentage	53.7%	(36)
Eagles (Holes per)	219.0	(83)
Birdie Average	3.75	(41)
All-Around Ranking	533	(34)
Scoring Avg. Before Cut	70.29	(21)
Round 3 Scoring Avg.	70.33	(49)
Final Round Scoring Average	71.87	(123)
Birdie Conversion Percentage	31.3%	(29)
Par Breakers	21.3%	(42)

MISCELLANEOUS PGA TOUR STATISTICS

2004 Low Round/Round: 64–Nissan Open/2
Career Low Round/Round: 62–2001 Genuity Championship/1
Career Largest Paycheck/Finish: $1,080,000–2003 Masters Tournament/1

SHOTLink
AN IBM ON DEMAND BUSINESS SOLUTION

HOT SHOTS

Par 5s where the Most Players Attempted to Reach the Green in Two Shots (2004)

Event/Course Name	Hole	Score Yard	Tries	Success	Success %	Avg Score
84 LUMBER Classic Nemacolin - Mystic Rock Course	8	565	357	36	10.08%	4.51
Chrysler Classic of Tucson Tucson Nat'l Golf	8	528	355	66	18.59%	4.43
John Deere Classic TPC at Deere Run	2	561	355	143	40.28%	4.27
BellSouth Classic TPC at Sugarloaf	10	608	350	40	11.43%	4.60
FedEx St. Jude Classic TPC at Southwind	5	527	350	89	25.43%	4.36

Par 5s with the Highest Success Percentage Reaching the Green in Two Shots (2004)

Event/Course Name	Hole	Score Yard	Tries	Success	Success %	Avg Score
Southern Farm Bureau Classic Annandale GC	18	532	235	139	59.15%	4.29
Michelin Championship at Las Vegas TPC at Summerlin**	3	492	199	109	54.77%	4.20
Michelin Championship at Las Vegas TPC at Summerlin**	16	560	169	88	52.07%	4.37
Sony Open in Hawaii Waialae CC	9	510	346	170	49.13%	4.15
Southern Farm Bureau Classic Annandale GC	5	522	294	140	47.62%	4.19

Par 5s where the Most Players Reached the Green in Two Shots (2004)

Event/Course Name	Hole	Score Yard	Tries	Success	Success %	Avg Score
Sony Open in Hawaii Waialae CC	9	510	346	170	49.13%	4.15
John Deere Classic TPC at Deere Run	2	561	355	143	40.28%	4.27
Southern Farm Bureau Classic Annandale GC	5	522	294	140	47.62%	4.19
Valero Texas Open LaCantera GC	14	527	311	140	45.02%	4.20
Southern Farm Bureau Classic Annandale GC	18	532	235	139	59.15%	4.29

Lee Westwood

EXEMPT STATUS: Top 125 on 2004 non-member money list
FULL NAME: Lee Westwood
HEIGHT: 6-0
WEIGHT: 205
BIRTHDATE: April 24, 1973
BIRTHPLACE: Worksop, England
RESIDENCE: Worksop, England

FAMILY: Wife, Laurae; Samuel (2001), Grace (2004)
SPECIAL INTERESTS: Films, snooker, cars, Nottingham Forest football club
TURNED PROFESSIONAL: 1993
JOINED TOUR: 2005

PGA TOUR VICTORIES (1):

1998 Freeport-McDermott Classic.

INTERNATIONAL VICTORIES (24):

1996 Volvo Scandinavian Masters [Eur], Sumitomo Visa Taiheiyo Masters [Jpn]. **1997** Volvo Masters Andalucia [Eur], Sumitomo Visa Taiheiyo Masters [Jpn]. **1998** Deutsche Bank-SAP Open-TPC of Europe [Eur]. National Car Rental English Open [Eur], The Standard Life Loch Lomond [Eur], Belgacom Open [Eur], Sumitomo Visa Taiheiyo Masters [Jpn], Holden Australian Open [Aus]. **1999** TNT Dutch Open [Eur], Smurfit European Open [Eur], Canon European Masters[Eur], Macau Open [Asia]. **2000** Dimension Data Pro-Am [SAf], Deutsche Bank-SAP Open TPC of Europe [Eur], Compaq European Grand Prix [Eur], Smurfit European Open [Eur], Volvo Scandinavian Masters [Eur], Belgacom Open [Eur], Cisco World Match Play Championship [Eur]. **2003** BMW International Open [Eur], dunhill links championship [Eur].

BEST 2004 PGA TOUR FINISHES:

4—British Open Championship; T9—WGC-NEC Invitational.

2004 SEASON:

Posted his best finish in a major championship and his fifth top-10 in 28 major championship appearances with his fourth-place showing at the British Open in Scotland, the highest finish by a European player at Royal Troon...Posted four rounds in the 60s at the WGC-NEC Invitational, just the ninth player in the event's six-year history to do so, in posting T9 finish....Placed second twice on the European Tour. Went 4-0-1 in the European Ryder Cup victory, sharing the high point total with teammate Sergio Garcia.

CAREER HIGHLIGHTS:

2003: Ended three years out of the limelight with an emotional victory in the BMW International Open with a back-nine 30 in the final round. A month later, beat Ernie Els by a shot to win the dunhill links championship at St Andrews. **2000:** Began year with win at Dimension Data Pro-Am in South Africa, which meant he had won a tournament on every continent — Africa, Asia, Australasia, Europe and North America...Captured the European Tour Volvo Order of Merit in the last tournament of the year. Winnings of 3,125,146 euro set a European Tour record after he captured five official titles. Westwood finished 407,181 euro ahead of Darren Clarke after overcoming a 107,768 euro deficit in the final event of the year, the WGC-American Express Championship. Successfully defended his Smurfit European Open title to go with wins in the Deutsche Bank SAP Open - TPC of Europe, the Compaq European Grand Prix, the Volvo Scandinavian Masters, the Belgacom Open and the Cisco World Match Play Championship. Joined Seve Ballesteros, Nick Faldo and Colin Montgomerie as the only players to win six times in a season in Europe. **1999:** Won three times on the European Tour and finished second on the Order of Merit behind Montgomerie. **1998:** Made his big breakthrough in the United States when he captured the Freeport McDermott Classic...Also won four times on the European Tour and finished third behind Montgomerie and Clarke. **1997:** Won the Volvo Masters Andalucia on the European Tour. **1996:** Picked up first European Tour win at the Volvo Scandinavian Masters in a playoff. **1994:** Finished 43rd on the European Tour's Order of Merit in his rookie season.

PERSONAL:

Took up the game at age 13 with a half set bought by his grandparents. Math teacher father, John, took up game at same time to give his son encouragement...Played rugby, cricket and soccer during his school days...Big supporter of Nottingham Forest FC... Married Laurae Coltart, sister of fellow European Tour player, Andrew, in January 1999.

PLAYER STATISTICS

2004 PGA TOUR STATISTICS

Scoring Average	70.40	(N/A)
Driving Distance	290.1	(N/A)
Driving Accuracy Percentage	59.7%	(N/A)
Total Driving	1,998	(N/A)
Greens in Regulation Pct.	60.6%	(N/A)
Putting Average	1.733	(N/A)
Sand Save Percentage	36.0%	(N/A)
Eagles (Holes per)	612.0	(N/A)
Birdie Average	3.71	(N/A)
Scoring Avg. Before Cut	71.65	(N/A)
Round 3 Scoring Avg.	70.71	(N/A)
Final Round Scoring Average	71.86	(N/A)
Birdie Conversion Percentage	32.1%	(N/A)
Par Breakers	20.8%	(N/A)

MISCELLANEOUS PGA TOUR STATISTICS

2004 Low Round/Round: 67–3 times, most recent British Open Championship/4
Career Low Round/Round: 66–2 times, most recent 2000 WGC-NEC Invitational/1
Career Largest Paycheck/Finish: $500,000–2000 WGC–American Express Championship/2

PGA TOUR CAREER SUMMARY — PLAYOFF RECORD: 0-0

Year	Events Played	Cuts Made	1st	2nd	3rd	Top 10	Top 25	Earnings	Rank
1995	1	1						$6,380	288
1996	1								
1997	5	5				1	4	155,645	138
1998	8	7	1			3	4	599,586	46
1999	11	10				3	5	384,097	106
2000	10	8		1		2	6	293,303	
2001	6	3					1	76,821	
2002	9	5					3	94,710	
2003	8	5						63,590	
2004	11	8				2	4	526,899	
Total	70	52	1	1		11	27	2,201,032	
EUROPEAN TOUR									
2004	15	12		2		6	9	1,306,684	

PGA TOUR TOP TOURNAMENT SUMMARY

Year	95	96	97	98	99	00	01	02	03	04
Masters			T24	44	T6	CUT		44		
U.S. Open			T19	T7	CUT	T5	CUT			T36
British Open	T96	CUT	T10	T64	T18	T64	T47	CUT	CUT	4
PGA			T29	CUT	T16	T15	T44	CUT	CUT	CUT
THE PLAYERS				T5	T6	T48	CUT	CUT		
WGC-Accenture Match Play					T33	T17		T17		T33
WGC-NEC Invitational					T33	T20	W/D	T15	T46	T9
WGC-American Express Champ					T4	2	CNL		T35	T13

SECTION 2 PLAYER BIOGRAPHIES

Jay Williamson

EXEMPT STATUS: 120th on 2004 money list
FULL NAME: Justin Arch Williamson IV
HEIGHT: 5-10
WEIGHT: 180
BIRTHDATE: February 7, 1967
BIRTHPLACE: St. Louis, MO
RESIDENCE: St. Louis, MO; plays out of Boone Valley GC
FAMILY: Wife, Marnie; Whitney Lain (5/11/99); Justin Thomas (8/5/02)
EDUCATION: Trinity College (1989, Political Science)
SPECIAL INTERESTS: Stock market, current events, sports
TURNED PROFESSIONAL: 1990
Q SCHOOL: 1994, 1995, 1998
Nationwide Tour Alumnus

BEST PGA TOUR CAREER FINISH:
T3—2003 BellSouth Classic.

BEST 2004 PGA TOUR FINISHES:
T7—Nissan Open; 8—Deutsche Bank Championship.

2004 SEASON:
Finished in the top 125 for the fifth consecutive season. Earned a career-high $660,038 on the strength of two top-10 finishes…A closing 64 at the Nissan Open moved him to T7. Had missed the cut at Riveria in his four previous starts…Next top-10` did not come until September, an eighth, at the Deutsche Bank Championship…One shot back of the lead thorugh 36 holes at the Michelin Championship at Las Vegas. Fired weekend rounds of 74-66 to finish T15. His $58,100 payday in Las Vegas was good enough to help secure his card for 2005.

CAREER HIGHLIGHTS:
2003: Only top-10 was T3 at the BellSouth Classic. Paycheck of $208,000 was largest of PGA TOUR career...Finished fourth on TOUR in Sand Saves. **2002:** Finished 125th on the money list thanks to T16 finish at the Buick Challenge and a T5 finish at the season-ending Southern Farm Bureau Classic, which pushed him past David Frost by $5,600 for the final fully-exempt spot on TOUR...Recorded hole-in-one on 196-yard, par-3 third hole, using a 7-iron, during third round of the Buick Invitational. **2001:** Started the season slow, but ended with a bang after changing his putting grip to "the claw"...Best effort of season came at the Marconi Pennsylvania Classic as rounds of 74-68-67-68 were good for T6, top career finish at the time. Was No. 131 going into the Pennsylvania event on money list, where he adopted "the claw," and jumped to 105th on money list...The next week at the Texas Open at LaCantera, opened with 65 and was one back of the lead through 18 holes, finish T11. **2000:** Earned $460,024 and finished 109th on the money list. Made the most of his exempt status, playing in 32 events and making the cut in 20 of those...Lone top-10 came at Bay Hill Invitational, a T7. **1999:** Only top-10 was a T4 at the rain-shortened AT&T Pebble Beach National Pro-Am. Made $263,618 and finished 144th on the money list...Returned to Qualifying Tournament to improve his position for the next season on the PGA TOUR and finished T2. **1998:** Member of the Nationwide Tour. Finished 18th on the money list thanks to two runner-up finishes...Lost to good friend Matt Gogel in a four-hole playoff at the Omaha Classic...Late in the season, finished alone in second at the Inland Empire Open in Moreno Valley, CA. **1995:** Rookie on the PGA TOUR...Best finish was a T4 at the Ideon Classic at Pleasant Valley. **1991:** Winner of Kansas Open. **Amateur:** Named Senior Scholar Athlete at Trinity College in 1989.

PERSONAL:
Played baseball and hockey in college.

PLAYER STATISTICS

2004 PGA TOUR STATISTICS

Scoring Average	71.40	(128)
Driving Distance	288.1	(85)
Driving Accuracy Percentage	69.3%	(33)
Total Driving	118	(13)
Greens in Regulation Pct.	65.4%	(89)
Putting Average	1.776	(91)
Sand Save Percentage	56.3%	(17)
Eagles (Holes per)	252.0	(99)
Birdie Average	3.43	(123)
All-Around Ranking	665	(67)
Scoring Avg. Before Cut	71.00	(96)
Round 3 Scoring Avg.	71.74	(154)
Final Round Scoring Average	71.00	(53)
Birdie Conversion Percentage	28.0%	(132)
Par Breakers	19.4%	(127)

MISCELLANEOUS PGA TOUR STATISTICS

2004 Low Round/Round: 62–Michelin Championship at Las Vegas/2
Career Low Round/Round: 62–2004 Michelin Championship at Las Vegas/2
Career Largest Paycheck/Finish: $208,000–2003 BellSouth Classic/T3

PGA TOUR CAREER SUMMARY — PLAYOFF RECORD: 0-0

Year	Events Played	Cuts Made	1st	2nd	3rd	Top 10	Top 25	Earnings	Rank
1995	22	11				3	3	$120,180	145
1996	27	13				1	2	82,773	175
1997	2	1						3,409	317
1999	32	12				1	4	263,618	144
2000	32	20				1	6	460,024	109
2001	35	13				3	4	476,031	106
2002	30	16				2	6	515,445	125
2003	31	17			1	1	4	627,132	101
2004	33	18				2	8	660,038	120
Total	244	121			1	14	37	3,208,650	
NATIONWIDE TOUR									
1992	1								
1994	2								
1995	8	2				1	2	11,133	114
1996	1								
1997	6	3					1	3,673	158
1998	28	17		2		6	8	110,921	18
Total	46	22		2		7	11	125,727	

PGA TOUR TOP TOURNAMENT SUMMARY

Year	99	00	01	02	03	04
U.S. Open	CUT		DQ		T20	
THE PLAYERS			T58	CUT	T27	CUT

Tiger Woods

EXEMPT STATUS: Winner, 2002 U.S. Open (through 2007)
FULL NAME: Eldrick T. Woods
HEIGHT: 6-2
WEIGHT: 180
BIRTHDATE: December 30, 1975
BIRTHPLACE: Cypress, CA
RESIDENCE: Orlando, FL

FAMILY: Wife, Elin
EDUCATION: Stanford University
SPECIAL INTERESTS: Basketball, fishing, all sports
TURNED PROFESSIONAL: 1996
JOINED TOUR: 1996

PGA TOUR VICTORIES (40):

1996 Las Vegas Invitational, Walt Disney World/Oldsmobile Classic. **1997** Mercedes Championships, Masters Tournament, GTE Byron Nelson Golf Classic, Motorola Western Open. **1998** BellSouth Classic. **1999** Buick Invitational, Memorial Tournament, Motorola Western Open, PGA Championship, WGC-NEC Invitational, National Car Rental Golf Classic/Disney, THE TOUR Championship, WGC-American Express Championship. **2000** Mercedes Championships, AT&T Pebble Beach National Pro-Am, Bay Hill Invitational, Memorial Tournament, U.S. Open Championship, British Open Championship, PGA Championship, WGC-NEC Invitational, Bell Canadian Open. **2001** Bay Hill Invitational, THE PLAYERS Championship, Masters Tournament, Memorial Tournament, WGC-NEC Invitational. **2002** Bay Hill Invitational presented by Cooper Tires, Masters Tournament, U.S. Open Championship, Buick Open, WGC-American Express Championship. **2003** Buick Invitational, WGC-Accenture Match Play Championship, Bay Hill Invitational presented by Cooper Tires, 100th Western Open presented by Golf Digest, WGC-American Express Championship. **2004** WGC-Accenture Match Play Championship.

INTERNATIONAL VICTORIES (8):

1997 Asian Honda Classic. **1998** Johnnie Walker Classic [Asia]. **1999** Deutsche Bank Open-TPC of Europe [Eur], World Cup of Golf [indiv]. **2000** Johnnie Walker Classic. **2001** Deutsche Bank-SAP Open TPC of Europe. **2002** Deutsche Bank-SAP Open TPC of Europe. **2004** Dunlop Phoenix [Jpn].

OTHER VICTORIES (9):

1998 PGA Grand Slam of Golf. **1999** World Cup [with Mark O'Meara], PGA Grand Slam of Golf. **2000** EMC World Cup [with David Duval]. PGA Grand Slam of Golf. **2001** Williams World Challenge, PGA Grand Slam of Golf. **2002** PGA Grand Slam of Golf. **2004** Target World Challenge

BEST 2004 PGA TOUR FINISHES:

1—WGC-Accenture Match Play Championship; 2—THE TOUR Championship presented by Coca-Cola, WGC-NEC Invitational, Deutsche Bank Championship; 3—the Memorial Tournament, Wachovia Championship, Buick Open; T4—Mercedes Championships, EDS Byron Nelson Championship; T7—Nissan Open, Cialis Western Open; 9—WGC-American Express Championship, British Open Championship; T10—Buick Invitational.

2004 SEASON:

Surpassed Greg Norman for most weeks at No. 1 in the Official World Golf Ranking following PGA Championship with his 332nd combined week at the top. Consecutive weeks reign at No. 1 ended at 264, as Vijay Singh took over world No. 1 on Sept. 6, the week following the Deutsche Bank Championship. Enters 2005 season with streak of 133 consecutive made cuts intact...T4 at the PGA TOUR's season-opening Mercedes Championships, earning $275,000 to surpass $40 million for career ($40,052,265)...With a T10, has finished in the top 10 in all seven starts at the Buick Invitational...Finished T7 at the Nissan Open, aided by a final-round, 7-under-par 64. In nine career starts (two as an amateur), Woods has yet to win a Nissan Open title...Captured second consecutive WGC-Accenture Match Play Championship for 40th career PGA TOUR win, tied with Cary Middlecoff for eighth all-time. Owns eight official World Golf Championships titles in 16 starts (nine in 18 starts including WGC-World Cup). With six match victories, including a 3-and-2 win over Davis Love III in the 36-hole finale, has won 12 consecutive matches, and overall Accenture Match Play Championship record is 20-3. Seventh event in which he successfully defended a title and 12th multi-win PGA TOUR event. His $1.2-million payday was largest in PGA TOUR history at the time, and Woods' 12th paycheck of at least $1 million on the PGA TOUR....At the Bay Hill Invitational, won the 2003 Mark McCormack Award, his sixth consecutive. The award goes to the player who has held the No. 1 ranking in the Official World Golf Ranking for the most weeks in a calendar year...Finished T3 at the Wachovia Championship after a final round, 4-under 68. Leader through 36 holes. Joey Sindelar's victory snapped Woods' streak of 18 consecutive wins when leading after 36 holes...For second consecutive week missed getting into the playoff by one stroke. Finished T4 at the EDS Byron Nelson Championship...Finished in third place at the Memorial Tournament. Finished in the top-10 for the fifth time in eight starts at Muirfield Village...In defense of Cialis Western Open title, finished T7, his fifth top-10 in nine appearances at Cog Hill G&CC...Posted his second consecutive top-10 at the British Open with a T9 in Scotland and his fifth in 10 British Open appearances...Finished T3 at the Buick Open, two shots behind champion Vijay Singh for fifth top-10 in six starts at Warwick Hills G&CC, with all 24 rounds being par or better. One of only two players who posted all four rounds in the 60s, with only one bogey for the week...Although he finished T24 at the PGA Championship, held on to the World No. 1 spot for a record-breaking 332nd week, passing Greg Norman for the most weeks at No. 1...Eleventh top-10 was T2 at NEC Invitational, sixth consecutive finish of T4 or better at the World Golf Championships event. Surpassed $4 million in season earnings for sixth consecutive season...Shared first-round lead with Ryan Palmer at Deutsche Bank Championship after opening-round 65. Paired with Vijay Singh in final round to determine who would be World No. 1 at the end of play on Labor Day. Entered Monday's final round needing to make up a three-stroke deficit to Singh but both players shot 2-under 69 and Woods ended up with his 14th career runner-up finish and the No.2 spot in the World for the first time since August 1999...Posted his fifth top-10 in five appearances at the WGC-American Express Championship with a ninth in Ireland despite battling through back pain in round one. Fell to third in the world, behind Singh and Els, for the first time since the Monday after the 1999 GTE Byron Nelson Classic (May 16, 1999)...In first tournament after Oct. 5 wedding to Elin Nordegren, finished second to Retief Goosen at THE TOUR Championship. Entered final round tied with Jay Haas for the lead at 9-under par, but bogeys on three of first seven holes ended title hopes. Rounds two and three (64-65) were best back-to-back rounds since 2000 Bell Canadian Open. Closing record stands at 30 of 33 when holding at least a share of the 54-hole lead. Jumped Ernie Els into No. 2 in Official World Golf Ranking. Won Dunlop Phoenix Tournament in November by eight strokes for first career victory in Japan.

CAREER HIGHLIGHTS:

2003: Continued his reign as the world's top-ranked player, earning PGA TOUR Player of the Year honors for the fifth consecutive season. Captured five events in 18 starts to lead TOUR in victories for the fifth consecutive season...Broke Byron Nelson's long-standing record for consecutive cuts made with his 114th straight at THE TOUR Championship...With victory at the WGC-American Express Championship, became the first player in PGA TOUR history to win five times in five consecutive seasons. Since 1981, Nick Price (1994) is the only other player to win five times in

PGA TOUR CAREER SUMMARY — PLAYOFF RECORD: 6-1

Year	Events Played	Cuts Made	1st	2nd	3rd	Top 10	Top 25	Earnings	Rank
1992A	1								
1993A	3								
1994A	3								
1995A	4	3							
1996A	3	2					1		
1996	8	8	2		2	5	7	$790,594	24
1997	21	20	4	1	1	9	14	2,066,833	1
1998	20	19	1	2	2	13	17	1,841,117	4
1999	21	21	8	1	2	16	18	6,616,585	1
2000	20	20	9	4	1	17	20	9,188,321	1
2001	19	19	5		1	9	18	5,687,777	1
2002	18	18	5	2	2	13	16	6,912,625	1
2003	18	18	5	2		12	16	6,673,413	2
2004	19	19	1	3	3	14	18	5,365,472	4
Total	178	167	40	15	14	108	145	45,142,737	
EUROPEAN TOUR									
2004	1	1				1	1	65,854	

PGA TOUR TOP TOURNAMENT SUMMARY

Year	95	96	97	98	99	00	01	02	03	04
Masters	T41	CUT	**1**	T8	T18	5	**1**	**1**	T15	T22
U.S. Open	W/D	T82	T19	T18	T3	**1**	T12	**1**	T20	T17
British Open	T68	T22	T24	3	T7	**1**	T25	T28	T4	T9
PGA			T29	T10	**1**	**1**	T29	2	T39	T24
THE PLAYERS			T31	T35	T10	2	**1**	T14	T11	T16
TOUR Championship		T21	T12	20	**1**	2	T13	T7	26	2
WGC-Accenture Match Play					T5	2		T33	**1**	**1**
WGC-NEC Invitational					**1**	**1**	**1**	4	T4	T2
WGC-American Express Champ					**1**	T5	CNL	**1**	**1**	9

NATIONAL TEAMS: World Amateur Team Championship, 1994; Walker Cup, 1995; Ryder Cup (4), 1997, 1999, 2002, 2004; Dunhill Cup, 1998; The Presidents Cup (3), 1998, 2000, 2003; World Cup (3) 1999-2001.

Tiger Woods (Continued)

a single season. Captured his record fifth consecutive Byron Nelson Award and the PGA of America's Vardon Trophy, based on each player's adjusted scoring average. Finished the season with an adjusted scoring average of 68.41, the second-lowest in TOUR history. Finished second on money list with $6,673,413, the fourth-highest single season amount and $900,494 behind Vijay Singh. . . Victory in the WGC-Accenture Match Play Championship completed a first-ever career sweep of the World Golf Championships events...Underwent arthroscopic surgery on his left knee on December 12, 2002 following Target World Challenge. Surgery was performed by Dr. Thomas Rosenberg at HealthSouth Surgical Center in Park City, UT. During the one-hour procedure, fluid on the outside and inside of anterior cruciate ligament was removed, and several benign cysts were removed. Missed first five events of 2003 due to subsequent rehabilitation. **2002:** Led the PGA TOUR in earnings and was named Player of the Year for the fourth consecutive season and the fifth time in six years. Won five times...Became the first player since Jack Nicklaus in 1972 to capture the Masters and U.S. Open in the same season...Earned third consecutive victory at the Bay Hill Invitational, the first player to win three different TOUR events (the Memorial Tournament [1999-2001] and the WGC-NEC Invitational [1999-2001]) three straight times. With 30th career PGA TOUR victory, surpassed Jack Nicklaus for most wins before the age of 30...Earned third Masters title, joining Jack Nicklaus (1965-66) and Nick Faldo (1989-90) as the only consecutive winners there. Only Nicklaus (six wins) and Arnold Palmer (four) have more Masters titles. Jimmy Demaret, Faldo, Gary Player and Sam Snead have also won three Masters. Tied with Retief Goosen at 11-under-par entering the final round, birdied two of the first three holes en route to a three-stroke victory over runner-up Goosen. Win was his 31st on TOUR...Earned his eighth major title with sixth wire-to-wire victory in U.S. Open history. Finished 3-under-par and won by three strokes over runner-up Phil Mickelson, the only other player to finish at par or better for the championship. Tied Tom Watson for fifth all-time with eight professional major victories. Became the fifth player to win the first two majors of the year - Craig Wood (1941), Ben Hogan (1951, '53), Arnold Palmer (1960) and Nicklaus ('72). In receiving a paycheck of $1 million, became the first player to surpass the $30-million mark in career earnings ($30,246,327), and the first player to exceed $4 million in four consecutive seasons. **2001:** Captured five PGA TOUR events to up his total to 29 wins in 110 career starts as a professional. Won the Masters to become the first player to hold all four professional major titles at once. Won PGA TOUR and PGA Player of the Year honors for the third consecutive year and fourth time in five seasons. Led TOUR in Scoring Average (68.81, adjusted) for third straight year and captured third straight Vardon Trophy. Also led TOUR in Scrambling, getting up and down 69.8 percent of the time, the highest percentage since Greg Norman's 72.8 percent in 1993. **2000:** One of the greatest years in the history of the game, setting or tying 27 PGA TOUR records and placing himself among the game's greats. Won three consecutive majors (U.S. and British Opens, PGA Championship) and career Grand Slam and totaled nine PGA TOUR victories. Non-adjusted scoring average of 68.17 best in golf history, surpassing Byron Nelson's 68.33 unofficial mark of 1945. Finished the year with 47 consecutive rounds of par or better and completing all 20 events started under par. Won PGA TOUR, PGA of America and GWAA player of the year honors...An eight-stroke victory in the British Open placed him in the same company with Gene Sarazen, Ben Hogan, Jack Nicklaus and Gary Player as winners of the career Grand Slam. Became the youngest to do so at age 24...Joined Ben Hogan (1953) as the only men to win three professional majors in one season...Was 53-under par in four majors, next-best mark was 18-under by Ernie Els...Nine TOUR victories most in one season since Sam Snead won 11 in 1950...20th career win at the U.S. Open made him youngest in TOUR history to win 20 times...Season-opening victories at Mercedes Championship and AT&T Pebble Beach National Pro-Am gave him wins in six consecutive starts, most since Hogan in 1948, and five behind Byron Nelson's record of 11 in a row. Beat Ernie Els in a playoff at Mercedes, then came from seven strokes back with seven holes to play at Pebble Beach, keyed by an eagle-birdie-par-birdie finish, for a 64 and a two-stroke win. Finished T2 at Buick Invitational...In Masters, started 75-72 and finished fifth. In first round, made double bogey on 10 and triple bogey on 12...At U.S. Open, won by a major championship record 15 strokes (old record: Tom Morris Sr., 13 at 1864 British Open) at Pebble Beach. His 12-under 272 total tied the Open record of Jack Nicklaus and Lee Janzen and broke the Open mark in relation to par...Completed career Grand Slam with eight-stroke victory at British Open. His 19-under total at St. Andrews broke the British Open and major championship record in relation to par...In head-to-head battle with fellow California junior star Bob May, won PGA in three-hole playoff. Became first player since Denny Shute in 1936-37 to defend PGA title. Woods and May each played the final-round back nine in 31, with Woods birdieing the final two holes to force the three-hole playoff. Woods went birdie-par-par to win. He finished 18-under, giving him a share of the PGA most under-par record with May...Won WGC-NEC Invitational the next week by a record 11 strokes. 21-under 259 total a record for Firestone South...In next start, out of a fairway bunker on the par-5 72nd hole, faded a 6-iron from 213 yards over water to within 15 feet to secure a one-stroke victory over Grant Waite. Outdueled third-round co-leader Waite 65-66 on final day. Joined Lee Trevino (1971) as only players to win U.S., British and Canadian Opens in same year...Named Sports Illustrated Sportsman of the Year, the first two-time recipient (also won in 1996) in the 46-year history of the award. Also named Associated Press Male Athlete of the Year, becoming only three-time winner of that award. **1999:** Earned a TOUR-record $6,616,585, nearly $3 million more than his nearest competitor, David Duval. Was named PGA TOUR Player of the Year, PGA of America and GWAA Player of the Year for second time...Earned his eighth career TOUR title and first since 1998 BellSouth Classic with two-stroke victory in Buick Invitational...Earned ninth TOUR victory at Memorial Tournament, defeating Vijay Singh by two strokes...Became youngest player since Seve Ballesteros to win two majors with his victory at PGA Championship at Medinah. Won by one stroke over Sergio Garcia...Became first player since Nick Price in 1994 to win five TOUR events in season with his win at WGC-NEC Invitational...Won his next start at National Car Rental Golf Classic at Walt Disney World Resort to become first player since Tom Watson in '80 to win six official TOUR titles in season...The next week won his third consecutive start at THE TOUR Championship, becoming the first player since Duval in '97 to accomplish that feat...Following week won the WGC-American Express Championship and became first player since Johnny Miller in '74 to win eight times in year and first since Ben Hogan in '53 to win four consecutive starts. **1998:** Earned second international victory at Johnnie Walker Classic in Thailand, defeating Ernie Els on second playoff hole, overcoming eight-stroke deficit to force playoff with Els...Earned seventh TOUR victory with one-stroke win over Jay Don Blake at BellSouth Classic. **1997:** PGA TOUR Player of the Year, a season that included four victories and nine top-10 finishes...Highlight of year came at Masters Tournament, where rounds of 70-66-65-69-270 set 72-hole record. Won by 12 strokes...In first start after Masters, won GTE Byron Nelson Classic and later in summer captured Motorola Western Open...Prior to Masters, won first event of 1997 season at rain-shortened Mercedes Championships, defeating Tom Lehman on first playoff hole...Member of Ryder Cup team, named PGA of America and Golf Writers Association of America Player of the Year. Associated Press chose his Masters win top sports story of 1997, and followed by his designation as AP's Male Athlete of the Year (first golfer to be so honored in 26 years). **1996:** Turned professional at Greater Milwaukee Open, where he finished T60, and followed with two victories and three top-10s in only eight starts...Began final round of Las Vegas Invitational four strokes back, closed with 64 to force playoff with Davis Love III, then parred first extra hole for first TOUR win. Earned $297,000 and was first sponsor's exemption to win TOUR event since Phil Mickelson at 1991 Northern Telecom Open...At Walt Disney World/Oldsmobile Classic, shot closing 66 for one-stroke win...Named PGA TOUR Rookie of the Year. Also named Sports Illustrated's Sportsman of the Year, becoming youngest to receive honor since gymnast Mary Lou Retton in 1984. **Amateur:** Won '91-93 U.S. Junior Amateur Championships when no one before or since has won more than one...In '94, at TPC at Sawgrass, became youngest winner of U.S. Amateur at age 18. The following year, became first to successfully defend U.S. Amateur title since Jay Sigel in '93. In '96, became first player to win three consecutive U.S. Amateur titles. Owns U.S. Amateur records for consecutive match-play victories (18) and winning percentage (.909). His six consecutive years of winning a USGA championship are second only to Bobby Jones' eight...Made cut in four of six major championships as amateur and was low amateur at 1995 Masters and 1996 British Open...Named year's top amateur player by Golf Digest and Golfweek in '92 and Golf World in '92 and '93. Golf World's "Man of the Year" in '94...Won '96 NCAA Championship at Stanford and was named Collegiate Player of the Year...Joined Jack Nicklaus and Phil Mickelson as the only players to win NCAA and U.S. Amateur in same year.

PERSONAL:

Nicknamed "Tiger" after a Vietnamese soldier who was a friend of his father's in Vietnam. . . Putted against Bob Hope on the "Mike Douglas Show" at age 2, shot 48 for nine holes at age 3 and was featured in Golf Digest at age 5. . . In Feb. 1998, named to Blackwell's Best-Dressed List. . . Eighth athlete to be named Wheaties permanent rep, following Bob Richards (1958), Bruce Jenner (1977), Mary Lou Retton (1984), Pete Rose (1985), Walter Payton (1986), Chris Evert (1987) and Michael Jordan (1988). . . Tiger Woods Foundation, chaired by father, Earl, created to provide minority participation in golf and related activities. Foundation has pledged its full support to World Golf Foundation's The First Tee program. . . In 1997 won Sports Star of the Year Award, given to athletes who combine excellence in their sports with significant charitable endeavors. . . In 2000, on the cover of Time magazine, 40 years after Arnold Palmer became first golfer so honored. . . Web site is www.tigerwoods.com.

PLAYER STATISTICS

2004 PGA TOUR STATISTICS

Scoring Average	69.04	(3)
Driving Distance	301.9	(9)
Driving Accuracy Percentage	56.1%	(182)
Total Driving	191	(87)
Greens in Regulation Pct.	66.9%	(47)
Putting Average	1.724	(2)
Sand Save Percentage	53.5%	(39)
Eagles (Holes per)	324.0	(141)
Birdie Average	4.38	(2)
All-Around Ranking	425	(8)
Scoring Avg. Before Cut	69.42	(3)
Round 3 Scoring Avg.	69.61	(14)
Final Round Scoring Average	70.28	(15)
Birdie Conversion Percentage	35.5%	(1)
Par Breakers	24.6%	(2)

MISCELLANEOUS PGA TOUR STATISTICS

2004 Low Round/Round: 64–2 times, most recent THE TOUR Championship presented by Coca-Cola/2
Career Low Round/Round: 61–2 times, most recent 2000 WGC-NEC Invitational/2
Career Largest Paycheck/Finish: $1,200,000–2004 WGC–Accenture Match Play Championship/1

BREHAUT, Jeff

FULL NAME: Jeffrey Alan Brehaut **BIRTHDATE:** June 13, 1963 **BIRTHPLACE:** Mountain View, CA **RESIDENCE:** Sunnyvale, CA, plays out of Los Altos G & CC **HEIGHT:** 6-0 **WEIGHT:** 170 **FAMILY:** Wife, Hilary; Riley Harrison (9/19/94), Natalie Bailey (7/12/99) **EDUCATION:** University of the Pacific (1986, Communications) **SPECIAL INTERESTS:** Landscaping, home renovations, stock market, 49ers football **TURNED PROFESSIONAL:** 1986 **JOINED TOUR:** 1999 **Q SCHOOL:** 1998, 1999, 2001, 2002, 2004 **OTHER INFORMATION:**
Improved 2005 status with T13 finish at 2004 PGA TOUR Qualifying Tournament. Made 17 cuts in a career-high 34 starts in 2004 and finished 149th on money list. Among the leaders all week at the 2004 John Deere Classic, thanks to a first-round 65. Finished T11. Lone top-10 of 2004 was T8 at Chrysler Classic of Greensboro. One shot off the 36-hole lead after opening 68-66. Made 23 cuts in 32 tournaments entered in 2003. Season's earnings were greater than the total of his three previous seasons on TOUR combined. Secured card down the stretch by making the cut in seven of his last eight starts and earning 41 percent of his total ($266,897) during that period. Stretch included a career-best T5 finish at the Chrysler Classic of Greensboro in his second-to-last start, which moved him from No. 122 to No. 97 on the money list. Medalist at 2002 TOUR Qualifying Tournament to retain TOUR card for 2003. Shot low round on each course, his lowest rounds of the year, with a tournament course record 64 on the TPC Stadium Course and a 63 on the Jack Nicklaus Tournament Course. Recorded a T7 at the 2002 SEI Pennsylvania Classic for his first top-10 since posting a T8 at the 1999 Westin Texas Open. T32 at TOUR Qualifying School to earn card for 2002. Had two 2002 events on his Major Medical Extension remaining to earn $231,306 (and equal No. 125 on the final 2001 money list) to remain in Major Medical Extension category. Participated in 26 events in 2001, making 14 cuts. Top 2001 finishes were T25 at Nissan Open and T21 at 2001 BellSouth Classic. Underwent shoulder surgery on Jan. 25, 2000. Did not make a cut on the PGA TOUR in 2000 and made three cuts in six Nationwide Tour starts. Earned his first TOUR card by finishing T23 at the 1997 Qualifying Tournament. Participated in his sixth Nationwide Tour Championship in six years on Tour in 1998. Tied for second all-time on the Nationwide Tour behind John Elliott's seven appearances in the season-ending event. Captured his second title on the Nationwide Tour, where he played from 1993-1998, at the 1997 Mississippi Gulf Coast Classic. Earned his first Nationwide Tour win at the 1995 Inland Empire Open. Named 1992 Golden State Tour Player of the Year after winning three times.
EXEMPT STATUS: T13 at 2004 PGA TOUR Qualifying Tournament
BEST PGA TOUR CAREER FINISH: T5—2003 Chrysler Classic of Greensboro.
NATIONWIDE TOUR VICTORIES (2): 1995 Inland Empire Open. **1997** Mississippi Gulf Coast Classic.
MONEY & POSITION:

1999 — 126,353 — 180	2001 — 175,046 — 181	2003 — 650,019 — 99
2000 — 0	2002 — 274,335 — 161	2004 — 448,914 — 149

BEST 2004 PGA TOUR FINISH: T8—Chrysler Classic of Greensboro.
PGA TOUR CAREER LOW ROUND: 63–2003 The Honda Classic/1
2004 SUMMARY: Tournaments Entered—34; in money—17; Top-10 finishes—1
CAREER SUMMARY: Tournaments Entered—150; in money—80; Top-10 finishes—5
CAREER EARNINGS: $1,674,666
Nationwide Tour Alumnus

BRIGGS, Danny

FULL NAME: Daniel Brian Briggs **BIRTHDATE:** November 30, 1960 **BIRTHPLACE:** Abilene, TX **RESIDENCE:** Cave Creek, AZ **HEIGHT:** 5-9 **WEIGHT:** 175 **FAMILY:** Wife, Kim; Sierra (12/31/86), Bailey (3/10/89), twins Alexa and Emma (6/28/91), Dallas (9/25/95) **EDUCATION:** Texas A&M University (1984, Parks and Recreation) **SPECIAL INTERESTS:** Music, family **TURNED PROFESSIONAL:** 1985 **Q SCHOOL:** 1985, 1987, 1998, 2003, 2004 **OTHER INFORMATION:**
Finished third at 2004 PGA TOUR Qualifying Tournament, fifth time he has earned his TOUR status through Q-school (1985, 1987, 1998, 2003, 2004). Played in 28 events in 2004 with one top-10, a T7 at the U.S. Bank Championship in Milwaukee. Top-10 was first since a T8 at the 1999 Doral-Ryder Open. Returned to Q-School after finishing 157th on 2004 money list. Member of the TOUR in 1986, 1988, 1999, 2000 and 2004 and member of the Nationwide Tour in 1991, 1993-96, 1998 and 2001-03. Four career runner-up finishes on Nationwide Tour. Split time playing both Tours in 2000 after receiving a special medical extension. Along with a second place at 1993 Nationwide Tour Championship, also has a pair of T2s at the 1994 Central Georgia Open and 1995 Inland Empire Open. Winner of the 1995 Arizona State Open. Three-time All-America at Texas A&M. Hosted golf tips segment on "Golf & Paradise" television program hosted by Johnny Bench.
EXEMPT STATUS: Third at 2004 PGA TOUR Qualifying Tournament
BEST PGA TOUR CAREER FINISH: T3—1986 Tallahassee Open.
MONEY & POSITION:

1985 — 0	1992 — 2,265 — 293	2000 — 72,354 — 205
1986 — 35,308 — 156	1995 — 46,415 — 207	2001 — 0
1987 — 4,713 — 228	1996 — 3,720 — 334	2003 — 11,712
1988 — 11,417 — 211	1997 — 0	2004 — 397,606 — 157
1991 — 0	1999 — 182,245 — 161	

BEST 2004 PGA TOUR FINISH: T7—U.S. Bank Championship in Milwaukee.
PGA TOUR CAREER LOW ROUND: 64–3 times, most recent 2003 Buick Open/2
2004 SUMMARY: Tournaments Entered—28; in money—15; Top-10 finishes—1
CAREER SUMMARY: Tournaments Entered—143; in money—65; Top-10 finishes—4
CAREER EARNINGS: $767,756
Nationwide Tour Alumnus

BRIGMAN, D.J.

FULL NAME: David Franklin Brigman, Jr. **BIRTHDATE:** May 3, 1976 **BIRTHPLACE:** Clovis, NM **RESIDENCE:** Albuquerque, NM; plays out of the University of New Mexico GC **HEIGHT:** 6-4 **WEIGHT:** 190 **FAMILY:** Wife: Marisa; Delaney Angelina (11/16/01), Sasha Darlington (9/27/04) **EDUCATION:** University of New Mexico (1999, Human Resources) **SPECIAL INTERESTS:** Skydiving, fishing, cooking, hanging out with family **TURNED PROFESSIONAL:** 1999 **JOINED TOUR:** 2004 **Q SCHOOL:** 2004 **OTHER INFORMATION:**
Regained TOUR card via T13 finish at 2004 PGA TOUR Qualifying School. Finished 160th on money list in rookie season. Had three top-25s in 27 starts, including T11 at both the Shell Houston Open and Bell Canadian Open. Jumped from 32nd to 16th on the 2003 Nationwide Tour by finishing second at the season-ending Nationwide Tour Championship. Made 15-foot putt on final hole to earn his first PGA TOUR card. A miss would have left him outside the top 20 on the final money list. Collected his first Nationwide Tour win at the 2003 Permian Basin Charity Golf Classic two weeks earlier, which helped him earn spot in season-ending event. Shot a bogey-free, 6-under 66 in the final round to wipe out a three-stroke deficit to Mark Hensby. Won the 2001 Chester's San Antonio Classic on the Hooters Tour. Winner of the 2000 New Mexico Open and the 1996 and 1998 New Mexico State Amateur titles. Twice named first-team All-Western Athletic Conference. Won the 1998 U.S. Collegiate Golf Championship thanks to final-round 68 to beat Charles Howell III by one stroke. Lists Oprah Winfrey as his hero. Wife is a television news anchor in Albuquerque. Says he washed dishes at local restaurants to pay for his wife's wedding ring.
EXEMPT STATUS: T13 at 2004 PGA TOUR Qualifying Tournament
BEST PGA TOUR CAREER FINISH: T11—2004 Shell Houston Open, Bell Canadian Open.
NATIONWIDE TOUR VICTORIES (1): 2003 Permian Basin Charity Golf Classic.
MONEY & POSITION:
2004 — 356,943 — 160
BEST 2004 PGA TOUR FINISHES: T11—Shell Houston Open, Bell Canadian Open; T24—Cialis Western Open.
PGA TOUR CAREER LOW ROUND: 65–2004 Sony Open in Hawaii/2
2004 SUMMARY: Tournaments Entered—27; in money—12; Top-10 finishes—0
CAREER SUMMARY: Tournaments Entered—27; in money—12; Top-10 finishes—0
CAREER EARNINGS: $356,943
Nationwide Tour Alumnus

BROWN, Billy Ray

FULL NAME: Billy Ray Brown **BIRTHDATE:** April 5, 1963 **BIRTHPLACE:** Missouri City, TX **RESIDENCE:** Missouri City, TX; plays out of Quail Valley CC **HEIGHT:** 6-3 **WEIGHT:** 205 **FAMILY:** Wife, Cindy; Kendall Lee (11/15/95), Kati Ray (10/7/99) **EDUCATION:** University of Houston **SPECIAL INTERESTS:** Hunting, fishing **TURNED PROFESSIONAL:** 1987 **Q SCHOOL:** 1987, 1995, 1996 **OTHER INFORMATION:** Did not play on the PGA TOUR in 2004. Has served as an on-course reporter for ABC's golf coverage since 1999. Golf career was cut short by third wrist surgery in seven years in 1999. Completed comeback from second wrist surgery with third PGA TOUR victory at 1997 Deposit Guaranty Golf Classic. Was two strokes off lead through 54 holes. After double bogey on par-4 17th, needed birdie on par-5 18th for win. Reached green in two and two-putted for victory worth $180,000. In 1992, closed with rounds of 64-66 to earn playoff at rain-shortened GTE Byron Nelson Classic. Beat Bruce Lietzke, Ben Crenshaw and Raymond Floyd in playoff. In 1991, sank 25-foot birdie putt on first extra hole of playoff with Rick Fehr and Corey Pavin to win Canon Greater Hartford Open. In 1990, tied for lead through 54 holes of U.S. Open at Medinah. Missed 15-foot putt on 72nd hole that would have put him in playoff with Hale Irwin and Mike Donald. Was a four-time All-America selection at Houston and was NCAA medalist as a freshman in 1982. Along with teammate Steve Elkington, led Houston to three NCAA team championships. Father, Charlie, was a tackle for the Oakland Raiders; brother Chuck played center for the St. Louis Cardinals.

EXEMPT STATUS: Past Champion

PLAYOFF RECORD: 2-0

PGA TOUR VICTORIES (3): 1991 Canon Greater Hartford Open. **1992** GTE Byron Nelson Golf Classic. **1997** Deposit Guaranty Golf Classic.

MONEY & POSITION:

1986 —	0		1992 —	485,151 —	29	1998 —	63,724 —	201
1987 —	3,000 —	246	1993 —	173,662 —	97	1999 —	301,472 —	132
1988 —	83,590 —	125	1994 —	4,254 —	284	2000 —	0	
1989 —	162,964 —	85	1995 —	56,111 —	196	2001 —	0	
1990 —	312,466 —	44	1996 —	67,203 —	185	2002 —	0	
1991 —	348,082 —	46	1997 —	268,709 —	91			

PGA TOUR CAREER LOW ROUND: 64–5 times, most recent 1996 United Airlines Hawaiian Open/4

CAREER SUMMARY: Tournaments Entered—315; in money—152; Top-10 finishes—16

CAREER EARNINGS: $2,330,389

BROWNE, Olin

FULL NAME: Olin Douglas Browne **BIRTHDATE:** May 22, 1959 **BIRTHPLACE:** Washington, D.C. **RESIDENCE:** Hobe Sound, FL. **HEIGHT:** 5-9 **WEIGHT:** 175 **FAMILY:** Wife, Pam; Olin, Jr. (7/9/88), Alexandra Grace (10/24/91) **EDUCATION:** Occidental College **SPECIAL INTERESTS:** Fly fishing, environment, some politics **TURNED PROFESSIONAL:** 1984 **Q SCHOOL:** 1995 **OTHER INFORMATION:** Made 15 cuts in 30 PGA TOUR starts in 2004, including two top-10s. Played in the final group with Adam Scott at the 2004 Booz Allen Classic, finished T7, his first top-10 since a T5 at the 2002 SEI Pennsylvania Classic, a span of 53 events. Next top-10, a T4, came a month later at the U.S. Bank Championship in Milwaukee. Shared first-round lead with seven others, tying a TOUR record for players sharing the lead through 18 holes (2000 Honda Classic). Missed the cut in the last two tournaments of the 2004 season and fell out of the top-125 to finish the year 127th. In 2003 finished out of the top 125 for the first time since 1994. Played in 34 tournaments and made 22 cuts to finish 130th on the final season money list. Best 2002 finish was a T5 at the 2002 SEI Pennsylvania Classic where he shot 65-66 on the weekend. In 2001 his best chance to earn first TOUR title since 1999 came in the AT&T Pebble Beach National Pro-Am. Shared third-round lead with Phil Mickelson at 14-under-par 202. Closed with 73 to finish T3. In 1999, earned his second TOUR victory in as many seasons with win at the MasterCard Colonial. Final-round 66, which included two eagles, produced a one-stroke victory. Win came on his 40th birthday and $504,000 payday largest of career. Also earned a spot in 2000 Mercedes Championships, which he had to miss in 1999 due to October surgery on his left arm. Leading up to victory, was not allowed to hit more than a small bucket of balls in practice. Went from late August 1998 to mid-February 1999 without touching his clubs. After 14 years as a professional, claimed his first TOUR title at the 1998 Canon Greater Hartford Open. Closed with 67 to earn a spot in playoff with Stewart Cink and Larry Mize. On the first extra hole, chipped in for birdie from 40 feet for the win, becoming the first player since Greg Norman at the 1995 NEC World Series of Golf to win a playoff by chipping in. His four Nationwide Tour career victories exceeded only by Sean Murphy and Matt Gogel with six and Chris Smith and Pat Bates with five. In 1993 won Monterrey Open and finished seventh on Nationwide money list to earn exempt status on PGA TOUR. Won Bakersfield Open and Hawkeye Open to finish second on Nationwide Tour money list in 1991 and earn exempt status on TOUR. After winning 1993 Monterrey Open in Mexico, gave victory speech in Spanish. Knows language because of his father's Chilean heritage. Did not start playing golf until he was 19. Got hooked on game while attending Occidental College in Los Angeles.

EXEMPT STATUS: 127th on 2004 money list

PLAYOFF RECORD: 1-0

PGA TOUR VICTORIES (2): 1998 Canon Greater Hartford Open. **1999** MasterCard Colonial.

NATIONWIDE TOUR VICTORIES (4): 1991 Bakersfield Open, Hawkeye Open. **1993** Monterrey Open. **1996** Dominion Open.

MONEY & POSITION:

1986 —	0		1994 —	101,580 —	154	2001 —	815,636 —	62
1988 —	0		1996 —	223,703 —	100	2002 —	615,828 —	111
1989 —	0		1997 —	261,810 —	94	2003 —	479,592 —	130
1991 —	0		1998 —	590,240 —	47	2004 —	597,034 —	127
1992 —	84,152 —	147	1999 —	834,331 —	51			
1993 —	2,738 —	290	2000 —	494,307 —	98			

BEST 2004 PGA TOUR FINISHES: T4—U.S. Bank Championship in Milwaukee; T7—Booz Allen Classic.

PGA TOUR CAREER LOW ROUND: 63–2 times, most recent 2001 Canon Greater Hartford Open/4

2004 SUMMARY: Tournaments Entered—30; in money—15; Top-10 finishes—2

CAREER SUMMARY: Tournaments Entered—338; in money—198; Top-10 finishes—20

CAREER EARNINGS: $5,100,952

Nationwide Tour Alumnus

BURNS, Bob

FULL NAME: Robert Donald Burns **BIRTHDATE:** April 5, 1968 **BIRTHPLACE:** Mission Hills, CA **RESIDENCE:** Valencia, CA **HEIGHT:** 5-8 **WEIGHT:** 165 **FAMILY:** Wife, Jayme Lynn; Charles James (6/28/03) **EDUCATION:** California State University-Northridge **SPECIAL INTERESTS:** Beer brewing, architecture, outdoors, NHRA, classic cars and engines **TURNED PROFESSIONAL:** 1991 **Q SCHOOL:** 1993, 1999, 2001 **OTHER INFORMATION:** Made 13 cuts in 30 PGA TOUR starts in 2004 and finished 130th on the money list to earn partial status for 2005. Earned T10 at 2004 PLAYERS Championship, first top-10 since capturing the 2002 Disney Golf Classic. Improved his position on the season money list with his T11 finish at the 2004 84 LUMBER Classic in late September. Moved from No. 127 to No. 112. Missed the cut in three of his last four starts to fall out of the top 125. In 2003, slipped to 158th. Made 28 starts with best effort coming at the John Deere Classic in September, a T21. Recorded the first hole-in-one of the 2003 TOUR season, acing the 176-yard fourth hole with a 6-iron at the TPC of Scottsdale. It was the third ace of his TOUR career. Won for the first time and earned over $1 million in a single season in 2002. Became the 14th first-time winner of the Disney Golf Classic, where he held off 54-hole leader Chris DiMarco by one stroke and Tiger Woods by two. Entered the week of Disney in a precarious position on the TOUR official money list at No. 118. Held a share of the lead with Hidemichi Tanaka and Jeff Sluman after opening with a 9-under-par 63. Entered final round two strokes off the lead, but fired a bogey-free 65. With a career-best paycheck of $666,000, moved from No. 118 to No. 49 on the season money list with $1,199,802, more than he has earned in his five previous years on TOUR ($1,119,649). Also jumped from 240th to 98th in the Official World Golf Ranking. In 2000, earned $391,075, 125th on the money list, with two top-10s and four top-25s. Led Nationwide Tour in earnings with $178,664 in 1998. Captured two events, the 1998 Dominion Open and 1998 TOUR Championship. Earned Nationwide Tour Player of the Year honors. In 1997, did not compete on either TOUR. Member of the Nationwide Tour in 1996. First qualified for the PGA TOUR by placing T11 in 1993 Qualifying Tournament. First year on TOUR got off to rocky start when his home in Northridge, CA was near the epicenter of massive earthquake in January 1994. Winner of 1990 NCAA Division II Championship and was an All-American selection that year.

EXEMPT STATUS: 130th on 2004 money list

PGA TOUR VICTORIES (1): 2002 Disney Golf Classic.

NATIONWIDE TOUR VICTORIES (2): 1998 Dominion Open, TOUR Championship.

MONEY & POSITION:

1992 —	0		1999 —	138,118 —	177	2002 —	1,199,802 —	51
1994 —	178,168 —	101	2000 —	391,075 —	125	2003 —	293,974 —	158
1995 —	59,243 —	191	2001 —	353,046 —	135	2004 —	581,421 —	130

BEST 2004 PGA TOUR FINISH: T10—THE PLAYERS Championship.

PGA TOUR CAREER LOW ROUND: 63–2 times, most recent 2004 Bob Hope Chrysler Classic/3

2004 SUMMARY: Tournaments Entered—30; in money—13; Top-10 finishes—1

CAREER SUMMARY: Tournaments Entered—233; in money—116; Top-10 finishes—9

CAREER EARNINGS: $3,194,846

Nationwide Tour Alumnus

BYRUM, Curt

FULL NAME: Curt Byrum **BIRTHDATE:** December 28, 1958 **BIRTHPLACE:** Onida, SD **RESIDENCE:** Scottsdale, AZ; plays out of Desert Mountain GC (Scottsdale, AZ) **HEIGHT:** 6-2 **WEIGHT:** 195 **FAMILY:** Wife, Cyndi, Christina (10/13/90), Jake (6/11/92) **EDUCATION:** University of New Mexico **SPECIAL INTERESTS:** Hunting and fishing **TURNED PROFESSIONAL:** 1982 **OTHER INFORMATION:** Continues work as analyst for The Golf Channel. Played in three Nationwide Tour events in 2004, making cut in all three starts including a T9 at the BellSouth Panama Championship. Member of the Nationwide Tour in 1992-93 and 1998-2000. Winning the 1989 Hardee's Golf Classic, coupled with brother Tom's victory at Kemper Open seven weeks earlier, made the Byrums the first brother pair to win on TOUR since Dave and Mike Hill (1972). Surgery on right elbow in 1992 caused a drop to 194th on TOUR money list. Also had elbow surgery in July 1996. Exceptional high school athlete, all-state in both football and basketball. Learned to play on nine-hole course in South Dakota he and brother Tom used to mow.

EXEMPT STATUS: Past Champion
PGA TOUR VICTORIES (1): 1989 Hardee's Golf Classic.
NATIONWIDE TOUR VICTORIES (2): 1993 White Rose Classic. **1999** South Florida Classic.
MONEY & POSITION:

1982	1,247	268	1989	221,702	64	1997	39,705	219
1983	30,772	130	1990	117,134	129	1998	88,734	188
1984	27,836	143	1991	78,725	148	1999	3,840	335
1985	6,943	193	1992	31,450	194	2000	12,041	235
1986	79,454	108	1994	137,587	128	2001	0	
1987	212,450	46	1995	173,838	107	2002	0	
1988	208,853	55	1996	104,226	160			

PGA TOUR CAREER LOW ROUND: 62–1996 Phoenix Open/4
2004 SUMMARY: Tournaments entered—2; in money—0; Top-10 finishes—0
CAREER SUMMARY: Tournaments Entered—371; in money—202; Top-10 finishes—19
CAREER EARNINGS: $1,576,535
Nationwide Tour Alumnus

C

CARTER, Jim

FULL NAME: Jim Laver Carter **BIRTHDATE:** June 24, 1961 **BIRTHPLACE:** Spring Lake, NC **RESIDENCE:** Scottsdale, AZ; plays out of Desert Mountain GC **HEIGHT:** 6-0 **WEIGHT:** 175 **FAMILY:** Wife, Cyndi; Shane (10/5/91), Brant (3/7/95), Race (4/3/97) **EDUCATION:** Arizona State University (1984, Business) **SPECIAL INTERESTS:** Family, sports **TURNED PROFESSIONAL:** 1985 **Q SCHOOL:** 1986, 1997, 2004 **OTHER INFORMATION:** Regained PGA TOUR card for 2005 by finishing T13 at 2004 Qualifying Tournament. Posted one top 25 in 2004, a T18 at the Buick Open. Finished 212th on the money list. Using an 8-iron, aced the 147-yard par-3 eighth hole in the second round of the 2004 FedEx St. Jude Classic. Finished out of the top 150 (172nd) on the money list in 2003 for the first time since 1990. Made 33 starts without a top-25. In 2002, finished among the top 100 on the money list for the seventh time in his career thanks to four top-10s. Finished among the top 50 on the 2000 PGA TOUR money list for the first time since 1989. Broke through to earn first TOUR title in his 13th year and 292nd TOUR start, a two-stroke win at the 2000 Touchstone Energy Tucson Open. Closing 66 brought him from four strokes back of third-round leader Tom Scherrer. During T57 at the MCI Classic, needed only 95 putts in four rounds at Harbour Town GL, tying for then-third-lowest total since TOUR began keeping stats in 1980. A victory at the 1994 New Mexico Charity Classic and three runner-up finishes that year helped him to fourth on Nationwide Tour money list, good for a spot on TOUR in 1995. Also a member of the Nationwide Tour in 1991 and 1993. Finished career-best 33rd on 1989 money list in a year that saw him record career-high six top-10s. After joining the Arizona State golf team as walk-on, won 1983 NCAA Championship during brilliant career. Twice named first-team All-America. Named school's Athlete of the Year in 1984. Two-time winner of Arizona State Amateur (1981, 1984), Southwest Amateur (1983, 1984) and Arizona Open (1989, 1996).

EXEMPT STATUS: T13 at 2004 PGA TOUR Qualifying Tournament
PGA TOUR VICTORIES (1): 2000 Touchstone Energy Tucson Open.
NATIONWIDE TOUR VICTORIES (1): 1994 New Mexico Charity Classic.
MONEY & POSITION:

1987	60,102	134	1994	0		2000	964,346	48
1988	191,489	60	1995	180,664	102	2001	345,926	138
1989	319,719	33	1996	223,696	101	2002	812,346	84
1990	54,392	172	1997	279,834	88	2003	218,061	172
1991	2,450	278	1998	407,184	71	2004	111,105	212
1993	2,753	289	1999	459,026	85			

BEST 2004 PGA TOUR FINISH: T18—Buick Open.
PGA TOUR CAREER LOW ROUND: 61–1989 Centel Classic/2
2004 SUMMARY: Tournaments Entered—18; in money—5; Top-10 finishes—0
CAREER SUMMARY: Tournaments Entered—424; in money—260; Top-10 finishes—26
CAREER EARNINGS: $4,633,091
Nationwide Tour Alumnus

CHAMBLEE, Brandel

FULL NAME: Brandel Eugene Chamblee **BIRTHDATE:** July 2, 1962 **BIRTHPLACE:** St. Louis, MO **RESIDENCE:** Scottsdale, AZ **HEIGHT:** 5-10 **WEIGHT:** 155 **FAMILY:** Wife, Karen; Brandel, Jr. (1/7/97), Brennan (7/30/02), Bergen (7/30/03) **EDUCATION:** University of Texas **SPECIAL INTERESTS:** Tennis, horses **TURNED PROFESSIONAL:** 1985 **JOINED TOUR:** 1988 **Q SCHOOL:** 1987,1990, 1991,1992 **OTHER INFORMATION:** Joined The Golf Channel full-time in 2004 as an analyst on Champions Tour events after working for ABC Sports part-time in 2003. Also a contributing analyst for The Golf Channel's Pre/Post Game Show. Played in one TOUR event, the Valero Texas Open where he finished 76th. Playing with partial status in 2003, played in 15 events with a best finish of T21 at the Bank of America Colonial. In 2002, finished outside the top 150 (195th) for the first time since 1991, making the cut in six of 15 starts. Was in a six-man Nissan Open playoff won by Robert Allenby in 2001. Finished among the top 100 on the TOUR money list for the seventh straight year. Earned his first PGA TOUR victory at 1998 Greater Vancouver Open. Shared second-round lead and made 36-foot birdie putt on the 72nd hole to cap a 5-under-par 66 and a 19-under 265 for a three-stroke victory over Payne Stewart. Won 1990 New England Classic as a member of the Nationwide Tour in its inaugural season. A first-team All-American in 1983 and second-team in 1982 and 1984 at Texas. Winner of 1983 Southwest Conference Championship. While growing up, rode cutting horses and roped calves on ranch at current site of TPC at Las Colinas in Irving, TX. After an unpleasant first experience with golf at age 7, didn't touch a club for five years. Taught himself golf swing by mimicking those he saw on television.

EXEMPT STATUS: Past Champion
PLAYOFF RECORD: 0-2
PGA TOUR VICTORIES (1): 1998 Greater Vancouver Open.
NATIONWIDE TOUR VICTORIES (1): 1990 New England Classic.
MONEY & POSITION:

1985	1,190	239	1993	126,940	119	1999	414,994	96
1987	0		1994	161,018	111	2000	493,906	99
1988	33,618	166	1995	213,796	86	2001	582,086	87
1989	0		1996	233,265	94	2002	372,263	146
1991	64,141	161	1997	334,664	70	2003	126,092	195
1992	97,921	133	1998	755,936	37	2004	6,580	257

BEST 2004 PGA TOUR FINISH: 76—Valero Texas Open.
PGA TOUR CAREER LOW ROUND: 62–1996 GTE Byron Nelson Golf Classic/2
2004 SUMMARY: Tournaments Entered—1; in money—1; Top-10 finishes—0
CAREER SUMMARY: Tournaments Entered—368; in money—188; Top-10 finishes—25
CAREER EARNINGS: $4,018,410
Nationwide Tour Alumnus

CLAMPETT, Bobby

FULL NAME: Bobby Clampett **BIRTHDATE:** April 22, 1960 **BIRTHPLACE:** Monterey, CA **RESIDENCE:** Cary, NC **HEIGHT:** 5-10 **WEIGHT:** 171 **FAMILY:** Wife, Marianna; Katelyn (10/30/87), Daniel (8/11/89), Michael (12/29/91); stepchildren, Nicholas (7/30/92), Anna (4/24/94) **EDUCATION:** Brigham Young University **SPECIAL INTERESTS:** Bible study, flying, snow skiing **TURNED PROFESSIONAL:** 1980 **Q SCHOOL:** 1990 **OTHER INFORMATION:** Joined CBS Sports in 1991 as an on-course reporter for the PGA Championship. Joined CBS golf team full-time upon retiring from PGA TOUR in 1995. Last event he played in on TOUR was in 2002. At 2000 U.S. Open, a first-day 68 was three strokes off Tiger Woods' first-round pace of 65. Shot in the 70s each succeeding day to finish T37. Captured the 1982 Southern Open. In 1984, became the youngest player to exceed $500,000 in career earnings. Active in golf course design. Winner 1978 and 1980 California State Amateurs. Low amateur 1978 U.S. Open. Winner 1978 World Amateur medal. Three-time All-American at Brigham Young 1978-80. Two-time winner of Fred Haskins Award, presented to top collegiate player. Member of 1982 World Cup team.

EXEMPT STATUS: Past Champion
PLAYOFF RECORD: 0-2
PGA TOUR VICTORIES (1): 1982 Southern Open.
MONEY & POSITION:

1980	19,801	127	1987	124,872	84	1994	105,710	152
1981	184,710	14	1988	88,067	118	1995	5,472	299
1982	184,600	17	1989	68,868	148	1996	0	
1983	86,575	64	1990	29,268	194	1997	10,092	272
1984	41,837	117	1991	127,817	116	1998	3,488	335
1985	81,121	94	1992	29,175	199	2000	22,056	227
1986	97,178	87	1993	112,293	131	2002	0	

PGA TOUR CAREER LOW ROUND: 63–1993 New England Classic/1
CAREER SUMMARY: Tournaments Entered—388; in money—223; Top-10 finishes—33
CAREER EARNINGS: $1,423,000

CLARK, Michael II

FULL NAME: Michael Clark II **BIRTHDATE:** May 4, 1969 **BIRTHPLACE:** Kingsport, TN **RESIDENCE:** Orlando, FL **HEIGHT:** 5-10 **WEIGHT:** 180 **FAMILY:** Wife, Ryndee; Austin (2/6/99), Darcy Leigh (3/9/01) **EDUCATION:** Georgia Tech **SPECIAL INTERESTS:** Hunting, fly fishing **TURNED PROFESSIONAL:** 1992 **Q SCHOOL:** 1999 **OTHER INFORMATION:** At the 2004 FedEx St. Jude Classic, posted a 10-over-par 81 in round one, but improved by 19 strokes in the second round with a career-best 9-under-par 62 to make the 36-hole cut on the number (143). Finished T33 after rounds of 70-69 on the weekend. Was one stroke back of the lead through 36 holes at the 2004 Chrysler Classic of Tucson after opening rounds of 68-65. Finished T15, best effort of the season. In four seasons following his win at the 2000 John Deere Classic, has yet to finish in the top 150 and has posted just two top-10s, a T7 at the 2003 FUNAI Classic at the WALT DISNEY WORLD Resort and a T8 at the 2001 Mercedes Championships. Named PGA TOUR Rookie of the Year in 2000 on strength of victory at the John Deere Classic, his 21st TOUR start. The final round was suspended in Moline, IL, until Monday due to heavy thunderstorms. Clark led by one at the suspension. Finishing Monday, he posted a then-tournament-record 19-under-par 265 at the TPC at Deere Run course, despite a bogey on the 72nd hole. Kirk Triplett birdied the 72nd hole to force a playoff, which Clark won with a birdie on the fourth extra hole. Earned PGA TOUR playing status with 11th-place finish at the 1999 PGA TOUR Qualifying Tournament. Member of the Nationwide Tour from 1996-1999. Won his second Nationwide Tour title at the 1998 Hershey Open. Winner on the Nationwide Tour for the first time at the 1996 Olympia Open. College teammate of David Duval, Charlie Rymer, Tom Shaw, Jr. and Jimmy Johnston at Georgia Tech.

EXEMPT STATUS: Past Champion
PLAYOFF RECORD: 1-0
PGA TOUR VICTORIES (1): 2000 John Deere Classic.
NATIONWIDE TOUR VICTORIES (2): 1996 Olympia Open. **1998** Hershey Open.
MONEY & POSITION:

1993 —	0		2000 —	854,822	56	2003 —	210,177	176
1994 —	0		2001 —	236,991	162	2004 —	101,639	216
1997 —	0		2002 —	239,422	167			

BEST 2004 PGA TOUR FINISH: T15—Chrysler Classic of Tucson.
PGA TOUR CAREER LOW ROUND: 62–2004 FedEx St. Jude Classic/2
2004 SUMMARY: Tournaments Entered—14; in money—5; Top-10 finishes—0
CAREER SUMMARY: Tournaments Entered—129; in money—50; Top-10 finishes—4
CAREER EARNINGS: $1,643,050
Nationwide Tour Alumnus

CLAXTON, Paul

FULL NAME: Paul Malcolm Claxton **BIRTHDATE:** February 9, 1968 **BIRTHPLACE:** Vidalia, GA **RESIDENCE:** Claxton, GA; plays out of Sea Island GC (Sea Island, GA) **HEIGHT:** 6-0 **WEIGHT:** 150 **FAMILY:** Wife, Paula; Parker (3/15/04) **EDUCATION:** University of Georgia (1992, Business) **SPECIAL INTERESTS:** Football, basketball, tennis **TURNED PROFESSIONAL:** 1993 **JOINED TOUR:** 1997 **Q SCHOOL:** 1996, 2001, 2004 **OTHER INFORMATION:** After playing on the Nationwide Tour the last two seasons, returns to the PGA TOUR in 2005 via a T4 finish at the 2004 Qualifying Tournament. Member of the PGA TOUR in 1997 and 2002 and the Nationwide Tour in 1995-96, 1998-2001 and 2003-04. Finished 61st on the Nationwide Tour money list in 2004 with two top-10s. Finished 27th on 2003 Nationwide Tour money list with four top-10s. In 2002, logged two top-25s and finished 184th on money list. Won first Nationwide Tour title of his career at the 2001 Louisiana Open. Two-time All-America selection at the University of Georgia. Won five college tournaments, including the Gator Invitational twice. Won the 1990 Cardinal Amateur. 1990 Sunnehanna Amateur Champion. Winner of the 1992 Georgia State Amateur Championship.

EXEMPT STATUS: T4 at 2004 PGA TOUR Qualifying Tournament
BEST PGA TOUR CAREER FINISH: 12—1997 CVS Charity Classic.
NATIONWIDE TOUR VICTORIES (1): 2001 Louisiana Open.
MONEY & POSITION:

1997 —	79,118	177	1998 —	0		2002 —	156,696	184

PGA TOUR CAREER LOW ROUND: 63–2002 FedEx St. Jude Classic/3
CAREER SUMMARY: Tournaments Entered—53; in money—23; Top-10 finishes—0
CAREER EARNINGS: $235,813
Nationwide Tour Alumnus

CLEARWATER, Keith

FULL NAME: Keith Allen Clearwater **BIRTHDATE:** September 1, 1959 **BIRTHPLACE:** Long Beach, CA **RESIDENCE:** Provo, UT **HEIGHT:** 6-0 **WEIGHT:** 195 **FAMILY:** Wife, Sue; Jennifer (3/8/85), Melissa (6/30/88), Nicholas (11/ 24/92), Amanda (7/12/94) **EDUCATION:** Brigham Young University **SPECIAL INTERESTS:** Family, church activities, home building, water sports, all sports **TURNED PROFESSIONAL:** 1982 **Q SCHOOL:** 1986, 2000 **OTHER INFORMATION:** Has earned two victories in his PGA TOUR career, both in his rookie season of 1987, the Colonial National Invitation and Centel Classic. Victory at Colonial came after he recorded a pair of 64s on a 36-hole Sunday. Named 1987 PGA TOUR Rookie of the Year. Winner of 1982 North and South Amateur and 1985 Alaska State Open. Member of winning 1981 NCAA Championship team at Brigham Young. Teammates at BYU included Rick Fehr, Richard Zokol and Bobby Clampett.

EXEMPT STATUS: Past Champion
PGA TOUR VICTORIES (2): 1987 Colonial National Invitation, Centel Classic.
MONEY & POSITION:

1982 —	0		1991 —	239,727	69	1998 —	18,465	249
1983 —	0		1992 —	609,273	22	1999 —	0	
1986 —	2,221	248	1993 —	348,763	44	2000 —	34,033	224
1987 —	320,007	31	1994 —	203,549	90	2001 —	66,178	208
1988 —	82,876	127	1995 —	34,354	219	2002 —	0	
1989 —	87,490	136	1996 —	137,617	139	2003 —	0	
1990 —	130,103	118	1997 —	51,043	203	2004 —	0	

PGA TOUR CAREER LOW ROUND: 61–2 times, most recent 1996 Deposit Guaranty Golf Classic/2
2004 SUMMARY: Tournaments Entered—5; in money—0; Top-10 finishes—0
CAREER SUMMARY: Tournaments Entered—390; in money—201; Top-10 finishes—27
CAREER EARNINGS: $2,365,698
Nationwide Tour Alumnus

COCHRAN, Russ

FULL NAME: Russell Earl Cochran **BIRTHDATE:** October 31, 1958 **BIRTHPLACE:** Paducah, KY **RESIDENCE:** Paducah, KY **HEIGHT:** 6-0 **WEIGHT:** 190 **FAMILY:** Wife, Jackie; Ryan (9/4/83), Reed (9/29/85), Case (4/5/89), Kelly Marie (2/21/92) **EDUCATION:** University of Kentucky **SPECIAL INTERESTS:** Basketball **TURNED PROFESSIONAL:** 1979 **Q SCHOOL:** 1982, 1995, 2001, 2003 **OTHER INFORMATION:** Finished out of the top 150 (No. 194) on the PGA TOUR money list for the third consecutive season. Best finishes were T24s at the Nissan Open and Ford Championship at Doral. Earned his TOUR card for the third time via Q-school with a T16 finish at the 2003 tournament. Also qualified in 2001, 1995 and 1982. Spent 2003 season on the Nationwide Tour for the first time in his career, finishing 69th on the money list with two top-10s, including a T3 at the Chitimacha Louisiana Open. Made cut in two of four starts on the TOUR with a T10 at the Southern Farm Bureau Classic. Held two-stroke lead over Mark Brooks and Vijay Singh through 54 holes at 1996 PGA Championship. Home-state victory eluded him as he shot final-round 77 to finish T17, five strokes out of Brooks-Kenny Perry playoff. Earned first PGA TOUR victory at 1991 Centel Western Open. Trailed Greg Norman by five strokes with eight holes to play. Was 2-under par down the stretch, while Norman played final nine in 40, and earned two-stroke victory to join Bob Charles, Sam Adams, Ernie Gonzalez and Phil Mickelson as left-handed TOUR winners at the time. Finished career-best 10th on the money list in 1991 thanks to the victory, two seconds and a third. Avid University of Kentucky basketball fan. Started playing with ladies' set because he couldn't find any other left-handed clubs. Son Ryan, also a left-hander, attends Florida on a golf scholarship.

EXEMPT STATUS: Past Champion
PLAYOFF RECORD: 0-1
PGA TOUR VICTORIES (1): 1991 Centel Western Open.
MONEY & POSITION:

1981 —	1,307	254	1990 —	230,278	65	1998 —	332,889	91
1983 —	7,968	188	1991 —	684,851	10	1999 —	314,423	129
1984 —	133,342	51	1992 —	326,290	46	2000 —	583,605	83
1985 —	87,331	87	1993 —	293,868	59	2001 —	362,556	134
1986 —	89,817	92	1994 —	239,827	77	2002 —	176,111	179
1987 —	148,110	74	1995 —	145,663	131	2003 —	103,400	208
1988 —	148,960	80	1996 —	330,183	62	2004 —	185,108	194
1989 —	132,678	107	1997 —	470,929	46			

BEST 2004 PGA TOUR FINISHES: T24—Nissan Open, Ford Championship at Doral.
PGA TOUR CAREER LOW ROUND: 63–1991 Deposit Guaranty Golf Classic/4
2004 SUMMARY: Tournaments Entered—25; in money—8; Top-10 finishes—0
CAREER SUMMARY: Tournaments Entered—594; in money—355; Top-10 finishes—58
CAREER EARNINGS: $5,529,494
Nationwide Tour Alumnus

COLES, Gavin

FULL NAME: Gavin James Coles **BIRTHDATE:** October 19, 1968 **BIRTHPLACE:** Bathurst, New South Wales, Australia **RESIDENCE:** Bathurst, New South Wales, Australia **HEIGHT:** 5-4 **WEIGHT:** 155 **FAMILY:** Wife, Robyn; Bradley (9/1/96), Matthew (4/3/99) **SPECIAL INTERESTS:** Family, social rounds of golf with his mates **TURNED PROFESSIONAL:** 1992 **JOINED TOUR:** 2003 **OTHER INFORMATION:** Made it back to the PGA TOUR for a second time grabbing the 20th and last spot from the 2004 Nationwide Tour graduating class. Won the 2004 New Zealand PGA Championship where his 6-under 282 equaled the highest winning total of the season and was good for a three-stroke win over Bradley Hughes, Brendan Jones and Bill Lunde. Collected $139,248 for his victory, the second-largest payout in Nationwide Tour history. A T4 at the Lake Erie Charity Classic was his only other top 10 of the season. During his rookie year on TOUR, shared the first-round lead at the 2003 84 Lumber Classic of Pennsylvania with Donnie Hammond after opening-round 7-under 65. Finished T58 but only played 36 holes due to reduction of field for a 36-hole-Sunday finish. Best finish was a T56 at The INTERNATIONAL. Finished 13th on the 2002 Nationwide Tour money list with $189,745. Won the season's first event, the Jacob's Creek Open Championship, by two strokes over Bryce Molder. The victory was his first after seven years as a professional, spent mostly on the PGA TOUR of Australasia. Added three other top-10s, including a T2 at the Fort Smith Classic. Has eight career top-10s on the PGA Tour of Australasia, including a T2 at the 2002 MasterCard Masters. Lost his full eligibility on the PGA Tour of Australasia at the end of the 2000 season but finished second on the secondary tour money list in 2001 to gain entrance into the 2002 Jacob's Creek Open where things turned around for him as a professional. Hometown of Bathurst is famous in Australia for having the biggest car race of the year. Normally the population of the town would be 30,000, however on the weekend of the race, the town swells to 150,000.

EXEMPT STATUS: 20th on 2004 Nationwide Tour money list
BEST PGA TOUR CAREER FINISH: T56—2003 The INTERNATIONAL.
NATIONWIDE TOUR VICTORIES (2): 2002 Jacob's Creek Open Championship. **2004** New Zealand PGA Championship.
MONEY & POSITION:
2003 — 55,350 — 227
CAREER SUMMARY: Tournaments Entered—28; in money—7; Top-10 finishes—0
CAREER EARNINGS: $55,350
Nationwide Tour Alumnus

D

DAVIDSON, Matt

FULL NAME: Matthew Donald Davidson **BIRTHDATE:** March 13, 1981 **BIRTHPLACE:** New Brunswick, NJ **RESIDENCE:** West Windsor, NJ; plays out of Furman University GC (Greenville, SC) **HEIGHT:** 5-9 **WEIGHT:** 155 **FAMILY:** Single **EDUCATION:** Furman University (2004, Political Science) **SPECIAL INTERESTS:** Reading, exercise, watching sports **TURNED PROFESSIONAL:** 2004 **Q SCHOOL:** 2004 **OTHER INFORMATION:** After graduating from Furman University in 2004, made it through all three stages of the 2004 PGA TOUR Qualifying Tournament in his first attempt. Finished T11 to become a rookie on the 2005 PGA TOUR. Played in two tournaments on the 2004 Tarheel Tour. Was the 2004 Southern Conference medalist and team won the Southern Conference championship. Won the 2004 Furman Intercollegiate. Named Southern Conference Player of the Year in 2001-02. Academic All-America 2002 and 2004. Won 2003 New Jersey Amateur. Mother Fran is an English professor at Mercer County Community College in Mercer, NJ, father Don is an attorney and brother Sean is in last year of law school at University of North Carolina.

EXEMPT STATUS: T11 at 2004 PGA TOUR Qualifying Tournament

DAVIS, Brian

FULL NAME: Brian Lester Davis **BIRTHDATE:** August 2, 1974 **BIRTHPLACE:** London, England **RESIDENCE:** Camberley, England; plays out of Vale Do Lobo (Portugal) **HEIGHT:** 5-11 **WEIGHT:** 185 **FAMILY:** Wife, Julie; Oliver (4/13/04) **SPECIAL INTERESTS:** All sports **TURNED PROFESSIONAL:** 1994 **Q SCHOOL:** 2004 **OTHER INFORMATION:** Rookie on the 2005 PGA TOUR after being the medalist in his first trip to TOUR Qualifying School since 1995. The first timer at final stage posted the highest final round (2-over 74) by a Q-School winner since and won by one stroke over Rob Rashell. Member of the European Tour from 1997-2004. Finished 31st on the European Tour's Volvo Order of Merit with three top-10s and his second career victory, at the ANZ Championship. T6 at the 2003 British Open, shooting 68-68 on the weekend. Recorded two seconds, a third and 10 top-10s on the European Tour in 2003. Won his first title, the Peugeot Open de España, at the PGA Golf de Catalunya in May 2000 when he met his wife to be, Julie, a former flight attendant and daughter of former England goalkeeper Ray Clemence. The couple married in October 2002 and in the week of his honeymoon, Davis played in the Telefonica Open de Madrid and finished T2, his best finish of the season. In 1998, missed the cut in five of his first six starts, then contracted chicken pox on flight home to the UK from South Africa. Taken ill with the virus in Dubai and spent a week in intensive care. Represented England at boy, youth and senior levels as an amateur. Won the 1992 Peter McEvoy Trophy as an amateur.

EXEMPT STATUS: First at 2004 PGA TOUR Qualifying Tournament
BEST PGA TOUR CAREER FINISH: T6—2003 British Open Championship.
MONEY & POSITION:

1998 — 0		2000 — 0	2004 — 110,250
1999 — 9,491	— 296	2003 — 228,611	

BEST 2004 PGA TOUR FINISH: T13—PGA Championship.
PGA TOUR CAREER LOW ROUND: 68–3 times, most recent 2003 WGC-American Express Championship/3
2004 SUMMARY: Tournaments Entered—7; in money—2; Top-10 finishes—0
CAREER SUMMARY: Tournaments Entered—14; in money—6; Top-10 finishes—1
CAREER EARNINGS: $348,352

DAY, Glen

FULL NAME: Glen Edward Day **BIRTHDATE:** November 16, 1965 **BIRTHPLACE:** Mobile, AL **RESIDENCE:** Alotian, AR; plays out of The Alotian Club **HEIGHT:** 5-10 **WEIGHT:** 170 **FAMILY:** Wife, Jennifer Ralston-Day; Whitney Elizabeth (7/26/94); Christina Francis (1/26/96) **EDUCATION:** University of Oklahoma **SPECIAL INTERESTS:** Hunting, tennis **TURNED PROFESSIONAL:** 1988 **Q SCHOOL:** 1993 **OTHER INFORMATION:** Fell out of the top-125 in 2004 for the first time since joining the PGA TOUR in 1994. Played in a career-high 33 events, making 17 cuts. Secured first top-10 in a year with his T3 at the 2004 Southern Farm Bureau Classic, where he finished T7 the prior season. Shared first-round lead with Harrison Frazar and John Senden. Finish jumped him from No. 146 on PGA TOUR money list to No. 130 with four events to go and ensured at least conditional status in 2005. In 2003, earned $379,153 of his $788,557 season total in the final seven tournaments, which included five top-25s. Earned runner-up finish at 2002 Tampa Bay Classic, seven strokes behind K.J. Choi. In 2001, finished 71st in earnings with $715,780. Posted best finish since winning the 1999 MCI Classic with a solo fourth at the 2001 MasterCard Colonial. Was the first of nine first-time winners during 1999 season with playoff victory at the MCI Classic. Sank 35-foot birdie putt on first extra hole to defeat Payne Stewart and Jeff Sluman. Shot 70-68-70 and was five strokes back of the lead heading into Sunday. Final-round 66 produced a tie with Stewart and Sluman. Made impressive jump as a legitimate contender in 1998. Led after 18 holes and was second through 54 holes before recording first career runner-up finish at THE PLAYERS Championship. A week later, T3 at 1998 Freeport-McDermott Classic and in next start was second at MCI Classic. In 1995, recorded a career-low round of 62 in first round of FedEx St. Jude Classic before finishing 21st. Finished third in rookie earnings in 1994 behind Ernie Els and Mike Heinen. Opened with season-low 64 on way to runner-up finish at 1994 Anheuser-Busch Classic, finishing three strokes behind winner Mark McCumber. T9 at 1994 Canon Greater Hartford Open same year, tournament in which he scored two holes-in-one. First earned membership on PGA TOUR by finishing 11th at 1993 Qualifying Tournament. Made first foray into golf-course design business with Salem Glen, near Winston-Salem, NC. Formed Glen Day-Alan Blalock Golf Course Design in 1999. Current projects include a course re-design at Oak Mountain State Park in Shelby County, AL and the Auburn Golf Building for Auburn University; also did course re-design at Vestavia Country Club, in Vestavia Hills, AL and working on re-design of the entrance at Vestavia CC. Credits grandfather with encouraging his pursuit of golf career. Grandfather co-signed loan so he could play in Asia and Europe. Father-in-law Bob Ralston is a Champions Tour and Nationwide Tour player. Has pictures of his daughters on buttons he wears on his cap while playing. Serves as host for annual Day For Charity Pro-Am in Little Rock, AR, in support of charities throughout central Arkansas.

EXEMPT STATUS: 138th on 2004 money list
PLAYOFF RECORD: 1-0
PGA TOUR VICTORIES (1): 1999 MCI Classic.

MONEY & POSITION:

1994	357,236	45	1998	1,283,416	15	2002	859,930	77
1995	201,809	91	1999	1,109,513	34	2003	788,557	81
1996	298,131	73	2000	617,242	75	2004	519,935	138
1997	248,323	98	2001	715,780	71			

BEST 2004 PGA TOUR FINISH: T3—Southern Farm Bureau Classic.
PGA TOUR CAREER LOW ROUND: 62–2 times, most recent 2004 Booz Allen Classic/2
2004 SUMMARY: Tournaments Entered—33; in money—17; Top-10 finishes—1
CAREER SUMMARY: Tournaments Entered—324; in money—201; Top-10 finishes—34
CAREER EARNINGS: $6,999,873

DELSING, Jay

FULL NAME: James Patrick Delsing **BIRTHDATE:** October 17, 1960 **BIRTHPLACE:** St. Louis, MO **RESIDENCE:** St. Louis, MO **HEIGHT:** 6-5 **WEIGHT:** 185 **FAMILY:** Wife, Kathy; MacKenzie (5/31/89), Gemma (12/9/91), Brennan (9/21/93), Joanna (10/2/03) **EDUCATION:** UCLA (1983, Economics) **SPECIAL INTERESTS:** Fishing, all sports **TURNED PROFESSIONAL:** 1984 **Q SCHOOL:** 1984, 1987, 1988, 1989, 1996, 1998, 2003 **OTHER INFORMATION:** Earned membership for the 2004 season with his T28 at PGA TOUR Qualifying Tournament. Played in 26 events and finished in the top-25 twice, a T24 at the Reno-Tahoe Open and T19 at the Chrysler Classic of Greensboro. In 2003, made nine starts on the PGA TOUR. Posted back-to-back top 20s, a T11 at the 2003 Greater Hartford Open and T19 at 2003 Buick Open. His T11 in Connecticut was his best finish since a T8 at the 1999 Michelob Championship at Kingsmill. Made three cuts in six events on the 2002 PGA TOUR and finished 18th on the 2002 Nationwide Tour money list. Won his second Nationwide Tour title at the 2002 Omaha Classic. Defeated Jeff Freeman in a four-hole Monday playoff at the 2001 Fort Smith Classic for his first TOUR-related victory. Father, Jim, was an outfielder for the New York Yankees, Chicago White Sox, St. Louis Browns and Kansas City A's from 1949-60. Father pinch-ran for midget Eddie Gaedel with the Browns in 1951.
EXEMPT STATUS: Veteran Member
BEST PGA TOUR CAREER FINISH: T2—1993 New England Classic, 1995 FedEx St. Jude Classic.
NATIONWIDE TOUR VICTORIES (2): 2001 Fort Smith Classic. **2002** Omaha Classic.
MONEY & POSITION:

1985	46,480	125	1992	296,740	52	1999	431,879	91
1986	65,850	123	1993	233,484	71	2000	132,843	182
1987	58,657	136	1994	143,738	124	2001	4,887	251
1988	45,504	152	1995	230,769	80	2002	22,430	228
1989	26,565	187	1996	117,246	153	2003	159,654	185
1990	207,740	74	1997	102,592	167	2004	190,184	193
1991	149,775	100	1998	154,683	160			

BEST 2004 PGA TOUR FINISHES: T19—Chrysler Classic of Greensboro; T24—Reno-Tahoe Open.
PGA TOUR CAREER LOW ROUND: 61–1993 Federal Express St. Jude Classic/4
2004 SUMMARY: Tournaments Entered—26; in money—11; Top-10 finishes—0
CAREER SUMMARY: Tournaments Entered—509; in money—253; Top-10 finishes—27
CAREER EARNINGS: $2,821,699
Nationwide Tour Alumnus

DODDS, Trevor

FULL NAME: Trevor George Dodds **BIRTHDATE:** September 26, 1959 **BIRTHPLACE:** Windhoek, Southwest Africa (Namibia) **RESIDENCE:** St. Louis, MO; plays out of Boone Valley GC (Augusta, MO) **HEIGHT:** 6-1 **WEIGHT:** 195 **FAMILY:** Wife, Kris; Audrey (2/11/96) **EDUCATION:** Lamar University (General Business and Industrial Engineering) **SPECIAL INTERESTS:** Books, sports **TURNED PROFESSIONAL:** 1985 **Q SCHOOL:** 1985, 1986, 1988, 1990, 1992, 2003 **OTHER INFORMATION:** In 2004, played in 20 events for the first time since 2000 but made just four cuts. Made it through the 2003 PGA TOUR Qualifying Tournament for the first time since 1992, finishing T26. Spent five seasons on the Nationwide Tour, including three consecutive from 2001-03. Finished 74th on the 2003 Nationwide Tour money list and made one of three cuts on the PGA TOUR. Won the 2001 Virginia Beach tournament on the Nationwide Tour. Closing 64 produced T10 at the 2001 B.C. Open, first top-10 since T10 at 1999 B.C. Open and 12th of his TOUR career. Earned his first TOUR victory at 1998 Greater Greensboro Chrysler Classic. In 1998, nominated for Comeback Player of the Year after season which not only included win in Greensboro, but three other top-10s and seven top-25s and return from bout with testicular cancer in summer of 1997. Has struggled to regain exempt status on TOUR eight of the nine times he has had it since 1986, but found success in late 1990s on Canadian Tour and Nationwide Tour. Won 1997 Miami Valley Open and added eight more top-10s to place fifth on Nationwide Tour money list, earning a spot on TOUR for 1998. Won six times on Canadian Tour from 1995-96 and finished first on that tour's Order of Merit both years. Represented Namibia in 1997 World Cup of Golf.
EXEMPT STATUS: Past Champion
PLAYOFF RECORD: 1-0
PGA TOUR VICTORIES (1): 1998 Greater Greensboro Chrysler Classic.
NATIONWIDE TOUR VICTORIES (3): 1990 Kansas City Classic. **1997** Miami Valley Open. **2001** Virginia Beach Open.
MONEY & POSITION:

1985	0		1991	57,786	169	1999	311,311	130
1986	14,694	190	1993	119,436	126	2000	191,044	166
1987	46,646	155	1994	92,734	160	2001	66,366	207
1988	16,179	202	1995	20,122	239	2002	27,352	224
1989	47,086	166	1996	6,638	301	2003	6,720	251
1990	74,544	153	1998	791,340	33	2004	45,015	231

BEST 2004 PGA TOUR FINISH: T29—Reno-Tahoe Open.
PGA TOUR CAREER LOW ROUND: 63–1987 Buick Open/3
2004 SUMMARY: Tournaments Entered—20; in money—4; Top-10 finishes—0
CAREER SUMMARY: Tournaments Entered—298; in money—143; Top-10 finishes—12
CAREER EARNINGS: $1,935,014
Nationwide Tour Alumnus

DRISCOLL, James

FULL NAME: James Edward Driscoll **BIRTHDATE:** October 9, 1977 **BIRTHPLACE:** Boston, MA **RESIDENCE:** Brookline, MA **HEIGHT:** 6-0 **WEIGHT:** 185 **FAMILY:** Single **EDUCATION:** University of Virginia **SPECIAL INTERESTS:** Fitness, reading **TURNED PROFESSIONAL:** 2001 **JOINED TOUR:** 2004 **OTHER INFORMATION:** Rookie on PGA TOUR after finishing seventh on the 2004 Nationwide Tour money list, where he was a member the past two seasons. Made the cut in 18 of 24 tournament appearances, with 12 top-25 finishes and $281,161 in earnings. Notched his first Tour victory with a 15-under-par 273 at the Virginia Beach Open. The former University of Virginia All-American finished four strokes ahead of his nearest challengers, including Tour money-leader Jimmy Walker. His 16-under 128 equaled the low final 36-hole score of the season. Also earned top-5 finishes at the Northeast Pennsylvania Classic, where he lost in a playoff, Miccosukee Championship (third), First Tee Arkansas Classic (T3) and Henrico County Open (T4). Finished season T7 in Birdie Average. Made the cut in six of nine events during his rookie Nationwide Tour season of 2003. Best finish came in his first event, T14 at the Chitimacha Louisiana Open. Received a sponsor's exemption into the 2002 Greater Richmond Open, where he finished T6 in his first career event on the Tour. Member of the Canadian Tour in 2002. Three-time All-American at Virginia. Recorded 23 career top-10 finishes for the Cavaliers. Winner of the 1998 Golf Digest Invitational. Runner-up to Jeff Quinney at the U.S. Amateur Championship in 2000. Runner-up finish got him into the field of the 2001 Masters Tournament, where rounds of 68-78 led to a missed cut by a single shot. His opening-round, 4-under-par 68 included just 23 putts. Member of the United States Walker Cup Team in 2001. Won a number of men's amateur events throughout the country, including the New England Amateur and the North and South Championship, before turning pro in 2001. Youngest of seven children.
EXEMPT STATUS: Seventh on 2004 Nationwide Tour money list
BEST PGA TOUR CAREER FINISH: T40—2002 B.C. Open.
NATIONWIDE TOUR VICTORIES (1): 2004 Virginia Beach Open.
MONEY & POSITION:

2001	7,208	2002	34,293

PGA TOUR CAREER LOW ROUND: 66–2002 Greater Milwaukee Open/2
2004 SUMMARY: Tournaments Entered—0; in money—0; Top-10 finishes—0
CAREER SUMMARY: Tournaments Entered—11; in money—6; Top-10 finishes—0
CAREER EARNINGS: $41,501
Nationwide Tour Alumnus

E

EDWARDS, David

FULL NAME: David Wayne Edwards **BIRTHDATE:** April 18, 1956 **BIRTHPLACE:** Neosho, MO **RESIDENCE:** Stillwater, OK; plays out of Karsten Creek GC **HEIGHT:** 5-8 **WEIGHT:** 165 **FAMILY:** Wife, Jonnie; Rachel Leigh (12/21/85), Abby Grace (11/22/93) **EDUCATION:** Oklahoma State University **SPECIAL INTERESTS:** Cars, motorcycles, radio-controlled miniture cars, flying **TURNED PROFESSIONAL:** 1978 **JOINED TOUR:** 1979 **Q SCHOOL:** Fall 1978 **OTHER INFORMATION:** Played in 13 PGA TOUR events, with nine made cuts in 2004. Best finish was T29 at the Reno-Tahoe Open. Most recent PGA TOUR victory came at the 1993 MCI Heritage Classic, where he closed with 69 on 37th birthday to defeat David Frost by two strokes. Finished that year 20th on money list, highest ranking of his career. A year earlier, defeated Rick Fehr on second playoff hole to win Memorial Tournament and end eight-year victory drought. First win on own came at 1984 Los Angeles Open, by two over Jack Renner. Teamed with older brother, Danny, for victory at 1980 Walt Disney World National Team Championship. All-America selection in 1978 and 1979 at Oklahoma State. Winner of 1994 and 1996 Oklahoma Opens.
EXEMPT STATUS: Past Champion
PLAYOFF RECORD: 1-1
PGA TOUR VICTORIES (4): 1980 Walt Disney World National Team Championship. **1984** Los Angeles Open. **1992** Memorial Tournament. **1993** MCI Heritage Golf Classic.
MONEY & POSITION:

1979 —	44,456 —	89	1988 —	151,513 —	76	1997 —	292,096 —	83
1980 —	35,810 —	95	1989 —	238,908 —	57	1998 —	97,252 —	184
1981 —	68,211 —	66	1990 —	166,028 —	95	1999 —	70,249 —	209
1982 —	49,896 —	93	1991 —	396,695 —	38	2000 —	44,194 —	218
1983 —	114,037 —	48	1992 —	515,070 —	27	2001 —	0	
1984 —	236,061 —	23	1993 —	653,086 —	20	2002 —	89,285 —	202
1985 —	21,506 —	157	1994 —	458,845 —	34	2003 —	129,370 —	194
1986 —	122,079 —	71	1995 —	225,857 —	83	2004 —	123,681 —	209
1987 —	148,217 —	73	1996 —	201,974 —	106			

BEST 2004 PGA TOUR FINISH: T29—Reno-Tahoe Open.
PGA TOUR CAREER LOW ROUND: 61–1987 Bob Hope Chrysler Classic/1
2004 SUMMARY: Tournaments Entered—13; in money—9; Top-10 finishes—0
CAREER SUMMARY: Tournaments Entered—536; in money—347; Top-10 finishes—65
CAREER EARNINGS: $4,694,375

EDWARDS, Joel

FULL NAME: Joel Ashley Edwards **BIRTHDATE:** November 22, 1961 **BIRTHPLACE:** Dallas, TX **RESIDENCE:** Coppell, TX **HEIGHT:** 6-0 **WEIGHT:** 190 **FAMILY:** Wife, Rhonda; Tanner Grant (4/23/97) **EDUCATION:** North Texas State University **SPECIAL INTERESTS:** Music, movies, flying **TURNED PROFESSIONAL:** 1984 **Q SCHOOL:** 1988, 1989, 1990, 1995 **OTHER INFORMATION:** Did not earn enough in his six starts from the Major Medical Extension category in 2004 to retain his card for the season. Played in 11 events, finishing 219th on the money list, the lowest in his 14-year TOUR career. Double bogeyed the final hole at 2004 TOUR Qualifying Tournament to miss his 2005 card by two strokes. Largely due to a torn tendon in elbow that required surgery, suffered through sub-par 2003 season with only seven made cuts in 23 starts. Received a Major Medical Extension for 2004. Coupled with $143,382 earned in 23 events in 2003, had the opportunity to play in six events to earn $344,113. Best finish was T18 at the 2003 B.C. Open. Battled with a bout of double pneumonia for two months at end of 2002 season and still felt effects at Sony Open in Hawaii in early 2003. Surpassed the $1-million mark in earnings for the second straight season in 2002, thanks to career-high four top-10s. Finished the 2001 season by making 10 of last 11 cuts and made $862,802 of his career-best $1,193,528. Earned first TOUR title in 316th career start at 2001 Air Canada Championship. Shared first- and second-round leads with Greg Kraft before taking three-stroke lead into final round. Led TOUR event after 54 holes for first time in career. Rounds of 65-67-68-65—265 produced share of tournament record. Earned $638,422 and was 73rd on the 2000 TOUR money list. In 1999, earned his 2000 TOUR card with a second-place finish on the Nationwide Tour money list. Brought home his first career victory with a come-from-behind win at the Mississippi Gulf Coast Open in February. Named Player of the Month for February. Had six top-10s in his last seven events. In 1996, broke into the Top 100 on the money list for the first time in career (No. 90, $248,450). Recorded a T2 at the 1992 B.C. Open to finish six strokes behind winner John Daly. Winner of 1988 North Dakota Open. Named to the All-Southland Conference team at North Texas State. American Junior Golf Association All-American. Had back surgery in January 1998, which kept him off the TOUR for most of the year.
EXEMPT STATUS: Past Champion
PGA TOUR VICTORIES (1): 2001 Air Canada Championship.
NATIONWIDE TOUR VICTORIES (1): 1999 Mississippi Gulf Coast Open.
MONEY & POSITION:

1984 —	0		1992 —	107,264 —	126	2000 —	638,422 —	73
1985 —	0		1993 —	150,623 —	106	2001 —	1,193,528 —	46
1987 —	0		1994 —	139,141 —	127	2002 —	1,077,651 —	61
1988 —	0		1995 —	114,285 —	149	2003 —	143,382 —	190
1989 —	46,851 —	167	1996 —	248,450 —	90	2004 —	83,572 —	219
1990 —	109,809 —	132	1997 —	114,856 —	158			
1991 —	106,820 —	131	1998 —	0				

BEST 2004 PGA TOUR FINISH: T29—Valero Texas Open.
PGA TOUR CAREER LOW ROUND: 62–2 times, most recent 2002 Invensys Classic at Las Vegas/3
2004 SUMMARY: Tournaments Entered—11; in money—5; Top-10 finishes—0
CAREER SUMMARY: Tournaments Entered—384; in money—192; Top-10 finishes—19
CAREER EARNINGS: $4,274,655
Nationwide Tour Alumnus

ELLIOTT, John

FULL NAME: John Elliott **BIRTHDATE:** September 5, 1963 **BIRTHPLACE:** Bristol, CT **RESIDENCE:** Glastonbury, CT; plays out of Mt. Snow (VT) **HEIGHT:** 5-11 **WEIGHT:** 225 **FAMILY:** Single **EDUCATION:** Central Connecticut State University **SPECIAL INTERESTS:** Fishing, skiing **TURNED PROFESSIONAL:** 1987 **JOINED TOUR:** 1992 **Q SCHOOL:** 1991, 1992, 1995, 1998, 2004 **OTHER INFORMATION:** Rejoins the TOUR in 2005 for the first time since 1999 with T4 finish at PGA TOUR Qualifying Tournament. Member of Nationwide Tour in 1991, 1994-95, 1997-98 and 2000-04. Member of PGA TOUR in 1992-94, 1996 and 1999. Two-time winner on the Nationwide Tour. First victory came in a playoff over Chris Perry at the 1994 Mississippi Gulf Coast Classic. Earned his second title in 1997 at the rain-shortened Alabama Classic. Made the cut in 14 of 26 events on the 2004 Nationwide Tour. Posted three top-10s and wrapped up the year No. 32 on the official money list, with $164,889. Had second-place finishes at the First Tee Arkansas Classic and the Cox Classic. Qualified for 2004 U.S. Open at Shinnecock Hills and missed cut. The only player to compete in all 30 events on the 2003 Nationwide Tour, making the cut in 12 events. Finished the year No. 43 on the money list, with $107,803. Best year on the PGA TOUR came in 1993 when he made the cut in 14 of 28 tournaments and finished No. 173 on the final money list. Also finished in the top 200 (No. 182) in 1999, making the cut in 11 of 28 tournaments. Grouped with Tiger Woods in Woods' first round as a professional at the 1996 Greater Milwaukee Open. Winner of the 1991 Massachusetts Open and 15 mini-tour events.

EXEMPT STATUS: T4 at 2004 PGA TOUR Qualifying Tournament

BEST PGA TOUR CAREER FINISH: T11—1993 H.E.B. Texas Open.

NATIONWIDE TOUR VICTORIES (2): 1994 Mississippi Gulf Coast Classic. **1997** Alabama Classic.

MONEY & POSITION:

1992 —	9,857 — 246	1996 —	26,926 — 226	2004 —	0
1993 —	60,378 — 173	1997 —	0		
1994 —	4,480 — 278	1999 —	120,083 — 182		

PGA TOUR CAREER LOW ROUND: 63–1993 H.E.B. Texas Open/4

2004 SUMMARY: Tournaments Entered—1; in money—0; Top-10 finishes—0

CAREER SUMMARY: Tournaments Entered—106; in money—37; Top-10 finishes—0

CAREER EARNINGS: $221,724

Nationwide Tour Alumnus

ELLIS, Danny

FULL NAME: Daniel James Ellis **BIRTHDATE:** September 15, 1970 **BIRTHPLACE:** Orlando, FL **RESIDENCE:** Heathrow, FL **HEIGHT:** 5-11 **WEIGHT:** 170 **FAMILY:** Wife, Brooke **EDUCATION:** Clemson University (1994, Parks, Recreation, Tourism Management) **SPECIAL INTERESTS:** Fishing **TURNED PROFESSIONAL:** 1994 **JOINED TOUR:** 2001 **Q SCHOOL:** 2000, 2001, 2003 **OTHER INFORMATION:** Recorded two top-10s and a career-best $490,413 in season earnings in 2004. Second top-10 of career was a T9 at the Ford Championship at Doral, good for $140,000, a career-best payday since joining the TOUR in 2001. Only player who finished in the top-10 at Doral without a PGA TOUR victory. 18- and 36-hole leader at the HP Classic of New Orleans after opening 63-66. Dropped from contention after a third-round 82 and finished 71st. Next top-10 did not come until October, a T7 at the Michelin Championship at Las Vegas. Shared the first-round lead with six others after a 63. Closed with a 63, as well, for his best TOUR finish since a career-best T6 at the 2001 National Car Rental Golf Classic at Walt Disney World Resort. Moved from 150th on the TOUR money list to 138th with three weeks remaining in season. Regained full playing privileges for 2004 by earning runner-up honors at 2003 PGA TOUR Qualifying Tournament. Played the 2003 season on a Major Medical Extension due to back surgery and subsequent rehabilitation. Made seven cuts in 10 starts, with a best finish of T27 at the 2003 Greater Milwaukee Open. After losing his card after rookie season in 2001, regained full playing privileges with a T10 finish at the 2001 Qualifying School. In first career full PGA TOUR season in 2001, played in 27 events and made 10 cuts. Best finish was T6 at the National Car Rental Golf Classic at Walt Disney World Resort. Runner-up finish in 1993 U.S. Amateur earned him spot in 1994 Masters, where he missed cut with rounds of 78-74. Lists those two accomplishments as biggest thrill in golf. Had back surgery in the spring of 2000 and did not play all summer. Member of the 1996 and 1997 Nationwide Tour. Three time All-America selection (1990, 1992-93) at Clemson. Runner-up at 1995 Canadian Masters. Played Canadian and Asian Tours in 1994-95.

EXEMPT STATUS: 144th on 2004 money list

BEST PGA TOUR CAREER FINISH: T6—2001 National Car Rental Golf Classic Disney.

MONEY & POSITION:

1994 —	0	2002 —	73,340 — 208	2004 —	490,413 — 144
2001 —	242,487 — 159	2003 —	101,443 — 209		

BEST 2004 PGA TOUR FINISHES: T7—Michelin Championship at Las Vegas; T9—Ford Championship at Doral.

PGA TOUR CAREER LOW ROUND: 63–4 times, most recent 2004 Michelin Championship at Las Vegas/1

2004 SUMMARY: Tournaments Entered—26; in money—14; Top-10 finishes—2

CAREER SUMMARY: Tournaments Entered—81; in money—36; Top-10 finishes—3

CAREER EARNINGS: $907,682

Nationwide Tour Alumnus

F

FALDO, Nick

FULL NAME: Nicholas Alexander Faldo **BIRTHDATE:** July 18, 1957 **BIRTHPLACE:** Welwyn Garden City, England **RESIDENCE:** Orlando, FL and Weybridge, England **HEIGHT:** 6-3 **WEIGHT:** 195 **FAMILY:** Wife, Valerie; Natalie (9/18/86), Matthew (3/17/89), Georgia (3/20/93), Emma (7/26/03) **SPECIAL INTERESTS:** Fly fishing, flying helicopters, photography **TURNED PROFESSIONAL:** 1976 **OTHER INFORMATION:** Will join ABC Sports in 2005 as an analyst in the booth alongside Mike Tirico and Paul Azinger. Played six events on the PGA TOUR in 2004. Past champion missed the cut at both the Masters Tournament and British Open. Also played nine events on the European Tour, finishing T4 at the Volvo PGA Championship. Streak of most consecutive majors played, dating back to 1987 British Open, ended at 65 when he withdrew from the 2003 PGA Championship to be at home in England for the birth of daughter Emma. Has earned six major championship titles — 1987-90-92 British Opens, 1989-90-96 Masters Tournaments. Shot closing 71 to defeat Rodger Davis and third-round leader Paul Azinger by one stroke in 1987 British Open at Muirfield. Made up five-stroke deficit with 65 on final day of 1989 Masters to force playoff with Scott Hoch, which he won with birdie on second playoff hole. Successfully defended Masters title with playoff victory over Raymond Floyd in 1990. Most memorable triumph may have come at 1996 Masters, where he entered final round trailing Greg Norman by six strokes, shot 67 to Norman's 78 and won by five. Gained share of lead at 1990 British Open at St. Andrews with second-round 65 and went five strokes ahead after third-round 67. Went on to five-stroke victory over Payne Stewart and Mark McNulty. Won second British Open at Muirfield in 1992, by a stroke over John Cook. Among active players, only Tom Watson and Tiger Woods (eight) have more major victories. Lost playoff to Curtis Strange in 1988 U.S. Open at The Country Club. First PGA TOUR victory came at 1984 Sea Pines Heritage Classic, beating Tom Kite by one stroke. After leaving PGA TOUR in 1989, returned full time in 1995 and promptly won Doral-Ryder Open by one stroke over Norman. Led Official World Golf Ranking for 81 weeks in 1993-94. Led European Tour Order of Merit in 1983 and 1992. 1977 European Tour Rookie of the Year. In 1990, became first international player to be named PGA of America Player of the Year. Won 1975 British Youths Amateur and English Amateur Championships. Holds Ryder Cup records for most matches played (46) and most points won (25). Operates Faldo Golf Institute at Marriott Grand Vista Resort in Orlando. Awarded MBE (Member of British Empire) in 1987.

EXEMPT STATUS: Winner, 1996 Masters Tournament (through 2006)

PLAYOFF RECORD: 2-1

PGA TOUR VICTORIES (9): 1984 Sea Pines Heritage. **1987** British Open Championship. **1989** Masters Tournament. **1990** Masters Tournament, British Open Championship. **1992** British Open Championship. **1995** Doral-Ryder Open. **1996** Masters Tournament. **1997** Nissan Open.

MONEY & POSITION:

1979 —	2,613 — 217	1989 —	327,981 — 31	1998 —	150,703 — 163
1981 —	35,349 — 102	1990 —	345,262 — 37	1999 —	221,544 — 151
1982 —	56,667 — 81	1991 —	127,156 — 117	2000 —	276,583 — 142
1983 —	67,851 — 79	1992 —	345,168 — 42	2001 —	215,961 — 165
1984 —	166,845 — 38	1993 —	188,886 — 91	2002 —	321,208
1985 —	54,060 — 117	1994 —	221,146 — 83	2003 —	262,258
1986 —	52,965 — 135	1995 —	790,961 — 19	2004 —	40,460
1987 —	36,281 — 169	1996 —	942,621 — 12		
1988 —	179,120 — 64	1997 —	431,326 — 58		

BEST 2004 PGA TOUR FINISH: T49—PGA Championship.

PGA TOUR CAREER LOW ROUND: 62–1981 Hawaiian Open/2

2004 SUMMARY: Tournaments Entered—6; in money—3; Top-10 finishes—0

CAREER SUMMARY: Tournaments Entered—287; in money—225; Top-10 finishes—52

CAREER EARNINGS: $5,860,978

WORLD GOLF HALL OF FAME MEMBER (Inducted 1997)

FORSMAN, Dan

FULL NAME: Daniel Bruce Forsman **BIRTHDATE:** July 15, 1958 **BIRTHPLACE:** Rhinelander, WI **RESIDENCE:** Provo, UT; plays out of Riverside CC **HEIGHT:** 6-4 **WEIGHT:** 210 **FAMILY:** Wife, Trudy; Ricky (1/18/85), Thomas (12/15/89) **EDUCATION:** Arizona State University **SPECIAL INTERESTS:** All sports, the arts, church activities, truth **TURNED PROFESSIONAL:** 1982 **Q SCHOOL:** 1982 **OTHER INFORMATION:** Finished out of the top 150 (No. 165) in 2004 for the first time in his 22-year PGA TOUR career. Had no top-10s for the first time since 1996 and returned to Q-School for the first time since 1982. Earned over $1 million for the second straight season in 2003 on the strength of four top-10s. Carded 9-under-par 62 at the TPC at Canyons during the first round of the 2003 Las Vegas Invitational to tie his career low, posted in the second round of the 1988 Bob Hope Chrysler Classic. Recorded an ace in the final round at TPC at Summerlin on the par-3 fifth hole en route to a T43 finish. With win at 2002 SEI Pennsylvania Classic, earned first TOUR victory since 1992 Buick Open, and more than doubled previous best year on TOUR in earnings with $1,318,570. Span of events between wins was 246 tournaments, or 10 years, one month and six days. Eagled the 72nd hole to win. Opened with a 73 but secured win by shooting 16-under the rest of the way. A 68 in the second round and a course-record-tying 64 in third round put him in position. Final-round 65 was good enough to finish one stroke ahead of Robert Allenby and Billy Andrade. Previous best season came in 1992, when he won the Buick Open and finished second three times on way to 10th-place finish on money list. T7 at PGA Championship and THE TOUR Championship that year, as well. Third victory came at 1990 Shearson Lehman Hutton Open, by two over Tommy Armour III. Winner of the 1987 MCI Long Distance Driving Competition. Won rain-shortened 1986 Bay Hill Classic with rounds of 68-67-67—202. First TOUR victory came at 1985 Lite Quad Cities Open. Two-time All-America at Arizona State.

EXEMPT STATUS: Past Champion

PLAYOFF RECORD: 1-1

PGA TOUR VICTORIES (5): 1985 Lite Quad Cities Open. **1986** Hertz Bay Hill Classic. **1990** Shearson Lehman Hutton Open. **1992** Buick Open. **2002** SEI Pennsylvania Classic.

MONEY & POSITION:

1982 —	0		1990 —	319,160 —	43	1998 —	312,058 —	99
1983 —	37,859 —	118	1991 —	214,175 —	78	1999 —	439,571 —	88
1984 —	52,152 —	105	1992 —	763,190 —	10	2000 —	379,349 —	128
1985 —	150,334 —	53	1993 —	410,150 —	36	2001 —	456,194 —	114
1986 —	169,445 —	54	1994 —	160,805 —	112	2002 —	1,305,790 —	44
1987 —	157,728 —	63	1995 —	194,539 —	93	2003 —	1,140,209 —	63
1988 —	269,440 —	40	1996 —	170,198 —	123	2004 —	315,540 —	165
1989 —	141,174 —	99	1997 —	443,034 —	56			

BEST 2004 PGA TOUR FINISH: T16—FUNAI Classic at the WALT DISNEY WORLD Resort.

PGA TOUR CAREER LOW ROUND: 62–2 times, most recent 2003 Las Vegas Invitational/1

2004 SUMMARY: Tournaments Entered—28; in money—10; Top-10 finishes—0

CAREER SUMMARY: Tournaments Entered—596; in money—395; Top-10 finishes—63

CAREER EARNINGS: $8,002,094

FREEMAN, Robin

FULL NAME: Robin Lee Freeman **BIRTHDATE:** May 7, 1959 **BIRTHPLACE:** St. Charles, MO **RESIDENCE:** Coronado, CA **HEIGHT:** 6-0 **WEIGHT:** 180 **FAMILY:** Wife, K.C.; Chase Kiner (6/20/93), Kyle Scott (8/8/95) **EDUCATION:** University of Central Oklahoma **SPECIAL INTERESTS:** Playing guitar, snow skiing, fast cars **TURNED PROFESSIONAL:** 1983 **Q SCHOOL:** 1988, 1991, 1992, 1993, 1999, 2001 **OTHER INFORMATION:** Made his only cut of the season in 13 starts on the PGA TOUR at the 2004 B.C. Open. Finished T3, his first top-10 since the 2002 Southern Farm Bureau Classic (T5). Made the cut in six of 15 appearances on the 2003 Nationwide Tour. Had two top-10s, including a season-best T2 at the Gila River Golf Classic at Wild Horse Pass Resort. Also made the cut in four of 12 events on the 2003 PGA TOUR. Made only one cut in first 11 starts of the 2002, but ended the year on a high note. Lone top 10 was T5 at season-ending, rain-shortened 2002 Southern Farm Bureau Classic. Placed T13 at 2001 Qualifying Tournament. Made 17 cuts in season-high 34 starts, but failed to finish in the top 125 in earnings despite two top-25s. In 2000, recorded the most single-season winnings of his career, $415,430, while making 17 cuts in 32 events played. Best effort of the season solo third at the Nissan Open, earning a career-best $210,800. Only two-time medalist in PGA TOUR Qualifying Tournament history, having won in 1988 and 1993. Best finish of career came at 1995 GTE Byron Nelson Classic, a T2, three strokes behind winner Ernie Els. Took up golf at age 14 after a fractured leg kept him from participating in other sports. Worked as a club professional for five years at Oak Tree and PGA West. Father-in-law is baseball Hall of Famer Ralph Kiner. Younger brother Jeff is a member of the Nationwide Tour.

EXEMPT STATUS: Veteran Member

BEST PGA TOUR CAREER FINISH: T2—1995 GTE Byron Nelson Golf Classic.

NATIONWIDE TOUR VICTORIES (2): 1998 Knoxville Open, San Jose Open.

MONEY & POSITION:

1983 —	0		1994 —	177,044 —	103	2000 —	415,430 —	115
1988 —	1,508 —	289	1995 —	283,756 —	68	2001 —	248,543 —	157
1989 —	26,517 —	188	1996 —	133,605 —	144	2002 —	227,179 —	169
1990 —	0		1997 —	135,702 —	147	2003 —	54,651 —	228
1992 —	101,642 —	128	1998 —	32,960 —	226	2004 —	144,000 —	203
1993 —	92,096 —	148	1999 —	62,495 —	219			

BEST 2004 PGA TOUR FINISH: T3—B.C. Open.

PGA TOUR CAREER LOW ROUND: 63–2 times, most recent 1994 United Airlines Hawaiian Open/1

2004 SUMMARY: Tournaments Entered—13; in money—1; Top-10 finishes—1

CAREER SUMMARY: Tournaments Entered—368; in money—171; Top-10 finishes—12

CAREER EARNINGS: $2,137,1

Nationwide Tour Alumnus

FROST, David

FULL NAME: David Laurence Frost **BIRTHDATE:** September 11, 1959 **BIRTHPLACE:** Cape Town, South Africa **RESIDENCE:** Dallas, TX; plays out of Preston Trail GC **HEIGHT:** 5-11 **WEIGHT:** 190 **FAMILY:** Wife, Corrie **SPECIAL INTERESTS:** All sports especially rugby, as well as good food and wine from his own vineyard (www.frost-wine.com) **TURNED PROFESSIONAL:** 1981 **Q SCHOOL:** 1984 **OTHER INFORMATION:** Finished outside the top 150 on the PGA TOUR money list for the second time in his 20-year career at No. 155. Lone top-10 was a T7 at the Michelin Championship at Las Vegas, his first top-10 since he finished fifth in Las Vegas a year earlier. Used top-50 career money winners exemption in 2001 after finishing No. 177 on the TOUR money list the previous year. Kept full exempt status for 2002 by finishing 101st on money list, his highest spot since 1997 when he ended the season at No. 50. Led TOUR in putting average (1.708) in 2001 for second time in career (first in 1993). Set course record at TPC at Deere Run with 9-under 62 during second round of 2000 John Deere Classic, since broken by J.P. Hayes in 2002 (61). Opened with back-to-back 63s at 1999 FedEx St. Jude Classic, tying PGA TOUR record for opening 36 holes with his 16-under-par 126 total.T7 at 1999 British Open was his best finish in a major since T5 in 1995 Masters and best finish in a British Open since T7 in 1988. Won 1998 Dunhill Cup for South Africa for second consecutive year. Teamed with Retief Goosen year after winning with Ernie Els. Following three years without a victory, earned his 10th PGA TOUR title in impressive form at 1997 MasterCard Colonial. Dedicated his win to Ben Hogan, who had inspired him since he came to America. Shared 36-hole lead after 66-63 with Brad Faxon and Paul Goydos for tournament record-tying 11-under 129. Fell three strokes out of lead with third-round 69 but fired front-nine 32 in final round on way to two-stroke victory over Faxon and Ogrin. In 1993, recorded back-to-back victories at Canadian Open and Hardee's Golf Classic. 259 total at Hardee's gained a seven-stroke victory and was two strokes off 72-hole TOUR record. Also a two-time winner in 1992, capturing Buick Classic and Hardee's Golf Classic. Won 1990 USF&G Classic in dramatic fashion, holing out from bunker on 72nd hole to defeat Greg Norman by one. Shot 60 in final round of 1990 Northern Telecom Open at Randolph Park GC. Won 1989 World Series of Golf and earned 10-year exemption by defeating Ben Crenshaw on second playoff hole. Earned first two TOUR victories in 1988. Both victories came in the fall, at the Southern Open and Seiko Tucson Open. Took up game with father while caddying for him at age 14. In 1994, established 300-acre vineyard with brother Michael in heart of wine-producing region of South Africa. Current David Frost Wines production is 7,000 bottles, consisting of Cabernet Sauvignon 1999, Merlot 1999, Chardonnay 2000 and Sauvignon Blanc 2001. Wine features an artist series by LeRoy

Neiman. Every vintage is dedicated to a golfer, and $1 from each bottle goes to the golfer's charity. Information may be found at frostwine.com.
EXEMPT STATUS: Past Champion
PLAYOFF RECORD: 2-3
PGA TOUR VICTORIES (10): 1988 Southern Open, Northern Telecom Tucson Open. **1989** NEC World Series of Golf. **1990** USF&G Classic. **1992** Buick Classic, Hardee's Golf Classic. **1993** Canadian Open, Hardee's Golf Classic. **1994** Canon Greater Hartford Open. **1997** MasterCard Colonial.
MONEY & POSITION:

1983 —	0		1991 —	171,262 —	93	1998 —	175,621 —	148
1985 —	118,537 —	70	1992 —	717,883 —	15	1999 —	360,452 —	117
1986 —	187,944 —	46	1993 —	1,030,717 —	5	2000 —	151,123 —	177
1987 —	518,072 —	11	1994 —	671,683 —	20	2001 —	504,376 —	101
1988 —	691,500 —	9	1995 —	357,658 —	50	2002 —	509,845 —	126
1989 —	620,430 —	12	1996 —	382,947 —	54	2003 —	583,177 —	114
1990 —	372,485 —	32	1997 —	458,700 —	50	2004 —	402,589 —	155

BEST 2004 PGA TOUR FINISH: T7—Michelin Championship at Las Vegas.
PGA TOUR CAREER LOW ROUND: 60–1990 Northern Telecom Tucson Open/2
2004 SUMMARY: Tournaments Entered—26; in money—13; Top-10 finishes—1
CAREER SUMMARY: Tournaments Entered—506; in money—325; Top-10 finishes—84
CAREER EARNINGS: $8,987,003

G

GALLAGHER, Jim Jr.

FULL NAME: James Thomas Gallagher, Jr. **BIRTHDATE:** March 24, 1961 **BIRTHPLACE:** Johnstown, PA **RESIDENCE:** Greenwood, MS **HEIGHT:** 6-0 **WEIGHT:** 200 **FAMILY:** Wife, Cissye; Mary Langdon (1/15/92), James Thomas III (12/1/93), Kathleen Meeks (7/20/96), Elizabeth Ruth (11/11/99) **EDUCATION:** University of Tennessee (1983, Marketing) **SPECIAL INTERESTS:** Hunting, coaching and watching his children play sports **TURNED PROFESSIONAL:** 1983 **Q SCHOOL:** Fall 1983, 1984 **OTHER INFORMATION:** Joined USA Network as a television analyst in 2003 and continues to work with the cable network. Played in nine events on the PGA TOUR in 2004, with two made cuts. Making his third start of the season, finished T10 at the B.C. Open, his first top-10 since a T5 at the 2002 Greater Greensboro Chrysler Classic. Member of PGA TOUR with full playing privileges in 1984, 1986-87, 89-99, and played at least 15 events annually between 1984 and 2002. Twice has reached the $1-million mark in earnings. First came in 1993, when he won Anheuser-Busch Golf Classic and THE TOUR Championship. Final-round 65 at Anheuser-Busch was good for two-stroke victory over Chip Beck and helped earn spot on first Ryder Cup team, where he defeated Seve Ballesteros, 3 and 2, to seal U.S. victory. Opened THE TOUR Championship at Olympic Club with course-record 63 en route to one-stroke victory over Greg Norman and David Frost. Second $1-million season came in 1995, when he again won twice. Stood in 10th place, seven strokes behind leader Jeff Sluman, entering final round of Kmart Greater Greensboro Open. Shot final-round 66 for one-stroke victory. Shot second-round 62 to take lead for good at FedEx St. Jude Classic. First TOUR victory came at 1990 Greater Milwaukee Open, where he defeated Ed Dougherty and Billy Mayfair on first playoff hole. Represented United States in 1994 at inaugural Presidents Cup, where his record was 3-1. Leading money winner on Tournament Players Series in 1985. The Gallaghers were selected National Golf Month Family for 1995 by PGA of America. Father, Jim, is a PGA professional in Marion, IN; wife, Cissye, is a former LPGA member; sister, Jackie Gallagher-Smith, and brother, Jeff, are both tour professionals.
EXEMPT STATUS: Past Champion
PLAYOFF RECORD: 1-1
PGA TOUR VICTORIES (5): 1990 Greater Milwaukee Open. **1993** Anheuser-Busch Golf Classic, THE TOUR Championship. **1995** KMart Greater Greensboro Open, FedEx St. Jude Classic.
MONEY & POSITION:

1984 —	22,249 —	148	1991 —	570,627 —	18	1998 —	153,992 —	161
1985 —	19,061 —	159	1992 —	638,314 —	19	1999 —	131,758 —	179
1986 —	79,967 —	107	1993 —	1,078,870 —	4	2000 —	240,514 —	151
1987 —	39,402 —	166	1994 —	325,976 —	51	2001 —	47,424 —	217
1988 —	83,766 —	124	1995 —	1,057,241 —	8	2002 —	191,403 —	175
1989 —	265,809 —	50	1996 —	277,740 —	76	2003 —	22,245 —	238
1990 —	476,706 —	25	1997 —	137,654 —	145	2004 —	82,385 —	220

BEST 2004 PGA TOUR FINISH: T10—B.C. Open.
PGA TOUR CAREER LOW ROUND: 61–1991 Las Vegas Invitational/4
2004 SUMMARY: Tournaments Entered—9; in money—2; Top-10 finishes—1
CAREER SUMMARY: Tournaments Entered—515; in money—299; Top-10 finishes—50
CAREER EARNINGS: $5,943,105
Nationwide Tour Alumnus

GIBSON, Kelly

FULL NAME: Kelly Michael Gibson **BIRTHDATE:** May 2, 1964 **BIRTHPLACE:** New Orleans, LA **RESIDENCE:** New Orleans, LA ; plays out of English Turn CC **HEIGHT:** 5-11 **WEIGHT:** 190 **FAMILY:** Wife, Elizabeth **EDUCATION:** Lamar University (1986, Speech Communications) **SPECIAL INTERESTS:** Cajun food, New Orleans Saints football **TURNED PROFESSIONAL:** 1986 **Q SCHOOL:** 1991, 1994 **OTHER INFORMATION:** Member of the Nationwide Tour in 1990, 1991, 1999, and 2001. Member of the PGA TOUR in 1992-98 and 2000. Split time on both Tours in 2002-04. Played in 10 PGA TOUR events in 2004, making four cuts. First-round leader at the 2004 B.C. Open with a 64. Three rounds in the 70s dropped him to T56. Made the cut in seven of 15 events on the 2003 Nationwide Tour. Finished T4 at the Samsung Canadian PGA Championship and T7 at the Miccosukee Championship in his only top-10s of the season. Made the cut in five of 13 appearances on the 2003 PGA TOUR. In addition to playing in 14 PGA TOUR events in 2002, made 13 starts on the Nationwide Tour. Posted T14 at the 2002 Valero Texas Open, his best effort on the PGA TOUR since he finished T6 at the 1997 Canon Greater Hartford Open. Earned full playing privileges for 2000 with 13th-place finish on 1999 Nationwide Tour. Second Nationwide Tour win came in wire-to-wire fashion at the 1999 Oregon Classic. Best career PGA TOUR finish came in the 1996 Las Vegas Invitational. Ended the five-day tournament with three straight 65s to finish T3 and earn a career-best paycheck of $95,700. Finished a career-best 69th on the 1996 final money list, with $307,228. After losing card following the 1994 season, regained exempt status with 26th-place finish at the Qualifying Tournament. Earned his first Nationwide Tour win at the 1991 season-ending Tri-Cities Open, where his final-round 63 gave him a two-stroke win over Jerry Anderson. Finished 14th on the 1991 money list. Four-year member of the Canadian Tour, where he won twice and was third on the Order of Merit in 1991. Led the Canadian Tour in scoring average in 1991 (69.75). Won the 1996 Erie (PA) Open. Associate design consultant at the TPC of Louisiana in hometown of New Orleans with Steve Elkington and Pete Dye. Course opened in 2004 and debuts as host site for Zurich Classic of New Orleans in 2005.
EXEMPT STATUS: Veteran Member
BEST PGA TOUR CAREER FINISH: T3—1996 Las Vegas Invitational.
NATIONWIDE TOUR VICTORIES (2): 1991 Tri-Cities Open. **1999** Oregon Classic.
MONEY & POSITION:

1989 —	502 —	298	1995 —	173,425 —	109	2001 —	0	
1990 —	0		1996 —	307,228 —	69	2002 —	154,459 —	186
1991 —	2,140 —	288	1997 —	267,230 —	92	2003 —	55,651 —	226
1992 —	137,984 —	105	1998 —	194,574 —	139	2004 —	34,511 —	237
1993 —	148,003 —	110	1999 —	38,105 —	233			
1994 —	134,841 —	129	2000 —	103,304 —	192			

BEST 2004 PGA TOUR FINISH: T50—HP Classic of New Orleans.
PGA TOUR CAREER LOW ROUND: 63–2 times, most recent 1999 Greater Milwaukee Open/3
2004 SUMMARY: Tournaments Entered—10; in money—4; Top-10 finishes—0
CAREER SUMMARY: Tournaments Entered—323; in money—169; Top-10 finishes—9
CAREER EARNINGS: $1,751,957
Nationwide Tour Alumnus

GILLIS, Tom

FULL NAME: Thomas Charles Gillis **BIRTHDATE:** July 16, 1968 **BIRTHPLACE:** Pontiac, MI **RESIDENCE:** Oxford, MI; plays out of Indianwood CC **HEIGHT:** 6-0 **WEIGHT:** 190 **FAMILY:** Wife, Jenny **EDUCATION:** Oakland Community College **SPECIAL INTERESTS:** Fishing, hunting **TURNED PROFESSIONAL:** 1990 **Q SCHOOL:** 2002, 2004 **OTHER INFORMATION:** Solidified status for 2005 with T26 finish at PGA TOUR Qualifying School. Did not play a PGA TOUR event in 2004 due to broken right wrist suffered on January 17, 2004. Granted Minor Medical Extension carryover (dating back to December 2002 left wrist surgery) for 2005, with one event to earn $55,395 to be elevated from Q-School category to Major Medical Extension category. Also has been granted Non-Exempt Major Medical Extension for missing entire 2004 season which provides him 18 additional starts to reach the amount earned by the No. 125 player on the money list (Tag Ridings $623,262) or else remain in Q-School category for remainder of 2005 season. Despite not starting 2003 campaign until Buick Invitational, enjoyed successful rookie campaign with five top-25s in 25 starts in 2003. Picked up his first career top-10 in 16th event on TOUR with a T7 at the FBR Capital Open. Was two back through 36 holes before finishing six behind winner Rory Sabbatini. Aced the 136-yard par-3 second hole at the TPC at Sugarloaf in the BellSouth Classic with a 9-iron. Earned initial PGA TOUR card via his T21 finish at the 2002 Qualifying Tournament. Played on the European Tour 1998-2002. Best finish in 2002 was a T11 at the Benson and Hedges International Open. Played the season on a Medical Extension after Chronic Fatigue Syndrome curtailed his 2001 season to six events. Has five career top-10s on the European Tour with a T3 best finish at the 2000 Belgacom Open. Won the 1994 Jamaican Open and has one victory on the Hooters Tour.

EXEMPT STATUS: T26 at 2004 PGA TOUR Qualifying Tournament.

BEST PGA TOUR CAREER FINISH: T7—2003 FBR Capital Open.

MONEY & POSITION:

1993	0		1997	13,330	255	2003	432,100	139
1995	0		1999	0				
1996	2,775	348	2002	18,414				

PGA TOUR CAREER LOW ROUND: 65–3 times, most recent 2003 John Deere Classic/2

2004 SUMMARY: Tournaments entered—25; in money—11; Top-10 finishes—1

CAREER SUMMARY: Tournaments Entered—33; in money—16; Top-10 finishes—1

CAREER EARNINGS: $466,619

GLASSON, Bill

FULL NAME: William Lee Glasson, Jr. **BIRTHDATE:** April 29, 1960 **BIRTHPLACE:** Fresno, CA **RESIDENCE:** Stillwater, OK **HEIGHT:** 5-11 **WEIGHT:** 175 **FAMILY:** Wife, Courtney; Maxwell Alexander (9/30/88); Dakota Jade (2/26/92); Reece (9/8/00) **EDUCATION:** Oral Roberts University (1982, Business) **SPECIAL INTERESTS:** Hunting, fishing, farm work **TURNED PROFESSIONAL:** 1983 **Q SCHOOL:** Fall 1983, 1984, 2002, 2004 **OTHER INFORMATION:** After placing 162nd on the 2004 PGA TOUR money list, went to the Qualifying Tournament and finished T4 after firing six rounds at par or better to retain his card for 2005. Posted two top-10s for the first time since 2000. In second start of season, finished T10 at the AT&T Pebble Beach National Pro-Am, his first top-10 since a T3 at the 2000 B.C. Open. In only his fourth start of the season posted a second top-10 with a T6 at the Chrysler Classic of Tucson. Played in 13 events and placed 179th on 2003 money list. Failed to keep exempt status for third consecutive season. Tied the TOUR record for most eagles (4) in a 90-hole event at the 2003 Bob Hope Chrysler Classic. Voted PGA TOUR Comeback Player of the Year in 1997 after returning from May 1996 surgery for detached right forearm muscle to earn seventh TOUR victory at Las Vegas Invitational. Qualified for THE TOUR Championship with victory, jumping from 54th on money list to 27th. First of eight TOUR victories came at 1985 Kemper Open. Earned second Kemper Open crown in 1992. Won twice in the fall of 1988, first at the B.C. Open and later a two-stroke victory at Centel Classic. Won 1989 Doral-Ryder Open by a stroke over Fred Couples. At 1994 Phoenix Open, shot a closing 64 to defeat Bob Estes by three. Two-time All-America at Oral Roberts. Medical history includes elbow surgeries, four sinus operations, four knee surgeries, lip surgery and forearm surgery. Nearly filed for permanent disability due to lower back problems in 1991. Flies own plane to many TOUR stops.

EXEMPT STATUS: T4 at 2004 PGA TOUR Qualifying Tournament

PGA TOUR VICTORIES (7): 1985 Kemper Open. **1988** B.C. Open, Centel Classic. **1989** Doral-Ryder Open. **1992** Kemper Open. **1994** Phoenix Open. **1997** Las Vegas Invitational.

MONEY & POSITION:

1984	17,845	162	1991	46,995	178	1998	353,222	84
1985	195,449	29	1992	283,765	54	1999	838,788	50
1986	121,516	72	1993	299,799	57	2000	552,795	86
1987	151,701	69	1994	689,110	17	2001	180,441	179
1988	380,651	30	1995	412,094	43	2002	4,599	248
1989	474,511	19	1996	50,028	198	2003	193,579	179
1990	156,791	100	1997	926,552	22	2004	346,030	162

BEST 2004 PGA TOUR FINISHES: T6—Chrysler Classic of Tucson; T10—AT&T Pebble Beach National Pro-Am.

PGA TOUR CAREER LOW ROUND: 62–1985 Panasonic Las Vegas Invitational/1

2004 SUMMARY: Tournaments Entered—17; in money—7; Top-10 finishes—2

CAREER SUMMARY: Tournaments Entered—434; in money—270; Top-10 finishes—65

CAREER EARNINGS: $6,676,261

Nationwide Tour Alumnus

GLOVER, Lucas

FULL NAME: Lucas Hendley Glover BIRTHDATE: November 12, 1979 **BIRTHPLACE:** Greenville, SC **RESIDENCE:** Greenville, SC; plays out of Berkeley Hall CC and The Thornblade Club **HEIGHT:** 6-2 **WEIGHT:** 188 **FAMILY:** Single **EDUCATION:** Clemson University **SPECIAL INTERESTS:** Music, fishing **TURNED PROFESSIONAL:** 2001 **JOINED TOUR:** 2004 **Q SCHOOL:** 2004 **OTHER INFORMATION:** After finishing 134th on money list in rookie season in 2004, improved status for 2005 with T26 finish at 2004 TOUR Qualifying School. On 108th and final hole, stuck approach shot to two feet and converted birdie putt to clinch TOUR card. Made 30 starts as a rookie in 2004 and played on the weekend 17 times. In only his 17th career start on TOUR, collected his first top-10 with a T10 finish at the Wachovia Championship. The Clemson graduate received a sponsor exemption into the event. Posted one of three aces during second round of Cialis Western Open. Used 5-iron from 220 yards on the 12th hole. For the first time in his TOUR career posted four rounds in the 60s at the Michelin Championship at Las Vegas to finish T15. Second top-10 was a T10 finish at the FUNAI Classic at the WALT DISNEY WORLD Resort, aided by four rounds of 68. After missing his 2003 PGA TOUR card by a stroke at the 2002 Qualifying Tournament, finished 17th on 2003 Nationwide Tour money list to earn first TOUR card. Jumped into the top 20 on the money list with three weeks remaining in the season, by earning his first Nationwide Tour title at the Gila River Golf Classic at Wild Horse Pass Resort. Posted four rounds in the 60s to finish at 18-under-par 270. Made the cut in seven of 12 tournaments on the 2002 Nationwide Tour, his rookie season. First-team All-American in 2000 and 2001 at Clemson. Was an honorable mention selection as a sophomore in 1999. First-team all-Atlantic Coast Conference from 1999-2001. Won three tournaments for Clemson during his career and was a member of two NCAA runners-up (1998 and 2001). Also a three-time South Carolina Amateur Champion from 1998-2000. Member of the 2001 U.S. Walker Cup team. Named to the 2000 and 2001 Palmer Cup teams. Lists Arnold Palmer as his hero. Biggest thrill in golf was playing in the 2002 U.S. Open. Credits his grandfather for giving him his start in golf. Avid Clemson sports fan.

EXEMPT STATUS: T26 at 2004 PGA TOUR Qualifying Tournament

BEST PGA TOUR CAREER FINISH: T10—2004 Wachovia Championship, FUNAI Classic at the WALT DISNEY WORLD Resort.

NATIONWIDE TOUR VICTORIES (1): 2003 Gila River Classic at Wild Horse Pass Resort.

MONEY & POSITION:

2001	6,180	2002	16,349		2004	557,454	134

BEST 2004 PGA TOUR FINISHES: T10—Wachovia Championship, FUNAI Classic at the WALT DISNEY WORLD Resort.

PGA TOUR CAREER LOW ROUND: 64–2 times, most recent 2004 Southern Farm Bureau Classic/3

2004 SUMMARY: Tournaments Entered—30; in money—17; Top-10 finishes—2

CAREER SUMMARY: Tournaments Entered—38; in money—20; Top-10 finishes—2

CAREER EARNINGS: $579,983

Nationwide Tour Alumnus

Other Prominent PGA TOUR Members

GOSSETT, David

FULL NAME: David Spencer Gossett **BIRTHDATE:** April 28, 1979 **BIRTHPLACE:** Phoenix, AZ **RESIDENCE:** Orlando, FL **HEIGHT:** 5-10 **WEIGHT:** 170 **FAMILY:** Single **EDUCATION:** University of Texas **SPECIAL INTERESTS:** Sports, fishing, reading, relaxing with friends and family **TURNED PROFESSIONAL:** 2000 **JOINED TOUR:** 2001 **OTHER INFORMATION:** Struggled with game and lost fully-exempt status in 2004. Made only two cuts in 25 starts and fell to No. 245 on the money list. Past champion posted an ace in the second round of the John Deere Classic on No. 12. In 2003, finished 84th on the money list; had compiled three straight seasons at No. 100 or better. Finished T3 at MCI Heritage with a final-round 66 to earn season-high $216,000. One stroke out of Davis Love III-Woody Austin playoff for best finish since T2 at 2002 Buick Classic. Followed up successful rookie year that included first TOUR victory with solid sophomore campaign in 2002, finishing 100th on money list. Notched best finish of season with a T2 at the Buick Classic, two strokes behind Chris Smith. One stroke behind leaders after both 36 and 54 holes. Had successful rookie PGA TOUR campaign in 2001, starting on the Nationwide Tour and ending as a TOUR winner. In fifth start of the year on TOUR, won John Deere Classic by one shot. Had a one-stroke lead after both 36 and 54 holes. Closed with a 66 to became the first sponsor exemption to win on TOUR since Tiger Woods at 1996 Las Vegas Invitational. Sank a four-foot par putt on the 18th green at the TPC at Deere Run to nip Briny Baird by one stroke. Was 14th on the Nationwide Tour money list thanks to six top-10s in 12 starts. Turned professional in July of 2000 during the weekend of the British Open. Posted a 59 in the fourth round of the PGA TOUR Qualifying Tournament, the first time any player has done that in Q-School. Finished T68 to earn status on Nationwide Tour. Won 1999 U.S. Amateur at Pebble Beach, defeating Sung Yoon Kim 9 and 8 in the final. Ended amateur career as No.1-ranked amateur in country, according to Golfweek. Played nine TOUR events as an amateur, making three cuts. Was low amateur with a T54 finish at 2000 Masters. At age 20, was the youngest member of the 1999 Walker Cup Team. Two-time first-team All-American in only two years of college. Winner of 1999 Big 12 Championship and Golf Digest Intercollegiate. 1999 NCAA Freshman of the Year and first-team All-American in 1999 and 2000. 1999 Big 12 Player of the Year, Freshman of the Year and Student Athlete of the Year. 1997 AJGA Player of the Year. Introduced to the game by his father, first competitive tournament was at age 10. Excelled in baseball growing up but changed focus to golf in high school. One of two biggest thrills was winning the 1999 U.S. Amateur at Pebble Beach. The other was playing with Jack Nicklaus during the final round of the 2000 Masters. Following victory at the 1999 U.S. Amateur, was honored by the Tennessee Sports Hall of Fame as its Amateur Athlete of the Year. Named Male Professional Athlete of the Year in 2001 after winning the John Deere Classic.
EXEMPT STATUS: Past Champion
PGA TOUR VICTORIES (1): 2001 John Deere Classic.
MONEY & POSITION:

2000 — 0	2002 — 676,308 — 100	2004 — 21,250 — 245
2001 — 748,126 — 68	2003 — 769,840 — 84	

BEST 2004 PGA TOUR FINISH: T59—The Honda Classic.
PGA TOUR CAREER LOW ROUND: 62–2003 Bob Hope Chrysler Classic/3
2004 SUMMARY: Tournaments Entered—25; in money—2; Top-10 finishes—0
CAREER SUMMARY: Tournaments Entered—113; in money—49; Top-10 finishes—7
CAREER EARNINGS: $2,215,524
Nationwide Tour Alumnus

GOW, Paul

FULL NAME: Paul Andrew Gow **BIRTHDATE:** November 10, 1970 **BIRTHPLACE:** Sydney, Australia **RESIDENCE:** Sydney, Australia **HEIGHT:** 5-10 **WEIGHT:** 185 **FAMILY:** Wife, Cherie; two children **SPECIAL INTERESTS:** Horse racing, rugby **TURNED PROFESSIONAL:** 1993 **JOINED TOUR:** 2000 **OTHER INFORMATION:** Spent 2004 on the Nationwide Tour after three seasons on the PGA TOUR. Finished 11th on the Nationwide Tour money list with $247,218 to earn his card. Equaled a Tour record with three playoff losses in one season, coming up just short at the BMW Charity Pro-Am at The Cliffs, SAS Carolina Classic and The Reese's Cup Classic. Had a hole-in-one on No. 15 during round two of the Price Cutter Charity Championship. Led the Tour in Sand Save Percentage. Finished 162nd on TOUR money list in 2003 with one top-10, a T8 finish at the Buick Open. Played in five Nationwide Tour events as well and shot a course-record, 10-under-par 61 in the third round of the Northeast Pennsylvania Classic, where he finished T6. Despite missing eight cuts in first nine starts in 2002, finished 134th on money list. On the Monday before the Bob Hope Chrysler Classic he banged into his hotel wall trying to walk from his bed to the bathroom. Was diagnosed with vertigo. As first player off the par-3 first hole during the third round of the 2002 Buick Classic, used a 5-iron from 200 yards to post just the third hole-in-one on that hole in tournament history and the first since 1990. Gow's ace was the fourth of the week (Steve Allan, Angel Cabrera, Larry Mize). The last time that happened at a TOUR event was the 1998 Bob Hope Chrysler Classic (Lee Janzen, J.L. Lewis, David Edwards and Joe Ozaki). After finishing second in a playoff to Jeff Sluman at the B.C. Open in 2001, finished T9 in Endicott in 2002, first top-10 finish since T5 at the 2001 Bell Canadian Open and the fourth of PGA TOUR career. Had a very successful rookie campaign on the PGA TOUR, finishing 83rd on the 2001 official TOUR money list with $608,382. Had three top-10 finishes highlighted by a solo second at the B.C. Open. Rounds of 69-65-66 produced share of 54-hole lead at B.C. Open with Jeff Sluman. Both players closed with 66, and Sluman won the playoff with birdie on the second extra hole. Shot 12-under-par 60 in first round of 2001 Canon Challenge to break Australian PGA Tour scoring record as defending champion. Did not play in the first five Nationwide Tour events in 2000, joining after competing in his native Australia. Played in 15 events and finished in the top-10 nine times, including winning the Hershey Open. Final round 1-over 71 left him at 3-under for the tournament, one shot better than runner-up Paul Claxton. Winner of the 2000 Canon Challenge. Had five top-10s during the 1999-2000 season and finished sixth on the Order of Merit. Played the Australasian PGA Tour in 1996-2000. Member of the Nationwide Tour from 1997-2000 and 2003-04.
EXEMPT STATUS: 11th on 2004 Nationwide Tour money list
PLAYOFF RECORD: 0-1
BEST PGA TOUR CAREER FINISH: 2—2001 B.C. Open.
NATIONWIDE TOUR VICTORIES (2): 1997 Permian Basin Open. **2000** Hershey Open.
MONEY & POSITION:

2000 — 13,627	2002 — 448,752 — 134
2001 — 608,382 — 83	2003 — 264,927 — 162

BEST 2004 PGA TOUR FINISH: T8—Buick Open.
PGA TOUR CAREER LOW ROUND: 64–2002 Canon Greater Hartford Open/3
2004 SUMMARY: Tournaments entered—21; in money—9; Top-10 finishes—1
CAREER SUMMARY: Tournaments Entered—85; in money—36; Top-10 finishes—6
CAREER EARNINGS: $1,335,688
Nationwide Tour Alumnus

GREEN, Ken

FULL NAME: Ken Green **BIRTHDATE:** July 23, 1958 **BIRTHPLACE:** Danbury, CT **RESIDENCE:** West Palm Beach, FL; plays out of Ridgewood CC (Danbury, CT) **HEIGHT:** 5-10 **WEIGHT:** 195 **FAMILY:** Ken Jr. (12/19/81), Hunter (9/30/88) **EDUCATION:** Palm Beach Junior College **SPECIAL INTERESTS:** Bowling **TURNED PROFESSIONAL:** 1980 **Q SCHOOL:** Fall 1981, 1982, 1984, 2002 **OTHER INFORMATION:** Played in 18 events with four made cuts. Best finish was a T37 at the Deutsche Bank Championship. Withdrew from five events and was disqualified from two. Will receive a Major Medical Extension carryover for 2005. Coupled with $113,989 earned in 2003-2004, has the opportunity to play in four events to earn $373,506 and match the $487,495 winnings of 2003's No. 125, Esteban Toledo. If he does so, will play out of the Major Medical Extension category for the remainder of the season. Limited to seven events in 2003 due to back problems. Received Major Medical Extension for the 2004 campaign. Best finish on the PGA TOUR in 2003 was T25 at the AT&T Pebble Beach National Pro-Am. Top-25 was first since a T12 at the 1997 Greater Milwaukee Open. Wrestled a 75-pound alligator to save his 2-year-old Alsatian dog, Nip, when the dog jumped into a canal at his home in West Palm Beach, FL, to retrieve a ball. Member of PGA TOUR since 1982 and a five-time winner on TOUR. Member of 1989 U.S. Ryder Cup squad. Winner of 1985 and 1992 Connecticut Opens, 1985 King Hassan Open (Morocco), 1988 Dunlop Phoenix and 1990 Hong Kong Open. Started playing golf at age 12 in Honduras, where father was principal of the American School and only sports choices were golf or soccer. Once described by Johnny Miller as best fairway wood player in game. An avid bowler who rolled a 300 game in September 1996.

EXEMPT STATUS: Major Medical Extension
PLAYOFF RECORD: 0-2
PGA TOUR VICTORIES (5): 1985 Buick Open. **1986** The International. **1988** Canadian Open, Greater Milwaukee Open. **1989** KMart Greater Greensboro Open.
MONEY & POSITION:

1982 —	11,899 —	170	1990 —	267,172 —	54	1998 —	16,858 —	253
1983 —	40,263 —	114	1991 —	263,034 —	65	1999 —	19,922 —	257
1984 —	20,160 —	156	1992 —	360,397 —	41	2000 —	14,513 —	233
1985 —	151,355 —	52	1993 —	229,750 —	75	2001 —	0	
1986 —	317,835 —	16	1994 —	155,156 —	116	2002 —	10,995 —	238
1987 —	273,271 —	36	1995 —	173,577 —	108	2003 —	70,633 —	221
1988 —	779,181 —	4	1996 —	161,663 —	133	2004 —	43,356 —	233
1989 —	304,754 —	37	1997 —	59,602 —	198			

BEST 2004 PGA TOUR FINISH: T37—Deutsche Bank Championship.
PGA TOUR CAREER LOW ROUND: 61–1988 Greater Milwaukee Open/3
2004 SUMMARY: Tournaments Entered—18; in money—4; Top-10 finishes—0
CAREER SUMMARY: Tournaments Entered—502; in money—274; Top-10 finishes—44
CAREER EARNINGS: $3,745,345
Nationwide Tour Alumnus

GRÖNBERG, Mathias

FULL NAME: Mathias Grönberg **BIRTHDATE:** March 12, 1970 **BIRTHPLACE:** Stockholm, Sweden **RESIDENCE:** Monaco **HEIGHT:** 6-0 **WEIGHT:** 185 **FAMILY:** Wife, Tara; Lars (2002) **EDUCATION:** Swedish Golf School (1988, Economics) **SPECIAL INTERESTS:** Family, reading **TURNED PROFESSIONAL:** 1990 **Q SCHOOL:** 2003 **OTHER INFORMATION:** Rookie on the PGA TOUR in 2004. Recorded first top-10 of his TOUR career in his 28th career start with a ninth-place finish at the 2004 Wachovia Championship. Earlier in the season finished T13 at the Bay Hill Invitational. Tied Duffy Waldorf for the most points on the weekend at the INTERNATIONAL and moved into the top-10. He collected $135,000 for his T9 finish and increased his season earnings to $565,014. Missed the cut in his last 10 starts of 2004 after the INTERNATIONAL and finished 132nd on the final money list. After seven previous attempts at PGA TOUR Qualifying Tournament, earned TOUR card for 2004 as medalist at the 2003 Qualifying Tournament. Finished 20-under-par with four of six rounds in the 60s. Played four events on the 2003 PGA TOUR, with two top-25s, a T18 at the British Open and a T15 at the John Deere Classic. Ended three years without a victory on the European Tour when he won the 60th Italian Open Telecom Italia. Finished 2003 with four top-10s in 22 events, and ranked 20th in earnings on the European Tour. In 2002, only played in 15 European Tour events due to the birth of his first child, Lars. Third victory on the European Tour came when he won the 2000 Mercedes-Benz South African Open. At the 1998 Smurfit European Open at The K Club, won by 10 strokes, the largest winning margin that year. Member of the Dunhill Cup and World Cup of Golf teams. Claimed his first European Tour victory when he won the 1995 Canon European Masters. In his amateur days he enrolled at the Gothenburg golf school as a 16-year-old 5-handicapper. Swedish Boys Champion in 1988, and British Youths champion two years later, then helped Sweden to win the Eisenhower Trophy by 12 strokes ahead of the United States in New Zealand where he won the individual title. Lists Monaco as home, but also has residences in New Jersey and Florida. Played soccer until the age of 16. Web site is mathiasgronberg.com.

EXEMPT STATUS: 132nd on 2004 money list
BEST PGA TOUR CAREER FINISH: 9—2004 Wachovia Championship, T9—The INTERNATIONAL.
MONEY & POSITION:

1995 —	0		2001 —	8,863		2004 —	565,014 —	132
1999 —	5,961 —	308	2002 —	0				
2000 —	0		2003 —	128,013				

BEST 2004 PGA TOUR FINISHES: 9—Wachovia Championship, The INTERNATIONAL.
PGA TOUR CAREER LOW ROUND: 66–2 times, most recent 2004 Buick Invitational/1
2004 SUMMARY: Tournaments Entered—32; in money—12; Top-10 finishes—2
CAREER SUMMARY: Tournaments Entered—48; in money—18; Top-10 finishes—2
CAREER EARNINGS: $707,850

GUTSCHEWSKI, Scott

FULL NAME: Scott Bernard Gutschewski **BIRTHDATE:** October 1, 1976 **BIRTHPLACE:** Omaha, NE **RESIDENCE:** Omaha, NE; plays out of Shadow Ridge CC **HEIGHT:** 6-0 **WEIGHT:** 260 **FAMILY:** Wife, Amy; Luke (3/31/03) **EDUCATION:** University of Nebraska **SPECIAL INTERESTS:** Spending time with family **TURNED PROFESSIONAL:** 1999 **JOINED TOUR:** 2005 **OTHER INFORMATION:** Rookie on the PGA TOUR after finishing 17th on the Nationwide Tour money list. Made the cut in 20 of 25 tournaments on the 2004 Nationwide Tour, including seven top-10s and earned $206,308 in his second year on that circuit. Finished T2 at the Mark Christopher Charity Classic for his best showing of the season. T5 at the Miccosukee Championship propelled him from No. 21 to No. 14 on the money list with one tournament to play. Also tallied top 5s at the Albertsons Boise Open (T4) and Jacob's Creek Open (T5). Ended season fifth in Total Driving and sixth in Driving Distance. Finished 26th on the 2003 Nationwide Tour money list during his rookie season. Had eight top-25s in 12 starts, including his first title at the Monterey Peninsula Classic. Tournament-record 12-under 276 was four shots better than the previous record and helped him garner a career-best $81,000. The victory assured him of a sponsor's exemption into the 2004 AT&T Pebble Beach National Pro-Am, where he T69 in his only previous start on the PGA TOUR. Was first on Tour in Birdie Average and second on Tour in Driving Distance and Scoring Average. Has also played on the Tight Lies Tour, Prairie Tour, Hooters Tour and the Canadian Tour. Played at the University of Nebraska from 1997-99 and was part of Nebraska's best team in school history in 1999. Helped lead the Huskers to a 14th-place finish at the NCAA Championships that season and had a runner-up finish at the Big 12 Championship. Lists his father and grandfather as giving him his start in golf.

EXEMPT STATUS: 17th on Nationwide Tour money list
BEST PGA TOUR CAREER FINISH: T69—2004 AT&T Pebble Beach National Pro-Am.
NATIONWIDE TOUR VICTORIES (1): 2003 Monterey Peninsula Classic.
MONEY & POSITION:
2004 — 9,858
BEST 2004 PGA TOUR FINISH: T69—AT&T Pebble Beach National Pro-Am.
PGA TOUR CAREER LOW ROUND: 69–2004 AT&T Pebble Beach National Pro-Am/3
2004 SUMMARY: Tournaments Entered—1; in money—1; Top-10 finishes—0
CAREER SUMMARY: Tournaments Entered—1; in money—1; Top-10 finishes—0
CAREER EARNINGS: $9,858
Nationwide Tour Alumnus

H

HAAS, Hunter

FULL NAME: Hunter Jefferson Huck Finn Haas **BIRTHDATE:** December 1, 1976 **BIRTHPLACE:** Fort Worth, TX **RESIDENCE:** Dallas, TX; plays out of Oak Cliff CC (Fort Worth, TX) **HEIGHT:** 5-10 **WEIGHT:** 171 **FAMILY:** Wife, Lorie **EDUCATION:** University of Oklahoma (2000, Sociology) **SPECIAL INTERESTS:** Wood working, yard work, cooking on the barbecue grill **TURNED PROFESSIONAL:** 2000 **Q SCHOOL:** 2000 **OTHER INFORMATION:** Returning for his second stint on the PGA TOUR after spending the past three seasons on the Nationwide Tour. Posted five top-10s and finished 16th on the 2004 Nationwide Tour money list, with $212,065. Broke through for his first career win at the Knoxville Open. Birdied the first extra hole to defeat Shane Bertsch and Justin Bolli for the $85,500 first-place check. Also lost a playoff to Bradley Hughes at the Preferred Health Systems Wichita Open. Finished 54th on the Nationwide Tour in 2003, with four top-10s. Was 44th in 2002, with two top-10s including a second-place showing at the Lake Erie Charity Classic at Peek 'n Peak Resort, one stroke behind winner Patrick Moore. Posted one of three double eagles on Tour in 2002 when his 3-iron from 234 yards found the bottom of the cup in the final round of the Gila River Golf Classic. Earned his PGA TOUR playing privileges with a T8 at the 2000 Qualifying Tournament. Made the cut in eight of 30 TOUR events in 2001, with his only top-25 finish coming in his first event of season and seventh career start, a T15 at the Touchstone Energy Tucson Classic. Best round of the year was a 65 in the second round of the Invensys Classic at Las Vegas. Summer of 1999, shortly after finishing his college golf eligiblity, won the U.S. Public Links and the Porter Cup in back-to-back weeks. The Public Links victory gave him an automatic exemption to the U.S. Amateur at Pebble Beach GL and the 2000 Masters. Was planning on playing professionally in 2000 while finishing up his degree, but could not pass up a guaranteed spot in the Masters, where he eventually missed the cut. Did manage to make a 35-foot putt on his final hole at the annual Masters Par-3 Contest to advance to four-person playoff. Chris Perry beat Haas, Jay Haas (no relation) and Steve Pate on the first playoff hole. Reached the semifinals at the 1999 U.S. Amateur. Member of the 1999 U.S. Walker Cup team. Has six bothers and sisters who all play competitive golf.

EXEMPT STATUS: 16th on 2004 Nationwide Tour money list
BEST PGA TOUR CAREER FINISH: T15—2001 Touchstone Energy Tucson Open.
NATIONWIDE TOUR VICTORIES (1): 2004 Knoxville Open.
MONEY & POSITION:

2000 —	6,685		2001 —	109,110 —	196	2002 —	13,545	

PGA TOUR CAREER LOW ROUND: 65–2001 Invensys Classic at Las Vegas/2
CAREER SUMMARY: Tournaments Entered—37; in money—10; Top-10 finishes—0
CAREER EARNINGS: $129,340
Nationwide Tour Alumnus

HALLBERG, Gary

FULL NAME: Gary Hallberg **BIRTHDATE:** May 31, 1958 **BIRTHPLACE:** Berwyn, IL **RESIDENCE:** Castle Rock, CO **HEIGHT:** 5-10 **WEIGHT:** 162 **FAMILY:** Wife, Shirley; Kristina (8/19/92), Eric Anders (1/10/94) **EDUCATION:** Wake Forest University (1980) **SPECIAL INTERESTS:** Family, sports, business **TURNED PROFESSIONAL:** 1980 **JOINED TOUR:** 1980 **OTHER INFORMATION:** Split the 2001-04 seasons playing both the PGA TOUR and the Nationwide Tour. Made a combined eight cuts in 18 appearances. Picked up first victory on the Nationwide Tour at the 2002 Northeast Pennsylvania Classic. Collected $81,000 for his victory, his biggest payday since winning the 1992 Buick Southern Open ($126,000). In 2001, finished solo second at the Nationwide Tour Samsung Canadian PGA Championship. In 1980, became first TOUR player to earn playing privileges without going through Qualifying Tournament. PGA TOUR Rookie of the Year for 1980. Won 1981 Lille Open in France and 1982 Chunichi Crowns Invitational in Japan. Winner 1986 Chrysler Team Championship (with Scott Hoch). Was first four-time first-team All-America selection. That feat later was matched by Phil Mickelson, David Duval and Bryce Molder. Won 1979 NCAA Championship and 1978-79 North and South Amateurs. Member 1977 U.S. Walker Cup team. Started Saturday Series Pro-Am held in conjunction with TOUR events. NBC and CNBC golf analyst in 2001.

EXEMPT STATUS: Past Champion
PLAYOFF RECORD: 0-2
PGA TOUR VICTORIES (3): 1983 Isuzu-Andy Williams San Diego Open. **1987** Greater Milwaukee Open. **1992** Buick Southern Open.
NATIONWIDE TOUR VICTORIES (1): 2002 Northeast Pennsylvania Classic.
MONEY & POSITION:

1980 —	75,844 —	56	1989 —	146,833 —	95	1998 —	167,540 —	156
1981 —	45,793 —	92	1990 —	128,954 —	121	1999 —	24,110 —	250
1982 —	36,192 —	113	1991 —	273,546 —	62	2000 —	19,212 —	228
1983 —	120,170 —	45	1992 —	236,629 —	67	2001 —	15,296 —	230
1984 —	187,260 —	30	1993 —	147,706 —	111	2002 —	0	
1985 —	108,872 —	75	1994 —	224,965 —	82	2003 —	24,417 —	236
1986 —	68,479 —	121	1995 —	99,332 —	160	2004 —	0	
1987 —	210,786 —	48	1996 —	2,544 —	358			
1988 —	28,551 —	179	1997 —	40,132 —	217			

BEST 2004 PGA TOUR FINISH: T47—AT&T Pebble Beach National Pro-Am.
PGA TOUR CAREER LOW ROUND: 63–5 times, most recent 1995 B.C. Open/2
2004 SUMMARY: Tournaments Entered—2; in money—0; Top-10 finishes—0
CAREER SUMMARY: Tournaments Entered—551; in money—284; Top-10 finishes—38
CAREER EARNINGS: $2,433,161
Nationwide Tour Alumnus

HAMMOND, Donnie

FULL NAME: Donald William Hammond **BIRTHDATE:** April 1, 1957 **BIRTHPLACE:** Frederick, MD **RESIDENCE:** Heathrow, FL **HEIGHT:** 5-10 **WEIGHT:** 170 **FAMILY:** Wife, Trenny; Matthew William (10/22/86), Brittany Marie (3/3/89), Brooke Haley (11/17/96), Halle Gracyn (7/14/99) **EDUCATION:** Jacksonville University **SPECIAL INTERESTS:** Astronomy, gardening, baseball **TURNED PROFESSIONAL:** 1979 **Q SCHOOL:** 1982, 1991, 1996, 2002 **OTHER INFORMATION:** Played in a combined 15 events in 2004 on the PGA TOUR and Nationwide Tour with best finish a T19 at the Nationwide Tour's Rheem Classic. In 2003, made cut in 19 of 27 events but posted just one top-25, a T23 at the BellSouth Classic. Finished T5 at 2002 TOUR Qualifying School to regain TOUR card for 2003 season, the fourth time in his career he has done so through Q-school. Collected 40th career top-10 on TOUR and first since 2000 Kemper Insurance Open (T10) with T9 at the 2002 Tampa Bay Classic. Longtime TOUR player who maintained his playing privileges from 1983-98. Finished 27th on the 2000 Nationwide Tour, thanks in part to his first victory on that Tour at the Lakeland Classic. Also a member in 1999. Winner of 1986 Bob Hope Chrysler Classic and 1989 Texas Open. In winning second PGA TOUR title at 1989 Texas Open, came within one stroke of the then PGA TOUR scoring record. Won the 2000 Lakeland Classic. Medalist by a record 14 strokes at 1982 Qualifying Tournament played at TPC at Sawgrass. Charter member of Jacksonville (FL) University Sports Hall of Fame.

EXEMPT STATUS: Past Champion
PLAYOFF RECORD: 1-0
PGA TOUR VICTORIES (2): 1986 Bob Hope Chrysler Classic. **1989** Texas Open.
NATIONWIDE TOUR VICTORIES (1): 2000 Lakeland Classic.
MONEY & POSITION:

1981 —	0		1989 —	458,741 —	20	1997 —	224,799 —	106
1982 —	0		1990 —	151,811 —	104	1998 —	141,843 —	167
1983 —	41,336 —	112	1991 —	102,668 —	135	1999 —	68,952 —	212
1984 —	67,874 —	87	1992 —	197,085 —	77	2000 —	96,938 —	194
1985 —	102,719 —	77	1993 —	340,432 —	47	2001 —	152,698 —	187
1986 —	254,987 —	28	1994 —	295,436 —	61	2002 —	263,366 —	165
1987 —	157,480 —	64	1995 —	141,150 —	136	2003 —	255,414 —	166
1988 —	256,010 —	44	1996 —	98,455 —	165	2004 —	65,024 —	225

BEST 2004 PGA TOUR FINISH: T35—Wachovia Championship.
PGA TOUR CAREER LOW ROUND: 63–4 times, most recent 2003 MCI Heritage/2
2004 SUMMARY: Tournaments Entered—13; in money—6; Top-10 finishes—0
CAREER SUMMARY: Tournaments Entered—481; in money—333; Top-10 finishes—40
CAREER EARNINGS: $3,935,217
Nationwide Tour Alumnus

HART, Jeff

FULL NAME: Jeffrey Robert Hart **BIRTHDATE:** May 5, 1960 **BIRTHPLACE:** Pomona, CA **RESIDENCE:** Solana Beach, CA; plays out of Lomas Sante Fe CC **HEIGHT:** 5-9 **WEIGHT:** 150 **FAMILY:** Wife, Carmen; Sabrina (2/13/91), Monique (12/9/98) **EDUCATION:** University of Southern California (1983, Physical Education) **SPECIAL INTERESTS:** Music, USC Trojans football **TURNED PROFESSIONAL:** 1983 **JOINED TOUR:** 1985 **Q SCHOOL:** 1984, 1988, 1989, 1995, 1996, 2004 **OTHER INFORMATION:** Rejoins PGA TOUR in 2005 after sixth successful trip through PGA TOUR Qualifying School in 2004, where he finished T26. Member of the Nationwide Tour in 1992-93, 1995, 2000 and 2002-04. Member of the PGA TOUR 1985, 1989-90, 1996-97 and 2001. On the Nationwide Tour in 2004, finished 85th on money list in 14 starts. Two top-10s were T5 at the Rheem Classic and T4 at the Cox Classic. In 157 career PGA TOUR starts, has one top-10, a T4 at the 1988 Deposit Guaranty Golf Classic. Nationwide Tour graduate in 2000 after finishing 15th on the money list, including his only victory on that circuit at the Steamtown Classic. Has 21 career top-10s on the Nationwide Tour, nine of which came in 1992. 1981 third-team All-American. 1982 first-team All-American.

EXEMPT STATUS: T26 at 2004 PGA TOUR Qualifying Tournament
BEST PGA TOUR CAREER FINISH: T4—1988 Deposit Guaranty Golf Classic.
NATIONWIDE TOUR VICTORIES (1): 2000 Steamtown Classic.
MONEY & POSITION:

1985 —	10,466 —	177	1991 —	1,866 —	303	1997 —	67,829 —	188
1988 —	7,875 —	223	1992 —	0		2001 —	219,386 —	164
1989 —	44,650 —	169	1994 —	0				
1990 —	57,189 —	171	1996 —	66,450 —	186			

PGA TOUR CAREER LOW ROUND: 65–3 times, most recent 1997 Walt Disney World/Oldsmobile Classic/2
2004 SUMMARY: Tournaments Entered—0; in money—0; Top-10 finishes—0
CAREER SUMMARY: Tournaments Entered—157; in money—75; Top-10 finishes—1
CAREER EARNINGS: $475,712
Nationwide Tour Alumnus

HAYES, J.P.

FULL NAME: John Patrick Hayes **BIRTHDATE:** August 2, 1965 **BIRTHPLACE:** Appleton, WI **RESIDENCE:** El Paso, TX; plays out of El Paso CC **HEIGHT:** 6-0 **WEIGHT:** 185 **FAMILY:** Wife, Laura; John Henry (9/27/01), Maggy Jean (12/8/03) **EDUCATION:** University of Texas-El Paso (1988, Marketing) **SPECIAL INTERESTS:** Fly Fishing **TURNED PROFESSIONAL:** 1989 **Q SCHOOL:** 1991, 1994, 1996, 1997, 2004 **OTHER INFORMATION:** Finished out of the top 125 (No. 174) for the first time on the PGA TOUR since 1997. Retained his privileges by finishing T26 at 2004 Qualifying Tournament. Closed with a 5-under 67 to make it on the number and finish in the top 30 and ties to earn a 2005 TOUR card. In 2002, finished in the top 125 for the sixth consecutive season with seven top-25s. Recorded career-best earnings of $955,271 capped by second career TOUR victory at 2002 John Deere Classic. T16 at Bob Hope Chrysler Classic was highlighted by TOUR record-tying eight consecutive birdies (13-18, 1-2) at the Palmer Course at PGA West. Wisconsin native finished in top five for the third consecutive year at the Greater Milwaukee Open with a T5 (T3-2000-01). Set tournament record with 7-under 28 on the front nine at Brown Deer Park Golf Course. Picked up second career victory at the John Deere Classic, four years, one month and 14 days after his first. Recorded 23 birdies and just one bogey over four rounds. Set tournament course record and tied the tournament record with a 10-under 61 in the second round. Steady year to finish in the top 100 on the 2001 money list for the fourth consecutive year. Recorded three top-10s, all in the second half of the season, a T3 in June at the Buick Classic, a T3 in the Greater Milwaukee Open and a T7 in the Reno-Tahoe Open. In 2000, recorded five top-10s, including the first runner-up finish of his career at the Honda Classic. Became the fourth first-time winner with playoff victory over Jim Furyk at rain-shortened 1994 Buick Classic. The week marked only the fifth time he had made the cut in 10 events. Also arrived at Westchester CC having broken 70 just once all year and with earnings of $16,712. Started road to victory with 66 in first round for T2, two strokes out of lead. Second round took place over Saturday and Sunday due to heavy rains. Birdied 17 and 18 Sunday morning to complete 67 and tie Furyk for lead. Both players recorded 68s in the third and final round, which included an eagle by Furyk and birdie by Hayes on 54th hole. In playoff, Hayes sank seven-foot birdie putt on first extra hole to earn two-year exemption and $324,000. Previous best finish on the PGA TOUR was T6 at the 1992 Anheuser-Busch Golf Classic. Earned first TOUR card by finishing 17th at 1991 Qualifying Tournament.

EXEMPT STATUS: T26 at 2004 PGA TOUR Qualifying Tournament
PLAYOFF RECORD: 1-0
PGA TOUR VICTORIES (2): 1998 Buick Classic. **2002** John Deere Classic.
NATIONWIDE TOUR VICTORIES (1): 1996 Miami Valley Open.
MONEY & POSITION:

1992 —	72,830 —	155	1997 —	160,722 —	135	2001 —	622,964 —	82
1993 —	6,650 —	253	1998 —	555,272 —	51	2002 —	955,271 —	66
1995 —	111,696 —	153	1999 —	436,302 —	89	2003 —	585,331 —	112
1996 —	0		2000 —	838,054 —	57	2004 —	260,816 —	174

BEST 2004 PGA TOUR FINISHES: T18—Buick Open; T22—THE PLAYERS Championship.
PGA TOUR CAREER LOW ROUND: 61–2002 John Deere Classic/2
2004 SUMMARY: Tournaments Entered—27; in money—11; Top-10 finishes—0
CAREER SUMMARY: Tournaments Entered—263; in money—143; Top-10 finishes—19
CAREER EARNINGS: $4,605,907
Nationwide Tour Alumnus

HEARN, David

FULL NAME: David Geoffrey Hearn **BIRTHDATE:** June 17, 1979 **BIRTHPLACE:** Brampton, Ontario, Canada **RESIDENCE:** Brantford, Ontario, Canada; plays out of Brantford G&CC **HEIGHT:** 6-1 **WEIGHT:** 165 **FAMILY:** Single **EDUCATION:** University of Wyoming **SPECIAL INTERESTS:** Music, movies, hockey, skiing, snowboarding **TURNED PROFESSIONAL:** 2001 **Q SCHOOL:** 2004 **OTHER INFORMATION:** Rookie on the 2005 PGA TOUR after making it through the 2004 Qualifying Tournament in his fourth try and first trip to the final stage, where he finished T21. Made the cut in eight of 12 appearances on the 2004 Nationwide Tour, finishing in the top 25 seven times. Ranked No. 35 on the official money list, with $161,706. Shot rounds of 70-65-67-71 to win the Alberta Classic at 15-under-par 273, finishing one stroke ahead of David McKenzie. Collected $81,000 for the victory. Posted four additional top-10s, including T6s at the Oregon Classic and the Permian Basin Charity Golf Classic and T7s at the Preferred Health Systems Wichita Open and the Albertsons Boise Open. Member of the Canadian Tour 2002-04. Finished No. 5 on the 2004 Order of Merit, including winning the Times Colonist Open. Has also played on the Asian Tour. Made it to the Round of 16 at the 1999 U.S. Amateur. Won the 1997 Ontario Match Play Championship. Teamed with Jon Mills to lead the Canadian Team to the title at the Four Nations Cup. Named All-Mountain West Conference during his senior season at the University of Wyoming. Winner of two collegiate tournaments. Grew up five blocks from Wayne Gretzky's home in Brantford, Ontario, Canada.

EXEMPT STATUS: T21 at 2004 PGA TOUR Qualifying Tournament
NATIONWIDE TOUR VICTORIES (1): 2004 Alberta Classic.
MONEY & POSITION:

2002 —	0	2003 —	0	2004 —	0

PGA TOUR CAREER LOW ROUND: 71–3 times, most recent 2003 Bell Canadian Open/2
2004 SUMMARY: Tournaments Entered—1; in money—0; Top-10 finishes—0
CAREER SUMMARY: Tournaments Entered—4; in money—0; Top-10 finishes—0
Nationwide Tour Alumnus

HEINEN, Mike

FULL NAME: William Michael Heinen, Jr. **BIRTHDATE:** January 17, 1967 **BIRTHPLACE:** Rayne, LA **RESIDENCE:** Lake Charles, LA **HEIGHT:** 6-1 **WEIGHT:** 215 **FAMILY:** Wife, Kathy; Olivia Kathryn (1/25/96), William Michael III (6/16/99) **EDUCATION:** University of Louisiana-Lafayette **SPECIAL INTERESTS:** Hunting, fishing **TURNED PROFESSIONAL:** 1989 **Q SCHOOL:** 1993, 2002 **OTHER INFORMATION:** Playing with partial status, made 17 starts on TOUR in 2004, with nine made cuts. In only second start of the season finished T8 at the Chrysler Classic of Tucson. Was one back of the lead through 54 holes, posted 2-under-par 70, for his best finish since he recorded a T5 at the 2002 John Deere Classic. Earned a career-best $432,417 in 2003 to finish 138th on the final money list. Best effort of the season was T11 at the Greater Hartford Open. Posted a hole-in-one on par-3 seventh hole at Pebble Beach GL during the AT&T Pebble Beach National Pro-Am. Recorded his career low round on Tour in his 458th round at the Greater Milwaukee Open. His 62 at Brown Deer Park Golf Course topped the 63s during the fourth round of the 1995 Buick Challenge and the first round of the 2002 John Deere Classic. Split time between PGA TOUR and Nationwide Tour in 2002. Made $138,041 and finished 26th on the Nationwide Tour money list in 2002. Turned in his first PGA TOUR top-10 since 1998 with his T5 at the 2002 John Deere Classic. Held first-round lead after a 63. Lone TOUR victory, a three-stroke win at the 1994 Shell Houston Open, came in 10th start. Lost playoff to Davis Love III at 1995 Freeport-McMoRan Classic. Prior to earning membership on PGA TOUR, played Canadian and Nationwide Tours. Two-time NCAA Division I All-American.

EXEMPT STATUS: Past Champion
PLAYOFF RECORD: 0-1
PGA TOUR VICTORIES (1): 1994 Shell Houston Open.
MONEY & POSITION:

1991 —	0		1997 —	3,000 —	330	2001 —	50,838 —	213
1994 —	390,963 —	40	1998 —	93,134 —	185	2002 —	246,853 —	166
1995 —	350,920 —	52	1999 —	0		2003 —	432,417 —	138
1996 —	102,588 —	161	2000 —	5,018 —	249	2004 —	166,185 —	195

BEST 2004 PGA TOUR FINISH: T8—Chrysler Classic of Tucson.
PGA TOUR CAREER LOW ROUND: 62–2003 Greater Milwaukee Open/4
2004 SUMMARY: Tournaments Entered—17; in money—9; Top-10 finishes—1
CAREER SUMMARY: Tournaments Entered—188; in money—89; Top-10 finishes—9
CAREER EARNINGS: $1,841,916
Nationwide Tour Alumnus

HEINTZ, Bob

FULL NAME: Robert Edward Heintz **BIRTHDATE:** May 1, 1970 **BIRTHPLACE:** Syosset, NY **RESIDENCE:** Dunedin, FL; plays out of Countryside CC (Clearwater, FL) **HEIGHT:** 6-0 **WEIGHT:** 210 **FAMILY:** Wife, Nancy; Eryn (5/20/96), Phillip John (6/8/99), Daniel Robert (3/28/02) **EDUCATION:** Yale University (1992, Economics) **SPECIAL INTERESTS:** Family, reading, travel, collecting chess sets **TURNED PROFESSIONAL:** 1992 **JOINED TOUR:** 2000 **Q SCHOOL:** 2001, 2004 **OTHER INFORMATION:** Rejoins the TOUR in 2005 after a T21 finish at Qualifying School. Played the TOUR in 2000 and 2002 and the Nationwide Tour in 1994, 1999, 2001 and 2003-04. Finished 77th on the Nationwide Tour money list in 2004 with top-10s at the Lake Erie Charity Classic (T7) and the Pete Dye West Virginia Classic (T8). Also logged two top-10s in 2003 where he finished 44th on money list. In last stint on TOUR in 2002, posted two top-25s and finished 192nd on money list. Recorded one TOUR top-10 in career, a T10, at B.C. Open in his rookie TOUR season of 2000. Won twice on Nationwide Tour in 1999, at the Shreveport Open and season-ending Nationwide Tour Championship. Playoff victory in final event moved him from 16th to sixth on final money list and gave him his first PGA TOUR card. From January 1996 through March 1997, gave up on golf to pursue career as a financial analyst. Three-time Ivy League champion at Yale. 1992 Academic All-America. Recruited to play basketball at Yale. Lists heroes as Jack Nicklaus in golf and former President George Bush in politics. Dad brought him to local muni at age 6 to learn golf.

EXEMPT STATUS: T21 at 2004 PGA TOUR Qualifying Tournament
BEST PGA TOUR CAREER FINISH: T10—2000 B.C. Open.
NATIONWIDE TOUR VICTORIES (2): 1999 Shreveport Open, TOUR Championship.
MONEY & POSITION:

1999 —	0		2002 —	127,346 —	192
2000 —	127,412 —	184	2004 —	0	

PGA TOUR CAREER LOW ROUND: 65–3 times, most recent 2002 Buick Classic/1
2004 SUMMARY: Tournaments Entered—1; in money—0; Top-10 finishes—0
CAREER SUMMARY: Tournaments Entered—64; in money—15; Top-10 finishes—1
CAREER EARNINGS: $254,758
Nationwide Tour Alumnus

HEND, Scott

FULL NAME: Scott Robert Hend **BIRTHPLACE:** Townsville, Queensland, Australia **RESIDENCE:** Brisbane, Queensland, Australia **HEIGHT:** 6-0 **WEIGHT:** 170 **FAMILY:** Wife, Leanne **SPECIAL INTERESTS:** Go-kart racing, Australian Rules football **TURNED PROFESSIONAL:** 1998 **Q SCHOOL:** 2003, 2004 **OTHER INFORMATION:** After finishing 136th on 2004 TOUR money list in rookie season, improved status for 2005 with T26 finish at TOUR Qualifying Tournament. Finished second in Driving Distance behind Hank Kuehne with a 312.6-yard average in 2004. Made the most of first made cut of career in sixth TOUR start, finishing solo third to earn $306,000 at the 2004 BellSouth Classic, two strokes behind champion Zach Johnson. Fired a career-best 64 in the first round of the 2004 FUNAI Classic at WALT DISNEY WORLD Resort. Was two back of the lead. Posted 78 in the second round and missed the cut. Earned inaugural TOUR card after finishing T21 at 2003 Qualifying Tournament. Captured the 2003 Order of Merit on the Von Nida Tour, Australia's secondary tour, thanks in part to a victory at the Queensland Open. Finished 21st on the 2002-03 PGA Tour of Australasia's Order of Merit, where he has been a member since 1998. Played in five 2003 Nationwide Tour events, posting two top-20s, including a season's-best T12 at the Alberta Calgary Classic. A member of the Canadian Tour since 2000. Won the 2002 Victoria Open and finished 10th on the Canadian Tour Order of Merit that season. Was a state representative at indoor cricket in his native Australia. Won tournament in Canada four days after being married, with bride Leanne serving as his caddie on their honeymoon.

EXEMPT STATUS: T26 at 2004 PGA TOUR Qualifying Tournament
BEST PGA TOUR CAREER FINISH: 3—2004 BellSouth Classic.
MONEY & POSITION:
2004 — 531,263 — 136
BEST 2004 PGA TOUR FINISH: 3—BellSouth Classic.
PGA TOUR CAREER LOW ROUND: 64–2004 FUNAI Classic at the WALT DISNEY WORLD Resort/1
2004 SUMMARY: Tournaments Entered—29; in money—11; Top-10 finishes—1
CAREER SUMMARY: Tournaments Entered—29; in money—11; Top-10 finishes—1
CAREER EARNINGS: $531,263

HENKE, Nolan

FULL NAME: Nolan Jay Henke **BIRTHDATE:** November 25, 1964 **BIRTHPLACE:** Battle Creek, MI **RESIDENCE:** Fort Myers, FL; plays out of Vines CC (Fort Myers, FL) **HEIGHT:** 6-0 **WEIGHT:** 165 **FAMILY:** Wife, Michelle; daughter, Hayden Reese (12/28/01) **EDUCATION:** Florida State University, 1987 **SPECIAL INTERESTS:** Fishing, Florida State football **TURNED PROFESSIONAL:** 1988 **Q SCHOOL:** 1988, 1989 **OTHER INFORMATION:** Made 10 Nationwide Tour starts and just one PGA TOUR start in 2004, missing cut in all but Rheem Classic (T53) on Nationwied Tour. Member of Nationwide Tour in 2002-2004. Never teed it up in a Nationwide Tour event until 2002. That year, made eight cuts in 19 starts, including a career-best T4 at the Nationwide Tour's Preferred Health Systems Wichita Open. Has three PGA TOUR victories, most recently 1993 BellSouth Classic. First TOUR victory came at 1990 B.C. Open, by three strokes over Mark Wiebe. Entered the final round of the 1991 Phoenix Open with four-stroke lead, then held on to defeat Tom Watson, Curtis Strange and Gil Morgan by one stroke. Won seven collegiate tournaments while at Florida State. 1987 All-America selection who finished second at NCAA Championship to Brian Watts. Holds charity events in Fort Myers each year to benefit Southwest Florida Children's Hospital and Hope Hospice House, as well as the Nolan Henke/Patty Berg, Jr. Masters to benefit junior golf.

EXEMPT STATUS: Past Champion
PLAYOFF RECORD: 0-1
PGA TOUR VICTORIES (3): 1990 B.C. Open. **1991** Phoenix Open. **1993** BellSouth Classic.
MONEY & POSITION:

1987 —	9,072 —	208	1994 —	278,419 —	70	2000 —	47,722 —	214
1989 —	57,465 —	159	1995 —	237,141 —	78	2001 —	25,420 —	224
1990 —	294,592 —	48	1996 —	302,726 —	71	2002 —	6,240 —	245
1991 —	518,811 —	28	1997 —	205,859 —	111	2003 —	13,970 —	247
1992 —	326,387 —	45	1998 —	444,561 —	65	2004 —	0	
1993 —	502,375 —	31	1999 —	335,804 —	122			

BEST 2004 PGA TOUR FINISH: T69—BellSouth Classic.
PGA TOUR CAREER LOW ROUND: 62–2 times, most recent 1998 Greater Milwaukee Open/2
2004 SUMMARY: Tournaments Entered—1; in money—0; Top-10 finishes—0
CAREER SUMMARY: Tournaments Entered—340; in money—190; Top-10 finishes—36
CAREER EARNINGS: $3,606,563
Nationwide Tour Alumnus

HENNINGER, Brian

FULL NAME: Brian Hatfield Henninger **BIRTHDATE:** October 19, 1962 **BIRTHPLACE:** Sacramento, CA **RESIDENCE:** Wilsonville, OR; plays out of Oregon GC **HEIGHT:** 5-8 **WEIGHT:** 150 **FAMILY:** Wife, Catherine; Carlin (6/10/93), Hunter (11/18/95), Mia (10/29/04) **EDUCATION:** University of Southern California (1987, Psychology) **TURNED PROFESSIONAL:** 1987 **JOINED TOUR:** 1993 **Q SCHOOL:** 1996 **OTHER INFORMATION:** Split time during the 2004 season playing on the PGA TOUR and Nationwide Tour. Made nine starts on both Tours. Played in 17 PGA TOUR events in 2003, with two top-25s. His T3 finish at 2002 B.C. Open was first top-10 since T4 at the 2000 Reno-Tahoe Open and best finish since T3 finish at the 1999 John Deere Classic. In 2001, failed to finish in the top 125 for first time since 1996 and didn't post a top-10 for the first time in his career. Collected second career PGA TOUR victory and second victory at Annandale GC in his final official event of 1999. Three-stroke victory over Chris DiMarco at Southern Farm Bureau Classic marked second time in five years he had won in Mississippi. Each of his wins has been over less than 72 holes. The 1999 tournament was reduced to 54 holes because of Payne Stewart memorial and rain that forced Monday finish. First TOUR victory came at rain-plagued 1994 Deposit Guaranty Golf Classic. After rain forced cancellation of Sunday's final round, birdied first playoff hole for victory. Playing in his first Masters in 1995, shared 54-hole lead with Ben Crenshaw before closing 76 left him T10. First joined PGA TOUR in 1993 after finishing second on 1992 Nationwide Tour money list with victories at South Texas Open, Macon Open and Knoxville Open. Leading money-winner on 1989 Golden State Tour. Outstanding prep tennis player who switched to golf as high school junior. Twice reached semifinals of state high school tennis tournament. Made University of Southern California golf team as a walk-on.

EXEMPT STATUS: Past Champion
PLAYOFF RECORD: 1-0
PGA TOUR VICTORIES (2): 1994 Deposit Guaranty Golf Classic. **1999** Southern Farm Bureau Classic.
NATIONWIDE TOUR VICTORIES (3): 1992 South Texas Open, Macon Open, Knoxville Open.
MONEY & POSITION:

1993 —	112,811 —	130	1997 —	329,864 —	71	2001 —	160,814 —	184
1994 —	294,075 —	63	1998 —	256,714 —	114	2002 —	281,614 —	158
1995 —	166,730 —	114	1999 —	774,486 —	55	2003 —	166,003 —	184
1996 —	135,680 —	142	2000 —	527,741 —	91	2004 —	6,240 —	261

BEST 2004 PGA TOUR FINISH: T65—Chrysler Classic of Tucson.
PGA TOUR CAREER LOW ROUND: 63–5 times, most recent 2000 Reno-Tahoe Open/2
2004 SUMMARY: Tournaments Entered—9; in money—1; Top-10 finishes—0
CAREER SUMMARY: Tournaments Entered—294; in money—162; Top-10 finishes—18
CAREER EARNINGS: $3,212,771
Nationwide Tour Alumnus

HJERTSTEDT, Gabriel

FULL NAME: Gabriel Hjertstedt **BIRTHDATE:** December 5, 1971 **BIRTHPLACE:** Umea, Sweden **RESIDENCE:** Atlantic Beach, FL **HEIGHT:** 5-9 **WEIGHT:** 160 **FAMILY:** Wife, Angela; Axel Gabriel (12/14/00) **SPECIAL INTERESTS:** Snow skiing, surfing, boating **TURNED PROFESSIONAL:** 1990 **Q SCHOOL:** 1996 **OTHER INFORMATION:** Split 2004 season between Nationwide Tour (18 events) and PGA TOUR (5), making 11 cuts in 23 starts. Has finished out of the top 150 for three consecutive years. Best finish since winning in 1999 was a T4 at the 2001 Greater Greensboro Classic, only top-10 since winning. In 1999, had career high in earnings of $933,033 (No. 41). Earned second PGA TOUR title at 1999 Touchstone Energy Tucson Open and became the first Swedish player to earn two victories on TOUR. Final-round 68, which included a double bogey on 72nd hole, earned a tie with Tommy Armour III. Sank a 25-foot birdie putt on first extra hole for victory that marked second time in three years he had won on TOUR. $495,000 payday more than he made in either of his first two seasons. Became first Swedish player to win on the PGA TOUR with victory at the 1997 B.C. Open in what likely would have been his last start of the year, earning $234,000. Trailed by one through 54 holes. Final-round 70 enough for win and moved him from 226th to 84th on season money list. In 1996, after overcoming dislocation of temporomandibular joint, which helped force him off European Tour in 1995, earned PGA TOUR card for following year via ninth-place finish in Qualifying Tournament. In 1990, competed on the PGA Tour of Australasia and earned Rookie of the Year honors. Born in Sweden, family emigrated to Queensland, Australia, when he was 11 and he learned to play golf there. Turned professional at age 18 and played on Australian, European and Japanese Tours prior to PGA TOUR.

EXEMPT STATUS: Past Champion
PLAYOFF RECORD: 1-0
PGA TOUR VICTORIES (2): 1997 B.C. Open. **1999** Touchstone Energy Tucson Open.
MONEY & POSITION:

1997 —	279,624 —	89	2000 —	296,189 —	138	2003 —	12,780 —	248
1998 —	167,072 —	157	2001 —	296,273 —	147	2004 —	22,870 —	243
1999 —	933,033 —	41	2002 —	69,186 —	210			

BEST 2004 PGA TOUR FINISH: T35—B.C. Open.
PGA TOUR CAREER LOW ROUND: 65–2 times, most recent 1999 National Car Rental Golf Classic/Disney/2
2004 SUMMARY: Tournaments Entered—5; in money—2; Top-10 finishes—0
CAREER SUMMARY: Tournaments Entered—170; in money—70; Top-10 finishes—7
CAREER EARNINGS: $2,077,026
Nationwide Tour Alumnus

HUGHES, Bradley

FULL NAME: Bradley Stuart Hughes **BIRTHDATE:** February 10, 1967 **BIRTHPLACE:** Melbourne, Australia **RESIDENCE:** Farmington, CT **HEIGHT:** 5-9 **WEIGHT:** 193 **FAMILY:** Wife, Laura; Madison (2/19/96), Evan (11/23/98), Nathan (10/8/01), Brennan (10/8/01), Georgia (7/7/03) **SPECIAL INTERESTS:** Computers, all sports **TURNED PROFESSIONAL:** 1988 **Q SCHOOL:** 1996, 1997 **OTHER INFORMATION:** Member of the Nationwide Tour in 2003-04 and the PGA TOUR from 1997-2002. Finished the year No. 12 on the Nationwide Tour money list, with $233,968. Claimed his first Tour victory at the Preferred Health Systems Wichita Open. Birdied the first playoff hole to hold off Erik Compton, Scott Harrington and Hunter Haas for the $85,500 first-place prize. Other top-5 finishes came at the New Zealand PGA Championship (T2) and the Albertsons Boise Open (T4). Finished 139th on Nationwide Tour money list in 2003, making just five of 20 cuts. Finished outside the top 200 on both the PGA TOUR (205) and Nationwide Tour (203) in 2002. Missed full PGA TOUR privileges for 2002 by $94, finishing No. 126 on money list. Earned $406,258 in 33 events, the third consecutive year with PGA TOUR earnings in excess of $400,000. Recorded two top-10s in 2001, including T3 at the Kemper Insurance Open. Second-round 63 tied career low on the PGA TOUR. Two career runner-up finishes, at the 1999 Kemper Insurance Open and 1998 CVS Charity Classic. Member of Australia's 1996 and 1997 World Cup team. Member of International Team in 1994 Presidents Cup competition, replacing an ill Greg Norman. Compiled a 1-3 overall record. Winner of 1996 Australian Players Championship, 1993 Microsoft Australian Masters, 1990 South Australian PGA, 1989 New Zealand Amateur, and 1987 and 1988 Victoria Amateurs. Shot 10-under-par 62 in his first round on European Tour (1989 Benson and Hedges International), where he was a member in 1989, 1990, 1994 and 1996. Played Japan Golf Tour from 1992-94. Won third tournament as a professional — the 1988 Western Australia Open. Made the first 10 cuts of his professional career. PGA TOUR of Australasia Rookie of the Year in 1988, when he finished 31st on money list. Played in the 1982 Victorian Open as a 14-year old amateur. Signed with Melbourne Football Club to play Australian Rules Football. Played at least one event on every major tour in rookie year. Same birthday as Greg Norman, but 12 years younger.
EXEMPT STATUS: 12th on Nationwide Tour money list
BEST PGA TOUR CAREER FINISH: T2—1998 CVS Charity Classic,1999 Kemper Open.
NATIONWIDE TOUR VICTORIES (1): 2004 Preferred Health Systems Wichita Open.
MONEY & POSITION:

1989 —	0		1997 —	142,793 —	142	2002 —	85,450 —	205
1993 —	28,125 —	200	1998 —	370,767 —	80	2003 —	0	
1994 —	29,891 —	212	1999 —	471,321 —	83	2004 —	0	
1995 —	7,146 —	281	2000 —	469,590 —	103			
1996 —	74,420 —	182	2001 —	406,258 —	126			

PGA TOUR CAREER LOW ROUND: 63–2 times, most recent 2001 Kemper Insurance Open/2
2004 SUMMARY: Tournaments Entered—1; in money—0; Top-10 finishes—0
CAREER SUMMARY: Tournaments Entered—193; in money—85; Top-10 finishes—13
CAREER EARNINGS: $2,085,761
Nationwide Tour Alumnus

HULBERT, Mike

FULL NAME: Michael Patrick Hulbert **BIRTHDATE:** April 14, 1958 **BIRTHPLACE:** Elmira, NY **RESIDENCE:** Orlando, FL; plays out of Bay Hill and Lake Nona **HEIGHT:** 6-0 **WEIGHT:** 175 **FAMILY:** Wife, Teresa; Justin Michael (7/25/93), Trevor (3/10/97) **EDUCATION:** East Tennessee State University (1980, Business Management) **SPECIAL INTERESTS:** Fishing, exercising **TURNED PROFESSIONAL:** 1981 **Q SCHOOL:** 1984, 1985 **OTHER INFORMATION:** Played in eight events on the PGA TOUR in 2004. Continued career in broadcasting for USA Network and ESPN. Served as assistant captain to Curtis Strange on the 2002 U.S. Ryder Cup team. Member of the PGA TOUR since 1985. Most recent of three TOUR victories came at 1991 Anheuser-Busch Golf Classic, where he beat Kenny Knox on the first hole of a playoff. Earned first win at 1986 Federal Express St. Jude Classic, beating childhood friend Joey Sindelar by one stroke. Second TOUR victory came at 1989 B.C. Open, where he topped Bob Estes in a playoff. Winner of several unofficial TOUR events, the 1991 Isuzu Kapalua Invitational, the 1991 JCPenney Classic, a mixed-team event, with Donna Andrews, and the 1987 Chrysler Team Championship with Bob Tway. 1979-80 All-America selection at East Tennessee State University.
EXEMPT STATUS: Past Champion
PLAYOFF RECORD: 2-0
PGA TOUR VICTORIES (3): 1986 Federal Express St. Jude Classic. **1989** B.C. Open. **1991** Anheuser-Busch Golf Classic.
MONEY & POSITION:

1983 —	0		1991 —	551,750 —	24	1998 —	335,954 —	88
1985 —	18,368 —	161	1992 —	279,577 —	55	1999 —	264,524 —	143
1986 —	276,687 —	21	1993 —	193,833 —	89	2000 —	59,878 —	209
1987 —	204,375 —	49	1994 —	221,007 —	84	2001 —	27,999 —	223
1988 —	127,752 —	94	1995 —	311,055 —	61	2002 —	46,148 —	217
1989 —	477,621 —	18	1996 —	235,131 —	93	2003 —	6,300 —	252
1990 —	216,002 —	67	1997 —	317,247 —	76	2004 —	0	

BEST 2004 PGA TOUR FINISH: 80—Greater Milwaukee Open.
PGA TOUR CAREER LOW ROUND: 63–3 times, most recent 1998 Phoenix Open/1
2004 SUMMARY: Tournaments Entered—8; in money—0; Top-10 finishes—0
CAREER SUMMARY: Tournaments Entered—577; in money—332; Top-10 finishes—43
CAREER EARNINGS: $4,171,208

I

IMADA, Ryuji

FULL NAME: Ryuji Imada **BIRTHDATE:** October 19, 1976 **BIRTHPLACE:** Mihara, Japan **RESIDENCE:** Tampa, FL **HEIGHT:** 5-8 **WEIGHT:** 150 **FAMILY:** Single **EDUCATION:** University of Georgia **SPECIAL INTERESTS:** Sports, music, movies **TURNED PROFESSIONAL:** 1999 **JOINED TOUR:** 2005 **OTHER INFORMATION:** Rookie on PGA TOUR after finishing third on 2004 Nationwide Tour money list. Member of that circuit for past five years and finished inside top 40 on money list four times. Had his best season in 2004 and was one of five players on Tour to surpass the $300,000 plateau with $313,185. Career-high seven top-10s, included his second his second career victory at the BMW Charity Pro-Am at The Cliffs. Birdied the fifth playoff hole to defeat Paul Gow and earned a career-best $108,000. Finished inside top-5 four other times—the Envirocare Utah Classic (T2), Northeast Pennsylvania Classic (third), First Tee Arkansas Classic (T3) and Henrico County Open (T4). Led the Tour in Scrambling and finished fourth in Scoring Average. Finished the 2003 Nationwide Tour season No. 37 on the money list, with $127,861 and a season-best third at the Northeast Pennsylvania Classic. Made his first and only cut in seven tries on the PGA TOUR at the 2003 BellSouth Classic, where he finished T74. Had a down season in 2002, finishing 105th on the Nationwide Tour money list after making the cut in eight of 20 tournaments. Had two runner-up finishes in 2001. Posted a tournament-record 64 in the second round of the Carolina Classic and fired final-round 69 to finish two strokes back of winner John Maginnes. Was 20-under through 54 holes of the Greater Cleveland Open. Held a three-stroke lead heading into the final round but managed just an even-par 72 and wound up second, one stroke behind Heath Slocum. Enjoyed solid rookie season in 2000, making the cut in 12 of 25 events. Shared second-round lead with Mike Heinen and David Berganio, Jr. at the Virginia Beach Open and trailed Todd Demsey by one after 54 holes. Defeated Demsey by five strokes to become first rookie winner of season. Final-round 76 at the 2000 PGA TOUR Qualifying Tournament left him three strokes short of earning his TOUR card. Left University of Georgia after his sophomore season. First-team All-American and All-SEC as a freshman in 1999. Helped lead the Bulldogs to their first national championship and finished runner-up to current PGA TOUR player Luke Donald in the individual competition. Won first collegiate title at Williams Intercollegiate in 1999. Had seven top-10 finishes during the 1998-99 collegiate season. Appeared as high as second in Golfweek/Titleist Men's Amateur Rankings. Reached match-play stage of 1998 U.S. Amateur but lost in first round. Has won six tournaments on major amateur circuit—1995 Porter Cup, 1996 Azalea Amateur, Dixie Amateur and Lakewood Invitational, 1997 Palatka Azalea Amateur and Southeastern Invitational. Finalist at 1997 U.S. Public Links. Excelled on junior level by twice being named to the AJGA All-American first team. 1995 Rolex Junior Player of the Year.
EXEMPT STATUS: Third on 2004 Nationwide Tour money list
BEST PGA TOUR CAREER FINISH: T74—2003 BellSouth Classic.
NATIONWIDE TOUR VICTORIES (2): 2000 Virginia Beach Open. **2004** BMW Charity Pro-Am at The Cliffs.
MONEY & POSITION:

1999 —	0	2001 —	0
2000 —	0	2003 —	7,600

BEST 2004 PGA TOUR FINISH: T74—BellSouth Classic.
PGA TOUR CAREER LOW ROUND: 67–2 times, most recent 2001 Sony Open in Hawaii/2
2004 SUMMARY: Tournaments entered—1; in money—1; Top-10 finishes—0
CAREER SUMMARY: Tournaments Entered—7; in money—1; Top-10 finishes—0
CAREER EARNINGS: $7,600
Nationwide Tour Alumnus

ISENHOUR, Tripp

FULL NAME: John Henry Isenhour III **BIRTHDATE:** April 6, 1968 **BIRTHPLACE:** Salisbury, NC **RESIDENCE:** Orlando, FL; plays out of Grand Cypress **HEIGHT:** 5-11 **WEIGHT:** 185 **FAMILY:** Wife, Kelly Lynn; two children **EDUCATION:** Georgia Tech (1990, Industrial Management) **SPECIAL INTERESTS:** Gourmet cooking **TURNED PROFESSIONAL:** 1990 **JOINED TOUR:** 2000 **OTHER INFORMATION:** Limited to 22 events on PGA TOUR in 2004 due to hand injury. Made eight cuts with a best finish of T37 at the Buick Invitational. Will receive a Minor Medical Extension for 2005. Coupled with $90,699 earned in 22 events in 2004, has the opportunity to play in seven events to earn $532,563 and match the $623,262 winnings of 2004's No. 125, Tag Ridings. Returned to TOUR in 2004 after earning TOUR card for second time in career after finishing eighth on the 2003 Nationwide Tour money list, the other was in 2000. Got off to a hot start in 2003 with nine top-25s in his first 11 events, including his second career win at the BMW Charity Pro-Am at The Cliffs. Collected $103,500 paycheck and surpassed the million-dollar mark ($1,055,469) in earnings on both tours. With three top-four finishes, was awarded Nationwide Tour Player of the Month honors in May. Had a hole-in-one during the first round of the Gila River Golf Classic. Finished No. 154 on the 2002 PGA TOUR money list with $319,210. Made the cut in 14 of 21 tournaments, with three top-25s. Best tournament was a T5 at the FedEx St. Jude Classic. In 2001, earned $299,452 as a rookie to rank No. 146 on the TOUR money list. Posted career-low final-round 63 for T7 at Canon Greater Hartford Open, his best finish of season. Member of Nationwide Tour in 1996 and 1998-2000. Recorded victory at Mississippi Gulf Coast Open in 2000 and received Player of the Month honors for March. In 1994, made the cut in his first PGA TOUR event, the BellSouth Classic, tying for 59th. Did not play in another PGA TOUR event until 2000. Winner of the 1998 Trinidad Open and Kansas Open. All-America selection in 1990 at Georgia Tech. Noted for his cooking expertise at home.

EXEMPT STATUS: Minor Medical Extension

BEST PGA TOUR CAREER FINISH: T5—2002 FedEx St. Jude Classic.

NATIONWIDE TOUR VICTORIES (2): 2000 Mississippi Gulf Coast Open. **2003** BMW Charity Pro-Am at the Cliffs.

MONEY & POSITION:

1994 —	2,604 —	300	2002 —	319,210 —	154
2001 —	299,452 —	146	2004 —	90,699 —	218

BEST 2004 PGA TOUR FINISH: T37—Buick Invitational.

PGA TOUR CAREER LOW ROUND: 63–2001 Canon Greater Hartford Open/4

2004 SUMMARY: Tournaments Entered—22; in money—8; Top-10 finishes—0

CAREER SUMMARY: Tournaments Entered—75; in money—39; Top-10 finishes—2

CAREER EARNINGS: $711,965

Nationwide Tour Alumnus

J

JOHANSSON, Per-Ulrik (pear ul-RIK yo-HAN-son)

FULL NAME: Per-Ulrik Johansson **BIRTHDATE:** December 6, 1966 **BIRTHPLACE:** Uppsala, Sweden **RESIDENCE:** Jupiter, FL; plays out of Valderama (Spain) **HEIGHT:** 5-8 **WEIGHT:** 155 **FAMILY:** Wife, Jill Parnevik; Stella (8/6/03) **EDUCATION:** Arizona State University (1990) **SPECIAL INTERESTS:** Music, ice hockey, cooking, wine, movies, books **TURNED PROFESSIONAL:** 1990 **Q SCHOOL:** 2000 **OTHER INFORMATION:** Limited to 12 events in 2004 due to April 2 hip surgery. Did not play after the Bay Hill Invitational until the Bell Canadian Open. Granted a Major Medical Extension for 2005. Coupled with $146,733 earned in 12 events in 2004 has the opportunity to play in seven events to earn $476,529 and match the $623,262 winnings of 2004's No. 125, Tag Ridings. If he does so, will play out of the Major Medical Extension category for the remainder of the season. Recorded four rounds in the 60s at the Omni Tucson National Golf Resort to finish T6 at the Chrysler Classic of Tucson, his only top-10 of the season. Missed the cut in all four fall events. Only top-10 of the 2003 season was a T6 at the EDS Byron Nelson Championship for the biggest payday of his career, $187,600. It was his first top-10 since the 2002 Nissan Open. Moved back into the top 125 on the money list after a T18 finish at the Chrysler Classic of Greensboro, but missed the cut in the last two events of the season and fell to the 126th position on the final money list. Enjoy a successful sophomore season in 2002 on the TOUR. Earned full exempt status on the strength of two top-10 finishes and five top-25s. In 2001, was sitting near the 125 bubble going into the Buick Challenge. A T7 finish advanced him from No. 122 to No. 97 and secured card for 2002 season. Began to show signs of a return to form with second-place finish in the 2000 Victor Chandler British Masters and two other top-three finishes at the Smurfit European Open and BBVA Open Turespana Masters. Earned membership to play on the PGA TOUR in 2001 with a T31 at the Qualifying Tournament in Palm Springs. Twice a winner in Europe in 1997, giving him five victories in his career and best Order of Merit finish, 11th. Two-stroke winner at 1997 Alamo English Open, where he shot third-round 64 and won Smurfit European Open by six strokes. First Swede to play in two Ryder Cups, at Oak Hill (1995) and Valderrama (1997). One of the fittest of the large Swedish contingent on the European Tour, but struck down by mystery virus toward the end of the 1997 season. Had to fly home to Sweden from World Cup in Kiawah Island, SC for tests. Weakened for several months by illness but gradually recovered health. Winner of 1996 Smurfit European Open. First career top-10 on PGA TOUR was T8 at 1996 PGA Championship. Winner of 1994 Chemapol Trophy Czech Open. In 1991, his first year on the European Tour, won Renault Belgian Open and Rookie of the Year honors. Winner of Sir Henry Cotton Rookie of the Year Award. Played on his first Dunhill Cup team and World Cup in 1991. As an amateur, represented his country at both junior and senior. Attended Arizona State, where he was on NCAA Championship team in 1990 and played with NCAA Champion Phil Mickelson. Attended Alabama Junior College before going to ASU. Has own Web site, p-uj.com, where he writes his own golf diary from PGA TOUR events. Married to Jill Parnevik, Jesper Parnevik's sister.

EXEMPT STATUS: Non-Exempt, Major Medical Extension

BEST PGA TOUR CAREER FINISH: T6—2001 Kemper Insurance Open, 2002 Nissan Open, 2003 EDS Byron Nelson Championship, 2004 Chrysler Classic of Tucson.

MONEY & POSITION:

1992 —	2,265 —	293	1997 —	66,151 —	191	2001 —	510,488 —	97
1993 —	0		1998 —	149,192 —	164	2002 —	556,064 —	121
1995 —	32,659 —	224	1999 —	70,073 —	211	2003 —	484,577 —	126
1996 —	79,100 —	179	2000 —	10,970		2004 —	146,733 —	202

BEST 2004 PGA TOUR FINISHES: T6—Chrysler Classic of Tucson.

PGA TOUR CAREER LOW ROUND: 64–2004 Bob Hope Chrysler Classic/3

2004 SUMMARY: Tournaments Entered—12; in money—5; Top-10 finishes—1

CAREER SUMMARY: Tournaments Entered—130; in money—70; Top-10 finishes—7

CAREER EARNINGS: $2,108,272

JOHNSON, Richard S. (RICK-ard)

FULL NAME: Richard Stanley Johnson **BIRTHDATE:** October 15, 1976 **BIRTHPLACE:** Stockholm, Sweden **RESIDENCE:** Jupiter, FL **HEIGHT:** 5-7 **WEIGHT:** 145 **FAMILY:** Single **SPECIAL INTERESTS:** Snowboarding, tennis, cars **TURNED PROFESSIONAL:** 1998 **Q SCHOOL:** 2002 **OTHER INFORMATION:** Made 18 cuts in 32 starts in his sophomore season on the PGA TOUR. Lone top-10 of the 2004 season was T8 at the Chrysler Classic of Greensboro. First top-10 finish of PGA TOUR career came in 14th start of 2003 at the FedEx St. Jude Classic. Carded a career-best 7-under 64 in the first round. Held or shared the lead for the first 54 holes and led David Toms by one entering the final round. Paired with Toms in the final group on Sunday, carded 2-under 69 to finish T3, four shots behind Toms. Earned a career-best $234,000 to jump to 108th on TOUR money list. Finished T7 at the 2003 Valero Texas Open moving from 124th on the season money list to 111th thanks to a $98,291 payday. Earned his card for 2003 by finishing T11 at the PGA TOUR Qualifying Tournament in La Quinta, CA. Made first TOUR start earlier in the season at 2002 THE INTERNATIONAL. Won for the first time at the 2002 ANZ Championship, beating Australians Craig Parry, Andre Stolz and Scott Laycock in the Modified Stableford format. Recorded T2 finishes in 2000 and 2001 on the European Tour. Played the European Challenge Tour in 1999, shooting a final-round 64 to come from four strokes back to win the 1999 Neuchatel Open Golf Trophy in his native Sweden. The 1998 season was his first professional season, making two cuts in four starts on the European Tour and three starts on the European Challenge Tour. Played handball at a high level in Sweden, having been a tennis player from age 6. Took up skateboarding and competed in the Swedish Championships. Suffered seven broken ribs, and also broke a hand and a foot doing stunts. Started golf at 15 as his girlfriend's family played. Won two national junior events but did not get picked for the Swedish Amateur side. Comes from a mixed background. His grandfather is an American (New Jersey), who married a Swede and settled in Sweden. Christian name pronounced Rick-ard.

EXEMPT STATUS: 148th on 2004 money list

BEST PGA TOUR CAREER FINISH: T3—2003 FedEx St. Jude Classic.

MONEY & POSITION:

2002 — 0 2003 — 559,021 — 120 2004 — 461,183 — 148

BEST 2004 PGA TOUR FINISH: T8—Chrysler Classic of Greensboro.

PGA TOUR CAREER LOW ROUND: 64–3 times, most recent 2004 Reno-Tahoe Open/4

2004 SUMMARY: Tournaments Entered—32; in money—18; Top-10 finishes—1

CAREER SUMMARY: Tournaments Entered—61; in money—34; Top-10 finishes—3

CAREER EARNINGS: $1,020,204

JONES, Brendan

FULL NAME: Brendan Jones **BIRTHDATE:** March 3, 1975 **BIRTHPLACE:** West Wyalong, New South Wales, Australia **RESIDENCE:** Canberra, Australia **HEIGHT:** 6-2 **WEIGHT:** 200 **FAMILY:** Wife, Adele **SPECIAL INTERESTS:** Sydney Swans Australian Rules Football team **TURNED PROFESSIONAL:** 1999 **JOINED TOUR:** 2005 **OTHER INFORMATION:** Rookie on PGA TOUR after finishing sixth on the 2004 Nationwide Tour money list, with $292,714. Averaged more than $36,000 per start in his eight appearances. Made the cut in six of those eight tournaments and finished inside the top four in five. Was T2 at the Jacob's Creek Open in his native Australia, followed by another T2 at the New Zealand Open. Third runner-up came three months later at the SAS Carolina Classic, losing in an eight-hole playoff to Chris Anderson. After a T4 at the Knoxville Open, broke through for his first Tour win at the LaSalle Bank Open with a tournament-record 16-under 268. Entered the event ranked No. 82 in the Official World Golf Ranking and became the second straight Australian to win the tournament, joining 2003 winner Andre Stolz. Winning total of $117,000 was the highest domestic payday in Nationwide Tour history and third-highest overall. Followed up his win at the LaSalle Bank Open with a missed cut at the U.S. Open Championship before heading back to the Japan Golf Tour to post his fourth career title, and second of the season, at the 2004 Mizuno Open. A member of the Japan Golf Tour from 2001-04, where he also won the 2004 Tsuruya Open, 2003 Sun Chlorella Classic and the 2002 Philip Morris KK Championship. Finished eighth on Japan Golf Tour money list in 2002 and sixth in 2003. Has played in three PGA TOUR events without making a cut entering the 2005 season.

EXEMPT STATUS: Sixth on 2004 Nationwide Tour money list

NATIONWIDE TOUR VICTORIES (1): 2004 LaSalle Bank Open.

MONEY & POSITION:

2004 — 0

PGA TOUR CAREER LOW ROUND: 71–2 times, most recent 2004 British Open Championship/1

2004 SUMMARY: Tournaments Entered—3; in money—0; Top-10 finishes—0

CAREER SUMMARY: Tournaments Entered—3; in money—0; Top-10 finishes—0

Nationwide Tour Alumnus

K

KOCH, Gary (COKE)

FULL NAME: Gary Koch **BIRTHDATE:** November 21, 1952 **BIRTHPLACE:** Baton Rouge, LA **RESIDENCE:** Tampa, FL **HEIGHT:** 5-11 **WEIGHT:** 170 **FAMILY:** Wife, Donna; Patricia (4/1/81), Rachel (7/30/83) **EDUCATION:** University of Florida (1974, Public Relations) **SPECIAL INTERESTS:** Golf course design, reading, music **TURNED PROFESSIONAL:** 1975 **Q SCHOOL:** Fall 1975 **OTHER INFORMATION:** Continued to split time between the Champions Tour and his duties on NBC Sports golf telecasts. Made 18 starts and played his best golf early in the season when he was a runner-up in two of his first five events. Six career PGA TOUR victories, the last coming in 1988. Finished among the top 100 money winners in six of seven years between 1982-88. Best financial year was 1988, with $414,694, 24th on the money list. Winner of 1968-70 Florida State Juniors. Was 1970 USGA Junior Amateur champion and added the Orange Bowl Juniors and the Florida State Open in 1969. Won the 1973 Trans-Mississippi Amateur and was 1973 and 1974 All-Southeastern Conference. First-team All-American from 1972-74. Member 1973 NCAA Championship team at Florida. Winner of 10 collegiate events. Member of 1973, 1975 Walker Cup and 1974 U.S. World Amateur teams. Was college teammate of Andy Bean. Also active in golf course design with Robbins/Koch Golf Designs, Inc.

EXEMPT STATUS: Past Champion

PLAYOFF RECORD: 2-0

PGA TOUR VICTORIES (6): 1976 Tallahassee Open. **1977** Florida Citrus Open. **1983** Doral-Eastern Open. **1984** Isuzu-Andy Williams San Diego Open, Bay Hill Classic. **1988** Panasonic Las Vegas Invitational.

MONEY & POSITION:

1974 —	0		1984 —	262,679	— 17	1993 —	702	— 329
1976 —	38,195	— 69	1985 —	121,566	— 68	1994 —	0	
1977 —	58,383	— 52	1986 —	180,693	— 50	1995 —	0	
1978 —	58,660	— 55	1987 —	33,727	— 175	1996 —	0	
1979 —	46,809	— 84	1988 —	414,694	— 24	1997 —	0	
1980 —	39,827	— 84	1989 —	86,348	— 138	1998 —	4,000	— 324
1981 —	11,999	— 165	1990 —	36,469	— 186	1999 —	5,250	— 318
1982 —	43,449	— 100	1991 —	7,189	— 243	2001 —	6,825	— 247
1983 —	168,330	— 27	1992 —	3,690	— 274	2002 —	0	

PGA TOUR CAREER LOW ROUND: 63–4 times, most recent 1986 Southern Open/2

CAREER SUMMARY: Tournaments Entered—401; in money—275; Top-10 finishes—44

CAREER EARNINGS: $1,629,482

KRAFT, Greg

FULL NAME: Gregory Thomas Kraft **BIRTHDATE:** April 4, 1964 **BIRTHPLACE:** Detroit, MI **RESIDENCE:** Clearwater, FL; plays out of Feather Sound CC **HEIGHT:** 5-11 **WEIGHT:** 190 **FAMILY:** Wife, Paula Jo **EDUCATION:** University of Tampa (1986, Business) **SPECIAL INTERESTS:** Sports **TURNED PROFESSIONAL:** 1986 **Q SCHOOL:** 1991, 1992, 1995 **OTHER INFORMATION:** Played only four times on the PGA TOUR and once on the Nationwide Tour in 2004. Made nine starts in 2003, with best finish of T28 at the AT&T Pebble Beach National Pro Am. In 2002, made 31 starts on TOUR with his best finish a T6 at the Touchstone Energy Tucson Open. Opened the 2001 season with two top-10s and secured his TOUR card for the 2002 season with seven straight made cuts to finish the year. Earned $503,605 and finished 103rd on the money list. In 2000, finished third at Advil Western Open. For the first time in his career, recorded a pair of runner-up finishes in a single season with second at 1999 Doral-Ryder Open and T2 at 1999 MasterCard Colonial. Held share of 54-hole lead at MasterCard Colonial after tying course record with third-round 61, then closing with 70. Best finish of the 1998 season was T4 at United Airlines Hawaiian Open. In contention for three rounds at Motorola Western Open before final-round 75 placed him T5. Fired third-round course-record 65 in 1998 PGA at Sahalee CC. Recorded career-best five top-10s in 1996. Led by four through 54 holes at Deposit Guaranty Golf Classic, but 71 on Sunday dropped him into T3, three behind winner Willie Wood. In 1993, captured the Deposit Guaranty Golf Classic to claim $54,000 when it was unofficial event in Hattiesburg, MS. Birdied 72nd hole to defeat Morris Hatalsky and Tad Rhyan by one stroke. Birdied last two holes to make cut in 1992 Qualifying Tournament, then fired 5-under-par 31 on back side of TPC at The Woodlands to earn TOUR card.

EXEMPT STATUS: Veteran Member

BEST PGA TOUR CAREER FINISH: 1—1993 Deposit Guaranty Golf Classic, 2—Walt Disney World/Oldsmobile Classic,1994 Motorola Western Open,1999 Doral-Ryder Open, T2—MasterCard Colonial.

MONEY & POSITION:

1992 — 88,824 — 140	1997 — 152,109 — 139	2002 — 222,614 — 171
1993 — 290,581 — 60	1998 — 326,571 — 94	2003 — 71,756 — 220
1994 — 279,901 — 69	1999 — 810,777 — 52	2004 — 0
1995 — 137,655 — 139	2000 — 597,021 — 81	
1996 — 331,708 — 61	2001 — 503,605 — 103	

BEST 2004 PGA TOUR FINISH: T28—AT&T Pebble Beach National Pro-Am.

PGA TOUR CAREER LOW ROUND: 61–1999 MasterCard Colonial/3

2004 SUMMARY: Tournaments Entered—4; in money—0; Top-10 finishes—0

CAREER SUMMARY: Tournaments Entered—340; in money—181; Top-10 finishes—24

CAREER EARNINGS: $3,813,122

Nationwide Tour Alumnus

KRATZERT, Billy

BIRTHDATE: June 29, 1952 **BIRTHPLACE:** Quantico, VA **RESIDENCE:** Ponte Vedra Beach, FL **HEIGHT:** 6-1 **WEIGHT:** 205 **FAMILY:** Wife, Janie; Rebecca Brea (9/6/78), Tyler Brennen (12/5/80), Thomas Andrew (4/29/91); one granddaughter **EDUCATION:** University of Georgia (1974, Business Finance) **SPECIAL INTERESTS:** Family, reading, country music, architecture, all sports **TURNED PROFESSIONAL:** 1974 **Q SCHOOL:** Spring, 1976 **OTHER INFORMATION:** Continued broadcasting work, primarily for ESPN and TNT. After competing in 14 events on the Champions Tour in 2003, did not participate in any Champions Tour events in 2004. Played the PGA TOUR from 1976-1996 and won four official events. Last TOUR appearance was at the 1997 AT&T Pebble Beach National Pro-Am. Had his best year in 1978 when he placed eighth on the money list with $183,683. Won the 1968 Indiana Amateur and 1969 Indiana Open. 1973 and 1974 All-American while at the University of Georgia. Inducted into the Indiana Golf Hall of Fame in 1993.

EXEMPT STATUS: Past Champion

PLAYOFF RECORD: 0-1

PGA TOUR VICTORIES (4): 1976 Walt Disney World National Team Championship. **1977** Sammy Davis Jr.-Greater Hartford Open. **1980** Greater Milwaukee Open. **1984** Pensacola Open.

MONEY & POSITION:

1976 — 21,253 — 102	1984 — 149,827 — 44	1992 — 16,439 — 217
1977 — 134,758 — 10	1985 — 180,331 — 37	1993 — 78,993 — 156
1978 — 183,683 — 8	1986 — 47,421 — 139	1994 — 42,127 — 196
1979 — 101,628 — 35	1987 — 78,232 — 114	1995 — 4,548 — 308
1980 — 175,771 — 12	1988 — 43,519 — 158	1996 — 3,030 — 344
1981 — 55,513 — 76	1989 — 7,773 — 220	1997 — 0
1982 — 22,779 — 140	1990 — 14,630 — 218	
1983 — 14,744 — 166	1991 — 19,819 — 208	

PGA TOUR CAREER LOW ROUND: 63–1988 Panasonic Las Vegas Invitational/3

CAREER SUMMARY: Tournaments Entered—466; in money—283; Top-10 finishes—59

CAREER EARNINGS: $1,396,819

KUCHAR, Matt

FULL NAME: Matthew Gregory Kuchar **BIRTHDATE:** June 21, 1978 **BIRTHPLACE:** Winter Park, FL **RESIDENCE:** Ponte Vedra Beach, FL **HEIGHT:** 6-4 **WEIGHT:** 195 **FAMILY:** Wife, Sybi **EDUCATION:** Georgia Tech (2000, Management) **SPECIAL INTERESTS:** Sports, boats, planes, hiking, skiing **TURNED PROFESSIONAL:** 2000 **JOINED TOUR:** 2001 **OTHER INFORMATION:** Shared first-round lead with J.J. Henry at the 2004 AT&T Pebble Beach National Pro-Am before finishing T48. T10 at 2004 HP Classic of New Orleans was lone top-10 of the season and first since a T9 at the 2002 Tampa Bay Classic. Struggled through a difficult season in 2003 which saw him fall out of the top 125 on the money list. Earned his best finish of the season at the 2003 FedEx St. Jude Classic with a 20th-place finish. Opened the 2002 season with a bang with a T4 at the Sony Open in Hawaii. Two months later earned his first victory at the 2002 Honda Classic. Victory jumped him from No. 149 in Official World Golf Ranking to No. 50 and qualified him for the 2002 Masters on the last day to qualify. Finished T5 at the 2002 Fed Ex St. Jude Classic, worth $133,475 to push him over the $1-million mark for the first time in a single season. Earned PGA TOUR card through sponsor exemptions in 2001. Ranked second behind Charles Howell III in TOUR non-member earnings with $572,669 in only 11 starts. Earnings would have ranked him 91st on TOUR official money list. After missing the cut in his first three TOUR starts, playing on a sponsor exemption, secured his card for 2002 with two big finishes. Earned first top-10 in TOUR event in sixth start as professional, a T3 at Air Canada Championship. Best effort of season came in San Antonio at Texas Open, a T2 two strokes behind winner Justin Leonard. Made three starts in Nationwide Tour events in 2001, including a T2 at the Siouxland Open in July. Played from Australia to Mexico, on the Nationwide Tour, Canadian Tour and the Golden Bear Tour. After finishing his collegiate career at Georgia Tech in May of 2000, decided to stay amateur and briefly took a job in finance. Played in the 2000 Westin Texas Open at LaCantera in October as an amateur and missed the cut. It was in Texas where he started to think about turning pro and giving the PGA TOUR a try. One month later, made his professional debut at the 2000 Australian Open (won by Aaron Baddeley). As an amateur, won the 1997 U.S. Amateur championship following three consecutive wins by Tiger Woods. Lost in the quarterfinals in 1998 when defending the U.S. Amateur crown at Oak Hill. As a sophomore in 1998 at Georgia Tech, finished 21st at Masters and 14th at U.S. Open. Finish at Masters was best 72-hole finish by an amateur in 20 years. Opted to finish his collegiate career at Georgia Tech, where he was a two-time first-team All-America selection and the Yellow Jackets' second player to be a four-time All-ACC selection (along with David Duval). Awarded Fred Haskins Award in 1998 as the nation's top collegiate golfer. 1998 ACC Player of the Year. Six career collegiate victories for Tech was bested only by Duval's eight. Father, Peter Kuchar, is an excellent tennis player who was ranked No. 1 in doubles at one time in Florida. Matt's wife, Sybi, was a standout tennis player at Georgia Tech, where they met. Got started in golf when his mother, Meg, upgraded the country club membership to include golf when he was age 12. Matt and his dad tried golf and were hooked.

EXEMPT STATUS: 139th on 2004 money list

PGA TOUR VICTORIES (1): 2002 The Honda Classic.

MONEY & POSITION:

2001 — 572,669	2003 — 176,047 — 182
2002 —1,237,725 — 49	2004 — 509,257 — 139

BEST 2004 PGA TOUR FINISH: T10—HP Classic of New Orleans.

PGA TOUR CAREER LOW ROUND: 63–2004 HP Classic of New Orleans/2

2004 SUMMARY: Tournaments Entered—28; in money—13; Top-10 finishes—1

CAREER SUMMARY: Tournaments Entered—100; in money—48; Top-10 finishes—7

CAREER EARNINGS: $2,495,698

L

LANGHAM, Franklin (LANG-um)

FULL NAME: James Franklin Langham **BIRTHDATE:** May 8, 1968 **BIRTHPLACE:** Thomson, GA **RESIDENCE:** Peachtree City, GA **HEIGHT:** 6-1 **WEIGHT:** 170 **FAMILY:** Wife, Ashley; Parker (4/29/97); Henry Carson (7/7/99); George Franklin (9/5/01) **EDUCATION:** University of Georgia (1991, Risk Management and Insurance) **SPECIAL INTERESTS:** Hunting, fishing **TURNED PROFESSIONAL:** 1992 **JOINED TOUR:** 1996 **Q SCHOOL:** 1997 **OTHER INFORMATION:** Member of the PGA TOUR in 1996 and 1998-2002 and the Nationwide Tour in 1993-95, 1997 and 2003-04. Wrapped up the 2004 Nationwide Tour season No. 4 on the official money list, with $312,896 and graduated to the PGA TOUR for second time in his career. Posted 13 top-25s in 16 made cuts. At the Rheem Classic, broke through for his second career Tour victory with a 72-hole total of 15-under 265, good for a two-stroke win over Keoke Cotner. A 9-under 61 in the second round was spurred on by the Tour's lowest nine-hole score of the season (28) and a season-best eight consecutive birdies (Nos. 3-10), one shy of the Nationwide Tour record of nine set by Omar Uresti in 1994. At the time, the win established a new record for time between victories on the Nationwide Tour, only to be surpassed later by Scott Gump's win in Boise. Langham's last win came at the 1993 Permian Basin Open, a gap of 10 years, 8 months and 17 days. Led Tour in Scoring Average, was second in Greens in Regulation and Birdie Average, third in Putting Average and seventh in All-Around Ranking. Finished the 2003 Nationwide Tour season No. 65 on the money list with $75,831. Finished No. 168 on the 2002 PGA TOUR money list, with $238,461. Played in only 22 events on the 2001 TOUR as season was cut short by left elbow surgery on Oct. 12. Achieved life-long dream by participating in his first Masters, finishing T40. Enjoyed breakthrough season in 2000 in fourth TOUR campaign. Eclipsed career-highs set the previous season in official money and ranking. Seven top-10s and three seconds also established career-highs. Ranking of 26th on the official money list marked his first top-30 finish in that category and qualified him for first TOUR Championship appearance. Produced second career runner-up at Doral-Ryder Open. Second-round 63 established a personal best. Had best seven-tournament stretch of short career during mid-season run in which he finished no worse than seventh in six of seven starts, including seventh-place finish at his first major, the PGA. Finished 76th on money list in 1999, his first time among the top 100. Had no exempt status on the 1997 PGA TOUR or Nationwide Tour but played in 16 Nationwide Tour events that year, with three top-10s and $27,550 in prize money. Regained his TOUR card with a sixth-place finish at the 1997 Qualifying Tournament. Finished 174th on the 1996 TOUR money list. Fourth-place finish on the 1995 Nationwide Tour money list secured his TOUR playing privileges for 1996 despite not winning a tournament. Three 1995 playoff losses a Nationwide Tour record that was tied in 2004 by Paul Gow. Captured the 1993 Permian Basin Open on the Nationwide Tour, where he defeated Doug Martin in a playoff. Was an All-American in 1991 at Georgia and was a member of the victorious 1991 U.S. Walker Cup team at Portmarnock GC in Dublin, Ireland. Walker Cup teammates included David Duval, Phil Mickelson and Jay Sigel.

EXEMPT STATUS: Fourth on 2004 Nationwide Tour money list
BEST PGA TOUR CAREER FINISH: 2—2000 Doral-Ryder Open, Greater Milwaukee Open, T2—1998 Deposit Guaranty Golf Classic, 2000 Kemper Insurance Open.
NATIONWIDE TOUR VICTORIES (2): 1993 Permian Basin Open. **2004** Rheem Classic.
MONEY & POSITION:

1992 —	0	1998 —	248,412 — 117	2002 —	238,461 — 168
1994 —	0	1999 —	535,652 — 76	2003 —	0
1996 —	83,632 — 174	2000 —	1,604,952 — 26	2004 —	18,450
1997 —	0	2001 —	332,538 — 141		

BEST 2004 PGA TOUR FINISH: T38—BellSouth Classic.
PGA TOUR CAREER LOW ROUND: 63–2 times, most recent 2002 Kemper Insurance Open/1
2004 SUMMARY: Tournaments Entered—1; in money—1; Top-10 finishes—0
CAREER SUMMARY: Tournaments Entered—173; in money—94; Top-10 finishes—12
CAREER EARNINGS: $3,062,095
Nationwide Tour Alumnus

LARDON, Brad

FULL NAME: Bradford Thomas Lardon **BIRTHDATE:** April 29, 1965 **BIRTHPLACE:** New York, NY **RESIDENCE:** Austin, TX; plays out of The Hills of Lakeway **HEIGHT:** 5-9 **WEIGHT:** 170 **FAMILY:** Wife, Kim; Nicklaus, Margot, Will, Lilly Ann **EDUCATION:** Rice University (1988, Political Science) **SPECIAL INTERESTS:** Economics, politics **TURNED PROFESSIONAL:** 1989 **Q SCHOOL:** 1990, 1993, 2001, 2002 **OTHER INFORMATION:** Member of PGA TOUR in 1990, 1994, 2002-04 and Nationwide Tour in 1990, '93, '96-97. Played in 17 events, with five made cuts in 2004. Best finish was T58 at the Cialis Western Open, where as an alternate was a late addition to the field and paired with Tiger Woods and Bob Estes. Will receive a Major Medical Extension carryover for 2005. Coupled with $56,653 earned in 2003-2004, has the opportunity to play in four events to earn $430,842 and match the $487,495 winnings of 2003's No. 125, Esteban Toledo. If he does so, will play out of the Major Medical Extension category for the remainder of the season. 2003 season cut short to eight events after suffering herniated disk. Best finish was T39 at the BellSouth Classic, his only made cut of the season. Did not play again after FBR Capital Open in June. Finished T26 at the National Qualifying Tournament to retain his TOUR card for 2003 after finishing 209th on 2002 money list. Only top-10 finish on Nationwide Tour was a T8 at 1993 Louisiana Open. Winner 1995-96 Texas State Open. Winner 1987 Sam Houston State Intercollegiate. Was U.S. top-five table-tennis player as junior. Teaching professional at Austin GC. Lists heroes as Lou Gehrig and Byron Nelson.

EXEMPT STATUS: Major Medical Extension
BEST PGA TOUR CAREER FINISH: T18—1991 Independent Insurance Agent Open.
MONEY & POSITION:

1991 —	20,926 — 205	1997 —	6,880 — 291	2004 —	40,253 — 235
1992 —	0	2002 —	71,511 — 209		
1994 —	21,429 — 223	2003 —	16,400 — 245		

BEST 2004 PGA TOUR FINISH: T51—Southern Farm Bureau Classic.
PGA TOUR CAREER LOW ROUND: 66–3 times, most recent 2004 Southern Farm Bureau Classic/3
2004 SUMMARY: Tournaments Entered—17; in money—5; Top-10 finishes—0
CAREER SUMMARY: Tournaments Entered—94; in money—31; Top-10 finishes—0
CAREER EARNINGS: $177,400
Nationwide Tour Alumnus

LONG, Michael

FULL NAME: Michael Richard Long **BIRTHDATE:** August 27, 1968 **BIRTHPLACE:** Cromwell, New Zealand **RESIDENCE:** Perth, Australia **HEIGHT:** 6-2 **WEIGHT:** 190 **FAMILY:** Single **EDUCATION:** Waikato University (1990, Management Studies) **SPECIAL INTERESTS:** Cooking, drawing, all sports, wine **TURNED PROFESSIONAL:** 1990 **JOINED TOUR:** 2002 **OTHER INFORMATION:** Returns to the PGA TOUR after graduating from the Nationwide Tour for the second time. Member of the Nationwide Tour in 1996, 2000-01 and 2003-04 and the PGA TOUR in 2002. Finished 19th on the 2004 Nationwide Tour with $199,943. Posted two runner-up finishes, losing in a playoff to Kevin Stadler at the Lake Erie Charity Classic and finishing two strokes behind Scott Gump at the Albertsons Boise Open. Finished the 2003 season No. 35 on the Nationwide Tour money list. Recorded the second victory of his career on that circuit at the rain-soaked Virginia Beach Open, his only top-10 of the season. In rainy conditions with wind chills in the 40s, finished his round with seven consecutive pars to hang on for two-stroke victory over Vaughn Taylor. Finished No. 183 on the 2002 TOUR money list. Made nine of 27 cuts. Cracked the top 25 on two occasions, a T15 at the SEI Pennsylvania Classic and T17 at the Disney Golf Classic. Earned first TOUR card by finishing 15th on the 2001 Nationwide Tour money list. Four rounds in the 60s gave him a one-stroke victory over Tjaart Van Der Walt at the Boise Open. Played on the PGA Tour of Australasia 1996-99. Won the 1999 Greg Norman Holden Classic and 1996 AMP Air New Zealand Open. Played the European Tour 1997-99. Has played in three British Opens (1997-99) and made the cut in 1998 (T66). Member of New Zealand's World Cup team in 1997 along with Grant Waite. Played on New Zealand's Dunhill Cup team in 1997-99. Only player to win all of the New Zealand Golf Association titles, Under-19, Under-21, Amateur and Open. Broke his neck in December 1999 boogie-boarding and says he is lucky to be walking, let alone playing golf.

EXEMPT STATUS: 19th on 2004 Nationwide Tour money list
BEST PGA TOUR CAREER FINISH: T15—2002 SEI Pennsylvania Classic.
NATIONWIDE TOUR VICTORIES (2): 2001 Boise Open. **2003** VB Open.
MONEY & POSITION:

1997 —	0	1999 —	0
1998 —	9,541 — 277	2002 —	157,723 — 183

PGA TOUR CAREER LOW ROUND: 65–2 times, most recent 2002 Buick Challenge/1
CAREER SUMMARY: Tournaments Entered—30; in money—10; Top-10 finishes—0
CAREER EARNINGS: $167,264
Nationwide Tour Alumnus

LYE, Mark

BIRTHDATE: November 13, 1952 **BIRTHPLACE:** Vallejo, CA **RESIDENCE:** Naples, FL **HEIGHT:** 6-2 **WEIGHT:** 195 **FAMILY:** Wife, Lisa **EDUCATION:** San Jose State University **SPECIAL INTERESTS:** Guitar, fishing, boating **TURNED PROFESSIONAL:** 1975 **Q SCHOOL:** Fall 1976 **OTHER INFORMATION:** Has served as the lead analyst for The Golf Channel the last few years and last played in a PGA TOUR event at the 1995 B.C. Open. Competed in 12 Champions Tour events in 2004, with best finish a solo ninth at the Greater Hickory Classic at Rock Barn, his best performance on the Champions Tour. Made 486 starts on TOUR in a career that began in 1977 after securing his card at the Fall Qualifying Tournament in 1976. Made 332 cuts and earned $1,800,654 in his three decades on the TOUR. Lone victory was a memorable one. Came from eight strokes down the final day with a closing-round 64 to earn a one-stroke win over John Mahaffey, Jim Thorpe and Sammy Rachels at the 1983 Bank of Boston Classic. Finished with birdies on three of the last four holes to claim the $63,000 first-place check, the largest of his career. Finest season came in 1989, when he earned $242,884 and was 56th on the money list. Closed that season with four straight top-10 finishes. Built a three-stroke lead after 36 holes at the 1984 Masters Tournament and trailed by only one after 54 holes before finishing T6. Won the 1976 Australian Order of Merit. College star at San Jose State, where he earned All-American honors in 1975. Diagnosed as a diabetic in high school. One of the few players to use an elongated putter while playing on TOUR. Often traveled with his guitar on TOUR, and at one point in his career teamed with Peter Jacobsen and the late Payne Stewart to form Jake Trout and The Flounders. Has battled melanoma in the past few years. First discovered a dime-sized mole on his left knee in 1991 and had surgery to remove the growth. After treatment and subsequent follow-ups, was cancer-free for five years before he discovered a small growth on his left thigh in 2002. Had surgery on his left leg in July 2002, followed by a series of chemotherapy treatments to treat the cancer. Remains on medication for the disease.

EXEMPT STATUS: Past Champion

PGA TOUR VICTORIES (1): 1983 Bank of Boston Classic.

MONEY & POSITION:

1977 —	22,034 —	101	1984 —	152,356 —	43	1991 —	147,530 —	104
1978 —	13,648 —	126	1985 —	112,735 —	72	1992 —	9,921 —	243
1979 —	51,184 —	75	1986 —	78,960 —	111	1993 —	106,936 —	139
1980 —	109,454 —	39	1987 —	73,625 —	121	1994 —	63,394 —	178
1981 —	76,044 —	57	1988 —	106,972 —	108	1995 —	0	
1982 —	67,460 —	62	1989 —	242,884 —	56			
1983 —	164,506 —	28	1990 —	201,011 —	77			

PGA TOUR CAREER LOW ROUND: 61–1984 Walt Disney World Golf Classic/3

CAREER SUMMARY: Tournaments Entered—486; in money—332; Top-10 finishes—41

CAREER EARNINGS: $1,800,654

LYLE, Sandy

FULL NAME: Alexander Walter Barr Lyle **BIRTHDATE:** February 9, 1958 **BIRTHPLACE:** Shrewbury, England **RESIDENCE:** United Kingdom and Ponte Vedra Beach, FL **HEIGHT:** 6-0 **WEIGHT:** 187 **FAMILY:** Wife, Jolande; Stuart (1983), James (1986), Alexandra Lonneke(1993), Quintin (1995) **SPECIAL INTERESTS:** Motorcycles, cars, airplanes **TURNED PROFESSIONAL:** 1977 **JOINED TOUR:** 1980 **OTHER INFORMATION:** Made the cut at both the Masters and British Open. Recorded one top-25 on the European Tour, a T11 at the Irish Open. Winner of 29 tournaments worldwide, including five on the PGA TOUR. Winner of 1985 British Open and 1988 Masters. Finished seventh on 1988 PGA TOUR money list after winning three times. Won individual title at 1980 World Cup of Golf. Led European Tour Order of Merit three times. Member of five consecutive European Ryder Cup teams (1979, '81, '83, '85, '87) and the 1977 Great Britain/Ireland Walker Cup team. Awarded Member of British Empire. After becoming first British winner of Masters, put Scottish dish haggis on menu at Champions' Dinner the next year.

EXEMPT STATUS: Past Champion

PLAYOFF RECORD: 3-1

PGA TOUR VICTORIES (6): 1985 British Open Championship. **1986** Greater Greensboro Open. **1987** Tournament Players Championship. **1988** Phoenix Open, KMart Greater Greensboro Open, Masters Tournament.

MONEY & POSITION:

1980 —	8,950 —	175	1989 —	292,293 —	43	1998 —	176,354 —	146
1981 —	2,350 —	225	1990 —	51,280 —	175	1999 —	113,004 —	190
1982 —	804 —	284	1991 —	59,794 —	166	2000 —	198,990 —	164
1983 —	0		1992 —	73,459 —	154	2001 —	11,551 —	238
1984 —	15,532 —	169	1993 —	86,121 —	153	2002 —	28,163 —	223
1985 —	40,452 —	132	1994 —	47,538 —	191	2003 —	0	
1986 —	143,415 —	64	1995 —	22,908 —	235	2004 —	49,142 —	229
1987 —	286,176 —	34	1996 —	94,490 —	168			
1988 —	726,934 —	7	1997 —	71,860 —	183			

BEST 2004 PGA TOUR FINISH: T37—Masters Tournament.

PGA TOUR CAREER LOW ROUND: 63–1988 KMart Greater Greensboro Open/2

2004 SUMMARY: Tournaments Entered—2; in money—2; Top-10 finishes—0

CAREER SUMMARY: Tournaments Entered—259; in money—137; Top-10 finishes—22

CAREER EARNINGS: $2,601,559

M

MACKENZIE, Will

FULL NAME: William Ruggles MacKenzie **BIRTHDATE:** September 28, 1974 **BIRTHPLACE:** Greenville, NC **RESIDENCE:** Greenville, NC; plays out of Brook Valley CC **HEIGHT:** 5-11 **WEIGHT:** 170 **FAMILY:** Single **SPECIAL INTERESTS:** Fishing, hunting, relaxing **TURNED PROFESSIONAL:** 2000 **Q SCHOOL:** 2004 **OTHER INFORMATION:** Rookie on the 2005 PGA TOUR after making it through the second and final stages of the 2004 Qualifying Tournament. Finished T26. Was his first trip to finals in three attempts. Has never played an event on the PGA TOUR and has made one cut in four attempts on the Nationwide Tour, a T48 at the 2004 Henrico County Open. Named 2004 Player of the Year on the Hooters Tour after finishing third on the money list and winning three times, at the Touchstone Energy Open in Greenville, NC; Buffalo Run Casino in Miami, OK; and Dothan (AL) Classic. Won the 2003 Canon U.S.A. Classic in West Palm Beach, FL on the Golden Bear Tour and finished ninth on the money list that year. Has also played the Canadian Tour. Is a professional kayaker.

EXEMPT STATUS: T26 at 2004 PGA TOUR Qualifying Tournament

MAGINNES, John

FULL NAME: John David Maginnes **BIRTHDATE:** July 14, 1968 **BIRTHPLACE:** Atlanta, GA **RESIDENCE:** Greensboro, NC **HEIGHT:** 6-1 **WEIGHT:** 195 **FAMILY:** Wife, Dena; Jack Bristol (11/14/98); Sophie (5/23/01) **EDUCATION:** East Carolina University **SPECIAL INTERESTS:** Reading, sports **TURNED PROFESSIONAL:** 1991 **Q SCHOOL:** 1995, 2002, 2003 **OTHER INFORMATION:** Member of the PGA TOUR 1996-97, 1999-2000 and 2003-04. Member of the Nationwide Tour 1994-95, 1998 and 2001-02. Due to elbow injury, limited to 12 PGA TOUR events in 2004, with two made cuts. Best finish was T41 in first start of season at Sony Open in Hawaii. Underwent season-ending right elbow surgery on June 30 of 2004 to remove bone spurs. Surgery was performed by former TOUR player Dr. Bill Mallon in Durham, NC. Did some on-course commentary for USA Network. Will receive a Major Medical Extension for 2005. Coupled with $26,420 earned in 12 events in 2004 has the opportunity to play in 17 events to earn $596,842 and match the $623,262 winnings of 2004's No. 125, Tag Ridings. If he does so, will play out of the Major Medical Extension category for the remainder of the season. Spent 2003 on the PGA TOUR, with one top-10, a T5 at the B.C. Open for eighth top-10 of his career on the PGA TOUR. Best finish since a T5 at the 1998 Deposit Guaranty Classic. Regained his PGA TOUR card by finishing T7 at the Qualifying Tournament. Finished 48th on the 2002 Nationwide Tour money list with two top-10s including a season's best second at the Greater Richmond Open. Three-time winner on the Nationwide Tour. Most recent victory came at the 2001 Carolina Classic in Raleigh, NC, just a short drive from his hometown of Durham and residence in Greensboro. Had emotional year during the 1999 TOUR season. His best finish came at the Motorola Western Open in July. Caddie Garland Dempsey collapsed on the 15th hole during the third round. Dempsey's heart stopped and Maginnes and ABC spotter Matt Moore performed CPR until paramedics arrived. Dempsey underwent successful quadruple bypass surgery. Maginnes was able to pull himself together and complete a 1-under-par 71 round. Fired a 2-under 70 on Sunday to finish in sixth place. Held the 36-hole lead the following week at the Greater Milwaukee Open on his way to a T10 showing. Career-best finish on the PGA TOUR came at the 1996 rain-shortened Buick Challenge. Was one of five players to share the 36-hole lead. Both the third and fourth rounds were rained out, resulting in a five-man playoff, which was won by Michael Bradley. First victory on the Nationwide Tour came in 1995 San Jose Open where he defeated Larry Silveira by three strokes. Won the 1998 Dakota Dunes Open, chipping in for birdie on the second playoff hole to defeat Ryan Howison and Sean Murphy. Shot 10-under-par 62 in the first round at Dakota Dunes. Ended 1998 season fifth on the money list to regain his TOUR card.

EXEMPT STATUS: Major Medical Extension

PLAYOFF RECORD: 0-1

BEST PGA TOUR CAREER FINISH: T2—1996 Buick Challenge.

NATIONWIDE TOUR VICTORIES (3): 1995 San Jose Open. **1998** Dakota Dunes Open. **2001** Carolina Classic.

MONEY & POSITION:

1992 —	0		1998 —	172,165 —	153	2002 —	21,701	
1995 —	2,807 —	324	1999 —	426,666 —	93	2003 —	308,928 —	155
1996 —	184,065 —	113	2000 —	211,749 —	158	2004 —	26,420 —	240
1997 —	110,166 —	164	2001 —	0				

BEST 2004 PGA TOUR FINISHE: T41—Sony Open in Hawaii.

PGA TOUR CAREER LOW ROUND: 63–1996 Greater Milwaukee Open/4

2004 SUMMARY: Tournaments Entered—12; in money—2; Top-10 finishes—0

CAREER SUMMARY: Tournaments Entered—179; in money—86; Top-10 finishes—8

CAREER EARNINGS: $1,464,667

Nationwide Tour Alumnus

MALTBIE, Roger

BIRTHDATE: June 30, 1951 **BIRTHPLACE:** Modesto, CA **RESIDENCE:** Los Gatos, CA **HEIGHT:** 5-10 **WEIGHT:** 200 **FAMILY:** Wife, Donna; Spencer Davis (3/3/87), Parker Travis (3/12/90) **EDUCATION:** San Jose State University **SPECIAL INTERESTS:** Music, 49ers football **TURNED PROFESSIONAL:** 1973 **Q SCHOOL:** 1974 **OTHER INFORMATION:** Continued work as a golf commentator for NBC golf telecasts. Missed the cut in lone TOUR appearance (AT&T Pebble Beach National Pro-Am). Teamed with Gary Koch to win the Raphael Division at 2003 Liberty Mutual Legends of Golf on the Champions Tour. During rookie year on TOUR in 1975, won back-to-back titles at Quad Cities Open and Pleasant Valley Classic.Two biggest career wins came in Ohio, the inaugural Memorial Tournament at Muirfield Village in Dublin in 1976 and the 1985 World Series of Golf at Firestone CC in Akron. Finished a career-best eighth on money list in 1985. Tied for 54-hole lead at the 1987 Masters, eventually finishing T4. Big San Francisco 49ers fan and possessor of Super Bowl rings given to him by former 49ers' owner Edward DeBartolo, Jr. Underwent two shoulder surgeries during playing career. Winner of 1972 and 1973 Northern California Amateur and 1974 California State Open.

EXEMPT STATUS: Past Champion
PLAYOFF RECORD: 2-1
PGA TOUR VICTORIES (5): 1975 Ed McMahon-Jaycees Quad Cities Open, Pleasant Valley Classic. **1976** Memorial Tournament. **1985** Manufacturers Hanover Westchester Classic, NEC World Series of Golf.
MONEY & POSITION:

1975 —	81,035 —	23	1985 —	360,554 —	8	1995 —	61,664 —	187
1976 —	117,737 —	18	1986 —	213,206 —	40	1996 —	48,800 —	199
1977 —	51,727 —	59	1987 —	157,023 —	65	1997 —	0	
1978 —	12,440 —	130	1988 —	150,602 —	77	1998 —	0	
1979 —	9,796 —	156	1989 —	134,333 —	105	1999 —	0	
1980 —	38,626 —	86	1990 —	58,536 —	169	2000 —	0	
1981 —	75,009 —	59	1991 —	37,962 —	188	2001 —	0	
1982 —	77,067 —	56	1992 —	109,742 —	125	2002 —	0	
1983 —	75,751 —	70	1993 —	155,454 —	103	2003 —	0	
1984 —	118,128 —	56	1994 —	67,686 —	174	2004 —	0	

PGA TOUR CAREER LOW ROUND: 63–4 times, most recent 1989 Walt Disney World/Oldsmobile Classic/2
2004 SUMMARY: Tournaments Entered—1; in money—0; Top-10 finishes—0
CAREER SUMMARY: Tournaments Entered—491; in money—327; Top-10 finishes—55
CAREER EARNINGS: $2,212,879

MAY, Bob

FULL NAME: Robert Anthony May **BIRTHDATE:** October 6, 1968 **BIRTHPLACE:** Lynwood, CA **RESIDENCE:** Las Vegas, NV **HEIGHT:** 5-7 **WEIGHT:** 155 **FAMILY:** Wife, Brenda; Trenton (9/14/97), Madelyn (9/25/00) **EDUCATION:** Oklahoma State University **SPECIAL INTERESTS:** Motorcycles, boats, hunting **TURNED PROFESSIONAL:** 1991 **JOINED TOUR:** 1994 **Q SCHOOL:** 1999 **OTHER INFORMATION:** Due to two bulging disks in his back, limited to only seven events in 2003 and none in 2004. Will receive a Non-Exempt Major Medical Extension carryover for 2005. Coupled with $134,308 earned in seven events in 2003, has the opportunity to play in 15 events to earn $353,187 and match the $487,495 winnings of 2003's No. 125, Esteban Toledo. If he does so, will play out of the Major Medical Extension category for the remainder of the season. In 2003, made six cuts, with a best finish of T21 at the Shell Houston Open. In 2002, fell out of the top 125 for the first time since 1999. His best finish in 2002 was T15 at the John Deere Classic. Early season play in 2001 limited by back that stiffened after third round of Bob Hope Chrysler Classic. Was forced to withdraw and diagnosed with two bulging discs in lower back. Took almost two months and returned to play a normal schedule the remainder of the year. Finished 94th in earnings and made 18 cuts in 25 starts. In what will be remembered as one of the great head-to-head duels in major championship history, lost a playoff to Tiger Woods in the 2000 PGA Championship at Valhalla GC. After opening with a 72, came back with 66-66-66. Paired with Woods in the final round, both players birdied 18. May drained a 15-footer to match Woods with a 31 on the back nine. In the three-hole playoff, May recorded three pars (4-4-5) while Woods birdied the first extra hole. In final three rounds, May produced 20 birdies and only two bogeys and shares the PGA Championship scoring record with Woods at 18-under-par 270. Played on the European Tour from 1996-1999 and won the 1999 Victor Chandler British Masters. Gained exempt status on TOUR in 1993 by virtue of his fourth-place finish on Nationwide Tour money list, where he had 11 top-10s, including two seconds. Three-time all-American at Oklahoma State, played on the 1991 NCAA championship team. Introduced to golf by aunt and uncle, then spent time at Big Tee Golf Center in Buena Park, CA, where he picked up range balls and in return was allowed to hit them back out. At age 11 began taking lessons from current teacher Eddie Merrins, the longtime head pro at Bel Air Country Club in Los Angeles. May's father, Jerry, who owned a gas station, would drive Bob every Sunday for 7 a.m. lesson with Merrin, an hour from the May's home in La Habra. At age 16, qualified to play in 1985 Los Angeles Open.

EXEMPT STATUS: Non-Exempt, Major Medical Extension
PLAYOFF RECORD: 0-1
BEST PGA TOUR CAREER FINISH: 2—2000 PGA Championship, T2—FedEx St. Jude Classic.
MONEY & POSITION:

1993 —	0		1999 —	50,000 —	225	2002 —	407,778 —	138
1994 —	31,079 —	209	2000 —	1,557,720 —	29	2003 —	134,308 —	193
1998 —	40,130 —	214	2001 —	534,936 —	94			

PGA TOUR CAREER LOW ROUND: 63–2 times, most recent 1999 Las Vegas Invitational/1
2004 SUMMARY: Tournaments entered—7; in money—6; Top-10 finishes—0
CAREER SUMMARY: Tournaments Entered—127; in money—72; Top-10 finishes—3
CAREER EARNINGS: $2,755,951
Nationwide Tour Alumnus

McCALLISTER, Blaine

FULL NAME: Blaine McCallister **BIRTHDATE:** October 17, 1958 **BIRTHPLACE:** Ft. Stockton, TX **RESIDENCE:** Ponte Vedra Beach, FL **HEIGHT:** 5-10 **WEIGHT:** 190 **FAMILY:** Wife, Claudia; Kelly, Paul **EDUCATION:** University of Houston **SPECIAL INTERESTS:** Hunting, fishing, tennis, baseball **TURNED PROFESSIONAL:** 1981 **Q SCHOOL:** Fall 1981, 1982, 1985, 1997, 1999, 2001 **OTHER INFORMATION:** Posted three top-25s in 2004, while making just six cuts in 27 events. Posted an ace in the first round of the 2004 Buick Championship, on No. 8 at the TPC at River Highlands from 202 yards with a 5-iron. Spent a season on the Nationwide Tour in 2003 for the first time in his career. Finished 12th on the money list after posting seven top-10s in 18 starts, including his first victory on that Tour at the Northeast Pennsylvania Classic. The victory was his first on any Tour since winning the 1993 B.C. Open. Kept TOUR card for 2002 with T32 finish at 2001 Qualifying School. Dropped from 49th to 149th on the 2001 official money list from the previous year, with a best finish of T5 at Greater Milwaukee Open. In 1999, finished 134th on season money list, leaving him non-exempt for the 2000 season. Instead he went to 1999 Qualifying Tournament and finished first, securing full privileges for 2000, a season that earned him a career-high $963,974, his most lucrative year in golf thanks to three top-10s, including a runner up and third-place finish. At Compaq Classic of New Orleans, narrowly missed first TOUR victory since 1993 B.C. Open. After sharing 54-hole led with Carlos Franco, closed with 68 to get into a playoff with Franco, which Franco won with par on second extra hole. Earned $367,200 for second-place finish, more than he made in any career year since 1991. Owns five victories on the PGA TOUR, including two in 1989 at The Honda Classic and Bank of Boston Classic. First TOUR win came at 1988 Hardee's Golf Classic. Middle rounds of 62-63 tied then-TOUR record for lowest consecutive rounds in TOUR history. Topped by Mark Calcavecchia (124) at the 2001 Phoenix Open. After 1983 season, spent a lot of time perfecting his left-handed putting style. First qualified to play on the TOUR in 1982. Natural left-hander who plays the game right-handed but putts southpaw. Is involved with eyesight organizations as a result of his wife, Claudia, suffering from pseudoxanthoma elasticum (PXE), a rare eye disease. Roomed with Fred Couples for one year and with CBS Sports golf host Jim Nantz for three while attending the University of Houston. Joined Couples and Nantz in Three Amigos Celebrity Tournament, first held in October 1994. One of the beneficiaries of the event was PXA research. Played with seven New York City firefighters at the Stadium Course at the TPC at Sawgrass in November of 2001 following Sept. 11 tragedy. The firefighters, who had spent the majority of their time at Ground Zero since the initial terrorist strikes, were part of a larger contingent honored by the city of Jacksonville for their heroics.

EXEMPT STATUS: Past Champion
PLAYOFF RECORD: 1-2
PGA TOUR VICTORIES (5): 1988 Hardee's Golf Classic. **1989** Honda Classic, Bank of Boston Classic. **1991** H.E.B. Texas Open. **1993** B.C. Open.
NATIONWIDE TOUR VICTORIES (1): 2003 Northeast Pennsylvania Classic.
MONEY & POSITION:

1982 —	7,894 —	186	1991 —	412,974 —	36	1999 —	295,932 —	134
1983 —	5,218 —	201	1992 —	261,187 —	59	2000 —	963,974 —	49
1984 —	0		1993 —	290,434 —	61	2001 —	280,589 —	149
1986 —	88,732 —	94	1994 —	351,554 —	47	2002 —	123,349 —	194
1987 —	120,005 —	87	1995 —	238,847 —	77	2003 —	65,820 —	223
1988 —	225,660 —	49	1996 —	179,427 —	117	2004 —	162,700 —	198
1989 —	523,891 —	15	1997 —	140,966 —	143			
1990 —	152,048 —	103	1998 —	228,304 —	125			

BEST 2004 PGA TOUR FINISHES: T20—Chrysler Classic of Tucson, BellSouth Classic; T24—Chrysler Classic of Greensboro.
PGA TOUR CAREER LOW ROUND: 62–1988 Hardee's Golf Classic/2
2004 SUMMARY: Tournaments Entered—27; in money—6; Top-10 finishes—0
CAREER SUMMARY: Tournaments Entered—585; in money—325; Top-10 finishes—40
CAREER EARNINGS: $5,119,505
Nationwide Tour Alumnus

McCORD, Gary

FULL NAME: Gary Dennis McCord **BIRTHDATE:** May 23, 1948 **BIRTHPLACE:** San Gabriel, CA **RESIDENCE:** Paradise Valley, AZ **HEIGHT:** 6-2 **WEIGHT:** 190 **FAMILY:** Wife, Diane, Krista (5/14/68), four grandchildren **EDUCATION:** University of California-Riverside (1971, Economics) **SPECIAL INTERESTS:** Acceleration, giving a name to each age spot on my body **TURNED PROFESSIONAL:** 1971 **JOINED TOUR:** 1974 **OTHER INFORMATION:** Played in 14 Champions Tour events in 2004, splitting time with his TV analyst position at CBS Sports. Has won twice on the Champions Tour, both in 1999. Writes for Golf Digest and has published three books: *Golf for Dummies*, *Golf For Dummies II* and *Just a Range Ball in a Box of Titleists*. Also hosted *Golf for Dummies* instructional DVD. Led U.S. Team as captain to victory in 2004 Tommy Bahama Challenge. Operates the Kostis-McCord Learning Center in Scottsdale, AZ, with Peter Kostis. Served as technical consultant for and appeared in the Kevin Costner movie "Tin Cup." Ran charity pro-am with Andrew Magee, the Santa Claus Classic, in Scottsdale for 10 years. Served as captain of the American team at the inaugural Tommy Bahama Challenge in late 2004. Was backed by the late Lawrence Welk early in his pro career and once appeared on the musical conductor's variety show. Played the PGA TOUR from 1974-98 with more than $600,000 in earnings in 376 tournaments. Top performances in his PGA TOUR career were a solo second at the 1975 Greater Milwaukee Open and a T2 at the 1977 Greater Milwaukee Open. Was a five-stroke victor at the 1991 Gateway Open. Two-time All-America selection at Cal-Riverside and the winner of the 1970 NCAA Division II Championship.

EXEMPT STATUS: Veteran Member
BEST PGA TOUR CAREER FINISH: 2—1975 Greater Milwaukee Open, T2—1977 Greater Milwaukee Open.
NATIONWIDE TOUR VICTORIES (1): 1991 Gateway Open.
MONEY & POSITION:

1973 —	499 —	265	1982 —	27,380 —	131	1991 —	7,365 —	241
1974 —	32,140 —	76	1983 —	55,756 —	94	1992 —	64,503 —	160
1975 —	43,028 —	59	1984 —	68,213 —	86	1993 —	16,456 —	225
1976 —	26,480 —	84	1985 —	32,198 —	140	1994 —	25,602 —	216
1977 —	46,318 —	65	1986 —	27,747 —	160	1995 —	15,813 —	245
1978 —	15,280 —	118	1987 —	3,689 —	240	1996 —	2,548 —	357
1979 —	36,843 —	105	1988 —	15,502 —	204	1997 —	2,880 —	332
1980 —	13,521 —	151	1989 —	29,629 —	181	1998 —	0	
1981 —	20,722 —	131	1990 —	32,249 —	191	1999 —	0	

PGA TOUR CAREER LOW ROUND: 63–1986 Provident Classic/3
CAREER SUMMARY: Tournaments Entered—378; in money—242; Top-10 finishes—24
CAREER EARNINGS: $662,359

McGOVERN, Jim

FULL NAME: James David McGovern **BIRTHDATE:** February 5, 1965 **BIRTHPLACE:** Teaneck, NJ **RESIDENCE:** Oradell, NJ; plays out of Hackensack GC **HEIGHT:** 6-1 **WEIGHT:** 200 **FAMILY:** Wife, Lauren; Melanie (2/5/95), Emily (4/6/96), Elizabeth Ann (2/24/99), Sean Harold (7/16/01) **EDUCATION:** Old Dominion University **SPECIAL INTERESTS:** Family, all sports **TURNED PROFESSIONAL:** 1988 **Q SCHOOL:** 1991, 1996, 1997 **OTHER INFORMATION:** Posted one top 25 in 2004, a T20 at the John Deere Classic. Ended the 2003 season with T13 at the Southern Farm Bureau Classic, best finish since T7 at the 2001 Michelob Championship. Also spent time playing on the Nationwide Tour, playing in 15 events and making eight cuts. Played 16 events on the PGA TOUR and 13 on the Nationwide Tour in 2002. Best finish on TOUR was T25 at the Valero Texas Open. On the Nationwide Tour, 13 starts yielded top-10s at Virginia Beach Open and the SAS Carolina Classic. Finished 76th on the Nationwide Tour money list with $52,472. Enjoyed his best season on the PGA TOUR in 1993 when he captured his lone victory, defeating John Huston with birdie on second playoff hole to win the rain-shortened Shell Houston Open. Had two other top-10s that year and finished No. 27 on the money list with $587,495. PGA TOUR member from 1991-99, playing an average of 32 tournaments a year from 1991 to 1998. Winner of 1994 Diners Club Matches with Jeff Maggert. Won Lake City, Texarkana and New Haven Opens en route to second-place finish on the 1990 Nationwide Tour money list. Brother Rob played linebacker in the NFL. Jim and his family were honored with the Metropolitan Golf Writers Family of the Year Award for 1996. Winner of the 1988 Metropolitan Open, 1987 Metropolitan Amateur. 1987 Virginia State Intercollegiate Champion. First exposed to the game when parents bought house adjacent to Hackensack (NJ) GC.

EXEMPT STATUS: Past Champion
PLAYOFF RECORD: 1-0
PGA TOUR VICTORIES (1): 1993 Shell Houston Open.
NATIONWIDE TOUR VICTORIES (3): 1990 Lake City Classic, New Haven Open, Texarkana Open.
MONEY & POSITION:

1989 —	0		1995 —	402,587 —	44	2000 —	266,647 —	143
1991 —	88,869 —	141	1996 —	116,727 —	154	2001 —	271,494 —	153
1992 —	169,888 —	92	1997 —	140,756 —	144	2002 —	86,862 —	203
1993 —	587,495 —	27	1998 —	106,726 —	180	2003 —	115,148 —	202
1994 —	227,764 —	79	1999 —	7,940 —	301	2004 —	72,377 —	223

BEST 2004 PGA TOUR FINISH: T20—John Deere Classic.
PGA TOUR CAREER LOW ROUND: 62–1992 Federal Express St. Jude Classic/2
2004 SUMMARY: Tournaments Entered—11; in money—4; Top-10 finishes—0
CAREER SUMMARY: Tournaments Entered—338; in money—181; Top-10 finishes—14
CAREER EARNINGS: $2,661,280
Nationwide Tour Alumnus

McLEAN, James

FULL NAME: James Hamilton McLean **BIRTHDATE:** September 16, 1978 **BIRTHPLACE:** Sydney, Australia **RESIDENCE:** Melbourne, Australia; Minneapolis, MN **HEIGHT:** 6-0 **WEIGHT:** 170 **FAMILY:** Single **EDUCATION:** University of Minnesota **SPECIAL INTERESTS:** Swimming, surfing, fishing **TURNED PROFESSIONAL:** 2000 **Q SCHOOL:** 2002 **OTHER INFORMATION:** Playing on a Minor Medical Extension in 2004, limited to only one event, a T20 at the HP Classic of New Orleans. Will receive a Minor Medical Extension carryover for 2005. Coupled with $174,506 earned in 20 events in 2003-04, has the opportunity to play in nine events to earn $312,989 and match the $487,495 winnings of 2003's No. 125, Esteban Toledo. If he does so, will play out of the Major Medical Extension category for the remainder of the season. Rookie played in only 19 events (with five made cuts) in 2003 due to bone spurs in wrist. Best finish was T18 at the Chrysler Classic of Tucson. Did not have enough official rounds to qualify for title, but Driving Distance average was 308.9, third behind Hank Kuehne and John Daly. Earned his card by finishing T2 at the 2002 PGA TOUR Qualifying Tournament. Also combats vision problems stemming from 2000 illness at Big 10 Championships, where he was hospitalized for an extended period. Rookie on the Nationwide Tour in 2001. Played in 19 Nationwide Tour events and made 10 cuts. Best finish was T7 at the 2002 Nationwide Arkansas Classic. Finished T54 at the 2001 PGA TOUR Qualifying Tournament at Bear Lakes CC. 1998 NCAA champion at Minnesota. His 17-under par finish at the University of New Mexico Championship Course tied a then-NCAA record held by John Inman, Phil Mickelson and Justin Leonard. His title helped lead the Gophers to a seventh-place finish. 1999 NCAA Regional Champion. 1998 and 1999 First-Team All-American. Winner of the 1998 Minnesota State Open and the Minnesota Amateur Championship. Cites winning medalist honors at the 1998 NCAA Championships as his biggest thrill in golf. Was introduced to golf by a friend at age 12. His father played professional football in Australia. Grew up in Wahgunyah, a town with a population of 500, in the Australian outback, where his family runs a motel.
EXEMPT STATUS: Minor Medical Extension
BEST PGA TOUR CAREER FINISH: T18—2003 Chrysler Classic of Tucson.
MONEY & POSITION:

2003 —	117,182 —	201	2004 —	57,324 —	228

BEST 2004 PGA TOUR FINISH: T20—HP Classic of New Orleans.
PGA TOUR CAREER LOW ROUND: 65–2003 Phoenix Open/1
2004 SUMMARY: Tournaments Entered—1; in money—1; Top-10 finishes—0
CAREER SUMMARY: Tournaments Entered—20; in money—6; Top-10 finishes—0
CAREER EARNINGS: $174,506
Nationwide Tour Alumnus

McROY, Spike

FULL NAME: Robert Lynn McRoy, Jr. **BIRTHDATE:** May 20, 1968 **BIRTHPLACE:** Huntsville, AL **RESIDENCE:** Huntsville, AL; plays out of Valley Hill CC **HEIGHT:** 5-11 **WEIGHT:** 155 **FAMILY:** Wife, Rica; Rily Alexander (2/27/99), Parker Kumar (4/17/01), Meera Sophia (9/3/2002) **EDUCATION:** University of Alabama (1991, Corporate Finance) **SPECIAL INTERESTS:** Guitar, fishing, stock market, Bible study **TURNED PROFESSIONAL:** 1991 **Q SCHOOL:** 1996, 1997 **OTHER INFORMATION:** Finished just outside the top 150 on the 2004 PGA TOUR money list at No. 159. Lone top-10 was a T8 at the final full-field event of the season, the Chrysler Championship in Tampa Bay, Florida. Had 35 starts in 2003, tied for most on TOUR with Pat Bates, Esteban Toledo and Neal Lancaster. Only top-10 of the 2003 season, was a T10 at the Greater Milwaukee Open. Finished a career-best 110th on 2002 TOUR money list with $616,814 after entering season with partial TOUR status. Earned first career PGA TOUR title in 115th career TOUR start at the B.C. Open, one of a record 18 first-time winners. Rolled in a 31-foot birdie putt on the 72nd hole to finish at 7-under-par 65 for the final round. The 19-under 269 total topped Fred Funk by a stroke, earning a career-high check of $378,000. Finished the year on a strong note with T5 finish at the season-ending Southern Farm Bureau Classic. After a two-year hiatus from the PGA TOUR, earned $401,654 to finish 127th on the 2001 money list. Needing $4,598 to retain PGA TOUR card for 2002, missed cut at final event, the Southern Farm Bureau Classic. Had one top-10 finish, a T3 at the Kemper Insurance Open. 2002 Nationwide Tour Player of the Year after winning the season-ending Nationwide Tour Championship at Highland Oaks GC in home state of Alabama. Earned $99,000 for second win of the season, pushing his season total to a then-Tour-record $300,638. First Nationwide Tour victory came at the Dakota Dunes Open. In 1999, split time between Nationwide Tour and PGA TOUR with 11 events on both Tours. Posted only one top 10 in 1998, a T6 at Buick Invitational, in 32 TOUR starts. Runner-up to Rafael Alarcon at the 1997 Compaq World Putting Championship. Finished T5 at 1997 Qualifying School to re-gain TOUR card. Winner of 1992 Alabama Open and two Hooters Tour events that year. Winner of the 1990 Cajun Classic. Earned his nickname from a great uncle who was a fan of the Detroit Tigers and star player Ty Cobb. Cobb was known for his aggressive baserunning, with spikes up going into bases. The great uncle sent Spike a miniature Tigers uniform when he was born. Wife obtained Doctorate in Optometry from Southern College of Optometry in Memphis in 1996.
EXEMPT STATUS: Past Champion
PGA TOUR VICTORIES (1): 2002 B.C. Open.
NATIONWIDE TOUR VICTORIES (2): 2000 Dakota Dunes Open, TOUR Championship.
MONEY & POSITION:

1991 —	0		1999 —	49,701 —	226	2003 —	480,773 —	129
1997 —	66,274 —	190	2001 —	401,654 —	127	2004 —	374,187 —	159
1998 —	179,770 —	145	2002 —	616,814 —	110			

BEST 2004 PGA TOUR FINISH: T8—Chrysler Championship.
PGA TOUR CAREER LOW ROUND: 62–2001 Bob Hope Chrysler Classic/4
2004 SUMMARY: Tournaments Entered—33; in money—13; Top-10 finishes—1
CAREER SUMMARY: Tournaments Entered—195; in money—76; Top-10 finishes—7
CAREER EARNINGS: $2,169,172
Nationwide Tour Alumnus

MILLER, Johnny

BIRTHDATE: April 29, 1947 **BIRTHPLACE:** San Francisco, CA **RESIDENCE:** Salt Lake City, UT **HEIGHT:** 6-2 **WEIGHT:** 205 **FAMILY:** Wife, Linda; John S. (6/2/70), Kelly (12/26/72), Casoi (7/30/74), Scott (5/12/76), Andy (2/3/78), Todd (1/2/80), 13 grandchildren **EDUCATION:** Brigham Young University (1969, Physical Education) **SPECIAL INTERESTS:** Fishing, ranching, church activities, course architecture, golf club design **TURNED PROFESSIONAL:** 1969 **Q SCHOOL:** Spring, 1969 **OTHER INFORMATION:** Played last official TOUR event at the 1997 AT&T Pebble Beach National Pro-Am. Participates in several unofficial events each year. Has played just two official events in his Champions Tour career since turning 50 in 1997. Works primarily as the lead analyst for NBC golf telecasts. Son Andy was a member of the PGA TOUR in 2003, earning his card through the National Qualifying Tournament. Andy qualified for the 2002 U.S. Open at Bethpage Black, and fired a hole-in-one on third hole in final round of NBC telecast, finishing T62. Played the PGA TOUR full time from 1969-1994 and won 24 official titles. Victory at 1994 AT&T Pebble Beach National Pro-Am made him the most recent grandfather to win a PGA TOUR event (first since Art Wall, Jr., at 1975 Greater Milwaukee Open). Biggest victory came when he won the 1973 U.S. Open at Oakmont, shooting 63 in the final round, the lowest score ever by a winner at that prestigious event. Was the PGA TOUR's leading money winner and Player of the Year in 1974 when he won eight times, the only player other than Jack Nicklaus or Tom Watson to win money title between 1971 and 1980. Member of 1975 and 1981 U.S. Ryder Cup teams, where he compiled a 2-2-2 record in the biennial matches. Winner 1964 U.S. Junior Amateur Championship. Elected to World Golf Hall of Fame in 1996. His family was the recipient of 1997 Jack Nicklaus Golf Family of the Year Award, presented by the National Golf Foundation. Is the co-founder of the Utah Junior Golf Association and is still its honorary chairman.

EXEMPT STATUS: Past Champion

PLAYOFF RECORD: 1-5

PGA TOUR VICTORIES (25): 1971 Southern Open Invitational. **1972** Sea Pines Heritage Classic. **1973** U.S. Open Championship. **1974** Bing Crosby National Pro-Am, Phoenix Open, Dean Martin Tucson Open, Sea Pines Heritage Classic, Tournament of Champions, Westchester Classic, World Open Golf Championship, Kaiser International Open Invitational. **1975** Phoenix Open, Dean Martin Tucson Open, Bob Hope Desert Classic, Kaiser International Open Invitational. **1976** NBC Tucson Open, Bob Hope Desert Classic, British Open Championship. **1980** Jackie Gleason-Inverrary Classic. **1981** Joe Garagiola-Tucson Open, Glen Campbell-Los Angeles Open. **1982** Wickes-Andy Williams San Diego Open. **1983** Honda Inverrary Classic. **1987** AT&T Pebble Beach National Pro-Am. **1994** AT&T Pebble Beach National Pro-Am.

MONEY & POSITION:

1969 —	8,203 —	125	1979 —	49,266 —	79	1989 —	66,174 —	150
1970 —	49,270 —	37	1980 —	127,117 —	30	1990 —	8,900 —	235
1971 —	80,459 —	18	1981 —	193,167 —	12	1991 —	2,864 —	269
1972 —	95,350 —	18	1982 —	169,065 —	20	1992 —	4,312 —	269
1973 —	124,766 —	9	1983 —	230,186 —	14	1993 —	0	
1974 —	346,302 —	1	1984 —	139,422 —	47	1994 —	225,000 —	81
1975 —	226,119 —	2	1985 —	126,616 —	64	1995 —	0	
1976 —	135,888 —	14	1986 —	71,444 —	118	1997 —	0	
1977 —	61,025 —	48	1987 —	139,398 —	78			
1978 —	17,440 —	112	1988 —	31,989 —	169			

PGA TOUR CAREER LOW ROUND: 61–3 times, most recent 1975 Dean Martin Tucson Open/4

CAREER SUMMARY: Tournaments Entered—385; in money—332; Top-10 finishes—105

CAREER EARNINGS: $2,747,484

WORLD GOLF HALL OF FAME MEMBER (Inducted 1996)

MIZE, Larry

FULL NAME: Larry Hogan Mize **BIRTHDATE:** September 23, 1958 **BIRTHPLACE:** Augusta, GA **RESIDENCE:** Columbus, GA **HEIGHT:** 6-0 **WEIGHT:** 165 **FAMILY:** Wife, Bonnie; David (4/17/86), Patrick (2/12/89), Robert (4/2/93) **EDUCATION:** Georgia Tech **SPECIAL INTERESTS:** Fishing, all sports, piano **TURNED PROFESSIONAL:** 1980 **Q SCHOOL:** Fall 1981 **OTHER INFORMATION:** Past Masters champion played in 13 events in 2004, with six made cuts. Lone top-25 was T21 at The Honda Classic, his best finish on the PGA TOUR since a T17 at the 2001 LaCantera Texas Open. Limited to 10 events due to injury in 2002, and did not finish in the top 125 for the first time in 21 seasons on TOUR. Granted Major Medical Extension for 2003 due to lower back injury suffered at the Greater Milwaukee Open. Did not play the remainder of the 2002 season. Got a late start to the 2002 season after suffering a cracked scapula in his shoulder, broken rib and a minor concussion in December 2001 when a horse he was riding on his parents' farm stepped into a hole and threw him. In 2001, placed among the top 125 on the PGA TOUR money list for the 20th consecutive season. Finished T3 at the 2000 MCI Classic, best finish since playoff loss to Olin Browne at 1998 Canon Greater Hartford Open. Another solid season in 1999, a year in which he earned $386,554, giving him 11 consecutive years in which he had made more than $200,000. Held four-stroke lead with four holes to play at 1998 Canon Greater Hartford Open, but fell into three-man playoff with Stewart Cink and Olin Browne. Browne won playoff with 30-foot birdie chip on first extra hole. After finishing 99th on money list in 1997 dedicated himself during off-season to work with instructor Chuck Cook on revamping his game for following season and placed 62nd on the money list. Enjoyed first two-victory season in 1993, his first wins since 1987 Masters triumph. Trailed Dudley Hart and Phil Mickelson by three strokes through 54 holes of Northern Telecom Open before closing 67 defeated Jeff Maggert by two. Came from four strokes off Fuzzy Zoeller's third-round lead to win Buick Open. Made 140-foot chip-in to win the 1987 Masters. Birdied the final hole at Augusta National to force playoff with Greg Norman and Seve Ballesteros. After Ballesteros was eliminated on first extra hole, used sand wedge from the right of the second hole, the par-4 11th, to chip in for birdie and defeat Norman. First TOUR victory came at 1983 Danny Thomas-Memphis Classic, where 25-foot birdie putt on final hole defeated Fuzzy Zoeller, Sammy Rachels and Chip Beck. Plays reduced schedule in order to spend more time with his family. Worked on a Masters scoreboard at the third hole during his early teen years.

EXEMPT STATUS: Past Champion

PLAYOFF RECORD: 1-3

PGA TOUR VICTORIES (4): 1983 Danny Thomas Memphis Classic. **1987** Masters Tournament. **1993** Northern Telecom Open, Buick Open.

MONEY & POSITION:

1980 —	1,189 —	252	1989 —	278,388 —	45	1998 —	464,294 —	62
1981 —	0		1990 —	668,198 —	14	1999 —	386,554 —	103
1982 —	28,787 —	125	1991 —	279,061 —	60	2000 —	425,624 —	111
1983 —	146,325 —	35	1992 —	316,428 —	47	2001 —	440,179 —	115
1984 —	172,513 —	36	1993 —	724,660 —	13	2002 —	7,634 —	244
1985 —	231,041 —	17	1994 —	386,029 —	42	2003 —	93,713 —	211
1986 —	314,051 —	17	1995 —	289,576 —	67	2004 —	136,020 —	206
1987 —	561,407 —	6	1996 —	317,468 —	67			
1988 —	187,823 —	62	1997 —	246,773 —	99			

BEST 2004 PGA TOUR FINISH: T21—The Honda Classic.

PGA TOUR CAREER LOW ROUND: 62–1985 Los Angeles Open/2

2004 SUMMARY: Tournaments Entered—13; in money—6; Top-10 finishes—0

CAREER SUMMARY: Tournaments Entered—538; in money—380; Top-10 finishes—83

CAREER EARNINGS: $7,103,733

SECTION 2 PLAYER BIOGRAPHIES

MORGAN, John E.

FULL NAME: John Edward Morgan **BIRTHDATE:** December 19, 1977 **BIRTHPLACE:** Bristol, England **RESIDENCE:** Bristol, Portishead, England; plays out of Clevedon GC **HEIGHT:** 6-2 **WEIGHT:** 195 **FAMILY:** Single **SPECIAL INTERESTS:** Music, dancing **TURNED PROFESSIONAL:** 2002 **Q SCHOOL:** 2002 **OTHER INFORMATION:** Played in 16 PGA TOUR events in 2004 and enters 2005 with partial status after finishing 145th on money list. In sixth start of season, finished second to Mark Hensby in a playoff at the 2004 John Deere Classic. Earned a career-best $410,000 after posting four rounds in the 60s. Final-round 6-under-par 65 included birdies on four of the final five holes. On second playoff hole, failed to get up-and-down from hazard as Hensby captured title with tap-in par on the par-3 16th hole at the TPC at Deere Run. The next week at the 2004 B.C. Open was one off the lead after 18, 36 and 54 holes, but a closing 72 dropped him to T13. The two weeks in July doubled his career money on the PGA TOUR. Also made six starts on the 2004 Nationwide Tour. Best finish was T15 at the Henrico County Open. Rookie on the PGA TOUR in 2003. Playing in only his 16th career event on TOUR, finished T5 at the 2003 B.C. Open. Prior to coming to the B.C. Open had just one top-25 in 15 starts, a T22 at the Buick Classic. Added a second top-10 with a T10 at the 2003 Southern Farm Bureau Classic in October. Late in the season finished T5 at the Chrysler Classic of Greensboro. Earned initial PGA TOUR card for the 2003 season via a T11 finish at the 2002 Qualifying Tournament, his first attempt at Q-School. After turning professional in April 2002, finished T2 at the Galeria Kaufhof Pokal Challenge in June, then won the Charles Church Challenge Tour Championship in July. Finished eighth on the European Challenge Tour's Order of Merit to earn his 2003 European Tour Card. Second rookie to earn card on both the PGA TOUR and European Tour in the same season (Richie Coughlan, 1998). Overcame dyslexia and epilepsy before turning professional in April 2002. Father has been a dock worker in England for more than 40 years. Lost a bet with founder of MTV in Miami in 2003 and dyed hair blue as a result. Switched to belly putter after conversation with Vijay Singh at the 2004 Zurich Classic of New Orleans.
EXEMPT STATUS: 145th on 2004 money list
PLAYOFF RECORD: 0-1
BEST PGA TOUR CAREER FINISH: 2—2004 John Deere Classic.
MONEY & POSITION:

2003 —	422,917	— 141	2004 —	487,032	— 145

BEST 2004 PGA TOUR FINISH: 2—John Deere Classic.
PGA TOUR CAREER LOW ROUND: 63–2003 Chrysler Classic of Tucson/2
2004 SUMMARY: Tournaments Entered—16; in money—4; Top-10 finishes—1
CAREER SUMMARY: Tournaments Entered—45; in money—15; Top-10 finishes—4
CAREER EARNINGS: $909,949

MORSE, John

FULL NAME: John Paul Morse **BIRTHDATE:** February 16, 1958 **BIRTHPLACE:** Marshall, MI **RESIDENCE:** Marshall, MI; plays out of Marshall CC **HEIGHT:** 5-10 **WEIGHT:** 180 **FAMILY:** Wife, Kelly; Christina (7/31/92) **EDUCATION:** University of Michigan **SPECIAL INTERESTS:** Fishing **TURNED PROFESSIONAL:** 1981 **JOINED TOUR:** 1994 **Q SCHOOL:** 1997 **OTHER INFORMATION:** Split time in 2004 between PGA TOUR (three events) and Nationwide Tour (16 events), including three top-10s on the Nationwide Tour. Made only one cut on the PGA TOUR, T60 at the B.C. Open. T4 finish at the 2002 Tampa Bay Classic presented by Buick marked the 1995 United Airlines Hawaiian Open champion's first top-10 since a T8 at the 1997 Shell Houston Open, and his best finish since a T3 at the 1995 LaCantera Texas Open (a span of 87 events). One top-10 finish on the Nationwide Tour in 2002, a T2 at the Hibernia Southern Open. Finished T73 in 2001 B.C. Open for first PGA TOUR start since 1998. Won 1995 United Airlines Hawaiian Open with closing 68 to defeat Tom Lehman and Duffy Waldorf by three strokes. Closed with 70 to finish fourth in 1996 U.S. Open at Oakland Hills CC in home state of Michigan. Earned first TOUR card by finishing fifth on 1993 Nationwide Tour money list. Winner of 1993 New England Classic. Played Australasian Tour from 1989-92. Winner 1990 Australian Open in playoff over Craig Parry. Big Ten champion at University of Michigan.
EXEMPT STATUS: Past Champion
PGA TOUR VICTORIES (1): 1995 United Airlines Hawaiian Open.
NATIONWIDE TOUR VICTORIES (1): 1993 New England Classic.
MONEY & POSITION:

1984 —	0		1995 —	416,803	— 42	2002 —	125,260	— 193
1987 —	0		1996 —	322,090	— 64	2003 —	22,361	— 237
1988 —	0		1997 —	161,363	— 134	2004 —	6,420	— 259
1991 —	9,117	— 230	1998 —	43,140	— 210			
1994 —	146,137	— 122	2001 —	3,880	— 255			

BEST 2004 PGA TOUR FINISHES: T60—B.C. Open.
PGA TOUR CAREER LOW ROUND: 64–2 times, most recent 1997 GTE Byron Nelson Golf Classic/2
2004 SUMMARY: Tournaments Entered—3; in money—1; Top-10 finishes—0
CAREER SUMMARY: Tournaments Entered—157; in money—74; Top-10 finishes—8
CAREER EARNINGS: $1,256,570
Nationwide Tour Alumnus

N

NOBILO, Frank (KNOB-il-o)

FULL NAME: Frank Ivan Joseph Nobilo **BIRTHDATE:** May 14, 1960 **BIRTHPLACE:** Auckland, New Zealand **RESIDENCE:** Auckland, New Zealand **HEIGHT:** 6-0 **WEIGHT:** 200 **FAMILY:** Wife, Selena; Bianca (1990) **SPECIAL INTERESTS:** Squash, motor racing **TURNED PROFESSIONAL:** 1979 **JOINED TOUR:** 1996 **Q SCHOOL:** 2000 **OTHER INFORMATION:** After finishing 135th on the money list in 2002, missed the 2003-04 seasons due to two ruptured disks in his back. Joined The Golf Channel as a full-time analyst in 2004, working primarily on Champions Tour broadcasts. Has the opportunity to play in 22 events in a Non-Exempt Major Medical Extension carryover. Missed several events at the end of 2002 due to a shoulder injury and finished No. 135. In 2001, the key to finishing in the top 125 for first time since 1998 was eight top-25s in 17 starts. Has participated in three Presidents Cups (1994, 1996, 1998). Captured first PGA TOUR title in second season on TOUR at the 1997 Greater Greensboro Chrysler Classic. Final-round 67, in cool and rainy conditions, moved him into tie with Brad Faxon. Parred first playoff hole for win. Also in 1997, captured the Hong Kong Open and Mexican Open,. Won 1996 Deutsche Bank Open on PGA European Tour and second consecutive Subaru Sarazen World Open, marking first successful defense of his career. Two-time New Zealand PGA Champion (1985-87). Has dealt with back problems relating to the fact his right leg is shorter than his left. Ancestors were Italian pirates who, after running out of things to pillage on the Adriatic, resettled in New Zealand in the early 1900s. Victim of a freak accident one week after marrying Selena Syer in Orlando in 1998. Errant tee shot at Lake Nona struck him above left eye, requiring 30 stitches and affecting his subsequent play.
EXEMPT STATUS: Non-Exempt, Major Medical Extension
PLAYOFF RECORD: 1-0
PGA TOUR VICTORIES (1): 1997 Greater Greensboro Chrysler Classic.
MONEY & POSITION:

1992 —	7,000	— 252	1996 —	262,292	— 81	2000 —	236,476	— 152
1993 —	14,500	— 230	1997 —	891,315	— 23	2001 —	462,650	— 108
1994 —	41,292	— 198	1998 —	269,134	— 108	2002 —	447,324	— 135
1995 —	52,119	— 203	1999 —	191,734	— 155			

PGA TOUR CAREER LOW ROUND: 63–2000 Doral-Ryder Open/2
CAREER SUMMARY: Tournaments Entered—173; in money—109; Top-10 finishes—12
CAREER EARNINGS: $2,875,836

NORTH, Andy

BIRTHDATE: March 9, 1950 **BIRTHPLACE:** Thorpe, WI **RESIDENCE:** Madison, WI **HEIGHT:** 6-4 **WEIGHT:** 200 **FAMILY:** Wife, Sue; Nichole (11/30/74), Andrea (8/22/78) **EDUCATION:** University of Florida (1972, B.S.) **SPECIAL INTERESTS:** All sports, gardening, snow shoeing, biking **TURNED PROFESSIONAL:** 1972 **OTHER INFORMATION:** Continues to serve as golf analyst for ESPN and on-course commentator for ABC Sports telecasts. Limited to two Champions Tour events in 2004. A two-time winner of the U.S. Open, one of 20 players with more than one Open win. First triumph came at Cherry Hills in Denver in 1978 and the second at Oakland Hills in Birmingham, MI, in 1985. Shares the PGA TOUR's nine-hole scoring record with Billy Mayfair and Mike Souchak with his 27 at the 1975 B.C. Open. Played on the 1985 U.S. Ryder Cup team and also represented the United States in the 1978 World Cup. Last PGA TOUR event was the 2000 AT&T Pebble Beach National Pro-Am. Earned a spot among the top 50 on the 2001 Champions Tour money list and secured a partial exemption for 2002. Turned in his top effort of the season in late March at the Emerald Coast Classic near Pensacola, losing a one-hole playoff to Mike McCullough. Teamed with Jim Colbert to win a second consecutive Liberty Mutual Legends of Golf title. Three-time All-America selection at Florida. Turned to golf in the seventh grade because bone in knee stopped growing and was disintegrating, causing him to give up football and basketball. Later returned to basketball, earning all-state honors. An avid follower of University of Wisconsin sports and at one time assisted the Badger football staff.
EXEMPT STATUS: Past Champion
PGA TOUR VICTORIES (3): 1977 American Express Westchester Classic. **1978** U.S. Open Championship. **1985** U.S. Open Championship.
MONEY & POSITION:

1972 —	923	— 259	1982 —	82,698	— 50	1992 —	16,360	— 218
1973 —	44,890	— 64	1983 —	52,416	— 99	1993 —	14,500	— 230
1974 —	55,455	— 43	1984 —	22,131	— 149	1994 —	3,165	— 292
1975 —	44,730	— 53	1985 —	212,268	— 24	1995 —	0	
1976 —	71,267	— 37	1986 —	41,652	— 146	1996 —	0	
1977 —	116,794	— 18	1987 —	42,876	— 163	1997 —	0	
1978 —	150,398	— 14	1988 —	10,759	— 212	1998 —	0	
1979 —	73,873	— 54	1989 —	13,620	— 204	1999 —	3,841	— 333
1980 —	55,212	— 70	1990 —	99,651	— 137	2000 —	0	
1981 —	111,401	— 30	1991 —	24,653	— 201			

PGA TOUR CAREER LOW ROUND: 63–1975 B.C. Open/1
CAREER SUMMARY: Tournaments Entered—482; in money—315; Top-10 finishes—50
CAREER EARNINGS: $1,365,530

O

OGRIN, David

FULL NAME: David Allen Ogrin **BIRTHDATE:** December 31, 1957 **BIRTHPLACE:** Waukegan, IL **RESIDENCE:** Canyon Lake, TX **HEIGHT:** 6-0 **WEIGHT:** 220 **FAMILY:** Wife, Sharon; Amy (6/20/88), Jessica (9/6/89), Dana (3/ 6/92), Clark Addison (10/18/93) **EDUCATION:** Texas A&M (1980, Economics) **SPECIAL INTERESTS:** Christianity, children, Chicago Cubs **TURNED PROFESSIONAL:** 1980 **JOINED TOUR:** 1983 **Q SCHOOL:** 1982, 1991, 1992 **OTHER INFORMATION:** Split time in 2004 playing on the PGA TOUR and Nationwide Tour. Played in only two PGA TOUR tournaments. Made the cut at the B.C. Open and finished T60. After 14 years and 405 tournaments, earned his first career title at 1996 LaCantera Texas Open. Part of six-man playoff at 1994 GTE Byron Nelson Classic, largest in TOUR history, won by Neal Lancaster. Also lost playoff to Hal Sutton in 1985 St. Jude Classic. Won unofficial 1997 Deposit Guaranty Golf Classic. Winner of 1980 Illinois Open and 1989 Chrysler Team Championship with Ted Schulz. Big Chicago Cubs fan, named his son Clark Addison after two streets that adjoin at Wrigley Field. Had childhood ambition of being a switch-hitting catcher. Given his first golf club at age 2. Met wife Sharon at 1985 Texas Open and married her at 1986 event.

EXEMPT STATUS: Past Champion

PLAYOFF RECORD: 0-2

PGA TOUR VICTORIES (1): 1996 LaCantera Texas Open.

MONEY & POSITION:

1983 —	36,003 —	121	1991 —	8,024 —	235	1999 —	141,082 —	175
1984 —	45,461 —	113	1992 —	33,971 —	193	2000 —	40,522 —	220
1985 —	76,294 —	95	1993 —	155,016 —	104	2001 —	6,030 —	248
1986 —	75,245 —	113	1994 —	199,199 —	92	2002 —	0	
1987 —	80,149 —	110	1995 —	151,419 —	123	2003 —	5,700 —	253
1988 —	138,807 —	86	1996 —	537,225 —	34	2004 —	6,420 —	259
1989 —	234,196 —	59	1997 —	593,683 —	36			
1990 —	64,190 —	167	1998 —	219,523 —	130			

BEST 2004 PGA TOUR FINISH: T60—B.C. Open.

PGA TOUR CAREER LOW ROUND: 62–1997 MasterCard Colonial/3

2004 SUMMARY: Tournaments Entered—2; in money—1; Top-10 finishes—0

CAREER SUMMARY: Tournaments Entered—499; in money—277; Top-10 finishes—32

CAREER EARNINGS: $2,848,159

Nationwide Tour Alumnus

O'HAIR, Sean

FULL NAME: Sean Marc O'Hair **BIRTHDATE:** July 11, 1982 **BIRTHPLACE:** Lubbock, TX **RESIDENCE:** Boothwyn, PA **HEIGHT:** 6-2 **WEIGHT:** 165 **FAMILY:** Wife, Jaclyn **SPECIAL INTERESTS:** Football, basketball, racing **TURNED PROFESSIONAL:** 1999 **Q SCHOOL:** 2004 **OTHER INFORMATION:** Rookie on the 2005 PGA TOUR after making it through all three stages of the 2004 Qualifying Tournament, including the final stage in his first attempt. Had been to Q-School every year since 1999. Has never played in a TOUR event but has made the cut in four of 18 career Nationwide Tour events (member in 2001) with his best finish a T28 at the 2004 First Tee Arkansas Classic. Spent time on the Cleveland Pro Tour and the Gateway Tour. Turned professional prior to graduating from high school.

EXEMPT STATUS: T4 at 2004 PGA TOUR Qualifying Tournament

Nationwide Tour Alumnus

OLAZABAL, Jose Maria (OH-lah-thah-bull)

FULL NAME: Jose Maria Olazabal **BIRTHDATE:** February 5, 1966 **BIRTHPLACE:** Fuenterrabia, Spain **RESIDENCE:** Fuenterrabia, Spain **HEIGHT:** 5-10 **WEIGHT:** 160 **FAMILY:** Single **SPECIAL INTERESTS:** Pop music, cinema, hunting, wildlife, ecology **TURNED PROFESSIONAL:** 1985 **JOINED TOUR:** 2000 **OTHER INFORMATION:** Full-time member of the PGA TOUR for the fourth season in 2004. Recorded a hole-in-one on the 13th hole in the second round of THE PLAYERS Championship with a 7-iron from 171 yards. It was the fifth ace at the 13th at THE PLAYERS Championship. Shared the 18-hole lead with Roger Tambellini at the BellSouth Classic, opening with a 7-under-par 65. Finished T45. First top-10 of the 2004 season was a T9 at the 84 LUMBER Classic, his first top-10 since a 10th at the 2003 Memorial Tournament. Made 16 starts in 2003 with his last tournament the PGA Championship in August. Finished T8 at the 2003 Masters, his second consecutive top-10 in Augusta and his seventh overall there. Finished solo 10th at the 2003 Memorial Tournament, aided by a bogey-free 6-under-par 66 in the third round, played in cold and wet conditions with winds up to 35 mph. Only round in the 60s on the day. In 2002, had a career year with seven top-10s and a victory. Captured sixth career PGA TOUR victory at the Buick Invitational, becoming the first player to win a TOUR event after being "on the cutline" (1-under-par 143) since Mike Sullivan at the 1989 Independent Insurance Agent Open. Erased a four-shot deficit with a final-round 65 to top J.L. Lewis and Mark O'Meara by one stroke, and joined Gary Player (1963) as only foreign-born champion in tournament's 50-year history. Played in the TOUR Championship for the first time in his career. First year as full-time member of the PGA TOUR came in 2001. Opened with rounds of 70-68 to trail 36-hole leader Chris DiMarco by four strokes at the Masters. Closing 71-72 dropped him to T15. In 36-hole finish, earned 19th career European Tour victory at French Open. In 2000, split time between European Tour and PGA TOUR. On European Tour, won the 2000 Benson & Hedges International Open. On PGA TOUR, missed the cut at the THE PLAYERS Championship and Masters, but rebounded later with T12 at the U.S. Open and T4 at the PGA. In 1999, completed one of the greatest triumphs over adversity when he added a second green jacket to the Masters title he won five years earlier. Finished two shots ahead of Davis Love III for an emotional victory, four years after watching the Masters from his bed due to back problem. Captured the 1998 Dubai Desert Classic. In 1997, after 18-month absence, during which he could not get out of bed, returned to European Tour at the Dubai Classic. He then won the Turespana Masters-Open de Canarias in his third tournament back. In 1997, started back therapy with Munich doctor Hans-Wilhelm Muller-Wohlfahrt and what was believed to be a foot problem was diagnosed as a back ailment. Withdrew from the 1995 Ryder Cup suffering from a foot problem, initially diagnosed as rheumatoid polyarthritis in three joints of right foot and two in left. Won the 1994 Masters by three strokes over third-round leader Tom Lehman, shooting final-round 69 to Lehman's 72. Moved into contention with third-round 69, to pull within one stroke of Lehman, who also shot 69 on Saturday. Later that season, won second NEC World Series of Golf by one over Scott Hoch — giving him his only multiple win season on PGA TOUR. Second PGA TOUR victory came at 1991 INTERNATIONAL. First victory on PGA TOUR came in record fashion at the 1990 NEC World Series of Golf. Opened with course-record 61, then added three consecutive 67s for tournament records following each round. Led Hale Irwin by eight strokes heading into final round and won by 12. Made debut in 1987 Ryder Cup at age 21. During storied Ryder Cup career, teamed with countryman Seve Ballesteros for pairing with most Ryder Cup victories (11-2-2 record). Won 1986 European Tour Qualifying School and claimed first European Tour title. As an amateur, won the British Boys, Youths and Amateur titles, the latter by beating Colin Montgomerie in the final. Born the day after a golf course opened next door (Real Golf Club de San Sebastian) where grandfather was greenskeeper. Mother and father also worked there. When grandfather died, Jose's father, Gaspar, took his place as greenskeeper. Father received a club to cut down and Jose, at age 2, used it to hit balls. Mother would take him out on golf course late in the afternoon starting at age 6. Sometimes called "Chemma," a short way to say Jose Maria in Spanish.

EXEMPT STATUS: 145th on 2004 money list

PGA TOUR VICTORIES (6): 1990 NEC World Series of Golf. **1991** The International. **1994** Masters Tournament, NEC World Series of Golf. **1999** Masters Tournament. **2002** Buick Invitational.

MONEY & POSITION:

1985 —	0		1993 —	60,160 —	174	2000 —	320,971	
1987 —	7,470 —	215	1994 —	969,900 —	7	2001 —	458,678 —	110
1989 —	56,039 —	160	1995 —	213,415 —	87	2002 —	1,987,027 —	24
1990 —	337,837 —	38	1997 —	173,589 —	126	2003 —	479,155 —	132
1991 —	382,124 —	43	1998 —	208,486 —	133	2004 —	495,050 —	142
1992 —	63,429 —	161	1999 —	865,167 —	46			

BEST 2004 PGA TOUR FINISH: T9—84 LUMBER Classic.

PGA TOUR CAREER LOW ROUND: 61–1990 NEC World Series of Golf/1

2004 SUMMARY: Tournaments Entered—17; in money—11; Top-10 finishes—1

CAREER SUMMARY: Tournaments Entered—163; in money—112; Top-10 finishes—33

CAREER EARNINGS: $7,078,495

OOSTERHUIS, Peter

FULL NAME: Peter Oosterhuis **BIRTHDATE:** May 3, 1948 **BIRTHPLACE:** London, England **RESIDENCE:** The Desert Mountain Club, Scottsdale, AZ **HEIGHT:** 6-5 **WEIGHT:** 235 **FAMILY:** Wife, Ruth Ann; two sons, Robert, Richard; two stepsons, Byron, Matt **SPECIAL INTERESTS:** Golf course architecture, dining out, bird watching **TURNED PROFESSIONAL:** 1968 **JOINED TOUR:** 1974 **OTHER INFORMATION:** In 2004, continued career as analyst for CBS Sports golf telecasts and also worked with The Golf Channel on its studio shows and live coverage of events. Joined CBS in 1998 after serving as lead analyst for The Golf Channel's coverage of the European Tour from 1995 to 1997. Amassed more than 20 victories worldwide, including a PGA TOUR victory at the 1981 Canadian Open. Competed on PGA TOUR full-time between 1975 and 1986. Participated in 314 PGA TOUR events during his career. Runner-up at the 1974 and 1982 British Opens and led the European Tour Order of Merit for four consecutive years (1971-74), a record that stood until broken by Colin Montgomerie in 1997. Played in six Ryder Cup matches for Great Britain and Europe between 1971 and 1981, sharing the European team mark for most singles victories. Member of the 1967 Walker Cup team. Between 1987 and 1993, served as Director of Golf at Forsgate CC in Jamesburg, NJ, and at Riviera CC in Pacific Palisades, CA. Son Robert, the former head professional at the TPC Four Seasons Resort at Las Colinas, site of the EDS Byron Nelson Championship, is now the Director of Golf at Four Seasons-Costa Rica's Peninsula Papagayo.

EXEMPT STATUS: Past Champion
PLAYOFF RECORD: 0-1
PGA TOUR VICTORIES (1): 1981 Canadian Open.
MONEY & POSITION:

1971 —	0		1978 —	50,480 —	66	1985 —	41,805 —	130
1972 —	1,675 —	222	1979 —	41,104 —	93	1986 —	15,364 —	188
1973 —	16,269 —	108	1980 —	30,662 —	107	1987 —	969 —	291
1974 —	21,914 —	93	1981 —	115,862 —	28	1988 —	0	
1975 —	59,936 —	34	1982 —	95,038 —	43	1989 —	0	
1976 —	41,323 —	66	1983 —	68,893 —	78			
1977 —	60,083 —	50	1984 —	74,314 —	79			

PGA TOUR CAREER LOW ROUND: 63–4 times, most recent 1986 Bob Hope Chrysler Classic/2
CAREER SUMMARY: Tournaments Entered—314; in money—234; Top-10 finishes—27
CAREER EARNINGS: $736,692

OWEN, Greg

FULL NAME: Gregory Clive Owen **BIRTHDATE:** February 19, 1972 **BIRTHPLACE:** Mansfield, Nottingham, England **RESIDENCE:** Mansfield, Nottinghamshire, England; plays out of Coxmoor GC **HEIGHT:** 6-4 **WEIGHT:** 200 **FAMILY:** Wife, Jacqui; Lauren (6/19/02) **SPECIAL INTERESTS:** Movies **TURNED PROFESSIONAL:** 1992 **OTHER INFORMATION:** Playing in his first PGA TOUR Qualifying Tournament, made it through all three stages to finish T4 and earn his initial TOUR card. The 2005 TOUR rookie has played the European Tour since 1996, where he finished in the top 40 on the Volvo Order of Merit from 2000-03. Finished 94th on the Volvo Order of Merit in 2004 with three top-10s, including a season-best seventh at the Qatar Masters. In 2003, posted his best finish in Europe at No. 21 on the Order of Merit. Picked up his first career victory on that tour with a win at The Daily Telegraph Damovo British Masters. Best finish in a major came at the 2001 British Open, where he finished T23 and posted a double eagle on the 11th hole in the third round. Won the 1996 Gosen Challenge on the European Challenge Tour. Was ranked No.1 tennis player in Nottinghamshire at age 13. Wife Jacqui was a national gymnast.

EXEMPT STATUS: T4 at 2004 PGA TOUR Qualifying Tournament
BEST PGA TOUR CAREER FINISH: T23—2001 British Open Championship.
MONEY & POSITION:

1999 —	0	2001 —	43,630	2003 —	0
2000 —	11,843	2002 —	0		

PGA TOUR CAREER LOW ROUND: 68–2001 British Open Championship/2
2004 SUMMARY: Tournaments entered—2; in money—0; Top-10 finishes—0
CAREER SUMMARY: Tournaments Entered—7; in money—2; Top-10 finishes—0
CAREER EARNINGS: $55,473

P

PAPPAS, Brenden

FULL NAME: Tyron Brenden Pappas **BIRTHDATE:** May 7, 1970 **BIRTHPLACE:** Phalaborwa, South Africa **RESIDENCE:** Ocala, FL; plays out of Golden Ocala Golf & Equestrian Club and Golden Hills Golf and Turf Club **HEIGHT:** 6-3 **WEIGHT:** 225 **FAMILY:** Wife: Berdene **EDUCATION:** University of Arkansas (1993, Retail Marketing) **SPECIAL INTERESTS:** Fishing, reading **TURNED PROFESSIONAL:** 1993 **JOINED TOUR:** 2002 **Q SCHOOL:** 2002 **OTHER INFORMATION:** Started the 2004 season by making eight straight cuts, including a T15 at the Sony Open in Hawaii, the first full-field event of the season. Two weeks later posted a T14 finish at the FBR Open. Best effort in 2004 was T12 at the Buick Open. Posted four rounds in the 60s at the 2004 Valero Texas Open and finished T22. A year after making less than $100,000, earned over $1.3 million in 2003 on the strength of five top-10s, including a second at the Southern Farm Bureau Classic and a third at the Chrysler Classic of Tucson. At Southern Farm Bureau, was 11-under for the day, 20-under for tournament, with one hole to play before settling for a 10-under 62 after a bogey on the 72nd hole. Sat as clubhouse leader (19-under) until John Huston birdied three of the final four holes for a one-stroke victory. Regained PGA TOUR for 2003 with T8th at 2002 PGA TOUR Qualifying Tournament. Rookie on the PGA TOUR in 2002. Played in 26 events and made six starts. Along with brother Deane, they became first brother combination to earn PGA TOUR cards by graduating from Nationwide Tour in 2001 via the Top 15. Began rookie year on Nationwide Tour with three top-5s in first seven starts. Finished second at 2001 Nationwide Tour Charity Pro-Am at The Cliffs, one stroke behind Jonathan Byrd. Struggled with game much of the season before a T2 at the Nationwide Tour Championship moved him from No. 23 to No. 10. Member of the Southern Africa Tour since 1994. Finished third on the Order of Merit in 1995-96. Named Rookie of the Year in 1993-94. Holds record for best front nine, 28 (8-under par), at Gary Player GC during the 1995-96 Dimension Data Pro-Am. Was the TearDrop Tour money winner in 2000 after winning the Virginia Beach Open. His other two brothers, Sean and Craigen, are also golf professionals. Gave $3,000 loan to fellow TOUR player Chris Couch in 2003 so he could keep playing on the Nationwide Tour. Couch went on to win twice and finish fourth on the money list.

EXEMPT STATUS: 137th on 2004 money list
BEST PGA TOUR CAREER FINISH: 2—2003 Southern Farm Bureau Classic.
MONEY & POSITION:

2002 —	83,519 —	206	2003 —	1,307,809 —	51	2004 —	524,905 — 137

BEST 2004 PGA TOUR FINISHES: T12—Buick Open; T14—FBR Open; T15—Sony Open in Hawaii; T21—B.C. Open; T22—Valero Texas Open; T25—The Honda Classic.
PGA TOUR CAREER LOW ROUND: 62–2003 Southern Farm Bureau Classic/4
2004 SUMMARY: Tournaments Entered—34; in money—21; Top-10 finishes—0
CAREER SUMMARY: Tournaments Entered—92; in money—46; Top-10 finishes—5
CAREER EARNINGS: $1,916,233
Nationwide Tour Alumnus

PATE, Steve

FULL NAME: Stephen Robert Pate **BIRTHDATE:** May 26, 1961 **BIRTHPLACE:** Ventura, CA **RESIDENCE:** Agoura Hills, CA; plays out of North Ranch CC (Westlake, CA) **HEIGHT:** 6-0 **WEIGHT:** 200 **FAMILY:** Wife, Sheri; Nicole (3/12/88), Sarah (10/8/90) **EDUCATION:** UCLA (1984, Psychology) **SPECIAL INTERESTS:** Fishing, reading, food **TURNED PROFESSIONAL:** 1983 **Q SCHOOL:** Fall 1984 **OTHER INFORMATION:** Finished 191st on the 2004 PGA TOUR money list after earning one top 25 in 24 starts, a T15 at the HP Classic of New Orleans. Made an appearance in 16 PGA TOUR events and six Nationwide Tour events in 2003. Playing on a Sponsor Exemption, carded four rounds in the 60s to finish T4 at the 2003 Greater Hartford Open, first top-10 since a T5 at the 2001 B.C. Open. Returned to PGA TOUR Qualifying tournament in 2003 and finished T21. Played in 21 TOUR events in 2002, with three top-25s. Held first-round lead at The 2002 INTERNATIONAL and finished 35th. David Duval's final-round 59 kept him from earning his seventh career PGA TOUR title at the 1999 Bob Hope Chrysler Classic. Finished T4 in 1999 Masters. During third-round 65, tied Augusta National record with seven consecutive birdies. Captain's Choice for 1999 U.S. Ryder Cup team. Named 1999 PGA TOUR Comeback Player of The Year. Earned first victory since 1992 Buick Invitational with one-stroke win at 1998 CVS Charity Classic. Win capped comeback from January 1996 car crash in California desert that left him with broken right hand, wrist and cheekbone. Ran into rear end of slow-moving truck while on way home from Phoenix Open. Made successful return to TOUR in 1997, following 1996 wrist injury, playing in 28 events and making cut 15 times. Ranked among top 100 on money list for first time since 1994. After fracturing right wrist in early season traffic accident in 1996, cracked bone in left wrist that August when he tripped on a dock. Won fog-curtailed 1992 Buick Invitational of California by one stroke over Chip Beck. Captured The Honda Classic en route to a career-best sixth on the money list in 1991. At 1991 Ryder Cup, played in only one match due to bruised hip suffered in traffic accident on way to team banquet. Won two events in 1988, the MONY Tournament of Champions and the Shearson Lehman Hutton-Andy Williams Open. Was 1983 PAC-10 champion and All-American at UCLA. Earned the nickname "Volcano" for his sometimes-volatile temper. Older brother John has competed in 1996 U.S. Amateur and 1996 and 2000 U.S. Mid-Amateur. Teammate of TOUR members Corey Pavin, Duffy Waldorf, Tom Pernice Jr. and Jay Delsing at UCLA.
EXEMPT STATUS: Past Champion
PLAYOFF RECORD: 0-3
PGA TOUR VICTORIES (6): 1987 Southwest Golf Classic. **1988** MONY Tournament of Champions, Shearson Lehman Hutton Andy Williams Open. **1991** Honda Classic. **1992** Buick Invitational of California. **1998** CVS Charity Classic.
MONEY & POSITION:

1985 —	89,358 —	86	1992 —	472,626 —	30	1999 —	1,755,960 —	13
1986 —	176,100 —	51	1993 —	254,841 —	64	2000 —	649,674 —	72
1987 —	335,728 —	26	1994 —	291,651 —	64	2001 —	271,967 —	151
1988 —	582,473 —	12	1995 —	89,758 —	168	2002 —	220,183 —	172
1989 —	306,554 —	35	1996 —	10,403 —	274	2003 —	192,518 —	180
1990 —	334,505 —	39	1997 —	261,436 —	95	2004 —	199,569 —	191
1991 —	727,997 —	6	1998 —	782,504 —	34			

BEST 2004 PGA TOUR FINISH: T15—HP Classic of New Orleans.
PGA TOUR CAREER LOW ROUND: 62–1989 Bob Hope Chrysler Classic/3
2004 SUMMARY: Tournaments Entered—24; in money—10; Top-10 finishes—0
CAREER SUMMARY: Tournaments Entered—533; in money—359; Top-10 finishes—67
CAREER EARNINGS: $8,005,806

PAULSON, Carl

FULL NAME: Carl Albert Paulson **BIRTHDATE:** December 29, 1970 **BIRTHPLACE:** Quantico, VA **RESIDENCE:** Orlando, FL **HEIGHT:** 5-9 **WEIGHT:** 180 **FAMILY:** Wife, Heather; Ned Maxwell (2/10/98), Robert Henry (6/7/01), Anastasia Wynn (8/10/04) **EDUCATION:** University of South Carolina (1994, Marketing) **SPECIAL INTERESTS:** Family, USC sports, fishing **TURNED PROFESSIONAL:** 1994 **Q SCHOOL:** 1994, 1995, 2004 **OTHER INFORMATION:** Regained TOUR card with T13 finish at 2004 PGA TOUR Qualifying School. With partial status in 2004, competed in 13 events with two made cuts. Best finish was T14 at John Deere Classic. Also played in 12 Nationwide Tour events. Best effort of the 2003 season came in first start of the year, a T15 finish at the Sony Open in Hawaii. Held a share of the first-round lead with J.J. Henry at Reno-Tahoe Open after a 6-under-par 66. Finished T39. Finished in the top 125 for third consecutive year on TOUR in 2002, despite missing five of six cuts down the stretch. Hospitalized in January for three days with viral meningitis and in late February, father Ned underwent triple bypass surgery. Then held solo 54-hole leader by one over eventual champion Craig Perks at 2002 PLAYERS Championship after third consecutive 69. Final-round 77 dropped him into a T4 finish. Second top-five of season came at the Greater Greensboro Chrysler Classic, where he finished T5. In honor of the Salesmanship Club, host organization for the Verizon Byron Nelson Classic, Paulson wore bright red trousers, a white golf shirt and a red cap in Sunday's final round. Salesmanship Club members wear that outfit all week each year. Had a solid 2001 season, finishing 99th in earnings to keep full exempt status on TOUR for the second consecutive season. Fired a second-round 63 at the 2001 WORLDCOM CLASSIC to highlight a T3 performance. Appeared to be in danger of losing his full exempt status as the TOUR headed into July 2000. Had earned $140,000 in first 18 starts and was 140th on the money list. However, a T9 at the Advil Western Open sparked a run in which he jumped to 64th on the TOUR money list and completed his best season on TOUR. Recorded career-high finish of second at Tampa Bay Classic. Earned fully exempt status on the 2000 PGA TOUR by finishing No. 1 on the 1999 Nationwide Tour money list with $223,051 and earning Player of the Year honors. Captured his first career victory at the 1999 Utah Classic. His five-stroke, 54-hole lead and six-stroke margin of victory were the largest on TOUR that year. After a week off, then won the Boise Open, adding another $58,500 to his earnings. Was a combined 40-under par for the two weeks. Medalist at the 1995 PGA TOUR Qualifying Tournament to re-gain card for the 1996 season. Made 14 cuts in 30 starts on PGA TOUR but finished 155th on 1996 money list. Played in 21 events, made 10 cuts and finished No. 183 on the 1995 money list. As an amateur, All-America selection and Southeastern Conference Player of the Year in 1993. Played select-level soccer until high school. Not related to TOUR member Dennis Paulson. Chronicled his first season on the PGA TOUR in the book, "Rookie on Tour."
EXEMPT STATUS: T13 at 2004 PGA TOUR Qualifying Tournament
BEST PGA TOUR CAREER FINISH: 2—2000 Tampa Bay Classic.
NATIONWIDE TOUR VICTORIES (2): 1999 Utah Classic, Boise Open.
MONEY & POSITION:

1995 —	64,501 —	183	2000 —	741,995 —	64	2003 —	365,177 —	147
1996 —	116,071 —	155	2001 —	508,208 —	99	2004 —	70,088 —	224
1999 —	0		2002 —	568,924 —	117			

BEST 2004 PGA TOUR FINISH: T14—John Deere Classic.
PGA TOUR CAREER LOW ROUND: 62–1995 Walt Disney World/Oldsmobile Classic/1
2004 SUMMARY: Tournaments Entered—13; in money—2; Top-10 finishes—0
CAREER SUMMARY: Tournaments Entered—189; in money—93; Top-10 finishes—9
CAREER EARNINGS: $2,434,965
Nationwide Tour Alumnus

POHL, Dan

FULL NAME: Danny Joe Pohl **BIRTHDATE:** April 1, 1955 **BIRTHPLACE:** Mt. Pleasant, MI **RESIDENCE:** Phoenix, AZ **HEIGHT:** 5-11 **WEIGHT:** 175 **FAMILY:** Wife, Mitzi; Michelle (2/2/78), Joshua Daniel (9/10/84), Taylor Whitney (9/10/86) **EDUCATION:** University of Arizona **SPECIAL INTERESTS:** Fishing, hunting, course design **TURNED PROFESSIONAL:** 1977 **Q SCHOOL:** Spring 1978, 1979 **OTHER INFORMATION:** Played in three TOUR events in 2004, with one made cut—T68 at the Bank of America Colonial. Also played five Nationwide Tour events, with a best finish of T19 at the Chitimacha Louisiana Open. Career has been sidetracked by numerous injuries, necessitating surgeries on back (1989), both knees (1994) and neck (1995). Despite setbacks has two TOUR victories, the 1986 Colonial Invitational and NEC World Series of Golf. Finished fifth on TOUR money list in 1986, with $463,630. Winner of the 1987 Vardon Trophy and Epson Stats All-Around title. Member of U.S. Ryder Cup squad in 1987. Led the PGA TOUR in Driving Distance in 1980-81. Lost playoff to Craig Stadler in 1982 Masters. Michigan State Amateur champion in 1975 and 1977. Named to the Michigan Golf Hall of Fame in May 2004. Has been involved in course design work, including the PohlCat Golf Course in Mt. Pleasant, MI.

EXEMPT STATUS: Past Champion

PLAYOFF RECORD: 1-2

PGA TOUR VICTORIES (2): 1986 Colonial National Invitation, NEC World Series of Golf.

MONEY & POSITION:

1978 —	1,047 —	237	1987 —	465,269 —	17	1997 —	12,047 —	260
1979 —	38,393 —	99	1988 —	396,400 —	27	1998 —	11,523 —	266
1980 —	105,008 —	44	1989 —	195,789 —	74	1999 —	15,008 —	266
1981 —	94,303 —	42	1991 —	163,438 —	95	2000 —	28,776 —	225
1982 —	97,213 —	40	1992 —	131,486 —	110	2001 —	0	
1983 —	89,830 —	62	1993 —	97,830 —	146	2002 —	24,570 —	226
1984 —	182,653 —	32	1994 —	21,734 —	221	2003 —	0	
1985 —	198,829 —	27	1995 —	166,219 —	117	2004 —	10,706 —	252
1986 —	463,630 —	5	1996 —	100,562 —	162			

BEST 2004 PGA TOUR FINISH: T68—Bank of America Colonial.

PGA TOUR CAREER LOW ROUND: 62–1989 Honda Classic/2

2004 SUMMARY: Tournaments Entered—3; in money—1; Top-10 finishes—0

CAREER SUMMARY: Tournaments Entered—424; in money—301; Top-10 finishes—70

CAREER EARNINGS: $3,112,263

Nationwide Tour Alumnus

POINTS, D.A.

FULL NAME: Darren Andrew Points **BIRTHDATE:** December 1, 1976 **BIRTHPLACE:** Pekin, IL **RESIDENCE:** Orlando, FL **HEIGHT:** 6-1 **WEIGHT:** 195 **FAMILY:** Single **EDUCATION:** University of Illinois (1999, Speech Communications) **SPECIAL INTERESTS:** Basketball, fishing, cars **TURNED PROFESSIONAL:** 1999 **JOINED TOUR:** 2005 **OTHER INFORMATION:** Rookie on PGA TOUR after finishing second on the 2004 Nationwide Tour money list with $332,815. Spent 2001-04 on that circuit. Posted his first Tour victory at the 2004 Northeast Pennsylvania Classic. Finished the tournament tied with James Driscoll at 14-under and then parred the first extra hole for the victory. A Glen Club course record 10-under 62 in the second round at the LaSalle Bank Open helped lead him to a runner-up finish the week prior to his win in Pennsylvania. The two strong showings helped earn June Player of the Month honors. Came back just a few weeks later and won the inaugural Pete Dye West Virginia Classic. His six-stroke lead after 36 and 54 holes marked the largest of the season in both categories on Tour. Led Tour in Birdie Average, finished third in All-Around Ranking and eighth in Putting Average. Finished No. 50 on the 2003 Nationwide Tour money list, with $95,614. Ended 2002 Nationwide Tour No. 66 on the money list, with $68,341. Had seven top-25 finishes and one top-10. Matched the Whirlwind GC record with a 10-under-par 61 in third round at Gila River. Finished T42 at the 2001 PGA TOUR Qualifying Tournament, missing his TOUR card by just two strokes. In rookie season on Nationwide Tour, won the Inland Empire Open. Ranked No. 30 on the final 2001 money list, with $126,366. Third-team All-America at Illinois. Three-time Illinois Amateur champion. Reached the quarterfinals of the 1996 U.S. Amateur at Pumpkin Ridge GC, where he lost to eventual champion Tiger Woods, 3 and 2, in the quarterfinals.

EXEMPT STATUS: Second on 2004 Nationwide Tour money list

NATIONWIDE TOUR VICTORIES (3): 2001 Inland Empire Open. **2004** Northeast Pennsylvania Classic, Pete Dye West Virginia Classic Presented by National Mining Assn..

MONEY & POSITION:

2004 — 0

PGA TOUR CAREER LOW ROUND: 70–2004 John Deere Classic/2

2004 SUMMARY: Tournaments Entered—2; in money—0; Top-10 finishes—0

CAREER SUMMARY: Tournaments Entered—2; in money—0; Top-10 finishes—0

Nationwide Tour Alumnus

PRICE, Philip

FULL NAME: John Phillip Price **BIRTHDATE:** October 21, 1966 **BIRTHPLACE:** Pontypridd, Wales **RESIDENCE:** Newport, Wales **HEIGHT:** 5-11 **WEIGHT:** 182 **FAMILY:** Wife, Sandra; John Edward (2000) **SPECIAL INTERESTS:** Rugby League - Leeds **TURNED PROFESSIONAL:** 1989 **Q SCHOOL:** 2004 **OTHER INFORMATION:** Rookie on 2005 PGA TOUR after making it through stage two and the final stage of the 2004 Qualifying Tournament, where he finished T13. Member of the European Tour 1991-2004. Finished 45th on 2004 Volvo Order of Merit, the eighth consecutive season he has been in the top 50 on their list. Best finish in 12 TOUR starts in 2004 was a T17 at the AT&T Pebble Beach National Pro-Am. T10 at the 2003 British Open and won the Smurfit European Open. Birdied the final hole at the K Club to capture his third European Tour title. Achieved his life-long ambition in September 2002 when he qualified in 10th place for The 34th Ryder Cup Matches. Beat Phil Mickelson 3 and 2 in singles. Earlier in the season won the Algarve Open de Portugal for a second time to help underline his credentials. Three years earlier, made a conscious decision to shed the 'journeyman' tag which followed him around during a decade on Tour, finishing 15th on the Volvo Order of Merit that year, 36th in 1999 and a career-best eighth in 2000. Created a big impact in 2000, finishing runner-up on four occasions, most notably in the WGC-NEC Invitational with a T2 behind Tiger Woods to collect the biggest check of his career. Credits his stronger mental approach to his 10-year association with psychologist Alan Fine, who lives in America and flew to Akron to lend his assistance during the WGC-NEC International event. Leading amateur for Wales, won Portuguese Open in 1994 and named 'Pontypridd Man of the Year'. Partnered with Ian Woosnam to second place in the 1991 World Cup.

EXEMPT STATUS: T13 at 2004 PGA TOUR Qualifying Tournament

BEST PGA TOUR CAREER FINISH: T2—2000 WGC-NEC Invitational.

MONEY & POSITION:

1998 —	0	2001 —	41,406	2004 —	150,749
1999 —	19,815 — 259	2002 —	54,133		
2000 —	0	2003 —	225,926		

BEST 2004 PGA TOUR FINISH: T17—AT&T Pebble Beach National Pro-Am.

PGA TOUR CAREER LOW ROUND: 65–2002 Bob Hope Chrysler Classic/1

2004 SUMMARY: Tournaments Entered—12; in money—7; Top-10 finishes—0

CAREER SUMMARY: Tournaments Entered—41; in money—25; Top-10 finishes—2

CAREER EARNINGS: $492,029

PRIDE, Dicky

FULL NAME: Richard Fletcher Pride III **BIRTHDATE:** July 15, 1969 **BIRTHPLACE:** Tuscaloosa, AL **RESIDENCE:** Orlando, FL **HEIGHT:** 6-0 **WEIGHT:** 175 **FAMILY:** Wife, Kim; Isabelle (10/12/99), Fletcher (10/2/01) **EDUCATION:** University of Alabama **SPECIAL INTERESTS:** Basketball, reading, University of Alabama football **TURNED PROFESSIONAL:** 1992 **Q SCHOOL:** 1993, 1997, 1998, 2000 **OTHER INFORMATION:** Finished 184th on 2004 PGA TOUR money list. Only top-10 of the season came in October, a T5 at the Michelin Championship at Las Vegas. Trailed Tom Lehman by one stroke after 54 holes and finished two strokes behind winner Andre Stolz after bogeying the 72nd hole. It was his best finish on TOUR since a fifth at the 1999 Motorola Western Open. In 2003, split time between the PGA TOUR and Nationwide Tour. Made 14 cuts on the PGA TOUR and finished in the top 20 six times. Earned a career-best $483,923 in a single season. Missed four months of the 2002 season due to an attack of gallstones and pancreatitis. Had to be fed through a tube for 2 months and had his gall bladder removed. After T25 finish at the Touchstone Energy Tucson Open in late February, did not play again until late June at the Canon Greater Hartford Open. Played in 27 events in 2001 and posted one top-10 in the last full-field events of the season, a T6 at Southern Farm Bureau Classic. Began the week at No. 190 on the PGA TOUR Money List and a $72,600 payday moved him the No. 170. Won 1994 Federal Express St. Jude Classic in rookie season. A 20-foot putt on 72nd hole earned spot in playoff with Hal Sutton and Gene Sauers. Holed 25-foot birdie putt on first extra hole to win. First top-10 finish of PGA TOUR career came at 1994 Deposit Guaranty Golf Classic two weeks earlier, a T8. Early in 1994, rescheduled his wedding day so it wouldn't conflict with PGA TOUR Qualifying Tournament. That year's victory at Federal Express St. Jude Classic made qualifying unnecessary. Later that season won a Buick for soon-to-be wife Kim with a hole-in-one at Buick Challenge. Despite not playing golf as a freshman at Alabama, and not seeing any action as a sophomore walk-on, still was twice named All-Southeastern Conference at Alabama. Semifinalist in 1991 U.S. Amateur.

EXEMPT STATUS: Past Champion

PLAYOFF RECORD: 1-0

PGA TOUR VICTORIES (1): 1994 Federal Express St. Jude Classic.

MONEY & POSITION:

1992 —	0		1997 —	45,830 —	207	2001 —	206,022 —	170
1994 —	305,769 —	57	1998 —	27,680 —	234	2002 —	142,556 —	190
1995 —	97,712 —	161	1999 —	381,040 —	109	2003 —	483,923 —	127
1996 —	167,852 —	125	2000 —	233,720 —	153	2004 —	230,329 —	184

BEST 2004 PGA TOUR FINISH: T5—Michelin Championship at Las Vegas.

PGA TOUR CAREER LOW ROUND: 64–2 times, most recent 2001 Bell Canadian Open/2

2004 SUMMARY: Tournaments Entered—23; in money—10; Top-10 finishes—1

CAREER SUMMARY: Tournaments Entered—297; in money—122; Top-10 finishes—11

CAREER EARNINGS: $2,322,431

R

RASHELL, Rob

FULL NAME: Robert Wayne Rashell **BIRTHDATE:** December 30, 1975 **BIRTHPLACE:** Richland, WA **RESIDENCE:** Scottsdale, AZ **HEIGHT:** 6-0 **WEIGHT:** 190 **FAMILY:** Single **EDUCATION:** University of Washington (1999, Business/Marketing) **SPECIAL INTERESTS:** Movies, Food, Business **TURNED PROFESSIONAL:** 1999 **Q SCHOOL:** 2004 **OTHER INFORMATION:** Rookie on the 2005 PGA TOUR after making it through all three stages of the 2004 Qualifying Tournament, including his first time at final stage. Finished second, one stroke behind Brian Davis. Has never played in a TOUR event and missed the cut in his only event on the Nationwide Tour, the 2001 Utah Classic. Spent the 2004 season as a rookie on the European Tour after making it through their qualifying tournament in 2003. Ended season 113th on the Volvo Order of Merit with his only two top-10s coming in his first two starts, a T10 at the Omega Hong Kong Open and a T2 at the Madeira Island Open. Had never been to Europe prior to heading to Germany in Fall 2003 for first stage of qualifying tournament. Second-team All Pac-10 in 1998 and '99. Won the 1997 Washington State Amateur.

EXEMPT STATUS: Second at PGA TOUR Qualifying Tournament

RUMMELLS, Dave

FULL NAME: David Lawrence Rummells **BIRTHDATE:** January 26, 1958 **BIRTHPLACE:** Cedar Rapids, IA **RESIDENCE:** Kissimmee, FL; plays out of St. Cloud GC **HEIGHT:** 6-0 **WEIGHT:** 165 **FAMILY:** Wife, Ira; Melissa (12/23/88), Eric (7/1/90) **EDUCATION:** University of Iowa (1981) **SPECIAL INTERESTS:** Fishing, bowling, basketball **TURNED PROFESSIONAL:** 1981 **Q SCHOOL:** 1985, 1990, 1992 **OTHER INFORMATION:** Made five cuts in 15 starts on the 2004 Nationwide Tour and missed cut in only PGA TOUR start at the B.C. Open. In addition to playing seven events on the PGA TOUR in 2003, made 10 starts on the Nationwide Tour. Played in four PGA TOUR events in 2002, making two cuts, including a T29 at the Valero Texas Open, his best finish since a T21 at the 1997 Greater Vancouver Open. Made the cut at the 2002 B.C. Open, his first made cut on PGA TOUR since the 1998 Westin Texas Open. Captured second title on the Nationwide Tour at 1997 Knoxville Open. Earned return trip to PGA TOUR in 1997 by virtue of sixth-place finish on 1996 Nationwide Tour money list. Won 1996 South Carolina Classic for first professional victory. Earned $108,000, largest paycheck of career, for second-place finish at 1993 Buick Invitational of California. Has carded four 61s in PGA TOUR events.

EXEMPT STATUS: Veteran Member
BEST PGA TOUR CAREER FINISH: 2—1993 Buick Invitational of California.
NATIONWIDE TOUR VICTORIES (2): 1996 South Carolina Classic. **1997** Knoxville Open.
MONEY & POSITION:

1986 —	83,227 —	103	1993 —	247,963 —	67	2000 —	0	
1987 —	154,720 —	67	1994 —	122,872 —	138	2001 —	0	
1988 —	274,800 —	38	1995 —	26,095 —	232	2002 —	27,349 —	225
1989 —	419,979 —	24	1996 —	3,045 —	343	2003 —	14,280 —	246
1990 —	111,539 —	131	1997 —	90,345 —	172	2004 —	0	
1991 —	213,627 —	79	1998 —	18,746 —	247			
1992 —	95,203 —	134	1999 —	0				

BEST 2004 PGA TOUR FINISH: T42—Bell Canadian Open.
PGA TOUR CAREER LOW ROUND: 61–2 times, most recent 1991 Chattanooga Classic/4
2004 SUMMARY: Tournaments Entered—1; in money—0; Top-10 finishes—0
CAREER SUMMARY: Tournaments Entered—334; in money—194; Top-10 finishes—23
CAREER EARNINGS: $1,903,790
Nationwide Tour Alumnus

S

SAUERS, Gene

FULL NAME: Gene Sauers **BIRTHDATE:** August 22, 1962 **BIRTHPLACE:** Savannah, GA **RESIDENCE:** Savannah, GA **HEIGHT:** 5-8 **WEIGHT:** 150 **FAMILY:** Wife, Tammy; Gene Jr. (1/23/89), Rhett (7/16/90), Dylan Thomas (8/30/93) **EDUCATION:** Georgia Southern University **SPECIAL INTERESTS:** Snow skiing, hunting, sport fishing **TURNED PROFESSIONAL:** 1983 **Q SCHOOL:** 1983 **OTHER INFORMATION:** Finished 170th on 2004 PGA TOUR money list after earning just one top 10 in 30 starts, a T5 at the Ford Championship at Doral. His third-round, 8-under-par 64 marked the best round for him on the PGA TOUR since a 64 in the opening round of the 1997 LaCantera Texas Open. Finished 159th on 2003 money list. One top-10 in 30 starts, a T10 at season-opening Mercedes Championships. Voted 2002 PGA TOUR Comeback Player of the Year. Jumped into top 100 in earnings for first time since 1995, thanks to a victory at Air Canada Championship after more than 13 years without a TOUR win. In only his fourth TOUR appearance of year, earned third career TOUR victory. Held one-stroke lead after 54 holes over Robert Allenby and Peter Lonard, and recorded a bogey-free round on Sunday to stave off runner-up Steve Lowery by one shot. First-place check of $630,000 was the largest paycheck of his career, and topped his previous PGA TOUR season-best of $374,485 in 1990. Span between 1989 Hawaiian Open victory and 2002 Air Canada title was 245 events, and the time between victories was 13 years, six months and 20 days, the fifth-longest in PGA TOUR history. Made 10 of 11 cuts on Nationwide Tour prior to Air Canada victory. Split time between the PGA TOUR and Nationwide Tour from 1998 to 2002. Earned his first Nationwide Tour win at the 1998 South Carolina Classic, becoming the first former PGA TOUR champion to win a Nationwide Tour event since Mark Carnevale won the 1997 Inland Empire Open. Finished a career-best 21st on Nationwide Tour money list that season. T2 at 1994 FedEx St. Jude Classic with Hal Sutton, falling in playoff to Dicky Pride. In 1993, for the first time in 10th year on TOUR, failed to increase money-won total over previous season. Held share of out outright lead first three rounds of 1992 PGA but finished T2. Finished second to Fred Couples at Nestle Invitational. Lost three-hole playoff to Mark Brooks at 1991 Kmart Greater Greensboro Open. Won unofficial 1990 Deposit Guaranty Golf Classic. Won the rain-shortened 1989 Hawaiian Open with rounds of 67-65-67. Recorded playoff victory over Blaine McCallister at 1986 Bank of Boston Classic. In 1984, was youngest player on TOUR out of PGA TOUR Qualifying School. Avid sport fisherman who has won a number of fishing tournaments. Youngest son, Dylan Thomas, is not named for Irish poet. Started the game at age 9 when he would tag along with father (who played at Columbus, GA, College) to the golf course on the weekends.

EXEMPT STATUS: Past Champion
PLAYOFF RECORD: 1-3
PGA TOUR VICTORIES (3): 1986 Bank of Boston Classic. **1989** Hawaiian Open. **2002** Air Canada Championship.
NATIONWIDE TOUR VICTORIES (1): 1998 South Carolina Classic.
MONEY & POSITION:

1984 —	36,537 —	128	1991 —	400,535 —	37	1998 —	47,917 —	206
1985 —	48,526 —	121	1992 —	434,566 —	32	1999 —	9,720 —	292
1986 —	199,044 —	42	1993 —	117,608 —	128	2000 —	28,217 —	226
1987 —	244,655 —	38	1994 —	250,654 —	73	2001 —	8,400 —	243
1988 —	280,719 —	35	1995 —	311,578 —	60	2002 —	715,605 —	99
1989 —	303,669 —	38	1996 —	123,904 —	148	2003 —	278,644 —	159
1990 —	374,485 —	31	1997 —	116,445 —	157	2004 —	287,151 —	170

BEST 2004 PGA TOUR FINISH: T5—Ford Championship at Doral.
PGA TOUR CAREER LOW ROUND: 62–2 times, most recent 1990 Southwestern Bell Colonial/4
2004 SUMMARY: Tournaments Entered—30; in money—10; Top-10 finishes—1
CAREER SUMMARY: Tournaments Entered—456; in money—287; Top-10 finishes—46
CAREER EARNINGS: $4,618,578
Nationwide Tour Alumnus

SCHERRER, Tom

FULL NAME: Thomas Cregg Scherrer **BIRTHDATE:** July 20, 1970 **BIRTHPLACE:** Skaneateles, NY **RESIDENCE:** Raleigh, NC **HEIGHT:** 6-0 **WEIGHT:** 210 **FAMILY:** Wife, Jennifer; Thomas William (7/14/99), Cregg James (6/18/01) **EDUCATION:** University of North Carolina **SPECIAL INTERESTS:** Family, reading **TURNED PROFESSIONAL:** 1992 **JOINED TOUR:** 1996 **OTHER INFORMATION:** Member of the PGA TOUR in 1996 and 1999-2003 and the Nationwide Tour 1994-95, 1997-98 and 2004. Made one start on the PGA TOUR in 2004 as a past champion at the Booz Allen Classic. Made the cut in 15 of 26 tournaments on the 2004 Nationwide Tour, including seven top-25s. Ranked No. 43 on the final money list, with $137,738. Opened the season with a runner-up finish at the BellSouth Panama Championship. At 2-under-par 278, was one of just three players to finish the event below par. Split time between the PGA TOUR and the Nationwide Tour in 2003. Entered 16 tournaments on the PGA TOUR and recorded two top-25s. Played in 10 Nationwide Tour events and finished T10 at the 2003 Lake Erie Charity Classic. Recorded only top-10 of the 2002 season in late August at the Air Canada Championship. Final-round 65 moved him up the leaderboard for a solo sixth. It was his best effort since a solo fourth at the 1999 Michelob Championship at Kingsmill. Began the 2001 season on a strong note, earning $76,500 combined in first two starts at WGC-Accenture Match Play Championship and Mercedes Championships. Made Masters debut after turning down invitation in 1993 as runner-up in 1992 U.S. Amateur. Turned professional then and joined the Nationwide Tour. Finished 25th at Augusta National in 2001. Earned his first PGA TOUR title in his 84th career start at the 2000 Kemper Insurance Open, where he defeated five players by two strokes. Only player to shoot sub-70 rounds each day and his 67-68-69-67—271 effort earned $540,000. Became ninth player to win first TOUR title at Kemper Insurance Open. Recorded a career-high four top-10s in 2000. Started 1999 season by making the cut in 12 of his first 15 events. As a member of 1998 Nationwide Tour, captured the Upstate Classic and finished 14th on money list to earn PGA TOUR card for 1999. Rookie on the PGA TOUR in 1996. Finished sixth on 1995 Nationwide Tour money list. Set Nationwide Tour record in 1995 by appearing in playoffs in three consecutive weeks. Won one of those playoffs at the Knoxville Open. Winner of 1990 North and South Amateur Championship. Runner-up to Justin Leonard in 1992 U.S. Amateur. Member of 1991 Walker Cup team. Captain of hockey team that won state high school championship in New York. Born in Syracuse, but hails from Skaneateles, NY.

EXEMPT STATUS: Past Champion
PGA TOUR VICTORIES (1): 2000 Kemper Insurance Open.
NATIONWIDE TOUR VICTORIES (2): 1995 Knoxville Open. **1998** Upstate Classic.
MONEY & POSITION:

1992	0		1999	427,849	92	2002	356,657	150
1996	136,323	141	2000	1,263,585	35	2003	122,431	198
1997	6,372	292	2001	212,091	167	2004	0	

PGA TOUR CAREER LOW ROUND: 63–1999 Canon Greater Hartford Open/1
2004 SUMMARY: Tournaments Entered—1; in money—0; Top-10 finishes—0
CAREER SUMMARY: Tournaments Entered—179; in money—84; Top-10 finishes—8
CAREER EARNINGS: $2,525,306
Nationwide Tour Alumnus

SHORT Jr., Wes

FULL NAME: Wesley Earl Short, Jr. **BIRTHDATE:** December 4, 1963 **BIRTHPLACE:** Austin, TX **RESIDENCE:** Austin, TX; plays out of The Hills of Lakeway **HEIGHT:** 6-0 **WEIGHT:** 190 **FAMILY:** Wife, Gail; Elizabeth Ann (11/25/83) **EDUCATION:** University of Texas **SPECIAL INTERESTS:** All sports **TURNED PROFESSIONAL:** 1987 **JOINED TOUR:** 2004 **Q SCHOOL:** 2003 **OTHER INFORMATION:** Rookie season on TOUR was limited to 12 events due to back injury. Best finish was T24 at the Buick Open. Will receive a Major Medical Extension for 2005. Coupled with $75,536 earned in 17 events in 2004 has the opportunity to play in 12 events to earn $547,726 and match the $623,262 winnings of 2004's No. 125, Tag Ridings. If he does so, will play out of the Major Medical Extension category for the remainder of the season. Finished T7 at PGA TOUR Qualifying Tournament to earn rookie PGA TOUR card. Member of the Nationwide Tour in 1998 and 2002-03. Made the cut in 17 of 28 events on the 2003 Nationwide Tour, with seven top-10s. Wrapped up the season No. 30 on the money list, with $146,997. Best finish was a runner-up at The Reese's Cup Classic. Finished No. 65 on the 2002 Nationwide Tour money list. Two top-10s, including a career-best T4 at the Louisiana Open. Lists Ben Hogan and Byron Nelson as his heroes. Cites his father as giving him his start in golf.

EXEMPT STATUS: Major Medical Extension
BEST PGA TOUR CAREER FINISH: T24—2004 Buick Open.
MONEY & POSITION:

2002	0		2004	75,536	222

BEST 2004 PGA TOUR FINISH: T24—Buick Open.
PGA TOUR CAREER LOW ROUND: 66–2004 U.S. Bank Championship in Milwaukee/1
2004 SUMMARY: Tournaments Entered—12; in money—4; Top-10 finishes—0
CAREER SUMMARY: Tournaments Entered—13; in money—4; Top-10 finishes—0
CAREER EARNINGS: $75,536
Nationwide Tour Alumnus

SIMPSON, Scott

FULL NAME: Scott William Simpson **BIRTHDATE:** September 17, 1955 **BIRTHPLACE:** San Diego, CA **RESIDENCE:** San Diego, CA **HEIGHT:** 6-2 **WEIGHT:** 205 **FAMILY:** Wife, Cheryl; Brea Yoshiko (10/10/82), Sean Tokuzo (10/14/86) **EDUCATION:** University of Southern California (1978, Business Administration) **SPECIAL INTERESTS:** Bible study, family activities, exercise, reading **TURNED PROFESSIONAL:** 1977 **JOINED TOUR:** 1979 **Q SCHOOL:** Fall 1978 **OTHER INFORMATION:** Past U.S. Open champion, who is eligible to join the Champions Tour in late 2005, competed in 18 TOUR events in 2004, with nine made cuts. T10 finish at Valero Texas Open was first top-10 since T2 at 2001 Greater Greensboro Chrysler Open. Finished outside top 125 in four of the last five seasons. In 2001, returned from broken ankle that sidelined him for all of 2000. Received a major medical exemption and had 29 tournaments to regain exempt status. Started season slowly with five missed cuts in first six starts. Held first-round lead after opening 66, stood one stroke back after 36 holes and two after 54 holes at Greater Greensboro Chrysler Classic. Finished T2 for first top-10 since T7 at 1999 Buick Invitational and his only one of the season. Earned $308,000 for the T2 finish or $200,000 more than he received for his Greensboro victory in 1987. Unable to play the PGA TOUR in 2000 due to broken ankle he suffered while skiing at the end of 1999. Prognosis was ankle could heal without surgery but did not and he underwent surgery in August, which involved inserting seven screws into the ankle and left him on crutches for two months. Most recent victory came in 1998 Buick Invitational. Posted final-round 64, then spent the next couple hours watching his 12-under-par 204 total stand up. Skip Kendall birdied the final hole of regulation to force playoff, but Scott won with birdie on first extra hole. Came from eight strokes back entering final round, at the time matching PGA TOUR best comeback since 1970. Victory came with former San Diego Chargers quarterback Stan Humphries on his bag. Also became third San Diego native to win Buick Invitational in six years (Phil Mickelson 1993, 2000, '01 and Craig Stadler 1994) and fifth overall (Gene Littler 1954 and Billy Casper 1966). Fell out of top 125 in 1997 for first time in his career. Made 16 of 25 cuts and finished in top-25 once. Chose to use one-time top-50 career money list ranking exemption to play in 1998. Impressive 1996 West Coast swing included T2 at Nissan Open, T3 Buick Invitational, T4 United Airlines Hawaiian Open and T6 at Phoenix Open. Named PGA TOUR Player of the Month for February, first to receive award without victory during that span. Earned more money in 1995 than in any other season on the heels of three runners-up paychecks: T2 at Northern Telecom Open, T2 at Motorola Western Open and second at Anheuser-Busch Golf Classic. Recorded a one-stroke victory over Corey Pavin, Billy Mayfair and D.A. Weibring at the 1993 GTE Byron Nelson Classic. Lost 18-hole playoff to Payne Stewart in 1991 U.S. Open at Hazeltine National. Defeated Bob Tway in playoff to win 1989 BellSouth Atlanta Classic. At 1987 U.S. Open, trailed Tom Watson by one stroke heading into final round at The Olympic Club, but closing 68, which included three birdies on back nine, good for one-stroke victory. Also won Greater Greensboro Open that year on way to fourth-place finish on money list. Final-round 65 gave him a five-stroke victory at the 1984 Manufacturers Hanover Westchester Classic. First TOUR victory came at 1980 Western Open, by five strokes over Andy Bean. NCAA Champion and All-American at University of Southern California in 1976 and 1977. Spends a great deal of time with family during season. Has served for 12 years as host of Scott Simpson HBIC Pro-Am in Los Angeles, which benefits Help for Brain-Injured Children. Partnered with actor Bill Murray every year at the AT&T Pebble Beach National Pro-Am.

EXEMPT STATUS: Past Champion
PLAYOFF RECORD: 2-3
PGA TOUR VICTORIES (7): 1980 Western Open. **1984** Manufacturers Hanover Westchester Classic. **1987** Greater Greensboro Open, U.S. Open Championship. **1989** BellSouth Atlanta Golf Classic. **1993** GTE Byron Nelson Golf Classic. **1998** Buick Invitational.
MONEY & POSITION:

1976	0		1986	202,223	41	1995	795,798	17
1978	3,100	189	1987	621,032	4	1996	309,648	68
1979	53,084	74	1988	108,301	106	1997	128,448	149
1980	141,323	24	1989	298,920	40	1998	449,777	64
1981	108,793	34	1990	235,309	63	1999	179,006	164
1982	146,903	24	1991	322,936	51	2001	512,530	96
1983	144,172	38	1992	155,284	97	2002	122,115	195
1984	248,581	22	1993	707,166	14	2003	78,153	217
1985	171,245	39	1994	307,884	56	2004	190,986	192

BEST 2004 PGA TOUR FINISH: T10—Valero Texas Open.
PGA TOUR CAREER LOW ROUND: 62–1991 United Hawaiian Open/1
2004 SUMMARY: Tournaments Entered—18; in money—9; Top-10 finishes—1
CAREER SUMMARY: Tournaments Entered—588; in money—400; Top-10 finishes—77
CAREER EARNINGS: $6,742,717

SNYDER, Joey III

FULL NAME: Joseph Andrew Snyder III **BIRTHDATE:** June 7, 1973 **BIRTHPLACE:** Springville, NY **RESIDENCE:** Scottsdale, AZ; plays out of Grayhawk **HEIGHT:** 6-2 **WEIGHT:** 225 **EDUCATION:** Arizona State University (1996, Business Management) **SPECIAL INTERESTS:** Fishing, outdoor activities **TURNED PROFESSIONAL:** 1996 **Q SCHOOL:** 2004 **OTHER INFORMATION:** Rookie on the 2005 PGA TOUR after making it through all three stages of the 2004 Qualifying Tournament, where he finished T13 in the final stage. Has attended Q-school every year since 1996, making it to finals in 1997 and 2004. Member of Nationwide TOUR in 1998-99, where he finished in the top 100 on the money list both years at No. 47 and 95, respectively. Posted two thirds in 1998, at the Carolina Classic and the Greensboro Open, his best finishes on that Tour. Played in just one PGA TOUR event, the 1996 LaCantera Texas Open, where he missed the cut. Played the Gateway Tour in 2002-04 and finished fifth in the 2004 Desert Series money list. Played Canadian Tour in 2000-01 and Asian Tour in 1997.

EXEMPT STATUS: T13 at 2004 PGA TOUR Qualifying Tournament

MONEY & POSITION:

1996 — 0

PGA TOUR CAREER LOW ROUND: 72–1996 LaCantera Texas Open/1

CAREER SUMMARY: Tournaments Entered—1; in money—0; Top-10 finishes—0

Nationwide Tour Alumnus

SPRINGER, Mike

FULL NAME: Michael Paul Springer **BIRTHDATE:** November 3, 1965 **BIRTHPLACE:** San Francisco, CA **RESIDENCE:** Fresno, CA **HEIGHT:** 5-11 **WEIGHT:** 210 **FAMILY:** Wife, Crystol; Haylee Danielle (5/26/93), Cody Michael (8/24/95), Mackenzie Brielle (5/11/01) **EDUCATION:** University of Arizona **SPECIAL INTERESTS:** Hunting, skiing **TURNED PROFESSIONAL:** 1988 **JOINED TOUR:** 1991 **Q SCHOOL:** 1999 **OTHER INFORMATION:** Split time between the PGA TOUR and Nationwide Tour for the fourth consecutive season in 2004. Posted three top-10s and finished No. 75 on the Nationwide Tour money list. Among his three top-10s was a T7 at the Chitimacha Louisiana Open, marking his first Top-10 finish in a PGA TOUR co-sponsored event since a T8 at the 1999 Greater Hartford Open. Had a season-best third-place showing at the LaSalle Bank Open. Tied his career low round with an opening-round 63 on the way to T8 at the 1999 Canon Greater Hartford Open, his most recent top-10 on the PGA TOUR. Wire-to-wire winner of the 1994 Kmart Greater Greensboro Open. Opened with an 8-under-par 64, held a four-stroke lead after the second and third rounds and won by three over Brad Bryant and Ed Humenik. Other career victory came later that year at the Greater Milwaukee Open, when he overcame a three-stroke deficit on the final day with a 5-under 67 to edge Loren Roberts by one shot. Finished 13th on the money list with $770,717. Has 22 career top-10s. Four-time winner on the Nationwide Tour. Won the first event contested on the Ben Hogan Tour, the 1990 Bakersfield Open.

EXEMPT STATUS: Past Champion

PGA TOUR VICTORIES (2): 1994 KMart Greater Greensboro Open, Greater Milwaukee Open.

NATIONWIDE TOUR VICTORIES (4): 1990 Bakersfield Open, Reno Open, El Paso Open. **1992** Fresno Open.

MONEY & POSITION:

1988 —	0		1995 —	55,146 —	198	2000 —	182,726 —	168
1991 —	178,587 —	91	1996 —	164,666 —	128	2001 —	81,141 —	202
1992 —	144,316 —	104	1997 —	191,422 —	119	2002 —	59,193 —	213
1993 —	214,729 —	79	1998 —	230,795 —	124	2003 —	53,453 —	229
1994 —	770,717 —	13	1999 —	165,675 —	168	2004 —	44,616 —	232

BEST 2004 PGA TOUR FINISHE: T35—Chrysler Classic of Greensboro.

PGA TOUR CAREER LOW ROUND: 63–3 times, most recent 1999 Canon Greater Hartford Open/1

2004 SUMMARY: Tournaments Entered—10; in money—4; Top-10 finishes—0

CAREER SUMMARY: Tournaments Entered—331; in money—154; Top-10 finishes—22

CAREER EARNINGS: $2,537,182

Nationwide Tour Alumnus

STADLER, Kevin

FULL NAME: Kevin Stadler **BIRTHDATE:** February 5, 1980 **BIRTHPLACE:** Reno, NV **RESIDENCE:** Scottsdale, AZ **HEIGHT:** 5-10 **WEIGHT:** 250 **FAMILY:** Single **EDUCATION:** University of Southern California (2002) **SPECIAL INTERESTS:** Hockey, Football, All Sports, Reading **TURNED PROFESSIONAL:** 2002 **JOINED TOUR:** 2005 **OTHER INFORMATION:** Rookie on the PGA TOUR after finishing 13th on the Nationwide Tour money list in his first season on that circuit. Made the cut in 11 of 13 tournament appearances on the 2004 Nationwide Tour, including six top-25 finishes. Won his first start of the season with a 9-under 279 at the Lake Erie Charity Classic, outlasting Bubba Watson and Michael Long in a four-hole playoff. His 2-over 74 was the highest final round by a winner all season. His father, Craig, won the Champions Tour's Bank of America Championship in Massachusetts just minutes earlier, making the father-son duo the first to accomplish such a feat since Bob Duval won the Emerald Coast Classic on March 28, 1999, the same day his son David won THE PLAYERS Championship. Became the first sponsor exemption to win on the Nationwide Tour since Chris Couch won the 2001 Florida Classic. Followed up his victory in Lake Erie with another win two weeks later at the Scholarship America Showdown, with a tournament record 11-under-par 269. Second win also came in extra holes, this time a three-hole affair with Kyle Thompson, Chris Tidland and Mathew Goggin. The win came in just his fourth career start on the Nationwide Tour, giving him the honor as the fastest player to two wins in Tour history. Dick Mast held the previous-best mark, winning his second career title in his sixth start back in 1990. Made the cut in four of five appearances on the 2004 PGA TOUR, including his first career cut at the AT&T Pebble Beach National Pro-Am, finishing T61. Came back the next week and shot an opening-round 64 to take a one-shot lead at the Buick Invitational, finishing the event T59. Was named Pac-10 player of the year as a senior at Southern California in 2002. Led the Trojans to their second consecutive Pac-10 championship and finished his senior year with six top-five finishes in NCAA play, including four seconds. As a senior at Kent Denver School in Englewood, CO, won the Colorado high school state championship and was a second-team 1997 AJGA Rolex All-American. He also won the 1997 Junior World Championships (he and father Craig are the only father/son champions in the history of the event).

EXEMPT STATUS: 13th on 2004 Nationwide Tour money list

BEST PGA TOUR CAREER FINISH: T40—2004 B.C. Open.

NATIONWIDE TOUR VICTORIES (2): 2004 Lake Erie Charity Classic at Peek 'n Peak Resort, Scholarship America Showdown.

MONEY & POSITION:

2003 — 0 2004 — 49,541

BEST 2004 PGA TOUR FINISH: T40—B.C. Open.

PGA TOUR CAREER LOW ROUND: 64–2004 Buick Invitational/1

2004 SUMMARY: Tournaments Entered—5; in money—4; Top-10 finishes—0

CAREER SUMMARY: Tournaments Entered—8; in money—4; Top-10 finishes—0

CAREER EARNINGS: $49,541

Nationwide Tour Alumnus

STANDLY, Mike

FULL NAME: Michael Dean Standly **BIRTHDATE:** May 19, 1964 **BIRTHPLACE:** Abilene, TX **RESIDENCE:** Houston, TX **HEIGHT:** 6-0 **WEIGHT:** 190 **FAMILY:** Wife, Nicole; Charles Allen, Suzanne Augusta **EDUCATION:** University of Houston **SPECIAL INTERESTS:** Fishing, hunting **TURNED PROFESSIONAL:** 1986 **JOINED TOUR:** 1990 **Q SCHOOL:** 1990 **OTHER INFORMATION:** Split time between the PGA TOUR (nine events) and the Nationwide Tour (10 events) in 2004. Lone TOUR victory came at 1993 Freeport-McMoRan Classic, where he posted a final-round 67 to come from two strokes off the lead. Finished second at 1997 Deposit Guaranty Golf Classic when Billy Ray Brown birdied the final hole to win by one. Has 29 top-25s in PGA TOUR career. Medalist in 1991 PGA TOUR Qualifying Tournament. Played Nationwide Tour in 1990, earning $10,446 in 28 events. Runner-up to Scott Verplank in 1986 NCAA tournament. 1986 All-American. Winner of the 1984 Boone Links Invitational.

EXEMPT STATUS: Past Champion

PGA TOUR VICTORIES (1): 1993 Freeport-McMoRan Golf Classic.

MONEY & POSITION:

1986 —	0		1994 —	179,850 —	99	2000 —	72,948 —	204
1987 —	0		1995 —	177,920 —	105	2001 —	5,766 —	249
1988 —	800 —	315	1996 —	99,034 —	164	2002 —	68,210 —	211
1991 —	55,846 —	171	1997 —	318,939 —	75	2003 —	62,991 —	224
1992 —	213,712 —	73	1998 —	191,976 —	140	2004 —	6,000 —	262
1993 —	323,886 —	49	1999 —	47,814 —	229			

BEST 2004 PGA TOUR FINISH: T69—B.C. Open.

PGA TOUR CAREER LOW ROUND: 62–1995 FedEx St. Jude Classic/1

2004 SUMMARY: Tournaments Entered—9; in money—1; Top-10 finishes—0

CAREER SUMMARY: Tournaments Entered—306; in money—149; Top-10 finishes—12

CAREER EARNINGS: $1,825,693

Nationwide Tour Alumnus

STILES, Darron

FULL NAME: Darron Gary Stiles **BIRTHDATE:** June 1, 1973 **BIRTHPLACE:** St. Petersburg, FL **RESIDENCE:** Pinehurst, NC **HEIGHT:** 6-3 **WEIGHT:** 215 **FAMILY:** Wife, Kim; Sydney Kalani (10/1/03) **EDUCATION:** Florida Southern College (1995, Accounting) **SPECIAL INTERESTS:** TV, Internet, darts, pool, video games **TURNED PROFESSIONAL:** 1995 **JOINED TOUR:** 2003 **OTHER INFORMATION:** Member of Nationwide Tour in 1997,1999-2002 and 2004 and PGA TOUR in 2003. Ended 2004 No. 15 on the money list, with $212,894. Despite not winning, was one of the most consistent players on Tour, with 15 top-25s in 2004. Posted more Top-10s (nine) and rounds in the 60s (43) than any other player on Tour in 2004. Placed third at the Pete Dye West Virginia Classic and fourth at the Northeast Pennsylvania Classic. Spent 2003 as a rookie on the PGA TOUR and finished 151st on the money list. Best effort was a T11 at the Greater Hartford Open, where he carded a TOUR career-best 63 in the second round. Finished ninth on the 2002 Nationwide Tour money list with $222,845 to earn his first TOUR card. Notched third win of his career at the Knoxville Open thanks to two eagles on par-4s in the final round that helped give him the two-stroke victory over Steve Ford and Aaron Baddeley. Posted three top-10s in 2001, including a third at the Richmond Open. Had a hole-in-one on the sixth hole at the Monterey Peninsula Classic (second round). Recorded four top-10s in 2000, including his second win at the Tri-Cities Open. Had four top-10s in 1999. Holed a 125-yard 9-iron for eagle on the final hole to win the Dominion Open, becoming the 11th player in Tour history to win as a Monday qualifier. Winner of two TearDrop Tour titles in 1999 and the 1996 Terciera Invitational Pro-Am in Portugal, setting course and tournament record. A three-time All-America at Florida Southern. Member of the 1995 Division II National Championship team. Had successful surgery to remove cancerous tumor from jaw in 1989. Has five career holes-in-one.

EXEMPT STATUS: 15th on 2004 Nationwide Tour money list

BEST PGA TOUR CAREER FINISH: T11—2003 Greater Hartford Open.

NATIONWIDE TOUR VICTORIES (3): 1999 Dominion Open. **2000** Tri-Cities Open. **2002** Knoxville Open.

MONEY & POSITION:

1999 —	0		2003 —	346,694 —	151

PGA TOUR CAREER LOW ROUND: 63–2003 Greater Hartford Open/2

2004 SUMMARY: Tournaments Entered—0; in money—0; Top-10 finishes—0

CAREER SUMMARY: Tournaments Entered—30; in money—17; Top-10 finishes—0

CAREER EARNINGS: $346,694

Nationwide Tour Alumnus

STRANGE, Curtis

FULL NAME: Curtis Northrop Strange **BIRTHDATE:** January 30, 1955 **BIRTHPLACE:** Norfolk, VA **RESIDENCE:** Morehead City, NC **HEIGHT:** 5-11 **WEIGHT:** 180 **FAMILY:** Wife Sarah; Thomas Wright III (8/25/82), David Clark (4/3/85) **EDUCATION:** Wake Forest University **SPECIAL INTERESTS:** Hunting, off-shore fishing **TURNED PROFESSIONAL:** 1976 **JOINED TOUR:** 1977 Q **SCHOOL:** Spring 1977 **OTHER INFORMATION:** Considered one of the premier players of the 1980s, with 16 of his 17 career PGA TOUR victories coming in that decade. In 1989, became first to successfully defend U.S. Open title since Ben Hogan (1950-51) at Oak Hill. Also played on five Ryder Cup squads during his career. Made four appearances on the PGA TOUR in 2004. Missed the cut in three events and withdrew from The Honda Classic. Left his role as the lead golf analyst for ABC Sports near the end of May to prepare for Champions Tour playing career. Began working for ABC in 1997. Served as captain for U.S. Ryder Cup team in 2002 when Captain Sam Torrance's European Team reclaimed the Cup. In 1989, earned one-stroke victory over Chip Beck, Mark McCumber and Ian Woosnam at Oak Hill for second consecutive U.S. Open title. Finished T2 at 1989 PGA Championship, one behind Payne Stewart. Won the 1988 U.S. Open at The Country Club, defeating Nick Faldo in an 18-hole playoff. U.S. Open victory was one of four on the 1988 season. Became first player to surpass $1 million in a season when he captured his third of three money titles. GWAA Player of the Year. Also Player of the Year in 1985 and 1987. As an amateur, was a three-time All-American, medalist at the 1974 NCAA and on the winning national championship team in 1974 and 1975 at Wake Forest. Teammates included Jay Haas and Scott Hoch. Started playing golf at age 7; father owned White Sands CC in Virginia Beach, VA. Identical twin, Allen, is a former TOUR member.

EXEMPT STATUS: Past Champion

PLAYOFF RECORD: 6-3

PGA TOUR VICTORIES (17): 1979 Pensacola Open. **1980** Michelob-Houston Open, Manufacturers Hanover Westchester Classic. **1983** Sammy Davis Jr.-Greater Hartford Open. **1984** Lajet Golf Classic. **1985** Honda Classic, Panasonic Las Vegas Invitational, Canadian Open. **1986** Houston Open. **1987** Canadian Open, Federal Express St. Jude Classic, NEC World Series of Golf. **1988** Independent Insurance Agent Open, Memorial Tournament, U.S. Open Championship, Nabisco Championship. **1989** U.S. Open Championship.

MONEY & POSITION:

1976 —	375 —	267	1986 —	237,700 —	32	1996 —	181,883 —	116
1977 —	30,928 —	81	1987 —	925,941 —	1	1997 —	171,092 —	129
1978 —	29,346 —	89	1988 —	1,147,644 —	1	1998 —	78,836 —	192
1979 —	138,368 —	21	1989 —	752,587 —	7	1999 —	118,138 —	183
1980 —	271,888 —	3	1990 —	277,172 —	53	2000 —	90,387 —	197
1981 —	201,513 —	9	1991 —	336,333 —	48	2001 —	148,632 —	188
1982 —	263,378 —	10	1992 —	150,639 —	99	2002 —	16,207 —	234
1983 —	200,116 —	21	1993 —	262,697 —	63	2003 —	0	
1984 —	276,773 —	14	1994 —	390,881 —	41	2004 —	0	
1985 —	542,321 —	1	1995 —	358,175 —	49			

PGA TOUR CAREER LOW ROUND: 62–2 times, most recent 1983 Sammy Davis Jr.-Greater Hartford Open/2

2004 SUMMARY: Tournaments Entered—4; in money—0; Top-10 finishes—0

CAREER SUMMARY: Tournaments Entered—596; in money—428; Top-10 finishes—129

CAREER EARNINGS: $7,599,951

STRICKER, Steve

FULL NAME: Steven Charles Stricker **BIRTHDATE:** February 23, 1967 **BIRTHPLACE:** Edgerton, WI **RESIDENCE:** Madison, WI **HEIGHT:** 6-0 **WEIGHT:** 185 **FAMILY:** Wife, Nicki; Bobbi Maria (8/31/98) **EDUCATION:** University of Illinois **SPECIAL INTERESTS:** Hunting **TURNED PROFESSIONAL:** 1990 **Q SCHOOL:** 1993 **OTHER INFORMATION:** Lost his fully-exempt card for the first time since the 1997 season after finishing 151st on the 2004 PGA TOUR money list and seeing his three-year exemption for winning the 2001 WGC-Accenture Match Play Championship expire. Co-leader through 36 holes at the rain-soaked 2004 Shell Houston Open. Finished T19 after a third-round 5-over-par 77 eliminated him from contention. With his wife Nicki on the bag, posted first top-10 since 2002 Verizon Byron Nelson Classic with a T4 at the 2004 John Deere Classic. Finished 189th on the 2003 TOUR money list, his lowest finish since he joined the TOUR in 1994. Best finish was a T18 at the Phoenix Open, his first start of the season, where he tied career low with a 62 during the second round. Defeated Pierre Fulke, 2 and 1, in 36-hole final of 2001 WGC-Accenture Match Play Championship. Third career victory jumped him from 91st to No. 47 in Official World Golf Ranking. Had not made a cut in TOUR event since July 2000. In 2000, managed to finish among top-10 only once. Finished fifth at 1999 U.S. Open for second consecutive year on strength of third-round 69, the only player under par that round. In 1998, recovered from off year in 1997 with strong campaign. In a limited schedule of 21 events, made 20 cuts. Played only four times after Aug. 1, due to birth of first child, and finished in top 10 each time. Tied for third-round lead with Vijay Singh at 1998 PGA Championship and closing 70 left him two strokes shy of Singh. Impressive 1996 season included seven top-10s, all either firsts, seconds or thirds. Earned $1,383,739 to finish fourth on money list. First TOUR victory came at 1996 Kemper Open, where he moved to within one stroke of Jay Williamson's lead with third-round 65 and closed with 68 for three-stroke victory. Won again that season at Motorola Western Open, with an eight-stroke victory. Was 2-3 in 1996 Presidents Cup. Was 5-0 on victorious 1996 Dunhill Cup team. In 1994, T2 in second event as a TOUR member at Northern Telecom Open. Finished 50th on the money list that year, fourth among rookies. All-American selection at University of Illinois in 1988-89. Wife Nicki, who had been his caddie throughout his professional career, gave up the bag in 1998 to deliver daughter Bobbi Maria. Returned to caddie in 1999 at Milwaukee. Father-in-law Dennis Tiziani, the former golf coach at University of Wisconsin, is his teacher. Brother-in-law Mario Tiziani is a 2005 PGA TOUR member.
EXEMPT STATUS: Past Champion
PGA TOUR VICTORIES (3): 1996 Kemper Open, Motorola Western Open. **2001** WGC-Accenture Match Play Championship.
MONEY & POSITION:

1990 —	3,974 —	255	1995 —	438,931 —	40	2000 —	418,780 —	113
1991 —	0		1996 —	1,383,739 —	4	2001 —	1,676,229 —	30
1992 —	5,550 —	261	1997 —	167,652 —	130	2002 —	789,713 —	88
1993 —	46,171 —	186	1998 —	1,313,948 —	13	2003 —	150,590 —	189
1994 —	334,409 —	50	1999 —	662,461 —	64	2004 —	440,906 —	151

BEST 2004 PGA TOUR FINISH: T4—John Deere Classic.
PGA TOUR CAREER LOW ROUND: 62–2 times, most recent 2003 Phoenix Open/2
2004 SUMMARY: Tournaments Entered—27; in money—13; Top-10 finishes—1
CAREER SUMMARY: Tournaments Entered—254; in money—173; Top-10 finishes—38
CAREER EARNINGS: $7,833,052
Nationwide Tour Alumnus

SUMMERHAYS, Boyd

FULL NAME: Boyd Preston Summerhays **BIRTHDATE:** June 16, 1979 **BIRTHPLACE:** Bountiful, UT **RESIDENCE:** Farmington, UT; plays out of Glenwild GC (Park City, UT) **HEIGHT:** 5-11 **WEIGHT:** 175 **FAMILY:** Wife, Barbara; Preston (7/22/02), Grace (7/9/04) **EDUCATION:** Oklahoma State University **SPECIAL INTERESTS:** Family **TURNED PROFESSIONAL:** 2001 **Q SCHOOL:** 2003 **OTHER INFORMATION:** Rookie season on TOUR was limited to eight events due to back injury. Best finish was T25 at the AT&T Pebble Beach National Pro-Am. Will receive a Major Medical Extension for 2005. Coupled with $37,127 earned in eight events in 2004 has the opportunity to play in 21 events to earn $586,135 and match the $623,262 winnings of 2004's No. 125, Tag Ridings. If he does so, will play out of the Major Medical Extension category for the remainder of the season. Qualified for PGA TOUR after finishing T26 at 2003 Qualifying Tournament. Medalist by six strokes over cousin Joseph Summerhays during first stage of tournament held at Bayonet Course in Seaside, CA. Only player to finish that stage below par (5-under). Four-time AJGA All-American, including first-team status in 1995-96. Winner of the 1996 AJGA Sportsmanship Award. Won Junior World Tournament in California three times at the age of 10-, 14- and 16-years old. Served a two-year Mormon mission to Argentina (1998-2000) and is fluent in Spanish. Uncle is Champions Tour player Bruce Summerhays.
EXEMPT STATUS: Major Medical Extension
BEST PGA TOUR CAREER FINISH: T25—2004 AT&T Pebble Beach National Pro-Am.
MONEY & POSITION:
2004 — 37,127 — 236
BEST 2004 PGA TOUR FINISH: T25—AT&T Pebble Beach National Pro-Am.
PGA TOUR CAREER LOW ROUND: 68–2004 Sony Open in Hawaii/1
2004 SUMMARY: Tournaments Entered—8; in money—1; Top-10 finishes—0
CAREER SUMMARY: Tournaments Entered—8; in money—1; Top-10 finishes—0
CAREER EARNINGS: $37,127

T

TANIHARA, Hideto

FULL NAME: Hideto Tanihara **BIRTHDATE:** November 16, 1978 **BIRTHPLACE:** Hiroshima, Japan **RESIDENCE:** Tokyo, Japan **HEIGHT:** 6-0 **WEIGHT:** 170 **FAMILY:** Single **EDUCATION:** Tohoku Univeristy (2000) **TURNED PROFESSIONAL:** 2000 **Q SCHOOL:** 2004 **OTHER INFORMATION:** Joins PGA TOUR as a rookie in 2005 after finishing T21 at the 2004 Qualifying Tournament. Had four career TOUR starts entering 2005. Made the cut in all three TOUR starts in 2004, with a top finish of T31 at the U.S. Bank Championship in Milwaukee. Played on the Japan Golf Tour the last three years (2002-04) and in his first year as a full-time member in 2003, was named the Tour's Rookie of the Year. Owns three professional victories, the 2002 Pro Gear Cup, 2003 Yomiyuri Open and the 2004 Asia Japan Okinawa Open. Tied the nine-hole Japan Golf Tour record with a 28 on the front nine (eight birdies) in the first round of the 2004 Sun Chlorella Classic. Introduced to game by father.
EXEMPT STATUS: T21 at 2004 PGA TOUR Qualifying Tournament
BEST PGA TOUR CAREER FINISH: T31—2004 U.S. Bank Championship in Milwaukee.
MONEY & POSITION:
2003 — 0 2004 — 41,729
BEST 2004 PGA TOUR FINISH: T31—U.S. Bank Championship in Milwaukee.
PGA TOUR CAREER LOW ROUND: 66–2004 Sony Open in Hawaii/2
2004 SUMMARY: Tournaments Entered—3; in money—3; Top-10 finishes—0
CAREER SUMMARY: Tournaments Entered—4; in money—3; Top-10 finishes—0
CAREER EARNINGS: $41,729

THATCHER, Roland

FULL NAME: Roland Churchill Thatcher IV **BIRTHDATE:** April 11, 1977 **BIRTHPLACE:** Hampton, VA **RESIDENCE:** The Woodlands, TX; plays out of The Club at Carolton Woods **HEIGHT:** 5-9 **WEIGHT:** 185 **FAMILY:** Wife, Lindsey **EDUCATION:** Auburn University (2000, Political Science, Criminal Justice) **TURNED PROFESSIONAL:** 2000 **Q SCHOOL:** 2003, 2004 **OTHER INFORMATION:** Earned 2005 card via T9 finish at PGA TOUR Qualifying School. Finished 177th on TOUR money list in rookie season. Recorded his first top-10 in his 17th career start, a T5 at the 2004 Reno-Tahoe Open and collected a career-best payday of $109,500. Closed with three birdies at Montreux G&CC in the third round to secure the 54-hole lead by one stroke over Vaughn Taylor. Missed a 7-foot birdie try on the last hole of regulation that would have put him in the playoff. Earned first TOUR card by finishing T28 at the 2003 Qualifying Tournament. Finished in the top 30 on the Nationwide Tour in 2002-03, including career-best 29th in 2003. Established a Kooyonga GC course record with a 6-under-par 65 in the opening round of the 2003 Jacob's Creek Open in Australia. Season's top finish was a T2 at the Price Cutter Charity Championship. Enjoyed standout rookie season on the 2002 Nationwide Tour, including his first victory at the Bank of America Monterey Peninsula Classic. Missed six straight cuts before a course-record 6-under 66 in the opening round of that tournament gave him a one-shot lead. Led by one after 36 holes and by five after 54 holes. Final-round 74 good enough to hold off Aaron Baddeley by two shots. One of two wire-to-wire winners on the 2002 Nationwide Tour. Finished T47 at the 2001 PGA TOUR Qualifying Tournament at Bear Lakes CC. Entered the final hole of Q-School needing a par to earn his TOUR card, but his approach hit a cart path and bounced on the top of the Bear Lakes clubhouse. He dropped into an unplayable lie and finished with a triple-bogey 7, missing his TOUR card by three strokes. Still shot final-round 69. Played the Golden Bear Tour in 2000-01. 2000 Southeastern Conference champion. Earned first-team All-SEC honors and second-team All-American honors. 1998 and 2000 Scholastic All-American. Named four consecutive years (1997-2000) to the Scholastic All-SEC team.
EXEMPT STATUS: T9 at 2004 PGA TOUR Qualifying Tournament
BEST PGA TOUR CAREER FINISH: T5—2004 Reno-Tahoe Open.
NATIONWIDE TOUR VICTORIES (1): 2002 Bank of America Monterey Peninsula Classic.
MONEY & POSITION:
2003 — 0 2004 — 247,987 — 177
BEST 2004 PGA TOUR FINISH: T5—Reno-Tahoe Open.
PGA TOUR CAREER LOW ROUND: 66–2 times, most recent 2004 Reno-Tahoe Open/1
2004 SUMMARY: Tournaments Entered—23; in money—9; Top-10 finishes—1
CAREER SUMMARY: Tournaments Entered—25; in money—9; Top-10 finishes—1
CAREER EARNINGS: $247,987
Nationwide Tour Alumnus

TIZIANI, Mario

FULL NAME: Mario Steven Tiziani **BIRTHDATE:** July 17, 1970 **BIRTHPLACE:** Ironwood, MI **RESIDENCE:** Shorewood, MN; plays out of Cherokee CC in Madison, WI **HEIGHT:** 6-0 **WEIGHT:** 175 **FAMILY:** Wife, Kressi; Alexa (1/29/01), McKella (3/25/03) **EDUCATION:** University of Wisconsin (1992, Sociology) **SPECIAL INTERESTS:** Hunting **TURNED PROFESSIONAL:** 1993 **Q SCHOOL:** 2004 **OTHER INFORMATION:** Rookie on 2005 PGA TOUR after making it through all three stages of the 2004 Qualifying Tournament. Finished T21. Has been to Q-School 12 times, but 2004 was his first trip to final stage. Has played in 14 TOUR events, making the cut in three with a career-best T32 at the 2003 Greater Milwaukee Open. Has also made the cut in eight of 23 events on the Nationwide Tour since 1993. Best finish was a T3 at the 2003 Alberta Calgary Classic. Played Canadian Tour from 1999-2004, where he won the 2003 Northern Ontario Open. Won 2002 Panama Open. Has six holes-in-one in competitive rounds. Father is the former golf coach at the University of Wisconsin. Mario is married to PGA TOUR player Steve Stricker's sister.

EXEMPT STATUS: T21 at 2004 PGA TOUR Qualifying Tournament

BEST PGA TOUR CAREER FINISH: T32—2003 Greater Milwaukee Open.

MONEY & POSITION:

1995 —	0	1999 —	0	2003 —	17,780
1996 —	0	2000 —	0	2004 —	0
1997 —	0	2002 —	22,603		

PGA TOUR CAREER LOW ROUND: 65–2002 Greater Milwaukee Open/2

2004 SUMMARY: Tournaments Entered—1; in money—0; Top-10 finishes—0

CAREER SUMMARY: Tournaments Entered—14; in money—3; Top-10 finishes—0

CAREER EARNINGS: $40,383

TRAHAN, D.J.

FULL NAME: Donald Roland Trahan, Jr. **BIRTHDATE:** December 18, 1980 **BIRTHPLACE:** Atlanta, GA **RESIDENCE:** Mt. Pleasant, SC; plays out of Rivertowne CC **HEIGHT:** 6-3 **WEIGHT:** 185 **FAMILY:** Single **EDUCATION:** Clemson University (2003, Sports Management) **SPECIAL INTERESTS:** Fishing, boating, most sports **TURNED PROFESSIONAL:** 2003 **Q SCHOOL:** 2004 **OTHER INFORMATION:** Rookie on the 2005 PGA TOUR after making it through the final stage of the 2004 Qualifying Tournament in his second attempt. Finished T11. Spent the 2004 season on the Nationwide Tour, where he finished 26th on the money list. Wrapped up the final full-field event of the season with his first Tour win at the Miccosukee Championship. Entered the final round four shots behind 54-hole leader Nick Watney, but a 6-under-par 65 catapulted him to a two-stroke win worth $90,000. Had a hole-in-one on No. 5 during the second round of the Envirocare Utah Classic. Turned professional at the FBR Capital Open in early June 2003. Posted rounds of 73-75 and missed the cut. Played a total of six events and made the cut in one, the Greater Hartford Open (T71). Played in the 2001 Masters as an amateur, missing the cut. Helped lead Clemson to the 2003 NCAA title, the first in school history. The No. 1-ranked Tigers became the first school in NCAA history to win its conference championship, an NCAA regional title and the NCAA Championship in the same year. Had one win among his nine top-10s in 13 starts as a senior. First-team All-American, first-team all-district and four-time All-ACC selection. Ben Hogan Award finalist. Had three wins among his nine top-10s during his junior year and was NCAA Player of the Year. Member of the 2001 U.S. Walker Cup team. Winner of the 2000 United States Public Links Championship, defeating Nationwide Tour members Bubba Watson in the 37-hole final and Kyle Thompson in the semifinal. ACC Rookie of the Year as a freshman. Former Clemson players Jonathan Byrd, Lucas Glover and Charles Warren are also on the PGA TOUR this year.

EXEMPT STATUS: T11 at 2004 PGA TOUR Qualifying Tournament

BEST PGA TOUR CAREER FINISH: T71—2003 Greater Hartford Open.

NATIONWIDE TOUR VICTORIES (1): 2004 Miccosukee Championship.

MONEY & POSITION:

2003 —	7,880	2004 —	0

BEST 2004 PGA TOUR FINISH: T71—Greater Hartford Open.

PGA TOUR CAREER LOW ROUND: 67–2003 Greater Hartford Open/2

2004 SUMMARY: Tournaments Entered—1; in money—0; Top-10 finishes—0

CAREER SUMMARY: Tournaments Entered—8; in money—1; Top-10 finishes—0

CAREER EARNINGS: $7,880

Nationwide Tour Alumnus

TRYBA, Ted (TREE-ba)

FULL NAME: Ted Nickolas Tryba BIRTHDATE: January 15, 1967 **BIRTHPLACE:** Wilkes-Barre, PA **RESIDENCE:** Orlando, FL **HEIGHT:** 6-4 **WEIGHT:** 205 **FAMILY:** Single **EDUCATION:** Ohio State University (1989, Marketing) **SPECIAL INTERESTS:** Basketball **TURNED PROFESSIONAL:** 1989 **Q SCHOOL:** 1989 **OTHER INFORMATION:** Will receive a Non-Exempt, Major Medical Extension carryover for 2005 from hip injury and subsequent surgery in 2002. Has played in only 18 events in the last three seasons. Played in nine events in 2004 with nine missed cuts. Missed all of 2003 due to recovery from 2002 hip surgery. Coupled with $17,706 earned in 2002, has the opportunity to play in two events to earn $497,739 and match the $515,445 winnings of 2002's No. 125. If he does so, will play out of the Major Medical Extension category for the remainder of the season. Due to hip surgery, did not make first 2002 start until the BellSouth Classic in April, and did not play again after the Buick Open in early August due to injury. In 2001, failed to post a top-10 for the second straight year after seven consecutive seasons with at least one. Spectacular year in 1999 as he posted career highs for earnings, money list position and top-10s. Earned $1,533,636 to more than triple his previous most lucrative year, $451,983 in 1995. Finished 20th on money list and recorded five top-10s. Earned second career victory at FedEx St. Jude Classic. Second-round 64 lifted him into contention, while third-round 67 produced a four-way tie for the lead. Final-round 66 featured pair of eagles, including one on No. 16 which ensured a two-stroke victory over Tom Lehman and Tim Herron. Set Riviera CC course record at Nissan Open with 10-under-par 61 (and career low) in third round. Broke through with first PGA TOUR victory at 1995 Anheuser-Busch Golf Classic. Trailed by one stroke through 54 holes, but final-round 68 earned one-stroke victory over Scott Simpson. Played Nationwide Tour from 1990-92 and won a tournament each year. Placed fourth on Nationwide Tour money list in 1992 to earn spot on PGA TOUR in 1993. Pennsylvania high school champion. Knew he wanted to be a professional golfer at age 7. Legally blind in left eye, which was punctured by stick at age 4.

EXEMPT STATUS: Non-Exempt, Major Medical Extension

PLAYOFF RECORD: 0-1

PGA TOUR VICTORIES (2): 1995 Anheuser-Busch Golf Classic. **1999** FedEx St. Jude Classic.

NATIONWIDE TOUR VICTORIES (3): 1990 Gateway Open. **1991** Utah Classic. 1992 Shreveport Open.

MONEY & POSITION:

1989 —	0		1996 —	162,944 —	131	2001 —	308,049 —	144
1990 —	10,708 —	226	1997 —	303,399 —	80	2002 —	17,706 —	232
1993 —	136,670 —	116	1998 —	421,786 —	67	2004 —	0	
1994 —	246,481 —	74	1999 —	1,533,636 —	20			
1995 —	451,983 —	39	2000 —	249,437 —	148			

PGA TOUR CAREER LOW ROUND: 61–1999 Nissan Open/3

2004 SUMMARY: Tournaments Entered—9; in money—0; Top-10 finishes—0

CAREER SUMMARY: Tournaments Entered—346; in money—180; Top-10 finishes—17

CAREER EARNINGS: $3,842,799

Nationwide Tour Alumnus

U

URESTI, Omar

FULL NAME: Omar David Uresti **BIRTHDATE:** August 3, 1968 **BIRTHPLACE:** Austin, TX **RESIDENCE:** Austin, TX; plays out of Onion Creek Club **HEIGHT:** 5-6 **WEIGHT:** 175 **FAMILY:** Wife, Anita; Omar David Jr. (8/18/04) **EDUCATION:** University of Texas (1991, Organizational Communication) **SPECIAL INTERESTS:** Billiards, ping-pong, going to movies, Stephen King novels **TURNED PROFESSIONAL:** 1991 **Q SCHOOL:** 1994, 1995, 2003, 2004 **OTHER INFORMATION:** Returned to Q-School after finishing 163rd on 2004 TOUR money list. Finished T21 to retain playing privileges for 2005. In first start of 2004, carded final-round 65 at the Sony Open in Hawaii to finish T10, his lone top-10 of season and best finish on the TOUR since a T8 at the 2000 Greater Greensboro Chrysler Classic. Finished T7 finish at 2003 Qualifying School. Third-round 63 tied Brendan Pappas' Crooked Cat course record at Orange County National. Began final round out of the top 30 at T34, but rallied with a 64 to place safely in the top 30. Member of the PGA TOUR in 1995-2000 and 2004 and the Nationwide Tour in 1993-94 and 2001-03. First earned PGA TOUR card by finishing 14th at 1994 Qualifying Tournament. Best TOUR season came in 1999 when he made the cut in 20 of 31 events and earned $405,201 to finish No. 99 on the money list. Best career PGA TOUR finish was T3 at the 1999 Bay Hill Invitational. Earned his only career Nationwide Tour title at the 1994 Shreveport Open, during which he posted nine consecutive birdies, a Nationwide Tour record that also bettered the all-time PGA TOUR mark by one. 1985 Texas Junior champion. Counts among biggest thrills in golf a hole-in-one at age 8. Named after actor Omar Sharif. Nickname is "O-man."

EXEMPT STATUS: T21 at 2004 PGA TOUR Qualifying Tournament

BEST PGA TOUR CAREER FINISH: T3—1997 Bay Hill Invitational.

NATIONWIDE TOUR VICTORIES (1): 1994 Shreveport Open.

MONEY & POSITION:

1991 —	0		1997 —	203,516 —	113	2000 —	213,433 — 157
1995 —	104,876 —	156	1998 —	281,347 —	107	2001 —	47,450
1996 —	171,797 —	122	1999 —	405,201 —	99	2004 —	345,797 — 163

BEST 2004 PGA TOUR FINISH: T10—Sony Open in Hawaii.

PGA TOUR CAREER LOW ROUND: 64–1998 Canon Greater Hartford Open/2

2004 SUMMARY: Tournaments Entered—28; in money—14; Top-10 finishes—1

CAREER SUMMARY: Tournaments Entered—227; in money—117; Top-10 finishes—9

CAREER EARNINGS: $1,773,418

Nationwide Tour Alumnus

UTLEY, Stan

FULL NAME: Stan Utley **BIRTHDATE:** January 16, 1962 **BIRTHPLACE:** Thayer, MO **RESIDENCE:** Scottsdale, Ariz. Plays out of Troon **HEIGHT:** 6-0 **WEIGHT:** 175 **FAMILY:** Wife, Elayna; Tatum Elayne (6/29/95), Jake Rhodes (8/11/97) **EDUCATION:** University of Missouri **SPECIAL INTERESTS:** Church, basketball, hunting, fishing **TURNED PROFESSIONAL:** 1984 **JOINED TOUR:** 1988 **OTHER INFORMATION:** Split time between the PGA TOUR (eight events) and the Nationwide Tour (four events). Played on the weekend three times on the PGA TOUR with his best finish coming at the John Deere Classic, a T32. In 2003, made seven cuts in 11 starts on the PGA TOUR. T26 at the 2003 Greater Hartford Open was best finish on the PGA TOUR since the 1998 Quad City Classic when he finished T17. Made a combined 11 of 16 cuts in 2002, including two top-10s on the Nationwide Tour. Also set a PGA TOUR record for fewest putts through nine holes. Needed just six putts over his first nine holes at the Northview G&CC during the second round of the 2002 Air Canada Championship. First qualified for PGA TOUR with victory at 1989 Chattanooga Classic. Won 1993 Cleveland Open en route to finishing third on Nationwide Tour money list. Finished 12th on 1995 Nationwide Tour money list with $108,270 after winning Louisiana Open and Miami Valley Open. Carded rounds of 62 in each of those victories. Three-time All-Big Eight selection and twice All-American. Won 1986 Kansas Open, 1988 and 1989 Missouri Opens, 1980 Missouri Junior Championship. His annual "Go For The Gold" skins game in Columbia, MO has been benefitting Rainbow House, a safe house for children, since 1991. Has own golf consulting business called Stan Utley's Tour-Tested Golf (stanutleygolf.com) where he teaches both professionals and amateurs.

EXEMPT STATUS: Past Champion

PGA TOUR VICTORIES (1): 1989 Chattanooga Classic.

NATIONWIDE TOUR VICTORIES (3): 1993 Cleveland Open. **1995** Louisiana Open, Miami Valley Open.

MONEY & POSITION:

1986 —	0		1992 —	14,964 —	222	1998 —	20,802 —	243
1987 —	0		1993 —	17,371 —	223	2000 —	15,336 —	232
1988 —	2,819 —	265	1994 —	63,345 —	179	2001 —	3,540 —	258
1989 —	107,400 —	118	1995 —	0		2002 —	28,423 —	221
1990 —	143,604 —	108	1996 —	4,438 —	325	2003 —	79,046 —	214
1991 —	127,849 —	115	1997 —	0		2004 —	45,610 —	230

BEST 2004 PGA TOUR FINISH: T32—John Deere Classic.

PGA TOUR CAREER LOW ROUND: 64–4 times, most recent 1991 Kemper Open/3

2004 SUMMARY: Tournaments Entered—8; in money—3; Top-10 finishes—0

CAREER SUMMARY: Tournaments Entered—196; in money—80; Top-10 finishes—6

CAREER EARNINGS: $674,546

Nationwide Tour Alumnus

V

VAN DER WALT, Tjaart (chart VAN-der-walt)

FULL NAME: Tjaart Nicolas van der Walt **BIRTHDATE:** September 25, 1974 **BIRTHPLACE:** Pretoria, South Africa **RESIDENCE:** Juno Beach, FL; plays out of Dainfern CC (Johannesburg, South Africa) **HEIGHT:** 6-1 **WEIGHT:** 189 **FAMILY:** Wife, Phillipa **EDUCATION:** Central Alabama Community College **SPECIAL INTERESTS:** Reading, exploring wildlife **TURNED PROFESSIONAL:** 1996 **Q SCHOOL:** 2003 **OTHER INFORMATION:** Rookie season on TOUR was limited to 12 events due to wrist injury. Did not play after British Open in July. Made six cuts, with a career-best finish of T21 at the EDS Byron Nelson Championship. Will receive a Major Medical Extension for 2005. Coupled with $138,785 earned in 12 events in 2004 has the opportunity to play in 17 events to earn $484,477 and match the $623,262 winnings of 2004's No. 125, Tag Ridings. If he does so, will play out of the Major Medical Extension category for the remainder of the season. Joined PGA TOUR for the first time in 2004 after T12 finish at 2003 PGA TOUR National Qualifying Tournament. Member of the Nationwide Tour 2000-2003. Made the cut in 17 of 24 events on the 2003 Nationwide Tour, with 11 top-25s. Finished the year No. 23 on the final money list, with $175,966. Best results were a solo third at the Omaha Classic and a T3 at the First Tee Arkansas Classic. Made the cut in 14 of 22 events in 2002, with four top-10s. Made the cut in 14 of 23 tournaments in 2001 and finished No. 18 on the Nationwide Tour money list, with $155,291. Best tournament was a second at the Boise Open. Prior to joining the Nationwide Tour, played primarily on South African Tour. Finished T50 at the 2000 WGC-American Express Championship at Valderrama GC in Sotogrande, Spain, in November, the only PGA TOUR event of his career entering 2004. Gained a berth in the WGC tournament by virtue of finishing in the top three on the 1999-2000 Southern Africa Tour Order of Merit. Runner-up to Nick Price in the 1998 Zimbabwe Open and third-place finisher at the Dimension Data Pro-Am. T2 at the 1997 Kalahari Classic and was fourth at the Zimbabwe Open and seventh on the Order of Merit that year. Runner-up Northern Transvaal U23 team in 1993. Received Northern Transvaal Colours in 1996. Attended Alexander City Junior College, a part of Central Alabama Community College, in the U.S., where he represented the college from 1993 to 1995 at the National Amateur Championships. Awarded All-American status by the National Junior College Athletic Association. Won the Willow Point Invitational in 1995 by a record nine strokes. Began playing golf at age 14. Enjoys fishing, tennis, cycling, reading and swimming.

EXEMPT STATUS: Major Medical Extension

BEST PGA TOUR CAREER FINISH: T21—2004 EDS Byron Nelson Championship.

MONEY & POSITION:

2000 —	0	2004 —	138,785 — 204

BEST 2004 PGA TOUR FINISH: T21—EDS Byron Nelson Championship.

PGA TOUR CAREER LOW ROUND: 65–2004 Buick Classic/2

2004 SUMMARY: Tournaments Entered—12; in money—6; Top-10 finishes—0

CAREER SUMMARY: Tournaments Entered—13; in money—7; Top-10 finishes—0

CAREER EARNINGS: $138,785

Nationwide Tour Alumnus

W

WADKINS, Lanny

FULL NAME: Jerry Lanston Wadkins **BIRTHDATE:** December 5, 1949 **BIRTHPLACE:** Richmond, VA **RESIDENCE:** Dallas, TX **HEIGHT:** 5-9 **WEIGHT:** 175 **FAMILY:** Wife, Penelope; Jessica (10/14/73), Travis (8/25/87), Tucker (8/19/92) **EDUCATION:** Wake Forest University **SPECIAL INTERESTS:** Bird hunting, scuba diving, watching sons play sports **TURNED PROFESSIONAL:** 1971 **JOINED TOUR:** 1971 **Q SCHOOL:** Fall 1971 **OTHER INFORMATION:** Assumed role of lead analyst for CBS golf telecasts in 2002 following the retirement of Ken Venturi. Played in 10 Champions Tour events for the second consecutive year in 2004. Best performance of the season was at the inaugural First Tee Open at Pebble Beach presented by Wal-Mart, where he T18. 1977 PGA Championship winner and 1995 Ryder Cup captain. Joined the Champions Tour in 2000, winning his only title in first event, the Emerald Coast Classic. In 1995, served as Ryder Cup captain at Oak Hill CC after playing on eight American teams. Last official victory came at the 1992 Canon Greater Hartford Open. In 1985, claimed three titles for the second time in his career. Named PGA of America Player of the Year when he finished second in earnings to Curtis Strange. Was also third on the 1983 money list, when he won twice and also had two seconds and a third. In 1982, won three times for the first time in his career. Braved windy conditions to win the 1979 Tournament Players Championship at Sawgrass CC by five strokes over Tom Watson. His biggest victory came in the 1977 PGA Championship at Pebble Beach GL, when he bested Gene Littler in a playoff. Three weeks later, defeated Hale Irwin and Tom Weiskopf by five strokes at the World Series of Golf. Finished third on the money list that year. In 1973, won twice in the same season for the first of five times he would have multi-victory campaigns. First of his 21 TOUR wins came at 1972 Sahara Invitational in his first full year on the PGA TOUR. 1968 and 1970 Southern Amateur, 1970 U.S. Amateur winner. Played on the Walker Cup teams in 1969 and 1971.

EXEMPT STATUS: Past Champion

PLAYOFF RECORD: 3-3

PGA TOUR VICTORIES (21): 1972 Sahara Invitational. **1973** Byron Nelson Golf Classic, USI Classic. **1977** PGA Championship, World Series of Golf. **1979** Glen Campbell-Los Angeles Open, Tournament Players Championship. **1982** Phoenix Open, MONY Tournament of Champions, Buick Open. **1983** Greater Greensboro Open, MONY Tournament of Champions. **1985** Bob Hope Classic, Los Angeles Open, Walt Disney World/Oldsmobile Classic. **1987** Doral-Ryder Open. **1988** Hawaiian Open, Colonial National Invitation. **1990** Anheuser-Busch Golf Classic. **1991** United Hawaiian Open. **1992** Canon Greater Hartford Open.

MONEY & POSITION:

1971 —	15,282 —	106	1982 —	306,827 —	7	1993 —	244,544 —	68
1972 —	113,063 —	10	1983 —	319,271 —	3	1994 —	54,114 —	185
1973 —	193,831 —	5	1984 —	198,996 —	29	1995 —	97,485 —	162
1974 —	45,660 —	57	1985 —	446,893 —	2	1996 —	64,995 —	189
1975 —	23,582 —	88	1986 —	264,931 —	23	1997 —	155,962 —	137
1976 —	42,850 —	64	1987 —	501,727 —	13	1998 —	32,436 —	227
1977 —	244,882 —	3	1988 —	616,596 —	10	1999 —	73,433 —	207
1978 —	53,811 —	62	1989 —	233,363 —	60	2000 —	0	
1979 —	195,710 —	10	1990 —	673,433 —	13	2001 —	0	
1980 —	67,778 —	60	1991 —	651,495 —	12			
1981 —	51,704 —	83	1992 —	366,837 —	40			

PGA TOUR CAREER LOW ROUND: 62–1989 Texas Open/1

CAREER SUMMARY: Tournaments Entered—690; in money—486; Top-10 finishes—139

CAREER EARNINGS: $6,355,681

WAITE, Grant

FULL NAME: Grant Osten Waite **BIRTHDATE:** August 11, 1964 **BIRTHPLACE:** Palmerston North, New Zealand **RESIDENCE:** Ocala, FL **HEIGHT:** 6-1 **WEIGHT:** 185 **FAMILY:** Wife, Lea; Osten Holland (6/1/94), Tanner Brian (6/2/95) **EDUCATION:** University of Oklahoma (1987, Finance) **SPECIAL INTERESTS:** Wind surfing, reading, skiing, fitness **TURNED PROFESSIONAL:** 1987 **Q SCHOOL:** 1989, 1992, 2003 **OTHER INFORMATION:** Posted two top-25s in 2004, including a season-best T11 at the BellSouth Classic. Finished T9 at the 2003 Holden New Zealand Open on the PGA TOUR of Australaisa. Best effort in 2003 on the PGA TOUR was T12 at the Greater Milwaukee Open. Regained TOUR card for 2004 with T28 finish at 2003 PGA TOUR Qualifying Tournament. In 2002 finished out of the top 150 (No. 152) for the first time since finishing No. 172 in 1994. Held first-round lead at 2002 Bell Canadian Open with a first-round 64. Closing 71 left him T6, his lone top-10 of the season. In 2001, made more than $500,000 for just second time in career. Shared first-round lead in Bay Hill Invitational with a 66, finished third. His 6-under 64 gave him first-round lead at 2001 PGA Championship but finished T59. In 2000, earned more than $1 million for the first time in his career on the strength of two runner-up finishes in Canada. Shared first-round lead and held 54-hole lead before finishing one stroke back of champion Rory Sabbatini at Air Canada Championship. Following week, lost to Tiger Woods by one stroke at Bell Canadian Open. Eagled the 18th hole for a 8-under-par 64 to claim sole possession of the 36-hole lead. Held share of 54-hole lead with Woods, who closed with 65 compared to his 66. Two-week Canadian stay produced earnings of $680,400. Had a T2 with Duffy Waldorf in 1997 Michelob Championship at Kingsmill The two lost a playoff to David Duval who birdied the first extra hole. Posted an 11-under-par 60 in the final round of the 1996 Phoenix Open. Was 11-under-par after 15 holes at the TPC of Scottsdale and needed only one birdie in his final three holes for a 59, but recorded three closing pars. Earned career-high spot on money list, No. 35, and first TOUR victory at 1993 Kemper Open. Was the first and second-round leader and just one stroke back of Tom Kite after 54 holes. Closing 70 gave him a one-stroke victory over Kite and the $234,000 winner's check. Three-time All-American at Oklahoma. Twice Australian Junior champion. Played on the New Zealand Junior soccer team.

EXEMPT STATUS: Past Champion

PLAYOFF RECORD: 0-1

PGA TOUR VICTORIES (1): 1993 Kemper Open.

MONEY & POSITION:

1988 —	1,494 —	290	1995 —	240,722 —	76	2001 —	539,227 —	93
1990 —	50,076 —	177	1996 —	302,288 —	72	2002 —	332,947 —	152
1991 —	9,307 —	229	1997 —	362,320 —	68	2003 —	150,999 —	188
1992 —	0		1998 —	245,636 —	118	2004 —	239,318 —	180
1993 —	411,405 —	35	1999 —	253,209 —	148			
1994 —	71,695 —	172	2000 —	1,142,789 —	38			

BEST 2004 PGA TOUR FINISHES: T11—BellSouth Classic; T14—Reno-Tahoe Open.

PGA TOUR CAREER LOW ROUND: 60–1996 Phoenix Open/4

2004 SUMMARY: Tournaments Entered—29; in money—10; Top-10 finishes—0

CAREER SUMMARY: Tournaments Entered—368; in money—192; Top-10 finishes—22

CAREER EARNINGS: $4,353,431

Nationwide Tour Alumnus

WALTERS, Euan (YOU-un)

FULL NAME: Euan Walters **BIRTHDATE:** November 12, 1970 **BIRTHPLACE:** Melbourne, Australia **RESIDENCE:** Melbourne, Australia **HEIGHT:** 6-0 **WEIGHT:** 200 **FAMILY:** Wife, Viktoria; Joshua, Elijah, Giverny **SPECIAL INTERESTS:** Christianity, family, working out **TURNED PROFESSIONAL:** 1994 **JOINED TOUR:** 2005 **OTHER INFORMATION:** Rookie on the PGA TOUR after finishing 14th on the Nationwide Tour money list in 2004, his first season on that circuit. Won the Jacob's Creek Open in his homeland of Australia. Drove 1,000 miles from Sydney to Adelaide in a car with 250,000 miles on the odometer in order to play in the event. His tournament-record 9-under 275 was good for a commanding five-stroke win over Brendan Jones, Anthony Painter and Wayne Grady. Collected a Tour record and personal best $145,587 for his efforts. Came back the following week with an impressive T5 finish at the New Zealand PGA Championship and garnered Player of the Month honors for February for his excellent play. Winner of the 1999 New South Wales PGA Championship and the 1999 Western Australian PGA Championship.

EXEMPT STATUS: 14th on 2004 Nationwide Tour money list

NATIONWIDE TOUR VICTORIES (1): 2004 Jacob's Creek Open.

Nationwide Tour Alumnus

WARREN, Charles

FULL NAME: Charles Otis Warren **BIRTHDATE:** June 21, 1975 **BIRTHPLACE:** Columbia, SC **RESIDENCE:** Columbia, SC; plays out of Thornblade Club, Greer, SC **HEIGHT:** 5-8 **WEIGHT:** 160 **FAMILY:** Wife, Kelly **EDUCATION:** Clemson University (1998, Marketing) **SPECIAL INTERESTS:** Hunting, fishing **TURNED PROFESSIONAL:** 1998 **Q SCHOOL:** 1998 **OTHER INFORMATION:** Member of the Nationwide Tour in 1998 and 2000-04 and a member of the PGA TOUR in 1999. Concluded the 2004 Nationwide Tour season No. 8 on the Tour money list, with $275,138 and two victories. At the Samsung Canadian PGA Championship, tallied his second career win with a final score of 19-under 269, seven strokes ahead of his closest competitor. His 7-under 65 in the second round was a course record. Earned Player of the Month honors for July. Became the eighth player (and second in 2004, along with Daniel Chopra) to win in consecutive starts on Tour when he came back in his next start to win the Cox Classic in Omaha, Nebraska. Finished the event at 21-under-par 267, one stroke ahead of John Elliott. Finished the 2003 Nationwide Tour No. 28 on the money list. Recorded a hole-in-one during the final round of the SAS Carolina Classic. Came back two weeks later and posted another ace during the first round of the Northeast Pennsylvania Classic. Best finish of the season was a T2 at the Albertsons Boise Open, six shots behind winner Roger Tambellini. Made the cut in 17 of 24 starts in 2002, with seven top-25s. Wound up No. 16 on the final money list, less than $10,000 behind Todd Barranger and the final exemption spot for the 2003 PGA TOUR. Earned his first career title at the BMW Charity Pro-Am at The Cliffs, with a record-tying 23-under-par total. Final-round 68 gave him a four-stroke win over Todd Fischer. Joined Jonathan Byrd (2001 winner) as the second consecutive Clemson University graduate to win in Greenville, about 45 minutes from campus. Had surgery on his left shoulder in late February 2001 and played in just 10 events on the Nationwide Tour. Posted five top-10s in 2000 on the Nationwide Tour. Rookie on the PGA TOUR in 1999 after making it through the 1998 Qualifying Tournament on his first attempt with a T17 finish. Made the cut in eight of 26 TOUR events, with one top-25 finish. Winner of 1997 NCAA Championship and 1997 and 1998 Atlantic Coast Conference Championship. First-team All-America selection in 1996-98. Winner of the 1998 Dave Williams Award as country's top collegiate player. One of only two Clemson Tigers to notch two top-10 finishes in the NCAA Championship during their career.

EXEMPT STATUS: Eighth on the 2004 Nationwide Tour money list

BEST PGA TOUR CAREER FINISH: T24—1999 Reno-Tahoe Open.
NATIONWIDE TOUR VICTORIES (3): 2002 BMW Charity Pro-Am at the Cliffs. **2004** Samsung Canadian PGA Championship, Cox Classic.
MONEY & POSITION:

1999 —	67,784 — 213	2003 —	11,984
2000 —	22,056	2004 —	0

BEST 2004 PGA TOUR FINISH: T62—Wachovia Championship.
PGA TOUR CAREER LOW ROUND: 66–1999 AT&T Pebble Beach National Pro-Am/2
2004 SUMMARY: Tournaments Entered—1; in money—0; Top-10 finishes—0
CAREER SUMMARY: Tournaments Entered—30; in money—10; Top-10 finishes—0
CAREER EARNINGS: $101,824
Nationwide Tour Alumnus

WATNEY, Nick

FULL NAME: Nicholas Alan Watney **BIRTHDATE:** April 25, 1981 **BIRTHPLACE:** Sacramento, CA **RESIDENCE:** Fresno, CA **HEIGHT:** 6-2 **WEIGHT:** 180 **FAMILY:** Single **EDUCATION:** Fresno State University (2003) **SPECIAL INTERESTS:** All sports, video games **TURNED PROFESSIONAL:** 2003 **JOINED TOUR:** 2005 **OTHER INFORMATION:** Rookie on the PGA TOUR after finishing fifth on the Nationwide Tour money list in 2004, his first season on that circuit. Made the cut in 19 of 25 tournaments, including 12 top-25 finishes. Entered the final event No. 19 on the official money list but posted his first career win at the Nationwide Tour Championship. Finished the event at 15-under-par 273, good for a three-stroke win and career-best $112,500 paycheck. After missing five cuts in his first seven starts, stormed back by making the cut in 15 of his last 16 events of the season. Had a second-place finish at the Miccosukee Championship just one week before his win, finishing two strokes behind champion D.J. Trahan, but winning $54,000 to jump 17 spots into the top 20 at the time. Held two-stroke lead after 54 holes, but an even-par 71 wasn't enough. Four top-10s in his final five starts helped lead him to Player of the Month honors in October. Turned professional in the summer of 2003 following outstanding collegiate career at Fresno State University. Made pro debut at the FBR Capital Open in June. Posted rounds of 74-74 and missed the cut. Second-round 66 helped him to a T10 finish at the Reno-Tahoe Open and a check for $66,500. First professional win came at the Lewis Chitengwa Memorial Championship on the Canadian Tour in August 2003. Posted four rounds in the 60s and won by five strokes in his only start on that tour. Was the No. 1-ranked college player during his senior year at Fresno State following four consecutive tournament wins in the fall season. Helped Fresno State to the Western Athletic Conference team title in the spring. Five wins during his senior year were more than any other player in the nation. Became the WAC's first three-time Player of the Year. Freshman of the Year in the WAC. Three-time All-America. Ben Hogan Award finalist in 2002. Palmer Cup team member in 2002. Set Fresno State single-season scoring record with a 70.53 average during junior year. Coached by his uncle, Mike, at Fresno State.
EXEMPT STATUS: Fifth on 2004 Nationwide Tour money list
BEST PGA TOUR CAREER FINISH: T10—2003 Reno-Tahoe Open.
NATIONWIDE TOUR VICTORIES (1): 2004 Nationwide Tour Championship.
MONEY & POSITION:

2003 —	73,255	2004 —	0

PGA TOUR CAREER LOW ROUND: 66–2003 Reno-Tahoe Open/2
2004 SUMMARY: Tournaments Entered—1; in money—0; Top-10 finishes—0
CAREER SUMMARY: Tournaments Entered—9; in money—2; Top-10 finishes—1
CAREER EARNINGS: $73,255
Nationwide Tour Alumnus

WATTS, Brian

FULL NAME: Brian Peter Watts **BIRTHDATE:** March 18, 1966 **BIRTHPLACE:** Montreal, Quebec, Canada **RESIDENCE:** Dallas, TX **HEIGHT:** 6-1 **WEIGHT:** 210 **FAMILY:** Wife, Debbye; Jason Bradshaw (7/25/97); Kelsie Diana (11/11/99), Kevin Peter (10/25/02) **EDUCATION:** Oklahoma State **SPECIAL INTERESTS:** Watching NHL's Dallas Stars, keeping up with NFL's Pittsburgh Steelers and Oklahoma State football and basketball; racing cars; participating in all of children's activities, especially sports **TURNED PROFESSIONAL:** 1988 **Q SCHOOL:** 1990, 2002 **OTHER INFORMATION:** Played in nine events on a Major Medical Extension. Made three cuts with best finish a T52 at the Valero Texas Open. Will receive a Major Medical Extension carryover for 2005. Coupled with $158,675 earned in 22 events in 2003-04, has the opportunity to play in seven events to earn $328,820 and match the $484,477 winnings of 2003's No. 125, Esteban Toledo. If he does so, will play out of the Major Medical Extension category for the remainder of the season. Having regained his TOUR card via 2002 PGA TOUR Qualifying School, was limited to 13 events in 2003 due to bulging disk in his back. Moved back into top 125 in 2001 after a year with conditional membership. Had surgery January 5, 2001 to repair a torn labrum in left hip. Posted lone top-10 in 29 starts with T9 at 2000 Westin Texas Open. Made successful transition from Japan Golf Tour to PGA TOUR in 1999, earning $767,409 in first full season since 1991 to rank 57th on money list. Played in only four PGA TOUR events in 1998 but made a name for himself around the world with his play at the British Open. Opened with 68-69 to capture 36-hole lead at Royal Birkdale GC. Third-round 73 maintained two-stroke advantage through 54 holes. Final-round 70 not enough to hold off eventual champion Mark O'Meara, who closed with 68. In four-hole playoff, O'Meara won by two strokes, 17-19. Won twice on Japanese Tour in 1998 at Casio World Open and Yomiuri Open, giving him 12 for his career in Japan. Two-time first-team, two-time second-team All-America and 1987 NCAA champion (individual and team) at Oklahoma State. Teammate of Scott Verplank, Jeff Maggert and Michael Bradley. Although Canadian-born, lived in Canada for only six months and was Naturalized as U.S. citizen at age 16. Son Jason given middle name of Bradshaw in honor of Brian's childhood sports idol, former Pittsburgh Steelers Hall of Fame quarterback Terry Bradshaw.
EXEMPT STATUS: Major Medical Extension
PLAYOFF RECORD: 0-1
BEST PGA TOUR CAREER FINISH: 2—1998 British Open Championship.
MONEY & POSITION:

1986 —	0	1993 —	23,235 — 209	2000 —	311,802 — 133
1988 —	816 — 314	1995 —	33,725 — 221	2001 —	457,293 — 112
1989 —	26,814 — 185	1996 —	6,000 — 303	2002 —	162,704 — 181
1990 —	12,535 — 224	1997 —	15,400 — 248	2003 —	134,905 — 192
1991 —	40,199 — 184	1998 —	335,735 — 90	2004 —	23,770 — 242
1992 —	663 — 314	1999 —	767,409 — 57		

BEST 2004 PGA TOUR FINISH: T52—Valero Texas Open.
PGA TOUR CAREER LOW ROUND: 63–2 times, most recent 2001 Verizon Byron Nelson Classic/3
2004 SUMMARY: Tournaments Entered—9; in money—3; Top-10 finishes—0
CAREER SUMMARY: Tournaments Entered—169; in money—93; Top-10 finishes—9
CAREER EARNINGS: $2,353,005

WETTERICH, Brett

FULL NAME: Brett Wetterich **BIRTHDATE:** August 9, 1973 **BIRTHPLACE:** Cincinnati, OH **RESIDENCE:** Jupiter, FL **HEIGHT:** 6-0 **WEIGHT:** 205 **FAMILY:** Single **EDUCATION:** Wallace State Community College **SPECIAL INTERESTS:** Hunting, fishing, all sports **TURNED PROFESSIONAL:** 1994 **Q SCHOOL:** 1999, 2001 **OTHER INFORMATION:** Member of the PGA TOUR in 2001-02 and the Nationwide Tour in 2003-4. Finished 10th on the 2004 Nationwide Tour money list, with one victory, a second and five top-10s, to earn TOUR card for 2005. Recorded his second career victory at the Envirocare Utah Classic with a 16-under-par 272. Rounds of 67-69-65-71 gave him a one-stroke win over Ryuji Imada and Franklin Langham and a first-place check worth $81,000. The win capped off the month of August in which he recorded four top-25s, good enough for Player of the Month honors. Finished second at the Nationwide Tour Championship, three strokes behind Nick Watney. Made the cut in 16 of 22 events on the 2003 Nationwide Tour, with seven top-25s. Wrapped up the year No. 24 on the money list, with $174,805. Won his first career tournament in his initial event of the 2003 season at the Chitimacha Louisiana Open. Opened with a 10-under-par 62, followed by rounds of 68-64-70 to finish with a season-best 24-under-par 264, three shots in front of Ken Duke. T20 at 2000 PGA TOUR Qualifying School to earn his 2001 PGA TOUR card. Granted Major Medical Extension carryover from 2001 after undergoing wrist surgery on Jan. 8, 2001 and spending the majority of the season rehabbing injury. Originally injured wrist during rookie PGA TOUR campaign in 2000 when he made only nine starts. Earned his first PGA TOUR card by way of T35 finish at the 1999 Q-School, the last player in the field to earn a card. His father got him interested in golf at age 2.
EXEMPT STATUS: 10th on 2004 Nationwide Tour money list
BEST PGA TOUR CAREER FINISH: T8—2002 The Honda Classic.
NATIONWIDE TOUR VICTORIES (2): 2003 Chitimacha Louisiana Open. **2004** Envirocare Utah Classic.
MONEY & POSITION:

1998 —	0	2001 —	0	2003 —	0
2000 —	7,174 — 242	2002 —	203,034 — 174		

PGA TOUR CAREER LOW ROUND: 63–2002 Canon Greater Hartford Open/2
2004 SUMMARY: Tournaments entered—1; in money—0; Top-10 finishes—0
CAREER SUMMARY: Tournaments Entered—44; in money—13; Top-10 finishes—1
CAREER EARNINGS: $210,208
Nationwide Tour Alumnus

WI, Charlie

FULL NAME: Charlie Wi **BIRTHDATE:** January 3, 1972 **BIRTHPLACE:** Seoul, South Korea **RESIDENCE:** North Hills, CA; plays out of Wood Ranch GC; Simi Valley, CA **HEIGHT:** 5-10 **WEIGHT:** 160 **FAMILY:** Single **EDUCATION:** University of California-Berkeley **SPECIAL INTERESTS:** Skiing, all sports **TURNED PROFESSIONAL:** 1995 **Q SCHOOL:** 2004 **OTHER INFORMATION:** Rookie on 2005 PGA TOUR after successfully navigating through all three stages of 2004 Qualifying Tournament. Finished T26 in his fourth attempt at finals. Winner of five Asian Tour events during career dating back to 2000, including three victories in 2001. Also member of Nationwide Tour (1996, 1998-2000) and European Tour (2002-2003). Best finish on European Tour was T5 at 2002 Dubai Desert Classic. Also made multiple starts on Japan Golf Tour during this period. One career PGA TOUR event, the 2002 WGC-NEC Invitational, where he finished T63. First-team All-America in 1995 at University of California, posting the third-lowest stroke average among collegians that season behind Tiger Woods and Stewart Cink. Won the 1990 California State Amateur at age 17 (second-youngest to accomplish that feat) and the 1995 Southern California Amateur Championship. Introduced to golf as a child by his father. Expert skier earned spending money during college by being a ski instructor. Student of martial arts, assisting with flexibility in golf swing.

EXEMPT STATUS: T26 at 2004 PGA TOUR Qualifying Tournament
BEST PGA TOUR CAREER FINISH: T63—2002 WGC-NEC Invitational.
MONEY & POSITION:
2002 — 0
PGA TOUR CAREER LOW ROUND: 72–2002 WGC-NEC Invitational/4
CAREER SUMMARY: Tournaments Entered—1; in money—1; Top-10 finishes—0
Nationwide Tour Alumnus

WIEBE, Mark

FULL NAME: Mark Charles Wiebe **BIRTHDATE:** September 13, 1957 **BIRTHPLACE:** Seaside, OR **RESIDENCE:** Denver, CO **HEIGHT:** 6-3 **WEIGHT:** 225 **FAMILY:** Wife, Cathy; Taylor (9/9/86), Gunner (1/1/89), Collier (4/17/92) **EDUCATION:** San Jose State University **SPECIAL INTERESTS:** Fishing, skiing **TURNED PROFESSIONAL:** 1980 **Q SCHOOL:** 1983, 1984 **OTHER INFORMATION:** Made 11 starts on the Nationwide Tour and six appearances including two made cuts on the PGA TOUR in 2004. Best effort was a T29 at the 2004 B.C. Open, his first made cut since finishing T10 at the 2001 Advil Western Open. Played primarily on the Nationwide Tour in 2003, making 18 starts. Best effort was T10 at the Permian Basin Classic. Had only two appearances on the PGA TOUR in 2003. Granted Special Medical Extension for first five events of the 2002 season. To keep Top-125 exemption status, had to earn $97,560 in those five events but missed cut in all five. Missed six other cuts as well as he tried to overcome elbow problems. Limited to 24 events in 2001 due to same injury. Underwent elbow surgery on Oct. 24, 2001. Earned $308,792 to rank 143rd on money list. Enjoyed best earning season of 16 years on TOUR in 2000, with $511,414. Recorded runner-up finish at the Westin Texas Open and four top-25s. Solo second was worth $280,800, a career payday. Narrowly missed third career PGA TOUR victory at the 1997 Kemper Open, finishing one stroke behind Justin Leonard. Tied for second at 1996 Nissan Open. Played under special medical extension in 1995. Missed most of 1994 season following March skiing accident. At the 1993 Buick Classic, closed 67-66 to pull even with Vijay Singh. Singh birdied third extra hole for victory. Winner of 1989 Colorado Open. Lost in extra holes to Tom Sieckmann at 1988 Anheuser-Busch Golf Classic. Shot 69-65-66-68—268 to win 1986 Hardee's Golf Classic by one stroke over Curt Byrum. Finished with career-best rank on money list (25th) and $260,180. First PGA TOUR victory came at 1985 Anheuser-Busch Golf Classic. Third-round 65 moved him to within one stroke of leader Danny Edwards. Shot 70 in final round to force playoff with John Mahaffey. Birdied first extra hole for title. Loves being a father of three very busy kids. A huge Denver sports fan, particularly of the Denver Broncos. Enjoys fly fishing.

EXEMPT STATUS: Past Champion
PLAYOFF RECORD: 1-2
PGA TOUR VICTORIES (2): 1985 Anheuser-Busch Golf Classic. **1986** Hardee's Golf Classic.
MONEY & POSITION:

1981 —	2,538	— 222	1989 —	296,269	— 41	1997 —	285,139	— 85
1982 —	0		1990 —	210,435	— 72	1998 —	282,211	— 106
1983 —	6,628	— 197	1991 —	100,046	— 136	1999 —	385,508	— 105
1984 —	16,257	— 166	1992 —	174,763	— 86	2000 —	511,414	— 94
1985 —	181,894	— 36	1993 —	360,213	— 42	2001 —	308,792	— 143
1986 —	260,180	— 25	1994 —	16,032	— 233	2002 —	0	
1987 —	128,651	— 82	1995 —	168,832	— 112	2003 —	0	
1988 —	392,166	— 28	1996 —	201,058	— 107	2004 —	25,435	— 241

BEST 2004 PGA TOUR FINISH: T29—B.C. Open.
PGA TOUR CAREER LOW ROUND: 61–1988 Northern Telecom Tucson Open/3
2004 SUMMARY: Tournaments Entered—6; in money—2; Top-10 finishes—0
CAREER SUMMARY: Tournaments Entered—498; in money—288; Top-10 finishes—47
CAREER EARNINGS: $4,314,460
Nationwide Tour Alumnus

WILLIS, Garrett

FULL NAME: Garrett Michael Willis **BIRTHDATE:** November 21, 1973 **BIRTHPLACE:** Charlotte, NC **RESIDENCE:** Knoxville, TN **HEIGHT:** 6-1 **WEIGHT:** 175 **FAMILY:** Wife, Jennifer **EDUCATION:** East Tennessee State University (1996, Communications) **SPECIAL INTERESTS:** Dining, TV and Video games **TURNED PROFESSIONAL:** 1996 **Q SCHOOL:** 2000 **OTHER INFORMATION:** Posted just two top-25s in 2004, including season-best T12 at the Chrysler Classic of Tucson, the event he won in 2001. Made the first hole-in-one in Reno Tahoe Open tournament history when he aced No. 16, using an 8-iron on the 156-yard hole. Best effort of the 2003 season was T11 at the Bell Canadian Open. Aced the par-3 11th hole with a 4-iron from 208 yards during the second round of the 2003 Deutsche Bank Championship. In 2002, fell out of the top 125 on the money list. Earned his only top-10 in his 26th start of the season in Valero Texas Open. Followed first-round 1-over-par 71 with a LaCantera course record 61. Rounds of 66-66 on the weekend earned $261,333, second-largest payday of TOUR career. Paycheck lifted him from 180th to 133rd on the TOUR money list. Needed only 96 putts on the week. Ended the 2002 season making eight consecutive cuts. In 2001 made first PGA TOUR start a winning one, defeating Kevin Sutherland by one stroke at Touchstone Energy Tucson Open. Third-round 64, after opening 71-69, lifted him to within two strokes of lead. Closed with 69. Third TOUR player to win his first start as a member, joining Ben Crenshaw (1973) and Robert Gamez (1990). Finished 66th on the 2000 Nationwide Tour money list with four top-25s. In 1999, made the cut in nine of 15 Nationwide Tour events with five top-25s. Monday qualifier who held the 36- and 54-hole lead at the 1999 Greensboro Open. Owned a three-stroke lead with three holes to play in the final round, but struggled down the stretch and finished second to winner Shaun Micheel. Qualified for the U.S. Open in 1998 and 1999, missing the cut both times. Won the 1997 Panama Open in January, coming from seven strokes back on the final day. Won 1996 Hooters Tour event in Decatur, AL in his first professional tournament. First-team All-American at East Tennessee State.

EXEMPT STATUS: Past Champion
PGA TOUR VICTORIES (1): 2001 Touchstone Energy Tucson Open.
MONEY & POSITION:

1998 —	0		2001 —	684,038	— 77	2003 —	467,213	— 134
1999 —	0		2002 —	444,483	— 136	2004 —	165,210	— 196

BEST 2004 PGA TOUR FINISHES: T12—Chrysler Classic of Tucson; T18—Reno-Tahoe Open.
PGA TOUR CAREER LOW ROUND: 61–2002 Valero Texas Open/2
2004 SUMMARY: Tournaments Entered—17; in money—7; Top-10 finishes—0
CAREER SUMMARY: Tournaments Entered—114; in money—48; Top-10 finishes—2
CAREER EARNINGS: $1,760,942
Nationwide Tour Alumnus

WILSON, Dean

FULL NAME: Dean Hiroshi Wilson **BIRTHDATE:** December 17, 1969 **BIRTHPLACE:** Kaneohe, HI **RESIDENCE:** Las Vegas, NV **HEIGHT:** 6-0 **WEIGHT:** 175 **FAMILY:** Single **EDUCATION:** Brigham Young University (1992, Secondary Education) **SPECIAL INTERESTS:** Fishing **TURNED PROFESSIONAL:** 1992 **Q SCHOOL:** 2002 **OTHER INFORMATION:** Made 16 cuts in a career-high 33 starts on the PGA TOUR in 2004. Posted first top-10 of 2004 with a T3 at the Valero Texas Open to earn $203,000. Jumped to No. 121 on money list with best career finish. Led by one stroke through 36 holes after opening 64-65 in Texas. In 2003, was one of seven rookie (out of 38 players) to retain full status out of the TOUR Qualifying School. In only his 10th career start on the PGA TOUR, finished T6 at the Chrysler Classic of Tucson. Earned status for the 2003 season by finishing T11 at the 2002 PGA TOUR Qualifying Tournament. Best 2002 PGA TOUR finish in four starts was T23 at Sony Open in Hawaii. Won twice on the Japan Golf Tour, at the 2002 Tsuruya Open and 2002 Gateway to the Open Mizuno Open. Came to PGA TOUR after garnering six victories on the Japan Golf Tour during three-year stretch (2000-2). Breakthrough year in Japan came in 2001 with three victories, including the Japan PGA match-play and stroke-play championships, both considered majors on that tour, and made it into the top 70 in the Official World Golf Ranking. Finished second on the 2001 Japan Golf Tour money list, earning over $950,361. Also finished T30 at the U.S. Open. JGT rookie of the year in 2000. Member of the Nationwide Tour in 1999, finishing with two top-25s in eight starts. Posted one top-25 in eight starts on the Nationwide Tour in 1996. As an amateur, was medalist at the 1991 Western Athletic Conference Championship. Member of the 1990-92 WAC championship teams at Brigham Young University. College teammate for three seasons at BYU with PGA TOUR member Mike Weir. Played in the historic first two rounds of the 2003 Bank of America Colonial with Annika Sorenstam and Aaron Barber. Wore a "Go Annika" button to pre-tournament press conference and was widely applauded for sportsmanship at the event. "A lot of people know me from playing with Annika. That's only positive for me. I'm proud to say I was the one with her."

EXEMPT STATUS: T13 at 2004 PGA TOUR Qualifying Tournament
BEST PGA TOUR CAREER FINISH: T3—2004 Valero Texas Open.
MONEY & POSITION:

2001 —	30,055		2003 —	654,345	— 98
2002 —	41,344		2004 —	561,340	— 133

BEST 2004 PGA TOUR FINISH: T3—Valero Texas Open.
PGA TOUR CAREER LOW ROUND: 63–2003 Las Vegas Invitational/2
2004 SUMMARY: Tournaments Entered—33; in money—16; Top-10 finishes—1
CAREER SUMMARY: Tournaments Entered—66; in money—34; Top-10 finishes—3
CAREER EARNINGS: $1,287,084
Nationwide Tour Alumnus

WILSON, Mark

FULL NAME: Mark Joseph Wilson **BIRTHDATE:** October 31, 1974 **BIRTHPLACE:** Menomonee Falls, WI **RESIDENCE:** Chicago, IL; plays out of Cog Hill G&CC **HEIGHT:** 5-8 **WEIGHT:** 145 **FAMILY:** Single **EDUCATION:** University of North Carolina (1997, Mathematics) **SPECIAL INTERESTS:** Skiing, watching Comedy Central **TURNED PROFESSIONAL:** 1997 **Q SCHOOL:** 2002, 2004
OTHER INFORMATION: Regained TOUR card for 2005 with T26 finish at PGA TOUR Qualifying Tournament. Playing with No. 126-150 status in 2004, participated in 19 events with one top-10, a T5 at the Reno-Tahoe Open. Also played in six 2004 Nationwide Tour events with two top-10s. As a rookie in 2003, playing in his 19th career event on TOUR, posted first top-10, a solo fourth at the HP Classic of New Orleans. Narrowly missed on retaining card in rookie season, finishing 128th on money list. Earned his first trip to the PGA TOUR via a T17 finish at the 2002 Qualifying Tournament. Spent 2002 season as a rookie on the Nationwide Tour. Only top-10 was a T8 at the SAS Carolina Classic. Played the Hooters Tour from 1998-2001 and won three times. Played the PGA Tour of Australasia from 2000-02. Has two career holes-in-one in competitive rounds both while playing with Doug LaBelle. Cites Ben Hogan as his hero. Got his start in golf from his father. Biggest thrill in golf was winning the state high school championship as a freshman.
EXEMPT STATUS: T26 at 2004 PGA TOUR Qualifying Tournament
BEST PGA TOUR CAREER FINISH: 4—2003 HP Classic of New Orleans.
MONEY & POSITION:

1998 —	0		2001 —	13,727		2004 —	300,317	— 167
1999 —	12,765	— 270	2002 —	0				
2000 —	8,500		2003 —	482,502	— 128			

BEST 2004 PGA TOUR FINISH: T5—Reno-Tahoe Open.
PGA TOUR CAREER LOW ROUND: 63–2004 Michelin Championship at Las Vegas/3
2004 SUMMARY: Tournaments Entered—19; in money—12; Top-10 finishes—1
CAREER SUMMARY: Tournaments Entered—57; in money—27; Top-10 finishes—2
CAREER EARNINGS: $817,812
Nationwide Tour Alumnus

WOOD, Willie

FULL NAME: Willie West Wood **BIRTHDATE:** October 1, 1960 **BIRTHPLACE:** Kingsville, TX **RESIDENCE:** Edmond, OK; plays out of Oak Tree GC **HEIGHT:** 5-7 **WEIGHT:** 145 **FAMILY:** Wife, Jenny; William (12/17/86), Kelby (6/15/88), Hayden (4/8/96) **EDUCATION:** Oklahoma State University **SPECIAL INTERESTS:** Fishing, physical fitness **TURNED PROFESSIONAL:** 1983 **Q SCHOOL:** 1983, 1992
OTHER INFORMATION: Split time between the PGA TOUR (nine events) and Nationwide Tour (five events). Made four cuts on the PGA TOUR, including a T18 at the 2004 Reno-Tahoe Open. Posted an ace in the third round of the 2004 John Deere Classic with a 7-iron on No. 16 from 168 yards and finished T59. Recorded a T18 at the 2003 Greater Hartford Open, best effort on the PGA TOUR since finishing 12th at the 2001 Southern Farm Bureau Classic. Aced No. 4 with a 5-iron from 186 yards in the final round of the FedEx St. Jude Classic. Made five cuts in six starts on the 2003 Nationwide Tour. In 2002, made a combined seven of 19 cuts, including one top-25 on each Tour. Member of the PGA TOUR since 1983. Enjoyed his best TOUR earnings season in 1998 when he finished 76th on the money list and made $397,110 on strength of a runner-up showing at the Sprint International and T4 at the CVS Charity Classic. Recorded a T12 at the 1997 Masters. First career victory came at the 1996 Deposit Guaranty Golf Classic. Came to Madison, MS after posting eight top-10s in 13 starts on the Nationwide Tour. Won in Mississippi by one stroke over Kirk Triplett. Lost playoff to Joey Sindelar at 1990 Hardees' Golf Classic. Medalist at 1983 PGA TOUR Qualifying Tournament. Winner of 1990 and 1995 Oklahoma Opens. Played in the 1982 Masters as an amateur. Made the cut and finished T41. Outstanding junior career featured victories at 1977 U.S. Junior, 1978 PGA Junior and 1979 Western Junior. Sister Deanie was member of LPGA Tour.
EXEMPT STATUS: Past Champion
PLAYOFF RECORD: 0-1
PGA TOUR VICTORIES (1): 1996 Deposit Guaranty Golf Classic.
MONEY & POSITION:

1983 —	8,400	— 185	1991 —	48,033	— 176	1999 —	115,884	— 185
1984 —	115,741	— 61	1992 —	57,748	— 168	2000 —	45,345	— 216
1985 —	153,706	— 49	1993 —	146,206	— 112	2001 —	196,113	— 173
1986 —	172,629	— 52	1994 —	87,102	— 165	2002 —	85,871	— 204
1987 —	95,917	— 98	1995 —	64,697	— 182	2003 —	118,280	— 200
1988 —	53,064	— 146	1996 —	255,158	— 87	2004 —	78,937	— 221
1989 —	9,677	— 212	1997 —	190,283	— 121			
1990 —	179,972	— 90	1998 —	397,110	— 76			

BEST 2004 PGA TOUR FINISH: T18—Reno-Tahoe Open.
PGA TOUR CAREER LOW ROUND: 63–3 times, most recent 1990 Hardee's Golf Classic/2
2004 SUMMARY: Tournaments Entered—9; in money—4; Top-10 finishes—0
CAREER SUMMARY: Tournaments Entered—457; in money—257; Top-10 finishes—23
CAREER EARNINGS: $2,675,872
Nationwide Tour Alumnus

Z

ZOKOL, Richard

FULL NAME: Richard Zokol **BIRTHDATE:** August 21, 1958 **BIRTHPLACE:** Kitimat, British Columbia **RESIDENCE:** White Rock, British Columbia **HEIGHT:** 5-10 **WEIGHT:** 180 **FAMILY:** Wife, Joanie; Conor and Garrett (10/14/87), Hayley (6/25/90) **EDUCATION:** Brigham Young University **SPECIAL INTERESTS:** Studying the human mind, family, hunting **TURNED PROFESSIONAL:** 1981 **Q SCHOOL:** Fall 1981, 1982, 1986, 1989, 1991, 2000 **OTHER INFORMATION:** Played in one event in 2004, the Bell Canadian Open. Combined with earnings from 2002 ($53,437), had eight 2003 events to equal or exceed 125th place on the 2002 Official PGA TOUR money list ($515,445) to be elevated to the Major Medical Extension category for the remainder of 2003. Made his first cut in his eighth event. PGA TOUR veteran made six of 20 cuts in 2002 before season-ending surgery to repair a severely arthritic joint in a right toe. Did not play after the 2002 Bell Canadian Open, and was granted a Minor Medical Extension for 2003. Earned 2002 TOUR card after finishing No. 13 on 2001 Nationwide Tour money list. Earned Nationwide Tour victory at 2001 Samsung Canadian PGA Championship, where he became first Canadian-born player to win the event since Ashley Chinner in 1996. Set tournament record with 17-under-par 271. Won the 1992 Deposit Guaranty Golf Classic (unofficial event), which was played opposite the Masters. Later that year, posted 19-under par total to win the Greater Milwaukee Open by two strokes over Dick Mast. Member of the 1980 Canada World Amateur Cup team. Winner of 1980 International Champions (Morocco). Won the 1981 Canadian Amateur. Member of the 1981 Brigham Young University NCAA Championship team. Roomed with Bobby Clampett for three years at BYU. Winner of 1982 British Columbia Open on the Canadian Tour, 1984 Utah State Open. Five-time Dunhill Cup team member. Interested in the mental aspects of the game. Once wore earphones to listen to music between shots while playing, earning nickname "Disco Dick."
EXEMPT STATUS: Past Champion
PGA TOUR VICTORIES (1): 1992 Greater Milwaukee Open.
NATIONWIDE TOUR VICTORIES (1): 2001 Samsung Canadian PGA Championship.
MONEY & POSITION:

1982 —	15,111	— 158	1990 —	191,634	— 84	1998 —	29,905	— 231
1983 —	38,107	— 117	1991 —	78,426	— 149	1999 —	27,022	— 246
1984 —	56,605	— 97	1992 —	311,909	— 48	2000 —	169,492	— 172
1985 —	71,192	— 102	1993 —	214,419	— 80	2001 —	32,803	— 220
1986 —	37,888	— 152	1994 —	78,074	— 169	2002 —	53,437	— 215
1987 —	114,406	— 89	1995 —	23,371	— 234	2003 —	19,155	— 241
1988 —	142,153	— 83	1996 —	30,260	— 221	2004 —	0	
1989 —	51,323	— 163	1997 —	53,705	— 201			

BEST 2004 PGA TOUR FINISH: T46—Reno-Tahoe Open.
PGA TOUR CAREER LOW ROUND: 63–1987 Georgia-Pacific Atlanta Golf Classic/2
2004 SUMMARY: Tournaments Entered—1; in money—0; Top-10 finishes—0
CAREER SUMMARY: Tournaments Entered—411; in money—198; Top-10 finishes—20
CAREER EARNINGS: $1,840,397
Nationwide Tour Alumnus

Prominent International Players

Includes top 100 in Official World Golf Ranking through Nov. 8, 2004, active World Golf Hall of Fame members, previous major championship winners and last-named Ryder Cup and Presidents Cup team members.

B

BALLESTEROS, Seve

HEIGHT: 6-0 **WEIGHT:** 195 **BIRTHDATE:** April 9, 1957 **BIRTHPLACE:** Pedrena, Spain **RESIDENCE:** Monaco **FAMILY:** Wife, Carmen; Baldomero (1990), Miguel (1992), Carmen (1994) **SPECIAL INTERESTS:** Cycling, fishing, gardening **TURNED PROFESSIONAL:** 1974 **OTHER INFORMATION:** Did not make a start in professional golf in 2004. Only made one of seven cuts on 2003 European Tour. Led Continental Europe to 13-12 victory over Great Britain and Ireland in April 2000 in the Seve Trophy. Inaugural event was played for Eurobet Seve Ballesteros Trophy at Sunningale GC. Colin Montgomerie was Great Britain-Ireland captain. Victorious European Ryder Cup captain in 1997. Winner of 72 tournaments worldwide, including 48 on European Tour. First victory came at 1976 Dutch Open, latest at 1995 Peugeot Spanish Open. Won five major championships: 1979, 1984 and 1988 British Opens; 1980 and 1983 Masters Tournaments. Has won Open Championships in nine countries: The Netherlands, France, Switzerland, Great Britain, Spain, Ireland, Germany, Japan and Kenya. Also won 1981 Australian PGA. Web site is www.seve-ballesteros.com.

PGA TOUR PLAYOFF RECORD: 1-2

PGA TOUR VICTORIES (9): 1978 Greater Greensboro Open. **1979** British Open Championship. **1980** Masters Tournament. **1983** Masters Tournament, Manufacturers Hanover Westchester Classic. **1984** British Open Championship. **1985** USF&G Classic. **1988** Manufacturers Hanover Westchester Classic, British Open Championship.

MONEY AND POSITION:

1977 —	9,450 —	154	1986 —	45,877 —	141	1995 —	64,345 —	184
1978 —	68,064 —	43	1987 —	305,058 —	32	1996 —	9,300 —	280
1979 —	8,490 —	165	1988 —	165,202 —	71	1997 —	0	
1980 —	87,917 —	48	1989 —	138,094 —	101	1998 —	0	
1981 —	10,299 —	172	1990 —	84,584 —	144	1999 —	0	
1982 —	105,828 —	35	1991 —	64,320 —	160	2000 —	0	
1983 —	210,933 —	18	1992 —	39,206 —	186	2001 —	0	
1984 —	132,660 —	52	1993 —	34,850 —	193	2002 —	0	
1985 —	206,638		1994 —	49,245 —	189	2003 —	0	

2004 PGA TOUR SUMMARY: Tournaments Entered—0; in money—0; Top-10 finishes—0

WORLD GOLF HALL OF FAME MEMBER (Inducted 1997)

BJORN, Thomas (bih-YORN)

HEIGHT: 6-2 **WEIGHT:** 194 **BIRTHDATE:** February 17, 1971 **BIRTHPLACE:** Silkeborg, Denmark **RESIDENCE:** Silkeborg, Denmark **FAMILY:** Wife, Pernilla; Filippa (5/28/99); Oliver and Julia (3/31/03) **SPECIAL INTERESTS:** Soccer **TURNED PROFESSIONAL:** 1993 **OTHER INFORMATION:** Retained his playing privileges on the PGA TOUR after finishing 73rd ($1,050,803) in his first official season on TOUR, but opted not to remain a member in 2005. In his initial event of the TOUR season, finished T4 at the Buick Invitational. Missed two months of action after suffering a neck injury at the British Open. Next top-10 did not come until October, a runner-up at the WGC-American Express Championship in Ireland, just his second top-10 in 13 WGC events (T9-2000 WGC-Accenture Match Play). One of two players (Ernie Els) to record four rounds in the 60s. Did not collect a win for the second straight season on the European Tour and finished 21st on the Volvo Order of Merit, his lowest finish in nine years on that Tour. Collected enough money as a non-member during the 2003 season and accepted his fully-exempt playing privileges on the 2004 PGA TOUR for the first time in his career. Finished T2 at the 2003 British Open where he made a double bogey on the par-3 16th hole and then bogey on No. 17 to fall one back of winner Ben Curtis. Was his fourth consecutive top-10 at the British Open. Did not post a win on the European Tour for the first time since 1997, breaking his streak of five consecutive years with a victory. Captured his second BMW International Open in 2002. Turned two-stroke third-round lead into four-stroke victory over John Bickerton and Bernhard Langer. Won once on 2001 European Tour, at Dubai Desert Classic, where he outdueled Tiger Woods. Also finished T2 at the Smurfit European Open and solo second at the Loch Lomond World Invitational. First European Tour victory came at 1996 Loch Lomond World Invitational, a win that helped him earn '96 Rookie of the Year honors. The Loch Lomond title also a catalyst toward his becoming first Danish golfer to play in Ryder Cup, in 1997. Captured two titles in 1998, Peugeot Open de Espana and Heineken Classic. In 2000, tied for second behind Tiger Woods in British Open and finished alone in third at PGA Championship, also won by Woods. With both parents playing the game, started in golf at age 6.

BEST PGA TOUR CAREER FINISH: 2—2004 WGC-American Express Championship, T2—2000 British Open Championship,2003 British Open Championship.

MONEY AND POSITION:

1996 —	0		1999 —	30,066 —	244	2002 —	360,629	
1997 —	13,118 —	256	2000 —	814,148		2003 —	548,412	
1998 —	92,838 —	186	2001 —	125,780		2004 —	1,050,803 —	73

BEST 2004 PGA TOUR FINISHES: 2—WGC-American Express Championship; T4—Buick Invitational.

2004 PGA TOUR SUMMARY: Tournaments Entered—12; in money—7; Top-10 finishes—2

C

CABRERA, Angel

HEIGHT: 6-0 **WEIGHT:** 210 **BIRTHDATE:** September 12, 1969 **BIRTHPLACE:** Cordoba, Argentina **RESIDENCE:** Cordoba, Argentina **FAMILY:** Wife, Silvia; Federico (5/6/89), Angel (10/3/91) **SPECIAL INTERESTS:** Soccer **TURNED PROFESSIONAL:** 1991 **OTHER INFORMATION:** Best PGA TOUR finish in 2004 was a T4 at the WGC-NEC Invitational, where he shot 67-68 on the weekend. Recorded two runner-up finishes on the European Tour in 2004, at the British Masters (T2) and the Volvo PGA Championship. Split his 2003 season between the PGA TOUR and the European Tour. Best PGA TOUR finish was a T15 at the Masters. Recorded two top-10s on European Tour. In 2002, placed T9 at the Masters. Won the Benson and Hedges International, beating England's Barry Lane by a stroke at The Belfry in England. Joined the PGA TOUR in 2001 as Special Temporary Member the week of The INTERNATIONAL. In 2001 Masters, shot first-round 66, one off the lead, and finished T10. Finished T7 in season's second major championship, U.S. Open. Caddied at Cordoba, home club of friend and mentor Eduardo Romero, until turning professional at age 20. Following three unsuccessful attempts at European Tour Qualifying School, received financial assistance from Romero. His countryman, who lived two blocks away from his young protege, had encouraged him to take up game at age 15. With Romero's support, secured card to play on European Tour in 1995. Shot 61 in 1991 Argentinian Open. Had a putt on 72nd hole of 1999 British Open to join Mark O'Meara-Brian Watts playoff. Claimed his first European title at the 2001 Open de Argentina. Winner of 1995 Paraguay Open and 1996 Volvo Masters of Latin America. Shot 61 in 1991 Argentine Open. Nicknamed "El Pato" (The Duck).

BEST PGA TOUR CAREER FINISH: T4—1999 British Open Championship,2004 WGC-NEC Invitational.

MONEY AND POSITION:

1997 —	10,315 —	268	2001 —	337,105		2004 —	237,839	
1999 —	167,480 —	167	2002 —	632,546				
2000 —	78,256		2003 —	372,252 —	145			

BEST 2004 PGA TOUR FINISH: T4—WGC-NEC Invitational.

2004 PGA TOUR SUMMARY: Tournaments Entered—8; in money—5; Top-10 finishes—1

CAMPBELL, Michael

HEIGHT: 5-10 **WEIGHT:** 189 **BIRTHDATE:** February 23, 1969 **BIRTHPLACE:** Hawera, New Zealand **RESIDENCE:** Wellington, New Zealand; London, England **FAMILY:** Wife, Julie; Thomas (1998), Jordan (2000) **SPECIAL INTERESTS:** Fishing, red wine collecting **TURNED PROFESSIONAL:** 1993 **OTHER INFORMATION:** Made four of six cuts on the PGA TOUR in 2004 and recorded a runner-up finish in the Barclays Scottish Open on the European Tour. In 2003, won Nissan Irish Open and placed second at the Omega European Masters on the European Tour. Playoff victory over Thomas Bjorn and Peter Hedblom at Irish Open was his sixth victory on the European Tour and 14th overall worldwide. In 2002, he won the Smurfit European Open at the K Club. Played on the 2003 PGA TOUR, but missed nine cuts in 14 starts. Earned $432,000 with a runner-up finish at the 2002 Bay Hill Invitational, thanks to a chip-in on the tournament's 72nd hole. Surpassed the previous year's No. 150 on the PGA TOUR Official Money List, and joined the TOUR as a Special Temporary Member for the remainder of 2002. In 1995, led British Open at St. Andrews by two strokes after three rounds. Closed with 76 for T3. Wrist injury produced lengthy fall before a resurgence in 1998. Ended 1999 by defeating Australian Geoff Ogilvy, Ernie Els and Tiger Woods to win first event of 2000 European Tour season, Johnnie Walker Classic in Taiwan. Continued return to form in 2000 by winning Crown Lager New Zealand Open in his home country, then won second successive European Tour event by claiming Heineken Classic in Perth. In October, captured Linde German Masters. Stayed in the race for the Volvo Order of Merit until the final week, eventually finishing a career-best fourth. Received Officer of New Zealand Order of Merit for services to New Zealand golf, called award the highlight of his career. His great-great-great-grandfather, Sir Logan Campbell, moved from Edinburgh to New Zealand in 1845. Winner of the 1992 Australia Amateur Championship. Web site is cambogolf.com.

BEST PGA TOUR CAREER FINISH: 2—2002 Bay Hill Invitational presented by Cooper Tires.

MONEY AND POSITION:

1995 —	141,388 —	135	1999 —	0		2002 —	614,250	
1996 —	66,338 —	187	2000 —	86,223		2003 —	107,814 —	205
1998 —	9,541 —	277	2001 —	213,192		2004 —	86,006	

BEST 2004 PGA TOUR FINISH: T20—British Open Championship.

2004 PGA TOUR SUMMARY: Tournaments Entered—6; in money—4; Top-10 finishes—0

D

DRUMMOND, Scott

HEIGHT: 5-11 **WEIGHT:** 168 **BIRTHDATE:** May 29, 1974 **BIRTHPLACE:** Shrewsbury, England **RESIDENCE:** Yelverton, Devon, England **FAMILY:** Wife, Claire; Keira (2004) **SPECIAL INTERESTS:** Cars, bodyboarding, music **TURNED PROFESSIONAL:** 1996 **OTHER INFORMATION:** Started the week of the 2004 Volvo PGA Championship in 396th position on the Official World Golf Ranking and finished it in 95th after claiming his first victory on the European Tour. Celebrated his 30th birthday during the week at Wentworth Club, then equaled the tournament record of 19-under 269, just four weeks after the birth of his first child, Keira. In four PGA TOUR starts, made three cuts, including sub-par first rounds at the PGA (T66), WGC-NEC Invitational (T61) and WGC-American Express Championship (T43). Has career similarities to Sandy Lyle. Both come from Shropshire, both played amateur golf for England and both took Scottish nationality from their father when they turned professional.

BEST PGA TOUR CAREER FINISH: T43—2004 WGC-American Express Championship.

MONEY AND POSITION:

2004 — 12,350

BEST 2004 PGA TOUR FINISH: T43—WGC-American Express Championship.

2004 PGA TOUR SUMMARY: Tournaments Entered—4; in money—3; Top-10 finishes—0

F

FORSYTH, Alastair

HEIGHT: 6-2 **WEIGHT:** 196 **BIRTHDATE:** February 5, 1976 **BIRTHPLACE:** Glasgow, Scotland **RESIDENCE:** Paisley, Scotland **SPECIAL INTERESTS:** Soccer **TURNED PROFESSIONAL:** 1988 **OTHER INFORMATION:** Recorded eight top-10s on the 2004 European Tour, including a T2 at the season-opening South African Airways Open and a third at the season-ending Volvo Masters Andalucia. Fired first-round 68 at the British Open on the way to T47 finish. Took up the game in Millport on the island of Cumbrae at age 8 and joined Ralston GC the following year. Dad, Alex, a retired police constable in Glasgow, encouraged him to play. Cousin, Calum Innes, formerly an assistant at Turnberry Hotel, is also a professional. Coached by Bill Lockie, who worked with the Scottish Golf Union. Played amateur golf for Scotland at boy, youth and senior level. Led the 2000 race for the Sir Henry Cotton Rookie of the Year Award until the last month, eventually losing out to Ian Poulter, but nevertheless finished 46th on the Volvo Order of Merit. Finished 116th in 2001 but was guaranteed a number of starts on the European Tour in 2002 and secured his first victory in the Carlsberg Malaysian Open after a playoff with Stephen Leaney. Finished the year in 42nd place and joined Paul Lawrie in the WGC-World Cup in Mexico after Andrew Oldcorn pulled out with an injury. Helped Scotland finish in a share of 12th place.

BEST PGA TOUR CAREER FINISH: T40—2003 WGC-American Express Championship.

MONEY AND POSITION:

2003 — 15,181　2004 — 22,404

BEST 2004 PGA TOUR FINISH: T47—British Open Championship.

2004 PGA TOUR SUMMARY: Tournaments Entered—1; in money—1; Top-10 finishes—0

G

GALLACHER, Stephen

HEIGHT: 6-2 **WEIGHT:** 192 **BIRTHDATE:** November 1, 1974 **BIRTHPLACE:** Dechmont, Scotland **RESIDENCE:** Bathgate, Scotland **FAMILY:** Wife, Helen; Jack (2001), Ellie (2004) **SPECIAL INTERESTS:** Soccer, fishing, cycling, snooker **TURNED PROFESSIONAL:** 1995 **OTHER INFORMATION:** Followed in the footsteps of Uncle Bernard Gallacher to win his first professional title at St. Andrews in the dunhill links championship after four rounds over St Andrews, Carnoustie and Kingsbarns. As an amateur, won the Scottish Amateur Match Play and Stroke Play Championships and the Lytham Trophy. Played in victorious Walker Cup side at Royal Porthcawl in 1995. Won his card at first attempt in 1995, but a back injury in the summer of 1996, sustained after removing his luggage from an airport carousel, meant he did not play from June onwards. Regained his card from the Challenge Tour in 1998, helped by victory in the KB Golf Challenge in the Czech Republic. Used acupuncturist and also Scottish Rugby Union trainer Ray McKinnon to help regain full fitness.

MONEY AND POSITION:

1999 — 0

H

HAEGGMAN, Joakim (YO-uh-keem HEG-mun)

HEIGHT: 6-1 **WEIGHT:** 190 **BIRTHDATE:** August 28, 1969 **BIRTHPLACE:** Kalmar, Sweden **RESIDENCE:** Monte Carlo, Monaco; plays out of Kalmar GC in Kalmar, Sweden **FAMILY:** Single **SPECIAL INTERESTS:** Fishing, wine, hunting **TURNED PROFESSIONAL:** 1989 **OTHER INFORMATION:** Won the 2004 Qatar Masters, his first European Tour victory in seven years. Went on to share third place in the Deutsche Bank-SAP Open TPC of Europe and outright third in the Volvo PGA Championship. Missed the first seven months of the 2003 season, recuperating from a broken ankle sustained while playing ice hockey in December 2002. As a result, started the 2004 season on a medical exemption. It was the second time he was injured playing ice hockey with friends. He was out of the game for nearly two years following an accident in 1994 which left him with a dislocated shoulder and broken ribs, an injury which effectively deprived him of the chance to retain his Ryder Cup berth. Served as one of Sam Torrance's captain's assistants at The Belfry during Europe's victory over the United States in The 34th Ryder Cup Matches in 2002. Took up golf at age 10 when parents sent him for personal instruction. Specializes in trick shots in golf clinics. Equaled record 27 for nine holes in the Alfred Dunhill Cup at St Andrews in 1997. Was the first Swede to play in The Ryder Cup Matches in 1993.

BEST PGA TOUR CAREER FINISH: T16—2004 British Open Championship.

MONEY AND POSITION:

1994 — 0　1998 — 13,736 — 259
1996 — 0　2004 — 105,316

BEST 2004 PGA TOUR FINISH: T16—British Open Championship.

2004 PGA TOUR SUMMARY: Tournaments Entered—5; in money—4; Top-10 finishes—0

HANSEN, Anders

HEIGHT: 6-1 **WEIGHT:** 165 **BIRTHDATE:** Sept. 16, 1970 **BIRTHPLACE:** Sonderborg, Denmark **RESIDENCE:** Monte Carlo **FAMILY:** Children, Marcus (1998), Filuca (2003) **SPECIAL INTERESTS:** Sports **TURNED PROFESSIONAL:** 1995 **OTHER INFORMATION:** Recorded a fourth and second on the European Tour at The Heritage and Open de Madrid, respectively, late in 2004 to jump into the top 100 in the world. Made his major breakthrough on the European Tour by winning the Volvo PGA Championship at Wentworth Club in 2002. Also finished T77 in the British Open and T58 and T57 in the WGC-NEC Invitational and WGC-American Express. Twice Danish Amateur champion and Eisenhower Trophy player, he started the game at age 10 influenced by the fact that his parents both played. Brother, Nicolai, is a scratch golfer. Anders attended University of Houston and won two college tournaments. Finished T2 in first professional tournament on the European Challenge Tour, the Team Erhverv Danish Open in 1995. No relation to his namesake, Soren. However, both made holes in one in successive weeks on the European Tour in 1999 and won their first European Tour titles within a month of each other in 2002.

BEST PGA TOUR CAREER FINISH: T33—2003 WGC-Accenture Match Play Championship.

MONEY AND POSITION:

1999 — 0　2003 — 0
2002 — 12,247　2004 — 0

BEST 2004 PGA TOUR FINISH: T33—WGC-Accenture Match Play Championship.

2004 PGA TOUR SUMMARY: Tournaments Entered—1; in money—0; Top-10 finishes—0

HO, S.K.

HEIGHT: 5-10 **WEIGHT:** 170 **BIRTHDATE:** August 20, 1973 **BIRTHPLACE:** Pusan, South Korea **RESIDENCE:** Kyong Ki-do, South Korea **FAMILY:** Single **SPECIAL INTERESTS:** Music **TURNED PROFESSIONAL:** 1995 **OTHER INFORMATION:** Won twice on the Japan Golf Tour in 2004 and placed third on the Order of Merit. As a result, played in two majors (cut at British Open, T55 at PGA) and two World Golf Championships events (T27 at WGC-NEC Invitational and 53rd at WGC-American Express Championship). Birdied final hole at the Japan PGA Championship in May to complete a 68 for a one-stroke victory and a five-year exemption on the Japan Golf Tour. In July, won the Japan Golf Tour Championship in a playoff. Claimed his first title on the Asian PGA Tour by winning the Shinhan Donghae Open on home soil in September 2002. Made a double eagle in the tournament and beat Simon Yates in a two-hole playoff. Also won his initial Japan Golf Tour event in July 2002, the first Korean winner in Japan since 1999. Played 2002 and 2003 WGC-World Cup for Korea with K.J. Choi. In 2002 in Mexico, they finished T3. Started playing golf at age 10.

BEST PGA TOUR CAREER FINISH: T27—2004 WGC-NEC Invitational.

MONEY AND POSITION:

2003 — 41,330　2004 — 13,200

BEST 2004 PGA TOUR FINISH: T27—WGC-NEC Invitational.

2004 PGA TOUR SUMMARY: Tournaments Entered—4; in money—3; Top-10 finishes—0

HOWELL, David

HEIGHT: 6-1 **WEIGHT:** 190 **BIRTHDATE:** June 23, 1975 **BIRTHPLACE:** Swindon, England **RESIDENCE:** Surrey, England **FAMILY:** Single **TURNED PROFESSIONAL:** 1995 **OTHER INFORMATION:** Ryder Cup rookie in 2004, posting a 1-1 record. Teamed with Paul Casey to win a Saturday Four-ball match and hold off an American rally. Birdied 16th and 17th holes at Oakland Hills to square the match before Casey parred the 18th hole to beat Chad Campbell and Jim Furyk 1-up. Lost to Furyk, 6 and 4, in singles. Posted his first top-10 in 12 career PGA TOUR events, a third at the 2004 WGC-American Express Championship in Ireland. Recorded nine top-10s and 17 top-25s in European Tour competition in 2004. Collected his first professional victory in November 1998 when he won the MasterCard Australian PGA Championship by seven strokes, three months before his win in Dubai. In his amateur days, won the British Boys Championship in 1993 before collecting 2 1/2 of three points in the 1995 Walker Cup victory over a Tiger Woods-led United States at Royal Porthcawl. Beat Notah Begay III in singles.

BEST PGA TOUR CAREER FINISH: 3—2004 WGC-American Express Championship.

MONEY AND POSITION:

1997 — 0	2001 — 0	2004 — 18,500
1998 — 12,471 — 263	2002 — 0	
1999 — 12,675 — 271	2003 — 0	

BEST 2004 PGA TOUR FINISH: 3—WGC-American Express Championship.

2004 PGA TOUR SUMMARY: Tournaments Entered—3; in money—2; Top-10 finishes—1

I

IMMELMAN, Trevor

HEIGHT: 5-10 **WEIGHT:** 159 **BIRTHDATE:** Dec. 16, 1979 **BIRTHPLACE:** Cape Town, South Africa **RESIDENCE:** Richmond, England and Orlando, FL **FAMILY:** Wife, Carminita **SPECIAL INTERESTS:** Music, movies **TURNED PROFESSIONAL:** 1999 **OTHER INFORMATION:** Followed in the footsteps of one of his heroes, Gary Player, when he became the first person since the Black Knight in 1976-77 to successfully defend the South African Airways Open in 2004. Came from two strokes back after three rounds to win by three strokes over Scotland's Alastair Forsyth and England's Steve Webster. Earned second win of the season at Deutsche Bank-SAP Open TPC of Europe. Tied for second with Padraig Harrington through 54 holes, two back of leader Gregory Havret. Final-round 65 was one better than Harrington's 66 to gain a one-stroke victory. Best PGA TOUR finish was a T17 at the WGC-Accenture Match Play Championship. In defense of WGC-World Cup title, finished T3 in 2004. In 2003, hit approach shot from 169 yards to six inches on the first playoff hole against Tim Clark at the South African Open. Tap-in birdie earned first career victory after three previous runner-up finishes, and $200,000 along with a two-year exemption on the European Tour. Shared first-round lead with five others at the Bay Hill Invitational but shot 8-over 80 in second round and missed cut. In third career World Golf Championships event, posted first career top-10 finish on the PGA TOUR with a T9 at the 2003 NEC Invitational. Won the 2003 WGC-World Cup with Rory Sabbatini. Recorded three seconds in 2002 on the European Tour: French Open, Volvo Scandinavian Masters and Omega European Masters. Also T43 at the British Open and T27 at the WGC-American Express. In 1996, made the South African team at the age of 17 and played in the Eisenhower Trophy in Chile. Perhaps 1997 was his defining year when he lost in three finals, the British Amateur at Royal St George's, the New Zealand Amateur and the US Junior. Made the cut as an amateur at the 1999 Masters and 2001 Memorial Tournament. Won the 2000 Vodacom Players Championship in his native South Africa. 1998 USGA Public Links champion. Started golf at age 5 and was a scratch player by age 12. Father, Johan, is the commissioner of the Sunshine Tour.

BEST PGA TOUR CAREER FINISH: T9—2003 WGC-NEC Invitational.

MONEY AND POSITION:

2002 — 21,728	2003 — 126,150	2004 — 109,560

BEST 2004 PGA TOUR FINISHES: T17—WGC-Accenture Match Play Championship; T23—WGC-American Express Championship.

2004 PGA TOUR SUMMARY: Tournaments Entered—12; in money—9; Top-10 finishes—0

IZAWA, Toshi (Toe-SHI ih-ZAH-wuh)

HEIGHT: 5-6 **WEIGHT:** 155 **BIRTHDATE:** March 2, 1968 **BIRTHPLACE:** Kanagawa, Japan **RESIDENCE:** Kanagawa, Japan **FAMILY:** Wife, Kazuko; Yumiko (7/21/97), Kyoko (12/12/99), Joichiro (8/26/02) **SPECIAL INTERESTS:** Listening to music **TURNED PROFESSIONAL:** 1989 **OTHER INFORMATION:** Missed cut in the Masters and U.S. Open and lost in the first round of the WGC-Accenture Match Play Championship in his only PGA TOUR starts. Won twice on the Japan Golf Tour in 2003, his first wins there since a five-win season in 2001. In 2002, recorded three top-25s on the PGA TOUR, including the WGC-Accenture Match Play, PGA Championship and WGC-NEC Invitational. Earned Special Temporary Member status on PGA TOUR in 2001, earning $469,180 in only four official events. Lost in six-man playoff at Nissan Open, which was won by Robert Allenby. In his Masters debut in 2001, T4 to gain Special Temporary status in only third official event, earning $246,400. Leading money-winner on 2001 Japan Golf Tour in with a career-high five victories. Has 14 career titles on the Japan Golf Tour.

PGA TOUR PLAYOFF RECORD: 0-1

BEST PGA TOUR CAREER FINISH: T2—2001 Nissan Open.

MONEY AND POSITION:

1999 — 0	2001 — 469,180	2003 — 73,000
2000 — 20,500	2002 — 69,204	2004 — 0

BEST 2004 PGA TOUR FINISH: T33—WGC-Accenture Match Play Championship.

2004 PGA TOUR SUMMARY: Tournaments Entered—3; in money—1; Top-10 finishes—0

J

JACQUELIN, Raphael (ra-FIE-ell JACK-uh-lan)

HEIGHT: 5-11 **WEIGHT:** 165 **BIRTHDATE:** May 8, 1974 **BIRTHPLACE:** Lyon, France **RESIDENCE:** Gland, Switzerland **FAMILY:** Wife, Fanny; Hugo (1997) **SPECIAL INTERESTS:** Soccer, tennis, music **TURNED PROFESSIONAL:** 1995 **OTHER INFORMATION:** Finished in the top five seven times on the 2004 European Tour in search of first European Tour title. Closest call was a sudden-death playoff loss to Marcel Siem at the Dunhill Championship in South Africa. Placed 29th on the Order of Merit. The 2003 season was the Frenchman's best on the European Tour since he graduated from the European Challenge Tour in 1997. Missed only five cuts in his 29 outings and placed a career-best 20th on the Order of Merit. Established three course records between August and October. Dreamed of being a professional soccer player until a knee injury at age 13 forced him to try other sports. Took up tennis, then switched to golf.

BEST PGA TOUR CAREER FINISH: T13—2001 British Open Championship.

MONEY AND POSITION:

1997 — 0	2002 — 0	2004 — 19,756
2001 — 57,310	2003 — 16,214	

BEST 2004 PGA TOUR FINISH: T54—British Open Championship.

2004 PGA TOUR SUMMARY: Tournaments Entered—2; in money—1; Top-10 finishes—0

JIMENEZ, Miguel Angel (ME-gehl ahn-HEL HIM-en-ez)

HEIGHT: 5-10 **WEIGHT:** 162 **BIRTHDATE:** January 5, 1964 **BIRTHPLACE:** Malaga, Spain **RESIDENCE:** Malaga, Spain **FAMILY:** Wife: Montserrat; Miguel Angel (5/7/95), Victor (1/5/99) **SPECIAL INTERESTS:** Cars **TURNED PROFESSIONAL:** 1982 **OTHER INFORMATION:** At age 40, won a season-high four times on the European Tour and placed fourth on the Order of Merit. Won the Johnnie Walker Classic, the Algarve Open, the BMW Asian Open and the BMW International. Capped the season by making his second European Ryder Cup team and teamed with Sergio Garcia to finish second for the WGC-World Cup competition in Spain. In seven PGA TOUR starts, his best finish was a T16 at the WGC-American Express Championship. In 2000, played in 11 PGA TOUR events and had two top-10 finishes, including a T2 with Ernie Els behind winner Tiger Woods at the U.S. Open. Finished fourth on the Volvo Order of Merit in 1998, the highlight coming in the Trophée Lancôme, where he chipped in for a birdie-2 at the 72nd hole to win. Also finished fourth in 1999, where apart from his win at Montecastillo and in the Turespaña Masters Open Andalucia, he also finished second in the WGC-American Express Championship at Valderrama, where he lost to Tiger Woods in a playoff. At the 1999 Ryder Cup, won once and halved two matches. One of seven brothers, he worked as a caddie in Malaga and did not take up the game until the age of 15. Nicknamed 'The Mechanic' but has a preference for driving, rather than repairing, high performance vehicles, especially his red Ferrari.

PGA TOUR PLAYOFF RECORD: 0-1

BEST PGA TOUR CAREER FINISHES: 2—1999 WGC-American Express Championship, T2—2000 U.S. Open Championship.

MONEY AND POSITION:

1995 — 57,196 — 193	1999 — 194,188 — 154	2003 — 0
1996 — 26,631 — 227	2000 — 488,848	2004 — 66,367
1997 — 0	2001 — 464,457 — 107	
1998 — 0	2002 — 280,568 — 160	

BEST 2004 PGA TOUR FINISH: T16—WGC-American Express Championship.

2004 PGA TOUR SUMMARY: Tournaments Entered—7; in money—6; Top-10 finishes—0

K

KATAYAMA, Shingo

HEIGHT: 5-7 **WEIGHT:** 160 **BIRTHDATE:** January 31, 1973 **BIRTHPLACE:** Ibaragi, Japan **RESIDENCE:** Tokyo, Japan **FAMILY:** Wife, Michiyo **SPECIAL INTERESTS:** Reading, skiing **TURNED PROFESSIONAL:** 1995 **OTHER INFORMATION:** Captured The Crowns and Woodone Open Hiroshima on Japan Golf Tour and made all three cuts in his PGA TOUR starts. Won 2003 Japan PGA Championship and ABC Championship on Japan Golf Tour. Played in a career-high eight PGA TOUR events in 2002, making the cut in two of the four majors. Became popular worldwide player at 2001 PGA Championship, smiling and joking on the way to a T4 finish. Displayed cowboy-style hat in performance. Won three times in Japan in 2001, at Token Corporation Cup, Asia Pacific Open and Suntory Open. Also had 12 top-10s on way to finishing second on money list. Showed strong "finishing kick" in closing out 2000, winning three starts in four weeks on Japan Golf Tour. Stretch drive gave him first money title. At 27, youngest earnings leader since 26-year-old Jumbo Ozaki in 1973. Captured Dunlop Phoenix in November, then in December won Nippon Series JT Cup and Okinawa Open back-to-back. Three victories lifted his season total to five. Earned third career title in April at Asian Tour Kirin Cup, followed by Munsingwear Open KSB Cup in May. First Japan Golf Tour win came at 1998 Sanko Grand Summer Championship. Followed with No. 2 in 1999, JCB Classic Sendai.

BEST PGA TOUR CAREER FINISH: T4—2001 PGA Championship.

MONEY AND POSITION:

1995 — 0
1999 — 9,374 — 297
2000 — 0
2001 — 254,685
2002 — 66,277
2003 — 61,499
2004 — 12,650

BEST 2004 PGA TOUR FINISH: T33—WGC-Accenture Match Play Championship.

2004 PGA TOUR SUMMARY: Tournaments Entered—3; in money—3; Top-10 finishes—0

L

LAWRIE, Paul

HEIGHT: 5-11 **WEIGHT:** 180 **BIRTHDATE:** January 1, 1969 **BIRTHPLACE:** Aberdeen, Scotland **RESIDENCE:** Aberdeen, Scotland **FAMILY:** Wife: Marian; Craig Robert (1995), Michael (1998) **SPECIAL INTERESTS:** Snooker, Aberdeen Football Club, cars **TURNED PROFESSIONAL:** 1986 **OTHER INFORMATION:** Only made cut in five PGA TOUR starts was a T37 at the Masters. Recorded one top-25 on the European Tour, a T11 at the Turespana Mallorca Classic. In 2003, finished T9 at the BellSouth Classic, his first PGA TOUR top-10 since a T5 at the 2000 WGC-Accenture Match Play Championship. Won 2002 Celtic Manor Resort Wales Open and placed T2 in the Omega European Masters the next week. Won 2001 Alfred dunhill links championship and finished second at Celtic Manor on European Tour. Played eight PGA TOUR events through 2000 after joining in November 1999, with his best finish being T5 in two World Golf Championships events — the Accenture Match Play and the World Cup. Defeated Jean Van de Velde and Justin Leonard in four-hole playoff to win 1999 British Open. Came from 10 strokes behind — the largest comeback in major championship history — with a final-round 67 to win at Carnoustie, just an hour from his home. Birdied the last two holes of the four-hole playoff. Worked as assistant under the late Doug Smart at Banchory, near Aberdeen, after leaving school at 17. The club has named the 14th hole after him. Backed by a consortium of local businessmen, won the 1992 UAP Under-25s Championship by eight strokes. Made superb Ryder Cup debut in 1999 at Brookline - hitting the opening tee shot and claiming 3 points, including a win over Jeff Maggert in the bottom singles tie. Awarded honorary law doctorate from Robert Gordon's University in his native Aberdeen. Made an Honorary Life Member of European Tour, then awarded the MBE in Queen's Birthday Honours List.

PGA TOUR PLAYOFF RECORD: 1-0

PGA TOUR VICTORIES (1): 1999 British Open Championship.

MONEY AND POSITION:

1995 — 8,733 — 263
1996 — 0
1998 — 0
1999 — 562,234 — 72
2000 — 249,735 — 147
2001 — 19,312
2002 — 50,335
2003 — 225,974
2004 — 32,663

BEST 2004 PGA TOUR FINISH: T37—Masters Tournament.

2004 PGA TOUR SUMMARY: Tournaments Entered—5; in money—1; Top-10 finishes—0

M

McDOWELL, Graeme (Grey-am)

HEIGHT: 5-11 **WEIGHT:** 168 **BIRTHDATE:** July 30, 1979 **BIRTHPLACE:** Portrush, Northern Ireland **RESIDENCE:** Cardiff, Wales **FAMILY:** Single **SPECIAL INTERESTS:** Reading, traveling **TURNED PROFESSIONAL:** 2002 **OTHER INFORMATION:** Captured the Telecom Italia Open in 2004 in a Monday playoff with Thomas Levet of France. Shot a record-tying 62 at St. Andrews in the first round of the dunhill links championship, where he placed second. Finished the European Tour season with nine top-10s, including a win, two seconds and two thirds to place sixth on the Order of Merit. Won his first European Tour title in only his fourth start as a professional when he won the 2002 Volvo Scandinavian Masters at Kunsängen Golf Club, the club he represents. Played a prominent role in Great Britain and Ireland's retention of the Walker Cup in 2001 at Sea Island, GA. At University of Alabama-Birmingham, McDowell was ranked the top collegiate golfer in the U.S.

BEST PGA TOUR CAREER FINISH: T30—2002 Air Canada Championship.

MONEY AND POSITION:

2001 — 0
2002 — 31,910
2003 — 9,620
2004 — 0

BEST 2004 PGA TOUR FINISH: T43—WGC-American Express Championship.

2004 PGA TOUR SUMMARY: Tournaments Entered—3; in money—1; Top-10 finishes—0

McGINLEY, Paul

HEIGHT: 5-7 **WEIGHT:** 165 **BIRTHDATE:** December 16, 1966 **BIRTHPLACE:** Dublin, Ireland **RESIDENCE:** Sunningdale, Berkshire, England **FAMILY:** Wife, Alison; Niamh (1999), Killian (2000), Maria (2002) **SPECIAL INTERESTS:** Soccer, music, Formula 1 racing **TURNED PROFESSIONAL:** 1991 **OTHER INFORMATION:** Best finish of the season on the PGA TOUR was a T6 at the PGA Championship. On the European Tour, placed second at the Dubai Desert Classic and T2 at the KLM Open. Totaled 2-0-1 record at the 2004 Ryder Cup. Teamed with Padraig Harrington to finish T3 at the WGC-World Cup. Scored the clinching point in the 2002 Ryder Cup by scoring a halve with American Jim Furyk. In 2001, won third European Tour title at The Celtic Manor Resort Wales Open. Earned first two titles at 1996 Hohe Brucke Open and 1997 Oki Pro-Am. Original sporting love was Gaelic football, but concentrated on golf after suffering broken left kneecap at age of 19. With Padraig Harrington, won World Cup of Golf at Kiawah Island, SC in November 1997.

BEST PGA TOUR CAREER FINISH: T6—2004 PGA Championship.

MONEY AND POSITION:

1993 — 0
1996 — 31,388 — 219
1997 — 9,131 — 279
1998 — 0
1999 — 0
2000 — 38,717
2001 — 57,079
2002 — 120,823
2003 — 41,330
2004 — 215,101

BEST 2004 PGA TOUR FINISH: T6—PGA Championship.

2004 PGA TOUR SUMMARY: Tournaments Entered—5; in money—4; Top-10 finishes—1

MONTGOMERIE, Colin

HEIGHT: 6-1 **WEIGHT:** 198 **BIRTHDATE:** June 23, 1963 **BIRTHPLACE:** Glasgow, Scotland **RESIDENCE:** London, England **FAMILY:** Children, Olivia (1993), Venetia (1996), Cameron (1998) **SPECIAL INTERESTS:** Music, cars, films **TURNED PROFESSIONAL:** 1987 **OTHER INFORMATION:** One of the premier golfers on the European Tour with 28 career titles and a record seven consecutive Order of Merit titles for yearly earnings from 1993-99. European Tour Player of the Year four times. In 2004, best PGA TOUR finish was a T9 at the WGC-Accenture Match Play Championship. Was in contention at the British Open at home course, Royal Troon, before shooting 72-76 on the weekend for T25 finish. Won the Caltex Masters on the European Tour, his 12th consecutive year with a professional victory. Went 3-0-1 in the 2004 Ryder Cup victory, improving his overall record to 19-8-5 in seven appearances, including 5-0-2 in singles. Shared the title in the 2002 season-ending Volvo Masters with Bernhard Langer after their playoff was stopped because of darkness after two holes. Hampered by an ailing back most of 2002, but still came back near end of season to lead European Team victory in the Ryder Cup, earning 4 points. Won the Skins Game at the end of 2000, his first victory on American soil. Born in Scotland, raised in Yorkshire where father, James, was a company director. Attended Houston Baptist University. Father retired as Royal Troon secretary in 1997. Lost in playoff for 1994 U.S. Open, and runner-up again to Ernie Els in 1997. Also defeated in sudden death by Steve Elkington for the PGA Championship in 1995.

PGA TOUR PLAYOFF RECORD: 0-2

BEST PGA TOUR CAREER FINISHES: 2—1995 PGA Championship,1997 U.S. Open Championship, T2—1994 U.S. Open Championship, 1996 THE PLAYERS Championship.

MONEY AND POSITION:

1992 — 98,045 — 132
1993 — 17,992 — 221
1994 — 213,828 — 87
1995 — 335,617 — 53
1996 — 421,011 — 48
1997 — 578,991 — 37
1998 — 321,823 — 97
1999 — 369,651 — 111
2000 — 409,044
2001 — 102,762
2002 — 188,095
2003 — 50,523
2004 — 96,479

BEST 2004 PGA TOUR FINISH: T9—WGC-Accenture Match Play Championship.

2004 PGA TOUR SUMMARY: Tournaments Entered—6; in money—5; Top-10 finishes—1

Prominent International Players

O

O'HERN, Nick

HEIGHT: 6-1 **WEIGHT:** 163 **BIRTHDATE:** October 18, 1971 **BIRTHPLACE:** Perth, Australia **RESIDENCE:** Perth, Australia **FAMILY:** Wife, Alana; Riley Matisse (2003) **SPECIAL INTERESTS:** Reading, Japanese language, basketball, wine collecting **TURNED PROFESSIONAL:** 1994 **OTHER INFORMATION:** Left-hander had best season on European Tour, with two seconds (French Open and Linde German Masters), two thirds and 11 top-10s. Made two 2004 PGA TOUR starts and finished T28 at the WGC-American Express Championship in Ireland and T31 in the PGA. Started golf at age 9, following his father, a 3-handicapper. Father played baseball for Australia and son for Western Australia. It was a tossup between turning professional at baseball, tennis or golf. Came through European Tour Qualifying School on first attempt in 1998.

BEST PGA TOUR CAREER FINISH: T5—2001 WGC-Accenture Match Play Championship.

MONEY AND POSITION:

2000 —	15,707	2003 —	0
2001 —	0	2004 —	34,250

BEST 2004 PGA TOUR FINISH: T28—WGC-American Express Championship.

2004 PGA TOUR SUMMARY: Tournaments Entered—2; in money—2; Top-10 finishes—0

R

ROMERO, Eduardo

HEIGHT: 6-2 **WEIGHT:** 185 **BIRTHDATE:** July 17, 1954 **BIRTHPLACE:** Cordoba, Argentina **RESIDENCE:** Cordoba, Argentina **FAMILY:** Wife: Adriana; Dolly (1981) **SPECIAL INTERESTS:** Hunting, fishing **TURNED PROFESSIONAL:** 1982 **OTHER INFORMATION:** Turned 50 and played on three Tours in 2004. Started all four majors, with two made cuts and a best finish of 39th at the Masters. Made three Champions Tour starts, with a best finish of T2 at the Senior British Open in his debut. Had a second and a third on the European Tour. T15 at the 2003 U.S. Open where he was three strokes back after 36 holes. Won the 2002 Barclays Scottish Open at Loch Lomond. Beat Fredrick Jacobson on the first playoff hole. With win at age 47 became the third-oldest winner in the history of the European Tour, behind Des Smyth and Neil Coles. Was also second at the dunhill links championship, losing to Padraig Harrington in a playoff. Nicknamed "El Gato" (The Cat) because of the way he stealthily stalks and overcomes opponents. Son of a club professional in Cordoba, where he still lives, he earned his PGA TOUR card in 1994 but returned to European Tour after one season. Used his own money to help sponsor friend Angel Cabrera on the European Tour and was rewarded in 1999 when Cabrera finished 10th on the Volvo Order of Merit. Attributed success over last few years to improved concentration, thanks to the study of an Indian yoga technique, Rhami Hayat.

BEST PGA TOUR CAREER FINISH: T2—1990 The International.

MONEY AND POSITION:

1986 —	21,749 —	172	1995 —	24,942 —	233	2001 —	54,374
1987 —	0		1996 —	12,158 —	264	2002 —	0
1990 —	74,667 —	152	1997 —	76,512 —	179	2003 —	156,515
1991 —	6,179 —	249	1998 —	35,945 —	223	2004 —	43,750
1992 —	0		1999 —	65,000 —	217		
1993 —	18,500 —	219	2000 —	23,534			

BEST 2004 PGA TOUR FINISH: T33—WGC-Accenture Match Play Championship.

2004 PGA TOUR SUMMARY: Tournaments Entered—6; in money—3; Top-10 finishes—0

T

TANIGUCHI, Toru (TOR-u Tan-a-goochi)

HEIGHT: 5-5 **WEIGHT:** 160 **BIRTHDATE:** February 10, 1968 **BIRTHPLACE:** Nara, Japan **RESIDENCE:** Nara, Japan **FAMILY:** Single **TURNED PROFESSIONAL:** 1992 **OTHER INFORMATION:** Won the Japan Open and Bridgestone Open on the Japan Golf Tour in late 2004 for his first victories in Japan since 2002 when he won four times and finished first in the Order of Merit. In 2001, finished third at the WGC-Accenture Match Play Championship. Defeated Bob Estes, Vijay Singh, Stuart Appleby and countryman Shigeki Maruyama before falling to eventual champion Steve Stricker in the semifinals. Received paycheck of $400,000. First career victory came in the 1998 Mitsubishi Galant Championship. Finished T88 at the 2000 PGA TOUR Qualifying Tournament, thereby missing qualifying for fully-exempt status on the 2001 Nationwide Tour by one stroke.

BEST PGA TOUR CAREER FINISH: 3—2001 WGC-Accenture Match Play Championship.

MONEY AND POSITION:

1998 —	0	2002 —	170,510
2001 —	187,914	2003 —	0

2004 PGA TOUR SUMMARY: Tournaments entered—4; in money—0; Top-10 finishes—0

W

WOOSNAM, Ian

HEIGHT: 5-5 **WEIGHT:** 160 **BIRTHDATE:** March 2, 1958 **BIRTHPLACE:** Oswestry, Wales **RESIDENCE:** Jersey, Channel Islands **FAMILY:** Wife, Glendryth; Daniel (1985), Rebecca (1988), Ami (1991) **SPECIAL INTERESTS:** Fishing, snooker, sports **TURNED PROFESSIONAL:** 1976 **OTHER INFORMATION:** Former Masters champion's best 2004 finish were two top-10s on the European Tour. Missed the cut at the Masters and PGA. Became the oldest winner in the history of the Cisco World Match Play Championship in 2001 (unofficial European Tour event) at the age of 43, defeating Padraig Harrington, 2 and 1, in the finals at Wentworth Club's famous West Course in Surrey, England. Victory was his third Cisco Match Play Championship title. T3 at 2001 British Open, matching best finish of career (1986) there. Entered final round tied for the lead with three other players. After making birdie from six inches on the par-3 first hole to re-claim a share of the lead, it was discovered that he had 15 clubs in his bag. Was penalized two strokes for the violation. Woosnam still managed a final-round 71. 28 career European Tour victories to go along with two PGA TOUR wins. Member of eight consecutive European Ryder Cup squads (1983-97). Both parents are Welsh and he learned the game on the local Llanmynech course (15 holes in Wales, three in England) on the border. Worked on family farm for six months after leaving school. Credits his stocky but powerful physique to lifting heavy hay bales. A rival of Sandy Lyle in Shropshire County Golf. Needed three attempts at Qualifying School to gain card. Used to travel in camper van and eat tins of beans to save money when an aspiring pro. Twice headed Volvo Order of Merit (1987, '90). European Tour Player of the Year in 1987. Won Masters in 1991. Lives in Jersey and commutes on own airplane.

PGA TOUR PLAYOFF RECORD: 1-0

PGA TOUR VICTORIES (2): 1991 USF&G Classic, Masters Tournament.

MONEY AND POSITION:

1984 —	0		1992 —	52,046 —	173	1999 —	104,478 —	195
1986 —	4,000 —	233	1993 —	55,426 —	176	2000 —	40,342	
1987 —	3,980 —	236	1994 —	51,895 —	188	2001 —	225,878	
1988 —	8,464 —	219	1995 —	174,464 —	106	2002 —	26,732	
1989 —	146,323 —	97	1996 —	41,696 —	203	2003 —	13,432	
1990 —	72,138 —	156	1997 —	40,738 —	216	2004 —	0	
1991 —	485,023 —	30	1998 —	123,005 —	174			

BEST 2004 PGA TOUR FINISH: T72—British Open Championship.

2004 PGA TOUR SUMMARY: Tournaments Entered—2; in money—0; Top-10 finishes—0

Definitions

Special Temporary Member:
A non-member of the PGA TOUR who wins an amount of official money, when combined with money earned in official money World Golf Championship events, equal to or greater than the amount won by the 150th finisher on the previous year's Official PGA TOUR Money List. He must join within 60 days after becoming eligible. The non-member is eligible to receive a maximum of seven Sponsor Exemptions before reaching Special Temporary Member status and unlimited Sponsor Exemptions thereafter.

Top 30 additional qualifiers for THE TOUR Championship:
Any Special Temporary Member whose official prize money, when combined with money earned in official money World Golf Championship events, is equal to or greater than 30th position on the 2005 Official PGA TOUR Money List through the Chrysler Championship (the final full-field event), provided such player applies for full PGA TOUR membership for the following year. He would be added to the field.

WGC money:
Players who are members of the PGA TOUR at the beginning of the year and those who become Regular Members during the year (win an event or earn an immediate promotion by winning three times on the Nationwide Tour) will appear on the Official PGA TOUR Money List ranked according to money won in PGA TOUR co-sponsored or approved tournaments. This includes any official money World Golf Championship events (WGCAccenture Match Play Championship, WGC-NEC Invitational and WGCAmerican Express Championship). Prize money earned by a non-member or Special Temporary Member in an official money World Golf Championship event will be deemed not to be official money and will not be included on the Official PGA TOUR Money List or Official PGA TOUR Career Money List.

Use Non-member Money List to determine:
Eligibility for Invitationals (i.e., Bay Hill, Colonial, Memorial)
Moving from Category 3 to Category 2 for groupings purposes (3 times a year)

Use Non-member Money plus WGC Earnings List to determine:
Special Temporary Membership
Membership for Next Year (Top 125 Non-member Category)
THE TOUR Championship
Qualifying Tournament Exemption into Final Stage

Tee Time Categories:

Category 1:
- PGA TOUR members currently in a tournament winners category. Non-members, who if they were members, would be in a tournament winners category.
- PGA TOUR Life Members (member for 15 years and won 20 events).
- Top 25 on Official PGA TOUR Career Money List through the end of the preceding year.

Category 1A:
- Tournament winners who no longer qualify for category 1 and who played in 5 or more PGA TOUR events or 10 or more combined PGA TOUR and Nationwide Tour events in the prior year.
- Former winners of THE PLAYERS Championship, Masters Tournament, U.S. Open, British Open and PGA Championship who no longer qualify for category 1.

Category 2:
- PGA TOUR members who play out of the Top 125 and Top 125 Non-members categories.
- Players with 50 or more career cuts and who played in 5 or more PGA TOUR events or 10 or more combined PGA TOUR and Nationwide Tour events in the prior year.
- Players within the top 50 on the current Official World Golf Ranking list.

Category 3: All others.

Voting Member:
A non-voting member can become a voting member by playing in at least 15 PGA TOUR co-sponsored or approved tournaments in a calendar year. He must play in at least 15 PGA TOUR co-sponsored or approved tournaments in each calendar year to retain voting membership. He must also attend at least one player meeting designated by the PGA TOUR during each calendar year.

Tournament Exemptions

Finishing at a certain point on the PGA TOUR Money List gains exemptions into other events as follows:

Top 20 on the final PGA TOUR Money List
British Open

Top 30
THE TOUR Championship presented by Coca-Cola U.S. Open

Top 40
Masters Tournament

Top 70
Bay Hill Invitational presented by MasterCard the Memorial Tournament

Top 80
Bank of America Colonial

2005 PGA TOUR Rookies

(Career cuts made-starts in parentheses)

2004 PGA TOUR Qualifying School (14)
Jason Allred (0-2), Matt Davidson (0-0), Brian Davis (6-14), David Hearn (0-4), Will MacKenzie (0-0), Sean O'Hair (0-0), Greg Owen (2-7), Phillip Price (14-41), Rob Rashell (0-0), Joey Snyder III (0-1), Hideto Tanihara (3-4), Mario Tiziani (3-14), D.J. Trahan (1-7 pro, 0-1 amateur), Charlie Wi (0-1)

* - As of January 1, 2005

2004 Nationwide Tour Graduates (10)
Justin Bolli (0-0), James Driscoll (5-8 pro, 1-3 amateur), Scott Gutschewski (1-1), Ryuji Imada (1-6 pro, 0-1 amateur), Brendan Jones (0-3), D.A. Points (0-2), Kevin Stadler (4-7 pro, 0-1 amateur), Jimmy Walker (1-6), Euan Walters (0-0), Nick Watney (2-9).

Oldest Rookie:	Phillip Price	38 years, two months, 11 days*
Youngest Rookie:	Sean O'Hair	22 years, five months, 21 days*

2005 International Players on the PGA TOUR

Argentina (1)
Jose Coceres

Australia (22)
Stephen Allan
Robert Allenby
Stuart Appleby
Aaron Baddeley
Gavin Coles
Steve Elkington
Paul Gow
Scott Hend
Mark Hensby
Bradley Hughes
Brendan Jones
Stephen Leaney
Peter Lonard
James McLean
Greg Norman
Geoff Ogilvy
Rod Pampling
Craig Parry
Adam Scott
John Senden
Andre Stolz
Euan Walters

Canada (5)
David Hearn
Glen Hnatiuk
Ian Leggatt
Mike Weir
Richard Zokol

England (8)
Paul Casey
Brian Davis
Luke Donald
John E. Morgan
Greg Owen
Ian Poulter
Justin Rose
Lee Westwood

Fiji (1)
Vijay Singh

France (1)
Thomas Levet

Germany (2)
Alex Cejka
Bernhard Langer

India (1)
Arjun Atwal

Ireland (1)
Padraig Harrington

Japan (4)
Ryuji Imada
Shigeki Maruyama
Hideto Tanihara
Hidemichi Tanaka

Namibia (1)
Trevor Dodds

New Zealand (4)
Michael Long
Craig Perks
Phil Tataurangi
Grant Waite

Northern Ireland (1)
Darren Clarke

Paraguay (1)
Carlos Franco

Scotland (1)
Sandy Lyle

South Africa (8)
Fulton Allem
Tim Clark
Ernie Els
David Frost
Retief Goosen
Brenden Pappas
Rory Sabbatini
Tjaart van der Walt

South Korea (3)
K.J. Choi
Kevin Na
Charlie Wi

Spain (2)
Sergio García
José María Olazábal

Sweden (8)
Mathias Gronberg
Daniel Chopra
Gabriel Hjertstedt
Frederik Jacobson
Per-Ulrik Johansson
Richard S. Johnson
Jesper Parnevik
Carl Pettersson

Trinidad & Tobago (1)
Stephen Ames

Wales (1)
Phillip Price

Zimbabwe (1)
Nick Price

2005 International Summary
78 international
players from 22 countries

(Clockwise, from left) Player of the Year **Craig Stadler**, Rookie of the Year **Mark McNulty** and Charles Schwab Cup winner **Hale Irwin** all turned in superb 2004 seasons.

2005 Champions Tour Eligibility Requirements

In order to be eligible for an official Champions Tour event, a player must be at least 50 years of ago prior to his first tournament obligation. The field size at the majority of Champions Tour events in 2005 will be 78 players and eligibility requirements modified as follows for standard 78-player fields:

Standard Field Size: 78 Players

1. **30 players** – Available from Prior-Year Money List, floor of 50
2. **30 players** – Available from All-Time Money List (not exempt in No.1), floor of net 70
3. **4 players** – PGA TOUR Career Victory Category, ages 50 and 51 (not exempt in No. 1 or No. 2)
4. **7 players** – Available from National Qualifying Tournament (Replaced by Reorder Category in August; see below)
5. **5 players** – Invited by the tournament
   - Two spots restricted: players with one PGA TOUR or Champions Tour win and Veteran Member status
   - Three spots unrestricted
6. **2 players** – Open Qualifying
   - Tournament winners not already in the field will reduce restricted and unrestricted Sponsor Exemptions in alternating order.
   - Special Medical is positioned as No. 8 Q-School.
   - National Qualifying Tournament No. 8 through net No. 15 access after categories 1 and 2 "floor out."
   - Past Champions access when National Qualifying Tournament "floors out."

Reorder Category

All Champions Tour members 75th or better on the Current Year Official Champions Tour Money List, along with the top 15 (net) finishers of the Champions Tour National Qualifying Tournament and members remaining eligible via the Special Medical Extension Category, shall be ranked upon each member's position on the current year Official Champions Tour Money List and replace the National Qualifying Tournament Category for the last eight full-field events of each season. The top seven available and not-otherwise-exempt players on the Reorder Category list, in order of their position on said List, shall be eligible to compete in open, full-field tournaments.

Alternates

After commitment deadline, withdrawals will be replaced by the first available player on the Prior-Year and All-Time Money Lists, in alternating order. If all available players from both lists are in the field ("floor out"), additional players from the standard priority order fill the field (i.e., Special Medical, second eight National Qualifying Tournament and Past Champions).

GEORGIA-PACIFIC GRAND CHAMPIONS ELIGIBILITY

The Georgia-Pacific Grand Champions competition consists of players within the starting field who are 60 years of age and older. The competition takes place over the first 36 holes of a 54-hole event or the first 54 holes of a 72-hole tournament. Georgia-Pacific Grand Champions' earnings are unofficial, but the participants earn official money for their position of finish in the overall tournament. The Georgia-Pacific Grand Champions Championship is the culminating event of the competition.

Jim Ahern (A-hurn)

EXEMPT STATUS: 43rd on 2004 Champions Tour Money List
FULL NAME: James Russell Ahern
HEIGHT: 5-9
WEIGHT: 160
BIRTHDATE: February 26, 1949
BIRTHPLACE: Duluth, MN
RESIDENCE: Phoenix, AZ

FAMILY: Wife, Tudy
CLUB AFFILIATION: Quintero G&CC (Lake Pleasant, AZ)
EDUCATION: Oklahoma State University (1972, Agronomy)
SPECIAL INTERESTS: Stock market, sports
TURNED PROFESSIONAL: 1972
JOINED PGA TOUR: 1973

JOINED CHAMPIONS TOUR: 1999

CHAMPIONS TOUR VICTORIES (2): 1999 AT&T Canada Senior Open Championship. **2003** Music City Championship at Gaylord Opryland.

2004 CHARLES SCHWAB CUP FINISH: 45th - 228 points

BEST PGA TOUR CAREER FINISH: T9—1973 Quad Cities Open.

OTHER VICTORIES (7): 1973 Yuma Open. **1986** Nebraska Open. **1986** North Dakota Open. **1990** Nebraska Open. **1991** North Dakota Open. **1992** South Dakota Open. **1997** Yamaha Pro-Pro Championship.

PGA TOUR CAREER EARNINGS: $13,412

BEST 2004 CHAMPIONS TOUR FINISHES: T3—Blue Angels Classic; T4—MasterCard Classic; T9—MasterCard Championship.

2004 SEASON:
All three of his top-10 finishes came in his first seven starts of the season...Used a final-round 65, his low round of the year, to vault into a T3 at the Blue Angels Classic in mid-April...T4 at MasterCard Classic near Mexico City a month earlier. Was among the leaders through nine holes in the final round before a disastrous double bogey on the 12th hole derailed his chances...Started his year with a T9 at the MasterCard Championship in Hawaii. Closed with a 6-under 66 at Hualalai.

CHAMPIONS TOUR CAREER HIGHLIGHTS:
2003: Found his winning ways for the first time since 1999 when he was a four-stroke victor over Jose Maria Canizares at the Music City Championship at Gaylord Opryland. Started with rounds of 64-63—127, the best opening 36-hole total for the season on the Champions Tour and held a six-stroke margin heading into Sunday's final round. Victory in Tennessee was one of three wire-to-wire events in 2003...Was the 54-hole leader at the JELD-WEN Tradition and eventually T2 at The Reserve, one stroke back of Tom Watson, after a final-round 72. Performance near Portland was his best-ever in a Champions Tour major. **2002:** Posted four top-10 finishes, highlighted by a fifth-place performance at the Bruno's Memorial Classic. Closing-round 66 at the Alabama event propelled him to his best finish since finishing second at the 2001 Farmers Charity Classic. **2001:** Was among the top-31 players on the money list for the first time on the Champions Tour...Neck problems during the middle of the summer forced him to miss almost a month of action. Returned at the U.S. Senior Open and recorded five top-10 finishes during a six-week stretch. Highlight of this run was a second-place effort at the Farmers Charity Classic near Grand Rapids, MI, one stroke short of Larry Nelson. **2000:** Finished second to Gil Morgan by a stroke at the rain-shortened Comfort Classic in Indianapolis. Moved into contention at Brickyard Crossing on Saturday with a sizzling 8-under 64, but never had the opportunity to challenge Morgan as bad weather washed out the final round. **1999:** Captured his first Champions Tour event in just his seventh start, defeating Hale Irwin in a playoff at the AT&T Canada Senior Open Championship. Made par on the second extra hole for the win after sinking a clutch 30-foot birdie putt on the 18th green in regulation to force the overtime session. Canadian triumph at Richelieu Valley near Montreal earned him an immediate exemption for a calendar year. Open qualified to get into the event and thus became just the seventh Monday qualifier in Champions Tour history to go on and win and the first since Dana Quigley in 1997...Selected by the PGA of America as the Senior Club Professional Player of the Year.

OTHER CAREER HIGHLIGHTS:
Was a member of the PGA TOUR between 1973 and 1975...Played a total of 60 PGA TOUR events...Played in the 1971 U.S. Amateur and finished in the top-20 at Wilmington CC...Also played in the 1972 U.S. Open at Pebble Beach, but missed the cut...Best career finish was a T9 at the 1973 Quad Cities Open...Biggest check of his PGA TOUR career was $2,400 for a T13 at the 1975 Phoenix Open...Finished second in the 1976 Queensland Open on the Australian Tour and also placed fifth in the 1976 Venezuela Open...Has had two career holes-in-one during competitive rounds.

PERSONAL:
Owns and operates Executive Golf Ltd., a company specializing in producing golf tournaments and clinics for a growing number of Fortune 500 corporations...Played collegiately at Oklahoma State with fellow Champions Tour players Mark Hayes and Doug Tewell...Was the head teaching professional from 1980 to 1985 at Des Moines (IA) G&CC, site of the 1999 U.S. Senior Open...Member of the South Dakota Sports Hall of Fame.

PLAYER STATISTICS

MISCELLANEOUS CHAMPIONS TOUR STATISTICS
2004 Low Round: 65–2 times, most recent 2004 Ford Senior Players Championship/2
Career Low Round: 63–2003 Music City Championship at Gaylord Opryland/2
Career Largest Paycheck: $210,000–2003 Music City Championship at Gaylord Opryland/1

MISCELLANEOUS PGA TOUR STATISTICS
Career Low Round: 67–2 times, most recent 1975 B.C. Open/2
Career Largest Paycheck: $2,400–1975 Phoenix Open/T13

CHAMPIONS TOUR CAREER SUMMARY — PLAYOFF RECORD: 1-0

Year	Events Played	1st	2nd	3rd	Top 10	Top 25	Earnings	Rank
1999	16	1		1	3	11	$478,963	41
2000	30		1		2	16	522,565	35
2001	31		1	1	9	17	831,480	24
2002	29				4	9	448,417	39
2003	26	1	1		3	7	626,958	31
2004	27			1	3	9	463,243	43
Total	159	2	3	3	24	69	3,371,624	

COMBINED ALL-TIME MONEY (3 TOURS): $3,385,036

CHAMPIONS TOUR TOP TOURNAMENT SUMMARY

Year	99	00	01	02	03	04
Senior PGA Championship		T8	T40	T18	CUT	CUT
U.S. Senior Open	T18	CUT	T7	T31	T35	T44
Ford Senior Players		T64	T28	T33	T71	T39
Senior British Open					70	
JELD-WEN Tradition		T19	T12	T57	T2	T36
Charles Schwab Cup Champ			T22			

CHAMPIONS TOUR YEAR-BY-YEAR STATISTICS (TOP 50 ON 2004 MONEY LIST)

	Scoring Average	Putting Average	Greens in Regulation	Driving Distance	Driving Accuracy
1999	70.42 (12)	1.793 (T38)	71.9 (8)	283.4 (2)	67.7 (T61)
2000	71.18 (34)	1.803 (T54)	68.7 (T28)	283.8 (4)	69.7 (T45)
2001	71.39 (T32)	1.818 (T65)	71.1 (10)	285.4 (2)	71.7 (T36)
2002	71.57 (39)	1.828 (T66)	70.7 (13)	281.0 (5)	72.9 (22)
2003	71.59 (46)	1.836 (T77)	70.2 (T20)	288.2 (4)	66.2 (55)
2004	71.94 (47)	1.839 (68)	71.0 (16)	282.4 (11)	67.6 (57)

SECTION 2 PLAYER BIOGRAPHIES

Jim Albus

EXEMPT STATUS: Net-70 on All-Time Money List
FULL NAME: James Christian Albus
HEIGHT: 6-1
WEIGHT: 215
BIRTHDATE: June 18, 1940
BIRTHPLACE: Staten Island, NY
RESIDENCE: Sarasota, FL

FAMILY: Wife, Brenda; Kathleen (5/3/71), Mark (2/7/73); two grandchildren
EDUCATION: Bucknell, UCLA (1965)
TURNED PROFESSIONAL: 1968
JOINED PGA TOUR: 1977

JOINED CHAMPIONS TOUR: 1990

CHAMPIONS TOUR VICTORIES (6): 1991 Mazda Presents THE SENIOR PLAYERS CHAMPIONSHIP. **1993** GTE Suncoast Classic. **1994** Vantage At The Dominion, Bank of Boston Senior Classic. **1995** SBC Presents The Dominion Seniors. **1998** GTE Classic.

OTHER SENIOR VICTORIES (1): 2001 Georgia-Pacific Super Seniors Match-Play Championship.

GEORGIA-PACIFIC GRAND CHAMPIONS VICTORIES (2): 2000 State Farm Senior Classic. **2001** SBC Championship.

BEST PGA TOUR CAREER FINISH: T26—1982 Manufacturers Hanover Westchester Classic.

OTHER VICTORIES (2): 1970 Metropolitan Open. **1985** Metropolitan Open.

PGA TOUR CAREER EARNINGS: $16,279

BEST 2004 CHAMPIONS TOUR FINISH: T24—Constellation Energy Classic.

2004 SEASON:

Registered just one top-25 performance during the campaign, a T24 late in the year at the Constellation Energy Classic near Baltimore...Opened with a 5-under 67 at the 3M Championship, his best round of the season, but eventually T32 in Minnesota after posting a pair of 74s on the weekend...Made his first career hole-in-one on the Champions Tour in the opening round of MasterCard Classic when he aced the par-3, 189-yard seventh hole at Bosque Real with a 6-iron shot...Finished 18th on the final Georgia-Pacific Grand Champions money list, with $50,833.

CHAMPIONS TOUR CAREER HIGHLIGHTS:

2003: Made 26 appearances, with best finish a T19 at the Long Island Classic in August. **2002:** T11 at the 3M Championship and T16 at the NFL Golf Classic...Missed nearly a month of the season after suffering minor injuries in a mountain biking accident in late August. **2001:** Enjoyed a productive first full season as a member of the Georgia-Pacific Grand Champions, finishing ninth on the final over-60 money list and winning the event at the SBC Championship...Also defeated Jim Dent 1-up to win the Grand Champions Match Play Championship near St. Louis...Best overall effort was a T6 at the Mexico Senior Classic. **2000:** Joined the ranks of the Georgia-Pacific Grand Champions in mid-June and won the first over-60 event he was eligible for at the State Farm Senior Classic. Nipped Lee Trevino for the victory near Baltimore by holing a pitch shot for an eagle on the final hole. Finished year with a playoff loss to Al Geiberger in the Georgia-Pacific Grand Champions Championship...Best overall finish was a T5 at the State Farm Senior Classic. **1999:** Underwent left hip replacement surgery after the last full-field event of the year. **1998:** Notched his first victory in three years, edging Simon Hobday, Kermit Zarley and Jose Maria Canizares by a stroke at the GTE Classic, his second victory in the Tampa Bay area. **1997:** Missed nearly two months of the season after he suffered a fractured ankle that kept him out of action from early May until early July...Best finish a T3 at the American Express Invitational in his hometown of Sarasota. **1996:** Underwent neck surgery early in the season and was out of action for two months before returning at Bruno's Memorial Classic. **1995:** One of only two players during the year to successfully defend a title, claiming a second consecutive SBC Dominion Seniors in San Antonio...Also second at the Senior Tournament of Champions, losing out on the third playoff hole to Jim Colbert...Named March Player of the Month. **1994:** One of six Champions Tour players over the million-dollar mark and the first former club professional to top $1 million in a season...Claimed the Bank of Boston Senior Classic, holding off Raymond Floyd and Lee Trevino...Also won the Vantage at The Dominion, going wire-to-wire for a one-stroke victory over Lee Trevino, Graham Marsh and George Archer...Set a then-Champions Tour record for most rounds in the 60s in a season (54) and most birdies in one year (453). **1993:** Captured the GTE Suncoast Classic, defeating Don Bies and Gibby Gilbert by two strokes. **1992:** Played every round in each of 37 official events. **1991:** Surprised the golf world by winning the 1991 Mazda Presents THE SENIOR PLAYERS Championship at the TPC of Michigan in only his sixth Champions Tour start. Came from three strokes back to defeat Bob Charles, Dave Hill and Charles Coody by one stroke. Became eligible to play in the event after shooting a final-round 64 at the NYNEX Commemorative and finishing T8 at Sleepy Hollow.

OTHER CAREER HIGHLIGHTS:

Head professional at the Piping Rock Club on Long Island for 14 years, but resigned to play the Champions Tour full-time...One of the top players in the Metropolitan PGA Section of New York...Was the runner-up in the 1990 PGA Senior Club Professional Championship...Did not play the PGA TOUR on a regular basis, but participated on the old winter TOUR in 1977 and 1978...Also played in six U.S. Opens and seven PGA Championships...Four-time Met Section Player of the Year...Member of the Metropolitan PGA Hall of Fame...Named Club Professional of the Year by the PGA of America in 1990.

PERSONAL:

Played basketball, baseball and was an intramural boxer at Bucknell University...Coaxed into golf by fraternity brothers while in college...Was an All-Middle Atlantic Conference outfielder in 1962, when he hit .421, the eighth-leading hitter in school history...Later transferred to UCLA, where he earned an undergraduate degree in 1965...First got into the golf business as an assistant pro at Mission Viejo CC...Moved back east two years later and was the head pro at Latourette GC on Staten Island, NY, from 1969-78...Honored in 1999 by the Met Golf Writers Association as its Comeback Player of the Year.

PLAYER STATISTICS

2004 CHAMPIONS TOUR STATISTICS

Scoring Average	73.92	(73)
Driving Distance	260.5	(70)
Driving Accuracy Percentage	76.0%	(15)
Total Driving	85	(48)
Greens in Regulation Pct.	61.4%	(69)
Putting Average	1.874	(79)
Sand Save Percentage	40.6%	(63)
Eagles (Holes per)	675.0	(62)
Birdie Average	2.23	(79)
All-Around Ranking	510	(76)

MISCELLANEOUS CHAMPIONS TOUR STATISTICS

2004 Low Round: 67–2004 3M Championship/1
Career Low Round: 63–1993 Ralphs Senior Classic/1
Career Largest Paycheck: $165,000–1998 GTE Classic/1

MISCELLANEOUS PGA TOUR STATISTICS

Career Low Round: 66–1978 American Express Westchester Classic/1
Career Largest Paycheck: $5,031–1984 U.S. Open Championship/T30

CHAMPIONS TOUR CAREER SUMMARY **PLAYOFF RECORD: 0-3**

Year	Events Played	1st	2nd	3rd	Top 10	Top 25	Earnings	Rank
1990	2					1	$14,433	95
1991	15	1			5	11	301,406	20
1992	37		1	2	7	24	404,693	16
1993	35	1		3	17	25	627,883	12
1994	35	2	6	3	18	32	1,237,128	3
1995	34	1	1	1	12	25	744,936	12
1996	31				3	11	244,833	56
1997	26			1	3	8	268,487	53
1998	34	1			8	15	643,380	27
1999	33				3	13	434,926	44
2000	33				4	9	418,398	43
2001	31				2	5	325,836	52
2002	28					4	202,553	72
2003	26					1	124,652	82
2004	25					1	104,312	85
Total	425	6	8	10	82	185	6,097,856	
COMBINED ALL-TIME MONEY (3 TOURS):							**$6,114,135**	

CHAMPIONS TOUR TOP TOURNAMENT SUMMARY

Year	90	91	92	93	94	95	96	97	98	99	00	01	02
Senior PGA Championship			T22	T7	T38	T10		T27	T39	T39	T51	79	CUT
U.S. Senior Open	T27	T29	T26	T35	T2	T29	T27		CUT	T13	T47	T59	CUT
Ford Senior Players		1	T18	T15	2	T35	T54	48	T24	T37	T60	T10	T30
Senior British Open													
JELD-WEN Tradition			T28	T17	T15	T54	T65		T53	T45	T43	T55	T44
Charles Schwab Cup Champ		T19	T21	T8	2	T14			T6				

Year	03	04
Senior PGA Championship	CUT	69
U.S. Senior Open	CUT	
Ford Senior Players	T48	T58
Senior British Open	CUT	
JELD-WEN Tradition	T42	T78
Charles Schwab Cup Champ		

Isao Aoki (ih-SAH-oh ay-OH-key)

WORLD GOLF HALL OF FAME MEMBER (Inducted 2004)
EXEMPT STATUS: Top 30 on All-Time Money List
FULL NAME: Isao Aoki
HEIGHT: 6-0
WEIGHT: 180
BIRTHDATE: August 31, 1942
BIRTHPLACE: Abiko, Chiba, Japan
RESIDENCE: Tokyo, Japan
FAMILY: Wife, Chie; Joanne (4/17/67)
SPECIAL INTERESTS: Fishing, golf course design
TURNED PROFESSIONAL: 1964
JOINED PGA TOUR: 1981

JOINED CHAMPIONS TOUR: 1992

CHAMPIONS TOUR VICTORIES (9): 1992 Nationwide Championship. **1994** Bank One Classic, Brickyard Crossing Championship. **1995** Bank of Boston Senior Classic. **1996** BellSouth Senior Classic at Opryland, Kroger Senior Classic. **1997** Emerald Coast Classic. **1998** BellSouth Senior Classic at Opryland. **2002** The Instinet Classic.

OTHER SENIOR VICTORIES (6): 1994 Japan Senior Open. **1995** American Express Grandslam, Japan Senior Open. **1996** Japan Senior Open. **1997** Japan Senior Open. **2000** Northern Cup Senior Open.

2004 CHARLES SCHWAB CUP FINISH: 67th - 58 points

GEORGIA-PACIFIC GRAND CHAMPIONS VICTORIES (3): 2003 Kroger Classic, Greater Hickory Classic at Rock Barn, Georgia-Pacific Grand Champions Championship.

PGA TOUR VICTORIES (1): 1983 Hawaiian Open.

OTHER VICTORIES (57): 1972 Kanto Open. **1973** Coldbeck, Chunichi Crowns, Pepsi Wilson, Sapporo Tokyu Open, KBC Augusta, Japan Pro. **1974** Kanto Pro, Nichie Taiko, Kanto Open, Sanpo Class, Tozai Taiko. **1975** Kanto Open, Chunichi Crowns. **1976** Tokai Classic. **1977** Tohoku Classic, Nichibei Taiko, Jun Classic. **1978** Chunichi Crowns, Japan Pro Match Play, Sapporo Tokyu Open, Kanto Pro, Nichibei Taiko, Japan Series, Colgate World Match Play. **1979** Chunichi Crowns, Japan Pro Match Play, Kanto Pro, Japan Series. **1980** Chunichi Crowns, Yomiuri Open, KBC Augusta, Kanto Open, Jun Classic. **1981** Japan Pro, Japan Pro Match Play, Shizuoka Open. **1982** Japan Pro Match Play. **1983** Kanto Pro, Sapporo Tokyu Open, Japan Open, Japan Series, Panasonic European Open. **1984** Sapporo Tokyu Open, Japan Open, KBC Augusta, Kanto Open. **1987** Dunlop Kokusai, ANA Open, Japan Open, Japan Series. **1989** Tokai Classic, Casio World Open. **1990** Mitsubishi Galant. **1991** Bridgestone Open. **1992** Mitsubishi Galant, Casio World Open.

PGA TOUR CAREER EARNINGS: $960,571

BEST 2004 CHAMPIONS TOUR FINISH: T6—FedEx Kinko's Classic.

2004 SEASON:

Finished out of the top 50 on the money list for the first time in his Champions Tour career...Highlight of his year was being elected into the World Golf Hall of Fame from the International ballot early in the year and inducted along with Tom Kite, Charlie Sifford and Marlene Streit in ceremonies in November...Lone top-10 finish of the season was a T6 at the FedEx Kinko's Classic near Austin. Trailed by just one stroke through 36 holes, but even-par 72 on Sunday left him three strokes back...Played in just six Georgia-Pacific Grand Champions events and came close to winning twice. Lost a playoff to J.C. Snead in the Georgia-Pacific competition at The ACE Group Classic and fell one stroke short of Bob Charles in the over-60 event at the FedEx Kinko's Classic...Qualified for the season-ending Grand Champions Championship, but chose to return home rather than make the trip to Sonoma. Placed 14th on the final Georgia-Pacific Grand Champions money list, with $79,375.

CHAMPIONS TOUR CAREER HIGHLIGHTS:

2003: T6 at the Royal Caribbean Golf Classic, his fifth top-10 finish at Crandon Park. Fell to Dale Douglass in a playoff for the Georgia-Pacific Grand Champions title at the Royal Caribbean event...Carded a bogey-free 64 in the third round of the JELD-WEN Tradition, his best score since posting the same number in the second round of the 2002 Royal Caribbean Classic...Enjoyed great success in his first full season in the Georgia-Pacific Grand Champions competition with three victories, including a win in the Georgia-Pacific Grand Champions Championship in Sonoma, CA, a six-stroke victory over Raymond Floyd and Tom Wargo. First won the Georgia-Pacific event at the Kroger Classic when he bested Jerry McGee in a three-hole playoff...Picked up a second Georgia-Pacific title at the inaugural Greater Hickory Classic at Rock Barn. Was bogey-free for 36 holes and finished one stroke better than Wargo...Finished the year second to Wargo on the Georgia-Pacific Grand Champions money list with $202,083. **2002:** Earned first victory since the 1998 season when he was a four-stroke winner over John Jacobs at The Instinet Classic in May. Had 13 birdies and one bogey on the weekend on his way to victory. Made up two strokes the final day to earn a career-best check for $225,000 while posting his ninth career win on the Champions Tour...Made a run at victory in the rain-shortened Royal Caribbean Classic before eventually finishing second for the third time at Crandon Park. 10-under total for 36 holes tied him with Tom Watson and Bruce Fleisher, one stroke behind winner John Jacobs...Earned a spot in the season-ending event in Oklahoma City for the second consecutive year, but chose to return to his native Japan and did not participate...Made his debut in the Georgia-Pacific Grand Champions competition (players 60 and older)in September. **2001:** Started the year with a runner-up finish at the Royal Caribbean Classic, one point short of Larry Nelson in the Modified Stableford event. Four-putted the first hole on Sunday, including a whiff for a double-bogey, that cost him either an outright victory or a spot in a playoff...Was the 36- and 54-hole leader at the U.S. Senior Open and eventually T2 along with Jim Colbert, one stroke back of Bruce Fleisher...Made his 1,000th professional start at the Ford Senior Players Championship. **2000:** Started the final round of the State Farm Senior Classic four shots behind Leonard Thompson, but forced a playoff with a final-round 65 that included birdies on three of the last four holes. Eventually lost to Thompson for the second time in his Champions Tour career on the second hole of overtime. **1999:** Injured his right shoulder early in the campaign and subsequently developed back problems that curtailed his season after the AT&T Canada Senior Open Championship at the end of August...Best finish was a runner-up performance to Bruce Fleisher at the Royal Caribbean Classic. **1998:** One of four players to go wire-to-wire, winning the BellSouth Senior Classic at Opryland with an 18-under-par 198 total, a tournament record at the time...Lost in a playoff to Leonard Thompson at the Coldwell Banker Burnet Classic and T2 at the Utah Showdown. **1997:** Had best year of his career with over $1.4 million in official money...Lone victory came at the Emerald Coast Classic. Fashioned a Champions Tour-record 60 (10-under-par) in the second round, and then, after a birdie on the final hole in regulation to tie Gil Morgan, came back with another birdie on

SECTION 2 PLAYER BIOGRAPHIES

CHAMPIONS TOUR CAREER SUMMARY — PLAYOFF RECORD: 1-4

Year	Events Played	1st	2nd	3rd	Top 10	Top 25	Earnings	Rank
1992	7	1	1	1	6	7	$324,650	26
1993	23		1	3	12	19	557,667	15
1994	22	2	2	1	10	16	632,975	13
1995	23	1	4	2	17	23	1,041,766	5
1996	26	2	4	1	16	24	1,162,581	4
1997	28	1	5	4	18	26	1,410,499	3
1998	22	1	2	3	10	17	1,042,200	9
1999	17		1		3	8	334,523	49
2000	19		1		3	10	374,353	51
2001	20		2		4	9	676,735	31
2002	19	1	1		4	12	653,836	31
2003	18				3	13	449,231	42
2004	21				1	5	265,036	56
Total	265	9	24	15	107	189	8,926,052	
ALL-TIME MONEY (3 TOURS):							**$9,886,623**	

CHAMPIONS TOUR TOP TOURNAMENT SUMMARY

Year	92	93	94	95	96	97	98	99	00	01	02	03	04
Senior PGA Championship		3	T5	T5	2	T20	T44	T15	T62	T20	CUT	CUT	T27
U.S. Senior Open		T20	10	T3	11	T49	T4	CUT	T47	T2	T18	T30	
Ford Senior Players		T5	T3	6	T30	T2	3	T14	T18	T17	21	T12	T28
Senior British Open												T14	T22
JELD-WEN Tradition		6	T9	2	T12	2	T13	T28	T47	T35	T20	T53	
Charles Schwab Cup Champ	T7	T15		T14	T8	3	T26						

Isao Aoki (Continued)

the first playoff hole to claim the title. 65 on Sunday, coupled with his record 60, helped him establish a then-Champions Tour mark for best consecutive rounds (60-65-125), breaking the record of 126 by Jim Colbert (62-64/1994) and Bob Murphy (63-63/1995)...Was second five times, with two of those coming in majors—The Tradition and PGA Seniors' Championship. **1996:** Won the BellSouth Senior Classic at Opryland and the Kroger Senior Classic...Named the Champions Tour Player of the Month in May and June. **1995:** Collected over $1 million for first time in his career, helped by a win at the Bank of Boston Senior Classic, where he birdied the final hole to nip Bob Charles and Hale Irwin...Was second four times, including playoff loss to Jack Nicklaus at The Tradition. **1994:** Caught fire in the fall, winning back-to-back events at the Bank One Classic and the rain-shortened Brickyard Crossing Championship...Almost earned a third win at The Transamerica, but lost on the first extra hole to Kermit Zarley...Played his final 10 holes at Silverado in 10-under-par (8 birdies, 1 eagle, 1 par) and carded an 8-under-par 29 on the back nine en route to a 63 that forced the playoff...Player of the Month for September. **1993:** T2 at the GTE West Classic. **1992:** Had impressive rookie year with six top-10 finishes in seven starts highlighted by victory at the Nationwide Championship. Shot a 66 on Saturday to take a one-stroke lead and was declared the winner when the final round was canceled by rain. Victory made him the first Japanese player to win on both the PGA TOUR and the Champions Tour...Made Champions Tour debut at the First of America Classic.

OTHER CAREER HIGHLIGHTS:

One of Japan's all-time greats, with 73 tournament victories worldwide...The only Japanese player to claim titles on six different Tours: PGA TOUR, Champions Tour, PGA European Tour, Australasian Tour, Japan Golf Tour and Japan Senior Tour...May be best known in the United States for holing a pitching wedge out of the rough from 128 yards for an eagle-3 on the 72nd hole at Waialae CC to leapfrog Jack Renner and win the 1983 Hawaiian Open, his only PGA TOUR title...Best year on TOUR was that same season, when he made $146,467 and placed 34th on the money list...Shadowed Jack Nicklaus for four days at Baltusrol GC in the 1980 U.S. Open, but eventually lost by two strokes when Nicklaus became the first player to record a 72-hole mark of 272 in a U.S. Open...Was a member of the 1982, 1983 and 1984 Japanese National teams that competed against the United States...Selected to the Japan team in 1985, 1987 and 1988 for the Kirin Cup competition...Was the leading money-winner five times on the Japan Golf Tour.

PERSONAL:

Was introduced to golf as a caddie at the Abiko GC while attending Abiko Junior High School...Earned the nickname "Tower" after the Tokyo Tower, because of his height (6 feet)...Uses an unorthodox putting stroke, but considers that to be the strongest part of his game.

PLAYER STATISTICS

2004 CHAMPIONS TOUR STATISTICS

Scoring Average	72.33	(54)
Driving Distance	264.8	(62)
Driving Accuracy Percentage	69.1%	(50)
Total Driving	112	(75)
Greens in Regulation Pct.	66.9%	(39)
Putting Average	1.827	(59)
Sand Save Percentage	63.5%	(1)
Eagles (Holes per)	1,188.0	(74)
Birdie Average	3.30	(37)
All-Around Ranking	376	(49)

MISCELLANEOUS CHAMPIONS TOUR STATISTICS

2004 Low Round: 67–2004 Bank of America Championship/2
Career Low Round: 60–1997 Emerald Coast Classic/2
Career Largest Paycheck: $225,000–2002 The Instinet Classic/1

MISCELLANEOUS PGA TOUR STATISTICS

Career Low Round: 64–2 times, most recent 1988 NEC World Series of Golf/3
Career Largest Paycheck: $58,500–1983 Hawaiian Open/1

25 MEMORABLE MOMENTS

The Champions Tour Is Born

1978 Liberty Mutual Legends of Golf

The idea that there may be a market for golfers age 50-plus competing on a national stage is born with the first Liberty Mutual Legends of Golf tournament. Played at the Onion Creek Golf Club in Austin, TX, the legendary Sam Snead and partner Gardner Dickinson steal the headlines with an NBC national television audience looking on. Snead birdies the 16th and 17th holes to tie the Australian team of Peter Thomson and Kel Nagle. Then, on 18, Snead's sensational fairway wedge shot stops four feet short of the hole, a putt he sinks for his third consecutive birdie and the title. Snead and Dickinson collect $50,000 each.

CHAMPIONS TOUR 25

George Archer

EXEMPT STATUS: Top 30 on All-Time Money List
FULL NAME: George William Archer
HEIGHT: 6-5 1/2
WEIGHT: 205
BIRTHDATE: October 1, 1939
BIRTHPLACE: San Francisco, CA
RESIDENCE: Incline Village, NV

FAMILY: Wife, Donna; Elizabeth (10/15/63), Marilyn (12/30/65); seven grandchildren
SPECIAL INTERESTS: Hunting, fishing, photography
TURNED PROFESSIONAL: 1964
JOINED PGA TOUR: 1964

JOINED CHAMPIONS TOUR: 1989

CHAMPIONS TOUR VICTORIES (19): **1989** Gatlin Brothers Southwest Classic. **1990** MONY Senior Tournament of Champions, Northville Long Island Classic, GTE Northwest Classic, Gold Rush at Rancho Murieta. **1991** Northville Long Island Classic, GTE North Classic, Raley's Senior Gold Rush. **1992** Murata Reunion Pro-Am, Northville Long Island Classic, Bruno's Memorial Classic. **1993** Ameritech Senior Open, First of America Classic, Raley's Senior Gold Rush, Ping Kaanapali Classic. **1995** Toshiba Senior Classic, Cadillac NFL Golf Classic. **1998** First of America Classic. **2000** MasterCard Championship.

OTHER SENIOR VICTORIES (4): **1990** Sports Shinko Cup, Princeville Classic. **1991** Sports Shinko Cup. **1994** Chrysler Cup [indiv].

GEORGIA-PACIFIC GRAND CHAMPIONS VICTORIES (8): **2000** Toshiba Senior Classic, Bruno's Memorial Classic, Boone Valley Classic, SBC Senior Open. **2001** Georgia-Pacific Super Seniors Championship. **2002** Royal Caribbean Classic, Bruno's Memorial Classic, SBC Championship.

PGA TOUR VICTORIES (12): **1965** Lucky International Open. **1967** Greater Greensboro Open. **1968** Pensacola Open Invitational, Greater New Orleans Open Invitational. **1969** Bing Crosby National Pro-Am, Masters Tournament. **1971** Andy Williams-San Diego Open Invitational, Greater Hartford Open Invitational. **1972** Glen Campbell-Los Angeles Open, Greater Greensboro Open. **1976** Sahara Invitational. **1984** Bank of Boston Classic.

OTHER VICTORIES (8): **1963** Trans-Mississippi Amateur, Northern California Open, Northern California Medal Play, San Francisco City Championship. **1968** PGA National Team Championship [with Bobby Nichols]. **1969** Argentine Masters. **1981** Colombian Open. **1982** Philippines Invitational.

PGA TOUR CAREER EARNINGS: $1,881,859

PGA TOUR PLAYOFF RECORD: 4-3

BEST 2004 CHAMPIONS TOUR FINISH: T30—Bruno's Memorial Classic.

2004 SEASON:
Appeared in just three official events during the season, with his last start coming at the FedEx Kinko's Classic near Austin in early May. Appearance in Texas was the 999th of his Tour career (625 PGA TOUR, 374 Champions Tour)...His T30 at the Bruno's Memorial Classic was best effort of the campaign...Teamed with Don Bies to T8 in the Raphael Division of the Liberty Mutual Legends of Golf.

CHAMPIONS TOUR CAREER HIGHLIGHTS:
2002: Won three Georgia-Pacific Grand Champions events and finished the year as the top money-winner with $318,925...Claimed the first over-60 event of the year at the Royal Caribbean Classic, defeating Dave Stockton and Al Geiberger with a birdie on the sixth hole of a playoff. Holed a six-foot downhill birdie putt on the final hole of regulation to get into the overtime session...Claimed his second crown at the Bruno's Memorial Classic, his second over-60 title in Birmingham. Went bogey free for 36 holes and defeated Bob Charles by two strokes with a 10-under-134 score...Added a third Georgia-Pacific title when he nipped Mike Hill by one stroke at the SBC Championship in San Antonio in October...Recorded hole-in-one, the seventh of his career, on the 17th hole in the final round of The Instinet Classic. **2001:** Ended his season with a victory in the Georgia-Pacific Grand Champions Championship, besting Bob Charles by three strokes. **2000:** Won his 19th career event on the Champions Tour at the season-opening MasterCard Championship in Hawaii. Became the first player over 60 to win the MasterCard event and the first Grand Champion to triumph in an official tournament since Gary Player claimed the 1998 Northville Long Island Classic at age 64. Also bested Miller Barber's record at age 57 of being the oldest player ever to claim the first event of any year. In windy conditions, triumphed by two strokes over Lee Trevino, Hale Irwin, Dana Quigley and Graham Marsh at Hualalai. Joined Barber and Al Geiberger as a multiple winner of the season-opening event and became the first to win at two different venues (1990 at LaCosta CC)...Took full advantage of his first full year among the Georgia-Pacific Grand Champions. Registered four victories in the first eight over-60 competitions and led the Georgia-Pacific Grand Champions in earnings with a single-season record $364,988. **1998:** Fired an 8-under-par 64 on Sunday to claim his second First of America Classic title. Five-stroke victory at Egypt Valley was his first title since 1995. **1997:** Rebounded from right hip replacement surgery in April 1996 to play a full schedule that included five top-10 performances...Named the Champions Tour's Comeback Player of the Year. **1996:** Played in just 12 events after undergoing right hip replacement surgery in April. Returned in late July at the Burnet Senior Classic, but played just twice after that. **1995:** Hinted at possible retirement early in year because of degenerative hip, but went on to post his fifth multiple-win season...Carded final-round 64 for a one-stroke triumph at inaugural Toshiba Senior Classic...Also notched a one-stroke win over Ray Floyd and Bob Murphy at Cadillac NFL Golf Classic. **1994:** Winless during the campaign, but out of the top 25 just twice and had year's best streak of par-or-better rounds (21)...Carded hole-in-one at GTE West Classic. **1993:** Finished among top four on money list for fourth straight year with three victories, including back-to-back wins at Ameritech Senior Open and First of America Classic...Also claimed third Raley's Senior Gold Rush title, edging Bob Charles and Chi Chi Rodriguez by one stroke. **1992:** Second on money list for second straight year...Had three wins, one second and five third-place finishes...Victory at Northville Long Island Classic was third in succession and won Murata Reunion in three-hole playoff with Tommy Aaron. Also claimed the inaugural Bruno's Memorial Classic, holding off the late Jack Kiefer and Rocky Thompson by a stroke. **1991:** Lost out to Mike Hill for the money title in the final week of the year, but still garnered Co-Player of the Year honors with Hill...Among his three titles were successful defenses at the Northville Long Island Classic and Raley's Senior Gold

CHAMPIONS TOUR CAREER SUMMARY **PLAYOFF RECORD: 4-2**

Year	Events Played	1st	2nd	3rd	Top 10	Top 25	Earnings	Rank
1989	5	1	1		4	5	$98,063	45
1990	32	4	4	1	23	30	749,691	4
1991	32	3	6	3	21	30	963,455	2
1992	32	3	2	5	19	30	860,175	2
1993	32	4	3	2	22	28	963,124	3
1994	30		2	2	17	28	717,578	10
1995	30	2		3	11	22	752,087	11
1996	12				3	7	160,213	67
1997	26		1		5	11	407,605	37
1998	29	1		1	6	18	660,076	25
1999	31		1	2	8	18	737,860	23
2000	29	1			5	17	713,079	29
2001	23					6	217,904	69
2002	23				2	7	276,667	63
2003	5					1	37,070	109
2004	3						15,000	131
Total	374	19	20	19	146	258	8,329,648	
COMBINED ALL-TIME MONEY (3 TOURS):							**$10,211,507**	

CHAMPIONS TOUR TOP TOURNAMENT SUMMARY

Year	90	91	92	93	94	95	96	97	98	99	00	01	02
Senior PGA Championship	5	5	13	T16	T10				T11	T22			
U.S. Senior Open	T13												
Ford Senior Players	T14	T13	T18	T17	T22	T30		T19	T50	T33	T69	T38	T73
JELD-WEN Tradition	T5	T6	T12	T25	T12	T17	T7	T8	T13	T14	T25	T63	
Charles Schwab Cup Champ	T9	T4	T2	T8	T12	T8			T16	T5	T14		

George Archer (Continued)

Rush...Also won GTE Classic in Indianapolis with then-record score 199...Had 18 top-five efforts, the most by any Champions Tour player that season. **1990:** Took advantage of his first full year, posting four wins and four runner-up finishes. **1989:** Became the sixth player in Champions Tour history to win their Champions Tour debut when he prevailed in a playoff over Orville Moody and Jimmy Powell at the Gatlin Brothers Southwest Classic. Won the event 14 days after his 50th birthday, making him youngest (at the time) winner in Champions Tour annals.

OTHER CAREER HIGHLIGHTS:

Last win on the PGA TOUR came at the 1984 Bank of Boston Classic at age 44, his first title in eight years...Biggest of his 12 PGA TOUR wins came at the 1969 Masters, where he outdueled Billy Casper, the late George Knudson and Tom Weiskopf down the stretch...First win as a professional, the 1965 Lucky International, came on the course on which he grew up, Harding Park GC in San Francisco...Finished among the TOUR's top-five money-winners in 1968, 1971 and 1972...Best earnings year was 1984 ($207,543)...Has had seven holes-in-one as a professional.

PERSONAL:

Has been hampered by various injuries throughout his career. Among seven major surgeries he has undergone have been left wrist (1975), back (1979), left shoulder (1987) and right hip replacement (1996)...Considered one of the game's all-time great putters, and at one time held the PGA TOUR record for fewest putts over four rounds (95/1980 Sea Pines Heritage Classic)...Daughter Elizabeth, the first female caddie at the Masters Tournament, is a Presbyterian minister who has earned a doctorate in theology...Another daughter, Lynne, teaches special education...Inducted into the California Golf Hall of Fame in 1991...Got started in golf by caddying at Peninsula CC near San Francisco at age 13...Biggest thrill was meeting his wife, Donna, on the golf course just over 40 years ago...Lists Mother Teresa as his biggest hero...Favorite golf courses include Pine Valley, Cypress Point and Shadow Creek...At 6-5 1/2, tallest man to win Masters...Spent a year working as a ranch hand in Gilroy, CA, before turning pro...Favorite entertainer is Bob Newhart, favorite athlete is Muhammad Ali and favorite TV show is "Law and Order."

PLAYER STATISTICS

2004 CHAMPIONS TOUR STATISTICS

Scoring Average	73.89	(N/A)
Driving Distance	268.7	(N/A)
Driving Accuracy Percentage	50.4%	(N/A)
Total Driving	1,998	(N/A)
Greens in Regulation Pct.	60.5%	(N/A)
Putting Average	1.827	(N/A)
Sand Save Percentage	47.1%	(N/A)
Birdie Average	2.89	(N/A)
All-Around Ranking	1,569	(N/A)

MISCELLANEOUS CHAMPIONS TOUR STATISTICS

2004 Low Round: 70–2 times, most recent 2004 Bruno's Memorial Classic/3

Career Low Round: 63–4 times, most recent 1993 Ping Kaanapali Classic/3

Career Largest Paycheck: $199,000–2000 MasterCard Championship/1

MISCELLANEOUS PGA TOUR STATISTICS

Career Low Round: 61–1983 Glen Campbell-Los Angeles Open/3

Career Largest Paycheck: $63,000–1984 Bank of Boston Classic/1

25 MEMORABLE MOMENTS

The Shootout at Onion Creek

1979 Liberty Mutual Legends of Golf

On the afternoon of April 30, 1979, there were fireworks galore at the Onion Creek Golf Club in Austin, TX, site of the second Liberty Mutual Legends of Golf. Birdies on the last two holes of regulation play by Roberto De Vicenzo and Julius Boros forced the tournament into sudden-death with Tommy Bolt and Art Wall. A national television audience on NBC marveled as the playoff produced one par and six birdies, with De Vicenzo and Bolt trading friendly barbs after each birdie. De Vicenzo and Bolt came away the champions, and a year later the Champions Tour was launched.

CHAMPIONS TOUR 25

Hugh Baiocchi (by-OCK-ee)

EXEMPT STATUS: Net-70 on All-Time Money List
FULL NAME: Hugh John Baiocchi
HEIGHT: 6-0
WEIGHT: 188
BIRTHDATE: August 17, 1946
BIRTHPLACE: Johannesburg, South Africa
RESIDENCE: Cape Town, South Africa

FAMILY: Wife, Joan; Lauren (2/19/73), Justin (3/11/75)
EDUCATION: University of Witwatersrand
SPECIAL INTERESTS: Travel, reading, fast cars
TURNED PROFESSIONAL: 1971

JOINED CHAMPIONS TOUR: 1997

CHAMPIONS TOUR VICTORIES (3): 1997 Pittsburgh Senior Classic. **1998** Comfort Classic, Kroger Senior Classic.

2004 CHARLES SCHWAB CUP FINISH: 55th - 144 points

BEST PGA TOUR CAREER FINISH: T22—1975 Masters Tournament.

OTHER VICTORIES (20): 1968 Brazil Amateur Championship. **1970** South African Amateur Championship. **1973** Western Province Open, South Africa International Classic. **1973** Swiss Open. **1974** ICL Transvaal Open. **1976** Scandinavian Enterprise Open, Rhodesian Dunlop Masters, Swaziland Holiday Inns Invitational, Transvaal Open. **1977** Sun Alliance PGA Match-Play Championship. **1978** South African Open. **1979** Swiss Open. **1980** Zimbabwe Open, South African PGA, Vaal Reefs Open. **1983** State Express Classic. **1989** Murphy's Cup, Twee Jongegezellen Masters.

PGA TOUR CAREER EARNINGS: $4,898

BEST 2004 CHAMPIONS TOUR FINISH: 3—MasterCard Classic.

2004 SEASON:

Nearly broke through with his first win in six years at MasterCard Classic near Mexico City in March. Trailed 36-hole leader Graham Marsh by just one stroke at the start of Sunday's final round and held a brief one-stroke lead after 10 holes, but consecutive bogeys on the next two holes dropped him from the lead. He went on to finish third, one shot out of a playoff with Marsh and eventual winner Ed Fiori. The third-place finish was his best since 2001 when he was T3 at the NFL Golf Classic,where he also finished one stroke shy of a playoff...Followed that effort with a T15 finish at the SBC Classic...Only other top-20 finish came in July when he was 17th at the Senior British Open.

CHAMPIONS TOUR CAREER HIGHLIGHTS:

2003: Played his best late in the summer when he was inside the top 10 in consecutive tournaments during a run of 10 straight rounds of par/better...Closed with his lowest score of the year, a 6-under 66, at The Reserve and improved 18 spots on the final day to T7 at the JELD-WEN Tradition, the final major championship of the season. Performance near Portland was his first top-10 in a major since a T8 at the 1999 U.S. Senior Open...Posted three straight sub-70 rounds the next week and T6 at the Kroger Classic near Cincinnati...Also T6 early in the year at the Music City Championship, his best performance on the Champions Tour in just over a year...Had an early season highlight when he made the seventh ace of his career during the final round of the Royal Caribbean Golf Classic, the first full-field event of the season. Holed a 9-iron shot at Key Biscayne's 131-yard eighth hole. **2002:** T7 at the NFL Golf Classic, thanks, in part, to rounds of 68-69 on the weekend. **2001:** T2 at the TD Waterhouse Championship, eight strokes back of Ed Dougherty and his best effort since a T2 at the 1998 EMC Kaanapali Classic...T3 at the NFL Golf Classic, one stroke out of a playoff with Allen Doyle and eventual winner John Schroeder...Made the first hole-in-one of the season at the SBC Senior Classic. Aced Valencia CC's 178-yard third hole with a 5-iron during the second round. **2000:** T5 at the Royal Caribbean Classic...Also solo fifth at the AT&T Canada Senior Open Championship...Had to withdraw from the Boone Valley Classic after undergoing an emergency appendectomy the night prior to the final round...Attended 2000 National Qualifying Tournament and finished T11, but did not participate in a playoff for a conditional card. **1999:** T6 at the State Farm Senior Classic and was solo sixth at the AT&T Canada Senior Open Championship where he was in contention until early in the final round. **1998:** Posted two victories and joined Hale Irwin as the only other player to win back-to-back events...Registered a tournament-record 20-under-par 196 score to defeat Bruce Summerhays by two strokes at the Comfort Classic and then came back a week later to win the rain-shortened Kroger Senior Classic in a playoff. Made birdie on the second extra hole to best four other players after Sunday's final round was canceled. **1997:** One of the real surprises on the Champions Tour, with a victory and 14 top-10 finishes in 25 starts (two as a Monday qualifier)...Began the year as a conditionally-exempt player (second eight at the 1996 National Qualifying Tournament) and did not play in his first event until the PGA Seniors' Championship (T35)...Lost to Bruce Crampton in a three-hole playoff at the Cadillac NFL Golf Classic...Also lost in a two-hole playoff to Bruce Summerhays at the Saint Luke's Classic where he opened with a 63 that included a 29 on the back nine...Won his first Champions Tour title at the Pittsburgh Senior Classic. Caught Bob Duval with birdies on the final two holes of regulation then prevailed in a playoff with a par on the sixth extra hole...Named Player of the Month for August. **1996:** Earned partially-exempt spot on the 1997 Champions Tour by finishing 10th at the National Qualifying Tournament...Involved in a six-man playoff for positions 9-14 before claiming 10th spot overall with a par on the fourth extra hole.

OTHER CAREER HIGHLIGHTS:

Has played tournament golf in 31 different countries around the world...Was a fixture for 23 years on the European Tour, where he won seven times after turning professional in November 1971. Best year was in 1977, when he finished second on the Order of Merit to Seve Ballesteros...Played in the Masters from 1974-76...Represented South Africa three times in the World Cup and was a South African PGA captain for three years...Winner of the 1977 PGA Match Play Championship in Europe...Owns 15 wins on the South African Tour, including the 1978 South Africa Open...Played an abbreviated PGA European Seniors Tour schedule in 1996, competing in just three events after turning 50 in August...Finished third at The Belfry PGA Seniors and T3 at the Scottish Seniors Open...Posted his career-low round of 61 at the 1985 Holiday Inn Invitational and again at the 1993 Royal Swazi Classic...Has had seven career holes-in-one in competitive rounds.

PERSONAL:

Credits his father as the person who most influenced his career...Was a scratch player by the age of 15...Golf hero is Gary Player...Is among a South African contingent on the Champions Tour that includes Player, John Bland, and Mark McNulty...Lists Cypress Point as his favorite golf course and Atlanta Brave Chipper Jones as his favorite athlete.

PLAYER STATISTICS

MISCELLANEOUS CHAMPIONS TOUR STATISTICS

2004 Low Round: 66–2004 MasterCard Classic/2
Career Low Round: 63–2 times, most recent 1998 Comfort Classic/2
Career Largest Paycheck: $172,500–1998 Comfort Classic/1

MISCELLANEOUS PGA TOUR STATISTICS

Career Low Round: 68–1974 Greater Greensboro Open/1
Career Largest Paycheck: $2,275–1975 Masters Tournament/T22

CHAMPIONS TOUR CAREER SUMMARY — PLAYOFF RECORD: 2-2

Year	Events Played	1st	2nd	3rd	Top 10	Top 25	Earnings	Rank
1997	25	1	2	1	14	17	$906,565	8
1998	35	2	1	2	13	25	1,183,959	5
1999	35				10	22	754,046	21
2000	36				4	12	499,608	37
2001	34		1	1	3	16	693,131	30
2002	32				2	9	341,909	52
2003	26				4	12	475,512	39
2004	26			1	1	4	327,791	50
Total	249	3	4	5	51	117	5,182,523	
COMBINED ALL-TIME MONEY (3 TOURS):							**$5,187,421**	

CHAMPIONS TOUR TOP TOURNAMENT SUMMARY

Year	97	98	99	00	01	02	03	04
Senior PGA Championship	T35	T36	7	T51	T40	CUT	T44	T57
U.S. Senior Open	T5	T7	T8	T41	T29	CUT		
Ford Senior Players	T10	T15	T14	T24	T14	T33	47	T28
Senior British Open								17
JELD-WEN Tradition		T25	T45	T47	T40	T42	T7	T70
Charles Schwab Cup Champ	T4	T8	T9		30			

CHAMPIONS TOUR YEAR-BY-YEAR STATISTICS (TOP 50 ON 2004 MONEY LIST)

	Scoring Average	Putting Average	Greens in Regulation	Driving Distance	Driving Accuracy
1997	70.66 (8)	1.814 (T52)	72.2 (4)	262.8 (39)	73.3 (17)
1998	70.86 (12)	1.801 (T35)	70.8 (6)	262.0 (T45)	74.6 (T8)
1999	70.86 (20)	1.794 (T40)	71.7 (T10)	262.8 (T54)	76.6 (9)
2000	71.41 (40)	1.812 (T63)	70.6 (T16)	264.7 (59)	72.2 (T25)
2001	71.38 (T30)	1.822 (72)	70.3 (11)	268.9 (56)	73.1 (T29)
2002	72.23 (T60)	1.867 (88)	67.4 (T34)	262.0 (71)	70.7 (T34)
2003	71.03 (31)	1.798 (T43)	69.3 (T27)	269.8 (52)	72.6 (21)
2004	72.78 (65)	1.855 (75)	65.8 (T50)	266.0 (60)	73.9 (23)

SECTION 2 PLAYER BIOGRAPHIES

Miller Barber

EXEMPT STATUS: Net-70 on All-Time Money List
FULL NAME: Miller Westford Barber, Jr.
HEIGHT: 5-9
WEIGHT: 216
BIRTHDATE: March 31, 1931
BIRTHPLACE: Shreveport, LA
RESIDENCES: Phoenix, AZ; Missoula, MT; Sherman, TX
FAMILY: Wife, Karen; Casey (8/24/62), Douglas (8/17/64), Brad (12/16/65), Larry (10/28/71), Richard (5/14/74); eight grandchildren
CLUB AFFILIATION: Preston Trail GC (Dallas, TX)
EDUCATION: Arkansas (1954, Business)
SPECIAL INTERESTS: Fly fishing
TURNED PROFESSIONAL: 1958
JOINED PGA TOUR: 1959

JOINED CHAMPIONS TOUR: 1981

CHAMPIONS TOUR VICTORIES (24): 1981 Peter Jackson Champions, Suntree Seniors Classic, PGA Seniors' Championship. **1982** U.S. Senior Open, Suntree Seniors Classic, Hilton Head Seniors International. **1983** Senior Tournament Players Championship, Merrill Lynch/Golf Digest Pro-Am, United Virginia Bank Seniors, Hilton Head Seniors International. **1984** Roy Clark Challenge, U.S. Senior Open, Greater Syracuse Senior Classic, Denver Post Champions of Golf. **1985** Sunrise Senior Classic, U.S. Senior Open, PaineWebber World Seniors Invitational. **1986** MONY Senior Tournament of Champions. **1987** Showdown Classic, Newport Cup. **1988** Showdown Classic, Fairfield-Barnett Space Coast Classic. **1989** MONY Senior Tournament of Champions, Vintage Chrysler Invitational.

OTHER SENIOR VICTORIES (4): 1985 Shootout at Jeremy Ranch [with Ben Crenshaw], Coca-Cola Grand Slam. **1987** Mazda Championship [with Nancy Lopez]. **1991** Fuji Electric Grandslam.

GEORGIA-PACIFIC GRAND CHAMPIONS VICTORIES (20): 1991 Bell Atlantic Classic, Kroger Senior Classic, Northville Long Island Classic, Bank One Classic, Raley's Senior Gold Rush. **1992** Royal Caribbean Classic, GTE West Classic, Vantage At The Dominion. **1993** GTE Suncoast Classic, Las Vegas Senior Classic, Southwestern Bell Classic, Quicksilver Classic, The Transamerica. **1994** Bank of Boston Senior Classic, Quicksilver Classic. **1995** GTE Suncoast Classic, Bell Atlantic Classic, Ralphs Senior Classic. **1996** Northville Long Island Classic. **1999** Las Vegas Senior Classic.

PGA TOUR VICTORIES (11): 1964 Cajun Classic Open Invitational. **1967** Oklahoma City Open Invitational. **1968** Byron Nelson Golf Classic. **1969** Kaiser International Open Invitational. **1970** Greater New Orleans Open Invitational. **1971** Phoenix Open Invitational. **1972** Dean Martin Tucson Open. **1973** World Open Golf Championship. **1974** Ohio Kings Island Open. **1977** Anheuser-Busch Golf Classic. **1978** Phoenix Open.

PGA TOUR CAREER EARNINGS: $1,564,204

PGA TOUR PLAYOFF RECORD: 3-4

BEST 2004 CHAMPIONS TOUR FINISH: T69—FedEx Kinko's Classic.

2004 SEASON:

Finished second with teammate Jim Ferree in the Demaret Division at the Liberty Mutual Legends of Golf...Bettered his age for the fifth time in his career when he had a final-round 72 at the FedEx Kinko's Classic in May...Matched his age two weeks later with a closing-round 73 at the Allianz Championship.

CHAMPIONS TOUR CAREER HIGHLIGHTS:

2003: Teamed with Jim Ferree to successfully defend Demaret Division title at the Liberty Mutual Legends of Golf...Became the first of five players to better their age for the season when he carded a 1-under 71 in the first round of the Bruno's Memorial Classic, the fourth time he's bettered his age. Matched his age one day later in Birmingham and again posted a 72 in the first round of the Farmers Charity Classic near Grand Rapids...Matched his age again with a 72 late in the year in the second round of the Greater Hickory Classic at Rock Barn. **2002:** Bettered his age by four strokes when he opened with a 5-under-par 67 at the BellSouth Senior Classic at Opryland. **2001:** Made the cut at the U.S. Senior Open at Salem CC in his final appearance at the event...Bettered his age when he carded a 2-under 68 in the second round of the Novell Utah Showdown. **2000:** Shot his age four times and was the first of five players to better his age when he carded a 4-under 68 in the opening round of the BellSouth Senior Classic at Opryland. **1999:** Played in his 500th Champions Tour event at the Bruno's Memorial Classic...Won his 20th Georgia-Pacific Grand Champions title during the 1999 Las Vegas Senior Classic at the TPC at Summerlin, his first over-60 win since the 1996 Northville Long Island Classic...Twice shot his age, firing 68 in the opening round of the Coldwell Banker Burnet Classic and again in the second round of the Comfort Classic. **1998:** Shot his age twice, carding a 67 in the opening round at the Vantage Championship and in the final round at The Transamerica. **1996:** Sank a 25-foot birdie putt on the final hole to best Tommy Jacobs for the MasterCard Champions crown at the Northville Long Island Classic. **1993:** Claimed five MasterCard Champions wins...Fired a career-low 62 in second round at the Gulfstream Aerospace Invitational, which helped him to a fourth-place finish. **1989:** Became first Champions Tour player to earn $2 million in combined career money...Also became first player to earn $2 million in Champions Tour career money, with victory at Vintage Chrysler Invitational. **1986:** Became the second player to pass the $1-million mark in Champions Tour earnings, when he placed 12th at the PGA Seniors' Championship. **1985:** Among three wins was defense of his title at the U.S. Senior Open at Edgewood Tahoe, his third win at the event. **1984:** Had four wins, including two-stroke victory

CHAMPIONS TOUR CAREER SUMMARY — PLAYOFF RECORD: 1-1

Year	Events Played	1st	2nd	3rd	Top 10	Top 25	Earnings	Rank
1981	6	3			6	6	$83,136	1
1982	10	3	1	1	9	9	106,890	1
1983	16	4	3	2	15	16	231,008	2
1984	22	4	3	3	20	22	299,099	2
1985	22	3	2	2	16	21	241,999	4
1986	27	1	2	1	15	27	204,837	9
1987	31	2	2	4	18	28	347,571	5
1988	30	2	2	4	16	23	329,833	9
1989	32	2	1	2	15	22	370,229	11
1990	33			1	9	19	274,184	21
1991	34			1	6	23	288,753	21
1992	33				3	14	170,798	40
1993	35				6	14	318,986	30
1994	33					6	126,327	60
1995	31				1	5	130,358	67
1996	33					4	103,174	76
1997	33					4	173,113	66
1998	30						79,594	82
1999	28					1	59,562	90
2000	27						49,024	98
2001	25						42,636	106
2002	11						10,104	131
2003	11						7,724	158
2004	10						9,924	148
Total	603	24	16	21	155	264	4,058,864	
COMBINED ALL-TIME MONEY (3 TOURS):							**$5,623,068**	

CHAMPIONS TOUR TOP TOURNAMENT SUMMARY

Year	81	82	83	84	85	86	87	88	89	90	91	92	93
Senior PGA Championship	1	T7		10		12		T3	T2	6	T20	WD	T37
U.S. Senior Open	6	1	3	1	1	7	13	WD	T37	T8	T24	T20	6
Ford Senior Players			1	3	T2	23	T8	T3	T4	T26	T13	T39	T56
JELD-WEN Tradition									T34	T7	T18	T20	T11
Charles Schwab Cup Champ										T11	T19		T24

Year	94	95	96	97	98	99	00	01
Senior PGA Championship	T56	WD	CUT	T59	CUT			CUT
U.S. Senior Open	T57	CUT	T43	CUT	CUT	62		
Ford Senior Players	74	T62	T44	67	76			
JELD-WEN Tradition	T49		74	T31	T73	64		

Miller Barber (continued)

over Arnold Palmer at the U.S. Senior Open at Oak Hill CC...Second on the money list behind Don January and finished in the top 10 in 20 of 22 starts...Was the only player to compete in every event that season. **1983:** Finished second again on the money list to January and had four victories...Was the first winner of the Senior Tournament Players Championship. Edged Gene Littler by a stroke at Canterbury GC after leading or sharing the lead for three of the four rounds. **1982:** Leading money-winner on the Champions Tour and winner of the U.S. Senior Open by four strokes over Gene Littler and Dan Sikes at Portland (OR) GC. **1981:** Led all players with $83,136 in earnings and won three events in six starts...Defeated Arnold Palmer by two strokes for the PGA Seniors' Championship at Turnberry Isle CC.

OTHER CAREER HIGHLIGHTS:

His 24 official Champions Tour wins are third behind Lee Trevino and Hale Irwin on the all-time victory list...Formerly shared Champions Tour record for most consecutive years winning at least one event (nine), but Hale Irwin now holds the record with 10 (1995-present)...Is the only three-time winner of the U.S. Senior Open...Played the PGA TOUR full-time from 1959-1983...Best year on the PGA TOUR was 1973, when he placed sixth in earnings with $184,014...Each of his 11 PGA TOUR wins came in a different season...Claimed at least one victory a year from 1967 to 1974, a feat matched only by Jack Nicklaus during that span...Shot 65-67 in freezing conditions in the final two rounds for his first PGA TOUR win, the 1964 Cajun Classic in Lafayette, LA...Was the 10th player to surpass the $1-million mark in official PGA TOUR career earnings..Has 24 career holes-in-one.

PERSONAL:

Inducted into the Arkansas Hall of Fame in 1977...Honored as a distinguished alumnus by Arkansas...Member of the Texas and Arkansas Sports Halls of Fame and both the Arkansas and Texas Golf Halls of Fame...Member of the United States Ryder Cup Team in 1969 and 1971 and lists his participation in those events as his biggest thrill in golf...A devoted follower of Arkansas Razorback athletic teams...Holds his own celebrity pro-am for charity in Montana each season...Served on the Sherman (TX) School Board from 1986-1992...Lists Cypress Point, Preston Trail and Whisper Rock as his favorite golf courses...Favorite entertainer is the late Bob Hope and favorite movie is "High Noon"...Nickname is "Mr. X."

PLAYER STATISTICS

2004 CHAMPIONS TOUR STATISTICS:

Scoring Average	79.43	(N/A)
Driving Distance	246.0	(N/A)
Driving Accuracy Percentage	69.5%	(N/A)
Total Driving	1,998	(N/A)
Greens in Regulation Pct.	44.8%	(N/A)
Putting Average	1.971	(N/A)
Sand Save Percentage	34.9%	(N/A)
Birdie Average	1.30	(N/A)
All-Around Ranking	1,569	(N/A)

MISCELLANEOUS CHAMPIONS TOUR STATISTICS

2004 Low Round: 72–2004 FedEx Kinko's Classic/3

Career Low Round: 62–1993 Gulfstream Aerospace Invitational/2

Career Largest Paycheck: $55,500–1989 Vintage Chrysler Invitational/1

MISCELLANEOUS PGA TOUR STATISTICS

Career Low Round: 63–2 times, most recent 1975 Sahara Invitational/1

Career Largest Paycheck: $100,000–1973 World Open Golf Championship/1

25 MEMORABLE MOMENTS

January Captures Inaugural Champions Tour Event in Atlantic City

1980 Atlantic City Senior International

Don January made history when he became the winner of the first Champions Tour tournament, the Atlantic City Senior International. The event brought together many of the legends of the game with a field that included the likes of Sam Snead, Julius Boros, Mike Souchak, Art Wall, Bob Goalby, Garner Dickinson and Dan Sikes. All would play prominent roles in the growth of the Champions Tour.

The tournament at Atlantic City Country Club even included a final-round 63 by Charles Sifford. But it would be January who etched his name in the record books. After opening with a 68, January followed with a 71-69 finish to post a two-stroke win and claim the $20,000 first prize.

CHAMPIONS TOUR 25

Dave Barr

EXEMPT STATUS: 46th on 2004 Champions Tour Money List
FULL NAME: David Allen Barr
HEIGHT: 6-1 1/2
WEIGHT: 215
BIRTHDATE: March 1, 1952
BIRTHPLACE: Kelowna, British Columbia, Canada
RESIDENCE: Westbank, British Columbia, Canada
FAMILY: Wife, Lu Ann; Brent Jason (10/11/80), Teryn Amber (4/13/83)
CLUB AFFILIATION: Kelowna G&CC (Kelowna, British Columbia, Canada)
EDUCATION: Oral Roberts University
SPECIAL INTERESTS: Hockey
TURNED PROFESSIONAL: 1974
JOINED PGA TOUR: 1978

JOINED CHAMPIONS TOUR: 2002

CHAMPIONS TOUR VICTORIES (1): 2003 Royal Caribbean Golf Classic.

2004 CHARLES SCHWAB CUP FINISH: 36th - 381 points

PGA TOUR VICTORIES (2): 1981 Quad Cities Open. **1987** Georgia-Pacific Atlanta Golf Classic.

OTHER VICTORIES (20): 1975 British Columbia Open. **1977** British Columbia Open, Alberta Open, Quebec Open. **1978** British Columbia Open. **1981** Victoria Open. **1983** World Cup [indiv]. **1985** CPGA Championship, Quebec Open, World Cup [with Dan Halldorson]. **1986** Quebec Open. **1987** Manitoba Open. **1988** Canadian TPC, Manitoba Open. **1989** Canadian Airlines International Mixed Team Championship [with Dawn Coe]. **1990** Canadian Airlines International Mixed Team Championship [with Dawn Coe]. **1991** Cadillac Skins Game. **1992** Cadillac Skins Game. **1993** Cadillac Skins Game. **1994** Dunhill Cup [with Rick Gibson and Ray Stewart].

PGA TOUR CAREER EARNINGS: $2,404,793

PGA TOUR PLAYOFF RECORD: 1-2

BEST 2004 CHAMPIONS TOUR FINISHES: T4—Senior PGA Championship; T6—Commerce Bank Long Island Classic; T9—Liberty Mutual Legends of Golf; T10—The ACE Group Classic.

2004 SEASON:

Finished T4 in the Senior PGA Championship at Valhalla, his first top-10 finish in a Champions Tour major. Trailed Hale Irwin by three strokes entering the final round, but shot 3-over 74...Initial top-10 finish of the 2004 season was a T10 at The ACE Group Classic in just his third start...Was only one stroke out of the lead after 36 holes at the Liberty Mutual Legends of Golf, but a final-round 75 dropped him seven spots to a T9 finish...Was also T6 at the Commerce Bank Long Island Classic.

CHAMPIONS TOUR CAREER HIGHLIGHTS:

2003: Became the first of seven first-time winners and the first Canadian to win on the Champions Tour event when he captured the first full-field event of the season, the Royal Caribbean Golf Classic. Birdied the final four holes, including the 18th from 35 feet, to overtake Gil Morgan and Bobby Wadkins by one stroke. Win in just his ninth start on the Champions Tour ended a victory drought of 16 years and earned him a check for $217,500, his largest ever as a professional...Continued his good play the next week when he was the 36-hole leader at The ACE Group Classic, but fell back into a T12 after posting a 75 on Sunday...T7 the following week at the Verizon Classic, thanks to a final-round 67...Earned February Player of the Month honors...Made his first ace on the Champions Tour and 10th hole-in-one of his career in the final round of the Allianz Championship. Holed a 4-iron shot on the 204-yard, par-3 fifth hole at Glen Oaks. Ace made him just the second player (Jim Thorpe is the other) to record a hole-in-one on the PGA TOUR, Champions Tour and Nationwide Tour. **2002:** Made eight Champions Tour appearances in his rookie year on the circuit, including three as a sponsor exemption...Debuted as an open qualifier at the Siebel Classic in Silicon Valley and finished T15...Posted a pair of top-10 finishes and his best effort came in his final start when he T9 at the Napa Valley Championship...Earned a full exemption for the 2003 season after finishing T5 at the 2002 National Qualifying Tournament at World Woods GC in Florida. Secured his spot in the top eight when he birdied the 72nd hole...Was the only member of the PGA TOUR to play on all three Tours during the season. Appeared in five events on the PGA TOUR, making four cuts, and made cuts in two tournaments on the Nationwide Tour.

OTHER CAREER HIGHLIGHTS:

Was a member of the PGA TOUR from 1978-2002, playing in 526 tournaments prior to the 2003 season...Made the cut in 320 of those, with career earnings totaling $2,404,793...Enjoyed his best year in 1994 when he earned $314,885 and finished 53rd on the money list...Also earned $291,244 in 1988 and was 33rd on the final money list that year, his highest position ever on the money list...Owns two PGA TOUR victories and both came in spectacular fashion. Won the 1987 Georgia-Pacific Atlanta Classic at the Atlanta CC with a sizzling 23-under-par 265 to beat Larry Mize by four strokes...Other win came at the 1981 Quad Cities Open where he outlasted Dan Halldorson, Victor Regalado, Frank Conner and Woody Blackburn in an eight-hole playoff. Had started the day five strokes back and closed with a 66 to earn a spot in the playoff...Was a runner-up on four occasions, including the 1985 U.S. Open at Oakland Hills where he was among three players (Denis Watson and T.C. Chen) who finished one stroke behind Andy North...Also lost playoffs to Corey Pavin at the 1986 Greater Milwaukee Open and Mark Brooks at the 1988 Canon Sammy Davis, Jr.-Greater Hartford Open (along with Joey Sindelar)...Has played in 39 events on the Nationwide Tour and T6 at the 1996 Louisiana Open...Won the Canadian Tour Order of Merit in 1977, 1985, 1986 and 1988 and owns a dozen wins on that tour...Won the individual title at the 1983 World Cup and teamed with Dan Halldorson to claim the team crown at the 1985 World Cup...In all, was on 13 Canadian World Cup teams and a nine-time member of Canadian Dunhill Cup teams (1985-89, 1991, 1993-95)...Captain of the winning 1994 squad, which included Rick Gibson and Ray Stewart...Member of 1972 Canadian World Amateur team...Winner of eight SCORE awards as Canada's top player...Inducted into the Canadian Golf Hall of Fame in 2000 and also a member of the B.C. Sports Hall of Fame...Has 10 career holes-in-one.

PERSONAL:

Biggest thrills in golf were winning his first PGA TOUR title at 1981 Quad Cities Open and being a part of Canada's upset win at the 1994 Dunhill Cup at St. Andrews...Outside of golf biggest thrill in his life was the birth of his two children...Two superstitions are using only white tees and carrying three coins in his pocket—quarter and two pennies...Favorite golf course is the Old Course at St. Andrews and favorite movie is "Caddyshack"...Enjoys cajun food and favorite athlete is Wayne Gretzky...Still uses a MacGregor CB-5 putter that was given to him by his college coach in 1971...Lists Danny Gans as his favorite entertainer and his favorite TV show is "CSI"...Favorite book is the *NHL Media Guide*...Best friend on the Champions Tour is Ed Fiori...The one course he'd like to play is Pine Valley...Enjoys any Tom Hanks movie.

PLAYER STATISTICS

MISCELLANEOUS CHAMPIONS TOUR STATISTICS
2004 Low Round: 66–3 times, most recent 2004 Commerce Bank Long Island Classic/2
Career Low Round: 65–2 times, most recent 2003 Columbus Southern Open/2
Career Largest Paycheck: $217,500–2003 Royal Caribbean Golf Classic/1

MISCELLANEOUS PGA TOUR STATISTICS
Career Low Round: 61–1988 Southern Open/3
Career Largest Paycheck: $108,000–1987 Georgia–Pacific Atlanta Golf Classic/1

CHAMPIONS TOUR CAREER SUMMARY — PLAYOFF RECORD: 0-0

Year	Events Played	1st	2nd	3rd	Top 10	Top 25	Earnings	Rank
2002	8				2	3	$132,259	87
2003	28	1			4	16	731,726	27
2004	28				4	8	436,531	46
Total	64	1			10	27	1,300,516	
COMBINED ALL-TIME MONEY (3 TOURS):							**$3,765,518**	

CHAMPIONS TOUR TOP TOURNAMENT SUMMARY

Year	02	03	04
Senior PGA Championship	T51	T57	T4
U.S. Senior Open	T31	CUT	T42
Ford Senior Players		T15	T71
JELD-WEN Tradition		T20	T61
Charles Schwab Cup Champ		T18	

CHAMPIONS TOUR YEAR-BY-YEAR STATISTICS (TOP 50 ON 2004 MONEY LIST)

	Scoring Average	Putting Average	Greens in Regulation	Driving Distance	Driving Accuracy
2002	71.92 (N/A)	1.879 (N/A)	68.8 (N/A)	268.8 (N/A)	68.1 (N/A)
2003	71.16 (38)	1.820 (66)	71.3 (13)	277.0 (21)	70.4 (37)
2004	71.83 (44)	1.828 (T60)	72.0 (11)	275.3 (24)	70.3 (40)

Andy Bean

EXEMPT STATUS: Top 30 on 2004 Champions Tour Money List
FULL NAME: Thomas Andrew Bean
HEIGHT: 6-4
WEIGHT: 260
BIRTHDATE: March 13, 1953
BIRTHPLACE: Lafayette, GA
RESIDENCE: Lakeland, FL
FAMILY: Wife, Debbie; Lauren Ashley (4/17/82), Lindsey Ann (8/10/84), Jordan Alisa (11/19/85)
EDUCATION: University of Florida (1976, Marketing/Business)
SPECIAL INTERESTS: Hunting, fishing
TURNED PROFESSIONAL: 1975
JOINED PGA TOUR: 1976

JOINED CHAMPIONS TOUR: 2003

BEST CHAMPIONS TOUR CAREER FINISH: T2—2004 Commerce Bank Long Island Classic.

2004 CHARLES SCHWAB CUP FINISH: 26th - 627 points

PGA TOUR VICTORIES (11): 1977 Doral-Eastern Open. **1978** Kemper Open, Danny Thomas Memphis Classic, Western Open. **1979** Atlanta Classic. **1980** Hawaiian Open. **1981** Bay Hill Classic. **1982** Doral-Eastern Open. **1984** Greater Greensboro Open. **1986** Doral-Eastern Open, Byron Nelson Golf Classic.

OTHER VICTORIES (7): 1974 Eastern Amateur, Falstaff Amateur. **1975** Dixie Amateur, Western Amateur. **1978** Dunlop Phoenix. **1986** Kapalua International. **1987** Kapalua International.

PGA TOUR CAREER EARNINGS: $3,531,780

PGA TOUR PLAYOFF RECORD: 3-3

BEST 2004 CHAMPIONS TOUR FINISHES:

T2—Commerce Bank Long Island Classic; T3—Bayer Advantage Celebrity Pro-Am; T4—JELD-WEN Tradition; T7—MasterCard Classic; T9—Liberty Mutual Legends of Golf; T10—3M Championship.

2004 SEASON:

Found himself in contention for his first Champions Tour victory at the Farmers Charity Classic but was forced to withdraw after having an allergic food reaction, which sent him to the hospital prior to the start of his final round. Had shared the 36-hole lead with Bob Gilder, three strokes over the field. Bounced back from his misfortune the next week by opening with a 7-under-par 65 and finishing T3 at the rain-shortened Bayer Advantage Celebrity Pro-Am...Challenged again at the Commerce Bank Long Island Classic, but eventually T2, one stroke shy of Jim Thorpe. Final-round 67 at Eisenhower Park earned him a career-best check of $110,000, but he missed on a playoff spot when his seven-foot birdie effort on the final hole didn't drop...Claimed a T4 finish at the JELD-WEN Tradition...Also T7 at MasterCard Classic in Mexico. Was the first-round leader after shooting a 5-under-par 67...Added T9 finish at the Liberty Mutual Legends of Golf after three straight sub-par rounds...Was the only player to shoot a round in the 60s in the final round of the Ford Senior Players Championship, where he finished T18...Ranked sixth in Driving Distance (286.6) and had the longest recorded drive during the season—a 375-yarder in the second round at the FedEx Kinko's Classic. His 320 birdies ranked fifth overall.

CHAMPIONS TOUR CAREER HIGHLIGHTS:

2003: Made Champions Tour debut in March and T26 at the Toshiba Senior Classic...Best finish of his rookie season was a T8 at the SAS Championship near Raleigh at the end of the campaign...Also T13 at Kinko's Classic of Austin after being among the leaders through 36 holes...Closed with his low round of the year, a 6-under 64, at the Columbus Southern Open...Withdrew prior to his start at the Senior British Open after an injury to his right calf muscle and the injury forced him to miss subsequent starts at the FleetBoston Classic and the 3M Championship...Ended his season by making his first hole-in-one on the Champions Tour at the SBC Championship in San Antonio. Just shortly after John Bland's ace, he holed a 6-iron shot from 195 yards on the par-3 18th hole at Oak Hills in the final round...Finished second to Tom Purtzer in Driving Distance, averaging 297.9 yards off the tee...Played in two PGA TOUR events, missing the cut at the Ford Championship at Doral and finishing 75th at the FedEx St. Jude Classic near Memphis.

OTHER CAREER HIGHLIGHTS:

Was an 11-time winner on PGA TOUR between 1977-86 and enjoyed a career that spanned four decades...Had battled injuries in the latter stages of his PGA TOUR career...First joined the PGA TOUR in 1976, making 586 starts with 343 cuts made in his career...Amassed $3,531,780 in career earnings...Five times he finished in the top 10 on the money list with third-place finishes in both 1978 and 1984...Was fourth in both 1980 and 1986 and was seventh in 1979...In a three-year span (1978-80), won five times, including three times in 1978 and finished in the top 10 a total of 32 times in 89 appearances...Most lucrative season in earnings came in 1986 when he won $491,938 with two victories and was fourth on the money list...Three-time winner of the Doral-Eastern Open...Claimed two victories in playoffs. Defeated Lee Trevino to win the 1978 Danny Thomas Memphis Classic and bested Bill Rogers to win the Western Open the same year...T2 with Hale Irwin at 1983 British Open, one stroke behind winner Tom Watson. Was a two-time runner-up at the PGA Championship (1980 and 1989)...Member of the 1979 and 1987 American Ryder Cup teams, also played for the U.S. squad in the 1984 U.S. vs. Japan matches...Low round of his career was a third-round 61 that was instrumental in his victory at the 1979 Atlanta Classic...Had an outstanding amateur career, winning 1974 Eastern and Falstaff Amateurs and 1975 Dixie and Western Amateurs...All-America at University of Florida...Winner of the 1978 Dunlop Phoenix in Japan...First played in a professional event in 1974 when he qualified for the U.S. Open as an amateur and finished T64 at Winged Foot.

PERSONAL:

Lived in Jekyll Island, GA, as a child where his father was associated with a golf course. His family moved to Lakeland when he was 15 and his father bought a golf course there...Dream would be to fly a jet and land it on a carrier...Lists Doral and Muirfield Village as his favorite golf courses...Favorite athletes are Jack Nicklaus and Arnold Palmer...Enjoys listening to Toby Keith and Garth Brooks.

PLAYER STATISTICS

MISCELLANEOUS CHAMPIONS TOUR STATISTICS

2004 Low Round: 65–3 times, most recent 2004 Commerce Bank Long Island Classic/2
Career Low Round: 64–2003 Columbus Southern Open/3
Career Largest Paycheck: $110,000–2004 Commerce Bank Long Island Classic/T2

MISCELLANEOUS PGA TOUR STATISTICS

2004 Low Round: 69–2 times, most recent FedEx St. Jude Classic/2
Career Low Round: 61–1979 Atlanta Classic/3
Career Largest Paycheck: $108,000–1986 Byron Nelson Golf Classic/1

CHAMPIONS TOUR CAREER SUMMARY — PLAYOFF RECORD: 0-0

Year	Events Played	1st	2nd	3rd	Top 10	Top 25	Earnings	Rank
2003	16				1	6	$230,493	59
2004	28		1	1	6	16	777,361	24
Total	44		1	1	7	22	1,007,855	
COMBINED ALL-TIME MONEY (3 TOURS):							**$4,542,484**	

CHAMPIONS TOUR TOP TOURNAMENT SUMMARY

Year	03	04
Senior PGA Championship	T32	T13
U.S. Senior Open		T25
Ford Senior Players		T18
Senior British Open		T13
JELD-WEN Tradition		T4
Charles Schwab Cup Champ		28

CHAMPIONS TOUR YEAR-BY-YEAR STATISTICS (TOP 50 ON 2004 MONEY LIST)

	Scoring Average	Putting Average	Greens in Regulation	Driving Distance	Driving Accuracy
2003	71.14 (37)	1.859 (85)	71.0 (14)	297.9 (2)	58.2 (80)
2004	71.22 (28)	1.815 (53)	71.1 (15)	286.6 (6)	57.9 (80)

John Bland

EXEMPT STATUS: Top 30 on All-Time Money List
FULL NAME: John Louis Bland
HEIGHT: 5-9
WEIGHT: 176
BIRTHDATE: September 22, 1945
BIRTHPLACE: Johannesburg, South Africa
RESIDENCE: Knysna, South Africa
FAMILY: Wife, Sonja; John-Mark (2/8/69), Bonney (5/7/71), Candice (3/8/75); three grandchildren
CLUB AFFILIATION: Fancourt G&CC (George, South Africa)
EDUCATION: St. John's Boscoe College
SPECIAL INTERESTS: Rugby, gardening, movies
TURNED PROFESSIONAL: 1969

JOINED CHAMPIONS TOUR: 1995

CHAMPIONS TOUR VICTORIES (5): 1995 Ralphs Senior Classic. **1996** Puerto Rico Senior Tournament of Champions, Bruno's Memorial Classic, Northville Long Island Classic, The Transamerica.

OTHER SENIOR VICTORIES (4): 1995 London Masters. **1997** Liberty Mutual Legends of Golf [with Graham Marsh], Franklin Templeton Senior South African Open. **1998** Franklin Templeton Senior South African Open.

2004 CHARLES SCHWAB CUP FINISH: 51st - 187 points

BEST PGA TOUR CAREER FINISH: 20—1978 World Series of Golf.

OTHER VICTORIES (23): 1970 Transvaal Open. **1977** Holiday Inns Champion of Champions. Victoria Falls Classic, South African PGA Championship. **1979** Holiday Inns Invitational. **1981** Sigma Series 2, Sigma Series 3. **1983** Benson & Hedges International Open, Holiday Inns Invitational, Kodak Classic. **1984** Goodyear Classic. **1986** Suze Open. **1987** Goodyear Classic. **1988** Trustbank Tournament of Champions, Safmarine Masters. **1989** Dewar's White Label Trophy. **1990** Dewar's White Label Trophy, Minolta Match Play, Spoomet Bloemfontein Classic. **1991** Palabora Classic, Bell's Cup, Trustbank Tournament of Champions, Martini Open.

PGA TOUR CAREER EARNINGS: $5,400

BEST 2004 CHAMPIONS TOUR FINISHES: T3—Royal Caribbean Golf Classic; T7—Outback Steakhouse Pro-Am; T9—Toshiba Senior Classic.

2004 SEASON:
Best finish came in his initial start of the season at the Royal Caribbean Golf Classic. Trailed after 36 holes by just one stroke before shooting a final-round, 1-over-par 73 in windy conditions to finish T3 with Gil Morgan. It was his best performance since earning a second-place finish at the 2002 Allianz Championship…Two weeks later added his second top-10 finish when he was T7 at the Outback Steakhouse Pro-Am in Tampa…For the ninth consecutive year, ranked among the Champions Tour's top 10 in Driving Accuracy. Hit the fairway off the tee 83.0 percent of the time to place second behind Allen Doyle.

CHAMPIONS TOUR CAREER HIGHLIGHTS:
2003: Finished out of the top 30 on the season-long money list for the first time since 1999…Registered just two top-10 finishes in 24 starts…Again played well at Glen Oaks CC in Des Moines, IA. Strung together three straight sub-70 rounds at the Allianz Championship and T8, his top effort of the season…Was one of just two players on the Champions Tour (Tom Jenkins) to make multiple aces during the season…First holed a 6-iron shot from 171 yards on the par-3 12th hole at Egypt Valley during the second round of the Farmers Charity Classic and then made his fourth career Champions Tour ace in the last round of his final start of the year at the SBC Championship. Again used a 6-iron, this time from 172 yards on the par-3 second hole at Oak Hills during the final round. Hole-in-one in San Antonio made him the first player since Bob Lendzion in 2000 to have multiple aces in the same season. **2002:** Top performance of the year came at the Allianz Championship, finishing second by one stroke to Bob Gilder. Had Champions Tour career-best 8-under 63 (course record) at Glen Oaks on Saturday with a hole-in-one (5-iron, 16th hole) that gave him a two-stroke lead after 36 holes. Was tied with Gilder with just three holes to play, but made a bogey at No. 17 and finished second. **2001:** Fired a final-round 66 to finish as the runner-up to Bruce Fleisher at the Home Depot Invitational, his best effort since barely losing to Graham Marsh at the 1997 U.S. Senior Open at Olympia Fields. **2000:** T4 at the SBC Senior Open near Chicago…Finished second to Christy O'Connor, Jr. for the second straight year at the unofficial Senior British Open at Royal County Down in Northern Ireland. **1999:** Had six top-10 performances, highlighted by a T4 at the Pacific Bell Senior Classic, three strokes short of Joe Inman. **1998:** Season was limited to just 18 events, including just two following the death of his first wife, Helen, in early August…Earlier in the year, put together four straight top-10s, including a fifth-place effort at the Pittsburgh Senior Classic. **1997:** Battled good friend Graham Marsh to the final hole before falling one stroke short at the U.S. Senior Open at Olympia Fields CC near Chicago…Contended all the way at Springhouse GC and was runner-up by two strokes to Gil Morgan at the BellSouth Senior Classic at Opryland…Finished one shy of Bob Eastwood at the Bell Atlantic Classic after the final round was canceled by heavy rain…Teamed with Marsh in March to win the Liberty Mutual Legends of Golf near Palm Springs, CA…Also lost in a playoff to Gary Player at Senior British Open at Royal Portrush. **1996:** Voted Champions Tour Rookie of the Year after earning $1,357,987 on the strength of four official wins…Claimed the first event of the year, the Puerto Rico Senior Tournament of Champions, when he birdied the final two holes to nip Jim Colbert…Also bested Colbert at The Transamerica, by one stroke, and at the Northville Long Island Classic, by three strokes…Also won the Bruno's Memorial Classic in a playoff over Kermit Zarley and John Paul Cain. **1995:** Made his Champions Tour debut at The Transamerica (tied for lead after 36 holes) and T5 at Silverado…Was the fourth player to Monday qualify and win an event (first since Rives McBee in 1989) when he claimed the Ralphs Senior Classic two weeks after joining the Champions Tour…Earned an immediate one-year exemption when he came from four strokes behind to beat Jim Colbert at Wilshire CC with a final-round 65.

OTHER CAREER HIGHLIGHTS:
A prolific winner in South Africa, he also played on the PGA European Tour from 1977 through 1994…First of two victories in Europe came at the 1983 Benson & Hedges International Open, where he defeated Bernhard Langer by one stroke…Also defeated Seve Ballesteros by four strokes to claim the 1986 Suze Open at Cannes Mougins…Represented South Africa in the 1975 World Cup and was on the South African team for the 1991 and 1992 Dunhill Cups…Led the South African Order of Merit in 1977, 1978, 1984 and 1986 and had his best year on the PGA European Tour in 1990, finishing in 16th place on the

CHAMPIONS TOUR CAREER SUMMARY **PLAYOFF RECORD: 1-0**

Year	Events Played	1st	2nd	3rd	Top 10	Top 25	Earnings	Rank
1995	3	1			3	3	$184,867	54
1996	35	4	1	2	17	32	1,357,987	3
1997	33		3	2	17	30	1,169,707	6
1998	18				5	12	321,752	52
1999	28				6	18	508,847	37
2000	32				8	24	777,887	21
2001	30		1		4	18	718,632	26
2002	29		1	2	7	16	824,405	25
2003	24				2	6	343,642	46
2004	26			1	3	13	516,605	38
Total	258	5	6	7	72	172	6,724,330	

COMBINED ALL-TIME MONEY (3 TOURS): **$6,729,730**

CHAMPIONS TOUR TOP TOURNAMENT SUMMARY

Year	96	97	98	99	00	01	02	03	04
Senior PGA Championship	T25	T7	T29	DQ	T10	T17	T51	T28	T42
U.S. Senior Open	T8	2			T21	CUT	T21	T40	
Ford Senior Players	T16	T10	T45	T22	T28	T45		T23	T46
Senior British Open								T32	T30
JELD-WEN Tradition	T7	T25	T25	T9	T9	T7	T57	T46	T24
Charles Schwab Cup Champ	T3	T22			T14	T18	T5		

CHAMPIONS TOUR YEAR-BY-YEAR STATISTICS (TOP 50 ON 2004 MONEY LIST)

	Scoring Average	Putting Average	Greens in Regulation	Driving Distance	Driving Accuracy
1995	68.25 (N/A)	1.691 (N/A)	76.4 (N/A)	260.6 (N/A)	77.7 (N/A)
1996	70.36 (6)	1.768 (6)	70.8 (6)	258.6 (T53)	78.0 (5)
1997	70.39 (5)	1.783 (T19)	72.0 (5)	255.5 (T66)	81.0 (1)
1998	71.69 (40)	1.807 (T41)	69.8 (11)	256.0 (T65)	78.3 (4)
1999	70.64 (16)	1.800 (T48)	72.0 (7)	261.6 (T60)	76.5 (T10)
2000	70.49 (17)	1.790 (T45)	72.3 (12)	263.4 (67)	78.3 (8)
2001	71.17 (25)	1.789 (T27)	68.9 (22)	269.3 (55)	81.4 (T1)
2002	71.51 (37)	1.802 (T47)	70.1 (18)	262.1 (70)	81.0 (4)
2003	71.32 (42)	1.812 (T58)	70.3 (T18)	263.6 (71)	79.1 (3)
2004	71.51 (37)	1.828 (T60)	69.7 (22)	261.5 (69)	83.0 (2)

John Bland (continued)

Order of Merit with £166,227...Selected as the Golfer of the Year in South Africa for 1996...Once shot 59 at the par-72 ERPM GC in Johannesburg...Has made 21 aces in his career.

PERSONAL:

Says the biggest thrill of his career came at the 1996 PGA Seniors' Championship when he played with Arnold Palmer for the first time and recorded his first hole-in-one on the Champions Tour...Lists Gary Player and Palmer as his heroes and his late wife, Helen, as the most influential person in his career...Son-in-law Hughie O'Shea is his caddie...Has worked with South African teacher Denis Hutchinson...Lists the Old Course at St. Andrews as his favorite course...Does not play with golf balls marked '3'...Lists Winston Churchill and Morne Du Plessis, a former captain of the South African rugby team, as his heroes...Enjoys eating South African barbecue.

PLAYER STATISTICS

MISCELLANEOUS CHAMPIONS TOUR STATISTICS

2004 Low Round: 65–2 times, most recent 2004 Toshiba Senior Classic/3
Career Low Round: 63–2002 Allianz Championship/2
Career Largest Paycheck: $162,800–2002 Allianz Championship/2

MISCELLANEOUS PGA TOUR STATISTICS

Career Low Round: 73–1978 World Series of Golf/4
Career Largest Paycheck: $5,400–1978 World Series of Golf/20

25 MEMERABLE MOMENTS

Palmer Wins Senior Debut

1980 Senior PGA Championship

The tournament, played at the Turnberry Isle Country Club in Miami, FL, marked the senior debut of the legendary Arnold Palmer, and he did not disappoint his legion of fans. A seven-foot birdie putt on the first hole of a sudden-death playoff with Paul Harney earned Palmer the title and $20,000 after the duo finished regulation at 1-over-par 289. "It's the PGA Championship I never won," said Palmer. The King would go on to claim nine more Champions Tour titles and ignite interest in the newly formed Tour in the same fashion he did for golf in America in the 1950s and '60s.

Brad Bryant

EXEMPT STATUS: 3rd at 2004 Champions Tour National Qualifying Tournament
FULL NAME: Bradley Dub Bryant
HEIGHT: 5-10
WEIGHT: 190
BIRTHDATE: December 11, 1954
BIRTHPLACE: Amarillo, TX
RESIDENCE: Lakeland, FL
FAMILY: Wife, Sue; William Jamieson (1/27/91), Jonathan David (4/26/93)
EDUCATION: University of New Mexico
SPECIAL INTERESTS: Bass fishing, hunting
TURNED PROFESSIONAL: 1976

JOINED CHAMPIONS TOUR: 2005

PGA TOUR VICTORIES (1): 1995 Walt Disney World/Oldsmobile Classic.

PGA TOUR CAREER EARNINGS: $3,558,804

PGA TOUR PLAYOFF RECORD: 0-1

BEST 2004 PGA TOUR FINISH: T37—Valero Texas Open.

2004 SEASON:

Is fully exempt for 2005 after finishing third at the Champions Tour National Qualifying Tournament at the King and Bear at World Golf Village near St. Augustine, FL, in November...Five of his six rounds were in the 60s, and he finished 22-under-par for the event...Played in six events during the year with four starts on the PGA TOUR and two on the Nationwide Tour...Earned $32,210 on the PGA TOUR and made three cuts, with a best finish a T37 at the Valero Texas Open where he shot four straight sub-par rounds...Was T10 at the Nationwide Tour's BMW Charity Pro-Am at The Cliffs.

OTHER CAREER HIGHLIGHTS:

Recorded lone PGA TOUR victory in his 18th season and 475th start when he won the rain-shortened 1995 Walt Disney World/Oldsmobile Classic. Held a share of the 36-hole lead following a 63 at Lake Buena Vista and his final-round 68 at the Magnolia Course gave him a one-stroke victory over Hal Sutton and Ted Tryba. Win helped him to his best earnings year on the PGA TOUR ($723,834/25th)...The previous season saw him finish a career-best 18th on the money list, with $687,803. Did not win but was second at the Doral-Ryder Open and the Kmart Greater Greensboro Open. Was also a third-place finisher twice that year...Held a one-stroke margin entering the final round of the 1993 Canadian Open before closing-round 74 left him third, three strokes behind David Frost...Was part of a five-man playoff at the Buick Southern Open later that year in an event won by John Inman...Prior to 2005, had made 558 starts on the PGA TOUR, enjoyed 49 top-10 finishes and made 211 cuts...Played full time on TOUR from 1979-1999 before he unofficially retired in 1999. Played a handful of events from 2000-2004. Played the 1999 season under a Special Medical Extension after missing almost all of the previous year...Battled various injuries in his career, including a degenerative disk in his lower back as well as shoulder problems...Finished in the top 125 on the money list for nine straight years from 1989-97. Led TOUR in birdies in 1994 (397).

PERSONAL:

Nickname "Dr. Dirt" bestowed upon him by Gary McCord in late 1970s. Younger brother Bart also played on the TOUR and won the 2004 Valero Texas Open at age 41...Biggest thrill in golf was watching Bart win the Valero Texas Open...Lists Bart as his favorite athlete...Has worked with David Leadbetter...His favorite course is Spyglass Hill and his favorite movie is "Chariots of Fire"...Enjoyed the "Lord of the Rings" trilogy...Favorite food is his mother's country-fried steak.

PLAYER STATISTICS

MISCELLANEOUS PGA TOUR STATISTICS
2004 Low Round: 66–Valero Texas Open/1
Career Low Round: 63–1995 Walt Disney World/Oldsmobile Classic/2
Career Largest Paycheck: $216,000–1995 Walt Disney World/Oldsmobile Classic/1

Jose Maria Canizares (CAN-ih-ZARE-us)

EXEMPT STATUS: Top 30 on 2004 Champions Tour Money List
FULL NAME: Jose Maria Canizares
HEIGHT: 5-11
WEIGHT: 165
BIRTHDATE: February 18, 1947
BIRTHPLACE: Madrid, Spain
RESIDENCE: Malaga, Spain
FAMILY: Wife, Felicidad; Genoveva (6/21/73), Gabriel (6/27/74), Jose Alejandro (1/9/83)
SPECIAL INTERESTS: All sports, reading, movies
TURNED PROFESSIONAL: 1967

JOINED CHAMPIONS TOUR: 1997

CHAMPIONS TOUR VICTORIES (1): 2001 Toshiba Senior Classic.

2004 CHARLES SCHWAB CUP FINISH: 12th - 1,314 points

OTHER VICTORIES (13): 1972 Lancia D'Oro. **1980** Avis-Jersey Open, Bob Hope British Classic. **1981** Italian Open. **1982** World Cup [with Manuel Pinero]. **1983** Bob Hope British Classic. **1984** World Cup [indiv], World Cup [with Jose Rivero], Kenya Open. **1988** Volvo Open. **1990** Benson & Hedges Mixed Team [with Tania Abitbol]. **1992** Roma Masters. **1998** Dubai Desert Classic.

BEST 2004 CHAMPIONS TOUR FINISHES: 2—Ford Senior Players Championship; T3—SAS Championship; T5—Charles Schwab Cup Championship; T6—FedEx Kinko's Classic; T8—Constellation Energy Classic; T9—Bayer Advantage Celebrity Pro-Am.

2004 SEASON:

Strong second half propelled him to his best year since 2001...Overall had six top-10s, one more than each of the last two years, and earned just over $225,000 more than he pocketed in 2003...Nearly claimed his first victory since 2001 in July when he battled Mark James for the top spot down the stretch at the Ford Senior Players Championship. Held a one-stroke advantage playing the par-5 17th hole at the TPC of Michigan, but dumped his third shot in the water and ended up with a double bogey that eventually left him one stroke shy of James. Earned $219,000 for his second-place finish, the largest check of his professional career. Was the 36-hole co-leader in Dearborn after closing his Friday round with six straight birdies...T3 at the SAS Championship in September, thanks to a final-round 66 at Prestonwood...Trailed by just two strokes heading into the final round of the season-ending Charles Schwab Cup Championship, but bogeyed three of his first four holes on Sunday and eventually T5 at Sonoma...First top-10 finish of the season didn't come until early May when he T6 at the FedEx Kinko's Classic. Was one of just two players (Morris Hatalsky) to post three consecutive sub-par rounds at The Hills CC.

CHAMPIONS TOUR CAREER HIGHLIGHTS:

2003: Had five top-10s highlighted by a runner-up finish at the Music City Championship at Gaylord Opryland, four strokes back of Jim Ahern...Also T3 at the Toshiba Senior Classic. **2002:** Troubled by a sore left shoulder for the majority of the season...Best effort came early in the year when he T4 at the Audi Senior Classic in Mexico...At U.S. Senior Open in Baltimore in July, finished T7, the fourth time he posted a top-10 finish in the event. **2001:** The top international player on the Champions Tour, eclipsing the million-dollar mark for the second consecutive season...Was top-10 in eight of his first 11 events, highlighted by first career victory on the Champions Tour at the Toshiba Senior Classic. Came from five strokes back on the final day, a best for the 2001 season. Sunk a 10-foot birdie putt on the final hole of regulation to force a playoff with Gil Morgan and then defeated Morgan on the ninth extra playoff hole with a 20-foot birdie putt. Victory came in his 109th start and was followed by a runner-up performance to Jim Colbert at the SBC Senior Classic. **2000:** Earned the most money without a win, pocketing $1,155,939 on the strength of 10 top-10 finishes...Along with Walter Hall and Tom Watson, lost out to Lanny Wadkins in a playoff at The ACE Group Classic...Finished third late in the year at The Transamerica and T3 at the season-ending IR SENIOR TOUR Championship after being the 36-hole leader...Fired a career-best 10-under 61 in the second round of the EMC Kaanapali Classic, equalling Jim Colbert's Kaanapali North Course record. **1999:** Came close to victory on several occasions...Along with Bruce Fleisher, lost in overtime to John Mahaffey at the Southwestern Bell Dominion...Also in contention at the PGA Seniors' Championship, but eventually T3 after a final-round 72...Was T3 at both the Nationwide Championship and Lightpath Long Island Classic. **1998:** One of 11 players to hit the $1-million mark in season earnings...Came close to the winner's circle twice...T2 at the GTE Classic after taking a two-stroke lead to the 16th tee on the final day and also lost in a playoff to Jay Sigel at the Bell Atlantic Classic on the third extra hole. **1997:** Debuted in April at the PGA Seniors' Championship and T35...Had four straight top-10 finishes at one point, starting with a T10 at the U.S. Senior Open, where he shot a third-round 66, the low round of the event...Nearly won the Northville Long Island Classic. Was tied for the 36-hole lead with Dana Quigley and Walter Hall. Contended until the final hole before missing a short putt that would have put him in a playoff with Jay Sigel and eventual winner Quigley...Also made five starts on the PGA European Seniors Tour, finishing seventh on the final Order of Merit...Earned fully-exempt status for the 1998 season by placing second at the National Qualifying Tournament.

OTHER CAREER HIGHLIGHTS:

A long-time standout on the PGA European Tour, where he won seven events...Finished in the top 10 on the Order of Merit six times, including three consecutive years (1983-85)...Best season was 1983, when he placed fourth...Had some record performances in Europe. Still shares the record for lowest nine-hole score with a 9-under-par 27 at the 1978 Ebel European Masters-Swiss Open in Crans-sur-Sierre. Eight years later, shot an 11-under-par 61 on the same course. Round included 11 birdies, which tied the PGA European Tour record at the time...Won more than 1.25 million pounds in his career...Enjoyed success in Ryder Cup play...Was a member of the European team in 1981, '83, '85 and '89...His 1985 singles victory over Fuzzy Zoeller helped the Europeans win their first Ryder Cup title in 28 years...Four years later at The Belfry, made a four-foot putt on the 18th hole to defeat Ken Green and assure Europe the Cup for another two years...Overall Ryder Cup record was 5-4-2...Teamed with countryman Manuel Pinero to help Spain win the 1982 World Cup in Acapulco, and two years later teamed with Jose Rivero for another Spanish victory in Rome. Was the medalist at the 1984 event...Has five career holes-in-one.

PERSONAL:

Began playing the game after working as a caddie as a youngster in Madrid...Says his biggest thrill in golf was winning his first event as a professional at South Sebastian in 1969...Son Alejandro won the individual title at the 2003 NCAA Golf Championship while playing for Arizona State.

PLAYER STATISTICS

MISCELLANEOUS CHAMPIONS TOUR STATISTICS
2004 Low Round: 66–3 times, most recent 2004 Constellation Energy Classic/2
Career Low Round: 61–2000 EMC Kaanapali Classic/2
Career Largest Paycheck: $219,000–2004 Ford Senior Players Championship/2

MISCELLANEOUS PGA TOUR STATISTICS
Career Low Round: 72–1986 PGA Championship/1

CHAMPIONS TOUR CAREER SUMMARY — PLAYOFF RECORD: 1-3

Year	Events Played	1st	2nd	3rd	Top 10	Top 25	Earnings	Rank
1997	7			1	4	5	202,908	63
1998	31		2	3	12	26	1,025,425	11
1999	33		1	3	14	27	1,087,284	10
2000	33		1	2	10	27	1,155,939	12
2001	30	1	2	1	12	20	1,191,094	14
2002	30				5	17	635,503	33
2003	27		1	1	5	12	680,895	30
2004	26		1	1	6	13	905,989	20
Total	217	1	8	12	68	147	6,885,036	

COMBINED ALL-TIME MONEY (3 TOURS): $6,885,036

CHAMPIONS TOUR TOP TOURNAMENT SUMMARY

Year	97	98	99	00	01	02	03	04
Senior PGA Championship	T35	T22	T3	T38	T61	T18	T26	T51
U.S. Senior Open	T10	T7	T27	T10	CUT	T7	T12	T12
Ford Senior Players		7	T5	T7	T26	T33	T40	2
Senior British Open							CUT	
JELD-WEN Tradition		T25	T20	T15	T12	T70	T62	T24
Charles Schwab Cup Champ		T11	T11	T3	T18		27	T5

CHAMPIONS TOUR YEAR-BY-YEAR STATISTICS (TOP 50 ON 2004 MONEY LIST)

	Scoring Average	Putting Average	Greens in Regulation	Driving Distance	Driving Accuracy
1997	71.09 (N/A)	1.816 (N/A)	71.0 (N/A)	263.3 (N/A)	73.3 (N/A)
1998	70.60 (8)	1.777 (T16)	69.2 (13)	261.9 (T47)	70.3 (T32)
1999	70.22 (7)	1.782 (T19)	70.7 (15)	269.6 (T24)	75.2 (17)
2000	70.04 (T10)	1.755 (10)	72.1 (14)	266.8 (T41)	75.4 (13)
2001	70.75 (17)	1.767 (16)	67.8 (31)	270.4 (52)	72.7 (32)
2002	71.19 (T30)	1.803 (49)	67.6 (32)	264.3 (T62)	71.5 (T27)
2003	71.17 (39)	1.795 (T39)	67.7 (T39)	262.4 (73)	71.5 (T28)
2004	71.11 (25)	1.774 (17)	66.4 (T44)	266.8 (58)	75.0 (19)

Bob Charles

EXEMPT STATUS: Top 30 on All-Time Money List
FULL NAME: Robert James Charles
HEIGHT: 6-1
WEIGHT: 175
BIRTHDATE: March 14, 1936
BIRTHPLACE: Carterton, New Zealand
RESIDENCE: Oxford, New Zealand; Palm Beach Gardens, FL
FAMILY: Wife, Verity; Beverly (1/22/66), David (8/29/68), four grandchildren
CLUB AFFILIATION: Millbrook Resort (Queenstown, New Zealand)
SPECIAL INTERESTS: Farming, golf course architecture
TURNED PROFESSIONAL: 1960
JOINED PGA TOUR: 1962

JOINED CHAMPIONS TOUR: 1986

CHAMPIONS TOUR VICTORIES (23): 1987 Vintage Chrysler Invitational, GTE Classic, Sunwest-Charley Pride Classic. **1988** NYNEX/Golf Digest Commemorative, Sunwest-Charley Pride Classic, Rancho Murieta Senior Gold Rush, Vantage Bank One Senior Golf Classic, Pepsi Senior Challenge. **1989** GTE Suncoast Classic, NYNEX/Golf Digest Commemorative, Digital Seniors Classic, Sunwest-Charley Pride Classic, Fairfield-Barnett Space Coast Classic. **1990** Digital Seniors Classic, GTE Kaanapali Classic. **1991** GTE Suncoast Classic. **1992** Raley's Senior Gold Rush, Transamerica Senior Golf Championship. **1993** Doug Sanders Celebrity Classic, Bell Atlantic Classic, Quicksilver Classic. **1995** Hyatt Regency Maui Kaanapali Classic. **1996** Hyatt Regency Maui Kaanapali Classic.

OTHER SENIOR VICTORIES (12): 1986 Mazda Championship [with Amy Alcott]. **1987** Mauna Lani Invitational. **1988** Fuji Electric Grandslam, 1st National Bank Classic. **1989** Fuji Electric Grandslam, Senior British Open. **1990** Fuji Electric Grandslam, Kintetsu Home Senior, Daikyo Senior Invitational. **1991** Kintetsu Home Senior. **1993** Senior British Open. **1998** Office Depot Father-Son Challenge [with David].

2004 CHARLES SCHWAB CUP FINISH:
T78th - 37 points

GEORGIA-PACIFIC GRAND CHAMPIONS VICTORIES (23): 1996 Las Vegas Senior Classic, Nationwide Championship, Ford Senior Players Championship, Hyatt Regency Maui Kaanapali Classic, MasterCard Champions Championship. **1997** Royal Caribbean Classic, LG Championship, GTE Classic, Toshiba Senior Classic, Las Vegas Senior Classic, Bruno's Memorial Classic, Nationwide Championship, Ford Senior Players Championship. **1998** The Home Depot Invitational, Kroger Senior Classic, MasterCard Champions Championship. **1999** Bell Atlantic Classic. **2001** Enterprise Rent-A-Car Match Play Championship, The Instinet Classic, AT&T Canada Senior Open Championship. **2003** Bruno's Memorial Classic, SAS Championship. **2004** FedEx Kinko's Classic.

PGA TOUR VICTORIES (6): 1963 Houston Classic, British Open Championship. **1965** Tucson Open Invitational. **1967** Atlanta Classic. **1968** Canadian Open. **1974** Greater Greensboro Open.

OTHER VICTORIES (24): 1954 New Zealand Open. **1961** New Zealand PGA Championship, The Daks Golf Tournament [tie]. **1961** Bowmaker Tournament, Caltex Open. **1962** Caltex Open, Swiss Open. **1963** Watties Open. **1966** Watties Open, New Zealand Open. **1967** Caltex Open. **1968** Watties Open. **1969** Picadilly World Match Play. **1970** New Zealand Open. **1972** Dunlop Masters, John Player Classic. **1973** Scandinavian Enterprise Open, South African Open, New Zealand Open. **1974** Swiss Open. **1978** Air New Zealand Shell Open. **1979** New Zealand PGA Championship. **1980** New Zealand PGA Championship. **1983** Tallahassee Open.

PGA TOUR CAREER EARNINGS: $546,868

PGA TOUR PLAYOFF RECORD: 0-2

BEST 2004 CHAMPIONS TOUR FINISH:
T10—Greater Hickory Classic at Rock Barn.

2004 SEASON:
Played in just 11 official Champions Tour events, his fewest tournaments in a single season...Made a farewell appearance in the New Zealand Open in January at Heretaunga, venue of his first win in that event as an 18-year-old in 1954...Did not start his year on the Champions Tour until late April...Had a productive outing in his initial Champions Tour appearance at the Liberty Mutual Legends of Golf in Savannah. Teamed with Stewart Ginn to claim the Raphael Division title. Drained a 54-foot birdie putt on the final hole to snag the team's $110,000 first prize...Two weeks later was tied for the lead after 36 holes at the FedEx Kinko's Classic before shooting a final-round 76 to slip to T27. Won the Georgia-Pacific Grand Champions title at the Austin event, the 23rd of his career in the over-60 competition...Lost to Jay Sigel in a playoff for the Georgia-Pacific title at the Greater Hickory Classic at Rock Barn but went on to finish T10 in the overall event, his best effort on the Champions Tour since T5 at the 2002 Greater Baltimore Classic. At 68, became the oldest player to register a top-10 finish on the Champions Tour since then 69-year-old Joe Jimenez finished T10 at the 1995 GTE Northwest Classic...Bettered his age for the second year in a row in Boston when he posted a 6-under 66 in the second round of the Bank of America Championship and then matched his age with a final-round 68 at the SBC Championship in October...Also made five appearances on the European Seniors Tour during the summer. Best effort was a T12 performance at the Travis Perkins Senior Masters in England...Made his 18th consecutive appearance in the Senior British Open and finished 65th at Royal Portrush...Runner-up with son, David, at Office Depot Father/Son Challenge in December.

CHAMPIONS TOUR CAREER HIGHLIGHTS:
2003: Did not make his first appearance until the Liberty Mutual Legends of Golf after straining a tendon in his right elbow in the fall of 2002...Bettered his age when he fired a 7-under 65 at age 67 in the second round of the Bruno's Memorial Classic and shot 65 again in the final round of the FleetBoston Classic...Won the Bruno's Georgia-Pacific Grand Champions competition when he rolled in an 18-foot birdie putt on the fifth playoff hole to defeat Jim Colbert...Claimed the 22nd Georgia-Pacific Grand Champions event of his career at the SAS Championship. Defeated Mike Hill with a par on the first playoff hole after both had finished 36 holes tied at 4-under 140. 67 in the second round of the SAS event matched his age. Made the fifth hole-in-one of his career in the second round of the Georgia-Pacific Grand Champions Championship in Sonoma, CA. **2002:** T5 at the Greater Baltimore Classic, just two strokes shy of J.C. Snead. Would have shot his age on Saturday, but was assessed a two-stroke penalty during his round and shot a 4-under-par 71. The two strokes also left him two strokes shy of Snead's winning total of 13-under-par 203...Performance was his best in a Champions Tour event since placing sixth at the 1999 Cadillac NFL Golf Classic...Runner-up to George Archer in the Georgia-Pacific Grand Champions competition at the Bruno's Memorial Classic and also a runner-up to Snead at the Greater Baltimore Classic over-60 event. **2001:**

CHAMPIONS TOUR CAREER SUMMARY — PLAYOFF RECORD: 2-7

Year	Events Played	1st	2nd	3rd	Top 10	Top 25	Earnings	Rank
1986	21		3	3	17	21	$261,160	7
1987	27	3	4	6	21	25	389,437	3
1988	28	5	5	1	22	27	533,929	1
1989	27	5	3		22	25	725,887	1
1990	27	2	1	4	15	22	584,318	7
1991	28	1	3	2	18	24	673,910	6
1992	28	2			12	22	473,903	10
1993	29	3	4	2	21	26	1,046,823	2
1994	25		1	1	11	21	511,737	23
1995	26	1	2	1	10	21	659,923	15
1996	29	1	1		14	22	760,179	12
1997	27			2	7	18	623,467	21
1998	26		2		4	9	402,284	45
1999	24				4	8	354,752	48
2000	23				1	10	282,370	60
2001	23				1	8	280,497	58
2002	19				2	6	198,959	73
2003	16					2	111,284	83
2004	11				1	1	86,370	88
Total	464	23	29	22	203	318	8,961,190	
COMBINED ALL-TIME MONEY (3 TOURS):							**$9,508,058**	

CHAMPIONS TOUR TOP TOURNAMENT SUMMARY

Year	86	87	88	89	90	91	92	93	94	95	96	97	98
Senior PGA Championship		T3	T11	T24	T29	3	T7	T4	T10	T5	T15	T7	T29
U.S. Senior Open	T10	T14	2	T9	T15	T8	T49	T13	DQ	T11	7	T18	T33
Ford Senior Players	16	T10	T6	T4	T18	T2	7	T5	T32	T23	T6	T16	T19
JELD-WEN Tradition				T4	T13	T12	T24	T11	T15	T12	T19	T17	T31
Charles Schwab Cup Champ					T7	3	T7	T13	11	7	T6	26	

Year	99	00	01	02	03	04
Senior PGA Championship	T32	T44	T59	T18	CUT	T57
U.S. Senior Open		T26	CUT			
Ford Senior Players	T14	T64				
Senior British Open					T20	65
JELD-WEN Tradition	75	36			72	

Bob Charles (continued)

Finished second on the final Georgia-Pacific money list with $315,533...Bettered his age for the first time when at age 65, he shot an 8-under 64 on the second day of the stroke-play portion of the Enterprise Rent-A-Car Match Play Championship and tied for medalist honors. Won the Georgia-Pacific Grand Champions competition at Boone Valley, defeating Mike Hill by five strokes. Eventually lost to Ted Goin in the round of 16, with the match going 23 holes...Claimed a second Georgia-Pacific title at The Instinet Classic, holding off Mike Hill and Rocky Thompson by two strokes...Recorded his 20th career Georgia-Pacific Grand Champions title and third of the 2001 campaign at the AT&T Canada Senior Open at Mississaugua...Made 34th and final appearance in the British Open at Royal Lytham & St. Annes, but missed the cut. **2000:** Won his only over-60 event at the Bell Atlantic Classic, besting Terry Dill by five strokes. **1998:** Fell in a two-hole playoff with Jim Dent at The Home Depot Invitational and then was one of five players in a playoff at the rain-shortened Kroger Senior Classic won by Hugh Baiocchi...Enjoyed success in the Grand Champions competition, finishing as the leading money-winner in the 60-and-over competition with $254,260...Posted Grand Champions victories at The Home Depot Invitational and Kroger Senior Classic...Fired a closing-round 66 to win the Grand Champions Championship in Myrtle Beach. **1997:** Finished third behind Hale Irwin and Gil Morgan in the season-opening event in Hawaii, the MasterCard Championship...Also T3 at the Toshiba Senior Classic, one stroke out of a playoff...Also won $252,690 in MasterCard Champions money and led the over-60 competition with eight wins...Claimed four consecutive MasterCard titles at the start of the season, eight in a row dating to 1996. **1996:** Outdueled Hale Irwin to successfully defend the Hyatt Regency Maui Kaanapali Classic, his third win in Hawaii and last of 23 official titles in his illustrious Champions Tour career...Was an easy eight-stroke winner in the MasterCard Champions event the day before, and become the third of just four players to complete the ultimate "double dip"...Claimed the season-ending MasterCard Champions Championship...Earned a then-record $266,100 along the way, breaking Jim Ferree's MasterCard Champions mark of $255,550 set in 1993. **1995:** Won second Hyatt Regency Maui Kaanapali Classic with a 10-foot birdie putt on third extra hole to defeat Dave Stockton. **1993:** Earned his third Byron Nelson Trophy for lowest scoring average (69.59) and, at the time, became quickest to reach $1 million in a single season (26 events)...Win at Quicksilver Classic produced largest check of his career: $157,500...Second-place finish to Dave Stockton on the money list tied Miller Barber's all-time record, at the time, of eight consecutive years among the top 10 in official earnings. **1992:** Won back-to-back events at Raley's Senior Gold Rush and Transamerica Senior Golf Classic, the first to complete the northern California double. **1991:** Won the GTE Suncoast Classic for the second time in three years and became the first multiple champion in the event. **1990:** Won twice, including defense of his Digital Seniors Classic title, and also surpassed Miller Barber for the top spot on the Champions Tour career money list during the season...Was only player to break par the final day at GTE Kaanapali Classic and recorded a four-stroke win in Hawaii. **1989:** Claimed five titles and was leading money-winner for second consecutive year with record $725,887...Won third straight Sunwest Bank/Charley Pride Classic, at the time, becoming only the second player to claim the same tournament for three consecutive years...Established a Champions Tour record for lowest 54-hole numerical score at the NYNEX/Golf Digest Commemorative (193, 17-under). **1988:** Five wins helped make him the leading money-winner...Posted back-to-back victories at NYNEX/Golf Digest Commemorative and Sunwest Bank/Charley Pride Classic...Lost to Gary Player in 18-hole playoff at U.S. Senior Open at Medinah CC. **1987:** Won three times and was third on money list.

OTHER CAREER HIGHLIGHTS:

One of the most successful lefthanded golfers of all-time, with 75 worldwide victories on five continents: North America, Australia, Europe, Africa and Asia...Won at least one event in nine of the 19 years on the Champions Tour...Owns 23 Champions Tour titles, fourth all-time behind Hale Irwin (40), Lee Trevino (29) and Miller Barber (24)...Was the first lefthander to win on the PGA TOUR when he captured the 1963 Houston Open by one stroke over Fred Hawkins...Last of six PGA TOUR victories came at the 1974 Greater Greensboro Open, by one stroke over Raymond Floyd and Lee Trevino...Biggest thrill in golf came when he defeated Phil Rodgers in a 36-hole playoff for the 1963 British Open Championship at Royal Lytham & St. Annes. Held the record for 40 years as the only left-hander ever to have won one of golf's four major championships until Canadian Mike Weir joined that exclusive club by winning the 2003 Masters...Most productive year on the PGA TOUR was 1967, when he pocketed $72,468 for 11th place on the money list...Won the 1954 New Zealand Open at age 18, the youngest champion of that event...Played on the 1962, 1963, 1964, 1965, 1966, 1967, 1968, 1971 and 1972 New Zealand World Cup teams and was also a member of New Zealand's team in the Alfred Dunhill Cup in 1985 and 1986...Has had five career holes-in-one in competition, including three on the Champions Tour.

PERSONAL:

Does everything righthanded except games requiring two hands...Designed two 18-hole resort courses (Millbrook) and a nine-hole course (Matarangi) in New Zealand...Received the prestigious Order of the British Empire from the Queen of England in 1972 and was honored as a Commander of the British Empire in 1992...Became Knight Companion of the New Zealand Order of Merit in 1999...Was the fifth recipient of the European Seniors Tour's Lladro Lifetime Achievement Award in 2002...Worked in the banking industry for six years (1954-60) before embarking on a golf career...Uses alternative medicine and takes deer velvet as a supplement to his diet...Son, David, is a tournament director for the PGA of America...Biggest thrill outside of golf was marrying his wife, Verity...Enjoys classical music, opera and stage productions...Is an avid tennis follower...Favorite athlete is Ben Hogan...Lists his favorite golf course as St. Andrews and favorite movie is "Out of Africa"...Favorite entertainer is Rowan Atkinson and favorite food is venison.

PLAYER STATISTICS

2004 CHAMPIONS TOUR STATISTICS:

Scoring Average	73.37	(N/A)
Driving Distance	255.2	(N/A)
Driving Accuracy Percentage	73.3%	(N/A)
Total Driving	1,998	(N/A)
Greens in Regulation Pct.	60.0%	(N/A)
Putting Average	1.812	(N/A)
Sand Save Percentage	51.4%	(N/A)
Birdie Average	2.86	(N/A)
All-Around Ranking	1,569	(N/A)

MISCELLANEOUS CHAMPIONS TOUR STATISTICS

2004 Low Round: 66–2004 Bank of America Championship/2
Career Low Round: 63–6 times, most recent 1992 Transamerica Senior Golf Championship/3
Career Largest Paycheck: $157,500–1993 Quicksilver Classic/1

MISCELLANEOUS PGA TOUR STATISTICS

Career Low Round: 63–1970 Danny Thomas Memphis Classic/4
Career Largest Paycheck: $44,066–1974 Greater Greensboro Open/1

SECTION 2 PLAYER BIOGRAPHIES

Jim Colbert

EXEMPT STATUS: Top 30 on All-Time Money List
FULL NAME: James Joseph Colbert
HEIGHT: 5-9
WEIGHT: 175
BIRTHDATE: March 9, 1941
BIRTHPLACE: Elizabeth, NJ
RESIDENCE: Las Vegas, NV
FAMILY: Wife, Marcia; Debbie (9/25/59); Christy (11/24/61); Kelly (7/19/65); six grandchildren
EDUCATION: Kansas State University (1964, Political Science)
TURNED PROFESSIONAL: 1965
JOINED PGA TOUR: 1966

JOINED CHAMPIONS TOUR: 1991

CHAMPIONS TOUR VICTORIES (20): 1991 Southwestern Bell Classic, Vantage Championship, First Development Kaanapali Classic. **1992** GTE Suncoast Classic, Vantage Championship. **1993** Royal Caribbean Classic, Ford Senior Players Championship. **1994** Kroger Senior Classic, Southwestern Bell Classic. **1995** Senior Tournament of Champions, Las Vegas Senior Classic, Bell Atlantic Classic, Energizer SENIOR TOUR Championship. **1996** Toshiba Senior Classic, Las Vegas Senior Classic, Nationwide Championship, Vantage Championship, Raley's Gold Rush Classic. **1998** The Transamerica. **2001** SBC Senior Classic.

OTHER SENIOR VICTORIES (5): 1995 Diners Club Matches [with Bob Murphy]. **1996** Diners Club Matches [with Bob Murphy]. **1998** Lexus Challenge [with Kevin Costner]. **2000** Liberty Mutual Legends of Golf [with Andy North]. **2001** Liberty Mutual Legends of Golf [with Andy North].

2004 CHARLES SCHWAB CUP FINISH:
46th - 176 points

GEORGIA-PACIFIC GRAND CHAMPIONS VICTORIES (8): 2001 Bruno's Memorial Classic, The Home Depot Invitational, Lightpath Long Island Classic, Kroger Senior Classic, Gold Rush Classic. **2002** Kroger Senior Classic, SAS Championship. **2004** SBC Classic.

PGA TOUR VICTORIES (8): 1969 Monsanto Open Invitational. **1972** Greater Milwaukee Open. **1973** Greater Jacksonville Open. **1974** American Golf Classic. **1975** Walt Disney World National Team Championship [with Dean Refram]. **1980** Joe Garagiola-Tucson Open. **1983** Colonial National Invitation, Texas Open.

OTHER VICTORIES (1): 1987 Jerry Ford Invitational.

PGA TOUR CAREER EARNINGS: $1,553,136

PGA TOUR PLAYOFF RECORD: 2-0

BEST 2004 CHAMPIONS TOUR FINISHES:
T18—SBC Classic; T23—MasterCard Classic.

2004 SEASON:

Best performances came in back-to-back starts in March. Was T23 at the MasterCard Classic and then T18 the week after at the SBC Classic...Was one stroke off the lead after the first round of the MasterCard event in Mexico but dropped back after a second-round 78...T18 the next week at Valencia CC, his top overall outing of the campaign. Birdied four of the last eight holes on Saturday to forge a tie with Jay Sigel in the Georgia-Pacific Grand Champions competition and then defeated Sigel with a par on the first playoff hole for his eighth career victory in the over-60 competition...Went on to finish 10th on the final Georgia-Pacific Grand Champions earnings list, with $117,667.

CHAMPIONS TOUR CAREER HIGHLIGHTS:

2003: T3 at the Bruno's Memorial Classic, his best performance in almost two years...Fired an 8-under 62 in the second round of the Senior British Open Championship, equalling the competitive course record at Turnberry. Round included 24 putts and made him the youngest player ever to match his age in a Champions Tour major. Score also tied Doug Tewell's final-round 62 at the 2001 Countrywide Tradition as the lowest round ever posted in a Champions Tour major...Followed Hugh Baiocchi's ace with a hole-in-one of his own in the final round of the Royal Caribbean Golf Classic. Aced the 178-yard 12th hole at Crandon Park GC with a 6-iron shot, the seventh ace in tournament history. **2002:** Posted back-to-back Georgia-Pacific Grand Champions titles when he defeated Isao Aoki in one-hole playoffs at the Kroger Senior Classic and the SAS Championship. **2001:** Oldest winner on the Champions Tour, finishing among the top 31 money-winners for an 11th straight year, the only player over 60 among that select group...Ended more than a two-year victory drought two days after turning 60 when he held off Jose Maria Canizares by one stroke for the SBC Senior Classic title, his 20th career victory on the Champions Tour. Holed an eight-foot birdie putt at the 15th hole to break out of a three-way logjam with Canizares and Gary McCord. Victory also made him the 10th player in Champions Tour history to win after turning 60...Teamed with Andy North to successfully defend their Liberty Mutual Legends of Golf title, the fifth time in tournament history a team had gone back to back. Better-ball score of 20-under 124 in the rain-shortened event clipped Bruce Fleisher and David Graham by three strokes...Won five Georgia-Pacific Grand Champions events, including the first two over-60 competitions he was eligible for (Bruno's Memorial Classic/The Home Depot Invitational). **2000:** Teamed with Andy North for victory in the Liberty Mutual Legends of Golf. Duo fired a better-ball team score of 25-under 191 and edged David Graham and Bruce Fleisher by one stroke...T2 at the Audi Senior Classic, five strokes back of Hubert Green after sharing the 36-hole lead with Jose Maria Canizares...Tied his Champions Tour career-low round of 61 on the first day of the TD Waterhouse Championship. Course record 11-under-par score at Tiffany Greens included eight straight birdies (holes 10-17) and equaled the Champions Tour's all-time best birdie streak (Chi Chi Rodriguez—1987 Silver Pages Classic). Led by two strokes after 36 holes, but finished third after a final-round 71...Opened Colbert Hills GC at Kansas State University in Manhattan on May 1. **1999:** Closed with 67 at Hualalai to T2 at the MasterCard Championship, three strokes back of John Jacobs. **1998:** Notched his 19th career victory on the Champions Tour by claiming The Transamerica. Birdied four of his last eight holes for a one-stroke win over David Lundstrom in Napa...Victory capped a successful comeback from prostate cancer surgery a year earlier...Named the Champions Tour's Comeback Player of the Year and is the only player to have garnered all three of the Champions Tour's major post-season awards. **1997:** Despite missing four months of the season while recuperating from prostate cancer surgery on June 23, still finished among the top-31 money-winners...Did not win for the first time in six years, but still had five top-five finishes, including a pair of seconds at the du Maurier Champions and the American Express Invitational...Recorded his third hole-in-one on the Champions Tour and fifth overall at the Bruno's Memorial Classic. **1996:** Won second Arnold Palmer Award as the leading money-winner with then-record $1,627,890...Earned title on last day of season when he birdied the final hole at the Energizer SENIOR TOUR Championship to help him to a T3 and a check for $121,000, good enough to beat Hale Irwin for the money

CHAMPIONS TOUR CAREER SUMMARY — PLAYOFF RECORD: 3-5

Year	Events Played	1st	2nd	3rd	Top 10	Top 25	Earnings	Rank
1991	22	3	5		16	22	880,749	3
1992	28	2	3	4	15	21	825,768	3
1993	31	2	3	1	10	24	779,889	7
1994	33	2	5	2	15	25	1,012,115	5
1995	34	4	3	2	17	27	1,444,386	1
1996	32	5	5	1	13	24	1,627,890	1
1997	19		2	1	6	12	556,000	27
1998	32	1	2	1	13	23	1,122,413	6
1999	30		1		6	18	638,621	28
2000	33		1	1	8	17	736,013	24
2001	29	1	1	1	8	15	930,096	19
2002	31					6	286,434	60
2003	29			1	2	7	344,011	45
2004	23					2	126,355	79
Total	406	20	31	15	129	243	11,310,740	
COMBINED ALL-TIME MONEY (3 TOURS):							**$12,863,876**	

CHAMPIONS TOUR TOP TOURNAMENT SUMMARY

Year	91	92	93	94	95	96	97	98	99	00	01	02	03
Senior PGA Championship	T8	T30	T45	2	9	T41	T32	T44	31	T54	T36	T27	62
U.S. Senior Open	T19	2	12	T20	53	T12		T16	T18	T10	T4	T31	CUT
Ford Senior Players	T8	T12	1	T14	T3	T16		T4	T14	T30	T38	T49	T68
Senior British Open													T10
JELD-WEN Tradition	T2	T33	T14	3	4	T31	T59	T11	WD	WD	T29	T31	T20
Charles Schwab Cup Champ	2	T7	T20	T26	1	T3	21	T11	T29	T19	25		

Year	04
Senior PGA Championship	CUT
Ford Senior Players	T71
JELD-WEN Tradition	T45

Jim Colbert (Continued)

crown by $12,121...Won $607,495 in his last seven starts, including two wins, a second, a T2 and a T3...Voted by his peers as Champions Tour Player of the Year for second year in succession...Had personal-best five wins...Highlights were defense of his title at the Las Vegas Senior Classic and a third Vantage Championship...Also named Player of the Month for October...Claimed Cadillac with hole-in-one at The Transamerica...Golf Writers Association Player of the Year. **1995:** Four victories included wire-to-wire triumph at the season-ending Energizer SENIOR TOUR Championship...Win helped him earn largest check of his career, $262,000, and also helped him to his first money title...Started the year with playoff triumph over Jim Albus in Puerto Rico at the Senior Tournament of Champions...Voted by his peers as the Player of the Year and also was named Player of the Year by the Golf Writers Association of America. **1994:** One of a then-record six Champions Tour players to win at least $1 million...July's Player of the Month after 30-day stretch that saw him post two wins and nine straight sub-70 rounds...Shot the then-lowest 36-hole number in Champions Tour history (126) at the GTE West Classic in Ojai, CA, but lost in a playoff to Jay Sigel. **1993:** Won year's first full-field event at the Royal Caribbean Classic, thanks in part to two of the best back-to-back rounds of the year—65-64 in the first two days of the competition...Held off Raymond Floyd for win at Ford Senior Players Championship, his only senior major. **1992:** Became first player to capture second consecutive Vantage Championship...Also defeated George Archer in playoff for win at GTE Classic. **1991:** Garnered Rookie of the Year honors after winning $880,749 and finishing third on money list...Had three wins and was second five times...First senior victory came in his hometown of Kansas City at Southwestern Bell Classic, a three-stroke triumph over Al Geiberger and Larry Laoretti...Matched Lee Elder's record at the time for all-time lowest 18-hole score when he fired second round 9-under 61 at First Development Kaanapali Classic and then claimed title by two strokes the next day.

OTHER CAREER HIGHLIGHTS:

Won eight PGA TOUR events in a career that ran from 1966-87...Was among the top-60 on the TOUR's official money list from 1969-1976...Best season on TOUR was 1983 when, at age 42, he earned $223,810 and had a pair of victories, including a playoff win over Fuzzy Zoeller at the Colonial National Invitation event.

PERSONAL:

Ran his own golf course management company, Jim Colbert Golf, prior to joining the Champions Tour...Spent several years as a color analyst for ESPN golf telecasts...Made his home in Kansas City from 1952-74 and earned a football scholarship to Kansas State...Had a limited career on the gridiron and turned to golf instead...A close friend of Kansas State football coach Bill Snyder and a big supporter of the school's sports program...Played a large role in helping the school build its new golf course (Colbert Hills GC) that is the home of the men's and women's teams, the First Tee National

PLAYER STATISTICS

2004 CHAMPIONS TOUR STATISTICS:

Scoring Average	73.51	(71)
Driving Distance	257.7	(73)
Driving Accuracy Percentage	76.7%	(11)
Total Driving	84	(46)
Greens in Regulation Pct.	61.3%	(70)
Putting Average	1.809	(45)
Sand Save Percentage	39.6%	(67)
Eagles (Holes per)	1,242.0	(76)
Birdie Average	3.04	(53)
All-Around Ranking	466	(69)

MISCELLANEOUS CHAMPIONS TOUR STATISTICS

2004 Low Round: 67–2004 Outback Steakhouse Pro-Am/1
Career Low Round: 61–2 times, most recent 2000 TD Waterhouse Championship/1
Career Largest Paycheck: $262,000–1995 Energizer SENIOR TOUR Championship/1

MISCELLANEOUS PGA TOUR STATISTICS

Career Low Round: 62–1983 Texas Open/2
Career Largest Paycheck: $72,000–1983 Colonial National Invitation/1

25 MEMORABLE MOMENTS

Palmer Claims Victory, His Last Official Win

1985 Crestar Classic

A last-minute decision to play in the Crestar Classic turned out to be a wise one for Arnold Palmer. The King's choice, made just hours before the entry deadline, provided a big spectator boost to the event near Richmond, VA. After opening with a 7-under-par 65 Friday, Palmer followed with rounds of 68 and 70 to cruise to a wire-to-wire, four-stroke win over the trio of Lee Elder, Jim Ferree and Larry Mowry. In winning his 10th title since turning 50, Palmer's winner's check for $48,750 was, astonishingly, his largest on the Champions Tour.

CHAMPIONS TOUR 25

Charles Coody (COO-dee)

EXEMPT STATUS: Net-70 on All-Time Money List
FULL NAME: Billy Charles Coody
HEIGHT: 6-2
WEIGHT: 225
BIRTHDATE: July 13, 1937
BIRTHPLACE: Stamford, TX
RESIDENCE: Abilene, TX

FAMILY: Wife, Lynette; Caryn (9/7/62), Kyle (8/21/64), Kristyn (5/4/70); seven grandchildren
CLUB AFFILIATION: Diamondback GC (Abilene, TX)
EDUCATION: Texas Christian University (1960, Business)
SPECIAL INTERESTS: Family activities, operating Diamondback GC
TURNED PROFESSIONAL: 1963
JOINED PGA TOUR: 1963

JOINED CHAMPIONS TOUR: 1987

CHAMPIONS TOUR VICTORIES (5): 1989 General Tire Las Vegas Classic. **1990** Vantage Championship. **1991** NYNEX Commemorative, Transamerica Senior Golf Championship. **1996** du Maurier Champions.

OTHER SENIOR VICTORIES (3): 1990 Liberty Mutual Legends of Golf [with Dale Douglass]. **1994** Liberty Mutual Legends of Golf [with Dale Douglass]. **1998** Liberty Mutual Legends of Golf [with Dale Douglass].

GEORGIA-PACIFIC GRAND CHAMPIONS VICTORIES (6): 1997 Pittsburgh Senior Classic, MasterCard Champions Championship. **1998** Utah Showdown, The Transamerica. **2002** BellSouth Senior Classic at Opryland, Napa Valley Championship.

PGA TOUR VICTORIES (3): 1964 Dallas Open Invitational. **1969** Cleveland Open Invitational. **1971** Masters Tournament.

OTHER VICTORIES (3): 1971 World Series of Golf. **1973** John Player Classic, W.B. & H.O. Wills Masters.

PGA TOUR CAREER EARNINGS: $1,187,762

BEST 2004 CHAMPIONS TOUR FINISH: T19—Liberty Mutual Legends of Golf.

2004 SEASON: Registered his first top-25 effort since 2002 when he T19 at the Liberty Mutual Legends of Golf in Savannah...Finished 19th on the final Georgia-Pacific Grand Champions money list, with $50,808...Made his 38th and final appearance in competition at The Masters, where he missed the cut.

CHAMPIONS TOUR CAREER HIGHLIGHTS:
2002: Two-time winner in the Georgia-Pacific Grand Champions competition. First title came when he defeated Dave Stockton in a one-hole playoff at the BellSouth Senior Classic at Opryland in Nashville. Second victory came when he easily won the over-60 event at the Napa Valley Championship by three strokes. **2001:** Returned to the Champions Tour for the first time since the 2000 SBC Senior Open after undergoing season-ending left knee surgery. Made his first start in seven months at the Verizon Classic...T25 at the BellSouth Senior Classic at Opryland. **1998:** Teamed with Dale Douglass to defeat Hugh Baiocchi and David Graham in a playoff for their third Liberty Mutual Legends of Golf title...Posted victories in the MasterCard Champions competition at the Utah Showdown and The Transamerica. **1997:** Joined the ranks of the MasterCard Champions midway through the season...Won his first MasterCard Champions event at the Pittsburgh Senior Classic...Saved best performance of the year for last, when he posted rounds of 70-68-72 and won the MasterCard Champions Championship by five strokes. **1996:** Ended a four-and-one-half-year victory drought by winning the inaugural du Maurier Champions in Canada. Rallied from four strokes down with a final-round 65 to defeat Larry Mowry by one stroke at Hamilton G&CC. **1994:** Teamed with Dale Douglass for a second unofficial Liberty Mutual Legends of Golf title. **1992:** Hampered by physical problems for the majority of the year that caused him to lose strength in his right arm and hand without warning...Best finish a T2 at Ko Olina Senior Invitational. **1991:** Won twice in a season for the only time in his career, with official victories at the NYNEX Commemorative and Transamerica Senior Golf Championship...At The Commemorative at Sleepy Hollow CC, matched Bob Charles' all-time numerical record at the time for lowest 54-hole score (193). **1990:** He and Dale Douglass captured their first Legends title in wire-to-wire fashion with a tournament-record 39-under-par total...Collected the largest check of his career, $202,500, for his three-stroke victory over Charles and Al Geiberger at the Vantage Championship. **1989:** Won his first Champions Tour title at the General Tire Las Vegas Classic in a playoff over Bob Charles and Chi Chi Rodriguez. **1987:** Made debut at MONY Syracuse Senior Classic.

OTHER CAREER HIGHLIGHTS:
Won three times on the PGA TOUR, including the 1971 Masters, where he birdied two of the last four holes to edge Jack Nicklaus and Johnny Miller...Among the top 60 on the PGA TOUR money list for 13 consecutive seasons...Best year on the PGA TOUR came in 1971, when he won $94,947 for 16th on the money list...Qualified for the 1960 and 1961 U.S. Open as an amateur and advanced to the semifinals of the 1962 U.S. Amateur...1971 U.S. Ryder Cup Team member...Has made 19 holes-in-one in his career.

PERSONAL:
A member of the Texas Golf Hall of Fame...Inducted into the Texas Sports Hall of Fame during the 2000 season...Named to the Class AA all-state basketball team in Texas in 1955...Had polio at age 13 and turned to golf for exercise after he was not allowed to play contact sports...Received his first set of golf clubs as a gift from his father, Richard, shortly thereafter...Has marked his ball since 1969 with an English half-penny coin, a gift from his daughter Caryn...Owner of Diamondback GC in Abilene and has been involved in a charity event at the club that has raised over $250,000 for several worthwhile organizations...Lists Pinehurst No. 2 as his favorite golf course...Biggest thrill in golf was winning the 1971 Masters, while his biggest thrills outside of golf were marrying his wife, Lynette, and the birth of their three children...Favorite movie is "Chariots of Fire" and his most-admired athlete is Jerry West.

PLAYER STATISTICS

2004 CHAMPIONS TOUR STATISTICS:

Scoring Average	74.53	(80)
Driving Distance	260.4	(71)
Driving Accuracy Percentage	69.6%	(46)
Total Driving	117	(77)
Greens in Regulation Pct.	59.1%	(75)
Putting Average	1.883	(80)
Sand Save Percentage	38.3%	(70)
Eagles (Holes per)	261.0	(27)
Birdie Average	2.14	(80)
All-Around Ranking	529	(78)

MISCELLANEOUS CHAMPIONS TOUR STATISTICS
2004 Low Round: 70–4 times, most recent 2004 Kroger Classic/1
Career Low Round: 62–1991 NYNEX Commemorative/2
Career Largest Paycheck: $202,500–1990 Vantage Championship/1

MISCELLANEOUS PGA TOUR STATISTICS
2004 Low Round: 79–Masters Tournament/2
Career Low Round: 62–1971 Cleveland Open Invitational/3
Career Largest Paycheck: $26,400–1980 Jackie Gleason–Inverrary Classic/T2

CHAMPIONS TOUR CAREER SUMMARY — PLAYOFF RECORD: 1-0

Year	Events Played	1st	2nd	3rd	Top 10	Top 25	Earnings	Rank
1987	15			3	5	8	$93,064	31
1988	31		1		7	21	161,286	20
1989	30	1	2	2	14	23	403,880	10
1990	32	1	3	6	14	29	762,901	3
1991	31	2	2		13	24	543,326	8
1992	29		1	1	6	17	286,294	28
1993	29				4	13	221,982	37
1994	30					16	219,295	39
1995	30				1	5	163,153	60
1996	29	1			3	6	328,054	42
1997	30					9	218,564	61
1998	26					1	141,258	71
1999	26					2	125,393	79
2000	9						24,959	110
2001	17					1	60,490	98
2002	24					1	117,487	88
2003	22						65,497	97
2004	19					1	62,608	95
Total	459	5	9	12	67	177	3,999,491	
COMBINED ALL-TIME MONEY (3 TOURS):							**$5,187,253**	

CHAMPIONS TOUR TOP TOURNAMENT SUMMARY

Year	88	89	90	91	92	93	94	95	96	97	98	99	00
Senior PGA Championship	T17	DQ	T38			T56	T19		T61	T52			
U.S. Senior Open	18	T5	T6	T6	T16	T35	T36		T22	T63	T26	T32	
Ford Senior Players	T10	2	T3	T2	T18	T22	T42	T58	T49	T60	T50	T59	
JELD-WEN Tradition		T4	T3	T6		T9	T12	T36	T31	T21	62	T50	60
Charles Schwab Cup Champ			T7	T26	T19								

Year	01	02	03	04
Senior PGA Championship		T45	CUT	
Senior British Open			T54	
JELD-WEN Tradition			T62	T78

Ben Crenshaw

WORLD GOLF HALL OF FAME MEMBER (Inducted 2002)
EXEMPT STATUS: Top 30 on All-Time Money List
FULL NAME: Ben Daniel Crenshaw
HEIGHT: 5-9
WEIGHT: 157
BIRTHDATE: January 11, 1952
BIRTHPLACE: Austin, TX
RESIDENCE: Austin, TX
FAMILY: Wife, Julie; Katherine Vail (10/6/87), Claire Susan (4/23/92), Anna Riley (2/12/98)
CLUB AFFILIATION: Austin GC (Austin, TX)
EDUCATION: University of Texas
SPECIAL INTERESTS: Fishing, bird watching, collecting golf artifacts, golf course architecture, country music
TURNED PROFESSIONAL: 1973
JOINED PGA TOUR: 1973

JOINED CHAMPIONS TOUR: 2002

BEST CHAMPIONS TOUR CAREER FINISH: T4—2003 3M Championship.

2004 CHARLES SCHWAB CUP FINISH: 52nd - 121 points

PGA TOUR VICTORIES (19): 1973 San Antonio Texas Open. **1976** Bing Crosby National Pro-Am, Hawaiian Open, Ohio Kings Island Open. **1977** Colonial National Invitation. **1979** Phoenix Open, Walt Disney World National Team Championship [with George Burns]. **1980** Anheuser-Busch Golf Classic. **1983** Byron Nelson Golf Classic. **1984** Masters Tournament. **1986** Buick Open, Vantage Championship. **1987** USF&G Classic. **1988** Doral-Ryder Open. **1990** Southwestern Bell Colonial. **1992** Centel Western Open. **1993** Nestle Invitational. **1994** Freeport-McMoRan Classic. **1995** Masters Tournament.

OTHER VICTORIES (5): 1972 NCAA Championship [indiv, tie]. **1976** Irish Open. **1981** Mexican Open. **1985** Shootout at Jeremy Ranch [with Miller Barber]. **1988** World Cup [indiv], World Cup [with Mark McCumber].

PGA TOUR CAREER EARNINGS: $7,091,166

PGA TOUR PLAYOFF RECORD: 0-8

BEST 2004 CHAMPIONS TOUR FINISHES: T20—Bruno's Memorial Classic; T23—Toshiba Senior Classic.

2004 SEASON:

Finished among the top 25 twice during a three-tournament span early in the season...T20 at the Bruno's Memorial Classic in May when he posted rounds of 69-70 on the weekend near Birmingham...T23 in late March at the Toshiba Senior Classic, thanks to rounds of 68-69 on the weekend at Newport Beach CC, his best back-to-back rounds of the season...Played in his 33rd consecutive Masters but missed the cut...Topped the Champions Tour in Putts Per Round (28.15).

CHAMPIONS TOUR CAREER HIGHLIGHTS:

2003: Best career performance on the Champions Tour came when he finished T4 at the 3M Championship near Minneapolis in August. Held the lead late in the final round, but had a double-bogey and bogey on two of the final five holes to slip back...Backed up his Minnesota performance two weeks later by placing T10 at the Allianz Championship in Iowa. Finish at Glen Oaks CC gave him back-to-back top 10s for the first time since 1995 campaign on the PGA TOUR (T5-Mercedes Championship/3-Phoenix Open)...Named as a Player Ambassador for the World Golf Hall of Fame midway through the season...Missed the cut at The Masters. **2002:** Champions Tour debut came at The ACE Group Classic in Naples, a T43 with a 1-under 215 total at The Club at TwinEagles...Debut was delayed one week by illness...T8 in early September at the Kroger Senior Classic near Cincinnati. Second-round 7-under-par 65 was his low round of the year...Went 281 holes without a three-putt at one point during the year and had only 15 three-putts in 61 rounds...Voted into the World Golf Hall of Fame via the PGA TOUR Ballot, and was inducted on Nov. 1.

OTHER CAREER HIGHLIGHTS:

Was the captain of the 1999 U.S. Ryder Cup team, which staged greatest comeback in event's history—winning 8 1/2 points in singles matches on final day to come from four points back for victory. His team was the first U.S. squad to win Ryder Cup since 1993...Played the PGA TOUR on a full-time basis from 1974-2001...Underwent foot surgery in 1997...Won his second Masters title in 1995. Earlier in week had served as pallbearer at funeral of long-time friend and teacher Harvey Penick. Closed with a 68 to defeat Davis Love III by one stroke...Produced a victory each year from 1992 through 1995. From July 1992 until April 1994, his only three top-10 finishes were victories. Received the Bob Jones Award from USGA in 1991 and was honored with the Old Tom Morris Award in 1997...Earned the second of two MasterCard Colonial titles in 1990, his fifth PGA TOUR win in his native state of Texas...Won William Richardson Award in 1989, given by Golf Writers Association of America...Earned his first Masters victory in 1984. Two strokes off lead entering final round, shot closing 68 to defeat Tom Watson by two strokes...Prevailed at the 1983 Byron Nelson Classic...Claimed the first of his two MasterCard Colonial titles in 1977...Won three events in 1976 (and finished second three times) on way to second-place finish on money list behind Jack Nicklaus. Despite opening 75, won Bing Crosby National Pro-Am by two over Mike Morley. The following week, closed with rounds of 65-66 to win Hawaiian Open by four over Larry Nelson and Hale Irwin. Third victory came at Ohio Kings Island Open. Had 14 top-10 finishes that year, a total he matched in 1987, when he placed third on the money list...Was the medalist in the 1973 PGA TOUR Qualifying Tournament by then-record 12-stroke margin...In his first start as a PGA TOUR member, defeated Orville Moody by two strokes in the San Antonio-Texas Open...Winner of three straight NCAA Championships (1971-73), sharing the 1972 title with University of Texas teammate Tom Kite...Winner of Fred Haskins Award as nation's outstanding collegiate golfer each of those years...Was a member of the United States Ryder Cup teams in 1981, 1983, 1987, 1995 and served as the captain of the 1999 American squad...Played on two U.S. World Cup teams (1985, 1988), was the captain of the American team in the 1988 Kirin Cup and played on the U.S. Dunhill Cup team in 1995...Has had five career holes-in-one in competitive rounds.

PERSONAL:

Noted golf historian...Also renowned as a golf course designer, having formed a partnership with Bill Coore in 1986. Duo created noted courses like Sand Hills Golf Club in Nebraska and The Plantation Course at Kapalua, site of the PGA TOUR's Mercedes Championships... Introduced to golf by his father and won his first tournament as a fourth-grader...Fought winning battle against Graves Disease (disease of the thyroid)in mid-1980s...1996 PGA National Golf Day Honorary Chairperson...His book, *A Feel for the Game*, reached No. 25 on the *New York Times* best-seller list in 2001...Appointed to President's Commission on White House Fellowships by President George W. Bush...Lists Bobby Jones as his hero and Pine Valley GC as his favorite course.

PLAYER STATISTICS

2004 CHAMPIONS TOUR STATISTICS:

Scoring Average	72.72	(64)
Driving Distance	263.2	(67)
Driving Accuracy Percentage	63.4%	(68)
Total Driving	135	(78)
Greens in Regulation Pct.	56.7%	(77)
Putting Average	1.772	(16)
Sand Save Percentage	50.0%	(20)
Eagles (Holes per)	324.0	(38)
Birdie Average	2.83	(62)
All-Around Ranking	412	(61)

MISCELLANEOUS CHAMPIONS TOUR STATISTICS
2004 Low Round: 68–2004 Toshiba Senior Classic/2
Career Low Round: 65–2002 Kroger Senior Classic/2
Career Largest Paycheck: $85,750–2003 3M Championship/T4

MISCELLANEOUS PGA TOUR STATISTICS
2004 Low Round: 74–Masters Tournament/1
Career Low Round: 61–1979 Phoenix Open/2
Career Largest Paycheck: $396,000–1995 Masters Tournament/1

CHAMPIONS TOUR CAREER SUMMARY — PLAYOFF RECORD: 0-0

Year	Events Played	1st	2nd	3rd	Top 10	Top 25	Earnings	Rank
2002	20				1	4	$204,528	71
2003	19				2	3	231,512	58
2004	18					2	113,343	83
Total	57				3	9	549,382	
COMBINED ALL-TIME MONEY (3 TOURS):							**$7,640,548**	

CHAMPIONS TOUR TOP TOURNAMENT SUMMARY

Year	02	03	04
Senior PGA Championship	T27	CUT	WD
U.S. Senior Open	CUT	CUT	CUT
Ford Senior Players	T53	T61	T56
Senior British Open			CUT
JELD-WEN Tradition	T64	T33	T55

Rodger Davis

EXEMPT STATUS: Special Medical Extension/45th on 2004 Champions Tour Money List
FULL NAME: Rodger Miles Davis
HEIGHT: 5-10
WEIGHT: 185
BIRTHDATE: May 18, 1951
BIRTHPLACE: Sydney, Australia
RESIDENCE: Queensland, Australia; Palm Beach, FL
FAMILY: Wife, Pamela; Nicole (1971), Kim (1975)
SPECIAL INTERESTS: Cards, fishing, theater
TURNED PROFESSIONAL: 1974

JOINED CHAMPIONS TOUR: 2001

CHAMPIONS TOUR VICTORIES (1): 2003 Toshiba Senior Classic.

2004 CHARLES SCHWAB CUP FINISH: 43rd - 282 points

BEST PGA TOUR CAREER FINISH: T5—1986 NEC World Series of Golf.

OTHER VICTORIES (29): 1977 McCallum's South Coast Open, Rosebud Invitational, Nedlands Masters. **1978** South Australian Open, Nedlands Masters, West Australia Open, Mandurah Open. **1979** Victoria Open. **1981** State Express Classic. **1985** Victoria PGA Championship. **1986** Whyte & Mackay PGA European Championship, National Panasonic Australian Open, Air New Zealand Open, New Zealand Open, Dunhill Cup [with Greg Norman and David Graham]. **1988** Bicentennial Classic, Wang Pro-Celebrity. **1989** Ford New South Wales Open. **1990** Palm Meadows Cup, Peugeot Spanish Open, Wang Pro-Celebrity, Four-Tours World Championship. **1991** Volvo Masters, SxL Sanctuary Cove Classic, AMP New Zealand Open. **1992** SxL Sanctuary Cove Classic, Coolum Classic. **1993** Cannes Open. **1996** Mauritius Open.

PGA TOUR CAREER EARNINGS: $113,579

BEST 2004 CHAMPIONS TOUR FINISHES: 2—Blue Angels Classic; 3—Constellation Energy Classic; T10—Kroger Classic.

2004 SEASON:

Battled back problems through much of the year and is expected to play a portion of 2005 under a Special Medical Extension...Did not play at The ACE Group Classic due to lower-back problems and then was forced to withdraw from the SBC Classic in his next start after 11 holes when he suffered an allergic reaction...Returned strong after a three-week break and finished solo second at the Blue Angels Classic, his best effort since winning the Toshiba Senior Classic in March of 2003. After playing his first six holes of the event in 3-over, rallied to play his last 48 holes in 12-under. Final-round 65 at The Moors, included five birdies in a six-hole stretch on the back nine...Did not record another top-10 finish until early October when he earned a solo third-place finish at the Constellation Energy Classic near Baltimore. Matched his low round of the year with an opening-round 7-under-par 65 and trailed first-round leader and eventual winner Wayne Levi by just one stroke after 18 holes. Made a spirited run in Sunday's closing round, shooting a 5-under-par 31 on the front nine to move near the top of the leaderboard, but an even-par 36 over the final nine holes doomed his chances. He finished three strokes behind Levi.

CHAMPIONS TOUR CAREER HIGHLIGHTS:

2003: Scattered five top-five performance among 22 starts, including his first Champions Tour career victory...Became the fourth of seven first-time winners when he secured a four-stroke victory at the Toshiba Senior Classic in late March. Set a new 36-hole tournament record at Newport Beach when he opened with rounds of 65-64—129 and then closed with a 3-under-par 68 on Sunday to easily defeat Larry Nelson...Had been in contention down the stretch in the first full-field event of the season at the Royal Caribbean Golf Classic and eventually finished solo fourth at Key Biscayne...Final-round 65 at the Farmers Charity Classic included a birdie-birdie-birdie-eagle-birdie finish, the best birdie/eagle stretch on the Champions Tour that year and the best run overall since the 2001 campaign...Had a run of seven straight rounds in the 60s (from the fourth round of the Senior British Open to the third round of the Allianz Championship)...Led the Champions Tour in both Putting (1.726) and Sand Saves (60 percent). **2002:** Had three top-five finishes and one of just two Australians (Stewart Ginn) among the top 31 money-winners...Shared the 36-hole lead with Dan O'Neill and eventual- winner Jay Sigel at the Farmers Charity Classic. Fired a 2-under-par 70 in the final round, but fell three strokes shy of Sigel and finished in sole possession of third place...Made a strong bid for his first Champions Tour victory at the Greater Baltimore Classic. Held a share of the lead on the 54th hole, but made a double bogey after hitting his tee shot into a hazard and T5. **2001:** Made debut shortly after turning 50 in May when he finished T27 at the Senior PGA Championship. Played in six events through open qualifying and sponsor's exemptions...Earned $66,990 and placed in the top 25 two times...In addition to his effort at the Senior PGA Championship, he also T21 at the Farmers Charity Classic and T21 at The Transamerica, his best performances of the year...Also made four starts on the Australasian Tour and made two cuts...Earned his initial exemption on the Champions Tour by finishing T3 at the Champions Tour National Qualifying Tournament at Calimesa, CA.

OTHER CAREER HIGHLIGHTS:

A long-time fixture on the European and Australian Tours...Won seven times as a member of the PGA European Tour and added 20 victories on the Australasian Tour to his resume...One of the finest players in Australia during his career, he represented the country on four World Cup teams and also participated in six Alfred Dunhill Cups, playing on the winning team in 1986...Was also a member of the winning team at the 1990 Four-Tours World Championship...Was the Australasian Order of Merit leader in both 1990 and 1991...First drew attention on the international stage in 1979 when he led the British Open with five holes to play before Seve Ballesteros emerged to grab the title. Still finished fifth at Royal Lytham that year...Turned in another stellar effort at the event in 1987, finishing T2 with Paul Azinger, one stroke behind Nick Faldo at Muirfield...Among his international titles were the 1986 Whyte & Mackay PGA European Championship where he defeated Des Smyth in a playoff, and the 1991 Volvo Masters at Valderrama.

PERSONAL:

Did not turn professional until age 23...Trained to be an accountant before turning to golf...Was considered one of the most popular and colorful players on both the European Tour and the Australasian Tour...Wears plus-fours when he plays, with socks that have his name running vertically.

PLAYER STATISTICS

MISCELLANEOUS CHAMPIONS TOUR STATISTICS

2004 Low Round: 65–2 times, most recent 2004 Constellation Energy Classic/1
Career Low Round: 64–2 times, most recent 2003 Toshiba Senior Classic/2
Career Largest Paycheck: $232,500–2003 Toshiba Senior Classic/1

MISCELLANEOUS PGA TOUR STATISTICS

Career Low Round: 68–3 times, most recent 1992 Masters Tournament/2
Career Largest Paycheck: $24,550–1986 NEC World Series of Golf/T5

CHAMPIONS TOUR CAREER SUMMARY — PLAYOFF RECORD: 0-0

Year	Events Played	1st	2nd	3rd	Top 10	Top 25	Earnings	Rank
2001	6					2	$66,990	97
2002	30			1	5	14	673,895	30
2003	22	1			8	13	885,781	22
2004	20		1	1	3	6	438,662	45
Total	78	1	1	2	16	35	2,065,328	
COMBINED ALL-TIME MONEY (3 TOURS):							**$2,178,907**	

CHAMPIONS TOUR TOP TOURNAMENT SUMMARY

Year	01	02	03	04
Senior PGA Championship	T27	T32	CUT	T47
U.S. Senior Open			T19	
Ford Senior Players		64	T30	
Senior British Open			T27	CUT
JELD-WEN Tradition		T35	T28	T55
Charles Schwab Cup Champ		WD	T13	

CHAMPIONS TOUR YEAR-BY-YEAR STATISTICS (TOP 50 ON 2004 MONEY LIST)

	Scoring Average	Putting Average	Greens in Regulation	Driving Distance	Driving Accuracy
2001	71.63 (N/A)	1.776 (N/A)	62.6 (N/A)	280.3 (N/A)	56.8 (N/A)
2002	71.16 (26)	1.789 (T32)	70.5 (14)	282.2 (4)	63.7 (66)
2003	70.41 (18)	1.726 (1)	69.3 (T27)	288.9 (3)	64.7 (61)
2004	71.67 (40)	1.796 (T35)	68.8 (30)	281.8 (12)	62.8 (70)

Jim Dent

EXEMPT STATUS: Top 30 on All-Time Money List
FULL NAME: James Lacey Dent
HEIGHT: 6-3
WEIGHT: 224
BIRTHDATE: May 9, 1939
BIRTHPLACE: Augusta, GA
RESIDENCE: Tampa, FL

FAMILY: Wife, Willye; Radiah (4/1/73), James Antonio (6/2/76), Jamie (8/15/94), Victoria (3/20/95), twins Joshua James and Joseph Samuel (8/11/99)
EDUCATION: Paine College
SPECIAL INTERESTS: Fishing, listening to jazz and blues, antique cars, cooking
TURNED PROFESSIONAL: 1966
JOINED PGA TOUR: 1970

JOINED CHAMPIONS TOUR: 1989

CHAMPIONS TOUR VICTORIES (12): 1989 MONY Syracuse Senior Classic, Newport Cup. **1990** Vantage At The Dominion, MONY Syracuse Senior Classic, Kroger Senior Classic, Crestar Classic. **1992** Newport Cup. **1994** Bruno's Memorial Classic. **1995** BellSouth Senior Classic at Opryland. **1996** Bank of Boston Senior Classic. **1997** The Home Depot Invitational. **1998** The Home Depot Invitational.

2004 CHARLES SCHWAB CUP FINISH: T64th - 66 points

GEORGIA-PACIFIC GRAND CHAMPIONS VICTORIES (9): 1999 Ameritech Senior Open, Coldwell Banker Burnet Classic, Vantage Championship. **2000** The Instinet Classic, Vantage Championship. **2001** SBC Senior Open. **2002** TD Waterhouse Championship, FleetBoston Classic. **2004** Administaff Small Business Classic.

BEST PGA TOUR CAREER FINISH: T2—1972 Walt Disney World Open Invitational.

OTHER VICTORIES (4): 1976 Florida PGA Championship. **1977** Florida PGA Championship. **1978** Florida PGA Championship. **1983** Michelob-Chattanooga Gold Club Classic.

PGA TOUR CAREER EARNINGS: $564,809

BEST 2004 CHAMPIONS TOUR FINISH: T5—Administaff Small Business Classic.

2004 SEASON:

Registered his lone top-10 finish of the year at the inaugural Administaff Small Business Classic and claimed his ninth career Georgia-Pacific Grand Champions title at Augusta Pines, as well. Was T5 in the overall event after opening with a 6-under 66 near Houston, one stroke away from matching his age. Made just one bogey in the 54-hole event. Cruised to an easy three-stroke win over Dave Stockton in the Georgia-Pacific competition, his first over-60 victory since the summer of 2002...Made his first career hole-in-one on the Champions Tour at The ACE Group Classic in Naples...Became the first player since Tom Jenkins in 2003 to have multiple aces in a season when he made his second hole-in-one of the 2004 campaign in the final round of the Commerce Bank Long Island Classic. Holed a 2-iron shot from 218 yards at the 13th hole on the Red Course at Eisenhower Park. They were his first aces on the Champions Tour after more than 400 starts.

CHAMPIONS TOUR CAREER HIGHLIGHTS:

2003: Lone top-10 finish proved to be his best effort in almost three Champions Tour seasons...Finished T2 behind Larry Nelson at the Constellation Energy Classic near Baltimore, his finest performance since a playoff loss to Nelson at the 2000 Vantage Championship. After opening with a 1-over-par 73, followed with a 7-under-par 65 in the second round and just missed shooting his age by one stroke. Spent the majority of his Sunday round lurking near the top and eventually closed with a 1-under-par 71 at Hayfields. His $120,000 check was more than a third of his official earnings on the year...Did not win a Georgia-Pacific Grand Champions event for the first time since 1999. **2002:** Was T3 at The ACE Group Classic, after firing three consecutive rounds in the 60s...Won Georgia-Pacific Grand Champions titles at the TD Waterhouse Championship and at the FleetBoston Classic. **2001:** Won Georgia Pacific Grand Champions competition at the SBC Senior Open. **2000:** Despite being out of action for most of April with a rotator cuff injury in his left shoulder, still had his best financial season since 1994...Was among the top 10 in a quarter of his 28 starts, highlighted by a playoff loss to Larry Nelson at the Vantage Championship. Shot three straight rounds of 66 at Tanglewood to join Gil Morgan and Nelson in the overtime session, but was eliminated on the first extra hole...Won a pair of Georgia-Pacific Grand Champions events and finished second to George Archer on the final money list with $309,391. **1999:** Made over $700,000 in official money for the first time since 1996 and joined the ranks of the Georgia-Pacific Grand Champions during the spring...Claimed three titles in the over-60 competition and placed second to Tom Shaw on the final Georgia-Pacific money list with $302,750. Best overall effort was a T2 at the Coldwell Banker Burnet Classic, two strokes back of Hale Irwin. **1998:** Successfully defended his Home Depot Invitational title in Charlotte, besting Bob Charles on the second hole of a sudden-death playoff. **1997:** Won 11th Champions Tour title when he defeated Lee Trevino and Larry Gilbert in a playoff at The Home Depot Invitational. Missed a two-foot birdie putt on the final hole of regulation, but sank a 10-footer on the second playoff hole to defeat Trevino after Gilbert had been eliminated one hole earlier. **1996:** Was 14th on final money list, thanks in part to victory at Bank of Boston Classic and 10 other top-10 finishes. **1995:** Won largest check of his career ($165,000) with his win at the BellSouth Senior Classic at Opryland, holding off Bob Murphy down the stretch for the title. **1994:** Easily enjoyed his best financial season and ended a two-year victory drought when he made up two strokes on the final day at the Bruno's Memorial Classic and won by two...Driving Distance leader for sixth straight year at 275.5, more than two yards per drive better than runner-up Tom Weiskopf. **1993:** Twice a runner-up, including a playoff loss to Dale Douglass at Ralphs Senior Classic. **1992:** Recorded win at the Newport Cup and reached $2 million in Champions Tour earnings during year. **1991:** Was second four times, including three losses by one stroke. **1990:** Defended title at MONY Syracuse Senior Classic and came from six strokes back to win the Crestar Classic. **1989:** Named Rookie of the Year by several publications after winning twice and finishing 12th on the money list...Came from five strokes back in each victory.

OTHER CAREER HIGHLIGHTS:

Played the old TPS series and picked up a victory in 1983 at the Michelob-Chattanooga Gold Cup Classic...Best year on the PGA TOUR was 1974 when he collected $48,486, 59th on the official money list...Came closest to a TOUR win at the 1972 Walt Disney World Classic, finishing T2 behind Jack Nicklaus...Won three consecutive Florida PGA Championships, starting in 1976.

PERSONAL:

Grew up in Augusta, GA, serving as a caddie at both Augusta National GC and Augusta CC...Played prep football at Laney High with former New York Jets star Emerson Boozer...Inducted into the Georgia Golf Hall of Fame in 1994...Nicknamed "Big Boy"...His two oldest children have worked as his caddie in the past...He and his wife adopted an infant son and daughter early in 1995, and adopted two infant sons in 1999.

PLAYER STATISTICS

2004 CHAMPIONS TOUR STATISTICS:

Scoring Average	72.87	(68)
Driving Distance	273.7	(31)
Driving Accuracy Percentage	59.4%	(76)
Total Driving	107	(73)
Greens in Regulation Pct.	59.4%	(74)
Putting Average	1.813	(49)
Sand Save Percentage	47.7%	(29)
Eagles (Holes per)	201.0	(18)
Birdie Average	2.82	(63)
All-Around Ranking	408	(60)

MISCELLANEOUS CHAMPIONS TOUR STATISTICS

2004 Low Round: 66–3 times, most recent 2004 Administaff Small Business Classic/1
Career Low Round: 62–1992 Bank One Classic/3
Career Largest Paycheck: $165,000–2 times, most recent 1998 The Home Depot Invitational/1

MISCELLANEOUS PGA TOUR STATISTICS

Career Low Round: 64–1981 Tallahassee Open/4
Career Largest Paycheck: $23,400–1988 Provident Classic/T3

CHAMPIONS TOUR CAREER SUMMARY — PLAYOFF RECORD: 2-2

Year	Events Played	1st	2nd	3rd	Top 10	Top 25	Earnings	Rank
1989	23	2	2	1	12	20	$337,691	12
1990	31	4	4	1	21	28	693,214	6
1991	32		4		13	27	529,315	9
1992	28	1	2	1	14	22	593,979	9
1993	28		2	1	9	19	513,515	18
1994	30	1		5	15	26	950,891	7
1995	24	1	1	1	7	18	575,603	19
1996	34	1			11	23	707,655	14
1997	31	1		1	5	12	590,646	22
1998	32	1	1		5	14	610,729	29
1999	31		1		9	17	715,035	25
2000	28		1	2	7	17	722,220	25
2001	28					7	291,548	56
2002	26			1	1	9	383,601	44
2003	22		1		1	4	304,812	50
2004	23				1	4	190,117	65
Total	451	12	19	14	131	267	8,710,572	
COMBINED ALL-TIME MONEY (3 TOURS):							**$9,275,381**	

CHAMPIONS TOUR TOP TOURNAMENT SUMMARY

Year	89	90	91	92	93	94	95	96	97	98	99	00	01
Senior PGA Championship		T38	T6	T14	T32	T29	T58	T46	CUT	T22	T34		T36
U.S. Senior Open	T3	10	T4	T8		T42		T22	WD		T8	CUT	T34
Ford Senior Players	T25	T3	T55	T36	T8	T6	T18	T13	T29	T50	T44	T52	T31
JELD-WEN Tradition		T43	T2	T24	T35	T17	T12	T43	T6		T60		
Charles Schwab Cup Champ		T11	T16	T4	T15	4	T12	5	T11	T8	T16	T19	

Year	02	03	04
Senior PGA Championship	T72	T34	CUT
U.S. Senior Open	T27	T12	CUT
Ford Senior Players	T58	T40	T71

SECTION 2 PLAYER BIOGRAPHIES

Terry Dill

EXEMPT STATUS: Net-70 on All-Time Money List
FULL NAME: Terrance Darby Dill
HEIGHT: 6-3
WEIGHT: 195
BIRTHDATE: May 13, 1939
BIRTHPLACE: Fort Worth, TX
RESIDENCE: Lakeway, TX
FAMILY: Wife, Linda; Terrance, Jr. (9/22/63), Jefferson (J.R., 8/7/64), Blake (12/22/64), Melinda (6/3/68), Andrew (8/28/73), Clarke (12/21/74); nine grandchildren
EDUCATION: University of Texas (B.A.,1962), University of Texas (J.D., 1976)
SPECIAL INTERESTS: Gardening, impressionist landscape painting
TURNED PROFESSIONAL: 1962
JOINED PGA TOUR: 1962

JOINED CHAMPIONS TOUR: 1989

CHAMPIONS TOUR VICTORIES (1): 1992 Bank One Classic.

GEORGIA-PACIFIC GRAND CHAMPIONS VICTORIES (3): 1999 State Farm Senior Classic. **2000** FleetBoston Classic, Kroger Senior Classic.

BEST PGA TOUR CAREER FINISH: T2—1970 Sahara Invitational.

PGA TOUR CAREER EARNINGS: $255,050

BEST 2004 CHAMPIONS TOUR FINISH: T23—MasterCard Classic.

2004 SEASON:

Lone top-25 finish came in Mexico when he was T23 at the MasterCard Classic at Bosque Real CC near Mexico City...Aced the par-3 11th hole at Valhalla during the opening round of the Senior PGA Championship, his second hole-in-one on the Champions Tour...Finished fourth in Driving Distance, the 16th straight year he has been among the leaders.

CHAMPIONS TOUR CAREER HIGHLIGHTS:

2003: Was among the top 20 in two of 26 events during the campaign...T18 at the Emerald Coast Classic, thanks to a 5-under 65 on Saturday, his best round since the second day of the 2001 Bruno's event (65)...T18 at the FleetBoston Classic, where he also finished second to Dave Stockton in the Georgia-Pacific Grand Champions event...Finished ninth on the final Georgia-Pacific Grand Champions money list with $97,883. **2002:** T10 at the FleetBoston Classic, thanks to three consecutive sub-par rounds...Twice a runner-up in the Georgia-Pacific Grand Champions competition. Fell one stroke shy of Jim Dent at the FleetBoston Classic and lost by one point to Walter Morgan in the Modified Stableford format at the Uniting Fore Care Classic...Was the only player over the age of 60 to finish in the top 10 in Driving Distance, finishing seventh with an average of 280.1. **2001:** Two best performances came in Champions Tour majors. Was among the early leaders at The Countrywide Tradition and eventually T16. Also T17 at the Senior PGA Championship...Was third in Driving Distance with an average of 284.3. **2000:** Became the oldest player to win the Driving Distance title when, at age 61, he averaged 286.2 yards per drive...Won both of his Georgia-Pacific Grand Champions titles within a four-week period late in the summer campaign. Defeated Lee Trevino by a stroke at the FleetBoston Classic and then bested Butch Baird and Simon Hobday by a stroke for the Grand Champions title at the Kroger Senior Classic. **1999:** Had four top-10 finishes, highlighted by a T2 at The Home Depot Invitational, one stroke short of Bruce Fleisher...Won the Georgia-Pacific Grand Champions title at the State Farm Senior Classic, holing a three-foot birdie putt on the last hole. **1998:** Enjoyed most-productive year of his Champions Tour career, finishing 20th on the final money list with career-best $701,210...Posted his senior career-low score of 62 on the last day of the Vantage Championship. **1997:** T2 at The Transamerica, his best effort since 1992...One of two players to have two eagles in a round twice, making a pair in the third round of The Tradition and again in the final round of the Vantage Championship. **1996:** Won the Driving Distance title for the first time with an average of 287.2 yards per-drive...Best finish was a T3 at American Express Invitational. **1992:** Recorded only Champions Tour victory when he prevailed by four strokes over Bruce Crampton and Dale Douglass at the Bank One Senior Classic in Lexington...One of only three wire-to-wire winners that year...Was second at the rain-shortened NYNEX Commemorative, losing a playoff on the first hole to Dale Douglass. **1991:** Took advantage of fully-exempt status for first time with seven top-10 finishes and over $200,000 in earnings. **1990:** Was 36-hole leader at Southwestern Bell Classic before finishing T2 in Oklahoma City...Also T2 at Greater Grand Rapids Open, missing a playoff by one stroke. **1989:** Made 15 starts, mostly as an open qualifier.

OTHER CAREER HIGHLIGHTS:

Played the PGA TOUR from 1962 to 1972 and again in 1975 and 1976...Was among the top 60 money-winners on TOUR five times from 1964 to 1970...Best year was 1970, when he earned $41,108 for 56th position on the money list...Southwest Conference medalist in 1960 while at Texas...Has had two holes-in-one in his professional career.

PERSONAL:

Graduated from the University of Texas Law School in 1976...Taught tax law at Texas A&M for three years but decided to resume his professional golf career when federal regulations changed...Was expected to begin a new career as a financial planner...Had surgery to remove a malignant tumor near his right ear in the fall of 1991 and has no hearing on that side...Enjoys painting and finished a landscape portrait of the third hole at Greystone G&C and presented it to the club as a gift from the players during the 2002 Bruno's Memorial Classic.

PLAYER STATISTICS

2004 CHAMPIONS TOUR STATISTICS:

Scoring Average	74.30	(75)
Driving Distance	287.6	(4)
Driving Accuracy Percentage	55.3%	(81)
Total Driving	85	(48)
Greens in Regulation Pct.	61.9%	(68)
Putting Average	1.857	(76)
Sand Save Percentage	22.2%	(81)
Eagles (Holes per)	270.0	(29)
Birdie Average	2.72	(68)
All-Around Ranking	482	(72)

MISCELLANEOUS CHAMPIONS TOUR STATISTICS

2004 Low Round: 67–2004 Farmers Charity Classic/2
Career Low Round: 62–1998 Vantage Championship/3
Career Largest Paycheck: $96,000–1999 The Home Depot Invitational/T2

MISCELLANEOUS PGA TOUR STATISTICS

Career Low Round: 64–1969 Phoenix Open Invitational/2
Career Largest Paycheck: $7,733–1970 Sahara Invitational/T2

CHAMPIONS TOUR CAREER SUMMARY — PLAYOFF RECORD: 0-1

Year	Events Played	1st	2nd	3rd	Top 10	Top 25	Earnings	Rank
1989	15				3	9	$82,332	50
1990	32		2	1	7	20	278,372	19
1991	33				7	15	242,191	31
1992	33	1	1		3	5	211,998	34
1993	33				1	12	179,976	50
1994	31				3	12	224,885	36
1995	34			1	6	9	289,652	40
1996	33			1	3	15	319,507	44
1997	31		1		2	13	325,522	48
1998	33			1	8	20	701,210	20
1999	34		1	1	4	17	583,637	33
2000	32				1	6	280,275	61
2001	30					8	251,150	64
2002	26				1	3	166,448	80
2003	26					3	155,834	76
2004	20					1	67,762	92
Total	476	1	5	5	49	168	4,360,750	
COMBINED ALL-TIME MONEY (3 TOURS):							**$4,617,713**	

CHAMPIONS TOUR TOP TOURNAMENT SUMMARY

Year	89	90	91	92	93	94	95	96	97	98	99	00	01
Senior PGA Championship		T16	T36	CUT	T45	CUT	T16	T46	CUT	T29	T24	CUT	T17
U.S. Senior Open	17	T11	WD		T23	T32	CUT				T32	T53	CUT
Ford Senior Players		T23	T5	T54	T40	T42	T55	T75	T34	T15	T68	T64	T59
JELD-WEN Tradition		T10	T40	T31	T17	T45	59	T31	T8	T17	T9	T61	T16
Charles Schwab Cup Champ		24	T12							T19			

Year	02	03	04
Senior PGA Championship		CUT	CUT
Ford Senior Players		T64	T58
JELD-WEN Tradition	T48	T69	T70

Ed Dougherty (DOCK-ur-tee)

EXEMPT STATUS: Top 30 on All-Time Money List
FULL NAME: Edward Matthew Dougherty
HEIGHT: 6-1
WEIGHT: 225
BIRTHDATE: November 4, 1947
BIRTHPLACE: Chester, PA
RESIDENCE: Port St. Lucie, FL

FAMILY: Wife, Carolyn
CLUB AFFILIATION: Ibis G&CC (Palm Beach Gardens, FL)
SPECIAL INTERESTS: Lionel toy trains, old Gottlieb pinball machines
TURNED PROFESSIONAL: 1969
JOINED PGA TOUR: 1975

JOINED CHAMPIONS TOUR: 1998

CHAMPIONS TOUR VICTORIES (2): 2000 Coldwell Banker Burnet Classic. **2001** TD Waterhouse Championship.

2004 CHARLES SCHWAB CUP FINISH: 63rd - 68 points

PGA TOUR VICTORIES (1): 1995 Deposit Guaranty Golf Classic.

PGA TOUR CAREER EARNINGS: $1,323,769

PGA TOUR PLAYOFF RECORD: 0-1

BEST 2004 CHAMPIONS TOUR FINISH: T7—The First Tee Open at Pebble Beach presented by Wal-Mart.

2004 SEASON:

Returned to action in late June following his off-season shoulder surgery and was T57 in his first start at the Bank of America Championship near Boston...Posted best finish of the year when he put together three straight sub-par rounds to finish T7 at The First Tee Open at Pebble Beach, his best finish in more than a year...Only other top-25 performance in 13 starts was a T23 at the SAS Championship.

CHAMPIONS TOUR CAREER HIGHLIGHTS:

2003: Finished out of the top 30 on the money list for the first time since 1998...Played his best golf during the month of June and early July, but then experienced shoulder problems later in the season...Closed with 66 in Nashville to T4 at the Music City Championship at Gaylord Opryland...T4 again three weeks later at the Farmers Charity Classic. Was the 36-hole leader in Grand Rapids, but fell back after posting an even-par 72 on Sunday...Opened with a 5-under-par 65, his low round of the year, at the Columbus Southern Open and shared the first-round lead before eventually finishing T16...Played in B.C. Open on the PGA TOUR, but missed the cut...Underwent right shoulder surgery in October. **2002:** Was the 36-hole leader by two strokes at the Audi Senior Classic after rounds of 71-65 and eventually T4...Was in contention at the U.S. Senior Open, trailing by four strokes after three rounds. Shot a 1-under 70 on Sunday and finished solo fourth at Caves Valley...Also T4 at the RJR Championship in September with three straight sub-70 rounds. **2001:** Enjoyed his finest season ever in professional golf...Went over the $1-million mark in earnings for the first time, due to a career-best 10 top-10 finishes...Recorded wire-to-wire victory at the TD Waterhouse Championship. Tied the Champions Tour record for lowest 54-hole score in relation to par (Raymond Floyd/1993 Gulfstream Aerospace Invitational) when he blitzed the Tiffany Greens GC course with a 22-under-par 194 total. His 36-hole score of 16-under 128 also tied the then-Champions Tour's all-time mark in relation to par (Hale Irwin/1997 Vantage Championship) for the first two rounds. His 10-under 62 on Friday was a Champions Tour career-best and was his lowest score since shooting 62 at the 1992 Chattanooga Classic on the PGA TOUR. Made a 12-foot birdie putt on the last hole to win by eight strokes over Walter Morgan, Hugh Baiocchi and Dana Quigley, the largest margin of victory in a 54-hole event since the 1993 Franklin Quest Championship...Almost won again at the AT&T Canada Senior Open. Fired a 6-under 65 on the last day to come from five strokes back and catch Walter Hall in regulation. Fell to Hall on the first playoff hole after making bogey for the second time on Mississauga's 18th hole on Sunday. **2000:** Registered his first victory in 69 Champions Tour starts at the Coldwell Banker Burnet Classic with a tournament record score of 19-under-par. The $240,000 first-place check was more than he made in his best year on the PGA TOUR (1992/$237,525). Was the August Player of the Month...Shot 19-under 197 again at the Gold Rush Classic but finished second to Jim Thorpe by two strokes...Had his first hole-in-one on the Champions Tour in the opening round of the SBC Championship. **1999:** Took advantage of his first full year on the Champions Tour by earning over $900,000 and a spot among the top 20 money-winners...Made headlines by being the 18-, 36- and 54-hole leader at the U.S. Senior Open. Lost to Dave Eichelberger on the final day...Took a one-stroke lead into the final round of the TD Waterhouse Championship, but finished two shots back of Allen Doyle despite a final-round 68...Was again the runner-up the next week at the Comfort Classic, falling two strokes short of Gil Morgan...Was also the 36-hole leader at the Kroger Senior Classic, but lost to Morgan again by two strokes despite posting a final-round 67. **1998:** Made debut on the Champions Tour in May at the Saint Luke's Classic and T19 in Kansas City...Best finish came near his home in the Philadelphia area. Playing on a sponsor exemption, he closed with a 64 to T3 at the Bell Atlantic Classic.

OTHER CAREER HIGHLIGHTS:

Long-time player on the PGA TOUR, where he competed from 1975-97...Had 460 starts in his career and made 243 cuts...No doubt the high point of his golf career came in 1995 when he prevailed at the Deposit Guaranty Golf Classic. Idled much of the early portion of the year by a shoulder injury suffered while lifting one of his vintage pinball machines, he shot rounds of 68-68-70 and stood in seventh place, three behind Dickey Thompson after 54 holes. Finished with a 66, which included 32 on the second nine and that was good enough to give him a two-stroke win over Gil Morgan. The victory, at age 47, made him the oldest first-time winner on the PGA TOUR since John Barnum captured the 1962 Cajun Classic at age 51...Lost in a playoff to Jim Gallagher, Jr. at the 1990 Greater Milwaukee Open and was also second at the Anheuser-Busch Golf Classic and the Chattanooga Classic in back-to-back weeks in 1992...Made three successful trips to the PGA TOUR National Qualifying Tournament in 1983, 1986 and 1989...Named PGA of America's Club Professional of the Year in 1985 after winning the Club Professional Championship at Mission Hills CC in Rancho Mirage, CA...Has had six holes-in-one during competitive rounds.

PERSONAL:

Is a serious model train enthusiast who has a vast collection of Lionel trains ranging from around 1900 to 1969. Houses his train collection in a two-story, 20-by-30 building. Usually makes it a point to visit train stores in cities while on TOUR...In recent years, has also begun refurbishing old pinball machines...Also collects cars and owns two 1958 Chevys and a 1963 Corvette...Served a tour in Vietnam and joins a host of players on the Champions Tour who served in the military...Returned from Southeast Asia and took up golf seriously at Fort Lewis, WA, when he wasn't allowed to play baseball...Played golf for the first time when he was working in the post office in Linwood, PA, at age 19...Follows the Philadelphia-area pro sports teams...Has started to learn to play the guitar and is a self-described "36-handicapper" with it...Nickname is "Doc.

PLAYER STATISTICS

2004 CHAMPIONS TOUR STATISTICS:

Scoring Average	72.70	(62)
Driving Distance	266.5	(59)
Driving Accuracy Percentage	79.0%	(8)
Total Driving	67	(20)
Greens in Regulation Pct.	63.2%	(60)
Putting Average	1.842	(71)
Sand Save Percentage	47.7%	(29)
Eagles (Holes per)	720.0	(63)
Birdie Average	2.50	(72)
All-Around Ranking	424	(64)

MISCELLANEOUS CHAMPIONS TOUR STATISTICS

2004 Low Round: 67–2004 Commerce Bank Long Island Classic/3
Career Low Round: 62–2001 TD Waterhouse Championship/1
Career Largest Paycheck: $240,000–2000 Coldwell Banker Burnet Classic/1

MISCELLANEOUS PGA TOUR STATISTICS

Career Low Round: 62–1992 Chattanooga Classic/3
Career Largest Paycheck: $126,000–1995 Deposit Guaranty Golf Classic/1

CHAMPIONS TOUR CAREER SUMMARY — PLAYOFF RECORD: 0-1

Year	Events Played	1st	2nd	3rd	Top 10	Top 25	Earnings	Rank
1998	19			1	6	15	$412,679	44
1999	25		4	1	7	18	951,072	16
2000	37	1	1		8	20	953,374	17
2001	36	1	1	4	10	21	1,330,818	13
2002	34				7	18	896,843	22
2003	29				4	12	565,146	33
2004	13				1	2	125,074	80
Total	193	2	6	6	43	106	5,235,007	
COMBINED ALL-TIME MONEY (3 TOURS):							**$6,559,216**	

CHAMPIONS TOUR TOP TOURNAMENT SUMMARY

Year	98	99	00	01	02	03	04
Senior PGA Championship		T11	T12	T49	T32	T40	
U.S. Senior Open	T7	2	T37	CUT	4	T17	CUT
Ford Senior Players	T56	T22	T36	T4	T6	T9	74
JELD-WEN Tradition		T50	T9	T24	T16	T69	T67
Charles Schwab Cup Champ		T22	29	T26	T10		

Dale Douglass

EXEMPT STATUS: Top 30 on All-Time Money List
FULL NAME: Dale Dwight Douglass
HEIGHT: 6-2
WEIGHT: 170
BIRTHDATE: March 5, 1936
BIRTHPLACE: Wewoka, OK
RESIDENCE: Castle Rock, CO

FAMILY: Wife, Joyce
CLUB AFFILIATION: The Wigwam Resort (Phoenix, AZ)
EDUCATION: University of Colorado (B.A., 1959)
TURNED PROFESSIONAL: 1960
JOINED PGA TOUR: 1963

JOINED CHAMPIONS TOUR: 1986

CHAMPIONS TOUR VICTORIES (11): 1986 Vintage Invitational, Johnny Mathis Senior Classic, U.S. Senior Open, Fairfield Barnett Senior Classic. **1988** GTE Suncoast Classic. **1990** Bell Atlantic Classic. **1991** Showdown Classic. **1992** NYNEX Commemorative, Ameritech Senior Open. **1993** Ralphs Senior Classic. **1996** Bell Atlantic Classic.

OTHER SENIOR VICTORIES (3): 1990 Liberty Mutual Legends of Golf [with Charles Coody]. **1994** Liberty Mutual Legends of Golf [with Charles Coody]. **1998** Liberty Mutual Legends of Golf [with Charles Coody].

GEORGIA-PACIFIC GRAND CHAMPIONS VICTORIES (12): 1996 Bell Atlantic Classic, Kroger Senior Classic, Ralphs Senior Classic. **1997** Boone Valley Classic. **1998** Las Vegas Senior Classic, Bell Atlantic Classic, State Farm Senior Classic, Ford Senior Players Championship, Raley's Gold Rush Classic. **1999** Nationwide Championship. **2001** Toshiba Senior Classic. **2003** Royal Caribbean Golf Classic.

PGA TOUR VICTORIES (3): 1969 Azalea Open Invitational, Kemper Open. **1970** Phoenix Open Invitational.

PGA TOUR CAREER EARNINGS: $573,351

PGA TOUR PLAYOFF RECORD: 0-3

BEST 2004 CHAMPIONS TOUR FINISH:
T39—Administaff Small Business Classic.

2004 SEASON:

Bettered his age for the second time in his career with a 5-under 66 in the final round of the Toshiba Senior Classic...Made his 18th career ace in the final round of the Allianz Championship, holing a 3-iron shot on the second hole at Glen Oaks, the Tour's eighth-hardest hole in 2004. It was also his first hole-in-one in 18 years and just his second on the Champions Tour.

CHAMPIONS TOUR CAREER HIGHLIGHTS:

2003: Became just the fifth player with at least 500 appearances on the Champions Tour when he made his 500th official start at the first full-field event of the year, the Royal Caribbean Golf Classic near Miami...Went on to win the Georgia-Pacific Grand Champions competition at Key Biscayne. Defeated Isao Aoki with a four-foot birdie putt on the first playoff hole after both players had finished 36 holes at 1-under 143...Georgia-Pacific victory was his first in the over-60 competition in almost two years...Best overall effort was a T18 at the rain-shortened SBC Classic at Valencia. **2002:** Bettered his age for the first time when he posted a 7-under 63 in the second round of the Emerald Coast Classic. Round was his best on the Champions Tour since he fashioned a 61 in the final round of the 1994 Ralphs Senior Classic. The score also made him, at the time, the second-youngest player in Champions Tour history to better his age (Joe Jimenez shot 63 at age 65 in the 1991 GTE Northwest Classic; Walter Morgan shot 60 at AT&T Canada Senior Open Championship at age 61 in July). T5 in the rain-shortened event in Milton, his best performance since the 1999 campaign...Later matched his age with a 5-under-par 66 in the second round of the Allianz Championship...Was the oldest player (66) in the field to make the cut at the U.S. Senior Open. **2001:** Won his 11th career Georgia-Pacific Grand Champions title at the Toshiba Senior Classic. Carded a pair of 69s on the first two days of the tournament to defeat Bob Charles and Lee Trevino by two strokes in the over-60 competition. **1999:** Won the over-60 event at the Nationwide Championship by one stroke over three other players. **1998:** Made 29 starts and finished 31st on the money list...Appeared headed for a playoff with Gil Morgan at the LG Championship before Morgan made eagle on the final hole to drop him into a second-place tie with Raymond Floyd...Continued to make his mark in the Georgia-Pacific Grand Champions competition, with five wins and a second-place finish behind Bob Charles on the Grand Champions money list with $249,790...Teamed with Charles Coody for their third Liberty Mutual Legends of Golf title. **1997:** Earned almost one-third of his season earnings at the PGA Seniors' Championship, making $105,000 for a distant T2 behind Hale Irwin. Runner-up performance at PGA National was his best in a major since the 1994 Tradition...Finished third on the Georgia-Pacific Grand Champions money list with $209,810 and recorded his only 60-and-over victory at the Boone Valley Classic, a two-stroke decision over Dick Hendrickson. **1996:** At the Bell Atlantic Classic, became the second of only four Grand Champions (60 and older) to double dip when he claimed the Georgia-Pacific event and won the overall tournament the next day in a playoff with Tom Wargo and John Schroeder. Made birdie on third extra hole after knocking a 6-iron five feet from the pin at Chester Valley. **1994:** Shot best score of his career, a final-round 61 at Rancho Park, in defense of his title at Ralphs Senior Classic, but still finished second at the event to Jack Kiefer...Also lost to Raymond Floyd on the first playoff hole at The Tradition despite four straight rounds in the 60s and a 17-under-par total for 72 holes. **1993:** Shot a sizzling 64 on Sunday and then defeated Jim Dent with birdie on first extra playoff hole to win the Ralphs Senior Classic at Rancho Park. **1992:** Posted 16 top-10 finishes, including wins at the rain-shortened NYNEX Commemorative (defeated Terry Dill in a playoff) and the Ameritech Senior Open...Was sixth on final money list with career-best $694,564. **1991:** Surpassed $600,000 in season earnings with victory at Showdown Classic in Utah...Trio of second places were among 17 top-10 finishes. **1990:** Went over half-million dollar mark for first time and was eighth on the final money list...Beat Gary Player in a playoff for Bell Atlantic title and also teamed with Charles Coody for first of three wins at unofficial Liberty Mutual Legends of Golf. **1988:** Victorious at GTE Suncoast Senior Classic, leading event from start to finish. **1986:** Had banner rookie year, finishing third on the money list and garnering four wins, including U.S. Senior Open at

CHAMPIONS TOUR CAREER SUMMARY — PLAYOFF RECORD: 4-4

Year	Events Played	1st	2nd	3rd	Top 10	Top 25	Earnings	Rank
1986	23	4	2	2	16	21	$309,760	3
1987	29		5	1	17	29	296,429	7
1988	29	1	1	2	13	22	280,457	12
1989	32		2	2	17	27	313,275	14
1990	31	1	4	2	15	23	568,198	8
1991	31	1	3	1	17	27	606,949	7
1992	32	2	2	1	16	25	694,564	6
1993	32	1	2	1	9	18	499,858	19
1994	33		2	1	9	27	543,886	18
1995	30			1	7	14	341,945	35
1996	29	1			2	9	318,507	45
1997	31		1		3	8	366,803	43
1998	29		1	2	5	12	569,293	31
1999	28		1		1	4	314,439	51
2000	29				1	8	260,695	62
2001	24					2	159,411	75
2002	27				3	6	313,254	55
2003	24					1	106,360	85
2004	23						59,856	98
Total	546	11	26	16	151	283	6,923,941	
COMBINED ALL-TIME MONEY (3 TOURS):							**$7,497,292**	

CHAMPIONS TOUR TOP TOURNAMENT SUMMARY

Year	86	87	88	89	90	91	92	93	94	95	96	97	98
Senior PGA Championship		2	T35	T31	7	T20	T14	T16	T5	T16	CUT	T2	T4
U.S. Senior Open	1	T6	T20	T3	CUT	T24	T14	T4	T25	T51	T22	CUT	T28
Ford Senior Players	T10	T24	T13	T18	T11	T8	T9	T51	T20	WD	T57	T34	T30
JELD-WEN Tradition				T22	T13	5	T60	T3	2	T8	T23	T46	T53
Charles Schwab Cup Champ					T2	23	T2	T8	17				29

Year	99	00	01	02	03	04
Senior PGA Championship		T46	T27	CUT	CUT	CUT
U.S. Senior Open	CUT	T45	CUT	T41	CUT	CUT
Ford Senior Players	T59	T18	T41	T68	T48	
Senior British Open					CUT	CUT
JELD-WEN Tradition	T28	T31	T40	T44	T52	77

Dale Douglass (continued)

Scioto CC by one stroke over Gary Player...Was the leader or co-leader in eight of his first 10 rounds on the Champions Tour, including seven straight. Of those seven, he held sole possession of the lead in six which was instrumental in back-to-back wins at The Vintage Invitational and the Johnny Mathis Seniors Classic...His streak could have been more impressive but after finishing tied with Charles Owens at the Del E. Webb SENIOR PGA TOUR Roundup in his first start, he lost in a playoff.

OTHER CAREER HIGHLIGHTS:

Joined the PGA TOUR in 1963, but his first official win did not come until the 1969 Azalea Open...Captured the Kemper Open that same season and went on to finish 12th on the official money list with $91,553, his best TOUR year...Won the 1970 Phoenix Open by one stroke over Gene Littler and Howie Johnson...Play was curtailed by assorted injuries throughout the '70s...Member of the 1969 United States Ryder Cup team...Has made 18 career holes-in-one.

PERSONAL:

Tournament Policy Board Player Director 1971-72...Vice President of the PGA in 1972...Served on the Champions Tour Division Board as a Player Director from 1990-1994 and again in 1996-97.

PLAYER STATISTICS

2004 CHAMPIONS TOUR STATISTICS:

Scoring Average	74.30	(75)
Driving Distance	255.9	(74)
Driving Accuracy Percentage	61.6%	(72)
Total Driving	146	(80)
Greens in Regulation Pct.	56.3%	(78)
Putting Average	1.842	(71)
Sand Save Percentage	53.3%	(12)
Eagles (Holes per)	1,206.0	(75)
Birdie Average	2.42	(75)
All-Around Ranking	532	(79)

MISCELLANEOUS CHAMPIONS TOUR STATISTICS

2004 Low Round: 66–2004 Toshiba Senior Classic/3
Career Low Round: 61–1994 Ralphs Senior Classic/3
Career Largest Paycheck: $135,000–1996 Bell Atlantic Classic/1

MISCELLANEOUS PGA TOUR STATISTICS

Career Low Round: 63–4 times, most recent 1973 Phoenix Open/1
Career Largest Paycheck: $30,000–1969 Kemper Open/1

25 MEMORABLE MOMENTS

Thomson Wins Record Ninth Tournament

1985

Five-time British Open champion Peter Thomson owned the Champions Tour in 1985, reeling off a record nine victories in 25 starts. With $386,724 in official earnings, the Australian topped that year's money list, and collected another $125,000 by winning the Mazda Bonus Pool. A 1988 World Golf Hall of Fame inductee, he added two second-place finishes to give him 22 top-10 finishes that year. Thomson came up just short of Don January in the Byron Nelson Award, which goes to the scoring leader (January was 70.11 to Thomson's 70.17). His victory record was matched in 1997 by Hale Irwin.

CHAMPIONS TOUR 25

SECTION 2 PLAYER BIOGRAPHIES

Allen Doyle

EXEMPT STATUS: Top 30 on 2004 Champions Tour Money List
FULL NAME: Allen Michael Doyle
HEIGHT: 6-3
WEIGHT: 210
BIRTHDATE: July 26, 1948
BIRTHPLACE: Woonsocket, RI
RESIDENCE: La Grange, GA

FAMILY: Wife, Kate; Erin (8/22/79), Michelle (10/26/80)
EDUCATION: Norwich University
SPECIAL INTERESTS: Family
TURNED PROFESSIONAL: 1995
JOINED PGA TOUR: 1996

JOINED CHAMPIONS TOUR: 1998

CHAMPIONS TOUR VICTORIES (9): 1999 ACE Group Classic, PGA Seniors' Championship, Cadillac NFL Golf Classic, TD Waterhouse Championship. **2000** Toshiba Senior Classic. **2001** Ford Senior Players Championship, State Farm Senior Classic. **2003** FleetBoston Classic. **2004** Bayer Advantage Celebrity Pro-Am.

OTHER SENIOR VICTORIES (2): 1999 Senior Slam. **2001** Senior Slam.

2004 CHARLES SCHWAB CUP FINISH:
6th - 1,888 points

BEST PGA TOUR CAREER FINISH: T7—1998 Deposit Guaranty Golf Classic.

OTHER VICTORIES (19): 1978 Georgia State Amateur. **1979** Georgia State Amateur. **1982** Georgia State Mid-Amateur Championship, Georgia State Four-Ball Tournament. **1986** Georgia State Four-Ball Tournament. **1987** Georgia State Amateur, Georgia State Mid-Amateur Championship, Georgia State Four-Ball Tournament. **1988** Georgia State Amateur, Georgia State Mid-Amateur Championship, Georgia State Four-Ball Tournament. **1989** Georgia State Four-Ball Tournament. **1990** Georgia State Mid-Amateur Championship, Georgia State Four-Ball Tournament. **1994** Porter Cup, Sunnehanna Amateur, Cardinal Amateur, Dogwood Amateur, Rice Planters Invitational.

NATIONWIDE TOUR VICTORIES (3): 1995 Mississippi Gulf Coast Classic, Texarkana Open, Tour Championship.

PGA TOUR CAREER EARNINGS: $245,923

BEST 2004 CHAMPIONS TOUR FINISHES:
1—Bayer Advantage Celebrity Pro-Am; T2—JELD-WEN Tradition; 3—Charles Schwab Cup Championship.

2004 SEASON:

Won for the eighth time in his career and for the second time near Kansas City when he claimed the rain-shortened Bayer Advantage Celebrity Pro-Am by a stroke over Jerry Pate. Made a short birdie putt on the 18th hole Saturday to give himself a one-stroke cushion over Pate and then was declared the winner when Sunday's final round was canceled due to course damage from overnight storms Saturday…Was among a handful of players who battled it out in Sunday's final round at the JELD-WEN Tradition in late August. Trailed by one stroke heading into Sunday's final round and remained in contention throughout the round but failed to birdie one of his final two holes to finish T2, one stroke behind Craig Stadler…Made nice showing at the season-ending Charles Schwab Cup Championship where he was a third-place finisher. Was T17 after two rounds but fired an impressive 5-under-par 67 in rainy conditions on Saturday and a 3-under-par 69 on Sunday to jump 14 places…His T11 finish at the SAS Championship earned him a check for $41,000 and pushed him over the $1-million mark for the sixth consecutive year…Champions Tour Player of the Month for June…After two straight years as the runner-up to Doug Tewell in Driving Accuracy, he finished first in that category, tying the all-time Champions Tour mark set in 1994 by Calvin Peete at 84.1 percent.

CHAMPIONS TOUR CAREER HIGHLIGHTS:

2003: Over the $1-million mark in earnings for a fifth straight season and was back among the top 10 on the money list after a year's absence, thanks to 13 top-10 finishes…Tied with Tom Jenkins for the most sub-par rounds on the Champions Tour with 64…Won for the first time in just over two years when he prevailed at the FleetBoston Classic. The native of nearby Norwood, MA, broke the 18-hole tournament record at Nashawtuc and equaled his career-low score with a second-round, 8-under-par 63 that included a 6-under-par 29 on the front nine. His 54-hole total of 198 also matched the tournament scoring mark, held by Chi Chi Rodriguez, and helped him defeat Bruce Fleisher and defending champion Bob Gilder by two strokes for his eighth career win on the Champions Tour…Contended earlier in the campaign for the Columbus Southern Open title near his home in Georgia and eventually finished one stroke short of Morris Hatalsky. Trailed by one stroke after 36 holes, but could not overtake Hatalsky despite closing with a 3-under-par 67 at Green Island CC…Also finished third late in the year at the SBC Championship in San Antonio and T4 at the U.S. Senior Open, his fourth consecutive top-10 finish in the event…Ranked among the top-five in Driving Accuracy for a fifth straight year, finishing second to Doug Tewell in that category (80.9 percent). **2002:** Had 13 top-10 finishes, including a second- and two third-place efforts…Runner-up to Hale Irwin at the Toshiba Senior Classic after owning sole possession of first place after the opening round. **2001:** Was the Champions Tour's mark of consistency, with 25 top-10 finishes in 34 starts, one top-10 short of Lee Trevino's all-time senior record (1990)…Battled Bruce Fleisher down the stretch for both the Charles Schwab Cup and the overall money title and claimed both honors…Received the Jack Nicklaus Player of the Year Award after a vote of his peers…Donated his entire $1 million annuity for winning the Charles Schwab Cup to six different charitable organizations…Earned $2,553,582, the third-highest single-season total in Champions Tour history…Was 236-under par, the most under by any player on the circuit for a season…Led the Champions Tour with 55 (out of 102) rounds in the 60s and had 81 sub-par rounds, one short of Tom Wargo's record (1994)…Won twice and came close to winning four other tournaments…Claimed both of his 2001 titles in playoffs over a span of three weeks, starting in mid-July. Holed a 35-foot birdie putt on the 72nd hole to jump into a playoff with Doug Tewell at the Ford Senior Players Championship and then defeated Tewell with a par on the first extra hole for his second major championship on the Champions Tour. The $375,000 paycheck was the largest of his career…Won again two weeks later at the State Farm Senior Classic. Rebounded from an opening-round 73 to get into a tie with Fleisher at the end of regulation and then outlasted Fleisher with a four-foot par putt on the third playoff hole. **2000:** Posted just one official victory during the season despite improving his scoring average

CHAMPIONS TOUR CAREER SUMMARY — PLAYOFF RECORD: 3-2

Year	Events Played	1st	2nd	3rd	Top 10	Top 25	Earnings	Rank
1998	6				2	5	$164,918	67
1999	31	4	4	1	16	24	1,911,640	3
2000	33	1		4	17	31	1,505,471	7
2001	34	2	5	3	25	30	2,553,582	1
2002	32		1	2	13	25	1,322,054	12
2003	30	1	1	1	13	23	1,349,272	9
2004	27	1	1	1	10	19	1,298,555	10
Total	193	9	12	12	96	157	10,105,491	

COMBINED ALL-TIME MONEY (3 TOURS): **$10,538,686**

CHAMPIONS TOUR TOP TOURNAMENT SUMMARY

Year	99	00	01	02	03	04
Senior PGA Championship	1	T17	4	T15	T7	T13
U.S. Senior Open	T13	T8	T4	T7	T4	T42
Ford Senior Players	T19	T12	1	T12	T15	T9
JELD-WEN Tradition	68		T10	T16	T42	T2
Charles Schwab Cup Champ	T9	T6	T22	T12	T25	3

CHAMPIONS TOUR YEAR-BY-YEAR STATISTICS (TOP 50 ON 2004 MONEY LIST)

	Scoring Average	Putting Average	Greens in Regulation	Driving Distance	Driving Accuracy
1998	69.29 (N/A)	1.758 (N/A)	72.9 (N/A)	260.2 (N/A)	77.9 (N/A)
1999	70.02 (5)	1.772 (T12)	71.8 (9)	259.3 (66)	78.6 (5)
2000	69.56 (6)	1.752 (8)	72.5 (10)	264.8 (58)	79.3 (5)
2001	69.41 (3)	1.743 (8)	72.2 (T4)	272.8 (35)	80.1 (3)
2002	70.21 (10)	1.781 (T23)	70.4 (T15)	259.8 (78)	82.7 (2)
2003	70.07 (12)	1.782 (29)	70.7 (17)	265.7 (65)	80.9 (2)
2004	70.31 (11)	1.810 (46)	69.2 (28)	263.8 (66)	84.1 (1)

Allen Doyle (continued)

by almost half a stroke from the previous season (69.56 vs. 70.02)...Claimed the rain-shortened Toshiba Senior Classic. Birdied the 18th hole of Saturday's second round to open a one-stroke lead over Howard Twitty and Jim Thorpe. Slim margin held up when heavy rains before and during Sunday's final round made the Newport Beach CC course unplayable...Matched his career low of 63 in the second round of the EMC Kaanapali Classic...Also had a rare double eagle in the second round of The Home Depot Invitational, holing a 3-wood second shot on the second hole at the TPC at Piper Glen. **1999:** Finished third on the final official earnings list despite occasional back problems...Won four times in his first full season and claimed his first senior major championship among those victories...Went wire-to-wire for his initial triumph at The ACE Group Classic, easily defeating Vicente Fernandez by five strokes. Win made him the first player ever to triumph on both the Champions Tour and Nationwide Tours...Returned to Florida just over a month later to defeat Fernandez again at the PGA Seniors' Championship at PGA National. Came from four strokes back on Sunday with an 8-under-par 64 and won by two shots, the best come-from-behind effort on the circuit that season...Despite having back problems throughout the final round, bested Joe Inman in a playoff for the Cadillac NFL Golf Classic title...Used a then-course-record 63, his lowest score of the campaign, in the opening round of the TD Waterhouse Championship to edge Ed Dougherty by two strokes. **1998:** Became fully exempt for the 1999 season by garnering medalist honors at the Champions Tour National Qualifying Tournament at Grenelefe...His 13-under-par 275 total was a Q-school record at the time...Made six appearances after turning 50 in June, and had his best finish at the Raley's Gold Rush Classic, finishing T4 near Sacramento.

OTHER CAREER HIGHLIGHTS:

Had a long and distinguished amateur career before turning professional in 1995...Member of two Walker Cup teams (1991-93), and also represented the United States on three World Amateur Cup teams (1990, 1992, 1994)...Joined the Nationwide Tour in March 1995 and made an immediate splash, winning three times: Mississippi Gulf Coast Classic, Texarkana Open and the Tour Championship...Was that circuit's only three-time winner, and two of those titles came in playoffs...Bested Franklin Langham in the first at the Mississippi event and then slipped by John Maginnes to win the Nationwide Tour Championship at Settindown Creek GC in Atlanta...Second to Jerry Kelly on the final money list and earned a full exemption to the 1996 PGA TOUR...At age 47, he was the oldest rookie in PGA TOUR history when he began play in 1996...In two seasons on the TOUR, he won slightly more than $200,000...Made 28 starts each year and won $136,789 in 1996, his best year on TOUR...In his final year as an amateur in 1994, he won five titles, including the Porter Cup and the Sunnehanna Amateur...Was a semifinalist at the 1992 U.S. Amateur, losing 2 and 1 to Justin Leonard at Muirfield Village...Was the medalist at the 1991 event.

PERSONAL:

A member of the Norwich (VT) University Sports Hall of Fame...Played both hockey and golf at the college and graduated as the top scoring defenseman in Norwich history and he was also the ECAC golf champion in 1970...Has been generous in support of his alma mater. Donated $1.1 million to the university in the summer of 2004 to help fund an ongoing athletic building project...Also sponsors an annual golf tournament (Allen Doyle Golf Classic) at the university which helps support the college hockey program...Says his unorthodox swing developed from practicing in a room with a low ceiling as a youngster in Massachusetts...Played on a number of amateur teams with fellow Champions Tour player Jay Sigel...Member of the Georgia Sports Hall of Fame and the Georgia Golf Hall of Fame...Once caddied for Bruce Fleisher in the late 1960s...Got started in golf while caddying at Spring Valley CC in Sharon, MA, when he was 14...Is a big sports fan, especially of the Boston Red Sox, and tries to see games whenever he is on the road...His favorite athlete of all-time is former Boston Bruins great Bobby Orr...His first car was a 1969 Mercury Montego, which he bought in 1972 for $2,500...Has carried a Scotty Cameron putter in his bag for more than a dozen years and has used only two putters in his career. Used to carry a copy of the old Tommy Armour Ironmaster before that. He has also used a Ping Eye-2 sand wedge for more than 20 years...Daughter Michelle qualified for the 2003 U.S. Women's Amateur.

PLAYER STATISTICS

MISCELLANEOUS CHAMPIONS TOUR STATISTICS

2004 Low Round: 64–2004 JELD-WEN Tradition/3
Career Low Round: 63–4 times, most recent 2003 FleetBoston Classic/2
Career Largest Paycheck: $375,000–2001 Ford Senior Players Championship/1

MISCELLANEOUS PGA TOUR STATISTICS

Career Low Round: 65–2 times, most recent 1997 Phoenix Open/2
Career Largest Paycheck: $36,150–1998 Deposit Guaranty Golf Classic/T7

25 MEMORABLE MOMENTS

Rodriguez Wins Fourth Tournament in a Row

1987

With nine holes remaining, things appeared bleak for Chi Chi Rodriguez in his bid to become the first player to record four consecutive victories. Facing a three-stroke deficit with nine holes to play, Rodriguez birdied four of the last nine holes to overtake Bruce Crampton at Bent Tree Country Club in Dallas and win the Senior Players Reunion Pro-Am. Rodriguez's decisive stroke came at the par-3 17th, where he nailed a 6-iron 12 feet from the hole before dropping in a birdie putt. Rodriguez sealed the win by two-putting for par from six feet on the 18th hole.

CHAMPIONS TOUR 25

R. W. Eaks

EXEMPT STATUS: T4 at 2004 Champions Tour National Qualifying Tournament
FULL NAME: Robert W. Eaks
HEIGHT: 6-0
WEIGHT: 200
BIRTHDATE: May 22, 1952
BIRTHPLACE: Colorado Springs, CO
RESIDENCE: Scottsdale AZ
FAMILY: Wife, Karen; Dawn (3/15/79), Jeremy (12/14/85)
CLUB AFFILIATION: Southern Dunes GC (Scottsdale, AZ)
EDUCATION: University of Northern Colorado
SPECIAL INTERESTS: Family, sports
TURNED PROFESSIONAL: 1976
JOINED PGA TOUR: 1980

JOINED CHAMPIONS TOUR: 2002

BEST CHAMPIONS TOUR CAREER FINISH: T7—2002 Farmers Charity Classic.

BEST PGA TOUR CAREER FINISH: T7—1998 United Airlines Hawaiian Open.

NATIONWIDE TOUR VICTORIES (3): **1990** Quicksilver Open. **1993** Louisiana Open. **1997** San Jose Open.

OTHER VICTORIES (2): **1995** Taco Bell Newport Classic. **1996** Taco Bell Newport Classic.

PGA TOUR CAREER EARNINGS: $291,734

BEST 2004 CHAMPIONS TOUR FINISHES: T12—Constellation Energy Classic; T13—Senior PGA Championship.

2004 SEASON:

Will be fully exempt in 2005 for the first time in his career after finishing T4 at the Champions Tour National Qualifying Tournament at the King and Bear at World Golf Village in Florida...Made seven appearances during the year, with three top-25 finishes...Best showing came in his final start at the Constellation Energy Classic near Baltimore when he open-qualified and finished T12...Was T13 at the Senior PGA Championship at Valhalla...Was conditionally exempt at the start of the year but lost his exempt status when Hajime Meshiai turned 50 in March.

CHAMPIONS TOUR CAREER HIGHLIGHTS:

2003: Played in eight events during the season, with two top-25 finishes...Was T13 at the Music City Championship in Nashville in May after open qualifying. Fired a second-round 8-under-par 64 at the Springhouse GC, matching his low round on the Champions Tour...Also open-qualified for the U.S. Senior Open and finished T19...Tied for 16th at the Champions Tour National Qualifying Tournament at the close of 2003, but dropped to 17th after making bogey on the second extra hole in a 10-man playoff for the final three spots. Earned conditional exemption until mid-March when Hajime Meshiai turned 50...**2002:** Conditionally exempt after finishing ninth at the 2001 Champions Tour National Qualifying Tournament...Played in 14 events and finished 65th on the money list...Twice finished in the top 10 during the season. Was T7 in his first start shortly after turning 50 in May at the Farmers Charity Classic and was T10 at the Allianz Championship in September...Created a buzz at the U.S. Senior Open at Caves Valley when he blistered the course with an opening-round 64 near Baltimore. Could not follow that up in his final 54 holes and eventually T37.

OTHER CAREER HIGHLIGHTS:

Has played on both the Nationwide Tour and PGA TOUR...Played the Nationwide Tour on a full-time basis from 1990-1997 before earning a spot on the PGA TOUR in both 1998 and 1999. Finished 13th on the Nationwide Tour money list in 1998 to earn his card, and then retained it for the following year...Also played some events on the PGA TOUR in 1981...Overall, had played in 258 events (made 147 cuts) on the Nationwide Tour and 77 events (made 23 cuts) on the PGA TOUR prior to the 2005 season. Had won $608,704 on the Nationwide Tour and $291,734 on the PGA TOUR...Ninth on the Nationwide Tour money list in 1997 when he won the last of three titles on that Tour at the San Jose Open...Other titles came at the 1990 Quicksilver Open and the 1993 Louisiana Open...Was a runner-up five times...Most lucrative year on the PGA TOUR came in 1998 when he played 34 events and earned $199,499 to place 137th on the money list...Best finish on the PGA TOUR came in 1998 when he was T7 at the United Airlines Hawaiian Open...Was also T9 that year at the B.C. Open...At one point in his career in 1997 (after T4 at Hershey Open) he passed Olin Browne as the career money leader on the Nationwide Tour...Was injured in an automobile accident following the 1996 Mississippi Gulf Coast Classic and missed nearly two months before returning and losing in a playoff to Stewart Cink at the Ozarks Open...Won the 1995 and 1996 Taco Bell Newport Classics...Has 19 career holes-in-one to his credit.

PERSONAL:

Was a high school All-America selection in basketball and was a member of a Colorado state high school championship team...Being a member of that state championship squad remains his biggest thrill outside of golf...Got started in golf as a caddie...Favorite golf course is Desert Mountain in Scottsdale...Enjoys the movie "Rudy."

PLAYER STATISTICS

2004 CHAMPIONS TOUR STATISTICS:

Scoring Average	71.67	(N/A)
Driving Distance	291.2	(N/A)
Driving Accuracy Percentage	60.3%	(N/A)
Total Driving	1,998	(N/A)
Greens in Regulation Pct.	65.1%	(N/A)
Putting Average	1.720	(N/A)
Sand Save Percentage	55.3%	(N/A)
Eagles (Holes per)	378.0	(N/A)
Birdie Average	3.67	(N/A)
All-Around Ranking	1,569	(N/A)

MISCELLANEOUS CHAMPIONS TOUR STATISTICS

2004 Low Round: 68–2004 Greater Hickory Classic at Rock Barn/2
Career Low Round: 64–2 times, most recent 2003 Music City Championship at Gaylord Opryland/2
Career Largest Paycheck: $51,000–2002 Farmers Charity Classic/T7

MISCELLANEOUS PGA TOUR STATISTICS

Career Low Round: 63–1998 United Airlines Hawaiian Open/2
Career Largest Paycheck: $54,225–1998 United Airlines Hawaiian Open/T7

CHAMPIONS TOUR CAREER SUMMARY **PLAYOFF RECORD: 0-0**

Year	Events Played	1st	2nd	3rd	Top 10	Top 25	Earnings	Rank
2002	14				2	7	$245,705	65
2003	8					2	83,607	90
2004	7					3	114,135	82
Total	29				2	12	443,447	

COMBINED ALL-TIME MONEY (3 TOURS): **$1,343,885**

CHAMPIONS TOUR TOP TOURNAMENT SUMMARY

Year	02	03	04
Senior PGA Championship			T13
U.S. Senior Open	T37	T19	CUT
Ford Senior Players		T40	

Bob Eastwood

EXEMPT STATUS: Net-70 on All-Time Money List
FULL NAME: Robert Fred Eastwood
HEIGHT: 5-10
WEIGHT: 185
BIRTHDATE: February 9, 1946
BIRTHPLACE: Providence, RI
RESIDENCE: Fort Worth, TX

FAMILY: Wife, Dell; Scott (8/19/71), Steven (12/29/73); stepchildren John, Jill, Tony; two grandchildren
EDUCATION: San Jose State University
SPECIAL INTERESTS: Hunting, fishing, wildlife conservation
TURNED PROFESSIONAL: 1969
JOINED PGA TOUR: 1969

JOINED CHAMPIONS TOUR: 1996

CHAMPIONS TOUR VICTORIES (2): 1997 Bell Atlantic Classic, Raley's Gold Rush Classic.

PGA TOUR VICTORIES (3): 1984 USF&G Classic, Danny Thomas Memphis Classic. **1985** Byron Nelson Golf Classic.

OTHER VICTORIES (8): 1965 Sacramento City Amateur Championship, Stockton City Championship. **1966** California State Amateur, Stockton City Championship. **1968** West Coast Athletic Conference Championship [indiv]. **1973** Mini-Kemper Open. **1976** Little Bing Crosby. **1981** Morocco Grand Prix.

PGA TOUR CAREER EARNINGS: $1,546,106

PGA TOUR PLAYOFF RECORD: 1-0

BEST 2004 CHAMPIONS TOUR FINISH:
T12—Toshiba Senior Classic.

2004 SEASON:

Was among the top 20 in three events for the second consecutive year...T12 at the Toshiba Senior Classic, with three straight sub-par rounds at Newport Beach CC...Also T19 at the Liberty Mutual Legends of Golf in late April and then T18 at the 3M Championship, with rounds of 69 on the first and last day of the event.

CHAMPIONS TOUR CAREER HIGHLIGHTS:

2002: T8 at the rain-shortened Emerald Coast Classic. **2001:** T2 at the Mexico Senior Classic. Shot 7-under 65 in the opening round to share the first-round lead with Ed Dougherty. Was the 36-hole co-leader as well, but came up one stroke short of Mike McCullough on Sunday. Missed out on a playoff opportunity when McCullough birdied the 17th hole and then made a four-foot par-saving putt to win the tournament. Runner-up effort at Puebla with Jim Colbert was his best performance on the Champions Tour since capturing at the 1997 Raley's Gold Rush Classic near Sacramento. **2000:** T4 at the Emerald Coast Classic. **1999:** T9 at the FORD SENIOR PLAYERS Championship. **1998:** T5 at the Nationwide Championship, his best performance out of five top-10 efforts...Tied his career-low round by opening with a 64 at the EMC Kaanapali Classic on Maui in October. **1997:** More than doubled the earnings from his rookie year, thanks to multiple wins for the first time since 1984...Picked up his first Champions Tour title at the rain-shortened Bell Atlantic Classic. A 27-foot birdie putt on the 18th hole Saturday gave him a one-stroke lead over John Bland and Bob E. Smith that proved to be the winning margin when the final round was washed out. Dedicated victory to his father, who had suffered a series of strokes the previous week...Won again late in the campaign in wire-to-wire fashion at the Raley's Gold Rush Classic. Defeated Rick Acton by two strokes after making two late birdies to secure the victory in front of a large gallery of family and friends...Tied his career-low round with a 6-under-par 64 on the second day of the Emerald Coast Classic. **1996:** Became eligible for his first Champions Tour event at the American Express Invitational, and turned in par/better scores in nine of his first 10 rounds...Made a serious bid for his first Champions Tour title at the Emerald Coast Classic, rallying from a four-stroke deficit to finish in a five-way tie for first before losing to Lee Trevino in the ensuing playoff.

OTHER CAREER HIGHLIGHTS:

Last of three PGA TOUR titles came at the 1985 Byron Nelson Classic...Was the beneficiary of Payne Stewart's double-bogey on the last hole, then defeated Stewart on the first hole of their playoff...Did not win his first title, the 1984 USF&G Classic, until his 13th year on the PGA TOUR...Captured a second title later that same season at the Danny Thomas-Memphis Classic and went on to have his best year on TOUR, with $232,742 and a spot among the top-25 money-winners...First earned his player's card in the spring 1969 PGA TOUR National Qualifying Tournament, capturing medalist honors...Didn't start full-time on TOUR until 1972 because of a stint in the U.S. military...Had four holes-in-one on the PGA TOUR and 11 overall in competition...Inducted into the Sacramento Golf Hall of Fame early in the 2005 season.

PERSONAL:

Started to play golf at age 4 as a result of his father being in the golf business...Helped his family construct Dry Creek Ranch GC near Sacramento in the late 1960s...Spent a stint in the U.S. Army during the '60s and served in Korea...Biggest thrill in golf was having his son Scott caddie for him when he won the 1997 Raley's Gold Rush Classic in Sacramento...Has never won a tournament without his wife, Dell, in attendance.

PLAYER STATISTICS

2004 CHAMPIONS TOUR STATISTICS:

Scoring Average	72.80	(66)
Driving Distance	272.5	(38)
Driving Accuracy Percentage	64.9%	(64)
Total Driving	102	(68)
Greens in Regulation Pct.	62.2%	(66)
Putting Average	1.811	(47)
Sand Save Percentage	57.0%	(5)
Eagles (Holes per)	585.0	(59)
Birdie Average	2.95	(58)
All-Around Ranking	403	(58)

MISCELLANEOUS CHAMPIONS TOUR STATISTICS

2004 Low Round: 67–2 times, most recent 2004 Commerce Bank Long Island Classic/2
Career Low Round: 64–3 times, most recent 1998 EMC Kaanapali Classic/1
Career Largest Paycheck: $150,000–1997 Bell Atlantic Classic/1

MISCELLANEOUS PGA TOUR STATISTICS

Career Low Round: 64–2 times, most recent 1990 Canon Greater Hartford Open/2
Career Largest Paycheck: $90,000–2 times, most recent 1985 Byron Nelson Golf Classic/1

CHAMPIONS TOUR CAREER SUMMARY **PLAYOFF RECORD: 0-1**

Year	Events Played	1st	2nd	3rd	Top 10	Top 25	Earnings	Rank
1996	27		2		5	11	$413,000	32
1997	28	2		1	10	15	833,908	11
1998	30				5	17	440,163	39
1999	27				1	8	288,789	55
2000	27				2	12	389,829	49
2001	29		1	1	3	12	482,993	40
2002	29				1	6	279,529	62
2003	24					4	207,867	63
2004	22					4	189,578	66
Total	243	2	3	2	27	89	3,525,656	
COMBINED ALL-TIME MONEY (3 TOURS):							**$5,071,762**	

CHAMPIONS TOUR TOP TOURNAMENT SUMMARY

Year	96	97	98	99	00	01	02	03	04
Senior PGA Championship	T61					CUT	T27		
U.S. Senior Open			T28						
Ford Senior Players	T72	T52	T39	T9	T49	T63	T40	T56	76
JELD-WEN Tradition	T37	T8	T20	T45	T19	T43	T31	T16	T45
Charles Schwab Cup Champ		T19							

David Eger (EE-gurr)

EXEMPT STATUS: Top 30 on 2004 Champions Tour Money List
FULL NAME: David Benjamin Eger
HEIGHT: 6-0
WEIGHT: 190
BIRTHDATE: March 17, 1952
BIRTHPLACE: Fort Meade, MD
RESIDENCE: Ponte Vedra Beach, FL
FAMILY: Dottie, Michael
EDUCATION: University of North Carolina, East Tennessee State University
SPECIAL INTERESTS: Reading, cooking, wine collecting, golf course design
TURNED PROFESSIONAL: 1978, 2001
JOINED PGA TOUR: 1978

JOINED CHAMPIONS TOUR: 2002

CHAMPIONS TOUR VICTORIES (1): 2003 MasterCard Classic.

2004 CHARLES SCHWAB CUP FINISH: 24th - 779 points

BEST PGA TOUR CAREER FINISH: T5—1979 American Optical Classic.

OTHER VICTORIES (14): 1988 U.S. Mid-Amateur. **1991** North and South Amateur. **1992** Crump Cup. **1995** Coleman Invitational. **1997** Crump Cup, Hugh Wilson. **1998** Hugh Wilson. **1997** Travis Memorial. **1999** Travis Memorial, Coleman Invitational. **1999** and **2000** Azalea Amateur, Travis Memorial, North and South Amateur. **2001** Travis Memorial.

PGA TOUR CAREER EARNINGS: $31,014

BEST 2004 CHAMPIONS TOUR FINISHES: T3—Bayer Advantage Celebrity Pro-Am; T5—The First Tee Open at Pebble Beach presented by Wal-Mart, Charles Schwab Cup Championship.

2004 SEASON:

Made a late push to secure his position among the top-30 money-winners for the second consecutive year. Started the month of September in 35th position on the money list but earned almost half of his 2004 money total in the last seven tournaments when he finished among the top 10 four times...Was the first-round leader at The First Tee Open at Pebble Beach and eventually T5, one of two top-five efforts during this stretch in the fall...Was on the leaderboard for most of the last 36 holes at the season-ending Charles Schwab Cup Championship and eventually T5 in Sonoma after a final-round 69...Best effort of the campaign came in mid-June when he T3 at the weather-shortened Bayer Advantage Celebrity Pro-Am. Was involved in a car accident on Sunday morning in Kansas City and suffered minor injuries that forced him to miss the Bank of America Championship in Boston just over a week later...Also T6 at both the Toshiba Senior Classic and 3M Championship, posting three consecutive sub-par rounds in each event.

CHAMPIONS TOUR CAREER HIGHLIGHTS:

2003: Among the top 30 for the first time in his career, placing 23rd on the final money list with $851,217...Birdied three of the final four holes to edge Hale Irwin, Eamonn Darcy, Tom Jenkins and Bruce Lietzke by one stroke for the MasterCard Classic title at Bosque Real CC near Mexico City. Started the final round four strokes back, but closed with a 7-under-par 65 for his first professional victory. Win earned him $300,000, the largest check of his career...Also made a late run at the Liberty Mutual Legends of Golf. Ended T2 along with Dana Quigley, one stroke back of Bruce Lietzke. Made just one bogey during the week and played his last 39 holes of the Legends event without a blemish...Champions Tour Player of the Month for March. **2002:** Made 13 appearances in his rookie season on the Champions Tour and finished 83rd on the money list with $154,510...Lone top-10 effort was a T9 at the SBC Senior Open...Earned fully-exempt status for 2003 after T5 at the National Qualifying Tournament in the fall. Was tied for the first-round lead at World Woods GC with Des Smyth and then slipped back in the pack before rallying with rounds of 67-69 on the final two days of the event...T6 at the regional qualifier at Marsh Creek CC in St. Augustine, FL, to move into the finals. **2001:** Was conditionally exempt for the 2002 season after finishing 14th at the National Qualifying Tournament in Calimesa, CA. Was one of four players who T14 at 3-under-par 285 and secured the 14th position when he made par on the 10th extra hole in a playoff with Mark Pfeil.

OTHER CAREER HIGHLIGHTS:

Played 58 events on the PGA TOUR from 1978-81 before being reinstated as an amateur in 1986. Earned $31,014 during that period, with his best finish a T5 at the 1979 American Optical Classic in Sutton, MA...Made 30 cuts in those 58 starts. Best money-earning season came in 1979 when he won $12,804, including a career-best $8,475 at American Optical...Enjoyed a stellar amateur career. Member of three Walker Cup teams in 1989, 1991 and 2001 and a two-time member (1990, 2000) of the United States team that competed in the World Amateur Team Championships, including the victorious 2000 team...Played in nine U.S. Amateur and eight Mid-Amateur Championships. Defeated Scott Mayne, 2 and 1, at Prairie Dunes CC to win the 1988 U.S. Mid-Amateur title. Was a semifinalist at both the 1990 and 2000 U.S. Amateur, losing to Phil Mickelson in 1990 (5 and 3) and Jeff Quinney in 2000 (3 and 1)...Competed as an amateur at the 1989 Masters and the 1998 U.S. Open...Has one career hole-in-one in competition.

PERSONAL:

Served two stints as a member of the PGA TOUR staff. The first was from 1982-92 when he was Director of Tournament Administration and the second was from 1995-96 when he was the TOUR's Vice President of Competition...Also served as Senior Director of Rules and Competition at the United States Golf Association from 1992-95...Says his biggest thrill in golf was playing on three Walker Cup teams...Favorite courses are Pine Valley and Cypress Point...Favorite athlete is Tiger Woods and favorite entertainer is Vince Gill...Lists "Caddyshack" and "Get Shorty" as his favorite movies and his favorite TV show is "Seinfeld"...Biggest thrill outside of golf is being the father of two children.

PLAYER STATISTICS

MISCELLANEOUS CHAMPIONS TOUR STATISTICS
2004 Low Round: 65–2004 Outback Steakhouse Pro-Am/1
Career Low Round: 65–3 times, most recent 2004 Outback Steakhouse Pro-Am/1
Career Largest Paycheck: $300,000–2003 MasterCard Classic/1

MISCELLANEOUS PGA TOUR STATISTICS
Career Low Round: 66–2 times, most recent 1980 Hawaiian Open/3
Career Largest Paycheck: $8,475–1979 American Optical Classic/T5

CHAMPIONS TOUR CAREER SUMMARY — PLAYOFF RECORD: 0-0

Year	Events Played	1st	2nd	3rd	Top 10	Top 25	Earnings	Rank
2002	13				1	4	$154,510	83
2003	25	1	1		4	11	851,217	23
2004	28			1	7	14	773,443	25
Total	66	1	1	1	12	29	1,779,170	
COMBINED ALL-TIME MONEY (3 TOURS):							**$1,810,184**	

CHAMPIONS TOUR TOP TOURNAMENT SUMMARY

Year	02	03	04
Senior PGA Championship		T17	T47
U.S. Senior Open		CUT	T37
Ford Senior Players		T35	T54
Senior British Open		T8	T33
JELD-WEN Tradition	T64	T46	T59
Charles Schwab Cup Champ		T10	T5

CHAMPIONS TOUR YEAR-BY-YEAR STATISTICS (TOP 50 ON 2004 MONEY LIST)

	Scoring Average	Putting Average	Greens in Regulation	Driving Distance	Driving Accuracy
2002	71.78 (T46)	1.843 (T84)	72.5 (7)	278.3 (13)	60.8 (79)
2003	71.04 (32)	1.790 (36)	67.2 (T44)	276.6 (23)	61.6 (71)
2004	71.38 (32)	1.790 (T29)	66.3 (46)	269.7 (52)	66.3 (62)

Dave Eichelberger (EYE-cull-bur-gurr)

EXEMPT STATUS: Top 30 on All-Time Money List
FULL NAME: Martin Davis Eichelberger, Jr.
HEIGHT: 6-1
WEIGHT: 195
BIRTHDATE: September 3, 1943
BIRTHPLACE: Waco, TX
RESIDENCE: Honolulu, HI

FAMILY: Wife, D.C.; Martin (9/28/69), Clint (3/14/73), twins Emalia and Davis (10/22/97), two grandchildren
CLUB AFFILIATION: Oahu CC (Honolulu, HI); The Stanwich Club (Greenwich, CT)
EDUCATION: Oklahoma State University (B.A., 1965)
SPECIAL INTERESTS: Hunting, fishing, cooking
TURNED PROFESSIONAL: 1966
JOINED PGA TOUR: 1967

JOINED CHAMPIONS TOUR: 1993

CHAMPIONS TOUR VICTORIES (6): 1994 Quicksilver Classic. **1996** VFW Senior Championship. **1997** The Transamerica. **1999** U.S. Senior Open, Novell Utah Showdown. **2002** Emerald Coast Classic.

OTHER SENIOR VICTORIES (1): 1994 Diners Club Matches [with Raymond Floyd].

2004 CHARLES SCHWAB CUP FINISH: 57th - 109 points

PGA TOUR VICTORIES (4): 1971 Greater Milwaukee Open. **1977** Greater Milwaukee Open. **1980** Bay Hill Classic. **1981** Tallahassee Open.

OTHER VICTORIES (1): 1979 JCPenney Mixed Team Classic [with Murle Breer].

PGA TOUR CAREER EARNINGS: $1,186,505

PGA TOUR PLAYOFF RECORD: 1-1

BEST 2004 CHAMPIONS TOUR FINISHES: T6—Blue Angels Classic; T7—MasterCard Championship.

2004 SEASON:

Improved 20 spots on the final money list, thanks to a pair of top-10 finishes early in the season that accounted for more than a third of his official earnings for the year...Trailed by two strokes after 36 holes of the season-opening MasterCard Championship on the strength of a 7-under 65 in the second round, his best score on the Champions Tour since the 2002 campaign. Eventually T7 at Hualalai and $59,500 paycheck was his largest in almost two years...T6 at the Blue Angels Classic in mid-April after posting three consecutive sub-70 rounds...Also finished ninth on the final Georgia-Pacific Grand Champions money list, with $125,437. Was a runner-up to Jay Sigel in the Grand Champions event at the Bruno's Memorial Classic and was second to Tom Wargo in the over-60 competition at the Allianz Championship in Iowa...Made his 13th career hole-in-one in the first round of the Constellation Energy Classic (No. 11, 7-iron, 169 yards), the 14th of 15 aces on the circuit in 2004...Started his year by open-qualifying for the Sony Open in Hawaii but missed the cut in his first PGA TOUR appearance since the 2000 U.S. Open after shooting rounds of 79-78 at Waialae.

CHAMPIONS TOUR CAREER HIGHLIGHTS:

2003: Best effort was a T12 at the Greater Hickory Classic at Rock Barn. **2002:** Captured the Emerald Coast Classic when the final round of the event was canceled by a heavy thunderstorm. Victory was his first on the Champions Tour since the 1999 Novell Utah Showdown and triumph at age 58 made him the Champions Tour's oldest champion since Jim Colbert won the 2001 SBC Senior Classic at 60 years, 2 days. Made the first hole-in-one of his Champions Tour career at The Moors, holing a 7-iron shot from 190 yards on the eighth hole in the opening round. **2001:** Placed solo fifth at the TD Waterhouse Championship, one of four top-10 performances. **2000:** T5 at the rain-shortened Toshiba Senior Classic after being the first-round co-leader...Made the cut at the U.S. Open and finished T57. His second-round 69 matched Tiger Woods for the day's lowest round...Made his 1,000th career start (PGA/Champions Tour combined) at the BellSouth Senior Classic at Opryland (T37)...Was inducted into the Waco High School Sports Hall of Fame late in the year. **1999:** In the span of three weeks in July, became a multiple winner in the same season for the first time in his professional career. First won his biggest tournament ever, claiming the U.S. Senior Open. Outdueled Ed Dougherty over the final nine holes and eventually triumphed by three strokes...Rebounded from a double-bogey down the stretch to win the Novell Utah Showdown title in a playoff over Dana Quigley. Two best rounds of the season came on consecutive days and 15-under-par 129 total for the first 36 holes was a '99 best. **1997:** Had only one top-10 finish in the first half of the season, but reeled off 10 in the second half after finding a new driver...Starting at the First of America Classic, was among the top-10 in eight of his last 11 tournaments...Runner-up at the Vantage Championship, when he equaled Hale Irwin's Tanglewood Park course record at the time and his career-low round of 62 on the last day of the tournament...Won his third Champions Tour title the next week at The Transamerica. Overcame a three-stroke deficit to win by four at Silverado. **1996:** Outdueled local favorite Jim Colbert to win the VFW Senior Championship by two strokes. **1995:** Did not win an event, but recorded 11 top-10 finishes, including a playoff loss to Bruce Devlin at the rain-shortened FHP Health Care Classic in Ojai, CA. **1994:** Selected by his peers as the Comeback Player of the Year after claiming his first win in 13 years at the Quicksilver Classic. Victory came in the midst of a 12-week run in which he missed the top 20 only once...Also fell to Bob Murphy in a five-hole playoff at the Raley's Senior Gold Rush. **1993:** Made the first of seven appearances at the GTE North Classic in Indianapolis after turning 50 in early September.

OTHER CAREER HIGHLIGHTS:

Has been one of the busiest players on the PGA TOUR in his career. Prior to the 2005 season, had played in 1,143 events on three Tours, including 779 on the PGA TOUR, 355 on the Champions Tour and nine on the Nationwide Tour...Prepped for the Champions Tour by playing in five PGA TOUR events in 1993. Had missed 22 cuts in a row prior to finishing T87 at the 1993 Buick Invitational of California...Won four titles between 1971 and 1981, with his last TOUR victory coming in the 1981 Tallahassee Open...Defeated Bob Murphy and Mark O'Meara in a playoff for the Tallahassee title...Strung together back-to-back $100,000 seasons in 1988-89...Braved horrible weather conditions to claim the 1980 Bay Hill Classic and went on to finish 31st on the money list. Led the TOUR in Eagles that year with 16...First title, at the 1971 Greater Milwaukee Open, helped him earn his only top-10 finish on the official money list (ninth)...Earned his first PGA TOUR player's card in the 1967 Qualifying Tournament...Semifinalist at the 1964 U.S. Amateur...Named to the 1965 Walker Cup and America's Cup teams...Has had 13 career holes-in-one.

PERSONAL:

Blossomed into one of the country's finest amateurs while at Oklahoma State...Started in the game at age 13 in the junior programs at his family's club in Waco, TX.

PLAYER STATISTICS

2004 CHAMPIONS TOUR STATISTICS:

Scoring Average	72.38	(56)
Driving Distance	270.5	(48)
Driving Accuracy Percentage	69.0%	(53)
Total Driving	101	(67)
Greens in Regulation Pct.	63.2%	(60)
Putting Average	1.791	(31)
Sand Save Percentage	36.1%	(76)
Eagles (Holes per)	237.0	(22)
Birdie Average	3.11	(48)
All-Around Ranking	394	(54)

MISCELLANEOUS CHAMPIONS TOUR STATISTICS
2004 Low Round: 65–2004 MasterCard Championship/2
Career Low Round: 62–2 times, most recent 1997 Vantage Championship/3
Career Largest Paycheck: $315,000–1999 U.S. Senior Open/1

MISCELLANEOUS PGA TOUR STATISTICS
2004 Low Round: 78–Sony Open in Hawaii/2
Career Low Round: 62–2 times, most recent 1978 Atlanta Classic/1
Career Largest Paycheck: $54,000–1980 Bay Hill Classic/1

CHAMPIONS TOUR CAREER SUMMARY — PLAYOFF RECORD: 1-2

Year	Events Played	1st	2nd	3rd	Top 10	Top 25	Earnings	Rank
1993	7						$11,927	100
1994	33	1	1	1	7	19	535,087	20
1995	33		2	1	11	24	610,866	16
1996	35	1			2	9	334,586	40
1997	34	1	1		11	19	794,322	13
1998	33			1	4	13	417,153	42
1999	33	2	1		3	11	882,532	17
2000	32				3	15	448,490	40
2001	31				4	13	479,724	41
2002	31	1	1	1	4	7	642,487	32
2003	28					1	178,622	72
2004	25				2	7	315,317	52
Total	355	6	6	4	51	138	5,651,112	

COMBINED ALL-TIME MONEY (3 TOURS): $6,838,217

CHAMPIONS TOUR TOP TOURNAMENT SUMMARY

Year	94	95	96	97	98	99	00	01	02	03	04
Senior PGA Championship		38	CUT	CUT	CUT	T67	CUT	T40	CUT	T57	T19
U.S. Senior Open	T13	T48	T35	T5	56	1	T34	T44	T47	CUT	T37
Ford Senior Players	T22	T38	T61	T56	T30	T48	68	T23	T33	T71	T46
Senior British Open											T54
JELD-WEN Tradition	72	T28	T50	T21	T49	T36	T15	T34	T60	T52	T19
Charles Schwab Cup Champ	22	6		T9		31					

Keith Fergus

EXEMPT STATUS: PGA TOUR Career Victory List
FULL NAME: Keith Carlton Fergus
HEIGHT: 6-2
WEIGHT: 200
BIRTHDATE: March 3, 1954
BIRTHPLACE: Temple, TX
RESIDENCE: Sugar Land, TX

FAMILY: Wife, Cindy; Steven (9/4/79), Laura (3/5/84)
EDUCATION: University of Houston
SPECIAL INTERESTS: Fishing
TURNED PROFESSIONAL: 1976
JOINED PGA TOUR: 1977

JOINED CHAMPIONS TOUR: 2004

BEST CHAMPIONS TOUR CAREER FINISH:
4—2004 Toshiba Senior Classic.

2004 CHARLES SCHWAB CUP FINISH:
59th - 96 points

PGA TOUR VICTORIES (3): 1981 Memorial Tournament. **1982** Georgia-Pacific Atlanta Golf Classic. **1983** Bob Hope Desert Classic.

OTHER VICTORIES (2): 1971 Texas State Junior. **1976** Texas State Open.

NATIONWIDE TOUR VICTORIES (2): 1994 Panama City Beach Classic, Boise Open.

PGA TOUR CAREER EARNINGS: $1,546,009

PGA TOUR PLAYOFF RECORD: 2-0

BEST 2004 CHAMPIONS TOUR FINISH: 4—Toshiba Senior Classic.

2004 SEASON:

Made 18 appearances after turning 50 in early March, primarily through the Career Victory Category...In contention for the first time on the Champions Tour when he found himself one stroke off the lead after 36 holes of the Toshiba Senior Classic. Eventually placed fourth at Newport Beach after a final-round 69...Had four other top-20 finishes, including a T14 at the Bank of America Championship and a T16 at the Blue Angels Classic...Had a run of nine straight par-or-better rounds early in the year, including five straight in the 60s—Toshiba Senior Classic (three) and Blue Angels Classic (two)...Fired a 7-under-par 65 in the second round of the Administaff Small Business Classic to move up 40 spots. The round was also his lowest since shooting a second-round 64 at the 1997 Quad City Classic...Made one start on the PGA TOUR and missed the cut at the Bob Hope Chrysler Classic.

CHAMPIONS TOUR CAREER HIGHLIGHTS:

2003: Finished ninth at the 2003 National Qualifying Tournament at the TPC at Eagle Trace. Shot 72-hole total of 3-under 285 but missed earning fully-exempt status by two strokes. Tied Rafael Navarro for the ninth spot and then claimed sole possession of ninth place with a par on the first playoff hole.

OTHER CAREER HIGHLIGHTS:

Originally played the PGA TOUR from 1977-1986 and then requalified for the PGA TOUR at the 1995 National Qualifying Tournament and played the circuit again full time from 1995-1998...Claimed the first of his three PGA TOUR victories at the 1981 Memorial Tournament, edging Jack Renner by a stroke at Muirfield Village. Won the Georgia-Pacific Atlanta Classic a year later when he beat Raymond Floyd in a playoff. Won another playoff with Rex Caldwell to claim the 1983 Bob Hope Desert Classic...Has three top-10 finishes in major championships, including a T3 at the 1980 U.S. Open...Was a member of the Nationwide Tour in 1994, 1998-2000...Returned to competitive golf on the 1994 Nationwide Tour and won two events that year, finishing 13th on the final money list with $107,053. Made back-to-back birdies on the final two holes of the Panama City Beach Classic to win by two shots over Tommy Armour III. Defeated Bill Murchison with a par on the second playoff hole to win the Boise Open later that season...Served as the golf coach at the University of Houston from 1988-1994...Is the only three-time All-American in golf at the University of Houston (1974-1976). Won more individual titles than any other Cougar in school history, amassing 19 in his collegiate career...Runner-up to Fred Ridley at the 1975 U.S. Amateur at The CC of Virginia.

PERSONAL:

Started playing golf at age 8...Played football and basketball in high school, but enjoyed practicing golf more than other sports...Was attacked by killer bees on the driving range prior to his third round at the 1996 Nortel Open and was stung 10-15 times. His caddie, Artie Granfield, was stung 50-100 times...Began using the long putter in 1988 while coaching at the University of Houston...Has done some golf course design work on the side...Did soap commericals on television in the 1980s.

PLAYER STATISTICS

2004 CHAMPIONS TOUR STATISTICS:

Scoring Average	71.16	(27)
Driving Distance	280.8	(14)
Driving Accuracy Percentage	69.7%	(45)
Total Driving	59	(14)
Greens in Regulation Pct.	69.5%	(25)
Putting Average	1.796	(35)
Sand Save Percentage	26.4%	(80)
Eagles (Holes per)	168.0	(11)
Birdie Average	3.52	(21)
All-Around Ranking	258	(26)

MISCELLANEOUS CHAMPIONS TOUR STATISTICS

2004 Low Round: 65–2004 Administaff Small Business Classic/2
Career Low Round: 65–2004 Administaff Small Business Classic/2
Career Largest Paycheck: $96,000–2004 Toshiba Senior Classic/4

MISCELLANEOUS PGA TOUR STATISTICS

2004 Low Round: 68–Bob Hope Chrysler Classic/4
Career Low Round: 62–1996 Las Vegas Invitational/1
Career Largest Paycheck: $67,500–1983 Bob Hope Desert Classic/1

CHAMPIONS TOUR CAREER SUMMARY — PLAYOFF RECORD: 0-0

Year	Events Played	1st	2nd	3rd	Top 10	Top 25	Earnings	Rank
2004	18				1	6	$321,717	51
Total	18				1	6	321,717	
COMBINED ALL-TIME MONEY (3 TOURS):							**$2,063,997**	

CHAMPIONS TOUR TOP TOURNAMENT SUMMARY

Year	04
Senior PGA Championship	T21
Ford Senior Players	T46
JELD-WEN Tradition	T36

Vicente Fernandez (vee-CEN-tay)

EXEMPT STATUS: Top 30 on 2004 Champions Tour Money List
FULL NAME: Vicente Fernandez
HEIGHT: 5-10
WEIGHT: 170
BIRTHDATE: April 5, 1946
BIRTHPLACE: Corrientes, Argentina
RESIDENCE: Buenos Aires, Argentina
FAMILY: Wife, Esther; Gustavo (7/31/74), Norberto (11/29/75)
SPECIAL INTERESTS: Sports, music
TURNED PROFESSIONAL: 1964

JOINED CHAMPIONS TOUR: 1996

CHAMPIONS TOUR VICTORIES (4): 1996 Burnet Senior Classic. **1997** Bank One Classic. **1999** Las Vegas Senior Classic. **2003** ACE Group Classic.

OTHER SENIOR VICTORIES (1): 2000 Chrysler Senior Match Play Challenge

2004 CHARLES SCHWAB CUP FINISH: 32nd - 460 points

BEST PGA TOUR CAREER FINISH:
T11—1977 Houston Open.

OTHER VICTORIES (18): 1968 Argentine Open. **1969** Argentine Open. **1970** Dutch Open. **1972** Ford Maracaibo Open. **1975** Benson & Hedges Festival. **1977** Brazil Open. **1979** Colgate PGA Championship. **1981** Argentine Open **1983** Brazil Open. **1984** Argentine Open, Brazil Open. **1985** Argentine Open. **1986** Argentine Open. **1987** Argentine Open. **1990** Argentine Open, Tenerife Open. **1992** Murphy's English Open. **2001** Argentine Open.

PGA TOUR CAREER EARNINGS: $13,986

BEST 2004 CHAMPIONS TOUR FINISHES: T3—3M Championship; T4—JELD-WEN Tradition; T7—Outback Steakhouse Pro-Am.

2004 SEASON:

Finished in the top 30 on the money list for the eighth time in nine years when he claimed the 30th spot, thanks in part to a late-season run. Earned nearly half his money ($301,340) in the last two months of the campaign to get into the season-ending Charles Schwab Cup Championship...Had two productive weeks in August. Made a spirited run for the title in the year's last major championship at the JELD-WEN Tradition late in the month. Entered the final round tied for the lead with Peter Jacobsen and held the lead for a large portion of Sunday's final round before consecutive bogeys on Nos. 16 and 17 knocked him from contention. He finished T4, two behind Craig Stadler...Strung together three consecutive sub-par rounds in his previous start at the 3M Championship to finish T3, three strokes back of Tom Kite. Performance in Minnesota was his best on the Champions Tour since 2003 U.S. Senior Open...Was T9 at the MasterCard Championship to start the year and then was T7 at the Outback Steakhouse Pro-Am one month later in Tampa...Only Tom Kite converted more par-5 birdie opportunities (43.9 percent to 43.1 percent).

CHAMPIONS TOUR CAREER HIGHLIGHTS:

2003: Returned to the top 30 after a year's absence despite missing just over a month of the season with family business in South America...Was among the top three in four events, one more than his combined top-three finishes in the last two seasons...Got his year started in a big way by winning The ACE Group Classic in his second appearance. Played all but the first hole of the event without a bogey and notched his first Champions Tour win in three years and nine months. Three-stroke win over Des Smyth and Tom Watson in Naples included holing a 61-foot birdie putt on the last hole. Hit 44 of 54 greens in regulation at The Club at TwinEagles, including all 18 greens on Sunday...Finished T2 at the Emerald Coast Classic, four strokes back of Bob Gilder, despite posting a 54-hole score of 13-under 197 that included just one bogey...Was also third at the Bayer Advantage Celebrity Pro-Am after being the 36-hole leader near Kansas City and third at the U.S. Senior Open, three behind Bruce Lietzke. Was the second-round leader at Inverness following a 7-under-par 64, the lowest second-round score in U.S. Senior Open history...Improved his putting, moving from T47 in 2002 to T13 and also added over 10 yards in driving distance from previous year. **2002:** Made a strong run to earn a spot in the year-end event, staying in contention all three days at the SBC Championship in San Antonio, but could only muster a solo third-place finish (two strokes behind winner Dana Quigley) in the year's final full-field event...Was plagued by off-course distractions during the year, including deaths in his family. **2001:** T2 at the Las Vegas Senior Classic. Trailed Jerry McGee by three strokes entering the final round, but shot an even-par 72 and was three strokes back of Bruce Fleisher at the end...Made it to the finals of the Enterprise Rent-A-Car Match Play Championship before losing, 1-up, to Leonard Thompson. **2000:** Finished second to Bruce Fleisher by two points at the Royal Caribbean Classic, a Modified Stableford event...Was also among the early leaders at the Nationwide Championship, but was edged out on the final day by Hale Irwin and T2 at the GC of Georgia...Capped his season by winning the Chrysler Senior Match Play Challenge at the Hyatt Dorado Beach in Puerto Rico. Went into the event as the lowest of 16 seeded players and upset Larry Nelson, John Jacobs and Raymond Floyd en route to the final match against Leonard Thompson. Birdied the first hole of a sudden-death playoff to beat Thompson for the title and $240,000 first-place check...Also won the Argentine Open for the seventh time, becoming the oldest ever to claim the biggest event in the country. **1999:** Among the circuit's top-10 money-winners for the first time in his career, eclipsing the seven-figure mark for the first time ever...Ended a 20-month victory drought with a two-stroke win at the Las Vegas Senior Classic. Broke a tie with Dave Eichelberger by making a 30-foot eagle putt at the 16th hole. The $210,000 winner's check in Vegas was his largest as a professional at the time...Also came close to victory earlier in the campaign at the PGA Seniors' Championship. Shared the lead heading into the final round at PGA National, but eventually second to Allen Doyle by two strokes...Was also a runner-up at The ACE Group Classic in Naples, a distant five strokes back of Doyle. **1998:** Closed with a 68 at the Las Vegas Senior Classic, but fell one stroke shy of Hale Irwin...Challenged Irwin again at the U.S. Senior Open at Riviera CC, but again came up one short. **1997:** Emerged victorious at the final Bank One Classic in Lexington when he seized the lead with three holes to play and went on to record a one-stroke victory over Isao Aoki. **1996:** First win was a memorable one...Posted a one-stroke victory at the Burnet Senior Classic in July and in the process, became just the fifth Monday qualifier in Champions Tour history to win a tournament. Breakthrough came in just his eighth start on the circuit...Was in contention with Hale Irwin in his first Champions Tour start before finishing third at the 1996 PGA Seniors' Championship.

CHAMPIONS TOUR CAREER SUMMARY — PLAYOFF RECORD: 0-0

Year	Events Played	1st	2nd	3rd	Top 10	Top 25	Earnings	Rank
1996	20	1		1	10	14	$605,251	18
1997	29	1		1	9	19	689,915	17
1998	24		2	2	9	20	996,338	12
1999	28	1	2	1	9	18	1,108,245	9
2000	27		2		6	22	758,048	23
2001	29		2		7	18	852,442	22
2002	28			1	4	15	572,233	35
2003	21	1	1	2	7	14	1,038,339	17
2004	26			1	4	16	657,367	30
Total	232	4	9	9	65	156	7,278,177	
COMBINED ALL-TIME MONEY (3 TOURS):							**$7,292,163**	

CHAMPIONS TOUR TOP TOURNAMENT SUMMARY

Year	96	97	98	99	00	01	02	03	04
Senior PGA Championship	3	T35	T6	2	T6	T25	CUT	T7	T19
U.S. Senior Open	T35	T32	2	CUT	T15	CUT	T25	3	CUT
Ford Senior Players	T16	15	T30	T29	WD	T17	T27	T33	T34
JELD-WEN Tradition		T46	3	T3	T19	T29	T44	T20	T4
Charles Schwab Cup Champ	T8	T11	T4	T11	T17	T16		T13	T20

CHAMPIONS TOUR YEAR-BY-YEAR STATISTICS (TOP 50 ON 2004 MONEY LIST)

	Scoring Average	Putting Average	Greens in Regulation	Driving Distance	Driving Accuracy
1996	70.85 (11)	1.749 (1)	67.9 (T21)	265.4 (T29)	66.2 (60)
1997	70.98 (13)	1.783 (T19)	69.1 (T9)	263.2 (36)	65.7 (T53)
1998	70.51 (5)	1.755 (6)	68.2 (15)	267.2 (T28)	67.4 (T58)
1999	70.25 (T8)	1.773 (T14)	70.3 (T17)	270.0 (23)	70.5 (40)
2000	70.38 (14)	1.770 (T18)	69.8 (20)	276.2 (14)	64.3 (81)
2001	70.93 (T20)	1.782 (T21)	69.6 (T17)	276.3 (21)	66.3 (T67)
2002	71.18 (29)	1.802 (T47)	67.0 (T38)	269.3 (42)	65.2 (T60)
2003	70.46 (T21)	1.769 (T13)	68.7 (31)	279.5 (T15)	60.1 (76)
2004	71.05 (23)	1.788 (28)	70.2 (19)	280.2 (17)	67.0 (59)

Vicente Fernandez (Continued)

OTHER CAREER HIGHLIGHTS:

Prior to joining the Champions Tour, played on the PGA European Tour for more than two decades and collected five official victories...Won the 1992 Murphy's English Open at The Belfry in dramatic fashion, sinking an 87-foot putt on the last hole for the victory. Triumph at age 46 made him the oldest winner on the European Tour since 48-year-old Neil Coles won the 1982 Sanyo Open...Initial European Tour win came in 1970, when he claimed the Heineken Dutch Open in Eindhoven...Also victorious at the Colgate PGA Championship in 1979 at St. Andrews, defeating Gary Player and Italy's Baldo Dassu by one stroke...Best season in Europe came in 1992, when he was 16th on the Order of Merit with winnings of £217,453 (well over $300,000)...Played in seven PGA TOUR events in 1977 and four the following year, making the cut in all 11 starts with winnings totaling $10,487...Best effort was a T11 at the 1977 Houston Open...Has won almost 100 tournaments in his career, including numerous South American titles...Member of five Argentine World Cup teams and also played on numerous other international teams...Once held the PGA European Tour record for most birdies in one round (10) at the 1983 Jersey Open on his way to a 62. Also had 62 in the 1971 French Open...Has 22 career holes-in-one.

PERSONAL:

The second Argentine to take a crack at the Champions Tour. Countryman Roberto De Vicenzo, winner of the 1967 British Open, played throughout the 1980s and early 1990s...Nickname is "Chino"...Competed on the European Tour with current Champions Tour players John Bland, Hugh Baiocchi and Jose Maria Canizares...Born with one leg shorter than the other and walks with a slight limp...Caddied for Chi Chi Rodriguez at the 1962 World Cup in Argentina...One of his sons, Gustavo, was his caddie for his first Champions Tour win at the Burnet Senior Classic.

PLAYER STATISTICS

MISCELLANEOUS CHAMPIONS TOUR STATISTICS

2004 Low Round: 66–5 times, most recent 2004 Charles Schwab Cup Championship/4
Career Low Round: 63–1997 Emerald Coast Classic/1
Career Largest Paycheck: $240,000–2003 ACE Group Classic/1

MISCELLANEOUS PGA TOUR STATISTICS

Career Low Round: 67–1977 Buick Open/4
Career Largest Paycheck: $3,800–1977 Houston Open/T11

25 MEMORABLE MOMENTS

Trevino Takes Champions Tour by Storm in Rookie Year

1990

Lee Trevino didn't waste any time making his mark on the Champions Tour when his chance came in 1990. Quick out of the gate, the Merry Mex won three times in his first four outings. He would go on to capture seven wins and earn both Rookie of the Year and Player of the Year honors, as well as the Byron Nelson Award as scoring leader. The 1981 World Golf Hall of Fame inductee became the first Champions Tour player to go over the $1-million mark in earnings and was the leading money winner in all of golf that season.

CHAMPIONS TOUR 25

Ed Fiori (fee-OR-ee)

EXEMPT STATUS: Top 30 on 2004 Champions Tour Money List
FULL NAME: Edward Ray Fiori
HEIGHT: 5-7
WEIGHT: 220
BIRTHDATE: April 21, 1953
BIRTHPLACE: Lynwood, CA
RESIDENCE: Sugar Land, TX
FAMILY: Wife, Debbie; Kelly Ann (1/29/82), Michael Ray (10/22/84)
EDUCATION: University of Houston
SPECIAL INTERESTS: Fishing, bird hunting
TURNED PROFESSIONAL: 1977
JOINED PGA TOUR: 1978

JOINED CHAMPIONS TOUR: 2003

CHAMPIONS TOUR VICTORIES (1): 2004 MasterCard Classic.

2004 CHARLES SCHWAB CUP FINISH: 35th - 392 points

PGA TOUR VICTORIES (4): 1979 Southern Open. **1981** Western Open. **1982** Bob Hope Desert Classic. **1996** Quad City Classic.

PGA TOUR CAREER EARNINGS: $2,270,198

PGA TOUR PLAYOFF RECORD: 2-0

BEST 2004 CHAMPIONS TOUR FINISHES: 1—MasterCard Classic; T9—Royal Caribbean Golf Classic, Liberty Mutual Legends of Golf.

2004 SEASON:

Broke through for his first professional victory in nearly eight years when he defeated Graham Marsh in a three-hole playoff to win the MasterCard Classic in March near Mexico City. Had birdied the final hole in regulation, which helped him close with a 5-under-par 67, one of only two players to finish below 70 on Sunday. Eventually earned a spot in the playoff with Marsh. Appeared to be out of contention when Marsh's lead on the field grew to three strokes with six holes to play, but found himself in a playoff when Marsh three-putted holes 16 and 17 to drop back into a tie with Fiori at the close of play. Finished the playoff with a par on the third extra hole to earn the $300,000 first prize, the largest check of his career. Victory was even more remarkable in that he had battled health issues (elevated blood pressure due to an alteration in his medication) in the second round, which nearly forced him out of the event. Medication was a result of a heart attack he suffered in January while undergoing a stress test...His seven-stroke comeback win against Marsh tied the second best come-from-behind effort in Champions Tour history...Other top-10 finishes were a pair of T9s at the Royal Caribbean Classic and Liberty Mutual Legends of Golf...Played in the Bob Hope Chrysler Classic shortly after his heart attack but missed the cut.

CHAMPIONS TOUR CAREER HIGHLIGHTS:

2003: Became eligible for the Champions Tour in April and debuted at the Kinko's Classic of Austin (T35)...Posted best finish of the year when he was T6 at the FleetBoston Classic after three straight rounds in the 60s...Second top-10 came in his last start of the campaign, a T9 at the Turtle Bay Championship in Hawaii...Led the Champions Tour in Scrambling, getting the ball up and down for par 66.4 percent of the time. **2002:** Attended the 2002 Champions Tour National Qualifying Tournament in November and finished T11 at the World Woods GC in Florida, earning a conditional exemption for the 2003 season. Also eligible for events via the PGA TOUR Career Victory category.

OTHER CAREER HIGHLIGHTS:

After enjoying three wins in a four-year span early in career, had to wait another 14 years, 8 months and 2 days for his fourth title, the 1996 Quad City Classic. Only Butch Baird, who went 15 years, 5 months and 10 days between his first and second TOUR victories, had a longer drought. Trailed Tiger Woods by one stroke after 54 holes but closed with a 67 for a two-stroke victory over Andrew Magee. His first-place check for $216,000 was more than he had won in any previous season on the PGA TOUR...Scored first victory in second season, winning playoff over Tom Weiskopf at 1979 Southern Open...Won 1981 Western Open by four-strokes over Jim Colbert, Greg Powers and Jim Simons despite an opening-round 74...Defeated Tom Kite in playoff to win 1982 Bob Hope Desert Classic...Prior to 2005 season, had played in 567 PGA TOUR events and made 349 cuts with earnings totaling $2,270,198...Best season from an earnings standpoint came in 1996 when he won $261,292...Best finish on the money list was 26th in 1983 when he won $175,619...Made three career starts on the Nationwide Tour, winning $1,890...Medalist at the 1977 PGA TOUR Qualifying Tournament at Pinehurst CC...Earned All-America honors at the University of Houston in 1977, the year the Cougars won the national championship. Played for the legendary coach Dave Williams.

PERSONAL:

Nicknamed "The Grip" because of his unusually strong grip on the club...Victory at Quad City postponed plans to retire from game and become a charter-boat captain...Got started in the game when he would sneak through the barbed wire onto a nine-hole course near his home in Downey, CA...Made his PGA TOUR debut in 1978 when he finished T66 at the Joe Garagiola-Tucson Open and won $325.

PLAYER STATISTICS

MISCELLANEOUS CHAMPIONS TOUR STATISTICS
2004 Low Round: 65–2004 JELD-WEN Tradition/2
Career Low Round: 65–2004 JELD-WEN Tradition/2
Career Largest Paycheck: $300,000–2004 MasterCard Classic/1

MISCELLANEOUS PGA TOUR STATISTICS
2004 Low Round: 72–Bob Hope Chrysler Classic/2
Career Low Round: 63–2 times, most recent 1992 Phoenix Open/2
Career Largest Paycheck: $216,000–1996 Quad City Classic/1

CHAMPIONS TOUR CAREER SUMMARY — PLAYOFF RECORD: 1-0

Year	Events Played	1st	2nd	3rd	Top 10	Top 25	Earnings	Rank
2003	18				2	6	$260,810	54
2004	28	1			3	9	689,420	27
Total	46	1			5	15	950,230	
COMBINED ALL-TIME MONEY (3 TOURS):							**$3,222,318**	

CHAMPIONS TOUR TOP TOURNAMENT SUMMARY

Year	03	04
Senior PGA Championship	CUT	T31
U.S. Senior Open	T47	WD
Ford Senior Players		T13
Senior British Open	T62	
JELD-WEN Tradition	T28	T29
Charles Schwab Cup Champ		27

CHAMPIONS TOUR YEAR-BY-YEAR STATISTICS (TOP 50 ON 2004 MONEY LIST)

	Scoring Average	Putting Average	Greens in Regulation	Driving Distance	Driving Accuracy
2003	71.38 (45)	1.819 (T64)	65.1 (56)	254.5 (84)	74.7 (14)
2004	71.74 (41)	1.817 (54)	62.1 (67)	248.3 (79)	80.7 (6)

Bruce Fleisher (FLY-shur)

EXEMPT STATUS: Top 30 on 2004 Champions Tour Money List
FULL NAME: Bruce Lee Fleisher
HEIGHT: 6-3
WEIGHT: 205
BIRTHDATE: October 16, 1948
BIRTHPLACE: Union City, TN
RESIDENCE: BallenIsles, FL

FAMILY: Wife, Wendy; Jessica (3/23/80)
EDUCATION: Miami-Dade Junior College, Furman University
SPECIAL INTERESTS: Music, fitness, nutrition
TURNED PROFESSIONAL: 1969
JOINED PGA TOUR: 1972

JOINED CHAMPIONS TOUR: 1999

CHAMPIONS TOUR VICTORIES (18): 1999 Royal Caribbean Classic, American Express Invitational, The Home Depot Invitational, BellSouth Senior Classic at Opryland, Lightpath Long Island Classic, The Transamerica, EMC Kaanapali Classic. **2000** Royal Caribbean Classic, GTE Classic, The Home Depot Invitational, Lightpath Long Island Classic. **2001** Las Vegas Senior Classic, The Home Depot Invitational, U.S. Senior Open. **2002** RJR Championship. **2003** Verizon Classic. **2004** Royal Caribbean Golf Classic, Bruno's Memorial Classic.

OTHER SENIOR VICTORIES (1): 2000 AIB Irish Seniors Open

2004 CHARLES SCHWAB CUP FINISH: 9th - 1,744 points

PGA TOUR VICTORIES (1): 1991 New England Classic.

OTHER VICTORIES (8): 1968 U.S. Amateur. **1971** Brazilian Open. **1977** Little Crosby Pro-Am. **1989** PGA Club Pro Championship, **1990** PGA Cup [team], Jamaican Open, Bahamas Open, Brazilian Open.

PGA TOUR CAREER EARNINGS: $1,695,111

PGA TOUR PLAYOFF RECORD: 1-0

BEST 2004 CHAMPIONS TOUR FINISHES: 1—Royal Caribbean Golf Classic, Bruno's Memorial Classic; 2—Greater Hickory Classic at Rock Barn; 3—Ford Senior Players Championship.

2004 SEASON:

Finished in the top 10 on the money list and went over $1 million in season earnings for the sixth consecutive year...Got off to a fast start early in the season when he prevailed by one stroke over Dana Quigley at the Royal Caribbean Golf Classic. Continued his mastery at the Crandon Park GC, winning the event for the third time in six tries. His 6-under-par total of 210 was the highest winning total in tournament history. He was the only player to finish all three rounds under par, including a final-round 71 in windy conditions. Birdied the final hole to hold off Quigley, and in the process became the first three-time winner in tournament history. The victory also marked the second time in his career he had won the same event three times, having done so at the Home Depot Invitational from 1999-01. Win near Miami marked the sixth straight year he had posted at least one victory...Became the first multiple winner of the 2004 season when he went wire-to-wire near Birmingham and cakewalked to a seven-stroke victory at the Bruno's Memorial Classic. Victory was his 18th career title on the Champions Tour, and he won his 12th different tournament. Made just two bogeys in the event and led the field by hitting 48 of 54 greens (90.7 percent). Winning margin at Greystone was his biggest ever...Was thwarted in his bid to win a third title at the Greater Hickory Classic at Rock Barn in August. Started the final round with a three-stroke advantage but was overtaken by Doug Tewell and finished second in Hickory despite posting a 4-under 68 on Sunday...His solo third-place finish at the Ford Senior Players Championship was his best ever in that event...Finished T4 at the JELD-WEN Tradition after a closing-round, 6-under-par 66. Was also T4 at the SBC Championship.

CHAMPIONS TOUR CAREER HIGHLIGHTS:

2003: After placing among the top three money-winners for four straight years, slipped to 10th in official earnings...Extended to five consecutive, his streak of years with at least one Champions Tour victory when he claimed his second Verizon Classic in the last four years early in the campaign. Outdueled Hale Irwin down the stretch at the TPC of Tampa Bay. Was the beneficiary of a two-stroke swing at the 17th hole on Sunday and went on to record his 16th career title on the circuit...Also challenged Tom Jenkins down the stretch at the Bruno's Memorial Classic, but finished solo second after making bogey on two of the last three holes...Made a spirited bid for another victory at the Columbus Southern Open, but his closing-round, 8-under-par 62 fell two strokes shy of eventual winner Morris Hatalsky...Opened with a 7-under-par 64 at the FleetBoston Classic in August and hung in contention for the duration before falling by three strokes to Allen Doyle and finishing T2 along with Bob Gilder...Also T2 at the Allianz Championship despite shooting a 7-under 64 in the second round, the low 18-hole score in the event...The week prior at the Long Island Classic, set a tournament mark by opening with an 8-under-par 62 on the Eisenhower Red course, but slipped to T16 after rounds of 72-71 on the weekend. **2002:** Recorded 20 top-10 finishes with 46 rounds in the 60s, both second to Hale Irwin (22/50)...Claimed his first title in more than 12 months when he had a record-setting performance at the RJR Championship. Was a five-stroke victor over Hale Irwin, and in the process, set Champions Tour 36- and 54-hole scoring records. His 54-hole total of 191 (19-under-par) broke the previous low by two strokes (set in 1989 by Bob Charles and matched by Charles Coody in 1991 and Gibby Gilbert in 1992) and his 36-hole score broke the old mark by two strokes, as well (set by Jim Colbert in 1994 and matched by Hale Irwin in 1997). Opened the tournament by tying the Champions Tour record with a 60 (10-under-par) that included pars on the last four holes. Had 10 birdies and 23 putts on the par-70 Tanglewood course. Victory made him the last of three wire-to-wire winners during the year (Tom Kite, MasterCard Championship, and Bob Gilder, FleetBoston Classic. **2001:** Earned over $2 million for the third straight year and went down to the wire with Allen Doyle for the top spot in the first Charles Schwab Cup competition and the money list...Among his three victories was his first major championship on the Champions Tour at the U.S. Senior Open...Joined Doyle as the only players to finish in the top 10 in all four senior major championships...Of his 94 rounds, 48 were in the 60s, and he had 70 sub-par rounds...Claimed his biggest career title at the U.S. Senior Open at Salem CC near Boston, one year after losing the 54-hole lead at Saucon Valley and finishing second to Hale Irwin. Was among four players four strokes back with one round to play, but carded a steady 68 in the final round to edge Gil Morgan and Isao Aoki by one stroke...Earlier in the year, overcame a two-stroke deficit entering the final round of the Las Vegas Senior Classic to win by three strokes...Became just the sixth player in Champions Tour history to win the same event three straight times when he triumphed at The Home Depot Invitational with a tournament-record score of 15-

CHAMPIONS TOUR CAREER SUMMARY — PLAYOFF RECORD: 1-2

Year	Events Played	1st	2nd	3rd	Top 10	Top 25	Earnings	Rank
1999	32	7	7	1	19	27	$2,515,705	1
2000	30	4	5	3	19	29	2,373,977	2
2001	31	3	3	4	20	29	2,411,543	2
2002	31	1	4	2	20	29	1,860,534	3
2003	29	1	3	1	10	23	1,306,013	10
2004	28	2	1	1	11	18	1,537,571	5
Total	181	18	23	12	99	155	12,005,344	
COMBINED ALL-TIME MONEY (3 TOURS):							**$13,739,228**	

CHAMPIONS TOUR TOP TOURNAMENT SUMMARY

Year	99	00	01	02	03	04
Senior PGA Championship	T3	T38	7	T6	T10	CUT
U.S. Senior Open	CUT	2	1	CUT	T43	T12
Ford Senior Players	T7	T18	T4	T12	T12	3
Senior British Open						T18
JELD-WEN Tradition	27	4	T7	T9	T20	T4
Charles Schwab Cup Champ	T2	T19	T18	T19	T10	T13

CHAMPIONS TOUR YEAR-BY-YEAR STATISTICS (TOP 50 ON 2004 MONEY LIST)

	Scoring Average	Putting Average	Greens in Regulation	Driving Distance	Driving Accuracy
1999	69.19 (1)	1.728 (1)	73.9 (2)	263.6 (T49)	79.4 (3)
2000	69.01 (3)	1.743 (6)	75.3 (T4)	274.0 (T22)	78.5 (T6)
2001	69.52 (4)	1.736 (3)	73.2 (2)	268.0 (61)	79.8 (4)
2002	69.73 (4)	1.761 (7)	72.9 (5)	262.2 (69)	79.4 (6)
2003	70.02 (9)	1.759 (7)	71.7 (T10)	264.1 (69)	75.5 (11)
2004	70.33 (12)	1.767 (13)	72.6 (10)	265.9 (61)	78.5 (9)

Bruce Fleisher (Continued)

under 201. Was the only player in the field to post three rounds in the 60s and was three strokes better than John Bland. **2000:** Successfully defended three titles during the year...Edged Vicente Fernandez by two points at the Royal Caribbean Classic, thanks to five birdies on Sunday in the Modified Stableford format event...Bested Hubert Green in a playoff at The Home Depot Invitational, making birdie on the third extra hole of overtime. Went wire-to-wire for the second year in a row to claim the Lightpath Long Island Classic, defeating Dana Quigley by two strokes...Had outdistanced Quigley by four strokes earlier in the year at the GTE Classic in Tampa and earned February Player of the Month honors. GTE Classic win gave him nine victories in his first 36 senior career starts and the nine wins came in a period of one year, 15 days, the fastest anyone has reached that mark in Champions Tour history...Suffered his most disappointing defeat of the season at the U.S. Senior Open at Saucon Valley. Fired a course-record, 7-under 64 on the first day and was also the 36- and 54-hole leader before being overtaken by Hale Irwin on Sunday. **1999:** Was the dominant player on the Champions Tour and collected all top post-season honors including Player of the Year, Rookie of the Year and the Byron Nelson Trophy for lowest scoring average (69.19)...Was the first rookie since Lee Trevino in 1990 to win the Arnold Palmer Award as the leading money-winner with $2,515,705 ($78,894/start), the second highest single-season total in the history of the circuit at the time...Also joined Trevino (1990), Bruce Crampton (1986) and Miller Barber (1981) as the only players to win seven official events in their first year on the Champions Tour...Had 56 rounds in the 60s, a record at the time, and was under par in 75 of his 96 rounds played (78.1 percent)...Became the eighth player in Champions Tour history to win his debut when he went wire-to-wire in claiming the Royal Caribbean Classic at Key Biscayne...Won the American Express Invitational in Sarasota by three strokes over Larry Nelson the very next week to become the first player ever to claim his first two starts on the circuit...Added a third title in late April at The Home Depot Invitational, edging Terry Dill and Jim Holtgrieve by a stroke in Charlotte...Used a 9-under-par 63 on Saturday, his low round of the year, to nip Al Geiberger by a shot for the BellSouth Senior Classic at Opryland title in Nashville...Went wire-to-wire in early August to clip Allen Doyle by two strokes at the Lightpath Long Island Classic...Outdueled Doyle again late in the season at The Transamerica, then clinched the money title two weeks later by edging Doyle again at the EMC Kaanapali Classic. **1998:** Earned a full exemption for the 1999 season after finishing second at the Champions Tour National Qualifying Tournament at Grenelefe...Fired four consecutive sub-par rounds and ended up three strokes back of Allen Doyle.

OTHER CAREER HIGHLIGHTS:

Played 410 events on the PGA TOUR, starting as an amateur in 1969 through the 1998 season, with earnings of nearly $1.7 million...Made 280 cuts in his career and probably enjoyed his greatest success in a three-year span in the early 1990s...Won his only PGA TOUR title in 1991 when he went seven extra holes to defeat Ian Baker-Finch, who would go on to win the British Open the next week. Rolled in 50-foot birdie putt on seventh playoff hole to defeat Baker-Finch...Had his best year in 1992 when he won $236,516 and finished 68th on the money list...Posted the first of four runner-up finishes when he was second at the 1974 Quad Cities Classic. Other second-place finishes were at the 1978 Magnolia Classic, the 1981 USF&G New Orleans Open and the 1993 New England Classic...Co-winner of the 1991 Hilton Bounceback Award...Joined the PGA TOUR on a full-time basis in 1972 after a much-heralded amateur career...Winner of the 1968 U.S. Amateur at Scioto CC in Columbus, OH...That victory earned him the honor of playing the first round of the 1969 Masters with Arnold Palmer, where he bested The King, 69-73...Won the 1989 PGA Club Pro Championship and was a member of the victorious U.S. team in the 1990 PGA Cup matches...Member of the 1969 Walker Cup team...Won a national junior college title...Won a gold medal in golf at the 1969 World Maccabiah Games in Israel and coached the team that represented the U.S. there in 1989...Has had two career holes-in-one in competition.

PERSONAL:

Worked as a club professional in the mid-to-late 1980s, including a stint at Williams Island CC in North Miami Beach...Lists Arnold Palmer and President George W. Bush as his heroes...Favorite golf course is Muirfield Village...Got started in golf at age 7 by working as a caddie with his two brothers...Says the biggest influence in his career was Henry Atkinson, an assistant pro in Wilmington, NC, and the person who helped teach him the golf swing and how to play the game...His favorite meal is his wife's fried chicken, with mashed potatoes on the side.

PLAYER STATISTICS

MISCELLANEOUS CHAMPIONS TOUR STATISTICS

2004 Low Round: 64–2004 Bruno's Memorial Classic/1
Career Low Round: 60–2002 RJR Championship/1
Career Largest Paycheck: $430,000–2001 U.S. Senior Open/1

MISCELLANEOUS PGA TOUR STATISTICS

Career Low Round: 63–2 times, most recent 1998 B.C. Open/3
Career Largest Paycheck: $180,000–1991 New England Classic/1

Raymond Floyd

WORLD GOLF HALL OF FAME MEMBER (Inducted 1989)
EXEMPT STATUS: Top 30 on All-Time Money List
FULL NAME: Raymond Loran Floyd
HEIGHT: 6-1
WEIGHT: 200
BIRTHDATE: September 4, 1942
BIRTHPLACE: Fort Bragg, NC
RESIDENCE: Palm Beach, FL
FAMILY: Wife, Maria; Raymond, Jr. (9/20/74), Robert Loran (1/23/76), Christina Loran (8/29/79)
CLUB AFFILIATION: Old Palm GC (Palm Beach Gardens, FL)
EDUCATION: University of North Carolina
SPECIAL INTERESTS: Sports, golf course design
TURNED PROFESSIONAL: 1961
JOINED PGA TOUR: 1963

JOINED CHAMPIONS TOUR: 1992

CHAMPIONS TOUR VICTORIES (14): 1992 GTE North Classic, Ralphs Senior Classic, SENIOR TOUR Championship. **1993** Gulfstream Aerospace Invitational, Northville Long Island Classic. **1994** The Tradition, Las Vegas Senior Classic, Cadillac NFL Golf Classic, GOLF MAGAZINE SENIOR TOUR Championship. **1995** PGA Seniors' Championship, Burnet Senior Classic, Emerald Coast Classic. **1996** Ford Senior Players Championship. **2000** Ford Senior Players Championship.

OTHER SENIOR VICTORIES (15): 1992 Fuji Electric Grandslam. **1994** Diners Club Matches [with Dave Eichelberger], Senior Skins Game. **1995** Senior Skins Game, Senior Slam at Los Cabos, Office Depot Father/Son Challenge [with Raymond, Jr.], Lexus Challenge [with Michael Chiklis]. **1996** Senior Skins Game, Senior Slam at Los Cabos, Office Depot Father/Son Challenge [with Raymond, Jr.]. **1997** Senior Skins Game, Office Depot Father/Son Challenge [with Raymond, Jr.], Lexus Challenge [with William Devane]. **1998** Senior Skins Game. **2000** Office Depot Father/Son Challenge [with Robert].

2004 CHARLES SCHWAB CUP FINISH: 47th - 207 points

GEORGIA-PACIFIC GRAND CHAMPIONS VICTORIES (2): 2003 SBC Championship. **2004** SAS Championship.

PGA TOUR VICTORIES (22): 1963 St. Petersburg Open Invitational. **1965** St. Paul Open Invitational. **1969** Greater Jacksonville Open, American Golf Classic, PGA Championship. **1975** Kemper Open. **1976** Masters Tournament, World Open Golf Championship. **1977** Byron Nelson Golf Classic, Pleasant Valley Classic. **1979** Greater Greensboro Open. **1980** Doral-Eastern Open. **1981** Doral-Eastern Open, Tournament Players Championship, Manufacturers Hanover Westchester Classic. **1982** Memorial Tournament, Danny Thomas Memphis Classic, PGA Championship. **1985** Houston Open. **1986** U.S. Open Championship, Walt Disney World/Oldsmobile Classic. **1992** Doral-Ryder Open.

OTHER VICTORIES (9): 1978 Brazilian Open. **1979** Costa Rica Open. **1981** Canadian PGA, Seiko Point Leader. **1982** Seiko Point Leader. **1985** Chrysler Team Championship [with Hal Sutton]. **1988** Skins Game. **1990** RMCC Invitational [with Fred Couples]. **1993** Franklin Funds Shark Shootout [with Steve Elkington].

PGA TOUR CAREER EARNINGS: $5,323,075

PGA TOUR PLAYOFF RECORD: 5-10

BEST 2004 CHAMPIONS TOUR FINISHES: T4—Allianz Championship; T10—Senior PGA Championship.

2004 SEASON:

Limited his schedule to just 12 events...Played his best golf during a three-week stretch in May. Was T4 at the Allianz Championship, thanks to a final-round 66 at Glen Oaks, the low round of the day and the performance near Des Moines was his best since 2001 campaign...One week earlier he played in the final group on Sunday at the FedEx Kinko's Classic but finished T27 after a final-round 75 at The Hills...On the leaderboard for most of the rain-soaked Senior PGA Championship and eventually T10 at Valhalla, his first top-10 effort in a major since 2001...Was sixth on the final Georgia-Pacific Grand Champions money list, with a victory at the SAS Championship...Was second to Mike Hill in the season-ending Georgia-Pacific Grand Champions Championship...Missed the cut in two PGA TOUR starts at the Masters and U.S. Open.

CHAMPIONS TOUR CAREER HIGHLIGHTS:

2003: Underwent successful prostate cancer surgery at Johns Hopkins Medical Center in late December 2002. In first start since the surgery, finished T9 at the SBC Classic in March and then T9 again a month later at the Liberty Mutual Legends of Golf...Played in only 11 official events and appeared in only three tournaments after the U.S. Senior Open in late June...Earned a spot in the Georgia-Pacific Grand Champions Championship in Sonoma, CA, by virtue of his runner-up finish in the Georgia-Pacific event at the SBC Championship. Lost in a playoff to Mike Hill in San Antonio but still netted $23,000 and vaulted from 18th into the top 16. T2 in the Georgia-Pacific Grand Champions Championship, six strokes back of Isao Aoki. Placed sixth on the final Georgia-Pacific money list with $116,100...Made one appearance on the PGA TOUR, missing the cut at the Masters. **2001:** A final-round 67 helped him to a T2 at the Verizon Classic in early February, three strokes back of winner Bob Gilder...Made a run at The Transamerica in late October only to come up one stroke short along with Doug Tewell, when Sammy Rachels eagled the final hole for victory. **2000:** Voted by his peers as the Comeback Player of the Year...Highlight of year came during July when he had sub-par scores in 10 consecutive rounds and was selected as the Player of the Month. Closed with a final-round 67 at Saucon Valley to place fourth in the U.S. Senior Open and then won his next start at the Ford Senior Players Championship, defeating Larry Nelson and Dana Quigley by a stroke. Second win in Dearborn ended a victory drought of four years and two days and at 57 years, 10 months and 12 days, made him the oldest ever at the time to claim a senior major championship since the Champions Tour started in 1980. Pocketed the largest check of his career, $345,000, when he rallied from six strokes back on the final day to win, the biggest margin in FORD SENIOR PLAYERS history and the best come-from-behind effort on the Champions Tour that year along with John Jacobs (Bruno's Memorial Classic)...Made the first of 16 holes-in-one on the Champions Tour that season when he aced the third hole in the opening round of the Royal Caribbean Classic, the second hole-in-one of his Champions Tour career. **1999:** T2 at the MasterCard Championship in Hawaii, three strokes back of John Jacobs...Also fell one stroke short of Hale Irwin at the Ameritech Senior Open. **1998:** Captured a fifth straight Senior Skins Game title in January...T2 at the LG Championship, two strokes short of Gil Morgan, who holed a sand wedge for eagle on the final hole for the victory. **1996:** Went over the million-dollar mark for third year in succession...A two-stroke winner over Hale Irwin at Ford Senior Players Championship...Also third at The Tradition and U.S. Senior Open. **1995:** Only out of top 10 twice in 21 events with wins at PGA Seniors' Championship, Burnet Senior Classic and Emerald Coast Classic...Earned second Byron Nelson Award for lowest

CHAMPIONS TOUR CAREER SUMMARY — **PLAYOFF RECORD: 3-1**

Year	Events Played	1st	2nd	3rd	Top 10	Top 25	Earnings	Rank
1992	7	3	1		6	6	$436,991	14
1993	14	2	4	2	12	14	713,168	9
1994	20	4	5	2	17	20	1,382,762	2
1995	21	3	7	1	19	21	1,419,545	2
1996	23	1		4	16	20	1,043,051	8
1997	20			3	10	16	584,755	23
1998	21		1	1	10	18	702,472	19
1999	19		2	1	9	15	683,314	27
2000	17	1			6	9	717,258	26
2001	14		2		5	9	546,190	34
2002	11					7	205,718	70
2003	11				2	5	201,675	66
2004	11				2	2	169,679	69
Total	209	14	22	14	114	162	8,806,576	
COMBINED ALL-TIME MONEY (3 TOURS):							**$14,129,651**	

CHAMPIONS TOUR TOP TOURNAMENT SUMMARY

Year	92	93	94	95	96	97	98	99	00	01	02	03	04
Senior PGA Championship		T13	T3	1	19	T35	15	T24	T51	T40	T15	T17	T10
U.S. Senior Open		T7	12	T8	3	T44	3	T11	4	T16	T21	T19	CUT
Ford Senior Players		2	T3	T10	1	T19	T19	T9	1	T6	T17		
JELD-WEN Tradition		T3	1	T6	3	T19	5	T20	WD	T16	T21		
Charles Schwab Cup Champ	1	T2	1	2	T14	T9	T11	8	T14				

Raymond Floyd (Continued)

scoring average (69.47)...Second to Jim Colbert on final money list when he fell just one stroke shy of defending title at Energizer SENIOR TOUR Championship...Birdied final hole at Burnet Senior Classic to edge Graham Marsh and bested Tom Wargo on second extra playoff hole to win Emerald Coast Classic. Recorded his first Champions Tour hole-in-one at that Pensacola event. **1994:** Earned over $1 million for first time in pro career and won four times, including dramatic victory at season-ending GOLF MAGAZINE SENIOR TOUR Championship. Overcame a six-stroke deficit on the final day and then holed a birdie putt on fifth extra hole to defeat Jim Albus...Won his first Champions Tour major at The Tradition, beating Dale Douglass in overtime...Also went wire-to-wire at the Cadillac NFL Golf Classic...Earned the Byron Nelson Trophy for lowest scoring average (69.08) and joined Don January and Lee Trevino as the only players at the time to win both a Byron Nelson Trophy and the Vardon Trophy (PGA TOUR-1983). **1993:** Split his time between the Champions Tour and PGA TOUR...Made just 14 Champions Tour starts, but still finished ninth on the final money list...Captured the Gulfstream Aerospace Invitational in record form when he finished 22-under-par 194 to set a Champions Tour mark in relation to par for 54 holes....Also won the Northville Long Island Classic by two strokes over five other players. **1992:** Won three times in just seven starts and capped the year by claiming the SENIOR TOUR Championship in Puerto Rico...During the fall campaign, had defeated Isao Aoki at the Ralphs Senior Classic with a 54-hole score of 18-under 198...Made history when he became the first player to win on both Tours (since matched by Craig Stadler) with his win at Ford Senior Players Championship and B.C. Open in 2003) in the same year...First captured his 22nd PGA TOUR event and third Doral-Ryder Open...With that title, he joined Sam Snead as the only players to win TOUR events in four different decades...Won the GTE North Classic title just 16 days after turning 50 and donated winner's check of $67,500 to Hurricane Andrew Relief Fund.

OTHER CAREER HIGHLIGHTS:

The winner of 36 TOUR events, including 14 on the Champions Tour...Has shown his mettle in the major championships on both Tours...Won a second Ford Senior Players Championship crown (2000/also won in 1996) to go with his victories at The Tradition (1994) and PGA Seniors' Championship (1995) title on the Champions Tour...On the PGA TOUR, earned wins at The Masters (1976), U.S. Open (1986), PGA Championship (1969, 1981) and THE PLAYERS Championship (1981)...Has enjoyed immense success in Florida, with nine TOUR victories...Became the oldest player to compete in the Ryder Cup matches and was instrumental in helping lead the United States to victory at The Belfry in his eighth appearance in 1993. Previously played for the American side in the biennial matches in 1969, 1975, 1977, 1981, 1985 and 1991, while serving as captain of the 1989 United States team at The Belfry...Won his 1976 Masters title by eight strokes, a record broken by Tiger Woods in 1997...Won the 1981 PLAYERS Championship in a playoff over Curtis Strange and Barry Jaeckel...Opened with a 63 at the 1982 PGA Championship at Southern Hills and went wire-to-wire...Came from behind with a 66 on Sunday at Shinnecock Hills to win the 1986 U.S. Open at age 43...Won his first event, the 1963 St. Petersburg Open, at age 20...Has had five holes-in-one on the PGA TOUR and two on the Champions Tour.

PERSONAL:

His family was named by *Golfweek* as the 1994 "Golf Family of the Year"...Also selected Golf World's "Man of the Year" for 1992...The son of L.B., a career Army man, he was exposed to golf at an early age in Fayetteville, NC, but chose to pursue baseball until capturing the National Jaycees golf title in 1960...Remains a devoted Chicago Cubs fan...Inducted into the World Golf Hall of Fame in 1989...He has two sons. Raymond, Jr., a Wake Forest graduate, works at the investment firm Lazard Freres in New York, and Robert, who is pursuing a professional golf career...His daughter Christina, also a Wake Forest graduate, works in public relations in New York City.

PLAYER STATISTICS

2004 CHAMPIONS TOUR STATISTICS:

Scoring Average	72.15	(N/A)
Driving Distance	272.8	(N/A)
Driving Accuracy Percentage	71.2%	(N/A)
Total Driving	1,998	(N/A)
Greens in Regulation Pct.	68.9%	(N/A)
Putting Average	1.841	(N/A)
Sand Save Percentage	56.8%	(N/A)
Eagles (Holes per)	297.0	(N/A)
Birdie Average	2.91	(N/A)
All-Around Ranking	1,569	(N/A)

MISCELLANEOUS CHAMPIONS TOUR STATISTICS

2004 Low Round: 66–2004 Allianz Championship/3
Career Low Round: 62–1992 Ralphs Senior Classic/3
Career Largest Paycheck: $345,000–2000 Ford Senior Players Championship/1

MISCELLANEOUS PGA TOUR STATISTICS

2004 Low Round: 73–Masters Tournament/1
Career Low Round: 63–2 times, most recent 1992 MCI Heritage Golf Classic/2
Career Largest Paycheck: $252,000–1992 Doral–Ryder Open/1

SECTION 2 PLAYER BIOGRAPHIES

John Fought (FOTE)

EXEMPT STATUS: PGA TOUR Career Victory List
FULL NAME: John Allen Fought III
HEIGHT: 6-0
WEIGHT: 230
BIRTHDATE: January 28, 1954
BIRTHPLACE: Portland, OR
RESIDENCE: Scottsdale, AZ

FAMILY: Wife, Mary; Tiffany (5/18/81), John IV (5/29/84), Natalie (5/19/89)
EDUCATION: Brigham Young University (1976, Accounting)
SPECIAL INTERESTS: Golf course architecture
TURNED PROFESSIONAL: 1977
JOINED PGA TOUR: 1978

JOINED CHAMPIONS TOUR: 2004

BEST CHAMPIONS TOUR CAREER FINISH: 70—2004 MasterCard Classic.

PGA TOUR VICTORIES (2): 1979 Buick-Goodwrench Open, Anheuser-Busch Golf Classic.

OTHER VICTORIES (3): 1975 Pacific Coast Amateur. **1976** Pacific Northwest Open. **1977** U.S. Amateur.

PGA TOUR CAREER EARNINGS: $387,036

PGA TOUR PLAYOFF RECORD: 1-0

BEST 2004 CHAMPIONS TOUR FINISH: 70—MasterCard Classic.

2004 SEASON:

Made just three starts, missing the cut at the Senior British Open and the U.S. Senior Open and finishing 70th in his first start on the Champions Tour at the MasterCard Classic in Mexico.

OTHER CAREER HIGHLIGHTS:

Played the PGA TOUR from 1979-1987 and earned his initial exemption on the circuit at the Q-School in the Fall of 1978...Recorded both TOUR victories in consecutive weeks during the 1979 season and earned Rookie of the Year honors. First TOUR victory at the Buick-Goodwrench Open came in dramatic fashion. Holed a 10-foot birdie putt on the last hole at Warwick Hills to get into a playoff with Jim Simons and then won the event on the second extra hole with a routine par...Rebounded from two strokes off the pace and birdied the 72nd hole again the next week at Silverado CC in Napa, CA, to break from a four-way tie with Alan Tapie, Bobby Wadkins and Buddy Gardner and win the Anheuser-Busch Classic...Earnings of $108,427 were the third highest total ever by a rookie at the time and proved to be the most he ever made in a single season as a professional...Turned his attention to golf course architecture after suffering a neck injury...Worked first with Bob Cupp in Portland, OR, before moving to Scottsdale in 2001 to work with PGA TOUR professional Tom Lehman on several design projects. Has his name on four courses ranked among Golfweek's Top 100 in the United States—both courses at Pumpkin Ridge near Portland (with Cupp), Crosswater in Sunriver, OR, (with Cupp) and The Gallery GC's North Course in Marana, AZ (with Lehman)...Won the 1977 U.S. Amateur at Aronimink near Philadelphia, defeating Doug Fischesser, 9 and 8, in the 36-hole final...Was a member of the 1977 United States Walker Cup team that defeated Great Britain and Ireland, 16-8, at Shinnecock Hills GC in New York.

PERSONAL:

Got started playing golf by his grandmother at age 7...Played collegiately at Brigham Young with fellow Champions Tour player Mike Reid and former PGA TOUR player Jim Nelford...Biggest thrill in golf was winning the U.S. Amateur and biggest thrill off the golf course is his design work that has produced four top-100 courses...Lists Mickey Mantle, Arnold Palmer and Ben Hogan as his heroes...Enjoys watching baseball and the Fox News Channel on television...Favorite movies are "The Natural" and the entire "Star Wars" trilogy...Best friend in golf is Mike Reid.

PLAYER STATISTICS

2004 CHAMPIONS TOUR STATISTICS:

Scoring Average	76.86	(N/A)
Driving Distance	275.0	(N/A)
Driving Accuracy Percentage	53.6%	(N/A)
Total Driving	1,998	(N/A)
Greens in Regulation Pct.	52.8%	(N/A)
Putting Average	1.842	(N/A)
Sand Save Percentage	100.0%	(N/A)
Birdie Average	2.14	(N/A)
All-Around Ranking	1,569	(N/A)

MISCELLANEOUS CHAMPIONS TOUR STATISTICS

2004 Low Round: 74–2004 U.S. Senior Open/1
Career Low Round: 74–2004 U.S. Senior Open/1
Career Largest Paycheck: $1,760–2004 MasterCard Classic/70

MISCELLANEOUS PGA TOUR STATISTICS

Career Low Round: 62–1983 Bob Hope Desert Classic/3
Career Largest Paycheck: $54,000–1979 Anheuser–Busch Golf Classic/1

CHAMPIONS TOUR CAREER SUMMARY — PLAYOFF RECORD: 0-0

Year	Events Played	1st	2nd	3rd	Top 10	Top 25	Earnings	Rank
2004	3						$1,760	198
Total	3						1,760	
COMBINED ALL-TIME MONEY (3 TOURS):							$388,796	

CHAMPIONS TOUR TOP TOURNAMENT SUMMARY

Year	04
U.S. Senior Open	CUT
Senior British Open	CUT

Al Geiberger (GUY-bur-gur)

EXEMPT STATUS: Top 30 on All-Time Money List
FULL NAME: Allen Lee Geiberger, Sr.
HEIGHT: 6-3
WEIGHT: 200
BIRTHDATE: September 1, 1937
BIRTHPLACE: Red Bluff, CA
RESIDENCE: Palm Desert, CA
FAMILY: Wife, Carolyn; Lee Ann (9/14/63), John (5/20/68), Brent (5/22/68), Bryan (9/28/76), Al, Jr. (1/2/88), Kathleen Marie (1/11/91)
CLUB AFFILIATION: Indian Ridge CC (Palm Desert, CA)
EDUCATION: University of Southern California (B.S., 1959)
SPECIAL INTERESTS: Boating, photography
TURNED PROFESSIONAL: 1959
JOINED PGA TOUR: 1960

CHAMPIONS TOUR VICTORIES (10): 1987 Vantage Championship, Hilton Head Seniors International, Las Vegas Senior Classic. **1988** The Pointe/Del E Webb Arizona Classic. **1989** GTE Northwest Classic. **1991** Kroger Senior Classic. **1992** Infiniti Senior Tournament of Champions. **1993** Infiniti Senior Tournament of Champions, GTE West Classic. **1996** Greater Naples IntelliNet Challenge.

OTHER SENIOR VICTORIES (1): 1989 Liberty Mutual Legends of Golf [with Harold Henning].

GEORGIA-PACIFIC GRAND CHAMPIONS VICTORIES (9): 1997 Bank One Classic. **1998** Royal Caribbean Classic, Pittsburgh Senior Classic, Ameritech Senior Open, BankBoston Classic. **1999** Toshiba Senior Classic, BellSouth Senior Classic at Opryland, The Transamerica. **2000** Georgia-Pacific Super Seniors Championship.

PGA TOUR VICTORIES (11): 1962 Ontario Open Invitational. **1963** Almaden Open Invitational. **1965** American Golf Classic. **1966** PGA Championship. **1974** Sahara Invitational. **1975** MONY Tournament of Champions, Tournament Players Championship. **1976** Greater Greensboro Open, Western Open. **1977** Danny Thomas Memphis Classic. **1979** Colonial National Invitation.

OTHER VICTORIES (4): 1961 Utah Open. **1962** Caracas Open. **1982** Frontier Airlines Open. **1985** Colorado Open.

PGA TOUR CAREER EARNINGS: $1,265,188

PGA TOUR PLAYOFF RECORD: 1-1

BEST 2004 CHAMPIONS TOUR FINISH: 74—Administaff Small Business Classic.

2004 SEASON:

Returned to the Champions Tour for the last two full-field events of the year...Appearance at the inaugural Administaff Small Business Classic was his first since the Toshiba Senior Classic in March, 2003. Finished 74th near Houston and then finished 75th at the SBC Championship in San Antonio the very next week...Highlight of his year was son Brent winning the Chrysler Classic of Greensboro event 28 years after his triumph in the same North Carolina city. Duo became the first father/son tandem to win the same PGA TOUR event.

CHAMPIONS TOUR CAREER HIGHLIGHTS:

2000: Won the season-ending Georgia-Pacific Grand Champions Championship. Defeated Jim Albus with a par on the second playoff hole and pocketed $138,000, his largest check as a professional. **1999:** Lost out in a four-man playoff with Allen Doyle, John Jacobs and eventual champion Gary McCord at the Toshiba Senior Classic...Also was second at the Boone Valley Classic, one stroke short of Bruce Fleisher at the BellSouth Senior Classic at Opryland...Had three wins in the Georgia-Pacific Grand Champions...Recorded a double eagle at the Novell Utah Showdown, his second albatross on the Champions Tour. **1998:** Won four Grand Champions events overall...Claimed the Grand Champions title at the Pittsburgh Senior Classic and then went on to finish fourth overall at Sewickley Heights GC...Also won the over-60 title at the BankBoston Classic and eventually finished T5 at Nashawtuc...Closed out the year with a solo second place finish at the MasterCard Champions Championship, just two strokes behind winner Bob Charles...Played in the PGA Championship at Sahalee CC with son Brent, the first time a father and son both competed in that prestigious event in the same year. **1997:** Top performance of the year came in the season's first official event, the MasterCard Championship at Hualalai, where he T4...Only other top-10 came at the final Bank One Classic, the same week he joined the ranks of the MasterCard Champions. Won the 60-and-over event in his debut, and was the 36-hole leader in the event, but faltered on the back nine on Sunday at Kearney Hill Links, eventually finishing T6. **1996:** Rebounded from off-season foot surgery (bone spurs in right big toe) to claim first title in almost three years in his first start at the Greater Naples Intellinet Challenge. Second-round 63 gave him a three-stroke lead after 36 holes, but he needed a birdie on 17th in final round to clinch one-stroke victory over Isao Aoki...Voted the Champions Tour Comeback Player of the Year. **1994:** Played in just seven events after missing most of the year with a torn rotator cuff in his left shoulder...Underwent surgery in March and did not return until October at Raley's Senior Gold Rush, where he finished T5. **1993:** Won second straight Infiniti Tournament of Champions to start the year, and had an additional victory at the GTE West Classic. **1992:** Started the year with a three-stroke win at the Infiniti Tournament of Champions. **1991:** Rallied to win the Kroger Senior Classic after a T2 at the Southwestern Bell Classic the week before. **1989:** Won GTE Northwest Classic and teamed with Harold Henning for win in unofficial Liberty Mutual Legends of Golf. **1988:** In first full season on Champions Tour, had a win at The Pointe/Del E. Webb Arizona Classic and five second-place finishes. **1987:** Found immediate success on the Champions Tour after turning 50 in September, posting three wins and a second-place effort...Fired senior career-best 62 in final round at Las Vegas Senior Classic that helped him to four-stroke win...The $135,000 he collected for his initial Champions Tour victory at the Vantage Championship, a two-stroke victory over Dave Hill, was nearly three times more than his biggest paycheck on the PGA TOUR ($54,000, 1979 Colonial)...Also defeated Jim Ferree in a playoff for the Hilton Head International title.

OTHER CAREER HIGHLIGHTS:

Won 11 times in 25 years on the PGA TOUR...On June 10, 1977, he became the first player to break 60 in an official PGA TOUR event, firing a 13-under-par 59 in the second round of the Danny Thomas-Memphis Classic (later

CHAMPIONS TOUR CAREER SUMMARY — PLAYOFF RECORD: 1-1

Year	Events Played	1st	2nd	3rd	Top 10	Top 25	Earnings	Rank
1987	10	3	1		7	10	$264,798	9
1988	24	1	5	2	15	22	348,735	6
1989	26	1	4	2	21	25	527,033	3
1990	25		1		8	17	373,624	13
1991	25	1	1	2	12	20	519,926	10
1992	26	1		3	10	22	385,339	19
1993	26	2	2	1	12	24	608,877	13
1994	7				2	3	72,729	69
1995	23			1	7	14	370,006	33
1996	21	1			4	16	372,301	36
1997	23				2	9	260,427	55
1998	22				2	12	310,350	53
1999	23		3		5	10	559,062	34
2000	17			1	1	2	160,249	75
2001	19					3	122,624	85
2002	5					1	26,914	109
2003	1							
2004	2						1,986	196
Total	325	10	17	12	108	210	5,284,981	
COMBINED ALL-TIME MONEY (3 TOURS):							**$6,550,169**	

CHAMPIONS TOUR TOP TOURNAMENT SUMMARY

Year	88	89	90	91	92	93	94	95	96	97	98	99	00
Senior PGA Championship	T3	T2	T29		T10								
U.S. Senior Open	T8	T7	T37	3	T3	T20					T28		
Ford Senior Players	2	T4	T14	T13	T18	3		T10	23	T39	T24	T48	
JELD-WEN Tradition		T7	T20	T44	T17	7		40	T5	T51	T23	T20	T43
Charles Schwab Cup Champ			T5	T4	13	18							

Year	01
Senior PGA Championship	T49
Ford Senior Players	T53

Al Geiberger (Continued)

equaled by Chip Beck at the 1991 Las Vegas Invitational at Sunrise GC and David Duval at the 1999 Bob Hope Chrysler Classic at PGA West). Carded 11 birdies and one eagle that day at Colonial CC to earn the nickname "Mr. 59." His run of six birdies and an eagle is still a PGA TOUR record...Saved his best efforts for the toughest courses, winning the 1965 American Golf Classic and 1966 PGA Championship at Firestone CC, the 1975 Tournament Players Championship and 1979 Colonial National Invitation at Colonial CC, and the 1976 Western Open at Butler National...1954 National Jaycee Champion...Member of the 1967 and 1975 United States Ryder Cup teams...Has six career holes-in-one.

PERSONAL:

Introduced to the game at age 5 by his parents and lists his dad and Byron Nelson as his biggest heroes...On the PGA TOUR, he endorsed Skippy peanut butter and still carries a peanut butter sandwich in his bag for snacking during competitive rounds...Received the 1999 Family of the Year Award from the Metropolitan Golf Writers Association in New York...Son, Brent, plays the PGA TOUR and won both the 1999 Canon Greater Hartford Open for his first TOUR win and last year's Chrysler Classic of Greensboro tournament. Another son, John, is the head golf coach at Pepperdine, the 1997 NCAA men's golf champion, and a third son, Bryan, played golf at Oregon State...Daughter Lee Ann is an assistant to a publisher for an Italian children's book publishing company in Milan, Italy...Lists Cypress Point as his favorite golf course and enjoys watching Everybody Loves Raymond and Cheers reruns on television...Favorite athletes are Jerry West and Sandy Koufax.

PLAYER STATISTICS

2004 CHAMPIONS TOUR STATISTICS:

Scoring Average	74.67	(N/A)
Driving Distance	262.3	(N/A)
Driving Accuracy Percentage	58.3%	(N/A)
Total Driving	1,998	(N/A)
Greens in Regulation Pct.	54.6%	(N/A)
Putting Average	1.898	(N/A)
Sand Save Percentage	33.3%	(N/A)
Birdie Average	1.83	(N/A)
All-Around Ranking	1,569	(N/A)

MISCELLANEOUS CHAMPIONS TOUR STATISTICS

2004 Low Round: 72–2004 Administaff Small Business Classic/2
Career Low Round: 62–1987 Las Vegas Senior Classic/3
Career Largest Paycheck: $135,000–1987 Vantage Championship/1

MISCELLANEOUS PGA TOUR STATISTICS

Career Low Round: 59–1977 Danny Thomas Memphis Classic/2
Career Largest Paycheck: $54,000–1979 Colonial National Invitation/1

25 MEMORABLE MOMENTS

President Bush Participates in Pro-Am

1990 Doug Sanders Kingwood Celebrity Classic

The 1990 Doug Sanders Kingwood Celebrity Classic had a special visitor in May 1990 when President George H.W. Bush participated in the pro-am at the Deerwood Club in suburban Houston. Bush's visit—along with a huge Secret Service detail—upstaged Lee Trevino, who went on to record a six-stroke victory over Gary Player. President Bush took time out from other activities during his Texas visit to play with his son and current President, George W., PGA TOUR Commissioner Deane Beman and host Doug Sanders, who had invited the Commander in Chief to play in the event he hosted each year.

CHAMPIONS TOUR 25

Gibby Gilbert

EXEMPT STATUS: Net-70 on All-Time Money List
FULL NAME: C.L. Gilbert, Jr.
HEIGHT: 5-9
WEIGHT: 190
BIRTHDATE: January 14, 1941
BIRTHPLACE: Chattanooga, TN
RESIDENCE: Chattanooga, TN

FAMILY: Wife, Judy; Jeff (11/14/62), Gibby (10/21/65), Mark (5/31/70), Melissa (3/4/84); three grandchildren
CLUB AFFILIATION: Valleybrook CC (Chattanooga, TN)
EDUCATION: University of Chattanooga
SPECIAL INTERESTS: Family
TURNED PROFESSIONAL: 1965
JOINED PGA TOUR: 1967

JOINED CHAMPIONS TOUR: 1991

CHAMPIONS TOUR VICTORIES (6): 1992 Southwestern Bell Classic, Kroger Senior Classic, First of America Classic. **1993** Las Vegas Senior Classic. **1996** Boone Valley Classic. **1997** Royal Caribbean Classic.

2004 CHARLES SCHWAB CUP FINISH: T74th - 36 points

GEORGIA-PACIFIC GRAND CHAMPIONS VICTORIES (2): 2002 SBC Senior Classic, Georgia-Pacific Super Seniors Championship.

PGA TOUR VICTORIES (3): 1970 Houston Champions International. **1976** Danny Thomas Memphis Classic. **1977** Walt Disney World National Team Championship [with Grier Jones].

OTHER VICTORIES (3): 1988 Tennessee Open. **1989** Tennessee Open. **1990** Tennessee Open.

PGA TOUR CAREER EARNINGS: $1,056,506

PGA TOUR PLAYOFF RECORD: 1-0

BEST 2004 CHAMPIONS TOUR FINISH: T42—Greater Hickory Classic at Rock Barn.

2004 SEASON:

Finished solo fifth, along with partner Jim Dent, in the Raphael Division at the Liberty Mutual Legends of Golf...Best individual effort was a T42 at the Greater Hickory Classic at Rock Barn.

CHAMPIONS TOUR CAREER HIGHLIGHTS:

2003: T9 at the Long Island Classic thanks to a closing 5-under-par 65. Underwent hip and lower-back surgery in the offseason. **2002:** Won the season-ending Georgia-Pacific event in Oklahoma City, defeating Dave Stockton and Mike Hill by one stroke. Win was worth $150,000 and vaulted him to a second place on the final Grand Champions money list...T8 at the SBC Senior Classic near Los Angeles. Defeated George Archer by one stroke at that event to win first Georgia-Pacific Grand Champions title of his career. **2000:** Missed almost three months of the summer season when he was operated on for bone spurs at the end of his collar bone and right rotator cuff. Did not play any events from mid-June until mid-September. **1998:** T2 at the MasterCard Championship. **1997:** Despite a hip injury, earned his sixth Champions Tour title at the year's first full-field event, a four-stroke win over David Graham at the Royal Caribbean Classic. **1996:** Captured first title in three years at the inaugural Boone Valley Classic. Was seemingly out of contention on the final day after a quadruple bogey on the second hole and trailed by six strokes on the front nine. Battled his way back with six birdies over the final 14 holes, including one at the 18th that forced a playoff with Hale Irwin. Won with a par on the first playoff hole and earned the largest check of his professional career: $180,000. **1993:** Won the Las Vegas Senior Classic thanks to a second-round 63, his lowest score of the year, to hold off Mike Hill by one stroke. **1992:** Posted back-to-back victories at the Southwestern Bell Classic and Kroger Senior Classic...Became the first of only two Champions Tour players to win back-to-back events with sub-200 scores. Never looked back after firing an 8-under-par 62 in the opening round of the Southwestern Bell event. In Kansas City, equaled a then-Champions Tour numerical record with a 17-under-par 193 total, and also tied the largest 54-hole victory margin ever on the Champions Tour (nine strokes). One week later, defeated good fried J.C. Snead on the second hole of a playoff to win the Kroger event after both had posted 15-under 198 totals...Matched his PGA TOUR career victory total with a late-summer triumph at the First of America Classic.

OTHER CAREER HIGHLIGHTS:

Collected more than $1 million in official earnings on the PGA TOUR from 1968-1985 and was exempt for 14 of those 17 years...First of his three PGA TOUR wins came at the 1970 Houston Champions International, where he defeated Bruce Crampton in a playoff...Best year was 1980, when he earned more than $100,000 for the only time in his TOUR career...A runner-up, with Jack Newton, to Seve Ballesteros in the 1980 Masters...Along with several others, owns the course record at the fabled Pinehurst No. 2 Course, shooting 62 during the 1973 World Open. At the time, the score shattered the old mark by three strokes...Has made nine aces in competition.

PERSONAL:

Lists Arnold Palmer as his hero...Enjoys spending time with his family...Got started in golf at age 13 by his father...Lists Los Angeles CC as his favorite golf course...Former member of Champions Tour Division Board...Son Gibby III has played on the Nationwide Tour...Biggest thrill was winning his first PGA TOUR event in Houston in 1970...Always marks his ball tails up with a penny.

PLAYER STATISTICS

2004 CHAMPIONS TOUR STATISTICS:

Scoring Average	74.96	(81)
Driving Distance	257.8	(72)
Driving Accuracy Percentage	72.0%	(28)
Total Driving	100	(66)
Greens in Regulation Pct.	57.7%	(76)
Putting Average	1.893	(81)
Sand Save Percentage	37.1%	(74)
Eagles (Holes per)	936.0	(71)
Birdie Average	2.27	(78)
All-Around Ranking	561	(81)

MISCELLANEOUS CHAMPIONS TOUR STATISTICS
2004 Low Round: 68–2004 Toshiba Senior Classic/2
Career Low Round: 62–1992 Southwestern Bell Classic/1
Career Largest Paycheck: $180,000–1996 Boone Valley Classic/1

MISCELLANEOUS PGA TOUR STATISTICS
Career Low Round: 64–2 times, most recent 1986 Deposit Guaranty Golf Classic/4
Career Largest Paycheck: $43,200–1980 Manufacturers Hanover Westchester Classic/2

CHAMPIONS TOUR CAREER SUMMARY — PLAYOFF RECORD: 2-1

Year	Events Played	1st	2nd	3rd	Top 10	Top 25	Earnings	Rank
1991	31		2	1	10	23	$392,351	14
1992	30	3	2	1	8	20	603,630	8
1993	32	1	2	2	10	25	661,378	11
1994	29				5	18	352,342	27
1995	31			1	3	15	361,645	34
1996	28	1	1		4	11	446,307	30
1997	30	1			4	15	440,533	34
1998	31		1		3	10	416,584	43
1999	26				1	8	270,484	57
2000	19					4	123,528	80
2001	21					1	134,828	82
2002	22				1	5	134,125	86
2003	21				1	2	100,290	87
2004	18						36,613	105
Total	369	6	8	5	50	157	4,474,638	
COMBINED ALL-TIME MONEY (3 TOURS):							**$5,531,144**	

CHAMPIONS TOUR TOP TOURNAMENT SUMMARY

Year	91	92	93	94	95	96	97	98	99	00	01	02	03
Senior PGA Championship		T19	T27	T29	13	CUT	T4	CUT	T18	T25		CUT	
U.S. Senior Open	T24	T11	T17	T20	T42		T21	T33					
Ford Senior Players	T25	T27	T33	T25	T23	T6	T26	T19	73			T65	
JELD-WEN Tradition	T35	T36	T3	T7	T36	T43	T51	T60	T50	T58			
Charles Schwab Cup Champ	T12	14	T15	T15		22							

Year	04
Senior PGA Championship	CUT

Bob Gilder

EXEMPT STATUS: Top 30 on 2004 Champions Tour Money List
FULL NAME: Robert Bryan Gilder
HEIGHT: 5-9
WEIGHT: 180
BIRTHDATE: December 31, 1950
BIRTHPLACE: Corvallis, OR
RESIDENCE: Corvallis, OR

FAMILY: Wife, Peggy; Bryan (3/24/75), Cammy Lynn (6/10/77), Brent (3/4/81)
CLUB AFFILIATION: Pumpkin Ridge GC (Cornelius, OR)
EDUCATION: Arizona State University (1973, Business Administration)
SPECIAL INTERESTS: Football, auto racing
TURNED PROFESSIONAL: 1973
JOINED PGA TOUR: 1976

JOINED CHAMPIONS TOUR: 2000

CHAMPIONS TOUR VICTORIES (7): 2001 Verizon Classic, SENIOR TOUR Championship. **2002** SBC Senior Open, FleetBoston Classic, Allianz Championship, Kroger Senior Classic. **2003** Emerald Coast Classic.

2004 CHARLES SCHWAB CUP FINISH: 27th - 583 points

PGA TOUR VICTORIES (6): 1976 Phoenix Open. **1980** Canadian Open. **1982** Byron Nelson Golf Classic, Manufacturers Hanover Westchester Classic, Bank of Boston Classic. **1983** Phoenix Open.

OTHER VICTORIES (6): 1973 Western Athletic Conference Championship [indiv]. **1974** New Zealand Open. **1982** Bridgestone International. **1988** Isuzu Kapalua International. **1988** Acom Team Championship [with Doug Tewell]. **1990** Acom P.T.

PGA TOUR CAREER EARNINGS: $3,032,108

PGA TOUR PLAYOFF RECORD: 1-0

BEST 2004 CHAMPIONS TOUR FINISHES: T3—FedEx Kinko's Classic, Farmers Charity Classic, Bayer Advantage Celebrity Pro-Am; 5—U.S. Senior Open.

2004 SEASON:

Finished outside the top-20 money-winners for the first time in his Champions Tour career...Played his best golf from May into early June, finishing third three times in five appearances... T3 for the second consecutive year at the FedEx Kinko's Classic in Austin. Helped his cause with a final-round, 7-under-par 65, the low round of the tournament and his best round of the year...Shared the 36-hole lead at the Farmers Charity Classic with Andy Bean before slipping back into a T3, with a final-round 71. Had a pair of eagles in carding an opening-round 66 in Grand Rapids...Followed with another strong showing the next week near Kansas City, T3 at the weather-shortened Bayer Advantage Celebrity Pro-Am...Also on the leaderboard throughout the U.S. Senior Open and finished solo fifth at Bellerive, his best performance in a senior major since the 2002 JELD-WEN Tradition.

CHAMPIONS TOUR CAREER HIGHLIGHTS:

2003: Among his nine top-10 finishes were a win, three seconds and a third...Played some of his best golf during a one-month stretch starting in late April with his seventh Champions Tour win at the Emerald Coast Classic. 54-hole 17-under 193 total shattered the tournament record by three strokes, and was also the lowest 54-hole winning score on the Champions Tour. Closing-round 63 in Pensacola was also the best finish by a winner in 2003. Used a second-round 64 to vault himself into a tie with Tom Watson after 36 holes and then cruised easily to the title after shooting a 7-under 63 on Easter Sunday. Made 23 birdies over 54 holes, the most by any player in the field, and birdied both par-5s at The Moors all three days...T4 the following week at the Liberty Mutual Legends of Golf and then placed T6 at the Bruno's Memorial Classic and solo third at the Kinko's Classic of Austin. Finish in Austin, one stroke shy of the Hale Irwin-Tom Watson playoff, was the first of two good efforts in Texas. Was a runner-up for a third consecutive year at the SBC Championship in San Antonio in October, losing to Craig Stadler by four strokes...Champions Tour's April Player of the Month...Came close to defending his title at the FleetBoston Classic in August after rounds of 68-65-68, but fell three strokes shy, finishing T2 with Bruce Fleisher behind Allen Doyle...Went head-to-head with Jim Thorpe at the Long Island Classic two weeks later but lost by one stroke. Had an opportunity to birdie the final hole and set up a potential playoff with Thorpe, but missed a six-foot birdie attempt on the final hole to finish second. **2002:** Had his most-productive season as a professional, with four wins and earnings totaling $2,367,637...Was the Champions Tour's Player of the Month for July and September after recording a pair of victories in consecutive weeks during each month...In July, became the first player since Jim Thorpe in 2001 to claim back-to-back events and the first professional since Lee Elder (1985) to win consecutive tournaments on the Champions Tour in playoffs. Defeated John Mahaffey with a birdie-3 on the third extra hole to win the FleetBoston Classic at Nashawtuc. Became the first wire-to-wire winner in the 22-year history of the event and just the second player ever to win both a PGA TOUR (1982 Bank of Boston Classic) and Champions Tour event in the Boston area (Arnold Palmer, the other). Fell into playoff after making bogey on the final hole, ending a run of 64 straight holes without a blemish...Defeated Hale Irwin a week earlier with a par on the first hole of a playoff to win the SBC Senior Open in Chicago. Trailed Irwin by one stroke with two holes to play in regulation, but made a crucial 15-foot birdie putt on the 16th hole to send the tournament to a playoff. Moved into the lead on Saturday with a course-record 63 on the Port Course at Harborside International...In September, rallied from two strokes down with eight holes to play to win the Allianz Championship. Dueled John Bland down the stretch and took the lead for good when Bland made bogey on the 17th hole at Glen Oaks. Victory in Des Moines was his third of the season, a first for him since claiming three PGA TOUR events in 1982...Added a fourth victory, and his third in a playoff, when he bested Tom Jenkins with a birdie-3 on the second extra hole to win the Kroger Senior Classic. Had just one bogey during the event at the TPC at River's Bend (No. 3, second round). Helped his cause by posting the first hole-in-one of his Champions Tour career on Friday...Became the second player to go over the $2-million mark after pocketing $50,700 for a T5 at the Napa Valley Championship...His eight consecutive rounds in the 60s was the best streak on the Champions Tour in 2002...Led all players with 399 birdies. **2001:** Was named Rookie of the Year, thanks to a pair of victories and 11 other top-10 finishes...Earnings of over $1.6 million were more than five times greater than his best year on the PGA TOUR (1982: $308,648)...Started and ended the season on a positive note...Closed with a 4-under 67 at the TPC of Tampa Bay to win the Verizon Classic by three strokes over four players. Only needed 75 total putts over three days for his Verizon title, his first win on TOUR in 18 years and 18 days (1983 Phoenix Open)...Became a multiple champion for the first time since 1982 when he closed the year with a victory at the SENIOR TOUR Championship at Gaillardia. Was the first-round leader in Oklahoma City and stayed

CHAMPIONS TOUR CAREER SUMMARY — PLAYOFF RECORD: 3-0

Year	Events Played	1st	2nd	3rd	Top 10	Top 25	Earnings	Rank
2001	30	2	1	1	13	24	$1,684,986	8
2002	34	4	2	3	16	24	2,367,637	2
2003	30	1	3	1	9	17	1,278,247	12
2004	28			3	4	16	791,452	22
Total	122	7	6	8	42	81	6,122,321	
COMBINED ALL-TIME MONEY (3 TOURS):							**$9,258,082**	

CHAMPIONS TOUR TOP TOURNAMENT SUMMARY

Year	01	02	03	04
Senior PGA Championship	3	T10	T10	CUT
U.S. Senior Open	T11	10	T43	5
Ford Senior Players	T63	T40	T30	T39
Senior British Open			CUT	T33
JELD-WEN Tradition	T29	T3	T28	T24
Charles Schwab Cup Champ	1	3	T20	T18

CHAMPIONS TOUR YEAR-BY-YEAR STATISTICS (TOP 50 ON 2004 MONEY LIST)

	Scoring Average	Putting Average	Greens in Regulation	Driving Distance	Driving Accuracy
2001	70.37 (11)	1.742 (T5)	66.8 (37)	272.6 (37)	73.9 (T21)
2002	70.26 (11)	1.760 (6)	68.5 (T27)	268.5 (45)	72.5 (23)
2003	70.46 (T21)	1.745 (3)	68.6 (T32)	275.6 (28)	71.6 (27)
2004	71.06 (24)	1.781 (21)	68.5 (31)	273.4 (32)	74.6 (22)

Bob Gilder (Continued)

close to the lead over the next two days. Eventually edged Doug Tewell by a stroke in windy conditions despite carding a 1-over 73, the highest finishing score by a winner since the 1999 Lightpath Long Island Classic. **2000:** Cruised to medalist honors at the 2000 Champions Tour National Qualifying Tournament despite playing all four days with a sprained left ankle and kidney stones. His 72-hole total of 19-under 269 shattered the Q-school scoring record and his seven-stroke margin of victory over Bill Holstead and Terry Mauney at Eagle Pines GC was the second-largest winning margin ever in a National Qualifying final.

OTHER CAREER HIGHLIGHTS:

Joined the PGA TOUR in 1976 after successfully earning his first player's card at the Qualifying School in the Fall of 1975 on his third try...Made 646 starts on the PGA TOUR and 42 more on the Nationwide Tour before embarking on his Champions Tour career...Played the Nationwide Tour on a full-time basis in 1997...First of six career victories on the PGA TOUR came in the 1976 Phoenix Open, where he overtook Roger Maltbie to win by two strokes. Victory came in his second start on the circuit (missed cut at Tucson the week before)...Last official win also came in Phoenix again in 1983, this time in a playoff with Johnny Miller, Rex Caldwell and Mark O'Meara...Had his best year on the PGA TOUR in 1982 when he won three times: Byron Nelson Classic, Manufacturers Hanover-Westchester Classic, Bank of Boston Classic. His four-round score of 22-under 266 at the Nelson was the lowest in the tournament's 16 years at Preston Trail GC...Posted a 19-under-par 261 score to win at Westchester. Highlight of that performance was a third-round double eagle on 509-yard 18th hole. Fairway marker commemorates the feat and marks the exact spot where he hit 3-wood...Was also a playoff winner over Jack Newton and Bob Charles in the 1974 New Zealand Open...Defeated John Mahaffey by two strokes in the 1988 Isuzu Kapalua International...Claimed three titles in Japan: 1982 Bridgestone International, 1988 Acom Team title (with Doug Tewell), 1990 Acom P.T...Was a member of the American team in the 1982 USA vs. Japan Team Matches and the 1983 Ryder Cup...Has two career holes-in-one.

PERSONAL:

A collegiate teammate of Tom Purtzer, Howard Twitty and Morris Hatalsky at Arizona State. Joined the team as a walk-on and eventually won the Western Athletic Conference individual title in 1973 and was an honorable mention All-America...Enjoys racing cars and raced seriously from 1985-92 in some Trans-Am races...Enjoys spy moves...Favorite golf course is Harbour Town GL in South Carolina...Says the best shot of his career was his double eagle in the third round on the 18th hole at Westchester in 1982.

PLAYER STATISTICS

MISCELLANEOUS CHAMPIONS TOUR STATISTICS

2004 Low Round: 65–2004 FedEx Kinko's Classic/3
Career Low Round: 63–3 times, most recent 2003 Emerald Coast Classic/3
Career Largest Paycheck: $440,000–2001 SENIOR TOUR Championship/1

MISCELLANEOUS PGA TOUR STATISTICS

Career Low Round: 62–1979 First NBC New Orleans Open/3
Career Largest Paycheck: $72,000–1982 Manufacturers Hanover Westchester Classic/1

25 MEMORABLE MOMENTS

Nicklaus Sets All-Time Scoring Record

1990 Ford Senior Players Championship

Jack Nicklaus made a shambles of the competition at Dearborn Country Club as he set a Champions Tour record score of 27-under-par 261. Nicklaus opened with a 7-under 65, his first competitive round in a month. On Friday, he shot 68 and took sole possession of the lead, a stroke in front of Lee Trevino and Terry Dill. The Golden Bear went on to tie the course record with a 64 on Saturday and then, starting at the third hole on Sunday, went eagle-birdie-birdie en route to a second straight 64. Nicklaus' four-round total eclipsed Orville Moody's 72-hole score at the 1988 Vintage Chrysler Invitational by two strokes.

CHAMPIONS TOUR 25

David Graham

EXEMPT STATUS: Net-70 on All-Time Money List
FULL NAME: Anthony David Graham
HEIGHT: 5-10
WEIGHT: 180
BIRTHDATE: May 23, 1946
BIRTHPLACE: Windsor, Australia
RESIDENCE: Whitefish, MT
FAMILY: Wife, Maureen; Andrew (11/8/74), Michael (10/1/77); three grandchildren
CLUB AFFILIATION: Preston Trail GC (Dallas, TX)
SPECIAL INTERESTS: Reading, wine collecting
TURNED PROFESSIONAL: 1962
JOINED PGA TOUR: 1971

JOINED CHAMPIONS TOUR: 1996

CHAMPIONS TOUR VICTORIES (5): **1997** GTE Classic, Southwestern Bell Dominion, Comfort Classic. **1998** Royal Caribbean Classic. **1999** Raley's Gold Rush Classic.

PGA TOUR VICTORIES (8): **1972** Cleveland Open. **1976** American Express Westchester Classic, American Golf Classic. **1979** PGA Championship. **1980** Memorial Tournament. **1981** Phoenix Open, U.S. Open Championship. **1983** Houston Coca-Cola Open.

OTHER VICTORIES (19): **1970** Thailand Open, French Open. **1971** Caracas Open, JAL Open. **1975** Wills Masters. **1976** Chunichi Crowns Invitational, Piccadilly World Match Play. **1977** Australian Open, South African PGA Championship. **1978** Mexico Cup. **1979** Westlakes Classic, New Zealand Open. **1980** Mexican Open, Rolex Japan, Brazilian Classic. **1981** Lancome Trophy. **1982** Lancome Trophy. **1985** Queensland Open. **1994** Australian Skins.

PGA TOUR CAREER EARNINGS: $1,888,731

PGA TOUR PLAYOFF RECORD: 2-1

BEST 2004 CHAMPIONS TOUR FINISH:
52—Liberty Mutual Legends of Golf.

2004 SEASON:

Withdrew during the final round of the Bank of America Championship in late June and was later diagnosed with congestive heart failure that sidelined him for the remainder of the year...Played in 12 events earlier in the season, with his best effort a 52nd in the Liberty Mutual Legends of Golf.

CHAMPIONS TOUR CAREER HIGHLIGHTS:

2002: Recorded the 10th hole-in-one of his professional career in the final round of the Ford Senior Players Championship. **2001:** Spent two months away from the circuit early in the year while his wife, Maureen, underwent open-heart surgery. Returned at the Liberty Mutual Legends of Golf in early April and, along with partner Bruce Fleisher, T2 in the rain-shortened better-ball event. **2000:** Finished third at the Boone Valley Classic, thanks to a second-round 64...Teamed with Bruce Fleisher to finish second at the Liberty Mutual Legends of Golf, one stroke behind Jim Colbert and Andy North. **1999:** Defeated Larry Mowry by four strokes at the Raley's Gold Rush Classic. Opened with a sizzling 9-under 63 then rebounded from a two-stroke deficit after 36 holes with a final-round 65. **1998:** Defeated Dave Stockton in a Champions Tour-record, 10-hole sudden-death playoff at the Royal Caribbean Classic...He and partner Hugh Baiocchi lost a two-hole playoff to Dale Douglass and Charles Coody at the Liberty Mutual Legends of Golf. **1997:** Secured three victories and was among the top five nine times...Won twice early in the year at the GTE Classic and the Southwestern Bell Dominion, then claimed his third title in September at the Comfort Classic...Picked up his first Champions Tour win by three strokes in Tampa, but his other two victories were nail-biters...Eagled the final hole at Dominion CC to slip past John Jacobs in San Antonio and then birdied the final hole in Indianapolis for a one-stroke victory over Larry Nelson and Bud Allin...Recorded his first Champions Tour hole-in-one at Ralphs Senior Classic. **1996:** Made his debut at the Bruno's Memorial Classic in June and competed in 19 events...Was one of the players in the record five-man playoff at the Emerald Coast Classic won on the first extra hole with a birdie by Lee Trevino.

OTHER CAREER HIGHLIGHTS:

Probably best known as a winner of two major championships, the 1979 PGA Championship and the 1981 U.S. Open...Birdied the third extra hole at Oakland Hills CC to defeat Ben Crenshaw for the PGA title...At Merion GC in the 1981 U.S. Open, he trailed George Burns by three strokes after 54 holes, but played one of the finest finishing rounds in Open history, a 3-under-par 67 that included hitting all 18 greens in regulation. Won by one stroke over Burns and Bill Rogers...First victory on the PGA TOUR came in the 1972 Cleveland Open, where he defeated close friend Bruce Devlin in a playoff...Made more than $100,000 in six consecutive TOUR campaigns (1979-84), with the high mark coming in 1983 when he collected $244,924. Claimed his last TOUR victory that year, coming from five strokes back on Sunday afternoon to win the Houston Coca-Cola Open...Teamed with Devlin to win the World Cup for Australia and was on the winning Australian Dunhill Cup team in 1985 and again in 1986...Was selected as the first captain of the International Team for the 1994 Presidents Cup...Has had 10 holes-in-one in his professional career.

PERSONAL:

Discovered the game of golf when he was 13...Found a set of left-handed clubs in his garage and played with them for two years before making the switch to a right-handed set...Worked in a golf shop in Melbourne, Australia, at age 16 and, after a three-year apprenticeship, took a head professional job at a nine-hole course in Tasmania...Became a touring professional in the late 1960s, first in Australia and then the Far East...Awarded the Order of Australia by Queen Elizabeth II in 1992 for contribution to the game...Inducted into the Australian Sports Hall of Fame and the Australian Golf Hall of Fame...A member of the Masters Tournament Cup & Tee Committee, which sets up the Augusta National layout each April...Involved in the golf design business, with a number of courses to his credit, including Grayhawk GC in Scottsdale, AZ, the Raven GC in Phoenix, AZ, and Grandover GC in Greensboro, NC...Considers his victory at the 1981 U.S. Open to be his biggest thrill in golf and credits Bruce Devlin as the person who most influenced his career...Loves to fly fish in his home state of Montana...Favorite TV show is "The Tonight Show" and favorite athlete is Andre Agassi...Top entertainer is Celine Dion and favorite golf courses are Augusta National and Cypress Point.

PLAYER STATISTICS

2004 CHAMPIONS TOUR STATISTICS:

Scoring Average	76.08	(N/A)
Driving Distance	265.3	(N/A)
Driving Accuracy Percentage	45.6%	(N/A)
Total Driving	1,998	(N/A)
Greens in Regulation Pct.	48.3%	(N/A)
Putting Average	1.850	(N/A)
Sand Save Percentage	47.8%	(N/A)
Birdie Average	2.00	(N/A)
All-Around Ranking	1,569	(N/A)

MISCELLANEOUS CHAMPIONS TOUR STATISTICS

2004 Low Round: 68–2004 Blue Angels Classic/2
Career Low Round: 63–2 times, most recent 1999 Raley's Gold Rush Classic/1
Career Largest Paycheck: $165,000–1999 Raley's Gold Rush Classic/1

MISCELLANEOUS PGA TOUR STATISTICS

Career Low Round: 63–3 times, most recent 1986 Bob Hope Chrysler Classic/3
Career Largest Paycheck: $72,000–1983 Houston Coca–Cola Open/1

CHAMPIONS TOUR CAREER SUMMARY — PLAYOFF RECORD: 1-1

Year	Events Played	1st	2nd	3rd	Top 10	Top 25	Earnings	Rank
1996	19		1		3	9	$271,415	52
1997	30	3	1	1	14	24	1,173,579	5
1998	31	1		3	12	20	945,300	13
1999	34	1		2	8	19	869,839	18
2000	26			1	3	8	421,347	42
2001	18					4	122,135	86
2002	21					4	175,620	77
2003	18					1	61,211	99
2004	12						22,063	116
Total	209	5	2	7	40	89	4,062,509	
COMBINED ALL-TIME MONEY (3 TOURS):							**$5,951,240**	

CHAMPIONS TOUR TOP TOURNAMENT SUMMARY

Year	96	97	98	99	00	01	02	03	04
Senior PGA Championship		T11	WD	T50	T28	CUT	CUT	T53	T65
U.S. Senior Open	T22	T40	19	CUT	T47	CUT	T31	CUT	
Ford Senior Players	T44	T10		T48	T41	WD	T49		
JELD-WEN Tradition		T21	WD	59	T31	T59	T13	77	
Charles Schwab Cup Champ		T14	T4	T18					

Hubert Green

EXEMPT STATUS: Top 30 on All-Time Money List
FULL NAME: Hubert Myatt Green
HEIGHT: 6-1
WEIGHT: 170
BIRTHDATE: December 28, 1946
BIRTHPLACE: Birmingham, AL
RESIDENCE: Birmingham, AL

FAMILY: Wife, Michelle; Hubert Myatt, Jr. (8/18/75), Patrick (10/17/78), James Thomas (2/11/84)
CLUB AFFILIATION: Birmingham CC (Birmingham, AL)
EDUCATION: Florida State University (1968, Marketing)
SPECIAL INTERESTS: Fishing, gardening
TURNED PROFESSIONAL: 1969
JOINED PGA TOUR: 1970

JOINED CHAMPIONS TOUR: 1996

CHAMPIONS TOUR VICTORIES (4): 1998 Bruno's Memorial Classic. **2000** Audi Senior Classic, Kroger Senior Classic. **2002** Lightpath Long Island Classic.

OTHER SENIOR VICTORIES (1): 1999 Liberty Mutual Legends of Golf [with Gil Morgan].

2004 CHARLES SCHWAB CUP FINISH:
31st - 411 points

PGA TOUR VICTORIES (19): 1971 Houston Champions International. **1973** Tallahassee Open, B.C. Open. **1974** Bob Hope Desert Classic, Greater Jacksonville Open, IVB-Philadelphia Golf Classic, Walt Disney World National Team Championship [with Mac McLendon]. **1975** Southern Open. **1976** Doral-Eastern Open, Greater Jacksonville Open, Sea Pines Heritage Classic. **1977** U.S. Open Championship. **1978** Hawaiian Open, Heritage Classic. **1979** Hawaiian Open, First NBC New Orleans Open. **1981** Sammy Davis Jr.-Greater Hartford Open. **1984** Southern Open. **1985** PGA Championship.

OTHER VICTORIES (3): 1975 Dunlop Phoenix. **1977** Irish Open. **1980** Jerry Ford Invitational [co-winner].

PGA TOUR CAREER EARNINGS: $2,591,959

PGA TOUR PLAYOFF RECORD: 2-3

BEST 2004 CHAMPIONS TOUR FINISH: T26—The First Tee Open at Pebble Beach presented by Wal-Mart.

2004 SEASON:

Returned to the Champions Tour at the season-opening MasterCard Championship in Hawaii (37th), but was forced to miss almost the next three months of the season after undergoing additional tests and treatments for a cancerous growth on his throat and tongue...Despite a loss of strength and weight, came back again in mid-April at the Blue Angels Classic in Pensacola, FL...Named Champions Tour Comeback Player of the Year...Finished third in Driving Accuracy.

CHAMPIONS TOUR CAREER HIGHLIGHTS:

2003: Season cut short in June after being diagnosed with a cancerous growth on his left tonsil and back of his tongue during a routine dental examination in May. Opted to begin radiation and chemotherapy sessions in early July and missed the remainder of the year while undergoing nearly six weeks of treatment for the disease at Shands Hospital in Gainesville, FL. Lost over 30 pounds during the treatment...In contention after 36 holes of the Royal Caribbean Golf Classic and eventually finished solo fifth at Key Biscayne, four strokes back of Dave Barr...Was just one stroke off the lead through 36 holes of the Farmers Charity Classic and eventually T4 in Grand Rapids, three strokes out of a playoff spot in his next-to-last start in June...T4 at the Liberty Mutual Legends of Golf...Made his third career ace on the Champions Tour during the final round of the Bayer Advantage Celebrity Pro-Am. **2002:** Voted Champions Tour Comeback Player of the Year...Returned from an inconsistent 2001 season in a big way, finishing 16th on the money list after dropping to 51st the previous year...Claimed his first title in nearly two years when he defeated Hale Irwin in a seven-hole playoff at the Lightpath Long Island Classic. Was tied for the 36-hole lead with Irwin, but fell behind by as many as four strokes with 12 holes to play. However, collected five birdies over the last 11 holes and then drained a 25-foot putt on the seventh extra hole for the victory. Earned $255,000 for his victory, the largest check of his pro career...Followed his victory in New York with another strong showing the following week at the 3M Championship, a solo second, three strokes behind Irwin...Prior to his win on Long Island, finished T2 at the Ford Senior Players Championship. Was the leader at the halfway point by three strokes after firing a second-round, 9-under-par 63 (tied tournament record). **2001:** T5 at the Turtle Bay Championship. Trailed Hale Irwin by two strokes entering the final round in Hawaii before losing by six strokes. **2000:** Won multiple tournaments in the same year for the first time since 1979...Collected a pair of official victories and pocketed almost as much official money as he made over the 1998 and 1999 seasons combined...His 14 top-10s overall equaled the combined total of his previous two Champions Tour campaigns...Posted his first victory in over 22 months at the inaugural Audi Senior Classic in Mexico. Birdied eight of his first 10 holes Sunday en route to a Champions Tour career-low round of 62 at LaVista CC and a five-stroke triumph over Jim Colbert, Dean Overturf and Doug Tewell...Also won the Kroger Senior Classic during the fall, holding off Larry Nelson by a stroke at Kings Island...Also lost to Bruce Fleisher on the fourth extra playoff hole at The Home Depot Invitational. Shot a course-record 63 at the TPC at Piper Glen in the second round...Played all 54 holes without a blemish at the Coldwell Banker Burnet Classic (T5) before the run came to an end during the first round of the FleetBoston Classic...Registered the second ace of his Champions Tour career in the final round of the State Farm Senior Classic. **1999:** Teamed with Gil Morgan to win the Liberty Mutual Legends of Golf. Duo went wire-to-wire on The Slammer & Squire course at World Golf Village and bested Tom Wargo and John Mahaffey by three strokes for the title...**1998:** Fired a final-round 64 in front of his hometown fans in Birmingham to win his first Champions Tour title at the Bruno's Memorial Classic. Made an eagle, par and four birdies over his last six holes to beat Hale Irwin by a stroke at Greystone G&CC...Carded his first ace on the Champions Tour in the opening round of the Comfort Classic. **1997:** During a streaky rookie season, posted nine top-10 finishes and collected more than $500,000 in official earnings, over twice what he made in his best year on the PGA TOUR (1978/$247,406)...Made a serious bid for his first Champions Tour title at the Northville Long Island Classic. Was one stroke off the lead after 36 holes before finishing T3, one stroke out of playoff contention...Sixth-place finish at the Ralphs Senior Classic netted him a $40,000 paycheck and vaulted him into the top 31 and a spot in the Energizer SENIOR TOUR Championship...Needed only 18 putts to shoot a 66 in his second official round on the Champions Tour at the Royal Caribbean Classic, one off the all-time record.

OTHER CAREER HIGHLIGHTS:

Is T36 among all-time winners with 19 victories during 26 years on the PGA TOUR...Sixteen of those wins came during the 1970s, when he was one of the top players in the world...Claimed the first of his two major titles in 1977 at the U.S. Open at Southern Hills...Defeated Lou Graham by one stroke, after playing the final four holes knowing a threat had been made on his life...Last victory was at the 1985 PGA Championship at Cherry Hills, where he outdueled Lee Trevino down the stretch...Claimed his first victory at the 1971 Houston Champions International. Tied Don January at the end of regulation, then birdied the first extra hole for the win...Named Rookie of the Year that season...Has won four events twice: Greater Jacksonville Open, Southern Open, Heritage Classic and Hawaiian Open...Biggest thrill in golf was when he won three consecutive events in 1976: Doral-Eastern Open, the Greater Jacksonville Open and Sea Pines Heritage

CHAMPIONS TOUR CAREER SUMMARY **PLAYOFF RECORD: 1-1**

Year	Events Played	1st	2nd	3rd	Top 10	Top 25	Earnings	Rank
1997	28			2	9	17	$556,402	26
1998	27	1	1		8	14	689,303	21
1999	30				6	14	631,046	30
2000	28	2	1		14	20	1,308,784	9
2001	27				2	8	337,108	51
2002	31	1	2		7	19	1,218,392	16
2003	16				6	7	514,575	35
2004	16						57,359	99
Total	203	4	4	2	52	99	5,312,969	
COMBINED ALL-TIME MONEY (3 TOURS):							**$7,904,928**	

CHAMPIONS TOUR TOP TOURNAMENT SUMMARY

Year	97	98	99	00	01	02	03	04
Senior PGA Championship	CUT	CUT	T39	T6	T27	T41	CUT	WD
U.S. Senior Open	T12	CUT	CUT	5	T29	T37	T30	CUT
Ford Senior Players	T10	T30	T5	T12	T20	T2		
JELD-WEN Tradition	T51	T47	WD		T10	T51		76
Charles Schwab Cup Champ	T7	31	T26	T8		T19		

SECTION 2 PLAYER BIOGRAPHIES

Hubert Green (continued)

Classic...Began the final round of the 1978 Masters with a three-stroke lead, only to fall victim to Gary Player's 64...Birdied the last hole of the 1978 World Series of Golf to tie Gil Morgan, but three-putted the first playoff hole...Was a member of the 1977, 1979 and 1985 U.S. Ryder Cup teams...Has 23 career holes-in-one.

PERSONAL:

Started to play golf at age 5, but participated in all sports as a teenager...Uses an unorthodox but effective swing...Turned professional in 1970 and worked one summer as an assistant pro at famed Merion GC in Ardmore, PA...Active in golf course design. Worked with Fuzzy Zoeller on the TPC at Southwind, venue for the PGA TOUR's FedEx St. Jude Classic. Also helped design Greystone G&CC in Birmingham with Bob Cupp, the site of the Bruno's Memorial Classic...His hero was baseball great Ted Williams...Biggest thrills in golf were his 1977 U.S. Open victory and winning three straight times in 1976...Favorite courses are Winged Foot, Pebble Beach, Cypress Point and Portmarnock in Ireland...Enjoys "The O'Reilly Factor" on the Fox News Channel.

PLAYER STATISTICS

2004 CHAMPIONS TOUR STATISTICS:

Scoring Average	74.41	(78)
Driving Distance	241.9	(81)
Driving Accuracy Percentage	82.3%	(3)
Total Driving	84	(46)
Greens in Regulation Pct.	49.8%	(81)
Putting Average	1.820	(57)
Sand Save Percentage	48.8%	(25)
Birdie Average	2.39	(76)
All-Around Ranking	479	(71)

MISCELLANEOUS CHAMPIONS TOUR STATISTICS

2004 Low Round: 69–2 times, most recent 2004 Administaff Small Business Classic/1

Career Low Round: 62–2000 Audi Senior Classic/3

Career Largest Paycheck: $255,000–2002 Lightpath Long Island Classic/1

MISCELLANEOUS PGA TOUR STATISTICS

Career Low Round: 62–1978 San Antonio Texas Open/1

Career Largest Paycheck: $125,000–1985 PGA Championship/1

25 MEMORABLE MOMENTS

Player Wins Final Major Title in The Dark

1990 Senior PGA Championship

Gary Player used a third-round 65 to spoil Jack Nicklaus and Lee Trevino's first appearances in a Senior PGA Championship and win the last of his six senior major titles. Player began the final round at PGA National Golf Club with a five-stroke lead over Nicklaus and a six-stroke advantage over Trevino. The trio played in the final grouping, but actually Player's only threat came from Chi Chi Rodriguez, who closed with a 66 to vault into second place. When play resumed after a rain delay, with darkness fast approaching, Player found the water and double-bogeyed No. 16. But he steadied himself and parred in for a two-shot victory.

CHAMPIONS TOUR 25

Jay Haas

EXEMPT STATUS: Top 30 on All-Time Money List
FULL NAME: Jay Dean Haas
HEIGHT: 5-10
WEIGHT: 180
BIRTHDATE: December 2, 1953
BIRTHPLACE: St. Louis, MO
RESIDENCE: Greenville, SC

FAMILY: Wife, Janice; Jay, Jr. (3/8/81), William Harlan (5/24/82), Winona Haley (1/18/84); Emily Frances (9/25/87), Georgia Ann (3/12/92)
CLUB AFFILIATION: Thornblade GC (Greer, SC)
EDUCATION: Wake Forest University
SPECIAL INTERESTS: All sports
TURNED PROFESSIONAL: 1976

JOINED CHAMPIONS TOUR: 2004

BEST CHAMPIONS TOUR CAREER FINISHES: 2—2004 Senior PGA Championship, The First Tee Open at Pebble Beach presented by Wal-Mart.

2004 CHARLES SCHWAB CUP FINISH: 13th - 1,274 points

PGA TOUR VICTORIES (9): 1978 Andy Williams-San Diego Open Invitational. **1981** Greater Milwaukee Open, B.C. Open. **1982** Hall Of Fame, Texas Open. **1987** Big "I" Houston Open. **1988** Bob Hope Chrysler Classic. **1992** Federal Express St. Jude Classic. **1993** H.E.B. Texas Open.

OTHER VICTORIES (4): 1975 NCAA Championship [indiv]. **1991** Mexican Open. **1996** Franklin Templeton Shootout [with Tom Kite]. **2004** CVS Charity Classic [with son, Bill].

PGA TOUR CAREER EARNINGS: $13,791,809

PGA TOUR PLAYOFF RECORD: 3-0

BEST 2004 CHAMPIONS TOUR FINISHES:
2—Senior PGA Championship, The First Tee Open at Pebble Beach presented by Wal-Mart; T3—U.S. Senior Open.

BEST 2004 PGA TOUR FINISHES:
3—Bob Hope Chrysler Classic; 5—The INTERNATIONAL; T6—THE PLAYERS Championship; T7—MCI Heritage, THE TOUR Championship presented by Coca-Cola.

2004 SEASON:

Made his Champions Tour debut at the Senior PGA Championship in Louisville, where he finished second, one stroke back of Hale Irwin after Irwin two-putted for birdie from 40 feet on the final hole...Among the leaders throughout the U.S. Senior Open before finishing T3, two strokes behind Peter Jacobsen. He and Jacobsen were the only two players in the field to post four consecutive sub-par scores at Bellerive...Was runner-up to Craig Stadler in his third and final start on the Champions Tour when he finished three strokes back at The First Tee Open at Pebble Beach. He was also T2 in the pro-junior competition, with his partner Sydney Burlison...Sank a 12-foot birdie putt on the 18th hole to give him and son Bill a victory in the two-day CVS Charity Classic at Rhode Island CC in late June...Appeared in 23 events on the PGA TOUR and finished 27th on the final money list, with $2,071,626, the second year in succession he earned over $2 million...Made the cut at the Wachovia Championship, the 566th time he made a cut in a PGA TOUR event, tying him with Gene Littler for third all-time. He since increased that to 575 heading into 2005...Was a captain's pick on the 2004 U.S. Ryder Cup team at Oakland Hills...Named the recipient of Payne Stewart Award at the close of the season. The award is presented annually to a player sharing Stewart's respect for the traditions of the game, his commitment to uphold the game's heritage of charitable support and his professional and meticulous presentation of himself and the sport through his dress and conduct...In first start of the year on the PGA TOUR, the past champion earned second consecutive top-three finish at the Bob Hope Chrysler Classic, posting five rounds in the 60s to finish one stroke out of playoff with Phil Mickelson and Skip Kendall...Was T6 at THE PLAYERS Championship, his second consecutive top-10 finish and the sixth of career in 27 starts in the event. The record for appearances at THE PLAYERS is 28 by Tom Kite and Ben Crenshaw. Was one of three players over the age of 50 who played in the tournament, along with Craig Stadler and Peter Jacobsen. All three made the cut...Made ninth straight cut of season and finished T7 at MCI Classic. The $144,600 paycheck moved him over the $1-million mark for just the second time in his 29 years on TOUR...Finished T8 at the Memorial Tournament...Son Bill qualified for the U.S. Open at Shinnecock Hills GC to join Jay as the first father-son duo to compete in the same U.S. Open twice...Collected his fifth career top-10 at the U.S. Open in 25 appearances with his T9 and his first since a T5 in 1997. Shared first-round lead after opening 4-under 66 with Shigeki Maruyama and Angel Cabrera...A week after making his second start on the Champions Tour at the U.S. Senior Open (T3), collected his seventh top-10 with a fifth-place finish at The INTERNATIONAL, moving him into the top-10 in Ryder Cup points with only one week remaining...Passed Chris DiMarco and Chris Riley to finish 12th on the Ryder Cup Team points list but was selected by Hal Sutton as one of two captain's choices...Eighth and final top-10 finish of the year came at THE TOUR Championship...Opened with rounds of 67-66-68 and was tied after 54 holes with Tiger Woods before closing-round 75 dropped him to a T7.

OTHER CAREER HIGHLIGHTS:

Won nine PGA TOUR titles in his 29-year career, with all wins coming between 1978 and 1993...Last TOUR win came at the 1993 H-E-B Texas Open when he defeated Bob Lohr in a playoff at Oak Hills CC in San Antonio...Easily enjoyed his finest financial season in golf in 2003, with over $2.5 million in official earnings, more than three times his previous-best, single-season year ($822,259/1995). Secured the 15th position on final money list, his highest standing since 1982...Earned first victory at the 1978 Andy Williams-San Diego Open, besting Andy Bean, Gene Littler and John Schroeder by three strokes at Torrey Pines GC...Before 2003, previous highest position ever on the TOUR money list was 13th ($229,746) in 1982 as a result of 10 top-10 finishes that included a pair of victories. Won playoff at the 1982 Hall of Fame Classic with John Adams and defeated Curtis Strange by three strokes at Texas Open that same year...T3 at both the 1995 Masters and 1999 PGA Championship at Medinah CC near Chicago, his top career performances in major championships...Was a captain's choice for the United States team at the inaugural Presidents Cup in 1994 and compiled a 3-2 record...Also played on the United States Ryder Cup squads in 1983, 1995 and 2004...Enters 2005 season with 575 career cuts made, third on the all-time PGA TOUR list behind Tom Kite (587) and Raymond Floyd (583)...Won the 1975 NCAA Championship at Wake Forest and received the Fred Haskins Award that year...Was a 1975 and 1976 All-America selection and a member of the 1975 United States Walker Cup team...Demon Deacon teammates included Curtis Strange and Scott Hoch.

PERSONAL:

Introduced to golf by his uncle, 1968 Masters Tournament winner Bob Goalby...Won first trophy at National Pee Wee Championship in Orlando at age 7...Brother Jerry is the golf coach at Wake Forest...Brother-in-law Dillard Pruitt played the PGA TOUR and is now a TOUR Rules Official...Appeared in a Hootie and the Blowfish music video...Son Jay, Jr. caddied for him in the 1999 PGA Championship and played college golf at Augusta State. Second son, Bill, was an All-American at Wake Forest and was the medalist and a semifinalist at the 2002 U.S. Amateur at Oakland Hills CC. He also won the 2004 Ben Hogan Award as the top collegiate male golfer. He'll play on the 2005 Nationwide Tour.

PLAYER STATISTICS

MISCELLANEOUS CHAMPIONS TOUR STATISTICS
2004 Low Round: 66–2004 The First Tee Open at Pebble Beach presented by Wal-Mart/2
Career Low Round: 66–2004 The First Tee Open at Pebble Beach presented by Wal-Mart/2
Career Largest Paycheck: $216,000–2004 Senior PGA Championship/2

MISCELLANEOUS PGA TOUR STATISTICS
2004 Low Round: 64–Bob Hope Chrysler Classic/3
Career Low Round: 61–2003 Bob Hope Chrysler Classic/2
Career Largest Paycheck: $572,000–2003 THE PLAYERS Championship/T2

CHAMPIONS TOUR CAREER SUMMARY — PLAYOFF RECORD: 0-0

Year	Events Played	1st	2nd	3rd	Top 10	Top 25	Earnings	Rank
2004	3		2	1	3	3	$541,920	34
Total	3		2	1	3	3	541,920	
COMBINED ALL-TIME MONEY (3 TOURS):							$14,333,729	

CHAMPIONS TOUR TOP TOURNAMENT SUMMARY

Year	04
Senior PGA Championship	2
U.S. Senior Open	T3

CHAMPIONS TOUR YEAR-BY-YEAR STATISTICS (TOP 50 ON 2004 MONEY LIST)

	Scoring Average	Putting Average	Greens in Regulation	Driving Distance	Driving Accuracy
2004	68.64 (N/A)	1.753 (N/A)	73.7 (N/A)	274.5 (N/A)	74.0 (N/A)

Walter Hall

EXEMPT STATUS: 32nd on 2004 Champions Tour Money List
FULL NAME: Walter Houston Hall
HEIGHT: 6-1
WEIGHT: 185
BIRTHDATE: June 12, 1947
BIRTHPLACE: Winston-Salem, NC
RESIDENCE: Clemmons, NC
FAMILY: Wife, Carol; Holly (8/14/77)
CLUB AFFILIATION: Bermuda Run CC (Bermuda Run, NC)
EDUCATION: University of Maryland
TURNED PROFESSIONAL: 1994

JOINED CHAMPIONS TOUR: 1997

CHAMPIONS TOUR VICTORIES (1): 2001 AT&T Canada Senior Open Championship.

OTHER SENIOR VICTORIES (1): 1997 Belfry PGA Seniors' Championship.

2004 CHARLES SCHWAB CUP FINISH: 37th - 359 points

OTHER VICTORIES (6): 1985 Carolinas Mid-Amateur. **1996** Hooters Tour Naturally Fresh Cup. **1997** Three Nitro Senior Series events [at Paradise Point in Smithville, MO; at Rarity Bay GC in Vonore, TN; at Chantilly G&CC in Centreville, VA].

BEST 2004 CHAMPIONS TOUR FINISHES:

T6—Commerce Bank Long Island Classic; T7—U.S. Senior Open; T8—Bruno's Memorial Classic, SAS Championship.

2004 SEASON:

Finished 32nd on the money list for the second straight year...Final season tally included four top-10 finishes...Best finish was a T6 at the Commerce Bank Long Island Classic, where he fired three straight rounds in the 60s...Had nice showing at the U.S. Senior Open. Was T7 after consecutive 69s on the weekend...T8 early in the year at the Bruno's Memorial Classic and then again in September at the SAS Championship...Had a fast start at the inaugural Administaff Small Business Classic in October, sharing the first-round lead with Wayne Levi after an 8-under-par 64, but slipped to a T12.

CHAMPIONS TOUR CAREER HIGHLIGHTS:

2003: Made a late run at a spot in the season-ending event in Sonoma, CA, but came up two spots short and finished outside the top-30 money-winners for the first time since becoming fully exempt in 1998. When he didn't qualify for the Charles Schwab Cup Championship, it ended a streak of 85 consecutive appearances in Champions Tour events that started at the 2001 NFL Golf Classic. Had four of his five top 10s on the season in his last eight starts of the year after mid-August...Best effort was a T4 in the SBC Championship in San Antonio, his last of 30 appearances in 2003. Strung together three consecutive sub-70 scores at Oak Hills, the only time during the campaign he posted three straight rounds in the 60s in the same event...Found himself T2 after 36 holes of the SAS Championship, three strokes back of Jim Ahern, but drifted back into a T12 at Prestonwood after a final-round 73...Early in the season, closed with 68-67 in Mexico to finish solo sixth at the MasterCard Classic...Low round came on the second day of the Senior British Open in Scotland, when he shot a sizzling 6-under 64 at Turnberry and improved his first-round number by 10 strokes. Went 340 consecutive holes without a three-putt during the season. **2002:** One of three players (Dana Quigley and Mike McCullough the others) to play in all 35 official events...T3 at the rain-shortened TD Waterhouse Championship his top finish of the year and his best since winning in Canada in 2000...Was the 36-hole leader at the U.S. Senior Open at Caves Valley and trailed by three strokes after 54 holes. Faded to a T11 after posting a 6-over 77 on Sunday. **2001:** After six career runner-up performances that included one playoff loss, won his only event on the Champions Tour at the AT&T Canada Senior Open. Victory in Canada made him the last of nine first-time winners and the fourth consecutive first-time winner, a first in Champions Tour history. Made a five-foot par putt on the last hole at Mississaugua G&CC to force a playoff with Ed Dougherty. Two-putted for par from 35 feet on the first extra hole for the victory. Was selected as the August Player of the Month after his Canadian victory along with two other top-10 finishes during the month. **2000:** Came close to victory three times...Was one of five players tied for the 36-hole lead at The ACE Group Classic, but along with Tom Watson and Jose Maria Canizares, fell to Lanny Wadkins in a playoff. Contended at the SBC Championship in San Antonio for the second straight year. Despite being hospitalized with kidney stones early in the week, emerged as the 36-hole leader, but fell one stroke short of Doug Tewell and was T2 despite a final-round 69...Made a run at Lee Trevino the next week at the Cadillac NFL Golf Classic and finished as the runner-up, two strokes short of the Merry Mex...Made his first hole-in-one on the Champions Tour in the second round of the Nationwide Championship. **1999:** Was solo third at the American Express Invitational, four strokes back of Bruce Fleisher...Challenged again at The Transamerica but again finished third, three strokes back of Fleisher...Fired a career-low, 9-under 62 on the last day of the EMC Kaanapali Classic. **1998:** Played in 28 events despite being conditionally exempt (11th at the National Qualifier)...Lost by one stroke to Bruce Summerhays at the State Farm Senior Classic despite rounds of 68-70-68...Also among the leaders down the stretch at the Northville Long Island Classic, but finished one stroke short of Gary Player. **1997:** Had some impressive outings after turning 50 in June...Despite playing in only eight events, won $161,796 with a pair of top-10 finishes...Made his debut after Monday qualifying at the Kroger Senior Classic and T8...Won The Belfry PGA Seniors Championship on the PGA European Seniors Tour...Recorded three victories on the Nitro Senior Series and was its leading money-winner with $89,889.

OTHER CAREER HIGHLIGHTS:

Turned professional in 1994, after which he played two years on the Asian Tour (1994-95) and one on the Hooters Tour (1996)...Made four unsuccessful attempts to earn his PGA TOUR card in the 1970s before regaining amateur status until 1994...Reached the U.S. Amateur round of 16 in 1985.

PERSONAL:

Began his golf career by playing for his high school team...Biggest thrill in golf was playing with Chi Chi Rodriguez for the first time and also winning The Belfry PGA Seniors Championship...Worked as a sales manager for an appliance distributor prior to embarking on his professional career.

PLAYER STATISTICS

MISCELLANEOUS CHAMPIONS TOUR STATISTICS

2004 Low Round: 64–2004 Administaff Small Business Classic/1
Career Low Round: 62–1999 EMC Kaanapali Classic/3
Career Largest Paycheck: $240,000–2001 AT&T Canada Senior Open Championship/1

CHAMPIONS TOUR CAREER SUMMARY — PLAYOFF RECORD: 1-1

Year	Events Played	1st	2nd	3rd	Top 10	Top 25	Earnings	Rank
1997	8			1	2	5	$161,796	71
1998	28		2	1	8	12	668,700	23
1999	36			2	11	22	816,342	20
2000	37		3		8	25	910,611	20
2001	35	1	1	1	13	23	1,339,059	11
2002	35			1	7	19	785,372	26
2003	30				5	13	578,806	32
2004	26				4	14	576,425	32
Total	235	1	6	6	58	133	5,837,110	
COMBINED ALL-TIME MONEY (3 TOURS):							**$5,837,110**	

CHAMPIONS TOUR TOP TOURNAMENT SUMMARY

Year	98	99	00	01	02	03	04
Senior PGA Championship	T47	T43	T17	T10	T10	CUT	T31
U.S. Senior Open		T32	T34	T19	T11	CUT	T7
Ford Senior Players	T30	T33	T49	T41	T30	T48	T16
Senior British Open						T32	
JELD-WEN Tradition	T35	T40	T34	T12	T51	T28	T19
Charles Schwab Cup Champ	T26	T24	T27	T7	T15		

CHAMPIONS TOUR YEAR-BY-YEAR STATISTICS (TOP 50 ON 2004 MONEY LIST)

	Scoring Average	Putting Average	Greens in Regulation	Driving Distance	Driving Accuracy
1997	70.21 (N/A)	1.779 (N/A)	71.3 (N/A)	271.7 (N/A)	65.8 (N/A)
1998	71.23 (19)	1.785 (21)	67.1 (24)	267.1 (30)	66.2 (T63)
1999	70.88 (T21)	1.775 (16)	68.3 (30)	267.3 (36)	67.0 (66)
2000	70.58 (18)	1.774 (T20)	69.7 (21)	276.3 (13)	65.8 (T71)
2001	70.58 (13)	1.744 (T9)	67.4 (35)	280.6 (T10)	61.9 (82)
2002	71.12 (25)	1.767 (11)	65.3 (T53)	272.4 (30)	61.3 (T74)
2003	71.11 (35)	1.758 (6)	63.7 (67)	268.5 (T55)	63.4 (64)
2004	71.00 (22)	1.769 (14)	66.5 (T42)	272.8 (T33)	67.2 (58)

John Harris

EXEMPT STATUS: 33rd on 2004 Champions Tour Money List
FULL NAME: John Richard Harris
HEIGHT: 6-0
WEIGHT: 190
BIRTHDATE: June 13, 1952
BIRTHPLACE: Minneapolis, MN
RESIDENCE: Edina, MN
FAMILY: Wife, Jenifer; Chris (3/24/78), Katie (10/5/79)
EDUCATION: University of Minnesota (1974, Business Administration)
SPECIAL INTERESTS: Insurance
TURNED PROFESSIONAL: 1976, 2002
JOINED PGA TOUR: 1976

JOINED CHAMPIONS TOUR: 2002

BEST CHAMPIONS TOUR CAREER FINISH: T5—2004 SAS Championship .

2004 CHARLES SCHWAB CUP FINISH: T39th - 331 points

BEST PGA TOUR CAREER FINISH: T26—1976 Hawaiian Open.

OTHER VICTORIES (14): **1974** Minnesota State Amateur. **1987** Minnesota State Amateur. **1988** Minnesota State Mid-Amateur. **1989** Minnesota State Amateur. **1990** Minnesota State Mid-Amateur. **1991** Minnesota State Mid-Amateur. **1992** Minnesota State Mid-Amateur. **1993** U.S. Amateur. **1994** Minnesota Open. **1995** Minnesota Open. **1999** Minnesota State Mid-Amateur. **2000** Minnesota State Amateur. **2001** Crump Cup. **2002** Terra Cotta Cup.

PGA TOUR CAREER EARNINGS: $2,347

BEST 2004 CHAMPIONS TOUR FINISHES: T5—SAS Championship; 7—Bayer Advantage Celebrity Pro-Am; 9—Senior PGA Championship; T10—Kroger Classic.

2004 SEASON:

Moved to his highest standing ever on the money list after compiling four top-10 finishes...It marked the first time in his three-year Champions Tour career he had recorded finishes in the top 10...Best showing came after he fired three straight sub-par rounds for a T5 at the SAS Championship in late September, his best performance ever on the Champions Tour...Was T7 at the weather-shortened Bayer Advantage Celebrity Pro-Am after being the first-round co-leader following a 7-under 65 at The National GC of Kansas City...Was among the leaders through three rounds of the Senior PGA Championship at Valhalla, but finished solo ninth after posting a final-round 76. Performance in Louisville was his first top-10 effort of Champions Tour career...After making a hole-in-one during the pro-am, made a double eagle in the second round of the 3M Championship. Holed a 5-wood second shot from 257 yards on the par-5 sixth hole, the first albatross on the Champions Tour since 2002 (John Jacobs/MasterCard Championship) and the 25th in the history of the circuit...Posted 11 straight sub-par rounds near the close of the year, starting at the Kroger Classic and ending in the final round of the Administaff Small Business Classic.

CHAMPIONS TOUR CAREER HIGHLIGHTS:

2003: Earned a conditional exemption for 2004 by virtue of his finish among the top 50 on the 2003 money list...Played in eight of his first 15 events through sponsor exemptions and was among the top 25 six times, including a T11 at the FleetBoston Classic, his highest Champions Tour finish ever at that point...Benefited from the re-order category following the Long Island Classic to compete in each of the last eight full-field events...Cracked the top 50 for good when he T16 at the inaugural Greater Hickory Classic at Rock Barn and earned $20,083...Returned to the National Qualifying Tournament in the fall to improve his position but missed the cut at the TPC at Eagle Trace in Florida. **2002:** Played in 12 events after mid-June, 10 through sponsor exemptions, and T63 in his debut on the Champions Tour at the Greater Baltimore Classic at Hayfields CC...In his third start on the circuit, T14 at the SBC Senior Open in Chicago, his top effort of the campaign. Rebounded from an opening-round 75 with 67-68 on the weekend at Harborside International...Made it to the finals of the National Qualifying Tournament, but did not earn any exemption for 2003 after a T61 at World Woods GC near Brooksville, FL.

OTHER CAREER HIGHLIGHTS:

Minnesota's dominant amateur player for nearly two decades, winning four state amateur titles and five state mid-amateur crowns as well as back-to-back state open championships. Was also on Minnesota's winning team at the 1997 and 2001 USGA Men's State Team Championship..Named as Minnesota Player of the Year 10 times (1987-1995 and 2000)...Biggest victory of his career came at age 41 at the 1993 U.S. Amateur Championship at Champions GC in Houston. Defeated Danny Ellis in the 36-hole final, 5 and 3, after both players were all square after 25 holes. Had rallied down the stretch to defeat defending champion Justin Leonard, 2 and 1, in a quarterfinal match earlier in the week...A four-time United States Walker Cup team member (1993, 1995, 1997, 2001) and had the victory-clinching match in both 1993 and 1997...First turned professional in 1976, then regained his amateur status in 1983 before turning professional again when he turned 50...Attempted to earn a PGA TOUR card three times, missing by a total of four strokes. Still played in 12 PGA TOUR events in his career, four as a professional in 1976, with a T26 at the Hawaiian Open that year at Waialae CC...Also played the Florida mini-tours in 1977 and 1978 and the Asian Tour in 1977...Has made seven holes-in-one in his career, all with a 6-iron.

PERSONAL:

Created the Harris-Homeyer Insurance Company in January 1979 with Bill Homeyer, father of former U.S. Women's Open champion, Hillary Lunke...Attended the University of Minnesota on a hockey scholarship, but also played golf, earning first team All-America honors in golf in 1974...Was legendary hockey coach Herb Brooks' first captain at Minnesota and was the second leading scorer for the 1974 team that won the NCAA Championship. Younger brother, Robby, was a linemate...Also started for Minnesota in 1971 when the Gophers were NCAA runners-up...Played briefly for the New England Whalers minor league team in 1975, but left hockey to pursue a golf career in 1976...Father started him playing golf and he grew up on a nine-hole course with sand greens in northern Minnesota...Is a member of the Minnesota Golf Hall of Fame and the University of Minnesota Hall of Fame...Received the Warren Rebholz Distinguished Service Award from the Minnesota Golf Association in 1999...Lists Augusta National GC as his favorite course.

PLAYER STATISTICS

MISCELLANEOUS CHAMPIONS TOUR STATISTICS

2004 Low Round: 65–2004 Bayer Advantage Celebrity /1
Career Low Round: 65–2004 Bayer Advantage Celebrity/1
Career Largest Paycheck: $74,400–2004 SAS Championship /T5

MISCELLANEOUS PGA TOUR STATISTICS

Career Low Round: 67–2 times, most recent 1994 Nestle Invitational/2
Career Largest Paycheck: $1,702–1976 Hawaiian Open/T26

CHAMPIONS TOUR CAREER SUMMARY — PLAYOFF RECORD: 1-0

Year	Events Played	1st	2nd	3rd	Top 10	Top 25	Earnings	Rank
2002	12					1	$100,637	91
2003	23					10	324,304	49
2004	25				4	14	557,479	33
Total	60				4	25	982,420	
COMBINED ALL-TIME MONEY (3 TOURS):							**$984,767**	

CHAMPIONS TOUR TOP TOURNAMENT SUMMARY

Year	02	03	04
Senior PGA Championship		T24	9
U.S. Senior Open	T41	T35	11
Ford Senior Players		T19	T51
Senior British Open		CUT	T38
JELD-WEN Tradition		T33	T24

CHAMPIONS TOUR YEAR-BY-YEAR STATISTICS (TOP 50 ON 2004 MONEY LIST)

	Scoring Average	Putting Average	Greens in Regulation	Driving Distance	Driving Accuracy
2002	72.12 (N/A)	1.811 (N/A)	67.3 (N/A)	283.5 (N/A)	63.3 (N/A)
2003	71.24 (40)	1.803 (T52)	69.4 (T25)	282.7 (9)	62.0 (70)
2004	71.34 (30)	1.784 (24)	69.4 (27)	284.5 (9)	68.9 (54)

Morris Hatalsky (huh-TALL-skee)

EXEMPT STATUS: Top 30 on 2004 Champions Tour Money List
FULL NAME: Morris Hatalsky
HEIGHT: 5-11
WEIGHT: 175
BIRTHDATE: November 10, 1951
BIRTHPLACE: San Diego, CA
RESIDENCE: Ponte Vedra Beach, FL
FAMILY: Wife, Tracy; Daniel Kenneth (12/11/80), Laura Rose(2/26/83)
CLUB AFFILIATION: Trillium Links & Lake Club (Cashiers, NC)
EDUCATION: U.S. International University, Arizona State University
SPECIAL INTERESTS: Family activities, Wake Forest and Bucknell basketball
TURNED PROFESSIONAL: 1973
JOINED PGA TOUR: 1976

JOINED CHAMPIONS TOUR: 2002

CHAMPIONS TOUR VICTORIES (2): 2002 Uniting Fore Care Classic. **2003** Columbus Southern Open.

2004 CHARLES SCHWAB CUP FINISH: 19th - 870 points

PGA TOUR VICTORIES (4): 1981 Hall Of Fame. **1983** Greater Milwaukee Open. **1988** Kemper Open. **1990** Bank of Boston Classic.

OTHER VICTORIES (1): 1968 Mexico National Junior Championship.

PGA TOUR CAREER EARNINGS: $1,707,280

PGA TOUR PLAYOFF RECORD: 2-1

BEST 2004 CHAMPIONS TOUR FINISHES: 2—Toshiba Senior Classic; 3—Greater Hickory Classic at Rock Barn, FedEx Kinko's Classic; T5—Bruno's Memorial Classic, Administaff Small Business Classic.

2004 SEASON:

Matched his previous year when he was 15th on the final money list and also equaled his previous year's total for top-10 finishes as well…Best finish came early in the campaign when he battled Tom Purtzer down the stretch at the Toshiba Senior Classic before eventually finishing second by one stroke at Newport Beach. Performance in Orange County was his best effort since finishing as a runner-up at 2003 3M Championship…Closed with a 66 to place solo third at the Greater Hickory Classic at Rock Barn, his second consecutive top-five effort in western North Carolina…Also was one of three players to finish T3 at the FedEx Kinko's Classic in Austin. Joined Jose Maria Canizares as the only players to post three straight sub-par rounds at the tournament…T5 the previous week at the Bruno's Memorial Classic…Finished his year on a positive note with three straight top-10 finishes in successive weeks. Was T5 at the Administaff Small Business Classic, T7 at the SBC Championship and then closed the year with a T7 at the Charles Schwab Cup Championship…Led all players in Putting with an average of 1.746 and was second to Ben Crenshaw in Putts Per Round at 28.27.

CHAMPIONS TOUR CAREER HIGHLIGHTS:

2003: Among the top five in five events, all after mid-May, and finished in the top 10 in a third of his starts…Highlight of his year was a victory at the Columbus Southern Open. Claimed second Champions Tour title when he defeated Allen Doyle by one stroke. Played all 54 holes without a bogey, and in the process became the first player to win an event without a bogey since Bruce Fleisher at the 1999 Transamerica…Extended his bogey-free streak to 98 holes to set a new Champions Tour standard, breaking the old record of 97 set by the late Jack Kiefer in 1994. Started his streak on the 12th hole of his second round at the Bayer Advantage Celebrity Pro-Am and saw it end at the second hole of his second-round at the Music City Championship…Nearly won a second title in August when he finished T2 with Gil Morgan at the 3M Championship, one stroke behind Wayne Levi. Narrowly missed a birdie putt at 18, which would have eventually earned him a playoff spot opposite Levi…Was the first-round leader at the Farmers Charity Classic and was in contention down the stretch on Sunday before coming up solo third in Grand Rapids, two strokes short of both Doug Tewell and Eamonn Darcy…Also was one stroke back after 54 holes of the JELD-WEN Tradition. Eventually T5 after a final-round 72. **2002:** Voted by his peers as the Rookie of the Year…Was one of the great success stories of the season…Began the year as a non-exempt player. However, took full advantage of open qualifying, sponsor exemptions and his Past Champion status to parlay those early appearances into exempt status via the Tour reshuffle…Registered his first Champions Tour victory at the Uniting Fore Care Classic. Pulled away from the field with five birdies on the front nine and won by 12 points in the Modified Stableford system event. Victory in Park City ended a drought of 12 years, one month and 10 days and put him over the $1-million mark in just his 16th event of the season…Enjoyed great early success as an open qualifier, posting four top 10s in five starts via that route, including a runner-up effort to Jay Sigel at the Farmers Charity Classic, one of three 2002 second-place finishes.

OTHER CAREER HIGHLIGHTS:

Played full-time on the PGA TOUR from 1977-94 and had four victories, the last coming at the 1990 Bank of Boston Classic. Birdied three of the last four holes on Sunday to nip Scott Verplank by one stroke…Twice won titles in playoffs. Beat George Cadle in a playoff at the 1983 Greater Milwaukee Open and defeated Tom Kite in a playoff at the 1988 Kemper Open…Played in 451 career events and made 284 cuts…Best years came in 1988 and 1990 when he earned $239,019 and $253,639, respectively…Was 47th on the 1988 money list, his highest position ever…Led all PGA TOUR players in Putting in 1983…Won the 1968 Mexico National Junior Championship…Member of NAIA national championship squad at U.S. International…San Diego High School Golfer of the Year as a senior…Has had three holes-in-one in competitive rounds.

PERSONAL:

Played collegiately at U.S. International University where he won NAIA All-America honors in 1972 and served as captain of the team…Originally started his career at Arizona State University as a freshman and was a teammate of current Champions Tour players Bob Gilder, Howard Twitty and Tom Purtzer…Daughter, Laura, played basketball at Bucknell University in Pennsylvania…Is a partner in the Trillium Links & Lake Club in western North Carolina…Lists the birth of his two children as his biggest thrill outside of golf and qualifying for the PGA TOUR in 1976 as his biggest thrill in golf…Got started in the sport when his older brother bought him a set of junior clubs when he was 10 years old…Favorite athletes as a youngster were Sandy Koufax and golf's Big Three—Arnold Palmer, Jack Nicklaus and Gary Player…Away from the course, enjoys following the activities of his two children…First car he ever owned was a 1963 Volvo with a stick shift…Considers making it through the PGA TOUR Qualifying School in 1976 as his greatest achievement because he had decided it would be the last time he was going to attempt to qualify…Favorite golf courses are Cypress Point, Pebble Beach and Pine Valley…He and his family have two West Highland White Terriers named Hazard and Niblick…Favorite actor is Sean Connery and favorite movie is "Chariots of Fire"…Best friend on the Champions Tour is Don Pooley.

PLAYER STATISTICS

MISCELLANEOUS CHAMPIONS TOUR STATISTICS
2004 Low Round: 65–2004 Toshiba Senior Classic/1
Career Low Round: 63–2002 RJR Championship/2
Career Largest Paycheck: $225,000–2 times, most recent 2003 Columbus Southern Open/1

MISCELLANEOUS PGA TOUR STATISTICS
Career Low Round: 64–11 times, most recent 2001 B.C. Open/2
Career Largest Paycheck: $162,000–1990 Bank of Boston Classic/1

CHAMPIONS TOUR CAREER SUMMARY — PLAYOFF RECORD: 0-0

Year	Events Played	1st	2nd	3rd	Top 10	Top 25	Earnings	Rank
2002	24	1	3	1	14	19	$1,391,044	10
2003	27	1	1	1	9	16	1,150,584	15
2004	27		1	2	9	19	1,066,506	15
Total	78	2	5	4	32	54	3,608,134	

COMBINED ALL-TIME MONEY (3 TOURS): $5,403,116

CHAMPIONS TOUR TOP TOURNAMENT SUMMARY

Year	02	03	04
Senior PGA Championship	T10	T28	T38
U.S. Senior Open	T5	T12	18
Ford Senior Players	T33	T35	T16
Senior British Open			T18
JELD-WEN Tradition		T5	T14
Charles Schwab Cup Champ	T5	T16	T7

CHAMPIONS TOUR YEAR-BY-YEAR STATISTICS (TOP 50 ON 2004 MONEY LIST)

	Scoring Average	Putting Average	Greens in Regulation	Driving Distance	Driving Accuracy
2002	69.85 (T5)	1.740 (2)	69.0 (T24)	268.9 (43)	71.2 (30)
2003	70.61 (23)	1.783 (30)	69.4 (T25)	267.6 (T58)	72.2 (T23)
2004	70.55 (14)	1.746 (1)	66.4 (T44)	264.3 (64)	76.2 (14)

Mike Hill

EXEMPT STATUS: Top 30 on All-Time Money List
FULL NAME: Michael Joseph Hill
HEIGHT: 5-9
WEIGHT: 180
BIRTHDATE: January 27, 1939
BIRTHPLACE: Jackson, MI
RESIDENCE: Brooklyn, MI

FAMILY: Wife, Sandra; Kimberly (5/16/63), Kristen (12/11/69), Michael Jr. (4/15/72); five grandchildren
CLUB AFFILIATION: Pelican Sound Golf & River Club (Estero, FL)
EDUCATION: Arizona State University
SPECIAL INTERESTS: Hunting and fishing
TURNED PROFESSIONAL: 1967
JOINED PGA TOUR: 1968

JOINED CHAMPIONS TOUR: 1989

CHAMPIONS TOUR VICTORIES (18): 1990 GTE Suncoast Classic, GTE North Classic, Fairfield-Barnett Space Coast Classic, Security Pacific Senior Classic, New York Life Champions. **1991** Doug Sanders Celebrity Classic, Ameritech Senior Open, GTE Northwest Classic, Nationwide Championship, New York Life Champions. **1992** Vintage Arco Invitational, Doug Sanders Celebrity Classic, Digital Seniors Classic. **1993** Better Homes & Gardens Real Estate Challenge, PaineWebber Invitational. **1994** The IntelliNet Challenge. **1995** Kroger Senior Classic. **1996** Bank One Classic.

OTHER SENIOR VICTORIES (5): 1988 Mazda Champions [with Patti Rizzo]. **1991** Liberty Mutual Legends of Golf [with Lee Trevino]. **1992** Liberty Mutual Legends of Golf [with Lee Trevino]. **1995** Liberty Mutual Legends of Golf [with Lee Trevino]. **1996** Liberty Mutual Legends of Golf [with Lee Trevino].

2004 CHARLES SCHWAB CUP FINISH: 60th - 94 points

GEORGIA-PACIFIC GRAND CHAMPIONS VICTORIES (17): 1999 The Home Depot Invitational, Bruno's Memorial Classic, Foremost Insurance Championship, Georgia-Pacific Super Seniors Championship. **2000** Royal Caribbean Classic, Las Vegas Senior Classic, Foremost Insurance Championship. **2001** Verizon Classic, BellSouth Senior Classic at Opryland, FleetBoston Classic, Farmers Charity Classic. **2002** The Instinet Classic, Lightpath Long Island Classic. **2003** Long Island Classic, SBC Championship. **2004** Commerce Bank Long Island Classic, Georgia-Pacific Grand Champions Championship.

PGA TOUR VICTORIES (3): 1970 Doral-Eastern Open Invitational. **1972** San Antonio Texas Open. **1977** Ohio Kings Island Open.

PGA TOUR CAREER EARNINGS: $573,724

BEST 2004 CHAMPIONS TOUR FINISHES: T6—Commerce Bank Long Island Classic; T8—Bruno's Memorial Classic.

2004 SEASON:

Played a limited schedule once again, with a pair of top-10 finishes to his credit...First came near Birmingham in April when he was T8 at Bruno's Memorial Classic...Continued to enjoy success on Long Island, where he was T6 at July's Commerce Bank Long Island Classic, his third straight top-10 effort in that event. Was T3 just three strokes behind Jerry Pate after 36 holes, but slipped three places with a 2-over 72 on Sunday. Cruised to a six-stroke victory in the Georgia-Pacific Grand Champions event at Eisenhower Park...Capped his year with a strong showing at the Georgia-Pacific Grand Champions Championship in Sonoma, CA. Fashioned three consecutive 3-under-par 69s to breeze to a five-stroke win over Raymond Floyd for his 17th career title. It was his second win at the season-ending event and the first since he won in 1999 in Myrtle Beach, SC...Was fourth on the final Georgia-Pacific Grand Champions money list, with $170,100, giving him $1,497,633 for his career in that category.

CHAMPIONS TOUR CAREER HIGHLIGHTS:

2003: Season highlighted by a solo third-place effort at the Verizon Classic, his best performance ever at the TPC of Tampa Bay and best showing in Tampa since winning at Tampa Palms in 1990. Final-round 66 included a hole-in-one on No. 6 with a 9-iron from 145 yards, his fifth ace overall, his first as a member of the Champions Tour and first ace since the 1980 Phoenix Open...Was again a force among the Georgia-Pacific Grand Champions event, finishing third on the final money list with $174,825...Won his 14th Georgia-Pacific Grand Champions title when he successfully defended his over-60 title at the Long Island Classic, defeating Jerry McGee and Lee Trevino by one stroke. His three straight rounds in the 60s were instrumental in his T5 overall finish on Long Island, his second consecutive top-10 effort at that tournament (was T8 in 2002)...Added a 15th Georgia-Pacific title near the end of the year at the SBC Championship when he birdied the first playoff hole to defeat Raymond Floyd. **2002:** Was T3 at The Instinet Classic, his best finish since the FleetBoston Classic in June 2001. Won the Georgia-Pacific Grand Champions competition at Princeton for his first of two victories in that category during the year...Carded a 7-under 64 on the first day of the Verizon Classic, his lowest round since posting 64 in the second round of the 1998 Boone Valley Classic...Fourth on the final Georgia-Pacific money list with $290,042. **2001:** Led the Georgia-Pacific Grand Champions money list with $325,137, the second-highest amount ever earned in that competition (George Archer won $364,988 in 2000)...Posted four victories in the over-60 events on the year and was first or second in his first eight starts in the Georgia-Pacific competition. Claimed his first Georgia-Pacific title at the Verizon Classic, defeating Gary Player by one stroke. Cruised to a five-stroke victory over Rocky Thompson and J.C. Snead in the 36-hole event at the BellSouth Senior Classic at Opryland. Won back-to-back G-P titles at the FleetBoston Classic and the Farmers Charity Classic, his third consecutive victory at that venue. Defeated Snead again by five strokes in the Georgia-Pacific event in Boston and bested Jim Dent in a playoff at Egypt Valley CC...Held a one-stroke lead over Larry Nelson after 36 holes of the FleetBoston Classic, but posted an even-par 72 on Sunday and T3, his best overall performance on the Champions Tour since 1997. **2000:** Won three Georgia-Pacific Grand Champions events and third on the G-P money list that year. **1999:** Enjoyed great success in the Georgia-Pacific Grand Champions competition with four wins and was third on the final money list...Won the season-ending Georgia-Pacific Super Seniors Championship. **1996:** Claimed 18th Champions Tour title with win at Bank One Classic in Lexington...Was also part of a record five-man playoff at Emerald Coast Classic, eventually won by Lee Trevino...Teamed with Trevino to win fourth Liberty Mutual Legends of Golf title. **1995:** Tossed aside chal-

SECTION 2 PLAYER BIOGRAPHIES

CHAMPIONS TOUR CAREER SUMMARY — PLAYOFF RECORD: 5-1

Year	Events Played	1st	2nd	3rd	Top 10	Top 25	Earnings	Rank
1989	32		1	1	19	26	$412,104	9
1990	32	5	4	3	21	29	895,678	2
1991	32	5	2	6	21	30	1,065,657	1
1992	29	3	3	2	22	27	802,423	4
1993	29	2	4	2	15	26	798,116	6
1994	25	1	1	1	10	21	580,621	16
1995	26	1		1	7	18	575,536	20
1996	19	1	2		7	15	528,130	22
1997	27		1	1	9	17	678,640	20
1998	20				1	12	274,359	58
1999	17				1	4	173,164	68
2000	19				2	6	239,395	66
2001	16			1	4	8	355,974	50
2002	16			1	4	8	351,284	47
2003	14			1	4	8	388,410	43
2004	15				2	3	169,255	70
Total	368	18	18	20	149	258	8,288,745	
COMBINED ALL-TIME MONEY (3 TOURS):							**$8,862,469**	

CHAMPIONS TOUR TOP TOURNAMENT SUMMARY

Year	89	90	91	92	93	94	95	96	97	98	99	00	01
Senior PGA Championship	T4	T16	T29	2	6	T15	WD		T35				
U.S. Senior Open	14	T3	T8			16							
Ford Senior Players	T18	T11	T8	T12	T13	T25	T18	T16	T49	T12	T44	40	T20
JELD-WEN Tradition	T29	T7	T23	T8	2	T7	WD		T19	T20			
Charles Schwab Cup Champ		1	1	T16	19	T8	T8	T10	T14				

Year	02	03	04
Ford Senior Players	T65	T23	75

Mike Hill (continued)

lenges by Isao Aoki and Graham Marsh to claim his first Champions Tour title in 17 months at the Kroger Senior Classic. Win at Kings Island made him the eighth man to win a Champions Tour and PGA TOUR event on the same layout. Had won the 1977 Ohio Kings Island Open on the same Grizzly Course. **1994:** Only player this year to successfully defend a title when he won the IntelliNet Challenge in Naples. **1993:** Captured two tournaments before the end of May and was among the top seven in more than one-third of his appearances during the season. **1992:** A trio of titles included a second consecutive official victory at the Doug Sanders Kingwood Celebrity Classic and second consecutive Liberty Mutual Legends of Golf title with Lee Trevino. **1991:** Shared Player of the Year honors with George Archer and won the Arnold Palmer Award as the leading money-winner on the Champions Tour after recording five victories...Went over $1 million in earnings for the only time in his career, and was the leading money-winner in all of golf that season...The $150,000 check at the season-ending New York Life Champions pushed him past the $1-million plateau in single-season earnings and made him the second Champions Tour player to top that level (Lee Trevino was the first in 1990) in a year. **1990:** Posted five wins and was runner-up to Trevino on the money list...First Champions Tour title came at the GTE Suncoast Classic near Tampa, a two-stroke victory over Trevino. **1989:** Was ninth on the final money list and was runner-up to Bob Charles at the Digital Seniors Classic.

OTHER CAREER HIGHLIGHTS:

Claimed three PGA TOUR titles...Defeated Jim Colbert by four strokes for his first win at the 1970 Doral-Eastern Open...Won the San Antonio-Texas Open late in 1972 with four consecutive rounds in the 60s...Last victory came at the 1977 Ohio Kings Island Open, where he fired a final-round 64 to edge Tom Kite by a stroke...Most profitable TOUR year was 1974, when he earned $76,802 and finished 28th on the money list...Needed three tries at the PGA TOUR National Qualifying Tournament before finally earning his card in the spring of 1968.

PERSONAL:

Younger brother of Dave Hill...Grew up on a dairy farm adjacent to a golf course and started the game as a caddie...Spent nearly four years in the Air Force and attended both Jackson (MI) Junior College and Arizona State prior to turning pro...Owns an 18-hole municipal golf course in Brooklyn, MI, known as Hill's Heart of the Lakes...Inducted into the Michigan Sports Hall of Fame in 1994...Lists Ben Hogan and Gordie Howe as his heroes...Got started in golf by working as a caddie at Jackson CC...Biggest thrill outside of golf is being married to his wife, Sandy, for 36 years and being around his children and grandchildren.

PLAYER STATISTICS

2004 CHAMPIONS TOUR STATISTICS:

Scoring Average	72.67	(61)
Driving Distance	268.7	(54)
Driving Accuracy Percentage	70.5%	(39)
Total Driving	93	(60)
Greens in Regulation Pct.	63.8%	(56)
Putting Average	1.850	(73)
Sand Save Percentage	40.0%	(65)
Eagles (Holes per)	828.0	(69)
Birdie Average	2.50	(72)
All-Around Ranking	489	(73)

MISCELLANEOUS CHAMPIONS TOUR STATISTICS

2004 Low Round: 66–2004 Commerce Bank Long Island Classic/1

Career Low Round: 63–3 times, most recent 1994 The IntelliNet Challenge/3

Career Largest Paycheck: $150,000–2 times, most recent 1991 New York Life Champions/1

MISCELLANEOUS PGA TOUR STATISTICS

Career Low Round: 63–1975 Phoenix Open/2

Career Largest Paycheck: $30,000–2 times, most recent 1977 Ohio Kings Island Open/1

25 MEMORABLE MOMENTS

Nicklaus Completes Senior Career Slam

1991 U.S. Senior Open

Four players were tied for the lead at Oakland Hills with two holes left in regulation, but only two emerged to play an extra round Monday. A five-foot birdie by Jack Nicklaus at the par-3 17th, coupled with Chi Chi Rodriguez's brilliant approach over a bunker at the 18th that rolled two feet from the cup for an easy birdie, left the two deadlocked after 72 holes. In the last 18-hole playoff in Champions Tour history, Rodriguez responded with a 69, but Nicklaus shot 65 for the victory. By winning, Nicklaus, at the time, became the first and only player to claim all four of the Champions Tour's major titles in his career.

Joe Inman

EXEMPT STATUS: Net-70 on All-Time Money List
FULL NAME: Joseph Cooper Inman, Jr.
HEIGHT: 5-11
WEIGHT: 165
BIRTHDATE: November 29, 1947
BIRTHPLACE: Indianapolis, IN
RESIDENCE: Marietta, GA

FAMILY: Wife, Nancy; Joseph Craig (4/13/77), Sally Anne (8/9/83), Kate (10/31/86)
CLUB AFFILIATION: Atlanta CC (Atlanta, GA)
EDUCATION: Wake Forest University (1970, History)
TURNED PROFESSIONAL: 1972
JOINED PGA TOUR: 1973

JOINED CHAMPIONS TOUR: 1998

CHAMPIONS TOUR VICTORIES (3): 1998 Pacific Bell Senior Classic. **1999** Pacific Bell Senior Classic. **2000** SBC Senior Classic.

2004 CHARLES SCHWAB CUP FINISH: T49th - 189 points

PGA TOUR VICTORIES (1): 1976 Kemper Open.

OTHER VICTORIES (3): 1968 Carolinas Open. **1969** North-South Amateur. **1970** North Carolina Amateur.

PGA TOUR CAREER EARNINGS: $729,249

BEST 2004 CHAMPIONS TOUR FINISHES: T4—SBC Classic; T5—Greater Hickory Classic at Rock Barn; T9—Allianz Championship.

2004 SEASON:

Among the top 10 in three events, one more than in his last two years combined...Also had his best earnings year since 2001 season, pocketing more than he made in both the 2002-2003 campaigns put together...Equaled the Valencia CC course record with a final-round 64 and vaulted into a T4 at the SBC Classic, his best Champions Tour finish since winning the same event at Wilshire CC in 2000....Opened with 64 the following week at the Toshiba Senior Classic, but eventually T18 at Newport Beach...Rebounded from an opening-round 73 with 67-68 on the weekend at the Greater Hickory Classic at Rock Barn to T5...Also T9 in late May at the Allianz Championship.

CHAMPIONS TOUR CAREER HIGHLIGHTS:

2003: Posted his lone top-10 finish in his final start, T9 at the Turtle Bay Championship...Two weeks earlier, vaulted into contention at the Greater Hickory Classic at Rock Barn after posting a course-record 9-under 63 in the second round, equaling his career-best round on the Champions Tour. Round included just 22 putts. Eventually slipped back into a T16 after a final-round 77...Fully exempt for 2004 by virtue of his T4 finish along with Lonnie Nielsen at the National Qualifying Tournament at the TPC at Eagle Trace. Fired four straight sub-par rounds at the National Qualifier, his first trip there since 1997. **2002:** T8 at the rain-shortened Emerald Coast Classic near Pensacola. **2001:** T6 at The Home Depot Invitational after trailing Jim Colbert by just one stroke entering the final round...Found himself again on the leaderboard through two rounds of the TD Waterhouse Championship, thanks to an 8-under 64 Saturday, his lowest round since the 1999 Kroger Senior Classic (63). Eventually T6 again after shooting a 2-under 70 at Tiffany Greens. **2000:** Among the top 10 in almost one-third of his starts and quickly recovered from an inner-ear infection to have his two best performances near the end of the season...Went all 54 holes of the EMC Kaanapali Classic without making a bogey and finished second to Hale Irwin by four strokes in Hawaii...Won for a third straight year at the SBC Senior Classic, becoming the fifth player in Champions Tour history to three-peat in an event. Bogey-free streak ended at 94 straight holes during the opening round of the Los Angeles event, the second-longest run in Champions Tour history, just three holes shy of Jack Kiefer's mark. **1999:** Successfully defended his Pacific Bell Senior Classic title. Rallied from three strokes back on Sunday with a sizzling 65 to edge Dave Stockton by two strokes. Almost won the Cadillac NFL Golf Classic, but lost to Allen Doyle on the fourth extra hole...Fired a Champions Tour career-low round of 7-under 63 on Saturday at the Kroger Senior Classic. **1998:** Won his first Champions Tour title late in the season at the Pacific Bell Senior Classic. Jumped from 42nd on the money list into the top 31 with the victory. Was a one-stroke winner over Lee Trevino at Wilshire CC, making birdie on three of his last five holes...Selected by his peers as the Champions Tour Rookie of the Year. **1997:** Earned fully-exempt status for 1998 after finishing T5 at the 1997 National Qualifying Tournament at the TPC of Sawgrass Valley Course in November.

OTHER CAREER HIGHLIGHTS:

High point came in 1976, when he won the Kemper Open by one stroke over Grier Jones and Tom Weiskopf at Quail Hollow CC in Charlotte, NC...Played a full schedule on the PGA TOUR from 1974-1986...In addition to his victory, was second at the following events: 1974 Tallahassee Open, 1977 Florida Citrus Open and 1979 Atlanta Classic...Enjoyed his best year financially in 1979, when he won $75,035 and finished 52nd on the money list...Enjoyed success as an amateur before beginning his professional career. Won the 1969 North-South Amateur and also played on the winning United States Walker Cup team in 1969, where his teammates included Bruce Fleisher, Steve Melnyk and Lanny Wadkins...Has had four career holes-in-one.

PERSONAL:

Worked as a Ping sales representative from 1989-97...Also was a member of the PGA TOUR Radio Network broadcast crew in 1997...His brother John is a two-time winner on the PGA TOUR and is now the golf coach at North Carolina...A college teammate of Leonard Thompson and Lanny Wadkins at Wake Forest...Served a brief stint in the U.S. Army following his graduation from Wake Forest...Lists Cypress Point as his favorite golf course and Arnold Palmer as his favorite athlete...Was inducted into the Wake Forest Sports Hall of Fame on Feb. 9, 2002 along with former Wake football players Ricky Proehl and Tony Mayberry.

PLAYER STATISTICS

MISCELLANEOUS CHAMPIONS TOUR STATISTICS

2004 Low Round: 64–2 times, most recent 2004 Toshiba Senior Classic/1
Career Low Round: 63–2 times, most recent 2003 Greater Hickory Classic at Rock Barn/2
Career Largest Paycheck: $210,000–2000 SBC Senior Classic/1

MISCELLANEOUS PGA TOUR STATISTICS

Career Low Round: 62–1978 Sammy Davis Jr.-Greater Hartford Open/2
Career Largest Paycheck: $50,000–1976 Kemper Open/1

CHAMPIONS TOUR CAREER SUMMARY — PLAYOFF RECORD: 0-1

Year	Events Played	1st	2nd	3rd	Top 10	Top 25	Earnings	Rank
1998	35	1		1	5	15	$653,902	26
1999	35	1	1	2	10	22	1,051,357	11
2000	34	1	1		11	18	973,504	16
2001	34				2	9	468,056	42
2002	26				1	3	183,700	76
2003	25				1	2	184,471	69
2004	26				3	10	420,051	47
Total	215	3	2	3	33	79	3,935,040	

COMBINED ALL-TIME MONEY (3 TOURS): $4,666,039

CHAMPIONS TOUR TOP TOURNAMENT SUMMARY

Year	98	99	00	01	02	03	04
Senior PGA Championship		T11	T54	T20	T57	CUT	T27
U.S. Senior Open		T3	T31	T48	T41	T40	
Ford Senior Players	T45	T22	T41	T17	T73		T63
Senior British Open							T66
JELD-WEN Tradition	DQ	T60	5	T52	68	T52	T59
Charles Schwab Cup Champ	T6	T18	T24				

CHAMPIONS TOUR YEAR-BY-YEAR STATISTICS (TOP 50 ON 2004 MONEY LIST)

	Scoring Average	Putting Average	Greens in Regulation	Driving Distance	Driving Accuracy
1998	71.52 (30)	1.807 (T41)	67.2 (23)	256.1 (64)	73.2 (T15)
1999	70.70 (19)	1.765 (T9)	69.2 (23)	255.5 (76)	71.2 (T35)
2000	70.77 (23)	1.767 (17)	68.5 (T31)	261.1 (72)	70.9 (T35)
2001	71.89 (44)	1.804 (50)	66.5 (39)	257.2 (81)	69.8 (T45)
2002	73.00 (T76)	1.831 (T70)	61.3 (T74)	250.3 (89)	69.0 (41)
2003	72.41 (66)	1.823 (68)	61.2 (T74)	252.2 (87)	66.7 (49)
2004	72.19 (50)	1.795 (34)	64.2 (55)	255.7 (75)	76.0 (T15)

Hale Irwin

WORLD GOLF HALL OF FAME MEMBER (Inducted 1992)
EXEMPT STATUS: Top 30 on 2004 Champions Tour Money List
FULL NAME: Hale S. Irwin
HEIGHT: 6-0
WEIGHT: 185
BIRTHDATE: June 3, 1945
BIRTHPLACE: Joplin, MO
RESIDENCE: Paradise Valley, AZ
FAMILY: Wife, Sally; Becky (12/15/71), Steven (8/6/74); two grandchildren
CLUB AFFILIATION: Hokuli'a (Kailua-Kona, HI)
EDUCATION: University of Colorado (1967, Marketing)
SPECIAL INTERESTS: Photography, golf course design
TURNED PROFESSIONAL: 1968
JOINED PGA TOUR: 1968

JOINED CHAMPIONS TOUR: 1995

CHAMPIONS TOUR VICTORIES (40): 1995 Ameritech Senior Open, Vantage Championship. **1996** American Express Invitational, PGA Seniors' Championship. **1997** MasterCard Championship, LG Championship, PGA Seniors' Championship, Las Vegas Senior Classic, Burnet Senior Classic, BankBoston Classic, Boone Valley Classic, Vantage Championship, Hyatt Regency Maui Kaanapali Classic. **1998** Toshiba Senior Classic, PGA Seniors' Championship, Las Vegas Senior Classic, Ameritech Senior Open, U.S. Senior Open, BankBoston Classic, Energizer SENIOR TOUR Championship. **1999** Nationwide Championship, Boone Valley Classic, Ford Senior Players Championship, Ameritech Senior Open, Coldwell Banker Burnet Classic. **2000** Nationwide Championship, BellSouth Senior Classic at Opryland, U.S. Senior Open, EMC Kaanapali Classic. **2001** Siebel Classic in Silicon Valley, Bruno's Memorial Classic, Turtle Bay Championship. **2002** ACE Group Classic, Toshiba Senior Classic, 3M Championship, Turtle Bay Championship. **2003** Kinko's Classic of Austin, Turtle Bay Championship. **2004** Liberty Mutual Legends of Golf, Senior PGA Championship.

OTHER SENIOR VICTORIES: (8): 1996 Lexus Challenge [with Sean Connery]. **1997** Senior Slam at Los Cabos. **1998** Senior Match Play Challenge. **1999** Senior Skins Game, Wendy's Three-Tour Challenge [with Jack Nicklaus and Tom Watson]. **2000** Our Lucaya Senior Slam. **2001** Senior Skins Game. **2002** Senior Skins Game.

2004 CHARLES SCHWAB CUP FINISH:
1st - 3,427 points

PGA TOUR VICTORIES (20): 1971 Sea Pines Heritage Classic. **1973** Sea Pines Heritage Classic. **1974** U.S. Open Championship. **1975** Atlanta Classic, Western Open. **1976** Glen Campbell-Los Angeles Open, Florida Citrus Open. **1977** Atlanta Classic, Colgate Hall of Fame Golf Classic, San Antonio Texas Open. **1979** U.S. Open Championship. **1981** Hawaiian Open, Buick Open. **1982** Honda Inverrary Classic. **1983** Memorial Tournament. **1984** Bing Crosby National Pro-Am. **1985** Memorial Tournament. **1990** U.S. Open Championship, Buick Classic. **1994** MCI Heritage Golf Classic.

OTHER VICTORIES (11): 1967 NCAA Championship [indiv]. **1974** Piccadilly World Match Play. **1975** Piccadilly World Match Play. **1978** Australian PGA. **1979** South African PGA, World Cup [indiv], World Cup [with John Mahaffey]. **1981** Bridgestone Classic. **1982** Brazilian Open. **1986** Bahamas Classic. **1987** Fila Classic.

PGA TOUR CAREER EARNINGS: $5,966,031

PGA TOUR PLAYOFF RECORD: 4-5

BEST 2004 CHAMPIONS TOUR FINISHES:
1—Liberty Mutual Legends of Golf, Senior PGA Championship; 2—U.S. Senior Open, Constellation Energy Classic, Administaff Small Business Classic presented by KBR; T3—The First Tee Open at Pebble Beach presented by Wal-Mart.

2004 SEASON:
Continued to defy the odds and again put together a remarkable season that contained multiple victories, despite having to deal with a tender lower back and assorted neck and shoulder pain late in the year...Was T7 at the Charles Schwab Cup Championship, which helped him hold off Craig Stadler by a mere 39 points in the season's final event to earn his second Charles Schwab Cup. Led the Schwab Cup race for 11 weeks during the summer and then slipped into second place for four weeks before regaining the top spot for good after his runner-up finish at the Administaff Small Business Classic...Was among the top 10 in 14 of 23 events, including three top-10 efforts in four of the senior major championships he entered...Had a Tour-best 40 rounds in the 60s out of 73 played (55 percent)...Went over $2-million mark in official money for the seventh time in the last eight years...Won multiple titles for an unprecedented 10th straight season, with both victories coming during the spring...Survived a grueling week at Valhalla in late May to claim his fourth Senior PGA Championship and his 40th career Champions Tour title. Two-putted from 40 feet to birdie the 72nd hole to claim the weather-plagued event by one stroke over Jay Haas. Led or was tied for the lead after each round, and victory came just three days short of his 59th birthday, making him the oldest winner of a major since the start of the Champions Tour and the oldest player ever to win multiple events. Win was his seventh senior major title and he joined Jack Nicklaus (JELD-WEN Tradition) as the only other player to win the same major four times. Triumph at Valhalla also gave him a major championship title in six of his nine full years on the Champions Tour...Held off Gil Morgan in late April for the Liberty Mutual Legends of Golf crown. Managed to eek out a one-stroke victory after making par on the final hole while Morgan two-putted from 20 feet for a bogey. Legends appearance was his first in a month and win in Savannah was his 21st different Champions Tour title...Had opportunities to win three other events during the year...Made a valiant bid to win his third U.S. Senior Open at Bellerive, but came up one stroke short of Peter Jacobsen. Posted rounds of 67-68 on 36-hole Sunday, but was derailed midway through the front nine of his final round by a bogey-double bogey stretch (holes 5 and 6)...Mounted a final-round charge at the Constellation Energy Classic, matching the tournament course record with a final-round 64, to finish second, two shots back of Wayne Levi. Birdied six of the last seven holes Sunday to post his lowest score since firing a 64 in the second round of the 2002 RJR Championship...Finished second again at the inaugural Administaff Small Business Classic, losing to Larry Nelson on the first hole of a playoff. Jumped into contention during the final round by holing a 4-iron second shot from 195 yards for an eagle on Augusta Pines' par-4 14th hole. Got into the overtime session after a two-putt birdie on the par-5 final hole...Missed the SAS Championship in Raleigh due to a neck strain...Ran off a string of 10 straight sub-par rounds from the Allianz Championship to the Bayer Advantage Celebrity Pro-Am and then had a 2004 Champions Tour-best 16 consecutive sub-par rounds over his last six starts of the year...Was also in contention early in the final round of the inaugural First Tee Open at Pebble Beach before eventually finishing T3 on the

CHAMPIONS TOUR CAREER SUMMARY **PLAYOFF RECORD: 2-6**

Year	Events Played	1st	2nd	3rd	Top 10	Top 25	Earnings	Rank
1995	12	2	3		11	12	$799,175	10
1996	23	2	7	2	21	23	1,615,769	2
1997	23	9	3	1	18	22	2,343,364	1
1998	22	7	6	2	20	22	2,861,945	1
1999	26	5	2	3	14	23	2,025,232	2
2000	24	4	4	1	17	23	2,128,968	3
2001	26	3	2	4	18	24	2,147,422	3
2002	27	4	6	4	22	27	3,028,304	1
2003	22	2	2	2	13	19	1,607,391	5
2004	23	2	3	1	14	20	2,035,397	2
Total	228	40	38	20	168	215	20,592,965	
COMBINED ALL-TIME MONEY (3 TOURS):							**$26,558,996**	

CHAMPIONS TOUR TOP TOURNAMENT SUMMARY

Year	95	96	97	98	99	00	01	02	03	04
Senior PGA Championship		1	1	1	T11	T2	T5	T2	T15	1
U.S. Senior Open	T5	2	T5	1	T3	1	T11	T11		2
Ford Senior Players	T10	2	T19	2	1	T4	3	T6	T12	T9
JELD-WEN Tradition		2	T13	4	T20	T37	3	6	T10	13
Charles Schwab Cup Champ	T8	T10	2	1	T18	T24	T7	4	T4	T7

CHAMPIONS TOUR YEAR-BY-YEAR STATISTICS (TOP 50 ON 2004 MONEY LIST)

	Scoring Average	Putting Average	Greens in Regulation	Driving Distance	Driving Accuracy
1995	68.85 (N/A)	1.730 (N/A)	78.1 (N/A)	253.8 (N/A)	82.2 (N/A)
1996	69.47 (1)	1.762 (3)	74.7 (1)	260.6 (T45)	79.0 (3)
1997	68.92 (1)	1.734 (1)	76.2 (1)	266.1 (T25)	76.5 (7)
1998	68.59 (1)	1.700 (1)	76.4 (1)	264.0 (42)	79.6 (3)
1999	69.58 (2)	1.756 (7)	73.4 (3)	264.6 (45)	79.1 (4)
2000	69.16 (4)	1.733 (3)	75.5 (3)	266.9 (40)	79.8 (3)
2001	69.29 (2)	1.728 (1)	72.2 (T4)	267.1 (63)	76.2 (T8)
2002	68.93 (1)	1.717 (1)	72.2 (9)	269.6 (39)	80.3 (5)
2003	69.59 (3)	1.772 (T17)	73.6 (2)	274.8 (32)	77.1 (5)
2004	69.58 (2)	1.753 (5)	76.0 (1)	269.8 (51)	80.9 (5)

Hale Irwin (continued)

Monterey Peninsula...Had at least one round in the 60s in 19 of 23 events played and has done so in 103 of his last 110 official events...Posted an ace during the first round of the PGA Championship at Whistling Straits. Used a 3-iron from 185 yards on the par-3 seventh hole. Ended up missing the cut by a stroke, ending his steak of consecutive cuts made at 16. Also only the second time in his career he has missed the cut at the PGA, the other being 1979...Did not participate in the U.S. Open Championship, ending a streak of 33 consecutive appearances in the event...Went over the $20-million mark in Champions Tour career earnings after T13 finish at the JELD-WEN Tradition ($46,000).

CHAMPIONS TOUR CAREER HIGHLIGHTS:

2003: Despite back woes for the final four months of the season, made history when he won his 38th career title at the Turtle Bay Championship. Made up two strokes on second-round leader Tom Kite the final day, and the pair battled down to the wire before he emerged victorious, thanks to a birdie on the 17th hole. In the process, became the first Champions Tour player to win the same event four times in succession and also became the first to win the same event five times. Win also increased his earnings in the Aloha State for all events to $3,503,975 and was his seventh official victory in Hawaii, including six on the Champions Tour...Overcame a triple bogey on the front nine in Sunday's final round to win the inaugural Kinko's Classic of Austin. Claimed his 37th career title after making birdie on the second playoff hole to defeat Tom Watson at The Hills CC., tying the all-time Champions Tour record held by Miller Barber for consecutive seasons with at least one title...Selected as the Champions Tour Player of the Month for May...Tied the Aronimink competitive course record with a closing-round, 5-under-par 65 at the Senior PGA Championship and T15...Earned a special exemption into the U.S. Open, his 33rd consecutive appearance in the event, but was forced to withdraw after 11 holes in the opening round with severe back spasms. Back injury kept him out of action for almost one month...Returned to action at the Ford Senior Players Championship and T12, thanks to a final-round 67. Earned $50,833 paycheck in Dearborn that vaulted him over the seven-figure mark in single-season earnings for an eighth consecutive year. Had at least one round in the 60s in 20 of 22 tournaments he played. **2002:** Voted by his peers as the Champions Tour's Player of the Year for a third time...Established a Champions Tour record for earnings in a season with $3,028,304, breaking his own mark of $2,861,945 and in the process became the oldest player to win the money title (Arnold Palmer Award) at age 57 (previous mark was by Peter Thomson, who won the 1985 money title at age 56)...Clinched his first Charles Schwab Cup and the money title with his fourth victory of the year at the Turtle Bay Championship in Hawaii, the 36th win of his Champions Tour career. Birdied the first extra playoff hole to defeat Gary McCord. Win allowed him to tie Jack Nicklaus (four wins at The Countrywide Tradition) for most victories in the same event and also was his first playoff win ever on the Champions Tour in six tries...Started the year by winning his third straight Senior Skins (1999, 2001, 2002; did not play in 2000) title on the island of Maui. Prevailed over Jack Nicklaus, Arnold Palmer and Fuzzy Zoeller at Wailea GC. Won five skins and $260,000 on the final hole to help him earn a record $450,000, breaking Raymond Floyd's mark of $420,000 in 1995....Captured his 33rd career title on the Champions Tour early on at The ACE Group Classic in Naples. Dueled Tom Watson down the stretch before defeating him by a stroke at The Club at TwinEagles...Set a Champions Tour record when he posted his 75th career top-three finish, a T2 at the Audi Senior Classic in Mexico, breaking Bob Charles' mark of 74...Won the Toshiba Senior Classic by five strokes with a record-setting 196 total, his second win in Newport Beach...Also won his third 3M Championship in Minnesota. Was tied with James Mason after 36 holes, but broke away from the pack for a three-stroke victory. Win at the TPC of the Twin Cities also marked the sixth consecutive season he had won at least three times...Became the first over the $3-million mark in season earnings with his fourth-place finish at the SENIOR TOUR Championship in Gaillardia...Also became the oldest player to claim the Byron Nelson Award as the Scoring leader (68.93)...Player of the Month for February and August...Played in his 32nd consecutive U.S. Open at Bethpage, but missed the cut. **2001:** Eclipsed the $2-million mark for an unprecedented fifth straight campaign at The Transamerica...Won three official events, the fifth straight year he's won at least three times in a season, tying him with Miller Barber and Lee Trevino for the most in Champions Tour history...Broke out of a tie with Lee Trevino atop the all-time victory list by claiming the inaugural Siebel Classic in Silicon Valley, his 30th career win in his 135th start on the Champions Tour...Posted three consecutive rounds of 65 and shattered the Bruno's Memorial Classic tournament record by six strokes with a 21-under 195 total. Easily outdistanced Stewart Ginn by four strokes for his 31st Champions Tour victory...Notched his 32nd title late in the campaign at the Turtle Bay Championship in Hawaii...Played in the U.S. Open at Southern Hills and T52 after being one stroke off the lead after an opening-round 67. **2000:** Claimed four official victories, the fourth straight year he won four or more titles in a season...Tied Lee Trevino atop the all-time victory list when he won his second EMC Kaanapali Classic, besting Joe Inman by four strokes. Victory in Hawaii gave him multiple wins in 10 different tournaments (since increased to 12)...Successfully defended his Nationwide Championship crown, at the time the sixth successful defense of his senior career. Made just one bogey over 54 holes and edged Tom Jenkins and Vicente Fernandez by one stroke...Picked up his second title three weeks later when he held off Gil Morgan by a stroke for the BellSouth Senior Classic at Opryland crown...Biggest victory of his season came in early July when he triumphed at the U.S. Senior Open for a second time. Carded rounds of 65-65 on the weekend at Saucon Valley and overtook Bruce Fleisher on the final day to win by three strokes. His 17-under 267 total was the lowest four-round score in any U.S. Senior Open Championship and gave him a sixth senior major title...Finished T27 at the U.S. Open at Pebble Beach and joined Tiger Woods as the only other player in the field to post at least two rounds in the 60s on the Monterey Peninsula...Underwent LASIK surgery the week prior to the GTE Classic and went on to T3 in Tampa. **1999:** Became the first player in the history of the Champions Tour to win five or more official tournaments three years in a row...Won all five of his events from early May until late August. During that four-month stretch, he was par/better in 34 of 37 rounds and had a scoring average of 68.51...Started the run with a dramatic victory at the Nationwide Championship. Holed a 74-yard wedge shot for an eagle on the final hole to break a tie with Bob Murphy...Closed with a 66 to defeat Al Geiberger by two strokes at the Boone Valley Classic...Biggest win of the year came at the Ford Senior Players Championship, when he captured his fifth senior major despite a sore right rotator cuff. Used a final-round 65 to blow away the field by seven shots, the largest margin of victory ever at the TPC of Michigan. His 72-hole score of 21-under 267 also equaled Gil Morgan's tournament record set in Dearborn in 1998...Rallied from an opening-round 73 to successfully defend his Ameritech Senior Open title by one stroke over Gary McCord, Bruce Fleisher and Raymond Floyd...Captured the Coldwell Banker Burnet Classic the next week in wire-to-wire fashion, defeating Jim Dent and Dale Douglass by two shots. Win in Minnesota moved him into solo second place on the all-time Champions Tour wins list...Set a Champions Tour record for consecutive sub-70 rounds with 13 in a row (second round/Ameritech Senior Open through second round/AT&T Canada Senior Open Championship)...Lost twice in playoffs. Fell to Tom McGinnis at BankBoston Classic and to Jim Ahern the following week at AT&T Canada Senior Open. **1998:** Voted the circuit's Player of the Year for the second straight season after seven victories, including two major championships...In 22 starts, amazingly finished in the top five in all but two tournaments...Posted a record 18 consecutive top-five finishes before string ended at the Boone Valley Classic (T13)...Won his second consecutive Arnold Palmer Award as the circuit's leading money-winner and averaged $130,088 per start...Also garnered his third straight Byron Nelson Award for the lowest scoring average (68.59), breaking Lee Trevino's all-time mark of 68.89 set in 1990...Each of his seven victories was significant...Fired a course-record 62 in the final round of the Toshiba Senior Classic to come from five strokes back and overtake Hubert Green for the title...Won his third consecutive PGA Seniors' Championship, matching Eddie Williams' mark for consecutive wins in the event (1942, 1945, 1946)...Successfully defended his title the next week at the Las Vegas Senior Classic...Fourth title of the campaign came in wire-to-wire fashion at the Ameritech Senior Open, his second senior victory in Chicago...Despite an opening-round 77, made birdie on the 72nd hole to nip Vicente Fernandez at the U.S. Senior Open at Riviera CC. Became just the 10th player to claim a PGA TOUR and Champions Tour event at the same venue. First-round score was also the highest ever by a winner in Champions Tour annals...Sixth victory at the BankBoston Classic was another successful title defense...Closed out the year with a five-stroke triumph at the Energizer SENIOR TOUR Championship in Myrtle Beach...Broke his own mark for fastest player to reach $1 million in a season when he went over seven figures in just his eighth official event ($101,200 for solo second place at the Bruno's Memorial Classic). **1997:** Had nine victories to tie Peter Thomson's 1985 record for most wins in one season...Became the first player to hit the $2-million mark in one season when he won his eighth title at the Vantage Championship and pocketed $225,000...Nine wins came in just 23 starts (18 top-10 finishes)...Got his year off to a great beginning with a two-stroke victory over Gil Morgan at the MasterCard Championship in Hawaii...Outdueled Bob Murphy a month later to win the LG Championship in Naples...Set a standard by successfully defending his PGA Seniors' Championship, winning by a Champions Tour-record 12 strokes...Edged Isao Aoki with a birdie putt at the final hole of the Las Vegas Senior Classic...Took control of the Burnet Senior Classic near Minneapolis with a birdie at the 17th hole and slipped past Lee Trevino...Made birdies on the final two holes for a two-stroke win at the BankBoston Classic...Claimed the Boone Valley Classic near his home in St. Louis, playing all 54 holes without a bogey...Played another bogey-free event at the Vantage Championship and used a 62 at Tanglewood in the second round to edge Dave Eichelberger...Tied Peter Thomson's record for wins in a single season with his ninth victory at the Hyatt Regency Maui Kaanapali Classic, defeating Mike Hill and Bruce Summerhays by three strokes...Claimed his first four titles in just seven starts, the fastest ever to that number...Of the 74 rounds he played, 57 were below par (77 percent) and only 13 were over par...More than half (41 of 74/55 percent) of his rounds were in the 60s...Won the Arnold Palmer Award as the leading money-winner and notched his second consecutive Byron Nelson Award as the Champions Tour scoring leader (68.92). **1996:** Just missed winning money title by $12,121 when he was passed by Jim Colbert on the final day at the Energizer SENIOR TOUR Championship, thanks to a birdie on the 72nd hole...Averaged $70,250 per start for the year with wins at PGA Seniors' Championship and American Express Invitational...Led the Champions Tour with 21 top-10 finishes and was under par in 21 of 23 events...Won his first Byron Nelson Award as the Champions Tour scoring leader (69.47)...Victory at the American Express Invitational pushed him past $1 million in Champions Tour earnings in his 16th event, the fastest to do so at the time. **1995:** Champions Tour Rookie of the Year after pair of victories and 10th-place finish on the money list in just 12 appear-

Hale Irwin (continued)

ances...Made debut at BellSouth Senior Classic at Opryland (T4)...Claimed first win at the Ameritech Senior Open in his fifth start...Victory was third of his career in Chicago area (also won '90 U.S. Open and '75 Western Open). Defeated Kermit Zarley by a whopping seven shots, equaling the largest winning margin on the Champions Tour in 1995...His 21-under-par 195 total smashed the tournament record by five and was just one shy of the all-time 54-hole scoring record in relation to par...Did not make a bogey all week at the Vantage Championship and defeated Dave Stockton by four strokes.

OTHER CAREER HIGHLIGHTS:

Has posted 98 top-three finishes (40 wins, 38 seconds, 20 thirds) in his 228 career appearances on the Champions Tour (43 percent) and going into the 2005 season has also finished in the top 10 168 times (74 percent)...Has won multiple events on the Champions Tour 12 times and has done it four times on the PGA TOUR...Had averaged $90,320 per start on the Champions Tour prior to 2005 season...His illustrious 29-year PGA TOUR career was highlighted by three U.S. Open titles, the last of which came in a grueling 19-hole playoff with Mike Donald at Medinah in 1990. Sank a 45-foot putt on the final hole to force overtime the next day, and then eventually won with a 10-foot birdie putt. Victory at 45 made him the oldest to win a U.S. Open...Followed that win with another the next week at the Buick Classic, and went on to have his finest earnings year on the PGA TOUR (sixth/ $838,249)...Other two Open victories came at Winged Foot in 1974 and Inverness in 1979...First and last of his 20 official TOUR wins (three total at Harbour Town) came at the MCI Heritage Classic. Defeated Greg Norman by two strokes at the 1994 event...Also was a two-time winner of the Atlanta Classic (1975-77) and the Memorial Tournament (1983, '85)...From early 1975 through 1978, he played 86 tournaments without missing a cut, third-best streak in TOUR history...Played on five Ryder Cup teams (1975, 1977, 1979, 1981 and 1991) and represented the United States twice in World Cup play (1974, 1979)...Claimed the individual title in the 1979 World Cup event...Was the United States Captain for the inaugural Presidents Cup, won by the Americans, 20-12...Has six career holes-in-one in competition.

PERSONAL:

Unusual two-sport participant at the University of Colorado: 1967 NCAA Champion in golf and two-time All-Big Eight selection as a football defensive back...Was also an Academic All-American...Member of Colorado's All-Century Football Team and inducted into the University of Colorado Athletic Hall of Fame in 2002...Son, Steve, also played on the Colorado golf team, and won the 2004 Colorado State Amateur Match Play Championship...Got his start in golf at age 4 through his father...Actively involved in his own course design business, including the TPC at Wakefield Plantation, site of the Nationwide Tour's SAS Carolina Classic...Inducted into the World Golf Hall of Fame in 1992...Biggest thrills in golf were his first TOUR win in 1971 at Hilton Head Island, SC, his three U.S. Open victories, his two U.S. Senior Open wins and playing on the victorious U.S. Ryder Cup team in 1991...Participates in a charity golf tournament in St. Louis each year to benefit the St. Louis Children's Hospital and Hale Irwin Center for Pediatric Hematology/Oncology...Says if he could meet one famous person dead or alive his choice would be Abraham Lincoln, because he came along at a very tumultuous time in our history and had a positive influence...His favorite golf course in the United States is Cypress Point, while overseas, he gives the nod Royal Melbourne in Australia...Leans toward the 2-iron he hit at the last hole to win the 1974 U.S. Open at Winged Foot as his all-time favorite shot...Broke 70 for the first time at age 14...Favorite all-time athlete is Byron "Whizzer" White, a fellow CU football standout and the former Chief Justice of the Supreme Court.

PLAYER STATISTICS

MISCELLANEOUS CHAMPIONS TOUR STATISTICS

2004 Low Round: 64–2004 Constellation Energy Classic/3
Career Low Round: 62–4 times, most recent 2000 EMC Kaanapali Classic/2
Career Largest Paycheck: $400,000–2000 U.S. Senior Open/1

MISCELLANEOUS PGA TOUR STATISTICS

2004 Low Round: 73–PGA Championship/2
Career Low Round: 61–1982 Southern Open/4
Career Largest Paycheck: $225,000–1994 MCI Heritage Golf Classic/1

25 MEMORABLE MOMENTS

Jimenez Becomes Youngest to Shoot His Age

1991 GTE Northwest Classic

Overshadowed in the wake of Mike Hill's fourth victory of 1991, 65-year-old Joe Jimenez made Champions Tour history at the Inglewood Country Club near Seattle in the second round when he fired a 9-under-par 63 to easily better his age for the first time in his career. In the process, Jimenez became the youngest player to ever accomplish the feat. His 63 led to a tie-for-15th finish in the tournament. Jimenez continued to amaze fans when, at age 69, he shot a 62 near Chicago in tying for seventh at the 1995 Ameritech Senior Open.

CHAMPIONS TOUR 25

John Jacobs

EXEMPT STATUS: Top 30 on All-Time Money List
FULL NAME: John Alexander Jacobs
HEIGHT: 6-3
WEIGHT: 225
BIRTHDATE: March 18, 1945
BIRTHPLACE: Los Angeles, CA
RESIDENCE: Scottsdale, AZ
FAMILY: Wife, Valerie; Paul, David; one grandchild
EDUCATION: University of Southern California
SPECIAL INTERESTS: Opera, classical music, horse racing, hiking
TURNED PROFESSIONAL: 1967
JOINED PGA TOUR: 1968

JOINED CHAMPIONS TOUR: 1995

CHAMPIONS TOUR VICTORIES (5): 1998 Nationwide Championship. **1999** MasterCard Championship. **2000** Bruno's Memorial Classic. **2002** Royal Caribbean Classic. **2003** Senior PGA Championship.

OTHER SENIOR VICTORIES (1): 1995 Senior Series Gulfport Open.

2004 CHARLES SCHWAB CUP FINISH: T39th - 331 points

BEST PGA TOUR CAREER FINISHES:
2—1971 United Air Lines-Ontario Open,1972 Greater Jacksonville Open,1976 Greater Milwaukee Open.

OTHER VICTORIES (4): 1984 Dunlop International, Republic of China Open. **1986** Singapore Rolex Open. **1991** Republic of China Open.

PGA TOUR CAREER EARNINGS: $119,776

PGA TOUR PLAYOFF RECORD: 0-1

BEST 2004 CHAMPIONS TOUR FINISHES:
3—Toshiba Senior Classic; T5—Royal Caribbean Golf Classic, Bank of America Championship.

2004 SEASON:

Failed to place in the top 30 on the money list for the first time in his career, finishing 39th overall...Recorded five top-10 finishes for the year but none after a T5 at the Bank of America Championship in late June where he was just two strokes off the lead after 36 holes before closing with a 71 near Boston...Most productive outing came early in the season when he was a third-place finisher at the Toshiba Senior Classic after being one stroke off the lead after 36 holes. It marked the third straight year he had finished in the top 10 at that event...Started the year with consecutive top-10 finishes. Was T9 at the MasterCard Championship and followed that with a T5 at the Royal Caribbean Golf Classic.

CHAMPIONS TOUR CAREER HIGHLIGHTS:

2003: Was among the top 10 in only four events, the fewest he's ever had in a full season on the Champions Tour, yet claimed the biggest prize of his career in early June near Philadelphia. Pulled away from Bobby Wadkins with birdies on the 15th and 16th holes to win the Senior PGA Championship at Aronimink GC by two strokes. Three of his four rounds were in the 60s, including a closing-round 68. In the process became the oldest winner of that event (58) since Pete Cooper, at age 61, in 1976. His $360,000 first-place check was his largest ever and was almost half of his total earnings on the season...Posted first top-10 finish in late March when he T3 at the Toshiba Senior Classic and then T6 at Bruno's Memorial Classic slightly more than a month later...Suffered left ankle sprain playing a practice round at the PGA Championship and missed one start in August. **2002:** Had a career-best year from an earnings standpoint, with $1,224,737...Made a crucial par save on the final hole to win the rain-shortened Royal Caribbean Classic, his first victory since the 2000 Bruno's Memorial Classic. Edged Isao Aoki, Tom Watson and Bruce Fleisher by a stroke at Crandon Park with an 11-under 133 total...Started the season by finishing second to Tom Kite at the MasterCard Championship. Final-round 68 at Hualalai included the first double eagle of his career on the par-5, 566-yard 10th hole (driver/8-iron, 189 yards)...Third-round leader at The Countrywide Tradition following a 66 and then finished tied with Jim Thorpe after 72 holes at Superstition Mountain. Lost to Thorpe in the year's first major championship when, on the first extra playoff hole, his four-foot birdie attempt lipped out. **2001:** Best effort came late in the year in Hawaii when he dueled Hale Irwin on the back nine of the Turtle Bay Championship before losing by three strokes. **2000:** Eclipsed the $1-million mark for the first time in his professional career...Defeated Gil Morgan in overtime at the Bruno's Memorial Classic. Came from six strokes back on Sunday with a final-round 64 at Greystone G&CC and then defeated Morgan with a par on the first playoff hole. Come-from-behind margin was the biggest by a Champions Tour player since Bruce Summerhays rallied from six shots back at the 1997 Saint Lukes Classic near Kansas City...Was the first player to post four straight rounds in the 60s at the IR SENIOR TOUR Championship and eventually finished second to Tom Watson by a stroke at the TPC of Myrtle Beach...Matched his career-low round with a 9-under 63 on Sunday at the Gold Rush Classic and finished third...Aced the eighth hole in the third round of the Ford Senior Players Championship, his second hole-in-one on the Champions Tour. **1999:** Went wire-to-wire at the beginning of the year for a three-stroke victory over Jim Colbert and Raymond Floyd at the MasterCard Championship...Was also the 18- and 36-hole leader at the Toshiba Senior Classic, but lost to good friend Gary McCord in an exciting four-way playoff at Newport Beach. First shot his career-low round, an 8-under 63, on Saturday at the EMC Kaanapali Classic. **1998:** Tasted victory for the first time in his Champions Tour career when he came from three strokes back on Sunday to claim the Nationwide Championship near Atlanta. Trailed Gil Morgan and Bob Eastwood by three strokes at the start of the final round, but jumped into contention with birdies on five of his first nine holes. Made a key birdie at the 17th hole down the stretch to nip Hale Irwin by a stroke for the title. **1997:** Nearly posted his first Champions Tour victory at the Southwestern Bell Dominion. Held a one-stroke lead over David Graham before Graham eagled the final hole to overtake him by one stroke...Knocked on the victory door again three weeks later when he was just two off the lead after 36 holes at the Las Vegas Senior Classic before finishing T3. **1996:** Was 23rd on the final money list, with best finish a solo second at the rain-shortened Brickyard Crossing

CHAMPIONS TOUR CAREER SUMMARY — PLAYOFF RECORD: 1-2

Year	Events Played	1st	2nd	3rd	Top 10	Top 25	Earnings	Rank
1995	3					1	$12,603	118
1996	35		1		8	18	510,263	23
1997	34		2	4	12	18	802,942	12
1998	34	1			8	21	799,654	15
1999	35	1	2	1	11	19	997,318	13
2000	34	1	1	3	9	16	1,124,589	14
2001	36		1		5	18	743,421	25
2002	32	1	3		10	17	1,224,737	14
2003	27	1		1	4	10	785,181	24
2004	28			1	5	9	508,682	39
Total	298	5	10	10	72	147	7,509,389	
COMBINED ALL-TIME MONEY (3 TOURS):							**$7,629,165**	

CHAMPIONS TOUR TOP TOURNAMENT SUMMARY

Year	96	97	98	99	00	01	02	03	04
Senior PGA Championship	T31	CUT	T13	T8	T38	T40	T64	1	T65
U.S. Senior Open	T17	T40	T48	T13	T10	T40	CUT	CUT	T54
Ford Senior Players	T33	T6	T24	3	T30	T20	T58	T61	69
Senior British Open								T73	T30
JELD-WEN Tradition	T31	3	T6	T36	8	T16	2	T66	T42
Charles Schwab Cup Champ	T14	27	22	T22	2	29	T17	30	

CHAMPIONS TOUR YEAR-BY-YEAR STATISTICS (TOP 50 ON 2004 MONEY LIST)

	Scoring Average	Putting Average	Greens in Regulation	Driving Distance	Driving Accuracy
1988	82.00 (N/A)	1.889 (N/A)	25.0 (N/A)	246.5 (N/A)	53.6 (N/A)
1995	71.67 (N/A)	1.821 (N/A)	69.1 (N/A)	283.4 (N/A)	46.0 (N/A)
1996	71.57 (25)	1.809 (30)	64.0 (51)	286.7 (2)	54.5 (86)
1997	71.19 (18)	1.813 (51)	67.6 (T17)	290.7 (1)	57.6 (88)
1998	71.56 (T32)	1.793 (30)	64.3 (54)	284.9 (1)	60.2 (83)
1999	71.15 (30)	1.811 (T58)	68.0 (T33)	285.7 (1)	60.0 (87)
2000	70.72 (21)	1.787 (T40)	68.4 (T35)	285.4 (2)	61.4 (86)
2001	71.41 (34)	1.788 (26)	65.9 (41)	279.3 (16)	61.8 (83)
2002	71.29 (35)	1.795 (42)	66.4 (44)	284.5 (3)	58.8 (84)
2003	71.71 (52)	1.806 (55)	67.1 (46)	282.5 (11)	57.8 (81)
2004	72.34 (55)	1.830 (64)	66.0 (T48)	286.0 (8)	60.0 (T74)

John Jacobs (continued)

Championship. **1995:** Earned fully-exempt status by finishing T2 at the 1995 Champions Tour National Qualifying Tournament...Made his debut on the Champions Tour in 1995, shortly after turning 50, and Monday-qualified for three events.

OTHER CAREER HIGHLIGHTS:

From 1968 through 1980, played numerous events on the PGA TOUR, recording three second-place finishes. One of those came at the 1972 Jacksonville Open, where he lost to Tony Jacklin in a playoff...Played in Asia during much of the 1980s...Was the first American to win the Asian golf circuit Order of Merit in 1984...From 1968 through 1991, won more than 100 long drive championships around the world.

PERSONAL:

Grew up on a golf course as a child as his father was director of parks and recreation for the city of Los Angeles...Was assisted in the development of his game by his brother, Tommy, a four-time winner on the PGA TOUR...His dream foursome would include his brother, Arnold Palmer and Walter Hagen, with maybe Ben Hogan thrown in to offset Hagen...Enjoys horse racing and says if he could have one job outside of golf it would be having the opportunity to call a race at a track...Enjoys Italian food...Favorite athletes are Michael Jordan and Arnold Palmer...Selects Winston Churchill and Franklin D. Roosevelt as the two people in history he would most like to meet because their decisions changed our world...Biggest thrills in golf were making the Champions Tour and winning 2003 Senior PGA Championship...Good friend of fellow Champions Tour player Gary McCord.

PLAYER STATISTICS

MISCELLANEOUS CHAMPIONS TOUR STATISTICS

2004 Low Round: 64–2004 MasterCard Championship/3
Career Low Round: 63–2 times, most recent 2000 Gold Rush Classic/3
Career Largest Paycheck: $360,000–2003 Senior PGA Championship/1

MISCELLANEOUS PGA TOUR STATISTICS

Career Low Round: 64–1971 United Air Lines-Ontario Open/2
Career Largest Paycheck: $14,820–1976 Greater Milwaukee Open/2

25 MEMORABLE MOMENTS

Floyd Makes History with Wins on Both Tours

1992 GTE North Classic

In March of 1992, Raymond Floyd claimed his 22nd and final PGA TOUR win at the Doral-Ryder Open. Then six months later and only two weeks after his 50th birthday, the North Carolinian fashioned rounds of 66-67-66 to march off with a two-shot victory in the GTE North Classic at the Broadmoor Country Club in Indianapolis, IN. Floyd became the first player in history to win tournaments on both the PGA TOUR and the Champions Tour in the same year. His feat would not be matched until Craig Stadler won the Ford Senior Players Championship and the B.C. Open in successive weeks in July 2003.

CHAMPIONS TOUR 25

Peter Jacobsen

EXEMPT STATUS: Top 30 on 2004 Champions Tour Money List
FULL NAME: Peter Erling Jacobsen
HEIGHT: 6-2
WEIGHT: 220
BIRTHDATE: March 4, 1954
BIRTHPLACE: Portland, OR
RESIDENCE: Bonita Springs, FL; Lake Oswego, OR
FAMILY: Wife, Jan; Amy (7/19/80), Kristen (2/23/82), Mick (10/12/84)
EDUCATION: University of Oregon
SPECIAL INTERESTS: Music
TURNED PROFESSIONAL: 1976

JOINED CHAMPIONS TOUR: 2004
CHAMPIONS TOUR VICTORIES (1): **2004** U.S. Senior Open.
2004 CHARLES SCHWAB CUP FINISH: 4th - 2,471 points

PGA TOUR VICTORIES (7): **1980** Buick-Goodwrench Open. **1984** Colonial National Invitation, Sammy Davis Jr.-Greater Hartford Open. **1990** Bob Hope Chrysler Classic. **1995** AT&T Pebble Beach National Pro-Am, Buick Invitational of California. **2003** Greater Hartford Open.

OTHER VICTORIES (7): **1974** Pacific-8 Conference Championship [indiv]. **1976** Oregon Open, Northern California Open. **1979** Western Australian Open. **1981** Johnnie Walker Cup. **1982** Johnnie Walker Cup. **1986** Fred Meyer Challenge [with Curtis Strange].

PGA TOUR CAREER EARNINGS: $7,572,970

PGA TOUR PLAYOFF RECORD: 1-3

BEST 2004 CHAMPIONS TOUR FINISHES:
1—U.S. Senior Open; 3—SBC Classic, Administaff Small Business Classic; 4—Charles Schwab Cup Championship, JELD-WEN Tradition.

BEST 2004 PGA TOUR FINISHES:
T14—AT&T Pebble Beach National Pro-Am; T15—Mercedes Championships.

2004 SEASON:
Officially joined the Champions Tour at the SBC Classic in March shortly after turning 50, but subsequent left hip surgery in April kept him out of action on the Tour for nearly three months...Highlight of his season came in his third start on the Champions Tour in late July when he was one-stroke victor over Hale Irwin in the U.S. Senior Open near St. Louis. Posted rounds of 69-68 Sunday, despite walking all 36 holes in 90-degree heat at Bellerive with a sore left hip. Became the second-youngest champion in Senior Open history at 50 years, 4 months, 28 days (Dale Douglass is youngest at 50/3/24)... Nearly won his second major title less than a month later. Shared the third-round lead with Vicente Fernandez at the JELD-WEN Tradition near his home in Portland, but couldn't hang on in Sunday's final round. Was among a half-dozen players slugging it out down the stretch on Sunday's back nine but saw his chances go awry when he made a double bogey at No. 17. Birdied the final hole, but his closing-round, 1-over-par 73 left him T4...Appeared to be in the driver's seat down the stretch at the inaugural Administaff Small Business Classic but dumped his second shot in the water from a fairway bunker on the par-5 final hole and fell one stroke short of a playoff with Hale Irwin and eventual winner Larry Nelson...Had to withdraw from both the Ford Senior Players Championship and the Senior British Open with hip problems prior to his Senior Open win...Finished third in his Champions Tour debut at the SBC Classic in early March. Was among the first-round leaders at Valencia after opening with 5-under 67...Also was tied for the first-round lead at the Commerce Bank Long Island Classic after firing a 6-under 64 on Friday. Eventually T26 at Eisenhower Park after experiencing pain in his left hip on the weekend...Made nice showing in the season-ending Charles Schwab Cup Championship, finishing fourth thanks to a closing-round 67...Played in 10 PGA TOUR events during the season as well, making six cuts and earning $232,851...T14 at the AT&T Pebble Beach National Pro-Am and T15 at the Mercedes Championships...Was one of three players over age 50 to make the cut at THE PLAYERS Championship and finished 80th at the TPC at Sawgrass...Withdrew from the MCI Heritage Classic in April and underwent left hip surgery to repair a torn labrum the following week. Did not play again until early July at the Commerce Bank Long Island Classic.

OTHER CAREER HIGHLIGHTS:
Qualified for the PGA TOUR in Fall 1976 and won seven times in 27 years on the circuit...Finished among the top 60 on the 2003 PGA TOUR's money list with a personal-best $1,162,726 for a single season. Highlight of his year was his seventh career victory on TOUR at the Greater Hartford Open. Held at least a share of the lead for all four days in carding four rounds in the 60s (63-67-69-67—266). Defeated Chris Riley by two strokes at the TPC at River Highlands. Victory came 19 years since last win at Hartford (1984), joining Arnold Palmer, Billy Casper, Paul Azinger and Phil Mickelson as multiple winners of the event. Triumph also came in his 27th season on the PGA TOUR (624th career tournament), making him the seventh-oldest winner in TOUR history at 49 years, 4 months, 23 days. First-place check of $720,000 was exactly 10 times more than he earned for his first GHO victory in 1984 ($72,000)...Named 2003 PGA TOUR Comeback Player of the Year...Highest finish on the money list came in 1995 when he was seventh ($1,075,057) on the strength of back-to-back victories at the AT&T Pebble Beach National Pro-Am and Buick Invitational of California. Shot a closing 65 for a two-stroke victory over David Duval at Pebble Beach and then used consecutive 68s on the weekend in San Diego for a four-stroke win over four players at Torrey Pines...First two-victory season came in 1984 when he defeated Payne Stewart in a playoff for the Colonial National Invitation title, which he dedicated to his father, who had just undergone serious surgery...Two-stroke triumph over Mark O'Meara at the Sammy Davis, Jr.-Greater Hartford Open later that year highlighted by a third-round 63...Came from six strokes off the pace in final round for first TOUR win at the 1990 Buick-Goodwrench Open in Michigan...A member of the United States Ryder Cup team in 1985 and 1995 and played for the American squad in the 1984 U.S. vs. Japan matches. Also played in the 1995 Dunhill Cup...Three-time All-America selection at University of Oregon.

PERSONAL:
Haw own event management company, Peter Jacobsen Productions, Inc. (pjp.com), which conducts the CVS Charity Classic, the Save Mart Shootout and two Champions Tour events, the JELD-WEN Tradition and the Constellation Energy Classic. PJP also conducted the 2003 U.S. Women's Open...Co-owns Jacobsen Hardy Golf Design Co. with former PGA TOUR player and swing instructor Jim Hardy.

PLAYER STATISTICS

MISCELLANEOUS CHAMPIONS TOUR STATISTICS
2004 Low Round: 64–2004 Commerce Bank Long Island Classic/1
Career Low Round: 64–2004 Commerce Bank Long Island Classic/1
Career Largest Paycheck: $470,000–2004 U.S. Senior Open/1

MISCELLANEOUS PGA TOUR STATISTICS
2004 Low Round: 67–3 times, most recent Nissan Open/2
Career Low Round: 62–1982 Manufacturers Hanover Westchester Classic/2
Career Largest Paycheck: $720,000–2003 Greater Hartford Open/1

CHAMPIONS TOUR CAREER SUMMARY — PLAYOFF RECORD: 0-0

Year	Events Played	1st	2nd	3rd	Top 10	Top 25	Earnings	Rank
2004	9	1		2	6	7	$1,040,690	16
Total	9	1		2	6	7	1,040,690	
COMBINED ALL-TIME MONEY (3 TOURS):							**$8,613,660**	

CHAMPIONS TOUR TOP TOURNAMENT SUMMARY

Year	04
U.S. Senior Open	1
JELD-WEN Tradition	T4
Charles Schwab Cup Champ	4

CHAMPIONS TOUR YEAR-BY-YEAR STATISTICS (TOP 50 ON 2004 MONEY LIST)

	Scoring Average	Putting Average	Greens in Regulation	Driving Distance	Driving Accuracy
2004	69.40 (N/A)	1.772 (N/A)	76.3 (N/A)	282.3 (N/A)	73.3 (N/A)

Mark James

EXEMPT STATUS: Top 30 on 2004 Champions Tour Money List
FULL NAME: Mark Hugh James
HEIGHT: 5-11
WEIGHT: 178
BIRTHDATE: October 28, 1953
BIRTHPLACE: Manchester, England
RESIDENCE: Ilkley, West Yorkshire, England
FAMILY: Wife, Jane
SPECIAL INTERESTS: All sports, science fiction, gardening, skiing
TURNED PROFESSIONAL: 1976

JOINED CHAMPIONS TOUR: 2004

CHAMPIONS TOUR VICTORIES (1): **2004** Ford Senior Players Championship.

2004 CHARLES SCHWAB CUP FINISH: 7th - 1,756 points

BEST PGA TOUR CAREER FINISH: T8—1995 British Open Championship.

OTHER VICTORIES (22): **1974** English Amateur Championship. **1977** Lusaka Open. **1978** Sun Alliance Match Play Championship. **1979** Welsh Classic, Carrolls Irish Open. **1980** Euro Masters Invitational, Carrolls Irish Open. **1981** Sao Paulo Open. **1982** Italian Open. **1983** Euro Masters Invitational, Tunisian Open. **1985** GSI Open. **1986** Benson & Hedges International Open. **1988** South African TPC, Peugeot Open de Espana. **1989** Karl Litten Desert Classic, AGF Open, NM English Open. **1990** Madeira Island Open, Turespana Iberia Open de Canarias. **1995** Moroccan Open. **1997** Peugeot Open de Espana.

PGA TOUR CAREER EARNINGS: $169,100

BEST 2004 CHAMPIONS TOUR FINISHES: 1—Ford Senior Players Championship; T3—Bayer Advantage Celebrity Pro-Am; 4—Senior British Open, Senior PGA Championship.

2004 SEASON:

Enjoyed highly successful rookie season and played some of his best golf in the Champions Tour majors...Claimed one of the year's biggest prizes when he was a one-stroke victor over Jose Maria Canizares at the Ford Senior Players Championship. Win near Detroit was the first by a European-born player in a Champions Tour major championship, and he earned a career-best check for $375,000 in Michigan. Started with three straight rounds in the 60s but a 1-over-par 73 was good enough to hold off Canizares by one stroke for the title...Followed his win in Michigan with another strong showing at the Senior British Open in Northern Ireland, placing fourth, two strokes behind winner Pete Oakley at Royal Portrush...Earned July Player of the Month honors as a result of his outstanding play...Also was par/better all four rounds at Bellerive and finished T15 in his first U.S. Senior Open...His closing-round, 2-under 69 at the Senior PGA Championship helped him to a T4 at Valhalla and he was also T19 at the JELD-WEN Tradition...In all, won nearly two thirds of his season earnings in the five major championships—$612,977...Made his debut on the Champions Tour at the Royal Caribbean Golf Classic and T18 at Crandon Park, six strokes back of winner Bruce Fleisher...Suffered a torn meniscus in his left knee while skiing in France prior to coming to America and had arthroscopic surgery in Fort Lauderdale, FL, after the Royal Caribbean event. Missed two other Florida tournaments, but returned to action at the MasterCard Classic in Mexico (T13)...Was T3 at the rain-shortened Bayer Advantage Celebrity Pro-Am, following rounds of 66-69...Led all players in Total Driving.

OTHER CAREER HIGHLIGHTS:

A mainstay on the European PGA Tour from 1976-2003, with 564 career appearances on the circuit and 18 victories between 1978-1997...Finished third on the European Tour Order of Merit in 1979 and fifth on the Order of Merit in 1989 when he won three times, his most victories ever in a single season...Finished among the top five in three of the six British Open Championships played between 1976-1981 and T3 in the 1981 event at Royal St. George's...Also T4 in the 1994 British Open at Turnberry...Earned his biggest check on the European Tour, 202,300, when he finished second to Colin Montgomerie in the 1999 Volvo PGA Championship...Received the Sir Henry Cotton Rookie of the Year Award in 1976 and also secured the Tooting Bec Cup that same year by firing a 66 at Royal Birkdale during the British Open...Served a stint as the chairman of the European Tour Tournament Committee...Played on seven European Ryder Cup teams (1977, 1979, 1981, 1989, 1991, 1993, 1995) and captained the 1999 squad at The Country Club in Brookline, MA...Also played for England in 10 World Cup competitions and seven Alfred Dunhill Cup matches...Played sparingly on the PGA TOUR, with 14 made cuts in 27 official events...Has made two holes-in-one in his career.

PERSONAL:

Nicknamed "Jesse" by his fellow professionals...Made a comeback in 2001 at the Volvo PGA Championships after he was diagnosed with testicular cancer and underwent chemotherapy and surgery in 2000...As an amateur, struck deal with his father that he would study hard for his A levels (he made two) in return for assistance to play one year of competitive golf as a full-time amateur...Passionate about his garden (refers to it as "ground under repair") in Yorkshire, England, and "Star Trek"...Started skiing in 1993...Lists Woodhall Spa in England as his favorite golf course...Favorite entertainer was Elvis Presley and favorite movie is "Total Recall"...Favorite food is roast chicken.

PLAYER STATISTICS

MISCELLANEOUS CHAMPIONS TOUR STATISTICS
2004 Low Round: 65–2004 Blue Angels Classic/2
Career Low Round: 65–2004 Blue Angels Classic/2
Career Largest Paycheck: $375,000–2004 Ford Senior Players Championship/1

MISCELLANEOUS PGA TOUR STATISTICS
Career Low Round: 67–2 times, most recent 1999 PGA Championship/4
Career Largest Paycheck: $53,167–1995 British Open Championship/T8

CHAMPIONS TOUR CAREER SUMMARY — PLAYOFF RECORD: 0-0

Year	Events Played	1st	2nd	3rd	Top 10	Top 25	Earnings	Rank
2004	20	1		1	5	14	$952,289	18
Total	20	1		1	5	14	952,289	
COMBINED ALL-TIME MONEY (3 TOURS):							$1,121,389	

CHAMPIONS TOUR TOP TOURNAMENT SUMMARY

Year	04
Senior PGA Championship	T4
U.S. Senior Open	T15
Ford Senior Players	1
Senior British Open	4
JELD-WEN Tradition	T19
Charles Schwab Cup Champ	T22

CHAMPIONS TOUR YEAR-BY-YEAR STATISTICS (TOP 50 ON 2004 MONEY LIST)

	Scoring Average	Putting Average	Greens in Regulation	Driving Distance	Driving Accuracy
2004	70.85 (T19)	1.819 (56)	71.9 (12)	276.1 (23)	75.6 (18)

Tom Jenkins

EXEMPT STATUS: Top 30 on 2004 Champions Tour Money List
FULL NAME: Thomas Wayne Jenkins
HEIGHT: 5-11
WEIGHT: 190
BIRTHDATE: December 14, 1947
BIRTHPLACE: Houston, TX
RESIDENCE: Austin, TX

FAMILY: Wife, Martha; Melani Anne (9/13/79), Thomas Wayne, Jr. (7/4/00), Weston Wyatt (12/2/02)
CLUB AFFILIATION: Barton Creek Resort (Austin, TX)
EDUCATION: University of Houston (1971, Business Administration)
SPECIAL INTERESTS: Computers
TURNED PROFESSIONAL: 1971
JOINED PGA TOUR: 1972

JOINED CHAMPIONS TOUR: 1998

CHAMPIONS TOUR VICTORIES (5): 1999 Bell Atlantic Classic. **2000** AT&T Canada Senior Open Championship. **2002** AT&T Canada Senior Open Championship. **2003** Bruno's Memorial Classic. **2004** Blue Angels Classic.

2004 CHARLES SCHWAB CUP FINISH: 23rd - 804 points

PGA TOUR VICTORIES (1): 1975 IVB-Philadelphia Golf Classic.

PGA TOUR CAREER EARNINGS: $470,019

PGA TOUR PLAYOFF RECORD: 0-1

BEST 2004 CHAMPIONS TOUR FINISHES: 1—Blue Angels Classic; 2—Allianz Championship, SAS Championship; 4—Bruno's Memorial Classic.

2004 SEASON:

Was a top-30 finisher for the sixth consecutive year when he was 13th on the final money list...Lone victory during the season came in April when his final-round 63 helped him cruise to a five-stroke win at the Blue Angels Classic, his fifth career title on the Champions Tour. Moved into contention with a second-round 65 at The Moors and then vaulted into the lead for good with birdies on three of his first four holes on Sunday...Twice a runner-up during the season. Second to Craig Stadler at the SAS Championship in September and finished three shots behind D.A. Weibring at the Allianz Championship in May...Finished fourth in defense of his Bruno's Memorial Classic title. Was in solo second place with one hole to go before making double bogey and dropping two spots in the final standings...Registered a pair of top-10 finishes in back-to-back starts early in the season. Was solo sixth at the Outback Steakhouse Pro-Am and then followed that with a T7 in his next outing at the MasterCard Classic near Mexico City. Had a strong finish in Mexico. After opening with a 4-over-par 76 on Friday, followed with rounds of 68-70 to jump into the top 10...Withdrew after the first round of The First Tee Open at Pebble Beach after having a reaction to some medication...Had his best year in the Greens in Regulation category, hitting 74.3 percent to finish third behind Hale Irwin and Tom Purtzer...Was eighth in Total Driving for the season, as well.

CHAMPIONS TOUR CAREER HIGHLIGHTS:

2003: Was perhaps the Champions Tour's most consistent player and may have had his finest year in golf, with 15 top-10 finishes in 30 starts, a 2003 Champions Tour best...Was seventh on the final earnings list, his highest ranking since 1999, with a personal-best $1.4 million in official earnings...Also tied with Allen Doyle for the most sub-par rounds during the year (64) and 41 of his 94 total rounds were in the 60s (T2)...Missed only the Senior British Open Championship during the year...Highlight of his season came in early May when he registered his fourth career win on the Champions Tour at the Bruno's Memorial Classic. Broke away from Bruce Fleisher and Hale Irwin with a final-round 67 for a three-stroke victory. Needed just 78 total putts over 54 holes at Greystone and became eligible for the Liberty Mutual Legends of Golf (five combined career titles) as a result of his triumph near Birmingham...Came close to winning earlier in the year in Mexico, but along with three other players, fell one stroke short of first-time winner David Eger at the MasterCard Classic...Was in contention for the majority of the season-ending Charles Schwab Cup Championship, before finishing T4 at Sonoma GC...His 7-under-par 63 in the final round at the Long Island Classic included a 6-under 28 on the front nine, the season's lowest numerical nine-hole score...Joined John Bland as the only other Champions Tour player with multiple aces during the year. First made a hole-in-one in the third round of the JELD-WEN Tradition when he aced No. 7 at The Reserve with a 4-iron from 203 yards and then notched his seventh career ace in the second round of the Charles Schwab Cup Championship when he used a 9-iron from 138 yards on No. 17 at Sonoma GC. **2002:** Won north of the border for the second time when he triumphed at the AT&T Canada Senior Open Championship. Opened with a 63 at Essex and closed with 64 to defeat Walter Morgan, Morris Hatalsky and Bruce Lietzke by three strokes. In winning, became first player since Don January (1983-84) to win multiple Champions Tour titles in Canada...Made strong bid for second win of the year, closing with a career-best 10-under-par 62 at the Kroger Senior Classic, which also tied the course record set earlier in the day by Bruce Lietzke. However, fell in a two-hole playoff with Bob Gilder, the second year in succession he lost in a playoff at the event...T10 at the Toshiba Senior Classic after playing all 54 holes without a bogey, the first senior to do so since Joe Inman at the 2000 EMC Kaanapali Classic. Bogey-free streak reached 67 holes before it ended the next week on the in sixth hole in the opening round of the Siebel Classic. **2001:** The only one of 16 millionaires to not win an event...Knocked on the victory door three times only to come up short with three runner-up finishes. Was in the hunt throughout The Instinet Classic, but finished two strokes back of Gil Morgan. One of only three players in the Novell Utah Showdown field to card three consecutive sub-70 rounds, but came up one stroke shy of Steve Veriato in Park City. Had victory snatched from his grasp at the Kroger Senior Classic. Closed with a then-career-best 7-under 63 at Kings Island on Sunday and was two strokes up on Jim Thorpe with one hole to play. Dramatic eagle by Thorpe forced a playoff and then a birdie by Thorpe on the first extra hole proved to be the winner. **2000:** Earned his second career title as a senior at the AT&T Canada Senior Open Championship. Made birdie on the final hole to nip Kermit Zarley by a stroke at St. Charles CC in Winnipeg. Victory came just over a month after his wife, Martha, delivered Tom Jr. **1999:** Voted by his peers as the Champions Tour's Comeback Player of the Year...Won the Bell Atlantic Classic in a playoff. Defeated Jim Thorpe with a birdie on the first extra hole for his first Champions Tour victory and first TOUR title since the 1975 IVB-Philadelphia Classic. Win at Hartefeld National made him the fifth of a record 11 first-time winners on the season. **1998:** Contended for the AT&T Canada Senior Open Championship crown in Calgary, but finished T2 behind Brian Barnes. **1997:** Earned a conditional exemption for 1998 by placing 10th at the Champions Tour National Qualifying Tournament in November.

OTHER CAREER HIGHLIGHTS:

Played the PGA TOUR full-time from 1973-85, with his busiest year coming in 1981, when he made 28 of 34 cuts. Earned a career-best $78,127, with his best finish that year a T2 at the Wickes-Andy Williams San Diego Open. Was one stroke off the lead after three rounds before fin-

CHAMPIONS TOUR CAREER SUMMARY — PLAYOFF RECORD: 1-2

Year	Events Played	1st	2nd	3rd	Top 10	Top 25	Earnings	Rank
1998	28		1		4	16	$455,212	36
1999	29	1		3	17	25	1,167,176	7
2000	36	1	1	1	11	26	1,298,244	10
2001	36		3	1	9	23	1,156,576	15
2002	34	1	1		10	24	1,220,872	15
2003	30	1	1		15	20	1,415,503	7
2004	27	1	2		8	17	1,138,843	13
Total	220	5	9	5	74	151	7,852,426	
COMBINED ALL-TIME MONEY (3 TOURS):							**$8,333,771**	

CHAMPIONS TOUR TOP TOURNAMENT SUMMARY

Year	98	99	00	01	02	03	04
Senior PGA Championship		T24	T12	T36	T36	T32	T13
U.S. Senior Open	T13	T18	T10	T26	T31	T10	T32
Ford Senior Players	T45	T29	T7	T31	T17	T5	T22
JELD-WEN Tradition	T68	13	T25	T38	T13	T60	T19
Charles Schwab Cup Champ		T26	13	T7	T17	T4	29

CHAMPIONS TOUR YEAR-BY-YEAR STATISTICS (TOP 50 ON 2004 MONEY LIST)

	Scoring Average	Putting Average	Greens in Regulation	Driving Distance	Driving Accuracy
1998	71.37 (24)	1.815 (T53)	69.1 (14)	263.9 (43)	71.5 (30)
1999	69.90 (4)	1.755 (6)	72.3 (5)	266.8 (37)	75.5 (T13)
2000	70.31 (13)	1.786 (T37)	72.4 (11)	271.3 (28)	72.1 (27)
2001	70.74 (16)	1.816 (T61)	71.8 (8)	271.4 (T45)	74.8 (13)
2002	70.56 (15)	1.805 (51)	71.8 (T10)	270.8 (T34)	73.6 (T17)
2003	69.99 (8)	1.779 (T22)	72.2 (T7)	273.5 (37)	70.9 (T33)
2004	70.66 (16)	1.813 (T49)	74.3 (3)	279.0 (18)	71.1 (T35)

Tom Jenkins (continued)

ishing in a tie with Bruce Lietzke and Raymond Floyd. Lietzke won with a birdie on the second extra hole...Made 315 career starts and made 223 cuts with 17 top-10 finishes...Claimed his only PGA TOUR victory in 1975 at the IVB-Philadelphia Classic, where he held off a late-charging Johnny Miller by one stroke...Had a T2 at the 1973 USI Classic...Played 29 events on the Nationwide Tour from 1992-94.

PERSONAL:

Biggest thrills in golf have been playing on the University of Houston's 1970 NCAA championship team, all of his victories on both the PGA TOUR and Champions Tour and playing with both Arnold Palmer and Jack Nicklaus...Biggest thrill outside of golf is being at the birth of his three children...Got started in golf by watching his father and older brother...A college teammate of John Mahaffey...His brother owns Winged Canyon, a winery in the Napa Valley...Favorite golf course is Pebble Beach...Enjoys watching "MASH" and "Seinfeld" reruns and lists Bob Hope as his favorite entertainer...American cyclist Lance Armstrong is his favorite athlete...Enjoys Mexican food...Best friend on the Champions Tour is Bruce Fleisher.

PLAYER STATISTICS

MISCELLANEOUS CHAMPIONS TOUR STATISTICS

2004 Low Round: 63–2004 Blue Angels Classic/3
Career Low Round: 62–2002 Kroger Senior Classic/3
Career Largest Paycheck: $240,000–2002 AT&T Canada Senior Open Championship/1

MISCELLANEOUS PGA TOUR STATISTICS

Career Low Round: 65–2 times, most recent 1981 Wickes/Andy Williams San Diego Open/1
Career Largest Paycheck: $30,000–1975 IVB–Philadelphia Golf Classic/1

25 MEMORABLE MOMENTS

Weiskopf Wins in Tribute to the Passing of Bert Yancey

1994 Franklin Quest Championship

Under other circumstances, Tom Weiskopf would have been delighted to win the Franklin Quest Championship in Park City, UT. Instead, his joy was tempered by the pall cast over the tournament by the death of his good friend, Bert Yancey, who died of cardiac arrest moments before his tee time in the opening round. By Sunday, Weiskopf was well off the pace, but he drained an 80-footer for birdie at the 16th, two-putted for eagle on the 17th and then knocked in an 18-foot birdie on the final hole to tie Dave Stockton. Weiskopf won on the first playoff hole when he made another 18-foot downhill birdie putt that Stockton couldn't match.

CHAMPIONS TOUR 25

SECTION 2 PLAYER BIOGRAPHIES

Mark Johnson

EXEMPT STATUS: 1st at 2004 Champions Tour National Qualifying Tournament
FULL NAME: Mark William Johnson
HEIGHT: 5-10
WEIGHT: 205
BIRTHDATE: May 22, 1954
BIRTHPLACE: Barstow, CA
RESIDENCE: Helendale, CA
FAMILY: Ryan (5/27/79), Heather (5/6/82)
CLUB AFFILIATION: Silver Lakes CC (Helendale, CA)
SPECIAL INTERESTS: Coaching kids, relaxing
TURNED PROFESSIONAL: 1998

JOINED CHAMPIONS TOUR: 2004

BEST CHAMPIONS TOUR CAREER FINISH: T8—2004 Administaff Small Business Classic.

2004 CHARLES SCHWAB CUP FINISH: 72nd - 44 points

BEST PGA TOUR CAREER FINISH: T43—2001 AT&T Pebble Beach National Pro-Am.

OTHER VICTORIES (9): 1972 CIF Championship [indiv]. **1989** SCGA Mid-Amateur. **1990** SCGA Tournament of Club Champions. **1993** SCGA Mid-Amateur. **1994** SCGA Mid-Amateur, Pacific Coast Amateur. **1996** California State Amateur, SCGA Tournament of Club Champions. **1997** SCGA Tournament of Club Champions.

PGA TOUR CAREER EARNINGS: $13,600

BEST 2004 CHAMPIONS TOUR FINISH: T8—Administaff Small Business Classic.

2004 SEASON:

Will be fully exempt for the 2005 season after capturing medalist honors at the National Qualifying Tournament at the King and Bear at World Golf Village in Florida, where he was a two-stroke winner over Tom McKnight. Earned $45,000 for his victory, the largest check of his professional career. Posted six consecutive sub-par rounds along the way, including a final-round, 8-under-par 64...Had finished 76th on the 2004 money list, appearing in just nine events, five of those through open qualifying...Open-qualified for the Administaff Small Business Classic near Houston in October and registered the best finish by a 2004 open qualifier when he was T8. Closed with rounds of 67-69 at Augusta Pines and earned a check for $44,000, largest in his nine appearances. Got into the event by shooting 67 on the Palmer Course at The Woodlands CC on Monday...Had also open-qualified earlier in the year at the Farmers Charity Classic, where he was T12...Was T14 at the Kroger Classic, where he fired an 8-under-par 64 in the second round, his low on the Champions Tour.

CHAMPIONS TOUR CAREER HIGHLIGHTS:

2003: Earned a conditional exemption for 2004 after finishing 14th at the 2003 Champions Tour National Qualifying Tournament at the TPC at Eagle Trace in Florida. One of two players tied for 14th after 72 holes at even-par 288, but claimed the 14th spot after a birdie on the second playoff hole. Opened with a 4-under-par 68, followed by a 2-under 70. Was just one stroke off the lead after 36 holes. However, a third-round, 6-over-par 78 dropped him into a tie for 16th after 54 holes before he closed with a 72 to secure conditional status for 2004. Earned a position in the Q-School finals after earning co-medalist honors at the Regional Qualifier in Calimesa, CA...Played on the Canadian Tour and was fourth on the Canadian Tour money list, with $47,451...Played in 10 events and made seven cuts, with his best finishes a pair of T2s at the TravelTex.com Canadian Tour Challenge and the Greater Vancouver Classic. Shared first-place money in Vancouver after an amateur, James Lepp, won the title...Named the Most Improved International Player...Made one start on the Nationwide Tour and was 46th at the Alberta Calgary Classic, where he earned $1,633...Also played at the Bell Canadian Open but missed the cut.

OTHER CAREER HIGHLIGHTS:

Played the Canadian Tour in 1999-2001...Played a full season on the Nationwide Tour in 2001 and earned $21,508 in 21 starts. His best finish was a T13 at the Siouxland Open...Overall has made 26 career starts on the Nationwide Tour, with earnings totaling $25,620...Owns two starts on the PGA TOUR, including a T43 at the 2001 AT&T Pebble Beach National Pro-Am, where he opened with a 65 and was just one stroke out of the lead...Won a number of amateur events in the Southern California area, including the 1996 California State Amateur.

PERSONAL:

Drove a Budweiser beer truck for 18 years before embarking on a professional golf career...His parents got him started in the game at age 9 in California...Biggest thrill in golf was winning the California State Amateur...Favorites include Pebble Beach GL, The Golf Channel, ESPN, Garth Brooks and "Titanic"...Top athlete is Tiger Woods and his favorite food is spaghetti.

PLAYER STATISTICS

2004 CHAMPIONS TOUR STATISTICS:

Scoring Average	71.88	(N/A)
Driving Distance	277.6	(N/A)
Driving Accuracy Percentage	70.5%	(N/A)
Total Driving	1,998	(N/A)
Greens in Regulation Pct.	73.2%	(N/A)
Putting Average	1.814	(N/A)
Sand Save Percentage	34.6%	(N/A)
Eagles (Holes per)	234.0	(N/A)
Birdie Average	3.65	(N/A)
All-Around Ranking	1,569	(N/A)

MISCELLANEOUS CHAMPIONS TOUR STATISTICS
2004 Low Round: 64–2004 Kroger Classic/2
Career Low Round: 64–2004 Kroger Classic/2
Career Largest Paycheck: $44,000–2004 Administaff Small Business Classic/T8

MISCELLANEOUS PGA TOUR STATISTICS
2004 Low Round: 72–Bell Canadian Open/2
Career Low Round: 65–2001 AT&T Pebble Beach National Pro-Am/1
Career Largest Paycheck: $13,600–2001 AT&T Pebble Beach National Pro–Am/T43

CHAMPIONS TOUR CAREER SUMMARY **PLAYOFF RECORD: 0-0**

Year	Events Played	1st	2nd	3rd	Top 10	Top 25	Earnings	Rank
2004	9				1	3	$134,261	76
Total	9				1	3	134,261	
COMBINED ALL-TIME MONEY (3 TOURS):							$173,481	

CHAMPIONS TOUR TOP TOURNAMENT SUMMARY

Year	04
U.S. Senior Open	CUT
Senior British Open	T53

Tom Kite

WORLD GOLF HALL OF FAME MEMBER (Inducted 2004)
EXEMPT STATUS: Top 30 on 2004 Champions Tour Money List
FULL NAME: Thomas Oliver Kite, Jr.
HEIGHT: 5-9
WEIGHT: 170
BIRTHDATE: December 9, 1949
BIRTHPLACE: McKinney, TX
RESIDENCE: Austin, TX
FAMILY: Wife, Christy; Stephanie Lee (10/7/81), twins David Thomas and Paul Christopher (9/1/84)
EDUCATION: University of Texas (1972, Business Administration)
SPECIAL INTERESTS: Landscaping
TURNED PROFESSIONAL: 1972
JOINED PGA TOUR: 1972

JOINED CHAMPIONS TOUR: 2000

CHAMPIONS TOUR VICTORIES (7): 2000 The Countrywide Tradition, SBC Senior Open. **2001** Gold Rush Classic. **2002** MasterCard Championship, SBC Senior Classic, Napa Valley Championship. **2004** 3M Championship.

2004 CHARLES SCHWAB CUP FINISH:
3rd - 2,981 points

PGA TOUR VICTORIES (19): 1976 IVB-Bicentennial Golf Classic. **1978** B.C. Open. **1981** American Motors Inverrary Classic. **1982** Bay Hill Classic. **1983** Bing Crosby National Pro-Am. **1984** Doral-Eastern Open, Georgia-Pacific Atlanta Golf Classic. **1985** MONY Tournament of Champions. **1986** Western Open. **1987** Kemper Open. **1989** Nestle Invitational, THE PLAYERS Championship, Nabisco Championship. **1990** Federal Express St. Jude Classic. **1991** Infiniti Tournament of Champions. **1992** BellSouth Classic, U.S. Open Championship. **1993** Bob Hope Chrysler Classic, Nissan Los Angeles Open.

OTHER VICTORIES (9): 1972 NCAA Championship [indiv, tie]. **1974** Air New Zealand Open. **1980** European Open. **1981** JCPenney Classic [with Beth Daniel]. **1987** Kirin Cup [indiv]. **1989** Dunhill Cup. **1992** Shark Shootout [with Davis Love III]. **1996** Oki Pro-Am, Franklin Templeton Shark Shootout [with Jay Haas].

PGA TOUR CAREER EARNINGS: $10,937,613

PGA TOUR PLAYOFF RECORD: 6-4

BEST 2004 CHAMPIONS TOUR FINISHES:
1—3M Championship; 2—Charles Schwab Cup Championship, Bank of America Championship, Senior British Open; T3—U.S. Senior Open, The First Tee Open at Pebble Beach presented by Wal-Mart; T4—Allianz Championship, JELD-WEN Tradition, SBC Championship.

BEST 2004 PGA TOUR FINISH: T57—U.S. Open Championship.

2004 SEASON:
Started slowly for the second consecutive year, but went on to finish third on the final earnings list, his highest standing ever, with more than $1.8 million, a career best. Also placed third on the final Charles Schwab Cup points list and is the only player to finish among the top five in the Schwab Cup race in each of the last three seasons...Had more top-five finishes than any other Champions Tour player, with all 10 top-fives coming after the start of May. Led the Champions Tour in Sub-Par Rounds (58) and also had 39 Rounds in the 60s (second to Irwin) out of 86 (45 percent) played...Ended nearly a 22-month victory drought by winning the 3M Championship, his seventh overall title on the Champions Tour, and came close to winning on several other occasions. One-stroke win over Craig Stadler at the TPC of the Twin Cities came during the midst of five consecutive top-five performances and was his first victory in 47 official starts on the Champions Tour. Took the lead with a 13-foot birdie putt on the 13th hole and then used a clutch two-putt birdie from 68 feet on the final green to notch the win...The week prior, had led for most of the last 36 holes of the U.S. Senior Open, but played the last four holes at Bellerive in 4-over to drop back into a T3 with Jay Haas...Was in contention the week earlier for all four days at the Senior British Open at Royal Portrush GC before falling one stroke short of eventual winner Pete Oakley in Northern Ireland...T2 at the Bank of America Championship, four strokes back of Craig Stadler and also finished second to Mark McNulty at the Charles Schwab Cup Championship despite shooting an 8-under 64 in the first round and holding a two-stroke advantage going into the final round...Low round of the campaign was an 8-under 63 on Friday at the Outback Steakhouse Pro-Am...Became one of the oldest players to earn a spot in the U.S. Open when he earned a berth at a qualifying tournament near Houston. Made the field in the prestigious event for the 31st consecutive year and 33rd time overall, tying Arnold Palmer and Gene Sarazen for third all-time. Made the cut at Shinnecock Hills and finished T57...Inducted into the World Golf Hall of Fame in November, along with Charlie Sifford, Marlene Streit and Isao Aoki.

CHAMPIONS TOUR CAREER HIGHLIGHTS:
2003: His $1,549,819 in earnings were the most money ever in a season without a victory, breaking Dana Quigley's mark of $1,327,659 set in 1999...Had just three top-10 finishes in the first six months, but closed with nine in his last 12 starts...Made a spirited run in the final round of the SAS Championship before eventually finishing T2 along with Bobby Wadkins, one stroke back of D.A. Weibring. Posted a career-best 11-under 61 on Sunday at Prestonwood and almost came from 11 strokes back to win. Final round included just 22 putts, with one-putts on each of the last nine holes...Also T2 at the JELD-WEN Tradition near Portland, one stroke back of Tom Watson. Missed sending the event into a playoff when he didn't convert a five-foot birdie putt on the final hole...Equaled the TPC of Michigan course record with a 63 and vaulted from 10th into a T2 at the Ford Senior Players Championship. His 9-under round was the lowest Sunday score in tournament history...Was the 36-hole leader at the Turtle Bay Championship before falling by two strokes to Hale Irwin in October. Traded leads with Irwin in the final round before hitting his second shot into the water on the 18th hole...Appeared to be in control at the Kinko's Classic in his hometown of Austin with two holes to play, but bogeys on 17 and 18 proved costly as he slipped into a T4, two strokes out of the Irwin-Watson playoff...Tied Larry Nelson for the best birdie average 4.30...Had more rounds in the 60s than any other player (42)...Played in the U.S. Open at Olympia Fields, but missed the cut. **2002:** Three victories, equaling the total of his first two years on the circuit, and a first for him since 1989...Was a six-stroke winner at the first official event, the MasterCard Championship. Became just the third player to go wire-to-wire in the tournament after opening with a Hualalai course-record 63 that included a pair of eagles on the front nine. Victory in Hawaii made him just the fourth player to claim the season-opening event on both the Champions Tour and the PGA TOUR (joining Jack Nicklaus, Al Geiberger and Don January)...Defeated Tom Watson in a playoff to win the SBC Senior Classic. Forced the overtime session with a birdie on the 18th hole and then made par on the second extra hole for the victory...Won his ninth TOUR title in the state of California near the end of the season. Held off Bruce Fleisher and Fred Gibson to win the Napa Valley Championship by one stroke despite shooting an even-par 72 on Sunday, the highest final-round score by a winner in 2002 and also the highest finish by a winner in the history of the event. Win at Silverado came 30 years after he successfully made it through the PGA TOUR Qualifying School at the same venue...Made consecutive eagles in the final round of the AT&T Canada Senior Open,

CHAMPIONS TOUR CAREER SUMMARY — PLAYOFF RECORD: 2-0

Year	Events Played	1st	2nd	3rd	Top 10	Top 25	Earnings	Rank
2000	20	2	1	1	9	18	$1,199,658	11
2001	23	1		4	16	22	1,398,802	10
2002	23	3		1	14	21	1,631,930	4
2003	27		4	1	12	20	1,549,819	6
2004	27	1	3	2	13	23	1,831,211	3
Total	120	7	8	9	64	104	7,611,419	
COMBINED ALL-TIME MONEY (3 TOURS):							**$18,549,032**	

CHAMPIONS TOUR TOP TOURNAMENT SUMMARY

Year	00	01	02	03	04
Senior PGA Championship	T2	T23	T15	T10	T21
U.S. Senior Open	3	15	3	T12	T3
Ford Senior Players	6	T10	T10	T2	T7
Senior British Open				4	T2
JELD-WEN Tradition	1	T24	T7	T2	T4
Charles Schwab Cup Champ	T8	T7	T21	3	2

CHAMPIONS TOUR YEAR-BY-YEAR STATISTICS (TOP 50 ON 2004 MONEY LIST)

	Scoring Average	Putting Average	Greens in Regulation	Driving Distance	Driving Accuracy
2000	69.63 (7)	1.775 (T22)	78.0 (1)	273.8 (24)	72.2 (T25)
2001	69.80 (5)	1.806 (T53)	74.1 (1)	282.5 (7)	73.7 (T24)
2002	69.64 (3)	1.779 (21)	75.9 (1)	279.4 (T9)	71.6 (26)
2003	69.79 (6)	1.797 (T41)	74.3 (1)	281.0 (13)	72.4 (22)
2004	69.98 (4)	1.785 (T25)	73.3 (6)	278.4 (T19)	72.8 (27)

Tom Kite (continued)

a Champions Tour first since Steve Veriato made back-to-back eagles at the 2002 Gold Rush Classic...Played in four PGA TOUR events, including first Masters since 1998, but missed the cut at Augusta National...Finished T36 at THE PLAYERS Championship, the 23rd time he made the cut in the event, a tournament record...Missed the cut at the MasterCard Colonial, ending a streak of 28 straight years in which he made the cut in the Fort Worth event. **2001:** Was among the top 10 in over two-thirds of his starts...Won the Gold Rush Classic by one stroke over Allen Doyle. Three-round total of 22-under 194 at Serrano CC tied an all-time 54-hole Champions Tour record in relation to par and included a 62 in the second round, his best score since closing with a 62 at the 1993 Bob Hope Chrysler Classic on the PGA TOUR. 17-under 127 score after two days was the lowest first 36-hole total of the year and 15-under 129 on Saturday and Sunday was the lowest last 36-hole total in 2001...Played in five events on the PGA TOUR...Rallied from 44th place after three rounds to T5 at the U.S. Open at Southern Hills, the best finish by a senior in a major championship since Sam Snead T3 in the 1974 PGA Championship. Along with Vijay Singh, fired a sizzling 6-under 64 in the final round, one shot off the 18-hole U.S. Open scoring record. **2000:** Posted first Champions Tour victory in his fifth start, a three-man playoff with Larry Nelson and Tom Watson at The Countrywide Tradition. Battled Watson for six holes (Nelson went out on the second extra hole) before prevailing with a birdie. Became the first player since Tom Wargo at the PGA Seniors' in 1993 to make his first victory a Champions Tour major...Also had a two-stroke win over Bruce Fleisher at the SBC Senior Open. Played the last four holes in 3-under-par to overtake Fleisher...Finished in the top 10 in all four Champions Tour majors. Finished T2 at he rain-shortened PGA Seniors' Championship, third at the U.S. Senior Open at Saucon Valley and sixth at the Ford Senior Players Championship after holding the lead going into the final round...Set a new Champions Tour standard by hitting 78.0 percent of Greens in Regulation, breaking the old mark of 77.0 percent by John Mahaffey in 1999.

OTHER CAREER HIGHLIGHTS:

Was the first player in PGA TOUR history to reach $6 million, $7 million, $8 million and $9 million in career earnings...Led the TOUR in career earnings from October 29, 1989 until August 27, 1995...Ranks T36 among PGA TOUR winners with 19 official titles...Most memorable was 1992 U.S. Open triumph at Pebble Beach. His even-par 72 in difficult conditions earned him a two-stroke victory over Jeff Sluman...Was the TOUR's leading money-winner in 1981 and 1989...Won the 1981 American Motors-Inverrary Classic by one stroke over Jack Nicklaus...Had his best year in 1989, when he won three times and set a single-season earnings record at the time, eclipsing the million-dollar mark in official money, the only time in his PGA TOUR career. Won the Nestle Invitational and THE PLAYERS Championship in consecutive weeks. Claimed the season-ending Nabisco Championships in a playoff with Payne Stewart and collected $450,000 for the win at Harbour Town GL, his largest TOUR payday...From 1981 through 1993, won at least one official tournament each year except 1988, and was runner-up three times that year...Last victories came in 1993, when he captured the Bob Hope Chrysler Classic with 10-under 62 in the final-round and Nissan Los Angeles Open. Set the TOUR record for most strokes under par in a 90-hole event by shooting 35-under-par 325 at the Hope Chrysler Classic. Won by three strokes at Riviera at the rain-shortened Nissan event in Los Angeles...Played on seven United States Ryder Cup teams (1979, 1981, 1983, 1985, 1987, 1989, 1993 and captained the 1997 American squad at Valderrama in Spain...Represented the United States in the World Cup in 1984 and 1985...Shared NCAA title with Texas teammate Ben Crenshaw in 1972...Played on the 1971 United States Walker Cup team at St. Andrews, Scotland...1973 *Golf Digest* Rookie of the Year...1979 Bob Jones Award recipient from the USGA...1981 Golf Writers Association Player of the Year...Earned the 1981 and 1982 Vardon Trophies for lowest scoring average...1989 PGA of America Player of the Year...Has had nine holes-in-one in competition.

PERSONAL:

After wearing glasses since age 12, had LASIK surgery in late January 1998 to correct acute nearsightedness...Started playing golf at age 6 by following his father around and won his first tournament at 11...Three of his last four PGA TOUR victories came on holidays—1992 BellSouth Classic (Mother's Day), 1992 U.S. Open (Father's Day), 1993 Bob Hope Chrysler Classic (Valentines Day)...Biggest thrill in golf was being selected as the Ryder Cup captain in 1997...Has worked with such teachers as Harvey Penick, Bob Toski, Peter Kostis, Chuck Cook, Jim McLean, Dave Pelz and Dave Phillips...His daughter, Stephanie, was a former gymnast at the University of Alabama and was a member of its national championship squad in 2002. Son David plays golf at South Carolina...Lists Pebble Beach as his favorite golf course and Michael Jordan as his favorite athlete...Dream foursome would include Bobby Jones, Ben Hogan, Byron Nelson and Walter Hagen "because they were the best players of all time that I never had a chance to play with."...The first car he owned was a 1957 Chevy...Enjoys Mexican food...He and his family have two dogs, Maja, a shepherd mix, and Mulligan, a fox-hound...Says the best shot of his career was when he holed his lob wedge for a birdie on the seventh hole at Pebble Beach during the last round of the 1992 U.S. Open that helped him to a two-stroke win...Would like to continue his golf course design work in the future with his son David joining him.

PLAYER STATISTICS

MISCELLANEOUS CHAMPIONS TOUR STATISTICS

2004 Low Round: 63–2004 Outback Steakhouse Pro-Am/1
Career Low Round: 61–2003 SAS Championship /3
Career Largest Paycheck: $262,500–2004 3M Championship/1

MISCELLANEOUS PGA TOUR STATISTICS

2004 Low Round: 71–U.S. Open Championship/2
Career Low Round: 62–4 times, most recent 1993 Bob Hope Chrysler Classic/5
Career Largest Paycheck: $450,000–1989 Nabisco Championship/1

Gary Koch (COKE)

EXEMPT STATUS: 41st on 2004 Champions Tour Money List
FULL NAME: Gary Donald Koch
HEIGHT: 5-11
WEIGHT: 170
BIRTHDATE: November 21, 1952
BIRTHPLACE: Baton Rouge, LA
RESIDENCE: Tampa, FL
FAMILY: Wife, Donna; Patricia (4/1/81), Rachel (7/30/83)
EDUCATION: University of Florida (1974, Public Relations)
SPECIAL INTERESTS: Golf course design, reading, music
TURNED PROFESSIONAL: 1975
JOINED PGA TOUR: 1976

JOINED CHAMPIONS TOUR: 2003

BEST CHAMPIONS TOUR CAREER FINISHES: T2—2004 The ACE Group Classic, Liberty Mutual Legends of Golf.

OTHER SENIOR VICTORIES (1): 2003 Liberty Mutual Legends of Golf [with Roger Maltbie].

2004 CHARLES SCHWAB CUP FINISH: 42nd - 323 points

PGA TOUR VICTORIES (6): 1976 Tallahassee Open. **1977** Florida Citrus Open. **1983** Doral-Eastern Open. **1984** Isuzu-Andy Williams San Diego Open, Bay Hill Classic. **1988** Panasonic Las Vegas Invitational.

OTHER VICTORIES (9): 1968 Florida State Junior. **1969** Florida State Junior, Orange Bowl Junior, Florida State Open. **1970** Florida State Junior, U.S. Junior Amateur. **1973** Trans-Mississippi Amateur, Southeastern Conference Championship [indiv]. **1974** Southeastern Conference Championship [indiv].

PGA TOUR CAREER EARNINGS: $1,629,482

PGA TOUR PLAYOFF RECORD: 2-0

BEST 2004 CHAMPIONS TOUR FINISHES: T2—The ACE Group Classic, Liberty Mutual Legends of Golf.

2004 SEASON:

Continued to split time between the Champions Tour and his duties on NBC Sports golf telecasts...Made 18 starts from the PGA TOUR Career Victory category and played his best golf early in the season when he was a runner-up in two of his first five events...Nearly won his first title in 16 years when he was involved in a three-man playoff with winner Craig Stadler and Tom Watson at The ACE Group Classic in Naples in February. Appeared to be in command with a three-stroke lead with five holes to play Sunday. However, he bogeyed the 14th and 17th holes to surrender his lead and then fell back into a playoff after missing a long birdie try. Watched Stadler sink a 27-foot birdie putt that eliminated him. Was the first-round leader after setting a new tournament course record at The Club at TwinEagles, a 10-under-par 62, his lowest round on either the PGA TOUR or Champions Tour, that included an 8-under 28 on the back nine...Added a second T2 finish in April at the Liberty Mutual Legends of Golf when he and Gil Morgan finished one stroke behind Hale Irwin in Savannah, GA...Only other top-15 performance during the rest of the campaign was a T14 at the inaugural First Tee Open at Pebble Beach presented bt Wal-Mart.

CHAMPIONS TOUR CAREER HIGHLIGHTS:

2003: Among the top-20 in five events...Made his Champions Tour debut at the Royal Caribbean Golf Classic and finished T17...Teamed with NBC colleague Roger Maltbie to win the unofficial Raphael Division at the Liberty Mutual Legends of Golf. Duo posted a bogey-free, 36-hole better-ball total of 14-under 130, two strokes better than both Chi Chi Rodriguez/Larry Ziegler and Mike Hill/Lee Trevino...T13 at the Kroger Classic, sandwiching rounds of 68-67 around a 73...Also T16 at the Music City Championship and T16 in his final start of the season at the SBC Championship in San Antonio.

OTHER CAREER HIGHLIGHTS:

Owns six career PGA TOUR victories, the last coming in 1988 at the Panasonic-Las Vegas Invitational...Finished among the top 100 money-winners in six of seven years between 1982-88...Best financial year was 1988 with $414,694, 24th on the money list...Highest finish on the money list was 17th in 1984 when he won both the Isuzu-Andy Williams San Diego Open and the Bay Hill Classic. On both occasions, he started the final round six strokes back and won in a playoff. Defeated Gary Hallberg in San Diego and George Burns in the Bay Hill Classic and in both cases won with a birdie on the second extra hole...Prior to 2004 had made 401 starts on the PGA TOUR, with 275 cuts and earnings totaling $1,629,482...Also played 14 events on the Nationwide Tour with additional earnings of $43,351. Best Nationwide Tour finish was a T4 at the 1998 Lakeland Classic...First-team All-American from 1972-74. Member of Florida's 1973 NCAA Championship team...Winner of 10 collegiate events...Member of 1973 and 1975 U.S. Walker Cup squads and 1974 U.S. World Amateur team...Was college teammate of Andy Bean, Andy North and Phil Hancock...Also active in golf course design with Robbins/Koch Golf Designs, Inc.

PERSONAL:

Began TV work with ESPN in 1990, working on Champions Tour telecasts before joining NBC Sports later in the decade...Gained his first taste of professional golf when he qualified for the 1973 U.S. Open at Oakmont as an amateur and finished 57th...Biggest thrill in golf was winning the USGA Junior Amateur Championship in 1970...Favorite golf course is Pebble Beach and favorite TV show is "Frasier."...Enjoys the music of Toby Keith and favorite athlete is Pete Sampras...Favorite movie is "The Sting" and favorite book is *The DaVinci Code.*

PLAYER STATISTICS

MISCELLANEOUS CHAMPIONS TOUR STATISTICS
2004 Low Round: 62–2004 The ACE Group Classic/1
Career Low Round: 62–2004 The ACE Group Classic/1
Career Largest Paycheck: $195,000–2004 Liberty Mutual Legends of Golf/T2

MISCELLANEOUS PGA TOUR STATISTICS
Career Low Round: 63–4 times, most recent 1986 Southern Open/2
Career Largest Paycheck: $250,000–1988 Panasonic Las Vegas Invitational/1

CHAMPIONS TOUR CAREER SUMMARY — PLAYOFF RECORD: 0-1

Year	Events Played	1st	2nd	3rd	Top 10	Top 25	Earnings	Rank
2003	19					7	$178,321	73
2004	18		2		2	4	485,129	41
Total	37		2		2	11	663,450	

COMBINED ALL-TIME MONEY (3 TOURS): $2,336,283

CHAMPIONS TOUR TOP TOURNAMENT SUMMARY

Year	03	04
Senior PGA Championship	CUT	T42
U.S. Senior Open	CUT	
Ford Senior Players		T39
Senior British Open	T51	
JELD-WEN Tradition		T36

CHAMPIONS TOUR YEAR-BY-YEAR STATISTICS (TOP 50 ON 2004 MONEY LIST)

	Scoring Average	Putting Average	Greens in Regulation	Driving Distance	Driving Accuracy
2003	72.18 (61)	1.800 (T48)	64.2 (61)	274.9 (31)	53.8 (87)
2004	71.79 (42)	1.765 (12)	67.3 (36)	274.0 (28)	64.2 (66)

Wayne Levi (LEV-ee)

EXEMPT STATUS: Top 30 on 2004 Champions Tour Money List
FULL NAME: Wayne John Levi
HEIGHT: 5-9
WEIGHT: 165
BIRTHDATE: February 22, 1952
BIRTHPLACE: Little Falls, NY
RESIDENCE: New Hartford, NY

FAMILY: Wife, Judy; Michelle (7/29/79), Lauren (1/20/83), Christine (1/30/84), Brian (5/1/88)
EDUCATION: State University of New York-Oswego
SPECIAL INTERESTS: Financial and stock markets, reading
TURNED PROFESSIONAL: 1973
JOINED PGA TOUR: 1977

JOINED CHAMPIONS TOUR: 2002

CHAMPIONS TOUR VICTORIES (2): **2003** 3M Championship. **2004** Constellation Energy Classic.

2004 CHARLES SCHWAB CUP FINISH: 17th - 1,009 points

PGA TOUR VICTORIES (12): **1978** Walt Disney World National Team Championship [with Bob Mann]. **1979** Houston Open. **1980** Pleasant Valley Jimmy Fund Classic. **1982** Hawaiian Open, Lajet Classic. **1983** Buick Open. **1984** B.C. Open. **1985** Georgia-Pacific Atlanta Golf Classic. **1990** BellSouth Atlanta Golf Classic, Centel Western Open, Canon Greater Hartford Open, Canadian Open.

OTHER VICTORIES (1): **1988** Chrysler Team Championship [with George Burns].

PGA TOUR CAREER EARNINGS: $4,716,842

PGA TOUR PLAYOFF RECORD: 2-1

BEST 2004 CHAMPIONS TOUR FINISHES: 1—Constellation Energy Classic; T2—Commerce Bank Long Island Classic; T3—Blue Angels Classic, FedEx Kinko's Classic, Administaff Small Business Classic.

BEST 2004 PGA TOUR FINISH: T21—B.C. Open.

2004 SEASON:

Enjoyed his finest season on the Champions Tour, surpassing the $1-million mark for the first time and finishing 11th overall on the money list, nine spots higher than 2003...Won for the second time in his career when he went wire-to-wire at the Constellation Energy Classic in early October. Tied the tournament record with an opening-round 64, followed by consecutive 68s. Held off a late charge from Hale Irwin for a two-stroke win near Baltimore. Opened with an 8-under-par 64 in his next start at the Administaff Small Business Classic and held a two-stroke margin over D.A. Weibring after 36 holes, but a closing-round 72 left him T3...Earlier in the year was a T2 at the Commerce Bank Long Island Classic. Besides eventual winner Jim Thorpe, was the only other player to post three straight rounds in the 60s on Eisenhower Park's Red Course. Missed a playoff with Thorpe when his uphill 15-foot birdie putt from the fringe on the last hole came up short...Shared the second-round lead at the Royal Caribbean Golf Classic with Don Pooley. Was in the thick of things until disaster struck during a five-hole span in Sunday's closing round. Was even-par for the day after 11 holes but bogeyed four of next five holes to close with a 3-over-par 75 to finish T5...Followed with a solo sixth-place finish the next week at The ACE Group Classic in Naples, FL...Posted back-to-back rounds of 67 on the weekend at The Moors to T3 at the Blue Angels Classic...Shared the second-round lead with Mark McNulty and Bob Charles at the FedEx Kinko's Classic in May, but slipped to a T3, two strokes behind Larry Nelson after never recovering from problems on the front nine (2-over)...Finished T8 at the SAS Championship...Made one start on the PGA TOUR at the B.C. Open. Made the cut after posting rounds of 72-67 and eventually T21.

CHAMPIONS TOUR CAREER HIGHLIGHTS:

2003: Highlight of the year was his first Champions Tour win, his first victory since the 1990 Canadian Open. Became the sixth of seven first-time winners on the Champions Tour when he triumphed by one stroke at the 3M Championship near Minneapolis in August. Put together three straight rounds in the 60s and sank a four-foot birdie putt on the final hole to nip Gil Morgan and Morris Hatalsky and earn $262,500, the largest check of his professional career. Victory at the TPC of the Twin Cities came in the midst of a run of 13 straight par-better rounds...Posted his career-low round on the Champions Tour when he shot 6-under 64 on Saturday at the Columbus Southern Open...Starting with a 67 at the Farmers Charity Classic on June 22, was under par in every final round the rest of the season (13 tournaments). **2002:** Finished a respectable 28th on the money list in his first full year on the Champions Tour...Made his debut in early March at the SBC Senior Classic near Los Angeles and T37 at Valencia CC...Posted first top-10 finish with a T10 the next week at the Toshiba Senior Classic...Best finish among seven top-10 efforts was a T4 at the Farmers Charity Classic in Michigan...Was the 36-hole leader at the Senior PGA Championship, but faded on Saturday with a 5-over 75 and eventually T6 at Firestone.

OTHER CAREER HIGHLIGHTS:

Played the PGA TOUR full time from 1977-1997...Had career year in 1990, for which he was selected by peers as the first PGA TOUR Player of the Year. Claimed four victories from May to September, making him the first since Curtis Strange in 1988 to win four times...Became the fifth player to earn more than $1 million in one season, finishing second to Greg Norman on the money list with $1,024,647...In near darkness, captured the BellSouth Atlanta Classic, an event he also won in 1985, by one stroke over Keith Clearwater, Larry Mize and Nick Price...Two weeks later, captured the Centel Western Open by four over Payne Stewart...Also shot four straight rounds in the 60s for a two-stroke victory at the Canon Greater Hartford Open...Fourth victory came at the Canadian Open, by one over Ian Baker-Finch and Jim Woodward...First TOUR victory came with Bob Mann in 1978 Walt Disney World Team Championship...Upstate New York native captured the 1984 B.C. Open...Won the 1982 Hawaiian Open with an orange ball, the first player to win with a ball that wasn't white...Was a member of the 1991 U.S. Ryder Cup team and represented the U.S. in the 1991 World Cup, as well.

PERSONAL:

Maintains a great interest in the stock market. Home office has numerous computers and financial documents...Favorite movie is "Contact"...Says best shot of his career was the sand wedge he hit to win 1990 BellSouth Atlanta Classic in near-darkness...Admires Tiger Woods...Favorite course is Butler National near Chicago...Says greatest accomplishment was winning four tournaments in 1990 and earning Player of the Year Award.

PLAYER STATISTICS

MISCELLANEOUS CHAMPIONS TOUR STATISTICS

2004 Low Round: 64–2 times, most recent 2004 Administaff Small Business Classic/1
Career Low Round: 64–3 times, most recent 2004 Administaff Small Business Classic /1
Career Largest Paycheck: $262,500–2003 3M Championship/1

MISCELLANEOUS PGA TOUR STATISTICS

2004 Low Round: 67–B.C. Open/4
Career Low Round: 62–1989 GTE Byron Nelson Golf Classic/1
Career Largest Paycheck: $180,000–4 times, most recent 1990 Canadian Open/1

CHAMPIONS TOUR CAREER SUMMARY — PLAYOFF RECORD: 0-0

Year	Events Played	1st	2nd	3rd	Top 10	Top 25	Earnings	Rank
2002	27				7	18	$725,822	28
2003	27	1			5	19	935,241	20
2004	27	1	1	3	10	19	1,244,064	11
Total	81	2	1	3	22	56	2,905,127	

COMBINED ALL-TIME MONEY (3 TOURS): **$7,621,969**

CHAMPIONS TOUR TOP TOURNAMENT SUMMARY

Year	02	03	04
Senior PGA Championship	T6	T17	T10
U.S. Senior Open		T6	T15
Ford Senior Players	T22	T40	T28
JELD-WEN Tradition	T21	T16	T19
Charles Schwab Cup Champ	T12	12	T20

CHAMPIONS TOUR YEAR-BY-YEAR STATISTICS (TOP 50 ON 2004 MONEY LIST)

	Scoring Average	Putting Average	Greens in Regulation	Driving Distance	Driving Accuracy
2002	70.76 (17)	1.789 (T32)	71.8 (T10)	267.9 (T47)	73.7 (16)
2003	70.37 (T16)	1.780 (T24)	71.6 (12)	273.4 (38)	78.2 (4)
2004	70.24 (T7)	1.786 (27)	73.1 (7)	271.4 (T41)	79.1 (7)

Bruce Lietzke (LITZ-key)

EXEMPT STATUS: Top 30 on 2004 Champions Tour Money List
FULL NAME: Bruce Alan Lietzke
HEIGHT: 6-2
WEIGHT: 205
BIRTHDATE: July 18, 1951
BIRTHPLACE: Kansas City, KS
RESIDENCE: Dallas, TX

FAMILY: Wife, Rosemarie; Stephen Taylor (10/5/83), Christine (10/11/85)
CLUB AFFILIATION: Bent Tree CC (Dallas, TX)
EDUCATION: University of Houston (1973)
SPECIAL INTERESTS: Serious fishing, sports car collection
TURNED PROFESSIONAL: 1974
JOINED PGA TOUR: 1975

JOINED CHAMPIONS TOUR: 2001

CHAMPIONS TOUR VICTORIES (7): 2001 3M Championship, SAS Championship. **2002** Audi Senior Classic, TD Waterhouse Championship, SAS Championship. **2003** Liberty Mutual Legends of Golf, U.S. Senior Open.

2004 CHARLES SCHWAB CUP FINISH: T21st - 842 points

PGA TOUR VICTORIES (13): 1977 Joe Garagiola-Tucson Open, Hawaiian Open. **1978** Canadian Open. **1979** Joe Garagiola-Tucson Open. **1980** Colonial National Invitation. **1981** Bob Hope Desert Classic, Wickes/Andy Williams San Diego Open, Byron Nelson Golf Classic. **1982** Canadian Open. **1984** Honda Classic. **1988** GTE Byron Nelson Golf Classic. **1992** Southwestern Bell Colonial. **1994** Las Vegas Invitational.

PGA TOUR CAREER EARNINGS: $6,474,794

PGA TOUR PLAYOFF RECORD: 6-6

BEST 2004 CHAMPIONS TOUR FINISHES: 2—FedEx Kinko's Classic, Bruno's Memorial Classic; 4—Ford Senior Players Championship; T6—3M Championship; T7—The First Tee Open at Pebble Beach presented by Wal-Mart.

2004 SEASON:

By his standards, did not enjoy the success he had in his previous three seasons on the Champions Tour, finishing with less than $1 million in earnings after surpassing that mark in his first two campaigns. Did not win for the first time ever on the Tour as well...Got off to a slow start after being plagued at the beginning of the year by so-called "frozen shoulder," or adhesive capsulitis, which caused him to miss the entire Florida swing and the MasterCard Classic in Mexico, where he won in 2002...Played in the season-opening MasterCard Championship (finished 38th) before missing the next four events. Returned to play at the SBC Classic where he was T33...Posted a final-round 67 at the Bruno's Memorial Classic to vault into a T2 at Greystone G&CC. Round equaled the lowest score shot on Sunday and gave him his best finish since T2 at the 2003 Allianz Championship...Followed his strong effort in Alabama with a runner-up finish the next week at the FedEx Kinko's Classic, where he fell one stroke shy of Larry Nelson...Made his second career hole-in-one on the Champions Tour in the final round of the Commerce Bank Long Island Classic. Aced the 179-yard 16th hole on the Red Course at Eisenhower Park with a 4-iron shot...Was fourth at the Ford Senior Players Championship, where his second round included a pair of eagles...Was T6 at 3M Championship, thanks to a final-round 66 that equaled the low round of the day at the TPC of the Twin Cities...Was one stroke behind 36-hole leader Peter Jacobsen at the JELD-WEN Tradition, but a third-round 73 eventually dropped him to a T11...Had nice effort the following week at The First Tee Open at Pebble Beach, finishing T7...Played in every event after mid-August (eight straight), a first for him since the early '80s.

CHAMPIONS TOUR CAREER HIGHLIGHTS:

2003: Won multiple titles on the Champions Tour for the third straight season and was in contention throughout the year for the Charles Schwab Cup. Eventually finished third in the Schwab Cup standings and placed fourth on the final 2003 money list with a personal-best $1.6 million, his highest ranking since placing fourth on the 1981 PGA TOUR earnings list...Made a strong bid for Player of the Year honors early on with eight of his nine top-10 finishes coming prior to July. Capped off the first half of the season by winning his first major title at the U.S. Senior Open. Was victorious by two strokes over Tom Watson at Toledo's Inverness Club, despite a closing-round 73. Helped position himself for his win with a 7-under-par 64 in the third round. Earned a check for $470,000, the largest of his professional career, and also was voted as the Player of the Month for June. Open victory ended a string of 16 consecutive events to begin a Champions Tour season without a repeat winner...Claimed his first victory of the year at the Liberty Mutual Legends of Golf despite playing the final 10 holes of the event without making a birdie. Held off David Eger and Dana Quigley by one stroke at the Westin Savannah Harbor course...Made another strong bid for victory in late August at the Allianz Championship, but finished T2 in Des Moines despite three straight rounds in the 60s, his third consecutive top-three performance in Iowa...Tied a Champions Tour record at the MasterCard Championship when he made a rare three eagles in the second round on his way to a T7 in Hawaii. Became just the fourth player in Champions Tour history to record three eagles in the same round and the first since Rocky Thompson at the 1992 Kaanapali Classic...Came close to defending his title at the MasterCard Classic in Mexico City, but fell one stroke shy of David Eger at Bosque Real CC...Was unable to defend again later in the season when he had to withdraw from the Bayer Advantage Celebrity Pro-Am midway through the first round due to elbow tendinitis...Showed his mettle when he bounced back from an opening-round, 5-over-par 75 to finish T3 at the Senior PGA Championship at Aronimink GC, closing with rounds of 67-70-67. **2002:** Rallied from a first-round 75 to win the Audi Senior Classic early in the season, beating Hale Irwin and Gary McCord by one stroke. Shot 66-67 on the weekend in Mexico City, capped by three birdies on his final nine holes. Opening round was the highest by an eventual winner since Hale Irwin opened with a 77 and won the 1998 U.S. Senior Open in Los Angeles...Also captured the rain-shortened TD Waterhouse Championship near Kansas City. Moved in front on Saturday with an 8-under 64 at Tiffany Greens and was declared the winner on Sunday when the golf course was deemed unplayable after a series of overnight thunderstorms...Claimed his third title when he defended at the SAS Championship. Helped his cause with a tournament-record, 9-under-par 63 in the second round and won by four shots. Became the first player to defend a title in 2002, and it also marked the fifth time in his career he has posted multiple victories in the same event...Moved into contention at the AT&T Canada Senior Open Championship with a 9-under 62 on Saturday, his low round on Tour since the 1998 Bob Hope Chrysler Classic. Led the event through 10 holes on Sunday, but eventually fell to Tom Jenkins by three strokes...Set a course record in the final round of the Kroger Senior Classic with a 10-under-par 62 at the TPC at River's Bend. **2001:** Became eligible for the Champions Tour in mid-July. Battled Bob Gilder for Rookie of the Year honors after posting a pair of victories and seven top-10s in just 10 senior appearances...Led the Champions Tour in most money won per start ($111,957) and became the last of 16 players to earn seven figures when he pocketed a check for $213,000 at the season-ending SENIOR TOUR Championship at Gaillardia...Debuted on the circuit at the SBC Senior Open near Chicago and won his first event, the 3M Championship, in his third appearance on the circuit.

CHAMPIONS TOUR CAREER SUMMARY — PLAYOFF RECORD: 0-0

Year	Events Played	1st	2nd	3rd	Top 10	Top 25	Earnings	Rank
2001	10	2	1	2	7	10	$1,119,573	16
2002	22	3	1	1	9	17	1,527,676	7
2003	22	2	2	1	9	14	1,610,826	4
2004	20		2		5	13	838,874	21
Total	74	7	6	4	30	54	5,096,949	
COMBINED ALL-TIME MONEY (3 TOURS):							**$11,571,743**	

CHAMPIONS TOUR TOP TOURNAMENT SUMMARY

Year	01	02	03	04
Senior PGA Championship		T45	T3	CUT
U.S. Senior Open		T21	1	T19
Ford Senior Players		T12	T33	4
JELD-WEN Tradition		T16	T46	T11
Charles Schwab Cup Champ	3	T10	T25	T16

CHAMPIONS TOUR YEAR-BY-YEAR STATISTICS (TOP 50 ON 2004 MONEY LIST)

	Scoring Average	Putting Average	Greens in Regulation	Driving Distance	Driving Accuracy
2001	68.73 (N/A)	1.751 (N/A)	77.8 (N/A)	292.3 (N/A)	77.3 (N/A)
2002	69.96 (8)	1.781 (T23)	70.4 (T15)	276.2 (T14)	73.4 (20)
2003	70.04 (10)	1.768 (T10)	71.7 (T10)	285.4 (7)	69.6 (39)
2004	70.85 (T19)	1.782 (T22)	70.4 (T17)	273.8 (T29)	74.8 (20)

Bruce Lietzke (continued)

Trailed by two strokes entering the final round, but fired a 69 at the TPC of the Twin Cities on Sunday to defeat Doug Tewell by two strokes. Made his first hole-in-one as a senior when he aced the 177-yard fourth hole with an 8-iron during the second round...Also won the inaugural SAS Championship in Raleigh, besting Allen Doyle and Gary McCord by three strokes, thanks to a final-round 66 at Prestonwood...Played two tournaments on the PGA TOUR prior to turning 50...Missed the cut at the Bob Hope Chrysler Classic and T58 at the MasterCard Colonial.

OTHER CAREER HIGHLIGHTS:

Winner of 13 events in his 24-year PGA TOUR career that began in 1975, including three wins in 1981 when he was fourth on the money list with $343,446. Held at least a share of the lead after each round of the Bob Hope Desert Classic in defeating Jerry Pate by two strokes. Two weeks later, bested Raymond Floyd and Tom Jenkins in playoff at Wickes-Andy Williams San Diego Open. Defeated Tom Watson in playoff for title at Byron Nelson Classic...First TOUR win came in playoff over Gene Littler at 1977 Joe Garagiola-Tucson Open and added second victory that year at Hawaiian Open three weeks later...Won four tournaments twice—Colonial (1980, 1992), Byron Nelson (1981, 1988), Tucson (1977, 1979) and Canadian Open (1978, 1982)...Nearly claimed a third Byron Nelson title in 1992, losing a playoff to Billy Ray Brown. Missed winning third Canadian Open, losing playoff to Greg Norman the same year...Most recent victory came at 1994 Las Vegas Invitational. Closing-round 65 defeated hometown product Robert Gamez by one stroke. With victory, earned a berth in 1995 Mercedes Championship, where he lost to Steve Elkington in a playoff...Had chance to claim first win since 1994 at the 1998 Bob Hope Chrysler Classic. Lost his one-stroke lead at the final hole when he missed a 15-foot birdie putt and Fred Couples converted a birdie opportunity to force a playoff. Lost on the first extra hole when Couples again birdied the 18th hole...Was only player in field at all three tournaments at which a player shot a 59—1977 Danny Thomas Memphis Classic (Al Geiberger), 1991 Las Vegas Invitational (Chip Beck) and 1999 Bob Hope Chrysler Classic (David Duval)...Best overall monetary year on the PGA TOUR was when he pocketed $703,805 and placed 16th on the 1992 earnings list...Was a member of the 1981 U.S. Ryder Cup team and served as the assistant to Ben Crenshaw at the 1999 Ryder Cup matches in Boston...Has had six holes-in-one in competition.

PERSONAL:

Playing schedule was envy of many on the PGA TOUR. Never played more than 25 events in any PGA TOUR season and never more than 20 tournaments in a single season after 1988...Lists Don January and Miller Barber as his heroes...Started in golf at age 5 by his brother, Duane. Credits Duane and Henry Homberg, a local Texas professional, for having the greatest influences on his game when he first started playing...Biggest thrill in golf was winning his first PGA TOUR event (1977 Tucson Open) and also being involved in the 1999 Ryder Cup as Assistant Captain to Ben Crenshaw...Favorite course is Muirfield Village...Is a big drag racing and auto racing fan...Has a large collection of muscle cars and built an 11-car garage at his home. The crown jewel of his collection is a 1967 yellow Corvette Stingray convertible, with the largest engine available—a 435-horse big block Chevrolet engine. Bought the car from Gil Morgan in 1982...His dream job would to be an engine builder for any race team. First car he ever owned was a 1970 bright orange Plymouth Roadrunner...Lists Tom Hanks and Bruce Springsteen as his favorite entertainers and drag racing legend Don Garlits as his favorite athlete...Best friend on the Champions Tour is Bill Rogers...Wife, Rose, and Jerry Pate's wife, Soozi, are sisters.

PLAYER STATISTICS

MISCELLANEOUS CHAMPIONS TOUR STATISTICS

2004 Low Round: 66–2 times, most recent 2004 3M Championship/3
Career Low Round: 62–2 times, most recent 2002 Kroger Senior Classic/3
Career Largest Paycheck: $470,000–2003 U.S. Senior Open/1

MISCELLANEOUS PGA TOUR STATISTICS

Career Low Round: 62–2 times, most recent 1998 Bob Hope Chrysler Classic/4
Career Largest Paycheck: $270,000–1994 Las Vegas Invitational/1

25 MEMORABLE MOMENTS

Nicklaus Wins 100th Title

1996 Tradition

Ten holes into the third round, it looked like a runaway for Hale Irwin, who led defending champion Jack Nicklaus by four strokes. Two holes later, Nicklaus was tied for the lead. After snaking in an 18-foot birdie at the par-3 11th hole as Irwin bogeyed, the Golden Bear made a double eagle at the par-5 12th. Nicklaus used the momentum for back-to-back 65s and a three-shot victory. Nicklaus made Champions Tour history, becoming the first player to win the same Champions Tour event four times. He also reached another milestone, the 100th victory of his professional career, going back to 1962.

CHAMPIONS TOUR 25

John Mahaffey

EXEMPT STATUS: Top 30 on All-Time Money List
FULL NAME: John Drayton Mahaffey
HEIGHT: 5-9
WEIGHT: 160
BIRTHDATE: May 9, 1948
BIRTHPLACE: Kerrville, TX
RESIDENCE: The Woodlands, TX

FAMILY: John D. Mahaffey III (8/8/88), Meagan (6/12/92)
CLUB AFFILIATION: Augusta Pines GC (Spring, TX)
EDUCATION: University of Houston (1970, Psychology)
SPECIAL INTERESTS: Fishing
TURNED PROFESSIONAL: 1971
JOINED PGA TOUR: 1971

JOINED CHAMPIONS TOUR: 1998

CHAMPIONS TOUR VICTORIES (1): 1999 Southwestern Bell Dominion.

PGA TOUR VICTORIES (10): 1973 Sahara Invitational. **1978** PGA Championship, American Optical Classic. **1979** Bob Hope Desert Classic. **1980** Kemper Open. **1981** Anheuser-Busch Golf Classic. **1984** Bob Hope Classic. **1985** Texas Open. **1986** Tournament Players Championship. **1989** Federal Express St. Jude Classic.

OTHER VICTORIES (4): 1970 NCAA Championship [indiv]. **1978** World Cup [indiv], World Cup [with Andy North]. **1979** World Cup [with Hale Irwin].

PGA TOUR CAREER EARNINGS: $3,876,852

PGA TOUR PLAYOFF RECORD: 3-2

BEST 2004 CHAMPIONS TOUR FINISH: T39—SBC Classic.

2004 SEASON:

Combined a playing schedule with some on-course announcing for The Golf Channel during Champions Tour events...Best effort was a T39 at the SBC Classic at Valencia...Continued to battle back problems throughout the season...Also suffered a broken toe in a freak hotel accident during the Blue Angels Classic and was forced to withdraw from the event Saturday morning.

CHAMPIONS TOUR CAREER HIGHLIGHTS:

2003: Battled a bad back for parts of the season...Lone top-25 finish was a T21 at the Verizon Classic in his third start of the year. **2002:** Played his best golf during a six-week span from mid-June until late July when he had two second-place finishes...First runner-up performance came at the Greater Baltimore Classic at Hayfields, one stroke behind J.C. Snead. Was on the leaderboard all three rounds and had his best effort since winning in San Antonio at the 1999 Southwestern Bell Dominion...Overcame back spasms to fire final-round 65 at FleetBoston Classic, but lost in a playoff to Bob Gilder. **2001:** Finished T4 in Napa after battling Allen Doyle and eventual winner Sammy Rachels to the wire. Vaulted into contention on Saturday when he fired his career-low round, a Silverado South course-record 10-under 62 that included a front-nine score of 28. Reeled off 11 birdies in the round and seven in a row (holes 1-7). **2000:** Finished solo third at the Kroger Senior Classic. **1999:** Won his first Champions Tour event at the Southwestern Bell Dominion. Victory in San Antonio came 14 years after he claimed the Texas Open in the same city on the PGA TOUR. Made a 30-foot birdie putt on the second playoff hole to beat Jose Maria Canizares and Bruce Fleisher. Holed a clutch 20-foot birdie putt at the 17th hole in regulation to get into the overtime session...Hit 77 percent of Greens in Regulation, the highest mark in the history of the Champions Tour at that time (since surpassed by Tom Kite's 78.0 in 2000). **1998:** Debuted at the Saint Luke's Classic and T26 at the Kansas City event...Best finish was a T2 at the Utah Showdown, where he finished four strokes behind Gil Morgan.

OTHER CAREER HIGHLIGHTS:

High point of 25-year career came at the 1978 PGA Championship at Oakmont CC, where he won a playoff over Tom Watson and Jerry Pate...Went on to claim the American Optical Classic in Sutton, MA, the following week...Earned a 10-year exemption with his one-stroke victory over Larry Mize at 1986 Tournament Players Championship (now THE PLAYERS Championship). Fired third-round 65 on Stadium Course at the TPC at Sawgrass to move into contention...Last victory came at the 1989 Federal Express St. Jude Classic, where he closed with rounds of 66-65 for a three-stroke win at TPC at Southwind...Led the PGA TOUR in Greens in Regulation in 1985 and 1986...Played on two U.S. World Cup teams, in 1978 and 1979, and was the medalist in 1978...Member of the U.S. Ryder Cup team in 1979 and the Nissan Cup squad in 1986...Was the 1970 NCAA champion while at the University of Houston, where he was a teammate of Tom Jenkins.

PERSONAL:

Early in his career, was sought out by other players to do imitations...Many thought his comic imitation of Chi Chi Rodriguez's swing was even better than the real thing.

PLAYER STATISTICS

2004 CHAMPIONS TOUR STATISTICS:

Scoring Average	74.14	(74)
Driving Distance	250.0	(78)
Driving Accuracy Percentage	77.0%	(10)
Total Driving	88	(53)
Greens in Regulation Pct.	60.2%	(72)
Putting Average	1.864	(78)
Sand Save Percentage	45.3%	(45)
Eagles (Holes per)	918.0	(70)
Birdie Average	2.10	(81)
All-Around Ranking	508	(75)

MISCELLANEOUS CHAMPIONS TOUR STATISTICS

2004 Low Round: 69–2004 Bank of America Championship/3
Career Low Round: 62–2001 The Transamerica/2
Career Largest Paycheck: $165,000–1999 Southwestern Bell Dominion/1

MISCELLANEOUS PGA TOUR STATISTICS

Career Low Round: 63–2 times, most recent 1985 USF&G Classic/1
Career Largest Paycheck: $180,000–1989 Federal Express St. Jude Classic/1

CHAMPIONS TOUR CAREER SUMMARY — PLAYOFF RECORD: 1-1

Year	Events Played	1st	2nd	3rd	Top 10	Top 25	Earnings	Rank
1998	23		1		2	11	$365,233	49
1999	32	1		1	13	23	988,778	15
2000	31			1	9	16	714,426	28
2001	25				4	13	467,985	43
2002	27		2		4	7	538,696	36
2003	20					1	73,306	95
2004	20						40,259	104
Total	178	1	3	2	32	71	3,188,683	
COMBINED ALL-TIME MONEY (3 TOURS):							**$7,065,535**	

CHAMPIONS TOUR TOP TOURNAMENT SUMMARY

Year	98	99	00	01	02	03	04
Senior PGA Championship		T18	T8		CUT	CUT	CUT
U.S. Senior Open	12	T29	T37	T7	T53	WD	CUT
Ford Senior Players		T22	T30	T51	T33	T56	
JELD-WEN Tradition		T28	T25	T73	T9		T64
Charles Schwab Cup Champ		T16	30				

Graham Marsh

EXEMPT STATUS: Top 30 on 2004 Champions Tour Money List
FULL NAME: Graham Vivian Marsh
HEIGHT: 5-11
WEIGHT: 187
BIRTHDATE: January 14, 1944
BIRTHPLACE: Kalgoorlie, Australia
RESIDENCE: Dalkeith, Australia
FAMILY: Tony (9/17/64), Jenni (3/14/69), Jeremy (5/5/81), Stephanie (11/24/82)
EDUCATION: University of Western Australia and Claremont Teachers College (1962)
SPECIAL INTERESTS: Skiing, tennis, watching cricket, golf course design
TURNED PROFESSIONAL: 1969
JOINED PGA TOUR: 1977

JOINED CHAMPIONS TOUR: 1994

CHAMPIONS TOUR VICTORIES (6): 1995 Bruno's Memorial Classic. **1996** World Seniors Invitational, Franklin Quest Championship. **1997** Nationwide Championship, U.S. Senior Open. **1999** The Tradition Presented by Countrywide.

OTHER SENIOR VICTORIES (3): 1997 Liberty Mutual Legends of Golf [with John Bland]. **1998** Japan Senior Open. **1999** Japan Senior Open.

2004 CHARLES SCHWAB CUP FINISH: 31st - 493 points

PGA TOUR VICTORIES (1): 1977 Heritage Classic.

OTHER VICTORIES (55): 1970 Watties Tournament, Swiss Open. **1971** Spaulding Masters, Indian Open. **1972** Swiss Open, German Open, Dunlop International. **1973** Sunbeam Electric Scottish Open, Thailand Open, Indian Open, Fuji Sankei Classic. **1974** Malaysian Open, Fuji Sankei Classic, Dunlop Wizard, Tokyo Open, Pepsi-Wilson. **1975** Dunlop Wizard, Tokyo Open, Malaysian Open. **1976** Benson & Hedges International, Dunlop Open, Suntory Open, Dunlop Phoenix, KBC Augusta, Dunhill Match-Play, Western Australia Open. **1977** Lancome Trophy, Colgate World Match-Play Championship, Dunhill Match-Play, Suntory Open, Dunlop Wizard, Chunichi Crowns. **1978** Western Australia PGA. **1979** Dutch Open, ANA Sapporo Open, Dunlop Masters. **1980** Benson & Hedges International. **1981** Dixcel Tissues European Open, Chunichi Open, Pepsi-Wilson. **1982** Ford Dealers South Australian Open, Australian Masters, Mayn Nickless Australian PGA Championship, Dunhill Queensland Open, Mitsubishi Galant. **1983** Yomiuri Open, Resch's Pilsner Tweed Classic, New Zealand PGA Championship. **1985** Lawrence Batley International, KLM Dutch Open, Tokai Classic. **1986** Suntory Open. **1987** Visa Taiheiyo Pacific Masters. **1989** Sapporo Tokyo Open. **1990** Tokai Classic.

PGA TOUR CAREER EARNINGS:$235,854

BEST 2004 CHAMPIONS TOUR FINISHES: 2—MasterCard Classic; T4—SBC Classic, Constellation Energy Classic; T8—Farmers Charity Classic; T9—Senior British Open.

2004 SEASON:

Recorded the highest finish on the money list by a player over age 60 last year and was among the top five in three events for the second consecutive year...Played his best golf during the month of March...Nearly won for the first time since his 1999 victory at The Tradition when he appeared in command at the MasterCard Classic near Mexico City. Led by three strokes with six holes to play, but three-putted for bogeys at the 16th and 17th holes in Sunday's final round and finished tied with Ed Fiori after 54 holes. Eventually lost the playoff to Fiori after making bogey on the third extra hole at Bosque Real CC. However, runner-up effort was his best on the Champions Tour since 2001 campaign. Saw a golden opportunity slip away on the first playoff hole when he mis-hit his second shot moments after Fiori hit his second shot out of bounds...Carded a final-round 65 at Valencia the next week to vault into a T4 at the SBC Classic...Made news in July when he finished T9 at the Senior British Open at Royal Portrush GC in Northern Ireland. Recorded holes-in-one on the 11th hole in both the first and third rounds of the event, a first on the Champions Tour on the same hole at the same tournament. Used a 9-iron in the opening round (171 yards) and an 8-iron on Saturday (182 yards). Two aces also earned him 340 bottles of Hardys Australian wine, one for every yard the shot covered (based on score-card yardage), and were his fourth and fifth aces since joining the Champions Tour (10th and 11th aces overall in competition). Also marked the second consecutive season he made a hole-in-one on the Champions Tour..Secured his spot among the top 30 on the money list when he earned $86,400 for a T4 late in the year at the Constellation Energy Classic. Trailed Wayne Levi by two strokes after 36 holes at The Hayfields, but ended up four strokes back of Levi after posting a final-round 70...Joined the ranks of the Georgia-Pacific Grand Champions at the start of the season and finished second on the final over-60 money list, with $170,646...Finished one stroke back of Jay Sigel in the Georgia-Pacific event at the Bank of America Championship near Boston.

CHAMPIONS TOUR CAREER HIGHLIGHTS:

2003: Among the top 30 for the first time since 1999, more than doubling his 2002 earnings. Highest total earnings in a season since 1999 as well...T3 at the Turtle Bay Championship near the end of the campaign thanks to a final-round 7-under-par 65 at the Palmer Course...Check for $98,625 clinched his position in the top 30 for the year. Aced No. 8 at Turtle Bay with a 9-iron from 140 yards during the second round...Finished T4 earlier in the season at the 3M Championship...Had a good showing at the Kroger Classic in September when he strung together three straight rounds in the 60s to finish fifth. Was on the leaderboard all three days before bogeys on two of the final four holes ended his chances...Strung together three straight rounds in the 60s at the Senior British Open at Turnberry in July and T10, his first top-10 effort in a major since placing second in the 1999 Ford Senior Players Championship. **2002:** Placed ninth in Mexico City at the Audi Senior Classic...Held a share of the first-round lead with Hale Irwin at the Allianz Championship, but rounds of 74-72 dropped him to a T42. **2001:** In the hunt at the Novell Utah Showdown before finishing T2 with three other players, one stroke back of Steve Veriato...Holed a 6-iron shot on the fourth hole at the TPC at the Twin Cities during the final round of the 3M Championship. Ace was his first since the 1997 Southwestern Bell Dominion event in San Antonio. **2000:** Missed a spot among the top 31 money-

CHAMPIONS TOUR CAREER SUMMARY — PLAYOFF RECORD: 0-1

Year	Events Played	1st	2nd	3rd	Top 10	Top 25	Earnings	Rank
1994	22		2		7	21	$492,402	24
1995	27	1	1	2	14	24	849,350	8
1996	28	2	2	2	16	25	1,024,290	9
1997	29	2		1	13	25	1,128,578	7
1998	28		1		7	19	664,432	24
1999	28	1	1	2	7	19	1,039,334	12
2000	30		1		6	19	599,008	32
2001	31		1		6	16	629,260	32
2002	26				1	9	356,100	46
2003	27			1	7	15	745,152	25
2004	30		1		5	15	756,048	26
Total	306	6	10	8	89	207	8,283,954	

COMBINED ALL-TIME MONEY (3 TOURS): $8,519,808

CHAMPIONS TOUR TOP TOURNAMENT SUMMARY

Year	94	95	96	97	98	99	00	01	02	03	04
Senior PGA Championship	T24	T5	T15	T20	T18	T18	T38	T27	WD	CUT	T38
U.S. Senior Open	T2	T8	4	1	CUT	T38	T19	T40	30	T28	T25
Ford Senior Players	T14	T14		T8	T60	2	T24	T23	T22	T30	T22
Senior British Open										T10	T9
JELD-WEN Tradition	T33	T17	T19	T6	T13	1	T19	T55	72	T20	63
Charles Schwab Cup Champ	T12	T8	T10	T24	24	T11				T13	T22

CHAMPIONS TOUR YEAR-BY-YEAR STATISTICS (TOP 50 ON 2004 MONEY LIST)

	Scoring Average	Putting Average	Greens in Regulation	Driving Distance	Driving Accuracy
1994	70.32 (11)	1.783 (14)	71.1 (T19)	256.6 (27)	77.1 (8)
1995	70.15 (6)	1.753 (T4)	72.2 (8)	257.4 (35)	75.2 (9)
1996	70.34 (5)	1.790 (T13)	72.6 (2)	265.7 (27)	76.8 (9)
1997	70.47 (7)	1.756 (3)	68.8 (T12)	268.0 (20)	71.4 (24)
1998	71.17 (T17)	1.782 (19)	67.7 (18)	266.1 (34)	72.8 (18)
1999	70.60 (15)	1.781 (18)	70.6 (16)	260.7 (64)	77.8 (7)
2000	70.80 (24)	1.777 (27)	69.4 (23)	265.3 (T52)	75.2 (14)
2001	71.20 (26)	1.791 (30)	67.5 (34)	270.9 (T48)	76.2 (T8)
2002	71.97 (51)	1.816 (58)	67.9 (31)	259.6 (79)	77.0 (T7)
2003	70.81 (26)	1.772 (T17)	66.8 (48)	271.0 (T46)	72.7 (20)
2004	71.44 (35)	1.791 (T31)	67.2 (37)	270.6 (47)	71.6 (33)

Graham Marsh (continued)

winners when David Lundstrom nipped him by $941...Was the 36-hole leader at the MasterCard Championship, but hit just 10 greens on Sunday and posted a final-round 74 to T2 at Hualalai. **1999:** Although only playing 36 holes, was declared the winner of The Tradition after a freak snowstorm wiped out the final rounds at Desert Mountain...Also battled Hale Irwin for most of the Ford Senior Players Championship before finishing a distant second at the TPC of Michigan. **1998:** Was solo second near St. Louis at the Boone Valley Classic. Finished two strokes short of Larry Nelson, despite a final-round 68 that included a pair of eagles. **1997:** Earned a career-best $1,128,578 for seventh on the final money list...Outdueled John Bland on the final day for a one-stroke win at the U.S. Senior Open at Olympia Fields CC in suburban Chicago. The victory, and a career-best $232,500, came just one week after he fought off a late challenge by Hale Irwin and earned a one-stroke win at the Nationwide Championship near Atlanta...Teamed with Bland earlier in the season to win the Liberty Mutual Legends of Golf...Recorded his first Champions Tour hole-in-one at the Southwestern Bell Dominion. **1996:** Was a one-stroke victor over Tom Wargo and Brian Barnes at the PaineWebber Invitational and fired a final-round 67 to win the Franklin Quest Championship by two strokes over Kermit Zarley. **1995:** Broke into the winner's circle at the Bruno's Memorial Classic. Used a second-round 63 to cruise to a five-stroke win over J.C. Snead at Greystone G&CC. **1994:** T2 at the Vantage at the Dominion and again at the U.S. Senior Open at Pinehurst, one stroke behind Simon Hobday. **1993:** Placed second to Bill Hall at the Champions Tour National Qualifying Tournament at Grenelefe to earn his initial exemption.

OTHER CAREER HIGHLIGHTS:

An accomplished world-class player, he owns 65 titles on five different tours (25 Japan Golf Tour, 16 Australasian Tour, 15 European Tour, one PGA TOUR, two Japanese Senior Tour and six Champions Tour)...Was among the top 10 on the Australasian Order of Merit for seven consecutive years from 1978-1984, finishing second in 1978 and 1982...Won a career-best six titles on three different Tours in 1977, including the Heritage Classic at Hilton Head on the PGA TOUR, where he edged Tom Watson by one stroke...A member of the Australian team in the 1973 Japan vs. Australia matches...Member of the 1985 and 1986 Nissan Cup teams and 1987 and 1988 Kirin Cup squads...Has 11 career holes-in-one, including five since joining the Champions Tour.

PERSONAL:

Has been honored by the Queen of England with the title Member of the British Empire (MBE)...Very active with his own junior golf foundation in Australia...Is managing director of Graham Marsh Golf Design. Has designed over 35 courses throughout Asia and Australia and is now doing design work in the United States...Nicknamed

PLAYER STATISTICS

MISCELLANEOUS CHAMPIONS TOUR STATISTICS

2004 Low Round: 65–2 times, most recent 2004 Bruno's Memorial Classic/2
Career Low Round: 63–2 times, most recent 1995 Kroger Senior Classic/2
Career Largest Paycheck: $232,500–1997 U.S. Senior Open/1

MISCELLANEOUS PGA TOUR STATISTICS

Career Low Round: 64–1983 World Series of Golf/2
Career Largest Paycheck: $45,000–1977 Heritage Classic/1

25 MEMORABLE MOMENTS

Open-Qualifier Quigley's Bittersweet Victory

1997 Northville Long Island Classic

Rarely has the final round of an event ended on a more somber note than the 1997 Northville Long Island Classic. Moments after earning his first victory as an open qualifier, Dana Quigley learned his father, Paul, had died after a lengthy battle with cancer. Earlier in the week, Quigley drove home to see his dad, who insisted he return and play in the event. After finishing with a 12-under-par 204, Quigley found himself in a playoff with Jay Sigel. After matching bogeys and pars on the first two playoff holes, Quigley finished off Sigel with a birdie on the third extra hole.

CHAMPIONS TOUR 25

Gary McCord

EXEMPT STATUS: 40th on 2004 Champions Tour Money List
FULL NAME: Gary Dennis McCord
HEIGHT: 6-2
WEIGHT: 190
BIRTHDATE: May 23, 1948
BIRTHPLACE: San Gabriel, CA
RESIDENCE: Paradise Valley, AZ
FAMILY: Wife, Diane, Krista (5/14/68), four grandchildren
CLUB AFFILIATION: Grayhawk GC (Scottsdale, AZ)
EDUCATION: University of California-Riverside (1971, Economics)
SPECIAL INTERESTS: Acceleration, giving a name to each age spot on my body
TURNED PROFESSIONAL: 1971
JOINED PGA TOUR: 1974

JOINED CHAMPIONS TOUR: 1998

CHAMPIONS TOUR VICTORIES (2): 1999 Toshiba Senior Classic, Ingersoll-Rand SENIOR TOUR Championship.

2004 CHARLES SCHWAB CUP FINISH: 29th - 539 points

BEST PGA TOUR CAREER FINISHES:
2—1975 Greater Milwaukee Open, T2—1977 Greater Milwaukee Open.

PGA TOUR CAREER EARNINGS: $662,359

BEST 2004 CHAMPIONS TOUR FINISHES:
2—SBC Championship; T5—Ford Senior Players Championship; T7—SBC Classic; T10—Kroger Classic.

NATIONWIDE TOUR VICTORIES (1): 1991
Gateway Open

2004 SEASON:
Continued to split time between the Champions Tour and CBS golf television commitments...Improved 48 spots on the money list from 2003...In his last official event of the season, was solo second at the SBC Championship, his best performance on the Champions Tour since losing in a playoff to Hale Irwin at the 2002 Turtle Bay Championship. Was one of just two players (Mark McNulty) to post three straight rounds in the 60s at Oak Hills, yet finished eight strokes back in San Antonio, the second time he's been a runner-up at this event (2001)...Also T5 at the Ford Senior Players Championship in July. Shared the 36-hole lead with Jose Maria Canizares, following a second-round, 8-under-par 64, his best round since 2001. Remained among the leaders for the next two days but watched his chances slip away Sunday with a 3-over-par 39 on the back nine on his way to a 74...First-round co-leader at the Kroger Classic after a 7-under 65 and eventually T10 at the TPC at River's Bend...Served as captain of the American team at the inaugural Tommy Bahama Challenge late in the year.

CHAMPIONS TOUR CAREER HIGHLIGHTS:
2003: Best outings came in his first and last starts of the season. T15 in his first appearance of the season at the Verizon Classic and T16 in his final event at the SBC Championship. **2002:** T2 at the Audi Senior Classic. Battled Bruce Lietzke down the stretch in Mexico City before falling one stroke short. Was also runnerup at the Turtle Bay Championship late in the year. Posted a final-round 69 to get into a playoff with Hale Irwin, but lost when he made a par on the first extra hole. **2001:** T2 at the inaugural SAS Championship in Raleigh, three strokes back of winner Bruce Lietzke. Also T2 at the SBC Championship, two strokes back of Larry Nelson, thanks to a Champions Tour career-low, 9-under 63 in the opening round. **2000:** Lost a three-man playoff at the LiquidGolf.com Invitational in Sarasota with J.C. Snead and eventual-winner Tom Wargo. **1999:** Won his first and last events of the year...Became the third of a record 11 first-time winners when he triumphed at the Toshiba Senior Classic. Received a sponsor's exemption into the event and eventually won the tournament in a four-way playoff. Made a four-foot birdie putt on the fifth extra hole to beat good friend John Jacobs after Al Geiberger and Allen Doyle had been eliminated earlier in the overtime session. Triumph at Newport Beach CC allowed him to join Doyle as the only other player to claim both a Nationwide Tour and a Champions Tour title. Capped his season with a thrilling victory at the Ingersoll-Rand SENIOR TOUR Championship and earned the largest paycheck of his career, $347,000. Moved into contention with a sizzling 64 at The Dunes Club on Saturday, and then fired a final-round 67 on Sunday to overtake Bruce Fleisher and Larry Nelson by one stroke. Victory at The Dunes came 26 years after he had earned PGA TOUR playing privileges there in the National Q-School. Voted Champions Tour's Player of the Month in March and November. **1998:** Earned a conditional exemption for the 1999 season by finishing 16th at the Champions Tour National Qualifying Tournament in the fall...Debuted at the U.S. Senior Open and T33 at Riviera CC near Los Angeles...Played five other events during the season on sponsor exemptions.

OTHER CAREER HIGHLIGHTS:
Played the PGA TOUR from 1974-98, with well over $600,000 in earnings in 376 tournaments...Made 242 cuts in that span with his best year financially coming in 1984 when he won $68,213, with a pair of top-10 finishes...Top performances in his PGA TOUR career were a solo second to Art Wall at the 1975 Greater Milwaukee Open and a T2 behind Dave Eichelberger at the 1977 Greater Milwaukee Open...Placed 59th on the official money list in 1975 with $43,028, his highest standing ever...Was a five-stroke victor at the 1991 Nationwide Gateway Open...Two-time All-America selection at Cal-Riverside and was the winner of the 1970 NCAA Division II Championship...Had had seven holes-in-one in competition.

PERSONAL:
Best known as a color analyst on CBS Sports' golf telecasts... Also writes for *Golf Digest*...Another of his efforts were three books: *Golf for Dummies, Golf For Dummies II* and *Just a Range Ball in a Box of Titleists*...Also hosted "Golf for Dummies" instructional DVD...Served as technical consultant for and appeared in the Kevin Costner movie "Tin Cup"...Was backed by the late Lawrence Welk early in his pro career and once appeared on the musical conductor's variety show...Got started in golf when he used to go with his mother to her golf class in Garden Grove, CA, when he was 12...Attended the same high school (Garden Grove HS) as comedian Steve Martin...Lists the smell of free range balls in the morning as his biggest thrill in golf...Favorite TV shows are "CSI" and "Vegas" and favorite athlete is Seabiscuit.

PLAYER STATISTICS

MISCELLANEOUS CHAMPIONS TOUR STATISTICS
2004 Low Round: 64–2004 Ford Senior Players Championship/2
Career Low Round: 63–2001 SBC Championship/1
Career Largest Paycheck: $347,000–1999 Ingersoll–Rand SENIOR TOUR Championship/1

MISCELLANEOUS PGA TOUR STATISTICS
Career Low Round: 63–1986 Provident Classic/3
Career Largest Paycheck: $28,600–1992 Northern Telecom Open/T10

CHAMPIONS TOUR CAREER SUMMARY — PLAYOFF RECORD: 1-2

Year	Events Played	1st	2nd	3rd	Top 10	Top 25	Earnings	Rank
1998	6				2	3	$112,173	73
1999	17	2	1		7	14	993,291	14
2000	22		1		9	14	584,477	33
2001	20		2	1	9	16	851,132	23
2002	22		2		4	11	681,960	29
2003	10					2	98,176	88
2004	14		1		4	10	497,325	40
Total	111	2	7	1	35	70	3,818,533	

COMBINED ALL-TIME MONEY (3 TOURS): $4,500,892

CHAMPIONS TOUR TOP TOURNAMENT SUMMARY

Year	98	99	00	01	02	03	04
Senior PGA Championship					T32	T40	
U.S. Senior Open	T33	52	T41	25	CUT	T50	
Ford Senior Players		T12	T41	T14	T33		T5
JELD-WEN Tradition		T5	T6		T27	73	T14
Charles Schwab Cup Champ		1		T11	T21		

CHAMPIONS TOUR YEAR-BY-YEAR STATISTICS (TOP 50 ON 2004 MONEY LIST)

	Scoring Average	Putting Average	Greens in Regulation	Driving Distance	Driving Accuracy
1998	71.53 (N/A)	1.765 (N/A)	66.1 (N/A)	277.7 (N/A)	68.4 (N/A)
1999	70.11 (6)	1.765 (T9)	70.3 (T17)	275.5 (9)	68.0 (T59)
2000	70.45 (16)	1.762 (12)	70.0 (19)	278.4 (7)	69.6 (T47)
2001	70.11 (8)	1.748 (T11)	71.2 (9)	278.3 (18)	71.1 (41)
2002	71.25 (33)	1.807 (52)	67.4 (T34)	278.8 (12)	69.6 (38)
2003	72.41 (N/A)	1.789 (N/A)	60.8 (N/A)	270.6 (N/A)	62.8 (N/A)
2004	70.16 (6)	1.761 (10)	73.0 (8)	271.4 (T41)	76.4 (13)

SECTION 2 PLAYER BIOGRAPHIES

Mike McCullough (muh-CULL-uh)

EXEMPT STATUS: Top 30 on All-Time Money List
FULL NAME: Michael McCullough
HEIGHT: 5-9
WEIGHT: 170
BIRTHDATE: March 21, 1945
BIRTHPLACE: Coshocton, OH
RESIDENCE: Scottsdale, AZ
FAMILY: Wife, Marilyn; Jason (4/24/75), Michelle (5/13/86), Mark (6/7/89)
EDUCATION: Bowling Green State University (1968, Education)
SPECIAL INTERESTS: Flying, outdoor activities
TURNED PROFESSIONAL: 1970
JOINED PGA TOUR: 1972

JOINED CHAMPIONS TOUR: 1995

CHAMPIONS TOUR VICTORIES (2): 2001 Mexico Senior Classic, Emerald Coast Classic.

2004 CHARLES SCHWAB CUP FINISH: T78th - 37 points

BEST PGA TOUR CAREER FINISH: 2—Tournament Players Championship.

OTHER VICTORIES (3): 1970 Ohio State Amateur. **1974** Mini-Kemper Open. **1977** Magnolia Classic.

PGA TOUR CAREER EARNINGS: $682,511

BEST 2004 CHAMPIONS TOUR FINISH: T9—Bank of America Championship.

2004 SEASON:

Finished out of the top 30 for the first time since 1999 after scoring average for the year went up nearly one stroke...Had just one top-10 performance, the fewest he's ever had in a full season on the Champions Tour. T9 at the Bank of America Championship after being near the top of the Friday leaderboard...Trailed by just one stroke after firing a 7-under 64 in the first round of the Outback Steakhouse Pro-Am, his best 18-hole score since 2002 campaign...Made the second of three holes-in-one during the opening round of the U.S. Senior Open, the first time three were made in the same day on the Champions Tour. Ace on the 179-yard 13th hole at Bellerive with a 5-iron was the first of his Champions Tour career.

CHAMPIONS TOUR CAREER HIGHLIGHTS:

2003: Dueled Jay Sigel down the stretch at the Bayer Advantage Celebrity Pro-Am near Kansas City before eventually falling one stroke shy. Missed a 20-foot birdie putt on the last hole that would have forced a playoff...Was a co-leader after 54 holes of the Ford Senior Players Championship along with Craig Stadler and Tom Watson. Final-round 73 snapped string of sub-par rounds at TPC of Michigan at nine consecutive and moved him into a T5, his fourth straight top-10 finish in Dearborn and fifth top-10 performance in his last six trips...Posted 18 straight rounds par-or-better during a run in late August and early September. Streak ended in opening round of the Constellation Energy Classic. **2002:** One of three players to play in every official event (Walter Hall and Dana Quigley were the others)...Third-round leader at the Ford Senior Players Championship before joining two others who finished one stroke behind Stewart Ginn...Also finished T2 at the BellSouth Senior Classic at Opryland where he was one of three players to finish three strokes behind his good friend Gil Morgan...Made 10 points on Sunday using the Modified Stableford Scoring system and T3 at the Uniting Fore Care Classic along with Hale Irwin, Jerry McGee and John Bland. **2001:** Had his finest season as a professional, claiming his first two victories on any TOUR in his first eight starts of the season. Rose to his highest level ever on any official money list, placing 12th on the final earnings list with more than $1.3 million, $400,000 more than his previous-best season (2000)...Triumphed for the first time in 612 combined events on the PGA TOUR (401), Champions Tour (178) and Nationwide Tour (33) when he edged Jim Colbert and Bob Eastwood for the Mexico Senior Classic title at Puebla. Birdied the 53rd hole to take the lead and then made a clutch four-foot par-saving putt on the last hole to seal the win...Returned to the winner's circle a month later at the Emerald Coast Classic in Florida. Battled Andy North down the stretch at The Moors and then two-putted for par on the first playoff hole for the victory. Win near Pensacola made him just the fifth player in Champions Tour history to record multiple victories despite the first title not coming until age 55 (Roberto De Vicenzo, Peter Thomson, Jim Ferree, Jimmy Powell)...Ended a record streak of consecutive events played for which he had been eligible at 177 in a row. Chose not to travel back across the country from his home in Arizona to play in the inaugural SAS Championship in Raleigh, the week after the Vantage Championship was canceled by the Sept. 11 tragedies. Began his run at the 1996 Hyatt Regency Maui Kaanapali Classic. **2000:** Closed the season with a bang, finishing T3 at the IR SENIOR TOUR Championship...Also T3 at the Cadillac NFL Golf Classic after posting three straight rounds in the 60s...Broke Bruce Summerhays' old mark of 96 consecutive eligible events when he teed it up in the Novell Utah Showdown...Fired his career-low on the second day of the Comfort Classic, a course-record 10-under-par 62 at Brickyard Crossing. Held the 36-hole lead in Indianapolis, but carded a 74 on the final day and finished T4. **1998:** Finished second at the Southwestern Bell Dominion, two strokes shy of Lee Trevino. **1997:** Earned fully-exempt status for 1998 after a T7 at the Champions Tour National Qualifying Tournament. **1996:** Played on all three Tours during the season...Competed at the Nationwide Tour South Carolina Classic and in three events on the PGA TOUR...Became fully exempt on the 1997 Champions Tour after finishing third at the 1996 National Qualifying Tournament. **1995:** Made his debut at the BellSouth Senior Classic at Opyland and T15...Earned conditional status for 1996 by beating six other players for the 16th spot at the Champions Tour Q-school.

OTHER CAREER HIGHLIGHTS:

Made 270 cuts in 405 starts on the PGA TOUR from 1973-96...Had 26 top-10 finishes during his TOUR career, including a second at the 1977 Tournament Players Championship (now THE PLAYERS Championship). Finished with a 75 at windy Sawgrass CC to end up two strokes behind winner Mark Hayes...Most lucrative year on TOUR was 1977, when he won $79,413 and had four top-10 finishes...Played a period of his career in Asia in 1970.

PERSONAL:

Inducted into the Toledo Golf Hall of Fame in 1999 and is also a member of the Bowling Green Athletic Hall of Fame...Has his pilot's license and is co-owner of two airplanes...Grandfather got him started in the game...Grew up next to a golf course in his hometown (Coshocton Town & CC)...Best friend on Champions Tour is Gil Morgan...Daughter plays golf at Trinity University in Texas.

PLAYER STATISTICS

MISCELLANEOUS CHAMPIONS TOUR STATISTICS
2004 Low Round: 64–2004 Outback Steakhouse Pro-Am/1
Career Low Round: 62–1999 Comfort Classic/2
Career Largest Paycheck: $225,000–2001 Mexico Senior Classic/1

MISCELLANEOUS PGA TOUR STATISTICS
Career Low Round: 63–1978 Atlanta Classic/3
Career Largest Paycheck: $34,200–1977 Tournament Players Championship/2

CHAMPIONS TOUR CAREER SUMMARY — PLAYOFF RECORD: 1-0

Year	Events Played	1st	2nd	3rd	Top 10	Top 25	Earnings	Rank
1995	8				1	6	$101,692	71
1996	21				2	11	193,960	63
1997	35				4	13	373,282	41
1998	37		1	1	7	21	741,735	16
1999	36				5	19	595,054	32
2000	37			2	8	20	928,420	18
2001	35	2	1		10	17	1,335,040	12
2002	35		2	1	7	17	918,340	21
2003	29		1		7	13	887,434	21
2004	28				1	12	370,263	48
Total	301	2	5	4	52	149	6,445,220	
COMBINED ALL-TIME MONEY (3 TOURS):							**$7,146,158**	

CHAMPIONS TOUR TOP TOURNAMENT SUMMARY

Year	95	96	97	98	99	00	01	02	03	04
Senior PGA Championship		T25	T46	T13	T24	T17	T65	WD	T34	WD
U.S. Senior Open	T21	T22	T44	T13	T53		T48	WD	T6	T19
Ford Senior Players		T44	T46	T9	T64	T4	T6	T2	T5	T34
Senior British Open									T37	CUT
JELD-WEN Tradition			T17	T6	T14	T9	2	T19	T20	T64
Charles Schwab Cup Champ				30		T3	15	T21	28	

CHAMPIONS TOUR YEAR-BY-YEAR STATISTICS (TOP 50 ON 2004 MONEY LIST)

	Scoring Average	Putting Average	Greens in Regulation	Driving Distance	Driving Accuracy
1995	70.80 (N/A)	1.818 (N/A)	70.1 (N/A)	262.2 (N/A)	63.1 (N/A)
1996	71.91 (T36)	1.854 (T75)	64.4 (46)	262.4 (T40)	70.5 (34)
1997	71.87 (T42)	1.809 (T46)	63.5 (52)	261.7 (42)	67.4 (44)
1998	71.42 (26)	1.800 (T33)	67.0 (T25)	265.6 (36)	70.9 (31)
1999	71.46 (38)	1.797 (46)	66.0 (49)	265.9 (T42)	72.1 (32)
2000	70.73 (22)	1.784 (T33)	69.1 (T24)	266.2 (47)	69.2 (T51)
2001	71.03 (23)	1.777 (20)	67.6 (T32)	275.3 (26)	67.8 (T58)
2002	71.23 (32)	1.768 (12)	65.6 (T51)	270.1 (T37)	67.6 (48)
2003	70.84 (27)	1.780 (T24)	67.9 (36)	279.7 (14)	66.3 (54)
2004	71.80 (43)	1.771 (15)	63.7 (T57)	274.5 (26)	67.8 (55)

Mark McCumber

EXEMPT STATUS: Top 30 on All-Time Money List
FULL NAME: Mark Randall McCumber
HEIGHT: 5-8
WEIGHT: 170
BIRTHDATE: September 7, 1951
BIRTHPLACE: Jacksonville, FL
RESIDENCE: Jacksonville, FL

FAMILY: Wife, Paddy; Addison (1/28/76), Megan (6/14/80), Mark Tyler (4/4/91)
SPECIAL INTERESTS: Family activities, golf course architecture
TURNED PROFESSIONAL: 1974
JOINED PGA TOUR: 1978

JOINED CHAMPIONS TOUR: 2001

BEST CHAMPIONS TOUR CAREER FINISH:
T4—2003 Verizon Classic.

2004 CHARLES SCHWAB CUP FINISH:
68th - 57 points

PGA TOUR VICTORIES (10): **1979** Doral-Eastern Open. **1983** Western Open, Pensacola Open. **1985** Doral-Eastern Open. **1987** Anheuser-Busch Golf Classic. **1988** THE PLAYERS Championship. **1989** Beatrice Western Open. **1994** Anheuser-Busch Golf Classic, Hardee's Golf Classic, THE TOUR Championship.

OTHER VICTORIES (1): **1988** World Cup [with Ben Crenshaw].

PGA TOUR CAREER EARNINGS: $5,309,688

PGA TOUR PLAYOFF RECORD: 2-0

BEST 2004 CHAMPIONS TOUR FINISH:
T5—Royal Caribbean Golf Classic.

2004 SEASON:

Had just one top-10 performance, and it came in his initial start of the season at the Royal Caribbean Golf Classic. His T5 at Crandon Park GC near Miami was best effort in almost a year on the Champions Tour...Only other top-20 performance of the season was a T18 in September at the inaugural First Tee Open at Pebble Beach presented by Wal-Mart.

CHAMPIONS TOUR CAREER HIGHLIGHTS:

2003: Among the early leaders at the Verizon Classic and finished T4 at the TPC of Tampa Bay, his best performance ever on the Champions Tour despite a second-round 75...Strung together 15 consecutive par-or-better rounds during the spring...Was near the top of the leaderboard for most of the Senior British Open before eventually T6 at Turnberry, his top effort in a senior major...Also T10 at the Senior PGA Championship. **2002:** T7 at the Verizon Classic. **2001:** Made Champions Tour debut at the inaugural SAS Championship in Raleigh and T48 at Prestonwood...Appeared in 11 events on the PGA TOUR on a Special Medical Exemption, missing the cut in eight tournaments and withdrew twice...Also did several stints as a golf analyst for Fox network broadcasts.

OTHER CAREER HIGHLIGHTS:

Had rotator cuff surgery on his right shoulder in the fall of 1996. While rehabbing shoulder, began to feel pain in neck, signaling on-going problem that finally was diagnosed as a spinal-cord lesion caused by a virus that may have settled in as long ago as 1995...Underwent extensive physical therapy to combat numbness in his left hand and fatigue in his legs...Posted three victories in 1994, including season-ending TOUR Championship and earned a career-best $1,208,209, third on the final money list. Defeated Glen Day by three strokes at Anheuser-Busch Golf Classic, followed by one-stroke win over Kenny Perry two months later at Hardee's Golf Classic. Two victories gave him first multiple-win season since 1983. At The TOUR Championship, sank 40-foot putt on first extra hole to defeat Fuzzy Zoeller...First TOUR victory came in his 12th tournament: the 1979 Doral-Eastern Open...Next wins came in 1983, at Western Open and Pensacola Open...Earned second Doral-Eastern crown in 1985...Won 1987 Anheuser-Busch Classic...Was hometown champion at 1988 PLAYERS Championship, defeating Mike Reid by four strokes...Earned first playoff victory at 1989 Beatrice Western Open over Peter Jacobsen...Also finished T2 to Tom Lehman at the 1996 British Open at Royal Lytham & St. Annes...Teamed with Ben Crenshaw to win 1988 World Cup title...U.S. finalist at 1995 Andersen Consulting World Championship of Golf.

PERSONAL:

Has made significant impact in golf-course design with Mark McCumber and Associates, design arm of McCumber Golf, which he operates with his brothers...Is a member of the American Society of Golf Architects, along with Jack Nicklaus...Grew up next to a golf course in Jacksonville, FL...Enjoys making soups, especially clam chowder, when he has time in the kitchen.

PLAYER STATISTICS

2004 CHAMPIONS TOUR STATISTICS:

Scoring Average	72.02	(49)
Driving Distance	264.4	(63)
Driving Accuracy Percentage	73.2%	(26)
Total Driving	89	(54)
Greens in Regulation Pct.	66.0%	(48)
Putting Average	1.835	(66)
Sand Save Percentage	45.9%	(38)
Birdie Average	2.82	(63)
All-Around Ranking	431	(65)

MISCELLANEOUS CHAMPIONS TOUR STATISTICS

2004 Low Round: 68–2004 Outback Steakhouse Pro-Am/2
Career Low Round: 65–2 times, most recent 2003 Senior British Open/3
Career Largest Paycheck: $78,400–2003 Verizon Classic/T4

MISCELLANEOUS PGA TOUR STATISTICS

Career Low Round: 63–1980 San Antonio Texas Open/2
Career Largest Paycheck: $540,000–1994 THE TOUR Championship/1

CHAMPIONS TOUR CAREER SUMMARY — PLAYOFF RECORD: 0-0

Year	Events Played	1st	2nd	3rd	Top 10	Top 25	Earnings	Rank
2001	3					1	$20,368	121
2002	17				1	4	191,661	74
2003	18				4	13	475,021	40
2004	16				1	5	200,020	64
Total	54				6	23	887,069	

COMBINED ALL-TIME MONEY (3 TOURS): $6,196,757

CHAMPIONS TOUR TOP TOURNAMENT SUMMARY

Year	02	03	04
Senior PGA Championship	T64	T10	T21
U.S. Senior Open	T51	T25	CUT
Ford Senior Players	T22	T15	T22
Senior British Open		T6	
JELD-WEN Tradition		T52	T70

Pat McGowan

EXEMPT STATUS: 7th at 2004 Champions Tour National Qualifying Tournament
FULL NAME: Patrick Ray McGowan
HEIGHT: 5-11
WEIGHT: 180
BIRTHDATE: November 27, 1954
BIRTHPLACE: Grand Forks, ND
RESIDENCE: Southern Pines, NC
FAMILY: Wife, Bonnie; Michael (10/22/90), Scotti (6/3/97)
EDUCATION: Brigham Young University
SPECIAL INTERESTS: Reading, sports psychology, fishing, duck hunting
TURNED PROFESSIONAL: 1977
JOINED PGA TOUR: 1978

JOINED CHAMPIONS TOUR: 2005

BEST PGA TOUR CAREER FINISHES: 2—1978 Canadian Open,1986 USF&G Classic, T2—1982 Miller High Life QCO.

OTHER VICTORIES (4): **1971** Mexican International Junior. **1976** Air Force Academy Invitational. **1977** Pacific Coast Intercollegiate. **1984** Sacramento Classic [TPS].

PGA TOUR CAREER EARNINGS: $915,577

2004 SEASON:

Earned seventh and final fully-exempt spot for 2005 after finishing seventh at the Champions Tour National Qualifying Tournament at the King and Bear at World Golf Village in St. Augustine, FL. Opened with a 1-over-par 73, which included a two-stroke penalty he called on himself because he believed his caddie had touched the line of his putt. Bounced back from that 73 to run off five consecutive rounds in the 60s to T7 with Norm Jarvis. Secured the final card when he birdied the third extra hole...Spent a portion of the year competing on the Sunbelt Senior Tour.

OTHER CAREER HIGHLIGHTS:

Played full time on the PGA TOUR from 1978-92 and overall appeared in 393 events in his career and made 235 cuts...Rookie of the Year in 1978...Did not win an event but was second three times and third four times...Was second to Bruce Lietzke at the 1978 Canadian Open at Glen Abbey and was a T2 along with Champions Tour rookie Brad Bryant at the 1982 Miller High Life Quad Cities Open in an event won by Payne Stewart. Added another second-place effort at the 1986 USF&G Classic...Highest finish on the money list came in 1983 when he was 57th, while best earnings year came in 1986 when he won $137,665.

PERSONAL:

Most recently has worked with his mother-in-law, Peggy Kirk Bell, and family as a golf instructor at Pine Needles Lodge and GC in Southern Pines, NC. The site hosted the U.S. Women's Open in 2001...Was a member of the PGA TOUR Policy Board from 1989-92...Played golf at BYU along with Mike Reid, John Fought and Jim Nelford...Biggest thrill in golf was finishing second at the 1978 Canadian Open and biggest thrills outside of golf was his marriage to wife, Bonnie, and the birth of his son and daughter...Favorite golf courses are Cypress Point, San Francisco GC, Riviera CC and Seminole GC...Enjoys Tom Hanks, "Big" and the TV channel Animal Planet...Favorite athlete is Arnold Palmer and one course he'd like to play is Shinnecock Hills...Avid fly fisherman...Got started playing golf as a nine-year-old at a nine-hole course in his hometown of Colusa, CA. He and his brothers had been avid tennis players at the club but after participating in a putting contest for kids at the club, became interested in the game and spent the next few years picking up golf balls on the range and learning the game.

PLAYER STATISTICS

MISCELLANEOUS PGA TOUR STATISTICS
Career Low Round: 62–1990 Northern Telecom Tucson Open/1
Career Largest Paycheck: $54,000–1986 USF&G Classic/2

Tom McKnight

EXEMPT STATUS: 2nd at 2004 Champions Tour National Qualifying Tournament
FULL NAME: Gene Thomas McKnight
HEIGHT: 6-1
WEIGHT: 190
BIRTHDATE: August 24, 1954
BIRTHPLACE: Roanoke, VA
RESIDENCE: Bluffton, SC
FAMILY: Wife, Vita; Tee (9/30/78), Jay (8/8/81), Tara (11/12/84)
EDUCATION: University of Virginia (1976, Commerce)
SPECIAL INTERESTS: Movies
TURNED PROFESSIONAL: 1976, 2001

JOINED CHAMPIONS TOUR: 2005

BEST CHAMPIONS TOUR CAREER FINISH: T12—2004 Constellation Energy Classic.

BEST PGA TOUR CAREER FINISH: T44—1999 Masters Tournament.

OTHER VICTORIES (1): 2001 Calabash Golf Links [Sunbelt].

BEST 2004 CHAMPIONS TOUR FINISH: T12—Constellation Energy Classic.

2004 SEASON:

Earned fully-exempt status for 2005 by finishing second at the Champions Tour National Qualifying Tournament at King and Bear at World Golf Village in Florida. Completed the six-round event 23-under-par and finished two strokes behind medalist Mark Johnson. Tied the course record in the final round when he fired a 9-under-par 63, his sixth consecutive sub-par round in the event near St. Augustine...Made one start during the year at the Constellation Energy Classic where he was T12 playing on a sponsor's exemption...Also played several events on the NGA Hooters Tour with four top-10 finishes on that circuit.

OTHER CAREER HIGHLIGHTS:

A long-time amateur player who turned professional for a second time in 2001. Had briefly turned professional in the mid-70s and tried qualifying for the PGA TOUR and playing mini-tour events before turning to the petroleum business in 1980...Regained his amateur standing in 1983 and began his amateur career in 1984, which lasted until turning professional again in 2001...Was the runner up at the 1998 U.S. Amateur to Hank Kuehne (lost 2 and 1) at Oak Hill CC in Rochester, NY. Defeated Sergio Garcia to reach the finals...Performance at that tournament earned him a berth in the 1999 Masters, where he finished T44. Among his victims in the early rounds of the 1992 U.S. Amateur were David Duval and Stewart Cink...Played for the United States team in the 1998 World Team Amateur competition in Chile...Also a member of the 1999 United States Walker Cup team...Played on the Sunbelt Senior Tour for three years after again turning professional in 2001.

PERSONAL:

Worked in the petroleum distributorship business for 20 years and was the former owner of a chain of On The Way convenience stores in the Carolinas...Biggest thrills in golf were playing on the U.S. team in the World Amateur and the Walker Cup...Biggest thrill away from golf was watching the birth of his three children...Lists his family as his heroes for their support over the years and for their persistence in pursuing their own dreams and goals...Favorites include Jimmy Buffett, Larry Bird, "CSI," "Top Gun" and any Patricia Cornwell book...Favorite golf course is Seminole GC. One course he'd like to play is St. Andrews...An all-district basketball player in high school.

PLAYER STATISTICS

2004 CHAMPIONS TOUR STATISTICS:

Scoring Average	69.33	(N/A)
Driving Distance	266.2	(N/A)
Driving Accuracy Percentage	76.2%	(N/A)
Total Driving	1,998	(N/A)
Greens in Regulation Pct.	77.8%	(N/A)
Putting Average	1.690	(N/A)
Sand Save Percentage	33.3%	(N/A)
Birdie Average	5.00	(N/A)
All-Around Ranking	1,569	(N/A)

MISCELLANEOUS CHAMPIONS TOUR STATISTICS

2004 Low Round: 68–2004 Constellation Energy Classic/2
Career Low Round: 68–2004 Constellation Energy Classic/2
Career Largest Paycheck: $30,720–2004 Constellation Energy Classic/T12

MISCELLANEOUS PGA TOUR STATISTICS

Career Low Round: 72–1999 U.S. Open Championship/1

CHAMPIONS TOUR CAREER SUMMARY — PLAYOFF RECORD: 0-0

Year	Events Played	1st	2nd	3rd	Top 10	Top 25	Earnings	Rank
2004	1					1	$30,720	106
Total	1					1	30,720	
COMBINED ALL-TIME MONEY (3 TOURS):							**$30,720**	

CHAMPIONS TOUR TOP TOURNAMENT SUMMARY

Mark McNulty

EXEMPT STATUS: Top 30 on 2004 Champions Tour Money List
FULL NAME: Mark William McNulty
HEIGHT: 5-10
WEIGHT: 160
BIRTHDATE: October 25, 1953
BIRTHPLACE: Bindwa, Zimbabwe

RESIDENCE: Sunningdale, Surrey, England
FAMILY: Wife, Allison; Matthew (1985), Catherine (1988)
SPECIAL INTERESTS: Piano, fine arts, koi fish
TURNED PROFESSIONAL: 1977

JOINED CHAMPIONS TOUR: 2004

CHAMPIONS TOUR VICTORIES (3): 2004 Outback Steakhouse Pro-Am, SBC Championship, Charles Schwab Cup Championship.

2004 CHARLES SCHWAB CUP FINISH: 5th - 2,417 points

BEST PGA TOUR CAREER FINISH: 4—1982 Danny Thomas Memphis Classic, T4—Sammy Davis Jr.-Greater Hartford Open.

OTHER VICTORIES: (55): 1974 Zimbabwe Amateur Championship, South African Amateur Stroke-Play Championship. **1979** Greater Manchester Open, Holiday Inns Royal Swazi Open. **1980** Braun German Open, Malaysian Open, Holiday Inns Invitational. **1981** SAB South African Masters, Sigma Series. **1982** SISA Classic, SAB Masters, Sharp Electronics Classic, Sun City Classic. **1984** Pan-Am Wild Coast Sun Classic. **1985** Safmarine Masters, Palabora Classic, Royal Swazi Sun Open. **1986** Quinta do Lago Portuguese Open, Safmarine Masters, Helix Wild Coast Sun Classic, Germiston Centenary, Barclays Bank Classic, Swazi Sun International, Trustbank Tournament of Champions, Million Dollar Challenge. **1987** London Standard 4-Stars Pro-Celebrity Classic, Dunhill British Masters, German Open, Southern Suns South African Open, AECI Charity Classic, Royal Swazi Sun Pro-Am, Trustbank Tournament of Champions, Million Dollar Challenge. **1988** Cannes Open, Benson & Hedges Trophy [with Marie Laure de Lorenz]. **1989** Torras Monte Carlo Open. **1990** Credit Lyonnais Cannes Open, Volvo German Open. **1991** Volvo German Open. **1992** Zimbabwe Open. **1993** Lexington PGA Championship, FNB Players' Championship. **1994** BMW International Open. **1996** Dimension Data Pro-Am, Sun Dutch Open, Volvo Masters Andalucia, Zimbabwe Open. **1997** San Lameer South African Masters, Nashua Wild Coast Challenge. **1998** Vodacom Players Championship. **2000** Stenham Swazi Open, Cabs Old Mutual Zimbabwe Open. 2001 Mercedes-Benz South African Open, Nashua Nedtel Cellular Masters. **2002** Vodacom Players Championship.

PGA TOUR CAREER EARNINGS: $657,737

BEST 2004 CHAMPIONS TOUR FINISHES:
1—Outback Steakhouse Pro-Am, SBC Championship, Charles Schwab Cup Championship; T5—Senior British Open.

2004 SEASON:

Overcame several health issues during the year and went on to earn Rookie of the Year honors on the Champions Tour, a first for a foreign-born player since South African John Bland in 1996...Became the first international player since David Graham (1997) to win three times in a single season on the Champions Tour and finished the year with a career-best $1.4 million in official earnings, the most by a first-year player since Bob Gilder in 2001 ($1.68 million)...Was unable to debut on the Champions Tour until the Outback Steakhouse Pro-Am due to shingles, but made the most of his initial start on the Champions Tour. Became just the 11th player in Champions Tour history, and first since Bobby Wadkins (2001 Lightpath Long Island Classic), to win in his first start on the circuit. Held off Larry Nelson and a hard-charging Fuzzy Zoeller for his initial triumph at the TPC of Tampa Bay...Missed almost two months (most of August and all of September) due to degenerative disks in his back, but returned to the circuit strong, posting back-to-back victories at the close of the season...Won his second title in record-setting fashion. Posted rounds of 63-65 on the weekend at Oak Hills CC and cruised to an easy victory at the SBC Championship in San Antonio. Eight-stroke win over Gary McCord was the largest victory margin on the Champions Tour since Ed Dougherty won by eight strokes at the 2001 TD Waterhouse Championship. His 18-under 195 at Oak Hills shattered the tournament record and was the lowest three-round numerical score on the circuit all season. Hit 45 of 54 greens in regulation for the week, including 24 in a row at one stretch, and needed just 81 total putts...Followed San Antonio win with a come-from-behind victory at the season-ending Charles Schwab Cup Championship in Sonoma. Trailed by five strokes entering the final round but carded a 66, the lowest Sunday score, to eke out a one-stroke victory over Kite. Became the fifth rookie to claim the Charles Schwab Cup Championship, and $440,000 check was easily his largest in the U.S. Vaulted into the fifth position in the final Charles Schwab Cup standings with his win in Sonoma and earned a $100,000 annuity...Voted as the Champions Tour's Player of the Month for October...Was also among a handful of players who battled for the title at the Senior British Open in July before eventually finishing T5, three strokes behind winner Pete Oakley...Started his season in early January in South Africa with T77 at the South African Airways Open and then T40 at the dunhill championship on the PGA European Tour.

CHAMPIONS TOUR CAREER HIGHLIGHTS:

2003: Came within a whisker of becoming the European Tour's oldest winner when, at age 49, he battled Welshman Philip Price down to the wire to T2, along with Scotland's Alastair Forsyth, at the Smurfit European Open in Ireland. Made only three bogeys over 72 holes and was tied for the lead with one hole to play before Price made birdie on the final hole for the victory at The K Club. Runner-up check for 250,793 was his largest ever in Europe...Became eligible for the Champions Tour in late October and earned fully-exempt status for 2004 by being the medalist at both the regional qualifier at Walt Disney World and the National Qualifying Tournament at the TPC at Eagle Trace near Fort Lauderdale, FL. Became the fifth international player, and second consecutive, to earn medalist honors at the Q-school final when he carded a bogey-free 68 in the final round to coast to a three-stroke victory over England's Mark James. His 72-hole total of 13-under 275 was the same as Ireland's Des Smyth a year earlier.

OTHER CAREER HIGHLIGHTS:

Since his first professional victory in 1979, became one of the world's most consistent winners, with 55 international titles over a span of more than two decades...Regarded as one of the sport's best putters...Played the European PGA Tour full time from 1978-2003 and ranks 19th on the career money list with 5,333,725...His 16 European Tour titles include four German Opens...Claimed three events in Europe during both the 1987 and 1996 seasons and finished second to Ian Woosnam on the European Tour Order of Merit in both 1987 and 1990...Biggest victory on the European Tour came at the 1996 Volvo Masters when he cruised to a seven-stroke victory over four players at Valderrama, Spain...Best performance in a major championship came in 1990 when he was T2, along with Payne Stewart, in the British Open Championship at St. Andrews, five strokes back of Nick Faldo...Also T8 in the 1990 PGA Championship at Shoal Creek in Alabama...Led the South African Tour's Order of Merit eight times: 1980-81, 1985-87, 1993, 1998, and 2001...Claimed a pair of South African Open titles, including the 2001 event at East

CHAMPIONS TOUR CAREER SUMMARY — PLAYOFF RECORD: 0-0

Year	Events Played	1st	2nd	3rd	Top 10	Top 25	Earnings	Rank
2004	20	3			7	16	$1,423,048	7
Total	20	3			7	16	1,423,048	
COMBINED ALL-TIME MONEY (3 TOURS):							**$2,080,785**	

CHAMPIONS TOUR TOP TOURNAMENT SUMMARY

Year	04
Senior PGA Championship	T7
U.S. Senior Open	T19
Ford Senior Players	T9
Senior British Open	T5
Charles Schwab Cup Champ	1

CHAMPIONS TOUR YEAR-BY-YEAR STATISTICS (TOP 50 ON 2004 MONEY LIST)

	Scoring Average	Putting Average	Greens in Regulation	Driving Distance	Driving Accuracy
2004	70.03 (5)	1.755 (T6)	69.6 (T23)	269.6 (53)	73.3 (25)

Mark McNulty (continued)

London GC at age 47. Holed a 20-foot birdie putt on the final green to nip Justin Rose by a stroke...Played in 112 PGA TOUR events from 1981-2001, made 69 cuts and earned $657,737...Made 57 starts on the PGA TOUR between 1982-1984 and finished fourth at the 1982 Danny Thomas-Memphis Classic and T4 at the Sammy Davis, Jr.-Greater Hartford Open...Represented Zimbabwe in eight World Cup competitions and also was a team member in seven Alfred Dunhill Cup matches...Played for the International team in both the 1994 and 1996 Presidents Cup, with a 3-4-2 record in the biennial event...Has made five holes-in-one in competition in his career.

PERSONAL:

Was a solid athlete is several sports as a youth, but excelled at golf...Has managed to rebound from a series of physical setbacks in his career. Escaped with facial injuries when his car collided with a bus near his parents' farm in 1980. While on vacation in Cape Town in December 1993, suffered a freak nerve injury in his neck while playing cricket with his kids. Knee injury curtailed his 1995 season...Best shot of his career was his pitch to nine feet from 68 yards on the final hole that beat Ian Woosnam at the 1987 British Masters...Favorite golf course is the Old Course at St. Andrews, but only when the weather is ideal...First modeled his game after Arnold Palmer and then refined it like Gary Player as he grew older...Plays the piano.

PLAYER STATISTICS

MISCELLANEOUS CHAMPIONS TOUR STATISTICS

2004 Low Round: 63–2004 SBC Championship/2
Career Low Round: 63–2004 SBC Championship/2
Career Largest Paycheck: $440,000–2004 Charles Schwab Cup Championship/1

MISCELLANEOUS PGA TOUR STATISTICS

Career Low Round: 65–3 times, most recent 1994 Texas Open/2
Career Largest Paycheck: $76,000–1994 NEC World Series of Golf/T5

25 MEMORABLE MOMENTS

Irwin Captures Nine Titles to Tie Thomson Record

1997

After two two-win seasons to launch his Champions Tour career, Hale Irwin caught fire in 1997, winning nine times to tie Peter Thomson's 1985 record. Irwin ran away with the money title, becoming the first Champions Tour player to go over the $2-million mark, was named the Player of the Year and won the Byron Nelson Award as scoring leader. His nine wins came in just 23 starts, earning him $101,885 per start. Of the 74 rounds Irwin played, 57 were below par. The 1992 World Golf Hall of Fame inductee would follow up his 1997 season with a seven-win campaign in 1998.

Hajime Meshiai (ha-JEE-me Mesh-E-eye)

EXEMPT STATUS: T4 at 2004 Champions Tour National Qualifying Tournament
FULL NAME: Hajime Meshiai
HEIGHT: 5-7
WEIGHT: 181
BIRTHDATE: March 12, 1954
BIRTHPLACE: Chiba, Japan
RESIDENCE: Chiba, Japan

FAMILY: Wife, Fukuko; Emiko (6/26/81), Yoko (4/6/83)
EDUCATION: Komazawa University (Law, 1976)
SPECIAL INTERESTS: Fishing
TURNED PROFESSIONAL: 1978

JOINED CHAMPIONS TOUR: 2004

BEST CHAMPIONS TOUR CAREER FINISH: T9—2004 FedEx Kinko's Classic.

2004 CHARLES SCHWAB CUP FINISH: T75th - 38 points

BEST PGA TOUR CAREER FINISH: T29—1988 Honda Classic.

OTHER VICTORIES (14): **1985** KBC Augusta. **1986** Pocari Sweat Open, Acom Doubles. **1987** Hiroshima Open. **1989** Yomiuri Sapporo Beer. **1991** Masaki Hirao Pro-Am. **1993** Asahi Beer Cup, Token Cup, Dunlop Open, Lark Cup. **1996** Sapporo Tokyu Open, Suntory Open. **1998** Token Cup. **1999** Jun Classic.

PGA TOUR CAREER EARNINGS: $33,033

BEST 2004 CHAMPIONS TOUR FINISH: T9—FedEx Kinko's Classic.

2004 SEASON:
Earned fully exempt status for 2005 after finishing T4 at the 2004 Champions Tour National Qualifying Tournament at the King and Bear at World Golf Village. Posted five straight rounds in the 60s and led or shared the lead for three rounds (rounds three to five) before shooting a final-round 71...Finished 74th on the money list and appeared in 14 events during the campaign after turning 50 in March...Debuted at the Toshiba Senior Classic and T41 at Newport Beach...Lone top-10 effort came at the FedEx Kinko's Classic in Austin in May when he was T9...Second in Driving Distance, with an average of 292.0.

CHAMPIONS TOUR CAREER HIGHLIGHTS:
2003: Played 22 events on the Japan Golf Tour and finished 63rd on the official money list, with $141,885...Best finish on the Japan Golf Tour was a T6 at the Japan Golf Tour Championship. Was also T11 at the Japan Open...As a 49-year-old, advanced to the Champions Tour's National Qualifying Tournament near Fort Lauderdale, FL, by being the co-medalist, along with Mark Johnson,at the regional qualifier in Calimesa, CA...Secured a full exemption for the 2004 season upon his 50th birthday March 12 by vaulting from T7 to solo third on the final day. Birdied five of his last six holes to shoot 66 at the TPC at Eagle Trace, equaling the low round of the event.

OTHER CAREER HIGHLIGHTS:
Won 11 career titles on the Japan Golf Tour... Joined the Japan PGA circuit in 1980 and improved every year on the money list before finishing third in 1987...Suffered a back injury in 1991, yet still maintained a spot among the top 50 on the money list...Had his best year in 1993 when he won four times and was the leading money-winner on the Japan Golf Tour, with $1,197,000...Suffered a slump for three seasons and then made another comeback in 1996, winning a pair of titles and finishing 12th on the money list with earnings of $471,000...Became the first qualifier for the World Finals of the 1997 Andersen Consulting World Championship of Golf when he defeated Kazuhiko Hosokawa, 1-up, to win the Japanese Championship at Golden Palm CC. Lost to Davis Love III in the World Semifinals at Grayhawk GC in Scottsdale in January 1998...Played in 18 events in his career on the PGA TOUR, including seven appearances in 1994, making eight cuts. Best finish was a T29 at the 1988 Honda Classic...Has made four holes-in-one in competition.

PERSONAL:
A powerful hitter off the tee and is nicknamed "Kong"...Close friend of Jumbo Ozaki, who helped him develop his game as a youth...Shigeo Nagashima, a Japanese baseball legend who played and managed the Tokyo Giants, is his hero...Played competitive baseball until his freshman year in college and then turned to golf...Favorite course is Augusta National and favorite athlete is Michael Jordan.

PLAYER STATISTICS

2004 CHAMPIONS TOUR STATISTICS:

Scoring Average	71.93	(46)
Driving Distance	292.0	(2)
Driving Accuracy Percentage	60.0%	(74)
Total Driving	76	(31)
Greens in Regulation Pct.	66.9%	(39)
Putting Average	1.851	(74)
Sand Save Percentage	40.0%	(65)
Eagles (Holes per)	396.0	(47)
Birdie Average	3.07	(50)
All-Around Ranking	397	(56)

MISCELLANEOUS CHAMPIONS TOUR STATISTICS
2004 Low Round: 67–2 times, most recent 2004 FedEx Kinko's Classic/3
Career Low Round: 67–2 times, most recent 2004 FedEx Kinko's Classic/3
Career Largest Paycheck: $38,400–2004 FedEx Kinko's Classic/T9

MISCELLANEOUS PGA TOUR STATISTICS
Career Low Round: 66–1994 Southwestern Bell Colonial/1
Career Largest Paycheck: $9,315–1994 Memorial Tournament/T30

CHAMPIONS TOUR CAREER SUMMARY — PLAYOFF RECORD: 0-0

Year	Events Played	1st	2nd	3rd	Top 10	Top 25	Earnings	Rank
2004	14				1	1	$150,863	74
Total	14				1	1	150,863	
COMBINED ALL-TIME MONEY (3 TOURS):							**$183,896**	

CHAMPIONS TOUR TOP TOURNAMENT SUMMARY

Year	04
Senior PGA Championship	T31
U.S. Senior Open	T50
Ford Senior Players	T28

Gil Morgan

EXEMPT STATUS: Top 30 on 2004 Champions Tour Money List
FULL NAME: Gilmer Bryan Morgan II
HEIGHT: 5-9
WEIGHT: 175
BIRTHDATE: September 25, 1946
BIRTHPLACE: Wewoka, OK
RESIDENCE: Edmond, OK
FAMILY: Wife, Jeanine; Molly (5/18/81), Maggie (8/10/82), Melanie (9/24/84)
CLUB AFFILIATION: Oak Tree GC (Edmond, OK)
EDUCATION: East Central State College (1968, B.S.), Southern College of Optometry (1972, Doctor of Optometry)
SPECIAL INTERESTS: Cars
TURNED PROFESSIONAL: 1972
JOINED PGA TOUR: 1973

JOINED CHAMPIONS TOUR: 1996

CHAMPIONS TOUR VICTORIES (23): **1996** Ralphs Senior Classic. **1997** The Tradition Presented by Countrywide, Ameritech Senior Open, BellSouth Senior Classic at Opryland, First of America Classic, Ralphs Senior Classic, Energizer SENIOR TOUR Championship. **1998** MasterCard Championship, LG Championship, The Tradition Presented by Countrywide, Ford Senior Players Championship, Utah Showdown, Vantage Championship. **1999** Comfort Classic, Kroger Senior Classic. **2000** Emerald Coast Classic, The Instinet Classic, Comfort Classic. **2001** ACE Group Classic, The Instinet Classic. **2002** BellSouth Senior Classic at Opryland. **2003** Kroger Classic. **2004** SBC Classic.

OTHER SENIOR VICTORIES (3): **1998** Senior Slam at Los Cabos. **1999** Senior Slam at Los Cabos. **1999** Liberty Mutual Legends of Golf [with Hubert Green].

2004 CHARLES SCHWAB CUP FINISH: 11th - 1,490 points

PGA TOUR VICTORIES (7): **1977** B.C. Open. **1978** Glen Campbell-Los Angeles Open, World Series of Golf. **1979** Danny Thomas Memphis Classic. **1983** Joe Garagiola-Tucson Open, Glen Campbell-Los Angeles Open. **1990** Kemper Open.

OTHER VICTORIES (3): **1978** Taiheiyo Masters. **1981** Oklahoma Open. **1997** Oklahoma Open.

PGA TOUR CAREER EARNINGS: $5,259,164

PGA TOUR PLAYOFF RECORD: 3-4

BEST 2004 CHAMPIONS TOUR FINISHES: 1—SBC Classic; T2—Liberty Mutual Legends of Golf, Kroger Classic; T3—Royal Caribbean Golf Classic, Blue Angels Classic, Farmers Charity Classic; T4—The ACE Group Classic.

2004 SEASON:

Over seven figures in official earnings for the eighth consecutive season on the strength of 14 top-10 finishes, the second most on the Champions Tour last year...Highlight of his season came early during the midst of 23 consecutive par-or-better rounds, a 2004 best...Extended to nine his streak of years winning at least one event (tied with Miller Barber, second only to Hale Irwin) when he redeemed himself by winning his third SBC Classic, one year after losing the event on the final hole. Cruised to a two-stroke victory over Larry Nelson at Valencia. Win was his fifth Tour title in the Los Angeles area on a fourth different course. SBC triumph was also his 23rd career victory on the Champions Tour, tying him with Bob Charles for fourth place on the all-time wins list...Was the 36-hole leader at the Liberty Mutual Legends of Golf in late April and battled Hale Irwin down the stretch before a bogey at the final hole dropped him to a T2 with Gary Koch, one stroke back of Hale Irwin. Bogey led to final-round 73 that ended streak of par-or-better scores...Celebrated his 200th career start on the Champions Tour when he almost successfully defended his Kroger Classic title late in the year. Closed with a 66 at the TPC at River's Bend, but lost to Bruce Summerhays by one stroke when he three-putted from 70 feet for a par-5 on the final hole...Was T3 twice in Florida (Royal Caribbean Golf Classic and Blue Angels Classic) and also T4 at The ACE Group Classic, where he was just one stroke shy of making the playoff...Made serious bid for another victory at the Farmers Charity Classic, with a spirited run in Sunday's final round, but a late bogey left him T3...Started the year by going 330 holes without three-putting (ended on the seventh hole of the first round of the Blue Angels Classic), a 2004 best, and also topped the Champions Tour in Second-Round Scoring Average (68.96)...Overall, was in the 60s in 37 of his 82 rounds (45 percent) and T2 in Sub-Par Rounds (55)...Improved his first-round score at the SBC Championship by 15 strokes with a Champions Tour career-best 9-under 62 on Saturday. Round equaled the Oak Hills course record (David Ogrin/1994 Texas Open pro-am) and included 10 birdies.

CHAMPIONS TOUR CAREER HIGHLIGHTS:

2003: Registered his highest standing on the money list since back-to-back second-place finishes in 1997-98. Ended the year third behind Tom Watson and Jim Thorpe as 14 top-10 finishes (T2 on Champions Tour) helped him reach the $1-million mark for the seventh straight year...Had a two-stroke, wire-to-wire victory over Doug Tewell at the Kroger Classic. Win was the 22nd of his illustrious career on the Champions Tour, tying him with Don January and Chi Chi Rodriguez for fifth place on the all-time victory list. Posted three straight rounds in the 60s and won the event near Cincinnati for the second time (1999). Fought off challenges from as many as four other players in the final round before sealing his victory with a birdie on the final hole. Win near Cincinnati made him just one of three wire-to-wire winners, joining Jim Ahern (Music City Championship) and Jim Thorpe (Charles Schwab Cup Championship)...Was also the 36-hole leader at the Royal Caribbean Golf Classic and led by one stroke with one hole to play before losing out to Dave Barr. Missed a seven-foot par putt on the final hole after an errant drive cost him a penalty stroke...Came close again at the SBC Classic. Was a victim of a three-shot turnaround at the final hole at Valencia CC. Three-putted the 18th hole after Tom Purtzer holed a 58-foot eagle putt...Was a contender at the 3M Championship in August, finishing T2 with Morris Hatalsky, one stroke behind Wayne Levi. Had a chance on the final hole but watched his second shot at 18 go awry, and then after hitting a good recovery shot, narrowly missed a birdie opportunity which would have gotten him into a playoff with Levi...Also finished T2 at the JELD-WEN Tradition with rounds of 67-68 on the weekend. **2002:** Moved into seventh place on the all-time victory list when he registered his 21st career title on the Champions Tour at the BellSouth Senior Classic at Opryland. Emerged from a pack of players with birdies on two of the last three holes for an eventual three-stroke triumph over Mike McCullough, Bruce Fleisher and Dana Quigley. Win was his second at Springhouse GC and gave him six top-five performances in six trips to Nashville. The victory marked the second year in succession he had won on Father's Day...Finished T2 at the SAS Championship, four strokes behind Bruce Lietzke, but $124,666 paycheck put him over the $1-million mark for the sixth straight season...Also finished the season as the runner-up to Tom Watson in the SENIOR TOUR Championship at Gaillardia. Dueled Watson head to head down the stretch, but eventually came up two strokes short after an errant drive on No. 16 led to a

SECTION 2 PLAYER BIOGRAPHIES

CHAMPIONS TOUR CAREER SUMMARY — PLAYOFF RECORD: 0-4

Year	Events Played	1st	2nd	3rd	Top 10	Top 25	Earnings	Rank
1996	5	1			1	3	$157,339	70
1997	25	6	4	2	19	23	2,160,562	2
1998	25	6	1	4	18	24	2,179,047	2
1999	27	2		6	15	22	1,493,282	5
2000	23	3	5		16	19	1,873,216	4
2001	24	2	4	1	14	23	1,885,871	5
2002	24	1	2	1	11	19	1,343,276	11
2003	25	1	4		14	21	1,620,206	3
2004	26	1	2	3	14	25	1,606,453	4
Total	204	23	22	17	122	179	14,319,252	

COMBINED ALL-TIME MONEY (3 TOURS): **$19,578,416**

CHAMPIONS TOUR TOP TOURNAMENT SUMMARY

Year	97	98	99	00	01	02	03	04
Senior PGA Championship	T15	3	T11	T32		T6	T7	T7
U.S. Senior Open	T3	T7	T3	T15	T2	T11	T12	T12
Ford Senior Players	T6	1	T7	T10	13	T40	T5	T9
JELD-WEN Tradition	1	1		T15	4	T35	T2	T11
Charles Schwab Cup Champ	1	2	28	T10	T5	2	T4	T13

CHAMPIONS TOUR YEAR-BY-YEAR STATISTICS (TOP 50 ON 2004 MONEY LIST)

	Scoring Average	Putting Average	Greens in Regulation	Driving Distance	Driving Accuracy
1996	70.87 (N/A)	1.801 (N/A)	68.9 (N/A)	283.7 (N/A)	73.4 (N/A)
1997	69.29 (2)	1.746 (2)	74.1 (2)	281.8 (4)	69.1 (T35)
1998	69.46 (2)	1.752 (5)	73.5 (3)	277.4 (8)	74.3 (11)
1999	69.69 (3)	1.773 (T14)	72.6 (4)	282.3 (3)	73.3 (27)
2000	68.83 (1)	1.740 (T4)	77.1 (2)	284.0 (3)	73.1 (16)
2001	69.20 (1)	1.742 (T5)	72.1 (6)	280.3 (13)	73.7 (T24)
2002	69.88 (7)	1.765 (10)	68.5 (T27)	276.2 (T14)	67.2 (51)
2003	69.71 (5)	1.768 (T10)	72.1 (9)	286.0 (6)	67.1 (48)
2004	69.76 (3)	1.759 (9)	72.7 (9)	289.6 (3)	70.1 (41)

Gil Morgan (continued)

bogey…Made the first ace of his Champions Tour career (10th overall) when he holed a 6-iron shot from 165 yards on Firestone's 12th hole during the second round of the Senior PGA Championship. **2001:** Earned his second consecutive Byron Nelson Trophy for best Scoring Average (69.20)…Held off Dana Quigley by two strokes to win The ACE Group Classic, his second senior victory in Naples. Final-round 66 at Pelican Marsh GC included a clutch birdie at the par-3 17th hole when his 7-iron shot stopped three feet from the hole. Followed his win in Naples with a runner-up performance at the Verizon Classic and then lost to Jose Maria Canizares in a nine-hole playoff at the Toshiba Senior Classic. Successfully defended his title at The Instinet Classic, going wire-to-wire to edge J.C. Snead and Tom Jenkins by two strokes. His 9-under 63 in the opening round at the TPC at Jasna Polana was a course record and included both a double eagle (No. 7-driver/3-iron) and eagle, a first on the Champions Tour since 1996. **2000:** Missed the first two months of the year following an off-season rib-cage injury…Earned his first Byron Nelson Award with a Scoring Average of 68.83, the second best mark in Champions Tour history…First of three victories came in his first official 2000 appearance near Pensacola, FL. Went wire-to-wire at the Emerald Coast Classic, winning by four strokes over Larry Nelson…Second victory came in late July when he came from behind at the The Instinet Classic…Added his third title at the rain-shortened Comfort Classic. Successfully defended his crown when he birdied the final two holes Saturday to overtake Jim Ahern. Was declared the winner on Sunday when bad weather washed out the final round at Brickyard Crossing…Set a Champions Tour standard when he put together an amazing 31 straight sub-par rounds. Started the streak at the Ford Senior Players Championship and saw it come to an end after one round of the SBC Senior Classic in Los Angeles. Had established the previous record of 26 consecutive in 1997. **1999:** Posted a pair of victories. Carded a final-round 69 at the Comfort Classic in Indianapolis and edged Ed Dougherty by two strokes. Came back two weeks later and won the Kroger Senior Classic title, defeating Dougherty again, thanks to a final-round 63…Also won his second straight Senior Slam in Los Cabos, Mexico, besting Hale Irwin by two strokes, and teamed with Hubert Green for the Liberty Mutual Legends of Golf crown. **1998:** Had six official victories that included a pair of Champions Tour majors…Successfully defended his Tradition title by coming from two strokes back of Tom Wargo to win by two at Desert Mountain…Also defeated Hale Irwin by three shots at the Ford Senior Players Championship with a whopping 21-under-par 267 total, a 72-hole record at the TPC of Michigan…Started the campaign with a victory at the MasterCard Championship at Hualalai and came from five strokes back to win the LG Championship in Naples…Played all 54 holes without a bogey at Park Meadows and cruised to a four-stroke victory at the Utah Showdown…Final win of the campaign came at the Vantage Championship. Used a closing-round 65 to outduel Irwin down the stretch…Claimed the unofficial Senior Slam at Los Cabos, defeating Hale Irwin by six strokes. **1997:** Voted by his peers as Rookie of the Year…Enjoyed a banner season, becoming just the second Champions Tour player at the time to go over $2 million in yearly earnings ($86,422/start)…Held off Irwin to win the season-ending Energizer SENIOR TOUR Championship…Made his first-ever successful title defense the week before at the Ralphs Senior Classic. One-stroke victory over George Archer at Wilshire CC gave him his fourth TOUR win in the Los Angeles area. First claimed back-to-back tournaments earlier in the year at the Ameritech Senior Open and BellSouth Senior Classic at Opryland. Was the first of three wire-to-wire winners when he nipped Irwin by one stroke at Kemper Lakes despite finishing bogey, bogey, double-bogey. Claimed a two-stroke win over John Bland at the BellSouth Senior Classic the week after…Won his first senior major in early April at The Tradition, finishing six strokes in front of Isao Aoki with a 22-under 266 score, the 72-hole tournament record at the time. Season's other victory came in the rain at the First of America Classic, where he birdied the 53rd hole to take a one-stroke lead over Bob Duval, then clinched the title with a scrambling par at No. 18…Broke Bob Murphy's all-time record of 24 consecutive sub-par rounds when he strung together 26 straight. **1996:** Earned his first Champions Tour title just 11 days after turning 50 at the Ralphs Senior Classic and became the youngest Champions Tour winner at the time…Debuted at the Vantage Championship (T16).

OTHER CAREER HIGHLIGHTS:

Played the PGA TOUR full-time from 1973-1995…Had one leg up on one of the great U.S. Opens of all time in 1992. At Pebble Beach, became the first player in Open history to reach 10-under-par early in third round, then climbed to 12-under through 43 holes before falling to an eventual T13 finish…Biggest of his seven PGA TOUR triumphs came in the 1978 World Series of Golf. Defeated Hubert Green in a playoff to emerge as the year's No. 2 money-winner behind Tom Watson…Had left shoulder rotator cuff surgery in September of 1986. After nine-month lay-off, returned to the TOUR in early May 1987 and was near the top of his game by midsummer…Most successful year was 1990, when he captured the Kemper Open in early June and placed in the top eight in seven consecutive events…Captured the first two tournaments of 1983, the Joe Garagiola-Tucson Open, in a playoff with Lanny Wadkins, and the Glen Campbell-Los Angeles Open…Was a runner-up 21 times in his PGA TOUR career…Named to the NAIA Hall of Fame in 1982 after being an NAIA All-American in 1968…Member of the 1979 and 1983 U.S. Ryder Cup teams…Has had 10 career holes-in-one.

PERSONAL:

Started playing golf at age 15…Holds a Doctor of Optometry degree and still keeps a current license, even though he has never practiced…Decided during his junior year at East Central State (OK) to pursue a career in golf, but waited until earning his optometry degree before turning professional…Has been a long-time follower of Oklahoma Sooners athletics.

PLAYER STATISTICS

MISCELLANEOUS CHAMPIONS TOUR STATISTICS

2004 Low Round: 62–2004 SBC Championship/2
Career Low Round: 62–2004 SBC Championship/2
Career Largest Paycheck: $328,000–1997 Energizer SENIOR TOUR Championship/1

MISCELLANEOUS PGA TOUR STATISTICS

Career Low Round: 62–3 times, most recent 1996 Deposit Guaranty Golf Classic/2
Career Largest Paycheck: $180,000–1990 Kemper Open/1

Walter Morgan

EXEMPT STATUS: Net-70 on All-Time Money List
FULL NAME: Walter Thomas Morgan
HEIGHT: 5-9
WEIGHT: 200
BIRTHDATE: May 31, 1941
BIRTHPLACE: Haddock, GA
RESIDENCE: Cornelius, NC

FAMILY: Wife, Geraldine; Felicia (11/12/75), Michel (7/9/84); stepchildren Ilene Parham, Wallace T. Parham, Keith L. Parham; seven grandchildren
EDUCATION: LaSalle College (1976)
SPECIAL INTERESTS: Fishing, lawn work
TURNED PROFESSIONAL: 1991

JOINED CHAMPIONS TOUR: 1991

CHAMPIONS TOUR VICTORIES (3): 1995 GTE Northwest Classic. **1996** FHP Health Care Classic, Ameritech Senior Open.

GEORGIA-PACIFIC GRAND CHAMPIONS VICTORIES (1): 2002 Uniting Fore Care Classic.

BEST 2004 CHAMPIONS TOUR FINISH: T60—Outback Steakhouse Pro-Am.

2004 SEASON:

Made 13 starts on the Champions Tour, his fewest number of appearances in a season since 1994, and didn't play after the Kroger Classic in mid-September...Best effort was a T60 at the Outback Steakhouse Pro-Am near Tampa...Finished 26th on the Georgia-Pacific Grand Champions money list, with $12,625.

CHAMPIONS TOUR CAREER HIGHLIGHTS:

2002: Posted best finish since the 2001 TD Waterhouse Championship (T2) with a T2 at the AT&T Canada Senior Open Championship, three strokes back of Tom Jenkins. Became the youngest player ever to better his age, when at 61, he equaled Isao Aoki's all-time Champions Tour record for lowest 18-hole score by firing an 11-under-par 60 (12 birdies) in the second round at Essex G&CC. Shot a 6-under 65 on Sunday despite making a bogey and double bogey. His 17-under 125 score over the last two days included 21 birdies and tied Aoki's all-time mark for best final 36 holes...Won his only Georgia-Pacific Grand Champions event at the Uniting Fore Care Classic in Park City. Scored 13 points on Saturday in the Modified Stableford event to total plus-17 for two days and nip Terry Dill by one point in the over-60 competition. **2001:** Turned in his best performance since the 1996 Ameritech Senior Open when he T2 at the TD Waterhouse Championship, eight strokes back of Ed Dougherty...Joined the ranks of the Georgia-Pacific Grand Champions in early June...Recorded the 23rd double eagle in Champions Tour history and the third of the 2001 season during the second round of the Gold Rush Classic. Holed a 5-wood second shot from 254 yards on the par-5 sixth hole at Serrano CC. **1997:** Earned the Champions Tour's "ironman" honor by playing 113 rounds in 36 events (Bobby Stroble also played 36, but with two fewer rounds). **1996:** Claimed a pair of titles and won a career-best $848,303...Rounds of 62-71-66 at the 1996 FHP Health Care Classic tied Gary Player after 54 holes. Birdied the first playoff hole to win for the second time...Went wire-to-wire at the Ameritech Senior Open with rounds of 63-70-72. **1995:** Voted by his peers as the Champions Tour's Comeback Player of the Year...Won his initial Champions Tour title at the GTE Northwest Classic. Held off Dave Stockton, Rocky Thompson, Al Geiberger and George Archer to claim the title near Seattle. Dedicated the win to the late Tommy Aycock, one of his fellow professionals, who had died of cancer at the beginning of the week...Carded his first hole-in-one as a senior during the third round of the Vantage Championship. **1994:** Regained fully-exempt status with a second-place finish at the 1994 Champions Tour National Qualifying Tournament. **1993:** Played 21 tournaments, mostly on partial exemption from the 1992 Champions Tour National Qualifying Tournament (13th place). **1992:** Fully exempt after a T6 in the 1991 Champions Tour National Qualifying Tournament, his first attempt. **1991:** Made his Champions Tour debut at the 1991 MONY Syracuse Senior Classic (T47) and open-qualified at three other events that year.

OTHER CAREER HIGHLIGHTS:

Won the 1996 Merrill Lynch Shoot-Out Championship when he birdied the final hole to defeat Bob Murphy at The Homestead in Hot Springs, VA...Has made nine career holes-in-one.

PERSONAL:

Served a 20-year stint in the U.S. Army, including two tours in Vietnam...Was the All-Service champion in 1975 and 1976...Also boxed in the military and won all 13 fights via KOs...Left the service in 1980 and tried for his PGA TOUR card, but missed the cut at the PGA TOUR National Qualifying Tournament by one stroke...Was a club professional in Texas until turning 50 in mid-1991...Is a self-taught player and didn't take up the game until age 29, spending most of his spare time playing baseball...Ventured onto a golf course in Hawaii and shot 79 in the first round he ever played...Credits Charlie Sifford with helping him make the transition to the Champions Tour, and his wife, Geraldine, for being the most influential person in his career...Chosen for the North Carolina Black Hall of Fame in 1995...Caddied for Chi Chi Rodriguez in the 1966 Hawaiian Open...His family has been quite involved in sports. His wife played college basketball, a stepson attended college on a track scholarship and his youngest son plays high school baseball. One of his cousins is former baseball great Joe Morgan...Biggest thrill in golf was winning his first Champions Tour event near Seattle in 1995.

PLAYER STATISTICS

2004 CHAMPIONS TOUR STATISTICS:

Scoring Average	76.62	(N/A)
Driving Distance	250.5	(N/A)
Driving Accuracy Percentage	74.2%	(N/A)
Total Driving	1,998	(N/A)
Greens in Regulation Pct.	50.2%	(N/A)
Putting Average	1.893	(N/A)
Sand Save Percentage	41.0%	(N/A)
Birdie Average	1.70	(N/A)
All-Around Ranking	1,569	(N/A)

MISCELLANEOUS CHAMPIONS TOUR STATISTICS

2004 Low Round: 68–2004 Blue Angels Classic/2
Career Low Round: 60–2002 AT&T Canada Senior Open Championship/2
Career Largest Paycheck: $165,000–1996 Ameritech Senior Open/1

CHAMPIONS TOUR CAREER SUMMARY — PLAYOFF RECORD: 1-0

Year	Events Played	1st	2nd	3rd	Top 10	Top 25	Earnings	Rank
1991	4					1	$10,430	100
1992	29				1	7	101,037	59
1993	21				4	7	138,700	57
1994	6					1	27,444	93
1995	35	1			5	15	423,756	27
1996	37	2			12	26	848,303	10
1997	36			1	11	22	687,676	18
1998	35			1	5	16	497,913	34
1999	36				1	13	309,068	52
2000	35				3	7	335,314	55
2001	34		1		2	6	421,687	46
2002	28		1		2	6	347,504	50
2003	24						39,302	107
2004	13						17,742	126
Total	373	3	2	2	46	127	$4,205,875	

CHAMPIONS TOUR TOP TOURNAMENT SUMMARY

Year	91	92	93	94	95	96	97	98	99	00	01	02	03
Senior PGA Championship					T55	T11	10	T6	CUT	T54	T27	CUT	
U.S. Senior Open	T40					T8	T21	T38	CUT				
Ford Senior Players		T74	T51	T69	T14	T24	T19	T30	T56	T73	T56	T40	76
JELD-WEN Tradition		T41			T50	T5	T15	T60	T14	T19	T43	T35	71
Charles Schwab Cup Champ					T24	T28	T17						

Year	04
Senior PGA Championship	CUT

Bob Murphy

EXEMPT STATUS: Top 30 on All-Time Money List
FULL NAME: Robert Joseph Murphy, Jr.
HEIGHT: 5-10
WEIGHT: 205
BIRTHDATE: February 14, 1943
BIRTHPLACE: Brooklyn, NY
RESIDENCE: Delray Beach, FL
FAMILY: Wife, Gail; Kimberly (1/11/69); two grandchildren
CLUB AFFILIATION: Delray Dunes Golf Club, Boynton Beach, FL
EDUCATION: University of Florida (1966, Physical Education)
SPECIAL INTERESTS: Fishing, stock market, collecting wine
TURNED PROFESSIONAL: 1967
JOINED PGA TOUR: 1968

JOINED CHAMPIONS TOUR: 1993

CHAMPIONS TOUR VICTORIES (11): 1993 Bruno's Memorial Classic, GTE North Classic. **1994** Raley's Senior Gold Rush, Hyatt Regency Maui Kaanapali Classic. **1995** The IntelliNet Challenge, PaineWebber Invitational, Nationwide Championship, VFW Senior Championship. **1996** Royal Caribbean Classic, Cadillac NFL Golf Classic. **1997** Toshiba Senior Classic.

OTHER SENIOR VICTORIES (2): 1995 Diners Club Matches [wih Jim Colbert]. **1996** Diners Club Matches [with Jim Colbert].

2004 CHARLES SCHWAB CUP FINISH: T62nd - 86 points

GEORGIA-PACIFIC GRAND CHAMPIONS VICTORIES (1): 2004 Kroger Classic.

PGA TOUR VICTORIES (5): 1968 Philadelphia Golf Classic, Thunderbird Classic. **1970** Greater Hartford Open Invitational. **1975** Jackie Gleason-Inverrary Classic. **1986** Canadian Open.

OTHER VICTORIES (5): 1965 U.S. Amateur. **1966** NCAA Championship [indiv]. **1967** Florida Open. **1970** Australian Masters. **1979** Jerry Ford Invitational.

PGA TOUR CAREER EARNINGS: $1,642,330

PGA TOUR PLAYOFF RECORD: 1-5

BEST 2004 CHAMPIONS TOUR FINISH: T13—Outback Steakhouse Pro-Am.

2004 SEASON:

Continued to juggle a playing schedule around his job as an analyst for NBC Sports…Started year with a T23 at the Royal Caribbean Golf Classic, his 300th career event on the Champions Tour…Two weeks later, closed with a final-round 66 to T13 at the Outback Steakhouse Pro-Am. His 5-under-par Sunday score was his best since 8-under 64 in second round of 2002 Ford Senior Players Championship…Finished 13th on the final Georgia-Pacific Grand Champions earnings list, with $102,083…Won his first-ever Georgia-Pacific Grand Champions competition at the Kroger Classic and went on to finish T23 in the overall event late in the year. His 36-hole score of 8-under 136 was one stroke better than Bruce Summerhays, the eventual winner of the overall Kroger tournament.

CHAMPIONS TOUR CAREER HIGHLIGHTS:

2003: T4 at the 3M Championship, his best finish on the Champions Tour since he was T2 at the 2000 Instinet Classic in Princeton, NJ…Made the 18th hole-in-one of his career (fourth on the Champions Tour) when he aced the fourth hole in the second round of the Turtle Bay Championship. Holed a 6-iron from 194 yards. **2002:** Aced the 202-yard, 12th hole at TwinEagles with a 7-wood during the second round of The ACE Group Classic. **2001:** Finished out of the top 50 on the money list for the first time…Best performance came in last start, a T8 at the SBC Championship, where he was tied for the 36-hole lead. **2000:** T2 at The Instinet Classic after Gil Morgan overtook him with a final-round 66. Shared the second-round lead with Tom Jenkins after rounds of 68-65. **1999:** Best performance was a runner-up at the Nationwide Championship. Appeared headed for a playoff with Hale Irwin before Irwin holed out from 74 yards for a dramatic eagle on No.18 to defeat him by two strokes at the GC of Georgia. **1997:** Scored a dramatic victory over Jay Sigel at the Toshiba Senior Classic. Went nine extra holes with Sigel before rolling in an 80-foot birdie putt to win the event, the second longest playoff in Champions Tour history. **1996:** Fired a final-round 67 to hold off Hale Irwin by four strokes at the Royal Caribbean Classic…Opened with a course-record 62 on his way to a two-stroke triumph over Jay Sigel at the Cadillac NFL Golf Classic. Victory at Upper Montclair made him the ninth of 10 players to win both a PGA TOUR (1968 Thunderbird Classic) and Champions Tour event at the same site…Registered his 16th career hole-in-one during the first round of the Energizer SENIOR TOUR Championship (12th hole). **1995:** Claimed four titles, tying Jim Colbert for the most victories by any Champions Tour player that season…Started with a victory in the rain-curtailed IntelliNet Challenge…Outlasted Raymond Floyd and Larry Ziegler at the PaineWebber Invitational…Avenged a runner-up finish the year before by claiming the Nationwide Championship over Hale Irwin and Bruce Summerhays…Had a Champions Tour record-tying 126 total over the final 36 holes for the VFW Senior Championship, defeating Jim Colbert by a stroke. **1994:** Defeated Dave Eichelberger to claim the Raley's Senior Gold Rush. Went wire-to-wire in Hawaii at the Hyatt Regency Maui Kaanapali Classic. Opened with a 62 on Maui and never looked back, equaling the tournament record of 195. **1993:** Voted the Champions Tour's Rookie of the Year on the strength of two tournament victories…Initial win came when he held off Lee Trevino and Bob Charles to claim the Bruno's Memorial Classic. Was also victorious at the rain-shortened GTE North Classic.

OTHER CAREER HIGHLIGHTS:

Last victory on the PGA TOUR came at the 1986 Canadian Open. Had not won since the 1975 Jackie Gleason-Inverrary Classic, but at age 43 defeated Greg Norman by three strokes at Glen Abbey GC…In his rookie year of 1968, he set a goal to win $40,000 but instead took home $105,595, a record at the time for a first-year player. Won back-to-back tournaments at the Philadelphia and Thunderbird Classics that season and was second at the Westchester Classic prior to his pair of victories…Also won the 1970 Greater Hartford Open…Defeated Bob Dickson to win the 1965 U.S. Amateur…Member of the 1966 U.S. World Amateur Cup and 1967 Walker Cup teams…Earned a spot on the 1975 U.S. Ryder Cup team…Has had 18 career holes-in-one, 12 in competition.

PERSONAL:

Initially coaxed out of the ESPN broadcast booth by Lee Trevino, who advised him to play the Champions Tour on a full-time basis…Recipient of the 1996 Ben Hogan Award from the Golf Writers Association of America for his comeback from arthritis…Serves as national spokesman for the Hook-A-Kid On Golf program…Returned to the booth in 2000, joining NBC for a number of events before becoming a full-time member of the broadcast team. Also worked on CBS golf telecasts during the 1980s…Was a standout pitcher and hitter in his youth and led his high school baseball team to the state championship in 1960…Got started in golf after suffering a football injury that forced him to the sidelines for baseball as well…Biggest thrill in golf was winning the U.S. Amateur title in 1965 after only playing golf for four years…Enjoys watching "CSI."

PLAYER STATISTICS

2004 CHAMPIONS TOUR STATISTICS:

Scoring Average	72.50	(59)
Driving Distance	254.0	(77)
Driving Accuracy Percentage	74.7%	(21)
Total Driving	98	(63)
Greens in Regulation Pct.	60.3%	(71)
Putting Average	1.797	(37)
Sand Save Percentage	57.6%	(4)
Eagles (Holes per)	486.0	(54)
Birdie Average	2.98	(57)
All-Around Ranking	380	(51)

MISCELLANEOUS CHAMPIONS TOUR STATISTICS

2004 Low Round: 66–2004 Outback Steakhouse Pro-Am/3
Career Low Round: 62–2 times, most recent 1996 Cadillac NFL Golf Classic/1
Career Largest Paycheck: $180,000–1995 Nationwide Championship/1

MISCELLANEOUS PGA TOUR STATISTICS

Career Low Round: 64–6 times, most recent 1983 Walt Disney World Golf Classic/3
Career Largest Paycheck: $108,000–1986 Canadian Open/1

CHAMPIONS TOUR CAREER SUMMARY — PLAYOFF RECORD: 2-0

Year	Events Played	1st	2nd	3rd	Top 10	Top 25	Earnings	Rank
1993	27	2	2	2	15	22	$768,743	8
1994	30	2	4	3	17	22	855,862	8
1995	28	4	3	3	20	23	1,241,524	4
1996	30	2	2	2	18	22	1,067,188	7
1997	30	1	1		7	15	685,611	19
1998	31				5	14	569,398	30
1999	30		1		4	12	472,956	43
2000	26		1		6	16	636,757	30
2001	25				1	7	261,924	62
2002	20					1	75,799	95
2003	22				1	5	239,158	57
2004	18					4	136,489	75
Total	317	11	14	10	94	163	7,011,409	
COMBINED ALL-TIME MONEY (3 TOURS):							**$8,653,739**	

CHAMPIONS TOUR TOP TOURNAMENT SUMMARY

Year	93	94	95	96	97	98	99	00	01	02	03	04
Senior PGA Championship	T39	T10	T10	T7	T27	T22	T39	T17	T13	WD	T63	WD
U.S. Senior Open	T15	T7	T3	T27	T32	T28	CUT	T26	T34	CUT	T17	T50
Ford Senior Players	T15	T10	T7	T33	T42	T4	T62	T16	T31	T40	T56	T63
JELD-WEN Tradition		T27	T8	4	T46	T17	T14		T67	T75	74	T45
Charles Schwab Cup Champ	5	WD	T14	T26	T11	T26		23				

Larry Nelson

EXEMPT STATUS: Top 30 on 2004 Champions Tour Money List
FULL NAME: Larry Gene Nelson
HEIGHT: 5-9
WEIGHT: 150
BIRTHDATE: September 10, 1947
BIRTHPLACE: Fort Payne, AL
RESIDENCE: Marietta, GA

FAMILY: Wife, Gayle; Drew (10/7/76), Josh (9/28/78); two grandchildren
EDUCATION: Kennesaw Junior College (1970)
SPECIAL INTERESTS: Golf course architecture
TURNED PROFESSIONAL: 1971
JOINED PGA TOUR: 1974

JOINED CHAMPIONS TOUR: 1997

CHAMPIONS TOUR VICTORIES (19): 1998 American Express Invitational, Pittsburgh Senior Classic, Boone Valley Classic. **1999** GTE Classic, Bruno's Memorial Classic. **2000** Las Vegas Senior Classic, Boone Valley Classic, FleetBoston Classic, Foremost Insurance Championship, Bank One Senior Championship, Vantage Championship. **2001** MasterCard Championship, Royal Caribbean Classic, FleetBoston Classic, Farmers Charity Classic, SBC Championship. **2003** Constellation Energy Classic. **2004** FedEx Kinko's Classic, Administaff Small Business Classic.

OTHER SENIOR VICTORIES (2): 1999 Chrysler Senior Match Play Challenge. **2004** Office Depot Father/Son Challenge [with Drew].

2004 CHARLES SCHWAB CUP FINISH:
14th - 1,269 points

PGA TOUR VICTORIES (10): 1979 Jackie Gleason-Inverrary Classic, Western Open. **1980** Atlanta Classic. **1981** Greater Greensboro Open, PGA Championship. **1983** U.S. Open Championship. **1984** Walt Disney World Golf Classic. **1987** PGA Championship, Walt Disney World/Oldsmobile Classic. **1988** Georgia-Pacific Atlanta Golf Classic.

OTHER VICTORIES (4): 1980 Tokai Classic. **1983** Dunlop International Open. **1989** Suntory Open. **1991** Dunlop Phoenix.

PGA TOUR CAREER EARNINGS: $3,827,401

PGA TOUR PLAYOFF RECORD: 3-2

BEST 2004 CHAMPIONS TOUR FINISHES:
1—FedEx Kinko's Classic, Administaff Small Business Classic; 2—Outback Steakhouse Pro-Am, SBC Classic; T3—3M Championship; T4—The ACE Group Classic; T5—Bruno's Memorial Classic, SAS Championship.

2004 SEASON:

With $1,428,224 in earnings, it was his best showing since the 2001 season when he went over $2 million for the season...Had multiple victories for the first time since 2001...Earned his 19th career Champions Tour title at the Administaff Small Business Classic near Houston in October. Matched the largest come-from-behind win of the season when he rallied from seven strokes back with a final-round 64, which included 10 birdies. Eventually defeated Hale Irwin with birdie on the first playoff hole for the victory at Augusta Pines. Win was his fourth overall title in the state of Texas and second of the year in the Lone Star State...Won in May in Austin at the FedEx Kinko's Classic, a one-stroke triumph over Bruce Lietzke at The Hills CC. After an opening-round, 1-over-par 73, followed with rounds of 69-67 and his final round was bogey-free...Saw his chance to win all three Champions Tour events in Texas go awry when he finished T7 at the SBC Championship in October...Was second to Mark McNulty at the Outback Steakhouse Pro-Am when he made birdie on the final hole near Tampa...Was T4 the week prior at The ACE Group Classic and narrowly missed joining a three-man playoff with Craig Stadler, Tom Watson and Gary Koch when he missed a par putt on the final hole...Also second to Gil Morgan by two strokes at the SBC Classic despite shooting three straight 68s at Valencia...Was in contention down the stretch at the 3M Championship and eventually posted a 6-under 66 to T3 at the TPC of the Twin Cities...Birdied more par-3 holes than any other player (20.2 percent) and also converted more birdie opportunities than any player at 32.6 precent...Shared the string for most consecutive sub-70 rounds during the year with Lonnie Nielsen as each had seven...Teamed with son Drew for three-stroke win at Office Depot Father/Son Challenge in December.

CHAMPIONS TOUR CAREER HIGHLIGHTS:

2003: Played well in spurts, especially late in the year when he registered five top-10 finishes in his last six starts to jump back into the top 10 on the final money list after a year's absence...Earned his first victory since October 2001 at the Constellation Energy Classic in mid-September. Forged a two-stroke victory over Doug Tewell and Jim Dent at Hayfields CC near Baltimore after being the 36-hole co-leader with Jay Sigel. Trailed at one point on the back nine before making a critical birdie on the 16th hole to tie Tewell. Pulled away on the final two holes when Tewell bogeyed both 17 and 18. Victory in Maryland was worth $225,000 and pushed him past the $1 million mark in single-season earnings for the sixth consecutive year. Win also propelled him to September Player of the Month honors...Battled Fuzzy Zoeller and eventual winner Dana Quigley down the stretch in the season-opening MasterCard Championship before eventually finishing second...Was also second at the Toshiba Senior Classic, finishing four strokes behind Rodger Davis. Helped his cause with a second-round 64...At the Emerald Coast Classic in April, finished as a runner-up—the third time that occurred in his first seven starts of the season. Ended four strokes back of Bob Gilder despite playing his last 36 holes at The Moors without making a bogey...Late in the season, held the 36-hole lead at the inaugural Greater Hickory Classic at Rock Barn, but finished second after a final-round 70...Withdrew from the Farmers Charity Classic before the start of the event due to the death of his mother-in-law...Had a penchant for going low several times in the first half of the year. Shot 64 in both the second rounds of the MasterCard Championship and Toshiba Senior Classic before matching his Champions Tour career-best round for a seventh time with a 7-under 63 on the final day of the Columbus Southern Open, his lowest score since the final day of the 2001 SBC Championship in San Antonio. Thanks to a run of six straight birdies, the best birdie streak on the Champions Tour in 2003, went on to post 64 in the final round of the Music City Championship a week later. **2002:** Did not record a victory for the first time since joining the Champions Tour late in the 1997 season...Two best events came in back-to-back starts during May. Was the 36-hole leader at the Bruno's Memorial Classic, but slipped to third, one stroke out of playoff contention, after a final-round 70 at

CHAMPIONS TOUR CAREER SUMMARY — PLAYOFF RECORD: 2-3

Year	Events Played	1st	2nd	3rd	Top 10	Top 25	Earnings	Rank
1997	6		1	1	4	6	$312,457	49
1998	23	3	5		11	20	1,442,476	3
1999	28	2	3	1	13	21	1,513,524	4
2000	30	6	7	1	23	26	2,708,005	1
2001	28	5	1	2	17	23	2,109,936	4
2002	25		1	1	11	20	1,143,224	18
2003	24	1	4	2	11	15	1,365,973	8
2004	25	2	2	1	11	14	1,428,224	6
Total	189	19	24	9	101	145	12,023,819	
COMBINED ALL-TIME MONEY (3 TOURS):							**$15,851,220**	

CHAMPIONS TOUR TOP TOURNAMENT SUMMARY

Year	98	99	00	01	02	03	04
Senior PGA Championship	2	T43	T2	T27	T6	T10	T57
U.S. Senior Open	WD	T23	T19	T7	T7	T40	T19
Ford Senior Players	T24	4	T2	T31	T8	29	T51
JELD-WEN Tradition	T44	2	T2	T5	T51	T33	T61
Charles Schwab Cup Champ	T16	T2	T10	T5	T5	T7	26

CHAMPIONS TOUR YEAR-BY-YEAR STATISTICS (TOP 50 ON 2004 MONEY LIST)

	Scoring Average	Putting Average	Greens in Regulation	Driving Distance	Driving Accuracy
1997	68.44 (N/A)	1.752 (N/A)	73.5 (N/A)	279.5 (N/A)	71.8 (N/A)
1998	69.87 (3)	1.748 (4)	70.5 (7)	271.2 (T18)	69.8 (T38)
1999	70.25 (T8)	1.750 (4)	71.2 (12)	272.6 (15)	68.6 (T55)
2000	68.87 (2)	1.724 (1)	73.5 (8)	278.6 (6)	74.2 (15)
2001	69.91 (6)	1.730 (2)	69.8 (16)	277.7 (19)	72.3 (T33)
2002	70.09 (9)	1.762 (8)	70.3 (17)	275.2 (T20)	68.5 (43)
2003	69.82 (7)	1.752 (5)	69.7 (24)	281.9 (12)	71.0 (32)
2004	70.62 (15)	1.747 (2)	68.1 (33)	284.3 (10)	69.9 (43)

Larry Nelson (continued)

Greystone...Backed up Birmingham performance with a solo second effort at the rain-shortened TD Waterhouse Championship. **2001:** Eclipsed the $2-million mark in earnings for a second straight year and again led the Champions Tour in official victories with five...Claimed the first two events of the season—the MasterCard Championship by one stroke over Jim Thorpe and the Royal Caribbean Classic by one point over Isao Aoki. Became the first player to win the first two tournaments in a season since Don January did so in 1981...Added a third victory in late June by defending his title at the FleetBoston Classic (by three strokes over Bruce Fleisher), the fifth player in the history of the Boston event to win in successive years. Defended again at the Farmers Charity Classic in Michigan, nipping Jim Ahern by one shot for his fourth victory of the season...Picked up his fifth win late in the campaign at the SBC Championship, defeating Bob Gilder and Gary McCord by two strokes. 54-hole total of 17-under-par 199 at The Dominion was a tournament record...Matched the low round of his career when he fired a second-round 63 at the Toshiba Senior Classic and also carded 63 in the final round of the SBC Championship. **2000:** Voted by his peers as the winner of the Jack Nicklaus Award, symbolizing the Champions Tour's Player of the Year...Earned $2,708,005, the third-highest money total in Champions Tour history, and claimed the Arnold Palmer Award as the leading money-winner on the Champions Tour. Averaged $90,267 per start over 30 appearances, thanks to a season-best six victories that included four wins in his final eight starts...Set an all-time Champions Tour record for most consecutive par/better rounds (32), starting the streak in the final round of the U.S. Senior Open in early July and ending it in the opening round of the SBC Senior Classic in late October...Won by five over Hale Irwin and Bruce Fleisher at the Las Vegas Senior Classic...Second win came near St. Louis when he posted a three-stroke victory over Tom Watson at the Boone Valley Classic, thanks to a dramatic eagle on the 17th hole...Was 4-under-par over his last nine holes at Nashawtuc and claimed the FleetBoston Classic by four over Jim Thorpe...Cruised to a wire-to-wire victory the following week and beat Dave Stockton by three strokes at the Foremost Insurance Championship in Grand Rapids. His 18-under 198 total at Egypt Valley included a course-record 63 on the final day...Took the lead in the money race for good when he edged Bill Brask and Jim Thorpe by a stroke at the Bank One Senior Championship in Dallas...Went on to best Gil Morgan and Jim Dent in a six-hole playoff at the Vantage Championship...Set Champions Tour standards for Rounds in the 60s (59/breaking Bruce Fleisher's old mark of 56 in 1999) and also for best Putting Average (1.724/breaking Jim Colbert's mark of 1.725 in 1991)...Raised eyebrows when he fired a 12-under-par 58 (29-29—58) in the Thursday Pro-Am at the Kroger Senior Classic (missed 15-footer on the last hole for 57)...Had just one round outside the 60s in his six victories (second round 70 at the FleetBoston Classic) and was over par in just one tournament all year (6-over at the GTE Classic). **1999:** Bothered by a herniated disc in his neck at several points during the year, but still won multiple official titles...Thwarted Bruce Fleisher's attempt at winning a third straight Champions Tour start when he prevailed by two strokes at the GTE Classic near Tampa...Birdied three of his last seven holes to edge Dana Quigley for the Bruno's Memorial Classic title near Birmingham. **1998:** Won three times in his first full year on the Champions Tour and lost two other events in playoffs...Missed seven weeks during the summer with a herniated disc near his neck...Initial victory came at the American Express Invitational in Sarasota...Opened with a sizzling 9-under 63 and cruised to a wire-to-wire, four-stroke win over Dave Stockton...Registered another easy start-to-finish win at the Pittsburgh Senior Classic. After building a Champions Tour record-tying eight-stroke lead after 36 holes, waltzed to a five-shot triumph over Bob Duval at Sewickley Heights...Used a pair of 65s on the weekend to ease past Graham Marsh for the Boone Valley Classic title near St. Louis. **1997:** Made his Champions Tour debut at the Boone Valley Classic, just two days after turning 50, and T16 after an opening-round 69...Made six starts and finished in the top 10 in four tournaments...Best effort was a T2 in his second career start at the Comfort Classic. In the hunt to the end at Brickyard Crossing before a final-hole birdie by winner David Graham...Prior to moving to the Champions Tour, played 18 events on the PGA TOUR, winning $196,981...T2 at the Doral-Ryder Open was his best TOUR finish that year and earned him his largest PGA TOUR career paycheck ($158,400).

OTHER CAREER HIGHLIGHTS:

Captured 10 PGA TOUR titles, including three majors. The native of Georgia won the 1981 PGA Championship at Atlanta Athletic Club. Opened with a 70, then shot consecutive 66s for a four-stroke lead after 54 holes. Finished with a 71 and four-stroke victory over Fuzzy Zoeller...Trailed Tom Watson and Seve Ballesteros by one stroke after three rounds of the 1983 U.S. Open at Oakmont, but fired a closing 67 for a one-stroke win over Watson. At the 1987 PGA Championship at PGA National GC, he used three different configurations of irons over four days of oppressive heat, but still managed to defeat Lanny Wadkins in a playoff...Recorded two victories (Jackie Gleason-Inverrary Classic and Western Open), two seconds and two thirds in 1979 en route to a second-place finish on the money list behind Watson with $281,022...Was named as Golf Digest's Most Improved Player that season...Best earnings year was 1987, when he made $501,292, 14th on the money list...Along with the PGA title, also was victorious at the 1987 Walt Disney World/Oldsmobile Classic...Last title came in 1988 at the Georgia-Pacific Atlanta Classic, where he defeated Chip Beck by one stroke...Played on three U.S. Ryder Cup teams (1979, 1981, 1987) and had a 9-3-1 record...In his final full year on the PGA TOUR in 1996, rebounded from four consecutive seasons in which he earned less than $100,000 to record the third-best earnings season of his 23-year career. In 21 starts, made $305,083 and finished 70th on the PGA TOUR money list.

PERSONAL:

Didn't begin playing golf until returning from his military service in Vietnam. Got his instruction from reading Ben Hogan's book, *The Five Fundamentals of Golf*...Broke 100 the first time he played and broke 70 within nine months...Active in golf course design, with 12 courses open for play worldwide...Has two sons who are aspiring golfers—Drew, his oldest, has played on the Hooters Tour, and Josh graduated from Auburn...Was a pitcher/shortstop for a Georgia Colt League Champion team as a youngster.

PLAYER STATISTICS

MISCELLANEOUS CHAMPIONS TOUR STATISTICS

2004 Low Round: 64–2 times, most recent 2004 Administaff Small Business Classic /3

Career Low Round: 63–7 times, most recent 2003 Columbus Southern Open/3

Career Largest Paycheck: $240,000–3 times, most recent 2004 Administaff Small Business Classic/1

MISCELLANEOUS PGA TOUR STATISTICS

Career Low Round: 63–5 times, most recent 1989 GTE Byron Nelson Golf Classic/1

Career Largest Paycheck: $158,400–1997 Doral–Ryder Open/T2

Jack Nicklaus

WORLD GOLF HALL OF FAME MEMBER (Inducted 1974)
EXEMPT STATUS: Top 30 on All-Time Money List
FULL NAME: Jack William Nicklaus
HEIGHT: 5-11
WEIGHT: 180
BIRTHDATE: January 21, 1940
BIRTHPLACE: Columbus, OH
RESIDENCE: North Palm Beach, FL
FAMILY: Wife, Barbara Bash; Jack II (9/23/61), Steven (4/11/63), Nancy Jean (5/5/65),Gary (1/15/69), Michael (7/24/73); 17 grandchildren
CLUB AFFILIATIONS: Muirfield VIllage GC (Dublin, OH), The Bear's Club (Jupiter, FL)
EDUCATION: Ohio State University
SPECIAL INTERESTS: Fishing, hunting, tennis
TURNED PROFESSIONAL: 1961
JOINED PGA TOUR: 1962

JOINED CHAMPIONS TOUR: 1990

CHAMPIONS TOUR VICTORIES (10): 1990 The Tradition at Desert Mountain, Mazda SENIOR TOURNAMENT PLAYERS Championship. **1991** The Tradition at Desert Mountain, PGA Seniors' Championship, U.S. Senior Open. **1993** U.S. Senior Open. **1994** Mercedes Championships. **1995** The Tradition. **1996** GTE Suncoast Classic, The Tradition.

OTHER SENIOR VICTORIES (5): 1991 Senior Skins Game. **1999** Wendy's Three-Tour Challenge [with Tom Watson, Hale Irwin]. Office Depot Father-Son Challenge [with Gary]. Diners Club Matches [with Tom Watson]. **2000** Hyundai Team Matches [with Tom Watson].

2004 CHARLES SCHWAB CUP FINISH:
62nd - 71 points

PGA TOUR VICTORIES (73): 1962 U.S. Open Championship, Seattle World's Fair Open Invitational, Portland Open Invitational. **1963** Palm Springs Golf Classic, Masters Tournament, Tournament of Champions, PGA Championship, Sahara Invitational. **1964** Phoenix Open Invitational, Tournament of Champions, Whitemarsh Open Invitational, Portland Open Invitational. **1965** Masters Tournament, Memphis Open Invitational, Thunderbird Classic, Philadelphia Golf Classic, Portland Open Invitational. **1966** Masters Tournament, British Open Championship, Sahara Invitational. **1967** Bing Crosby National Pro-Am, U.S. Open Championship, Western Open, Westchester Classic, Sahara Invitational. **1968** Western Open, American Golf Classic. **1969** Andy Williams-San Diego Open Invitational, Sahara Invitational, Kaiser International Open Invitational. **1970** Byron Nelson Golf Classic, British Open Championship, National Four-Ball Championship [with Arnold Palmer]. **1971** PGA Championship, Tournament of Champions, Byron Nelson Golf Classic, National Team Championship [with Arnold Palmer], Walt Disney World Open Invitational. **1972** Bing Crosby National Pro-Am, Doral-Eastern Open, Masters Tournament, U.S. Open Championship, Westchester Classic, U.S. Professional Match Play Championship, Walt Disney World Open Invitational. **1973** Bing Crosby National Pro-Am, Greater New Orleans Open, Tournament of Champions, Atlanta Classic, PGA Championship, Ohio Kings Island Open, Walt Disney World Golf Classic. **1974** Hawaiian Open, Tournament Players Championship. **1975** Doral-Eastern Open, Sea Pines Heritage Classic, Masters Tournament, PGA Championship, World Open Golf Championship. **1976** Tournament Players Championship, World Series of Golf. **1977** Jackie Gleason-Inverrary Classic, MONY Tournament of Champions, Memorial Tournament. **1978** Jackie Gleason-Inverrary Classic, Tournament Players Championship, British Open Championship, IVB-Philadelphia Golf Classic. **1980** U.S. Open Championship, PGA Championship. **1982** Colonial National Invitation. **1984** Memorial Tournament. **1986** Masters Tournament.

OTHER VICTORIES (25): 1959 U.S. Amateur. **1961** U.S. Amateur, NCAA Championship [indiv]. **1962** World Series of Golf. **1963** World Series of Golf, Canada Cup [with Arnold Palmer], Canada Cup [indiv]. **1964** Australian Open, Canada Cup [with Arnold Palmer], Canada Cup [indiv]. **1966** PGA Team Championship [with Arnold Palmer]. Canada Cup [with Arnold Palmer]. **1967** World Series of Golf, World Cup [with Arnold Palmer]. **1968** Australian Open. **1970** World Series of Golf, Piccadilly World Match Play Championship. **1971** Australian Open, World Cup [with Lee Trevino], Canada Cup [indiv]. **1973** World Cup [with Johnny Miller]. **1975** Australian Open. **1976** Australian Open. **1978** Australian Open. **1983** Chrysler Team Championship [with Johnny Miller].

PGA TOUR CAREER EARNINGS: $5,734,322

PGA TOUR PLAYOFF RECORD: 13-10

BEST 2004 CHAMPIONS TOUR FINISH: 6—MasterCard Championship.

BEST 2004 PGA TOUR FINISH: T63—the Memorial Tournament.

2004 SEASON:
Solo sixth-place effort at the season-opening MasterCard Championship in Hawaii was his best on the Champions Tour since a T4 at the 2001 U.S. Senior Open. Carded three consecutive rounds in the 60s at Hualalai, a first in a 54-hole Champions Tour event for him...Finished in third place at the Wendy's Champions Skins Game. Earned three skins and $60,000 over the first nine holes, but was shut out on the back nine at Wailea's Gold Course...Was T15 at The ACE Group Classic and T36 at the Toshiba Senior Classic...Played three rounds at the Senior PGA Championship before withdrawing...Became the second-oldest player to make a cut on the PGA TOUR when he finished T63 at the Memorial after a final-round 71, his lowest score on the PGA TOUR in two years...Played in his 44th Masters, tying Sam Snead and Billy Casper for number of appearances in the tournament, but missed the cut...Also competed in the Nationwide Tour's BMW Charity Pro-Am at The Cliffs, along with sons Gary, Jackie and Michael. All missed the cut at The Cliffs in Traveler's Rest, SC.

CHAMPIONS TOUR CAREER HIGHLIGHTS:
2003: Was in contention for 36 holes of the Kinko's Classic of Austin before finishing T7 after an even-par 72 on Sunday...Also was in contention on Sunday at the JELD-WEN Tradition before eventually T10 in Portland, his eighth top-10 performance in 13 appearances in the event...Started the season with a nice showing at the MasterCard Championship. Was T11 at Hualalai after closing with a 6-under-par 66, his best score since posting 65 on the last day of the 1996 Tradition...Made his debut on the Nationwide Tour at the BMW Charity Pro-Am at The Cliffs and T45 in event near Greenville, SC. Appearance at The Cliffs with four sons marked the first time all five played together in a professional event...Captained the U.S. Presidents Cup team for a second time in the biennial matches in South Africa. **2002:** Made just two official appearances due to persistent lower back pain. Played in April at The Countrywide Tradition and finished 69th. Arizona appearance was his first official event since July 2001 when he was forced to WD from the Ford Senior Players Championship with a hamstring injury...Bad back forced him to miss the Masters, only the second time the six-time champion didn't start in the tournament since his debut in 1959. Hip replacement surgery forced him to miss the 1999 tournament...Made the cut at the Senior PGA Championship at Firestone, but was forced to withdraw on Saturday morning with lower back pain... Lone appearance on the PGA TOUR was at The Memorial Tournament where he made the cut and finished 71st. **2001:**

CHAMPIONS TOUR CAREER SUMMARY **PLAYOFF RECORD: 2-1**

Year	Events Played	1st	2nd	3rd	Top 10	Top 25	Earnings	Rank
1990	4	2	1	1	4	4	$340,000	15
1991	5	3			4	5	343,734	17
1992	4		1	1	3	3	114,548	53
1993	6	1			3	5	206,028	42
1994	6	1			5	5	239,278	34
1995	7	1	2	1	7	7	538,800	22
1996	7	2			3	7	360,861	38
1997	6		1		3	6	239,932	58
1998	6				3	5	205,723	61
1999	3					1	19,673	110
2000	7				1	5	166,422	74
2001	7				2	4	266,127	61
2002	2						1,880	176
2003	9				2	6	221,593	62
2004	4				1	2	105,464	84
Total	83	10	5	3	41	65	3,370,062	
COMBINED ALL-TIME MONEY (3 TOURS):							**$9,106,497**	

CHAMPIONS TOUR TOP TOURNAMENT SUMMARY

Year	90	91	92	93	94	95	96	97	98	99	00	01	02
Senior PGA Championship	T3	1	T10	T9	9	8	T22	T2	T6		T12	12	WD
U.S. Senior Open	2	1	T3	1	T7	2	16	T5	T13		T21	T4	
Ford Senior Players	1	T22		T22	T6	2	T24	T8	6	WD	T34	WD	
JELD-WEN Tradition	1	1	2	T9	T4	1	1	T25	T25		T9	T29	69

Year	03	04
Senior PGA Championship	CUT	WD
U.S. Senior Open	T25	
Ford Senior Players	T40	
Senior British Open	T14	
JELD-WEN Tradition	T10	

Jack Nicklaus (continued)

Registered two top-10 finishes...T4 at the U.S. Senior Open and finished fourth at the Siebel Classic in Silicon Valley...Made a spirited run at the U.S. Senior Open before bogeys on the 15th and 16th holes the final day ended his chances. **1999:** Underwent hip replacement surgery in January and played in only three official tournaments on the Champions Tour...Did not play until midway thru the year at the Bell Atlantic Classic. Carded two rounds of 70 on the weekend at Hartefeld National and finished 18th near Philadelphia. **1998:** Hobbled by a painful left hip for the majority of the year...Closed with 68 at Augusta National and T6 at The Masters, four strokes back of eventual winner Mark O'Meara...Ended his remarkable run of 154 straight appearances in major championships when he chose not to compete in the PGA Championship at Sahalee CC. **1997:** Broke Sam Snead's record for most rounds played at the Masters with his 147th on Sunday...Played his 10,000th hole at the U.S. Open at Congressional CC. **1996:** Became the first player to win the same Champions Tour event four times when he claimed The Tradition. Victory in Arizona was his 100th as a professional and was his eighth senior major championship, the most by any player over 50. Shot 65 in the final round at Desert Mountain to best Hale Irwin by three strokes. Carded his third career double eagle on Saturday at The Tradition, his first since the 1965 Greater Jacksonville Open...Also claimed his only 54-hole event on the Champions Tour, rallying from five strokes back to edge J.C. Snead for the GTE Suncoast Classic title. **1995:** Defeated Isao Aoki in a playoff to win his third Tradition title and, at the time, became only the fifth man to win the same tournament three times. **1994:** Came from three strokes back of Bob Murphy to win the Mercedes Championships at LaCosta by a stroke. **1993:** Claimed his second U.S. Senior Open title, holding off rival Tom Weiskopf by a shot at Cherry Hills CC near Denver. **1991:** Made just five appearances on the Champions Tour, but won three official events, including his only PGA Seniors' Championship and first U.S. Senior Open title...Shot 17-under 271 at PGA National GC, the lowest 72-hole score on the Champions Tour that year, to claim the PGA Seniors' crown by six strokes over Bruce Crampton...U.S. Senior Open victory over Chi Chi Rodriguez came in an 18-hole playoff at Oakland Hills CC, 65 to 69, making him the first player ever to win USGA titles in five different decades and the first and only player to win all of the Champions Tour's four major championships at the time...Also came from five strokes back to successfully defend his Tradition title by one over Jim Colbert, Jim Dent and Phil Rodgers. **1990:** Played in just four official Champions Tour events but won twice, finished second once and T3 in his only other tournament...Four-stroke win over Gary Player at The Tradition made him the seventh of just 10 players ever to claim a title in their Champions Tour debut...Finished solo sixth at the Masters a week later, at the time, the best finish by a senior in a major since Sam Snead (T3 at1974 PGA Championship)...Cruised to a six-stroke victory at the Mazda Senior Tournament Players Championship in record-setting fashion by shooting a 27-under-par 261 at Dearborn CC, the lowest 72-hole total in Champions Tour history.

OTHER CAREER HIGHLIGHTS:

Considered by many to be the greatest player in the history of the sport...Cited as Golfer of the Millenium or Golfer of the Century from such publications or media outlets as Associated Press, PGATOUR.COM, *Golf World*, BBC and *Golfweek*...Finished ninth in ESPN's Greatest Athlete of the Century voting...Honored by *Sports Illustrated* as Best Individual Male Athlete of the Century...Named Golfer of the Century by the Associated Press and *Golf* and by *Golf Monthly U.K.* in 1996, Sports Illustrated's Athlete of the Decade for the 1970s, 1978 *Sports Illustrated* Sportsman of the Year and PGA Player of the Year five times (1967, 1972, 1973, 1975, 1976)...PGA TOUR, Champions Tour and Nationwide Tour Player of the Year trophies all bear his name...Ranks second only to Sam Snead (81) on the PGA TOUR victory list with 70 official titles...First TOUR player to reach $2 million (12/1/73), $3 million (5/2/77), $4 million (2/6/83) and $5 million (8/20/88) in career earnings...Co-holds, with Arnold Palmer, the PGA TOUR record for most years winning at least one TOUR event, 17 (1962-78)...105 consecutive cuts made (11/70-9/76) is third behind Byron Nelson's 113 and Tiger Woods' 114...Dominated golf in the 1960s and 1970s...From 1962-1969 finished in top 10 in 122 of 186 events (66 percent); 1970-79 finished among top 10 in 121 of 171 events (71 percent)...In remarkable three-year period from 1971 to 1973, finished in top 10 in 45 of 55 events (82 percent)...Winning performance in professional majors is unmatched: six Masters, five PGA Championships, four U.S. Opens, three British Opens and three PLAYERS Championships...The only player who has won all four major championships on the both PGA TOUR and Champions Tour...Became the oldest player (46) to win the Masters when he won in 1986...First professional win came in the 1962 U.S. Open at Oakmont, where he defeated Arnold Palmer in a playoff...Had an outstanding amateur record...Won five consecutive Ohio State Junior Championships, beginning at age 12. Won the 1959 U.S. Amateur by defeating Charles Coe, 1-up. Claimed a second U.S. Amateur in 1961 by defeating Dudley Wysong, 8 and 6...That same year, he was a member of the victorious U.S. Walker Cup squad, won the Western Amateur, NCAA Championship and Big Ten title and finished fourth in the U.S. Open...Finished runner-up to Palmer in the 1960 U.S. Open at Cherry Hills by two strokes, establishing the amateur record score of 282...Posted a 17-8-3 Ryder Cup record...Received the 1982 Card Walker Award for outstanding contributions to junior golf...Inducted into the World Golf Hall of Fame in 1974...Walker Cup selection in 1959 and 1961...World Cup team member in 1963, 1964, 1966, 1967, 1971 and 1973...Named to the U.S. Ryder Cup squad in 1969, 1971, 1973, 1975, 1977 and 1981...Ryder Cup captain in 1983 and 1987...Presidents Cup captain in 1998 in Australia and again in 2003 in South Africa...Joined Palmer and Byron Nelson as the first recipients of the Payne Stewart Award in 2000...Selected for membership into the Augusta National GC in the fall of 2001, joining Arnold Palmer as only the second professional golfer to be admitted into the exclusive club.

PERSONAL:

Remains one of golf's driving forces off the course...Founder and host of The Memorial Tournament...One of the world's leading golf course designers...The Nicklaus companies' global business includes golf course design, development and licensing...Over 300 professional golf tournaments have been staged on as many as 62 Nicklaus courses, including 12 current PGA TOUR and Champions Tour events as well as Ryder Cup, PGA Championship and World Cups...Selected as *Golf World's* Golf Course Architect of the Year in 1993...At age 10, carded a 51 in the first nine holes he played...Jack Nicklaus Museum on campus of Ohio State, his alma mater, opened in May 2002....Named 1999 Father of the Year by Minority Golf Association...Named co-chair with Juli Inkster of The First Tee's Capital Campaign, More Than A Game, in November 2000.

PLAYER STATISTICS

2004 CHAMPIONS TOUR STATISTICS:

Scoring Average	70.42	(N/A)
Driving Distance	270.0	(N/A)
Driving Accuracy Percentage	67.9%	(N/A)
Total Driving	1,998	(N/A)
Greens in Regulation Pct.	68.5%	(N/A)
Putting Average	1.743	(N/A)
Sand Save Percentage	55.0%	(N/A)
Eagles (Holes per)	108.0	(N/A)
Birdie Average	3.50	(N/A)
All-Around Ranking	1,569	(N/A)

MISCELLANEOUS CHAMPIONS TOUR STATISTICS

2004 Low Round: 66–2004 MasterCard Championship/2
Career Low Round: 64–2 times, most recent 1990 Mazda SENIOR TOURNAMENT PLAYERS Championship/4
Career Largest Paycheck: $150,000–3 times, most recent 1996 The Tradition/1

MISCELLANEOUS PGA TOUR STATISTICS

2004 Low Round: 71–the Memorial Tournament/4
Career Low Round: 62–2 times, most recent 1973 Ohio Kings Island Open/3
Career Largest Paycheck: $144,000–1986 Masters Tournament/1

Lonnie Nielsen

EXEMPT STATUS: 36th on 2004 Champions Tour Money List
FULL NAME: Lonnie D. Nielsen
HEIGHT: 5-11
WEIGHT: 200
BIRTHDATE: June 29, 1953
BIRTHPLACE: Belle Plaine, IA
RESIDENCE: Orchard Park, NY
FAMILY: Wife, Mary Jo; Sarah (2/17/81), Mollie (9/3/83), Andy (3/10/87)
CLUB AFFILIATION: Crag Burn GC (East Aurora, NY)
EDUCATION: University of Iowa (1976, Business)
SPECIAL INTERESTS: Playing cards
TURNED PROFESSIONAL: 1976

JOINED CHAMPIONS TOUR: 2003

BEST CHAMPIONS TOUR CAREER FINISH: T5—2004 SAS Championship.

OTHER SENIOR VICTORIES (2): 2003 Otesago Senior Open Championship, Turning Stone Seniors Championship.

2004 CHARLES SCHWAB CUP FINISH: 44th - 258 points

BEST PGA TOUR CAREER FINISH: T5—1979 Ed McMahon-Jaycees Quad Cities Open.

OTHER VICTORIES (32): 1984 Western New York PGA Match Play Championship. **1985** New York State Open, Western New York Section PGA Championship. **1986** Western New York PGA Match Play Championship, Western New York Section PGA Championship. **1987** Western New York Section PGA Championship. **1988** PGA Match Play Championship, PGA Stroke Play Championship. **1989** New York State Open, Western New York Open, Western New York Section PGA Championship, PGA Match Play Championship. **1990** Western New York Open, Western New York PGA Match Play Championship, Western New York Section PGA Championship. **1991** Western New York PGA Match Play Championship. **1993** Western New York PGA Match Play Championship, Western New York Open, Western New York Section PGA Championship. **1994** Western New York PGA Match Play Championship, Western New York Section PGA Championship. **1995** Western New York Open. **1996** Western New York Section PGA Championship. **1997** Western New York Open. **1998** Western New York Open, Western New York PGA Match Play Championship. **1999** Western New York PGA Match Play Championship. **2000** Western New York Section PGA Championship. 2001 Western New York PGA Match Play Championship. **2002** Western New York PGA Match Play Championship. **2002** Western New York Open. **2003** Western New York Open.

PGA TOUR CAREER EARNINGS: $119,416

BEST 2004 CHAMPIONS TOUR FINISHES: T5—SAS Championship; T6—Toshiba Senior Classic; T9—The First Tee Open at Pebble Beach presented by Wal-Mart; T10—The ACE Group Classic, Greater Hickory Classic at Rock Barn.

2004 SEASON:

Earned over a half million dollars in his first full year on the Champions Tour...His best performance of the season came in late September when he finished T5 at the SAS Championship near Raleigh...Was T6 at the Toshiba Senior Classic in California where he started a run of seven straight sub-70 rounds...Had impressive showing at The ACE Group Classic when he opened with a 9-under-par 63 and eventually finished T10...Was two strokes off the lead after the first round of the Bruno's Memorial Classic but shot a second-round, 3-over-par 75 and eventually was T11. His opening round included a string of four birdies and an eagle, the best birdie-eagle streak on the Champions Tour for the year...His other top-10 finishes were a T10 at the Greater Hickory Classic at Rock Barn and a T9 at The First Tee Open at Pebble Beach...His string of seven consecutive rounds in the 60s was the best on the Champions Tour, sharing that honor with Larry Nelson...Attempted to improve his exempt status at the National Qualifying Tournament in the fall. Finished in a tie with Des Smyth after six rounds at the King and Bear in St. Augustine, FL, and eventually placed ninth when Smyth did not participate in a playoff.

CHAMPIONS TOUR CAREER HIGHLIGHTS:

2003: Earned fully exempt status for 2004 by finishing T4 at the Champions Tour National Qualifying Tournament at the TPC at Eagle Trace in Florida. Was just one of five players in the field to record four sub-par rounds and finished with a 72-hole total of 7-under-par 281. Earned a spot in the finals by virtue of his third-place finish at the PGA Senior Club Pro Championship...Twice open-qualified on the Champions Tour after turning 50 in June. Was T47 at the Constellation Energy Classic near Baltimore and T31 at the Turtle Bay Championship in Hawaii.

OTHER CAREER HIGHLIGHTS:

Played the PGA TOUR on a full-time basis from 1978-83 before giving up TOUR golf to become a club professional and Director of Golf at Crag Burn GC in East Aurora, NY, near Buffalo...Career earnings on the PGA TOUR totaled $119,416 in 124 events from 1978-1996. Made 75 cuts and had two top-10 finishes during that span...Was T5 at the 1979 Ed McMahon-Jaycees Quad City Open, T8 at the 1980 Danny Thomas Memphis Classic and T11 at the 1986 PGA Championship at Inverness...Made 14 appearances on the Nationwide Tour from 1990-96, with total earnings of $14,389...Finished T3 at the 1993 Hawkeye Open...Winner of numerous club professional titles in his career, including the 1988 PGA Stroke Play Championship...A nine-time winner of the Western New York PGA Section Championship and a two-time winner of the PGA Match Play Championship (1988-89)...Claimed the New York State Open in both 1985 and 1989...A 10-time winner of the Western New York PGA Match Play Championship and was selected as the Western New York PGA Player of the Year 12 times. Led the Western New York PGA Section money list 13 times, including six consecutive years (1993-98). Is that sections all-time leading money-winner, with over $310,000 in career earnings...Chosen as the PGA National Club Professional of the Year in 1986, 1987 and 1989...Established more than 40 course records in his career, with a career-low round of 61, which he shot on two occasions—at Pima CC in Scottsdale, AZ, and Dragon Ridge CC in Las Vegas...Has 11 career holes-in-one.

PERSONAL:

Has worked with such teachers as Butch Harmon, Chuck Zweiner and Bob Fry...Biggest thrill in golf was finishing 11th at the 1986 PGA Championship and biggest thrill away from golf was the birth of his three children...Father got him started in the game as a youngster in Iowa and he grew up playing on sand greens in Belle Plaine, IA (population 2,000)...His father owned the local bowling alley in his hometown...Favorite courses are Pebble Beach, Spyglass, Butler National and Merion...Enjoys "Seinfeld," entertainer Robin Williams and "The Sting"...Favorite athlete is Wayne Gretzky and favorite book is *The Firm*...A close friend of fellow Champions Tour member John Harris.

PLAYER STATISTICS

MISCELLANEOUS CHAMPIONS TOUR STATISTICS
2004 Low Round: 63–2004 The ACE Group Classic/1
Career Low Round: 63–2004 The ACE Group Classic/1
Career Largest Paycheck: $74,400–2004 SAS Championship/T5

MISCELLANEOUS PGA TOUR STATISTICS
Career Low Round: 63–1981 Sammy Davis Jr.-Greater Hartford Open/1
Career Largest Paycheck: $12,000–1986 PGA Championship/T11

CHAMPIONS TOUR CAREER SUMMARY — PLAYOFF RECORD: 0-0

Year	Events Played	1st	2nd	3rd	Top 10	Top 25	Earnings	Rank
2003	2						$15,225	131
2004	26				5	12	529,262	36
Total	28				5	12	544,487	
COMBINED ALL-TIME MONEY (3 TOURS):							**$678,742**	

CHAMPIONS TOUR TOP TOURNAMENT SUMMARY

Year	04
Senior PGA Championship	T31
Ford Senior Players	T46
Senior British Open	T22
JELD-WEN Tradition	T45

CHAMPIONS TOUR YEAR-BY-YEAR STATISTICS (TOP 50 ON 2004 MONEY LIST)

	Scoring Average	Putting Average	Greens in Regulation	Driving Distance	Driving Accuracy
2003	73.33 (N/A)	1.844 (N/A)	71.3 (N/A)	271.3 (N/A)	63.1 (N/A)
2004	71.43 (34)	1.777 (18)	70.4 (T17)	278.4 (T19)	66.5 (61)

SECTION 2 PLAYER BIOGRAPHIES

Greg Norman

WORLD GOLF HALL OF FAME MEMBER (Inducted 2001)
EXEMPT STATUS: Top 30 on All-Time Money List
FULL NAME: Gregory John Norman
HEIGHT: 6-0
WEIGHT: 180
BIRTHDATE: February 10, 1955
BIRTHPLACE: Mt. Isa, Queensland, Australia
RESIDENCE: Hobe Sound, FL
FAMILY: Wife, Laura; Morgan-Leigh (10/5/82), Gregory (9/19/85)
CLUB AFFILIATION: Medalist GC (Hobe Sound, FL)
SPECIAL INTERESTS: Fishing, hunting, scuba diving
TURNED PROFESSIONAL: 1976
JOINED PGA TOUR: 1983
JOINED CHAMPIONS TOUR: 2005

PGA TOUR VICTORIES (20): 1984 Kemper Open, Canadian Open. **1986** Panasonic Las Vegas Invitational, Kemper Open, British Open Championship. **1988** MCI Heritage Golf Classic. **1989** The International, Greater Milwaukee Open. **1990** Doral-Ryder Open, Memorial Tournament. **1992** Canadian Open. **1993** Doral-Ryder Open, British Open Championship. **1994** THE PLAYERS Championship. **1995** Memorial Tournament, Canon Greater Hartford Open, NEC World Series of Golf. **1996** Doral-Ryder Open. **1997** FedEx St. Jude Classic, NEC World Series of Golf.

OTHER VICTORIES (68): 1976 Westlakes Classic [Aus]. **1977** Martini International [Eur], Kuzuhz International [Jpn]. **1978** New South Wales Open [Aus], Traralgon Classic [Aus], Caltex Festival of Sydney Open [Aus], South Seas Classic [Fiji]. **1979** Traralgon Classic [Aus], Martini International [Eur], Hong Kong Open. **1980** Australian Open [Aus], French Open [Eur], Scandinavian Open [Eur], Suntory World Match Play Championship [Eur], State Express Classic, Benson & Hedges International. **1981** Australian Masters [Aus], Martini International [Eur], Dunlop Masters [Eur]. **1982** Dunlop Masters [Eur], State Express Classic [Eur], Benson & Hedges International [Eur]. **1983** Australian Masters [Aus], Stefan Queensland Open [Aus], National Panasonic New South Wales Open [Aus], Hong Kong Open, Cannes Invitational [Eur], Suntory World Match Play Championship [Eur], Kapalua International. **1984** Victorian Open [Aus], Australian Masters [Aus], Australian PGA [Aus].**1985** Toshiba Australian PGA Championship [Aus], National Panasonic Australian Open [Aus], Dunhill Cup. **1986** Stefan Queensland Open [Aus], National Panasonic New South Wales Open [Aus], West End Jubilee South Australian Open [Aus], National Panasonic Western Australian Open [Aus], European Open [Eur], Suntory World Matchplay Championship [Eur], Dunhill Cup, PGA Grand Slam of Golf. **1987** Australian Masters [Aus], National Panasonic Australian Open [Aus]. **1988** Palm Meadows Cup [Aus], ESP Open [Aus], PGA National Tournament Players Championship [Aus], Panasonic New South Wales Open [Aus], Lancia Italian Open [Eur]. **1989** Australian Masters [Aus], PGA National Tournament Players Championship [Aus], Chunichi Crowns [Jpn]. **1990** Australian Masters [Aus]. **1993** Taiheyo Masters [Jpn], PGA Grand Slam of Golf. **1994** Johnnie Walker Asian Classic [Eur], PGA Grand Slam of Golf. **1995** Australian Open [Aus], Fred Meyer Challenge [with Brad Faxon]. **1996** Ford South Australian Open [Aus], Australian Open [Aus], Fred Meyer Challenge [with Brad Faxon]. **1997** Fred Meyer Challenge [with Brad Faxon], Andersen Consulting World Championship. **1998** Greg Norman Holden International [Aus], Franklin Templeton Shootout [with Steve Elkington]. **2001** Skins Game.

PGA TOUR CAREER EARNINGS: $13,946,089

PGA TOUR PLAYOFF RECORD: 4-7

BEST 2004 PGA TOUR FINISH: T81—THE PLAYERS Championship.

2004 SEASON:

Made seven starts on PGA TOUR and made one cut—THE PLAYERS Championship (T81)...Also made one appearance in Australia (Heineken Classic) and in Asia (BMW Asian Open)...Was T4 with Scott McCarron at Franklin Templeton Shootout.

OTHER CAREER HIGHLIGHTS:

The winner of 88 titles worldwide, including 20 championships on the PGA TOUR...Named to the World Golf Hall of Fame in 2001...A three-time winner of the Arnold Palmer Award as the PGA TOUR's leading money winner in 1986, 1990 and 1995, he was also a five-time winner of the Byron Nelson Award for the best adjusted scoring average...In addition, he won three Vardon Trophies from the PGA of America for the lowest adjusted scoring average...Was also the winner of the Jack Nicklaus Trophy as the 1995 PGA TOUR Player of the Year, as well as the PGA of America's Player of the Year...Held the No. 1 spot in the Official World Golf Ranking for 331 weeks at one point in his career in the 1990s and positioned himself in the top 50 in the World Ranking for 700 weeks before falling out in 1999...Three-time member of the International team in The Presidents Cup (1998, 2000 and 2002)...Owns 29 top-10 finishes in major championships, with victories at the 1986 and 1993 British Opens. First PGA TOUR victory came at the 1984 Kemper Open, where he defeated Mark O'Meara by five strokes. Added a second title four weeks later by two strokes over Jack Nicklaus at the Canadian Open...Won his first money title in 1986 when he defended his title at the Kemper Open, claimed the Panasonic Las Vegas Invitational and won his first British Open crown at Turnberry. After an opening round 74, shot tournament-record-tying 63 to take a two-stroke lead after 36 holes and followed with rounds of 74-69 to defeat Gordon Brand by two strokes...Second money crown came in 1990 when he won twice, including the Memorial Tournament...Captured second British Open in 1993. Trailed Corey Pavin and Nick Faldo by one stroke after 54 holes but closed with a 64 to defeat Faldo by one stroke...Earned at least $1 million five times (1990, 1993-95 and 1997) and was first player to earn $1 million four times (1990, 1993-95)...Tied the Masters scoring record with an opening-round 63 in 1996 and led by six after 54 holes but lost when he shot 78 in the final round as Nick Faldo shot 67. That marked the eighth time in his career he had finished as a runner-up in a major championship...Won the 2001 Skins Game, shutting out Tiger Woods, Colin Montgomerie and Jesper Parnevik...Battled various injuries in his career, including a left shoulder problem in 1998 which required April surgery by Dr. Richard Steadman in Colorado. Procedure involved the shaving of bone spurs, which caused tendinitis in his rotator cuff, and the use of a heat probe to shrink the shoulder socket capsule. Followed a seven-month rehabilitation period with a victory at the Franklin Templeton Shootout with partner Steve Elkington...Sidelined by arthroscopic hip surgery in June, 2000 after being troubled by a bothersome right hip for a number of years. Pain was linked to previous shoulder woes. In amazing show of physical perseverance, returned to action at The INTERNATIONAL just five weeks later to record second top-10 of year. Finished alone in fourth with 38 points after returning to hitting balls just eight days prior to event...Had dramatic victory at the 1997 FedEx St. Jude Classic, where he birdied final three holes for a 66 to earn one-stroke victory over Dudley Hart. Became first to surpass $10 million in career earnings during the 1996 season...Four times in his career he played a season without missing a cut (1983, 1987, 1994-95)...In 1995 won three titles—the Memorial Tournament, Canon Greater Hartford Open and NEC World Series of Golf—and then-record $1,654,959.

PERSONAL:

Serves as chairman and CEO of Great White Shark Enterprises, a multi-national corporation with offices in Jupiter, FL, and Sydney, Australia. The company's interests are primarily focused around golf and the golf lifestyle. Established in 1987, Greg Norman Golf Course Design is recognized as one of the premier signature design groups. Medallist Developments is an international developer of premier residential golf course communities. Established in 1995, Greg Norman Turf Company licenses proprietary turfgrasses for golf courses, athletic fields and home lawns. Greg Norman Collection is a leading worldwide marketer and distributor of men's sportswear, golf apparel and accessories. Greg Norman Estates produces a line of highly rated wines. Greg Norman's Australian Grille in North Myrtle Beach, SC, offers indoor and outdoor dining with authentic Australian fare. The Greg Norman Production Company, which is devoted to event management, operates the Franklin Templeton Shootout...Began playing at age 16 caddieing for his mother. Was a scratch player two years later...Initial ambition was to become a pilot in the Australian Air Force but opted for golf and took just four tournaments to record first of more than 80 titles worldwide.

PLAYER STATISTICS

MISCELLANEOUS PGA TOUR STATISTICS
2004 Low Round: 72–4 times, most recent Cialis Western Open/1
Career Low Round: 62–4 times, most recent 1993 Doral-Ryder Open/3
Career Largest Paycheck: $450,000–1994 THE PLAYERS Championship/1

Pete Oakley

EXEMPT STATUS: 2004 Tournament Winner
FULL NAME: Peter H. Oakley
HEIGHT: 5-7
WEIGHT: 155
BIRTHDATE: June 28, 1949
BIRTHPLACE: Panama City, FL
RESIDENCE: Lincoln, DE
FAMILY: Zachary (7/25/82), Jeremy (10/24/83)

CLUB AFFILIATION: The Rookery (Milton, DE)
EDUCATION: Santa Fe Community College (1971)
SPECIAL INTERESTS: Current events, guitar, Christian music, literature
TURNED PROFESSIONAL: 1974

JOINED CHAMPIONS TOUR: 2004

CHAMPIONS TOUR VICTORIES (1): 2004 Senior British Open.

OTHER SENIOR VICTORIES (2): 1999 PGA Senior Club Pro Championship. **2000** PGA Senior Stroke Play Championship.

2004 CHARLES SCHWAB CUP FINISH: 20th - 867 points

OTHER VICTORIES (6): 1980 Delaware State Open. **1982** Delaware State Open. **1989** Philadelphia Open. **1990** Delaware State Open, Philadelphia Open. **1995** Delaware State Open.

BEST 2004 CHAMPIONS TOUR FINISHES: 1—Senior British Open.

2004 SEASON:

Joined the Champions Tour on a full-time basis after claiming the Senior British Open in July. Earned a full year's exemption from that point when he won at Royal Portrush in Northern Ireland. Sank a 10-foot par putt on the final hole to hold off Tom Kite and Eduardo Romero by one stroke for the title. Had blasted out of a deep greenside bunker moments before sinking his winning putt. Victory at Portrush made him the 10th open qualifier to win a Champions Tour event. Successfully open-qualified for the event earlier that week out of a 132-man field. Earned $289,152 for his win, the largest payday of his pro career. Had been a fully-exempt player on the European Seniors Tour prior to his victory, after finishing fourth at that Tour's qualifying tournament in the fall of 2003 in Portugal...Best finishes on the European Seniors Tour prior to his win in Northern Ireland were a pair of T8s at the Open de France Seniors and the Ryder Cup Wales Senior Open...After his win in Northern Ireland, he played the 10 remaining Champions Tour events, with his best finish a T34 at the SAS Championship near Raleigh in late September.

CHAMPIONS TOUR CAREER HIGHLIGHTS:

2003: Played in two events, missing the cut at the Senior PGA Championship and finishing T35 at the U.S. Senior Open...Finished fourth at the European Seniors Tour Qualifying Tournament in Portugal. **2002:** Finished T32 at the U.S. Senior Open...Played one event on the European Seniors Tour and finished T73 at the De Vere PGA Seniors Championship. **2001:** Made one start on the Champions Tour and was T61 at the Senior PGA Championship...Was T35 at the Champions Tour National Qualifying Tournament. **2000:** Finished T41 at the U.S. Senior Open and T66 at the Senior PGA Championship...Was T31 at the Champions Tour National Qualifying Tournament. **1999:** Made one appearance and was T32 at the U.S. Senior Open...Also T36 at the Champions Tour National Qualifying Tournament.

OTHER CAREER HIGHLIGHTS:

Was a long-time club professional who won numerous sectional titles in the Philadelphia-Delaware area, including four Delaware State Open crowns. Also claimed the 1999 PGA Senior Club Pro Championship by three strokes despite starting his final round with a double bogey...Represented the U.S. at the 1994 PGA Cup Matches...Won the 2000 PGA Senior Stroke Play title.

PERSONAL:

Got started in the game as an 11-year-old by his mother who thought the nearby nine-hole golf course would be a great babysitter for him and his brother, David, a former Champions Tour player...Calls his 2004 Senior British Open victory his biggest thrill in golf...Serves as the Director of Golf at The Rookery in Delaware, a daily fee course where he is a managing partner...Considers consistency the strongest part of his game...One of his superstitions is staying with the same golf ball when he is playing well.

PLAYER STATISTICS

MISCELLANEOUS CHAMPIONS TOUR STATISTICS
2004 Low Round: 66–2004 U.S. Senior Open/2
Career Low Round: 66–2004 U.S. Senior Open/2
Career Largest Paycheck: $289,153–2004 Senior British Open/1

MISCELLANEOUS PGA TOUR STATISTICS
Career Low Round: 71–2 times, most recent 1995 PGA Championship/1

CHAMPIONS TOUR CAREER SUMMARY — PLAYOFF RECORD: 0-0

Year	Events Played	1st	2nd	3rd	Top 10	Top 25	Earnings	Rank
1999	1						$11,035	119
2000	2						13,810	125
2001	1						3,913	172
2002	1						10,750	129
2003	2						14,801	133
2004	12	1			1	1	342,990	49
Total	19	1			1	1	397,299	
COMBINED ALL-TIME MONEY (3 TOURS):							**$397,827**	

CHAMPIONS TOUR TOP TOURNAMENT SUMMARY

Year	99	00	01	02	03	04
Senior PGA Championship	T66	T61	T32	CUT	CUT	
U.S. Senior Open	T32	T41	T35	T37		
Senior British Open						1
JELD-WEN Tradition						T73

CHAMPIONS TOUR YEAR-BY-YEAR STATISTICS (TOP 50 ON 2004 MONEY LIST)

	Scoring Average	Putting Average	Greens in Regulation	Driving Distance	Driving Accuracy
1999	74.25 (N/A)	2.000 (N/A)	59.7 (N/A)	251.6 (N/A)	64.3 (N/A)
2000	73.57 (N/A)	1.963 (N/A)	65.1 (N/A)	248.8 (N/A)	75.5 (N/A)
2001	74.50 (N/A)	1.800 (N/A)	55.6 (N/A)	238.9 (N/A)	67.9 (N/A)
2002	72.50 (N/A)	1.821 (N/A)	54.2 (N/A)	255.8 (N/A)	71.4 (N/A)
2003	74.00 (N/A)	2.000 (N/A)	58.3 (N/A)	262.5 (N/A)	76.1 (N/A)
2004	73.21 (N/A)	1.843 (N/A)	60.5 (N/A)	257.9 (N/A)	75.4 (N/A)

Arnold Palmer

WORLD GOLF HALL OF FAME MEMBER (Inducted 1974)
EXEMPT STATUS: 75 or more All-Time Victories
FULL NAME: Arnold Daniel Palmer
HEIGHT: 5-10
WEIGHT: 185
BIRTHDATE: September 10, 1929
BIRTHPLACE: Latrobe, PA
RESIDENCES: Latrobe, PA; Bay Hill, FL
FAMILY: Peggy (2/26/56), Amy (8/4/58); seven grandchildren
CLUB AFFILIATIONS: Latrobe CC (Latrobe, PA), Laurel Valley GC (Ligonier, PA), Bay Hill Club (Orlando, FL)
EDUCATION: Wake Forest University
SPECIAL INTERESTS: Flying, business, clubmaking
TURNED PROFESSIONAL: 1954
JOINED PGA TOUR: 1955

JOINED CHAMPIONS TOUR: 1980

CHAMPIONS TOUR VICTORIES (10): 1980 PGA Seniors' Championship. **1981** U.S. Senior Open. **1982** Marlboro Classic, Denver Post Champions of Golf. **1983** Boca Grove Classic. **1984** General Foods PGA Seniors' Championship, Senior Tournament Players Championship, Quadel Senior Classic. **1985** Senior Tournament Players Championship. **1988** Crestar Classic.

OTHER SENIOR VICTORIES (5): 1984 Doug Sanders Celebrity Pro-Am. **1986** Union Mutual Classic. **1990** Senior Skins Game. **1992** Senior Skins Game. **1993** Senior Skins Game.

PGA TOUR VICTORIES (62): 1955 Canadian Open. **1956** Insurance City Open, Eastern Open. **1957** Houston Open, Azalea Open Invitational, Rubber City Open Invitational, San Diego Open Invitational. **1958** St. Petersburg Open Invitational, Masters Tournament, Pepsi Championship. **1959** Thunderbird Invitational, Oklahoma City Open Invitational, West Palm Beach Open Invitational. **1960** Palm Springs Desert Golf Classic, Texas Open Invitational, Baton Rouge Open Invitational, Pensacola Open Invitational, Masters Tournament, U.S. Open Championship, Insurance City Open Invitational, Mobile Sertoma Open Invitational. **1961** San Diego Open Invitational, Phoenix Open Invitational, Baton Rouge Open Invitational, Texas Open Invitational, Western Open, British Open Championship. **1962** Palm Springs Golf Classic, Phoenix Open Invitational, Masters Tournament, Texas Open Invitational, Tournament of Champions, Colonial National Invitation, British Open Championship, American Golf Classic. **1963** Los Angeles Open, Phoenix Open Invitational, Pensacola Open Invitational, Thunderbird Classic Invitational, Cleveland Open Invitational, Western Open, Whitemarsh Open Invitational. **1964** Masters Tournament, Oklahoma City Open Invitational. **1965** Tournament of Champions. **1966** Los Angeles Open, Tournament of Champions, Houston Champions International. **1967** Los Angeles Open, Tucson Open Invitational, American Golf Classic, Thunderbird Classic. **1968** Bob Hope Desert Classic, Kemper Open. **1969** Heritage Golf Classic, Danny Thomas-Diplomat Classic. **1970** National Four-Ball Championship [with Jack Nicklaus]. **1971** Bob Hope Desert Classic, Florida Citrus Invitational, Westchester Classic, National Team Championship [with Jack Nicklaus]. **1973** Bob Hope Desert Classic.

OTHER VICTORIES (19): 1954 U.S. Amateur. **1955** Panama Open, Colombia Open. **1960** Canada Cup [with Sam Snead]. **1962** Canada Cup [with Sam Snead]. **1963** Australian Wills Masters Tournament, Canada Cup [with Jack Nicklaus]. **1964** Piccadilly World Match Play Championship, Canada Cup [with Jack Nicklaus]. **1966** Australian Open, Canada Cup [with Jack Nicklaus], PGA Team Championship [with Jack Nicklaus]. **1967** Piccadilly World Match Play Championship, World Cup [with Jack Nicklaus], World Cup [indiv]. **1971** Lancome Trophy. **1975** Spanish Open, British PGA Championship. **1980** Canadian PGA Championship.

PGA TOUR CAREER EARNINGS: $1,861,857

PGA TOUR PLAYOFF RECORD: 14-10

BEST 2004 CHAMPIONS TOUR FINISH: 39—MasterCard Championship.

2004 SEASON:
Celebrated his 50th year in professional golf...Finished second to Tom Watson at the Wendy's Champions Skins Game, earning five skins and $140,000 at Wailea. Lost out on a golden opportunity for victory on the final hole of regulation when, with five skins and $260,000 on the line, he missed an eight-foot birdie putt. Overall performance was still his best since winning the 1993 event...Played in his 26th consecutive Bay Hill Invitational and appeared in the Masters Tournament for a 50th straight year...Served as captain of the U.S. team once again at the UBS Cup.

CHAMPIONS TOUR CAREER HIGHLIGHTS:
2003: Matched his age three times (seventh, eighth and ninth times in his career) and also bettered his age (second time in his career) during the campaign...Shot one better than his age in the opening round of the SBC Championship when he carded a 73. Later matched his age in the same event when he closed with a 74 in San Antonio...Earlier in the year he had matched his age with an opening-round 73 at the MasterCard Championship in Hawaii and a first-round 73 at the Liberty Mutual Legends of Golf in Savannah, GA...Made his 23rd consecutive appearance in the U.S. Senior Open at the Inverness Club in Toledo...Captained the United States team to victory for the second consecutive year in the UBS Cup Matches at Sea Island, GA. **2002:** Matched his age in the final round of the Napa Valley Championship when he shot a 1-over 73. It was the first time he shot his age since opening with a 1-under 71 at the 2001 Senior PGA Championship at Ridgewood CC in New Jersey. Accomplishment in Napa made him the eighth and final player to shoot or better his age on the Champions Tour during the season. **2001:** Became just the third player in PGA TOUR history to shoot his age when he fired a 1-under-par 71 in the fourth round of the Bob Hope Chrysler Classic...Shot his age again on the Champions Tour when he opened with another 1-under-par 71 in May at the

CHAMPIONS TOUR CAREER SUMMARY **PLAYOFF RECORD: 2-1**

Year	Events Played	1st	2nd	3rd	Top 10	Top 25	Earnings	Rank
1980	1	1			1	1	$20,000	4
1981	4	1	1	2	4	4	55,100	4
1982	7	2		1	5	7	73,848	4
1983	12	1	1	1	8	12	106,590	6
1984	13	3	3		9	12	184,582	4
1985	13	1	1	2	9	12	137,024	11
1986	15		1	1	6	13	99,056	21
1987	17			1	8	13	128,910	19
1988	18	1		1	8	14	185,373	17
1989	17				4	11	119,907	38
1990	17					5	66,519	65
1991	17				4	7	143,967	46
1992	18					4	70,815	72
1993	18				1	5	106,232	64
1994	13					1	34,471	91
1995	12					1	51,526	86
1996	16					1	48,192	89
1997	13						29,052	101
1998	13						20,454	111
1999	10						8,185	135
2000	14						15,338	122
2001	7						4,384	167
2002	8						5,596	150
2003	9						19,311	126
2004	7						14,812	133
Total	309	10	7	9	67	123	1,749,244	
COMBINED ALL-TIME MONEY (3 TOURS):							**$3,611,101**	

CHAMPIONS TOUR TOP TOURNAMENT SUMMARY

Year	80	81	82	83	84	85	86	87	88	89	90	91	92
Senior PGA Championship	1	2	T3		1			T16	T5	T11	T13	CUT	T47
U.S. Senior Open		1	6	T11	2	T11	T25	T14	T22	T53	CUT	CUT	T32
Ford Senior Players				T5	1	1	T3	T5	T32	T4	T48	T43	T36
JELD-WEN Tradition										T26	T61		

Year	93	94	95	96	97	98	99	00	01	02	03	04
Senior PGA Championship	T27	CUT	CUT	CUT	CUT	CUT	CUT	CUT	CUT	CUT	CUT	WD
U.S. Senior Open	T52	T57	T51	T43	68	51	CUT	CUT	CUT	CUT	CUT	CUT
Ford Senior Players	T44	T65	T46									
Senior British Open											CUT	
JELD-WEN Tradition	T57		T25	T43								

Arnold Palmer (continued)

Senior PGA Championship at Ridgewood CC in New Jersey. **2000:** Reached a milestone in July when he played his 1,000th TOUR event at The Instinet Classic...Bettered his age for the first time when he fired a 3-under-par 69 in the second round of the FleetBoston Classic. One week earlier had matched his age with a final-round 70 at the Novell Utah Showdown, the first time he had shot his age since posting a final-round 66 at the 1995 GTE Northwest Classic. Also matched his age with a 71 at the Vantage Championship. Joined Jack Nicklaus and Byron Nelson as the first recipients of the Payne Stewart Award presented at The TOUR Championship. **1997:** Underwent surgery for prostate cancer in mid-January and made his first start after the surgery at the PGA TOUR's Bay Hill Invitational in late March. **1996:** Captained the United States team to victory in The Presidents Cup near Washington, D.C. **1995:** Shot his age for the first time in the final round of the GTE Northwest Classic in Seattle, carding a 66 on his birthday...Made triumphant return to St. Andrews for his final British Open appearance on the 35th anniversary of his first Open Championship in 1960. **1994:** Played in his last U.S. Open at Oakmont CC near Pittsburgh, 40 years after competing in his first one. **1993:** Pocketed $190,000 at the Senior Skins Game and was the event's leading money-winner for a second straight year...Was the designated honoree at The Memorial at Muirfield Village. **1992:** Racked up $205,000 in winning the Senior Skins Game at Mauna Lani...Carded the 16th hole-in-one of his career, and last in competition, in the opening round of the GTE Northwest Classic. **1988:** Had his finest earnings year as a Champions Tour player, placing 17th on the final money list with $185,373...Recorded his last official win near Richmond, claiming the Crestar Classic title in wire-to-wire fashion by four strokes over Lee Elder, Larry Mowry and Jim Ferree. **1986:** Made holes-in-one on consecutive days at the par-3 third hole at the TPC at Avenel during the Chrysler Cup pro-am competition, a first for a professional player. **1985:** Ran away from the field with an 11-shot win at the Senior Tournament Players Championship at Canterbury GC near Cleveland, and established an all-time record for largest margin of victory, not broken until Hale Irwin's 12-shot win at the 1997 PGA Seniors' Championship. **1984:** His three victories during the campaign were the most in any single season of his Champions Tour career and marked the first time since 1971 that he claimed a trio of titles in a year...Won a pair of Champions Tour major championships: the PGA Seniors' Championship by two strokes over Don January, and the Senior Tournament Players Championship where he bested Peter Thomson by three shots...Also edged Orville Moody and Lee Elder by one at the Quadel Seniors Classic near the end of the campaign. **1983:** Ended a 15-month victory drought by capturing the season-ending Boca Grove Senior Classic. **1982:** Collected a pair of titles, the first coming at the Marlboro Classic by four strokes over Billy Casper and Bob Rosburg. Added the Denver Post Champions of Golf title when he held off Bob Goalby by a stroke. **1981:** Became the first player to claim both a U.S. Open and U.S. Senior Open title with his playoff victory over Bob Stone and Billy Casper at Oakland Hills CC near Detroit. **1980:** Playoff victory over Paul Harney at the PGA Seniors' Championship made him the first of only 10 men to claim the first official Champions Tour event he entered...Debuted on the circuit at the unofficial World Seniors Invitational, finishing as runner-up to Gene Littler in Charlotte.

OTHER CAREER HIGHLIGHTS:

Owns 91 victories worldwide...A winner of eight major championships in his career: four Masters, two British Opens, one U.S. Open and one U.S Amateur...Ranks fourth on the all-time PGA TOUR victory list with 62 titles...Was the first player in PGA TOUR history to reach $1 million in official earnings, achieving that feat with a T2 at the PGA Championship in San Antonio on July 21, 1968...Tied with Jack Nicklaus for most consecutive years winning at least one tournament (17)...Named PGA TOUR Player of the Year in 1960 and 1962...Led the PGA TOUR in earnings in 1958, 1960, 1962 and 1963...Appropriately, the annual award for leading money-winner on both the PGA TOUR and Champions Tour is named for him...Four-time Vardon Trophy winner (1961, 1962, 1964, 1967)...Recipient of the USGA's Bob Jones Award in 1971 and the Byron Nelson Award in 1957, 1960, 1961, 1962 and 1963...Member of the World Golf Hall of Fame, American Golf Hall of Fame, All-American Collegiate Golf Hall of Fame...Named Associated Press Athlete of the Decade for the 1960s, Hickok Professional Athlete of the Year (1960), *Sports Illustrated* Sportsman of the Year (1960)...Awarded the PGA of America's Distinguished Service Award in 1994...Springboard to professional fame was his victory in the 1954 U.S. Amateur...Last PGA TOUR victory was at the 1973 Bob Hope Desert Classic, an event he won five times...In addition to 1996 Presidents Cup captaincy, was Ryder Cup captain in 1963 and 1975 and a member of the U.S. Ryder Cup team in 1961, 1963, 1965, 1967, 1971 and 1973...Once held the record for most Ryder Cup matches won with 22 (22-8-2 lifetime record), since surpassed by Nick Faldo with 23...Member of the American World Cup team in 1960, 1962, 1963, 1964, 1965, 1966 and 1967...Has had 17 holes-in-one in his career, the latest of which came at Latrobe (PA) CC on 9/6/97...Recipient of the Francis Ouimet Award from the Francis Ouimet Caddie Scholarship Foundation...Received the Donald Ross Award from the American Society of Golf Course Architects in March 1999...Received the Presidential Medal of Freedom from President George W. Bush in White House ceremony on June 23, 2004.

PERSONAL:

Maintains an active business schedule with golf course design, construction and development...A pilot of considerable renown, he once held one world aviation record and was the first person to receive a Citation X aircraft off the production line. Got a newer version of the Citation X just prior to last year's Verizon Classic in February...Chairman of the Board of The Golf Channel...Collaborated with Jack Nicklaus on the King and Bear at the World Golf Village that opened in November 2000.

PLAYER STATISTICS

2004 CHAMPIONS TOUR STATISTICS:

Scoring Average	80.78	(N/A)
Driving Distance	232.4	(N/A)
Driving Accuracy Percentage	70.6%	(N/A)
Total Driving	1,998	(N/A)
Greens in Regulation Pct.	30.2%	(N/A)
Putting Average	1.939	(N/A)
Sand Save Percentage	48.9%	(N/A)
Birdie Average	1.33	(N/A)
All-Around Ranking	1,569	(N/A)

MISCELLANEOUS CHAMPIONS TOUR STATISTICS

2004 Low Round: 75–2 times, most recent 2004 Bank of America Championship/3
Career Low Round: 63–1984 General Foods PGA Seniors' Championship/2
Career Largest Paycheck: $48,750–1988 Crestar Classic/1

MISCELLANEOUS PGA TOUR STATISTICS

2004 Low Round: 79–Bay Hill Invitational/2
Career Low Round: 62–1966 Los Angeles Open/3
Career Largest Paycheck: $50,000–1971 Westchester Classic/1

SECTION 2 PLAYER BIOGRAPHIES

Jerry Pate

EXEMPT STATUS: Top 30 on 2004 Champions Tour Money List
FULL NAME: Jerome Kendrick Pate
HEIGHT: 5-11
WEIGHT: 180
BIRTHDATE: September 16, 1953
BIRTHPLACE: Macon, GA
RESIDENCE: Pensacola, FL
FAMILY: Wife, Soozi; Jennifer Kaye (10/5/78), Wesley Nelson (9/5/80), James Kendrick (10/12/83)
CLUB AFFILIATION: Pensacola, CC (Pensacola, FL)
EDUCATION: University of Alabama (2001, Administrative Science)
SPECIAL INTERESTS: Golf course design, agronomy, music, charity work, Boy Scouts, The First Tee
TURNED PROFESSIONAL: 1975
JOINED PGA TOUR: 1975

JOINED CHAMPIONS TOUR: 2004

BEST CHAMPIONS TOUR CAREER FINISHES: 2—2004 Bayer Advantage Celebrity Pro-Am, T2—2004 JELD-WEN Tradition.

2004 CHARLES SCHWAB CUP FINISH: 16th - 1,115 points

PGA TOUR VICTORIES (8): 1976 U.S. Open Championship, Canadian Open. **1977** Phoenix Open, Southern Open. **1978** Southern Open. **1981** Danny Thomas Memphis Classic, Pensacola Open. **1982** Tournament Players Championship.

OTHER VICTORIES (7): 1974 U.S. Amateur. **1974** Florida Amateur. **1976** Pacific Masters. **1977** Mixed Team Championship [with Hollis Stacy]. **1980** Brazilian Open. **1981** Colombia Open, ABC Sports Shinko.

PGA TOUR CAREER EARNINGS: $1,634,246

PGA TOUR PLAYOFF RECORD: 1-2

BEST 2004 CHAMPIONS TOUR FINISHES:

2—Bayer Advantage Celebrity Pro-Am, JELD-WEN Tradition; 4—Greater Hickory Classic at Rock Barn; 5—Commerce Bank Long Island Classic.

2004 SEASON:

Made Champions Tour debut at the Royal Caribbean Golf Classic and was T23 at The Links at Key Biscayne, posting the best 36-hole score of anyone in the field on the weekend...Played in an event in his hometown for the first time since the 1988 Pensacola Open on the PGA TOUR, finishing T12 at the Blue Angels Classic...Made a serious bid for his first victory on the Champions Tour when he was the 36-hole leader at the Commerce Bank Long Island Classic. Led by two strokes entering the final round, but eventually finished fifth on the Red Course at Eisenhower Park, two strokes back of eventual winner Jim Thorpe. Had made just one bogey over his first 36 holes, but started with four bogeys over his first nine holes Sunday and posted a 3-over 73 in the final round...Came close again in late August when he took the lead at the JELD-WEN Tradition with two holes to play following an eagle at No. 16, but finished bogey-bogey to T2, one stroke behind Craig Stadler...Finished second to Allen Doyle at the Bayer Advantage Celebrity Pro-Am near Kansas City. Did not get the chance to battle Doyle on Sunday after the final round was canceled due to weather-related damage to the course the previous night.

CHAMPIONS TOUR CAREER HIGHLIGHTS:

2003: Was expected to make his Champions Tour debut in September shortly after turning 50, but July surgery forced him to postpone plans...Underwent surgery on his left shoulder, the same one he had done in 1987. Dr. James Andrews performed the "cleaning out" surgery in July. Pate spent the remainder of the year undergoing rehabilitation, with plans to be ready to go at the start of the 2004 season. Made three starts on PGA TOUR and missed cut in all three.

OTHER CAREER HIGHLIGHTS:

Played the PGA TOUR on a full-time basis from 1976-1995, with the exception of the 1993 season. Finished sixth on the money list in both 1980 ($222,976) and 1981 ($280,627)...Won eight times on the PGA TOUR, with his biggest victory coming at the 1976 U.S. Open Championship at the Atlanta Athletic Club. Was a runnerup 15 times in his PGA TOUR career, including the 1978 PGA Championship at Oakmont where he and Tom Watson lost in a playoff to John Mahaffey. Was also second with Gary Player at the 1979 U.S. Open at Inverness two strokes behind Hale Irwin. First gained attention as a PGA TOUR rookie in 1976. Last swing in the U.S. Open, a 5-iron from the rough, left him a two-foot birdie putt for a two-shot victory over Tom Weiskopf and Al Geiberger...Closed with 63 at the Canadian Open that same season to best Jack Nicklaus by four strokes...Official earnings of $153,102 in 1976 were the most ever won by a rookie until Hal Sutton bettered the mark in 1982...Claimed the first Tournament Players Championship staged at the TPC at Sawgrass in dramatic fashion in 1982, using an orange golf ball. Played the final seven holes in 4-under and birdied both the 17th (15-foot putt) and 18th (5-iron to two feet) to register a two-stroke victory over Brad Bryant and Scott Simpson. Celebrated the win by pushing former TOUR Commissioner Deane Beman and course architect Pete Dye into the large lake left of No. 18 green and then diving in himself...PGA TOUR career was cut short by three surgeries in three years on left shoulder. Tore cartilage in 1982 and had surgery in 1985. Tore rotator cuff in 1986 and had surgery that year and again in 1987...Was the medalist at the 1975 PGA TOUR Fall Qualifying Tournament after an All-American career at Alabama concluded in 1975...Defeated John Grace, 2 and 1, to win the 1974 U.S. Amateur at Ridgewood CC in New Jersey...Played on the victorious U.S. Walker Cup team in 1975 at St. Andrews and also was on the winning American team in the 1981 Ryder Cup at Walton Heath, England...Has had two holes-in-one in competitive rounds.

PERSONAL:

Served as a color analyst on CBS, ABC and BBC golf broadcasts during the decade of the 1990s...Wife, Soozi, and Bruce Lietzke's wife, Rose, are sisters...Received degree from Alabama in summer of 2001, walking through graduation ceremonies with daughter, Jenni...Involved in the golf course design business and also owns and operates a wholesale distributorship for Toro, Echo and Lawnboy outdoor power and irrigation products that services seven southeastern states...Biggest thrill in golf was winning the 1976 U.S. Open...Lists his favorite golf shot as the 5-iron he hit to win THE PLAYERS Championship...Biggest thrills away from golf were the birth of his children and his graduation from Alabama...Always marks his ball with coin on tails...Favorite golf courses are Cypress Point, St. Andrews and National GL...Enjoys watching The Discovery Channel and The Weather Channel. His all-time favorite movie is "Animal House"...Favorite athlete is Arnold Palmer. Likes watching Clint Eastwood...Enjoys Italian food. His alma mater opened the Jerry Pate Golf Center at Tuscaloosa's Ol' Colony Club last November. It will be the home of the men's and women's golf teams.

PLAYER STATISTICS

MISCELLANEOUS CHAMPIONS TOUR STATISTICS
2004 Low Round: 64–2004 Commerce Bank Long Island Classic/1
Career Low Round: 64–2004 Commerce Bank Long Island Classic/1
Career Largest Paycheck: $183,540–2004 JELD–WEN Tradition/T2

MISCELLANEOUS PGA TOUR STATISTICS
2004 Low Round: 65–Bob Hope Chrysler Classic/3
Career Low Round: 63–1976 Canadian Open/4
Career Largest Paycheck: $90,000–1982 Tournament Players Championship/1

CHAMPIONS TOUR CAREER SUMMARY — PLAYOFF RECORD: 0-0

Year	Events Played	1st	2nd	3rd	Top 10	Top 25	Earnings	Rank
2004	27		2		7	14	$946,940	19
Total	27		2		7	14	946,940	
COMBINED ALL-TIME MONEY (3 TOURS):							**$2,581,186**	

CHAMPIONS TOUR TOP TOURNAMENT SUMMARY

Year	04
Senior PGA Championship	T10
U.S. Senior Open	CUT
Ford Senior Players	T34
JELD-WEN Tradition	T2
Charles Schwab Cup Champ	T18

CHAMPIONS TOUR YEAR-BY-YEAR STATISTICS (TOP 50 ON 2004 MONEY LIST)

	Scoring Average	Putting Average	Greens in Regulation	Driving Distance	Driving Accuracy
2004	70.88 (21)	1.764 (11)	67.4 (T34)	280.4 (16)	67.7 (56)

Gary Player

WORLD GOLF HALL OF FAME MEMBER (Inducted 1974)
EXEMPT STATUS: Top 30 on All-Time Money List
FULL NAME: Gary Player
HEIGHT: 5-7
WEIGHT: 146
BIRTHDATE: November 1, 1935
BIRTHPLACE: Johannesburg, South Africa
RESIDENCES: Johannesburg, South Africa; Palm Beach, FL
FAMILY: Wife, Vivienne Verwey; Jennifer, Marc, Wayne, Michele, Theresa, Amanda; 13 grandchildren
CLUB AFFILIATION: Blair Atholl (Johannesburg, South Africa)
SPECIAL INTERESTS: Breeding thoroughbred race horses, ranching and farming, education, golf course design, family, health and fitness
TURNED PROFESSIONAL: 1953
JOINED PGA TOUR: 1957

WORLD GOLF HALL of FAME

JOINED CHAMPIONS TOUR: 1985

CHAMPIONS TOUR VICTORIES (19): **1985** Quadel Senior Classic. **1986** General Foods PGA Seniors' Championship, United Hospitals Senior Golf Championship, Denver Post Champions of Golf. **1987** Mazda SENIOR TOURNAMENT PLAYERS Championship, U.S. Senior Open, PaineWebber World Seniors Invitational. **1988** General Foods PGA Seniors' Championship, Aetna Challenge, Southwestern Bell Classic, U.S. Senior Open, GTE North Classic. **1989** GTE North Classic, The RJR Championship. **1990** PGA Seniors' Championship. **1991** Royal Caribbean Classic. **1993** Bank One Classic. **1995** Bank One Classic. **1998** Northville Long Island Classic.

OTHER SENIOR VICTORIES (12): **1986** Nissan Senior Skins. **1987** Northville Invitational, German PGA Team Championship. **1988** Nissan Senior Skins, Senior British Open. **1990** Senior British Open. **1991** Nissan Senior Skins. **1993** Irish Senior Masters. **1997** Daiichi Seimei Cup, Senior British Open, Shell Wentworth Senior Masters. **2000** Senior Skins Game.

GEORGIA-PACIFIC GRAND CHAMPIONS VICTORIES (11): **1996** FHP Health Care Classic, Franklin Quest Championship, Vantage Championship. **1997** Raley's Gold Rush Classic. **1998** Nationwide Championship, BellSouth Senior Classic at Opryland, First of America Classic, Northville Long Island Classic. **1999** Pacific Bell Senior Classic. **2000** BellSouth Senior Classic at Opryland. **2002** Farmers Charity Classic.

PGA TOUR VICTORIES (24): **1958** Kentucky Derby Open. **1959** British Open Championship. **1961** Lucky International Open, Sunshine Open Invitational, Masters Tournament. **1962** PGA Championship. **1963** San Diego Open Invitational. **1964** Pensacola Open Invitational, 500 Festival Open Invitation. **1965** U.S. Open Championship. **1968** British Open Championship. **1969** Tournament of Champions. **1970** Greater Greensboro Open. **1971** Greater Jacksonville Open, National Airlines Open Invitational. **1972** Greater New Orleans Open, PGA Championship. **1973** Southern Open. **1974** Masters Tournament, Danny Thomas Memphis Classic, British Open Championship. **1978** Masters Tournament, MONY Tournament of Champions, Houston Open.

OTHER VICTORIES (53): **1956** South African Open, East Rand Amateur and Open, Ampol Tournament. **1957** Australian PGA Championship. **1958** Australian Open. **1959** Transvaal Open. **1960** Sprite Tournament, Transvaal Open, South African Open. **1962** Australian Open, Transvaal Open. **1963** Australian Open, Transvaal Open. **1965** Australian Open, Piccadilly World Match Play Championship, South African Open, World Cup [indiv], World Cup [with Harold Henning], World Series of Golf. **1966** Piccadilly World Match Play Championship, Transvaal Open, South African Open. **1967** South African Open. **1968** Piccadilly World Match Play Championship, World Series of Golf, South African Open. **1969** Australian Open, South African Open, South African PGA Championship. **1970** Australian Open. **1971** South Africa Masters, Piccadilly World Match Play Championship, General Motors Open Golf Tournament. **1972** South African Masters, South African Open, Brazilian Open, World Series of Golf. **1973** Piccadilly World Match Play Championship. **1974** Australian Open, Brazilian Open, Ibergolf Tournament. **1975** Lancome Trophy, South African Open. **1976** South African Masters, South African Open. **1977** South African Open, World Cup [indiv]. **1979** South African Open. **1980** Chile Open, Trophy Felix Houphonet-Boigny. **1981** South African Open. **1984** Johnnie Walker. **1994** Skills Challenge.

PGA TOUR CAREER EARNINGS: $1,834,482

PGA TOUR PLAYOFF RECORD: 3-10

BEST 2004 CHAMPIONS TOUR FINISH:
T24—Outback Steakhouse Pro-Am.

2004 SEASON:
For the second consecutive year, matched his age at the MasterCard Championship in Hawaii with a final-round 68 at Hualalai...Bettered his age for the first time in his career when he closed with 5-under 66 in the final round of the Outback Steakhouse Pro-Am, where he posted his top finish, a T24...Made his 47th start in the Masters, moving into second place on the all-time list for starts behind Arnold Palmer (50), but did not make the cut...Competed at the BMW Charity Pro-Am at The Cliffs on the Nationwide Tour (missed cut)...Served as captain of the Rest of the World squad at the UBS Cup.

CHAMPIONS TOUR CAREER HIGHLIGHTS:
2003: Shot his age for the second time in his career when he fashioned a second-round 67 at the MasterCard Championship in Hawaii, and eventually finished T29...Best finish came in Mexico City where he was T22 at the MasterCard Classic...Served as captain of the International Team at the Presidents Cup in South Africa. **2002:** Turned in strong performance at the Farmers Charity Classic in May. Was a one-stroke victor in the Georgia-Pacific Grand Champions competition and then finished T9 in the tournament, his best effort since a T8 at the 2001 Senior PGA Championship...Entered the open qualifier for the British Open, but was forced to withdraw due to a pulled rib muscle. **2001:** Appeared in his 46th and final British Open at Royal Lytham & St. Annes, site of his 1974 victory...Named as the World Golf Hall of Fame's Global Ambassador late in the year. **2000:** Opened with an 8-under 64 at the BellSouth Senior Classic at Opryland, at the time, the youngest ever to shoot his age on the Champions Tour. His 36-hole total of 11-under-par 133 was good enough to win the Georgia-Pacific Grand Champions title in Nashville...Had a dramatic victory at the Senior Skins competition in January. Birdied the first extra hole to claim four skins and $220,000, good enough to defeat Tom Watson, Jack Nicklaus and Arnold Palmer at Mauna Lani. **1999:** Claimed the Georgia-Pacific Grand Champions title at the Pacific Bell Senior Classic, defeating Al Geiberger by four strokes...In July, received a third doctorate from the University of Dundee, Scotland. **1998:** Just two months shy of his 63rd birthday, became the second-oldest

CHAMPIONS TOUR CAREER SUMMARY — **PLAYOFF RECORD: 4-2**

Year	Events Played	1st	2nd	3rd	Top 10	Top 25	Earnings	Rank
1985	1	1			1	1	$30,000	44
1986	17	3	4	2	13	17	291,190	5
1987	20	3	2	3	16	20	333,439	6
1988	20	5	2	3	16	18	435,914	2
1989	18	2	1	1	11	17	514,116	4
1990	22	1	4	2	13	20	507,268	9
1991	20	1	1	2	9	17	337,253	18
1992	21		2	3	9	16	346,798	23
1993	22	1	1		6	15	360,272	26
1994	22		1	1	4	12	309,776	30
1995	20	1			2	11	309,251	38
1996	23		3		7	13	494,714	24
1997	22				1	10	208,615	62
1998	18	1			5	15	455,206	37
1999	20				2	7	235,181	61
2000	21					7	199,579	70
2001	21				3	4	256,013	63
2002	18				1	1	109,006	90
2003	15					1	78,690	93
2004	15					1	62,287	96
Total	376	19	21	17	119	223	5,874,569	

COMBINED ALL-TIME MONEY (3 TOURS): **$7,709,051**

CHAMPIONS TOUR TOP TOURNAMENT SUMMARY

Year	86	87	88	89	90	91	92	93	94	95	96	97	98
Senior PGA Championship	1	8	1	T8	1	T8	5	T16	T19	T60	T31	T20	T39
U.S. Senior Open	2	1	1	T9	T3	T8	T3	T17	T13	T19	T60	T21	
Ford Senior Players	T14	1	T3	3	T18	T43	T18	T33	T42		T49	T49	
JELD-WEN Tradition				2	2	T15	T20	T17	T27	T17	T9	T51	T17
Charles Schwab Cup Champ											T26		

Year	99	00	01	02	03	04
Senior PGA Championship	T43	T46	T8	T45	CUT	CUT
U.S. Senior Open		CUT	57	CUT	T54	CUT
Ford Senior Players	T29	T57	T56			T58
Senior British Open					T51	CUT
JELD-WEN Tradition	T50	T34	T19	T62	75	T64

Gary Player (continued)

winner in the history of the Champions Tour with his one-stroke victory over J.C. Snead and Walter Hall at the Northville Long Island Classic...Captured his fourth consecutive MasterCard Champions title the day before and thus became the fourth player (fifth time) to "double dip," claiming both events in the same week. **1997:** Received an honorary Doctor of Science award from the University of Ulster in Ireland...Inducted into the Captains Club at the 1997 Memorial Tournament. **1996:** Won three MasterCard Champions titles in his first year in the over-60 competition...Fell to Walter Morgan on the first hole of a playoff at the FHP Health Care Classic at Ojai, CA. **1995:** Captured his second Bank One Classic in three years when he returned to Lexington and shot a final-round 64. Came from four strokes back on Sunday, thanks to eight birdies...Received an honorary Doctor of Laws degree from St. Andrews University in Scotland and was the recipient of the Hilton Hotel Lifetime Achievement Award. **1994:** Competed in his 40th consecutive British Open at Turnberry in Scotland...Named an Honorary Member of the Royal & Ancient GC of St. Andrews. **1993:** Celebrated his 40th year as a professional with his 38th TOUR victory, a three-stroke win over Dale Douglass at the Bank One Classic in Lexington, KY. **1991:** Started the year with a victory at the Royal Caribbean Classic, his seventh straight season capturing at least one Champions Tour title. **1990:** Outdueled Jack Nicklaus and Lee Trevino for his third PGA Seniors' Championship, the last of his six senior majors...Received the South African Sportsman of the Century Award. **1989:** Had his biggest earnings year in golf, thanks to a $202,500 paycheck for winning the Vantage Championship, the largest first prize of his illustrious career...Also successfully defended his crown at the rain-shortened GTE North Classic in Indianapolis, beating Al Geiberger, Joe Jimenez and Billy Casper by a stroke. **1988:** Won a career-high five times in 20 starts, including his second PGA Seniors' Championship and second U.S. Senior Open...Was three strokes better than Chi Chi Rodriguez at PGA National and defeated good friend Bob Charles in an 18-hole playoff at Medinah for the U.S. Senior Open crown. **1987:** Sank an eight-foot birdie putt on the 72nd hole for the Mazda Senior Tournament Players Championship at Sawgrass FL...Cruised to a six-shot victory at the U.S. Senior Open at Brooklawn CC in Fairfield, CT and became the third man to hold both the U.S. Open and U.S. Senior Open titles. **1986:** Defeated Lee Elder by two strokes for his first Champions Tour major, the General Foods PGA Seniors' Championship, and went on to claim two other events in consecutive weeks—the United Hospitals Seniors and the Denver Post Champions. **1985:** Fifth of 10 men to win his first Champions Tour start when he claimed the Quadel Seniors Classic at Boca Grove Plantation by three strokes over Ken Still and Jim Ferree.

OTHER CAREER HIGHLIGHTS:

One of the most successful international golfers of all time, he has 163 tournament wins worldwide...His nine major titles include three Masters Tournaments, three British Opens, two PGA Championships and one U.S. Open...Last Masters victory came in 1978, when he began the final round seven strokes behind Hubert Green and shot 64, winning by one after birdies on seven of the final 10 holes...One week later, he came from seven strokes back in the final round to win the Tournament of Champions...Won three consecutive tournaments on the PGA TOUR when he captured the Houston Open the week following his Tournament of Champions victory in 1978...Only player in the 20th century to win a British Open in three different decades...Completed his Grand Slam in 1965 at age 29 with his U.S. Open victory at Bellerive near St. Louis...Won at least one TOUR event in five different decades...Had his best year on the PGA TOUR in 1978, earning $177,336...Leading money-winner on the PGA TOUR in 1961...Inducted into the World Golf Hall of Fame in 1974...Has 23 career holes-in-one...Once shot a 59 in a round at the 1974 Brazilian Open.

PERSONAL:

Dubbed the Black Knight, Mr. Fitness and the International Ambassador of Golf...A renowned golf course architect with over 200 design projects located throughout the world. Designer of the course at the TPC at Jasna Polana near Princeton, NJ, and The Links at Fancourt in South Africa—the site of the 2003 Presidents Cup...Operates Black Knight International, which includes Gary Player Group, Gary Player Design, Gary Player Golf Academy and Gary Player Enterprises—aspects of which include licensing, publishing, videos, apparel, golf equipment and memorabilia...Gary Player Stud Farm has received worldwide acclaim for breeding top horses...Operates The Player Foundation, with its primary objective to promote education for underprivileged children. The Foundation built the Blair Atholl Schools in Johannesburg, South Africa, which has educational facilities for more than 500 students from kindergarten through the seventh grade and also supports other educational projects throughout the world...Says his biggest thrill in golf is being the third player in history after Gene Sarazen and Ben Hogan to win all four Grand Slam events...Has traveled more miles than any athlete in history - more than 14 million and counting...At one point in his career, traveled with his six children and more than 30 pieces of luggage that sometimes took as many as three taxis to transport...Among his heroes are Winston Churchill, Mother Teresa, Nelson Mandela and Mahatma Gandhi...Among his favorite golf courses are The Links at Fancourt in his native South Africa, Cypress Point, Carnoustie and the TPC at Jasna Polana...One of his superstitions or lucky charms is wearing black...Favorite athletes are Michael Jordan and Pele...Web site is GaryPlayer.com.

PLAYER STATISTICS

2004 CHAMPIONS TOUR STATISTICS:

Scoring Average	74.39	(77)
Driving Distance	246.7	(80)
Driving Accuracy Percentage	73.5%	(24)
Total Driving	104	(69)
Greens in Regulation Pct.	55.1%	(79)
Putting Average	1.814	(52)
Sand Save Percentage	45.9%	(38)
Eagles (Holes per)	792.0	(68)
Birdie Average	2.50	(72)
All-Around Ranking	490	(74)

MISCELLANEOUS CHAMPIONS TOUR STATISTICS

2004 Low Round: 66–2004 Outback Steakhouse Pro-Am/3
Career Low Round: 63–1993 GTE West Classic/1
Career Largest Paycheck: $202,500–1989 The RJR Championship/1

MISCELLANEOUS PGA TOUR STATISTICS

2004 Low Round: 80–Masters Tournament/2
Career Low Round: 62–1976 Florida Citrus Open/3
Career Largest Paycheck: $62,500–1984 PGA Championship/T2

Dan Pohl (POLE)

EXEMPT STATUS: PGA TOUR Career Victory List
FULL NAME: Danny Joe Pohl
HEIGHT: 5-11
WEIGHT: 175
BIRTHDATE: April 1, 1955
BIRTHPLACE: Mt. Pleasant, MI
RESIDENCE: Phoenix, AZ
FAMILY: Wife, Mitzi; Michelle (2/2/78), Joshua Daniel (9/10/84), Taylor Whitney (9/10/86)
EDUCATION: University of Arizona
SPECIAL INTERESTS: Fishing, hunting, course design
TURNED PROFESSIONAL: 1977
JOINED PGA TOUR: 1978

JOINED CHAMPIONS TOUR: 2005

PGA TOUR VICTORIES (2): 1986 Colonial National Invitation, NEC World Series of Golf.

OTHER VICTORIES (2): 1975 Michigan Amateur. **1977** Michigan Amateur.

PGA TOUR CAREER EARNINGS: $3,112,263

PGA TOUR PLAYOFF RECORD: 1-2

BEST 2004 PGA TOUR FINISH: T68—Bank of America Colonial.

2004 SEASON:
Competed on both the PGA TOUR and Nationwide Tours...Made three starts on the PGA TOUR—Bank of America Colonial (T68), John Deere Classic (missed cut) and the B.C. Open (missed cut)—and earned $10,706...Made cut in his initial appearance on the Nationwide Tour at the Chitimacha Louisiana Open, where he finished T19. Failed to make the cut in three other starts.

OTHER CAREER HIGHLIGHTS:
Played full-time on the PGA TOUR from 1979-1996, with 386 of his 424 career starts coming in that in that span. Made 301 cuts, with 70 top-10 finishes...Owns two career victories, both of which came in 1986. The first was in a playoff at the rain-shortened Colonial National Invitation where he birdied the first extra hole to defeat Payne Stewart. Three months later was victorious at the NEC World Series of Golf, which earned him an automatic 10-year exemption on the PGA TOUR. Was tied with Lanny Wadkins after 54 holes, and despite a bogey on the final hole, held on for a one-stroke victory over Wadkins at Firestone CC...Finished second a total of seven times, including a pair of playoff losses at the 1982 Masters and the 1985 Canon-Sammy Davis Jr.-Greater Hartford Open. Watched Craig Stadler make a par on the first extra hole to fall at Augusta and was one of three in a playoff near Hartford (Jodie Mudd the other) when Phil Blackmar birdied the first extra hole for the win...Second-most lucrative season on the PGA TOUR came in 1986, with earnings totaling $463,630. In addition to his wins, he was also second to Greg Norman at the Las Vegas Invitational that year...The following year enjoyed a career-best season, with earnings of $465,269, highlighted by a career-best nine top-10 finishes. Made the cut in 24 of 26 starts and was fifth on the money list...Third-place finisher at the 1981 PGA Championship...Career has been sidetracked by numerous injuries, necessitating surgeries on back (1989), both knees (1994) and neck (1995). Missed all of the 1990 season due to back surgery...Winner of the 1987 Vardon Trophy for the lowest scoring average and Epson Stats All-Around title...Led the PGA TOUR in Driving Distance in 1980-81...Member of U.S. Ryder Cup squad in 1987.

PERSONAL:
Named to the Michigan Golf Hall of Fame in May 2004...Has been involved in course design work, including the PohlCat Golf Course in Mt. Pleasant, MI...Starred as a collegian at the University of Arizona.

PLAYER STATISTICS

MISCELLANEOUS PGA TOUR STATISTICS
2004 Low Round: 69–John Deere Classic/1
Career Low Round: 62–1989 Honda Classic/2
Career Largest Paycheck: $126,000–1986 NEC World Series of Golf/1

SECTION 2 PLAYER BIOGRAPHIES

Don Pooley

EXEMPT STATUS: Net-70 on All-Time Money List
FULL NAME: Sheldon George Pooley, Jr.
HEIGHT: 6-3
WEIGHT: 195
BIRTHDATE: August 27, 1951
BIRTHPLACE: Phoenix, AZ
RESIDENCE: Tucson, AZ
FAMILY: Wife, Margaret; Lynn (1/19/80), Kerri (5/19/82)
EDUCATION: University of Arizona (1973, Business Administration)
SPECIAL INTERESTS: Family, reading, shooting sports
TURNED PROFESSIONAL: 1973
JOINED PGA TOUR: 1975

JOINED CHAMPIONS TOUR: 2001

CHAMPIONS TOUR VICTORIES (2): 2002 U.S. Senior Open. **2003** Allianz Championship.

2004 CHARLES SCHWAB CUP FINISH: 33rd - 424 points

PGA TOUR VICTORIES (2): 1980 B.C. Open. **1987** Memorial Tournament.

OTHER VICTORIES (2): 1989 Ebel Match Play. **1992** Amoco Centel Championship.

PGA TOUR CAREER EARNINGS: $3,296,615

BEST 2004 CHAMPIONS TOUR FINISHES: T4—Liberty Mutual Legends of Golf; T5—Senior British Open; T7—The ACE Group Classic; T10—3M Championship.

2004 SEASON:

Moved up one spot on the money list from the previous season, with earnings just over a half-million dollars despite injury problems during the year. Underwent hernia surgery in the spring and also battled back problems in the latter stages of the campaign...Made nice showing at the Senior British Open. Shared the first- and second-round leads at Royal Portrush GC and remained in the hunt all four days before eventually finishing T5 in Northern Ireland, three behind winner Pete Oakley. His opening-round, 3-under-par 69 included consecutive eagles on Nos. 9 and 10...Finished T4 at the Liberty Mutual Legends of Golf in his last start before undergoing hernia surgery in late April...Shared the second-round lead at the Royal Caribbean Golf Classic with Wayne Levi but shot a closing-round 77 and finished T13...Was T7 the following week at The ACE Group Classic in Naples, FL...Other top-10 finish came in August at the 3M Championship where he was T10.

CHAMPIONS TOUR CAREER HIGHLIGHTS:

2003: Underwent surgery on January 3 at the Hughston Clinic in Columbus, GA, to repair a labrum tear in his left shoulder. Originally injured the shoulder in the spring of 2002, hitting balls on a wet surface at Bruno's Memorial Classic...Was scheduled to return to the circuit in April but re-injured the shoulder during rehab and did not start his season until the Columbus Southern Open in mid-May with a T45 in Georgia...Completed his comeback with a three-stroke victory at the Allianz Championship in Iowa, thanks to three consecutive sub-70 rounds. Used an eagle on the par-5 11th hole at Glen Oaks to overtake former major league baseball pitcher Rick Rhoden and then cruised to an easy victory despite playing his last seven holes of the event in even par...Showed signs that he was ready to contend again two weeks earlier in Minnesota. Set a new course and tournament record at the 3M Championship in August when he shot a 9-under-par 63 in the second round at the TPC of the Twin Cities. Was just one stroke off the pace after his record round, but shot a 1-over-par 73 on Sunday to finish T10...Voted by his peers as Comeback Player of the Year. **2002:** One of only two players (Rodger Davis) to finish among the top 31 money-winners after earning exempt status at the 2001 National Qualifying Tournament. Was one of a record 17 millionaires on the Champions Tour and earned more than twice his best year on the PGA TOUR ($450,005, 1987)...Won the biggest event of his career in his 22nd start on the Champions Tour. Became the first qualifier to win the U.S. Senior Open and just the sixth player to claim the prestigious event in his first attempt. Holed a dramatic 10-foot birdie putt on the fifth extra hole of a playoff to beat Tom Watson. Moved into the lead in the third round by shooting a course-record 8-under 63 at Caves Valley GC near Baltimore, the lowest 18-hole score ever posted in U.S. Senior Open history. Got into the championship through the USGA qualifier in Nashville (116 players for five spots). Made a two-foot birdie putt on the last hole to advance into a three-man playoff for the final two spots. Secured a spot with a 15-foot birdie putt on the first extra hole. Victory at Caves Valley also ended a TOUR victory drought of 15 years, one month. **2001:** Debuted on the Champions Tour at the Kroger Senior Classic and T4 at the rain-shortened event near Cincinnati...Also T4 later in the fall campaign at the Gold Rush Classic near Sacramento. Prepped for the Champions Tour by playing in three PGA TOUR and seven Nationwide Tour events...T5 at the Charity Pro-Am at The Cliffs near Greenville, SC...Earned a full exemption for the 2002 season by virtue of his sixth-place finish at the National Qualifying Tournament in the fall.

OTHER CAREER HIGHLIGHTS:

Played in 540 events on the PGA TOUR from 1976-2000, making 354 cuts...Best season came in 1987 when he earned a career-best $450,005, thanks to a win at The Memorial Tournament...Battled various injuries in the early '90s. Suffered a ruptured disc in his neck taking practice swings and underwent surgery in January of 1992. Followed with lower back surgery in October of 1993...Went from Oct. 1993-April 1994 and May-September 1994 without touching a club...First career victory came at 1980 B.C. Open, where he closed with 68 for one-stroke win over Peter Jacobsen...Came from four strokes behind on final day of the 1987 Memorial Tournament to overtake Scott Hoch...Made a Million-Dollar Hole-in-One at 1987 Bay Hill Classic...His 192-yard 4-iron hit 17th hole flagstick two feet the above cup and dropped in. Arnold Palmer Children's Hospital received $500,000 with his effort...Winner of 1992 Amoco Centel Championship...Won 1985 Vardon Trophy...Led PGA TOUR in Putting in 1988 and again in 1997...Recorded three eagles in one round of the 1992 Texas Open...Has made four career holes-in-one.

PERSONAL:

Has been involved in the PGA TOUR Bible study throughout his career and has been involved with the Fellowship of Christian Athletes...Helped coach his daughter's basketball teams at one point. Daughter, Kerri, played point guard at Biola University near Los Angeles...Likes Mexican food....Among his other interests are all kinds of shooting (trap, skeet and sporting clay)...Got started in golf at age 6. Caddie Cliff Moore used to be his club professional and has been his instructor since he was a junior in high school...Favorite golf course is Pebble Beach...Member of the University of Arizona Hall of Fame and the Riverside (CA) Hall of Fame.

PLAYER STATISTICS

MISCELLANEOUS CHAMPIONS TOUR STATISTICS
2004 Low Round: 65–2004 MasterCard Championship/2
Career Low Round: 63–2 times, most recent 2003 3M Championship/2
Career Largest Paycheck: $450,000–2002 U.S. Senior Open/1

MISCELLANEOUS PGA TOUR STATISTICS
2004 Low Round: 70–Chrysler Classic of Tucson/2
Career Low Round: 61–1986 Phoenix Open/2
Career Largest Paycheck: $140,000–1987 Memorial Tournament/1

CHAMPIONS TOUR CAREER SUMMARY — PLAYOFF RECORD: 1-0

Year	Events Played	1st	2nd	3rd	Top 10	Top 25	Earnings	Rank
2001	7				4	6	$266,976	60
2002	29	1		1	8	18	1,155,456	17
2003	15	1			3	7	491,012	38
2004	21				4	9	524,974	37
Total	72	2		1	19	40	2,438,418	
COMBINED ALL-TIME MONEY (3 TOURS):							**$5,775,168**	

CHAMPIONS TOUR TOP TOURNAMENT SUMMARY

Year	02	03	04
Senior PGA Championship	T18	CUT	
U.S. Senior Open	1	T43	T15
Ford Senior Players	T22	T40	T13
Senior British Open		T27	T5
JELD-WEN Tradition	T9	T14	T53
Charles Schwab Cup Champ	27		

CHAMPIONS TOUR YEAR-BY-YEAR STATISTICS (TOP 50 ON 2004 MONEY LIST)

	Scoring Average	Putting Average	Greens in Regulation	Driving Distance	Driving Accuracy
2001	69.40 (N/A)	1.720 (N/A)	73.1 (N/A)	280.9 (N/A)	68.4 (N/A)
2002	70.59 (16)	1.756 (4)	66.7 (T42)	267.9 (T47)	66.4 (T55)
2003	70.94 (29)	1.791 (37)	68.9 (30)	266.7 (62)	71.9 (26)
2004	71.35 (31)	1.785 (T25)	65.5 (52)	270.2 (49)	69.1 (T50)

Tom Purtzer

EXEMPT STATUS: Top 30 on 2004 Champions Tour Money List
FULL NAME: Thomas Warren Purtzer
HEIGHT: 6-0
WEIGHT: 210
BIRTHDATE: December 5, 1951
BIRTHPLACE: Des Moines, IA
RESIDENCE: Green Valley, AZ

FAMILY: Wife, Lori; Laura (7/3/80); Ashley (12/5/83), Eric (11/5/85), Liza Jane (2/10/96), twins Jay Warren and Jennifer Ann (5/7/98), twins Robin and Juli (8/25/02)
CLUB AFFILIATION: Desert Mountain GC (Scottsdale, AZ)
EDUCATION: Arizona State University (1973, Business)
SPECIAL INTERESTS: All sports, music, auto racing, muscle cars
TURNED PROFESSIONAL: 1973
JOINED PGA TOUR: 1975

JOINED CHAMPIONS TOUR: 2001

CHAMPIONS TOUR VICTORIES (2): 2003 SBC Classic. **2004** Toshiba Senior Classic.

2004 CHARLES SCHWAB CUP FINISH: T21st - 842 points

PGA TOUR VICTORIES (5): 1977 Glen Campbell-Los Angeles Open. **1984** Phoenix Open. **1988** Gatlin Brothers-Southwest Golf Classic. **1991** Southwestern Bell Colonial, NEC World Series of Golf.

OTHER VICTORIES (3): 1991 Shark Shootout [with Lanny Wadkins]. **1993** Fred Meyer Challenge [with Steve Elkington]. **1996** JCPenney Mixed Team Classic [with Juli Inkster].

PGA TOUR CAREER EARNINGS: $4,134,028

PGA TOUR PLAYOFF RECORD: 2-0

BEST 2004 CHAMPIONS TOUR FINISHES:

1—Toshiba Senior Classic; T2—Bank of America Championship; T3—Outback Steakhouse Pro-Am, 3M Championship; 5—MasterCard Championship.

2004 SEASON:

Narrowly missed hitting the $1-million mark in season earnings for the second straight year when he closed the year with $997,367 in official money. However, played in seven fewer events mainly due to back problems (sliding disc in lower back), which troubled him for most of the season...Tied the Champions Tour's all-time record and set a course record with an 11-under 60 (nine birdies and an eagle) in the first round of the Toshiba Senior Classic before going on to win at Newport Beach CC by one stroke over Morris Hatalsky. Used birdies on two of the last four holes to secure the Toshiba victory, his second title on the Champions Tour...Was the 18- and 36-hole leader at the Bank of America Championship, but eventually T2 near Boston, four strokes back of Craig Stadler, after posting an even-par 72 on Sunday...Also was the 36-hole leader at the 3M Championship for the second consecutive year, but eventually T3 after carding a final-round 74...Was T3 at the Outback Steakhouse Pro-Am, two strokes behind eventual winner Mark McNulty...Champions Tour Player of the Month in March, thanks to his win and a solo sixth-place finish at the SBC Classic the previous week...Led all players once again in Driving Distance at 294.8 yards per drive and was also second in Greens in Regulation behind Hale Irwin.

CHAMPIONS TOUR CAREER HIGHLIGHTS:

2003: Was among 17 players to earn over $1 million for the season...Earned his first Champions Tour victory when he drained an eagle putt of 58 feet, 3 inches to edge Gil Morgan at the SBC Classic by one stroke. Came to the final hole trailing Morgan by two strokes, but became the first player to make an eagle on the final hole and win an event since Sammy Rachels did so at the 2001 Transamerica. Had a hole-in-one in the opening round, the first player to do so and win the event since Bob Gilder at the 2002 Kroger Senior Classic...Was the second-round leader at the 3M Championship and was tied for the lead the final day until hitting two balls into the water for a quadruple bogey at the 17th hole. Eventually finished T10...Reeled off nine straight sub-70 rounds from the final day of the Verizon Classic through the last round of the Emerald Coast Classic (a cumulative 34-under-par). His string of sub-70 rounds stood as the best run on the 2003 Champions Tour until Craig Stadler raised it to 10 late in the year...Led all players in Driving Distance at 298.3, the best number posted in Champions Tour history. Also led the PGA TOUR in that category in 1990 at 279. **2002:** Official earnings of $760,056 topped his best year on the PGA TOUR (1991: $750,568)...Balanced eight top-10 finishes among 23 starts...Debuted on the Champions Tour at the Royal Caribbean Classic and T7. It was his first top 10 since finishing T4 at the 1998 Walt Disney World Classic on the PGA TOUR. Was in contention early in the final round, but faded after playing the back nine on Sunday in 1-over par. Was the early leader in the event on Friday before steady rains washed out the round. Rebounded with a 67 in the opening round at Crandon Park on Saturday...Best performance of the season was a T3 at the SBC Senior Classic near Los Angeles in early March. Was the first-round leader at Valencia CC and one of just two players to break par, after carding a 2-under 70 in cool, windy conditions on Friday...Vaulted into the top 31 for good when he T5 at the Napa Valley Championship and earned a $50,700 paycheck.

OTHER CAREER HIGHLIGHTS:

Five TOUR victories in 25-year career included two in 1991. Made up four-stroke deficit at 1991 Southwestern Bell Colonial with closing 64, good for three-stroke victory. NEC World Series of Golf win that season earned him a 10-year exemption that expired when he turned 50...Won first TOUR title at Riviera in 1977 at the Glen Campbell-Los Angeles Open, edging Lanny Wadkins by a shot...Other wins came at 1984 Phoenix Open and 1988 Gatlin Brothers-Southwest Classic...Was the medalist in the 1979 U.S. vs. Japan event and played for the PGA TOUR in the Four Tours Championship in 1991...Has had seven career holes-in-one in competitive rounds.

PERSONAL:

Has been described as having "sweetest" swing on TOUR...Brother Paul played PGA TOUR in 1970s and early 1980s...Close friend of former Milwaukee Brewer star and Hall of Famer Robin Yount as well as country singer Vince Gill...Lists the births of his kids as his biggest thrill outside of golf...Favorite golf course is Riviera CC near Los Angeles...Enjoys Mexican food.

PLAYER STATISTICS

MISCELLANEOUS CHAMPIONS TOUR STATISTICS
2004 Low Round: 60–2004 Toshiba Senior Classic/1
Career Low Round: 60–2004 Toshiba Senior Classic/1
Career Largest Paycheck: $240,000–2004 Toshiba Senior Classic/1

MISCELLANEOUS PGA TOUR STATISTICS
Career Low Round: 62–1988 Northern Telecom Tucson Open/2
Career Largest Paycheck: $216,000–2 times, most recent 1991 NEC World Series of Golf/1

CHAMPIONS TOUR CAREER SUMMARY — PLAYOFF RECORD: 0-0

Year	Events Played	1st	2nd	3rd	Top 10	Top 25	Earnings	Rank
2002	23			1	8	12	$760,056	27
2003	24	1			11	18	1,043,977	16
2004	19	1	1	2	8	11	997,367	17
Total	66	2	1	3	27	41	2,801,401	
COMBINED ALL-TIME MONEY (3 TOURS):							**$6,935,429**	

CHAMPIONS TOUR TOP TOURNAMENT SUMMARY

Year	02	03	04
Senior PGA Championship	CUT		
U.S. Senior Open	T56	CUT	T29
Ford Senior Players	T17	T5	T54
JELD-WEN Tradition	T7	T16	T29
Charles Schwab Cup Champ	T5	T7	T22

CHAMPIONS TOUR YEAR-BY-YEAR STATISTICS (TOP 50 ON 2004 MONEY LIST)

	Scoring Average	Putting Average	Greens in Regulation	Driving Distance	Driving Accuracy
2002	70.87 (19)	1.824 (T62)	73.0 (4)	280.6 (6)	65.9 (57)
2003	70.05 (11)	1.780 (T24)	73.1 (3)	298.3 (1)	63.6 (T62)
2004	70.24 (T7)	1.805 (42)	75.2 (2)	294.8 (1)	63.7 (67)

Dana Quigley

EXEMPT STATUS: Top 30 on 2004 Champions Tour Money List
FULL NAME: Dana C. Quigley
HEIGHT: 6-2
WEIGHT: 190
BIRTHDATE: April 14, 1947
BIRTHPLACE: Lynnfield Centre, MA
RESIDENCE: West Palm Beach, FL
FAMILY: Wife, Angie; Nicole (8/25/81), Devon (8/18/84)
CLUB AFFILIATION: Crestwood CC (Rehoboth, MA)
EDUCATION: University of Rhode Island (1969, Business)
SPECIAL INTERESTS: Baseball, hockey, all sports, planes, boats
TURNED PROFESSIONAL: 1971
JOINED PGA TOUR: 1973

JOINED CHAMPIONS TOUR: 1997

CHAMPIONS TOUR VICTORIES (8): 1997 Northville Long Island Classic. **1998** Emerald Coast Classic, Raley's Gold Rush Classic. **2000** TD Waterhouse Championship. **2001** SBC Senior Open. **2002** Siebel Classic in Silicon Valley, SBC Championship. **2003** MasterCard Championship.

OTHER SENIOR VICTORIES (2): 2001 Hyundai Team Matches [with Allen Doyle]. **2002** Hyundai Team Matches [with Allen Doyle].

2004 CHARLES SCHWAB CUP FINISH:
18th - 922 points

BEST PGA TOUR CAREER FINISH:
6—1980 Greater Milwaukee Open.

OTHER VICTORIES (16): 1973 Rhode Island Open. **1981** Rhode Island Open. **1982** Massachusetts Open. **1983** Massachusetts Open. **1984** Massachusetts Open. **1985** New England PGA Championship. **1986** Vermont Open. **1987** Vermont Open. **1989** New England PGA Championship. **1991** New England PGA Championship. **1992** Rhode Island Open. **1993** Rhode Island Open, New England PGA Championship. **1995** Rhode Island Open. **1996** Rhode Island Open, New England PGA Championship.

PGA TOUR CAREER EARNINGS: $92,298

BEST 2004 CHAMPIONS TOUR FINISHES:
2—MasterCard Championship, Royal Caribbean Golf Classic; T5—Bank of America Championship, Ford Senior Players Championship.

2004 SEASON:

Played in all 30 events and has now teed it up in every Champions Tour event for the last seven seasons...Appearance at the season-ending Charles Schwab Cup Championship was his 262nd consecutive start for which he's been eligible and his 248th straight event overall...Went over seven figures in official earnings for the seventh straight season as a result of top-10 performances in almost a third of his events...Did not win an event for the first time in four years...Best two performances of the year came in his first two starts...Fell one stroke short of Fuzzy Zoeller in defense of his MasterCard Championship title in Hawaii, despite a final-round 65 that included four birdies in his last six holes...Followed runner-up performance at Hualalai with another strong outing two weeks later at the Royal Caribbean Golf Classic near Miami. Began the final round five strokes off the lead, but made a spirited run at Bruce Fleisher before ending up one stroke back despite a 4-under-par 68 in windy conditions...Made 22 birdies at Nashawtuc in the Bank of America Championship, yet finished T5 near Boston...Had strong performance at the Ford Senior Players Championship, with a T5 finish, his top effort in a major championship since T2 in Dearborn in 2000. Performance in Michigan came in his 250th consecutive start for which he was eligible...Led the Champions Tour in Birdies for the second straight year with 363 and T2 in Sub-Par Rounds with 55.

CHAMPIONS TOUR CAREER HIGHLIGHTS:

2003: Led the Champions Tour in Birdies with 381...Won the season-opener at the MasterCard Championship. Birdied two of the last three holes in Sunday's final round, including the 18th, to nip Larry Nelson by two strokes for his eighth career Champions Tour title. Earned a career-best $250,000 for the victory at Hualalai...T2 along with David Eger at the Liberty Mutual Legends of Golf, one stroke back of Bruce Lietzke. Performance in Savannah came during a run of 13 straight par/better rounds. **2002:** Claimed more than one event in a season for the first time since 1998. Had 11 of his 12 top 10s in the first half of the year, but his lone top-10 performance in the second half of the season was a big one. Celebrated his 200th consecutive start by winning the SBC Championship in San Antonio. Seventh victory of his career came by one stroke over Bob Gilder at Oak Hills CC...Named Player of the Month for March after claiming his sixth career title. Edged Bob Gilder and Fuzzy Zoeller by one stroke at the Siebel Classic in Silicon Valley. Finished with a 2-under-par 70 on Sunday in cold, rainy conditions at Coyote Creek GC...At Bruno's Memorial Classic, lost to Sammy Rachels on second hole of playoff. Tournament was his 178th consecutive start for which he was eligible, a new Champions Tour record, surpassing Mike McCullough's mark of 177...Made his second career hole-in-one on the Champions Tour in the second round of the SBC Senior Open. Holed a 7-iron shot from 163 yards on the 13th hole of the Port Course at Harborside International. **2001:** The busiest player on the Champions Tour, with 37 official starts (112 rounds)...Won his fifth Champions Tour title at the SBC Senior Open near Chicago. Three consecutive sub-70 rounds gave him a five-stroke victory over Jay Sigel at Kemper Lakes...Had the year's final hole-in-one at the SENIOR TOUR Championship at Gaillardia in the third round. **2000:** Had his finest financial season, finishing fourth on the money list with $1,802,063...Set a new mark when he played in all 39 official events, breaking old record of 38, held by four players, including himself. Played more rounds than any other player (114)...Drained a 12-foot birdie putt on the final hole to defeat hometown favorite Tom Watson for the TD Waterhouse Championship title in Kansas City. Winning putt came just moments after Watson had placed his 8-iron approach shot within a foot of the cup, setting up a possible playoff. **1999:** The Champions Tour "ironman," he played every round (119) of every official event (38)...Registered 18 top 10s (second to Bruce Fleisher)...Set an all-time record for lowest 36-hole score in relation to par (18-under 126) at the Novell Utah Showdown when he posted his two lowest rounds of the season on successive days. Achieved a personal best on the Champions Tour when he set the Park Meadows CC course record on Saturday with a sizzling 10-under 62, then added a 64 on Sunday to move into a tie with Dave Eichelberger at the end of regulation. Lost to Eichelberger in overtime when he missed a short par putt on the first extra hole...Led the circuit in Sub-Par Rounds (77) and Total Birdies (418). **1998:** Won a pair of titles and was over the $1-million mark in official earnings for the

CHAMPIONS TOUR CAREER SUMMARY — PLAYOFF RECORD: 1-2

Year	Events Played	1st	2nd	3rd	Top 10	Top 25	Earnings	Rank
1997	20	1			3	10	$427,774	36
1998	38	2	1		15	28	1,103,882	7
1999	38		2	3	18	27	1,327,658	6
2000	39	1	5	2	18	28	1,802,063	5
2001	37	1	2	2	14	27	1,537,931	9
2002	35	2	2		12	24	1,569,972	6
2003	31	1	1	1	12	25	1,303,304	11
2004	30		2		9	20	1,090,649	14
Total	268	8	15	8	101	189	10,163,233	

COMBINED ALL-TIME MONEY (3 TOURS): **$10,255,531**

CHAMPIONS TOUR TOP TOURNAMENT SUMMARY

Year	97	98	99	00	01	02	03	04
Senior PGA Championship	T40	T6	T5	T2	T15	T10	T17	CUT
U.S. Senior Open	T12	T16	T11	T26	T11	T25	T50	24
Ford Senior Players	T26	T41	T37	T2	T23	T27	11	T5
Senior British Open							T10	T22
JELD-WEN Tradition		T31	T36	T37	T34	T27	T7	T33
Charles Schwab Cup Champ		25	T5	T27	24	T21	T20	12

CHAMPIONS TOUR YEAR-BY-YEAR STATISTICS (TOP 50 ON 2004 MONEY LIST)

	Scoring Average	Putting Average	Greens in Regulation	Driving Distance	Driving Accuracy
1997	71.29 (T22)	1.814 (T52)	67.1 (21)	261.8 (41)	73.1 (18)
1998	70.94 (14)	1.763 (8)	65.4 (T38)	265.0 (37)	73.2 (T15)
1999	70.39 (10)	1.787 (T33)	70.9 (14)	268.6 (29)	75.1 (T18)
2000	69.85 (9)	1.764 (T13)	72.2 (13)	281.0 (5)	71.0 (T32)
2001	70.43 (12)	1.771 (18)	68.6 (24)	280.6 (T10)	74.3 (T16)
2002	70.50 (14)	1.759 (5)	67.1 (37)	272.9 (27)	70.3 (37)
2003	70.21 (15)	1.772 (T17)	68.1 (T34)	275.7 (T26)	72.2 (T23)
2004	70.76 (17)	1.758 (8)	68.3 (32)	271.3 (43)	75.9 (17)

Chi Chi Rodriguez

WORLD GOLF HALL OF FAME MEMBER (Inducted 1992)
EXEMPT STATUS: Top 30 on All-Time Money List
FULL NAME: Juan Antonio Rodriguez
HEIGHT: 5-7
WEIGHT: 150
BIRTHDATE: October 23, 1935
BIRTHPLACE: Rio Piedras, Puerto Rico
RESIDENCE: Dorado, Puerto Rico; Palm City, FL
FAMILY: Wife, Iwalani; Donnette (4/6/62)
CLUB AFFILIATION: El Legado (Guayama, Puerto Rico)
SPECIAL INTERESTS: Helping kids, bird watching
TURNED PROFESSIONAL: 1960
JOINED PGA TOUR: 1960

JOINED CHAMPIONS TOUR: 1985

CHAMPIONS TOUR VICTORIES (22): 1986 Senior Tournament Players Championship, Digital Seniors Classic, United Virgina Bank Seniors. **1987** General Foods PGA Seniors' Championship, Vantage At The Dominion, United Hospitals Senior Golf Championship, Silver Pages Classic, Senior Players Reunion Pro-Am, Digital Seniors Classic, GTE Northwest Classic. **1988** Doug Sanders Kingwood Celebrity Classic, Digital Seniors Classic. **1989** Crestar Classic. **1990** Las Vegas Senior Classic, Ameritech Senior Open, Sunwest-Charley Pride Classic. **1991** GTE West Classic, Vintage Arco Invitational, Las Vegas Senior Classic, Murata Reunion Pro-Am. **1992** Ko Olina Senior Invitational. **1993** Burnet Senior Classic.

OTHER SENIOR VICTORIES (2): 1988 Senior Skins Game. **1989** Senior Skins Game.

PGA TOUR VICTORIES (8): 1963 Denver Open Invitational. **1964** Lucky International Open, Western Open. **1967** Texas Open Invitational. **1968** Sahara Invitational. **1972** Byron Nelson Golf Classic. **1973** Greater Greensboro Open. **1979** Tallahassee Open.

OTHER VICTORIES (2): 1976 Pepsi Mixed Team Championship [with JoAnn Washam]. **1979** Bahamas Open.

PGA TOUR CAREER EARNINGS: $1,037,106

PGA TOUR PLAYOFF RECORD: 3-1

BEST 2004 CHAMPIONS TOUR FINISH: 75—Kroger Classic.

2004 SEASON:

Appeared in just seven events, the fewest he has played in his career on the Champions Tour. Finished T12 in Raphael Division at Liberty Mutual Legends of Golf.

CHAMPIONS TOUR CAREER HIGHLIGHTS:

2003: Played in just nine official events...Competed in the Raphael Division at the Liberty Mutual Legends of Golf, and along with partner Larry Ziegler, finished T2 in the 36-hole event, two strokes back of winners Gary Koch/Roger Maltbie. **2002:** Came within a shot of shooting his age when he posted a 5-under 67 on the last day of the Bruno's Memorial Classic, his best score since the 2000 Gold Rush Classic (65). **2000:** T3 at the FleetBoston Classic after three straight sub-par rounds, his best finish since T2 at the 1996 Ralphs Senior Classic in Los Angeles. **1998:** Year came to a halt after a mild heart attack in mid-October. Scheduled to play in Sacramento at the Raley's Gold Rush Classic, but was forced to withdraw after having an angioplasty performed. **1996:** Made his fourth hole-in-one on the Champions Tour in the opening round of the Raley's Gold Rush Classic. **1994:** Served as the Grand Marshal for the Tournament of Roses Parade in Pasadena, CA. **1993:** Last of his 22 official victories came at the inaugural Burnet Senior Classic, when he closed with 65 to beat Jim Colbert and Bob Murphy by two strokes...Received the Herb Graffis Award. **1992:** Won the Ko Olina Senior Invitational in Hawaii by six strokes near the end of the year...Inducted into the World Golf Hall of Fame. **1991:** Won all four of his events within seven weeks early in the season and finished the year fourth on the final money list...Claimed the rain-shortened GTE West Classic with a pair of 66s...Birdied the last hole to win the Vintage ARCO Invitational near Palm Springs...Successfully defended his Las Vegas Senior Classic title and then defeated Jim Colbert in a playoff for the Murata Reunion title, his 20th Champions Tour career victory...Almost won the U.S. Senior Open, but fell to Jack Nicklaus in an 18-hole playoff at Oakland Hills CC near Detroit. **1990:** Won three events and was among the top three in nine events overall...Breezed to a seven-stroke victory at the Ameritech Senior Open at Grand Traverse, MI...Also triumphed at the Las Vegas Senior Classic and the Sunwest Bank/Charley Pride Classic. **1989:** Came from two strokes back to defeat Jim Dent and Dick Rhyan for the Crestar Classic title near Richmond...Received the Bob Jones Award, the highest honor bestowed by the USGA. **1988:** Became the first player in Champions Tour annals to win the same event three consecutive years when he claimed the Digital Seniors Classic in Concord, MA...Also won the Doug Sanders Kingwood Celebrity Classic by two strokes over Walt Zembriski and Bob Charles...Received the 1988 Fred Raphael Award for his service to the game, and was honored by the Golf Course Superintendents Association with the Old Tom Morris Award. **1987:** Became the first Champions Tour player to surpass the half-million dollar mark in single-season earnings and earned his second consecutive Byron Nelson Award for the lowest scoring average on the circuit...Won a career-high seven times, including three in a row and a Champions Tour-record four consecutive events that he entered...Claimed his last Champions Tour major championship title, the General Foods PGA Seniors' Championship, coming from six strokes back on the final day to overtake Dale Douglass...Set a Champions Tour record with eight straight birdies (holes 6-13) en route to a win at the Silver Pages Classic in Oklahoma City...Earned his second consecutive Byron Nelson Award with a scoring average of 70.07...Honored by former President Ronald Reagan with the National Puerto Rican Coalition Life Achievement Award. **1986:** Had an outstanding rookie year, winning three tournaments and finishing second seven times...First Champions Tour win was a major, the Senior Tournament Players Championship at Canterbury GC near Cleveland...Edged Gary Player by a stroke for the Digital Seniors Classic and was a three-stroke victor over Don January at the United Virginia Bank Seniors...Received the Card Walker Award from the PGA TOUR for his contributions to junior golf...Earned his first Byron Nelson Award with a scoring average of 69.65. **1985:** Debuted on the Champions Tour in the final event on the schedule, T5 at the Quadel Seniors Classic in Boca Raton, FL.

CHAMPIONS TOUR CAREER SUMMARY — PLAYOFF RECORD: 1-7

Year	Events Played	1st	2nd	3rd	Top 10	Top 25	Earnings	Rank
1985	1				1	1	$7,700	71
1986	25	3	7	3	23	24	399,172	2
1987	27	7	4	3	20	27	509,145	1
1988	27	2	3		14	25	313,940	10
1989	25	1	2		10	16	275,414	17
1990	31	3	2	4	21	27	729,788	5
1991	32	4	5	1	17	27	794,013	4
1992	32	1	4	4	18	24	711,095	5
1993	32	1	4	1	16	27	798,857	5
1994	30		1	2	12	19	571,598	17
1995	28				1	10	194,922	53
1996	27		1		6	13	390,900	33
1997	28				4	16	372,359	42
1998	22				1	2	115,684	72
1999	20				1	4	150,407	73
2000	20			1	2	2	191,170	72
2001	19						31,870	110
2002	19					1	68,177	96
2003	9						8,527	154
2004	7						4,346	183
Total	461	22	33	19	167	265	6,639,084	

COMBINED ALL-TIME MONEY (3 TOURS): $7,676,190

CHAMPIONS TOUR TOP TOURNAMENT SUMMARY

Year	86	87	88	89	90	91	92	93	94	95	96	97	98
Senior PGA Championship	T5	1	2	T19	2	T12	3	T32	T5	T26	T4	T27	CUT
U.S. Senior Open	T10	3	T6	T18	T3	2	7	T4	T32	T29	T17	T21	CUT
Ford Senior Players	1	T2	T26	T10	T5	T25	4	T20	T32		T13	T34	T50
JELD-WEN Tradition				T7	T48	T6	3	T30	T37	WD	T12	T43	70
Charles Schwab Cup Champ					4	T26	T7	T24	T26				

Year	99	00	01	02	03
Senior PGA Championship				CUT	
U.S. Senior Open	CUT	T37	CUT		
Ford Senior Players	T33	T60	73		
JELD-WEN Tradition	T65	WD	T67		78

Chi Chi Rodriguez (continued)

OTHER CAREER HIGHLIGHTS:

Played the PGA TOUR from 1960-81...First PGA TOUR win came at the 1963 Denver Open...Came back from elbow surgery in 1971 with a playoff victory over Billy Casper at the 1972 Byron Nelson Classic...Last PGA TOUR victory came in 1979 at the Tallahassee Open with a tournament-record 19-under-par 269, a mark equaled by Jeff Sluman six years later...Most productive year on TOUR was 1972 with $113,503 in official earnings...Member of the 1973 U.S. Ryder Cup team...Represented Puerto Rico on 12 World Cup teams.

PERSONAL:

One of the most popular figures in all of sports...Has raised more than $5 million for his Chi Chi Rodriguez Foundation in Clearwater, FL, with his "Chi Chi and the Bear" and "Chi Chi and the Zinger" golf outings, featuring Jack Nicklaus and Paul Azinger...Recipient of the Ambassador of Golf Award in 1981...Became a member of the World Humanitarian Sports Hall of Fame in 1994...As a boy in Puerto Rico, gravitated to golf by hitting tin cans with a guava tree stick...Worked as a caddie until joining the U.S. Army at age 19...Biggest thrill in golf was winning his first professional event, the Denver Open Invitational, at Denver CC in 1963...Favorite movie is "Boys Town" and favorite book is False Witness...Says one of his biggest thrills outside of golf was meeting Mother Teresa in the Philippines and talking with her for 45 minutes...Some of his favorite entertainers are Paul Anka and the late Sammy Davis, Jr...Favorite all-time pro athlete is Babe Ruth and enjoys the TV show "America's Most Wanted."...Lists favorite foods as rice and beans, pork chops and buffalo...Among his heroes are Mother Teresa, General George Patton and Mahatma Gandhi.

PLAYER STATISTICS

2004 CHAMPIONS TOUR STATISTICS:

Scoring Average	79.00	(N/A)
Driving Distance	232.8	(N/A)
Driving Accuracy Percentage	73.1%	(N/A)
Total Driving	1,998	(N/A)
Greens in Regulation Pct.	39.2%	(N/A)
Putting Average	1.896	(N/A)
Sand Save Percentage	20.5%	(N/A)
Birdie Average	1.47	(N/A)
All-Around Ranking	1,569	(N/A)

MISCELLANEOUS CHAMPIONS TOUR STATISTICS

2004 Low Round: 73–2004 Toshiba Senior Classic/2
Career Low Round: 62–1992 GTE West Classic/1
Career Largest Paycheck: $157,500–1993 Burnet Senior Classic/1

MISCELLANEOUS PGA TOUR STATISTICS

Career Low Round: 63–1974 Canadian Open/2
Career Largest Paycheck: $42,000–1973 Greater Greensboro Open/1

25 MEMORABLE MOMENTS

Irwin Holes 74-Yard Wedge Shot on Final Hole to Win

1999 Nationwide Championship

With a one-birdie, no-bogey round underway, Hale Irwin went to the par-5 18th hole assuming he needed a birdie. Irwin heard a roar and thought Bob Murphy had made birdie on the final hole. So Irwin hit a 3-wood into the center of the fairway and then laid up short of the water with a 5-iron. He hit a sand wedge onto the front of the green and watched as it hopped forward and spun into the cup for an eagle that gave him a two-stroke win over Murphy. Irwin re-enacted his famous U.S. Open victory lap, trotting to the green and slapping gallery members' hands.

CHAMPIONS TOUR 25

Jay Sigel (SIG-ul)

EXEMPT STATUS: Top 30 on All-Time Money List
FULL NAME: Robert Jay Sigel
HEIGHT: 6-1
WEIGHT: 212
BIRTHDATE: November 13, 1943
BIRTHPLACE: Bryn Mawr, PA
RESIDENCE: Berwyn, PA

FAMILY: Wife, Betty; Jennifer (12/29/72), Amy (12/30/74), Megan (1/3/79)
CLUB AFFILIATIONS: Aronimink GC (Newtown Square, PA), Pine Valley GC (Pine Valley, NJ)
EDUCATION: Wake Forest University (1967, Sociology)
SPECIAL INTERESTS: Charity work, insurance business
TURNED PROFESSIONAL: 1993

JOINED CHAMPIONS TOUR: 1994

CHAMPIONS TOUR VICTORIES (8): **1994** GTE West Classic. **1996** Energizer SENIOR TOUR Championship. **1997** Bruno's Memorial Classic, Kroger Senior Classic. **1998** Bell Atlantic Classic, EMC Kaanapali Classic. **2002** Farmers Charity Classic. **2003** Bayer Advantage Celebrity Pro-Am.

2004 CHARLES SCHWAB CUP FINISH: 38th - 335 points

GEORGIA-PACIFIC GRAND CHAMPIONS VICTORIES (3): **2004** Bruno's Memorial Classic, Bank of America Championship, Greater Hickory Classic at Rock Barn.

BEST PGA TOUR CAREER FINISH: T18—1979 IVB-Philadelphia Golf Classic.

OTHER VICTORIES (15): **1975** Porter Cup. **1976** Sunnehanna Amateur. **1978** Sunnehanna Amateur. **1979** British Amateur. **1981** Porter Cup. **1982** U.S. Amateur. **1983** U.S. Amateur, U.S. Mid-Amateur. **1984** Northeastern Amateur. **1985** U.S. Mid-Amateur, Northeastern Amateur. **1987** Porter Cup, U.S. Mid-Amateur. **1988** Sunnehanna Amateur. **1991** Northeastern Amateur.

BEST 2004 CHAMPIONS TOUR FINISHES: T4—MasterCard Classic, Allianz Championship; T8—Bruno's Memorial Classic; T9—3M Championship, FedEx Kinko's Classic, Bank of America Championship.

2004 SEASON:

Fell out of the top 30 on the money list in the final full-field event of the year yet put together another solid season that included six top-10 finishes, the most he's had in one season since 1999. All six top-10 efforts came prior to mid-August...Was T8 at the Bruno's Memorial Classic and then closed with a 66, the second-lowest round of the day, to T9 at the FedEx Kinko's Classic...Followed performance in Austin with a T4 at the Allianz Championship in Iowa. Final-round 68 was just one of eight scores in the 60s on Sunday at Glen Oaks...Earlier in the year, was in contention through much of the final round of the MasterCard Classic in Mexico before three bogeys on the back nine derailed him, leading to a T4 finish...The leading player among the Georgia-Pacific Grand Champions, with three over-60 titles and $219,292. Won his first Grand Champions event at the Bruno's Memorial Classic, edging Dave Eichelberger by one stroke when Eichelberger made bogey on the 18th hole Saturday...Claimed his second Grand Champions event near Boston at the Bank of America Championship. Birdied four consecutive holes midway through the back nine to overtake Graham Marsh...Won his third Georgia-Pacific title at the Greater Hickory Classic at Rock Barn. Made birdie on the 36th hole to tie Bob Charles, and then defeated Charles on the first playoff hole when he got up and down from the bunker for a par while Charles three-putted for a bogey.

CHAMPIONS TOUR CAREER HIGHLIGHTS:

2003: Was 29th on the final money list, the first time he had finished in the top 30 in back-to-back seasons since 1997-98...Won for the eighth time in his career when he made a nine-foot birdie putt on the last hole to defeat Mike McCullough at the Bayer Advantage Celebrity Pro-Am. Came from two strokes back on the final day with a course-record tying 7-under 65 at The National GC of Kansas City. Victory was his first top-10 finish of the season and, at age 59, made him the oldest Champions Tour winner ever in Kansas City. His opening-round 72 in Kansas City was the highest start by a winner in 2003...Was tied for the 36-hole lead with Larry Nelson at the Constellation Energy Classic before closing with a 1-over-par 73 to slip to a T4 near Baltimore. **2002:** Voted as the Champions Tour's Comeback Player of the Year...Earned first victory since October 1998 with a two-stroke win over Morris Hatalsky at the Farmers Charity Classic. Was tied for lead after 36 holes with Rodger Davis and Dan O'Neill and closed with a 5-under-par 67 at Egypt Valley. Helped his cause with a pair of eagles in the final round...Also finished a distant second to Hatalsky at the Uniting Fore Care Classic. Made 24 points on the weekend in the Modified Stableford System and finished 12 points back in Park City. **2001:** Missed the first five months of the season, recovering from rotator cuff surgery on both shoulders (left shoulder in Nov. 2000; right shoulder in Jan. 2001)...Returned to action at the BellSouth Senior Classic at Opryland (T58)...Finished second at the SBC Senior Classic. **2000:** Troubled most of the year by a left shoulder problem and underwent arthroscopic surgery in November. **1999:** The 36-hole leader at the BankBoston Classic before finishing T3 after missing birdie opportunities on the 53rd and 54th hole...Third- place finisher at the Vantage Campionship. **1998:** Defeated Jose Maria Canizares with a birdie on the third extra hole of a playoff for the Bell Atlantic Classic title. Course-record 62 at Hartefeld National on Saturday that included an amazing 27 on the front nine. Champions Tour-record nine-hole score featured an eagle and seven straight birdies, the best eagle-birdie run in the history of the circuit...Went wire-to-wire for victory at the EMC Kaanapali Classic. Fired a career-best 10-under 61 in the opening round. **1997:** Tied Gil Morgan for the most top-10 finishes (19) in the campaign, while compiling multiple wins for the first time as a professional...Captured his first victory of the year in Birmingham at the Bruno's Memorial Classic, holding off Gil Morgan by three strokes...Six consecutive top 10s from mid-June to mid-July were highlighted by a win at the Kroger Senior Classic. Waltzed to a seven-stroke victory over Isao Aoki at Kings Island, setting a tournament record with an 18-under-par 195 total...Came close to winning two other events...Lost to Bob Murphy in a nine-hole playoff at the Toshiba Senior Classic when Murphy sank an 80-foot birdie putt...Also fell to open qualifier Dana Quigley in a three-hole playoff at the Northville Long Island Classic. **1996:** Posted the biggest victory of his Champions Tour career in the year's final official event, a

CHAMPIONS TOUR CAREER SUMMARY — PLAYOFF RECORD: 2-2

Year	Events Played	1st	2nd	3rd	Top 10	Top 25	Earnings	Rank
1994	29	1		3	14	20	$634,130	12
1995	31		1	2	9	22	567,557	21
1996	32	1	3		15	26	1,094,630	6
1997	31	2	2	1	19	25	1,294,838	4
1998	32	2	1	6	14	25	1,403,912	4
1999	31			2	6	15	549,061	35
2000	32				2	13	362,707	52
2001	18		1		4	8	516,027	37
2002	30	1	1		4	16	843,526	24
2003	30	1			4	10	721,989	29
2004	28				6	12	593,815	31
Total	324	8	9	14	97	192	8,582,191	

COMBINED ALL-TIME MONEY (3 TOURS): **$8,582,191**

CHAMPIONS TOUR TOP TOURNAMENT SUMMARY

Year	94	95	96	97	98	99	00	01	02	03	04
Senior PGA Championship	13	T30	T11	T40	T6	T22	T12		T57	T17	T27
U.S. Senior Open	T7	T21	T5	T10	T28	CUT	CUT	T11	T21	T30	T54
Ford Senior Players	9	T18	T16	T10	T12	T37	T52	T8	T17	T35	T34
Senior British Open										T27	
JELD-WEN Tradition	T52	T6	11	5	66	T28	T19		T75	T28	T45
Charles Schwab Cup Champ	3	T20	1	T4	3				T21	29	

CHAMPIONS TOUR YEAR-BY-YEAR STATISTICS (TOP 50 ON 2004 MONEY LIST)

	Scoring Average	Putting Average	Greens in Regulation	Driving Distance	Driving Accuracy
1994	70.51 (14)	1.807 (T33)	72.9 (9)	272.0 (2)	70.7 (T28)
1995	70.96 (17)	1.816 (T42)	73.2 (4)	277.4 (1)	71.1 (T26)
1996	70.47 (7)	1.801 (T26)	71.8 (4)	283.4 (3)	67.4 (49)
1997	70.37 (4)	1.809 (T46)	73.3 (3)	285.3 (3)	67.6 (T42)
1998	70.55 (7)	1.786 (22)	72.3 (4)	278.3 (6)	69.1 (T44)
1999	71.24 (31)	1.802 (52)	72.2 (6)	272.9 (T13)	66.8 (T68)
2000	71.35 (38)	1.806 (59)	70.2 (18)	274.4 (T19)	69.0 (T53)
2001	71.09 (24)	1.748 (T11)	70.2 (T12)	274.5 (27)	69.8 (T45)
2002	71.17 (T27)	1.808 (53)	71.2 (12)	276.2 (T14)	69.4 (39)
2003	71.13 (36)	1.793 (38)	68.1 (T34)	275.9 (25)	65.7 (58)
2004	71.33 (29)	1.804 (41)	69.8 (21)	278.1 (21)	71.4 (34)

Jay Sigel (continued)

two-stroke win over Kermit Zarley at the Energizer SENIOR TOUR Championship in Myrtle Beach, SC. Helped his cause with a hole-in-one in the third round (10th of his career). **1995:** Broke Jim Dent's run as the Champions Tour's longest hitter, winning that statistical category with an average of 277.4 yards per drive. **1994:** Garnered Rookie of the Year honors after completing one of the most remarkable come-from-behind victories in golf history at the GTE West Classic in Ojai, CA. Rallied from 10 strokes down to catch Jim Colbert in regulation and then defeated him on the fourth extra playoff hole for his first professional win...Final-round course-record 63 at The Dunes Club came on his 51st birthday during the GOLF MAGAZINE SENIOR TOUR Championship and included both an eagle and rare double-eagle (15th/5-wood/220 yards). **1993:** Earned a conditional card at the Champions Tour National Qualifying Tournament, finishing 11th at Grenelefe Resort.

OTHER CAREER HIGHLIGHTS:

One of the country's all-time finest amateur golfers...Captured back-to-back U.S. Amateur crowns in 1982-83, three U.S. Mid-Amateur titles and the 1979 British Amateur title...Served as playing captain of the 1983 and 1985 United States Walker Cup teams and was a member of the 1977, 1979, 1981, 1983, 1985, 1987, 1989, 1991 and 1993 squads. Holds record for most appearances and total points won in Walker Cup history...Played on a recod seven American teams in the World Amateur Team Championship...Was low amateur in the 1981, 1982 and 1988 Masters, as well as the 1980 British Open and 1984 U.S. Open...Captured three Porter Cups, three Northeast Amateur titles, four Pennsylvania Open Championships, 11 Pennsylvania Amateur titles and seven Philadelphia Open Championships...Also won three Sunnehanna Amateur titles and had the 11th hole at Sunnehanna CC dedicated to him in 1979...Nine-time Crump Cup champion at Pine Valley GC...Received the Bob Jones Award and Ben Hogan Award in 1984...Also received the 1984 Marine Corps Scholarship Foundation's Athlete of the Year Award...Included in the list of 100 Heroes of American Golf, and was inducted into the Collegiate Golf Coaches of America Hall of Fame in 1988...Was selected to Pennsylvania's Sports Hall of Fame in 1993...Selected as the Philadelphia Sportswriters Professional Athlete of the Year in 1994...Named the Most Courageous Athlete by the Philadelphia Sportswriters Association in 2000...Has 18 career holes-in-one.

PERSONAL:

Is Senior Vice President of Century Business Services...Serves as President of the Greater Philadelphia Scholastic Golf Association and is the President of the First Tee of Philadelphia chapter...Works part-time as a fee-paid consultant on golf course design projects...Biggest thrills in golf were winning back-to-back U.S. Amateur titles, serving as a two-time playing captain of the U.S. Walker Cup team and also winning the Ben Hogan and Bobby Jones awards ...He and his family have a Brittany Spaniel named Replace All Divots...Has worked with such golf instructors as Mitchell Spearman and Bill Davis...Heroes are Bobby Jones, Jack Nicklaus and Arnold Palmer...Father got him started in the sport...Collects Ping putters and Wilson Black Dot wedges...Is an honorary member at the following golf clubs: Bala GC, Philadelphia, PA; Stonewall GC, Bulltown, PA; Rolling Green GC, Springfield, PA; Wild Dunes Beach and Racquet Club, Charleston, SC; Cherry Hills CC, Denver, CO; Wannamoisett CC, Rumford, RI; The Dunes Golf & Beach Club, Myrtle Beach, SC; Egypt Valley CC, Grand Rapids, MI...Favorite courses are Pine Valley and Cypress Point...Favorite number is 13. When he won the 1997 Bruno's Memorial Classic, he played in the 13th group the last two days. In addition, he was born on the 13th of November, his first hole-in-one was on hole 13 on July 13th. He was also the 13th player to win both the U.S. and British Amateurs and wears size 13 shoes.

PLAYER STATISTICS

MISCELLANEOUS CHAMPIONS TOUR STATISTICS

2004 Low Round: 66–2 times, most recent 2004 FedEx Kinko's Classic/3
Career Low Round: 61–1998 EMC Kaanapali Classic/1
Career Largest Paycheck: $280,000–1996 Energizer SENIOR TOUR Championship/1

MISCELLANEOUS PGA TOUR STATISTICS

Career Low Round: 68–1979 IVB-Philadelphia Golf Classic/4

25 MEMORABLE MOMENTS

Duvals' Dual Victory on Same Weekend

1999 Emerald Coast Classic

Sitting on a 36-hole total of 11-under-par 129 and a three-shot lead going into the final round of the 1999 Emerald Coast Classic, Bob Duval called his son David, the world's No. 1 player at the time, who also held a one-shot lead at THE PLAYERS Championship 350 miles away. In a conversation with his son, the elder Duval was told to take it one shot at a time. The advice paid off Sunday as he edged Bruce Fleisher and then watched on TV as his son recorded a two-stroke victory over Scott Gump. The two became the first father-son tandem to win TOUR titles on the same weekend.

CHAMPIONS TOUR 25

Scott Simpson

EXEMPT STATUS: Top 30 on All-Time Money List
FULL NAME: Scott William Simpson
HEIGHT: 6-2
WEIGHT: 205
BIRTHDATE: September 17, 1955
BIRTHPLACE: San Diego, CA
RESIDENCE: San Diego, CA

FAMILY: Wife, Cheryl; Brea Yoshiko (10/10/82), Sean Tokuzo (10/14/86)
EDUCATION: University of Southern California (1978, Business Administration)
SPECIAL INTERESTS: Bible study, family activities, exercise, reading
TURNED PROFESSIONAL: 1977
JOINED PGA TOUR: 1979

JOINED CHAMPIONS TOUR: 2005

PGA TOUR VICTORIES (7): 1980 Western Open. **1984** Manufacturers Hanover Westchester Classic. **1987** Greater Greensboro Open, U.S. Open Championship. **1989** BellSouth Atlanta Golf Classic. **1993** GTE Byron Nelson Golf Classic. **1998** Buick Invitational.

OTHER VICTORIES (4): 1984 Chunichi Crowns (Jpn), Dunlop Phoenix (Jpn). **1988** Chunichi Crowns (Jpn). **1990** Perrier Invitational (Eur).

PGA TOUR CAREER EARNINGS: $6,742,717

PGA TOUR PLAYOFF RECORD: 2-3

BEST 2004 PGA TOUR FINISH:
T10—Valero Texas Open.

2004 SEASON:
Played in 18 events on the PGA TOUR, making the cut in half of his starts...Was on the leaderboard throughout the weekend at the Valero Texas Open and eventually T10 in San Antonio, his first top-10 performance since T2 at the 2001 Greater Greensboro Chrysler Open...Also T18 at the Reno-Tahoe Open after being one stroke off the lead after the first round.

OTHER CAREER HIGHLIGHTS:
Played the PGA TOUR regularly from 1979-2004...Prior to 2005 season, appeared in 588 events with 400 cuts made...Won seven times on the PGA TOUR with his biggest victory coming at the 1987 U.S. Open. Trailed Tom Watson by one stroke heading into the final round at The Olympic Club, but closed with a 68, which included three birdies on the back nine, good for a one-stroke victory...Also won the Greater Greensboro Open that year on way to fourth-place finish on money list, his highest ranking ever...Lost 18-hole playoff to Payne Stewart in 1991 U.S. Open at Hazeltine National...Most recent victory came in 1998 Buick Invitational when he defeated Skip Kendall with a birdie on the first playoff hole. Posted a final-round 64 at the Buick Invitational and came from eight strokes back entering the final round, at the time matching PGA TOUR best comeback since 1970. Victory came with former San Diego Chargers quarterback Stan Humphries on his bag. Also became third San Diego native to win Buick Invitational in six years (Phil Mickelson-1993, Craig Stadler-1994) and fifth overall (Gene Littler-1954, Billy Casper-1966)...Recorded one-stroke victory over Corey Pavin, Billy Mayfair and D.A. Weibring at the 1993 GTE Byron Nelson Classic...First TOUR victory came in 1980 Western Open, by five strokes over Andy Bean...Won second tournament on TOUR by five as well, at 1984 Manufacturers Hanover Westchester Classic...Defeated Bob Tway in playoff to win 1989 BellSouth Atlanta Classic...In 1996, impressive West Coast swing included T2 at Nissan Open, T3 Buick Invitational, T4 United Airlines Hawaiian Open and T6 at Phoenix Open. Named PGA TOUR Player of the Month for February, 1996, first to receive award without victory during that month...Was unable to play the PGA TOUR in 2000 due to a broken ankle he suffered while skiing during the New Year holiday. Prognosis was ankle could heal without surgery but did not. Underwent surgery in August, 2000, which involved placing seven screws into the ankle...Received a major medical extension in 2001...NCAA champion and All-American at University of Southern California in 1976 and 1977...Played on victorious U.S. Walker Cup team in 1977 and was also a member of the American Ryder Cup team in 1987.

PERSONAL:
Spends a great deal of time with family during season...Has served 15 years as host of Scott Simpson HBIC Pro-Am in Los Angeles, which benefits Help For Brain-Injured Children.

PLAYER STATISTICS

MISCELLANEOUS PGA TOUR STATISTICS
2004 Low Round: 65–Valero Texas Open/1
Career Low Round: 62–1991 United Hawaiian Open/1
Career Largest Paycheck: $378,000–1998 Buick Invitational/1

SECTION 2 PLAYER BIOGRAPHIES

Des Smyth (SMITH)

EXEMPT STATUS: 35th on 2004 Champions Tour Money List
FULL NAME: Desmond John Smyth
HEIGHT: 5-10
WEIGHT: 175
BIRTHDATE: February 12, 1953
BIRTHPLACE: Drogheda, County Louth, Ireland
RESIDENCE: Drogheda, Ireland
FAMILY: Wife, Vicki; Karen (10/3/81), Gregory (2/13/84), Shane (4/18/88)
SPECIAL INTERESTS: Tennis, horse racing, rugby
TURNED PROFESSIONAL: 1974

JOINED CHAMPIONS TOUR: 2003

BEST CHAMPIONS TOUR CAREER FINISH:
T2—2003 The ACE Group Classic.

2004 CHARLES SCHWAB CUP FINISH:
48th - 196 points

BEST PGA TOUR CAREER FINISH: T13—2001 British Open Championship.

OTHER VICTORIES (19): **1979** Irish National PGA Championship, Sun Alliance European Match Play Championship. **1980** Newcastle Brown "900" Open, Cold Shield Greater Manchester Open, Hennessy Cognac Cup. **1981** Coral Classic. **1982** Hennessy Cognac Cup. **1983** Sanyo Open. **1985** Irish National PGA Championship. **1986** Irish National PGA Championship. **1987** Guinness Pro-Am. **1988** BNP Jersey Open, Dunhill Cup. **1990** Irish National PGA Championship. **1993** Madrid Open. **1995** Glen Dimplex Irish Matchplay Championship. **1996** Irish National PGA Championship. 2001 Irish National PGA Championship, Madeira Island Open.

PGA TOUR CAREER EARNINGS: $134,139

BEST 2004 CHAMPIONS TOUR FINISHES:
T5—Kroger Classic; T6—Blue Angels Classic; T8—Administaff Small Business Classic; T9—Bank of America Championship.

2004 SEASON:
Made a late run at a spot among the top-30 money-winners, but came up short. Was in 44th position on the money list at the start of September and eventually finished 35th, thanks to two of his four overall top-10 performances coming in his last five starts of the season...Best overall effort was a T5 at the Kroger Classic near Cincinnati in early September. Was just one stroke off the lead after 36 holes but slipped back after an even-par 72 on Sunday at the TPC at River's Bend. Was the opening-round co-leader with Gary McCord after firing a 7-under 65 on Friday...Early in the campaign, posted his career-low round on the Champions Tour, a bogey-free, 6-under 64 on Sunday at the Blue Angels Classic and moved up 33 spots on the final day into a T6 near Pensacola...Played in the National Qualifying Tournament during the fall in an attempt to improve his conditional status. Finished in a tie with Lonnie Nielsen after six rounds, but placed 10th after electing not to participate in a playoff.

CHAMPIONS TOUR CAREER HIGHLIGHTS:
2003: One of three rookies to finish in the top 30 on the money list, joining Craig Stadler and D.A. Weibring. Also joined 2002 Q-School graduates David Eger and Dave Barr among the top 30 money-winners...Raised eyebrows in his Champions Tour debut at The ACE Group Classic. Closed the Naples event with birdies on five of his last six holes and T2 in the event with Tom Watson...Three consecutive rounds in the 60s helped him to a T3 finish at the Columbus Southern Open, one week after he was T6 at the Bayer Advantage Celebrity Pro-Am...Was the 54-hole leader at the Senior PGA Championship, but closed with a 4-over-par 74 to slip to a T5 at Aronimink GC. Fired a course-record 5-under-par 65 in the third round. **2002:** Joined Doug Dalziel of Scotland (1987), Simon Hobday of South Africa (1990) and Masaru Amano (1995) as the fourth international player to earn medalist honors at the Champions Tour's National Qualifying Tournament at World Woods GC in Brooksville, FL. Overcame a four-stroke deficit on the last day at World Woods and made an eight-foot birdie putt on the final hole to overtake Japan's Seiji Ebihara for top honors. His 72-hole score of 13-under 275 earned him a check for $42,000...Advanced to the finals after being the low man at the regional site at Marsh Creek CC in St. Augustine, FL. Shot 11-under 277 over 72 holes, six shots better than Bill Thorpe and Doug Johnson.

OTHER CAREER HIGHLIGHTS:
Played 29 years on the European PGA Tour and won eight official tournaments on the circuit...Best known as the European Tour's oldest winner. Won the 2001 Madeira Island Open in Portugal by two strokes over John Bickerton at 48 years, 1 month and 4 days, 20 days older than the previous-oldest champion, Neil Coles...Finished seventh on the European PGA Tour Order of Merit in 1988 with £171,951...T4 at the 1982 British Open Championship at Troon...Shot a final-round 62 in the 1990 Mitsubishi Austrian Open and placed third in the event...Played on the European Ryder Cup team in 1979 and 1981 and represented Ireland on five World Cup teams (1979, 1980, 1982, 1988, 1989)...Has made eight holes-in-one in competition.

PERSONAL:
Started playing golf at age 6...Lists Jack Nicklaus as his hero and the birth of his children as his biggest thrill outside of golf...Favorite golf course is Carnoustie in Scotland and favorite entertainer is singer Neil Diamond...Enjoys Italian food...Favorite athlete is boxer Muhammad Ali...Designed Ballykisteen G&CC in Limerick Junction, Ireland.

PLAYER STATISTICS

MISCELLANEOUS CHAMPIONS TOUR STATISTICS
2004 Low Round: 64–2004 Blue Angels Classic/3
Career Low Round: 64–2004 Blue Angels Classic/3
Career Largest Paycheck: $128,000–2003 ACE Group Classic/T2

MISCELLANEOUS PGA TOUR STATISTICS
Career Low Round: 65–2001 British Open Championship/2
Career Largest Paycheck: $57,310–2001 British Open Championship/T13

CHAMPIONS TOUR CAREER SUMMARY PLAYOFF RECORD: 0-0

Year	Events Played	1st	2nd	3rd	Top 10	Top 25	Earnings	Rank
2003	23		1	2	10	18	$959,600	18
2004	27				4	14	536,904	35
Total	50		1	2	14	32	1,496,503	
COMBINED ALL-TIME MONEY (3 TOURS):							**$1,630,642**	

CHAMPIONS TOUR TOP TOURNAMENT SUMMARY

Year	03	04
Senior PGA Championship	T5	T57
U.S. Senior Open	T19	T29
Ford Senior Players	T48	T51
Senior British Open	13	T13
JELD-WEN Tradition	T14	T40
Charles Schwab Cup Champ	T20	

CHAMPIONS TOUR YEAR-BY-YEAR STATISTICS (TOP 50 ON 2004 MONEY LIST)

	Scoring Average	Putting Average	Greens in Regulation	Driving Distance	Driving Accuracy
2003	70.19 (13)	1.786 (33)	69.8 (23)	275.7 (T26)	70.9 (T33)
2004	71.41 (33)	1.813 (T49)	69.5 (T25)	272.7 (36)	72.0 (T28)

J.C. Snead

EXEMPT STATUS: Top 30 on All-Time Money List
FULL NAME: Jesse Carlyle Snead
HEIGHT: 6-2
WEIGHT: 215
BIRTHDATE: October 14, 1940
BIRTHPLACE: Hot Springs, VA
RESIDENCE: Hobe Sound, FL

FAMILY: Jason (10/10/78)
EDUCATION: East Tennessee State University
SPECIAL INTERESTS: Hunting, farming
TURNED PROFESSIONAL: 1964
JOINED PGA TOUR: 1968

JOINED CHAMPIONS TOUR: 1990

CHAMPIONS TOUR VICTORIES (4): 1993 Vantage at The Dominion. **1995** Royal Caribbean Classic, Ford Senior Players Championship. **2002** Greater Baltimore Classic.

2004 CHARLES SCHWAB CUP FINISH:
T78th - 37 points

GEORGIA-PACIFIC GRAND CHAMPIONS VICTORIES (4): 2001 Novell Utah Showdown. **2002** Greater Baltimore Classic. **2003** Music City Championship at Gaylord Opryland. **2004** The ACE Group Classic.

PGA TOUR VICTORIES (8): 1971 Tucson Open Invitational, Doral-Eastern Open Invitational. **1972** IVB-Philadelphia Golf Classic. **1975** Andy Williams-San Diego Open Invitational. **1976** Andy Williams-San Diego Open Invitational, Kaiser International Open Invitational. **1981** Southern Open. **1987** Manufacturers Hanover Westchester Classic.

OTHER VICTORIES (2): 1973 Australian Open. **1980** Jerry Ford Invitational [co-winner].

PGA TOUR CAREER EARNINGS: $2,197,545

PGA TOUR PLAYOFF RECORD: 3-1

BEST 2004 CHAMPIONS TOUR FINISH:
T10—The ACE Group Classic.

2004 SEASON:
Finished among the top 20 in two of his first four starts of the year...T10 at The ACE Group Classic in Naples was his first top-10 performance since win in 2002...Continued his good play in Florida, with a T13 at the Outback Steakhouse Pro-Am in Tampa. Final-round 66 at the TPC of Tampa Bay was his best round on the Champions Tour since 2002...Finished fifth on the final Georgia-Pacific Grand Champions money list, with $153,791 and won the Georgia-Pacific title at The ACE Group Classic, defeating Isao Aoki in a one-hole playoff.

CHAMPIONS TOUR CAREER HIGHLIGHTS:
2003: Made his fifth career hole-in-one on the Champions Tour at the Bayer Advantage Celebrity Pro-Am, tying him with Charlie Sifford for most career aces on the over-50 circuit. Holed a 6-iron shot from 162 yards on No. 4 at The National GC of Kansas City in the final round...Also made consecutive eagles during the third round of the JELD-WEN Tradition. Holed a pitch shot on the par-5 15th hole at The Reserve and then followed by hitting the par-5 16th green in two and making a 22-foot putt...Inducted into the Virginia Sports Hall of Fame in late April, along with former college basketball coach Terry Holland and all-pro NFL linebacker Lawrence Taylor...Posted a one-stroke victory over Dave Stockton in the Georgia-Pacific Grand Champions competition at the Music City Championship at Gaylord Opryland. **2002:** Ended nearly a seven-year victory drought when he prevailed by one stroke at the Greater Baltimore Classic. Sank a 10-foot par putt on the final hole to nip John Mahaffey, Doug Tewell and Bobby Wadkins. Set a Hayfields Club course record in the second round with his 8-under-par 64. Became only the fifth player, and first since Gary Player in 1998, to win both the Georgia-Pacific Grand Champions title and the overall tournament. Victory at 61 years, 8 months and 9 days made him the third oldest player to win a Champions Tour event behind Mike Fetchick (63 years) and Player (62 years, 9 months, 22 days). The win was also his first since the 1995 Ford Senior Players Championship and set a record for longest time between Champions Tour victories (6 years, 11 months, 7 days), eclipsing the old record of 6 years, 10 months and 3 days by Larry Ziegler (1991 Newport Cup-1998 Saint Lukes Classic). **2001:** T2 at The Instinet Classic, two strokes behind Gil Morgan...Lone victory in the Georgia-Pacific Grand Champions competition came at the Novell Utah Showdown, a two-stroke win over Walter Morgan. **2000:** Along with Gary McCord, lost to Tom Wargo (won with birdie on third extra hole) in a playoff at the LiquidGolf.com Invitational. **1999:** Closed with a final-round 65 at Serrano CC and T3 at the Raley's Gold Rush Classic. **1998:** T2 at the Northville Long Island Classic along with Walter Hall, one stroke short of Gary Player. Recorded a hole-in-one in the final round of The Home Depot Invitational. **1995:** Enjoyed his most lucrative season with more than $950,000 in official money...Defeated Raymond Floyd in a playoff for the Royal Caribbean Classic title and then bested Jack Nicklaus in overtime for the Ford Senior Players Championship title, the biggest win of his career. **1993:** Broke into the Champions Tour winner's circle when he braved the elements for a one-stroke victory at the Vantage at The Dominion in San Antonio. His 54-hole score of 2-under 214 was impressive, considering a fluke winter storm that moved through south Texas during the event. **1990:** T21 in his debut on the Champions Tour at The Transamerica Senior Golf Championship in Napa, site of his victory in the Kaiser International in 1976.

OTHER CAREER HIGHLIGHTS:
Collected the last of his eight PGA TOUR titles at the 1987 Manufacturer's Hanover-Westchester Classic, defeating Seve Ballesteros in a playoff...Captured his first two TOUR victories in a three-week span, winning the 1971 Tucson Open and the Doral-Eastern Open immediately before and after the PGA Championship...Member of the U.S. Ryder Cup teams in 1971, 1973 and 1975...Has 15 career holes-in-one.

PERSONAL:
Nephew of the legendary Sam Snead, who passed away in 2002...Was an excellent all-around athlete as a youngster, winning all-state honors in three sports. Spent nearly four years playing baseball in the Washington Senators' farm system before becoming a professional golfer in 1964...Biggest thrill in his career was his first TOUR victory in Tucson.

PLAYER STATISTICS

2004 CHAMPIONS TOUR STATISTICS:

Scoring Average	72.00	(48)
Driving Distance	270.1	(50)
Driving Accuracy Percentage	69.3%	(48)
Total Driving	98	(63)
Greens in Regulation Pct.	64.7%	(54)
Putting Average	1.824	(58)
Sand Save Percentage	47.7%	(29)
Eagles (Holes per)	612.0	(60)
Birdie Average	2.94	(60)
All-Around Ranking	407	(59)

MISCELLANEOUS CHAMPIONS TOUR STATISTICS
2004 Low Round: 66–2004 Outback Steakhouse Pro-Am/3
Career Low Round: 62–1996 Kroger Senior Classic/1
Career Largest Paycheck: $225,000–1995 Ford Senior Players Championship/1

MISCELLANEOUS PGA TOUR STATISTICS
Career Low Round: 62–1973 Phoenix Open/1
Career Largest Paycheck: $108,000–1987 Manufacturers Hanover Westchester Classic/1

CHAMPIONS TOUR CAREER SUMMARY — PLAYOFF RECORD: 2-3

Year	Events Played	1st	2nd	3rd	Top 10	Top 25	Earnings	Rank
1990	4				3	4	$47,494	74
1991	30		1		8	20	302,287	19
1992	29		2		8	19	383,698	20
1993	28	1		1	10	19	487,500	20
1994	31			3	14	28	584,864	15
1995	28	2	3	2	12	21	978,137	6
1996	31		3		10	23	763,382	11
1997	33				6	19	476,149	33
1998	32		1		8	21	612,307	28
1999	31			1	11	19	743,841	22
2000	30		1		3	11	411,634	45
2001	26		1		4	10	500,854	38
2002	23	1			2	6	439,713	42
2003	26					2	204,250	65
2004	23				1	5	234,469	59
Total	405	4	12	7	100	227	7,170,578	
COMBINED ALL-TIME MONEY (3 TOURS):							**$9,368,123**	

CHAMPIONS TOUR TOP TOURNAMENT SUMMARY

Year	91	92	93	94	95	96	97	98	99	00	01	02	03
Senior PGA Championship	CUT	T30	T9	T15	T16	T20	26	T36	T8	T28		T27	CUT
U.S. Senior Open	T15	T26	T40	T50	T5		T32	T22	T13	T58	T29		T30
Ford Senior Players	T17	T2	T20	T16	1	T13	T60	T9	T53	T57	16	T30	T53
JELD-WEN Tradition	T23	T8	T23	T17	T20	T9	T13	T25	T14	T51	T5	T48	T66
Charles Schwab Cup Champ	T12	30	12	T20	26	17		23	T11				

Year	04
Senior PGA Championship	DQ
U.S. Senior Open	CUT
Ford Senior Players	T56
JELD-WEN Tradition	T42

Craig Stadler

EXEMPT STATUS: Top 30 on 2004 Champions Tour Money List
FULL NAME: Craig Robert Stadler
HEIGHT: 5-10
WEIGHT: 255
BIRTHDATE: June 2, 1953
BIRTHPLACE: San Diego, CA
RESIDENCE: Evergreen, CO

FAMILY: Wife, Sue; Kevin (2/5/80), Chris (11/23/82)
EDUCATION: University of Southern California (1975)
SPECIAL INTERESTS: Hunting, wine collecting
TURNED PROFESSIONAL: 1975
JOINED PGA TOUR: 1977

JOINED CHAMPIONS TOUR: 2003

CHAMPIONS TOUR VICTORIES (8): **2003** Ford Senior Players Championship, Greater Hickory Classic at Rock Barn, SBC Championship. **2004** The ACE Group Classic, Bank of America Championship, JELD-WEN Tradition, The First Tee Open at Pebble Beach presented by Wal-Mart, SAS Championship.

2004 CHARLES SCHWAB CUP FINISH: 2nd - 3,388 points

PGA TOUR VICTORIES (13): **1980** Bob Hope Desert Classic, Greater Greensboro Open. **1981** Kemper Open. **1982** Joe Garagiola-Tucson Open, Masters Tournament, Kemper Open, World Series of Golf. **1984** Byron Nelson Golf Classic. **1991** THE TOUR Championship. **1992** NEC World Series of Golf. **1994** Buick Invitational of California. **1996** Nissan Open. **2003** B.C. Open.

OTHER VICTORIES (6): **1985** Canon European Masters. **1987** Dunlop Phoenix. **1990** Scandinavian Enterprise Open. **1992** Argentine Open. **1999** Champions Challenge [with son, Kevin]. **2002** Office Depot Father/Son Challenge [with Kevin].

PGA TOUR CAREER EARNINGS: $9,730,968

PGA TOUR PLAYOFF RECORD: 3-3

BEST 2004 CHAMPIONS TOUR FINISHES: 1—The ACE Group Classic, Bank of America Championship, JELD-WEN Tradition, The First Tee Open at Pebble Beach presented by Wal-Mart, SAS Championship; 2—3M Championship; 3—Senior PGA Championship, MasterCard Championship.

BEST 2004 PGA TOUR FINISH: T21—B.C. Open.

2004 SEASON:
Was voted by his peers as the Champions Tour's Player of the Year after a career-best five victories in a single season, the most wins by any player in a year since Larry Nelson in 2001...Also topped the Champions Tour earnings list for 2004 and received the Arnold Palmer Award as the circuit's leading money-winner, with a personal-best $2,306,606, the 10th-highest money total ever...Joined Lee Trevino and Tom Watson as the third player to earn money titles on both the Champions Tour and the PGA TOUR...Had 35 Rounds in the 60s out of 67 played (52 percent) and earned the Byron Nelson Trophy for best scoring average, 69.30...Also finished second in the Charles Schwab Cup competition. Led the season-long race during the month of September before finishing 39 points back of Hale Irwin at season's end...Was among the top three in over a third of his 21 starts, and five victories included three consecutive wins during the summer, a first on the Champions Tour since Gil Morgan won three consecutive starts on the Champions Tour (1997-1998)...Started the run by earning his second major championship on the Champions Tour at the JELD-WEN Tradition. Closed with four straight birdies in the final round to win by one stroke over Jerry Pate and Allen Doyle. Took over the lead in the money race for good with his $345,000 first-place check near Portland. Helped his cause when he made a rare double eagle on the 16th hole Saturday, nailing a perfect 4-iron from 207 yards. Was 11-under-par on the critical par 5s at The Reserve...Made it two straight wins the following week by capturing the inaugural First Tee Open at Pebble Beach presented by Wal-Mart. Won by three strokes over Jay Haas, after opening with an even-par 72 at the Bayonet Golf Course. Played his last 37 holes in 16-under-par and teamed with his junior partner, Aaron Woodard from Denver, to post a four-stroke victory in the pro-junior competition, as well. Back-to-back victories were the first on the Champions Tour since Bob Gilder in 2002 (Allianz Championship/Kroger Classic)...Made it three wins in three consecutive starts when he cruised to a six-stroke, wire-to-wire victory over Tom Jenkins at the SAS Championship in Raleigh. Was 14-under-par on the back nine en route to a tournament-record score of 17-under-par 199. Check for $270,000 at the SAS event pushed his season earnings past the $2-million mark, the first player to do so in two years...Started the year by winning The ACE Group Classic in Naples. Prevailed by making a 27-foot birdie putt on the first hole of a playoff with Tom Watson and Gary Koch at TwinEagles. Appeared to be out of contention after a double bogey at the 13th hole on Sunday left him three behind leader Koch. However, a birdie at 15, coupled with bogeys by Koch at 14 and 17, opened the door...Also rallied from four strokes back on the final day to win by four at the Bank of America Championship near Boston. Final-round 64 at Nashawtuc was the lowest Sunday score in tournament history and victory became extra special when son Kevin claimed the Lake Erie Charity Classic on the Nationwide Tour in a four-hole playoff just an hour later, marking the second time a father and son won on the same day in PGA TOUR-sponsored events (David Duval/Bob Duval on March 28, 1999)...Also finished second at the 3M Championship in Minnesota. Made a run at Tom Kite in the final round at the TPC of the Twin Cities, but missed a 14-foot eagle putt on the last hole and fell one stroke short. His 8-under 64 in the opening round at the TPC of the Twin Cities was best-ever start on the circuit..Eagled the final hole to finish solo third at the Senior PGA Championship at Valhalla...Opened his 2004 Champions Tour season by finishing T3 at the MasterCard Championship. Only made one bogey in the 54-hole event and equaled the Hualalai course record on the final day, with a 9-under 63...Champions Tour Player of the Month in both August and September...Led the Champions Tour in Eagles (14) and Birdie Average (4.18)...Played in two PGA TOUR events in Hawaii at the start of the season. Was T28 at the Mercedes Championships and then missed the cut at the Sony Open in Hawaii...Also played in the AT&T Pebble Beach National Pro-Am with his son, Kevin, and T35 in the event...Made an appearance at THE PLAYERS Championship, where he made the cut and finished T66...Was T21 in defense of his title at the B.C. Open in July.

CHAMPIONS TOUR CAREER HIGHLIGHTS:
2003: The Champions Tour Rookie of the Year thanks to three wins and seven top-10 finishes...Did not become eligible until turning 50 on June 2...Made history when he became the first Champions Tour player to win a PGA TOUR event, a one-stroke victory in the B.C.Open at the En-Joie GC. Used a final-round, 9-under-par 63 to make up eight strokes (largest comeback in tournament history) to defeat Steve Lowery and Alex Cejka by one stroke. Had four straight rounds in the 60s, the first time he had done so in a PGA TOUR event since the 1995 B.C. Open. Victory in New York made him just the second player in history to win a PGA TOUR and Champions Tour event in the same year. (Raymond Floyd-1992 Doral-Ryder Open at 49, and the GTE North Classic). Victory in Endicott also made him just the fifth player in PGA TOUR history to win an event over the age of 50 (fifth oldest at 51 years, 1 month, 18

CHAMPIONS TOUR CAREER SUMMARY — **PLAYOFF RECORD: 1-0**

Year	Events Played	1st	2nd	3rd	Top 10	Top 25	Earnings	Rank
2003	14	3			7	13	$1,192,278	14
2004	21	5	1	2	12	19	2,306,066	1
Total	35	8	1	2	19	32	3,498,344	
COMBINED ALL-TIME MONEY (3 TOURS):							**$13,229,312**	

CHAMPIONS TOUR TOP TOURNAMENT SUMMARY

Year	03	04
Senior PGA Championship	T15	3
U.S. Senior Open	T10	T7
Ford Senior Players	1	T18
Senior British Open	19	
JELD-WEN Tradition	T10	1
Charles Schwab Cup Champ	9	T7

CHAMPIONS TOUR YEAR-BY-YEAR STATISTICS (TOP 50 ON 2004 MONEY LIST)

	Scoring Average	Putting Average	Greens in Regulation	Driving Distance	Driving Accuracy
2003	69.38 (2)	1.779 (T22)	73.0 (4)	287.0 (5)	70.6 (35)
2004	69.30 (1)	1.749 (3)	73.8 (4)	286.1 (7)	70.6 (T37)

Craig Stadler (continued)

days) and the first since Art Wall at the 1975 Greater Milwaukee Open...One week earlier, broke through for his first Champions Tour victory at the Ford Senior Players Championship, a three-stroke win over Tom Watson, Tom Kite and Jim Thorpe. Became the 14th player in history to record his first victory at a major championship and became the youngest winner in Ford Senior Players Championship history (50 years, 1 month, 19 days). Trailed by six strokes at the halfway point, but rebounded with rounds of 65-66, with only 51 putts in the final two rounds at the TPC of Michigan...Added a second Champions Tour title at the inaugural Greater Hickory Classic at Rock Barn. Started two strokes back in the final round, but made birdie on five of his first seven holes and cruised to a two-stroke win over Larry Nelson, his first in North Carolina since the 1991 TOUR Championship...Joined Tom Watson as the only other player on the Champions Tour to win in consecutive starts when he cruised to a four-stroke win over Bob Gilder at the SBC Championship in San Antonio, two weeks after winning in North Carolina. Win was his first in Texas since the 1984 Byron Nelson Classic and gave him four overall TOUR victories in a season for the first time since 1982...T15 in his Champions Tour debut at the Senior PGA Championship...Second to Tom Watson in Scoring (69.38). Also had the best Final-Round Scoring average, at 68.43.

OTHER CAREER HIGHLIGHTS:

Won 13 times on the PGA TOUR, with his biggest triumph coming at the 1982 Masters. After opening with a 75, came back to win at Augusta National in a playoff over Dan Pohl...His B.C. Open win came seven years after his previous win at the 1996 Nissan Open...In 1992, captured the NEC World Series of Golf by one stroke over Corey Pavin, 10 years after winning same event. In 1982, made up five strokes with closing 65 and then defeated Raymond Floyd in a playoff...Was the PGA TOUR's leading money-winner in 1982 thanks to four victories, a personal best for a single season...Finished second on money list in 1991 after winning THE TOUR Championship at Pinehurst No. 2 in a playoff with Russ Cochran...Shot the low round of his career, an 11-under 61, on the final day of the 1990 Scandinavian Enterprise Open to win by four strokes over Craig Parry...Was a two-time All-America selection at the University of Southern California...Defeated David Strawn to win the 1973 U.S. Amateur at Inverness...Has four career holes-in-one.

PERSONAL:

Nicknamed "The Walrus" and is one of golf's most colorful and popular personalities...A California native who lives in Denver and is an ardent fan of NHL's Colorado Avalanche...Inducted into San Diego's Breithard Hall of Fame in February of 1996..Son Kevin turned professional and won the 2002 Colorado Open in a playoff with his father as his caddie...Kevin is now a member of the PGA TOUR...Younger son, Chris, played college football at Lake Forest College in Illinois and served as his dad's caddie when he won the B.C. Open...Got started in golf at age 4 by his father...Favorite golf course is Harbour Town on Hilton Head Island, SC...Favorite athlete is Wayne Gretzky...Enjoys reading any book authored by Wilbur Smith...Always uses a dull penny for a ball marker...Lists Arnold Palmer as his hero.

PLAYER STATISTICS

MISCELLANEOUS CHAMPIONS TOUR STATISTICS

2004 Low Round: 63–2 times, most recent 2004 The First Tee Open at Pebble Beach presented by Wal-Mart/2
Career Low Round: 63–2 times, most recent 2004 The First Tee Open at Pebble Beach presented by Wal-Mart/2
Career Largest Paycheck: $375,000–2003 Ford Senior Players Championship/1

MISCELLANEOUS PGA TOUR STATISTICS

2004 Low Round: 67–B.C. Open/1
Career Low Round: 62–4 times, most recent 1987 Shearson Lehman Brothers Andy Williams Open/2
Career Largest Paycheck: $540,000–2003 B.C. Open/1

25 MEMORABLE MOMENTS

Doyle Donates Entire Winnings To Charity

2001 Charles Schwab Cup

When Allen Doyle won the inaugural Charles Schwab Cup in 2001 and its $1-million annuity that went to the champion, he quickly reminded everyone what the human spirit is all about. The man who just a few years earlier was making $30,000 a year running the Doyle Driving Center in LaGrange, GA, announced his donation to seven national and LaGrange charitable organizations over the 10-year period. Doyle finished 216 points ahead of Bruce Fleisher in the first season-long competition, thanks to 25 top-10 performances that included wins at the Ford Senior Players Championship and the State Farm Senior Classic.

CHAMPIONS TOUR 25

Dave Stockton

EXEMPT STATUS: Top 30 on All-Time Money List
FULL NAME: David Knapp Stockton
HEIGHT: 5-11
WEIGHT: 190
BIRTHDATE: November 2, 1941
BIRTHPLACE: San Bernardino, CA
RESIDENCE: Redlands, CA
FAMILY: Wife, Catherine; David (7/31/68), Ronald (9/16/70); four grandchildren
EDUCATION: University of Southern California (1964, General Management)
SPECIAL INTERESTS: Bison ranching, hunting, fishing
TURNED PROFESSIONAL: 1964
JOINED PGA TOUR: 1964

JOINED CHAMPIONS TOUR: 1991

CHAMPIONS TOUR VICTORIES (14): 1992 Mazda Presents THE SENIOR PLAYERS Championship. **1993** Murata Reunion Pro-Am, Southwestern Bell Classic, Franklin Quest Championship, GTE Northwest Classic, The Transamerica. **1994** Nationwide Championship, Ford Senior Players Championship, Burnet Senior Classic. **1995** GTE Suncoast Classic, Quicksilver Classic. **1996** U.S. Senior Open, First of America Classic. **1997** Franklin Quest Championship.

2004 CHARLES SCHWAB CUP FINISH: 46th - 208 points

GEORGIA-PACIFIC GRAND CHAMPIONS VICTORIES (1): 2003 FleetBoston Classic.

PGA TOUR VICTORIES (10): 1967 Colonial National Invitation. **1968** Cleveland Open Invitational, Greater Milwaukee Open. **1970** PGA Championship. **1971** Massachusetts Classic. **1973** Greater Milwaukee Open. **1974** Glen Campbell-Los Angeles Open, Quad Cities Open, Sammy Davis Jr.-Greater Hartford Open. **1976** PGA Championship.

OTHER VICTORIES (1): 1967 Haig Scotch Foursome Invitational [with Laurie Hammer].

PGA TOUR CAREER EARNINGS: $1,303,281

PGA TOUR PLAYOFF RECORD: 0-1

BEST 2004 CHAMPIONS TOUR FINISHES: T3—Farmers Charity Classic; T4—SBC Championship; T9—FedEx Kinko's Classic.

2004 SEASON:
Finished among the top 50 money-winners for an unprecedented 12th consecutive season...Secured a spot among the top 50 in San Antonio, his last official event of the season. Was tied for the opening-round lead at the SBC Championship and eventually T4 at Oak Hills...Posted best showing of the season in June when he was T3 at the Farmers Charity Classic in Michigan (nine top-10 finishes, including 1996 victory there), two strokes back of Jim Thorpe...Also T9 earlier in the year at the FedEx Kinko's Classic in Austin...Finished seventh on the final Georgia-Pacific Grand Champions money list, with $145,250...Finished second to Jim Dent in the Georgia-Pacific event at the Administaff Small Business Classic and T2 in the over-60 competition at the Commerce Bank Long Island Classic.

CHAMPIONS TOUR CAREER HIGHLIGHTS:
2003: T8 at the Music City Championship at Gaylord Opryland and also finished second to J.C. Snead in the Georgia-Pacific Grand Champions competition in Nashville...Was also second in the Georgia-Pacific competition at the Toshiba Senior Classic, losing in a playoff to Tom Wargo...Finished second again to Wargo by a stroke in the over-60 competition at the Farmers Charity Classic. Eventually T8 in the overall event in Grand Rapids, his seventh top-10 finish in western Michigan in 12 appearances...Moved to the other side of the state and was T9 at the Ford Senior Players Championship in Dearborn, his seventh top-10 performance in the event, tying him with Bob Charles, Raymond Floyd and Hale Irwin for the most in tournament history...Fifth on the final Georgia-Pacific Grand Champions money chart with $142,833...Struggled with the putter, dropping from a T18 in 2002 to a T69 in Putting and also slipped from T9 to T46 in Putts Per Round (28.90 to 29.60). **2002:** Had his highest finish on the money list since 1998...Birdied the final three holes at the TPC of Tampa Bay to close with a 68 and T3 at the Verizon Classic, his best finish in a Champions Tour event since placing second at the 2000 Foremost Insurance Championship...T3 again at the Toshiba Senior Classic after posting three straight sub-70 scores at Newport Beach...Closed with 8-under 64 at the Napa Valley Championship, his low round since the 2000 Novell Utah Showdown...Joined the ranks of the Georgia-Pacific Grand Champions at the start of the year and finished third on the over-60 money list with $304,291...Along with Al Geiberger, lost to George Archer in a six-hole playoff for the Georgia-Pacific title at the Royal Caribbean Classic and suffered another overtime loss to Charles Coody at the BellSouth Senior Classic at Opryland. One of three players who lost to Jim Dent in overtime for the Georgia-Pacific title at the TD Waterhouse Championship. Missed a playoff opportunity with Gibby Gilbert in the Georgia-Pacific Super Seniors Championship in Oklahoma City when he three-putted the final hole. **2001:** Led all players in fewest putts per round (28.46). **2000:** Finished solo second at the Foremost Insurance Championship, three strokes back of wire-to-wire winner Larry Nelson. **1999:** Led by two strokes heading into the final round of the Pacific Bell Senior Classic, but a 70 on Sunday left him T2 behind Joe Inman. **1998:** Went over the million-dollar mark ($1,040,524) in yearly earnings for a fifth time, the first Champions Tour player to do so for five consecutive years...Opened with a 7-under 64 at the Royal Caribbean Classic, but eventually lost to David Graham in a 10-hole playoff, the longest sudden-death affair in Champions Tour history...Also finished second to Larry Nelson at the American Express Invitational. **1997:** Birdied three of the final four holes to post a two-stroke win over Kermit Zarley at the Franklin Quest Championship. **1996:** Victorious at

CHAMPIONS TOUR CAREER SUMMARY — PLAYOFF RECORD: 0-6

Year	Events Played	1st	2nd	3rd	Top 10	Top 25	Earnings	Rank
1991	1					1	$12,965	94
1992	32	1	3	2	14	27	656,458	7
1993	34	5	5	2	22	29	1,175,944	1
1994	32	3	3	5	21	30	1,402,519	1
1995	34	2	6	3	24	31	1,415,847	3
1996	29	2	3	1	17	23	1,117,685	5
1997	29	1	1	2	9	21	854,611	10
1998	27		2	2	16	21	1,040,524	10
1999	25		1		2	14	428,234	45
2000	25		1		4	14	513,640	36
2001	24				7	11	522,444	36
2002	26			2	4	15	594,943	34
2003	20				3	9	339,468	47
2004	21			1	3	9	440,423	44
Total	359	14	25	20	146	255	10,515,705	
COMBINED ALL-TIME MONEY (3 TOURS):							**$11,818,986**	

CHAMPIONS TOUR TOP TOURNAMENT SUMMARY

Year	92	93	94	95	96	97	98	99	00	01	02	03	04
Senior PGA Championship	4	T23	T3	CUT		T15	T4	T32	CUT	T56		T53	CUT
U.S. Senior Open	T3	T30	T4	T21	1	CUT	6	T29	T6	T7	CUT	CUT	T29
Ford Senior Players	1	T11	1	T7	T8	T2	T24	T22	T28	T70	T8	T9	T66
JELD-WEN Tradition	T5	T14	T9	T12	T19	T15	T6	T20	T31	T52	T35	65	T14
Charles Schwab Cup Champ	T27	4	6	5	18	T19	T8						

CHAMPIONS TOUR YEAR-BY-YEAR STATISTICS (TOP 50 ON 2004 MONEY LIST)

	Scoring Average	Putting Average	Greens in Regulation	Driving Distance	Driving Accuracy
1991	67.67 (N/A)	1.864 (N/A)	81.5 (N/A)	264.3 (N/A)	69.0 (N/A)
1992	70.27 (5)	1.739 (1)	68.9 (25)	245.4 (61)	67.3 (47)
1993	69.71 (2)	1.742 (1)	71.6 (10)	254.0 (42)	69.6 (T28)
1994	69.41 (2)	1.730 (1)	74.6 (3)	254.8 (T34)	73.8 (T16)
1995	69.85 (3)	1.744 (3)	72.1 (9)	249.1 (60)	70.6 (30)
1996	70.25 (4)	1.763 (4)	69.4 (8)	255.6 (64)	72.5 (T20)
1997	70.78 (10)	1.762 (4)	64.8 (43)	253.3 (75)	71.1 (25)
1998	70.49 (4)	1.740 (2)	65.0 (T43)	254.6 (70)	72.0 (T24)
1999	71.28 (33)	1.782 (T19)	66.6 (47)	256.1 (75)	70.2 (41)
2000	70.93 (29)	1.764 (T13)	67.1 (43)	260.3 (74)	71.6 (30)
2001	71.51 (T36)	1.748 (T11)	61.6 (T74)	260.1 (T75)	71.3 (38)
2002	71.00 (23)	1.775 (T18)	66.3 (45)	256.7 (82)	67.3 (50)
2003	71.70 (51)	1.825 (69)	66.3 (51)	258.1 (82)	72.0 (25)
2004	71.53 (38)	1.779 (20)	63.3 (59)	255.6 (76)	72.0 (T28)

Dave Stockton (continued)

the U.S. Senior Open at Canterbury GC near Cleveland. After opening with a 70, fired back-to-back 67s to open a seven-shot lead after 54 holes and then held off a late charge by Hale Irwin to win by two strokes...Came from four strokes back a month later to win the First of America Classic near Grand Rapids. **1995:** Claimed the earliest win of his Champions Tour career when he triumphed at the GTE Suncoast Classic near Tampa, defeating three players by two strokes...Also came from four shots back to win the Pittsburgh Senior Classic by one shot over Isao Aoki. **1994:** Claimed a second consecutive Arnold Palmer Award as the circuit's leading money-winner, the first player to do so since Bob Charles in 1988-89...Earnings of over $1.4 million were more than his total amount in 27 years on the PGA TOUR...Voted Player of the Year by the Golf Writers Association of America...Nabbed wins at the Nationwide Championship and a second Ford Senior Players Championship title, where he was six strokes better than Jim Albus...Also won the Burnet Senior Classic by one over Albus. **1993:** Collected both the Arnold Palmer Award and the Champions Tour Player of the Year Award after winning a career-high five tournaments...Won back-to-back events at the Franklin Quest Championship and the GTE Northwest Classic...Tied a 54-hole Champions Tour record for largest victory margin, winning by nine strokes in Utah...Was the circuit's only wire-to-wire winner of the season at the GTE Northwest event near Seattle...Voted Player of the Year by the Golf Writers Association of America and other assorted publications. **1992:** Voted Champions Tour Rookie of the Year...Won his first event at the Mazda Presents THE SENIOR PLAYERS Championship, coming from behind to edge J.C Snead and Lee Trevino on the last hole. **1991:** Debuted on the circuit at the First Development Kaanapali Classic. Shot three sub-70 rounds and finished 12th at the final full-field event of the year in Hawaii.

OTHER CAREER HIGHLIGHTS:

Won 10 times on the PGA TOUR and was among the top 60 on the money list from 1967-78...A two-time winner of the PGA Championship. Claimed his first PGA Championship in 1970 at Southern Hills CC in Tulsa, OK, foiling Arnold Palmer and Bob Murphy. Last TOUR win came in the 1976 PGA Championship when he defeated Raymond Floyd and Don January at Congressional CC...Was runner-up at the 1975 Masters, 1975 PLAYERS Championship and 1978 U.S. Open...Most productive year was 1974, when he won three events and finished sixth on the money list with $155,104...Captained the 1991 U.S. Ryder Cup team to victory at Kiawah Island, SC...Also played on the 1971 and 1977 Ryder Cup teams...Has made 16 career holes-in-one.

PERSONAL:

Made history in March 1996, when he and his two sons each played a different TOUR event on the same weekend...Dave was at the FHP Health Care Classic, Dave Jr. was playing at the Doral-Ryder Open and youngest son, Ronnie, was playing in the Inland Empire Open on the Nationwide Tour...Became co-owner of a bison ranch in northern California in 1996...Served as honorary chairman for the 1995 Heartland of America Pro-Am that raised more than $400,000 to build a new day-care center for Oklahoma City...Was known as "King of the Corporate Outings" during the 1980s when he averaged more than 90 days a year mixing business with the game of golf...Father was a golf professional and got him started in the game of golf...Broke his back at age 15 and as a result, stopped playing basketball and baseball to concentrate of golf...Favorite athlete was Ted Williams. Favorite meal is Mexican food. Also admires Byron Nelson...Biggest golf thrill was winning 1970 PGA Championship.

PLAYER STATISTICS

MISCELLANEOUS CHAMPIONS TOUR STATISTICS

2004 Low Round: 66–2 times, most recent 2004 SBC Championship/1

Career Low Round: 62–2 times, most recent 1996 Cadillac NFL Golf Classic/2

Career Largest Paycheck: $212,500–1996 U.S. Senior Open/1

MISCELLANEOUS PGA TOUR STATISTICS

Career Low Round: 63–2 times, most recent 1987 Hardee's Golf Classic/2

Career Largest Paycheck: $45,000–1976 PGA Championship/1

25 MEMORABLE MOMENTS

Kite Wins Head-To-Head Dual with Watson

2002 SBC Classic

Tom Watson's dramatic 41-yard chip-in for eagle on the final hole forced Tom Kite to make an eight-foot birdie putt to send the tournament into overtime at the 2002 SBC Classic. Watson's eagle prompted him to run with arms in the air, reminiscent of his dance after chipping in at the 17th at Pebble Beach in the 1982 U.S. Open. All of a sudden Kite went from leading to trailing by one and had to get up and down to force a playoff. He was up to the task and then managed to two-putt for a par on the second extra hole for his fifth career victory on the Champions Tour.

CHAMPIONS TOUR 25

Curtis Strange

EXEMPT STATUS: Top 30 on All-Time Money List
FULL NAME: Curtis Northrop Strange
HEIGHT: 5-11
WEIGHT: 180
BIRTHDATE: January 30, 1955
BIRTHPLACE: Norfolk, VA
RESIDENCE: Morehead City, NC

FAMILY: Wife Sarah; Thomas Wright III (8/25/82), David Clark (4/3/85)
EDUCATION: Wake Forest University
SPECIAL INTERESTS: Hunting, off-shore fishing
TURNED PROFESSIONAL: 1976
JOINED PGA TOUR: 1977

JOINED CHAMPIONS TOUR: 2005

PGA TOUR VICTORIES (17): **1979** Pensacola Open. **1980** Michelob-Houston Open, Manufacturers Hanover Westchester Classic. **1983** Sammy Davis Jr.-Greater Hartford Open. **1984** Lajet Golf Classic. **1985** Honda Classic, Panasonic Las Vegas Invitational, Canadian Open. **1986** Houston Open. **1987** Canadian Open, Federal Express St. Jude Classic, NEC World Series of Golf. **1988** Independent Insurance Agent Open, Memorial Tournament, U.S. Open Championship, Nabisco Championship. **1989** U.S. Open Championship.

OTHER VICTORIES (4): **1986** ABC Cup (Jpn). **1988** Sanctuary Cove Classic (Aus). **1989** Palm Meadows Cup (Aus). **1993** Greg Norman's Holden Classic (Aus).

PGA TOUR CAREER EARNINGS: $7,599,951

PGA TOUR PLAYOFF RECORD: 6-3

2004 SEASON: Made four appearances on the PGA TOUR...Missed the cut in three events and withdrew from The Honda Classic...Left his role as the lead golf analyst for ABC Sports near the end of May.

OTHER CAREER HIGHLIGHTS:
Considered one of the premier players of the 1980s, with 16 of his 17 career PGA TOUR victories coming in that decade...Won at least one tournament a year for seven straight years (1983-1989)...In 1989 at Oak Hill CC, became the first player to successfully defend a U.S. Open title since Ben Hogan (1950-51) with a one-stroke victory over Chip Beck, Mark McCumber and Ian Woosnam...Also finished T2 at the 1989 PGA Championship...Came close to a third U.S. Open crown in 1994, finishing one stroke out of Ernie Els, Loren Roberts, Colin Montgomerie playoff at Oakmont...Best year on TOUR came when he won four times in 1988, including his first U.S. Open at The Country Club, defeating Nick Faldo in an 18-hole playoff...Became the first player to surpass $1 million in a season when he captured his third of three money titles (1985, 1987-88)...Voted as Player of the Year for a third time by the Golf Writers Association of America...Biggest payday ($360,000) came with playoff victory over Tom Kite at 1988 Nabisco Championships...Selected as the 1988 PGA of America Player of the Year...Edged Bill Kratzert by a stroke for his first PGA TOUR title at the 1979 Pensacola Open...Served as captain for U.S. Ryder Cup team in 2002 when Captain Sam Torrance's European Team reclaimed the Cup...Also played on five American Ryder Cup squads (1983, 1985, 1987, 1989, 1995), the 1975 Walker Cup team and the 1974 World Amateur team...Set course record at Old Course at St. Andrews (62) during the 1987 Dunhill Cup...Exemplary amateur career included victories at the 1973 Southeastern Amateur, 1974 Western Amateur, 1975-76 Virginia Amateurs, 1975-76 North & South Amateurs...Was a three-time All-America selection at Wake Forest, the medalist at the 1974 NCAA Championship and on the winning national championship team in 1974 and 1975...Also won the Virginia State Junior at age 15...Worked on ABC Sports golf telecasts from 1997-2004.

PERSONAL:
Started playing golf at age 7; father owned White Sands CC in Virginia Beach, VA...Identical twin, Allen, is a former TOUR member.

PLAYER STATISTICS

MISCELLANEOUS PGA TOUR STATISTICS
2004 Low Round: **73**–MCI Heritage/1
Career Low Round: **62**–2 times, most recent 1983 Sammy Davis Jr.-Greater Hartford Open/2
Career Largest Paycheck: **$360,000**–1988 Nabisco Championship/1

Ron Streck

EXEMPT STATUS: PGA TOUR Career Victory List
FULL NAME: Ronald Raymond Streck
HEIGHT: 5-11
WEIGHT: 185
BIRTHDATE: July 17, 1954
BIRTHPLACE: Tulsa, OK
RESIDENCE: Tulsa, OK

FAMILY: Wife, Jody; Juliane (7/6/90), Justin (10/27/91), Reagan (3/23/99)
EDUCATION: University of Tulsa (1976, Education)
SPECIAL INTERESTS: Skiing, cars, motorcycles
TURNED PROFESSIONAL: 1976
JOINED PGA TOUR: 1977

JOINED CHAMPIONS TOUR: 2004

BEST CHAMPIONS TOUR CAREER FINISH: T28—2004 SBC Championship.

PGA TOUR VICTORIES (2): 1978 San Antonio Texas Open. **1981** Michelob-Houston Open.

NATIONWIDE TOUR VICTORIES (1): 1993 Yuma Open.

PGA TOUR CAREER EARNINGS: $815,348

PGA TOUR PLAYOFF RECORD: 0-1

BEST 2004 CHAMPIONS TOUR FINISH: T28—SBC Championship.

2004 SEASON:

Made five appearances on the Champions Tour and debuted on the circuit at the Senior British Open (missed cut)...Played in events through the PGA TOUR Career Victory category, with best finish a T28 at the SBC Championship in San Antonio.

OTHER CAREER HIGHLIGHTS:

Played the PGA TOUR from 1977-99, with 329 starts and 215 cuts to his credit. Most of those came during a 10-year span (1979-88) when he played in 268 events. His best year financially came in 1985 when he earned $142,848 and finished 55th on the money list. Had five top-10 finishes that season, including a playoff loss to Woody Blackburn at the Isuzu-Andy Williams San Diego Open...Won twice on the PGA TOUR. The first came in 1978 when he fired back-to-back rounds on the weekend of 63-62—125 to claim the San Antonio Texas Open by one stroke over Hubert Green and Lon Hinkle. He earned $40,000. His consecutive rounds of 63-62 still ranks among the best consecutive rounds in PGA TOUR history (tied for second). Only Mark Calcavecchia (60-64—124/second and third rounds at 2001 Phoenix Open) has done better. Began Saturday's round 12 strokes behind 36-hole leader Ben Crenshaw before his scorching weekend play. Had earned just $6,616 during the 1978 season before capturing the San Antonio victory...Added his second TOUR win three years later by again prevailing in Texas, posting a three-stroke victory over Hale Irwin and Jerry Pate at the rain-shortened Michelob-Houston Open at Woodlands CC. Shot a third-round 62, which gave him a three-stroke margin after 54 holes and held up when bad weather reduced the event to 54 holes...Was second at the MONY Tournament of Champions at LaCosta in 1982...His career earnings total $815,348...Has also played the Nationwide Tour, making 75 starts, with earnings totaling $128,094. Was victorious at the 1993 Yuma Open, defeating Chris DiMarco in a playoff...College standout at University of Tulsa, where he won All-American honors for the Golden Hurricanes and was a four-time All-Missouri Valley Conference selection...Has 12 holes-in-one overall and eight in competition.

PERSONAL:

His dad got him started in the game at age 3 1/2...Biggest thrill in golf came in 1978 when his parents were on hand to see him capture his first PGA TOUR victory in San Antonio...Won all-state honors in basketball while in high school and was also a member of a state championship team...Named his youngest son after former President Ronald Reagan and says his biggest thrill outside of golf was the day his son, Reagan, was born...Is an owner of a water-treatment business...Favorite TV show is "Hannity & Colmes," while favorite athlete is the late Sam Snead...Favorite movie is "The Sound of Music"...His favorite golf course is Hillcrest CC in Bartlesville, OK...Heroes are Ronald Reagan, George W. Bush and all members of our military who fight for our freedom.

PLAYER STATISTICS

2004 CHAMPIONS TOUR STATISTICS:

Scoring Average	72.57	(N/A)
Driving Distance	287.7	(N/A)
Driving Accuracy Percentage	76.8%	(N/A)
Total Driving	1,998	(N/A)
Greens in Regulation Pct.	66.2%	(N/A)
Putting Average	1.881	(N/A)
Sand Save Percentage	50.0%	(N/A)
Birdie Average	2.86	(N/A)
All-Around Ranking	1,569	(N/A)

MISCELLANEOUS CHAMPIONS TOUR STATISTICS

2004 Low Round: 69–3 times, most recent 2004 SBC Championship/2
Career Low Round: 69–3 times, most recent 2004 SBC Championship/2
Career Largest Paycheck: $12,150–2004 SBC Championship/T28

MISCELLANEOUS PGA TOUR STATISTICS

Career Low Round: 62–4 times, most recent 1990 Chattanooga Classic/3
Career Largest Paycheck: $47,250–1981 Michelob Houston Open/1

CHAMPIONS TOUR CAREER SUMMARY — PLAYOFF RECORD: 0-0

Year	Events Played	1st	2nd	3rd	Top 10	Top 25	Earnings	Rank
2004	5						$29,592	107
Total	5						29,592	
COMBINED ALL-TIME MONEY (3 TOURS):							**$973,034**	

CHAMPIONS TOUR TOP TOURNAMENT SUMMARY

Year	04
Senior British Open	CUT

Mike Sullivan

EXEMPT STATUS: PGA TOUR Career Victory List
FULL NAME: Mike Sullivan
HEIGHT: 6-2
WEIGHT: 220
BIRTHDATE: January 1, 1955
BIRTHPLACE: Gary, IN
RESIDENCE: Greenville, TN
FAMILY: Wife, Lucy; Rebecca (6/13/85)
EDUCATION: University of Florida
SPECIAL INTERESTS: Flying, hunting, fishing
TURNED PROFESSIONAL: 1975
JOINED PGA TOUR: 1977

JOINED CHAMPIONS TOUR: 2005

PGA TOUR VICTORIES (3): 1980 Southern Open. **1989** Independent Insurance Agent Open. **1994** B.C. Open.

OTHER VICTORIES (1): 1984 Shootout at Jeremy Ranch [with Don January].

PGA TOUR CAREER EARNINGS: $2,301,255

PGA TOUR PLAYOFF RECORD: 0-4

BEST 2004 PGA TOUR FINISH: 78—B.C. Open.

2004 SEASON:

Made one appearance on the PGA TOUR and finished 78th at the B.C. Open...Played 15 events on the Nationwide Tour and recorded one top-10 finish, a solo fourth at the Rheem Classic in late April. Strung together four consecutive sub-70 rounds in Fort Smith, AR, and was five strokes back of Franklin Langham.

OTHER CAREER HIGHLIGHTS:

Entering the 2005 season, has made 532 career appearances on the PGA TOUR, with 332 cuts made. Played the circuit full-time from 1977-1999...First of three PGA TOUR titles came at the 1980 Southern Open, a five-stroke triumph over Dave Eichelberger and Johnny Miller at Green Island CC...Captured second career title as early starter in 1989 Independent Insurance Agent Open. Barely made the cut and began final round seven strokes back. Proceeded to fire 7-under 65 at the TPC at The Woodlands and 8-under 280 total was good enough for a one-shot victory over Craig Stadler...Enjoyed best season on TOUR in 1994, when he won the B.C. Open by four strokes over Jeff Sluman. Also lost in a playoff to Brian Henninger at the weather-shortened Deposit Guaranty Golf Classic. Finished the year with $298,586, leaving him 60th on the money list...Posted 7-under 28 for nine holes in 1988 Texas Open...Teamed with Don January to win 1984 Shootout at Jeremy Ranch in Park City, UT...Has played the Nationwide Tour from 1997-2004, with 117 career starts and 49 cuts made. Best-ever Nationwide Tour finish came in 1998 when he finished second at the Dominion Open. Was third-round co-leader at Dominion, but fired a final-round 74 to wind up two strokes back of Bob Burns...Collected a third-place check at the rain-shortened Upstate Classic.

PERSONAL:

Briefly attended University of Florida, where Andy Bean was a roommate...Has been plagued by back trouble throughout his career.

PLAYER STATISTICS

MISCELLANEOUS PGA TOUR STATISTICS
2004 Low Round: 71–B.C. Open/2
Career Low Round: 62–2 times, most recent 1992 Federal Express St. Jude Classic/3
Career Largest Paycheck: $162,000–1994 B.C. Open/1

Bruce Summerhays

EXEMPT STATUS: Top 30 on 2004 Champions Tour Money List
FULL NAME: Bruce Patton Summerhays
HEIGHT: 5-9
WEIGHT: 175
BIRTHDATE: February 14, 1944
BIRTHPLACE: St. Louis, MO
RESIDENCE: Farmington, UT
FAMILY: Wife, Carolyn; Shelly (7/4/65), Bryan (10/2/67), Joseph (9/16/71), William (2/16/73), Rachel (7/10/74), Susanna (3/2/76), Bruce, Jr. (12/23/77), Carrie (6/21/80); 26 grandchildren
CLUB AFFILIATION: Promontory-The Ranch Club (Park City, UT)
EDUCATION: University of Utah
SPECIAL INTERESTS: Family, fishing, music, sports, church service
TURNED PROFESSIONAL: 1966

JOINED CHAMPIONS TOUR: 1994

CHAMPIONS TOUR VICTORIES (3): **1997** Saint Luke's Classic. **1998** State Farm Senior Classic. **2004** Kroger Classic.

2004 CHARLES SCHWAB CUP FINISH: 34th - 417 points

BEST PGA TOUR CAREER FINISH: T3—1974 Bing Crosby National Pro-Am.

OTHER VICTORIES (16): **1966** Provo Open. **1974** Northern California Medal Play. **1975** Northern California Match Play. **1976** Northern California Open. **1977** Northern California Match Play, Northern California Medal Play. **1979** Wasatch Open. **1981** Wasatch Open, Rocky Mountain PGA Championship. **1982** Rocky Mountain PGA Championship. **1986** Wasatch Open. **1991** Provo Open, Utah PGA Championship. **1992** Dixie Open, Wendover Open. **1993** Provo Open. **2001** Champions Challenge [with son, Joseph].

PGA TOUR CAREER EARNINGS: $9,602

BEST 2004 CHAMPIONS TOUR FINISHES:

1—Kroger Classic; 8—Bayer Advantage Celebrity Pro-Am; T9—Bank of America Championship, Senior British Open.

2004 SEASON:

Returned to the top-30 on the money list for the first time since the 2001 season and was one of just two players 60 or older (Graham Marsh, the other) to qualify for the season-ending Charles Schwab Cup Championship...Won for the third time on the Champions Tour at the Kroger Classic near Cincinnati late in the year. Win ended a victory drought of 6 years, 2 months and 7 days (209 starts). At 60 years, 6 months and 28 days old, he became the eighth oldest winner in Champions Tour history (13th player over 60 to win) and the oldest champion since 61-year-old J.C. Snead's triumph at the 2002 Greater Baltimore Classic. Rallied from six strokes back for victory, thanks to a final-round 64 at the TPC at River's Bend, his best round in over four years. Got up and down for a clutch birdie on the last hole to post a 15-under-par 201 total and then watched his closest pursuers fail in their bids to catch him...Initial top-10 performance of the season was a T8 at the rain-shortened Bayer Advantage Celebrity Pro-Am...Also finished T9 two weeks later at the Bank of America Championship and T9 again at the Senior British Open, the second straight year in the top 10 in that major championship...Finished fourth on the final Georgia-Pacific Grand Champions money list, with $154,983...Finished second to Bob Murphy in the Georgia-Pacific event at the Kroger Classic and was a distant third at the Georgia-Pacific Grand Champions Championship in Sonoma.

CHAMPIONS TOUR CAREER HIGHLIGHTS:

2003: Top performance came overseas in July. One of six players to post four consecutive rounds in the 60s on the Ailsa course at Turnberry and placed solo third at the Senior British Open, thanks to a final-round 65. Performance in Scotland was his best effort in a Champions Tour event since T3 at the 2002 Countrywide Tradition...Matched that finish nearly three months later when he closed with a 6-under-par 66 at the Turtle Bay Championship to finish T3 with along Graham Marsh. **2002:** Was among the leaders for the first two days of the Verizon Classic, but faded into T7 with a final-round 75 at the TPC of Tampa Bay...Closed with a 68 on Sunday at The Countrywide Tradition and fell just one stroke shy of earning a berth in a playoff with John Jacobs and eventual winner Jim Thorpe. Third-place effort in Arizona was his best performance since the SBC Senior Open in July 2000 (solo third). **2001:** Was T4 at both the Kroger Senior Classic and Allianz Championship...Held sole possession of the 36-hole lead at the Novell Utah Showdown before seeing his quest for his first win since 1998 go awry with a double bogey at the par-5 17th hole on Sunday...Led all players in Eagles, with 19. **2000:** Opened with a career-low 10-under 62 at the LiquidGolf.com Invitational and was the 36-hole leader at the TPC at Prestancia before eventually T8 in Sarasota...Best overall finish was a solo third at SBC Senior Open near Chicago. **1999:** Finished second at the inaugural Bank One Championship, five strokes back of Tom Watson...T2 at the Pacific Bell Senior Classic, two strokes behind Joe Inman. **1998:** Tasted victory at the State Farm Senior Classic near Baltimore. Made a 20-foot birdie putt on the 18th green at Hobbit's Glen to avert a playoff with Walter Hall and Hale Irwin...Led the Champions Tour in Total Birdies (430). **1997:** Earned his first Champions Tour victory in his 102nd start. Claimed the Saint Luke's Classic in suburban Kansas City in a playoff over Hugh Baiocchi. Trailed by six strokes entering the final round, but made birdie on two of the last three holes to tie Baiocchi, then defeated him with a par on the second extra playoff hole. Saw his string of consecutive official events end at 96 straight when he skipped the BankBoston Classic in August due to a back problem. **1996:** Earned the "ironman" title after setting a Champions Tour record by playing an amazing 119 rounds (the old mark was 115 by Rives McBee and John Paul Cain in 1990). **1995:** Blitzed the GC of Georgia with a course-record 63 in the first round of the Nationwide Championship. Eventually settled for a T2 with Hale Irwin, two behind Bob Murphy...Came close again in his native Utah, but was one of six players to fall one stroke short of Tony Jacklin at the Franklin Quest Championship...Also led with six holes to play at The Transamerica, but lost to Lee Trevino down the stretch. **1994:** Earned a full exemption for 1995 after a fourth-place finish at the National Qualifying Tournament...Played in four events (three Monday qualifying/one sponsor exemption).

OTHER CAREER HIGHLIGHTS:

One of the top players in the Utah PGA section for a number of years prior to joining the Champions Tour...Twice selected as the Rocky Mountain PGA Section Player of the Year...Never qualified for the PGA TOUR on a full-time basis, but played in nine PGA TOUR events when he was living in northern California and made eight cuts...T3 in the 1974 Bing Crosby National Pro-Am...Also qualified for

SECTION 2 PLAYER BIOGRAPHIES

CHAMPIONS TOUR CAREER SUMMARY — PLAYOFF RECORD: 1-1

Year	Events Played	1st	2nd	3rd	Top 10	Top 25	Earnings	Rank
1994	4					1	$20,711	96
1995	36		3	1	14	27	729,021	13
1996	38				5	20	449,659	29
1997	35	1	1	2	8	23	776,804	14
1998	37	1	3	2	12	24	1,098,942	8
1999	36		2	2	13	26	1,118,377	8
2000	38			1	10	24	914,554	19
2001	34				10	23	904,617	20
2002	33			1	4	12	530,760	37
2003	28			2	4	8	509,194	36
2004	28	1			4	12	677,459	28
Total	347	3	9	11	84	200	7,730,098	

COMBINED ALL-TIME MONEY (3 TOURS): $7,740,400

CHAMPIONS TOUR TOP TOURNAMENT SUMMARY

Year	95	96	97	98	99	00	01	02	03	04
Senior PGA Championship	T26	T37	T23	T47	T5	T25	T10	T45	CUT	T31
U.S. Senior Open	T29	T8	T12	T20	7	CUT	T21	CUT	CUT	T32
Ford Senior Players	T38	T24	T34	T19	T19	T41	T59	T40	T23	T18
Senior British Open									3	T9
JELD-WEN Tradition	T8	T23	T25	9	T14	T9	T24	T3	T5	T45
Charles Schwab Cup Champ	T14	25	T14	T16	4	26	21			T22

CHAMPIONS TOUR YEAR-BY-YEAR STATISTICS (TOP 50 ON 2004 MONEY LIST)

	Scoring Average	Putting Average	Greens in Regulation	Driving Distance	Driving Accuracy
1994	71.33 (N/A)	1.804 (N/A)	68.5 (N/A)	265.8 (N/A)	68.5 (N/A)
1995	70.57 (9)	1.782 (T13)	70.5 (15)	267.6 (9)	65.5 (59)
1996	71.76 (30)	1.815 (T37)	65.5 (38)	272.1 (9)	65.6 (T62)
1997	71.18 (17)	1.782 (T17)	66.2 (29)	269.5 (14)	63.1 (T70)
1998	71.17 (T17)	1.767 (T11)	65.1 (42)	273.8 (11)	63.8 (T77)
1999	70.57 (14)	1.782 (T19)	69.6 (21)	276.8 (7)	63.2 (83)
2000	70.67 (19)	1.783 (32)	71.0 (15)	277.5 (11)	65.0 (78)
2001	70.93 (T20)	1.786 (25)	69.5 (19)	283.2 (5)	65.4 (72)
2002	71.78 (T46)	1.786 (T30)	65.1 (56)	271.5 (33)	63.1 (70)
2003	71.68 (50)	1.799 (T46)	66.4 (50)	276.8 (22)	62.1 (69)
2004	71.62 (39)	1.778 (19)	65.8 (T50)	271.2 (44)	69.6 (T46)

Bruce Summerhays (continued)

four U.S. Open Championships and four PGA Championships...Was a member of two U.S. teams in PGA Cup matches...Named the 1977 Northern California PGA Section Player of the Year...A collegiate All-American at the University of Utah...Was an assistant professional at the Olympic Club in San Francisco from 1968-1976 and set the Ocean Course record with a 60...Was Pac-8 Coach of the Year at Stanford University, where he served as golf coach in 1978-79...Has three career holes-in-one.

PERSONAL:

Was inducted into the University of Utah Athletic Hall of Fame prior to the start of the 1998 season...Father, Pres, was the head baseball coach at the University of Utah and also served as an assistant football coach at the school...Favorite golf courses are The Olympic Club, Pebble Beach, Cypress Point and the TPC of Tampa Bay...Likes the Discovery Channel...His favorite athletes are John Stockton and Cal Ripken, Jr...Favorite movies are "Hoosiers" and "Field of Dreams"...Biggest thrill in golf was winning the 2001 Champions Challenge with his son Joseph...Favorite books are *The Book of Mormon* and *The Bible*...Daughter, Carrie, has played on the LPGA.

PLAYER STATISTICS

MISCELLANEOUS CHAMPIONS TOUR STATISTICS

2004 Low Round: 64–2004 Kroger Classic/3
Career Low Round: 62–2000 LiquidGolf.com Invitational/1
Career Largest Paycheck: $225,000–2004 Kroger Classic/1

MISCELLANEOUS PGA TOUR STATISTICS

Career Low Round: 69–3 times, most recent 1976 Kaiser International Open Invitational/1
Career Largest Paycheck: $6,764–1974 Bing Crosby National Pro–Am/T3

25 MEMORABLE MOMENTS

Pooley Outlasts Watson In Playoff For First Champions Tour Win

2002 U.S. Senior Open

After making 17 consecutive pars in regulation, Don Pooley made a 10-foot birdie putt on the fifth playoff hole to end his epic five-hour duel with Tom Watson and become the first-ever qualifier to win a U.S. Senior Open title. Pooley played himself into a three-stroke lead with a rousing 63 on Saturday, the lowest 18-hole score in U.S. Senior Open history. He got into the championship through a regional qualifier, where he made a birdie to force a playoff and a birdie to earn a spot into the field. Pooley became just the sixth golfer to win the U.S. Senior Open on his first try.

CHAMPIONS TOUR 25

Doug Tewell (TOOL)

EXEMPT STATUS: Top 30 on 2004 Champions Tour Money List
FULL NAME: Douglas Fred Tewell
HEIGHT: 5-10
WEIGHT: 215
BIRTHDATE: August 27, 1949
BIRTHPLACE: Baton Rouge, LA
RESIDENCE: Edmond, OK

FAMILY: Wife, Pam; Kristi (9/24/69), Jay (3/31/75); four grandchildren
CLUB AFFILIATION: Oak Tree GC (Edmond, OK)
EDUCATION: Oklahoma State University (1971, Speech Communications)
SPECIAL INTERESTS: Family, broadcasting, auto racing
TURNED PROFESSIONAL: 1971
JOINED PGA TOUR: 1975

JOINED CHAMPIONS TOUR: 1999

CHAMPIONS TOUR VICTORIES (8): 2000 PGA Seniors' Championship, SBC Championship, Novell Utah Showdown. **2001** The Countrywide Tradition. **2002** Verizon Classic, Liberty Mutual Legends of Golf. **2003** Farmers Charity Classic. **2004** Greater Hickory Classic at Rock Barn.

2004 CHARLES SCHWAB CUP FINISH:
15th - 1,173 points

PGA TOUR VICTORIES (4): 1980 Sea Pines Heritage, IVB-Golf Classic. **1986** Los Angeles Open. **1987** Pensacola Open.

OTHER VICTORIES (3): 1978 South Central PGA Championship. **1982** Oklahoma Open. **1988** Acom Team Championship [with Bob Gilder].

PGA TOUR CAREER EARNINGS: $2,713,623

PGA TOUR PLAYOFF RECORD: 1-0

BEST 2004 CHAMPIONS TOUR FINISHES:
1—Greater Hickory Classic at Rock Barn; T2—Kroger Classic; T3—MasterCard Championship, SAS Championship presented by Forbes; T4—JELD-WEN Tradition; T5—Bank of America Championship.

2004 SEASON:

Improved one spot on the money list from 2003 and surpassed the $1-million mark in earnings for the fifth straight year...Ended a drought of just over a year when, after borrowing a Ping Anser putter from the stash of surplus clubs at the home of close friend Walter Hall, used the club to win the Greater Hickory Classic at Rock Barn. Made a clutch 13-foot birdie putt on the last hole to edge Bruce Fleisher by one stroke and win the western North Carolina event. Shot an 8-under-par 64 in the last round to come from three strokes back of Fleisher on Sunday. Victory was his eighth on the Champions Tour and gave him five straight years with at least one win and also began a string of five straight top-10 finishes. Went bogey-free over his 54 holes at Rock Barn, a first since Morris Hatalsky won the 2003 Columbus Southern Open without making a bogey...Started his opening round at the JELD-WEN Tradition with a string of 59 holes without a bogey, but made one on the first hole to end that streak. Eventually finished T4 at the Oregon event, thanks to four straight sub-par rounds...After a T9 at The First Tee Open at Pebble Beach presented by Wal-Mart, came back with another strong outing the next week near Cincinnati. Was the 36-hole leader at the Kroger Classic but eventually fell one stroke short of a charging Bruce Summerhays at the TPC at River's Bend...Followed with another strong performance in his next start, grabbing a T3 at the SAS Championship, his fifth consecutive top-10 finish...Led the season-opening MasterCard Championship by two strokes after 36 holes, but eventually finished T3 in Hawaii despite a final-round 69 at Hualalai. His 64-65-129 (15-under) total over the first two rounds were the low first-36 holes total on the Champions Tour for the year...Three consecutive rounds in the 60s earned him a T5 at the Bank of America Championship near Boston. Plagued for a portion of the year with an elbow problem, which forced him to withdraw from the season-ending Charles Schwab Cup Championship...After three straight years of leading or sharing the Driving Accuracy category, he slipped to fourth.

CHAMPIONS TOUR CAREER HIGHLIGHTS:

2003: Got off to a slow start, but ended up with top-10 finishes in a third of his 27 appearances. Earned seven figures for the fourth straight year, yet slipped out of the top 10 money-winners for the first time since joining the Champions Tour...Victory near Grand Rapids came in dramatic fashion and extended his number of years with at least one win to four straight seasons. Came from three strokes back on Sunday to claim his seventh career title at the Farmers Charity Classic. Tied Eamonn Darcy after 54 holes as a result of a clutch 18-foot eagle putt on the 17th hole at Egypt Valley. Eventually defeated Darcy with a 15-foot birdie putt on the third playoff hole. Victory made him the 16th different winner in 2003, tying the all-time Champions Tour record for longest span without a repeat winner...Had finished in third place a month earlier at the Columbus Southern Open on the strength of a second-round 64, his lowest score of the year...Played his best golf of the campaign from late August to late September when he had four top-five performances in five starts and put together a streak of 12 straight sub-par rounds during that period...Had back-to-back runner-up efforts in consecutive weeks. First battled fellow Edmond, OK, resident Gil Morgan throughout the Kroger Classic. Got within one stroke of Morgan, but missed birdie chances at the last two holes and eventually came up two strokes shy at the TPC at River's Bend...T2 for the second straight year the following week at the Constellation Energy Classic near Baltimore. Made up three strokes on 36-hole co-leaders Larry Nelson and Jay Sigel on the final day, and briefly grabbed the lead late in the final round. Fell back after missing a birdie opportunity on No. 16 and then bogeyed the last two holes to finish two strokes shy of Nelson...Had another chance for a win the following week at the SAS Championship. Led the Champions Tour in Driving Accuracy for the third straight year (81.5 percent). **2002:** The third of six multiple winners...Came from three strokes back to win the Verizon Classic by one stroke over Hale Irwin. Was the only player in the field to record three consecutive rounds in the 60s at the TPC of Tampa Bay and hit 41 of 42 fairways...Held off Bobby Wadkins by a stroke to win the Liberty Mutual Legends of Golf. Again drove the ball in 41 of 42 fairways at the King & Bear course...Made the first hole-in-one of the 2002 season when he aced the 217-yard eighth hole with a 4-iron at Hualalai GC during the opening round of the MasterCard Championship. Ace was the first in MasterCard Championship history...Made first PGA TOUR start since 1999 and made his fifth consecutive cut, finishing T68 at the WORLDCOM CLASSIC-The Heritage of Golf at Harbour Town, site of his first TOUR victory in 1980. **2001:** In April, closed with a Cochise course-record 10-under-par 62 at Desert Mountain, the lowest score ever shot in a major championship on the Champions Tour, and completed a wire-to-wire victory at The Countrywide Tradition. Victory at Desert Mountain GC was his second major victory on the Champions Tour. Needed just 19 putts in his final round and his 72-hole total of 23-under-par 265 was the best four-round score on the Champions Tour since Jack

CHAMPIONS TOUR CAREER SUMMARY — PLAYOFF RECORD: 1-1

Year	Events Played	1st	2nd	3rd	Top 10	Top 25	Earnings	Rank
1999	5					2	$59,162	91
2000	27	3	1	1	9	19	1,408,194	8
2001	28	1	5		14	20	1,721,339	7
2002	27	2	2	1	12	24	1,579,988	5
2003	27	1	2	1	9	21	1,237,681	13
2004	27	1	1	2	8	20	1,179,440	12
Total	141	8	11	5	52	106	7,185,804	

COMBINED ALL-TIME MONEY (3 TOURS): **$9,910,396**

CHAMPIONS TOUR TOP TOURNAMENT SUMMARY

Year	00	01	02	03	04
Senior PGA Championship	1	T8	T18	T5	T25
U.S. Senior Open	T21	T34	T11	T54	T7
Ford Senior Players	T34	2	5	T23	T22
JELD-WEN Tradition	T25	1	T21	T46	T4
Charles Schwab Cup Champ	T19	2	T21	T16	WD

CHAMPIONS TOUR YEAR-BY-YEAR STATISTICS (TOP 50 ON 2004 MONEY LIST)

	Scoring Average	Putting Average	Greens in Regulation	Driving Distance	Driving Accuracy
1999	70.47 (N/A)	1.848 (N/A)	73.0 (N/A)	265.9 (N/A)	85.5 (N/A)
2000	70.09 (12)	1.805 (T57)	74.4 (T6)	269.7 (32)	79.4 (4)
2001	69.94 (7)	1.773 (19)	72.9 (3)	270.6 (50)	81.4 (T1)
2002	69.85 (T5)	1.776 (20)	73.3 (3)	263.4 (66)	83.6 (1)
2003	70.45 (20)	1.798 (T43)	72.8 (5)	266.6 (63)	81.5 (1)
2004	70.30 (10)	1.790 (T29)	73.5 (5)	266.9 (57)	82.1 (4)

Doug Tewell (continued)

Nicklaus posted an all-time record of 27-under 261 at the 1990 Ford Senior Players Championship. The nine-stroke win was also the largest margin of victory since Hale Irwin won the 1997 PGA Seniors' Championship by 12 strokes. Victory near Phoenix was his fourth Champions Tour title, coming in his 40th career start. Did not register his fourth win on the PGA TOUR until his 541st start...Almost claimed a second major title at the Ford Senior Players Championship, but fell in a one-hole playoff to Allen Doyle. Appeared on the verge of winning the title before Doyle drained a 35-foot putt on the 72nd hole to force the overtime session...Closed the season with a solo second-place finish at the SENIOR TOUR CHAMPIONSHIP at Gaillardia. **2000:** Earned Rookie of the Year honors, thanks to three victories, including a win in a Champions Tour major...Broke through in a big way with his first Champions Tour title, the rain-shortened PGA Seniors' Championship. Victory was his first since the '87 Pensacola Open. Became just the 10th player ever to make his first victory on the Champions Tour a major when he waltzed to a seven-shot triumph over Dana Quigley, Tom Kite, Larry Nelson and Hale Irwin at PGA National...Added his second victory at the SBC Championship in San Antonio, holing a birdie putt on the final hole for a one-stroke win over Walter Hall and Larry Nelson...Claimed his third title at the Novell Utah Showdown, outdistancing his neighbor Gil Morgan by two strokes in Park City. **1999:** Turned 50 in August, but did not play his first event until early October due to a back injury he sustained right before he was eligible to play...Made debut on the Champions Tour at the Vantage Championship and finished T15.

OTHER CAREER HIGHLIGHTS:

Won four times in a PGA TOUR career that started in June of 1975...Last victory came at the 1987 Pensacola Open, a three-stroke triumph over Danny Edwards and Phil Blackmar...Had his best earnings year in 1986 when he finished the season with $310,285 (No. 18)...Had a run-away victory (seven strokes) over Clarence Rose in the Los Angeles Open that year...Highest money standing came in 1980 when he placed 17th with $161,684...Won two titles in 1980, defeating Jerry Pate in a playoff for the Sea Pines Heritage Classic crown and coming from behind to defeat Tom Kite at the IVB-Philadelphia Classic...Went over $2 million in PGA TOUR earnings with his T21 at the 1992 PLAYERS Championship...Led the PGA TOUR in Driving Accuracy in both 1992 and 1993...Never attended a TOUR Q-School. Entered as a PGA of America member after serving as a club professional from 1971-1975. First worked as an assistant pro at Kicking Bird GC in Edmond, OK, before moving to Pinetop CC in Pinetop, AZ, first as an assistant and then the head professional. Also taught lessons in the off season at Camelback CC near Phoenix...Underwent major elbow surgery in September of 1995 that caused him to miss all of the 1996 season...Has had 12 career holes-in-one.

PERSONAL:

Daughter, Kristi, is married to Pat Bates, a member of the PGA TOUR. Bates was a three-time winner on the Nationwide Tour in 2001, including the season-ending Nationwide Tour Championship...Biggest thrills in golf were winning the 1980 MCI Heritage Classic, his first TOUR victory and his first Champions Tour win at the 2000 PGA Seniors' Championship, each by seven strokes...Lists his father and Labron Harris, Sr. as the most influential people in his golf career...Got started in the game by working as a caddie for his father in Stillwater, OK...Has worked with such instructors as Gary Smith, Jim Flick, Stan Utley and Labron Harris...Attended Oklahoma State his freshman year on a basketball scholarship from the legendary coach Henry Iba...Has worked as an on-course commentator for The Golf Channel, ESPN and Fox Sports...Favorite golf course is Harbour Town GL in Hilton Head, SC...Biggest thrill outside of golf was attending Race Driving School with Rick Mears, Bobby Rahal and Al Unser, Sr...Always keeps a penny in his pocket for good luck...Nickname is "Tewell Time."

PLAYER STATISTICS

MISCELLANEOUS CHAMPIONS TOUR STATISTICS

2004 Low Round: 64–3 times, most recent 2004 Administaff Small Business Classic/3
Career Low Round: 62–2001 The Countrywide Tradition/4
Career Largest Paycheck: $324,000–2000 PGA Seniors' Championship/1

MISCELLANEOUS PGA TOUR STATISTICS

Career Low Round: 62–1987 Phoenix Open/3
Career Largest Paycheck: $82,667–1998 Canon Greater Hartford Open/T4

25 MEMORABLE MOMENTS

Watson Captures Bittersweet Major Championship Win

2003 JELD-WEN Tradition

Playing all year knowing his caddie and longtime friend was dying from ALS, Tom Watson was committed to winning at least one tournament in 2003 with Bruce Edwards on the bag. Watson had won in July at the Senior British Open in Northern Ireland, but Edwards did not make the trip. On at least five other occasions with Edwards at his side, Watson had come close yet failed to win. But Watson fulfilled his promise by capturing the JELD-WEN Tradition near Portland, OR, with a clutch up-and-down from a greenside bunker on the 72nd hole. The pair embraced on the green for what would be their last win together. Edwards died the following spring.

Leonard Thompson

EXEMPT STATUS: Top 30 on All-Time Money List
FULL NAME: Leonard Stephen Thompson
HEIGHT: 6-1
WEIGHT: 215
BIRTHDATE: January 1, 1947
BIRTHPLACE: Laurinburg, NC
RESIDENCE: Ponte Vedra Beach, FL

FAMILY: Wife, Lea; Marti (6/7/67), Stephen (4/6/74); three grandchilden
CLUB AFFILIATION: Pablo Creek Club (Jacksonville, FL)
EDUCATION: Wake Forest University (1969)
SPECIAL INTERESTS: Fishing
TURNED PROFESSIONAL: 1971
JOINED PGA TOUR: 1971

JOINED CHAMPIONS TOUR: 1997

CHAMPIONS TOUR VICTORIES (3): 1998 Coldwell Banker Burnet Classic. **2000** State Farm Senior Classic. **2001** Enterprise Rent-A-Car Match Play Championship.

2004 CHARLES SCHWAB CUP FINISH: 73rd - 42 points

PGA TOUR VICTORIES (3): 1974 Jackie Gleason-Inverrary Classic. **1977** Pensacola Open. **1989** Buick Open.

PGA TOUR CAREER EARNINGS: $1,819,028

BEST 2004 CHAMPIONS TOUR FINISH: T9—Toshiba Senior Classic.

2004 SEASON:

Finished 60th on the money list, with a Champions Tour career-low $228,672...Posted lone top-10 finish in March when he fashioned three straight sub-par rounds to finish T9 at the Toshiba Senior Classic...Slipped in Driving Accuracy from 18th in 2003 to 37th.

CHAMPIONS TOUR CAREER HIGHLIGHTS:

2003: Made just 25 starts, the fewest events he's played in a season since joining the Champions Tour...Had both of his top-10 finishes in the first third of the campaign...Shared the first-round lead at the Emerald Coast Classic, thanks to a Champions Tour career-low-tying round of 63. Eventually T2 in the event after posting a final-round 66 at The Moors. Credited a change to the long putter for his runner-up performance in Pensacola, his best overall effort since winning near St. Louis in May 2001. **2002:** T5 at the BellSouth Senior Classic at Opryland on the strength of a closing 5-under 67 at Springhouse GC. **2001:** Claimed his third career Champions Tour title when he bested Vicente Fernandez, 2-up, in the final of the Enterprise Rent-A-Car Match Play Championship near St. Louis. Victory was worth a career-best $300,000 and also avenged his loss to Fernandez in the finals of the unofficial 2000 Chrysler Senior Match Play Championship in Puerto Rico. Played 104 competitive holes on his way to the victory, the most of any player in the field. **2000:** Collected his second Champions Tour crown when he ended almost a two-year victory drought with victory at the State Farm Senior Classic in Columbia, MD. Birdied the third playoff hole to defeat Isao Aoki at Hobbit's Glen. **1999:** Recorded his two best efforts of the campaign in first third of the season...Closed with a final-round 66 at the Royal Caribbean Classic to finish T3...Shot two rounds of 70 at Desert Mountain and T3 at The Tradition after the event was shortened to 36 holes. **1998:** Won the rain-shortened Coldwell Banker Burnet Classic. Birdied the second hole of a sudden-death playoff to defeat Isao Aoki for the title at Bunker Hills GC. **1997:** As a rookie, played in 30 events and two of those appearances were as a Monday qualifier (Toshiba Senior Classic and Nationwide Championship)...T5 at the U.S. Senior Open at Olympia Fields CC outside of Chicago.

OTHER CAREER HIGHLIGHTS:

Played the PGA TOUR from 1971-1996 and also made 17 appearances on the Nationwide Tour from 1993-1996...Won three PGA TOUR events, with the last victory in 1989 at the Buick Open. Prevailed by one stroke over Billy Andrade, Doug Tewell and Payne Stewart at Warwick Hills in Grand Blanc. After a first-round 65, trailed by three entering the final round, but rallied with a 4-under-par 68 for a one-stroke triumph. Win ended an 11-year, nine-month drought, the third-longest stretch between victories in PGA TOUR history. Buick Open victory also helped him to a personal PGA TOUR-best $261,397, more than triple his earnings total from the previous season ($84,659)...Prior to the Michigan win, previous victory came at the 1977 Pensacola Open, where he rolled in a 50-foot birdie putt on the 72nd hole to edge rookie Curtis Strange...First PGA TOUR win came in 1974 at the Jackie Gleason-Inverrary Classic, where he nipped Hale Irwin by one stroke...Set a course record at the 1981 Canadian Open, shooting a 62 (31-31) at Glen Abbey GC. Hit every green in regulation except one, but birdied that hole with a chip-in from off the green. Used the same ball for all 18 holes. The ball then was presented to the Royal Canadian Golf Association for display in its museum at Glen Abbey...Also turned in a stellar performance at the 1977 Colgate Hall of Fame at Pinehurst No. 2. Shot a nine-hole record 7-under-par 29 on the back nine of the fabled course in his native North Carolina...Highest money position on the PGA TOUR came in 1973 and 1974 when he finished 15th...Recorded one top-10 finish on the Nationwide Tour when he placed sixth at the 1996 Tallahassee Open...Has one hole-in-one in his career.

PERSONAL:

Played collegiately at Wake Forest University, where he was a teammate of Joe Inman and Lanny Wadkins...Inducted into Wake Forest Athletic Hall of Fame in 1997...Has worked with instructor Jimmy Ballard...Got started in golf by his father...His hero is fellow Wake Forest product Arnold Palmer...Was a standout high school basketball player who turned down scholarship opportunities to play college golf...His daughter is an attorney and his son is a biomedical engineer...Lists "The Andy Griffith Show" as his favorite TV program and basketball star Tim Duncan as his favorite athlete...Best friend on the Champions Tour is Bill Kratzert.

PLAYER STATISTICS

2004 CHAMPIONS TOUR STATISTICS:

Scoring Average	72.81	(67)
Driving Distance	272.8	(33)
Driving Accuracy Percentage	70.6%	(37)
Total Driving	70	(26)
Greens in Regulation Pct.	69.1%	(29)
Putting Average	1.858	(77)
Sand Save Percentage	37.2%	(73)
Eagles (Holes per)	480.0	(53)
Birdie Average	2.81	(66)
All-Around Ranking	435	(67)

MISCELLANEOUS CHAMPIONS TOUR STATISTICS

2004 Low Round: 66–2004 The ACE Group Classic/1
Career Low Round: 63–2 times, most recent 2003 Emerald Coast Classic/1
Career Largest Paycheck: $300,000–2001 Enterprise Rent–A–Car Match Play Championship/1

MISCELLANEOUS PGA TOUR STATISTICS

Career Low Round: 62–2 times, most recent 1991 Hardee's Golf Classic/2
Career Largest Paycheck: $180,000–1989 Buick Open/1

CHAMPIONS TOUR CAREER SUMMARY — PLAYOFF RECORD: 2-0

Year	Events Played	1st	2nd	3rd	Top 10	Top 25	Earnings	Rank
1997	30				7	13	$384,806	40
1998	35	1		3	10	21	927,753	14
1999	36			2	4	17	635,095	29
2000	34	1		2	10	17	1,013,837	15
2001	31	1			5	17	893,881	21
2002	32				1	5	308,813	56
2003	25		1		2	8	372,079	44
2004	26				1	3	228,672	60
Total	249	3	1	7	40	101	4,764,936	
COMBINED ALL-TIME MONEY (3 TOURS):							**$6,597,854**	

CHAMPIONS TOUR TOP TOURNAMENT SUMMARY

Year	97	98	99	00	01	02	03	04
Senior PGA Championship		T22	CUT	T66	CUT	T36	T50	T51
U.S. Senior Open	T5	T38	T23	T26	T19	CUT		49
Ford Senior Players	T29	T54	T19	T36	T28	T58	T53	T22
JELD-WEN Tradition	T51	42	T3	46	T47	T21	T52	T29
Charles Schwab Cup Champ		T19	T18	T3	14			

Rocky Thompson

EXEMPT STATUS: Net-70 on All-Time Money List
FULL NAME: Hugh Delane Thompson
HEIGHT: 5-11
WEIGHT: 174
BIRTHDATE: October 14, 1939
BIRTHPLACE: Shreveport, LA
RESIDENCE: Plano, TX
FAMILY: Roxanne (4/14/68), Delana Lynn (5/26/76)
CLUB AFFILIATION: Paris G&CC (Paris, TX)
EDUCATION: University of Houston (B.B.A.,1962)
SPECIAL INTERESTS: Pool, dancing, ping-pong, fishing, tennis
TURNED PROFESSIONAL: 1964
JOINED PGA TOUR: 1964

JOINED CHAMPIONS TOUR: 1989

CHAMPIONS TOUR VICTORIES (3): 1991 MONY Syracuse Senior Classic, Digital Seniors Classic. **1994** GTE Suncoast Classic.

GEORGIA-PACIFIC GRAND CHAMPIONS VICTORIES (1): 2000 Nationwide Championship.

BEST PGA TOUR CAREER FINISHES: 2—1969 Western Open, T2—1970 Kiwanis Peninsula Open Invitational.

PGA TOUR CAREER EARNINGS: $146,391

BEST 2004 CHAMPIONS TOUR FINISH: T33—Allianz Championship.

2004 SEASON:

Played in 22 events, the fewest since joining the Champions Tour full time in 1990...Was among the first-round leaders at the Bank of America Championship when he opened with 5-under 67 at Nashawtuc. Eventually finished T54 after posting consecutive rounds of 75 on the weekend...Best finish was a T33 at the Allianz Championship.

CHAMPIONS TOUR CAREER HIGHLIGHTS:

2003: Did not register a top-25 finish for the first time since joining the Champions Tour in 1989...Best effort was a T33 at the SAS Championship, when he closed with a 69 at Prestonwood CC...Lowest rounds of the year were 67s on the final day of the Royal Caribbean Golf Classic and the second round of the Long Island Classic...Won a golf cart in the final round of the Long Island Classic when he made a hole-in-one on the 16th hole. Used a 6-iron on the 167-yard hole for the 12th ace of his career...Finished 10th on the Georgia-Pacific Grand Champions money list with $97,708. **2002:** Lone top-10 performance was a T7 at the Siebel Classic in Silicon Valley in March. **2000:** Defeated Bob Charles by a stroke for his only Georgia-Pacific Grand Champions win at the Nationwide Championship. **1996:** T2 at the Kroger Senior Classic, a distant five strokes back of Isao Aoki. **1995:** Had his finest financial season with over $600,000 in earnings...Was runner-up to Jim Colbert at the Las Vegas Senior Classic after being the 36-hole leader. **1994:** Came from seven strokes back on the last day to win the GTE Suncoast Classic. 10-under 61 on Sunday was the lowest finish ever by a winner on the Champions Tour. **1993:** Played in 37 tournaments, more than anyone else that year...Finished T2 at the Nationwide Championship. **1992:** Appeared in 35 tournaments and finished T2 at the inaugural Bruno's Memorial Classic...Recorded three eagles in a round at the Kaanapali Classic, the first player to do so since Jimmy Powell at the 1985 Greenbrier/American Express Championship. **1991:** Collected multiple wins for the only time in his TOUR career...Used a course-record 62 in the opening round of the MONY Syracuse Senior Classic to go wire-to-wire and capture his first victory in 611 attempts by his own calculations...Took the Digital Seniors Classic title later in the season, when he made an eight-foot birdie putt on the final hole. **1990:** Had a solid rookie campaign with nine top-10s...Had two of his best outings in his native state of Texas (fourth at the Murata Reunion Pro-Am and T5 at the Gatlin Brothers-Southwest Senior Classic). **1989:** Earned medalist honors at the Champions Tour National Qualifying Tournament at the Ravines G&CC. Was the only player under par in that event and won by a record 10 strokes.

OTHER CAREER HIGHLIGHTS:

Played the PGA TOUR full-time from 1965-1982, but was never exempt...Earned the nickname "King Rabbit" for his uncanny success at open qualifying for events...Best year on the PGA TOUR was in 1968, when he collected $20,685 and recorded two top-five finishes: T3 at the Atlanta Classic and T4 at the Buick Open...Was the runner-up at the 1969 Western Open...Has claimed 60 golf tournaments in his career: 12 junior titles, 25 amateur events and 18 professional events...Has 12 career holes-in-one.

PERSONAL:

Officially resigned as the mayor of Toco, TX, on Sept. 10, 1998. Was voted Mayor Emeritus by the city council and renders advice on matters when called...Helped design the Killer Bee driver...Took up golf at the age of 12, and within two years was shooting par...Has won tournaments in tennis, ping-pong and billiards...Biggest thrill in golf was posting his first victory at the MONY Syracuse Senior Classic...Favorite golf courses are Cypress Point, Brookhollow CC in Dallas and Greystone G&CC near Birmingham...Favorite entertainer is James Brown...Favorite athletes are Arnold Palmer and Julius Erving.

PLAYER STATISTICS

2004 CHAMPIONS TOUR STATISTICS:

Scoring Average	74.51	(79)
Driving Distance	267.2	(56)
Driving Accuracy Percentage	69.1%	(50)
Total Driving	106	(71)
Greens in Regulation Pct.	54.7%	(80)
Putting Average	1.841	(70)
Sand Save Percentage	45.9%	(38)
Eagles (Holes per)	1,170.0	(72)
Birdie Average	2.32	(77)
All-Around Ranking	522	(77)

MISCELLANEOUS CHAMPIONS TOUR STATISTICS

2004 Low Round: 67–2004 Bank of America Championship/1
Career Low Round: 61–1994 GTE Suncoast Classic/3
Career Largest Paycheck: $115,500–1995 Energizer SENIOR TOUR Championship/T3

MISCELLANEOUS PGA TOUR STATISTICS

Career Low Round: 64–1964 Dallas Open Invitational/2
Career Largest Paycheck: $14,800–1969 Western Open/2

CHAMPIONS TOUR CAREER SUMMARY **PLAYOFF RECORD: 0-0**

Year	Events Played	1st	2nd	3rd	Top 10	Top 25	Earnings	Rank
1989	3				1	2	$17,300	84
1990	31				9	24	308,915	18
1991	35	2	1		12	25	435,794	12
1992	36		1	1	10	26	432,778	15
1993	37		1	1	14	27	571,844	14
1994	31	1	1	1	8	19	529,073	22
1995	32		1	3	9	19	666,521	14
1996	31		1		5	14	385,719	35
1997	29				2	12	273,037	52
1998	29				1	5	181,301	65
1999	32			1	2	5	305,275	54
2000	32					2	187,333	73
2001	33				3	7	283,594	57
2002	30				1	3	173,586	79
2003	25						64,182	98
2004	22						62,163	97
Total	468	3	6	7	77	190	4,878,413	
COMBINED ALL-TIME MONEY (3 TOURS):							**$5,024,804**	

CHAMPIONS TOUR TOP TOURNAMENT SUMMARY

Year	90	91	92	93	94	95	96	97	98	99	00	01	02
Senior PGA Championship		T6	T14	T16	T19	T26	T20	T46	T39		T32	T61	CUT
U.S. Senior Open	T15	T24	T32	T23	T13	T14	CUT	T21	61	T58	CUT	63	
Ford Senior Players	T11	T34	T33	4	T16	T18	T8	T60	75	T37	T60	T45	T71
JELD-WEN Tradition	T13	T44	T36	T40	73	T12	T17	T67	T39	T40	T37	T47	T60
Charles Schwab Cup Champ	T5	30	T23	T20	10	T3							

Year	03	04
Senior PGA Championship		CUT
U.S. Senior Open	CUT	
JELD-WEN Tradition	76	T73

Jim Thorpe

EXEMPT STATUS: Top 30 on 2004 Champions Tour Money List
FULL NAME: Jimmy Lee Thorpe
HEIGHT: 6-0
WEIGHT: 205
BIRTHDATE: February 1, 1949
BIRTHPLACE: Roxboro, NC
RESIDENCE: Heathrow, FL

FAMILY: Wife, Carol; Sheronne (3/6/77), Chera (12/3/88)
EDUCATION: Morgan State University
SPECIAL INTERESTS: Football, basketball, hunting
TURNED PROFESSIONAL: 1972
JOINED PGA TOUR: 1976

JOINED CHAMPIONS TOUR: 1999

CHAMPIONS TOUR VICTORIES (9): 2000 The Transamerica, Gold Rush Classic. **2001** Kroger Senior Classic, Allianz Championship. **2002** The Countrywide Tradition. **2003** Long Island Classic, Charles Schwab Cup Championship. **2004** Farmers Charity Classic, Commerce Bank Long Island Classic.

2004 CHARLES SCHWAB CUP FINISH: 10th - 1,493 points

PGA TOUR VICTORIES (3): 1985 Greater Milwaukee Open, Seiko-Tucson Match Play Championship. **1986** Seiko-Tucson Match Play Championship.

OTHER VICTORIES (1): 1982 Canadian PGA Championship.

PGA TOUR CAREER EARNINGS: $1,935,566

PGA TOUR PLAYOFF RECORD: 0-1

BEST 2004 CHAMPIONS TOUR FINISHES: 1—Farmers Charity Classic, Commerce Bank Long Island Classic; T2—Kroger Classic; T4—Allianz Championship, Constellation Energy Classic; T5—Royal Caribbean Golf Classic, Administaff Small Business Classic.

2004 SEASON:

Finished among the top-10 money winners for the fifth straight season and won multiple victories for the fourth time in six seasons...Got his year jump-started when he was a one-stroke victor over Fred Gibson at the Farmers Charity Classic, despite a double bogey on the final hole. Came from three strokes back in the final round, thanks to seven birdies in the first 14 holes on Sunday...Rallied from four strokes back to win his second straight Commerce Bank Long Island Classic title a month later. Joined Bruce Fleisher, Lee Trevino and George Archer on the list of players who have successfully defended titles on Long Island. Win on the Red Course at Eisenhower Park was his ninth career title on the Champions Tour. Final-round 67 included three birdies on the front nine that allowed him to overtake 54-hole leader Jerry Pate. Avoided a playoff with a clutch par save from 19 feet on the last hole. Had just 23 putts in his opening-round 65, including one-putts on seven straight holes (No. 8-14). Win in New York made him the only player to successfully defend a title in 2004...Made a bid to win a second Kroger Classic title on the final day. Closed with 66 at the TPC at River's Bend but came up one stroke short. Was T2 when he missed 20-foot bid for eagle on the final hole...His closing-round 64 at the Constellation Energy Classic tied the tournament record and helped him to a T4 finish near Baltimore in early October...Also placed T7 at the Ford Senior Players Championship and ran his Champions Tour-best (at the time) string of sub-par rounds for the year to 14 before a closing-round 73 ended that streak...Made a big move Sunday in Iowa to T4 at the Allianz Championship, his third top-five performance in four trips to Des Moines. After opening with a 76, made 12 birdies in his last 36 holes to move up the leaderboard at Glen Oaks...Opened the campaign with a T9 at the MasterCard Championship in Hawaii and followed that with another top-10 finish in his next start when he was T5 at the Royal Caribbean Golf Classic...Plagued for several weeks in the early spring with a back problem, which caused him to miss three straight events...Second in Eagles, with 13...His Final-Round Scoring Average of 69.56 was third best on the Champions Tour. Fourteen times in 26 starts he finished with a round in the 60s.

CHAMPIONS TOUR CAREER HIGHLIGHTS:

2003: Had perhaps his finest season in professional golf when he was among the top three six times starting in mid-July...Appeared to be out of the Charles Schwab Cup competition through the first half of the season, but eventually finished second in the Schwab Cup race behind Tom Watson when he became the Champions Tour's hottest player after mid-August...Was voted the Champions Tour Player of the Month for both August and October...Also placed second behind Watson in the final money standings with a personal-best $1,830,306...Had two victories on the Champions Tour for the third time in the last four years and was the last of only five multiple winners on the circuit in 2003...In the winner's circle for the first time in 16 months when he slipped by Bob Gilder for a one-stroke victory at the Long Island Classic with a tournament-record score of 15-under 195. Tied a Champions Tour record in the second round when he shot a 10-under-par 60 on the Red Course at Eisenhower Park. Record-tying score gave him a two-stroke cushion entering Sunday's final round and 3-under-par 67 proved to be good enough for the win. Short birdie putts on 16 and 17 clinched title. Win in Long Island came during a run of 16 consecutive sub-par rounds, a 2003 best streak of sub-par scores..Capped his year with a wire-to-wire victory at the Charles Schwab Cup Championship in Sonoma, CA, a first in the season-ending event since Jim Colbert in 1995. His 20-under-par total over 72 holes at Sonoma GC, included playing the par-5s in 13-under, was the lowest 72-hole score in relation to par on the Champions Tour in 2003 and the lowest four-round total in event history. Was locked in a duel with Tom Watson down the stretch, but holed a 67-foot eagle putt from the fringe on the par-5 16th and then made a 10-foot birdie putt on No. 17 to seal the win. Third Champions Tour win in northern California came with a $440,000 first-place check, his largest ever as a professional...In between wins, was second once and third twice in a span of six events. Followed up his Long Island performance with a T2 at the Allianz Championship. Shot three consecutive rounds in the 60s in Des Moines, but came up three strokes short of Don Pooley. **2002:** Won the first major championship of his career at The Tradition. Bested John Jacobs on first hole of a playoff at Superstition Mountain. Made birdie on the 72nd hole of the event to forge the overtime session and then added another birdie on the first extra hole to claim the title. Victory in Arizona was the first of his TOUR career before September 1...Was voted as the circuit's Player of the Month for April...Nearly claimed a second major title, finishing one stroke shy of Stewart Ginn at the Ford Senior Players Championship in July despite shooting a 7-under 65 on Sunday...Had a bizarre finish at the FleetBoston Classic. Had a chance to win outright on the final hole, but T3 after three-putting from five feet. **2001:** Posted back-to-back victories early in the fall. Won a playoff for the rain-shortened Kroger Senior Classic title. Made a dramatic eagle on the final hole of regulation at the Kroger event to set up a playoff with Tom Jenkins and then won with a birdie on the first extra hole. Hit 3-wood from 245 yards for

CHAMPIONS TOUR CAREER SUMMARY — PLAYOFF RECORD: 2-1

Year	Events Played	1st	2nd	3rd	Top 10	Top 25	Earnings	Rank
1999	36		2	1	9	21	$857,746	19
2000	37	2	3	2	18	30	1,656,747	6
2001	35	2	2	2	13	25	1,827,223	6
2002	32	1	1	2	11	22	1,511,591	9
2003	30	2	2	2	14	19	1,830,306	2
2004	26	2	1		12	19	1,378,343	9
Total	196	9	11	9	77	136	9,061,956	
COMBINED ALL-TIME MONEY (3 TOURS):							**$11,007,557**	

CHAMPIONS TOUR TOP TOURNAMENT SUMMARY

Year	99	00	01	02	03	04
Senior PGA Championship	T34	T32	2	T4	T60	CUT
U.S. Senior Open	T27	T6	T21	T11	T30	T19
Ford Senior Players	T22	T10	T26	T2	T2	T7
JELD-WEN Tradition	T7	T15	T19	1	T7	T14
Charles Schwab Cup Champ	7	T17	T11	T15	1	T7

CHAMPIONS TOUR YEAR-BY-YEAR STATISTICS (TOP 50 ON 2004 MONEY LIST)

	Scoring Average	Putting Average	Greens in Regulation	Driving Distance	Driving Accuracy
1999	70.88 (T21)	1.795 (T42)	71.7 (T10)	271.1 (22)	72.4 (T29)
2000	69.73 (8)	1.749 (7)	73.4 (9)	277.9 (T8)	69.6 (T47)
2001	70.15 (9)	1.761 (15)	69.9 (15)	280.7 (9)	68.1 (T55)
2002	70.28 (12)	1.793 (T40)	69.0 (T24)	278.9 (11)	67.5 (49)
2003	70.20 (14)	1.760 (8)	70.1 (22)	279.5 (T15)	66.6 (50)
2004	70.44 (13)	1.752 (4)	69.9 (20)	280.8 (T14)	65.1 (63)

Jim Thorpe (continued)

a one-foot tap-in eagle putt...Then claimed the inaugural Allianz Championship the following week. Used seven birdies in an 11-hole stretch to win by two strokes at Glen Oaks...Also lost by a stroke to Tom Watson at the Senior PGA Championship. Missed an uphill six-foot birdie putt to tie on Ridgewood CC's final hole. **2000:** Claimed the first two victories of his Champions Tour career and yearly winnings of $1.6 million almost matched his entire earnings total in 25 years on the PGA TOUR...Claimed back-to-back victories in northern California at The Transamerica and the Gold Rush Classic. Win in the Napa Valley ended a victory drought of just over 14 years ('86 Seiko Tucson Match Play Championship). 18-under-par 198 score at Silverado was three better than Bruce Fleisher and was a tournament record...Cruised to a two-stroke victory over Ed Dougherty at the Gold Rush Classic with a 21-under 195 total for 54 holes, a tournament record at the time, and the lowest 54-hole score on the Champions Tour that season. Second-round 62 at the Gold Rush event was a course record at Serrano. Victory near Sacramento allowed him to become the first player since Gibby Gilbert in 1992 to win consecutive starts with sub-200 scores...Recorded his second hole-in-one on the Champions Tour in the opening round of the Boone Valley Classic. **1999:** Came closest to a victory at the Bell Atlantic Classic. Fired a final-round 65 on Sunday at Hartefeld National to come from four strokes off the pace and catch Tom Jenkins, but eventually lost to Jenkins on the first playoff hole...Made his first hole-in-one on the Champions Tour in the final round of the Royal Caribbean Classic. **1998:** Earned full exemption for 1999 by finishing T6 at the National Qualifying Tournament at Grenelefe Golf and Tennis Resort. After carding rounds of 67-76-72, fired a 3-under-par 69 on the final day to secure his top-eight finish.

OTHER CAREER HIGHLIGHTS:

Played on the PGA TOUR from 1976-98, with 459 tournaments to his credit and nearly $2 million in career earnings...Enjoyed his greatest success in a two-year span in 1985-86, when he earned three wins and was among the leading money-winners on the circuit...Was fourth on the money list in 1985 with $379,091, including wins at the Greater Milwaukee Open and the Seiko-Tucson Match Play Championship, where he bested Jack Renner in the final...Just missed adding a third victory when he lost in a playoff to Scott Verplank at the Western Open...In 1985, won $326,087 and ranked 15th on the money list with a victory at the Seiko Tucson Match Play Championship, besting Scott Simpson in the finals. Was unable to make it three in a row in 1987 when the event switched back to a stroke-play format...Underwent surgery on his left wrist and thumb in September 1987, and missed much of 1988 recuperating...Had runner-up finishes in 1989 (Kemper Open) and 1990 (Phoenix Open)...Co-medalist at the 1978 PGA TOUR Fall National Qualifying Tournament with John Fought...First earned card in 1975, but returned home after making just $2,000 in 1976...Is one of only two players (Dave Barr is the other) to record holes-in-one on the PGA TOUR, Champions Tour and Nationwide Tour. Has one Nationwide Tour ace to go with the three aces he had on the PGA TOUR and two on the Champions Tour.

PERSONAL:

Is the ninth of 12 children...Grew up next to eighth fairway at Roxboro (NC) CC, where father, Elbert Sr., was the superintendent...One of his brothers, Chuck, played for a period on the PGA TOUR and in several events on the Champions Tour in 1998, while another brother, Bill, has been through the National Qualifying Tournament several times...Earned a football scholarship to Morgan State as a running back.

PLAYER STATISTICS

MISCELLANEOUS CHAMPIONS TOUR STATISTICS

2004 Low Round: 64–2004 Constellation Energy Classic/3
Career Low Round: 60–2003 Long Island Classic/2
Career Largest Paycheck: $440,000–2003 Charles Schwab Cup Championship/1

MISCELLANEOUS PGA TOUR STATISTICS

Career Low Round: 62–1985 Greater Milwaukee Open/3
Career Largest Paycheck: $150,000–2 times, most recent 1986 Seiko–Tucson Match Play Championship/1

25 MEMORABLE MOMENTS

Stadler Wins on Both Tours in Consecutive Weeks

2003 Ford Senior Players Championship

Only one month after reaching 50, and in his fourth start on the Champions Tour, Craig Stadler won his first-ever title, a three-stroke win over Tom Watson, Tom Kite and Jim Thorpe. Stadler's rounds of 65-66 on the weekend included just 51 total putts. He then traveled to Endicott, NY, for the B.C. Open as a favor to the sponsor. Four days and one 63 later, Stadler became the first player to win a Champions Tour event one week and a PGA TOUR title the next. Stadler's birdie on the last hole completed his 9-under-par round and helped him beat Alex Cejka and Steve Lowery.

CHAMPIONS TOUR 25

Lee Trevino

WORLD GOLF HALL OF FAME MEMBER (Inducted 1981)
EXEMPT STATUS: Top 30 on All-Time Money List
FULL NAME: Lee Buck Trevino
HEIGHT: 5-7
WEIGHT: 180
BIRTHDATE: December 1, 1939
BIRTHPLACE: Dallas, TX
RESIDENCE: Dallas, TX
FAMILY: Wife, Claudia; Richard (11/21/62), Tony Lee (4/13/69), Troy (9/13/73), Olivia Leigh (2/3/89), Daniel Lee (10/20/92)
SPECIAL INTERESTS: Fishing
TURNED PROFESSIONAL: 1960
JOINED PGA TOUR: 1967

JOINED CHAMPIONS TOUR: 1989

CHAMPIONS TOUR VICTORIES (29): 1990 Royal Caribbean Classic, Aetna Challenge, Vintage Chrysler Invitational, Doug Sanders Kingwood Celebrity Classic, NYNEX Commemorative, U.S. Senior Open, Transamerica Senior Golf Championship. **1991** Aetna Challenge, Vantage at The Dominion, Charley Pride Classic. **1992** Vantage at The Dominion, The Tradition, PGA Seniors' Championship, Las Vegas Senior Classic, Bell Atlantic Classic. **1993** Cadillac NFL Golf Classic, Nationwide Championship, Vantage Championship. **1994** Royal Caribbean Classic, PGA Seniors' Championship, PaineWebber Invitational, Bell Atlantic Classic, BellSouth Senior Classic at Opryland, Northville Long Island Classic. **1995** Northville Long Island Classic, The Transamerica. **1996** Emerald Coast Classic. **1998** Southwestern Bell Dominion. **2000** Cadillac NFL Golf Classic.

OTHER SENIOR VICTORIES (9): 1991 Liberty Mutual Legends of Golf [with Mike Hill]. **1992** Mitsukoshi Classic, Liberty Mutual Legends of Golf [with Mike Hill]. **1993** American Express Grandslam. **1994** American Express Grandslam. **1995** Liberty Mutual Legends of Golf [with Mike Hill]. **1996** Liberty Mutual Legends of Golf [with Mike Hill], Australian PGA Seniors' Championship. **2003** ConAgra Foods Champions Skins Game.

GEORGIA-PACIFIC GRAND CHAMPIONS VICTORIES (1): 2000 Gold Rush Classic.

PGA TOUR VICTORIES (29): 1968 U.S. Open Championship, Hawaiian Open. **1969** Tucson Open Invitational. **1970** Tucson Open Invitational, National Airlines Open Invitational. **1971** Tallahassee Open Invitational, Danny Thomas Memphis Classic, U.S. Open Championship, Canadian Open, British Open Championship, Sahara Invitational. **1972** Danny Thomas Memphis Classic, British Open Championship, Greater Hartford Open Invitational, Greater St. Louis Golf Classic. **1973** Jackie Gleason Inverrary-National Airlines Classic, Doral-Eastern Open. **1974** Greater New Orleans Open, PGA Championship. **1975** Florida Citrus Open. **1976** Colonial National Invitation. **1977** Canadian Open. **1978** Colonial National Invitation. **1979** Canadian Open. **1980** Tournament Players Championship, Danny Thomas Memphis Classic, San Antonio Texas Open. **1981** MONY Tournament of Champions. **1984** PGA Championship.

OTHER VICTORIES (12): 1969 World Cup [with Orville Moody]. **1971** World Cup [with Jack Nicklaus]. **1974** World Series of Golf. **1975** Mexican Open. **1977** Morocco Grand Prix. **1978** Benson & Hedges Lancome Trophy, International Open. **1979** Canadian PGA Championship. **1980** Lancome Trophy. **1981** Sun City Classic. **1983** Canadian PGA Championship. **1985** British Masters. **1987** Skins Game.

PGA TOUR CAREER EARNINGS: $3,478,328

PGA TOUR PLAYOFF RECORD: 5-5

BEST 2004 CHAMPIONS TOUR FINISH: T11—Bruno's Memorial Classic.

2004 SEASON:
Competition was limited to 12 official events, the fewest he has ever played in a season...Bothered by a nerve problem in his lower back and did not play after mid-July. Withdrew from the Bank of America Championship during the second round and then was forced to withdraw from the Ford Senior Players Championship after an opening-round 77, even though he played as a marker for Dana Quigley in the second round...His T11 at the Bruno's Memorial Classic near Birmingham was his best performance on the Champions Tour since T9 at the 2002 Napa Valley Championship. His 4-under 68 in the opening round at Greystone was his best since shooting 65 on Saturday at 2003 Long Island Classic...Co-honoree at the Memorial Tournament with prominent women's amateur golfer Joyce Wethered...Also was honored by Northern Ohio Charities with the 2004 Ambassador of Golf Award, which he received at the World Golf Championships-NEC Invitational.

CHAMPIONS TOUR CAREER HIGHLIGHTS:
2003: Played in only 13 official events, at the time the fewest number of appearances in a single season since joining the Champions Tour, and for the first time since turning 50, did not register a top-10 finish during the season...Highlight of his year came early when he captured the ConAgra Foods Champions Skins Game in January. Defeated Hale Irwin with a birdie on the third extra hole for his first victory in the unofficial event. Birdie was worth $100,000 and helped push his earnings in the event to $240,000, $40,000 more than Irwin's total...Also teamed with Mike Hill to finish T2, two strokes back of Gary Koch/Roger Maltbie in the Raphael Division at the Liberty Mutual Legends of Golf...Best overall finish was a T22 at the MasterCard Championship at Hualalai...Finished second to Mike Hill by one stroke in the Georgia-Pacific Grand Champions competition at the Long Island Classic after carding a second-round 65, his lowest score since posting a 65 on Saturday at the 2000 FleetBoston Classic...Finished 16th on the final Georgia-Pacific Grand Champions money list with $69,583. **2002:** Lone top-10 performance came late in the season with a T9 at the Napa Valley Championship, thanks to a pair of 3-under 69s on the weekend...Finished eighth on the final Georgia-Pacific Grand Champions money list with $207,375. **2001:** Earned a $1-million prize when he made a hole-in-one at the Par-3 Challenge at Treetops Resort in Michigan. **2000:** Ended a victory drought of more than two years when he prevailed by two strokes over Walter Hall at the Cadillac NFL Golf Classic in New Jersey. Became just the second player to win in five different decades (Gary Player is the other). Victory at Upper Montclair CC made him, at the time, the seventh-oldest player to win a Champions Tour event...Finished third on the Georgia-Pacific Grand Champions money list and picked up his only win in the over-60 competition at the Gold Rush Classic. Defeated Chi Chi Rodriguez and Rocky Thompson by three strokes at Serrano for the Georgia-Pacific crown...Made his second hole-in-one on the Champions Tour at the Nationwide Championship...Made one final appearance at the British Open, but failed to make the cut at St. Andrews. **1998:**

CHAMPIONS TOUR CAREER SUMMARY — PLAYOFF RECORD: 3-3

Year	Events Played	1st	2nd	3rd	Top 10	Top 25	Earnings	Rank
1989	1				1	1	9,258	93
1990	28	7	8	1	26	28	1,190,518	1
1991	28	3	4	4	20	25	723,163	5
1992	27	5	3	1	21	26	1,027,002	1
1993	25	3	3	1	14	20	956,591	4
1994	23	6	1	3	15	21	1,202,369	4
1995	29	2	3	1	17	26	943,993	7
1996	28	1		2	11	17	662,753	16
1997	27		2		10	19	733,912	15
1998	27	1	1	1	7	14	716,366	18
1999	25			1	5	15	500,103	39
2000	25	1	1		3	12	545,186	34
2001	17				2	5	215,426	70
2002	17				1	4	189,762	75
2003	13					1	71,559	96
2004	12					1	70,810	90
Total	352	29	26	15	153	235	9,758,773	
COMBINED ALL-TIME MONEY (3 TOURS):							**$13,237,101**	

CHAMPIONS TOUR TOP TOURNAMENT SUMMARY

Year	90	91	92	93	94	95	96	97	98	99	00	01	02
Senior PGA Championship	T3	11	1	T23	1	T2	T22	T27	CUT	T15	WD	T59	
U.S. Senior Open	1	T4	T18	9	11	7		T15			T31		
Ford Senior Players	2	T8	T2	T40	T3	T30	T8	T19	8	T12		T36	T65
JELD-WEN Tradition	T24	T33	1	13	T21	T20	T37	T25					
Charles Schwab Cup Champ	T2	T12	T7	T6		T22	19	T4	T11				

Year	03	04
Ford Senior Players		WD

Lee Trevino (continued)

Claimed his third Southwestern Bell Dominion title, a two-stroke win over Mike McCullough. Victory in San Antonio was his seventh overall title in his native state. **1996:** Emerged victorious from a record five-man playoff at the Emerald Coast Classic. Holed a 35-foot birdie putt on the first extra hole to nip Mike Hill, Dave Stockton, David Graham and Bob Eastwood...Teamed with Mike Hill to win a fourth Liberty Mutual Legends of Golf title. **1995:** Captured an unprecedented third Liberty Mutual Legends of Golf title with Mike Hill...Became the Champions Tour's all-time victory leader at the time when he successfully defended his Northville Long Island Classic title, the 25th win of his Champions Tour career...Also became the first two-time winner of The Transamerica. **1994:** Notched six victories before August and was chosen by his peers as the Champions Tour Player of the Year for a third time...Earnings of $1,202,369 were the most of his illustrious career for a single season...Caught Miller Barber on the all-time victory list when he triumphed at the Northville Long Island Classic...Also benefited from a late collapse by Raymond Floyd for his second PGA Seniors' Championship...Played hurt for the majority of the summer with a bulging disc in his neck, and underwent surgery in October. **1993:** Won three times, despite not starting the season until the last week of March due to surgery for ligament damage near his left thumb. Won the Cadillac NFL Golf Classic in his seventh start of the year, then claimed back-to-back events at the Nationwide and Vantage Championships. **1992:** Secured his second Arnold Palmer Award after becoming the first golfer to earn over $1 million in a season twice...Easily garnered Player of the Year honors, as well, on the strength of five official victories...Claimed three straight titles in the spring: The Tradition, PGA Seniors' Championship and Las Vegas Senior Classic...Also teamed with Mike Hill to win a second consecutive Liberty Mutual Legends of Golf crown...Earned his third straight Byron Nelson Award with a 69.46 scoring average. **1991:** Won three times...Defended his title at the Aetna Challenge, nipping Dale Douglass with a birdie at the final hole...Triumphed at the Vantage at The Dominion when he eagled the final hole...Cruised to a four-stroke victory at the Sunwest Bank/Charley Pride Senior Classic in Albuquerque...Teamed with Mike Hill to win the Liberty Mutual Legends of Golf...Earned a second consecutive Byron Nelson Award with a scoring average of 69.50. **1990:** Was the leading money-winner in all of golf and became the first Champions Tour player to earn over $1 million in single-season earnings...Easily took home the Arnold Palmer Award, as well as Player of the Year and Rookie of the Year honors...His seven victories, a personal best for one season, were the second highest total in a year at the time...Won three of his first four starts, including the Royal Caribbean Classic, his first, where he made up seven strokes over the last nine holes to defeat Jim Dent...Shot 67 on the final day at Ridgewood CC to beat Jack Nicklaus for the U.S. Senior Open title...Posted back-to-back wire-to-wire wins at the Aetna Challenge and The Vintage Chrysler Invitational...Finished out of the top 10 only twice all year and won the Byron Nelson Award with a stroke average of 68.89, the lowest in Champions Tour history until Hale Irwin's 68.59 in 1998. **1989:** Joined the Champions Tour at the last official money event of the year, the GTE Kaanapali Classic. Carded back-to-back 69s at that rain-shortened event and finished T7.

OTHER CAREER HIGHLIGHTS:

Won 29 times on the PGA TOUR and is ranked T17 on the all-time victory list...Voted PGA TOUR Rookie of the Year in 1967...Was the leading money-winner in 1970 with $157,037 and was voted as the Player of the Year in 1971...Made his debut at the 1966 U.S. Open, but first got national attention the next year at Baltusrol when he finished fifth and made $6,000...Gained headlines with his first TOUR win at the 1968 U.S. Open at Oak Hill CC, becoming the first player in Open history to play all four rounds under par and in the 60s...Won the Open again in 1971, defeating Jack Nicklaus in an 18-hole playoff at Merion...Won back-to-back British Open titles in 1971 and 1972...Collected a record fifth Vardon Trophy in 1980 with a scoring average of 69.73, the lowest since Sam Snead's 69.23 in 1950...Won a second PGA Championship in 1984 at Shoal Creek in Birmingham, AL, at the age of 44. Ended a three-plus-year victory drought with that title, outlasting Gary Player and Lanny Wadkins down the stretch...Member of six American Ryder Cup teams and was captain of the 1985 squad...Teamed with Orville Moody to win the 1969 World Cup for the United States, and joined Nicklaus for another World Cup title in 1971...Hampered throughout his career by back problems and underwent surgery for a herniated disc in November of 1976...Struck by lightning, along with Bobby Nichols and Jerry Heard, at the 1975 Western Open...Inducted into the World Golf Hall of Fame in 1981...*Sporting News* Man of the Year in 1971...Won the Ben Hogan Award from the Golf Writers Association of America in 1980.

PERSONAL:

Entirely self-taught and, as a youth, became the protege of Hardy Greenwood, owner of Hardy's Driving Range in Dallas...Was raised next door to the Glen Lakes CC in Dallas where he got started in the game...Served in the Marine Corps for four years from the age of 17 to 21...Became a golf professional in 1960 and got his first job working as an assistant professional in El Paso, TX...Between PGA TOUR and Champions Tour, served a stint as golf analyst for NBC...Favorite courses are Pine Valley, Oak Hill and Cypress Point...Favorite entertainer is Alan King and also enjoys George Lopez...Other favorites include "Chariots of Fire," Michael Jordan and steak...Biggest thrill was winning the 1971 U.S. Open...Enjoys spending time with his family...One of his superstitions is not using a yellow tee.

PLAYER STATISTICS

2004 CHAMPIONS TOUR STATISTICS:

Scoring Average	72.58	(N/A)
Driving Distance	260.3	(N/A)
Driving Accuracy Percentage	76.5%	(N/A)
Total Driving	1,998	(N/A)
Greens in Regulation Pct.	60.0%	(N/A)
Putting Average	1.854	(N/A)
Sand Save Percentage	42.4%	(N/A)
Birdie Average	2.97	(N/A)
All-Around Ranking	1,569	(N/A)

MISCELLANEOUS CHAMPIONS TOUR STATISTICS

2004 Low Round: 68–2004 Bruno's Memorial Classic/1
Career Low Round: 63–1991 First Development Kaanapali Classic/2
Career Largest Paycheck: $225,000–1993 Vantage Championship/1

MISCELLANEOUS PGA TOUR STATISTICS

Career Low Round: 64–12 times, most recent 1989 Canon Greater Hartford Open/2
Career Largest Paycheck: $125,000–1984 PGA Championship/1

Howard Twitty

EXEMPT STATUS: Net-70 on All-Time Money List
FULL NAME: Howard Allen Twitty
HEIGHT: 6-5
WEIGHT: 210
BIRTHDATE: January 15, 1949
BIRTHPLACE: Phoenix, AZ
RESIDENCE: Scottsdale, AZ

FAMILY: Wife, Sheree; Jocelyn Noel (11/20/80), Charles Barnes Barris (6/7/89), Mary Caroline Claire (9/11/90), William Howard Hudson (2/23/94), Alicia Anne Marie (1/22/92), Samantha Rose Reeves (1/20/97)
EDUCATION: Arizona State University (1972, Business Administration)
SPECIAL INTERESTS: All sports
TURNED PROFESSIONAL: 1974
JOINED PGA TOUR: 1975

JOINED CHAMPIONS TOUR: 1999

BEST CHAMPIONS TOUR CAREER FINISH: T2—2000 Toshiba Senior Classic.

PGA TOUR VICTORIES (3): **1979** B.C. Open. **1980** Sammy Davis Jr.-Greater Hartford Open. **1993** United Airlines Hawaiian Open.

OTHER VICTORIES (3): **1970** Porter Cup, Sunnehanna Amateur. **1975** Thailand Open.

PGA TOUR CAREER EARNINGS: $2,713,551

PGA TOUR PLAYOFF RECORD: 1-0

BEST 2004 CHAMPIONS TOUR FINISH: T18—3M Championship.

2004 SEASON:

Had just one top 25 finish in 22 starts, the fewest in his Champions Tour career...Best showing came in August when he sandwiched rounds of 69-68 around a second-round 74 for a T18 at the TPC of the Twin Cities near Minneapolis.

CHAMPIONS TOUR CAREER HIGHLIGHTS:

2003: Was among the top 25 three times and had his best finish late in the year at the Turtle Bay Championship in Hawaii, when he was T19...Returned to the National Qualifying Tournament in an attempt to improve his playing status for 2004 but missed the cut at the TPC at Eagle Trace. **2002:** T18 at the SBC Senior Classic at Valencia CC...Missed a month of the season due to the tragic drowning death of his oldest son, Kevin, on March 23. Returned to action at The Countrywide Tradition in late April. **2001:** T7 at The Countrywide Tradition...Returned to the Champions Tour National Qualifying Tournament in the fall and ended up as the medalist at the event. Easily outdistanced Larry Ziegler by three strokes for top honors in Calimesa, CA. Was tied with Rodger Davis for the top spot heading into the final round, but birdied five of his first nine holes to seize the lead and never looked back. **2000:** Best Champions Tour career showing came at the rain-shortened Toshiba Senior Classic when he had rounds of 67-70 to finish T2, just one stroke back of Allen Doyle. **1999:** Went to the Champions Tour National Qualifying Tournament and regained fully-exempt status after finishing in the top eight. Played 72 holes in 6-under-par 282 and finished T2 with Stewart Ginn at Tucson National, five strokes back of medalist Mark Hayes. **1998:** Fully exempt for 1999 after finishing sixth at the 1998 Champions Tour Qualifying Tournament.

OTHER CAREER HIGHLIGHTS:

Had a long and successful career on the PGA TOUR from 1974-98, playing in 634 tournaments with three victories and $2.7 million in official earnings...Enjoyed his finest year in 1993 when, at age 44, he won the United Airlines Hawaiian Open by four strokes and went on to win a career-best $416,833 and finish 34th on the money list. Victory established a TOUR record for longest period between wins: 12 years and seven months. Prior to that, his last win had come in 1980 at the Sammy Davis, Jr.-Greater Hartford Open, where he won a playoff against Jim Simons. Win came during a hot streak in the summer that featured a run of 13 of 14 rounds in the 60s, with a cumulative total of 57-under-par. Victory also helped him to a career-best 14th-place finish on the money chart...Posted his first TOUR victory at the 1979 B.C. Open, holding off Doug Tewell and Tom Purtzer down the stretch...Earned over $200,000 for the first time in his career in 1991, a year which featured 11 straight cuts made and five straight events in which he finished no worse than 20th...College standout at Arizona State University and a two-time All-America selection for the Sun Devils in 1970 and 1972...Played the Asian Tour at one point in his career and won the 1975 Thailand Open...Amateur wins included the 1970 Porter Cup and the Sunnehanna Amateur.

PERSONAL:

Has done some consulting on course design, collaborating with Roger Maltbie on the well-received redesign of the TPC at River Highlands in Connecticut, site of the Buick Championship, and with Tom Weiskopf on the TPC of Scottsdale, site of the FBR Open...Missed a portion of the 1996 season following surgery on his feet. Wears sandals with golf spikes on the bottom while he plays.

PLAYER STATISTICS

2004 CHAMPIONS TOUR STATISTICS:

Scoring Average	73.55	(72)
Driving Distance	262.3	(68)
Driving Accuracy Percentage	58.2%	(79)
Total Driving	147	(81)
Greens in Regulation Pct.	59.9%	(73)
Putting Average	1.840	(69)
Sand Save Percentage	43.5%	(55)
Eagles (Holes per)	1,170.0	(72)
Birdie Average	2.65	(71)
All-Around Ranking	559	(80)

MISCELLANEOUS CHAMPIONS TOUR STATISTICS

2004 Low Round: 66–2004 Bank of America Championship/2
Career Low Round: 65–2001 Novell Utah Showdown/1
Career Largest Paycheck: $104,000–2000 Toshiba Senior Classic/T2

MISCELLANEOUS PGA TOUR STATISTICS

Career Low Round: 62–2 times, most recent 1990 Buick Southern Open/1
Career Largest Paycheck: $216,000–1993 United Airlines Hawaiian Open/1

CHAMPIONS TOUR CAREER SUMMARY — PLAYOFF RECORD: 0-0

Year	Events Played	1st	2nd	3rd	Top 10	Top 25	Earnings	Rank
1999	32				1	10	$308,655	53
2000	32		1	1	2	10	428,874	41
2001	29				3	10	431,932	44
2002	30					5	206,890	69
2003	25					3	151,555	77
2004	22					1	97,037	87
Total	170		1	1	6	39	1,624,943	

COMBINED ALL-TIME MONEY (3 TOURS): **$4,339,993**

CHAMPIONS TOUR TOP TOURNAMENT SUMMARY

Year	99	00	01	02	03	04
Senior PGA Championship		T46	T13	CUT	CUT	CUT
U.S. Senior Open						CUT
Ford Senior Players	T48	T52	T66	T58	77	T66
JELD-WEN Tradition	T9	T25	T7	T64	T62	T67

SECTION 2 PLAYER BIOGRAPHIES

Bobby Wadkins

EXEMPT STATUS: Top 30 on 2004 Champions Tour Money List
FULL NAME: Robert Edwin Wadkins
HEIGHT: 6-1
WEIGHT: 205
BIRTHDATE: July 26, 1951
BIRTHPLACE: Richmond, VA
RESIDENCE: Richmond, VA

FAMILY: Wife, Linda; Casey Tanner (2/14/90)
EDUCATION: East Tennessee State University (1973, Health and Physical Education)
SPECIAL INTERESTS: Deer, big-game hunting and bass fishing
TURNED PROFESSIONAL: 1973
JOINED PGA TOUR: 1974

JOINED CHAMPIONS TOUR: 2000

CHAMPIONS TOUR VICTORIES (1): 2001 Lightpath Long Island Classic.

2004 CHARLES SCHWAB CUP FINISH: 41st - 325 points

BEST PGA TOUR CAREER FINISHES: 2—1978 Joe Garagiola-Tucson Open,1979 IVB-Philadelphia Golf Classic,1985 Sea Pines Heritage, T2—1979 Anheuser-Busch Golf Classic,1987 Shearson Lehman Brothers Andy Williams Open,1994 Kemper Open.

OTHER VICTORIES (7): 1971 Virginia State Amateur. **1978** European Open. **1979** Dunlop Phoenix [Jpn]. **1982** Virginia State Open. **1986** Dunlop Phoenix [Jpn]. Virginia State Open. **1990** Fred Meyer Challenge [with Lanny Wadkins].

PGA TOUR CAREER EARNINGS: $2,822,418

PGA TOUR PLAYOFF RECORD: 0-2

BEST 2004 CHAMPIONS TOUR FINISHES: T2—Commerce Bank Long Island Classic; 3—SBC Championship; T5—Greater Hickory Classic at Rock Barn; T10—The ACE Group Classic.

2004 SEASON:

Vaulted into the season-ending Charles Schwab Cup Championship with a solo third-place finish at the SBC Championship the week prior. Was in the 37th position and moved up into the 29th spot on the money list after posting consecutive rounds of 67 on the weekend at Oak Hills that earned him a $108,000 check in San Antonio...T2 on July 4 at the Commerce Bank Long Island Classic, one stroke shy of Jim Thorpe. Stood in the fairway on the final hole with a chance to win the event but pushed his 5-iron approach right of the 18th green and could not get up and down for par. Shared the first-round lead at Eisenhower Park with Jerry Pate and Peter Jacobsen after firing 6-under 64 on the Red Course...Was among the first-round leaders at the Greater Hickory Classic at Rock Barn and eventually T5...In contention at the Kroger Classic before having to withdraw from the event after 11 holes Saturday with back spasms...Also withdrew from the SAS Championship in Raleigh two weeks later.

CHAMPIONS TOUR CAREER HIGHLIGHTS:

2003: Had a trio of second-place finishes...Battled through back spasms at the Royal Caribbean Golf Classic in his second start and eventually T2 at Key Biscayne. Missed a seven-foot birdie putt on the final hole which would have forced a playoff...Runner-up for second consecutive year at the Senior PGA Championship, finishing two strokes behind John Jacobs at Aronimink GC near Philadelphia...Made a strong bid for a win at the SAS Championship in Raleigh in September before eventually coming up one stroke short of D.A. Weibring. Was tied for the lead with two holes to play but par-par finish at Prestonwood left him T2 with Tom Kite...Fired a 9-under 61 (6-under-par 29 on the back nine) in the second round of the Emerald Coast Classic, his career best as a professional in 823 TOUR events. The 61 moved him within one stroke of the 36-hole lead, but he eventually T7 at The Moors GC after posting a 69 on Easter Sunday. **2002:** Only Allen Doyle earned more money during the year without posting a victory. Came close to the winner's circle in three events and played his best golf from May-June when he was among the top 10 in five straight tournaments...Closed with a final-round 66 at the Liberty Mutual Legends of Golf, but placed second to Doug Tewell by one stroke. Had caught Tewell midway through the back nine on Sunday, but made a bogey at the 16th hole...Was the 54-hole leader at the Senior PGA Championship at Firestone, but lost to Fuzzy Zoeller by two strokes, T2 along with Hale Irwin after posting a 1-over 71 on Sunday...T2 again at the Greater Baltimore Classic, one of three players to fall one stroke shy of J.C. Snead despite closing with a 6-under-par 66 on Sunday...Opened the campaign with a third-place finish at the MasterCard Championship...Was only one stroke out of the lead through two rounds of the SBC Senior Open, but three double bogeys on Sunday dropped him into a T14. **2001:** Made his first appearance on the circuit a memorable one. Became the youngest winner in Champions Tour history when he claimed the Lightpath Long Island Classic 10 days after turning 50. Edged Allen Doyle and Larry Nelson by one stroke and broke Gil Morgan's record as the youngest winner (50 years, 11 days/ 1996 Ralphs Senior Classic). His 12-foot birdie putt on the final hole at the Meadow Brook Club gave him his first win in TOUR event in his 778th start. Helped his cause early in the final round when he rebounded from a double bogey with a double eagle on the third hole (driver, pitching wedge from 135 yards). Became just the 10th player, and first since brother Lanny, to win in his debut on the Champions Tour. Win also enabled the Wadkins brothers to become just the second set of siblings to triumph on the Champions Tour (Dave and Mike Hill).

OTHER CAREER HIGHLIGHTS:

Played the PGA TOUR on a full-time basis from 1975-1998...Made 465 cuts in 712 starts before joining the Champions Tour in August, 2001...Also played in 65 events on the Nationwide Tour from 1993-2001...Earned $2,882,418 on the PGA TOUR and $195,495 on the Nationwide Tour...Never won an event on either TOUR, but had six second-place finishes on the PGA TOUR and three more on the Nationwide Tour...Best year on the PGA TOUR came in 1987 when he won $342,173 and finished 25th on the money list, thanks to seven top 10s. Earned largest check on the PGA TOUR in 1994, $114,000, when he T2 at the Kemper Open, three strokes behind Mark Brooks...Made his first cut as a member of the PGA TOUR at the Dean Martin-Tucson Open, finishing T25 and earning $1,510...Winner of 1978 European Open and 1979 and 1986 Dunlop Phoenix (Japan) titles...Has five career holes-in-one and two double eagles.

PERSONAL:

After attending the University of Houston for one year, won All-American honors in 1972-73 at East Tennessee State...Along with older brother, Lanny, kept Richmond, VA, city junior title in family for six consecutive years (Lanny four, Bobby two)...Biggest thrill in golf was posting first Champions Tour victory at the Lightpath Long Island Classic and biggest thrill outside golf was when his son, Casey, was born. Son has played in five national baseball tournaments...Favorite athletes are Mickey Mantle and Arnold Palmer...Favorite golf course is Cypress Point...Was eight when his father got him started in golf.

PLAYER STATISTICS

MISCELLANEOUS CHAMPIONS TOUR STATISTICS
2004 Low Round: 64–2004 Commerce Bank Long Island Classic/1
Career Low Round: 61–2003 Emerald Coast Classic/2
Career Largest Paycheck: $255,000–2001 Lightpath Long Island Classic/1

MISCELLANEOUS PGA TOUR STATISTICS
Career Low Round: 64–9 times, most recent 1996 Buick Challenge/1
Career Largest Paycheck: $114,400–1994 Kemper Open/T2

CHAMPIONS TOUR CAREER SUMMARY — PLAYOFF RECORD: 0-0

Year	Events Played	1st	2nd	3rd	Top 10	Top 25	Earnings	Rank
2001	10	1			4	7	$549,657	33
2002	30		3	1	11	19	1,270,336	13
2003	28		3		6	13	942,109	19
2004	26		1	1	4	14	676,461	29
Total	94	1	7	2	25	53	3,438,562	
COMBINED ALL-TIME MONEY (3 TOURS):							**$6,456,475**	

CHAMPIONS TOUR TOP TOURNAMENT SUMMARY

Year	02	03	04
Senior PGA Championship	T2	2	T25
U.S. Senior Open	T11	T35	CUT
Ford Senior Players	T12	T40	T34
Senior British Open		T32	
JELD-WEN Tradition	T13	T52	T24
Charles Schwab Cup Champ	29	T18	T13

CHAMPIONS TOUR YEAR-BY-YEAR STATISTICS (TOP 50 ON 2004 MONEY LIST)

	Scoring Average	Putting Average	Greens in Regulation	Driving Distance	Driving Accuracy
2001	69.70 (N/A)	1.816 (N/A)	75.1 (N/A)	286.9 (N/A)	69.2 (N/A)
2002	70.47 (13)	1.792 (T38)	72.8 (6)	279.4 (T9)	68.2 (44)
2003	70.89 (28)	1.799 (T46)	70.3 (T18)	277.4 (T19)	66.5 (T51)
2004	71.12 (26)	1.799 (38)	69.6 (T23)	281.4 (13)	66.8 (60)
2004	71.53 (38)	1.779 (20)	63.3 (59)	255.6 (76)	72.0 (T28)

Lanny Wadkins

EXEMPT STATUS: Top 30 on All-Time Money List
FULL NAME: Jerry Lanston Wadkins
HEIGHT: 5-9
WEIGHT: 175
BIRTHDATE: December 5, 1949
BIRTHPLACE: Richmond, VA
RESIDENCE: Dallas, TX

FAMILY: Wife, Penelope; Jessica (10/14/73), Travis (8/25/87), Tucker (8/19/92)
EDUCATION: Wake Forest University
SPECIAL INTERESTS: Bird hunting, scuba diving, watching sons play sports
TURNED PROFESSIONAL: 1971
JOINED PGA TOUR: 1971

JOINED CHAMPIONS TOUR: 2000

CHAMPIONS TOUR VICTORIES (1): 2000 The ACE Group Classic.

2004 CHARLES SCHWAB CUP FINISH: 44th - 210 points

PGA TOUR VICTORIES (21): 1972 Sahara Invitational. **1973** Byron Nelson Golf Classic, USI Classic. **1977** PGA Championship, World Series of Golf. **1979** Glen Campbell-Los Angeles Open, Tournament Players Championship. **1982** Phoenix Open, MONY Tournament of Champions, Buick Open. **1983** Greater Greensboro Open, MONY Tournament of Champions. **1985** Bob Hope Classic, Los Angeles Open, Walt Disney World/Oldsmobile Classic. **1987** Doral-Ryder Open. **1988** Hawaiian Open, Colonial National Invitation. **1990** Anheuser-Busch Golf Classic. **1991** United Hawaiian Open. **1992** Canon Greater Hartford Open.

OTHER VICTORIES (8): 1968 Southern Amateur. **1970** U.S. Amateur, Southern Amateur. **1978** Victorian PGA Championship, Canadian PGA Championship. **1979** Bridgestone Open. **1984** World Nissan Championship. **1990** Fred Meyer Challenge [with Bobby Wadkins].

PGA TOUR CAREER EARNINGS: $6,355,681

PGA TOUR PLAYOFF RECORD: 3-3

BEST 2004 CHAMPIONS TOUR FINISH: T18—The First Tee Open at Pebble Beach presented by Wal-Mart.

2004 SEASON:

Due to broadcasting commitments with CBS Sports, played in just 10 events for the second consecutive year...Best performance of the season was at the inaugural First Tee Open at Pebble Beach presented by Wal-Mart, where he was T18.

CHAMPIONS TOUR CAREER HIGHLIGHTS:

2003: Lone top-10 finish was a T8 at the U.S. Senior Open at the Inverness Club in Toledo. Got off to a nice start at the Toshiba Senior Classic, opening with his low round of the year, a 6-under-par 65. **2002:** Managed to record three top-10 finishes, all before the end of March...Placed solo third at the rain-shortened Emerald Coast Classic, thanks to a 7-under 63 in the second round, his career-low 18-hole score on the Champions Tour and best round since shooting a 62 at the 1989 Texas Open on the PGA TOUR. Performance at The Moors was his best since winning the 2000 ACE Group Classic in his initial Champions Tour appearance...Assumed the role of lead analyst for CBS golf telecasts at the SBC Senior Open following the retirement of Ken Venturi and continued in that capacity in 2003. **2001:** Played the Champions Tour despite several injuries (wrist and elbow) and broadcasting commitments on CBS golf telecasts...Was grouped with his brother, Bobby, in the second round of the 3M Championship, the first time the two had played an official round together since the 1999 MCI Classic in Hilton Head...T9 at the Enterprise Rent-A-Car Match Play Championship. **2000:** Troubled for a portion of the year with right elbow problems...Became just the ninth of 10 players ever to win in his Champions Tour debut (brother, Bobby, became the 10th during the 2001 season). Defeated Tom Watson, Walter Hall and Jose Maria Canizares in a playoff for The ACE Group Classic title. Rallied from three strokes down to get into overtime on the final day with an 8-under-par 64, then won the event when he eliminated Canizares with a par on the third extra hole...Made first hole-in-one on the Champions Tour during the opening round of the Nationwide Championship.

OTHER CAREER HIGHLIGHTS:

Won 21 official events on the PGA TOUR in a 29-year career and is in the top 30 on the all-time victory list...First win came at the 1972 Sahara Invitational in his first full year on the PGA TOUR...Won twice in the same season five times (1973, '77, '79, '83 and '88) and three times in a season twice (1982 and '85)...Biggest victory came in the 1977 PGA Championship at Pebble Beach, when he bested Gene Littler in a playoff...Three weeks later, defeated Hale Irwin and Tom Weiskopf by five strokes at the World Series of Golf...Finished third on the money list that year...Also was third on the 1983 money list, when he won twice and also had two seconds and a third...Named PGA of America Player of the Year in 1985, when he finished second in earnings to Curtis Strange...Braved windy conditions to win the 1979 Tournament Players Championship at Sawgrass CC by five strokes over Tom Watson...Last official victory came at the 1992 Canon Greater Hartford Open. Entered the final round five strokes back of Donnie Hammond, but used a final-round 65 to post a 6-under-par 274 total and defeat Hammond, Nick Price and Dan Forsman by two strokes...Served as the 1995 U.S. Ryder Cup captain at Oak Hill CC and played on the American team eight times. Also played on the Walker Cup team in 1969 and 1971.

PERSONAL:

Enjoys well-deserved reputation as a fierce competitor...Along with brother, Bobby, kept Richmond, VA, junior championship trophy in Wadkins household for six consecutive years (Lanny won four times, Bobby twice)...Is now the lead analyst for CBS golf telecasts...Served as the player consultant on the TPC of Myrtle Beach, the venue of the Charles Schwab Cup Championship in 2000... Biggest thrill in golf was winning the 1977 PGA Championship, and his biggest thrill outside of golf is watching his sons play sports...Favorite golf course is Pebble Beach GL.

PLAYER STATISTICS

2004 CHAMPIONS TOUR STATISTICS:

Scoring Average	71.53	(N/A)
Driving Distance	265.8	(N/A)
Driving Accuracy Percentage	62.9%	(N/A)
Total Driving	1,998	(N/A)
Greens in Regulation Pct.	64.4%	(N/A)
Putting Average	1.807	(N/A)
Sand Save Percentage	40.4%	(N/A)
Eagles (Holes per)	540.0	(N/A)
Birdie Average	2.93	(N/A)
All-Around Ranking	1,569	(N/A)

MISCELLANEOUS CHAMPIONS TOUR STATISTICS

2004 Low Round: 68–2004 Bank of America Championship/1
Career Low Round: 63–2002 Emerald Coast Classic/2
Career Largest Paycheck: $180,000–2000 ACE Group Classic/1

MISCELLANEOUS PGA TOUR STATISTICS

Career Low Round: 62–1989 Texas Open/1
Career Largest Paycheck: $198,000–1991 United Hawaiian Open/1

CHAMPIONS TOUR CAREER SUMMARY — PLAYOFF RECORD: 1-0

Year	Events Played	1st	2nd	3rd	Top 10	Top 25	Earnings	Rank
2000	23	1			2	10	$413,048	44
2001	18				1	3	164,833	73
2002	20			1	3	5	294,124	58
2003	10				1	2	150,953	78
2004	10					1	84,604	89
Total	81	1		1	7	21	1,107,562	

COMBINED ALL-TIME MONEY (3 TOURS): $7,463,243

CHAMPIONS TOUR TOP TOURNAMENT SUMMARY

Year	00	01	02	03
Senior PGA Championship	T54	T15	T27	T53
U.S. Senior Open			T37	T8
Ford Senior Players	T24		T49	
JELD-WEN Tradition	T25	46		T39

Tom Wargo

EXEMPT STATUS: Top 30 on All-Time Money List
FULL NAME: Amos Tom Wargo
HEIGHT: 6-0
WEIGHT: 205
BIRTHDATE: September 16, 1942
BIRTHPLACE: Marlette, MI
RESIDENCE: Centralia, IL

FAMILY: Wife, Irene; Michelle (12/12/65); two grandchildren
CLUB AFFILIATION: Greenview GC (Centralia, IL)
SPECIAL INTERESTS: Harley-Davidson motorcycles
TURNED PROFESSIONAL: 1976

JOINED CHAMPIONS TOUR: 1993

CHAMPIONS TOUR VICTORIES (4): 1993 PGA Seniors' Championship. **1994** Doug Sanders Celebrity Classic. **1995** Dallas Reunion Pro-Am. **2000** LiquidGolf.com Invitational.

OTHER SENIOR VICTORIES (1): 1994 Senior British Open.

2004 CHARLES SCHWAB CUP FINISH: T72nd - 39 points

GEORGIA-PACIFIC GRAND CHAMPIONS VICTORIES (3): 2003 Toshiba Senior Classic, Farmers Charity Classic. **2004** Allianz Championship.

BEST PGA TOUR CAREER FINISH: T28—1992 PGA Championship.

OTHER VICTORIES (3): 1990 Gateway PGA Sectional Championship. **1991** PGA Club Professional Winter Stroke Play Championship, Gateway PGA Sectional Championship.

PGA TOUR CAREER EARNINGS: $16,058

BEST 2004 CHAMPIONS TOUR FINISHES: T20—Bruno's Memorial Classic; T22—Ford Senior Players Championship.

2004 SEASON:

Among the top 25 in just two events, both coming in the middle third of the season...Closed with a 68 near Birmingham to T20 at the Bruno's Memorial Classic and then T22 at the Ford Senior Players Championship...Was among the early leaders at the Allianz Championship but eventually slipped back into a T27 in Iowa...Finished eighth on the final Georgia-Pacific money list, with $133,062...Claimed his third career Georgia-Pacific title at the Allianz event, defeating Dave Eichelberger by a stroke.

CHAMPIONS TOUR CAREER HIGHLIGHTS:

2003: Lone top-10 finish was T9 at rain-shortened SBC Classic in California. A week later won his first Georgia-Pacific Grand Champions title when he defeated Dave Stockton in two extra holes at the Toshiba Senior Classic and also finished T13 overall...Claimed his second Georgia-Pacific Grand Champions title when he edged Stockton again by one stroke at the Farmers Charity Classic...Was the leading money-winner in the Georgia-Pacific Grand Champions competition, with $219,312, including $46,000 for his T2 finish at the Georgia-Pacific Grand Champions Championship in Sonoma, CA, at the end of the year. **2002:** Had his season cut short in mid-September when he suffered a heart attack just prior to the start of the final round at the RJR Championship. Underwent angioplasty shortly after in Winston-Salem, NC, and did not play the remainder of the year...Best showing came near Kansas City where he vaulted from a T25 into a T3 at the rain-shortened TD Waterhouse Championship, thanks to a 7-under 65 in the second round. It was his best performance since a T3 at the rain-shortened Comfort Classic in 2000...Had a rare feat at the AT&T Canada Senior Open when he eagled the par-5 13th hole at Essex all three days. Was 6-under on that hole, but played his other 51 holes for the week 1-over par. Made his third hole-in-one on the Champions Tour (12th overall) in the opening round of the Ford Senior Players Championship. Aced the 192-yard fourth hole with a 5-iron. **2001:** Best finish a T6 at the Emerald Coast Classic...Plagued much of the year with back problems. **2000:** Ended a victory drought of nearly five years when he defeated Gary McCord and J.C. Snead in a three-hole playoff at the LiquidGolf.com Invitational, his first Champions Tour title since the 1995 Dallas Reunion Pro-Am (120 starts). Came from three strokes back of Bruce Summerhays with a final-round 68 at The TPC at Prestancia. **1998:** Second by two strokes to Gil Morgan at The Tradition. **1997:** T3 at the U.S. Senior Open at Olympia Fields CC near Chicago. Shared the first-round lead after opening with a 69, and followed with rounds of 70-73-70 to finish two strokes behind Graham Marsh. **1996:** Lost to Dale Douglass on the third playoff hole for the Bell Atlantic Classic title near Philadelphia. **1995:** Easily won the Dallas Reunion Pro-Am with the first of only two wire-to-wire performances on the circuit that year. 54-hole score of 13-under 197 was seven shots better than Dave Stockton and Dave Eichelberger...Almost captured the Emerald Coast Classic, but fell to Raymond Floyd in a playoff. **1994:** Was the Champions Tour's "ironman," playing in 36 tournaments and 112 rounds...Defeated Bob Murphy at the Doug Sanders Kingwood Celebrity Classic...Journeyed across the pond and won the Senior British Open at Royal Lytham & St. Annes in England. **1993:** First Champions Tour victory was memorable. Made a par on the second playoff hole to defeat Bruce Crampton at the PGA Seniors' Championship in just his sixth senior start. **1992:** Initially earned a conditional exemption with a 10th-place finish at the Champions Tour National Qualifying Tournament. Shot rounds of 69-66-77-74—286 and then made birdie on the first playoff hole to earn his position.

OTHER CAREER HIGHLIGHTS:

Was the low club professional at the 1992 PGA Championship at Bellerive CC (T28) and was the only senior to make the cut at the 1993 PGA Championship at Inverness (T31)...Won 10 events on the Founders Club PGA Tournament Series...Named 1992 PGA Club Professional of the Year...Was the Gateway PGA Section's Player of the Year in 1991 and 1992 and a member of every PGA Cup squad from 1988-92...Also won the 1991 Winter Stroke-Play Championship and the 1990 and 1991 PGA Section Championships in Illinois.

PERSONAL:

Raised on a Michigan dairy farm...Didn't play golf until he taught himself at age 25...Owner of Greenview GC in Centralia, IL...Jobs prior to golf included iron worker, assembly-line auto worker, bartende, and commercial fisherman in Alaska...An accomplished bowler who once thought about a professional career in that sport...Says biggest thrill in golf was winning the 1993 PGA Seniors' Championship...Enjoys the History and Discovery Channels, and his favorite entertainer is the late Red Skelton...Favorite movie is "The Sting"...List all members of the armed forces as his heroes.

PLAYER STATISTICS

2004 CHAMPIONS TOUR STATISTICS:

Scoring Average	72.70	(62)
Driving Distance	272.6	(37)
Driving Accuracy Percentage	60.2%	(73)
Total Driving	110	(74)
Greens in Regulation Pct.	62.4%	(65)
Putting Average	1.792	(33)
Sand Save Percentage	42.6%	(58)
Eagles (Holes per)	310.5	(36)
Birdie Average	3.01	(55)
All-Around Ranking	419	(62)

MISCELLANEOUS CHAMPIONS TOUR STATISTICS

2004 Low Round: 65–2004 SBC Classic/3
Career Low Round: 63–1995 FHP Health Care Classic/2
Career Largest Paycheck: $180,000–2000 LiquidGolf.com Invitational/1

MISCELLANEOUS PGA TOUR STATISTICS

Career Low Round: 70–1993 PGA Championship/2
Career Largest Paycheck: $9,000–1992 PGA Championship/T28

CHAMPIONS TOUR CAREER SUMMARY — PLAYOFF RECORD: 2-2

Year	Events Played	1st	2nd	3rd	Top 10	Top 25	Earnings	Rank
1993	32	1		1	15	24	$557,270	16
1994	36	1	3		25	32	1,005,344	6
1995	33	1	2	2	14	24	844,687	9
1996	35		3	1	10	21	695,705	15
1997	33			1	8	15	567,419	24
1998	33		1	1	7	19	679,579	22
1999	32				5	13	498,621	40
2000	32	1		1	7	12	777,838	22
2001	23				1	10	314,188	54
2002	23			1	4	9	515,440	38
2003	23				1	7	277,301	53
2004	23					2	160,813	72
Total	358	4	9	8	97	188	6,894,204	
COMBINED ALL-TIME MONEY (3 TOURS):							**$6,913,320**	

CHAMPIONS TOUR TOP TOURNAMENT SUMMARY

Year	93	94	95	96	97	98	99	00	01	02	03	04
Senior PGA Championship	1	T10	T30	T15	CUT	T11	T39	74	T20	CUT	T34	CUT
U.S. Senior Open	T17	T4	T27	T35	T3	T43	6	T34	T59	T51	CUT	CUT
Ford Senior Players	T13	T10	T30	T16	T39	T41	T44	T12	T28	T12	T73	T22
JELD-WEN Tradition	T17	T9	T45	T37	T11	2	T28	T61	T19	T48	T42	T55
Charles Schwab Cup Champ	T8	5	T3	T10	T17	21		T6				

Denis Watson

EXEMPT STATUS: PGA TOUR Career Victory List
FULL NAME: Denis Leslie Watson
HEIGHT: 6-0
WEIGHT: 170
BIRTHDATE: October 18, 1955
BIRTHPLACE: Salisbury, Rhodesia (Zimbabwe)
RESIDENCE: Fort Lauderdale, FL

FAMILY: Kyle (9/23/86), Paige (4/22/89), Ross (8/31/91)
CLUB AFFILIATION: Old Head GC (Kinsale, Ireland)
EDUCATION: Rhodesia (English System)
SPECIAL INTERESTS: Golf course design, fishing, cooking, farming
TURNED PROFESSIONAL: 1976
JOINED PGA TOUR: 1981

JOINED CHAMPIONS TOUR: 2005

PGA TOUR VICTORIES (3): 1984 Buick Open, NEC World Series of Golf, Panasonic Las Vegas Invitational.

OTHER VICTORIES (1): 1975 World Amateur Team Championship [with George Harvey].

PGA TOUR CAREER EARNINGS: $1,288,621

PGA TOUR PLAYOFF RECORD: 0-1

OTHER CAREER HIGHLIGHTS:

Played the PGA TOUR on a regular basis from 1981-1996 and made a total of 834 starts (139 cuts made)...Easily had his best season in 1984 when he won all three of his titles on the and finished fourth on the final money list, with $408,562...Came close to winning PGA Player of the Year honors by joining Tom Watson as the only three-time winner that year...Had brilliant seven-week spurt late in the summer of 1984. Won his first TOUR title at the Buick Open, thanks to a 63-68 finish at Warwick Hills. Then placed 33rd at the PGA Championship. Shot course-record 8-under-par 62 in the second round of the NEC World Series of Golf at Firestone, then stayed in front the rest of the way to collect $126,000 and 10-year exemption. Three events later, earned TOUR's richest payday ($162,000) when he won the Las Vegas Invitational, edging Andy Bean by one stroke...Followed stellar 1984 season with a solid 1985 campaign that included a pair of runner-up finishes. T2 in the U.S. Open, one shot behind Andy North. Also finished second to Roger Maltbie in defense of World Series title...Did not play on the PGA TOUR in 1995 due to surgery on right arm to repair ulnar nerve damage...Also played in 24 Nationwide Tour events and made four cuts...Best effort on the Nationwide circuit was a T9 at the 1998 Greater Austin Open.

PERSONAL:

Named Rhodesian Sportsman of the Year in 1975...Twice represented South Africa in World Series of Golf (1980 and 1982)...Has recently done segments on "The Golf Channel Academy" with good friend David Leadbetter.

PLAYER STATISTICS

MISCELLANEOUS PGA TOUR STATISTICS
2004 Low Round: 76–B.C. Open/1
Career Low Round: 62–1984 NEC World Series of Golf/2
Career Largest Paycheck: $162,000–1984 Panasonic Las Vegas Invitational/1

Tom Watson

WORLD GOLF HALL OF FAME MEMBER (Inducted 1988)
EXEMPT STATUS: Top 30 on All-Time Money List
FULL NAME: Thomas Sturges Watson
HEIGHT: 5-9
WEIGHT: 175
BIRTHDATE: September 4, 1949
BIRTHPLACE: Kansas City, MO
RESIDENCE: Stilwell, KS
FAMILY: Wife, Hilary; Meg (9/13/79), Michael Barrett (12/15/82), stepchildren Kyle (9/23/86), Paige (4/22/89), Ross (8/31/91)
EDUCATION: Stanford University (1971, Psychology)
SPECIAL INTERESTS: Current affairs, outdoor life
TURNED PROFESSIONAL: 1971
JOINED PGA TOUR: 1971

JOINED CHAMPIONS TOUR: 1999

CHAMPIONS TOUR VICTORIES (6): 1999 Bank One Championship. **2000** IR SENIOR TOUR Championship. **2001** Senior PGA Championship. **2002** SENIOR TOUR Championship at Gaillardia. **2003** Senior British Open, JELD-WEN Tradition.

OTHER SENIOR VICTORIES (4): 1999 Wendy's Three-Tour Challenge [with Jack Nicklaus and Hale Irwin]. **1999** Diner's Club Matches [with Jack Nicklaus]. **2000** Hyundai Team Matches [with Jack Nicklaus]. **2004** Wendy's Champions Skins Game.

2004 CHARLES SCHWAB CUP FINISH: 28th - 551 points

PGA TOUR VICTORIES (39): 1974 Western Open. **1975** Byron Nelson Golf Classic, British Open Championship. **1977** Bing Crosby National Pro-Am, Andy Williams-San Diego Open Invitational, Masters Tournament, Western Open, British Open Championship. **1978** Joe Garagiola-Tucson Open, Bing Crosby National Pro-Am, Byron Nelson Golf Classic, Colgate Hall of Fame Classic, Anheuser-Busch Golf Classic. **1979** Sea Pines Heritage Classic, MONY Tournament of Champions, Byron Nelson Golf Classic, Memorial Tournament, Colgate Hall of Fame Classic. **1980** Andy Williams-San Diego Open Invitational, Glen Campbell-Los Angeles Open, MONY Tournament of Champions, Greater New Orleans Open, Byron Nelson Golf Classic, British Open Championship, World Series of Golf. **1981** Masters Tournament, USF&G New Orleans Open, Atlanta Classic. **1982** Glen Campbell-Los Angeles Open, Sea Pines Heritage, U.S. Open Championship, British Open Championship. **1983** British Open Championship. **1984** Seiko-Tucson Match Play Championship, MONY Tournament of Champions, Western Open. **1987** Nabisco Championship. **1996** Memorial Tournament. **1998** MasterCard Colonial.

OTHER VICTORIES (5):
1980 Dunlop Phoenix [Jpn]. **1984** Australian Open. **1992** Hong Kong Open. **1994** Skins Game. **1997** Dunlop Phoenix [Jpn].

PGA TOUR CAREER EARNINGS: $9,892,128

PGA TOUR PLAYOFF RECORD: 8-4

BEST 2004 CHAMPIONS TOUR FINISHES: T2—The ACE Group Classic; 3—Allianz Championship; T4—Senior PGA Championship; T9—FedEx Kinko's Classic; T10—Constellation Energy Classic.

BEST 2004 PGA TOUR FINISH: T66—Bay Hill Invitational.

2004 SEASON:

Made just 12 official starts on the Champions Tour and was troubled by hip and shoulder problems throughout the season...Did not register an official victory for the first time in his Champions Tour career and also finished outside the top 30 money-winners for the first time...Won his first Wendy's Champions Skins Game early in the season when he two-putted for a par from 25 feet on the third extra playoff hole and then watched Lee Trevino three-putt from 25 feet for a bogey. Finished with eight birdies and an eagle to collect 10 skins and $400,000 at Wailea...Continued to be snakebit at The ACE Group Classic, losing in a three-way playoff with winner Craig Stadler and Gary Koch. Got himself into position with birdies on 16 and 17 Sunday and nearly earned the win at the final hole, but missed a nine-foot birdie putt which would have given him a one-stroke win. After Stadler drained a 27-foot birdie putt on the first extra hole, missed a chance to keep the playoff going when his birdie bid from 10 feet missed. Runner-up finish in Naples was his fourth in five starts at this event and was his second loss in a playoff...Also contended down the stretch at the Allianz Championship, but eventually finished third after posting a final-round 71, four strokes back of D.A. Weibring...T9 the week prior at the FedEx Kinko's Classic after being just one stroke off the pace after the opening round...T4 at the Senior PGA Championship after being tied with Hale Irwin for the first-round lead at Valhalla...Finished T10 in his final start of the season at the Constellation Energy Classic in early October...Shortly after playing near Baltimore, reconsidered his initial decision to undergo both left hip and right shoulder surgery, opting for rehab instead...Made an appearance at the Bay Hill Invitational on the PGA TOUR, where he made the cut and finished T66, his first made cut on the PGA TOUR since the 2002 Colonial...Also played in his 31st Masters Tournament with a heavy heart, learning about the death of his longtime caddie, Bruce Edwards, just hours before his scheduled first-round tee time. Missed the cut at Augusta National...Forced to withdraw from the British Open Championship at Troon, missing the prestigious event for the first time since 1996.

CHAMPIONS TOUR CAREER HIGHLIGHTS:

2003: Experienced a bittersweet season as he had his finest year on the Champions Tour at the same time he was teaming with long-time caddie and friend Bruce Edwards in his battle against Lou Gehrig's disease...Was either first or second in half of his 14 appearances on the Champions Tour, and as a result of his stellar play throughout the campaign, earned all of the circuit's top honors, including the Charles Schwab Cup, the Jack Nicklaus Player of the Year Award, the Arnold Palmer Award and the Byron Nelson Trophy...Donated his $1-million annuity for winning the Schwab Cup to ALS research and patient care and other charities. Throughout the course of the season, helped raise nearly $3 million for ALS-related causes and other charities...Was the leading money-winner for the first time since 1984, with a personal-best $1,853,108, and earned the most money per start on the Champions Tour last year, $132,365...Earned first Player of the Year honor since 1984...Was under par in 37 of 48 rounds and stroke average of 68.81 was the second lowest in Champions Tour history (Hale Irwin, 68.59, 1998)...Became the first player ever to compete in all nine major championships on the PGA TOUR/Champions Tour combined in a single season...Won multiple major titles in a season for the first time on the Champions Tour since Gil Morgan in 1998 and for the first time in his career since 1982. In July, won his second career major on the Champions Tour when he outdueled Englishman Carl Mason on the Ailsa course at Turnberry for an emotional win at the Senior British Open Championship in Scotland. Only had one three-putt over his 74 holes and posted a final-round 64, the lowest finish ever by a winner in Senior

CHAMPIONS TOUR CAREER SUMMARY — PLAYOFF RECORD: 1-6

Year	Events Played	1st	2nd	3rd	Top 10	Top 25	Earnings	Rank
1999	2	1			1	2	$208,240	62
2000	13	1	4		10	13	1,146,361	13
2001	13	1	1		8	11	986,547	17
2002	14	1	5		10	12	1,522,437	8
2003	14	2	5		10	13	1,853,108	1
2004	12		1	1	5	7	475,203	42
Total	68	6	16	1	44	58	6,191,895	
COMBINED ALL-TIME MONEY (3 TOURS):							**$16,084,023**	

CHAMPIONS TOUR TOP TOURNAMENT SUMMARY

Year	00	01	02	03	04
Senior PGA Championship	T17	1	T18	T17	T4
U.S. Senior Open	T10	T16	2	2	T25
Ford Senior Players	T18	T8		T2	
Senior British Open				1	T22
JELD-WEN Tradition	T2		5	1	T55
Charles Schwab Cup Champ	1	4	1	2	

CHAMPIONS TOUR YEAR-BY-YEAR STATISTICS (TOP 50 ON 2004 MONEY LIST)

	Scoring Average	Putting Average	Greens in Regulation	Driving Distance	Driving Accuracy
1999	67.67 (N/A)	1.600 (N/A)	74.1 (N/A)	286.3 (N/A)	82.1 (N/A)
2000	69.23 (5)	1.731 (2)	75.3 (T4)	272.8 (25)	72.6 (T20)
2001	70.21 (10)	1.738 (4)	70.2 (T12)	272.0 (42)	74.3 (T16)
2002	69.57 (2)	1.781 (T23)	74.9 (2)	268.8 (44)	75.3 (13)
2003	68.81 (1)	1.736 (2)	72.2 (T7)	284.0 (8)	69.2 (41)
2004	71.36 (N/A)	1.819 (N/A)	71.9 (N/A)	278.7 (N/A)	75.2 (N/A)

Tom Watson (continued)

British Open history. His 6-under Sunday score, coupled with Mason's double bogey at the 72nd hole, allowed Watson to get into a playoff. Eventually defeated Mason with a par-4 on the second extra hole to become just the 11th player, and first since Hale Irwin in 1998, to win an official event on both the PGA TOUR and Champions Tour at the same venue...In his next start in late August, became the first player since Hale Irwin in 1998 to win consecutive majors when he claimed the JELD-WEN Tradition, the first fifth major in Champions Tour history, near Portland, OR. With Edwards on the bag, edged Jim Ahern, Tom Kite and Gil Morgan by a stroke when he got his ball up and down from a greenside bunker for birdie on the final hole. Roller coaster event included a second-round, 10-under 62 at The Reserve, tying the lowest round ever posted in a major on the Champions Tour, and a 1-over 73 on Saturday that made him just the third Tradition winner ever with an over-par score among the four rounds...Was also the runner-up to Bruce Lietzke at the U.S. Senior Open, falling two strokes short at the Inverness Club in Toledo, OH. Had opened with a 5-under-par 66 at the event and held a three-stroke advantage over Lietzke after the first round before rounds of 72-70-71 to close the tournament...Finished second again, along with Tom Kite and Jim Thorpe, in his next start at the Ford Senior Players Championship. Moved into contention in adverse weather conditions Friday with an 8-under 64, the low round of the day by four strokes, and his best score ever at the TPC of Michigan. Was tied for the 54-hole lead with Mike McCullough and Craig Stadler, but eventually lost by three strokes to Stadler, despite a final-round 69...Edged Jim Thorpe for the money title and also clinched the Charles Schwab Cup at the end of the season with a solo second-place finish at the Charles Schwab Cup Championship in Sonoma, CA...Received a special exemption to play in his first U.S. Open since 2000 and made headlines on Thursday when he was tied for the first-round lead after posting a 5-under 65. Eventually T28 at Olympia Fields after shooting 7-over 147 on the weekend...Turned in masterful performance at the British Open at Royal St. George's, finishing T18 thanks in part to a closing-round 69...Received the Card Walker Award during the week of the Bayer Advantage Celebrity Pro-Am and was honored with the Payne Stewart Award at THE TOUR Championship in Houston. **2002:** For the second time, saved his best for last and won the season-ending SENIOR TOUR Championship at Gaillardia. Opened with a 2-over 74, but played the last 52 holes of the event without making a bogey (17-under) despite cold, rainy weather in Oklahoma City. His $440,000 paycheck was largest as a professional. Earned 440 Charles Schwab Cup points and vaulted from 10th position into fourth in the final points standings (1,582 points: $200,000 annuity)...Contended down the stretch at the rain-shortened Royal Caribbean Classic before eventually T2 along with Isao Aoki and Bruce Fleisher, one stroke behind John Jacobs...Also went head to head down the stretch with Hale Irwin at The ACE Group Classic before losing by one stroke. Went for the green in two at the par-5 17th hole, but came up short in the water and eventually made a bogey. Made his first hole-in-one on the Champions Tour and 13th of his career in the opening round (16th hole, 6-iron, 156 yards) at TwinEagles...Recorded third consecutive runner-up finish after losing in a playoff to Tom Kite at SBC Senior Classic. Chipped in for eagle from 123 feet on the 54th hole to force Kite to make a five-foot birdie putt to tie. Kite won with a par on the second playoff hole...Lost to Don Pooley in a playoff for the U.S. Senior Open at Caves Valley. Played his last 10 holes in 5-under to catch Pooley and then matched him with three pars and a birdie in overtime before finally falling to Pooley's birdie on No. 18, the fifth extra hole...Was also one of three players to T2 at the SAS Championship behind Bruce Lietzke...Finished solo seventh at the MasterCard Colonial, his 11th career top-10 effort at Colonial and his best PGA TOUR finish since T9 at the 2000 PGA Championship. **2001:** Won his first Champions Tour major title. Triumphed at the Senior PGA Championship in New Jersey. After opening with a 72, followed with rounds of 69-66-67 to edge Jim Thorpe by one stroke at Ridgewood CC...Troubled much of the early portion of the year with a strained ligament in his right elbow that he injured while working out just prior to the Masters...Inducted into the Bay Area Sports Hall of Fame during the week of the Siebel Classic in Silicon Valley. **2000:** Saved his best for the last official event of the season, claiming the IR SENIOR TOUR Championship in Myrtle Beach. Was T3 after 54 holes, but fired a 6-under-par 66 on the final day for the victory. Held off a late charge by John Jacobs for a one-stroke win. Win at TPC of Myrtle Beach made him the first to claim season-ending events on both TOURs (won '87 Nabisco Championship of Golf)...Lost twice in playoffs. Was one of four players involved in the overtime session at The ACE Group Classic, eventually falling to Lanny Wadkins...Along with Larry Nelson, lost in a three-way playoff to Tom Kite at The Countrywide Tradition...Also battled Larry Nelson until the final hole at the Boone Valley Classic before finishing solo second in St. Louis...T9 at the PGA Championship near Louisville, the best performance by a senior in that event since Sam Snead T3 in 1974. Matched his career-best round in a PGA Championship when he posted a 65 on Saturday at Valhalla. **1999:** Claimed his first Champions Tour win in his second start, the Bank One Championship in Dallas...At the time, became the third-youngest player ever to win a Champions Tour event at 50 years, 15 days. Gil Morgan (50 years, 11 days/1996 Ralphs Senior Classic) and George Archer (50 years, 14 days/1989 Gatlin Brothers Southwest Classic)...Made debut on the Champions Tour at the Comfort Classic in Indianapolis just six days after turning 50.

OTHER CAREER HIGHLIGHTS:

Ranks T9 on the PGA TOUR's all-time victory list, with 39 official titles...Had a remarkable run from 1977 through 1982, when he won at least three titles per year...Has been a runner-up 31 times in his PGA TOUR career...First victory came at the 1974 Western Open, when he defeated Tom Weiskopf and J.C. Snead by two strokes...Winner of eight major championships (1975, '77, '80, '82, '83 British Opens, 1977, '81 Masters Tournaments and 1982 U.S. Open)...In 1982, became one of just six players to win the U.S. Open and British Open in the same year (Bobby Jones, Gene Sarazen, Ben Hogan, Lee Trevino and Tiger Woods are the others)...Was the PGA TOUR's leading money winner five times, including four years in a row (1977-80, 1984)...In 1980, became the first player to earn $500,000 in a season when he captured six TOUR events to go along with a third British Open crown...Went 27 consecutive years earning at least $100,000 (1974-2000), a TOUR record...In 1987, won the season-ending Nabisco Championship (now THE TOUR Championship) and earned $360,000...After a nine-year absence from the winner's circle, claimed the 1996 Memorial Tournament. Had a one-stroke lead over Ernie Els through 54 holes and closed with a 70 to post a one-stroke victory over David Duval...Finished 25th on the money list, his highest ranking since 1987, and made his first trip to THE TOUR Championship since winning it in 1987...Earned 39th PGA TOUR title with victory in 1998 MasterCard Colonial. At 48, became the oldest player ever to win the event (previous oldest: Ben Hogan was 46 when he captured his last of five Colonial titles). Stretch between first victory (1974) and last victory—23 years, 11 months, 24 days—third-longest in TOUR history...Winner of three Vardon Trophies (1977-79)...Six-time PGA of America Player of the Year...Played on four American Ryder Cup teams and captained the 1993 squad to victory at The Belfry...Also played for the United States against Japan in 1982 and 1984...Elected to the World Golf Hall of Fame in 1988.

PERSONAL:

Big fan of hometown Kansas City Royals...Active in Kansas City area charitable endeavors and development of golf courses for junior players...In 1999, was made an honorary member of the Royal & Ancient GC of St. Andrews, joining fellow Americans Arnold Palmer, Jack Nicklaus, former President George Bush and the late Gene Sarazen.

PLAYER STATISTICS

MISCELLANEOUS CHAMPIONS TOUR STATISTICS

2004 Low Round: 66–2004 MasterCard Championship/3
Career Low Round: 62–2 times, most recent 2003 JELD-WEN Tradition/2
Career Largest Paycheck: $440,000–2002 SENIOR TOUR Championship at Gaillardia/1

MISCELLANEOUS PGA TOUR STATISTICS

2004 Low Round: 70–Bay Hill Invitational Presented by MasterCard/1
Career Low Round: 63–3 times, most recent 1992 Buick Invitational of California/1
Career Largest Paycheck: $414,000–1998 MasterCard Colonial/1

D.A. Weibring (Y-bring)

EXEMPT STATUS: Top 30 on 2004 Champions Tour Money List
FULL NAME: Donald Albert Weibring, Jr.
HEIGHT: 6-1
WEIGHT: 200
BIRTHDATE: May 25, 1953
BIRTHPLACE: Quincy, IL
RESIDENCE: Frisco, TX
FAMILY: Wife, Kristy; Matt (12/4/79), Katey (12/29/82), Allison Paige (10/3/87)
EDUCATION: Illinois State University (1975, Business Administration)
SPECIAL INTERESTS: Basketball, golf course design
TURNED PROFESSIONAL: 1975
JOINED PGA TOUR: 1977

JOINED CHAMPIONS TOUR: 2003

CHAMPIONS TOUR VICTORIES (2): **2003** SAS Championship. **2004** Allianz Championship.

2004 CHARLES SCHWAB CUP FINISH: 8th - 1,754 points

PGA TOUR VICTORIES (5):
1979 Ed McMahon-Jaycees Quad Cities Open. **1987** Beatrice Western Open. **1991** Hardee's Golf Classic. **1995** Quad City Classic. **1996** Canon Greater Hartford Open.

OTHER VICTORIES (3):
1985 Golf Digest Polaroid Cup, Shell-Air New Zealand Open. **1989** Family House Invitational.

PGA TOUR CAREER EARNINGS: $4,770,705

PGA TOUR PLAYOFF RECORD: 0-2

BEST 2004 CHAMPIONS TOUR FINISHES:
1—Allianz Championship; T2—Bruno's Memorial Classic, Bank of America Championship; T4—JELD-WEN Tradition; 5—Outback Steakhouse Pro-Am, The First Tee Open at Pebble Beach presented by Wal-Mart.

2004 SEASON:
Led the Champions Tour with 15 top-10 finishes in 25 appearances. Earnings of $1.4 million were almost twice what he made in his abbreviated rookie season...Got an early birthday present when he went wire to wire at the Allianz Championship for his fifth Tour victory in the Midwest. Three-stroke win over Tom Jenkins near Des Moines was his second Champions Tour career title and propelled him to May Player of the Month honors. Made just one bogey for the week on the back nine and led the field in Greens in Regulation (47 of 54)...Came within two strokes of Bruce Fleisher after four holes in Sunday's final round of the Bruno's Memorial Classic before eventually finishing T2, along with Bruce Lietzke, seven strokes back...Also closed with 65 at Nashawtuc and T2 in the Bank of America Championship near Boston, four strokes back of Craig Stadler...Made a run for the title at the JELD-WEN Tradition, hanging among the leaders all four days before finishing T4. Faltered on the back nine Sunday, making critical bogeys at Nos. 13 and 18 to end his chances...Followed that effort the next week with a T5 at The First Tee Open at Pebble Beach presented by Wal-Mart...Continued his strong play in his next three starts, finishing T10 at the Kroger Classic, T8 at the SAS Championship and T6 at the Constellation Energy Classic, giving him five straight top-10 finishes.

CHAMPIONS TOUR CAREER HIGHLIGHTS:
2003: Did not become eligible for the Champions Tour until June, yet was one of three rookies to finish among the top 30 money-winners...Among the top five in two events before he became the seventh first-time winner on the Champions Tour at Prestonwood CC near Raleigh, NC. Despite suffering from flu-like symptoms, rallied from five strokes back to claim the SAS Championship. Appeared to be out of contention after a three-putt at No. 16, but finished eagle-birdie to defeat Bobby Wadkins and Tom Kite by a stroke. Victory was his first in over seven years on TOUR and also made him the 25th different winner in 2003, tying the all-time Champions Tour record for most different champions in a season (25 in 1995)...Played in the final group on Sunday at the Senior British Open, but faltered on the back nine at Turnberry and finished solo fifth. Moved into early contention with a second-round, 7-under-par 63, his career-best as a professional.

OTHER CAREER HIGHLIGHTS:
Winner of five PGA TOUR events in his career, which began in 1977. A three-time TOUR winner in Moline, IL. First career victory at the 1979 Ed McMahon-Jaycees Quad Cities Open came after a final-round 65. Also won the 1991 Hardee's Golf Classic and 1995 Quad City Classic. Captured a fourth TOUR title in Illinois at the 1987 Beatrice Western Open where a closing 68 produced a one-stroke win...Lone TOUR victory outside of Illinois came at 1996 Canon-Greater Hartford Open. Hartford victory, a four-stroke win over Tom Kite, came while he was battling the effects of Bell's Palsy...Was inducted into Illinois PGA Hall of Fame in 2001 and is also a member of the Illinois State University Hall of Fame and the Quincy Notre Dame High School Hall of Fame...Has own design and management company, D.A. Weibring/Golf Resources Group, which has been in business for 18 years. Company has been involved in some 60 projects, one of which is the TPC at Deere Run, which became the host course for the John Deere Classic in 2000. Firm has 20 projects in various stages of design and development...Co-winner of 1991 Hilton Bounceback Award, thanks to successful recovery from Nov. 1989 right wrist surgery.

PERSONAL:
Son, Matt, was a two-time All-America at Georgia Tech and turned pro following graduation. Played in some Nationwide Tour events in 2002, 2003 and 2004...Daughter Katey is pursuing a professional dancing career. Daughter Allison also participates in dance...Was an all-state basketball player in Illinois...Became a good friend of former NBA basketball star Doug Collins while at Illinois State...Enjoys watching "The West Wing," "Will & Grace" and reruns of "Seinfeld"...Best friend in golf is Peter Jacobsen...Got started in golf when his dad cut down a wooden-shafted putter for him when he was five.

PLAYER STATISTICS

MISCELLANEOUS CHAMPIONS TOUR STATISTICS
2004 Low Round: 65–6 times, most recent 2004 Charles Schwab Cup Championship/4
Career Low Round: 63–2003 Senior British Open/2
Career Largest Paycheck: $270,000–2003 SAS Championship/1

MISCELLANEOUS PGA TOUR STATISTICS
2004 Low Round: 69–3 times, most recent John Deere Classic/2
Career Low Round: 64–10 times, most recent 1998 Quad City Classic/1
Career Largest Paycheck: $270,000–1996 Canon Greater Hartford Open/1

CHAMPIONS TOUR CAREER SUMMARY — PLAYOFF RECORD: 0-0

Year	Events Played	1st	2nd	3rd	Top 10	Top 25	Earnings	Rank
2003	14	1			7	10	$729,852	28
2004	25	1	2		15	19	1,413,795	8
Total	39	2	2		22	29	2,143,647	
COMBINED ALL-TIME MONEY (3 TOURS):							**$6,914,352**	

CHAMPIONS TOUR TOP TOURNAMENT SUMMARY

Year	03	04
Senior PGA Championship	T48	T17
U.S. Senior Open		6
Ford Senior Players		T13
Senior British Open	5	T61
JELD-WEN Tradition	T10	T4
Charles Schwab Cup Champ	T20	T7

CHAMPIONS TOUR YEAR-BY-YEAR STATISTICS (TOP 50 ON 2004 MONEY LIST)

	Scoring Average	Putting Average	Greens in Regulation	Driving Distance	Driving Accuracy
2003	69.70 (4)	1.768 (T10)	72.4 (6)	278.2 (17)	75.6 (T9)
2004	70.28 (9)	1.755 (T6)	71.6 (13)	270.9 (45)	71.7 (32)

Kermit Zarley (ZAR-lee)

EXEMPT STATUS: Net-70 on All-Time Money List
FULL NAME: Kermit Millard Zarley, Jr.
HEIGHT: 6-0
WEIGHT: 175
BIRTHDATE: September 29, 1941
BIRTHPLACE: Seattle, WA
RESIDENCE: Scottsdale, AZ

FAMILY: Christine (7/25/67), Monica (12/11/68), Michael (10/20/70); four grandchildren
EDUCATION: University of Houston (B.B.A, 1963)
SPECIAL INTERESTS: Bible study, writing, weightlifting
TURNED PROFESSIONAL: 1963
JOINED PGA TOUR: 1963

JOINED CHAMPIONS TOUR: 1991

CHAMPIONS TOUR VICTORIES (1): 1994 The Transamerica.

PGA TOUR VICTORIES (2): 1968 Kaiser International Open Invitational. **1970** Canadian Open.

OTHER VICTORIES: (3): 1962 NCAA Championship [indiv]. **1972** National Team Championship [with Babe Hiskey]. **1984** Tallahassee Open.

PGA TOUR CAREER EARNINGS: $715,721

PGA TOUR PLAYOFF RECORD: 0-1

BEST 2004 CHAMPIONS TOUR FINISHES:
T45—SAS Championship.

2004 SEASON:

Played in just 10 events, with best finish a T45 at the SAS Championship...First appearance came at Bruno's Memorial Classic in May.

CHAMPIONS TOUR CAREER HIGHLIGHTS:

2002: Returned to action for the first time in nearly a year at the 3M Championship in August. Sidelined most of year due to complications from 2001 surgery on his left shoulder...Joined the ranks of the Georgia-Pacific Grand Champions at the Napa Valley Championship and T2 in the over-60 competition. Shot 6-under 66 in the opening round thanks to his second career ace on the Champions Tour. Holed a 4-iron shot from 196 yards on No. 7 of the South course at Silverado. Eventually T16 overall in the Napa event, his first top-20 finish on the Champions Tour since the 2000 Bank One Championship (T13). **2001:** Troubled by shoulder problems for most of the season...Did not make his first appearance until the first week of July at the U.S. Senior Open after surgery. **2000:** Battled Tom Jenkins down to the wire at the AT&T Canada Senior Open before falling one stroke short. Had tied Jenkins at 13-under par when he completed his final-round 66, but Jenkins, playing one group behind, birdied the final hole for the win. **1999:** In the final round at Boone Valley GC, aced the 177-yard, par-3 third hole for the first hole-in-one of his Champions Tour career. **1998:** Finished second to Jim Albus at the GTE Classic near Tampa. **1997:** Second to Dave Stockton at Franklin Quest Championship in Utah. **1996:** Lost to John Bland in a three-way playoff at the Bruno's Memorial Classic...Also was a runner-up at the season-ending Energizer SENIOR TOUR Championship at Myrtle Beach and earned a career-best $160,000 paycheck...Carded one of three double-eagles on the Champions Tour during the second round of the Boone Valley Classic. **1994:** Claimed his first TOUR win in more than 24 years when he captured The Transamerica. Defeated Isao Aoki on the first hole of a sudden-death playoff. Victory came at Silverado CC near Napa, CA, the same venue where he claimed his first PGA TOUR win in 1968...Lost in overtime to Lee Trevino at the Royal Caribbean Classic. **1993:** Fired a career-low and year-best round of 10-under 62 at the Desert Inn on the opening day of the Las Vegas Senior Classic. **1991:** Made his Champions Tour debut at the Raley's Senior Gold Rush and finished T15 at Rancho Murieta CC...Had not played in any PGA TOUR event since 1987, with 1982 being his last full year on the circuit.

OTHER CAREER HIGHLIGHTS:

Turned professional in 1963 and won twice on the PGA TOUR...Waited five years for his first victory at the 1968 Kaiser International, topping Dave Marr by a stroke with a final-round 65...Closed with a 67 to edge Gibby Gilbert for the Canadian Open title in 1970...Also teamed with Babe Hiskey to win the unofficial 1972 PGA National Team Championship...Lost to Hale Irwin in a playoff for the 1976 Florida Citrus Open title...Later won the 1984 Tallahassee Open, a satellite event on the old Tournament Players Series circuit...At the 1962 NCAA Championship, he won the individual title and helped lead Houston to the team title...Has made 16 career holes-in-one.

PERSONAL:

Co-founded the PGA TOUR Bible Study group in 1965...In the period between the PGA TOUR and Champions Tour, he authored three books on religion and world affairs: *The Gospel*, *The Gospels Interwoven* and *Palestine is Coming*...Has his own Web site: kermitzarley.com...Received an honorary doctorate in the spring of 2001 from North Park University.

PLAYER STATISTICS

2004 CHAMPIONS TOUR STATISTICS:

Scoring Average	74.93	(N/A)
Driving Distance	253.6	(N/A)
Driving Accuracy Percentage	71.4%	(N/A)
Total Driving	1,998	(N/A)
Greens in Regulation Pct.	55.0%	(N/A)
Putting Average	1.855	(N/A)
Sand Save Percentage	44.4%	(N/A)
Birdie Average	2.30	(N/A)
All-Around Ranking	1,569	(N/A)

MISCELLANEOUS CHAMPIONS TOUR STATISTICS
2004 Low Round: 69–2004 SBC Championship/3
Career Low Round: 62–1993 Las Vegas Senior Classic/1
Career Largest Paycheck: $160,000–1996 Energizer SENIOR TOUR Championship/2

MISCELLANEOUS PGA TOUR STATISTICS
Career Low Round: 64–6 times, most recent 1979 Colonial National Invitation/4
Career Largest Paycheck: $25,000–2 times, most recent 1970 Canadian Open/1

CHAMPIONS TOUR CAREER SUMMARY — PLAYOFF RECORD: 1-2

Year	Events Played	1st	2nd	3rd	Top 10	Top 25	Earnings	Rank
1991	2					1	$6,858	113
1992	28			1	10	21	341,647	24
1993	33			1	8	25	414,715	23
1994	28	1	2		8	20	538,274	19
1995	29		2		6	23	525,789	23
1996	28		4		6	18	710,110	13
1997	30		1		5	15	429,442	35
1998	30		1		4	11	357,978	50
1999	31			1	8	13	536,146	36
2000	26		1		2	9	392,604	47
2001	7						19,518	123
2002	7					1	40,896	101
2003	8						29,479	113
2004	10						20,227	120
Total	297	1	11	3	57	157	4,363,683	
COMBINED ALL-TIME MONEY (3 TOURS):							**$5,079,404**	

CHAMPIONS TOUR TOP TOURNAMENT SUMMARY

Year	92	93	94	95	96	97	98	99	00	01	02	03
Senior PGA Championship		T21	CUT	T21	DQ	T11	T39	T58	T10			
U.S. Senior Open	T24	3	T17	T14	CUT	T21	T38	T46	CUT	CUT		
Ford Senior Players	T16	T22	T25	T14	T33	T34	T9	T9	T52	WD		
JELD-WEN Tradition	T5	T25	T27	T20	T27	T38	T35	T50	T66			T52
Charles Schwab Cup Champ	T23	T6	T20	T20	2							

Fuzzy Zoeller (ZELL-er)

EXEMPT STATUS: Top 30 on 2004 Champions Tour Money List
FULL NAME: Frank Urban Zoeller
HEIGHT: 5-10
WEIGHT: 190
BIRTHDATE: November 11, 1951
BIRTHPLACE: New Albany, IN
RESIDENCE: Floyds Knobs, IN
FAMILY: Wife, Diane; Sunnye Noel (5/5/79), Heide Leigh (8/23/81), Gretchen Marie (3/27/84), Miles Remington (6/1/89)
CLUB AFFILIATION: Naples National (Naples, FL)
EDUCATION: Edison (FL) Junior College; University of Houston
SPECIAL INTERESTS: All sports, golf course design
TURNED PROFESSIONAL: 1973
JOINED PGA TOUR: 1974

JOINED CHAMPIONS TOUR: 2002

CHAMPIONS TOUR VICTORIES (2): 2002 Senior PGA Championship. **2004** MasterCard Championship.

OTHER SENIOR VICTORIES: 2002 Senior Slam.

2004 CHARLES SCHWAB CUP FINISH: 25th - 636 points

PGA TOUR VICTORIES (10): 1979 Andy Williams-San Diego Open Invitational, Masters Tournament. **1981** Colonial National Invitation. **1983** Sea Pines Heritage, Panasonic Las Vegas Pro Celebrity Classic. **1984** U.S. Open Championship. **1985** Hertz Bay Hill Classic. **1986** AT&T Pebble Beach National Pro-Am, Sea Pines Heritage, Anheuser-Busch Golf Classic.

OTHER VICTORIES (6): 1972 Florida State Junior College Championship [indiv]. **1973** Indiana State Amateur. **1985** Skins Game. **1986** Skins Game. **1987** Merrill Lynch Shoot-Out Championship. **2003** Tylenol Par-3 Challenge.

PGA TOUR CAREER EARNINGS: $5,803,343

PGA TOUR PLAYOFF RECORD: 2-2

BEST 2004 CHAMPIONS TOUR FINISHES: 1—MasterCard Championship; T3—Outback Steakhouse Pro-Am; T6—Blue Angels Classic; T7—U.S. Senior Open.

2004 SEASON:

Won his first event on the Champions Tour in just over 19 months when he started the 2004 season with a come-from-behind victory at the MasterCard Championship. Shot 64 in the final round and outdueled Dana Quigley down the stretch, thanks to birdies on the last three holes, including a clutch 18-foot putt on No. 18 for the win. Had 23 total birdies for the week...Made a strong run at another victory at the Outback Steakhouse Pro-Am a month later. Birdied 11 of his first 14 holes, including seven straight, at the TPC of Tampa Bay on Sunday and briefly held the lead before a bogey on the final hole eventually left him in a T3. Final-round 61 was a career best and equaled the TPC of Tampa Bay course record...Voted as the Champions Tour's February Player of the Month...Shot 6-under 29 on the front side of Glen Oaks during the second round of the Allianz Championship, a nine-hole record at the course...Had strong performance at the U.S. Senior Open, where he finished T7 at Bellerive CC...Other top-10 finish was a T6 at the Blue Angels Classic near Pensacola in April...Showed some marked improvement with his putting statistics from the previous season. Moved from 69th (29.98) to 17th (29.13) in Putts Per Round and his Putting average dropped from 56th in 2003 to 22nd...Made his 26th appearance at the Masters but did not make the cut.

CHAMPIONS TOUR CAREER HIGHLIGHTS:

2003: In 22 starts netted $741,830 and was 26th on the final money list, earning himself a second straight trip to the season-ending Charles Schwab Cup Championship...Got off to a good start in his first outing of the season. Opened with a third-place finish at the MasterCard Championship. Moved into contention with a course-record-tying, 9-under-par 63 in the second round, but could not hold off a late charge by Dana Quigley on Sunday and finished three strokes back...Had two strong performances in major championships...Made a spirited defense of his Senior PGA Championship title and was the only player in the field to shoot par or better for all four rounds. Was leading early in the final round, but eventually finished T3 at Aronimink GC, three strokes behind winner John Jacobs...Finished T4 in his next start at the U.S. Senior Open in June, where he was under par in three of his four rounds...Easily won the Tylenol Par-3 Challenge at Treetops Resort in Michigan, banking $330,000. **2002:** Among the top 10 in one-third of his starts as a Champions Tour rookie...Became the 11th player to make his first Champions Tour title a major when he held off Bobby Wadkins and Hale Irwin for the Senior PGA Championship crown. Was the only player in the 144-man field to finish under par (2-under) over 72 holes at Firestone and ended a TOUR victory drought of 15 years, 10 months and 27 days dating back to the 1986 Anheuser-Busch Golf Classic...Challenged Dana Quigley earlier in the year for the Siebel Classic in Silicon Valley title before eventually T2 in San Jose with Bob Gilder...Held off Don Pooley by one stroke to win the Senior Slam on the Lost Gold course at Superstition Mountain in early November. His 36-hole score of 6-under 138 in the event, pitting the winners of the four major championships, earned him a $300,000 check...Made his official debut on the Champions Tour at the Royal Caribbean Classic, tying for 51st at Crandon Park with a 1-under 143 total in the rain-shortened event...Played in both the Masters and PGA Championship at Hazeltine in Minnesota, but missed the cut in both events.

OTHER CAREER HIGHLIGHTS:

Has played in 566 events on the PGA TOUR and made cuts in 399 tournaments...Owner of two major titles, 1979 Masters and the 1984 U.S. Open...Claimed Masters title on second extra hole of playoff with Ed Sneed and Tom Watson. Became just the third player (Horton Smith in 1934, Gene Sarazen in 1935) to win the prestigious event at Augusta National in his first attempt... Bested Greg Norman in an 18-hole playoff for 1984 U.S. Open Championship at Winged Foot GC in New York...Was also the runner-up to Larry Nelson in the 1981 PGA Championship at the Atlanta Athletic Club and finished third in the 1994 British Open Championship at Turnberry, Scotland...Has won 10 PGA TOUR titles, including three in 1986...Best season from a financial standpoint came in 1994 when he went over the $1 million mark for the only time in his career ($1,016,804). Although he didn't win that season, recorded five runner-up finishes (at the time the most since Jack Nicklaus and Arnold Palmer had six in 1964), including a playoff loss to Mark McCumber in the season-ending TOUR Championship. Earned a career-best $324,000 at that event which pushed him over seven figures in single-season earnings...First TOUR win came at the 1979 Wickes-Andy Williams San Diego Open. Came back after an opening-round 76 to defeat Bill Kratzert, Wayne Levi, Artie McNickle and Tom Watson by five strokes...Has long history of back trouble, which first became known at 1984 PGA Championship when he was hospitalized before first round. Underwent surgery for ruptured discs later that year and was sidelined until February of 1985...In third start after return, won the Bay Hill Classic...Played on three American Ryder Cup teams

CHAMPIONS TOUR CAREER SUMMARY — PLAYOFF RECORD: 0-0

Year	Events Played	1st	2nd	3rd	Top 10	Top 25	Earnings	Rank
2002	21	1	1		7	12	$945,211	20
2003	22			2	6	12	741,830	26
2004	21	1		1	4	11	787,838	23
Total	64	2	1	3	17	35	2,474,879	
COMBINED ALL-TIME MONEY (3 TOURS):							**$8,278,222**	

CHAMPIONS TOUR TOP TOURNAMENT SUMMARY

Year	02	03	04
Senior PGA Championship	1	T3	T27
U.S. Senior Open	T41	T4	T7
Ford Senior Players	T10	T23	T58
Senior British Open		T14	
JELD-WEN Tradition	T19	T20	T33
Charles Schwab Cup Champ	T5	T20	T16

CHAMPIONS TOUR YEAR-BY-YEAR STATISTICS (TOP 50 ON 2004 MONEY LIST)

	Scoring Average	Putting Average	Greens in Regulation	Driving Distance	Driving Accuracy
2002	71.28 (34)	1.798 (45)	68.2 (29)	275.2 (T20)	66.7 (54)
2003	70.68 (25)	1.810 (56)	70.8 (T15)	276.4 (24)	71.5 (T28)
2004	70.82 (18)	1.782 (T22)	67.0 (38)	274.2 (27)	70.0 (42)

Fuzzy Zoeller (continued)

(1979, 1983, 1985)...Also won the 1985 and 1986 Skins Game and claimed the 1987 Merrill Lynch Shoot-Out Championship...Won 1972 Florida State Junior College and 1973 Indiana State Amateur titles...Member of the National Junior College Athletic Association (NJCAA) Hall of Fame.

PERSONAL:

Always a gallery favorite because of his relaxed approach to the game...Has an interest in golf course design and one of his projects is the TPC at Summerlin, host course of the PGA TOUR's Las Vegas event...Won USGA's Bob Jones Award in 1985. Award given in recognition of distinguished sportsmanship in golf...Lists Wayne Gretzky and Michael Jordan as his favorite athletes and Arnold Palmer as his idol growing up...Enjoys the outdoors and went on a sheep hunt to Alaska in 2001...Web site is fuz.com.

PLAYER STATISTICS

MISCELLANEOUS CHAMPIONS TOUR STATISTICS

2004 Low Round: 61–2004 Outback Steakhouse Pro-Am/3
Career Low Round: 61–2004 Outback Steakhouse Pro-Am/3
Career Largest Paycheck: $360,000–2002 Senior PGA Championship/1

MISCELLANEOUS PGA TOUR STATISTICS

2004 Low Round: 79–Masters Tournament/1
Career Low Round: 62–1982 B.C. Open/2
Career Largest Paycheck: $324,000–1994 THE TOUR Championship/2

In Memoriam

The Champions Tour fondly remembers two former members who passed away in 2004, Harold Henning and Fred Haas. These players will be greatly missed.

Harold Henning (1934-2004)

Fred Haas (1916-2004)

Other Prominent Members

B

BEMAN, Deane (BE-man)

BIRTHDATE: April 22, 1938 **BIRTHPLACE:** Washington, D.C. **RESIDENCE:** Ponte Vedra Beach, FL **JOINED PGA TOUR:** 1967 **OTHER INFORMATION:** Replaced Joseph C. Dey, Jr. as Commissioner of the PGA TOUR on March 1, 1974 and served in that role until June 1, 1994. Oversaw the most explosive period of growth in TOUR history. Was instrumental in the development of Tournament Players Clubs and the births of the Champions Tour in 1980 and the Nationwide Tour in 1990. Last of four official TOUR titles came when he defeated Bunky Henry and Bob Dickson by one stroke at Crawford County CC to claim the 1973 Shrine-Robinson Open. Runner-up at 1969 U.S. Open. In 1967, at age 29, left a prosperous insurance brokerage firm in Bethesda, MD, to join the PGA TOUR as a full-time player. Member of four Walker Cup teams, four World Amateur teams and three U.S. America's Cup teams. Selected to the World Golf Hall of Fame in 2000.

PGA TOUR VICTORIES (4): 1969 Texas Open Invitational. **1970** Greater Milwaukee Open. **1972** Quad Cities Open. **1973** Shrine-Robinson Open Golf Classic.

PGA TOUR CAREER EARNINGS: $370,003

ALL-TIME CAREER EARNINGS: $635,429

BEST CHAMPIONS TOUR CAREER FINISH: 5—1996 Hyatt Regency Kaanapali Classic

CHAMPIONS TOUR CAREER EARNINGS: $265,426

CHAMPIONS TOUR CAREER LOW ROUND: 66—3 times, most recent 1996 Hyatt Regency Maui Kaanapali Classic/3

WORLD GOLF HALL OF FAME MEMBER (Inducted 2000)

BOLT, Tommy

BIRTHDATE: March 31, 1918 **BIRTHPLACE:** Haworth, OK **RESIDENCE:** Cherokee Village, AR; Lecanto, FL **JOINED PGA TOUR:** 1950 **OTHER INFORMATION:** Named to the World Golf Hall of Fame in 2002...Did not join the PGA TOUR until age 32 after serving four years in the Army in World War II and 10 years of construction work...Won 15 career titles on the PGA TOUR, including the 1958 U.S. Open at age 40 where he prevailed by four shots over Gary Player in 95-degree heat during a double-round final day...Won the 1980 Liberty Mutual Legends of Golf with Art Wall, a year after the pair fell to Julius Boros and Roberto De Vicenzo in a six-hole playoff...One of the foundering members of the Champions Tour...Long considered one of golf's most colorful personalities.

PGA TOUR VICTORIES (15): 1951 North & South Open Championship. **1952** Los Angeles Open. **1953** San Diego Open, Tucson Open. **1954** Miami Beach Intl Four-Ball, Insurance City Open, Rubber City Open. **1955** Convair-San Diego Open, Tucson Open, St. Paul Open. **1957** Eastern Open Invitational. **1958** Colonial National Invitational, U.S. Open Championship. **1960** Memphis Open Invitational. **1961** Pensacola Open Invitational.

PGA TOUR CAREER EARNINGS: $320,811

ALL-TIME CAREER EARNINGS: $356,901

BEST CHAMPIONS TOUR CAREER FINISH: T3—1980 Suntree Senior PGA Tour Classic.

CHAMPIONS TOUR CAREER EARNINGS: $36,090

CHAMPIONS TOUR CAREER LOW ROUND: 67—1985 Vintage Invitational/3

WORLD GOLF HALL OF FAME MEMBER (Inducted 2002)

BURNS, George

BIRTHDATE: July 29, 1949 **BIRTHPLACE:** Brooklyn, NY **RESIDENCE:** Boynton Beach, FL **SPECIAL INTERESTS:** Financial markets **JOINED PGA TOUR:** 1975 **OTHER INFORMATION:** Made three appearances in 2004, with best finish a T64 at the Allianz Championship. Won four times on the PGA TOUR, with his biggest victory coming at the 1980 Bing Crosby National Pro-Am. Was two strokes back of David Edwards entering the final round at Pebble Beach, but shot a closing 69 for a one-stroke victory over Dan Pohl. Had 11 other top-10 finishes in 1980 and placed seventh on the final money list, his highest standing ever. Played defensive end at Maryland for one season before quitting football to concentrate solely on golf. Was a force in amateur golf, with a victory in the 1973 Canadian Amateur. Also claimed the Porter Cup, North-South Amateur and New York State Amateur in 1974. Member of the 1975 Walker Cup team and 1975 World Amateur team. Has had six career holes-in-one.

PGA TOUR VICTORIES (4): 1979 Walt Disney World National Team Championship. **1980** Bing Crosby National Pro-Am. **1985** Bank of Boston Classic. **1987** Shearson Lehman Brothers Andy Williams Open.

PGA TOUR CAREER EARNINGS: $1,781,090

ALL-TIME CAREER EARNINGS: $2,153,523

BEST CHAMPIONS TOUR CAREER FINISH: T9—2000 Comfort Classic.

CHAMPIONS TOUR CAREER EARNINGS: $369,349

CHAMPIONS TOUR CAREER LOW ROUND: 64—2000 EMC Kaanapali Classic/3

BYMAN, Bob

BIRTHDATE: April 21, 1955 **BIRTHPLACE:** Poughkeepsie, NY **RESIDENCE:** Las Vegas, NV **JOINED PGA TOUR:** 1978 **OTHER INFORMATION:** Played the PGA TOUR on a full-time basis from 1979-84...Career totals include 139 starts, with 65 cuts made...Best season came in 1979 when he won his only TOUR victory in a playoff against John Schroeder at the Bay Hill Citrus Classic...Earned $94,243 that season and made the cut in all 20 starts...Won the 1977 and 1978 Dutch Opens, as well as the 1977 New Zealand and Scandinavian Opens...Attended Wake Forest.

PGA TOUR VICTORIES (1): 1979 Bay Hill Citrus Classic.

PGA TOUR CAREER EARNINGS: $161,884

ALL-TIME CAREER EARNINGS: $161,884

C

CASPER, Billy

BIRTHDATE: June 24, 1931 **BIRTHPLACE:** San Diego, CA **RESIDENCE:** Chula Vista, CA **OTHER INFORMATION:** Won the last of his nine Champions Tour titles at the 1989 Transamerica Senior Golf Championship at Silverado CC. Three-stroke victory over Al Geiberger came 18 years after he claimed the 1971 Kaiser International on the PGA TOUR at Silverado. Won a pair of senior major championships. Bested Rod Funseth in an 18-hole playoff for the 1983 U.S. Senior Open title at Hazeltine National GC. Defeated Al Geiberger by two strokes at the TPC at Sawgrass Valley Course for the Mazda SENIOR TOURNAMENT PLAYERS Championship. Ranks sixth on the PGA TOUR's all-time victory list, with 51 titles. Was the second player to reach $1 million in career TOUR earnings (Arnold Palmer the first in 1968), attaining that mark on January 11, 1970, with his win at the Los Angeles Open, his 43rd TOUR title. Was the PGA TOUR's top money-winner in 1966 and again in 1968, when he was the first player to surpass $200,000 in single-season earnings. A two-time U.S. Open champion, in 1959 at Winged Foot and 1966 at the Olympic Club. Rallied from seven strokes down with nine holes to play at the '66 Open to tie Arnold Palmer before winning the ensuing 18-hole playoff. Beat Gene Littler in a playoff for the 1970 Masters title, the last 18-hole playoff at Augusta National. PGA Player of the Year in 1966 and 1970. Member of the U.S. Ryder Cup teams in 1961, 1963, 1965, 1967, 1969, 1971, 1973, 1975 and non-playing captain in 1979. Winner of the Vardon Trophy in 1960, 1963, 1965, 1966 and 1968 and the Byron Nelson Award in 1966, 1968 and 1970. Inducted into the World Golf Hall of Fame in 1978 and the PGA Hall of Fame in 1982. Has made 21 holes-in-one in his professional career, with two coming on the Champions Tour. Named *Golfweek's* Father of the Year for 1996 and was selected as the Memorial Tournament's honoree that same season. Also received the Jimmy Demaret Award at the 1996 Liberty Mutual Legends of Golf. Was also the honoree at the 1997 Nissan Open in Los Angeles.

PGA TOUR VICTORIES (51): 1956 Labatt Open. **1957** Phoenix Open Invitational, Kentucky Derby Open Invitational. **1958** Bing Crosby National Pro-Am Golf Championship, Greater New Orleans Open Invitational, Buick Open Invitational. **1959** U.S. Open Championship, Portland Centennial Open Invitational, Lafayette Open Invitational, Mobile Sertoma Open Invitational. **1960** Portland Open Invitational, Hesperia Open Invitational, Orange County Open Invitational. **1961** Portland Open Invitational. **1962** Doral Country Club Open Invitational, Greater Greensboro Open, 500 Festival Open Invitation, Bakersfield Open Invitational. **1963** Bing Crosby National Pro-Am, Insurance City Open Invitational. **1964** Doral Open Invitational, Colonial National Invitation, Greater Seattle Open Invitational, Almaden Open Invitational. **1965** Bob Hope Desert Classic, Western Open, Insurance City Open Invitational, Sahara Invitational. **1966** San Diego Open Invitational, U.S. Open Championship, Western Open, 500 Festival Open Invitation. **1967** Canadian Open, Carling World Open. **1968** Los Angeles Open, Greater Greensboro Open, Colonial National Invitation, 500 Festival Open Invitation, Greater Hartford Open Invitational, Lucky International Open. **1969** Bob Hope Desert Classic, Western Open, Alcan Open. **1970** Los Angeles Open, Masters Tournament, IVB-Philadelphia Golf Classic, Avco Classic. **1971** Kaiser International Open Invitational. **1973** Western Open, Sammy Davis Jr.-Greater Hartford Open. **1975** First NBC New Orleans Open.

PGA TOUR CAREER EARNINGS: $1,691,583

ALL-TIME CAREER EARNINGS: $3,410,255

CHAMPIONS TOUR VICTORIES (9): 1982 The Shootout at Jeremy Ranch, Merrill Lynch/Golf Digest Pro-Am. **1983** U.S. Senior Open. **1984** SENIOR PGA TOUR Roundup. **1987** Del E. Webb Arizona Classic, Greater Grand Rapids Open. **1988** Vantage At The Dominion, Mazda SENIOR TOURNAMENT PLAYERS Championship. **1989** Transamerica Senior Golf Championship.

CHAMPIONS TOUR CAREER EARNINGS: $1,718,672

CHAMPIONS TOUR CAREER LOW ROUND: 64—1987 Greater Grand Rapids Open/3

WORLD GOLF HALL OF FAME MEMBER (Inducted 1978)

D

DE VICENZO, Roberto (dee-vi-CHEN-so)

BIRTHDATE: April 14, 1923 **BIRTHPLACE:** Buenos Aires, Argentina **RESIDENCE:** Buenos Aires, Argentina **JOINED PGA TOUR:** 1947 **OTHER INFORMATION:** Enjoyed great success around the world, with more than 100 international victories and well over 200 total career wins. Probably his greatest triumph came in 1967 when he won the British Open at Hoylake by two strokes over Jack Nicklaus. Won five times on the PGA TOUR, the last coming at the 1968 Houston Champions by one stroke over Lee Trevino. The win came just three weeks after he signed an incorrect scorecard at the Masters, voiding an apparent tie with Bob Goalby. Posted two wins on the Champions Tour in 84 appearances, including the inaugural U.S. Senior Open in 1980 at Winged Foot where he was a four-stroke victor over William Campbell. Teamed with Julius Boros to win the Liberty Mutual Legends of Golf in 1979. Again won the event in 1983 with Rod Funseth. Represented Argentina in the World Cup 17 times and won the individual title in 1969 and 1972. Teamed with Antonio Cerda to win the team crown in 1953.

PGA TOUR VICTORIES (5): 1957 Colonial National Invitation Tournament, All American Open. **1966** Dallas Open Invitational. **1967** British Open Championship. **1968** Houston Champions International.
PGA TOUR CAREER EARNINGS: $201,100
ALL-TIME CAREER EARNINGS: $611,458
CHAMPIONS TOUR VICTORIES (2): 1980 U.S. Senior Open. **1984** Merrill Lynch/Golf Digest Pro-Am.
CHAMPIONS TOUR CAREER EARNINGS: $410,358
CHAMPIONS TOUR CAREER LOW ROUND: 65—3 times, most recent 1987 Mazda SENIOR TOURNAMENT PLAYERS Championship/3
WORLD GOLF HALL OF FAME MEMBER (Inducted 1989)

DICKSON, Bob

BIRTHDATE: January 25, 1944 **BIRTHPLACE:** McAlester, OK **RESIDENCE:** Ponte Vedra Beach, FL **OTHER INFORMATION:** Made three starts in 2004, with best finish a T39 at the MasterCard Classic in Mexico. Began his Champions Tour career in 1994 and lone victory came at the 1998 Cadillac NFL Golf Classic, nipping both Jim Colbert and Larry Nelson with a birdie on the first playoff hole. Earned fully-exempt status for 1997 by being the medalist at the Champions Tour National Qualifying Tournament. Started working for the PGA TOUR in 1979 as the Director of Marketing for the TPC at Sawgrass and was also a Rules Official on the Champions Tour from 1986-1988. Appointed as the Tournament Director of the Nationwide Tour in 1989 and was instrumental in its development from the outset. Played the PGA TOUR from 1968-1978. Won his first TOUR title in his rookie season at the 1968 Haig Open, defeating Chi Chi Rodriguez by two strokes. Had his best year in 1973, when he was among the top 30 on the money list, with $89,182 and won the Andy Williams-San Diego Open by three strokes over Billy Casper, Bruce Crampton, Grier Jones and Phil Rodgers. One of only four men to have claimed both the U.S. Amateur and the British Amateur in the same year (1967). Defeated Rod Cerrudo, 2 and 1, at Formby GC in England for the British Amateur title and then topped Vinnie Giles by one stroke at The Broadmoor in Colorado Springs for the U.S. Amateur crown. Recipient of the 1968 Bob Jones Award from the USGA. A member of the victorious 1967 Walker Cup team and the successful U.S. America's Cup team that season. Has had eight career holes-in-one as a professional, including two on the Champions Tour.

PGA TOUR VICTORIES (2): 1968 Haig Open Invitational. **1973** Andy Williams-San Diego Open Invitational.
PGA TOUR CAREER EARNINGS: $296,640
ALL-TIME CAREER EARNINGS: $2,898,107
CHAMPIONS TOUR VICTORIES (1): 1998 Cadillac NFL Golf Classic.
CHAMPIONS TOUR CAREER EARNINGS: $2,601,467
CHAMPIONS TOUR CAREER LOW ROUND: 64—1994 Ralphs Senior Classic/2

DONALD, Mike

BIRTHDATE: July 11, 1955 **BIRTHPLACE:** Grand Rapids, MI **RESIDENCE:** Hollywood, FL **OTHER INFORMATION:** Made 549 starts in his career on the PGA TOUR while playing from 1980-2004, making 250 cuts. Lone TOUR win came in the 1989 Anheuser Busch Classic, where he beat Hal Sutton and Tim Simpson in a playoff, thanks to a final-round 65. Finished second to Hale Irwin at the 1990 U.S. Open at Medinah CC. Both shot 74 in the playoff, but in the first sudden-death playoff hole in Open history, Irwin rolled in a 10-foot birdie putt for win. Earlier that year, led after a first-round 64 at the Masters. Best year on TOUR was in 1989 when he won $430,232 with five top-10 finishes. In addition to his playoff win, he was second and third that year. In 1990 earned $348,328 with a pair of runner-up finishes, including the U.S. Open. Won the 1984 JCPenney Classic with Vicki Alvarez. Teamed with Fred Couples to win 1990 Sazale Classic. Won the 1974 National Junior College Athletic Association (NJCAA) title while playing at Broward Community College. Member of the NJCAA Hall of Fame. Also played at Georgia Southern University.

PGA TOUR VICTORIES (1): 1989 Anheuser-Busch Golf Classic.
PGA TOUR CAREER EARNINGS: $1,970,260
ALL-TIME CAREER EARNINGS: $2,027,834

F

FERGUSON, Mike

BIRTHDATE: January 26, 1952 **BIRTHPLACE:** Brisbane, Australia **RESIDENCE:** Queensland, Australia **OTHER INFORMATION:** Earned conditional status on the 2005 Champions Tour by securing the 13th spot at the National Qualifying Tournament. Finished the six-round event in a tie with John Ross at 15-under-par 417, but placed 13th after making a par on the first extra playoff hole while Ross made bogey. First attempted to qualify for the Champions Tour at the 2002 national qualifier but missed the cut. Played 20 events on the 2004 European Seniors Tour and finished 37th on the Order of Merit, with £51,311. Finished T9 at both the Bosch Italian Seniors Open and The Mobile Cup. Also played partially on the European Seniors Tour in 2002 and 2003 and T8 at the 2002 DeVere PGA Seniors Championship. Winner of the 2002 Australian PGA Seniors Championship, and in 2003 won both the Malaysian Seniors Open and the Northern Territory Senior PGA Championship. Played five events on the PGA TOUR and made the cut at the 1984 Southern Open (T40) and Pensacola Open (T52). Appears in the Australian edition of the Guinness Book of World Records, having teamed with Simon Owen to play the fastest round in a major Australian tournament while still scoring par or better. Duo took just one hour, 56 minutes to achieve the feat at the 1985 Australian Masters at Huntingdale GC in Melbourne. Brother-in-law of the late Payne Stewart. Was a champion swimmer, boxer and rugby league player as a youth who concentrated on golf after suffering an injury. Winner of the North Queensland Championship in 1972 and was runner-up in the 1969 Australian Boys Championship. Enjoys fishing and physical fitness.

BEST PGA TOUR CAREER FINISH: T40—1984 Southern Open.
PGA TOUR CAREER EARNINGS: $1,755
ALL-TIME CAREER EARNINGS: $19,571
BEST CHAMPIONS TOUR CAREER FINISH: T22—2004 Senior British Open.
CHAMPIONS TOUR CAREER EARNINGS: $17,816
CHAMPIONS TOUR CAREER LOW ROUND: 69—2004 Senior British Open/4

G

GIBSON, Fred

BIRTHDATE: September 12, 1947 **BIRTHPLACE:** Washington, D.C. **RESIDENCE:** Orlando, FL **OTHER INFORMATION:** Played in 23 events in 2004, with best finish a solo second to Jim Thorpe at the Farmers Charity Classic, his best finish on Champions Tour since 2002 when he was second at Napa Valley Championship. Joined the Champions Tour in 1998 and prior to 2005, had made 186 starts. Lone victory came in 1999 when he was the last of 11 first-time winners. Birdied four of his last five holes to cruise to a three-stroke victory over Bruce Fleisher at the Vantage Championship at Tanglewood when he carded back-to-back rounds of 62-64—126 and tied Dana Quigley's mark for best consecutive rounds that year. Official earnings of over $600,000 were better than twice what he pocketed in his 1998 rookie season. Played in seven PGA TOUR events after turning professional in 1977, including five Kemper Opens. Won the 1996 Tobago Open.

BEST PGA TOUR CAREER FINISH: 82—1980 Kemper Open.
PGA TOUR CAREER EARNINGS: $704
ALL-TIME CAREER EARNINGS: $2,353,856
CHAMPIONS TOUR VICTORIES (1): 1999 Vantage Championship.
CHAMPIONS TOUR CAREER EARNINGS: $2,353,152
CHAMPIONS TOUR CAREER LOW ROUND: 62—1999 Vantage Championship/2

GINN, Stewart (GHIN)

BIRTHDATE: June 2, 1949 **BIRTHPLACE:** Melbourne, Australia **RESIDENCE:** Kuala Lumpur, Malaysia **OTHER INFORMATION:** Competed in 25 events in 2004. Teamed with Bob Charles to win the Legends Division at the Liberty Mutual Legends of Golf. Best finish in official event came at the MasterCard Championship (T9). Best year on Champions Tour came in 2002 when he finished 18th on the money list, with $950,055. Along with Isao Aoki (The Instinet Classic), was the only other international player to win an event in 2002. Broke through for his first victory at the Ford Senior Players Championship, where he was a one-stroke victor over Jim Thorpe, Mike McCullough and Hubert Green. His birdie on the 17th hole proved to be the difference and earned him a career-best $375,000. Also became the 13th player to win his first Champions Tour title in a major championship and the fourth of five to earn his first Champions Tour victory in that tournament (Chi Chi Rodriguez, Jim Albus, Dave Stockton and Craig Stadler were the others). Three straight sub-70 rounds at the 2001 Bruno's Memorial Classic, including a 7-under 65 Saturday, earned him a second-place finish, four strokes back of Hale Irwin. Finished 28th on the final money list, while year earlier in 2000 he came on late in the year to finish 27th on the money list. Primarily played on the PGA European Seniors Tour and the Japan PGA Tour prior to joining Champions Tour in 2002. Earned a full exemption on the 2000 Champions Tour by finishing T2 at the National Qualifying Tournament at the Omni Tucson National Resort & Spa. Was a mainstay on the Australasian and Japan PGA Golf Tours for more than 20 years. Won 16 times around the world as a professional, including the Tasmanian Open three times. Was a semifinalist in the Australian Amateur in 1970 and was the Victorian Junior champion.

Was talked out of attempting to play the PGA TOUR by his peers in the early 1970s and regretted his decision. Has used up an estimated 20 passports to play golf throughout the world and has won tournaments on three different tours in his career. Came from a non-golf family, although they lived behind the 12th green at famed Royal Melbourne GC. Began caddying at Royal Melbourne at age 10 and fell in love with the game after watching the old Canada Cup competition in 1959 from his backyard. Played Australian Rules Football as a youth, but chose to pursue a career in golf on advice from his uncle and turned professional at age 20 and was an assistant secretary manager at Royal Melbourne for a short time.
BEST PGA TOUR CAREER FINISH: 29—1980 World Series of Golf.
PGA TOUR CAREER EARNINGS: $26,095
ALL-TIME CAREER EARNINGS: $3,240,828
CHAMPIONS TOUR VICTORIES (1): 2002 Ford Senior Players Championship.
CHAMPIONS TOUR CAREER EARNINGS: $3,214,733
CHAMPIONS TOUR CAREER LOW ROUND: 65—5 times, most recent 2003 Music City Championship at Gaylord Opryland/3

H

HAYES, Mark

BIRTHDATE: July 12, 1949 **BIRTHPLACE:** Stillwater, OK **RESIDENCE:** Edmond, OK **OTHER INFORMATION:** Made three starts in 2004, with best effort a T53 at the MasterCard Classic in Mexico. Joined the Champions Tour at the 1999 Coldwell Banker Burnet Classic via sponsor exemption. Best career finish on the circuit came when he T10 at the 2001 Siebel Classic in Silicon Valley. Was the medalist at the 1999 Champions Tour National Qualifying Tournament in Tucson and also finished among the top eight at the 2000 National Q-School at Walt Disney World. Was among the top 25 on the PGA TOUR money list from 1976-79 and had his best year in 1976, with earnings of $151,699. Finished 11th on the money list that year, with a pair of victories at the Byron Nelson Classic and the Pensacola Open. Biggest victory of his career came at the 1977 Tournament Players Championship at Sawgrass CC. Braved gale-force winds to defeat Mike McCullough by two strokes and earn a 10-year TOUR exemption. Played on the 1979 U.S. Ryder Cup team. A two-time collegiate All-American at Oklahoma State in 1970-71. Member of the 1972 World Amateur Cup squad. Has had 13 competitive holes-in-one. Involved in the golf course design business since 1990. Served a stint in the U.S. Army from 1971-1973.
PGA TOUR VICTORIES (3): 1976 Byron Nelson Golf Classic, Pensacola Open. **1977** Tournament Players Championship.
PGA TOUR CAREER EARNINGS: $1,555,739
ALL-TIME CAREER EARNINGS: $2,092,201
BEST CHAMPIONS TOUR CAREER FINISH: T10—2001 Siebel Classic in Silicon Valley.
CHAMPIONS TOUR CAREER EARNINGS: $534,352
CHAMPIONS TOUR CAREER LOW ROUND: 65—2 times, most recent 2000 ACE Group Classic/2

J

JACKLIN, Tony

BIRTHDATE: July 7, 1944 **BIRTHPLACE:** Scunthorpe, England **RESIDENCE:** Lewisburg, WV **OTHER INFORMATION:** Outlasted six players for the 1995 Franklin Quest Championship title in Park City, UT, the second of two Champions Tour titles. The other came in 1994, when he triumphed at the rain-shortened First of America Classic in Grand Rapids, MI, in only his fourth start on the Champions Tour. Widely recognized as the man who helped re-establish European competitiveness in the Ryder Cup matches. Captained the European team to its first victory in the Ryder Cup in 28 years in 1985, and in 1987 again led the Europeans to a surprise win at Muirfield Village, OH, their first win in America. Owns 24 victories worldwide, including two major championships. His win at the 1969 British Open at Royal Lytham made him the first home-grown champion since Max Faulkner in 1951. Conquered high winds at Hazeltine GC to claim the U.S. Open 11 months later, a first by a Briton in 50 years. Also won Greater Jacksonville Open titles in 1968 and 1972. Member of the European Ryder Cup teams in 1967, 1969, 1971, 1973, 1975, 1977, 1979 and captained the team in 1983, 1985, 1987 and 1989. Named to the British World Cup team in 1966, 1970, 1971 and 1972. Elected to the World Golf Hall of Fame and inducted in November 2002.
PGA TOUR VICTORIES (4): 1968 Jacksonville Open Invitational. **1969** British Open Championship. **1970** U.S. Open Championship. **1972** Greater Jacksonville Open.
PGA TOUR CAREER EARNINGS: $336,530
ALL-TIME CAREER EARNINGS: $1,486,593
CHAMPIONS TOUR VICTORIES (2): 1994 First of America Classic. **1995** Franklin Quest Championship.
CHAMPIONS TOUR CAREER EARNINGS: $1,150,063
CHAMPIONS TOUR CAREER LOW ROUND: 64—1996 Franklin Quest Championship/2
WORLD GOLF HALL OF FAME MEMBER (Inducted 2002)

JARVIS, Norm

BIRTHDATE: January 28, 1952 **BIRTHPLACE:** Prince Albert, Saskatchewan, Canada **RESIDENCE:** Surrey, British Columbia, Canada **OTHER INFORMATION:** Earned a conditional exemption on the 2005 Champions Tour after placing eighth at the National Qualifying Tournament in St. Augustine, FL. Vaulted into a tie with Pat McGowan when he chipped in for an eagle on the final hole. Both finished six rounds at 19-under 413 on the King and Bear layout. Lost the seventh position after McGowan made birdie on the third playoff hole. First attempted to qualify for the Champions Tour at the 2001 National Qualifying Tournament (T50) at age 49. Tried again in both the 2002 and 2003 national qualifiers but did not advance out of the regionals. Played two Champions Tour events in 2002 and recorded his best-ever performance when he T15 at the AT&T Canada Senior Open Championship at Essex G&CC that year. Also open-qualified for the Lightpath Long Island Classic that year and T57 in New York. Open-qualified for the 2003 Verizon Classic and T68 near Tampa. Winner of two professional events in Canada—1994 Victoria Payless Open and the 1989 Canadian Club Professional Championship. Heroes are the late George Knudson and Moe Norman and favorite athletes are Mario Lemieux and Wayne Gretzky. Got started in golf at a nine-hole, sand-greens golf course in Indian Head, Saskatchewan. Has made four holes-in-one in his career. Favorite golf courses are Winged Foot GC, Pinehurst No. 2 and the TPC of Tampa Bay. Favorite entertainer is Harrison Ford.
ALL-TIME CAREER EARNINGS: $28,835
BEST CHAMPIONS TOUR CAREER FINISH: T15—2002 AT&T Canada Senior Open Championship.
CHAMPIONS TOUR CAREER EARNINGS: $28,835
CHAMPIONS TOUR CAREER LOW ROUND: 67—2002 AT&T Canada Senior Open Championship/3

K

KRATZERT, Bill

BIRTHDATE: June 29, 1952 **BIRTHPLACE:** Quantico, VA **RESIDENCE:** Ponte Vedra Beach, FL **JOINED PGA TOUR:** 1976 **OTHER INFORMATION:** Had played in just 15 Champions Tour events prior to 2005, including 14 in 2003. Owns one top-10 finish—at the 2003 Royal Caribbean Golf Classic. Played the PGA TOUR from 1976-1996. Overall, made 466 starts, with 283 cuts and earned $1,396,819 in his career. Also won $13,648 in 12 events on the Nationwide Tour. Last PGA TOUR appearance was at the 1997 AT&T Pebble Beach National Pro-Am. Had his best year in 1978 when he placed eighth on the money list, with $183,683. Won for the first time in 1976 when he teamed with Woody Blackburn to win the Walt Disney World Team Championship in a playoff over Bobby Nichols and Gay Brewer. Added subsequent wins at the 1977 Greater Hartford Open, where he was a three-stroke victor over Grier Jones and Larry Nelson, and in 1980, a four-stroke margin over Howard Twitty at the Greater Milwaukee Open. Last victory came in 1984 at the Pensacola Open, where he came from two strokes behind with four to go to win by two strokes. Shared the first-round lead at the 1986 Masters with Ken Green. A 1973 and 1974 All-American while at the University of Georgia. Inducted into the Indiana Golf Hall of Fame in 1993. Winner of the Indiana State Amateur as a 16-year-old. Father, Bill, was the head professional for more than 40 years at the Fort Wayne CC and got him started in the game at age 13. When he failed to earn his PGA TOUR card in 1974, he went to work as a forklift operator for $4 per hour before eventually earning his card at the spring qualifying school in 1976. A good friend of Texas Tech basketball coach Bob Knight and former Vice President Dan Quayle.
PGA TOUR VICTORIES (4): 1976 Walt Disney World National Team Championship. **1977** Sammy Davis Jr.-Greater Hartford Open. **1980** Greater Milwaukee Open. **1984** Pensacola Open.
PGA TOUR CAREER EARNINGS: $1,396,819
ALL-TIME CAREER EARNINGS: $1,549,913
BEST CHAMPIONS TOUR CAREER FINISH: T10—2003 Royal Caribbean Golf Classic.
CHAMPIONS TOUR CAREER EARNINGS: $139,446
CHAMPIONS TOUR CAREER LOW ROUND: 67—3 times, most recent 2003 FleetBoston Classic/3

L

LITTLER, Gene

BIRTHDATE: July 21, 1930 **BIRTHPLACE:** San Diego, CA **RESIDENCE:** Rancho Santa Fe, CA **OTHER INFORMATION:** Last of his eight Champions Tour wins came in 1989, when he won the Aetna Challenge. Was a two-stroke victor over Harold Henning. When he played in the 2001 Gold Rush Classic, it was his 1,000th TOUR event (615 PGA TOUR, 385 Champions Tour). Three times in his career he won twice in the same season. Set a Champions Tour record for lowest nine-hole score, an 8-under-par 28 (broken by Jay Sigel in 1998; record is now 27 by Seiji Ebihara in 2002). Opened his third round at the 1983 Suntree Classic with seven consecutive birdies, narrowly missing birdie on the eighth hole. Then birdied the ninth hole. Made debut on the Champions Tour at the 1981 Michelob-Egypt Temple Senior Classic. Joined the PGA TOUR shortly after winning the 1954 San Diego Open as an amateur and never had to qualify for a TOUR event. Winner of the 1961 U.S. Open at Oakland Hills CC by one

stroke over Bob Goalby and Doug Sanders. Fell to Billy Casper in an 18-hole playoff at the 1970 Masters, the last 18-hole playoff at Augusta National. Also lost to Lanny Wadkins in a playoff at Pebble Beach for the 1977 PGA Championship. Won three times in 1975 and earned $182,883, his best earnings season on the PGA TOUR. Inducted into the PGA Hall of Fame in 1982 and the World Golf Hall of Fame in 1990. Selected to the U.S. Ryder Cup teams in 1961, 1963, 1965, 1967, 1969, 1971 and 1975. Underwent surgery for cancer of the lymph system in spring 1972 and miraculously returned that fall. Received the 1973 Bob Jones and Ben Hogan Awards for his courageous comeback that culminated with a win at the St. Louis Children's Hospital Classic that same year. Nicknamed "The Machine" because of his smooth tempo swinging the golf club.
PGA TOUR VICTORIES (29): 1954 San Diego Open. **1955** Los Angeles Open, Phoenix Open, Tournament of Champions, Labatt Open. **1956** Texas Open Invitational, Tournament of Champions, Palm Beach Round Robin. **1957** Tournament of Champions. **1959** Phoenix Open Invitational, Tucson Open Invitational, Arlington Hotel Open, Insurance City Open Invitational, Miller Open Invitational. **1960** Oklahoma City Open Invitational, Eastern Open Invitational. **1961** U.S. Open Championship. **1962** Lucky International Open, Thunderbird Classic Invitational. **1965** Canadian Open. **1969** Phoenix Open Invitational, Greater Greensboro Open. **1971** Monsanto Open Invitational, Colonial National Invitational. **1973** St. Louis Children's Hospital. **1975** Bing Crosby National Pro-Am, Danny Thomas Memphis Classic, Westchester Classic. **1977** Houston Open.
PGA TOUR CAREER EARNINGS: $1,584,210
ALL-TIME CAREER EARNINGS: $3,901,444
CHAMPIONS TOUR VICTORIES (8): 1983 Daytona Beach Seniors Golf Classic, Greater Syracuse Classic. **1984** Senior Seiko/Tucson Match Play Champ. **1986** Sunwest Bank Classic, Bank One Senior Golf Classic. **1987** NYNEX/Golf Digest Commemorative, Gus Machado Classic. **1989** Aetna Challenge.
CHAMPIONS TOUR CAREER EARNINGS: $2,317,234
CHAMPIONS TOUR CAREER LOW ROUND: 63—2 times, most recent 1986 Bank One Senior Golf Classic/2
WORLD GOLF HALL OF FAME MEMBER (Inducted 1990)

LYE, Mark

BIRTHDATE: November 13, 1952 **BIRTHPLACE:** Vallejo, CA **RESIDENCE:** Naples, FL **JOINED PGA TOUR:** 1977 **OTHER INFORMATION:** Competed in 12 events in 2004, with best finish a solo ninth place at the Greater Hickory Classic at Rock Barn, his best performance on the Champions Tour. Made Champions Tour debut at the 2003 Senior British Open, with a T27 at Turnberry, his first Tour appearance in over four years. Has served as the lead analyst for The Golf Channel the last few years. Last played in a PGA TOUR event at the 1995 B.C. Open. Made 486 starts on the PGA TOUR in a career that began in 1977 after securing his card at the PGA TOUR's Fall Qualifying Tournament in 1976. Made 332 cuts and earned $1,800,654 in his three decades on the TOUR. Lone victory was a memorable one. Came from eight strokes down the final day with a closing-round 64 to earn a one-stroke win over John Mahaffey, Jim Thorpe and Sammy Rachels at the 1983 Bank of Boston Classic. Finished with birdies on three of the last four holes to claim the $63,000 first-place check, the largest of his career. Finest season came in 1989, when he earned $242,884 and was 56th on the money list. Closed that season with four straight top-10 finishes. Built a three-stroke lead after 36 holes at the 1984 Masters Tournament and trailed by only one after 54 holes before finishing T6. Won the 1976 Australian Order of Merit. College star at San Jose State, where he earned All-American honors in 1975. Diagnosed as a diabetic in high school. One of the few players to use an elongated putter while playing on the PGA TOUR. Often traveled with his guitar on the PGA TOUR, and at one point in his career teamed with Peter Jacobsen and the late Payne Stewart to form Jake Trout and The Flounders. Has battled melanoma in the past few years. First discovered a dime-sized mole on his left knee in 1991 and had surgery to remove the growth. After treatment and subsequent follow-ups, was cancer-free for five years before he discovered a small growth on his left thigh in 2002. Had surgery on his left leg in July 2002, followed by a series of chemotherapy treatments to treat the cancer. Remains on medication for the disease...Suffered a left knee injury while working the UBS Cup in November 2004.
PGA TOUR VICTORIES (1): 1983 Bank of Boston Classic.
PGA TOUR CAREER EARNINGS: $1,800,654
ALL-TIME CAREER EARNINGS: $1,991,455
BEST CHAMPIONS TOUR CAREER FINISH: 9—2004 Greater Hickory Classic at Rock Barn.
CHAMPIONS TOUR CAREER EARNINGS: $183,403
CHAMPIONS TOUR CAREER LOW ROUND: 66—2 times, most recent 2004 Greater Hickory Classic at Rock Barn/1

M

MALTBIE, Roger

BIRTHDATE: June 30, 1951 **BIRTHPLACE:** Modesto, CA **RESIDENCE:** Los Gatos, CA **OTHER INFORMATION:** Has appeared in several Champions Tour events in the last few years, but primarily works as a golf commentator for NBC Sports' golf telecasts. Teamed with Gary Koch to win the Raphael Division at 2003 Liberty Mutual Legends of Golf. Played the PGA TOUR from 1975-1996 and during his rookie year, won back-to-back titles at the 1975 Quad Cities Open and Pleasant Valley Classic. Came back the following year to prevail at the inaugural Memorial Tournament, where he defeated Hale Irwin on the fourth playoff hole. Did not win again for nine years when he claimed a pair of titles in 1985—Manufacturers Hanover Westchester Classic and the NEC World Series of Golf. Defeated George Burns and Raymond Floyd for his win in New York. Also claimed the unofficial Magnolia Classic in 1980 in Hattiesburg, MS. In his PGA TOUR career, made 489 starts and made 327 cuts. Best year was in 1985 when he won $360,554 for eighth place on the money list. At one time in his career was a member of the PGA Tour's Policy Board.
PGA TOUR VICTORIES (5): 1975 Ed McMahon-Jaycees Quad Cities Open, Pleasant Valley Classic. **1976** Memorial Tournament. **1985** Manufacturers Hanover Westchester Classic, NEC World Series of Golf.
PGA TOUR CAREER EARNINGS: $2,212,879
ALL-TIME CAREER EARNINGS: $2,252,236
BEST CHAMPIONS TOUR CAREER FINISH: T20—2003 Bayer Advantage Celebrity Pro-Am.
CHAMPIONS TOUR CAREER EARNINGS: $34,434
CHAMPIONS TOUR CAREER LOW ROUND: 68—2002 Napa Valley Championship/3

MAST, Dick

BIRTHDATE: March 23, 1951 **BIRTHPLACE:** Bluffton, OH **RESIDENCE:** Winter Garden, FL **OTHER INFORMATION:** Earned conditional status for the 2005 Champions Tour season after placing 12th at the National Qualifying Tournament near St. Augustine, FL. Posted 16-under 416 total over six rounds at the King and Bear course at World Golf Village. Made five appearances on the Champions Tour in 2004, open-qualifying for his first three starts. Best effort was a T18 in his first appearance at the Royal Caribbean Golf Classic. First joined the Champions Tour in the spring of 2001 and made his debut at the Bruno's Memorial Classic (T38). Was fully exempt for the 2002 Champions Tour after finishing eighth at the 2001 Champions Tour National Qualifying Tournament. Grabbed the eighth and final fully-exempt position when he birdied the second playoff hole. Best finish of his Champions Tour career was T3 at the 2002 Turtle Bay Championship in Hawaii, one stroke out of a playoff with Hale Irwin and Gary McCord. His $90,000 check in Hawaii was his largest ever on the Champions Tour. Played primarily on the PGA TOUR from 1974-2001, with 328 total starts. Made 176 cuts on the PGA TOUR during that period with earnings totaling $1,110,985. Also played in 103 events on the Nationwide Tour and made 63 cuts, with total earnings of $311,028. Best year on the PGA TOUR came in 1993 when he earned a career-best $210,125 and finished 82nd on the money list. Finished second to Richard Zokol at the 1992 Greater Milwaukee Open. Owns four Nationwide Tour victories, including three in 1990—Mississippi Gulf Coast Classic, Pensacola Open and the Fort Wayne Open. Added a fourth in 1999 when he captured the New Mexico Classic. Finished third on the money list on the Nationwide Tour in 1990 to earn his PGA TOUR card again. Has one career hole-in-one. Biggest thrill in golf was finishing 32-under-par in a regional PGA TOUR qualifier in 1985. Heroes are Arnold Palmer, Jack Nicklaus and Gary Player. His father, a former club pro, got him started in golf as a child.
BEST PGA TOUR CAREER FINISH: 2—1992 Greater Milwaukee Open.
PGA TOUR CAREER EARNINGS: $1,110,985
ALL-TIME CAREER EARNINGS: $2,348,112
BEST CHAMPIONS TOUR CAREER FINISH: T3—2002 Turtle Bay Championship.
CHAMPIONS TOUR CAREER EARNINGS: $926,099
CHAMPIONS TOUR CAREER LOW ROUND: 64—2002 SBC Senior Open/2

McGEE, Jerry

BIRTHDATE: July 21, 1943 **BIRTHPLACE:** New Lexington, OH **RESIDENCE:** East Palestine, OH **OTHER INFORMATION:** Played in 13 events in 2004. A regular on the Champions Tour starting in 1993, with 317 career starts prior to 2005. Owns 29 top-10 finishes, with his best effort a T2 at the 1997 BankBoston Classic..Had his best season that year by earning $562,974, placing him 25th on money list. In March, 1999 was diagnosed with cancer (squamous cell carcinoma) and was operated on by Dr. Eugene Myers at the University of Pittsburgh Medical Center (March 24). Operation lasted six and a half hours for the removal of two malignant tumors on the left side of his neck and at the base of his tongue. Went through seven weeks of radiation before returning in July that year at the Ameritech Senior Open in Chicago in July, but only played in two events before returning home for more rehab before returning late in the year. Has battled various injuries throughout his career. Played the PGA TOUR from 1967-1981 before being forced off because of hypoglycemia. Worked for 12 years as director of golf at Oak Tree CC in West Middlesex, PA, until becoming eligible for the Champions Tour. Finest year on PGA TOUR was 1979, when he won the Kemper Open by one stroke over Jerry Pate. Victory at Quail Hollow CC in Charlotte came on wife, Jill's, birthday. Later captured the Sammy Davis, Jr.-Greater Hartford Open by one stroke over Jack Renner. Won five cars at various 1978 tournaments for being closest to the pin. Among the top 60 on the PGA TOUR money list eight times, including six consecutive seasons from 1974-1979. First victory came at the 1975 Pensacola Open, eight seasons after joining the TOUR. Was a member of the 1977 United States Ryder Cup team. Has had 20 career holes-in-one, including seven in tournament play. Marks his ball with an Indian-head penny.
PGA TOUR VICTORIES (4): 1975 Pensacola Open. **1977** IVB-Philadelphia Golf Classic. **1979** Kemper Open, Sammy Davis Jr.-Greater Hartford Open.
PGA TOUR CAREER EARNINGS: $871,753
ALL-TIME CAREER EARNINGS: $4,141,158
BEST CHAMPIONS TOUR CAREER FINISH: T2—1997 BankBoston Classic.
CHAMPIONS TOUR CAREER EARNINGS: $3,269,405
CHAMPIONS TOUR CAREER LOW ROUND: 63—1998 Vantage Championship/2

MILLER, Johnny

BIRTHDATE: April 29, 1947 **BIRTHPLACE:** San Francisco, CA **RESIDENCE:** Salt Lake City, UT **OTHER INFORMATION:** Has played just two official events in his Champions Tour career. Debuted on the circuit at the 1997 Franklin Quest Championship in Utah and T44. Also T23 at The Transamerica that year. Works primarily as the lead analyst for NBC Sports' golf telecasts. Played the PGA TOUR full time from 1969-1994 and won 24 official titles. His 1994 AT&T Pebble Beach National Pro-Am victory made him the most recent grandfather to win a PGA TOUR event (first since Art Wall, Jr. at 1975 Greater Milwaukee Open). Biggest victory came when he won the 1973 U.S. Open at Oakmont, shooting 63 in the final round, the lowest score ever by a winner at that prestigious event. Was the PGA TOUR's leading money winner in 1974, the only player other than Jack Nicklaus or Tom Watson to win money title between 1971 and 1980. Was a member of the 1975 and 1981 U.S. Ryder Cup teams. Played on 1973, '75 and '80 U.S. World Cup teams. Winner of 1974 PGA Player of Year. Winner 1964 U.S. Junior Amateur Championship. Ranks eighth on the all-time list for victories in a single season with eight in 1974. First player elected to PGA TOUR Hall of Fame, part of World Golf Hall of Fame, in 1996.

PGA TOUR VICTORIES (25): 1971 Southern Open Invitational. **1972** Sea Pines Heritage Classic. **1973** U.S. Open Championship. **1974** Bing Crosby National Pro-Am, Phoenix Open, Dean Martin Tucson Open, Sea Pines Heritage Classic, Tournament of Champions, Westchester Classic, World Open Golf Championship, Kaiser International Open Invitational. **1975** Phoenix Open, Dean Martin Tucson Open, Bob Hope Desert Classic, Kaiser International Open Invitational. **1976** NBC Tucson Open, Bob Hope Desert Classic, British Open Championship. **1980** Jackie Gleason-Inverrary Classic. **1981** Joe Garagiola-Tucson Open, Glen Campbell-Los Angeles Open. **1982** Wickes-Andy Williams San Diego Open. **1983** Honda Inverrary Classic. **1987** AT&T Pebble Beach National Pro-Am. **1994** AT&T Pebble Beach National Pro-Am.

PGA TOUR CAREER EARNINGS: $2,747,484
ALL-TIME CAREER EARNINGS: $2,759,200
BEST CHAMPIONS TOUR CAREER FINISH: T23—1997 The Transamerica.
CHAMPIONS TOUR CAREER EARNINGS: $11,716
CHAMPIONS TOUR CAREER LOW ROUND: 70—3 times, most recent 1997 The Transamerica/3
WORLD GOLF HALL OF FAME MEMBER (Inducted 1996)

N

NORTH, Andy

BIRTHDATE: March 9, 1950 **BIRTHPLACE:** Thorpe, WI **RESIDENCE:** Madison, WI **OTHER INFORMATION:** Made just three appearances in 2004 while still battling injuries. Has made 89 starts on Champions Tour since joining in 2000. Best finish was a solo second at the 2001 Emerald Coast Classic, where he lost in a one-hole playoff with Mike McCullough near Pensacola. In all had 10 top-10 finishes on the Champions Tour. Teamed with Jim Colbert to win a second consecutive Liberty Mutual Legends of Golf title in 2001. Joined the PGA TOUR in 1973 and played full-time until the 1992 season when he was slowed by various physical woes. Underwent six knee surgeries and operations to remove skin cancers from his nose and cheek, suffered from right elbow bone spurs and also battled shoulder and neck problems, as well. Two-time winner of the U.S. Open and one of 19 players with more than one Open win. First victory came at Cherry Hills CC in Colorado in 1978 and the second at Oakland Hills CC in Birmingham, MI, in 1985. Had four-stroke lead at Cherry Hills with five holes to play. By the time he reached the 18th hole, needed only bogey to win. He secured that for victory over Dave Stockton and J.C. Snead. Victory at Oakland Hills came with a 279 total, one stroke better than international runner-up trio of Tze-Chung Chen of Taiwan, Dave Barr of Canada and Denis Watson of Zimbabwe. Other PGA TOUR victory came in 1977 when he prevailed in the Westchester Classic. Shares the PGA TOUR's nine-hole scoring record with Billy Mayfair and Mike Souchak. Shot a 27 at the 1975 B.C. Open. Played on the 1985 U.S. Ryder Cup team and also represented the United States in the 1978 World Cup. Still serves as an analyst on ESPN's telecasts and has also done work for ABC Sports. Was a color analyst on ESPN telecasts prior to joining the Champions Tour in 2000. Three-time All-America selection at the University of Florida. Avid follower of University of Wisconsin sports and, at one time, assisted the Badger football staff. Won the 1969 Wisconsin Amateur and 1971 Western Amateur.

PGA TOUR VICTORIES (3): 1977 American Express Westchester Classic. **1978** U.S. Open Championship. **1985** U.S. Open Championship.
PGA TOUR CAREER EARNINGS: $1,365,530
ALL-TIME CAREER EARNINGS: $2,657,076
BEST CHAMPIONS TOUR CAREER FINISH: 2—2001 Emerald Coast Classic.
CHAMPIONS TOUR CAREER EARNINGS: $1,291,546
CHAMPIONS TOUR CAREER LOW ROUND: 64—2 times, most recent 2002 Kroger Senior Classic/1

P

POWELL, Jimmy

BIRTHDATE: January 17, 1935 **BIRTHPLACE:** Dallas, TX **RESIDENCE:** La Quinta, CA **OTHER INFORMATION:** Made four starts in 2004, including the Liberty Mutual Legends of Golf, where he and teammate Frank Beard placed T2 in the Raphael Division. Played the Champions Tour full time from 1985-2002 and won four events. Became the Champions Tour's second-oldest winner (61 years, 8 months, 5 days) when he defeated John Jacobs by a stroke at the rain-shortened Brickyard Crossing Championship in 1996. Also claimed the Georgia-Pacific Grand Champions event in Indianapolis, becoming the first player to "double dip" twice on the Champions Tour. His $112,500 paycheck was the largest of his career. Recorded the fifth hole-in-one of his Champions Tour career at the 1996 Kroger Senior Classic when he aced the Grizzly course's 16th hole at Kings Island on Saturday. Made Champions Tour history at the First of America Classic in Grand Rapids, MI, by becoming the first player to win both a Georgia-Pacific Grand Champions event and the overall tournament. Won the Georgia-Pacific competition in Grand Rapids by six over Ken Still and Gay Brewer and then cruised to a five-stroke victory over Babe Hiskey in the 54-hole tournament at The Highlands. Blistered the Vineyards CC layout en route to the 1992 Aetna Challenge title in Naples by four strokes over Lee Trevino. At the time, his 19-under-par 197 score equaled the 54-hole scoring record in relation to par. Notched his first Champions Tour victory at the 1990 Southwestern Bell Classic in Oklahoma City, when he came from four strokes back with a closing 65 to win by three. Initially earned his exemption for the Champions Tour in 1989 by virtue of his T4 finish at the 1988 National Qualifying Tournament at the TPC at Prestancia. Joined the Champions Tour early in the 1985 season and T4 at the Greenbrier/American Express Championship. Final-round, 10-under-par 62 included three eagles and was the best round of his professional career. Played the PGA TOUR from 1959 through 1963 and again in 1980-81. Was the oldest player to qualify for the PGA TOUR at age 46 until Allen Doyle topped him at age 47 in 1996. 1973 Southern California PGA Player of the Year. Former head professional at Stevens Park GC in Dallas, the same course where he learned to play the game.

BEST PGA TOUR CAREER FINISH: 6—1968 Andy Williams-San Diego Open Invitational.
PGA TOUR CAREER EARNINGS: $27,871
ALL-TIME CAREER EARNINGS: $3,794,774
CHAMPIONS TOUR VICTORIES (4): 1990 Southwestern Bell Classic. **1992** Aetna Challenge. **1995** First of America Classic. **1996** Brickyard Crossing Championship.
CHAMPIONS TOUR CAREER EARNINGS: $3,766,903
CHAMPIONS TOUR CAREER LOW ROUND: 62—1985 Greenbrier American Express Championship/3

R

RACHELS, Sammy

BIRTHDATE: September 23, 1950 **BIRTHPLACE:** DeFuniak Springs, FL **RESIDENCE:** DeFuniak Springs, FL **OTHER INFORMATION:** Earned third Champions Tour career victory at 2002 Bruno's Memorial Classic, with a playoff win over Dana Quigley. Holed a downhill, 10-foot birdie putt on the second playoff hole to win on his 31st wedding anniversary. Victory near Birmingham, along with two other top-10 performances during the month of May, earned him Champions Tour Player of the Month honors. Enjoyed an impressive rookie season in 2001, with two victories and a spot in the top 31 on the money list. First win came in May in Nashville where he closed with a then career-best 63 to win the BellSouth Senior Classic at Opryland by four strokes over Hale Irwin at Springhouse GC. Helped his cause Sunday when he holed wedges for eagles on the first and 10th holes and also had a chip-in birdie on the eighth hole. Second title came in dramatic fashion in mid-October when he holed a 30-foot eagle putt on the final hole at Silverado to overtake Raymond Floyd and Doug Tewell for The Transamerica title. Trailed Floyd and Tewell by a stroke heading to the final hole, but hit 5-iron to within 30 feet and then sunk the putt for the win. Became the first player since Hale Irwin (1999 Nationwide Championship) to claim an event by posting an eagle on the final hole. Utilized two styles of putters in his victories. Used a normal-length putter in Nashville, but had switched to a long putter just prior to winning in Napa. First earned a spot on the Champions Tour after finishing sixth in the National Qualifying Tournament at Walt Disney World. Secured the sixth position after making birdie on the second playoff hole. Despite four back operations, played on the PGA TOUR from 1975-1985 and had 11 top-10 finishes in 123 career events. Had his best year on the PGA TOUR in 1983, earning $75,238 in 15 events. T2 in both the Danny Thomas-Memphis Classic and the Bank of Boston Classic, with four rounds in the 60s in both events. Also was the runner-up to Russ Cochran at the Magnolia Classic in Hattiesburg, MS, that year. Has had six career holes-in-one in competition.

BEST PGA TOUR CAREER FINISH: T2—1983 Danny Thomas Memphis Classic, Bank of Boston Classic.
OTHER VICTORIES: (2): **1994** PGA Club Professional Championship. **2000** Southern PGA Club Professional Championship.
PGA TOUR CAREER EARNINGS: $226,796
ALL-TIME CAREER EARNINGS: $2,457,329
CHAMPIONS TOUR VICTORIES (3): 2001 BellSouth Senior Classic at Opryland, The Transamerica. **2002** Bruno's Memorial Classic.
CHAMPIONS TOUR CAREER EARNINGS: $2,219,378
CHAMPIONS TOUR CAREER LOW ROUND: 63—2 times, most recent 2001 The Transamerica/2

ROBISON, Gary

BIRTHDATE: March 27, 1954 **BIRTHPLACE:** Fort Eustis, VA **RESIDENCE:** Canton, OH **OTHER INFORMATION:** Earned a conditional exemption on the 2005 Champions Tour after placing 11th at the National Qualifying Tournament in St. Augustine, FL. Posted a 17-under-par 415 total over six rounds at the King and Bear layout at World Golf Village. Finished T8 at the 2004 Senior PGA Club Professional Championship after being the first-round leader in the event. First attempted to qualify for the Champions Tour at the 2003 National Q-School, but ended up T30 at the TPC at Eagle Trace. Is the director of golf at Firestone CC and was the 1999 Merchandiser of the Year. A nine-time Northern Ohio PGA Section Player of the Year and winner of the 1986 Ohio State Open. Played in four PGA Championships, but missed the cut in each event. Has made seven holes-in-one, including four in competition. Enjoys flying airplanes and auto racing. Favorite movie is "Caddyshack."
ALL-TIME CAREER EARNINGS: $1,400

ROGERS, Bill

BIRTHDATE: September 10, 1951 **BIRTHPLACE:** Waco, TX **RESIDENCE:** San Antonio, TX **OTHER INFORMATION:** Played 11 times in 2004, with best effort a T12 at the Administaff Small Business Classic. Also T14 in Texas at the FedEx Kinkos Classic. Joined the Champions Tour in 2001 and played the circuit primarily through the PGA TOUR Victory Category until the end of the 2003 season. Teamed with Bruce Lietzke to easily win the Raphael Division at the 2002 Liberty Mutual Legends of Golf. Duo posted a better-ball score of 20-under 124 for 36 holes, nine strokes better than Tommy Aaron/Don Bies. Played the PGA TOUR from 1975-88 and enjoyed his greatest success in 1981, with four victories that year. Biggest win of his career came at the 1981 British Open, defeating Bernhard Langer by four stokes at Royal St. George's. Named to the 1981 U.S. Ryder Cup squad and was the PGA Player of the Year the same year. Chosen for the University of Houston Hall of Honor in 1981 after earning All-America honors for the Cougars as a collegian. Roomed with Bruce Lietzke at UH. Amateur career also included a Southern Amateur title in 1972 and a spot on the 1973 United States Walker Cup team. Served as the Director of Golf at San Antonio CC for 11 years after his PGA TOUR career. Biggest thrill in golf was representing the U.S. as an amateur and professional player. Started playing golf as a 9-year-old in Montgomery, AL, and lived at various locales around the world while his father was a lieutenant colonel in the Air Force. Spent time in Germany and Morocco as a youngster
PGA TOUR VICTORIES (6): 1978 Bob Hope Desert Classic. **1981** Sea Pines Heritage, British Open Championship, World Series of Golf, Texas Open. **1983** USF&G Classic.
PGA TOUR CAREER EARNINGS: $1,384,710
ALL-TIME CAREER EARNINGS: $1,731,940
BEST CHAMPIONS TOUR CAREER FINISH: T7—2003 3M Championship.
CHAMPIONS TOUR CAREER EARNINGS: $347,230
CHAMPIONS TOUR CAREER LOW ROUND: 66—2004 SBC Championship/3

ROSS, John

BIRTHDATE: April 18, 1952 **BIRTHPLACE:** Burlington, VT **RESIDENCE:** Freeman, WV **OTHER INFORMATION:** Earned conditional status for the 2005 Champions Tour by finishing 14th at the National Qualifying Tournament. Finished six rounds tied with Mike Ferguson at 15-under-par 417, but lost out for the 13th position when he made a bogey on the first playoff hole. Played two Champions Tour events in 2004. Finished T46 at the U.S. Senior Open and open-qualified for the SAS Championship, where he T71. Qualified for the 2003 U.S. Senior Open, but missed the cut. Was T57 at the 2003 National Q-School. Debuted on the Champions Tour after open-qualifying for the 2002 NFL Golf Classic and T70. Also open-qualified for the SAS Championship later in the year and T64 at Prestonwood. At 2002 National Qualifying Tournament, T33. Played in 48 events on the PGA TOUR from 1989-1993 and made 24 cuts. Fully-exempt in 1992 after finishing T13 at the 1991 Q-School, the oldest rookie to qualify that year. Career-best finish was a T16 at the 1992 Buick Open in Michigan. Also played 88 events on the Nationwide Tour from 1990-98 and made 40 cuts. Finished T2 at the 1991 Hawkeye Open, two strokes back of Olin Browne. In 2003, won two tournaments on the Sunbelt Senior Tour—the Gainesville Open and Myrtle Beach Classic. Also won the Albany Senior Invitational that year. Winner of the West Virginia Open in 1997 and 1999. In 1999 on the Teardrop Tour, won the Tour Championship in Alabama. Won seven mini-tour events in Florida on the Space Coast Tour. Served several stints as a club professional from 1977-1987. Has had three career holes-in-one. Favorite golf course is Pinehurst No. 2. Lists Jesus Christ as his hero and The Bible as his favorite book.
BEST PGA TOUR CAREER FINISH: T16—1992 Buick Open.
PGA TOUR CAREER EARNINGS: $126,453
ALL-TIME CAREER EARNINGS: $213,299
BEST CHAMPIONS TOUR CAREER FINISH: T46—2004 U.S. Senior Open.
CHAMPIONS TOUR CAREER EARNINGS: $14,131
CHAMPIONS TOUR CAREER LOW ROUND: 70—2004 U.S. Senior Open/2

S

SAN FILIPPO, Mike (fuh-LEAP-oh)

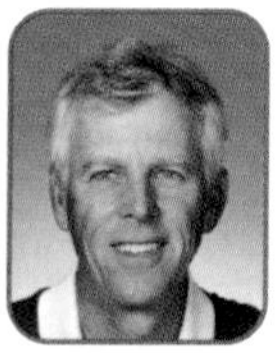

BIRTHDATE: October 10, 1952 **BIRTHPLACE:** Miami, FL **RESIDENCE:** Hobe Sound, FL **OTHER INFORMATION:** Secured the final conditionally-exempt spot on the 2005 Champions Tour at the 2004 National Qualifying Tournament. Was the first-round leader at the King and Bear after firing a 7-under 65, but eventually finished six rounds in a three-way tie for 15th with a 14-under 418 total. Made birdie on the first playoff hole with Daniel Talbot. Played in three official Champions Tour events in 2004. Open-qualified at the Royal Caribbean Golf Classic and T35 at Crandon Park GC. Also T31 at the Senior PGA Championship at Valhalla and T37 at the Bank of America Championship after receiving a sponsor exemption into the Boston event. Also T11 at the 2004 Senior PGA Club Professional Championship. Missed on a conditional exemption for 2004 after finishing T16 at the 2003 National Q-School at the TPC at Eagle Trace. Played in 13 Champions Tour events in 2003 and T34 at the Senior PGA Championship at Aronomink after sharing the first-round lead. Also T4 at the 2003 PGA Senior Club Professional event. Conditionally-exempt on the Champions Tour in 2003 after placing 16th at the 2002 National Q-School. Finished 72 holes at World Woods GC in a five-way tie for 15th at 6-under 282. Eventually got the 16th spot when he lost to Jerry McGee with a bogey on the fourth playoff hole. Won the 2002 PGA Senior Club Professional Championship in a playoff. Made birdie on the third hole of sudden-death to defeat Bob Ralston at PGA GC in Port St. Lucie. Played in 22 events on the PGA TOUR from 1988-1998 and made only one cut. Finished 74th at the 1998 Doral-Ryder Open and earned a check for $3,840. Competed in 14 PGA Club Professional Championships and finished fourth in the 1991 event at Doral, two strokes back of Larry Gilbert. Was 1993 PGA Club Professional Player of the Year, 1992 PGA Stroke-Play Champion and winner of the 1993 Maine Open. Member of the 1992 PGA Cup team. Has made 11 holes-in-one, three in competition. Was the 1990 and 1999 New England PGA Player of the Year and New England PGA Section champion. Father got him started playing golf. Lists the Teeth of the Dog in the Dominican Republic as his favorite golf course. Was a pre-med student at Florida State. After college, once held a job as a lab technician for a medical diagnostic company. Served a stint as the teaching professional at Nashawtuc CC, the venue for the Champions Tour's Bank of America Championship. Biggest thrill outside of golf was watching the Boston Red Sox win the 2004 World Series. Lists Dan Marino as his favorite athlete.
BEST PGA TOUR CAREER FINISH: 74—1998 Doral-Ryder Open.
PGA TOUR CAREER EARNINGS: $3,840
ALL-TIME CAREER EARNINGS: $96,424
BEST CHAMPIONS TOUR CAREER FINISH: T31—2004 Senior PGA Championship.
CHAMPIONS TOUR CAREER EARNINGS: $76,308
CHAMPIONS TOUR CAREER LOW ROUND: 67—2003 Columbus Southern Open/1

SCHROEDER, John

BIRTHDATE: November 12, 1945 **BIRTHPLACE:** Great Barrington, MA **RESIDENCE:** Rancho Santa Fe, CA **OTHER INFORMATION:** Made six appearances in 2004, with best finish a T20 at the MasterCard Classic in Mexico. A regular on the Champions Tour from 1996-2003. Selected as the Champions Tour's Comeback Player of the Year in 2001 after gaining first Champions Tour victory when he defeated Allen Doyle in a two-hole playoff to capture the NFL Golf Classic in New Jersey. Birdied the 18th hole in regulation at Upper Montclair to help set up the playoff, and then got up and down for a par-3 on the second extra hole to earn the win. Win was his first TOUR victory since the 1973 Liggett & Myers Open Match Play Championship, ending a drought of 27 years, 9 months and 15 days, the second-longest gap between a final PGA TOUR victory and first Champions Tour triumph (Mike Fetchick: 28 years, 9 months and 27 days). Almost won the 1996 Bell Atlantic Classic, but lost along with Tom Wargo to Dale Douglass in a playoff near Philadelphia. Captured his only PGA TOUR title at the 1973 Liggett & Myers Open Match Play Championship. Defeated Grier Jones, Bud Allin, Lee Trevino and DeWitt Weaver in the 18-hole final. Came close to a second TOUR victory at the inaugural Bay Hill Classic in 1979. A par on the final hole would have won it for him, however, he and Bob Byman both bogeyed, and Byman won with a par on the second playoff hole..Is the son of tennis star Ted Schroeder, winner of the 1942 U.S. Open and 1949 Wimbledon Championship and standout performer on 10 American Davis Cup teams. All-America selection at the University of Michigan in 1968 and a member of its Hall of Fame. Has worked as a golf commentator for ABC, ESPN and was a member of NBC's golf broadcast team for more than a dozen years before joining the Champions Tour in 1996. One of the original owners of Cobra Golf.
PGA TOUR VICTORIES (1): 1973 U.S. Professional Match Play Championship.
PGA TOUR CAREER EARNINGS: $546,569
ALL-TIME CAREER EARNINGS: $3,228,237
CHAMPIONS TOUR VICTORIES (1): 2001 NFL Golf Classic.
CHAMPIONS TOUR CAREER EARNINGS: $2,670,538
CHAMPIONS TOUR CAREER LOW ROUND: 63—2001 Kroger Senior Classic/2

SIECKMANN, Tom (SEEK-mun)

BIRTHDATE: January 14, 1955 **BIRTHPLACE:** York, NE **RESIDENCE:** Omaha, NE **OTHER INFORMATION:** Had 313 starts and made 168 cuts in his PGA TOUR career. Played full-time on TOUR from 1985-94, with one career victory. Won the 1988 Anheuser-Busch Golf Classic in a playoff with Mark Wiebe at Kingsmill CC. His victory led to 54th place on the PGA TOUR money list, the highest finish of his career. Enjoyed his most lucrative year in 1991 when his earnings totaled $278,598 and he was 61st on the money list. In back-to-back starts that year, was second at the Nestle Invitational and third at the USF&G Classic. Won the 1981 Philipines, Thailand and Brazilian Opens, the 1982 Rolex Open (Switzerland), the 1984 Singapore Open, as well as the 1992 Mexican Open. Medalist at the 1985 PGA TOUR National Qualifying Tournament. Began his college career at Nebraska before finishing at Oklahoma State.
PGA TOUR VICTORIES (1): 1988 Anheuser-Busch Golf Classic.
PGA TOUR CAREER EARNINGS: $1,310,647
ALL-TIME CAREER EARNINGS: $1,310,647

SIFFORD, Charles

BIRTHDATE: June 2, 1922 **BIRTHPLACE:** Charlotte, NC **RESIDENCE:** Kingwood, TX **OTHER INFORMATION:** Inducted into the World Golf Hall of Fame in November 2004, along with Tom Kite, Marlene Stewart Streit and Isao Aoki. Holds the distinction of being the oldest player to earn an exemption on the Champions Tour from the prior year's money list when he finished in the top 28 in 1986 at the age of 64. In 1980, shot a closing, 8-under-par 63 at the Atlantic City International to T6 in the first Champions Tour event ever played. Won the other cosponsored event that season, the Suntree Classic at Melbourne, FL, by four strokes over Don January. Played 422 PGA TOUR events in his career and made 399 cuts. Won the Hartford Open in 1967. Also defeated Harold Henning in a playoff for the 1969 Los Angeles Open. title. Among the top-60 money-winners on the PGA TOUR from 1960-69. Won six Negro National Open titles. Honored as one of the top 100 people in the first Century of Golf. Also a member of both the North Carolina Sportswriters Hall of Fame and the Northern Ohio Sports Hall of Fame. Published his autobiography, *Just Let Me Play*, during the summer of 1992. Started in golf as a caddie in Charlotte, NC, and began playing professionally at age 17 on the United Golf Association Tour. Was singer Billy Eckstine's personal pro and was nicknamed "Little Horse" by Eckstine.
PGA TOUR VICTORIES (2): 1967 Greater Hartford Open Invitational. **1969** Los Angeles Open.
PGA TOUR CAREER EARNINGS: $341,224
ALL-TIME CAREER EARNINGS: $1,271,817
CHAMPIONS TOUR VICTORIES (1): 1980 Suntree Senior PGA Tour Classic.
CHAMPIONS TOUR CAREER EARNINGS: $930,593
CHAMPIONS TOUR CAREER LOW ROUND: 63—1980 Atlantic City Senior International/3
WORLD GOLF HALL OF FAME MEMBER (Inducted 2004)

T

THOMSON, Peter

BIRTHDATE: August 23, 1929 **BIRTHPLACE:** Melbourne, Australia **RESIDENCE:** Melbourne, Australia **OTHER INFORMATION:** Involved in design and development of more than 30 golf courses, mainly in Japan. Set the original Champions Tour record for victories in a year with nine in 1985. Won British Open five times (1954-56, 1958 and 1965), a feat matched by Tom Watson and bettered only by the legendary Harry Vardon's six titles. Played part-time on the PGA TOUR in the 1950s and 1960s and collected his only win at the 1956 Texas International Open, when he beat Gene Littler and Cary Middlecoff in a playoff. Ran for Australian Parliament in 1982 and lost by only four-percent of the vote. Inducted into the World Golf Hall of Fame in 1988. Captain of the International Team in the 1996, 1998 and 2000 Presidents Cups.
PGA TOUR VICTORIES (5): 1955 British Open Championship. **1956** Texas International Open, British Open Championship. **1958** British Open Championship. **1965** British Open Championship.
PGA TOUR CAREER EARNINGS: $78,501
ALL-TIME CAREER EARNINGS: $1,139,618
CHAMPIONS TOUR VICTORIES (11): 1984 WBTV World Seniors Invitational, General Foods PGA Seniors' Championship. **1985** Vintage Invitational, American Golf Carta Blanca Johnny Mathis, MONY Senior Tournament of Champions, Champions Classic, Senior Players Reunion Pro-Am, MONY Syracuse Senior Classic, du Maurier Champions, United Virgina Bank Seniors, Suntree Senior Classic.
CHAMPIONS TOUR CAREER EARNINGS: $1,061,117
CHAMPIONS TOUR CAREER LOW ROUND: 64—3 times, most recent 1985 du Maurier Champions/1
WORLD GOLF HALL OF FAME MEMBER (Inducted 1988)

Z

ZEMBRISKI, Walter

BIRTHDATE: May 24, 1935 **BIRTHPLACE:** Mahwah, NJ **RESIDENCE:** Orlando, FL **OTHER INFORMATION:** Made three starts in 2004, with T54 at the Bayer Advantage Celebrity Pro-Am his best outing. Won the last of his three Champions Tour victories at the 1989 GTE West Classic. Fired rounds of 64-68-65 to best George Archer and Jim Dent by two strokes. Surprised the golf world by winning the Vantage Championship in 1988. Bested Al Geiberger, Dave Hill and Dick Rhyan by three strokes to claim the $135,000 first-place check, the largest on the Champions Tour at the time. Earned fully-exempt status on the Champions Tour at the 1985 National Qualifying Tournament by finishing third. Had brief stint on the PGA TOUR after earning his card in 1967. Qualified for the U.S. Open in 1978 and 1982. Played by himself in the final round of the 1978 event at Cherry Hills CC near Denver, and had the fastest round in Open history: two hours, 13 minutes. Won 10 tournaments on the 1982 Space Coast mini-tour in Florida. Grew up near Out of Bounds Club in Mahwah, NJ, a public course where his father once caddied for Babe Ruth and where he taught himself to play golf while working as a caddie. Was the only public course player to win the "Ike" Championship, a prestigious amateur tournament in the Northeast, capturing the event in 1964 at Winged Foot GC. Spent several years as a construction worker reinforcing steel beams.
BEST PGA TOUR CAREER FINISH: T26—1967 Carling World Open.
PGA TOUR CAREER EARNINGS: $3,088
ALL-TIME CAREER EARNINGS: $3,145,593
CHAMPIONS TOUR VICTORIES (3): 1988 Newport Cup, Vantage Championship. **1989** GTE West Classic.
CHAMPIONS TOUR CAREER EARNINGS: $3,142,505
CHAMPIONS TOUR CAREER LOW ROUND: 63—1995 VFW Senior Championship/2

ZIEGLER, Larry

BIRTHDATE: August 12, 1939 **BIRTHPLACE:** St. Louis, MO **RESIDENCE:** Orlando, FL **OTHER INFORMATION:** Made four appearances in 2004, with a T33 at the Greater Hickory Classic at Rock Barn his best showing. Had highly successful outing at the 2001 National Qualifying Tournament, when he finished second to Howard Twitty and earned fully-exempt status for the year. At age 62 years, 3 months, became the second-oldest player behind the late J.C. Goosie (62 years, 6 months) to earn his card. Bogeyed the final three holes but still won the 1998 Saint Luke's Classic near Kansas City with a 2-under-par 208, the highest winning 54-hole total in relation to par during the year. Triumph at Loch Lloyd CC came six years, 10 months and 3 days after his initial victory on the Champions Tour at the 1991 Newport Cup, the longest span between wins on the circuit. Equaled the largest winning margin of the year when he won by six strokes at the 1991 Newport Cup. Initial Champions Tour title over George Archer, Tom Shaw and Jim Dent in Rhode Island ended a 25-year victory drought. First of three PGA TOUR victories came at the 1969 Michigan Golf Classic, where he defeated Homero Blancas in a playoff. Fell to Lou Graham in a playoff at the 1972 Liggett & Myers Open. Most productive year was 1976, when he collected $84,165, won the First NBC New Orleans Open and finished T3 in the Masters. Winner of the 1975 Greater Jacksonville Open. One of 14 children, he grew up with seven brothers and six sisters. Started in golf as a caddie and worked his way through the ranks to caddiemaster, assistant professional and finally head professional. Once held a position on the Board of Directors of the St. Louis Blues hockey team. An avid fan of NASCAR racing, he has considered becoming involved in the sport in the future.
PGA TOUR VICTORIES (3): 1969 Michigan Golf Classic. **1975** Greater Jacksonville Open. **1976** First NBC New Orleans Open.
PGA TOUR CAREER EARNINGS: $726,197
ALL-TIME CAREER EARNINGS: $3,329,278
CHAMPIONS TOUR VICTORIES (2): 1991 Newport Cup. **1998** Saint Luke's Classic.
CHAMPIONS TOUR CAREER EARNINGS: $2,603,081
CHAMPIONS TOUR CAREER LOW ROUND: 63—1993 Ralphs Senior Classic/1

Phil Mickelson captured his first major championship at the Masters Tournament and also won the Bob Hope Chrysler Classic for the second time on the way to a third-place finish on the money list.

2004 Mercedes Championships [First of 48 official events]

Mercedes Championships

APPLEBY

Winner: STUART APPLEBY
66-67-66-71 270 (-22) $1,060,000

The Plantation Course

Kapalua, Maui, HI

January 8-11, 2004

Purse: $5,300,000
Par: 36-37—73
Yards: 7,263

LEADERS: First Round—Stuart Appleby posted a 7-under-par 66 and led by one over Darren Clarke. Four players were two shots back.
Second Round—Vijay Singh was at 14-under 132 and led Appleby by one. Clarke was four off the lead.
Third Round—Appleby, at 20-under 199, led Singh by two. Retief Goosen was third, five off the pace.

CUT: There was no cut. All 30 players completed 72 holes.

PRO-AM: $10,000. Tommy Armour III, 51, $2,000.

WEATHER: Mostly sunny, warm and breezy all week. High temperatures 80-82. Winds SW 10-25 mph.

Check out the 2005 Mercedes Championships, January 6-9 on ESPN

ORDER OF FINISH

Stuart Appleby	1	66-67-66-71	270	$1,060,000.00
Vijay Singh	2	68-64-69-70	271	600,000.00
Darren Clarke	3	67-69-69-70	275	400,000.00
Retief Goosen	T4	70-70-64-73	277	275,000.00
Tiger Woods	T4	71-70-65-71	277	275,000.00
Kirk Triplett	6	68-69-71-70	278	204,000.00
Adam Scott	7	69-74-68-68	279	180,000.00
Scott Hoch	8	68-71-69-72	280	170,000.00
Ben Crane	T9	71-74-66-70	281	155,000.00
Davis Love III	T9	69-71-69-72	281	$155,000.00
Jim Furyk	11	70-71-68-74	283	140,000.00
Jonathan Kaye	12	74-70-66-74	284	130,000.00
Justin Leonard	T13	68-73-71-73	285	115,000.00
Shaun Micheel	T13	70-71-69-75	285	115,000.00
Tommy Armour III	T15	73-71-73-70	287	89,166.67
Steve Flesch	T15	73-72-72-70	287	89,166.67
Peter Jacobsen	T15	70-71-73-73	287	89,166.67
Shigeki Maruyama	T15	69-72-72-74	287	89,166.67
Chad Campbell	T15	71-76-65-75	287	89,166.66
Kenny Perry	T15	73-71-68-75	287	89,166.66
Fred Couples	T21	69-72-72-75	288	$79,000.00
Ernie Els	T21	73-70-73-72	288	79,000.00
J.L. Lewis	T21	70-71-69-78	288	79,000.00
Mike Weir	24	71-70-73-75	289	75,000.00
Rory Sabbatini	25	73-74-74-70	291	73,000.00
John Huston	T26	69-72-71-81	293	70,000.00
Frank Lickliter II	T26	73-76-70-74	293	70,000.00
Craig Stadler	T28	73-78-68-75	294	67,500.00
Bob Tway	T28	76-74-72-72	294	67,500.00
Ben Curtis	30	73-80-70-74	297	66,000.00

(T) = Tie

NOTES

After his Mercedes win, ***Stuart Appleby*** *had taken a lead into the final round three times during his career and came away with victory each time. In addition to winning the 2004 Mercedes Championships, Appleby also prevailed after taking a lead into the final round of the 2003 Las Vegas Invitational and the 1997 Honda Classic. His other two victories were in come-from-behind fashion.*

Stuart Appleby*, who earned a career-best $1,060,000 in winning in 2004, had finished inside the top two in four of his last six starts on the PGA TOUR, dating back to the 2003 84 Lumber Classic of Pennsylvania. Furthermore, he had won twice in his last four starts on TOUR.*

TOURNAMENT HISTORY

Year	Winner	Score	Runner-up	Score	Location	Par/Yards
TOURNAMENT OF CHAMPIONS						
1953	Al Besselink	280	Chandler Harper	281	Desert Inn CC, Las Vegas, NV	72/7,209
1954	Art Wall	278	Al Besselink	284	Desert Inn CC, Las Vegas, NV	72/7,209
			Lloyd Mangrum			
1955	Gene Littler	280	Jerry Barber	293	Desert Inn CC, Las Vegas, NV	72/7,209
			Pete Cooper			
			Bob Toski			
1956	Gene Littler	281	Cary Middlecoff	285	Desert Inn CC, Las Vegas, NV	72/7,209
1957	Gene Littler	285	Billy Casper	288	Desert Inn CC, Las Vegas, NV	72/7,209
			Jimmy Demaret			
			Dow Finsterwald			
			Billy Maxwell			
1958	Stan Leonard	275	Billy Casper	276	Desert Inn CC, Las Vegas, NV	72/7,209
1959	Mike Souchak	281	Art Wall	283	Desert Inn CC, Las Vegas, NV	72/7,209
1960	Jerry Barber	268	Jay Hebert	272	Desert Inn CC, Las Vegas, NV	72/7,209
1961	Sam Snead	273	Tommy Bolt	280	Desert Inn CC, Las Vegas, NV	72/7,209
1962	Arnold Palmer	276	Billy Casper	277	Desert Inn CC, Las Vegas, NV	72/7,209
1963	Jack Nicklaus	273	Tony Lema	278	Desert Inn CC, Las Vegas, NV	72/7,209
			Arnold Palmer			
1964	Jack Nicklaus	279	Al Geiberger	281	Desert Inn CC, Las Vegas, NV	72/7,209
			Doug Sanders			
1965	Arnold Palmer	277	Chi Chi Rodriguez	279	Desert Inn CC, Las Vegas, NV	72/7,209
1966	Arnold Palmer*	283	Gay Brewer	283	Desert Inn CC, Las Vegas, NV	72/7,209
1967	Frank Beard	278	Arnold Palmer	279	Stardust CC, Las Vegas, NV	71/6,725
1968	Don January	276	Julius Boros	277	Stardust CC, Las Vegas, NV	71/6,725
1969	Gary Player	284	Lee Trevino	286	La Costa CC, Carlsbad, CA	72/6,911
1970	Frank Beard	273	Billy Casper	280	La Costa CC, Carlsbad, CA	72/6,911
			Tony Jacklin			
			Gary Player			
1971	Jack Nicklaus	279	Bruce Devlin	287	La Costa CC, Carlsbad, CA	72/6,911
			Gary Player			
			Dave Stockton			
1972	Bobby Mitchell*	280	Jack Nicklaus	280	La Costa CC, Carlsbad, CA	72/6,911
1973	Jack Nicklaus	276	Lee Trevino	277	La Costa CC, Carlsbad, CA	72/6,911
1974	Johnny Miller	280	Bud Allin	281	La Costa CC, Carlsbad, CA	72/6,911
			John Mahaffey			
MONY TOURNAMENT OF CHAMPIONS						
1975	Al Geiberger*	277	Gary Player	277	La Costa CC, Carlsbad, CA	72/6,911
1976	Don January	277	Hubert Green	282	La Costa CC, Carlsbad, CA	72/6,911
1977	Jack Nicklaus*	281	Bruce Lietzke	281	La Costa CC, Carlsbad, CA	72/6,911
1978	Gary Player	281	Andy North	283	La Costa CC, Carlsbad, CA	72/6,911

Mercedes Championships

NOTES

By finishing T4, ***Tiger Woods*** *earned $275,000 and moved over the $40-million mark in career earnings on the PGA TOUR ($40,052,265).*

TIGER WOODS

Four of the top-five finishers in 2004 were international players, including ***Stuart Appleby****,* ***Vijay Singh****,* ***Darren Clarke*** *and* ***Retief Goosen****.* ***Tiger Woods*** *was the only player born in the United States to crack the top five.*

Since 1986, when the Mercedes Championships moved to the early portion of the PGA TOUR schedule, all but two of the winners have finished the season inside the top 30. The only two not to crack the top 30 at the end of the season were ***Mac O'Grady*** *(No. 35) in 1987 and* ***Tom Kite*** *(No. 39) in 1991. Dating back to 1953, the first year of the Tournament of Champions, the lowest any winner of this tournament has finished a season was 43rd (****Art Wall*** *in 1954).*

Since 1953, 10 of the Mercedes Championships' winners have finished the season in the No. 1 spot on the money list. ***Jack Nicklaus*** *and* ***Tom Watson*** *lead in that category with three wins and three No. 1 finishes. The only person to win and finish atop the money list since the tournament moved to the early portion of the schedule is* ***Tiger Woods*** *in 1997 and 2000.*

Tournament Record:
261, Ernie Els, 2003
Current Course Record:
62, K.J. Choi, 2003

TOURNAMENT HISTORY

Year	Winner	Score	Runner-up	Score	Location	Par/Yards
1979	Tom Watson	275	Lee Trevino Bruce Lietzke	281	La Costa CC, Carlsbad, CA	72/6,911
1980	Tom Watson	276	Jerry Pate Jim Colbert	279	La Costa CC, Carlsbad, CA	72/6,911
1981	Lee Trevino	273	Raymond Floyd	275	La Costa CC, Carlsbad, CA	72/6,911
1982	Lanny Wadkins	280	Andy Bean	283	La Costa CC, Carlsbad, CA	72/6,911
1983	Lanny Wadkins	280	David Graham Craig Stadler Ron Streck Raymond Floyd	281	La Costa CC, Carlsbad, CA	72/6,911
1984	Tom Watson	274	Bruce Lietzke	279	La Costa CC, Carlsbad, CA	72/7,022
1985	Tom Kite	275	Mark McCumber	281	La Costa CC, Carlsbad, CA	72/7,022
1986	Calvin Peete	267	Mark O'Meara	273	La Costa CC, Carlsbad, CA	72/7,022
1987	Mac O'Grady	278	Rick Fehr	279	La Costa CC, Carlsbad, CA	72/7,022
1988	Steve Pate~	202	Larry Nelson	203	La Costa CC, Carlsbad, CA	72/7,022
1989	Steve Jones	279	David Frost	282	La Costa CC, Carlsbad, CA	72/7,022
1990	Paul Azinger	272	Jay Haas Ian Baker-Finch	273	La Costa CC, Carlsbad, CA	72/7,022
INFINITI TOURNAMENT OF CHAMPIONS						
1991	Tom Kite	272	Lanny Wadkins	273	La Costa CC, Carlsbad, CA	72/7,022
1992	Steve Elkington*	279	Brad Faxon	279	La Costa CC, Carlsbad, CA	72/7,022
1993	Davis Love III	272	Tom Kite	273	La Costa CC, Carlsbad, CA	72/7,022
MERCEDES CHAMPIONSHIPS						
1994	Phil Mickelson*	276	Fred Couples	276	La Costa CC, Carlsbad, CA	72/7,022
1995	Steve Elkington*	278	Bruce Lietzke	278	La Costa CC, Carlsbad, CA	72/7,022
1996	Mark O'Meara	271	Nick Faldo	274	La Costa CC, Carlsbad, CA	72/7,022
1997	Tiger Woods*~	202	Scott Hoch Tom Lehman	202	La Costa CC, Carlsbad, CA	72/7,022
1998	Phil Mickelson	271	Mark O'Meara	272	La Costa CC, Carlsbad, CA	72/7,022
1999	David Duval	266	Tiger Woods Billy Mayfair	275	The Plantation Course, Kapalua, HI	73/7,263
2000	Tiger Woods*	276	Mark O'Meara Ernie Els	276	The Plantation Course, Kapalua, HI	73/7,263
2001	Jim Furyk	274	Rory Sabbatini	275	The Plantation Course, Kapalua, HI	73/7,263
2002	Sergio Garcia*	274	David Toms	274	The Plantation Course, Kapalua, HI	73/7,263
2003	Ernie Els	261	K.J. Choi	269	The Plantation Course, Kapalua, HI	73/7,263
2004	Stuart Appleby	270	Rocco Mediate Vijay Singh	271	The Plantation Course, Kapalua, HI	73/7,263

*KEY: * = Playoff ~ = Weather-shortened*

Stuart Appleby checks yardage during 2004 Mercedes Championships.

SECTION 3 TOURNAMENT HISTORIES

2004 Sony Open in Hawaii

[Second of 48 official events]

Winner: ERNIE ELS #
67-64-66-65 262 (-18) $864,000

Waialae Country Club

Honolulu, HI

January 15-18, 2004

Purse: $4,800,000
Par: 35-35—70
Yards: 7,060

LEADERS: First Round—Carlos Franco, at 7-under 63, led by two over Jesper Parnevik. Six players were three shots back.

Second Round—Steve Allan was at 11-under 129 and led by one over Harrison Frazar. Ernie Els was two back and Luke Donald three behind.

Third Round—Frazar was at 14-under 196 and led Els by one. Davis Love III and Frank Lickliter II were two back.

CUT: 79 players at 1-under 139 from a field of 142 professionals and two amateurs.

PRO-AM: $10,000. Front nine: Brett Quigley, 24, $2,000; Back nine: Steve Flesch, 26, $2000.

WEATHER: Mostly sunny and warm all week. More humid on Sunday with a few light sprinkles. Highs of 80-82. Winds mainly out of the south 5-15 mph.

Check out the 2005 Sony Open in Hawaii, January 13-16 on ESPN

ORDER OF FINISH

 # Won playoff with a birdie-2 on third extra hole

Ernie Els #	1	67-64-66-65	262	$864,000.00
Harrison Frazar	2	67-63-66-66	262	518,400.00
Davis Love III	3	70-65-63-67	265	326,400.00
Frank Lickliter II	4	71-62-65-68	266	230,400.00
Briny Baird	T5	68-66-66-67	267	182,400.00
Jerry Kelly	T5	68-65-69-65	267	182,400.00
John Riegger	7	68-66-67-67	268	160,800.00
Stephen Ames	T8	66-70-65-68	269	144,000.00
Craig Barlow	T8	66-69-66-68	269	144,000.00
Paul Azinger	T10	67-66-66-71	270	110,400.00
Retief Goosen	T10	67-69-65-69	270	110,400.00
John Huston	T10	67-67-69-67	270	110,400.00
Vijay Singh	T10	69-68-67-66	270	110,400.00
Omar Uresti	T10	72-66-67-65	270	110,400.00
Aaron Baddeley	T15	66-72-67-66	271	76,800.00
Craig Bowden	T15	70-64-69-68	271	76,800.00
Brenden Pappas	T15	67-69-69-66	271	76,800.00
Jesper Parnevik	T15	65-68-70-68	271	76,800.00
Bo Van Pelt	T15	71-65-67-68	271	76,800.00
Joe Durant	T20	70-66-69-67	272	50,057.15
Chris Riley	T20	69-69-67-67	272	50,057.15
Michael Allen	T20	68-69-65-70	272	50,057.14
Luke Donald	T20	66-66-71-69	272	50,057.14
Carlos Franco	T20	63-72-68-69	272	50,057.14
Shaun Micheel	T20	72-64-68-68	272	50,057.14
Corey Pavin	T20	68-67-66-71	272	$50,057.14
Steve Allan	T27	67-62-70-74	273	34,800.00
Cameron Beckman	T27	70-69-66-68	273	34,800.00
Robert Gamez	T27	67-66-72-68	273	34,800.00
Charles Howell III	T27	68-68-69-68	273	34,800.00
Jonathan Byrd	T31	67-69-66-72	274	28,464.00
Ben Crane	T31	68-70-68-68	274	28,464.00
Mark Hensby	T31	68-69-68-69	274	28,464.00
Tim Herron	T31	67-69-69-69	274	28,464.00
Pat Perez	T31	70-69-65-70	274	28,464.00
D.J. Brigman	T36	69-65-72-69	275	22,608.00
Bart Bryant (S)	T36	68-70-70-67	275	22,608.00
Fred Funk	T36	69-64-74-68	275	22,608.00
Brian Gay	T36	69-67-73-66	275	22,608.00
Duffy Waldorf	T36	70-67-68-70	275	22,608.00
Tommy Armour III	T41	72-67-70-67	276	16,800.00
Pat Bates	T41	68-65-72-71	276	16,800.00
Jason Dufner	T41	69-70-65-72	276	16,800.00
Brent Geiberger	T41	70-67-68-71	276	16,800.00
John Maginnes	T41	68-68-69-71	276	16,800.00
Shigeki Maruyama	T41	71-67-69-69	276	16,800.00
Kevin Na	T41	68-67-70-71	276	16,800.00
Olin Browne (S)	T48	70-68-73-66	277	12,064.00
Russ Cochran	T48	69-69-71-68	277	12,064.00
Peter Jacobsen	T48	69-70-69-69	277	12,064.00
Ted Purdy	T48	66-71-71-69	277	12,064.00
Hideto Tanihara (S)	T48	67-66-72-72	277	12,064.00
Tjaart Van der Walt	T48	69-68-69-71	277	12,064.00
Danny Briggs	T54	71-67-69-71	278	$10,944.00
Jonathan Kaye	T54	67-68-68-75	278	10,944.00
Kenichi Kuboya (S)	T54	73-66-70-69	278	10,944.00
Rod Pampling	T54	72-67-72-67	278	10,944.00
Andre Stolz	T54	68-70-70-70	278	10,944.00
Bob Burns	T59	71-67-70-71	279	10,464.00
Ken Duke	T59	70-69-68-72	279	10,464.00
David Ishii	T59	66-71-74-68	279	10,464.00
Tom Lehman	T59	72-67-71-69	279	10,464.00
Scott Simpson (S)	T59	70-66-73-70	279	10,464.00
Arjun Atwal	T64	71-68-68-73	280	9,648.00
Woody Austin	T64	69-70-71-70	280	9,648.00
Jason Bohn	T64	69-66-72-73	280	9,648.00
Todd Fischer	T64	69-70-70-71	280	9,648.00
Lucas Glover	T64	71-68-74-67	280	9,648.00
Richard S. Johnson	T64	68-67-71-74	280	9,648.00
Bobby Kalinowski (Q)	T64	70-68-71-71	280	9,648.00
Brad Lardon (S)	T64	69-69-69-73	280	9,648.00
Joe Ogilvie	T64	71-68-73-68	280	9,648.00
Ryan Palmer	T64	70-66-70-74	280	9,648.00
John Senden	T64	71-67-69-73	280	9,648.00
Hidemichi Tanaka	T64	67-70-71-72	280	9,648.00
Jeff Brehaut	76	69-69-71-72	281	9,024.00
Heath Slocum	77	67-71-72-73	283	8,928.00
Loren Roberts	78	71-68-75-70	284	8,832.00
Tom Carter	79	70-69-75-72	286	8,736.00

(Q) = Open Qualifier; (S) = Sponsor Exemption; (T) = Tie

The following players did not finish (C=cut, W=withdrew, A=amateur)

C—140-Stuart Appleby, Rich Barcelo, Chad Campbell, Daniel Chopra, Darren Clarke, Ben Curtis, Jim Furyk, Jeff Maggert, David Morland IV, Craig Perks, Kenny Perry, Brett Quigley, Gene Sauers, Boyd Summerhays, Grant Waite, Michelle Wie (A), Dean Wilson. **141-**David Branshaw, Ron Castillo, Jr., John Cook, Kris Cox, Scott Hoch, Tripp Isenhour, Zach Johnson, Brian Kortan, Tom Pernice, Jr., Roger Tambellini, Esteban Toledo. **142-**Chris Couch, Steve Flesch, Spike McRoy, Greg Meyer, David Peoples, Vaughn Taylor. **143-**Notah Begay III, Hunter Mahan, Dan Olsen, Tim Petrovic, Adam Scott, Chris Smith, Craig Stadler, Roland Thatcher. **144-**Brian Bateman, Skip Kendall, Matt Kuchar, Blaine McCallister, Patrick Sheehan, Wes Short, Jr., Jeff Sluman. **145-**Todd Hamilton, Kevin Hayashi, J.P. Hayes, Tetsuji Hiratsuka, Hirofumi Miyase, Yusaku Miyazato, John Morse. **146-**Scott Hend, Kevin Muncrief, Carl Pettersson, **148-**Guy Boros, Jonathan Ota (A), Myung Jun Park. **150-**Tom Byrum. **157-**Dave Eichelberger. **W—78-**Rory Sabbatini.

HARRISON FRAZAR

TOURNAMENT HISTORY

Year	Winner	Score	Runner-up	Score	Location	Par/Yards
HAWAIIAN OPEN						
1965	Gay Brewer*	281	Bob Goalby	281	Waialae CC, Honolulu, HI	72/7,234
1966	Ted Makalena	271	Gay Brewer	274	Waialae CC, Honolulu, HI	72/7,234
			Billy Casper			
1967	Dudley Wysong*	284	Billy Casper	284	Waialae CC, Honolulu, HI	72/7,234
1968	Lee Trevino	272	George Archer	274	Waialae CC, Honolulu, HI	72/7,234
1969	Bruce Crampton	274	Jack Nicklaus	278	Waialae CC, Honolulu, HI	72/7,234
1970	No Tournament					
1971	Tom Shaw	273	Miller Barber	274	Waialae CC, Honolulu, HI	72/7,234
1972	Grier Jones*	274	Bob Murphy	274	Waialae CC, Honolulu, HI	72/7,234
1973	John Schlee	273	Orville Moody	275	Waialae CC, Honolulu, HI	72/7,234
1974	Jack Nicklaus	271	Eddie Pearce	274	Waialae CC, Honolulu, HI	72/7,234
1975	Gary Groh	274	Al Geiberger	275	Waialae CC, Honolulu, HI	72/7,234
1976	Ben Crenshaw	270	Hale Irwin	274	Waialae CC, Honolulu, HI	72/7,234
			Larry Nelson			
1977	Bruce Lietzke	273	Don January	276	Waialae CC, Honolulu, HI	72/7,234
			Takashi Murakami			
1978	Hubert Green*	274	Bill Kratzert	274	Waialae CC, Honolulu, HI	72/7,234
1979	Hubert Green	267	Fuzzy Zoeller	270	Waialae CC, Honolulu, HI	72/7,234
1980	Andy Bean	266	Lee Trevino	269	Waialae CC, Honolulu, HI	72/7,234
1981	Hale Irwin	265	Don January	271	Waialae CC, Honolulu, HI	72/7,234
1982	Wayne Levi	277	Scott Simpson	278	Waialae CC, Honolulu, HI	72/7,234
1983	Isao Aoki	268	Jack Renner	269	Waialae CC, Honolulu, HI	72/7,234
1984	Jack Renner*	271	Wayne Levi	271	Waialae CC, Honolulu, HI	72/7,234
1985	Mark O'Meara	267	Craig Stadler	268	Waialae CC, Honolulu, HI	72/6,975
1986	Corey Pavin	272	Paul Azinger	274	Waialae CC, Honolulu, HI	72/6,975
1987	Corey Pavin*	270	Craig Stadler	270	Waialae CC, Honolulu, HI	72/6,975
1988	Lanny Wadkins	271	Richard Zokol	272	Waialae CC, Honolulu, HI	72/6,975

Sony Open in Hawaii

NOTES

With his win at the 2004 Sony Open in Hawaii, **Ernie Els** became the first player to win the same event in consecutive years in playoffs since **Nick Faldo** won the 1989 and 1990 Masters.

Ernie Els' victory over **Harrison Frazar** was the 10th playoff in the history of the Sony Open in Hawaii. Els was involved in the last one as well, defeating **Aaron Baddeley** on the second extra hole in 2003.

Ernie Els posted a final-round, 5-under-par 65 last year, bringing his consecutive rounds in the 60s streak at the Sony Open in Hawaii to 16. During that span, he is 56-under par. He has finished in the top five in his last four appearances at the Sony Open in Hawaii (fifth in 2000, fourth in 2001, first in 2003, first in 2004).

14-year-old **Michelle Wie** fired a 2-under-par 68 in the second round to finish the tournament at even-par 140, just one shot shy of making the cut. Wie had the putter working in round two, making birdie putts from 58 feet on No. 7, 52 feet on No. 11, 17 feet on No. 16 and 4 feet on No. 18. Her only bogeys came on Nos. 1 and 13.

MICHELLE WIE

The biggest winners of the Sony Open in Hawaii were the 91 charity beneficiaries who received a total of $700,000 in grants from the Friends of Hawaii Charities, the Sony Open in Hawaii host for the past four years. During this time, over 200 worthy Hawaii non-profit entities have received a total of $2 million in charity funds from the Friends. Friends of Hawaii Charities was incorporated in 1998 to benefit not-for-profit organizations serving Hawaii's children, youth, and women through health and education oriented projects.

Tournament Record:
260, John Huston, 1998; Brad Faxon, 2001
Current Course Record: (Par 70)
62, John Cook, 2002; Steve Allan, Frank Lickliter II, 2004
Other Course Record: (Par 72)
60, Davis Love III, 1994

TOURNAMENT HISTORY

Year	Winner	Score	Runner-up	Score	Location	Par/Yards
1989	Gene Sauers	197	David Ogrin	198	Waialae CC, Honolulu, HI	72/6,975
1990	David Ishii	279	Paul Azinger	280	Waialae CC, Honolulu, HI	72/6,975
UNITED HAWAIIAN OPEN						
1991	Lanny Wadkins	270	John Cook	274	Walalae CC, Honolulu, HI	72/6,975
UNITED AIRLINES HAWAIIAN OPEN						
1992	John Cook	265	Paul Azinger	267	Walalae CC, Honolulu, HI	72/6,975
1993	Howard Twitty	269	Joey Sindelar	273	Walalae CC, Honolulu, HI	72/6,975
1994	Brett Ogle	269	Davis Love III	270	Walalae CC, Honolulu, HI	72/6,975
1995	John Morse	269	Tom Lehman Duffy Waldorf	272	Walalae CC, Honolulu, HI	72/6,975
1996	Jim Furyk*	277	Brad Faxon	277	Walalae CC, Honolulu, HI	72/6,975
1997	Paul Stankowski*	271	Jim Furyk Mike Reid	271	Walalae CC, Honolulu, HI	72/7,012
1998	John Huston	260	Tom Watson	267	Walalae CC, Honolulu, HI	72/7,012
SONY OPEN IN HAWAII						
1999	Jeff Sluman	271	Davis Love III Jeff Maggert Len Mattiace Chris Perry Tommy Tolles	273	Waialae CC, Honolulu, HI	70/7,060
2000	Paul Azinger	261	Stuart Appleby	268	Waialae CC, Honolulu, HI	70/7,060
2001	Brad Faxon	260	Tom Lehman	264	Waialae CC, Honolulu, HI	70/7,060
2002	Jerry Kelly	266	John Cook	267	Waialae CC, Honolulu, HI	70/7,060
2003	Ernie Els*	264	Aaron Baddeley	264	Waialae CC, Honolulu, HI	70/7,060
2004	Ernie Els*	262	Harrison Frazar	262	Waialae CC, Honolulu, HI	70/7,060

KEY: * = Playoff

Waialae Country Club, site of the Sony Open in Hawaii.

2004 Bob Hope Chrysler Classic

[Third of 48 official events]

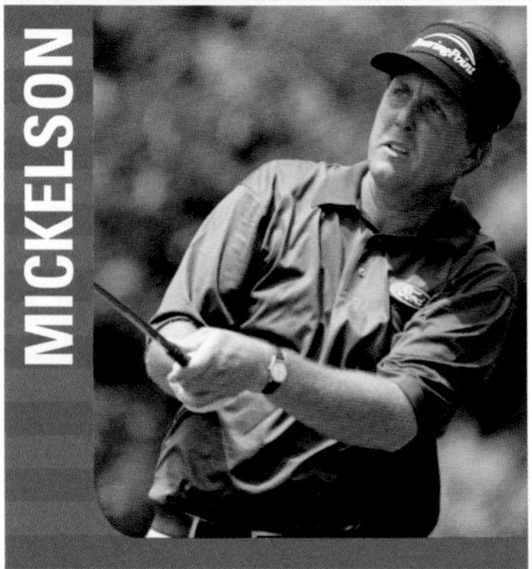

Winner: PHIL MICKELSON #
68-63-64-67-68 330 (-30) $810,000

Check out the 2005 Bob Hope Chrysler Classic, January 26-30 on USA/ABC

Arnold Palmer Private Course at PGA West

LaQuinta, CA

January 21-25, 2004

Purse: $4,500,000
Host Course (HC):
Par: 36-36—72 Yards: 6,930
Bermuda Dunes CC (BD):
Par: 36-36—72 Yards: 6,962
Indian Wells CC (IW):
Par: 36-36—72 Yards: 6,478
La Quinta CC (LQ):
Par: 36-36—72 Yards: 7,060

LEADERS: First Round—Skip Kendall (HC) and Mark Hensby (IW) shared the lead at 9-under-par 63. Kenny Perry (IW) was one back.
Second Round—Perry (HC) added a 66 to move to 14-under 130. Phil Mickelson (IW), Kendall (BD) and Kirk Triplett (BD) were one back.
Third Round—Mickelson (HC) jumped to 21-under 195 to lead Jay Haas (IW) and Ben Crane (LQ) by two.
Fourth Round—Mickelson (BD) and Triplett (IW) shared the lead at 26-under 262. Perry (LQ) was one back and Haas (HC) two.

CUT: 79 players at 11-under-par 277 after 72 holes from a field of 128 professionals.

PRO-AM: $5,000. Fredrik Jacobson and Brenden Pappas, 57, $1,750 each.

WEATHER: On Wednesday, mostly cloudy with light rain in the morning. Partly sunny and breezy in the afternoon with gusts up to 25 mph. Temperatures in the low 60s. Mostly cloudy, temperatures in the high 60s and winds below 20 mph on Thursday. Friday, mostly sunny with temperatures in the low 70s. Mostly cloudy with temperatures in the low-to mid-60s on Saturday. Sun on Sunday with temperatures in the high 60s.

ORDER OF FINISH

 # Won playoff with a birdie-4 on first extra hole

Phil Mickelson #	1	68-63-64-67-68 330	$810,000.00
Skip Kendall	2	63-68-68-66-65 330	486,000.00
Jay Haas	3	65-68-64-67-67 331	306,000.00
Jonathan Kaye	4	67-70-66-65-64 332	216,000.00
Ben Crane	T5	68-64-65-69-68 334	164,250.00
Jesper Parnevik	T5	67-68-66-65-68 334	164,250.00
Kenny Perry	T5	64-66-69-64-71 334	164,250.00
Bernhard Langer	8	67-67-69-68-64 335	139,500.00
Harrison Frazar	T9	73-67-66-63-67 336	104,142.86
Kent Jones	T9	69-65-68-68-66 336	104,142.86
J.L. Lewis	T9	68-68-69-64-67 336	104,142.86
Rod Pampling	T9	70-67-67-66-66 336	104,142.86
Chris Riley	T9	68-64-69-70-65 336	104,142.86
Paul Azinger	T9	67-65-66-69-69 336	104,142.85
Kirk Triplett	T9	66-65-68-63-74 336	104,142.85
Steve Flesch	T16	72-66-63-68-68 337	69,750.00
Rocco Mediate	T16	70-67-65-69-66 337	69,750.00
Mark O'Meara	T16	72-69-67-65-64 337	69,750.00
Jeff Sluman	T16	68-67-66-70-66 337	69,750.00
Stephen Ames	T20	68-72-64-69-65 338	48,750.00
Zach Johnson	T20	66-67-70-66-69 338	48,750.00
Geoff Ogilvy	T20	69-67-63-71-68 338	48,750.00
Loren Roberts	T20	67-67-66-66-72 338	48,750.00
Scott Verplank	T20	70-64-71-68-65 338	48,750.00
Duffy Waldorf	T20	71-67-65-69-66 338	48,750.00
Joe Durant	T26	74-67-68-65-65 339	$33,975.00
Danny Ellis	T26	71-63-67-64-74 339	33,975.00
Retief Goosen	T26	71-64-70-67-67 339	33,975.00
Dean Wilson	T26	67-65-69-68-70 339	33,975.00
John Daly	T30	68-68-65-72-67 340	27,337.50
Richard S. Johnson	T30	66-70-64-68-72 340	27,337.50
Jerry Kelly	T30	65-71-70-67-67 340	27,337.50
Justin Leonard	T30	65-71-69-68-67 340	27,337.50
Joe Ogilvie	T30	66-67-68-68-71 340	27,337.50
John Riegger	T30	69-63-71-70-67 340	27,337.50
Robert Damron	T36	72-67-64-70-68 341	21,195.00
Bob Estes	T36	69-68-71-66-67 341	21,195.00
Lee Janzen	T36	66-73-67-68-67 341	21,195.00
Stephen Leaney	T36	69-71-67-68-66 341	21,195.00
Tom Pernice, Jr.	T36	70-65-68-69-69 341	21,195.00
Billy Andrade	T41	69-68-71-63-71 342	16,200.00
Notah Begay III	T41	68-66-67-71-70 342	16,200.00
Bob Burns	T41	68-69-63-71-71 342	16,200.00
Steve Pate (S)	T41	67-67-67-72-69 342	16,200.00
John Senden	T41	66-72-62-73-69 342	16,200.00
Mike Weir	T41	70-67-68-70-67 342	16,200.00
Marco Dawson	T47	69-73-66-66-69 343	12,360.00
Kevin Na (S)	T47	68-68-68-71-68 343	12,360.00
Paul Stankowski	T47	68-69-69-69-68 343	12,360.00
Michael Allen	T50	70-67-68-71-68 344	10,770.00
Stewart Cink	T50	71-68-68-70-67 344	10,770.00
Robert Gamez	T50	71-69-60-69-75 344	10,770.00
Fredrik Jacobson	T50	67-69-66-71-71 344	10,770.00
Peter Jacobsen	T50	67-70-69-71-67 344	$10,770.00
Carl Pettersson	T50	74-69-69-64-68 344	10,770.00
Chad Campbell	T56	70-68-70-67-70 345	10,035.00
Steve Elkington	T56	68-70-68-71-68 345	10,035.00
Todd Fischer	T56	68-67-63-70-77 345	10,035.00
Donnie Hammond	T56	68-72-68-67-70 345	10,035.00
Neal Lancaster	T56	70-69-68-70-68 345	10,035.00
Scott McCarron	T56	76-64-69-65-71 345	10,035.00
Mark Calcavecchia	T62	72-65-68-67-74 346	9,450.00
Chris Couch	T62	66-67-70-70-73 346	9,450.00
Mathias Gronberg	T62	67-66-71-73-69 346	9,450.00
John Huston	T62	70-70-66-68-72 346	9,450.00
Spike McRoy	T62	74-67-67-69-69 346	9,450.00
Kevin Sutherland	T62	74-67-66-68-71 346	9,450.00
Grant Waite (S)	T62	68-67-68-73-70 346	9,450.00
J.J. Henry	T69	72-70-70-65-70 347	8,955.00
Per-Ulrik Johansson (S)	T69	67-74-64-68-74 347	8,955.00
Corey Pavin	T69	70-71-68-68-70 347	8,955.00
Tim Petrovic	T69	69-68-73-66-71 347	8,955.00
Patrick Sheehan	73	69-69-72-66-72 348	8,730.00
Glen Hnatiuk	T74	67-74-65-71-72 349	8,595.00
Steve Lowery	T74	73-70-69-65-72 349	8,595.00
Cameron Beckman	T76	72-68-69-68-73 350	8,415.00
Brenden Pappas	T76	67-69-71-70-73 350	8,415.00
Ian Leggatt	78	73-70-68-65-75 351	8,280.00
Patrick Moore	79	72-71-68-66-76 353	8,190.00

(Q) = Open Qualifier; (S) = Sponsor Exemption; (T) = Tie

The following players did not finish (C=cut, W=withdrew)

C—278-Steve Allan, David Branshaw, Dan Forsman, Mark Hensby, Gene Sauers, Esteban Toledo, Jay Williamson. **279-**Craig Barlow, Jay Delsing, Keith Fergus, Carlos Franco, Matt Gogel, Tim Herron, Chris Smith. **280-**Briny Baird, Mark Brooks, Daniel Chopra, John Cook, Brent Geiberger, Dudley Hart, David Morland IV. **281-**Billy Mayfair, Bo Van Pelt. **282-**Rich Beem, Jeff Brehaut, J.P. Hayes, Brandt Jobe, Ryan Palmer, David Peoples, Heath Slocum. **283-**Glen Day, Chris DiMarco. **284-**Fred Funk, Charles Howell III, Steve Stricker, Hal Sutton. **285-**Olin Browne, Joey Sindelar. **287-**Pat Bates. **288-**David Gossett, Pat Perez. **289-**Tommy Armour III, Cliff Kresge. **294-**Tom Carter, Geoffrey Dean. **295-**Ed Fiori. **296-**Michael Beard. **303-**Mark Hayes. **W—150-**Chris Perry.

PHIL MICKELSON

TOURNAMENT HISTORY

Year	Winner	Score	Runner-up	Score	Location	Par/Yards
PALM SPRINGS GOLF CLASSIC						
1960	Arnold Palmer	338	Fred Hawkins	341	Bermuda Dunes CC, Palm Springs, CA Indian Wells CC, Indian Wells, CA Tamarisk CC, Palm Springs, CA Thunderbird CC, Palm Springs, CA (H)	72/6,837 72/6,478 72/6,869 N/A
1961	Billy Maxwell	345	Doug Sanders	347	Bermuda Dunes CC, Palm Springs, CA Indian Wells CC, Indian Wells, CA Tamarisk CC, Palm Springs, CA (H) Thunderbird CC, Palm Springs, CA Eldorado CC, Palm Springs, CA	72/6,837 72/6,478 72/6,869 N/A 72/6,708
1962	Arnold Palmer	342	Jay Hebert Gene Littler	345	Bermuda Dunes CC, Palm Springs, CA (H) Indian Wells CC, Indian Wells, CA Tamarisk CC, Palm Springs, CA Thunderbird CC, Palm Springs, CA Eldorado CC, Palm Springs, CA	72/6,837 72/6,478 72/6,869 N/A 72/6,708
1963	Jack Nicklaus*	345	Gary Player	345	Bermuda Dunes CC, Palm Springs, CA Indian Wells CC, Indian Wells, CA (H) Tamarisk CC, Palm Springs, CA Eldorado CC, Palm Springs, CA	72/6,837 72/6,478 72/6,869 72/6,708
1964	Tommy Jacobs*	353	Jimmy Demaret	353	Bermuda Dunes CC, Palm Springs, CA Indian Wells CC, Indian Wells, CA Eldorado CC, Palm Springs, CA (H) La Quinta CC, La Quinta, CA	72/6,837 72/6,478 72/6,708 72/6,911

*KEY: * = Playoff (H) = Host course*

Bob Hope Chrysler Classic

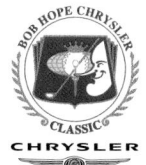

NOTES

*When **Phil Mickelson** won last year at the Bob Hope Chrysler Classic it marked the fifth time in his career that he won his initial start of the season. The others were the Tucson Open (1991), Mercedes Championships (1994 and 1998) and the Bob Hope Chrysler Classic (2002).*

*How about 51-year old **Jay Haas**. In his last four starts at the Bob Hope Chrysler Classic, Haas is 100-under par.*

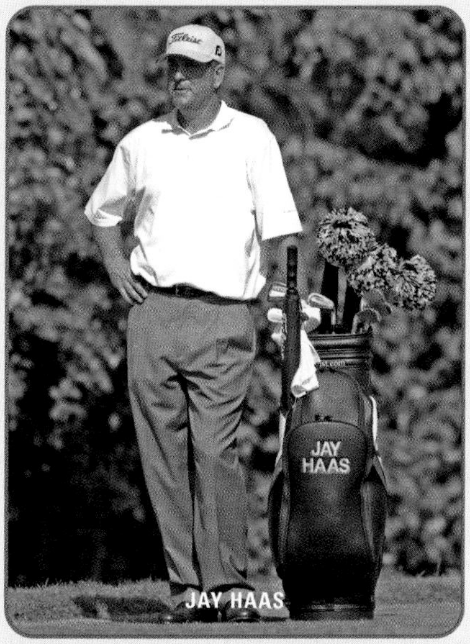

JAY HAAS

Go low or don't go was true once again in the California desert in 2004. There were 61 rounds of 65 or better posted during the 2004 Bob Hope Chrysler Classic, including one 60, two 62s and 12 63s.

*With **Phil Mickelson**'s victory last year, it made the Bob Hope Chrysler Classic the first PGA TOUR event ever won three consecutive years by a lefty. Mickelson won in 2002, **Mike Weir** in 2003 and Mickelson in 2004.*

Tournament Record:
324, Joe Durant, 2001

Tournament Course Record:
59, David Duval, 1999 (PGA West/Palmer Course)
60, Robert Gamez, 2004 (Indian Wells CC)
61, Lennie Clements, 1994 (La Quinta CC)
61, Pat Perez, 2003 (Bermuda Dunes CC)
62, Jonathan Kaye, 1999 (Tamarisk CC)
63, Kenny Perry, 1995; Payne Stewart, 1996 (Indian Ridge CC)

TOURNAMENT HISTORY

Year	Winner	Score	Runner-up	Score	Location	Par/Yards
BOB HOPE DESERT CLASSIC						
1965	Billy Casper	348	Tommy Aaron	349	Bermuda Dunes CC, Palm Springs, CA (H)	72/6,837
			Arnold Palmer		Indian Wells CC, Indian Wells, CA	72/6,478
					Eldorado CC, Palm Springs, CA	72/6,708
					La Quinta CC, La Quinta, CA	72/6,911
1966	Doug Sanders*	349	Arnold Palmer	349	Bermuda Dunes CC, Palm Springs, CA	72/6,837
					Indian Wells CC, Indian Wells, CA (H)	72/6,478
					Eldorado CC, Palm Springs, CA	72/6,708
					La Quinta CC, La Quinta. CA	72/6,911
1967	Tom Nieporte	349	Doug Sanders	350	Bermuda Dunes CC, Palm Springs, CA	72,6,837
					Indian Wells CC, Indian Wells, CA	72/6,478
					Eldorado CC, Palm Springs, CA	72/6,708
					La Quinta CC, La Quinta, CA (H)	72/6,911
1968	Arnold Palmer*	348	Deane Beman	348	Bermuda Dunes CC, Palm Springs, CA (H)	72/6,837
					Indian Wells CC, Indian Wells, CA	72/6,478
					Eldorado CC, Pa!m Springs, CA	72/6,708
					La Quinta CC, La Quinta, CA	72/6,911
1969	Billy Casper	345	Dave Hill	348	Bermuda Dunes CC, Palm Springs, CA	72/6,837
					Indian Wells CC, Indian Wells, CA (H)	72/6,478
					Tamarisk CC, Palm Springs, CA	72/6,869
					La Quinta CC, La Quinta, CA	72/6,911
1970	Bruce Devlin	339	Larry Ziegler	343	Bermuda Dunes CC, Palm Springs, CA	72/6,837
					Indian Wells CC, Indian Wells, CA	72/6,478
					Eldorado CC, Palm Springs, CA	72/6,708
					La Quinta CC, La Quinta, CA (H)	72/6,911
1971	Arnold Palmer*	342	Raymond Floyd	342	Bermuda Dunes CC, Palm Springs, CA (H)	72/6,837
					Indian Wells CC, Indian Wells, CA	72/6,478
					Tamarisk CC, Palm Springs, CA	72/6,869
					La Quinta CC, La Quinta, CA	72/6,911
1972	Bob Rosburg	344	Lanny Wadkins	345	Bermuda Dunes CC, Palm Springs, CA	72/6,837
					Indian Wells CC, Indian Wells, CA (H)	72/6,478
					Eldorado CC, Palm Springs, CA	72/6,708
					La Quinta CC, La Quinta, CA	72/6,911
1973	Arnold Palmer	343	Johnny Miller	345	Bermuda Dunes CC, Palm Springs, CA (H)	72/6,837
			Jack Nicklaus		Indian Wells CC, Indian Wells, CA	72/6,478
					Tamarisk CC, Palm Springs, CA	72/6,869
					La Quinta CC, La Quinta, CA	72/6,911
1974	Hubert Green	341	Bert Yancey	343	Bermuda Dunes CC, Palm Springs, CA	72/6,837
					Indian Wells CC, Indian Wells, CA (H)	72/6,478
					Eldorado CC, Palm Springs, CA	72/6,708
					La Quinta CC, La Quinta, CA	72/6,911
1975	Johnny Miller	339	Bob Murphy	342	Bermuda Dunes CC, Palm Springs, CA (H)	72/6,837
					Indian Wells CC, Indian Wells, CA	72/6,478
					Tamarisk CC, Palm Springs, CA	72/6,869
					La Quinta CC, La Quinta, CA	72/6,911
1976	Johnny Miller	344	Rik Massengale	347	Bermuda Dunes CC, Palm Springs, CA	72/6,837
					Indian Wells CC, Indian Wells, CA (H)	72/6,478
					Eldorado CC, Palm Springs, CA	72/6,708
					La Quinta CC, La Quinta, CA	72/6,911
1977	Rik Massengale	337	Bruce Lietzke	343	Bermuda Dunes CC, Palm Springs, CA	72/6,837
					Indian Wells CC, Indian Wells, CA	72/6,478
					Tamarisk CC, Palm Springs, CA	72/6,869
					La Quinta CC, La Quinta, CA (H)	72/6,911
1978	Bill Rogers	339	Jerry McGee	341	Bermuda Dunes CC, Palm Springs, CA (H)	72/6,837
					Indian Wells CC, Indian Wells, CA	72/6,478
					Eldorado CC, Palm Springs, CA	72/6,708
					La Quinta CC, La Quinta, CA	72/6,911
1979	John Mahaffey	343	Lee Trevino	344	Bermuda Dunes CC, Palm Springs, CA	72/6,837
					Indian Wells CC, Indian Wells, CA (H)	72/6,478
					Tamarisk CC, Palm Springs, CA	72/6,869
					La Quinta CC, La Quinta, CA	72/6,911
1980	Craig Stadler	343	Tom Purtzer	345	Bermuda Dunes CC, Palm Springs, CA	72/6,837
			Mike Sullivan		Indian Wells CC, Indian Wells, CA	72/6,478
					Eldorado CC, Palm Springs, CA	72/6,708
					La Quinta CC, La Quinta, CA (H)	72/6,911
1981	Bruce Lietzke	335	Jerry Pate	337	Bermuda Dunes CC, Palm Springs, CA (H)	72/6,837
					Indian Wells CC, Indian Wells, CA	72/6,478
					Tamarisk CC, Palm Springs, CA	72/6,869
					La Quinta CC, La Quinta, CA	72/6,911
1982	Ed Fiori*	335	Tom Kite	335	Bermuda Dunes CC, Palm Springs, CA	72/6,837
					Indian Wells CC, Indian Wells, CA (H)	72/6,478
					Eldorado CC, Palm Springs, CA	72/6,708
					La Quinta CC, La Quinta, CA	72/6,911
1983	Keith Fergus*	335	Rex Caldwell	335	Bermuda Dunes CC, Palm Springs, CA	72/6,837
					Indian Wells CC, Indian Wells, CA	72/6,478
					Tamarisk CC, Palm Springs, CA	72/6,869
					La Quinta CC, La Quinta, CA (H)	72/6,911

*KEY: * = Playoff (H) = Host course*

Bob Hope Chrysler Classic

NOTES

Phil Mickelson's playoff victory makes him the second player in tournament history to win two playoffs. **Arnold Palmer** won playoffs in 1968 and 1971.

Coming into the 2004 tournament, only nine players had ever reached the 30-under mark. Last year, two accomplished the feat – **Phil Mickelson** (30-under) and **Skip Kendall** (30-under). Mickelson became the second player to do it twice. The nine were **Mike Weir** (30-under/2003), Mickelson (30-under/2002), **David Berganio, Jr.** (30-under/2002), **Joe Durant** (36-under/2001), **Paul Stankowski** (32-under/2001), **Mark Calcavecchia** (30-under/2001,32-under/1997), **John Cook** (33-under/1997) and **Tom Kite** (35-under/1993).

In 2004 10 players managed to finish the week without posting a round in the 70s, including **Phil Mickelson** (W), **Skip Kendall** (2nd), **Jay Haas** (3rd), **Ben Crane** (T5), **Jesper Parnevik** (T5), **Bernhard Langer** (8th), **Kent Jones** (T9), **J.L. Lewis** (T9), **Paul Azinger** (T9) and **Paul Stankowski** (T47). In tournament history, 95 players have posted five rounds in the 60s.

ARNOLD PALMER

Four times an age 40-plus player has won the Bob Hope Chrysler Classic – twice by **Arnold Palmer** in 1973 (44 years, 6 month, 29 days) and 1971 (42 years, 6 months, 26 days), **Tom Kite** in 1993 (44 years, 9 month, 25 days) and **Bob Rosburg** in 1972 (46 years, 8 months, 8 days).

With the veteran **Phil Mickelson**'s 22nd TOUR victory at the Bob Hope Chrysler Classic, **Donnie Hammond** (1986) remains the last player to earn his first TOUR victory at the Hope, a streak of 19 years. Hammond and **Bill Rogers** (1978) are the only two first-time winners in the 45 years of the Hope.

TOURNAMENT HISTORY

Year	Winner	Score	Runner-up	Score	Location	Par/Yards
BOB HOPE CLASSIC						
1984	John Mahaffey*	340	Jim Simons	340	Bermuda Dunes CC, Palm Springs, CA (H)	72/6,837
					Indian Wells CC, Indian Wells, CA	72/6,478
					Eldorado CC, Palm Springs, CA	72/6,708
					La Quinta CC, La Quinta, CA	72/6,911
1985	Lanny Wadkins*	333	Craig Stadler	333	Bermuda Dunes CC, Palm Springs, CA	72/6,837
					Indian Wells CC, Indian Wells, CA (H)	72/6,478
					Tamarisk CC, Palm Springs, CA	72/6,869
					La Quinta CC, La Quinta, CA	72/6,911
BOB HOPE CHRYSLER CLASSIC						
1986	Donnie Hammond*	335	John Cook	335	Bermuda Dunes CC, Palm Springs, CA (H)	72/6,837
					Indian Wells CC, Indian Wells, CA	72/6,478
					Eldorado CC, Palm Springs, CA	72/6,708
					La Quinta CC, La Quinta, CA	72/6,911
1987	Corey Pavin	341	Bernhard Langer	342	Bermuda Dunes CC, Palm Springs, CA	72/6,837
					Indian Wells CC, Indian Wells, CA	72/6,478
					PGA West/Stadium Course, La Quinta, CA (H)	72/7,114
					Eldorado CC, Palm Springs, CA	72/6,708
1988	Jay Haas	338	David Edwards	340	Bermuda Dunes CC, Palm Springs, CA	72/6,837
					Indian Wells CC, Indian Wells, CA (H)	72/6,478
					La Quinta CC, La Quinta, CA	72/6,911
					PGA West/Palmer Course, La Quinta, CA	72/6,924
1989	Steve Jones*	343	Paul Azinger	343	Bermuda Dunes CC, Palm Springs, CA (H)	72/6,837
			Sandy Lyle		Indian Wells CC, Indian Wells, CA	72/6,478
					Eldorado CC, Palm Springs, CA	72/6,708
					PGA West/Palmer Course, La Quinta, CA	72/6,924
1990	Peter Jacobsen	339	Scott Simpson	340	PGA West/Palmer Course, La Quinta, CA (H)	72/6,924
			Brian Tennyson		Bermuda Dunes CC, Palm Springs, CA	72/6,927
					Indian Wells CC, Indian Wells, CA	72/6,478
					Tamarisk CC, Palm Springs, CA	72/6,875
1991	Corey Pavin*	331	Mark O'Meara	331	PGA West/Palmer Course, La Quinta, CA	72/6,924
					Bermuda Dunes CC, Palm Springs, CA	72/6,927
					Indian Wells CC, Indian Wells, CA (H)	72/6,478
					La Quinta CC, La Quinta, CA	72/6,911
1992	John Cook*	336	Rick Fehr	336	PGA West/Palmer Course, La Quinta, CA	72/6,924
			Tom Kite		Bermuda Dunes CC, Palm Springs, CA (H)	72/6,927
			Mark O'Meara		Indian Wells CC, Indian Wells, CA	72/6,478
			Gene Sauers		La Quinta CC, La Quinta, CA	72/6,911
1993	Tom Kite	325	Rick Fehr	331	PGA West/Palmer Course, La Quinta, CA (H)	72/6,924
					Bermuda Dunes CC, Palm Springs, CA	72/6,927
					Indian Wells CC, Indian Wells, CA	72/6,478
					Tamarisk CC, La Quinta, CA	72/6,881
1994	Scott Hoch	334	Lennie Clements	337	PGA West/Palmer Course, La Quinta, CA	72/6,924
			Jim Gallagher, Jr.		Bermuda Dunes CC, Palm Springs, CA	72/6,927
			Fuzzy Zoeller		Indian Wells CC, Indian Wells, CA (H)	72/6,478
					La Quinta CC, La Quinta, CA	72/6,888
1995	Kenny Perry	335	David Duval	336	Bermuda Dunes CC, Palm Springs, CA (H)	72/6,927
					Indian Wells CC, Indian Wells, CA	72/6,478
					La Quinta CC, La Quinta, CA	72/6,901
					Indian Ridge CC, Palm Desert, CA	72/7,037
1996	Mark Brooks	337	John Huston	338	Indian Ridge CC, Palm Desert, CA (H)	72/7,037
					Bermuda Dunes CC, Palm Springs, CA	72/6,927
					Indian Wells CC, Indian Wells, CA	72/6,478
					Tamarisk CC, Palm Springs, CA	72/6,881
1997	John Cook	327	Mark Calcavecchia	328	Indian Wells CC, Indian Wells, CA (H)	72/6,478
					Indian Ridge CC, Palm Desert, CA	72/7,037
					Bermuda Dunes CC, Palm Springs, CA	72/6,927
					La Quinta CC, La Quinta, CA	72/6,901
1998	Fred Couples*	332	Bruce Lietzke	332	Bermuda Dunes CC, Palm Springs, CA (H)	72/6,927
					Indian Wells CC, Indian Wells, CA	72/6,478
					PGA West/Palmer Course, La Quinta, CA	72/6,931
					La Quinta CC, La Quinta, CA	72/6,901
1999	David Duval	334	Steve Pate	335	PGA West/Palmer Course, La Quinta, CA (H)	72/6,931
					Bermuda Dunes CC, Palm Springs, CA	72/6,927
					Tamarisk CC, Palm Springs, CA	72/6,881
					Indian Wells CC, Indian Wells, CA	72/6,478
2000	Jesper Parnevik	331	Rory Sabbatini	332	Bermuda Dunes CC, Palm Springs, CA (H)	72/6,829
					PGA West/Palmer Course, La Quinta, CA	72/6,950
					Indian Wells CC, Indian Wells, CA	72/6,478
					La Quinta CC, La Quinta, CA	72/7,060
2001	Joe Durant	324	Paul Stankowski	328	PGA West/Palmer Course, La Quinta, CA (H)	72/6,950
					Bermuda Dunes CC, Palm Springs, CA	72/6,829
					Indian Wells CC, Indian Wells, CA	72/6,478
					La Quinta CC, La Quinta, CA	72/7,060

KEY: * = Playoff (H) = Host course

KEY: * = Playoff (H) = Host course

Bob Hope Chrysler Classic

DUVAL'S 59

***David Duval** was the last player to shoot 59 on the PGA TOUR and the third in history, joining **Al Geiberger** (1977) and **Chip Beck** (1991). His feat came at the 1999 Bob Hope Chrysler Classic. Duval shot his 59 in the final round at PGA West's Palmer Course on Jan. 24. Duval recorded one eagle and 11 birdies in his round and won by one stroke over **Steve Pate**. He rallied from a seven-stroke deficit after four rounds.*

A shot-by-shot account of Duval's 59:

No. 1:	*Driver, pitching wedge, 5 feet, BIRDIE*
No. 2:	*Driver, 4-iron left of green, sand wedge to 3 feet, BIRDIE*
No. 3:	*6-iron to 3 feet, BIRDIE*
No. 4:	*2-iron, 9-iron to 15 feet, two-putt, PAR*
No. 5:	*5-iron to 5 feet, BIRDIE*
No. 6:	*Driver, 5-iron, sand wedge to 30 feet, two putt, PAR*
No. 7:	*2-iron, 7-iron to 40 feet, two-putt, PAR*
No. 8:	*3-wood, sand wedge over the green, 3-iron chip to 6 feet, PAR*
No. 9:	*3-wood, 8-iron to 8 feet, BIRDIE*
OUT:	***31 (5-under par)***
No. 10:	*3-wood, sand wedge to 5 feet, BIRDIE*
No. 11:	*Driver, 4-iron left of green, pitched to 4 inches, BIRDIE*
No. 12:	*6-iron to 2 feet, BIRDIE*
No. 13:	*3-wood, 7-iron to 12 feet, two-putt, PAR*
No. 14:	*Driver into bunker, 5-iron, sand wedge to 10 feet, BIRDIE*
No. 15:	*8-iron to 1 foot, BIRDIE*
No. 16:	*2-iron, sand wedge to 6 inches, BIRDIE*
No. 17:	*9-iron to 20 feet, two-putt, PAR*
No. 18:	*Driver, 5-iron to 6 feet, EAGLE*
IN:	***28 (8-under par)***
TOTAL:	***59 (13-under par)***

TOURNAMENT HISTORY

Year	Winner	Score	Runner-up	Score	Location	Par/Yards
2002	Phil Mickelson*	330	David Berganio, Jr.	330	PGA West/Palmer Course, La Quinta, CA (H)	72/6,930
					Bermuda Dunes CC, Palm Springs, CA	72/6,927
					Indian Wells CC, Indian Wells, CA	72/6,881
					Tamarisk CC, La Quinta, CA	72/6,478
2003	Mike Weir	330	Jay Haas	332	PGA West/Palmer Course, La Quinta, CA (H)	72/6,930
					Bermuda Dunes CC, Palm Springs, CA	72/6,927
					Indian Wells CC, Indian Wells, CA	72/6,478
					La Quinta CC, La Quinta, CA	72/7,060
2004	Phil Mickelson*	330	Skip Kendall	330	PGA West/Palmer Course, La Quinta, CA (H)	72/6,930
					Bermuda Dunes CC, Palm Springs, CA	72/6,927
					Indian Wells CC, Indian Wells, CA	72/6,478
					La Quinta CC, La Quinta, CA	72/7,060

*KEY: * = Playoff (H) = Host course*

ELIGIBILITY REQUIREMENTS FOR THE 2005 BOB HOPE CHRYSLER CLASSIC

Eligible players in the 128-player field are:

- Winners of THE PLAYERS Championship prior to 1996.
- Winners of THE PLAYERS Championship (only since 1996), Masters Tournament, U.S. Open, British Open and PGA Championship from 1995 to 1997 and from 2000 to 2004. Beginning with the 1998 winners of these events, winners are eligible for five years.
- Winners of the NEC World Series of Golf in the last 10 years (1995-1997).
- Winners of THE TOUR Championship in the last three years (2002-2004).
- Winners of official money World Golf Championship events in the last three years (2002-2004).
- The leader from the final Official PGA TOUR Money List in each of the last five calendar years (2000-2004).
- Playing members of the last-named U.S. Ryder Cup team (2004).
- Current PGA TOUR members who were playing members from the last named U.S. and International Presidents Cup teams (2003).
- PGA TOUR members who use an exemption for 2005 as one of the leaders (either top 25 or top 50) from the Official PGA TOUR Career Money List.
- Winners of the Bob Hope Chrysler Classic prior to 1999, and winners of the Bob Hope Chrysler Classic in 1999 and beyond, for a period of 10 years following their win.
- Either the current winner of the PGA Section Championship or the current PGA Section Player of the Year where the tournament is played, as determined by the Section.
- Eight sponsor exemptions, restricted as follows:
- Two from among the current year's PGA TOUR membership
  - Two from among the 2004 PGA TOUR Qualifying Tournament's top 30 finishers and ties and the first through 20th finishers from the 2004 Official Nationwide Tour Money List.
  - Two foreign players designated by the Commissioner.
- Life members of the PGA TOUR.
- PGA TOUR members from the current Tournament Winners category.
- If necessary to complete the field, those PGA TOUR members among the top 125 finishers on the 2004 Official PGA TOUR Money List, in order of their position on such list.
- If necessary to complete the field, PGA TOUR members from the 2005 priority ranking of eligible players after the top 125, in order of their positions on such list.

SECTION 3 TOURNAMENT HISTORIES

2004 FBR Open

[Fourth of 48 official events]

FBR OPEN

Winner: JONATHAN KAYE
65-68-66-67 266 (-18) $936,000

Tournament Players Club of Scottsdale

Scottsdale, AZ

January 29 – February 1, 2004

Purse: $5,200,000
Par: 35-36—71
Yards: 7,216

LEADERS: First Round—Scott Verplank used an 8-under 63 to hold a one-stroke lead over Phil Mickelson. Jonathan Kaye and Mike Weir were two back.
Second Round—Mickelson moved to 10-under 132 and held a one-stroke lead over Kaye, Verplank and Jeff Sluman.

Third Round—Chris DiMarco and Kaye sat at 14-under 199, while Mickelson was one behind.

CUT: 70 players at even-par 142 from a field of 131 professionals and one amateur.

PRO-AM: $10,000. Briny Baird and Vijay Singh, 53, $1,800 each.

WEATHER: Tournament began Thursday with a 20-minute frost delay. Sunny with a high of 65. Sunny all day Friday with temperatures reaching the high 60s. Mostly cloudy and cool on Saturday with temperatures in the 50s and W-SW gusts up to 20 mph in the afternoon. Sunny on Sunday with temperatures reaching the low 60s.

Check out the 2005 FBR Open, February 3-6 on USA/CBS

ORDER OF FINISH

Johnathan Kaye 1	65-68-66-67	266	$936,000.00
Chris DiMarco 2	68-67-64-69	268	561,600.00
Steve Flesch T3	66-69-68-66	269	301,600.00
Vijay Singh T3	71-69-63-66	269	301,600.00
Duffy Waldorf T5	70-68-68-65	271	197,600.00
Mike Weir T5	65-69-68-69	271	197,600.00
Phil Mickelson T7	64-68-68-72	272	167,700.00
Scott Verplank T7	63-70-70-69	272	167,700.00
Sergio Garcia T9	71-67-65-70	273	130,000.00
Retief Goosen T9	70-68-68-67	273	130,000.00
Fredrik Jacobson T9	68-68-67-70	273	130,000.00
Justin Leonard T9	69-67-66-71	273	130,000.00
Kevin Sutherland T9	72-65-68-68	273	130,000.00
Robert Allenby T14	71-68-68-67	274	78,115.56
Rod Pampling T14	66-71-69-68	274	78,115.56
Brenden Pappas T14	66-70-70-68	274	78,115.56
Heath Slocum T14	71-69-67-67	274	78,115.56
Bo Van Pelt (Q) T14	66-69-70-69	274	78,115.56
Stephen Ames T14	72-64-69-69	274	78,115.55
Ricky Barnes (S) T14	67-67-68-72	274	78,115.55
Alex Cejka T14	70-67-68-69	274	78,115.55
Stewart Cink T14	69-70-67-68	274	78,115.55
Tom Lehman 23	71-69-66-69	275	54,080.00
Tim Herron T24	72-70-68-66	276	$45,760.00
Charles Howell III T24	68-71-68-69	276	45,760.00
Bob Tway T24	69-71-67-69	276	45,760.00
Marco Dawson T27	71-69-68-69	277	36,140.00
Bob Estes T27	68-72-66-71	277	36,140.00
Glen Hnatiuk T27	68-71-69-69	277	36,140.00
Brandt Jobe T27	70-65-71-71	277	36,140.00
Bernhard Langer T27	69-67-66-75	277	36,140.00
Jeff Sluman T27	66-67-71-73	277	36,140.00
Paul Azinger T33	71-66-70-71	278	27,473.34
Mark Calcavecchia T33	71-66-70-71	278	27,473.34
Glen Day T33	72-68-67-71	278	27,473.33
Jay Haas T33	68-72-67-71	278	27,473.33
Kent Jones T33	67-70-68-73	278	27,473.33
Chris Riley T33	66-69-75-68	278	27,473.33
Chad Campbell T39	70-70-70-69	279	22,360.00
Brent Geiberger T39	71-66-70-72	279	22,360.00
Lee Janzen T39	68-67-70-74	279	22,360.00
Tom Byrum T42	71-69-67-73	280	18,720.00
Jim Carter (S) T42	72-69-69-70	280	18,720.00
Mark O'Meara T42	68-68-71-73	280	18,720.00
Joey Sindelar T42	70-70-69-71	280	18,720.00
J.P. Hayes T46	72-70-66-73	281	15,149.34
Arron Oberholser T46	75-66-70-70	281	15,149.33
Carl Pettersson T46	73-69-70-69	281	15,149.33
Steve Elkington T49	69-68-72-73	282	$12,833.60
Carlos Franco T49	68-70-70-74	282	12,833.60
Jesper Parnevik T49	70-72-70-70	282	12,833.60
Tim Petrovic T49	68-73-70-71	282	12,833.60
Paul Stankowski T49	70-70-69-73	282	12,833.60
Notah Begay III T54	68-70-73-72	283	11,908.00
John Daly T54	71-70-71-71	283	11,908.00
Steve Lowery T54	70-70-70-73	283	11,908.00
John Senden T54	69-71-73-70	283	11,908.00
Briny Baird 58	70-69-70-75	284	11,648.00
Jeff Brehaut T59	70-70-73-72	285	11,388.00
Scott McCarron T59	66-72-68-79	285	11,388.00
Tom Pernice, Jr. T59	69-72-70-74	285	11,388.00
John Riegger T59	71-69-71-74	285	11,388.00
Shigeki Maruyama T63	73-66-77-70	286	10,972.00
John Rollins T63	72-68-72-74	286	10,972.00
Steve Stricker T63	69-73-71-73	286	10,972.00
Esteban Toledo T63	69-72-77-68	286	10,972.00
Tommy Armour III 67	70-70-72-75	287	10,712.00
Fred Funk T68	69-73-76-72	290	10,556.00
Chris Smith T68	69-72-70-79	290	10,556.00
David Gossett 70	70-72-74-75	291	10,400.00

(Q) = Open Qualifier; (S) = Sponsor Exemption; (T) = Tie

The following players did not finish (C=cut, W=withdrew, A=amateur)

C—143-Steve Allan, Woody Austin, Pat Bates, Rich Beem, K.J. Choi, Fred Couples, Ben Crane, Robert Gamez, Dudley Hart, J.J. Henry, Per-Ulrik Johansson, Richard S. Johnson, Skip Kendall, Matt Kuchar, Stephen Leaney, Spike McRoy, David Peoples, Craig Perks, Kirk Triplett, Jay Williamson. **144-**Aaron Baddeley, Bob Burns, Jonathan Byrd, Tim Clark, Luke Donald, John Huston, Neal Lancaster, Rocco Mediate, Ted Purdy, Dean Wilson. **145-**Cameron Beckman, Joe Durant, Matt Gogel, Ian Leggatt, Frank Lickliter II, Jeff Maggert, Rory Sabbatini. **146-**Paul Casey, Niclas Fasth, Hank Kuehne, J.L. Lewis, Billy Mayfair, Geoff Ogilvy, Patrick Sheehan, Steven Tate (A). **147-**Robert Damron, Todd Fischer, Bill Glasson, Don Yrene. **148-**GW Cable, Dan Forsman, Pat Perez, Gene Sauers. **149-**Harrison Frazar. **150-**Billy Andrade. **151-**Mark Brooks, Hal Sutton. **152-**Cliff Kresge. **154-**Tony Rohlik. **155-**Brett Upper. **W—75-**Kenny Perry. **72-**Jose Maria Olazabal.

Scenic hole at the TPC of Scottsdale.

TOURNAMENT HISTORY

Year	Winner	Score	Runner-up	Score	Location	Par/Yards
ARIZONA OPEN						
1932	Ralph Guldahl	285	John Perelli	290	Phoenix CC, Phoenix, AZ	71/6,726
1933	Harry Cooper	281	Ray Mangrum	283	Phoenix CC, Phoenix, AZ	71/6,726
			Horton Smith			
PHOENIX OPEN INVITATIONAL						
1935	Ky Laffoon	281	Craig Wood	285	Phoenix CC, Phoenix, AZ	71/6,726
1936	No Tournament					
1937	No Tournament					
1938	No Tournament					
1939	Byron Nelson	198	Ben Hogan	210	Phoenix CC, Phoenix, AZ	71/6,726
1940	Ed Oliver	205	Ben Hogan	206	Phoenix CC, Phoenix, AZ	71/6,726
1941	No Tournament					
1942	No Tournament					
1943	No Tournament					
1944	Harold McSpaden*	273	Byron Nelson	273	Phoenix CC, Phoenix, AZ	71/6,726
1945	Byron Nelson	274	Denny Shute	276	Phoenix CC, Phoenix, AZ	71/6,726
1946	Ben Hogan*	273	Herman Keiser	273	Phoenix CC, Phoenix, AZ	71/6,726
1947	Ben Hogan	270	Lloyd Mangrum	277	Phoenix CC, Phoenix, AZ	71/6,726
			Ed Oliver			
1948	Bobby Locke	268	Jimmy Demaret	269	Phoenix CC, Phoenix, AZ	71/6,726
1949	Jimmy Demaret*	278	Ben Hogan	278	Phoenix CC, Phoenix, AZ	71/6,726
1950	Jimmy Demaret	269	Sam Snead	270	Phoenix CC, Phoenix, AZ	71/6,726
1951	Lew Worsham	272	Lawson Little	273	Phoenix CC, Phoenix, AZ	71/6,726
1952	Lloyd Mangrum	274	E.J. Harrison	279	Phoenix CC, Phoenix, AZ	71/6,726
1953	Lloyd Mangrum	272	Johnny Bulla	278	Phoenix CC, Phoenix, AZ	71/6,726
			Ted Kroll			
			Bo Wininger			

FBR Open

FBR OPEN

NOTES

The new sponsor of this event, Friedman, Billings, Ramsey Group, Inc. and The Thunderbirds, the organization hosting the tournament, went the extra mile with their "Birdies for Charity" program last year. The pair donated $100 for every birdie, $1,000 for every eagle and $10,000 for every double eagle or hole-in-one. With 1,399 birdies and 28 eagles the total amount donated last year was $167,900.

***Jonathan Kaye** collected a career-high paycheck of $936,000 and jumped to the top of the PGA TOUR season money list for the first time in his career with $1,292,944. He earned over $1 million in a season for the fourth time in his career.*

*Three lefties finished in the Top-10 last year at the FBR Open—**Steve Flesch** (T3), **Mike Weir** (T5) and **Phil Mickelson** (T7). That hasn't happened since the 2000 Phoenix Open when the same three players accomplished the feat.*

MARK CALCAVECCHIA

*Think the purses have changed much over the past 13 years on the PGA TOUR? Three-time Phoenix Open champion **Mark Calcavecchia** took home a check worth $720,000 after winning the 2001 Phoenix Open. The first time Calcavecchia captured the Phoenix title, in 1989, the entire purse was $700,000. His share that year was $126,000. **Vijay Singh** received $720,000 for his win at the 2003 Phoenix Open, with an overall purse of $4 million for the field. When Singh won here in 1995, he earned $234,000 from a purse of $1.3 million.*

Tournament Record:
256, Mark Calcavecchia, 2001
Current Course Record:
60, Grant Waite, 1996; Mark Calcavecchia, 2001

TOURNAMENT HISTORY

Year	Winner	Score	Runner-up	Score	Location	Par/Yards
1954	Ed Furgol*	272	Cary Middlecoff	272	Phoenix CC, Phoenix, AZ	71/6,726
1955	Gene Littler	275	Billy Maxwell	276	Arizona CC, Phoenix, AZ	70/6,216
			Johnny Palmer			
1956	Cary Middlecoff	276	Mike Souchak	279	Phoenix CC, Phoenix, AZ	71/6,726
1957	Billy Casper	271	Cary Middlecoff	274	Arizona CC, Phoenix, AZ	70/6,216
			Mike Souchak			
1958	Ken Venturi	274	Walter Burkemo	275	Phoenix CC, Phoenix, AZ	71/6,726
			Jay Hebert			
1959	Gene Littler	268	Art Wall	269	Arizona CC, Phoenix, AZ	70/6,216
1960	Jack Fleck*	273	Bill Collins	273	Phoenix CC, Phoenix, AZ	71/6,726
1961	Arnold Palmer*	270	Doug Sanders	270	Arizona CC, Phoenix, AZ	70/6,216
1962	Arnold Palmer	269	Billy Casper	281	Phoenix CC, Phoenix, AZ	71/6,726
			Don Fairfield			
			Bob McCallister			
			Jack Nicklaus			
1963	Arnold Palmer	273	Gary Player	274	Arizona CC, Phoenix, AZ	70/6,216
1964	Jack Nicklaus	271	Bob Brue	274	Phoenix CC, Phoenix, AZ	71/6,726
1965	Rod Funseth	274	Bert Yancey	277	Arizona CC, Phoenix, AZ	70/6,216
1966	Dudley Wysong	278	Gardner Dickinson	279	Phoenix CC, Phoenix, AZ	71/6,726
1967	Julius Boros	272	Ken Still	273	Arizona CC, Phoenix, AZ	70/6,216
1968	George Knudson	272	Julius Boros	275	Phoenix CC, Phoenix, AZ	71/6,726
			Sam Carmichael			
			Jack Montgomery			
1969	Gene Littler	263	Miller Barber	265	Arizona CC, Phoenix, AZ	70/6,216
			Don January			
			Billy Maxwell			
1970	Dale Douglass	271	Howie Johnson	272	Phoenix CC, Phoenix, AZ	71/6,726
			Gene Littler			
1971	Miller Barber	261	Billy Casper	263	Arizona CC, Phoenix, AZ	70/6,216
			Dan Sikes			
1972	Homero Blancas*	273	Lanny Wadkins	273	Phoenix CC, Phoenix, AZ	71/6,726
1973	Bruce Crampton	268	Steve Melnyk	269	Arizona CC, Phoenix, AZ	70/6,216
			Lanny Wadkins			
1974	Johnny Miller	271	Lanny Wadkins	272	Phoenix CC, Phoenix, AZ	71/6,726
1975	Johnny Miller	260	Jerry Heard	274	Phoenix CC, Phoenix, AZ	71/6,726
1976	Bob Gilder	268	Roger Maltbie	270	Phoenix CC, Phoenix, AZ	71/6,726
1977	Jerry Pate*	277	Dave Stockton	277	Phoenix CC, Phoenix, AZ	71/6,726
1978	Miller Barber	272	Jerry Pate	273	Phoenix CC, Phoenix, AZ	71/6,726
			Lee Trevino			
1979	Ben Crenshaw~	199	Jay Haas	200	Phoenix CC, Phoenix, AZ	71/6,726
1980	Jeff Mitchell	272	Rik Massengale	276	Phoenix CC, Phoenix, AZ	71/6,726
1981	David Graham	268	Lon Hinkle	269	Phoenix CC, Phoenix, AZ	71/6,726
1982	Lanny Wadkins	263	Jerry Pate	269	Phoenix CC, Phoenix, AZ	71/6,726
1983	Bob Gilder*	271	Rex Caldwell	271	Phoenix CC, Phoenix, AZ	71/6,726
			Johnny Miller			
			Mark O'Meara			
1984	Tom Purtzer	268	Corey Pavin	269	Phoenix CC, Phoenix, AZ	71/6,726
1985	Calvin Peete	270	Morris Hatalsky	272	Phoenix CC, Phoenix, AZ	71/6,726
			Doug Tewell			
1986	Hal Sutton	267	Calvin Peete	269	Phoenix CC, Phoenix, AZ	71/6,726
			Tony Sills			
1987	Paul Azinger	268	Hal Sutton	269	TPC of Scottsdale, Scottsdale, AZ	71/6,992
1988	Sandy Lyle*	269	Fred Couples	269	TPC of Scottsdale, Scottsdale, AZ	71/6,992
1989	Mark Calcavecchia	263	Chip Beck	270	TPC of Scottsdale, Scottsdale, AZ	71/6,992
1990	Tommy Armour III	267	Jim Thorpe	272	TPC of Scottsdale, Scottsdale, AZ	71/6,992
1991	Nolan Henke	268	Gil Morgan	269	TPC of Scottsdale, Scottsdale, AZ	71/6,992
			Curtis Strange			
			Tom Watson			
1992	Mark Calcavecchia	264	Duffy Waldorf	269	TPC of Scottsdale, Scottsdale, AZ	71/6,992
1993	Lee Janzen	273	Andrew Magee	275	TPC of Scottsdale, Scottsdale, AZ	71/6,992
1994	Bill Glasson	268	Bob Estes	271	TPC of Scottsdale, Scottsdale, AZ	71/6,992
1995	Vijay Singh*	269	Billy Mayfair	269	TPC of Scottsdale, Scottsdale, AZ	71/6,992
1996	Phil Mickelson*	269	Justin Leonard	269	TPC of Scottsdale, Scottsdale, AZ	71/6,992
1997	Steve Jones	258	Jesper Parnevik	269	TPC of Scottsdale, Scottsdale, AZ	71/6,992
1998	Jesper Parnevik	269	Tommy Armour III	272	TPC of Scottsdale, Scottsdale, AZ	71/7,059
			Brent Geiberger			
			Steve Pate			
			Tom Watson			
1999	Rocco Mediate	273	Justin Leonard	275	TPC of Scottsdale, Scottsdale, AZ	71/7,059
2000	Tom Lehman	270	Robert Allenby	271	TPC of Scottsdale, Scottsdale, AZ	71/7,083
			Rocco Mediate			
2001	Mark Calcavecchia	256	Rocco Mediate	264	TPC of Scottsdale, Scottsdale, AZ	71/7,083
2002	Chris DiMarco	267	Kenny Perry	268	TPC of Scottsdale, Scottsdale, AZ	71/7,089
			Kaname Yokoo			
2003	Vijay Singh	261	John Huston	264	TPC of Scottsdale, Scottsdale, AZ	71/7,089
FBR OPEN						
2004	Jonathan Kaye	266	Chris DiMarco	268	TPC of Scottsdale, Scottsdale, AZ	71/7,216

*KEY: * = Playoff ~ = Weather-shortened*

2004 AT&T Pebble Beach National Pro-Am

[Fifth of 48 official events]

Winner: VIJAY SINGH
67-68-68-69 272 (-16) $954,000

Pebble Beach Golf Links

Pebble Beach, CA

February 5-8, 2004

Purse: $5,300,000
Host Course (HC)
Par: 36-36—72 Yards: 6,816
Spyglass Hill GC (SP)
Par: 36-36—72 Yards: 6,862
Poppy Hills GC (PH)
Par: 36-36—72 Yards: 6,833

LEADERS: First Round—Matt Kuchar (PH) and J.J. Henry (HC) carded 7-under 65s to lead Tommy Tolles (HC) by one. Eight players were two shots back.
Second Round—Luke Donald (HC) moved to 10-under-par 134 to lead Tom Pernice, Jr. (SP), Ken Duke (HC), Henry (PH) and Vijay Singh (SP) by one.
Third Round—Singh (HC) and Arron Oberholser (SP) at 13-under-par 203 held the lead by three strokes over Donald (PH), Phillip Price (HC) and Jeff Maggert (HC). Phil Mickelson (HC) was four behind.

CUT: 68 players at 1-under-par 215 from a field of 180 professionals.

WEATHER: Due to heavy rains, players were granted preferred lies on the Poppy Hills and Spyglass Hill courses during the first three rounds. Sunny and pleasant on Thursday with a high of 61. Sunny and pleasant on Friday, turning cloudy by late afternoon. Temperatures reached 62 degrees. Mostly sunny and breezy on Saturday with a high temperature of 58. NW winds up to 12-18 mph. Mostly sunny with a high of 62 on Sunday.

Check out the 2005 AT&T Pebble Beach National Pro-Am, February 9-13 on USA/CBS

ORDER OF FINISH

Vijay Singh	1	67-68-68-69	272	$954,000.00
Jeff Maggert	2	71-68-67-69	275	572,400.00
Phil Mickelson	3	68-68-71-69	276	360,400.00
K.J. Choi	T4	67-70-71-71	279	219,066.67
Mike Weir	T4	73-70-66-70	279	219,066.67
Arron Oberholser	T4	69-67-67-76	279	219,066.66
Jesper Parnevik	T7	70-67-73-70	280	165,183.34
Mark Hensby	T7	70-67-73-70	280	165,183.33
Tom Pernice, Jr.	T7	67-68-73-72	280	165,183.33
Bill Glasson	T10	73-69-66-73	281	127,200.00
Kent Jones	T10	67-71-74-69	281	127,200.00
Scott McCarron	T10	69-68-71-73	281	127,200.00
Corey Pavin	T10	69-68-73-71	281	127,200.00
Todd Fischer	T14	72-70-72-68	282	95,400.00
Peter Jacobsen	T14	70-71-70-71	282	95,400.00
Kirk Triplett	T14	69-70-70-73	282	95,400.00
Mark Brooks	T17	71-72-68-72	283	76,850.00
Luke Donald	T17	69-65-72-77	283	76,850.00
Phillip Price	T17	67-70-69-77	283	76,850.00
Ted Purdy	T17	68-73-70-72	283	76,850.00
Arjun Atwal	T21	72-70-72-70	284	57,240.00
Rich Barcelo	T21	72-69-73-70	284	57,240.00
Tim Petrovic	T21	71-71-70-72	284	57,240.00
Paul Stankowski	T21	69-71-72-72	284	57,240.00
Woody Austin	T25	69-71-72-73	285	37,126.50
Brian Bateman	T25	69-71-69-76	285	37,126.50
Daniel Chopra	T25	71-71-68-75	285	37,126.50
Fred Couples	T25	70-71-73-71	285	37,126.50
Niclas Fasth	T25	69-71-72-73	285	$37,126.50
Todd Hamilton	T25	71-69-73-72	285	37,126.50
Tom Lehman	T25	70-69-72-74	285	37,126.50
Carl Pettersson	T25	69-74-72-70	285	37,126.50
Boyd Summerhays	T25	69-74-70-72	285	37,126.50
Bo Van Pelt	T25	72-68-73-72	285	37,126.50
Craig Barlow	T35	67-75-71-73	286	25,572.50
Charles Howell III	T35	69-73-72-72	286	25,572.50
Jerry Kelly	T35	71-72-70-73	286	25,572.50
Ryan Palmer	T35	74-72-68-72	286	25,572.50
Craig Stadler	T35	68-71-71-76	286	25,572.50
Willie Wood	T35	72-70-71-73	286	25,572.50
Jay Don Blake	T41	71-74-70-72	287	18,550.00
Greg Chalmers	T41	71-70-72-74	287	18,550.00
Jay Delsing	T41	73-66-73-75	287	18,550.00
David Edwards	T41	74-68-72-73	287	18,550.00
Steve Friesen (Q)	T41	69-70-73-75	287	18,550.00
J.J. Henry	T41	65-70-75-77	287	18,550.00
Loren Roberts	T41	72-68-72-75	287	18,550.00
Tom Byrum	T48	74-68-72-74	288	13,320.67
Joel Kribel	T48	68-73-72-75	288	13,320.67
Matt Kuchar	T48	65-74-74-75	288	13,320.67
John Senden	T48	71-68-73-76	288	13,320.67
Danny Briggs	T48	70-70-74-74	288	13,320.66
Mark Wilson	T48	70-74-71-73	288	13,320.66
Ken Duke	T54	67-68-76-78	289	12,084.00
J.P. Hayes	T54	72-70-73-74	289	12,084.00
Joe Ogilvie	T54	71-67-77-74	289	12,084.00
David Sutherland	T54	74-70-69-76	289	12,084.00
Kevin Sutherland	T54	70-69-73-77	289	12,084.00
Zach Johnson	T59	71-71-72-76	290	$11,713.00
Neal Lancaster	T59	72-72-71-75	290	11,713.00
Robert Gamez	T61	67-69-76-79	291	11,501.00
Kevin Stadler (S)	T61	69-73-72-77	291	11,501.00
David Branshaw	T63	71-71-73-77	292	11,236.00
Dennis Paulson	T63	69-68-78-77	292	11,236.00
Patrick Sheehan	T63	71-67-75-79	292	11,236.00
Trevor Dodds	66	74-72-69-78	293	11,024.00
Deane Pappas	67	68-73-74-80	295	10,918.00
Per-Ulrik Johansson	68	73-71-71-81	296	10,812.00
Steve Allan	T69	68-77-71	216	9,858.00
Jason Bohn	T69	74-69-73	216	9,858.00
Glen Day	T69	70-70-76	216	9,858.00
Steve Elkington	T69	72-72-72	216	9,858.00
Scott Gutschewski (S)	T69	74-73-69	216	9,858.00
Donnie Hammond	T69	75-70-71	216	9,858.00
Tim Herron	T69	73-68-75	216	9,858.00
Tripp Isenhour	T69	74-72-70	216	9,858.00
Frank Lickliter II	T69	74-74-68	216	9,858.00
Steve Lowery	T69	75-69-72	216	9,858.00
Casey Martin (S)	T69	71-74-71	216	9,858.00
David Morland IV	T69	77-69-70	216	9,858.00
Kevin Na	T69	74-74-68	216	9,858.00
Mark O'Meara	T69	75-72-69	216	9,858.00
Brett Quigley	T69	76-70-70	216	9,858.00
Chris Smith	T69	71-71-74	216	9,858.00
Vaughn Taylor	T69	70-73-73	216	9,858.00

(Q) = Open Qualifier; (S) = Sponsor Exemption; (T) = Tie

The following players did not finish (C=cut, W=withdrew)

C—217-Billy Andrade, Aaron Barber, Craig Bowden, Chris Couch, Jason Gore, Richard S. Johnson, Davis Love III, Rory Sabbatini, Andre Stolz, Stan Utley. **218-**Marco Dawson, Brad Faxon, Mathias Gronberg, Mike Hulbert, Rocco Mediate, Larry Mize, Bryce Molder, John E. Morgan, Steve Pate, Tag Ridings, Scott Simpson, Nick Watney, Brian Watts. **219-**Jim Carter, Robert Damron, Lucas Glover, David Gossett, Jose Maria Olazabal, Rod Pampling, Tommy Tolles. **220-**Olin Browne, Michael Clark II, Harrison Frazar, Scott Hend, Brian Kortan, J.L. Lewis, Paul McGinley, Jim McGovern, Kris Moe, Dan Olsen, Mike Springer, Roger Tambellini, Grant Waite, Mark Wiebe. **221-**Aaron Baddeley, Jeff Brehaut, Dan Forsman, Robin Freeman, Matt Gogel, Mike Grob, Esteban Toledo. **222-**Todd Barranger, Mark Calcavecchia, Robert Hamilton, Blaine McCallister, D.A. Points, Kevin Streelman, Roland Thatcher. **223-**Russ Cochran, Brian Henninger, Hunter Mahan, Omar Uresti. **224-**Tom Carter, Keith Clearwater, Hank Kuehne, Brad Lardon, Kevin Muncrief, Mike Standly. **225-**John Ellis, Ian Leggatt. **226-**D.J. Brigman, Kris Cox. **227-**Jonathan Byrd, Kelly Gibson. **228-**Mike Heinen, David Lebeck, Jin Park, Dicky Pride, Dave Stockton, Jr. **229-**Ken Green, John Maginnes, John Rollins. **230-**Guy Boros, Hirofumi Miyase, Pat Perez, Tjaart Van der Walt. **231-**Shawn Kelly, John Morse. **233-**George Burns, Jason Dufner, Garrett Willis. **234-**Roger Maltbie. **237-**Rick Leibovich. **W—75-**John Cook. **150-**Wes Short, Jr.

TOURNAMENT HISTORY

Year	Winner	Score	Runner-up	Score	Location	Par/Yards
BING CROSBY PROFESSIONAL-AMATEUR						
1937	Sam Snead	68	George Von Elm	72	Rancho Santa Fe CC, Rancho Santa Fe, CA	73/6,769
1938	Sam Snead	139	Jimmy Hines	141	Rancho Santa Fe CC, Rancho Santa Fe, CA	73/6,769
1939	Dutch Harrison	138	Byron Nelson Horton Smith	139	Rancho Santa Fe CC, Rancho Santa Fe, CA	73/6,769
1940	Ed Oliver	135	Vic Ghezzi	138	Rancho Santa Fe CC, Rancho Santa Fe, CA	73/6,769
1941	Sam Snead	136	Craig Wood	137	Rancho Santa Fe CC, Rancho Santa Fe, CA	73/6,769
1942	John Dawson#	133	Leland Gibson Lloyd Mangrum	136	Rancho Santa Fe CC, Rancho Santa Fe, CA	73/6,769
1943	No Tournament					
1944	No Tournament					
1945	No Tournament					
1946	No Tournament					
1947	Ed Furgol George Fazio	213	Tied		Cypress Point CC, Pebble Beach, CA Monterey Peninsula CC, Pebble Beach, CA Pebble Beach GL, Pebble Beach, CA	72/6,506 71/6,356 72/6,815
1948	Lloyd Mangrum	205	Stan Leonard	210	Cypress Point CC, Pebble Beach, CA Monterey Peninsula CC, Pebble Beach, CA Pebble Beach GL, Pebble Beach, CA	72/6,506 71/6,356 72/6,815
1949	Ben Hogan	208	Jim Ferrier	210	Cypress Point CC, Pebble Beach, CA Monterey Peninsula CC, Pebble Beach, CA Pebble Beach GL, Pebble Beach, CA	72/6,506 71/6,356 72/6,815
1950	Sam Snead Jack Burke, Jr. Smiley Quick Dave Douglas	214	Tied		Cypress Point CC, Pebble Beach, CA Monterey Peninsula CC, Pebble Beach, CA Pebble Beach GL, Pebble Beach, CA	72/6,506 71/6,356 72/6,815

AT&T Pebble Beach National Pro-Am

NOTES

With his 16th career PGA TOUR victory at the 2004 AT&T Pebble Beach National Pro-Am, ***Vijay Singh*** *became the eighth player over the age of 40 to win the event. The others:* ***Payne Stewart*** *(1999),* ***Mark O'Meara*** *(1997),* ***Peter Jacobsen*** *(1995),* ***Johnny Miller*** *(1994),* ***Gene Littler*** *(1975),* ***E.J. (Dutch) Harrison*** *(1954) and* ***Jimmy Demaret*** *(1952). Miller was the oldest at 46 years, nine months and seven days.*

Vijay Singh*'s 2004 victory came in his 10th appearance at the AT&T Pebble Beach National Pro-Am. He has five top-10 finishes at the AT&T, all five of those in the last six years. The winner's check of $954,000 was the second-largest payday in his career at the time.*

PETER JACOBSEN

Tournament Record:
268, Mark O'Meara

Tournament Course Record:
62, Tom Kite, 1983; David Duval, 1997 (Pebble Beach GL)
62, Matt Gogel, 2001 (Poppy Hills GC)
64, Dan Forsman, 1993; Steve Lowery, 1995; David Berganio, Jr., 2001 (Spyglass Hill GC)

TOURNAMENT HISTORY

Year	Winner	Score	Runner-up	Score	Location	Par/Yards
1951	Byron Nelson	209	Cary Middlecoff	212	Cypress Point CC, Pebble Beach, CA Monterey Peninsula CC, Pebble Beach, CA Pebble Beach GL, Pebble Beach, CA	72/6,506 71/6,356 72/6,815
1952	Jimmy Demaret	145	Art Bell	147	Cypress Point CC, Pebble Beach, CA Monterey Peninsula CC, Pebble Beach, CA Pebble Beach GL, Pebble Beach, CA	72/6,506 71/6,356 72/6,815
THE BING CROSBY PROFESSIONAL-AMATEUR INVITATIONAL						
1953	Lloyd Mangrum	204	Julius Boros	208	Cypress Point CC, Pebble Beach, CA Pebble Beach GL, Pebble Beach, CA	72/6,506 72/6,815
1954	Dutch Harrison	210	Jimmy Demaret	211	Cypress Point CC, Pebble Beach, CA Monterey Peninsula CC, Pebble Beach, CA Pebble Beach GL, Pebble Beach, CA	72/6,506 71/6,356 72/6,815
1955	Cary Middlecoff	209	Julius Boros Paul McGuire	213	Cypress Point CC, Pebble Beach, CA Monterey Peninsula CC, Pebble Beach, CA Pebble Beach GL, Pebble Beach, CA	72/6,506 71/6,356 72/6,815
BING CROSBY NATIONAL PROFESSIONAL-AMATEUR GOLF CHAMPIONSHIP						
1956	Cary Middlecoff	202	Mike Souchak	207	Cypress Point CC, Pebble Beach, CA Monterey Peninsula CC, Pebble Beach, CA Pebble Beach GL, Pebble Beach, CA	72/6,506 71/6,356 72/6,815
1957	Jay Hebert	213	Cary Middlecoff	215	Cypress Point CC, Pebble Beach, CA Monterey Peninsula CC, Pebble Beach, CA Pebble Beach GL, Pebble Beach, CA	72/6,506 71/6,356 72/6,815
1958	Billy Casper	277	Dave Marr	281	Cypress Point CC, Pebble Beach, CA Monterey Peninsula CC, Pebble Beach, CA Pebble Beach GL, Pebble Beach, CA	72/6,506 71/6,356 72/6,815
BING CROSBY NATIONAL						
1959	Art Wall	279	Jimmy Demaret Gene Littler	281	Cypress Point CC, Pebble Beach, CA Monterey Peninsula CC, Pebble Beach, CA Pebble Beach GL, Pebble Beach, CA	72/6,506 71/6,356 72/6,815
1960	Ken Venturi	286	Julius Boros Tommy Jacobs	289	Cypress Point CC, Pebble Beach, CA Monterey Peninsula CC, Pebble Beach, CA Pebble Beach GL, Pebble Beach, CA	72/6,506 71/6,356 72/6,815
1961	Bob Rosburg	282	Roberto De Vicenzo Dave Ragan	283	Cypress Point CC, Pebble Beach, CA Monterey Peninsula CC, Pebble Beach, CA Pebble Beach GL, Pebble Beach, CA	72/6,506 71/6,356 72/6,815
1962	Doug Ford*	286	Joe Campbell	286	Cypress Point CC, Pebble Beach, CA Monterey Peninsula CC, Pebble Beach, CA Pebble Beach GL, Pebble Beach, CA	72/6,506 71/6,356 72/6,815
1963	Billy Casper	285	Dave Hill Jack Nicklaus Gary Player Bob Rosburg Art Wall	286	Cypress Point CC, Pebble Beach, CA Monterey Peninsula CC, Pebble Beach, CA Pebble Beach GL, Pebble Beach, CA	72/6,506 71/6,356 72/6,815
BING CROSBY NATIONAL PROFESSIONAL-AMATEUR						
1964	Tony Lema	284	Gay Brewer Bo Wininger	287	Cypress Point CC, Pebble Beach, CA Monterey Peninsula CC, Pebble Beach, CA Pebble Beach GL, Pebble Beach, CA	72/6,506 71/6,356 72/6,815
1965	Bruce Crampton	284	Tony Lema	287	Cypress Point CC, Pebble Beach, CA Monterey Peninsula CC, Pebble Beach, CA Pebble Beach GL, Pebble Beach, CA	72/6,506 71/6,356 72/6,815
1966	Don Massengale	283	Arnold Palmer	284	Cypress Point CC, Pebble Beach, CA Monterey Peninsula CC, Pebble Beach, CA Pebble Beach GL, Pebble Beach, CA	72/6,506 71/6,356 72/6,815
1967	Jack Nicklaus	284	Billy Casper	289	Pebble Beach GL, Pebble Beach, CA Cypress Point CC, Pebble Beach, CA Spyglass Hill GC, Pebble Beach, CA	72/6,815 72/6,506 72/6,810
1968	Johnny Pott*	285	Billy Casper Bruce Devlin	285	Pebble Beach GL, Pebble Beach, CA Cypress Point CC, Pebble Beach, CA Spyglass Hill GC, Pebble Beach, CA	72/6,815 72/6,506 72/6,810
1969	George Archer	283	Bob Dickson Dale Douglass Howie Johnson	284	Pebble Beach GL, Pebble Beach, CA Cypress Point CC, Pebble Beach, CA Spyglass Hill GC, Pebble Beach, CA	72/6,815 72/6,506 72/6,810
1970	Bert Yancey	278	Jack Nicklaus	279	Pebble Beach GL, Pebble Beach, CA Cypress Point CC, Pebble Beach, CA Spyglass Hill GC, Pebble Beach, CA	72/6,815 72/6,506 72/6,810
1971	Tom Shaw	278	Arnold Palmer	280	Pebble Beach GL, Pebble Beach, CA Cypress Point CC, Pebble Beach, CA Spyglass Hill GC, Pebble Beach, CA	72/6,815 72/6,506 72/6,810
1972	Jack Nicklaus*	284	Johnny Miller	284	Pebble Beach GL, Pebble Beach, CA Cypress Point CC, Pebble Beach, CA Spyglass Hill GC, Pebble Beach, CA	72/6,815 72/6,506 72/6,810
1973	Jack Nicklaus*	282	Raymond Floyd Orville Moody	282	Pebble Beach GL, Pebble Beach, CA Cypress Point CC, Pebble Beach, CA Spyglass Hill GC, Pebble Beach, CA	72/6,815 72/6,506 72/6,810
1974	Johnny Miller~	208	Grier Jones	212	Pebble Beach GL, Pebble Beach, CA Cypress Point CC, Pebble Beach, CA Spyglass Hill GC, Pebble Beach, CA	72/6,815 72/6,506 72/6,810

AT&T Pebble Beach National Pro-Am

NOTES

Vijay Singh*'s victory at the 2004 AT&T Pebble Beach National Pro-Am extended his consecutive top-10 streak to 12, dating back to the 2003 WGC-NEC Invitational. The streak, which ended the following week at the Buick Invitational, was the longest on TOUR since* ***Jack Nicklaus*** *had 14 in a row in 1977. The following is a list of the longest consecutive top-10 streaks since 1970:*

Jack Nicklaus	*14*	*1977*
Jack Nicklaus	*13*	*1973*
Jack Nicklaus	*12*	*1971, 1975*
Vijay Singh	*12*	*2003-04*

JACK NICKLAUS

During his streak of 12 consecutive top-10 finishes that began at the 2003 WGC-NEC Invitational and ran through the 2004 AT&T Pebble Beach National Pro-Am, ***Vijay Singh*** *was a cumulative 146-under par. His scoring average for the streak was 67.95 and he earned $5,016,683 (with a weekly average earning of $418,056.92).*

Vijay Singh and caddie

TOURNAMENT HISTORY

Year	Winner	Score	Runner-up	Score	Location	Par/Yards
1975	Gene Littler	280	Hubert Green	284	Pebble Beach GL, Pebble Beach, CA Cypress Point CC, Pebble Beach, CA Spyglass Hill GC, Pebble Beach, CA	72/6,815 72/6,506 72/6,810
1976	Ben Crenshaw	281	Mike Morley	283	Pebble Beach GL, Pebble Beach, CA Cypress Point CC, Pebble Beach, CA Spyglass Hill GC, Pebble Beach, CA	72/6,815 72/6,506 72/6,810
1977	Tom Watson	273	Tony Jacklin	274	Pebble Beach GL, Pebble Beach, CA Cypress Point CC, Pebble Beach, CA Monterey Peninsula CC, Pebble Beach, CA	72/6,815 72/6,506 71/6,400
1978	Tom Watson*	280	Ben Crenshaw	280	Pebble Beach GL, Pebble Beach, CA Cypress Point CC, Pebble Beach, CA Spyglass Hill GC, Pebble Beach, CA	72/6,815 72/6,506 72/6,810
1979	Lon Hinkle*	284	Andy Bean Mark Hayes	284	Pebble Beach GL, Pebble Beach, CA Cypress Point CC, Pebble Beach, CA Spyglass Hill GC, Pebble Beach, CA	72/6,815 72/6,506 72/6,810
1980	George Burns	280	Dan Pohl	281	Pebble Beach GL, Pebble Beach, CA Cypress Point CC, Pebble Beach, CA	72/6,815 72/6,506
1981	John Cook~*	209	Bobby Clampett Ben Crenshaw Hale Irwin Barney Thompson	209	Pebble Beach GL, Pebble Beach, CA Cypress Point CC, Pebble Beach, CA Spyglass Hill GC, Pebble Beach, CA	72/6,815 72/6,506 72/6,810
1982	Jim Simons	274	Craig Stadler	276	Pebble Beach GL, Pebble Beach, CA Cypress Point CC, Pebble Beach, CA Spyglass Hill GC, Pebble Beach, CA	72/6,815 72/6,506 72/6,810
1983	Tom Kite	276	Rex Caldwell Calvin Peete	278	Pebble Beach GL, Pebble Beach, CA Cypress Point CC, Pebble Beach, CA Spyglass Hill GC, Pebble Beach, CA	72/6,815 72/6,506 72/6,810
1984	Hale Irwin*	278	Jim Nelford	278	Pebble Beach GL, Pebble Beach, CA Cypress Point CC, Pebble Beach, CA Spyglass Hill GC, Pebble Beach, CA	72/6,815 72/6,506 72/6,810
1985	Mark O'Meara	283	Kikuo Arai Larry Rinker Curtis Strange	284	Pebble Beach GL, Pebble Beach, CA Cypress Point CC, Pebble Beach, CA Spyglass Hill GC, Pebble Beach, CA	72/6,815 72/6,506 72/6,810
AT&T PEBBLE BEACH NATIONAL PRO-AM						
1986	Fuzzy Zoeller~	205	Payne Stewart	210	Pebble Beach GL, Pebble Beach, CA Cypress Point CC, Pebble Beach, CA Spyglass Hill GC, Pebble Beach, CA	72/6,815 72/6,506 72/6,810
1987	Johnny Miller	278	Payne Stewart	279	Pebble Beach GL, Pebble Beach, CA Cypress Point CC, Pebble Beach, CA Spyglass Hill GC, Pebble Beach, CA	72/6,815 72/6,506 72/6,810
1988	Steve Jones*	280	Bob Tway	280	Pebble Beach GL, Pebble Beach, CA Cypress Point CC, Pebble Beach, CA Spyglass Hill GC, Pebble Beach, CA	72/6,815 72/6,506 72/6,810
1989	Mark O'Meara	277	Tom Kite	278	Pebble Beach GL, Pebble Beach, CA Cypress Point CC, Pebble Beach, CA Spyglass Hill GC, Pebble Beach, CA	72/6,815 72/6,506 72/6,810
1990	Mark O'Meara	281	Kenny Perry	283	Pebble Beach GL, Pebble Beach, CA Cypress Point CC, Pebble Beach, CA Spyglass Hill GC, Pebble Beach, CA	72/6,815 72/6,506 72/6,810
1991	Paul Azinger	274	Brian Claar Corey Pavin	278	Pebble Beach GL, Pebble Beach, CA Spyglass Hill GC, Pebble Beach, CA Poppy Hills GC, Pebble Beach, CA	72/6,815 72/6,810 72/6,865
1992	Mark O'Meara*	275	Jeff Sluman	275	Pebble Beach GL, Pebble Beach, CA Spyglass Hill GC, Pebble Beach, CA Poppy Hills GC, Pebble Beach, CA	72/6,815 72/6,810 72/6,865
1993	Brett Ogle	276	Billy Ray Brown	279	Pebble Beach GL, Pebble Beach, CA Spyglass Hill GC, Pebble Beach, CA Poppy Hills GC, Pebble Beach, CA	72/6,815 72/6,810 72/6,865
1994	Johnny Miller	281	Jeff Maggert Corey Pavin Kirk Triplett Tom Watson	282	Pebble Beach GL, Pebble Beach, CA Spyglass Hill GC, Pebble Beach, CA Poppy Hills GC, Pebble Beach, CA	72/6,815 72/6,810 72/6,865
1995	Peter Jacobsen	271	David Duval	273	Pebble Beach GL, Pebble Beach, CA Spyglass Hill GC, Pebble Beach, CA Poppy Hills GC, Pebble Beach, CA	72/6,799 72/6,810 72/6,865
1996	No Tournament+					
1997	Mark O'Meara	268	David Duval Tiger Woods	269	Pebble Beach GL, Pebble Beach, CA Spyglass Hill GC, Pebble Beach, CA Poppy Hills GC, Pebble Beach, CA	72/6,799 72/6,859 72/6,861
1998	Phil Mickelson~	202	Tom Pernice, Jr.	203	Pebble Beach GL, Pebble Beach, CA Spyglass Hill GC, Pebble Beach, CA Poppy Hills GC, Pebble Beach, CA	72/6,799 72/6,859 72/6,861
1999	Payne Stewart~	206	Frank Lickliter	207	Pebble Beach GL, Pebble Beach, CA Spyglass Hill GC, Pebble Beach, CA Poppy Hills GC, Pebble Beach, CA	72/6,799 72/6,859 72/6,861
2000	Tiger Woods	273	Matt Gogel Vijay Singh	275	Pebble Beach GL, Pebble Beach, CA Spyglass Hill GC, Pebble Beach, CA Poppy Hills GC, Pebble Beach, CA	72/6,816 72/6,817 72/6,833
2001	Davis Love III	272	Vijay Singh	273	Pebble Beach GL, Pebble Beach, CA Spyglass Hill GC, Pebble Beach, CA	72/6,816 72/6,817

AT&T Pebble Beach National Pro-Am

NOTES

Jeff Maggert *birdied the final two holes in the final round at the 2004 AT&T Pebble Beach National Pro-Am to finish in solo second place. It was Maggert's first runner-up effort since finishing tied for second at the 2000 Buick Challenge – a span of 85 starts.*

Craig Stadler and Kevin Stadler

Playing in the same pairing, Sponsor Exemption ***Kevin Stadler*** *and his father* ***Craig*** *both made the 54-hole cut and finished T61 and T35, respectively. It was the first made cut of Kevin's career in four starts, third as a professional. One week later, Kevin was the first-round leader at the Buick Invitational after an 8-under-par 64 (before finishing T59), while Craig went on to win The ACE Group Classic on the Champions Tour.*

Bill Glasson *finished T10 at the 2004 AT&T Pebble Beach National Pro-Am, his first top-10 on TOUR since a T3 at the 2000 B.C. Open, a span of 60 events between top-10s. Glasson's top-10 earned him a start the following week at the Buick Invitational.*

BILL GLASSON

TOURNAMENT HISTORY

Year	Winner	Score	Runner-up	Score	Location	Par/Yards
2002	Matt Gogel	274	Pat Perez	277	Poppy Hills GC, Pebble Beach, CA Pebble Beach GL, Pebble Beach, CA Spyglass Hill GC, Pebble Beach, CA	72/6,833 72/6,816 72/6,862
2003	Davis Love III	274	Tom Lehman	275	Poppy Hills GC, Pebble Beach, CA Pebble Beach GL, Pebble Beach, CA Spyglass Hill GC, Pebble Beach, CA	72/6,833 72/6,816 72/6,862
2004	Vijay Singh	272	Jeff Maggert	275	Poppy Hills GC, Pebble Beach, CA Pebble Beach GL, Pebble Beach, CA Spyglass Hill GC, Pebble Beach, CA Poppy Hills GC, Pebble Beach, CA	72/6,833 72/6,816 72/6,862 72/6,833

*KEY: * = Playoff ~ = Weather-shortened # = Amateur + = Canceled after two rounds due to unplayable course conditions*

ELIGIBILITY REQUIREMENTS FOR 2005 AT&T PEBBLE BEACH NATIONAL PRO-AM

Eligible players in the 180-professional field are those players listed in order of priority under Section III-A of the Tournament Regulations, except that prior to such players, the following shall first be eligible:

- Winners of the AT&T Pebble Beach National Pro-Am prior to 2000, and winners of the AT&T Pebble Beach National Pro-Am in 2000 and beyond for a period of five years following their win.
- Winners of THE PLAYERS Championship, Masters Tournament, U.S. Open, British Open and PGA Championship prior to 2000, and winners of these events in 2000 and beyond for a period of five years following their win.
- 16 sponsor exemptions, restricted as follows:
  - Four from the current year's PGA TOUR membership.
  - Eight from among the 2004 PGA TOUR Qualifying Tournament's top 30 finishers and ties and the first through 20th finishers on the 2004 Official Nationwide Tour Money List.
  - Four "unrestricted" that must be awarded to professionals.

NOTE: The sponsor will team each professional player with an amateur player. The PGA TOUR shall group the professional players and assign starting times. After three rounds, the field will be cut to the low 60 professionals and ties and exactly the low 25 pro-am teams. Professionals placing 61st to 70th and ties will receive official prize money normally distributed to those places.

Hole No. 7 at the Pebble Beach Golf Links.

2004 Buick Invitational

[Sixth of 48 official events]

BUICK INVITATIONAL

Winner: JOHN DALY #
69-66-68-75 278 (-10) $864,000

Torrey Pines Golf Course

La Jolla, CA

February 12-15, 2004

Purse: $4,800,000
South Course (Host Course)
Par: 36-36—72 Yards: 7,568
North Course
Par: 36-36—72 Yards: 6,874

LEADERS: First Round—Kevin Stadler (N) carded an 8-under-par 64 to lead Jesper Parnevik (N) and Ted Purdy (N) by one. Five players were two strokes back.
Second Round—Stewart Cink (N) moved to 11-under-par 133 to lead Steve Flesch (S) and John Daly (S) by two. Bo Van Pelt was three back.

Third Round—Daly at 13-under-par 203 led Cink by one. Dennis Paulson was two back and Flesch was three behind.

CUT: 82 players at 1-under-par from a field of 154 professionals and two amateurs.

WEATHER: On Thursday, mostly sunny and warm, with a high of 69. Winds N-NW up to 15 mph. Friday, a mix of sun and high clouds. High temperatures reached 68 with winds primarily N-NW 7-12 mph. Saturday, variably cloudy most of the day with rain in the late morning. Slightly cooler temperatures with a high of 64. Westerly winds up to 10-15 mph. Warm and sunny on Sunday with a high of 65.

Check out the 2005 Buick Invitational, January 20-23 on USA/ABC

ORDER OF FINISH

 # Won playoff with a birdie-4 on first extra hole

John Daly #	1	69-66-68-75	278	$864,000.00
Luke Donald	T2	69-69-71-69	278	422,400.00
Chris Riley	T2	67-71-71-69	278	422,400.00
Thomas Bjorn	T4	70-69-72-68	279	174,000.00
Shigeki Maruyama	T4	72-67-71-69	279	174,000.00
Phil Mickelson	T4	74-69-69-67	279	174,000.00
Jesper Parnevik	T4	65-73-70-71	279	174,000.00
Bo Van Pelt	T4	68-68-73-70	279	174,000.00
Duffy Waldorf	T4	68-70-71-70	279	174,000.00
Stewart Cink	T10	70-63-71-76	280	106,400.00
Jay Haas	T10	70-69-70-71	280	106,400.00
Brandt Jobe	T10	69-69-70-72	280	106,400.00
Billy Mayfair	T10	72-65-72-71	280	106,400.00
Tom Pernice, Jr.	T10	71-68-69-72	280	106,400.00
Tiger Woods	T10	71-68-72-69	280	106,400.00
Craig Barlow	T16	66-73-71-71	281	72,000.00
Niclas Fasth	T16	70-68-74-69	281	72,000.00
Steve Flesch	T16	67-68-72-74	281	72,000.00
Tom Lehman	T16	66-73-70-72	281	72,000.00
Brett Quigley	T16	70-68-72-71	281	72,000.00
Hank Kuehne	T21	73-67-71-71	282	51,840.00
Stephen Leaney	T21	72-65-71-74	282	51,840.00
Rory Sabbatini	T21	69-73-71-69	282	51,840.00
Bob Tway	T21	66-73-71-72	282	51,840.00
Woody Austin	T25	70-71-70-73	284	37,440.00
K.J. Choi	T25	68-73-74-69	284	37,440.00
Dennis Paulson (S)	T25	69-69-67-79	284	$37,440.00
Roger Tambellini	T25	68-71-70-75	284	37,440.00
Vaughn Taylor	T25	74-65-72-73	284	37,440.00
Danny Ellis	T30	71-71-71-72	285	28,525.72
Joey Sindelar	T30	67-73-72-73	285	28,525.72
Tommy Tolles	T30	68-73-71-73	285	28,525.72
Arjun Atwal	T30	73-70-75-67	285	28,525.71
Sergio Garcia	T30	67-71-73-74	285	28,525.71
Jonathan Kaye	T30	71-68-73-73	285	28,525.71
David Peoples	T30	73-70-72-70	285	28,525.71
Briny Baird	T37	72-69-73-72	286	22,560.00
Tripp Isenhour	T37	74-67-73-72	286	22,560.00
Heath Slocum	T37	67-73-75-71	286	22,560.00
Robert Allenby	T40	74-67-70-76	287	18,720.00
Stuart Appleby	T40	73-70-70-74	287	18,720.00
Aaron Baddeley	T40	68-74-72-73	287	18,720.00
Zach Johnson	T40	73-70-75-69	287	18,720.00
Grant Waite (S)	T40	73-69-74-71	287	18,720.00
Michael Allen	T45	72-69-75-72	288	13,212.00
Stephen Ames	T45	73-69-77-69	288	13,212.00
Tom Carter	T45	76-66-73-73	288	13,212.00
Mathias Gronberg	T45	66-73-74-75	288	13,212.00
Kent Jones	T45	70-73-72-73	288	13,212.00
Brenden Pappas	T45	69-70-72-77	288	13,212.00
Tim Petrovic	T45	67-74-77-70	288	13,212.00
Kevin Sutherland	T45	66-74-75-73	288	13,212.00
Chad Campbell	T53	69-73-74-73	289	11,008.00
Todd Fischer	T53	68-71-76-74	289	11,008.00
Neal Lancaster	T53	71-70-76-72	289	11,008.00
Bernhard Langer	T53	71-70-72-76	289	$11,008.00
Hidemichi Tanaka	T53	69-72-74-74	289	11,008.00
Jay Williamson	T53	70-69-78-72	289	11,008.00
Craig Bowden	T59	70-70-74-76	290	10,368.00
Bob Burns	T59	71-70-72-77	290	10,368.00
Ken Duke	T59	70-70-76-74	290	10,368.00
Jose Maria Olazabal	T59	76-67-73-74	290	10,368.00
Corey Pavin	T59	70-73-75-72	290	10,368.00
Kevin Stadler (S)	T59	64-74-75-77	290	10,368.00
Hal Sutton	T59	67-70-76-77	290	10,368.00
Brian Bateman	T66	70-73-74-74	291	9,744.00
Jason Bohn	T66	74-67-74-76	291	9,744.00
Jason Dufner	T66	70-71-72-78	291	9,744.00
Charles Howell III	T66	69-74-75-73	291	9,744.00
Fredrik Jacobson	T66	67-74-79-71	291	9,744.00
Rod Pampling	T66	70-70-75-76	291	9,744.00
Billy Andrade	T72	72-68-77-75	292	9,216.00
Jay Delsing (S)	T72	71-72-76-73	292	9,216.00
Kevin Na	T72	72-69-78-73	292	9,216.00
Arron Oberholser	T72	71-70-70-81	292	9,216.00
Ted Purdy	T72	65-75-71-81	292	9,216.00
Chris Smith	T77	71-72-77-73	293	8,880.00
Dean Wilson	T77	70-68-77-78	293	8,880.00
Robert Damron	79	68-71-77-78	294	8,736.00
Keiichiro Fukabori	T80	70-67-83-75	295	8,592.00
Patrick Sheehan	T80	72-65-77-81	295	8,592.00
Spike McRoy	82	72-71-77-80	300	8,448.00

(Q) = Open Qualifier; (S) = Sponsor Exemption; (T) = Tie

The following players did not finish (C=cut, W=withdrew, D=disqualified, A=amateur)

C—144-Rich Barcelo, Tim Clark, Kris Cox, Bob Estes, J.J. Henry, Craig Perks, Vijay Singh. **145-**Chris Heintz (A), Scott Hend, Brian Kortan, Cliff Kresge, Mark O'Meara, Ryan Palmer, Pat Perez, Andre Stolz, Roland Thatcher, Lee Westwood. **146-**Rich Beem, Jay Don Blake, Brad Faxon, Robin Freeman, Bill Glasson, Lee Janzen, Skip Kendall, Shaun Micheel, Dan Olsen, John Rollins, Esteban Toledo, Omar Uresti. **147-**David Branshaw, Jeff Brehaut, Russ Cochran, Brent Geiberger, Matt Kuchar, Hunter Mahan, Blaine McCallister, Hirofumi Miyase, Kevin Muncrief, Geoff Ogilvy, John Riegger, Ron Skayhan, Boyd Summerhays. **148-**Darren Clarke, Marco Dawson, David Morland IV, Steve Pate. **149-**D.J. Brigman, Daniel Chopra, Trevor Dodds, Todd Hamilton, Dudley Hart, Joe Ogilvie, Carl Pettersson, Gene Sauers, David Schnider (A). **150-**John Maginnes, Steve Stricker. **151-**Guy Boros, Alex Cejka, Geoffrey Dean, Paul Holtby, Tim Parun. **152-**Joe Durant. **153-**Lucas Glover, Scott Simpson. **155-**Mike Lavery. **156-**Chris Couch, J.B. Sneve. **160-**David Oh. **W—**Tjaart Van der Walt, Tommy Armour III, **83-**Mark Hensby, **70-**Mark Calcavecchia. **D—80-**J.L. Lewis.

TOURNAMENT HISTORY

Year	Winner	Score	Runner-up	Score	Location	Par/Yards
SAN DIEGO OPEN						
1952	Ted Kroll	276	Jimmy Demaret	279	San Diego CC, San Diego, CA	72/6,931
1953	Tommy Bolt	274	Doug Ford	277	San Diego CC, San Diego, CA	72/6,931
1954	Gene Littler#	274	E. J. Harrison	278	Rancho Santa Fe GC, Rancho Santa Fe, CA	72/6,797
CONVAIR-SAN DIEGO OPEN						
1955	Tommy Bolt	274	Johnny Palmer	276	Mission Valley CC, San Diego, CA	72/6,619
1956	Bob Rosburg	270	Dick Mayer	272	Singing Hills GC, El Cajon, CA	72/6,573
SAN DIEGO OPEN INVITATIONAL						
1957	Arnold Palmer	271	Al Balding	272	Mission Valley CC, San Diego, CA	72/6,619
1958	No Tournament					
1959	Marty Furgol	274	Joe Campbell	275	Mission Valley CC, San Diego, CA	72/6,619
			Billy Casper			
			Dave Ragan			
			Mike Souchak			
			Bo Wininger			
1960	Mike Souchak	269	Johnny Pott	270	Mission Valley CC, San Diego, CA	72/6,619
1961	Arnold Palmer*	271	Al Balding	271	Mission Valley CC, San Diego, CA	72/6,619
1962	Tommy Jacobs*	277	Johnny Pott	277	Stardust CC, San Diego, CA	71/6,725
1963	Gary Player	270	Tony Lema	271	Stardust CC, San Diego, CA	71/6,725
1964	Art Wall	274	Tony Lema	276	Rancho Bernardo CC, San Diego, CA	72/6,455
			Bob Rosburg			
1965	Wes Ellis*	267	Billy Casper	267	Stardust CC, San Diego, CA	71/6,725
1966	Billy Casper	268	Tommy Aaron	272	Stardust CC, San Diego, CA	71/6,725
			Tom Weiskopf			
1967	Bob Goalby	269	Gay Brewer	270	Stardust CC, San Diego, CA	71/6,725
ANDY WILLIAMS-SAN DIEGO OPEN INVITATIONAL						
1968	Tom Weiskopf	273	Al Geiberger	274	Torrey Pines GC, La Jolla, CA	72/N-6,659, S-7,021

Buick Invitational

BUICK INVITATIONAL

NOTES

*2004 Buick Invitational winner **John Daly** went 189 starts and 8 years, 6 months, and 22 days between PGA TOUR wins, his last coming at the 1995 British Open.*

*The 278 total (10-under-par) total for **John Daly** was the highest Buick Invitational winning 72-hole total since **Phil Mickelson**'s 278 won the event in 1993. The highest winning total in Buick Invitational history was 284 by **Jack Nicklaus** in 1969.*

***John Daly** defeated **Chris Riley** and **Luke Donald** in the first hole of sudden death, nearly holing a bunker shot on No. 18 that he converted for a birdie-4. The playoff was the 13th in Buick Invitational history and the first since **Phil Mickelson** topped **Davis Love III** and **Frank Lickliter II** in sudden death in 2001. The last time there was a three-way playoff on the PGA TOUR was the 2002 Bell Canadian Open, where **John Rollins** defeated **Neal Lancaster** and **Justin Leonard**.*

***John Daly**'s winning 3-over-par score of 75 was the highest final-round score for a champion on the PGA TOUR since **Steve Pate** carded a 3-over-par 75 in a winning effort at the 1991 Honda Classic.*

PHIL MICKELSON

Tournament Record:
266, George Burns, 1987; Tiger Woods, 1999

Tournament Course Record:
61, Mark Brooks, 1990 (Torrey Pines North)
62, Tiger Woods, 1999 (Torrey Pines South)

TOURNAMENT HISTORY

Year	Winner	Score	Runner-up	Score	Location	Par/Yards
1969	Jack Nicklaus	284	Gene Littler	285	Torrey Pines GC, La Jolla, CA	72/N-6,659, S-7,021
1970	Pete Brown*	275	Tony Jacklin	275	Torrey Pines GC, La Jolla, CA	72/N-6,659, S-7,021
1971	George Archer	272	Dave Eichelberger	275	Torrey Pines GC, La Jolla, CA	72/N-6,659, S-7,021
1972	Paul Harney	275	Hale Irwin	276	Torrey Pines GC, La Jolla, CA	72/N-6,659, S-7,021
1973	Bob Dickson	278	Billy Casper	281	Torrey Pines GC, La Jolla, CA	72/N-6,659, S-7,021
			Bruce Crampton			
			Grier Jones			
			Phil Rodgers			
1974	Bobby Nichols	275	Rod Curl	276	Torrey Pines GC, La Jolla, CA	72/N-6,659, S-7,021
			Gene Littler			
1975	J.C. Snead*	279	Raymond Floyd	279	Torrey Pines GC, La Jolla, CA	72/N-6,659, S-7,021
			Bobby Nichols			
1976	J.C. Snead	272	Don Bies	273	Torrey Pines GC, La Jolla, CA	72/N-6,659, S-7,021
1977	Tom Watson	269	Larry Nelson	274	Torrey Pines GC, La Jolla, CA	72/N-6,659, S-7,021
			John Schroeder			
1978	Jay Haas	278	Andy Bean	281	Torrey Pines GC, La Jolla, CA	72/N-6,659, S-7,021
			Gene Littler			
			John Schroeder			
1979	Fuzzy Zoeller	282	Bill Kratzert	287	Torrey Pines GC, La Jolla, CA	72/N-6,659, S-7,021
			Wayne Levi			
			Artie McNickle			
			Tom Watson			
1980	Tom Watson*	275	D.A. Weibring	275	Torrey Pines GC, La Jolla, CA	72/N-6,659, S-7,021
WICKES/ANDY WILLIAMS SAN DIEGO OPEN						
1981	Bruce Lietzke*	278	Raymond Floyd	278	Torrey Pines GC, La Jolla, CA	72/N-6,659, S-7,021
			Tom Jenkins			
1982	Johnny Miller	270	Jack Nicklaus	271	Torrey Pines GC, La Jolla, CA	72/N-6,659, S-7,021
ISUZU/ANDY WILLIAMS SAN DIEGO OPEN						
1983	Gary Hallberg	271	Tom Kite	272	Torrey Pines GC, La Jolla, CA	72/N-6,659, S-7,021
1984	Gary Koch*	272	Gary Hallberg	272	Torrey Pines GC, La Jolla, CA	72/N-6,659, S-7,021
1985	Woody Blackburn*	269	Ron Streck	269	Torrey Pines GC, La Jolla, CA	72/N-6,659, S-7,021
SHEARSON LEHMAN BROTHERS ANDY WILLIAMS OPEN						
1986	Bob Tway~*	204	Bernhard Langer	204	Torrey Pines GC, La Jolla, CA	72/N-6,659, S-7,021
1987	George Burns	266	J.C. Snead	270	Torrey Pines GC, La Jolla, CA	72/N-6,659, S-7,021
			Bobby Wadkins			
SHEARSON LEHMAN HUTTON ANDY WILLIAMS OPEN						
1988	Steve Pate	269	Jay Haas	270	Torrey Pines GC, La Jolla, CA	72/N-6,659, S-7,021
SHEARSON LEHMAN HUTTON OPEN						
1989	Greg Twiggs	271	Steve Elkington	273	Torrey Pines GC, La Jolla, CA	72/N-6,659, S-7,021
			Brad Faxon			
			Mark O'Meara			
			Mark Wiebe			
1990	Dan Forsman	275	Tommy Armour III	277	Torrey Pines GC, La Jolla, CA	72/N-6,659, S-7,021
SHEARSON LEHMAN BROTHERS OPEN						
1991	Jay Don Blake	268	Bill Sander	270	Torrey Pines GC, La Jolla, CA	72/N-6,659, S-7,021
BUICK INVITATIONAL OF CALIFORNIA						
1992	Steve Pate~	200	Chip Beck	201	Torrey Pines GC, La Jolla, CA	72/N-6,659, S-7,021
1993	Phil Mickelson	278	Dave Rummells	282	Torrey Pines GC, La Jolla, CA	72/N-6,659, S-7,021
1994	Craig Stadler	268	Steve Lowery	269	Torrey Pines GC, La Jolla, CA	72/N-6,592, S-7,000
1995	Peter Jacobsen	269	Mark Calcavecchia	273	Torrey Pines GC, La Jolla, CA	72/N-6,592, S-7,000
			Mike Hulbert			
			Hal Sutton			
			Kirk Triplett			
BUICK INVITATIONAL						
1996	Davis Love III	269	Phil Mickelson	271	Torrey Pines GC, La Jolla, CA	72/N-6,592, S-7,022
1997	Mark O'Meara	275	Donnie Hammond	277	Torrey Pines GC, La Jolla, CA	72/N-6,592, S-7,022
			David Ogrin			
			Mike Hulbert			
			Lee Janzen			
			Jesper Parnevik			
			Craig Stadler			
			Duffy Waldorf			
1998	Scott Simpson~*	204	Skip Kendall	204	Torrey Pines GC, La Jolla, CA	72/N-6,592, S-7,000
1999	Tiger Woods	266	Billy Ray Brown	268	Torrey Pines GC, La Jolla, CA	72/N-6,854, S-7,000
2000	Phil Mickelson	270	Shigeki Maruyama	274	Torrey Pines GC, La Jolla, CA	72/N-6,874, S-7,055
			Tiger Woods			
2001	Phil Mickelson*	269	Frank Lickliter	269	Torrey Pines GC, La Jolla, CA	72/N-6,874, S-7,055
			Davis Love III			
2002	Jose M. Olazabal	275	J.L. Lewis	276	Torrey Pines GC, La Jolla, CA	72/N-6,874, S-7,568
			Mark O'Meara			
2003	Tiger Woods	272	Carl Pettersson	276	Torrey Pines GC, La Jolla, CA	72/N-6,874, S-7,568
2004	John Daly*	278	Luke Donald	278	Torrey Pines GC, La Jolla, CA	72/N-6,874, S-7,568
			Chris Riley			

*KEY: * = Playoff N = North S = South ~ = Weather-shortened # = Amateur*

2004 Nissan Open

[Seventh of 48 official events]

Winner: MIKE WEIR
66-64-66-71 267 (-17) $864,000

Riviera Country Club

Pacific Palisades, CA

February 19-22, 2004

Purse: $4,800,000
Par: 35-36—71
Yards: 7,260

LEADERS: First Round—Shaun Micheel and Shigeki Maruyama carded 7-under-par 64s to lead Hank Kuehne by one. Four players were two back. **Second Round**—Maruyama and Mike Weir equaled the 36-hole tournament record at 12-under-par 130. Briny Baird and Scott McCarron were one back. **Third Round**—Weir moved to a 54-hole tournament record 17-under-par 196 to take a five-stroke lead over Maruyama. Jeff Maggert was six shots back.

CUT: 78 players at 1-under-par 141 from a field of 144 professionals.

PRO-AM: $10,000. Jay Haas and Jonathan Kaye, 56, $1,800 each.

WEATHER: Mostly cloudy Thursday with high temperatures of 62. Winds E-NE 5-15 mph. Play was suspended due to darkness at 5:33 p.m. with 10 players still on the course. Those players were back in position Friday at 7:30 a.m. with the second round resuming as scheduled at 7a.m. Mostly cloudy with occasional rain showers, some moderate, Friday through Sunday. Highs in the upper-50s with low temperatures in the upper-40s.

Check out the 2005 Nissan Open, February 17-20 on USA/ABC

ORDER OF FINISH

Mike Weir	1	66-64-66-71	267	$864,000.00
Shigeki Maruyama	2	64-66-71-67	268	518,400.00
Stuart Appleby	3	70-64-70-66	270	326,400.00
John Daly	4	68-64-72-67	271	230,400.00
Hank Kuehne	5	65-72-68-67	272	192,000.00
Kirk Triplett	6	66-67-72-68	273	172,800.00
J.J. Henry	T7	71-69-65-69	274	149,600.00
Jay Williamson	T7	69-69-72-64	274	149,600.00
Tiger Woods	T7	72-66-72-64	274	149,600.00
Briny Baird	T10	69-62-73-71	275	110,400.00
Tim Clark	T10	72-69-64-70	275	110,400.00
Jeff Maggert	T10	67-66-69-73	275	110,400.00
Loren Roberts	T10	70-65-69-71	275	110,400.00
Bob Tway	T10	68-67-71-69	275	110,400.00
Robert Allenby	T15	66-69-72-69	276	76,800.00
Brent Geiberger	T15	70-67-69-70	276	76,800.00
Brandt Jobe	T15	72-69-66-69	276	76,800.00
Corey Pavin	T15	68-69-72-67	276	76,800.00
Rory Sabbatini	T15	70-67-71-68	276	76,800.00
Sergio Garcia	T20	71-65-72-69	277	55,920.00
Neal Lancaster	T20	69-68-72-68	277	55,920.00
Scott McCarron	T20	66-65-72-74	277	55,920.00
Tim Petrovic	T20	68-68-74-67	277	55,920.00
Stephen Ames	T24	70-67-72-69	278	37,140.00
Russ Cochran (Q)	T24	67-66-73-72	278	37,140.00
Joe Durant	T24	71-65-72-70	278	$37,140.00
Mathias Gronberg	T24	68-69-71-70	278	37,140.00
Shaun Micheel	T24	64-70-73-71	278	37,140.00
Carl Pettersson	T24	68-69-68-73	278	37,140.00
Vijay Singh	T24	71-70-68-69	278	37,140.00
Hidemichi Tanaka	T24	72-68-71-67	278	37,140.00
Steve Elkington	T32	73-68-68-70	279	25,988.58
Aaron Baddeley	T32	70-66-69-74	279	25,988.57
Stewart Cink	T32	69-67-70-73	279	25,988.57
Fred Funk	T32	71-66-71-71	279	25,988.57
Tim Herron	T32	69-64-73-73	279	25,988.57
Jose Maria Olazabal	T32	71-65-74-69	279	25,988.57
Paul Stankowski	T32	69-68-70-72	279	25,988.57
Michael Allen	T39	71-66-70-73	280	19,680.00
Chad Campbell	T39	70-71-69-70	280	19,680.00
Jay Haas	T39	71-66-70-73	280	19,680.00
Fredrik Jacobson	T39	72-69-73-66	280	19,680.00
Kevin Sutherland	T39	69-69-71-71	280	19,680.00
Paul Azinger	T44	74-64-73-70	281	14,166.86
Chris DiMarco	T44	70-67-72-72	281	14,166.86
Joe Ogilvie	T44	67-73-69-72	281	14,166.86
Bo Van Pelt	T44	68-73-69-71	281	14,166.86
Lee Westwood (S)	T44	73-67-67-74	281	14,166.86
Carlos Franco	T44	69-72-70-70	281	14,166.85
Hal Sutton	T44	72-68-71-70	281	14,166.85
Billy Andrade	T51	69-68-73-72	282	11,366.40
Tom Byrum	T51	69-72-70-71	282	11,366.40
Tom Carter	T51	70-71-68-73	282	$11,366.40
Per-Ulrik Johansson (S)	T51	71-68-71-72	282	11,366.40
Bernhard Langer	T51	73-68-69-72	282	11,366.40
Rich Beem	T56	73-67-71-72	283	10,848.00
Zach Johnson	T56	71-68-77-67	283	10,848.00
Tom Lehman	T56	70-70-72-71	283	10,848.00
Woody Austin	T59	67-69-71-77	284	10,416.00
Fred Couples	T59	66-70-77-71	284	10,416.00
Ben Crane	T59	73-67-73-71	284	10,416.00
Frank Lickliter II	T59	74-65-70-75	284	10,416.00
Spike McRoy	T59	71-69-71-73	284	10,416.00
Justin Rose	T59	75-65-67-77	284	10,416.00
K.J. Choi	T65	69-72-71-73	285	10,032.00
Phillip Price (S)	T65	68-73-74-70	285	10,032.00
Luke Donald	T67	69-71-74-72	286	9,792.00
Steve Flesch	T67	70-69-72-75	286	9,792.00
Lee Janzen	T67	70-66-76-74	286	9,792.00
Thomas Bjorn	T70	69-71-73-74	287	9,504.00
Jeff Brehaut	T70	69-72-70-76	287	9,504.00
Brenden Pappas	T70	68-73-73-73	287	9,504.00
Charles Howell III	73	70-71-75-72	288	9,312.00
Matt Gogel	T74	70-70-72-77	289	9,120.00
Jerry Kelly	T74	71-69-76-73	289	9,120.00
Pat Perez	T74	71-68-75-75	289	9,120.00
John Riegger	77	68-71-73-78	290	8,928.00
Jesper Parnevik	78	69-69-83-74	295	8,832.00

(Q) = Open Qualifier; (S) = Sponsor Exemption; (T) = Tie

The following players did not finish (C=cut, W=withdrew)

C—142-Steve Allan, Tommy Armour III, Peter Jacobsen, Kent Jones, Peter Lonard, David Toms. **143-**Cameron Beckman, Notah Begay III, David Berganio, Jr., Angel Cabrera, Ben Curtis, Robert Damron, Niclas Fasth, Cliff Kresge, Mark O'Meara, Arron Oberholser, Ryan Palmer, Eduardo Romero, Dean Wilson. **144-**Craig Barlow, Pat Bates, Bob Burns, Daniel Chopra, Geoffrey Dean, Brad Faxon, Todd Fischer, Stephen Leaney, Billy Mayfair, David Peoples, Tom Pernice, Jr., Nick Price, Brett Quigley, Steve Stricker. **145-**Alex Cejka, Jonathan Kaye, Skip Kendall, Rocco Mediate, Craig Perks, Esteban Toledo. **146-**Glen Hnatiuk, Gene Sauers. **147-**Fulton Allem, Mark Brooks, Danny Ellis, Paul Holtby, Richard S. Johnson, Steve Lowery, Daisuke Maruyama, Hirofumi Miyase, Geoff Ogilvy, Heath Slocum. **148-**Olin Browne, Scott Heyn, Tetsuji Hiratsuka, Kevin Na. **149-**David Gossett, Patrick Sheehan. **150-**Darren Clarke, Bob Estes, Ian Leggatt, John Rollins. **151-**David Frost. **152-**Patrick Moore. **153-**Robin Freeman, John Senden. **W—**Duffy Waldorf.

Fellow Canadians rooting for Mike Weir.

TOURNAMENT HISTORY

Year	Winner	Score	Runner-up	Score	Location	Par/Yards
LOS ANGELES OPEN						
1926	Harry Cooper	279	George Von Elm	282	Los Angeles CC (North), Los Angeles, CA	71/6,895
1927	Bobby Cruickshank	282	Ed Dudley	288	El Caballero CC, Tarzana, CA	71/6,830
			Charles Guest			
1928	Macdonald Smith	284	Harry Cooper	287	Wilshire CC, Los Angeles, CA	71/6,442
1929	Macdonald Smith	285	Tommy Armour	291	Riviera CC, Pacific Palisades, CA	71/7,029
1930	Densmore Shute	296	Bobby Cruickshank	300	Riviera CC, Pacific Palisades, CA	71/7,029
			Horton Smith			
1931	Ed Dudley	285	Al Espinosa	287	Wilshire CC, Los Angeles, CA	71/6,442
			Eddie Loos			
1932	Macdonald Smith	281	Leo Diegel	285	Hillcrest CC, Los Angeles, CA	71/6,911
			Olin Dutra			
			Joe Kirkwood, Sr.			
			Dick Metz			
1933	Craig Wood	281	Leo Diegel	285	Wilshire CC, Los Angeles, CA	71/6,442
			Willie Hunter			
1934	Macdonald Smith	280	Willie Hunter	288	Los Angeles CC (North), Los Angeles, CA	71/6,895
			Bill Mehlhorn			
1935	Vic Ghezzi*	285	Johnny Revolta	285	Los Angeles CC (North), Los Angeles, CA	71/6,895
1936	Jimmy Hines	280	Henry Picard	284	Los Angeles CC (North), Los Angeles, CA	71/6,895
			Jimmy Thomson			
1937	Harry Cooper	274	Ralph Guldahl	279	Griffith Park (Wilson), Los Angeles, CA	72/6,802
			Horton Smith		Griffith Park (Harding), Los Angeles, CA	72/6,488
1938	Jimmy Thomson	273	Johnny Revolta	277	Griffith Park (Wilson), Los Angeles, CA	72/6,802
					Griffith Park (Harding), Los Angeles, CA	72/6,488
1939	Jimmy Demaret	274	Harold McSpaden	281	Griffith Park (Wilson), Los Angeles, CA	72/6,802
					Griffith Park (Harding), Los Angeles, CA	72/6,488
1940	Lawson Little	282	Clayton Heafner	283	Los Angeles CC (North), Los Angeles, CA	71/6,895
1941	Johnny Bulla	281	Craig Wood	283	Riviera CC, Pacific Palisades, CA	71/7,029
1942	Ben Hogan*	282	Jimmy Thomson	282	Hillcrest CC, Los Angeles, CA	71/6,911

Nissan Open

NOTES

With his win at the 2004 Nissan Open, ***Mike Weir*** *became the second-winningest left-hander in PGA TOUR history with seven career wins, surpassing* ***Bob Charles'*** *six.* ***Phil Mickelson*** *leads all southpaws with 23 PGA TOUR victories.*

With his second consecutive victory at the Nissan Open, ***Mike Weir*** *became the sixth player in tournament history to notch back-to-back wins and the first since* ***Corey Pavin*** *(1994-95). The others were* ***Macdonald Smith*** *(1928-29),* ***Ben Hogan*** *(1947-48),* ***Paul Harney*** *(1964-65) and* ***Arnold Palmer*** *(1966-67). Weir is the 20th player to post multiple wins at the Nissan Open.*

Fourteen of the last 15 winners at the Nissan Open have been over age 30. ***Ernie Els****, at age 29, won the 1999 Nissan Open and was the last player under age 30 to win at Riviera Country Club.*

In 2004, ***Mike Weir*** *set the 54-hole tournament record at 17-under-par 196 to take a commanding five-stroke advantage over* ***Shigeki Maruyama*** *into the final round. The previous 54-hole record of 16-under-par 197 was set by* ***Fred Couples*** *in 1990.*

FRED COUPLES

Tournament Record:
264, Lanny Wadkins, 1985

Current Course Record:
61, Ted Tryba, 1999

Other Course Record:
61, George Archer, 1983 (Rancho Municipal GC)

TOURNAMENT HISTORY

Year	Winner	Score	Runner-up	Score	Location	Par/Yards
1943	No Tournament					
1944	Harold McSpaden	278	Johnny Bulla	281	Wilshire CC, Los Angeles, CA	71/6,442
1945	Sam Snead	283	Harold McSpaden	284	Riviera CC, Pacific Palisades, CA	71/7,029
			Byron Nelson			
1946	Byron Nelson	284	Ben Hogan	289	Riviera CC, Pacific Palisades, CA	71/7,029
1947	Ben Hogan	280	Toney Penna	283	Riviera CC, Pacific Palisades, CA	71/7,029
1948	Ben Hogan	275	Lloyd Mangrum	279	Riviera CC, Pacific Palisades, CA	71/7,029
1949	Lloyd Mangrum	284	E.J. Harrison	287	Riviera CC, Pacific Palisades, CA	71/7,029
1950	Sam Snead*	280	Ben Hogan	280	Riviera CC, Pacific Palisades, CA	71/7,029
1951	Lloyd Mangrum	280	Henry Ransom	281	Riviera CC, Pacific Palisades, CA	71/7,029
1952	Tommy Bolt*	289	Jack Burke, Jr.	289	Riviera CC, Pacific Palisades, CA	71/7,029
1953	Lloyd Mangrum	280	Jack Burke, Jr.	285	Riviera CC, Pacific Palisades, CA	71/7,029
1954	Fred Wampler	281	Jerry Barber	282	Fox Hills CC, Culver City, CA	N/A
			Chick Harbert			
1955	Gene Littler	276	Ted Kroll	278	Inglewood CC, Inglewood, CA	N/A
1956	Lloyd Mangrum	272	Jerry Barber	275	Rancho Municipal GC, Los Angeles, CA	71/6,827
1957	Doug Ford	280	Jay Hebert	281	Rancho Municipal GC, Los Angeles, CA	71/6,827
1958	Frank Stranahan	275	E. J. Harrison	278	Rancho Municipal GC, Los Angeles, CA	71/6,827
1959	Ken Venturi	278	Art Wall	280	Rancho Municipal GC, Los Angeles, CA	71/6,827
1960	Dow Finsterwald	280	Bill Collins	283	Rancho Municipal GC, Los Angeles, CA	71/6,827
			Jay Hebert			
			Dave Ragan			
1961	Bob Goalby	275	Eric Brown	278	Rancho Municipal GC, Los Angeles, CA	71/6,827
			Art Wall			
1962	Phil Rodgers	268	Bob Goalby	277	Rancho Municipal GC, Los Angeles, CA	71/6,827
			Fred Hawkins			
1963	Arnold Palmer	274	Al Balding	277	Rancho Municipal GC, Los Angeles, CA	71/6,827
			Gary Player			
1964	Paul Harney	280	Bobby Nichols	281	Rancho Municipal GC, Los Angeles, CA	71/6,827
1965	Paul Harney	276	Dan Sikes	279	Rancho Municipal GC, Los Angeles, CA	71/6,827
1966	Arnold Palmer	273	Miller Barber	276	Rancho Municipal GC, Los Angeles, CA	71/6,827
			Paul Harney			
1967	Arnold Palmer	269	Gay Brewer	274	Rancho Municipal GC, Los Angeles, CA	71/6,827
1968	Billy Casper	274	Arnold Palmer	277	Brookside GC, Pasadena, CA	71/7,021
1969	Charles Sifford*	276	Harold Henning	276	Rancho Municipal GC, Los Angeles, CA	71/6,827
1970	Billy Casper*	276	Hale Irwin	276	Rancho Municipal GC. Los Angeles, CA	71/6,827
GLEN CAMPBELL LOS ANGELES OPEN						
1971	Bob Lunn*	274	Billy Casper	274	Rancho Municipal GC, Los Angeles, CA	71/6,827
1972	George Archer*	270	Tommy Aaron	270	Rancho Municipal GC, Los Angeles, CA	71/6,827
			Dave Hill			
1973	Rod Funseth	276	Don Bies	279	Riviera CC, Pacific Palisades, CA	71/7,029
			David Graham			
			Dave Hill			
			Tom Weiskopf			
1974	Dave Stockton	276	John Mahaffey	278	Riviera CC, Pacific Palisades, CA	71/7,029
			Sam Snead			
1975	Pat Fitzsimons	275	Tom Kite	279	Riviera CC, Pacific Palisades, CA	71/7,029
1976	Hale Irwin	272	Tom Watson	274	Riviera CC, Pacific Palisades, CA	71/7,029
1977	Tom Purtzer	273	Lanny Wadkins	274	Riviera CC, Pacific Palisades, CA	71/7,029
1978	Gil Morgan	278	Jack Nicklaus	280	Riviera CC, Pacific Palisades, CA	71/7,029
1979	Lanny Wadkins	276	Lon Hinkle	277	Riviera CC, Pacific Palisades, CA	71/7,029
1980	Tom Watson	276	Bob Gilder	277	Riviera CC, Pacific Palisades, CA	71/7,029
			Don January			
1981	Johnny Miller	270	Tom Weiskopf	272	Riviera CC, Pacific Palisades, CA	71/7,029
1982	Tom Watson*	271	Johnny Miller	271	Riviera CC, Pacific Palisades, CA	71/7,029
1983	Gil Morgan	270	Gibby Gilbert	272	Rancho Municipal GC, Los Angeles, CA	71/6,827
			Mark McCumber			
			Lanny Wadkins			
LOS ANGELES OPEN						
1984	David Edwards	279	Jack Renner	282	Riviera CC, Pacific Palisades, CA	71/7,029
1985	Lanny Wadkins	264	Hal Sutton	271	Riviera CC, Pacific Palisades, CA	71/7,029
1986	Doug Tewell	270	Clarence Rose	277	Riviera CC, Pacific Palisades, CA	71/7,029
LOS ANGELES OPEN PRESENTED BY NISSAN						
1987	Tze-Chung Chen*	275	Ben Crenshaw	275	Riviera CC, Pacific Palisades, CA	71/7,029
1988	Chip Beck	267	Mac O'Grady	271	Riviera CC, Pacific Palisades, CA	71/7,029
			Bill Sander			
NISSAN LOS ANGELES OPEN						
1989	Mark Calcavecchia	272	Sandy Lyle	273	Riviera CC, Pacific Palisades, CA	71/7,029
1990	Fred Couples	266	Gil Morgan	269	Riviera CC, Pacific Palisades, CA	71/7,029
1991	Ted Schulz	272	Jeff Sluman	273	Riviera CC, Pacific Palisades, CA	71/7,029
1992	Fred Couples*	269	Davis Love III	269	Riviera CC, Pacific Palisades, CA	71/7,029
1993	Tom Kite~	206	Dave Barr	209	Riviera CC, Pacific Palisades, CA	71/7,029
			Fred Couples			
			Donnie Hammond			
			Payne Stewart			
1994	Corey Pavin	271	Fred Couples	273	Riviera CC, Pacific Palisades, CA	71/6,946
NISSAN OPEN						
1995	Corey Pavin	268	Jay Don Blake	271	Riviera CC, Pacific Palisades, CA	71/6,946

SECTION 3 TOURNAMENT HISTORIES

Nissan Open

NOTES

*Holding a five-stroke lead heading into the final round, **Mike Weir** was able to hold off **Shigeki Maruyama** by a single stroke with an even-par 71 on Sunday – his first win in six attempts when holding at least a share of the 54-hole lead on the PGA TOUR.*

BRINY BAIRD

***Briny Baird**'s 9-under-par 62 in the second round was just one shot off of the Riviera Country Club and Nissan Open record. **Ted Tryba** shot 61 at Riviera in 1999. **George Archer** shot 61 in 1983 when the tournament was held at the Rancho Park Country Club. Baird's round equaled the best second round in tournament history, previously set by **Larry Mize** in 1985 and **Kenny Perry** in 1995.*

*Five of the six past Nissan Open champions in the field made the cut in 2004: **Mike Weir** (2003), **Kirk Triplett** (2000), **Robert Allenby** (2001), **Fred Couples** (1990, 1992) and **Corey Pavin** (1994-95). **Billy Mayfair** (1998) was the only former winner to miss the cut.*

*Two-time champion **Fred Couples** has played in every Nissan Open since 1982 and has a total of 11 top-10s in 23 starts.*

***Tiger Woods** has played the Nissan Open nine times, having made his debut on the PGA TOUR in 1992 as a 16-year-old amateur playing on a Sponsor Exemption. As a professional, Woods has played in the Nissan Open seven times with four top-10 finishes. His best performance was solo second, losing in a playoff to **Billy Mayfair** in 1998 at Valencia Country Club.*

TOURNAMENT HISTORY

Year	Winner	Score	Runner-up	Score	Location	Par/Yards
1996	Craig Stadler	278	Kenny Perry Mark Brooks Fred Couples Scott Simpson Mark Wiebe	279	Riviera CC, Pacific Palisades, CA	71/6,946
1997	Nick Faldo	272	Craig Stadler	275	Riviera CC, Pacific Palisades, CA	71/6,946
1998	Billy Mayfair*	272	Tiger Woods	272	Valencia CC, Valencia, CA	71/6,987
1999	Ernie Els	270	Ted Tryba Tiger Woods Davis Love III	272	Riviera CC, Pacific Palisades, CA	71/6,953
2000	Kirk Triplett	272	Jesper Parnevik	273	Riviera CC, Pacific Palisades, CA	71/7,055
2001	Robert Allenby*	276	Brandel Chamblee Toshi Izawa Dennis Paulson Jeff Sluman Bob Tway	276	Riviera CC, Pacific Palisades, CA	71/7,055
2002	Len Mattiace	269	Brad Faxon Rory Sabbatini Scott McCarron	270	Riviera CC, Pacific Palisades, CA	71/7,174
2003	Mike Weir*	275	Charles Howell	275	Riviera CC, Pacific Palisades, CA	71/7,222
2004	Mike Weir	267	Shigeki Maruyama	268	Riviera CC, Pacific Palisades, CA	71/7,222

*KEY: * = Playoff ~ = Weather-shortened*

Mike Weir tees off during the 2004 Nissan Open.

2004 WGC-Accenture Match Play Championship

[Eighth of 48 official events]

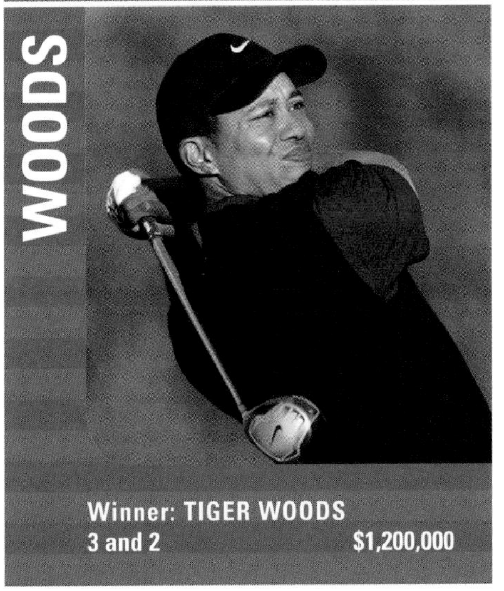

Winner: TIGER WOODS
3 and 2 $1,200,000

La Costa Resort and Spa

Carlsbad, CA

February 25-29, 2004

Purse: $7,000,000
Par: 36-36—72
Yards: 7,247

WEATHER: On Wednesday, partly sunny with increasing clouds in the afternoon and temperatures reaching 60 degrees. Winds out of the SW up to 12 mph. Heavy rains overnight, 1.5 inches that forced Thursday postponement. Friday morning, play was delayed 10 minutes due to thunderstorms in the area. High of 58 degrees on Friday with winds W-NW up to 12 mph in the late afternoon. On Saturday, cool in the early morning warming up to 58 degrees in the afternoon. Winds W-NW up to 12 mph. Sunday, sunny and pleasant, with a high of 64 degrees. Light winds W-NW up to eight mph.

Check out the 2005 WGC-Accenture Match Play Championship, February 23-27 on ESPN/ABC

RESULTS

First-Round Results

Match #1	Padraig Harrington (9) def. Toshi Izawa (56)	2 and 1
Match #2	Bob Estes (41) def. Scott Verplank (24)	19 holes
Match #3	Duffy Waldorf (53) def. Jonathan Kaye (12)	5 and 4
Match #4	Ian Poulter (44) def. Chris Riley (21)	1-up
Match #5	Darren Clarke (10) def. Eduardo Romero (55)	25 holes
Match #6	Alex Cejka (42) def. Justin Leonard (23)	4 and 3
Match #7	Stuart Appleby (11) def. Justin Rose (54)	5 and 4
Match #8	Chris DiMarco (22) def. Michael Campbell (43)	2-up
Match #9	David Toms (8) def. Niclas Fasth (57)	19 holes
Match #10	Shaun Micheel (40) def. Paul Casey (25)	21 holes
Match #11	John Huston (60) def. Retief Goosen (5)	2 and 1
Match #12	Peter Lonard (28) def. Rocco Mediate (37)	1-up
Match #13	Kenny Perry (7) def. Jeff Sluman (58)	6 and 4
Match #14	Steve Flesch (39) def. Brad Faxon (26)	19 holes
Match #15	Phil Mickelson (6) def. Lee Westwood (59)	3 and 1
Match #16	Ben Curtis (38) def. Charles Howell III (27)	2-up
Match #17	Thomas Bjorn (16) def. Scott Hoch (49)	4 and 3
Match #18	Fredrik Jacobson (17) def. Phillip Price (48)	5 and 4
Match #19	Colin Montgomerie (52) def. Nick Price (13)	20 holes
Match #20	Stewart Cink (45) def. K.J. Choi (20)	4 and 2
Match #21	Chad Campbell (15) def. Tim Herron (50)	3 and 2
Match #22	Loren Roberts (47) def. Jay Haas (18)	1-up
Match #23	Robert Allenby (14) def. Brian Davis (51)	3 and 2
Match #24	Adam Scott (19) def. Miguel Angel Jimenez (46)	2 and 1
Match #25	Tiger Woods (1) def. John Rollins (64)	1-up
Match #26	Trevor Immelman (32) def. Shigeki Maruyama (33)	2 and 1
Match #27	Mike Weir (4) def. Rich Beem (61)	3 and 2
Match #28	Stephen Leaney (29) def. Fred Funk (36)	1-up
Match #29	Vijay Singh (2) def. Shingo Katayama (63)	5 and 3
Match #30	Jerry Kelly (31) def. Sergio Garcia (34)	1-up
Match #31	Davis Love III (3) def. Briny Baird (62)	2-up
Match #32	Fred Couples (35) def. Bob Tway (30)	3 and 2

Players losing in the first round earned $35,000 each.

Second-Round Results

Match #33	Toms def. Micheel	4 and 3
Match #34	Harrington def. Estes	3 and 2
Match #35	Huston def Lonard	1-up
Match #36	Poulter def. Waldorf	7 and 5
Match #37	Perry def. Flesch	1-up
Match #38	Clarke def. Cejka	6 and 5
Match #39	Mickelson def. Curtis	7 and 6
Match #40	DiMarco def. Appleby	19 holes
Match #41	Woods def. Immelman	5 and 4
Match #42	Jacobson def. Bjorn	5 and 4
Match #43	Leaney def. Weir	4 and 2
Match #44	Montgomerie def. Cink	5 and 4
Match #45	Kelly def. Singh	4 and 2
Match #46	Campbell def. Roberts	3 and 1
Match #47	Love def. Couples	3 and 2
Match #48	Scott def. Allenby	23 holes

Players losing in the second round earned $75,000 each.

Third-Round Results

Match #49	Woods def. Jacobson	5 and 4
Match #50	Harrington def. Toms	1-up
Match #51	Leaney def. Montgomerie	1-up
Match #52	Poulter def. Huston	2 and 1
Match #53	Kelly def. Campbell	1-up
Match #54	Clarke def. Perry	3 and 2
Match #55	Love def. Scott	4 and 3
Match #56	Mickelson def. DiMarco	3 and 2

Players losing in the third round earned $115,000 each.

Quarterfinals Results

Match #57	Woods def. Harrington	2 and 1
Match #58	Leaney def. Poulter	1-up
Match #59	Clarke def. Kelly	5 and 3
Match #60	Love def. Mickelson	1-up

Players losing in the quarterfinals earned $225,000 each.

Semifinal Results

Match #61	Woods def. Leaney	2 and 1
Match #62	Love def. Clarke	21 holes

Third-place Match

Match #64	Clarke ($530,000) def. Leaney ($430,000)	2-up

Championship Match - 36 holes

Match #63	Woods ($1,200,000) def. Love ($700,000)	3 and 2

NOTES

*The 2004 first-round match between **Loren Roberts** (age 48) and **Jay Haas** (50), won by Roberts 1-up, pitted two of the three oldest players in last year's field. Haas is the oldest player to tee it up in the history of the WGC-Accenture Match Play Championship. **Eduardo Romero** (49 years) was the second-oldest player in the 2004 field.*

Six of the 32 first-round matches went extra holes, tying the record at the Accenture Match Play Championship set in 2001.

*Of the eight first-time participants at the 2004 WGC-Accenture Match Play Championship, five won at least one match: **Shaun Micheel**, **Ben Curtis**, **Fredrik Jacobson**, **Chad Campbell** and **Ian Poulter**. **Briny Baird**, **John Rollins** and **Brian Davis** did not win.*

TOURNAMENT HISTORY

Year	Winner	Score	Runner-up	Score	Location	Par/Yards
WORLD GOLF CHAMPIONSHIPS–ACCENTURE MATCH PLAY CHAMPIONSHIP						
1999	Jeff Maggert	38 Holes	Andrew Magee		La Costa Resort and Spa, Carlsbad, CA	72/7,022
2000	Darren Clarke	4 and 3	Tiger Woods		La Costa Resort and Spa, Carlsbad, CA	72/7,022
2001	Steve Stricker	2 and 1	Pierre Fulke		The Metropolitan Club, South Oakleigh, Victoria, Australia	72/7,066
2002	Kevin Sutherland	1-up	Scott McCarron		La Costa Resort and Spa, Carlsbad, CA	72/7,022
2003	Tiger Woods	2 and 1	David Toms		La Costa Resort and Spa, Carlsbad, CA	72/7,278
2004	Tiger Woods	3 and 2	Davis Love III		La Costa Resort and Spa, Carlsbad, CA	72/7,247

Tiger Woods on the way to victory.

Woods with the Walter Hagen Cup.

2004 Chrysler Classic of Tucson *[Ninth of 48 official events]*

Winner: HEATH SLOCUM
67-64-70-65 266 (-22) $540,000

Omni Tucson National Golf Resort

Tucson, AZ

February 26-29, 2004

Purse: $3,000,000
Par: 36-36—72
Yards: 7,109

LEADERS: First Round—Frank Lickliter II fired a 9-under 63 to lead Carlos Franco, Steve Allan, Mark Hensby and Per-Ulrik Johansson by two.
Second Round—Heath Slocum moved to 13-under, one ahead of Bill Glasson. Michael Clark II, Geoff Ogilvy, Harrison Frazar and Hensby were two back.
Third Round—Aaron Baddeley and Slocum shared the lead at 15-under 201. Mike Heinen, Franco and Hensby were one back.

CUT: 72 players at 4-under-par 140 from a field of 143 professionals and one amateur.

PRO-AM: $10,000. Rory Sabbatini, 49, $2,000.

WEATHER: Sunny with temperatures reaching the 70s on Thursday. Cloudy with light rain on Friday morning. Temperatures in the 50s-60s with SW winds 10-20 mph. Play suspended at 3:31 p.m. MT and then postponed at 4:25 p.m. for the day. Second round resumed at 7:45 a.m. Saturday. A mix of sun and clouds with temperatures in the 50s and W winds 10-15 mph. Partly cloudy Sunday with temperatures in the upper 50s. Winds out of the W 10-15 mph.

Check out the 2005 Chrysler Classic of Tucson, February 24-27 on USA

ORDER OF FINISH

Heath Slocum	1	67-64-70-65	266	$540,000.00
Aaron Baddeley	2	68-69-64-66	267	324,000.00
Harrison Frazar	T3	66-67-71-66	270	156,000.00
Mark Hensby	T3	65-68-69-68	270	156,000.00
Rory Sabbatini	T3	69-68-69-64	270	156,000.00
Bill Glasson	T6	66-66-71-68	271	104,250.00
Per-Ulrik Johansson	T6	65-69-69-68	271	104,250.00
Tim Clark	T8	66-68-72-66	272	84,000.00
Todd Fischer	T8	68-68-69-67	272	84,000.00
Carlos Franco	T8	65-69-68-70	272	84,000.00
Mike Heinen	T8	66-71-65-70	272	84,000.00
Angel Cabrera	T12	66-71-68-68	273	63,000.00
Dan Olsen	T12	69-69-66-69	273	63,000.00
Garrett Willis	T12	71-69-67-66	273	63,000.00
Notah Begay III	T15	68-70-69-67	274	52,500.00
Michael Clark II	T15	68-65-72-69	274	52,500.00
Mark Calcavecchia	T17	67-69-69-70	275	45,000.00
Hunter Mahan	T17	69-68-69-69	275	45,000.00
Geoff Ogilvy	T17	67-66-72-70	275	45,000.00
Brian Bateman	T20	73-66-69-68	276	31,285.72
Dennis Paulson	T20	67-72-69-68	276	31,285.72
Hidemichi Tanaka	T20	69-70-69-68	276	31,285.72
Danny Briggs	T20	67-72-70-67	276	31,285.71
Brian Gay	T20	69-70-70-67	276	$31,285.71
Blaine McCallister	T20	71-67-69-69	276	31,285.71
Ted Purdy	T20	69-66-72-69	276	31,285.71
Cameron Beckman	T27	70-68-70-69	277	20,400.00
David Branshaw	T27	70-67-71-69	277	20,400.00
Frank Lickliter II	T27	63-73-72-69	277	20,400.00
Billy Mayfair	T27	71-68-70-68	277	20,400.00
Larry Mize (S)	T27	68-72-70-67	277	20,400.00
Patrick Sheehan	T27	68-69-72-68	277	20,400.00
Chris Smith	T27	68-70-70-69	277	20,400.00
Olin Browne	T34	66-72-70-70	278	15,150.00
David Edwards	T34	69-68-71-70	278	15,150.00
Steve Elkington	T34	69-66-70-73	278	15,150.00
J.L. Lewis	T34	71-67-69-71	278	15,150.00
Steve Pate	T34	71-69-68-70	278	15,150.00
Vaughn Taylor	T34	66-68-69-75	278	15,150.00
Brent Geiberger	T40	67-70-72-70	279	12,300.00
Todd Hamilton	T40	70-68-70-71	279	12,300.00
Dean Wilson	T40	69-71-69-70	279	12,300.00
Russ Cochran	T43	67-70-72-71	280	9,620.00
Tripp Isenhour	T43	71-69-70-70	280	9,620.00
Cliff Kresge	T43	70-67-71-72	280	9,620.00
John Maginnes	T43	70-69-68-73	280	9,620.00
Brenden Pappas	T43	70-69-75-66	280	9,620.00
Omar Uresti	T43	68-70-71-71	280	9,620.00
Ricky Barnes (S)	T49	68-72-75-66	281	$7,404.00
David Frost	T49	68-71-70-72	281	7,404.00
Steve Lowery	T49	71-67-73-70	281	7,404.00
Deane Pappas	T49	70-70-75-66	281	7,404.00
Tag Ridings	T49	67-68-72-74	281	7,404.00
Pat Bates	T54	71-69-72-70	282	6,780.00
Guy Boros	T54	68-71-71-72	282	6,780.00
D.J. Brigman	T54	70-67-71-74	282	6,780.00
Kris Cox	T54	69-69-75-69	282	6,780.00
Keiichiro Fukabori	T54	72-67-73-70	282	6,780.00
Dicky Pride	T54	71-68-72-71	282	6,780.00
Brian Watts	T54	67-72-72-71	282	6,780.00
Jason Bohn	T61	71-68-69-75	283	6,480.00
Andre Stolz	T61	69-70-72-72	283	6,480.00
Don Yrene	T61	68-72-71-72	283	6,480.00
Tom Lehman	64	67-70-72-75	284	6,360.00
Steve Allan	T65	65-72-76-72	285	6,240.00
Greg Chalmers	T65	70-70-70-75	285	6,240.00
Brian Henninger	T65	66-71-72-76	285	6,240.00
Roger Tambellini	68	69-69-75-73	286	6,120.00
John Daly	T69	67-73-76-74	290	6,000.00
Joel Kribel	T69	69-70-75-76	290	6,000.00
Casey Martin (S)	T69	69-70-77-74	290	6,000.00

(Q) = Open Qualifier; (S) = Sponsor Exemption; (T) = Tie

The following players did not finish (C=cut, W=withdrew, A=amateur)

C—141-Arjun Atwal, Craig Bowden, Glen Day, John Douma, Hirofumi Miyase, Joe Ogilvie, Don Pooley, Boyd Summerhays, Ted Tryba, Willie Wood. **142**-Rich Barcelo, Jeff Brehaut, Jim Carter, Jason Dufner, Lucas Glover, Mathias Gronberg, Donnie Hammond, Kevin Muncrief, Sean Murphy, Roland Thatcher. **143**-Mark Brooks, Tom Carter, Daniel Chopra, Jay Delsing, Ken Duke, Kevin Na, David Peoples, David Sutherland, Kevin Sutherland, Stan Utley, Mark Wiebe, Mark Wilson. **144**-Jay Don Blake, Trevor Dodds, Matt Gogel, Mike Grob, Scott Harrington, Brian Kortan, Chris Nallen (A), Ryan Palmer, Pat Perez, Scott Simpson, Paul Stankowski. **145**-Bob Burns, Carl Paulson, Tommy Tolles, Grant Waite. **146**-Michael Allen, David Berganio, Jr., Bart Bryant, Chris Couch, Scott Hend. **147**-Benoit Beisser, Tom Byrum, Mike Standly. **148**-Patrick Moore, David Morland IV, Jose Maria Olazabal, Brett Upper. **150**-Richard S. Johnson. **153**-John E. Morgan. **157**-Fulton Allem. **W—77**-Jim McGovern, **76**-Tony Rohlik, **74**-Glen Hnatiuk, Robin Freeman, **73**-Jeff Maggert, **72**-Wes Short, Jr., Ian Leggatt, Brad Lardon, Ken Green, **71**-Aaron Barber, **217**-Jay Williamson.

AARON BADDELEY

TOURNAMENT HISTORY

Year	Winner	Score	Runner-up	Score	Location	Par/Yards
TUCSON OPEN						
1945	Ray Mangrum	268	Byron Nelson	269	El Rio G&CC, Tucson, AZ	70/6,418
1946	Jimmy Demaret	268	Herman Barron	272	El Rio G&CC, Tucson, AZ	70/6,418
1947	Jimmy Demaret	264	Ben Hogan	267	El Rio G&CC, Tucson, AZ	70/6,418
1948	Skip Alexander	264	Johnny Palmer	265	El Rio G&CC, Tucson, AZ	70/6,418
1949	Lloyd Mangrum	263	Al Smith	268	El Rio G&CC, Tucson, AZ	70/6,418
1950	Chandler Harper	267	Sam Snead	269	El Rio G&CC, Tucson, AZ	70/6,418
1951	Lloyd Mangrum	269	Jack Burke, Jr	271	El Rio G&CC, Tucson, AZ	70/6,418
			Jim Turnesa			
			Lew Worsham			
1952	Henry Williams	274	Cary Middlecoff	276	El Rio G&CC, Tucson, AZ	70/6,418
1953	Tommy Bolt	265	Chandler Harper	266	El Rio G&CC, Tucson, AZ	70/6,418
1954	No Tournament					
1955	Tommy Bolt	265	Bud Holscher	269	El Rio G&CC, Tucson, AZ	70/6,418
			Art Wall			
1956	Ted Kroll	264	Dow Finsterwald	267	El Rio G&CC, Tucson, AZ	70/6,418
1957	Dow Finsterwald*	269	Don Whitt	269	El Rio G&CC, Tucson, AZ	70/6,418
1958	Lionel Hebert	265	Don January	267	El Rio G&CC, Tucson, AZ	70/6,418
1959	Gene Littler	266	Joe Campbell	267	El Rio G&CC, Tucson, AZ	70/6,418
			Art Wall			
1960	Don January	271	Bob Harris	274	El Rio G&CC, Tucson, AZ	70/6,418
HOME OF THE SUN INVITATIONAL						
1961	Dave Hill*	269	Tommy Bolt	269	El Rio G&CC, Tucson, AZ	70/6,418
			Bud Sullivan			
TUCSON OPEN						
1962	Phil Rodgers	263	Jim Ferrier	266	El Rio G&CC, Tucson, AZ	70/6,418
1963	Don January	266	Gene Littler	277	49er CC, Tucson, AZ	72/6,722
			Phil Rodgers			
1964	Jack Cupit	274	Rex Baxter	276	49er CC, Tucson, AZ	72/6,722
1965	Bob Charles	271	Al Geiberger	275	Tucson National GC, Tucson, AZ	72/7,305
1966	Joe Campbell*	278	Gene Littler	278	Tucson National GC, Tucson, AZ	72/7,305

Chrysler Classic of Tucson

NOTES

*Arizona State University student **Benoit Beisser** Monday qualified for the tournament after his mother Deana signed him up and did not inform him until the night before. Beisser, who was a professional and did not play golf for Arizona State University, missed the cut after rounds of 72-75 in his first PGA TOUR event.*

*2004 winner **Heath Slocum** was the third-round leader in 2002 before finishing in a tie for sixth after a final-round even-par 72. In 2004, after sharing the 54-hole lead with **Aaron Baddeley**, Slocum fired a 7-under 65 to win by a stroke over Baddeley. Slocum, who joined the TOUR in 2001 after winning three times in one season on the Nationwide Tour, earned his first TOUR victory in his 78th start on TOUR.*

FRANK LICKLITER II

*__Heath Slocum__ became the 13th first-time winner in tournament history and the fourth of five since 2000. The only non first-time winner since 2000 was 2003 champion **Frank Lickliter II**.*

*Runner-up **Aaron Baddeley** had played his last 39 holes without a bogey before bogeying the final hole to finish one stroke behind Heath Slocum. Baddeley's three-putt on the final hole was his first of the week. Baddeley led the tournament with a putting average of 1.523 and needed just 95 putts over four rounds to become the second player in 2004 to finish a tournament with less than 100 putts. **Mike Weir** used 99 putts to win the Nissan Open the week prior.*

Tournament Record:
263, Loyd Mangrum, 1949 (El Rio G&CC); Phil Rodgers, 1962 (El Rio G&CC); Johnny Miller, 1975 (Tucson National)
Current Course Record:
61, Johnny Miller, 1975
Tournament Course Record:
60, David Frost, 1990 (Randolph Park GC)

TOURNAMENT HISTORY

Year	Winner	Score	Runner-up	Score	Location	Par/Yards
1967	Arnold Palmer	273	Chuck Courtney	274	Tucson National GC, Tucson, AZ	72/7,305
1968	George Knudson	273	Frank Beard Frank Boynton	274	Tucson National GC, Tucson, AZ	72/7,305
1969	Lee Trevino	271	Miller Barber	278	Tucson National GC, Tucson, AZ	72/7,305
1970	Lee Trevino*	275	Bob Murphy	275	Tucson National GC, Tucson, AZ	72/7,305
1971	J.C. Snead	273	Dale Douglass	274	Tucson National GC, Tucson, AZ	72/7,305
1972	Miller Barber*	273	George Archer	273	Tucson National GC, Tucson, AZ	72/7,305
DEAN MARTIN TUCSON OPEN						
1973	Bruce Crampton	277	George Archer Gay Brewer Labron Harris, Jr	282	Tucson National GC, Tucson, AZ	72/7,305
1974	Johnny Miller	272	Ben Crenshaw	275	Tucson National GC, Tucson, AZ	72/7,305
1975	Johnny Miller	263	John Mahaffey	272	Tucson National GC, Tucson, AZ	72/7,305
NBC TUCSON OPEN						
1976	Johnny Miller	274	Howard Twitty	277	Tucson National GC, Tucson, AZ	72/7,305
JOE GARAGIOLA TUCSON OPEN						
1977	Bruce Lietzke*	275	Gene Littler	275	Tucson National GC, Tucson, AZ	72/7,305
1978	Tom Watson	276	Bobby Wadkins	277	Tucson National GC, Tucson, AZ	72/7,305
1979	Bruce Lietzke	265	Buddy Gardner Jim Thorpe Tom Watson	267	Randolph Park Muncipal GC, Tucson, AZ	70/6,860
1980	Jim Colbert	270	Dan Halldorson	274	Tucson National GC, Tucson, AZ	72/7,305
1981	Johnny Miller	265	Lon Hinkle	267	Randolph Park Municipal GC, Tucson, AZ	70/6,860
1982	Craig Stadler	266	Vance Heafner John Mahaffey	269	Randolph Park Municipal GC, Tucson, AZ	70/6,860
1983	Gil Morgan*	271	Curtis Strange Lanny Wadkins	271	Randolph Park Municipal GC, Tucson, AZ	70/6,860
SEIKO-TUCSON MATCH PLAY CHAMPIONSHIP						
1984	Tom Watson	2 and 1	Gil Morgan		Randolph Park Municipal GC, Tucson, AZ	70/6,860
1985	Jim Thorpe	4 and 3	Jack Renner		Randolph Park Municipal GC, Tucson, AZ	70/6,860
1986	Jim Thorpe##	67	Scott Simpson	71	Randolph Park Municipal GC, Tucson, AZ	70/6,860
SEIKO-TUCSON OPEN						
1987	Mike Reid	268	Chip Beck Mark Calcavecchia Hal Sutton Fuzzy Zoeller	272	TPC at StarPass, Tucson, AZ	72/7,010
NORTHERN TELECOM TUCSON OPEN						
1988	David Frost	266	Mark Calcavecchia Mark O'Meara	271	TPC at StarPass, Tucson, AZ	72/7,010
1989	No tournament					
1990	Robert Gamez	270	Mark Calcavecchia Jay Haas	274	TPC at StarPass, Tucson, AZ (H) Randolph Park Municipal GC, Tucson, AZ	72/7,010 72/6,902
NORTHERN TELECOM OPEN						
1991	Phil Mickelson#	272	Tom Purtzer Bob Tway	273	TPC at StarPass, Tucson, AZ (H) Tucson National GC, Tucson, AZ	72/7,010 72/7,305
1992	Lee Janzen	270	Bill Britton	271	TPC at StarPass, Tucson, AZ (H) Tucson National GC, Tucson, AZ	72/7,010 72/7,305
1993	Larry Mize	271	Jeff Maggert	273	Tucson National GC, Tucson, AZ (H) Starr Pass GC, Tucson, AZ	72/7,148 72/7,010
1994	Andrew Magee	270	Jay Don Blake Loren Roberts Vijay Singh Steve Stricker	272	Tucson National GC, Tucson, AZ (H) Starr Pass GC, Tucson, AZ	72/7,148 72/7,010
1995	Phil Mickelson	269	Jim Gallagher, Jr Scott Simpson	270	Tucson National GC, Tucson, AZ (H) Starr Pass GC, Tucson, AZ	72/7,148 72/7,010
NORTEL OPEN						
1996	Phil Mickelson	273	Bob Tway	275	Tucson National GC, Tucson, AZ (H) Starr Pass GC, Tucson, AZ	72/7,148 71/6,942
TUCSON CHRYSLER CLASSIC						
1997	Jeff Sluman	275	Steve Jones	276	Omni Tucson National Resort, Tucson, AZ	72/7,148
1998	David Duval	269	Justin Leonard David Toms	273	Omni Tucson National Resort, Tucson, AZ	72/7,148
TOUCHSTONE ENERGY TUCSON OPEN						
1999	Gabriel Hjertstedt*	276	Tommy Armour III	276	Omni Tucson National Resort, Tucson, AZ	72/7,148
2000	Jim Carter	269	Chris DiMarco Tom Scherrer Jean Van de Velde	271	Omni Tucson National Resort, Tucson, AZ	72/7,109
2001	Garrett Willis	273	Kevin Sutherland	274	Omni Tucson National Resort, Tucson, AZ The Gallery GC, Marana, AZ	72/7,109 71/7,360
2002	Ian Leggatt	268	David Peoples Loren Roberts	270	Omni Tucson National Resort, Tucson, AZ	72/7,109
2003	Frank Lickliter II	269	Chad Campbell	271	Omni Tucson National Resort, Tucson, AZ	72/7,109
2004	Heath Slocum	266	Aaron Baddeley	267	Omni Tucson National Resort, Tucson, AZ	72/7,109

*KEY: * = Playoff # = Amateur (H) = Host Course ## = Match Medal Play Format*

SECTION 3 TOURNAMENT HISTORIES

2004 Ford Championship at Doral *[10th of 48 official events]*

Winner: CRAIG PARRY #
71-65-67-68 271 (-17) $900,000

Doral Golf Resort & Spa (Blue Course)

Miami, FL

March 4-7, 2004

Purse: $5,000,000
Par: 36-36—72
Yards: 7,266

LEADERS: First Round—Chris Smith recorded a 7-under 65 to lead Joe Durant by one. Phil Mickelson, Retief Goosen and Scott Verplank were two back.
Second Round—Goosen moved to 9-under-par 135, one ahead of Mickelson, Craig Parry and Todd Hamilton.

Third Round—Parry's 5-under 67 moved him to 13-under-par 203, one in front of Verplank and Gene Sauers. Six players were two shots back.

CUT: 79 players at 1-over-par 145 from a field of 144 professionals.

PRO-AM: $10,000. Scott Hoch, 54, $2,000.

WEATHER: Partly cloudy Thursday. High of 83. Winds SE 15-25 mph. Mostly sunny on Friday with temperatures in the lower 80s. Winds SE 15-25 mph with gusts up to 32 mph. Partly cloudy Saturday, with afternoon sun. High of 84. Winds S-SE 5-15 mph. Morning clouds on Sunday, then mostly sunny. Temperatures in the upper 80s, with W winds 5-12 mph.

Check out the 2005 Ford Championship at Doral, March 3-6 on USA/NBC

ORDER OF FINISH

 # Won playoff with an eagle-2 on first extra hole

Player	Pos.	Scores	Total	Money
Craig Parry #	1	71-65-67-68	271	$900,000.00
Scott Verplank	2	67-72-65-67	271	540,000.00
Retief Goosen	3	67-68-71-66	272	340,000.00
Joe Durant	4	66-72-67-68	273	240,000.00
K.J. Choi	T5	70-69-66-69	274	175,625.00
Bernhard Langer	T5	75-68-66-65	274	175,625.00
Gene Sauers	T5	70-70-64-70	274	175,625.00
David Toms	T5	72-68-65-69	274	175,625.00
Mark Calcavecchia	T9	68-69-70-68	275	140,000.00
Danny Ellis	T9	69-69-67-70	275	140,000.00
Chris DiMarco	T11	68-70-67-71	276	110,000.00
Neal Lancaster	T11	71-68-72-65	276	110,000.00
Shigeki Maruyama	T11	70-69-69-68	276	110,000.00
Nick Price	T11	72-70-65-69	276	110,000.00
Alex Cejka	T15	69-68-69-71	277	87,500.00
Todd Hamilton	T15	68-68-71-70	277	87,500.00
Woody Austin	T17	73-69-70-66	278	65,428.58
Angel Cabrera	T17	70-69-69-70	278	65,428.57
Stewart Cink	T17	70-69-69-70	278	65,428.57
Fred Funk	T17	71-69-70-68	278	65,428.57
Robert Gamez	T17	73-71-66-68	278	65,428.57
John Riegger	T17	68-73-66-71	278	65,428.57
Heath Slocum	T17	70-74-68-66	278	65,428.57
Russ Cochran	T24	74-71-66-68	279	44,000.00
Phil Mickelson	T24	67-69-69-74	279	44,000.00
Dennis Paulson (S)	T24	68-70-71-70	279	$44,000.00
Stephen Ames	T27	71-69-70-70	280	36,250.00
Jesper Parnevik	T27	71-70-67-72	280	36,250.00
Craig Perks	T27	68-69-73-70	280	36,250.00
Chris Smith	T27	65-76-71-68	280	36,250.00
Ryan Palmer	T31	72-70-73-66	281	31,000.00
Kenny Perry	T31	72-70-68-71	281	31,000.00
Bo Van Pelt	T31	70-74-70-67	281	31,000.00
Briny Baird	T34	68-75-70-69	282	23,150.00
Brian Bateman	T34	70-75-71-66	282	23,150.00
Jay Haas	T34	73-67-71-71	282	23,150.00
Cliff Kresge	T34	74-71-70-67	282	23,150.00
Peter Lonard	T34	74-69-66-73	282	23,150.00
Shaun Micheel	T34	72-71-70-69	282	23,150.00
Rod Pampling	T34	74-71-66-71	282	23,150.00
Brett Quigley	T34	73-70-67-72	282	23,150.00
Patrick Sheehan	T34	71-74-70-67	282	23,150.00
Jeff Sluman	T34	70-72-69-71	282	23,150.00
Tommy Armour III	T44	71-72-68-72	283	14,450.00
Jose Coceres	T44	71-72-67-73	283	14,450.00
Jerry Kelly	T44	70-74-70-69	283	14,450.00
Skip Kendall	T44	69-70-76-68	283	14,450.00
Justin Leonard	T44	70-69-74-70	283	14,450.00
Billy Mayfair	T44	70-74-69-70	283	14,450.00
Dan Olsen	T44	72-71-71-69	283	14,450.00
Joey Sindelar	T44	74-71-70-68	283	14,450.00
Paul Azinger	T52	71-70-71-72	284	11,725.00
Craig Barlow	T52	70-74-68-72	284	11,725.00
Olin Browne (S)	T52	70-74-71-69	284	$11,725.00
David Peoples	T52	71-71-72-70	284	11,725.00
Michael Allen	T56	72-71-69-73	285	11,050.00
Erik Compton (S)	T56	73-70-70-72	285	11,050.00
Marco Dawson	T56	72-72-68-73	285	11,050.00
Scott Hoch	T56	70-74-71-70	285	11,050.00
Hank Kuehne	T56	72-71-69-73	285	11,050.00
Hunter Mahan	T56	74-69-73-69	285	11,050.00
Sven Struver (Q)	T56	73-70-74-68	285	11,050.00
Dean Wilson	T56	72-71-73-69	285	11,050.00
Arjun Atwal	T64	77-68-75-66	286	10,350.00
Notah Begay III	T64	76-69-72-69	286	10,350.00
Lee Janzen	T64	72-70-69-75	286	10,350.00
Joe Ogilvie	T64	72-73-71-70	286	10,350.00
John Senden	T64	71-73-70-72	286	10,350.00
Omar Uresti	T64	73-72-71-70	286	10,350.00
Bill Glasson	T70	73-72-73-69	287	9,900.00
J.L. Lewis	T70	73-72-71-71	287	9,900.00
Ted Purdy	T70	71-73-70-73	287	9,900.00
Niclas Fasth	73	73-72-71-72	288	9,700.00
Tom Carter	T74	74-71-72-72	289	9,450.00
Carlos Franco	T74	71-74-70-74	289	9,450.00
J.J. Henry	T74	73-70-71-75	289	9,450.00
Brenden Pappas	T74	71-72-69-77	289	9,450.00
Tim Clark	78	68-76-75-71	290	9,200.00
Tripp Isenhour	79	70-75-73-74	292	9,100.00

(Q) = Open Qualifier; (S) = Sponsor Exemption, (T) = Tie

The following players did not finish (C=cut, W=withdrew)

C—146-John Cook, Ben Curtis, David Frost, Brian Gay, David Gossett, J.P. Hayes, Mark Hensby, John Huston, Spike McRoy, Tim Petrovic. **147-**Billy Andrade, Cameron Beckman, Rich Beem, David Branshaw, Glen Day, Harrison Frazar, Mathias Gronberg, Zach Johnson, Boyd Summerhays, Jay Williamson. **148-**Ricky Barnes, Craig Bowden, D.J. Brigman, Daniel Chopra, Robert Damron, Ken Duke, Todd Fischer, Dudley Hart, Scott Hend, Scott McCarron, Chris Riley, Steve Stricker, Hal Sutton, Tommy Tolles, Bob Tway. **149-**Fulton Allem, Glen Hnatiuk, Brandt Jobe, Per-Ulrik Johansson, Blaine McCallister, Vaughn Taylor. **150-**Steve Allan, Pat Bates, Jason Bohn, Ben Crane, Bob Ford, Mike Heinen, Kevin Na, Esteban Toledo. **151-**Rich Barcelo, Steve Burns, Steve Elkington, Matt Kuchar, Steve Pate. **152-**Patrick Moore, Alan Morin, Tatsuaki Nakamura, Dicky Pride. **153-**Richard S. Johnson, Dean Prowse. **154-**Danny Briggs, Roger Tambellini. **156-**Steve Lowery. **W—81-**Brent Geiberger, **79-**Michael Bradley.

TOURNAMENT HISTORY

Year	Winner	Score	Runner-up	Score	Location	Par/Yards
DORAL CC OPEN INVITATIONAL						
1962	Billy Casper	283	Paul Bondeson	284	Doral CC (Blue), Miami, FL	72/6,939
1963	Dan Sikes	283	Sam Snead	284	Doral CC (Blue), Miami, FL	72/6,939
1964	Billy Casper	277	Jack Nicklaus	278	Doral CC (Blue), Miami, FL	72/6,939
1965	Doug Sanders	274	Bruce Devlin	275	Doral CC (Blue), Miami, FL	72/6,939
1966	Phil Rodgers	278	Jay Dolan Kermit Zarley	279	Doral CC (Blue), Miami, FL	72/6,939
1967	Doug Sanders	275	Harold Henning Art Wall	276	Doral CC (Blue), Miami, FL	72/6,939
1968	Gardner Dickinson	275	Tom Weiskopf	276	Doral CC (Blue), Miami, FL	72/6,939
1969	Tom Shaw	276	Tommy Aaron	277	Doral CC (Blue), Miami, FL	72/6,939
DORAL-EASTERN OPEN INVITATIONAL						
1970	Mike Hill	279	Jim Colbert	283	Doral CC (Blue), Miami, FL	72/6,939
1971	J.C. Snead	275	Gardner Dickinson	276	Doral CC (Blue), Miami, FL	72/6,939
1972	Jack Nicklaus	276	Bob Rosburg Lee Trevino	278	Doral CC (Blue), Miami, FL	72/6,939
1973	Lee Trevino	276	Bruce Crampton Tom Weiskopf	277	Doral CC (Blue), Miami, FL	72/6,939
1974	Bud Allin	272	Jerry Heard	273	Doral CC (Blue), Miami, FL	72/6,939
1975	Jack Nicklaus	276	Forrest Fezler Bert Yancey	279	Doral CC (Blue), Miami, FL	72/6,939
1976	Hubert Green	270	Mark Hayes Jack Nicklaus	276	Doral CC (Blue), Miami, FL	72/6,939
1977	Andy Bean	277	David Graham	278	Doral CC (Blue), Miami, FL	72/6,939
1978	Tom Weiskopf	272	Jack Nicklaus	273	Doral CC (Blue), Miami, FL	72/6,939
1979	Mark McCumber	279	Bill Rogers	280	Doral CC (Blue), Miami, FL	72/6,939
1980	Raymond Floyd*	279	Jack Nicklaus	279	Doral CC (Blue), Miami, FL	72/6,939
1981	Raymond Floyd	273	Keith Fergus David Graham	274	Doral CC (Blue), Miami, FL	72/6,939

Ford Championship at Doral

NOTES

*In one of the most exciting finishes in PGA TOUR history, **Craig Parry** holed a 6-iron from 176 yards on the first playoff hole to defeat **Scott Verplank** at the 2004 Ford Championship at Doral.*

*Coincidence? The last memorable hole-out from the fairway to win on the PGA TOUR was by **Robert Gamez** on the final hole of the 1990 Bay Hill Invitational. Gamez, just like Parry, holed out from 176 yards. The 18th hole at Bay Hill was the toughest on TOUR in 1989 and the 18th at Doral was the toughest on TOUR in 2004. Need more? Both Gamez and Parry had their brothers caddying for them. It was also the second career win for each. Parry's previous victory came at the 2002 WGC-NEC Invitational.*

STEVE ELKINGTON

*With **Craig Parry**'s victory, every winner of the Ford Championship at Doral since 1990, except **Steve Elkington** in 1997 and 1999, has had ties to the state of Florida at the time of his victory. Prior to Elkington, 1989 winner **Bill Glasson** was the last tournament champion at Doral who did not have a connection to Florida (birthplace, resident). Parry has residences in Sydney, Australia and Orlando, FL.*

***Craig Parry**'s win last season marked the second consecutive season the Ford Championship at Doral ended in a playoff. **Scott Hoch** outlasted **Jim Furyk** in a three-hole playoff to win the 2003 title. In all, the tournament has needed extra holes to determine a victor six times (1980, 1986, 1990, 1991, 2003 and 2004).*

Tournament Record:
265, Greg Norman, 1993; Jim Furyk, 2000
Current Course Record:
61, Stephen Ames, 2000

TOURNAMENT HISTORY

Year	Winner	Score	Runner-up	Score	Location	Par/Yards
1982	Andy Bean	278	Scott Hoch Mike Nicolette Jerry Pate	279	Doral CC (Blue), Miami, FL	72/6,939
1983	Gary Koch	271	Ed Fiori	276	Doral CC (Blue), Miami, FL	72/6,939
1984	Tom Kite	272	Jack Nicklaus	274	Doral CC (Blue), Miami, FL	72/6,939
1985	Mark McCumber	284	Tom Kite	285	Doral CC (Blue), Miami, FL	72/6,939
1986	Andy Bean*	276	Hubert Green	276	Doral CC (Blue), Miami, FL	72/6,939
DORAL-RYDER OPEN						
1987	Lanny Wadkins	277	Seve Ballesteros Tom Kite Don Pooley	280	Doral CC (Blue), Miami, FL	72/6,939
1988	Ben Crenshaw	274	Chip Beck Mark McCumber	275	Doral CC (Blue), Miami, FL	72/6,939
1989	Bill Glasson	275	Fred Couples	276	Doral CC (Blue), Miami, FL	72/6,939
1990	Greg Norman*	273	Paul Azinger Mark Calcavecchia Tim Simpson	273	Doral CC (Blue), Miami, FL	72/6,939
1991	Rocco Mediate^	276	Curtis Strange	276	Doral CC (Blue), Miami, FL	72/6,939
1992	Raymond Floyd	271	Keith Clearwater Fred Couples	273	Doral CC (Blue), Miami, FL	72/6,939
1993	Greg Norman	265	Paul Azinger Mark McCumber	269	Doral CC (Blue), Miami, FL	72/6,939
1994	John Huston	274	Billy Andrade Brad Bryant	277	Doral CC (Blue), Miami, FL	72/6,939
1995	Nick Faldo	273	Peter Jacobsen Greg Norman	274	Doral CC (Blue), Miami, FL	72/6,939
1996	Greg Norman	269	Michael Bradley Vijay Singh	271	Doral CC (Blue), Miami, FL	72/6,939
1997	Steve Elkington	275	Nick Price Larry Nelson	277	Doral CC (Blue), Miami, FL	72/6,939
1998	Michael Bradley	278	John Huston Billy Mayfair	279	Doral CC (Blue), Miami, FL	72/7,125
1999	Steve Elkington	275	Greg Kraft	276	Doral CC (Blue), Miami, FL	72/7,125
2000	Jim Furyk	265	Franklin Langham	267	Doral CC (Blue), Miami, FL	72/7,125
GENUITY CHAMPIONSHIP						
2001	Joe Durant	270	Mike Weir	272	Doral CC (Blue), Miami, FL	72/7,125
2002	Ernie Els	271	Tiger Woods	273	Doral CC (Blue), Miami, FL	72/7,125
FORD CHAMPIONSHIP AT DORAL						
2003	Scott Hoch^	271	Jim Furyk	271	Doral CC (Blue), Miami, FL	72/7,125
2004	Craig Parry*	271	Scott Verplank	271	Doral CC (Blue), Miami, FL	72/7,266

*KEY: * = Playoff ^ = Monday playoff*

Fans watch the action on hole No. 18, the toughest hole on the PGA TOUR in 2004.

2004 The Honda Classic [11h of 48 official events]

The Honda Classic

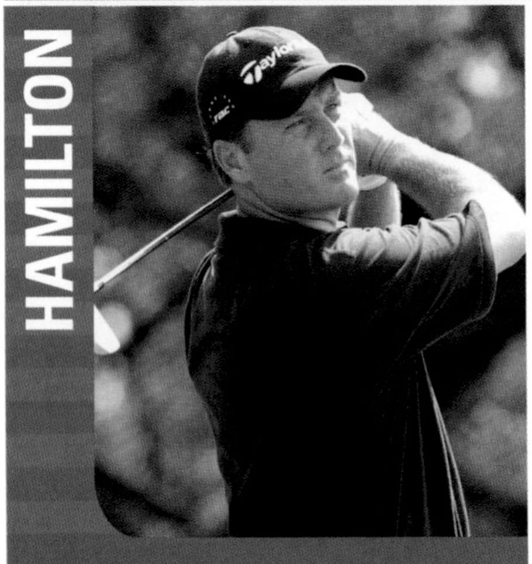

Winner: TODD HAMILTON
68-66-68-74 276 (-12) $900,000

The Country Club at Mirasol (Sunrise Course)

Palm Beach Gardens, FL

March 11-14, 2004

Purse: $5,000,000
Par: 36-36—72
Yards: 7,468

LEADERS: First Round—Carl Pettersson set the course record with a 9-under-par 63 to lead Mark Hensby by two strokes. Rory Sabbatini, Steve Flesch and Jesper Parnevik were three behind. **Second Round**—Pettersson moved to 13-under-par 131 to lead Brad Faxon and Todd Hamilton by three. Fredrik Jacobson was four back. **Third Round**—Hamilton improved to 14-under-par 202 to lead Jacobson by four. Pettersson and Chris Riley were five back while Aaron Baddeley, Davis Love III and Tom Pernice, Jr., were six behind.

CUT: 73 players at even-par 144 from a field of 144 professionals.

PRO-AM: $10,000. David Toms, 55, $2,000.

WEATHER: Mostly sunny on Thursday, with a high of 72 in mid-afternoon. NE winds 5-12 mph. Friday, mostly sunny with temperatures reaching 77. Winds E 5-15 mph. Warm and sunny on Saturday, with temperatures reaching 78. E winds 10-15 mph. Partly cloudy most of Sunday, with temperatures reaching 81. Stronger E winds up to 20 mph. Light rain for part of the afternoon.

Check out the 2005 Honda Classic, March 10-13 on USA/NBC

ORDER OF FINISH

Todd Hamilton	1	68-66-68-74	276	$900,000.00
Davis Love III	2	69-69-70-69	277	540,000.00
Brian Bateman	3	71-69-70-68	278	340,000.00
Robert Allenby	T4	68-74-67-70	279	196,875.00
Woody Austin	T4	71-69-69-70	279	196,875.00
Fredrik Jacobson	T4	67-69-70-73	279	196,875.00
Kevin Na	T4	67-72-71-69	279	196,875.00
Brad Faxon	8	68-66-76-70	280	155,000.00
Tommy Armour III	T9	69-69-73-70	281	130,000.00
Chad Campbell	T9	71-70-71-69	281	130,000.00
Lee Janzen	T9	74-66-70-71	281	130,000.00
Rory Sabbatini	T9	66-72-71-72	281	130,000.00
Craig Bowden	T13	69-69-72-72	282	83,125.00
Mark Hensby	T13	65-73-71-73	282	83,125.00
Zach Johnson	T13	69-75-66-72	282	83,125.00
Geoff Ogilvy	T13	73-70-70-69	282	83,125.00
Rod Pampling	T13	75-67-67-73	282	83,125.00
Tom Pernice, Jr.	T13	70-68-70-74	282	83,125.00
Carl Pettersson	T13	63-68-76-75	282	83,125.00
Chris Riley	T13	72-67-68-75	282	83,125.00
Aaron Baddeley	T21	72-69-67-75	283	54,000.00
Briny Baird	T21	68-71-73-71	283	54,000.00
Luke Donald	T21	70-69-75-69	283	54,000.00
Larry Mize (S)	T21	68-71-70-74	283	54,000.00
Fred Couples	T25	68-70-73-73	284	$39,000.00
Justin Leonard	T25	71-73-69-71	284	39,000.00
Brenden Pappas	T25	69-72-70-73	284	39,000.00
Brett Quigley	T25	69-74-71-70	284	39,000.00
David Toms	T25	72-72-69-71	284	39,000.00
Chris DiMarco	T30	74-68-74-69	285	30,375.00
Steve Flesch	T30	66-76-71-72	285	30,375.00
Ryan Palmer	T30	72-68-74-71	285	30,375.00
Jesper Parnevik	T30	66-72-74-73	285	30,375.00
Ted Purdy	T30	69-73-70-73	285	30,375.00
John Senden	T30	72-66-75-72	285	30,375.00
Cliff Kresge	T36	73-70-72-71	286	24,583.34
Craig Parry	T36	73-68-72-73	286	24,583.33
Justin Rose	T36	71-70-71-74	286	24,583.33
Notah Begay III	T39	72-72-72-71	287	22,000.00
Roger Tambellini	T39	70-70-74-73	287	22,000.00
D.J. Brigman	T41	72-69-73-74	288	18,500.00
Billy Mayfair	T41	70-69-73-76	288	18,500.00
Craig Perks	T41	72-70-74-72	288	18,500.00
Patrick Sheehan	T41	71-71-76-70	288	18,500.00
Hidemichi Tanaka	T41	71-68-72-77	288	18,500.00
Ken Duke	T46	68-74-71-76	289	13,371.43
Carlos Franco	T46	67-75-73-74	289	13,371.43
Glen Hnatiuk	T46	69-72-72-76	289	13,371.43
Brandt Jobe	T46	69-73-74-73	289	13,371.43
Mark O'Meara	T46	71-73-74-71	289	13,371.43
Chris Smith	T46	70-73-73-73	289	$13,371.43
John Riegger	T46	67-75-71-76	289	13,371.42
Joe Durant	T53	73-71-70-76	290	11,700.00
Charles Howell III	T53	72-71-75-72	290	11,700.00
Craig Barlow	T55	73-70-72-76	291	11,350.00
J.J. Henry	T55	74-68-79-70	291	11,350.00
Per-Ulrik Johansson (S)	T55	74-70-70-77	291	11,350.00
Dean Wilson	T55	70-73-72-76	291	11,350.00
Pat Bates	T59	72-72-69-79	292	10,850.00
Robert Damron	T59	69-72-74-77	292	10,850.00
Glen Day	T59	69-70-74-79	292	10,850.00
David Gossett	T59	69-74-73-76	292	10,850.00
Skip Kendall	T59	71-73-76-72	292	10,850.00
Jeff Sluman	T59	72-68-80-72	292	10,850.00
Danny Ellis	T65	71-69-75-78	293	10,350.00
Mathias Gronberg	T65	71-72-75-75	293	10,350.00
Bernhard Langer	T65	71-71-75-76	293	10,350.00
Scott McCarron	T65	69-74-73-77	293	10,350.00
Jason Dufner	69	72-72-79-71	294	10,100.00
Jay Delsing	T70	72-72-73-78	295	9,900.00
Joe Ogilvie	T70	71-70-77-77	295	9,900.00
Gene Sauers	T70	68-73-76-78	295	9,900.00
Michael Allen	73	69-73-76-80	298	9,700.00

(Q) = Open Qualifier; (S) = Sponsor Exemption; (T) = Tie

The following players did not finish (C=cut, W=withdrew, D=disqualified)

C—145-Paul Azinger, Jeff Brehaut, Daniel Chopra, Brian Gay, Richard S. Johnson, Kent Jones, Dan Olsen, Steve Stricker, Vaughn Taylor. **146-**Cameron Beckman, Jason Bohn, David Branshaw, Alex Cejka, Jose Coceres, Bob Estes, Todd Fischer, Neal Lancaster, John Rollins, Joey Sindelar, Paul Stankowski, Omar Uresti. **147-**Fulton Allem, Stephen Ames, Arjun Atwal, Olin Browne, Tom Byrum, Hank Kuehne, Spike McRoy, Dean Prowse, Hal Sutton, Jay Williamson. **148-**Danny Briggs, Bob Burns, David Frost, Robert Gamez, Matt Gogel, Tim Herron, Hunter Mahan, Steve Pate. **149-**Steve Allan, Rich Barcelo, John Cook, Todd Gleaton, Bob Heintz, Andy Morse, Pat Perez. **150-**Ramon Bescansa, Greg Chalmers, Fred Funk, Matt Kuchar, Boyd Summerhays, Tommy Tolles. **151-**Ricky Barnes, Russ Cochran, Blaine McCallister, Kenny Perry, Lee Rinker, Bo Van Pelt. **152-**Grant Waite. **154-**Billy Andrade, Tom Carter. **157-**J.P. Hayes, Len Mattiace. **160-**John Bungert. **163-**Esteban Toledo. **W—**Mark Calcavecchia. **82-**Curtis Strange. **77-**Marco Dawson, Mark Brooks. **76-**Tripp Isenhour. **D—72-**Greg Norman.

18th hole at Sunrise Course

TOURNAMENT HISTORY

Year	Winner	Score	Runner-up	Score	Location	Par/Yards
JACKIE GLEASON'S INVERRARY CLASSIC						
1972	Tom Weiskopf	278	Jack Nicklaus	279	Inverrary G&CC (East), Lauderhill, FL	72/7,128
JACKIE GLEASON'S INVERRARY NATIONAL AIRLINES CLASSIC						
1973	Lee Trevino	279	Forrest Fezler	280	Inverrary G&CC (East), Lauderhill, FL	72/7,128
JACKIE GLEASON'S INVERRARY CLASSIC						
1974	Leonard Thompson	278	Hale Irwin	279	Inverrary G&CC (East), Lauderhill, FL	72/7,128
1975	Bob Murphy	273	Eddie Pearce	274	Inverrary G&CC (East), Lauderhill, FL	72/7,128
1976	No Tournament+					
1977	Jack Nicklaus	275	Gary Player	280	Inverrary G&CC (East), Lauderhill, FL	72/7,128
1978	Jack Nicklaus	276	Grier Jones	277	Inverrary G&CC (East), Lauderhill, FL	72/7,128
1979	Larry Nelson	274	Grier Jones	277	Inverrary G&CC (East), Lauderhill, FL	72/7,128
1980	Johnny Miller	274	Charles Coody	276	Inverrary G&CC (East), Lauderhill, FL	72/7,128
			Bruce Lietzke			
AMERICAN MOTORS INVERRARY CLASSIC						
1981	Tom Kite	274	Jack Nicklaus	275	Inverrary G&CC (East), Lauderhill, FL	72/7,128
HONDA INVERRARY CLASSIC						
1982	Hale Irwin	269	Tom Kite	270	Inverrary G&CC (East), Lauderhill, FL	72/7,128
			George Burns			
1983	Johnny Miller	278	Jack Nicklaus	280	Inverrary G&CC (East), Lauderhill, FL	72/7,128
THE HONDA CLASSIC						
1984	Bruce Lietzke*	280	Andy Bean	280	TPC at Eagle Trace, Coral Springs, FL	72/7,030
1985	Curtis Strange*	275	Peter Jacobsen	275	TPC at Eagle Trace, Coral Springs, FL	72/7,030
1986	Kenny Knox	287	Andy Bean	288	TPC at Eagle Trace, Coral Springs, FL	72/7,030
			John Mahaffey			
			Jodie Mudd			
			Clarence Rose			
1987	Mark Calcavecchia	279	Bernhard Langer	282	TPC at Eagle Trace, Coral Springs, FL	72/7,030
			Payne Stewart			

NOTES

Todd Hamilton *earned his first career PGA TOUR victory in 2004 in his 18th career event on the PGA TOUR at the age of 38 years, four months and 26 days. He was the second first-time winner of 2004, joining* ***Heath Slocum*** *(Chrysler Classic of Tucson), and the first rookie to win since* ***Adam Scott*** *at the 2003 Deutsche Bank Championship.*

2004 Honda Classic champion ***Todd Hamilton*** *became the eighth player to win his first PGA TOUR event at The Honda Classic in 32 years. The others:* ***Leonard Thompson*** *(1974),* ***Larry Nelson*** *(1979),* ***Kenny Knox*** *(1986),* ***John Huston*** *(1990),* ***Tim Herron*** *(1996),* ***Stuart Appleby*** *(1997) and* ***Matt Kuchar*** *(2002).*

Todd Hamilton *entered The Honda Classic No. 96 in the Official World Golf Ranking and jumped to No. 38 with his maiden victory. His rank after THE PLAYERS Championship (No. 40) earned an invitation to his first Masters.*

Brian Bateman *enjoyed his career-best finish with a solo third in his 66th career start. His previous best was a T11 at the 2003 HP Classic of New Orleans, where he also collected $106,000. Bateman earned $340,000 for his third-place finish, which tops his best year on the PGA TOUR – 2002, 31 starts, $281,421.*

Davis Love III *earned his second consecutive runner-up finish at The Honda Classic. Starting the day six shots behind* ***Todd Hamilton****, Love took the clubhouse lead at 11-under-par before Hamilton's birdies on the 71st and 72nd holes edged Love by one stroke.*

DAVIS LOVE III

Tournament Record:
264, Justin Leonard, 2003 (The CC of Mirasol-Sunset)
Current Course Record:
63, Carl Petterson, 2004
Other Course Records:
62, Hale Irwin, 1979 (Inverrary G&CC)
62, Dan Pohl, 1989, Tim Herron, 1996 (TPC at Eagle Trace)
62, Jerry Kelly, Adam Scott, 2003 (The CC of Mirasol-Sunset)

TOURNAMENT HISTORY

Year	Winner	Score	Runner-up	Score	Location	Par/Yards
1988	Joey Sindelar	276	Ed Fiori Sandy Lyle Payne Stewart	278	TPC at Eagle Trace, Coral Springs, FL	72/7,030
1989	Blaine McCallister	266	Payne Stewart	270	TPC at Eagle Trace, Coral Springs, FL	72/7,030
1990	John Huston	282	Mark Calcavecchia	284	TPC at Eagle Trace, Coral Springs, FL	72/7,030
1991	Steve Pate	279	Paul Azinger Dan Halldorson	282	TPC at Eagle Trace, Coral Springs, FL	72/7,030
1992	Corey Pavin*	273	Fred Couples	273	Weston Hills G&CC, Ft. Lauderdale, FL	72/7,069
1993	Fred Couples~*	207	Robert Gamez	207	Weston Hills G&CC, Ft. Lauderdale, FL	72/7,069
1994	Nick Price	276	Craig Parry	277	Weston Hills G&CC, Ft. Lauderdale, FL	71/6,964
1995	Mark O'Meara	275	Nick Faldo	276	Weston Hills G&CC, Ft. Lauderdale, FL	71/6,964
1996	Tim Herron	271	Mark McCumber	275	TPC at Eagle Trace, Coral Springs, FL	72/7,037
1997	Stuart Appleby	274	Michael Bradley Payne Stewart	275	TPC at Heron Bay, Coral Springs, FL	72/7,268
1998	Mark Calcavecchia	270	Vijay Singh	273	TPC at Heron Bay, Coral Springs, FL	72/7,268
1999	Vijay Singh	277	Payne Stewart	279	TPC at Heron Bay, Coral Springs, FL	72/7,268
2000	Dudley Hart	269	J.P. Hayes Kevin Wentworth	270	TPC at Heron Bay, Coral Springs, FL	72/7,268
2001	Jesper Parnevik	270	Craig Perks Mark Calcavecchia Geoff Ogilvy	271	TPC at Heron Bay, Coral Springs, FL	72/7,268
2002	Matt Kuchar	269	Brad Faxon Joey Sindelar	271	TPC at Heron Bay, Coral Springs, FL	72/7,268
2003	Justin Leonard	264	Chad Campbell Davis Love III	265	CC at Mirasol, Palm Beach Gardens, FL (Sunset Course)	72/7,157
2004	Todd Hamilton	276	Davis Love III	277	CC at Mirasol, Palm Beach Gardens, FL (Sunrise Course)	72/7,468

*KEY: * = Playoff ~ = Weather-shortened + = Inverrary served as site for Tournament Players Championship*

Fans enjoy the play during The Honda Classic.

2004 Bay Hill Invitational

presented by MasterCard *[12th of 48 official events]*

BAY HILL INVITATIONAL
Presented by MasterCard

CAMPBELL

Winner: CHAD CAMPBELL
66-68-70-66 270 (-18) $900,000

Bay Hill Club and Lodge

Orlando, FL

March 18-21, 2004

Purse: $5,000,000
Par: 36-36—72
Yards: 7,267

LEADERS: First Round—Darren Clarke, Chad Campbell and Shigeki Maruyama shared the lead at 6-under 66. Zach Johnson, Tiger Woods, Stuart Appleby and Jerry Kelly were one back.
Second Round—Maruyama moved to 12-under 132, two ahead of Clarke, Campbell and Appleby.

Third Round—Appleby sat at 16-under 200, four ahead of Campbell. Adam Scott was six back.

CUT: 73 players at even-par 144 from a field of 120 professionals and one amateur.

PRO-AM: $10,000. 52 players, $193.30 each. Canceled due to heavy rain.

WEATHER: Sunny with temperatures reaching the low 80s on Thursday. Similar conditions on Friday, a little warmer. A mix of sun and clouds on Saturday with E winds up to 20 mph. Mostly sunny and warm on Sunday.

Check out the 2005 Bay Hill Invitational presented by MasterCard, March 17-20 on USA/NBC

ORDER OF FINISH

Chad Campbell	1	66-68-70-66	270	$900,000.00
Stuart Appleby	2	67-67-66-76	276	540,000.00
Adam Scott	T3	68-70-68-71	277	290,000.00
Scott Verplank	T3	68-68-73-68	277	290,000.00
Jerry Kelly	5	67-69-73-69	278	200,000.00
Stephen Ames	T6	72-65-73-70	280	161,875.00
Darren Clarke	T6	66-68-74-72	280	161,875.00
Zach Johnson	T6	67-68-75-70	280	161,875.00
Shigeki Maruyama	T6	66-66-75-73	280	161,875.00
John Daly	T10	68-70-70-73	281	130,000.00
Dennis Paulson	T10	72-67-72-70	281	130,000.00
Tom Lehman	12	70-74-70-68	282	115,000.00
Mathias Gronberg (S)	T13	69-72-72-70	283	100,000.00
Bo Van Pelt	T13	72-72-70-69	283	100,000.00
Charles Howell III	T15	71-71-71-71	284	70,333.34
Kenny Perry	T15	69-72-72-71	284	70,333.34
Lee Westwood	T15	73-69-74-68	284	70,333.34
Fred Couples	T15	76-67-68-73	284	70,333.33
Mark Hensby	T15	72-70-70-72	284	70,333.33
Fredrik Jacobson	T15	70-69-70-75	284	70,333.33
J.L. Lewis	T15	71-70-71-72	284	70,333.33
Steve Lowery (S)	T15	70-67-71-76	284	70,333.33
John Riegger	T15	72-67-72-73	284	70,333.33
Craig Barlow	T24	72-68-72-73	285	39,571.43
Brad Faxon	T24	68-73-77-67	285	$39,571.43
Tim Herron	T24	70-73-71-71	285	39,571.43
Ryan Palmer	T24	71-72-72-70	285	39,571.43
Justin Rose (S)	T24	71-70-69-75	285	39,571.43
Jeff Sluman	T24	72-68-73-72	285	39,571.43
Rod Pampling	T24	69-70-69-77	285	39,571.42
Thomas Bjorn	T31	71-70-73-72	286	27,166.67
Lee Janzen	T31	70-66-78-72	286	27,166.67
Frank Lickliter II	T31	74-67-73-72	286	27,166.67
Davis Love III	T31	69-74-71-72	286	27,166.67
Brett Quigley	T31	71-70-72-73	286	27,166.67
Kirk Triplett	T31	72-68-73-73	286	27,166.67
Niclas Fasth	T31	71-71-70-74	286	27,166.66
Sergio Garcia	T31	73-66-70-77	286	27,166.66
Vijay Singh	T31	68-72-70-76	286	27,166.66
Ben Curtis	T40	69-69-77-72	287	19,000.00
Joe Durant	T40	72-70-73-72	287	19,000.00
Steve Flesch	T40	73-68-72-74	287	19,000.00
Bernhard Langer	T40	72-70-71-74	287	19,000.00
Jose Maria Olazabal	T40	73-71-71-72	287	19,000.00
Patrick Sheehan	T40	70-71-74-72	287	19,000.00
Alex Cejka	T46	72-70-71-75	288	12,850.00
Stewart Cink	T46	73-71-74-70	288	12,850.00
Brian Gay (S)	T46	68-71-71-78	288	12,850.00
Trevor Immelman	T46	73-69-76-70	288	12,850.00
Kent Jones	T46	72-70-75-71	288	12,850.00
Neal Lancaster	T46	76-67-75-70	288	$12,850.00
Arron Oberholser	T46	71-73-70-74	288	12,850.00
Loren Roberts	T46	70-71-72-75	288	12,850.00
Gene Sauers	T46	75-69-72-72	288	12,850.00
Tiger Woods	T46	67-74-74-73	288	12,850.00
Aaron Baddeley	T56	68-74-71-76	289	11,250.00
Danny Ellis	T56	70-67-77-75	289	11,250.00
Mark O'Meara	T56	69-73-73-74	289	11,250.00
Omar Uresti	T56	71-71-73-74	289	11,250.00
Ben Crane	T60	72-71-73-74	290	10,950.00
Harrison Frazar	T60	76-68-71-75	290	10,950.00
Woody Austin	T62	73-70-77-71	291	10,650.00
Hunter Mahan (S)	T62	69-69-79-74	291	10,650.00
Tim Petrovic	T62	72-72-69-78	291	10,650.00
Phillip Price (S)	T62	73-71-72-75	291	10,650.00
Billy Andrade (S)	T66	72-72-73-75	292	10,350.00
Tom Watson (S)	T66	70-74-75-73	292	10,350.00
Nick Faldo	68	70-72-77-74	293	10,200.00
Todd Hamilton	T69	71-70-77-76	294	10,050.00
Mike Heinen	T69	71-71-75-77	294	10,050.00
Scott McCarron	71	69-71-82-74	296	9,900.00
Stephen Leaney	72	72-71-78-76	297	9,800.00
Dicky Pride (S)	73	72-71-80-75	298	9,700.00

(Q) = Open Qualifier; (S) = Sponsor Exemption; (T) = Tie

The following players did not finish (C=cut, W=withdrew)

C—145-Arjun Atwal, Brian Bateman, Ernie Els, Retief Goosen, David Gossett, Mike Hulbert, Tripp Isenhour, Len Mattiace, Carl Pettersson. **146-**Robert Allenby, Patrick Damron, Todd Fischer, J.J. Henry, Hank Kuehne, Jeff Maggert, Craig Parry, Joey Sindelar, Duffy Waldorf. **147-**Robert Gamez, Skip Kendall, Rory Sabbatini. **148-**K.J. Choi, Nick Flanagan, Geoff Ogilvy, Hidemichi Tanaka. **149-**Peter Lonard, Tom Pernice, Jr. **150-**Tommy Armour III, Scott Hoch, Dan Olsen, Ian Poulter, Steve Stricker, Dean Wilson. **151-**Paul Azinger, Mark Brooks, Olin Browne, Ted Purdy. **152-**Robert Damron, Per-Ulrik Johansson. **153-**Craig Bowden. **154-**Craig Perks, Jay Williamson. **160-**Dean A. Wilson. **167-**Arnold Palmer. **W—**Russ Cochran. **79-**Bob Byman. **77-**Paul Casey. **74-**Peter Jacobsen.

STUART APPLEBY

TOURNAMENT HISTORY

Year	Winner	Score	Runner-up	Score	Location	Par/Yards
FLORIDA CITRUS OPEN INVITATIONAL						
1966	Lionel Hebert	279	Charles Coody	281	Rio Pinar CC, Orlando, FL	72/7,012
			Dick Lytle			
			Jack Nicklaus			
1967	Julius Boros	274	George Knudson	275	Rio Pinar CC, Orlando, FL	72/7,012
			Arnold Palmer			
1968	Dan Sikes	274	Tom Weiskopf	275	Rio Pinar CC, Orlando, FL	72/7,012
1969	Ken Still	278	Miller Barber	279	Rio Pinar CC, Orlando, FL	72/7,012
1970	Bob Lunn	271	Rives McBee	282	Rio Pinar CC, Orlando, FL	72/7,012
1971	Arnold Palmer	270	Julius Boros	271	Rio Pinar CC, Orlando, FL	72/7,012
1972	Jerry Heard	276	Bobby Mitchell	278	Rio Pinar CC, Orlando, FL	72/7,012
1973	Bud Allin	265	Charles Coody	273	Rio Pinar CC, Orlando, FL	72/7,012
1974	Jerry Heard	273	Homero Blancas	276	Rio Pinar CC, Orlando, FL	72/7,012
			Jim Jamieson			
1975	Lee Trevino	276	Hale Irwin	277	Rio Pinar CC, Orlando, FL	72/7,012
1976	Hale Irwin*	270	Kermit Zarley	270	Rio Pinar CC, Orlando, FL	72/7,012
1977	Gary Koch	274	Dale Hayes	276	Rio Pinar CC, Orlando, FL	72/7,012
			Joe Inman			
1978	Mac McLendon	271	David Graham	273	Rio Pinar CC, Orlando, FL	72/7,012
BAY HILL CITRUS CLASSIC						
1979	Bob Byman*	278	John Schroeder	278	Bay Hill Club & Lodge, Orlando, FL	71/7,103
BAY HILL CLASSIC						
1980	Dave Eichelberger	279	Leonard Thompson	282	Bay Hill Club & Lodge, Orlando, FL	71/7,103
1981	Andy Bean	266	Tom Watson	273	Bay Hill Club & Lodge, Orlando, FL	71/7,103
1982	Tom Kite*	278	Jack Nicklaus	278	Bay Hill Club & Lodge, Orlando, FL	71/7,103
			Denis Watson			
1983	Mike Nicolette*	283	Greg Norman	283	Bay Hill Club & Lodge, Orlando, FL	71/7,103
1984	Gary Koch*	272	George Burns	272	Bay Hill Club & Lodge, Orlando, FL	71/7,103
HERTZ BAY HILL CLASSIC						
1985	Fuzzy Zoeller	275	Tom Watson	277	Bay Hill Club & Lodge, Orlando, FL	71/7,103

NOTES

Chad Campbell *became the first player to come from behind and win at Bay Hill since* ***Phil Mickelson*** *came from two back of* ***Omar Uresti*** *in 1997.*

Chad Campbell *turned in the best final-round score (6-under 66) by a winner at Bay Hill since* ***Phil Mickelson*** *posted a 7-under 65 in his 1997 win.*

With his win from four strokes back through 54 holes, ***Chad Campbell*** *turned in the biggest come-from-behind victory at Bay Hill since* ***Gary Koch*** *came from six strokes back of third-round leader* ***Hal Sutton*** *in 1984 and defeated* ***George Burns*** *in a playoff.*

Chad Campbell *became the second winner in 2004 to record a bogey-free final round (****Heath Slocum*** *at the Chrysler Classic of Tucson was the first).*

TOMMY ARMOUR III

Chad Campbell*'s six-stroke victory was the largest of the season through 12 events and largest on TOUR since* ***Tommy Armour III****'s seven-stroke win at the 2003 Valero Texas Open.*

Chad Campbell *was the second player in 2004 through 12 events to hold or share the first-round lead and go on to victory (****Stuart Appleby*** *at the Mercedes Championships was the first).*

After going his first 67 tournaments without a victory on TOUR, ***Chad Campbell*** *picked up his second win in 10 tournaments by winning the Bay Hill Invitational. Campbell's first victory came at the 2003 season-ending TOUR Championship.*

Tournament Record:
264, Payne Stewart, 1987
Current Course Record:
62, Andy Bean, 1981; Greg Norman, 1984

TOURNAMENT HISTORY

Year	Winner	Score	Runner-up	Score	Location	Par/Yards
1986	Dan Forsman~	202	Raymond Floyd	203	Bay Hill Club & Lodge, Orlando, FL	71/7,103
			Mike Hulbert			
1987	Payne Stewart	264	David Frost	267	Bay Hill Club & Lodge, Orlando, FL	71/7,103
1988	Paul Azinger	271	Tom Kite	276	Bay Hill Club & Lodge, Orlando, FL	71/7,103
THE NESTLE INVITATIONAL						
1989	Tom Kite*	278	Davis Love III	278	Bay Hill Club & Lodge, Orlando, FL	71/7,103
1990	Robert Gamez	274	Greg Norman	275	Bay Hill Club & Lodge, Orlando, FL	72/7,114
1991	Andrew Magee~	203	Tom Sieckmann	205	Bay Hill Club & Lodge, Orlando, FL	72/7,114
1992	Fred Couples	269	Gene Sauers	278	Bay Hill Club & Lodge, Orlando, FL	72/7,114
1993	Ben Crenshaw	280	Davis Love III	282	Bay Hill Club & Lodge, Orlando, FL	72/7,114
			Rocco Mediate			
			Vijay Singh			
1994	Loren Roberts	275	Nick Price	276	Bay Hill Club & Lodge, Orlando, FL	72/7,114
			Vijay Singh			
			Fuzzy Zoeller			
1995	Loren Roberts	272	Brad Faxon	274	Bay Hill Club & Lodge, Orlando, FL	72/7,114
BAY HILL INVITATIONAL PRESENTED BY OFFICE DEPOT						
1996	Paul Goydos	275	Jeff Maggert	276	Bay Hill Club & Lodge, Orlando, FL	72/7,196
1997	Phil Mickelson	272	Stuart Appleby	275	Bay Hill Club & Lodge, Orlando, FL	72/7,207
BAY HILL INVITATIONAL PRESENTED BY COOPER TIRES						
1998	Ernie Els	274	Bob Estes	278	Bay Hill Club & Lodge, Orlando, FL	72/7,207
			Jeff Maggert			
1999	Tim Herron*	274	Tom Lehman	274	Bay Hill Club & Lodge, Orlando, FL	72/7,207
2000	Tiger Woods	270	Davis Love III	274	Bay Hill Club & Lodge, Orlando, FL	72/7,208
2001	Tiger Woods	273	Phil Mickelson	274	Bay Hill Club & Lodge, Orlando, FL	72/7,208
2002	Tiger Woods	275	Michael Campbell	279	Bay Hill Club & Lodge, Orlando, FL	72/7,239
2003	Tiger Woods	269	Stewart Cink	280	Bay Hill Club & Lodge, Orlando, FL	72/7,239
			Brad Faxon			
			Kenny Perry			
			Kirk Triplett			
2004	Chad Campbell	270	Stuart Appleby	276	Bay Hill Club & Lodge, Orlando, FL	72/7,239

*KEY: * = Playoff ~ = Weather-shortened*

ELIGIBILITY REQUIREMENTS FOR THE 2005 BAY HILL INVITATIONAL

Eligible players are:

- Winners of the Bay Hill Invitational prior to 2000, and winners of the Bay Hill Invitational in 2000 and beyond for a period of five years following their win.
- Winners of THE PLAYERS Championship, Masters Tournament, U.S. Open, British Open and PGA Championship from 1995 to1997 and from 2000 to 2004. Beginning with the 1998 winners of these events, winners will be eligible for five years.
- Winners of the NEC World Series of Golf in the last 10 years (1995-1997).
- Winners of THE TOUR Championship in the last three years (2002-2004).
- Winners of the WGC-Accenture Match Play Championship in the last three years (2003-2005).
- Winners of the WGC-NEC Invitational and WGC-American Express Championship in the last three years (2002-2004).
- Winners of PGA TOUR cosponsored or approved tournaments, whose victories are considered official, since the previous year's Bay Hill Invitational.
- Playing members of the last-named U.S. Ryder Cup team (2004).
- Current PGA TOUR members who were playing members of the last named U.S. and International Presidents Cup teams (2003).
- The winner of the 2004 U.S. Amateur Championship, if still an amateur player.
- The top 50 players from the Official World Golf Ranking through the Ford Championship.
- 18 sponsor exemptions, restricted as follows:
  - Two from among the 2004 PGA TOUR Qualifying Tournament's top 30 finishers and ties, and the first through 20th finishers on the 2004 Official Nationwide Tour Money List.
  - Eight from among the current year's PGA TOUR membership.
  - Eight "unrestricted".
- Two foreign players designated by the Commissioner.
- The top 70 players from the 2004 Official PGA TOUR Money List.
- Members in the Top 125-Nonmembers category whose official money for the previous year equals or exceeds the amount of official money earned by the player finishing in 70th position on the 2004 Official PGA TOUR Money List.
- The top 70 players from the 2005 Official PGA TOUR Money List through the Ford Championship.
- Either the current winner of the PGA Section Championship or the current PGA Section Player of the Year where the tournament is played, as determined by the Section.
- If necessary to complete a field of 120 players, those players below 70th position from the 2005 Official PGA TOUR Money List through the Ford Championship, in order of their positions on such list.
- In recognition of his remarkable career achievements, indelible contributions to golf and his role as host of the Bay Hill Invitational, a lifetime exemption for Arnold Palmer. (Such exemption will be an addition to the field.)

2004 THE PLAYERS Championship

[13th of 48 official events]

THE PLAYERS CHAMPIONSHIP

Winner: ADAM SCOTT
65-72-69-70 276 (-12) $1,440,000

Tournament Players Club at Sawgrass (Stadium Course)

Ponte Vedra Beach, FL

March 25-28, 2004

Purse: $8,000,000
Par: 36-36—72
Yards: 7,093

LEADERS: First Round—Adam Scott carded a 7-under-par 65 to lead Duffy Waldorf and Kevin Sutherland by one shot. K.J. Choi, Thomas Bjorn and Bob Burns were two behind. Five players were three back.
Second Round—Sutherland and Jerry Kelly moved to 9-under-par 135 to lead Scott and Ernie Els by two strokes. Vijay Singh and Padraig Harrington where three back.

Third Round—Scott at 10-under 206 led Sutherland and Frank Lickliter II by two strokes. Els, Kelly, Paul Stankowski, Kenny Perry and Phil Mickelson were three back.

CUT: 83 players at 2-over-par from a field of 148 professionals.

WEATHER: On Thursday, variably cloudy and windy with a high of 69, E winds 15-20 mph. Friday, partly cloudy and breezy with a high of 75, cooling off in late afternoon. Intermittent showers during the afternoon. Winds 10-20 mph. Saturday, warm and sunny in the morning with a high of 75. Partly cloudy in the afternoon. NE winds 10-15 mph. Sunday, partly cloudy and warm with a high of 78 and SE winds 5-10 mph.

Check out the 2005 PLAYERS Championship, March 24-27 on ESPN/NBC

ORDER OF FINISH

Adam Scott	1	65-72-69-70	276	$1,440,000.00
Padraig Harrington	2	68-70-73-66	277	864,000.00
Frank Lickliter II	T3	69-71-68-72	280	416,000.00
Phil Mickelson	T3	70-69-70-71	280	416,000.00
Kenny Perry	T3	69-71-69-71	280	416,000.00
Jay Haas	T6	72-73-70-66	281	268,000.00
Jerry Kelly	T6	69-66-74-72	281	268,000.00
Kevin Sutherland	T6	66-69-73-73	281	268,000.00
Shaun Micheel	9	70-76-69-67	282	232,000.00
Bob Burns	T10	67-72-72-72	283	200,000.00
Paul Casey	T10	72-70-69-72	283	200,000.00
Fred Funk	T10	73-71-68-71	283	200,000.00
Stephen Ames	T13	75-69-72-68	284	154,666.67
Vijay Singh	T13	70-68-72-74	284	154,666.67
Craig Parry	T13	74-72-64-74	284	154,666.66
Woody Austin	T16	76-69-66-74	285	116,000.00
Tom Byrum	T16	74-71-71-69	285	116,000.00
Matt Kuchar	T16	74-67-71-73	285	116,000.00
Geoff Ogilvy	T16	73-70-72-70	285	116,000.00
Paul Stankowski	T16	73-70-66-76	285	116,000.00
Tiger Woods	T16	75-69-68-73	285	116,000.00
Thomas Bjorn	T22	67-76-73-70	286	80,000.00
Stewart Cink	T22	70-73-74-69	286	80,000.00
Glen Day	T22	71-75-67-73	286	80,000.00
J.P. Hayes	T22	72-73-72-69	286	80,000.00
Cameron Beckman	T26	70-71-72-74	287	56,800.00
Darren Clarke	T26	71-74-73-69	287	56,800.00
Steve Elkington	T26	69-76-70-72	287	$56,800.00
Ernie Els	T26	68-69-72-78	287	56,800.00
John Huston	T26	72-71-71-73	287	56,800.00
Jeff Sluman	T26	69-70-73-75	287	56,800.00
Scott Verplank	T26	68-75-73-71	287	56,800.00
Jeff Maggert	T33	73-73-70-72	288	39,644.45
Len Mattiace	T33	74-69-74-71	288	39,644.45
Jesper Parnevik	T33	72-71-73-72	288	39,644.45
Corey Pavin	T33	74-67-74-73	288	39,644.45
Robert Allenby	T33	71-73-70-74	288	39,644.44
Briny Baird	T33	71-74-70-73	288	39,644.44
Alex Cejka	T33	69-71-73-75	288	39,644.44
Davis Love III	T33	77-68-70-73	288	39,644.44
Ian Poulter	T33	70-73-71-74	288	39,644.44
Pat Bates	T42	73-73-73-70	289	24,087.28
Scott Hoch	T42	70-71-77-71	289	24,087.28
Colin Montgomerie	T42	73-73-73-70	289	24,087.28
Chad Campbell	T42	75-69-71-74	289	24,087.27
K.J. Choi	T42	67-79-69-74	289	24,087.27
Brad Faxon	T42	70-75-73-71	289	24,087.27
Justin Leonard	T42	75-69-72-73	289	24,087.27
David Peoples	T42	72-72-73-72	289	24,087.27
Nick Price	T42	75-69-73-72	289	24,087.27
Brett Quigley	T42	73-73-69-74	289	24,087.27
Rory Sabbatini	T42	73-68-75-73	289	24,087.27
Sergio Garcia	T53	68-73-72-77	290	18,432.00
Matt Gogel	T53	72-71-70-77	290	18,432.00
Shigeki Maruyama	T53	70-73-74-73	290	18,432.00
Scott McCarron	T53	76-70-69-75	290	18,432.00
Tim Petrovic	T53	71-72-74-73	290	$18,432.00
Joe Durant	T58	74-71-72-74	291	17,360.00
Carlos Franco	T58	74-70-74-73	291	17,360.00
Todd Hamilton	T58	71-72-76-72	291	17,360.00
Billy Mayfair	T58	76-70-70-75	291	17,360.00
Rod Pampling	T58	73-71-72-75	291	17,360.00
Justin Rose	T58	73-73-70-75	291	17,360.00
John Senden	T58	73-72-70-76	291	17,360.00
Heath Slocum	T58	73-73-72-73	291	17,360.00
Mark Calcavecchia	T66	71-72-72-77	292	16,240.00
Ben Crane	T66	71-72-71-78	292	16,240.00
Spike McRoy	T66	74-71-75-72	292	16,240.00
Arron Oberholser	T66	73-73-75-71	292	16,240.00
Loren Roberts	T66	73-70-79-70	292	16,240.00
Craig Stadler	T66	70-76-74-72	292	16,240.00
Nick Faldo	T72	71-75-71-76	293	15,600.00
Tom Pernice, Jr.	T72	72-71-70-80	293	15,600.00
Brandt Jobe	T74	68-75-76-75	294	15,200.00
Joey Sindelar	T74	73-70-73-78	294	15,200.00
Duffy Waldorf	T74	66-73-71-84	294	15,200.00
Bernhard Langer	T77	71-74-73-77	295	14,800.00
Bob Tway	T77	69-71-78-77	295	14,800.00
John Daly	79	69-73-76-80	298	14,560.00
Peter Jacobsen	80	72-73-71-83	299	14,400.00
Greg Norman	T81	72-73-77-79	301	14,160.00
Hidemichi Tanaka	T81	72-71-74-84	301	14,160.00
Neal Lancaster	83	72-71-80-79	302	13,920.00

(T) = Tie

The following players did not finish (C=cut, W=withdrew)

C—147-Stuart Appleby, Lee Janzen, Jonathan Kaye, Skip Kendall, Cliff Kresge, Paul Lawrie, J.L. Lewis, John Rollins, Patrick Sheehan, Kirk Triplett. **148-**Jonathan Byrd, Ben Curtis, Luke Donald, Todd Fischer, Brenden Pappas, Pat Perez, John Riegger, Gene Sauers, Esteban Toledo, David Toms. **149-**Robert Damron, Robert Gamez, J.J. Henry, Tom Lehman, Craig Perks, Mike Weir. **150-**Notah Begay III, Tim Clark, Bob Estes, Steve Flesch, Charles Howell III, Jose Maria Olazabal, Carl Pettersson, Steve Stricker, Dean Wilson. **151-**Steve Allan, Tommy Armour III, Rich Beem, Brian Davis, Chris DiMarco, Fredrik Jacobson, Kent Jones, Hal Sutton. **152-**Fred Couples, Retief Goosen, Chris Smith. **153-**Jeff Brehaut. **154-**Mark Brooks, David Frost, Tim Herron, Hank Kuehne, Stephen Leaney, Steve Lowery, Chris Riley. **155-**Aaron Baddeley, Richard S. Johnson, Peter Lonard, Jay Williamson. **156-**Billy Andrade, Harrison Frazar, David Gossett, Glen Hnatiuk. **159-**Craig Barlow. **W—**Trevor Immelman. **75-**Brent Geiberger.

The 9th hole at The Stadium Course.

TOURNAMENT HISTORY

Year	Winner	Score	Runner-up	Score	Location	Par/Yards
TOURNAMENT PLAYERS CHAMPIONSHIP						
1974	Jack Nicklaus	272	J.C. Snead	274	Atlanta CC, Marietta, GA	72/6,883
1975	Al Geiberger	270	Dave Stockton	273	Colonial CC, Fort Worth, TX	70/7,160
1976	Jack Nicklaus	269	J.C. Snead	272	Inverrary G&CC, Lauderhill, FL	72/7,127
1977	Mark Hayes	289	Mike McCullough	291	Sawgrass CC, Ponte Vedra Beach, FL	72/7,174
1978	Jack Nicklaus	289	Lou Graham	290	Sawgrass CC, Ponte Vedra Beach, FL	72/7,174
1979	Lanny Wadkins	283	Tom Watson	288	Sawgrass CC, Ponte Vedra Beach, FL	72/7,174
1980	Lee Trevino	278	Ben Crenshaw	279	Sawgrass CC, Ponte Vedra Beach, FL	72/7,174
1981	Raymond Floyd*	285	Barry Jaeckel	285	Sawgrass CC, Ponte Vedra Beach, FL	72/7,174
			Curtis Strange			
1982	Jerry Pate	280	Brad Bryant	282	TPC at Sawgrass, Ponte Vedra Beach, FL	72/6,857
			Scott Simpson			
1983	Hal Sutton	283	Bob Eastwood	284	TPC at Sawgrass, Ponte Vedra Beach, FL	72/6,857
1984	Fred Couples	277	Lee Trevino	278	TPC at Sawgrass, Ponte Vedra Beach, FL	72/6,857
1985	Calvin Peete	274	D.A. Weibring	277	TPC at Sawgrass, Ponte Vedra Beach, FL	72/6,857
1986	John Mahaffey	275	Larry Mize	276	TPC at Sawgrass, Ponte Vedra Beach, FL	72/6,857
1987	Sandy Lyle*	274	Jeff Sluman	274	TPC at Sawgrass, Ponte Vedra Beach, FL	72/6,857
THE PLAYERS CHAMPIONSHIP						
1988	Mark McCumber	273	Mike Reid	277	TPC at Sawgrass, Ponte Vedra Beach, FL	72/6,857
1989	Tom Kite	279	Chip Beck	280	TPC at Sawgrass, Ponte Vedra Beach, FL	72/6,857
1990	Jodie Mudd	278	Mark Calcavecchia	279	TPC at Sawgrass, Ponte Vedra Beach, FL	72/6,857
1991	Steve Elkington	276	Fuzzy Zoeller	277	TPC at Sawgrass, Ponte Vedra Beach, FL	72/6,857
1992	Davis Love III	273	Ian Baker-Finch	277	TPC at Sawgrass, Ponte Vedra Beach, FL	72/6,857
			Phil Blackmar			
			Nick Faldo			
			Tom Watson			
1993	Nick Price	270	Bernhard Langer	275	TPC at Sawgrass, Ponte Vedra Beach, FL	72/6,857
1994	Greg Norman	264	Fuzzy Zoeller	268	TPC at Sawgrass, Ponte Vedra Beach, FL	72/6,857

NOTES

With the 2004 PLAYERS Championship title, ***Adam Scott*** *had won six times in seven attempts when holding at least a share of the 54-hole lead, including four on the European Tour. His only blemish was the 2001 Compass Group English Open, when he carded a final-round 73 to finish third behind fellow Australian* ***Peter O'Malley*** *and Frenchman* ***Raphael Jacquelin****. Scott has posted final rounds in the 70 or better in all six of his professional victories, with a scoring average for the final round at these six events of 68.50.*

Adam Scott *became the sixth international player to win THE PLAYERS Championship and the third Aussie, joining* ***Greg Norman*** *(1994) and two-time champion* ***Steve Elkington*** *(1991, 1997).*

FRED COUPLES

At the age of 23 years, 8 months and 12 days, Adam Scott became the youngest winner in the history of THE PLAYERS Championship. ***Fred Couples****—at the age of 24 years, five months and 28 days – won the 1984 PLAYERS Championship.*

Padraig Harrington*'s back-nine 6-under-par 30 was the low nine-hole score at THE PLAYERS in 2004. It was the first time since 1997 (****Taylor Smith****, 1997 Round 1) that a player posted a 30 on the final nine, and the seventh player all-time to do so at the TPC at Sawgrass. The round started out inauspiciously, as he had three bogeys and a birdie in his first five holes. Over the next 13 holes, Harrington posted six birdies and an eagle to finish at 6-under-par 66 on the day—11-under-par for the tournament for his second consecutive runner-up finish at THE PLAYERS. Starting out five behind Scott, his comeback would have tied the largest comeback in the final 18 holes at THE PLAYERS Championship since* ***Justin Leonard*** *made up five strokes on* ***Lee Janzen*** *on the final day in 1998.*

Tournament Record:
264, Greg Norman, 1994

Current Course Record:
63, Fred Couples, 1992, Greg Norman, 1994

TOURNAMENT HISTORY

Year	Winner	Score	Runner-up	Score	Location	Par/Yards
1995	Lee Janzen	283	Bernhard Langer	284	TPC at Sawgrass, Ponte Vedra Beach, FL	72/6,857
1996	Fred Couples	270	Colin Montgomerie Tommy Tolles	274	TPC at Sawgrass, Ponte Vedra Beach, FL	72/6,896
1997	Steve Elkington	272	Scott Hoch	279	TPC at Sawgrass, Ponte Vedra Beach, FL	72/6,896
1998	Justin Leonard	278	Glen Day Tom Lehman	280	TPC at Sawgrass, Ponte Vedra Beach, FL	72/6,950
1999	David Duval	285	Scott Gump	287	TPC at Sawgrass, Ponte Vedra Beach, FL	72/7,093
2000	Hal Sutton	278	Tiger Woods	279	TPC at Sawgrass, Ponte Vedra Beach, FL	72/7,093
2001	Tiger Woods	274	Vijay Singh	275	TPC at Sawgrass, Ponte Vedra Beach, FL	72/7,093
2002	Craig Perks	280	Stephen Ames	282	TPC at Sawgrass, Ponte Vedra Beach, FL	72/7,093
2003	Davis Love III	271	Jay Haas Padraig Harrington	277	TPC at Sawgrass, Ponte Vedra Beach, FL	72/7,093
2004	Adam Scott	276	Padraig Harrington	277	TPC at Sawgrass, Ponte Vedra Beach, FL	72/7,093

KEY: * = Playoff

ELIGIBILITY REQUIREMENTS FOR THE 2005 THE PLAYERS CHAMPIONSHIP

Eligible players are:

- Winners of PGA TOUR cosponsored or approved tournaments, whose victories are considered official, since the previous year's PLAYERS Championship.
- The top 125 finishers on the 2004 Official PGA TOUR Money List.
- For the duration of their exemption, PGA TOUR members who earned a Tournament Winner exemption prior to March 1, 2004.
- Winners of THE PLAYERS Championship, Masters Tournament, U.S. Open, British Open and PGA Championship from 1995 to 1997 and from 2000 to 2004. Beginning with 1998, winners will be eligible for five years.
- Winners of the NEC World Series of Golf in the last 10 years (1995-1997).
- Winners of THE TOUR Championship in the last three years (2002-2004).
- Winners of the WGC-Accenture Match Play Championship in the last three years (2003-2005).
- Winners of the WGC-NEC Invitational and WGC-American Express Championship in the last three years (2002-2004).
- Any player(s), not otherwise eligible, among the top 50 leaders from the Official World Golf Ranking through the Bay Hill Invitational.
- Any player(s), not otherwise eligible, among the top 10 leaders from the 2005 Official PGA TOUR Money List through the Bay Hill Invitational.
- If necessary to complete a field of 144 players, PGA TOUR members from the 2005 Official PGA TOUR Money List below 10th position through the Bay Hill Invitational, in order of their positions on such list.
- The PLAYERS Championship Committee may invite a player(s), not otherwise eligible, who is a current inductee of the World Golf Hall of Fame. (NOTE: Such a player would be added to the field.)

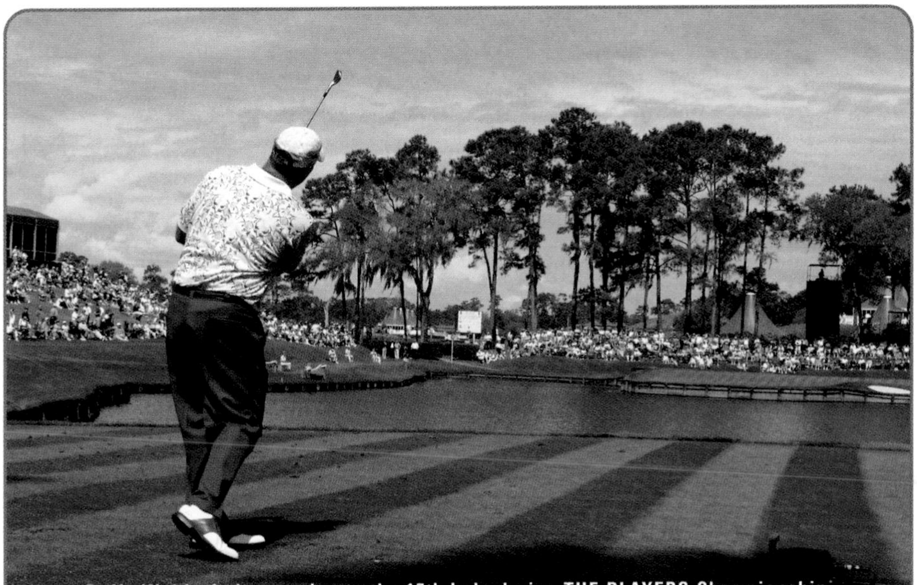

Duffy Waldorf plays a shot to the 17th hole during THE PLAYERS Championship.

2004 BellSouth Classic [14th of 48 official events]

BELLSOUTH CLASSIC

JOHNSON

Winner: ZACH JOHNSON
69-66-68-72 275 (-12) $810,000

Tournament Players Club at Sugarloaf

Duluth, GA

April 1-4, 2004

Purse: $4,500,000
Par: 36-36—72
Yards: 7,293

LEADERS: First Round—Roger Tambellini and Jose Maria Olazabal shot 7-under 65s to lead Craig Bowden by one. Tim Petrovic and Shaun Micheel were two back.
Second Round—Zach Johnson fired a 6-under par 66 to take a two-stroke lead at 9-under-par 135. Bowden, Petrovic and Ben Crane were all at 7-under-par 137.
Third Round—Johnson moved to 13-under 203 to extend his lead to three strokes over Padraig Harrington and Scott Hend.

CUT: 71 players at 1-over-par 145 from a field of 143 professionals and one amateur

PRO-AM: Billy Andrade, Rory Sabbatini, 56, $1,150 each. Stewart Cink, Steve Elkington, 28, $900 each. Lee Janzen, David Gossett, 28, $900 each.

WEATHER: Cold and windy on Thursday with temperatures in the low 50s and winds 15-25 mph. Cold and windy again on Friday with temperatures in the high 50s. Lots of sunshine on Saturday with temperatures reaching the high 60s. Turning cold and windy again on Sunday with temperatures in the low 60s. Afternoon winds 15-20 mph

Check out the 2005 BellSouth Classic, March 31-April 3 on USA/NBC

ORDER OF FINISH

Zach Johnson	1	69-66-68-72	275	$810,000.00
Mark Hensby	2	73-70-66-67	276	486,000.00
Scott Hend	3	72-66-68-71	277	306,000.00
Padraig Harrington	4	70-69-67-72	278	216,000.00
Peter Lonard	5	73-67-69-71	280	180,000.00
Ben Crane	T6	68-69-71-73	281	156,375.00
Lee Janzen	T6	75-67-68-71	281	156,375.00
Stewart Cink	T8	75-67-69-71	282	135,000.00
Luke Donald	T8	72-70-71-69	282	135,000.00
Phil Mickelson	10	69-72-71-71	283	121,500.00
David Peoples	T11	73-72-66-73	284	103,500.00
Tim Petrovic	T11	67-70-75-72	284	103,500.00
Grant Waite	T11	73-72-70-69	284	103,500.00
Steve Allan	T14	71-72-71-71	285	74,250.00
Craig Bowden	T14	66-71-72-76	285	74,250.00
Brian Gay	T14	68-70-69-78	285	74,250.00
Neal Lancaster	T14	70-75-66-74	285	74,250.00
Tag Ridings (S)	T14	73-69-71-72	285	74,250.00
Roger Tambellini	T14	65-78-72-70	285	74,250.00
Briny Baird	T20	74-69-70-73	286	45,393.75
Jeff Brehaut	T20	71-74-69-72	286	45,393.75
Chris DiMarco	T20	75-70-72-69	286	45,393.75
Glen Hnatiuk	T20	70-72-68-76	286	45,393.75
Blaine McCallister	T20	71-69-71-75	286	$45,393.75
Arron Oberholser	T20	72-68-71-75	286	45,393.75
Chris Smith	T20	70-70-74-72	286	45,393.75
Duffy Waldorf	T20	73-70-71-72	286	45,393.75
Larry Mize (S)	T28	76-69-70-72	287	32,625.00
Kevin Na	T28	73-71-69-74	287	32,625.00
Kris Cox (S)	T30	71-70-70-77	288	27,945.00
Steve Lowery	T30	71-73-67-77	288	27,945.00
Shaun Micheel	T30	67-72-75-74	288	27,945.00
David Morland IV	T30	72-70-72-74	288	27,945.00
Steve Stricker	T30	69-76-73-70	288	27,945.00
Rich Beem	T35	69-75-73-72	289	23,175.00
Steve Elkington	T35	70-75-71-73	289	23,175.00
Harrison Frazar	T35	71-74-69-75	289	23,175.00
Steve Flesch	T38	71-73-71-75	290	18,450.00
Robert Gamez	T38	71-70-76-73	290	18,450.00
Brent Geiberger	T38	73-70-72-75	290	18,450.00
John Huston	T38	70-73-72-75	290	18,450.00
Franklin Langham (S)	T38	74-70-72-74	290	18,450.00
Joe Ogilvie	T38	70-75-69-76	290	18,450.00
Pat Perez	T38	73-71-74-72	290	18,450.00
Brian Bateman	T45	73-70-75-73	291	12,612.86
Bob Burns	T45	76-69-73-73	291	12,612.86
Spike McRoy	T45	70-73-74-74	291	12,612.86
Brett Quigley	T45	73-71-74-73	291	12,612.86
Mike Weir	T45	73-70-73-75	291	$12,612.86
Jose Maria Olazabal	T45	65-77-73-76	291	12,612.85
Deane Pappas	T45	72-72-71-76	291	12,612.85
Guy Boros	T52	72-73-71-76	292	10,552.50
Chris Couch	T52	72-69-75-76	292	10,552.50
Richard S. Johnson	T52	72-73-73-74	292	10,552.50
Carl Pettersson	T52	76-68-73-75	292	10,552.50
Kevin Durkin (Q)	T56	71-73-72-77	293	9,945.00
Lucas Glover	T56	75-70-72-76	293	9,945.00
Jonathan Kaye	T56	73-72-71-77	293	9,945.00
Billy Mayfair	T56	68-76-73-76	293	9,945.00
Scott McCarron	T56	74-71-72-76	293	9,945.00
Dennis Paulson	T56	72-73-71-77	293	9,945.00
Rory Sabbatini	T56	68-75-75-75	293	9,945.00
Scott Simpson (S)	T56	68-76-70-79	293	9,945.00
David Branshaw	T64	72-73-72-77	294	9,495.00
Danny Briggs	T64	70-74-75-75	294	9,495.00
Brian Kortan	T66	69-73-73-80	295	9,315.00
Bo Van Pelt	T66	75-70-74-76	295	9,315.00
Roland Thatcher	68	72-71-72-81	296	9,180.00
Daniel Chopra	69	71-73-76-77	297	9,090.00
Hirofumi Miyase	70	70-73-75-80	298	9,000.00
Brian Watts	71	71-73-77-79	300	8,910.00

(Q) = Open Qualifier; (S) = Sponsor Exemption; (T) = Tie

The following players did not finish

(C=cut, W=withdrew, A=amateur)

C—146-Michael Allen, Cliff Kresge, Paul Stankowski. **147-**Rich Barcelo, Bart Bryant, Jason Dufner, J.J. Henry, Joel Kribel, Matt Kuchar, Brenden Pappas, Ted Purdy, Adam Scott, Joey Sindelar, Heath Slocum, Andre Stolz, Tim Weinhart. **148-**Cameron Beckman, Dan Forsman, David Gossett, Skip Kendall, Patrick Sheehan, Boyd Summerhays, Hal Sutton, Hidemichi Tanaka, Tjaart Van der Walt. **149-**Jason Bohn, Mark Brooks, Ken Duke, Esteban Toledo, Bob Tway. **150-**Pat Bates, Notah Begay III, Jim Carter, Glen Day, Trevor Dodds, Kevin Muncrief, Dan Olsen, Corey Pavin, Vaughn Taylor, Jay Williamson. **151-**Billy Andrade, Nick Cassini, Niclas Fasth, Kent Jones, Hunter Mahan, Greg Norman, Tom Pernice, Jr., John Rollins, Omar Uresti. **152-**Paul Azinger, Ricky Barnes, Tom Carter, Ryan Palmer, Phillip Price. **153-**D.J. Brigman, Paul Lawrie, John Maginnes. **154-**Matt Gogel, Tripp Isenhour, David Noll (A), Craig Stevens. **155-**Thomas Bjorn, Jay Delsing, Patrick Moore, David Toms. **156-**Arjun Atwal, Brad Lardon. **157-**Bryce Molder. **158-**Brian Dixon, Tommy Tolles. **160-**Steve Pate. **W**—Kevin Sutherland, Roger Rowland.

MARK HENSBY

TOURNAMENT HISTORY

Year	Winner	Score	Runner-up	Score	Location	Par/Yards
ATLANTA CLASSIC						
1967	Bob Charles	282	Tommy Bolt	284	Atlanta CC, Marietta, GA	72/7,007
			Richard Crawford			
			Gardner Dickinson			
1968	Bob Lunn	280	Lee Trevino	283	Atlanta CC, Marietta, GA	72/7,007
1969	Bert Yancey*	277	Bruce Devlin	277	Atlanta CC, Marietta, GA	72/7,007
1970	Tommy Aaron	275	Dan Sikes	276	Atlanta CC, Marietta, GA	72/7,007
1971	Gardner Dickinson*	275	Jack Nicklaus	275	Atlanta CC, Marietta, GA	72/7,007
1972	Bob Lunn	275	Gary Player	277	Atlanta CC, Marietta, GA	72/7,007
1973	Jack Nicklaus	272	Tom Weiskopf	274	Atlanta CC, Marietta, GA	72/7,007
1974	No Tournament+					
1975	Hale Irwin	271	Tom Watson	275	Atlanta CC, Marietta, GA	72/7,007
1976	No Tournament++					
1977	Hale Irwin	273	Steve Veriato	274	Atlanta CC, Marietta, GA	72/7,007
1978	Jerry Heard	269	Lou Graham	271	Atlanta CC, Marietta, GA	72/7,007
			Bob Murphy			
			Tom Watson			
1979	Andy Bean	265	Joe Inman	273	Atlanta CC, Marietta, GA	72/7,007
1980	Larry Nelson	270	Andy Bean	277	Atlanta CC, Marietta, GA	72/7,007
			Don Pooley			
1981	Tom Watson*	277	Tommy Valentine	277	Atlanta CC, Marietta, GA	72/7,007
GEORGIA-PACIFIC ATLANTA GOLF CLASSIC						
1982	Keith Fergus*	273	Raymond Floyd	273	Atlanta CC, Marietta, GA	72/7,007
1983	Calvin Peete~	206	Chip Beck	208	Atlanta CC, Marietta, GA	72/7,007
			Jim Colbert			
			Don Pooley			
1984	Tom Kite	269	Don Pooley	274	Atlanta CC, Marietta, GA	72/7,007
1985	Wayne Levi*	273	Steve Pate	273	Atlanta CC, Marietta, GA	72/7,007
1986	Bob Tway	269	Hal Sutton	271	Atlanta CC, Marietta, GA	72/7,007
1987	Dave Barr	265	Larry Mize	269	Atlanta CC, Marietta, GA	72/7,007
1988	Larry Nelson	268	Chip Beck	269	Atlanta CC, Marietta, GA	72/7,007

NOTES

Zach Johnson *became the fourth player to win his first PGA TOUR event at the BellSouth Classic, joining* ***Ben Crane*** *(2003),* ***Paul Stankowski*** *(1996) and* ***Tommy Aaron*** *(1970).*

ZACH JOHNSON

Zach Johnson *tried to become just the third player since the BellSouth Classic moved to TPC at Sugarloaf to string together four rounds in the 60s in a single event. A final-round 72 kept him from the mark.* ***David Duval*** *accomplished the feat when he won the 1999 tournament. That same year* ***Davis Love III*** *finished T7 and posted four rounds in the 60s.*

Zach Johnson *became the 16th rookie in TOUR history to earn $1 million in his first season.* ***Todd Hamilton*** *did it earlier in 2004. Johnson surpassed the $1-million mark in just nine events.*

Stewart Cink *posted his sixth top-10 finish at the TPC at Sugarloaf in eight appearances with his T8. He missed the cut in the other two starts.* ***Phil Mickelson*** *added his fifth at the course. The pair are tops in that category since the tournament moved to this course in 1997. Cink's sixth top-10 at the BellSouth Classic moved him into second on the all-time list behind* ***Jack Nicklaus*** *and* ***Don Pooley****.*

Australian rookie ***Scott Hend*** *made the first cut of his career in his sixth career event on the PGA TOUR. He made the most of it with his first top-10, a T3, that earned him his first TOUR paycheck of $306,000.*

Phil Mickelson *became the new leading money winner at the BellSouth Classic thanks to his 10th-place finish. Mickelson passed* ***Scott McCarron*** *($1,070,277) with earnings of $1,133,416 in seven appearances.*

Tournament Record:
265, Andy Bean, 1979; Dave Barr, 1987 (Atlanta CC)

Current Course Record:
63, Tiger Woods, 1998; Duffy Waldorf, 1999; Ben Crane, 2003

Tournament Course Record:
61, Andy Bean, 1979 (Atlanta CC)

TOURNAMENT HISTORY

Year	Winner	Score	Runner-up	Score	Location	Par/Yards
ATLANTA CLASSIC						
1967	Bob Charles	282	Tommy Bolt Richard Crawford Gardner Dickinson	284	Atlanta CC, Marietta, GA	72/7,007
1968	Bob Lunn	280	Lee Trevino	283	Atlanta CC, Marietta, GA	72/7,007
1969	Bert Yancey*	277	Bruce Devlin	277	Atlanta CC, Marietta, GA	72/7,007
1970	Tommy Aaron	275	Dan Sikes	276	Atlanta CC, Marietta, GA	72/7,007
1971	Gardner Dickinson*	275	Jack Nicklaus	275	Atlanta CC, Marietta, GA	72/7,007
1972	Bob Lunn	275	Gary Player	277	Atlanta CC, Marietta, GA	72/7,007
1973	Jack Nicklaus	272	Tom Weiskopf	274	Atlanta CC, Marietta, GA	72/7,007
1974	No Tournament+					
1975	Hale Irwin	271	Tom Watson	275	Atlanta CC, Marietta, GA	72/7,007
1976	No Tournament++					
1977	Hale Irwin	273	Steve Veriato	274	Atlanta CC, Marietta, GA	72/7,007
1978	Jerry Heard	269	Lou Graham Bob Murphy Tom Watson	271	Atlanta CC, Marietta, GA	72/7,007
1979	Andy Bean	265	Joe Inman	273	Atlanta CC, Marietta, GA	72/7,007
1980	Larry Nelson	270	Andy Bean Don Pooley	277	Atlanta CC, Marietta, GA	72/7,007
1981	Tom Watson*	277	Tommy Valentine	277	Atlanta CC, Marietta, GA	72/7,007
GEORGIA-PACIFIC ATLANTA GOLF CLASSIC						
1982	Keith Fergus*	273	Raymond Floyd	273	Atlanta CC, Marietta, GA	72/7,007
1983	Calvin Peete~	206	Chip Beck Jim Colbert Don Pooley	208	Atlanta CC, Marietta, GA	72/7,007
1984	Tom Kite	269	Don Pooley	274	Atlanta CC, Marietta, GA	72/7,007
1985	Wayne Levi*	273	Steve Pate	273	Atlanta CC, Marietta, GA	72/7,007
1986	Bob Tway	269	Hal Sutton	271	Atlanta CC, Marietta, GA	72/7,007
1987	Dave Barr	265	Larry Mize	269	Atlanta CC, Marietta, GA	72/7,007
1988	Larry Nelson	268	Chip Beck	269	Atlanta CC, Marietta, GA	72/7,007
BELLSOUTH ATLANTA GOLF CLASSIC						
1989	Scott Simpson	278	Bob Tway	278	Atlanta CC, Marietta, GA	72/7,007
1990	Wayne Levi	275	Keith Clearwater Larry Mize Nick Price	276	Atlanta CC, Marietta, GA	72/7,007
1991	Corey Pavin*	272	Steve Pate	272	Atlanta CC, Marietta, GA	72/7,007
BELLSOUTH CLASSIC						
1992	Tom Kite	272	Jay Don Blake	275	Atlanta CC, Marietta, GA	72/7,007
1993	Nolan Henke	271	Mark Calcavecchia Nick Price Tom Sieckmann	273	Atlanta CC, Marietta, GA	72/7,007
1994	John Daly	274	Nolan Henke Brian Henninger	275	Atlanta CC, Marietta, GA	72/7,007
1995	Mark Calcavecchia	271	Jim Gallagher, Jr.	273	Atlanta CC, Marietta, GA	72/7,007
1996	Paul Stankowski*	280	Brandel Chamblee	280	Atlanta CC, Marietta, GA	72/7,018
1997	Scott McCarron	274	David Duval Brian Henninger Lee Janzen	277	TPC at Sugarloaf, Duluth, GA	72/7,259
1998	Tiger Woods	271	Jay Don Blake	272	TPC at Sugarloaf, Duluth, GA	72/7,259
1999	David Duval	270	Stewart Cink	272	TPC at Sugarloaf, Duluth, GA	72/7,259
2000	Phil Mickelson~*	205	Gary Nicklaus	205	TPC at Sugarloaf, Duluth, GA	72/7,259
2001	Scott McCarron	280	Mike Weir	283	TPC at Sugarloaf, Duluth, GA	72/7,259
2002	Retief Goosen	272	Jesper Parnevik	276	TPC at Sugarloaf, Duluth, GA	72/7,259
2003	Ben Crane	272	Bob Tway	276	TPC at Sugarloaf, Duluth, GA	72/7,293
2004	Zach Johnson	275	Mark Hensby	276	TPC at Sugarloaf, Duluth, GA	72/7,293

*KEY: * = Playoff ~ = Weather-shortened + = Served as site for Tournament Players Championship ++ = Served as site for U.S. Open*

SECTION 3 TOURNAMENT HISTORIES

2004 Masters Tournament [15th of 48 official events]

Winner: PHIL MICKELSON
72-69-69-69 279 (-9) $1,170,000

Augusta National Golf Club

Augusta, GA

April 8-11, 2003

Purse: $6,500,000
Par: 36-36—72
Yards: 7,290

LEADERS: First Round—Justin Rose's 5-under 67 gave him a two-stroke lead over Chris DiMarco and Jay Haas.
Second Round—Rose moved to 6-under 138, two ahead of Alex Cejka and Jose Maria Olazabal. K.J. Choi and Phil Mickelson were three back.
Third Round—DiMarco and Mickelson sat at 6-under 210, while Paul Casey trailed by one. Bernhard Langer, Ernie Els and Choi were three behind.

CUT: 42 professionals and two amateurs at 4-over-par 148 from a field of 88 professionals and five amateurs.

WEATHER: Cloudy with light rain off and on throughout Thursday. Temperatures in the 60s-70s, and SW winds reaching 18 mph. Play was suspended at 4:09 p.m. due to severe weather in the area for two hours and six minutes. Play was suspended for the day at 7:45 p.m. due to darkness. There were 18 players left on the course. First-round resumed at 8 a.m. Friday with the second round resuming at 8:45 a.m. A mix of sun and clouds on Friday with temperatures in the 70s. Plenty of sun and temperatures in the 80s on Saturday. Hazy and humid on Sunday with temperatures in the high 70s.

Check out the 2005 Masters Tournament, April 7-10 on USA/CBS

ORDER OF FINISH

Phil Mickelson	1	72-69-69-69	279	$1,170,000.00
Ernie Els	2	70-72-71-67	280	702,000.00
K.J. Choi	3	71-70-72-69	282	442,000.00
Sergio Garcia	T4	72-72-75-66	285	286,000.00
Bernhard Langer	T4	71-73-69-72	285	286,000.00
Paul Casey	T6	75-69-68-74	286	189,893.00
Fred Couples	T6	73-69-74-70	286	189,893.00
Chris DiMarco	T6	69-73-68-76	286	189,893.00
Davis Love III	T6	75-67-74-70	286	189,893.00
Nick Price	T6	72-73-71-70	286	189,893.00
Vijay Singh	T6	75-73-69-69	286	189,893.00
Kirk Triplett	T6	71-74-69-72	286	189,893.00
Retief Goosen	T13	75-73-70-70	288	125,667.00
Padraig Harrington	T13	74-74-68-72	288	$125,667.00
Charles Howell III	T13	71-71-76-70	288	125,667.00
Casey Wittenberg	T13	76-72-71-69	288	Amateur
Stewart Cink	T17	74-73-69-73	289	97,500.00
Steve Flesch	T17	76-67-77-69	289	97,500.00
Jay Haas	T17	69-75-72-73	289	97,500.00
Fredrik Jacobson	T17	74-74-67-74	289	97,500.00
Stephen Leaney	T17	76-71-73-69	289	97,500.00
Stuart Appleby	T22	73-74-73-70	290	70,200.00
Shaun Micheel	T22	72-76-72-70	290	70,200.00
Justin Rose	T22	67-71-81-71	290	70,200.00
Tiger Woods	T22	75-69-75-71	290	70,200.00
Alex Cejka	26	70-70-78-73	291	57,200.00
Mark O'Meara	T27	73-70-75-74	292	51,025.00
Bob Tway	T27	75-71-74-72	292	51,025.00
Scott Verplank	29	74-71-76-72	293	48,100.00
Jose Maria Olazabal	30	71-69-79-75	294	$46,150.00
Bob Estes	T31	76-72-73-74	295	41,275.00
Brad Faxon	T31	72-76-76-71	295	41,275.00
Jerry Kelly	T31	74-72-73-76	295	41,275.00
Ian Poulter	T31	75-73-74-73	295	41,275.00
Justin Leonard	T35	76-72-72-76	296	35,913.00
Phillip Price	T35	71-76-73-76	296	35,913.00
Paul Lawrie	T37	77-70-73-77	297	32,663.00
Sandy Lyle	T37	72-74-75-76	297	32,663.00
Eduardo Romero	39	74-73-74-77	298	30,550.00
Todd Hamilton	40	77-71-76-75	299	29,250.00
Tim Petrovic	T41	72-75-75-78	300	27,950.00
Brandt Snedeker	T41	73-75-75-77	300	Amateur
Jeff Sluman	43	73-70-82-77	302	26,650.00
Chris Riley	44	70-78-78-78	304	25,350.00

(T) = Tie

The following players did not finish (C=cut, A=amateur)

C—149-Robert Allenby, Michael Campbell, Darren Clarke, Ben Crenshaw, John Daly, Raymond Floyd, J.L. Lewis, Zhang Lian-wei, Peter Lonard, Craig Perks, John Rollins, Craig Stadler, Mike Weir. **150-**Briny Baird, Rich Beem, Ben Curtis, Fred Funk, Jeff Maggert, Larry Mize, Jack Nicklaus, Craig Parry, Nathan T. Smith (A). **151-**Angel Cabrera, Nick Faldo, Jonathan Kaye, Len Mattiace, Rocco Mediate, Colin Montgomerie, David Toms, Ian Woosnam. **152-**Nick Flanagan (A), Toshi Izawa, Kenny Perry, Tom Watson. **153-**Jonathan Byrd, Chad Campbell, Trevor Immelman, Shigeki Maruyama, Adam Scott, Gary Wolstenholme (A). **154-**Tim Clark, Tim Herron. **155-**Brian Davis. **157-**Thomas Bjorn. **160-**Fuzzy Zoeller. **162-**Gary Player. **167-**Charles Coody. **168-**Arnold Palmer. **170-**Tommy Aaron.

Phil Mickelson on the Tonight Show.

TOURNAMENT HISTORY

Year	Winner	Score	Runner-up	Score	Location	Par/Yards
MASTERS TOURNAMENT						
1934	Horton Smith	284	Craig Wood	285	Augusta National GC, Augusta, GA	72/6,925
1935	Gene Sarazen*	282	Craig Wood	282	Augusta National GC, Augusta, GA	72/6,925
1936	Horton Smith	285	Harry Cooper	286	Augusta National GC, Augusta, GA	72/6,925
1937	Byron Nelson	283	Ralph Guldahl	285	Augusta National GC, Augusta, GA	72/6,925
1938	Henry Picard	285	Ralph Guldahl Harry Cooper	287	Augusta National GC, Augusta, GA	72/6,925
1939	Ralph Guldahl	279	Sam Snead	280	Augusta National GC, Augusta, GA	72/6,925
1940	Jimmy Demaret	280	Lloyd Mangrum	284	Augusta National GC, Augusta, GA	72/6,925
1941	Craig Wood	280	Byron Nelson	283	Augusta National GC, Augusta, GA	72/6,925
1942	Byron Nelson*	280	Ben Hogan	280	Augusta National GC, Augusta, GA	72/6,925
1943	No Tournament ++					
1944	No Tournament ++					
1945	No Tournament ++					
1946	Herman Keiser	282	Ben Hogan	283	Augusta National GC, Augusta, GA	72/6,925
1947	Jimmy Demaret	281	Byron Nelson Frank Stranahan	283	Augusta National GC, Augusta, GA	72/6,925
1948	Claude Harmon	279	Cary Middlecoff	284	Augusta National GC, Augusta, GA	72/6,925
1949	Sam Snead	282	Johnny Bulla Lloyd Mangrum	285	Augusta National GC, Augusta, GA	72/6,925
1950	Jimmy Demaret	283	Jim Ferrier	285	Augusta National GC, Augusta, GA	72/6,925
1951	Ben Hogan	280	Skee Riegel	282	Augusta National GC, Augusta, GA	72/6,925
1952	Sam Snead	286	Jack Burke, Jr.	290	Augusta National GC, Augusta, GA	72/6,925
1953	Ben Hogan	274	Ed Oliver, Jr.	279	Augusta National GC, Augusta, GA	72/6,925
1954	Sam Snead*	289	Ben Hogan	289	Augusta National GC, Augusta, GA	72/6,925
1955	Cary Middlecoff	279	Ben Hogan	286	Augusta National GC, Augusta, GA	72/6,925
1956	Jack Burke, Jr.	289	Ken Venturi	290	Augusta National GC, Augusta, GA	72/6,925
1957	Doug Ford	282	Sam Snead	286	Augusta National GC, Augusta, GA	72/6,925
1958	Arnold Palmer	284	Doug Ford Fred Hawkins	285	Augusta National GC, Augusta, GA	72/6,925
1959	Art Wall	284	Cary Middlecoff	285	Augusta National GC, Augusta, GA	72/6,925
1960	Arnold Palmer	282	Ken Venturi	283	Augusta National GC, Augusta, GA	72/6,925
1961	Gary Player	280	Charles R. Coe Arnold Palmer	281	Augusta National GC, Augusta, GA	72/6,925
1962	Arnold Palmer*	280	Gary Player Dow Finsterwald	280	Augusta National GC, Augusta, GA	72/6,925
1963	Jack Nicklaus	286	Tony Lema	287	Augusta National GC, Augusta, GA	72/6,925
1964	Arnold Palmer	276	Dave Marr Jack Nicklaus	282	Augusta National GC, Augusta, GA	72/6,925

NOTES

Phil Mickelson's 5-under 31 on the back nine in 2004 was the lowest final-round back nine by a winner since **Jack Nicklaus**' 30 in 1986. **Gary Player** also had a 30 in 1978.

Phil Mickelson became the second consecutive first-time major championship winner at the Masters, following 2003 champion **Mike Weir**, and the sixth consecutive in the majors dating back to **Ernie Els** becoming a repeat major winner at the 2002 British Open (**Rich Beem**/2002 PGA; Weir/2003 Masters; **Jim Furyk**/2003 U.S. Open; **Ben Curtis**/2003 British Open; **Shaun Micheel**/2003 PGA).

When **Phil Mickelson** sank the winning putt on the 18th hole on Sunday, it was the sixth time a winner had birdied the final hole to win the Masters. The others include **Mark O'Meara** (1998), **Sandy Lyle** (1988), **Gary Player** (1978), **Arnold Palmer** (1960) and **Art Wall** (1959). It was also the fourth time the birdie has come on the final putt of the tournament—Palmer, Lyle and O'Meara.

Phil Mickelson became the 14th straight player to come from the final round's last pairing at the Masters and win. **Nick Faldo** was the last player to come from outside the last group and win the Masters, in 1990.

Phil Mickelson had the third-most victories (22) by a player prior to earning his first major championship victory. **Ben Hogan** won 30 times prior to winning the 1946 PGA Championship, while **Sam Snead** won 27 times before winning the 1942 PGA Championship.

With **Phil Mickelson**'s win, it was the first time that left-handers have won the same major championship in back-to-back years, following **Mike Weir** in 2003. Mickelson became the third left-hander to win a major following Weir and **Bob Charles** at the 1963 British Open.

Tournament Record:
270, Tiger Woods, 1997
Current Course Record:
63, Nick Price, 1986; Greg Norman, 1996

TOURNAMENT HISTORY

Year	Winner	Score	Runner-up	Score	Location	Par/Yards
1965	Jack Nicklaus	271	Arnold Palmer Gary Player	280	Augusta National GC, Augusta, GA	72/6,925
1966	Jack Nicklaus*	288	Tommy Jacobs Gay Brewer, Jr.	288	Augusta National GC, Augusta, GA	72/6,925
1967	Gay Brewer, Jr.	280	Bobby Nichols	281	Augusta National GC, Augusta, GA	72/6,925
1968	Bob Goalby	277	Roberto De Vicenzo	278	Augusta National GC, Augusta, GA	72/6,925
1969	George Archer	281	Billy Casper George Knudson Tom Weiskopf	282	Augusta National GC, Augusta, GA	72/6,925
1970	Billy Casper*	279	Gene Littler	279	Augusta National GC, Augusta, GA	72/6,925
1971	Charles Coody	279	Johnny Miller Jack Nicklaus	281	Augusta National GC, Augusta, GA	72/6,925
1972	Jack Nicklaus	286	Bruce Crampton Bobby Mitchell Tom Weiskopf	289	Augusta National GC, Augusta, GA	72/6,925
1973	Tommy Aaron	283	J. C. Snead	284	Augusta National GC, Augusta, GA	72/6,925
1974	Gary Player	278	Tom Weiskopf Dave Stockton	280	Augusta National GC, Augusta, GA	72/6,925
1975	Jack Nicklaus	276	Johnny Miller Tom Weiskopf	277	Augusta National GC, Augusta, GA	72/6,925
1976	Raymond Floyd	271	Ben Crenshaw	279	Augusta National GC, Augusta, GA	72/6,925
1977	Tom Watson	276	Jack Nicklaus	278	Augusta National GC, Augusta, GA	72/6,925
1978	Gary Player	277	Hubert Green Rod Funseth Tom Watson	278	Augusta National GC, Augusta, GA	72/6,925
1979	Fuzzy Zoeller*	280	Ed Sneed Tom Watson	280	Augusta National GC, Augusta, GA	72/6,925
1980	Seve Ballesteros	275	Gibby Gilbert Jack Newton	279	Augusta National GC, Augusta, GA	72/6,925
1981	Tom Watson	280	Johnny Miller Jack Nicklaus	282	Augusta National GC, Augusta, GA	72/6,925
1982	Craig Stadler*	284	Dan Pohl	284	Augusta National GC, Augusta, GA	72/6,925
1983	Seve Ballesteros	280	Ben Crenshaw Tom Kite	284	Augusta National GC, Augusta, GA	72/6,925
1984	Ben Crenshaw	277	Tom Watson	279	Augusta National GC, Augusta, GA	72/6,925
1985	Bernhard Langer	282	Curtis Strange Seve Ballesteros Raymond Floyd	284	Augusta National GC, Augusta, GA	72/6,925
1986	Jack Nicklaus	279	Greg Norman Tom Kite	280	Augusta National GC, Augusta, GA	72/6,925
1987	Larry Mize*	285	Seve Ballesteros Greg Norman	285	Augusta National GC, Augusta, GA	72/6,925
1988	Sandy Lyle	281	Mark Calcavecchia	282	Augusta National GC, Augusta, GA	72/6,925
1989	Nick Faldo*	283	Scott Hoch	283	Augusta National GC, Augusta, GA	72/6,925
1990	Nick Faldo*	278	Raymond Floyd	278	Augusta National GC, Augusta, GA	72/6,925
1991	Ian Woosnam	277	Jose Maria Olazabal	278	Augusta National GC, Augusta, GA	72/6,925
1992	Fred Couples	275	Raymond Floyd	277	Augusta National GC, Augusta, GA	72/6,925
1993	Bernhard Langer	277	Chip Beck	281	Augusta National GC, Augusta, GA	72/6,925
1994	Jose Maria Olazabal	279	Tom Lehman	281	Augusta National GC, Augusta, GA	72/6,925
1995	Ben Crenshaw	274	Davis Love III	275	Augusta National GC, Augusta, GA	72/6,925
1996	Nick Faldo	276	Greg Norman	281	Augusta National GC, Augusta, GA	72/6,925
1997	Tiger Woods	270	Tom Kite	282	Augusta National GC, Augusta, GA	72/6,925
1998	Mark O'Meara	279	David Duval Fred Couples	280	Augusta National GC, Augusta, GA	72/6,925
1999	Jose Maria Olazabal	280	Davis Love III	282	Augusta National GC, Augusta, GA	72/6,985
2000	Vijay Singh	278	Ernie Els	281	Augusta National GC, Augusta, GA	72/6,985
2001	Tiger Woods	272	David Duval	274	Augusta National GC, Augusta, GA	72/6,985
2002	Tiger Woods	276	Retief Goosen	279	Augusta National GC, Augusta, GA	72/7,270
2003	Mike Weir*	281	Len Mattiace	281	Augusta National GC, Augusta, GA	72/7,290
2004	Phil Mickelson	279	Ernie Els	280	Augusta National GC, Augusta, GA	72/7,290

*KEY: * = Playoff ++ = World War II*

ELIGIBILITY REQUIREMENTS FOR THE 2005 MASTERS TOURNAMENT

- Masters Champions (Lifetime).
- U.S. Open Champions (Honorary, non-competing after 5 years).
- British Open Champions (Honorary, non-competing after 5 years).
- PGA Champions (Honorary, non-competing after 5 years).
- Winners of THE PLAYERS Championship (3 years).
- Current U.S. Amateur Champion (6-A) (Honorary, non-competing after 1 year); Runner-up to the current U.S. Amateur Champion.
- Current British Amateur Champion (Honorary, non-competing after 1 year).
- Current U.S. Amateur Public Links Champion.
- Current U.S. Mid-Amateur Champion.
- The first 16 players, including ties, in the previous year's Masters.
- The first 8 players, including ties, in the previous year's U.S. Open.
- The first 4 players, including ties, in the previous year's British Open.
- The first 4 players, including ties, in the previous year's PGA.
- The 40 leaders on the Final PGA TOUR Money List for the previous year.
- The 10 leaders on the PGA TOUR Money List through THE PLAYERS Championship.
- The 50 leaders on the Final Official World Golf Ranking for the previous year.
- The 50 leaders on the Official World Golf Ranking through THE PLAYERS Championship.

The Masters Committee, at its discretion, also invites International players not otherwise qualified.

SECTION 3 TOURNAMENT HISTORIES

2004 MCI Heritage [16th of 48 official events]

MCI Heritage

Winner: STEWART CINK #
72-69-69-64 274 (-10) $864,000

Harbour Town Golf Links

Hilton Head, SC

April 15-18, 2004

Purse: $4,800,000
Par: 36-35—71
Yards: 6,973

LEADERS: First Round—Cameron Beckman shot a 4-under 67 to take a one-stroke lead over Heath Slocum, Jonathan Byrd, Ben Curtis, Rod Pampling and Jay Haas.
Second Round—Curtis, at 8-under 134, moved one stroke ahead of Slocum and two in front of Ted Purdy.
Third Round—Purdy, after a 6-under 65, moved to 12-under 201. He was four strokes ahead of Slocum and five better than Stephen Ames.

CUT: 72 players at 2-over-par 144 from a field of 132 professionals and one amateur.

PRO-AM: $10,000. Bob Tway and Brad Faxon, 55, $1,800 each

WEATHER: Breezy and cool Thursday morning, with temperatures warming to 70 and N winds 10-20 mph. Sunny and warmer Friday after a cool morning with high temperature of 73 and SE winds 10-15 mph. Sunny on Saturday with a high in the mid-70s, with S-SE ocean breezes at 10-15 mph. On Sunday, bright sunshine with a high temperature of 76 and S-SE winds at 5-10 mph.

Check out the 2005 MCI Heritage, April 14-17 on USA/CBS

ORDER OF FINISH

 # Won playoff with a birdie-3 on fifth playoff hole

Stewart Cink #	1	72-69-69-64	274	$864,000.00
Ted Purdy	2	69-67-65-73	274	518,400.00
Ernie Els	T3	69-70-68-69	276	249,600.00
Carl Pettersson	T3	72-71-66-67	276	249,600.00
Patrick Sheehan	T3	71-66-69-70	276	249,600.00
Fred Funk	6	69-69-69-70	277	172,800.00
Stephen Ames	T7	70-68-68-72	278	144,600.00
Jay Haas	T7	68-69-70-71	278	144,600.00
Scott Hoch	T7	70-68-71-69	278	144,600.00
Justin Rose	T7	73-69-66-70	278	144,600.00
Darren Clarke	T11	71-66-71-72	280	101,760.00
Jose Coceres	T11	71-68-72-69	280	101,760.00
Jonathan Kaye	T11	70-70-68-72	280	101,760.00
Kevin Na	T11	69-68-70-73	280	101,760.00
Geoff Ogilvy	T11	71-73-70-66	280	101,760.00
Bob Burns	T16	73-70-67-71	281	63,040.00
Jonathan Byrd	T16	68-71-70-72	281	63,040.00
Lucas Glover (S)	T16	73-70-66-72	281	63,040.00
Fredrik Jacobson	T16	73-69-68-71	281	63,040.00
Kent Jones	T16	72-72-68-69	281	63,040.00
Cliff Kresge	T16	71-70-74-66	281	63,040.00
Rod Pampling	T16	68-72-69-72	281	63,040.00
Tim Petrovic	T16	69-72-71-69	281	63,040.00
Jay Williamson	T16	71-72-69-69	281	$63,040.00
John Huston	T25	69-68-74-71	282	35,862.86
Skip Kendall	T25	72-71-69-70	282	35,862.86
Mark O'Meara	T25	71-67-73-71	282	35,862.86
Dennis Paulson	T25	73-70-70-69	282	35,862.86
Nick Price	T25	69-71-74-68	282	35,862.86
Alex Cejka	T25	70-71-68-73	282	35,862.85
Ben Curtis	T25	68-66-75-73	282	35,862.85
Scott Verplank	T32	73-69-72-69	283	25,988.58
Woody Austin	T32	71-71-69-72	283	25,988.57
Tom Byrum	T32	74-68-69-72	283	25,988.57
Chad Campbell	T32	69-69-70-75	283	25,988.57
Matt Kuchar	T32	72-70-70-71	283	25,988.57
Davis Love III	T32	72-70-69-72	283	25,988.57
Heath Slocum	T32	68-67-70-78	283	25,988.57
Craig Bowden	T39	70-72-74-68	284	19,200.00
David Frost	T39	71-68-75-70	284	19,200.00
Lee Janzen	T39	71-72-70-71	284	19,200.00
Bernhard Langer	T39	71-71-70-72	284	19,200.00
Justin Leonard	T39	71-72-73-68	284	19,200.00
Spike McRoy	T39	69-71-71-73	284	19,200.00
Cameron Beckman	T45	67-72-74-72	285	13,212.00
Jeff Brehaut	T45	74-66-73-72	285	13,212.00
Tim Clark	T45	70-71-72-72	285	13,212.00
Ben Crane	T45	74-67-74-70	285	13,212.00
Robert Gamez	T45	69-70-73-73	285	13,212.00
Dudley Hart	T45	74-68-70-73	285	$13,212.00
Jeff Maggert	T45	73-66-70-76	285	13,212.00
John Rollins	T45	71-70-71-73	285	13,212.00
Billy Andrade	T53	77-64-71-74	286	10,908.00
Brian Bateman	T53	69-71-75-71	286	10,908.00
Glen Day	T53	72-68-72-74	286	10,908.00
Zach Johnson	T53	69-72-75-70	286	10,908.00
J.L. Lewis	T53	69-75-72-70	286	10,908.00
Frank Lickliter II	T53	71-71-71-73	286	10,908.00
Scott Simpson	T53	73-69-72-72	286	10,908.00
Dean Wilson	T53	72-71-67-76	286	10,908.00
Craig Barlow	T61	71-71-76-69	287	10,320.00
Scott Hend	T61	73-70-66-78	287	10,320.00
Ian Poulter	T61	70-70-73-74	287	10,320.00
Loren Roberts	T61	69-73-72-73	287	10,320.00
Bob Estes	65	71-72-71-74	288	10,080.00
Robert Damron	66	74-69-72-74	289	9,984.00
Matt Gogel	T67	71-71-76-72	290	9,840.00
Dan Olsen	T67	71-72-73-74	290	9,840.00
Brad Faxon	T69	71-71-81-68	291	9,648.00
Billy Mayfair	T69	76-68-73-74	291	9,648.00
Tommy Armour III	T71	76-68-77-71	292	9,456.00
Todd Fischer	T71	72-72-75-73	292	9,456.00

(S) = Sponsor Exemption; (T) = Tie

The following players did not finish
(C=cut, W=withdrew, A=amateur)

C—145-Steve Allan, Notah Begay III, Joe Durant, Niclas Fasth, Trevor Immelman, Richard S. Johnson, Stephen Leaney, Blaine McCallister, Joe Ogilvie, Jesper Parnevik, John Riegger, Jeff Sluman. **146-**Pat Bates, Mathias Gronberg, Corey Pavin, David Peoples, Tom Pernice, Jr., Roger Tambellini. **147-**Fulton Allem, Mark Brooks, Mark Calcavecchia, Luke Donald, Todd Hamilton, Mark Hensby, Glen Hnatiuk, Peter Lonard, Larry Mize, Joey Sindelar, Esteban Toledo. **148-**Brian Gay, Retief Goosen, Greg Norman, Ryan Palmer, Kevin Sutherland. **149-**Michael Allen, Tom Carter, John Cook, Dan Forsman, Neal Lancaster, Bob Tway, Grant Waite. **150-**Arron Oberholser, Curtis Strange, D.J. Trahan. **151-**Jeffrey Lankford, Pat Perez, Gene Sauers, Chris Smith. **152-**George Bryan, Brenden Pappas, Omar Uresti. **153-**Len Mattiace, Lee Westwood. **154-**Paul Azinger, Steve Flesch. **155-**Mike Harmon. **156-**John Maginnes. **157-**Brian Harman (A). **158-**David Gossett. **W—76-**Steve Elkington. **74-**Peter Jacobsen.

TED PURDY

TOURNAMENT HISTORY

Year	Winner	Score	Runner-up	Score	Location	Par/Yards
HERITAGE CLASSIC						
1969	Arnold Palmer	283	Richard Crawford Bert Yancey	286	Harbour Town GL, Hilton Head, SC	71/6,657
1970	Bob Goalby	280	Lanny Wadkins	284	Harbour Town GL, Hilton Head, SC	71/6,657
SEA PINES HERITAGE CLASSIC						
1971	Hale Irwin	279	Bob Lunn	280	Harbour Town GL, Hilton Head, SC	71/6,657
1972	Johnny Miller	281	Tom Weiskopf	282	Ocean Course, Hilton Head, SC (first two rounds) Harbour Town GL, Hilton Head, SC (second two rounds)	72/6,600 71/6,657
1973	Hale Irwin	272	Jerry Heard Grier Jones	277	Harbour Town GL, Hilton Head, SC	71/6,657
1974	Johnny Miller	276	Gibby Gilbert	279	Harbour Town GL, Hilton Head, SC	71/6,657
1975	Jack Nicklaus	271	Tom Weiskopf	274	Harbour Town GL, Hilton Head, SC	71/6,657
1976	Hubert Green	274	Jerry McGee	279	Harbour Town GL, Hilton Head, SC	71/6,657
1977	Graham Marsh	273	Tom Watson	274	Harbour Town GL, Hilton Head, SC	71/6,657
1978	Hubert Green	277	Hale Irwin	280	Harbour Town GL, Hilton Head, SC	71/6,657
1979	Tom Watson	270	Ed Sneed	275	Harbour Town GL, Hilton Head, SC	71/6,657
1980	Doug Tewell*	280	Jerry Pate	280	Harbour Town GL, Hilton Head, SC	71/6,657
1981	Bill Rogers	278	Bruce Devlin Hale Irwin Gil Morgan Craig Stadler	279	Harbour Town GL, Hilton Head, SC	71/6,657
1982	Tom Watson*	280	Frank Conner	280	Harbour Town GL, Hilton Head, SC	71/6,657
1983	Fuzzy Zoeller	275	Jim Nelford	277	Harbour Town GL, Hilton Head, SC	71/6,657
1984	Nick Faldo	270	Tom Kite	271	Harbour Town GL, Hilton Head, SC	71/6,657
1985	Bernhard Langer*	273	Bobby Wadkins	273	Harbour Town GL, Hilton Head, SC	71/6,657
1986	Fuzzy Zoeller	276	Chip Beck Roger Maltbie Greg Norman	277	Harbour Town GL, Hilton Head, SC	71/6,657

NOTES

*Last year's playoff between **Ted Purdy** and **Stewart Cink** was the third in the last four years at the MCI Heritage. The playoff between **Jose Coceres** and **Billy Mayfair** in 2001 ended with Coceres winning with a par on the fifth hole. In 2003, **Davis Love III** outlasted **Woody Austin** on the fourth hole.*

JOSE COCERES

*Last year marked the second five-hole playoff in MCI Heritage history. The first came in 2001 when **Jose Coceres** outlasted **Billy Mayfair** with a par. The 2001 event was also the last time a TOUR event had a five-hole playoff.*

*With his victory last year, **Stewart Cink** joined a stellar group of players who have won the MCI Heritage at least twice. **Davis Love III** has five titles, followed by **Hale Irwin**'s three. **Johnny Miller**, **Hubert Green**, **Tom Watson** and **Payne Stewart** all won twice at Harbour Town.*

*Five times in history a player 40 or over has won the MCI Heritage. The first player to do it was **Arnold Palmer** at the inaugural 1969 tournament. He was 40 years, 2 months and 20 days when he edged **Richard Crawford** and **Bert Yancey** by three strokes. The next year, **Bob Goalby** (41 years, 8 months, 15 days) prevailed. No player in his 40s won the tournament for the next 24 years until **Hale Irwin** began a trend where the tournament crowned three 40-somethings in a four-tournament span. Irwin was 48 years, 10 months and 14 days in 1994. Two years later, **Loren Roberts** (40 years, 9 months, 27 days) won, followed by **Nick Price** a year later (40 years, 20 months, 22 days).*

*The youngest winner in MCI Heritage history is **Davis Love III**. He was 23 years and 6 days when he won the first of his five titles.*

Tournament Record:
265, Loren Roberts, 1996
Current Course Record:
61, David Frost, 1994

TOURNAMENT HISTORY

Year	Winner	Score	Runner-up	Score	Location	Par/Yards
MCI HERITAGE CLASSIC						
1987	Davis Love III	271	Steve Jones	272	Harbour Town GL, Hilton Head, SC	71/6,657
1988	Greg Norman	271	David Frost Gil Morgan	272	Harbour Town GL, Hilton Head, SC	71/6,657
1989	Payne Stewart	268	Kenny Perry	273	Harbour Town GL, Hilton Head, SC	71/6,657
1990	Payne Stewart*	276	Steve Jones Larry Mize	276	Harbour Town GL, Hilton Head, SC	71/6,657
1991	Davis Love III	271	Ian Baker-Finch	273	Harbour Town GL, Hilton Head, SC	71/6,657
1992	Davis Love III	269	Chip Beck	273	Harbour Town GL, Hilton Head, SC	71/6,657
1993	David Edwards	273	David Frost	275	Harbour Town GL, Hilton Head, SC	71/6,657
1994	Hale Irwin	266	Greg Norman	268	Harbour Town GL, Hilton Head, SC	71/6,657
MCI CLASSIC						
1995	Bob Tway*	275	David Frost Nolan Henke	275	Harbour Town GL, Hilton Head, SC	71/6,657
1996	Loren Roberts	265	Mark O'Meara	268	Harbour Town GL, Hilton Head, SC	71/6,912
1997	Nick Price	269	Brad Faxon Jesper Parnevik	275	Harbour Town GL, Hilton Head, SC	71/6,915
1998	Davis Love III	266	Glen Day	273	Harbour Town GL, Hilton Head, SC	71/6,916
1999	Glen Day*	274	Jeff Sluman Payne Stewart	274	Harbour Town GL, Hilton Head, SC	71/6,916
2000	Stewart Cink	270	Tom Lehman	272	Harbour Town GL, Hilton Head, SC	71/6,916
WORLDCOM CLASSIC-THE HERITAGE OF GOLF						
2001	Jose Coceres*	273	Billy Mayfair	273	Harbour Town GL, Hilton Head, SC	71/6,916
2002	Justin Leonard	270	Heath Slocum	271	Harbour Town GL, Hilton Head, SC	71/6,916
MCI HERITAGE						
2003	Davis Love III*	271	Woody Austin	271	Harbour Town GL, Hilton Head, SC	71/6,973
2004	Stewart Cink*	274	Ted Purdy	274	Harbour Town GL, Hilton Head, SC	71/6,973

*KEY: * = Playoff ~ = Weather-shortened*

ELIGIBILITY REQUIREMENTS FOR THE 2005 MCI HERITAGE

Eligible players are:

- Winners of MCI Heritage prior to 2000, and winners of MCI Heritage in 2000 and beyond for a period of five years following their win.
- Winners of the U.S. Open or PGA Championship who played in a minimum of 15 PGA TOUR cosponsored or approved tournaments in 2004.
- Winners of THE PLAYERS Championship and Masters Tournament from 1996 to 1997 and from 2001 to 2005. Beginning with the 1998 winners of these events, winners are eligible for five years.
- Winners of the British Open from 1995 to 1997 and from 2000 to 2004. Beginning with the 1998 winner, winners are eligible for five years.
- Winners of the NEC World Series of Golf in the last 10 years (1995-1997).
- Winners of THE TOUR Championship in the last three years (2002-2004).
- Winners of the WGC-Accenture Match Play Championship in the last three years (2003-2005).
- Winners of the WGC-NEC Invitational and WGC-American Express Championship in the last three years (2002-2004).
- Winner of the 2004 U.S. Amateur Championship, if still an amateur player.
- The leader from the final Official PGA TOUR Money List in each of the last five calendar years (2000-2004).
- Playing members of the last-named U.S. Ryder Cup team (2004).
- Current PGA TOUR members who were playing members from the last-named U.S. and International Presidents Cup teams (2003).
- The 20 players who are leading on the 2005 Official PGA TOUR Money List through the BellSouth Classic.
- Five players not otherwise eligible who are leading on the 2005 Official PGA TOUR Money List through the BellSouth Classic.
- The top 50 players from the Official World Golf Ranking through completion of the Bay Hill Invitational.
- Eight sponsor exemptions, restricted as follows:
  - Two from among the current year's PGA TOUR membership.
  - Two from among the 2004 PGA TOUR Qualifying Tournament's top 30 finishers and ties and the first through 20th finishers from the 2004 Official Nationwide Tour Money List.
- Two foreign players designated by the Commissioner.
- Either the current winner of the PGA Section Championship or the current PGA Section Player of the Year where the tournament is played, as determined by the Section.
- PGA TOUR members who use an exemption for 2005 as one of the leaders (either top 25 or top 50) on the Official PGA TOUR Career Money List.
- Life members of the PGA TOUR.
- Those PGA TOUR members among the top 125 finishers on the 2004 Official PGA TOUR Money List.
- Members in the Top 125-Nonmembers category whose official money for the previous year equals or exceeds the amount of official money earned by the player finishing in 125th position on the 2004 Official PGA TOUR Money List.
- PGA TOUR members from the current Tournament Winners category.
- If necessary to complete a field of 132 players, PGA TOUR members from the 2005 priority ranking of eligible players, after the top 125, in order of their positions on such list.

2004 Shell Houston Open [17th of 48 official events]

Winner: VIJAY SINGH
74-66-69-68 277 (-11) $900,000

Redstone Golf Club

Humble, TX

April 22-26, 2004

Purse: $5,000,000
Par: 35-37—72
Yards: 7,508

LEADERS: First Round—Rod Pampling at 6-under 66 led Chris Riley by one.
Second Round—Zach Johnson, Steve Stricker and Steve Lowery at 6-under-par 138 led Patrick Sheehan, Paul Azinger and Vijay Singh by one stroke.
Third Round—John Huston and Singh at 7-under 209 led Joe Ogilvie and Jose Coceres by one. Geoff Ogilvy, Scott Hoch, John Daly, Dudley Hart and Azinger were three back.

CUT: 71 players at 1-over-par 145 from a field of 156 professionals.

PRO-AM: $10,000. Blaine McCallister, 53, $2,000.

WEATHER: Thursday had a high of 84. On Friday, thunderstorms suspended play at 3:43 p.m. Play resumed at 5:49 p.m. and was halted due to darkness at 7:38 p.m. Round three began on Saturday at 4:40 p.m., with players allowed "preferred lies". Play was suspended for the day at 6:38 p.m. with a re-start of the third round at 7:30 a.m. on Sunday. Sunday had scattered thunderstorms most of the day. Play was suspended at 10:38 a.m. with 56 of the 71 players yet to complete the third round. Play was officially suspended at 4 p.m. Monday temperatures reached 79 degrees. Players were allowed "preferred lies" for the final round.

Check out the 2005 Shell Houston Open, April 21-24 on USA/CBS

ORDER OF FINISH

Vijay Singh	1	74-66-69-68	277	$900,000.00
Scott Hoch	2	73-68-71-67	279	540,000.00
John Huston	3	71-71-67-71	280	340,000.00
Stephen Ames	T4	68-76-69-69	282	220,000.00
Dudley Hart	T4	69-72-71-70	282	220,000.00
Paul Azinger	T6	73-67-72-71	283	161,875.00
Jose Coceres	T6	73-69-68-73	283	161,875.00
John Daly	T6	76-69-67-71	283	161,875.00
Rory Sabbatini	T6	74-70-69-70	283	161,875.00
Geoff Ogilvy	10	71-70-71-72	284	135,000.00
D.J. Brigman	T11	71-72-70-72	285	96,250.00
K.J. Choi	T11	74-70-72-69	285	96,250.00
Tim Herron	T11	73-71-70-71	285	96,250.00
Zach Johnson	T11	71-68-74-72	285	96,250.00
David Peoples	T11	70-71-73-71	285	96,250.00
Ted Purdy	T11	72-73-71-69	285	96,250.00
Patrick Sheehan	T11	69-71-74-71	285	96,250.00
Paul Stankowski	T11	72-70-71-72	285	96,250.00
Jason Bohn	T19	71-72-73-70	286	52,611.12
Mark Calcavecchia	T19	72-69-72-73	286	52,611.11
Carlos Franco	T19	73-72-69-72	286	52,611.11
Steve Lowery	T19	70-69-76-71	286	52,611.11
Kevin Na	T19	72-70-72-72	286	52,611.11
Joe Ogilvie	T19	72-70-68-76	286	$52,611.11
Tim Petrovic	T19	69-73-72-72	286	52,611.11
Steve Stricker	T19	69-70-77-70	286	52,611.11
Bo Van Pelt	T19	74-71-69-72	286	52,611.11
Brian Bateman	28	77-68-71-71	287	37,000.00
Tom Carter	T29	71-73-71-73	288	30,437.50
Lucas Glover	T29	68-77-75-68	288	30,437.50
Neal Lancaster	T29	70-71-76-71	288	30,437.50
Justin Leonard	T29	71-70-72-75	288	30,437.50
Len Mattiace	T29	75-70-71-72	288	30,437.50
Billy Mayfair	T29	74-71-72-71	288	30,437.50
Tom Pernice, Jr.	T29	70-73-73-72	288	30,437.50
John Riegger	T29	69-71-74-74	288	30,437.50
Russ Cochran	T37	70-74-70-75	289	22,000.00
Ben Crane	T37	72-72-72-73	289	22,000.00
Hank Kuehne	T37	74-70-72-73	289	22,000.00
Blaine McCallister	T37	74-70-74-71	289	22,000.00
Chris Riley	T37	67-74-76-72	289	22,000.00
Hal Sutton	T37	69-73-74-73	289	22,000.00
Mathias Gronberg	T43	73-72-72-73	290	16,033.34
Arron Oberholser	T43	73-71-70-76	290	16,033.34
Jeff Brehaut	T43	71-74-73-72	290	16,033.33
Danny Briggs	T43	73-72-71-74	290	16,033.33
Jay Haas	T43	72-73-70-75	290	16,033.33
Rod Pampling	T43	66-79-73-72	290	16,033.33
Robert Allenby	T49	72-71-76-72	291	$12,340.00
Alex Cejka	T49	72-71-72-76	291	12,340.00
Fred Couples	T49	71-74-74-72	291	12,340.00
Frank Lickliter II	T49	68-77-73-73	291	12,340.00
Lee Westwood	T49	76-69-73-73	291	12,340.00
David Frost	T54	71-73-72-76	292	11,400.00
Brian Kortan	T54	71-74-74-73	292	11,400.00
Edward Loar (Q)	T54	74-71-72-75	292	11,400.00
Dennis Paulson	T54	71-74-73-74	292	11,400.00
Heath Slocum	T54	73-70-74-75	292	11,400.00
Robert Gamez	T59	74-71-75-73	293	10,850.00
Mike Heinen	T59	73-72-71-77	293	10,850.00
Scott Hend	T59	73-71-72-77	293	10,850.00
J.J. Henry	T59	71-74-76-72	293	10,850.00
Joel Kribel	T59	71-72-77-73	293	10,850.00
Roger Tambellini	T59	71-74-78-70	293	10,850.00
Aaron Baddeley	T65	71-72-77-74	294	10,450.00
Daniel Chopra	T65	72-73-74-75	294	10,450.00
Brian Gay	T67	72-73-74-76	295	10,250.00
Tjaart Van der Walt	T67	71-74-75-75	295	10,250.00
Phil Blackmar	69	76-67-76-78	297	10,100.00
Deane Pappas	T70	68-77-78-75	298	9,950.00
Dicky Pride	T70	71-73-76-78	298	9,950.00

(Q) = Open Qualifier; (S) = Sponsor Exemption; (T) = Tie

The following players did not finish
(C=cut, W=withdrew, D=disqualified)

C—146-Steve Allan, Billy Andrade, Notah Begay III, Craig Bowden, Greg Chalmers, Ken Green, Mark Hensby, Cliff Kresge, Joey Sindelar, Andre Stolz, Kevin Sutherland, Jimmy Walker. **147-**Arjun Atwal, Cameron Beckman, Olin Browne, Bob Burns, Robert Damron, Jay Delsing, Jason Dufner, Kent Jones, Matt Kuchar, Jeff Maggert, Scott McCarron, Steve Pate, Hidemichi Tanaka, Grant Waite, Garrett Willis. **148-**Briny Baird, Mark Brooks, David Gossett, Todd Hamilton, Spike McRoy, Dan Olsen, Pat Perez, Justin Rose, Victor Schwamkrug. **149-**Tommy Armour III, David Branshaw, Ken Duke, John Maginnes, Hunter Mahan, Brenden Pappas. **150-**Rich Beem, Niclas Fasth, Charles Howell III, David Lundstrom, Jim McGovern, David Morland IV, Ryan Palmer, Tag Ridings, John Senden, Brandt Snedeker, Esteban Toledo, Dean Wilson. **151-**Guy Boros, Bart Bryant, Chris Couch, Todd Fischer, Hirofumi Miyase, Patrick Moore, Kevin Muncrief, Tommy Tolles. **152-**Ty Armstrong, Kris Cox, Tripp Isenhour, Brett Quigley, Brian K. Smith, Roland Thatcher, Mark Wilson. **153-**Craig Perks. **154-**Tom Byrum. **155-**Lonny Alexander, Steve Elkington, Ken Kelley, Jason Laing. **157-**Aaron Barber. **158-**Dan Forsman. **W—81-**Trevor Dodds. **77-**Brad Lardon. **76-**Vaughn Taylor, Brent Geiberger. **75-**Rich Barcelo. **73-**Jay Williamson. **72-**Duffy Waldorf. **D—77-**David Sutherland.

TOURNAMENT HISTORY

Year	Winner	Score	Runner-up	Score	Location	Par/Yards
TOURNAMENT OF CHAMPIONS						
1946	Byron Nelson	274	Ben Hogan	276	River Oaks CC, Houston, TX	71/6,588
1947	Bobby Locke	277	Johnny Palmer Ellsworth Vines	282	Memorial Park GC, Houston, TX	72/7,421
1948	No Tournament					
1949	Johnny Palmer	272	Cary Middlecoff	273	Pine Forest CC, Houston, TX	72/6,510
HOUSTON OPEN						
1950	Cary Middlecoff	277	Pete Cooper	280	Brae Burn CC, Houston, TX	72/6,725
1951	Marty Furgol	277	Jack Burke, Jr.	278	Memorial Park GC, Houston, TX	70/7,212
1952	Jack Burke, Jr.	277	Frank Stranahan	283	Memorial Park GC, Houston, TX	70/7,212
1953	Cary Middlecoff*	283	Jim Ferrier Shelley Mayfield Earl Stewart Bill Nary	283	Memorial Park GC, Houston, TX	70/7,212
1954	Dave Douglas	277	Cary Middlecoff	279	Memorial Park GC, Houston, TX	70/7,212
1955	Mike Souchak	273	Jerry Barber	275	Memorial Park GC, Houston, TX	70/7,212
1956	Ted Kroll	277	Jack Burke, Jr. Dave Douglas	280	Memorial Park GC, Houston, TX	70/7,212
1957	Arnold Palmer	279	Doug Ford	280	Memorial Park GC, Houston, TX	70/7,212
1958	Ed Oliver	281	Roberto De Vicenzo Jay Hebert	282	Memorial Park GC, Houston, TX	70/7,212
HOUSTON CLASSIC						
1959	Jack Burke, Jr.*	277	Julius Boros	277	Memorial Park GC, Houston, TX	70/7,212
1960	Bill Collins*	280	Arnold Palmer	280	Memorial Park GC, Houston, TX	70/7,212
1961	Jay Hebert*	276	Ken Venturi	276	Memorial Park GC, Houston, TX	72/7,122
1962	Bobby Nichols*	278	Jack Nicklaus Dan Sikes	278	Memorial Park GC, Houston, TX	72/7,021
1963	Bob Charles	268	Fred Hawkins	269	Memorial Park GC, Houston, TX	72/7,021
1964	Mike Souchak	278	Jack Nicklaus	279	Sharpstown CC, Houston, TX	71/7,021
1965	Bobby Nichols	273	Bruce Devlin Chi Chi Rodriguez	274	Sharpstown CC, Houston, TX	71/7,021

NOTES

*The key to victory for **Vijay Singh** in 2004 at the Shell Houston Open? Greens in Regulation. He entered the week No. 1 on the PGA TOUR in GIR (72.9 percent) and led the field last year at 84.7 percent, hitting 61 of 72 greens. He also led the field in Driving Distance (318.3 yards). In his bogey-free final round, Singh was near-perfect, hitting 13 of 14 fairways and 16 of 18 greens.*

__Vijay Singh__ and __Scott Hoch__, the champion and runner-up, respectively, did not record a bogey in the final round in 2004. In fact, Singh went bogey-free over the final 36 holes.

SCOTT HOCH

*Prior to the 2004 Shell Houston Open, **Vijay Singh** had won the last Monday finish on the PGA TOUR, at the 2003 John Deere Classic.*

*With his victory, **Vijay Singh** becomes the eighth multiple winner of the Shell Houston Open, joining **Cary Middlecoff** (1950, 1953), **Mike Souchak** (1955, 1964), **Jack Burke, Jr.** (1952, 1958), **Arnold Palmer** (1957, 1966), **Bobby Nichols** (1963, 1965), **Bruce Crampton** (1973, 1975) and **Curtis Strange** (1980, 1986, 1988).*

__John Daly__ was attempting to pull off a rare feat, winning a PGA TOUR event after beginning his final round on No. 10. __Keith Clearwater__ was the last player to win after starting on the back nine in the final round, having done so at the 1987 Colonial. Playing the final 36 holes on Sunday, Clearwater carded rounds of 64-64 to seize the title from 54-hole leader __Ben Crenshaw__. Daly pulled within one of eventual champion __Vijay Singh__ on his final nine, but bogeys on three of his last five holes dashed his chance for victory.

Tournament Record:
266, Curtis Strange, Lee Trevino, 1980 (Woodlands CC); Vijay Singh, 2002 (TPC at The Woodlands)

Current Course Record:
64, Hank Kuehne, Greg Chalmers, Jeff Maggert, 2003

Tournament Course Record:
62, Ron Streck, 1981 (Woodlands CC); Fred Funk, 1992 (TPC at The Woodlsnds)

TOURNAMENT HISTORY

Year	Winner	Score	Runner-up	Score	Location	Par/Yards
HOUSTON CHAMPIONS INTERNATIONAL						
1966	Arnold Palmer+	275	Gardner Dickinson	276	Champions GC, Houston, TX	71/7,166
1967	Frank Beard	274	Arnold Palmer	275	Champions GC, Houston, TX	71/7,166
1968	Roberto De Vicenzo	274	Lee Trevino	275	Champions GC, Houston, TX	71/7,166
1969	No Tournament++					
1970	Gibby Gilbert*	282	Bruce Crampton	282	Champions GC, Houston, TX	70/7,166
1971	Hubert Green*	280	Don January	280	Champions GC, Houston, TX	70/7,166
HOUSTON OPEN						
1972	Bruce Devlin	278	Tommy Aaron Lou Graham Doug Sanders	280	Westwood CC, Houston, TX	72/6,998
1973	Bruce Crampton	277	Dave Stockton	278	Quail Valley GC, Missouri City, TX	72/6,905
1974	Dave Hill	276	Rod Curl Steve Melnyk Andy North	277	Quail Valley GC, Missouri City, TX	72/6,905
1975	Bruce Crampton	273	Gil Morgan	275	Woodlands CC, The Woodlands, TX	72/6,929
1976	Lee Elder	278	Forrest Fezler	279	Woodlands CC, The Woodlands, TX	72/6,997
1977	Gene Littler	276	Lanny Wadkins	279	Woodlands CC, The Woodlands, TX	72/6,997
1978	Gary Player	270	Andy Bean	271	Woodlands CC, The Woodlands, TX	72/6,997
1979	Wayne Levi	268	Michael Brannan	270	Woodlands CC, The Woodlands, TX	71/6,918
MICHELOB HOUSTON OPEN						
1980	Curtis Strange*	266	Lee Trevino	266	Woodlands CC, The Woodlands, TX	71/6,918
1981	Ron Streck~	198	Hale Irwin Jerry Pate	201	Woodlands CC, The Woodlands, TX	71/7,071
1982	Ed Sneed*	275	Bob Shearer	275	Woodlands CC, The Woodlands, TX	71/7,031
HOUSTON COCA-COLA OPEN						
1983	David Graham	275	Lee Elder Jim Thorpe Lee Trevino	280	Woodlands CC, The Woodlands, TX	71/7,031
1984	Corey Pavin	274	Buddy Gardner	275	Woodlands CC, The Woodlands, TX	71/7,031
HOUSTON OPEN						
1985	Raymond Floyd	277	David Frost Bob Lohr	278	TPC at The Woodlands, The Woodlands, TX	72/7,042
1986	Curtis Strange*	274	Calvin Peete	274	TPC at The Woodlands, The Woodlands, TX	72/7,045
BIG I HOUSTON OPEN						
1987	Jay Haas*	276	Buddy Gardner	276	TPC at The Woodlands, The Woodlands, TX	72/7,042
INDEPENDENT INSURANCE AGENT OPEN						
1988	Curtis Strange*	270	Greg Norman	270	TPC at The Woodlands, The Woodlands, TX	72/7,045
1989	Mike Sullivan	280	Craig Stadler	281	TPC at The Woodlands, The Woodlands, TX	72/7,042
1990	Tony Sills~*	204	Gil Morgan	204	TPC at The Woodlands, The Woodlands, TX	72/7,042
1991	Fulton Allem+++	273	Billy Ray Brown Mike Hulbert Tom Kite	274	TPC at The Woodlands, The Woodlands, TX	72/7,042
SHELL HOUSTON OPEN						
1992	Fred Funk	272	Kirk Triplett	274	TPC at The Woodlands, The Woodlands, TX	72/7,042
1993	Jim McGovern~*	199	John Huston	199	TPC at The Woodlands, The Woodlands, TX	72/7,042
1994	Mike Heinen	272	Tom Kite Jeff Maggert Hal Sutton	275	TPC at The Woodlands, The Woodlands, TX	72/7,042
1995	Payne Stewart*	276	Scott Hoch	276	TPC at The Woodlands, The Woodlands, TX	72/7,042
1996	Mark Brooks*	274	Jeff Maggert	274	TPC at The Woodlands, The Woodlands, TX	72/7,042
1997	Phil Blackmar*	276	Kevin Sutherland	276	TPC at The Woodlands, The Woodlands, TX	72/7,042
1998	David Duval	276	Jeff Maggert	277	TPC at The Woodlands, The Woodlands, TX	72/7,018
1999	Stuart Appleby	279	John Cook Hal Sutton	280	TPC at The Woodlands, The Woodlands, TX	72/7,018
2000	Robert Allenby*	275	Craig Stadler	275	TPC at The Woodlands, The Woodlands, TX	72/7,018
2001	Hal Sutton	278	Joe Durant Lee Janzen	281	TPC at The Woodlands, The Woodlands, TX	72/7,018
2002	Vijay Singh	266	Darren Clarke	272	TPC at The Woodlands, The Woodlands, TX	72/7,018
2003	Fred Couples	267	Stuart Appleby Mark Calcavecchia Hank Kuehne	271 271 271	Redstone GC, Humble, TX	72/7,508
2004	Vijay Singh	277	Scott Hoch	279	Redstone GC, Humble, TX	72/7,508

*KEY: * = Playoff ~ = Weather-shortened + = Tournament postponed in April 1966; rescheduled to November ++ = Champions served as site for U.S. Open +++ = Tournament postponed in April 1991; rescheduled to October*

2004 HP Classic of New Orleans [18th of 48 official events]

HP CLASSIC OF NEW ORLEANS

Winner: VIJAY SINGH
70-65-68-63 266 (-22) $918,000

English Turn Golf & Country Club

New Orleans, LA

April 29 – May 3, 2004

Purse: $5,100,000
Par: 36-36—72
Yards: 7,078

LEADERS: First Round—Danny Ellis fired a 9-under 63 to lead Ken Duke by one.
Second Round—Ellis moved to 15-under 129, one ahead of Charles Howell III. Phil Mickelson, Matt Kuchar, Craig Bowden, Duke, Paul Azinger and Ryan Palmer were three back.
Third Round—Joe Ogilvie sat at 17-under 199, two ahead of Howell and Mickelson. Justin Rose and Hidemichi Tanaka trailed by three.

CUT: 80 players at 4-under-par 140 from a field of 156 professionals on Sunday.

PRO-AM: $10,000. K.J. Choi, 54, $2,000.

WEATHER: Light rain Thursday morning with temperatures in the high 70s. There was a weather delay due to lightning at 2:08 p.m. Play resumed at 5:30 p.m. and was suspended at 7:30 p.m. Bad weather continued on Friday with play suspended at 2 p.m. First round resumed at 7 a.m. on Saturday. Second round began at 8:15 a.m. with "preferred lies" and was delayed at 4:29 p.m. Play was suspended for the day at 5:35 p.m. Second round resumed at 7 a.m. on Sunday and concluded at 10:04 a.m. Third round began at 10:40 a.m. with "preferred lies". Final round concluded on Monday.

Check out the 2005 Zurich Classic of New Orleans, April 28-May 1 on USA/CBS

ORDER OF FINISH

Vijay Singh	1	70-65-68-63	266	$918,000.00
Phil Mickelson	T2	67-65-69-66	267	448,800.00
Joe Ogilvie	T2	66-67-66-68	267	448,800.00
Hidemichi Tanaka	4	69-64-69-67	269	244,800.00
Charles Howell III	T5	66-64-71-70	271	193,800.00
Justin Rose	T5	67-70-65-69	271	193,800.00
Stephen Ames	T7	67-69-71-65	272	158,950.00
Brian Bateman	T7	67-67-69-69	272	158,950.00
K.J. Choi	T7	67-68-68-69	272	158,950.00
Joe Durant	T10	67-70-67-69	273	132,600.00
Matt Kuchar	T10	69-63-71-70	273	132,600.00
Ken Duke	T12	64-68-72-70	274	107,100.00
David Frost	T12	69-69-70-66	274	107,100.00
Ryan Palmer	T12	68-64-72-70	274	107,100.00
Paul Azinger	T15	66-66-71-72	275	81,600.00
Bob Burns	T15	69-64-75-67	275	81,600.00
Steve Pate	T15	75-65-68-67	275	81,600.00
Carl Pettersson	T15	68-68-73-66	275	81,600.00
David Sutherland	T15	66-67-72-70	275	81,600.00
Dan Forsman	T20	71-68-69-68	276	57,324.00
James H. McLean	T20	70-67-71-68	276	57,324.00
Pat Perez	T20	70-70-70-66	276	57,324.00
John Senden	T20	70-67-72-67	276	57,324.00
Steve Stricker	T20	71-69-67-69	276	57,324.00
Bob Estes	T25	69-65-75-68	277	36,493.34
Mathias Gronberg	T25	67-70-72-68	277	$36,493.34
Geoff Ogilvy	T25	68-69-72-68	277	36,493.34
Briny Baird	T25	73-67-71-66	277	36,493.33
Jonathan Byrd	T25	70-70-71-66	277	36,493.33
Robert Damron	T25	66-70-70-71	277	36,493.33
J.L. Lewis	T25	69-67-71-70	277	36,493.33
Ted Purdy	T25	68-68-68-73	277	36,493.33
Hal Sutton	T25	69-66-76-66	277	36,493.33
Steve Allan	T34	72-68-68-70	278	23,089.10
Daniel Chopra	T34	73-65-67-73	278	23,089.09
Russ Cochran	T34	70-69-70-69	278	23,089.09
Jerry Kelly	T34	69-67-71-71	278	23,089.09
Skip Kendall	T34	71-64-73-70	278	23,089.09
Steve Lowery	T34	70-65-72-71	278	23,089.09
Deane Pappas	T34	68-69-68-73	278	23,089.09
Dennis Paulson	T34	66-72-72-68	278	23,089.09
Joey Sindelar	T34	71-69-72-66	278	23,089.09
Andre Stolz	T34	70-69-71-68	278	23,089.09
David Toms	T34	69-66-72-71	278	23,089.09
Steve Flesch	T45	68-67-74-70	279	14,932.80
Scott Hoch	T45	70-69-71-69	279	14,932.80
Kent Jones	T45	68-71-69-71	279	14,932.80
Chris Riley	T45	68-68-73-70	279	14,932.80
Bob Tway	T45	67-70-70-72	279	14,932.80
Craig Bowden	T50	66-66-73-75	280	12,418.50
Harrison Frazar	T50	74-66-68-72	280	12,418.50
Kelly Gibson (S)	T50	68-67-76-69	280	12,418.50
Hirofumi Miyase	T50	69-68-73-70	280	$12,418.50
Olin Browne (S)	T54	70-68-73-70	281	11,526.00
Greg Chalmers	T54	67-72-70-72	281	11,526.00
Ken Green	T54	70-66-76-69	281	11,526.00
Joel Kribel	T54	72-64-72-73	281	11,526.00
Andrew McLardy (Q)	T54	70-69-73-69	281	11,526.00
Scott Verplank	T54	68-70-71-72	281	11,526.00
Dean Wilson	T54	70-68-71-72	281	11,526.00
Guy Boros	T61	70-70-63-79	282	11,016.00
Chris Smith	T61	72-68-68-74	282	11,016.00
Kirk Triplett	T61	66-69-75-72	282	11,016.00
Pat Bates	T64	71-69-70-73	283	10,761.00
Omar Uresti	T64	69-69-70-75	283	10,761.00
Blaine McCallister	T66	68-71-68-77	284	10,557.00
Esteban Toledo	T66	69-69-72-74	284	10,557.00
John E. Morgan	T68	69-71-74-71	285	10,302.00
Dan Olsen	T68	68-69-75-73	285	10,302.00
Vaughn Taylor	T68	69-70-72-74	285	10,302.00
Danny Ellis	71	63-66-82-75	286	10,098.00
D.J. Brigman	T72	70-68-73-76	287	9,945.00
John Riegger	T72	68-69-75-75	287	9,945.00
Fulton Allem	74	69-67-78-74	288	9,792.00
Jeff Brehaut	75	69-70-73-77	289	9,690.00
Chris DiMarco	T76	69-69-72-80	290	9,537.00
Mike Heinen	T76	74-65-79-72	290	9,537.00
Tommy Tolles	78	69-71-73-79	292	9,384.00

(Q) = Open Qualifier; (S) = Sponsor Exemption; (T) = Tie

The following players did not finish (C=cut, W=withdrew)

C—141-Ricky Barnes, Jim Carter, Jose Coceres, Jay Delsing, Brian Gay, J.P. Hayes, Richard S. Johnson, Tom Pernice, Jr., Gene Sauers, Patrick Sheehan, Mike Standly, Garrett Willis, Mark Wilson. **142**-Jason Bohn, Danny Briggs, Mark Brooks, Bart Bryant, Jason Dufner, Dudley Hart, Brad Lardon, John Maginnes, Patrick Moore, Kevin Muncrief, Roland Thatcher. **143**-Woody Austin, Aaron Barber, Rich Barcelo, David Branshaw, Todd Hamilton, Tripp Isenhour, Cliff Kresge, Craig Perks, Roger Tambellini, Tjaart Van der Walt. **144**-Glen Day, Trevor Dodds, Lucas Glover, Scott Hend, Hank Kuehne, Kevin Na, Dicky Pride, Heath Slocum, Jeff Sluman, Bo Van Pelt. **145**-Todd Fischer, Carlos Franco, Brian Kortan, Hunter Mahan, Brent Schwarzrock, Scott Simpson, Brandt Snedeker. **146**-Spike McRoy, Patrick Prince, Brett Quigley. **147**-Arjun Atwal, Niclas Fasth, Brenden Pappas. **148**-Tom Carter, David Church, Michael Pearson. **150**-Stuart Appleby, Kris Cox, Tim Thelen. **153**-Bryant MacKellar. **163**-Derek Sanders. **W**—Grant Waite, Neal Lancaster, Cliff Bailey. **76**-David Morland IV. **74**-Brent Geiberger, Alex Cejka. **72**-Chris Couch, Michael Allen. **71**-David Peoples, Tom Byrum. **136**-John Rollins. **207**-Jay Williamson.

TOURNAMENT HISTORY

Year	Winner	Score	Runner-up	Score	Location	Par/Yards
GREATER NEW ORLEANS OPEN INVITATIONAL						
1938	Harry Cooper	285	Harold McSpaden	289	City Park GC, New Orleans, LA	72/6,656
1939	Henry Picard	284	Dick Metz	289	City Park GC, New Orleans, LA	72/6,656
1940	Jimmy Demaret	286	Ralph Guldahl	287	City Park GC, New Orleans, LA	72/6,656
			Harold McSpaden			
			Sam Snead			
1941	Henry Picard	276	Ben Hogan	278	City Park GC, New Orleans, LA	72/6,656
1942	Lloyd Mangrum	281	Lawson Little	282	City Park GC, New Orleans, LA	72/6,656
			Sam Snead			
1943	No Tournament					
1944	Sammy Byrd	285	Byron Nelson	290	City Park GC, New Orleans, LA	72/6,656
1945	Byron Nelson*	284	Harold McSpaden	284	City Park GC, New Orleans, LA	72/6,656
1946	Byron Nelson	277	Ben Hogan	282	City Park GC, New Orleans, LA	72/6,656
1947	No Tournament					
1948	Bob Hamilton	280	Roberto De Vicenzo	281	City Park GC, New Orleans, LA	72/6,656
			Fred Haas			
			Lawson Little			
1949	No Tournament					
1950	No Tournament					
1951	No Tournament					
1952	No Tournament					
1953	No Tournament					
1954	No Tournament					
1955	No Tournament					
1956	No Tournament					
1957	No Tournament					
1958	Billy Casper*	278	Ken Venturi	278	City Park GC, New Orleans, LA	72/6,656
1959	Bill Collins	280	Jack Burke, Jr.	283	City Park GC, New Orleans, LA	72/6,656
			Tom Nieporte			

Zurich Classic of New Orleans

ZURICH Classic OF NEW ORLEANS

NOTES

DAVID TOMS

***Vijay Singh** matched the 72-hole course record at English Turn Golf & Country Club with his 22-under 266 (**David Toms** 2001).*

*The tournament record is 262 by **Chip Beck** in 1988 at Lakewood Country Club.*

***Vijay Singh**'s back nine 7-under 29 tied the back-nine course record at English Turn set by **Harrison Frazar** during the third round of the 2000 event. There have been two other players to post 29 on the back nine, **Kelly Grunewald** (first round) in 2001 and **Rich Beem** (first round) in 2002.*

*The Tournament Players Club of Louisiana, a **Pete Dye** design, will debut this year as the tournament site. PGA TOUR players **Steve Elkington** and **Kelly Gibson** were design consultants on the 7,520-yard, par-72 public course.*

***Vijay Singh** was the first player to record back-to-back Monday victories since the TOUR began keeping track of such things in 1980. He also won the last three Monday finishes on TOUR, beginning with the 2003 John Deere Classic and including the 2004 Shell Houston Open and the 2004 HP Classic of New Orleans. The Monday finish victories don't end there as he also won the 1997 Memorial Tournament.*

*At age 41 years, 2 months, 12 days, **Vijay Singh** became the sixth player over age 40 to win in New Orleans. The last player over 40 to win was **Ben Crenshaw** in 1994 at age 42 years, 2 months and 22 days. The other four include: 1986, **Calvin Peete** (42 years, 8 months, 5 days); 1975, **Billy Casper** (43 years, 10 days, 24 days); 1972, **Gary Player** (42 years, 6 months, 16 days); and 1965, **Dick Mayer** (40 years, 8 months, 17 days).*

Tournament Record:
262, Chip Beck, 1988 (Lakewood CC)

Tournament Course Record:
61, Paul Stankowski, 2001

TOURNAMENT HISTORY

Year	Winner	Score	Runner-up	Score	Location	Par/Yards
1960	Dow Finsterwald	270	Al Besselink	276	City Park GC, New Orleans, LA	72/6,656
1961	Doug Sanders	272	Gay Brewer Mac Main	277	City Park GC, New Orleans, LA	72/6,656
1962	Bo Wininger	281	Bob Rosburg	283	City Park GC, New Orleans, LA	72/6,656
1963	Bo Wininger	279	Tony Lema Bob Rosburg	282	Lakewood CC, New Orleans, LA	72/7,080
1964	Mason Rudolph	283	Jack Nicklaus Chi Chi Rodriguez Glenn Stuart	284	Lakewood CC, New Orleans, LA	72/7,080
1965	Dick Mayer	273	Bruce Devlin Bill Martindale	274	Lakewood CC, New Orleans, LA	72/7,080
1966	Frank Beard	276	Gardner Dickinson	278	Lakewood CC, New Orleans, LA	72/7,080
1967	George Knudson	277	Jack Nicklaus	278	Lakewood CC, New Orleans, LA	72/7,080
1968	George Archer	271	Bert Yancey	273	Lakewood CC, New Orleans, LA	72/7,080
1969	Larry Hinson*	275	Frank Beard	275	Lakewood CC, New Orleans, LA	72/7,080
1970	Miller Barber*	278	Bob Charles Howie Johnson	278	Lakewood CC, New Orleans, LA	72/7,080
1971	Frank Beard	276	Hubert Green	277	Lakewood CC, New Orleans, LA	72/7,080
1972	Gary Player	279	Dave Eichelberger Jack Nicklaus	280	Lakewood CC, New Orleans, LA	72/7,080
1973	Jack Nicklaus*	280	Miller Barber	280	Lakewood CC, New Orleans, LA	72/7,080
1974	Lee Trevino	267	Bobby Cole Ben Crenshaw	275	Lakewood CC, New Orleans, LA	72/7,080
FIRST NBC NEW ORLEANS OPEN						
1975	Billy Casper	271	Peter Oosterhuis	273	Lakewood CC, New Orleans, LA	72/7,080
1976	Larry Ziegler	274	Victor Regalado	275	Lakewood CC, New Orleans, LA	72/7,080
1977	Jim Simons	273	Stan Lee	276	Lakewood CC, New Orleans, LA	72/7,080
1978	Lon Hinkle	271	Gibby Gilbert Fuzzy Zoeller	272	Lakewood CC, New Orleans, LA	72/7,080
1979	Hubert Green	273	Frank Conner Bruce Lietzke Steve Melnyk Lee Trevino	274	Lakewood CC, New Orleans, LA	72/7,080
GREATER NEW ORLEANS OPEN						
1980	Tom Watson	273	Lee Trevino	275	Lakewood CC, New Orleans, LA	72/7,080
USF&G NEW ORLEANS OPEN						
1981	Tom Watson	270	Bruce Fleisher	272	Lakewood CC, New Orleans, LA	72/7,080
USF&G CLASSIC						
1982	Scott Hoch~	206	Bob Shearer Tom Watson	208	Lakewood CC, New Orleans, LA	72/7,080
1983	Bill Rogers	274	David Edwards Jay Haas Vance Heafner	277	Lakewood CC, New Orleans, LA	72/7,080
1984	Bob Eastwood	272	Larry Rinker	275	Lakewood CC, New Orleans, LA	72/7,080
1985	Seve Ballesteros~	205	Peter Jacobsen John Mahaffey	207	Lakewood CC, New Orleans, LA	72/7,080
1986	Calvin Peete	269	Pat McGowan	274	Lakewood CC, New Orleans, LA	72/7,080
1987	Ben Crenshaw	268	Curtis Strange	271	Lakewood CC, New Orleans, LA	72/7,080
1988	Chip Beck	262	Lanny Wadkins	269	Lakewood CC, New Orleans, LA	72/7,080
1989	Tim Simpson	274	Greg Norman Hal Sutton	276	English Turn G&CC, New Orleans, LA	72/7,106
1990	David Frost	276	Greg Norman	277	English Turn G&CC, New Orleans, LA	72/7,106
1991	Ian Woosnam*	275	Jim Hallet	275	English Turn G&CC, New Orleans, LA	72/7,106
FREEPORT-MCMORAN CLASSIC						
1992	Chip Beck	276	Greg Norman Mike Standly	277	English Turn G&CC, New Orleans, LA	72/7,106
1993	Mike Standly	281	Russ Cochran Payne Stewart	282	English Turn G&CC, New Orleans, LA	72/7,106
1994	Ben Crenshaw	273	Jose Maria Olazabal	276	English Turn G&CC, New Orleans, LA	72/7,106
1995	Davis Love III*	274	Mike Heinen	274	English Turn G&CC, New Orleans, LA	72/7,106
FREEPORT•MCDERMOTT CLASSIC						
1996	Scott McCarron	275	Tom Watson	280	English Turn G&CC, New Orleans, LA	72/7,116
1997	Brad Faxon	272	Bill Glasson Jesper Parnevik	275	English Turn G&CC, New Orleans, LA	72/7,116
1998	Lee Westwood	273	Steve Flesch	276	English Turn G&CC, New Orleans, LA	72/7,116
COMPAQ CLASSIC OF NEW ORLEANS						
1999	Carlos Franco	269	Steve Flesch Harrison Frazar	271	English Turn G&CC, New Orleans, LA	72/7,116
2000	Carlos Franco*	270	Blaine McCallister	270	English Turn G&CC, New Orleans, LA	72/7,116
2001	David Toms	266	Phil Mickelson	268	English Turn G&CC, New Orleans, LA	72/7,116
2002	K.J. Choi	271	Dudley Hart Geoff Ogilvy	275	English Turn G&CC, New Orleans, LA	72/7,116
HP CLASSIC OF NEW ORLEANS						
2003	Steve Flesch*	267	Bob Estes	267	English Turn G&CC, New Orleans, LA	72/7,116
2004	Vijay Singh	266	Phil Mickelson Joe Ogilvie	267	English Turn G&CC, New Orleans, LA	72/7,116

*KEY: * = Playoff ~ = Weather-shortened*

2004 Wachovia Championship

[19th of 48 official events]

WACHOVIA CHAMPIONSHIP

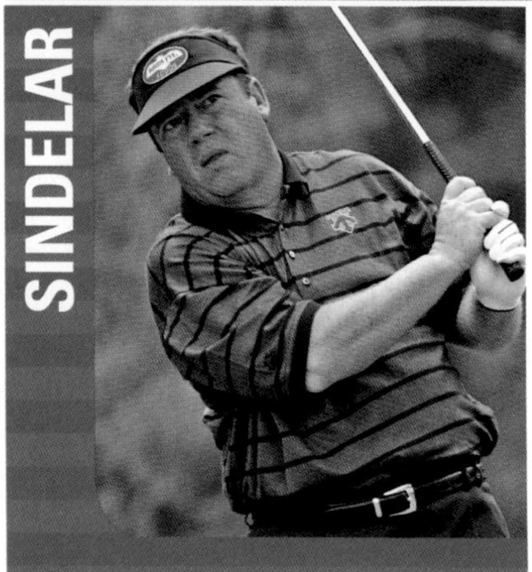

Winner: JOEY SINDELAR #
69-69-70-69 277 (-11) $1,008,000

Quail Hollow Club

Charlotte, NC

May 6-9, 2004

Purse: $5,600,000
Par: 36-36—72
Yards: 7,442

LEADERS: First Round—Kirk Triplett shot a tournament-record 8-under-par 64 to lead a group of four players by two strokes.
Second Round—Tiger Woods moved into the lead with a second-round 66 to lead Triplett, Notah Begay III and Arron Oberholser by two.
Third Round— Oberholser shot a third-round 68 to finish one stroke ahead of Geoff Ogilvy and Notah Begay III.

CUT: 72 players at even-par from a field of 156.

PRO-AM: $10,000. Rory Sabbatini, 59, $2,000

WEATHER: Mostly sunny on Thursday with a high of 87 in the afternoon. Sunny and hot again on Friday with a high of 91. Hot and mostly sunny on Saturday with a high of 90. Warm, slightly cloudy on Sunday with highs in the low 90s.

Check out the 2005 Wachovia Championship, May 5-8 on USA/CBS

ORDER OF FINISH

 # Won playoff with a par-4 on second playoff hole

Joey Sindelar #	1	69-69-70-69	277	$1,008,000.00
Arron Oberholser	2	69-68-68-72	277	604,800.00
Carlos Franco	T3	68-71-69-70	278	324,800.00
Tiger Woods	T3	69-66-75-68	278	324,800.00
Notah Begay III	T5	67-70-69-73	279	196,700.00
Steve Flesch	T5	72-72-66-69	279	196,700.00
Jeff Maggert	T5	71-69-67-72	279	196,700.00
Phil Mickelson	T5	70-70-72-67	279	196,700.00
Mathias Gronberg	9	69-71-71-69	280	162,400.00
Lucas Glover (S)	T10	74-70-68-69	281	128,800.00
Geoff Ogilvy	T10	69-71-66-75	281	128,800.00
Vijay Singh	T10	68-70-71-72	281	128,800.00
Heath Slocum	T10	67-75-67-72	281	128,800.00
Kevin Sutherland	T10	71-68-71-71	281	128,800.00
Stuart Appleby	T15	66-72-70-74	282	86,800.00
Tom Byrum	T15	74-69-71-68	282	86,800.00
Luke Donald	T15	67-73-73-69	282	86,800.00
Matt Gogel	T15	69-72-70-71	282	86,800.00
Jonathan Kaye	T15	68-74-69-71	282	86,800.00
Kirk Triplett	T15	64-73-71-74	282	86,800.00
Chad Campbell	T21	70-74-66-73	283	54,160.00
Todd Hamilton	T21	71-71-70-71	283	54,160.00
J.J. Henry	T21	72-70-70-71	283	54,160.00
Davis Love III	T21	73-66-72-72	283	$54,160.00
Pat Perez	T21	73-70-70-70	283	54,160.00
Nick Price	T21	74-69-70-70	283	54,160.00
Mike Weir	T21	67-72-75-69	283	54,160.00
Cameron Beckman	T28	67-72-71-74	284	38,920.00
Jay Haas	T28	71-73-71-69	284	38,920.00
Spike McRoy	T28	69-74-71-70	284	38,920.00
Joe Ogilvie	T28	68-71-76-69	284	38,920.00
Gene Sauers	T32	70-72-71-72	285	33,133.34
Jason Bohn	T32	71-70-72-72	285	33,133.33
John Senden	T32	69-73-71-72	285	33,133.33
Ben Curtis	T35	71-71-74-70	286	25,293.34
Donnie Hammond (Q)	T35	72-70-73-71	286	25,293.34
John Riegger	T35	74-70-73-69	286	25,293.34
Pat Bates	T35	75-68-72-71	286	25,293.33
Rich Beem	T35	70-73-68-75	286	25,293.33
K.J. Choi	T35	71-73-69-73	286	25,293.33
Daniel Chopra	T35	73-68-71-74	286	25,293.33
John Cook	T35	74-70-67-75	286	25,293.33
Stephen Leaney	T35	71-72-71-72	286	25,293.33
Scott Hend	T44	73-71-71-72	287	16,930.67
Peter Lonard	T44	73-68-72-74	287	16,930.67
Shaun Micheel	T44	70-72-74-71	287	16,930.67
Dean Wilson	T44	73-71-74-69	287	16,930.67
Brett Quigley	T44	66-72-74-75	287	16,930.66
Jeff Sluman	T44	70-73-70-74	287	16,930.66
Robert Allenby	T50	72-68-74-74	288	$13,402.67
Chris DiMarco	T50	69-70-76-73	288	13,402.67
Tripp Isenhour	T50	71-71-75-71	288	13,402.67
Richard S. Johnson	T50	72-69-76-71	288	13,402.67
Rich Barcelo	T50	74-68-72-74	288	13,402.66
Rory Sabbatini	T50	66-74-74-74	288	13,402.66
Steve Allan	T56	69-74-72-74	289	12,544.00
Brad Faxon	T56	73-71-72-73	289	12,544.00
Shigeki Maruyama	T56	69-75-72-73	289	12,544.00
Kelly Mitchum	T56	72-69-77-71	289	12,544.00
David Peoples	T56	70-71-75-73	289	12,544.00
Sergio Garcia	T61	73-71-76-70	290	12,096.00
Brent Geiberger	T61	70-74-74-72	290	12,096.00
Billy Mayfair	T61	70-74-76-70	290	12,096.00
Tom Carter	T64	73-70-73-75	291	11,816.00
Tim Clark	T64	73-69-71-78	291	11,816.00
Michael Allen	T66	74-69-70-79	292	11,536.00
Robert Damron	T66	72-71-73-76	292	11,536.00
Jerry Kelly	T66	69-74-75-74	292	11,536.00
Grant Waite	69	72-71-76-74	293	11,312.00
Matt Kuchar	T70	76-68-73-78	295	11,144.00
Blaine McCallister	T70	70-74-78-73	295	11,144.00
Hidemichi Tanaka	72	72-71-77-80	300	10,976.00

(Q) = Open Qualifier; (S) = Sponsor Exemption; (T) = Tie

The following players did not finish ((C=cut, W=withdrew)

C—145-Woody Austin, Russ Cochran, Ben Crane, Jay Delsing, Jason Dufner, J.P. Hayes, Tim Herron, Zach Johnson, J.L. Lewis, Frank Lickliter II, Mark O'Meara, Jesper Parnevik, Ted Purdy. **146-**Billy Andrade, Danny Briggs, Stewart Cink, Joe Durant, Danny Ellis, Fred Funk, Robert Gamez, Brandt Jobe, Kent Jones, Justin Leonard, David Morland IV, Kevin Na, Carl Pettersson, John Rollins, Chris Smith, Esteban Toledo, David Toms. **147-**Tommy Armour III, Jeff Brehaut, D.J. Brigman, Todd Fischer, Harrison Frazar, David Frost, Scott Hoch, Cliff Kresge, John Maginnes, Dan Olsen, Ryan Palmer, Vaughn Taylor, Duffy Waldorf. **148-**Ricky Barnes, Olin Browne, Bob Burns, Jonathan Byrd, Ken Duke, Brian Gay, Jerry Haas, Charles Howell III, Lee Janzen, Skip Kendall, Len Mattiace, Corey Pavin, Tim Petrovic. **149-**Glen Day, Tom Pernice, Jr. **150-**Aaron Baddeley, Dan Forsman, Hank Kuehne, Dicky Pride, Paul Stankowski, Roger Tambellini. **151-**Arjun Atwal, Craig Bowden, Hunter Mahan, Patrick Moore, Omar Uresti. **152-**David Gossett, Neal Lancaster, Jeffrey Lankford, Craig Perks, Charles Warren. **153-**David Branshaw, Steve Lowery. **154-**Jose Coceres, Scott Piercy. **155-**Andy Crain. **157-**Fulton Allem, Michael Clark II. **163-**Todd Gleaton. **W—73-**Scott McCarron. **66-**Fredrik Jacobson.

Tournament Record:
277, Joey Sindelar, Arron Oberholser, 2004
Current Course Record:
64, Kirk Triplett, 2004

TOURNAMENT HISTORY

Year	Winner	Score	Runner-up	Score	Location	Par/Yards
WACHOVIA CHAMPIONSHIP						
2003	David Toms	278	Vijay Singh Robert Gamez Brent Geiberger	280	Quail Hollow Club, Charlotte, NC	72/7,396
2004	Joey Sindelar*	277	Arron Oberholser	277	Quail Hollow Club, Charlotte, NC	72/7,442

*KEY: * = Playoff*

2004 EDS Byron Nelson Championship

[20th of 48 official events]

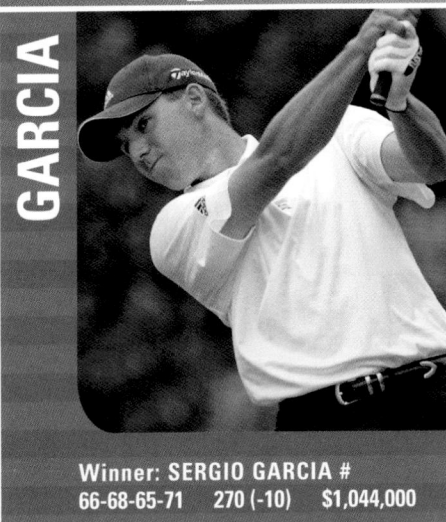

EDS Byron Nelson CHAMPIONSHIP

GARCIA

Winner: SERGIO GARCIA #
66-68-65-71 270 (-10) $1,044,000

Tournament Players Course at Four Seasons

Las Colinas; Irving, TX

May 13-16, 2004

Purse: $5,800,000
Host Course (HC)
Par: 35-35—70 Yards: 7,016
Cottonwood Valley Course (CV)
Par: 34-36—70 Yards: 6,847

LEADERS: First Round—Peter Lonard (CV) and J.L. Lewis (CV) sat at 6-under 64, one stroke ahead of Tiger Woods (HC) and Dudley Hart (CV). **Second Round**—Woods (CV) moved to 8-under 132 to hold a one-stroke lead over Mark O'Meara (CV). Sergio Garcia (HC), Daniel Chopra (CV), Jerry Kelly (CV), Jonathan Byrd (CV) and Lonard (HC) were two behind. **Third Round**—Garcia sat at 11-under 199, two ahead of Kelly. Deane Pappas and Woods trailed by two.

PRO-AM: $20,000. TPC Four Seasons—Jerry Kelly and Spike McRoy, 53, $1,800 each. Cottonwood Valley Course—Carl Pettersson and Zach Johnson, 53, $1,800 each.

CUT: 80 players at even-par 140 from a field of 155 professional and one amateur.

WEATHER: Rain at times on Thursday with the sun breaking through in the afternoon. Mostly cloudy on Friday with temperatures in the high 60s. Saturday temperatures reached the high 70s. Mix of sun and clouds on Sunday.

Check out the 2005 EDS Byron Nelson Championship, May 12-15 on USA/CBS

ORDER OF FINISH

 # Won playoff with a par-4 on first playoff hole

Player	Pos.	Rounds	Total	Money
Sergio Garcia #	1	66-68-65-71	270	$1,044,000.00
Robert Damron	T2	67-69-68-66	270	510,400.00
Dudley Hart	T2	65-71-67-67	270	510,400.00
Tim Herron	T4	69-70-68-64	271	239,733.34
Duffy Waldorf	T4	67-70-66-68	271	239,733.33
Tiger Woods	T4	65-67-70-69	271	239,733.33
Ernie Els	T7	69-70-66-67	272	174,725.00
Stephen Leaney	T7	66-69-69-68	272	174,725.00
Shigeki Maruyama	T7	70-70-66-66	272	174,725.00
Nick Price	T7	66-71-69-66	272	174,725.00
Jerry Kelly	T11	66-68-67-72	273	133,400.00
Mark O'Meara	T11	67-66-70-70	273	133,400.00
Deane Pappas	T11	67-69-66-71	273	133,400.00
Brian Bateman	T14	69-69-69-67	274	92,800.00
David Branshaw	T14	70-69-67-68	274	92,800.00
Chris DiMarco	T14	69-70-65-70	274	92,800.00
Luke Donald	T14	68-71-64-71	274	92,800.00
Carlos Franco	T14	70-70-67-67	274	92,800.00
Matt Gogel	T14	69-69-68-68	274	92,800.00
Scott Verplank	T14	71-66-67-70	274	92,800.00
Briny Baird	T21	69-69-65-72	275	58,000.00
Tom Carter	T21	68-69-69-69	275	58,000.00
Rod Pampling	T21	66-72-66-71	275	58,000.00
Rory Sabbatini	T21	69-69-70-67	275	58,000.00
Tjaart Van der Walt (S)	T21	69-68-68-70	275	58,000.00
Bo Van Pelt	T21	70-69-66-70	275	$58,000.00
Jonathan Byrd	T27	67-67-70-72	276	39,440.00
John Daly	T27	68-71-71-66	276	39,440.00
Harrison Frazar	T27	68-69-70-69	276	39,440.00
Shaun Micheel	T27	67-68-71-70	276	39,440.00
Ted Purdy	T27	68-69-67-72	276	39,440.00
Chris Smith	T27	66-72-70-68	276	39,440.00
Brandt Snedeker (S)	T27	70-66-71-69	276	39,440.00
Jesper Parnevik	T34	67-73-69-68	277	28,668.58
Russ Cochran	T34	70-68-68-71	277	28,668.57
Kent Jones	T34	68-72-67-70	277	28,668.57
Hank Kuehne	T34	70-69-65-73	277	28,668.57
Justin Leonard	T34	69-70-68-70	277	28,668.57
Kevin Na	T34	71-66-69-71	277	28,668.57
Carl Pettersson	T34	67-71-69-70	277	28,668.57
Robert Allenby	T41	69-67-68-74	278	20,300.00
Tommy Armour III	T41	73-65-68-72	278	20,300.00
J.J. Henry	T41	68-71-66-73	278	20,300.00
Zach Johnson	T41	68-69-68-73	278	20,300.00
John Senden	T41	72-68-71-67	278	20,300.00
Kevin Sutherland	T41	68-71-68-71	278	20,300.00
Bob Tway	T41	68-69-69-72	278	20,300.00
Bart Bryant	T48	70-70-70-69	279	14,577.34
Chad Campbell	T48	73-67-69-70	279	14,577.34
Cameron Beckman	T48	70-67-71-71	279	14,577.33
Jason Bohn	T48	69-69-67-74	279	14,577.33
J.L. Lewis	T48	64-74-68-73	279	14,577.33
Peter Lonard	T48	64-70-71-74	279	14,577.33
Rich Barcelo	T54	68-71-69-72	280	$13,224.00
Tom Byrum	T54	71-69-68-72	280	13,224.00
Daniel Chopra	T54	66-68-72-74	280	13,224.00
Craig Perks	T54	70-69-71-70	280	13,224.00
Jay Williamson	T54	66-71-73-70	280	13,224.00
Notah Begay III	T59	68-72-70-71	281	12,470.00
Jay Delsing	T59	69-68-69-75	281	12,470.00
Todd Fischer	T59	70-67-70-74	281	12,470.00
Todd Hamilton	T59	74-65-70-72	281	12,470.00
Neal Lancaster	T59	70-67-71-73	281	12,470.00
Kenny Perry	T59	67-70-71-73	281	12,470.00
Vijay Singh	T59	68-67-68-78	281	12,470.00
Mike Weir	T59	69-69-69-74	281	12,470.00
Greg Chalmers (S)	T67	68-68-73-73	282	11,716.00
John Cook	T67	67-73-75-67	282	11,716.00
Mark Hensby	T67	68-71-67-76	282	11,716.00
Lee Janzen	T67	70-68-71-73	282	11,716.00
Pat Perez	T67	71-68-71-72	282	11,716.00
Billy Andrade	T72	70-70-71-72	283	11,252.00
Kevin Durkin (Q)	T72	66-70-73-74	283	11,252.00
Steve Lowery	T72	68-69-70-76	283	11,252.00
Scott Simpson (S)	75	71-69-74-71	285	11,020.00
Tommy Tolles	76	69-69-68-80	286	10,904.00
Ken Duke	77	70-70-73-74	287	10,788.00
Gene Sauers	78	71-69-75-73	288	10,672.00
Vaughn Taylor	79	71-69-73-77	290	10,556.00
Aaron Baddeley	80	70-69-79-77	295	10,440.00

(Q) = Open Qualifier; (S) = Sponsor Exemption; (T) = Tie

The following players did not finish (C=cut, W=withdrew, A=amateur)

C—141-Rich Beem, D.J. Brigman, Bob Burns, Jim Carter, Glen Day, Jason Dufner, Brian Gay, Jason Hartwick (A), Frank Lickliter II, Phil Mickelson, Tim Petrovic, Loren Roberts, John Rollins, Jeff Sluman, Steve Stricker. **142-**Danny Ellis, Bob Estes, Brent Geiberger, Richard S. Johnson, Cliff Kresge, Jeff Maggert, Hunter Mahan, David Peoples, Esteban Toledo. **143-**Steve Allan, Stuart Appleby, Tim Clark, Ben Crane, Brad Faxon, Fred Funk, Brandt Jobe, Billy Mayfair, Spike McRoy, Dan Olsen, Jin Park, Dean Wilson. **144-**Michael Allen, JC Anderson, Chris Couch, Chris Riley, Hidemichi Tanaka. **145-**Woody Austin, Kris Cox, Brad Elder, Robert Gamez, Scott Hend, Paul Stankowski, David Toms. **146-**Jeff Brehaut, Olin Browne, Cameron Doan, Jamie Elliott, Lucas Glover, J.P. Hayes, John Maginnes, Hal Sutton, Roger Tambellini. **147-**Dan Forsman, Mike Henderson, Blaine McCallister, Scott McCarron, Ryan Palmer, Omar Uresti, Brian Watts. **148-**Pat Bates. **149-**Danny Briggs, John Huston, Tripp Isenhour, Patrick Moore. **150-**Fulton Allem, Mark Brooks, Grant Waite. **155-**David Morland IV. **W—78-**Joe Ogilvie. **77-**Tag Ridings. **73-**Arron Oberholser.

TOURNAMENT HISTORY

Year	Winner	Score	Runner-up	Score	Location	Par/Yards
DALLAS OPEN						
1944	Byron Nelson	276	Harold McSpaden	286	Lakewood CC, Dallas, TX	N/A
1945	Sam Snead	276	Harold McSpaden	280	Dallas CC, Dallas, TX	N/A
1946	Ben Hogan	284	Herman Keiser Paul Runyan	286	Brook Hollow CC, Dallas, TX	N/A
1947	No Tournament					
1948	No Tournament					
1949	No Tournament					
1950	No Tournament					
1951	No Tournament					
1952	No Tournament					
1953	No Tournament					
1954	No Tournament					
1955	No Tournament					
1956	Don January	268	Dow Finsterwald Doug Ford	269	Preston Hollow CC, Dallas, TX	N/A
1956A	Peter Thomson*	267	Gene Littler Cary Middlecoff	267	Preston Hollow CC, Dallas, TX	N/A
1957	Sam Snead	264	Bob Inman Billy Maxwell Cary Middlecoff	274	Glen Lakes CC, Dallas, TX	N/A
1958	Sam Snead*	272	Julius Boros John McMullen Gary Player	272	Oak Cliff CC, Dallas, TX	71/6,836
1959	Julius Boros	274	Dow Finsterwald Earl Stewart, Jr. Bo Wininger	275	Oak Cliff CC, Dallas, TX	71/6,836
1960	Johnny Pott*	275	Ted Kroll Bo Wininger	275	Oak Cliff CC, Dallas, TX	71/6,836

EDS Byron Nelson Championship

NOTES

***Sergio Garcia** collected his first win at the tournament where he made his professional PGA TOUR debut in 1999. It was his third top-10 in six appearances after a T3 in 1999 and T8 in 2001.*

***Sergio Garcia** (24) became the youngest winner at the tournament since **Tiger Woods** won the 1997 event at the age of 21 years, four months and 18 days.*

*2004 champion **Sergio Garcia** led the tournament in Greens In Regulation hitting 59 of 72 (81.2 percent) of the greens.*

*Winning the 2004 tournament helped **Sergio Garcia** move into third on the all-time tournament earnings list with $1,382,500.*

*The win was **Sergio Garcia**'s 12th worldwide including nine official money events, four on the PGA TOUR, four on the European Tour and one on the Asian PGA.*

***Sergio Garcia** collected his second playoff win in three career playoff appearances.*

*Coupled with the 2001 victory at the MasterCard Colonial, **Sergio Garcia** became the 13th player to win both the Byron Nelson and the Colonial in his career. **Phil Mickelson** (1996 GTE Byron Nelson Golf Classic/2000 MasterCard Colonial) was the last player to win both events.*

*The playoff was the 18th in the history of the EDS Byron Nelson Championship, and the first since 2001 when **Robert Damron** topped **Scott Verplank** in the fourth extra hole.*

ROBERT DAMRON

Tournament Record:
262, Loren Roberts, Steve Pate, 1999

Current Course Record:
61, Billy Mayfair, 1993; Charlie Rymer, 1996; Justin Leonard, 2001 (TPC at Los Colinas)
61, Ernie Els, 1995; Tiger Woods, 1999 (Cottonwood Valley Course)

TOURNAMENT HISTORY

Year	Winner	Score	Runner-up	Score	Location	Par/Yards
1961	Earl Stewart, Jr.	278	Gay Brewer Arnold Palmer Doug Sanders	279	Oak Cliff CC, Dallas, TX	71/6,836
1962	Billy Maxwell	277	Johnny Pott	281	Oak Cliff CC, Dallas, TX	71/6,836
1963	No Tournament					
1964	Charles Coody	271	Jerry Edwards	272	Oak Cliff CC, Dallas, TX	71/6,836
1965	No Tournament					
1966	Roberto De Vicenzo	276	Joe Campbell Raymond Floyd Harold Henning	277	Oak Cliff CC, Dallas, TX	71/6,836
1967	Bert Yancey	274	Roberto De Vicenzo Kermit Zarley	275	Oak Cliff CC, Dallas, TX	71/6,836
BYRON NELSON GOLF CLASSIC						
1968	Miller Barber	270	Kermit Zarley	271	Preston Trail GC, Dallas, TX	70/6,993
1969	Bruce Devlin	277	Frank Beard Bruce Crampton	278	Preston Trail GC, Dallas, TX	70/6,993
1970	Jack Nicklaus*	274	Arnold Palmer	274	Preston Trail GC Dallas, TX	70/6,993
1971	Jack Nicklaus	274	Frank Beard Jerry McGee	276	Preston Trail GC, Dallas, TX	70/6,993
1972	Chi Chi Rodriguez*	273	Billy Casper	273	Preston Trail GC, Dallas, TX	70/6,993
1973	Lanny Wadkins*	277	Dan Sikes	277	Preston Trail GC, Dallas, TX	70/6,993
1974	Bud Allin	269	Homero Blancas Charles Coody Lee Trevino Tom Watson	273	Preston Trail GC, Dallas, TX	70/6,993
1975	Tom Watson	269	Bob E. Smith	271	Preston Trail GC, Dallas, TX	70/6,993
1976	Mark Hayes	273	Don Bies	275	Preston Trail GC, Dallas, TX	70/6,993
1977	Raymond Floyd	276	Ben Crenshaw	278	Preston Trail GCS, Dallas, TX	70/6,993
1978	Tom Watson	272	Lee Trevino	273	Preston Trail GC, Dallas, TX	70/6,993
1979	Tom Watson*	275	Bill Rogers	275	Preston Trail GC, Dallas, TX	70/6,993
1980	Tom Watson	274	Bill Rogers	275	Preston Trail GC, Dallas, TX	70/6,993
1981	Bruce Lietzke*	281	Tom Watson	281	Preston Trail GC, Dallas, TX	70/6,993
1982	Bob Gilder	266	Curtis Strange	271	Preston Trail GC, Dallas, TX	70/6,993
1983	Ben Crenshaw	273	Brad Bryant Hal Sutton	274	Las Colinas Sports Club, Irving, TX	71/6,982
1984	Craig Stadler	276	David Edwards	277	Las Colinas Sports Club, Irving, TX	71/6,982
1985	Bob Eastwood*	272	Payne Stewart	272	Las Colinas Sports Club, Irving, TX	71/6,982
1986	Andy Bean	269	Mark Wiebe	270	TPC at Las Colinas, Irving, TX	70/6,767
1987	Fred Couples*	266	Mark Calcavecchia	266	TPC at Las Colinas, Irving, TX	70/6,767
GTE BYRON NELSON GOLF CLASSIC						
1988	Bruce Lietzke*	271	Clarence Rose	271	TPC at Las Colinas, Irving, TX	70/6,767
1989	Jodie Mudd*	265	Larry Nelson	265	TPC at Las Colinas, Irving, TX	70/6,767
1990	Payne Stewart~	202	Lanny Wadkins	204	TPC at Las Colinas, Irving, TX	70/6,767
1991	Nick Price	270	Craig Stadler	271	TPC at Las Colinas, Irving, TX	70/6,767
1992	Billy Ray Brown*~	199	Ben Crenshaw Raymond Floyd Bruce Lietzke	199	TPC at Las Colinas, Irving, TX	70/6,850
1993	Scott Simpson	270	Billy Mayfair Corey Pavin D.A. Weibring	271	TPC at Las Colinas, Irving, TX	70/6,850
1994	Neal Lancaster*~	132	Tom Byrum Mark Carnevale David Edwards Yoshinori Mizumaki David Ogrin	132	TPC at Las Colinas, Irving, TX (H) Cottonwood Valley Course, Irving, TX	70/6,850 71/6,862
1995	Ernie Els	263	Mike Heinen D.A. Weibring Robin Freeman	266	TPC at Las Colinas, Irving, TX (H) Cottonwood Valley Course, Irving, TX	70/6,850 70/6,862
1996	Phil Mickelson	265	Craig Parry	267	TPC at Las Colinas, Irving, TX (H) Cottonwood Valley Course, Irving, TX	70/6,899 70/6,846
1997	Tiger Woods	263	Lee Rinker	265	TPC at Las Colinas, Irving, TX (H) Cottonwood Valley Course, Irving, TX	70/6,899 70/6,846
1998	John Cook	265	Fred Couples Hal Sutton Harrison Frazar	268	TPC at Las Colinas, Irving, TX (H) Cottonwood Valley Course, Irving, TX	70/6,924 70/6,846
1999	Loren Roberts*	262	Steve Pate	262	TPC at Las Colinas, Irving, TX (H) Cottonwood Valley Course, Irving, TX	70/6,924 70/6,846
2000	Jesper Parnevik*	269	Davis Love III Phil Mickelson	269	TPC at Las Colinas, Irving, TX (H) Cottonwood Valley Course, Irving, TX	70/6,994 70/6,846
VERIZON BYRON NELSON CLASSIC						
2001	Robert Damron*	263	Scott Verplank	263	TPC at Las Colinas, Irving, TX (H) Cottonwood Valley Course, Irving, TX	70/7,017 70/6,846
2002	Shigeki Maruyama	266	Ben Crane	268	TPC at Las Colinas, Irving, TX (H) Cottonwood Valley Course, Irving, TX	70/7,017 70/6,846
EDS BYRON NELSON CHAMPIONSHIP						
2003	Vijay Singh	265	Nick Price	267	TPC at Las Colinas, Irving, TX (H) Cottonwood Valley Course, Irving, TX	70/7,022 70/6,846
2004	Sergio Garcia*	270	Robert Damron Dudley Hart	270	TPC at Las Colinas, Irving, TX (H) Cottonwood Valley Course, Irving, TX	70/7,016 70/6,847

*KEY: * = Playoff (H) = Host Course*

2004 Bank of America Colonial [21st of 48 official events]

FLESCH

Winner: STEVE FLESCH
66-69-67-67 269 (-11) $954,000

Colonial Country Club

Fort Worth, TX

May 20-23, 2004

Purse: $5,300,000
Par: 35-35—70
Yards: 7,054

LEADERS: First Round—Craig Perks posted a 6-under 64 to lead Jesper Parnevik by a stroke. Tim Petrovic, Steve Flesch, Stewart Cink, Jeff Maggert and John Senden stood two back.
Second Round—J.L. Lewis and Justin Leonard sat at 6-under 134, one ahead of Robert Gamez, Maggert, Perks and Flesch.

Third Round— Chad Campbell tied the course record with a 9-under 61 to join a three-way tie with Brian Gay and Flesch at 8-under 202. Zach Johnson trailed by two.

CUT: 74 players at 3-over-par 143 from a field of 114 professionals.

PRO-AM: $10,000. Jonathan Byrd, 52, $2,000.

WEATHER: Partly cloudy, windy (S 15-25 mph), warm (high 80s) and humid all four days. Some higher gusts up to 30 mph on Friday, Saturday and Sunday afternoons.

Check out the 2005 Bank of America Colonial, May 19-22 on USA/CBS

ORDER OF FINISH

Steve Flesch	1	66-69-67-67	269	$954,000.00
Chad Campbell	2	70-71-61-68	270	572,400.00
Stephen Ames	3	70-69-68-64	271	360,400.00
Craig Perks	4	64-71-70-68	273	254,400.00
Robert Gamez	T5	71-64-71-68	274	186,162.50
Skip Kendall	T5	68-71-68-67	274	186,162.50
Tim Petrovic	T5	66-71-69-68	274	186,162.50
Bo Van Pelt	T5	68-69-72-65	274	186,162.50
Mark Brooks	T9	71-68-67-69	275	143,100.00
Jeff Maggert	T9	66-69-73-67	275	143,100.00
John Senden (S)	T9	66-74-70-65	275	143,100.00
Kenny Perry	T12	67-71-70-68	276	116,600.00
Loren Roberts	T12	68-70-71-67	276	116,600.00
Tom Byrum	T14	68-69-71-69	277	72,433.34
Lee Janzen	T14	70-66-71-70	277	72,433.34
Joe Ogilvie	T14	71-70-68-68	277	72,433.34
Kirk Triplett	T14	69-69-71-68	277	72,433.34
Brian Bateman	T14	69-69-68-71	277	72,433.33
Stewart Cink	T14	66-70-71-70	277	72,433.33
Tim Clark	T14	68-70-69-70	277	72,433.33
Brian Gay (S)	T14	70-67-65-75	277	72,433.33
Zach Johnson	T14	71-65-68-73	277	72,433.33
Justin Leonard	T14	70-64-72-71	277	72,433.33
Jesper Parnevik	T14	65-72-68-72	277	72,433.33
Chris Riley	T14	67-71-69-70	277	$72,433.33
Fred Funk	26	70-72-65-71	278	42,400.00
Stephen Leaney	T27	70-68-71-70	279	38,425.00
J.L. Lewis	T27	68-66-75-70	279	38,425.00
Peter Lonard	T27	71-71-67-70	279	38,425.00
Bob Tway	T27	70-69-68-72	279	38,425.00
Glen Day (S)	T31	72-71-67-70	280	32,131.25
Dennis Paulson	T31	67-70-71-72	280	32,131.25
Corey Pavin	T31	70-70-72-68	280	32,131.25
Rory Sabbatini	T31	72-69-67-72	280	32,131.25
Joe Durant	T35	70-73-69-69	281	25,572.50
Sergio Garcia	T35	72-67-73-69	281	25,572.50
Davis Love III	T35	74-67-72-68	281	25,572.50
Phil Mickelson	T35	71-66-70-74	281	25,572.50
Brett Quigley (S)	T35	70-68-68-75	281	25,572.50
Scott Verplank	T35	72-68-67-74	281	25,572.50
Dudley Hart (S)	T41	73-70-66-73	282	20,670.00
Joey Sindelar	T41	71-69-72-70	282	20,670.00
Hal Sutton	T41	71-67-73-71	282	20,670.00
Tommy Armour III	T44	69-74-71-69	283	16,023.67
Chris DiMarco	T44	69-71-72-71	283	16,023.67
Todd Hamilton	T44	72-71-70-70	283	16,023.67
Rod Pampling	T44	72-71-69-71	283	16,023.67
Frank Lickliter II	T44	68-70-68-77	283	16,023.66
David Toms	T44	72-70-68-73	283	16,023.66
Aaron Baddeley	T50	68-71-74-71	284	12,905.50
Briny Baird	T50	71-69-71-73	284	$12,905.50
Brad Faxon	T50	70-68-75-71	284	12,905.50
Kent Jones	T50	70-69-73-72	284	12,905.50
Robert Allenby	T54	67-76-73-69	285	11,978.00
Steve Elkington	T54	71-71-73-70	285	11,978.00
Matt Gogel	T54	70-73-76-66	285	11,978.00
Mathias Gronberg	T54	70-70-71-74	285	11,978.00
Neal Lancaster	T54	73-70-70-72	285	11,978.00
Rocco Mediate	T54	72-71-71-71	285	11,978.00
Carl Pettersson	T54	67-74-73-71	285	11,978.00
Scott Hend	T61	69-74-72-71	286	11,501.00
Mike Weir	T61	68-73-71-74	286	11,501.00
Luke Donald	T63	69-74-73-71	287	11,130.00
Tim Herron	T63	69-72-72-74	287	11,130.00
Hunter Mahan (S)	T63	70-71-71-75	287	11,130.00
Geoff Ogilvy	T63	74-69-69-75	287	11,130.00
Patrick Sheehan	T63	71-70-69-77	287	11,130.00
Steve Lowery	T68	69-74-75-70	288	10,706.00
Dan Pohl	T68	71-72-72-73	288	10,706.00
Jeff Sluman	T68	72-70-74-72	288	10,706.00
Len Mattiace	T71	71-71-74-73	289	10,441.00
Brenden Pappas	T71	73-70-72-74	289	10,441.00
Mark Calcavecchia	73	72-68-75-75	290	10,282.00
Bob Estes	74	68-74-72-77	291	10,176.00

(Q) = Open Qualifier; (S) = Sponsor Exemption; (T) = Tie

The following players did not finish (C=cut, W=withdrew)

C—144-Fulton Allem, Stuart Appleby, Woody Austin, Pat Bates, D.J. Brigman, Olin Browne, Dan Forsman, J.J. Henry, Tripp Isenhour, Heath Slocum. **145-**Bob Burns, Danny Ellis, Harrison Frazar, John Huston, Jonathan Kaye, Shigeki Maruyama, Ted Purdy, John Rollins. **146-**Jonathan Byrd, Brent Geiberger, Billy Mayfair, Ryan Palmer. **147-**Duffy Waldorf. **148-**Keith Clearwater, Lucas Glover. **149-**Hank Kuehne, Esteban Toledo, Jay Williamson. **150-**Craig Bowden, David Frost. **151-**Mark Hensby, Dean Wilson. **153-**Notah Begay III. **154-**Bill Glasson. **160-**Rod Curl. **W—**Kevin Na. **77-**Ben Crane. **75-**John Riegger. **74-**Hidemichi Tanaka. **71-**Rich Beem.

STEVE FLESCH

TOURNAMENT HISTORY

Year	Winner	Score	Runner-up	Score	Location	Par/Yards
COLONIAL NATIONAL INVITATION TOURNAMENT						
1946	Ben Hogan	279	Harry Todd	280	Colonial CC, Fort Worth, TX	70/7,035
1947	Ben Hogan	279	Toney Penna	280	Colonial CC, Fort Worth, TX	70/7,035
1948	Clayton Heafner	272	Skip Alexander Ben Hogan	278	Colonial CC, Fort Worth, TX	70/7,035
1949	No Tournament					
1950	Sam Snead	277	Skip Alexander	280	Colonial CC, Fort Worth, TX	70/7,035
1951	Cary Middlecoff	282	Jack Burke, Jr.	283	Colonial CC, Fort Worth, TX	70/7,035
1952	Ben Hogan	279	Lloyd Mangrum	283	Colonial CC, Fort Worth, TX	70/7,035
1953	Ben Hogan	282	Doug Ford Cary Middlecoff	287	Colonial CC, Fort Worth, TX	70/7,035
1954	Johnny Palmer	280	Fred Haas	282	Colonial CC, Fort Worth, TX	70/7,035
1955	Chandler Harper	276	Dow Finsterwald	284	Colonial CC, Fort Worth, TX	70/7,035
1956	Mike Souchak	280	Tommy Bolt	281	Colonial CC, Fort Worth, TX	70/7,035
1957	Roberto De Vicenzo	284	Dick Mayer	285	Colonial CC, Fort Worth, TX	70/7,021
1958	Tommy Bolt	282	Ken Venturi	283	Colonial CC, Fort Worth, TX	70/7,021
1959	Ben Hogan*	285	Fred Hawkins	285	Colonial CC, Fort Worth, TX	70/7,021
1960	Julius Boros	280	Gene Littler Kel Nagle	281	Colonial CC, Fort Worth, TX	70/7,021
1961	Doug Sanders	281	Kel Nagle	282	Colonial CC, Fort Worth, TX	70/7,021
1962	Arnold Palmer*	281	Johnny Pott	281	Colonial CC, Fort Worth, TX	70/7,021
1963	Julius Boros	279	Gary Player	283	Colonial CC, Fort Worth, TX	70/7,021
1964	Billy Casper	279	Tommy Jacobs	283	Colonial CC, Fort Worth, TX	70/7,021
1965	Bruce Crampton	276	George Knudson	279	Colonial CC, Fort Worth, TX	70/7,021
1966	Bruce Devlin	280	R.H. Sikes	281	Colonial CC, Fort Worth, TX	70/7,021
1967	Dave Stockton	278	Charles Coody	280	Colonial CC, Fort Worth, TX	70/7,021
1968	Billy Casper	275	Gene Littler	280	Colonial CC, Fort Worth, TX	70/7,021
1969	Gardner Dickinson	278	Gary Player	279	Colonial CC, Fort Worth, TX	70/7,142
1970	Homero Blancas	273	Gene Littler Lee Trevino	274	Colonial CC, Fort Worth, TX	70/7,142
1971	Gene Littler	283	Bert Yancey	284	Colonial CC, Fort Worth, TX	70/7,142

Bank of America Colonial

NOTES

Steve Flesch *earned his second career PGA TOUR victory in his 209th start on his 37th birthday at the 2004 Bank of America Colonial. Of active PGA TOUR players, the only other player to win on his birthday is* ***David Edwards*** *at the 1993 MCI Heritage Golf Classic.*

With his 2004 Bank of America Colonial victory, ***Steve Flesch*** *became the second left-handed player to win at Colonial Country Club (****Phil Mickelson*** *in 2000).*

2004 Bank of America Colonial winner ***Steve Flesch*** *was the only player in the field to post four rounds in the 60s (66-69-67-67) in 2004.*

Steve Flesch*'s 11-under-par 269 total was the highest total by a winner at the Bank of America Colonial since* ***Olin Browne*** *won with a score of 8-under 272 in 1999.*

Seven players have earned their maiden PGA TOUR victory at the Bank of America Colonial: ***Roberto DeVicenzo*** *(1957),* ***Dave Stockton*** *(1967),* ***Rod Curl*** *(1974),* ***Dan Pohl*** *(1986),* ***Keith Clearwater*** *(1987),* ***Ian Baker-Finch*** *(1989) and* ***Sergio Garcia*** *(2001). Five players searching for their first TOUR win at the time finished among the top-10 at the 2004 event:* ***Stephen Ames*** *(3),* ***Bo Van Pelt*** *(T5),* ***Skip Kendall*** *(T5),* ***Tim Petrovic*** *(T5) and* ***John Senden*** *(T9).*

Ten past champions of the Bank of America Colonial competed at the 2004 Bank of America Colonial: ***Fulton Allem*** *(1993),* ***Olin Browne*** *(1999),* ***Keith Clearwater*** *(1987),* ***Rod Curl*** *(1974),* ***David Frost*** *(1997),* ***Sergio Garcia*** *(2001),* ***Phil Mickelson*** *(2000),* ***Corey Pavin*** *(1985/1996),* ***Kenny Perry*** *(2003) and* ***Dan Pohl*** *(1986). Six of the 10 made the 36-hole cut, the exceptions being Allem, Clearwater, Curl and Frost.*

Tournament Record:
261, Kenny Perry, 2003

Current Course Record:
61, Keith Clearwater, Lee Janzen, 1993; Greg Kraft, 1999; Kenny Perry, Justin Leonard, 2003; Chad Campbell, 2004

TOURNAMENT HISTORY

Year	Winner	Score	Runner-up	Score	Location	Par/Yards
1972	Jerry Heard	275	Fred Marti	277	Colonial CC, Fort Worth, TX	70/7,142
1973	Tom Weiskopf	276	Bruce Crampton	277	Colonial CC, Fort Worth, TX	70/7,142
			Jerry Heard			
1974	Rod Curl	276	Jack Nicklaus	277	Colonial CC, Fort Worth, TX	70/7,142
1975	No Tournament+					
1976	Lee Trevino	273	Mike Morley	274	Colonial CC, Fort Worth, TX	70/7,142
1977	Ben Crenshaw	272	John Schroeder	273	Colonial CC, Fort Worth, TX	70/7,142
1978	Lee Trevino	268	Jerry Heard	272	Colonial CC, Fort Worth, TX	70/7,142
			Jerry Pate			
1979	Al Geiberger	274	Don January	275	Colonial CC, Fort Worth, TX	70/7,096
			Gene Littler			
1980	Bruce Lietzke	271	Ben Crenshaw	272	Colonial CC, Fort Worth, TX	70/7,096
1981	Fuzzy Zoeller	274	Hale Irwin	278	Colonial CC, Fort Worth, TX	70/7,096
1982	Jack Nicklaus	273	Andy North	276	Colonial CC, Fort Worth, TX	70/7,096
1983	Jim Colbert*	278	Fuzzy Zoeller	278	Colonial CC, Fort Worth, TX	70/7,096
1984	Peter Jacobsen*	270	Payne Stewart	270	Colonial CC, Fort Worth, TX	70/7,096
1985	Corey Pavin	266	Bob Murphy	270	Colonial CC, Fort Worth, TX	70/7,096
1986	Dan Pohl*~	205	Payne Stewart	205	Colonial CC, Fort Worth, TX	70/7,096
1987	Keith Clearwater	266	Davis Love III	269	Colonial CC, Fort Worth, TX	70/7,096
1988	Lanny Wadkins	270	Mark Calcavecchia	271	Colonial CC, Fort Worth, TX	70/7,096
			Ben Crenshaw			
			Joey Sindelar			
SOUTHWESTERN BELL COLONIAL						
1989	Ian Baker-Finch	270	David Edwards	274	Colonial CC, Fort Worth, TX	70/7,096
1990	Ben Crenshaw	272	John Mahaffey	275	Colonial CC, Fort Worth, TX	70/7,096
			Corey Pavin			
			Nick Price			
1991	Tom Purtzer	267	David Edwards	270	Colonial CC, Fort Worth, TX	70/7,096
			Scott Hoch			
			Bob Lohr			
1992	Bruce Lietzke*	267	Corey Pavin	267	Colonial CC, Fort Worth, TX	70/7,096
1993	Fulton Allem	264	Greg Norman	265	Colonial CC, Fort Worth, TX	70/7,096
1994	Nick Price*	266	Scott Simpson	266	Colonial CC, Fort Worth, TX	70/7,096
COLONIAL NATIONAL INVITATION						
1995	Tom Lehman	271	Craig Parry	272	Colonial CC, Fort Worth, TX	70/7,096
MASTERCARD COLONIAL						
1996	Corey Pavin	272	Jeff Sluman	274	Colonial CC, Fort Worth, TX	70/7,010
1997	David Frost	265	Brad Faxon	267	Colonial CC, Fort Worth, TX	70/7,010
			David Ogrin			
1998	Tom Watson	265	Jim Furyk	267	Colonial CC, Fort Worth, TX	70/7,010
1999	Olin Browne	272	Fred Funk	273	Colonial CC, Fort Worth, TX	70/7,010
			Paul Goydos			
			Tim Herron			
			Greg Kraft			
			Jeff Sluman			
2000	Phil Mickelson	268	Stewart Cink	270	Colonial CC, Fort Worth, TX	70/7,080
			Davis Love III			
2001	Sergio Garcia	267	Brian Gay	269	Colonial CC, Fort Worth, TX	70/7,080
			Phil Mickelson			
2002	Nick Price	267	Kenny Perry	272	Colonial CC, Fort Worth, TX	70/7,080
			David Toms			
2003	Kenny Perry	261	Justin Leonard	267	Colonial CC, Fort Worth, TX	70/7,080
2004	Steve Flesch	269	Chad Campbell	270	Colonial CC, Fort Worth, TX	70/7,054

*KEY: * = Playoff ~ = Weather-shortened + = Served as site for Tournament Players Championship*

Phil Mickelson putts during the 2004 Bank of America Colonial.

2004 FedEx St. Jude Classic [22nd of 48 official events]

FedEx St. Jude Classic

TOMS

Winner: DAVID TOMS
67-63-65-73 268 (-16) $846,000

Tournament Players Club at Southwind

Memphis, TN

May 27-30, 2004

Purse: $4,700,000
Par: 36-35—71
Yards: 7,103

LEADERS: First Round—Vaughn Taylor at 5-under-par 66 led David Toms and Paul Stankowski by one stroke. Stewart Cink, Lian-wei Zhang and Hirofumi Miyase were two back.
Second Round—Toms moved to 12-under-par 130 to lead Taylor by one and Ben Crane by two.
Third Round—Toms at 18-under-par 195 led Taylor by seven and Brian Gay by eight.

CUT: 74 players at 1-over-par 143 from a field of 156 professionals.

PRO-AM: $10,000. Kevin Sutherland, 51, $2,000.

WEATHER: On Thursday, early clouds with partly sunny conditions in the afternoon, S winds up to 25 mph and high temperature of 86. Friday, showers off and on most of the morning. Clearing with some sunshine in the afternoon with high temperatures of 82. Winds SW up to 15 mph. Saturday, cloudy with calmer conditions and high temperatures of 82. 3 p.m. finish on Sunday due to expected severe late-afternoon weather. Cloudy and warm (84-degree high) with light sprinkles and gusts reaching 25 mph.

Check out the 2005 FedEx St. Jude Classic, May 26-29 on USA/CBS

ORDER OF FINISH

David Toms	1	67-63-65-73	268	$846,000.00
Bob Estes	2	74-64-67-69	274	507,600.00
Tim Herron	T3	72-64-69-70	275	272,600.00
Steve Lowery	T3	74-64-70-67	275	272,600.00
Stewart Cink	T5	68-70-69-69	276	165,087.50
Brian Gay	T5	71-66-66-73	276	165,087.50
Fredrik Jacobson	T5	75-68-64-69	276	165,087.50
Vaughn Taylor	T5	66-65-71-74	276	165,087.50
Craig Bowden	T9	72-68-66-71	277	122,200.00
Charles Howell III	T9	70-70-68-69	277	122,200.00
Hirofumi Miyase	T9	68-69-67-73	277	122,200.00
Paul Stankowski	T9	67-69-71-70	277	122,200.00
Michael Allen	T13	71-68-70-69	278	85,540.00
Michael Bradley	T13	70-70-67-71	278	85,540.00
Brian Kortan	T13	75-67-66-70	278	85,540.00
Joel Kribel	T13	73-65-70-70	278	85,540.00
Dennis Paulson	T13	72-68-67-71	278	85,540.00
Steve Allan	T18	70-67-69-73	279	61,288.00
Kris Cox	T18	72-67-68-72	279	61,288.00
Tom Pernice, Jr.	T18	75-68-63-73	279	61,288.00
Loren Roberts	T18	71-71-67-70	279	61,288.00
John Senden	T18	74-69-65-71	279	61,288.00
Hank Kuehne	T23	73-66-70-71	280	45,120.00
Joe Ogilvie	T23	74-69-66-71	280	45,120.00
Ted Purdy	T23	72-64-71-73	280	$45,120.00
Billy Andrade	T26	75-67-67-72	281	33,370.00
Danny Briggs	T26	74-68-67-72	281	33,370.00
Fred Funk	T26	73-68-66-74	281	33,370.00
Matt Kuchar	T26	73-66-70-72	281	33,370.00
Hunter Mahan	T26	73-67-70-71	281	33,370.00
David Peoples	T26	71-69-68-73	281	33,370.00
Patrick Sheehan	T26	69-70-70-72	281	33,370.00
Notah Begay III	T33	75-65-69-73	282	23,291.12
Doug Barron (S)	T33	76-67-67-72	282	23,291.11
Rich Beem	T33	73-64-68-77	282	23,291.11
Michael Clark II	T33	81-62-70-69	282	23,291.11
Ben Crane	T33	70-65-73-74	282	23,291.11
Joel Edwards	T33	73-68-67-74	282	23,291.11
Brent Geiberger	T33	69-72-74-67	282	23,291.11
Mike Grob	T33	75-67-66-74	282	23,291.11
J.P. Hayes	T33	70-71-70-71	282	23,291.11
Cameron Beckman	T42	73-68-70-72	283	16,450.00
John Daly	T42	71-65-72-75	283	16,450.00
Robert Damron	T42	71-69-69-74	283	16,450.00
Robert Gamez	T42	72-71-68-72	283	16,450.00
Matt Gogel	T42	72-69-69-73	283	16,450.00
Bart Bryant	T47	72-68-69-75	284	12,072.29
Ken Duke	T47	74-66-70-74	284	12,072.29
Zhang Lian-wei	T47	68-72-70-74	284	12,072.29
Gene Sauers	T47	74-66-69-75	284	12,072.29
Jim McGovern	T47	75-66-71-72	284	$12,072.28
Brett Quigley	T47	75-68-68-73	284	12,072.28
Tjaart Van der Walt	T47	72-69-70-73	284	12,072.28
Brian Bateman	T54	73-65-73-74	285	10,716.00
Jay Delsing	T54	72-70-67-76	285	10,716.00
J.J. Henry	T54	70-70-71-74	285	10,716.00
Bryce Molder (Q)	T54	74-69-69-73	285	10,716.00
Kirk Triplett	T54	73-69-70-73	285	10,716.00
Tom Lehman	59	70-70-71-75	286	10,434.00
David Edwards	T60	73-70-69-75	287	10,246.00
Brenden Pappas	T60	71-69-71-76	287	10,246.00
Stan Utley	T60	72-70-69-76	287	10,246.00
Jose Coceres	T63	74-64-74-76	288	9,964.00
Scott Hend	T63	73-70-72-73	288	9,964.00
Tripp Isenhour	T63	70-67-73-78	288	9,964.00
Vance Veazey (S)	66	71-70-73-75	289	9,776.00
Greg Chalmers	T67	70-70-72-78	290	9,635.00
Pat Perez	T67	72-70-70-78	290	9,635.00
Tom Carter	69	72-66-74-79	291	9,494.00
Rich Barcelo	T70	70-71-73-78	292	9,353.00
Chris Smith	T70	74-69-77-72	292	9,353.00
Brandt Snedeker (S)	T72	74-69-76-75	294	9,165.00
Mike Springer	T72	75-67-72-80	294	9,165.00
Deane Pappas	74	72-69-74-83	298	9,024.00

(Q) = Open Qualifier; (S) = Sponsor Exemption; (T) = Tie

The following players did not finish
(C=cut, W=withdrew, D=disqualified)

C—144-Glen Day, Jason Dufner, Jim Gallagher, Jr., Mathias Gronberg, Steve Pate. **145-**Paul Azinger, Jason Bohn, Jeff Brehaut, Bob Burns, Jim Carter, Rick Fehr, Todd Fischer, Robin Freeman, David Frost, Kelly Gibson, Ken Green, Mike Heinen, Greg Kraft, Len Mattiace, Billy Mayfair, Carl Paulson, John Riegger, Esteban Toledo.**146-**Mark Brooks, Daniel Chopra, Trevor Dodds, Richard S. Johnson, Blaine McCallister, Geoff Ogilvy, Kevin Sutherland. **147-**Guy Boros, Joe Durant, Bill Glasson, David Gossett, Donnie Hammond, John Maginnes, John E. Morgan, David Sutherland, Tommy Tolles, Mark Wilson. **148-**Arjun Atwal, Aaron Barber, Chris Couch, Keiichiro Fukabori, David Howser, Mike Hulbert, Cliff Kresge, Spike McRoy, Heath Slocum, Roland Thatcher, Jay Williamson. **149-**Mark Hensby, Brad Lardon, Roger Tambellini, Grant Waite, Garrett Willis. **150-**David Branshaw, Danny Ellis, Brian Henninger, Shaun Micheel, David Morland IV, Craig Parry, Dicky Pride, Andre Stolz, Ted Tryba. **151-**Jay Don Blake, Lucas Glover, Brian Wilson. **152-**Zeb Patten, Willie Wood. **154-**Tim Petrovic. **155-**Bobby Cochran, Kevin Muncrief. **156-**Mike Standly. **157-**Pat Bates. **158-**Brett Paquet. **159-**Matt Loving. **161-**Loren Personett. **176-**Tim Tims. **W—74-**Russ Cochran. **D—83-**Randy Helton. **73-**Dan Olsen.

TOURNAMENT HISTORY

Year	Winner	Score	Runner-up	Score	Location	Par/Yards
MEMPHIS INVITATIONAL OPEN						
1958	Billy Maxwell	267	Cary Middlecoff	268	Colonial CC, Memphis, TN	70/6,466
1959	Don Whitt*	272	Al Balding Gary Player	272	Colonial CC, Memphis, TN	70/6,466
1960	Tommy Bolt*	273	Ben Hogan Gene Littler	273	Colonial CC, Memphis, TN	70/6,466
1961	Cary Middlecoff	266	Gardner Dickinson Mike Souchak	271	Colonial CC, Memphis, TN	70/6,466
1962	Lionel Hebert*	267	Gene Littler Gary Player	267	Colonial CC, Memphis, TN	70/6,466
1963	Tony Lema*	270	Tommy Aaron	270	Colonial CC, Memphis, TN	70/6,466
1964	Mike Souchak	270	Billy Casper Tommy Jacobs	271	Colonial CC, Memphis, TN	70/6,466
1965	Jack Nicklaus*	271	Johnny Pott	271	Colonial CC, Memphis, TN	70/6,466
1966	Bert Yancey	265	Gene Littler	270	Colonial CC, Memphis, TN	70/6,466
1967	Dave Hill	272	Johnny Pott	274	Colonial CC, Memphis, TN	70/6,466
1968	Bob Lunn	268	Monty Kaser	269	Colonial CC, Memphis, TN	70/6,466
1969	Dave Hill	265	Lee Elder	267	Colonial CC, Memphis, TN	70/6,466
DANNY THOMAS MEMPHIS CLASSIC						
1970	Dave Hill	267	Frank Beard Homero Blancas Bob Charles	268	Colonial CC, Memphis, TN	70/6,466
1971	Lee Trevino	268	Lee Elder Jerry Heard Hale Irwin Randy Wolff	272	Colonial CC, Memphis, TN	70/6,466
1972	Lee Trevino	281	John Mahaffey	285	Colonial CC (South), Cordova, TN	72/6,883
1973	Dave Hill	283	Allen Miller Lee Trevino	284	Colonial CC (South), Cordova, TN	72/7,282
1974	Gary Player	273	Lou Graham	275	Colonial CC (South), Cordova, TN	72/7,282

FedEx St. Jude Classic

NOTES

***David Toms**' six-stroke win at the 2004 FedEx St. Jude Classic matched **Chad Campbell** (Bay Hill Invitational) for the largest on the PGA TOUR in 2004. The largest margin of victory at the FedEx was seven by **John Cook** over **John Adams** in 1996.*

*The 2004 FedEx St. Jude Classic marked the second time **David Toms** has won a PGA TOUR event in his career with an over-par final round. In 2003 at the Wachovia Championship, Toms held a five-stroke lead entering Sunday and posted a 1-over-par 73 to win by two over three players.*

*In 2004, **David Toms** became the third player to win back-to-back titles at the FedEx St. Jude Classic. **Dave Hill** (1969-70) and **Lee Trevino** (1971-72) both won in consecutive seasons. Toms also won the Michelob Championship at Kingsmill in back-to-back seasons (2000 and 2001).*

***David Toms**' streak of 11 consecutive rounds in the 60s at the FedEx St. Jude Classic came to an end with his 2-over-par 73 in the final round of the 2004 event.*

*Seven players in the top 10 earned their first top-10 finish of the 2004 season at the FedEx St. Jude Classic: **Bob Estes** (2), **Steve Lowery** (T3), **Vaughn Taylor** (T5), **Brian Gay** (T5), **Paul Stankowski** (T9), **Craig Bowden** (T9) and **Hirofumi Miyase** (T9). Three players—Taylor, Miyase and Bowden – posted the first top-10s of their respective careers on the PGA TOUR.*

*Past champion **Bob Estes** closed his second round in 2004 with seven consecutive birdies, tying Vijay Singh for most consecutive birdies on the season (Mercedes Championships).*

BOB ESTES

Tournament Record:
258, John Cook, 1996
Current Course Record:
61, Jay Delsing, 1993; Bob Estes, 2001
Tournament Course Record:
59, Al Geiberger, 1977 (Colonial CC)

TOURNAMENT HISTORY

Year	Winner	Score	Runner-up	Score	Location	Par/Yards
1975	Gene Littler	270	Hubert Green John Mahaffey	275	Colonial CC (South), Cordova, TN	72/7,282
1976	Gibby Gilbert	273	Forrest Fezler	277	Colonial CC (South), Cordova, TN	72/7,282
1977	Al Geiberger	273	John Lister Gil Morgan Jerry McGee Gary Player	276	Colonial CC (South), Cordova, TN	72/7,282
1978	Andy Bean*	277	Lee Trevino	277	Colonial CC (South), Cordova, TN	72/7,282
1979	Gil Morgan*	278	Larry Nelson	278	Colonial CC (South), Cordova, TN	72/7,282
1980	Lee Trevino	272	Tom Purtzer	273	Colonial CC (South), Cordova, TN	72/7,282
1981	Jerry Pate	274	Tom Kite Bruce Lietzke	276	Colonial CC (South), Cordova, TN	72/7,282
1982	Raymond Floyd	271	Mike Holland	277	Colonial CC (South), Cordova, TN	72/7,282
1983	Larry Mize	274	Chip Beck	275	Colonial CC (South), Cordova, TN	72/7,282
1984	Bob Eastwood	280	Sammy Rachels Fuzzy Zoeller Ralph Landrum Mark O'Meara Tim Simpson	282	Colonial CC (South), Cordova, TN	72/7,282
ST. JUDE MEMPHIS CLASSIC						
1985	Hal Sutton*	279	David Ogrin	279	Colonial CC (South), Cordova, TN	72/7,282
FEDERAL EXPRESS ST. JUDE CLASSIC						
1986	Mike Hulbert	280	Joey Sindelar	281	Colonial CC (South), Cordova, TN	72/7,282
1987	Curtis Strange	275	Russ Cochran	276	Colonial CC (South), Cordova, TN	72/7,282
1988	Jodie Mudd	273	Mike Donald Tom Kite Denis Watson Peter Jacobsen Nick Price	274	Colonial CC (South), Cordova, TN	72/7,282
1989	John Mahaffey	272	Bob Gilder Hubert Green Bernhard Langer Bob Tway	275	TPC at Southwind, Germantown, TN	71/7,006
1990	Tom Kite*	269	John Cook	269	TPC at Southwind, Germantown, TN	71/7,006
1991	Fred Couples	269	Rick Fehr	272	TPC at Southwind, Germantown, TN	71/7,006
1992	Jay Haas	263	Dan Forsman	266	TPC at Southwind, Germantown, TN	71/7,006
1993	Nick Price	266	Robert Gamez Rick Fehr Jeff Maggert	269	TPC at Southwind, Germantown, TN	71/7,006
1994	Dicky Pride*	267	Gene Sauers Hal Sutton	267	TPC at Southwind, Germantown, TN	71/7,006
FEDEX ST. JUDE CLASSIC						
1995	Jim Gallagher, Jr.	267	Jay Delsing Ken Green	268	TPC at Southwind, Germantown, TN	71/7,006
1996	John Cook	258	John Adams	265	TPC at Southwind, Germantown, TN	71/7,006
1997	Greg Norman	268	Dudley Hart	269	TPC at Southwind, Germantown, TN	71/7,006
1998	Nick Price*	268	Jeff Sluman	268	TPC at Southwind, Germantown, TN	71/7,006
1999	Ted Tryba	265	Tim Herron Tom Lehman	268	TPC at Southwind, Germantown, TN	71/7,006
2000	Notah Begay III	271	Chris DiMarco Bob May	272	TPC at Southwind, Germantown, TN	71/7,030
2001	Bob Estes	267	Bernhard Langer	268	TPC at Southwind, Germantown, TN	71/7,030
2002	Len Mattiace	266	Tim Petrovic	267	TPC at Southwind, Germantown, TN	71/7,006
2003	David Toms	264	Nick Price	267	TPC at Southwind, Germantown, TN	71/7,030
2004	David Toms	268	Bob Estes	274	TPC at Southwind, Germantown, TN	71/7,103

*KEY: * = Playoff ~ = Weather-shortened*

2004 the Memorial Tournament [23rd of 48 official events]

Winner: ERNIE ELS
68-70-66-66 270 (-18) $945,000

Muirfield Village Golf Club

Dublin, OH

June 3-6, 2004

Purse: $5,250,000
Par: 36-36—72
Yards: 7,265

LEADERS: First Round—Ernie Els and Ben Curtis shared the lead at 4-under 68. Eight players trailed by one.
Second Round—Curtis, Justin Rose and Stephen Ames sat at 7-under 137, one ahead of K.J. Choi, Fred Couples and Els. Todd Hamilton was two back.
Third Round—Els moved to 12-under 204, two ahead of Couples, Choi and Rose. Ames and Tiger Woods were three behind.

CUT: 76 players at 4-over-par 148 from a field of 105 professionals.

PRO-AM: $10,000. Nick Price, 59, $2,000.

WEATHER: Thursday, a mix of sun and clouds with temperatures in the mid-70s. A little cooler and cloudier on Friday and Saturday. Similar conditions on Sunday with temperatures a touch warmer.

Check out the 2005 Memorial Tournament, June 2-5 on ESPN/CBS

ORDER OF FINISH

Ernie Els	1	68-70-66-66	270	$945,000.00
Fred Couples	2	69-69-68-68	274	567,000.00
Tiger Woods	3	72-68-67-69	276	357,000.00
Justin Rose (S)	4	70-67-69-71	277	252,000.00
K.J. Choi	5	71-67-68-72	278	210,000.00
Stephen Ames	T6	69-68-70-72	279	182,437.50
Kenny Perry	T6	72-72-66-69	279	182,437.50
Ben Curtis	T8	68-69-73-72	282	152,250.00
Retief Goosen	T8	70-72-69-71	282	152,250.00
Jay Haas	T8	70-72-69-71	282	152,250.00
John Daly	T11	72-69-73-69	283	111,300.00
Stephen Leaney	T11	71-71-71-70	283	111,300.00
J.L. Lewis	T11	70-72-70-71	283	111,300.00
Peter Lonard	T11	71-73-70-69	283	111,300.00
Rory Sabbatini	T11	71-71-71-70	283	111,300.00
Jerry Kelly	T16	74-70-70-70	284	84,000.00
Davis Love III	T16	70-73-72-69	284	84,000.00
Tom Pernice, Jr.	T16	73-71-71-69	284	84,000.00
John Cook (S)	T19	71-74-71-69	285	65,887.50
Brad Faxon	T19	72-74-71-68	285	65,887.50
Tim Herron	T19	76-71-66-72	285	65,887.50
Scott McCarron	T19	72-69-75-69	285	65,887.50
Harrison Frazar	23	73-72-69-72	286	54,600.00
Chad Campbell	T24	72-73-74-68	287	39,725.00
Chris DiMarco	T24	71-74-72-70	287	$39,725.00
Dan Forsman	T24	73-73-67-74	287	39,725.00
Sergio Garcia	T24	73-69-72-73	287	39,725.00
Zach Johnson	T24	69-73-70-75	287	39,725.00
Tom Lehman	T24	74-69-73-71	287	39,725.00
Geoff Ogilvy	T24	74-68-71-74	287	39,725.00
Ted Purdy	T24	74-70-72-71	287	39,725.00
Vijay Singh	T24	73-72-71-71	287	39,725.00
Robert Allenby	T33	74-74-74-66	288	27,150.00
Steve Flesch	T33	72-73-72-71	288	27,150.00
Todd Hamilton	T33	69-70-73-76	288	27,150.00
Lee Janzen	T33	69-73-72-74	288	27,150.00
Jeff Sluman	T33	70-73-73-72	288	27,150.00
Kevin Sutherland	T33	71-70-72-75	288	27,150.00
Hidemichi Tanaka	T33	73-75-72-68	288	27,150.00
Rich Beem	T40	71-71-72-75	289	19,950.00
Stewart Cink	T40	70-74-75-70	289	19,950.00
Tim Clark	T40	73-75-69-72	289	19,950.00
Padraig Harrington	T40	71-74-74-70	289	19,950.00
Tim Petrovic	T40	75-69-71-74	289	19,950.00
John Rollins	T40	69-74-74-72	289	19,950.00
Mark Hensby	T46	74-74-73-69	290	14,553.00
Trevor Immelman (S)	T46	73-73-69-75	290	14,553.00
Shigeki Maruyama	T46	71-71-76-72	290	14,553.00
Len Mattiace	T46	70-73-73-74	290	14,553.00
Jesper Parnevik	T46	75-71-74-70	290	14,553.00
Briny Baird	T51	76-69-71-75	291	$12,521.25
Niclas Fasth	T51	75-70-73-73	291	12,521.25
Jeff Maggert	T51	73-69-76-73	291	12,521.25
Nick Price	T51	74-73-72-72	291	12,521.25
Tommy Armour III	T55	72-72-72-76	292	11,812.50
Keiichiro Fukabori	T55	72-74-74-72	292	11,812.50
Skip Kendall	T55	77-71-69-75	292	11,812.50
Rocco Mediate	T55	71-73-73-75	292	11,812.50
Arron Oberholser	T55	69-74-72-77	292	11,812.50
Brenden Pappas	T55	73-74-72-73	292	11,812.50
Hunter Mahan	61	74-70-75-74	293	11,445.00
Mark Calcavecchia	62	74-72-73-75	294	11,340.00
Billy Andrade (S)	T63	71-73-75-76	295	11,130.00
Stuart Appleby	T63	73-74-70-78	295	11,130.00
Jack Nicklaus	T63	74-73-77-71	295	11,130.00
Woody Austin	T66	73-74-78-72	297	10,815.00
Paul Azinger	T66	69-74-78-76	297	10,815.00
Craig Parry	T66	71-72-79-75	297	10,815.00
Aaron Baddeley (S)	T69	74-74-78-72	298	10,552.50
Shaun Micheel	T69	73-73-80-72	298	10,552.50
Frank Lickliter II	T71	71-75-73-80	299	10,342.50
Corey Pavin	T71	71-75-76-77	299	10,342.50
Thomas Bjorn	T73	71-76-78-75	300	10,132.50
Darren Fichardt (S)	T73	70-78-74-78	300	10,132.50
Hirofumi Miyase (S)	75	73-75-77-78	303	9,975.00

(S) = Sponsor Exemption; (T) = Tie

The following players did not finish (C=cut, W=withdrew)

C—149-Charles Howell III, Hank Kuehne, Joey Sindelar, Brandt Snedeker. **150-**Luke Donald, Fred Funk, Robert Gamez, Thongchai Jaidee, Jonathan Kaye, Justin Leonard, Rod Pampling, Craig Perks. **151-**Alex Cejka, Nick Flanagan, Mathias Gronberg, Joe Ogilvie, Heath Slocum, Bo Van Pelt. **152-**Kirk Triplett. **153-**Arjun Atwal, Ben Crane, Mark O'Meara, Bob Tway. **154-**Lian-wei Zhang. **156-**Jonathan Byrd, Duffy Waldorf. **W—86-**Andre Stolz. **81-**David Edwards. **75-**Dudley Hart. **148-**Steve Elkington.

TOURNAMENT HISTORY

Year	Winner	Score	Runner-up	Score	Location	Par/Yards
THE MEMORIAL TOURNAMENT						
1976	Roger Maltbie*	288	Hale Irwin	288	Muirfield Village GC, Dublin, OH	72/7,027
1977	Jack Nicklaus	281	Hubert Green	283	Muirfield Village GC, Dublin, OH	72/7,101
1978	Jim Simons	284	Bill Kratzert	285	Muirfield Village GC, Dublin, OH	72/7,101
1979	Tom Watson	285	Miller Barber	288	Muirfield Village GC, Dublin, OH	72/7,101
1980	David Graham	280	Tom Watson	281	Muirfield Village GC, Dublin, OH	72/7,116
1981	Keith Fergus	284	Jack Renner	285	Muirfield Village GC, Dublin, OH	72/7,116
1982	Raymond Floyd	281	Peter Jacobsen	283	Muirfield Village GC, Dublin, OH	72/7,116
			Wayne Levi			
			Roger Maltbie			
			Gil Morgan			
1983	Hale Irwin	281	Ben Crenshaw	282	Muirfield Village GC, Dublin, OH	72/7,116
			David Graham			
1984	Jack Nicklaus*	280	Andy Bean	280	Muirfield Village GC, Dublin, OH	72/7,116
1985	Hale Irwin	281	Lanny Wadkins	282	Muirfield Village GC, Dublin, OH	72/7,106
1986	Hal Sutton	271	Don Pooley	275	Muirfield Village GC, Dublin, OH	72/7,106
1987	Don Pooley	272	Curt Byrum	275	Muirfield Village GC, Dublin, OH	72/7,104
1988	Curtis Strange	274	David Frost	276	Muirfield Village GC, Dublin, OH	72/7,104
			Hale Irwin			
1989	Bob Tway	277	Fuzzy Zoeller	279	Muirfield Village GC, Dublin, OH	72/7,104
1990	Greg Norman~	216	Payne Stewart	217	Muirfield Village GC, Dublin, OH	72/7,104
1991	Kenny Perry*	273	Hale Irwin	273	Muirfield Village GC, Dublin, OH	72/7,104
1992	David Edwards*	273	Rick Fehr	273	Muirfield Village GC, Dublin, OH	72/7,104
1993	Paul Azinger	274	Corey Pavin	275	Muirfield Village GC, Dublin, OH	72/7,104
1994	Tom Lehman	268	Greg Norman	273	Muirfield Village GC, Dublin, OH	72/7,104
1995	Greg Norman	269	David Duval	273	Muirfield Village GC, Dublin, OH	72/7,104
			Mark Calcavecchia			
			Steve Elkington			
1996	Tom Watson	274	David Duval	276	Muirfield Village GC, Dublin, OH	72/7,118
1997	Vijay Singh~	202	Jim Furyk	204	Muirfield Village GC, Dublin, OH	72/7,163
			Greg Norman			

Fred Funk signs autographs for fans.

the Memorial Tournament

NOTES

June has been kind to ***Ernie Els****. Five of his PGA TOUR wins have come during this month. Besides his 2004 Memorial Tournament victory, Els has won two U.S. Opens and two Buick Classics in June.*

Ernie Els *posted two of the five lowest rounds of the tournament last year at Muirfield Village Golf Club with rounds of 66 on the weekend. The other 6-under 66s were turned in by* ***Tim Herron****,* ***Kenny Perry*** *and* ***Robert Allenby****.*

Tournament host ***Jack Nicklaus*** *finished at 7-over 297 (T63) for the tournament. At age 64 years, 4 months and 13 days, he made the cut for the 22nd time at the Memorial Tournament. The oldest player to make the cut in a PGA TOUR event was* ***Sam Snead*** *when he made the cut at the 1979 Manufacturers Hanover Westchester Classic at age 67 years, 2 months, 21 days.*

In the history of the Memorial Tournament, only four players have won the event in their 40s. They include ***Jack Nicklaus*** *(1984),* ***Greg Norman*** *(1995),* ***Tom Watson*** *(1996) and* ***Kenny Perry*** *(2003). Watson is the oldest champion at 46 years, 271 days.*

In the 29-year history of the Memorial Tournament, only seven times has a player managed to record all four rounds in the 60s. ***Fred Couples*** *has managed four sub-70 rounds twice, in 1998 when he won and in 2004 when he finished second. The others include* ***Tiger Woods*** *(2001),* ***Steve Elkington*** *(1995) (finished 2nd),* ***Tom Lehman*** *(1994),* ***Paul Azinger*** *(1993) and* ***Hal Sutton*** *(1986).*

Tiger Woods *made his eighth start in the Memorial Tournament, having played in it each year since he turned professional. He won the Memorial Tournament from 1999-2001 and finished third in 2004. Coupled with his success in the WGC-NEC Invitational in Akron, he has won six times in the state of Ohio, second only to the seven times he has won in both California and Florida.*

Tournament Record:
268, Tom Lehman, 1994

Current Course Record:
61, John Huston, 1996

TOURNAMENT HISTORY

Year	Winner	Score	Runner-up	Score	Location	Par/Yards
1998	Fred Couples	271	Andrew Magee	275	Muirfield Village GC, Dublin, OH	72/7,163
1999	Tiger Woods	273	Vijay Singh	275	Muirfield Village GC, Dublin, OH	72/7,163
2000	Tiger Woods	269	Ernie Els Justin Leonard	274	Muirfield Village GC, Dublin, OH	72/7,018
2001	Tiger Woods	271	Paul Azinger Sergio Garcia	278	Muirfield Village GC, Dublin, OH	72/7,018
2002	Jim Furyk	274	John Cook David Peoples	276	Muirfield Village GC, Dublin, OH	72/7,224
2003	Kenny Perry	275	Lee Janzen	277	Muirfield Village GC, Dublin, OH	72/7,265
2004	Ernie Els	270	Fred Couples	274	Muirfield Village GC, Dublin, OH	72/7,265

*KEY: * = Playoff ~ = Weather-shortened*

Jack Nicklaus and spectators watch approach shot during the 2004 Memorial.

Winner: SERGIO GARCIA #
70-66-68-67 272 (-12) $945,000

Westchester Country Club (West Course)

Harrison, NY

June 10-13, 2004

Purse: $5,250,000
Par: 36-35—71
Yards: 6,751

LEADERS: First Round—Vijay Singh shot an 8-under 63 to lead Fredrik Jacobson by one stroke. David Frost was three strokes off the lead while eight players were four behind.
Second Round—Fred Couples at 10-under-par 132 led Singh, Jacobson and Luke Donald by a stroke.
Third Round—Loren Roberts, at 12-under-par 201, held a one-stoke lead over Rory Sabbatini and Cameron Beckman. Tom Byrum and Donald were two strokes back.

CUT: 83 players at 1-under-par from a field of 156 professionals.

PRO-AM: $10,000. Loren Roberts, 53, $2,000.

WEATHER: On Thursday, cloudy skies with a high of 79 and NE winds up to 10 mph. Light rain in the afternoon. Friday was cool and slightly overcast with temperatures in the low 70s. North winds 5-10 mph. Saturday was sunny reaching 82 degrees with NE winds 5-12 mph. Sunday was overcast and cooler with temperatures in the 70s and NE winds 5-12 mph.

Check out the 2005 Barclays Classic, June 23-26 on USA/ABC

ORDER OF FINISH

 # Won playoff with a birdie-4 on the third extra hole

Sergio Garcia #	1	70-67-68-67	272	$945,000.00
Padraig Harrington	T2	68-68-68-68	272	462,000.00
Rory Sabbatini	T2	69-68-65-70	272	462,000.00
Tom Byrum	T4	71-64-68-71	274	217,000.00
Fred Couples	T4	67-65-74-68	274	217,000.00
Vijay Singh	T4	63-70-71-70	274	217,000.00
Luke Donald	7	67-66-70-72	275	175,875.00
Fredrik Jacobson	8	64-69-74-69	276	162,750.00
Cameron Beckman	T9	68-68-66-75	277	131,250.00
Tim Clark	T9	68-72-68-69	277	131,250.00
Chris DiMarco	T9	69-69-69-70	277	131,250.00
Kenny Perry	T9	69-71-71-66	277	131,250.00
Bo Van Pelt	T9	68-71-68-70	277	131,250.00
Robert Allenby	T14	69-71-69-69	278	97,125.00
Scott Hend	T14	68-68-72-70	278	97,125.00
Ernie Els	T16	68-69-72-70	279	73,650.00
J.J. Henry	T16	68-73-69-69	279	73,650.00
Phil Mickelson	T16	69-68-69-73	279	73,650.00
Joe Ogilvie	T16	72-66-70-71	279	73,650.00
Craig Parry	T16	73-66-69-71	279	73,650.00
Brett Quigley	T16	69-68-72-70	279	73,650.00
Loren Roberts	T16	67-70-64-78	279	73,650.00
Stuart Appleby	T23	69-70-69-72	280	46,725.00
Kris Cox	T23	67-71-68-74	280	46,725.00
Brad Faxon	T23	68-73-67-72	280	46,725.00
Zach Johnson	T23	74-66-70-70	280	46,725.00
Dennis Paulson	T23	70-68-68-74	280	$46,725.00
Brian Gay	T28	70-68-68-75	281	36,487.50
Davis Love III	T28	68-71-70-72	281	36,487.50
Tim Petrovic	T28	69-69-71-72	281	36,487.50
Scott Verplank	T28	69-70-69-73	281	36,487.50
Bart Bryant	T32	72-68-72-70	282	26,670.00
Dan Forsman	T32	70-71-69-72	282	26,670.00
Dudley Hart	T32	67-71-73-71	282	26,670.00
Jerry Kelly	T32	71-69-72-70	282	26,670.00
Neal Lancaster	T32	70-71-70-71	282	26,670.00
Steve Lowery	T32	69-70-72-71	282	26,670.00
Ted Purdy	T32	69-70-69-74	282	26,670.00
Adam Scott	T32	71-70-72-69	282	26,670.00
Joey Sindelar	T32	68-72-70-72	282	26,670.00
Kevin Sutherland	T32	68-70-73-71	282	26,670.00
Glen Day	T42	71-70-73-69	283	15,807.28
Peter Lonard	T42	67-74-72-70	283	15,807.28
Tom Pernice, Jr.	T42	71-70-72-70	283	15,807.28
Pat Bates	T42	72-69-67-75	283	15,807.27
D.J. Brigman (S)	T42	71-69-71-72	283	15,807.27
Daniel Chopra (S)	T42	69-70-71-73	283	15,807.27
Skip Kendall	T42	68-71-68-76	283	15,807.27
Rocco Mediate	T42	71-67-71-74	283	15,807.27
David Morland IV	T42	69-70-70-74	283	15,807.27
Pat Perez	T42	73-66-70-74	283	15,807.27
John Senden	T42	70-68-71-74	283	15,807.27
Stephen Leaney	T53	73-67-73-71	284	12,285.00
Omar Uresti	T53	70-71-74-69	284	12,285.00
Craig Bowden	T55	71-69-72-73	285	11,865.00
Todd Fischer	T55	69-71-70-75	285	$11,865.00
David Frost	T55	66-72-70-77	285	11,865.00
John Rollins	T55	72-66-74-73	285	11,865.00
Bob Tway	T55	71-69-71-74	285	11,865.00
Arjun Atwal	T60	73-67-76-70	286	11,287.50
Jose Coceres	T60	69-68-70-79	286	11,287.50
Robert Damron	T60	67-70-73-76	286	11,287.50
Danny Ellis	T60	75-66-75-70	286	11,287.50
Carlos Franco	T60	68-69-74-75	286	11,287.50
Tjaart Van der Walt	T60	71-65-75-75	286	11,287.50
Niclas Fasth	T66	69-71-75-72	287	10,815.00
Richard S. Johnson	T66	69-72-73-73	287	10,815.00
Esteban Toledo	T66	71-69-72-75	287	10,815.00
Jonathan Byrd	T69	67-70-71-80	288	10,552.50
Alex Cejka	T69	70-69-73-76	288	10,552.50
Billy Andrade	T71	70-70-75-74	289	10,237.50
Notah Begay III	T71	69-72-73-75	289	10,237.50
Jason Bohn	T71	72-68-76-73	289	10,237.50
Chris Smith	T71	71-70-70-78	289	10,237.50
Billy Mayfair	75	68-68-76-78	290	9,975.00
Brad Adamonis (Q)	T76	69-72-73-77	291	9,712.50
Tom Carter	T76	70-69-77-75	291	9,712.50
Joel Edwards	T76	69-72-71-79	291	9,712.50
Miguel A. Jimenez	T76	70-67-76-78	291	9,712.50
Jonathan Kaye	T80	73-66-73-80	292	9,397.50
Grant Waite	T80	72-69-75-76	292	9,397.50
Patrick Sheehan	82	71-69-76-78	294	9,240.00

Q) = Open Qualifier; (S) = Sponsor Exemption; (T) = Tie

The following players did not finish
(C=cut, W=withdrew, D=disqualified)

C—142-David Branshaw, Chad Campbell, Russ Cochran, Fred Funk, Lee Janzen, Tom Lehman, Spike McRoy, Dan Olsen, Deane Pappas, Jesper Parnevik, Chris Riley, Vaughn Taylor, Mike Weir. **143-**Olin Browne, Darren Clarke, Jason Dufner, Ken Duke, Jay Haas, Todd Hamilton, J.P. Hayes, Kent Jones, Cliff Kresge, Shigeki Maruyama, Arron Oberholser, Corey Pavin, Paul Stankowski, Roger Tambellini.**144-**Michael Allen, Stephen Ames, Jim Carter, Jay Delsing, Matt Kuchar, Len Mattiace, Patrick Moore, Tommy Tolles. **145-**Mathias Gronberg, J.L. Lewis, Kevin Na, Ryan Palmer, Craig Perks, Brandt Snedeker, David Toms. **146-**Craig Barlow, Jeff Brehaut, Bob Burns, Stewart Cink, Jeff Maggert, Brenden Pappas, Steve Pate.**147-**Briny Baird, Danny Briggs, Darrell Kestner, Carl Pettersson, John Riegger. **148-**Carl Alexander, Rich Barcelo, Mark Brooks, Lucas Glover, Blaine McCallister. **150-**John Maginnes, Jay Williamson. **151-**Steve Allan, Thomas Bjorn. **152-**Woody Austin, Craig Thomas, **153-**Keith Clearwater, Hirofumi Miyase. **156-**Heath Wassem. **157-**David Gossett. **160-**Fulton Allem. **163-**Robert Deruntz. **W—75-**Duffy Waldorf. **D—75-**Guy Boros. **138-**Jeff Sluman.

Sergio Garcia charges to victory.

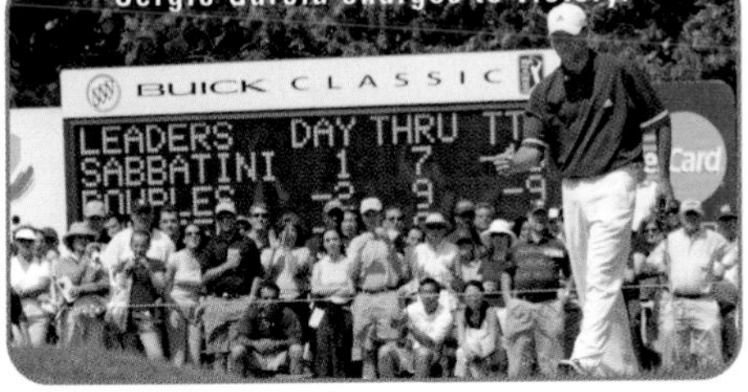

TOURNAMENT HISTORY

Year	Winner	Score	Runner-up	Score	Location	Par/Yards
WESTCHESTER CLASSIC						
1967	Jack Nicklaus	272	Dan Sikes	273	Westchester CC, Harrison, NY	72/6,573
1968	Julius Boros	272	Bob Murphy Jack Nicklaus Dan Sikes	273	Westchester CC, Harrison, NY	72/6,648
1969	Frank Beard	275	Bert Greene	276	Westchester CC, Harrison, NY	72/6,677
1970	Bruce Crampton	273	Larry Hinson Jack Nicklaus	274	Westchester CC, Harrison, NY	72/6,700
1971	Arnold Palmer	270	Gibby Gilbert Hale Irwin	275	Westchester CC, Harrison, NY	72/6,700
1972	Jack Nicklaus	270	Jim Colbert	273	Westchester CC, Harrison, NY	72/6,700
1973	Bobby Nichols*	272	Bob Murphy	272	Westchester CC, Harrison, NY	72/6,614
1974	Johnny Miller	269	Don Bies	271	Westchester CC, Harrison, NY	72/6,614
1975	Gene Littler*	271	Julius Boros	271	Westchester CC, Harrison, NY	72/6,614
AMERICAN EXPRESS WESTCHESTER CLASSIC						
1976	David Graham	272	Ben Crenshaw Tom Watson Fuzzy Zoeller	275	Westchester CC, Harrison, NY	71/6,603
1977	Andy North	272	George Archer	274	Westchester CC, Harrison, NY	71/6,603
1978	Lee Elder	274	Mark Hayes	275	Westchester CC, Harrison, NY	71/6,603
MANUFACTURERS HANOVER WESTCHESTER CLASSIC						
1979	Jack Renner	277	David Graham Howard Twitty	278	Westchester CC, Harrison, NY	71/6,603
1980	Curtis Strange	273	Gibby Gilbert	275	Westchester CC, Harrison, NY	71/6,603
1981	Raymond Floyd	275	Bobby Clampett Gibby Gilbert Craig Stadler	277	Westchester CC, Harrison, NY	71/6,603

Barclays Classic

NOTES

The 2004 cut of 1-under-par 141 was the first time in tournament history that the cut fell under par, although the 141 total (1-over-par) was matched in 1982 when the course played at 6,329 yards and at par 70. Since the course was reconfigured in 1982 to a par 71 at approximately 6,700 yards, the low cut had been even-par in 2003. The 83 players that made the 36-hole cut matched the high of the 2004 season to date at THE PLAYERS Championship.

The 2004 playoff between ***Sergio Garcia****,* ***Padraig Harrington*** *and* ***Rory Sabbatini*** *was the 13th in Buick Classic history, and the fifth in the last seven years. With his victory, Garcia improved to 3-1 in playoffs on the PGA TOUR. His first two victories in 2004 came in three-way playoffs. The Buick Classic victory was the second time Garcia has defeated Harrington in a playoff. He defeated Harrington at the 1999 Linde German Masters.*

Sergio Garcia*'s final round 4-under-par 67 extended his streak of consecutive rounds of par or better in the Buick Classic to 19.*

Sergio Garcia*'s victory at the 2004 Buick Classic came 28 days after his last TOUR victory, a three-way playoff win over* ***Robert Damron*** *and* ***Dudley Hart*** *at the EDS Byron Nelson Championship.*

Sergio Garcia *became the fifth multiple winner of the Buick Classic, joining* ***Jack Nicklaus*** *(1967, 1972),* ***Seve Ballesteros*** *(1983, 1988),* ***Vijay Singh*** *(1993, 1995) and* ***Ernie Els*** *(1996, 1997). Garcia has four consecutive top 10s at the Buick Classic, including two victories.*

Runner-up ***Padraig Harrington*** *was the only player to record four rounds in the 60s in 2004.*

Brad Faxon *set the Buick Classic consecutive cuts made streak by making his 16th consecutive in 2004. He was tied with* ***J.C. Snead****. Faxon has made 17 of 20 cuts at Westchester Country Club in his career dating back to 1984.*

Tournament Record:
261, Bob Gilder, 1982
Current Course Record:
62, Dan Sikes, 1967; Jim Wright, 1976; Peter Jacobsen, 1982

TOURNAMENT HISTORY

Year	Winner	Score	Runner-up	Score	Location	Par/Yards
1982	Bob Gilder	261	Peter Jacobsen Tom Kite	266	Westchester CC, Harrison, NY	70/6,329
1983	Seve Ballesteros	276	Andy Bean Craig Stadler	278	Westchester CC, Harrison, NY	71/6,687
1984	Scott Simpson	269	David Graham Jay Haas Mark O'Meara	274	Westchester CC, Harrison, NY	71/6,687
1985	Roger Maltbie*	275	George Burns Raymond Floyd	275	Westchester CC, Harrison, NY	71/6,722
1986	Bob Tway	272	Willie Wood	273	Westchester CC, Harrison, NY	71/6,723
1987	J.C. Snead*	276	Seve Ballesteros	276	Westchester CC, Harrison, NY	71/6,769
1988	Seve Ballesteros*	276	David Frost Ken Green Greg Norman	276	Westchester CC, Harrison, NY	71/6,779
1989	Wayne Grady*	277	Ronnie Black	277	Westchester CC, Harrison, NY	71/6,779
BUICK CLASSIC						
1990	Hale Irwin	269	Paul Azinger	271	Westchester CC, Harrison, NY	71/6,779
1991	Billy Andrade	273	Brad Bryant	275	Westchester CC, Harrison, NY	71/6,779
1992	David Frost	268	Duffy Waldorf	276	Westchester CC, Harrison, NY	71/6,779
1993	Vijay Singh*	280	Mark Wiebe	280	Westchester CC, Harrison, NY	71/6,779
1994	Lee Janzen	268	Ernie Els	271	Westchester CC, Harrison, NY	71/6,779
1995	Vijay Singh*	278	Doug Martin	278	Westchester CC, Harrison, NY	71/6,779
1996	Ernie Els	271	Steve Elkington	279	Westchester CC, Harrison, NY	71/6,779
1997	Ernie Els	268	Jeff Maggert	270	Westchester CC, Harrison, NY	71/6,722
1998	J.P. Hayes~*	201	Jim Furyk	201	Westchester CC, Harrison, NY	71/6,722
1999	Duffy Waldorf*	276	Dennis Paulson	276	Westchester CC, Harrison, NY	71/6,722
2000	Dennis Paulson*	276	David Duval	276	Westchester CC, Harrison, NY	71/6,722
2001	Sergio Garcia	268	Scott Hoch	271	Westchester CC, Harrison, NY	71/6,722
2002	Chris Smith	272	David Gossett Pat Perez Loren Roberts	274	Westchester CC, Harrison, NY	71/6,722
2003	Jonathan Kaye*	271	John Rollins	271	Westchester CC, Harrison, NY	71/6,783
2004	Sergio Garcia*	272	Padraig Harrington Rory Sabbatini	272	Westchester CC, Harrison, NY	71/6,751

*KEY: * = Playoff ~ = Weather-shortened*

Fans watch the action at the 2004 Buick Classic.

2004 U.S. Open Championship

[25th of 48 official events]

GOOSEN

Winner: RETIEF GOOSEN
70-66-69-71 276 (-4) $1,125,000

Shinnecock Hills Golf Club

Southampton, NY

June 17-20, 2004

Purse: $6,250,000
Par: 35-35—70
Yards: 6,996

LEADERS: First Round—Jay Haas, Shigeki Maruyama and Angel Cabrera held the lead at 4-under-par 66. Corey Pavin was one shot back, while nine players were two shots behind.
Second Round—Maruyama and Phil Mickelson moved to 6-under-par 134 to lead Jeff Maggert by one. Retief Goosen and Fred Funk were two back. Ernie Els and Cabrera were three behind.
Third Round—Goosen at 5-under-par 205 led Els and Mickelson by two strokes and Funk and Maruyama by three.

CUT: 62 professionals and four amateurs at 5-over 145 from a field of 148 professionals and eight amateurs.

WEATHER: Warm, overcast and humid on Thursday with a high of 78. Light S winds 5-12 mph. Slight drizzle in the afternoon. Play suspended at 4:43 p.m. due to a dangerous weather situation. Play resumed at 6:55 p.m. Play was suspended for the day at 7:40 p.m. due to fog/darkness. Play resumed at 7 a.m. on Friday with the second round beginning at 7:30 a.m. Mostly sunny and warmer on Friday with a high of 82. E winds 5-12 mph. Cloudy in the morning on Saturday, partly cloudy in the afternoon. Temperatures reached 74 in the afternoon. NW winds between 10-15 mph. Sunday, sunny and warm with a high of 79. Slightly stronger winds up to 18 mph.

Check out the 2005 U.S. Open, June 16-19 on ESPN/NBC

ORDER OF FINISH

Retief Goosen	1	70-66-69-71	276	$1,125,000.00
Phil Mickelson	2	68-66-73-71	278	675,000.00
Jeff Maggert	3	68-67-74-72	281	424,604.00
Shigeki Maruyama	T4	66-68-74-76	284	267,756.00
Mike Weir	T4	69-70-71-74	284	267,756.00
Fred Funk	6	70-66-72-77	285	212,444.00
Robert Allenby	T7	70-72-74-70	286	183,828.00
Steve Flesch	T7	68-74-70-74	286	183,828.00
Stephen Ames	T9	74-66-73-74	287	145,282.00
Chris DiMarco	T9	71-71-70-75	287	145,282.00
Ernie Els	T9	70-67-70-80	287	145,282.00
Jay Haas	T9	66-74-76-71	287	145,282.00
Tim Clark	T13	73-70-66-79	288	119,770.00
Tim Herron	T13	75-66-73-74	288	119,770.00
Spencer Levin	T13	69-73-71-75	288	Amateur
Angel Cabrera	16	66-71-77-75	289	109,410.00
Skip Kendall	T17	68-75-74-73	290	98,477.00
Corey Pavin	T17	67-71-73-79	290	98,477.00
Tiger Woods	T17	72-69-73-76	290	98,477.00
Mark Calcavecchia	T20	71-71-74-75	291	80,644.00
Sergio Garcia	T20	72-68-71-80	291	80,644.00
David Toms	T20	73-72-70-76	291	$80,644.00
Kirk Triplett	T20	71-70-73-77	291	80,644.00
Daniel Chopra	T24	73-68-76-75	292	63,328.00
Lee Janzen	T24	72-70-71-79	292	63,328.00
Tim Petrovic	T24	69-75-72-76	292	63,328.00
Nick Price	T24	73-70-72-77	292	63,328.00
Shaun Micheel	T28	71-72-70-80	293	51,774.00
Vijay Singh	T28	68-70-77-78	293	51,774.00
Ben Curtis	30	68-75-72-79	294	46,089.00
K.J. Choi	T31	76-68-76-75	295	41,759.00
Padraig Harrington	T31	73-71-76-75	295	41,759.00
Peter Lonard	T31	71-73-77-74	295	41,759.00
David Roesch	T31	68-73-74-80	295	41,759.00
Bo Van Pelt	T31	69-73-73-80	295	41,759.00
Charles Howell III	T36	75-70-68-83	296	36,813.00
Hidemichi Tanaka	T36	70-74-73-79	296	36,813.00
Lee Westwood	T36	73-71-73-79	296	36,813.00
Casey Wittenberg	T36	71-71-75-79	296	Amateur
Jerry Kelly	T40	76-69-71-81	297	30,672.00
Stephen Leaney	T40	72-70-71-84	297	30,672.00
Spike McRoy	T40	72-72-72-81	297	30,672.00
Joe Ogilvie	T40	70-75-74-78	297	30,672.00
Pat Perez	T40	73-67-76-81	297	30,672.00
Geoffrey Sisk	T40	72-72-71-82	297	$30,672.00
Scott Verplank	T40	71-71-72-83	297	30,672.00
Bill Haas	T40	72-73-71-81	297	Amateur
Kris Cox	T48	68-74-77-79	298	23,325.00
Jim Furyk	T48	72-72-75-79	298	23,325.00
Zach Johnson	T48	70-73-75-80	298	23,325.00
Chris Riley	T48	72-71-72-83	298	23,325.00
John Rollins	T48	76-68-76-78	298	23,325.00
Dudley Hart	T53	71-73-70-85	299	19,390.00
Scott Hoch	T53	75-70-73-81	299	19,390.00
Tom Carter	T55	74-71-70-85	300	18,405.00
Trevor Immelman	T55	69-70-79-82	300	18,405.00
Joakim Haeggman	T57	74-69-76-83	302	17,304.00
Tom Kite	T57	72-71-75-84	302	17,304.00
Phillip Price	T57	70-73-75-84	302	17,304.00
Alex Cejka	T60	75-70-73-85	303	16,353.00
Craig Parry	T60	70-73-75-85	303	16,353.00
Cliff Kresge	T62	72-73-77-82	304	15,888.00
Chez Reavie	T62	73-72-71-88	304	Amateur
J.J. Henry	64	75-69-86-76	306	15,630.00
Kevin Stadler	65	68-72-82-85	307	15,372.00
Billy Mayfair	66	70-70-81-89	310	15,089.00

(T) = Tie

The following players did not finish
(C=cut, W=withdrew, A=Amateur)

C—146-Rich Beem, Tom Byrum, Chad Campbell, Michael Campbell, Brian Davis, Bob Estes, Brad Faxon, Dan Forsman, J.P. Hayes, Justin Hicks, Miguel A. Jimenez, Jonathan Kaye, Justin Leonard, Ian Poulter, Eduardo Romero, Rory Sabbatini, John Senden, Bob Tway, Omar Uresti, Duffy Waldorf. **147-**Briny Baird, Craig Bowden, Paul Casey, Darren Clarke, Tripp Isenhour, Dan Olsen, Kevin Sutherland, Bubba Watson. **148-**Thomas Bjorn, John Douma, Robert Garrigus, Brian Gay, Toshi Izawa, Brad Lardon, J.L. Lewis, Dennis Paulson, Tom Pernice, Jr., Joey Sindelar, Chris Smith, Steve Stricker. **149-**Steve Allan, Stuart Appleby, Eric Axley, Stewart Cink, John Elliott, Brendan Jones, Brock Mackenzie (A), Parker McLachlin, Nathan T. Smith (A), Andrew Tschudin, Camilo Villegas. **150-**Charleton Dechert, Raymond Floyd, Thomas Levet, David Morland IV, Adam Scott, Scott Weatherly. **151-**Aaron Baddeley, Nick Faldo, David Faught, Matt Gogel, Todd Hamilton, Pete Jordan, Davis Love III, Kenny Perry. **152-**Mark Brooks, Jonathan Byrd, John Connelly, Fred Couples, Jeff Gove, Jimmy Green, Gabriel Hjertstedt, Fredrik Jacobson, Roger Tambellini. **153-**Scott Hend, Paul Lawrie, Leif Olson, Payton Osborn, Carl Paulson. **154-**Nick Flanagan (A), Steve Gotsche, Steve Sokol, Johnson Wagner. **155-**Justin Rose. **157-**Casey Bourque. **158-**Oscar Alvarez (A). **160-**Joey Maxon. **165-**David Duval. **166-**David Carr.
W—Carlos Franco.

TOURNAMENT HISTORY

Year	Winner	Score	Runner-up	Score	Location
U.S. OPEN CHAMPIONSHIP					
1895	Horace Rawlins	173	Willie Dunn	175	Newport GC, Newport, RI
1896	James Foulis	152	Horace Rawlins	155	Shinnecock Hills GC, Southhampton, NY
1897	Joe Lloyd	162	Willie Anderson	163	Chicago GC, Wheaton, IL
	(Competition extended from 36 to 72 holes after 1897)				
1898	Fred Herd	328	Alex Smith	335	Myopia Hunt Club, Hamilton, MA
1899	Willie Smith	315	George Low Val Fitzjohn W. H. Way	326	Baltimore CC, Baltimore, MD
1900	Harry Vardon	313	J.H. Taylor	315	Chicago GC, Wheaton, IL
1901	Willie Anderson*	331	Alex Smith	331	Myopia Hunt Club, Hamilton, MA
1902	Laurie Auchterlonie	307	Stewart Gardner	313	Garden City GC, Garden City, NY
1903	Willie Anderson*	307	David Brown	307	Baltusrol GC (Lower), Short Hills, NJ
1904	Willie Anderson	303	Gil Nicholls	308	Glen View Club, Golf, IL
1905	Willie Anderson	314	Alex Smith	316	Myopia Hunt Club, Hamilton, MA
1906	Alex Smith	295	Willie Smith	302	Onwentsia Club, Lake Forest, IL
1907	Alex Ross	302	Gil Nicholls	304	Philadelphia Cricket Club, Chestnut Hill, PA
1908	Fred McLeod*	322	Willie Smith	322	Myopia Hunt Club, Hamilton, MA
1909	George Sargent	290	Tom McNamara	294	Englewood GC, Englewood, NJ
1910	Alex Smith*	298	John McDermott Macdonald Smith	298	Philadelphia Cricket Club, Chestnut Hill, PA
1911	John McDermott*	307	Mike Brady George Simpson	307	Chicago GC, Wheaton, IL
1912	John McDermott	294	Tom McNamara	296	CC of Buffalo, Buffalo, NY
1913	Francis Ouimet*	304	Harry Vardon Edward Ray	304	The Country Club, Brookline, MA
1914	Walter Hagen	290	Charles Evans, Jr.	291	Midlothian CC, Blue Island, IL
1915	Jerome Travers	297	Tom McNamara	298	Baltusrol GC (Lower), Short Hills, NJ
1916	Charles Evans, Jr.	286	Jock Hutchison	288	Minikahda Club, Minneapolis, MN
1917	No tournament+				
1918	No Tournament+				
1919	Walter Hagen*	301	Mike Brady	301	Brae Burn CC, West Newton, MA

SECTION 3 TOURNAMENT HISTORIES

NOTES

Key to victory in 2004? On the week, ***Retief Goosen*** *used 111 putts but did not three-putt once in 72 holes. Goosen led the field with only 24 putts in the final round – including 12 one-putts.*

After his 2004 U.S. Open victory, ***Retief Goosen*** *has won four of five PGA TOUR events when holding at least a share of the 54-hole lead. His final-round scoring average when holding at least a share of the lead is 71.2.*

In 104 U.S. Opens, the leader/co-leader through 54 holes has gone on to win on 47 occasions, including the last six: ***Payne Stewart*** *(1999),* ***Tiger Woods*** *(2000),* ***Retief Goosen*** *(2001),* ***Tiger Woods*** *(2002),* ***Jim Furyk*** *(2003) and* ***Retief Goosen*** *(2004).*

The final-round scoring average (78.727) at the 2004 U.S. Open was the highest Round 4 scoring average at the U.S. Open since the 1972 U.S. Open won by ***Jack Nicklaus*** *at Pebble Beach Golf Links, where the scoring average was 78.80. The scoring average on Sunday was also the highest single-round average on the PGA TOUR since the field averaged 79.383 at Pebble Beach Golf Links in the third round of the 1999 AT&T Pebble Beach National Pro-Am.*

Overall on the week, the scoring average of 74.081 was the highest on the PGA TOUR since Oak Hill Country Club averaged 74.309 for the 2003 PGA Championship. The highest tournament scoring average on the 2004 season had been the Masters Tournament at 73.974.

Robert Allenby *(70) was the only player to post a score at par or better in the final round. He jumped from T34 to T7 with his first top-10 U.S. Open finish. The last time no player broke par in the final round of the U.S. Open was 1963.*

There have been 22 international winners of the U.S. Open on 28 different occasions. The last non-South African international player to win the U.S. Open was Australia's ***David Graham*** *in 1981. Three South Africans have won the U.S. Open:* ***Gary Player*** *(1965),* ***Ernie Els*** *(1994, 1997) and* ***Retief Goosen*** *(2001, 2004).*

TOURNAMENT HISTORY

Year	Winner	Score	Runner-up	Score	Location
1920	Edward Ray	295	Harry Vardon	296	Inverness CC, Toledo, OH
			Jack Burke		
			Leo Diegel		
			Jock Hutchison		
1921	James M. Barnes	289	Walter Hagen	298	Columbia CC, Chevy Chase, MD
			Fred McLeod		
1922	Gene Sarazen#	288	John L. Black	289	Skokie CC, Glencoe, IL
			Robert T. Jones, Jr.		
1923	Robert T. Jones, Jr.*	296	Bobby Cruickshank	296	Inwood CC, Inwood, NY
1924	Cyril Walker#	297	Robert T. Jones, Jr.	300	Oakland Hills CC (South), Birmingham, MI
1925	Willie Macfarlane*	291	Robert T. Jones, Jr.	291	Worcester CC, Worcester, MA
1926	Robert T. Jones, Jr.	293	Joe Turnesa	294	Scioto CC, Columbus, OH
1927	Tommy Armour*	301	Harry Cooper	301	Oakmont CC, Oakmont, PA
1928	Johnny Farrell*	294	Robert T. Jones, Jr.	294	Olympia Fields CC, Matteson, IL
1929	Robert T. Jones, Jr.*	294	Al Espinosa	294	Winged Foot GC (West), Mamaroneck, NY
1930	Robert T. Jones, Jr.	287	Macdonald Smith	289	Interlachen CC, Hopkins, MN
1931	Billy Burke*	292	George Von Elm	292	Inverness Club, Toledo, OH
1932	Gene Sarazen	286	Phil Perkins	289	Fresh Meadows CC, Flushing, NY
			Bobby Cruickshank		
1933	Johnny Goodman	287	Ralph Guldahl	288	North Shore CC, Glenview, IL
1934	Olin Dutra	293	Gene Sarazen	294	Merion Cricket Club, Ardmore, PA
1935	Sam Parks, Jr.	299	Jimmy Thomson	301	Oakmont CC, Oakmont, PA
1936	Tony Manero	282	Harry Cooper	284	Baltusrol GC (Lower), Springfield, NJ
1937	Ralph Guldahl	281	Sam Snead	283	Oakland Hills CC (South), Birmingham, MI
1938	Ralph Guldahl	284	Dick Metz	290	Cherry Hills CC, Englewood, CO
1939	Byron Nelson*	284	Craig Wood	284	Philadelphia CC, Gladwyne, PA
			Denny Shute		
1940	Lawson Little*	287	Gene Sarazen	287	Canterbury GC, Beachwood, OH
1941	Craig Wood	284	Denny Shute	287	Colonial CC, Fort Worth, TX
1942	No Tournament++				
1943	No Tournament++				
1944	No Tournament++				
1945	No Tournament++				
1946	Lloyd Mangrum*	284	Vic Ghezzi	284	Canterbury GC, Beachwood, OH
			Byron Nelson		
1947	Lew Worsham*	282	Sam Snead	282	St. Louis CC, Clayton, MO
1948	Ben Hogan	276	Jimmy Demaret	278	Riviera CC, Pacific Palisades, CA
1949	Cary Middlecoff	286	Sam Snead	287	Medinah CC, Medinah, IL
			Clayton Heafner		
1950	Ben Hogan*	287	Lloyd Mangrum	287	Merion GC, Ardmore, PA
			George Fazio		
1951	Ben Hogan	287	Clayton Heafner	289	Oakland Hills CC (South), Birmingham, MI
1952	Julius Boros	281	Ed Oliver	285	Northwood CC, Dallas, TX
1953	Ben Hogan	283	Sam Snead	289	Oakmont CC, Oakmont, PA
1954	Ed Furgol	284	Gene Littler	285	Baltusrol GC (Lower), Springfield, NJ
1955	Jack Fleck*	287	Ben Hogan	287	Olympic Club (Lake), San Francisco, CA
1956	Cary Middlecoff	281	Ben Hogan	282	Oak Hill CC, Rochester, NY
			Julius Boros		
1957	Dick Mayer*	282	Cary Middlecoff	282	Inverness Club, Toledo, OH
1958	Tommy Bolt	283	Gary Player	287	Southern Hills CC, Tulsa, OK
1959	Billy Casper	282	Bob Rosburg	283	Winged Foot GC (West), Mamaroneck, NY
1960	Arnold Palmer	280	Jack Nicklaus	282	Cherry Hills CC, Englewood, CO
1961	Gene Littler	281	Bob Goalby	282	Oakland Hills CC, Birmingham, MI
			Doug Sanders		
1962	Jack Nicklaus*	283	Arnold Palmer	283	Oakmont CC, Oakmont PA
1963	Julius Boros*	293	Jacky Cupit	293	The Country Club, Brookline, MA
			Arnold Palmer		
1964	Ken Venturi	278	Tommy Jacobs	282	Congressional CC (Blue), Bethesda, MD
1965	Gary Player*	282	Kel Nagle	282	Bellerive CC, St Louis, MO
1966	Billy Casper*	278	Arnold Palmer	278	Olympic Club (Lake), San Francisco, CA
1967	Jack Nicklaus	275	Arnold Palmer	279	Baltusrol GC, Springfield, NJ
1968	Lee Trevino	275	Jack Nicklaus	279	Oak Hill CC, Rochester NY
1969	Orville Moody	281	Deane Beman	282	Champions GC, Houston, TX
			Al Geiberger		
			Bob Rosburg		
1970	Tony Jacklin	281	Dave Hill	288	Hazeltine GC, Chaska, MN
1971	Lee Trevino*	280	Jack Nicklaus	280	Merion GC, Ardmore, PA
1972	Jack Nicklaus	290	Bruce Crampton	293	Pebble Beach GL, Pebble Beach, CA
1973	Johnny Miller	279	John Schlee	280	Oakmont CC, Oakmont, PA
1974	Hale Irwin	287	Forrest Fezler	289	Winged Foot GC (West), Mamaroneck, NY
1975	Lou Graham*	287	John Mahaffey	287	Medinah CC, Medinah, IL
1976	Jerry Pate	277	Tom Weiskopf	279	Atlanta Athletic Club, Duluth, GA
			Al Geiberger		
1977	Hubert Green	278	Lou Graham	279	Southern Hills CC, Tulsa, OK
1978	Andy North	285	Dave Stockton	286	Cherry Hills CC, Englewood, CO
			J.C. Snead		
1979	Hale Irwin	284	Gary Player	286	Inverness Club, Toledo, OH
			Jerry Pate		
1980	Jack Nicklaus	272	Isao Aoki	274	Baltusrol GC (Lower), Springfield NJ

U.S. Open Championship

NOTES

Last year, at 6-under-par 134, ***Shigeki Maruyama*** *and* ***Phil Mickelson*** *were one stroke short of the U.S. Open 36-hole record set by* ***Jim Furyk*** *and* ***Vijay Singh*** *in 2003 at Olympia Fields Country Club.*

Playing in his 33rd U.S. Open, past champion ***Tom Kite*** *made the cut in the 2004 U.S. Open at 3-over-par and played on the weekend for the 24th time at the age of 54 years, 6 months, and 9 days. Kite qualified for the 2004 U.S. Open, marking his 31st consecutive appearance in the tournament. Kite's streak began at the 1974 U.S. Open at Winged Foot, where he tied for eighth.* ***Jack Nicklaus*** *made the most consecutive U.S. Open starts (44, 1957-2000), followed by Hale Irwin (33, 1971-2003) and Kite, Gene Sarazen and Arnold Palmer (31).*

Retief Goosen *has posted all final-round scores during his four PGA TOUR wins in the 70s (1-over 71 at 2001 U.S. Open, 2-under 70 at BellSouth Classic, 1-under 70 at Chrysler Championship, 1-over 71 at 2004 U.S. Open).*

Retief Goosen *joins the club of 21 players that have multiple victories at the U.S. Open. There are 16 players with two victories, and five more players with three or more.*

Jay *(T9) and* ***Bill Haas*** *(T40), playing in the U.S. Open together for the second consecutive year, became the second father-son duo out of five to make the cut at the U.S. Open. The Kirkwood father-son combination made the cut at Riviera Country Club in 1947, with Joe Sr. finishing T28, while Joe Jr. edged him at T21. The Haases also became the first father-son team to play in the same U.S. Open more than once.*

Raymond Floyd *was the oldest player in the 2004 field at 61 years, 9 months, and 13 days.* ***Casey Wittenberg*** *was the youngest at 19 years, 6 months, and 17 days.*

Tournament Record:
272, Jack Nicklaus, 1980 (Baltusrol GC); Lee Janzen, 1993 (Baltusrol GC); Tiger Woods, 2000 (Pebble Beach GL); Jim Furyk, 2003 (Olympia Fields CC)

18-Hole Record:
63, Johnny Miller, 1973 (Oakmont CC); Tom Weiskopf, 1980 (Baltusrol GC); Jack Nicklaus, 1980 (Baltusrol GC)

TOURNAMENT HISTORY

Year	Winner	Score	Runner-up	Score	Location
1981	David Graham	273	George Burns	276	Merion GC, Ardmore, PA
			Bill Rogers		
1982	Tom Watson	282	Jack Nicklaus	284	Pebble Beach GL, Pebble Beach, CA
1983	Larry Nelson	280	Tom Watson	281	Oakmont CC, Oakmont, PA
1984	Fuzzy Zoeller*	276	Greg Norman	276	Winged Foot GC (West), Mamaroneck, NY
1985	Andy North	279	Dave Barr	280	Oakland Hills CC (South), Birmingham, MI
			Tze-Chung Chen		
			Denis Watson		
1986	Raymond Floyd	279	Lanny Wadkins	281	Shinnecock Hills GC, Southampton, NY
			Chip Beck		
1987	Scott Simpson	277	Tom Watson	278	Olympic Club (Lake), San Francisco, CA
1988	Curtis Strange*	278	Nick Faldo	278	The Country Club, Brookline, MA
1989	Curtis Strange	278	Chip Beck	279	Oak Hill CC, Rochester, NY
			Mark McCumber		
			Ian Woosnam		
1990	Hale Irwin*	280	Mike Donald	280	Medinah CC, Medinah, IL
1991	Payne Stewart*	282	Scott Simpson	282	Hazeltine National GC, Chaska, MN
1992	Tom Kite	285	Jeff Sluman	287	Pebble Beach GL, Pebble Beach, CA
1993	Lee Janzen	272	Payne Stewart	274	Baltusrol GC (Lower), Springfield, NJ
1994	Ernie Els*	279	Loren Roberts	279	Oakmont CC, Oakmont, PA
			Colin Montgomerie		
1995	Corey Pavin	280	Greg Norman	282	Shinnecock Hills GC, Southampton, NY
1996	Steve Jones	278	Tom Lehman	279	Oakland Hills CC, Bloomfield Hills, MI
			Davis Love III		
1997	Ernie Els	276	Colin Montgomerie	277	Congressional CC (Blue), Bethesda, MD
1998	Lee Janzen	280	Payne Stewart	281	Olympic Club (Lake), San Francisco, CA
1999	Payne Stewart	279	Phil Mickelson	280	Pinehurst (No. 2), Pinehurst, NC
2000	Tiger Woods	272	Ernie Els	287	Pebble Beach GL, Pebble Beach, CA
			Miguel A. Jiminez		
2001	Retief Goosen*	276	Mark Brooks	276	Southern Hills CC, Tulsa, OK
2002	Tiger Woods	277	Phil Mickelson	280	Bethpage State Park (Black), Farmingdale, NY
2003	Jim Furyk	272	Stephen Leaney	275	Olympia Fields CC, Olympia Fields, IL
2004	Retief Goosen	276	Phil Mickelson	278	Shinnecock Hills GC, Southampton, NY

*KEY: * = Playoff + = World War I ++ = World War II*

Retief Goosen, on "Regis and Kelly," displays the U.S. Open trophy.

2004 Booz Allen Classic [26th of 48 official events]

Booz | Allen Classic

SCOTT

Winner: ADAM SCOTT
66-62-67-68 263 (-21) $864,000

Tournament Players Club at Avenel

Potomac, MD

June 24-27, 2004

Purse: $4,800,000
Par: 36-35—71
Yards: 6,987

LEADERS: First Round—Charles Howell III recorded a course-record, 10-under-par 61 to lead Rich Beem and Olin Browne by three strokes. **Second Round**—Adam Scott's 62 moved him to 14-under-par 128, two ahead of Howell and Browne. **Third Round**—Scott, at 18-under-par 195, held a six-shot advantage over Browne

CUT: 80 players at 1-under-par 141 from a field of 156 professionals.

PRO-AM: $10,000. Chris Riley and John Daly, 51, $1,800 each.

WEATHER: On Thursday, partly sunny and warm. High of 90. Winds S-SE 4-8 mph. On Friday, increasing clouds and humid with scattered afternoon showers. Play was suspended due to lightning in the area at 4:05 p.m. with 78 players yet to complete their round. Play resumed at 5:56 p.m. and the second round was complete at 8:31 p.m. High of 86. Winds S-SE 6-12 mph. On Saturday, sunny with gusty winds. High of 84. Winds NW 12-18 mph. On Sunday, mostly sunny and pleasant. Cooler temperatures with a high of 80. Winds W-SW 6-12 mph.

Check out the 2005 Booz Allen Classic, June 9-12 on USA/ABC

ORDER OF FINISH

Adam Scott	1	66-62-67-68	263	$864,000.00
Charles Howell III	2	61-69-72-65	267	518,400.00
Rory Sabbatini	3	67-67-69-66	269	326,400.00
Tim Herron	T4	69-68-68-67	272	198,400.00
Arron Oberholser	T4	69-65-68-70	272	198,400.00
Bo Van Pelt	T4	69-68-68-67	272	198,400.00
Olin Browne	T7	64-66-71-72	273	154,800.00
Alex Cejka	T7	74-63-67-69	273	154,800.00
Aaron Barber	T9	70-68-68-68	274	134,400.00
Frank Lickliter II	T9	67-69-72-66	274	134,400.00
Harrison Frazar	T11	67-69-70-69	275	101,760.00
Tom Lehman	T11	66-67-71-71	275	101,760.00
Ryan Palmer	T11	70-69-68-68	275	101,760.00
Jeff Sluman	T11	65-71-69-70	275	101,760.00
Duffy Waldorf	T11	67-71-66-71	275	101,760.00
Rich Barcelo	T16	71-69-69-67	276	79,200.00
Tom Pernice, Jr.	T16	68-71-69-68	276	79,200.00
Guy Boros	T18	68-69-71-69	277	67,200.00
J.J. Henry	T18	68-69-70-70	277	67,200.00
Kevin Na	T18	68-71-64-74	277	67,200.00
Billy Andrade	T21	68-71-72-67	278	45,060.00
Bart Bryant	T21	71-67-67-73	278	45,060.00
Ben Crane	T21	70-70-66-72	278	45,060.00
Joe Durant	T21	69-71-68-70	278	45,060.00
Danny Ellis	T21	67-69-71-71	278	45,060.00
Scott Hend	T21	66-72-69-71	278	45,060.00
David Morland IV	T21	69-71-72-66	278	$45,060.00
Vaughn Taylor	T21	68-71-68-71	278	45,060.00
Michael Allen	T29	70-71-69-69	279	31,920.00
Craig Barlow	T29	69-68-69-73	279	31,920.00
Matt Gogel	T29	69-70-71-69	279	31,920.00
Hidemichi Tanaka	T29	70-65-73-71	279	31,920.00
Notah Begay III	T33	72-65-71-72	280	23,280.00
Brent Geiberger	T33	71-68-72-69	280	23,280.00
Bill Glasson	T33	72-69-67-72	280	23,280.00
Bill Haas (S)	T33	69-65-73-73	280	23,280.00
Pete Jordan (Q)	T33	72-67-72-69	280	23,280.00
Shaun Micheel	T33	67-72-66-75	280	23,280.00
Chris Riley	T33	72-66-69-73	280	23,280.00
Steve Stricker	T33	67-68-71-74	280	23,280.00
Esteban Toledo	T33	69-71-68-72	280	23,280.00
Mark Wilson	T33	69-72-69-70	280	23,280.00
Michael Bradley	T43	70-65-70-76	281	14,616.00
David Branshaw	T43	69-70-71-71	281	14,616.00
Danny Briggs	T43	70-69-69-73	281	14,616.00
John Cook	T43	71-69-69-72	281	14,616.00
Glen Day	T43	69-62-79-71	281	14,616.00
Luke Donald	T43	72-68-70-71	281	14,616.00
Mark Hensby	T43	68-72-70-71	281	14,616.00
Corey Pavin	T43	70-68-70-73	281	14,616.00
Rich Beem	T51	64-67-72-79	282	11,296.00
Jeff Brehaut	T51	70-69-71-72	282	11,296.00
Brad Faxon	T51	74-66-71-71	282	11,296.00
Charley Hoffman (Q)	T51	69-70-71-72	282	11,296.00
Richard S. Johnson	T51	72-67-72-71	282	$11,296.00
Carl Pettersson	T51	67-71-70-74	282	11,296.00
Steve Allan	T57	69-67-75-72	283	10,512.00
Pat Bates	T57	70-71-72-70	283	10,512.00
Cameron Beckman	T57	70-68-79-66	283	10,512.00
Daniel Chopra	T57	72-69-70-72	283	10,512.00
David Edwards	T57	68-73-71-71	283	10,512.00
Len Mattiace	T57	71-69-71-72	283	10,512.00
Tommy Tolles	T57	69-72-71-71	283	10,512.00
Garrett Willis	T57	71-68-70-74	283	10,512.00
Billy Mayfair	65	66-70-75-73	284	10,080.00
Cliff Kresge	T66	71-68-74-72	285	9,888.00
Kelly Mitchum (S)	T66	72-69-76-68	285	9,888.00
Heath Slocum	T66	70-69-74-72	285	9,888.00
Tom Byrum	T69	72-69-76-69	286	9,648.00
Jonathan Kaye	T69	70-70-71-75	286	9,648.00
Aaron Baddeley	T71	67-74-74-72	287	9,312.00
Kelly Gibson	T71	71-70-72-74	287	9,312.00
Hunter Mahan	T71	69-70-73-75	287	9,312.00
Geoff Ogilvy	T71	70-68-74-75	287	9,312.00
Patrick Sheehan	T71	68-71-77-71	287	9,312.00
Mike Grob	76	72-68-72-77	289	9,024.00
Steve Pate	T77	68-73-76-73	290	8,880.00
Dicky Pride	T77	68-71-76-75	290	8,880.00
John Daly	79	70-70-76-77	293	8,736.00
Jay Don Blake (S)	80	69-70-77-85	301	8,640.00

(Q) = Open Qualifier; (S) = Sponsor Exemption; (T) = Tie

The following players did not finish (C=cut, W=withdrew)

C—142-D.J. Brigman, Mark Brooks, Russ Cochran, Jay Delsing, Trevor Dodds, Joel Edwards, Robert Gamez, Joel Kribel, Blaine McCallister, Rod Pampling, Deane Pappas, Tom Scherrer. **143-**Matt Hendrix, Hank Kuehne, Brad Lardon, Spike McRoy, Brenden Pappas, Jay Williamson, Willie Wood. **144-**Tim Clark, Jason Dufner, Todd Fischer, Brian Gay, Mathias Gronberg, Donnie Hammond, Justin Leonard, Dean Wilson. **145-**Arjun Atwal, Tom Carter, Kris Cox, Scott Hoch, Scott McCarron, Hirofumi Miyase, Gene Sauers, Chris Smith, Paul Stankowski, Omar Uresti, Stan Utley, Tjaart Van der Walt. **146-**Fred Funk, Carl Paulson, Roland Thatcher. **147-**Jim Carter, Greg Chalmers, Ken Duke, Mike Hulbert, Tripp Isenhour, Kent Jones, Patrick Moore, Dennis Paulson, Brett Quigley, Joey Sindelar, Andre Stolz, David Sutherland. **148-**Jason Bohn, Lucas Glover, Brandon Knaub, Brian Kortan, Ricky Touma. **149-**Jim McGovern, Del Ponchock. **150-**John E. Morgan, Ted Tryba. **151-**Michael Clark II. **153-**George Bradford, Mike Heinen, Jim Schouller, Jr. **155-**Kevin Muncrief. **W—81-**Lee Janzen. **79-**Dan Olsen. **76-**Chris Couch. **75-**Ken Green. **74-**Boyd Summerhays, Pat Perez, Craig Bowden. **72-**Neal Lancaster.

TOURNAMENT HISTORY

Year	Winner	Score	Runner-up	Score	Location	Par/Yards
KEMPER OPEN						
1968	Arnold Palmer	276	Bruce Crampton Art Wall	280	Pleasant Valley CC, Sutton, MA	71/7,110
1969	Dale Douglass	274	Charles Coody	278	Quail Hollow CC, Charlotte, NC	72/7,205
1970	Dick Lotz	278	Lou Graham Larry Hinson Grier Jones Tom Weiskopf	280	Quail Hollow CC, Charlotte, NC	72/7,205
1971	Tom Weiskopf*	277	Dale Douglass Gary Player Lee Trevino	277	Quail Hollow CC, Charlotte, NC	72/7,205
1972	Doug Sanders	275	Lee Trevino	276	Quail Hollow CC, Charlotte, NC	72/7,205
1973	Tom Weiskopf	271	Lanny Wadkins	274	Quail Hollow CC, Charlotte, NC	72/7,205
1974	Bob Menne*	270	Jerry Heard	270	Quail Hollow CC, Charlotte, NC	72/7,205
1975	Raymond Floyd	278	John Mahaffey Gary Player	281	Quail Hollow CC, Charlotte, NC	72/7,205
1976	Joe Inman	277	Grier Jones Tom Weiskopf	278	Quail Hollow CC, Charlotte, NC	72/7,205
1977	Tom Weiskopf	277	George Burns Bill Rogers	279	Quail Hollow CC, Charlotte, NC	72/7,205
1978	Andy Bean	273	Mark Hayes Andy North	278	Quail Hollow CC, Charlotte, NC	72/7,205
1979	Jerry McGee	272	Jerry Pate	273	Quail Hollow CC, Charlotte, NC	72/7,205
1980	John Mahaffey	275	Craig Stadler	278	Congressional CC, Bethesda, MD	72/7,173
1981	Craig Stadler	270	Tom Watson Tom Weiskopf	276	Congressional CC, Bethesda, MD	72/7,173
1982	Craig Stadler	275	Seve Ballesteros	282	Congressional CC, Bethesda, MD	72/7,173

NOTES

The Booz Allen Classic returns to the Congressional Country Club in 2005 for the first time since ***Greg Norman*** *won the tournament in 1986 in a playoff over* ***Larry Mize****. This year will mark the eighth time the tournament has been played at the famed course. Of the seven previous tournaments at Congressional,* ***Norman*** *and* ***Craig Stadler*** *each won twice.*

The 2005 Booz Allen Classic is scheduled to finish on Congressional's 190-yard, par-3 18th hole, a rarity on the PGA TOUR. Only THE TOUR Championship presented by Coca-Cola finishes on a par 3, the 235-yard 18th at East Lake Golf Club in Atlanta.

The Booz Allen Classic dates back to 1968 and has been held at four different courses over that time span (Pleasant Valley Country Club, Quail Hollow Country Club, Congressional Country Club and TPC at Avenel). ***Bill Glasson*** *is the only player to win on two different courses, winning in 1985 at Congressional and in 1992 at the TPC at Avenel.*

*Four players—***Tom Weiskopf***,* ***Craig Stadler****,* ***Bill Glasson*** *and* ***Greg Norman****—have won the Booz Allen Classic more than once.*

All three of ***Adam Scott****'s PGA TOUR victories have come at Tournament Players Club venues. In addition to his victory at the 2004 Booz Allen Classic (TPC at Avenel), he also won the 2004 PLAYERS Championship at the TPC at Sawgrass and the 2003 Deutsche Bank Championship at the TPC of Boston.*

Adam Scott*'s 21-under-par 263 winning score in 2004 equaled the tournament record held by* ***Billy Andrade*** *and* ***Jeff Sluman*** *in 1991. Andrade went on to defeat Sluman on the first playoff hole that year.*

Tournament Record:
263, Billy Andrade, Jeff Sluman, 1991; Adam Scott, 2004
Current Course Record:
61, Charles Howell, 2004
Other Course Record:
61, Jerry McGee, 1979 (Quail Hollow CC)

TOURNAMENT HISTORY

Year	Winner	Score	Runner-up	Score	Location	Par/Yards
1983	Fred Couples*	287	Tze-Chung Chen	287	Congressional CC, Bethesda, MD	72/7,173
			Barry Jaeckel			
			Gil Morgan			
			Scott Simpson			
1984	Greg Norman	280	Mark O'Meara	285	Congressional CC, Bethesda, MD	72/7,173
1985	Bill Glasson	278	Larry Mize	279	Congressional CC, Bethesda, MD	72/7,173
			Corey Pavin			
1986	Greg Norman*	277	Larry Mize	277	Congressional CC, Bethesda, MD	72/7,173
1987	Tom Kite	270	Chris Perry	277	TPC at Avenel, Potomac, MD	71/6,864
			Howard Twitty			
1988	Morris Hatalsky*	274	Tom Kite	274	TPC at Avenel, Potomac, MD	71/6,867
1989	Tom Byrum	268	Tommy Armour III	273	TPC at Avenel, Potomac, MD	71/6,917
			Billy Ray Brown			
			Jim Thorpe			
1990	Gil Morgan	274	Ian Baker-Finch	275	TPC at Avenel, Potomac, MD	71/6,917
1991	Billy Andrade*	263	Jeff Sluman	263	TPC at Avenel, Potomac, MD	71/6,904
1992	Bill Glasson	276	John Daly	277	TPC at Avenel, Potomac, MD	71/7,005
			Ken Green			
			Mike Springer			
			Howard Twitty			
1993	Grant Waite	275	Tom Kite	276	TPC at Avenel, Potomac, MD	71/7,005
1994	Mark Brooks	271	Bobby Wadkins	274	TPC at Avenel, Potomac, MD	71/7,005
			D.A. Weibring			
1995	Lee Janzen*	272	Corey Pavin	272	TPC at Avenel, Potomac, MD	71/7,005
1996	Steve Stricker	270	Brad Faxon	273	TPC at Avenel, Potomac, MD	71/7,005
			Scott Hoch			
			Mark O'Meara			
			Grant Waite			
1997	Justin Leonard	274	Mark Wiebe	275	TPC at Avenel, Potomac, MD	71/7,005
1998	Stuart Appleby	274	Scott Hoch	275	TPC at Avenel, Potomac, MD	71/7,005
1999	Rich Beem	274	Bill Glasson	275	TPC at Avenel, Potomac, MD	71/7,005
			Bradley Hughes			
KEMPER INSURANCE OPEN						
2000	Tom Scherrer	271	Greg Chalmers	273	TPC at Avenel, Potomac, MD	71/7,005
			Kazuhiko Hosokawa			
			Franklin Langham			
			Justin Leonard			
			Steve Lowery			
2001	Frank Lickliter	268	J.J. Henry	269	TPC at Avenel, Potomac, MD	71/7,005
2002	Bob Estes	273	Rich Beem	274	TPC at Avenel, Potomac, MD	71/6,987
FBR CAPITAL OPEN						
2003	Rory Sabbatini	270	Joe Durant	274	TPC at Avenel, Potomac, MD	71/6,987
			Fred Funk			
			Duffy Waldorf			
BOOZ ALLEN CLASSIC						
2004	Adam Scott	263	Charles Howell III	267	TPC at Avenel, Potomac, MD	71/6,987

*KEY: * = Playoff ~ = Weather-shortened*

2004 Cialis Western Open [27th of 48 official events]

Cialis (tadalafil) WESTERN OPEN

AMES

Winner: STEPHEN AMES
67-73-64-70 274 (-10) $864,000

Cog Hill Golf & Country Club (Dubsdread)

Lemont, IL

July 1-4, 2004

Purse: $4,800,000
Par: 35-36—71
Yards: 7,326

LEADERS: First Round—Loren Roberts used a 7-under 64 to hold a one-stroke lead over Robert Allenby. Seven players were three back.
Second Round—Steve Lowery, Matt Gogel and Charles Howell III sat at 6-under 136. Geoff Ogilvy and Mark Hensby trailed by one.
Third Round—Stephen Ames and Hensby moved to 9-under 204, one ahead of Ogilvy. Stuart Appleby and Lowery were two behind.

CUT: 82 players at 2-over-par 144 from a field of 155 professionals.

PRO-AM: $10,000. Ben Crane, 53, $2,000.

WEATHER: Mostly sunny on Thursday with temperatures reaching the mid-80s and variable light winds. Mostly sunny again on Friday with temperatures topping at 81 and slightly stronger winds 10-15 mph out of the E-NE. Saturday tee times moved to 7-9 a.m. in threesomes due to expected afternoon thunderstorms. Light rain at times. Temperatures in high 70s and winds out of SE up to 18 mph. Players in threesomes again on Sunday beginning at 10 a.m. Mostly cloudy throughout the day with temperatures in the 70s and W winds up to 20 mph.

Check out the 2005 Cialis Western Open, June 30-July 3 on USA/ABC

ORDER OF FINISH

Stephen Ames	1	67-73-64-70	274	$864,000.00
Steve Lowery	2	68-68-70-70	276	518,400.00
Luke Donald	T3	72-68-70-67	277	278,400.00
Mark Hensby	T3	67-70-67-73	277	278,400.00
Stuart Appleby	T5	71-68-67-72	278	182,400.00
Geoff Ogilvy	T5	68-69-68-73	278	182,400.00
Jim Furyk	T7	69-71-68-71	279	144,600.00
Davis Love III	T7	70-74-67-68	279	144,600.00
Carl Pettersson	T7	71-70-69-69	279	144,600.00
Tiger Woods	T7	70-73-65-71	279	144,600.00
Robert Allenby	T11	65-73-71-71	280	98,400.00
Scott Hoch	T11	69-69-73-69	280	98,400.00
Shigeki Maruyama	T11	70-72-67-71	280	98,400.00
Pat Perez	T11	69-73-71-67	280	98,400.00
Loren Roberts	T11	64-75-73-68	280	98,400.00
Scott Verplank	T11	72-71-67-70	280	98,400.00
Carlos Franco	T17	74-69-70-68	281	64,960.00
Robert Gamez	T17	67-71-72-71	281	64,960.00
Matt Gogel	T17	72-64-74-71	281	64,960.00
Charles Howell III	T17	69-67-74-71	281	64,960.00
John Rollins	T17	71-69-69-72	281	64,960.00
Vijay Singh	T17	72-71-68-70	281	64,960.00
J.J. Henry	23	69-73-68-72	282	49,920.00
D.J. Brigman	T24	68-70-75-70	283	42,240.00
Peter Lonard	T24	72-70-70-71	283	42,240.00
Billy Mayfair	T24	69-74-69-71	283	42,240.00
Michael Allen	T27	68-72-72-72	284	33,360.00
David Branshaw	T27	68-74-72-70	284	$33,360.00
Bart Bryant	T27	71-71-71-71	284	33,360.00
Bob Burns	T27	74-68-72-70	284	33,360.00
Jonathan Byrd	T27	67-72-71-74	284	33,360.00
Mike Small	T27	69-70-69-76	284	33,360.00
Tom Carter	T33	71-72-71-71	285	24,822.86
Jose Coceres	T33	72-69-74-70	285	24,822.86
Richard S. Johnson	T33	70-71-73-71	285	24,822.86
Kevin Na	T33	70-69-75-71	285	24,822.86
Steve Stricker	T33	69-75-71-70	285	24,822.86
Jason Bohn	T33	71-73-71-70	285	24,822.85
Jerry Kelly	T33	72-72-72-69	285	24,822.85
Briny Baird	T40	70-73-70-73	286	17,760.00
Rich Beem	T40	69-73-71-73	286	17,760.00
K.J. Choi	T40	68-71-74-73	286	17,760.00
David Frost	T40	75-68-71-72	286	17,760.00
Steve Pate	T40	73-70-67-76	286	17,760.00
Brett Quigley	T40	73-71-71-71	286	17,760.00
Mark Wilson (S)	T40	72-71-71-72	286	17,760.00
Skip Kendall	T47	68-75-71-73	287	12,912.00
Stephen Leaney	T47	76-66-70-75	287	12,912.00
Scott McCarron	T47	71-72-74-70	287	12,912.00
Jeff Sluman	T47	72-70-71-74	287	12,912.00
Chad Campbell	T51	67-76-73-72	288	11,232.00
Jason Dufner (S)	T51	71-72-75-70	288	11,232.00
Steve Elkington	T51	72-72-72-72	288	11,232.00
Patrick Sheehan	T51	73-70-69-76	288	11,232.00
Scott Simpson (S)	T51	68-71-73-76	288	11,232.00
Chris Smith	T51	68-72-70-78	288	11,232.00
Jay Williamson	T51	69-73-74-72	288	$11,232.00
Steve Allan	T58	72-69-72-76	289	10,560.00
Aaron Baddeley	T58	75-69-73-72	289	10,560.00
Pat Bates	T58	72-70-77-70	289	10,560.00
Todd Fischer	T58	70-74-72-73	289	10,560.00
Brad Lardon	T58	76-68-71-74	289	10,560.00
Brian Bateman	T63	74-67-74-75	290	9,936.00
Robert Damron	T63	70-74-73-73	290	9,936.00
Dan Forsman	T63	68-72-72-78	290	9,936.00
Hank Kuehne	T63	70-73-76-71	290	9,936.00
Len Mattiace	T63	74-70-72-74	290	9,936.00
Gene Sauers	T63	73-68-75-74	290	9,936.00
Joey Sindelar	T63	72-70-77-71	290	9,936.00
Vaughn Taylor	T63	71-69-72-78	290	9,936.00
Tommy Armour III	T71	72-72-73-74	291	9,264.00
Craig Bowden	T71	69-72-73-77	291	9,264.00
Glen Day	T71	74-69-73-75	291	9,264.00
Brent Geiberger	T71	72-70-74-75	291	9,264.00
Lucas Glover	T71	75-68-79-69	291	9,264.00
Kevin Sutherland	T71	68-73-71-79	291	9,264.00
Heath Slocum	77	71-68-75-78	292	8,928.00
J.P. Hayes	78	74-68-74-77	293	8,832.00
Joel Edwards	T79	74-70-76-74	294	8,688.00
J.L. Lewis	T79	67-74-78-75	294	8,688.00
Trevor Dodds	T81	73-71-75-76	295	8,496.00
Ryan Palmer	T81	74-69-76-76	295	8,496.00

(S) = Sponsor Exemption; (T) = Tie

The following players did not finish
(C=cut, W=withdrew, D=disqualified)

C—145-Craig Barlow, Notah Begay III, Ben Curtis, Jay Delsing, Dudley Hart, Zach Johnson, Hunter Mahan, Blaine McCallister, Ted Purdy, **146**-Joe Affrunti, Guy Boros, Greg Chalmers, Kris Cox, Bob Estes, Steve Flesch, Mathias Gronberg, Todd Hamilton, Cliff Kresge, Joe Ogilvie, Brenden Pappas, Brandt Snedeker, Roland Thatcher, Dean Wilson, **147**-Woody Austin, Danny Briggs, Olin Browne, Tom Byrum, Brian Gay, Shaun Micheel, Rod Pampling, Deane Pappas, John Senden, Tjaart van der Walt, Camilo Villegas, Grant Waite, **148**-Daniel Chopra, Ken Duke, Joe Durant, Ken Green, Neal Lancaster, Tommy Tolles, **149**-Arjun Atwal, Rich Barcelo, Jeff Brehaut, Brian Kortan, Hirofumi Miyase, David Morland IV, Craig Perks, Andre Stolz, **150**-Russ Cochran, Danny Ellis, Frank Lickliter II, Rocco Mediate, Greg Norman, Dan Olsen, **151**-Chris Botsford, Joel Kribel, Derek Lamely, Omar Uresti, **152**-Kent Jones, Esteban Toledo, Mike Weir, Casey Wittenberg, **153**-Aaron Barber, Brett Melton, **154**-David Gossett, Scott Hend, Patrick Moore, **155**-Roy Biancalana, **157**-Danny Mulhearn. **W—82**-Chris Couch, **72**-Cameron Beckman. **D—73**-John Riegger.

TOURNAMENT HISTORY

Year	Winner	Score	Runner-up	Score	Location	Par/Yards
WESTERN OPEN						
1899	Willie Smith*	156	Laurie Auchterlonie	156	Glen View GC, Chicago, IL	72/6362
1900	No Tournament					
1901	Laurie Auchterlonie	160	David Bell	162	Midlothian CC, Midlothian, IL	71/6654
1902	Willie Anderson	299	Willie Smith	304	Euclid Club, Euclid, OH	N/A
1903	Alex Smith	318	Laurie Auchterlonie David Brown	320	Milwaukee CC, Milwaukee, WI	72/6867
1904	Willie Anderson	304	Alex Smith	308	Kent CC, Grand Rapids, MI	71/6514
1905	Arthur Smith	278	James Maiden	280	Cincinnati GC, Cincinnati, OH	71/6231
1906	Alex Smith	306	Jack Hobens	309	Homewood CC, Homewood, IL	70/6311
1907	Robert Simpson	307	Willie Anderson Fred McCloud	309	Hinsdale GC, Hinsdale, IL	71/6475
1908	Willie Anderson	299	Fred McCloud	300	Normandie GC, St. Louis, MO	71/6534
1909	Willie Anderson	288	Stewart Gardner	297	Skokie CC, Glencoe, IL	72/6913
1910	Charles Evans, Jr.#	6 and 5	George Simpson		Beverly CC, Chicago, IL	72/6754
1911	Robert Simpson	2 and 1	Tom MacNamara		Kent CC, Grand Rapids, MI	71/6514
1912	Macdonald Smith	299	Alex Robertson	302	Idlewild CC, Flossmoor, IL	72/6754
1913	John McDermott	295	Mike Brady	302	Memphis CC, Memphis, TN	70/6695
1914	Jim Barnes	293	Willie Kidd	294	Interlachen CC, Edina, MN	73/6733
1915	Tom McNamara	304	Alex Cunningham	306	Glen Oak CC, Glen Ellyn, IL	72/6503
1916	Walter Hagen	286	Jock Hutchison George Sargent	287	Blue Mound CC, Milwaukee, WI	N/A
1917	Jim Barnes	283	Walter Hagen	285	Westmoreland CC, Wilmette, IL	72/6798
1918	No Tournament					
1919	Jim Barnes	283	Leo Diegel	286	Mayfield CC, Cleveland, OH	72/6609
1920	Jock Hutchison	296	James Barnes Clarence Hackney Harry Hampton	297	Olympia Fields CC, Olympia Fields, IL	71/6749
1921	Walter Hagen	287	Jock Hutchison	292	Oakwood Club, Cleveland Heights, OH	71/6709

NOTES

***Stephen Ames** became the first player age 40 or older to collect his initial TOUR victory since **Brad Bryant** (41 years, 9 months, 28 days) won the 1995 Walt Disney World/Oldsmobile Golf Classic.*

*Acefest: University of Illinois men's golf coach **Mike Small** posted a hole-in-one with a 6-iron on the 180-yard second hole in Friday's second round in 2004. **Lucas Glover** aced the 218-yard 12th hole with a 5-iron. **Scott Hoch** temporarily grabbed a share of the lead at 6-under-par with an ace on the 196-yard 14th hole with a 4-iron. It was the first time in tournament history that three aces were recorded in the same round. The last time three holes-in-one occurred on the PGA TOUR in a single round was the third round at the 2002 Buick Classic.*

*Since 1916, when TOUR records are available for this statistic, **Stephen Ames** became the 12th player to win his first PGA TOUR event at the Cialis Western Open. The others: **Abe Espinosa** (1928), **Herman Barron** (1942), **Hugh Royer** (1970), **Jim Jamieson** (1972), **Tom Watson** (1974), **Scott Simpson** (1980), **Scott Verplank**-a (1985), **D.A. Weibring** (1987), **Jim Benepe** (1988), **Russ Cochran** (1991) and **Joe Durant** (1998).*

***Stephen Ames** posted the highest winning total in relation to par at the tournament (10-under 274) since **Billy Mayfair** won the 1995 event with a total of 9-under 279. Also, the total of 9-under 204 by co-leaders **Stephen Ames** and **Mark Hensby** was the highest third-round total at the Cialis Western Open since 1997, when **Tiger Woods**, **Justin Leonard** and **Loren Roberts** sat at 9-under 207.*

*In winning the 2004 Cialis Western Open, **Stephen Ames** collected his eighth top-10 finish in his last 10 events earning $2,392,212 during that period. Ames, who finished with 11 top-10s, had never posted more than four top-10s in a season during his first six years on TOUR.*

***Stephen Ames** became the fifth consecutive international player to win on the PGA TOUR and was one of 26 wins by international players in 48 events during the 2004 season.*

TOURNAMENT HISTORY

Year	Winner	Score	Runner-up	Score	Location	Par/Yards
1922	Mike Brady	291	Laurie Ayton	301	Oakland Hills CC, Birmingham, MI	72/7052
			Jock Hutchison			
1923	Jock Hutchison	281	Bobby Cruickshank	287	Colonial CC, Memphis, TN	70/7116
			Leo Diegel			
			Walter Hagen			
			Joe Kirkwood, Sr.			
1924	Bill Mehlhorn	293	Al Watrous	301	Calumet CC, Homewood, IL	72/6524
1925	Macdonald Smith	281	Leo Diegel	287	Youngstown CC, Youngstown, OH	71/6,597
			Johnny Farrell			
			Emmet French			
			Walter Hagen			
			Bill Mehlhorn			
1926	Walter Hagen	279	Harry Cooper	288	Highland G&CC, Indianapolis, IN	70/6,501
			Gene Sarazen			
1927	Walter Hagen	281	Al Espinosa	285	Olympia Fields CC, Olympia Fields, IL	71/6,749
			Bill Mehlhorn			
1928	Abe Espinosa	291	Johnny Farrell	294	North Shore GC, Chicago, IL	72/7,024
1929	Tommy Armour	273	Horton Smith	281	Ozaukee CC, Mequon, WI	70/6,553
1930	Gene Sarazen	278	Al Espinosa	285	Indianwood G&CC, Lake Orion, MI	N/A
1931	Ed Dudley	280	Walter Hagen	284	Miami Valley GC, Dayton, OH	71/6,589
1932	Walter Hagen	287	Olin Dutra	288	Canterbury GC, Beechwood, OH	72/6,877
1933	Macdonald Smith	282	Tommy Armour	288	Olympia Fields CC, Olympia Fields, IL	71/6,749
1934	Harry Cooper*	274	Ky Laffoon	274	CC of Peoria, Peoria, IL	70/6,068
1935	John Revolta	290	Willie Goggin	294	South Bend CC, South Bend, IN	71/6,455
1936	Ralph Guldahl	274	Ray Mangrum	277	Davenport CC, Davenport, IA	71/6,458
1937	Ralph Guldahl*	288	Horton Smith	288	Canterbury CC, Beachwood, OH	72/6,877
1938	Ralph Guldahl	279	Sam Snead	286	Westwood CC, St. Louis, MO	72/6,785
1939	Byron Nelson	281	Lloyd Mangrum	282	Medinah CC, Medinah, IL	71/7,104
1940	Jimmy Demaret*	293	Toney Penna	293	River Oaks CC, Houston, TX	72/6,868
1941	Ed Oliver	275	Ben Hogan	278	Phoenix GC, Phoenix, AZ	71/6,726
			Byron Nelson			
1942	Herman Barron	276	Henry Picard	278	Phoenix GC, Phoenix, AZ	71/6,726
1943	No Tournament++					
1944	No Tournament++					
1945	No Tournament++					
1946	Ben Hogan	271	Lloyd Mangrum	275	Sunset CC, St. Louis, MO	72/6,323
1947	Johnny Palmer	270	Bobby Locke	271	Salt Lake City CC, Salt Lake City, UT	72/6,891
			Ed Oliver			
1948	Ben Hogan*	281	Ed Oliver	281	Brookfield CC, Buffalo, NY	72/6,813
1949	Sam Snead	268	Cary Middlecoff	272	Keller GC, St. Paul, MN	72/6,542
1950	Sam Snead	282	Jim Ferrier	283	Brentwood CC, Brentwood, CA	72/6,729
			E. J. Harrison			
1951	Marty Furgol	270	Cary Middlecoff	271	Davenport CC, Davenport, IA	71/6,450
1952	Lloyd Mangrum	274	Bobby Locke	282	Westwood CC, St. Louis, MO	72/6,785
1953	Dutch Harrison	278	Ed Furgol	282	Bellerive CC, St. Louis, MO	71/7,305
			Fred Haas			
			Lloyd Mangrum			
1954	Lloyd Mangrum*	277	Ted Kroll	277	Kenwood CC, Cincinnati, OH	72/6,950
1955	Cary Middlecoff	272	Mike Souchak	274	Portland GC, Portland, OR	72/6,564
1956	Mike Fetchick*	284	Doug Ford	284	Presidio CC, San Francisco, CA	72/6,488
			Jay Hebert			
			Don January			
1957	Doug Ford*	279	George Bayer	279	Plum Hollow GC, Southfield, MI	72/6,854
			Gene Littler			
			Billy Maxwell			
1958	Doug Sanders	275	Dow Finsterwald	276	Red Run GC, Royal Oak, MI	72/6,801
1959	Mike Souchak	272	Arnold Palmer	273	Pittsburgh Field Club, Fox Chapel, PA	71/6,586
1960	Stan Leonard*	278	Art Wall	278	Western G&CC, Redford, MI	72/6,808
1961	Arnold Palmer	271	Sam Snead	273	Blythefield CC, Belmont, MI	71/6,730
1962	Jacky Cupit	281	Billy Casper	283	Medinah CC, Medinah, IL	71/7,014
1963	Arnold Palmer*	280	Julius Boros	280	Beverly CC, Chicago, IL	71/6,923
			Jack Nicklaus			
1964	Chi Chi Rodriguez	268	Arnold Palmer	269	Tam O'Shanter CC, Niles, IL	71/6,686
1965	Billy Casper	270	Jack McGowan	272	Tam O'Shanter CC, Niles, IL	71/6,686
			Chi Chi Rodriguez			
1966	Billy Casper	283	Gay Brewer	286	Medinah CC, Medinah, IL	71/7,014
1967	Jack Nicklaus	274	Doug Sanders	276	Beverly CC, Chicago, IL	71/6,923
1968	Jack Nicklaus	273	Miller Barber	276	Olympia Fields CC, Olympia Fields, IL	71/6,749
1969	Billy Casper	276	Rocky Thompson	280	Midlothian CC, Midlothian, IL	71/6,654
1970	Hugh Royer	273	Dale Douglass	274	Beverly CC, Chicago, IL	71/6,923
1971	Bruce Crampton	279	Bobby Nichols	281	Olympia Fields CC, Olympia Fields, IL	71/6,749
1972	Jim Jamieson	271	Labron Harris, Jr.	277	Sunset Ridge, Winnetka, IL	71/6,716
1973	Billy Casper	272	Larry Hinson	273	Midlothian CC, Midlothian, IL	71/6,654
			Hale Irwin			
1974	Tom Watson	287	J.C. Snead	289	Butler National GC, Oak Brook, IL	71/7,002
			Tom Weiskopf			
1975	Hale Irwin	283	Bobby Cole	284	Butler National GC, Oak Brook, IL	71/7,002
1976	Al Geiberger	288	Joe Porter	289	Butler National GC, Oak Brook, IL	71/7,002
1977	Tom Watson	283	Wally Armstrong	284	Butler National GC, Oak Brook, IL	72/7,097
			Johnny Miller			

NOTES

Stephen Ames *became the first player from Trinidad and Tobago to win a PGA TOUR tournament and the second player from a Caribbean nation after* ***Chi Chi Rodriguez****, of Puerto Rico who won eight times on the PGA TOUR.*

Steve Lowery *holed a huge putt on the 72nd hole in 2004 from eight feet, six inches. Not only did he earn a British Open exemption with the made putt, he also made $160,000 with the putt, the difference between solo second ($518,000) and a three-way tie for third ($358,400).*

Davis Love III *posted his fourth consecutive top-10 at the Cialis Western Open in 2004. His T7 in 2004 follows runner-up finishes in 2001 and 2002 and a T7 in 1997.*

Jim Furyk*'s T7 finish in 2004 was his fifth top-10 finish at the Cialis Western Open in his last six appearances. Furyk finished sixth in 1997, T7 in 1998 and T3 in 2000 and 2003.*

Third-round leaders go on to win at this tournament almost half the time. Since 1902 (95 72-hole events), 55 of the players who have held/shared the third-round lead have won; since 1950 (53 events), 27 players have gone on to win; and over the last 10 years, five players have gone on to victory, including last year's winner ***Stephen Ames****.*

The cut of 82 players at 2-over-par 144 was the highest in relation to par since 1998 when 78 players made the cut at 2-over 146.

Tournament Record:
267, Scott Hoch, 2001; Tiger Woods, 2003

Current Course Record:
63, Jeff Sluman, 1992; John Adams, 1993; Dudley Hart, 1998; Nick Price, Brian Henninger, Stephen Ames, 2000

TOURNAMENT HISTORY

Year	Winner	Score	Runner-up	Score	Location	Par/Yards
1978	Andy Bean*	282	Bill Rogers	282	Butler National GC, Oak Brook, IL	72/7,097
1979	Larry Nelson*	286	Ben Crenshaw	286	Butler National GC, Oak Brook, IL	72/7,097
1980	Scott Simpson	281	Andy Bean	286	Butler National GC, Oak Brook, IL	72/7,097
1981	Ed Fiori	277	Jim Colbert Greg Powers Jim Simons	281	Butler National GC, Oak Brook, IL	72/7,097
1982	Tom Weiskopf	276	Larry Nelson	277	Butler National GC, Oak Brook, IL	72/7,097
1983	Mark McCumber	284	Tom Watson	285	Butler National GC, Oak Brook, IL	72/7,097
1984	Tom Watson*	280	Greg Norman	280	Butler National GC, Oak Brook, IL	72/7,097
1985	Scott Verplank*#	279	Jim Thorpe	279	Butler National GC, Oak Brook, IL	72/7,097
1986	Tom Kite*	286	Fred Couples David Frost Nick Price	286	Butler National GC, Oak Brook, IL	72/7,097
BEATRICE WESTERN OPEN						
1987	D.A. Weibring~	207	Larry Nelson Greg Norman	208	Butler National GC, Oak Brook, IL**	72/6,752
1988	Jim Benepe	278	Peter Jacobsen	279	Butler National GC, Oak Brook, IL	72/7,097
1989	Mark McCumber*	275	Peter Jacobsen	275	Butler National GC, Oak Brook, IL	72/7,097
CENTEL WESTERN OPEN						
1990	Wayne Levi	275	Payne Stewart	279	Butler National GC, Oak Brook, IL	72/7,097
1991	Russ Cochran	275	Greg Norman	277	Cog Hill G&CC (Dubsdread), Lemont, IL	72/7,040
1992	Ben Crenshaw	276	Greg Norman	277	Cog Hill G&CC (Dubsdread), Lemont, IL	72/7,040
SPRINT WESTERN OPEN						
1993	Nick Price	269	Greg Norman	274	Cog Hill G&CC (Dubsdread), Lemont, IL	72/7,040
MOTOROLA WESTERN OPEN						
1994	Nick Price	277	Greg Kraft	278	Cog Hill G&CC (Dubsdread), Lemont, IL	72/7,040
1995	Billy Mayfair	279	Jay Haas Justin Leonard Jeff Maggert	280	Cog Hill G&CC (Dubsdread), Lemont, IL	72/7,040
1996	Steve Stricker	270	Billy Andrade Jay Don Blake	278	Cog Hill G&CC (Dubsdread), Lemont, IL	72/7,073
1997	Tiger Woods	275	Frank Nobilo	278	Cog Hill G&CC (Dubsdread), Lemont, IL	72/7,073
1998	Joe Durant	271	Vijay Singh	273	Cog Hill G&CC (Dubsdread), Lemont, IL	72/7,073
1999	Tiger Woods	273	Mike Weir	276	Cog Hill G&CC (Dubsdread), Lemont, IL	72/7,073
ADVIL WESTERN OPEN						
2000	Robert Allenby*	274	Nick Price	274	Cog Hill G&CC (Dubsdread), Lemont, IL	72/7,073
2001	Scott Hoch	267	Davis Love III	268	Cog Hill G&CC (Dubsdread), Lemont, IL	72/7,073
2002	Jerry Kelly	269	Davis Love III	271	Cog Hill G&CC (Dubsdread), Lemont, IL	72/7,224
100TH WESTERN OPEN						
2003	Tiger Woods	267	Rich Beem	272	Cog Hill G&CC (Dubsdread), Lemont, IL	72/7,320
CIALIS WESTERN OPEN						
2004	Stephen Ames	274	Steve Lowery	276	Cog Hill G&CC (Dubsdread), Lemont, IL	72/7,326

*KEY: * = Playoff ~ = Weather-shortened # = Amateur*

*** Rain forced play to be held on nine holes of Butler National and nine holes at adjacent Oak Brook Village course.*

2004 John Deere Classic [28th of 48 official events]

JOHN DEERE CLASSIC

HENSBY

Winner: MARK HENSBY #
68-65-69-66 268 (-16) $684,000

Tournament Players Club at Deere Run

Silvis, IL

July 8-11, 2004

Purse: $3,800,000
Par: 35-36—71
Yards: 7,193

LEADERS: First Round—Jose Coceres posted a 9-under-par 62 to lead Vaughn Taylor by one stroke. Greg Chalmers and Daniel Chopra were two behind. **Second Round**—Coceres moved to 12-under-par 130 to lead Chalmers by one, Taylor by two and Mark Hensby by three. **Third Round**—Coceres at 15-under-par 198 led Chalmers by two and seven players by four.

CUT: 76 players at 2-under-par 140 from a field of 156 professionals.

PRO-AM: $10,000. Notah Begay III, 53, $2,000.

WEATHER: Thursday, mostly sunny with a high of 78 degrees. Friday, play was suspended at 9:34 a.m. and resumed at 12:30 p.m. Play for the day was suspended at 6:16 p.m. with 78 players yet to complete the second round. Play of the second round was delayed until 8:30 a.m. due to fog. The third round tee times ran from noon – 1:48 p.m. off Nos. 1 and 10 on Saturday. Partly sunny on Saturday with a high of 84. On Sunday, the start of the final round was delayed one hour, 15 minutes due to fog. Partly cloudy with a high of 80. Play was suspended at 3:47 p.m. on the first hole of the sudden-death playoff. Play resumed at 4:57.

Check out the 2005 John Deere Classic, July 7-10 on USA/ABC

ORDER OF FINISH

 # Won playoff with a par-3 on second hole of sudden-death

Mark Hensby #	1	68-65-69-66	268	$684,000.00
John E. Morgan	2	66-69-68-65	268	410,400.00
Jose Coceres	3	62-68-68-71	269	258,400.00
Greg Chalmers	T4	64-67-69-70	270	149,625.00
Joel Kribel	T4	70-65-70-65	270	149,625.00
Vijay Singh	T4	69-67-67-67	270	149,625.00
Steve Stricker	T4	71-67-64-68	270	149,625.00
Stewart Cink	T8	70-65-67-69	271	110,200.00
John Rollins	T8	66-69-69-67	271	110,200.00
Jeff Sluman	T8	69-68-66-68	271	110,200.00
Jeff Brehaut	T11	65-70-68-69	272	87,400.00
Jay Haas	T11	67-68-67-70	272	87,400.00
Scott Hoch	T11	68-68-68-68	272	87,400.00
Jason Bohn	T14	67-71-68-67	273	62,700.00
Robert Gamez	T14	67-68-67-71	273	62,700.00
Scott McCarron	T14	70-69-65-69	273	62,700.00
Carl Paulson	T14	68-72-67-66	273	62,700.00
Patrick Sheehan	T14	69-66-69-69	273	62,700.00
Vaughn Taylor	T14	63-69-70-71	273	62,700.00
Zach Johnson	T20	70-69-65-70	274	44,270.00
Len Mattiace	T20	68-68-69-69	274	44,270.00
Jim McGovern	T20	67-69-68-70	274	44,270.00
Casey Wittenberg (S)	T20	68-71-66-69	274	44,270.00
Olin Browne	T24	68-71-68-68	275	33,440.00
Glen Day	T24	70-68-70-67	275	$33,440.00
Joe Durant	T24	66-69-67-73	275	33,440.00
Hank Kuehne	T27	69-68-68-71	276	26,980.00
J.L. Lewis	T27	67-73-68-68	276	26,980.00
Shigeki Maruyama	T27	70-70-69-67	276	26,980.00
David Morland IV	T27	71-69-66-70	276	26,980.00
Tom Pernice, Jr.	T27	68-68-67-73	276	26,980.00
Joel Edwards	T32	71-68-70-68	277	20,574.29
Lucas Glover	T32	68-67-72-70	277	20,574.29
Kevin Sutherland	T32	67-69-73-68	277	20,574.29
Stan Utley	T32	70-69-67-71	277	20,574.29
Aaron Barber	T32	66-70-76-65	277	20,574.28
Ben Crane	T32	69-71-70-67	277	20,574.28
Chris DiMarco	T32	72-66-72-67	277	20,574.28
Bart Bryant	T39	70-68-69-71	278	14,820.00
Daniel Chopra	T39	64-72-73-69	278	14,820.00
Harrison Frazar	T39	69-71-70-68	278	14,820.00
Neal Lancaster	T39	70-70-69-69	278	14,820.00
John Senden	T39	70-69-72-67	278	14,820.00
Wes Short, Jr.	T39	68-71-71-68	278	14,820.00
Mark Wilson	T39	68-68-70-72	278	14,820.00
Woody Austin	T46	69-70-68-72	279	9,880.00
Briny Baird	T46	69-68-68-74	279	9,880.00
Kris Cox	T46	69-71-68-71	279	9,880.00
Jason Dufner	T46	68-72-71-68	279	9,880.00
Todd Fischer	T46	69-70-69-71	279	9,880.00
Mike Heinen	T46	70-66-71-72	279	9,880.00
Nick Price	T46	68-70-69-72	279	$9,880.00
Ted Purdy	T46	65-71-73-70	279	9,880.00
Hidemichi Tanaka	T46	72-67-70-70	279	9,880.00
Carlos Franco	T55	70-67-73-70	280	8,626.00
Donnie Hammond	T55	71-67-72-70	280	8,626.00
J.P. Hayes	T55	69-68-68-75	280	8,626.00
Mike Springer	T55	70-70-71-69	280	8,626.00
Todd Hamilton	T59	67-70-71-73	281	8,284.00
Chris Smith	T59	67-73-73-68	281	8,284.00
Kirk Triplett	T59	68-72-68-73	281	8,284.00
Camilo Villegas (S)	T59	71-68-68-74	281	8,284.00
Willie Wood	T59	70-68-74-69	281	8,284.00
Jonathan Byrd	T64	67-72-70-73	282	8,018.00
Richard S. Johnson	T64	68-68-72-74	282	8,018.00
Pat Perez	66	70-69-75-69	283	7,904.00
David Edwards	T67	69-70-73-72	284	7,752.00
Kevin Na	T67	70-70-71-73	284	7,752.00
Roland Thatcher	T67	70-68-73-73	284	7,752.00
D.J. Brigman	T70	69-71-74-71	285	7,486.00
J.J. Henry	T70	68-72-74-71	285	7,486.00
Tripp Isenhour	T70	70-70-71-74	285	7,486.00
Roger Tambellini	T70	68-70-74-73	285	7,486.00
Matt Kuchar	T74	69-70-72-75	286	7,258.00
Patrick Moore	T74	72-68-68-78	286	7,258.00

(S) = Sponsor Exemption; (T) = Tie

The following players did not finish (C=cut; W=withdrew)

C—141-Tommy Armour III, Jay Don Blake, Guy Boros, Mathias Gronberg, Bill Haas, Hunter Mahan, Steve Pate, Gene Sauers, Esteban Toledo, Garrett Willis, Dean Wilson. **142-**Notah Begay III, Michael Clark II, Keith Clearwater, Trevor Dodds, Jim Gallagher, Jr., Brian Gay, Brent Geiberger, Kelly Gibson, Brian Kortan, Brad Lardon, Blaine McCallister, Spike McRoy, Hirofumi Miyase, Geoff Ogilvy, Jay Williamson. **143-**Rich Barcelo, Craig Barlow, Pat Bates, Michael Bradley, Bill Glasson, Joe Ogilvie, Dan Pohl, Dicky Pride, Loren Roberts, Andre Stolz, Tommy Tolles, Ted Tryba, Omar Uresti. **144-**Joe Affrunti, Jim Carter, Robert Damron, D.A. Points. **145-**Jay Delsing, Ken Duke, Robin Freeman, David Frost, Hiroyuki Fujita, Mike Grob, Rocco Mediate, Grant Waite. **146-**Paul Azinger, Kent Jones, Deane Pappas. **147-**Bob Burns, Russ Cochran, David Gossett, Kevin Muncrief, Scott Simpson. **148-**John Bermel, Brian Henninger, Brenden Pappas, Heath Slocum. **149-**Brock Mackenzie, Ryan Palmer, David Sutherland. **150-**Chris Couch, Jamie Rogers. **151-**Tom Carter. **152-**Bradley Heaven. **153-**Chris Winkel. **154-**Kevin Haefner. **155-**John Shawver. **W—79-**Dan Olsen. **77-**Ken Green. **76-**Mike Standly. **75-**Billy Mayfair, Gary March. **73-**Dan Forsman. **71-**Scott Hend. **214-**Jeff Maggert.

TOURNAMENT HISTORY

Year	Winner	Score	Runner-up	Score	Location	Par/Yards
QUAD CITIES OPEN						
1972	Deane Beman	279	Tom Watson	280	Crow Valley CC, Bettendorf, IA	71/6,501
1973	Sam Adams	268	Dwight Nevil	271	Crow Valley CC, Bettendorf, IA	71/6,501
			Kermit Zarley			
1974	Dave Stockton	271	Bruce Fleisher	272	Crow Valley CC, Bettendorf, IA	71/6,501
ED MCMAHON-JAYCEES QUAD CITY OPEN						
1975	Roger Maltbie	275	Dave Eichelberger	276	Oakwood CC, Coal Valley, IL	70/6,602
1976	John Lister	268	Fuzzy Zoeller	270	Oakwood CC, Coal Valley, IL	70/6,602
1977	Mike Morley	267	Bob Murphy	269	Oakwood CC, Coal Valley, IL	70/6,602
			Victor Regalado			
1978	Victor Regalado	269	Fred Marti	270	Oakwood CC, Coal Valley, IL	70/6,602
1979	D.A. Weibring	266	Calvin Peete	268	Oakwood CC, Coal Valley, IL	70/6,602
QUAD CITIES OPEN						
1980	Scott Hoch	266	Curtis Strange	269	Oakwood CC, Coal Valley, IL	70/6,602
1981	Dave Barr*	270	Woody Blackburn	270	Oakwood CC, Coal Valley, IL	70/6,602
			Frank Conner			
			Dan Halldorson			
			Victor Regalado			
MILLER HIGH-LIFE QUAD CITIES OPEN						
1982	Payne Stewart	268	Brad Bryant	270	Oakwood CC, Coal Valley, IL	70/6,602
			Pat McGowan			
1983	Danny Edwards*	266	Morris Hatalsky	266	Oakwood CC, Coal Valley, IL	70/6,602
1984	Scott Hoch	266	George Archer	271	Oakwood CC, Coal Valley, IL	70/6,602
			Vance Heafner			
			Dave Stockton			
LITE QUAD CITIES OPEN						
1985	Dan Forsman	267	Bob Tway	268	Oakwood CC, Coal Valley, IL	70/6,602
HARDEE'S GOLF CLASSIC						
1986	Mark Wiebe	268	Curt Byrum	269	Oakwood CC, Coal Valley, IL	70/6,602

John Deere Classic

JOHN DEERE CLASSIC

NOTES

Australian ***Mark Hensby*** *became the sixth international champion of the John Deere Classic, joining New Zealand's* ***John Lister*** *(1976), Mexico's* ***Victor Regalado*** *(1978), Canada's* ***Dave Barr*** *(1981), South Africa's* ***David Frost*** *(1992-93) and Fiji's* ***Vijay Singh*** *(2003).*

Mark Hensby *became the 16th player to collect his first PGA TOUR win at the John Deere Classic, joining* ***Sam Adams*** *(1973),* ***Roger Maltbie*** *(1975),* ***John Lister*** *(1976),* ***Mike Morley*** *(1977),* ***D.A. Weibring*** *(1979),* ***Scott Hoch*** *(1980),* ***Dave Barr*** *(1981),* ***Payne Stewart*** *(1982),* ***Dan Forsman*** *(1985),* ***Blaine McCallister*** *(1988),* ***Curt Byrum*** *(1989),* ***David Toms*** *(1997),* ***J.L. Lewis*** *(1999),* ***Michael Clark II*** *(2000) and* ***David Gossett*** *(2001).*

2004 John Deere Classic champion ***Mark Hensby*** *collected his second consecutive top-10, having finished T3 the previous week at the Cialis Western Open. It marked the first time he logged back-to-back top-10s in his career on the PGA TOUR.*

The round of 8-under-par 62 in the first round of the 2004 John Deere Classic by ***Jose Coceres*** *was one off the course record of 10-under-par 61 by* ***J.P. Hayes*** *in 2002. Hayes' 61 came in the second round en route to his second TOUR victory. Coceres was on track through 54 holes to become the first wire-to-wire winner on the PGA TOUR since Davis Love III did so at the 2003 INTERNATIONAL, but a double-bogey on the eighth hole in the final round dropped him from the lead. He finished solo third, his best finish since winning the 2002 National Car Rental Golf Classic at WALT DISNEY WORLD Resort.*

Vaughn Taylor *posted two eagles in the first round, on No. 2 and No. 17, both par-5s en route to his career low of 8-under-par 63. His previous low was 65 in the second round at the 2004 FedEx St. Jude Classic where he finished T5.*

TOURNAMENT HISTORY

Year	Winner	Score	Runner-up	Score	Location	Par/Yards
1987	Kenny Knox	265	Gil Morgan	266	Oakwood CC, Coal Valley, IL	70/6,606
1988	Blaine McCallister	261	Dan Forsman	264	Oakwood CC, Coal Valley, IL	70/6,606
1989	Curt Byrum	268	Bill Britton	269	Oakwood CC, Coal Valley, IL	70/6,606
			Brian Tennyson			
1990	Joey Sindelar*	268	Willie Wood	268	Oakwood CC, Coal Valley, IL	70/6,606
1991	D.A. Weibring	267	Paul Azinger	268	Oakwood CC, Coal Valley, IL	70/6,796
			Peter Jacobsen			
1992	David Frost	266	Tom Lehman	269	Oakwood CC, Coal Valley, IL	70/6,796
			Loren Roberts			
1993	David Frost	259	Payne Stewart	266	Oakwood CC, Coal Valley, IL	70/6,796
			D.A. Weibring			
1994	Mark McCumber	265	Kenny Perry	266	Oakwood CC, Coal Valley, IL	70/6,796
QUAD CITY CLASSIC						
1995	D.A. Weibring~	197	Jonathan Kaye	198	Oakwood CC, Coal Valley, IL	70/6,796
1996	Ed Fiori	268	Andrew Magee	270	Oakwood CC, Coal Valley, IL	70/6,762
1997	David Toms	265	Brandel Chamblee	268	Oakwood CC, Coal Valley, IL	70/6,762
			Robert Gamez			
			Jimmy Johnston			
1998	Steve Jones	263	Scott Gump	264	Oakwood CC, Coal Valley, IL	70/6,762
JOHN DEERE CLASSIC						
1999	J.L. Lewis*	261	Mike Brisky	261	Oakwood CC, Coal Valley, IL	70/6,762
2000	Michael Clark II*	265	Kirk Triplett	265	TPC at Deere Run, Silvis, IL	71/7,183
2001	David Gossett	265	Briny Baird	266	TPC at Deere Run, Silvis, IL	71/7,183
2002	J.P. Hayes	262	Robert Gamez	266	TPC at Deere Run, Silvis, IL	71/7,183
2003	Vijay Singh	268	Chris Riley	272	TPC at Deere Run, Silvis, IL	71/7,193
			Jonathan Byrd			
			J.L. Lewis			
2004	Mark Hensby*	268	John E. Morgan	268	TPC at Deere Run, Silvis, IL	71/7,193

*KEY: * = Playoff ~ = Weather-shortened*

Tournament Record:
259, David Frost, 1993 (Oakwood CC)
Current Course Record:
61, J.P. Hayes, 2002
Other Course Record:
61, Mike Smith, 1987 (Oakwood CC)

Fans look on from behind the green at the TPC at Deere Run.

2004 British Open Championship

[29th of 48 official events]

THE OPEN CHAMPIONSHIP

HAMILTON

Winner: TODD HAMILTON #
71-67-67-69 274 (-10) $1,348,272

Royal Troon Golf Club

Troon, Ayrshire, Scotland

July 15-18, 2004

Purse: $7,490,400
Par: 36-35—71
Yards: 7,175

LEADERS: First Round—Paul Casey and Thomas Levet sat at 5-under 66, one ahead of Michael Campbell. Nine players were two back.
Second Round—Skip Kendall moved to 7-under 135 to hold a one stroke lead over Levet. Barry Lane and K.J. Choi trailed by two.
Third Round—Todd Hamilton sat at 8-under 205, one stroke ahead of Ernie Els and two ahead of Phil Mickelson and Retief Goosen.

CUT: 73 players at 3-over-par 145 from a field of 151 professionals and five amateurs.

WEATHER: On Thursday, mostly cloudy with temperatures in the high 50s/low 60s and winds out of the SW 5-12 mph. A mix of sun and clouds on Friday with temperatures making it into the low 60s and winds out of SW 8-18 mph. A mix of sun and clouds with light rain in the morning and a couple of quick showers in the afternoon on Saturday. Temperatures reaching the mid-60s and winds out of the SW 8-15 mph. Sunday, variably cloudy, breezy and cool with temperatures into the low 60s.

Check out the 2005 British Open, July 14-17 on TNT/ABC

ORDER OF FINISH

 # Won four-hole playoff with four pars (Total: Hamilton 15, Els 16)

Todd Hamilton #	1	71-67-67-69	274	$1,348,272.00
Ernie Els	2	69-69-68-68	274	805,218.00
Phil Mickelson	3	73-66-68-68	275	514,965.00
Lee Westwood	4	72-71-68-67	278	393,246.00
Thomas Levet	T5	66-70-71-72	279	298,679.70
Davis Love III	T5	72-69-71-67	279	298,679.70
Retief Goosen	T7	69-70-68-73	280	220,030.50
Scott Verplank	T7	69-70-70-71	280	220,030.50
Mike Weir	T9	71-68-71-71	281	167,597.70
Tiger Woods	T9	70-71-68-72	281	167,597.70
Mark Calcavecchia	T11	72-73-69-68	282	129,833.59
Darren Clarke	T11	69-72-73-68	282	129,833.59
Skip Kendall	T11	69-66-75-72	282	129,833.59
Stewart Cink	T14	72-71-71-69	283	105,801.90
Barry Lane	T14	69-68-71-75	283	105,801.90
K.J. Choi	T16	68-69-74-73	284	88,012.20
Joakim Haeggman	T16	69-73-72-70	284	88,012.20
Justin Leonard	T16	70-72-71-71	284	88,012.20
Kenny Perry	T16	69-70-73-72	284	88,012.20
Michael Campbell	T20	67-71-74-73	285	71,346.06
Paul Casey	T20	66-77-70-72	285	71,346.06
Bob Estes	T20	73-72-69-71	285	71,346.06
Gary Evans	T20	68-73-73-71	285	71,346.06
Vijay Singh	T20	68-70-76-71	285	$71,346.06
Colin Montgomerie	T25	69-69-72-76	286	60,391.35
Ian Poulter	T25	71-72-71-72	286	60,391.35
Takashi Kamiyama	T27	70-73-71-73	287	54,305.40
Rod Pampling	T27	72-68-74-73	287	54,305.40
Jyoti Randhawa	T27	73-72-70-72	287	54,305.40
Keiichiro Fukabori	T30	73-71-70-74	288	45,878.70
Shigeki Maruyama	T30	71-72-74-71	288	45,878.70
Mark O'Meara	T30	71-74-68-75	288	45,878.70
Nick Price	T30	71-71-69-77	288	45,878.70
David Toms	T30	71-71-74-72	288	45,878.70
Bo Van Pelt	T30	72-71-71-74	288	45,878.70
Stuart Appleby	T36	71-70-73-75	289	35,111.25
Kim Felton	T36	73-67-72-77	289	35,111.25
Tetsuji Hiratsuka	T36	70-74-70-75	289	35,111.25
Steve Lowery	T36	69-73-75-72	289	35,111.25
Hunter Mahan	T36	74-69-71-75	289	35,111.25
Tjaart van der Walt	T36	70-73-72-74	289	35,111.25
Kenneth Ferrie	T42	68-74-73-75	290	27,714.48
Charles Howell III	T42	75-70-72-73	290	27,714.48
Trevor Immelman	T42	69-74-71-76	290	27,714.48
Andy Oldcorn	T42	73-70-71-76	290	27,714.48
Adam Scott	T42	73-68-74-75	290	27,714.48
Paul Bradshaw	T47	75-67-72-77	291	22,404.33
Alastair Forsyth	T47	68-74-79-70	291	22,404.33
Mathias Gronberg	T47	70-74-73-74	291	22,404.33
Miguel A. Jimenez	T47	74-71-71-75	291	$22,404.33
Jerry Kelly	T47	75-70-73-73	291	22,404.33
Shaun Micheel	T47	70-72-70-79	291	22,404.33
Sean Whiffin	T47	73-72-71-75	291	22,404.33
Steve Flesch	T54	75-70-70-77	292	19,755.93
Ignacio Garrido	T54	71-74-72-75	292	19,755.93
Raphael Jacquelin	T54	72-72-73-75	292	19,755.93
James Kingston	T57	73-72-74-74	293	19,100.52
Paul McGinley	T57	69-76-75-73	293	19,100.52
Carl Pettersson	T57	68-77-74-74	293	19,100.52
Paul Broadhurst	T60	71-74-72-77	294	18,538.74
Gary Emerson	T60	70-71-76-77	294	18,538.74
Brad Faxon	T60	74-68-73-79	294	18,538.74
Chris DiMarco	T63	71-71-78-76	296	18,070.59
Mark B. Foster	T63	71-72-76-77	296	18,070.59
Stuart Wilson	T63	68-75-77-76	296	Amateur
Marten Olander	T66	68-74-78-77	297	17,696.07
Rory Sabbatini	T66	71-72-73-81	297	17,696.07
Martin Erlandsson	T68	73-70-77-78	298	17,321.55
Paul Wesselingh	T68	73-72-76-77	298	17,321.55
Bob Tway	70	76-68-73-82	299	17,040.66
Rich Beem	T71	69-73-77-81	300	16,759.77
Christian Cevaer	T71	70-74-74-82	300	16,759.77
Sandy Lyle	73	70-73-81-79	303	16,478.88

(T) = Tie

The following players did not finish (C=cut, A-amateur)

C—146-Scott Barr, Chad Campbell, Tim Clark, Luke Donald, Klas Eriksson, Jim Furyk, Mathew Goggin, Jay Haas, S.K. Ho, Fredrik Jacobson, Euan Little. **147-**Robert Allenby, Lloyd Campbell (A), Jonathan Cheetham, Glen Day, Padraig Harrington, Barry Hume, Brendan Jones, Stephen Leaney, Peter Lonard, Grant Muller, Peter O'Malley, Craig Parry, Jean-Francois Remesy, Chris Riley, Paul Sheehan, Sven Struver, Steven Tiley (A). **148-**Arjun Atwal, John Daly, Nick Flanagan (A), Sergio Garcia, Tim Herron, John Huston, Maarten Lafeber, Phillip Price, Daniel Sugrue, Ben Willman. **149-**Stephen Ames, Aaron Baddeley, Cameron Beckman, Ben Curtis, Brian Davis, Zach Johnson, Spike McRoy, Greg Norman, Miles Tunnicliff. **150-**Richard Green, Anders Hansen, Matthew Hazelden, Hidemasa Hoshino, Jonathan Kaye, Simon Wakefield. **151-**Simon Dyson, Darren Fichardt, Peter Hedblom, Tom Lehman, Hennie Otto, Craig Perks. **152-**Scott Drummond, Graeme McDowell, Brian McElhinney (A), Eduardo Romero. **153-**Thomas Bjorn, Nick Faldo, Jimmy Green, David Griffiths. **154-**Dinesh Chand, Nicolas Colsaerts, David Howell, Frank Lickliter II. **155-**Paul Lawrie. **156-**Louis Oosthuizen, Andrew Willey. **157-**Adam Le Vesconte, Ian Spencer. **158-**Andrew Buckle. **159-**Yoshinobu Tsukada. **160-**Tom Weiskopf. **161-**Brett Taylor. **163-**Neil Evans. **164-**Lewis Atkinson, Anthony Millar.

TOURNAMENT HISTORY

Year	Winner	Score	Runner-up	Score	Location
BRITISH OPEN CHAMPIONSHIP					
1860	Willie Park	174	Tom Morris, Sr.	176	Prestwick, Scotland
	(The first Open was open only to professional golfers)				
1861	Tom Morris, Sr.,	163	Willie Park	167	Prestwick, Scotland
	(The second Open was open to amateurs also)				
1862	Tom Morris, Sr.	163	Willie Park	176	Prestwick, Scotland
1863	Willie Park	168	Tom Morris, Sr.	170	Prestwick, Scotland
1864	Tom Morris, Sr.	167	Andrew Strath	169	Prestwick, Scotland
1865	Andrew Strath	162	Willie Park	164	Prestwick, Scotland
1866	Willie Park	169	David Park	171	Prestwick, Scotland
1867	Tom Morris, Sr.	170	Willie Park	172	Prestwick, Scotland
1868	Tom Morris, Jr.	157	Robert Andrew	159	Prestwick, Scotland
1869	Tom Morris, Jr.	154	Tom Morris, Sr.	157	Prestwick, Scotland
1870	Tom Morris, Jr.	149	David Strath Bob Kirk	161	Prestwick, Scotland
1871	No Tournament**				
1872	Tom Morris, Jr.	166	David Strath	169	Prestwick, Scotland
1873	Tom Kidd	179	Jamie Anderson	180	St. Andrews, Scotland
1874	Mungo Park	159	Tom Morris, Jr.	161	Musselburgh, Scotland
1875	Willie Park	166	Bob Martin	168	Prestwick, Scotland
1876	Bob Martin	176	David Strath***	176	St. Andrews, Scotland
1877	Jamie Anderson	160	Robert Pringle	162	Musselburgh, Scotland
1878	Jamie Anderson	157	Bob Kirk	159	Prestwick, Scotland
1879	Jamie Anderson	169	Andrew Kirkaldy James Allan	172	St. Andrews, Scotland
1880	Robert Ferguson	162	Peter Paxton	167	Musselburgh, Scotland
1881	Robert Ferguson	170	Jamie Anderson	173	Prestwick, Scotland
1882	Robert Ferguson	171	Willie Fernie	174	St. Andrews, Scotland
1883	Willie Fernie*	159	Robert Ferguson	159	Musselburgh, Scotland
1884	Jack Simpson	160	Douglas Rolland Willie Fernie	164	Prestwick, Scotland

*KEY: * = Playoff ** = Canceled because Tom Morris, Jr. retired championship belt*

British Open Championship

THE OPEN CHAMPIONSHIP

NOTES

The playoff between ***Todd Hamilton*** *and* ***Ernie Els*** *was the 17th in Open Championship history. It was Hamilton's first on the PGA TOUR. He participated in five playoffs on the Japan Golf Tour and won only once. Els moved to 4-3 lifetime on the PGA TOUR in playoffs.*

BEN CURTIS

Todd Hamilton *became the second consecutive rookie on the PGA TOUR to win the British Open following in the footsteps of* ***Ben Curtis****.*

Todd Hamilton *became the seventh first-time winner of a major championship in the last eight championships and first since* ***Phil Mickelson*** *at the 2004 Masters Tournament.*

Todd Hamilton *is the eighth player to win his first major championship at the British Open in the last 20 years. The others:* ***Ben Curtis*** *(2003),* ***David Duval*** *(2001),* ***Paul Lawrie*** *(1999),* ***Justin Leonard*** *(1997),* ***Tom Lehman*** *(1996),* ***Greg Norman*** *(1986) and* ***Sandy Lyle*** *(1985).*

Coming into the 2004 British Open, ***Todd Hamilton****'s previous best finish at The British Open was a T44 in 1996 and in a major championship, T29 at the 2003 PGA Championship.*

Todd Hamilton *began the year World No. 81, but dropped to No. 96 prior to his victory at The Honda Classic and moved to 38th after the win. He came into The British Open ranked World No. 56 and improved 40 spots to No. 16, his highest career ranking.*

Todd Hamilton *became the sixth multiple winner on the PGA TOUR in 2004 and first player to win twice in his rookie season since Jose Coceres in 2001. He was just the 10th rookie to win twice on the PGA TOUR in the same season since 1970. The others:* ***Jose Coceres*** *(2001),* ***Carlos Franco*** *and* ***Notah Begay III*** *(1999),* ***Tiger Woods*** *(1996),* ***Robert Gamez*** *(1990),* ***Keith Clearwater*** *(1987),* ***John Fought*** *(1979),* ***Jerry Pate*** *(1976) and* ***Roger Maltbie*** *(1975).*

TOURNAMENT HISTORY

Year	Winner	Score	Runner-up	Score	Location
1885	Bob Martin	171	Archie Simpson	172	St. Andrews, Scotland
1886	David Brown	157	Willie Campbell	159	Musselburgh, Scotland
1887	Willie Park, Jr.	161	Bob Martin	162	Prestwick, Scotland
1888	Jack Burns	171	Ben Sayers	172	St. Andrews, Scotland
			David Anderson		
1889	Willie Park, Jr.*	155	Andrew Kirkaldy	155	Musselburgh, Scotland
1890	John Ball, Jr.	164	Willie Fernie	167	Prestwick, Scotland
			Archie Simpson		
1891	Hugh Kirkaldy	166	Andrew Kirkaldy	168	St. Andrews, Scotland
			Willie Fernie		
	(Competition extended from 36 to 72 holes after 1891)				
1892	Harold H. Hilton	305	John Ball, Jr.	308	Muirfield, Scotland
			Hugh Kirkaldy		
			Alexander Herd		
1893	William Auchterlonie	322	John E. Laidlay	324	Prestwick, Scotland
1894	John H. Taylor	326	Douglas Rolland	331	Royal St. George's, England
1895	John H. Taylor	322	Alexander Herd	326	St. Andrews, Scotland
1896	Harry Vardon*	316	John H. Taylor	316	Muirfield, Scotland
1897	Harold H. Hilton	314	James Braid	315	Hoylake, England
1898	Harry Vardon	307	Willie Park, Jr.	308	Prestwick, Scotland
1899	Harry Vardon	310	Jack White	315	Royal St. George's, England
1900	John H. Taylor	309	Harry Vardon	317	St Andrews, Scotland
1901	James Braid	309	Harry Vardon	312	Muirfield, Scotland
1902	Alexander Herd	307	Harry Vardon	308	Hoylake, England
			James Braid		
1903	Harry Vardon	300	Tom Vardon	306	Prestwick, Scotland
1904	Jack White	296	John H. Taylor	297	Royal St. George's, England
			James Braid		
1905	James Braid	318	John H. Taylor	323	St. Andrews, Scotland
			Rowland Jones		
1906	James Braid	300	John H. Taylor	304	Muirfield, Scotland
1907	Arnaud Massy	312	John H. Taylor	314	Hoylake, England
1908	James Braid	291	Tom Ball	299	Prestwick, Scotland
1909	John H. Taylor	295	James Braid	301	Cinque Ports, England
			Tom Ball		
1910	James Braid	299	Alexander Herd	303	St. Andrews, Scotland
1911	Harry Vardon*	303	Arnaud Massy	303	Royal St. George's, England
1912	Edward (Ted) Ray	295	Harry Vardon	299	Muirfield, Scotland
1913	John H. Taylor	304	Edward (Ted) Ray	312	Hoylake, England
1914	Harry Vardon	306	John H. Taylor	309	Prestwick, Scotland
1915	No Tournament+				
1916	No Tournament+				
1917	No Tournament+				
1918	No Tournament+				
1919	No Tournament+				
1920	George Duncan	303	Alexander Herd	305	Cinque Ports, England
1921	Jock Hutchison*	296	Roger Wethered	296	St. Andrews, Scotland
1922	Walter Hagen	300	George Duncan	301	Royal St. George's, England
			James M. Barnes		
1923	Arthur G. Havers	295	Walter Hagen	296	Royal Troon, Scotland
1924	Walter Hagen	301	Ernest Whitcombe	302	Hoylake, England
1925	James M. Barnes	300	Archie Compston	301	Prestwick, Scotland
			Edward (Ted) Ray		
1926	Robert T. Jones, Jr.	291	Al Watrous	293	Royal Lytham & St. Annes, England
1927	Robert T. Jones, Jr.	285	Aubrey Boomer	291	St. Andrews, Scotland
			Fred Robson		
1928	Walter Hagen	292	Gene Sarazen	294	Royal St. George's, England
1929	Walter Hagen	292	Johnny Farrell	298	Muirfield, Scotland
1930	Robert T. Jones, Jr.	291	Macdonald Smith	293	Hoylake, England
			Leo Diegel		
1931	Tommy D. Armour	296	Jose Jurado	297	Carnoustie, Scotland
1932	Gene Sarazen	283	Macdonald Smith	288	Prince's, England
1933	Denny Shute*	292	Craig Wood	292	St. Andrews, Scotland
1934	Henry Cotton	283	Sidney F. Brews	288	Royal St. George's, England
1935	Alfred Perry	283	Alfred Padgham	287	Muirfield, Scotland
1936	Alfred Padgham	287	James Adams	288	Hoylake, England
1937	Henry Cotton	290	R. A. Whitcombe	292	Carnoustie, Scotland
1938	R. A. Whitcombe	295	James Adams	297	Royal St. George's, England
1939	Richard Burton	290	Johnny Bulla	292	St. Andrews, Scotland
1940	No Tournament++				
1941	No Tournament++				
1942	No Tournament++				
1943	No Tournament++				
1944	No Tournament++				
1945	No Tournament++				
1946	Sam Snead	290	Bobby Locke	294	St. Andrews, Scotland
			Johnny Bulla		
1947	Fred Daly	293	R. W. Horne	294	Hoylake, England
			Frank Stranahan		

*KEY: * = Playoff ** = Canceled because Tom Morris, Jr. retired championship belt + = World War I ++ = World War II*

NOTES

With an exchange rate of $1.8726 in the United States, the 4,000,000 sterling purse in the United Kingdom translates into a $7,490,400 purse in the United States. As such, ***Todd Hamilton*** *received 720,000 sterling or $1,348,272 towards the PGA TOUR money list. The purse and winner's share become the second richest in TOUR history behind THE PLAYERS Championship earlier this year, which had a purse of $8,000,000 and a winner's share of $1,440,000.*

Todd Hamilton*'s win broke a streak of six consecutive international winners on the PGA TOUR.*

The win gave ***Todd Hamilton*** *his second career top-10 finish on the PGA TOUR in 33 starts and both of them were victories.*

PHIL MICKELSON

Phil Mickelson *finished first, second and third in 2004's first three major championships. He and* ***Ernie Els*** *were the only players to post top-10s in all four majors in 2004. Els finished as the runner-up for the second time in a major championship last season. He finished one stroke behind* ***Phil Mickelson*** *at the Masters Tournament. He also finished T9 at the U.S. Open. Mickelson finished T6 at the PGA and Els T4.*

Players from the United States have won eight of the last 10 British Opens.

Stuart Wilson *was the only amateur to make the cut at the 2004 British Open. Wilson finished the tournament at 12-over par in a tie for 63rd.*

Retief Goosen *recorded his third straight top-10 at the British Open with his T7 finish. Goosen finished T10 and T8 the past two seasons. He is the only player to finish inside the top 10 over the last three seasons.*

Along with being just the sixth player to record four rounds in the 60s at the British Open, Els became the 23rd player to do so in a major. It has happened six times at the British Open, 15 times at the PGA Championship, two times at the U.S. Open and none at the Masters Tournament.

TOURNAMENT HISTORY

Year	Winner	Score	Runner-up	Score	Location
1948	Henry Cotton	284	Fred Daly	289	Muirfield, Scotland
1949	Bobby Locke*	283	Harry Bradshaw	283	Royal St. George's, England
1950	Bobby Locke	279	Roberto De Vicenzo	281	Royal Troon, Scotland
1951	Max Faulkner	285	Antonio Cerda	287	Portrush, Ireland
1952	Bobby Locke	287	Peter Thomson	288	Royal Lytham & St. Annes, England
1953	Ben Hogan	282	Frank Stranahan	286	Carnoustie, Scotland
			Dai Rees		
			Peter Thomson		
			Antonio Cerda		
1954	Peter Thomson	283	Sidney S. Scott	284	Royal Birkdale, England
			Dai Rees		
			Bobby Locke		
1955	Peter Thomson	281	John Fallon	283	St. Andrews, Scotland
1956	Peter Thomson	286	Flory Van Donck	289	Hoylake, England
1957	Bobby Locke	279	Peter Thomson	282	St Andrews, Scotland
1958	Peter Thomson*	278	Dave Thomas	278	Royal Lytham & St. Annes, England
1959	Gary Player	284	Fred Bullock	286	Muirfield, Scotland
			Flory Van Donck		
1960	Kel Nagle	278	Arnold Palmer	279	St. Andrews, Scotland
1961	Arnold Palmer	284	Dai Rees	285	Royal Birkdale, England
1962	Arnold Palmer	276	Kel Nagle	282	Royal Troon, Scotland
1963	Bob Charles*	277	Phil Rodgers	277	Royal Lytham & St. Annes, England
1964	Tony Lema	279	Jack Nicklaus	284	St. Andrews, Scotland
1965	Peter Thomson	285	Brian Huggett	287	Southport, England
			Christy O'Connor		
1966	Jack Nicklaus	282	Doug Sanders	283	Muirfield, Scotland
			Dave Thomas		
1967	Roberto De Vicenzo	278	Jack Nicklaus	280	Hoylake, England
1968	Gary Player	289	Jack Nicklaus	291	Carnoustie, Scotland
			Bob Charles		
1969	Tony Jacklin	280	Bob Charles	282	Royal Lytham & St. Annes, England
1970	Jack Nicklaus*	283	Doug Sanders	283	St. Andrews, Scotland
1971	Lee Trevino	278	Lu-Liang Huan	279	Royal Birkdale, England
1972	Lee Trevino	278	Jack Nicklaus	279	Muirfield, Scotland
1973	Tom Weiskopf	276	Johnny Miller	279	Royal Troon, Scotland
			Neil Coles		
1974	Gary Player	282	Peter Oosterhuis	286	Royal Lytham & St. Annes, England
1975	Tom Watson*	279	Jack Newton	279	Carnoustie, Scotland
1976	Johnny Miller	279	Jack Nicklaus	285	Royal Birkdale, England
			Seve Ballesteros		
1977	Tom Watson	268	Jack Nicklaus	269	Turnberry, Scotland
1978	Jack Nicklaus	281	Ben Crenshaw	283	St. Andrews, Scotland
			Simon Owen		
			Tom Kite		
			Raymond Floyd		
1979	Seve Ballesteros	283	Ben Crenshaw	286	Royal Lytham & St. Annes, England
			Jack Nicklaus		
1980	Tom Watson	271	Lee Trevino	275	Muirfield, Scotland
1981	Bill Rogers	276	Bernhard Langer	280	Royal St. George's, England
1982	Tom Watson	284	Nick Price	285	Royal Troon, Scotland
			Peter Oosterhuis		
1983	Tom Watson	275	Andy Bean	276	Royal Birkdale, England
			Hale Irwin		
1984	Seve Ballesteros	276	Tom Watson	278	St. Andrews, Scotland
			Bernhard Langer		
1985	Sandy Lyle	282	Payne Stewart	283	Royal St. George's, England
1986	Greg Norman	280	Gordon Brand	285	Turnberry, Scotland
1987	Nick Faldo	279	Paul Azinger	280	Muirfield, Scotland
			Rodger Davis		
1988	Seve Ballesteros	273	Nick Price	275	Royal Lytham & St. Annes, England
1989	Mark Calcavecchia*	275	Wayne Grady	275	Royal Troon, Scotland
			Greg Norman		
1990	Nick Faldo	270	Payne Stewart	275	St. Andrews, Scotland
			Mark McNulty		
1991	Ian Baker-Finch	272	Mike Harwood	274	Royal Birkdale, England
1992	Nick Faldo	272	John Cook	273	Muirfield, Scotland
1993	Greg Norman	267	Nick Faldo	269	Royal St. George's, England
1994	Nick Price	268	Jesper Parnevik	269	Turnberry, Scotland
1995	John Daly*	282	Costantino Rocca	282	St. Andrews, Scotland
1996	Tom Lehman	271	Ernie Els	273	Royal Lytham & St. Annes, England
			Mark McCumber		
1997	Justin Leonard	272	Darren Clarke	275	Royal Troon, Scotland
			Jesper Parnevik		
1998	Mark O'Meara*	280	Brian Watts	280	Royal Birkdale, England
1999	Paul Lawrie*	290	Justin Leonard	290	Carnoustie, Scotland
			Jean Van de Velde		
2000	Tiger Woods	269	Thomas Bjorn	277	St. Andrews, Scotland
			Ernie Els		
2001	David Duval	274	Niclas Fasth	277	Royal Lytham & St. Annes, England

*KEY: * = Playoff ** = Canceled because Tom Morris, Jr. retired championship belt + = World War I ++ = World War II*

British Open Championship

THE OPEN CHAMPIONSHIP

NOTES

***Phil Mickelson**'s bogey-free streak came to an end at 49 on Sunday. Mickelson bogeyed the par-4 13th hole to stop the longest streak of the week. He did not record a bogey during rounds two and three.*

*Those turning in career bests at the British Open: **Todd Hamilton** (1st/T44 in 1996), **Phil Mickelson** (3rd/T11 in 2000), **Scott Verplank** (T7/T15 in 1999), **Retief Goosen** (T7/T8 in 2002) and **Mike Weir** (T9/T28 in 2003).*

*Those turning in career bests in a major championship: **Todd Hamilton** (1st/T29 2003 PGA Championship) and **Scott Verplank**, who matched his best with his T7. He previously finished T7 at the 2001 PGA Championship.*

For the week, No. 11 finished as the most difficult with a scoring average of 4.413 or .413-over par. That made it the fifth most difficult hole on the PGA TOUR last season. The par-4 18th hole at Doral for the Ford Championship at Doral played to an average of 4.480, the hardest on TOUR in 2004.

***Ben Curtis** became the first British Open defending champion to miss the cut since 1999 winner **Paul Lawrie** missed in 2000. In fact, he was just the fifth Open defending champion to miss the cut in the last 50 years. The others: **Mark O'Meara** (1998 winner), **Mark Calcavecchia** (1989 winner) and **Tom Watson** (1975 winner).*

*Through round one, there was not an American player inside the top 10 on the leaderboard. The last time that happened was in 1959 when Bob Sweeny was tied for 69th through 18 holes. The highest-placed American players after round one were **Rich Beem**, **Skip Kendall**, **Scott Verplank**, **Kenny Perry** and **Steve Lowery**, who sat in a tie for 13th at 2-under par. In fact, since 1987, there had been at least one American inside the top three on the leaderboard through 18 holes.*

Tournament Record:
267, Greg Norman, 1993 (Royal St. George's)

18-Hole Record:
63, Mark Hayes, 1977 (Turnberry); Isao Aoki, 1980 (Muirfield); Greg Norman, 1986 (Turnberry); Paul Broadhurst, 1990 (St. Andrews); Jodie Mudd, 1991 (Royal Birkdale); Nick Faldo, 1993 (Royal St. George's); Payne Stewart, 1993 (Royal St. George's)

TOURNAMENT HISTORY

Year	Winner	Score	Runner-up	Score	Location
2002	Ernie Els*	278	Stuart Appleby Steve Elkington Thomas Levet	278	Muirfield, Scotland
2003	Ben Curtis	283	Thomas Bjorn Vijay Singh	284	Royal St. George's, England
2004	Todd Hamilton*	274	Ernie Els	274	Royal Troon, Scotland

*KEY: * = Playoff ** = Canceled because Tom Morris, Jr. retired championship belt + = World War I ++ = World War II*
[NOTE: Became an official PGA TOUR victory/money became official in 1995]

ELIGIBILITY REQUIREMENTS FOR THE 2005 BRITISH OPEN CHAMPIONSHIP

Players exempt from both qualifying stages are:

- The top 10 finishers and ties from the 2004 British Open.
- Former winners of the British Open who are under the age of 65 on July 17, 2005.
- The top 50 players from the Official World Golf Ranking as of May 9, 2005.
- The top 20 players from the final 2004 PGA European Tour Order of Merit.
- Winners of the Volvo PGA Championship in the last three years (2003-2005).
- The top three players, not otherwise exempt, from among the top 20 players on the 2004 PGA European Tour Order of Merit as of May 29, 2005.
- The top two players, not otherwise exempt, who have earned the most PGA European Tour official prize money from the 2005 British Masters through the 2005 French Open, including the U.S. Open.
- The leading player, not otherwise exempt, in the 2005 Smurfit European Open and 2005 Barclays Scottish Open. Ties for last places will be decided by better final round score, and if still tied, better third-round score, better second-round score. If still tied, all players still tied will be exempt.
- Winners of the U.S. Open in the last five years (2001-2005).
- Winners of the Masters in the last five years (2001-2005).
- Winners of the PGA Championship in the last five years (2000-2004).
- Winners of THE PLAYERS Championship in the last three years (2003-2005).
- The top 20 players from the 2004 Official PGA TOUR Money List.
- The top three players, not otherwise exempt, from among the top 20 players on the 2005 Official PGA TOUR Money List through May 29, 2005.
- The top two players, not otherwise exempt, who have earned the most PGA TOUR Official Money from the 2005 PLAYERS Championship and the five cosponsored and approved events leading up to and including the Cialis Western Open.
- The leading player, not otherwise exempt, in the 2005 Cialis Western Open and the 2005 John Deere Classic. Ties for last places will be decided by better final round score, and if still tied, better third round score, better second round score. If still tied, all players still tied will be exempt.
- Playing members of the 2004 Ryder Cup teams.
- Winner of the 2004 Bell Canadian Open.
- Winner of the 2004 Japan Open
- The player who leads the 2004 Asian Tour Official Money List.
- The top two players from the 2004 Australasian Tour Official Money List.
- The top two players from the 2004 Japan Golf Tour Official Money List.
- The player who leads the 2004/2005 Southern Africa Tour Official Money List.
- The top four players, not otherwise exempt, from among the Top 20 players who have earned the most Japan Golf Tour official prize money from the 2005 Japan PGA Championship through the Mizuno Open.
- The leading four players, not otherwise exempt, from the 2005 Mizuno Open.
- Winner of the 2004 Senior British Open.
- Winner of the 2005 British Amateur, if still an amateur.
- Winner of the 2004 U.S. Amateur, if still an amateur.
- The individual winner of the 2004 European Amateur Championship, if still an amateur.

2004 B.C. Open

[30th of 48 official events]

Winner: JONATHAN BYRD
67-65-68-68 268 (-20) $540,000

En-Joie Golf Club

Endicott, NY

July 15-18, 2004

Purse: $3,000,000
Par: 37-35—72
Yards: 6,974

LEADERS: First Round—Kelly Gibson opened with an 8-under-par 64 and led Camilo Villegas, Todd Fischer, John E. Morgan and Kevin Stadler by one stroke. Four players were two back.
Second Round—Jonathan Byrd was at 12-under 132, one stroke ahead of Morgan and Daniel Chopra. Fischer, Chris Smith, Roland Thatcher and Neal Lancaster were two back.
Third Round—Byrd added a 4-under-par 68 and led by one stroke at 16-under-par 200. Ted Purdy, Robert Gamez, Tommy Tolles, Notah Begay III and Morgan were tied for second.

Check out the 2005 B.C. Open, July 14-17 on USA

CUT: 78 players at 2-under-par 142 from a field of 132 professionals.

PRO-AM: Hidemichi Tanaka, Blaine McCallister, 9-under, $1,800 each.

WEATHER: Cloudy and wet on Thursday. Play was suspended from 11:04-11:32. Mostly cloudy with scattered showers on Friday, highs in the high 60s. Play was suspended for 34 minutes on Friday afternoon due to dangerous weather and at 6:37 p.m. due to heavy rain. The second round completed at 7:32 p.m. Sunny and warm most of Saturday. Play was suspended for 38 minutes on Saturday afternoon due to dangerous weather. Round three was completed at 6:43 p.m. Sunday's tee times were moved to 7:15-9:03 a.m. in threesomes due to expected afternoon thunderstorms. Play was suspended at 9:49 a.m. due thunderstorms and heavy rain. The round was completed at 8:21 p.m.

ORDER OF FINISH

Jonathan Byrd	1	67-65-68-68	268	$540,000.00
Ted Purdy	2	69-67-65-68	269	324,000.00
Notah Begay III	T3	73-62-66-69	270	144,000.00
Todd Fischer	T3	65-69-71-65	270	144,000.00
Robin Freeman	T3	70-67-67-66	270	144,000.00
Hidemichi Tanaka	T3	68-68-68-66	270	144,000.00
Neal Lancaster	T7	67-67-69-68	271	93,500.00
Vaughn Taylor	T7	71-66-68-66	271	93,500.00
Camilo Villegas	T7	65-70-67-69	271	93,500.00
Jim Gallagher, Jr.	T10	70-68-66-68	272	75,000.00
Robert Gamez	T10	75-61-65-71	272	75,000.00
John Senden	T10	71-66-67-68	272	75,000.00
Hank Kuehne	T13	70-68-67-68	273	56,250.00
John E. Morgan	T13	65-68-68-72	273	56,250.00
Chris Smith	T13	69-65-69-70	273	56,250.00
Tommy Tolles	T13	67-69-65-72	273	56,250.00
Steve Allan	T17	72-68-64-70	274	43,500.00
Bill Haas (S)	T17	74-66-66-68	274	43,500.00
Joey Sindelar	T17	68-69-68-69	274	43,500.00
Jay Williamson	T17	68-67-70-69	274	43,500.00
Pat Bates	T21	70-68-67-70	275	28,162.50
Jason Bohn	T21	67-68-69-71	275	28,162.50
Wayne Levi	T21	72-67-69-67	275	28,162.50
Brenden Pappas	T21	66-73-67-69	275	28,162.50
John Rollins	T21	71-65-72-67	275	28,162.50
Craig Stadler	T21	67-69-71-68	275	$28,162.50
Esteban Toledo	T21	71-66-70-68	275	28,162.50
Omar Uresti	T21	71-67-67-70	275	28,162.50
Jim Carter	T29	70-68-68-70	276	19,075.00
Greg Chalmers	T29	68-71-70-67	276	19,075.00
Daniel Chopra	T29	68-65-72-71	276	19,075.00
John Cook	T29	69-68-68-71	276	19,075.00
Jason Dufner	T29	69-71-69-67	276	19,075.00
Mark Wiebe	T29	69-70-69-68	276	19,075.00
David Edwards	T35	71-71-66-69	277	14,790.00
Gabriel Hjertstedt	T35	67-68-70-72	277	14,790.00
Richard S. Johnson	T35	69-68-70-70	277	14,790.00
David Peoples	T35	70-66-69-72	277	14,790.00
Stan Utley	T35	68-69-71-69	277	14,790.00
Fred Funk	T40	74-68-68-68	278	12,300.00
Lucas Glover	T40	67-74-70-67	278	12,300.00
Kevin Stadler (S)	T40	65-70-71-72	278	12,300.00
Michael Clark II	T43	70-69-71-69	279	9,900.00
Mike Grob	T43	71-71-67-70	279	9,900.00
Brian Kortan	T43	69-68-73-69	279	9,900.00
Wes Short, Jr.	T43	72-69-68-70	279	9,900.00
Roland Thatcher	T43	66-68-76-69	279	9,900.00
Craig Bowden	T48	68-71-71-70	280	7,387.50
Olin Browne	T48	67-71-70-72	280	7,387.50
Tom Carter	T48	67-72-70-71	280	7,387.50
Hiroyuki Fujita	T48	72-70-68-70	280	7,387.50
Brock Mackenzie (S)	T48	69-71-69-71	280	7,387.50
Carl Paulson	T48	69-70-74-67	280	$7,387.50
Brett Quigley	T48	66-69-71-74	280	7,387.50
Garrett Willis	T48	66-71-70-73	280	7,387.50
Kelly Gibson	T56	64-74-71-72	281	6,750.00
Matt Hendrix (S)	T56	72-70-68-71	281	6,750.00
Kevin Muncrief	T56	70-71-69-71	281	6,750.00
Roger Tambellini	T56	69-69-70-73	281	6,750.00
Billy Andrade	T60	72-68-73-69	282	6,420.00
Tim Conley (S)	T60	72-70-72-68	282	6,420.00
Trevor Dodds	T60	74-68-70-70	282	6,420.00
Ken Duke	T60	73-68-74-67	282	6,420.00
John Morse	T60	71-70-69-72	282	6,420.00
David Ogrin	T60	73-68-70-71	282	6,420.00
Mark Wilson	T60	70-69-71-72	282	6,420.00
Danny Briggs	T67	72-69-73-69	283	6,150.00
Kevin Na	T67	70-70-70-73	283	6,150.00
Mike Heinen	T69	67-75-70-72	284	6,000.00
Mike Springer	T69	71-71-73-69	284	6,000.00
Mike Standly	T69	72-68-71-73	284	6,000.00
Jim Benepe	T72	67-68-76-74	285	5,820.00
Ken Green	T72	69-71-71-74	285	5,820.00
Grant Waite	T72	71-69-74-71	285	5,820.00
David Sutherland	75	73-69-68-76	286	5,700.00
Brad Bryant	T76	72-70-71-74	287	5,610.00
Brandt Snedeker (Q)	T76	69-73-71-74	287	5,610.00
Mike Sullivan	78	71-71-73-74	289	5,520.00

(Q) = Open Qualifier; (S) = Sponsor Exemption; (T) = Tie

The following players did not finish (C=cut, W=withdrew)

C—143-Joel Edwards, Rick Fehr, Bill Glasson, Kent Jones, Blaine McCallister, David Morland IV, Dan Pohl, Dicky Pride, **144-**Jay Don Blake, Michael Bradley, David Branshaw, Bill Britton, Keith Clearwater, Greg Kraft, Matt Kuchar, Dave Rummells, Scott Simpson, Mike Sposa, Phil Tataurangi, Dean Wilson, **145-**John Adams, Alex Cejka, Nolan Henke, Mike Hulbert, Jim McGovern, Akio Sadakata, Willie Wood, **146-**Brad Fabel, Donnie Hammond, Bradley Heaven, Dan Olsen, **147-**Michael Allen, Aaron Barber, Guy Boros, Kenny Knox, William Link IV, Tag Ridings, Larry Rinker, **148-**Dan Halldorson, Mac O'Grady, Sam Randolph, **149-**David Branham, Dennis Colligan, Mike Donald, David Frost, Gary Hallberg, J.P. Hayes, Brian Henninger, Ted Tryba, **151-**David Gossett, **160-**Kevin Savage, **165-**Bob Lohr. **W—77-**Hirofumi Miyase, **73-**Tripp Isenhour.

TOURNAMENT HISTORY

Year	Winner	Score	Runner-up	Score	Location	Par/Yards
BROOME COUNTY OPEN						
1971	Claude Harmon, Jr.**	69	Chuck Courtney Norman Rack Hal Underwood	69	En-Joie GC, Endicott, NY	71/6,966
B.C. OPEN						
1972	Bob Payne**	136	Dave Marad	137	En-Joie GC, Endicott, NY	71/6,966
1973	Hubert Green	266	Dwight Nevil	272	En-Joie GC, Endicott, NY	71/6,966
1974	Richie Karl*	273	Bruce Crampton	273	En-Joie GC, Endicott, NY	71/6,966
1975	Don Iverson	274	Jim Colbert David Graham	275	En-Joie GC, Endicott, NY	71/6,966
1976	Bob Wynn	271	Bob Gilder	272	En-Joie GC, Endicott, NY	71/6,966
1977	Gil Morgan	270	Lee Elder	275	En-Joie GC, Endicott, NY	71/6,966
1978	Tom Kite	267	Mark Hayes	272	En-Joie GC, Endicott, NY	71/6,966
1979	Howard Twitty	270	Tom Purtzer	271	En-Joie GC, Endicott, NY	71/6,966
1980	Don Pooley	271	Peter Jacobsen	272	En-Joie GC, Endicott, NY	71/6,966
1981	Jay Haas	270	Tom Kite	273	En-Joie GC, Endicott, NY	71/6,966
1982	Calvin Peete	265	Jerry Pate	272	En-Joie GC, Endicott, NY	71/6,966
1983	Pat Lindsey	268	Gil Morgan	272	En-Joie GC, Endicott, NY	71/6,966
1984	Wayne Levi	275	Russ Cochran Hal Sutton	276	En-Joie GC, Endicott, NY	71/6,966
1985	Joey Sindelar	274	Mike Reid	275	En-Joie GC, Endicott, NY	71/6,966
1986	Rick Fehr	267	Larry Mize	269	En-Joie GC, Endicott, NY	71/6,966
1987	Joey Sindelar	266	Jeff Sluman	270	En-Joie GC, Endicott, NY	71/6,966
1988	Bill Glasson	268	Wayne Levi Bruce Lietzke	270	En-Joie GC, Endicott, NY	71/6,966
1989	Mike Hulbert*	268	Bob Estes	268	En-Joie GC, Endicott, NY	71/6,966
1990	Nolan Henke	268	Mark Wiebe	271	En-Joie GC, Endicott, NY	71/6,966
1991	Fred Couples	269	Peter Jacobsen	272	En-Joie GC, Endicott, NY	71/6,966

B.C. Open

NOTES

***Jonathan Byrd**'s victory at the 2004 B.C. Open was the 150th win by a former Nationwide Tour player on the PGA TOUR.*

*There have been 12 players who have earned their maiden PGA TOUR victory at the B.C. Open: **Richie Karl** (1974), **Don Iverson** (1975), **Bob Wynn** (1976), **Gil Morgan** (1977), **Howard Twitty** (1979), **Don Pooley** (1980), **Pat Lindsey** (1983), **Rick Fehr** (1986), **Nolan Henke** (1990), **Gabriel Hjertstedt** (1997), **Chris Perry** (1998) and **Spike McRoy** (2002).*

*With his victory in the 2003 B.C. Open, **Craig Stadler** became the second player in PGA TOUR history to win a PGA TOUR and Champions Tour event in the same season. Stadler won the Ford Seniors Players Championship on the Champions Tour the week before. The only other player to do so was Ray Floyd in 1992 when he won the Ryder-Doral Open at age 49 and the GTE North Classic later in the season on the Champions Tour.*

CRAIG STADLER

*In 2003, **Craig Stadler**, at age 50 years, 1 month, 18 days, became the fifth-oldest player to win a PGA TOUR event, and the first player over age 50 to win since Art Wall won the 1975 Greater Milwaukee Open at age 51 years, 7 months, 10 days.*

***Craig Stadler**'s eight-stroke come-from-behind win in 2003 was the largest in B.C. Open history, surpassing the 2002 mark of seven by Spike McRoy over Shaun Micheel. The PGA TOUR record is 10 by Paul Lawrie at the 1999 British Open.*

*In capturing the 2003 B.C. Open, **Craig Stadler** posted four consecutive rounds in the 60s (67-69-68-63—267). It was the first time Stadler had done so in a PGA TOUR event since the 1995 B.C. Open when he finished in a T3.*

Tournament Record:
265, Calvin Peete, 1982
Tournament Course Record:
61, Hal Sutton, 1995; Fred Funk, 1999; Robert Gamez, 2004

TOURNAMENT HISTORY

Year	Winner	Score	Runner-up	Score	Location	Par/Yards
1992	John Daly	266	Joel Edwards Ken Green Jay Haas Nolan Henke	272	En-Joie GC, Endicott, NY	71/6,966
1993	Blaine McCallister	271	Denis Watson	272	En-Joie GC, Endicott, NY	71/6,966
1994	Mike Sullivan	266	Jeff Sluman	270	En-Joie GC, Endicott, NY	71/6,966
1995	Hal Sutton	269	Jim McGovern	270	En-Joie GC, Endicott, NY	71/6,966
1996	Fred Funk~*	202	Pete Jordan	202	En-Joie GC, Endicott, NY	71/6,920
1997	Gabriel Hjertstedt	275	Chris Perry Lee Rinker Andrew Magee	276	En-Joie GC, Endicott, NY	72/6,994
1998	Chris Perry	273	Peter Jacobsen	276	En-Joie GC, Endicott, NY	72/6,994
1999	Brad Faxon*	273	Fred Funk	273	En-Joie GC, Endicott, NY	72/6,994
2000	Brad Faxon	270	Esteban Toledo	271	En-Joie GC, Endicott, NY	72/6,974
2001	Jeff Sluman*	266	Paul Gow	266	En-Joie GC, Endicott, NY	72/6,974
2002	Spike McRoy	269	Fred Funk	270	En-Joie GC, Endicott, NY	72/6,974
2003	Craig Stadler	267	Alex Cejka Steve Lowery	268	En-Joie GC, Endicott, NY	72/6,974
2004	Jonathan Byrd	268	Ted Purdy	269	En-Joie GC, Endicott, NY	72/6,974

*KEY: * = Playoff ~ = Weather-shortened ** = Unofficial tournament*

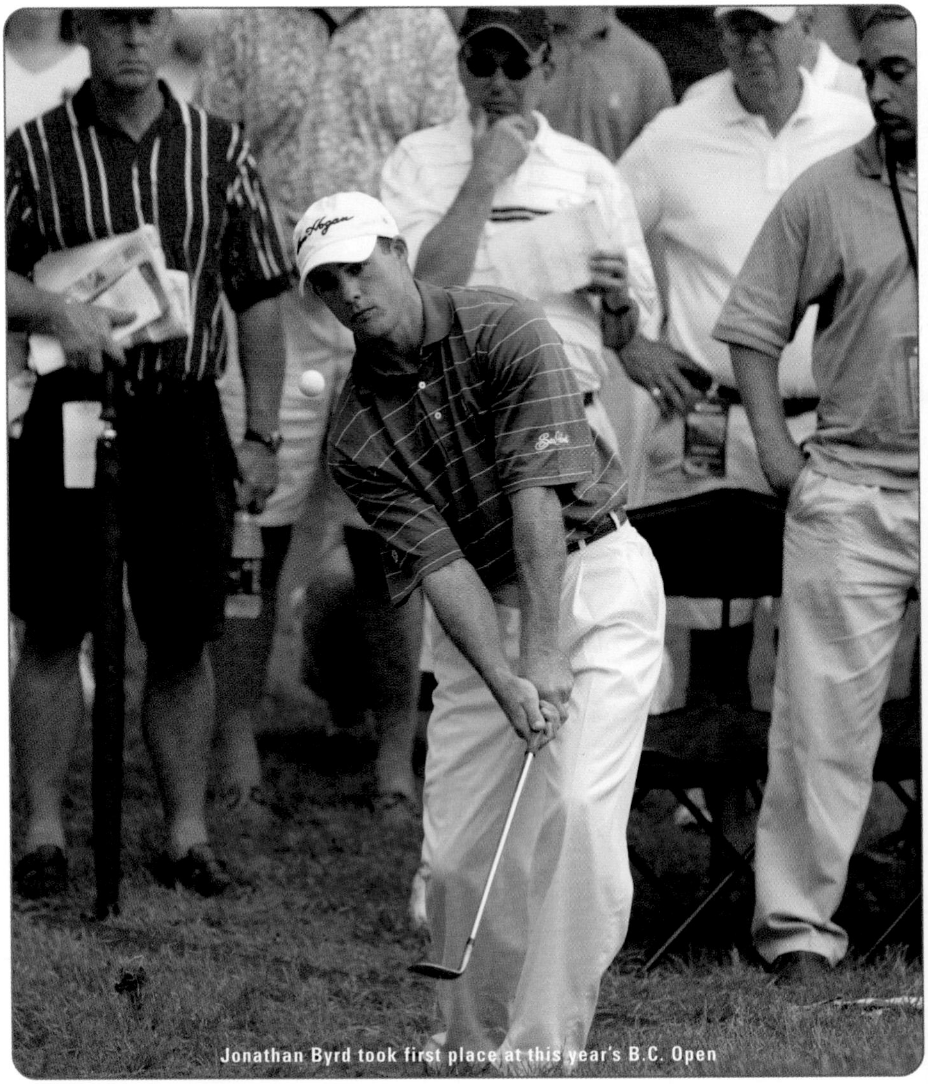
Jonathan Byrd took first place at this year's B.C. Open

2004 U.S. Bank Championship in Milwaukee

[31st of 48 official events]

Winner: CARLOS FRANCO
68-63-69-67 267 (-13) $630,000

Brown Deer Park Golf Course

Milwaukee, WI

July 22-25, 2004

Purse: $3,500,000
Par: 34-36—70
Yards: 6,759

LEADERS: First Round—Eight players were tied for the lead at 5-under-par 65: Bo Van Pelt, Todd Fischer, Brett Quigley, Patrick Sheehan, Brian Kortan, Robert Gamez, Danny Briggs and Olin Browne.

Second Round—Carlos Franco at 9-under-par 131 led Rich Beem by one and Scott Hoch by two. Van Pelt and Sheehan were three behind.

Third Round—Franco, Quigley and Sheehan shared the lead at 10-under-par 200. Kenny Perry was one back while Jason Dufner and Scott Verplank were two behind.

CUT: 86 players at 1-over-par 141 from a field of 156 professionals.

PRO-AM: Reduced to nine holes with front- and back-nine winners. $10,000. Front nine, Robert Gamez, $1,200. Back nine, Billy Mayfair, $1,200.

WEATHER: Mostly sunny on Thursday with a high of 83. Cooler and less humid in the afternoon. Cooler on Friday with a high of 70. Sunny skies all day. Saturday, partly cloudy and cool with a high of 67. Sunday, sunny with a high of 72.

Check out the 2005 U.S. Bank Championship in Milwaukee, July 21-24 on USA/CBS

ORDER OF FINISH

Carlos Franco	1	68-63-69-67	267	$630,000.00
Fred Funk	T2	68-68-67-66	269	308,000.00
Brett Quigley	T2	65-71-64-69	269	308,000.00
Billy Andrade	T4	72-64-67-67	270	144,666.67
Olin Browne	T4	65-70-68-67	270	144,666.67
Patrick Sheehan	T4	65-68-67-70	270	144,666.66
Bo Van Pelt	T7	65-68-71-67	271	109,083.34
Danny Briggs	T7	65-70-68-68	271	109,083.33
Kenny Perry	T7	69-67-65-70	271	109,083.33
Scott Hoch	10	68-65-70-69	272	94,500.00
Jason Dufner	T11	67-67-68-71	273	84,000.00
Scott Verplank	T11	66-69-67-71	273	84,000.00
Tom Byrum	T13	69-70-65-70	274	63,700.00
Jerry Kelly	T13	66-72-67-69	274	63,700.00
Frank Lickliter II	T13	70-69-68-67	274	63,700.00
Scott McCarron	T13	70-68-69-67	274	63,700.00
Corey Pavin	T13	70-68-66-70	274	63,700.00
Craig Bowden	T18	66-70-69-70	275	47,250.00
Bart Bryant	T18	70-68-71-66	275	47,250.00
Todd Fischer	T18	65-70-72-68	275	47,250.00
Kirk Triplett	T18	68-67-70-70	275	47,250.00
Aaron Barber	T22	73-68-69-66	276	33,600.00
Lucas Glover	T22	69-72-64-71	276	33,600.00
Jeff Sluman	T22	66-72-71-67	276	33,600.00
Jay Williamson	T22	67-68-68-73	276	33,600.00
Dean Wilson	T22	67-71-68-70	276	33,600.00
Brad Faxon	T27	71-68-67-71	277	25,375.00
Dan Forsman	T27	66-68-71-72	277	25,375.00
Brian Gay	T27	70-66-67-74	277	$25,375.00
Richard S. Johnson	T27	70-70-66-71	277	25,375.00
Cameron Beckman	T31	66-72-68-72	278	20,755.00
J.J. Henry	T31	69-71-70-68	278	20,755.00
Ryan Palmer	T31	67-73-68-70	278	20,755.00
Roger Tambellini	T31	73-65-70-70	278	20,755.00
Hideto Tanihara	T31	69-70-69-70	278	20,755.00
Rich Barcelo	T36	68-70-74-67	279	14,365.91
Robert Gamez	T36	65-71-73-70	279	14,365.91
Brent Geiberger	T36	68-72-69-70	279	14,365.91
Kent Jones	T36	69-71-70-69	279	14,365.91
Matt Kuchar	T36	68-70-70-71	279	14,365.91
Brenden Pappas	T36	69-71-70-69	279	14,365.91
Wes Short, Jr.	T36	66-71-74-68	279	14,365.91
Steve Stricker	T36	75-66-68-70	279	14,365.91
Tommy Tolles	T36	70-70-68-71	279	14,365.91
Mark Wilson	T36	71-70-66-72	279	14,365.91
Daniel Chopra	T36	68-69-68-74	279	14,365.90
Greg Chalmers	T47	67-69-73-71	280	8,708.00
John Cook	T47	72-66-70-72	280	8,708.00
Jay Delsing	T47	70-70-66-74	280	8,708.00
Steve Elkington	T47	68-72-70-70	280	8,708.00
Bob Estes	T47	72-69-70-69	280	8,708.00
Mike Grob	T47	70-71-70-69	280	8,708.00
Tripp Isenhour	T47	68-71-71-70	280	8,708.00
Len Mattiace	T47	69-72-72-67	280	8,708.00
Spike McRoy	T47	71-69-70-70	280	8,708.00
Joey Sindelar	T47	69-70-69-72	280	8,708.00
Steve Allan	T57	69-70-71-71	281	7,770.00
Paul Azinger	T57	66-72-70-73	281	7,770.00
Rich Beem	T57	66-66-76-73	281	$7,770.00
Harrison Frazar	T57	70-70-70-71	281	7,770.00
Kevin Muncrief	T57	66-73-73-69	281	7,770.00
Jonathan Byrd	T62	68-72-72-70	282	7,385.00
Jim Carter	T62	69-68-72-73	282	7,385.00
Jim Gallagher, Jr.	T62	71-65-73-73	282	7,385.00
Ted Purdy	T62	74-65-68-75	282	7,385.00
Loren Roberts	T62	71-70-71-70	282	7,385.00
Scott Simpson (S)	T62	71-70-67-74	282	7,385.00
Tom Carter	68	70-70-71-72	283	7,140.00
J.L. Lewis	T69	69-72-73-70	284	7,000.00
Steve Lowery	T69	70-71-76-67	284	7,000.00
Camilo Villegas	T69	72-68-75-69	284	7,000.00
Mark Calcavecchia	T72	69-70-71-75	285	6,790.00
Joe Durant	T72	71-70-73-71	285	6,790.00
Skip Kendall	T72	71-68-72-74	285	6,790.00
Jason Bohn	T75	70-70-74-72	286	6,510.00
Kris Cox	T75	68-73-71-74	286	6,510.00
Nick Gilliam (S)	T75	70-69-75-72	286	6,510.00
Ken Green	T75	70-66-72-78	286	6,510.00
Dan Olsen	T75	69-70-73-74	286	6,510.00
Steve Pate	T80	69-72-74-72	287	6,265.00
David Roesch (S)	T80	74-67-69-77	287	6,265.00
Cliff Kresge	T82	72-67-75-76	290	6,125.00
Kevin Na	T82	71-70-78-71	290	6,125.00
Brad Lardon	84	70-71-73-77	291	6,020.00
David Edwards	85	70-70-72-82	294	5,950.00

(Q) = Open Qualifier; (S) = Sponsor Exemption; (T) = Tie

The following players did not finish
(C=cut, W=withdrew, D=disqualified)

C—142-Pat Bates, K.J. Choi, Robert Damron, Joel Edwards, Robin Freeman, Mike Heinen, John E. Morgan, David Peoples, Heath Slocum, Hidemichi Tanaka, Tim Thelen, Grant Waite. **143-**Notah Begay III, Gene Sauers, Omar Uresti, Garrett Willis. **144-**Woody Austin, Brian Bateman, Jeff Brehaut, Glen Day, Ken Duke, Nathan Fritz, Brian Kortan, Neal Lancaster, Patrick Moore, David Morland IV, Deane Pappas, Dennis Paulson, Chris Smith, Roland Thatcher, Esteban Toledo. **145-**Joe Affrunti, Michael Allen, Arjun Atwal, Craig Barlow, David Branshaw, D.J. Brigman, Danny Ellis, J.P. Hayes, Hunter Mahan, Blaine McCallister, Sean Murphy, Tag Ridings, Jerry Smith. **146-**Jay Don Blake, Michael Clark II, Trevor Dodds, Donnie Hammond, Billy Mayfair, Larry Mize, Carl Paulson. **147-**David Frost, Joel Kribel, Hirofumi Miyase, Mike Springer, David Sutherland, Ted Tryba. **148-**Vaughn Taylor. **149-**Jim Schuman, Mario Tiziani. **150-**Charlie Brown, Mike Standly, Casey Wittenberg. **151-**Chris Couch. **153-**Jon Turcott. **154-**Dicky Pride. **162-**Andy Barrett. **163-**David Gossett. **W—76-**Bill Glasson. **214-**Alex Cejka. **D—149-**Guy Boros.

TOURNAMENT HISTORY

Year	Winner	Score	Runner-up	Score	Location	Par/Yards
GREATER MILWAUKEE OPEN						
1968	Dave Stockton	275	Sam Snead	279	Northshore CC, Mequon, WI	71/7,075
1969	Ken Still	277	Gary Player	279	Northshore CC, Mequon, WI	71/7,075
1970	Deane Beman	276	Richard Crawford	279	Northshore CC, Mequon, WI	71/7,075
			Ted Hayes			
			Don Massengale			
1971	Dave Eichelberger	270	Ralph Johnston	271	Tripoli GC, Milwaukee, WI	71/6,514
			Bob Shaw			
1972	Jim Colbert	271	Bud Allin	272	Tripoli GC, Milwaukee, WI	71/6,514
			Chuck Courtney			
			George Johnson			
			Grier Jones			
1973	Dave Stockton	276	Homero Blancas	277	Tuckaway CC, Franklin, WI	72/7,030
			Hubert Green			
1974	Ed Sneed	276	Grier Jones	280	Tuckaway CC, Franklin, WI	72/7,030
1975	Art Wall	271	Gary McCord	272	Tuckaway CC, Franklin, WI	72/7,030
1976	Dave Hill	270	John Jacobs	273	Tuckaway CC, Franklin, WI	72/7,030
1977	Dave Eichelberger	278	Morris Hatalsky	280	Tuckaway CC, Franklin, WI	72/7,030
			Gary McCord			
			Mike Morley			
1978	Lee Elder*	275	Lee Trevino	275	Tuckaway CC, Franklin, WI	72/7,030
1979	Calvin Peete	269	Victor Regalado	274	Tuckaway CC, Franklin, WI	72/7,030
			Jim Simons			
			Lee Trevino			
1980	Bill Kratzert	266	Howard Twitty	270	Tuckaway CC, Franklin, WI	72/7,030
1981	Jay Haas	274	Chi Chi Rodriguez	277	Tuckaway CC, Franklin, WI	72/7,030
1982	Calvin Peete	274	Victor Regalado	276	Tuckaway CC, Franklin, WI	72/7,030

U.S. Bank Championship in Milwaukee

NOTES

*The eight co-leaders through 18 holes (**Bo Van Pelt, Todd Fischer, Brett Quigley, Patrick Sheehan, Brian Kortan, Robert Gamez, Danny Briggs** and **Olin Browne**) tied a PGA TOUR record for the most players tied for the 18-hole lead dating back to 1970. The 2000 Honda Classic also had eight co-leaders through 18 holes.*

*Co-leader **Brett Quigley**'s father Paul caddied for fellow Rhode Island native **Brad Faxon** at the 2003 U.S. Bank Championship. Growing up, Faxon often caddied for Paul in events in Rhode Island. Paul is a part-time caddie for his brother Dana on the Champions Tour as well as Brett on the PGA TOUR.*

*Eight of the 10 past champions competing at the 2004 U.S. Bank Championship made the cut: **Kenny Perry** (2003), **Jeff Sluman** (1998 and 2002), **Loren Roberts** (1996 and 2000), **Carlos Franco** (1999), **Scott Hoch** (1995 and 1997), **Jim Gallagher Jr.** (1990), **Ken Green** (1988) and **Corey Pavin** (1986). The two missing the cut were **Billy Mayfair** (1993) and **Mike Springer** (1994).*

*In 2004, two-time champion **Scott Hoch** continued his tournament leading streak of 12 consecutive cuts made here, dating back to the 1993 season. The all-time tournament record is 13 by **Dave Eichelberger** (1970-1982).*

SCOTT HOCH

*En route to victory, **Carlos Franco** tied his 18-hole career low with a 7-under-par 63 in the second round. He also posted a 7-under-par 63 in the first round of the 2004 Sony Open in Hawaii but finished T20.*

Tournament Record:
260, Loren Roberts, 2000
Current Course Record:
61, Steve Lowery, 1999
Other Course Record:
61, Ken Green, 1988 (Tuckaway CC); Robert Gamez, 1991 (Tuckaway CC)

TOURNAMENT HISTORY

Year	Winner	Score	Runner-up	Score	Location	Par/Yards
1983	Morris Hatalsky*	275	George Cadle	275	Tuckaway CC, Franklin, WI	72/7,030
1984	Mark O'Meara	272	Tom Watson	277	Tuckaway CC, Franklin, WI	72/7,030
1985	Jim Thorpe	274	Jack Nicklaus	277	Tuckaway CC, Franklin, WI	72/7,030
1986	Corey Pavin*	272	Dave Barr	272	Tuckaway CC, Franklin, WI	72/7,030
1987	Gary Hallberg	269	Wayne Levi Robert Wrenn	271	Tuckaway CC, Franklin, WI	72/7,030
1988	Ken Green	268	Mark Calcavecchia Jim Gallagher, Jr. Donnie Hammond Dan Pohl	274	Tuckaway CC, Franklin, WI	72/7,030
1989	Greg Norman	269	Andy Bean	272	Tuckaway CC, Franklin, WI	72/7,030
1990	Jim Gallagher, Jr.*	271	Ed Dougherty Billy Mayfair	271	Tuckaway CC, Franklin, WI	72/7,030
1991	Mark Brooks	270	Robert Gamez	271	Tuckaway CC, Franklin, WI	72/7,030
1992	Richard Zokol	269	Dick Mast	271	Tuckaway CC, Franklin, WI	72/7,030
1993	Billy Mayfair*	270	Mark Calcavecchia Ted Schulz	270	Tuckaway CC, Franklin, WI	72/7,030
1994	Mike Springer	268	Loren Roberts	269	Brown Deer Park GC, Milwaukee, WI	71/6,716
1995	Scott Hoch	269	Marco Dawson	272	Brown Deer Park GC, Milwaukee, WI	71/6,716
1996	Loren Roberts*	265	Jerry Kelly	265	Brown Deer Park GC, Milwaukee, WI	71/6,739
1997	Scott Hoch	268	Loren Roberts David Sutherland	269	Brown Deer Park GC, Milwaukee, WI	71/6,739
1998	Jeff Sluman	265	Steve Stricker	266	Brown Deer Park GC, Milwaukee, WI	71/6,739
1999	Carlos Franco	264	Tom Lehman	266	Brown Deer Park GC, Milwaukee, WI	71/6,739
2000	Loren Roberts	260	Franklin Langham	268	Brown Deer Park GC, Milwaukee, WI	71/6,759
2001	Shigeki Maruyama*	266	Charles Howell III	266	Brown Deer Park GC, Milwaukee, WI	71/6,759
2002	Jeff Sluman	261	Tim Herron Steve Lowery	265	Brown Deer Park GC, Milwaukee, WI	71/6,759
2003	Kenny Perry	267	Steve Allan Heath Slocum	269	Brown Deer Park GC, Milwaukee, WI	70/6,759
U.S. BANK CHAMPIONSHIP IN MILWAUKEE						
2004	Carlos Franco	267	Fred Funk Brett Quigley	269	Brown Deer Park GC, Milwaukee, WI	70/6,759

*KEY: * = Playoff*

Carlos Franco, the 2004 winner of the U.S. Bank Championship in Milwaukee.

Winner: VIJAY SINGH
63-70-65-67 265 (-23) $810,000

Warwick Hills Golf & Country Club

Grand Blanc, MI

July 29-August 1, 2004

Purse: $4,500,000
Par: 36-36—72
Yards: 7,127

LEADERS: First Round—Vijay Singh posted a 9-under-par 63 to lead Olin Browne by one stroke and Mike Grob by two. Five players were three shots behind.
Second Round—Singh, Jim Furyk and Billy Andrade were tied for the lead at 11-under-par 133. Browne, Carlos Franco, John Daly and Stewart Cink were one behind. Four players were two back.

Third Round—Singh at 18-under-par 198 led Daly by two and Tiger Woods and Franco by three. Daniel Chopra was four behind.

CUT: 71 players at 4-under-par from a field of 156 professionals.

PRO-AM: $10,000. Brendan Pappas, Jeff Sluman, Cliff Kresge, 52, $1,666.67.

WEATHER: Mostly sunny on Thursday morning, turning cloudy in the afternoon. High of 84 degrees and S winds 5-10 mph. Cloudy with off and on drizzle most of the afternoon with patches of heavy rain. High temperature of 76 with S winds 5-10 mph. Mostly sunny on Saturday with a high of 84 in mid-afternoon. Stronger winds W 10-15 mph. Mostly sunny on Sunday with a high of 83. S-SW winds 10-15 mph.

Check out the 2005 Buick Open, July 28-31 on USA/CBS

ORDER OF FINISH

Vijay Singh	1	63-70-65-67	265	$810,000.00
John Daly	2	70-64-66-66	266	486,000.00
Carlos Franco	T3	67-67-67-66	267	261,000.00
Tiger Woods	T3	67-68-66-66	267	261,000.00
Stewart Cink	5	69-65-70-66	270	180,000.00
Jim Furyk	T6	66-67-70-68	271	156,375.00
Jeff Sluman	T6	70-67-68-66	271	156,375.00
Daniel Chopra	T8	68-68-66-70	272	135,000.00
Jerry Kelly	T8	71-66-69-66	272	135,000.00
Mark O'Meara	T10	67-70-70-66	273	117,000.00
Scott Verplank	T10	70-67-70-66	273	117,000.00
Craig Barlow	T12	66-69-72-68	275	94,500.00
Jose Maria Olazabal	T12	70-67-69-69	275	94,500.00
Brenden Pappas	T12	66-73-69-67	275	94,500.00
Billy Andrade	T15	68-65-73-70	276	76,500.00
Chris DiMarco	T15	69-68-73-66	276	76,500.00
Kenny Perry	T15	69-68-72-67	276	76,500.00
Jim Carter (S)	T18	69-69-70-69	277	56,700.00
Paul Casey (S)	T18	72-66-69-70	277	56,700.00
J.P. Hayes	T18	72-68-69-68	277	56,700.00
Hank Kuehne	T18	69-69-68-71	277	56,700.00
Geoff Ogilvy	T18	69-70-69-69	277	56,700.00
Bob Tway	T18	68-67-73-69	277	56,700.00
Woody Austin	T24	72-68-69-69	278	$36,450.00
Olin Browne	T24	64-70-69-75	278	36,450.00
Glen Day	T24	68-71-71-68	278	36,450.00
Brian Gay	T24	68-70-69-71	278	36,450.00
Justin Rose	T24	68-70-71-69	278	36,450.00
Wes Short, Jr.	T24	70-68-71-69	278	36,450.00
Steve Allan	T30	67-72-68-72	279	25,600.00
Paul Azinger	T30	72-68-70-69	279	25,600.00
Rich Barcelo	T30	70-69-70-70	279	25,600.00
Danny Briggs	T30	68-72-72-67	279	25,600.00
Bob Burns	T30	70-70-71-68	279	25,600.00
Neal Lancaster	T30	71-68-70-70	279	25,600.00
Hunter Mahan	T30	70-68-77-64	279	25,600.00
Scott McCarron	T30	68-69-70-72	279	25,600.00
Brett Quigley	T30	72-68-69-70	279	25,600.00
Tom Byrum	T39	71-69-72-68	280	19,350.00
Matt Gogel	T39	68-68-68-76	280	19,350.00
Patrick Sheehan	T39	71-69-70-70	280	19,350.00
Bill Glasson	42	75-63-71-72	281	17,550.00
Jeff Brehaut	T43	70-69-72-71	282	13,410.00
Robert Damron	T43	67-71-73-71	282	13,410.00
Jason Dufner	T43	71-69-71-71	282	13,410.00
Steve Flesch	T43	69-71-69-73	282	13,410.00
Billy Mayfair	T43	71-69-73-69	282	13,410.00
Larry Mize (S)	T43	70-70-71-71	282	13,410.00
David Peoples	T43	66-71-71-74	282	$13,410.00
Tom Pernice, Jr.	T43	70-70-69-73	282	13,410.00
Jay Williamson	T43	70-69-72-71	282	13,410.00
Pat Bates	T52	70-65-74-74	283	10,552.50
Greg Chalmers	T52	69-71-73-70	283	10,552.50
Dan Forsman	T52	68-71-76-68	283	10,552.50
Mathias Gronberg	T52	69-71-73-70	283	10,552.50
John E. Morgan	T56	70-70-73-71	284	10,080.00
Dan Olsen	T56	72-68-70-74	284	10,080.00
Pat Perez	T56	73-67-70-74	284	10,080.00
Carl Pettersson	T56	69-71-73-71	284	10,080.00
Roland Thatcher	T56	69-71-72-72	284	10,080.00
Lucas Glover	T61	70-69-76-70	285	9,765.00
Steve Stricker	T61	69-71-71-74	285	9,765.00
Bill Haas (S)	T63	72-65-76-73	286	9,585.00
Joe Ogilvie	T63	73-67-72-74	286	9,585.00
Robert Gamez	T65	68-68-78-73	287	9,405.00
J.L. Lewis	T65	72-67-75-73	287	9,405.00
Ken Duke	T67	69-71-71-77	288	9,180.00
Mike Grob	T67	65-73-74-76	288	9,180.00
David Morland IV	T67	70-70-78-70	288	9,180.00
Len Mattiace	70	66-73-73-77	289	9,000.00
Hideto Tanihara	71	73-67-77-74	291	8,910.00

(Q) = Open Qualifier; (S) = Sponsor Exemption; (T) = Tie

The following players did not finish (C=cut)

C—141-Arjun Atwal, Briny Baird, Jose Coceres, Kris Cox, David Edwards, Mark Hensby, Scott Hoch, Spike McRoy, Sean Pacetti, Ryan Palmer, Steve Pate, Tim Petrovic, Miguel Rivera, John Senden, Roger Tambellini, Tommy Tolles. **142-**Tommy Armour III, Michael Bradley, John Cook, Brent Geiberger, Tripp Isenhour, Skip Kendall, Matt Kuchar. **143-**Aaron Barber, Craig Bowden, D.J. Brigman, Bart Bryant, Michael Clark II, Joe Durant, Dudley Hart, Mike Heinen, Greg Kraft, Shaun Micheel, Dennis Paulson, Loren Roberts, Matt Seppanen, Chris Smith, Esteban Toledo. **144-**Aaron Baddeley, Jason Bohn, Tom Carter, K.J. Choi, Russ Cochran, Jay Delsing, Danny Ellis, Brian Kortan, Kevin Na, Carl Paulson, Tag Ridings, Jeff Roth, Omar Uresti, Mark Wilson. **145-**Guy Boros, David Branshaw, Craig Perks, Heath Slocum, Garrett Willis. **146-**Ken Green, John Huston, Jeff Maggert, Hirofumi Miyase, David Sutherland, Grant Waite, Brian Watts. **147-**Fulton Allem, Kevin Muncrief, Dean Wilson. **148-**Brian Bateman, Trevor Dodds, Cliff Kresge, Brad Lardon, Gene Sauers, Ted Tryba. **149-**Deane Pappas, Phil Tataurangi. **150-**Stephen Ames, Scott Hend. **151-**Mike Austin, Chris Couch, Bradley Heaven, Dicky Pride, Ryan Welborn, Casey Wittenberg. **152-**Steve Vecellio. **158-**Bob Ackerman.

TOURNAMENT HISTORY

Year	Winner	Score	Runner-up	Score	Location	Par/Yards
BUICK OPEN INVITATIONAL						
1958	Billy Casper	285	Ted Kroll Arnold Palmer	286	Warwick Hills CC, Grand Blanc, MI	72/7,014
1959	Art Wall*	282	Dow Finsterwald	282	Warwick Hills CC, Grand Blanc, MI	72/7,014
1960	Mike Souchak	282	Gay Brewer Art Wall	283	Warwick Hills CC, Grand Blanc, MI	72/7,014
1961	Jack Burke, Jr.*	284	Billy Casper Johnny Pott	284	Warwick Hills CC, Grand Blanc, MI	72/7,014
1962	Bill Collins	284	Dave Ragan	285	Warwick Hills CC, Grand Blanc, MI	72/7,014
1963	Julius Boros	274	Dow Finsterwald	279	Warwick Hills CC, Grand Blanc, MI	72/7,014
1964	Tony Lema	277	Dow Finsterwald	280	Warwick Hills CC, Grand Blanc, MI	72/7,014
1965	Tony Lema	280	Johnny Pott	282	Warwick Hills CC, Grand Blanc, MI	72/7,014
1966	Phil Rodgers	284	Johnny Pott Kermit Zarley	286	Warwick Hills CC, Grand Blanc, MI	72/7,014
1967	Julius Boros	283	Bob Goalby R.H. Sikes Bert Yancey	286	Warwick Hills CC, Grand Blanc, MI	72/7,014
1968	Tom Weiskopf	280	Mike Hill	281	Warwick Hills CC, Grand Blanc, MI	72/7,014
1969	Dave Hill	277	Frank Beard	279	Warwick Hills CC, Grand Blanc, MI	72/7,014
1970	No tournament					
1969	No tournament					
VERN PARSELL BUICK OPEN						
1972	Gary Groh**	273	John Mahaffey	275	Flint Elks CC, Flint, MI	72/6,902
LAKE MICHIGAN CLASSIC						
1973	Wilf Homenuik* **	215	Jim Ferriell	215	Benton Harbor Elks CC, Benton Harbor, MI	71/6,690
FLINT ELKS OPEN						
1974	Bryan Abbott**	135	Joe Porter	136	Flint Elks CC, Flint, MI	72/6,902
1975	Spike Kelley**	208	Randy Erskine Jim Marshall Mike McCullough	209	Flint Elks CC, Flint, MI	72/6,902

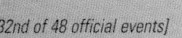

Buick Open

NOTES

*2004 Buick Open champion **Vijay Singh** joined the short list of players who have managed to win the Buick Open multiple times, including **Tony Lema** who is the only player to win consecutive championships in 1964 and 1965. **Julius Boros** won the event in 1963 and 1967. It was also the fourth event with multiple TOUR victories for Singh (Shell Houston Open, Phoenix Open, Buick Classic, Buick Open).*

*With his win at the 2004 Buick Open, **Vijay Singh** won the 11th time in 18 tries when holding at least a share of the 54-hole lead on the PGA TOUR, including seven straight beginning with the 2002 Shell Houston Open. The last time he failed to do so was the 2001 WORLDCOM Classic where he shot 74 in the final round and finished T3.*

JIM FURYK

***Jim Furyk** (T6) has never missed a cut in 10 starts at the Buick Open and has top-10s in five of his last six starts, including top honors in 2003. In 40 career rounds at Warwick Hills, Furyk has 39 rounds of par or better, including 24 rounds in the 60s.*

***Tiger Woods** (T3) has five top-10 finishes in six starts at the Buick Open, including a victory in 2002. All 24 rounds at Warwick Hills G&CC have been at par or better.*

*Seven champions in Buick Open history have posted all four rounds in the 60s, including just three in the last 10 years: **Jim Furyk**/2003, **Kenny Perry**/2001 and **Justin Leonard**/1996.*

***Daniel Chopra** (T8) posted his first career top-10 at the 2004 Buick Open.*

***Briny Baird** aced the 197-yard, par-3 third hole in the first round of the 2004 Buick Open. His father, Butch, posted the first hole-in-one in the inaugural Buick Open in 1962, also on No. 3.*

Tournament Record:
262, Robert Wrenn, 1987
Current Course Record:
61, Billy Mayfair, 2001

TOURNAMENT HISTORY

Year	Winner	Score	Runner-up	Score	Location	Par/Yards
1976	Ed Sabo* **	279	Randy Erskine	279	Flint Elks CC, Flint, MI	72/6,902
1977	Bobby Cole	271	Fred Marti	272	Flint Elks CC, Flint, MI	72/6,902
BUICK GOODWRENCH OPEN						
1978	Jack Newton*	280	Mike Sullivan	280	Warwick Hills G&CC, Grand Blanc, MI	72/7,014
1979	John Fought*	280	Jim Simons	280	Warwick Hills G&CC, Grand Blanc, MI	72/7,014
1980	Peter Jacobsen	276	Bill Kratzert	277	Warwick Hills G&CC, Grand Blanc, MI	72/7,014
			Mark Lye			
BUICK OPEN						
1981	Hale Irwin*	277	Bobby Clampett	277	Warwick Hills G&CC, Grand Blanc, MI	72/7,014
			Peter Jacobsen			
			Gil Morgan			
1982	Lanny Wadkins	273	Tom Kite	274	Warwick Hills G&CC, Grand Blanc, MI	72/7,014
1983	Wayne Levi	272	Isao Aoki	273	Warwick Hills G&CC, Grand Blanc, MI	72/7,014
			Calvin Peete			
1984	Denis Watson	271	Payne Stewart	272	Warwick Hills G&CC, Grand Blanc, MI	72/7,014
1985	Ken Green	268	Wayne Grady	272	Warwick Hills G&CC, Grand Blanc, MI	72/7,014
1986	Ben Crenshaw	270	J.C. Snead	271	Warwick Hills G&CC, Grand Blanc, MI	72/7,014
			Doug Tewell			
1987	Robert Wrenn	262	Dan Pohl	269	Warwick Hills G&CC, Grand Blanc, MI	72/7,014
1988	Scott Verplank	268	Doug Tewell	270	Warwick Hills G&CC, Grand Blanc, MI	72/7,014
1989	Leonard Thompson	273	Billy Andrade	274	Warwick Hills G&CC, Grand Blanc, MI	72/7,014
			Payne Stewart			
			Doug Tewell			
1990	Chip Beck	272	Mike Donald	273	Warwick Hills G&CC, Grand Blanc, MI	72/7,014
			Hale Irwin			
			Fuzzy Zoeller			
1991	Brad Faxon*	271	Chip Beck	271	Warwick Hills G&CC, Grand Blanc, MI	72/7,014
1992	Dan Forsman*	276	Steve Elkington	276	Warwick Hills G&CC, Grand Blanc, MI	72/7,014
			Brad Faxon			
1993	Larry Mize	272	Fuzzy Zoeller	273	Warwick Hills G&CC, Grand Blanc, MI	72/7,014
1994	Fred Couples	270	Corey Pavin	272	Warwick Hills G&CC, Grand Blanc, MI	72/7,014
1995	Woody Austin*	270	Mike Brisky	270	Warwick Hills G&CC, Grand Blanc, MI	72/7,014
1996	Justin Leonard	266	Chip Beck	271	Warwick Hills G&CC, Grand Blanc, MI	72/7,105
1997	Vijay Singh	273	Tom Byrum	277	Warwick Hills G&CC, Grand Blanc, MI	72/7,105
			Russ Cochran			
			Ernie Els			
			Brad Fabel			
			Joe Ozaki			
			Curtis Strange			
1998	Billy Mayfair	271	Scott Verplank	273	Warwick Hills G&CC, Grand Blanc, MI	72/7,105
1999	Tom Pernice, Jr.	270	Ted Tryba	271	Warwick Hills G&CC, Grand Blanc, MI	72/7,105
			Tom Lehman			
			Bob Tway			
2000	Rocco Mediate	268	Chris Perry	270	Warwick Hills G&CC, Grand Blanc, MI	72/7,105
2001	Kenny Perry	263	Chris DiMarco	265	Warwick Hills G&CC, Grand Blanc, MI	72/7,105
			Jim Furyk			
2002	Tiger Woods	271	Fred Funk	275	Warwick Hills G&CC, Grand Blanc, MI	72/7,127
			Brian Gay			
			Mark O'Meara			
			Esteban Toledo			
2003	Jim Furyk	267	Briny Baird	269	Warwick Hills G&CC, Grand Blanc, MI	72/7,127
			Chris DiMarco			
			Geoff Ogilvy			
			Tiger Woods			
2004	Vijay Singh	265	John Daly	266	Warwick Hills G&CC, Grand Blanc, MI	72/7,127

*KEY: * = Playoff ~ = Weather-shortened ** = Unofficial tournament*

The 17th hole of the Warwick Hills Golf & Country Club.

2004 The INTERNATIONAL [33rd of 48 official events]

The INTERNATIONAL at Castle Pines Golf Club

Winner: ROD PAMPLING
+15 +7 +7 +2 +31 $900,000

Castle Pines Golf Club

Castle Rock, CO

August 5-8, 2004

Purse: $5,000,000
Par: 36-36—72
Yards: 7,619

LEADERS: First Round—Rod Pampling with 15 points held a one-stroke lead over Geoff Ogilvy, Jose Coceres and Chris DiMarco. Stephen Leaney trailed by three.
Second Round—DiMarco moved to 31 points, nine ahead of Pampling. Bob Tway and Danny Briggs were 13 back.
Third Round—DiMarco and Pampling sat at 29 points, one ahead of Alex Cejka. Tom Pernice, Jr. and Tway were three behind.

CUT: Starting field of 144 professionals cut to 72 players at 6 points or better after 36 holes. After 54 holes, the field was cut to 44 players at +14 or better.

PRO-AM: $5,000 Morning: John Huston, 34, $1,000. $5,000 Afternoon: Rich Beem, 21, $1,000.

WEATHER: Thursday, partly cloudy with temperatures in the low 80s. Play was delayed at 3:03 p.m. MT and suspended for the day at 5:55 p.m. First round resumed Friday at 7 a.m. The second round was moved back to a 9:30 a.m. start. Mostly sunny on Friday with temperatures into the mid-80s. First round finished at 11:01 a.m. Play was delayed at 3:30 p.m. Play was delayed again at 5:28 p.m. Play was suspended for the day at 8:03 p.m. Second-round play resumed at 7 a.m. on Saturday and concluded at 10:30 a.m. Third round started at 11:10 a.m. Mostly sunny with light rain at times. Temperatures into the mid-80s. Mostly sunny on Sunday with temperatures in the mid-80s.

Check out the 2005 INTERNATIONAL, August 4-7 on USA/CBS

ORDER OF FINISH

Rod Pampling	1	+15	+7	+7	+2	+31	$900,000.00
Alex Cejka	2	+8	+9	+11	+1	+29	540,000.00
Tom Pernice, Jr.	3	+5	+10	+11	+1	+27	340,000.00
Duffy Waldorf	4	+8	+3	+7	+8	+26	240,000.00
Jay Haas	5	+10	+3	+8	+4	+25	200,000.00
Stewart Cink	T6	+6	+5	+11	+2	+24	167,500.00
Chris DiMarco	T6	+14	+17	-2	-5	+24	167,500.00
Tim Petrovic	T6	+9	+5	+8	+2	+24	167,500.00
Mathias Gronberg	T9	+2	+6	+9	+6	+23	135,000.00
Bernhard Langer	T9	+7	+7	+5	+4	+23	135,000.00
Bob Tway	T9	+9	+9	+8	-3	+23	135,000.00
Todd Hamilton	T12	+6	+8	+7	+1	+22	105,000.00
Jose Maria Olazabal	T12	+11	+3	+9	-1	+22	105,000.00
Kevin Sutherland	T12	+5	+10	+4	+3	+22	105,000.00
Justin Leonard	T15	+6	+7	+1	+7	+21	82,500.00
Davis Love III	T15	+8	+8	+5	0	+21	82,500.00
Rocco Mediate	T15	+7	+7	+7	0	+21	82,500.00
Corey Pavin	T15	+4	+6	+8	+3	+21	82,500.00
Stuart Appleby	T19	+2	+6	+6	+6	+20	60,600.00
Notah Begay III	T19	+1	+13	0	+6	+20	60,600.00
Chad Campbell	T19	+6	+3	+7	+4	+20	60,600.00
Kevin Na	T19	+5	+4	+8	+3	+20	60,600.00
Justin Rose	T19	+9	+2	+10	-1	+20	60,600.00
Olin Browne (S)	T24	-1	+18	-1	+3	+19	$41,500.00
John Cook	T24	+3	+5	+6	+5	+19	41,500.00
Harrison Frazar	T24	+2	+9	+3	+5	+19	41,500.00
Mark Hensby	T24	+2	+8	+4	+5	+19	41,500.00
John Rollins	T24	+8	+6	+4	+1	+19	41,500.00
Ernie Els	29	+4	+8	+4	+2	+18	35,500.00
Bart Bryant	30	+8	+1	+6	+2	+17	34,000.00
Danny Ellis	T31	+1	+15	+5	-5	+16	31,000.00
Brad Faxon	T31	+9	-1	+9	-1	+16	31,000.00
Bill Haas (S)	T31	+10	0	+4	+2	+16	31,000.00
Brian Bateman	T34	-2	+12	+6	-1	+15	27,000.00
Lucas Glover	T34	+4	+2	+8	+1	+15	27,000.00
Arron Oberholser	T34	+6	+7	+9	-7	+15	27,000.00
J.P. Hayes	37	+6	+10	+4	-6	+14	24,500.00
Billy Mayfair	38	+4	+6	+4	-1	+13	23,500.00
Danny Briggs	39	+8	+10	0	-6	+12	22,500.00
Tom Lehman	T40	+11	-5	+9	-5	+10	20,500.00
Brett Quigley	T40	+6	+4	+4	-4	+10	20,500.00
Kirk Triplett	T40	+3	+4	+7	-4	+10	20,500.00
Jose Coceres	43	+14	-1	+1	-5	+9	18,500.00
Geoff Ogilvy	44	+14	+3	-1	-8	+8	17,500.00
Brent Geiberger	T45	+3	+4	+6		+13	16,000.00
John Senden	T45	-3	+9	+7		+13	16,000.00
Robert Allenby	T47	+8	-1	+5		+12	13,220.00
Brenden Pappas	T47	0	+11	+1		+12	13,220.00
Craig Perks	T47	+5	+4	+3		+12	$13,220.00
Dicky Pride (S)	T47	0	+9	+3		+12	13,220.00
Rory Sabbatini	T47	+5	+6	+1		+12	13,220.00
Jason Bohn	T52	+4	+3	+4		+11	11,600.00
Steve Elkington	T52	+4	+6	+1		+11	11,600.00
Ryan Palmer	T52	+5	+1	+5		+11	11,600.00
Tag Ridings	T52	+7	+4	0		+11	11,600.00
David Toms	T52	+6	+2	+3		+11	11,600.00
Bo Van Pelt	T52	+4	+3	+4		+11	11,600.00
Cameron Beckman	T58	+1	+7	+2		+10	11,150.00
Carl Pettersson	T58	+3	+4	+3		+10	11,150.00
D.J. Brigman	T60	+5	+4	0		+9	10,900.00
Brian Kortan	T60	+8	+5	-4		+9	10,900.00
Roger Tambellini	T60	+7	-1	+3		+9	10,900.00
Neal Lancaster	T63	+2	+6	0		+8	10,650.00
Chris Riley	T63	-1	+9	0		+8	10,650.00
Tom Carter	T65	+7	+1	-1		+7	10,350.00
Jay Delsing (S)	T65	+4	+2	+1		+7	10,350.00
Stephen Leaney	T65	+12	-2	-3		+7	10,350.00
Steve Stricker	T65	+6	+6	-5		+7	10,350.00
John Huston	69	+8	-1	-1		+6	10,100.00
Steve Allan	T70	-3	+11	-6		+2	9,950.00
Rich Beem	T70	+4	+3	-5		+2	9,950.00
Frank Lickliter II	72	+2	+7	-10		-1	9,800.00

(S) = Sponsor Exemption, (T) = Tie

The following players did not finish (C=cut)

C—(+5)-Michael Allen, Briny Baird, David Branshaw, Bob Burns, Tripp Isenhour, Joel Kribel, Scott McCarron, Larry Mize, David Peoples, Phil Tataurangi, Esteban Toledo. **(+4)**-Ken Duke, Brian Gay, Matt Gogel. **(+3)**-Daniel Chopra, Brian Davis, Todd Fischer, Charles Howell III, Cliff Kresge, Hank Kuehne, Spike McRoy, Craig Parry, Mark Wiebe, Jay Williamson. **(+2)**-Stephen Ames, Pat Bates, Glen Day, Dan Forsman, Dudley Hart, Lee Janzen, Zach Johnson, Patrick Sheehan, Grant Waite. **(+1)**-Jonathan Byrd, Steve Flesch, Mike Hulbert, Jonathan Kaye, Joe Ogilvie, Steve Pate. **(-1)**-Ricardo Gonzalez, Ken Green, Greg Norman, Phillip Price, Clarence Rose, Joey Sindelar, Heath Slocum, Kevin Stadler, Hal Sutton, Vaughn Taylor. **(-2)**-Arjun Atwal, Jeff Brehaut, Gary Hallberg, Brian Watts. **(-3)**-Nick Flanagan, Kent Jones, Gene Sauers. **(-4)**-Rich Barcelo, Craig Barlow, Mark Brooks, Ben Curtis, Steve Lowery, Hirofumi Miyase. **(-5)**-David Duval, Dan Olsen, Pat Perez, Ted Purdy. **(-6)**-Thongchai Jaidee. **(-7)**-Kris Cox. **(-9)**-Scott Hend, Deane Pappas. **(-10)**-Aaron Baddeley. **(-11)**-Bill Loeffler.

Tournament Record:
48 points, Phil Mickelson, 1997; Ernie Els, 2000
Tournament Course Record:
20 points, Greg Whisman, 1992; Tom Purtzer, 1997

TOURNAMENT HISTORY

Year	Winner	Score	Runner-up	Score	Location	Par/Yards
THE INTERNATIONAL						
1986	Ken Green	+12	Bernhard Langer	+9	Castle Pines GC, Castle Rock, CO	72/7,559
1987	John Cook	+11	Ken Green	+9	Castle Pines GC, Castle Rock, CO	72/7,559
1988	Joey Sindelar	+17	Steve Pate Dan Pohl	+13	Castle Pines GC, Castle Rock, CO	72/7,559
1989	Greg Norman	+13	Clarence Rose	+11	Castle Pines GC, Castle Rock, CO	72/7,559
1990	Davis Love III	+14	Steve Pate Eduardo Romero Peter Senior	+11	Castle Pines GC, Castle Rock, CO	72/7,559
1991	Jose Maria Olazabal	+10	Ian Baker-Finch Scott Gump Bob Lohr	+7	Castle Pines GC, Castle Rock, CO	72/7,559
1992	Brad Faxon	+14	Lee Janzen	+12	Castle Pines GC, Castle Rock, CO	72/7,559
1993	Phil Mickelson	+45	Mark Calcavecchia	+37	Castle Pines GC, Castle Rock, CO	72/7,559
SPRINT INTERNATIONAL						
1994	Steve Lowery*	+35	Rick Fehr	+35	Castle Pines GC, Castle Rock, CO	72/7,559
1995	Lee Janzen	+34	Ernie Els	+33	Castle Pines GC, Castle Rock, CO	72/7,559
1996	Clarence Rose*	+31	Brad Faxon	+31	Castle Pines GC, Castle Rock, CO	72/7,559
1997	Phil Mickelson	+48	Stewart Appleby	+41	Castle Pines GC, Castle Rock, CO	72/7,559
1998	Vijay Singh	+47	Phil Mickelson Willie Wood	+41	Castle Pines GC, Castle Rock, CO	72/7,559
1999	David Toms	+47	David Duval	+44	Castle Pines GC, Castle Rock, CO	72/7,559
INTERNATIONAL PRESENTED BY QWEST						
2000	Ernie Els	+48	Phil Mickelson	+44	Castle Pines GC, Castle Rock, CO	72/7,559
2001	Tom Pernice	+34	Chris Riley	+33	Castle Pines GC, Castle Rock, CO	72/7,559
2002	Rich Beem	+44	Steve Lowery	+43	Castle Pines GC, Castle Rock, CO	72/7,594
THE INTERNATIONAL						
2003	Davis Love III	+46	Retief Goosen Vijay Singh	+34	Castle Pines GC, Castle Rock, CO	72/7,594
2004	Rod Pampling	+31	Alex Cejka	+29	Castle Pines GC, Castle Rock, CO	72/7,619

[NOTE: Prior to 1993, winning score was for fourth round only. Beginning in 1993, winning score has been total for four rounds.]
*KEY: * = Playoff ~ = Weather-shortened*

2004 PGA Championship *[34th of 48 official events]*

Winner: VIJAY SINGH #
67-68-69-76 280 (-8) $1,125,000

Whistling Straits Golf Club

Kohler, WI

August 12-15, 2004

Purse: $6,250,000
Par: 36-36—72
Yards: 7,514

LEADERS: First Round—Darren Clarke, at 7-under-par 65, led Justin Leonard and Ernie Els by one stroke. Vijay Singh, Scott Verplank, Luke Donald and Briny Baird were two behind. Nine players were three back.
Second Round—Leonard and Singh moved to 9-under-par 135 to lead Clarke, Els and Baird by one. Chris DiMarco was two behind.

Third Round—Singh at 12-under-par 204 led Leonard by one. Els, Clarke, Chris Riley, Phil Mickelson and Chris Riley were four back.

CUT: 73 players at 1-over-par 145 from a field of 156 professionals.

WEATHER: On Thursday, variably cloudy, breezy and cool with a high of 63. Winds N-NE 10-20 mph. Friday, slightly warmer and partly cloudy with a high of 65. NE winds 10-15 mph. Saturday, mostly sunny and breezy with NE winds reaching 10-15 mph. Warmer temperatures reached a high of 67. Sunday, sunny and warm with a high of 73. Winds SE 10-15 mph.

Check out the 2005 PGA Championship, August 11-14 on TNT/CBS

ORDER OF FINISH

 # Won three-hole playoff with a birdie and two pars.

Vijay Singh #	1	67-68-69-76	280	$1,125,000.00
Chris DiMarco	T2	68-70-71-71	280	550,000.00
Justin Leonard	T2	66-69-70-75	280	550,000.00
Ernie Els	T4	66-70-72-73	281	267,500.00
Chris Riley	T4	69-70-69-73	281	267,500.00
K.J. Choi	T6	68-71-73-70	282	196,000.00
Paul McGinley	T6	69-74-70-69	282	196,000.00
Phil Mickelson	T6	69-72-67-74	282	196,000.00
Robert Allenby	T9	71-70-72-70	283	152,000.00
Stephen Ames	T9	68-71-69-75	283	152,000.00
Ben Crane	T9	70-74-69-70	283	152,000.00
Adam Scott	T9	71-71-69-72	283	152,000.00
Darren Clarke	T13	65-71-72-76	284	110,250.00
Brian Davis	T13	70-71-69-74	284	110,250.00
Brad Faxon	T13	71-71-70-72	284	110,250.00
Arron Oberholser	T13	73-71-70-70	284	110,250.00
Stuart Appleby	T17	68-75-72-70	285	76,857.15
Jean-Francois Remesy	T17	72-71-70-72	285	76,857.15
Stewart Cink	T17	73-70-70-72	285	76,857.14
Matt Gogel	T17	71-71-69-74	285	76,857.14
Fredrik Jacobson	T17	72-70-70-73	285	76,857.14
Loren Roberts	T17	68-72-70-75	285	76,857.14
David Toms	T17	72-72-69-72	285	76,857.14
Tom Byrum	T24	72-73-71-70	286	$46,714.29
Chad Campbell	T24	73-70-71-72	286	46,714.29
J.L. Lewis	T24	73-69-72-72	286	46,714.29
Shaun Micheel	T24	77-68-70-71	286	46,714.29
Luke Donald	T24	67-73-71-75	286	46,714.28
Geoff Ogilvy	T24	68-73-71-74	286	46,714.28
Tiger Woods	T24	75-69-69-73	286	46,714.28
Carlos Franco	T31	69-75-72-71	287	34,250.00
Charles Howell III	T31	70-71-72-74	287	34,250.00
Miguel A. Jimenez	T31	76-65-75-71	287	34,250.00
Nick O'Hern	T31	73-71-68-75	287	34,250.00
Chip Sullivan	T31	72-71-73-71	287	34,250.00
Bo Van Pelt	T31	74-71-70-72	287	34,250.00
Briny Baird	T37	67-69-75-77	288	24,687.50
Steve Flesch	T37	73-72-67-76	288	24,687.50
Jay Haas	T37	68-72-71-77	288	24,687.50
Todd Hamilton	T37	72-73-75-68	288	24,687.50
Trevor Immelman	T37	75-69-72-72	288	24,687.50
Zach Johnson	T37	75-70-69-74	288	24,687.50
Ian Poulter	T37	73-72-70-73	288	24,687.50
Brett Quigley	T37	74-69-73-72	288	24,687.50
Tommy Armour III	T45	72-71-74-72	289	18,500.00
Niclas Fasth	T45	74-70-73-72	289	18,500.00
Padraig Harrington	T45	68-71-72-78	289	18,500.00
David Howell	T45	72-72-70-75	289	18,500.00
Michael Campbell	T49	71-73-69-77	290	14,660.00
Nick Faldo	T49	72-70-74-74	290	$14,660.00
Joe Ogilvie	T49	75-68-70-77	290	14,660.00
Patrick Sheehan	T49	70-71-75-74	290	14,660.00
Duffy Waldorf	T49	69-72-70-79	290	14,660.00
Carl Pettersson	54	71-71-76-73	291	13,600.00
Paul Azinger	T55	74-71-74-73	292	13,200.00
S.K. Ho	T55	72-73-73-74	292	13,200.00
Rod Pampling	T55	73-69-70-80	292	13,200.00
Craig Parry	T55	70-75-71-76	292	13,200.00
Eduardo Romero	T55	72-73-70-77	292	13,200.00
Hidemichi Tanaka	T55	72-71-71-78	292	13,200.00
Bob Tway	T55	71-70-74-77	292	13,200.00
Woody Austin	T62	74-71-74-74	293	12,650.00
Shingo Katayama	T62	74-70-76-73	293	12,650.00
Jeff Sluman	T62	72-72-79-70	293	12,650.00
Scott Verplank	T62	67-76-77-73	293	12,650.00
Scott Drummond	T66	71-72-76-75	294	12,350.00
Bernhard Langer	T66	74-70-75-75	294	12,350.00
Robert Gamez	T68	72-73-76-75	296	12,150.00
Mark Hensby	T68	74-69-77-76	296	12,150.00
Colin Montgomerie	70	73-72-78-74	297	12,000.00
Roy Biancalana	71	73-72-75-79	299	11,900.00
Jeff Coston	72	77-68-79-77	301	11,800.00
Skip Kendall	73	72-73-79-80	304	11,700.00

(Q) = Open Qualifier; (S) = Sponsor Exemption; (T) = Tie

The following players did not finish
(C=cut, W=withdrew, D=disqualified)

C—146-Brian Bateman, Jonathan Byrd, Paul Casey, Alex Cejka, Joe Durant, Fred Funk, Sergio Garcia, Hale Irwin, Raphael Jacquelin, Thomas Levet, Peter Lonard, Rocco Mediate, Jose Maria Olazabal, Tim Petrovic, Heath Slocum, Kevin Sutherland, Mike Weir, Lee Westwood, **147**-Bill Britton, Ben Curtis, Quinn Griffing, Stephen Leaney, Jesper Parnevik, Tom Pernice, Jr., Phillip Price, Ted Purdy, Justin Rose, Hal Sutton, **148**-Mark Brooks, Tim Clark, Bob Estes, Ricardo Gonzalez, Davis Love III, Scott McCarron, Brenden Pappas, Joey Sindelar, Craig Thomas, Kirk Triplett, Zane Zwemke, **149**-Tim Fleming, Harrison Frazar, Mark O'Meara, Kenny Perry, **150**-Angel Cabrera, John Huston, Shigeki Maruyama, **151**-Rich Beem, Brendan Jones, Alan Schulte, Mike Small, **152**-Frank Bensel, Graeme McDowell, **153**-Billy Andrade, Jim Furyk, Joakim Haeggman, Cary Hungate, Jerry Kelly, Steve Schneiter, Ian Woosnam, **154**-Tetsuji Hiratsuka, Steve Lowery, Rory Sabbatini, Bruce Smith, **155**-Jonathan Kaye, Mike Northern, Ron Philo, Jr., Bob Sowards, **156**-Tim Herron, Jeff Roth, David Tentis, Robert Thompson, **157**-Mike Baker, John Daly, **158**-David Duval, Thongchai Jaidee, Mike Schuchart, **159**-Sean English, **160**-Jeffrey Lankford, ***162***-Mark Evenson. **W**—Dudley Hart, **80**-Frank Lickliter II, **76**-Scott Hoch. **D—147**-Mark Calcavecchia.

TOURNAMENT HISTORY

Year	Winner	Score	Runner-up	Score	Location
PGA CHAMPIONSHIP					
1916	James M. Barnes	1-up	Jock Hutchison		Siwanoy CC, Bronxville, NY
1917	No Tournament+				
1918	No Tournament+				
1919	James M. Barnes	6 and 5	Fred McLeod		Engineers CC, Roslyn, NY
1920	Jock Hutchison	1-up	J. Douglas Edgar		Flossmoor CC, Flossmoor, IL
1921	Walter Hagen	3 and 2	James M. Barnes		Inwood CC, Far Rockaway, NY
1922	Gene Sarazen	4 and 3	Emmet French		Oakmont CC, Oakmont, PA
1923	Gene Sarazen*	1-up	Walter Hagen		Pelham CC, Pelham, NY
1924	Walter Hagen	2 up	James M. Barnes		French Lick CC, French Lick, IN
1925	Walter Hagen	6 and 5	William Mehlhorn		Olympia Fields CC, Olympia Fields, IL
1926	Walter Hagen	5 and 3	Leo Diegel		Salisbury GC, Westbury, NY
1927	Walter Hagen	1-up	Joe Turnesa		Cedar Crest CC, Dallas, TX
1928	Leo Diegel	6 and 5	Al Espinosa		Five Farms CC, Baltimore, MD
1929	Leo Diegel	6 and 4	Johnny Farrell		Hillcrest CC, Los Angeles, CA
1930	Tommy Armour	1-up	Gene Sarazen		Fresh Meadow CC, Flushing, NY
1931	Tom Creavy	2 and 1	Denny Shute		Wannamoisett CC, Rumford, RI
1932	Olin Dutra	4 and 3	Frank Walsh		Keller GC, St. Paul, MN
1933	Gene Sarazen	5 and 4	Willie Goggin		Blue Mound CC, Milwaukee, WI
1934	Paul Runyan*	1-up	Craig Wood		Park CC, Williamsville, NY
1935	Johnny Revolta	5 and 4	Tommy Armour		Twin Hills CC, Oklahoma City, OK
1936	Denny Shute	3 and 2	Jimmy Thomson		Pinehurst CC, Pinehurst, NC
1937	Denny Shute*	1-up	Harold McSpaden		Pittsburgh Field Club, Aspinwall, PA
1938	Paul Runyan	8 and 7	Sam Snead		Shawnee CC, Shawnee-on-Delaware, PA
1939	Henry Picard*	1-up	Byron Nelson		Pomonok CC, Flushing, NY
1940	Byron Nelson	1-up	Sam Snead		Hershey CC, Hershey, PA
1941	Vic Ghezzi*	1-up	Byron Nelson		Cherry Hills CC, Englewood, CO
1942	Sam Snead	2 and 1	Jim Turnesa		Seaview CC, Atlantic City, NJ
1943	No Tournament++				
1944	Bob Hamilton	1-up	Byron Nelson		Manito G&CC, Spokane, WA
1945	Byron Nelson	4 and 3	Sam Byrd		Moraine CC, Dayton, OH

NOTES

With his victory at the 2004 PGA Championship, ***Vijay Singh*** *moved to 12-of-19 when holding the 54-hole lead on the PGA TOUR, including 3-3 in major championships. The last time Singh failed to hold the 54-hole lead was the 2001 WORLDCOM Classic, where he finished T3 after leading Jose Coceres and Billy Mayfair by two strokes through 54 holes. With the PGA win, Singh has won eight consecutive times when holding at least a share of the 54-hole lead.*

In 2004, ***Vijay Singh*** *became the 18th different player to win at least two PGA Championships and the first since Tiger Woods (1999, 2000). He also became the 41st player to win three or more major championships in his career.*

With his 2004 PGA Championship victory, ***Vijay Singh*** *became the fourth-oldest player to win the PGA Championship at 41 years, 5 months and 23 days. The oldest in order: 1. Julius Boros (48 years, 4 months, 18 days), 1968 PGA Championship; 2. Jerry Barber (45 years, 3 months, 6 days), 1961; 3. Lee Trevino (44 years, 8 months, 18 days), 1984.*

Vijay Singh*'s final-round 4-over-par 76 was the highest final-round 18-hole score by a PGA champion and the highest final-round score for a winner at a major since Reg Whitcombe shot a closing 78 at Royal St. George's in winning the 1938 British Open. The all-time highest final-round score for a major champion is 84 by Fred Herd in 1898 at the U.S. Open. The previous highest PGA Championship final-round score for the winner since the event became a stroke-play event in 1958 was 74 by Raymond Floyd in 1969 at NCR Country Club in Dayton, OH.*

With his win at the 2004 PGA Championship, ***Vijay Singh*** *became the fourth different player since 1980 to collect five or more wins in a season, joining Tiger Woods (1999, 2000, 2001, 2002, 2003), Nick Price (1994) and Tom Watson (1980).*

Tournament Record:
265, David Toms, 2001

18-Hole Record:
63, Bruce Crampton, 1975 (Firestone CC); Raymond Floyd, 1982 (Southern Hills CC); Gary Player, 1984 (Shoal Creek); Vijay Singh, 1993 (Inverness); Brad Faxon, Michael Bradley, 1995 (Riviera CC); Jose Maria Olazabal, 2000 (Valhalla); Mark O'Meara, 2001 (Atlanta Athletic Club)

TOURNAMENT HISTORY

Year	Winner	Score	Runner-up	Score	Location
1946	Ben Hogan	6 and 4	Ed Oliver		Portland GC, Portland, OR
1947	Jim Ferrier	2 and 1	Chick Harbert		Plum Hollow CC, Detroit, MI
1948	Ben Hogan	7 and 6	Mike Turnesa		Norwood Hills CC, St. Louis, MO
1949	Sam Snead	3 and 2	Johnny Palmer		Hermitage CC, Richmond, VA
1950	Chandler Harper	4 and 3	Henry Williams, Jr.		Scioto CC, Columbus, OH
1951	Sam Snead	7 and 6	Walter Burkemo		Oakmont CC, Oakmont, PA
1952	Jim Turnesa	1-up	Chick Harbert		Big Spring CC, Louisville, KY
1953	Walter Burkemo	2 and 1	Felice Torza		Birmingham CC, Birmingham, MI
1954	Chick Harbert	4 and 3	Walter Burkemo		Keller GC, St. Paul, MN
1955	Doug Ford	4 and 3	Cary Middlecoff		Meadowbrook CC, Detroit, MI
1956	Jack Burke	3 and 2	Ted Kroll		Blue Hill CC, Boston, MA
1957	Lionel Hebert	2 and 1	Dow Finsterwald		Miami Valley CC, Dayton, OH
1958	Dow Finsterwald	276	Billy Casper	278	Llanerch CC, Havertown, PA
1959	Bob Rosburg	277	Jerry Barber	278	Minneapolis GC, St. Louis Park, MN
			Doug Sanders		
1960	Jay Hebert	281	Jim Ferrier	282	Firestone CC, Akron, OH
1961	Jerry Barber*	277	Don January	277	Olympia Fields CC, Olympia Fields, IL
1962	Gary Player	278	Bob Goalby	279	Aronimink GC, Newtown Square, PA
1963	Jack Nicklaus	279	Dave Ragan, Jr.	281	Dallas Athletic Club, Dallas, TX
1964	Bobby Nichols	271	Jack Nicklaus	274	Columbus CC, Columbus, OH
			Arnold Palmer		
1965	Dave Marr	280	Billy Casper	282	Laurel Valley CC, Ligonier, PA
			Jack Nicklaus		
1966	Al Geiberger	280	Dudley Wysong	284	Firestone CC, Akron, OH
1967	Don January*	281	Don Massengale	281	Columbine CC, Littleton, CO
1968	Julius Boros	281	Bob Charles	282	Pecan Valley CC, San Antonio, TX
			Arnold Palmer		
1969	Raymond Floyd	276	Gary Player	277	NCR CC, Dayton, OH
1970	Dave Stockton	279	Arnold Palmer	281	Southern Hills CC, Tulsa, OK
			Bob Murphy		
1971	Jack Nicklaus	281	Billy Casper	283	PGA National GC, Palm Beach Gardens, FL
1972	Gary Player	281	Tommy Aaron	283	Oakland Hills CC (South), Birmingham, MI
			Jim Jamieson		
1973	Jack Nicklaus	277	Bruce Crampton	281	Canterbury GC, Beachwood, OH
1974	Lee Trevino	276	Jack Nicklaus	277	Tanglewood GC, Winston-Salem, NC
1975	Jack Nicklaus	276	Bruce Crampton	278	Firestone CC, Akron, OH
1976	Dave Stockton	281	Raymond Floyd	282	Congressional CC (Blue), Bethesda, MD
			Don January		
1977	Lanny Wadkins*	282	Gene Littler	282	Pebble Beach GL, Pebble Beach, CA
1978	John Mahaffey*	276	Jerry Pate	276	Oakmont CC (South), Oakmont, PA
			Tom Watson		
1979	David Graham*	272	Ben Crenshaw	272	Oakland Hills CC, Birmingham, MI
1980	Jack Nicklaus	274	Andy Bean	281	Oak Hill CC, Rochester, NY
1981	Larry Nelson	273	Fuzzy Zoeller	277	Atlanta Athletic Club, Duluth, GA
1982	Raymond Floyd	272	Lanny Wadkins	275	Southern Hills CC, Tulsa, OK
1983	Hal Sutton	274	Jack Nicklaus	275	Riviera CC, Pacific Palisades, CA
1984	Lee Trevino	273	Gary Player	277	Shoal Creek, Birmingham, AL
			Lanny Wadkins		
1985	Hubert Green	278	Lee Trevino	280	Cherry Hills CC, Englewood, CO
1986	Bob Tway	276	Greg Norman	278	Inverness Club, Toledo, OH
1987	Larry Nelson*	287	Lanny Wadkins	287	PGA National, Palm Beach Gardens, FL
1988	Jeff Sluman	272	Paul Azinger	275	Oak Tree GC, Edmond, OK
1989	Payne Stewart	276	Andy Bean	277	Kemper Lakes GC, Hawthorn Woods, IL
			Mike Reid		
			Curtis Strange		
1990	Wayne Grady	282	Fred Couples	285	Shoal Creek, Birmingham, AL
1991	John Daly	276	Bruce Lietzke	279	Crooked Stick GC, Carmel, IN
1992	Nick Price	278	John Cook	281	Bellerive CC, St. Louis, MO
			Jim Gallagher, Jr.		
			Gene Sauers		
			Nick Faldo		
1993	Paul Azinger*	272	Greg Norman	272	Inverness Club, Toledo, OH
1994	Nick Price	269	Corey Pavin	275	Southern Hills CC, Tulsa, OK
1995	Steve Elkington*	267	Colin Montgomerie	267	Riviera CC, Pacific Palisades, CA
1996	Mark Brooks*	277	Kenny Perry	277	Valhalla GC, Louisville, KY
1997	Davis Love III	269	Justin Leonard	274	Winged Foot GC (West), Mamaroneck, NY
1998	Vijay Singh	271	Steve Stricker	273	Sahalee CC, Redmond, WA
1999	Tiger Woods	277	Sergio Garcia	278	Medinah CC, Medinah, IL
2000	Tiger Woods*	270	Bob May	270	Valhalla GC, Louisville, KY
2001	David Toms	265	Phil Mickelson	266	Atlanta Athletic Club, Duluth, GA
2002	Rich Beem	278	Tiger Woods	279	Hazeltine GC, Chaska, MN
2003	Shaun Micheel	276	Chad Campbell	278	Oak Hill CC, Rochester, NY
2004	Vijay Singh	280	Chris DiMarco	280	Whistling Straits, Kohler, WI
			Justin Leonard		

*KEY: * = Playoff + = World War I ++ = World War II*

2004 WGC-NEC Invitational

[35th of 48 official events]

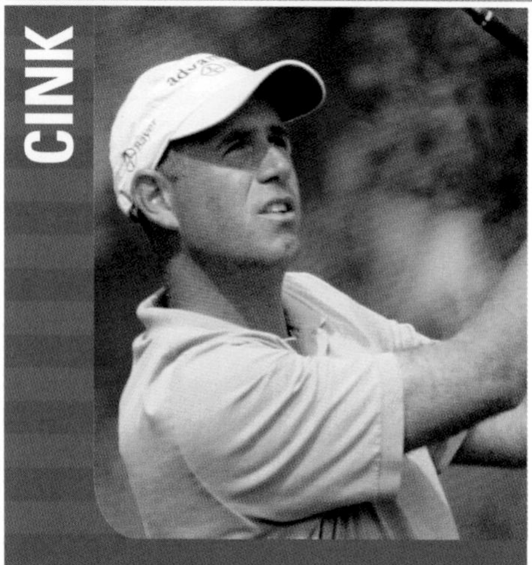

CINK

Winner: STEWART CINK
63-68-68-70 269 (-11) $1,200,000

Firestone Country Club (South Course)

Akron, OH

August 19-22, 2004

Purse: $7,000,000
Par: 35-35—70
Yards: 7,360

LEADERS: First Round—Stewart Cink shot a 7-under-par 63 to lead Zach Johnson by two strokes. Bob Tway and Barry Lane were four behind. Eight players were five back.
Second Round—Cink at 9-under-par 121 led Rory Sabbatini and Tiger Woods by three strokes. David Toms and Rod Pampling were four behind.
Third Round—Cink moved to 11-under-par 199 to lead Woods, David Toms and Chris DiMarco by five shots. Three players were six behind.

CUT: There was no cut. 75 of the 76 players completed 72 holes.

WEATHER: Due to heavy rainfall on Wednesday, players were allowed preferred lies all four rounds. The start of the first round was delayed from 9:35 a.m. to 2:45 p.m. due to heavy rain and lightning. The players played in threesomes off two tees instead of twosomes off No. 1. Warm and partly sunny, cloudy in late afternoon. Play was suspended at 5:05 p.m. Play resumed at 5:45 p.m. and was suspended due to darkness at 8:05 p.m. Sixteen players completed the first round, and 60 didn't. There was a 7:30 a.m. re-start on Friday. Second round beginning at 10:20 after players were re-paired in threesomes. Mostly cloudy on Friday, temperatures in the 60s. Mid-afternoon, heavy and steady rainfall. Play was suspended at 3:09 p.m. and suspended for the day at 4:34 p.m. 1.5 inches of rain fell on Friday. Saturday, partly cloudy and cooler in the morning. Mostly sunny in the afternoon, high of 71 degrees. Sunny and clear on Sunday, high of 77.

Check out the 2005 WGC-NEC Invitational, August 18-21 on ESPN/CBS

ORDER OF FINISH

Stewart Cink	1	63-68-68-70	269	$1,200,000.00
Rory Sabbatini	T2	68-66-71-68	273	552,500.00
Tiger Woods	T2	68-66-70-69	273	552,500.00
Angel Cabrera	T4	69-70-67-68	274	282,500.00
Davis Love III	T4	68-68-72-66	274	282,500.00
Bob Tway	T6	67-73-67-68	275	178,333.34
Chris DiMarco	T6	68-69-67-71	275	178,333.33
David Toms	T6	69-66-69-71	275	178,333.33
Robert Allenby	T9	71-67-69-69	276	116,000.00
Stuart Appleby	T9	69-70-69-68	276	116,000.00
Alex Cejka	T9	72-67-71-66	276	116,000.00
Charles Howell III	T9	71-67-68-70	276	116,000.00
Lee Westwood	T9	69-69-69-69	276	116,000.00
Darren Clarke	T14	71-70-68-68	277	87,500.00
Rod Pampling	T14	68-67-70-72	277	87,500.00
Paul Casey	T16	72-70-68-68	278	79,333.34
Luke Donald	T16	71-70-65-72	278	79,333.33
Sergio Garcia	T16	68-70-70-70	278	79,333.33
Jerry Kelly	T19	69-73-64-73	279	74,000.00
Scott Verplank	T19	69-69-67-74	279	74,000.00
Todd Hamilton	21	69-67-71-73	280	71,000.00
Stephen Ames	T22	69-70-69-73	281	65,000.00
Jim Furyk	T22	68-72-71-70	281	65,000.00
Zach Johnson	T22	65-73-73-70	281	65,000.00
Stephen Leaney	T22	73-67-68-73	281	$65,000.00
Jesper Parnevik	T22	69-72-70-70	281	65,000.00
S.K. Ho	T27	70-67-73-72	282	58,000.00
Miguel A. Jimenez	T27	71-70-72-69	282	58,000.00
Shigeki Maruyama	T27	69-68-72-73	282	58,000.00
Kenny Perry	T27	72-75-69-66	282	58,000.00
Brett Rumford	T27	71-73-69-69	282	58,000.00
Fred Couples	T32	72-68-69-74	283	51,000.00
Brad Faxon	T32	72-72-69-70	283	51,000.00
Trevor Immelman	T32	73-69-72-69	283	51,000.00
Fredrik Jacobson	T32	69-72-68-74	283	51,000.00
Thongchai Jaidee	T32	71-71-76-65	283	51,000.00
Thomas Levet	T32	68-73-70-72	283	51,000.00
Peter Lonard	T32	71-69-76-67	283	51,000.00
Joey Sindelar	T32	70-70-71-72	283	51,000.00
Vijay Singh	T32	73-73-67-70	283	51,000.00
Jay Haas	T41	70-69-71-74	284	45,500.00
Mike Weir	T41	70-67-73-74	284	45,500.00
John Daly	T43	71-69-74-71	285	43,000.00
Phil Mickelson	T43	70-75-68-72	285	43,000.00
Chris Riley	T43	72-69-71-73	285	43,000.00
Paul McGinley	T46	73-72-69-72	286	40,750.00
Nick Price	T46	69-73-72-72	286	40,750.00
Tim Clark	T48	71-70-72-74	287	39,750.00
Steve Flesch	T48	75-70-71-71	287	39,750.00
Tommy Armour III	T50	76-72-70-70	288	38,000.00
Ricardo Gonzalez	T50	73-75-70-70	288	$38,000.00
Justin Leonard	T50	73-71-72-72	288	38,000.00
Shaun Micheel	T50	71-72-73-72	288	38,000.00
Phillip Price	T50	72-70-74-72	288	38,000.00
Barry Lane	T55	67-77-73-72	289	36,000.00
J.L. Lewis	T55	73-71-73-72	289	36,000.00
Adam Scott	T55	71-67-75-76	289	36,000.00
K.J. Choi	T58	71-73-69-77	290	34,500.00
Carlos Franco	T58	69-73-75-73	290	34,500.00
Colin Montgomerie	T58	69-71-75-75	290	34,500.00
Scott Drummond	T61	69-75-73-75	292	32,750.00
Niclas Fasth	T61	75-68-70-79	292	32,750.00
Fred Funk	T61	69-75-71-77	292	32,750.00
Bernhard Langer	T61	74-69-75-74	292	32,750.00
Ernie Els	T65	72-77-72-72	293	30,750.00
Mark Hensby	T65	71-70-78-74	293	30,750.00
Jonathan Kaye	T65	71-75-72-75	293	30,750.00
Craig Parry	T65	79-69-71-74	293	30,750.00
Chad Campbell	T69	74-74-71-75	294	29,250.00
Kirk Triplett	T69	73-67-79-75	294	29,250.00
Andrew McLardy	71	73-83-69-70	295	28,500.00
Mark O'Meara	T72	71-72-77-76	296	27,750.00
Peter Senior	T72	69-77-74-76	296	27,750.00
Padraig Harrington	74	77-74-70-76	297	27,000.00
Pierre Fulke	75	73-77-78-76	304	26,500.00

(T) = Tie

The following player did not finish (W=withdrew)
W—80-Joakim Haeggman.

TOURNAMENT HISTORY

From 1962 through 1975, the World Series of Golf was played as a four-man, 36-hole exhibition. All money won in the tournament was unofficial. The winners in those years (with winning totals in parentheses):

1962 Jack Nicklaus (135)
1963 Jack Nicklaus (140)
1964 Tony Lema (138)
1965 Gary Player (139)
1966 Gene Littler (143)
1967 Jack Nicklaus (144)
1968 Gary Player (143)
1969 Orville Moody (141)
1970 Jack Nicklaus (136)
1971 Charles Coody (141)
1972 Gary Player (142)
1973 Tom Weiskopf (137)
1974 Lee Trevino (139)
1975 Tom Watson (140)

Year	Winner	Score	Runner-up	Score	Location	Par/Yards
WORLD SERIES OF GOLF						
1976	Jack Nicklaus	275	Hale Irwin	279	Firestone CC (South), Akron, OH	70/7,149
1977	Lanny Wadkins	267	Hale Irwin Tom Weiskopf	272	Firestone CC (South), Akron, OH	70/7,149
1978	Gil Morgan*	278	Hubert Green	278	Firestone CC (South), Akron, OH	70/7,149
1979	Lon Hinkle	272	Larry Nelson Bill Rogers Lee Trevino	273	Firestone CC (South), Akron, OH	70/7,149
1980	Tom Watson	270	Raymond Floyd	272	Firestone CC (South), Akron, OH	70/7,149
1981	Bill Rogers	275	Tom Kite	276	Firestone CC (South), Akron, OH	70/7,149
1982	Craig Stadler*	278	Raymond Floyd	278	Firestone CC (South), Akron, OH	70/7,149
1983	Nick Price	270	Jack Nicklaus	274	Firestone CC (South), Akron, OH	70/7,149
NEC WORLD SERIES OF GOLF						
1984	Denis Watson	271	Bruce Lietzke	273	Firestone CC (South), Akron, OH	70/7,149
1985	Roger Maltbie	268	Denis Watson	272	Firestone CC (South), Akron, OH	70/7,149
1986	Dan Pohl	277	Lanny Wadkins	278	Firestone CC (South), Akron, OH	70/7,149
1987	Curtis Strange	275	Fulton Allem	278	Firestone CC (South), Akron, OH	70/7,149
1988	Mike Reid*	275	Tom Watson	275	Firestone CC (South), Akron, OH	70/7,149

WGC-NEC Invitational

NOTES

***Stewart Cink**'s first-round, 7-under-par 63 sets a new opening round WGC-NEC Invitational low. Three players have started the WGC-NEC Invitational at Firestone Country Club with 64 - **Tiger Woods** (2001), **Ben Curtis** (2003) and **Sergio Garcia** (2003). Cink's 63 also tied his career low round. He also shot at the 2004 Buick Invitational and the 2000 WGC-NEC Invitational.*

Players were allowed preferred lies in the first three rounds at the 2004 WGC-NEC Invitational due to severe weather. There were four weather- and darkness-related suspensions on Thursday and Friday and the field had a two-tee start in rounds two and three due to the various delays.

*In his six-year career at the WGC-NEC Invitational, **Tiger Woods** has three wins and six finishes of T4 or better, the only player in the tournament's six-year history with six top-10s. **Jim Furyk**'s string of five consecutive WGC-NEC Invitational top-10s was broken as Furyk finished T22.*

***Stewart Cink** became the first wire-to-wire victor on the PGA TOUR in 2004, and the first since **Davis Love III** did so at the 2003 INTERNATIONAL. **Tiger Woods** won the 2000 WGC-NEC Invitational in wire-to-wire fashion when he won by 11 strokes over Justin Leonard and Phillip Price at Firestone Country Club. Woods also won the 2002 WGC-American Express Championship wire-to-wire.*

***Lee Westwood** became just the ninth player in WGC-NEC Invitational history in 2004 to post all four rounds in the 60s, shooting 69-69-69-69—276 en route to a T9 finish.*

Stewart Cink *earned his first multiple-victory season on the PGA TOUR with his win at the 2004 WGC-NEC Invitational. He won the MCI Classic earlier in the season.*

WGC-NEC Invitational Record:
259, Tiger Woods, 2000
NEC World Series of Golf Record:
262, Jose Maria Olazabal, 1990
Current Course Record:
61, Jose Maria Olazabal, 1990; Tiger Woods, 2000

TOURNAMENT HISTORY

Year	Winner	Score	Runner-up	Score	Location	Par/Yards
1989	David Frost*	276	Ben Crenshaw	276	Firestone CC (South), Akron, OH	70/7,149
1990	Jose Maria Olazabal	262	Lanny Wadkins	274	Firestone CC (South), Akron, OH	70/7,149
1991	Tom Purtzer*	279	Jim Gallagher, Jr.	279	Firestone CC (South), Akron, OH	70/7,149
			Davis Love III			
1992	Craig Stadler	273	Corey Pavin	274	Firestone CC (South), Akron, OH	70/7,149
1993	Fulton Allem	270	Jim Gallagher, Jr.	275	Firestone CC (South), Akron, OH	70/7,149
			Nick Price			
			Craig Stadler			
1994	Jose Maria Olazabal	269	Scott Hoch	270	Firestone CC (North), Akron, OH	70/6,918
1995	Greg Norman*	278	Billy Mayfair	278	Firestone CC (South), Akron, OH	70/7,149
			Nick Price			
1996	Phil Mickelson	274	Billy Mayfair	277	Firestone CC (South), Akron, OH	70/7,149
			Steve Stricker			
			Duffy Waldorf			
1997	Greg Norman	273	Phil Mickelson	277	Firestone CC (South), Akron, OH	70/7,189
1998	David Duval	269	Phil Mickelson	271	Firestone CC (South), Akron, OH	70/7,189
WORLD GOLF CHAMPIONSHIPS–NEC INVITATIONAL						
1999	Tiger Woods	270	Phil Mickelson	271	Firestone CC (South), Akron, OH	70/7,139
2000	Tiger Woods	259	Justin Leonard	270	Firestone CC (South), Akron, OH	70/7,139
			Phillip Price			
2001	Tiger Woods*	268	Jim Furyk	268	Firestone CC (South), Akron, OH	70/7,139
2002	Craig Parry	268	Robert Allenby	272	Sahalee CC; Sammamish, WA	72/6,949
			Fred Funk			
2003	Darren Clarke	268	Jonathan Kaye	272	Firestone CC (South), Akron, OH	70/7,230
2004	Stewart Cink	269	Rory Sabbatini	273	Firestone CC (South), Akron, OH	70/7,360
			Tiger Woods			

*KEY: * = Playoff ~ = Weather-shortened*

The par-5 16th at Firestone County Club.

ELIGIBILITY REQUIREMENTS FOR THE 2005 WGC-NEC INVITATIONAL

Players exempt from both qualifying stages are:

- Playing members of the 2005 U.S. and International teams from The Presidents Cup.
- Playing members of the 2004 U.S. and European teams from the Ryder Cup.
- The top 50 players, including any tied for 50th place, from the Official World Golf Ranking as of Monday, August 8, 2005 (i.e. through completion of The International).
- The top 50 players, including any tied for 50th place, from the Official World Golf Ranking as of Monday, August 15, 2005 (i.e. through completion of the PGA Championship).
- Tournament winners, whose victories are considered official, of tournaments from the Federation Tours since the prior year's NEC Invitational through December 31, 2004 with an Official World Golf Ranking Strength of Field Rating of 100 points or more.
- The winner of the following tournament from each of the following TOURs:
  - Japan Golf Tour: 2005 Japan Golf Tour Championship
  - Australian Tour: 2004 Australian PGA Championship
  - South Africa Tour: 2005 Tour Championship
  - Asian Tour: 2004 Volvo Masters of Asia
- Tournament Winners, whose victories are considered official of tournaments from teh Federation of Tours from January 1, 2005 through the 2005 NEC Invitational, with an Official World Golf Ranking Strength of Field Rating of 115 points or more.

2004 Reno-Tahoe Open [36th of 48 official events]

Reno·Tahoe Open

TAYLOR

Winner: VAUGHN TAYLOR #
67-67-69-75 278 (-10) $540,000

Montreux Golf & Country Club

Reno, NV

August 19-22, 2004

Purse: $3,000,000
Par: 36-36—72
Yards: 7,472

LEADERS: First Round—Roland Thatcher opened with a 6-under-par 66 and led Mark Wiebe, Mark Calcavecchia, Vaughn Taylor, Mark Wilson, Scott Simpson and Daniel Chopra by one stroke.
Second Round—Corey Pavin, after a 7-under-par 65, took the lead at 11-under-par 133. Taylor and Thatcher trailed by one stroke.
Third Round—Thatcher, at 14-under-par 202, led Taylor by one stroke. Steve Allan and Hunter Mahan trailed by two strokes.

CUT: 72 players at even-par 144 from a field of 132 professionals.

WEATHER: Thursday sunny and warm, scattered afternoon thunderstorms forced two stoppages of play. Play was suspended due to darkness at 7:46 p.m. with 66 players still on the course. The first round resumed at 7 a.m. on Friday and was completed at 10:19 a.m. Sunny and pleasant on Friday before, thunderstorms again caused a suspension of play. Play was suspended for the day due to darkness at 7:45 with 65 players on the course. The second round resumed at 7 a.m. on Saturday and was completed at 11:19 a.m. Partly cloudy and breezy on Saturday, highs in the upper 80s. Mostly cloudy and windy on Sunday, highs in the upper 70s. Wind gusts reaching 45 mph.

Check out the 2005 Reno-Tahoe Open, August 18-21 on The Golf Channel

ORDER OF FINISH

 # Won playoff with a birdie-3 on first hole of sudden death

Vaughn Taylor #	1	67-67-69-75	278	$540,000.00
Steve Allan	T2	68-68-68-74	278	224,000.00
Hunter Mahan	T2	69-67-68-74	278	224,000.00
Scott McCarron	T2	69-67-71-71	278	224,000.00
Carl Pettersson	T5	69-67-74-69	279	109,500.00
Roland Thatcher	T5	66-68-68-77	279	109,500.00
Mark Wilson	T5	67-71-69-72	279	109,500.00
Woody Austin	8	71-67-70-72	280	93,000.00
Michael Allen	T9	71-66-75-71	283	75,000.00
Daniel Chopra	T9	67-70-73-73	283	75,000.00
Ken Duke	T9	71-67-73-72	283	75,000.00
Joe Ogilvie	T9	72-64-72-75	283	75,000.00
Dennis Paulson	T9	68-75-69-71	283	75,000.00
Corey Pavin	T14	68-65-76-75	284	52,500.00
John Rollins	T14	69-70-74-71	284	52,500.00
Grant Waite	T14	70-69-72-73	284	52,500.00
Dean Wilson	T14	74-69-67-74	284	52,500.00
Craig Barlow	T18	72-69-69-75	285	37,800.00
Steve Elkington	T18	71-69-70-75	285	37,800.00
Spike McRoy	T18	73-69-72-71	285	37,800.00
Scott Simpson	T18	67-71-71-76	285	37,800.00
Garrett Willis	T18	72-66-74-73	285	37,800.00
Willie Wood	T18	72-70-70-73	285	$37,800.00
Jason Bohn	T24	70-71-73-72	286	24,900.00
Jay Delsing	T24	76-68-69-73	286	24,900.00
John Senden	T24	73-65-73-75	286	24,900.00
Hidemichi Tanaka	T24	68-68-75-75	286	24,900.00
Jay Williamson	T24	73-68-71-74	286	24,900.00
Cameron Beckman	T29	72-69-77-69	287	19,075.00
Ben Crane	T29	73-68-71-75	287	19,075.00
Trevor Dodds	T29	71-71-71-74	287	19,075.00
David Edwards	T29	73-70-73-71	287	19,075.00
Matt Gogel	T29	71-73-73-70	287	19,075.00
J.J. Henry	T29	69-75-69-74	287	19,075.00
Rich Beem	T35	68-71-75-74	288	14,790.00
John Cook	T35	75-69-68-76	288	14,790.00
Danny Ellis	T35	71-69-75-73	288	14,790.00
Brent Geiberger	T35	71-67-75-75	288	14,790.00
Duffy Waldorf	T35	71-68-75-74	288	14,790.00
David Branshaw	T40	72-72-71-74	289	11,700.00
Jeff Brehaut	T40	70-74-70-75	289	11,700.00
Lucas Glover	T40	70-71-75-73	289	11,700.00
J.P. Hayes	T40	71-72-71-75	289	11,700.00
Richard S. Johnson	T40	72-71-82-64	289	11,700.00
Todd Fischer	T45	71-72-72-75	290	9,030.00
Brian Gay	T45	73-70-73-74	290	9,030.00
Bill Haas (S)	T45	71-68-67-84	290	9,030.00
Jose Maria Olazabal	T45	69-72-72-77	290	$9,030.00
Guy Boros	49	73-71-74-73	291	7,800.00
Jay Don Blake	T50	70-69-74-79	292	7,305.00
Olin Browne	T50	70-67-74-81	292	7,305.00
Chris Smith	T50	74-69-70-79	292	7,305.00
Roger Tambellini	T50	73-69-73-77	292	7,305.00
Arjun Atwal	T54	74-70-76-73	293	6,930.00
Glen Day	T54	70-69-79-75	293	6,930.00
Mark Calcavecchia	T56	67-77-74-76	294	6,750.00
Mike Heinen	T56	70-73-80-71	294	6,750.00
Len Mattiace	T56	71-69-76-78	294	6,750.00
Gene Sauers	T56	72-71-77-74	294	6,750.00
Michael Clark II	T60	74-70-78-73	295	6,540.00
David Morland IV	T60	76-68-77-74	295	6,540.00
Phil Tataurangi	T60	73-71-71-80	295	6,540.00
Dicky Pride	T63	72-71-76-77	296	6,360.00
Jyoti Randhawa	T63	74-69-77-76	296	6,360.00
Mark Wiebe	T63	67-73-79-77	296	6,360.00
Michael Bradley	T66	73-70-79-75	297	6,180.00
Nick Flanagan	T66	72-72-80-73	297	6,180.00
Matt Kuchar	T66	72-72-72-81	297	6,180.00
Ryan Palmer	69	71-73-80-75	299	6,060.00
Jim McGovern	70	69-72-84-75	300	6,000.00
Scott Hend	71	70-74-85-80	309	5,940.00

(Q) = Open Qualifier; (S) = Sponsor Exemption; (T) = Tie

The following players did not finish
(C=cut, W=withdrew, D=disqualified)

C—145-Danny Briggs, Tom Carter, Jason Dufner, Joel Kribel, Pat Perez, Ted Purdy, Andre Stolz. **146-**Bart Bryant, Dan Forsman, Harrison Frazar, David Frost, Matt Hendrix, Gabriel Hjertstedt, Cliff Kresge, Hank Kuehne, Brad Lardon, Steve Pate, Tag Ridings, Kevin Sutherland. **147-**Aaron Barber, Kelly Gibson, Mike Grob, Peter Jacobsen, Greg Kraft, Rocco Mediate, Carl Paulson, Stan Utley. **148-**D.J. Brigman, Mark Brooks, Greg Chalmers, Joel Edwards, Billy Mayfair, Kevin Muncrief, Kevin Na, David Sutherland. **149-**Rich Barcelo, Notah Begay III, Robin Freeman, Brian Henninger, Blaine McCallister, Hirofumi Miyase, Wes Short, Jr., Esteban Toledo. **150-**Kris Cox, Jim Gallagher, Jr., Kent Jones. **151-**Larry Mize. **152-**Mathias Gronberg, **154-**Mike Springer, Tim Thelen, Ted Tryba. **155-**Brian Kortan. **156-**Jim Carter. **W—**Rick Leibovich, Tripp Isenhour. **77-**Chris Couch. **76-**Tommy Tolles, David Peoples, John E. Morgan, Craig Bowden. **D—217-**Donnie Hammond.

TOURNAMENT HISTORY

Year	Winner	Score	Runner-up	Score	Location	Par/Yards
RENO-TAHOE OPEN						
1999	Notah Begay III	274	Chris Perry	277	Montreux G&CC, Reno, NV	72/7,552
2000	Scott Verplank*	275	Jean Van de Velde	275	Montreux G&CC, Reno, NV	72/7,552
2001	John Cook	271	Jerry Kelly	272	Montreux G&CC, Reno, NV	72/7,552
2002	Chris Riley*	271	Jonathan Kaye	271	Montreux G&CC, Reno, NV	72/7,472
2003	Kirk Triplett	271	Tim Herron	274	Montreux G&CC, Reno, NV	72/7,472
2004	Vaughn Taylor*	278	Steve Allen Hunter Mahan Scott McCarron	278	Montreux G&CC, Reno, NV	72/7,472

*KEY: * = Playoff ~ = Weather-shortened*

Tournament Record:
271, John Cook, 2001; Chris Riley, Jonathan Kaye, 2002; Kirk Triplett, 2003
Tournament Course Record:
63, Notah Begay III, 1999; Brian Henninger, 2000; Kirk Triplett, 2003

Vaughn Taylor studies putt.

2004 Buick Championship [37th of 48 official events]

BUICK CHAMPIONSHIP

AUSTIN

Winner: WOODY AUSTIN #
68-70-66-66 270 (-10) $756,000

Tournament Players Club at River Highlands

Cromwell, CT

August 26-29, 2004

Purse: $4,200,000
Par: 35-35—70
Yards: 6,820

LEADERS: First Round—Corey Pavin fired a 62 to take a three-shot lead over Bob Burns and Matt Weibring.
Second Round—Fred Funk and Zach Johnson were tied at 8-under 132, one stroke ahead of Hank Kuehne and two ahead of Jose Coceres and Pavin.
Third Round—Funk shot a 1-under 69 and took a one-stroke advantage over Tom Byrum and Pavin. Hunter Mahan and Joey Sindelar were two back.

CUT: 80 players at 1-over-par 141 from a field of 155 professionals and one amateur.

PRO-AM: Tom Pernice, Jr., 52, $2,000

WEATHER: On Thursday, dense fog delayed the start of play for one hour until 8 a.m. Clear and sunny after the fog broke, with highs in the mid-80s. Overcast and warmer Friday, with higher humidity and temperatures reaching the high 80s. Hazy, warm and humid all day Saturday, with the high temperature reaching 90. Warm, hot and humid again Sunday, with the high temperature reaching 90. SW winds, gusting to 15 mph.

Check out the 2005 Buick Championship, August 25-28 on USA/CBS

ORDER OF FINISH

 # Won playoff with a birdie-3 on first hole of sudden death

Player	Pos.	Scores	Total	Money
Woody Austin #	1	68-70-66-66	270	$756,000.00
Tim Herron	2	70-69-65-66	270	453,600.00
Fred Funk	T3	66-66-69-70	271	218,400.00
Zach Johnson	T3	67-65-73-66	271	218,400.00
Tom Pernice, Jr.	T3	70-66-68-67	271	218,400.00
Jason Bohn	T6	71-67-69-65	272	140,700.00
Matt Gogel	T6	67-69-69-67	272	140,700.00
Corey Pavin	T6	62-72-68-70	272	140,700.00
Tom Byrum	T9	69-66-67-71	273	109,200.00
Todd Fischer	T9	71-69-67-66	273	109,200.00
Jeff Sluman	T9	72-69-70-62	273	109,200.00
Kevin Sutherland	T9	70-70-67-66	273	109,200.00
Arjun Atwal	T13	68-72-70-64	274	69,825.00
Robert Damron	T13	71-68-68-67	274	69,825.00
Brad Faxon	T13	69-68-70-67	274	69,825.00
Jerry Kelly	T13	66-71-70-67	274	69,825.00
Hank Kuehne	T13	68-65-71-70	274	69,825.00
Hidemichi Tanaka	T13	68-69-67-70	274	69,825.00
Kirk Triplett	T13	68-67-69-70	274	69,825.00
Omar Uresti	T13	68-70-67-69	274	69,825.00
Craig Barlow	T21	73-66-69-67	275	42,000.00
Jose Coceres	T21	68-66-70-71	275	42,000.00
Frank Lickliter II	T21	73-68-67-67	275	42,000.00
Hunter Mahan	T21	71-67-65-72	275	42,000.00
Loren Roberts	T21	67-72-69-67	275	42,000.00
Bo Van Pelt	T21	69-68-68-70	275	$42,000.00
Olin Browne	T27	69-68-71-68	276	29,820.00
Brent Geiberger	T27	71-67-68-70	276	29,820.00
David Peoples	T27	66-70-73-67	276	29,820.00
Tim Wilkinson (Q)	T27	67-71-74-64	276	29,820.00
Garrett Willis	T27	72-66-71-67	276	29,820.00
Cameron Beckman	T32	71-69-67-70	277	20,440.00
Craig Bowden	T32	66-73-71-67	277	20,440.00
Daniel Chopra	T32	71-68-65-73	277	20,440.00
Joe Durant	T32	69-69-68-71	277	20,440.00
J.L. Lewis	T32	71-70-67-69	277	20,440.00
Kevin Na	T32	72-67-69-69	277	20,440.00
Tim Petrovic	T32	68-70-74-65	277	20,440.00
Ted Purdy	T32	73-66-68-70	277	20,440.00
John Senden	T32	69-70-70-68	277	20,440.00
Joey Sindelar	T32	68-67-68-74	277	20,440.00
Heath Slocum	T32	70-71-69-67	277	20,440.00
Jay Williamson	T32	68-71-67-71	277	20,440.00
Billy Andrade	T44	72-67-71-68	278	13,053.60
Jonathan Byrd	T44	72-67-70-69	278	13,053.60
Jason Dufner	T44	66-70-70-72	278	13,053.60
Brian Kortan	T44	70-71-69-68	278	13,053.60
Billy Mayfair	T44	68-71-69-70	278	13,053.60
Aaron Barber	T49	70-69-70-70	279	10,365.60
Pat Bates	T49	70-70-71-68	279	10,365.60
Ken Duke	T49	68-69-70-72	279	10,365.60
Skip Kendall	T49	69-69-66-75	279	10,365.60
Chris Nallen (S)	T49	69-70-74-66	279	10,365.60
Bart Bryant	T54	70-69-69-72	280	$9,618.00
Mike Heinen	T54	70-69-72-69	280	9,618.00
J.J. Henry	T54	69-72-71-68	280	9,618.00
Vaughn Taylor	T54	71-69-70-70	280	9,618.00
Bob Burns	T58	65-70-70-76	281	9,324.00
Bill Haas (S)	T58	70-69-69-73	281	9,324.00
Matt Weibring (S)	T58	65-72-74-70	281	9,324.00
Michael Allen	T61	69-72-68-73	282	8,946.00
Aaron Baddeley	T61	68-70-71-73	282	8,946.00
Ryan Palmer	T61	68-73-71-70	282	8,946.00
Pat Perez	T61	69-69-70-74	282	8,946.00
Craig Perks	T61	69-71-75-67	282	8,946.00
Esteban Toledo	T61	69-66-74-73	282	8,946.00
Russ Cochran	T67	68-73-71-71	283	8,526.00
Robert Gamez	T67	69-66-70-78	283	8,526.00
Hirofumi Miyase	T67	72-68-73-70	283	8,526.00
Steve Pate	T67	71-70-69-73	283	8,526.00
Justin Rose	T71	71-70-71-72	284	8,232.00
Scott Simpson (S)	T71	67-69-76-72	284	8,232.00
Roland Thatcher	T71	70-69-75-70	284	8,232.00
Brian Harman (S)	T71	73-67-71-73	284	Amateur
Tag Ridings	T75	67-71-77-70	285	8,022.00
Patrick Sheehan	T75	70-71-73-71	285	8,022.00
Deane Pappas	T77	68-73-73-72	286	7,854.00
Dicky Pride	T77	71-70-78-67	286	7,854.00
Scott Hend	79	71-70-71-80	292	7,728.00

(Q) = Open Qualifier; (S) = Sponsor Exemption; (T) = Tie

The following players did not finish
(C=cut, W=withdrew, D=disqualified)

C—142-Steve Allan, David Branshaw, Kris Cox, Niclas Fasth, David Frost, Brian Gay, Bradley Hughes, Joe Ogilvie, Carl Paulson, Brett Quigley, David Sutherland, Hal Sutton, Grant Waite, **143-**Guy Boros, Tim Clark, Glen Day, Nick Flanagan, Lee Janzen, Neal Lancaster, Nick Price, Jyoti Randhawa, Chris Smith, **144-**Danny Briggs, Mark Calcavecchia, Tom Carter, Mathias Gronberg, Cliff Kresge, Matt Kuchar, Peter Lonard, Len Mattiace, Brenden Pappas, Dennis Paulson, Wes Short, Jr., Steve Stricker, **145-**Jim Carter, Danny Ellis, Kent Jones, Brad Lardon, John Rollins, Gene Sauers, Eli Zackheim, **146-**Rich Barcelo, Blaine McCallister, Spike McRoy, Casey Wittenberg, **147-**Jeff Brehaut, Jay Delsing, Roger Tambellini, Dean Wilson, **148-**Chris Couch, Trevor Dodds, Mike Grob, Richard S. Johnson, Tommy Tolles, **149-**Greg Chalmers, Fred Couples, **150-**Kevin Giancola, Lucas Glover, David Morland IV, Andre Stolz, Ted Tryba, **151-**Dan Forsman, Tom Gleeton, Uly Grisette, Joel Kribel, Phil Tataurangi, Brian Watts, Mark Wilson, **152-**Mark Brooks, Kevin Muncrief, **154-**Frank Graziosa, **157-**Bob Mucha. **W—**John E. Morgan, **81-**Dan Olsen, **138-**Arron Oberholser. **D—77-**Ken Green, **71-**Dudley Hart.

TOURNAMENT HISTORY

Year	Winner	Score	Runner-up	Score	Location	Par/Yards
INSURANCE CITY OPEN						
1952	Ted Kroll	273	Lawson Little Skee Riegel Earl Stewart, Jr.	277	Wethersfield CC, Wethersfield, CT	71/6,568
1953	Bob Toski	269	Jim Ferrier	270	Wethersfield CC, Wethersfield, CT	71/6,568
1954	Tommy Bolt*	271	Earl Stewart, Jr.	271	Wethersfield CC, Wethersfield, CT	71/6,568
1955	Sam Snead	269	Fred Hawkins Mike Souchak	276	Wethersfield CC, Wethersfield, CT	71/6,568
1956	Arnold Palmer*	274	Ted Kroll	274	Wethersfield CC, Wethersfield, CT	71/6,568
1957	Gardner Dickinson	272	George Bayer	274	Wethersfield CC, Wethersfield, CT	71/6,568
1958	Jack Burke, Jr.	268	Dow Finsterwald Art Wall	271	Wethersfield CC, Wethersfield, CT	71/6,568
1959	Gene Littler	272	Tom Nieporte	273	Wethersfield CC, Wethersfield, CT	71/6,568
1960	Arnold Palmer*	270	Bill Collins Jack Fleck	270	Wethersfield CC, Wethersfield, CT	71/6,568
1961	Billy Maxwell*	271	Ted Kroll	271	Wethersfield CC, Wethersfield, CT	71/6,568
1962	Bob Goalby*	271	Art Wall	271	Wethersfield CC, Wethersfield, CT	71/6,568
1963	Billy Casper	271	George Bayer	272	Wethersfield CC, Wethersfield, CT	71/6,568
1964	Ken Venturi	273	Al Besselink Paul Bondeson Sam Carmichael Jim Grant	274	Wethersfield CC, Wethersfield, CT	71/6,568
1965	Billy Casper*	274	Johnny Pott	274	Wethersfield CC, Wethersfield, CT	71/6,568
1966	Art Wall	266	Wes Ellis	268	Wethersfield CC, Wethersfield, CT	71/6,568
GREATER HARTFORD OPEN INVITATIONAL						
1967	Charlie Sifford	272	Steve Oppermann	273	Wethersfield CC, Wethersfield, CT	71/6,568
1968	Billy Casper	266	Bruce Crampton	269	Wethersfield CC, Wethersfield, CT	71/6,568
1969	Bob Lunn*	268	Dave Hill	268	Wethersfield CC, Wethersfield, CT	71/6,568

NOTES

*A couple of interesting similarities between **Woody Austin**'s two PGA TOUR wins: Both have come in Buick-sponsored tournaments played in August, and both came in a two-man playoff.*

*The key to **Woody Austin**'s two victories was putting. Austin had struggled throughout his career finishing T57, T145, T129, T161 and T162 from 2003 back to 1999 but managed to finish sixth in putting (1.654) at the Buick Championship after entering the week with an average of 1.796 (137th). During his 1995 Buick Open win, Austin came into the week ranked 126th (1.800) and finished first that week with an average of 1.576.*

***Woody Austin** became the first player to record a round in the 70s (68-70-66-66) and win the Buick Championship since **D.A. Weibring** in 1996. He also recorded the highest 72-hole total at the tournament (10-under 270) since Weibring won in 1996 with a total of 10-under 270.*

***Woody Austin**'s win came nine years and 23 days since his last victory at the 1995 Buick Open, a span of 274 tournaments between wins.*

***Woody Austin** improved his playoff record to 2-1 by recording birdie on the first extra hole to defeat **Tim Herron**. Austin defeated **Mike Brisky** at the 1995 Buick Open on the second extra hole. The win helped Austin to earn Rookie of the Year honors that season.*

There were only 13 eagles during the 2004 Buick Championship. It's the fewest number of eagles in one Buick Championship since 1994, when the field recorded 11. In fact, there were no eagles at the TPC at River Highlands during round three. It was the first time since the final round of the 1993 tournament that no eagles were posted during a round at the Buick Championship.

Tournament Record:
259, Tim Norris, 1982 (Wethersfield CC)
Current Course Record:
61, Kirk Triplett, 2000; Phil Mickelson, Scott Verplank, 2001
Other Course Record:
61, Dana Quigley, 1982 (Wethersfield CC)

TOURNAMENT HISTORY

Year	Winner	Score	Runner-up	Score	Location	Par/Yards
1970	Bob Murphy	267	Paul Harney	271	Wethersfield CC, Wethersfield, CT	71/6,568
1971	George Archer*	268	Lou Graham J.C. Snead	268	Wethersfield CC, Wethersfield, CT	71/6,568
1972	Lee Trevino*	269	Lee Elder	269	Wethersfield CC, Wethersfield, CT	71/6,568
SAMMY DAVIS, JR.-GREATER HARTFORD OPEN						
1973	Billy Casper	264	Bruce Devlin	265	Wethersfield CC, Wethersfield, CT	71/6,568
1974	Dave Stockton	268	Raymond Floyd	272	Wethersfield CC, Wethersfield, CT	71/6,568
1975	Don Bies*	267	Hubert Green	267	Wethersfield CC, Wethersfield, CT	71/6,568
1976	Rik Massengale	266	Al Geiberger J.C. Snead	268	Wethersfield CC, Wethersfield, CT	71/6,568
1977	Bill Kratzert	265	Grier Jones Larry Nelson	268	Wethersfield CC, Wethersfield, CT	71/6,568
1978	Rod Funseth	264	Dale Douglass Lee Elder Bill Kratzert	268	Wethersfield CC, Wethersfield, CT	71/6,568
1979	Jerry McGee	267	Jack Renner	268	Wethersfield CC, Wethersfield, CT	71/6,568
1980	Howard Twitty*	266	Jim Simons	266	Wethersfield CC, Wethersfield, CT	71/6,568
1981	Hubert Green	264	Bobby Clampett Fred Couples Roger Maltbie	265	Wethersfield CC, Wethersfield, CT	71/6,568
1982	Tim Norris	259	Raymond Floyd Hubert Green	265	Wethersfield CC, Wethersfield, CT	71/6,568
1983	Curtis Strange	268	Jay Haas Jack Renner	269	Wethersfield CC, Wethersfield, CT	71/6,568
1984	Peter Jacobsen	269	Mark O'Meara	271	TPC of Connecticut, Cromwell, CT	71/6,786
CANON SAMMY DAVIS, JR.-GREATER HARTFORD OPEN						
1985	Phil Blackmar*	271	Jodie Mudd Dan Pohl	271	TPC of Connecticut, Cromwell, CT	71/6,786
1986	Mac O'Grady*	269	Roger Maltbie	269	TPC of Connecticut, Cromwell, CT	71/6,786
1987	Paul Azinger	269	Dan Forsman Wayne Levi	270	TPC of Connecticut, Cromwell, CT	71/6,786
1988	Mark Brooks*	269	Dave Barr Joey Sindelar	269	TPC of Connecticut, Cromwell, CT	71/6,786
CANON GREATER HARTFORD OPEN						
1989	Paul Azinger	267	Wayne Levi	268	TPC of Connecticut, Cromwell, CT	71/6,786
1990	Wayne Levi	267	Mark Calcavecchia Brad Fabel Rocco Mediate Chris Perry	269	TPC of Connecticut, Cromwell, CT	70/6,531
1991	Billy Ray Brown*	271	Rick Fehr Corey Pavin	271	TPC at River Highlands, Cromwell, CT	70/6,820
1992	Lanny Wadkins	274	Dan Forsman Donnie Hammond Nick Price	276	TPC at River Highlands, Cromwell, CT	70/6,820
1993	Nick Price	271	Dan Forsman Roger Maltbie	272	TPC at River Highlands, Cromwell, CT	70/6,820
1994	David Frost	268	Greg Norman	269	TPC at River Highlands, Cromwell, CT	70/6,820
1995	Greg Norman	267	Dave Stockton, Jr. Kirk Triplett Grant Waite	269	TPC at River Highlands, Cromwell, CT	70/6,820
1996	D.A. Weibring	270	Tom Kite	274	TPC at River Highlands, Cromwell, CT	70/6,820
1997	Stewart Cink	267	Tom Byrum Brandel Chamblee Jeff Maggert	268	TPC at River Highlands, Cromwell, CT	70/6,820
1998	Olin Browne*	266	Stewart Cink Larry Mize	266	TPC at River Highlands, Cromwell, CT	70/6,820
1999	Brent Geiberger	262	Skip Kendall	265	TPC at River Highlands, Cromwell, CT	70/6,820
2000	Notah Begay III	260	Mark Calcavechia	261	TPC at River Highlands, Cromwell, CT	70/6,820
2001	Phil Mickelson	264	Billy Andrade	265	TPC at River Highlands, Cromwell, CT	70/6,820
2002	Phil Mickelson	266	Jonathan Kaye Davis Love III	267	TPC at River Highlands, Cromwell, CT	70/6,820
GREATER HARTFORD OPEN						
2003	Peter Jacobsen	266	Chris Riley	268	TPC at River Highlands, Cromwell, CT	70/6,820
BUICK CHAMPIONSHIP						
2004	Woody Austin*	270	Tim Herron	270	TPC at River Highlands, Cromwell, CT	70/6,820

*KEY: * = Playoff ~ = Weather-shortened*

2004 Deutsche Bank Championship

[38th of 48 official events]

Deutsche Bank CHAMPIONSHIP

SINGH

Winner: VIJAY SINGH
68-63-68-69 268 (-16) $900,000

Tournament Players Club of Boston

Norton, MA

September 3-6, 2004

Purse: $5,000,000
Par: 36-35—71
Yards: 7,415

LEADERS: First Round—Ryan Palmer and Tiger Woods sat at 6-under 65, one ahead of Mark O'Meara, Cameron Beckman and Jonathan Byrd. **Second Round**—Vijay Singh used a 63 to move to 11-under 131. John Rollins, Woods and Bill Haas trailed by two. **Third Round**—Singh sat at 14-under 199, three ahead of Woods. Haas was five back.

CUT: 70 players at even-par 142 from a field of 155 professionals and one amateur.

PRO-AM: $10,000. Kevin Sutherland, 54, $2,000

WEATHER: Friday, a mix of sun and clouds with winds out of the SW 6-14 mph and temperatures from 58-80 degrees. Mostly sunny and warm on Saturday with temperatures reaching the low 80s and light winds out of the north. Sunday, mostly cloudy and breezy with a high of 70 and E-NE winds at 10-20 mph. Mostly sunny and pleasant on Monday with temperatures from the 60s to mid-70s and winds out of the SE 4-12 mph.

Check out the 2005 Deutsche Bank Championship, September 2-5 on USA/ABC

ORDER OF FINISH

Vijay Singh	1	68-63-68-69	268	$900,000.00
Adam Scott	T2	69-67-70-65	271	440,000.00
Tiger Woods	T2	65-68-69-69	271	440,000.00
Daniel Chopra	T4	68-69-70-67	274	220,000.00
John Rollins	T4	67-66-75-66	274	220,000.00
Hank Kuehne	T6	68-68-71-68	275	173,750.00
Shigeki Maruyama	T6	68-66-71-70	275	173,750.00
Jay Williamson	8	68-68-70-70	276	155,000.00
Brad Faxon	T9	72-69-68-68	277	135,000.00
Bill Haas (Q)	T9	69-64-71-73	277	135,000.00
Charles Howell III	T9	67-68-76-66	277	135,000.00
Camilo Villegas (S)	12	69-68-72-69	278	115,000.00
David Duval	T13	72-70-70-67	279	93,750.00
Zach Johnson	T13	68-72-71-68	279	93,750.00
Dennis Paulson	T13	69-70-71-69	279	93,750.00
David Toms	T13	69-71-73-66	279	93,750.00
Dan Forsman	T17	68-72-69-71	280	70,000.00
Richard S. Johnson	T17	70-69-73-68	280	70,000.00
Matt Kuchar	T17	69-73-70-68	280	70,000.00
Ryan Palmer	T17	65-69-74-72	280	70,000.00
Deane Pappas	T17	67-70-72-71	280	70,000.00
Skip Kendall	T22	69-69-71-72	281	52,000.00
Neal Lancaster	T22	72-69-70-70	281	52,000.00
Tim Petrovic	T22	70-68-71-72	281	$52,000.00
Todd Fischer	T25	72-67-73-70	282	39,875.00
Frank Lickliter II	T25	68-67-76-71	282	39,875.00
Hunter Mahan	T25	72-69-71-70	282	39,875.00
David Peoples	T25	73-66-73-70	282	39,875.00
Aaron Baddeley	T29	68-70-74-71	283	31,791.67
Brent Geiberger	T29	72-70-70-71	283	31,791.67
Jesper Parnevik	T29	70-71-73-69	283	31,791.67
Justin Rose	T29	72-70-74-67	283	31,791.67
Jonathan Byrd	T29	66-71-72-74	283	31,791.66
Dean Wilson	T29	71-71-68-73	283	31,791.66
Jeff Brehaut	T35	71-68-78-67	284	26,375.00
Jim Furyk	T35	69-70-77-68	284	26,375.00
John Daly	T37	71-70-73-71	285	19,500.00
Jason Dufner	T37	71-69-75-70	285	19,500.00
Ken Green	T37	72-68-74-71	285	19,500.00
Mike Heinen	T37	72-70-74-69	285	19,500.00
J.J. Henry	T37	70-71-75-69	285	19,500.00
Mark Hensby	T37	69-70-73-73	285	19,500.00
Lee Janzen	T37	70-69-74-72	285	19,500.00
Kent Jones	T37	71-68-74-72	285	19,500.00
Arron Oberholser	T37	70-69-71-75	285	19,500.00
Jeff Sluman	T37	70-68-77-70	285	19,500.00
Hidemichi Tanaka	T37	70-72-72-71	285	19,500.00
John Senden	T48	71-69-79-68	287	12,428.58
Cameron Beckman	T48	66-71-76-74	287	$12,428.57
Jason Bohn	T48	72-70-73-72	287	12,428.57
Tim Clark	T48	70-67-75-75	287	12,428.57
Robert Gamez	T48	71-71-74-71	287	12,428.57
Steve Pate	T48	71-71-72-73	287	12,428.57
Craig Perks	T48	67-71-74-75	287	12,428.57
Danny Briggs	T55	68-73-73-74	288	11,350.00
Trevor Immelman	T55	71-70-74-73	288	11,350.00
Billy Mayfair	T55	67-72-77-72	288	11,350.00
Joey Sindelar	T55	72-69-74-73	288	11,350.00
Michael Allen	T59	72-69-77-71	289	11,000.00
Robert Damron	T59	69-72-71-77	289	11,000.00
Mark Wilson	T59	73-68-73-75	289	11,000.00
Briny Baird	T62	72-69-76-73	290	10,700.00
Ben Crane	T62	69-72-75-74	290	10,700.00
Danny Ellis	T62	72-68-74-76	290	10,700.00
Bob Burns	T65	71-66-77-77	291	10,450.00
Harrison Frazar	T65	70-71-74-76	291	10,450.00
Pat Bates	67	70-72-78-73	293	10,300.00
Brian Kortan	68	72-70-74-78	294	10,200.00
Guy Boros	69	72-70-74-79	295	10,100.00
Mark O'Meara	70	66-74-82-76	298	10,000.00

(Q) = Open Qualifier; (S) = Sponsor Exemption; (T) = Tie

The following players did not finish (C=cut, W=withdrew)

C—143-Billy Andrade, Tommy Armour III, Arjun Atwal, Aaron Barber, D.J. Brigman, Tom Carter, Russ Cochran, Nick Flanagan, Scott Hend, Spike McRoy, Geoff Ogilvy, Pat Perez, Brett Quigley, Wes Short, Jr., Marcel Siem, Roland Thatcher. **144-**Rich Barcelo, Brian Bateman, Mark Brooks, Glen Day, Dudley Hart, Tim Herron, Ted Purdy, Chris Smith, Bo Van Pelt, Casey Wittenberg. **145-**Niclas Fasth, Brian Gay, Lucas Glover, Brian Henninger, Blaine McCallister, Kevin Na, Dan Olsen, Tom Pernice, Jr., Patrick Sheehan, Heath Slocum, David Sutherland, Kevin Sutherland, Grant Waite, Garrett Willis. **146-**Craig Bowden, Jason Caron, Jose Coceres, David Frost, Mathias Gronberg, Steve Lowery, Hirofumi Miyase. **147-**Woody Austin, Bart Bryant, Greg Chalmers, Kris Cox, Ben Curtis, Shaun Micheel, Chris Nallen, Jamie Neher, Phillip Price, Dicky Pride, Tag Ridings, Steve Stricker. **148-**Kevin Muncrief, Gene Sauers, Roger Tambellini. **149-**John Cook, Len Mattiace, Brenden Pappas, Geoffrey Sisk, Phil Tataurangi, Esteban Toledo. **150-**Olin Browne, Ken Duke. **151-**Ron Philo, Jr. **152-**David Branshaw, Chris Couch, Frank Vana (A). **153-**Paul Azinger. **154-**Cliff Kresge. **156-**Mike Baker. **157-**Steve Allan, Trevor Dodds. **158-**Jeffery W. Martin. **168-**David Gossett. **W—80-**Joe Durant. **77-**John E. Morgan. **75-**Andre Stolz, Carlos Franco. **72-**Steve Flesch.

Tournament Record:
264, Adam Scott, 2003
18-Hole Record:
62, Adam Scott, 2003

TOURNAMENT HISTORY

Year	Winner	Score	Runner-up	Score	Location	Par/Yards
DEUTSCHE BANK CHAMPIONSHIP						
2003	Adam Scott	264	Rocco Mediate	268	TPC of Boston, Norton, MA	71/7,415
2004	Vijay Singh	268	Adam Scott	271	TPC of Boston, Norton, MA	71/7,415
			Tiger Woods			

Fans gathered to watch Vijay Singh win at the Deutsche Bank Championship.

2004 Bell Canadian Open [39th of 48 official events]

BELL CANADIAN OPEN

Winner: VIJAY SINGH #
68-66-72-69 275 (-9) $810,000

Glen Abbey Golf Club

Oakville, Ontario, Canada

September 9-12, 2004

Purse: $4,500,000
Par: 35-36—71
Yards: 7,222

LEADERS: First Round—Joey Sindelar, at 5-under-par 66, led Billy Andrade, Craig Barlow and D.J. Brigman by one stroke. Pat Perez, Mike Weir, Vijay Singh and Tag Ridings were two back.
Second Round—Weir moved to 9-under-par 133 to lead Singh by one and Jesper Parnevik by two. Perez, Barlow and David Branshaw where three back.
Third Round—Weir, at 10-under-par 203, led Singh, Parnevik and Cliff Kresge by three strokes. Brigman and Joe Ogilvie were four behind.

CUT: 3-over-par 145 from a field of 151 professionals and five amateurs.

PRO-AM: $10,000. Scott McCarron, 56, $2,000.

WEATHER: Heavy rains overnight (2.56 inches) caused a four-hour delay on Thursday, moving first-round tee times to a 12:15 p.m. start. Warm and clear in the afternoon with temperatures in the low 70s. High winds with NW gusts up to 30 mph. 77 of the 156 players completed the first round. The remaining 79 players completed the first round at 1 p.m. Friday after beginning at 7:31 a.m. The second round commenced at 11:45 a.m. Warm and sunny on Friday with a high of 72. Play for the day was halted at 7:31 p.m. due to darkness. Second-round play resumed at 7:33 a.m. on Saturday and was completed at 11:13 a.m. Third-round tee times ran from 11:45 a.m. to 1:45 p.m. in threesomes off two tees. Mostly sunny and warm on the weekend with temperatures in the mid 70s.

Check out the 2005 Bell Canadian Open, September 8-11 on ESPN

ORDER OF FINISH

 # Won playoff with a par-5 on the third hole of sudden death

Vijay Singh #	1	68-66-72-69	275	$810,000.00
Mike Weir	2	68-65-70-72	275	486,000.00
Joe Ogilvie	3	70-69-69-69	277	306,000.00
Stewart Cink	T4	72-68-69-69	278	177,187.50
Tom Lehman	T4	74-70-70-64	278	177,187.50
Hunter Mahan	T4	72-69-69-68	278	177,187.50
Justin Rose	T4	70-70-75-63	278	177,187.50
Robert Damron	8	72-71-70-66	279	139,500.00
Mark Hensby	T9	70-69-70-71	280	126,000.00
Jesper Parnevik	T9	69-66-71-74	280	126,000.00
Billy Andrade	T11	67-75-71-68	281	103,500.00
D.J. Brigman	T11	67-74-67-73	281	103,500.00
David Sutherland	T11	69-72-68-72	281	103,500.00
David Branshaw	T14	71-65-75-71	282	76,500.00
Cliff Kresge	T14	69-70-67-76	282	76,500.00
Steve Lowery	T14	70-69-70-73	282	76,500.00
Pat Perez	T14	68-68-78-68	282	76,500.00
Dean Wilson	T14	71-70-69-72	282	76,500.00
Arjun Atwal	T19	71-67-75-70	283	54,540.00
Jose Coceres	T19	72-70-74-67	283	54,540.00
Glen Day	T19	70-69-70-74	283	54,540.00
Bill Haas	T19	71-71-67-74	283	54,540.00
Kenny Perry	T19	71-67-74-71	283	54,540.00
Chris DiMarco	T24	69-71-73-71	284	41,400.00
Casey Wittenberg (S)	T24	73-72-71-68	284	41,400.00
Craig Barlow	T26	67-69-75-74	285	$29,992.50
Chad Campbell	T26	73-68-72-72	285	29,992.50
Bill Glasson	T26	72-70-73-70	285	29,992.50
Corey Pavin	T26	73-70-72-70	285	29,992.50
David Peoples	T26	69-70-73-73	285	29,992.50
Craig Perks	T26	70-72-75-68	285	29,992.50
Brett Quigley	T26	69-71-73-72	285	29,992.50
Joey Sindelar	T26	66-73-74-72	285	29,992.50
Roland Thatcher	T26	72-72-71-70	285	29,992.50
Bob Tway	T26	74-71-70-70	285	29,992.50
David Edwards	T36	72-69-74-71	286	21,656.25
Dudley Hart	T36	72-73-73-68	286	21,656.25
Richard S. Johnson	T36	73-70-71-72	286	21,656.25
Roger Tambellini	T36	71-71-69-75	286	21,656.25
Jason Bohn	T40	73-70-72-72	287	18,000.00
Greg Chalmers	T40	71-72-70-74	287	18,000.00
David Frost	T40	73-71-71-72	287	18,000.00
Davis Love III	T40	72-73-68-74	287	18,000.00
Jonathan Byrd	T44	72-70-69-77	288	14,850.00
Esteban Toledo	T44	76-68-72-72	288	14,850.00
Tommy Tolles	T44	72-70-78-68	288	14,850.00
Mark Brooks	T47	69-73-76-71	289	11,898.00
Fred Funk	T47	74-70-72-73	289	11,898.00
Tim Petrovic	T47	72-70-73-74	289	11,898.00
Jim Rutledge (S)	T47	74-71-75-69	289	11,898.00
Mark Wilson	T47	74-70-71-74	289	11,898.00
David Duval	T52	71-72-76-71	290	10,494.00
Todd Fischer	T52	71-71-75-73	290	10,494.00
Steve Flesch	T52	73-71-75-71	290	$10,494.00
Tag Ridings	T52	68-76-72-74	290	10,494.00
Omar Uresti	T52	74-70-74-72	290	10,494.00
Neal Lancaster	T57	71-70-75-75	291	10,035.00
Billy Mayfair	T57	70-74-72-75	291	10,035.00
Jim McGovern	T57	71-72-76-72	291	10,035.00
Phil Mickelson	T57	75-69-79-68	291	10,035.00
Paul Azinger	T61	72-68-74-78	292	9,630.00
Tom Carter	T61	72-71-76-73	292	9,630.00
Brian Kortan	T61	71-74-70-77	292	9,630.00
Dennis Paulson	T61	69-72-75-76	292	9,630.00
Garrett Willis	T61	71-74-75-72	292	9,630.00
Aaron Barber	T66	72-73-75-73	293	9,225.00
Danny Briggs	T66	69-73-77-74	293	9,225.00
Jim Carter	T66	72-69-78-74	293	9,225.00
Justin Leonard	T66	76-66-77-74	293	9,225.00
Larry Mize	T70	76-68-74-76	294	8,865.00
David Morland IV	T70	70-73-73-78	294	8,865.00
Dicky Pride	T70	72-72-77-73	294	8,865.00
Grant Waite	T70	75-70-73-76	294	8,865.00
Dirk Ayers (Q)	T74	72-71-79-73	295	8,550.00
John Rollins	T74	74-71-74-76	295	8,550.00
Kevin Sutherland	T74	74-71-75-75	295	8,550.00
Andre Stolz	77	71-74-77-74	296	8,370.00
Chris Couch	78	71-71-79-83	304	8,280.00

(Q) = Open Qualifier; (S) = Sponsor Exemption; (T) = Tie

The following players did not finish
(C=cut, W=withdrew, A=Amateur)

C—146-Aaron Baddeley, Tom Byrum, Michael Clark II, Jason Dufner, Brian Gay, Mathias Gronberg, Fredrik Jacobson, J.L. Lewis, Len Mattiace, Wes Short, Jr., Brad Sutterfield, Brian Watts, **147**-Tommy Armour III, Jay Don Blake, Craig Bowden, Scott Dunlap, Jim Gallagher, Jr., Marc Girouard, Mike Grob, Clint Jensen, Blaine McCallister, Hirofumi Miyase, Ted Purdy, Scott Simpson, **148**-Michael Allen, Jeff Brehaut, Steve Elkington, David Faught, Dan Forsman, Jon Mills, John E. Morgan, Tom Pernice, Jr., Richard Scott (A), Stephen Woodard, **149**-Stephen Ames, Erik Compton, Jay Delsing, Kelly Gibson, Charles Howell III, Per-Ulrik Johansson, Mike Springer, **150**-Daniel Chopra, Kris Cox, Mike Heinen, Scott McCarron, Spike McRoy, Kevin Muncrief, Steve Scott, Richard Zokol, **151**-Ken Duke, Camilo Villegas, **152**-Joel Edwards, Derek Gillespie, Rob McMillan, **153**-Trevor Dodds, David Hearn, Gabriel Hjertstedt, Hank Kuehne, Dan Olsen, Chris Smith, **154**-Rich Barcelo, Guy Boros, Marc Bourgeois (A), Craig Doell (A), Steve Stricker, **155**-Bob Burns, **156**-David Mathis, **157**-Robin Freeman, **159**-James Lepp (A), **165**-Darren Wallace (A). **W**—Ken Green, Brent Geiberger, **80**-Carl Paulson, Briny Baird, **78**-Olin Browne, Michael Bradley, **75**-Arron Oberholser, **71**-Mark Calcavecchia.

TOURNAMENT HISTORY

Year	Winner	Score	Runner-up	Score	Location	Par/Yards
CANADIAN OPEN						
1904	John H. Oke	156	Percy Barrett	158	Royal Montreal GC, Dixie, Quebec	N/A
1905	George Cumming	148	Percy Barrett	151	Toronto GC, Mississauga, Ontario	N/A
1906	Charles Murray	170	George Cumming Alex Robertson Tom Reith	171	Royal Ottawa GC, Aylmer, Quebec	N/A
1907	Percy Barrett	306	George Cumming	308	Lambton GC, Toronto, Ontario	N/A
1908	Albert Murray	300	George Sargent	304	Royal Montreal GC, Dixie, Quebec	N/A
1909	Karl Keffer	309	George Cumming	312	Toronto GC, Mississauga, Ontario	N/A
1910	Daniel Kenny	303	George S. Lyon	307	Lambton GC, Toronto, Ontario	70/N/A
1911	Charles Murray	314	Davie Black	316	Royal Ottawa GC, Aylmer, Quebec	N/A
1912	George Sargent	299	James M. Barnes	302	Rosedale GC, Toronto, Ontario	N/A
1913	Albert Murray	295	Nicol Thompson Jack Burke, Sr.	301	Royal Montreal GC, Dixie, Quebec	N/A
1914	Karl Keffer	300	George Cumming	301	Toronto GC, Mississauga, Ontario	N/A
1915	No Tournament					
1916	No Tournament					
1917	No Tournament					
1918	No Tournament					
1919	J. Douglas Edgar	278	James Barnes Robert T. Jones, Jr. Karl Keffer	294	Hamilton GC, Ancaster, Ontario	N/A
1920	J. Douglas Edgar*	298	Tommy Armour Charles R. Murray	298	Rivermead GC, Aylmer, Quebec	N/A
1921	W. H. Trovinger	293	Mike Brady Bob MacDonald	296	Toronto GC, Mississauga, Ontario	N/A
1922	Al Watrous	303	Tom Kerrigan	304	Mt. Bruno GC, St. Bruno, Quebec	72/6,643

Bell Canadian Open

BELL CANADIAN OPEN

NOTES

With his victory in 2004, ***Vijay Singh*** *became the eighth player over the age of 40 to win the Bell Canadian Open, joining the following seven: 1942,* ***Craig Wood*** *(40 years, 8 months, 20 days); 1962,* ***Ted Kroll*** *(42 years, 11 months, 15 days); 1963,* ***Doug Ford*** *(40 years, 11 months); 1964,* ***Kel Nagle*** *(43 years, 7 months, 11 days); 1972,* ***Gay Brewer*** *(40 years, 3 months, 20 days); 1986,* ***Bob Murphy*** *(43 years, 4 months, 15 days) and 2003,* ***Bob Tway*** *(44 years, 4 months, 3 days).*

Vijay Singh*'s 2004 victory came in his seventh appearance in the Bell Canadian Open. His best finish before 2004 was a T6 in 2002 and 2003. With the $810,000 paycheck, Singh cracked $1 million in career earnings at the Bell Canadian Open.*

Of the past six champions of the Bell Canadian Open in the field in 2004, five made the cut: ***Bob Tway*** *(2003),* ***John Rollins*** *(2002),* ***Billy Andrade*** *(1998),* ***Dudley Hart*** *(1996) and* ***David Frost*** *(1993).* ***Ken Green*** *(1988) withdrew prior to completing his first round.*

JOEY SINDELAR

Joey Sindelar *extended his streak of made cuts at the Bell Canadian Open to 10 dating back to 1995. Sindelar has made 15 career cuts at the Bell Canadian Open in 20 starts with five top-10 finishes. The 1996 champion,* ***Dudley Hart****, made his fifth straight cut at the Bell Canadian Open and has made 10 of 12 cuts at the Bell Canadian Open in his career.*

Vijay Singh *joined four players (****Tiger Woods****,* ***Tom Watson****,* ***Johnny Miller****, and* ***Jack Nicklaus****) who have won seven or more PGA TOUR events in a single season since 1970. Woods (8/1999, 9/2000) and Nicklaus (7/1972, 7/1973) did it twice, while Watson (7/1980), Miller (8/1974) and Singh (7/2004) have managed the feat once.*

With his win at the 2004 Bell Canadian Open, ***Vijay Singh*** *won his fourth event in five starts. During this period, Singh earned $3,696,000.*

TOURNAMENT HISTORY

Year	Winner	Score	Runner-up	Score	Location	Par/Yards
1923	C. W. Hackney	295	Tom Kerrigan	300	Lakeview GC, Mississauga, Ontario	N/A
1924	Leo Diegel	285	Gene Sarazen	287	Mt. Bruno GC, St. Bruno, Quebec	72/6,643
1925	Leo Diegel	295	Mike Brady	297	Lambton GC, Toronto, Ontario	N/A
1926	Macdonald Smith	283	Gene Sarazen	286	Royal Montreal GC, Dixie, Quebec	N/A
1927	Tommy Armour	288	Macdonald Smith	289	Toronto GC, Mississauga, Ontario	N/A
1928	Leo Diegel	282	Archie Compston	284	Rosedale GC, Toronto, Ontario	N/A
			Walter Hagen			
			Macdonald Smith			
1929	Leo Diegel	274	Tommy Armour	277	Kanawaki GC, Kahnawake, Quebec	N/A
1930	Tommy Armour*	273	Leo Diegel	277	Hamilton GC, Ancaster, Ontario	N/A
1931	Walter Hagen*	292	Percy Alliss	292	Mississaugua G&CC, Mississauga, Ontario	N/A
1932	Harry Cooper	290	Al Watrous	293	Ottawa Hunt Club, Ottawa, Ontario	N/A
1933	Joe Kirkwood	282	Harry Cooper	290	Royal York GC, Toronto, Ontario	N/A
			Lex Robson			
1934	Tommy Armour	287	Ky Laffoon	289	Lakeview CG, Toronto, Ontario	N/A
1935	Gene Kunes	280	Vic Ghezzi	282	Summerlea GC, Montreal, Quebec	N/A
1936	Lawson Little	271	Jimmy Thomson	279	St. Andrews GC, Toronto, Ontario	70/N/A
1937	Harry Cooper	285	Ralph Guldahl	287	St. Andrews GC, Toronto, Ontario	70/N/A
1938	Sam Snead*	277	Harry Cooper	277	Mississaugua G&CC, Mississauga, Ontario	N/A
1939	Harold McSpaden	282	Ralph Guldahl	287	Riverside CC, St. John, New Brunswick	70/6,231
1940	Sam Snead*	281	Harold McSpaden	281	Scarborough G&CC, Scarborough, Ontario	/6,685
1941	Sam Snead	274	Bob Gray, Jr.	276	Lambton GC, Toronto, Ontario	70/N/A
1942	Craig Wood	275	Mike Turnesa	279	Mississaugua G&CC, Mississauga, Ontario	N/A
1943	No Tournament					
1944	No Tournament					
1945	Byron Nelson	280	Herman Barron	284	Thornhill GC, Thornhill, Ontario	N/A
1946	George Fazio*	278	Dick Metz	278	Beaconsfield GC, Montreal, Quebec	N/A
1947	Bobby Locke	268	Ed Oliver	270	Scarborough G&CC, Scarborough, Ontario	N/A
1948	C.W. Congdon	280	Vic Ghezzi	283	Shaughnessy Heights GC, Vancouver, B.C.	N/A
			Ky Laffoon			
			Dick Metz			
1949	Dutch Harrison	271	Jim Ferrier	275	St. George's G&CC, Etobicoke, Ontario	N/A
1950	Jim Ferrier	271	Ted Kroll	274	Royal Montreal GC, Dixie, Quebec	N/A
1951	Jim Ferrier	273	Fred Hawkins	275	Mississaugua G&CC, Mississauga, Ontario	N/A
			Ed Oliver			
1952	Johnny Palmer	263	Fred Haas	274	St. Charles CC, Winnipeg, Manitoba	N/A
			Dick Mayer			
1953	Dave Douglas	273	Wally Ulrich	274	Scarborough G&CC, Scarborough, Ontario	N/A
1954	Pat Fletcher	280	Gordon Brydson	284	Point Grey GC, Vancouver, B.C.	N/A
			Bill Welch			
1955	Arnold Palmer	265	Jack Burke, Jr.	269	Weston GC, Toronto, Ontario	N/A
1956	Doug Sanders*#	273	Dow Finsterwald	273	Beaconsfield GC, Montreal, Quebec	N/A
1957	George Bayer	271	Bo Wininger	273	Westmount G&CC, Kitchener, Ontario	N/A
1958	Wesley Ellis, Jr.	267	Jay Hebert	268	Mayfair G&CC, Edmonton, Alberta	N/A
1959	Doug Ford	276	Dow Finsterwald	278	Islesmere G&CC, Montreal, Quebec	N/A
			Art Wall			
			Bo Wininger			
1960	Art Wall	269	Bob Goalby	275	St. George's G&CC, Etobicoke, Ontario	N/A
			Jay Hebert			
1961	Jacky Cupit	270	Buster Cupit	275	Niakwa CC, Winnipeg, Manitoba	N/A
			Dow Finsterwald			
			Bobby Nichols			
1962	Ted Kroll	278	Charles Sifford	280	Le Club Laval-sur-le-Lac, Laval-sur-le-Lac, Quebec	N/A
1963	Doug Ford	280	Al Geiberger	281	Scarborough G&CC, Scarborough, Ontario	N/A
1964	Kel Nagle	277	Arnold Palmer	279	Pinegrove CC, St. Luc, Quebec	N/A
1965	Gene Littler	273	Jack Nicklaus	274	Mississaugua G&CC, Mississauga, Ontario	N/A
1966	Don Massengale	280	Chi Chi Rodriguez	283	Shaughnessy G&CC, Vancouver, B.C.	N/A
1967	Billy Casper*	279	Art Wall	279	Montreal Municipal GC, Montreal, Quebec	N/A
1968	Bob Charles	274	Jack Nicklaus	276	St. George's G&CC, Etobicoke, Ontario	70/6,792
1969	Tommy Aaron*	275	Sam Snead	275	Pinegrove G&CC, St. Luc, Quebec	72/7,076
1970	Kermit Zarley	279	Gibby Gilbert	282	London Hunt & CC, London, Ontario	72/7,168
1971	Lee Trevino*	275	Art Wall	275	Richelieu Valley G&CC, Ste. Julie de Vercheres, Quebec	72/6,920
1972	Gay Brewer	275	Sam Adams	276	Cherry Hill Club, Ridgeway, Ontario	71/6,751
			Dave Hill			
1973	Tom Weiskopf	278	Forrest Fezler	280	Richelieu Valley G&CC, Ste. Julie de Vercheres, Quebec	72/6,905
1974	Bobby Nichols	270	John Schlee	274	Mississaugua G&CC, Mississauga, Ontario	70/6,788
			Larry Ziegler			
1975	Tom Weiskopf*	274	Jack Nicklaus	274	Royal Montreal GC, Ile Bizard, Quebec	70/6,628
1976	Jerry Pate	267	Jack Nicklaus	271	Essex G&CC,Windsor, Ontario.	70/6,696
1977	Lee Trevino	280	Peter Oosterhuis	284	Glen Abbey GC, Oakville, Ontario	72/7,096
1978	Bruce Lietzke	283	Pat McGowan	284	Glen Abbey GC, Oakville, Ontario	71/7,050
1979	Lee Trevino	281	Ben Crenshaw	284	Glen Abbey GC, Oakville, Ontario	71/7,059
1980	Bob Gilder	274	Jerry Pate	276	Royal Montreal GC, Ile Bizard, Quebec	70/6,628
			Leonard Thompson			

*KEY: *=Playoff #=Amateur = Weather-shortened*

SECTION 3 TOURNAMENT HISTORIES

Bell Canadian Open

BELL CANADIAN OPEN

NOTES

There have been 18 tournaments decided by playoffs in the 95 Bell Canadian Opens, including the last three years. With his 2004 victory, ***Vijay Singh*** *improved his record to 5-1 in playoffs on the PGA TOUR – having also won the PGA Championship in a three-hole playoff over Justin Leonard and Chris DiMarco in 2004. Mike Weir is 3-2 in playoffs on the PGA TOUR.*

The 275 total for the champion ***Vijay Singh*** *was the highest winning score at the Bell Canadian Open since 1999 when* ***Hal Sutton*** *also totaled 275 at Glen Abbey Golf Club.*

JUSTIN ROSE

Justin Rose *tied his career-low round on the PGA TOUR with an 8-under-par 63 in the final round. He matched his 63 posted in the first round of the 2003 Deutsche Bank Championship. Rose's 63 was also the low round of the 2004 Bell Canadian Open. He made the largest jump of the day into the top 10, from T34 to T4.*

All seven U.S. Ryder Cup members playing at the 2004 Bell Canadian Open made the cut. Here are their respective finishes: ***Stewart Cink*** *(T4),* ***Chris DiMarco*** *(T24),* ***Chad Campbell*** *(T26),* ***Davis Love III*** *(T40),* ***Fred Funk*** *(T47) and* ***Phil Mickelson*** *(T57).*

Tournament Record:
268, John Palmer, 1952 (St. Charles CC)

Course Record:
62, Leonard Thompson, 1981 (Par 71); Andy Bean, 1983 (Par 71); Greg Norman, 1986 (par 72) (Glen Abbey)

TOURNAMENT HISTORY

Year	Winner	Score	Runner-up	Score	Location	Par/Yards
1981	Peter Oosterhuis	280	Bruce Lietzke	281	Glen Abbey GC, Oakville, Ontario	71/7,060
			Jack Nicklaus			
			Andy North			
1982	Bruce Lietzke	277	Hal Sutton	279	Glen Abbey GC, Oakville, Ontario	71/7,060
1983	John Cook*	277	Johnny Miller	277	Glen Abbey GC, Oakville, Ontario	71/7,055
1984	Greg Norman	278	Jack Nicklaus	280	Glen Abbey GC, Oakville, Ontario	72/7,102
1985	Curtis Strange	279	Jack Nicklaus	281	Glen Abbey GC, Oakville, Ontario	72/7,102
			Greg Norman			
1986	Bob Murphy	280	Greg Norman	283	Glen Abbey GC, Oakville, Ontario	72/7,102
1987	Curtis Strange	276	David Frost	279	Glen Abbey GC, Oakville, Ontario	72/7,102
			Jodie Mudd			
			Nick Price			
1988	Ken Green	275	Bill Glasson	276	Glen Abbey GC, Oakville, Ontario	72/7,102
			Scott Verplank			
1989	Steve Jones	271	Clark Burroughs	273	Glen Abbey GC, Oakville, Ontario	72/7,102
			Mark Calcavecchia			
			Mike Hulbert			
1990	Wayne Levi	278	Ian Baker-Finch	279	Glen Abbey GC, Oakville, Ontario	72/7,102
			Jim Woodward			
1991	Nick Price	273	David Edwards	274	Glen Abbey GC, Oakville, Ontario	72/7,102
1992	Greg Norman*	280	Bruce Lietzke	280	Glen Abbey GC, Oakville, Ontario	72/7,102
1993	David Frost	279	Fred Couples	280	Glen Abbey GC, Oakville, Ontario	72/7,102
BELL CANADIAN OPEN						
1994	Nick Price	275	Mark Calcavecchia	276	Glen Abbey GC, Oakville, Ontario	72/7,102
1995	Mark O'Meara*	274	Bob Lohr	274	Glen Abbey GC, Oakville, Ontario	72/7,102
1996	Dudley Hart~	202	David Duval	203	Glen Abbey GC, Oakville, Ontario	72/7,112
1997	Steve Jones	275	Greg Norman	276	Royal Montreal GC, Ile-Bizard, Quebec	70/6,810
1998	Billy Andrade*	275	Bob Friend	275	Glen Abbey GC, Oakville, Ontario	72/7,112
1999	Hal Sutton	275	Dennis Paulson	278	Glen Abbey GC, Oakville, Ontario	72/7,112
2000	Tiger Woods	266	Grant Waite	267	Glen Abbey GC, Oakville, Ontario	72/7,112
2001	Scott Verplank	266	Bob Estes	269	Royal Montreal GC, Ile-Bizard, Quebec	70/6,859
			Joey Sindelar			
2002	John Rollins*	272	Neal Lancaster	272	Angus Glen GC, Markham, Ontario	72/7,372
			Justin Leonard			
2003	Bob Tway*	272	Brad Faxon	272	Hamilton G&CC, Hamilton, Ontario	70/6,985
2004	Vijay Singh*	275	Mike Weir	275	Glen Abbey GC, Oakville, Ontario	71/7,222

*KEY: *=Playoff #=Amateur = Weather-shortened*

Mike Weir lining up a putt.

ELIGIBILITY REQUIREMENTS FOR THE 2005 BELL CANADIAN OPEN

Eligible players are:

- Players in the 156-player field are those players listed in order of priority under Article III, Section A of the Tournament Regulations, except that prior to such players, the following shall first be eligible:
- 20 sponsor exemptions, restricted as follows:
  - 2 from among the current year's membership.
  - 2 from among the 2004 PGA TOUR Qualifying Tournament's top 30 finishers and ties and the first through 20th finishers on the 2004 Official Nationwide Tour Money List.

2004 Valero Texas Open [40th of 48 official events]

BRYANT

Winner: BART BRYANT
67-67-60-67 261 (-19) $630,000

The Resort Course at LaCantera

San Antonio, TX

September 16-19, 2004

Purse: $3,500,000
Par: 35-35—70
Yards: 6,881

LEADERS: First Round—Ted Purdy tied the course record with a 9-under-par 61 to lead Jim McGovern, Tim Clark, Dean Wilson and J.J. Henry by three strokes. Six players were four behind. **Second Round**—Wilson moved to 11-under-par 129 to lead Purdy by one stroke and Henry and Ryan Palmer by two. **Third Round**—Bart Bryant set the course record with a 10-under-par 60, moving to 16-under-par 194. He led Hunter Mahan by three strokes and eight players by four.

CUT: 79 players at 2-under-par 138 from a field of 144 professionals.

PRO-AM: Justin Leonard, 49, $2,000.

WEATHER: Thursday, hot and humid with a high of 95 in mid-afternoon. Partly cloudy skies with winds N-NE 5-12 mph. On Friday, a high of 97 with partly cloudy skies. Saturday, warm and mostly sunny with a high of 95. On Sunday, partly cloudy skies and slightly cooler temperatures with a high of 92.

Check out the 2005 Valero Texas Open, September 22-25 on ESPN

ORDER OF FINISH

Player	Pos.	Scores	Total	Money
Bart Bryant	1	67-67-60-67	261	$630,000.00
Patrick Sheehan	2	65-68-65-66	264	378,000.00
Todd Fischer	T3	68-67-63-67	265	203,000.00
Dean Wilson	T3	64-65-70-66	265	203,000.00
Tim Clark	T5	64-70-64-68	266	118,650.00
J.J. Henry	T5	64-67-67-68	266	118,650.00
Jerry Kelly	T5	66-67-68-65	266	118,650.00
Hunter Mahan	T5	68-67-62-69	266	118,650.00
Ted Purdy	T5	61-69-71-65	266	118,650.00
Justin Leonard	T10	65-68-68-66	267	84,000.00
J.L. Lewis	T10	69-67-68-63	267	84,000.00
Scott Simpson	T10	65-67-66-69	267	84,000.00
Heath Slocum	T10	66-69-64-68	267	84,000.00
Brent Geiberger	T14	66-68-67-67	268	63,000.00
Joe Ogilvie	T14	67-70-61-70	268	63,000.00
Duffy Waldorf	T14	66-67-67-68	268	63,000.00
Olin Browne	T17	69-67-66-67	269	50,750.00
Bob Estes	T17	68-66-70-65	269	50,750.00
Tom Lehman	T17	66-70-68-65	269	50,750.00
Justin Rose	T17	68-68-65-68	269	50,750.00
John Senden	21	66-65-69-70	270	42,000.00
Scott McCarron	T22	65-69-68-69	271	31,550.00
Brenden Pappas	T22	68-69-65-69	271	31,550.00
Jesper Parnevik	T22	69-65-67-70	271	31,550.00
Pat Perez	T22	66-69-63-73	271	31,550.00
Loren Roberts	T22	66-68-69-68	271	$31,550.00
Vaughn Taylor	T22	70-68-67-66	271	31,550.00
Jay Williamson	T22	71-66-64-70	271	31,550.00
Jay Delsing	T29	65-72-64-71	272	21,306.25
Joel Edwards	T29	70-67-69-66	272	21,306.25
Brian Gay	T29	66-70-65-71	272	21,306.25
Jason Hartwick (S)	T29	70-66-69-67	272	21,306.25
Fredrik Jacobson	T29	68-68-64-72	272	21,306.25
Ryan Palmer	T29	66-65-67-74	272	21,306.25
Tim Thelen	T29	68-70-66-68	272	21,306.25
Bo Van Pelt	T29	66-69-69-68	272	21,306.25
Brad Bryant	T37	66-68-68-71	273	16,100.00
Daniel Chopra	T37	68-69-70-66	273	16,100.00
Kent Jones	T37	69-67-68-69	273	16,100.00
David Peoples	T37	67-64-70-72	273	16,100.00
Tommy Armour III	T41	67-70-68-69	274	11,917.50
D.J. Brigman	T41	66-72-66-70	274	11,917.50
Tom Byrum	T41	68-68-67-71	274	11,917.50
Tom Carter	T41	69-68-67-70	274	11,917.50
Ben Crane	T41	66-72-68-68	274	11,917.50
Matt Kuchar	T41	68-68-67-71	274	11,917.50
Corey Pavin	T41	67-69-71-67	274	11,917.50
Bob Tway	T41	70-68-64-72	274	11,917.50
Mark Wilson	T49	65-72-70-68	275	8,843.34
Arjun Atwal	T49	67-67-66-75	275	8,843.33
Deane Pappas	T49	67-70-68-70	275	8,843.33
Jim Benepe	T52	70-67-68-71	276	8,080.00
Steve Elkington	T52	68-69-70-69	276	$8,080.00
Lucas Glover	T52	71-66-69-70	276	8,080.00
Gabriel Hjertstedt	T52	69-69-72-66	276	8,080.00
Dan Olsen	T52	68-69-67-72	276	8,080.00
Rod Pampling	T52	70-68-68-70	276	8,080.00
Brian Watts	T52	69-69-68-70	276	8,080.00
Shaun Micheel	T59	67-69-72-69	277	7,735.00
Tim Petrovic	T59	67-67-70-73	277	7,735.00
Brian Bateman	T61	70-68-70-70	278	7,490.00
Pat Bates	T61	68-70-69-71	278	7,490.00
Guy Boros	T61	68-69-73-68	278	7,490.00
Adam Meyer (Q)	T61	70-68-68-72	278	7,490.00
Andre Stolz	T61	71-66-69-72	278	7,490.00
Willie Wood	66	69-69-67-74	279	7,280.00
Briny Baird	T67	70-66-69-75	280	7,140.00
David Branshaw	T67	69-68-74-69	280	7,140.00
Kevin Muncrief	T67	66-68-73-73	280	7,140.00
Brad Lardon	T70	68-68-74-71	281	6,965.00
David Sutherland	T70	68-69-70-74	281	6,965.00
Aaron Baddeley	72	67-69-70-76	282	6,860.00
Jose Coceres	T73	68-67-70-78	283	6,755.00
Hank Kuehne	T73	68-67-72-76	283	6,755.00
Jeff Brehaut	75	71-66-73-74	284	6,650.00
Brandel Chamblee	76	68-69-74-74	285	6,580.00
Omar Uresti	77	68-69-72-77	286	6,510.00
Jeff Maggert	78	67-68-70-82	287	6,440.00

(Q) = Open Qualifier; (S) = Sponsor Exemption; (T) = Tie

The following players did not finish
(C=cut, W=withdrew, D=disqualified)

C—139-Mark Brooks, Jim Carter, Michael Clark II, Russ Cochran, Glen Day, David Edwards, Bill Glasson, Mike Heinen, Scott Hend, Frank Lickliter II, David Lundstrom, Hirofumi Miyase, Larry Mize, John E. Morgan, Jose Maria Olazabal, Gene Sauers, Mike Standly, **140**-Steve Allan, Rich Beem, Bob Burns, Greg Chalmers, Danny Ellis, Kelly Gibson, J.P. Hayes, Brian Henninger, Richard S. Johnson, Cliff Kresge, Jim McGovern, Carl Paulson, Dicky Pride, Mike Springer, Roger Tambellini, Tommy Tolles, **141**-Cameron Beckman, Jay Don Blake, Danny Briggs, Chris Couch, Robin Freeman, Mike Grob, David Ogrin, Roland Thatcher, JJ Wall, **142**-Robert Allenby, David Morland IV, Wes Short, Jr., Camilo Villegas, **143**-Brian Kortan, Esteban Toledo, Grant Waite, Mark Wiebe, **144**-Robert Gamez, **145**-Ken Duke, David Gossett, Blaine McCallister, **146**-Mike Hulbert, **147**-Rich Barcelo, Per-Ulrik Johansson, Larry Rinker, **148**-Kris Cox, **149**-Donnie Hammond, **150**-Jim Gallagher, Jr. **W—75**-Craig Bowden, **73**-Garrett Willis, Dennis Paulson, **211**-Aaron Barber. **D—70**-Jason Dufner.

TOURNAMENT HISTORY

Year	Winner	Score	Runner-up	Score	Location	Par/Yards
TEXAS OPEN						
1922	Bob MacDonald	281	Cyril Walker	282	Brackenridge Park GC, San Antonio, TX	71/6,185
1923	Walter Hagen*	279	Bill Mehlhorn	279	Brackenridge Park GC, San Antonio, TX	71/6,185
1924	Joe Kirkwood	279	George Kerrigan	286	Brackenridge Park GC, San Antonio, TX	71/6,185
			James Ockenden			
1925	Joe Turnesa	284	Macdonald Smith	285	Brackenridge Park GC, San Antonio, TX	71/6,185
1926	Macdonald Smith	288	Bobby Cruickshank	289	Brackenridge Park GC, San Antonio, TX	71/6,185
1927	Bobby Cruickshank	272	Larry Nabholtz	295	Willow Springs GC, San Antonio, TX	72/6,930
1928	Bill Mehlhorn	297	Harry Cooper	298	Willow Springs GC, San Antonio, TX	72/6,930
1929	Bill Mehlhorn	277	Horton Smith	281	Brackenridge Park GC, San Antonio, TX	71/6,185
1930	Denny Shute	277	Ed Dudley	280	Brackenridge Park GC, San Antonio, TX	71/6,185
			Al Espinosa			
			Neil McIntyre			
1931	Abe Espinosa	281	Harry Cooper	283	Brackenridge Park GC, San Antonio, TX	71/6,185
			Joe Turnesa			
			Frank Walsh			
1932	Clarence Clark	287	Gus Moreland	288	Brackenridge Park GC, San Antonio, TX	71/6,185
			Gene Sarazen			
1933	No Tournament					
1934	Wiffy Cox	283	Byron Nelson	284	Brackenridge Park GC, San Antonio, TX	71/6,185
			Craig Wood			
1935	No Tournament					
1936	No Tournament					
1937	No Tournament					
1938	No Tournament					
1939	Dutch Harrison	271	Sam Byrd	273	Brackenridge Park GC, San Antonio, TX	71/6,185
1940	Byron Nelson*	271	Ben Hogan	271	Brackenridge Park GC, San Antonio, TX	71/6,185
1941	Lawson Little	273	Ben Hogan	276	Willow Springs GC, San Antonio, TX	72/6,930
1942	Chick Harbert*	272	Ben Hogan	272	Willow Springs GC, San Antonio, TX	72/6,930
1943	No Tournament					

Valero Texas Open

VALERO TEXAS OPEN at LACANTERA

NOTES

BART BRYANT

***Bart Bryant**'s 10-under-par 60 in the third round of the 2004 Valero Texas Open was a career low and bettered the course record of 61 set by **Garrett Willis** in 2002 and later matched by **Bob Tway** (2003), **Heath Slocum** (2003) and **Ted Purdy** (2004). Bryant's previous career low was 63 in the final round of the 2002 Greater Milwaukee Open. Bryant's 60 matched the Valero Texas Open's 18-hole record total, as well as the 2004 18-hole low total posted by **Robert Gamez** in the third round of the Bob Hope Chrysler Classic at Indian Wells Country Club.*

*Of the 15 60s shot in PGA TOUR history, four have been recorded at the Texas Open, including **Al Brosch** (1951/Brackenridge Park GC), **Ted Kroll** (1954/Brackenridge Park), **Mike Souchak** (1955/Brackenridge Park) and **Bart Bryant** (2004/LaCantera GC).*

***Bart Bryant** won his first PGA TOUR event at the 2004 Valero Texas Open at age 41 years, 10 months and one day, the oldest first-time winner since **Ed Dougherty** claimed his lone TOUR title at the 1995 Deposit Guaranty Golf Classic at 47 years, 8 months and 19 days.*

***Bart Bryant** became the 14th first-time winner in the history of the Valero Texas Open, joining **Chick Harbert** (1942), **Tony Holguin** (1953), **Mike Souchak** (1955), **Jay Hebert** (1957), **Bill Johnston** (1958), **Harold Henning** (1966), **Deane Beman** (1969), **Ben Crenshaw** (1973), **Terry Diehl** (1974), **Ron Streck** (1978), **Bob Estes** (1994), **Duffy Waldorf** (1995) and **David Ogrin** (1996).*

TOURNAMENT HISTORY

Year	Winner	Score	Runner-up	Score	Location	Par/Yards
1944	Johnny Revolta	273	Harold McSpaden	274	Willow Springs GC, San Antonio, TX	72/6,930
			Byron Nelson			
1945	Sam Byrd	268	Byron Nelson	269	Willow Springs GC, San Antonio, TX	72/6,930
1946	Ben Hogan	264	Sam Byrd	270	Willow Springs GC, San Antonio, TX	72/6,930
1947	Ed Oliver	265	Jimmy Demaret	266	Willow Springs GC, San Antonio, TX	72/6,930
1948	Sam Snead	264	Jimmy Demaret	266	Willow Springs GC, San Antonio, TX	72/6,930
1949	Dave Douglas	268	Sam Snead	269	Willow Springs GC, San Antonio, TX	72/6,930
1950	Sam Snead	265	Jimmy Demaret	266	Brackenridge Park GC, San Antonio, TX	71/6,185
					Fort Sam Houston GC, San Antonio, TX	72/6,566
1951	Dutch Harrison*	265	Doug Ford	265	Brackenridge Park GC, San Antonio, TX	71/6,185
					Fort Sam Houston GC, San Antonio, TX	72/6,881
1952	Jack Burke, Jr.	260	Doug Ford	266	Brackenridge Park GC, San Antonio, TX	71/6,185
1953	Tony Holguin	264	Doug Ford	265	Brackenridge Park GC, San Antonio, TX	71/6,185
1954	Chandler Harper	259	Johnny Palmer	261	Brackenridge Park GC, San Antonio, TX	71/6,185
1955	Mike Souchak	257	Fred Haas	264	Brackenridge Park GC, San Antonio, TX	71/6,185
1956	Gene Littler	276	Mike Fetchick	278	Fort Sam Houston GC, San Antonio, TX	72/6,566
			Frank Stranahan			
			Ernie Vossler			
1957	Jay Hebert	271	Ed Furgol	272	Brackenridge Park GC, San Antonio, TX	71/6,185
1958	Bill Johnston	274	Bob Rosburg	277	Brackenridge Park GC, San Antonio, TX	71/6,185
1959	Wes Ellis	276	Bill Johnston	278	Brackenridge Park GC, San Antonio, TX	71/6,185
			Tom Nieporte			
1960	Arnold Palmer	276	Doug Ford	278	Fort Sam Houston GC, San Antonio, TX	72/6,566
			Frank Stranahan			
1961	Arnold Palmer	270	Al Balding	271	Oak Hills CC, San Antonio, TX	70/6,576
1962	Arnold Palmer	273	Joe Campbell	274	Oak Hills CC, San Antonio, TX	70/6,576
			Gene Littler			
			Mason Rudolph			
			Doug Sanders			
1963	Phil Rodgers	268	Johnny Pott	270	Oak Hills CC, San Antonio, TX	70/6,576
1964	Bruce Crampton	273	Bob Charles	274	Oak Hills CC, San Antonio, TX	70/6,576
			Chi Chi Rodriguez			
1965	Frank Beard	270	Gardner Dickinson	273	Oak Hills CC, San Antonio, TX	70/6,576
1966	Harold Henning	272	Wes Ellis	275	Oak Hills CC, San Antonio, TX	70/6,576
			Gene Littler			
			Ken Still			
1967	Chi Chi Rodriguez	277	Bob Charles	278	Pecan Valley CC, San Antonio, TX	71/7,183
			Bob Goalby			
1968	No Tournament					
1969	Deane Beman*	274	Jack McGowan	274	Pecan Valley CC, San Antonio, TX	71/7,183
SAN ANTONIO TEXAS OPEN						
1970	Ron Cerrudo	273	Dick Lotz	278	Pecan Valley CC, San Antonio, TX	71/7,183
1971	No Tournament					
1972	Mike Hill	273	Lee Trevino	275	Woodlake GC, San Antonio, TX	72/7,143
1973	Ben Crenshaw	270	Orville Moody	272	Woodlake GC, San Antonio, TX	71/6,990
1974	Terry Diehl	269	Mike Hill	270	Woodlake GC, San Antonio, TX	72/7,143
1975	Don January*	275	Larry Hinson	275	Woodlake GC, San Antonio, TX	72/7,143
1976	Butch Baird*	273	Miller Barber	273	Woodlake GC, San Antonio, TX	72/7,143
1977	Hale Irwin	266	Miller Barber	268	Oak Hills CC, San Antonio, TX	70/6,576
1978	Ron Streck	265	Hubert Green	266	Oak Hills CC, San Antonio, TX	70/6,576
			Lon Hinkle			
1979	Lou Graham	268	Eddie Pearce	269	Oak Hills CC, San Antonio, TX	70/6,576
			Bill Rogers			
			Doug Tewell			
1980	Lee Trevino	265	Terry Diehl	266	Oak Hills CC, San Antonio, TX	70/6,576
TEXAS OPEN						
1981	Bill Rogers*	266	Ben Crenshaw	266	Oak Hills CC, San Antonio, TX	70/6,576
1982	Jay Haas	262	Curtis Strange	265	Oak Hills CC, San Antonio, TX	70/6,576
1983	Jim Colbert	261	Mark Pfeil	266	Oak Hills CC, San Antonio, TX	70/6,576
1984	Calvin Peete	266	Bruce Lietzke	269	Oak Hills CC, San Antonio, TX	70/6,576
1985	John Mahaffey*	268	Jodie Mudd	268	Oak Hills CC, San Antonio, TX	70/6,576
VANTAGE CHAMPIONSHIP						
1986	Ben Crenshaw~	196	Payne Stewart	197	Oak Hills CC, San Antonio, TX	70/6,576
TEXAS OPEN PRESENTED BY NABISCO						
1988	Corey Pavin	259	Robert Wrenn	267	Oak Hills CC, San Antonio, TX	70/6,576
1989	Donnie Hammond	258	Paul Azinger	265	Oak Hills CC, San Antonio, TX	70/6,576
H-E-B TEXAS OPEN						
1990	Mark O'Meara	261	Gary Hallberg	262	Oak Hills CC, San Antonio, TX	70/6,576
1991	Blaine McCallister*	269	Gary Hallberg	269	Oak Hills CC, San Antonio, TX	70/6,576
1992	Nick Price*	263	Steve Elkington	263	Oak Hills CC, San Antonio, TX	71/6,650
1993	Jay Haas*	263	Bob Lohr	263	Oak Hills CC, San Antonio, TX	71/6,650
TEXAS OPEN						
1994	Bob Estes	265	Gil Morgan	266	Oak Hills CC, San Antonio, TX	71/6,650
LACANTERA TEXAS OPEN						
1995	Duffy Waldorf	268	Justin Leonard	274	LaCantera GC (Resort), San Antonio, TX	72/6,899
1996	David Ogrin	275	Jay Haas	276	LaCantera GC (Resort), San Antonio, TX	72/7,001

*KEY: *=Playoff #=Amateur = Weather-shortened*

Valero Texas Open

NOTES

***Bart Bryant**, a native of Gatesville, TX, became the 16th Texas native/resident to win the Valero Texas Open: **Byron Nelson** (Fort Worth, 1940), **Ben Hogan** (Fort Worth, 1946), **Jack Burke, Jr.** (Houston, 1952), **Tony Holguin** (San Antonio, 1953), **Wesley Ellis** (San Antonio, 1959), **Ben Crenshaw** (Austin, 1973, 1986), **Don January** (Denton, 1975), **Lee Trevino** (Dallas, 1980), **Bill Rogers** (Texarkana/San Antonio, 1981), **John Mahaffey** (The Woodlands, 1985), **Blaine McCallister** (Fort Stockton, 1991), **Bob Estes** (Austin, 1994), **David Ogrin** (Garden Ridge, 1996), **Justin Leonard** (Dallas, 2000, 2001) and **Tommy Armour III** (Irving, 2003).*

Bart Bryant *(187th start) and his brother Brad (556th start) were playing in their 743rd combined event on the PGA TOUR at the 2004 Valero Texas Open. Bart and Brad (1995 Walt Disney World/Oldsmobile Classic winner) joined 10 other brother combinations that have captured PGA TOUR events. They include:*

- ***Lloyd Mangrum-Ray Mangrum***
- ***Alex Smith-Macdonald Smith-Willie Smith***
- ***Jim Turnesa-Joe Turnesa-Mike Turnesa-Phil Turnesa***
- ***Lionel Hebert-Jay Hebert***
- ***Al Espinosa-Abe Espinosa***
- ***Don Massengale-Rik Massengale***
- ***Dave Hill-Mike Hill***
- ***Danny Edwards-David Edwards***
- ***Joe Inman-John Inman***
- ***Curt Byrum-Tom Byrum***

***Bart Bryant**'s victory came in his 187th start on the PGA TOUR. His previous-best finish on TOUR was seventh at the 1991 Honda Classic. Prior to the 2004 Valero Texas Open victory, he only had a total of four top-10 performances in his TOUR career.*

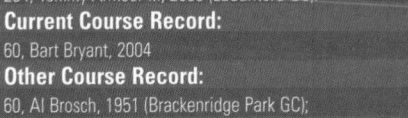

Tournament Record:
254, Tommy Armour III, 2003 (LaCantera GC).
Current Course Record:
60, Bart Bryant, 2004
Other Course Record:
60, Al Brosch, 1951 (Brackenridge Park GC);
Ted Kroll, 1954 (Brackenridge Park);
Mike Souchak, 1955 (Brackenridge Park);

TOURNAMENT HISTORY

Year	Winner	Score	Runner-up	Score	Location	Par/Yards
1997	Tim Herron	271	Rick Fehr Brent Geiberger	273	LaCantera GC (Resort), San Antonio, TX	72/7,001
WESTIN TEXAS OPEN						
1998	Hal Sutton	270	Jay Haas Justin Leonard	271	LaCantera GC (Resort), San Antonio, TX	72/7,001
1999	Duffy Waldorf*	270	Ted Tryba	270	LaCantera GC (Resort), San Antonio, TX	72/7,001
2000	Justin Leonard	261	Mark Wiebe	266	LaCantera GC (Resort), San Antonio, TX	70/6,905
TEXAS OPEN AT LACANTERA						
2001	Justin Leonard	266	J.J. Henry Matt Kuchar	268	LaCantera GC (Resort), San Antonio, TX	71/6,929
VALERO TEXAS OPEN						
2002	Loren Roberts	261	Fred Couples Fred Funk Garrett Willis	264	LaCantera GC (Resort), San Antonio, TX	70/6,881
2003	Tommy Armour III	254	Loren Roberts Bob Tway	261	LaCantera GC (Resort), San Antonio, TX	70/6,881
2004	Bart Bryant	261	Patrick Sheehan	264	LaCantera GC (Resort), San Antonio, TX	70/6,881

*KEY: * = Playoff ~ = Weather-shortened*

Patrick Sheehan placed second at last year's Valero Texas Open.

2004 84 LUMBER Classic *[41st of 48 official events]*

84 LUMBER Classic
NEMACOLIN WOODLANDS RESORT

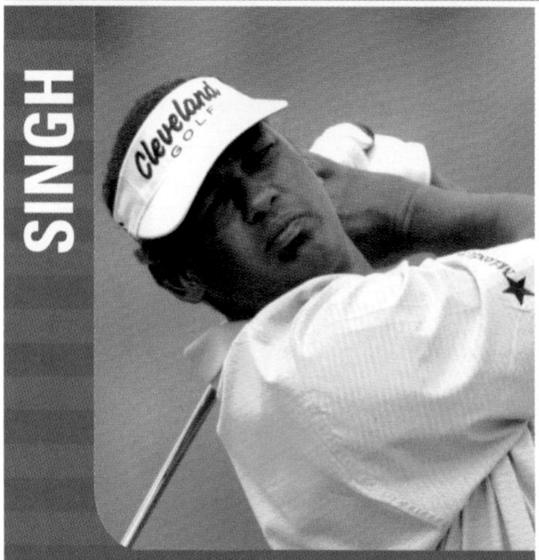

Winner: VIJAY SINGH
64-68-72-69 273 (-15) $756,000

Nemacolin Woodlands Resort & Spa (Mystic Rock Golf Course)

Farmington, PA

September 23-26, 2004

Purse: $4,200,000
Par: 36-36—72
Yards: 7,471

LEADERS: First Round—Vijay Singh opened with 8-under-par 64 to take a three-stroke lead over Richard S. Johnson, Pat Perez, Cameron Beckman, Ben Curtis and Robert Allenby.
Second Round—Singh moved to 12-under 132 and led Curtis by two and Chris DiMarco by three.
Third Round—Singh sat at 12-under 204, two ahead of DiMarco. Jonathan Byrd and Matt Gogel were three back.

CUT: 74 players at 1-under-par 143 from a field of 143 professionals.

PRO-AM: $10,000. John Daly, 53, $2,000.

WEATHER: Cool to low 80s. Sunday's reached only the mid-70s. Fog delay on Thursday. Play was suspended because of darkness Thursday. Players returned on Friday at 7:15 a.m. to complete the first round and start the second round on schedule. Fog delay. Afternoon times were delayed 30 minutes. Fog delayed Saturday. Tee times were adjusted to a 10:32 a.m. start with players grouped in threesomes off No. 1 and No. 10 tees. Sunday's final round pairings were adjusted to threesomes off No. 1 and No. 10.

Check out the 2005 84 LUMBER Classic, September 15-18 on ESPN

ORDER OF FINISH

Vijay Singh	1	64-68-72-69	273	$756,000.00
Stewart Cink	2	71-71-67-65	274	453,600.00
Jonathan Byrd	T3	68-72-67-69	276	201,600.00
Chris DiMarco	T3	70-65-71-70	276	201,600.00
Zach Johnson	T3	69-69-70-68	276	201,600.00
Pat Perez	T3	67-73-69-67	276	201,600.00
K.J. Choi	T7	71-68-73-65	277	135,450.00
Duffy Waldorf	T7	70-69-70-68	277	135,450.00
Frank Lickliter II	T9	71-72-67-68	278	117,600.00
Jose Maria Olazabal	T9	73-70-70-65	278	117,600.00
Bob Burns	T11	73-68-68-70	279	100,800.00
Matt Gogel	T11	71-68-68-72	279	100,800.00
Cameron Beckman	T13	67-73-73-67	280	72,000.00
John Daly	T13	68-72-70-70	280	72,000.00
Robert Gamez	T13	69-70-70-71	280	72,000.00
Kent Jones	T13	69-68-71-72	280	72,000.00
Billy Mayfair	T13	71-69-71-69	280	72,000.00
Tim Petrovic	T13	75-67-70-68	280	72,000.00
Tag Ridings	T13	71-71-68-70	280	72,000.00
Robert Allenby	T20	67-74-72-68	281	47,208.00
Jonathan Kaye	T20	73-69-71-68	281	47,208.00
Shigeki Maruyama	T20	72-71-68-70	281	47,208.00
John Rollins	T20	72-70-69-70	281	47,208.00
Chris Smith	T20	69-72-71-69	281	47,208.00
Jeff Brehaut	T25	69-71-72-70	282	$31,380.00
Charles Howell III	T25	70-70-70-72	282	31,380.00
Richard S. Johnson	T25	67-71-72-72	282	31,380.00
Ted Purdy	T25	73-70-70-69	282	31,380.00
Patrick Sheehan	T25	72-69-69-72	282	31,380.00
Roland Thatcher	T25	72-70-70-70	282	31,380.00
David Toms	T25	70-71-72-69	282	31,380.00
Mark Brooks	T32	70-73-68-72	283	24,307.50
Ben Curtis	T32	67-67-81-68	283	24,307.50
Lee Janzen	T32	68-73-71-71	283	24,307.50
Jerry Kelly	T32	76-67-70-70	283	24,307.50
Tim Clark	T36	71-71-69-73	284	19,355.00
Len Mattiace	T36	70-68-71-75	284	19,355.00
Brenden Pappas	T36	72-68-72-72	284	19,355.00
David Peoples	T36	71-69-73-71	284	19,355.00
Justin Rose	T36	69-72-71-72	284	19,355.00
Steve Stricker	T36	71-71-70-72	284	19,355.00
Jason Bohn	T42	72-68-70-75	285	13,513.50
Glen Day	T42	72-71-70-72	285	13,513.50
Brian Gay	T42	75-67-71-72	285	13,513.50
Brent Geiberger	T42	69-69-73-74	285	13,513.50
J.P. Hayes	T42	68-69-73-75	285	13,513.50
Joey Sindelar	T42	68-69-72-76	285	13,513.50
Vaughn Taylor	T42	74-69-73-69	285	13,513.50
Grant Waite	T42	72-70-73-70	285	13,513.50
Carlos Franco	T50	71-71-71-73	286	10,332.00
Skip Kendall	T50	72-71-71-72	286	$10,332.00
Rod Pampling	T50	70-73-70-73	286	10,332.00
Steve Allan	T53	71-69-71-76	287	9,544.50
Mark Calcavecchia	T53	72-71-71-73	287	9,544.50
Robert Damron	T53	70-73-70-74	287	9,544.50
Steve Flesch	T53	71-72-68-76	287	9,544.50
Todd Hamilton	T53	72-68-72-75	287	9,544.50
Fredrik Jacobson	T53	72-70-74-71	287	9,544.50
Kevin Na	T53	68-73-69-77	287	9,544.50
Omar Uresti	T53	72-70-73-72	287	9,544.50
Billy Andrade	T61	69-73-71-75	288	9,072.00
Gene Sauers	T61	74-67-75-72	288	9,072.00
Mike Weir	T61	69-72-74-73	288	9,072.00
Tom Carter	T64	72-69-76-72	289	8,862.00
David Frost	T64	72-71-76-70	289	8,862.00
Greg Chalmers (Q)	T66	71-71-71-77	290	8,652.00
Tom Pernice, Jr.	T66	69-74-71-76	290	8,652.00
Roger Tambellini	T66	68-75-73-74	290	8,652.00
Dan Forsman	T69	68-73-73-77	291	8,442.00
Cliff Kresge	T69	72-71-73-75	291	8,442.00
Neal Lancaster	71	71-71-75-75	292	8,316.00
Tommy Armour III	72	68-74-73-78	293	8,232.00
Kris Cox	73	68-72-75-80	295	8,148.00
Tim Herron	74	72-71-73-80	296	8,064.00

(Q) = Open Qualifier, (T) = Tie

The following players did not finish(C=cut, W=withdrew)

C—144-Michael Allen, Craig Barlow, Guy Boros, Ken Duke, Brad Faxon, Dudley Hart, Scott Hend, Brian Kortan, Shaun Micheel, Dicky Pride, Esteban Toledo, Tommy Tolles, **145**-Arjun Atwal, Woody Austin, Ben Crane, Jay Delsing, David Duval, Steve Elkington, Danny Ellis, Niclas Fasth, Mathias Gronberg, Mark Hensby, Stephen Leaney, Peter Lonard, Dan Olsen, Ryan Palmer, Rory Sabbatini, John Senden, Scott Simpson, Heath Slocum, Scott Verplank, Camilo Villegas, **146**-Rich Beem, Bart Bryant, Jason Dufner, Lucas Glover, J.J. Henry, Matt Kuchar, Scott McCarron, John E. Morgan, Bo Van Pelt, **147**-Daniel Chopra, Hidemichi Tanaka, Phil Tataurangi, Dean Wilson, **148**-Pat Bates, Jay Don Blake, David Gossett, Andre Stolz, **149**-Steve Lowery, Deane Pappas, Steve Pate, **150**-Chris Couch, Spike McRoy, Brett Quigley, **151**-Aaron Baddeley, John Cook, Sean Farren, David Morland IV, **152**-D.J. Brigman, J.L. Lewis, **153**-David Branshaw, **154**-Kevin Muncrief, Curtis Strange, **164**-John Aber. **W**—Russ Cochran, **76**-Jay Williamson, Rocco Mediate, **75**-Ken Green, **72**-Danny Briggs.

Tournament Record:
264, J.L. Lewis, 2003 (Nemacolin Woodlands Resort and Spa)
Current Course Record:
62, J.L. Lewis, 2003
Other Course Record:
64, Jim Carter, 2000 (Waynesboro CC)
64, Stuart Appleby, Kevin Sutherland, Robert Gamez (Laurel Valley CC), 2001

TOURNAMENT HISTORY

Year	Winner	Score	Runner-up	Score	Location	Par/Yards
SEI PENNSYLVANIA CLASSIC						
2000	Chris DiMarco	270	Mark Calcavecchia Brad Elder Scott Hoch Jonathan Kaye Chris Perry	276	Waynesborough CC, Paoli, PA	71/6,939
MARCONI PENNSYLVANIA CLASSIC						
2001	Robert Allenby	269	Rocco Mediate Larry Mize	272	Laurel Valley CC, Ligonier, PA	72/7,261
SEI PENNSYLVANIA CLASSIC						
2002	Dan Forsman	270	Robert Allenby Billy Andrade	271	Waynesborough CC, Paoli, PA	71/6,939
84 LUMBER CLASSIC OF PENNSYLVANIA						
2003	J.L. Lewis	266	Stuart Appleby Frank Lickliter II Tim Petrovic	268	Mystic Rock GC, Farmington, PA	72/7,276
84 LUMBER CLASSIC						
2004	Vijay Singh	273	Stewart Cink	274	Mystic Rock GC, Farmington, PA	72/7,471

2004 WGC–American Express Championship

[42nd of 48 official events]

American Express Championship

Winner: ERNIE ELS
69-64-68-69 270 (-18) $1,200,000

Mount Juliet Conrad

Thomastown, Co. Kilkenny, Ireland

September 30-October 3, 2004

Purse: $7,000,000
Par: 36-36—72
Yards: 7,256

LEADERS: First Round—Todd Hamilton posted a 6-under-par 66 to lead Miguel Angel Jimenez, Steve Flesch, Stuart Appleby, Luke Donald, Sergio Garcia and Adam Scott by one stroke. Eight players were two behind.

Second Round—Ernie Els moved to 11-under-par 133 to lead Jimenez and Hamilton by two strokes. Justin Leonard was three back.

Third Round—Els maintained the lead at 15-under-par 201 to lead Thomas Bjorn by two and David Howell, Hamilton and Padraig Harrington by three.

CUT: There was no cut; all 68 professionals completed 72 holes.

WEATHER: Due to rain on Wednesday, players were allowed preferred lies all four rounds. Thursday, dry and cool with temperatures in the high 50s. Sunny spells with increased clouds in the late afternoon. Friday, high 50s, breezy and overcast with heavy rains in the morning and occasional showers the rest of the day. Winds gusts up to 25 mph. Occasional patches of sunshine. Saturday, cool and partly cloudy with temperatures reaching 60. Light shower in the early afternoon. On Sunday, players teed off Nos. 1 and 10 in threesomes due to impending threatening weather. Cool and cloudy with steady rain mid-morning. Temperatures in the low 50s.

Check out the 2005 WGC-American Express Championship, October 6-9 on ESPN/ABC

ORDER OF FINISH

Ernie Els	1	69-64-68-69	270	$1,200,000.00
Thomas Bjorn	2	68-69-66-68	271	675,000.00
David Howell	3	69-69-66-71	275	450,000.00
Darren Clarke	T4	71-72-65-68	276	308,000.00
Sergio Garcia	T4	67-72-67-70	276	308,000.00
Retief Goosen	T6	68-69-68-72	277	200,000.00
Todd Hamilton	T6	66-69-69-73	277	200,000.00
Padraig Harrington	T6	69-69-66-73	277	200,000.00
Tiger Woods	9	68-70-70-70	278	155,000.00
Zach Johnson	10	68-71-69-71	279	135,000.00
Luke Donald	T11	67-71-71-71	280	112,500.00
Mark Hensby	T11	73-73-69-65	280	112,500.00
Brad Faxon	T13	70-68-72-71	281	90,000.00
David Toms	T13	70-74-68-69	281	90,000.00
Lee Westwood	T13	68-69-71-73	281	90,000.00
Stuart Appleby	T16	67-74-70-72	283	79,000.00
Angel Cabrera	T16	69-69-74-71	283	79,000.00
Miguel A. Jimenez	T16	67-68-75-73	283	79,000.00
Jerry Kelly	T16	69-73-69-72	283	79,000.00
Shigeki Maruyama	T16	70-70-73-70	283	79,000.00
Paul Casey	T21	72-70-71-71	284	72,000.00
Rory Sabbatini	T21	71-70-70-73	284	72,000.00
Stewart Cink	T23	71-73-67-74	285	$65,000.00
Steve Flesch	T23	67-70-74-74	285	65,000.00
Trevor Immelman	T23	71-71-72-71	285	65,000.00
Barry Lane	T23	69-72-72-72	285	65,000.00
Peter Lonard	T23	69-70-70-76	285	65,000.00
Alex Cejka	T28	70-74-69-73	286	54,625.00
Carlos Franco	T28	69-72-75-70	286	54,625.00
Richard Green	T28	72-70-72-72	286	54,625.00
Justin Leonard	T28	68-68-77-73	286	54,625.00
Thomas Levet	T28	73-71-73-69	286	54,625.00
Paul McGinley	T28	70-75-71-70	286	54,625.00
Nick O'Hern	T28	68-73-75-70	286	54,625.00
Bob Tway	T28	71-70-72-73	286	54,625.00
Stephen Ames	T36	73-72-70-72	287	48,000.00
Fred Couples	T36	73-67-70-77	287	48,000.00
Chris DiMarco	T36	69-75-70-73	287	48,000.00
Jim Furyk	T36	70-70-71-76	287	48,000.00
Adam Scott	T36	67-74-73-73	287	48,000.00
Thongchai Jaidee	T41	71-75-71-71	288	44,500.00
Davis Love III	T41	74-69-69-76	288	44,500.00
Arjun Atwal	T43	71-78-70-70	289	42,000.00
Scott Drummond	T43	69-71-73-76	289	42,000.00
Jay Haas	T43	72-71-70-76	289	42,000.00
Graeme McDowell	T43	73-70-75-71	289	42,000.00
Peter Senior	T43	69-74-74-72	289	$42,000.00
Desvonde Botes	T48	70-72-75-74	291	40,250.00
Joakim Haeggman	T48	71-71-73-76	291	40,250.00
Chad Campbell	T50	70-79-71-72	292	39,000.00
Andrew McLardy	T50	73-73-70-76	292	39,000.00
Chris Riley	T50	70-75-73-74	292	39,000.00
S.K. Ho	53	71-76-72-74	293	38,000.00
Robert Allenby	T54	68-74-75-77	294	37,000.00
Tim Herron	T54	73-75-72-74	294	37,000.00
Scott Verplank	T54	71-82-72-69	294	37,000.00
K.J. Choi	T57	71-76-75-73	295	35,750.00
Jean-Francois Remesy	T57	72-71-75-77	295	35,750.00
Darren Fichardt	T59	76-71-74-75	296	34,250.00
Charles Howell III	T59	74-73-71-78	296	34,250.00
Fredrik Jacobson	T59	74-76-72-74	296	34,250.00
Jonathan Kaye	T59	70-73-73-80	296	34,250.00
Stephen Leaney	63	73-75-71-78	297	33,000.00
Yong Eun Yang	64	75-76-71-77	299	32,500.00
Andre Stolz	65	70-76-75-79	300	32,000.00
Michael Campbell	66	74-77-73-80	304	31,500.00
Shingo Katayama	67	79-76-76-75	306	31,000.00
Lian-wei Zhang	68	75-77-76-79	307	30,500.00

NOTES

*With his victory at the 2004 WGC-American Express Championship, **Ernie Els** jumped to No. 2 in the Official World Golf Ranking ahead of **Tiger Woods**. The last time Els was No. 2 was after the 2003 Chrysler Classic of Greensboro. One week later, he fell to No. 3 when **Vijay Singh** won the FUNAI Classic at The WALT DISNEY WORLD Resort. The last time Woods was No. 3 in the Official World Golf Ranking was May 16, 1999 after the GTE Byron Nelson Classic, when he was passed by **Davis Love III**.*

Tournament Record:
263, Tiger Woods, 2002 (Mount Juliet Estate)

18-Hole Record:
62, Sergio Garcia, Retief Goosen, 2002 (Mount Juliet Estate)

TOURNAMENT HISTORY

Year	Winner	Score	Runner-up	Score	Location	Par/Yards
WORLD GOLF CHAMPIONSHIPS-AMERICAN EXPRESS CHAMPIONSHIP						
1999	Tiger Woods*	278	Miguel A. Jimenez	278	Valderrama GC, Andalucia, Spain	71/6,830
2000	Mike Weir	277	Lee Westwood	279	Valderrama GC, Andalucia, Spain	72/6,974
2001	No Tournament				Bellerive CC, St. Louis, MO	
2002	Tiger Woods	263	Retief Goosen	264	Mount Juliet Estate, Kilkenny, Ireland	72/7,246
2003	Tiger Woods	274	Stuart Appleby Tim Herron Vijay Singh	276	Capital City Club (Crabapple), Woodstock, GA	70/7,189
2004	Ernie Els	270	Thomas Bjorn	271	Mount Juliet Conrad, Kilkenny, Ireland	72/7,256

*KEY: * = Playoff*

ELIGIBILITY REQUIREMENTS FOR THE 2005 WGC-AMERICAN EXPRESS CHAMPIONSHIP

Eligible players are:

- The top 50 players, including any players tied for 50th place, from the Official World Golf Ranking as of September 26, 2005.
- The top 50 players, including any players tied for 50th place, from the Official World Golf Ranking as of October 3, 2005
- The top 30 players from the 2005 Official PGA TOUR Money List, as of September 26, 2005.
- The top 30 players from the 2005 Official PGA TOUR Money List, as of October 3, 2005.
- The top 20 players from the 2005 European Tour Volvo (Order of Merit) as of Monday, September 26, 2005.
- The top 20 players from the 2005 European Tour Volvo (Order of Merit) as of Monday October 3, 2005.
- The top 3 players from the Japan Golf Tour Order of Merit as of September 26, 2005.
- The top 3 players from the Japan Golf Tour Order of Merit as of October 3, 2005.
- The top three players from the final 2004 Australasian Tour Order of Merit.
- The top three players from the final 2004/2005 Southern Africa Tour Order of Merit.
- The top three players from the final 2004 Asian Tour Order of Merit.

2004 Southern Farm Bureau Classic

[43rd of 48 official events]

FUNK

Winner: FRED FUNK
69-67-64-66 266 (-22) $540,000

Annandale Golf Club

Madison, MS

September 30 – October 3, 2004

Purse: $3,000,000
Par: 36-36—72
Yards: 7,199

LEADERS: First Round—Harrison Frazar, Glen Day and John Senden opened with 7-under 65s. Loren Roberts, Bill Glasson, Brenden Pappas, Deane Pappas, David Sutherland and Patrick Sheehan trailed by one.

Second Round—Frazar and Steve Pate sat at 12-under 132, one ahead of John Senden, Patrick Sheehan and Chris Couch.

Third Round—Fred Funk at 16-under 200 led Couch and Pate by a stroke. Kevin Na, Greg Chalmers and Senden trailed by two.

CUT: 70 players at 4-under-par 140 from a field of 132 professionals.

PRO-AM: $10,000. Matt Gogel, 50, $2,000.

WEATHER: Sunny with temperatures reaching the mid to high 80s. Same on Friday. Cloudy on Saturday with a patch of very light rain in the morning. Temperatures in the mid-80s. Mostly sunny on Sunday with temperatures in the low 80s.

Check out the 2005 Southern Farm Bureau Classic, October 6-9 on The Golf Channel

ORDER OF FINISH

Fred Funk	1	69-67-64-66	266	$540,000.00
Ryan Palmer	2	69-68-66-64	267	324,000.00
Glen Day	T3	65-70-70-63	268	144,000.00
J.J. Henry	T3	70-67-66-65	268	144,000.00
Kevin Na	T3	71-65-66-66	268	144,000.00
Loren Roberts	T3	66-69-68-65	268	144,000.00
Kirk Triplett	7	69-69-65-66	269	100,500.00
Jonathan Byrd	T8	70-69-66-65	270	90,000.00
Tim Clark	T8	68-69-67-66	270	90,000.00
Pat Bates	T10	69-66-68-68	271	72,000.00
Greg Chalmers	T10	68-67-67-69	271	72,000.00
Chris Couch	T10	70-63-68-70	271	72,000.00
Carl Pettersson	T10	67-69-67-68	271	72,000.00
Steve Allan	T14	69-69-67-67	272	52,500.00
Danny Briggs	T14	72-65-69-66	272	52,500.00
Rod Pampling	T14	69-71-68-64	272	52,500.00
John Senden	T14	65-68-69-70	272	52,500.00
Heath Slocum	18	70-67-70-66	273	45,000.00
Robert Damron	T19	70-65-71-68	274	33,857.15
Brent Geiberger	T19	71-66-72-65	274	33,857.15
Craig Barlow	T19	67-71-68-68	274	33,857.14
Tom Carter	T19	69-69-67-69	274	33,857.14
Bill Glasson	T19	66-70-68-70	274	33,857.14
Ted Purdy	T19	69-69-66-70	274	$33,857.14
Patrick Sheehan	T19	66-67-72-69	274	33,857.14
Woody Austin	T26	72-64-70-69	275	21,750.00
Aaron Barber	T26	69-68-71-67	275	21,750.00
Daniel Chopra	T26	70-70-66-69	275	21,750.00
Lucas Glover	T26	73-67-64-71	275	21,750.00
Richard S. Johnson	T26	73-66-68-68	275	21,750.00
Steve Pate	T26	67-65-69-74	275	21,750.00
Joe Durant	T32	68-69-70-69	276	18,150.00
Chris Smith	T32	67-71-69-69	276	18,150.00
Billy Andrade	T34	67-70-71-69	277	14,200.00
Jason Bohn	T34	69-71-68-69	277	14,200.00
Harrison Frazar	T34	65-67-73-72	277	14,200.00
Shaun Micheel	T34	70-68-69-70	277	14,200.00
David Morland IV	T34	68-67-70-72	277	14,200.00
Deane Pappas	T34	66-70-70-71	277	14,200.00
Omar Uresti	T34	70-70-70-67	277	14,200.00
Camilo Villegas (S)	T34	72-64-68-73	277	14,200.00
Jay Williamson	T34	68-71-68-70	277	14,200.00
Cameron Beckman	T43	72-68-66-72	278	10,500.00
Brad Bryant	T43	69-70-69-70	278	10,500.00
Dan Forsman	T43	69-69-70-70	278	10,500.00
Olin Browne	T46	69-68-71-71	279	8,316.00
Jay Delsing	T46	73-67-72-67	279	8,316.00
David Frost	T46	71-69-66-73	279	8,316.00
Brenden Pappas	T46	66-72-72-69	279	$8,316.00
Joey Sindelar	T46	70-69-69-71	279	8,316.00
Jay Don Blake (S)	T51	68-67-71-74	280	7,060.00
Matt Gogel	T51	71-66-70-73	280	7,060.00
Kent Jones	T51	68-71-69-72	280	7,060.00
Brad Lardon	T51	70-70-66-74	280	7,060.00
Tommy Tolles	T51	71-67-72-70	280	7,060.00
Garrett Willis	T51	69-70-71-70	280	7,060.00
Rich Beem	T57	70-67-72-72	281	6,720.00
Larry Mize	T57	68-71-72-70	281	6,720.00
Dicky Pride	T57	72-67-72-70	281	6,720.00
Kris Cox	T60	70-69-73-70	282	6,570.00
David Sutherland	T60	66-73-69-74	282	6,570.00
Jeff Brehaut	T62	68-69-74-72	283	6,420.00
J.P. Hayes	T62	71-69-73-70	283	6,420.00
Craig Perks	T62	72-68-71-72	283	6,420.00
Paul Azinger	T65	71-68-74-71	284	6,240.00
Brian Bateman	T65	71-66-73-74	284	6,240.00
Grant Waite	T65	72-68-72-72	284	6,240.00
David Peoples	68	71-69-71-74	285	6,120.00
Ken Duke	T69	70-69-73-74	286	6,030.00
Kelly Gibson (S)	T69	71-69-70-76	286	6,030.00

(S) = Sponsor Exemption

The following players did not finish (C=cut, W=withdrew)

C—141-Michael Allen, Mark Brooks, John Cook, Jason Dufner, Mike Grob, Scott Hend, Cliff Kresge, Hirofumi Miyase, Carl Paulson, Brett Quigley, Hidemichi Tanaka, Roland Thatcher, Esteban Toledo, Stan Utley, Mark Wilson, **142**-Craig Bowden, Danny Ellis, Bob Estes, Niclas Fasth, Brian Henninger, Neal Lancaster, Blaine McCallister, Spike McRoy, Kevin Muncrief, Dan Olsen, Mike Standly, Dean Wilson, **143**-Guy Boros, David Branshaw, Bart Bryant, David Duval, Donnie Hammond, John Huston, Tim Thelen, **144**-Jim Carter, David Edwards, Joel Edwards, Matt Kuchar, Jim McGovern, Corey Pavin, Gene Sauers, Steve Stricker, Vaughn Taylor, **145**-Mathias Gronberg, Scott Simpson, **146**-Trevor Dodds, Brian Gay, Brian Kortan, Hank Kuehne, Steve Lowery, **147**-Michael Clark II, Robin Freeman, John E. Morgan, **148-**Michael Bradley, David Church, Rett Crowder, Jim Gallagher, Jr., Willie Wood, **149**-David Gossett, Mike Springer. **W**—Russ Cochran, **75**-Phil Tataurangi.

NOTES

Fred Funk *became the second player to win the Southern Farm Bureau Classic twice since it became an official PGA TOUR event in 1994.* ***Brian Henninger*** *(1994, 1999) and* ***Dwight Nevil*** *(Magnolia Golf Classic at Hattiesburg Country Club/1972-73/unofficial event) are other multiple winners of the tournament.*

TOURNAMENT HISTORY

Year	Winner	Score	Runner-up	Score	Location	Par/Yards
MAGNOLIA STATE CLASSIC						
1968	Mac McLendon*	269	Pete Fleming	269	Hattiesburg CC, Hattiesburg, MS	70/6,280
1969	Larry Mowry	272	Larry Hinson Alvin Odom	273	Hattiesburg CC, Hattiesburg, MS	70/6,280
1970	Chris Blocker	271	Roy Pace Martin Roesink	272	Hattiesburg CC, Hattiesburg, MS	70/6,280
1971	Roy Pace	270	Jack Lewis, Jr.	271	Hattiesburg CC, Hattiesburg, MS	70/6,280
1972	Mike Morley	269	Rick Rhoads	272	Hattiesburg CC, Hattiesburg, MS	70/6,280
1973	Dwight Nevil	268	Bert Greene	271	Hattiesburg CC, Hattiesburg, MS	70/6,280
1974	Dwight Nevil~	133	Bunky Henry Gil Morgan	135	Hattiesburg CC, Hattiesburg, MS	70/6,280
1975	Bob Wynn	270	Mike Morley	272	Hattiesburg CC, Hattiesburg, MS	70/6,280
1976	Dennis Meyer	271	Artie McNickle Tom Purtzer	273	Hattiesburg CC, Hattiesburg, MS	70/6,280
1977	Mike McCullough	269	Orville Moody Gary Groh	272	Hattiesburg CC, Hattiesburg, MS	70/6,280
1978	Craig Stadler	268	Bob Eastwood Bruce Fleisher	269	Hattiesburg CC, Hattiesburg, MS	70/6,280
1979	Bobby Walzel*	272	Buddy Gardner	272	Hattiesburg CC, Hattiesburg, MS	70/6,280
1980	Roger Maltbie~	65	Lee Carter	66	Hattiesburg CC, Hattiesburg, MS	70/6,280
1981	Tom Jones*	268	Mike Smith	268	Hattiesburg CC, Hattiesburg, MS	70/6,280
1982	Payne Stewart	270	Jay Cudd Bruce Douglass	273	Hattiesburg CC, Hattiesburg, MS	70/6,280
1983	Russ Cochran~#	203	Sammy Rachels	205	Hattiesburg CC, Hattiesburg, MS	70/6,280
1984	Lance Ten Broeck~*#	201	Mike Smith	201	Hattiesburg CC, Hattiesburg, MS	70/6,280
1985	Jim Gallagher, Jr.~*#	131	Paul Azinger	131	Hattiesburg CC, Hattiesburg, MS	70/6,280
DEPOSIT GUARANTY GOLF CLASSIC						
1986	Dan Halldorson	263	Paul Azinger	265	Hattiesburg CC, Hattiesburg, MS	70/6,594
1987	David Ogrin	267	Nick Faldo	268	Hattiesburg CC, Hattiesburg, MS	70/6,594
1988	Frank Conner	267	Brian Mogg	272	Hattiesburg CC, Hattiesburg, MS	70/6,594
1989	Jim Booros~*	199	Mike Donald	199	Hattiesburg CC, Hattiesburg, MS	70/6,594

Southern Farm Bureau Classic

NOTES

Fred Funk *matched the 72-hole tournament record of 22-under 266 at Annandale Golf Club set by* ***Steve Lowery*** *and* ***Skip Kendall*** *in 2000 and matched the low final round by a winner since 1994 (****Ed Dougherty****/1995) with his 6-under 66.*

Fred Funk *is the tournament's all-time money winner with $1,028,465 and top-10 leader with six in 11 appearances dating back to 1985. He has earned $996,152 since the event became an official TOUR event in 1994 with two wins and a third in 2001.*

KIRK TRIPLETT

Kirk Triplett *posted a T7 at Annandale Golf Club to move ahead of* ***David Ogrin*** *for second on the all-time top-10 list at the Southern Farm Bureau Classic with five. He also has yet to miss a cut in nine appearances at the tournament dating back to 1990.*

At age 48, ***Fred Funk*** *became the oldest player to win on TOUR since* ***Peter Jacobsen*** *(49 years, four months, 23 days) won the 2003 Greater Hartford Open.*

Fred Funk *was one of four players in 2004 that ended a winless streak of over six years—****John Daly*** *(eight years),* ***Joey Sindelar*** *(13 years) and* ***Woody Austin*** *(nine years).*

Fred Funk *collected his first victory in over six years. Ironically, his last win also came at Annandale GC in July 1998, a span of six years, two months and 14 days, including 196 events and 10 runner-up finishes in between.*

*Two rookies finished in the top-10 at the 2004 Southern Farm Bureau Classic and posted their career-best finishes on TOUR—****Ryan Palmer*** *(runner-up) and* ***Kevin Na*** *(T3).*

Tournament Record:
266, Steve Lowery, Skip Kendall, 2000; Fred Funk, 2004 (Annandale GC)

Current Course Record:
61, Keith Clearwater, 1996

TOURNAMENT HISTORY

Year	Winner	Score	Runner-up	Score	Location	Par/Yards
1990	Gene Sauers	268	Jack Ferenz	270	Hattiesburg CC, Hattiesburg, MS	70/6,594
1991	Larry Silveira*	266	Russ Cochran	266	Hattiesburg CC, Hattiesburg, MS	70/6,594
			Mike Nicolette			
1992	Richard Zokol	267	Mike Donald	268	Hattiesburg CC, Hattiesburg, MS	70/6,594
			Bob Eastwood			
			Mike Nicolette			
			Greg Twiggs			
1993	Greg Kraft	267	Morris Hatalsky	268	Hattiesburg CC, Hattiesburg, MS	70/6,594
			Tad Rhyan			
1994	Brian Henninger~*	135	Mike Sullivan	135	Annandale GC, Madison, MS	72/7,157
1995	Ed Dougherty	272	Gil Morgan	274	Annandale GC, Madison, MS	72/7,157
1996	Willie Wood	268	Kirk Triplett	269	Annandale GC, Madison, MS	72/7,157
1997	Billy Ray Brown	271	Mike Standly	272	Annandale GC, Madison, MS	72/7,157
1998	Fred Funk	270	Paul Goydos	272	Annandale GC, Madison, MS	72/7,157
			Franklin Langham			
			Tim Loustalot			
SOUTHERN FARM BUREAU CLASSIC						
1999	Brian Henninger+	202	Chris DiMarco	205	Annandale GC, Madison, MS	72/7,157
2000	Steve Lowery*	266	Skip Kendall	266	Annandale GC, Madison, MS	72/7,199
2001	Cameron Beckman	269	Chad Campbell	270	Annandale GC, Madison, MS	72/7,199
2002	Luke Donald~	201	Deane Pappas	202	Annandale GC, Madison, MS	72/7,199
2003	John Huston	268	Brenden Pappas	269	Annandale GC, Madison, MS	72/7,199
2004	Fred Funk	266	Ryan Palmer	267	Annandale GC, Madison, MS	72/7,199

*KEY: * = Playoff ~ = Weather-shortened # = Tournament Players Series (TPS) event 1983-1985 (1994 first year as official event) + = The tournament was shortened to 54 holes due to the death of Payne Stewart*

Fred Funk took home the trophy at the 2004 Southern Farm Bureau Classic.

2004 Michelin Championship at Las Vegas

[44th of 48 official events]

MICHELIN CHAMPIONSHIP at Las Vegas

Winner: ANDRE STOLZ
67-67-65-67 266 (-21) $720,000

Tournament Players Club at Summerlin

Las Vegas, NV

October 7-10, 2004

Purse: $4,000,000
Host Course (HC)
Par: 36-36—72/Yards: 7,243
TPC at The Canyons (TC)
Par: 36-35—71/Yards: 7,019
Bear's Best (BB)
Par: 36-36—72/Yards: 7,219

LEADERS: First Round—Danny Ellis (TC), Scott Verplank (HC), Harrison Frazar (HC) Kent Jones (BB), Billy Mayfair (BB) and Jason Bohn (TC) each fired an 8-under-par 64. Justin Leonard (HC), Tom Lehman (TC) and Danny Briggs (HC) were one shot back. **Second Round**—J.L. Lewis (HC) moved to 14-under-par 130 to take a one-stroke lead over Chez Reavie (HC), Alex Cejka (HC) and Olin Browne (BB). **Third Round**—Lehman (BB), at 17-under-par 198, led Dicky Pride (HC) and Andre Stolz (HC) by one stroke.

CUT: 72 players at 8-under-par 207 from a field of 144 professionals.

WEATHER: Sunny and warm on Thursday. High of 91. Winds SE 4-8 mph. Mostly sunny, warm and a slight breeze on Friday. High of 91. Winds SE 5-10 mph. Mostly sunny and warm on Saturday. Winds gusting S 15-25 mph. Partly sunny and slightly breezy on Sunday. High of 87. Winds NE 5-15 mph.

Check out the 2005 Michelin Championship at Las Vegas, October 13-16 on USA/ABC

ORDER OF FINISH

Andre Stolz	1	67-67-65-67	266	$720,000.00
Harrison Frazar	T2	64-68-68-67	267	298,666.67
Tag Ridings	T2	67-66-73-61	267	298,666.67
Tom Lehman	T2	64-68-66-69	267	298,666.66
Carl Pettersson	T5	68-68-65-67	268	152,000.00
Dicky Pride	T5	66-67-66-69	268	152,000.00
Danny Ellis	T7	63-70-73-63	269	120,500.00
David Frost	T7	69-71-67-62	269	120,500.00
Lee Janzen	T7	68-66-70-65	269	120,500.00
Tim Petrovic	T7	66-66-68-69	269	120,500.00
Bob Estes	T11	67-65-68-70	270	88,000.00
Jim Furyk	T11	67-67-70-66	270	88,000.00
Brian Gay	T11	68-70-65-67	270	88,000.00
Duffy Waldorf	T11	65-66-69-70	270	88,000.00
Greg Chalmers	T15	69-67-64-71	271	58,100.00
Jose Coceres	T15	66-68-69-68	271	58,100.00
Ben Crane	T15	68-65-69-69	271	58,100.00
Lucas Glover	T15	68-68-67-68	271	58,100.00
Kent Jones	T15	64-68-70-69	271	58,100.00
Scott Verplank	T15	64-72-66-69	271	58,100.00
Jay Williamson	T15	69-62-74-66	271	58,100.00
Mark Wilson	T15	68-73-63-67	271	58,100.00
Stuart Appleby	T23	69-67-69-67	272	32,133.34
Danny Briggs	T23	65-71-68-68	272	$32,133.34
Omar Uresti	T23	67-65-72-68	272	32,133.34
Briny Baird	T23	72-63-70-67	272	32,133.33
Jason Bohn	T23	63-70-70-69	272	32,133.33
Olin Browne	T23	67-64-69-72	272	32,133.33
Justin Leonard	T23	65-70-67-70	272	32,133.33
J.L. Lewis	T23	67-63-70-72	272	32,133.33
Pat Perez	T23	70-68-66-68	272	32,133.33
Tom Byrum	T32	66-70-65-72	273	22,640.00
Alex Cejka	T32	65-65-72-71	273	22,640.00
Dudley Hart	T32	69-70-65-69	273	22,640.00
Billy Mayfair	T32	64-69-71-69	273	22,640.00
Scott McCarron	T32	66-71-67-69	273	22,640.00
Billy Andrade	T37	68-68-68-70	274	16,800.00
Woody Austin	T37	74-66-66-68	274	16,800.00
Paul Azinger	T37	69-65-71-69	274	16,800.00
David Duval	T37	67-68-68-71	274	16,800.00
Robert Gamez	T37	67-66-70-71	274	16,800.00
Geoff Ogilvy	T37	66-67-70-71	274	16,800.00
Chris Smith	T37	70-66-67-71	274	16,800.00
Bo Van Pelt	T37	72-68-65-69	274	16,800.00
Steve Allan	T45	67-70-68-70	275	11,211.43
Robert Allenby	T45	69-68-68-70	275	11,211.43
Craig Barlow	T45	66-71-69-69	275	11,211.43
Donnie Hammond (S)	T45	68-65-71-71	275	11,211.43
Corey Pavin	T45	68-70-68-69	275	$11,211.43
Tom Pernice, Jr.	T45	66-72-69-68	275	11,211.43
Rich Barcelo	T45	69-66-72-68	275	11,211.42
Cameron Beckman	T52	67-66-69-74	276	9,104.00
David Branshaw	T52	67-66-71-72	276	9,104.00
Glen Day	T52	68-64-72-72	276	9,104.00
Paul Goydos	T52	66-68-70-72	276	9,104.00
Richard S. Johnson	T52	66-69-71-70	276	9,104.00
Jonathan Kaye	T52	65-71-69-71	276	9,104.00
Ryan Palmer	T52	71-71-65-69	276	9,104.00
Deane Pappas	T52	74-70-63-69	276	9,104.00
Craig Perks	T52	69-70-66-71	276	9,104.00
Dean Wilson	T52	68-64-72-72	276	9,104.00
Daniel Chopra	T62	72-64-70-72	278	8,520.00
Ted Purdy	T62	71-67-69-71	278	8,520.00
Jeff Sluman	T62	70-67-68-73	278	8,520.00
Steve Stricker	T62	68-72-67-71	278	8,520.00
John Rollins	66	72-65-69-74	280	8,320.00
Skip Kendall	T67	66-72-66-77	281	8,160.00
Frank Lickliter II	T67	69-69-69-74	281	8,160.00
Spike McRoy	T67	66-70-70-75	281	8,160.00
Kris Cox	70	68-71-67-76	282	8,000.00
Mark Brooks	71	70-73-64-76	283	7,920.00
Chez Reavie (S)	72	66-64-75-85	290	7,840.00

(S) = Sponsor Exemption

The following players did not finish
(C=cut, W=withdrew, D=disqualified)

C—208-Craig Bowden, Jason Dufner, Dan Forsman, Bill Glasson, Steve Lowery, Blaine McCallister, Arron Oberholser, Joe Ogilvie, Dan Olsen, Jesper Parnevik, Brett Quigley, Esteban Toledo, Bob Tway, **209**-Pat Bates, Bart Bryant, Jay Delsing, Joe Durant, Steve Flesch, J.P. Hayes, **210**-Brent Geiberger, Matt Gogel, Mathias Gronberg, Charles Howell III, Mike Hulbert, John Huston, Len Mattiace, Rocco Mediate, Kevin Sutherland, Grant Waite, **211**-Mark Calcavecchia, Nick Flanagan, Edward Fryatt, Scott Hend, Brian Kortan, Steve Pate, John Senden, Tommy Tolles, **212**-Michael Allen, Shaun Micheel, Chris Riley, Roger Tambellini, Kirk Triplett, **213**-Bob Burns, Trevor Dodds, Hirofumi Miyase, David Morland IV, Michael Ruiz, Roland Thatcher, **214**-Guy Boros, Chris Couch, **215**-Arjun Atwal, D.J. Brigman, Tom Carter, Matt Kuchar, Neal Lancaster, Garrett Willis, **216**-Jay Don Blake, Robin Freeman, Gene Sauers, **217**-Jeff Brehaut, Russ Cochran, Per-Ulrik Johansson, Cliff Kresge, Brenden Pappas, **218**-Tommy Armour III, Hunter Mahan, **219**-Ken Green, **220**-Kevin Muncrief, **223**-Todd Fischer, **225**-Ken Duke. **W—134**-Phil Mickelson. **D—135**-Kevin Na.

TOURNAMENT HISTORY

Year	Winner	Score	Runner-up	Score	Location	Par/Yards
PANASONIC LAS VEGAS PRO-CELEBRITY CLASSIC						
1983	Fuzzy Zoeller	340	Rex Caldwell	344	Las Vegas CC, Las Vegas, NV (H) Desert Inn CC, Las Vegas, NV Dunes CC, Las Vegas, NV Showboat CC, Las Vegas, NV	72/7,164 72/7,111 72/7,240 72/7,045
PANASONIC LAS VEGAS INVITATIONAL						
1984	Denis Watson	341	Andy Bean	342	Las Vegas CC, Las Vegas, NV (H) Desert Inn CC, Las Vegas, NV Showboat CC, Las Vegas, NV Tropicana CC, Las Vegas, NV	72/7,164 72/7,111 72/7,045 71/6,481
1985	Curtis Strange	338	Mike Smith	339	Las Vegas CC, Las Vegas, NV (H) Desert Inn CC, Las Vegas, NV Tropicana CC, Las Vegas, NV	72/7,164 72/7,111 71/6,481
1986	Greg Norman	333	Dan Pohl	340	Las Vegas CC, Las Vegas, NV (H) Desert Inn CC, Las Vegas, NV Spanish Trail G&CC, Las Vegas, NV	72/7,164 72/7,111 72/7,088
1987	Paul Azinger~	271	Hal Sutton	272	Las Vegas CC, Las Vegas, NV (H) Desert Inn CC, Las Vegas, NV Spanish Trail G&CC, Las Vegas, NV	72/7,164 72/7,111 72/7,088
1988	Gary Koch~	274	Peter Jacobsen Mark O'Meara	275	Las Vegas CC, Las Vegas, NV (H) Desert Inn CC, Las Vegas, NV Spanish Trail G&CC, Las Vegas, NV	72/7,164 72/7,111 72/7,088
LAS VEGAS INVITATIONAL						
1989	Scott Hoch*	336	Robert Wrenn	336	Las Vegas CC, Las Vegas, NV (H) Desert Inn CC, Las Vegas, NV Spanish Trail G&CC, Las Vegas, NV	72/7,164 72/7,111 72/7,088
1990	Bob Tway*	334	John Cook	334	Las Vegas CC, Las Vegas, NV (H) Desert Inn CC, Las Vegas, NV Spanish Trail G&CC, Las Vegas, NV	72/7,164 72/7,111 72/7,088

Michelin Championship at Las Vegas

MICHELIN CHAMPIONSHIP at Las Vegas

NOTES

Andre Stolz *was the third consecutive, and fifth overall, international player to win the Michelin Championship at Las Vegas. He joined South African* ***Denis Watson*** *(1984), Australian* ***Greg Norman*** *(1986), New Zealand's* ***Phil Tataurangi*** *(2002) and Aussie* ***Stuart Appleby*** *(2003) as international players who have won in Las Vegas.*

Andre Stolz *became the fourth player to notch his first career win at the Michelin Championship at Las Vegas, joining* ***Phil Tataurangi*** *(2002),* ***Tiger Woods*** *(1996) and* ***Jim Furyk*** *(1995).*

Andre Stolz *collected a career-best $720,000 for his 2004 win and jumped from No. 217 to No. 89 on the PGA TOUR official money list. It wasn't his only big leap, as the victory also lifted Stolz 205 spots from No. 341 to No. 136 in the Official World Golf Ranking.*

Mark Brooks *and* ***Russ Cochran*** *have started a tournament-record 21 consecutive Michelin Championships at Las Vegas. Each missed the inaugural tournament in 1983, but have played every year since to hold the record for most tournament appearances.*

TOM LEHMAN

Tom Lehman*'s payday of $298,666 for his T2 finish at the 2004 Michelin Championship at Las Vegas moved him over the $1-million mark for the season for the eighth time in his career. It is the second time that Lehman, who was making his ninth start in Las Vegas, has come up just short in Las Vegas. In 2001, he finished one stroke behind winner* ***Bob Estes****.*

Tournament Record:
328, Stuart Appleby, Scott McCarron, 2003

Current Course Record:
61, Davis Love III, 2001, (TPC at Summerlin)
61, Chris DiMarco, 2001, (Southern Highlands GC)
62, John Daly, 2001; Craig Barlow, Dan Forsman, 2003; Jay Williamson, 2004 (TPC at The Canyons)
63, Briny Baird, 2004 (Bear's Best)

Tournament Course Record:
59, Chip Beck, 1991 (Sunrise CC)

TOURNAMENT HISTORY

Year	Winner	Score	Runner-up	Score	Location	Par/Yards
1991	Andrew Magee*	329	D.A. Weibring	329	Las Vegas CC, Las Vegas, NV (H) Desert Inn CC, Las Vegas, NV Sunrise GC, Las Vegas, NV	72/7,164 72/7,111 72/6,914
1992	John Cook	334	David Frost	336	Las Vegas CC, Las Vegas, NV Desert Inn CC, Las Vegas, NV TPC at Summerlin, Las Vegas, NV (H)	72/7,164 72/7,111 72/7,243
1993	Davis Love III	331	Craig Stadler	339	Las Vegas CC, Las Vegas, NV Desert Inn CC, Las Vegas, NV TPC at Summerlin, Las Vegas, NV (H)	72/7,164 72/7,111 72/7,243
1994	Bruce Lietzke	332	Robert Gamez	333	Las Vegas CC, Las Vegas, NV Las Vegas Hilton CC, Las Vegas, NV TPC at Summerlin, Las Vegas, NV (H)	72/7,164 71/6,815 72/7,243
1995	Jim Furyk	331	Billy Mayfair	332	Las Vegas CC, Las Vegas, NV Las Vegas Hilton CC, Las Vegas, NV TPC at Summerlin, Las Vegas, NV (H)	72/7,162 71/6,815 72/7,243
1996	Tiger Woods*	332	Davis Love III	332	TPC at Summerlin, Las Vegas, NV (H) Desert Inn CC, Las Vegas, NV Las Vegas Hilton CC, Las Vegas, NV	72/7,243 72/7,095 71/6,815
1997	Bill Glasson	340	David Edwards Billy Mayfair	341	TPC at Summerlin, Las Vegas, NV (H) Desert Inn CC, Las Vegas, NV Las Vegas Hilton CC, Las Vegas, NV	72/7,243 72/7,200 72/7,164
1998	Jim Furyk	335	Mark Calcavecchia	336	TPC at Summerlin, Las Vegas, NV (H) Desert Inn CC, Las Vegas, NV Las Vegas CC, Las Vegas, NV	72/7,243 72/7,193 72/7,164
1999	Jim Furyk	331	Jonathan Kaye	332	TPC at Summerlin, Las Vegas, NV (H) Desert Inn CC, Las Vegas, NV Las Vegas CC, Las Vegas, NV	72/7,243 72/7,193 72/7,164
INVENSYS CLASSIC AT LAS VEGAS						
2000	Billy Andrade	332	Phil Mickelson	333	TPC at Summerlin, Las Vegas, NV (H) Desert Inn CC, Las Vegas, NV Southern Highlands GC, Las Vegas, NV	72/7,243 72/7,193 72/7,247
2001	Bob Estes	329	Tom Lehman Rory Sabbatini	330	TPC at Summerlin, Las Vegas, NV (H) TPC at The Canyons, Las Vegas, NV Southern Highlands GC, Las Vegas, NV	72/7,243 71/7,019 72/7,247
2002	Phil Tataurangi	330	Stuart Appleby Jeff Sluman	331	TPC at Summerlin, Las Vegas, NV (H) TPC at The Canyons, Las Vegas, NV Southern Highlands GC, Las Vegas, NV	72/7,243 71/7,063 72/7,440
2003	Stuart Appleby*	328	Scott McCarron	328	TPC at Summerlin, Las Vegas, NV (H) TPC at The Canyons, Las Vegas, NV Southern Highlands GC, Las Vegas, NV	72/7,243 71/7,063 72/7,440
MICHELIN CHAMPIONSHIP AT LAS VEGAS						
2004	Andre Stolz	266	Harrison Frazar Tag Ridings Tom Lehman	267	TPC at Summerlin, Las Vegas, NV (H) TPC at The Canyons, Las Vegas, NV Bear's Best GC, Las Vegas, NV	72/7,243 71/7,019 72/7,219

*KEY: * = Playoff ~ = Weather-shortened*

View of the 16th hole at the TPC at Summerlin.

SECTION 3 TOURNAMENT HISTORIES

2004 Chrysler Classic of Greensboro

[45th of 48 official events]

GEIBERGER

Winner: BRENT GEIBERGER
66-67-71-66 270 (-18) $828,000

Forest Oaks Country Club

Greensboro, NC

October 14-17, 2004

Purse: $4,600,000
Par: 36-36—72
Yards: 7,311

LEADERS: First Round—Jason Dufner posted a 7-under-par 65 to lead Brent Geiberger, Tom Pernice, Jr., Bo Van Pelt, Brenden Pappas and Brett Quigley by one stroke.
Second Round—Geiberger moved to 11-under-par 133 to lead Jeff Brehaut, David Toms and Pernice by one. Five players were two behind.
Third Round—Geiberger and Tom Lehman at 12-under-par 204 led Toms, Matt Gogel, Michael Allen and Joe Ogilvie by one. Chris Smith and Shigeki Maruyama were two behind.

CUT: 71 players at 3-under-par 141 from a field of 131 professionals and one amateur.

PRO-AM: $10,000. Two nine-hole competitions due to rain. First tee: Brenden Pappas, 23, $1,000. Tenth Tee: John Daly, Robert Gamez, Kevin Sutherland, 26, $833.34.

WEATHER: Thursday, partly cloudy and comfortable with a high of 71. Friday, showers in the early morning followed by mix of clouds and sunshine. Cooler temperatures with a high of 61 degrees. High winds in the afternoon. Saturday temperatures in the 40s, warming to mid-60s in the afternoon. Sunday, cool and sunny in the morning warming up with temperatures reaching 69 in the afternoon.

Check out the 2005 Chrysler Classic of Greensboro, September 29-October 2 on USA/ABC

ORDER OF FINISH

Brent Geiberger	1	66-67-71-66	270	$828,000.00
Michael Allen	2	70-67-68-67	272	496,800.00
Chris Smith	3	70-69-67-67	273	312,800.00
Tom Lehman	T4	69-66-69-70	274	202,400.00
David Toms	T4	69-65-71-69	274	202,400.00
Arjun Atwal	6	71-70-68-66	275	165,600.00
Tom Pernice, Jr.	7	66-68-73-69	276	154,100.00
Jeff Brehaut	T8	68-66-73-70	277	110,975.00
Ben Crane	T8	68-69-70-70	277	110,975.00
Jason Dufner	T8	65-70-73-69	277	110,975.00
Matt Gogel	T8	70-69-66-72	277	110,975.00
Richard S. Johnson	T8	67-71-69-70	277	110,975.00
Jerry Kelly	T8	70-65-72-70	277	110,975.00
Joe Ogilvie	T8	68-67-70-72	277	110,975.00
Ted Purdy	T8	71-68-74-64	277	110,975.00
Cameron Beckman	T16	71-67-71-69	278	73,600.00
Rod Pampling	T16	69-71-70-68	278	73,600.00
Bo Van Pelt	T16	66-69-74-69	278	73,600.00
Jay Delsing	T19	67-72-73-68	280	55,752.00
Carlos Franco	T19	70-70-69-71	280	55,752.00
Hank Kuehne	T19	67-69-73-71	280	55,752.00
Shigeki Maruyama	T19	68-70-68-74	280	55,752.00
Brett Quigley	T19	66-71-72-71	280	55,752.00
David Frost	T24	70-66-71-74	281	$42,320.00
Blaine McCallister (S)	T24	67-70-70-74	281	42,320.00
Ryan Moore (S)	T24	68-69-73-71	281	Amateur
Jason Bohn	T27	70-70-71-71	282	31,970.00
Brad Faxon	T27	68-70-71-73	282	31,970.00
Fred Funk	T27	69-71-69-73	282	31,970.00
Jesper Parnevik	T27	72-68-69-73	282	31,970.00
John Rollins	T27	68-73-72-69	282	31,970.00
Jeff Sluman	T27	68-71-72-71	282	31,970.00
Steve Stricker	T27	70-71-71-70	282	31,970.00
Roland Thatcher	T27	70-69-73-70	282	31,970.00
Todd Fischer	T35	67-74-71-71	283	20,825.46
Arron Oberholser	T35	71-70-71-71	283	20,825.46
Tag Ridings	T35	69-71-72-71	283	20,825.46
Mike Springer	T35	70-68-74-71	283	20,825.46
Kevin Sutherland	T35	70-71-72-70	283	20,825.46
Billy Andrade	T35	67-71-72-73	283	20,825.45
Mark Calcavecchia	T35	69-69-71-74	283	20,825.45
Cliff Kresge	T35	69-72-70-72	283	20,825.45
Deane Pappas	T35	70-70-70-73	283	20,825.45
Corey Pavin	T35	70-69-72-72	283	20,825.45
Carl Pettersson	T35	67-72-72-72	283	20,825.45
Robert Allenby	T46	71-69-73-71	284	13,468.80
Danny Ellis	T46	69-72-73-70	284	13,468.80
Skip Kendall	T46	70-71-71-72	284	13,468.80
Dan Olsen	T46	67-73-74-70	284	$13,468.80
Brenden Pappas	T46	66-71-76-71	284	13,468.80
D.J. Brigman	T51	67-74-77-67	285	11,009.34
Tim Petrovic	T51	69-69-79-68	285	11,009.34
Ken Duke	T51	72-69-72-72	285	11,009.33
Fredrik Jacobson	T51	70-69-73-73	285	11,009.33
Steve Pate	T51	69-70-75-71	285	11,009.33
Mark Wilson	T51	68-72-72-73	285	11,009.33
Lucas Glover	T57	70-68-73-75	286	10,350.00
Hunter Mahan	T57	70-69-75-72	286	10,350.00
Geoff Ogilvy	T57	69-72-78-67	286	10,350.00
Chris Stroud (S)	T57	69-71-73-73	286	10,350.00
Zach Johnson	61	68-73-72-74	287	10,120.00
Guy Boros	T62	70-70-75-73	288	9,844.00
Niclas Fasth	T62	70-71-73-74	288	9,844.00
Scott Hend	T62	71-69-77-71	288	9,844.00
Frank Lickliter II	T62	70-70-74-74	288	9,844.00
Rocco Mediate	T62	70-71-73-74	288	9,844.00
Craig Parry	67	69-69-75-76	289	9,568.00
Jose Coceres	68	69-72-71-79	291	9,476.00
Robert Damron	69	71-70-79-73	293	9,384.00
Billy Mayfair	70	73-68-81-73	295	9,292.00

(S) = Sponsor Exemption

The following players did not finish
(C=cut, W=withdrew, D=disqualified)

C—**142**-Briny Baird, Pat Bates, Bob Burns, Tom Carter, Tim Clark, John Daly, Mathias Gronberg, Jay Haas, Dudley Hart, Lee Janzen, Kent Jones, Neal Lancaster, Dicky Pride, Justin Rose, Joey Sindelar, Heath Slocum, **143**-Danny Briggs, Mark Brooks, Chris Couch, Kris Cox, Luke Donald, J.P. Hayes, J.J. Henry, **144**-Jonathan Byrd, Robert Gamez, Brian Gay, Davis Love III, Roger Tambellini, Vaughn Taylor, Duffy Waldorf, Dean Wilson, **145**-Ben Curtis, Trevor Dodds, Dan Forsman, Jim Furyk, Matt Kuchar, J.L. Lewis, Len Mattiace, Spike McRoy, Kevin Na, Esteban Toledo, Omar Uresti, **146**-Rich Barcelo, David Branshaw, Jim Gallagher, Jr., Gene Sauers, **147**-Russ Cochran, Glen Day, Brian Kortan, David Morland IV, Patrick Sheehan, **149**-Per-Ulrik Johansson, Tommy Tolles, Grant Waite, **150**-Curtis Strange, **151**-Craig Bowden, David Gossett, Hirofumi Miyase, Ryan Palmer, **152**-Jeffrey Lankford. **W**—**140**-Steve Elkington. **D**—Ken Green.

TOURNAMENT HISTORY

Year	Winner	Score	Runner-up	Score	Location	Par/Yards
GREATER GREENSBORO OPEN						
1938	Sam Snead	272	Johnny Revolta	276	Starmount Forest CC, Greensboro, NC Sedgefield CC, Greensboro, NC	71/6,630 70/6,680
1939	Ralph Guldahl	280	Clayton Heafner Lawson Little	283	Starmount Forest CC, Greensboro, NC Sedgefield CC, Greensboro, NC	71/6,630 70/6,680
1940	Ben Hogan	270	Craig Wood	279	Starmount Forest CC, Greensboro, NC Sedgefield CC, Greensboro, NC	71/6,630 70/6,680
1941	Byron Nelson	276	Vic Ghezzi	278	Starmount Forest CC, Greensboro, NC Sedgefield CC, Greensboro, NC	71/6,630 70/6,680
1942	Sam Byrd	279	Ben Hogan Lloyd Mangrum	281	Starmount Forest CC, Greensboro, NC	71/6,630
1943	No Tournament					
1944	No Tournament					
1945	Byron Nelson	271	Sam Byrd	279	Starmount Forest CC, Greensboro, NC	71/6,630
1946	Sam Snead	270	Herman Keiser	270	Sedgefield CC, Greensboro, NC	70/6,680
1947	Vic Ghezzi	286	Frank Stranahan	288	Starmount Forest CC, Greensboro, NC	71/6,630
1948	Lloyd Mangrum	278	Lew Worsham	279	Sedgefield CC, Greensboro, NC	70/6,680
1949	Sam Snead*	276	Lloyd Mangrum	276	Starmount Forest CC, Greensboro, NC	71/6,630
1950	Sam Snead	269	Jimmy Demaret	279	Sedgefield CC, Greensboro, NC	70/6,680
1951	Art Doering	279	Jim Ferrier	284	Starmount Forest CC, Greensboro, NC	71/6,630
1952	Dave Douglas	277	Bobby Locke	278	Starmount Forest CC, Greensboro, NC	71/6,630
1953	Earl Stewart, Jr.*	275	Sam Snead	275	Sedgefield CC, Greensboro, NC	70/6,680
1954	Doug Ford*	283	Marty Furgol	283	Starmount Forest CC, Greensboro, NC	71/6,630
1955	Sam Snead	273	Julius Boros Art Wall	274	Sedgefield CC, Greensboro, NC	70/6,680
1956	Sam Snead*	279	Fred Wampler	279	Starmount Forest CC, Greensboro, NC	71/6,630
1957	Stan Leonard	276	Mike Souchak	279	Sedgefield CC, Greensboro, NC	70/6,680
1958	Bob Goalby	275	Dow Finsterwald Don January Tony Lema Sam Snead	277	Starmount Forest CC, Greensboro, NC	71/6,630

Chrysler Classic of Greensboro

NOTES

Brent Geiberger *captured his second career TOUR victory with his two-stroke win over* ***Michael Allen*** *in Greensboro in 2004. Geiberger entered the week at No. 144 on the TOUR money list, looking to secure his card for 2005. With the win, Geiberger earned a two-year PGA TOUR exemption and jumped to No. 52 with his $828,000 payday. He opened 66-67-71 and held a share of the lead at 12-under-par with* ***Tom Lehman*** *entering the final round, and posted final-round bogey-free 66 to secure two-stroke victory over Allen. With the victory, Brent joined father Al (1976 champion) in becoming the first father-son combination in modern history to win the same PGA TOUR event.*

Steve Stricker *(Round 3) and* ***Ted Purdy*** *(Round 4) each posted two eagles in a round at the 2004 Chrysler Classic of Greensboro. Purdy shot an 8-under-par 64 in the final round, the low round of the week, and jumped from T48 to T8 in the final standings.*

Brad Faxon*'s streak of holes without a three-putt ended at 362 with a three-putt bogey on the third hole of his third round at the 2004 Chrysler Classic of Greensboro. His last three-putt occurred on the last hole of the PGA Championship in August. The streak lasted over 19 rounds.*

Ryan Moore*, who completed one of the top amateur seasons in history in 2004, winning the NCAA Championship, the Public Links, the Western Amateur and the U.S. Amateur, became the first amateur to make the cut at the Chrysler Classic of Greensboro since* ***Gary Pinns*** *in 1980. Moore (T24) had the lowest finish for an amateur in Greensboro since* ***Bill Harvey*** *finished T23 in 1961.*

Tournament Record:
265, Jesper Parnevik, 1999
Current Course Record:
(Old Design)
62, Davis Love III, 1992; Mark O'Meara, 1996; Jeff Maggert, 1999
(Redesign)
63, Peter Jacobsen, 2003

TOURNAMENT HISTORY

Year	Winner	Score	Runner-up	Score	Location	Par/Yards
			Art Wall			
1959	Dow Finsterwald	278	Art Wall	280	Starmount Forest CC, Greensboro, NC	71/6,630
1960	Sam Snead	270	Dow Finsterwald	272	Starmount Forest CC, Greensboro, NC	71/6,630
1961	Mike Souchak	276	Sam Snead	283	Sedgefield CC, Greensboro, NC	70/6,680
1962	Billy Casper	275	Mike Souchak	276	Sedgefield CC, Greensboro, NC	70/6,680
1963	Doug Sanders	270	Jimmy Clark	274	Sedgefield CC, Greensboro, NC	70/6,680
1964	Julius Boros*	277	Doug Sanders	277	Sedgefield CC, Greensboro, NC	70/6,680
1965	Sam Snead	273	Billy Casper	278	Sedgefield CC, Greensboro, NC	70/6,680
			Jack McGowan			
			Phil Rodgers			
1966	Doug Sanders*	276	Tom Weiskopf	276	Sedgefield CC, Greensboro, NC	70/6,680
1967	George Archer	267	Doug Sanders	269	Sedgefield CC, Greensboro, NC	70/6,680
1968	Billy Casper	267	George Archer	271	Sedgefield CC, Greensboro, NC	70/6,680
			Gene Littler			
			Bobby Nichols			
1969	Gene Littler*	274	Julius Boros	274	Sedgefield CC, Greensboro, NC	70/6,680
			Orville Moody			
			Tom Weiskopf			
1970	Gary Player	271	Miller Barber	273	Sedgefield CC, Greensboro, NC	71/7,034
1971	Bud Allin*	275	Dave Eichelberger	275	Sedgefield CC, Greensboro, NC	71/7,034
			Rod Funseth			
1972	George Archer*	272	Tommy Aaron	272	Sedgefield CC, Greensboro, NC	71/7,034
1973	Chi Chi Rodriguez	267	Lou Graham	268	Sedgefield CC, Greensboro, NC	71/7,012
			Ken Still			
1974	Bob Charles	270	Raymond Floyd	271	Sedgefield CC, Greensboro, NC	71/7,012
			Lee Trevino			
1975	Tom Weiskopf	275	Al Geiberger	278	Sedgefield CC, Greensboro, NC	71/6,643
1976	Al Geiberger	268	Lee Trevino	270	Sedgefield CC, Greensboro, NC	71/6,643
1977	Danny Edwards	276	George Burns	280	Forest Oaks CC, Greensboro, NC	72/7,075
			Larry Nelson			
1978	Seve Ballesteros	282	Jack Renner	283	Forest Oaks CC, Greensboro, NC	72/6,958
			Fuzzy Zoeller			
1979	Raymond Floyd	282	George Burns	283	Forest Oaks CC, Greensboro, NC	72/6,958
			Gary Player			
1980	Craig Stadler	275	George Burns	281	Forest Oaks CC, Greensboro, NC	72/6,958
			Bill Kratzert			
			Jack Newton			
			Jerry Pate			
1981	Larry Nelson*	281	Mark Hayes	281	Forest Oaks CC, Greensboro, NC	72/6,984
1982	Danny Edwards	285	Bobby Clampett	286	Forest Oaks CC, Greensboro, NC	72/6,984
1983	Lanny Wadkins	275	Craig Stadler	280	Forest Oaks CC, Greensboro, NC	72/6,984
			Denis Watson			
1984	Andy Bean	280	George Archer	282	Forest Oaks CC, Greensboro, NC	72/6,984
1985	Joey Sindelar	285	Isao Aoki	286	Forest Oaks CC, Greensboro, NC	72/6,984
			Craig Stadler			
1986	Sandy Lyle	275	Andy Bean	277	Forest Oaks CC, Greensboro, NC	72/6,984
1987	Scott Simpson	282	Clarence Rose	284	Forest Oaks CC, Greensboro, NC	72/6,984
KMART GREATER GREENSBORO OPEN						
1988	Sandy Lyle*	271	Ken Green	271	Forest Oaks CC, Greensboro, NC	72/6,984
1989	Ken Green	277	John Huston	279	Forest Oaks CC, Greensboro, NC	72/6,984
1990	Steve Elkington	282	Mike Reid	284	Forest Oaks CC, Greensboro, NC	72/6,984
			Jeff Sluman			
1991	Mark Brooks*	275	Gene Sauers	275	Forest Oaks CC, Greensboro, NC	72/6,984
1992	Davis Love III	272	John Cook	278	Forest Oaks CC, Greensboro, NC	72/6,984
1993	Rocco Mediate*	281	Steve Elkington	281	Forest Oaks CC, Greensboro, NC	72/6,984
1994	Mike Springer	275	Brad Bryant	278	Forest Oaks CC, Greensboro, NC	72/6,984
			Ed Humenik			
			Hale Irwin			
1995	Jim Gallagher, Jr.	274	Peter Jacobsen	275	Forest Oaks CC, Greensboro, NC	72/6,984
			Jeff Sluman			
GREATER GREENSBORO CHRYSLER CLASSIC						
1996	Mark O'Meara	274	Duffy Waldorf	276	Forest Oaks CC, Greensboro, NC	72/7,062
1997	Frank Nobilo*	274	Brad Faxon	274	Forest Oaks CC, Greensboro, NC	72/7,062
1998	Trevor Dodds*	276	Scott Verplank	276	Forest Oaks CC, Greensboro, NC	72/7,062
1999	Jesper Parnevik	265	Jim Furyk	267	Forest Oaks CC, Greensboro, NC	72/7,062
2000	Hal Sutton	274	Andrew Magee	277	Forest Oaks CC, Greensboro, NC	72/7,062
2001	Scott Hoch	272	Brett Quigley	273	Forest Oaks CC, Greensboro, NC	72/7,062
			Scott Simpson			
2002	Rocco Mediate	272	Mark Calcavecchia	275	Forest Oaks CC, Greensboro, NC	72/7,062
CHRYSLER CLASSIC OF GREENSBORO						
2003	Shigeki Maruyama	266	Brad Faxon	271	Forest Oaks CC, Greensboro, NC	72/7,311
2004	Brent Geiberger	270	Michael Allen	272	Forest Oaks CC, Greensboro, NC	72/7,311

*KEY: * = Playoff ~ = Weather-shortened*

2004 FUNAI Classic at the WALT DISNEY WORLD Resort

[46th of 48 official events]

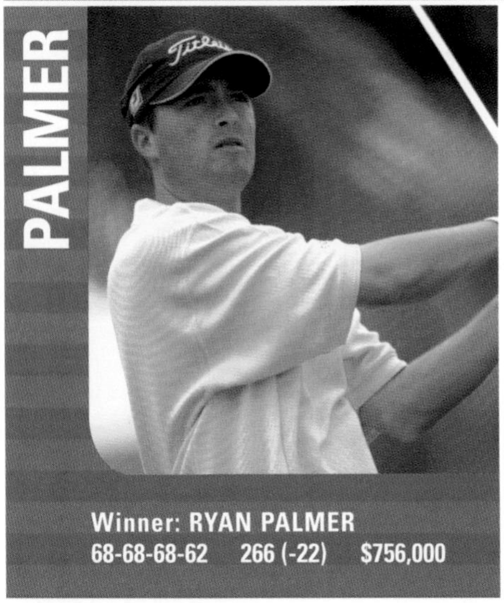

Winner: RYAN PALMER
68-68-68-62 266 (-22) $756,000

WALT DISNEY WORLD Resort

Lake Buena Vista, FL

October 21-24, 2004

Magnolia Course (Host)
Par: 36-36—72 Yards: 7,200
Palm Course
Par: 36-36—72 Yards: 7,015

LEADERS: First Round—J.L Lewis (MG) opened with a 10-under-par 62 and led Mark Hensby (PG), John Huston (MG) and Scott Hend (MG) by two strokes.
Second Round—Briny Baird (PG) moved into the lead at 13-under-par 131 after a 6-under-par 66, leading Tom Lehman (MG) by one stroke.

Third Round— Lehman and Baird shared the lead at 17-under-par 199. Scott Verplank trailed by one stroke.

CUT: 86 players at 4-under-par 140 from a field of 144 professionals.

WEATHER: Mostly sunny and warm on Thursday with temperatures reaching the mid to upper 80's. Friday partly cloudy and humid with a shower in the afternoon, temperatures reaching the low 80s. Mostly sunny and breezy on Saturday with highs in the low 80s and winds from the NE at 10-15 mph. Partly cloudy on Sunday with temperatures in the mid-80s. E winds at 10-15 mph.

Check out the 2005 FUNAI Classic at WALT DISNEY WORLD Resort, October 20-23 on ESPN/ABC

ORDER OF FINISH

Ryan Palmer	1	68-68-68-62	266	$756,000.00
Briny Baird	T2	65-66-68-70	269	369,600.00
Vijay Singh	T2	66-71-65-67	269	369,600.00
Cameron Beckman	T4	68-65-68-69	270	184,800.00
Joey Sindelar	T4	66-70-67-67	270	184,800.00
Mark Calcavecchia	T6	71-66-65-69	271	135,975.00
Tim Clark	T6	69-69-64-69	271	135,975.00
Mark Hensby	T6	64-71-68-68	271	135,975.00
Tom Lehman	T6	66-66-67-72	271	135,975.00
Lucas Glover	T10	68-68-68-68	272	93,100.00
John Huston	T10	64-71-69-68	272	93,100.00
Neal Lancaster	T10	69-69-67-67	272	93,100.00
Geoff Ogilvy	T10	68-67-67-70	272	93,100.00
Carl Pettersson	T10	70-70-68-64	272	93,100.00
Vaughn Taylor	T10	68-66-72-66	272	93,100.00
Billy Andrade	T16	69-69-69-66	273	57,015.00
Bart Bryant	T16	66-71-67-69	273	57,015.00
Ben Curtis	T16	66-71-66-70	273	57,015.00
Chris DiMarco	T16	69-65-70-69	273	57,015.00
Dan Forsman	T16	68-70-66-69	273	57,015.00
Jerry Kelly	T16	67-68-71-67	273	57,015.00
Skip Kendall	T16	66-67-72-68	273	57,015.00
Scott Verplank	T16	70-65-65-73	273	57,015.00
J.L. Lewis	T24	62-73-72-67	274	35,805.00
Loren Roberts	T24	71-67-66-70	274	35,805.00
Justin Rose	T24	71-68-69-66	274	35,805.00
Kirk Triplett	T24	66-67-72-69	274	35,805.00
Stephen Ames	T28	65-71-67-72	275	28,560.00
Richard S. Johnson	T28	68-67-71-69	275	$28,560.00
Zach Johnson	T28	68-72-68-67	275	28,560.00
Scott McCarron	T28	69-67-68-71	275	28,560.00
Spike McRoy	T28	68-72-71-64	275	28,560.00
Steve Allan	T33	67-72-71-66	276	21,262.50
Arjun Atwal	T33	68-71-73-64	276	21,262.50
Brian Bateman	T33	68-70-67-71	276	21,262.50
Joe Durant	T33	69-70-71-66	276	21,262.50
Stephen Leaney	T33	70-69-68-69	276	21,262.50
Steve Lowery	T33	72-67-67-70	276	21,262.50
Pat Perez	T33	69-71-66-70	276	21,262.50
Craig Perks	T33	73-65-70-68	276	21,262.50
Michael Allen	T41	73-67-69-68	277	14,301.00
Bob Estes	T41	69-70-69-69	277	14,301.00
Steve Flesch	T41	67-71-71-68	277	14,301.00
Fred Funk	T41	69-69-71-68	277	14,301.00
Brian Gay	T41	67-72-68-70	277	14,301.00
Fredrik Jacobson	T41	69-70-68-70	277	14,301.00
Jose Maria Olazabal	T41	65-72-69-71	277	14,301.00
Brenden Pappas	T41	67-67-74-69	277	14,301.00
Daniel Chopra	T49	67-71-68-72	278	10,262.00
Carlos Franco	T49	69-71-69-69	278	10,262.00
Paul Goydos	T49	70-70-66-72	278	10,262.00
Hank Kuehne	T49	69-64-71-74	278	10,262.00
John Rollins	T49	68-71-70-69	278	10,262.00
Omar Uresti	T49	67-71-70-70	278	10,262.00
Chad Campbell	T55	69-67-70-73	279	9,408.00
Michael Clark II (S)	T55	67-71-72-69	279	9,408.00
Danny Ellis	T55	69-71-70-69	279	9,408.00
Harrison Frazar	T55	67-67-70-75	279	9,408.00
Robert Gamez	T55	68-71-70-70	279	$9,408.00
J.J. Henry	T55	69-68-70-72	279	9,408.00
Deane Pappas	T55	70-70-69-70	279	9,408.00
John Cook	T62	68-70-71-71	280	8,862.00
David Frost	T62	71-68-68-73	280	8,862.00
Charles Howell III	T62	67-71-72-70	280	8,862.00
Matt Kuchar	T62	69-70-71-70	280	8,862.00
Jeff Maggert	T62	68-71-70-71	280	8,862.00
Dean Wilson	T62	69-71-68-72	280	8,862.00
Stuart Appleby	T68	69-66-73-73	281	8,358.00
Ben Crane	T68	71-69-72-69	281	8,358.00
Lee Janzen	T68	71-69-70-71	281	8,358.00
Kent Jones	T68	69-70-71-71	281	8,358.00
Hunter Mahan	T68	69-70-71-71	281	8,358.00
Rod Pampling	T68	69-69-71-72	281	8,358.00
Rich Beem	T74	70-70-70-72	282	7,896.00
Shaun Micheel	T74	69-71-72-70	282	7,896.00
Arron Oberholser	T74	69-71-72-70	282	7,896.00
Tom Pernice, Jr.	T74	67-69-74-72	282	7,896.00
Bob Tway	T74	69-71-72-70	282	7,896.00
Bob Burns	T79	69-70-75-70	284	7,602.00
Esteban Toledo	T79	73-67-71-73	284	7,602.00
Tom Carter	T81	69-70-72-74	285	7,434.00
Jay Williamson	T81	68-68-76-73	285	7,434.00
David Branshaw	T83	67-73-73-73	286	7,266.00
Jose Coceres	T83	70-70-70-76	286	7,266.00
Gene Sauers	85	69-71-73-75	288	7,140.00
Ken Duke	86	72-64-75-80	291	7,056.00

(S) = Sponsor Exemption

The following players did not finish (C=cut)

C—141-Tommy Armour III, Woody Austin, Jason Bohn, Jeff Brehaut, Jonathan Byrd, John Daly, Niclas Fasth, Brad Faxon, Dudley Hart, J.P. Hayes, Rocco Mediate, Jesper Parnevik, Tag Ridings, Hidemichi Tanaka, **142**-Craig Barlow, D.J. Brigman, Olin Browne, Robert Damron, Glen Day, Jason Dufner, Rick Fehr, Jim Furyk, Scott Hend, Peter Lonard, Craig Parry, Ian Poulter, Chris Smith, Bo Van Pelt, **143**-Paul Azinger, Danny Briggs, David Gossett, Brett Quigley, Patrick Sheehan, Heath Slocum, **144**-Brad Bryant, Mathias Gronberg, Cliff Kresge, Len Mattiace, Jeff Sluman, Kevin Sutherland, **145**-Fulton Allem, Mark Brooks, Todd Fischer, Billy Mayfair, **146**-Aaron Baddeley, Craig Bowden, Tim Herron, **147**-Pat Bates, Duffy Waldorf, **148**-Nick Price, **149**-Hirofumi Miyase, Joe Ogilvie, Tim Petrovic, **150**-David Duval, Brad Hauer, Bernhard Langer, Kevin Na, **151**-Ted Purdy.

TOURNAMENT HISTORY

Year	Winner	Score	Runner-up	Score	Location	Par/Yards
WALT DISNEY WORLD OPEN INVITATIONAL						
1971	Jack Nicklaus	273	Deane Beman	276	Walt Disney World Resort, (Magnolia) Lake Buena Vista, FL	72/7,190
1972	Jack Nicklaus	267	Jim Dent Bobby Mitchell Larry Wood	276	Walt Disney World Resort, (Palm) Walt Disney World Resort, (Magnolia) Lake Buena Vista, FL	72/6,941 72/7,190
1973	Jack Nicklaus	275	Mason Rudolph	276	Walt Disney World Resort, (Palm) Walt Disney World Resort, (Magnolia) Lake Buena Vista, FL	72/6,941 72/7,190
WALT DISNEY WORLD NATIONAL TEAM CHAMPIONSHIP						
1974	Hubert Green/ Mac McLendon	255	J.C. Snead/ Sam Snead Ed Sneed/ Bert Yancey	256	Walt Disney World Resort, (Palm) Walt Disney World Resort, (Magnolia) Lake Buena Vista, FL	72/6,941 72/7,190
1975	Jim Colbert/ Dean Refram	252	Bobby Cole/ Victor Regalado John Schlee/ Curtis Sifford	255	Walt Disney World Resort, (Palm) Walt Disney World Resort, (Magnolia) Lake Buena Vista, FL	72/6,941 72/7,190
1976	Woody Blackburn/ Bill Kratzert*	260	Gay Brewer/ Bobby Nichols	260	Walt Disney World Resort, (Palm) Walt Disney World Resort, (Magnolia) Lake Buena Vista, FL	72/6,941 72/7,190
1977	Gibby Gilbert/ Grier Jones	253	Steve Melnyk/ Andy North	254	Walt Disney World Resort, (Palm) Walt Disney World Resort, (Magnolia)	72/6,941 72/7,190
1978	Wayne Levi/ Bob Mann	254	Bobby Wadkins/ Lanny Wadkins	257	Walt Disney World Resort, (Palm) Walt Disney World Resort, (Magnolia) Lake Buena Vista, FL	72/6,941 72/7,190

FUNAI Classic at the WALT DISNEY WORLD Resort

NOTES

Since turning professional in 1996, ***Tiger Woods*** *has six victories in 16 TOUR events in his adopted hometown of Orlando, with four wins coming at the Bay Hill Invitational and two at the FUNAI Classic at the WALT DISNEY WORLD Resort. In eight career appearances at Disney, Woods has two wins and six top 10s.*

Five different players have won this event more than once, led by ***Jack Nicklaus****, who captured three titles at Disney (1971-73).* ***Larry Nelson*** *(1984, 1987),* ***Tim Simpson*** *(1989-90),* ***John Huston*** *(1992, 1998) and* ***Tiger Woods*** *(1996, 1999) are the other multiple winners. Nelson also has the largest final-round comeback in tournament history, making up a six-stroke deficit in 1987 to defeat* ***Morris Hatalsky*** *and* ***Mark O'Meara*** *by one stroke after a 63 on Sunday.*

VIJAY SINGH

Four players have won the FUNAI Classic at the WALT DISNEY WORLD Resort after turning 40: ***Vijay Singh*** *in 2003 (40 years, 8 months, 4 days),* ***Raymond Floyd*** *in 1986 (44 years, 1 month, 15 days),* ***Larry Nelson*** *in 1987 (40 years, 1 month, 8 days) and* ***Brad Bryant*** *in 1995 (40 years, 9 months, 27 days) all won in their 40s.*

Ryan Palmer *became the 15th player to earn his initial PGA TOUR victory at the FUNAI Classic, joining* ***Mac McLendon*** *(1974),* ***Woody Blackburn*** *(1976),* ***Bill Kratzert*** *(1976),* ***Wayne Levi*** *(1978),* ***Bob Mann*** *(1978),* ***George Burns*** *(1979),* ***David Edwards*** *(1980),* ***Vance Heafner*** *and* ***Mike Holland*** *(1981),* ***Hal Sutton*** *(1982),* ***Bob Lohr*** *(1988),* ***Jeff Maggert*** *(1993),* ***Brad Bryant*** *(1995) and* ***Bob Burns*** *(2002).*

TOURNAMENT HISTORY

Year	Winner	Score	Runner-up	Score	Location	Par/Yards
1979	George Burns/ Ben Crenshaw	255	Scott Bess/ Dan Halldorson Jeff Hewes/ Peter Jacobsen Sammy Rachels/ D.A. Weibring	258	Walt Disney World Resort, (Palm) Walt Disney World Resort, (Magnolia) Lake Buena Vista, FL	72/6,941 72/7,190
1980	Danny Edwards/ David Edwards	253	Gibby Gilbert/ Dan Halldorson Mike Harmon/ Barry Harwell Grier Jones/ Dana Quigley	255	Walt Disney World Resort, (Palm) Walt Disney World Resort, (Magnolia) Lake Buena Vista, FL	72/6,941 72/7,190
1981	Vance Heafner/ Mike Holland	246	Chip Beck/ Rex Caldwell	251	Walt Disney World Resort, (Palm) Walt Disney World Resort, (Magnolia) Lake Buena Vista, FL	72/6,941 72/7,190
WALT DISNEY WORLD GOLF CLASSIC						
1982	Hal Sutton*	269	Bill Britton	269	Walt Disney World Resort, (Palm) Walt Disney World Resort, (Magnolia) Walt Disney World Res., (Lake Buena Vista) Lake Buena Vista, FL	72/6,941 72/7,190 72/6,706
1983	Payne Stewart	269	Nick Faldo Mark McCumber	271	Walt Disney World Resort, (Palm) Walt Disney World Resort, (Magnolia) Walt Disney World Res., (Lake Buena Vista) Lake Buena Vista, FL	72/6,941 72/7,190 72/6,706
1984	Larry Nelson	266	Hubert Green	267	Walt Disney World Resort, (Palm) Walt Disney World Resort, (Magnolia) Walt Disney World Res., (Lake Buena Vista) Lake Buena Vista, FL	72/6,941 72/7,190 72/6,706
WALT DISNEY WORLD/OLDSMOBILE CLASSIC						
1985	Lanny Wadkins	267	Mike Donald Scott Hoch	268	Walt Disney World Resort, (Palm) Walt Disney World Resort, (Magnolia) Walt Disney World Res., (Lake Buena Vista) Lake Buena Vista, FL	72/6,941 72/7,190 72/6,706
1986	Raymond Floyd*	275	Lon Hinkle Mike Sullivan	275	Walt Disney World Resort, (Palm) Walt Disney World Resort, (Magnolia) Walt Disney World Res., (Lake Buena Vista) Lake Buena Vista, FL	72/6,941 72/7,190 72/6,706
1987	Larry Nelson	268	Morris Hatalsky Mark O'Meara	269	Walt Disney World Resort, (Palm) Walt Disney World Resort, (Magnolia) Walt Disney World Res., (Lake Buena Vista) Lake Buena Vista, FL	72/6,941 72/7,190 72/6,706
1988	Bob Lohr*	263	Chip Beck	263	Walt Disney World Resort, (Palm) Walt Disney World Resort, (Magnolia) Walt Disney World Res., (Lake Buena Vista) Lake Buena Vista, FL	72/6,941 72/7,190 72/6,706
1989	Tim Simpson	272	Donnie Hammond	273	Walt Disney World Resort, (Palm) Walt Disney World Resort, (Magnolia) Walt Disney World Res., (Lake Buena Vista) Lake Buena Vista, FL	72/6,941 72/7,190 72/6,706
1990	Tim Simpson	264	John Mahaffey	265	Walt Disney World Resort, (Palm) Walt Disney World Resort, (Magnolia) Walt Disney World Res., (Lake Buena Vista) Lake Buena Vista, FL	72/6,941 72/7,190 72/6,706
1991	Mark O'Meara	267	David Peoples	268	Walt Disney World Resort, (Palm) Walt Disney World Resort, (Magnolia) Walt Disney World Res., (Lake Buena Vista) Lake Buena Vista, FL	72/6,941 72/7,190 72/6,706
1992	John Huston	262	Mark O'Meara	265	Walt Disney World Resort, (Palm) Walt Disney World Resort, (Magnolia) Walt Disney World Res., (Lake Buena Vista) Lake Buena Vista, FL	72/6,941 72/7,190 72/6,706
1993	Jeff Maggert	265	Greg Kraft	268	Walt Disney World Resort, (Palm) Walt Disney World Resort, (Magnolia) Walt Disney World Res., (Lake Buena Vista) Lake Buena Vista, FL	72/6,941 72/7,190 72/6,706
1994	Rick Fehr	265	Craig Stadler Fuzzy Zoeller	271	Walt Disney World Resort, (Palm) Walt Disney World Resort, (Magnolia) Walt Disney World Res., (Eagle Pines)	72/6,941 72/7,190 72/6,772
1995	Brad Bryant~	198	Hal Sutton Ted Tryba	199	Walt Disney World Resort, (Palm) Walt Disney World Resort, (Magnolia) Walt Disney World Res., (Lake Buena Vista) Lake Buena Vista, FL	72/6,941 72/7,190 72/6,819
1996	Tiger Woods	267	Payne Stewart	268	Walt Disney World Resort, (Palm) Walt Disney World Resort, (Magnolia) Walt Disney World Res., (Lake Buena Vista) Lake Buena Vista, FL	72/6,957 72/7,190 72/6,819

*KEY: * = Playoff ~ = Weather-shortened*

SECTION 3 TOURNAMENT HISTORIES

FUNAI Classic at the WALT DISNEY WORLD Resort

NOTES

JOHN HUSTON

***Ryan Palmer** came from five strokes back on Sunday in 2004 to win. It marked the third time that a player has recorded a final-round 62 at the Magnolia Course and went on to win the tournament. **John Huston** did it in 1992, when he won his first of two titles at Disney, and **Duffy Waldorf** matched the feat, when he won in 2000.*

***Vijay Singh**'s four-stroke victory over **Stewart Cink**, **John Rollins** and **Scott Verplank** in 2003 was the largest margin of victory at the FUNAI Classic at the WALT DISNEY WORLD Resort since 1972 when **Jack Nicklaus** rolled to a nine-stroke victory over **Bobby Mitchell**. Singh's margin ended a string of eight years where the margin was either one stroke or sudden-death in Orlando.*

***Briny Baird** tied a PGA TOUR record in 2003 for his eagle-birdie streak during the second round at Disney's Palm Course. He started the streak with an eagle on the 13th hole and then proceeded to birdie the next seven holes (15-18 and 1-3). That eight-hole stretch tied the TOUR mark set by **Billy Mayfair** at the 2001 Buick Open.*

***Ryan Palmer**'s victory last year at the FUNAI Classic on the PGA TOUR was the a record fifth victory by a member of the graduating Nationwide Tour class of 2003, joining **Zach Johnson**, **Mark Hensby**, **Vaughn Taylor** and **Andre Stolz**.*

*With **David Duval**'s playoff victory over **Dan Forsman** at the 1997 Walt Disney World/Oldsmobile Classic, Duval became the first player in PGA TOUR history to win playoffs in consecutive weeks. The week before, Duval won the Michelob Championship at Kingsmill in a playoff over **Duffy Waldorf** and **Grant Waite**.*

Tournament Record:
262, John Huston, 1992
Current Course Record:
61, Mark Lye, 1984 (Palm)
61, Payne Stewart, 1990 (Magnolia)

TOURNAMENT HISTORY

Year	Winner	Score	Runner-up	Score	Location	Par/Yards
1997	David Duval*	270	Dan Forsman	270	Walt Disney World Resort, (Palm) Walt Disney World Resort, (Magnolia) Walt Disney World Res., (Lake Buena Vista) Lake Buena Vista, FL	72/6,957 72/7,190 72/6,819
NATIONAL CAR RENTAL GOLF CLASSIC AT WALT DISNEY WORLD RESORT						
1998	John Huston	272	Davis Love III	273	Walt Disney World Resort, (Palm) Walt Disney World Resort, (Magnolia) Lake Buena Vista, FL	72/6,967 72/7,190
1999	Tiger Woods	271	Ernie Els	272	Walt Disney World Resort, (Palm) Walt Disney World Resort, (Magnolia) Lake Buena Vista, FL	72/6,967 72/7,190
2000	Duffy Waldorf	262	Steve Flesch	263	Walt Disney World Resort, (Palm) Walt Disney World Resort, (Magnolia) Lake Buena Vista, FL	72/7,193 72/7,243
2001	Jose Coceres	265	Davis Love III	266	Walt Disney World Resort, (Palm) Walt Disney World Resort, (Magnolia) Lake Buena Vista, FL	72/7,193 72/7,201
DISNEY GOLF CLASSIC						
2002	Bob Burns	263	Chris DiMarco	264	Walt Disney World Resort, (Palm) Walt Disney World Resort, (Magnolia) Lake Buena Vista, FL	72/6,957 72/7,200
FUNAI CLASSIC AT WALT DISNEY WORLD RESORT						
2003	Vijay Singh	265	Scott Verplank Tiger Woods Stewart Cink	269	Walt Disney World Resort, (Palm) Walt Disney World Resort, (Magnolia) Lake Buena Vista, FL	72/6,957 72/7,200
2004	Ryan Palmer	266	Briny Baird Vijay Singh	269	Walt Disney World Resort, (Palm) Walt Disney World Restort, (Magnolia) Lake Buena Vista, FL	72/7,015 72/7,200

*KEY: * = Playoff ~ = Weather-shortened*

Briny Baird took second place at the 2004 FUNAI Classic at the WALT DISNEY WORLD Resort

2004 Chrysler Championship *[47th of 48 official events]*

Winner: VIJAY SINGH
65-69-67-65 266 (-18) $900,000

The Westin Innisbrook Resort (Copperhead Course)

Tampa Bay, FL

October 28-31, 2004

Purse: $5,000,000
Par: 36-35—71
Yards: 7,340

LEADERS: First Round—Jeff Sluman fired a course-record, 9-under 62 to take a two-stroke lead over Jonathan Kaye, Kent Jones and Kirk Triplett. Vijay Singh trailed by three.
Second Round—Jonathan Byrd and Sluman sat at 10-under 132, while Tommy Armour III, Rod Pampling and Singh were two back.

Third Round—Singh moved to 12-under 201, one ahead of Armour and two in front of Jesper Parnevik and Triplett.

CUT: 73 players at even-par 142 from a field of 132 professionals.

PRO-AM: $10,000. Dan Forsman, 58, $2,000.

WEATHER: Mostly sunny and warm all week with temperatures in the mid-80s and light winds.

Check out the 2005 Chrysler Championship, October 27-30 on USA/ABC

ORDER OF FINISH

Vijay Singh	1	65-69-67-65	266	$900,000.00
Tommy Armour III	T2	70-64-68-69	271	440,000.00
Jesper Parnevik	T2	68-67-68-68	271	440,000.00
Joe Durant	4	68-71-70-63	272	240,000.00
Kirk Triplett	5	64-71-68-70	273	200,000.00
Robert Allenby	T6	70-67-69-68	274	173,750.00
David Toms	T6	70-69-67-68	274	173,750.00
Spike McRoy	T8	69-72-66-68	275	145,000.00
Kenny Perry	T8	70-68-70-67	275	145,000.00
Carl Pettersson	T8	68-68-70-69	275	145,000.00
Tim Clark	T11	69-69-70-68	276	120,000.00
Tag Ridings	T11	72-69-71-64	276	120,000.00
Tom Carter	T13	73-67-65-72	277	93,750.00
Jay Haas	T13	67-70-70-70	277	93,750.00
Lee Janzen	T13	67-72-70-68	277	93,750.00
Kevin Na	T13	70-70-68-69	277	93,750.00
Bob Estes	T17	70-70-70-68	278	75,000.00
Kent Jones	T17	64-71-75-68	278	75,000.00
Craig Parry	T17	68-72-69-69	278	75,000.00
Retief Goosen	T20	69-73-66-71	279	58,250.00
Matt Kuchar	T20	69-72-66-72	279	58,250.00
Geoff Ogilvy	T20	72-67-70-70	279	58,250.00
Jeff Sluman	T20	62-70-74-73	279	58,250.00
Briny Baird	T24	70-68-72-70	280	$40,500.00
Tim Herron	T24	70-69-67-74	280	40,500.00
Bernhard Langer	T24	70-69-71-70	280	40,500.00
Shaun Micheel	T24	73-69-70-68	280	40,500.00
Jose Maria Olazabal	T24	67-71-67-75	280	40,500.00
Hidemichi Tanaka	T24	70-70-70-70	280	40,500.00
Woody Austin	T30	68-71-70-72	281	29,062.50
Pat Bates	T30	72-68-73-68	281	29,062.50
Jeff Brehaut	T30	72-69-69-71	281	29,062.50
Harrison Frazar	T30	68-74-70-69	281	29,062.50
Chris Riley	T30	68-72-67-74	281	29,062.50
Justin Rose	T30	65-71-71-74	281	29,062.50
Vaughn Taylor	T30	70-65-73-73	281	29,062.50
Dean Wilson	T30	72-68-68-73	281	29,062.50
David Frost	T38	73-69-73-67	282	21,000.00
Stephen Leaney	T38	67-70-72-73	282	21,000.00
Justin Leonard	T38	71-71-68-72	282	21,000.00
Rocco Mediate	T38	76-66-69-71	282	21,000.00
Arron Oberholser	T38	71-68-73-70	282	21,000.00
Tom Pernice, Jr.	T38	71-71-70-70	282	21,000.00
Bart Bryant	T44	70-71-71-71	283	15,116.67
Tom Byrum	T44	68-70-72-73	283	15,116.67
Mark Calcavecchia	T44	68-71-73-71	283	15,116.67
Fred Funk	T44	70-70-76-67	283	15,116.67
Jonathan Byrd	T44	66-66-75-76	283	15,116.66
John Huston	T44	70-68-71-74	283	$15,116.66
Brian Gay	T50	69-73-73-69	284	11,966.67
Charles Howell III	T50	68-71-72-73	284	11,966.67
Neal Lancaster	T50	70-72-70-72	284	11,966.67
Duffy Waldorf	T50	69-73-72-70	284	11,966.67
Stephen Ames	T50	70-71-69-74	284	11,966.66
Patrick Sheehan	T50	71-71-68-74	284	11,966.66
Skip Kendall	T56	70-70-69-76	285	11,350.00
Billy Mayfair	T56	69-71-73-72	285	11,350.00
Glen Day	T58	71-70-70-75	286	11,050.00
Peter Jacobsen	T58	71-70-73-72	286	11,050.00
Ryan Palmer	T58	70-69-75-72	286	11,050.00
Brenden Pappas	T58	70-72-70-74	286	11,050.00
Brian Bateman	T62	69-70-78-70	287	10,600.00
Chad Campbell	T62	70-72-72-73	287	10,600.00
Rod Pampling	T62	69-65-76-77	287	10,600.00
Brett Quigley	T62	69-73-73-72	287	10,600.00
Bo Van Pelt	T62	75-67-73-72	287	10,600.00
Aaron Baddeley	67	70-70-74-74	288	10,300.00
Loren Roberts	68	71-68-81-70	290	10,200.00
Len Mattiace	69	71-71-74-77	293	10,100.00
Carlos Franco	T70	73-67-73-82	295	9,950.00
J.L. Lewis	T70	68-72-77-78	295	9,950.00
Jay Williamson	72	72-69-77-82	300	9,800.00

The following players did not finish
(C=cut, W=withdrew, D=disqualified)

C—143-Paul Azinger, Stewart Cink, Jose Coceres, Jim Furyk, J.P. Hayes, Richard S. Johnson, Ted Purdy, **144**-K.J. Choi, Cliff Kresge, Pat Perez, Craig Perks, **145**-Billy Andrade, Craig Barlow, Daniel Chopra, Todd Fischer, Dan Forsman, Robert Gamez, Davis Love III, Tim Petrovic, Steve Stricker, **146**-Stuart Appleby, Ben Crane, Robert Damron, Lucas Glover, Mathias Gronberg, J.J. Henry, Fredrik Jacobson, Jerry Kelly, Steve Lowery, Joey Sindelar, Chris Smith, Hal Sutton, Esteban Toledo, **147**-Cameron Beckman, Bob Burns, Alex Cejka, Brad Faxon, Brent Geiberger, Phil Mickelson, Heath Slocum, **148**-Steve Allan, Greg Chalmers, Niclas Fasth, Bill Glasson, Jay Overton, Mike Weir, **149**-Olin Browne, Frank Lickliter II, Hunter Mahan, **150**-Rich Beem, Peter Lonard, **152**-Mark Hensby, **153**-Gene Sauers, **154**-Hank Kuehne, **157**-David Gossett, Brad Hauer. **W—78**-Fulton Allem, **76**-Mark Brooks, **220**-Jonathan Kaye. **D—80**-Joe Ogilvie.

TOURNAMENT HISTORY

Year	Winner	Score	Runner-up	Score	Location	Par/Yards
TAMPA BAY CLASSIC						
2000	John Huston	271	Carl Paulson	274	Westin Innisbrook Resort, (Copperhead) Palm Harbor, FL	71/7,295
2001	No Tournament					
2002	K.J. Choi	267	Glen Day	274	Westin Innisbrook Resort, (Copperhead) Palm Harbor, FL	71/7,295
CHRYSLER CHAMPIONSHIP						
2003	Retief Goosen	272	Vijay Singh	275	Westin Innisbrook Resort, (Copperhead) Palm Harbor, FL	71/7,315
2004	Vijay Singh	266	Tommy Armour III Jesper Parnevik	271	Westin Innisbrook Resort, (Copperhead) Palm Harbor, FL	71/7,340

Tournament Record:
266, Vijay Singh, 2004
Tournament Course Record:
62, Jeff Sluman, 2004

2004 THE TOUR Championship

presented by Coca-Cola *[48th of 48 official events]*

Winner: RETIEF GOOSEN
70-66-69-64 269 (-11) $1,080,000

East Lake Golf Club

Atlanta, GA

November 4-7, 2004

Purse: $6,000,000
Par: 35-35—70
Yards: 7,141

LEADERS: First Round—Jay Haas, Jerry Kelly and Darren Clarke shared the lead at 3-under-par 67. David Toms and Zach Johnson were one stroke behind.
Second Round—Haas moved to 7-under-par 133 to lead Stephen Ames by two and Tiger Woods and Retief Goosen by three.
Third Round—Haas and Woods, at 9-under-par 201, led Mike Weir, Goosen and Ames by four strokes.

CUT: There was no cut; 29 of the 31 starters completed 72 holes.

PRO-AM: $10,000. Kenny Perry, Fred Funk, Chad Campbell, Darren Clarke, 56, $1,550.

WEATHER: Heavy rain early in the week. More than one inch fell prior to start of play on Thursday. Partly cloudy with temperatures reaching 66 degrees. W Winds 15-20 mph. Friday, sunny skies and cooler temperatures reaching a high of 62 degrees. N-NW winds up to 20 mph. Saturday, sunny skies and warmer temperatures in the afternoon with a high of 68 degrees. NW winds 10-15 mph. Sunday, sunny and warm with a high of 70. Calm W winds 10-15 mph.

Check out the 2005 TOUR Championship presented by Coca-Cola, November 3-6, on ESPN/ABC

ORDER OF FINISH

Retief Goosen	1	70-66-69-64	269	$1,080,000.00
Tiger Woods	2	72-64-65-72	273	648,000.00
Jerry Kelly	3	67-71-71-65	274	414,000.00
Stephen Ames	T4	69-66-70-70	275	248,000.00
Mark Hensby	T4	69-70-69-67	275	248,000.00
Mike Weir	T4	69-69-67-70	275	248,000.00
Jay Haas	T7	67-66-68-75	276	198,000.00
Scott Verplank	T7	74-67-68-67	276	198,000.00
Vijay Singh	9	69-73-70-65	277	180,000.00
Ernie Els	T10	72-71-68-67	278	$158,200.00
Rory Sabbatini	T10	71-68-71-68	278	158,200.00
David Toms	T10	68-73-70-67	278	158,200.00
Zach Johnson	13	68-71-71-69	279	141,600.00
Padraig Harrington	14	69-75-68-68	280	134,400.00
Stuart Appleby	T15	69-72-71-69	281	123,800.00
Darren Clarke	T15	67-73-70-71	281	123,800.00
Sergio Garcia	T15	71-70-69-71	281	123,800.00
John Daly	18	69-72-71-70	282	117,000.00
Shigeki Maruyama	T19	73-76-67-68	284	112,500.00
Phil Mickelson	T19	71-72-67-74	284	112,500.00
Stewart Cink	T21	70-73-71-71	285	$105,600.00
Steve Flesch	T21	69-78-67-71	285	105,600.00
Adam Scott	T21	75-71-69-70	285	105,600.00
Chris DiMarco	T24	72-71-70-73	286	98,400.00
Carlos Franco	T24	72-68-78-68	286	98,400.00
Fred Funk	T24	73-70-75-68	286	98,400.00
K.J. Choi	27	73-73-72-70	288	94,800.00
Todd Hamilton	28	72-72-76-70	290	93,600.00
Kenny Perry	29	76-72-70-73	291	92,400.00

The following players did not finish (W=withdrew)
W—Davis Love III, **146**-Chad Campbell.

NOTES

***Retief Goosen** fired a bogey-free, final-round 64 to come from four strokes behind to win the 2004 TOUR Championship presented by Coca-Cola by four strokes. The win marked Goosen's fourth consecutive year with a victory and his first PGA TOUR season with multiple wins. He won the U.S. Open in June 2004.*

Tournament Record:
267, Phil Mickelson, 2000 (East Lake GC)
18-Hole Record:
61, Chad Campbell, 2003 (Champions GC)

TOURNAMENT HISTORY

Year	Winner	Score	Runner-up	Score	Location	Par/Yards
NABISCO CHAMPIONSHIPS OF GOLF						
1987	Tom Watson	268	Chip Beck	270	Oak Hills CC, San Antonio, TX	70/6,576
NABISCO GOLF CHAMPIONSHIPS						
1988	Curtis Strange*	279	Tom Kite	279	Pebble Beach GL, Pebble Beach, CA	72/6,815
NABISCO CHAMPIONSHIPS						
1989	Tom Kite*	276	Payne Stewart	276	Harbour Town GL, Hilton Head, SC	71/6,657
1990	Jodie Mudd*	273	Billy Mayfair	273	Champions GC, Houston, TX	71/7,187
THE TOUR CHAMPIONSHIP						
1991	Craig Stadler*	279	Russ Cochran	279	Pinehurst (No. 2), Pinehurst, NC	71/7,005
1992	Paul Azinger	276	Lee Janzen Corey Pavin	279	Pinehurst (No. 2), Pinehurst, NC	71/7,005
1993	Jim Gallagher, Jr.	277	David Frost John Huston Greg Norman Scott Simpson	278	Olympic Club (Lake), San Francisco, CA	71/6,812
1994	Mark McCumber*	274	Fuzzy Zoeller	274	Olympic Club (Lake), San Francisco, CA	71/6,812
THE TOUR CHAMPIONSHIP PRESENTED BY MERCEDES-BENZ AND MICHELOB						
1995	Billy Mayfair	280	Steve Elkington Corey Pavin	283	Southern Hills CC, Tulsa, OK	70/6,834
1996	Tom Lehman	268	Brad Faxon	274	Southern Hills CC, Tulsa, OK	70/6,834
1997	David Duval	273	Jim Furyk	274	Champions GC, Houston, TX	71/7,200
THE TOUR CHAMPIONSHIP PRESENTED BY SOUTHERN COMPANY AND MERCEDES-BENZ						
1998	Hal Sutton*	274	Vijay Singh	274	East Lake GC, Atlanta, GA	70/6,980
THE TOUR CHAMPIONSHIP PRESENTED BY SOUTHERN COMPANY						
1999	Tiger Woods	269	Davis Love III	273	Champions GC, Houston, TX	71/7,220
2000	Phil Mickelson	267	Tiger Woods	269	East Lake GC, Atlanta, GA	70/6,980
2001	Mike Weir *	270	Ernie Els Sergio Garcia David Toms	270	Champions GC, Houston, TX	71/7,220
THE TOUR CHAMPIONSHIP PRESENTED BY COCA-COLA						
2002	Vijay Singh	268	Charles Howell III	270	East Lake GC, Atlanta, GA	70/6,980
2003	Chad Campbell	268	Charles Howell III	271	Champions GC, Houston, TX	71/7,220
2004	Retief Goosen	269	Tiger Woods	273	East Lake GC, Atlanta, GA	70/7,141

*KEY: * = Playoff ~ = Weather-shortened*

2004 Franklin Templeton Shootout *[Unofficial event]*

Franklin Templeton Shootout

KUEHNE/SLUMAN

Winner: HANK KUEHNE/JEFF SLUMAN
64-62-61 187 (-29) $300,000 EACH

Tiburon Golf Club

Naples, FL

November 12-14, 2004

Purse: $2,500,000
Par: 36-36—72
Yards: 7,288

LEADERS: First Round—Steve Flesch and Justin Leonard opened with a 9-under-par 63 and led Hank Kuehne and Jeff Sluman by one stroke in the modified alternate-shot format.
Second Round—Flesch and Leonard followed with a better-ball score of 9-under-par 63 and shared the leaderboard with Kuehne and Flesch at 18-under-par 126.

WEATHER: Sunny and warm Friday and Saturday, with highs in the low 80s. Mostly cloudy, breezy and cooler Sunday, with brief intermittent showers in the afternoon. Highs were in the upper 70s.

FORMAT: Round 1: Modified Alternate Shot
Round 2: Better Ball
Round 3: Scramble

Check out the 2005 Franklin Templeton Shootout, November 11-13 on USA/CBS

ORDER OF FINISH

Hank Kuehne/Jeff Sluman	64-62-61	187	-29	$300,000 each
Steve Flesch/Justin Leonard	63-63-63	189	-27	187,500 each
Mark Calcavecchia/Loren Roberts	66-63-61	190	-26	112,500 each
Greg Norman/Scott McCarron	65-64-62	191	-25	87,500 each
Bill Haas/Jay Haas	69-61-61	191	-25	87,500 each
Scott Hoch/Kenny Perry	67-65-60	192	-24	$77,500 each
John Daly/Rory Sabbatini	65-68-60	193	-23	72,500 each
Paul Azinger/Olin Browne	68-65-62	195	-21	70,000 each
Chad Campbell/Chris Riley	71-66-59	196	-20	67,500 each
Steve Elkington/Rocco Mediate	70-65-64	199	-17	63,750 each
Nick Faldo/Fred Funk	70-66-63	199	-17	63,750 each
Charles Howell III/Lee Janzen	71-65-64	200	-16	60,000 each

NOTES

*After winning in 2003 in a three-team playoff, **Hank Kuehne** and **Jeff Sluman** finished strong in 2004 to reclaim the title at the Franklin Templeton Shootout. They became just the second team in 16 years to defend the Franklin Templeton Shootout title, winning by two strokes over **Justin Leonard** and **Steve Flesch**. They made consecutive birdies on Nos. 15, 16, 17 and 18 in the scramble format to split $600,000 of the $2.5 million purse.*

Tournament Record:
182, Raymond Floyd/Fred Couples (Sherwood CC), 1990
18-Hole Record:
55, Greg Norman/Nick Price (Sherwood CC) 1993; John Cook/Peter Jacobsen (Sherwood CC) 1998

TOURNAMENT HISTORY

Year	Winner	Score	Runner-up	Score	Location	Par/Yards
RMCC INVITATIONAL						
1989	Curtis Strange, Mark O'Meara	190	Tom Weiskopf, Lanny Wadkins	196	Sherwood CC	72/7,025
			Bernhard Langer, John Mahaffey		Thousand Oaks, CA	
1990	Raymond Floyd, Fred Couples	182	Peter Jacobsen, Arnold Palmer	187	Sherwood CC	72/7,025
					Thousand Oaks, CA	
SHARK SHOOTOUT BENEFITING RMCC						
1991	Tom Purtzer, Lanny Wadkins	189	Greg Norman, Jack Nicklaus	193	Sherwood CC	72/7,025
FRANKLIN FUNDS SHARK SHOOTOUT						
1992	Davis Love III, Tom Kite	191	Fred Couples, Raymond Floyd	192	Sherwood CC	72/7,025
			Nick Price, Billy Ray Brown		Thousand Oaks, CA	
			Hale Irwin, Bruce Lietzke			
1993	Steve Elkington, Raymond Floyd	188	Hale Irwin, Bruce Lietzke	189	Sherwood CC	72/7,025
			Mark O'Meara, Curtis Strange		Thousand Oaks, CA	
			Mark Calcavecchia, Brad Faxon			
			Tom Kite, Davis Love III			
1994	Fred Couples, Brad Faxon	190	Curtis Strange, Mark O'Meara	192	Sherwood CC	72/7,025
					Thousand Oaks, CA	
FRANKLIN TEMPLETON SHARK SHOOTOUT						
1995	Mark Calcavecchia, Steve Elkington	184	Lee Janzen, Chip Beck	185	Sherwood CC	72/7,025
					Thousand Oaks, CA	
1996	Jay Haas, Tom Kite	187	Craig Stadler, Lanny Wadkins	189	Sherwood CC	72/7,025
			Hale Irwin, Lee Janzen		Thousand Oaks, CA	
1997	Scott McCarron, Bruce Lietzke	186	David Duval, Scott Hoch	188	Sherwood CC	72/7,025
					Thousand Oaks, CA	
1998	Steve Elkington, Greg Norman*	189	John Cook, Peter Jacobsen	189	Sherwood CC	72/7,025
					Thousand Oaks, CA	
1999	Fred Couples, David Duval	184	Scott McCarron, Scott Hoch	190	Sherwood CC	72/7,025
					Thousand Oaks, CA	
2000	Brad Faxon, Scott McCarron*	190	Carlos Franco, Scott Hoch	190	Doral Resort & Spa	72/7,171
					Miami, FL	
2001	Brad Faxon, Scott McCarron	183	John Daly, Frank Lickliter	185	Tiburon GC, Naples, FL	72/7,277
FRANKLIN TEMPLETON SHOOTOUT						
2002	Rocco Mediate, Lee Janzen	185	Matt Kuchar, David Gossett	186	Tiburon GC, Naples, FL	72/7,288
			John Huston, Jeff Maggert			
2003	Jeff Sluman, Hank Kuehne*	193	Shaun Micheel, Chad Campbell	193	Tiburon GC, Naples, FL	72/7,288
			Brad Faxon, Scott McCarron			
2004	Jeff Sluman, Hank Kuehne	187	Steve Flesch, Justin Leonard	189	Tiburon GC, Naples, FL	72/7,288

*KEY: * = Playoff*

2004 World Golf Championships–World Cup *[Unofficial event]*

WORLD CUP

ENGLAND

Winner: ENGLAND
Luke Donald/Paul Casey
61-64-68-68 257(-31) $700,000

Real Club de Golf de Sevilla

Seville, Spain

November 18-21, 2004

Purse: $4,000,000
Par: 36-36—72
Yards: 7,013

LEADERS: First Round—Ireland's Padraig Harrington/Paul McGinley and Austria's Markus Brier/Martin Wiegele shot 12-under-par 60s to lead Paul Casey/Luke Donald of England by one stroke. Shigeki Maruyama/Hidemichi Tanaka of Japan were two back.

Second Round—Casey/Donald of England moved to 19-under-par 125 to take a five-stroke lead over Brier/Wiegele of Austria. Six teams were six strokes behind.

Third Round—With an 11-under-par 61, Sergio Garcia/Miguel Angel Jimenez of Spain moved to 24-under-par 192 to take a one-stroke lead over Casey/Donald of England. Four teams were three back.

FORMAT: Thursday/Saturday—Four-ball; Friday/Sunday—Foursomes

WEATHER: Sunny and cool each morning, warming to the low 70s during the afternoon.

Check out the 2005 WGC-World Cup, November 17-20 on ESPN/ABC

ORDER OF FINISH

Country / Team	Pos.	Scores	Total	Money
England				
Paul Casey/Luke Donald	1	61-64-68-64	257	700,000.00
Spain				
Sergio Garcia/Miguel A. Jimenez	2	63-68-61-66	258	350,000.00
Ireland				
Padraig Harrington/Paul McGinley	3	60-71-64-65	260	200,000.00
South Africa				
Trevor Immelman/Rory Sabbatini	4	66-65-64-68	263	100,000.00
Austria				
Markus Brier/Martin Wiegele	T5	60-70-68-67	265	67,500.00
Holland				
Robert-Jan Derksen/Maarten Lafeber	T5	65-69-63-68	265	67,500.00
Germany				
Kariem Baraka/Marcel Siem	T7	64-69-66-68	267	47,500.00
Sweden				
Joakim Haeggman/Fredrik Jacobson	T7	64-67-64-72	267	47,500.00
United States				
Bob Tway/Scott Verplank	T7	64-67-64-72	267	47,500.00
South Korea				
Kim Dae-sub/Shin Yong-jin	T10	65-70-64-70	269	31,250.00
Wales				
Bradley Dredge/Philip Price	T10	65-69-64-71	269	31,250.00
Australia				
Stephen Leaney/Nick O'Hern	T10	64-68-65-72	269	31,250.00
Japan				
Shigeki Maruyama/Hidemichi Tanaka	T10	62-69-65-73	269	31,250.00
Denmark				
Anders Hansen/Soren Kjeldsen	14	64-73-67-66	270	25,000.00
France				
Raphael Jacquelin/Thomas Levet	T15	68-68-66-70	272	24,250.00
New Zealand				
Craig Perks/David Smail	T15	69-73-62-68	272	24,250.00
Italy				
Andrea Maestroni/Alessandro Tadini	17	70-71-64-68	273	23,500.00
Scotland				
Scott Drummond/Alastair Forsyth	18	64-72-66-72	274	23,000.00
Argentina				
Angel Cabrera/Eduardo Romero	19	70-71-65-70	276	22,500.00
Canada				
Stuart Anderson/Darren Griff	20	68-71-65-73	277	22,000.00
Colombia				
Jose Garrido/Manuel Merizalde	21	67-73-65-75	280	21,500.00
Myanmar				
Kyi Hla Han/Soe Kyaw Naing	22	69-73-67-73	282	21,000.00
Taiwan				
Wang Ter-Chang/Lu Wei-chih	23	70-70-68-75	283	20,500.00
Mexico				
Pablo Del Olmo/Alejandro Quiroz	24	74-72-68-74	288	20,000.00

NOTES

*The winning team of **Paul Casey/Luke Donald** of England shared $1,400,000 ($700,000) in prize money. Casey's largest previous payday was $350,000 when he paired with **Justin Rose** and finished second at the 2003 WGC-World Cup, while Donald's best previous payday came when he collected $468,000 upon winning his first PGA TOUR title, the Southern Farm Bureau Classic in 2002.*

***Paul Casey** has finished T5, T3, second and first in the last four WGC-World Cups, respectively. With his $700,000 payday, he eclipsed the $1-million mark in earnings at the WGC-World Cup, with $1,220,000. He is the only player to earn over $1 million in the event. Second on the WGC-World Cup money list is **Rory Sabbatini** of South Africa with $800,000 thanks to a fourth-place finish in Sevilla, Spain.*

TOURNAMENT HISTORY

Year	Country	Winning Team Members	Individual Medalist
CANADA CUP			
1953	Argentina	Antonio Cerda, Roberto De Vicenzo	Antonio Cerda, Argentina
1954	Australia	Peter Thomson, Kel Nagle	Stan Leonard, Canada
1955	United States	Chick Harbert, Ed Furgol	Ed Furgol, United States
1956	United States	Ben Hogan, Sam Snead	Ben Hogan, United States
1957	Japan	Torakichi Nakamura, Koichi Ono	Torakichi Nakamura, Japan
1958	Ireland	Harry Bradshaw, Christy O'Connor	Angel Miguel, Spain
1959	Australia	Peter Thomson, Kel Nagle	Stan Leonard, Canada
1960	United States	Sam Snead, Arnold Palmer	Flory Von Donck, Belgium
1961	United States	Sam Snead, Jimmy Demaret	Sam Snead, United States
1962	United States	Sam Snead, Arnold Palmer	Roberto De Vicenzo, Argentina
1963	United States	Arnold Palmer, Jack Nicklaus	Jack Nicklaus, United States
1964	United States	Arnold Palmer, Jack Nicklaus	Jack Nicklaus, United States
1965	South Africa	Gary Player, Harold Henning	Gary Player, South Africa
1966	United States	Jack Nicklaus, Arnold Palmer	George Knudson, Canada
WORLD CUP			
1967	United States	Jack Nicklaus, Arnold Palmer	Arnold Palmer, United States
1968	Canada	Al Balding, George Knudson	Al Balding, Canada
1969	United States	Orville Moody, Lee Trevino	Lee Trevino, United States
1970	Australia	Bruce Devlin, David Graham	Roberto De Vicenzo, Argentina
1971	United States	Jack Nicklaus, Lee Trevino	Jack Nicklaus, United States
1972	Taiwan	Hsieh Min Nan, Lu Liang Huan	Hsieh Min Nan, Taiwan
1973	United States	Jack Nicklaus, Johnny Miller	Johnny Miller, United States
1974	South Africa	Bobby Cole, Dale Hayes	Bobby Cole, South Africa
1975	United States	Johnny Miller, Lou Graham	Johnny Miller, United States
1976	Spain	Seve Ballesteros, Manuel Pinero	Ernesto Acosta, Mexico
1977	Spain	Seve Ballesteros, Antonio Garrido	Gary Player, South Africa
1978	United States	John Mahaffey, Andy North	John Mahaffey, United States
1979	United States	John Mahaffey, Hale Irwin	Hale Irwin, United States
1980	Canada	Dan Halldorson, Jim Nelford	Sandy Lyle, Scotland

World Golf Championships–World Cup

WORLD GOLF CHAMPIONSHIPS
WORLD CUP

NOTES

The Arnold Palmer-designed Victoria Clube de Golfe Course at Vilamoura in Algarve, Portugal will host the 2005 World Golf Championships-Algarve World Cup. This will be the first time that the WGC-World Cup has been played in Portugal and the second time in Europe since the event came under the umbrella of the World Golf Championships and underwent a title and format change. The course, which opened for play in early 2004, is, at 7,174 yards (6,560 meters), the longest 18-hole layout in Portugal.

The English team of **Paul Casey/Luke Donald** *carded a final-round, 8-under-par 64, the lowest foursomes total in tournament history. The previous mark of 7-under 65 was held by the United States team of* **Phil Michelson/David Toms** *(2002 World Cup in Mexico) and the Denmark team of* **Thomas Bjorn/Soren Hansen** *(2001 World Cup in Japan).*

The South Africa Team of **Trevor Immelman/ Rory Sabbatini***, who won the World Cup in 2003 at Kiawah Island, SC, carded a 4-under-par 68 foursomes total on Sunday to finish fourth.*

There were 19 players on the 24 two-man teams at the 2004 WGC-World Cup that made their first appearance in a World Golf Championships-World Cup event, including 13 players who made their debut in a World Golf Championships event.

Four teams in the 2004 event in Seville, Spain — Argentina, Ireland, France and Japan —had players who played in all four previous WGC-World Cup events. They were **Angel Cabrera** *and* **Eduardo Romero** *(Argentina),* **Padraig Harrington** *and* **Paul McGinley** *(Ireland), and* **Thomas Levet** *(France) and* **Shigeki Maruyama** *(Japan).*

Jose Maria Olazabal *designed the Real Club de Golf de Sevilla, site of the 2004 tournament. Previously, Olazabal played in one WGC-World Cup, the 2000 tournament in Argentina. Paired with* **Miguel Angel Jimenez***, Olazabal's team tied for seventh in 2000.*

TOURNAMENT HISTORY

Year	Country	Winning Team members	Individual Medalist
1981	No tournament		
1982	Spain	Manuel Pinero, Jose Maria Canizares	Manuel Pinero, Spain
1983	United States	Rex Caldwell, John Cook	Dave Barr, Canada
1984	Spain	Jose Maria Canizares, Jose Rivero	Jose Maria Canizares
1985	Canada	Dan Halldorson, Dave Barr	Howard Clark, England
1986	No tournament		
1987	Wales	Ian Woosnam, David Llewellyn	Ian Woosnam, Wales
1988	United States	Ben Crenshaw, Mark McCumber	Ben Crenshaw, United States
1989	Australia	Wayne Grady, Peter Fowler	Peter Fowler, Australia
1990	Germany	Bernhard Langer, Torsten Gideon	Payne Stewart, United States
1991	Sweden	Anders Forsbrand, Per Ulrik Johansson	Ian Woosnam, Wales
1992	United States	Fred Couples, Davis Love III	Brett Ogle, Australia
1993	United States	Fred Couples, Davis Love III	Bernhard Langer, Germany
1994	United States	Fred Couples, Davis Love III	Fred Couples, United States
1995	United States	Fred Couples, Davis Love III	Davis Love III, United States
1996	South Africa	Ernie Els, Wayne Westner	Ernie Els, South Africa
1997	Ireland	Padraig Harrington, Paul McGinley	Colin Montgomerie, Scotland
1998	England	David Carter, Nick Faldo	Scott Verplank, United States
1999	United States	Tiger Woods, Mark O'Meara	Tiger Woods, United States

Year	Country	Winning Team Members	Score	Location	Par/Yards
WGC–EMC WORLD CUP					
2000	United States	Tiger Woods, David Duval	254	Buenos Aires GC, Buenos Aires, Argentina	72/6,939
2001	South Africa	Ernie Els, Retief Goosen	264	Taiheiyo Club (Gotemba), Gotemba City, Japan	72/7,247
2002	Japan	Shigeki Maruyama, Toshi Izawa	252	Vista Vallarta, Puerto Vallarta, Mexico	72/7,057
WGC–WORLD CUP					
2003	South Africa	Trevor Immelman, Rory Sabbatini	275	Kiawah Island Resorts (Ocean), Kiawah, SC	72/7,296
2004	England	Paul Casey, Luke Donald	257	Real Club de Golf de Sevilla, Seville, Spain	72/7,013

The Victoria Club de Golfe Course at Vilamoura, site of the 2005 World Golf Championships-Algarve World Cup.

2004 UBS Cup [Unofficial Event]

UBS CUP
Sea Island

NOTES

*After playing to a draw last year, the United States team claimed its third UBS Cup outright with a 14-10 win over the Rest of the World squad. The four-point margin of victory for the American team was the second-largest winning margin in UBS Cup history, surpassed only by a five-point triumph by the U.S. squad in the 2002 UBS Cup at Sea Island, GA. **Arnold Palmer**, the captain of the United States team, remained undefeated as a skipper in international team competition (2-0 in the Ryder Cup, 1-0 in The Presidents Cup and 3-0-1 as UBS Cup captain).*

*The U.S.'s **Fred Couples**, playing in his first UBS Cup, was the only player to earn three full points during the competition. Couples teamed with **Hal Sutton** in the Friday foursomes to defeat **Peter Senior** and **Rodger Davis**. He partnered with **Raymond Floyd** in the Saturday four-ball matches, defeating **Ian Woosnam** and **Sandy Lyle**. On the final day, Couples defeated **Colin Montgomerie** in his singles match.*

***Hal Sutton** halved his singles match with fellow 2004 Ryder Cup captain **Bernhard Langer** on Sunday and remains undefeated in UBS Cup play. Sutton is 5-0-1 (2-0 in foursomes, 2-0 in four-ball and 1-0-1 in singles) as a member of two American UBS Cup squads.*

***Sam Torrance**'s four straight birdies (holes 4-7) during final-day play tied the UBS Cup record for most consecutive birdies in a singles match. In 2001, **Ian Woosnam** made four straight birdies (holes 9-12) in his singles match on the Ocean Course at Kiawah Island. **Hale Irwin** birdied four consecutive holes twice (2-5) and (8-11) in his singles match at Sea Island Golf Club in 2003.*

*For the second consecutive year in the UBS Cup, **Scott Hoch** earned the deciding point for the American team. Hoch's 20-foot birdie putt on the 17th hole Sunday gave him a 2-and-1 victory over **Carl Mason** and allowed the U.S. to retain the UBS Cup. In 2003, Hoch sunk a 12-foot birdie putt on the last hole to halve his match with Eduardo Romero and salvage a 12-12 draw, allowing the U.S. to keep the UBS Cup.*

Kiawah Island Club (Cassique)

Kiawah Island, SC

November 19-21, 2004

Purse: $3,000,000
Par: 36-36—72
Yards: 6,965

WEATHER: Sunny and pleasant on Friday, with highs in the mid-70s and a gentle breeze from the southwest at 5 mph. Cloudy Saturday, with highs in the low-70s and light winds from the southwest at 5 mph. Light showers early Sunday and then cloudy for the remainder of the day. Temperatures were in the low-70s, with westerly breezes at 5-10 mph in the afternoon.

FINAL RESULTS: U.S. 14, Rest of the World 10. U.S. players received $150,000 each. Rest of the World players received $100,000 each.

Check out the 2005 UBS Cup, November 18-20 on The Golf Channel

FIRST DAY
Foursomes Matches – Rest of the World 3½, U.S. 2½
Arnold Palmer/Jay Haas (U.S.) halved with Gary Player/Mark McNulty (ROW)
Colin Montgomerie/Bernhard Langer (ROW) defeated Tom Kite/Raymond Floyd (U.S.), 1-up
Hale Irwin/Fred Funk (U.S.) defeated Sam Torrance/Barry Lane (ROW), 5 and 3
Ian Woosnam/Sandy Lyle (ROW) defeated Tom Watson/Scott Hoch (U.S.), 4 and 3
John Chillas/Carl Mason (ROW) defeated Curtis Strange/Craig Stadler (U.S.), 4 and 3
Hal Sutton/Fred Couples (U.S.) defeated Peter Senior/Rodger Davis (ROW), 3 and 2

SECOND DAY
Four-Ball Matches – U.S. 4, Rest of the World 2
Arnold Palmer/Jay Haas (U.S.) halved with Gary Player/Mark McNulty (ROW)
Craig Stadler/Tom Kite (U.S.) halved with Sam Torrance/Barry Lane (ROW)
Hal Sutton/Tom Watson (U.S.) defeated Rodger Davis/Peter Senior (ROW), 4 and 2
Scott Hoch/Curtis Strange (U.S.) defeated Carl Mason/John Chillas (ROW), 2 and 1
Ray Floyd/Fred Couples (U.S.) defeated Ian Woosnam/Sandy Lyle (ROW), 4 and 2
Colin Montgomerie/Bernhard Langer (U.S.) defeated Hale Irwin/Fred Funk (U.S.), 2 and 1

THIRD DAY
Individual Matches – U.S. 7½, Rest of the World 4½
Gary Player (ROW) defeated Arnold Palmer (U.S.), 6 and 5
Jay Haas (U.S.) defeated Barry Lane (ROW), 5 and 3
Craig Stadler (U.S.) defeated Ian Woosnam (ROW), 5 and 4
Tom Kite (U.S.) defeated Rodger Davis (ROW), 1-up
Sam Torrance (ROW) defeated Curtis Strange (U.S.), 5 and 3
Peter Senior (ROW) defeated Fred Funk (U.S.), 1-up
Raymond Floyd (U.S.) halved with Mark McNulty (ROW)
Tom Watson (U.S.) defeated Sandy Lyle (ROW), 1-up
Scott Hoch (U.S.) defeated Carl Mason (ROW), 2 and 1
Hale Irwin (U.S.) halved with John Chillas (ROW)
Fred Couples (U.S.) defeated Colin Montgomerie (ROW), 5 and 3
Hal Sutton (U.S.) halved with Bernhard Langer (ROW)

TOURNAMENT HISTORY

Year	Winner/Score	Location	Par/Yards
UBS WARBURG CUP			
2001	United States 12½, Rest of the World 11½	Kiawah Island (Ocean Course), SC	72/7,296
UBS CUP			
2002	United States 14½, Rest of the World 8½	Sea Island GC, Sea Island, GA	70/6,985
2003	United States 12, Rest of the World 12	Sea Island GC, Sea Island, GA	70/6,985
2004	United States 14, Rest of the World 10	Kiawah Island (Ocean Course), SC	72/6,965

2004 The Merrill Lynch Skins Game *[Unofficial Event]*

Merrill Lynch Skins Game

COUPLES

Winner: FRED COUPLES
11 Skins $640,000

Trilogy Golf Club at La Quinta

La Quinta, CA

November 27-28, 2004

Purse: $1,000,000
Par: 36-36—72
Yards: 7,038

WEATHER: Sunny on Saturday with temperatures in the low 70s. Sunny, but cooler (low 60s) and windy (N-NW 12-20 mph) on Sunday.

Holes 1-6:	Worth $25,000 each
Holes 7-12:	Worth $50,000 each
Holes 13-17:	Worth $70,000 each
Hole 18:	Worth $200,000

Check out the 2005 Merrill Lynch Skins Game, November 26-27 on ABC

Hole	Par	Result
1	4	Three players halve with par
2	4	Scott wins with birdie/collects $50,000 (two skins)
3	5	Three players halve with birdie
4	4	Four players halve with par
5	4	Four players halve with par
6	3	Two players halve with birdie
7	4	Two players halve with birdie
8	3	Two players halve with par
9	5	Two players halve with birdie
10	4	Couples wins with birdie/collects $300,000 (eight skins)
11	3	Four players halve with par
12	4	Three players halve with birdie
13	4	Four players halve with par
14	4	Four players halve with par
15	4	Woods wins with birdie/collects $310,000 (five skins)
16	5	Two players halve with birdie
17	3	Three players halve with par
18	5	Two players halve with birdie

Playoff:

18	5	Couples, Woods advance with birdie/Scott, Sorenstam eliminated
17	3	Both players advance with par
18	5	Both players advance with par
17	3	Couples wins with par/collects $340,000 (three skins)

FINAL STANDINGS:

PLAYER	SKINS WON	MONEY WON
Fred Couples	11	$640,000
Tiger Woods	5	$310,000
Adam Scott	2	$50,000
Annika Sorenstam	0	$0

NOTES

With his birdie on the 10th hole to begin day two of the 2004 Merrill Lynch Skins Game, ***Fred Couples*** *earned eight skins and $300,000 to move over the $3-million mark in career earnings at the tournament. Couples came into the event with $2,875,000 in his previous 10 appearances. Couples also brought his tournament-leading career skins total to 74.*

Fred Couples *picked up three more skins (77) and $340,000 by winning the four-hole playoff over* ***Tiger Woods*** *(****Adam Scott*** *and* ***Annika Sorenstam*** *were eliminated after the first hole) to bring his career-total to $3,515,000. The next closest competitor in tournament history is* ***Greg Norman*** *with $1,115,000 in four appearances. It was also Couples' fifth title in the event.*

Tournament Record:
$1,000,000, Greg Norman, 2001

TOURNAMENT HISTORY

Year	Winner	Earnings	Location	Par/Yards
1983	Gary Player	$170,000	Desert Highlands CC, Scottsdale, AZ	72/7,100
1984	Jack Nicklaus	240,000	Desert Highlands CC, Scottsdale, AZ	72/7,100
1985	Fuzzy Zoeller	255,000	Bear Creek CC, Murietta, CA	72/7,024
1986	Fuzzy Zoeller	370,000	TPC at PGA West, La Quinta, CA	72/7,271
1987	Lee Trevino	310,000	TPC at PGA West, La Quinta, CA	72/7,271
1988	Raymond Floyd	290,000	TPC at PGA West, La Quinta, CA	72/7,271
1989	Curtis Strange	265,000	TPC at PGA West, La Quinta, CA	72/7,271
1990	Curtis Strange	225,000	TPC at PGA West, La Quinta, CA	72/7,271
1991	Payne Stewart	260,000	TPC at PGA West, La Quinta, CA	72/7,271
1992	Payne Stewart	220,000	Bighorn GC, Palm Desert, CA	72/6,848
1993	Payne Stewart	280,000	Bighorn GC, Palm Desert, CA	72/6,848
1994	Tom Watson	210,000	Bighorn GC, Palm Desert, CA	72/6,848
1995	Fred Couples	270,000	Bighorn GC, Palm Desert, CA	72/6,848
1996	Fred Couples	280,000	Rancho La Quinta GC, La Quinta, CA	72/7,087
1997	Tom Lehman	300,000	Rancho La Quinta GC, La Quinta, CA	72/6,983
1998	Mark O'Meara	430,000	Rancho La Quinta GC, La Quinta, CA	72/6,983
1999	Fred Couples	635,000	Landmark Golf Club, Indio, CA	72/7,258
2000	Colin Montgomerie	415,000	Landmark Golf Club, Indio, CA	72/7,068
2001	Greg Norman	1,000,000	Landmark Golf Club, Indio, CA	72/7,068
2002	Mark O'Meara	405,000	Landmark Golf Club, Indio, CA	72/7,068
2003	Fred Couples	605,000	Trilogy GC at La Quinta, La Quinta, CA	72/7,113
2004	Fred Couples	640,000	Trilogy GC at La Quinta, La Quinta, CA	72/7,038

2004 Tommy Bahama Challenge

[Unofficial event]

Tommy Bahama CHALLENGE

Chris Riley, member of the U.S. Team

Grayhawk Golf Club

Scottsdale, AZ

November 8, 2004 (Competition date)
January 1, 2005 (TV date)

Purse: $700,000
Par: 36-36—72
Yards: 7,108

FORMAT: 4 head-to-head singles matches, using a medal-play format.

Check out the 2005 Tommy Bahama Challenge, January 2, 2006 on CBS

First Place: United States, $400,000
2 Points
* Chad Campbell, ½ point
Hank Kuehne, 0 points
Zach Johnson, ½ point
Chris Riley, 1 point

Second Place: International, $280,000
2 Points
Paul Casey, 0 points
David Howell, ½ point
Kevin Na, ½ point
Ian Poulter, 1 point

Match Results
Campbell (66) and Howell (66), halved
Poulter (68) def. Kuehne (70)
Johnson (70) and Na (70), halved
Riley (69) def. Casey (72)

• United States won on the first hole of alternate shot sudden-death playoff.

• Campbell won an additional $20,000 and an automobile for winning the medalist playoff with Howell.

TOURNAMENT HISTORY

Year	Winner	Score	Location	Par/Yards
2004	United States 2, International	2*	Grayhawk GC, Scottsdale, AZ	72/7,108

*KEY: * = Playoff*

2004 Shinhan Korea Golf Championship

OBERHOLSER

Winner: ARRON OBERHOLSER
72-73-70-69 284 (-4) $1,000,000

Jungmun Golf Club

Jeju Island, South Korea

Nov. 25-28, 2004

Purse: $3,550,000
Par: 36-36—72
Yards: 7,454

LEADERS: First Round—Ted Purdy at 7-under-par 65 led Padraig Harrington and Yong Eun Yang by one. Tom Pernice, Jr. and Brian Bateman were tied for fourth at 68.
Second Round—Yong Eun Yang at 3-under 141 led Harrington and Bateman by two. Three others were three back.
Third Round—Miguel Jimenez at 2-under 214 led Arron Oberholser by one shot. Kevin Na and Bateman were two off the pace.

CUT: There was no cut. All 38 players completed 72 holes.

PRO-AM: Team: Robert Gamez, 61.

WEATHER: Thursday, mostly sunny and warm. High of 72. Winds E 10 mph. Friday, cloudy, windy and colder with intermittent rain. High of 49. Winds NW 35-40 mph and gusting. Saturday, mostly sunny. High of 60. Winds NW 15-20 mph. Sunday, sunny and warmer. High of 64. Winds NW 5-10 mph.

ORDER OF FINISH

Arron Oberholser	1	72-73-70-69	284	$1,000,000.00
Miguel A. Jimenez	T2	70-75-69-72	286	325,000.00
Kevin Na	T2	70-74-72-70	286	325,000.00
Trevor Immelman	4	70-74-78-65	287	200,000.00
Daniel Chopra	T5	71-76-71-71	289	147,500.00
Tim Petrovic	T5	70-77-72-70	289	147,500.00
Brian Bateman	T7	68-75-73-74	290	110,000.00
Mathias Gronberg	T7	74-75-71-70	290	110,000.00
Matt Kuchar	T7	72-74-74-70	290	110,000.00
Duffy Waldorf	T7	73-78-71-68	290	110,000.00
Padraig Harrington	T11	66-77-76-72	291	71,250.00
J.J. Henry	T11	73-73-72-73	291	71,250.00
Billy Mayfair	T11	72-77-74-68	291	$71,250.00
Yong Eun Yang	T11	66-75-80-70	291	71,250.00
Carlos Franco	15	71-73-76-72	292	55,000.00
Harrison Frazar	16	70-80-76-67	293	50,000.00
Mark Calcavecchia	T17	70-76-76-72	294	40,000.00
Frank Lickliter II	T17	73-80-73-68	294	40,000.00
Joe Ogilvie	T17	71-76-72-75	294	40,000.00
Mark Hensby	20	73-77-76-69	295	31,500.00
Zach Johnson	T21	70-80-74-72	296	29,500.00
John Rollins	T21	71-80-71-74	296	29,500.00
Brian Gay	T23	77-78-70-72	297	27,000.00
Shaun Micheel	T23	71-78-76-72	297	27,000.00
Tom Pernice, Jr.	T23	68-80-78-71	297	27,000.00
Nick Faldo	T26	74-80-73-71	298	24,500.00
ik-Jae Jang	T26	77-76-73-72	298	$24,500.00
K.J. Choi	28	76-77-78-68	299	23,000.00
Cameron Beckman	T29	73-73-80-75	301	22,084.00
Brett Quigley	T29	74-83-72-72	301	22,083.00
Bo Van Pelt	T29	73-77-74-77	301	22,083.00
Rich Beem	32	69-81-78-75	303	21,500.00
Craig Bowden	T33	73-83-76-72	304	21,000.00
No-Seok Park	T33	74-80-77-73	304	21,000.00
Ted Purdy	T33	65-84-80-75	304	21,000.00
Robert Gamez	36	74-78-76-77	305	20,500.00
Paul Stankowski	37	79-78-74-75	306	20,250.00
Alex Cejka	38	72-80-81-75	308	20,000.00

NOTES

*Champion **Arron Oberholser** collected $1 million for his victory. In the currency exchange from dollars to won, he collected roughly $1 billion won.*

TOURNAMENT HISTORY

Year	Winner	Score	Runner-up	Score	Location	Par/Yards
2004	Arron Oberholser	284	Miguel A. Jimenez Kevin Na	286	Jungmun GC, South Korea	72/7,454

2004 PGA TOUR Qualifying Tournament

[Unofficial event]

Winner: BRIAN DAVIS
72-65-67-69-68-74 415 (-20) $50,000

PGA West

La Quinta, CA

Dec. 1-6, 2004

Purse: $1,187,500
TPC Stadium Course (Host Course)
Par: 36-36—72
Yards: 7,300
Jack Nicklaus Tournament Course
Par: 36-36—72
Yards: 7,204

1,240 players participated in the 2004 PGA TOUR Qualifying Tournament. Twelve first- and six second-stage regionals were held to reduce the field. A total of 169 players competed in the final qualifying stage, which consisted of six rounds with no cut.

The top 30 players and ties (a total of 35 players) received PGA TOUR cards for 2005. The next 51 finishers earned fully exempt Nationwide Tour cards for 2005, and the remainder of the field received conditional Nationwide Tour status.

Nine players qualified by making it through all three stages – Rob Rashell, Sean O'Hair, Greg Owen, Matt Davidson, Jason Allred, Joey Snyder III, Mario Tiziani, Charlie Wi and Will MacKenzie.

Check out the 2005 PGA TOUR Qualifying Tournament, November 30-December 5 on The Golf Channel

ORDER OF FINISH

Brian Davis	1	72-65-67-69-68-74	415	$50,000.00
Rob Rashell	2	68-68-70-67-74-69	416	40,000.00
Danny Briggs	3	74-73-69-66-69-68	419	35,000.00
Paul Claxton	T4	71-70-71-71-70-67	420	26,500.00
John Elliott	T4	70-73-65-71-68-73	420	26,500.00
Bill Glasson	T4	72-71-68-70-68-71	420	26,500.00
Sean O'Hair	T4	70-71-68-72-71-68	420	26,500.00
Greg Owen	T4	72-64-70-69-72-73	420	26,500.00
Jason Bohn	T9	71-74-71-66-69-70	421	25,000.00
Roland Thatcher	T9	73-70-66-71-71-70	421	25,000.00
Matt Davidson	T11	73-71-65-70-72-71	422	25,000.00
D.J. Trahan	T11	67-69-73-72-74-67	422	$25,000.00
Jason Allred	T13	71-69-73-71-70-69	423	25,000.00
Jeff Brehaut	T13	71-68-61-72-78-73	423	25,000.00
D.J. Brigman	T13	69-79-74-66-69-66	423	25,000.00
Jim Carter	T13	70-72-71-67-70-73	423	25,000.00
Carl Paulson	T13	72-72-69-66-72-72	423	25,000.00
Phillip Price	T13	67-69-71-72-73-71	423	25,000.00
Joey Snyder III	T13	70-72-69-73-65-74	423	25,000.00
Dean Wilson	T13	68-70-69-73-71-72	423	25,000.00
David Hearn	T21	73-64-73-70-67-77	424	25,000.00
Bob Heintz	T21	69-71-72-76-64-72	424	25,000.00
Hideto Tanihara	T21	72-70-69-75-70-68	424	25,000.00
Mario Tiziani	T21	70-67-72-76-68-71	424	25,000.00
Omar Uresti	T21	68-68-68-75-73-72	424	$25,000.00
Craig Barlow	T26	80-65-69-73-68-70	425	25,000.00
Doug Barron	T26	73-71-70-72-70-69	425	25,000.00
Tom Gillis	T26	73-75-68-70-68-71	425	25,000.00
Lucas Glover	T26	69-71-73-71-70-71	425	25,000.00
Jeff Hart	T26	72-72-74-64-71-72	425	25,000.00
J.P. Hayes	T26	74-71-72-71-70-67	425	25,000.00
Scott Hend	T26	69-70-73-71-70-72	425	25,000.00
Will MacKenzie	T26	72-70-68-68-70-77	425	25,000.00
Charlie Wi	T26	68-72-73-70-74-68	425	25,000.00
Mark Wilson	T26	71-70-69-77-69-69	425	25,000.00

The following 51 players earned fully exempt 2005 Nationwide Tour status as the next number of finishers nearest 50 after the Qualifying Tournament graduates:

Olin Browne	T36	73-72-72-70-66-73	426	$5,000.00
Bob Burns	T36	67-73-78-70-69-69	426	5,000.00
Kyle Gallo	T36	70-70-74-72-66-74	426	5,000.00
David McKenzie	T36	72-64-72-75-72-71	426	5,000.00
Tim O'Neal	T36	68-74-70-74-70-70	426	5,000.00
Tjaart van der Walt	T36	69-71-66-74-74-72	426	5,000.00
Scott Weatherly	T36	68-73-73-66-76-70	426	5,000.00
Joel Edwards	T43	70-73-67-74-70-73	427	5,000.00
Bill Haas	T43	75-68-70-70-73-71	427	5,000.00
Richard S. Johnson	T43	74-70-70-70-69-74	427	5,000.00
Jim Rutledge	T43	69-73-72-73-71-69	427	5,000.00
Paul Stankowski	T43	72-73-71-68-74-69	427	5,000.00
Guy Boros	T48	73-71-73-70-70-71	428	5,000.00
Russ Cochran	T48	71-73-68-71-72-73	428	5,000.00
Joel Kribel	T48	70-74-72-72-69-71	428	5,000.00
Steve Larick	T48	77-69-73-72-67-70	428	5,000.00
Dan Olsen	T48	70-65-67-76-75-75	428	5,000.00
Sean Pacetti	T48	77-70-71-65-70-75	428	$5,000.00
Scott Petersen	T48	75-69-73-71-73-67	428	5,000.00
Dicky Pride	T48	70-74-70-72-70-72	428	5,000.00
Boo Weekley	T48	72-71-79-68-71-67	428	5,000.00
Tyler Williamson	T48	71-71-74-74-67-71	428	5,000.00
Nick Cassini	T58	71-70-69-74-75-70	429	5,000.00
Kevin Durkin	T58	71-73-76-72-67-70	429	5,000.00
Danny Ellis	T58	72-73-72-70-71-71	429	5,000.00
Hiroyuki Fujita	T58	68-73-71-71-74-72	429	5,000.00
Per-Ulrik Johansson	T58	73-69-70-73-70-74	429	5,000.00
Troy Matteson	T58	74-70-74-65-76-70	429	5,000.00
Tom Scherrer	T58	74-73-74-69-70-69	429	5,000.00
Brian Smock	T58	70-75-73-69-73-69	429	5,000.00
Kyle Thompson	T58	72-73-73-69-71-71	429	5,000.00
Jeremy Anderson	T67	71-72-68-76-72-71	430	5,000.00
Brendon de Jonge	T67	69-75-72-70-75-69	430	5,000.00
Jeff Freeman	T67	72-75-74-74-69-66	430	5,000.00
Scott Gardiner	T67	74-66-69-73-71-77	430	$5,000.00
Doug LaBelle II	T67	70-74-71-75-70-70	430	5,000.00
Steve Pleis	T67	73-69-77-74-66-71	430	5,000.00
Scott Simpson	T67	71-73-71-75-74-66	430	5,000.00
Jerry Smith	T67	74-69-71-69-72-75	430	5,000.00
Mike Sposa	T67	70-72-73-75-72-68	430	5,000.00
Tim Wilkinson	T67	71-75-70-73-73-68	430	5,000.00
Arjun Atwal	T77	70-71-70-70-77-73	431	5,000.00
Aaron Barber	T77	68-77-71-67-75-73	431	5,000.00
Shane Bertsch	T77	71-77-73-72-72-66	431	5,000.00
Jaxon Brigman	T77	71-73-73-70-73-71	431	5,000.00
Chad Collins	T77	69-74-71-75-71-71	431	5,000.00
Keoke Cotner	T77	67-74-67-74-74-75	431	5,000.00
Jim McGovern	T77	73-70-71-75-69-73	431	5,000.00
Alan McLean	T77	73-74-72-70-73-69	431	5,000.00
David Morland IV	T77	72-70-71-71-69-78	431	5,000.00
Jason Schultz	T77	76-77-72-67-74-65	431	5,000.00

The following players are non-exempt members of the 2005 Nationwide Tour:

Ben Bates	T87	71-73-71-76-70-71	432
Dave Cunningham	T87	72-72-76-71-72-69	432
Jason Enloe	T87	73-71-75-69-72-72	432
Jeff Gove	T87	73-70-72-72-70-75	432
Fran Quinn	T87	70-70-70-75-70-77	432
Scott Sterling	T87	72-71-71-79-71-68	432
Vance Veazey	T87	71-73-74-68-73-73	432
Brian Watts	T87	73-72-69-74-71-73	432
Chris Wollmann	T87	71-71-77-72-70-71	432
Craig Bowden	T96	75-69-69-76-74-70	433
Jamie Broce	T96	70-71-75-71-72-74	433
Chris Kamin	T96	75-70-75-72-73-68	433
Cliff Kresge	T96	72-77-72-70-73-69	433
Martin Laird	T96	74-74-73-71-76-65	433
Chris Tidland	T96	74-72-77-69-70-71	433
Dan Forsman	T102	70-74-71-74-78-67	434
Brian Kortan	T102	68-70-77-71-77-71	434
John E. Morgan	T102	71-69-73-76-74-71	434
Brent Schwarzrock	T102	76-66-70-74-78-70	434
Johnson Wagner	T102	76-73-71-73-73-68	434
Matt Weibring	T102	77-69-73-67-78-70	434
Mark Wurtz	T102	68-73-73-71-72-77	434
Jay Don Blake	T109	72-71-73-74-74-71	435
Matt Kuchar	T109	71-73-73-73-75-70	435
Jason Buha	T111	70-71-71-79-75-70	436
Bubba Dickerson	T111	68-72-73-74-76-73	436
Robert Garrigus	T111	80-71-74-69-73-69	436
Kevin Gessino-Kraft	T111	80-72-76-66-69-73	436
Scott Gump	T111	66-74-76-72-68-80	436
Ryan Hietala	T111	71-77-76-71-70-71	436
Andrew Johnson	T111	76-71-74-71-73-71	436
Cameron Percy	T111	74-72-76-71-72-71	436
Jeff Quinney	T111	73-76-76-68-74-69	436
Joseph Alfieri	T120	71-79-74-70-70-73	437
Billy Harvey	T120	71-74-72-68-75-77	437
Steve Haskins	T120	71-73-75-72-71-75	437
Brad Ott	T120	75-72-71-72-75-72	437
Jon Rusk	T120	74-73-74-75-71-70	437
Esteban Toledo	T120	70-67-72-79-72-77	437
Richie Coughlan	T126	73-71-74-74-72-74	438
Glen Day	T126	74-74-70-73-75-72	438
Jason Gore	T126	74-69-73-75-75-72	438
Tom Johnson	T126	79-63-76-75-69-76	438
Steve Runge	T126	70-73-74-74-78-69	438
Kris Blanks	T131	76-75-75-73-69-71	439
Craig Carmichael	T131	73-69-74-71-74-78	439
Tripp Isenhour	T131	71-73-73-73-75-74	439
Kenneth Staton	T131	72-76-76-70-73-72	439
Sean Whiffin	T131	73-73-72-74-73-74	439
Keith Huber	T136	70-72-74-74-76-74	440
Will Moore	T136	71-70-76-74-75-74	440
Ryan Armour	T138	73-72-72-74-74-76	441
Jay Delsing	T138	71-74-80-68-74-74	441
Charley Hoffman	T138	73-78-70-74-72-74	441
Chris Nallen	T138	74-77-81-70-72-67	441
Todd Pinneo	T138	77-75-73-69-77-70	441
Ewan Porter	T143	70-77-76-74-78-67	442
Warren Schutte	T143	72-78-71-73-79-69	442
Scott Parel	T145	70-77-70-71-79-77	444
Chad Wilfong	T145	72-80-73-72-76-71	444
Jeff Burns	T147	76-75-81-70-74-69	445
Jason Caron	T147	72-76-79-74-74-70	445
Kim Felton	T147	76-75-72-69-81-72	445
Justin Hicks	T147	71-72-77-78-75-72	445
Todd Rossetti	T147	76-69-80-72-75-73	445
David Carter	T152	78-69-77-72-71-79	446
Carl Desjardins	T152	72-72-75-77-72-78	446
Jim Gallagher, Jr.	154	71-79-79-76-72-70	447
Dave Christensen	T155	71-72-71-76-80-78	448
Paul Curry	T155	76-76-74-75-76-71	448
Alex Rodger	T155	77-73-81-70-76-71	448
Alex Aragon	158	68-73-75-79-83-72	450
Dustin White	159	71-81-74-74-79-72	451
Jeff Klauk	T160	71-74-76-75-80-78	454
Payton Osborn	T160	76-76-84-72-74-72	454
Brian Henninger	162	73-76-79-69-79-80	456
Keith Nolan	163	76-82-83-73-73-73	460
Tim Turpen	164	71-77-81-81-79-72	461

The following players did not finish (W=withdrew, D=disqualified)

W—David Peoples, **303**-Steve Collins, **293**-Soren Kjeldsen, **367**-Mathew Goggin, **D—363**-Ken Green, **144**-S.K. Ho

SECTION 3 TOURNAMENT HISTORIES

TOURNAMENT HISTORY

Year	Medalist	Cards Granted	Applicants	Final Field	Format	Location
PGA TOUR QUALIFYING TOURNAMENT						
1965	John Schlee	17	49	49	144 holes	PGA National GC, Palm Beach Gardens, FL
1966	Harry Toscano	32	99	99	144 holes	PGA National GC, Palm Beach Gardens, FL
1967	Bobby Cole	30	111	111	144 holes	PGA National GC, Palm Beach Gardens, FL
1968 (Spring)	Bob Dickson	15	81	81	144 holes	PGA National GC, Palm Beach Gardens, FL
1968 (Fall)	Grier Jones	30	79	79	144 holes	PGA National GC, Palm Beach Gardens, FL
1969 (Spring)	Bob Eastwood	15	91	91	144 holes	PGA National GC, Palm Beach Gardens, FL
1969 (Fall)	Doug Olson	12	182	48	144 holes	PGA National GC, Palm Beach Gardens, FL
1970	Robert Barbarossa	18	250	60	72 holes, after nine 54-hole District Qualifiers	Tucson CC, Tucson, AZ
1971	Bob Zender	23	357	75	108 holes, after three 72-hole Regional Qualifiers	PGA National GC, Palm Beach Gardens, FL
1972	Larry Stubblefield/	25	468	81	108 holes, after three 72-hole Regional Qualifiers	Silverado CC, Napa, CA
	John Adams					
1973	Ben Crenshaw	23	373	78	144 holes, after three 72-hole Regional Qualifiers	Perdido Bay CC, Pensacola, FL
						Dunes GC, N. Myrtle Beach, SC
1974	Fuzzy Zoeller	19	447	78	144 holes, after three 72-hole Regional Qualifiers	Silverado CC, Napa CA
						Canyon CC, Palm Springs, CA
1975 (Spring)	Joey Dills	13	233	233	108 holes	Bay Tree Plantation, N. Myrtle Beach, SC
1975 (Fall)	Jerry Pate	25	380	380	108 holes	Walt Disney World, Lake Buena Vista, FL
1976 (Spring)	Bob Shearer	15	276	276	108 holes	Bay Tree Plantation, N. Myrtle Beach, SC
	Woody Blackburn					
1976 (Fall)	Keith Fergus	29	349	349	108 holes	Rancho Viejo CC, Brownsville, TX
						Valley International CC, Brownsville, TX
1977 (Spring)	Phil Hancock	26	408	408	108 holes	Pinehurst CC, Pinehurst, NC
1977 (Fall)	Ed Fiori	34	660	144	72 holes, after Sectional Qualifiers	Pinehurst CC, Pinehurst, NC
1978 (Spring)	Wren Lum	28	502	150	72 holes, after five 72-hole Regional Qualifiers	U. of New Mexico GC, Albuquerque, NM
1978 (Fall)	Jim Thorpe/	27	606	120	72 holes, after five 72-hole Regional Qualifiers	Waterwood National CC, Huntsville, TX
	John Fought					
1979 (Spring)	Terry Mauney	25	521	150	72 holes, after five 72-hole Regional Qualifiers	Pinehurst CC, Pinehurst, NC
1979 (Fall)	Tom Jones	27	652	120	72 holes, after five 72-hole Regional Qualifiers	Waterwood National CC, Huntsville, TX
1980 (Spring)	Jack Spradlin	27	553	150	72 holes, after five 72-hole Regional Qualifiers	Pinehurst CC, Pinehurst, NC
1980 (Fall)	Bruce Douglass	27	621	120	72 holes, after five 72-hole Regional Qualifiers	Fort Washington G&CC, Fresno, CA
1981 (Spring)	Billy Glisson	25	556	150	72 holes, after five 72-hole Regional Qualifiers	Walt Disney World Golf Resort, Lake Buena Vista, FL
1981 (Fall)	Robert Thompson/	34	513	120	72 holes, after six 72-hole Regional Qualifiers	Waterwood National CC, Huntsville, TX
	Tim Graham					
1982	Donnie Hammond	50	696	200	108 holes, after eight Regional Qualifiers	TPC at Sawgrass, Ponte Vedra, F
						Sawgrass CC, Ponte Vedra, FL
1983	Willie Wood	57	624	144	108 holes, after nine Regional Qualifiers	TPC at Sawgrass, Ponte Vedra, FL
1984	Paul Azinger	50	800	160	108 holes, after 10 Regional Qualifiers	La Quinta Hotel and GC
						Mission Hills CC, La Quinta, CA
1985	Tom Sieckmann	50	825	162	108 holes, after 11 Regional Qualifiers	Grenelefe Resort, Haines City, FL
1986	Steve Jones	53	750	186	108 holes, after 14 Regionals	PGA West (Stadium Course) La Quinta, CA
						La Quinta Hotel Golf & Tennis Resort (Dunes Course)
1987	John Huston	54	800	183	108 holes, after 11 Regionals	Matanzas Woods GC
						Pine Lakes CC; Palm Coast, FL
1988	Robin Freeman	52	750	183	108 holes after 11 Regionals	La Quinta Hotel (Dunes Course)
						PGA West Jack Nicklaus Resort Course; La Quinta, CA
1989	David Peoples	59	825	180	108 holes, after 11 Regionals	TPC at The Woodlands, The Woodlands, TX
1990	Duffy Waldorf	49	835	182	108 holes, after 11 Regionals	La Quinta Hotel (Dunes Course)
						PGA West (Nicklaus Course), La Quinta, CA
1991	Mike Standly	48	850	181	108 holes after 12 Regionals	Grenelefe Resort, Haines City, FL
1992	Massy Kuramato	43	800	186	108 holes after 13 Regionals	TPC at The Woodlands, The Woodlands, TX
	Skip Kendall					
	Brett Ogle					
	Perry Moss					
	Neale Smith					
1993	Ty Armstrong	46	800	191	108 holes after 13 Regionals	La Quinta Hotel (Dunes Course)
	Dave Stockton, Jr.					PGA West Jack Nicklaus Resort Course
	Robin Freeman					La Quinta, CA
1994	Woody Austin	46	1000	185	108 holes after 13 Regionals	Grenelefe Resort, Haines City, FL
1995	Carl Paulson	42	1000	190	108 holes after 15 Regionals	Bear Lakes CC (Lakes and Links Courses)
						West Palm Beach, FL
1996	Allen Doyle~	49	1153	188	90 holes after 17 Regionals	La Purisma GC; Lompoc, CA
	Jimmy Johnston					Sandpiper GC; Goleta, CA
1997	Scott Verplank	38	1200	168	108 holes after 17 Regionals	Grenelefe Resort (West and South Courses)
						Grenelefe, FL
1998	Mike Weir	41	1100	169	108 holes after 19 Regionals	PGA West (Weiskopf Private Course)
						La Quinta Resort (Dunes Course)
1999	Blaine McCallister	40	1100	169	108 holes after 19 Regionals	Doral Golf Resort & Spa (Gold Course and Silver Course)
2000	Stephen Allan	36	1100	169	108 holes after 18 Regionals	PGA West (Nicklaus Tournament and Private Courses)
						La Quinta, CA

PGA TOUR Qualifying Tournament

TOURNAMENT HISTORY

Year	Medalist	Cards Granted	Applicants	Final Field	Format	Location
2001	Pat Perez	36	1200	167	108 holes after 18 Regionals	Bear Lakes CC (Lakes and Links Courses) West Palm Beach, FL
2002	Jeff Brehaut	38	1300	170	108 holes after 19 Regionals	PGA West (TPC Stadium and Nicklaus Courses) La Quinta, CA
2003	Mathias Gronberg	34	1200	170	108 holes after 19 Regionals	Orange County National (Panther Lake and Crooked Cat Courses) Winter Garden, FL
2004	Brian Davis	35	1240	169	108 holes after 18 Regionals	PGA West (TPC Stadium and Nicklaus Courses) La Quinta, CA

Key: ~ Tournament shortened to 90 holes because of continuing rain and unplayable course conditions

NOTE: The American Professional Golfers also held a School in the fall of 1968, graduating 21. The 144-hole competition was played at Doral CC. The medalist was Martin Roesink.

SECTION 3 TOURNAMENT HISTORIES

2004 Office Depot Father/Son Challenge *[Unofficial Event]*

Office DEPOT Father/Son Challenge at ChampionsGate

NELSON

Winners: LARRY/DREW NELSON
60-59 119 (-25) $200,000/TEAM

ChampionsGate Golf Resort (International)

ChampionsGate, FL

December 4-5, 2004

Purse: $1,000,000
Par: 37-35—72
Yards: 7,111

LEADERS: First Round—Larry and Drew Nelson combined for a 12-under-par 60 and led Jerry/Wesley Pate by one stroke. Bob/David Charles trailed by two strokes.

FORMAT: 36-hole scramble; all 16 teams completed 36 holes.

WEATHER: Mostly cloudy, breezy and cool Saturday, with highs in the low 60s. Winds were from the north at 10-15 mph, with higher gusts. Mostly sunny and warmer Sunday, with highs in 70s.

Check out the 2005 Father/Son Challenge, December 3-4 on NBC

ORDER OF FINISH

Larry Nelson/Drew Nelson	1	60-59—119	$200,000/team
Bob Charles/David Charles	2	62-60—122	105,000/team
Jerry Pate/Wesley Pate	T3	61-64—125	59,800/team
Tom Kite/David Kite	T3	63-62—125	59,800/team
Raymond Floyd/Raymond Floyd, Jr.	T3	63-62—125	$59,800/team
Bill Rogers/Ben Rogers	T3	64-61—125	59,800/team
Curtis Strange/Thomas Strange	T3	66-59—125	59,800/team
Dave Stockton/Ronnie Stockton	8	65-61—126	48,000/team
Vijay Singh/Qass Singh	T9	66-62—128	46,500/team
Bernhard Langer/Stefan Langer	T9	63-65—128	46,500/team
Lee Trevino/Rick Trevino	11	66-63—129	$45,000/team
Arnold Palmer/Sam Saunders	T12	65-65—130	43,000/team
Hale Irwin/Steve Irwin	T12	65-65—130	43,000/team
Lee Janzen/Aaron Stewart	T12	64-66—130	43,000/team
Lanny Wadkins/Travis Wadkins	15	67-65—132	41,000/team
Craig Stadler/Chris Stadler	16	67-67—134	40,000/team

NOTES

*Team Nelson's winning total of 60-59—119 tied the tournament record set by Team Floyd (**Ray** and son **Ray Jr.**) in 1995 and tied by Team Charles (**Bob** and son **Dave**) in 1998, Team Nicklaus (**Jack** and **Gary**) in 1999 and the Floyds (**Ray** and **Robert**) in 1999. The 59 was one of two shot on Sunday and it was the product of the Nelsons birdieing the entire back nine en route to a 27.*

*Two-time U.S. Open winner (1993, 1998) **Lee Janzen** played with **Aaron Stewart**, the 15-year-old son of the late Payne Stewart, who won three major championships (1989 PGA and 1991 and 1999 U.S. Opens).*

TOURNAMENT HISTORY

Year	Winner	Score	Runner-up	Score	Location	Par/Yards
OFFICE DEPOT FATHER/SON CHALLENGE						
1995	Raymond Floyd/ Raymond Floyd, Jr.	119	Hale Irwin/ Steve Irwin	125	Windsor Club, Orchid Island, FL	72/6,709
1996	Raymond Floyd/ Raymond Floyd, Jr.	124	Dave Stockton/ Ron Stockton	126	Windsor Club, Orchid Island, FL	72/6,709
1997	Raymond Floyd/ Raymond Floyd, Jr.	120	Dave Stockton/ Ron Stockton	121	Windsor Club, Orchid Island, FL	72/6,709
1998	Bob Charles/ David Charles	119	Craig Stadler/ Kevin Stadler	123	Windsor Club, Orchid Island, FL	72/6,709
1999	Jack Nicklaus/ Gary Nicklaus*	119	Raymond Floyd/ Robert Floyd	119	TwinEagles G&CC, Naples, FL	72/7,214
2000	Raymond Floyd/ Robert Floyd*	122	Johnny Miller/ Scott Miller	122	Ocean Club Paradise Island, Bahamas	72/6,907
2001	Raymond Floyd/ Robert Floyd	124	Hale Irwin/ Steve Irwin	125	Ocean Club Paradise Island, Bahamas	72/6,907
2002	Craig Stadler/ Kevin Stadler*	120	Hale Irwin/ Steve Irwin	125	Ocean Club Paradise Island, Bahamas	72/6,928
2003	Hale Irwin/ Steve Irwin	123	Jack Nicklaus/ Jack Nicklaus II	124	ChampionsGate Golf Resort ChampionsGate, FL	72/7,069
2004	Larry Nelson/ Drew Nelson	119	Bob Charles/ David Charles	122	ChampionsGate Golf Resort ChampionsGate, FL	72/7,111

*KEY: * = Playoff*

2004 PGA Grand Slam of Golf [Unofficial event]

MICKELSON

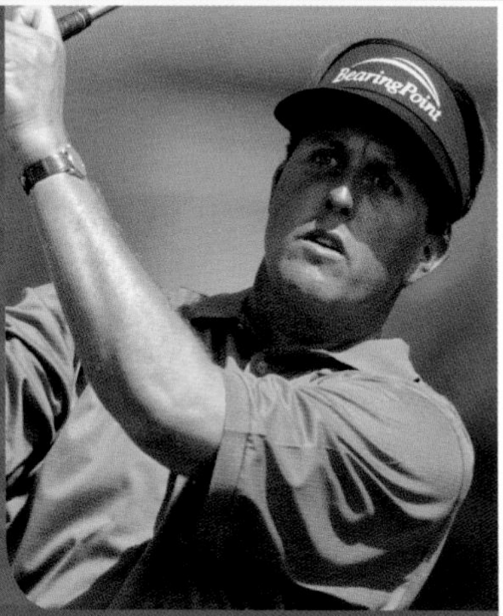

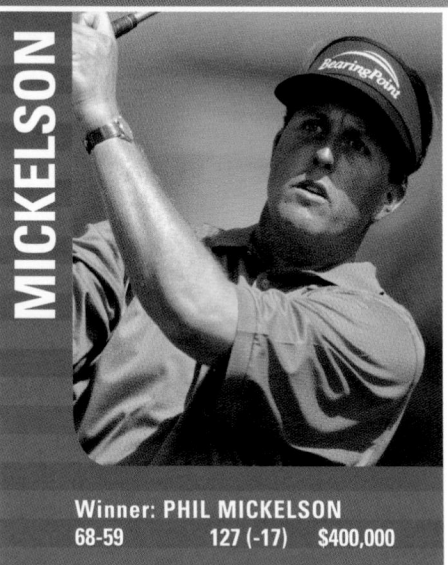

Winner: PHIL MICKELSON
68-59 127 (-17) $400,000

Poipu Bay GC & Hyatt Regency Kauai Resort & Spa

Koloa, Kauai, HI

November 23-24, 2004

Purse: $1,000,000
Par: 36-36–72
Yards: 7,108

FORMAT: Two days of medal play. A sudden-death playoff is conducted in the event of a tie after 36 holes.

LEADERS: First Round—Retief Goosen shot a 7-under-par 65 to open a one-stroke lead over Vijay Singh. Phil Mickelson was three strokes back and Todd Hamilton five strokes behind.

Second Round—Mickelson went out in an event record 28, building a two-stroke lead over Singh and Goosen. Mickelson's front nine featured six birdies and an eagle. Mickelson added five back-nine birdies to finish with an event and career-record 59. Singh was runner-up, five strokes back at 132 after a second straight 66. Goosen finished third with a 68 and 133, and Hamilton fourth after a closing 75 and 145 total.

WEATHER: Sunny to open first-round play, with a SE wind of 2-12 mph and 89-degree temperature. In the second round, partly cloudy with temperature of 79 degrees and a NW wind 2-4 mph.

Check out the 2005 PGA Grand Slam of Golf, November 22-23 on TNT

ORDER OF FINISH

Phil Mickelson	1	68-59	127	$400,000
Vijay Singh	2	66-66	132	250,000
Retief Goosen	3	65-68	133	200,000
Todd Hamilton	4	70-75	145	150,000

NOTES

***Phil Mickelson** posted a 59 on day two for a two-day total of 127, tying the tournament record. He topped PGA champion **Vijay Singh** by five strokes. Mickelson had 11 birdies, an eagle and no bogeys. He had just 24 putts, including 11 on the front nine. Mickelson's previous competitive career low was 61 at the 2001 Greater Hartford Open. His 2004 season low was a 63 at the Bob Hope Chrysler Classic.*

A capsule look at Mickelson's 59, which is an unofficial TOUR score:

***No. 1:** Driver, wedge, 40 feet, two-putt, PAR*
***No. 2:** Driver, 5-iron over green, two-putt, BIRDIE*
***No. 3:** 4-iron, 30 feet, one-putt, BIRDIE*
***No. 4:** Driver, wedge, eight feet, one-putt, BIRDIE*
***No. 5:** Driver, wedge, six feet, one-putt, BIRDIE*
***No. 6:** Driver, 3-wood, 20 feet, one-putt, EAGLE*
***No. 7:** 8-iron, four feet, one-putt, BIRDIE*
***No. 8:** 3-wood, sand wedge into greenside bunker, six feet, one-putt, PAR*
***No. 9:** Driver, 9-iron, 15 feet, one-putt, BIRDIE*
OUT: 28 (8-under par)
***No. 10:** Driver, 9-iron, six feet, two-putt, PAR*
***No. 11:** 5-iron, 30 feet, two-putt, PAR*
***No. 12:** Driver, wedge, 4-feet, one-putt, BIRDIE*
***No. 13:** 3-wood, sand wedge, 50 feet, one-putt, BIRDIE*
***No. 14:** Driver, 3-wood, chip, eight feet, one-putt, BIRDIE*
***No. 15:** Driver, wedge, 40 feet, two-putt, PAR*
***No. 16:** 3-wood, 4-iron, 30 feet, one-putt, BIRDIE*
***No. 17:** 4-iron right of green, chip, two feet, one-putt, PAR*
***No. 18:** Driver, 6-iron, nine feet, two-putt, BIRDIE*
IN: 31 (5-under par)
TOTAL: 59 (13-under par)

TOURNAMENT HISTORY

Year	Winner	Score	Runner-up	Score	Location	Par/Yards
PGA GRAND SLAM OF GOLF						
[Conducted as an 18-hole event from 1979-90, inclusive]						
1979	Andy North+	73	John Mahaffey	77	Oak Hill CC, Rochester, NY	70/6,974
	Gary Player	73	Jack Nicklaus	77		
1980	Lanny Wadkins	71	Hale Irwin	73	Hazeltine National GC, Chaska, MN	72/7,148
1981	Lee Trevino	68	Tom Watson	71	Breakers West GC, West Palm Beach, FL	71/7,100
1982	Bill Rogers	71	Larry Nelson	75	PGA National GC (Champion) Palm Beach Gardens, FL	72/7,137
1986	Greg Norman	70	Fuzzy Zoeller	72	Kemper Lakes GC Hawthorn Woods, IL	72/7,127
1988	Larry Nelson	69	Larry Mize	70	Kemper Lakes GC Hawthorn Woods, IL	72/7,127
			Scott Simpson	70		
1989	Curtis Strange	73	Craig Stadler	75	Kemper Lakes GC, Hawthorn Woods, IL	
1990	Andy North	70	Craig Stadler	74	Kemper Lakes GC Hawthorn Woods, IL	
[Conducted as a 36-hole stroke-play event from 1991 to present, with the exception of 1998-99, when it was match play]						
1991	Ian Woosnam	135	Ian Baker-Finch	139	Kauai Lagoons Resort, Kauai, HI	72/7,035
1992	Nick Price*	137	Tom Kite	137	PGA West (Nicklaus Resort) La Quinta, CA	72/7,126
1993	Greg Norman	145	Paul Azinger	147	PGA West (Nicklaus Resort) La Quinta, CA	72/7,126
1994	Greg Norman	136	Nick Price	139	Poipu Bay GC, Kauai, HI	72/6,957
1995	Ben Crenshaw	140	Steve Elkington	141	Poipu Bay GC, Kauai, HI	72/6,957
1996	Tom Lehman	134	Steve Jones	136	Poipu Bay GC, Kauai, HI	72/6,957
1997	Ernie Els	133	Tiger Woods	136	Poipu Bay GC, Kauai, HI	72/6,957
1998	Tiger Woods	2-Up	Vijay Singh		Poipu Bay GC, Kauai, HI;	72/6,957
1999	Tiger Woods	3 and 2	David Love III		Poipu Bay GC, Kauai, HI;	72/6,957
2000	Tiger Woods*	139	Vijay Singh	139	Poipu Bay GC, Kauai, HI	72/6,957
2001	Tiger Woods	132	David Toms	135	Poipu Bay GC, Kauai, HI	72/6,957
2002	Tiger Woods#	127	Justin Leonard	141	Poipu Bay GC, Kauai, HI	72/7,081
			Davis Love III			
2003	Jim Furyk	135	Mike Weir	143	Poipu Bay GC, Kauai, HI	72/7,081
2004	Phil Mickelson#	127	Vijay Singh	132	Poipu Bay GC, Kauai, HI	72/7,108

*KEY: + = No sudden-death playoff was conducted * = Won sudden-death playoff # = 36-hole scoring record*

2004 Target World Challenge

Presented by Williiams *[Unofficial event]*

Winner: TIGER WOODS
67-66-69-66 268 (-16) $1,250,000

Sherwood Country Club

Thousand Oaks, CA

December 9-12, 2004

Purse: $5,250,000
Par: 36-35—71
Yards: 6,988

LEADERS: First Round—Jim Furyk, Tiger Woods and Colin Montgomerie posted 4-under-par 66s to take a one-stroke lead over Fred Couples, Miguel Angel Jimenez and Padraig Harrington.

Second Round—Woods and Montgomerie moved to 9-under par 133 to lead Haas and Furyk by two strokes.
Third Round—Montgomerie was at 13-under 200, two strokes ahead of Woods, Haas and Furyk.

CUT: There was no 36-hole cut; All 16 players completed 72 holes.

WEATHER: Sunny all week, with cool temperatures in the early morning. Afternoon highs reached the upper 70s.

Check out the 2005 Target World Challenge, December 8-11 on USA/ABC

ORDER OF FINISH

Player	Pos.	Scores	Money
Tiger Woods	1	67-66-69-66—268	$1,250,000
Padraig Harrington	2	68-69-67-66—270	750,000
Colin Montgomerie	T3	67-66-67-71—271	447,500
Jay Haas	T3	69-66-67-69—271	447,500
Miguel Angel Jimenez	5	68-69-66-70—273	$290,000
Jim Furyk	6	67-68-67-74—276	240,000
Stewart Cink	7	70-69-69-70—278	220,000
Fred Couples	T8	68-70-71-70—279	205,000
Vijay Singh	T8	74-69-68-68—279	205,000
Chad Campbell	10	70-68-69-73—280	190,000
Chris DiMarco	11	69-67-70-75—281	$185,000
Davis Love III	T12	70-66-74-72—282	172,500
John Daly	T12	73-69-75-65—282	172,500
Kenny Perry	14	73-73-69-69—284	165,000
Todd Hamilton	T15	73-69-74-73—289	155,000
Stephen Ames	T15	74-69-74-72—289	155,000

NOTES

Since the Target World Challenge moved to Sherwood Country Club in 2000, only four times has a player managed to record four rounds in the 60s. ***Tiger Woods*** *did it in 2000 when he finished second to* ***Davis Love III****. While Woods,* ***Padraig Harrington*** *and* ***Jay Haas*** *all accomplished the feat in 2004.*

In 2003, ***Davis Love III*** *became the first multiple winner of the Target World Challenge.* ***Tiger Woods*** *matched him in 2004 with his second victory at Sherwood Country Club.*

Tiger Woods *leads the career money list at the Target World Challenge with $4,080,000. Woods donates his earnings from the Target World Challenge back to his foundation.*

TOURNAMENT HISTORY

Year	Winner	Score	Runner-up	Score	Location	Par/Yards
WILLIAMS WORLD CHALLENGE PRESENTED BY TARGET						
1999	Tom Lehman	267	David Duval	270	Grayhawk GC, Scottsdale, AZ	70/7,066
2000	Davis Love III	266	Tiger Woods	268	Sherwood CC, Thousand Oaks, CA	72/7,025
2001	Tiger Woods	273	Vijay Singh	276	Sherwood CC, Thousand Oaks, CA	72/7,025
2002	Padraig Harrington	268	Tiger Woods	270	Sherwood CC, Thousand Oaks, CA	72/7,025
TARGET WORLD CHALLENGE PRESENTED BY WILLIAMS						
2003	Davis Love III	277	Tiger Woods	279	Sherwood CC, Thousand Oaks, CA	72/7,025
2004	Tiger Woods	268	Padraig Harringon	270	Sherwood CC, Thousand Oaks, CA	71/6,988

2004 Wendy's 3-Tour Challenge *[Unofficial event]*

Jay Haas, PGA TOUR Team

Reflection Bay GC

Henderson, NV

November 9, 2004 (Competition date)
December 18-19, 2004 (TV Dates)

Purse: $900,000
Par: 36-36—72
Yards: PGA TOUR - 7,225
Champions Tour - 7,040
LPGA - 6,319

First Place: LPGA, $340,000
Juli Inkster
Cristie Kerr
Grace Park

Second Place: Champions Tour, $335,000
Peter Jacobsen
Tom Kite
Craig Stadler

Third Place: PGA TOUR, $225,000
Fred Couples
John Daly
Jay Haas

Victories By Tour

PGA TOUR	6
Champions Tour	4
LPGA	3

NOTE: The three LPGA team members made six birdies in the last three holes to rally past the PGA TOUR and Champions Tour.

Check out the 2005 Wendy's Three-Tour Challenge, December 17-18 on ABC

NOTES

The Wendy's 3-Tour Challenge is an annual tournament pitting three-member teams representing the PGA TOUR, Champions Tour and LPGA Tour against each other with $900,000 in prize money.

TOURNAMENT HISTORY

WENDY'S 3-TOUR CHALLENGE

Year	Winner	Team Members	Location
1992	LPGA	Nancy Lopez, Dottie Pepper, Patty Sheehan	New Albany CC, New Albany, OH
1993	Champions Tour	Raymond Floyd, Jack Nicklaus, Chi Chi Rodriguez	Colleton River Plantation, Hilton Head, SC
1994	PGA TOUR	Paul Azinger, Fred Couples, Greg Norman	PGA West (Nicklaus Resort Course), La Quinta, CA
1995	Champions Tour	Raymond Floyd, Hale Irwin, Jack Nicklaus	Muirfield Village GC, Dublin, OH
1996	PGA TOUR	Fred Couples, Davis Love III, Payne Stewart	SouthShore GC, Lake Las Vegas Resort, Henderson, NV
1997	PGA TOUR	Fred Couples, Tom Lehman, Phil Mickelson	SouthShore GC, Lake Las Vegas Resort, Henderson, NV
1998	Champions Tour	Hale Irwin, Gil Morgan, Larry Nelson	Reflection Bay GC, Lake Las Vegas Resort, Henderson, NV
1999	Champions Tour	Hale Irwin, Jack Nicklaus, Tom Watson	Reflection Bay GC, Lake Las Vegas Resort, Henderson, NV
2000	PGA TOUR	Notah Begay III, Rocco Mediate, Phil Mickelson	Reflection Bay GC, Lake Las Vegas Resort, Henderson, NV
2001	LPGA	Dottie Pepper, Annika Sorenstam, Karrie Webb	SouthShore GC, Las Vegas Resort, Henderson, NV
2002	PGA TOUR	John Daly, Jim Furyk, Rich Beem	DragonRidge CC, Henderson, NV
2003	PGA TOUR	Mark Calcavecchia, Peter Jacobsen, John Daly	Reflection Bay GC, Henderson, NV
2004	LPGA	Juli Inkster, Cristie Kerr, Grace Park	Reflection Bay GC, Henderson, NV

Tiger Woods won the World Golf Championships-Accenture Match Play Championship for the second consecutive season and placed fourth on the money list.

International Federation of PGA Tours/World Golf Championships

Tiger Woods is the only player to capture all four World Golf Championships titles in his career.

At the 1996 Presidents Cup, golf's five world governing bodies—the European Tour, Japan Golf Tour Organization, PGA TOUR, PGA Tour of Australasia and Sunshine Tour (South Africa)—reached agreement on several key elements of professional golf designed to create new international events, beginning in 1999.

Three major initiatives were outlined at Robert Trent Jones Golf Club, site of the second Presidents Cup:

- Formation of the International Federation of PGA Tours.
- Joint sanctioning by the members of the International Federation of PGA Tours of significant competitions, including some at the world championship level for the game's top players.
- A structure for a generally accepted worldwide ranking system.

Those "significant competitions" were announced in October 1997 when the Federation introduced the World Golf Championships.

The first three jointly sanctioned championships—the Accenture Match Play Championship, the NEC Invitational and the American Express Championship—were launched in 1999. Jeff Maggert won the first event and Tiger Woods the latter two. The addition of the World Cup was announced in December 1999 and debuted in December 2000.

The 2005 World Golf Championships will begin in February with the Accenture Match Play Championship at La Costa Resort and Spa in Carlsbad, CA. In August, the NEC Invitational will be held at Firestone CC's South Course in Akron, OH. In September, the American Express Championship will return to the United States for the second time when it is held at San Francisco's Harding Park Golf Course. The series will conclude in November as Portugal's Victoria Clube de Golfe at Vilamoura Golf Resort will play host to the Algarve World Cup.

The World Golf Championships events feature players from around the world competing against one another in varied formats (match and stroke play and team competition). The championships rotate through a variety of outstanding venues worldwide. Roughly half of the golf courses are in the United States and half at venues represented by the International Federation of PGA Tours. World Golf Championships events have been contested on five continents.

The Asian Tour joined the International Federation of PGA Tours as a full-fledged member in November 1999, while the Canadian Tour was named an associate member in March 2000.

Accenture, NEC and American Express are the umbrella sponsors of the World Golf Championships. JELD-WEN is an official sponsor of all four events, while Kohler is a sponsor for all except the WGC-NEC Invitational.

Fields for the World Golf Championships are filled primarily through the Official World Golf Ranking, which is endorsed by all the sport's major professional organizations and governing bodies and individual Tour's Official Money Lists/Orders of Merit.

www.worldgolfchampionships.com

Accenture Match Play Championship

Dates: February 21-27, 2005
Site: La Costa Resort and Spa, Carlsbad, CA, USA
Format: Match play (hole-by-hole competition)
Field: Top 64 available players based on the Official World Golf Ranking released Monday, Feb. 14, 2005
Champion: Tiger Woods, 2004
Contact: Michael Garten, Executive Director
Phone: 858-481-6291 Fax: 858-481-9464

About Accenture:
Accenture is a global management consulting, technology services and outsourcing company. Committed to delivering innovation, Accenture collaborates with its clients to help them become high-performance businesses and governments. With deep industry and business process expertise, broad global resources and a proven track record, Accenture can mobilize the right people, skills and technologies to help clients improve their performance. With more than 100,000 people in 48 countries, the company generated net revenues of US$13.67 billion for the fiscal year ended Aug. 31, 2004. Its home page is www.accenture.com.

World Golf Championships® accenture Match Play Championship

NEC Invitational

Dates: August 16-21, 2005
Site: Firestone Country Club (South Course), Akron, OH, USA
Format: 72 holes, stroke play
Field: Approx. 75 players, consisting of members of the last-named United States and International Presidents Cup teams; members of the last-named U.S. and European Ryder Cup teams; if not otherwise eligible, players ranked among the top 50, including any players tied for 50th place, on the Official World Golf Ranking as of Monday of tournament week; if not otherwise eligible, winners of worldwide events since the prior year's NEC Invitational with an Official World Golf Ranking strength-of-field rating of 100 points or more; and if not otherwise eligible, the winner of one selected tournament from the PGA Tour of Australasia, Sunshine Tour (South Africa), Asian Tour and Japan Golf Tour.
Champion: Stewart Cink, 2004
Contact: Tom Strong, Executive Director
Phone: 330-644-2299 Fax: 330-644-7187

About NEC Corporation:
NEC Corporation (NASDAQ: NIPNY) (FTSE: 6701q.l)is one of the world's leading providers of Internet, broadband network and enterprise business solutions dedicated to meeting the specialized needs of its diverse and global base of customers. Ranked as one of the world's top patent-producing companies, NEC delivers tailored solutions in the key fields of computer, networking and electron devices, by integrating its technical strengths in IT and Networks, and by providing advanced semiconductor solutions through NEC Electronics Corporation. The NEC Group employs more than 143,000 people worldwide and had net sales of approximately $47 billion in the fiscal year ended March 2004. For additional information, please visit the NEC home page at: http://www.nec.com .

World Golf Championships® NEC INVITATIONAL

American Express Championship

Dates: October 4-9, 2005
Site: Harding Park Golf Course, San Francisco, CA, USA
Format: 72 holes, stroke play
Field: Approx. 70 players, including the top 50 available from the Official World Golf Ranking the week prior and leaders of the six Tours' Official Money Lists/Orders of Merit.
Champion: Ernie Els, 2004
Contact: Ron Cross, Executive Director
Phone: 415-278-9989 Fax: 415-278-9780

About American Express:
American Express Company is a diversified worldwide travel, financial and network services company founded in 1850. It is a world leader in charge and credit cards, Travelers Cheques, travel, financial planning, business services, insurance and international banking.

World Golf Championships® American Express Championship

Algarve World Cup

Dates: November 15-20, 2005
Site: Victoria Clube de Golfe, Vilamoura Golf Resort, Algarve, Portugal
Format: 72 holes, team competition consisting of two rounds of four-ball medal play (better ball) and two rounds of foursomes medal play (alternate shot).
Field: 24 two-man teams representing 24 countries.
Champions: England (Paul Casey/Luke Donald), 2004
Contact: Peter Adams/James Cramer
Phone: 011-44-134-484-0400/904-273-3293

World Golf Championships® WORLD CUP

The Presidents Cup

The Presidents Cup will return to the United States and the Robert Trent Jones Golf Club in Lake Manassas, Virginia this year for the fourth time, with Jack Nicklaus and Gary Player serving as Captains of the United States and International Teams, respectively.

History

The Presidents Cup, which will be played for the sixth time in 2005, was developed to give the world's best non-European players an opportunity to compete in international team match-play competition.

A biennial event played in non-Ryder Cup years, the first Presidents Cup was played Sept. 16-18, 1994 at Robert Trent Jones Golf Club. The U.S. Team, captained by Hale Irwin, defeated Captain David Graham's International side, 20-12.

The 2003 Presidents Cup was originally scheduled for November 2002, but was postponed one year in the wake of the September 11, 2001 terrorist attacks on the United States. Played at The Links at Fancourt Hotel and Country Club Estate in George, South Africa, the competition ended in a tie. After both teams completed regulation tied at 17 points, Ernie Els of the International Team and Tiger Woods of the U.S. were designated to represent their teams in a sudden-death playoff. After three playoff holes, and as darkness was descending, Captains Player and Jack Nicklaus, in the spirit of the competition, decided that the two teams would share the Cup.

Former U.S. President Gerald Ford presided over the first Presidents Cup as Honorary Chairman. Former President George Bush, like Ford an avid golfer, served as Honorary Chairman for the 1996 Presidents Cup. Australian Prime Minister John Howard was Honorary Chairman for the 1998 event. In 2000, President Bill Clinton made history when he became the first sitting president to serve as Honorary Chairman. In 2003, Thabo Mbeki, President of the Republic of South Africa, was Honorary Chairman. Current President George W. Bush will be the Honorary Chairman of the 2005 Presidents Cup.

Jack Nicklaus (L) and Gary Player return as captains after the 2003 Presidents Cup tie.

Eligibility

Members of the 2005 U.S. Team will be selected based on official earnings from the start of the 2004 season through the 2005 PGA Championship. International Team players for the 2005 Presidents Cup will be chosen on the basis of the Official World Golf Ranking. International Teams do not include players eligible for the European Ryder Cup Team.

The eligibility rankings are used to select 10 members for both squads. The 12-man teams are rounded out by two Captain's Choices per team.

Structure and Scoring

The Presidents Cup competition consists of 34 matches—11 foursomes (alternate shot) and 11 four-ball (better ball) matches. There are 12 singles matches involving all players on the final Sunday. All matches are worth one point each, for a total of 34 points. There are no playoffs for foursomes or four-ball, with each side receiving ½-point. Singles matches all square after 18 holes will go to extra holes until a team winner is determined. In a change inspired by the events of the 2003 Presidents Cup, if the match is deadlocked at the end of singles play, the competition will be deemed a tie and the teams will share The Presidents Cup.

The Presidents Cup follows the PGA TOUR creed of giving back. There is no purse for the players. Net revenues are divided into equal shares that the players and Captains designate for charities or golf-related projects of their choice. Contributions in their names are made through PGA TOUR Charities, Inc. The first five Presidents Cups generated $10.05 million for charities worldwide.

The Presidents Cup – 2003

The Links Course at Fancourt Hotel and Country Club Estate

George, Western Cape Province, South Africa
Par: 36-37—73; Yards: 6,858 Nov. 20-23, 2003
Honorary Chairman: President Thabo Mbeki
Captains: Jack Nicklaus, Gary Player

DAY ONE

Foursomes—International 3½, United States 2½

Nick Price/Mike Weir (Int.) def. David Toms/Phil Mickelson, 1-up
Retief Goosen/Vijay Singh (Int.) def. Chris DiMarco/Jerry Kelly, 3 and 2
Davis Love III/Kenny Perry (U.S.) def. Peter Lonard/Tim Clark, 4 and 2
Ernie Els/Adam Scott (Int.) def. Justin Leonard/Jim Furyk, 1-up
Jay Haas/Fred Funk (U.S.) halved with Robert Allenby/Stephen Leaney
Tiger Woods/Charles Howell III (U.S.) def. Stuart Appleby/K.J. Choi, 4 and 3

DAY TWO

Four-ball—United States 3, International 2

Allenby/Weir (Int.) def. Mickelson/Toms, 3 and 1
Perry/Love III (U.S.) def. Goosen/Choi, 2 and 1
Furyk/Haas (U.S.) def. Appleby/Scott, 6 and 5
DiMarco/Leonard (U.S.) def. Singh/Price, 1-up
Els/Clark (Int.) def. Woods/Howell III, 5 and 3

Totals: International 5½, United States 5½

Foursomes—United States 4; International 1

Perry/Kelly (U.S.) def. Choi/Lonard, 2 and 1
Funk/Toms (U.S.) def. Allenby/Leaney, 4 and 3
Woods/Howell III (U.S.) def. Clark/Goosen, 1-up
Els/Scott (Int.) def. DiMarco/Mickelson, 1-up
Furyk/Leonard (U.S.) def. Singh/Weir, 5 and 4

Totals: United States 9½, International 6½

DAY THREE

Four-ball—International 6, United States 0

Lonard/Leaney (Int.) def. Funk/Mickelson, 2 and 1
Els/Clark (Int.) def. Furyk/Haas, 3 and 2
Scott/Choi (Int.) def. Perry/Kelly, 5 and 4
Singh/Goosen (Int.) def. Woods/Howell, 2 and 1
Weir/Allenby (Int.) def. DiMarco/Leonard, 1-up
Price/Appleby (Int.) def Love/Toms, 2 and 1

Totals: International 12½, United States 9½

DAY FOUR

Singles—United States 7½, International 4½

Furyk (U.S.) def. Weir, 3 and 1
Kelly (U.S.) def. Clark, 1-up
Perry (U.S.) def. Price, 1-up
Choi (Int.) def. Leonard, 4 and 2
Howell (U.S.) def. Scott, 5 and 4
Haas (U.S.) def. Leaney, 4 and 3
Goosen (Int.) def. Mickelson, 2 and 1
Lonard (Int.) def. Funk, 4 and 3
DiMarco (U.S.) def. Appleby, 1-up
Singh (Int.) def. Toms, 4 and 3
Woods (U.S.) def. Els, 4 and 3
Love (U.S.) halved with Allenby

Final Total: International 17, United States 17

Playoff: Woods (U.S.) and Els (Int.) halved three sudden-death holes with pars. The match was called because of darkness and deemed a tie. The teams opted to share The Presidents Cup for the next two years.

The Presidents Cup – 2000

Robert Trent Jones GC

Prince William County, VA
Par: 36-36—72 Yards: 7,315 October 19-22, 2000
Honorary Chairman: President Bill Clinton
Captains: Ken Venturi, Peter Thomson

FIRST DAY
Foursomes—United States 5, International 0
Phil Mickelson/Tom Lehman (U.S.) def. Steve Elkington/Greg Norman, 5 and 4
Hal Sutton/Jim Furyk (U.S.) def. Robert Allenby/Stuart Appleby, 1-up
Stewart Cink/Kirk Triplett (U.S.) def. Mike Weir/Retief Goosen, 3 and 2
Tiger Woods/Notah Begay III (U.S.) def. Vijay Singh/Ernie Els, 1-up
David Duval/Davis Love III (U.S.) def. Nick Price/Carlos Franco, 1-up

SECOND DAY
Four-Ball—International 4, United States 1
Michael Campbell/Goosen (Int.) def. Sutton/Paul Azinger, 4 and 3
Weir/Elkington (Int.) def. Lehman/Loren Roberts, 3 and 2
Price/Norman (Int.) def. Furyk/Duval, 6 and 5
Shigeki Maruyama/Franco (Int.) def. Woods/Begay, 3 and 2
Mickelson/Love (U.S.) def. Singh/Els, 2 and 1
Totals: United States 6, International 4

Foursomes—United States 4, International 1
Cink/Triplett (U.S.) def. Allenby/Appleby, 2 and 1
Roberts/Azinger (U.S.) def. Franco/Maruyama, 5 and 4
Woods/Begay (U.S.) def. Singh/Els, 6 and 5
Sutton/Lehman (U.S.) def. Campbell/Goosen, 4 and 2
Price/Weir (Int.) def. Mickelson/Duval, 6 and 4
Totals: United States 10, International 5

THIRD DAY
Four-Ball—United States 4, International 1
Sutton/Furyk (U.S.) def. Campbell/Norman, 6 and 5
Lehman/Mickelson (U.S.) def. Weir/Elkington, 2 and 1
Love/Duval (U.S.) def. Price/Els, 3 and 2
Triplett/Cink (U.S.) def. Allenby/Franco, 1-up
Singh/Goosen (Int.) def. Woods/Begay, 2 and 1
Totals: United States 14, International 6

FOURTH DAY
Singles—United States 7½, International 4½
Allenby (Int.) def. Azinger, 2 and 1
Duval (U.S.) def. Price, 2 and 1
Roberts (U.S.) def. Appleby, 3 and 2
Weir (Int.) def. Mickelson, 4 and 3
Love (U.S.) def. Els, 4 and 3
Elkington (Int.) def. Lehman, 1-up
Woods (U.S.) def. Singh, 2 and 1
Cink (U.S.) def. Norman, 2 and 1
Franco (Int.) def. Sutton, 6 and 5
Furyk (U.S.) def. Maruyama, 5 and 4
Triplett (U.S.) halved with Campbell
Begay (U.S.) def. Goosen, 1-up
Totals: United States 21½, International 10½

The Presidents Cup – 1998

Royal Melbourne GC

Melbourne, Victoria, Australia
Par: 36-36—72 Yards: 6,981 December 11-13, 1998
Honorary Chairman: Prime Minister John Howard
Captains: Jack Nicklaus, Peter Thomson

FIRST DAY
Foursomes—International 3½, United States 1½
Frank Nobilo/Greg Turner (Int.) def. Mark O'Meara/David Duval, 1-up
Greg Norman/Steve Elkington (Int.) def. Jim Furyk/John Huston, 2-up
Shigeki Maruyama/Craig Parry (Int.) def Lee Janzen/Scott Hoch, 3 and 2
Tiger Woods/Fred Couples (U.S.) def. Ernie Els/Vijay Singh, 5 and 4
Davis Love III/Justin Leonard (U.S.) halved with Stuart Appleby/Nick Price

Four-Ball—International 3½, United States 1½
Norman/Elkington (Int.) def. O'Meara/Furyk, 2 and 1
Maruyama/Joe Ozaki (Int.) def. Mark Calcavecchia/Huston, 4 and 3
Duval/Phil Mickelson (U.S.) halved with Els/Price
Couples/Love (U.S.) def. Parry/Carlos Franco, 1-up
Appleby/Singh (Int.) def. Leonard/Woods, 2 and 1
Totals: International 7, United States 3

SECOND DAY
Foursomes—International 4½, United States ½
Nobilo/Turner (Int.) def. Leonard/Love, 2-up
Janzen/Calcavecchia (U.S.) halved with Norman/Elkington
Maruyama/Parry (Int.) def. Woods/Couples, 1-up
Appleby/Price (Int.) def. Duval/Mickelson, 1-up
Els/Singh (Int.) def. Hoch/Furyk, 6 and 4

Four-Ball—International 3, United States 2
O'Meara/Hoch (U.S.) def. Nobilo/Turner, 1-up
Els/Singh (Int.) def. Woods/Huston, 1-up
Maruyama/Ozaki (Int.) def. Duval/Mickelson, 1-up
Janzen/Calcavecchia (U.S.) def. Price/Franco, 3 and 2
Norman/Elkington (Int.) def. Couples/Love, 2 and 1
Totals: International 14½, United States 5½

THIRD DAY
Singles—United States 6, International 6
Parry (Int.) def. Leonard, 5 and 3
Price (Int.) def. Duval, 2 and 1
Furyk (U.S.) def. Nobilo, 4 and 2
Mickelson (U.S.) halved with Franco
Maruyama (Int.) def. Huston, 3 and 2
Hoch (U.S.) def. Ozaki, 4 and 3
Calcavecchia (U.S.) halved with Turner
Janzen (U.S.) halved with Elkington
Els (Int.) def. Love, 1-up
Couples (U.S.) halved with Singh
Woods (U.S.) def. Norman, 1-up
O'Meara (U.S.) def. Appleby, 1-up
Totals: International 20½, United States 11½

Formats

Match play: Competition where the winner of holes is the determining factor as opposed to total strokes in medal play.
Four-ball: A match where two play their own balls against the other twosome's two balls, with the better-ball score of each side winning the hole.
Foursomes: A match where two play against two and each side plays one ball, with partners alternating shots from the tee until completion of the hole.
Singles: One-on-one competition using a match-play format.

The Presidents Cup – 1996

Robert Trent Jones GC

Prince William County, VA
Par: 36-36—72 Yards: 7,239 September 13-15, 1996
Honorary Chairman: Former President George H.W. Bush
Captains: Arnold Palmer, Peter Thomson

FIRST DAY

Four-Ball—United States 4, International 1
Fred Couples/Davis Love III (U.S.) def. Greg Norman/Robert Allenby, 2 and 1
Ernie Els/Mark McNulty (Int.) def. Scott Hoch/Mark Brooks, 2-up
Phil Mickelson/Corey Pavin (U.S.) def. Vijay Singh/Jumbo Ozaki, 2 and 1
Mark O'Meara/David Duval (U.S.) def. Steve Elkington/Frank Nobilo, 3 and 2
Tom Lehman/Steve Stricker (U.S.) def. Nick Price/Peter Senior, 4 and 2

Foursomes—United States 3½, International 1½
Kenny Perry/Justin Leonard (U.S.) def. Price/David Frost, 3 and 2
O'Meara/Duval (U.S.) def. Nobilo/Craig Parry, 2 and 1
Elkington/Singh (Int.) def. Lehman/Stricker, 2-up
Mickelson/Pavin (U.S.) halved with Els/McNulty
Couples/Love (U.S.) def. Norman/Allenby, 1-up
Totals: United States 7½, International 2½

SECOND DAY

Four-Ball—International 3, United States 2
Price/Elkington (Int.) def. Leonard/Lehman, 2-up
Norman/Allenby (Int.) def. Stricker/Pavin, 1-up
Perry/Hoch (U.S.) def. Parry/Nobilo, 2 and 1
Ozaki/Singh (Int.) def. Love/Couples, 2 and 1
O'Meara/Duval (U.S.) def. Els/McNulty, 4 and 3
Totals: United States 9½, International 5½

Foursomes—International 4, United States 1
Senior/Frost (Int.) def. Pavin/Mickelson, 3 and 2
Nobilo/Allenby (Int.) def. Love/Brooks, 3 and 2
Price/McNulty (Int.) def. Perry/Leonard, 3 and 1
Norman/Els (Int.) def. Lehman/Stricker, 1-up
O'Meara/Hoch (U.S.) def. Elkington/Singh, 1-up
Totals: United States 10½, International 9½

THIRD DAY

Singles—United States 6, International 6
Parry (Int.) def. Brooks, 5 and 4
Duval (U.S.) def. Senior, 3 and 2
O'Meara (U.S.) def. Price, 1-up
Frost (Int.) def. Perry, 7 and 6
Stricker (U.S.) def. Allenby, 6 and 5
Hoch (U.S.) def. McNulty, 1-up
Love (U.S.) def. Ozaki, 5 and 4
Elkington (Int.) def. Leonard, 1-up
Els (Int.) def. Mickelson, 3 and 2
Norman (Int.) def. Pavin, 3 and 1
Nobilo (Int.) def. Lehman, 3 and 2
Couples (U.S.) def. Singh, 2 and 1
Totals: United States 16½, International 15½

The Presidents Cup – 1994

Robert Trent Jones GC

Prince William County, VA
Par: 36-36—72 Yards: 7,239 September 16-18, 1994
Honorary Chairman: Former President Gerald R. Ford
Captains: Hale Irwin, David Graham

FIRST DAY

Four-Ball—United States 5, International 0
Corey Pavin/Jeff Maggert (U.S.) def. Steve Elkington/Vijay Singh, 2 and 1
Jay Haas/Scott Hoch (U.S.) def. Fulton Allem/David Frost, 6 and 5
Davis Love III/Fred Couples (U.S.) def. Nick Price/Bradley Hughes, 1-up
John Huston/Jim Gallagher, Jr. (U.S.) def. Craig Parry/Robert Allenby, 4 and 2
Tom Lehman/Phil Mickelson (U.S.) def. Frank Nobilo/Peter Senior, 3 and 2

Foursomes—United States 2½, International 2½
Hale Irwin/Loren Roberts (U.S.) def. Frost/Allem, 3 and 1
Haas/Hoch (U.S.) def. Parry/Tsukasa Watanabe, 4 and 3
Nobilo/Allenby (Int.) def. Pavin/Maggert, 2 and 1
Elkington/Singh (Int.) def. Mickelson/Lehman, 2 and 1
Price/Mark McNulty (Int.) halved with Love/Gallagher
Totals: United States 7½, International 2½

SECOND DAY

Four-Ball—International 3½, United States 1½
Allem/McNulty (Int.) def. Gallagher/Huston, 4 and 3
Watanabe/Singh (Int.) def. Haas/Hoch, 3 and 1
Parry/Hughes (Int.) def. Roberts/Lehman, 4 and 3
Couples/Love (U.S.) def. Nobilo/Allenby, 2-up
Price/Elkington (Int.) halved with Mickelson/Pavin
Totals: United States 9, International 6

Foursomes—United States 3, International 2
Frost/Senior (Int.) def. Irwin/Haas, 6 and 5
Pavin/Roberts (U.S.) def. Parry/Allem, 1-up
Singh/Elkington (Int.) def. Maggert/Huston, 3 and 2
Love/Gallagher (U.S.) def. Nobilo/Allenby, 7 and 5
Mickelson/Lehman (U.S.) def. Hughes/McNulty, 3 and 2
Totals: United States 12, International 8

THIRD DAY

Singles—United States 8, International 4
Irwin (U.S.) def. Allenby, 1-up
Haas (U.S.) def. McNulty, 4 and 3
Gallagher (U.S.) def. Watanabe, 4 and 3
Mickelson (U.S.) halved with Allem
Singh (Int.) halved with Lehman
Senior (Int.) def. Huston, 3 and 2
Hoch (U.S.) halved with Frost
Maggert (U.S.) def. Hughes, 2 and 1
Nobilo (Int.) halved with Roberts
Couples (U.S.) def. Price, 1-up
Love (U.S.) def. Elkington, 1-up
Parry (Int.) def. Pavin, 1-up
Totals: United States 20, International 12

All-Time Presidents Cup Records

U.S. Team

Player (Years)	Overall (Win-Loss-Halve)	Four-Ball (W-L-H)	Foursomes (W-L-H)	Singles (W-L-H)
Paul Azinger (2000)	1-2-0	0-1-0	1-0-0	0-1-0
Notah Begay III (2000)	3-2-0	0-2-0	2-0-0	1-0-0
Mark Brooks (1996)	0-3-0	0-1-0	0-1-0	0-1-0
Mark Calcavecchia (1998)	1-1-2	1-1-0	0-0-1	0-0-1
Stewart Cink (2000)	4-0-0	1-0-0	2-0-0	1-0-0
Fred Couples (1994, 1996, 1998)	8-3-1	4-2-0	2-1-0	2-0-1
Chris DiMarco (2003)	2-3-0	1-1-0	0-2-0	1-0-0
David Duval (1996, 1998, 2000)	7-6-1	3-2-1	2-3-0	2-1-0
Fred Funk (2003)	1-2-1	0-1-0	1-0-1	0-1-0
Jim Furyk (1998, 2000, 2003)	7-6-0	2-3-0	2-3-0	3-0-0
Jim Gallagher, Jr. (1994)	3-1-1	1-1-0	1-0-1	1-0-0
Jay Haas (1994, 2003)	5-3-1	2-2-0	1-0-2	2-0-0
Scott Hoch (1994, 1996, 1998)	7-4-1	3-2-0	2-2-0	2-0-1
Charles Howell III (2003)	3-2-0	0-2-0	2-0-0	1-0-0
John Huston (1994, 1998)	1-7-0	1-3-0	0-2-0	0-2-0
Hale Irwin (1994)	2-1-0	0-0-0	1-1-0	1-0-0
Lee Janzen (1998)	1-1-2	1-0-0	0-1-1	0-0-1
Jerry Kelly (2003)	2-2-0	0-1-0	1-1-0	1-0-0
Tom Lehman (1994, 1996, 2000)	6-8-1	3-3-0	3-3-0	0-2-1
Justin Leonard (1996, 1998, 2003)	3-9-1	1-3-0	2-3-1	0-3-0
Davis Love III (1994, 1996, 1998, 2000, 2003)	14-6-3	7-3-0	4-2-2	3-1-1
Jeff Maggert (1994)	2-2-0	1-0-0	0-2-0	1-0-0
Phil Mickelson (1994, 1996, 1998, 2000, 2003)	6-12-5	4-2-2	2-2-1	0-3-2
Mark O'Meara (1996, 1998)	7-2-0	3-1-0	2-1-0	2-0-0
Corey Pavin (1994, 1996)	3-5-2	2-1-1	1-2-1	0-2-0
Kenny Perry (1996, 2003)	6-3-0	2-1-0	3-1-0	1-1-0
Loren Roberts (1994, 2000)	4-2-1	0-2-0	3-0-0	1-0-1
Steve Stricker (1996)	2-3-0	1-1-0	0-2-0	1-0-0
Hal Sutton (2000)	3-2-0	1-1-0	2-0-0	0-1-0
David Toms (2003)	1-4-0	0-2-0	1-1-0	0-1-0
Kirk Triplett (2000)	3-0-1	1-0-0	2-0-0	0-1-0
Tiger Woods (1998, 2000, 2003)	8-7-0	0-6-0	5-1-0	3-0-0

International Team

Player (Years)	Overall (W-L-H)	Four-Ball (W-L-H)	Foursomes (W-L-H)	Singles (W-L-H)
Fulton Allem (1994)	1-1-1	1-1-0	0-2-0	0-0-1
Robert Allenby (1994, 1996, 2000, 2003)	6-11-2	3-4-0	2-5-1	1-2-1
Stuart Appleby (1998, 2000, 2003)	3-7-1	2-1-0	1-3-1	0-3-0
Michael Campbell (2000)	1-1-1	1-1-0	0-1-0	0-0-1
K.J. Choi (2003)	2-3-0	1-1-0	0-2-0	1-0-0
Tim Clark (2003)	2-3-0	2-0-0	0-2-0	0-1-0
Steve Elkington (1994, 1996, 1998)	8-4-3	3-2-1	4-1-1	1-1-1
Ernie Els (1996, 1998, 2000, 2003)	10-8-2	4-3-1	4-3-1	2-2-0
Carlos Franco (1998, 2000)	2-5-1	1-3-0	0-2-0	1-0-1
David Frost (1994, 1996)	3-3-1	0-1-0	2-2-0	1-0-1
Retief Goosen (2000, 2003)	5-5-0	3-1-0	1-3-0	1-1-0
Bradley Hughes (1994)	1-3-0	1-1-0	0-1-0	0-1-0
Stephen Leaney (2003)	1-2-1	1-0-0	0-1-1	0-1-0
Peter Lonard (2003)	2-2-0	1-0-0	0-2-0	1-0-0
Shigeki Maruyama (1998, 2000)	6-2-0	3-0-0	2-1-0	1-1-0
Mark McNulty (1994, 1996)	3-4-2	2-1-0	1-1-2	0-2-0
Frank Nobilo (1994, 1996, 1998)	5-8-1	0-5-0	4-2-0	1-1-1
Greg Norman (1996, 1998, 2000)	7-6-1	4-2-0	2-2-1	1-2-0
Joe Ozaki (1998)	2-1-0	2-0-0	0-0-0	0-1-0
Jumbo Ozaki (1996)	1-2-0	1-1-0	0-0-0	0-1-0
Craig Parry (1994, 1996, 1998)	6-6-0	1-3-0	2-3-0	3-0-0
Nick Price (1994, 1996, 1998, 2000, 2003)	8-11-4	3-5-2	4-2-2	1-4-0
Adam Scott (2003)	3-2-0	1-1-0	2-0-0	0-1-0
Peter Senior (1994, 1996)	3-3-0	0-2-0	2-0-0	1-1-0
Vijay Singh (1994, 1996, 1998, 2000, 2003)	12-11-2	6-4-0	5-5-0	1-2-2
Greg Turner (1998)	2-1-1	0-1-0	2-0-0	0-0-1
Tsukasa Watanabe (1994)	1-2-0	1-0-0	0-1-0	0-1-0
Mike Weir (2000, 2003)	6-4-0	3-1-0	2-2-0	1-1-0

Ryder Cup Matches

Oakland Hills CC, Bloomfield Hills, MI
Par: 35-35—70
Yards: 7,077
September 17-19, 2004
Captains: Hal Sutton (U.S.), Bernhard Langer (Europe)

FRIDAY

Morning Four-Ball—Europe 3½, United States ½
Colin Montgomerie-Padraig Harrington (Eur.) def. Phil Mickelson-Tiger Woods, 2 and 1
Darren Clarke-Miguel Angel Jimenez (Eur.) def. Davis Love III-Chad Campbell, 5 and 4
Chris Riley-Stewart Cink (U.S.) halved with Paul McGinley-Luke Donald
Sergio Garcia-Lee Westwood (U.S.) def. David Toms-Jim Furyk, 5 and 3

Afternoon Foursomes—Europe 3, United States 1
DiMarco-Jay Haas (U.S.) def. Jimenez-Thomas Levet, 3 and 2
Montgomerie-Harrington (Eur.) def. Love-Fred Funk, 4 and 2
Clarke-Westwood (Eur.) def. Mickelson-Woods, 1-up
Garcia-Donald (Eur.) def. Cink-Kenny Perry, 2 and 1

Totals: Europe 6½, United States 1½

SATURDAY

Morning Four-ball—United States 2½, Europe 1½
Haas-DiMarco (U.S.) halved with Garcia-Westwood
Woods-Riley (U.S.) def. Clarke-Ian Poulter, 4 and 3
Paul Casey-David Howell (Eur.) def. Furyk-Campbell, 1-up
Cink-Love (U.S.) def. Montgomerie-Harrington, 3 and 2

Afternoon Foursomes—Europe 3, United States 1
Clarke-Westwood (Eur.) def. Haas-DiMarco, 5 and 4
Mickelson-Toms (U.S.) def. Jimenez-Levet, 4 and 3
Garcia-Donald (Eur.) def. Furyk-Funk, 1-up
Harrington-McGinley (Eur.) def. Love-Woods, 4 and 3

Totals: Europe 11, United States 5

SUNDAY

Singles—Europe 7½, United States 4½
Woods (U.S.) def. Casey, 3 and 2
Garcia (Eur.) def. Mickelson, 3 and 2
Love III (U.S.) halved with Clarke
Furyk (U.S.) def. Howell, 6 and 4
Westwood (Eur.) def. Perry, 1-up
Montgomerie (Eur.) def. Toms, 1-up
Campbell (U.S.) def. Donald, 5 and 3
DiMarco (U.S.) def. Jimenez, 1-up
Levet (Eur.) def. Funk, 1-up
Poulter (Eur.) def. Riley, 3 and 2
Harrington (Eur.) def. Haas, 1-up
McGinley (Eur.) def. Cink, 3 and 2

Totals: Europe 18½, United States 9½

Year	Location	Date	Results			
1927	Worcester Country Club, Worcester, MA	June 3-4	U.S.	9½	Britain	2½
1929	Moortown, England	April 26-27	Britain	7	U.S.	5
1931	Scioto Country Club, Columbus, OH	June 26-27	U.S.	9	Britain	3
1933	Southport & Ainsdale Courses, England	June 26-27	Britain	6½	U.S.	5½
1935	Ridgewood Country Club, Ridgewood, NJ	Sept. 28-29	U.S.	9	Britain	3
1937	Southport & Ainsdale Courses, England	June 29-30	U.S.	8	Britain	4
	Ryder Cup Matches not held during World War II years.					
1947	Portland Golf Club, Portland, OR	Nov. 1-2	U.S.	11	Britain	1
1949	Ganton Golf Course, Scarborough, England	Sept. 16-17	U.S.	7	Britain	5
1951	Pinehurst Country Club, Pinehurst, NC	Nov. 2-4	U.S.	9½	Britain	2½
1953	Wentworth, England	Oct. 2-3	U.S.	6½	Britain	5½
1955	Thunderbird Ranch and Country Club, Palm Springs, CA	Nov. 5-6	U.S.	8	Britain	4
1957	Lindrick Golf Club, Yorkshire, England	Oct. 4-5	Britain	7½	U.S	4½
1959	Eldorado Country Club, Palm Desert, CA	Nov. 6-7	U.S.	8½	Britain	3½
1961	Royal Lytham and St. Annes Golf Club, St. Annes-On-The-Sea, England	Oct. 13-14	U.S.	14½	Britain	9½
1963	East Lake Country Club, Atlanta, GA	Oct. 11-13	U.S.	23	Britain	9
1965	Royal Birkdale Golf Club, Southport, England	Oct. 7-9	U.S.	19½	Britain	12½
1967	Champions Golf Club, Houston, TX	Oct. 20-22	U.S.	23½	Britain	8½
1969	Royal Birkdale Golf Club, Southport, England	Sept. 18-20	U.S.	16	Britain	16 (Tie)
1971	Old Warson Country Club, St. Louis, MO	Sept. 16-18	U.S.	18½	Britain	13½
1973	Muirfield, Scotland	Sept. 20-22	U.S.	19	Britain	13
1975	Laurel Valley Golf Club, Ligonier, PA	Sept. 19-21	U.S.	21	Britain	11
1977	Royal Lytham and St. Annes Golf Club, St. Annes-On-The-Sea, England	Sept. 15-17	U.S	12½	Britain	7½
1979	Greenbrier, White Sulphur Springs, WV	Sept. 13-15	U.S.	17	Europe	11
1981	Walton Heath Golf Club, Surrey, England	Sept. 18-20	U.S.	18½	Europe	9½
1983	PGA National Golf Club, Palm Beach Gardens, FL	Oct. 14-16	U.S.	14½	Europe	13½
1985	The Belfry Golf Club, Sutton Coldfield, England	Sept. 13-15	Europe	16½	U.S.	11½
1987	Muirfield Village Golf Club, Dublin, OH	Sept. 24-27	Europe	15	U.S.	13
1989	The Belfry Golf Club, Sutton Coldfield, England	Sept. 22-24	U.S.	14	Europe	14 (Tie)
1991	The Ocean Course, Kiawah Island, SC	Sept. 26-29	U.S.	14½	Europe	13½
1993	The Belfry Golf Club, Sutton Coldfield, England	Sept. 24-26	U.S.	15	Europe	13
1995	Oak Hill Country Club, Rochester, NY	Sept. 22-24	Europe	14½	U.S.	13½
1997	Valderrama Golf Club, Sotogrande, Spain	Sept. 26-28	Europe	14½	U.S.	13½
1999	The Country Club, Brookline, MA	Sept. 24-26	U.S.	14½	Europe	13½
2002	The Belfry Golf Club, Sutton Coldfield, England	Sept. 27-29	Europe	15½	U.S.	12½
2004	Oakland Hills, Bloomfield Hills, MI	Sept. 17-19	Europe	18½	U.S.	9½

(The United States leads the series, 24-9-2.)

Ryder Cup Player Records (Active PGA TOUR Players)

Player (Years)	Overall W-L-H	Four-Ball W-L-H	Foursomes W-L-H	Singles W-L-H
Paul Azinger (1989, 1991, 1993, 2002)	5-8-3	1-5-1	2-3-0	2-0-2
Mark Calcavecchia (1987, 1989, 1991, 2002)	6-7-1	1-4-0	4-1-0	1-2-1
Chad Campbell (2004)	1-2-0	0-2-0	0-0-0	1-0-0
Paul Casey (2004)	1-1-0	1-0-0	0-0-0	0-1-0
Stewart Cink (2002, 2004)	2-4-1	1-0-1	1-2-0	0-2-0
Darren Clarke (1997, 1999, 2002, 2004)	7-7-3	4-3-1	3-2-0	0-2-2
John Cook (1993)	1-1-0	1-0-0	0-0-0	0-1-0
Fred Couples (1989, 1991,1993, 1995, 1997)	7-9-4	4-3-2	1-5-0	2-1-2
Chris DiMarco (2004)	2-1-1	0-0-1	1-1-0	1-0-0
Luke Donald (2004)	2-1-1	0-0-1	2-0-0	0-1-0
David Duval (1999, 2002)	2-3-2	1-2-1	0-1-0	1-0-1
Nick Faldo (1977, 1979, 1981,1983, 1985, 1987, 1989, 1991,1993, 1995, 1997)	23-19-4	7-9-1	10-6-2	6-4-1
Brad Faxon (1995 1997)	2-4-0	2-2-0	0-0-0	0-2-0
Fred Funk (2004)	0-3-0	0-0-0	0-2-0	0-1-0
Jim Furyk (1997, 1999, 2002, 2004)	4-9-2	0-5-1	1-4-0	3-0-1
Jim Gallagher, Jr. (1993)	2-1-0	1-1-0	0-0-0	1-0-0
Sergio García (1999, 2002, 2004)	10-3-2	3-1-2	6-0-0	1-2-0
Ken Green (1989)	2-2-0	0-1-0	2-0-0	0-1-0
Jay Haas (1983, 1995, 2004)	4-6-2	2-0-2	2-3-0	0-3-0
Padraig Harrington (1999, 2000, 2002, 2004)	7-4-1	2-2-0	2-2-1	3-0-0
Scott Hoch (1997, 2002)	2-3-2	0-1-1	2-1-0	0-1-1
Peter Jacobsen (1985, 1995)	2-4-0	0-2-0	2-0-0	0-2-0
Lee Janzen (1993, 1997)	2-3-0	0-1-0	1-1-0	1-1-0
Miguel Angel Jimenez (1999, 2004)	2-5-2	2-0-1	0-3-1	0-2-0
Per-Ulrik Johansson (1995, 1997)	3-2-0	1-1-0	1-0-0	1-1-0
Bernhard Langer (1981, 1983, 1985, 1987, 1989, 1991, 1993, 1995, 1997, 2002)	21-15-6	6-6-2	11-6-1	4-3-0
Tom Lehman (1995, 1997, 1999)	5-3-2	1-1-1	1-2-1	3-0-0
Justin Leonard (1997, 1999)	0-3-5	0-1-2	0-2-1	0-0-2
Davis Love III (1993, 1995, 1997, 1999, 2002, 2004)	9-12-5	3-6-2	3-5-1	3-1-2
Sandy Lyle (1979, 1981, 1983, 1985, 1987)	7-9-2	3-2-1	3-3-1	1-4-0
Jeff Maggert (1995, 1997, 1999)	6-5-0	1-1-0	4-2-0	1-2-0
Phil Mickelson (1995, 1997, 1999, 2002, 2004)	9-8-3	4-4-1	2-2-2	3-2-0
Larry Mize (1987)	1-1-2	1-0-0	0-1-1	0-0-1
Mark O'Meara (1985, 1989, 1991,1997, 1999)	4-9-1	2-2-1	1-3-0	1-4-0
José María Olazábal (1987, 1989, 1991, 1993, 1995, 1999)	15-8-5	7-2-3	7-2-1	1-5-0
Jesper Parnevik (1997, 1999, 2002)	4-3-4	2-1-1	2-0-2	0-2-1
Steve Pate (1991, 1999)	2-2-1	0-2-0	1-0-0	1-0-1
Corey Pavin (1991, 1993, 1995)	8-5-0	4-2-0	2-2-0	2-1-0
Kenny Perry (2004)	0-2-0	0-0-0	0-1-0	0-1-0
Ian Poulter (2004)	1-1-0	0-1-0	0-0-0	1-0-0
Chris Riley (2004)	1-1-1	1-0-1	0-0-0	0-1-0
Loren Roberts (1995)	3-1-0	2-0-0	1-0-0	0-1-0
Scott Simpson (1987)	1-1-0	0-1-0	0-0-0	1-0-0
Craig Stadler (1983, 1985)	4-2-2	1-0-2	1-2-0	2-0-0
Curtis Strange (1983, 1985, 1987, 1989, 1995)	6-12-2	0-5-1	4-4-1	2-3-0
Hal Sutton (1985, 1987, 1999, 2002)	7-5-4	1-2-2	5-1-1	1-2-1
David Toms (2002, 2004)	4-3-1	1-2-0	2-0-1	1-1-0
Scott Verplank (2002)	2-1-0	0-0-0	1-1-0	1-0-0
Tiger Woods (1997, 1999, 2002, 2004)	7-11-2	3-5-0	2-5-1	2-1-1

Future Ryder Cup Sites

2006	The K Club, Straffan, Co. Kildare, Ireland
2008	Valhalla Golf Club, Louisville, KY
2010	Celtic Manor, Newport, Wales
2012	Medinah Country Club, Medinah, IL
2014	Gleneagles, Pershire, Scotland
2016	Hazeltine National Golf Club, Chaska, MN

Lehman 2006 U.S. Ryder Cup Captain

Tom Lehman, the 1996 British Open champion and a five-time PGA TOUR winner, will captain the 2006 United States Ryder Cup Team at The K Club in Straffan, County Kildaire, Ireland. Lehman was named captain on Nov. 3, 2004. Lehman, 45, competed on three consecutive Ryder Cup Teams (1995, '97 and '99).

Official World Golf Ranking

The Official World Golf Ranking, which is endorsed by the four major championships and six professional Tours that make up the International Federation of PGA Tours, is issued every Monday following the completion of the previous week's tournaments from around the world.

Results from events on the world's leading professional tours—the Asian Tour, PGA Tour of Australasia, European Tour, Japan Golf Tour, PGA TOUR, Nationwide Tour, Sunshine Tour, Canadian Tour and European Challenge Tour—are evaluated, and points are awarded according to the players' finishing positions. Tournaments are "rated" according to the strength of field based on the number and ranking of the world's top players in respective tournament fields (event "ratings").

In addition, some strength-of-field weighting is given to the inclusion in each field of a significant percentage of the top 30 on the host Tour's prior year Official Money Lists. The four major championships and THE PLAYERS Championship are rated separately to reflect the higher field quality of the events. In addition, the Volvo PGA Championship in Europe and the Australian, Japanese and South African Open Championships are allocated higher minimum point levels to reflect their status.

The Official World Golf Ranking points for each player are accumulated over a two-year "rolling" period, with the points awarded in the most recent 13-week period doubled. Each player then is ranked according to his average points per tournament, which is determined by dividing his total number of points by the tournaments he has played over that two-year period. There is a minimum requirement of 40 tournaments for the two-year period.

The winners of the Masters Tournament, U.S. Open, British Open and PGA Championship are awarded 50 points (30 points for second place, 20 for third, 15 for fourth, down to 0.75 points for a player completing the final round), and the winner of THE PLAYERS Championship is awarded 40 points (points are awarded down to 60th place).

The Volvo PGA Championship has a minimum of 32 points for the winner (points down to 56th place). In addition, the Open Championships of Australia, Japan and South Africa have a minimum of 16 points for the winner (points awarded down to 37th place).

Minimum points levels of all the other official Tour events have been set at three points for the Asian Nationwide, European Challenge and Canadian Tours; six points for the Sunshine (points to 14th place); eight points for Australasia and Japan (points to 19th place); and 12 points for Europe and the United States (points to 27th place).

Beginning in September 2001, a new feature was added to the ranking system—any applicable two-year time period is divided into eight 13-week segments. Ranking points in each player's record will be reduced in value by one-eighth at the conclusion of each segment, thereby cutting the sudden and sometimes dramatic impact of the reduction of one-half that previously occurred at the one- and two-year anniversaries of events in which players earn points. Full Ranking points are awarded for tournaments reduced to 54 holes because of inclement weather or other reasons. For events completing only 36 holes, Ranking points are reduced by 25 percent.

The Official World Golf Ranking is available each week at PGA TOUR sites or by going to www.officialworldgolfranking.com or www.owgr.com. The top 75 as of Nov. 8, 2004 (last ranking of official 2004 PGA TOUR season) follows:

Rank	Player	Points
1.	Vijay Singh *	13.80
2.	Tiger Woods *	12.21
3.	Ernie Els *	12.01
4.	Retief Goosen *	8.08
5.	Phil Mickelson *	7.48
6.	Mike Weir *	6.25
7.	Padraig Harrington *	6.19
8.	Davis Love III *	6.11
9.	Sergio Garcia *	5.88
10.	Stewart Cink *	5.22
11.	Adam Scott *	5.00
12.	Darren Clarke *	4.49
13.	Kenny Perry *	4.27
14.	Chris DiMarco *	4.26
15.	Miguel A. Jimenez	4.21
16.	Jim Furyk *	4.18
17.	Chad Campbell *	4.14
18.	Stuart Appleby *	4.02
19.	David Toms *	3.97
20.	Todd Hamilton *	3.93
21.	Stephen Ames *	3.89
22.	Scott Verplank *	3.74
23.	Jay Haas *	3.47
24.	Shigeki Maruyama *	3.34
25.	Luke Donald *	3.32
26.	Fred Couples *	3.29
27.	Lee Westwood *	3.28
28.	K.J. Choi *	3.27
29.	Angel Cabrera	3.27
30.	Paul Casey *	3.22
31.	Rory Sabbatini *	3.20
32.	Thomas Bjorn *	3.11
33.	Robert Allenby *	3.08
34.	Justin Leonard *	3.08
35.	Jerry Kelly *	3.05
36.	Ian Poulter *	2.92
37.	Steve Flesch *	2.91
38.	Fredrik Jacobson *	2.78
39.	David Howell	2.69
40.	Mark Hensby *	2.68
41.	Zach Johnson *	2.68
42.	Jonathan Kaye *	2.66
43.	John Daly *	2.64
44.	Nick Price *	2.63
45.	Chris Riley *	2.62
46.	Thomas Levet *	2.59
47.	Joakim Haeggman	2.53
48.	Fred Funk *	2.45
49.	Stephen Leaney *	2.43
50.	Trevor Immelman	2.42
51.	Alex Cejka *	2.40
52.	Kirk Triplett *	2.40
53.	Nick O'Hern	2.39
54.	Brad Faxon *	2.34
55.	Charles Howell III *	2.31
56.	Bob Tway *	2.27
57.	Jeff Maggert *	2.25
58.	Tim Herron *	2.22
59.	Tom Lehman *	2.19
60.	Graeme McDowell	2.16
61.	Shingo Katayama	2.14
62.	Duffy Waldorf *	2.13
63.	Shaun Micheel *	2.12
64.	Toru Taniguchi	2.09
65.	Rod Pampling *	2.07
66.	Peter Lonard *	2.04
67.	Justin Rose *	2.02
68.	Paul McGinley	1.98
69.	Tim Clark *	1.94
70.	Briny Baird *	1.92
71.	Loren Roberts *	1.90
72.	Stephen Gallacher	1.90
73.	Jesper Parnevik *	1.85
74.	Carlos Franco *	1.83
75.	Colin Montgomerie	1.81

* PGA TOUR Member

officialworldgolfranking.com

Mark H. McCormack Award

The Mark H. McCormack Award has been presented annually since 1998 to the player who holds the No. 1 position on the Official World Golf Ranking for the greatest number of weeks in each calendar year. Tiger Woods has won the award every year since its inception. He held the top position on the Official World Golf Ranking in 2004 until the Ranking of Sept. 6, when Vijay Singh became No. 1. The award was created in 1998 by the Governing Board of the Official World Golf Ranking to honor McCormack for the significant role he played in founding a world ranking system for professional golf. McCormack founded IMG, a premier worldwide sports and lifestyle management and marketing firm in the early 1960's. He passed away May 16, 2003.

Official World Golf Ranking Records

RECORDS FOR WORLD NO. 1 IN THE OFFICIAL WORLD GOLF RANKING (released each Monday through Dec. 27, 2004)
Through Nov. 8, 2004

PLAYER	INCLUSIVE DATES	LENGTH (WEEKS)
Bernhard Langer	April 6-20, 1986	**3 weeks**
Seve Ballesteros	April 27-September 7, 1986	20 weeks
	November 22, 1987	1 week
	October 30, 1988	1 week
	November 13, 1988-March 19, 1989	19 weeks
	April 2-August 13, 1989	20 weeks
		Total: 61 weeks
Greg Norman	September 14, 1986-November 15, 1987	62 weeks
	November 29, 1987-October 23, 1988	48 weeks
	November 6, 1988	1 week
	March 26, 1989	1 week
	August 20, 1989-August 26, 1990	54 weeks
	October 14, 1990-January 27, 1991	16 weeks
	February 6-August 7, 1994	27 weeks
	June 18, 1995-April 13, 1997	96 weeks
	April 27-June 8, 1997	7 weeks
	June 29, 1997	1 week
	September 7, 1997-January 4, 1998	18 weeks
		Total: 331 weeks
Nick Faldo	September 2-October 7, 1990	6 weeks
	February 3-March 31, 1991	9 weeks
	March 29, 1992	1 week
	July 19, 1992-January 30, 1994	82 weeks
		Total: 98 weeks
Ian Woosnam	April 7, 1991-March 15, 1992	**50 weeks**
Fred Couples	March 22, 1992	1 week
	April 5-July 12, 1992	15 weeks
		Total: 16 weeks
Nick Price	August 14, 1994-June 11, 1995	**43 weeks**
Tom Lehman	April 20, 1997	**1 week**
Tiger Woods	June 15, 1997	1 week
	July 6-August 31, 1997	9 weeks
	January 11-April 5, 1998	13 weeks
	May 10, 1998	1 week
	June 14, 1998-March 21, 1999	41 weeks
	July 4-August 1, 1999	5 weeks
	Aug. 15, 1999 to Aug. 30, 2004	264 weeks##
		Total: 334 weeks **
Ernie Els	June 22, 1997	1 week
	April 12-May 3, 1998	4 weeks
	May 17-June 7, 1998	4 weeks
		Total: 9 weeks
David Duval	March 28-June 27, 1999	14 weeks
	August 8, 1999	1 week
		Total: 15 weeks
Vijay Singh	Sept. 6, 2004-Nov. 8, 2004	**10 weeks**
		Total of 971 weeks

** Record number of weeks at No. 1
Record consecutive weeks at No.1

Winners of Major U.S. Amateur Events

U.S. Amateur Champions (Since 1949)	
1949	Charles R. Coe
1950	Sam Urzetta
1951	Billy Maxwell
1952	Jack Westland
1953	Gene Littler
1954	Arnold Palmer
1955	Harvie Ward
1956	Harvie Ward
1957	Hillman Robbins
1958	Charles R. Coe
1959	Jack Nicklaus
1960	Deane Beman
1961	Jack Nicklaus
1962	Labron Harris Jr.
1963	Deane Beman
1964	William C. Campbell
1965	Bob Murphy (291)
1966	Gary Cowan (285)
1967	Bob Dickson (285)
1968	Bruce Fleisher (284)
1969	Steve Melnyk (286)
1970	Lanny Wadkins (279)
1971	Gary Cowan (280)
1972	Vinny Giles (285)
1973	Craig Stadler
1974	Jerry Pate
1975	Fred Ridley
1976	Bill Sander
1977	John Fought
1978	John Cook
1979	Mark O'Meara
1980	Hal Sutton
1981	Nathaniel Crosby
1982	Jay Sigel
1983	Jay Sigel
1984	Scott Verplank
1985	Sam Randolph
1986	Buddy Alexander
1987	Bill Mayfair
1988	Eric Meeks
1989	Chris Patton
1990	Phil Mickelson
1991	Mitch Voges
1992	Justin Leonard
1993	John Harris
1994	Tiger Woods
1995	Tiger Woods
1996	Tiger Woods
1997	Matt Kuchar
1998	Hank Kuehne
1999	David Gossett
2000	Jeff Quinney
2001	Ben (Bubba) Dickerson
2002	Ricky Barnes
2003	Nick Flanagan
2004	Ryan Moore

NCAA Champions (Since 1949)	
1949	Harvie Ward, North Carolina
1950	Fred Wampler, Purdue
1951	Tom Nieporte, Ohio State
1952	Jim Vickers, Oklahoma
1953	Earl Moeller, Oklahoma State
1954	Hillman Robbins, Memphis State
1955	Joe Campbell, Purdue
1956	Rick Jones, Ohio State
1957	Rex Baxter Jr. Houston
1958	Phil Rodgers, Houston
1959	Dick Crawford, Houston
1960	Dick Crawford, Houston
1961	Jack Nicklaus, Ohio State
1962	Kermit Zarley, Houston
1963	R.H. Sikes, Arkansas
1964	Terry Small, San Jose State
1965	Marty Fleckman, Houston
1966	Bob Murphy, Florida
1967	Hale Irwin, Colorado
1968	Grier Jones, Oklahoma State
1969	Bob Clark, Los Angeles State
1970	John Mahaffey, Houston
1971	Ben Crenshaw, Texas
1972	Ben Crenshaw, Texas; Tom Kite, Texas
1973	Ben Crenshaw, Texas
1974	Curtis Strange, Wake Forest
1975	Jay Haas, Wake Forest
1976	Scott Simpson, USC
1977	Scott Simpson, USC
1978	David Edwards, Oklahoma State
1979	Gary Hallberg, Wake Forest
1980	Jay Don Blake, Utah State
1981	Ron Commans, USC
1982	Billy Ray Brown, Houston
1983	Jim Carter, Arizona State
1984	John Inman, North Carolina
1985	Clark Burroughs, Ohio State
1986	Scott Verplank, Oklahoma State
1987	Brian Watts, Oklahoma State
1988	E.J. Pfister, Oklahoma State
1989	Phil Mickelson, Arizona State
1990	Phil Mickelson, Arizona State
1991	Warren Schutte, Nevada-Las Vegas
1992	Phil Mickelson, Arizona State
1993	Todd Demsey, Arizona State
1994	Justin Leonard, Texas
1995	Chip Spratlin, Auburn
1996	Tiger Woods, Stanford
1997	Charles Warren, Clemson
1998	James McLean, Minnesota
1999	Luke Donald, Northwestern
2000	Charles Howell III, Oklahoma State
2001	Nick Gilliam, Florida
2002	Troy Matteson, Georgia Tech
2003	Alejandro Canizares, Arizona State
2004	Ryan Moore, Nevada-Las Vegas

U.S. Public Links Champions (Since 1949)	
1949	Kenneth J. Towns
1950	Stanley Bielat
1951	Dave Stanley
1952	Omer L. Bogan
1953	Ted Richards, Jr.
1954	Gene Andrews
1955	Sam D. Kocsis
1956	James H. Buxbaum
1957	Don Essig, III
1958	Daniel D. Sikes, Jr.
1959	William A Wright
1960	Verne Callison
1961	R.H. Sikes
1962	R.H. Sikes
1963	Robert Lunn
1964	William McDonald
1965	Arne Dokka
1966	Lamont Kaser
1967	Verne Callison (287)
1968	Gene Towry (292)
1969	J.M. Jackson (292)
1970	Robert Risch (293)
1971	Fred Haney (290)
1972	Bob Allard (285)
1973	Stan Stopa (294)
1974	Chas. Barenaba (290)
1975	Randy Barenaba
1976	Eddie Mudd
1977	Jerry Vidovic
1978	Dean Prince
1979	Dennis Walsh
1980	Jodie Mudd
1981	Jodie Mudd
1982	Billy Tuten
1983	Billy Tuten
1984	Bill Malley
1985	Jim Sorenson
1986	Billy Mayfair
1987	Kevin Johnson
1988	Ralph Howe
1989	Tim Hobby
1990	Mike Combs
1991	David Berganio, Jr.
1992	Warren Schutte
1993	David Berganio, Jr.
1994	Guy Yamamoto
1995	Chris Wollman
1996	Tim Hogarth
1997	Tim Clark
1998	Trevor Immelman
1999	Hunter Haas
2000	D.J. Trahan
2001	Chez Reavie
2002	Ryan Moore
2003	Brandt Snedeker
2004	Ryan Moore

** Parentheses indicates stroke play*

In 2004, **Stewart Cink** won multiple events for the first time in his career, the MCI Heritage and the World Golf Championships-NEC Invitational, on the way to a career-high finish of fifth on the money list.

2004 Official PGA TOUR Money List

Player	Events	Wins	Money
1. Vijay Singh	29	9	$10,905,166
2. Ernie Els	16	3	5,787,225
3. Phil Mickelson	22	2	5,784,823
4. Tiger Woods	19	1	5,365,472
5. Stewart Cink	28	2	4,450,270
6. Retief Goosen	16	2	3,885,573
7. Adam Scott	16	2	3,724,984
8. Stephen Ames	27	1	3,303,205
9. Sergio Garcia	18	2	3,239,215
10. Davis Love III	24		3,075,092
11. Todd Hamilton+	27	2	3,063,778
12. Chris DiMarco	27		2,971,842
13. Stuart Appleby	25	1	2,949,235
14. Mike Weir	22	1	2,761,536
15. Mark Hensby@	29	1	2,718,766
16. Rory Sabbatini	26		2,500,397
17. Jerry Kelly	29		2,496,222
18. Steve Flesch	31	1	2,461,787
19. Zach Johnson@	30	1	2,417,685
20. Scott Verplank	24		2,365,592
21. John Daly	22	1	2,359,507
22. David Toms	24	1	2,357,531
23. Shigeki Maruyama	26		2,301,692
24. Chad Campbell	28	1	2,264,985
25. Fred Funk	29	1	2,103,731
26. K.J. Choi	24		2,077,775
27. Jay Haas	23		2,071,626
28. Darren Clarke	16		2,009,819
29. Carlos Franco	27	1	1,955,395
30. Kenny Perry	23		1,952,043
31. Rod Pampling	26	1	1,737,725
32. Tim Herron	26		1,727,577
33. Charles Howell III	30		1,703,485
34. Jonathan Kaye	25	1	1,695,332
35. Luke Donald	21		1,646,268
36. Ted Purdy@	35		1,636,876
37. Ryan Palmer@	33	1	1,592,344
38. Kirk Triplett	24		1,566,426
39. Bo Van Pelt@	30		1,553,825
40. Jesper Parnevik	24		1,550,135
41. Joey Sindelar	31	1	1,536,881
42. Justin Leonard	25		1,531,023
43. Jeff Maggert	20		1,527,884
44. Robert Allenby	26		1,513,537
45. Woody Austin	29	1	1,495,980
46. Duffy Waldorf	26		1,487,912
47. Tom Pernice, Jr.	31		1,475,274
48. Harrison Frazar	25		1,446,764
49. Joe Ogilvie@	32		1,443,363
50. Fred Couples	16		1,396,109
51. Carl Pettersson	28		1,367,962
52. Arron Oberholser	23		1,355,433
53. Tom Lehman	19		1,343,277
54. Alex Cejka	24		1,313,483
55. Craig Parry	16	1	1,308,586
56. Chris Riley	23		1,292,732
57. Brent Geiberger	31	1	1,259,779
58. Frank Lickliter II	27		1,259,234
59. Fredrik Jacobson	24		1,259,048
60. Scott Hoch	17		1,239,360
61. Geoff Ogilvy	26		1,236,910

Player	Events	Wins	Money
62. Justin Rose	22		$1,236,764
63. Patrick Sheehan	33		1,234,344
64. Skip Kendall	29		1,206,438
65. Tim Petrovic	32		1,193,354
66. Steve Lowery	28		1,191,245
67. Vaughn Taylor@	27	1	1,176,434
68. Stephen Leaney	24		1,166,560
69. Briny Baird	30		1,156,517
70. Jonathan Byrd	27	1	1,133,165
71. Tim Clark	26		1,108,190
72. Heath Slocum	31	1	1,066,837
73. Thomas Bjorn	12		1,050,803
74. Bob Estes	23		1,046,064
75. Ben Crane	27		1,036,958
76. Brad Faxon	28		1,016,898
77. Jeff Sluman	28		1,007,635
78. Loren Roberts	22		998,677
79. Bob Tway	26		966,553
80. Bart Bryant	23	1	962,167
81. Joe Durant	26		952,547
82. Shaun Micheel	27		949,919
83. Bernhard Langer	15		943,589
84. Robert Damron	28		933,388
85. Kevin Sutherland	27		928,760
86. Brian Bateman#	24		919,255
87. Kevin Na#	32		901,158
88. Michael Allen+	28		882,872
89. Corey Pavin	23		881,938
90. John Huston	20		874,280
91. Tom Byrum	25		873,139
92. Dudley Hart	23		854,638
93. J.J. Henry	30		848,823
94. Todd Fischer	33		847,996
95. Tommy Armour III	28		844,634
96. Lee Janzen	25		837,482
97. Brett Quigley	31		836,380
98. Matt Gogel	25		817,117
99. Hank Kuehne	30		816,889
100. Hunter Mahan#	30		813,089
101. Andre Stolz@	20	1	808,373
102. J.L. Lewis	32		807,345
103. Nick Price	15		796,086
104. Hidemichi Tanaka	27		795,206
105. Scott McCarron	27		790,720
106. Jose Coceres	20		779,196
107. Cameron Beckman	30		779,189
108. Daniel Chopra+	33		763,253
109. John Rollins	29		737,957
110. Robert Gamez	31		725,368
111. Pat Perez	32		723,724
112. Mark Calcavecchia	24		717,876
113. Neal Lancaster	33		701,239
114. John Senden	28		698,203
115. Chris Smith	33		692,785
116. Jim Furyk	14		691,675
117. Dennis Paulson	21		677,035
118. Peter Lonard	23		675,189
119. Kent Jones	32		674,909
120. Jay Williamson	33		660,038
121. Steve Allan	33		648,480
122. Brian Gay#	32		645,194

Player	Events	Money
123. Aaron Baddeley	27	$632,876
124. Billy Andrade	31	631,143
125. Tag Ridings	18	623,262
126. Paul Azinger	23	601,438
127. Olin Browne	30	597,034
128. Craig Barlow	25	595,820
129. Notah Begay III	23	583,537
130. Bob Burns	30	581,421
131. Jason Bohn@	29	567,930
132. Mathias Gronberg#	32	565,014
133. Dean Wilson	33	561,340
134. Lucas Glover@	30	557,454
135. Mark O'Meara	17	543,866
136. Scott Hend#	29	531,263
137. Brenden Pappas	34	524,905
138. Glen Day	33	519,935
139. Matt Kuchar	28	509,257
140. Billy Mayfair	32	503,251
141. Ben Curtis	20	500,818
142. Jose Maria Olazabal	17	495,050
143. Craig Bowden@	30	494,568
144. Danny Ellis#	26	490,413
145. John E. Morgan	16	487,032
146. Arjun Atwal#	30	486,052
147. David Peoples	26	479,464
148. Richard S. Johnson	32	461,183
149. Jeff Brehaut	34	448,914
150. Paul Stankowski	14	442,872
151. Steve Stricker	27	440,906
152. Craig Perks	27	423,748
153. John Riegger#	17	423,263
154. Thomas Levet	5	404,305
155. David Frost	26	402,589
156. Greg Chalmers	22	402,380
157. Danny Briggs+	28	397,606
158. Tom Carter@	35	395,780
159. Spike McRoy	33	374,187
160. D.J. Brigman@	27	356,943
161. Deane Pappas#	22	346,633
162. Bill Glasson	17	346,030
163. Omar Uresti+	28	345,797
164. Jason Dufner@	28	317,770
165. Dan Forsman	28	315,540
166. Ken Duke+	30	301,309
167. Mark Wilson	19	300,317
168. Pat Bates	32	299,384
169. David Branshaw+	30	293,617
170. Gene Sauers	30	287,151
171. Joel Kribel	13	276,862
172. Niclas Fasth	22	265,423
173. Mark Brooks	31	264,076
174. J.P. Hayes	27	260,816
175. Cliff Kresge	33	258,062
176. Rocco Mediate	19	257,692
177. Roland Thatcher+	23	247,987
178. Brandt Jobe	9	247,911
179. Steve Elkington	20	243,238
180. Grant Waite#	29	239,318
181. Roger Tambellini+	28	234,164
182. Peter Jacobsen	10	232,851
183. Rich Beem	28	230,499

2004 Official PGA TOUR Money List (cont.)

Player	Events	Money
184. Dicky Pride	23	$230,329
185. Aaron Barber	17	229,915
186. Rich Barcelo+	26	223,597
187. David Sutherland	16	216,419
188. Len Mattiace	25	213,707
189. John Cook	19	210,448
190. Kris Cox#	26	205,171
191. Steve Pate#	24	199,569
192. Scott Simpson	18	190,986
193. Jay Delsing+	26	190,184
194. Russ Cochran+	25	185,108
195. Mike Heinen	17	166,185
196. Garrett Willis	17	165,210
197. David Morland IV@	27	164,435
198. Blaine McCallister@	27	162,700
199. Hirofumi Miyase#	27	162,120
200. Brian Kortan#	24	159,939
201. Tommy Tolles@	25	151,852
202. Per-Ulrik Johansson	12	146,733
203. Robin Freeman	13	144,000
204. Tjaart van der Walt+	12	138,785
205. Craig Stadler	6	137,475
206. Larry Mize	13	136,020
207. Dan Olsen#	31	135,731
208. Guy Boros@	24	130,783
209. David Edwards	13	123,681
210. David Duval	9	121,044

Player	Events	Money
211. Esteban Toledo	36	$115,185
212. Jim Carter	18	111,105
213. Michael Bradley	9	106,336
214. Hal Sutton	16	103,698
215. Glen Hnatiuk	9	103,500
216. Michael Clark II	14	101,639
217. Chris Couch@	24	100,283
218. Tripp Isenhour@	22	90,699
219. Joel Edwards	11	83,572
220. Jim Gallagher, Jr.	9	82,385
221. Willie Wood	9	78,937
222. Wes Short, Jr.+	12	75,536
223. Jim McGovern	11	72,377
224. Carl Paulson	13	70,088
225. Donnie Hammond	13	65,024
226. Mike Grob	13	60,103
227. Marco Dawson	6	59,550
228. James H. McLean	1	57,324
229. Sandy Lyle	2	49,142
230. Stan Utley	8	45,610
231. Trevor Dodds+	20	45,015
232. Mike Springer	10	44,616
233. Ken Green	18	43,356
234. Jay Don Blake	14	41,555
235. Brad Lardon	17	40,253
236. Boyd Summerhays#	8	37,127
237. Kelly Gibson	10	34,511

Player	Events	Money
238. Brad Bryant	4	$32,210
239. Wayne Levi	1	28,163
240. John Maginnes#	12	26,420
241. Mark Wiebe	6	25,435
242. Brian Watts	9	23,770
243. Gabriel Hjertstedt	5	22,870
244. Kevin Muncrief+	21	21,660
245. David Gossett	25	21,250
246. Paul Goydos	2	19,366
247. Tom Kite	1	17,304
248. Patrick Moore	14	15,448
249. Greg Norman	7	14,160
250. Jim Benepe	2	13,900
251. Jack Nicklaus	2	11,130
252. Dan Pohl	3	10,706
253. Tom Watson	2	10,350
254. Phil Blackmar	1	10,100
255. Fulton Allem	13	9,792
256. Ian Leggatt	5	8,280
257. Brandel Chamblee	1	6,580
258. Phil Tataurangi	8	6,540
T259. John Morse	3	6,420
T259. David Ogrin	2	6,420
261. Brian Henninger	9	6,240
262. Mike Standly	9	6,000
263. Mike Sullivan	1	5,520

@ = Top 20 Nationwide Tour # = 2003 Qualifying Tournament Grad + = Q-School Grad/Nationwide Tour

2004 PGA TOUR Non-Member Money List

Player	Events	Money
1. Padraig Harrington*	12	$1,882,276
2. Lee Westwood	11	526,899
3. Paul Casey*	11	517,939
4. Bill Haas	10	315,259
5. Camilo Villegas	10	237,984
6. Angel Cabrera	8	237,839
7. Paul McGinley	5	215,101
8. Ian Poulter*	9	176,318
9. Phillip Price	12	150,749
10. Brian Davis	7	110,250
11. Trevor Immelman	12	109,560
12. Barry Lane	3	105,802
13. Joakim Haeggman	5	105,316
14. Colin Montgomerie	6	96,479
15. Michael Campbell	6	86,006
16. Casey Wittenberg	9	85,670
17. Ricky Barnes	7	85,520
18. Jean-Francois Remesy	3	76,857
19. Keiichiro Fukabori	5	73,063
20. Gary Evans	1	71,346
21. Miguel A. Jimenez	7	66,367
22. Jyoti Randhawa	3	60,665
23. Takashi Kamiyama	1	54,305
24. Brandt Snedeker	9	54,215
25. Kevin Stadler	5	49,541
26. David Roesch	2	48,024

Player	Events	Money
27. Eduardo Romero	6	$43,750
28. Hideto Tanihara	3	41,729
29. Nick Faldo	6	40,460
T30. Kim Felton	1	35,111
T30. Tetsuji Hiratsuka	4	35,111
T32. Nick O'Hern	2	34,250
T32. Chip Sullivan	1	34,250
34. Mike Small	2	33,360
35. Paul Lawrie	5	32,663
36. Geoffrey Sisk	2	30,672
37. Tim Wilkinson	1	29,820
T38. Kenneth Ferrie	1	27,714
T38. Andy Oldcorn	1	27,714
40. Doug Barron	1	23,291
41. Pete Jordan	2	23,280
42. Kelly Mitchum	2	22,432
T43. Paul Bradshaw	1	22,404
T43. Alastair Forsyth	1	22,404
T43. Sean Whiffin	1	22,404
T46. Jason Hartwick	2	21,306
T46. Tim Thelen	5	21,306
48. Kevin Durkin	2	21,197
T49. Ignacio Garrido	1	19,756
T49. Raphael Jacquelin	2	19,756
51. James Kingston	1	19,101
52. Steve Friesen	1	18,550

Player	Events	Money
T53. Paul Broadhurst	1	$18,539
T53. Gary Emerson	1	18,539
55. David Howell	3	18,500
56. Franklin Langham	1	18,450
57. Mark B. Foster	1	18,071
58. Marten Olander	1	17,696
T59. Martin Erlandsson	1	17,322
T59. Paul Wesselingh	1	17,322
61. Christian Cevaer	1	16,760
62. Casey Martin	2	15,858
63. S.K. Ho	4	13,200
64. Shingo Katayama	3	12,650
65. Scott Drummond	4	12,350
66. Lian-Wei Zhang	4	12,072
67. Roy Biancalana	2	11,900
68. Jim Rutledge	1	11,898
69. Jeff Coston	1	11,800
70. Andrew McLardy	3	11,526
71. Edward Loar	1	11,400
72. Charley Hoffman	1	11,296
T73. Erik Compton	2	11,050
T73. Sven Struver	2	11,050
75. Kenichi Kuboya	1	10,944
76. Bryce Molder	3	10,716
77. David Ishii	1	10,464
78. Chris Nallen	3	10,366

* Special Temporary Member

2004 PGA TOUR Tournament Summary

	Tournament	Course(s)	Winner	Score	To Par	Margin	Earnings	Runner(s)-Up
1.	**Mercedes Championships§**	Plantation Course at Kapalua Lahaina, HI	Stuart Appleby	270	22-under	1 stroke	$1,060,000	Vijay Singh
2.	**Sony Open in Hawaii§**	Waialae CC Honolulu, HI	Ernie Els	262	18-under	Playoff	$864,000	Harrison Frazar
3.	**Bob Hope Chrysler Classic§**	Palmer Private Course At PGA West (Host Course) Indian Wells CC Bermuda Dunes CC La Quinta CC La Quinta, CA	Phil Mickelson	330	30-under	Playoff	$810,000	Skip Kendall
4.	**FBR Open§**	TPC of Scottsdale Scottsdale, AZ	Jonathan Kaye	266	18-under	2 strokes	$936,000	Chris DiMarco
5.	**AT&T Pebble Beach§ National Pro-Am**	Pebble Beach GL (Host Course) Spyglass Hill GC Poppy Hills GC Pebble Beach, CA	Vijay Singh	272	16-under	3 strokes	$954,000	Jeff Maggert
6.	**Buick Invitational§**	Torrey Pines GC South Course (Host Course) North Course LaJolla, CA	John Daly	278	10-under	Playoff	$864,000	Luke Donald Chris Riley
7.	**Nissan Open§**	Riviera CC Pacific Palisades, CA	Mike Weir	267	17-under	1 stroke	$864,000	Shigeki Maruyama
8.	**WGC-Accenture Match Play Championship§**	La Costa Resort and Spa Carlsbad, CA	Tiger Woods	3&2			$1,200,000	Davis Love III
9.	**Chrysler Classic of Tucson§**	Omni Tucson National Golf Resort and Spa Tucson, AZ	Heath Slocum	266	22-under	1 stroke	$540,000	Aaron Baddeley
10.	**Ford Championship at Doral**	Doral Golf Resort & Spa Blue Course Miami, FL	Craig Parry	271	17-under	Playoff	$900,000	Scott Verplank
11.	**The Honda Classic**	The CC at Mirasol Sunrise Course Palm Beach Gardens, FL	Todd Hamilton	276	12-under	1 stroke	$900,000	Davis Love III
12.	**Bay Hill Invitational Presented by MasterCard**	Bay Hill Club and Lodge Orlando, FL	Chad Campbell	270	18-under	6 strokes	$900,000	Stuart Appleby
13.	**THE PLAYERS Championship**	TPC at Sawgrass Ponte Vedra Beach, FL	Adam Scott	276	12-under	1 stroke	$1,440,000	Padraig Harrington
14.	**BellSouth Classic**	TPC at Sugarloaf Duluth, GA	Zach Johnson	275	13-under	1 stroke	$810,000	Mark Hensby
15.	**Masters Tournament**	Augusta National GC Augusta, GA	Phil Mickelson (2)	279	9-under	1 stroke	$1,170,000	Ernie Els
16.	**MCI Heritage**	Harbour Town GL Hilton Head Island, SC	Stewart Cink	274	10-under	Playoff	$860,000	Ted Purdy
17.	**Shell Houston Open**	Redstone GC Humble, TX	Vijay Singh (2)	277	11-under	2 strokes	$900,000	Scott Hoch
18.	**HP Classic of New Orleans**	English Turn G&CC New Orleans, LA	Vijay Singh (3)	266	22-under	1 stroke	$918,000	Joe Ogilvie Phil Mickelson

( ) Indicates number of victories through that event   § PGA TOUR West Coast Swing Presented by The St. Paul

2004 PGA TOUR Tournament Summary (cont.)

	Tournament	Course(s)	Winner	Score	To Par	Margin	Earnings	Runner(s)-Up
19.	**Wachovia Championship**	Quail Hallow Club Charlotte, NC	Joey Sindelar	277	11-under	Playoff	$1,008,000	Arron Oberholser
20.	**EDS Byron Nelson Championship**	Four Seasons Resort and Club Las Colinas TPC at Four Seasons (Host Course) Cottonwood Valley Course Irving, TX	Sergio Garcia	270	10-under	Playoff	$1,044,000	Robert Damron Dudley Hart
21.	**Bank of America Colonial**	Colonial CC Fort Worth, TX	Steve Flesch	269	11-under	1 stroke	$954,000	Chad Campbell
22.	**FedEx St. Jude Classic**	TPC at Southwind Memphis, TN	David Toms	268	16-under	6 strokes	$846,000	Bob Estes
23.	**the Memorial Tournament**	Muirfield Village GC Dublin, OH	Ernie Els (2)	270	18-under	4 strokes	$945,000	Fred Couples
24.	**Buick Classic**	Westchester CC West Course Harrison, NY	Sergio Garcia (2)	272	12-under	Playoff	$945,000	Padraig Harrington Rory Sabbatini
25.	**U.S. Open Championship**	Shinnecock Hills GC Southampton, NY	Retief Goosen	276	4-under	2 strokes	$1,125,000	Phil Mickelson
26.	**Booz Allen Classic**	TPC at Avenel Potomac, MD	Adam Scott (2)	263	21-under	4 strokes	$864,000	Charles Howell III
27.	**Cialis Western Open**	Cog Hill G&CC Lemont, IL	Stephen Ames	274	10-under	2 strokes	$864,000	Steve Lowery
28.	**John Deere Classic**	TPC at Deere Run Silvis, IL	Mark Hensby	268	16-under	Playoff	$684,000	John E. Morgan
29.	**British Open Championship**	Royal Troon GC Ayshire, Scotland	Todd Hamilton (2)	274	10-under	Playoff	$1,348,272	Ernie Els
30.	**B.C. Open**	En-Joie GC Endicott, NY	Jonathan Byrd	268	20-under	1 stroke	$540,000	Ted Purdy
31.	**U.S. Bank Championship in Milwaukee**	Brown Deer Park GC Milwaukee, WI	Carlos Franco	267	13-under	2 strokes	$630,000	Fred Funk Brett Quigley
32.	**Buick Open**	Warwick Hills G&CC Grand Blanc, MI	Vijay Singh (4)	265	23-under	1 stroke	$810,000	John Daly
33.	**The INTERNATIONAL**	Castle Pines GC Castle Rock, CO	Rod Pampling	31 points		2 points	$900,000	Alex Cejka
34.	**PGA Championship**	Whistling Straits GC Haven, WI	Vijay Singh (5)	280	8-under	Playoff	$1,125,000	Chris DiMarco Justin Leonard
35.	**WGC-NEC Invitational**	Firestone CC South Course Akron, OH	Stewart Cink (2)	269	11-under	4 strokes	$1,200,000	Tiger Woods Rory Sabbatini
36.	**Reno-Tahoe Open**	Montreux G&CC Reno, NV	Vaughn Taylor	278	10-under	Playoff	$540,000	Scott McCarron Steve Allan Hunter Mahan
37.	**Buick Championship**	TPC at River Highlands Cromwell, CT	Woody Austin	270	10-under	Playoff	$756,000	Tim Herron
38.	**Deutsche Bank Championship‡**	TPC at Boston Norton, MA	Vijay Singh (6)	268	16-under	3 strokes	$900,000	Adam Scott Tiger Woods
39.	**Bell Canadian Open‡**	Glen Abbey GC Oakville, Ontario, Canada	Vijay Singh (7)	275	9-under	Playoff	$810,000	Mike Weir

( ) Indicates number of victories through that event ‡ FallFinish Presented by PricewaterhouseCoopers

2004 PGA TOUR Tournament Summary (cont.)

	Tournament	Course(s)	Winner	Score	To Par	Margin	Earnings	Runner(s)-Up
40.	**Valero Texas Open‡**	The Resort Course at LaCantera San Antonio, TX	Bart Bryant	261	19-under	3 strokes	$630,000	Patrick Sheehan
41.	**84 LUMBER Classic‡**	Nemacolin Woodlands Resort & Spa Mystic River GC Farmington, PA	Vijay Singh (8)	273	15-under	1 stroke	$756,000	Stewart Cink
42.	**WGC-American Express Championship‡**	Mount Juliet Estate Thomastown, Co. Kilkenny Ireland	Ernie Els (3)	270	18-under	1 stroke	$1,200,000	Thomas Bjorn
43.	**Southern Farm Bureau Classic‡**	Annandale GC Madison, MS	Fred Funk	266	22-under	1 stroke	$540,000	Ryan Palmer
44.	**Michelin Championship at Las Vegas‡**	TPC at Summerlin (Host Course) TPC at The Canyons Bear's Best Las Vegas, NV	Andre Stolz	266	21-under	1 stroke	$720,000	Tag Ridings Harrison Frazar Tom Lehman
45.	**Chrysler Classic of Greensboro‡**	Forest Oaks CC Greensboro, NC	Brent Geiberger	270	18-under	2 strokes	$828,000	Michael Allen
46.	**FUNAI Classic at the WALT DISNEY WORLD Resort‡**	Magnolia Course (Host Course) Palm Course Lake Buena Vista, FL	Ryan Palmer	266	22-under	3 strokes	$756,000	Vijay Singh Briny Baird
47.	**Chrysler Championship‡**	Westin Innisbrook Resort Copperhead Course Tampa Bay, FL	Vijay Singh (9)	266	18-under	5 strokes	$900,000	Tommy Armour III Jesper Parnevik
48.	**THE TOUR Championship presented by Coca-Cola‡**	East Lake GC Atlanta, GA	Retief Goosen (2)	269	11-under	4 strokes	$1,080,000	Tiger Woods

( ) Indicates number of victories through that event ‡ FallFinish Presented by PricewaterhouseCoopers

LOW 9:
27 (9-under), **Robert Gamez**, Indian Wells CC (front nine), third round, Bob Hope Chrysler Classic. (Tied PGA TOUR Record)
28 (8-under), **Charles Howell III**, TPC at Avenel (front nine), first round, Booz Allen Classic
28 (8-under), **Vijay Singh**, Abbey Glen GC (front nine), first round, Bell Canadian Open

LOW 18:
60 (12-under), **Robert Gamez,** Indian Wells CC, third round, Bob Hope Chrysler Classic
60 (10-under), **Bart Bryant**, third round, Valero Texas Open

LOW FIRST 18:
61 (10-under), **Charles Howell III**, TPC at Avenel, Booz Allen Classic
61 (9-under), **Ted Purdy**, Valero Texas Open

LOW FIRST 36:
128 (14-under), **Adam Scott** (66-62), Booz Allen Classic
129 (15-under), **Danny Ellis** (63-66), HP Classic of New Orleans
129 (11-under), **Steve Allan** (67-62), Sony Open in Hawaii
129 (11-under), **Dean Wilson** (64-65), Valero Texas Open

LOW 36 (any rounds):
126 (18-under), **Robert Gamez** (61-65), B.C. Open, second, third rounds
127 (17-under), **Phil Mickelson** (63-64), Bob Hope Chrysler Classic, second, third rounds
127 (13-under), **Frank Lickliter II** (62-65), Sony Open in Hawaii, second, third rounds
127 (13-under), **Bart Bryant** (67-60), Valero Texas Open, second, third rounds

LOW FIRST 54:
194 (16-under), **Bart Bryant** (67-67-60), Valero Texas Open
195 (21-under), **Phil Mickelson** (68-63-64), Bob Hope Chrysler Classic
195 (18-under), **David Toms** (67-63-65), FedEx St. Jude Classic
195 (18-under), **Adam Scott** (66-62-67), Booz Allen Classic

LOW 54 (any rounds):
194 (22-under), **Phil Mickelson** (63-64-67), Bob Hope Chrysler Classic, second, third and fourth rounds
194 (22-under), **Danny Ellis** (63-67-64), Bob Hope Chrysler Classic, second, third and fourth rounds
194 (16-under), **Bart Bryant** (67-67-60), Valero Texas Open, first, second and third rounds

LOW 72:
261 (19-under), **Bart Bryant**, Valero Texas Open
262 (26-under), **Phil Mickelson**, Bob Hope Chrysler Classic
262 (26-under), **Kirk Triplett**, Bob Hope Chrysler Classic
262 (18-under), **Ernie Els**, Sony Open in Hawaii
262 (18-under), **Harrison Frazar**, Sony Open in Hawaii

LOW 90:
330 (30-under), **Phil Mickelson**, four courses (par-72), 2004 Bob Hope Chrysler Classic
330 (30-under), **Skip Kendall**, four courses (par-72), 2004 Bob Hope Chrysler Classic

HIGH 72:
280 (8-under), **Vijay Singh**, PGA Championship
279 (9-under), **Phil Mickelson**, Masters Tournament

LARGEST WINNING MARGIN:
6 strokes, **Chad Campbell**, Bay Hill Invitational presented by MasterCard
5 strokes, **Vijay Singh**, Chrysler Championship

LOW START BY WINNER:
63 (9-under), **Vijay Singh**, Buick Open
63 (7-under), **Stewart Cink**, WGC-NEC Invitational
64 (8-under), **Vijay Singh**, 84 LUMBER Classic

HIGH START BY WINNER:
74 (2-over), **Vijay Singh**, Shell Houston Open
72 (1-over), **Stewart Cink**, MCI Heritage
72 (even), **Phil Mickelson**, Masters Tournament

LOW FINISH BY WINNER:
62 (10-under), **Ryan Palmer**, FUNAI Classic at the WALT DISNEY WORLD Resort
63 (9-under), **Vijay Singh**, HP Classic of New Orleans

HIGH FINISH BY WINNER:
76 (4-over), **Vijay Singh**, PGA Championship
75 (3-over), **John Daly**, Buick Invitational
75 (3-over), **Vaughn Taylor**, Reno-Tahoe Open

LARGEST 18-HOLE LEAD:
3 strokes, **Charles Howell III**, Booz Allen Classic; **Corey Pavin**, Buick Championship, **Ted Purdy**, Valero Texas Open, **Vijay Singh**, 84 LUMBER Classic

LARGEST 36-HOLE LEAD:
3 strokes, **Carl Pettersson**, The Honda Classic, **Stewart Cink**, WGC-NEC Invitational

LARGEST 54-HOLE LEAD:
7 strokes, **David Toms**, FedEx St. Jude Classic
6 strokes, **Adam Scott**, Booz Allen Classic

LOW 36-HOLE CUT:
4-under-par 140, Chrysler Classic of Tucson, HP Classic of New Orleans, Buick Open, Southern Farm Bureau Classic, FUNAI Classic at the WALT DISNEY WORLD Resort

HIGH 36-HOLE CUT:
4-over-par 148, the Memorial Tournament, Masters Tournament

LOW 54-HOLE CUT:
8-under 207, Michelin Championship at Las Vegas

HIGH 54-HOLE CUT:
even-par 216, AT&T Pebble Beach National Pro-Am

LOW 72-HOLE CUT:
11-under-par 277, Bob Hope Chrysler Classic

FEWEST TO MAKE 36-HOLE CUT:
66, U.S. Open
70, FBR Open, Deutsche Bank Championship, Southern Farm Bureau Classic

MOST TO MAKE 36-HOLE CUT:
86, U.S. Bank Championship in Milwaukee, FUNAI Classic at the WALT DISNEY WORLD Resort

FEWEST TO MAKE 54-HOLE CUT:
72, Michelin Championship at Las Vegas

MOST TO MAKE 54-HOLE CUT:
85, AT&T Pebble Beach National Pro-Am

MOST TO MAKE 72-HOLE CUT:
79, Bob Hope Chrysler Classic

MOST TIED FOR LEAD, 18 HOLES:
8, U.S. Bank Championship in Milwaukee, Michelin Championship at Las Vegas

MOST TIED FOR LEAD, 36 HOLES:
3, Shell Houston Open, the Memorial Tournament, Cialis Western Open

MOST TIED FOR LEAD, 54 HOLES:
3, Bank of America Colonial

MOST CONSECUTIVE EVENTS IN THE MONEY:
133, **Tiger Woods** (PGA TOUR Record)*

*Key: * - Active streak*

CONSECUTIVE YEARS WITH WIN:
9, **Tiger Woods** (1996-2004)

HOLES-IN-ONE (34):
Carl Pettersson (No. 14, Round 2), Nissan Open; **Jose Maria Olazabal** (No. 13, Round 2), THE PLAYERS Championship; **Chris DiMarco** (No. 6, Round 1), **Padraig Harrington** (No. 16, Round 4), **Kirk Triplett** (No. 16, Round 4), Masters Tournament; **Brian Gay** (No. 3, Round 4), Shell Houston Open; **Jim Carter** (No. 8, Round 2), **Michael Allen** (No. 4, Round 3), Fed Ex St. Jude Classic; **Tom Pernice, Jr** (No. 12, Round 2), the Memorial Tournament; **Spencer Levin** – Amateur (No. 17, Round 1), U.S. Open; **Ryan Palmer** (No. 9, Round 3), Booz Allen Classic; **Mike Small** (No. 2, Round 2), **Scott Hoch** (No. 14, Round 2), **Lucas Glover** (No. 12, Round 2), Cialis Western Open; **Mark Hensby** (No. 3, Round 1), **David Gossett** (No. 12, Round 2), **Willie Wood** (No. 16, Round 3), **John Rollins** (No. 7, Round 4), **Greg Chalmers** (No. 7, Round 4), John Deere Classic; **Ernie Els** (No. 8, Round 3), British Open; **Briny Baird** (No. 3, Round 1), Buick Open; **Steve Flesch** (No. 7, Round 1), The INTERNATIONAL; **Hale Irwin** (No. 7, Round 1), **Robert Gamez** (No. 17, Round 2), PGA Championship; **Garrett Willis** (No. 16, Round 4), Reno-Tahoe Open; **Blaine McCallister** (No. 8, Round 1), Buick Championship; **David Peoples** (No. 12, Round 1), **Ben Curtis** (No. 12, Round 4), 84 LUMBER Classic; **Thongchai Jaidee**, (No. 11, Round 2), WGC American Express Championship; **Justin Rose** (No. 17, Round 1), Chrysler Classic of Greensboro; **Tim Clark** (No. 3 Palm Course, Round 1), **Vaughn Taylor** (No. 3, Magnolia Course Round 4), FUNAI Classic at the WALT DISNEY WORLD Resort; **Jonathan Kaye** (No. 17, Round 1), **Mathias Gronberg** (No. 15, Round 2), Chrysler Championship.

DOUBLE EAGLES (3):
John Daly (#2, Par 5, PGA West/Palmer Course), Bob Hope Chrysler Classic
John Douma (#8, Par 5), Chrysler Classic of Tucson
Gary Evans (#4, Par 5), British Open

THREE EAGLES IN ONE ROUND (1):
Harrison Frazar (#5, #7, #14), Indian Wells CC, Bob Hope Chrysler Classic

TWO EAGLES IN ONE ROUND (43):
Chad Campbell, Mercedes Championships; **John Senden** (BD), **Danny Ellis** (IW), **Kenny Perry** (LQ), **Harrison Frazar** (IW), Bob Hope Chrysler Classic; **Arron Oberholser**, **Charles Howell III**, **Alex Cejka**, **John Daly** FBR Open; **John Senden** (SP), AT&T Pebble Beach National Pro-Am; **Jeff Sluman**, Ford Championship at Doral.; **Ken Duke**, The Honda Classic; **Craig Parry**, THE PLAYERS Championship; **Jimmy Walker**, **Paul Stankowski**, Shell Houston Open; **Jeff Maggert**, **Mathias Gronberg, Vaughn Taylor**, Wachovia Championship; **Rich Beem**, **Jason Dufner**, **Michael Clark II**, Fed Ex St. Jude Classic; **Charles Howell III**, Booz Allen Classic; **Vaughn Taylor**, John Deere Classic; **Camilo Villegas**, **Mike Heinen**, **Ted Purdy**, B.C. Open.; **Tag Ridings**, U.S. Bank Championship in Milwaukee; **Geoff Ogilvy**, The INTERNATIONAL; **Ryan Palmer**, Deutsche Bank Championship; **Phil Mickelson**, Bell Canadian Open; **Ben Curtis**, 84 LUMBER Classic; **John Senden**, **Harrison Frazar**, **Rod Pampling**, Southern Farm Bureau Classic; **Lee Janzen** (TS), **Jonathan Kaye** (BB), **Craig Barlow** (TS), **Jim Furyk** (TS), **Kent Jones** (TS), Michelin Championship at Las Vegas; **Steve Stricker**, **Ted Purdy**, Chrysler Classic of Greensboro; **Hank Kuehne** (PC), **Tom Lehman** (MG), FUNAI Classic at the WALT DISNEY WORLD Resort.

BACK-TO-BACK EAGLES (3):
Kenny Perry (#5, #6, La Quinta CC), Bob Hope Chrysler Classic; **Ken Duke** (#5, #6), The Honda Classic; **Jim Furyk** (#15, #16, TPC at Summerlin) Michelin Championship at Las Vegas.

BEST BIRDIE STREAK:
7, **Vijay Singh** (#12-18/second round), Mercedes Championships
7, **Bob Estes** (#12-18/second round), FedEx St. Jude Classic
7, **Neal Lancaster** (#15-3/first round), U.S. Bank Championship in Milwaukee

BEST BIRDIE/EAGLE STREAK:
7-under, **Robert Gamez** (B-B-B-B-B-E/#18-5/third round), Indian Wells CC, Bob Hope Chrysler Classic
7-under, **Billy Andrade** (E-B-B-B-B-B/#6-11/fourth round), PGA West/Palmer Course, Bob Hope Chrysler Classic

BEST COME-FROM-BEHIND LAST DAY TO WIN:
9 strokes, **Stewart Cink**, MCI Heritage
5 strokes, **Ryan Palmer**, FUNAI Classic at the WALT DISNEY WORLD Resort

MOST CONSECUTIVE ROUNDS PAR OR BETTER (SEASON):
22, **Retief Goosen**

CURRENT:
21, **Carl Pettersson**

MULTIPLE WINNERS (8):
Vijay Singh (9), AT&T Pebble Beach National Pro-Am, Shell Houston Open, HP Classic of New Orleans, Buick Open, PGA Championship, Deutsche Bank Championship, Bell Canadian Open, 84 LUMBER Classic, Chrysler Championship
Ernie Els (3), Sony Open in Hawaii, the Memorial Tournament, WGC-American Express Championship
Phil Mickelson (2), Bob Hope Chrysler Classic, Masters Tournament
Sergio Garcia (2), EDS Byron Nelson Championship, Buick Classic
Adam Scott (2), THE PLAYERS Championship, Booz Allen Classic
Todd Hamilton (2), The Honda Classic, British Open
Stewart Cink (2), MCI Heritage, WGC-NEC Invitational
Retief Goosen (2), U.S. Open, THE TOUR Championship presented by Coca-Cola

WIRE-TO-WIRE WINNERS (2):
Stewart Cink, WGC-NEC Invitational
Vijay Singh, 84 LUMBER Classic

FIRST-TIME WINNERS (10): (Rookies underlined)
Heath Slocum, Chrysler Classic of Tucson
Todd Hamilton, The Honda Classic
Zach Johnson, BellSouth Classic
Stephen Ames, Cialis Western Open
Mark Hensby, John Deere Classic
Rod Pampling, The INTERNATIONAL
Vaughn Taylor, Reno Tahoe Open
Bart Bryant, Valero Texas Open
Andre Stolz, Michelin Championship at Las Vegas
Ryan Palmer, FUNAI Classic at the WALT DISNEY WORLD Resort

COURSE RECORDS (no ties):
60 (12-under), **Robert Gamez,** Indian Wells CC, third round, Bob Hope Chrysler Classic
63 (9-under), **Carl Pettersson**, The CC at Mirasol, Sunrise Course, first round, The Honda Classic
64 (8-under), **Kirk Triplett**, Quail Hollow Club, first round, Wachovia Championship
61 (10-under), **Charles Howell III**, TPC at Avenel, first round, Booz Allen Classic
60 (10-under), **Bart Bryant**, The Resort Course at LaCantera, third round, Valero Texas Open
63 (9-under), **Briny Baird**, Bear's Best, second round, Michelin Championship at Las Vegas
62 (9-under), **Jeff Sluman**, Innisbrook Resort, Copperhead Course, first round, Chrysler Championship

TOURNAMENT RECORDS:
277 (11-under), **Joey Sindelar**, **Arron Oberholser**, Wachovia Championship
266 (18-under), **Vijay Singh**, Chrysler Championship

2004 Facts and Figures (cont.)

PLAYOFFS (14):

Sony Open in Hawaii, **Ernie Els** def. **Harrison Frazar** with a birdie-2 on the third extra hole.

Bob Hope Chrysler Classic, **Phil Mickelson** def. **Skip Kendall** with a birdie-4 on the first extra hole.

Buick Invitational, **John Daly** def. **Chris Riley** and **Luke Donald** with a birdie-4 on the first extra hole.

Ford Championship at Doral, **Craig Parry** def. **Scott Verplank** with an eagle-2 on the first extra hole.

MCI Heritage, **Stewart Cink** def. **Ted Purdy** with a birdie-3 on the fifth extra hole

Wachovia Championship, **Joey Sindelar** def. **Arron Olberholser** with a par-4 on the second extra hole.

EDS Byron Nelson Championship, **Sergio Garcia** def. **Dudley Hart** and **Robert Damron** with a par-4 on the first extra hole.

Buick Classic, **Sergio Garcia** def. **Rory Sabbatini** with a birdie-4 on the third extra hole. **Padraig Harrington** was eliminated on the second playoff hole.

John Deere Classic, **Mark Hensby** def. **John E. Morgan** with a par-3 on the second extra hole.

British Open, **Todd Hamilton** def. **Ernie Els** 15 to 16 in a four-hole playoff.

PGA Championship, **Vijay Singh** def. **Justin Leonard** and **Chris DiMarco** in a three-hole playoff at 1-under-par with a 3-3-4 finish on Nos. 10-17-18. Leonard and DiMarco did not finish the 18th hole in the playoff.

Reno-Tahoe Open, **Vaughn Taylor** def. **Scott McCarron**, **Steve Allan**, **Hunter Mahan** with a birdie-3 on the first extra hole.

Buick Championship, **Woody Austin** def. **Tim Herron** with a birdie-3 on the first extra hole.

Bell Canadian Open, **Vijay Singh** def. **Mike Weir** with par-5 on the third extra hole.

EDS Byron Nelson Championship, **Sergio Garcia** def. **Robert Damron** and **Dudley Hart** with a par-4 on the first extra hole.

MONDAY FINISHES:

Shell Houston Open – weather related
HP Classic of New Orleans – weather related
Deutsche Bank Championship – Labor Day scheduled finish

PLAYERS OF THE MONTH:

January	**Jonathan Kaye**
February	**John Daly**
March	**Adam Scott**
April	**Phil Mickelson**
May	**Steve Flesch**
June	**Retief Goosen**
July	**Todd Hamilton**
August	**Vijay Singh**
September	**Vijay Singh**
October/November	**Vijay Singh**

Glossary of Statistics

Driving Distance
The average number of yards per measured drive. Driving distance is measured on two holes per round. Care is taken to select holes which face in opposite directions to counteract the effects of wind. Drives are measured to the point they come to rest, regardless of whether they are in the fairway or not.

Driving Accuracy
The percentage of time a player is able to hit the fairway with his tee shot.

Greens in Regulation
The percentage of time a player was able to hit the green in regulation (greens hit in regulation/holes played). Note: A green is considered hit in regulation if any part of the ball is touching the putting surface and the number of strokes taken is two less than par or fewer.

Putting Average
Measures putting performance on greens hit in regulation. For each green hit in regulation, the total number of putts is divided by the number of greens hit in regulation. By using greens hit in regulation, we are able to eliminate the affects of chipping close and one-putting in the computation.

Total Driving
Total Driving is computed by totaling a player's rank in driving distance and driving accuracy.

Eagles (holes per)
The average number of holes between each eagle.

Birdie Leaders
The average number of birdies made per round played.

Sand Saves Percentage
The percentage of time a player is able to get up and down once in a green-side sand bunker. Note: This up and down is computed regardless of score on the hole.

All Around
This statistic is computed by totaling a player's rank in each of the following statistics: Scoring Leaders, Putting Leaders, Eagle Leaders, Birdie Leaders, Sand Saves, Greens in Regulation, Driving Distance and Driving Accuracy.

Note: See Statistical Leaders, pages 5-10 and 5-11

2004 Statistical Leaders

Driving Distance

	Name	Rounds	Avg.
1.	Hank Kuehne	89	314.4
2.	Scott Hend	79	312.6
3.	John Daly	79	306.0
4.	Mike Heinen	53	305.2
5.	Chris Smith	105	304.0
6.	Lucas Glover	91	303.4
7.	Geoff Ogilvy	87	303.3
8.	Chris Couch	55	302.1
9.	Tiger Woods	72	301.9
10.	J.J. Henry	103	301.3
	TOUR AVG.		**287.3**

Driving Accuracy Percentage

	Name	Rounds	%
1.	Fred Funk	96	77.2
2.	Scott Verplank	91	77.1
3.	Craig Bowden	83	76.1
4.	Joe Durant	85	75.1
5.	Tom Byrum	83	74.7
6.	Jose Coceres	64	74.3
7.	Bart Bryant	69	74.2
8.	Olin Browne	88	73.5
9.	John Cook	53	73.4
10.	Omar Uresti	85	73.1
	TOUR AVG.		**64.2**

Greens In Regulation

	Name	Rounds	Avg.
1.	Joe Durant	85	73.3
2.	Vijay Singh	110	73.0
3.	Tom Lehman	66	71.4
4.	Sergio Garcia	64	70.8
5.	Briny Baird	97	70.6
6.	John Senden	96	70.5
7.	Chris Smith	105	70.4
8.	Robert Allenby	88	70.3
9.	Duffy Waldorf	73	69.9
10.	Phil Mickelson	79	69.5
	TOUR AVG.		**65.1**

Putting Average

	Name	Rounds	Avg.
1.	Stewart Cink	97	1.723
2.	Tiger Woods	72	1.724
3.	Greg Chalmers	70	1.726
4.	Carl Pettersson	97	1.733
5.	John Daly	79	1.736
6.	Brian Gay	94	1.737
T7.	Mark Hensby	93	1.738
T7.	Loren Roberts	79	1.738
T9.	Ben Crane	92	1.740
T9.	Ernie Els	58	1.740
	TOUR AVG.		**1.777**

Total Driving

	Name	Rounds	%
1.	Jeff Brehaut	34	79
2.	John Senden	28	93
3.	Ted Purdy	35	98
4.	Lucas Glover	30	99
T5.	Joe Durant	26	101
T5.	J.J. Henry	30	101
7.	Jason Bohn	29	109
8.	Craig Barlow	25	110
9.	Brian Bateman	24	113
T10.	Robert Allenby	26	114
T10.	Harrison Frazar	25	114
T10.	Bo Van Pelt	30	114
	TOUR AVG.		**196**

Eagles (Holes Per)

	Name	Rounds	Holes
1.	Nick Price	50	90.0
2.	Geoff Ogilvy	87	92.1
3.	Harrison Frazar	82	92.3
4.	John Daly	79	101.6
5.	Vaughn Taylor	82	105.4
6.	Mike Heinen	53	106.0
7.	John Senden	96	108.0
8.	Vijay Singh	110	116.5
9.	Scott Hend	79	118.5
10.	Tom Lehman	66	118.8
	TOUR AVG.		**222.1**

Birdie Average

	Name	Rounds	Avg.
1.	Vijay Singh	110	4.40
2.	Tiger Woods	72	4.38
3.	Phil Mickelson	79	4.20
4.	Ernie Els	58	4.07
5.	Retief Goosen	55	4.05
6.	Carl Pettersson	97	4.00
7.	John Daly	79	3.99
8.	Geoff Ogilvy	87	3.97
T9.	Woody Austin	94	3.96
T9.	Adam Scott	52	3.96
T9.	Scott Verplank	91	3.96
	TOUR AVG.		**3.53**

Sand Save Percentage

	Name	Rounds	%
1.	Dan Forsman	77	62.3
2.	Jose Coceres	64	61.7
3.	Dennis Paulson	71	61.1
4.	Geoff Ogilvy	87	61.0
5.	Len Mattiace	75	60.2
6.	David Frost	78	60.1
T7.	Hank Kuehne	89	59.3
T7.	Loren Roberts	79	59.3
T7.	Adam Scott	52	59.3
10.	Rod Pampling	94	58.9
	TOUR AVG.		**49.1**

Scoring Average

	Name	Rounds	Avg.
1.	Vijay Singh	110	68.84
2.	Ernie Els	58	68.98
3.	Tiger Woods	72	69.04
4.	Phil Mickelson	79	69.16
5.	Retief Goosen	55	69.32
6.	Sergio Garcia	64	69.80
7.	Stewart Cink	97	69.82
8.	Stephen Ames	95	69.90
9.	Scott Verplank	91	69.92
T10.	Jay Haas	79	70.05
T10.	David Toms	74	70.05
	TOUR AVG.		**71.13**

All-Around Ranking

	Name	Rounds	Pts.
1.	Geoff Ogilvy	26	268
2.	Vijay Singh	29	282
3.	Phil Mickelson	22	296
4.	John Daly	22	359
5.	Stephen Ames	27	370
6.	Retief Goosen	16	374
7.	Harrison Frazar	25	375
8.	Tiger Woods	19	425
T9.	Tom Lehman	19	426
T9.	David Toms	24	426
	TOUR AVG.		**783**

Note: See Glossary, page 5-9

2004 PGA TOUR Statistical High/Low

Those with 50 rounds or more based on 196 ranked players.

	Highest	Average	Lowest
Driving Distance	314.4	287.3	268.2
Driving Accuracy	77.2	64.2	49.9
Total Driving	79	196	353
Greens In Regulation	73.3	65.1	54.7
Putting	1.723	1.777	1.847
Eagles	90.0	222.1	1350.0
Birdies	4.40	3.53	2.40
Sand Saves	62.3	49.1	31.8
Scoring	68.84	71.13	75.01
All-Around	268	783	1319

Year-By-Year Statistical Leaders

Driving Distance

1980	Dan Pohl	274.3
1981	Dan Pohl	280.1
1982	Bill Calfee	275.3
1983	John McComish	277.4
1984	Bill Glasson	276.5
1985	Andy Bean	278.2
1986	Davis Love III	285.7
1987	John McComish	283.9
1988	Steve Thomas	284.6
1989	Ed Humenik	280.9
1990	Tom Purtzer	279.6
1991	John Daly	288.9
1992	John Daly	283.4
1993	John Daly	288.9
1994	Davis Love III	283.8
1995	John Daly	289.0
1996	John Daly	288.8
1997	John Daly	302.0
1998	John Daly	299.4
1999	John Daly	305.6
2000	John Daly	301.4
2001	John Daly	306.7
2002	John Daly	306.8
2003	**Hank Kuehne**	**321.4**
2004	Hank Kuehne	314.4

Driving Accuracy Pct.

1980	Mike Reid	79.5
1981	Calvin Peete	81.9
1982	**Calvin Peete**	**84.6**
1983	Calvin Peete	81.3
1984	Calvin Peete	77.5
1985	Calvin Peete	80.6
1986	Calvin Peete	81.7
1987	Calvin Peete	83.0
1988	Calvin Peete	82.5
1989	Calvin Peete	82.6
1990	Calvin Peete	83.7
1991	Hale Irwin	78.3
1992	Doug Tewell	82.3
1993	Doug Tewell	82.5
1994	David Edwards	81.6
1995	Fred Funk	81.3
1996	Fred Funk	78.7
1997	Allen Doyle	80.8
1998	Bruce Fleisher	81.4
1999	Fred Funk	80.2
2000	Fred Funk	79.7
2001	Joe Durant	81.1
2002	Fred Funk	81.2
2003	Fred Funk	77.9
2004	Fred Funk	77.2

Greens In Regulation Pct.

1980	Jack Nicklaus	72.1
1981	Calvin Peete	73.1
1982	Calvin Peete	72.4
1983	Calvin Peete	71.4
1984	Andy Bean	72.1
1985	John Mahaffey	71.9
1986	John Mahaffey	72.0
1987	Gil Morgan	73.3
1988	John Adams	73.9
1989	Bruce Lietzke	72.6
1990	Doug Tewell	70.9
1991	Bruce Lietzke	73.3
1992	Tim Simpson	74.0
1993	Fuzzy Zoeller	73.6
1994	Bill Glasson	73.0
1995	Lennie Clements	72.3
1996	Mark O'Meara	71.783*
1997	Tom Lehman	72.7
1998	Hal Sutton	71.3
1999	Tiger Woods	71.4
2000	**Tiger Woods**	**75.2**
2001	Tom Lehman	74.5
2002	Tiger Woods	74.0
2003	Joe Durant	72.9
2004	Joe Durant	73.3

Putting Average

1980	Jerry Pate	28.81
1981	Alan Tapie	28.70
1982	Ben Crenshaw	28.65
1983	Morris Hatalsky	27.96
1984	Gary McCord	28.57
1985	Craig Stadler	28.627*
1986	Greg Norman	1.736
1987	Ben Crenshaw	1.743
1988	Don Pooley	1.729
1989	Steve Jones	1.734
1990	Larry Rinker	1.7467*
1991	Jay Don Blake	1.7326*
1992	Mark O'Meara	1.731
1993	David Frost	1.739
1994	Loren Roberts	1.737
1995	Jim Furyk	1.708
1996	Brad Faxon	1.709
1997	Don Pooley	1.718
1998	Rick Fehr	1.722
1999	Brad Faxon	1.723
2000	Brad Faxon	1.704
2001	David Frost	1.708
2002	**Bob Heintz**	**1.682**
2003	John Huston	1.713
2004	Stewart Cink	1.723

Total Driving

1991	Bruce Lietzke	42
1992	Bruce Lietzke	50
1993	Greg Norman	41
1994	Nick Price	43
1995	**Nick Price**	**40**
1996	David Duval	47
1997	Joe Durant	67
1998	Hal Sutton	62
1999	Tiger Woods	52
2000	Tiger Woods	56
2001	Sergio Garcia	46
2002	Charles Howell III	70
2003	Mike Heinen	51
2004	Jeff Brehaut	79

Eagles (Holes Per)

1980	Dave Eichelberger	16
1981	Bruce Lietzke	12
1982	Tom Weiskopf	10
	J.C. Snead	10
	Andy Bean	10
1983	Chip Beck	15
1984	Gary Hallberg	15
1985	Larry Rinker	14
1986	Joey Sindelar	16
1987	Phil Blackmar	20
1988	Ken Green	21
1989	Lon Hinkle	14
	Duffy Waldorf	14
1990	Paul Azinger	14
1991	Andy Bean	15
	John Huston	15
1992	Dan Forsman	18
1993	Davis Love III	15
1994	Davis Love III	18
1995	Kelly Gibson	16#
1996	Tom Watson	97.2
1997	Tiger Woods	104.1
1998	Davis Love III	83.3
1999	Vijay Singh	104.8
2000	**Tiger Woods**	**72.0**
2001	Phil Mickelson	73.8
2002	John Daly	78.4
2003	Tiger Woods	76.5
2004	Nick Price	90.0

Birdie Average

1980	Andy Bean	388
1981	Vance Heafner	388
1982	Andy Bean	392
1983	Hal Sutton	399
1984	Mark O'Meara	419
1985	Joey Sindelar	411
1986	Joey Sindelar	415
1987	Dan Forsman	409
1988	Dan Forsman	465
1989	Ted Schulz	415
1990	Mike Donald	401
1991	Scott Hoch	446
1992	Jeff Sluman	417
1993	John Huston	426
1994	Brad Bryant	397
1995	Steve Lowery	410+
1996	Fred Couples	4.20
1997	Tiger Woods	4.25
1998	David Duval	4.29
1999	Tiger Woods	4.46
2000	**Tiger Woods**	**4.92**
2001	Phil Mickelson	4.54
2002	Tiger Woods	4.47
2003	Vijay Singh	4.41
2004	Vijay Singh	4.40

Sand Save Pct.

1980	Bob Eastwood	65.4
1981	Tom Watson	60.1
1982	Isao Aoki	60.2
1983	Isao Aoki	62.3
1984	Peter Oosterhuis	64.7
1985	Tom Purtzer	60.8
1986	Paul Azinger	63.8
1987	Paul Azinger	63.2
1988	Greg Powers	63.5
1989	Mike Sullivan	66.0
1990	Paul Azinger	67.2
1991	Ben Crenshaw	64.9
1992	Mitch Adcock	66.9
1993	Ken Green	64.4
1994	Corey Pavin	65.4
1995	Billy Mayfair	68.6
1996	Gary Rusnak	64.0
1997	Bob Estes	70.3
1998	**Keith Fergus**	**71.0**
1999	Jeff Sluman	67.3
2000	Fred Couples	67.0
2001	Franklin Langham	68.9
2002	Jóse María Olazábal	64.9
2003	Stuart Appleby	62.1
2004	Dan Forsman	62.3

Scoring Average

1980	Lee Trevino	69.73
1981	Tom Kite	69.80
1982	Tom Kite	70.21
1983	Raymond Floyd	70.61
1984	Calvin Peete	70.56
1985	Don Pooley	70.36
1986	Scott Hoch	70.08
1987	David Frost	70.09
1988	Greg Norman	69.38
1989	Payne Stewart	69.485*
1990	Greg Norman	69.10
1991	Fred Couples	69.59
1992	Fred Couples	69.38
1993	Greg Norman	68.90
1994	Greg Norman	68.81
1995	Greg Norman	69.06
1996	Tom Lehman	69.32
1997	Nick Price	68.98
1998	David Duval	69.13
1999	Tiger Woods	68.43
2000	**Tiger Woods**	**67.79**
2001	Tiger Woods	68.81
2002	Tiger Woods	68.56
2003	Tiger Woods	68.41
2004	Vijay Singh	68.84

All-Around

1987	Dan Pohl	170
1988	Payne Stewart	170
1989	Paul Azinger	250
1990	Paul Azinger	162
1991	Scott Hoch	283
1992	Fred Couples	256
1993	Gil Morgan	252
1994	Bob Estes	227
1995	Justin Leonard	323
1996	Fred Couples	215
1997	Bill Glasson	282
1998	John Huston	151
1999	Tiger Woods	120
2000	**Tiger Woods**	**113**
2001	Phil Mickelson	174
2002	Phil Mickelson	259
2003	Tiger Woods	206
2004	Geoff Ogilvy	268

* = carried a decimal farther to determine winner
\# = changed to frequency
\+ = changed to average per round

Category records are boldfaced

Note: See Glossary, page 5-9

West Coast Swing Presented By Allianz

Phil Mickelson captured the 2004 PGA TOUR West Coast Swing presented by The St. Paul. Mickelson, who won the Bob Hope Chrysler Classic in January, received a $500,000 winner's bonus, presented to the player who accumulates the most points during the nine-tournament West Coast Swing, based on top-10 performances. Vijay Singh finished runner-up and collected $300,000, while third-place finisher Mike Weir earned $200,000. Mickelson finished with 241.250 points, Singh had 212.500 and Weir, 175.000.

In addition to his victory, Mickelson finished tied for seventh at the FBR Open, third at AT&T Pebble Beach National Pro-Am, tied for fourth in the Buick Invitational and tied for fifth at the World Golf Championships-Accenture Match Play Championship.

Mickelson won the inaugural "King of the Swing" title in 1998. Tiger Woods earned the title the next two years, Davis Love III captured the 2001 title, Chris DiMarco in 2002 and Mike Weir won in 2003.

Allianz Life (the U.S. life subsidiary of the Allianz Group), a leading provider of annuities, life and health coverage, will be the presenting sponsor of the competition beginning this year.

Final 2004 West Coast Swing Standings

	Player	Events	Points
1.	Phil Mickelson	5	241.250
2.	Vijay Singh	7	227.000
3.	Mike Weir	6	175.000
4.	Tiger Woods	4	166.666
5.	Stuart Appleby	5	160.000
6.	John Daly	5	150.000
6.	Jonathan Kaye	7	150.000
8.	Davis Love III	4	142.500
9.	Harrison Frazar	5	123.571
10.	Darren Clarke	5	120.000

Fall Finish Presented By PricewaterhouseCoopers

On the strength of four wins and top-10s in all five starts, Vijay Singh won his third consecutive Fall Finish Presented by PricewaterhouseCoopers. Singh received a bonus of $500,000.

Now in its sixth year, the Fall Finish Presented by PricewaterhouseCoopers is an 11-tournament series (that begins at the Deutsche Bank Championship and will end with the conclusion of THE TOUR Championship presented by Coca-Cola) that includes enhanced purses and bonus awards totaling $1 million. Points are awarded for each top-10 finish, from 100 points for first place to 10 for 10th. Singh also won the title in 2002 and 2003. Bob Estes won the series in 2001, and Tiger Woods won in 2000.

Singh finished the 2004 season with 480 points to earn the $500,000 bonus. Ryan Palmer placed second with 170 points to win $300,000 and Tom Lehman third with 163.750 points to win $200,000. In six starts, Singh won the Deutsche Bank Championship, Bell Canadian Open, the 84 LUMBER Classic and the Chrysler Championship, was second at the FUNAI Classic at the WALT DISNEY WORLD Resort and ninth at THE TOUR Championship presented by Coca-Cola.

Final 2004 Fall Finish Standings

	Player	Events	Points
1.	Vijay Singh	6	480.000
2.	Ryan Palmer	8	170.000
3.	Tom Lehman	5	163.750
4.	Tiger Woods	3	150.000
5.	Retief Goosen	3	125.000
6.	Mike Weir	4	110.000
7.	Stewart Cink	5	106.250
8.	Ernie Els	2	103.333
9.	Bart Bryant	7	100.000
9.	Fred Funk	6	100.000
9.	Brent Geiberger	8	100.000
9.	Andre Stolz	6	100.000

2004 Scoring Average By Event

The scoring average, by round, for the field during the course of the 2004 season, with cumulative average:

Tournament	Round 1	Round 2	Round 3	Round 4	Round 5	Total
Mercedes Championships	70.600	71.800	69.500	72.867		71.192
Sony Open in Hawaii	70.271	69.000	69.215	69.329		69.508
Bob Hope Chrysler Classic	69.688	69.188	68.528	69.016	69.114	69.107
FBR Open	70.894	70.754	69.329	70.757		70.552
AT&T Pebble Beach National Pro-Am	72.272	72.458	73.067	73.662		72.717
Buick Invitational	71.536	72.040	73.171	73.134		72.265
Nissan Open	71.469	69.783	71.256	71.064		70.814
Chrysler Classic of Tucson	70.132	70.634	70.833	69.901		70.373
Ford Championship at Doral	72.347	72.754	69.671	69.924		71.570
The Honda Classic	72.119	72.529	72.342	73.247		72.482
Bay Hill Invitational Presented by MasterCard	72.142	71.667	72.781	72.767		72.238
THE PLAYERS Championship	72.810	73.548	71.928	73.470		73.004
BellSouth Classic	73.106	73.507	71.493	74.141		73.143
Masters Tournament	75.172	73.785	73.273	72.545		73.974
MCI Heritage	72.797	71.534	71.056	71.375		71.833
Shell Houston Open	73.160	73.405	72.549	72.606		73.056
HP Classic of New Orleans	70.405	69.801	71.291	70.538		70.388
Wachovia Championship	72.391	72.714	71.806	72.139		72.368
EDS Byron Nelson Championship	69.949	71.033	69.138	71.000		70.343
Bank of America Colonial	70.876	71.266	70.405	70.784		70.878
FedEx St. Jude Classic	74.461	69.908	69.446	73.081		71.890
the Memorial Tournament	73.133	72.882	72.267	72.267		72.697
Buick Classic	71.276	70.771	71.171	72.756		71.351
U.S. Open Championship	73.361	73.026	73.515	78.727		74.068
Booz Allen Classic	70.897	70.845	70.963	71.313		70.963
Cialis Western Open	71.910	72.789	71.707	72.366		72.238
John Deere Classic	70.558	70.638	69.711	69.973		70.346
B.C. Open	71.220	70.346	69.526	69.962		70.397
British Open Championship	72.910	73.551	72.425	73.918		73.212
U.S. Bank Championship in Milwaukee	70.321	71.260	70.093	70.753		70.657
Buick Open	70.968	70.712	71.085	70.197		70.778
The INTERNATIONAL	72.569	72.271	71.736	74.000		72.470
PGA Championship	73.329	73.268	71.986	73.767		73.163
Reno-Tahoe Open	72.415	71.528	73.458	74.352		72.671
WGC-NEC Invitational	70.803	70.853	70.987	71.720		71.090
Buick Championship	71.297	70.711	70.000	69.557		70.589
Deutsche Bank Championship	71.814	71.543	73.186	71.186		71.839
Bell Canadian Open	73.227	72.432	72.923	72.128		72.731
Valero Texas Open	68.861	69.329	68.139	69.923		69.068
84 LUMBER Classic	71.930	71.835	71.230	71.716		71.742
Southern Farm Bureau Classic	70.641	69.700	69.314	69.557		69.915
WGC-American Express Championship	70.515	72.235	71.426	73.044		71.805
Michelin Championship at Las Vegas	68.542	68.806	70.599	69.875		69.390
Chrysler Classic of Greensboro	70.107	71.443	72.243	71.100		71.087
FUNAI Classic at the WALT DISNEY WORLD Resort	69.382	70.694	69.663	69.826		69.928
Chrysler Championship	71.432	71.202	71.123	71.292		71.278
THE TOUR Championship presented by Coca-Cola	70.633	70.867	69.931	69.345		70.203

2004 Player Performance Chart (1-25)

LEGEND

- (blank) Did not play
- T7 Final position
- P1 P2 Involved in playoff
- DQ Disqualified
- CUT Missed cut
- WD Withdrew
- DNS Did not start

Tournament	1. Vijay Singh	2. Ernie Els	3. Phil Mickelson	4. Tiger Woods	5. Stewart Cink	6. Retief Goosen	7. Adam Scott	8. Stephen Ames	9. Sergio Garcia	10. Davis Love III	11. Todd Hamilton	12. Chris DiMarco	13. Stuart Appleby	14. Mike Weir	15. Mark Hensby	16. Rory Sabbatini	17. Jerry Kelly	18. Steve Flesch	19. Zach Johnson	20. Scott Verplank	21. John Daly	22. David Toms	23. Shigeki Maruyama	24. Chad Campbell	25. Fred Funk
Mercedes Championships	2	T21		T4		T4	7			T9			1	24		25		T15				DNS	T15	T15	DNS
Sony Open in Hawaii	T10	P1				T10	CUT	T8		3	CUT		CUT		T31	WD	T5	CUT	CUT				T41	CUT	T36
Bob Hope Chrysler Classic			P1		T50	T26		T20				CUT		T41	CUT		T30	T16	T20	T20	T30			T56	CUT
FBR Open	T3		T7		T14	T9		T14	T9			2		T5		CUT		T3		T7	T54		T63	T39	T68
AT&T Pebble Beach National Pro-Am	1		3							CUT	T25			T4	T7	CUT	T35		T59						
Buick Invitational	CUT		T4	T10	T10			T45	T30		CUT		T40		WD	T21		T16	T40		P1		T4	T53	
Nissan Open	T24			T7	T32			T24	T20			T44	3	1		T15	T74	T67	T56		4	CUT	2	T39	T32
Chrysler Classic of Tucson											T40				T3	T3					T69				
WGC-Accenture Match Play Champ	T17		T5	1	T17	T33	T9		T33	2		T9	T17	T17			T5	T17		T33		T9	T33	T9	T33
Ford Championship at Doral			T24		T17	3		T27			T15	T11			CUT		T44		CUT	P2		T5	T11		T17
The Honda Classic								CUT		2	1	T30			T13	T9		T30	T13			T25		T9	CUT
Bay Hill Invitational	T31	CUT		T46	T46	CUT	T3	T6	T31	T31	T69		2		T15	CUT	5	T40	T6	T3	T10		T6	1	
THE PLAYERS Championship	T13	T26	T3	T16	T22	CUT	1	T13	T53	T33	T58	CUT	CUT	CUT		T42	T6	CUT		T26	79	CUT	T53	T42	T10
BellSouth Classic			10		T8		CUT					T20		T45	2	T56		T38	1			CUT			
Masters Tournament	T6	2	1	T22	T17	T13	CUT		T4	T6	40	T6	T22	CUT			T31	T17		29	CUT	CUT	CUT	CUT	CUT
MCI Heritage		T3			P1	CUT		T7		T32	CUT				CUT			CUT	T53	T32				T32	6
Shell Houston Open	1							T4			CUT				CUT	T6			T11		T6				
HP Classic of New Orleans	1		T2					T7			CUT	T76	CUT				T34	T45		T54		T34			
Wachovia Championship	T10		T5	T3	CUT				T61	T21	T21	T50	T15	T21		T50	T66	T5	CUT			CUT	T56	T21	CUT
EDS Byron Nelson Championship	T59	T7	CUT	T4					P1		T59	T14	CUT	T59	T67	T21	T11		T41	T14	T27	CUT	T7	T48	CUT
Bank of America Colonial			T35		T14			3	T35	T35	T44	T44	CUT	T61	CUT	T31		1	T14	T35		T44	CUT	2	26
FedEx St. Jude Classic					T5										CUT						T42	1			T26
the Memorial Tournament	T24	1		3	T40	T8		T6	T24	T16	T33	T24	T63		T46	T11	T16	T33	T24		T11		T46	T24	CUT
Buick Classic	T4	T16	T16		CUT		T32	CUT	P1	T28	CUT	T9	T23	CUT		P2	T32		T23	T28		CUT	CUT	CUT	CUT
U.S. Open Championship	T28	T9	2	T17	CUT	1	CUT	T9	T20	CUT	CUT	T9	CUT	T4		CUT	T40	T7	T48	T40		T20	T4	CUT	6
Booz Allen Classic							1								T43	3					79				CUT
Cialis Western Open	T17			T7				1		T7	CUT		T5	CUT	T3		T33	CUT	CUT	T11			T11	T51	
John Deere Classic	T4				T8						T59	T32			P1				T20				T27		
B.C. Open																									T40
British Open Championship	T20	P2	3	T9	T14	T7	T42	CUT	CUT	T5	P1	T63	T36	T9		T66	T47	T54	CUT	T7	CUT	T30	T30	CUT	
U.S. Bank Championship in Milwaukee																	T13			T11					T2
Buick Open	1			T3	5			CUT				T15			CUT		T8	T43		T10	2				
The INTERNATIONAL		29			T6			CUT		T15	T12	T6	T19		T24	T47		CUT	CUT			T52		T19	
PGA Championship	P1	T4	T6	T24	T17		T9	T9	CUT	CUT	T37	P2	T17	CUT	T68	CUT	CUT	T37	T37	T62	CUT	T17	CUT	T24	CUT
Reno-Tahoe Open																									
WGC-NEC Invitational	T32	T65	T43	T2	1	DNS	T55	T22	T16	T4	21	T6	T9	T41	T65	T2	T19	T48	T22	T19	T43	T6	T27	T69	T61
Buick Championship																	T13		T3						T3
Deutsche Bank Championship	1			T2			T2								T37			WD	T13		T37	T13	T6		
Bell Canadian Open	P1		T57		T4			CUT		T40		T24		P2	T9			T52						T26	T47
Valero Texas Open																	T5								
84 LUMBER Classic	1				2						T53	T3		T61	CUT	CUT	T32	T53	T3	CUT	T13	T25	T20		
Southern Farm Bureau Classic																									1
WGC-American Express Championship		1		9	T23	T6	T36	T36	T4	T41	T6	T36	T16		T11	T21	T16	T23	10	T54		T13	T16	T50	
Michelin Championship at Las Vegas			WD										T23					CUT		T15					
Chrysler Classic of Greensboro										CUT							T8		61		CUT	T4	T19		T27
FUNAI Classic							T28				T16	T68		T6		T16	T41	T28	T16	CUT			T55	T41	
Chrysler Championship	1		CUT		CUT	T20		T50		CUT			CUT	CUT	CUT		CUT					T6		T62	T44
THE TOUR Championship	9	T10	T19	2	T21	1	T21	T4	T15	WD	28	T24	T15	T4	T4	T10	3	T21	13	T7	18	T10	T19	WD	T24

Note: Players listed according to place on the final 2004 PGA TOUR Money List.

2004 Player Performance Chart (26-50)

LEGEND

	Did not play
T7	Final position
P1 P2	Involved in playoff
DQ	Disqualified
CUT	Missed cut
WD	Withdrew
DNS	Did not start

Tournament	26. K.J. Choi	27. Jay Haas	28. Darren Clarke	29. Carlos Franco	30. Kenny Perry	31. Rod Pampling	32. Tim Herron	33. Charles Howell III	34. Jonathan Kaye	35. Luke Donald	36. Ted Purdy	37. Ryan Palmer	38. Kirk Triplett	39. Bo Van Pelt	40. Jesper Parnevik	41. Joey Sindelar	42. Justin Leonard	43. Jeff Maggert	44.Robert Allenby	45. Woody Austin	46. Duffy Waldorf	47. Tom Pernice, Jr.	48. Harrison Frazar	49. Joe Ogilvie	50. Fred Couples
Mercedes Championships			3		T15				12				6				T13								T21
Sony Open in Hawaii			CUT	T20	CUT	T54	T31	T27	T54	T20	T48	T64		T15	T15			CUT		T64	T36	CUT	P2	T64	
Bob Hope Chrysler Classic		3		CUT	T5	T9	CUT	CUT	4			CUT	T9	CUT	T5	CUT	T30				T20	T36	T9	T30	
FBR Open	CUT	T33		T49	WD	T14	T24	T24	1	CUT	CUT		CUT	T14	T49	T42	T9	CUT	T14	CUT	T5	T59	CUT	DNS	CUT
AT&T Pebble Beach National Pro-Am	T4					CUT	T69	T35		T17	T17	T35	T14	T25	T7			2		T25		T7	CUT	T54	T25
Buick Invitational	T25	T10	CUT			T66		T66	T30	P2	T72	CUT		T4	T4	T30			T40	T25	T4	T10		CUT	
Nissan Open	T65	T39	CUT	T44			T32	73	CUT	T67		CUT	6	T44	78			T10	T15	T59	WD	CUT		T44	T59
Chrysler Classic of Tucson				T8							T20	CUT						WD					T3	CUT	
WGC-Accenture Match Play Champ	T33	T33	3		T9		T33	T33	T33								T33		T17		T17				T17
Ford Championship at Doral	T5	T34		T74	T31	T34					T70	T31		T31	T27	T44	T44			T17			CUT	T64	
The Honda Classic				T46	CUT	T13	CUT	T53		T21	T30	T30		CUT	T30	CUT	T25		T4	T4		T13		T70	T25
Bay Hill Invitational	CUT		T6		T15	T24	T24	T15			CUT	T24	T31	T13		CUT		CUT	CUT	T62	CUT	CUT	T60		T15
THE PLAYERS Championship	T42	T6	T26	T58	T3	T58	CUT	CUT	CUT	CUT			CUT		T33	T74	T42	T33	T33	T16	T74	T72	CUT		CUT
BellSouth Classic									T56	T8	CUT	CUT		T66		CUT					T20	CUT	T35	T38	
Masters Tournament	3	T17	CUT		CUT		CUT	T13	CUT				T6				T35	CUT	CUT						T6
MCI Heritage		T7	T11			T16			T11	CUT	P2	CUT			CUT	CUT	T39	T45		T32		CUT		CUT	
Shell Houston Open	T11	T43		T19		T43	T11	CUT			T11	CUT		T19		CUT	T29	CUT	T49		WD	T29		T19	T49
HP Classic of New Orleans	T7			CUT				T5			T25	T12	T61	CUT		T34				CUT		CUT	T50	T2	
Wachovia Championship	T35	T28		T3			CUT	CUT	T15	T15	CUT	CUT	T15		CUT	P1	CUT	T5	T50	CUT	CUT	CUT	CUT	T28	
EDS Byron Nelson Championship				T14	T59	T21	T4			T14	T27	CUT		T21	T34		T34	CUT	T41	CUT	T4		T27	WD	
Bank of America Colonial					T12	T44	T63		CUT	T63	CUT	CUT	T14	T5	T14	T41	T14	T9	T54	CUT	CUT		CUT	T14	
FedEx St. Jude Classic							T3	T9			T23		T54									T18		T23	
the Memorial Tournament	5	T8			T6	CUT	T19	CUT	CUT	CUT	T24		CUT	CUT	T46	CUT	CUT	T51	T33	T66	CUT	T16	23	CUT	2
Buick Classic		CUT	CUT	T60	T9				T80	7	T32	CUT		T9	CUT	T32		CUT	T14	CUT	WD	T42		T16	T4
U.S. Open Championship	T31	T9	CUT	WD	CUT		T13	T36	CUT				T20	T31		CUT	CUT	3	T7		CUT	CUT		T40	CUT
Booz Allen Classic						CUT	T4	2	T69	T43		T11		T4		CUT	CUT				T11	T16	T11		
Cialis Western Open	T40			T17		CUT		T17		T3	CUT	T81				T63			T11	CUT				CUT	
John Deere Classic		T11		T55							T46	CUT	T59					WD		T46		T27	T39	CUT	
B.C. Open											2					T17									
British Open Championship	T16	CUT	T11		T16	T27	CUT	T42	CUT	CUT				T30			T16		CUT						
U.S. Bank Championship in Milwaukee	CUT			1	T7						T62	T31	T18	T7		T47				CUT			T57		
Buick Open	CUT			T3	T15							CUT						CUT		T24		T43		T63	
The INTERNATIONAL		5				1		CUT	CUT		CUT	T52	T40	T52		CUT	T15		T47		4	3	T24	CUT	
PGA Championship	T6	T37	T13	T31	CUT	T55	CUT	T31	CUT	T24	CUT		CUT	T31	CUT	CUT	P2		T9	T62	T49	CUT	CUT	T49	
Reno-Tahoe Open											CUT	69								8	T35		CUT	T9	
WGC-NEC Invitational	T58	T41	T14	T58	T27	T14		T9	T65	T16			T69		T22	T32	T50		T9						T32
Buick Championship							P2				T32	T61	T13	T21		T32				P1		T3		CUT	CUT
Deutsche Bank Championship				WD			CUT	T9			CUT	T17		CUT	T29	T55				CUT		CUT	T65		
Bell Canadian Open					T19			CUT			CUT				T9	T26	T66					CUT		3	
Valero Texas Open						T52					T5	T29		T29	T22		T10	78	CUT		T14			T14	
84 LUMBER Classic	T7			T50		T50	74	T25	T20		T25	CUT		CUT		T42			T20	CUT	T7	T66			
Southern Farm Bureau Classic						T14					T19	2	7			T46				T26			T34		
WGC-American Express Championship	T57	T43	T4	T28			T54	T59	T59	T11							T28		T54						T36
Michelin Championship at Las Vegas								CUT	T52		T62	T52	CUT	T37	CUT		T23		T45	T37	T11	T45	T2	CUT	
Chrysler Classic of Greensboro		CUT		T19		T16				CUT	T8	CUT		T16	T27	CUT			T46		CUT	7		T8	
FUNAI Classic				T49		T68	CUT	T62			CUT	1	T24	CUT	CUT	T4		T62		CUT	CUT	T74	T55	CUT	
Chrysler Championship	CUT	T13		T70	T8	T62	T24	T50	WD		CUT	T58	5	T62	T2	CUT	T38		T6	T30	T50	T38	T30	DQ	
THE TOUR Championship	27	T7	T15	T24	29																				

Note: Players listed according to place on the final 2004 PGA TOUR Money List.

2004 Player Performance Chart (51-75)

LEGEND

(blank)	Did not play
T7	Final position
P1 P2	Involved in playoff
DQ	Disqualified
CUT	Missed cut
WD	Withdrew
DNS	Did not start

Tournament	51. Carl Pettersson	52. Arron Oberholser	53. Tom Lehman	54. Alex Cejka	55. Craig Parry	56. Chris Riley	57. Brent Geiberger	58. Frank Lickliter II	59. Fredrik Jacobson	60. Scott Hoch	61. Geoff Ogilvy	62. Justin Rose	63. Patrick Sheehan	64. Skip Kendall	65. Tim Petrovic	66. Steve Lowery	67. Vaughn Taylor	68. Stephen Leaney	69. Briny Baird	70. Jonathan Byrd	71. Tim Clark	72. Heath Slocum	73. Thomas Bjorn	74. Bob Estes	75.Ben Crane
Mercedes Championships								T26		8															T9
Sony Open in Hawaii	CUT		T59			T20	T41	4		CUT			CUT	CUT	CUT		CUT		T5	T31		77			T31
Bob Hope Chrysler Classic	T50					T9	CUT		T50		T20		73	P2	T69	T74		T36	CUT			CUT		T36	T5
FBR Open	T46	T46	23	T14		T33	T39	CUT	T9		CUT		CUT	CUT	T49	T54		CUT	58	CUT	CUT	T14		T27	CUT
AT&T Pebble Beach National Pro-Am	T25	T4	T25					T69					T63		T21	T69	T69			CUT					
Buick Invitational	CUT	T72	T16	CUT		P2	CUT		T66		CUT		T80	CUT	T45		T25	T21	T37		CUT	T37	T4	CUT	
Nissan Open	T24	CUT	T56	CUT			T15	T59	T39		CUT	T59	CUT	CUT	T20	CUT		CUT	T10		T10	CUT	T70	CUT	T59
Chrysler Classic of Tucson			64				T40	T27			T17		T27			T49	T34				T8	1			
WGC-Accenture Match Play Champ				T17		T33			T9	T33		T33						4	T33				T17	T17	
Ford Championship at Doral				T15	P1	CUT	WD			T56			T34	T44	CUT	CUT	CUT		T34		78	T17			CUT
The Honda Classic	T13			CUT	T36	T13			T4		T13	T36	T41	T59			CUT		T21					CUT	
Bay Hill Invitational	CUT	T46	12	T46	CUT			T31	T15	CUT	CUT	T24	T40	CUT	T62	T15		72					T31		T60
THE PLAYERS Championship	CUT	T66	CUT	T33	T13	CUT	WD	T3	CUT	T42	T16	T58	CUT	CUT	T53	CUT		CUT	T33	CUT	CUT	T58	T22	CUT	T66
BellSouth Classic	T52	T20					T38						CUT	CUT	T11	T30	CUT		T20			CUT	CUT		T6
Masters Tournament				26	CUT	44			T17			T22			T41			T17	CUT	CUT	CUT		CUT	T31	
MCI Heritage	T3	CUT		T25				T53	T16	T7	T11	T7	T3	T25	T16			CUT		T16	T45	T32		65	T45
Shell Houston Open		T43		T49		T37	WD	T49		2	10	CUT	T11		T19	T19	WD		CUT			T54			T37
HP Classic of New Orleans	T15			WD		T45	WD			T45	T25	T5	CUT	T34		T34	T68		T25	T25		CUT		T25	
Wachovia Championship	CUT	P2					T61	CUT	WD	CUT	T10			CUT	CUT	CUT	CUT	T35		CUT	T64	T10			CUT
EDS Byron Nelson Championship	T34	WD				CUT	CUT	CUT							CUT	T72	79	T7	T21	T27	CUT			CUT	CUT
Bank of America Colonial	T54					T14	CUT	T44			T63		T63	T5	T5	T68		T27	T50	CUT	T14	CUT		74	WD
FedEx St. Jude Classic			59		CUT	T33			T5		CUT		T26		CUT	T3	T5					CUT		2	T33
the Memorial Tournament		T55	T24	CUT	T66			T71			T24	4		T55	T40			T11	T51	CUT	T40	CUT	T73		CUT
Buick Classic	CUT	CUT	CUT	T69	T16	CUT			8				82	T42	T28	T32	CUT	T53	CUT	T69	T9		CUT		
U.S. Open Championship				T60	T60	T48			CUT	T53		CUT		T17	T24			T40	CUT	CUT	T13		CUT	CUT	
Booz Allen Classic	T51	T4	T11	T7		T33	T33	T9		CUT	T71		T71				T21				CUT	T66			T21
Cialis Western Open	T7						T71	CUT		T11	T5		T51	T47		2	T63	T47	T40	T27		77		CUT	DNS
John Deere Classic							CUT			T11	CUT		T14				T14		T46	T64		CUT			T32
B.C. Open				CUT													T7			1					
British Open Championship	T57		CUT		CUT	CUT		CUT	CUT					T11		T36		CUT			CUT		CUT	T20	
U.S. Bank Championship in Milwaukee				WD			T36	T13		10			T4	T72		T69	CUT			T62		CUT		T47	
Buick Open	T56						CUT			CUT	T18	T24	T39	CUT	CUT				CUT			CUT			
The INTERNATIONAL	T58	T34	T40	2	CUT	T63	T45	72			44	T19	CUT		T6	CUT	CUT	T65	CUT	CUT		CUT			
PGA Championship	54	T13		CUT	T55	T4		WD	T17	WD	T24	CUT	T49	73	CUT	CUT		CUT	T37	CUT	CUT	CUT		CUT	T9
Reno-Tahoe Open	T5						T35										P1								T29
WGC-NEC Invitational				T9	T65	T43			T32									T22			T48		DNS		
Buick Championship		WD					T27	T21				T71	T75	T49	T32		T54			T44	CUT	T32			
Deutsche Bank Championship		T37					T29	T25			CUT	T29	CUT	T22	T22	CUT			T62	T29	T48	CUT			T62
Bell Canadian Open		WD	T4				WD		CUT			T4			T47	T14			WD	T44					
Valero Texas Open			T17				T14	CUT	T29			T17	2		T59		T22		T67		T5	T10		T17	T41
84 LUMBER Classic							T42	T9	T53			T36	T25	T50	T13	CUT	T42	CUT		T3	T36	CUT			CUT
Southern Farm Bureau Classic	T10						T19						T19			CUT	CUT			T8	T8	18		CUT	
WGC-American Express Championship				T28		T50			T59									63					2		
Michelin Championship at Las Vegas	T5	CUT	T2	T32		CUT	CUT	T67			T37			T67	T7	CUT			T23					T11	T15
Chrysler Classic of Greensboro	T35	T35	T4		67		1	T62	T51		T57	CUT	CUT	T46	T51		CUT		CUT	CUT	CUT	CUT			T8
FUNAI Classic	T10	T74	T6		CUT				T41		T10	T24	CUT	T16	CUT	T33	T10	T33	T2	CUT	T6	CUT		T41	T68
Chrysler Championship	T8	T38		CUT	T17	T30	CUT	CUT	CUT		T20	T30	T50	T56	CUT	CUT	T30	T38	T24	T44	T11	CUT		T17	CUT
THE TOUR Championship																									

Note: Players listed according to place on the final 2004 PGA TOUR Money List.

2004 Player Performance Chart (76-100)

LEGEND

- (blank) Did not play
- T7 Final position
- P1 P2 Involved in playoff
- DQ Disqualified
- CUT Missed cut
- WD Withdrew
- DNS Did not start

Tournament	76. Brad Faxon	77. Jeff Sluman	78. Loren Roberts	79. Bob Tway	80. Bart Bryant	81. Joe Durant	82. Shaun Micheel	83. Bernhard Langer	84. Robert Damron	85. Kevin Sutherland	86. Brian Bateman	87. Kevin Na	88. Michael Allen	89. Corey Pavin	90. John Huston	91. Tom Byrum	92. Dudley Hart	93. J.J. Henry	94. Todd Fischer	95. Tommy Armour III	96. Lee Janzen	97. Brett Quigley	98. Matt Gogel	99. Hank Kuehne	100. Hunter Mahan
Mercedes Championships				T28			T13								T26					T15					
Sony Open in Hawaii		CUT	78		T36	T20	T20				CUT	T41	T20	T20	T10	CUT			T64	T41		CUT			CUT
Bob Hope Chrysler Classic		T16	T20			T26		8	T36	T62		T47	T50	T69	T62		CUT	T69	T56	CUT	T36		CUT		
FBR Open		T27		T24		CUT		T27	CUT	T9					CUT	T42	CUT	CUT	CUT	67	T39		CUT	CUT	
AT&T Pebble Beach National Pro-Am	CUT		T41						CUT	T54	T25	T69		T10		T48		T41	T14			T69	CUT	CUT	CUT
Buick Invitational	CUT			T21		CUT	CUT	T53	79	T45	T66	T72	T45	T59			CUT	CUT	T53	WD	CUT	T16		T21	CUT
Nissan Open	CUT		T10	T10		T24	T24	T51	CUT	T39		CUT	T39	T15		T51		T7	CUT	CUT	T67	CUT	T74	5	
Chrysler Classic of Tucson					CUT					CUT	T20	CUT	CUT			CUT			T8				CUT		T17
WGC-Accenture Match Play Champ	T33	T33	T17	T33			T17								T9										
Ford Championship at Doral		T34		CUT		4	T34	T5	CUT		T34	CUT	T56		CUT		CUT	T74	CUT	T44	T64	T34		T56	T56
The Honda Classic	8	T59			DNS	T53		T65	T59		3	T4	73			CUT		T55	CUT	T9	T9	T25	CUT	CUT	CUT
Bay Hill Invitational	T24	T24	T46			T40		T40	CUT		CUT							CUT	CUT	CUT	T31	T31		CUT	T62
THE PLAYERS Championship	T42	T26	T66	T77		T58	9	T77	CUT	T6				T33	T26	T16		CUT	CUT	CUT	CUT	T42	T53	CUT	
BellSouth Classic				CUT	CUT		T30			WD	T45	T28	CUT	CUT	T38			CUT			T6	T45	CUT		CUT
Masters Tournament	T31	43		T27			T22	T4																	
MCI Heritage	T69	CUT	T61	CUT		CUT		T39	66	CUT	T53	T11	CUT	CUT	T25	T32	T45		T71	T71	T39		T67		
Shell Houston Open					CUT				CUT	CUT	28	T19			3	CUT	T4	T59	CUT	CUT		CUT		T37	CUT
HP Classic of New Orleans		CUT		T45	CUT	T10			T25		T7	CUT	WD			WD	CUT		CUT			CUT		CUT	CUT
Wachovia Championship	T56	T44				CUT	T44		T66	T10		CUT	T66	CUT		T15		T21	CUT	CUT	CUT	T44	T15	CUT	CUT
EDS Byron Nelson Championship	CUT	CUT	CUT	T41	T48		T27		P2	T41	T14	T34	CUT		CUT	T54	P2	T41	T59	T41	T67		T14	T34	CUT
Bank of America Colonial	T50	T68	T12	T27		T35					T14	WD		T31	CUT	T14	T41	CUT		T44	T14	T35	T54	CUT	T63
FedEx St. Jude Classic			T18		T47	CUT	CUT		T42	CUT	T54		T13					T54	CUT			T47	T42	T23	T26
the Memorial Tournament	T19	T33		CUT			T69			T33				T71			WD			T55	T33			CUT	61
Buick Classic	T23	DQ	T16	T55	T32				T60	T32		CUT	CUT	CUT		T4	T32	T16	T55		CUT	T16			
U.S. Open Championship	CUT			CUT			T28			CUT				T17		CUT	T53	64			T24		CUT		
Booz Allen Classic	T51	T11			T21	T21	T33					T18	T29	T43		T69		T18	CUT		WD	CUT	T29	CUT	T71
Cialis Western Open		T47	T11		T27	CUT	CUT		T63	T71	T63	T33	T27			CUT	CUT	23	T58	T71		T40	T17	T63	CUT
John Deere Classic		T8	CUT		T39	T24			CUT	T32		T67						T70	T46	CUT				T27	CUT
B.C. Open												T67	CUT						T3			T48		T13	
British Open Championship	T60			70			T47								CUT										T36
U.S. Bank Championship in Milwaukee	T27	T22	T62		T18	T72			CUT		CUT	T82	CUT	T13		T13		T31	T18			T2			CUT
Buick Open		T6	CUT	T18	CUT	CUT	CUT		T43		CUT	CUT			CUT	T39	CUT			CUT		T30	T39	T18	T30
The INTERNATIONAL	T31			T9	30			T9		T12	T34	T19	CUT	T15	69		CUT		CUT		CUT	T40	CUT	CUT	
PGA Championship	T13	T62	T17	T55		CUT	T24	T66		CUT	CUT				CUT	T24	WD			T45		T37	T17		
Reno-Tahoe Open					CUT					CUT		CUT	T9	T14				T29	T45				T29	CUT	P2
WGC-NEC Invitational	T32			T6			T50	T61												T50					
Buick Championship	T13	T9	T21		T54	T32			T13	T9		T32	T61	T6		T9	DQ	T54	T9		CUT	CUT	T6	T13	T21
Deutsche Bank Championship	T9	T37			CUT	WD	CUT		T59	CUT	CUT	CUT	T59				CUT	T37	T25	CUT	T37	CUT		T6	T25
Bell Canadian Open				T26					8	T74			CUT	T26		CUT	T36		T52	CUT		T26		CUT	T4
Valero Texas Open			T22	T41	1		T59				T61			T41		T41		T5	T3	T41				T73	T5
84 LUMBER Classic	CUT				CUT		CUT		T53			T53	CUT				CUT	CUT		72	T32	CUT	T11		
Southern Farm Bureau Classic			T3		CUT	T32	T34		T19		T65	T3	CUT	CUT	CUT			T3				CUT	T51	CUT	
WGC-American Express Championship	T13			T28																					
Michelin Championship at Las Vegas		T62		CUT	CUT	CUT	CUT			CUT		DQ	CUT	T45	CUT	T32	T32		CUT	CUT	T7	CUT	CUT		CUT
Chrysler Classic of Greensboro	T27	T27							69	T35		CUT	2	T35			CUT	CUT	T35		CUT	T19	T8	T19	T57
FUNAI Classic	CUT	CUT	T24	T74	T16	T33	T74	CUT	CUT	CUT	T33	CUT	T41		T10		CUT	T55	CUT	CUT	T68	CUT		T49	T68
Chrysler Championship	CUT	T20	68		T44	4	T24	T24	CUT		T62	T13			T44	T44		CUT	CUT	T2	T13	T62		CUT	CUT
THE TOUR Championship																									

Note: Players listed according to place on the final 2004 PGA TOUR Money List.

2004 Player Performance Chart (101-125)

LEGEND

(blank box)	Did not play
T7	Final position
P1, P2	Involved in playoff
DQ	Disqualified
CUT	Missed cut
WD	Withdrew
DNS	Did not start

Tournament	101. Andre Stolz	102. J.L. Lewis	103. Nick Price	104. Hidemichi Tanaka	105. Scott McCarron	106. Jose Coceres	107. Cameron Beckman	108. Daniel Chopra	109. John Rollins	110. Robert Gamez	111. Pat Perez	112. Mark Calcavecchia	113. Neal Lancaster
Mercedes Championships		T21											
Sony Open in Hawaii	T54			T64			T27	CUT		T27	T31		
Bob Hope Chrysler Classic		T9			T56		T76	CUT		T50	CUT	T62	T56
FBR Open		CUT			T59		CUT		T63	CUT	CUT	T33	CUT
AT&T Pebble Beach National Pro-Am	CUT	CUT			T10			T25	CUT	T61	CUT	CUT	T59
Buick Invitational	CUT	DQ		T53				CUT	CUT		CUT	WD	T53
Nissan Open			CUT	T24	T20		CUT	CUT	CUT		T74		T20
Chrysler Classic of Tucson	T61	T34		T20			T27	CUT			CUT	T17	
WGC-Accenture Match Play Champ			T33						T33				
Ford Championship at Doral		T70	T11		CUT	T44	CUT	CUT		T17		T9	T11
The Honda Classic				T41	T65	CUT	CUT	CUT	CUT	CUT	CUT	WD	CUT
Bay Hill Invitational		T15		CUT	71					CUT			T46
THE PLAYERS Championship		CUT	T42	T81	T53		T26		CUT	CUT	CUT	T66	83
BellSouth Classic	CUT			CUT	T56		CUT	69	CUT	T38	T38		T14
Masters Tournament		CUT	T6						CUT				
MCI Heritage		T53	T25			T11	T45		T45	T45	CUT	CUT	CUT
Shell Houston Open	CUT			CUT	CUT	T6	CUT	T65		T59	CUT	T19	T29
HP Classic of New Orleans	T34	T25		4	CUT	CUT		T34	WD		T20		WD
Wachovia Championship		CUT	T21	72	WD	CUT	T28	T35	CUT	CUT	T21		CUT
EDS Byron Nelson Championship		T48	T7	CUT	CUT		T48	T54	CUT	CUT	T67		T59
Bank of America Colonial		T27		WD					CUT	T5		73	T54
FedEx St. Jude Classic	CUT					T63	T42	CUT		T42	T67		
the Memorial Tournament	WD	T11	T51	T33	T19				T40	CUT		62	
Buick Classic		CUT				T60	T9	T42	T55		T42		T32
U.S. Open Championship		CUT	T24	T36				T24	T48		T40	T20	
Booz Allen Classic	CUT			T29	CUT		T57	T57		CUT	WD		WD
Cialis Western Open	CUT	T79			T47	T33	WD	CUT	T17	T17	T11		CUT
John Deere Classic	CUT	T27	T46	T46	T14	3		T39	T8	T14	66		T39
B.C. Open				T3				T29	T21	T10			T7
British Open Championship			T30				CUT					T11	
U.S. Bank Championship in Milwaukee		T69		CUT	T13		T31	T36		T36		T72	CUT
Buick Open		T65			T30	CUT		T8		T65	T56		T30
The INTERNATIONAL					CUT	43	T58	CUT	T24		CUT		T63
PGA Championship		T24		T55	CUT					T68		DQ	
Reno-Tahoe Open	CUT			T24	P2		T29	T9	T14		CUT	T56	
WGC-NEC Invitational		T55	T46										
Buick Championship	CUT	T32	CUT	T13		T21	T32	T32	CUT	T67	T61	CUT	CUT
Deutsche Bank Championship	WD			T37		CUT	T48	T4	T4	T48	CUT		T22
Bell Canadian Open	77	CUT			CUT	T19		CUT	T74		T14	WD	T57
Valero Texas Open	T61	T10			T22	T73	CUT	T37		CUT	T22		
84 LUMBER Classic	CUT	CUT		CUT	CUT		T13	CUT	T20	T13	T3	T53	71
Southern Farm Bureau Classic				CUT			T43	T26					CUT
WGC-American Express Championship	65												
Michelin Championship at Las Vegas	1	T23			T32	T15	T52	T62	66	T37	T23	CUT	CUT
Chrysler Classic of Greensboro		CUT				68	T16		T27	CUT		T35	CUT
FUNAI Classic		T24	CUT	CUT	T28	T83	T4	T49	T49	T55	T33	T6	T10
Chrysler Championship		T70		T24		CUT	CUT	CUT		CUT	CUT	T44	T50
THE TOUR Championship													

Tournament	114. John Senden	115. Chris Smith	116. Jim Furyk	117. Dennis Paulson	118. Peter Lonard	119. Kent Jones	120. Jay Williamson	121. Steve Allan	122. Brian Gay	123. Aaron Baddeley	124. Billy Andrade	125. Tag Ridings
Mercedes Championships			11								DNS	
Sony Open in Hawaii	T64	CUT	CUT					T27	T36	T15		
Bob Hope Chrysler Classic	T41	CUT				T9	CUT	CUT			T41	
FBR Open	T54	T68				T33	CUT	CUT		CUT	CUT	
AT&T Pebble Beach National Pro-Am	T48	T69		T63		T10		T69		CUT	CUT	CUT
Buick Invitational		T77		T25		T45	T53			T40	T72	
Nissan Open	CUT				CUT	CUT	T7	CUT		T32	T51	
Chrysler Classic of Tucson		T27		T20			WD	T65	T20	2		T49
WGC-Accenture Match Play Champ					T17							
Ford Championship at Doral	T64	T27		T24	T34		CUT	CUT	CUT		CUT	
The Honda Classic	T30	T46				CUT	CUT	CUT	CUT	T21	CUT	
Bay Hill Invitational				T10	CUT	T46	CUT		T46	T56	T66	
THE PLAYERS Championship	T58	CUT			CUT	CUT	CUT	CUT		CUT	CUT	
BellSouth Classic		T20		T56	5	CUT	CUT	T14	T14		CUT	T14
Masters Tournament					CUT							
MCI Heritage		CUT		T25	CUT	T16	T16	CUT	CUT		T53	
Shell Houston Open	CUT			T54		CUT	WD	CUT	T67	T65	CUT	CUT
HP Classic of New Orleans	T20	T61		T34		T45	WD	T34	CUT			
Wachovia Championship	T32	CUT			T44	CUT		T56	CUT	CUT	CUT	
EDS Byron Nelson Championship	T41	T27			T48	T34	T54	CUT	CUT	80	T72	WD
Bank of America Colonial	T9			T31	T27	T50	CUT		T14	T50		
FedEx St. Jude Classic	T18	T70		T13			CUT	T18	T5		T26	
the Memorial Tournament					T11					T69	T63	
Buick Classic	T42	T71		T23	T42	CUT	CUT	CUT	T28		T71	
U.S. Open Championship	CUT	CUT	T48	CUT	T31			CUT	CUT	CUT		
Booz Allen Classic		CUT		CUT		CUT	CUT	T57	CUT	T71	T21	
Cialis Western Open	CUT	T51	T7		T24	CUT	T51	T58	CUT	T58		
John Deere Classic	T39	T59				CUT	CUT		CUT			
B.C. Open	T10	T13				CUT	T17	T17			T60	CUT
British Open Championship			CUT		CUT					CUT		
U.S. Bank Championship in Milwaukee		CUT		CUT		T36	T22	T57	T27		T4	CUT
Buick Open	CUT	CUT	T6	CUT			T43	T30	T24	CUT	T15	CUT
The INTERNATIONAL	T45					CUT	CUT	T70	CUT	CUT		T52
PGA Championship			CUT		CUT						CUT	
Reno-Tahoe Open	T24	T50		T9		CUT	T24	P2	T45			CUT
WGC-NEC Invitational			T22		T32							
Buick Championship	T32	CUT		CUT	CUT	CUT	T32	CUT	CUT	T61	T44	T75
Deutsche Bank Championship	T48	CUT	T35	T13		T37	8	CUT	CUT	T29	CUT	CUT
Bell Canadian Open		CUT		T61					CUT	CUT	T11	T52
Valero Texas Open	21			WD		T37	T22	CUT	T29	72		
84 LUMBER Classic	CUT	T20			CUT	T13	WD	T53	T42	CUT	T61	T13
Southern Farm Bureau Classic	T14	T32				T51	T34	T14	CUT		T34	
WGC-American Express Championship			T36		T23							
Michelin Championship at Las Vegas	CUT	T37	T11			T15	T15	T45	T11		T37	T2
Chrysler Classic of Greensboro		3	CUT			CUT			CUT		T35	T35
FUNAI Classic		CUT	CUT		CUT	T68	T81	T33	T41	CUT	T16	CUT
Chrysler Championship		CUT	CUT		CUT	T17	72	CUT	T50	67	CUT	T11
THE TOUR Championship												

Note: Players listed according to place on the final 2004 PGA TOUR Money List.

2004 Player Performance Chart (126-150)

LEGEND

- (blank) Did not play
- T7 Final position
- P1 P2 Involved in playoff
- DQ Disqualified
- CUT Missed cut
- WD Withdrew
- DNS Did not start

	126. Paul Azinger	127. Olin Browne	128. Craig Barlow	129. Notah Begay III	130. Bob Burns	131. Jason Bohn	132. Mathias Gronberg	133. Dean Wilson	134. Lucas Glover	135. Mark O'Meara	136. Scott Hend	137. Brenden Pappas	138. Glen Day	139. Matt Kuchar	140. Billy Mayfair	141. Ben Curtis	142. Jose Maria Olazabal	143. Craig Bowden	144. Danny Ellis	145. John E. Morgan	146. Arjun Atwal	147. David Peoples	148. Richard S. Johnson	149. Jeff Brehaut	150. Paul Stankowski
Mercedes Championships																30									
Sony Open in Hawaii	T10	T48	T8	CUT	T59	T64		CUT	T64		CUT	T15		CUT		CUT		T15			T64	CUT	T64	76	
Bob Hope Chrysler Classic	T9	CUT	CUT	T41	T41		T62	T26		T16		T76	CUT		CUT				T26			CUT	T30	CUT	T47
FBR Open	T33			T54	CUT			CUT		T42		T14	T33	CUT	CUT		W/D	DNS				CUT	CUT	T59	T49
AT&T Pebble Beach National Pro-Am		CUT	T35			T69	CUT		CUT	T69	CUT		T69	T48			CUT	CUT		CUT	T21		CUT	CUT	T21
Buick Invitational			T16		T59	T66	T45	T77	CUT	CUT	CUT	T45		CUT	T10		T59	T59	T30		T30	T30		CUT	
Nissan Open	T44	CUT	CUT	CUT	CUT		T24	CUT		CUT		T70			CUT	CUT	T32		CUT			CUT	CUT	T70	T32
Chrysler Classic of Tucson		T34		T15	CUT	T61	CUT	T40	CUT		CUT	T43	CUT		T27		CUT	CUT		CUT	CUT	CUT	CUT	CUT	CUT
WGC-Accenture Match Play Champ																T17									
Ford Championship at Doral	T52	T52	T52	T64		CUT	CUT	T56			CUT	T74	CUT	CUT	T44	CUT		CUT	T9		T64	T52	CUT		
The Honda Classic	CUT	CUT	T55	T39	CUT	CUT	T65	T55		T46		T25	T59	CUT	T41			T13	T65		CUT		CUT	CUT	CUT
Bay Hill Invitational	CUT	CUT	T24				T13	CUT		T56						T40	T40	CUT	T56		CUT				
THE PLAYERS Championship			CUT	CUT	T10			CUT				CUT	T22	T16	T58	CUT	CUT					T42	CUT	CUT	T16
BellSouth Classic	CUT			CUT	T45	CUT			T56		3	CUT	CUT	CUT	T56		T45	T14			CUT	T11	T52	T20	CUT
Masters Tournament										T27						CUT	30								
MCI Heritage	CUT		T61	CUT	T16		CUT	T53	T16	T25	T61	CUT	T53	T32	T69	T25		T39				CUT	CUT	T45	
Shell Houston Open	T6	CUT		CUT	CUT	T19	T43	CUT	T29		T59	CUT		CUT	T29			CUT			CUT	T11		T43	T11
HP Classic of New Orleans	T15	T54			T15	CUT	T25	T54	CUT		CUT	CUT	CUT	T10				T50	71	T68	CUT	W/D	CUT	75	
Wachovia Championship		CUT		T5	CUT	T32	9	T44	T10	CUT	T44		CUT	T70	T61	T35		CUT	CUT		CUT	T56	T50	CUT	CUT
EDS Byron Nelson Championship		CUT		T59	CUT	T48		CUT	CUT	T11	CUT		CUT		CUT				CUT			CUT	CUT	CUT	CUT
Bank of America Colonial		CUT		CUT	CUT		T54	CUT	CUT		T61	T71	T31		CUT			CUT	CUT			DNS			
FedEx St. Jude Classic	CUT			T33	CUT	CUT	CUT		CUT		T63	T60	CUT	T26	CUT			T9	CUT	CUT	CUT	T26	CUT	CUT	T9
the Memorial Tournament	T66						CUT			CUT		T55				T8					CUT				
Buick Classic		CUT	CUT	T71	CUT	T71	CUT		CUT		T14	CUT	T42	CUT	75			T55	T60		T60		T66	CUT	CUT
U.S. Open Championship											CUT				66	30		CUT							
Booz Allen Classic		T7	T29	T33		CUT	CUT	CUT	CUT		T21	CUT	T43		65			W/D	T21	CUT	CUT		T51	T51	CUT
Cialis Western Open		CUT	CUT	CUT	T27	T33	CUT	CUT	T71		CUT	CUT	T71		T24	CUT		T71	CUT		CUT		T33	CUT	
John Deere Classic	CUT	T24	CUT	CUT	CUT	T14	CUT	CUT	T32		W/D	CUT	T24	T74	W/D					P2			T64	T11	
B.C. Open		T48		T3		T21		CUT	T40			T21		CUT				T48		T13		T35	T35		
British Open Championship							T47			T30			CUT			CUT					CUT				
U.S. Bank Championship in Milwaukee	T57	T4	CUT	CUT		T75		T22	T22			T36	CUT	T36	CUT			T18	CUT	CUT	CUT	CUT	T27	CUT	
Buick Open	T30	T24	T12		T30	CUT	T52	CUT	T61	T10	CUT	T12	T24	CUT	T43		T12	CUT	CUT	T56	CUT	T43		T43	
The INTERNATIONAL		T24	CUT	T19	CUT	T52	T9		T34		CUT	T47	CUT		38	CUT	T12		T31		CUT	CUT		CUT	
PGA Championship	T55									CUT		CUT				CUT	CUT								
Reno-Tahoe Open		T50	T18	CUT		T24	CUT	T14	T40		71		T54	T66	CUT		T45	W/D	T35	W/D	T54	W/D	T40	T40	
WGC-NEC Invitational										T72															
Buick Championship		T27	T21		T58	T6	CUT	CUT	CUT		79	CUT	CUT	CUT	T44			T32	CUT	W/D	T13	T27	CUT	CUT	
Deutsche Bank Championship	CUT	CUT			T65	T48	CUT	T29	CUT	70	CUT	CUT	CUT	T17	T55	CUT		CUT	T62	W/D	CUT	T25	T17	T35	
Bell Canadian Open	T61	W/D	T26		CUT	T40	CUT	T14					T19		T57			CUT		CUT	T19	T26	T36	CUT	
Valero Texas Open		T17			CUT			T3	T52		CUT	T22	CUT	T41			CUT	W/D	CUT	CUT	T49	T37	CUT	75	
84 LUMBER Classic			CUT		T11	T42	CUT	CUT	CUT		CUT	T36	T42	CUT	T13	T32	T9		CUT	CUT	CUT	T36	T25	T25	
Southern Farm Bureau Classic	T65	T46	T19			T34	CUT	CUT	T26		CUT	T46	T3	CUT				CUT	CUT	CUT		68	T26	T62	
WGC-American Express Championship																					T43				
Michelin Championship at Las Vegas	T37	T23	T45		CUT	T23	CUT	T52	T15		CUT	CUT	T52	CUT	T32			CUT	T7		CUT		T52	CUT	
Chrysler Classic of Greensboro					CUT	T27	CUT	CUT	T57		T62	T46	CUT	CUT	70	CUT		CUT	T46		6		T8	T8	
FUNAI Classic	CUT	CUT	CUT		T79	CUT	CUT	T62	T10		CUT	T41	CUT	T62	CUT	T16	T41	CUT	T55		T33		T28	CUT	
Chrysler Championship	CUT	CUT	CUT		CUT	DNS	CUT	T30	CUT			T58	T58	T20	T56		T24						CUT	T30	
THE TOUR Championship																									

Toughest Holes on the 2004 PGA TOUR

RANK	GOLF COURSE	HOLE #	PAR	AVG. SCORE	AVG. OVER PAR	EAGLES	BIRDIES	PARS	BOGEYS	DOUBLE BOGEYS	TRIPLE BOGEY+	TOURNAMENT NAME
1.	Doral Golf Resort & Spa	18	4	4.480	.480		31	231	125	53	4	Ford Championship at Doral
2.	Torrey Pines (South Course)	12	4	4.462	.462		13	160	128	14	1	Buick Invitational
3.	Shinnecock Hills GC	10	4	4.446	.446		38	217	153	25	9	U.S. Open Championship
4.	TPC at Southwind	11	3	3.442	.442		52	249	85	51	18	FedEx St. Jude Classic
5.	Royal Troon GC	11	4	4.413	.413		35	264	108	38	13	British Open Championship
6.	Shinnecock Hills GC	07	3	3.410	.410		20	249	149	20	4	U.S. Open Championship
7.	Shinnecock Hills GC	06	4	4.391	.391		25	243	153	18	3	U.S. Open Championship
8.	Whistling Straits	15	4	4.385	.385		29	247	155	20	3	PGA Championship
9.	Cottonwood Valley GC	01	4	4.383	.383		5	94	46	9		EDS Byron Nelson Championship
10.	Glen Abbey GC	14	4	4.382	.382		24	276	121	33	4	Bell Canadian Open
11.	Glen Abbey GC	16	4	4.369	.369		43	227	168	17	3	Bell Canadian Open
12.	East Lake GC	16	4	4.364	.364		4	73	36	4	1	THE TOUR Championship
13.	Quail Hollow CC	18	4	4.363	.363		37	255	126	32	4	Wachovia Championship
14.	Mount Juliet	18	4	4.357	.357		8	176	74	12	2	WGC-American Express Championship
15.	Augusta National GC	01	4	4.354	.354		13	165	85	8	3	Masters Tournament
16.	Brown Deer Park GC	04	4	4.351	.351		28	273	164	15	1	U.S. Bank Championship in Milwaukee
T17.	TPC at Sugarloaf	15	4	4.347	.347	1	26	236	151	11	1	BellSouth Classic
T17.	Augusta National GC	18	4	4.347	.347		20	156	84	11	3	Masters Tournament
T19.	TPC at Sugarloaf	05	4	4.345	.345		55	223	101	41	6	BellSouth Classic
T19.	Redstone GC (Fall Creek)	07	4	4.345	.345		32	253	136	25		Shell Houston Open
21.	Waialae CC	01	4	4.337	.337		19	279	128	16	3	Sony Open in Hawaii
22.	Montreux G&CC	08	4	4.332	.332		45	231	84	28	10	Reno-Tahoe Open
23.	Shinnecock Hills GC	11	3	3.330	.330		55	244	103	28	12	U.S. Open Championship
24.	TPC at Sugarloaf	01	4	4.329	.329		32	244	133	13	4	BellSouth Classic
25.	Westchester CC	12	4	4.328	.328		40	258	156	18	1	Buick Classic
T26.	Shinnecock Hills GC	04	4	4.326	.326		24	275	123	17	3	U.S. Open Championship
T26.	Palm GC	18	4	4.326	.326		5	90	46	3		FUNAI Classic
28.	Pebble Beach GL	09	4	4.320	.320		17	148	71	9	2	AT&T Pebble Beach National Pro-Am
29.	Whistling Straits	18	4	4.319	.319		30	279	120	23	2	PGA Championship
30.	Westchester CC	11	4	4.313	.313		31	280	146	15	1	Buick Classic
31.	Shinnecock Hills GC	18	4	4.312	.312	1	23	276	123	17	2	U.S. Open Championship
32.	The Country Club at Mirasol	14	4	4.311	.311		35	246	124	22		The Honda Classic
T33.	Torrey Pines (South Course)	15	4	4.310	.310		22	189	91	13	1	Buick Invitational
T33.	Shinnecock Hills GC	14	4	4.310	.310		34	258	133	14	3	U.S. Open Championship
T33.	Royal Troon GC	12	4	4.310	.310		34	285	109	24	6	British Open Championship
36.	Torrey Pines (North Course)	11	4	4.309	.309		16	83	44	8	1	Buick Invitational
37.	Westin Innisbrook (Copperhead)	16	4	4.308	.308		45	221	117	17	6	Chrysler Championship
T38.	Spyglass Hill GC	05	3	3.307	.307		8	114	51	6		AT&T Pebble Beach National Pro-Am
T38.	Spyglass Hill GC	16	4	4.307	.307		13	111	44	9	2	AT&T Pebble Beach National Pro-Am
40.	Torrey Pines (South Course)	04	4	4.304	.304		22	190	92	10	2	Buick Invitational
41.	Colonial CC	09	4	4.303	.303		33	222	88	24	3	Bank of America Colonial
42.	Royal Troon GC	10	4	4.301	.301		31	277	133	15	2	British Open Championship
T43.	Cog Hill G&CC	06	3	3.299	.299		26	290	143	12		Cialis Western Open
T43.	Cog Hill G&CC	18	4	4.299	.299	1	45	266	132	25	2	Cialis Western Open
45.	Waialae CC	13	4	4.297	.297		23	276	137	9		Sony Open in Hawaii
T46.	Shinnecock Hills GC	09	4	4.296	.296		45	246	130	18	3	U.S. Open Championship
T46.	TPC at Deere Run	09	4	4.296	.296	1	35	267	137	14	2	John Deere Classic
T48.	Plantation Course at Kapalua	01	4	4.292	.292		7	79	27	6	1	Mercedes Championships
T48.	Riviera CC	08	4	4.292	.292		44	255	120	18	5	Nissan Open
T48.	Augusta National GC	11	4	4.292	.292	1	19	165	78	10	1	Masters Tournament
T48.	TPC at Four Seasons Resort	03	4	4.292	.292		28	189	80	14	4	EDS Byron Nelson Championship

South African **Retief Goosen** recorded his first multiple-win season on the PGA TOUR, taking home a second U.S. Open championship and completing the season with a victory in THE TOUR Championship presented by Coca-Cola.

Scoring Records

72 holes:

254 **Tommy Armour III** (64-62-63-65), The Resort at LaCantera (par 70), 2003 Valero Texas Open (26-under-par)

Tommy Armour III

256 **Mark Calcavecchia** (65-60-64-67), TPC of Scottsdale (par 71), 2001 Phoenix Open (28-under-par)

257 **Mike Souchak** (60-68-64-65), Brackenridge Park GC (par 71), 1955 Texas Open (27-under-par)

258 **Donnie Hammond** (65-64-65-64), Oak Hills CC (par 70), 1989 Texas Open (22-under-par)
John Cook (64-62-63-69), TPC at Southwind (par 71), 1996 FedEx St. Jude Classic (26-under-par)
Steve Jones (62-64-65-67), TPC of Scottsdale (par 71), 1997 Phoenix Open (26-under-par)

259 **Byron Nelson** (62-68-63-66), Broadmoor GC (par 70), 1945 Seattle Open (21-under-par)
Chandler Harper (70-63-63-63), Brackenridge Park GC (par 71), 1954 Texas Open (25-under-par)
Tim Norris (63-64-66-66), Wethersfield CC (par 71), 1982 Sammy Davis, Jr. Greater Hartford Open (25-under-par)
Corey Pavin (64-63-66-66), Oak Hills CC (par 70), 1988 Texas Open (21-under-par)
David Frost (68-63-64-64), Oakwood CC (par 70), 1993 Hardee's Golf Classic (21-under-par)
Tiger Woods (64-61-67-67), Firestone CC (par 70), 2000 World Golf Championships-NEC Invitational (21-under-par)
Joe Durant* (65-61-67-66), four courses (all courses, par 72), 2001 Bob Hope Chrysler Classic (29-under-par)
Tim Herron* (69-64-61-65), four courses (all courses, par 72), 2003 Bob Hope Chrysler Classic (29-under-par)
(* Through first four rounds of 90-hole tournament.)

90 holes:

324 **Joe Durant** (65-61-67-66-65), four courses (all courses, par 72), 2001 Bob Hope Chrysler Classic (36-under-par), Won

Joe Durant

325 **Tom Kite** (67-67-64-65-62), four courses (all courses, par 72), 1993 Bob Hope Chrysler Classic (35-under-par), Won

327 **John Cook** (66-69-67-62-63), four courses (all courses, par 72), 1997 Bob Hope Chrysler Classic (33-under-par), Won

328 **Mark Calcavecchia** (64-67-66-64-67), four courses (all courses, par 72), 1997 Bob Hope Chrysler Classic (32-under-par), Finished 2nd
Paul Stankowski (67-64-65-69-63), four courses (all courses, par 72), 2001 Bob Hope Chrysler Classic (32-under-par), Finished 2nd
Stuart Appleby (62-68-63-66-69), three courses (TPC Summerlin/par 72, TPC Canyons/par 71, Southern Highlands/par 72), 2003 Las Vegas Invitational (31-under-par), Won
Scott McCarron (69-62-64-67-66), three courses (TPC Summerlin/par 72, TPC Canyons/par 71, Southern Highlands/par 72), 2003 Las Vegas Invitational (31-under-par), Lost playoff

329 **Andrew Magee** (69-65-67-62-66), three courses (all courses, par 72), 1991 Las Vegas Invitational (31-under-par), Won
D.A. Weibring (70-64-65-64-66), three courses (all courses, par 72), 1991 Las Vegas Invitational (31-under-par), Lost playoff

Most strokes under par
72 holes:

31 **Ernie Els**, 2003 Mercedes Championship, 261, par 73 (won)

29 **Joe Durant***, 2001 Bob Hope Chrysler Classic, 259, four courses, par 72 (won)
Tim Herron*, 2003 Bob Hope Chrysler Classic, 259, four courses, par 72 (T3)

28 **John Huston**, 1998 United Airlines Hawaiian Open, 260, par 72 (won)
Mark Calcavecchia, 2001 Phoenix Open, 256, par 71 (won)
Stuart Appleby*, 2003 Las Vegas Invitational, 259, three courses -TPC Summerlin/par 72, TPC Canyons/par 71, Southern Highlands/par 72 (won)

27 **Ben Hogan**, 1945 Portland Invitational, 261, par 72 (won)
Mike Souchak, 1955 Texas Open, 257, par 71 (won)
Mark Calcavecchia*, 1997 Bob Hope Chrysler Classic, 261, four courses, par 72 (2nd)
Jonathan Byrd, 2002 Buick Challenge, 261, par 72 (won)
Steve Flesch*, 2003 Las Vegas Invitational, 260, three courses-TPC Summerlin/par 72, TPC Canyons/par 71, Southern Highlands/par 72, (T6)

26 **Gay Brewer**, 1967 Pensacola Open, 262, par 72 (won)
Robert Wrenn, 1987 Buick Open, 262, par 72 (won)
Chip Beck, 1988 USF&G Classic, 262, par 72 (won)
John Huston, 1992 Walt Disney World/Oldsmobile Classic, 262, two courses, par 72 (won)
John Cook, 1996 FedEx St. Jude Classic, 258, par 71 (won)
Steve Jones, 1997 Phoenix Open, 258, par 71 (won)
David Duval, 1999 Mercedes Championships, 266, par 73 (won)
Duffy Waldorf, 2000 National Car Rental Golf Classic at Walt Disney World Resort, 262, two courses, par 72 (won)
Jay Haas*, 2002 Bob Hope Chrysler Classic, 262, four courses, par 72 (T16)
David Toms, 2002 Buick Challenge, 262, par 72 (2nd)
Tommy Armour III, 2003 Valero Texas Open, 254, par 70 (won)
Phil Mickelson*, 2004 Bob Hope Chrysler Classic, 262, four courses, par 72 (won)
Kirk Triplett*, 2004 Bob Hope Chrysler Classic, 262, four courses, par 72 (T9)
(* Through first four rounds of 90-hole tournament.)

90 holes:

36 **Joe Durant**, 2001 Bob Hope Chrysler Classic, 324, four courses, par 72 (won)

35 **Tom Kite**, 1993 Bob Hope Chrysler Classic, 325, four courses, par 72 (won)

33 **John Cook**, 1997 Bob Hope Chrysler Classic, 327, four courses, par 72 (won)

32 **Mark Calcavecchia**, 1997 Bob Hope Chrysler Classic, 328, four courses, par 72 (2nd)
Paul Stankowski, 2001 Bob Hope Chrysler Classic, 328, four courses, par 72 (2nd)

31 **Andrew Magee**, 1991 Las Vegas Invitational, 329, three courses, par 72 (won)
D.A. Weibring, 1991 Las Vegas Invitational, 329, three courses, par 72 (lost playoff)
Stuart Appleby, 2003 Las Vegas Invitational, 328, three courses (won)
Scott McCarron, 2003 Las Vegas Invitational, 328, three courses (Lost playoff)

54 holes:
Opening rounds:

189 **John Cook** (64-62-63), TPC at Southwind (par 71), 1996 FedEx St. Jude Classic (24-under-par)
Mark Calcavecchia (65-60-64), TPC of Scottsdale (par 71), 2001 Phoenix Open, (24-under-par)
Tommy Armour III (64-62-63), The Resort at LaCantera (par 70), 2003 Valero Texas Open, (21-under-par)

191 **Johnny Palmer** (65-62-64), Brackenridge Park GC (par 71), 1954 Texas Open (22-under-par)
Gay Brewer (66-64-61), Pensacola CC (par 72), 1967 Pensacola Open (25-under-par)
Steve Jones (62-64-65), TPC of Scottsdale (par 71), 1997 Phoenix Open (22-under-par)

192 **Mike Souchak** (60-68-64), Brackenridge Park GC (par 71), 1955 Texas Open (21-under-par)
Bob Gilder (64-63-65), Westchester CC (par 70), 1982 Manufacturers Hanover Westchester Classic (18-under-par)
Tiger Woods (64-61-67), Firestone CC (par 70), 2000 World Golf Championships-NEC Invitational (18-under-par)
Steve Flesch (62-64-66), Southern Highlands GC (par 72)/TPC at Canyons (par 71)/TPC at Summerlin (par 72), 2003 Las Vegas Invitational (23-under-par)
Scott Verplank (64-62-66), TPC at Canyons (par 71)/TPC at Summerlin (par 72)/ Southern Highlands GC (par 72), 2003 Las Vegas Invitational (23-under-par)

Consecutive rounds:

189 **Chandler Harper** (63-63-63), Brackenridge Park GC (par 71), rounds 2-4, 1954 Texas Open, (24-under-par)
John Cook (64-62-63), TPC at Southwind (par 71), rounds 1-3, 1996 FedEx St. Jude Classic, (24-under-par)
Mark Calcavecchia (65-60-64), TPC of Scottsdale (par 71), rounds 1-3, 2001 Phoenix Open, (24-under-par)
Tommy Armour III (64-62-63), The Resort at LaCantera (par 70), rounds 1-3, 2003 Valero Texas Open, (21-under-par)

36 holes:

Opening rounds:

125 **Tiger Woods** (64-61), Firestone CC (par 70), 2000 World Golf Championships-NEC Invitational (15-under-par)
Mark Calcavecchia (65-60), TPC of Scottsdale (par 71), 2001 Phoenix Open (17-under-par)
Tom Lehman (63-62), TPC of Summerlin (par 72)/Southern Highlands GC (par 72), 2001 Invensys Classic at Las Vegas (19-under-par)

126 **Tommy Bolt** (64-62), Cavalier Yacht & CC (par 69), 1954 Virginia Beach Open (12-under-par)
Paul Azinger (64-62), at Oak Hills CC (par 70), 1989 Texas Open presented by Nabisco (14-under-par)
John Cook (64-62), TPC at Southwind (par 71), 1996 FedEx St. Jude Classic (16-under-par)
Rick Fehr (64-62), Las Vegas Hilton CC (par 71)/TPC at Summerlin (par 72), 1996 Las Vegas Invitational (17-under-par)
Steve Jones (62-64), TPC of Scottsdale (par 71), 1997 Phoenix Open (16-under-par)
David Frost (63-63), TPC at Southwind (par 71), 1999 FedEx St. Jude Classic (16-under-par)
Joe Durant (65-61), La Quinta CC (par 72)/Indian Wells CC (par 72), 2001 Bob Hope Chrysler Classic (18-under-par)
Tommy Armour III (64-62), The Resort at LaCantera (par 70), 2003 Valero Texas Open, (14-under-par)
Steve Flesch (62-64), Southern Highlands GC (par 72)/TPC at Canyons (par 71), 2003 Las Vegas Invitational (17-under-par)
Scott Verplank (64-62), TPC at Canyons (par 71)/TPC at Summerlin (par 72), 2003 Las Vegas Invitational (17-under-par)

Consecutive rounds:

124 **Mark Calcavecchia** (60-64), TPC of Scottsdale (par 71), Rounds 2-3, 2001 Phoenix Open, (18-under-par)

125 **Gay Brewer** (64-61), Pensacola CC (par 72), Rounds 2-3, 1967 Pensacola Open, (19-under-par)
Ron Streck (63-62), Oak Hills CC (par 70), Rounds 3-4, 1978 Texas Open, (15-under-par)
Blaine McCallister (62-63), Oakwood CC (par 70), Rounds 2-3, 1988 Hardee's Golf Classic, (15-under-par)
John Cook (62-63), TPC at Southwind (par 71), Rounds 2-3, 1996 FedEx St. Jude Classic, (17-under-par)
John Cook (62-63), Indian Wells CC (par 72), Rounds 4-5, 1997 Bob Hope Chrysler Classic, (19-under-par)
Tiger Woods (64-61), Firestone CC (par 70), Rounds 1-2, 2000 World Golf Championships-NEC Invitational, (15-under-par)
Mark Calcavecchia (65-60), TPC of Scottsdale (par 71), Rounds 1-2, 2001 Phoenix Open, (17-under-par)
Tom Lehman (63-62), TPC of Summerlin (par 72)/Southern Highlands GC (par 72), Rounds 1-2, 2001 Invensys Classic at Las Vegas, (19-under-par)
Tim Herron (64-61), Bermuda Dune CC (par 72)/PGA West/Palmer Course (par 72), Rounds 2-3, 2003 Bob Hope Chrysler Classic, (19-under-par)
Kenny Perry (64-61), Colonial CC (par 70), Rounds 2-3, 2003 Bank of America Colonial, (15-under-par)
Tommy Armour III (64-61), The Resort at LaCantera (par 70), Rounds 2-3, 2003 Valero Texas Open, (15-under-par)

Al Geiberger

Chip Beck

David Duval

18 holes:

59 **Al Geiberger** (29-30), Colonial CC (par 72), June 10, second round, 1977 Memphis Classic (13-under-par), 1 eagle, 11 birdies. Began on back nine, sank eight-foot birdie putt on ninth hole. Won by three strokes
Chip Beck (30-29), Sunrise GC (par 72), October 11, third round, 1991 Las Vegas Invitational (13-under-par), 13 birdies. Began on back nine, birdied his last three holes, including three-footer on ninth hole. Finished T3
David Duval (31-28), PGA West (Palmer Course) (par 72), January 24, final round, 1999 Bob Hope Chrysler Classic (13-under-par), 1 eagle, 11 birdies. Made six-foot eagle putt on 18th hole. Won by one stroke

60 **Al Brosch**, Brackenridge Park GC, third round, 1951 Texas Open (11-under-par)
Bill Nary, El Paso CC, third round, 1952 El Paso Open (11-under-par)
Ted Kroll (30-30), Brackenridge Park GC, third round, 1954 Texas Open (11-under-par)
Wally Ulrich (29-31), Cavalier Yacht & CC, second round, 1954 Virginia Beach Open (9-under-par)
Tommy Bolt (30-30), Wethersfield CC, second round, 1954 Insurance City Open (11-under-par)
Mike Souchak (27-33), Brackenridge Park GC, San Antonio, TX, first round, 1955 Texas Open (11-under-par)
Sam Snead, Glen Lakes CC, second round, 1957 Dallas Open (11-under-par)
David Frost (29-31), Randolph Park GC, second round, 1990 Northern Telecom Tucson Open (12-under-par)
Davis Love III (31-29), Waialae CC, second round, 1994 United Airlines Hawaiian Open (12-under-par)
Grant Waite (31-29), TPC of Scottsdale, final round, 1996 Phoenix Open (11-under-par)
Steve Lowery (29-31), Callaway Gardens (Mountain View Course), final round, 1997 Buick Challenge (12-under-par)
Tommy Armour III (30-30), Las Vegas CC, second round, 1999 Las Vegas Invitational (12-under-par)
Mark Calcavecchia (29-31), TPC of Scottsdale, second round, 2001 Phoenix Open (11-under-par)
Robert Gamez (27-33), Indian Wells CC, third round, 2004 Bob Hope Chrysler Classic (12-under)
Bart Bryant (29-31), The Resort Course at LaCantera, third round, 2004 Valero Texas Open (10-under)

9 holes:

27 **Mike Souchak**, Brackenridge Park GC (par-35), back nine, first round, 1955 Texas Open (8-under-par)
Andy North, En-Joie GC (par-34), back nine, first round, 1975 B.C. Open (7-under-par)
Billy Mayfair, Warwick Hills G&CC (par-36), back nine, final round, 2001 Buick Open, (9-under-par)
Robert Gamez, Indian Wells CC (par-36), front nine, third round, 2004 Bob Hope Chrysler Classic (9-under-par)

Most strokes under par, 9 holes:

9 **Billy Mayfair**, 27, Warwick Hills G&CC (par-36), back nine, final round, 2001 Buick Open
Robert Gamez, 27, Indian Wells CC (par-36), front nine, third round, 2004 Bob Hope Chrysler Classic

Best Vardon Trophy scoring average

Non-adjusted:

68.17, **Tiger Woods**, 2000 (5,181 strokes, 76 rounds)
68.87, **Tiger Woods**, 2001 (5,234 strokes, 76 rounds)
69.00, **Tiger Woods**, 2002 (4,692 strokes, 68 rounds)
69.03, **Davis Love III**, 2001 (5,177 strokes, 75 rounds)
69.11, **Vijay Singh**, 2003 (7,049 strokes, 102 rounds)
69.16, **Phil Mickelson**, 2001 (5,671 strokes, 82 rounds)
69.19, **Vijay Singh**, 2004 (7,611 strokes, 110 rounds)
69.23, **Sam Snead**, 1950 (6,646 strokes, 96 rounds)
69.28, **Jim Furyk**, 2003 (6,997 strokes, 101 rounds)
69.30, **Ben Hogan**, 1948 (5,267 strokes, 76 rounds)
69.33, **Greg Norman**, 1994 (4,368 strokes, 63 rounds)
69.34, **Vijay Singh**, 2001 (6,379 strokes, 92 rounds)
69.37, **Sam Snead**, 1949 (5,064 strokes, 73 rounds)

Adjusted (since 1988):

67.79, **Tiger Woods**, 2000
68.41, **Tiger Woods**, 2003
68.43, **Tiger Woods**, 1999
68.56, **Tiger Woods**, 2002
68.65, **Vijay Singh**, 2003
68.81, **Greg Norman**, 1994
68.81, **Tiger Woods**, 2001
68.84, **Vijay Singh**, 2004
68.90, **Greg Norman**, 1993

[NOTE: Byron Nelson's stroke average in 1945 was 68.34 (7,657 strokes in 112 rounds). However, the Vardon Trophy was not awarded from 1942-46 because of World War II.]

Most birdies a in row:
8 **Bob Goalby**, Pasadena GC, final round, 65, 1961 St. Petersburg Open (won)
Fuzzy Zoeller, Oakwood CC, first round, 63, 1976 Quad Cities Open (won)
Dewey Arnette, Warwick Hills GC, first round, 65, 1987 Buick Open (T47)
Edward Fryatt, Doral Golf Resort and Spa (Blue Course), second round, 62, 2000 Doral-Ryder Open (T9)
J.P. Hayes, Palmer Course at PGA West, first round, 65, 2002 Bob Hope Chrysler Classic (T16)
Jerry Kelly, TPC at Summerlin, third round, 65, 2003 Las Vegas Invitational (T9)

Best birdie-eagle streak (by holes):
8 **Billy Mayfair**, 7 birdies, 1 eagle, Warwick Hills G&CC, final round, 2001 Buick Open
Briny Baird, 7 birdies, 1 eagle, Disney Palm Course, second round, 2003 FUNAI Classic at the WALT DISNEY WORLD Resort
7 **Al Geiberger**, 6 birdies, 1 eagle, Colonial CC, second round, 1977 Danny Thomas Memphis Classic
Webb Heintzelman, 5 birdies, 1 eagle, 1 birdie, Spanish Trail G&CC, third round, 1989 Las Vegas Invitational
Davis Love III, 6 birdies, 1 eagle, Pebble Beach GC, final round, 2001 AT&T Pebble Beach National Pro-Am

Most birdies in a row to win:
6 **Mike Souchak**, 1956 St. Paul Open (last 6 holes)
5 **Jack Nicklaus**, 1978 Jackie Gleason Inverrary Classic (last 5 holes)
Tom Weiskopf, 1971 Kemper Open (last 4 holes plus 1 playoff hole)
[NOTE: John Cook birdied final hole of regulation at 1992 Bob Hope Chrysler Classic, then birdied first 3 holes of playoff and eagled fourth hole to win]

Most birdies, 72 holes:
32 **Mark Calcavecchia**, 2001 Phoenix Open
Paul Gow, 2001 B.C. Open
31 **John Huston**, 1998 United Airlines Hawaiian Open

Most birdies, 90 holes:
37 **Joe Durant**, 2001 Bob Hope Chrysler Classic
Phil Mickelson, 2004 Bob Hope Chrysler Classic

Most under-par, consecutive starts:
54-under, **Joe Durant**, 2001 Bob Hope Chrysler Classic (36-under) and Genuity Championship (18-under)

Most consecutive rounds par or better:
52 **Tiger Woods**, third round, 2000 GTE Byron Nelson Classic, through first round, 2001 Phoenix Open

Victory Records

Most victories during career (PGA TOUR cosponsored and/or approved tournaments only):
82 **Sam Snead**
73 **Jack Nicklaus**
64 **Ben Hogan**
62 **Arnold Palmer**
52 **Byron Nelson**
51 **Billy Casper**

Most consecutive years winning at least one tournament:
17 **Jack Nicklaus** (1962-78)
Arnold Palmer (1955-71)
16 **Billy Casper** (1956-71)

Most consecutive victories: (Tournament, site, dates, score, purse)
11 **Byron Nelson**, March 8-11, 1945, to August 2-4, 1945; 1945 Miami Four Ball with **Jug McSpaden**, Miami Springs Course, March 8-11, won 8-6, $1,500; 1945 Charlotte Open, Myers Park GC, March 16-21, 272, $2,000; 1945 Greensboro Open, Starmount CC, March 23-25, 271, $1,000; 1945 Durham Open, Hope Valley CC, March 30-April 1, 276, $1,000; 1945 Atlanta Open, Capital City Course, April 5-8, 263, $2,000, 1945 Montreal Open, Islemere G&CC, June 7-10, 268, $2,000; 1945 Philadelphia Inquirer Invitational, Llanerch CC, June 14-17, 269, $3,000; 1945 Chicago Victory National Open, Calumet CC, June 29-July 1, 275, $2,000; 1945 PGA Championship, Moraine CC, Dayton, OH, July 9-15,won 4-3, $3,750; 1945 Tam O'Shanter Open, Tam O'Shanter CC, Chicago, IL, July 26-30, 269, $10,000; 1945 Canadian Open, Thornhill CC, Toronto, Ont., August 2-4, 280, $2,000; Winnings during streak: $30,250; [NOTE: Nelson won a 12th event in Spring Lake, NJ, which is not counted as official as its purse was below the PGA minimum]
6 **Ben Hogan**, June 9-12, 1948 to August 19-22, 1948; 1948 U.S. Open, Riviera CC, June 9-12, 276, $2,000; 1948 Inverness Round Robin (Jimmy Demaret), Inverness CC, June 24-27, Plus 16, $1,500; 1948 Motor City Open, Meadowbrook CC, July 1-4, 275, $2,600; 1948 Reading Open, Berkshire CC, July 22-25, 269, $2,600; 1948 Western Open, Brookfield CC, July 29-August 1, 281, $2,500; 1948 Denver Open Invitational, Wellshire CC, August 19-22, 270, $2,150; Winnings during streak: $11,350
6 **Tiger Woods**, August 26-29, 1999 to February 3-6, 2000; 1999 World Golf Championships-NEC Invitational, Firestone CC, August 26-29, 270, $1,000,000; 1999 National Car Rental Golf Classic at Walt Disney World Resort, Disney Magnolia/Disney Palm, October 21-24, 271, $450,000; 1999 THE TOUR Championship, Champions GC, October 28-31, 269, $900,000; 1999 World Golf Championships-American Express Championship, Valderrama GC, November 4-7, 278, $1,000,000; 2000 Mercedes Championships, Kapalua GC, January 6-9, 276, $522,000; 2000 AT&T Pebble Beach National Pro-Am, Pebble Beach GL, February 3-6, 273, $720,000; Winnings during streak: $4,592,000

Tiger Woods

Byron Nelson

4 **Byron Nelson**, October 11-14, 1945 to January 10-13, 1946; 1945 Seattle Open; 1945 Glen Garden Invitational; 1946 Los Angeles Open; 1946 San Francisco Open.
4 **Jack Burke, Jr.**, February 14-17, 1952 to March 6-9, 1952; 1952 Texas Open; 1952 Houston Open; 1952 Baton Rouge Open; 1952 St. Petersburg Open (four consecutive weeks).
4 **Ben Hogan**, April 9-12, 1953 to June 10-13, 1953: 1953 Masters Tournament, 1953 Pan American, 1953 Colonial, 1953 U.S. Open.
3 **Walter Hagen**, 1923
Joe Kirkwood, Sr., 1924
Bill Mehlhorn, 1929
Horton Smith, 1929
Paul Runyan, 1933
Henry Picard, 1939
Jimmy Demaret, 1940
Ben Hogan, 1940
Byron Nelson, 1944, 1945-46
Sam Snead, 1945
Ben Hogan, 1946 (twice)
Bobby Locke, 1947
Cary Middlecoff, 1951
Jim Ferrier, 1951
Ben Hogan, 1953
Billy Casper, 1960
Arnold Palmer, 1960, 1962
Johnny Miller, 1974
Jack Nicklaus, 1975
Hubert Green, 1976
Gary Player, 1978
Tom Watson, 1980
Nick Price, 1993
David Duval, 1997
Tiger Woods, 2000-2001
Vijay Singh, 2004

Most victories in single event:
8 **Sam Snead**, Greater Greensboro Open: 1938, 1946, 1949, 1950, 1955, 1956, 1960, 1965 (27-year span also record for time between first and last victories in same event)
6 **Harry Vardon**, British Open: 1896, 1898, 1899, 1903, 1911, 1914
Alex Ross, North & South Open: 1902, 1904, 1907, 1908, 1910, 1915
Sam Snead, Miami Open: 1937, 1939, 1946, 1950, 1951, 1955
Jack Nicklaus, Masters: 1963, 1965, 1966, 1972, 1975, 1986

5 **J.H. Taylor**, British Open: 1894, 1895, 1900, 1909, 1913
James Braid, British Open: 1901, 1905, 1906, 1908, 1910
Walter Hagen, Western Open: 1916, 1921, 1926, 1927, 1932
Walter Hagen, PGA Championship: 1921, 1924, 1925, 1926, 1927
Sam Snead, Goodall Palm Beach Round Robin: 1938, 1952, 1954, 1955, 1957
Ben Hogan, Colonial NIT: 1946, 1947, 1952, 1953, 1959
Peter Thomson, British Open: 1954, 1955, 1956, 1958, 1965
Arnold Palmer, Bob Hope Desert Classic: 1960, 1962, 1968, 1971, 1973
Jack Nicklaus, Tournament of Champions: 1963, 1964, 1971, 1973, 1977
Jack Nicklaus, PGA Championship: 1963, 1971, 1973, 1975, 1980
Tom Watson, British Open: 1975, 1977, 1980, 1982, 1983
Mark O'Meara, AT&T Pebble Beach National Pro-Am: 1985, 1989, 1990, 1992, 1997
Davis Love III, MCI Heritage: 1987, 1991, 1992, 1998, 2003

Major Championship Wins

(Amateur and Professional)
20 **Jack Nicklaus**, 1959-86 (6 Masters, 4 U.S. Opens, 3 British Opens, 5 PGAs, 2 U.S. Amateurs)
13 **Bobby Jones**, 1923-30 (4 U.S. Opens, 3 British Opens, 5 U.S. Amateurs, 1 British Amateur)
11 **Walter Hagen**, 1914-29 (2 U.S. Opens, 4 British Opens, 5 PGAs)
Tiger Woods, 1994-2002 (3 Masters, 2 U.S. Opens, 1 British Open, 2 PGAs, 3 U.S. Amateurs)
9 **John Ball**, 1888-1912 (1 British Open, 8 British Amateurs)
Ben Hogan, 1946-53 (2 Masters, 4 U.S. Opens, 1 British Open, 2 PGAs)
Gary Player, 1959-78 (3 Masters, 1 U.S. Open, 3 British Opens, 2 PGAs)
8 **Arnold Palmer**, 1954-64 (4 Masters, 1 U.S. Open, 2 British Opens, 1 U.S. Amateur)
Tom Watson, 1975-83 (2 Masters, 1 U.S. Open, 5 British Opens)

Jack Nicklaus

(Professional Only)
18 **Jack Nicklaus**
11 **Walter Hagen**
9 **Ben Hogan**; **Gary Player**
8 **Tom Watson**; **Tiger Woods**
7 **Harry Vardon**; **Bobby Jones**; **Gene Sarazen**; **Sam Snead**; **Arnold Palmer**
6 **Lee Trevino**; **Nick Faldo**
5 **James Braid**; **John H. Taylor**; **Byron Nelson**; **Peter Thomson**; **Seve Ballesteros**
4 **Old Tom Morris**, **Young Tom Morris**, **Willie Park**, **Willie Anderson**, **James Barnes**, **Bobby Locke**, **Ray Floyd**
3 **James Anderson**, **Robert Ferguson**, **Tommy Armour**, **Ralph Guldahl**, **Denny Shute**, **Henry Cotton**, **Jimmy Demaret**, **Cary Middlecoff**, **Julius Boros**, **Billy Casper**, **Larry Nelson**, **Hale Irwin**, **Nick Price**, **Payne Stewart**, **Ernie Els**, **Vijay Singh**.

Most consecutive victories in single event:
4 **Tom Morris, Jr.**, British Open, 1868-70 (no event 1871), 1872
Walter Hagen, PGA Championship, 1924-1927
Gene Sarazen, Miami Open, 1926 (schedule change), 1928-1930;
Tiger Woods, Bay Hill Invitational, 2000-2003
3 **Willie Anderson**, U.S. Open, 1903-1905
Walter Hagen, Metropolitan Open, 1916, 1919-1920 (no event held 1917-1918 due to World War I)
Gene Sarazen, Miami Beach Open, 1927-1929
Henry Picard, Tournament of the Gardens, 1935-37
Ralph Guldahl, Western Open, 1936-1938
Ben Hogan, Asheville Land of the Sky Open, 1940-1942
Gene Littler, Tournament of Champions, 1955-1957
Billy Casper, Portland Open, 1959-1961
Arnold Palmer, Texas Open, 1960-1962
Arnold Palmer, Phoenix Open, 1961-1963
Jack Nicklaus, Disney World Golf Classic, 1971-1973
Johnny Miller, Tucson Open, 1974-1976
Tom Watson, Byron Nelson Classic, 1978-1980
Tiger Woods, Memorial Tournament, 1999-2001
Tiger Woods, World Golf Championships-NEC Invitational, 1999-2001

Most victories in calendar year:
18 **Byron Nelson**, 1945
13 **Ben Hogan**, 1946
11 **Sam Snead**, 1950
10 **Ben Hogan**, 1948
9 **Paul Runyan**, 1933
Tiger Woods, 2000
Vijay Singh, 2004
8 **Horton Smith**, 1929
Gene Sarazen, 1930
Byron Nelson, 1944
Arnold Palmer, 1960
Arnold Palmer, 1962
Johnny Miller, 1974
Sam Snead, 1938
Tiger Woods, 1999
7 12 times, most recently **Tom Watson**, 1980

Arnold Palmer

Winners of Career Grand Slam (in the event of multiple victories in a major championship, only the first is listed):
Gene Sarazen: 1922 U.S. Open, 1922 PGA Championship, 1932 British Open, 1935 Masters Tournament
Ben Hogan: 1946 PGA Championship, 1948 U.S. Open, 1951 Masters Tournament, 1953 British Open
Gary Player: 1959 British Open, 1961 Masters Tournament, 1962 PGA Championship, 1965 U.S. Open
Jack Nicklaus: 1962 U.S. Open, 1963 Masters Tournament, 1963 PGA Championship, 1966 British Open
Tiger Woods: 1997 Masters Tournament, 1999 PGA Championship, 2000 U.S. Open, 2000 British Open

Longest time between first and last victory in same event (won other times in that event):
27 years, **Sam Snead**, Greater Greensboro Open (1938-1965) (won six other GGOs in between)

Longest time between victories in same event, and no other wins in that tournament in between:
21 years, **Hale Irwin**, Heritage Classic (1973-1994)

Most first-time winners during calendar year:
18, 2002
14, 1991
13, 1996
12, 1979, 1980, 1986
11, 1977, 1985, 1988
10, 1968, 1969, 1971, 1974, 1983, 1987, 1990, 1994, 2001, 2004

Most years between victories:
15 years, 5 months, 10 days, **Butch Baird** (May 7, 1961-October 17, 1976), 240 starts
14 years, 8 months, 2 days, **Ed Fiori** (January 17, 1982-September 15, 1996), 409 starts
13 years, 8 months, **Tommy Armour III** (January 28, 1990-September 28, 2003), 366 starts
13 years, 8 months, **Joey Sindelar** (September 9, 1990 – May 9, 2004), 370 starts
13 years, 6 months, 20 days, **Gene Sauers** (February 12, 1989-September 1, 2002), 245 starts
12 years, 5 months, 21 days, **Howard Twitty** (July 27, 1980-January 17, 1993), 307 starts
12 years, 27 days, **Scott Verplank** (July 31, 1988-August 27, 2000), 253 starts
11 years, 9 months, **Leonard Thompson** (October 30, 1977-July 30, 1989), 357 starts
11 years, 3 months, 27 days, **Bob Murphy** (March 2, 1975-June 29, 1986), 266 starts
11 years, 22 days, **Bob Rosburg** (January 22, 1961-February 13, 1972), 198 starts

Most years from first victory to last:
28 years, 11 months, 20 days, **Raymond Floyd** (March 17, 1963-March 8, 1992)
28 years, 2 months, 17 days, **Sam Snead** (January 17, 1937-April 4, 1965)

23 years, 11 months, 24 days, **Tom Watson** (June 30, 1974-May 24, 1998)
23 years, 11 months, 5 days, **Macdonald Smith** (August 28, 1912-August 2, 1936)
23 years, 9 months, 27 days, **Jack Nicklaus** (June 17, 1962-April 13, 1986)
23 years, 6 months, 7 days, **Craig Stadler** (January 13, 1980-July 20, 2003)
23 years, 3 months, 7 days, **Gene Littler** (January 24, 1954-May 1, 1977)
22 years, 11 months, 3 days, **Peter Jacobsen** (August 24, 1980-July 27, 2003)
22 years, 10 months, 19 days, **Jim Barnes** (August 26, 1914-July 15, 1937)
22 years, 7 months, 21 days, **Scott Hoch** (July 20, 1980-March 10, 2003)
22 years, 4 months, 25 days, **Johnny Miller** (September 12, 1971-February 6, 1994)
22 years, 4 months, 20 days, **Hale Irwin** (November 28, 1971-April 17, 1994)

Most wins by players in their 20s:
40 **Tiger Woods**
30 **Jack Nicklaus**

Most wins by players in their 30s:
42 **Arnold Palmer**
40 **Ben Hogan**

Most wins by players after 40:
17 **Sam Snead**
12 **Vijay Singh**
10 **Julius Boros**
7 **Gene Littler, E.J. (Dutch) Harrison**
6 **Ben Hogan, Tom Kite, Greg Norman, Loren Roberts, Hal Sutton**
5 **Jack Nicklaus, Lee Trevino, Miller Barber**

Sam Snead

Youngest winners:
19 years, 10 months, **Johnny McDermott**, 1911 U.S. Open
20 years, 5 days, **Gene Sarazen**, 1922 Southern Open
20 years, 1 month, 15 days, **Charles Evans, Jr.** (amateur), 1910 Western Open
20 years, 4 months, 12 days, **Francis Ouimet**, (amateur), 1913 U.S. Open
20 years, 4 months, 18 days, **Gene Sarazen**, 1922 U.S. Open
20 years, 5 months, 13 days, **Horton Smith**, 1928 Oklahoma City Open
20 years, 5 months, 22 days, **Gene Sarazen**, 1922 PGA Championship
20 years, 6 months, 13 days, **Raymond Floyd**, 1963 St. Petersburg Open
20 years, 6 months, 28 days, **Phil Mickelson** (amateur), 1991 Northern Telecom Open
20 years, 7 months, 1 day, **Horton Smith**, 1928 Catalina Island Open
20 years, 7 months, 16 days, **Tom Creavy**, 1931 PGA Championship

Youngest to make cut:
15 years, 8 months, 20 days, **Bob Panasik**, 1957 Canadian Open
16 years, 9 months, 7 days, **Ty Tryon**, 2001 Honda Classic
17 years, 1 month, 22 days, **Tommy Jacobs**, 1952 Masters Tournament

Oldest to make cut:
67 years, 2 months, 21 days, **Sam Snead**, 1979 Manufacturers Hanover Westchester Classic

Oldest winners:
52 years, 10 months, 8 days, **Sam Snead**, 1965 Greater Greensboro Open
51 years, 7 months, 10 days, **Art Wall**, 1975 Greater Milwaukee Open
51 years, 3 months, 7 days, **Jim Barnes**, 1937 Long Island Open
51 years, 1 month, 5 days, **John Barnum**, 1962 Cajun Classic
50 years, 1 month, 18 days, **Craig Stadler**, 2003 B.C. Open
49 years, 6 months, 4 days, **Raymond Floyd**, 1992 Doral-Ryder Open
49 years, 4 months, 23 days, **Peter Jacobsen**, 2003 Greater Hartford Open

Oldest first-time winner:
51 years, 1 month, 5 days, **John Barnum**, 1962 Cajun Classic

Most recent amateur winners of PGA TOUR events:
Gene Littler, 1954 San Diego Open
Doug Sanders, 1956 Canadian Open
Scott Verplank, 1985 Western Open
Phil Mickelson, 1991 Northern Telecom Open

Widest winning margin (strokes):
16 **J.D. Edgar**, 1919 Canadian Open
Joe Kirkwood, Sr., 1924 Corpus Christi Open
Bobby Locke, 1948 Chicago Victory National Championship
15 **Tiger Woods**, 2000 U.S. Open
14 **Ben Hogan**, 1945 Portland Invitational
Johnny Miller, 1975 Phoenix Open
13 **Byron Nelson**, 1945 Seattle Open
Gene Littler, 1955 Tournament of Champions
12 **Byron Nelson**, 1939 Phoenix Open
Arnold Palmer, 1962 Phoenix Open
Jose Maria Olazabal, 1990 NEC World Series of Golf
Tiger Woods, 1997 Masters Tournament

Best come-from-behind in final round to win (strokes):
10 **Paul Lawrie**, 1999 British Open
9 **Stewart Cink**, 2004 MCI Heritage
8 **Jack Burke, Jr.**, 1956 Masters Tournament
Ken Venturi, 1959 Los Angeles Open
Mark Lye, 1983 Bank of Boston Classic
Hal Sutton, 1985 St. Jude Memphis Classic
Chip Beck, 1990 Buick Open
Scott Simpson, 1998 Buick Invitational
Craig Stadler, 2003 B.C. Open

Largest lead with 18 holes to play (strokes):
13 **Bobby Locke**, 1948 Chicago Victory National Championship (won by 16)
11 **Gene Sarazen**, 1927 Long Island Open (won by 11)
10 **Walter Hagen**, 1920 Florida West Coast Open (won by 12)
Ben Hogan, 1945 Portland Invitational (won by 14)
Gene Littler, 1955 Tournament of Champions (won by 13)
Tiger Woods, 2000 U.S. Open (won by 15)

Tiger Woods

Largest lead with 18 holes to play and lost (strokes):
6 **Bobby Cruickshank**, 1928 Florida Open
Gay Brewer, 1969 Danny Thomas-Diplomat Classic
Hal Sutton, 1983 Anheuser-Busch Golf Classic
Greg Norman, 1996 Masters Tournament

Playoff Records

Longest sudden-death playoffs (holes):
11 1949 Motor City Open: **Cary Middlecoff** and **Lloyd Mangrum** were declared co-winners by mutual agreement
8 1965 Azalea Open: **Dick Hart** def. **Phil Rodgers**
1978 Greater Milwaukee Open: **Lee Elder** def. **Lee Trevino**
1981 Quad Cities Open: **Dave Barr** def. **Woody Blackburn**, **Dan Halldorson**, **Frank Conner**, **Victor Regalado**
1983 Phoenix Open: **Bob Gilder** def. **Rex Caldwell**, **Johnny Miller**, **Mark O'Meara**

Most players in sudden-death playoff:
6 1994 GTE Byron Nelson Classic: **Neal Lancaster** def. **Tom Byrum**, **Mark Carnevale**, **David Edwards**, **Yoshinori Mizumaki** and **David Ogrin**
2001 Nissan Open: **Robert Allenby** def. **Toshi Izawa**, **Brandel Chamblee**, **Bob Tway**, **Jeff Sluman** and **Dennis Paulson**
5 Six times, (most recently 1996 Buick Challenge: **Michael Bradley** def. **Fred Funk**, **Davis Love III**, **John Maginnes** and **Len Mattiace**)
Teams at the 1985 Chrysler Team Championship

Most playoffs, season:
16 1988, 1991
15 1972
14 2004

Putting Records

Fewest putts, one round:

18 **Sam Trahan**, Whitemarsh Valley CC, final round, 1979 IV Philadelphia Golf Classic
Mike McGee, Colonial CC, first round, 1987 Federal Express St. Jude Classic
Kenny Knox, Harbour Town GL, first round, 1989 MCI Heritage Classic
Andy North, Kingsmill GC, second round, 1990 Anheuser-Busch Golf Classic
Jim McGovern, TPC at Southwind, second round, 1992 Federal Express St. Jude Classic
Corey Pavin, Glen Abbey GC, second round, 2000 Bell Canadian Open

Fewest putts, four rounds:

93 **Kenny Knox**, Harbour Town GL, 1989 MCI Heritage Classic
Mark Calcavecchia, Forest Oaks CC, 2002 Greater Greensboro Chrysler Classic
94 **Bob Tway**, Harbour Town GL, 1986 MCI Heritage Classic
95 **George Archer**, Harbour Town GL, 1980 Sea Pines Heritage Classic
Mark O'Meara, TPC at Las Colinas, 1989 GTE Byron Nelson Classic
Andy Bean, Harbour Town GL, 1990 MCI Heritage Classic
Payne Stewart, Harbour Town GL, 1999 MCI Classic
Jim Carter, Harbour Town GL, 2000 MCI Classic
Davis Love III, Harbour Town GL, 2000 MCI Classic
Bob Heintz, Forest Oaks CC, 2002 Greater Greensboro Chrysler Classic
Chris Riley, CC at Mirasol, 2003 Honda Classic
Aaron Baddeley, Omni Tucson National, 2004 Chrysler Classic of Tucson

Kenny Knox

Fewest putts, nine holes:

6 **Stan Utley**, Northview G&CC, front nine, second round, 2002 Air Canada Championship
7 **Bill Nary**, El Paso CC, back nine, third round, 1952 El Paso Open
8 **Jim Colbert**, Deerwood, front nine, final round, 1967 Greater Jacksonville Open
Sam Trahan, Whitemarsh Valley CC, back nine, final round, 1979 IVB Philadelphia Golf Classic
Bill Calfee, Forest Oaks CC, back nine, third round, 1980 Greater Greensboro Open
Kenny Knox, Harbour Town GL, back nine, first round, 1989 MCI Heritage Classic
John Inman, Harbour Town GL, front nine, final round, 1994 MCI Heritage Classic

Miscellaneous Records

Most consecutive events without missing cut:

133 **Tiger Woods***, Buick Invitational, February 5-8, 1998, through THE TOUR Championship, November 4-7, 2004
113 **Byron Nelson**, Bing Crosby National Pro-Am, January 26, 1941, through Colonial National Invitation, May 27-30, 1948 (withdrew after two rounds of 1949 Bing Crosby National Pro-Am)
105 **Jack Nicklaus**, Sahara Open, October 29-November 1,1970, through World Series of Golf, September 2-5, 1976 (missed cut 1976 World Open)
86 **Hale Irwin**, Bing Crosby National Pro-Am, January 23-26, 1975, through conclusion of 1978 season (missed cut in first start of 1979 season at Bing Crosby National Pro-Am)
72 **Dow Finsterwald**, Carling Golf Classic, September 22-25, 1955, through Houston Invitational, February 21-24, 1958 (missed the cut at Baton Rouge Open Invitational)
53 **Tom Kite**, Western Open, July 3-6, 1980, through Manufacturers Hanover Westchester Classic, June 24-27, 1982 (missed cut at 1982 Canadian Open)
Vijay Singh, NEC World Series of Golf, August 24-27, 1995, through THE PLAYERS Championship, March 26-29, 1998 (missed cut at 1998 Masters)
* Streak intact through end of 2004 season.

Most career cuts made:

587 **Tom Kite**
583 **Raymond Floyd**
575 **Jay Haas**
566 **Gene Littler**
561 **Doug Ford**
543 **Arnold Palmer**

Most top-10s in a season:

31 **Harold (Jug) McSpaden**, 1945

Most top-10s in a career:

358 **Sam Snead**

Most consecutive top-10s in a career:

65 **Byron Nelson**, 1942 Texas Open through 1946 New Orleans Open

Youngest professional shooting his age or below:

66 (4-under, fourth round), **Sam Snead** (age 67), 1979 Quad Cities Open
67 (3-under, second round), **Sam Snead** (age 67), 1979 Quad Cities Open

Most victories before 21st birthday:

7 **Horton Smith**

Youngest to win five titles:

20 years, 10 months, 1 day, **Horton Smith**
21 years, 5 months, 20 days, **Tiger Woods**

First African-American to play PGA TOUR:

Bill Spiller, 1948 Los Angeles Open

First African-American to win official PGA TOUR title:

Pete Brown, 1964 Waco Turner Open

Pete Brown

Women who played in PGA TOUR events:

Babe Didrikson Zaharias: 1938 Los Angeles Open (Jan. 7-10), 81-84 (missed cut). Note: Sponsor invitation; 1945 Los Angeles Open (Jan. 5-8) 76-81-79 (missed cut). Note: Qualified with 76-76; 1945 Phoenix Open (Jan. 11-14) 77-72-75-80—304 (33rd). Note: Sponsor invitation; 1945 Tucson Open (Jan. 18-21) 307 total (42nd). Note: Qualified with 74-81.
Annika Sorenstam: 2003 Bank of America Colonial (May 22-25) 71-74—145 (missed cut) Note: Sponsor exemption.
Suzy Whaley: 2003 Greater Hartford Open (July 24-27), 75-78—153 (missed cut). Note: Qualified by winning 2002 Connecticut PGA Section Championship.
Michelle Wie: 2004 Sony Open in Hawaii (Jan.15-18) 72-68 (missed cut). Note: Sponsor exemption.

Lefthanders who have won:

23 **Phil Mickelson**, 1991 Northern Telecom Open. 1993 Buick Invitational of California, The International. 1994 Mercedes Championships. 1995 Northern Telecom Open. 1996 Nortel Open, Phoenix Open, GTE Byron Nelson Golf Classic, NEC World Series of Golf. 1997 Bay Hill Invitational, Sprint International. 1998 Mercedes Championships, AT&T Pebble Beach National Pro-Am. 2000 Buick Invitational, BellSouth Classic, MasterCard Colonial, THE TOUR Championship. 2001 Buick Invitational, Canon Greater Hartford Open. 2002 Bob Hope Chrysler Classic, Canon Greater Hartford Open. 2004 Bob Hope Chrysler Classic, Masters Tournament.
7 **Mike Weir**, 1999 Air Canada Championship. 2000 WGC-American Express Championship. 2001 THE TOUR Championship. 2003 Bob Hope Chrysler Classic, Nissan Open, Masters Tournament. 2004 Nissan Open.
6 **Bob Charles**, 1963 Houston Classic. British Open. 1965 Tucson Open Invitational. 1967 Atlanta Classic. 1968 Canadian Open. 1974 Greater Greensboro Open
2 **Steve Flesch**, 2003 HP Classic of New Orleans. 2004 Bank of America Colonial
1 **Sam Adams**, 1973 Quad Cities Open
Ernie Gonzalez, 1986 Pensacola Open
Russ Cochran, 1991 Centel Western Open

Father-son winners:
Tom Morris Sr.-Tom Morris Jr.
Willie Park-Willie Park Jr.
Joe Kirkwood Sr.-Joe Kirkwood Jr.
Clayton Heafner-Vance Heafner
Julius Boros-Guy Boros
Al Geiberger-Brent Geiberger

Brothers who have won:
(Year of first official victory/career wins in parentheses)
Lloyd Mangrum (1940/36)-Ray Mangrum (1936/5)
Alex Smith (1906/2)-Macdonald Smith (1924/24)-Willie Smith (1899/1)
Jim Turnesa (1951/2)-Joe Turnesa (1924/15)-Mike Turnesa (1931/6)-Phil Turnesa (1932/1)
Lionel Hebert (1957/5)-Jay Hebert (1957/5)
Al Espinosa (1924/8)-Abe Espinosa (1928/3)
Don Massengale (1966/2)-Rik Massengale (1975/3)
Dave Hill (1961/13)-Mike Hill (1970/3)
Danny Edwards (1977/5)-David Edwards (1980/4)
Joe Inman (1976/1)-John Inman (1987/2)
Curt Byrum (1989/1)-Tom Byrum (1989/1)
Brad Bryant (1995/1)-Bart Bryant (2004/1)

Hole-in-one on par 4:
Andrew Magee, driver, on 332-yard par-4 17th hole, TPC of Scottsdale, AZ, in first round of the 2001 Phoenix Open

Money-Winning Records

Most money won in a season:
$10,905,166, **Vijay Singh**, 2004
$9,188,321, **Tiger Woods**, 2000
$7,573,907, **Vijay Singh**, 2003
$6,912,625, **Tiger Woods**, 2002
$6,673,413, **Tiger Woods**, 2003

Most money won by a rookie:
$3,063,778, **Todd Hamilton**, 2004
$2,417,685, **Zach Johnson**, 2004
$1,864,584, **Carlos Franco**, 1999
$1,592,344, **Ryan Palmer**, 2004
$1,520,632, **Charles Howell III**, 2001

Most money won by a second-year player:
$3,912,064, **Chad Campbell**, 2003
$3,724,984, **Adam Scott**, 2004
$2,702,747, **Charles Howell III**, 2002
$2,617,004, **Retief Goosen**, 2002
$2,066,833, **Tiger Woods**, 1997

Most money won in first two seasons:
$4,963,720, **Adam Scott**, 2003-2004
$4,727,538, **Chad Campbell**, 2002-2003
$4,223,379, **Charles Howell III**, 2001-2002
$3,743,989, **Retief Goosen**, 2001-2002
$3,415,176, **Carlos Franco**, 1999-2000

Most consecutive years with $100,000 or more in earnings:
27 **Tom Watson**, 1974-2000
26 **Jay Haas**, 1979-2004
25 **Craig Stadler**, 1980-2004
23 **Tom Kite**, 1976-1998

Most consecutive years with $200,000 or more in earnings
21 **Mark O'Meara**, 1984-2004
19 **Nick Price**, 1986-2004
18 **Mark Calcavecchia**, 1987-2004
Fred Couples, 1987-2004

Most consecutive years with $500,000 or more in earnings:
12 **Mark Calcavecchia**, 1993-2004
Jeff Maggert, 1993-2004
Phil Mickelson, 1993-2004
11 **Ernie Els**, 1994-2004
Scott Hoch, 1994-2004
Tom Lehman, 1994-2004

Most consecutive years with $1,000,000 or more in earnings:
10 **Davis Love III**, 1995-2004
9 **Scott Hoch**, 1996-2004
Phil Mickelson, 1996-2004
8 **Vijay Singh**, 1997-2004
Tiger Woods, 1997-2004
Justin Leonard, 1997-2004

Most years with $1,000,000 or more in earnings:
11 **Davis Love III**
10 **Nick Price**
9 **Scott Hoch**
Vijay Singh
Phil Mickelson

David Toms

Most money won in a season without victory:
$3,459,740, **David Toms**, 2002
$3,440,829, **Vijay Singh**, 2001
$3,075,092, **Davis Love III**, 2004
$2,971,842, **Chris DiMarco**, 2004
$2,718,445, **Brad Faxon**, 2003

Most consecutive years finishing top 10 on money list:
17 **Jack Nicklaus**, 1962-78
11 **Arnold Palmer**, 1957-67

Most years finishing top 10 money list:
18 **Jack Nicklaus**
15 **Sam Snead**
13 **Arnold Palmer**

Most years leading money list:
8 **Jack Nicklaus**

Most consecutive years leading money list:
4 **Tom Watson**, 1977-80
Tiger Woods, 1999-2002

Youngest to win $1 million in earnings in a season:
21 years, 5 months, 21 days, **Tiger Woods**, 1997

Quickest to $1 million in earnings in a career:
5 events, **Retief Goosen**

Quickest to $2 million in earnings in a career:
16 events, **Tiger Woods**

Number of players to win over $2 million in a single season:
29 2003
28 2004
23 2002
16 2001
15 2000
9 1999
3 1998
1 1997

Number of players to win over $1 million in a single season:

77	2004
72	2003
61	2002
56	2001
45	2000
36	1999
26	1998
18	1997
9	1995, 1996
6	1994
5	1993
4	1992
2	1989, 1990

First-year players to win $1 million or more:

$3,063,778, **Todd Hamilton**, 2004
$2,417,685, **Zach Johnson**, 2004
$1,864,584, **Carlos Franco**, 1999
$1,592,344, **Ryan Palmer**, 2004
$1,520,632, **Charles Howell III**, 2001
$1,502,888, **Jose Coceres**, 2001
$1,462,713, **Jonathan Byrd**, 2002
$1,451,726, **Pat Perez**, 2002
$1,434,911, **Ben Curtis**, 2003
$1,413,113, **Peter Lonard**, 2002
$1,255,314, **Notah Begay III**, 1999
$1,238,736, **Adam Scott**, 2003
$1,207,104, **Shigeki Maruyama**, 2000
$1,182,883, **Alex Cejka**, 2003
$1,176,434, **Vaughn Taylor**, 2004
$1,126,985, **Retief Goosen**, 2001
$1,088,205, **Luke Donald**, 2002
$1,073,847, **J.J. Henry**, 2001

Biggest One-Season Gains

Rank	Player	Season	Money	Season	Money	Gain
1.	Tiger Woods	1998	$1,841,117	1999	$6,616,585	$4,775,468
2.	Phil Mickelson	2003	$1,623,137	2004	$5,784,823	$4,161,686
3.	Mike Weir	2002	$ 843,890	2003	$4,918,910	$4,075,020
4.	Davis Love III	2002	$2,056,160	2003	$6,081,896	$4,025,736
5.	Vijay Singh	2002	$3,756,563	2003	$7,573,907	$3,817,344

Money Levels on the PGA TOUR

Year	#1 Final Money List		#30 Final Money List		#125 Final Money List	
2004	Vijay Singh	$10,905,166	Kenny Perry	$1,952,043	Tag Ridings	$623,262
2003	Vijay Singh	7,573,907	K.J. Choi	1,999,663	Esteban Toledo	487,495
2002	Tiger Woods	6,912,625	Steve Lowery	1,882,553	Jay Williamson	515,445
2001	Tiger Woods	5,687,777	Steve Stricker	1,676,229	Woody Austin	406,352
2000	Tiger Woods	9,188,321	Carlos Franco	1,550,592	Bob Burns	391,075
1999	Tiger Woods	6,616,585	Loren Roberts	1,258,745	Charles Raulerson	326,893
1998	David Duval	2,591,031	Andrew Magee	964,302	Blaine McCallister	228,304
1997	Tiger Woods	2,066,833	Andrew Magee	752,007	Neal Lancaster	179,273
1996	Tom Lehman	1,780,159	Duffy Waldorf	604,382	Dicky Pride	167,852
1995	Greg Norman	1,654,959	Nick Price	611,700	John Wilson	149,280
1994	Nick Price	1,499,927	Mark Calcavecchia	533,201	Dennis Paulson	142,515
1993	Nick Price	1,478,557	Billy Mayfair	513,072	Ronnie Black	120,041
1992	Fred Couples	1,344,188	Steve Pate	472,626	Roger Maltbie	109,742
1991	Corey Pavin	979,430	Ian Woosnam	485,023	John Adams	117,549
1990	Greg Norman	1,165,477	John Huston	435,690	Bob Eastwood	123,908

All-Time PGA TOUR Money List

	Player	Money
1.	Tiger Woods	$45,142,737
2.	Vijay Singh	36,760,089
3.	Phil Mickelson	29,557,928
4.	Davis Love III	29,207,838
5.	Ernie Els	24,466,992
6.	Jim Furyk	19,731,382
7.	Nick Price	19,715,533
8.	David Toms	18,942,915
9.	Scott Hoch	18,455,984
10.	Justin Leonard	17,639,781
11.	Fred Couples	16,544,574
12.	Mark Calcavecchia	16,412,462
13.	David Duval	16,356,349
14.	Kenny Perry	15,909,178
15.	Mike Weir	15,606,744
16.	Jeff Sluman	15,502,142
17.	Tom Lehman	15,473,541
18.	Brad Faxon	15,327,693
19.	Hal Sutton	15,249,365
20.	Fred Funk	15,019,306
21.	Stewart Cink	14,104,588
22.	Loren Roberts	14,081,948
23.	Greg Norman	13,946,089
24.	Jay Haas	13,791,809
25.	Mark O'Meara	13,687,545
26.	Scott Verplank	13,646,851
27.	Chris DiMarco	13,609,377
28.	Bob Estes	13,286,333
29.	Paul Azinger	13,281,971
30.	Stuart Appleby	13,233,506
31.	Bob Tway	13,116,936
32.	John Huston	13,005,980
33.	Jeff Maggert	12,281,068
34.	Lee Janzen	12,101,457
35.	Kirk Triplett	$11,850,516
36.	Payne Stewart	11,737,008
37.	Jesper Parnevik	11,396,995
38.	Rocco Mediate	11,361,822
39.	Jerry Kelly	11,327,398
40.	John Cook	11,295,153
41.	Corey Pavin	11,139,031
42.	Retief Goosen	11,119,459
43.	Sergio Garcia	11,045,484
44.	Tom Kite	10,937,613
45.	Robert Allenby	10,767,108
46.	Steve Lowery	10,541,382
47.	Steve Flesch	10,486,622
48.	Billy Mayfair	10,483,744
49.	Steve Elkington	10,262,170
50.	Duffy Waldorf	10,183,668
51.	Tom Watson	9,892,128
52.	Craig Stadler	9,730,968
53.	Tim Herron	9,689,490
54.	Billy Andrade	9,439,702
55.	Shigeki Maruyama	9,154,398
56.	Joey Sindelar	8,988,650
57.	David Frost	8,987,003
58.	Charles Howell III	8,759,352
59.	Scott McCarron	8,446,847
60.	Mark Brooks	8,387,257
61.	Jonathan Kaye	8,171,506
62.	Dudley Hart	8,075,956
63.	Steve Pate	8,005,806
64.	Frank Lickliter II	8,004,359
65.	Dan Forsman	8,002,094
66.	Andrew Magee	7,959,025
67.	Stephen Ames	7,847,124
68.	Steve Stricker	7,833,052
69.	Chris Riley	$7,730,581
70.	Rory Sabbatini	7,724,208
71.	Curtis Strange	7,599,951
72.	Peter Jacobsen	7,572,970
73.	Kevin Sutherland	7,554,453
74.	Craig Parry	7,481,976
75.	K.J. Choi	7,388,417
76.	Bernhard Langer	7,297,104
77.	Carlos Franco	7,277,434
78.	Chad Campbell	7,277,092
79.	Larry Mize	7,103,733
80.	Ben Crenshaw	7,091,166
81.	Jose Maria Olazabal	7,078,495
82.	Glen Day	6,999,873
83.	Skip Kendall	6,887,822
84.	Chris Perry	6,866,671
85.	John Daly	6,852,695
86.	Scott Simpson	6,742,717
87.	Bill Glasson	6,676,261
88.	Tom Pernice, Jr.	6,598,090
89.	Joe Durant	6,577,188
90.	Bruce Lietzke	6,474,794
91.	Len Mattiace	6,435,955
92.	Lanny Wadkins	6,355,681
93.	Brent Geiberger	6,216,995
94.	Chip Beck	6,199,550
95.	Steve Jones	6,052,026
96.	Robert Gamez	5,971,568
97.	Hale Irwin	5,966,031
98.	Woody Austin	5,959,094
99.	Jim Gallagher, Jr.	5,943,105
100.	J.L. Lewis	5,937,693

Top 50 All-Time PGA TOUR Winners

1.	Sam Snead	82
2.	Jack Nicklaus	73
3.	Ben Hogan	64
4.	Arnold Palmer	62
5.	Byron Nelson	52
6.	Billy Casper	51
7.	Walter Hagen	44
T8.	Cary Middlecoff	40
T8.	Tiger Woods	40
T10.	Gene Sarazen	39
T10.	Tom Watson	39
12.	Lloyd Mangrum	36
13.	Horton Smith	32
T14.	Harry Cooper	31
T14.	Jimmy Demaret	31
16.	Leo Diegel	30
T17.	Gene Littler	29
T17.	Paul Runyan	29
T17.	Lee Trevino	29
20.	Henry Picard	26
T21.	Tommy Armour	25
T21.	Johnny Miller	25
T23.	Gary Player	24
T23.	Vijay Singh	24
T23.	Macdonald Smith	24
26.	Phil Mickelson	23
T27.	Johnny Farrell	22
T27.	Raymond Floyd	22
T29.	Willie Macfarlane	21
T29.	Phil Mickelson	21
T29.	Lanny Wadkins	21
T29.	Craig Wood	21
T33.	James Barnes	20
T33.	Hale Irwin	20
T33.	Bill Mehlhorn	20
T33.	Greg Norman	20
T33.	Doug Sanders	20
T38.	Ben Crenshaw	19
T38.	Doug Ford	19
T38.	Hubert Green	19
T38.	Tom Kite	19
T42.	Julius Boros	18
T42.	Jim Ferrier	18
T42.	E.J. Harrison	18
T42.	Davis Love III	18
T42.	Nick Price	18
T42.	Johnny Revolta	18
T48.	Jack Burke, Jr.	17
T48.	Bobby Cruickshank	17
T48.	Harold McSpaden	17
T48.	Curtis Strange	17

Past Leading Money Winners

Year	Player	Money
1934	Paul Runyan	$6,767.00
1935	Johnny Revolta	9,543.00
1936	Horton Smith	7,682.00
1937	Harry Cooper	14,138.69
1938	Sam Snead	19,534.49
1939	Henry Picard	10,303.00
1940	Ben Hogan	10,655.00
1941	Ben Hogan	18,358.00
1942	Ben Hogan	13,143.00
1943	No Statistics Compiled	
1944	Byron Nelson (War Bonds)	37,967.69
1945	Byron Nelson (War Bonds)	63,335.66
1946	Ben Hogan	42,556.16
1947	Jimmy Demaret	27,936.83
1948	Ben Hogan	32,112.00
1949	Sam Snead	31,593.83
1950	Sam Snead	35,758.83
1951	Lloyd Mangrum	26,088.83
1952	Julius Boros	37,032,97
1953	Lew Worsham	34,002.00
1954	Bob Toski	65,819.81
1955	Julius Boros	63,121.55
1956	Ted Kroll	72,835.83
1957	Dick Mayer	65,835.00

Year	Player	Money
1958	Arnold Palmer	$42,607.50
1959	Art Wall	53,167.60
1960	Arnold Palmer	75,262.85
1961	Gary Player	64,540.45
1962	Arnold Palmer	81,448.33
1963	Arnold Palmer	128,230.00
1964	Jack Nicklaus	113,284.50
1965	Jack Nicklaus	140,752.14
1966	Billy Casper	121,944.92
1967	Jack Nicklaus	188,998.08
1968	Billy Casper*	205,168.67
1969	Frank Beard	164,707.11
1970	Lee Trevino	157,037.63
1971	Jack Nicklaus	244,490.50
1972	Jack Nicklaus	320,542.26
1973	Jack Nicklaus	308,362.10
1974	Johnny Miller	353,021.59
1975	Jack Nicklaus	298,149.17
1976	Jack Nicklaus	266,438.57
1977	Tom Watson	310,653.16
1978	Tom Watson	362,428.93
1979	Tom Watson	462,636.00
1980	Tom Watson	530,808.33
1981	Tom Kite	375,698.84

Year	Player	Money
1982	Craig Stadler	$446,462.00
1983	Hal Sutton	426,668.00
1984	Tom Watson	476,260.00
1985	Curtis Strange	542,321.00
1986	Greg Norman	653,296.00
1987	Curtis Strange	925,941.00
1988	Curtis Strange	1,147,644.00
1989	Tom Kite	1,395,278.00
1990	Greg Norman	1,165,477.00
1991	Corey Pavin	979,430.00
1992	Fred Couples	1,344,188.00
1993	Nick Price	1,478,557.00
1994	Nick Price	1,499,927.00
1995	Greg Norman	1,654,959.00
1996	Tom Lehman	1,780,159.00
1997	Tiger Woods	2,066,833.00
1998	David Duval	2,591,031.00
1999	Tiger Woods	6,616,585.00
2000	Tiger Woods	9,188,321.00
2001	Tiger Woods	5,687,777.00
2002	Tiger Woods	6,912,625.00
2003	Vijay Singh	7,573,907.00
2004	Vijay Singh	10,905,166.00

* Total money listed from 1968 through 1974. Official money listed beginning in 1975.

$1 Million-plus Paydays on the PGA TOUR

There have been 42 $1 million-plus official winners' checks on the PGA TOUR. Tiger Woods has the most with 12 of his 40 victories reaching $1 million or more. Vijay Singh, Mike Weir, Darren Clarke, Ernie Els and Retief Goosen have two each. Jeff Maggert received the first $1 million check at the 1999 WGC-Accenture Match Play Championship and Adam Scott picked up the largest, $1,440,000, at the 2004 PLAYERS Championship.

1999			
2/28	Jeff Maggert	WGC-Accenture Match Play Champ.	$1,000,000
8/29	Tiger Woods	WGC-NEC Invitational	1,000,000
11/7	Tiger Woods	WGC-American Express	1,000,000

2000			
2/27	Darren Clarke	WGC-Accenture Match Play Champ.	$1,000,000
3/26	Hal Sutton	THE PLAYERS Championship	1,080,000
8/27	Tiger Woods	WGC-NEC Invitational	1,000,000
11/12	Mike Weir	WGC-American Express	1,000,000

2001			
1/7	Steve Stricker	WGC-Accenture Match Play Champ.	$1,000,000
3/25	Tiger Woods	THE PLAYERS Championship	1,080,000
4/8	Tiger Woods	Masters Tournament	1,008,000
8/26	Tiger Woods	WGC-NEC Invitational	1,000,000

Note: The 2001 WGC-American Express Championship, a scheduled $1-million first prize, was canceled.

2002			
2/24	Kevin Sutherland	WGC-Accenture Match Play Champ.	$1,000,000
3/24	Craig Perks	THE PLAYERS Championship	1,080,000
4/14	Tiger Woods	Masters Tournament	1,008,000
6/16	Tiger Woods	U.S. Open	1,000,000
7/21	Ernie Els	British Open	1,106,140
8/25	Craig Parry	WGC-NEC Invitational	1,000,000
9/22	Tiger Woods	WGC-American Express	1,000,000

2003			
1/12	Ernie Els	Mercedes Championship	$1,000,000
3/2	Tiger Woods	WGC-Accenture Match Play Champ.	1,050,000
3/30	Davis Love III	THE PLAYERS Championship	1,170,000
4/13	Mike Weir	Masters Tournament	1,080,000
5/11	David Toms	Wachovia Championship	1,008,000
5/18	Vijay Singh	EDS Byron Nelson Championship	1,008,000
6/15	Jim Furyk	U.S. Open	1,080,000
7/20	Ben Curtis	British Open	1,112,720
8/17	Shaun Micheel	PGA Championship	1,080,000
8/24	Darren Clarke	WGC-NEC Invitational	1,050,000
10/5	Tiger Woods	WGC-American Express	1,050,000
11/9	Chad Campbell	THE TOUR Championship	1,080,000

2004			
1/11	Stuart Appleby	Mercedes Championship	$1,060,000
2/29	Tiger Woods	WGC-Accenture Match Play Champ.	1,200,000
3/28	Adam Scott	THE PLAYERS Championship	1,440,000
4/11	Phil Mickelson	Masters Tournament	1,170,000
5/9	Joey Sindelar	Wachovia Championship	1,008,000
5/16	Sergio Garcia	EDS Byron Nelson Championship	1,044,000
6/20	Retief Goosen	U.S. Open Championship	1,125,000
7/18	Todd Hamilton	British Open Championship	1,348,272
8/15	Vijay Singh	PGA Championship	1,125,000
8/22	Stewart Cink	WGC-NEC Invitational	1,200,000
10/3	Ernie Els	WGC-American Express Championship	1,200,000
11/7	Retief Goosen	THE TOUR Championship	1,080,000

Growth of the Purses on the PGA TOUR

Year	No. of Events	Total Money
1938	38	$158,000
1939	28	121,000
1940	27	117,000
1941	30	169,200
1942	21	116,650
1943	3	17,000
1944	22	150,500
1945	36	435,380
1946	37	411,533
1947	31	352,500
1948	34	427,000
1949	25	338,200
1950	33	459,950
1951	30	460,200
1952	32	498,016
1953	32	562,704
1954	26	600,819
1955	36	782,010
1956	36	847,070
1957	32	820,360
1958	39	1,005,800
1959	43	1,225,205
1960	41	1,335,242
1961	45	$1,461,830
1962	49	1,790,320
1963	43	2,044,900
1964	41	2,301,063
1965	36	2,848,515
1966	36	3,704,445
1967	37	3,979,162
1968	45	5,077,600
1969	47	5,465,875
1970	55	6,751,523
1971	63	7,116,000
1972	71	7,596,749
1973	75	8,657,225
1974	57	8,165,941
1975	51	7,895,450
1976	49	9,157,522
1977	48	9,688,977
1978	48	10,337,332
1979	46	12,801,200
1980	45	13,371,786
1981	45	14,175,393
1982	46	15,089,576
1983	45	17,588,242
1984	46	$21,251,382
1985	47	25,290,526
1986	46	25,442,242
1987	46	32,106,093
1988	47	36,959,307
1989	44	41,288,787
1990	44	46,251,831
1991	44	49,628,203
1992	44	49,386,906
1993	43	53,203,611
1994	43	56,416,080
1995	44	61,650,000
1996	45	70,700,000
1997	45	80,550,000
1998	45	96,150,000
1999	47	135,808,500
2000	49	164,350,000
2001	49	175,900,000
2002	49	198,950,000
2003	48	224,700,000
2004	48	241,320,400
2005	48	252,350,400 *

* Prior to the start of 2005 season. Purses for 2004 major championships and THE PLAYERS Championship have been used; total will increase as purses are announced. PGA TOUR events occasionally will increase previously announced purses. Official events only.

Most PGA TOUR Wins Year-by-Year

1916	James Barnes	3
	Walter Hagen	3
1917	James Barnes	2
	Mike Brady	2
1918	Jock Hutchison	1
	Walter Hagen	1
	Patrick Doyle	1
1919	James Barnes	5
1920	Jock Hutchison	4
1921	James Barnes	4
1922	Walter Hagen	4
1923	Walter Hagen	5
	Joe Kirkwood, Sr	5
1924	Walter Hagen	5
1925	Leo Diegel	5
1926	Bill Mehlhorn	5
	Macdonald Smith	5
1927	Johnny Farrell	7
1928	Bil Mehlhorn	7
1929	Horton Smith	8
1930	Gene Sarazen	8
1931	Wiffy Cox	4
1932	Gene Sarazen	4
1933	Paul Runyan	9
1934	Paul Runyan	7
1935	Johnny Revolta	5
	Henry Picard	5
1936	Ralph Guldahl	3
	Henry Picard	3
	Jimmy Hines	3
1937	Harry Cooper	8
1938	Sam Snead	8
1939	Henry Picard	8
1940	Jimmy Demaret	6
1941	Sam Snead	7
1942	Ben Hogan	6
1943	Sam Byrd	1
	Harold McSpaden	1
	Steve Warga	1
1944	Byron Nelson	8
1945	Byron Nelson	18
1946	Ben Hogan	13
1947	Ben Hogan	7
1948	Ben Hogan	10
1949	Cary Middlecoff	7
1950	Sam Snead	11
1951	Cary Middlecoff	6
1952	Jack Burke, Jr	5
	Sam Snead	5
1953	Ben Hogan	5
1954	Bob Toski	4
1955	Cary Middlecoff	6
1956	Mike Souchak	4
1957	Arnold Palmer	4
1958	Ken Venturi	4
1959	Gene Littler	5
1960	Arnold Palmer	8
1961	Arnold Palmer	6
1962	Arnold Palmer	8
1963	Arnold Palmer	7
1964	Tony Lema	5
1965	Jack Nicklaus	5
1966	Billy Casper	4
1967	Jack Nicklaus	5
1968	Billy Casper	6
1969	Dave Hill	3
	Billy Casper	3
	Jack Nicklaus	3
	Ray Floyd	3
1970	Billy Casper	4
1971	Lee Trevino	6
1972	Jack Nicklaus	7
1973	Jack Nicklaus	7
1974	Johnny Miller	8
1975	Jack Nicklaus	5
1976	Ben Crenshaw	3
	Hubert Green	3
1977	Tom Watson	5
1978	Tom Watson	5
1979	Tom Watson	5
1980	Tom Watson	7
1981	Bill Rogers	4
1982	Craig Stadler	4
	Tom Watson	4
	Calvin Peete	4
1983	Fuzzy Zoeller	2
	Lanny Wadkins	2
	Calvin Peete	2
	Hal Sutton	2
	Gil Morgan	2
	Mark McCumber	2
	Jim Colbert	2
	Seve Ballesteros	2
1984	Tom Watson	3
	Denis Watson	3
1985	Lanny Wadkins	3
	Curtis Strange	3
1986	Bob Tway	4
1987	Curtis Strange	3
	Paul Azinger	3
1988	Curtis Strange	4
1989	Tom Kite	3
	Steve Jones	3
1990	Wayne Levi	4
1991	Ian Woosnan	2
	Corey Pavin	2
	Billy Andrade	2
	Tom Purtzer	2
	Mark Brooks	2
	Nick Price	2
	Fred Couples	2
	Andrew Magee	2
1992	Fred Couples	3
	Davis Love III	3
	John Cook	3
1993	Nick Price	4
1994	Nick Price	6
1995	Greg Norman	3
	Lee Janzen	3
1996	Phil Mickelson	4
1997	Tiger Woods	4
1998	David Duval	4
1999	Tiger Woods	8
2000	Tiger Woods	9
2001	Tiger Woods	5
2002	Tiger Woods	5
2003	Tiger Woods	5
2004	Vijay Singh	9

PGA TOUR Wins By Former Nationwide Tour Players

1.	Bruce Fleisher	1991 New England Classic
2.	John Daly	1991 PGA Championship
3.	John Daly	1992 B.C. Open
4.	Jim McGovern	1993 Shell Houston Open
5.	Mike Standly	1993 Freeport-McMoRan Classic
6.	Jeff Maggert	1993 Walt Disney World/Oldsmobile Classic
7.	Mike Springer	1994 Kmart Greater Greensboro Open
8.	Mike Heinen	1994 Shell Houston Open
9.	John Daly	1994 BellSouth Classic
10.	Tom Lehman	1994 Memorial Tournament
11.	Ernie Els	1994 U.S. Open
12.	Brian Henninger	1994 Deposit Guaranty Classic
13.	Steve Lowery	1994 Sprint International
14.	Mike Springer	1994 Greater Milwaukee Open
15.	John Morse	1995 United Airlines Hawaiian Open
16.	Ernie Els	1995 GTE Byron Nelson Classic
17.	Tom Lehman	1995 Colonial National Invitation
18.	Ted Tryba	1995 Anheuser-Busch Golf Classic
19.	John Daly	1995 British Open
20.	Woody Austin	1995 Buick Open
21.	Jim Furyk	1995 Las Vegas Invitational
22.	Jim Furyk	1996 United Airlines Hawaiian Open
23.	Tim Herron	1996 Honda Classic
24.	Paul Goydos	1996 Bay Hill Invitational
25.	Steve Stricker	1996 Kemper Open
26.	Ernie Els	1996 Buick Classic
27.	Steve Stricker	1996 Motorola Western Open
28.	Tom Lehman	1996 British Open
29.	Willie Wood	1996 Deposit Guaranty Classic
30.	Clarence Rose	1996 Sprint International
31.	Guy Boros	1996 Greater Vancouver Open
32.	Tom Lehman	1996 TOUR Championship
33.	Stuart Appleby	1997 Honda Classic
34.	Ernie Els	1997 U.S. Open
35.	Ernie Els	1997 Buick Classic
36.	David Toms	1997 Quad City Classic
37.	Stewart Cink	1997 Canon Greater Hartford Open
38.	Tim Herron	1997 LaCantera Texas Open
39.	David Duval	1997 Michelob Championship at Kingsmill
40.	David Duval	1997 Walt Disney World/Oldsmobile Classic
41.	David Duval	1997 TOUR Championship
42.	David Duval	1998 Tucson Chrysler Classic
43.	Ernie Els	1998 Bay Hill Invitational
44.	Trevor Dodds	1998 Greater Greensboro Chrysler Classic
45.	David Duval	1998 Shell Houston Open
46.	Stuart Appleby	1998 Kemper Open
47.	J.P. Hayes	1998 Buick Classic
48.	Joe Durant	1998 Motorola Western Open
49.	Olin Browne	1998 Canon Greater Hartford Open
50.	David Duval	1998 NEC World Series of Golf
51.	Brandel Chamblee	1998 Greater Vancouver Open
52.	Chris Perry	1998 B.C. Open
53.	David Duval	1998 Michelob Championship at Kingsmill
54.	Jim Furyk	1998 Las Vegas Invitational
55.	David Duval	1999 Mercedes Championships
56.	David Duval	1999 Bob Hope Chrysler Classic
57.	Ernie Els	1999 Nissan Open
58.	Jeff Maggert	1999 WGC-Accenture Match Play Championship
59.	Tim Herron	1999 Bay Hill Invitational
60.	David Duval	1999 PLAYERS Championship
61.	David Duval	1999 BellSouth Classic
62.	Stuart Appleby	1999 Shell Houston Open
63.	Olin Browne	1999 MasterCard Colonial
64.	Ted Tryba	1999 FedEx St. Jude Classic
65.	J.L. Lewis	1999 John Deere Classic
66.	Brent Geiberger	1999 Canon Greater Hartford Open
67.	Tom Pernice Jr.	1999 Buick Open
68.	David Toms	1999 Sprint International
69.	Notah Begay	1999 Reno-Tahoe Open
70.	David Toms	1999 Buick Challenge
71.	Notah Begay	1999 Michelob Championship at Kingsmill
72.	Jim Furyk	1999 Las Vegas Invitational
73.	Brian Henninger	1999 Southern Farm Bureau Classic
74.	Tom Lehman	2000 Phoenix Open
75.	Jim Carter	2000 Touchstone Energy Tucson Open
76.	Jim Furyk	2000 Doral-Ryder Open
77.	Stewart Cink	2000 MCI Classic
78.	Tom Scherrer	2000 Kemper Insurance Open
79.	Dennis Paulson	2000 Buick Classic
80.	Notah Begay	2000 FedEx St. Jude Classic
81.	Notah Begay	2000 Canon Greater Hartford Open
82.	Michael Clark	2000 John Deere Classic
83.	Ernie Els	2000 International
84.	Chris DiMarco	2000 SEI Pennsylvania Classic
85.	David Duval	2000 Buick Challenge
86.	David Toms	2000 Michelob Championship at Kingsmill
87.	Steve Lowery	2000 Southern Farm Bureau Classic
88.	Steve Stricker	2001 WGC-Accenture Match Play Championship
89.	Jim Furyk	2001 Mercedes Championships
90.	Garrett Willis	2001 Touchstone Energy Tucson Open
91.	Joe Durant	2001 Bob Hope Chrysler Classic
92.	Joe Durant	2001 Genuity Championship
93.	David Toms	2001 Compaq Classic of New Orleans
94.	Frank Lickliter	2001 Kemper Insurance Open
95.	David Duval	2001 British Open
96.	David Gossett	2001 John Deere Classic
97.	Tom Pernice Jr.	2001 International
98.	David Toms	2001 PGA Championship
99.	Joel Edwards	2001 Air Canada Championship
100.	David Toms	2001 Michelob Championship at Kingsmill
101.	Chris DiMarco	2001 Buick Challenge
102.	Cameron Beckman	2001 Southern Farm Bureau Classic
103.	Jerry Kelly	2002 Sony Open in Hawaii
104.	Chris DiMarco	2002 Phoenix Open
105.	Matt Gogel	2002 AT&T Pebble Beach National Pro-Am
106.	Len Mattiace	2002 Nissan Open
107.	Kevin Sutherland	2002 WGC-Accenture Match Play Championship
108.	Ian Leggatt	2002 Touchstone Energy Tucson Open
109.	Ernie Els	2002 Genuity Championship
110.	Craig Perks	2002 PLAYERS Championship
111.	Jim Furyk	2002 Memorial
112.	Chris Smith	2002 Buick Classic
113.	Len Mattiace	2002 FedEx St. Jude Classic
114.	Jerry Kelly	2002 Advil Western Open

PGA TOUR Wins By Former Nationwide Tour Players (cont.)

115.	Ernie Els	2002 British Open
116.	Spike McRoy	2002 B.C. Open
117.	J.P. Hayes	2002 John Deere Classic
118.	Chris Riley	2002 Reno-Tahoe Open
119.	Gene Sauers	2002 Air Canada Championship
120.	John Rollins	2002 Bell Canadian Open
121.	Phil Tataurangi	2002 Invensys Classic at Las Vegas
122.	Bob Burns	2002 Disney Golf Classic
123.	Jonathan Byrd	2002 Buick Challenge
124.	Ernie Els	2003 Mercedes Championships
125.	Ernie Els	2003 Sony Open
126.	Frank Lickliter	2003 Chrysler Classic of Tucson
127.	Ben Crane	2003 BellSouth Classic
128.	Steve Flesch	2003 HP Classic of New Orleans
129.	David Toms	2003 Wachovia Championship
130.	Jim Furyk	2003 U.S. Open
131.	David Toms	2003 FedEx St. Jude Classic
132.	Jim Furyk	2003 Buick Open
133.	Shaun Micheel	2003 PGA Championship
134.	J.L. Lewis	2003 84 Lumber Classic of Pennsylvania
135.	Tommy Armour III	2003 Valero Texas Open
136.	Stuart Appleby	2003 Las Vegas Invitational
137.	Chad Campbell	2003 TOUR Championship
138.	Stuart Appleby	2004 Mercedes Championships
139.	Ernie Els	2004 Sony Open
140.	John Daly	2004 Buick Invitational
141.	Heath Slocum	2004 Chrysler Classic of Tucson
142.	Chad Campbell	2004 Bay Hill Invitational
143.	Zach Johnson	2004 BellSouth Classic
144.	Stewart Cink	2004 MCI Heritage
145.	Steve Flesch	2004 Bank of America Colonial
146.	David Toms	2004 FedEx St. Jude Classic
147.	Ernie Els	2004 Memorial Tournament
148.	Stephen Ames	2004 Cialis Western Open
149.	Mark Hensby	2004 John Deere Classic
150.	Jonathan Byrd	2004 B.C. Open
151.	Rod Pampling	2004 International
152.	Stewart Cink	2004 WGC-NEC Invitational
153.	Vaughn Taylor	2004 Reno-Tahoe Open
154.	Woody Austin	2004 Buick Championship
155.	Bart Bryant	2004 Valero Texas Open
156.	Ernie Els	2004 WGC-American Express Championship
157.	Andre Stolz	2004 Michelin Las Vegas Invitational
158.	Brent Geiberger	2004 Chrysler Classic of Greensboro
159.	Ryan Palmer	2004 FUNAI Classic at the WALT DISNEY WORLD Resort

Total PGA TOUR Wins By Former Nationwide Tour Players (73 players)

15	Ernie Els
13	David Duval
10	David Toms
10	Jim Furyk
5	Tom Lehman
5	John Daly
5	Stuart Appleby
4	Notah Begay
4	Stewart Cink
3	Joe Durant
3	Tim Herron
3	Steve Stricker
3	Chris DiMarco
2	Woody Austin
2	Brent Geiberger
2	Jonathan Byrd
2	Steve Flesch
2	Chad Campbell
2	Olin Browne
2	Frank Lickliter
2	Brian Henninger
2	J.L. Lewis
2	Steve Lowery
2	Jeff Maggert
2	Tom Pernice, Jr.
2	Mike Springer
2	Ted Tryba
2	Jerry Kelly
2	Len Mattiace
2	J.P. Hayes
1	Tommy Armour III
1	Cameron Beckman
1	Guy Boros
1	Jim Carter
1	Brandel Chamblee
1	Michael Clark II
1	Trevor Dodds
1	Joel Edwards
1	Bruce Fleisher
1	David Gossett
1	Paul Goydos
1	Mike Heinen
1	Jim McGovern
1	John Morse
1	Dennis Paulson
1	Chris Perry
1	Clarence Rose
1	Tom Scherrer
1	Mike Standly
1	Garrett Willis
1	Willie Wood
1	Matt Gogel
1	Ian Leggatt
1	Kevin Sutherland
1	Craig Perks
1	Chris Smith
1	Spike McRoy
1	Chris Riley
1	Gene Sauers
1	John Rollins
1	Phil Tataurangi
1	Bob Burns
1	Ben Crane
1	Shaun Micheel
1	Heath Slocum
1	Zach Johnson
1	Bart Bryant
1	Ryan Palmer
1	Vaughn Taylor
1	Andre Stolz
1	Rod Pampling
1	Stephen Ames
1	Mark Hensby

Single Tournament Stat Records (1980-2004)

Records for single tournaments since 1980:

72-Hole Events				
Driving Distance	Hank Kuehne	343.6 yards	2003	Valero Texas Open
Driving Accuracy	Calvin Peete	56 of 56	1986	Memorial
	Calvin Peete	56 of 56	1987	Memorial
	David Frost	56 of 56	1988	Tucson
	Brian Claar	56 of 56	1992	Memorial
Greens in Reg.	Peter Jacobsen	69 of 72	1995	AT&T
Putts	Kenny Knox	93	1989	MCI
	Mark Calcavecchia	93	2002	Greensboro
Birdies	Mark Calcavecchia	32	2001	Phoenix
	Paul Gow	32	2001	B.C. Open
Eagles	Dave Eichelberger	5	1980	Hawaii
	Davis Love III	5	1994	Hawaii
Total Driving	Fuzzy Zoeller	2	1981	PGA

54-Hole Events				
Driving Distance	John Daly	306.3 yards	1993	Houston
Driving Accuracy	Keith Fergus	41 of 42	1981	AT&T
	Fulton Allem	41 of 42	1993	Houston
	John Dowdall	41 of 42	1993	Houston
Greens In Reg.	Mike Heinen	53 of 54	1995	Walt Disney World
Putts	Jonathan Kaye	70	1995	Quad City
Birdies	Hale Irwin	20	1981	Houston
	Robert Wrenn	20	1992	San Diego
	John Huston	20	1993	Houston
	Blaine McCallister	20	1993	Houston
Eagles	Bob Eastwood	3	1986	San Diego
	Bill Glasson	3	1986	San Diego
	Dan Forsman	3	1992	San Diego
Total Driving	Hal Sutton	4	1996	B.C. Open
	Guy Hill	4	1998	Buick Classic

90-Hole Events				
Driving Distance	Tiger Woods	322.6 yards	1996	Las Vegas
Driving Accuracy	Doug Tewell	64 of 70	1992	Las Vegas
Greens In Reg.	Kent Jones	83 of 90	2003	Las Vegas
Putts	Paul Azinger	126	2004	Bob Hope
Birdies	Tom Kite	37	1993	Bob Hope
	Phil Mickeson	37	2004	Bob Hope
Eagles (18)*	Harrison Frazar	4	2004	Bob Hope
Total Driving	Buddy Gardner	7	1983	Las Vegas
	Joey Sindelar	7	1986	Bob Hope

All Events				
Longest Drive	Davis Love III	476 yards	2004	Mercedes Champ
Scrambling	Robert Gamez	21 of 21	1992	FedEx St. Jude Clas.
	D.A. Weibring	21 of 21	1993	John Deere Classic
	Shigeki Maruyama	21 of 21	2002	Shell Houston Open
Birdie Conversion	Brett Upper	60.9% (14 of 23)	1986	MCI Heritage

* 18 players, with Frazar being the most recent.

Winners

Last to win back-to-back starts
Vijay Singh, 2004 Deutsche Bank Championship, Bell Canadian Open

Last to win three consecutive events
Tiger Woods, 1999 National Car Rental/Disney, TOUR Championship, WGC-American Express

Last to win three consecutive starts
Vijay Singh, 2004 Deutsche Bank Championship, Bell Canadian Open, 84 LUMBER Classic

Last to win four consecutive events
Jack Burke, Jr., 1952 Texas Open, Houston Open, Baton Rouge Open, St. Petersburg Open

Last to win same event four consecutive years
Tiger Woods, 2000-2003, Bay Hill Invitational

Last to successfully defend title
David Toms, 2003-04 Fed Ex St. Jude Classic

Last to successfully defend title week after winning another event
Tiger Woods, 2000 WGC-NEC Invitational (after winning PGA Championship)

Last to win first two starts of season
Ernie Els, 2003 Mercedes Championships, Sony Open in Hawaii

Last to win same event three times
Tiger Woods, 1999, 2002-2003 WGC- American Express Championship

Last to win same event for first two victories
Brian Henninger, 1994, 1999 Southern Farm Bureau Classic

Last left-hander to win
Steve Flesch, 2004 Bank of America Colonial

Last Monday Open Qualifier to win
Fred Wadsworth, 1986 Southern Open

Last to receive sponsor's exemption and win
Phil Mickelson (amateur), 1991 Northern Telecom Open; **Adam Scott** (professional), 2003 Deutsche Bank Championship

Last alternate to win
Gene Sauers, 2002 Air Canada Championship

Last rookie to win
Ryan Palmer, 2004 FUNAI Classic at WALT DISNEY WORLD Resort

Last rookie to win twice
Todd Hamilton, 2004 Honda Classic, British Open Championship

Last amateur to win
Phil Mickelson, 1991 Northern Telecom Open

Last to win in first TOUR start
Jim Benepe, 1988 Beatrice Western Open

Last to win in first start as official member of PGA TOUR
Garrett Willis, 2001 Touchstone Energy Tucson Open

Last time five consecutive first-time winners
2002, **Charles Howell III**, Michelob Championship at Kingsmill; **Phil Tataurangi**, Invensys Classic at Las Vegas; **Bob Burns**, Disney Golf Classic; **Jonathan Byrd**, Buick Challenge; **Luke Donald**, Southern Farm Bureau Classic.

Last wire-to-wire winner (no ties)
Vijay Singh, 2004 84 LUMBER Classic

Last back-to-back wire-to-wire winner, same event
Ernie Els, 1996-97 Buick Classics

Last rookie wire-to-wire winner
Tim Herron, 1996 Honda Classic

Last to win with even-par score
Mark O'Meara, 1998 British Open

Last to win with over-par score
Paul Lawrie, 1999 British Open Championship (+6)

Last to win in which they failed to record a birdie in the final round
Vijay Singh, 2004 PGA Championship

Last to win with no bogeys over 72 holes
Lee Trevino, 1974 Greater New Orleans Open

Last time player shot 80 and won
Kenny Knox, 1986 Honda Classic (third round)

Last to win by holing final shot from off green
Craig Parry, 2004 Ford Championship at Doral

Last to win first three consecutive titles in playoffs
Robert Allenby, 2000 Shell Houston Open, Advil Western Open, 2001 Nissan Open

Last to win playoffs in consecutive weeks
David Duval, 1997 Michelob Championship at Kingsmill, Walt Disney World/Oldsmobile Classic

Last time a player won event when teeing off No.10 in final round:
Keith Clearwater, 1987 Colonial

Tournament Finishes

Last 36-hole event
1996 Buick Challenge

Last 54-hole event
2002 Southern Farm Bureau Classic

Last Monday finish (unscheduled)
2004 HP Classic of New Orleans

Last Monday U.S. Open playoff finish
2001 **Retief Goosen** defeated **Mark Brooks**

Last Tuesday finish
1980 Joe Garagiola-Tucson Open

Last 36-hole final day
2003 84 Lumber Classic of Pennsylvania

Last 54-hole final day
1925 Shawnee Open (**Willie Macfarlane/Willie Klein** 18-hole playoff after field completed 36 holes)

Last time cut made after 18 holes
1987 Beatrice Western Open

Last time cut made closest to 60
2003 84 Lumber Classic of Pennsylvania (57)

Last time full final round played Monday (unscheduled)
2004 HP Classic of New Orleans

Weather

Last time tournament rained out
1991 Independent Insurance Agent Open

Last time it snowed during tournament
2001 Touchstone Energy Tucson Open

Last time tournament canceled and not rescheduled
1996 AT&T Pebble Beach National Pro-Am

Last tournament canceled for reasons other than weather
2001 WGC-American Express, Tampa Bay Classic (Sept. 11 terrorist tragedy)

Last time final round postponed and played later in season
1998 AT&T Pebble Beach National Pro-Am

Last tournament round suspended by wind
Round 2, 1999 Bob Hope Chrysler Classic

Last round canceled, then restarted
2001 BellSouth Classic, first round

Double Eagles, Eagles and Aces

Last time back-to-back eagles
Jim Furyk, 2004 Michelin Championship at Las Vegas

Last time double eagle
Gary Evans, 2004 British Open (#4, Par 5. Royal Troon GC)

Last time three eagles in same round
Harrison Frazar (#5, #7, #14), Indian Wells CC, 2004 Bob Hope Chrysler Classic

Last time four aces same day, same hole
1989 U.S. Open, **Doug Weaver, Mark Wiebe, Jerry Pate, Nick Price** on hole No. 6, 159 yards, all with a 7-iron, second round

Last time three aces in one round
2004 Cialis Western Open, **Mike Small** (No. 2), **Scott Hoch** (No. 14), **Lucas Glover** (No. 12), second round

Last to make hole-in-one while winning tournament
Mark Hensby, 2004 John Deere Classic, first round

Last ace on par 4
Andrew Magee, No. 17, TPC of Scottsdale, 2001 Phoenix Open

Last time consecutive eagle 2s, same group
Joe Durant and **J.L. Lewis**, 2002 Kemper Open, TPC at Avenel (par-4 fifth hole)

Playoffs

Last one-hole playoff
2004 Buick Championship (Woody Austin def. Tim Herron)

Last two-hole playoff
2004 John Deere Classic (Mark Hensby def. John E. Morgan)

Last three-hole playoff
2004 Bell Canadian Open (Vijay Singh def. Mike Weir)

Last four-hole playoff
2004 British Open (Todd Hamilton def. Ernie Els), Scheduled for four holes.

Last five-hole playoff
2004 MCI Heritage (Stewart Cink def. Ted Purdy)

Last six-hole playoff
1986 Kemper Open (Greg Norman def. Larry Mize)

Last seven-hole playoff
2001 WGC-NEC Invitational (Tiger Woods def. Jim Furyk)

Last eight-hole playoff
1983 Phoenix Open (Bob Gilder def. Johnny Miller, Mark O'Meara and Rex Caldwell)

Last 11-hole playoff (PGA TOUR record for sudden death)
1949 Motor City Open (Cary Middlecoff and Lloyd Mangrum declared co-winners)

Last 18-hole playoff
2001 U.S. Open (Retief Goosen def. Mark Brooks)

Last 18-hole-plus playoff
1994 U.S. Open (Ernie Els def. Loren Roberts and Colin Montgomerie; Montgomerie eliminated via 18-hole playoff; Els won on 20th extra hole)

Last 18-hole-plus playoff in non-major championship
1972 Tucson Open (21 holes) (Miller Barber def. George Archer)

Last 36-hole playoff in PGA TOUR event
1947 All-American Open (Bobby Locke def. Ed Oliver)

Last 54-hole playoff in PGA TOUR event
1926 Metropolitan Open (Macdonald Smith def. Gene Sarazen)

Last 72-hole playoff (two 36-hole rounds)
1931 U.S. Open Championship (Billy Burke def. George Von Elm)

Last playoff won with eagle
2004 Ford Championship at Doral (Craig Parry def. Scott Verplank, first extra hole)

Last playoff won with birdie
2004 Buick Championship (Woody Austin def. Tim Herron, first extra hole)

Last playoff won with bogey
2003 Masters (Mike Weir def. Len Mattiace, first extra hole)

Last playoff won with double bogey
2001 Buick Invitational (Phil Mickelson def. Frank Lickliter, third extra hole)

Last two-man playoff
2004 Bell Canadian Open (Vijay Singh def. Mike Weir)

Last three-man playoff
2004 PGA (Vijay Singh def. Chris DiMarco and Justin Leonard)

Last four-man playoff
2004 Reno Tahoe Open (Vaughn Taylor def. Scott McCarron, Steve Allan and Hunter Mahan)

Last five-man playoff
1996 Buick Challenge (Michael Bradley def. Fred Funk, Davis Love III, John Maginnes and Len Mattiace)

Last six-man playoff
2001 Nissan Open (Robert Allenby def. Toshi Izawa, Brandel Chamblee, Bob Tway, Jeff Sluman and Dennis Paulson)

Last five-team playoff
1985 Chrysler Team Championship

Last tie/no playoff in PGA TOUR event
1952 Jacksonville Open (Sam Snead forfeited to Doug Ford after 72 holes)

Last time three consecutive multi-hole playoffs
2000 Shell Houston Open, Compaq Classic of New Orleans, GTE Byron Nelson Classic

Last time five consecutive playoffs
1946 Goodall Round-Robin, Philadelphia Inquirer Open, U.S. Open, Inverness 4-Ball, Canadian Open

Miscellaneous

Last to repeat as money leader
Vijay Singh, 2003-2004

Last son of past PGA TOUR champion to win TOUR event
Brent Geiberger, 2004 Chrysler Classic of Greensboro

Last grandfather to win
Johnny Miller, 1994 AT&T Pebble Beach National Pro-Am

The Last Time (cont.)

Last to win with wife as caddie
Steve Stricker, 1996 Motorola Western Open

Last to win with sister as caddie
John Huston, 1998 United Airlines Hawaiian Open

Last to eagle first hole first two rounds
Nick Price, 1996 BellSouth Classic, Atlanta CC (par-4 first hole)

Last to record hole-in-one, eagle-2 and eagle-3 same week
Tiger Woods, 1998 Sprint International

Last to shoot his age
Arnold Palmer, 2001 Bob Hope Chrysler Classic (PGA West), fourth round, 71

Last to be even par or better in each tournament in a single season
Tiger Woods, 2000, 2002

Individual Playoff Records

AARON, Tommy (0-4)
Lost to Tony Lema, 1963 Memphis Open; lost to Arnold Palmer, 1963 Cleveland Open; lost to George Archer, 1972 Glen Campbell Los Angeles Open; lost to George Archer, 1972 Greater Greensboro Open.

ADAMS, John (0-1)
Lost to Jay Haas, 1982 Hall of Fame Classic.

ALEXANDER, Skip (1-0)
Defeated Ky Laffoon, 1950 Empire State Open.

ALLAN, Steve (0-1)
Lost to Vaughn Taylor, 2004 Reno-Tahoe Open.

ALLENBY, Robert (3-0)
Defeated Craig Stadler, 2000 Shell Houston Open; defeated Nick Price, 2000 Advil Western Open; defeated Toshi Izawa, Brandel Chamblee, Bob Tway, Jeff Sluman and Dennis Paulson, 2001 Nissan Open.

ALLIN, Buddy (1-0)
Defeated Dave Eichelberger and Rod Funseth, 1971 Greater Greensboro Open.

ALLISS, Percy (0-1)
Lost to Walter Hagen, 1931 Canadian Open.

ANDERSON, Willie (2-0)
Defeated Alex Smith, 1901 U.S. Open; defeated David Brown, 1903 U.S. Open.

ANDRADE, Billy (2-1)
Defeated Jeff Sluman, 1991 Kemper Open; lost to John Inman, 1993 Buick Southern Open; defeated Bob Friend, 1998 Bell Canadian Open.

APPLEBY, Stuart (1-1)
Lost to Ernie Els, 2002 British Open Championship; defeated Scott McCarron, 2003 Las Vegas Invitational.

ARCHER, George (4-3)
Defeated Bob Charles, 1965 Lucky International Open; lost to Jack Nicklaus, 1969 Kaiser International; lost to George Knudson, 1970 Robinson Open; defeated Lou Graham and J.C. Snead, 1971 Greater Hartford Open; defeated Tommy Aaron and Dave Hill, 1972 Glen Campbell Los Angeles Open; lost to Miller Barber, 1972 Dean Martin Tucson Open; defeated Tommy Aaron, 1972 Greater Greensboro Open.

ARMOUR, Tommy (2-2)
Lost to J. Douglas Edgar, 1920 Canadian Open; defeated Harry Cooper, 1927 U.S. Open; defeated Leo Diegel, 1930 Canadian Open; lost to Willie Macfarlane, 1936 Walter Olson Open.

ARMOUR III, Tommy (1-1)
Lost to Gabriel Hjertstedt, 1999 Touchstone Energy Tucson Open.

AUCHTERLONIE, Laurie (0-1)
Lost to Willie Smith, 1899 Western Open.

AUSTIN, Woody (2-1)
Defeated Mike Brisky, 1995 Buick Open; lost to Davis Love III, 2003 MCI Heritage; defeated Tim Herron, 2004 Buick Championship.

AZINGER, Paul (1-2)
Lost to Steve Jones, 1989 Bob Hope Chrysler Classic; lost to Greg Norman, 1990 Doral-Ryder Open; defeated Greg Norman, 1993 PGA Championship.

BADDELEY, Aaron (0-1)
Lost to Ernie Els, 2003 Sony Open in Hawaii.

BAIRD, Butch (1-0)
Defeated Miller Barber, 1976 San Antonio Texas Open.

BAKER-FINCH, Ian (0-1)
Lost to Bruce Fleisher, 1991 New England Classic.

BALDING, Al (1-3)
Defeated Al Besselink, 1957 Havana Invitational; lost to Don Whitt, 1959 Memphis Open; lost to Arnold Palmer, 1961 San Diego Open; lost to George Knudson, 1964 Fresno Open.

BALLESTEROS, Seve (1-2)
Lost to Larry Mize, 1987 Masters Tournament; lost to J.C. Snead, 1987 Manufacturers Hanover Westchester Classic; defeated David Frost, Greg Norman and Ken Green, 1988 Manufacturers Hanover Westchester Classic.

BARBER, Jerry (1-0)
Defeated Don January, 1961 PGA Championship.

BARBER, Miller (3-4)
Lost to Gary Player, 1964 Pensacola Open; defeated Gary Player, 1967 Oklahoma City Open; defeated Bob Charles and Howie Johnson, 1970 Greater New Orleans Open; defeated George Archer, 1972 Dean Martin Tucson Open; lost to Jack Nicklaus, 1973 Greater New Orleans Open; lost to Bert Greene, 1973 Liggett and Myers Open; lost to Butch Baird, 1976 San Antonio Texas Open.

BARNES, James (0-3)
Lost to Walter Hagen, 1916 Metropolitan Open; lost to Walter Hagen, 1920 Metropolitan Open; lost to Robert MacDonald, 1923 Metropolitan Open.

BARR, Dave (1-2)
Defeated Woody Blackburn, Frank Conner, Dan Halldorson and Victor Regalado, 1981 Quad Cities Open; lost to Corey Pavin, 1986 Greater Milwaukee Open; lost to Mark Brooks, 1988 Canon Sammy Davis, Jr.-Greater Hartford Open.

BARRON, Herman (1-0)
Defeated Lew Worsham, 1946 Philadelphia Inquirer Open.

BAYER, George (2-2)
Lost to Doug Ford, 1957 Western Open; defeated Sam Snead, 1958 Havana International; defeated Jack Fleck, 1960 St. Petersburg Open; lost to Eric Monti, 1961 Ontario Open.

BEAN, Andy (3-3)
Defeated Lee Trevino, 1978 Danny Thomas Memphis Classic; defeated Bill Rogers, 1978 Western Open; lost to Lon Hinkle, 1979 Bing Crosby National Pro-Am; lost to Bruce Lietzke, 1984 Honda Classic; lost to Jack Nicklaus, 1984 Memorial Tournament; defeated Hubert Green, 1986 Doral-Eastern Open.

BEARD, Frank (0-3)
Lost to Jack Nicklaus, 1968 American Golf Classic; lost to Larry Hinson, 1969 Greater New Orleans Open; lost to Johnny Miller, 1974 World Open.

BECK, Chip (0-2)
Lost to Bob Lohr, 1988 Walt Disney World/Oldsmobile Classic; lost to Brad Faxon, 1991 Buick Open.

BEGAY III, Notah (1-0)
Defeated Tom Byrum, 1999 Michelob Championship at Kingsmill.

BEMAN, Deane (1-1)
Lost to Arnold Palmer, 1968 Bob Hope Desert Classic; defeated Jack McGowan, 1969 Texas Open.

BERGANIO, Jr., David (0-1)
Lost to Phil Mickelson, 2002 Bob Hope Chrysler Classic.

BESSELINK, Al (2-2)
Defeated Don Fairfield, 1955 West Palm Beach Open; lost to Ed Furgol, 1957 Caliente Open; defeated Bob Rosburg, 1957 Caracas Open; lost to Al Balding, 1957 Havana Invitational.

BIES, Don (1-0)
Defeated Hubert Green, 1975 Sammy Davis, Jr.-Greater Hartford Open.

BLACK, Ronnie (1-1)
Defeated Sam Torrance, 1983 Southern Open; lost to Wayne Grady, 1989 Manufacturers Hanover Westchester Classic.

BLACKBURN, Woody (1-1)
Lost to Dave Barr, 1981 Quad Cities Open; defeated Ron Streck, 1985 Isuzu-Andy Williams-San Diego Open. (Also won playoff with Bill Kratzert to win unofficial 1976 Walt Disney World National Team Championship).

BLACKMAR, Phil (3-0)
Defeated Jodie Mudd and Dan Pohl, 1985 Canon Sammy Davis, Jr.-Greater Hartford Open; defeated Payne Stewart, 1988 Provident Classic; defeated Kevin Sutherland, 1997 Shell Houston Open.

BLANCAS, Homero (1-1)
Lost to Larry Ziegler, 1969 Michigan Golf Classic; defeated Lanny Wadkins, 1972 Phoenix Open.

BLOCKER, Chris (0-1)
Lost to Doug Sanders, 1970 Bahama Islands Open.

BOLT, Tommy (3-3)
Defeated Jack Burke, Jr. and Dutch Harrison, 1952 Los Angeles Open; lost to Jack Burke, Jr., 1952 Baton Rouge Open; defeated Earl Stewart, 1954 Insurance City Open; lost to Sam Snead, 1955 Miami Beach Open; defeated Ben Hogan and Gene Littler, 1960 Memphis Open; lost to Dave Hill, 1961 Home of the Sun Open.

BOROS, Julius (4-5)
Defeated Cary Middlecoff, 1952 World Championship of Golf; defeated George Fazio, 1954 Carling's World Open; lost to Sam Snead, 1958 Dallas Open; lost to Jack Burke Jr., 1959 Houston Classic; defeated Arnold Palmer and Jacky Cupit, 1963 U.S. Open; lost to Arnold Palmer, 1963 Western Open; defeated Doug Sanders, 1964 Greater Greensboro Open; lost to Gene Littler, 1969 Greater Greensboro Open; lost to Gene Littler, 1975 Westchester Classic.

BRADLEY, Jackson (0-1)
Lost to Henry Ransom, 1955 Rubber City Open.

BRADLEY, Michael (1-0)
Defeated Fred Funk, Davis Love III, John Maginnes and Len Mattiace, 1996 Buick Challenge.

BRADSHAW, Harry (0-1)
Lost to Bobby Locke, 1949 British Open.

BRADY, Mike (1-2)
Lost to John McDermott, 1911 U.S. Open; defeated Patrick Doyle, 1916 Massachusetts Open; lost to Walter Hagen, 1919 U.S. Open.

BRANCA, Tee (0-1)
Lost to Al Zimmerman, 1938 Utah Open.

BREWER, Gay (2-5)
Lost to Arnold Palmer, 1959 West Palm Beach Open; defeated Doug Sanders, 1965 Greater Seattle Open; defeated Bob Goalby, 1965 Hawaiian Open; lost to Jack Nicklaus, 1966 Masters Tournament; lost to Arnold Palmer, 1966 Tournament of Champions; lost to Dave Hill, 1969 IVB-Philadelphia Classic; lost to Jim Colbert, 1974 American Golf Classic.

BRISKY, Mike (0-2)
Lost to Woody Austin, 1995 Buick Open; lost to J.L. Lewis, 1999 John Deere Classic.

BRITTON, Bill (0-1)
Lost to Hal Sutton, 1982 Walt Disney World Golf Classic.

BROOKS, Mark (4-3)
Defeated Dave Barr and Joey Sindelar, 1988 Canon Sammy Davis, Jr.-Greater Hartford Open; lost to Tom Purtzer, 1988 Gatlin Brothers Southwest Classic; defeated Gene Sauers, 1991 Kmart Greater Greensboro Open; lost to John Inman, 1993 Buick Southern Open; defeated Jeff Maggert, 1996 Shell Houston Open; defeated Kenny Perry, 1996 PGA Championship; lost to Retief Goosen, 2001 U.S. Open.

BROWN, Billy Ray (2-0)
Defeated Corey Pavin and Rick Fehr, 1991 Canon Greater Hartford Open; defeated Raymond Floyd, Ben Crenshaw and Bruce Lietzke, 1992 GTE Byron Nelson Classic.

BROWN, David (0-1)
Lost to Willie Anderson, 1903 U.S. Open.

BROWN, Pete (1-1)
Lost to Billy Casper, 1964 Alamden Open; defeated Tony Jacklin, 1964 Andy Williams San Diego Open.

BROWNE, Olin (1-0)
Defeated Stewart Cink and Larry Mize, 1998 Canon Greater Hartford Open.

BRYANT, Brad (0-1)
Lost to John Inman, 1993 Buick Southern Open.

BURKE, Billy (2-0)
Defeated Bill Mehlhorn, 1929 Glens Falls Open; defeated George Von Elm, 1931 U.S.Open.

BURKE, Jack Jr. (4-4)
Lost to Tommy Bolt, 1952 Los Angeles Open; defeated Bill Nary and Tommy Bolt, 1952 Baton Rouge Open; defeated Dick Mayer, 1952 Miami Open; lost to Cary Middlecoff, 1952 Kansas City Open; lost to Henry Ransom, 1955 Rubber City Open; lost to Art Wall, 1958 Rubber City Open; defeated Julius Boros, 1959 Houston Classic; defeated Billy Casper and Johnny Pott, 1961 Buick Open.

BURNS, George (0-2)
Lost to Gary Koch, 1984 Bay Hill Classic; lost to Roger Maltbie, 1985 Manufacturers Hanover Westchester Classic.

BYMAN, Bob (1-0)
Defeated John Schroeder, 1979 Bay Hill Citrus Classic.

BYRD, Sam (1-0)
Defeated Dutch Harrison, 1945 Mobile Open.

BYRUM, Tom (0-2)
Lost to Neal Lancaster, 1994 GTE Byron Nelson Classic; lost to Notah Begay III, 1999 Michelob Championship at Kingsmill.

CADLE, George (0-1)
Lost to Morris Hatalsky, 1983 Greater Milwaukee Open.

CALCAVECCHIA, Mark (1-3)
Defeated Wayne Grady and Greg Norman, 1985 British Open; lost to Fred Couples, 1987 Byron Nelson Classic; lost to Greg Norman, 1990 Doral-Ryder Open; lost to Billy Mayfair, 1993 Greater Milwaukee Open.

CALDWELL, Rex (0-2)
Lost to Keith Fergus, 1983 Bob Hope Desert Classic; lost to Bob Gilder, 1983 Phoenix Open.

CAMPBELL, Joe (1-2)
Lost to Doug Ford, 1962 Bing Crosby National Pro-Am; defeated Gene Littler, 1966 Tucson Open; lost to Randy Glover, 1967 Azalea Open.

CARNEVALE, Mark (0-1)
Lost to Neal Lancaster, 1994 GTE Byron Nelson Classic.

CASPER, Billy (8-8)
Defeated Ken Venturi, 1958 Greater New Orleans Open; lost to Jack Burke, Jr., 1961 Buick Open; defeated Pete Brown and Jerry Steelsmith, 1964 Almaden Open; lost to Wes Ellis, 1965 San Diego Open; defeated Johnny Pott, 1965 Insurance City Open; defeated Arnold Palmer, 1966 U.S. Open; defeated Art Wall, 1967 Canadian Open; defeated Al Geiberger, 1967 Carling World Open; lost to Dudley Wysong, 1967 Hawaiian Open; lost to Johnny Pott, 1968 Bing Crosby National Pro-Am; lost to Jack Nicklaus, 1969 Kaiser International; defeated Hale Irwin, 1970 Los Angeles Open; defeated Gene Littler, 1970 Masters Tournament; lost to Bob Lunn, 1971 Glen Campbell Los Angeles Open; lost to Chi Chi Rodriguez, 1972 Byron Nelson Classic; lost to Jack Nicklaus, 1975 World Open.

CHAMBLEE, Brandel (0-2)
Lost to Paul Stankowski, 1996 BellSouth Classic; lost to Robert Allenby, 2001 Nissan Open.

CHARLES, Bob (1-2)
Defeated Phil Rodgers, 1963 British Open; lost to George Archer, 1965 Lucky International Open; lost to Miller Barber, 1970 Greater New Orleans Open.

CHEN, Tze-Chung (1-1)
Lost to Fred Couples, 1983 Kemper Open; defeated Ben Crenshaw, 1987 Los Angeles Open.

CHRISTIAN, Neil (0-1)
Lost to Lawson Little, 1937 San Francisco Match Play.

CINK, Stewart (1-1)
Lost to Olin Browne, 1998 Canon Greater Hartford Open; defeated Ted Purdy, 2004 MCI Heritage.

CLAMPETT, Bobby (0-2)
Lost to John Cook, 1981 Bing Crosby National Pro-Am; lost to Hale Irwin, 1981 Buick Open.

CLARK, Jimmy (1-1)
Defeated Jim Turnesa, 1952, Fort Wayne Open; lost to Bo Wininger, 1955 Baton Rouge Open.

CLARK, Michael II (1-0)
Defeated Kirk Triplett, 2000 John Deere Classic.

COCHRAN, Russ (0-1)
Lost to Craig Stadler, 1991 THE TOUR Championship.

COLBERT, Jim (2-0)
Defeated Raymond Floyd, Gay Brewer and Forrest Fezler, 1974 American Golf Classic; defeated Fuzzy Zoeller, 1983 Colonial National Invitation.

COLLINS, Bill (1-3)
Lost to Jack Fleck, 1960 Phoenix Open; defeated Arnold Palmer, 1960 Houston Classic; lost to Arnold Palmer, 1960 Insurance City Open; lost to Al Johnston, 1962 Hot Springs Open.

CONGDON, Charles (0-1)
Lost to Ed Oliver, 1948 Tacoma Open.

CONNER, Frank (0-2)
Lost to Dave Barr, 1981 Quad Cities Open; lost to Tom Watson, 1982 Sea Pines Heritage Classic.

COOK, John (3-3)
Defeated Hale Irwin, Ben Crenshaw, Bobby Clampett and Barney Thompson, 1981 Bing Crosby National Pro-Am; defeated Johnny Miller, 1983 Canadian Open; lost to Donnie Hammond, 1986 Bob Hope Chrysler Classic; lost to Tom Kite, 1990 Federal Express St. Jude Classic; lost to Bob Tway, 1990 Las Vegas Invitational; defeated Gene Sauers, Rick Fehr, Mark O'Meara and Tom Kite, 1992 Bob Hope Chrysler Classic.

COOPER, Harry (3-4)
Lost to Tommy Armour, 1927 U.S. Open; defeated Ky Laffoon, 1934 Western Open; lost to Johnny Revolta, 1934 St. Paul Open; defeated Dick Metz, 1936 St. Paul Open; lost to Leonard Dodson, 1936 St. Petersburg Open; defeated Horton Smith and Ralph Guldahl, 1937 St. Petersburg Open; lost to Sam Snead, 1938 Canadian Open.

COOPER, Pete (1-1)
Defeated Wes Ellis, Jr., 1958 West Palm Beach Open; lost to Arnold Palmer, 1959 West Palm Beach Open.

COCERES, Jose (1-0)
Defeated Billy Mayfair, 2001 WORLDCOM CLASSIC.

COUPLES, Fred (5-4)
Defeated Tze-Chung Chen, Barry Jaeckel, Gil Morgan and Scott Simpson, 1983 Kemper Open; lost to Tom Kite, 1986 Western Open; defeated Mark Calcavecchia, 1987 Byron Nelson Classic; lost to Sandy Lyle, 1988 Phoenix Open; defeated Davis Love III, 1992 Nissan Los Angeles Open; lost to Corey Pavin, 1992 Honda Classic; defeated Robert Gamez, 1993 Honda Classic; lost to Phil Mickelson, 1994 Mercedes Championships; defeated Bruce Lietzke, 1998 Bob Hope Chrysler Classic.

COURTNEY, Chuck (0-1)
Lost to DeWitt Weaver, 1972 Southern Open.

COX, Wiffy (1-1)
Defeated Joe Turnesa, 1931 North & South Open; defeated Bill Mehlhorn, 1936 Sacramento Open.

CRAMPTON, Bruce (0-2)
Lost to Gibby Gilbert, 1970 Houston Champions International; lost to Richie Karl, 1974 B.C. Open.

CRENSHAW, Ben (0-8)
Lost to Tom Watson, 1978 Bing Crosby National Pro-Am; lost to Larry Nelson, 1979 Western Open; lost to David Graham, 1979 PGA Championship; lost to John Cook, 1981 Bing Crosby National Pro-Am; lost to Bill Rogers, 1981 Texas Open; lost to Tze-Chung Chen, 1987 Los Angeles Open; lost to David Frost, 1989 NEC World Series of Golf; lost to Billy Ray Brown, 1992 GTE Byron Nelson Classic.

CRUICKSHANK, Bobby (1-3)
Lost to Robert T. Jones, Jr., 1923 U.S. Open; lost to Johnny Farrell, 1926 Florida Open; lost to Bill Mehlhorn, 1926 South Central Open; defeated Johnny Revolta, 1935 Orlando Open.

CUPIT, Jacky (1-2)
Lost to Dave Marr, 1961 Greater Seattle Open; lost to Julius Boros, 1963 U.S. Open; defeated Chi Chi Rodriguez, 1966 Cajun Classic Open.

DALY, John (2-0)
Defeated Costantino Rocca, 1995, British Open; defeated Chris Riley and Luke Donald, 2004 Buick Invitational.

DAMRON, Robert (1-1)
Defeated Scott Verplank, 2001 Verizon Byron Nelson Classic; lost to Sergio Garcia, 2004 EDS Byron Nelson Championship.

DAY, Glen (1-0)
Defeated Jeff Sluman and Payne Stewart, 1999 MCI Classic.

DEMARET, Jimmy (4-5)
Defeated Toney Penna, 1940 Western Open; lost to Dave Douglas, 1947 Orlando Open; lost to Lloyd Mangrum, 1948 Lower Rio Grande Open; defeated Otto Greiner, 1948 St. Paul Open; lost to Ben Hogan, 1949 Long Beach Open; defeated Ben Hogan, 1949 Phoenix Open; lost to Johnny Palmer, 1949 World Championship of Golf; defeated Ken Venturi and Mike Souchak, 1957 Thunderbird Invitational; lost to Tommy Jacobs, 1964 Palm Springs Golf Classic.

DEVLIN, Bruce (0-3)
Lost to Johnny Pott, 1968 Bing Crosby National Pro-Am; lost to Bert Yancey, 1969 Atlanta Classic; lost to David Graham, 1972 Cleveland Open.

DICKINSON, Gardner (1-2)
Lost to Art Wall, 1956 Fort Wayne Open; lost to Raymond Floyd, 1969 Greater Jacksonville Open; defeated Jack Nicklaus, 1971 Atlanta Golf Classic.

DIEGEL, Leo (3-2)
Lost to Abe Mitchell, 1922 Southern Open; defeated Will MacFarlane, 1924 Shawnee Open; defeated Fred McLeod, 1927 Middle Atlantic Open; lost to Tommy Armour, 1930 Canadian Open; defeated Gene Sarazen, 1930 Oregon Open.

DIEHL, Terry (0-1)
Lost to Tom Kite, 1976 IVB-Bicentennial Golf Classic.

DiMARCO, Chris (1-1)
Defeated David Duval, 2001 Buick Challenge; lost to Vijay Singh, 2004 PGA Championship.

DODDS, Trevor (1-0)
Defeated Scott Verplank, 1998 Greater Greensboro Chrysler Classic.

DODSON, Leonard (3-1)
Lost to Ray Mangrum, 1936 Wildwood New Jersey Open; defeated Harry Cooper, 1936 St. Petersburg Open; defeated Horton Smith, 1937 Hollywood Open; defeated Dutch Harrison and Ben Hogan, 1941 Oakland Open.

DONALD, Luke (0-1)
Lost to John Daly, 2004 Buick Invitational.

DONALD, Mike (1-1)
Defeated Tim Simpson and Hal Sutton, 1989 Anheuser-Busch Golf Classic; lost to Hale Irwin, 1990 U.S. Open.

DOUGHERTY, Ed (0-1)
Lost to Jim Gallagher, Jr., 1990 Greater Milwaukee Open.

DOUGLAS, Dave (1-1)
Defeated Jimmy Demaret and Herman Keiser, 1947 Orlando Open; lost to Cary Middlecoff, 1951 Kansas City Open.

DOUGLASS, Dale (0-3)
Lost to Chi Chi Rodriguez, 1968 Sahara Invitational; lost to Don January, 1970 Greater Jacksonville Open; lost to Tom Weiskopf, 1971 Kemper Open.

DOW, Willie (0-1)
Lost to Ralph Stonehouse, 1934 Miami Open.

DOYLE, Patrick (0-1)
Lost to Mike Brady, 1916 Massachusetts Open.

DUDLEY, Ed (1-1)
Defeated Charles Lacey, 1936 Philadelphia Open; lost to Dick Metz, 1937 Thomasville Open.

DUTRA, Olin (1-0)
Defeated Joe Kirkwood, Sr., 1930 Long Beach Open.

DUVAL, David (2-2)
Defeated Grant Waite and Duffy Waldorf, 1997 Michelob Championship at Kingsmill; defeated Dan Forsman, 1997 Walt Disney World/Oldsmobile Classic; lost to Dennis Paulson, 2000 Buick Classic; lost to Chris DiMarco, 2001 Buick Challenge.

EASTWOOD, Bob (1-0)
Defeated Payne Stewart, 1985 Byron Nelson Classic.

EDGAR, J. Douglas (1-0)
Defeated Tommy Armour and Charles Murray, 1920 Canadian Open.

EDWARDS, Danny (1-0)
Defeated Morris Hatalsky, 1983 Miller High Life-Quad Cities Open.

EDWARDS, David (1-1)
Defeated Rick Fehr, 1992 Memorial Tournament; lost to Neal Lancaster, 1994 GTE Byron Nelson Classic.

EICHELBERGER, Dave (1-1)
Lost to Buddy Allin, 1971 Greater Greensboro Open; defeated Bob Murphy and Mark O'Meara, 1981 Tallahassee Open.

ELDER, Lee (2-2)
Lost to Jack Nicklaus, 1968 American Golf Classic; lost to Lee Trevino, 1972 Greater Hartford Open; defeated Peter Oosterhuis, 1974 Monsanto Open; defeated Lee Trevino, 1978 Greater Milwaukee Open.

ELKINGTON, Steve (4-4)
Defeated Brad Faxon, 1992 Infiniti Tournament of Champions; lost to Dan Forsman, 1992 Buick Open; lost to Nick Price, 1992 H-E-B Texas Open; lost to Rocco Mediate, 1993 Kmart Greater Greensboro Open; defeated Bruce Lietzke, 1995 Mercedes Championships; defeated Colin Montgomerie, 1995 PGA Championship; defeated Fred Funk, 1998 Buick Challenge; lost to Ernie Els, 2002 British Open Championship.

ELLIS, Wes (1-1)
Lost to Pete Cooper, 1958 West Palm Beach Open; defeated Billy Casper, 1965 San Diego Open.

ELS, Ernie (4-3)
Defeated Loren Roberts and Colin Montgomerie, 1994 U.S. Open; lost to Tiger Woods, 2000 Mercedes Championships; lost to Mike Weir, 2001 THE TOUR Championship; defeated Stuart Appleby, Steve Elkington and Thomas Levet, 2002 British Open Championship; defeated Aaron Baddeley, 2003 Sony Open in Hawaii; defeated Harrison Frazar, 2004 Sony Open in Hawaii; lost to Todd Hamilton, 2004 British Open.

ESPINOSA, Al (0-1)
Lost to Robert T. Jones, Jr., 1929 U.S. Open.

ESPINOSA, Abe (0-1)
Lost to Macdonald Smith, 1924 Northern California Open.

ESTES, Bob (0-3)
Lost to Mike Hulbert, 1989 B.C. Open; lost to John Inman, 1993 Buick Southern Open; lost to Steve Flesch, 2003 HP Classic of New Orleans.

FAIRFIELD, Don (0-2)
Lost to Al Besselink, 1955 West Palm Beach Open; lost to Dow Finsterwald, 1959 Kansas City Open.

FALDO, Nick (2-1)
Lost to Curtis Strange, 1988 U.S. Open; defeated Scott Hoch, 1989 Masters Tournament; defeated Raymond Floyd, 1990 Masters Tournament.

FARRELL, Johnny (3-2)
Defeated Bobby Cruickshank, 1926 Florida Open; lost to Gene Sarazen, 1928 Nassau Bahamas Open; defeated Robert T. Jones, Jr., 1928 U.S. Open; lost to Willie Macfarlane, 1930 Metropolitan Open; defeated Vic Ghezzi, 1936 New Jersey Open.

FAXON, Brad (2-6)
Defeated Chip Beck, 1991 Buick Open; lost to Steve Elkington, 1992 Infiniti Tournament of Champions; lost to Dan Forsman, 1992 Buick Open; lost to Jim Furyk, 1996 United Airlines Hawaiian Open; lost to Clarence Rose, 1996 Sprint International; lost to Frank Nobilo, 1997 Greater Greensboro Chrysler Classic; defeated Fred Funk, 1999 B.C. Open; lost to Bob Tway, 2003 Bell Canadian Open.

FAZIO, George (1-3)
Defeated Dick Metz, 1946 Canadian Open; lost to Lloyd Mangrum, 1948 Utah Open; lost to Ben Hogan, 1950 U.S. Open; lost to Julius Boros, 1954 Carling's World Open.

FEHR, Rick (0-4)
Lost to Billy Ray Brown, 1991 Canon Greater Hartford Open; lost to John Cook, 1992 Bob Hope Chrysler Classic; lost to David Edwards, 1992 Memorial Tournament; lost to Steve Lowery, 1994 Sprint International.

FERGUS, Keith (2-0)
Defeated Raymond Floyd, 1982 Georgia-Pacific Atlanta Classic; defeated Rex Caldwell, 1983 Bob Hope Desert Classic.

FERRIER, Jim (2-1)
Defeated Fred Haas, Jr., 1947 St. Paul Open; defeated Sam Snead, 1950 St. Paul Open; lost to Cary Middlecoff, 1953 Houston Open.

FETCHICK, Mike (2-0)
Defeated Lionel Hebert, 1956 St. Petersburg Open; defeated Jay Hebert, Don January and Doug Ford, 1956 Western Open.

FEZLER, Forrest (0-1)
Lost to Jim Colbert, 1974 American Golf Classic.

FINSTERWALD, Dow (2-4)
Lost to Doug Sanders, 1956 Canadian Open; defeated Don Whitt, 1957 Tucson Open; lost to Art Wall, 1958 Rubber City Open; lost to Art Wall, 1959 Buick Open; defeated Don Fairfield, 1959 Kansas City Open; lost to Arnold Palmer, 1962 Masters Tournament.

FIORI, Ed (2-0)
Defeated Tom Weiskopf, 1979 Southern Open; defeated Tom Kite, 1982 Bob Hope Desert Classic.

FLECK, Jack (3-2)
Defeated Ben Hogan, 1955 U.S. Open; defeated Bill Collins, 1960 Phoenix Open; lost to George Bayer, 1960 St. Petersburg Open; lost to Arnold Palmer, 1960 Insurance City Open; defeated Bob Rosburg, 1961 Bakersfield Open.

FLECKMAN, Marty (1-0)
Defeated Jack Montgomery, 1967 Cajun Classic Open.

FLEISHER, Bruce (1-0)
Defeated Ian Baker-Finch, 1991 New England Classic.

FLESCH, Steve (1-0)
Defeated Bob Estes, 2003 HP Classic of New Orleans.

FLOYD, Raymond (5-10)
Defeated Gardner Dickinson, 1969 Greater Jacksonville Open; lost to Arnold Palmer, 1971 Bob Hope Desert Classic; lost to Jack Nicklaus, 1973 Bing Crosby National Pro-Am; lost to Jim Colbert, 1974 American Golf Classic; lost to J.C.Snead, 1975 Andy Williams San Diego Open; defeated Jerry McGee, 1976 World Open; defeated Jack Nicklaus, 1980 Doral-Eastern Open; lost to Bruce Lietzke, 1981 Wickes Andy Williams-San Diego Open; defeated Barry Jaeckel and Curtis Strange, 1981 Tournament Players Championship; lost to Keith Fergus, 1982 Georgia-Pacific Atlanta Classic; lost to Craig Stadler, 1982 World Series of Golf; lost to Roger Maltbie, 1985 Manufacturers Hanover Westchester Classic; defeated Mike Sullivan and Lon Hinkle, 1986 Walt Disney World/Oldsmobile Classic; lost to Nick Faldo, 1990 Masters Tournament; lost to Billy Ray Brown, 1992 GTE Byron Nelson Classic.

FORD, Doug (5-7)
Lost to Dutch Harrison, 1951 Texas Open; lost to Cary Middlecoff, 1951 Kansas City Open; defeated Sam Snead, 1952 Jacksonville Open; lost to Earl Stewart, 1953 Greensboro Open; defeated Marty Furgol, 1954 Greater Greensboro Open; lost to Henry Ransom, 1955 Rubber City Open; lost to Ted Kroll, 1955 Philadelphia Daily News Open; lost to Mike Fetchick, 1956 Western Open; lost to Arnold Palmer, 1957 Rubber City Open; defeated George Bayer, Gene Littler and Billy Maxwell, 1957 Western Open; defeated Arnold Palmer, 1961 "500" Festival Open; defeated Joe Campbell, 1962 Bing Crosby National Pro-Am.

FORSMAN, Dan (1-1)
Defeated Steve Elkington and Brad Faxon, 1992 Buick Open; lost to David Duval, 1997 Walt Disney World/Oldsmobile Classic.

FOUGHT, John (1-0)
Defeated Jim Simons, 1979 Buick Goodwrench Open.

FRANCO, Carlos (1-0)
Defeated Blaine McCallister, 2000 Compaq Classic of New Orleans.

FRAZAR, Harrison (0-1)
Lost to Ernie Els, 2004 Sony Open in Hawaii.

FRIEND, Bob (0-1)
Lost to Billy Andrade, 1998 Bell Canadian Open.

FROST, David (2-3)
Lost to Tom Kite, 1986 Western Open; lost to Seve Ballesteros, 1988 Manufacturers Hanover Westchester Classic; defeated Bob Tway, 1988 Southern Open; defeated Ben Crenshaw, 1989 NEC World Series of Golf; lost to Bob Tway, 1995 MCI Classic.

FUNK, Fred (1-3)
Defeated Pete Jordan, 1996 B.C. Open; lost to Michael Bradley, 1996 Buick Challenge; lost to Steve Elkington, 1998 Buick Challenge; lost to Brad Faxon, 1999 B.C. Open.

FUNSETH, Rod (0-1)
Lost to Buddy Allin, 1971 Greater Greensboro Open.

FURGOL, Ed (2-1)
Defeated Cary Middlecoff, 1954 Phoenix Open; lost to Bob Rosburg, 1956 Motor City Open; defeated Al Besselink, 1957 Caliente Open.

FURGOL, Marty (0-1)
Lost to Doug Ford, 1954 Greater Greensboro Open.

FURYK, Jim (1-4)
Defeated Brad Faxon, 1996 United Airlines Hawaiian Open; lost to Paul Stankowski, 1997 United Airlines Hawiian Open; lost to J.P. Hayes, 1998 Buick Classic; lost to Tiger Woods, 2001 World Golf Championships-NEC Invitational; lost to Scott Hoch, 2003 Ford Championship at Doral.

GALLAGHER, Jim Jr. (1-1)
Defeated Ed Dougherty and Billy Mayfair, 1990 Greater Milwaukee Open; lost to Tom Purtzer, 1991 NEC World Series of Golf.

GAMEZ, Robert (0-1)
Lost to Fred Couples, 1993 Honda Classic.

GARCIA, Sergio (3-1)
Lost to Mike Weir, 2001 THE TOUR Championship; defeated David Toms, 2002 Mercedes Championships; defeated Dudley Hart and Robert Damron, 2004 EDS Byron Nelson Championship; defeated Rory Sabbatini and Padraig Harrington, 2004 Buick Classic.

GARDNER, Buddy (0-1)
Lost to Jay Haas, 1987 Big "I" Houston Open.

GEIBERGER, Al (1-1)
Lost to Billy Casper, 1967 Carling World Open; defeated Gary Player, 1975 MONY Tournament of Champions.

GHEZZI, Vic (2-4)
Defeated Johnny Revolta, 1935 Los Angeles Open; lost to Johnny Farrell, 1936 New Jersey Open; lost to Henry Picard, 1939 Metropolitan Open; defeated Byron Nelson, 1941 PGA Championship; lost to Lloyd Mangrum, 1946 U.S. Open; lost to Ed Oliver, 1948 Tacoma Open.

GILBERT, Gibby (1-0)
Defeated Bruce Crampton, 1970 Houston Champions International.

GILDER, Bob (1-0)
Defeated, Rex Caldwell, Johnny Miller and Mark O'Meara, 1983 Phoenix Open.

GLOVER, Randy (1-0)
Defeated Joe Campbell, 1967 Azalea Open.

GOALBY, Bob (2-1)
Defeated Art Wall, 1962 Insurance City Open; lost to Gay Brewer, 1965 Hawaiian Open; defeated Jim Wiechers, 1969 Robinson Open.

GOLDEN, John (2-0)
Defeated George Von Elm, 1931 Agua Caliente Open; defeated Craig Wood, 1932 North & South Open.

GOOSEN, Retief (1-0)
Defeated Mark Brooks, 2001 U.S. Open.
GOW, Paul (0-1)
Lost to Jeff Sluman, 2001 B.C. Open.
GRADY, Wayne (1-1)
Lost to Mark Calcavecchia, 1985 British Open; defeated Ronnie Black, 1989 Manufacturers Hanover Westchester Classic.
GRAHAM, David (2-1)
Defeated Bruce Devlin, 1972 Cleveland Open; lost to Lou Graham, 1972 Liggett and Myers Open; defeated Ben Crenshaw, 1979 PGA Championship.
GRAHAM, Lou (3-1)
Lost to George Archer, 1971 Greater Hartford Open; defeated Hale Irwin, David Graham and Larry Ziegler, 1972 Liggett and Myers Open; defeated John Mahaffey, 1975 U.S. Open; defeated Bobby Wadkins, 1979 IVB-Philadelphia Classic.
GREEN, Hubert (2-3)
Defeated Don January, 1971 Houston Champions International; lost to Don Bies, 1975 Sammy Davis, Jr.-Greater Hartford Open; defeated Bill Kratzert, 1978 Hawaiian Open; lost to Gil Morgan, 1978 World Series of Golf; lost to Andy Bean, 1986 Doral-Eastern Open.
GREEN, Ken (0-2)
Lost to Sandy Lyle, 1988 Kmart Greater Greensboro Open; lost to Seve Ballesteros, 1988 Manufacturers Hanover Westchester Classic.
GREENE, Bert (1-0)
Defeated Miller Barber, 1973 Liggett and Myers Open.
GREINER, Otto (0-1)
Lost to Jimmy Demaret, 1948 St. Paul Open.
GULDAHL, Ralph (2-2)
Lost to Macdonald Smith, 1936 Seattle Open; lost to Harry Cooper, 1937 St. Petersburg Open; defeated Horton Smith, 1937 Western Open; defeated Denny Shute and Gene Sarazen, 1939 Dapper Dan Open.
HAAS, Fred Jr. (2-3)
Lost to Jim Ferrier, 1947 St. Paul Open; lost to Ed Oliver, 1948 Tacoma Open; defeated Ben Hogan and Johnny Palmer, 1948 Portland Open; defeated Bob Hamilton, 1949 Miami Open: lost to Shelly Mayfield, 1955 Thunderbird Invitational.
HAAS, Jay (3-0)
Defeated John Adams, 1982 Hall of Fame Classic; defeated Buddy Gardner, 1987 Big "I" Houston Open; defeated Bob Lohr, 1993 H-E-B Texas Open.
HAGEN, Walter (5-1)
Defeated James Barnes and Charles Hoffner, 1916 Metropolitan Open; defeated Mike Brady, 1919 U.S. Open; defeated James Barnes, 1920 Metropolitan Open; lost to Gene Sarazen, 1923 PGA Championship; defeated Bill Mehlhorn, 1923 Texas Open; defeated Percy Alliss, 1931 Canadian Open.
HALLBERG, Gary (0-2)
Lost to Gary Koch, 1984 Isuzu-Andy Williams-San Diego Open; lost to Blaine McCallister, 1991 H-E-B Texas Open.
HALLDORSON, Dan (0-1)
Lost to Dave Barr, 1981 Quad Cities Open.
HALLET, Jim (0-2)
Lost to Kenny Knox, 1990 Buick Southern Open: lost to Ian Woosnam, 1991 USF&G Classic.
HAMILTON, Bob (0-1)
Lost to Fred Haas, Jr., 1949 Miami Open.
HAMILTON, Todd (1-0)
Defeated Ernie Els, 2004 British Open.
HAMMOND, Donnie (1-0)
Defeated John Cook, 1986 Bob Hope Chrysler Classic.
HAMPTON, Harry (0-1)
Lost to George McLean, 1923 Shawnee Open.
HARBERT, Chick (2-1)
Defeated Ben Hogan, 1942 Texas Open; defeated Dutch Harrison, 1942 St. Paul Open; lost to Henry Ransom, 1950 World Championship of Golf.
HARNEY, Paul (0-1)
Lost to Arnold Palmer, 1963 Thunderbird Classic.
HARPER, Chandler (1-1)
Lost to Johnny Revolta, 1938 St. Petersburg Open; defeated Ted Kroll, 1953 El Paso Open.
HARRINGTON, Padraig (0-1)
Lost to Sergio Garcia, 2004 Buick Classic.
HARRIS, Labron Jr. (1-1)
Lost to Bob Murphy, 1968 Philadelphia Golf Classic; defeated Bert Yancey, 1971 Robinson Open.
HARRISON, Dutch (1-8)
Lost to Dick Metz, 1939 Oakland Open; lost to Leonard Dodson, 1941 Oakland Open; lost to Chick Harbert, 1942 St. Paul Open; lost to Sam Byrd, 1945 Mobile Open; lost to Johnny Palmer, 1946 Nashville Invitational; lost to Ben Hogan, 1948 Motor City Open; lost to Lloyd Mangrum, 1948 World's Championship of Golf; defeated Doug Ford, 1951 Texas Open; lost to Tommy Bolt, 1952 Los Angeles Open.
HART, Dick (1-0)
Defeated Phil Rogers, 1965 Azalea Open.
HART, Dudley (0-1)
Lost to Sergio Garcia, 2004 EDS Byron Nelson Championship.
HATALSKY, Morris (2-1)
Defeated George Cadle, 1983 Greater Milwaukee Open; lost to Danny Edwards, 1983 Miller High Life-Quad Cities Open; defeated Tom Kite, 1988 Kemper Open.
HAWKINS, Fred (0-1)
Lost to Ben Hogan, 1959 Colonial National Invitation.
HAYES, J.P. (1-0)
Defeated Jim Furyk, 1998 Buick Challenge.
HAYES, Mark (0-2)
Lost to Lon Hinkle, 1979 Bing Crosby National Pro-Am; lost to Larry Nelson, 1981 Greater Greensboro Open.
HEAFNER, Clayton (1-1)
Lost to Byron Nelson, 1942 Tam O' Shanter Open; defeated Lew Worsham, 1947 Jacksonville Open.
HEARD, Jerry (0-1)
Lost to Bob Menne, 1974 Kemper Open.
HEBERT, Jay (2-1)
Lost to Mike Fetchick, 1956 Western Open; defeated Ken Venturi, 1961 Houston Classic; defeated Gary Player, 1961 American Golf Classic.
HEBERT, Lionel (1-1)
Lost to Mike Fetchick, 1956 St. Petersburg Open; defeated Gary Player and Gene Littler, 1962 Memphis Open.
HEINEN, Mike (0-1)
Lost to Davis Love III, 1995 Freeport-McMoRan Classic.
HENKE, Nolan (0-1)
Lost to Bob Tway, 1995 MCI Classic.
HENNING, Harold (0-1)
Lost to Charles Sifford, 1969 Los Angeles Open.
HENNINGER, Brian (1-0)
Defeated Mike Sullivan, 1994 Deposit Guaranty Classic.
HENSBY, Mark (1-0)
Defeated John E. Morgan, 2004 John Deere Classic.
HERRON, Tim (1-1)
Defeated Tom Lehman, 1999 Bay Hill Invitational; lost to Woody Austin, 2004 Buick Championship.
HILL, Dave (4-2)
Defeated Tommy Bolt and Bud Sullivan, 1961 Home of the Sun Open; defeated Mike Souchak, 1963 Hot Springs Open; defeated Gay Brewer, Tommy Jacobs and R.H. Sikes, 1969 IVB-Philadelphia Classic; lost to Bob Lunn, 1969 Greater Hartford Open; lost to George Archer, 1972 Glen Campbell Los Angeles Open; defeated Rik Massengale, 1975 Sahara Invitational.
HINKLE, Lon (1-2)
Lost to Ed Sneed, 1977 Tallahassee Open; defeated Andy Bean and Mark Hayes, 1979 Bing Crosby National Pro-Am; lost to Raymond Floyd, 1986 Walt Disney World/Oldsmobile Classic.
HINSON, Larry (1-1)
Defeated Frank Beard, 1969 Greater New Orleans Open; lost to Don January, 1975 San Antonio Texas Open.
HISKEY, Babe (1-0)
Defeated Dudley Wysong, 1965 Cajun Classic.
HJERTSTEDT, Gabriel (1-0)
Defeated Tommy Armour III, 1999 Touchstone Energy Tucson Open.
HOCH, Scott (2-2)
Lost to Nick Faldo, 1989 Masters Tournament; defeated Robert Wrenn, 1989 Las Vegas Invitational; lost to Payne Stewart, 1995 Shell Houston Open; Defeated Jim Furyk, 2003 Ford Championship at Doral.
HOFFNER, Charles (0-1)
Lost to Walter Hagen, 1916 Metropolitan Open.

HOGAN, Ben (8-12)
Lost to Byron Nelson, Texas Open, 1940; lost to Leonard Dodson, 1941 Oakland Open; defeated Jimmy Thomson, 1942 Los Angeles Open; lost to Chick Harbert, 1942 Texas Open; lost to Byron Nelson, 1942 Masters Tournament; lost to Harold McSpaden, 1944 Chicago Victory Open; defeated Harold McSpaden, 1945 Montgomery Invitational; defeated Herman Keiser, 1946 Phoenix Open; lost to Ray Mangrum, 1946 Pensacola Open; defeated Dutch Harrison, 1948 Motor City Open; defeated Ed Oliver, 1948 Western Open; lost to Fred Haas, Jr., 1948 Portland Open; defeated Jimmy Demaret, 1949 Long Beach Open; lost to Jimmy Demaret, 1949 Phoenix Open; lost to Sam Snead, 1950 Los Angeles Open; defeated Lloyd Mangrum and George Fazio, 1950 U.S. Open; lost to Sam Snead, 1954 Masters Tournament; lost to Jack Fleck, 1955 U.S. Open; defeated Fred Hawkins, 1959 Colonial National Invitation; lost to Tommy Bolt, 1960 Memphis Open.

HOLSCHER, Bud (0-1)
Lost to Dick Mayer, 1956 Philadelphia Daily News Open.

HOWELL, Charles III (0-2)
Lost to Shigeki Maruyama, 2001 Greater Milwaukee Open; lost to Mike Weir, 2003 Nissan Open.

HULBERT, Mike (2-0)
Defeated Bob Estes, 1989 B.C. Open; defeated Kenny Knox, 1991 Anheuser-Busch Golf Classic.

HUNTER, Willie (1-0)
Defeated Harold Sampson, 1927 California Open.

HUSTON, John (0-1)
Lost to Jim McGovern, 1993 Shell Houston Open.

INMAN, John (1-0)
Defeated Bob Estes, Mark Brooks, Brad Bryant and Billy Andrade, 1993 Buick Southern Open.

IRWIN, Hale (4-5)
Lost to Billy Casper, 1970 Los Angeles Open; lost to Lou Graham, 1972 Liggett and Myers Open; defeated Kermit Zarley, 1976 Florida Citrus Open; lost to Roger Maltbie, 1976 Memorial Tournament; lost to John Cook, 1981 Bing Crosby National Pro-Am; defeated Bobby Clampett, Peter Jacobsen and Gil Morgan, 1981 Buick Open; defeated Jim Nelford, 1984 Bing Crosby National Pro-Am; defeated Mike Donald, 1990 U.S. Open; lost to Kenny Perry, 1991 Memorial Tournament.

IZAWA, Toshi (0-1)
Lost to Robert Allenby, 2001 Nissan Open.

JACKLIN, Tony (1-1)
Lost to Pete Brown, 1970 Andy Williams San Diego Open; defeated John Jacobs, 1972 Greater Jacksonville Open.

JACOBS, John (0-1)
Lost to Tony Jacklin, 1972 Greater Jacksonville Open.

JACOBS, Tommy (2-2)
Defeated Johnny Pott, 1962 San Diego Open; defeated Jimmy Demaret, 1964 Palm Springs Golf Classic; lost to Jack Nicklaus, 1966 Masters Tournament; lost to Dave Hill, 1969 IVB-Philadelphia Classic.

JACOBSEN, Peter (1-3)
Lost to Hale Irwin, 1981 Buick Open; defeated Payne Stewart, 1984 Colonial National Invitation; lost to Curtis Strange, 1985 Honda Classic; lost to Mark McCumber, 1989 Beatrice Western Open.

JAECKEL, Barry (1-2)
Defeated Bruce Lietzke, 1978 Tallahassee Open; lost to Raymond Floyd, 1981 Tournament Players Championship; lost to Fred Couples, 1983 Kemper Open.

JANUARY, Don (3-5)
Lost to Mike Fetchick, 1956 Western Open; lost to Jerry Barber, 1961 PGA Championship; lost to Chi Chi Rodriguez, 1964 Lucky International Open; defeated Don Massengale, 1967 PGA Championship; lost to Jack Nicklaus, 1969 Kaiser International; defeated Dale Douglass, 1970 Greater Jacksonville Open; lost to Hubert Green, 1971 Houston Champions International; defeated Larry Hinson, 1975 San Antonio Texas Open.

JANZEN, Lee (1-0)
Defeated Corey Pavin, 1995 Kemper Open.

JENKINS, Tom (0-1)
Lost to Bruce Lietzke, 1981 Wickes Andy Williams-San Diego Open.

JIMENEZ, Miguel Angel (0-1)
Lost to Tiger Woods, 1999 World Golf Championships-American Express Championship.

JOHNSON, Howie (1-1)
Defeated Arnold Palmer, 1958 Azalea Open; lost to Miller Barber, 1970 Greater New Orleans Open.

JOHNSTON, Al (1-0)
Defeated Bill Collins, 1962 Hot Springs Open.

JONES, Grier (2-0)
Defeated Bob Murphy, 1972 Hawaiian Open; defeated Dave Marad, 1972 Robinson's Fall Classic.

JONES, Robert T. Jr. (2-2)
Defeated Bobby Cruickshank, 1923 U.S. Open; lost to Willie Macfarlane, 1925 U.S. Open; lost to Johnny Farrell, 1928 U.S. Open; defeated Al Espinosa, 1929 U.S. Open.

JONES, Steve (2-1)
Defeated Bob Tway, 1988 AT&T Pebble Beach National Pro-Am; defeated Sandy Lyle and Paul Azinger, 1989 Bob Hope Chrysler Classic; lost to Payne Stewart, 1990 MCI Heritage Classic.

JORDAN, Pete (0-1)
Lost to Fred Funk, 1996 B.C. Open.

KARL, Richie (1-0)
Defeated Bruce Crampton, 1974 B.C. Open.

KAYE, Jonathan (1-1)
Lost to Chris Riley, 2002 Reno-Tahoe Open; defeated John Rollins, 2003 Buick Classic.

KEISER, Herman (0-2)
Lost to Ben Hogan, 1946 Phoenix Open; lost to Dave Douglas, 1947 Orlando Open.

KELLY, Jerry (0-1)
Lost to Loren Roberts, 1996 Greater Milwaukee Open.

KENDALL, Skip (0-3)
Lost to Scott Simpson, 1998 Buick Invitational; lost to Steve Lowery, 2000 Southern Farm Bureau Classic; lost to Phil Mickelson, 2004 Bob Hope Chrysler Classic.

KIRKWOOD, Joe Sr. (1-1)
Defeated Macdonald Smith, 1923 California Open; lost to Olin Dutra, 1930 Long Beach Open.

KITE, Tom (6-4)
Defeated Terry Diehl, 1976 IVB-Bicentennial Golf Classic; lost to Ed Fiori, 1982 Bob Hope Desert Classic; defeated Jack Nicklaus and Denis Watson, 1982 Bay Hill Classic; defeated Fred Couples, David Frost and Nick Price, 1986 Western Open; lost to Morris Hatalsky, 1988 Kemper Open; lost to Curtis Strange, 1988 Nabisco Championships; defeated Davis Love III, 1989 Nestle Invitational; defeated Payne Stewart, 1989 Nabisco Championships; defeated John Cook, 1990 Federal Express St. Jude Classic; lost to John Cook, 1992 Bob Hope Chrysler Classic.

KLEIN, Willie (0-1)
Lost to Willie Macfarlane, 1925 Shawnee Open.

KNOX, Kenny (1-1)
Defeated Jim Hallet, 1990 Buick Southern Open; lost to Mike Hulbert, 1991 Anheuser-Busch Golf Classic.

KNUDSON, George (3-0)
Defeated Mason Rudolph, 1963 Portland Open; defeated Al Balding, 1964 Fresno Open; defeated George Archer, 1970 Robinson Open.

KOCH, Gary (2-0)
Defeated Gary Hallberg, 1984 Isuzu-Andy Williams-San Diego Open; defeated George Burns, 1984 Bay Hill Classic.

KRATZERT, Bill (0-1)
Lost to Hubert Green, 1978 Hawaiian Open.

KROLL, Ted (1-7)
Lost to Cary Middlecoff, 1952 Motor City Open; lost to Chandler Harper, 1953 El Paso Open; lost to Cary Middlecoff, 1953 Carling's Open; lost to Lloyd Mangrum, 1954 Western Open; defeated Doug Ford, 1955 Philadelphia Daily News Open; lost to Arnold Palmer, 1956 Insurance City Open; lost to Johnny Pott, 1960 Dallas Open; lost to Billy Maxwell, 1961 Insurance City Open.

LACEY, Charles (0-1)
Lost to Ed Dudley, 1936 Philadelphia Open.

LAFFOON, Ky (1-3)
Defeated Paul Runyan, 1934 Glens Falls Open; lost to Harry Cooper, 1934 Western Open; lost to Johnny Revolta, 1934 St. Paul Open; lost to Skip Alexander, 1950 Empire State Open.

LANCASTER, Neal (1-1)
Defeated Tom Byrum, Mark Carnevale, David Edwards, Yoshinori Mizumaki and David Ogrin, 1994 GTE Byron Nelson Classic; lost to John Rollins, 2002 Bell Canadian Open.

LANGER, Bernhard (1-1)
Defeated Bobby Wadkins, 1985 Sea Pines Heritage Classic; lost to Bob Tway, 1986 Shearson Lehman Brothers-Andy Williams Open.

LAWRIE, Paul (1-0)
Defeated Jean Van de Velde and Justin Leonard, 1999 British Open.

LEHMAN, Tom (0-2)
Lost to Tiger Woods, 1997 Mercedes Championships; lost to Tim Herron, 1999 Bay Hill Invitational.

LEMA, Tony (3-1)
Defeated Bob Rosburg, 1962 Orange County Open; defeated Tommy Aaron, 1963 Memphis Open; lost to Arnold Palmer, 1963 Cleveland Open; defeated Arnold Palmer, 1964 Cleveland Open.
LEONARD, Justin (0-4)
Lost to Phil Mickelson, 1996 Phoenix Open; lost to Paul Lawrie, 1999 British Open; lost to John Rollins, 2002 Bell Canadian Open; lost to Vijay Singh, 2004 PGA Championship.
LEONARD, Stan (1-1)
Lost to Gene Littler, 1955 Labatt Open; defeated Art Wall, 1960 Western Open.
LEVET, Thomas (0-1)
Lost to Ernie Els, 2002 British Open Championship.
LEVI, Wayne (2-1)
Defeated Gil Morgan, 1980 Pleasant Valley Jimmy Fund Classic; lost to Jack Renner, 1984 Hawaiian Open; defeated Steve Pate, 1985 Georgia Pacific Atlanta Classic.
LEWIS, J.L. (1-0)
Defeated Mike Brisky, 1999 John Deere Classic.
LICKLITER, Frank II (0-1)
Lost to Phil Mickelson, 2001 Buick Invitational.
LIETZKE, Bruce (6-6)
Defeated Gene Littler, 1977 Joe Garagiola-Tucson Open; lost to Jack Nicklaus, 1977 MONY Tournament of Champions; lost to Barry Jaeckel, 1978 Tallahassee Open; defeated Raymond Floyd and Tom Jenkins, 1981 Wickes Andy Williams-San Diego Open; defeated Tom Watson, 1981 Byron Nelson Classic; defeated Andy Bean, 1984 Honda Classic; defeated Clarence Rose, 1988 GTE Byron Nelson Classic; lost to Billy Ray Brown, 1992 GTE Byron Nelson Classic; defeated Corey Pavin, 1992 Southwestern Bell Colonial; lost to Greg Norman, 1992 Canadian Open; lost to Steve Elkington, 1995 Mercedes Championships; lost to Fred Couples, 1998 Bob Hope Chrysler Classic.
LITTLE, Lawson (2-0)
Defeated Neil Christian, 1937 San Francisco Match Play; defeated Gene Sarazen, 1940 U.S. Open.
LITTLER, Gene (3-8)
Defeated Stan Leonard, 1955 Labatt Open; lost to Peter Thomson, 1955 Texas International Open; lost to Doug Ford, 1957 Western Open; lost to Tommy Bolt, 1960 Memphis Open; lost to Lionel Hebert, 1962 Memphis Open; lost to Joe Campbell, 1966 Tucson Open; defeated Orville Moody, Julius Boros and Tom Weiskopf, 1969 Greater Greensboro Open; lost to Billy Casper, 1970 Masters Tournament; defeated Julius Boros, 1975 Westchester Classic; lost to Bruce Lietzke, 1977 Joe Garagiola-Tucson Open; lost to Lanny Wadkins, 1977 PGA Championship.
LOCKE, Bobby (4-0)
Defeated Ed Oliver, 1947 All American Open; defeated Frank Stranahan, 1949 Cavalier Specialist Tournament; defeated Harry Bradshaw, 1949 British Open; defeated Lloyd Mangrum, 1950 All American Tournament.
LOHR, Bob (1-2)
Defeated Chip Beck, 1988 Walt Disney World/Oldsmobile Classic; lost to Jay Haas, 1993 H-E-B Texas Open; lost to Mark O'Meara, 1995 Bell Canadian Open.
LOVE, Davis III (2-7)
Lost to Tom Kite, 1989 Nestle Invitational; lost to Tom Purtzer, 1991 NEC World Series of Golf; lost to Fred Couples, 1992 Nissan Los Angeles Open; defeated Mike Heinen, 1995 Freeport McMoRan Classic; lost to Michael Bradley, 1996 Buick Challenge; lost to Tiger Woods, 1996 Las Vegas Invitational; lost to Jesper Parnevik, 2000 GTE Byron Nelson Classic; lost to Phil Mickelson, 2001 Buick Invitational; defeated Woody Austin, 2003 MCI Heritage.
LOWERY, Steve (2-0)
Defeated Rick Fehr, 1994 Sprint International; defeated Skip Kendall, 2000 Southern Farm Bureau Classic.
LUNN, Bob (2-0)
Defeated Dave Hill, 1969 Greater Hartford Open; defeated Billy Casper, 1971 Glen Campbell Los Angeles Open.
LUTHER, Ted (1-0)
Defeated Felix Serafin, 1935 Hershey Open.
LYLE, Sandy (3-1)
Defeated Jeff Sluman, 1987 Tournament Players Championship; defeated Fred Couples, 1988 Phoenix Open; defeated Ken Green, 1988 Kmart Greater Greensboro Open; lost to Steve Jones, 1989 Bob Hope Chrysler, Classic.
MacDONALD, Robert (1-0)
Defeated James Barnes, 1923 Metropolitan Open.

MACFARLANE, Willie (4-2)
Lost to Leo Diegel, 1924 Shawnee Open; defeated Robert T. Jones, Jr., 1925 U.S. Open; defeated Willie Klein, 1925 Shawnee Open; defeated Johnny Farrell, 1930 Metropolitan Open; lost to Denny Shute, 1933 Gasparilla Open; defeated Tommy Armour, 1936 Walter Olson Open.
MAGEE, Andrew (1-0)
Defeated D.A. Weibring, 1991 Las Vegas Invitational.
MAGGERT, Jeff (0-1)
Lost to Mark Brooks, 1996 Shell Houston Open.
MAGINNES, John (0-1)
Lost to Michael Bradley, 1996 Buick Challenge.
MAHAFFEY, John (3-2)
Lost to Lou Graham, 1975 U.S. Open; defeated Jerry Pate and Tom Watson, 1978 PGA Championship; defeated Jim Simons, 1984 Bob Hope Desert Classic; lost to Mark Wiebe, 1985 Anheuser-Busch Golf Classic; defeated Jodie Mudd, 1985 Texas Open.
MAHAN, Hunter (0-1)
Lost to Vaughn Taylor, 2004 Reno-Tahoe Open.
MALTBIE, Roger (2-1)
Defeated Hale Irwin, 1976 Memorial Tournament; defeated George Burns and Raymond Floyd, 1985 Manufacturers Hanover Westchester Classic; lost to Mac O'Grady, 1986 Canon Sammy Davis, Jr.-Greater Hartford Open.
MANERO, Tony (0-1)
Lost to Ray Mangrum, 1937 Miami Open.
MANGRUM, Lloyd (5-3-1)
Defeated Vic Ghezzi and Byron Nelson, 1946 U.S. Open; defeated Jimmy Demaret, 1948 Lower Rio Grande Open; defeated Sam Snead and Dutch Harrison, 1948 World's Championship of Golf; defeated George Fazio, 1948 Utah Open; lost to Sam Snead, 1949 Greater Greensboro Open; tied Cary Middlecoff, 1949 Motor City Open; lost to Ben Hogan, 1950 U.S. Open; lost to Bobby Locke, 1950 All American Tournament; defeated Ted Kroll, 1954 Western Open.
MANGRUM, Ray (3-1)
Lost to Henry Picard, 1936 North & South Open; defeated Leonard Dodson, 1936 Wildwood New Jersey Open; defeated Tony Manero, 1937 Miami Open; defeated Ben Hogan, 1946 Pensacola Open.
MARAD, Dave (0-1)
Lost to Grier Jones, 1972 Robinson's Fall Classic.
MARR, Dave (2-0)
Defeated Bob Rosburg and Jacky Cupit, 1961 Greater Seattle Open; defeated Jerry Steelsmith, 1962 Azalea Open.
MARTIN, Doug (0-1)
Lost to Vijay Singh, 1995 Buick Classic.
MARUYAMA, Shigeki (1-0)
Defeated Charles Howell III, 2001 Greater Milwaukee Open.
MASSENGALE, Don (0-1)
Lost to Don January, 1967 PGA Championship.
MASSENGALE, Rik (0-1)
Lost to Dave Hill, 1975 Sahara Invitational.
MATTIACE, Len (0-2)
Lost to Michael Bradley, 1996 Buick Challenge; lost to Mike Weir, 2003 Masters Tournament.
MAXWELL, Billy (1-2)
Lost to Bo Wininger, 1955 Baton Rouge Open; lost to Doug Ford, 1957 Western Open; defeated Ted Kroll, 1961 Insurance City Open.
MAY, Bob (0-1)
Lost to Tiger Woods, 2000 PGA Championship.
MAYFAIR, Billy (2-5)
Lost to Jim Gallagher, Jr., 1990 Greater Milwaukee Open; lost to Jodie Mudd, 1990 Nabisco Championship; defeated Mark Calcavecchia and Ted Schulz, 1993 Greater Milwaukee Open; lost to Vijay Singh, 1995 Phoenix Open; lost to Greg Norman, 1995 NEC World Series of Golf; defeated Tiger Woods, 1998 Nissan Open; lost to Jose Coceres, 2001 WORLDCOM CLASSIC.
MAYER, Dick (2-1)
Lost to Jack Burke, Jr., 1952 Miami Open; defeated Bud Holscher, 1956 Philadelphia Daily News Open; defeated Cary Middlecoff, 1957 U.S. Open.
MAYFIELD, Shelley (1-1)
Lost to Cary Middlecoff, 1953 Houston Open; defeated Mike Souchak and Fred Haas, Jr., 1955 Thunderbird Invitational.
McCALLISTER, Blaine (1-2)
Lost to Gene Sauers, 1986 Bank of Boston Classic; defeated Gary Hallberg, 1991 H-E-B Texas Open; lost to Carlos Franco, 2000 Compaq Classic of New Orleans.

McCARRON, Scott (0-2)
Lost to Stuart Appleby, 2003 Las Vegas Invitational; lost to Vaughn Taylor, 2004 Reno-Tahoe Open.

McCUMBER, Mark (2-0)
Defeated Peter Jacobsen, 1989 Beatrice Western Open; defeated Fuzzy Zoeller, 1994 THE TOUR Championship.

McDERMOTT, John (1-1)
Lost to Alex Smith, 1910 U.S. Open; defeated Mike Brady and George Simpson, 1911 U.S. Open.

McGEE, Jerry (0-1)
Lost to Raymond Floyd, 1976 World Open.

McGOVERN, Jim (1-0)
Defeated John Huston, 1993 Shell Houston Open.

McGOWAN, Jack (0-1)
Lost to Deane Beman, 1969 Texas Open.

McLEAN, George (1-0)
Defeated Harry Hampton, 1923 Shawnee Open.

McLENDON, Mac (1-0)
Defeated Mike Reid, 1978 Pensacola Open.

McLEOD, Fred (1-1)
Defeated Willie Smith, 1908 U.S. Open; lost to Leo Diegel, 1927 Middle Atlantic Open.

McMULLIN, John (0-1)
Lost to Sam Snead, 1958 Dallas Open.

McSPADEN, Harold (3-4)
Lost to Denny Shute, 1937 PGA Championship; lost to Sam Snead, 1940 Canadian Open; defeated Buck White, 1943 All American Open; defeated Byron Nelson, 1944 Phoenix Open; defeated Ben Hogan, 1944 Chicago Victory Open; lost to Byron Nelson, 1945 New Orleans Open; lost to Ben Hogan, 1945 Montgomery Invitational.

MEDIATE, Rocco (2-0)
Defeated Curtis Strange, 1991, Doral-Ryder Open; defeated Steve Elkington, 1993 Kmart Greater Greensboro Open.

MEHLHORN, Bill (4-3)
Lost to Walter Hagen, 1923, Texas Open; defeated Bobby Cruickshank, 1926 South Central Open; defeated Gene Sarazen, 1926 South Florida Open; defeated Fred Morrison, 1928 Hawaiian Open; defeated Bobby Cruickshank and Horton Smith, 1929 South Central Open; lost to Billy Burke, 1929 Glens Falls Open; lost to Wiffy Cox, 1936 Sacramento Open.

MENNE, Bob (1-1)
Lost to Lee Trevino, 1970 National Airlines Open; defeated Jerry Heard, 1974 Kemper Open.

METZ, Dick (2-2)
Lost to Harry Cooper, 1936 St. Paul Open; defeated Ed Dudley, 1937 Thomasville Open; defeated Dutch Harrison, 1939 Oakland Open; lost to George Fazio, 1946 Canadian Open.

MICKELSON, Phil (6-1)
Defeated Fred Couples, 1994 Mercedes Championships; defeated Justin Leonard, 1996 Phoenix Open; defeated Gary Nicklaus, 2000 BellSouth Classic; lost to Jesper Parnevik, 2000 GTE Byron Nelson Classic; defeated Davis Love III and Frank Lickliter II, 2001 Buick Invitational; defeated David Berganio, Jr., 2002 Bob Hope Chrysler Classic; defeated Skip Kendall, 2004 Bob Hope Chrysler Classic.

MIDDLECOFF, Cary (7-6-1)
Defeated George Schoux, 1947 Charlotte Open; lost to Ed Oliver, 1948 Tacoma Open; tied Lloyd Mangrum, 1949 Motor City Open; defeated Ed Oliver, 1950 St. Louis Open; defeated Doug Ford and Dave Douglas, 1951 Kansas City Open; defeated Ted Kroll, 1952 Motor City Open; lost to Julius Boros, 1952 World Championship of Golf; defeated Jack Burke, Jr., 1952 Kansas City Open; defeated Shelley Mayfield, Jim Ferrier, Earl Stewart and Bill Nary, 1953 Houston Open; defeated Ted Kroll, 1953 Carling's Open; lost to Art Wall, 1953 Fort Wayne Open; lost to Ed Furgol, 1954 Phoenix Open; lost to Peter Thomson, 1956 Texas International Open; lost to Dick Mayer, 1957 U.S. Open.

MILLER, Johnny (1-5)
Lost to Jack Nicklaus, 1972 Bing Crosby National Pro-Am; defeated Frank Beard, Bob Murphy and Jack Nicklaus, 1974 World Open; lost to Tom Watson, 1979 Colgate Hall of Fame Classic; lost to Tom Watson, 1982 Glen Campbell Los Angeles Open; lost to Bob Gilder, 1983 Phoenix Open; lost to John Cook, 1983 Canadian Open.

MILLER, Massie (0-1)
Lost to Joe Turnesa, 1929 Lannin Memorial Tournament.

MITCHELL, Abe (1-0)
Defeated Leo Diegel, 1922 Southern Open.

MITCHELL, Bobby (1-0)
Defeated Jack Nicklaus, 1972 Tournament of Champions.

MIZE, Larry (1-3)
Lost to Greg Norman, 1986 Kemper Open; defeated Greg Norman and Seve Ballesteros, 1987 Masters Tournament; lost to Payne Stewart, 1990 MCI Heritage Classic; lost to Olin Browne, 1998 Canon Greater Hartford Open.

MIZUMAKI, Yoshinori (0-1)
Lost to Neal Lancaster, 1994 GTE Byron Nelson Classic.

MONTGOMERIE, Colin (0-2)
Lost to Ernie Els, 1994 U.S. Open; lost to Steve Elkington, 1995 PGA Championship.

MONTGOMERY, Jack (0-1)
Lost to Marty Fleckman, 1967 Cajun Classic Open.

MONTI, Eric (1-0)
Defeated George Bayer and Bobby Nichols, 1961 Ontario Open.

MOODY, Orville (0-2)
Lost to Gene Littler, 1969 Greater Greensboro Open; lost to Jack Nicklaus, 1973 Bing Crosby National Pro-Am.

MORGAN, Gil (3-4)
Defeated Hubert Green, 1978 World Series of Golf; defeated Larry Nelson, 1979 Danny Thomas-Memphis Classic; lost to Wayne Levi, 1980 Pleasant Valley Jimmy Fund Classic; lost to Hale Irwin, 1981 Buick Open; defeated Lanny Wadkins and Curtis Strange, 1983 Joe Garagiola-Tucson Open; lost to Fred Couples, 1983 Kemper Open; lost to Tony Sills, 1990 Independent Insurance Agent Open.

MORGAN, John E. (0-1)
Lost to Mark Hensby, 2004 John Deere Classic.

MORRISON, Fred (0-1)
Lost to Bill Mehlhorn, 1928 Hawaiian Open.

MUDD, Jodie (2-2)
Lost to Phil Blackmar, 1985 Canon Sammy Davis, Jr.-Greater Hartford Open; lost to John Mahaffey, 1985 Texas Open; defeated Larry Nelson, 1989 GTE Byron Nelson Classic; defeated Billy Mayfair, 1990 Nabisco Championships.

MURPHY, Bob (1-5)
Defeated Labron Harris, Jr., 1968 Philadelphia Golf Classic; lost to Lee Trevino, 1970 Tucson Open; lost to Grier Jones, 1972 Hawaiian Open; lost to Bobby Nichols, 1973 Westchester Classic; lost to Johnny Miller, 1974 World Open; lost to Dave Eichelberger, 1981 Tallahassee Open.

MURRAY, Charles (0-1)
Lost to J. Douglas Edgar, 1920 Canadian Open.

NAGLE, Kel (0-1)
Lost to Gary Player, 1965 U.S. Open.

NARY, Bill (0-2)
Lost to Jack Burke, Jr., 1952 Baton Rouge Open; lost to Cary Middlecoff, 1953 Houston Open.

NELFORD, Jim (0-1)
Lost to Hale Irwin, 1984 Bing Crosby National Pro-Am.

NELSON, Byron (6-6)
Defeated Craig Wood and Denny Shute, 1939 U.S. Open; lost to Henry Picard, 1939 PGA Championship; defeated Ben Hogan, 1940 Texas Open; lost to Horton Smith, 1941 Florida West Coast Open; lost to Vic Ghezzi, 1941 PGA Championship; defeated Ben Hogan, 1942 Masters Tournament; defeated Clayton Heafner, 1942 Tam O' Shanter Open; lost to Harold McSpaden, 1944 Phoenix Open; defeated Sam Snead, 1945 Charlotte Open; defeated Harold McSpaden, 1945 New Orleans Open; lost to Sam Snead, 1945 Gulfport Open; lost to Lloyd Mangrum, 1946 U.S. Open.

NELSON, Larry (3-2)
Lost to Gil Morgan, 1979 Danny Thomas-Memphis Classic; defeated Ben Crenshaw, 1979 Western Open; defeated Mark Hayes, 1981 Greater Greensboro Open; defeated Lanny Wadkins, 1987 PGA Championship; lost to Jodie Mudd, 1989 GTE Byron Nelson Classic.

NEWTON, Jack (1-1)
Lost to Tom Watson, 1975 British Open; defeated Mike Sullivan, 1978 Buick-Goodwrench Open.

NICHOLS, Bobby (2-2)
Lost to Eric Monti, 1961 Ontario Open; defeated Dan Sikes and Jack Nicklaus, 1962 Houston Classic; defeated Bob Murphy, 1973 Westchester Classic; lost to J.C. Snead, 1975 Andy Williams San Diego Open.

NICKLAUS, Gary (0-1)
Lost to Phil Mickelson, 2000 BellSouth Classic.

NICKLAUS, Jack (14-11)
Lost to Bobby Nichols, 1962 Houston Classic; defeated Arnold Palmer, 1962 U.S. Open; defeated Gary Player, 1963 Palm Springs Golf Classic; lost to Arnold Palmer, 1963 Western Open; lost to Doug Sanders, 1965 Pensacola Open; defeated Johnny Pott, 1965 Memphis Open; defeated Tommy Jacobs and Gay Brewer, 1966 Masters Tournament; defeated Frank Beard and Lee Elder, 1968 American Golf Classic; defeated George Archer, Billy Casper and Don January, 1969 Kaiser International; defeated Arnold Palmer, 1970 Byron Nelson Classic, defeated Doug Sanders, 1970 British Open; lost to Gardner Dickinson, 1971 Atlanta Golf Classic; lost to Lee Trevino, 1971 U.S. Open; defeated Johnny Miller, 1972 Bing Crosby National Pro-Am; lost to Bobby Mitchell, 1972 Tournament of Champions; defeated Raymond Floyd and Orville Moody, 1973 Bing Crosby National Pro-Am; defeated Miller Barber, 1973 Greater New Orleans Open; lost to Johnny Miller, 1974 World Open; lost to Tom Weiskopf, 1975 Canadian Open; defeated Billy Casper, 1975 World Open; defeated Bruce Lietzke, 1977 MONY Tournament of Champions; lost to Raymond Floyd, 1980 Doral-Eastern Open; lost to Tom Kite, 1982 Bay Hill Classic; defeated Andy Bean, 1984 Memorial Tournament.

NICOLETTE, Mike (1-0)
Defeated Greg Norman, 1983 Bay Hill Classic.

NOBILO, Frank (1-0)
Defeated Brad Faxon, 1997 Greater Greensboro Chrysler Classic.

NORMAN, Greg (4-8)
Lost to Mike Nicolette, 1983 Bay Hill Classic; lost to Fuzzy Zoeller, 1984 U.S. Open; lost to Tom Watson, 1984 Western Open; lost to Mark Calcavecchia, 1985 British Open; defeated Larry Mize, 1986 Kemper Open; lost to Larry Mize, 1987 Masters Tournament; lost to Curtis Strange, 1988 Independent Insurance Agent Open; lost to Seve Ballesteros, 1988 Manufacturers Hanover Westchester Classic; defeated Paul Azinger, Mark Calcavecchia and Tim Simpson, 1990 Doral-Ryder Open; defeated Bruce Lietzke, 1992 Canadian Open; lost to Paul Azinger, 1993 PGA Championship; defeated Billy Mayfair and Nick Price, 1995 NEC World Series of Golf.

OBERHOLSER, Arron (0-1)
Lost to Joey Sindelar, 2004 Wachovia Championship.

O'GRADY, Mac (1-0)
Defeated Roger Maltbie, 1986 Canon Sammy Davis, Jr.-Greater Hartford Open.

OGRIN, David (0-2)
Lost to Hal Sutton, 1985 St. Jude Memphis Classic; lost to Neal Lancaster, 1994 GTE Byron Nelson Classic.

OLIVER, Ed (1-3)
Lost to Bobby Locke, 1947 All American Open; lost to Ben Hogan, 1948 Western Open; defeated Cary Middlecoff, Fred Haas, Jr., Charles Congdon and Vic Ghezzi, 1948 Tacoma Open; lost to Cary Middlecoff, 1950 St. Louis Open.

O'MEARA, Mark (3-4)
Lost to Dave Eichelberger, 1981 Tallahassee Open; lost to Bob Gilder, 1983 Phoenix Open; lost to Corey Pavin, 1991 Bob Hope Chrysler Classic; lost to John Cook, 1992 Bob Hope Chrysler Classic; defeated Jeff Sluman, 1992 AT&T Pebble Beach National Pro-Am; defeated Bob Lohr, 1995 Bell Canadian Open; defeated Brian Watts, 1998 British Open.

OOSTERHUIS, Peter (0-1)
Lost to Lee Elder, 1974 Monsanto Open.

OUIMET, Francis (1-0)
Defeated Harry Vardon and Edward Ray, 1913 U.S. Open.

PALMER, Arnold (14-10)
Defeated Ted Kroll, 1956 Insurance City Open; defeated Doug Ford, 1957 Rubber City Open; lost to Howie Johnson, 1958 Azalea Open; defeated Gay Brewer and Pete Cooper, 1959 West Palm Beach Open; lost to Bill Collins, 1960 Houston Classic; defeated Bill Collins and Jack Fleck, 1960 Insurance City Open; defeated Al Balding, 1961 San Diego Open; defeated Doug Sanders, 1961 Phoenix Open; lost to Doug Ford, 1961 "500" Festival Open; defeated Gary Player and Dow Finsterwald, 1962 Masters Tournament; defeated Johnny Pott, 1962 Colonial National Invitation; lost to Jack Nicklaus, 1962 U.S. Open; defeated Paul Harney, 1963 Thunderbird Classic; lost to Julius Boros, 1963 U.S. Open; defeated Tommy Aaron and Tony Lema, 1963 Cleveland Open; defeated Julius Boros and Jack Nicklaus, 1963 Western Open; lost to Gary Player, 1964 Pensacola Open; lost to Tony Lema, 1964 Cleveland Open; lost to Doug Sanders, 1966 Bob Hope Desert Classic; defeated Gay Brewer, 1966 Tournament of Champions; lost to Billy Casper, 1966 U.S. Open; defeated Deane Beman, 1968 Bob Hope Desert Classic; lost to Jack Nicklaus, 1970 Byron Nelson Classic; defeated Raymond Floyd, 1971 Bob Hope Desert Classic.

PALMER, Johnny (2-1)
Defeated Dutch Harrison, 1946 Nashville Invitational; lost to Fred Haas, Jr., 1948 Portland Open; defeated Jimmy Demaret, 1949 World Championship of Golf.

PARNEVIK, Jesper (1-0)
Defeated Davis Love III and Phil Mickelson, 2000 GTE Byron Nelson Classic.

PARRY, Craig (1-0)
Defeated Scott Verplank, 2004 Ford Championship at Doral.

PATE, Jerry (1-2)
Defeated Dave Stockton, 1977 Phoenix Open; lost to John Mahaffey, 1978 PGA Championship; lost to Doug Tewell, 1980 Sea Pines Heritage Classic.

PATE, Steve (0-3)
Lost to Wayne Levi, 1985 Georgia Pacific Atlanta Classic; lost to Corey Pavin, 1991 BellSouth Atlanta Classic; lost to Loren Roberts, 1999 GTE Byron Nelson Classic.

PAULSON, Dennis (1-2)
Lost to Duffy Waldorf, 1999 Buick Classic; defeated David Duval, 2000 Buick Classic; lost to Robert Allenby, 2001 Nissan Open.

PAVIN, Corey (5-3)
Defeated Dave Barr, 1986 Greater Milwaukee Open; defeated Craig Stadler, 1987 Hawaiian Open; defeated Mark O'Meara, 1991 Bob Hope Chrysler Classic; defeated Steve Pate, 1991 BellSouth Atlanta Classic; lost to Billy Ray Brown, 1991 Canon Greater Hartford Open; defeated Fred Couples, 1992 Honda Classic; lost to Bruce Lietzke, 1992 Southwestern Bell Colonial; lost to Lee Janzen, 1995 Kemper Open.

PEETE, Calvin (0-1)
Lost to Curtis Strange, 1986 Houston Open.

PENNA, Toney (0-1)
Lost to Jimmy Demaret, 1940 Western Open.

PERRY, Kenny (1-1)
Defeated Hale Irwin, 1991 Memorial Tournament; lost to Mark Brooks, 1996 PGA Championship.

PICARD, Henry (3-1)
Defeated Ray Mangrum, 1936 North & South Open; lost to Sam Snead, 1939 St. Petersburg Open; defeated Paul Runyan and Vic Ghezzi, 1939 Metropolitan Open; defeated Byron Nelson, 1939 PGA Championship.

PLAYER, Gary (3-10)
Lost to Sam Snead, 1958 Dallas Open; lost to Don Whitt, 1959 Memphis Open; lost to Jay Hebert, 1961 American Golf Classic; lost to Arnold Palmer, 1962 Masters Tournament; lost to Lionel Hebert, 1962 Memphis Open; lost to Jack Nicklaus, 1963 Palm Springs Golf Classic; defeated Arnold Palmer and Miller Barber, 1964 Pensacola Open; defeated Kel Nagle, 1965 U.S. Open; lost to Miller Barber, 1967 Oklahoma City Open; lost to Steve Reid, 1968 Azalea Open; defeated Hal Underwood, 1971 Greater Jacksonville Open; lost to Tom Weiskopf, 1971 Kemper Open; lost to Al Geiberger, 1975 MONY Tournament of Champions.

POHL, Dan (1-2)
Lost to Craig Stadler, 1982 Masters Tournament; lost to Phil Blackmar, 1985 Canon Sammy Davis, Jr.-Greater Hartford Open; defeated Payne Stewart, 1986 Colonial National Invitation.

POTT, Johnny (2-5)
Defeated Bo Wininger and Ted Kroll, 1960 Dallas Open; lost to Jack Burke, Jr., 1961 Buick Open; lost to Tommy Jacobs, 1962 San Diego Open; lost to Arnold Palmer, 1962 Colonial National Invitation; lost to Jack Nicklaus, 1965 Memphis Open; lost to Billy Casper, 1965 Insurance City Open; defeated Billy Casper and Bruce Devlin, 1968 Bing Crosby National Pro-Am.

PRICE, Nick (3-3)
Lost to Tom Kite, 1986 Western Open; defeated Steve Elkington, 1992 H-E-B Texas Open; defeated Scott Simpson, 1994 Southwestern Bell Colonial; lost to Greg Norman, 1995 NEC World Series of Golf; defeated Jeff Sluman, 1998 FedEx St. Jude Classic; lost to Robert Allenby, 2000 Advil Western Open.

PRIDE, Dicky (1-0)
Defeated Gene Sauers and Hal Sutton, 1994 Federal Express St. Jude Classic.

PURDY, Ted (0-1)
Lost to Stewart Cink, 2004 MCI Heritage.

PURTZER, Tom (2-0)
Defeated Mark Brooks, 1988 Gatlin Brothers Southwest Classic; defeated Davis Love III and Jim Gallagher, 1991 NEC World Series of Golf.

RAGAN, Dave Jr. (1-0)
Defeated Doug Sanders, 1962 West Palm Beach Open.

RANSOM, Henry (2-0)
Defeated Chick Harbert, 1950 World Championship of Golf; defeated Jack Burke, Jr., Doug Ford and Jackson Bradley, 1955 Rubber City Open.

RAY, Edward (0-1)
Lost to Francis Ouimet, 1913 U.S. Open.

REGALADO, Victor (0-1)
Lost to Dave Barr, 1981 Quad Cities Open.

REID, Mike (1-3)
Lost to Mac McLendon, 1978 Pensacola Open; lost to Hal Sutton, 1985 Southwest Golf Classic; defeated Tom Watson, 1988 NEC World Series of Golf; lost to Paul Stankowski, 1997 United Airlines Hawaiian Open.

REID, Steve (1-0)
Defeated Gary Player, 1968 Azalea Open.

RENNER, Jack (1-0)
Defeated Wayne Levi, 1984 Hawaiian Open.

REVOLTA, Johnny (2-2)
Defeated Ky Laffoon and Harry Cooper, 1934 St. Paul Open; lost to Vic Ghezzi, 1935 Los Angeles Open; lost to Bobby Cruickshank, 1935 Orlando Open; defeated Chandler Harper, 1938 St. Petersburg Open.

RILEY, Chris (1-1)
Defeated Jonathan Kaye, 2002 Reno-Tahoe Open; lost to John Daly, 2004 Buick Invitational.

ROBERTS, Loren (2-1)
Lost to Ernie Els, 1994 U.S. Open; defeated Jerry Kelly, 1996 Greater Milwaukee Open; defeated Steve Pate, 1999 GTE Byron Nelson Classic.

ROCCA, Costantino (0-1)
Lost to John Daly, 1995 British Open.

RODGERS, Phil (0-2)
Lost to Bob Charles, 1963 British Open; lost to Dick Hart, 1965 Azalea Open.

RODRIGUEZ, Chi Chi (3-1)
Defeated Don January, 1964 Lucky International Open; lost to Jacky Cupit, 1966 Cajun Classic Open; defeated Dale Douglass, 1968 Sahara Invitational; defeated Billy Casper, 1972 Byron Nelson Classic.

ROGERS, Bill (1-2)
Lost to Andy Bean, 1978 Western Open; lost to Tom Watson, 1979 Byron Nelson Classic; defeated Ben Crenshaw, 1981 Texas Open.

ROLLINS, John (1-1)
Defeated Justin Leonard and Neal Lancaster, 2002 Bell Canadian Open; lost to Jonathan Kaye, 2003 Buick Classic.

ROSBURG, Bob (1-5)
Defeated Ed Furgol, 1956 Motor City Open; lost to Al Besselink, 1957 Caracas Open; lost to Art Wall, 1958 Eastern Open; lost to Dave Marr, 1961 Greater Seattle Open; lost to Jack Fleck, 1961 Bakersfield Open; lost to Tony Lema, 1962 Orange County Open.

ROSE, Clarence (1-1)
Lost to Bruce Lietzke, 1988 GTE Byron Nelson Classic; defeated Brad Faxon, 1996 Sprint International.

RUDOLPH, Mason (0-1)
Lost to George Knudson, 1963 Portland Open.

RUNYAN, Paul (1-2)
Lost to Ky Laffoon, 1934 Glens Falls Open; defeated Craig Wood, 1934 PGA Championship; lost to Henry Picard, 1939 Metropolitan Open.

SABBATINI, Rory (0-1)
Lost to Sergio Garcia, 2004 Buick Classic.

SAMPSON, Harold (0-1)
Lost to Willie Hunter, 1927 California Open.

SANDERS, Doug (5-5)
Defeated Dow Finsterwald, 1956 Canadian Open; lost to Arnold Palmer, 1961 Phoenix Open; lost to Dave Ragan, Jr., 1962 West Palm Beach Open; lost to Julius Boros, 1964 Greater Greensboro Open; defeated Jack Nicklaus, 1965 Pensacola Open; lost to Gay Brewer, 1965 Greater Seattle Open; defeated Arnold Palmer, 1966 Bob Hope Desert Classic; defeated Tom Weiskopf, 1966 Greater Greensboro Open; lost to Jack Nicklaus, 1970 British Open; defeated Chris Blocker, Bahama Islands Open.

SARAZEN, Gene (3-7)
Defeated Walter Hagen, 1923 PGA Championship; lost to Macdonald Smith, 1926 Metropolitan Open; lost to Bill Mehlhorn, 1926 South Florida Open; lost to Joe Turnesa, 1927 Ridgewood CC Open; defeated Johnny Farrell, 1928 Nassau Bahamas Open; lost to Leo Diegel, 1930 Oregon Open; defeated Craig Wood, 1935 Masters Tournament; lost to Sam Snead, 1938 Goodall Round Robin; lost to Ralph Guldahl, 1939 Dapper Dan Open; lost to Lawson Little, 1940 U.S. Open.

SAUERS, Gene (1-3)
Defeated Blaine McCallister, 1986 Bank of Boston Classic; lost to Mark Brooks, 1991 Kmart Greater Greensboro Open; lost to John Cook, 1992 Bob Hope Chrysler Classic; lost to Dicky Pride, 1994 Federal Express St. Jude Classic.

SCHLEE, John (0-1)
Lost to Ed Sneed, 1973 Kaiser International.

SCHOUX, George (0-1)
Lost to Cary Middlecoff, 1947 Charlotte Open.

SCHROEDER, John (0-1)
Lost to Bob Byman, 1979 Bay Hill Citrus Classic.

SCHULZ, Ted (0-1)
Lost to Billy Mayfair, 1993 Greater Milwaukee Open.

SERAFIN, Felix (0-1)
Lost to Ted Luther, 1935 Hershey Open.

SHEARER, Bob (0-1)
Lost to Ed Sneed, 1982 Michelob-Houston Open.

SHEPPARD, Charles (0-1)
Lost to Al Zimmerman, 1938 Utah Open.

SHUTE, Denny (5-3)
Lost to Horton Smith, 1929 Fort Myers Open; defeated Craig Wood, 1933 British Open; defeated Willie Macfarlane, 1933 Gasparilla Open; defeated Horton Smith, 1934 Gasparilla Open; defeated Jug McSpaden, 1937 PGA Championship; lost to Byron Nelson, 1939 U.S. Open; lost to Ralph Guldahl, 1939 Dapper Dan Open; defeated Horton Smith, 1939 Glens Falls Open.

SIECKMANN, Tom (1-0)
Defeated Mark Wiebe, 1988 Anheuser-Busch Golf Classic.

SIFFORD, Charles (1-0)
Defeated Harold Henning, 1969 Los Angeles Open.

SIKES, Dan (0-2)
Lost to Bobby Nichols, 1962 Houston Classic; lost to Lanny Wadkins, 1973 Byron Nelson Golf Classic.

SIKES, R.H. (0-1)
Lost to Dave Hill, 1969 IVB-Philadelpha Classic.

SILLS, Tony (1-0)
Defeated Gil Morgan, 1990 Independent Insurance Agent Open.

SIMONS, Jim (0-3)
Lost to John Fought, 1979 Buick Goodwrench Open; lost to Howard Twitty, 1980 Sammy Davis, Jr.-Greater Hartford Open; lost to John Mahaffey, 1984 Bob Hope Desert Classic.

SIMPSON, George (0-1)
Lost to John McDermott, 1911 U.S. Open.

SIMPSON, Scott (2-3)
Lost to Fred Couples, 1983 Kemper Open; defeated Bob Tway, 1989 BellSouth Atlanta Golf Classic; lost to Payne Stewart, 1991 U.S. Open; lost to Nick Price, 1994 Southwestern Bell Colonial; defeated Skip Kendall, 1998 Buick Invitational.

SIMPSON, Tim (0-2)
Lost to Mike Donald, 1989 Anheuser-Busch Golf Classic; lost to Greg Norman, 1990 Doral-Ryder Open.

SINDELAR, Joey (2-1)
Lost to Mark Brooks, 1988 Canon Sammy Davis, Jr.-Greater Hartford Open; defeated Willie Wood, 1990 Hardee's Golf Classic; defeated Arron Oberholser, 2004 Wachovia Championship.

SINGH, Vijay (5-1)
Defeated Mark Wiebe, 1993 Buick Classic; defeated Billy Mayfair, 1995 Phoenix Open; defeated Doug Martin, 1995 Buick Classic; lost to Hal Sutton, 1998 THE TOUR Championship; defeated Justin Leonard and Chris DiMarco, 2004 PGA Championship; defeated Mike Weir, 2004 Bell Canadian Open.

SLUMAN, Jeff (1-6)
Lost to Sandy Lyle, 1987 Tournament Players Championship; lost to Billy Andrade, 1991 Kemper Open; lost to Mark O'Meara, 1992 AT&T Pebble Beach National Pro-Am; lost to Nick Price, 1998 FedEx St. Jude Classic; lost to Glen Day, 1999 MCI Classic; lost to Robert Allenby, 2001 Nissan Open; defeated Paul Gow, 2001 B.C. Open.

SMITH, Alex (1-1)
Lost to Willie Anderson, 1901 U.S. Open; defeated John McDermott and Macdonald Smith, 1910 U.S. Open.

SMITH, Horton (3-6)
Lost to Bill Mehlhorn, 1929 South Central Open; defeated Denny Shute, 1929 Fort Myers Open; lost to Denny Shute, 1934 Gasparilla Open; lost to Harry Cooper, 1937 St. Petersburg Open; lost to Ralph Guldahl, 1937 Western Open; lost to Leonard Dodson, 1937 Hollywood Open; lost to Denny Shute, 1939 Glens Falls Open; defeated Byron Nelson, 1941 Florida West Coast Open.

SMITH, Macdonald (3-2)
Lost to Alex Smith, 1910 U.S. Open; lost to Joe Kirkwood, Sr., 1923 California Open; defeated Abe Espinosa, 1924 Northern California Open; defeated Gene Sarazen, 1926 Metropolitan Open; defeated Ralph Guldahl, 1936 Seattle Open.

SMITH, Willie (1-1)
Defeated Laurie Auchterlonie, 1899 Western Open; lost to Fred McLeod, 1908 U.S. Open.

SNEAD, J.C. (3-1)
Lost to George Archer, 1971 Greater Hartford Open; defeated Raymond Floyd and Bobby Nichols, 1975 Andy Williams San Diego Open; defeated Mike Sullivan, 1981 Southern Open; defeated Seve Ballesteros, 1987 Manufacturers Hanover Westchester Classic.

SNEAD, Sam (12-5)
Won 1936 West Virginia Closed Pro; defeated Harry Cooper, 1938 Canadian Open; defeated Henry Picard, 1939 St. Petersburg Open; defeated Harold McSpaden, 1940 Canadian Open; lost to Byron Nelson, 1945 Charlotte Open; defeated Byron Nelson, 1945 Gulfport Open; won 1946 Virginia Open; lost to Lew Worsham, 1947 U.S. Open; defeated Lloyd Mangrum, 1949 Greater Greensboro Open; defeated Ben Hogan, 1950 Los Angeles Open; lost to Jim Ferrier, 1950 St. Paul Open; lost to Doug Ford, 1952 Jacksonville Open; lost to Earl Stewart, 1953 Greensboro Open; defeated Ben Hogan, 1954 Masters Tournament; defeated Tommy Bolt, 1955 Miami Open; defeated Fred Wampler, 1956 Greater Greensboro Open; defeated Gary Player, Julius Boros and John McMullin, 1958 Dallas Open.
SNEED, Ed (3-1)
Defeated John Schlee, 1973 Kaiser International; defeated Lon Hinkle, 1977 Tallahassee Open; lost to Fuzzy Zoeller, 1979 Masters Tournament; defeated Bob Shearer, 1982 Michelob-Houston Open.
SOUCHAK, Mike (0-3)
Lost to Shelley Mayfield, 1955 Thunderbird Invitational; lost to Jimmy Demaret, 1957 Thunderbird Invitational; lost to Dave Hill, 1963 Hot Springs Open.
STADLER, Craig (3-3)
Defeated Dan Pohl, 1982 Masters Tournament; defeated Raymond Floyd, 1982 World Series of Golf; lost to Lanny Wadkins, 1985 Bob Hope Desert Classic; lost to Corey Pavin, 1987 Hawaiian Open; defeated Russ Cochran, 1991 THE TOUR Championship; lost to Robert Allenby, 2000 Shell Houston Open.
STANKOWSKI, Paul (2-0)
Defeated Brandel Chamblee, 1996 BellSouth Classic; defeated Jim Furyk and Mike Reid, 1997 United Airlines Hawaiian Open.
STEELSMITH, Jerry (0-2)
Lost to Dave Marr, 1962 Azalea Open; lost to Billy Casper, 1964 Almaden Open.
STEWART, Earl Jr. (1-2)
Lost to Cary Middlecoff, 1953 Houston Open; defeated Sam Snead, Doug Ford and Art Wall, 1953 Greensboro Open; lost to Tommy Bolt, 1954 Insurance City Open.
STEWART, Payne (3-6)
Lost to Peter Jacobsen, 1984 Colonial National Invitation; lost to Bob Eastwood, 1985 Byron Nelson Classic; lost to Dan Pohl, 1986 Colonial National Invitation; lost to Phil Blackmar, 1988 Provident Classic; lost to Tom Kite, 1989 Nabisco Championships; defeated Steve Jones and Larry Mize, 1990 MCI Heritage Classic; defeated Scott Simpson, 1991 U.S. Open; defeated Scott Hoch, 1995 Shell Houston Open; lost to Glen Day, 1999 MCI Classic.
STILL, Ken (1-0)
Defeated Lee Trevino and Bert Yancey, 1977 Kaiser International.
STOCKTON, Dave (0-1)
Lost to Jerry Pate, 1977 Phoenix Open.
STONEHOUSE, Ralph (1-0)
Defeated Willie Dow, 1934 Miami Open.
STRANAHAN, Frank (0-1)
Lost to Bobby Locke, 1949 Cavalier Specialist Tournament.
STRANGE, Curtis (6-3)
Defeated Lee Trevino, 1980 Michelob Houston Open; lost to Raymond Floyd, 1981 Tournament Players Championship; lost to Gil Morgan, 1983 Joe Garagiola-Tucson Open; defeated Peter Jacobsen, 1985 Honda Classic; defeated Calvin Peete, 1986 Houston Open; defeated Greg Norman, 1988 Independent Insurance Agent Open; defeated Nick Faldo, 1988 U.S. Open; defeated Tom Kite, 1988 Nabisco Championships; lost to Rocco Mediate, 1991 Doral-Ryder Open.
STRECK, Ron (0-1)
Lost to Woody Blackburn, 1985 Isuzu-Andy Williams-San Diego Open.
SULLIVAN, Bud (0-1)
Lost to Dave Hill, 1961 Home of the Sun Open.
SULLIVAN, Mike (0-4)
Lost to Jack Newton, 1978 Buick-Goodwrench Open; lost to J.C. Snead, 1981 Southern Open; lost to Raymond Floyd, 1986 Walt Disney World/Oldsmobile Classic; lost to Brian Henninger, 1994 Deposit Guaranty Golf Classic.
SUTHERLAND, Kevin (0-1)
Lost to Phil Blackmar, 1997 Shell Houston Open.
SUTTON, Hal (4-2)
Defeated Bill Britton, 1982 Walt Disney World Golf Classic; defeated David Ogrin, 1985 St. Jude Memphis Classic; defeated Mike Reid, 1985 Southwest Golf Classic; lost to Mike Donald, 1989 Anheuser-Busch Golf Classic; lost to Dicky Pride, 1994 Federal Express St. Jude Classic; defeated Vijay Singh, 1998 THE TOUR Championship.
TAYLOR, Vaughn (1-0)
Defeated Scott McCarron, Steve Allan and Hunter Mahan, 2004 Reno-Tahoe Open.
TEWELL, Doug (1-0)
Defeated Jerry Pate, 1980 Sea Pines Heritage Classic.
THOMAS, Dave (0-1)
Lost to Peter Thomson, 1958 British Open.
THOMPSON, Barney (0-1)
Lost to John Cook, 1981 Bing Crosby National Pro-Am.
THOMSON, Jimmy (0-1)
Lost to Ben Hogan, 1942 Los Angeles Open.
THOMSON, Peter (2-0)
Defeated Gene Littler and Cary Middlecoff, 1956 Texas International Open; defeated Dave Thomas, 1958 British Open.
THORPE, Jim (0-1)
Lost to Scott Verplank, 1985 Western Open.
TOMS, David (1-2)
Defeated Mike Weir, 2000 Michelob Championship at Kingsmill; lost to Mike Weir, 2001 THE TOUR Championship; lost to Sergio Garcia, 2002 Mercedes Championships.
TORRANCE, Sam (0-1)
Lost to Ronnie Black, 1983 Southern Open.
TREVINO, Lee (5-5)
Defeated Bob Murphy, 1970 Tucson Open; defeated Bob Menne, 1970 National Airlines Open; lost to Ken Still, 1970 Kaiser International; defeated Jack Nicklaus, 1971 U.S. Open; lost to Tom Weiskopf, 1971 Kemper Open; defeated Art Wall, 1971 Canadian Open; defeated Lee Elder, 1972 Greater Hartford Open; lost to Andy Bean, 1978 Danny Thomas-Memphis Classic; lost to Lee Elder, 1978 Greater Milwaukee Open; lost to Curtis Strange, 1980 Michelob Houston Open.
TRIPLETT, Kirk (0-1)
Lost to Michael Clark II, 2000 John Deere Classic.
TROMBLEY, Bill (0-1)
Lost to Art Wall, 1956 Fort Wayne Open.
TRYBA, Ted (0-1)
Lost to Duffy Waldorf, 1999 Westin Texas Open.
TWAY, Bob (4-4)
Defeated Bernhard Langer, 1986 Shearson Lehman Brothers-Andy Williams Open; lost to Steve Jones, 1988 AT&T Pebble Beach National Pro-Am; lost to David Frost, 1988 Southern Open; lost to Scott Simpson, 1989 BellSouth Atlanta Golf Classic; defeated John Cook, 1990 Las Vegas Inviational; defeated Nolan Henke and David Frost, 1995 MCI Classic; lost to Robert Allenby, 2001 Nissan Open; defeated Brad Faxon, 2003 Bell Canadian Open.
TWITTY, Howard (1-0)
Defeated Jim Simons, 1980 Sammy Davis, Jr.-Greater Hartford Open.
TURNESA, Jim (0-1)
Lost to Jimmy Clark, 1952 Fort Wayne Open.
TURNESA, Joe (2-1)
Defeated Gene Sarazen, 1927 Ridgewood CC Open; defeated Massie Miller, 1929 Lannin Memorial Tournament; lost to Wiffy Cox, 1931 North & South Open.
ULOZAS, Tom (0-1)
Lost to Bert Yancey, 1972 American Golf Classic.
UNDERWOOD, Hal (0-1)
Lost to Gary Player, 1971 Greater Jacksonville Open.
VAN de VELDE, Jean (0-2)
Lost to Paul Lawrie, 1999 British Open; lost to Scott Verplank, 2000 Reno-Tahoe Open.
VALENTINE, Tommy (0-1)
Lost to Tom Watson, 1981 Atlanta Classic.
VARDON, Harry (0-1)
Lost to Francis Ouimet, 1913 U.S. Open.
VENTURI, Ken (0-3)
Lost to Jimmy Demaret, 1957 Thunderbird Invitational; lost to Billy Casper, 1958 Greater New Orleans Open; lost to Jay Hebert, 1961 Houston Classic.
VERPLANK, Scott (2-3)
Defeated Jim Thorpe, 1985 Western Open; lost to Trevor Dodds, 1998 Greater Greensboro Chrysler Classic; defeated Jean Van de Velde, 2000 Reno-Tahoe Open; lost to Robert Damron, 2001 Verizon Byron Nelson Classic; lost to Craig Parry, 2004 Ford Championship at Doral.
VON ELM, George (0-2)
Lost to John Golden, 1931 Agua Caliente Open; lost to Billy Burke, 1931 U.S. Open.
WADKINS, Bobby (0-2)
Lost to Lou Graham, 1979 IVB-Philadelphia Classic; lost to Bernhard Langer, 1985 Sea Pines Heritage Classic.

WADKINS, Lanny (3-3)
Lost to Homero Blancas, 1972 Phoenix Open; defeated Dan Sikes, 1973 Byron Nelson Golf Classic; defeated Gene Littler, 1977 PGA Championship; lost to Gil Morgan, 1983 Joe Garagiola-Tucson Open; defeated Craig Stadler, 1985 Bob Hope Desert Classic; lost to Larry Nelson, 1987 PGA Championship.

WAITE, Grant (0-1)
Lost to David Duval, 1997 Michelob Championship at Kingsmill.

WALDORF, Duffy (2-1)
Lost to David Duval, 1997 Michelob Championship at Kingsmill; defeated Dennis Paulson, 1999 Buick Classic; defeated Ted Tryba, 1999 Westin Texas Open.

WALL, Art Jr. (5-5)
Lost to Earl Stewart, 1953 Greensboro Open; defeated Cary Middlecoff, 1953 Fort Wayne Open; defeated Bill Trombley and Gardner Dickinson, Jr., 1956 Fort Wayne Open; defeated Dow Finsterwald, 1958 Rubber City Open; defeated Jack Burke, Jr. and Bob Rosburg, 1958 Eastern Open; defeated Dow Finsterwald, 1959 Buick Open; lost to Stan Leonard, 1960 Western Open; lost to Bob Goalby, 1962 Insurance City Open; lost to Billy Casper, 1967 Canadian Open; lost to Lee Trevino, 1971 Canadian Open.

WAMPLER, Fred (0-1)
Lost to Sam Snead, 1956 Greater Greensboro Open.

WATSON, Denis (0-1)
Lost to Tom Kite, 1982 Bay Hill Classic.

WATSON, Tom (9-4)
Defeated Jack Newton, 1975 British Open; defeated Ben Crenshaw, 1978 Bing Crosby National Pro-Am; lost to John Mahaffey, 1978 PGA Championship; lost to Fuzzy Zoeller, 1979 Masters Tournament; defeated Bill Rogers, 1979 Byron Nelson Classic; defeated Johnny Miller, 1979 Colgate Hall of Fame Classic; defeated D.A. Weibring, 1980 Andy Williams-San Diego Open; lost to Bruce Lietzke, 1981 Byron Nelson Classic; defeated Tommy Valentine, 1981 Atlanta Classic; defeated Johnny Miller, 1982 Glen Campbell Los Angeles Open; defeated Frank Conner, 1982 Sea Pines Heritage Classic; defeated Greg Norman, 1984 Western Open; lost to Mike Reid, 1988 NEC World Series of Golf.

WATTS, Brian (0-1)
Lost to Mark O'Meara, 1998 British Open

WEAVER, DeWitt (1-0)
Defeated Chuck Courtney, 1972 Southern Open.

WEIBRING, D.A. (0-2)
Lost to Tom Watson, 1980 Andy Williams-San Diego Open; lost to Andrew Magee, 1991 Las Vegas Invitational.

WEIR, Mike (3-2)
Lost to David Toms, 2000 Michelob Championship at Kingsmill; defeated Ernie Els, Sergio Garcia and David Toms, 2001 THE TOUR Championship; defeated Charles Howell III, 2003 Nissan Open; defeated Len Mattiace, 2003 Masters Tournament; lost to Vijay Singh, 2004 Bell Canadian Open

WEISKOPF, Tom (2-3)
Lost to Doug Sanders, 1966 Greater Greensboro Open; lost to Gene Littler, 1969 Greater Greensboro Open; defeated Dale Douglass, Gary Player and Lee Trevino, 1971 Kemper Open; defeated Jack Nicklaus, 1975 Canadian Open; lost to Ed Fiori, 1979 Southern Open.

WHITE, Buck (0-1)
Lost to Harold McSpaden, 1943 All American Open.

WHITT, Don (1-1)
Lost to Dow Finsterwald, 1957 Tucson Open; defeated Gary Player and Al Balding, 1959 Memphis Open.

WIEBE, Mark (1-2)
Defeated John Mahaffey, 1985 Anheuser-Busch Golf Classic; lost to Tom Sieckmann, 1988 Anheuser-Busch Golf Classic; lost to Vijay Singh, 1993 Buick Classic.

WIECHERS, Jim (0-1)
Lost to Bob Goalby, 1969 Robinson Open.

WININGER, Bo (1-1)
Defeated Jimmy Clark and Billy Maxwell, 1955 Baton Rouge Open; lost to Johnny Pott, 1960 Dallas Open.

WOOD, Craig (0-5)
Lost to John Golden, 1932 North & South Open; lost to Denny Shute, 1933 British Open; lost to Paul Runyan, 1934 PGA Championship; lost to Gene Sarazen, 1935 Masters Tournament; lost to Byron Nelson, 1939 U.S. Open.

WOOD, Willie (0-1)
Lost to Joey Sindelar, 1990 Hardee's Golf Classic.

WOODS, Tiger (6-1)
Defeated Davis Love III, 1996 Las Vegas Invitational; defeated Tom Lehman, 1997 Mercedes Championships; lost to Billy Mayfair, 1998 Nissan Open; defeated Miguel Angel Jimenez, 1999 World Golf Championships-American Express Championship; defeated Ernie Els, 2000 Mercedes Championships; defeated Bob May, 2000 PGA Championship; defeated Jim Furyk, 2001 World Golf Championships-NEC Invitational.

WOOSNAM, Ian (1-0)
Defeated Jim Hallet, 1991 USF&G Classic.

WORSHAM, Lew (1-2)
Lost to Herman Barron, 1946 Philadelphia Inquirer Open; lost to Clayton Heafner, 1947 Jacksonville Open; defeated Sam Snead, 1947 U.S. Open.

WRENN, Robert (0-1)
Lost to Scott Hoch, 1989 Las Vegas Invitational.

WYSONG, Dudley (1-1)
Lost to Babe Hiskey, 1965 Cajun Classic; defeated Billy Casper, 1967 Hawaiian Open.

YANCEY, Bert (2-2)
Defeated Bruce Devlin, 1969 Atlanta Classic; lost to Ken Still, 1970 Kaiser International; lost to Labron Harris, Jr., 1971 Robinson Open. defeated Tom Ulozas, 1972 American Golf Classic.

ZARLEY, Kermit (0-1)
Lost to Hale Irwin, 1976 Florida Citrus Open.

Mercedes Championships

1966 Arnold Palmer (63) def. Gay Brewer (79) by 16 strokes in an 18-hole playoff.
1972 Bobby Mitchell def. Jack Nicklaus with a birdie on the first playoff hole.
1975 Al Geiberger def. Gary Player with a birdie on the first playoff hole.
1977 Jack Nicklaus def. Bruce Lietzke with a birdie on the third playoff hole.
1992 Steve Elkington def. Brad Faxon with a birdie on the first playoff hole.
1994 Phil Mickelson def. Fred Couples with a par on the second playoff hole.
1995 Steve Elkington def. Bruce Lietzke with a birdie on the second playoff hole.
1997 Tiger Woods def. Tom Lehman with a birdie on the first playoff hole.
2000 Tiger Woods def. Ernie Els with a birdie on the second playoff hole.
2002 Sergio Garcia def. David Toms with a birdie on the first playoff hole.

Sony Open in Hawaii

1965 Gay Brewer def. Bob Goalby with a par on the first playoff hole.
1967 Dudley Wysong def. Billy Casper with a par on the first playoff hole.
1972 Grier Jones def. Bob Murphy with a par on the first playoff hole.
1978 Hubert Green def. Bill Kratzert with a par on the second playoff hole.
1984 Jack Renner def. Wayne Levi with a par on the second playoff hole.
1987 Corey Pavin def. Craig Stadler with a birdie on the second playoff hole.
1996 Jim Furyk def. Brad Faxon with a birdie on the third playoff hole.
1997 Paul Stankowski def. Jim Furyk, Mike Reid and Tom Watson with a birdie on the fourth playoff hole.
2003 Ernie Els def. Aaron Baddeley with a birdie on the second playoff hole.
2004 Ernie Els def. Harrison Frazar with a birdie on the third playoff hole.

Bob Hope Chrysler Classic

1963 Jack Nicklaus (65) def. Gary Player (73) by eight strokes in an 18-hole playoff.
1964 Tommy Jacobs def. Jimmy Demaret with a par on the second playoff hole.
1966 Doug Sanders def. Arnold Palmer with a birdie on the first playoff hole.
1968 Arnold Palmer def. Deane Beman with a par on the second playoff hole.
1971 Arnold Palmer def. Raymond Floyd with a birdie on the first playoff hole.
1982 Ed Fiori def. Tom Kite with a birdie on the second playoff hole.
1983 Keith Fergus def. Rex Caldwell with a par on the first playoff hole.
1984 John Mahaffey def. Jim Simons with a par on the second playoff hole.
1985 Lanny Wadkins def. Craig Stadler with a birdie on the fifth playoff hole.
1986 Donnie Hammond def. John Cook with a birdie on the first playoff hole.
1989 Steve Jones def. Paul Azinger and Sandy Lyle with a birdie on the first playoff hole.
1991 Corey Pavin def. Mark O'Meara with a birdie on the first playoff hole.
1992 John Cook def. Rick Fehr, Tom Kite, Mark O'Meara and Gene Sauers with an eagle on the fourth playoff hole.
1998 Fred Couples def. Bruce Lietzke with a birdie on the first playoff hole.
2002 Phil Mickelson def. David Berganio, Jr. with a birdie on the first playoff hole.
2004 Phil Mickelson def. Skip Kendall with a birdie on the first playoff hole.

FBR Open

1944 Harold McSpaden (70) def. Byron Nelson (72) by two strokes in an 18-hole playoff.
1946 Ben Hogan (68) def. Herman Keiser (70) by two strokes in an 18-hole playoff.
1949 Jimmy Demaret (67) def. Ben Hogan (70) by three strokes in an 18-hole playoff.
1954 Ed Furgol (71) and Cary Middlecoff (71) tied in an 18-hole playoff. Furgol def. Middlecoff with a par on the first sudden-death playoff hole.
1960 Jack Fleck (68) def. Bill Collins (71) by three strokes in an 18-hole playoff.
1961 Arnold Palmer (67) def. Doug Sanders (70) by three strokes in an 18-hole playoff.
1972 Homero Blancas def. Lanny Wadkins with a birdie on the first playoff hole.
1977 Jerry Pate def. Dave Stockton with a par on the first playoff hole.
1983 Bob Gilder def. Rex Caldwell, Johnny Miller and Mark O'Meara with a par on the eighth playoff hole.
1988 Sandy Lyle def. Fred Couples with a bogey on the third playoff hole.
1995 Vijay Singh def. Billy Mayfair with a par on the first playoff hole.
1996 Phil Mickelson def. Justin Leonard with a birdie on the third playoff hole.

AT&T Pebble Beach National Pro-Am

1962 Doug Ford def. Joe Campbell with a par on the first playoff hole.
1968 Johnny Pott def. Billy Casper and Bruce Devlin with a birdie on the first playoff hole.
1972 Jack Nicklaus def. Johnny Miller with a birdie on the first playoff hole.
1978 Tom Watson def. Ben Crenshaw with a par on the second playoff hole.
1979 Lon Hinkle def. Andy Bean and Mark Hayes with a birdie on the third playoff hole.
1981 John Cook def. Bobby Clampett, Ben Crenshaw, Hale Irwin and Barney Thompson with a par on the third playoff hole.
1984 Hale Irwin def. Jim Nelford with a birdie on the second playoff hole.
1988 Steve Jones def. Bob Tway with a birdie on the second playoff hole.
1992 Mark O'Meara def. Jeff Sluman with a par on the first playoff hole.

Buick Invitational

1961 Arnold Palmer def. Al Balding with a birdie on the first playoff hole.
1962 Tommy Jacobs def. Johnny Pott with a birdie on the first playoff hole.
1965 Wes Ellis def. Billy Casper with a birdie on the first playoff hole.
1970 Pete Brown def. Tony Jacklin with a par on the first playoff hole.
1975 J.C. Snead def. Raymond Floyd and Bobby Nichols with a birdie on the second playoff hole.
1980 Tom Watson def. D.A. Weibring with a par on the first playoff hole.
1984 Gary Koch def. Gary Hallberg with a birdie on the second playoff hole.
1985 Woody Blackburn def. Ron Streck with a par on the fourth playoff hole.
1986 Bob Tway def. Bernhard Langer with a par on the second playoff hole.
1998 Scott Simpson def. Skip Kendall with a birdie on the first playoff hole.
2001 Phil Mickelson def. Frank Lickliter and Davis Love III with a double-bogey on the third playoff hole.
2004 John Daly def. Chris Riley and Luke Donald with a birdie on the first playoff hole.

Nissan Open

1935 Vic Ghezzi (73) def. Johnny Revolta (75) by two strokes in an 18-hole playoff.
1942 Ben Hogan (72) def. Jimmy Thomson (73) by one stroke in an 18-hole playoff.
1950 Sam Snead (72) def. Ben Hogan (76) by four strokes in an 18-hole playoff.
1952 Tommy Bolt (69) def. Jack Burke, Jr. (71) by two strokes in an 18-hole playoff.
1969 Charles Sifford def. Harold Henning with a birdie on the first playoff hole.
1970 Billy Casper def. Hale Irwin with a birdie on the first playoff hole.
1971 Bob Lunn def. Billy Casper with a birdie on the fourth playoff hole.
1972 George Archer (66) def. Tommy Aaron (68) and Dave Hill (68) by two strokes in an 18-hole playoff.
1982 Tom Watson def. Johnny Miller with a birdie on the third playoff hole.
1987 Tze-Chung Chen def. Ben Crenshaw with a par on the first playoff hole.
1992 Fred Couples def. Davis Love III with a birdie on the second playoff hole.
1998 Billy Mayfair def. Tiger Woods with a birdie on the first playoff hole.
2001 Robert Allenby def. Brandel Chamblee, Toshi Izawa, Dennis Paulson, Jeff Sluman and Bob Tway with a birdie on the first playoff hole.
2003 Mike Weir def. Charles Howell III with a birdie on the second playoff hole.

Chrysler Classic of Tucson

1957 Dow Finsterwald (65) def. Don Whitt (69) by four strokes in an 18-hole playoff.
1961 Dave Hill def. Tommy Bolt and Bud Sullivan with a birdie on the third playoff hole.
1966 Joe Campbell def. Gene Littler with a birdie on the first playoff hole.
1970 Lee Trevino def. Bob Murphy with a birdie on the first playoff hole.
1972 Miller Barber (72) tied with George Archer (72) in an 18-hole playoff. Barber def. Archer with a birdie on the third playoff hole.
1977 Bruce Lietzke def. Gene Littler with a birdie on the fourth playoff hole.
1983 Gil Morgan def. Curtis Strange and Lanny Wadkins with a birdie on the second playoff hole.
1999 Gabriel Hjertstedt def. Tommy Armour III, Chris DiMarco, Tom Scherrer and Jean Van de Velde with a birdie on the first playoff hole.

Ford Championship at Doral

1980 Raymond Floyd def. Jack Nicklaus with a birdie on the second playoff hole.
1986 Andy Bean def. Hubert Green with a birdie on the fourth playoff hole.
1990 Greg Norman def. Paul Azinger, Mark Calcavecchia and Tim Simpson with an eagle on the first playoff hole.
1991 Rocco Mediate def. Curtis Strange with a birdie on the first playoff hole.
2003 Scott Hoch def. Jim Furyk with a birdie on the third playoff hole.
2004 Craig Parry def. Scott Verplank with an eagle on the first playoff hole.

The Honda Classic

1984 Bruce Lietzke def. Andy Bean with a par on the first playoff hole.
1985 Curtis Strange def. Peter Jacobsen with a par on the first playoff hole.
1992 Corey Pavin def. Fred Couples with a birdie on the second playoff hole.
1993 Fred Couples def. Robert Gamez with a birdie on the second playoff hole.

Bay Hill Invitational

1976 Hale Irwin def. Kermit Zarley with a par on the sixth playoff hole.
1979 Bob Byman def. John Schroeder with a par on the second playoff hole.
1982 Tom Kite def. Jack Nicklaus and Denis Watson with a birdie on the first playoff hole.
1983 Mike Nicolette def. Greg Norman with a par on the first playoff hole.
1984 Gary Koch def. George Burns with a birdie on the second playoff hole.
1989 Tom Kite def. Davis Love III with a par on the second playoff hole.
1999 Tim Herron def. Tom Lehman with a birdie on the first playoff hole.

THE PLAYERS Championship

1981 Raymond Floyd def. Barry Jaeckel and Curtis Strange with a par on the second playoff hole.
1987 Sandy Lyle def. Jeff Sluman with a par on the third playoff hole.

Shell Houston Open

1953 Cary Middlecoff (69) def. Jim Ferrier (71) and Shelley Mayfield (71) by two strokes Earl Stewart (72) by three strokes and Bill Nary (75) by six strokes in an 18-hole playoff.
1959 Jack Burke, Jr. (64) def. Julius Boros (69) by five strokes in an 18-hole playoff.
1960 Bill Collins (69) def. Arnold Palmer (71) by two strokes in an 18-hole playoff.
1961 Jay Hebert (69) and Ken Venturi (69) tied in an 18-hole playoff. Hebert def. Venturi with a birdie on the first sudden-death playoff hole.
1962 Bobby Nichols (71) and Dan Sikes (71) def. Jack Nicklaus (76) by five strokes in an 18-hole playoff. Nichols def. Sikes with a birdie on the first sudden-death playoff hole.
1970 Gibby Gilbert def. Bruce Crampton with a birdie on the third playoff hole.
1971 Hubert Green def. Don January with a birdie on the first playoff hole.
1980 Curtis Strange def. Hale Irwin and Lee Trevino with a birdie on the first playoff hole.
1982 Ed Sneed def. Bob Shearer with a birdie on the first playoff hole.
1986 Curtis Strange def. Calvin Peete with a birdie on the third playoff hole.
1987 Jay Haas def. Buddy Gardner with a par on the first playoff hole.
1988 Curtis Strange def. Greg Norman with a birdie on the third playoff hole.
1990 Tony Sills def. Gil Morgan with a par on the first playoff hole.
1993 Jim McGovern def. John Huston with a birdie on the second playoff hole.
1995 Payne Stewart def. Scott Hoch with a par on the first playoff hole.
1996 Mark Brooks def. Jeff Maggert with a birdie on the first playoff hole.
1997 Phil Blackmar def. Kevin Sutherland with a birdie on the first playoff hole.
2000 Robert Allenby def. Craig Stadler with a par on the fourth playoff hole.

BellSouth Classic

1969 Bert Yancey def. Bruce Devlin with a birdie on the second playoff hole.
1971 Gardner Dickinson def. Jack Nicklaus with a par on the first playoff hole.
1981 Tom Watson def. Tommy Valentine with a par on the third playoff hole.
1982 Keith Fergus def. Raymond Floyd with a birdie on the first playoff hole.
1985 Wayne Levi def. Steve Pate with a birdie on the second playoff hole.
1989 Scott Simpson def. Bob Tway with a par on the first playoff hole.
1990 Corey Pavin def. Steve Pate with a par on the first playoff hole.
1996 Paul Stankowski def. Brandel Chamblee with a birdie on the first playoff hole.
2000 Phil Mickelson def. Gary Nicklaus with a birdie on the first playoff hole.

The Masters

1935 Gene Sarazen (144) def. Craig Wood (149) by five strokes in a 36-hole playoff.
1942 Byron Nelson (69) def. Ben Hogan (70) by one stroke in an 18-hole playoff.
1954 Sam Snead (70) def. Ben Hogan (71) by one stroke in an 18-hole playoff.
1962 Arnold Palmer (68) def. Gary Player (71) by three strokes and Dow Finsterwald (77) by nine strokes in an 18-hole playoff.
1966 Jack Nicklaus (70) def. Tommy Jacobs (72) by two strokes and Gay Brewer (78) by eight strokes in an 18-hole playoff.
1970 Billy Casper (69) def. Gene Littler (74) by five strokes in an 18-hole playoff.
1979 Fuzzy Zoeller def. Ed Sneed and Tom Watson with a birdie on the second playoff hole.
1982 Craig Stadler def. Dan Pohl with a par on the first playoff hole.
1987 Larry Mize def. Seve Ballesteros and Greg Norman with a birdie on the second playoff hole.
1989 Nick Faldo def. Scott Hoch with a birdie on the second playoff hole.
1990 Nick Faldo def. Raymond Floyd with a par on the second playoff hole.
2003 Mike Weir def. Len Mattiace with a bogey on the first playoff hole.

MCI Heritage

1980 Doug Tewell def. Jerry Pate with a par on the first playoff hole.
1982 Tom Watson def. Frank Conner with a par on the third playoff hole.
1985 Bernhard Langer def. Bobby Wadkins with a par on the first playoff hole.
1990 Payne Stewart def. Steve Jones and Larry Mize with a birdie on the second playoff hole.
1995 Bob Tway def. David Frost and Nolan Henke with a par on the second playoff hole.
1999 Glen Day def. Jeff Sluman and Payne Stewart with a birdie on the first playoff hole.
2001 Jose Coceres def. Billy Mayfair with a par on the fifth playoff hole.
2003 Davis Love III def. Woody Austin with a birdie on the fourth playoff hole.
2004 Stewart Cink def. Ted Purdy with a birdie on the fifth playoff hole.

Zurich Classic of New Orleans

1945 Byron Nelson def. Harold McSpaden with a birdie on the first playoff hole.
1958 Billy Casper def. Ken Venturi with an eagle on the third playoff hole.
1969 Larry Hinson def. Frank Beard with a par on the third playoff hole.
1970 Miller Barber def. Bob Charles, Hubert Green and Howie Johnson with a birdie on the first playoff hole.
1973 Jack Nicklaus def. Miller Barber with a birdie on the second playoff hole.
1991 Ian Woosnam def. Jim Hallet with a par on the second playoff hole.
1995 Davis Love III def. Mike Heinen with a birdie on the second playoff hole.
2000 Carlos Franco def. Blaine McCallister with a par on the second playoff hole.
2003 Steve Flesch def. Bob Estes with a birdie on the first playoff hole.

Wachovia Championship

2004 Joey Sindelar def. Arron Oberholser with a par on the second playoff hole.

EDS Byron Nelson Championship

1956 Peter Thomson def. Gene Littler and Cary Middlecoff with a birdie on the first playoff hole.
1958 Sam Snead def. Julius Boros, John McMullen and Gary Player with a birdie on the first playoff hole.
1960 Johnny Pott def Ted Kroll and Bo Wininger with a birdie on the third playoff hole.
1970 Jack Nicklaus def. Arnold Palmer with a birdie on the first playoff hole.
1972 Chi Chi Rodriguez def. Billy Casper with a birdie on the first playoff hole.
1973 Lanny Wadkins def. Dan Sikes with a par on the first playoff hole.
1979 Tom Watson def. Bill Rogers with a birdie on the first playoff hole.
1981 Bruce Lietzke def. Tom Watson with a par on the first playoff hole.
1985 Bob Eastwood def. Payne Stewart with a bogey on the first playoff hole.
1987 Fred Couples def. Mark Calcavecchia with a par on the third playoff hole.
1988 Bruce Lietzke def. Clarence Rose with a birdie on the first playoff hole.
1989 Jodie Mudd def. Larry Nelson with a birdie on the first playoff hole.
1992 Billy Ray Brown def. Ben Crenshaw, Raymond Floyd and Bruce Lietzke with a birdie on the first playoff hole.
1994 Neal Lancaster def. Tom Byrum, Mark Carnevale, David Edwards, Yoshinori Mizumaki and David Ogrin with a birdie on the first playoff hole.
1999 Loren Roberts def. Steve Pate with a par on the first playoff hole.
2000 Jesper Parnevik def. Davis Love III and Phil Mickelson with a par on the third playoff hole.
2001 Robert Damron def. Scott Verplank with a birdie on the fourth playoff hole.
2004 Sergio Garcia def. Dudley Hart and Robert Damron with a par on the first playoff hole.

Bank of America Colonial

1959 Ben Hogan (69) def. Fred Hawkins (73) by four strokes in an 18-hole playoff.
1962 Arnold Palmer (69) def. Johnny Pott (73) by four strokes in an 18-hole playoff.
1983 Jim Colbert def. Fuzzy Zoeller with a par on the sixth playoff hole.
1984 Peter Jacobsen def. Payne Stewart with a birdie on the first playoff hole.
1986 Dan Pohl def. Payne Stewart with a birdie on the first playoff hole.
1992 Bruce Lietzke def. Corey Pavin with a birdie on the first playoff hole.
1994 Nick Price def. Scott Simpson with a birdie on the first playoff hole.

the Memorial Tournament

1976 Roger Maltbie def. Hale Irwin with a birdie on the fourth playoff hole.
1984 Jack Nicklaus def. Andy Bean with a par on the third playoff hole.
1991 Kenny Perry def. Hale Irwin with a birdie on the first playoff hole.
1992 David Edwards def. Rick Fehr with a par on the second playoff hole.

Booz Allen Classic

1971 Tom Weiskopf def. Dale Douglass and Gary Player with a birdie on the first playoff hole.
1974 Bob Menne def. Jerry Heard with a birdie on the first playoff hole.
1983 Fred Couples def. Tze-Chung Chen, Barry Jaeckel, Gil Morgan and Scott Simpson with a birdie on the second playoff hole.
1986 Greg Norman def. Larry Mize with a par on the sixth playoff hole.
1988 Morris Hatalsky def. Tom Kite with a par on the second playoff hole.
1991 Billy Andrade def. Jeff Sluman with a birdie on the first playoff hole.
1995 Lee Janzen def. Corey Pavin with a birdie on the first playoff hole.

Barclays Classic

1973 Bobby Nichols def. Bob Murphy with a birdie on the first playoff hole.
1975 Gene Littler def. Julius Boros with a par on the first playoff hole.
1985 Roger Maltbie def. George Burns with a birdie on the first playoff hole.
1987 J.C. Snead def. Seve Ballesteros with a par on the first playoff hole.
1988 Seve Ballesteros def. David Frost and Ken Green with a birdie on the first playoff hole.
1989 Wayne Grady def. Ronnie Black with a birdie on the first playoff hole.
1993 Vijay Singh def. Mark Wiebe with a birdie on the third playoff hole.
1995 Vijay Singh def. Doug Martin with a birdie on the fifth playoff hole.
1998 J.P. Hayes def. Jim Furyk with a birdie on the first playoff hole.
1999 Duffy Waldorf def. Dennis Paulson with a birdie on the first playoff hole.
2000 Dennis Paulson def. David Duval with a par on the fourth playoff hole.
2003 Jonathan Kaye def. John Rollins with an eagle on the first playoff hole.
2004 Sergio Garcia def. Rory Sabbatini and Padraig Harrington with a birdie on the third playoff hole.

U.S. Open

1901 Willie Anderson (85) def. Alex Smith (86) by one stroke in an 18-hole playoff.
1903 Willie Anderson (82) def. David Brown (84) by two strokes in an 18-hole playoff.
1908 Fred McLeod (77) def. Willie Smith (83) by six strokes in an 18-hole playoff.
1910 Alex Smith (71) def. John McDermott (75) by four strokes and Macdonald Smith (77) by six strokes in an 18-hole playoff.
1913 Francis Ouimet (72) def. Harry Vardon (77) by five strokes and Edward Ray (78) by six strokes in an 18-hole playoff.
1919 Walter Hagen (77) def. Mike Brady (78) by one stroke in an 18-hole playoff.
1923 Robert T. Jones (76) def. Bobby Cruickshank (78) by two strokes in an 18-hole playoff.
1925 Willie McFarlane (147) def. Robert T. Jones (148) by one stroke in a 36-hole playoff.
1927 Tommy Armour (76) def. Harry Cooper (79) by three strokes in an 18-hole playoff.
1928 Johnny Farrell (143) def. Robert T. Jones (144) by one stroke in a 36-hole playoff.
1929 Robert T. Jones (141) def. Al Espinosa (164) by 23 strokes in an 36-hole playoff.
1931 Billy Burke (297) def. George Von Elm (298) by one stroke in a 72-hole playoff.
1939 Byron Nelson (138) def. Craig Wood (141) by three strokes in a 36-hole playoff. Denny Shute (76) was eliminated after the first 18 holes.
1940 Lawson Little (70) def. Gene Sarazen (73) by three strokes in an 18-hole playoff.
1946 Lloyd Mangrum (144) def. Vic Ghezzi (145) and Byron Nelson (145) by one stroke in an 36-hole playoff.
1947 Lew Worsham (69) def. Sam Snead (70) by one stroke in an 18-hole playoff.
1950 Ben Hogan (69) def. Lloyd Mangrum (73) by four strokes and George Fazio (75) by six strokes in an 18-hole playoff.
1955 Jack Fleck (69) def. Ben Hogan (72) by three strokes in an 18-hole playoff.
1957 Dick Mayer (72) def. Cary Middlecoff (79) by seven strokes in an 18-hole playoff.
1962 Jack Nicklaus (71) def. Arnold Palmer (74) by three strokes in an 18-hole playoff.
1963 Julius Boros (70) def. Jacky Cupit (73) by three strokes and Arnold Palmer (76) by six strokes in an 18-hole playoff.
1965 Gary Player (71) def. Kel Nagle (74) by three strokes in an 18-hole playoff.
1966 Billy Casper (69) def. Arnold Palmer (73) by four strokes in an 18-hole playoff.
1971 Lee Trevino (68) def. Jack Nicklaus (71) by three strokes in an 18-hole playoff.
1975 Lou Graham (71) def. John Mahaffey (73) by two strokes in an 18-hole playoff.
1984 Fuzzy Zoeller (67) def. Greg Norman (75) by eight strokes in an 18-hole playoff.
1988 Curtis Strange (71) def. Nick Faldo (75) by four strokes in an 18-hole playoff.
1990 Hale Irwin (77) def. Mike Donald (78) by one stroke in 19-hole playoff.
1991 Payne Stewart (75) def. Scott Simpson (77) by two strokes in an 18-hole playoff.
1994 Ernie Els (82) def. Loren Roberts (83) by one stroke in a 20-hole playoff. Colin Montgomerie (78) was eliminated after the first 18 holes.
2001 Retief Goosen (70) def. Mark Brooks (72) by two strokes in an 18-hole playoff.

Buick Championship

1954 Tommy Bolt def. Earl Stewart when Stewart conceded on the first playoff hole.
1956 Arnold Palmer def. Ted Kroll with a birdie on the second playoff hole.
1960 Arnold Palmer def. Bill Collins and Jack Fleck with a birdie on the third playoff hole.
1961 Billy Maxwell def. Ted Kroll with a birdie on the seventh playoff hole.
1962 Bob Goalby def. Art Wall with a birdie on the seventh playoff hole.
1965 Billy Casper def. Johnny Pott with a birdie on the first playoff hole.
1969 Bob Lunn def. Dave Hill with a birdie on the fourth playoff hole.
1971 George Archer def. Lee Elder, Lou Graham and J.C. Snead with a birdie on the first playoff hole.
1972 Lee Trevino def Lee Elder with a birdie on the first playoff hole.
1975 Don Bies def. Hubert Green with a birdie on the second playoff hole.
1980 Howard Twitty def. Jim Simons with a birdie on the sixth playoff hole.
1985 Phil Blackmar def. Jodie Mudd and Dan Pohl with a birdie on the first playoff hole.
1986 Mac O'Grady def. Roger Maltbie with a par on the first playoff hole.
1988 Mark Brooks def. Dave Barr and Joey Sindelar with a birdie on the second playoff hole.
1991 Billy Ray Brown def. Rick Fehr and Corey Pavin with a birdie on the first playoff hole.
1998 Olin Browne def. Stewart Cink and Larry Mize with a birdie on the first playoff hole.
2004 Woody Austin def. Tim Herron with a birdie on the first playoff hole.

FedEx St. Jude Classic

1959 Don Whitt def. Al Balding and Gary Player with a birdie on the second playoff hole.
1960 Tommy Bolt def. Ben Hogan and Gene Littler with a birdie on the first playoff hole.
1962 Lionel Hebert def. Gene Littler and Gary Player with a birdie on the first playoff hole.
1963 Tony Lema def. Tommy Aaron with a par on the first playoff hole.
1965 Jack Nicklaus def. Johnny Pott with a par on the first playoff hole.
1978 Andy Bean def. Lee Trevino with a birdie on the first playoff hole.
1979 Gil Morgan def. Larry Nelson with a birdie on the second playoff hole.
1985 Hal Sutton def. David Ogrin with a birdie on the first playoff hole.
1990 Tom Kite def. John Cook with a birdie on the first playoff hole.
1994 Dicky Pride def. Gene Sauers and Hal Sutton with a birdie on the first playoff hole.
1998 Nick Price def. Jeff Sluman with a birdie on the second playoff hole.

Cialis Western Open

1899 Willie Smith (74) def. Laurie Auchterlonie (84) by 10 strokes in an 18-hole playoff.
1934 Harry Cooper (133) def. Ky Laffoon (136) by three strokes in a 36-hole playoff.
1937 Ralph Guldahl (72) def. Horton Smith (76) by four strokes in an 18-hole playoff.
1940 Jimmy Demaret (69) def. Toney Penna (72) by three strokes in an 18-hole playoff.
1948 Ben Hogan (64) def. Ed Oliver (73) by nine strokes in an 18-hole playoff.
1954 Lloyd Mangrum def. Ted Kroll with a birdie on the first playoff hole.
1956 Mike Fetchick (66) def. Jay Hebert (71) by five strokes, Doug Ford (72) by six strokes and Don January (75) by nine strokes in an 18-hole playoff.
1957 Doug Ford def. George Bayer, Gene Littler and Billy Maxwell with a par on the third playoff hole.
1960 Stan Leonard def. Art Wall with a birdie on the first playoff hole.
1963 Arnold Palmer (70) def. Julius Boros (71) by one stroke and Jack Nicklaus (73) by three strokes in an 18-hole playoff.
1978 Andy Bean def. Bill Rogers with a par on the first playoff hole.
1979 Larry Nelson def. Ben Crenshaw with a birdie on the first playoff hole.

1984 Tom Watson def. Greg Norman with a birdie on the third playoff hole.
1985 Scott Verplank def. Jim Thorpe with a par on the second playoff hole.
1986 Tom Kite def. Fred Couples, David Frost and Nick Price with a birdie on the first playoff hole.
1989 Mark McCumber def. Peter Jacobsen with a par on the first playoff hole.
2000 Robert Allenby def. Nick Price with a par on the first playoff hole.

U.S. Bank Championship in Milwaukee

1978 Lee Elder def. Lee Trevino with a par on the eighth playoff hole.
1983 Morris Hatalsky def. George Cadle with a par on the second playoff hole.
1986 Corey Pavin def. Dave Barr with a birdie on the fourth playoff hole.
1990 Jim Gallagher, Jr. def. Ed Dougherty and Billy Mayfair with a par on the first playoff hole.
1993 Billy Mayfair def. Mark Calcavecchia and Ted Schulz with a birdie on the fourth playoff hole.
1996 Loren Roberts def. Jerry Kelly with a birdie on the first playoff hole.
2001 Shigeki Maruyama def. Charles Howell III with a birdie on the first playoff hole.

B.C. Open

1974 Richie Karl def. Bruce Crampton with a birdie on the first playoff hole.
1989 Mike Hulbert def. Bob Estes with a par on the first playoff hole.
1996 Fred Funk def. Pete Jordan with a birdie on the first playoff hole.
1999 Brad Faxon def. Fred Funk with a par on the second playoff hole.
2001 Jeff Sluman def. Paul Gow with a birdie on the second playoff hole.

British Open

1883 Willie Fernie (158) def. Robert Ferguson (159) by one stroke in a 36-hole playoff.
1889 Willie Park, Jr. (158) def. Andrew Kirkaldy (163) by five strokes in a 36-hole playoff.
1896 Harry Vardon (157) def. John H. Taylor (161) by four strokes in a 36-hole playoff.
1911 Harry Vardon (143) in 35 holes def. Arnaud Massy (148) in 34 holes.
1921 Jock Hutchison (150) def. Roger Wethered (159) by nine strokes in a 36-hole playoff.
1933 Denny Shute (149) def. Craig Wood (154) by five strokes in a 36-hole playoff.
1949 Bobby Locke (135) def. Harry Bradshaw (147) by 12 strokes in a 36-hole playoff.
1958 Peter Thomson (139) def. Dave Thomas (143) by four strokes in a 36-hole playoff.
1963 Bob Charles (140) def. Phil Rodgers (148) by eight strokes in a 36-hole playoff.
1970 Jack Nicklaus (72) def. Doug Sanders (73) by one stroke in an 18-hole playoff.
1975 Tom Watson (71) def. Jack Newton (72) by one stroke in an 18-hole playoff.
1989 Mark Calcavecchia (13) def. Wayne Grady (16) by three strokes and Greg Norman (no final total) in a four-hole playoff.
1995 John Daly (15) def. Costantino Rocca (19) by four strokes in a four-hole playoff.
1998 Mark O'Meara (17) def. Brian Watts (19) by two strokes in a four-hole playoff.
1999 Paul Lawrie (15) def. Justin Leonard (18) and Jean Van de Velde (18) by three strokes in a four-hole playoff.
2002 Ernie Els (16) and Thomas Levet (16) def. Stuart Appleby (17) and Steve Elkington (17) in a four-hole playoff. Els def. Levet with a par on the first sudden-death hole.
2004 Todd Hamilton (15) def. Ernie Els (16) in a four-hole playoff.

John Deere Classic

1981 Dave Barr def. Woody Blackburn, Frank Conner, Dan Halldorson and Victor Regalado with a par on the eighth playoff hole.
1983 Danny Edwards def. Morris Hatalsky with a birdie on the first playoff hole.
1990 Joey Sindelar def. Willie Wood with a par on the first playoff hole.
1999 J.L. Lewis def. Mike Brisky with a birdie on the fifth playoff hole.
2000 Michael Clark II def. Kirk Triplett with a birdie on the fourth playoff hole.
2004 Mark Hensby def. John E. Morgan with a par on the second playoff hole.

The INTERNATIONAL

1994 Steve Lowery def. Rick Fehr with a par on the first playoff hole.
1996 Clarence Rose def. Brad Faxon with an eagle on the third playoff hole.

Buick Open

1959 Art Wall (71) def. Dow Finsterwald (73) by two strokes in an 18-hole playoff.
1961 Jack Burke, Jr. (71) def. Billy Casper (74) and Johnny Pott (74) by three strokes in an 18-hole playoff.
1978 Jack Newton def. Mike Sullivan with a birdie on the first playoff hole.
1979 John Fought def. Jim Simons with a par on the second playoff hole.
1981 Hale Irwin def. Bobby Clampett, Peter Jacobsen and Gil Morgan with a birdie on the second playoff hole.
1991 Brad Faxon def. Chip Beck with a par on the first playoff hole.
1992 Dan Forsman def. Steve Elkington and Brad Faxon with a par on the second playoff hole.
1995 Woody Austin def. Mike Brisky with a par on the second playoff hole.

PGA Championship

1923 Gene Sarazen def. Walter Hagen with a birdie on the second playoff hole.
1934 Paul Runyan def. Craig Wood with a par on the second playoff hole.
1937 Denny Shute def. Harold McSpaden with a par on the first playoff hole.
1939 Henry Picard def. Byron Nelson with a birdie on the first playoff hole.
1941 Vic Ghezzi def. Byron Nelson with a par on the second playoff hole.
1961 Jerry Barber (67) def. Don January (68) by one stroke in an 18-hole playoff.
1967 Don January (69) def. Don Massengale (71) by three strokes in an 18-hole playoff.
1977 Lanny Wadkins def. Gene Littler with a par on the third playoff hole.
1978 John Mahaffey def. Jerry Pate and Tom Watson with a birdie on the second playoff hole.
1979 David Graham def. Ben Crenshaw with a birdie on the third playoff hole.
1987 Larry Nelson def. Lanny Wadkins with a par on the first playoff hole.
1993 Paul Azinger def. Greg Norman with a par on the second playoff hole.
1995 Steve Elkington def. Collin Montgomerie with a birdie on the first playoff hole.
1996 Mark Brooks def. Kenny Perry with a birdie on the first playoff hole.
2000 Tiger Woods (12) def. Bob May (13) by one stroke in a three-hole playoff.
2004 Vijay Singh (10) def. Justin Leonard and Chris DiMarco in a three-hole playoff.

WGC-NEC Invitational

1978 Gil Morgan def. Hubert Green with a par on the first playoff hole.
1982 Craig Stadler def. Raymond Floyd with a par on the fourth playoff hole.
1988 Mike Reid def. Tom Watson with a par on the first playoff hole.
1989 David Frost def. Ben Crenshaw with a par on the second playoff hole.
1991 Tom Purtzer def. Jim Gallagher Jr. and Davis Love III with a par on the second playoff hole.
1995 Greg Norman def. Billy Mayfair and Nick Price with a birdie on the first playoff hole.
2001 Tiger Woods def. Jim Furyk with a birdie on the seventh playoff hole.

Reno-Tahoe Open

2000 Scott Verplank def. Jean Van de Velde with a birdie on the fourth playoff hole.
2004 Vaughn Taylor def. Scott McCarron, Steve Allan and Hunter Mahan with a birdie on the first playoff hole.

Bell Canadian Open

1920 J. Douglas Edgar (73) def. Charles R. Murray (74) by one stroke and Tommy Armour (75) by two strokes in an 18-hole playoff.
1930 Tommy Armour (138) def. Leo Diegel (141) by three strokes in a 36-hole playoff.
1931 Walter Hagen (141) def. Percy Alliss (142) by one stroke in an 18-hole playoff.
1938 Sam Snead (67) tied Harold McSpaden (67) in an 18-hole playoff. Snead defeated McSpaden by five strokes in a nine-hole playoff.
1940 Sam Snead (71) def. Harold McSpaden (72) by one stroke in an 18-hole playoff.
1946 George Fazio (70) def. Dick Metz (71) by one stroke in an 18-hole playoff.
1956 Doug Sanders def. Dow Finsterwald with a par on the first playoff hole.
1967 Billy Casper (65) def. Art Wall (69) by four strokes in an 18-hole playoff.
1969 Tommy Aaron (70) def. Sam Snead (72) by two strokes in an 18-hole playoff.
1971 Lee Trevino def. Art Wall with a birdie on the first playoff hole.
1975 Tom Weiskopf def. Jack Nicklaus with a birdie on the first playoff hole.
1983 John Cook def. Johnny Miller with a birdie on the sixth playoff hole.
1992 Greg Norman def. Bruce Lietzke with a par on the second playoff hole.
1995 Mark O'Meara def. Bob Lohr with a par on the first playoff hole.
1998 Billy Andrade def. Bob Friend with a par on the first playoff hole.
2002 John Rollins def. Neal Lancaster and Justin Leonard with a birdie on the first playoff hole.
2003 Bob Tway def. Brad Faxon with a bogey on the third playoff hole.
2004 Vijay Singh def. Mike Weir with a par on the third playoff hole.

Tournament Playoff Records (cont.)

WGC-American Express Championship

1999 Tiger Woods def. Miguel Angel Jimenez with a birdie on the first playoff hole.

Valero Texas Open

1923 Walter Hagen (71) def. Bill Mehlhorn (74) by three strokes in an 18-hole playoff.
1940 Byron Nelson (70) def. Ben Hogan (71) by one stroke in an 18-hole playoff.
1942 Chick Harbert (69) def. Ben Hogan (72) by three strokes in an 18-hole playoff.
1951 Dutch Harrison def. Doug Ford with a birdie on the first playoff hole.
1969 Deane Beman def. Jack McGowan with a birdie on the first playoff hole.
1975 Don January def. Larry Hinson with a birdie on the second playoff hole.
1976 Butch Baird def. Miller Barber with a birdie on the first playoff hole.
1981 Bill Rogers def. Ben Crenshaw with a birdie on the first playoff hole.
1985 John Mahaffey def. Jodie Mudd with a par on the second playoff hole.
1991 Blaine McCallister def. Gary Hallberg with a birdie on the second playoff hole.
1992 Nick Price def. Steve Elkington with a par on the second playoff hole.
1993 Jay Haas def. Bob Lohr with a birdie on the second playoff hole.
1999 Duffy Waldorf def. Ted Tryba with a birdie on the first playoff hole.

Michelin Championship at Las Vegas

1989 Scott Hoch def. Robert Wrenn with a birdie on the fifth playoff hole.
1990 Bob Tway def. John Cook with a par on the first playoff hole.
1991 Andrew Magee def. D.A. Weibring with a par on the second playoff hole.
1996 Tiger Woods def. Davis Love III with a par on the first playoff hole.
2003 Stuart Appleby def. Scott McCarron with a birdie on the first playoff hole.

Chrysler Classic of Greensboro

1949 Sam Snead (69) def. Lloyd Mangrum (71) by two strokes in an 18-hole playoff.
1953 Earl Stewart (68) and Sam Snead (68) def. Doug Ford (70) by two strokes and Art Wall (72) by four strokes in an 18-hole playoff. Stewart def. Snead with a par on the first sudden-death hole.
1954 Doug Ford (72) def. Marty Furgol (75) by three strokes in an 18-hole playoff.
1956 Sam Snead def. Fred Wampler with a birdie on the second playoff hole.
1964 Julius Boros def. Doug Sanders with a par on the first playoff hole.
1966 Doug Sanders def. Tom Weiskopf with a par on the second playoff hole.
1969 Gene Littler def. Julius Boros, Orville Moody and Tom Weiskopf with a birdie on the fifth playoff hole.
1971 Bud Allin def. Dave Eichelberger and Rod Funseth with a birdie on the first playoff hole.
1972 George Archer def. Tommy Aaron with a par on the second playoff hole.
1981 Larry Nelson def. Mark Hayes with a birdie on the second playoff hole.
1988 Sandy Lyle def. Ken Green with a birdie on the first playoff hole.
1991 Mark Brooks def. Gene Sauers with a par on the third playoff hole.
1993 Rocco Mediate def. Steve Elkington with a birdie on the fourth playoff hole.
1997 Frank Nobilo def. Brad Faxon with a par on the first playoff hole.
1998 Trevor Dodds def. Scott Verplank with a par on the first playoff hole.

FUNAI Classic at the WALT DISNEY WORLD Resort

1982 Hal Sutton def. Bill Britton with a birdie on the fourth playoff hole.
1986 Raymond Floyd def. Lon Hinkle and Mike Sullivan with a par on the first playoff hole.
1988 Bob Lohr def. Chip Beck with a par on the fifth playoff hole.
1997 David Duval def. Dan Forsman with a par on the first playoff hole.

Southern Farm Bureau Classic

1994 Brian Henninger def. Mike Sullivan with a birdie on the first playoff hole.
2000 Steve Lowery def. Skip Kendall with a birdie on the first playoff hole.

THE TOUR Championship

1988 Curtis Strange def. Tom Kite with a birdie on the second playoff hole.
1989 Tom Kite def. Payne Stewart with a par on the second playoff hole.
1990 Jodie Mudd def. Billy Mayfair with a birdie on the first playoff hole.
1991 Craig Stadler def. Russ Cochran with a birdie on the second playoff hole.
1994 Mark McCumber def. Fuzzy Zoeller with a birdie on the first playoff hole.
1998 Hal Sutton def. Vijay Singh with a birdie on the first playoff hole.
2001 Mike Weir def. Ernie Els, Sergio Garcia and David Toms with a birdie on the first playoff hole.

Facts and Figures (1970-2004)

Low 9:

2004	27 (9-under)	**Robert Gamez**, Bob Hope Chrysler Classic.
	28 (8-under)	**Charles Howell III**, Booz Allen Classic; **Vijay Singh**, Bell Canadian Open
2003	28 (8-under)	**Pat Perez**, Bob Hope Chrysler Classic; **Craig Barlow**, MCI Heritage
	28 (7-under)	**Chris DiMarco**, Phoenix Open
2002	28 (8-under)	**Brent Schwarzrock**, AT&T Pebble Beach National Pro-Am, **Joel Edwards**, Fed Ex St. Jude Classic
	28 (7-under)	**Charles Howell III**, Nissan Open; **J.P. Hayes**, Greater Milwaukee Open
2001	27 (9-under)	**Billy Mayfair**, Buick Open
2000	29 (8-under)	**Jerry Kelly**, B.C. Open
	29 (7-under)	**Paul Goydos**, **Barry Cheesman**, Bob Hope Chrysler Classic; **Paul Azinger**, AT&T Pebble Beach National Pro-Am; **Edward Fryatt**, Doral-Ryder Open; **Harrison Frazar**, Compaq Classic of New Orleans; **David Howser**, FedEx St. Jude Classic; **Tom Scherrer**, Michelob Championship at Kingsmill; **Chris DiMarco**, **Paul Stankowski**, Invensys Classic at Las Vegas; **Brian Watts**, Southern Farm Bureau Classic
	29 (6-under)	**Chris Perry**, MCI Classic; **Carl Paulson**, MasterCard Colonial; **Jay Williamson**, Kemper Insurance Open; **Greg Kraft**, Buick Classic; **Brian Henninger**, Canon Greater Hartford Open; **Tim Herron**, Air Canada Championship; **Steve Gotsche**, Bell Canadian Open; **Tom Lehman**, **Rocco Mediate**, SEI Pennsylvania Classic; **Paul Goydos**, **Harrison Frazar**, Westin Texas Open
1999	28 (8-under)	**David Duval**, Bob Hope Chrysler Classic
	28 (6-under)	**Paul Goydos**, GTE Byron Nelson Classic
1998	28 (8-under)	**David Duval**, Tucson Chrysler Classic; **Loren Roberts**, Greater Milwaukee Open
	28 (7-under)	**Vijay Singh**, Canon Greater Hartford Open
1997	28 (8-under)	**David Duval**, AT&T Pebble Beach National Pro-Am
1996	28 (8-under)	**Jeff Julian**, Buick Invitational; **Nolan Henke**, Walt Disney World/Oldsmobile Golf Classic
	28 (6-under)	**Gil Morgan**, GTE Byron Nelson Classic
1995	28 (7-under)	**Brad Faxon**, PGA
	29 (7-under)	**Jim Gallagher, Jr.**, **Mark Brooks**, **Kenny Perry**, Bob Hope Chrysler Classic; **Jay Delsing**, FedEx St. Jude Classic; **Dave Stockton, Jr.**, **Brad Bryant**, Walt Disney World/Oldsmobile Golf Classic
	29 (6-under)	**Mike Brisky**, **Fuzzy Zoeller**, Canon Greater Hartford Open
	30 (7-under)	**Hal Sutton**, B.C. Open
1994	29 (7-under)	**Davis Love III**, Hawaiian; **Lennie Clements**, Bob Hope; **Ronnie Black**, Buick Invitational; **Larry Nelson**, Doral-Ryder; **Dennis Paulson**, Freeport-McMoRan; **Brian Henninger**, New England
	29 (6-under)	**Steve Lamontagne**, Honda; **Guy Boros**, Southwestern Bell Colonial
	29 (5-under)	**Glen Day**, B.C. Open
1993	28 (7-under)	**Keith Clearwater**, **Wayne Levi**, Southwestern Bell Colonial
	29 (7-under)	**Fuzzy Zoeller**, **Tom Kite**, Bob Hope; **Greg Norman**, Buick Open; **Dan Halldorson**, Milwaukee
1992	29 (7-under)	**Gil Morgan**, **Neal Lancaster**, Bob Hope; **Greg Norman**, Buick Open; **Mark Calcavecchia**, Masters, **Jim McGovern**, Federal Express; **John Cook**, Las Vegas
	29 (6-under)	**Dillard Pruitt**, Phoenix; **Robin Freeman**, Byron Nelson; **David Frost**, Hardee's; **Donnie Hammond**, **David Edwards**, Texas
1991	28 (7-under)	**Andrew Magee**, Los Angeles
	28 (6-under)	**Emlyn Aubrey**, Chattanooga

1990	28 (7-under)	**Kenny Knox**, Chattanooga
	29 (7-under)	**Tom Kite**, Bob Hope
	29 (6-under)	**David Frost**, Tucson; **Mike Hulbert**, Colonial; **Kirk Triplett**, Buick Classic; **Howard Twitty**, **David Peoples**, Southern; **Steve Jones**, **Billy Ray Brown**, **John Dowdall**, Texas
	29 (5-under)	**Chris Perry**, **Brad Fabel**, Canon GHO
1989	28 (8-under)	**Steve Pate**, Bob Hope; **Webb Heintzelman**, Las Vegas
1988	28 (7-under)	**Mike Sullivan**, Texas
	29 (7-under)	**Sandy Lyle**, Pebble Beach; **Dave Eichelberger**, Hawaiian; **Gil Morgan**, Andy Williams; **Ken Green**, Milwaukee; **Mike Donald**, Walt Disney; **Mark Wiebe**, **Ken Green**, Tucson
1987	29 (7-under)	**Dewey Arnette**, **Trevor Dodds**, Buick
	30 (7-under)	**Joey Sindelar**, B.C. Open
	29 (6-under)	**Payne Stewart**, Phoenix; **David Frost**, Andy Williams; **Wayne Levi**, Hartford; **Curtis Strange**, Anheuser-Busch; **Dave Rummells**, **Dave Stockton**, Hardee's; **Robert Thompson**, Provident
1986	29 (7-under)	**Hubert Green**, Doral; **Mike Sullivan**, Houston; **Charles Bolling**, Las Vegas
	29 (6-under)	**Willie Wood**, Westchester; **Mike Smith**, Hardee's; **Mike Donald**, Southern
1985	29 (7-under)	**Jim Thorpe**, Milwaukee
	29 (6-under)	**John Mahaffey**, Bob Hope; **Larry Mize**, Los Angeles; **Tom Watson**, Colonial; **Roger Maltbie**, Westchester; **Brad Fabel**, Quad Cities; **Mike Gove**, Texas; **Ken Brown**, Pensacola
1984	29 (6-under)	**George Burns**, Colonial; **Mike McCullough**, Canadian; **Mark O'Meara**, Hartford
	30 (6-under)	**Gibby Gilbert**, Bob Hope; **Willie Wood**, Phoenix; **Greg Norman**, Bay Hill; **David Graham**, T of C; **Payne Stewart**, Memorial; **Tom Kite**, Westchester; **Tommy Valentine**, **Mike Donald**, Atlanta; **Gary Player**, PGA; **Rod Nuckolls**, **Steve Brady**, **Denis Watson**, Buick; **Lon Hinkle**, **Scott Simpson**, Las Vegas; **George Archer**, Bank of Boston; **Mark Lye**, **Larry Rinker**, Walt Disney
1983	28 (7-under)	**Jeff Sluman**, Quad Cities
	28 (6-under)	**Mark O'Meara**, B.C. Open
	29 (7-under)	**Hubert Green**, Bob Hope; **Craig Stadler**, Buick
	29 (6-under)	**Jon Chaffee**, **Rick Pearson**, Quad Cities; **Gibby Gilbert**, PGA; **Lanny Wadkins**, Anheuser-Busch; **George Cadle**, **Jim Colbert**, Texas; **Gary Hallberg**, Pensacola.
1982	29 (7-under)	**George Burns**, Hartford
	29 (6-under)	**Scott Hoch**, Houston; **Gary Koch**, **Bob Eastwood**, **Allen Miller**, Quad Cities; **Fred Couples**, PGA; **Isao Aoki**, Hartford
1981	29 (6-under)	**Mike Holland**, Anheuser-Busch; **Fuzzy Zoeller**, Hartford; **Bob Gilder**, Southern
1980	29 (7-under)	**Bob Murphy**, Tallahassee; **Curtis Strange**, Houston; **John Fought**, Buick
	29 (6-under)	**Gary Koch**, Byron Nelson
1979	29 (7-under)	**Kermit Zarley**, Doral-Eastern; **Andy Bean**, Atlanta
	29 (6-under)	**Pat McGowan**, Phoenix; **Brad Bryant**, Quad Cities; **Allen Miller**, Hartford
1978	29 (7-under)	**Gary Koch**, Houston
	29 (6-under)	**Rod Funseth**, Hartford; **Ron Streck**, Texas
	29 (5-under)	**Rod Curl**, B.C. Open
1977	29 (7-under)	**Graham Marsh**, T of C; **Bobby Wadkins**, Memorial; **Al Geiberger**, Memphis; **Lanny Wadkins**, Milwaukee; **Rik Massengale**, Pleasant Valley; **Florentino Molina**, Hartford; **Leonard Thompson**, Hall of Fame
	29 (6-under)	**Fred Marti**, Pleasant Valley; **Rod Curl**, IVB; **Bruce Lietzke**, Hartford; **Tom Weiskopf**, World Series
1976	28 (8-under)	**Jim Colbert**, Bob Hope; **Fuzzy Zoeller**, Quad Cities
1975	27 (7-under)	**Andy North**, B.C. Open
	28 (7-under)	**Bruce Crampton**, Sahara
	29 (7-under)	**Hale Irwin**, Phoenix; **Tom Weiskopf**, Westchester
	29 (6-under)	**Jim Simons**, Hartford
1974	29 (7-under)	**Tom Kite**, Doral-Eastern; **Dan Sikes**, New Orleans; **Tom Watson**, Hartford
	29 (6-under)	**Raymond Floyd**, American Classic
1973	28 (7-under)	**Bert Yancey**, American Classic
1972	29 (7-under)	**Babe Hiskey**, Inverrary; **Bert Yancey**, Walt Disney
	29 (7-under)	**Dwight Nevil**, Southern; **Cesar Sanudo**, Sahara
1971	28 (7-under)	**Jim Jamieson**, Robinson
1970	29 (6-under)	**Dave Hill**, Cleveland; **George Knudson**, Robinson; **Wilf Homenuik**, Azalea
	29 (5-under)	**Lou Graham**, Memphis

Low 18:

2004	60 (12-under)	**Robert Gamez**, Bob Hope Chrysler Classic
	60 (10-under)	**Bart Bryant**, Valero Texas Open
	61 (11-under)	**Robert Gamez**, B.C. Open; **Tag Ridings**, Michelin Championship at Las Vegas
	61 (10-under)	**Charles Howell III**, Booz Allen Classic
	61 (9-under)	**Chad Campbell**, Bank of America Colonial; **Ted Purdy**, **Joe Ogilvie**, Valero Texas Open
2003	61 (11-under)	**Pat Perez**, **Jay Haas**, **Tim Herron**, Bob Hope Chrysler Classic
	61 (10-under)	**Chad Campbell**, THE TOUR Championship
	61 (9-under)	**Kenny Perry**, **Justin Leonard**, Bank of America Colonial; **Heath Slocum**, **Bob Tway**, Valero Texas Open
2002	61 (10-under)	**J.P. Hayes**, John Deere Classic; **John Huston**, Buick Challenge
	61 (9-under)	**Garrett Willis**, Valero Texas Open
	62 (10-under)	**Kenny Perry**, Bob Hope Chrysler Classic (Palmer Private at PGA West); **Cliff Kresge**, B.C. Open; **Sergio Garcia**, **Retief Goosen**, WGC-American Express Championship; **Phil Tataurangi**, Invensys Classic at Las Vegas.
	62 (9-under)	**Davis Love III**, WORLDCOM CLASSIC; **Pat Bates**, John Deere Classic; **Robert Allenby**, Air Canada Championship; **Tim Herron**, Buick Challenge; **Steve Jones**, **Lee Janzen**, **Joel Edwards**, Invensys Classic at Las Vegas
2001	60 (11-under)	**Mark Calcavecchia**, Phoenix Open
	61 (11-under)	**Joe Durant**, **Robert Gamez**, Bob Hope Chrysler Classic; **Paul Stankowski**, Compaq Classic of New Orleans; **Billy Mayfair** Buick Open; **Chris DiMarco**, **Davis Love III**, Invensys Classic at Las Vegas.
2000	61 (11-under)	**Brent Geiberger**, Bob Hope Chrysler Classic; **Stephen Ames**, Doral-Ryder Open
	61 (9-under)	**Kirk Triplett**, Canon Greater Hartford Open; **Tiger Woods**, World Golf Championships–NEC Invitational
1999	59 (13-under)	**David Duval**, Bob Hope Chrysler Classic
1998	62 (10-under)	**Bruce Lietzke**, Bob Hope Chrysler Classic; **Davis Love III**, Buick Invitational; **David Duval**, Tucson Chrysler Classic
	62 (9-under)	**Loren Roberts**, **Nolan Henke**, Greater Milwaukee Open
	62 (8-under)	**Scott Gump**, **Vijay Singh**, Canon Greater Hartford Open; **John Cook**, NEC World Series of Golf
1997	60 (12-under)	**Steve Lowery**, Buick Challenge
1996	60 (11-under)	**Grant Waite**, Phoenix Open
	61 (11-under)	**John Huston**, Memorial Tournament; **Keith Clearwater**, Deposit Guaranty Golf Classic
1995	61 (10-under)	**Hal Sutton**, B.C. Open
	61 (9-under)	**Ernie Els**, GTE Byron Nelson Classic
	62 (10-under)	**Jim Furyk**, Buick Open; **Carl Paulson**, Walt Disney World/Oldsmobile Golf Classic
	62 (9-under)	**Kenny Perry**, Nissan Open
1994	60 (12-under)	**Davis Love III**, Hawaiian
1993	61 (10-under)	**Jay Delsing**, Federal Express
	61 (9-under)	**Billy Mayfair**, Byron Nelson; **Keith Clearwater**, **Lee Janzen**, Colonial
1992	62 (10-under)	**Davis Love III**, Kmart GGO; **Fred Funk**, Houston; **John Cook**, Las Vegas; **Lee Janzen**, **John Huston**, Walt Disney
	62 (8-under)	**David Frost**, Hardee's; **Nick Price**, Texas
1991	59 (13-under)	**Chip Beck**, Las Vegas
1990	60 (12-under)	**David Frost**, Tucson
1989	61 (11-under)	**Jim Carter**, Centel; **Bob Tway**, Walt Disney
1988	61 (11-under)	**Ken Green**, Milwaukee; **Mark Wiebe**, Tucson
	61 (9-under)	**Dave Barr**, Southern
1987	61 (11-under)	**David Edwards**, Bob Hope
	61 (9-under)	**Mike Smith**, Hardee's
1986	61 (10-under)	**Don Pooley**, Phoenix
	61 (9-under)	**Rod Curl**, Southern
	62 (10-under)	**George Burns**, Las Vegas; **Greg Norman**, Canadian
1985	62 (10-under)	**Jim Thorpe**, Milwaukee
	62 (9-under)	**Larry Mize**, Los Angeles; **Jay Delsing**, B.C. Open
	62 (8-under)	**Bill Glasson**, Las Vegas; **Ron Streck**, Quad Cities
1984	61 (11-under)	**Mark Lye**, Walt Disney
1983	61 (10-under)	**George Archer**, Los Angeles
	62 (10-under)	**John Fought**, Bob Hope; **Tom Kite**, Bing Crosby
	62 (9-under)	**Andy Bean**, Canadian; **Curtis Strange**, Hartford
	62 (8-under)	**Jon Chaffee**, Quad Cities; **Craig Stadler**, **Jim Colbert**, Texas
1982	61 (10-under)	**Dana Quigley**, Hartford
	61 (9-under)	**Hale Irwin**, Southern
	62 (10-under)	**Larry Rinker**, Tallahassee

1981	62 (10-under)	**Nick Faldo**, **Hale Irwin**, Hawaiian
	62 (9-under)	**Andy Bean**,Bay Hill; **Ron Streck**, Houston; **Leonard Thompson**, Canadian; **Mark O'Meara**, Hartford
1980	62 (9-under)	**Jim Simons**, Hartford
	62 (8-under)	**George Burns**, Texas
	63 (9-under)	**Andy Bean**, Hawaiian; **Bob Shearer**, Atlanta; **Bob Mann**, Pensacola
1979	61 (11-under)	**Jerry McGee**, Kemper; **Andy Bean**, Atlanta
	61 (10-under)	**Ben Crenshaw**, Phoenix
1978	62 (10-under)	**Dave Eichelberger**, Atlanta
	62 (9-under)	**Joe Inman**, Hartford
	62 (8-under)	**Hubert Green**, **Ron Streck**, San Antonio
1977	59 (13-under)	**Al Geiberger**, Memphis
1976	62 (10-under)	**Gary Player**, Florida Citrus
1975	61 (11-under)	**Johnny Miller**, Tucson
	61 (10-under)	**Johnny Miller**, Phoenix
1974	61 (11-under)	**Bert Yancey**, Bob Hope
1973	62 (9-under)	**Jack Nicklaus**, Ohio Kings Island; **Gibby Gilbert**, **Tom Watson**, World Open
	62 (8-under)	**J.C. Snead**, Phoenix
	63 (9-under)	**Dave Stockton**, Milwaukee; **Hubert Green**, Disney
	63 (8-under)	**Johnny Miller**, U.S. Open; **Hubert Green** (2), Hartford; **John Schroeder**, Quad Cities
	63 (7-under)	**Dick Rhyan**, Southern
1972	61 (10-under)	**Homero Blancas**, Phoenix
1971	62 (9-under)	**Billy Casper**, Phoenix; **Charles Coody**, Cleveland
	62 (8-under)	**Larry Ziegler**, **Dave Eichelberger**, Memphis; **Bobby Mitchell**, Southern
1970	61 (10-under)	**Johnny Miller**, Phoenix

Low First 18:

2004	61 (10-under)	**Charles Howell III**, Booz Allen Classic
	61 (9-under)	**Ted Purdy**, Valero Texas Open
	62 (10-under)	**J.L. Lewis**, FUNAI Classic at WALT DISNEY WORLD Resort
	62 (9-under)	**Jose Coceres**, John Deere Classic; **Jeff Sluman**, Chrysler Championship
	62 (8-under)	**Corey Pavin**, Buick Championship
2003	61 (9-under)	**Heath Slocum**, **Bob Tway**, Valero Texas Open
	62 (10-under)	**Steve Flesch**, **Stuart Appleby**, Las Vegas Invitational
	62 (9-under)	**Harrison Frazar**, Phoenix Open
	62 (8-under)	**Aaron Baddeley**, Valero Texas Open
2002	62 (9-under)	**Davis Love III**, WORLDCOM CLASSIC; **Steve Jones**, Invensys Classic at Las Vegas
	63 (10-under)	**Mike Weir**, Mercedes Championships
2001	61 (10-under)	**Bob Estes**, FedEx St. Jude Classic
	62 (10-under)	**Mike Weir**, Genuity Championship
2000	63 (9-under)	**David Toms**, Bob Hope Chrysler Classic; **Nick Price**, Advil Western Open; **Woody Austin**, Buick Open; **Jeff Maggert**, Buick Challenge; **Bruce Lietzke**, Invensys Classic at Las Vegas; **Steve Flesch**, **Tiger Woods**, National Car Rental Golf Classic; **Nick Price**, WGC–American Express Championship
	63 (8-under)	**Tom Lehman**, **Phil Mickelson**, Phoenix Open
	63 (7-under)	**Paul Azinger**, Sony Open in Hawaii
1999	61 (11-under)	**Craig Barlow**, Las Vegas Invitational
	61 (9-under)	**Tiger Woods**, GTE Byron Nelson Classic
	62 (9-under)	**Ben Bates**, Greater Milwaukee Open
1998	62 (10-under)	**Davis Love III**, Buick Invitational
	62 (9-under)	**Loren Roberts**, Greater Milwaukee Open
1997	62 (10-under)	**Steve Jones**, Phoenix Open; **Brian Claar**, **Mike Reid**, United Airlines Hawaiian Open; **Sonny Skinner**, Buick Open
1996	62 (10-under)	**Tim Herron**, Honda Classic
	62 (9-under)	**Nolan Henke**, Greater Milwaukee Open
1995	62 (10-under)	**Carl Paulson**, Walt Disney World/Oldsmobile Golf Classic
	62 (9-under)	**Glen Day**, **Mike Standly**, FedEx St. Jude Classic
1994	61 (10-under)	**Bob Lohr**, Anheuser-Busch
1993	62 (9-under)	**Mike Smith**, Texas
	63 (9-under)	**Howard Twitty**, Hawaiian; **Billy Andrade**, Northern Telecom
	63 (8-under)	**Jim Gallagher, Jr.**, TOUR Championship
	63 (7-under)	**Jeff Woodland**, Hardee's
1992	62 (10-under)	**Lee Janzen**, Walt Disney
	62 (8-under)	**David Frost**, Hardee's
1991	61 (11-under)	**Robert Gamez**, Milwaukee
	61 (9-under)	**Marco Dawson**, Chattanooga
1990	61 (9-under)	**Jose Maria Olazabal**, World Series
	62 (10-under)	**Pat McGowan**, Tucson
	62 (9-under)	**Larry Silveira**, Federal Express
	62 (8-under)	**Howard Twitty**, Southern
1989	61 (11-under)	**Bob Tway**, Walt Disney
1988	62 (10-under)	**Bob Lohr**, Walt Disney
1987	61 (11-under)	**David Edwards**, Bob Hope
1986	62 (8-under)	**Ernie Gonzalez**, Deposit Guaranty
	63 (9-under)	**George Burns**, Hawaiian
	63 (8-under)	**Hubert Green**, Phoenix
	63 (7-under)	**Bob Lohr**, Hardee's
1985	62 (8-under)	**Bill Glasson**, Las Vegas
	63 (9-under)	**Fred Couples**, Honda; **John Mahaffey**, USF&G
	63 (8-under)	**Lanny Wadkins**, Los Angeles; **Mac O'Grady**, Byron Nelson; **John Cook**, Pensacola
1984	62 (9-under)	**Lon Hinkle**, Las Vegas
1983	62 (8-under)	**Craig Stadler**, Texas
	63 (9-under)	**Craig Stadler**, Bob Hope, **Fuzzy Zoeller**, Las Vegas
	63 (8-under)	**Mark O'Meara**, B.C. Open, **Mark Lye**, Pensacola
	63 (7-under)	**Tom Byrum**, Quad Cities
1982	62 (10-under)	**Larry Rinker**, Tallahassee
1981	63 (8-under)	**Lon Nielsen**, Hartford
	63 (7-under)	**Dan Halldorson**, Tucson; **Craig Stadler**, Texas
	64 (8-under)	**Skip Dunaway**, USF&G
	64 (7-under)	**Tom Watson**, Bay Hill; **Calvin Peete**, B.C. Open
1980	62 (9-under)	**Jim Simons**, Hartford
	63 (9-under)	**Bob Shearer**, Atlanta
	63 (7-under)	**Bruce Lietzke**, Colonial; **Jack Nicklaus**, **Tom Weiskopf**, U.S. Open; **Scott Hoch**, Quad Cities
1979	61 (11-under)	**Jerry McGee**, Greensboro
1978	62 (10-under)	**Dave Eichelberger**, Atlanta
	62 (8-under)	**Hubert Green**, Texas
1977	63 (8-under)	**J.C. Snead**, Hall of Fame
	63 (7-under)	**Charles Coody**, Texas
	64 (8-under)	**Rik Massengale**, Bob Hope; **George Burns**, Buick
	64 (7-under)	**Fred Marti**, Pleasant Valley; **Lee Elder**, Hartford
	64 (6-under)	**Jerry Pate**, Southern
1976	63 (9-under)	**Johnny Miller**, Kaiser International
	63 (8-under)	**Fuzzy Zoeller**, Quad Cities; **David Graham**, **Carlton White**, Westchester; **Buddy Allin**, B.C. Open
	64 (8-under)	**Rod Curl**, Hawaiian; **Ken Still**, Milwaukee
1975	63 (8-under)	**Andy North**, B.C. Open; **Miller Barber**, Sahara
	64 (8-under)	**Johnny Miller**, Bob Hope; Bob Stanton, Inverrary
	64 (7-under)	**Tom Weiskopf**, Greensboro; **Andy North**, Pensacola; **Dennis Meyer**, Hartford
1974	62 (10-under)	**Johnny Miller**, Tucson
1973	62 (9-under)	**Gibby Gilbert**, World Open
	62 (8-under)	**J.C. Snead**, Phoenix
	63 (8-under)	**Hubert Green**, Hartford
	64 (8-under)	**Jack Nicklaus**, Bob Hope; **Gibby Gilbert**, **Chi Chi Rodriguez**, Florida Citrus; **Lee Trevino**, Doral-Eastern; **Tom Weiskopf**, Westchester
1972	63 (8-under)	**Bert Yancey**, Hartford
	64 (8-under)	**DeWitt Weaver**, Westchester
	64 (7-under)	**Dave Hill**, Monsanto
	64 (6-under)	**Deane Beman**, St. Louis
1971	63 (9-under)	**Joel Goldstrand**, Hartford
1970	63 (7-under)	**Dave Hill**, Memphis
	64 (8-under)	**Arnold Palmer**, Florida Citrus; **Bob Menne**, National Airlines
	64 (7-under)	**Bert Greene**, Phoenix; **Arnold Palmer**, **Tommy Aaron**, Greensboro; **Tommy Aaron**, Sahara

Low First 36:

2004	128 (14-under)	**Adam Scott**, Booz Allen Classic;
	129 (15-under)	**Danny Ellis**, HP Classic of New Orleans;
	129 (11-under)	**Steve Allan**, Sony Open in Hawaii;
		Dean Wilson, Valero Texas Open
2003	126 (17-under)	**Steve Flesch**, **Scott Verplank**, Las Vegas Invitational;
	126 (14-under)	**Tommy Armour III**, Valero Texas Open
2002	127 (17-under)	**Chris DiMarco**, Walt Disney World Resort Golf Classic
2001	125 (17-under)	**Mark Calcavecchia**, Phoenix Open
	125 (19-under)	**Tom Lehman**, Invensys Classic at Las Vegas
2000	125 (15-under)	**Tiger Woods**, WGC–NEC Invitational
	127 (15-under)	**David Frost**, John Deere Classic
	128 (16-under)	**Steve Flesch**, National Car Rental Golf Classic
1999	126 (16-under)	**David Frost**, FedEx St. Jude Classic
1998	128 (16-under)	**John Huston**, United Airlines Hawaiian Open;
		David Duval, Tucson Chrysler Classic
1997	126 (16-under)	**Steve Jones**, Phoenix Open
1996	126 (16-under)	**John Cook**, FedEx St. Jude Classic
	126 (17-under)	**Rick Fehr**, Las Vegas Invitational
1995	127 (15-under)	**Jim Gallagher, Jr.**, FedEx St. Jude Classic
1994	127 (15-under)	**Bob Estes**, Texas
	128 (16-under)	**Davis Love III**, Hawaiian; **Scott Hoch**, Bob Hope
1993	129 (15-under)	**Blaine McCallister**, Houston
	129 (11-under)	**Dan Forsman**, Byron Nelson; **Fulton Allem**, Colonial
1992	128 (14-under)	**Roger Maltbie**, Texas
	130 (10-under)	**David Frost**, Hardee's
	130 (12-under)	**Davis Love III**, Los Angeles; **Dan Forsman**, Federal Express
	131 (13-under)	**Tom Watson**, **Brad Faxon**, **Mike Springer**, Buick Invitational
1991	127 (17-under)	**Robert Gamez**, Milwaukee
	127 (13-under)	**Lennie Clements**, Chattanooga
1990	128 (16-under)	**Tim Simpson**, Walt Disney
	128 (12-under)	**Jose Maria Olazabal**, World Series;
		Peter Persons, Chattanooga; **Steve Jones**, Texas
1989	126 (14-under)	**Paul Azinger**, Texas
	128 (16-under)	**Dan Pohl**, Honda
1988	127 (13-under)	**Corey Pavin**, Texas
	129 (15-under)	**Jeff Sluman**, Greensboro; **Larry Nelson**, Atlanta;
		Bob Lohr, Disney
1987	128 (16-under)	**Robert Wrenn**, Buick
	128 (14-under)	**Joey Sindelar**, B.C. Open
1986	128 (12-under)	**Hal Sutton**, Phoenix; **Ernie Gonzalez**, Pensacola
1985	128 (12-under)	**Tim Simpson**, Southern
1984	130 (14-under)	**Chip Beck**, Walt Disney
	130 (11-under)	**Lon Hinkle**, Las Vegas
	130 (10-under)	**Jim Colbert**, Texas
1983	128 (12-under)	**Jim Colbert**, Texas
	129 (15-under)	**Craig Stadler**, Bob Hope
1982	127 (15-under)	**Tim Norris**, Hartford
	127 (13-under)	**Bob Gilder**, Westchester
1981	129 (13-under)	**Lon Nielsen**, Hartford
1980	129 (13-under)	**Curtis Strange**, Houston
	129 (11-under)	**Scott Hoch**, Quad Cities
	131 (13-under)	**Tom Watson**, T of C
	131 (9-under)	**Mike Sullivan**, Southern
1979	128 (14-under)	**Ben Crenshaw**, Phoenix
1978	128 (14-under)	**Phil Hancock**, Hartford
	128 (12-under)	**Ben Crenshaw**, Texas
1977	127 (15-under)	**Hale Irwin**, Hall of Fame
1976	130 (12-under)	**Roger Maltbie**, Phoenix; **Buddy Allin**, B.C. Open;
		Rik Massengale, Hartford
	131 (13-under)	**Raymond Floyd**, Masters
	132 (12-under)	**Fuzzy Zoeller**, Milwaukee
1975	128 (14-under)	**Johnny Miller**, Phoenix
	129 (15-under)	**Tom Weiskopf**, Westchester
	129 (13-under)	**Jack Nicklaus**, Heritage
1974	130 (12-under)	**Dave Stockton**, Hartford
	132 (12-under)	**Jack Nicklaus**, Hawaiian; **Hubert Green**, Memphis
1973	129 (11-under)	**J.C. Snead**, Phoenix
	131 (13-under)	**Buddy Allin**, Florida Citrus
	131 (11-under)	**Jim Wiechers**, Hartford
	133 (11-under)	**John Schlee**, Kaiser International
1972	131 (13-under)	**Dwight Nevil**, Westchester
	131 (9-under)	**Deane Beman**, St. Louis
1971	129 (13-under)	**Miller Barber**, **Paul Harney**, **Gene Littler**, Phoenix
1970	130 (12-under)	**Bobby Mitchell**, Azalea

Low First 54:

2004	194 (16-under)	**Bart Bryant**, Valero Texas Open
	195 (21-under)	**Phil Mickelson**, Bob Hope Chrysler Classic
	195 (18-under)	**David Toms**, FedEx St. Jude Classic;
		Adam Scott, Booz Allen Classic
2003	189 (21-under)	**Tommy Armour III**, Valero Texas Open
	192 (23-under)	**Steve Flesch**, **Scott Verplank**, Las Vegas Invitational
2002	193 (20-under)	**Jeff Sluman**, Greater Milwaukee Open
	195 (20-under)	**Jim Furyk**, Invensys Classic at Las Vegas
2001	189 (24-under)	**Mark Calcavecchia**, Phoenix Open
2000	192 (18-under)	**Tiger Woods**, WGC–NEC Invitational
	194 (19-under)	**Loren Roberts**, Greater Milwaukee Open
	194 (22-under)	**Steve Flesch**, National Car Rental Golf Classic
1999	193 (17-under)	**Brian Henninger**, John Deere Classic
1998	194 (22-under)	**John Huston**, United Airlines Hawaiian Open
1997	191 (22-under)	**Steve Jones**, Phoenix Open
1996	189 (24-under)	**John Cook**, FedEx St. Jude Classic
1995	195 (18-under)	**Jim Gallagher, Jr.**, FedEx St. Jude Classic
	195 (18-under)	**Fred Funk**, Ideon Classic
	195 (15-under)	**Ernie Els**, GTE Byron Nelson Classic
	196 (20-under)	**Harry Taylor**, Bob Hope Chrysler Classic
1994	195 (18-under)	**Bob Estes**, Texas
	197 (19-under)	**Lennie Clements**, Bob Hope; **Greg Norman**, PLAYERS
1993	195 (21-under)	**Greg Norman**, Doral-Ryder
	195 (15-under)	**David Frost**, Hardee's
1992	194 (16-under)	**David Frost**, Hardee's
	196 (20-under)	**Ted Schulz**, **Mark O'Meara**, Walt Disney
	197 (16-under)	**Nick Price**, Texas
1989	194 (16-under)	**John Daly**, Chattanooga; **Donnie Hammond**, Texas
1991	195 (18-under)	**Hal Sutton**, Kemper
	195 (15-under)	**Lance Ten Broeck**, Chattanooga
	196 (20-under)	**Chip Beck**, **Bruce Lietzke**, Las Vegas
1990	193 (23-under)	**Tim Simpson**, Walt Disney
	193 (17-under)	**Peter Persons**, Chattanooga
	197 (19-under)	**Gene Sauers**, Hawaiian
1988	193 (17-under)	**Blaine McCallister**, Hardee's; **Corey Pavin**, Texas
1987	195 (21-under)	**Robert Wrenn**, Buick
1986	196 (17-under)	**Hal Sutton**, Phoenix
	196 (14-under)	**Ben Crenshaw**, Vantage
	199 (17-under)	**Calvin Peete**, T of C
1985	197 (13-under)	**Jodie Mudd**, Texas; **Tim Simpson**, Southern
	198 (18-under)	**Craig Stadler**, Bob Hope; **Mark O'Meara**, Hawaiian;
		Woody Blackburn, San Diego
1984	196 (20-under)	**Larry Nelson**, Walt Disney
1983	194 (16-under)	**Jim Colbert**, Texas
	198 (15-under)	**Jack Renner**, Hartford
	199 (17-under)	**Craig Stadler**, Bob Hope
1982	192 (18-under)	**Bob Gilder**, Westchester
	193 (20-under)	**Tim Norris**, Hartford
1981	196 (20-under)	**Bruce Lietzke**, Bob Hope; **Hale Irwin**, Hawaiian
1980	195 (18-under)	**Curtis Strange**, Houston
	200 (19-under)	**Jim Colbert**, Tucson
1979	197 (16-under)	**Wayne Levi**, Houston
	197 (13-under)	**Doug Tewell**, Texas
	198 (18-under)	**Hubert Green**, Hawaiian; **Andy Bean**, Atlanta
1978	198 (18-under)	**Andy Bean**, Houston
	198 (12-under)	**Ben Crenshaw**, Texas
1977	196 (17-under)	**Bill Kratzert**, Hartford; **Hale Irwin**, Hall of Fame
1976	200 (16-under)	**J.C. Snead**, San Diego
	200 (13-under)	**Roger Maltbie**, Phoenix; **Al Geiberger**, Greensboro;
		Rik Massengale, **J.C. Snead**, Hartford
	200 (10-under)	**Lee Trevino**, Colonial
1975	196 (17-under)	**Johnny Miller**, Phoenix
1974	198 (18-under)	**Terry Diehl**, Texas
1973	198 (18-under)	**Buddy Allin**, Florida Citrus
1972	198 (12-under)	**Deane Beman**, St. Louis
	201 (15-under)	**George Knudson**, Kaiser International
1971	194 (19-under)	**Paul Harney**, Phoenix
1970	198 (15-under)	**Bob Murphy**, Hartford; Bobby Mitchell, Azalea
	198 (12-under)	**Homero Blancas**, Memphis

Low First 72:

2004	261 (19-under)	**Bart Bryant**, Valero Texas Open
	262 (26-under)	**Phil Mickelson**; **Kirk Triplett**, Bob Hope Chrysler Classic
	262 (18-under)	**Ernie Els**; **Harrison Frazar**, Sony Open in Hawaii
2003	254 (26-under)	**Tommy Armour III**, Valero Texas Open (PGA TOUR Record)
	259 (29-under)	**Tim Herron**, Bob Hope Chrysler Classic
2002	261 (27-under)	**Jonathan Byrd**, Buick Challenge
	261 (23-under)	**Jeff Sluman**, Greater Milwaukee Open
	261 (19-under)	**Loren Roberts**, Valero Texas Open
2001	254 (29-under)	**Joe Durant**, Bob Hope Chrysler Classic
	256 (28-under)	**Mark Calcavecchia**, Phoenix Open
2000	259 (21-under)	**Tiger Woods**, World Golf Championships–NEC Invitational
	260 (24-under)	**Loren Roberts**, Greater Milwaukee Open
	262 (26-under)	**Duffy Waldorf**, National Car Rental Golf Classic
	264 (23-under)	**Rory Sabbatini**, Bob Hope Chrysler Classic
1999	261 (19-under)	**J.L. Lewis**, John Deere Classic
	261 (19-under)	**Mike Brisky**, John Deere Classic
1998	260 (28-under)	**John Huston**, United Airlines Hawaiian Open
1997	258 (26-under)	**Steve Jones**, Phoenix Open
	261 (27-under)	**Mark Calcavecchia**, Bob Hope Chrysler Classic
1996	258 (26-under)	**John Cook**, FedEx St. Jude Classic
1995	263 (17-under)	**Ernie Els**, GTE Byron Nelson Classic
	268 (20-under)	**Duffy Waldorf**, LaCantera Texas Open
	264 (23-under)	**Billy Mayfair**, **Jim Furyk**, Las Vegas Invitational
	265 (23-under)	**Kenny Perry**, Bob Hope
1994	264 (24-under)	**Scott Hoch**, Bob Hope; **Greg Norman**, PLAYERS
1993	259 (21-under)	**David Frost**, Hardee's
	263 (25-under)	**Tom Kite**, Bob Hope
1992	262 (26-under)	**John Huston**, Walt Disney
1991	260 (20-under)	**Dillard Pruitt**, Chattanooga
	263 (21-under)	**Billy Andrade**, **Jeff Sluman**, Kemper
	263 (25-under)	**Bruce Lietzke**, **Craig Stadler**, **D.A. Weibring**, **Andrew Magee**, Las Vegas
1990	260 (20-under)	**Peter Persons**, Chattanooga
	264 (24-under)	**Bob Tway**, Las Vegas; **Tim Simpson**, Walt Disney
1989	258 (22-under)	**Donnie Hammond**, Texas
	266 (22-under)	**Blaine McCallister**, Honda; **Scott Hoch**, Las Vegas
1988	259 (21-under)	**Corey Pavin**, Texas
	262 (26-under)	**Chip Beck**, USF&G
1987	262 (26-under)	**Robert Wrenn**, Buick
1986	267 (21-under)	**Calvin Peete**, T of C
	267 (17-under)	**Hal Sutton**, Phoenix; **Rick Fehr**, B.C. Open
1985	264 (20-under)	**Lanny Wadkins**, Los Angeles
	264 (16-under)	**Tim Simpson**, Southern
	267 (21-under)	**Mark O'Meara**, Hawaiian; **Lanny Wadkins**, Disney World
1984	265 (15-under)	**Hubert Green**, Southern
	266 (22-under)	**Larry Nelson**, Disney World
1983	261 (19-under)	**Jim Colbert**, Texas
	266 (18-under)	**Mark McCumber**, Pensacola
	267 (20-under)	**Fuzzy Zoeller**, Las Vegas
	268 (20-under)	**Isao Aoki**, Hawaiian
1982	259 (25-under)	**Tim Norris**, Hartford
1981	264 (20-under)	**Hubert Green**, Hartford
	265 (23-under)	**Hale Irwin**, Hawaiian
	265 (15-under)	**Johnny Miller**, Tucson
1980	265 (15-under)	**Lee Trevino**, Texas
	266 (22-under)	**Andy Bean**, Hawaiian; **Bill Kratzert**, Milwaukee
	270 (22-under)	**Jim Colbert**, Tucson
	266 (18-under)	**Curtis Strange**, **Lee Trevino**, Houston; **Howard Twitty**, **Jim Simons**, Hartford
1979	265 (23-under)	**Andy Bean**, Atlanta
1978	264 (24-under)	**Rod Funseth**, Hartford
1977	264 (20-under)	**Hale Irwin**, Hall of Fame
1976	266 (18-under)	**Rik Massengale**, Hartford
	268 (16-under)	**Bob Gilder**, Phoenix; **Al Geiberger**, Greensboro; **John Lister**, Quad Cities
	269 (19-under)	**Jack Nicklaus**, TPC
1975	260 (24-under)	**Johnny Miller**, Phoenix
	263 (25-under)	**Johnny Miller**, Tucson
1974	267 (21-under)	**Lee Trevino**, New Orleans
1973	264 (20-under)	**Billy Casper**, Hartford
	265 (23-under)	**Buddy Allin**, Florida Citrus
1972	267 (21-under)	**Jack Nicklaus**, Walt Disney
1971	261 (23-under)	**Miller Barber**, Phoenix
1970	267 (17-under)	**Bob Murphy**, Hartford
	267 (13-under)	**Dave Hill**, Memphis

Low 90:

2004	330 (30-under)	**Phil Mickelson**, **Skip Kendall**, Bob Hope Chrysler Classic
	331 (29-under)	**Jay Haas**, Bob Hope Chrysler Classic
2003	328 (31-under)	**Stuart Appleby**, **Scott McCarron**, Las Vegas Invitational
	330 (30-under)	**Mike Weir**, Bob Hope Chrysler Classic
2002	330 (30-under)	**Phil Mickelson**, **David Berganio, Jr.**, Bob Hope Chrysler Classic
2001	324 (36-under)	**Joe Durant**, Bob Hope Chrysler Classic
2000	331 (27-under)	**Jesper Parnevik**, Bob Hope Chrysler Classic
	332 (28-under)	**Billy Andrade**, Invensys Classic at Las Vegas
1999	331 (29-under)	**Jim Furyk**, Las Vegas Invitational
1998	332 (28-under)	**Fred Couples**, **Bruce Lietzke**, Bob Hope Chrysler Classic
1997	327 (33-under)	**John Cook**, Bob Hope Chrysler Classic
1996	332 (27-under)	**Tiger Woods**, Las Vegas Invitational
1995	331 (28-under)	**Jim Furyk**, Las Vegas
1994	332 (27-under)	**Bruce Lietzke**, Las Vegas
1993	325 (35-under)	**Tom Kite**, Bob Hope
1992	336 (24-under)	**John Cook**, **Gene Sauers**, **Rick Fehr**, **Mark O'Meara**, **Tom Kite**, Bob Hope
1991	329 (31-under)	**Andrew Magee**, **D.A. Weibring**, Las Vegas
1990	334 (26-under)	**Bob Tway**, Las Vegas
1989	336 (24-under)	**Scott Hoch**, Robert Wrenn, Las Vegas
1988	338 (22-under)	**Jay Haas**, Bob Hope
1987	341 (19-under)	**Corey Pavin**, Bob Hope
1986	333 (27-under)	**Greg Norman**, Las Vegas
1985	333 (27-under)	**Lanny Wadkins**, Bob Hope
1984	340 (20-under)	**John Mahaffey**, **Jim Simons**, Bob Hope
1983	335 (25-under)	**Keith Fergus**, **Rex Caldwell**, Bob Hope
1982	335 (25-under)	**Ed Fiori**, Bob Hope
1981	335 (25-under)	**Bruce Lietzke**, Bob Hope
1980	343 (17-under)	**Craig Stadler**, Bob Hope
1979	343 (17-under)	**John Mahaffey**, Bob Hope
1978	339 (21-under)	**Bill Rogers**, Bob Hope
1977	337 (23-under)	**Rik Massengale**, Bob Hope
1976	344 (16-under)	**Johnny Miller**, Bob Hope
1975	339 (21-under)	**Johnny Miller**, Bob Hope
1974	341 (19-under)	**Hubert Green**, Bob Hope
1973	343 (17-under)	**Arnold Palmer**, Bob Hope
1972	344 (16-under)	**Bob Rosburg**, Bob Hope
1971	342 (18-under)	**Arnold Palmer**, Bob Hope
1970	339 (21-under)	**Bruce Devlin**, Bob Hope

Highest Winning Score:

2004	280 (8-under)	**Vijay Singh**, PGA Championship
	279 (9-under)	**Phil Mickelson**, Masters Tournament
	278 (10-under)	**Vaughn Taylor**, Reno-Tahoe Open; **John Daly**, Buick Invitational
	277 (11-under)	**Joey Sindelar**, Wachovia Championship
2003	283 (1-under)	**Ben Curtis**, British Open
	281 (7-under)	**Mike Weir**, Masters Tournament
2002	280 (8-under)	**Craig Perks**, THE PLAYERS Championship
	278 (10-under)	**Rich Beem**, PGA Championship
2001	280 (8-under)	**Scott McCarron**, BellSouth Classic
	276 (4-under)	**Retief Goosen**, U.S. Open
2000	276 (8-under)	**David Duval**, Dennis Paulson, Buick Classic
	278 (10-under)	**Hal Sutton**, THE PLAYERS Championship
1999	290 (6-over)	**Paul Lawrie**, British Open
1998	280 (even-par)	**Lee Janzen**, U.S. Open
1997	276 (4-under)	**Ernie Els**, U.S. Open
	276 (12-under)	**Phil Blackmar**, Shell Houston Open
1996	280 (8-under)	**Paul Stankowski**, BellSouth Classic
	278 (2-under)	**Steve Jones**, U.S. Open
1995	280 (even-par)	**Corey Pavin**, U.S. Open, **Billy Mayfair**, TOUR Championship
	283 (5-under)	**Lee Janzen**, THE PLAYERS
1994	281 (7-under)	**Johnny Miller**, AT&T
	279 (5-under)	**Ernie Els**, U.S. Open
1993	281 (7-under)	**Mike Standly**, Freeport-McMoRan; **Rocco Mediate**, Kmart GGO
	280 (4-under)	**Vijay Singh**, Buick Classic

1992	285 (3-under)	**Tom Kite**, U.S. Open
1991	282 (6-under)	**Payne Stewart**, U.S. Open
	279 (1-under)	**Tom Purtzer**, World Series
	279 (5-under)	**Craig Stadler**, TOUR Championship
	279 (9-under)	**Steve Pate**, Honda
1990	282 (6-under)	**John Huston**, Honda; **Steve Elkington**, Kmart GGO; **Wayne Grady**, PGA
1989	283 (5-under)	**Nick Faldo**, Masters
	278 (2-under)	**Curtis Strange**, U.S. Open
1988	281 (7-under)	**Sandy Lyle**, Masters
1987	287 (1-under)	**Larry Nelson**, PGA
1986	287 (1-under)	**Kenny Knox**, Honda
	279 (1-under)	**Raymond Floyd**, U.S. Open
1985	285 (3-under)	**Joey Sindelar**, Greensboro
	279 (1-under)	**Andy North**, U.S. Open
1984	276 (4-under)	**Fuzzy Zoeller**, U.S. Open
	280 (8-under)	**Bruce Lietzke**, Honda; **Jack Nicklaus**, Memorial; **Greg Norman**, Kemper; **Tom Watson**, Western
1983	287 (1-under)	**Fred Couples**, Kemper
1982	278 (2-under)	**Craig Stadler**, World Series
	285 (3-under)	**Danny Edwards**, Greensboro
1981	281 (1-over)	**Bruce Lietzke**, Byron Nelson
1980	280 (4-under)	**Doug Tewell**, Heritage
1979	284 (even-par)	**Hale Irwin**, U.S. Open
1978	289 (1-over)	**Jack Nicklaus**, TPC
1977	289 (1-over)	**Mark Hayes**, TPC
1976	288 (4-over)	**Al Geiberger**, Western
	288 (even-par)	**Roger Maltbie**, Memorial
	281 (1-over)	**Dave Stockton**, PGA
1975	287 (3-over)	**Lou Graham**, U.S. Open
1974	287 (7-over)	**Hale Irwin**, U.S. Open
	287 (3-over)	**Tom Watson**, Western
1973	283 (5-under)	**Tommy Aaron**, Masters; **Dave Hill**, Memphis
	277 (3-under)	**Lanny Wadkins**, Byron Nelson
1972	290 (2-over)	**Jack Nicklaus**, U.S. Open
1971	283 (3-over)	**Gene Littler**, Colonial
1970	282 (2-over)	**Gibby Gilbert**, Houston

Largest Winning Margin:

2004	6 strokes	**Chad Campbell**, Bay Hill Invitational
	5 strokes	**Vijay Singh**, Chrysler Championship
2003	11 strokes	**Tiger Woods**, Bay Hill Invitational
	8 strokes	**Ernie Els**, Mercedes Championships
2002	7 strokes	**K.J. Choi**, Tampa Bay Classic
2001	8 strokes	**Mark Calcavecchia**, Phoenix Open
2000	15 strokes	**Tiger Woods**, U.S. Open
1999	9 strokes	**David Duval**, Mercedes Championships
1998	7 strokes	**John Huston**, United Airlines Hawaiian Open; **Davis Love III**, MCI Classic
1997	12 strokes	**Tiger Woods**, Masters Tournament
1996	8 strokes	**Ernie Els**, Buick Classic; **Steve Stricker**, Motorola Western Open
1995	6 strokes	**Duffy Waldorf**, LaCantera Texas Open
1994	6 strokes	**Nick Price**, PGA
1993	8 strokes	**Davis Love III**, Las Vegas
1992	9 strokes	**Fred Couples**, Nestle
1991	4 strokes	**Lanny Wadkins**, Hawaiian; **Paul Azinger**, Pebble Beach
1990	12 strokes	**Jose Maria Olazabal**, World Series
1989	7 strokes	**Mark Calcavecchia**, Phoenix; **Donnie Hammond**, Texas
1988	8 strokes	**Corey Pavin**, Texas
1987	7 strokes	**Tom Kite**, Kemper; **Robert Wrenn**, Buick; **Ken Brown**, Southern
1986	7 strokes	**Doug Tewell**, Los Angeles; **Greg Norman**, Las Vegas
1985	7 strokes	**Lanny Wadkins**, Los Angeles
1984	6 strokes	**George Archer**, Bank of Boston; **Hubert Green**, Southern
1983	5 strokes	**Gary Koch**, Doral; **Lanny Wadkins**, Greensboro; **David Graham**, Houston; **Jim Colbert**, Texas
1982	7 strokes	**Craig Stadler**, Kemper; **Calvin Peete**, B.C. Open; **Calvin Peete**, Pensacola
1981	7 strokes	**Andy Bean**, Bay Hill
1980	7 strokes	**Larry Nelson**, Atlanta; **Jack Nicklaus**, PGA
1979	8 strokes	**Andy Bean**, Atlanta
1978	5 strokes	**Andy Bean**, Kemper; **Tom Kite**, B.C. Open
1977	7 strokes	**Jerry Pate**, Southern; **Rik Massengale**, Bob Hope
1976	8 strokes	**Raymond Floyd**, Masters
1975	14 strokes	**Johnny Miller**, Phoenix
1974	8 strokes	**Lee Trevino**, New Orleans; **Johnny Miller**, Kaiser International
1973	8 strokes	**Buddy Allin**, Florida Citrus
1972	9 strokes	**Jack Nicklaus**, Walt Disney
1971	8 strokes	**Jack Nicklaus**, T of C
1970	7 strokes	**Frank Beard**, T of C; **Tony Jacklin**, U.S. Open

Low Start By A Winner:

2004	63 (9-under)	**Vijay Singh**, Buick Open
	63 (7-under)	**Stewart Cink**, WGC-NEC Invitational
	64 (8-under)	**Vijay Singh**, 84 LUMBER Classic
2003	62 (10-under)	**Stuart Appleby**, Las Vegas Invitational
2002	63 (8-under)	**K.J. Choi**, Tampa Bay Classic
2001	61 (10-under)	**Bob Estes**, FedEx St. Jude Classic
2000	63 (8-under)	**Tom Lehman**, Phoenix Open
	63 (7-under)	**Paul Azinger**, Sony Open in Hawaii
1999	65 (7-under)	**Jesper Parnevik**, Greater Greensboro Chrysler Classic
	65 (6-under)	**Carlos Franco**, Greater Milwaukee Open
1998	63 (9-under)	**John Huston**, United Airlines Hawaiian Open
1997	62 (10-under)	**Steve Jones**, Phoenix Open
1996	62 (10-under)	**Tim Herron**, Honda Classic
1995	63 (9-under)	**Kenny Perry**, Bob Hope; **Woody Austin**, Buick Open
1994	62 (9-under)	**Bob Estes**, Texas
1993	63 (9-under)	**Howard Twitty**, Hawaiian
	63 (8-under)	**Jim Gallagher, Jr.**, TOUR Championship
1992	62 (8-under)	**David Frost**, Hardee's
1991	63 (9-under)	**Mark Brooks**, Milwaukee
1990	61 (9-under)	**Jose Maria Olazabal**, World Series
1989	64 (8-under)	**Greg Norman**, Milwaukee
1988	62 (10-under)	**Bob Lohr**, Walt Disney
1987	64 (8-under)	**Mike Reid**, Tucson
1986	64 (7-under)	**Hal Sutton**, Phoenix
1985	63 (8-under)	**Lanny Wadkins**, Los Angeles
	64 (8-under)	**Tom Kite**, T of C
1984	64 (6-under)	**Peter Jacobsen**, Colonial
1983	63 (9-under)	**Fuzzy Zoeller**, Las Vegas
1982	63 (8-under)	**Tim Norris**, Hartford
	63 (7-under)	**Jay Haas**, Texas
1981	65 (7-under)	**Bruce Lietzke**, Bob Hope; **Hale Irwin**, Buick
	65 (6-under)	**David Graham**, Phoenix; **Morris Hatalsky**, Hall of Fame
1980	63 (7-under)	**Bruce Lietzke**, Colonial; **Jack Nicklaus**, U.S. Open; **Scott Hoch**, Quad Cities
	65 (7-under)	**Tom Watson**, T of C
	66 (7-under)	**Jim Colbert**, Tucson
1979	61 (11-under)	**Jerry McGee**, Kemper
1978	63 (9-under)	**Tom Watson**, Tucson
1977	64 (8-under)	**Rik Massengale**, Bob Hope
	64 (6-under)	**Jerry Pate**, Southern
	65 (6-under)	**Graham Marsh**, Heritage; **Hale Irwin**, Hall of Fame
	66 (6-under)	**Tom Watson**, Bing Crosby, San Diego
1976	63 (8-under)	**David Graham**, Westchester
1975	64 (8-under)	**Johnny Miller**, Bob Hope
1974	62 (10-under)	**Johnny Miller**, Tucson
1973	64 (8-under)	**Lee Trevino**, Doral-Eastern
1972	64 (7-under)	**Dave Hill**, Monsanto
	65 (7-under)	**Grier Jones**, Hawaiian
1971	64 (8-under)	**Arnold Palmer**, Westchester
	64 (7-under)	**Dave Eichelberger**, Milwaukee
1970	63 (7-under)	**Dave Hill**, Memphis

High Start By A Winner:

2004	74 (2-over)	**Vijay Singh**, Shell Houston Open
	72 (1-over)	**Stewart Cink**, MCI Heritage
	72 (even)	**Phil Mickelson**, Masters Tournament
2003	73 (1-over)	**Ben Crane**, BellSouth Classic
	72 (1-over)	**Mike Weir**, Nissan Open
2002	73 (even)	**Sergio Garcia**, Mercedes Championships
	73 (2-over)	**Dan Forsman**, SEI Pennsylvania Classic
2001	73 (2-over)	**Robert Allenby**, Nissan Open; **Mike Weir**, THE TOUR Championship

2000	72 (even)	**Vijay Singh**, Masters Tournament; **Tiger Woods**, Bell Canadian Open
	71 (even)	**Stewart Cink**, MCI Classic
	71 (1-under)	**Tiger Woods**, Memorial Tournament
1999	73 (2-over)	**Paul Lawrie**, British Open
1998	74 (2-over)	**Mark O'Meara**, Masters Tournament
	73 (3-over)	**Lee Janzen**, U.S. Open
1997	75 (3-over)	**Jeff Sluman**, Tucson Chrysler Classic
1996	75 (3-over)	**Mark O'Meara**, Greater Greensboro Chrysler Classic
	74 (4-over)	**Steve Jones**, U.S. Open
1995	73 (3-over)	**Greg Norman**, NEC World Series of Golf
	73 (1-over)	**Payne Stewart**, Shell Houston Open; **Billy Mayfair**, Motorola Western
1994	74 (2-over)	**Jose Maria Olazabal**, Masters
1993	75 (3-over)	**Phil Mickelson**, Buick Invitational
1992	73 (1-over)	**Greg Norman**, Canadian
1991	73 (1-over)	**Ian Woosnam**, USF&G
	72 (2-over)	**Tom Purtzer**, World Series
1990	72 (even-par)	**David Ishii**, Hawaiian
1989	76 (4-over)	**Steve Jones**, Bob Hope; **Mike Sullivan**, IIAO
1988	73 (1-over)	**Curtis Strange**, Memorial
1987	75 (3-over)	**Lanny Wadkins**, Doral
1986	75 (5-over)	**Raymond Floyd**, U.S. Open
1985	72 (even-par)	**Bernhard Langer**, Masters; **Bill Glasson**, Kemper
1984	73 (1-over)	**Greg Norman**, Canadian
	71 (1-over)	**Fuzzy Zoeller**, U.S. Open
1983	75 (4-over)	**Larry Nelson**, U.S. Open
1982	75 (3-over)	**Craig Stadler**, Masters
1981	74 (2-over)	**Ed Fiori**, Western
1980	74 (2-over)	**Raymond Floyd**, Doral-Eastern
1979	76 (4-over)	**Fuzzy Zoeller**, San Diego
1978	76 (4-over)	**Bruce Lietzke**, Canadian
	75 (4-over)	**John Mahaffey**, PGA
1977	72 (even-par)	**Mark Hayes**, TPC; **Jack Nicklaus**, Memorial; **Al Geiberger**, Memphis
1976	75 (3-over)	**Ben Crenshaw**, Pebble Beach
	73 (3-over)	**Lee Trevino**, Colonial
1975	74 (3-over)	**Lou Graham**, U.S. Open
1974	73 (3-over)	**Hale Irwin**, U.S. Open; **Lee Trevino**, PGA
1973	73 (2-over)	**Rod Funseth**, Los Angeles
1972	73 (1-over)	**Gary Player**, New Orleans
	72 (1-over)	**Deane Beman**, Quad Cities
	71 (1-over)	**Gary Player**, PGA
1971	75 (4-over)	**Buddy Allin**, Greensboro
1970	76 (4-over)	**Pete Brown**, San Diego

Low Finish By A Winner:

2004	62 (10-under)	**Ryan Palmer**, FUNAI Classic at WALT DISNEY WORLD Resort
	63 (9-under)	**Vijay Singh**, HP Classic of New Orleans
2003	62 (10-under)	**J.L. Lewis**, 84 Lumber Classic of Pennsylvania
2002	62 (10-under)	**Phil Tataurangi**, Invensys Classic at Las Vegas
2001	63 (9-under)	**Davis Love III**, AT&T Pebble Beach National Pro-Am; **Bob Estes**, Invensys Classic at Las Vegas
	63 (7-under)	**Sergio Garcia**, MasterCard Colonial
2000	62 (10-under)	**Duffy Waldorf**, National Car Rental Golf Classic
	63 (7-under)	**Phil Mickelson**, MasterCard Colonial
1999	59 (13-under)	**David Duval**, Bob Hope Chrysler Classic
1998	64 (8-under)	**Scott Simpson**, Buick Invitational; **David Duval**, Shell Houston Open
1997	63 (9-under)	**John Cook**, Bob Hope Chrysler Classic
1996	63 (8-under)	**Fred Funk**, B.C. Open
	64 (8-under)	**Davis Love III**, Buick Invitational; **Fred Couples**, THE PLAYERS Championship; **Tiger Woods**, Las Vegas Invitational
1995	61 (10-under)	**Hal Sutton**, B.C. Open
1994	64 (7-under)	**Bill Glasson**, Phoenix
	65 (7-under)	**Bruce Lietzke**, Las Vegas
	64 (6-under)	**Nick Price**, Colonial
1993	62 (10-under)	**Tom Kite**, Bob Hope
	62 (8-under)	**Fulton Allem**, World Series
1992	62 (10-over)	**Davis Love III**, Greensboro; **John Huston**, Disney
1991	64 (8-under)	**Mark Brooks**, Greensboro; **Mark O'Meara**, Disney
	64 (7-under)	**Bruce Fleisher**, New England
	64 (6-under)	**Tom Purtzer**, Colonial; **D.A. Weibring**, Hardee's
	64 (6-under)	**Dillard Pruitt**, Chattanooga
1990	62 (10-under)	**Greg Norman**, Doral
1989	63 (9-under)	**Bill Britton**, Centel
1988	64 (8-under)	**Tom Purtzer**, Southwest; **Chip Beck**, USF&G
1987	63 (9-under)	**Larry Nelson**, Walt Disney
1986	62 (9-under)	**Mac O'Grady**, Hartford
1985	63 (9-under)	**Lanny Wadkins**, Walt Disney
1984	63 (8-under)	**Gary Koch**, Bay Hill, **Ronnie Black**, Anheuser-Busch
1983	63 (9-under)	**Calvin Peete**, Atlanta
1982	63 (7-under)	**Payne Stewart**, Quad Cities
	65 (7-under)	**Lanny Wadkins**, Buick Open
1981	62 (9-under)	**Ron Streck**, Houston
1980	65 (5-under)	**Lee Trevino**, Texas; **Tom Watson**, WSOG
	66 (6-under)	**Andy Bean**, Hawaiian; **Raymond Floyd**, Doral-Eastern; **Bill Kratzert**, Milwaukee
1979	64 (7-under)	**Lou Graham**, IVB
	65 (7-under)	**Calvin Peete**, Milwaukee
1978	62 (8-under)	**Ron Streck**, Texas
1977	64 (6-under)	**Mike Hill**, Ohio Kings Island
	65 (7-under)	**Miller Barber**, Anheuser-Busch
1976	63 (9-under)	**Johnny Miller**, Bob Hope
	63 (7-under)	**Jerry Pate**, Canadian
	65 (7-under)	**Jack Nicklaus**, TPC
1975	61 (11-under)	**Johnny Miller**, Tucson
1974	64 (7-under)	**Dave Stockton**, Quad Cities
	65 (7-under)	**Hubert Green**, Bob Hope; **Lee Trevino**, New Orleans; **Dave Hill**, Houston
1973	63 (8-under)	**Johnny Miller**, U.S. Open
1972	64 (8-under)	**Grier Jones**, Hawaiian; **Jack Nicklaus**, Walt Disney
1971	65 (7-under)	**George Archer**, San Diego
	65 (6-under)	**Miller Barber**, Phoenix; **Bobby Mitchell**, Cleveland
1970	63 (8-under)	**George Knudson**, Robinson Open

High Finish By A Winner:

2004	76 (4-over)	**Vijay Singh**, PGA Championship
	75 (3-over)	**John Daly**, Buick Invitational; **Vaughn Taylor**, Reno Tahoe Open
2003	73 (1-over)	**David Toms**, Wachovia Championship
	72 (2-over)	**Tiger Woods**, WGC-American Express Championship
	72 (1-over)	**Jim Furyk**, U.S. Open
2002	73 (2-over)	**Justin Leonard**, WORLDCOM CLASSIC
2001	73 (1-over)	**Scott McCarron**, BellSouth Classic
2000	72 (even)	**Robert Allenby**, Shell Houston Open
1999	73 (1-over)	**David Duval**, THE PLAYERS Championship; **Tiger Woods**, National Car Rental Golf Classic at Walt Disney World Resort
1998	73 (1-over)	**David Duval**, Tucson Chrysler Classic; **Ernie Els**, Bay Hill Invitational
1997	71 (1-under)	**Mark O'Meara**, Buick Invitational, **Stuart Appleby**, Honda Classic
	69 (1-under)	**Ernie Els**, U.S. Open; **Steve Jones**, Bell Canadian Open
1996	72 (even-par)	**David Ogrin**, LaCantera Texas Open
	71 (even-par)	**Guy Boros**, Greater Vancouver Open
	70 (even-par)	**Phil Mickelson**, NEC World Series of Golf
1995	73 (3-over)	**Billy Mayfair**, TOUR Championship
	73 (2-over)	**Fred Funk**, Ideon Classic
1994	74 (2-over)	**Johnny Miller**, AT&T
1993	71 (1-over)	**Scott Simpson**, Byron Nelson
	71 (1-under)	**Brett Ogle**, Pebble Beach
1992	72 (even-par)	**Steve Elkington**, T of C; **Tom Kite**, U.S. Open; **David Frost**, Hardee's
1991	75 (3-over)	**Steve Pate**, Honda
1990	72 (even-par)	**Mark O'Meara**, Pebble Beach; **David Ishii**, Hawaiian; **Dan Forsman**, Shearson Lehman
	71 (even-par)	**Payne Stewart**, MCI
1989	72 (1-over)	**Wayne Grady**, Westchester
	72 (even-par)	**Bill Glasson**, Doral-Ryder
	70 (even-par)	**Curtis Strange**, U.S. Open
1988	74 (2-over)	**Steve Jones**, Pebble Beach; **Curtis Strange**, Nabisco
1987	72 (1-over)	**Paul Azinger**, Hartford
	71 (1-over)	**Curtis Strange**, World Series
	72 (even-par)	**Larry Nelson**, PGA
1986	71 (1-over)	**Dan Pohl**, World Series
	71 (even-par)	**Hal Sutton**, Phoenix
	71 (1-under)	**John Mahaffey**, TPC; **Bob Murphy**, Canadian

1985	74 (2-over)	**Curtis Strange**, Honda; **Scott Verplank**, Western
	74 (4-over)	**Andy North**, U.S. Open
1984	73 (1-over)	**Greg Norman**, Kemper
1983	77 (5-over)	**Fred Couples**, Kemper
1982	75 (3-over)	**Danny Edwards**, Greensboro
1981	75 (3-over)	**Larry Nelson**, Greensboro
1980	74 (3-over)	**Dave Eichelberger**, Bay Hill
1979	77 (5-over)	**Lon Hinkle**, Bing Crosby
1978	75 (3-over)	**Jack Nicklaus**, TPC
1977	74 (2-over)	**Gene Littler**, Houston; **Lee Trevino**, Canadian
	73 (2-over)	**Jerry Pate**, Phoenix
1976	76 (4-over)	**Roger Maltbie**, Memorial
1975	73 (2-over)	**Lou Graham**, U.S. Open
	73 (1-over)	**Gene Littler**, Bing Crosby
	72 (1-over)	**Tom Jenkins**, IVB
	71 (1-over)	**Jack Nicklaus**, PGA
1974	73 (3-over)	**Hale Irwin**, U.S. Open
	73 (1-over)	**Allen Miller**, Tallahassee
1973	75 (4-over)	**Homero Blancas**, Monsanto
1972	74 (2-over)	**Jack Nicklaus**, Masters, U.S. Open; **Gary Player**, PGA
	73 (3-over)	**Jerry Heard**, Colonial
1971	74 (4-over)	**Jerry Heard**, American Classic
1970	72 (1-over)	**Billy Casper**, Los Angeles
	72 (even-par)	**Bob Stone**, Citrus Open; **Ken Still**, Kaiser International

Largest 18-Hole Lead:

2004	3 strokes	**Charles Howell III**, Booz Allen Classic; **Corey Pavin**, Buick Championship; **Ted Purdy**, Valero Texas Open; **Vijay Singh**, 84 LUMBER Classic
2003	3 strokes	**Fred Funk**, Nissan Open; **Darren Clarke**, Masters Tournament; **Briny Baird**, Buick Classic
2002	3 strokes	**Mike Weir**, Mercedes Championships
2001	3 strokes	**Paul Stankowski**, Compaq Classic of New Orleans; **Bob Estes**, FedEx St. Jude Classic
2000	3 strokes	**Harrison Frazar**, Memorial Tournament; **Nick Price**, Advil Western Open; **Esteban Toledo**, B.C. Open; **Jeff Maggert**, Buick Challenge
1999	2 strokes	**Tommy Tolles**, Sony Open in Hawaii; **Ben Bates**, Greater Milwaukee Open; **Sergio Garcia**, PGA Championship; **Robert Friend**, Buick Challenge
1998	3 strokes	**Loren Roberts**, Greater Milwaukee Open
1997	4 strokes	**Sonny Skinner**, Buick Open
1996	2 strokes	**Tim Herron**, Honda Classic; **Nolan Henke**, Greater Milwaukee Open; **Scott Dunlap**, Bell Canadian Open
1995	2 strokes	**John Huston**, Mercedes Championships; **Duffy Waldorf**, Phoenix Open; **Mark Brooks**, Nestle Invitational; **Woody Austin**, Buick Open
1994	4 strokes	**Jose Maria Olazabal**, Freeport-McMoRan
1993	5 strokes	**Jim Gallagher, Jr.**, TOUR Championship
1992	3 strokes	**Billy Ray Brown**, PLAYERS
1991	3 strokes	**Lanny Wadkins**, T of C, **Scott Hoch**, Buick Open
1990	4 strokes	**Fred Couples**, Memorial; **Jose Maria Olazabal**, World Series
1989	4 strokes	**Bob Tway**, Disney World
1988	3 strokes	**Davis Love III**, Phoenix; **Jeff Sluman**, Southern
1987	4 strokes	**Mike Sullivan**, Honda
1986	3 strokes	**Fred Couples**, Kemper
1985	4 strokes	**Tom Kite**, T of C
1984	3 strokes	**David Graham**, T of C; **Ralph Landrum**, Pensacola
1983	4 strokes	**George Burns**, Kemper
1982	4 strokes	**Terry Mauney**, Los Angeles; **Larry Rinker**, Tallahassee
1981	3 strokes	**Calvin Peete**, B.C. Open
1980	2 strokes	**Dan Pohl**, Bay Hill; **Jerry Pate**, Heritage; **Tom Purtzer**, Greensboro; **Bob Murphy**,Tallahassee; **Tom Watson**, Byron Nelson, World Series; **Bruce Lietzke**, Colonial; **Bob Shearer**, Atlanta; **Scott Hoch**, Quad Cities; **Jim Simons**, Hartford; **Barry Jaeckel**,Hall of Fame
1979	4 strokes	**Mark Lye**, Atlanta; **Dana Quigley**, Hall of Fame
1978	3 strokes	**Tom Watson**, Tucson, Bing Crosby; **Jeff Hewes**, Canadian
1977	3 strokes	**Rik Massengale**, Bob Hope; **Fred Marti**, Pleasant Valley
1976	3 strokes	**Mike Reid** (amateur), U.S. Open
1975	3 strokes	**Bob Stanton**, Inverrary; **Jack Nicklaus**, Heritage; **Tom Weiskopf**, Greensboro; **David Graham**, Western
1974	4 strokes	**Johnny Miller**, Tucson
1973	5 strokes	**Gibby Gilbert**, World
1972	3 strokes	**Jack Nicklaus**, Bing Crosby
1971	3 strokes	**Charles Coody**, Masters
1970	3 strokes	**Rod Funseth**, San Antonio

Largest 36-Hole Lead:

2004	3 strokes	**Carl Pettersson**, The Honda Classic, **Stewart Cink**, WGC-NEC Invitational
2003	5 strokes	**Tiger Woods**, WGC-American Express Championship; **Shigeki Maruyama**, Chrysler Classic of Greensboro
2002	4 strokes	**Pat Perez**, AT&T Pebble Beach National Pro-Am; **Tiger Woods**, Bay Hill Invitational, Buick Open
2001	5 strokes	**Brad Faxon**, Sony Open in Hawaii; **Mark Calcavecchia**, Phoenix Open
2000	7 strokes	**Tiger Woods**, World Golf Championships–NEC Invitational
1999	5 strokes	**David Duval**, Mercedes Championships; **Fred Funk**, B.C. Open
1998	7 strokes	**David Duval**, Tucson Chrysler Classic
1997	5 strokes	**Steve Jones**, Phoenix Open
1996	6 strokes	**Tim Herron**, Honda Classic
1995	4 strokes	**Tom Lehman**, MCI Classic; **D.A. Weibring**, Quad City Classic
1994	5 strokes	**Nick Price**, PGA
1993	3 strokes	**Payne Stewart**, Buick Invitational; **Steve Stricker**, Canadian; **Tom Lehman**, Buick Southern
1992	4 strokes	**Davis Love III**, Los Angeles; **Chip Beck**, Freeport-McMoRan; **Bruce Lietzke**, Canadian
1991	4 strokes	**Blaine McCallister**, Texas; **Jeff Maggert**, IIAO
1990	9 strokes	**Jose Maria Olazabal**, World Series
1989	5 strokes	**Fuzzy Zoeller**, Memorial
1988	4 strokes	**Paul Azinger**, Bay Hill; **Larry Nelson**, Atlanta
1987	7 strokes	**Joey Sindelar**, B.C. Open
1986	5 strokes	**Sandy Lyle**, Greensboro
1985	5 strokes	**Calvin Peete**, Phoenix
1984	6 strokes	**Nick Price**, Canadian
1983	6 strokes	**Hal Sutton**, Anheuser-Busch
1982	6 strokes	**Roger Maltbie**, Colonial
1981	4 strokes	**Jack Nicklaus**, Masters; **Leonard Thompson**, Canadian
1980	5 strokes	**Rex Caldwell**, Buick
1979	4 strokes	**Ben Crenshaw**, Phoenix; **Tom Watson**, Memorial
1978	5 strokes	**Mac McLendon**, Pensacola
1977	6 strokes	**Al Geiberger**, Memphis
1976	6 strokes	**Bob Dickson**, Western
1975	7 strokes	**Tom Weiskopf**, Westchester
1974	6 strokes	**Johnny Miller**, Heritage
1973	4 strokes	**Billy Casper**, Bing Crosby; **Tom Watson**, Hawaiian; **Lee Trevino**, Doral-Eastern; **Jack Nicklaus**, Atlanta; **Forrest Fezler**, American Classic
1972	4 strokes	**Homero Blancas**, Phoenix; **Chris Blocker**, Florida Citrus; **Dave Hill**, Monsanto
1971	3 strokes	**Jerry Heard**, American Classic; **Billy Casper**, Kaiser International
1970	4 strokes	**Grier Jones**, Monsanto

Largest 54-Hole Lead:

2004	7 strokes	**David Toms**, FedEx St. Jude Classic
2003	8 strokes	**Kenny Perry**, Bank of America Colonial
2002	8 strokes	**Ernie Els**, Genuity Championship
2001	6 strokes	**Mark Calcavecchia**, Phoenix Open
2000	10 strokes	**Tiger Woods**, U.S. Open
1999	6 strokes	**Rocco Mediate**, Phoenix Open
1998	7 strokes	**David Duval**, Tucson Chrysler Classic
1997	9 strokes	**Tiger Woods**, Masters Tournament
1996	9 strokes	**Tom Lehman**, THE TOUR Championship
1995	5 strokes	**Scott Hoch**, Shell Houston Open
1994	5 strokes	**Steve Elkington**, Buick Southern
1993	6 strokes	**Greg Norman**, Doral-Ryder
1992	6 strokes	**Fred Couples**, Nestle
1991	5 strokes	**Steve Pate**, Honda
1990	8 strokes	**Jose Maria Olazabal**, World Series
1989	4 strokes	**Ian Baker-Finch**, Colonial; **Greg Norman**, Milwaukee; **John Daly**, Chattanooga
1988	5 strokes	**Corey Pavin**, Texas
1987	8 strokes	**Joey Sindelar**, Buick

1986	5 strokes	**Fuzzy Zoeller**, Pebble Beach; **Calvin Peete**, USF&G; **Mark Calcavecchia**, Southwest
1985	5 strokes	**Corey Pavin**, Colonial
1984	7 strokes	**Greg Norman**, Kemper
1983	6 strokes	**Mike Nicolette**, Bay Hill; **Hal Sutton**, Anheuser-Busch
1982	7 strokes	**Craig Stadler**, Tucson
1981	5 strokes	**Bruce Lietzke**, Bob Hope; **Hale Irwin**, Hawaiian; **Jay Haas**, Milwaukee
1980	7 strokes	**Jim Colbert**, Tucson; **Seve Ballesteros**, Masters
1979	8 strokes	**Tom Watson**, Heritage
1978	5 strokes	**Tom Watson**, PGA; **Tom Kite**, B.C. Open
1977	6 strokes	**Lee Trevino**, Canadian
1976	8 strokes	**Raymond Floyd**, Masters
1975	7 strokes	**Johnny Miller**, Phoenix
1974	6 strokes	**Jack Nicklaus**, Hawaiian
1973	9 strokes	**Jack Nicklaus**, Ohio Kings Island
1972	8 strokes	**Jim Jamieson**, Western
1971	5 strokes	**Jack Nicklaus**, T of C; **Jerry Heard**, American Classic
1970	4 strokes	**Ron Cerrudo**, San Antonio; **Bob Stone**, Citrus Open; **Tony Jacklin**, U.S. Open; **Bob Murphy**, Hartford; **Bobby Mitchell**, Azalea

Low 36-Hole Cut:

2004	140 (4-under)	Chrysler Classic of Tucson; HP Classic of New Orleans; Buick Open; Southern Farm Bureau Classic; FUNAI Classic at the WALT DISNEY WORLD Resort
2003	138 (6-under)	The Honda Classic
2002	138 (6-under)	Walt Disney World Resort Golf Classic
	139 (5-under)	Buick Challenge
	140 (4-under)	Touchstone Energy Tucson Open, The Honda Classic
	139 (3-under)	Greater Milwaukee Open, John Deere Classic
2001	139 (5-under)	National Car Rental Golf Classic at Walt Disney World Resort
	139 (1-under)	Sony Open in Hawaii
2000	139 (1-under)	Canon Greater Hartford Open
	140 (4-under)	Honda Classic; National Car Rental Golf Classic; Southern Farm Bureau Classic
1999	138 (4-under)	FeEx St. Jude Classic
1998	139 (5-under)	United Airlines Hawaiian Open
	138 (3-under)	Greater Milwaukee Open
1997	140 (4-under)	United Airlines Hawaiian Open
	138 (2-under)	GTE Byron Nelson Classic
1996	139 (3-under)	Greater Milwaukee Open
	140 (4-under)	Buick Invitational
1995	139 (3-under)	FedEx St. Jude Classic
	139 (1-under)	GTE Byron Nelson Classic
	140 (4-under)	Buick Open
1994	139 (3-under)	Texas
	140 (even-par)	Hardee's
	141 (3-under)	Hawaiian, Buick Invitational
1993	140 (4-under)	Shell Houston
	140 (2-under)	H-E-B Texas
1992	139 (1-under)	Byron Nelson
	139 (3-under)	Federal Express, Texas
	140 (4-under)	Buick Invitational
1991	137 (3-under)	Chattanooga
	140 (4-under)	Milwaukee, Shearson Lehman
	140 (2-under)	Phoenix, Anheuser-Busch, New England
1990	138 (2-under)	Chattanooga, Texas
	141 (3-under)	Milwaukee
1989	137 (3-under)	Byron Nelson, Texas
1988	141 (3-under)	Andy Williams, USF&G
	139 (1-under)	Hardee's, Provident, Texas
1987	140 (4-under)	Andy Williams
	139 (1-under)	Byron Nelson, Hardee's
1986	141 (3-under)	Buick
	139 (1-under)	Vantage
1985	139 (5-under)	San Diego
1984	141 (3-under)	San Diego
	141 (1-under)	Phoenix
1983	139 (3-under)	Hartford
	139 (1-under)	Texas
1982	139 (3-under)	Hartford
1981	139 (3-under)	Hartford
1980	140 (2-under)	Hartford
	141 (3-under)	Milwaukee
1979	140 (even-par)	Tucson
	141 (1-under)	Phoenix, Houston
	142 (2-under)	Hawaiian, Pensacola
1978	140 (2-under)	Hartford
	142 (2-under)	Anheuser-Busch
	140 (even-par)	Texas
1977	142 (2-under)	Buick
1976	142 (even-par)	Phoenix, Hartford
	143 (1-under)	Hawaiian, San Diego
	144 (even-par)	Florida Citrus
1975	142 (even-par)	Hartford, Sahara
	144 (even-par)	Inverrary, Houston, Westchester, Texas, Kaiser International
1974	141 (1-under)	Greensboro, Hartford
	142 (2-under)	Kemper, Texas
	143 (1-under)	San Diego
1973	140 (2-under)	Hartford
1972	141 (1-under)	Hartford
1971	137 (5-under)	Phoenix
1970	140 (even-par)	Memphis
	141 (1-under)	Azalea
	141 (1-over)	Magnolia
	143 (1-under)	Citrus Invitational

High 36-Hole Cut:

2004	148 (4-over)	the Memorial Tournament; Masters Tournament
	145 (3-over)	British Open; Bell Canadian Open
2003	150 (8-over)	British Open
	148 (8-over)	PGA Championship
2002	150 (10-over)	U.S. Open
2001	147 (3-over)	THE PLAYERS Championship, Memorial Tournament
	146 (6-over)	U.S. Open
2000	150 (6-over)	THE PLAYERS Championship
	149 (7-over)	U.S. Open
1999	154 (12-over)	British Open
1998	150 (6-over)	Masters Tournament
1997	149 (5-over)	Masters Tournament
	147 (7-over)	U.S. Open
1996	148 (8-over)	U.S. Open
1995	149 (5-over)	THE PLAYERS
	148 (4-over)	British Open
	146 (6-over)	U.S. Open
1994	148 (4-over)	Doral-Ryder
	147 (5-over)	Honda, U.S. Open
1993	152 (8-over)	Freeport-McMoRan
1992	148 (4-over)	Nestle
	148 (6-over)	PGA
1991	149 (5-over)	USF&G
1990	157 (13-over)	Memorial
1989	150 (6-over)	Memorial
1988	149 (5-over)	Memorial
1987	151 (7-over)	Honda, PGA
1986	150 (10-over)	U.S. Open
	150 (6-over)	St. Jude Classic
1985	150 (6-over)	Memorial
1984	151 (9-over)	Los Angeles
	151 (7-over)	Memorial
1983	152 (10-over)	Bay Hill
1982	149 (5-over)	Memorial, Kemper, Western
	147 (7-over)	Colonial
1981	152 (8-over)	Memorial
1980	150 (6-over)	Memorial, Western
	149 (9-over)	PGA
1979	157 (13-over)	Memorial
1978	153 (9-over)	TPC
1977	155 (11-over)	TPC
1976	157 (13-over)	Memorial
1975	151 (9-over)	Western
1974	151 (9-over)	Heritage
	149 (9-over)	PGA
1973	151 (7-over)	Masters
	149 (9-over)	American Classic
1972	154 (10-over)	U.S. Open
	150 (10-over)	PGA

1971	152 (10-over)	Heritage
1970	153 (9-over)	U.S. Open
	151 (9-over)	Heritage
	151 (7-over)	Masters
	150 (10-over)	PGA

Fewest To Make 36-Hole Cut:

2004	66	U.S. Open
2003	68	U.S. Open
2002	70	Phoenix Open, Valero Texas Open
2001	70	Sony Open in Hawaii, Memorial Tournament, FedEx St. Jude Classic, British Open Championship, Reno-Tahoe Open
2000	70	MasterCard Colonial, Buick Open
1999	70	Buick Challenge
1998	70	AT&T Pebble Beach National Pro-Am, Buick Challenge
1997	70	United Airlines Hawaiian Open, Kemper Open, British Open, Michelob Championship at Kingsmill
1996	70	Phoenix Open, B.C. Open
1995	70	Phoenix Open
1994	70	Buick Classic, Federal Express
1993	70	New England
1992	70	Texas
1991	70	Buick Classic, Chattanooga
1990	70	Canadian, Texas
1989	70	Doral-Ryder, Memorial, Atlanta, Hardee's, PGA
1988	70	Phoenix
1987	70	Buick, Centel
1986	70	Hawaiian, Heritage, Buick, Anhueser-Busch
1985	70	Atlanta, Quad Cities
1984	70	Atlanta, PGA, Milwaukee
1983	70	Hawaii, Atlanta, Memorial
1982	70	Houston, Disney World
1981	70	Inverrary
1980	70	Doral-Eastern
1979	70	Byron Nelson, Pensacola
1978	70	Tucson, San Diego, Byron Nelson, American Optical, Westchester
1977	70	Hawaiian
1976	70	Heritage
1975	70	B.C. Open
1974	70	Greensboro, American Classic, Sahara
1973	70	Jacksonville, IVB, Southern, Kaiser International
1972	70	Monsanto, Colonial, Cleveland
1971	70	Los Angeles, Tucson, Kaiser International
1970	70	San Diego, Canadian, PGA

Fewest To Make 54-Hole Cut:

2004	72	Michelin Championship at Las Vegas
2003	74	AT&T Pebble Beach National Pro-Am
2002	70	Invensys Classic at Las Vegas
2001	74	Invensys Classic at Las Vegas
2000	70	AT&T Pebble Beach National Pro-Am
1999	70	AT&T Pebble Beach National Pro-Am
1998	74	Las Vegas Invitational
1997	70	Las Vegas Invitational
1996	77	Walt Disney World
1995	70	Walt Disney World
1994	72	AT&T Pebble Beach
1993	73	Walt Disney World
1992	72	Las Vegas Invitational
1991	73	AT&T Pebble Beach
1990	78	AT&T Pebble Beach
1989	73	Las Vegas Invitational
1988	72	Las Vegas Invitational
1987	70	Las Vegas Invitational
1986	71	AT&T Pebble Beach
1985	70	Las Vegas Invitational
1984	73	Bing Crosby
1983	75	Bing Crosby
1982	70	Walt Disney World
1981	77	Bing Crosby
1980	75	Bing Crosby
1979	78	Bing Crosby
1978	70	Bing Crosby
1977	73	Bing Crosby
1976	76	Bing Crosby
1975	75	Bing Crosby
1974	71	Bing Crosby
1973	71	Bing Crosby
1972	70	Bing Crosby
1971	80	Bing Crosby
1970	71	Bing Crosby

Most To Make 36-Hole Cut:

2004	86	U.S. Bank Championship in Milwaukee; FUNAI Classic at the WALT DISNEY WORLD Resort
2003	89	Chrysler Classic of Greensboro
2002	89	Buick Invitational
2001	88	Greater Milwaukee Open
2000	87	Air Canada Championship
1999	88	Greater Milwaukee Open
1998	84	MCI Classic
1997	88	Quad City Classic
1996	103	U.S. Open (10-stroke rule)
	88	Buick Open
1995	103	British Open (10-stroke rule)
	88	Quad City Classic
1994	88	Buick Southern Open
1993	90	Buick Invitational
1992	85	PGA
1991	84	Hardee's
1990	88	Buick Classic
1989	85	Phoenix
1988	89	Milwaukee
1987	87	USF&G
1986	86	Phoenix, Southern
1985	83	Buick
1984	89	LaJet
1983	87	PGA
1982	90	Texas
1981	91	Hartford
1980	83	Phoenix
1979	88	Quad Cities
1978	85	New Orleans
1977	86	Doral-Eastern
1976	85	Westchester
1975	86	San Diego
1974	84	B.C. Open
1973	90	Phoenix
1972	86	St. Louis
1971	88	Hartford
1970	85	Kaiser International, Sahara

Most To Make 54-Hole Cut:

2004	85	AT&T Pebble Beach National Pro-Am
2003	80	Las Vegas Invitational
2002	72	AT&T Pebble Beach National Pro-Am
2001	75	Bob Hope Chrysler Classic
2000	74	Invensys Classic at Las Vegas
1999	71	Bob Hope Chrysler Classic, Las Vegas Invitational
1998	74	Las Vegas Invitational
1997	77	AT&T Pebble Beach
1996	79	Las Vegas Invitational
1995	80	Las Vegas Invitational
1994	77	Walt Disney World
1993	82	AT&T Pebble Beach
1992	82	AT&T Pebble Beach
1991	80	Walt Disney World
1990	86	Las Vegas Invitational
1989	82	Walt Disney World
1988	76	AT&T Pebble Beach
1987	82	AT&T Pebble Beach
1986	81	Las Vegas Invitational
1985	74	Walt Disney World
1984	83	Walt Disney World
1983	80	Walt Disney World

1982	77	Bing Crosby
1981	77	Bing Crosby
1980	75	Bing Crosby
1979	78	Bing Crosby
1978	70	Bing Crosby
1977	73	Bing Crosby
1976	76	Bing Crosby
1975	72	Bing Crosby
1974	71	Bing Crosby
1973	71	Bing Crosby
1972	70	Bing Crosby
1971	80	Bing Crosby
1970	71	Bing Crosby

Most Tied For Lead, 18 Holes:

2004	8	U.S. Bank Championship in Milwaukee; Michelin Championship at Las Vegas
2003	6	The Honda Classic
2002	6	Bay Hill Invitational
2001	6	Touchstone Energy Tucson Open
2000	8	The Honda Classic
1999	5	Compaq Classic of New Orleans
1998	5	Doral-Ryder Open
1997	7	Greater Milwaukee Open
1996	4	MCI Classic, FedEx St. Jude Classic
1995	5	Buick Invitational of California
1994	5	Western, Deposit Guaranty, Federal Express St. Jude
1993	7	Phoenix
1992	6	Kmart Greater Greensboro
1991	5	USF&G
1990	4	Bob Hope Chrysler, Phoenix, USF&G
1989	5	Kmart Greater Greensboro
1988	6	Buick Open
1987	7	Western
1986	6	Shearson Lehman-Andy Williams
1985	4	Bob Hope, Isuzu Andy Williams, Hawaiian, Colonial
1984	7	Los Angeles
1983	4	Phoenix
1982	5	Greater Milwaukee
1981	5	Hawaiian
1980	4	Kemper
1979	5	Greater Greensboro, U.S. Open
1978	7	TPC
1977	7	U.S. Open
1976	4	Houston, Pensacola
1975	6	Tallahassee
1974	5	B.C. Open
1973	6	Southern
1972	6	U.S. Open
1971	4	Canadian, Greater Hartford
1970	7	Coral Springs

Most Tied For Lead, 36 Holes:

2004	3	Shell Houston Open, the Memorial Tournament, Cialis Western Open
2003	3	Shell Houston Open
2002	5	British Open Championship, PGA Championship
2001	8	Canon Greater Hartford Open
2000	3	Buick Invitational, Shell Houston Open, Canon Greater Hartford Open
1999	3	National Car Rental Golf Classic at Walt Disney World Resort, Buick Challenge, Buick Open, U.S. Open
1998	6	National Car Rental Golf Classic at Walt Disney World Resort
1997	3	Las Vegas, B.C. Open, Greater Vancouver, MasterCard Colonial
1996	5	Greater Vancouver Open, Buick Challenge
1995	5	B.C. Open
1994	4	Northern Telecom
1993	4	Nissan Los Angeles, Deposit Guaranty, H-E-B Texas, Las Vegas
1992	4	Kemper
1991	3	Honda, Buick Classic
1990	3	Bob Hope Chrysler, AT&T Pebble Beach
1989	4	Kmart Greater Greensboro
1988	6	Honda
1987	5	Doral-Ryder
1986	4	Memorial
1985	3	Los Angeles, Doral-Eastern, Masters, St. Jude Memphis
1984	3	Los Angeles, Doral-Eastern, PGA
1983	3	MONY T of C, Miller High Life Quad Cities, Panasonic Las Vegas, Walt Disney World
1982	6	TPC
1981	3	Danny Thomas Memphis, Pleasant Valley
1980	4	Memorial, B.C. Open
1979	3	Hawaiian, Tallahassee
1978	5	Sea Pines Heritage
1977	7	Westchester
1976	4	Greater Greensboro, Pleasant Valley
1975	6	Sahara
1974	4	U.S. Open
1973	6	Liggett & Myers, Shrine Robinson
1972	6	U.S. Open
1971	6	National Airlines
1970	3	Colonial, Dow Jones

Most Tied For Lead, 54 Holes:

2004	3	Bank of America Colonial
2003	4	Buick Classic, FUNAI Classic at the WALT DISNEY WORLD Resort
2002	3	Bob Hope Chrysler Classic (90-hole event), Buick Invitational, Reno-Tahoe Open
2001	4	British Open
2000	2	Mercedes Championships, AT&T Pebble Beach National Pro-Am, BellSouth Classic, GTE Byron Nelson Classic, Compaq Classic of New Orleans, Advil Western Open, B.C. Open, Bell Canadian Open, THE TOUR Championship
1999	4	FedEx St. Jude Classic
1998	3	Greater Greensboro Chrysler Classic, MasterCard Colonial, Canon GHO
1997	4	THE TOUR Championship
1996	4	Walt Disney World/Oldsmobile Classic
1995	4	MCI
1994	3	Northern Telecom, Phoenix, Shell Houston, Federal Express St. Jude, Las Vegas
1993	4	NEC World Series, H-E-B Texas
1992	4	GTE Byron Nelson
1991	4	Las Vegas
1990	3	Nestle, Buick Southern
1989	3	Manufacturers Hanover Westchester, Canon Greater Hartford, NEC World Series
1988	4	Provident, Centel
1987	4	Las Vegas
1986	4	Buick Open, Federal Express St. Jude
1985	3	Doral-Eastern, TPC, Houston, Pensacola
1984	5	Las Vegas
1983	5	Colonial
1982	3	Miller High-Life Quad Cities
1981	3	Memorial, Anheuser-Busch
1980	3	Doral-Eastern, World Series
1979	3	Glen Campbell Los Angeles
1978	5	First NBC New Orleans
1977	3	Kemper, Western
1976	5	IVB-Philadelphia
1975	4	San Antonio-Texas
1974	4	Glen Campbell Los Angeles, Houston, Southern
1973	4	U.S. Open
1972	3	Jackie Gleason's Inverrary, Greater Jacksonville, Liggett & Myers, Southern
1971	5	Andy Williams San Diego
1970	4	Greater Greensboro

Most Consecutive Events In The Money:

2004	133	**Tiger Woods**
2003	114	**Tiger Woods**
2002	96	**Tiger Woods**
2001	78	**Tiger Woods**
2000	59	**Tiger Woods**
1999	38	**Tiger Woods**
1998	53	**Vijay Singh**
1997	46	**Vijay Singh**
1996	24	**Vijay Singh**
1995	14	**Jay Haas**
1994	25	**Fred Couples**
1993	25	**Steve Elkington**
1992	19	**Tom Kite**
1991	18	**Fred Couples**
1990	17	**Larry Mize**
1989	33	**Tom Kite**
1988	15	**Ben Crenshaw**
1987	19	**Greg Norman**
1986	16	**Gene Sauers**
1985	14	**Tom Kite**, **Scott Hoch**
1984	21	**Jack Nicklaus**
1983	26	**Hale Irwin**
1982	53	**Tom Kite**
1981	35	**Tom Kite**
1980	28	**Tom Watson**
1979	17	**Hubert Green**, **Bill Rogers**
1978	86	**Hale Irwin**
1977	54	**Hale Irwin**
1976	105	**Jack Nicklaus**
1975	91	**Jack Nicklaus**
1974	74	**Jack Nicklaus**
1973	56	**Jack Nicklaus**
1972	37	**Jack Nicklaus**

Consecutive Years With Win:

2004	9	**Tiger Woods** (1996-2003)
2003	8	**Tiger Woods** (1996-2003)
2002	7	**Tiger Woods** (1996-2002)
2001	6	**Tiger Woods** (1996-2001)
2000	7	**Ernie Els** (1994-2000)
1999	6	**Ernie Els** (1994-99)
1998	6	**Phil Mickelson** (1993-98)
1997	6	**Greg Norman** (1992-97)
1996	5	**Greg Norman** (1992-96)
1995	4	**Ben Crenshaw**, **Lee Janzen**, **Greg Norman** (1992-95)
1994	5	**Fred Couples** (1990-94)
1993	7	**Paul Azinger** (1987-93)
1992	6	**Paul Azinger** (1987-92)
1991	5	**Paul Azinger** (1987-91)
1990	4	**Paul Azinger** (1987-90)
1989	7	**Curtis Strange** (1983-89)
1988	6	**Curtis Strange** (1983-88)
1987	7	**Tom Kite** (1981-87)
1986	6	**Tom Kite** (1981-86)
1985	5	**Hale Irwin**, **Tom Kite** (1981-85)
1984	4	**Hale Irwin**, **Tom Kite** (1981-84)
1983	4	**Johnny Miller** (1980-83)
1982	6	**Bruce Lietzke**, **Tom Watson** (1977-82)
1981	14	**Lee Trevino** (1968-81)
1980	13	**Lee Trevino** (1968-80)
1979	12	**Lee Trevino** (1968-79)
1978	17	**Jack Nicklaus** (1962-78)
1977	16	**Jack Nicklaus** (1962-77)
1976	15	**Jack Nicklaus** (1962-76)
1975	14	**Jack Nicklaus** (1962-75)
1974	13	**Jack Nicklaus** (1962-74)
1973	12	**Jack Nicklaus** (1962-73)
1972	11	**Jack Nicklaus** (1962-72)
1971	17	**Arnold Palmer** (1955-71)
1970	16	**Arnold Palmer** (1955-70)

Holes-In-One By Year:

2004 – 34	1999 – 27	1994 – 44	1989 – 32
2003 – 32	1998 – 27	1993 – 25	1988 – 22
2002 – 40	1997 – 31	1992 – 33	1987 – 30
2001 – 27	1996 – 39	1991 – 29	1986 – 21
2000 – 31	1995 – 35	1990 – 34	1985 – 35

Three Eagles In One Round:

2004	**Harrison Frazar** (#5, #7, #14), Indian Wells CC, Bob Hope Chrysler Classic
2003	**Davis Love III** (#1, #14, #17), Castle Pines GC, The INTERNATIONAL
2001	**Rocky Walcher**, AT&T Pebble Beach National Pro-Am; **Mathew Goggin**, Invensys Classic at Las Vegas
1998	**Brian Kamm**, Kemper Open
1995	**Tommy Tolles**, Bell Canadian; **John Adams**, Buick Challenge
1994	**Davis Love III**, Hawaiian; **Dave Stockton, Jr.**, Disney
1992	**Dan Forsman**, Honda; **Don Pooley**, Texas
1990	**David Frost**, Las Vegas
1981	**Bruce Lietzke**, Hawaiian; **Howard Twitty**, Pensacola

Double Eagles:

2004	**John Daly** (#2, Par 5, PGA West/Palmer Course), Bob Hope Chrysler Classic; **John Douma** (#8, Par 5), Chrysler Classic of Tucson; **Gary Evans** (#4, Par 5), British Open
2003	**James McLean** (#17, Par 5, CC at Mirasol, Sunset Course), The Honda Classic; **Dave Stockton, Jr.** (#5, Par 5, Cog Hill G&CC), 100th Western Open
2002	**Deane Pappas**, Bob Hope Chrysler Classic (Indian Wells CC, #18); **Tim Petrovic**, The Honda Classic, (TPC at Heron Bay, #16); **Steve Lowery**, The International Presented By Qwest, (Castle Pines CC, #17); **John Riegger**, Michelob Championship at Kingsmill, (Kingsmill GC, #3)
2001	**Andrew Magee**, Phoenix Open, (TPC of Scottsdale, #17); **Jeff Maggert**, The British Open, (Royal Lytham and St. Annes, #6); **Greg Owen**, The British Open, (Royal Lytham and St. Annes, #11); **Jimmy Green**, B.C. Open, (En-Joie GC, #12); **Craig Parry**, Invensys Classic at Las Vegas, (TPC at Summerlin, #3).
2000	**David Sutherland**, Honda Classic (TPC at Heron Bay, #14); **Craig Stadler**, Shell Houston Open (TPC at The Woodlands, #15); **Bill Glasson**, FedEx St. Jude Classic (TPC at Southwind, #5); **Frank Lickliter II**, John Deere Classic (TPC at Deere Run, #2); **Ernie Els**, World Golf Championships–NEC Invitational (Firestone CC, #2); **Jim Gallagher, Jr.**, Southern Farm Bureau Classic (Annandale GC, #5)
1999	**Jerry Kelly** (Indian Wells CC, #14), Bob Hope Chrysler Classic; **Tommy Tolles** (Omni Tucson National, #2),Touchstone Energy Tucson Open; **Charles Raulerson** (Doral, #1) Doral-Ryder Open; **Scott Dunlap** (TPC at Avenel, #6), Kemper Open; **Carlos Franco** (Muirfield Village, #7), Memorial Tournament
1998	**Woody Austin** (TPC at Avenel, #6), Kemper Open
1997	**David Duval** (Tucson National, #2), Tucson Chrysler Classic; **Peter Teravainen** (Muirfield Village, #11), Memorial Tournament
1996	**Guy Hill**, Bell Canadian Open (Glen Abbey GC, #18)
1995	**Per-Ulrik Johansson**, PGA Championship (Riviera CC, #11); **J.L. Lewis**, Milwaukee (Brown Deer Park GC, #4)
1994	**Olin Browne**, Northern Telecom (Tucson National, #2); **Jeff Maggert**, Masters (Augusta National, #13); **Mike Donald**, Texas (Oak Hills, #15)
1993	**Massy Kuramoto**, Deposit Guaranty (Hattiesburg, #3); **Tom Sieckmann**, Kmart GGO (Forest Oaks, #9); **Bobby Wadkins**, Memorial (Muirfield Village, #15); **Darrell Kestner**, PGA (Inverness, #13)
1992	**Mark O'Meara**, Bob Hope (Indian Wells, #18); **Billy Andrade**, Las Vegas (LVCC, #2)
1991	**Payne Stewart**, Pebble Beach (Spyglass, #7); **Mark Brooks**, Kemper (TPC Avenel, #6); **Lon Hinkle**, Anheuser-Busch (Kingsmill, #13); **John Daly**, Western (Cog Hill, #5); **Davis Love III**, World Series (Firestone, #2)
1990	**Tom Pernice**, Phoenix (TPC Scottsdale, #15); **Gary Koch**, Anheuser-Busch (Kingsmill, #3); **Steve Pate**, **Jim Gallagher, Jr.**, International (Castle Pines, #17); **Greg Bruckner**, Southern (Green Island, #18)
1989	**Bill Britton**, Anheuser-Busch (Kingsmill, #3)
1988	**Mike Reid**, Los Angeles (Riviera, #1); **Jim Booros**, Provident (Valleybrook, #17)
1987	**David Edwards**, Andy Williams (Torrey Pines South, #17); **Dan Halldorson**, Provident (Valleybrook, #8)
1986	**Mike Hulbert**, Pebble Beach (Cypress Point, #10)
1985	**T.C. Chen**, U.S. Open (Oakland Hills, #2)
1984	**Hal Sutton**, Byron Nelson (Las Colinas, #7); **John Adams**, Canadian (Glen Abbey, #16)
1983	None

1982	**Bob Gilder**, Westchester (Westchester, #18); **Pat McGowan**, Walt Disney (Palm Course, #1)
1981	**Jim Thorpe**, LaJet (Fairway Oaks)
1980	**Bruce Lietzke**, Inverrary (Inverrary); **Fred Marti**, Milwaukee (Tuckaway); **Stanton Altgelt**, IVB (Whitemarsh Valley)
1979	**Rik Massengale**, Tucson (Randolph North); **Bob Murphy**, Tallahassee (Killearn)
1978	**Terry Mauney**, Hawaiian (Waialae); **George Burns**, Colonial (Colonial); **Jim Nelford**, Tommy Valentine, Atlanta (Atlanta CC)
1977	**Joe Inman**, Bob Hope (La Quinta)
1976	**Lyn Lott**, World (Pinehurst No. 2, #16)
1975	**Lee Elder**, Greensboro (Sedgefield); **Miller Barber**, Canadian (Royal Montreal)
1974	**George Knudson**, Bob Hope (Indian Wells); **Larry Wise**, Greensboro (Sedgefield)
1973	**Jerry Heard**, Milwaukee (Tuckaway)
1972	**Bob Murphy**, Bing Crosby (Pebble Beach, #2); **Roy Pace**, Houston (Westwood, #13)
1971	**Rod Curl**, Greensboro (Sedgefield); **Larry Ziegler**, Westchester (Westchester)
1970	**Rod Curl**, Memphis (Colonial); **Mike Hill**, AVCO (Pleasant Valley)

Longest Birdie Streak:

2004	7	**Vijay Singh** (#12-18/Round 2), Mercedes Championships; **Bob Estes** (#12-18/Round 2), FedEx St. Jude Classic; **Neal Lancaster** (#15-3/Round 1), U.S. Bank Championship in Milwaukee
2003	8	**Jerry Kelly** (#7-14/Rd. 3), Las Vegas Invitational
2002	8	**J.P. Hayes**, Bob Hope Chrysler Classic
2001	6	**Brad Elder**, **Spike McRoy**, AT&T Pebble Beach National Pro-Am; Robert Allenby, **Billy Mayfair**, **Joe Durant**, **J.L. Lewis**, **Mark Wiebe**, Bob Hope Chrysler Classic; **Stuart Appleby**, Kemper Insurance Open; **Brian Claar**, Greater Milwaukee Open; **Trevor Dodds**, B.C. Open; **Billy Mayfair**, Buick Open; **Davis Love III**, Invensys Classic at Las Vegas
2000	8	**Edward Fryatt**, Doral-Ryder Open
1999	7	**Steve Pate**, Masters Tournament; **Ted Tryba**, Buick Open
1998	6	**David Toms**, Masters Tournament
1997	6	**John Cook**, Bob Hope Chrysler Classic; **Don Pooley**, Bob Hope Chrysler Classic; **Brian Claar**, United Airlines Hawaiian Open; **Glen Day**, MCI Classic; **David Ogrin**, MasterCard Colonial; **David Sutherland**, B.C. Open
1996	7	**Greg Norman**, Mercedes Championships; **Kirk Triplett**, Buick Invitational
1995	7	**Jay Delsing**, FedEx St. Jude Classic
1994	7	**Keith Clearwater**, Colonial
1992	6	**Gil Morgan**, Bob Hope; **Ed Fiori**, Phoenix; **Mark Calcavecchia**, Masters; **Fred Funk**, Houston; **Tom Kite**, BellSouth; **Andy Dillard**, U.S. Open; **Andy Bean**, Chattanooga
1991	6	**Mark Lye**, Phoenix; **Bill Sander**, Shearson Lehman; **Mark Brooks**, Kmart GGO; **Karl Kimball**, Milwaukee; **Chip Beck**, Las Vegas
1990	7	**Steve Elkington**, Bob Hope; **Scott Verplank**, Milwaukee
1989	7	**Wayne Grady**, Shearson Lehman
1988	7	**Nick Faldo**, T of C
1987	8	**Dewey Arnette**, Buick
1986	6	**Doug Tewell**, Los Angeles; **Don Pooley**, USF&G; **Dave Rummells**, TPC; **Jack Nicklaus**, Memorial; **Kenny Knox**, Buick; **Mark Calcavecchia**, Milwaukee
1985	7	**Hubert Green**, Western
1984	7	**Tommy Valentine**, Atlanta; **Mike McCullough**, Canadian; **Rod Nuckolls**, Buick
1983	6	**Bill Kratzert**, Los Angeles; **Mike Sullivan**, **David Graham**, Buick
1982	7	**Scott Hoch**, Bob Hope
1981	6	**Tom Kite**, Pensacola
1980	7	**George Burns**, Westchester; **John Fought**, Buick
1979	7	**John Mahaffey**, Bob Hope
1978	6	**Bob Gilder**, Doral-Eastern
1977	7	**Bobby Walzel**, Pensacola
1976	8	**Fuzzy Zoeller**, Quad Cities
1975	6	**Johnny Miller**, Masters
1974	6	**Gary McCord**, Bing Crosby; **Mike McCullough**, Bob Hope; **Ben Crenshaw**, San Diego
1973	6	**Dan Sikes**, Westchester; **Hale Irwin**, World Open
1972	7	**Bert Yancey**, Walt Disney
1971	6	**Gibby Gilbert**, Westchester
1970	6	**Frank Beard**, T of C; **Wilf Homenuik**, Azalea

Longest Birdie/Eagle Streak (5 or more):

2004	6	**Robert Gamez** (B-B-B-B-B-E/#18-5/Rd. 3), Indian Wells C.C., Bob Hope Chrysler Classic; **Billy Andrade** (E-B-B-B-B-B/#6-11/Rd 4), PGA West/Palmer Course, Bob Hope Chrysler Classic
2003	8	**Briny Baird** (B-B-B-B-B-B-B-E/#14-#3/Rd 2), FUNAI Classic at the WALT DISNEY WORLD Resort
2002	6	**Peter Lonard** (E-B-B-B-B-B), Compaq Classic of New Orleans
2001	8	**Billy Mayfair** (B-E-B-B-B-B-B-B), Buick Open
2000	6	**Blaine McCallister** (B-B-B-B-E-B), Compaq Classic of New Orleans; **Skip Kendall** (E-B-B-B-B-B), Buick Open
1999	6	**Barry Cheesman** (B-E-B-B-B-B), GTE Byron Nelson Classic
1998	5	**John Daly** (B-B-B-B-E), **J.L. Lewis** (B-B-E-B-B), Bob Hope Chrysler Classic; **Donnie Hammond** (B-B-B-B-E), **Vijay Singh** (B-E-B-B-B), Canon Greater Hartford Open; **Clarence Rose** (E-B-B-B-B), B.C. Open
1997	6	**Andrew Magee** (B-B-B-B-E-B), Bob Hope Chrysler Classic; **Tom Purtzer** (B-B-B-E-B-B), Sprint International
1996	5	**Grant Waite** (E,B,E,B,B), Phoenix Open; **Neal Lancaster** (B,E,B,B,B), U.S. Open; **Steve Stricker** (B,E,B,B,B), Motorola Western Open
1995	5	**Keith Fergus** (B,B,B,B,E,), Hawaiian; **Ben Crenshaw** (B,E,B,B,B), Phoenix
1994	5	**Ken Green**, Phoenix (B,E,B,E,B)
1993	5	**Rick Fehr**, Bob Hope (B,E,B,B,B)
1992	5	**Chris Tucker**, Federal Express (B,E,B,B,B); **Lee Janzen**, Disney, (E,B,B,B,B)
1991	6	**Robert Gamez**, Milwaukee (B,B,B,E,B,B)
1990	6	**David Frost**, Tucson (B,B,B,B,B,E)
1989	7	**Webb Heintzelman**, Las Vegas (B,B,B,B,B,E,B)
1986	5	**Raymond Floyd**, Bob Hope (E,B,B,B,B); **Denis Watson**, Hartford (B,E,B,B,B)
1983	6	**Craig Stadler**, Buick (B,B,E,B,B,B)
1977	7	**Al Geiberger**, Memphis (B,B,B,B,E,B,B)
1975	5	**Bob Mitchell**, Memphis (B,B,B,B,E)

Best Come-From-Behind, Final-Round Win:

2004	9 strokes	**Stewart Cink**, MCI Heritage
2003	8 strokes	**Craig Stadler**, B.C. Open
2002	7 strokes	**Len Mattiace**, Fed Ex St. Jude Classic; **Spike McRoy**, B.C. Open; **John Rollins**, Bell Canadian Open
2001	7 strokes	**Davis Love III**, AT&T Pebble Beach National Pro-Am
2000	6 strokes	**Phil Mickelson**, MasterCard Colonial; **Duffy Waldorf**, National Car Rental Golf Classic
1999	10 strokes	**Paul Lawrie**, British Open (PGA TOUR record)
1998	8 strokes	**Scott Simpson**, Buick Invitational
1997	5 strokes	**Frank Nobilo**, Greater Greensboro Chrysler Classic; **Justin Leonard**, Kemper Open; **Justin Leonard**, British Open
1996	6 strokes	**Nick Faldo**, Masters Tournament
1995	7 strokes	**Jim Gallagher, Jr.**, Kmart GGO; **Payne Stewart**, Shell Houston Open
1994	7 strokes	**Nick Price**, Colonial
1993	5 strokes	**Vijay Singh**, Buick Classic
1992	5 strokes	**Lanny Wadkins**, Canon GHO; **David Edwards**, Memorial; **Mark Carnevale**, Chattanooga
1991	7 strokes	**Mark Brooks**, Kmart GGO; **Fulton Allem**, IIAO
1990	8 strokes	**Chip Beck**, Buick Open
1989	7 strokes	**Mike Sullivan**, IIAO
1988	7 strokes	**Sandy Lyle**, Phoenix
1987	6 strokes	**Corey Pavin**, Hawaiian; **Larry Nelson**, Walt Disney
1986	7 strokes	**Tom Kite**, Western
1985	8 strokes	**Hal Sutton**, Memphis
1984	7 strokes	**Ronnie Black**, Anheuser-Busch
1983	8 strokes	**Mark Lye**, Bank of Boston
1982	6 strokes	**Tom Kite**, Bay Hill
1981	6 strokes	**Raymond Floyd**, TPC
1980	6 strokes	**Peter Jacobsen**, Buick
1979	6 strokes	**Raymond Floyd**, Greensboro; **Lou Graham**, IVB; **Fuzzy Zoeller**, Masters
1978	7 strokes	**Gary Player**, Masters, T of C; **John Mahaffey**, PGA
1977	6 strokes	**Lanny Wadkins**, PGA; **Miller Barber**, Anheuser-Busch
1976	5 strokes	**Al Geiberger**, Western
1975	7 strokes	**Roger Maltbie**, Quad Cities
1974	6 strokes	**Tom Watson**, Western
1973	6 strokes	**Johnny Miller**, U.S. Open
1972	5 strokes	**Grier Jones**, Hawaiian
1971	5 strokes	**Gene Littler**, Colonial
1970	7 strokes	**Pete Brown**, San Diego

Three Or More Victories:

2004	9	**Vijay Singh**, AT&T Pebble Beach National Pro-Am, Shell Houston Open, HP Classic of New Orleans, Buick Open, PGA Championship, Deutsche Bank Championship, Bell Canadian Open, 84 LUMBER Classic, Chrysler Championship
	3	**Ernie Els**, Sony Open in Hawaii, the Memorial Tournament, WGC-American Express Championship
2003	5	**Tiger Woods**, Buick Invitational, WGC-Accenture Match Play, Bay Hill Invitational, Western Open, WGC-American Express
	4	**Davis Love III**, AT&T Pebble Beach National Pro Am, THE PLAYERS, MCI Heritage, The INTERNATIONAL
		Vijay Singh, Phoenix Open, EDS Byron Nelson, John Deere Classic, FUNAI Classic at WALT DISNEY WORLD Resort
	3	**Mike Weir**, Bob Hope Chrysler Classic, Nissan Open, Masters
		Kenny Perry, Bank of America Colonial, Memorial, Greater Milwaukee Open
2002	5	**Tiger Woods**, Bay Hill Invitational, Masters, U.S. Open,Buick Open, WGC-American Express
2001	5	**Tiger Woods**, Bay Hill, THE PLAYERS, Masters, Memorial, WGC-NEC Invitational
	3	**David Toms**, Compaq Classic of New Orleans, PGA, Michelob Championship
2000	9	**Tiger Woods**, Mercedes, AT&T Pebble Beach, Bay Hill, Memorial, U.S. Open, British Open, PGA, WGC– NEC Invitational, Bell Canadian Open
	4	**Phil Mickelson**, Buick Invitational, BellSouth Classic, MasterCard Colonial, THE TOUR Championship
1999	8	**Tiger Woods**, Buick Invitational, Memorial, Motorola Western Open, PGA, WGC-NEC Invitational, National Car Rental Golf Classic at Walt Disney World Resort, THE TOUR Championship, WGC-AmericanExpress
	4	**David Duval**, Mercedes Championships, Bob Hope Chrysler Classic, THE PLAYERS, BellSouth Classic
1998	4	**David Duval**, Tucson Chrysler Classic, Shell Houston Open, NEC World Series of Golf, Michelob Championship
1997	4	**Tiger Woods**, Mercedes, Masters, GTE Byron Nelson,Motorola Western Open
	3	**David Duval**, Michelob Championship, Walt Disney World/Oldsmobile, THE TOUR Championship
1996	4	**Phil Mickelson**, Nortel Open, Phoenix Open, GTE Byron Nelson Classic, NEC World Series of Golf
	3	**Mark Brooks**, Bob Hope Chrysler Classic, Shell Houston Open, PGA
1995	3	**Lee Janzen**, PLAYERS, Kemper, Sprint;
		Greg Norman, Memorial, Hartford, NEC World Series of Golf
1994	6	**Nick Price**, Honda, Colonial, Western, British Open, PGA, Canadian
	3	**Mark McCumber**, Anheuser-Busch, Hardee's, TOUR Championship
1993	4	**Nick Price**, PLAYERS, Canon GHO, Western, Federal Express
	3	**Paul Azinger**, Memorial, New England, PGA
1992	3	**Fred Couples**, Los Angeles, Nestle, Masters; **Davis Love III**, PLAYERS, MCI, Kmart GGO; **John Cook**, Bob Hope, Hawaiian, Las Vegas
1991		None
1990	4	**Wayne Levi**, Atlanta, Western, Canon GHO, Canadian
1989	3	**Tom Kite**, Nestle, PLAYERS, Nabisco;
		Mark Calcavecchia, Phoenix, Los Angeles, British Open
1988	4	**Curtis Strange**, Houston, Memorial, U.S. Open, Nabisco
	3	**Sandy Lyle**, Phoenix, Greensboro, Masters
1987	3	**Curtis Strange**, Canadian, St. Jude, World Series;
		Paul Azinger, Phoenix, Las Vegas, Hartford
1986	4	**Bob Tway**, Andy Williams, Westchester, Atlanta, PGA
	3	**Fuzzy Zoeller**, Pebble Beach, Heritage, Anheuser-Busch;
		Greg Norman, Las Vegas, Kemper, British Open
1985	3	**Curtis Strange**, Honda, Las Vegas, Canadian;
		Lanny Wadkins, Bob Hope, Los Angeles, Disney
1984	3	**Tom Watson**, Tucson Match Play, TofC, Western;
		Denis Watson, Buick, World Series, Las Vegas
1983		None
1982	4	**Calvin Peete**, Milwaukee, Anheuser-Busch, B.C. Open, Pensacola;
		Craig Stadler, Tucson, Masters, Kemper, World Series;
		Tom Watson, Los Angeles, Heritage, U.S. Open, British Open
	3	**Raymond Floyd**, Memorial, Memphis, PGA; **Lanny Wadkins**, Phoenix, TofC, Buick; **Bob Gilder**, Byron Nelson, Westchester, Bank of Boston
1981	4	**Bill Rogers**, Heritage, British Open, World Series, Texas
	3	**Bruce Lietzke**, Bob Hope, San Diego, Byron Nelson;
		Tom Watson, Masters, New Orleans, Atlanta;
		Raymond Floyd, Doral-Eastern, TPC, Westchester
1980	7	**Tom Watson**, San Diego, Los Angeles, T of C, New Orleans, Byron Nelson, British Open, World Series
	3	**Lee Trevino**, TPC, Memphis, Texas
1979	5	**Tom Watson**, Heritage, T of C, Byron Nelson, Memorial, Hall of Fame
	3	**Lou Graham**, IVB, American Optical, Texas
1978	5	**Tom Watson**, Tucson, Bing Crosby, Byron Nelson, Hall of Fame, Anheuser-Busch
	4	**Jack Nicklaus**, Inverrary, TPC, IVB, British Open
	3	**Gary Player**, Masters, T of C, Houston;
		Andy Bean, Kemper, Memphis, Western
1977	5	**Tom Watson**, Pebble Beach, San Diego, Masters, Western, British Open
	3	**Jack Nicklaus**, Inverrary, T of C, Memorial;
		Hale Irwin, Atlanta, Hall of Fame, Texas
1976	3	**Hubert Green**, Doral-Eastern, Jacksonville, Heritage;
		Ben Crenshaw,Pebble Beach, Hawaiian, Ohio Kings Island;
		Johnny Miller, Tucson, Hope, British Open
1975	5	**Jack Nicklaus**, Doral-Eastern, Heritage, Masters, PGA, World
	4	**Johnny Miller**, Phoenix, Tucson, Bob Hope, Kaiser International
	3	**Gene Littler**, Bing Crosby, Memphis, Westchester
1974	8	**Johnny Miller**, Bing Crosby, Phoenix, Tucson, Heritage, T of C, Westchester, World, Kaiser International
	3	**Hubert Green**, Bob Hope, Jacksonville, IVB;
		Dave Stockton, Los Angeles, Quad Cities, Hartford;
		Gary Player, Masters, Danny Thomas, British Open
1973	7	**Jack Nicklaus**, Bing Crosby, New Orleans, TofC, Atlanta, PGA, Ohio Kings Island, Walt Disney
	5	**Tom Weiskopf**, Colonial, Kemper, IVB, British Open, Canadian Open
	4	**Bruce Crampton**, Phoenix, Tucson, Houston, American Classic
1972	7	**Jack Nicklaus**, Bing Crosby, Doral-Eastern, Masters, U.S. Open, Westchester, Match Play, Walt Disney
	4	**Lee Trevino**, Memphis, Hartford, St. Louis, British Open
1971	6	**Lee Trevino**, Tallahassee, Memphis, U.S. Open, British Open, Canadian, Sahara
	5	**Jack Nicklaus**, PGA, TofC, Byron Nelson, National Team, Walt Disney
	4	**Arnold Palmer**, Bob Hope, Florida Citrus, Westchester, National Team
1970	4	**Billy Casper**, Los Angeles, Masters, IVB, AVCO
	3	**Jack Nicklaus**, Nelson, British Open, National Four-Ball

Wire-To-Wire Winners (leader after every round, no ties):

2004	**Stewart Cink**, WGC-NEC Invitational; **Vijay Singh**, 84 LUMBER Classic
2003	**Tiger Woods**, 100th Western Open; **Davis Love III**, The INTERNATIONAL
2002	**Tiger Woods**, U.S. Open, WGC-American Express Championship;
	K.J. Choi, Tampa Bay Classic
2001	**Bob Estes**, FedEx St. Jude Classic
2000	**Paul Azinger**, Sony Open in Hawaii;
	Hal Sutton, THE PLAYERS Championship;
	Tiger Woods, U.S. Open, World Golf Championships–NEC Invitational
1999	**Jesper Parnevik**, Greater Greensboro Chrysler Classic;
	David Toms, Sprint International
1998	None
1997	**Steve Jones**, Phoenix Open; **Steve Elkington**, THE PLAYERS Championship;
	Nick Price, MCI Classic; **Ernie Els**, Buick Classic
1996	**Tim Herron**, Honda Classic; **Ernie Els**, Buick Classic;
	Scott Hoch, Michelob Championship at Kingsmill
1995	None
1994	**Greg Norman**, PLAYERS; Mike Springer, Kmart GGO; **Bob Estes**, Texas
1993	**Howard Twitty**, Hawaiian; **Nick Price**, Western
1992	**Fred Couples**, Nestle; **David Frost**, Hardee's
1991	None
1990	**Jose Maria Olazabal**, World Series; **Tim Simpson**, Disney
1989	**Ian Baker-Finch**, Colonial
1988	Steve Pate, T of C; **Larry Nelson**, Atlanta; **Bob Lohr**, Disney;
	Curtis Strange, Nabisco
1987	**Joey Sindelar**, B.C. Open; **Tom Watson**, Nabisco
1986	None
1985	**Tom Kite**, T of C
1984	**Greg Norman**, Kemper
1983	**Hal Sutton**, PGA; **Nick Price**, World Series
1982	**Bob Gilder**, Westchester; **Raymond Floyd**, PGA; **Tim Norris**, Hartford
1981	None
1980	**Tom Watson**, T of C, Byron Nelson; **Bruce Lietzke**, Colonial;
	Scott Hoch, Quad Cities
1979	**Bruce Lietzke**, Tucson; **Tom Watson**, Heritage, T of C
1978	**Tom Watson**, Tucson

1977	**Rik Massengale**, Bob Hope; **Andy Bean**, Doral-Eastern; **Lee Trevino**, Canadian; **Jerry Pate**, Southern
1976	**Raymond Floyd**, Masters; **Mark Hayes**, Byron Nelson
1975	**Johnny Miller**, Tucson; **Tom Weiskopf**, Greensboro; **Al Geiberger**, TPC
1974	**Johnny Miller**, Tucson, Heritage; **Allen Miller**, Tallahassee; **Ed Sneed**, Milwaukee
1973	**Lee Trevino**, Doral-Eastern; **Homero Blancas**, Monsanto
1972	**Jack Nicklaus**, Masters; **Dave Hill**, Monsanto
1971	**Jack Nicklaus**, PGA; **Arnold Palmer**, Westchester
1970	**Tony Jacklin**, U.S. Open

First-Time Winners Since 1970:

(Rookies underlined)

2004	10	Heath Slocum, Todd Hamilton; Zach Johnson; Stephen Ames; Mark Hensby; Rod Pampling; Vaughn Taylor; Bart Bryant; Andre Stolz; Ryan Palmer
2003	7	Ben Crane, Steve Flesch, Jonathan Kaye, Ben Curtis, Shaun Micheel, Adam Scott, Chad Campbell
2002	18	Jerry Kelly, Matt Gogel, Len Mattiace, Kevin Sutherland, Ian Leggatt, Matt Kuchar, Craig Perks, K.J. Choi, Chris Smith, Spike McRoy, Chris Riley, Craig Parry, John Rollins, Charles Howell III, Phil Tataurangi, Bob Burns, Jonathan Byrd, Luke Donald
2001	10	Garrett Willis, Jose Coceres (2), Robert Damron, Sergio Garcia, Frank Lickliter II, Retief Goosen, Shigeki Maruyama, David Gossett, Joel Edwards, Cameron Beckman
2000	8	Kirk Triplett, Jim Carter, Darren Clarke, Tom Scherrer, Dennis Paulson, Michael Clark II, Rory Sabbatini, Chris DiMarco
1999	9	Glen Day, Carlos Franco (2), Rich Beem, Paul Lawrie, J.L. Lewis, Brent Geiberger, Tom Pernice Jr., Notah Begay III (2), Mike Weir
1998	8	Jesper Parnevik, Lee Westwood, Trevor Dodds, J.P. Hayes, Joe Durant, Olin Browne, Brandel Chamblee, Chris Perry
1997	6	Stuart Appleby, Frank Nobilo, David Toms, Stewart Cink, Gabriel Hjerstedt, David Duval
1996	13	Tim Herron, Paul Goydos, Scott McCarron, Paul Stankowski, Steve Stricker, Willie Wood, Justin Leonard, Clarence Rose, Guy Boros, Dudley Hart, Michael Bradley, Tiger Woods (2), David Ogrin
1995	7	John Morse, Ted Tryba, Ed Dougherty, Woody Austin, Brad Bryant, Jim Furyk, Duffy Waldorf
1994	10	Loren Roberts, Mike Springer, Mike Heinen, Neal Lancaster, Tom Lehman, Ernie Els, Brian Henninger, Dicky Pride, Steve Lowery, Bob Estes
1993	7	Brett Ogle, Mike Standly, Jim McGovern, Grant Waite, Vijay Singh, Billy Mayfair, Jeff Maggert
1992	4	Lee Janzen, Fred Funk, Mark Carnevale, Richard Zokol
1991	14	Phil Mickelson, Jay Don Blake, Rocco Mediate, Ian Woosnam, Kenny Perry, Billy Andrade, Russ Cochran, Bruce Fleisher, Dillard Pruitt, Billy Ray Brown, Brad Faxon, John Daly, David Peoples, Fulton Allem
1990	10	Robert Gamez (2), Tommy Armour III, David Ishii, John Huston, Tony Sills, Steve Elkington, Peter Persons, Jose Maria Olazabal, Jim Gallagher, Jr., Nolan Henke
1989	9	Greg Twiggs, Ian Baker-Finch, Tom Byrum, Wayne Grady, Mike Donald, Curt Byrum, Stan Utley, Ted Schulz, Bill Britton
1988	11	Steve Jones, Chip Beck, Jim Benepe, Tom Sieckmann, Blaine McCallister, Mark Brooks, Jodie Mudd, Jeff Sluman, David Frost, Andrew Magee, Bob Lohr
1987	10	Paul Azinger, T.C. Chen, Davis Love III, Keith Clearwater (2), Robert Wrenn, John Inman, Sam Randolph, Steve Pate, Ken Brown, Mike Reid
1986	12	Donnie Hammond, Bob Tway, Kenny Knox, Sandy Lyle, Dan Pohl, Mac O'Grady, Mike Hulbert, Rick Fehr, Gene Sauers, Mark Calcavecchia, Fred Wadsworth, Ernie Gonzalez
1985	11	Woody Blackburn, Joey Sindelar, Bernhard Langer, Bill Glasson, Mark Wiebe, Dan Forsman, Phil Blackmar, Scott Verplank, Ken Green, Jim Thorpe, Tim Simpson
1984	6	Bob Eastwood, Nick Faldo, Corey Pavin, Greg Norman, Denis Watson, Mark O'Meara
1983	10	Isao Aoki, Gary Hallberg, Mike Nicolette, Fred Couples, Larry Mize, Nick Price, Pat Lindsey, Mark Lye, Rex Caldwell, Ronnie Black
1982	5	Bob Shearer, Payne Stewart, Tim Norris, Bobby Clampett, Hal Sutton
1981	5	John Cook, Keith Fergus, Dave Barr, Peter Oosterhuis, Morris Hatalsky
1980	12	Craig Stadler, Jeff Mitchell, Mark Pfeil, Scott Simpson, Scott Hoch, Peter Jacobsen, Don Pooley, Phil Hancock, Mike Sullivan, Dan Halldorson, David Edwards, Doug Tewell
1979	12	Fuzzy Zoeller, Bob Byman, Larry Nelson, Mark McCumber, Calvin Peete, D.A. Weibring, Jack Renner, Howard Twitty, John Fought (2), Ed Fiori, Curtis Strange, George Burns
1978	9	Jay Haas, Bill Rogers, Seve Ballesteros, Barry Jaeckel, Lon Hinkle, Jack Newton, Ron Streck, Wayne Levi, Bob Mann
1977	10	Bruce Lietzke, Tom Purtzer, Andy Bean, Graham Marsh, Danny Edwards, Jim Simons, Mike Morley, Andy North, Bobby Cole, Gil Morgan
1976	9	Bob Gilder, Gary Koch, Mark Hayes, Tom Kite, Joe Inman, Jerry Pate (2), John Lister, Bob Wynn, Bill Kratzert
1975	8	Gary Groh, Pat Fitzsimons, Jerry McGee, Rik Massengale, Tom Jenkins, Roger Maltbie (2), Don Bies, Don Iverson
1974	11	Leonard Thompson, Lee Elder, Allen Miller, Rod Curl, Bob Menne, Tom Watson, Richie Karl, Victor Regalado, Forrest Fezler, Terry Diehl, Mac McLendon
1973	6	John Schlee, Bert Greene, Sam Adams, Ed Sneed, John Mahaffey, Ben Crenshaw
1972	5	Grier Jones, Bob Shaw, Jim Jamieson, David Graham, Lanny Wadkins
1971	10	J.C. Snead, Bud Allin, Hubert Green, Bobby Mitchell, Dave Eichelberger, Jerry Heard, DeWitt Weaver, Johnny Miller, Labron Harris, Hale Irwin
1970	6	Mike Hill, Bob Stone, Gibby Gilbert, Tommy Aaron, Hugh Royer, Bill Garrett

Average Driving Distance Since 1980:

2004 – 287.3	1997 – 267.6	1990 – 262.7	1983 – 258.7
2003 – 286.3	1996 – 266.4	1989 – 261.8	1982 – 256.8
2002 – 279.8	1995 – 263.6	1988 – 263.5	1981 – 259.7
2001 – 279.4	1994 – 261.8	1987 – 262.5	1980 – 256.8
2000 – 273.2	1993 – 260.3	1986 – 261.5	
1999 – 272.4	1992 – 260.5	1985 – 260.4	
1998 – 270.6	1991 – 261.4	1984 – 259.6	